THE
GOOD PUB
GUIDE 2021

THE TOP 5,000 PUBS FOR FOOD AND DRINK IN THE UK

Editor: Cath Phillips
Consultant Editor: Fiona Stapley
Commissioning Editor: Ben West

The Good Pub Guide
was founded by Alisdair Aird in 1982

Please send reports on pubs to:

Freepost THE GOOD PUB GUIDE, Random House Publishing,
20 Vauxhall Bridge Road, London SW1V 2SA

or feedback@goodguides.com

or visit our website: www.thegoodpubguide.co.uk

If you would like to advertise in the next edition of The Good Pub Guide,
please email goodpubguide@tbs-ltd.co.uk

1

Published in 2020 by Ebury Press, an imprint of Ebury Publishing

Ebury Press, an imprint of Ebury Publishing
20 Vauxhall Bridge Road,
London, SW1V 2SA

www.penguin.co.uk

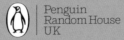

Penguin
Random House
UK

MIX
Paper from
responsible sources
FSC® C018179

Penguin Random House is committed to a sustainable future for
our business, our readers and our planet. This book is made from
Forest Stewardship Council® certified paper.

To buy books by your favourite authors and register for offers,
visit www.penguin.co.uk

Typesetter: Integra
Designer: Jerry Goldie Graphic Design
Proofreader: Tamsin Shelton
Good Pub Guide icons: William Collins

Printed and bound in Great Britain by Clays Ltd, Elcograf S.p.A.

The authorised representative in the EEA is Penguin Random House Ireland,
Morrison Chambers, 32 Nassau Street, Dublin D02 YH68

ISBN 9781529106503

Contents

RIDLEY INNS

Welcome back, we can't wait to see you all...

Enjoy a broad selection of delicious, high quality food to suit all tastes and dietary requirements, all home-made and locally-sourced. You'll also find a great selection of drinks including some personally selected real ales.

THE COCK INN
RINGMER

www.cockpub.co.uk

01273 812040

FOOD SERVICE TIMES

Monday & Tuesday: 12-2.30pm
Wednesday & Thursday: 12-2.30pm & 6-9pm
Friday & Saturday: 12-9pm
Sunday: 12-7:30pm

THE HIGHLANDS INN
UCKFIELD

www.highlandsinn.co.uk

01825 762989

FOOD SERVICE TIMES

Monday - Thursday 12-2 30pm & 6-9:pm
Friday & Saturday: 12-9pm
Sunday: 12-7:30pm

HEATHFIELD TAVERN
HEATHFIELD

www.theheathfieldtavern.co.uk

01435 864847

FOOD SERVICE TIMES

Monday & Tuesday: Closed
Wednesday & Thursday: 12-2.30pm & 6-9pm
Friday & Saturday: 12-9pm
Sunday: 12-4pm

www.ridleyinns.co.uk

Timings subject to change – please check websites and Facebook

Join the Butcombe Loyalty Club
and enjoy 25% off food in our pubs
every Wednesday. We'll even give
you £5 to spend as a welcome gift:
loyalty.butcombe.com

Find your local:
butcombe.com/pubs-rooms

Introduction & The Good Pub Guide Awards 2021

By Fiona Stapley

'I do accept that what we're doing is extraordinary. We're taking away the ancient, inalienable right of freeborn people of the United Kingdom to go to the pub.' So said Prime Minister Boris Johnson when he announced the closure of all pubs, restaurants, bars and cafés on 20 March 2020, as part of the nationwide lockdown imposed to combat the coronavirus pandemic. Even during two world wars, the pubs stayed open, and their total closure is the first time this has happened in our country's history – though some are thought to have shut during the Great Plague of 1665. With 48,000 pubs in Britain, these shutdowns were an unmitigated disaster for everyone concerned.

'For us, the shutdown came just as we had paid the bills for the 2019 Christmas period and were looking forward to the cash inflow from our busy season, which starts with Mother's Day, Easter and the May bank holidays and then runs through to the end of September. We are going to lose all that income,' Jeannette Goodrich from the Rose & Crown in Snettisham, Norfolk told us. For some pubs, missing out on these big, money-making events meant they had to shut their doors immediately and for good. Thousands of others wondered how on earth they were going to save their businesses. 'A total nightmare' is how many described the situation. With a good pub being at the heart of any community, this was a devastating blow for customers too.

But a first-class publican is entrepreneurial and positive by nature, so standing still was never going to be an option. Many decided to take the opportunity provided by forced closure to refresh and update their businesses – redecorating and refurbishing bars and bedrooms, often so hard to do in normal circumstances. We even heard of a state-of-the-art, Covid-bashing air-con system being installed. Outdoor space became precious and as around 27,000 pubs in Britain have gardens, these were expanded as much as was possible. New outdoor bars were added, barbecues and pizza ovens installed, gazebos and marquees erected and car parks were turned over to outdoor dining. The centre of some towns and cities were transformed into continental-style alfresco dining areas by pavements being widened and roads closed for part of the day. All that was needed was good weather – and luckily, we got it.

We're all in this together

As a way of coping without trade, pubs opened village shops on their premises to sell home-baked bread, household essentials and local farm produce. Since up to 70 million pints of beer were about to be poured down the drain, the sight of customers queuing with empty milk containers outside the side window of a pub to buy cut-price ale became a familiar one. Publicans said that it was lovely to hear (socially distanced) laughter and chat again. Curtailed online menus offered home-made ready meals, which kept kitchen staff busy and were often delivered to people who were unable to get out. Alcohol was provided to make hand sanitiser for NHS and social care workers; some landlords even offered bedrooms to NHS staff who needed

living quarters near hospitals. As one landlord put it, 'This is all about the community, it's not just every man for himself. We are all in this together, so everyone should help out where they can.' Websites were updated to help with online drink and food ordering, digital sales and payment, and virtual quizzes, online home-brew classes and Zoom evenings between customers became the norm. One enterprising pub even turned a large van into a mobile alehouse where the back doors opened to reveal a working bar with beer taps.

Many of our top pubs went that extra mile. Mary McLaughlin and Tim Bird (who own Cheshire Cat Pubs & Bars and run half a dozen excellent inns), together with their staff, have done wonders in supporting their communities. Their 'hub shops' kept their local butcher, brewer, egg producers, potato farmers, beekeepers, cheesemakers and bakers all busy. They kept their staff in work by starting up the 'Pub Hub Shrub' selling hundreds of jasmine, lavender and geranium plants and compost to locals when garden centres were closed. They created a wine shop in one pub (which has since become a permanent feature) and, as well as offering their 'just heat' meals to pub customers, they also sent food to nursing homes and schools and looked after their dustmen, postie and local taxi firm who did all their deliveries. As Tim said, 'The fear of losing one's 11-year-old dream makes you do everything within your grasp to ensure survival. But it has been physically and mentally exhausting.'

On 4 July, pubs were allowed to open again. But before this could happen, licensees had to work out how the various rules and regulations would apply to them in the day-to-day running of their pubs. This became increasingly complicated as government guidelines were packed with vague terms such as 'where possible' and 'if appropriate'. To interpret this means checking with the relevant local authority, licensing body and police licensing officer – who all had the power to close pubs down. These regulations included hand sanitiser stations, regular 15-minute cleaning and physical distancing rules (fewer tables, one-way systems, appropriate floor and wall signage, and masks, visors and screens). Some pubs carried out temperature checks and took contact details from their customers. A sadness for many was that the bar area was now out of bounds to customers, so it was going to be impossible and impractical to just pop in for a quick pint and a chat any more.

Help came for pubs from a number of sources including industry bodies and some breweries, and there's been warm praise for the government's support: this has included the furlough scheme (which ran out at the end of October 2020), the Eat Out to Help Out discount (throughout August) and the Job Support Scheme (in place from 1 November for six months). Chancellor Rishi Sunak also extended the reduction in VAT (from 20% to 5%) on food, soft drinks and accommodation, which will now last until the end of March 2021.

The IFBB (Independent Family Brewers of Great Britain), an association of 29 family-owned breweries, invested more than £20 million in pubs during lockdown. This support has included cancelling rent payments and suspending service charge and loan repayments. Some of the larger pubcos have not been so generous and have deferred rents rather than scrapping them; as a result, tenants have had to give up their pubs to avoid accruing huge debts that they will be unable to repay.

Hopes and fears

As we went to press (and the rules were changing every few days), the government unveiled three new levels of restrictions for pubs across England in an attempt to stem the pandemic tide (Scotland and Wales have their own regulations).

This ongoing rollercoaster period has tested those in the pub trade to the very limit and beyond, and led one licensee to state, 'I am really fearful for our industry,' while another (fingers crossed behind her back) said, 'I just wish we could see a way of getting back to life as normal with a jostling queue at the bar and not a face mask in sight.' A hopeful Oliver Thain from Cambscuisine told us, 'There will, of course, be many challenges ahead but we can't wait until hospitality is back at the heart of our lives once more.' Fingers tightly crossed indeed.

October 2020

Top Ten Awards 2021

Shepherd Neame has been brewing beer in Faversham, Kent since 1698, which makes it the oldest continuous brewer in the country. Family-run since 1864, it owns more than 300 pubs and inns, mainly in Kent, London and south-east England. It supplies its ales to around 2,000 other outlets and exports to more than 35 countries.

Beers include its flagship Master Brew, as well as Bishops Finger, Spitfire and seasonal ales; under their Faversham Steam Brewery moniker, they brew Whitstable Bay Pale Ale, Black Stout, Blonde Lager, Organic Ale and Ruby Ale. There are also Bear Island craft ales (East Coast Pale Ale and Triple Hopped Lager) and a Cask Club that offers a monthly choice described as 'a new range of contemporary cask ales designed to satisfy the beer-curious drinker'.

The brewing process uses only chalk-filtered water from an artesian well deep beneath the brewery, with British malted barley and hops that come mainly from Kent. Sustainability is high on the company's list of priorities: waste oil from pub kitchens is converted into biofuel, grain and hop waste is recycled as animal food, all cardboard packaging is 100% recyclable, and high-tech cask, keg and bottling lines minimise the use of natural resources.

'Sheps', as the brewery is fondly known, employs nearly 300 people with some local workers being the fourth or fifth generation of the same family to work for the company. Shepherd Neame also supports a network of farmers, fishermen and food producers throughout Kent and the South East to ensure their pub menus champion fresh local food, and by investing in their listed buildings they aim to preserve ancient crafts including thatching, stonemasonry, traditional carpentry and glass etching.

In order to help protect employees, licensees and the company during the coronavirus lockdown in 2020, the directors took a temporary 20% pay cut, suspended rent receipts, cancelled the shareholder dividend and ceased all non-contractual capital expenditure in the brewery and throughout the pub estate. They have been reviewing all these precautionary actions on a weekly basis and hope to return to normal business as soon as possible. **Shepherd Neame** is our *Brewery of the Year 2021*.

This year's Top Ten Beer Pubs are spread all over the country and include the **Bhurtpore** in Aston (Cheshire), **Beer Hall at Hawkshead**

Brewery in Staveley (Cumbria), **Tom Cobley** in Spreyton (Devon), **Fat Cat** in Norwich (Norfolk), **Halfway House** at Pitney (Somerset), **Fat Cat** in Ipswich (Suffolk), **Nags Head** in Malvern (Worcestershire), **Maltings** in York (Yorkshire), **Harp** in London and **Guildford Arms** in Edinburgh (Scotland). All these pubs keep an extraordinarily interesting list of real ales, but it's Colin Keatley's collection of at least 32 ales that wins the **Fat Cat** in Norwich the title *Beer Pub of the Year 2021*.

You'll find that the beers are significantly cheaper at the own-brew pubs featured in the Guide. Our Top Ten Own-Brew Pubs are the **Brewery Tap** in Peterborough (Cambridgeshire), **Beer Hall at Hawkshead Brewery** in Staveley, **Drunken Duck** near Hawkshead and **Watermill** at Ings (all Cumbria), **Boot** in Repton (Derbyshire), **Church Inn** at Uppermill (Lancashire), **Dipton Mill Inn** at Diptonmill and **Ship** in Newton-by-the-Sea (both Northumbria), **Gribble Inn** at Oving (Sussex) and **Weighbridge Brewhouse** in Swindon (Wilshire). From the on-site Hexhamshire microbrewery the quality of their beers makes the **Dipton Mill Inn** at Diptonmill (Northumbria) winner of *Own-Brew Pub of the Year 2021*.

Nowadays, wine in pubs can be extraordinarily good and quite a few places have their own little wine shop on the premises. Our Top Ten Wine Pubs are the **Old Bridge Hotel** in Huntingdon (Cambridgeshire), **George & Dragon** at Clifton and **Drunken Duck** near Hawkshead (both in Cumbria), **Acorn** at Evershot (Dorset), **Inn at Whitewell** at Whitewell (Lancashire), **Olive Branch** in Clipsham (Leicestershire & Rutland), **Duncombe Arms** at Ellastone (Staffordshire), **Woods in Dulverton** (Somerset), **Unruly Pig** in Bromeswell (Suffolk) and **Griffin** in Felinfach (Wales). The exceptionally knowledgeable and generous spirited Paddy Groves reckons he could put 1,000 wines up on the bar and will open any of them for just a glass – **Woods** in Dulverton is our *Wine Pub of the Year 2021*.

Stocking quite amazing collections of malt whiskies, our Top Ten Whisky Pubs are the **Bhurtpore** in Aston and **Old Harkers Arms** in Chester (both in Cheshire), **Acorn** in Evershot (Dorset), **Red Fox** at Thornton Hough (Lancashire), **Angel** in Larling (Norfolk), **Black Jug** in Horsham (Sussex), **Pack Horse** in Widdop (Yorkshire), **Bow Bar** in Edinburgh, **Bon Accord** in Glasgow and **Sligachan Hotel** on the Isle of Skye (Scotland). With more than 500 whiskies on their gantry, the **Bon Accord** in Glasgow is our *Whisky Pub of the Year 2021*.

The nation's love affair with gin continues unabated, and our Top Ten Gin Pubs this year are the **Bhurtpore** in Aston and **Cholmondeley**

Arms in Cholmondeley (both in Cheshire), **Old Courthouse** in Cheltenham and **Bell** in Selsley (both in Gloucestershire), **Mill House** in North Warnborough (Hampshire), **Red Fox** at Thornton Hough (Lancashire), **Maytime** at Asthall (Oxfordshire), **Oakley** at Brewood (Staffordshire), **Haycutter** in Oxted (Surrey) and **Falcon** at Warmington (Warwickshire). For their vast collection of more than 400 gins, the **Cholmondeley Arms** in Cholmondeley is our *Gin Pub of the Year 2021*.

The best pubs in town and country

Genuinely unspoilt and unchanging pubs run by dedicated landlords and landladies can be found all over Britain. Our Top Ten contenders are the **Blacksmiths Arms** in Broughton Mills (Cumbria), **White Lion** in Barthomley (Cheshire), **Flying Childers** at Stanton in Peak (Derbyshire), **Digby Tap** in Sherborne and **Square & Compass** at Worth Matravers (both in Dorset), **Three Horseshoes** in Warham (Norfolk), **Crown** in Churchill and **Halfway House** in Pitney (both in Somerset), **Kings Head** in Laxfield (Suffolk) and **Olde Mitre** in London. The **White Lion** at Barthomley is our *Unspoilt Pub of the Year 2021*.

A roaring log fire, appealing food and a genuinely warm welcome conjure up a perfect country pub and our Top Ten this year are the **White Horse** in Hedgerley and **Crown** at Little Missenden (both in Buckinghamshire), **Pheasant** in Burwardsley (Cheshire), **Rugglestone** in Widecombe (Devon), **Brace of Pheasants** in Plush (Dorset), **Royal Oak** in Fritham (Hampshire), **Hatchet** at Lower Chute and **Malet Arms** in Newton Tony (both Wiltshire), **Fleece** at Bretforton (Worcestershire) and **Harp** in Old Radnor (Wales). Part of a working farm and with proper traditional character in its bar rooms, the thatched, family-run **Royal Oak** in Fritham is *Country Pub of the Year 2021*.

If you are a stranger in a town or city, there's no better place to feel less alone than a friendly and cheerful pub. Our Top Ten Town Pubs are the **Old Harkers Arms** in Chester (Cheshire), **Lion** in Winchcombe (Gloucestershire), **Wykeham Arms** in Winchester (Hampshire), **Wharf** in Manchester (Lancashire), **Bank House** in King's Lynn (Norfolk), **Victoria** in Durham (Northumbria), **Lion & Pheasant** in Shrewsbury (Shropshire), **Old Green Tree** in Bath (Somerset), **Old Joint Stock** in Birmingham (Warwickshire) and **Olde Mitre** (London). In a fine town, the historic, friendly and gently civilised **Lion** in Winchcombe is *Town Pub of the Year 2021*.

For somewhere special to spend a few days in beautiful countryside or in a lovely old town, many people head for an inn with enjoyable food, a convivial bar and sumptuous bedrooms. Our Top Ten Inns are the **Drunken Duck** near Hawkshead (Cumbria), **Rock** in Haytor Vale (Devon), **New Inn** in Cerne Abbas (Dorset), **Kings Head** in Bledington (Gloucestershire), **Wellington Arms** at Baughurst (Hampshire), **Inn at Whitewell** in Whitewell (Lancashire), **Lord Crewe Arms** in Blanchland (Northumbria), **Cat** in West Hoathly (Sussex), **Blue Lion** in East Witton (Yorkshire) and **Red Lion** in East Chisenbury (Wiltshire). Dating from the 16th century, the very atmospheric **Kings Head** in Bledington is our *Inn of the Year 2021*.

Looking for value and taste

To produce good, interesting food at keen prices, rather than just cheap, standard fare, is not easy, but our Top Ten Value Pubs manage it. They are the **Drake Manor** in Buckland Monachorum (Devon), **Digby Tap** in Sherborne (Dorset), **Red Lion** in Preston (Hertfordshire), **Church Inn** at Uppermill (Lancashire), **Butcher & Beast** in Heighington (Lincolnshire), **Dipton Mill Inn** at Diptonmill (Northumbria), **Rose & Crown** in Oxford (Oxfordshire), **Queen**

Victoria at Priddy (Somerset), **Blue Boar** in Aldbourne (Wiltshire) and **Crown & Trumpet** in Broadway (Worcestershire). For their very popular food using their own pork and honey, **Drake Manor** in Buckland Monachorum is *Value Pub of the Year 2021*.

Exceptional food cooked by first-class chefs using the best local, seasonal produce can be found in these Top Ten Dining Pubs. They are the **Punch Bowl** at Crosthwaite (Cumbria), **Wellington Arms** in Baughurst (Hampshire), **Stagg** in Titley (Herefordshire), **Olive Branch** at Clipsham (Leicestershire & Rutland), **Martins Arms** in Colston Bassett (Nottinghamshire), **Swan** in Swinbrook (Oxfordshire), **Unruly Pig** at Bromeswell (Suffolk), **Red Lion** in East Chisenbury (Wiltshire), **Shibden Mill** in Halifax (Yorkshire) and **Bunch of Grapes** at Pontypridd (Wales). 'Inspired' and 'impeccable' are just two words used by our readers to describe the wonderful meals at the **Unruly Pig** at Bromeswell, which is our *Dining Pub of the Year 2021*.

The best of the very best

It's always exciting to discover brilliant pubs and our new entries this year are spread across Britain. Our Top Ten New Pubs are the **Pointer** in Brill (Buckinghamshire), **Three Hills** in Bartlow (Cambridgeshire), **Fox & Barrel** at Cotebrook (Cheshire), **Baiting House** at Upper Sapey (Herefordshire), **Five Bells** at Brabourne (Kent), **Kings Arms** at Great Stainton (Northumbria), **Swan** in Ascott-under-Wychwood and **Chequers** in Churchill (both in Oxfordshire), **Queens Arms** in Corton Denham (Somerset) and the **Boat** at Erbistock (Wales). Graham Price, co-owner of the Boat at Erbistock, is also the co-founder of Brunning & Price and knows a thing or two about excellent pubs. A lovely 17th-century golden-stone inn with top-notch attributes, the **Boat** at Erbistock is our *New Pub of the Year 2021*.

At the heart of every special pub, be it a simple tavern or stylish dining pub, are landlords and landladies that are the driving force behind these gems. This year's Top Ten Licensees are **Philip and Lauren Davison** from the Fox in Peasemore (Berkshire), **Alex Clarke** who owns both the Black Bull in Balsham and the Red Lion in Hinxton (Cambridgeshire), **John Vereker** of the Bell at Horndon-on-the-Hill (Essex), **Claire and Jim Alexander** of the Ebrington Arms in Ebrington (Gloucestershire), **Jeannette and Anthony Goodrich** of the Rose & Crown in Snettisham (Norfolk), **Paddy Groves** from Woods in Dulverton (Somerset), **Colin and Teresa Ombler** of the Bell in Welford-on-Avon (Warwickshire), **Nigel Stevens** of the Wyvill Arms in Constable Barton (Yorkshire), **Judith Fish** of the Applecross

Inn in Applecross (Scotland) and the **Key family** of the Nags Head in Usk (Wales). For long-term dedication and unwavering support and love for their pub, their staff and their community, **Jeannette and Anthony Goodrich** of the Rose & Crown in Snettisham (Norfolk) are *Licensees of the Year 2021*.

There are so many wonderful pubs in Britain that to pick the absolute best is not an easy task. But the ones that shine the brightest are the **Cock** at Hemingford Grey (Cambridgeshire), **Old Coastguard** in Mousehole (Cornwall), **Bell** at Horndon-on-the-Hill (Essex), **Kings Head** in Bledington (Gloucestershire), **Inn at Whitewell** at Whitewell (Lancashire), **Olive Branch** in Clipsham (Leicestershire & Rutland), **Rose & Crown** in Snettisham (Norfolk), **Rose & Crown** at Romaldkirk (Northumbria), **Woods** in Dulverton (Somerset) and **Durham Ox** in Crayke (Yorkshire). As every aspect of this pub is first class, the **Olive Branch** in Clipsham (Leicestershire & Rutland) is *Pub of the Year 2021*.

Top Ten Pubs 2021

(in county order)

Cock Hemingford Grey (Cambridgeshire)

Old Coastguard Mousehole (Cornwall)

Bell Horndon-on-the-Hill (Essex)

Kings Head Bledington (Gloucestershire)

Inn at Whitewell Whitewell (Lancashire)

Olive Branch Clipsham (Leicestershire & Rutland)

Rose & Crown Snettisham (Norfolk)

Rose & Crown Romaldkirk (Northumbria)

Woods Dulverton (Somerset)

Durham Ox Crayke (Yorkshire)

61 DEEP PALE ALE

drinkaware.co.uk for the facts

[UK'S BEST —GOLDEN— ALE 2019]

W19 WORLD BEER AWARDS UNITED KINGDOM WINNER

61 Metres. That's the depth of the well at the Brewery that gives this refreshing pale ale its name. The five American and Australian hops gives it its fresh, zesty aroma, whilst the tropical fruit and citrus notes make it extremely drinkable.

61 DEEP 3.8% ALC/VOL PALE ALE

MARSTON'S BREWERY

BURTON ON TRENT

61 DEEP PALE ALE

MARSTON'S BREWERY BURTON ON TRENT

EST. 1834

DE14

marstonsbrewery.co.uk

f 🅾 @marstonsbrewery

In the pub, my boy!

By **James Blunt**

I should like to be able to say that when Armageddon came, I was in the pub. But when, in 2020, a global pandemic hit and pub-goers across the land screamed 'lock in!', some spod in government misheard and ordered a lockdown instead. And so, fundamentally, the greatest opportunity of our lifetime – the chance, in the future, to be able to answer a grandchild's question, 'Grandfather, where were you during the Great Pandemic of 2020?' with the answer, 'In the pub, my boy' – has been taken from us.

Instead, forced closure was thrust upon us, and pub owners questioned why they'd ever bothered with insurance in the first place if the one exception in the small print is always the thing that's just happened. It was the same for music touring. I had comprehensive coverage, with one exception – communicable diseases. How did they know!?

At the **Fox & Pheasant**, my pub in Chelsea, we used the time to do things you don't usually get a chance to do in a business that runs seven days a week, 365 days a year: clean, purify and perfect. Our chefs dreamt up exciting new menus, and our front of house staff polished the dartboard. We made urinals look like crime scenes. But we also learnt something deeper and more important – that we were missed and yearned for, and when our doors opened again, people were happy. Because pubs are the greatest indicators that not just existence and survival, but *life* had returned.

When London, in its 'modern' form, was created, the first buildings to go up weren't nail salons or fried chicken takeaways – they were pubs, to which workers would retire each evening to be sated and fed, while the rest of the street was being built. Of the homes and houses around the Fox & Pheasant, the first to be built was the Fox & Pheasant itself. At more than 170 years old, it has seen war, disease and depressions come and go, but it has endured. For we are social beasts, who thrive on human interaction. And while I understand that pubs are the antithesis of 'social distancing',

each year much have its catchphrase. 2021's catchphrase will be different, and if we're lucky it will incorporate the word 'beer'. And even if it doesn't, I am still full of hope. Because out of hard times comes innovation and creativity. Someone might have used lockdown to invent something kinder than Twitter. Someone else might have painted something more profound than a Damien Hirst coloured dot, and someone out there, through accident or design, might just have used the pandemic to brew something fantastically, end-of-worldly, you're beautifully, delicious – and just in case they have, you know where I'll be…

James Blunt is an English singer, songwriter, musician, record producer and pub landlord. He rose to fame with his 2004 debut album *Back to Bedlam*, including the singles 'You're Beautiful' and 'Goodbye My Lover'. He bought the Fox & Pheasant in 2017, one of his favourite pubs in London, to save it from being converted into flats.

Fox & Pheasant 1 Billing Road, SW10 9UJ, www.thefoxandpheasant.com

My recipe for the Great British Pub

By **Candice Brown**

My parents ran pubs for 25 years, so I suppose they really do run in my blood. I'm used to all the variations that pub life has to offer: the different kinds of establishment, people from all walks of life, the beer and drinks – and of course, the food. Pub grub! For me, the best kind of food served in a pub is good old-fashioned comfort food. Simple classics, revisited and brought up to date. Straightforward food cooked perfectly will always win out over soulless and overcomplicated dishes. Food that evokes nostalgic memories, leaves you feeling warm, contented and wanting seconds.

You can think of a pub as somewhere for a pint and a packet of scampi fries (and I'm in no way adverse to that kind of pub experience), but nowadays we're lucky enough to have an abundance of beautiful, independently minded pubs serving an array of real ales and craft beers, in sumptuous yet cosy surroundings, and delivering delicious, high-quality food.

This for me is the epitome of a Great British Pub. Food that is well thought out, sourced as close to home as possible to support local and small businesses, and making the best of the seasonal produce the UK is lucky enough to have. Winter gives us hand-raised pies filled with melt-in-the-mouth beef cooked in ale and served with creamy mash and gravy. Spring offers lamb dishes of all kinds, locally grown asparagus and vegetables made into light yet satisfying soups. Summer provides stunning fruits and berries, woven into delicious puddings and cakes. This harvest is something I look forward to each year, whether it's for a simple victoria sponge with strawberries and fresh cream or for making jam to be used at a later date. Not to mention fresh seafood: crab at its sweetest and simply grilled salmon. Autumn is my favourite season for food;

as the nights grow darker and cooler, the produce reflects this. Rich game, apples and blackberries picked fresh from the tree or bush and put straight into crumbles and pies.

Running my own pub

In 2018, my brother Ben and I took over the **Green Man** pub in Eversholt, Buckinghamshire. Having my own pub has given me the opportunity to put my love for (and memories of) the Great British Pub into a place I'm truly proud of. We've turned a small village pub into a thriving centre for the community, decked out with antiques and cosy chesterfields. We serve local ales, wines to suit all tastes and have the pickings from our own fruit trees and bramble bushes to include on our menu. Our food is simple, comforting and big. Desserts cause arguments and nearly everyone has a second helping. Our pub is the sort of pub I'd like to go to! A place where you start with a quick drink and a little bit of lunch, but end up settling down in front of the fire, drinking red wine and staying for dinner, with the promise of returning sooner rather than later.

Born in North London, **Candice Brown** grew up in the pubs that her parents ran. Taught to bake by her beloved Nan, she won *The Great British Bake Off* TV series in 2016 and has since become a regular columnist for the *Sunday Times'* food magazine *Dish*. In her spare time, you can find Candice walking her dogs Dennis, Albus and Sybil, in the stands at Tottenham, at the rugby with her dad or settling down to a great big Sunday roast with her family. Her book *Comfort: Delicious Bakes and Family Treats* is published by Ebury Press.

Favourite pub Swan Inn 2 Hare Lane, Claygate, Surrey KT10 9B, josepizarro.com

My dear friend José Pizarro, the Spanish chef and restaurateur, has recently opened this gastropub in Surrey and it really is a stunner. Beautiful, cosseting, the ambience is perfect and the food – well, it's to die for.

The haunted pubs of London

By **Christopher Winn**

You never know who you're going to meet in a pub, that is one of their joys. Although in London, possibly the most haunted capital city in the world, the chances are that many of the characters you might come across in some of the city's best loved pubs will have been propping up the bar for a lot longer than you can imagine.

For instance, should you find yourself standing next to Cedric at the **Grenadier** in Belgravia, then mind you don't burn your hand on his cigarette, as happened to a Scotland Yard detective a while back – a nasty surprise considering that smoking is no longer allowed in pubs and Cedric died 200 years ago.

The Grenadier was built in 1720 as an officers' mess for the 1st Royal Regiment of Foot Guards, later known as the Grenadier Guards, and while such luminaries as the Duke of Wellington and George IV were entertained by the officers upstairs, lower-ranking soldiers would drink and gamble in the cellar. One of these soldiers, Cedric, was caught cheating at a game of cards and was beaten to death by his comrades. Despite the fact that concerned drinkers have been trying to pay off his debts ever since by attaching dollar bills to the pub ceiling, Cedric haunts the Grenadier to this day, moving objects around overnight, moaning in the cellar, smoking at the bar and even being pictured with his face pressed up against the pub window.

Don't be shocked if you are ordered to stand and deliver at the **Spaniards Inn** on Hampstead Heath. The father of highwayman Dick Turpin was said to have been the landlord of this historic 16th-century tavern and Turpin used it as a hideout. He now clatters around upstairs while his horse, Black Bess, gallops around the car park. Downstairs, you may have your sleeve pulled by Black Dick, a regular who was run down and killed by a horse and cart outside the pub and has been trying to get served ever since.

When it comes to getting served, bar presence is important, although not perhaps the type of presence frequently seen hanging around in Victorian garb behind the bar down at the **Old Bull & Bush** in Hampstead. Originally a farmhouse built in the 17th century and granted a liquor licence in 1721, the pub was being restored in the 1980s when the builders discovered a skeleton bricked up in a wall, along with a selection of Victorian medical equipment. He was taken away and given a proper burial, but seems reluctant to leave his old haunt. One thought is that he could have been Jack the Ripper who got trapped while hiding in the basement along with his tools.

Jack the Ripper turns up again at the **Ten Bells** in Spitalfields. Not in person, but one of his victims, Mary Kelly, is alleged to have picked up clients here while another, Annie Chapman, is thought to have had a drink here before she was murdered in a nearby street. And then there was landlord George Roberts who was murdered with an axe, and reports of a baby found dead upstairs. It could be any of them who terrorises staff in the upper rooms or moves objects around in the bar and stirs up sudden blasts of icy wind, felt by bar staff and customers alike.

Chills and thrills

If, after all this talk of ghouls and ghosts, you could murder a pint, then try the **Rising Sun** near St Bartholomew's Hospital in Smithfield, the pub of choice for a gang of 19th-century body snatchers, who would drug well-oiled customers, kill them and then sell the bodies to the hospital for medical research. The ghostly snatchers are still at it, apparently, going after the barmaids living upstairs by pulling the duvets off their beds and running icy hands down their backs while they are showering.

Barmaids often seem to feature. A Spanish barmaid at the **Flask** in Highgate in the 18th century hanged herself in the pub cellar after an affair with the landlord. She now plays with the lights, smashes glasses and breathes down customers' necks, while her presence is said to send a chill running through you quicker than a cold lager.

Always fun, of course, is a lock-in, when the landlord invites favoured customers to a private drinking session after hours. One particular lock-in, however, proved less than enjoyable. This occurred at the **Viaduct Tavern** in Holborn, the last original Victorian gin palace in the City of London, built to celebrate the opening of the world's first flyover, Holborn Viaduct, in 1869. The building that was demolished to make way for the pub was a jail and some of the prison cells were left intact and are now used as cellars. Both staff and customers claim to have heard bangs and tortured screams coming up from down below, and one night in 1996 the manager went down to tidy up and was locked in when a ghostly hand slammed the cellar door shut behind him and the lights went out. He was trapped there for hours until his wife came down to see where he was and pushed the door open quite easily from the outside.

Last orders goes to the oldest pub in London's Mayfair, the **Coach & Horses**, an 18th-century coaching inn where some customers still arrive the old-fashioned way. Many a time patrons have looked on indulgently as a coach and four pulls up outside before realising with horror that the coachman is headless and the grinning passengers are grisly skulls. One way to drive people to drink.

As you can see, London certainly has no shortage of haunted pubs for those who like to chase down their tipple with a spirit or two. And if you start talking to a stranger in a

London pub, don't try to spin them a yarn because they will probably see right through you.

Grenadier 18 Wilton Row, SW1X 7NR,
  www.grenadierbelgravia.com
Spaniards Inn Spaniards Road, NW3 7JJ,
  www.thespaniardshampstead.co.uk
Old Bull & Bush North End Way, NW3 7HE,
  www.thebullandbush.co.uk
Ten Bells 84 Commercial Street, E1 6LY,
  www.tenbells.com
Rising Sun 38 Cloth Fair, EC1A 7JQ,
  risingsunbarbican.co.uk
Flask 77 Highgate West Hill, N6 6BU,
  www.theflaskhighgate.com
Viaduct Tavern 126 Newgate Street, EC1A 7AA,
  www.viaducttavern.co.uk
Coach & Horses 5 Hill Street, W1J 5LD,
  www.coachandhorsesmayfair.co.uk

Christopher Winn is the author of the bestselling I Never Knew That book series, which began with *I Never Knew That About England* and was followed by volumes on Scotland, Ireland, Wales, London, the River Thames and many more. The latest in the series is *I Never Knew That About Coastal England* (Ebury Press, 2019).

Favourite pub Refectory Milford, Surrey GU8 5HJ,
www.brunningandprice.co.uk/refectory

Drinking when you're not drinking

By **Ben Branson**

G rowing up in the Lincolnshire countryside, you could be sure of two things: the village pub was the rock-steady feature and social centre for all the gossip and goings-on of the community; and, first published a year before I was born in 1982, there was always a copy of *The Good Pub Guide* at home. I think pubs are brilliant, so what a privilege – and perhaps a sign of the times – for the founder of a non-alcoholic drinks company to help introduce this year's edition of the Guide!

The role of the public house has shifted significantly over the last 30 years, with much of the penny-counting and bar-propping updated to meet the needs of the modern

punter. These days, we want good coffee, more veggie options, we have allergies, children in tow, we like craft beer with pizza, we'll start with a cocktail and we want to know where the food comes from. We want better, we're willing to pay for it – and publicans have answered our call.

Historically, if you weren't drinking alcohol, for whatever reason, you drew the shortest, saddest straw. 'Um, I don't know… oh, I'll just have a lime and soda' (we've all been there). Those apologetic words, uttered quietly, were met with either the refrain 'Are you feeling OK?' or a despondent glance that screamed: poor you! But those days of fluorescent lime-coloured pints are over, and a new dawn of proper non-alcoholic drinks has arrived. Pubs up and down the country now offer some of the best options if you're not drinking. The driver isn't forgotten, the pregnant lady not ignored and, instead of a compromise or an apology, people are now openly ordering a Seedlip & Tonic or a Nanny State (BrewDog's alcohol-free beer) or an Ӕcorn Spritz (Ӕcorn Bitter plus sparkling water).

I'd go as far as to say that pubs now are what pubs were always destined to be. Diverse, inclusive, multifaceted and more social than they ever were before – and that's a great thing. Congratulations to all those featured in this book, thank you for all your hard work.

Ben Branson is the founder of Seedlip (seedlipdrinks.com), producer of the world's first distilled non-alcoholic spirits. His mission is twofold: solve the dilemma of 'what to drink when you're not drinking'® and continue his family's 300 years of farming heritage.

Favourite pub Coach West Street, Marlow, Buckinghamshire SL7 2LS, www.thecoachmarlow.co.uk

Located round the corner from where I developed Seedlip in my kitchen, this was one of the first pubs that Seedlip was served in. Try the triple-cooked chips with béarnaise sauce and a Seedlip & Tonic!

What is a good pub?

We hear about possible new entries for this Guide from our many thousands of correspondents who keep us in touch with pubs they visit – by post, by email at feedback@goodguides.com or via our website, www.thegoodpubguide.co.uk. These might be places they visit regularly (and it's their continued approval that reassures us about keeping a pub as a full entry for another year) or pubs they have discovered on their travels and that perhaps we know nothing about. And it's from these new discoveries that we make up a shortlist, to be considered for possible inclusion as new Main Entries.

What marks a pub out for special attention could be an out of the ordinary choice of drinks – a wide range of real ales (perhaps even brewed by the pub), several hundred whiskies, a remarkable wine list, interesting spirits from small distillers or proper farm ciders and perries. It could be delicious food (often outclassing many restaurants in the area) or even remarkable value meals. Maybe as a place to stay it's pretty special, with lovely bedrooms and obliging service. Or the building itself might be stunning (from golden-stone Georgian houses to part of centuries-old monasteries or extravagant Victorian gin palaces) or in a stunning setting, amid beautiful countryside or situated by water.

Above all, what makes a good pub is its atmosphere. You should feel at home and genuinely welcomed by the landlord or landlady – it's their influence that can make or break a pub. It follows from this that a lot of ordinary local pubs, perfectly good in their own right, don't earn a place in the Guide. What makes them attractive to their regulars could make strangers feel a bit left out.

Another point is that there's not necessarily any link between charm and luxury. A basic unspoilt tavern may be worth travelling miles for, while a too smartly refurbished dining pub may not be worth crossing the street for.

The pubs featured as Main Entries do pay a fee, which helps to cover the Guide's production costs. But no pub can gain an entry simply by paying this fee. Only pubs that have been inspected anonymously, and approved by us, are invited to join.

Using the Guide

The Counties

England has been split alphabetically into counties. Each chapter starts by picking out the pubs that are currently doing best in the area, or are specially attractive for one reason or another.

The county boundaries we use are those for the administrative counties (not the old traditional counties, which were changed back in 1976). We have left the new unitary authorities within the counties that they formed part of until their creation in the most recent local government reorganisation. Metropolitan areas have been included in the counties around them – for example, Merseyside in Lancashire. And occasionally we have grouped counties together – for example, Rutland with Leicestershire, and Durham with Northumberland to make Northumbria. If in doubt, check the Contents pages.

Scotland, Wales and London have each been covered in single chapters. This year we've changed the county and area names in Wales, to bring them into line with modern nomenclature. Pubs are listed alphabetically (except in London, which is split into Central, East, North, South, West and Outer), under the name of the town or village where they are. If the village is so small that you might not find it on a road map, we've listed it under the name of the nearest sizeable village or town. The maps use the same town and village names, and additionally include a few big cities that don't have any listed pubs – for orientation.

We list pubs in their true county, not their postal county. Just once or twice, when the village itself is in one county but the pub is just over the border in the next-door county, we have used the village county, not the pub one.

Star ★

Really outstanding pubs are awarded a star, and in one case two: these are the aristocrats among pubs. The stars do NOT signify extra luxury or specially good food – in fact, some of the pubs that appeal most distinctively and strongly are decidedly basic in terms of food and surroundings. The detailed description of each pub shows what its particular appeal is, and this is what the stars refer to.

Food Award 🍽

Pubs where food is really outstanding.

Stay Award 🛏

Pubs that are good as places to stay at (obviously, you can't expect the same level of luxury at £60 a head as you'd get for £100 a head). Pubs with bedrooms are marked on the maps as a square.

Wine Award ♀

Pubs with particularly enjoyable wines by the glass – and/or carafe – often an extensive and interesting range.

Beer Award ◀

Pubs where the quality of the beer is quite exceptional, or pubs that keep a particularly interesting range of beers in good condition.

Value Award £

This distinguishes pubs that offer really good value food. In all the award-winning pubs, you will find an interesting choice of main course options for around £12.

Also Worth a Visit

The Also Worth a Visit section at the end of each county chapter includes brief descriptions of pubs that we feel are worthy of inclusion – many of them, indeed, as good in their way as the featured pubs (these are picked out by a star). Many of these are recommended by our reader-reporters. The descriptions of these other pubs, written by us, usually reflect the experience of several different people.

The pubs in Also Worth a Visit may become featured entries in future editions. So do please help us know which are hot prospects for our inspection programme (and which are not!), by reporting on them. There are report forms at the back of the Guide, or you can email us at feedback@goodguides.com, or write to us at:

Freepost THE GOOD PUB GUIDE, Random House Publishing, 20 Vauxhall Bridge Road, London SW1V 2SA.

Locating Pubs

We include a postcode for every pub. Pubs outside London are given a British Grid four-figure map reference. Where a pub is exceptionally difficult to find, we include a six-figure reference in the directions. The Map number (Main Entries only) refers to the maps at the back of the Guide.

Motorway Pubs

If a pub is within four or five miles of a motorway junction, we give special directions for finding it from the motorway. These are listed at the end of the book, motorway by motorway.

Prices and Other Factual Details

The Guide went to press in late autumn of 2020, after each pub was sent a checking sheet to get up-to-date food, drink and bedroom prices and other factual information. By the summer of 2021 prices are bound to have increased, but if you find a significantly different price please let us know.

Breweries or independent chains to which pubs are 'tied' are named at the beginning of the italic-print rubric after each Main Entry. That generally means the pub has to get most if not all its drinks from that brewery or chain. If the brewery is not an independent one but just part of a combine, we name the combine in brackets. When the pub is tied, we have spelled out whether the landlord or landlady is a tenant, has the pub on a lease, or is a manager. Tenants and leaseholders of breweries generally have considerably greater freedom to do things their own way, and in particular are allowed to buy drinks including a beer from sources other than their tied brewery.

Free houses are pubs not tied to a brewery. In theory they can shop around, but in practice many free houses have loans from the big brewers, on terms that bind them to sell those breweries' beers. So don't be too surprised to find that so-called free houses may be stocking a range of beers restricted to those from a single brewery.

Real ale is used by us to mean beer that has been maturing naturally in its cask. We do not count as real ale beer that has been pasteurised or filtered to remove its natural yeasts.

Other drinks. As well as wine lists, we've also looked out particularly for pubs doing enterprising non-alcoholic drinks (including good tea or coffee), interesting spirits (especially gins and malt whiskies), country wines, freshly squeezed juices and good farm ciders.

Bar food usually refers to what is sold in the bar, though this is often the same food as served in a separate restaurant. If we know that a pub serves sandwiches, we say so – if you don't see them mentioned, assume you can't get them. Food listed is an example of the sort of thing you'd find served in the bar on a normal day.

Children. If we don't mention children at all, assume that they are not welcome. All but one or two pubs allow children in their garden if they have one. 'Children welcome' means the pub has told us that it lets them in with no special restrictions. In other cases, we report exactly what arrangements pubs say they make for children. However, we have to note that sometimes pubs make restrictions that they haven't told us about (children allowed only if eating, for example). If you find this, please let us know, so that we can clarify with the pub concerned for the next edition.

The absence of any reference to children in an Also Worth a Visit entry means we don't know either way. Children are allowed into some part of most pubs in this Guide (there is no legal restriction on the movement of children over 14 in any pub). Children under 16 cannot have alcoholic drinks. Children aged 16 and 17 can drink beer, wine or cider with a meal if it is bought by an adult and they are accompanied by an adult.

Dogs. If Main Entry licensees have told us they allow dogs in their bar, restaurant or bedrooms, we say so; absence of reference to dogs means dogs are not welcome. If you take a dog into a pub, you should have it on a lead. We also mention in the text any pub dogs or cats (or indeed other animals) that we know about.

Parking. If we know there is a problem with parking, we say so; otherwise assume there is a car park.

Credit cards. The vast majority of pubs these days accept debit and credit cards; we say if a pub does not accept them.

Telephone numbers are given for all pubs if possible.

Wi-fi. We don't mention free wi-fi, because it's standard in most pubs these days – though not universal. And don't expect a good signal in remote rural locations.

Opening hours are for summer; we say if we know of differences in winter, or on particular days of the week. In rural areas, many pubs may open rather later and close earlier than their details show. Pubs are allowed to stay open all day if licensed to do so.

However, outside cities many pubs in England and Wales close during the afternoon. We'd be grateful to hear of any differences from the hours we quote.

Bedroom prices can vary considerably, and it is always worth asking for special deals. The price we give, for guidance only, is for a standard double room in high season. This will usually include a full English breakfast (if available), VAT and any automatic service charge.

Meal times. Bar food is commonly served between the hours of 12-2 and 7-9, at least from Monday to Saturday. We spell out the times if they are significantly different. To be sure of a table it's best to book before you go. Sunday hours vary considerably from pub to pub, so it's advisable to check before you leave.

Disabled access. It is often hard to get a reliable picture of how easy access is for visitors with disabilities, so we depend on readers' direct experience. If you can help with such information, we would be very grateful for your reports.

Website, iPhone and iPad

You can read and search *The Good Pub Guide* via our website (www.thegoodpubguide.co.uk), which includes every pub in this Guide. You can also write reviews and let us know about undiscovered gems. The Guide is also available as an app for your iPhone or iPad and as an eBook for your Kindle.

Changes during the year – please tell us

Changes are inevitable during the course of the year. Licensees change, and so do their policies. We hope that you will find everything just as we say, but if not please let us know. You can email us at feedback@goodguides.com. The General Data Protection Regulation (GPDR) requires that we have your consent to use your name in future editions of the Guide; the easiest way to do this is to use one of the report forms at the back of the book.

Many thanks to all the writers on *The Good Pub Guide 2021*
Ismay Atkins, Jack Barker, Claire Dodd, Jan Fuscoe, Ronnie Haydon, Kirsten Henton, Ruth Jarvis, Yasemen Kaner-White, Lucy Margetts, Bridget McGrouther, Laurence Mitchell, Mari Nicholson, Juliet Rix, Louise Simpson, Luke Waterson, Celia Welfare, Ben West, Jerusha West, Antonia Windsor, Joel Wyllie and Yolanda Zappaterra.

Editors' acknowledgements

We could not produce the Guide without the huge help we have from the many thousands of readers who report to us on the pubs they visit, often in great detail. Particular thanks to these greatly valued correspondents: Chris and Angela Buckell, John Pritchard, Tony and Wendy Hobden, Susan and John Douglas, Clive and Fran Dutson, Gerry and Rosemary Dobson, Liz Bell, Tracey and Stephen Groves, Ian Herdman, Neil and Angela Huxter, Simon King, Steve Whalley, Michael Butler, Ann and Colin Hunt, Richard Tilbrook, Tony Scott, Richard and Penny Gibbs, Mrs Margo Finlay, Jörg Kasprowski, Edward Mirzoeff, Guy Vowles, Paul Humphreys, David Lamb, Revd R P Tickle, Mike and Mary Carter, Michael Doswell, R K Phillips, Simon Collett-Jones, Peter Meister, Tony and Jill Radnor, Dave Braisted, Sara Fulton and Roger Baker, Dr W I C Clark, Dr and Mrs A K Clarke, Derek and Sylvia Stephenson, Pete and Sarah, John Wooll, Christopher and Elise Way, GSB, Ian Malone, Steve and Claire Harvey, Mike and Eleanor Anderson, John Beeken, Stephen Funnell, M G Hart, David Jackman, Miss B D Picton, Mr and Mrs Richard Osborne, Sheila Topham, Lesley Broadbent, Gordon and Margaret Ormondroyd, Nigel and Jean Eames, Kevin Chesson, Ian Phillips, Christian Mole, Giles and Annie Francis, Robert Wivell, John Coatsworth, Paul Griffiths, Hugh Roberts, Roger and Anne Newbury, John Gibbon, Katharine Cowherd, Audrey Young, Minda and Stanley Alexander, Richard Kennell, R L Borthwick, Derek Stafford, Michael Sargent, I D Barnett, Brian and Anna Marsden, Anthony Bradbury, Gail Plews, David and Judy Robison, MJ, Mark Sheard, Lucien Perring, William and Ann Reid, Martin and Anne Muers, Hunter and Christine Wright, Richard Tingle, Laura Bennett, Mr and Mrs P R Thomas, Dr Simon Barley, David Fowler, David Barras, Jayne Francis, M A Borthwick, M and GR, Christopher Buckmaster, Miss A E Dare, Roy and Gill Payne, Mike and Margaret Banks, W K Wood, John and Hilary Murphy, Ian Cuttle, Margaret and Peter Staples, Guy Smith, Caroline Warwick, Jonathon Caswell, Liz Nicholas, Stuart Norris, Bernice Walsh, Paul Desborough, Penny Shinfield, Sharon Butler, Kim Ryan Skuse, Ammie Thorne, Tim Buckley, Steven Haworth, Colin Gooch, Christopher Warren, Colin and Angela Boocock, Paul Baxter, S G N Bennett, Helene Grygar, David and Stella Martin, Andrew Shaw, Fran Panrucker, Tim and Wendy Lloyd, R&H A-V, Peter Hesketh-Roberts, Hugh Duncan, Nick Hales, Paul Westwood, Malcolm and Pauline Pellatt, Janet and Peter Race, Dr and Mrs J D Abell, Iceman, Peter and Anne Hollindale, Phil and Anne Nash, Adam Bellinger, David and Gill Carrington, Baz Manning, Daniel Nixon, Stephen Shepherd, Robert Lester, Richard and Judy Winn, Gene and Kitty Rankin, MC, Steve Harvey, Mark O'Sullivan, John Kendall, Dr Martin Owton, Chloe and Tim Hodge, B and F A Hannam, John Coatsworth, Jon Neighbour, Demelza Hill, Colin McLachlan, Stephen Saunders, James Corbett, Frosty, Diana and Richard Gibbs, John Hunter Wright, David and Sally Frost, Carl Smith, Stevie Hart, PL, Brian and Margaret Merritt, Gordon and Barbara Illingworth, John Evans, Tom and Ruth Rees, Alan Cowell, Steve Thomas, Edward King, Andrew Bosi, Neil Hammacott, Mrs P R Sykes, Mick and Moira Brummell, Don Humphries, John Harvey, John and Sharon Hancock, Vinnie Grewell, Nick Higgins, Cherry Dainty, Martin Hughes, Dr D J & Mrs S C Walker, Eddie Edwards, Liz and Martin Eldon, Christopher Mobbs, Rod and Chris Pring, Philip Kavanagh, M G Trotter, Mrs P Sumner, Jamie and Sue May, S Holder, Pat and Tony Martin, Max Simons, Roy Shutz, Ian Wilson, Alistair Forsyth, Peter Cole, Clive Adams, Gillian Longman, Julian Richardson, Joe Oakley, Jo Kavaney, Gordon Parry, Susan Robinson, Mrs P Sumner, David Dore, Roy and Lindsey Fentiman, Robert Watt, Mrs J Ekins-Daukes, Mrs Edna Jones, D W Stokes, Franklyn Roberts, Barry Collett, Angela and Steve Heard, R J Herd, David Longhurst, Mr and Mrs J Watkins, E A Eaves, Richard Cole, Patric Curwen, Tony Smaithe, Alan Johnson.

Many thanks to Maria Byrne, Adam Clilverd, Joelle Dickens, Michelle Luk Hang, Keesha Blundell and Hayley Reed at The Book Service for their cheerful dedication. Also thanks to Parastou Khiaban from Penguin Random House and Rob and Mel Harrison from Thinking Fox, who together built and look after our lovely new database. Finally, heartfelt thanks to Fiona Stapley, Fiona Wright and Patrick Stapley for their invaluable help and encouragement throughout.

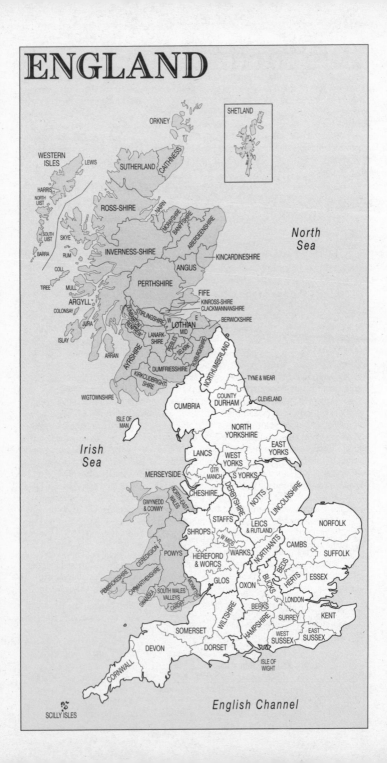

Bedfordshire

 IRELAND   TL1341 MAP 5

Black Horse 🍽 🛏 🍷

(01462) 811398 – www.blackhorseireland.com

Off A600 Shefford–Bedford; SG17 5QL

●●●

Bedfordshire Dining Pub of the Year

Contemporary décor in old building, excellent food, good wine list and lovely garden with attractive terraces; bedrooms

This enticing 17th-c pub mixes the old with the new, with its modern, welcoming décor and contemporary, imaginative cuisine and first class choice of drinks. The relaxing bar has inglenook fireplaces, beams in low ceilings and timbering, with ales such as Adnams Southwold, Sharps Doom Bar and Woodfordes Wherry on handpump, 27 wines by the glass from a well described list, a dozen malt whiskies, Weston's cider and good coffee from the long green-slate bar counter. There are leather armchairs and comfortable wall seats, a mix of elegant wooden and high-backed leather dining chairs around attractive tables on polished oak boards or sandstone flooring, original artwork and fresh flowers; background music. French windows open from the restaurant on to various terraces with individual furnishings and pretty flowering pots and beds. The chalet-style bedrooms (just across a courtyard in a separate building) are comfortable and well equipped; continental breakfasts are included and taken in your room. The Birch at Woburn is under the same ownership.

🍽 Delicious, seasonal food includes sandwiches, sharing boards, steamed bao bun with crispy pork belly, hoisin sauce, stir-fried vegetables, pickled mooli and sriracha mayonnaise, Cromer crab thermidor and crab apple salad, charred aubergine with romesco sauce, almonds, sherry and crispy buckwheat salad, steak burger with toppings and french fries, baked sea bass fillet with spiced Thai sauce, wild rice and kohlrabi salad, local venison steak with celeriac purée, pickled carrots, crispy shallots and blackberry jus, and puddings such as banana sticky toffee pudding with salted caramel sauce and banana ice-cream and a chef's soufflé of the day. *Benchmark main dish: lager-battered fish and chips £14.95. Two-course evening meal £24.95.*

Free house ~ Licensee Darren Campbell ~ Real ale ~ Open 12-3, 6-11; 12-11 Sat; 12-5 Sun ~ Bar food 12-2.30, 6-9.30; 12-5 Sun ~ Restaurant ~ Children welcome ~ Bedrooms £95

Post Office address codings confusingly give the impression that some pubs are in Bedfordshire, when they're really in Buckinghamshire or Cambridgeshire (which is where we list them).

WOBURN
SP9433 MAP 4

Birch 🏮 ❦ ❦

(01525) 290295 – www.birchwoburn.com

3.5 miles from M1 junction 13; follow Woburn signs via A507 and A4012, right in village then A5130 (Newport Road); MK17 9HX

Well run dining establishment with focus on imaginative food and drinks, plus attentive service

Bright, bustling and modern, this very pleasant hostelry boasts several individually and elegantly furnished linked rooms with contemporary décor and furnishings. The upper dining area has high-backed leather or wooden dining chairs around tables on stripped and polished floorboards, while the lower part occupies a light and airy conservatory with a pitched glazed roof, ceramic floor tiles, light coloured furnishings, original artwork and fresh flowers. The bustling bar is similarly furnished and has a few high bar stools against the sleek, smart counter where they serve beers such as Adnams Ghost Ship and St Austell Tribute on handpump, 24 good wines by the glass, a dozen malt whiskies and quite a few teas and coffees; background music. There are tables out on a sheltered deck, and in summer the front of the pub has masses of flowering hanging baskets and tubs. This is sister pub to the Black Horse at Ireland.

 Appealing food includes lunchtime baguettes, goats cheese arancini with beetroot purée and rocket leaves, smoked paprika whitebait with herb aioli and crispy potato julienne, pork and apple scotch egg, pan-fried chicken breast with chorizo, asparagus and gnocchi in tarragon cream, grilled swordfish steak with white wine, prawn and cream sauce, Thai-spiced red pepper and butternut squash risotto with pine nuts, braised rolled pork belly with mash potato, hispi cabbage and cider, bacon and mustard cream, and puddings such as Italian meringue lemon tart and raspberry and white chocolate cheesecake. *Benchmark main dish: beer-battered fillet of fish with chunky chips £15.95. Two-course evening meal £25.00.*

Free house ~ Licensee Mark Campbell ~ Real ale ~ Open 12-3, 6-11; 12-5 Sun ~ Bar food 12-2.30, 6-9.30; 12-5 Sun ~ Restaurant ~ Children welcome ~ Pianist or singer some Fri evenings

WOOTTON
TL0046 MAP 4

Legstraps

(01234) 854112 – www.thelegstraps.co.uk

Keeley Lane; MK43 9HR

Bustling village pub with a nice range of food from open kitchen, local ales and wines by the glass

A highlight here is the top quality food – though there are plenty of drinkers too and the kind, efficient staff welcome everyone. The low-ceilinged bar has an elegant feel with contemporary and comfortable upholstered chairs around all sizes of table, big flagstones, a woodburning stove in a brick fireplace with a leather sofa and box wall seats to either side, and leather-topped stools against the pale planked counter. They have two guest ales changing each week on handpump, good wines by the glass and 27 gins; background music, TV and board games. The dining rooms have bold paintwork, similar furnishings to the bar, polished bare boards and flower prints on one end wall with butterflies wallpaper on another.

🍴 From the open kitchen, the well thought-of modern food includes Devon white crab with avocado purée, pork and chorizo scotch egg with salad, BBQ chicken croquettes, roasted chicken supreme with sweet potato rösti, pak choi and romanesco sauce, rib-eye steak and triple-cooked chips with watercress peppercorn sauce, pork tenderloin with dijon dill cream sauce, fondant potato and crackling, sweet potato and chickpea curry with raita and onion bhaji, and puddings such as chocolate mousse and stout sticky toffee pudding with vanilla ice-cream. *Benchmark main dish: beer-battered Cornish haddock and skinny fries £15.00. Two-course evening meal £22.50.*

Free house ~ Licensee Laura Osbourne ~ Real ale ~ Open 3-7pm Mon for drinks only; 12-11; 12-8 Sun ~ Bar food 12-9; 12-5 Sun ~ Restaurant ~ Children welcome ~ Dogs allowed in bar

Also Worth a Visit in Bedfordshire

Besides the fully inspected pubs, you might like to try these pubs that have been recommended to us and described by readers. Do tell us what you think of them: feedback@goodguides.com

AMPTHILL   TL0337
Albion (01525) 634857
Dunstable Street; MK45 2JT Drinkers' pub with up to 12 well kept ales including local B&T and Everards, real ciders and a perry, no food apart from bar snacks; occasional live music; dogs welcome, paved beer garden, open all day.

BEDFORD   TL0549
Castle (01234) 353295
Newnham Street; MK40 3JR Modernised 19th-c two-bar pub; Courage Directors, Eagle IPA, Youngs and guests, generous helpings of enjoyable good value pubby food from baguettes up, some themed evenings, friendly helpful service; Mon open mike night; children welcome, no dogs inside at meal times, courtyard garden, five bedrooms, open all day, no evening food Sat-Mon.

BEDFORD   TL0550
★ **Park** (01234) 273929
Corner of Kimbolton Road (B660) and Park Avenue, out past Bedford Hospital; MK40 2PA Recently refurbished Edwardian local on outskirts of town with bar with heavy beams and leaded lights in big windows, an airy conservatory, garden room and softly lit dining areas; sheltered brick-paved terrace. Bombardier, Eagle IPA and guests, and excellent choice of wines by the glass; background music. Children welcome in bar and restaurant areas, dogs in bar. Imaginative, varied predominantly British menu. Open all day (midnight Thurs-Sat), food all day Fri/Sat.

BEDFORD   TL0450
Wellington Arms (01234) 308033
Wellington Street; MK40 2JX Friendly no-frills backstreet local; a dozen well kept ales including Adnams, Bass, B&T and guests real cider and occasional guest perries, and a good range of continental beers; wooden tables and chairs on bare boards, lots of breweriana; no food, live music about once a month; dogs allowed; seats in backyard, open all day from midday, and perhaps at its best in the evening.

BIDDENHAM   TL0249
Three Tuns (01234) 354847
Off A428; MK40 4BD Refurbished part-thatched village dining pub with bar, lounge and restaurant extension; good food (not Sun evening, Tues) from traditional favourites up, well kept Three Tuns and Greene King ales and plenty of wines by the glass, friendly service; children welcome, spacious garden with picnic-sets, more contemporary furniture on terrace and decked area, open all day.

BLETSOE   TL0157
Falcon (01234) 781222
Rushden Road (A6 N of Bedford); MK44 1QN 17th-c building with comfortable opened-up bar; low beams and joists, seating from cushioned wall/window seats to high-backed settles, woodburner in double-aspect fireplace, snug with sofas and old pews, panelled dining room, popular food from pub standards and burgers up (plenty of gluten-free choices), selection of cask ales from Wells and Youngs, decent choice of wines by the glass; background music; children welcome, dogs in bar, decked and paved terrace in lovely big garden down to the Great Ouse, open (and food) all day.

BOLNHURST   TL0858
★ **Plough** (01234) 376274
Kimbolton Road; MK44 2EX Stylishly converted Tudor building with thriving atmosphere, charming professional staff and top notch cooking from chef-landlord (must book), Adnams and a couple of interesting guests, more than 15 wines by the glass from good carefully annotated wine list (including organic vintages and plenty of pudding wines), airy dining extension, log fires; children welcome, dogs in bar, attractive tree-shaded garden with decking overlooking pond, remains of old moat, closed Mon and maybe for two weeks after Christmas.

BROOM   TL1743
Cock (01767) 314411
*High Street; from A1 opposite
Biggleswade turn-off, follow 'Old Warden
3, Aerodrome 2' signpost, first left signed
Broom; SG18 9NA* Friendly and unspoilt
19th-c village-green pub; four changing
ales tapped from casks by cellar steps off
central corridor (no counter), proper cider
and enjoyable traditional home-made food,
including themed nights and meal deals,
original latch doors linking one quietly cosy
little room to the next (four in all), low
ceilings, stripped panelling, farmhouse tables
and chairs on old tiles, open fires, games
room with table skittles, bar billiards and
darts; children and dogs welcome, picnic-sets
on terrace by back lawn, camping field, open
all day, no food Sun evening.

CARDINGTON   TL0847
Kings Arms · (01234) 838533
*The Green; off A603 E of Bedford;
MK44 3SP* Spacious Mitchells & Butlers
village dining pub with refurbished linked
areas; extensive choice of enjoyable food
from light lunches up including a vegan
menu, meal deal Tues and Weds evenings,
Sharps Doom Bar and a couple of guests
from well stocked bar, helpful friendly
service; background music; children and
dogs (in bar) welcome, disabled facilities,
modern tables and chairs on front terrace,
picnic-sets under willows to the side, open
(and food) all day.

CLOPHILL   TL0838
Stone Jug (01525) 860526
*N on A6 from A507 roundabout, after
200 metres, second turn on right into
backstreet; MK45 4BY* Secluded old stone-
built local (originally three cottages), cosy
and welcoming with traditional old-fashioned
atmosphere, well kept Otter, St Austell and
three local guests, popular good value pubby
lunchtime food (not Sun, Mon), various
rooms around L-shaped bar, darts in small
games extension; background music; children
and dogs welcome, roadside picnic-sets
and pretty little back terrace, open all day
Fri-Sun, closed Mon lunchtime.

FLITTON   TL0535
White Hart (01525) 862022
Village signed off A507; MK45 5EJ
Friendly family-managed village dining
pub; front bar with dark leather tub chairs
around low tables, contemporary leather and
chrome seats at pedestal tables, steps down
to good-sized, simply furnished back dining
area with dark wooden floorboards, a real
ale or two such as local B&T, good popular
food (booking advised) including afternoon
teas; children and dogs (in bar) welcome,
neatly kept garden with teak furniture on tree-
shaded terrace, 13th-c church next door, open
all weekends (Sun till 8pm), closed Mon.

GREAT BARFORD   TL1351
Anchor (01234) 870364
High Street; off A421; MK44 3LF
Open-plan pub by medieval arched bridge
and church; good sensibly priced food from
snacks up, Eagle IPA, Youngs Bitter and
guests kept well, friendly staff, river views
from main bar, back restaurant where
children allowed; background music; picnic-
sets in front looking across to Great Ouse,
open (and food) all day weekends.

HARLINGTON   TL0330
Carpenters Arms (01525) 872384
*Sundon Road: a mile from M1 junction
12; A5120, first right to Harlington,
right in village; LU5 6LS* Old low-beamed
village local; well kept ales including Greene
King IPA and Woodfordes Wherry as regulars
plus a couple of guests; generous helpings
of enjoyable home-cooked food (not Sun
evening), good friendly service, bare boards
or carpeted floors, log fires; dogs welcome
and children until 9pm, open all day Fri-Sun.

HENLOW   TL1738
Crown (01462) 812433
High Street; SG16 6BS Modernised
beamed dining pub with good choice of
popular food including children's menu, well
kept Caledonian Deuchars IPA, Courage
Directors and a guest, craft beers, several
wines by the glass, friendly helpful staff,
woodburners (one in inglenook); quiet
background music, daily newspapers; terrace
and small garden, five well appointed
bedrooms in converted stables, open (and
food) all day, breakfasts and Sat brunch for
non-residents.

HENLOW   TL1738
★ Engineers Arms (01462) 812284
*A6001 S of Biggleswade; High Street;
SG16 6AA* Traditional 19th-c village pub
with up to ten well kept changing ales and
eight proper ciders/perries, also bottled
international beers and good choice of wines/
gins, helpful knowledgeable staff, bar snacks;
comfortable carpeted front room with old
local photographs, various bric-a-brac and
nice open fire, smaller tiled inner area and
another carpeted one; beer/cider festivals,
poker, quiz and music nights, sports TVs; dogs
allowed in bar, plenty of outside seating, open
all day (till 1am Fri, Sat).

HENLOW   TL1738
Five Bells (01462) 811125
High Street; SG16 6AE Long flower-
decked pub with busy opened-up bar and
restaurant; enjoyable generously served
food from extensive reasonably priced menu
including bargain OAP weekday lunch, well
kept Greene King ales, guest beers and
decent range of wines, friendly helpful staff;
children welcome, garden with play area,
open all day, food all day Sat, till 7pm Sun.

HOUGHTON CONQUEST   TL0342
Chequers   (01525) 404853
B530 towards Ampthill; MK45 3JP
Refurbished roadside country dining pub
(Little Gems); enjoyable fairly pubby food
from pizzas and burgers up, three real ales
and plenty of wines by the glass, friendly
helpful service; children welcome, garden
with play area, open (and food) all day,
weekend brunch from 9am.

HOUGHTON CONQUEST   TL0441
Knife & Cleaver   (01234) 930789
*Between B530 (old A418) and A6, S of
Bedford; MK45 3LA* Updated and extended
17th-c village dining pub opposite church;
good variety of well liked food from separate
bar and restaurant menus, extensive choice
of wines by the glass including champagne;
Charles Wells IPA and a couple of guests;
friendly staff; children welcome, dogs allowed
in bar area only, nine chalet bedrooms
arranged around courtyard and garden, good
breakfast, free charging of electric cars for
guests, open all day from 7am Mon-Fri, 8am
Sat, Sun for breakfast.

HUSBORNE CRAWLEY   SP9635
White Horse   (01525) 280565
Mill Road, just off A507; MK43 0XE
Open-plan village pub arranged
around central servery; two real ales and
good reasonably priced home-made food
(vegetarians and special diets well catered
for), friendly attentive staff, beams, wood and
quarry-tiled floors, some stripped brickwork
and woodburner; children and dogs (in bar)
welcome, tables outside and lovely hanging
baskets, close to Woburn Safari Park, open
(and food) all day, till 9pm (6pm) Sun.

LITTLE GRANSDEN   TL2755
Chequers   (01767) 677348
Main Road; SG19 3DW Welcoming village
local in same family for over 60 years and
keeping its 1950s feel; simple bar with coal
fire, darts and framed historical information
about the pub, interesting range of own-
brewed Son of Sid ales, step down to cosy
snug with another fire and bench seats,
comfortable back lounge with fish tank, no
food apart from excellent fish and chips Fri
evening (must book); open all day Fri, Sat.

MILTON BRYAN   SP9730
Red Lion   (01525) 210044
*Toddington Road, off B528 S of Woburn;
MK17 9HS* Refurbished red-brick village
dining pub; Greene King ales and a guest,
several wines by the glass, cocktails and good
range of gins, well liked nicely presented food
from bar snacks and sharing boards up, Weds
steak night, Thurs burgers, good friendly
service, central bar with dining areas either
side, beams and open fire; children and dogs
welcome, pretty views from big garden, open
all day Sat, till 7pm Sun.

NORTHILL   TL1446
★Crown   (01767) 627337
*Ickwell Road; off B658 W of Biggleswade;
SG18 9AA* Popular prettily situated village
pub dating from the 17th c; cosy flagstoned
bar with copper-topped counter, heavy low
beams and bay window seats, woodburner
here and in restaurant with modern furniture
on light wood floor, steps up to another
dining area with exposed brick and high
ceiling, good brasserie-style food (not Sun
evening) including lunchtime baguettes/
panini, Greene King and several guests,
plenty of wines by the glass, prompt friendly
service; soft background music; children
welcome, no dogs inside, tables out at front
and on sheltered side terrace, more in big
back garden with play area, open all day Fri
and Sat, till 7pm Sun.

OAKLEY   TL0053
★Bedford Arms   (01234) 822280
High Street; MK43 7RH 16th-c village
inn with interesting contemporary décor
in several interconnected rooms, pubbiest
part with wooden furniture on bare boards,
flower prints and a woodburner, four cosy,
individually decorated rooms lead off, one
has farmhouse chairs and a cushioned pew
beside a small fireplace, another very much
Victorian in style, Eagle IPA and a couple of
guests, 25 or so wines by the glass and well
regarded food (not Sun evening), stone-
floored dining rooms with tartan-covered
seating or wicker chairs, airy conservatory;
daily papers, TV, darts and board games;
children welcome till 7pm, dogs in bar, pretty
garden, open all day (till 7pm Sun).

ODELL   SP9657
Bell   (01234) 910850
*Off A6 S of Rushden, via Sharnbrook;
High Street; MK43 7AS* Popular and
welcoming thatched village pub; several
comfortable low-beamed rooms around
central servery, log fire and inglenook
woodburner, good reasonably priced
home-made food (not Sun evening, booking
advised) including Mon steak, Tues pie
and Thurs curry nights, well kept Greene
King Abbot Ale and three guests and good
selection of wines/gins, friendly helpful young
staff; children and dogs welcome, big garden
backing on to river, handy for Harrold-Odell
Country Park, open all day.

OLD WARDEN   TL1343
Hare & Hounds   (01767) 627225
*Village signposted off A600 S of
Bedford and B658 W of Biggleswade;
SG18 9HQ* Four cosy rooms, inglenook
woodburner in one; tweed upholstered
chairs at light wood tables on stripped
wood, tiled or carpeted floors, prints and
old photographs including aircraft in the
Shuttleworth Collection (just up the road),
good food using local ingredients from

sharing boards up, Eagle IPA and two guests, several wines by the glass, cocktails, friendly attentive service; background music; children and dogs welcome, garden stretching up to pine woods behind, nice thatched village and good local walks, open all day, no food Sun evening.

RAVENSDEN   TL0754

★ **Horse & Jockey** (01234) 772319

Village signed off B660 N of Bedford; pub at Church End, off village road; MK44 2RR Pleasantly modern brick pub decorated in olive greys and deep reds; leather easy chairs in bar with wall of old local photographs, Adnams Southwold, a couple of guests, more than 20 wines by the glass, good gin selection, bright dining room with chunky tables and high-backed seats, good food cooked by landlord-chef from shortish but varied menu including weekday set lunch, friendly service; background music, board games, children welcome, dogs in bar (limited dining space), modern tables and chairs under parasols on sheltered deck, a few picnic-sets on grass, handsome medieval church next door, open till 6pm Sun, closed Mon.

RISELEY   TL0462

Fox & Hounds (01234) 709714

Off A6 from Sharnbrook/Bletsoe roundabout; High Street, just E of Gold Street; MK44 1DT Modernised village pub dating from the 16th c; low beams, stripped boards and imposing stone fireplace, Bombardier and two guests, signature flame-grilled steaks cut to weight and other enjoyable food including good value set menu, separate dining room; children and dogs (in bar) welcome, seats out in front and in back garden with terrace, open all day, food all day Sat, till 6pm Sun.

SALFORD   SP9339

Swan (01908) 281008

Not far from M1 junction 13 – left off A5140; MK17 8BD Popular Edwardian country dining pub (Peach group); well liked food from sandwiches and deli boards to dry-aged steaks, also fixed-price lunchtime menu Mon-Sat, ales such as Greene King and Hook Norton, good range of wines, gins and cocktails, friendly accommodating staff, updated interior with drinking area to right of central servery, sofas and leather chairs on wood floor, restaurant to left with modern country cottage feel and window view into kitchen; background music; children welcome, dogs in bar, seats out on decking, open (and food) all day.

SHEFFORD   TL1439

Brewery Tap (01462) 628448

North Bridge Street; SG17 5DH No-nonsense L-shaped bar notable for its well kept/priced B&T ales brewed nearby and guest beers; bare boards and low ceiling,

beer bottle collection and other brewerania, simple lunchtime rolls, friendly helpful staff; occasional live music, darts and dominoes; children (in family area) and dogs welcome, picnic-sets out behind, open all day.

SHILLINGTON   TL1234

Crown (01462) 711667

High Road, S end; SG5 3LP Under same ownership as the Chequers at Westoning; emphasis on good food in smart comfortable surroundings including sandwiches, sharing plates and pub classics, also a cosy bar area serving ales such as Otter and Adnams Ghost Ship alongside an excellent range of wines, 21 whiskies and 12 gins, large restaurant/ conservatory, cheerful enthusiastic staff; children and dogs welcome, garden tables, open all day, food all day weekends.

SOULDROP   SP9861

Bedford Arms (01234) 781384

Village signposted off A6 Rushden– Bedford; High Street; MK44 1EY Village pub dating from the 17th c; cosy low-beamed bar with snug and alcove, Black Sheep, Greene King IPA and three guests, several wines by the glass, tasty well priced pubby food, cottagey dining area has more low beams, broad floorboards and woodburner in central fireplace, also roomy mansard-ceilinged part with big inglenook; occasional live music, table skittles, shove-ha'penny and darts; children and dogs (in bar) welcome, garden tables, open all day Fri-Sun, closed Mon.

STEPPINGLEY   TL0135

French Horn (01525) 721225

Off A507 just N of Flitwick; Church End; MK45 5AU Comfortable dining pub next to church; linked rooms with stippled beams, standing posts and wall timbers, two inglenooks (one with woodburner), eclectic mix of chesterfields, leather armchairs, cushioned antique dining chairs and other new and old furniture on flagstones or bare boards, Greene King IPA and a changing guest such as Timothy Taylors Landlord, good range of wines by the glass and malt whiskies, well liked freshly made food with French influences, friendly staff, elegant dining room; background music, TV; children and dogs (in bar) welcome, seats outside overlooking small green, open all day, no food Sun evening, Mon.

STOTFOLD   TL2136

Fox & Duck (01462) 732434

Arlesey Road; SG5 4HE Welcoming roadside pub-restaurant with light modern interior; good variety of enjoyable generously served food from lunchtime ciabattas and bar snacks up, Sharps Atlantic and a guest ale and over a dozen wines by the glass, friendly accommodating staff, separate coffee lounge; occasional live music, pool table, children and dogs welcome, big enclosed garden with play area, open (and food) all day.

STUDHAM TL0215

Bell (01582) 872460

Dunstable Road; LU6 2QG Village pub dating from the 16th c; timbered bar and restaurant, wide choice of food from sandwiches to main dishes and good value Sun lunch, Greene King, Sharps and guests, decent choice of wines by the glass including champagne, lots of gifts and other items for sale; background music, open mike night every other Weds, quiz Thurs; children and dogs (in bar) welcome, seats out at front and in big back garden with giant blackboard to doodle on, nice country views and good walks, handy for Whipsnade Zoo and the Tree Cathedral (NT), open all day, food all day weekends.

STUDHAM TL0215

Red Lion (01582) 872530

Church Road; LU6 2QA Character community pub with hands-on landlord and friendly staff; public bar and eating areas filled with pictures and bits and pieces collected over many years, house plants, wood flooring, carpeting and old red and black tiles, open fire, ales such as Adnams, Fullers, Greene King and Timothy Taylors, enjoyable pubby food (not Sun, Mon or Tues evenings); background music, quiz/curry night first Tues of month; children and dogs welcome, green picnic-sets in front under pretty window boxes, more on side grass, play house, open all day.

SUTTON TL2247

★**John O'Gaunt** (01767) 260377

Off B1040 Biggleswade–Potton; SG19 2NE Friendly bustling village pub just up from 14th-c packhorse bridge and ford; beams and timbering, flagstoned bar with leather seats and banquettes around iron-framed tables, open fire, ales such as Adnams and Woodfordes, local cider and 15 wines by the glass, good food cooked by landlord-chef including Thurs fish and chips, dining rooms with mix of furniture on wood flooring, logburner; background music; children and dogs (in bar) welcome, picnic-sets in sheltered garden, closed Sun evening, Mon, Tues (open lunchtime bank holiday Mon).

TILSWORTH SP9824

Anchor (01525) 211404

Just off A5 NW of Dunstable; LU7 9PU Comfortably modernised 19th-c red-brick village pub now run by welcoming Greek family; popular authentic Greek dishes, Greene King ales, Greek and international wines and ouzo, cheerful attentive service, dining conservatory; monthly live music; children and dogs welcome, picnic-sets in large garden, open (and food) all day except Mon, closed Mon lunchtime.

TOTTERNHOE SP9721

Cross Keys (01525) 220434

Off A505 W of A5; Castle Hill Road; LU6 2DA Restored thatched and timbered two-bar pub below remains of a motte and bailey fort; low beams and cosy furnishings, good reasonably priced food (not Sun evening, Mon) from sandwiches up, well kept Adnams Broadside, Greene King IPA and guests, dining room; children and dogs (in bar) welcome, good views from attractive big garden, plenty of walks nearby, open all day Fri-Sun.

TURVEY SP9452

Three Cranes (01234) 881365

Off A428 W of Bedford; MK43 8EP Renovated stone-built village pub on two levels, good food (not Sun evening) from sandwiches and sharing boards to daily specials, up to five well kept ales, friendly staff; children and dogs (in bar) welcome, secluded tree-shaded garden, five bedrooms, open all day Wed-Sun.

TURVEY SP9352

★**Three Fyshes** (01234) 881463

A428 NW of Bedford; Bridge Street, W end of village; MK43 8ER Well maintained early 17th-c beamed village pub; big inglenook with woodburner, mix of easy and upright chairs around tables on tiles or ancient flagstones, a couple of changing real ales, decent choice of wines and good food, friendly staff, carpeted side restaurant; background music; children and dogs (in bar) welcome, charming garden with decking overlooking bridge and mill on the Great Ouse (note the flood marks), car park further along the street, open all day, no food Sun evening, Mon.

WESTONING SP0332

Chequers (01525) 712967

Park Road (A5120 N of M1 junction 12); MK45 5LA Updated 17th-c thatched village pub under same owners as the Crown at Shillington; enjoyable food including vegan menu, good value set lunch, steak night Weds, seafood evening Thurs; Otter and Purity plus guest ale, good choice of wines by the glass and of other drinks, various teas/coffees, helpful friendly service, low-beamed front bar and good-sized stables restaurant; occasional live music; children and dogs welcome, courtyard tables, open all day from 9am (10am weekends) for breakfast.

WOBURN SP9433

Bell (01525) 290280

Bedford Street; MK17 9QJ Traditional and comfortable with small beamed bar and longer bare-boards dining lounge up steps, enjoyable good value food, Greene King,

---

If you know a pub is ever open all day, please tell us.

guest beers and several gins, friendly helpful service; background music; children and dogs welcome, back terrace, hotel part across busy road, handy for Woburn Abbey/Safari Park, open (and food) all day.

WOBURN   SP9433
Black Horse (01525) 290210
Bedford Street; MK17 9QB Long and narrow 18th-c dining pub (Peach group); enjoyable food from deli boards up including weekday set menu till 6pm, well kept Greene King ales and a guest, good choice of wines, gins and cocktails, several bare-boards areas ranging from bar with old leather settles and coal fire through more contemporary furnishings, steps down to pleasant back restaurant; background music; children welcome, attractive sheltered courtyard, open (and food) all day.

Berkshire

BRAY
Crown 🌟 🍷

SU9079 Map 2

(01628) 621936 – www.thecrownatbray.co.uk

1.75 miles from M4 junction 9; A308 towards Windsor, then left at Bray signpost on to B3028; High Street; SL6 2AH

Ancient low-beamed pub with open-plan rooms, highly regarded food, real ales and seats in the large garden

This 16th-c pub is a favourite with locals and promises a warm welcome to visitors, with high stools around an equally high table, simple tables and chairs beside an open fire and regulars who drop in for a chat and a drink. Most emphasis is, of course, on dining – which is not surprising given that the owner is Heston Blumenthal. The snug rooms have panelling, heavy old beams (some so low you may have to mind your head), plenty of timbers at elbow height where walls have been knocked through, a second log fire and neatly upholstered dining chairs and cushioned settles. Courage Best and Directors, a beer named for the pub and a quickly changing guest on handpump and around 18 wines by the glass; board games. The garden, complete with an outdoor kitchen and bar, is open from May to September.

🌟 The first class, seasonal food is properly pubby rather than restauranty, with dishes such as fish and chips with home-made tartare sauce, 32-day aged bavette or rib-eye steak with a choice of sauce, skate wing with samphire and butter sauce, squash salad with cavolo nero and goats curd, and puddings such as poached plums with yoghurt sorbet and rum and raisin crème brûlée. *Benchmark main dish: burger with toppings and fries £19.00. Two-course evening meal £27.00.*

Star Pubs & Bars ~ Tenant Matt Larcombe ~ Real ale ~ Open 11.30-11; 11.30-10.30 Sun ~ Bar food 12-2.15, 6-9.15 (9.45 Fri); 12-2.45, 6-9.45; 12-4.45 Sun ~ Children welcome ~ Dogs allowed in bar

CHAPEL ROW
Bladebone 🌟 🍷

SU5769 Map 2

(0118) 971 4000 – www.thebladebone.com

Centre of village; RG7 6PD

Popular village pub with appealing food, simply furnished bar and dining rooms and seats on terrace and in garden

Run by an enthusiastic young couple, the Sandersons, this is a lovingly renovated red-brick dining pub. The main focus is placed on the very good, well presented food cooked by the landlord, but the atmosphere is relaxed and friendly and there's a proper bar for those just wanting a pint and a chat. Furnishings are quirky and contemporary: green wallpaper with a pheasant design, a mix of leather and tartan upholstered or wooden dining chairs around chunky farmhouse or carved timber tables on bare boards, high metal chairs by the bar counter, a couple of sofas, unusual light fittings and a couple of brick fireplaces. Sharps Doom Bar and West Berkshire Mr Chubbs on handpump, Aspall's cider and 17 wines by the glass from a well chosen list; background music. The airy little dining conservatory leads to a terrace with rattan-style furniture and there are more seats arranged on the lawn.

 The impressive food, including a weekday set menu, offers such dishes as Cornish cock crab tian, goats cheese tartlet with red onion jam, pan-fried hake with gnocchi and sauce vierge, chicken supreme with garlic and potato terrine and leeks, market fish with Thai red sauce, sticky jasmine rice and pak choi, Windsor Estate pork (confit belly, roast tenderloin) with celeriac remoulade, weekend specials such as moules frites, plus puddings. *Benchmark main dish: beer-battered haddock and chips £16.00. Two-course evening meal £24.00.*

Free house ~ Licensees Richie and Charlotte Sanderson ~ Real ale ~ Open 12-midnight; 12-11 Sun ~ Bar food 12-3, 5.30-9.30; 12-6 Sun ~ Restaurant ~ Children welcome ~ Dogs welcome

CHIEVELEY   SU4574   Map 2
Crab & Boar ♥ ⛵
(01635) 247550 – www.crabandboar.com
North Heath, W of village; RG20 8UE

Welcoming inn with enjoyable food, a good drinks choice, charming staff and seats outside; lovely bedrooms

Dog lovers enjoy this civilised country pub, where all of the 14 comfortable and well equipped bedrooms welcome canine guests; they come with private courtyards and some have hot tubs too. The various bar and dining rooms are smartly furnished. One end of the bar is light and airy with tall chairs lining a high shelf, a couple of unusual, equally high tables with garden planter bases, a contemporary chandelier and stools lining the counter. The other end is cosier, with leather armchairs and sofas facing one another across a low table in front of a woodburning stove; background music and TV. There's West Berkshire Good Old Boy and a guest on handpump, 18 good wines by the glass, a dozen gins and a dozen malt whiskies. The first room leading off has beams and timbering, tartan-upholstered stall seating and leather banquettes, and framed race tickets on the walls. Dining rooms, linked by timbering and steps, are decorated with old fishing reels, a large boar's head, photos and prints, with an eclectic mix of attractive chairs and tables on bare floorboards or carpet. An end room is just right for a private party. Outside, the garden has elegant metal or teak tables and chairs on gravel and grass; there's also a fountain and an outside bar.

Good food includes Scottish smoked salmon with watercress and shaved fennel, truffle mac 'n' cheese fritters, chicken, tarragon and leek pie with mash and buttered greens, Moving Mountain vegan burger with vegan cheddar, guacamole and fries, pan-fried 8oz rump steak with chips and garlic and parsley butter, roast cauliflower with Persian-spiced lentils, spinach and chickpeas, and puddings such as rhubarb and custard crumble pie and lemon tart. *Benchmark main dish: crispy battered haddock and chips £14.00. Two-course evening meal £21.00.*

Cirrus Inns ~ Licensee Ed Nelson ~ Real ale ~ Open 12-10.30 ~ Bar food 12-3, 6-9; 12-3, 6-9.30 Fri, Sat ~ Restaurant ~ Children welcome ~ Dogs allowed in bar & bedrooms ~ Bedrooms: £150

CURRIDGE

SU4871 Map 2

Bunk 🛏

(01635) 200400 – www.thebunkinn.co.uk

Handy for M4 junction 13, off A34 S; RG18 9DS

Popular pub with attractive bar and dining rooms, good modern food and seats outside; bedrooms

You can indeed bunk up at the Bunk Inn – there are nine well equipped and comfortable bedrooms to choose from. The bustling bar has chunky wooden armchairs and sofa alongside an open fire, leather-seated wall banquettes, and farmhouse chairs and stools around pine tables on wide boards. More stools line the counter where they keep Red Rock Devon County, Two Cocks 1643 Cavalier and a changing guest on handpump and good wines by the glass; background music and board games. The candlelit dining room has painted, wooden and high-backed leather chairs around a mix of tables, rustic stable door partitioning, a pale green dado with mirrors and artwork on brick walls above, fresh flowers and little plants in pots; there's also a spacious dining conservatory. Outside, terraces (heated in chilly weather) have tables and chairs and picnic-sets under parasols.

🍴 Tasty food starts with breakfast (7.30-11am, 8-11am at weekends) and includes panko-breaded squid with roasted garlic aioli, buffalo chicken wings with a choice of sauce, caesar salad, ale-battered haddock and chips, gnocchi with triple-cheese sauce, basil and truffle oil, a choice of steaks, a pie and a fish of the day, and puddings such as crumble of the day and sticky toffee pudding. *Benchmark main dish: half roasted chicken with fries and a choice of sauce £13.50. Two-course evening meal £21.00.*

Upham ~ Real ale ~ Open 7.30am-3pm, 5-11pm Weds, Thurs; 7.30am-11pm Fri; 8am-11pm Sat; 8am-7pm Sun; closed Mon, Tues ~ Bar food 12-9.30; 12-8 Sun ~ Restaurant ~ Well behaved children welcome ~ Dogs allowed in bar & bedrooms

HARE HATCH

SU8077 Map 2

Horse & Groom 🍷 🍺

(0118) 940 3136 – www.brunningandprice.co.uk/horseandgroom

A4 Bath Road W of Maidenhead; RG10 9SB

Spreading pub with attractively furnished timbered rooms, enjoyable food and seats outside

This attractive, 300-year-old coaching inn stands on what was the major thoroughfare between London and the West Country. There are plenty of signs of great age in the interconnected rooms and much of interest too: beams and timbering, a pleasing variety of well spread individual tables and chairs on mahogany-stained boards, oriental rugs and some carpet to soften the acoustics, and open fires in attractive tiled fireplaces. Also, a profusion of mainly old or antique prints and mirrors, book-lined shelves, house plants and daily papers. Well trained, courteous staff serve a splendid range of drinks including Brakspears Bitter, Marstons Pedigree, Thwaites Lancaster Bomber and Wychwood Hobgoblin on handpump, 15 wines by the glass, two farm ciders, 110 gins and 50 malt whiskies; background music and board games. There are picnic-sets in the sheltered back garden, and teak tables and chairs under parasols on the front terrace.

🍴 Rewarding food from a daily changing menu includes sandwiches and 'light bites', crispy baby squid with sweet chilli sauce, chicken caesar croquettes, cauliflower, chickpea and squash tagine with couscous, king prawn linguine, steak burger with coleslaw and chips, braised feather of beef bourguignon with horseradish mash and kale, and puddings such as triple chocolate brownie and lemon tart with blackcurrant sorbet. There's a separate gluten-free menu. *Benchmark main dish: chicken, ham and leek pie with mash and buttered greens £15.25. Two-course evening meal £22.00.*

Brunning & Price ~ Manager John Nicholson ~ Real ale ~ Open 11.30-11; 11.30-10.30 Sun ~ Bar food 12-9; 12-9.30 Fri, Sat ~ Children welcome ~ Dogs allowed in bar

 KINTBURY   SU3866 Map 2

Dundas Arms ♀ ⇔

(01488) 658263 – www.dundasarms.co.uk
Village signposted off A4 Newbury–Hungerford about a mile W of Halfway; Station Road – pub just over humpback canal bridge, at start of village itself; RG17 9UT

Waterside inn with plenty of outside seats, nicely furnished bar and dining rooms and good choice of food and drinks; stylish bedrooms

This handsome early 19th-c inn sits on a pretty islet between the River Kennet and the Kennet & Avon Canal. Arrive early if you want to sit outside; although the riverside terrace and mature garden have lots of seats and tables under large white parasols, they fill up fast. Inside, the simply furnished bar has a counter decorated in old pennies, traditional furniture on bare boards and Ramsbury Gold and a changing local guest on handpump, local cider and 17 wines by the glass (including fizz) served by helpful, friendly staff. There are various dining areas: the main one is decorated in classic country style with green panelled walls, decorative tiled flooring and a pretty fireplace, while the Potting Shed has garden tools, little watering cans and books on a dresser and large windows overlooking the garden. The eight well appointed riverside bedrooms are stylish and contemporary; all are dog-friendly and five come with their own private terrace.

Good food includes dishes such as heritage tomato and mozzarella salad, truffle mac 'n' cheese fritters, roast cauliflower with Persian-spiced lentils, spinach and chickpeas, seared bream with Cornish new potato niçoise, pan-fried 8oz rump steak with chips and garlic and parsley butter, crispy battered haddock with chips, and puddings such as eton mess pavlova and dark chocolate brownie. *Benchmark main dish: British brisket burger with ruby slaw and fries £12.50. Two-course evening meal £21.00.*

Cirrus Inns ~ Licensee Lee Hart ~ Real ale ~ Open 11-11; 11-10 Sun ~ Bar food 12-3, 6-9.30; 12-7 Sun ~ Restaurant ~ Children welcome ~ Dogs allowed in bar & bedrooms ~ Bedrooms: £160

 MAIDENS GREEN   SU9072 Map 2

Winning Post ⇔

(01344) 882242 – www.winningpostwinkfield.co.uk
Follow signs to Winkfield Plain W of Winkfield off A330, then first right; SL4 4SW

18th-c inn with beams and timbering in character rooms, interesting food and drinks choice, friendly feel and seats in garden; bedrooms

If you're heading to Ascot or Henley, the 12 quiet and comfortable bedrooms overlooking the garden are a useful place to stay – dogs are welcome too. A gently civilised place, it's popular with chatty locals and families too, especially at weekends. The beamed, open-plan rooms are connected by timbering (some with crash pads). The main bar area has leather and wood tub chairs around a table in one window, a long cushioned settle in another, and big flagstones and stools by the bar where they keep Otter Bitter and a changing guest on handpump and good wines by the glass. An end room, also with flagstones, has more tub chairs, wall seating and contemporary paintwork on planked walls; TV. The dining rooms are to the left of the bar: one long room has huge wall photos of horses and there are tartan banquettes, cushioned dining chairs around wooden tables on bare boards, a woodburning stove, hanging lanterns and bowler-hat lights. A room to the back of the inn called the Winning Enclosure has horse-racing wall photos and a large raised fireplace. The partly covered terrace has good quality seats and tables under parasols.

Food is good and includes buffalo chicken wings, mushroom shawarma with vegan mayonnaise and pickled vegetables, assorted burgers and steaks, half roasted chicken with a choice of sauce, ale-battered haddock and chips, three-cheese gnocchi with basil and white truffle oil, and puddings such as crumble of the day with custard and dark chocolate brownie with vanilla ice-cream. *Benchmark main dish: pie of the day £14.50. Two-course evening meal £22.00.*

Upham ~ Manager Zach Leach ~ Real ale ~ Open 11-10; 11-11 Fri, Sat ~ Bar food 12-2.30, 6-9; 12-9 Sat; 12-8 Sun ~ Restaurant ~ Children welcome ~ Dogs allowed in bar & bedrooms

NEWBURY

SU4767   Map 2

Newbury 🏵️ 🍽️ 🍷 🍺

(01635) 49000 – www.thenewburypub.co.uk
Bartholomew Street; RG14 5HB

Lively pub with plenty of bar and dining space, rewarding food and regular events

This popular town-centre pub has lots of different seating areas to suit whatever mood you're in – from a rooftop terrace with a cocktail bar, a pizza oven and an electric folding canopy roof to a downstairs courtyard with seats and tables. The inviting bar has an assortment of wooden dining chairs around sturdy farmhouse and other solid tables on bare boards, comfortable leather sofas, big paintings, church candles and an open fire. Light and airy dining rooms have wall benches and church chairs around more rustic tables on more bare boards, local artwork and an open kitchen; background music and board games. There's a brilliant range of drinks, a highlight being gin from their own 137 Gin Distillery (you can buy a bottle to take home with you). Also, a beer named for them (from Greene King), Timothy Taylors Landlord and guests on handpump, 20 malt whiskies, 28 wines (including champagne and sparkling) by the glass, an extensive cocktail list (using their own gin) and a fine range of coffees and teas (including tea grown in Cornwall). The distillery is also a private dining room for hire.

The grazing-style menu offers a choice of small and large plates under headings such as 'Fish', 'Meat', 'Vegetable' and 'Sweet', with customers encouraged to share and special deals at lunchtime. Typical dishes include padrón peppers, smoked pork and bacon sliders, roast scallop with sweetcorn and chorizo, pan-fried salmon fillet with sauce vierge, roast pork with sage and onion stuffing and mash, lamb faggot with pea fritter, roasted beets with whipped blue cheese, sweet potato gratin with chilli jam, and grilled peaches with vanilla cream. *Benchmark main dish: barbecue smoked brisket with flatbread £12.00. Two-course evening meal £22.00.*

Greene King ~ Lease Peter Lumber ~ Real ale ~ Open 5-11 Mon; 11.30-11 Tues, Weds; 11.30-midnight Thurs; 11.30am-1am Fri; 12pm-2am Sat; 11.30-10.30 Sun ~ Bar food 11-3, 5-9; 12-6 Sun ~ Restaurant ~ Children welcome ~ Dogs allowed in bar

PEASEMORE

SU4577 Map 2

Fox

(01635) 248480 – www.foxatpeasemore.co.uk

4 miles from M4 junction 13, via Chieveley: keep on through Chieveley to Peasemore, turning left into Hillgreen Lane at small sign to Fox Inn; village also signposted from B4494 Newbury–Wantage; RG20 7JN

Friendly downland pub on top form under its expert licensees

Mr and Mrs Davison are always on hand to offer a genuine welcome to all the customers to their consistently good and popular pub. The long bare-boards bar has strategically placed high-backed chairs (comfort guaranteed by plenty of colourful cushions), a warm woodburning stove in a stripped-brick chimney breast and, for real sybarites, two luxuriously carpeted end areas, one with velour tub armchairs. Friendly, efficient, neatly dressed staff serve West Berkshire Good Old Boy and a couple of changing guests on handpump, 16 wines by the glass and summer farm cider; background music. This is downland horse-training country, and picnic-sets outside at the front on grass look across to the rolling fields beyond the quiet country lane – on a clear day you can see as far as the Hampshire border hills some 20 miles south. There is more seating under parasols on a smallish sheltered back terrace. They offer a self-catering one-bedroom apartment. Enjoyable surrounding walks.

Popular pubby food includes whitebait with garlic mayo, goats cheese and beetroot tart, roasted Mediterranean vegetable and chickpea pie, burger (beef or mushroom and halloumi) and chips, steak and ale pie, confit of duck with sautéed potatoes and braised red cabbage, and puddings such as honey and coconut cheesecake and apple and berry crumble with custard or vanilla pod ice-cream. *Benchmark main dish: fish pie £12.95. Two-course evening meal £20.00.*

Free house ~ Licensees Philip and Lauren Davison ~ Real ale ~ Open 12-2.30, 6-11; 12-11 Sat; 12-6 Sun ~ Bar food 12-2, 6-9; 12-3, 5.30-9 Sat; 12-4 Sun ~ Children welcome ~ Dogs allowed in bar

RUSCOMBE

SU7976 Map 2

Royal Oak

(0118) 934 5190 – www.burattas.co.uk

Ruscombe Lane (B3024 just E of Twyford); RG10 9JN

Wide choice of food at welcoming pub with interesting furnishings and paintings and local beer and wine

---

Known locally as Buratta's (after the friendly couple who run the place), this much loved pub is usually full of chatty customers having a fine old time. The carpeted bars are open-plan but carefully laid out so that each area is fairly snug but still feels part of the action. A good variety of furniture runs from dark oak tables to big chunky pine ones with mixed seating to match; the two sofas facing each other are popular. Contrasting with the old exposed ceiling joists, mostly unframed modern paintings and prints decorate the walls, which are painted in grey and white. Binghams (the brewery is just across the road) Twyford Tipple, Fullers London Pride and a guest from Loddon on handpump, 16 wines by the glass (they stock wines from the village's Stanlake Park vineyard), 14 malt whiskies, six gins and attentive service. Picnic-sets are arranged around a venerable central hawthorn in the garden behind (where there are ducks and chickens); summer barbecues. The pub is on the annual Henley Arts Trail. Do visit the landlady's antiques and collectables shop, which is open during pub hours.

🍴 Enjoyable food from a regularly updated menu includes sandwiches and paninis, Thai-style fishcakes with sweet chilli sauce, chicken liver and pancetta parfait, ploughman's, a pie of the day, ham, egg and chips, falafel and spinach burger with sautéed potatoes, chilli con carne, mushroom ravioli with marinara sauce, crispy-skin salmon with crushed new potatoes and confit fennel, and puddings. *Benchmark main dish: twice-cooked pork belly with black pudding mash £13.00. Two-course evening meal £22.00.*

Enterprise ~ Lease Jenny and Stefano Buratta ~ Real ale ~ Open 12-3, 6-11; 12-4 Sun; closed Mon ~ Bar food 12-2.30, 7-9.30; 12-3 Sun ~ Restaurant ~ Children welcome ~ Dogs allowed in bar

SONNING

Bull 🍷 🛏

SU7575   Map 2

(0118) 969 3901 – www.bullinnsonning.co.uk
Off B478, by church; village signed off A4 E of Reading; RG4 6UP

Attractive spot for pretty timbered inn with plenty of character in old-fashioned bars, friendly staff and good food; bedrooms

Dating from the 16th c, this appealing Fullers pub appears in Jerome K Jerome's 1889 comic novel *Three Men in a Boat* as 'a veritable picture of an old country inn'. The two old-fashioned bar rooms certainly have plenty of character: low ceilings and heavy beams, cosy alcoves, leather armchairs and sofas, cushioned antique settles and low wooden chairs on bare boards, and open fires. You'll find Fullers HSB and London Pride and a couple of guest ales on handpump served by helpful staff, about 20 good wines by the glass, cocktails and a farm cider. The light dining room has coral-coloured walls above panelling, a mix of wooden chairs and tables, parquet flooring and shelves of books; TV. The seven modern boutique-style bedrooms do get booked up well in advance. If you bear left through the ivy-clad churchyard opposite, then turn left along the bank of the river, you come to a very pretty lock. The Thames Valley Park is close by. The wisteria across the building's front is a lovely sight in full bloom.

🍴 Pleasing food includes sandwiches and dishes such as roast beetroot and fennel salad, beef burger and triple-cooked chips, aubergine and tomato ragoût with flatbread, caesar salad, hot smoked salmon niçoise with egg, lemon and thyme roast chicken with chorizo, courgettes and cannellini beans, and puddings such as molasses, date and hops sticky toffee pudding and bakewell tart with raspberries and vanilla ice-cream. *Benchmark main dish: Fullers Frontier-battered haddock and chips £15.75. Two-course evening meal £23.00.*

Fullers ~ Manager Sian and Jason Smith ~ Real ale ~ Open 10am-11pm; 12-10.30 Sun ~ Bar food 12-9.30; 12-8.30 Sun; 12-3, 6-9 in winter ~ Restaurant ~ Children welcome ~ Dogs allowed in bar ~ Bedrooms: £129

WOOLHAMPTON
Rowbarge 🍺 🍷

SU5766   Map 2

(0118) 971 2213 – www.brunningandprice.co.uk/rowbarge
Station Road; RG7 5SH

Canalside pub with plenty of interest in rambling rooms, six real ales, good quality food and lots of outside seating

This reliably good Brunning & Price pub is always popular but especially in summer, when people spill out on to the shaded terrace with its wooden chairs and tables or grab a picnic-set on the sizeable grassy expanse overlooking the Kennet & Avon Canal. Six rambling rooms with beams and timbering are connected by open doorways and knocked-through walls. The décor is gently themed to represent the canal with hundreds of prints and photographs (some of rowing and boats) and oars on the walls, as well as old glass and stone bottles in nooks and crannies, big house plants and fresh flowers, plenty of candles and several open fires; the many large mirrors create an impression of even more space. Throughout there are antique dining chairs around various nice old tables, settles, built-in cushioned wall seating, armchairs, a group of high stools around a huge wooden barrel table, and rugs on polished boards, stone tiles or carpeting. You'll find St Austell Brunning & Price Traditional Bitter, Rowbarge Ruby (named for them from Loddon), Frome Funky Monkey and three quickly changing guest beers on handpump, 21 wines by the glass (including fizz), 90 gins and 65 malt whiskies; background music and board games. Friendly, efficient young staff keep things running smoothly even when busy.

Enjoyable food (with a separate gluten-free menu) includes sandwiches, 'light bites', chicken caesar croquettes, baked camembert with apple, celery and walnut salad, beer-battered cod with chips, crispy beef salad, braised shoulder of lamb with crushed new potatoes and rosemary gravy, Malaysian chicken curry with coconut rice and pak choi, pea and mint tortellini with pea velouté and asparagus, and desserts such as hot waffle and caramelised banana with toffee sauce and honeycomb ice-cream and a choice of British cheeses. *Benchmark main dish: pork and leek sausages with mash and buttered greens £13.95. Two-course evening meal £22.00.*

Brunning & Price ~ Manager Steve Butt ~ Real ale ~ Open 10am-11pm; 10am-10.30pm Sun ~ Bar food 10-9.30; 10-10 Fri, Sat; 10-9 Sun ~ Restaurant ~ Children welcome ~ Dogs allowed in bar

YATTENDON
SU5574   Map 2
Royal Oak ★ ♥ 🛏

(01635) 201325 – www.royaloakyattendon.co.uk

The Square; B4009 NE from Newbury; right at Hampstead Norreys, village signed on left; RG18 0UG

Berkshire Dining Pub of the Year

Civilised old pub with lovely new dining room, imaginative food and seats in pretty garden; bedrooms

This handsome red-brick inn is only ten minutes from the racecourse at Newbury, so it can get busy on race days. It's also a popular place to stay, with ten smart bedrooms in the main house or a separate cottage, overlooking the garden or the village square. But the main reason customers visit is for the excellent food from head chef Nick MacGregor. New this year is the lovely Orangery dining room, with a central skylight above a maple tree and an open kitchen (complete with three-tiered rotisserie, Argentine parilla grill and pizza oven). It's a stylish space, with olive green paintwork, contemporary light wood and upholstered seating around matching tables, and colourful insect prints; bi-fold doors open out to the charming walled garden. Newly re-landscaped, this has wicker seats and wooden tables on a terrace, under a pergola and elsewhere; boules. There are also picnic-sets with parasols at the front of the pub. The bar rooms have beams and panelling, an appealing mix of wooden dining chairs and tables, some half-panelled wall seating, rugs on quarry tiles or wooden floorboards, plenty of prints on brick, cream or red walls, lovely flower arrangements and four log fires; background music and TV. Well kept ales from the local area include the likes of Ramsbury Gold, Ringwood Razorback and a changing guest on handpump, and around 20 wines by the glass.

🍽️ Imaginative food with international influences includes crispy bang-bang chicken with ponzu mayo, sweetcorn and coriander fritters with smashed avocado and pico de gallo, a choice of pizzas, beer-battered fish and chips, cauliflower, black dhal and spinach butter masala, seafood laksa (salmon, prawn, mussels) with glass noodles and pak choi, steaks with peppercorn sauce or garlic butter, roast shoulder of lamb with garlic and rosemary potatoes, and desserts such as treacle and chocolate tart with clotted cream and sticky date pudding with butterscotch sauce. *Benchmark main dish: fish pie (salmon, cod, prawns) £19.00. Two-course evening meal £26.00.*

Free house ~ Licensee Rob McGill ~ Real ale ~ Open 12-2.30, 6-9; 12.30-3, 6.30-9.30 Sat; 12.30-3, 6.30-9.30 Sun ~ Restaurant ~ Children welcome ~ Dogs welcome ~ Bedrooms: £130

Also Worth a Visit in Berkshire

Besides the fully inspected pubs, you might like to try these pubs that have been recommended to us and described by readers. Do tell us what you think of them: feedback@goodguides.com

ALDWORTH   SU5579
★**Bell** (01635) 578272 *A329*
Reading–Wallingford; left on to B4009 at Streatley; RG8 9SE Unspoilt and unchanging village pub in same family for over 250 years; Grade-II listed interior with simply furnished panelled rooms, beams in ochre ceiling, old photographs and ancient one-handed clock, woodburner, glass-panelled hatch serving well kept Arkells, West Berkshire and a monthly guest, Upton cider and nice house wines, good value rolls, ploughman's and winter soup, traditional pub games; no mobile phones or credit cards; well behaved children and dogs welcome, seats in quiet cottagey garden by cricket ground, animals in paddock behind pub, closed Mon (open lunchtime bank holidays), can get busy weekends.

ALDWORTH   SU5579
Four Points (01635) 578367
B4009 towards Hampstead Norreys; RG8 9RL Attractive 17th-c thatched roadside pub with relaxed family vibe; low beams, standing timbers and panelling, nice fire in bar with more formal seating area to the left and restaurant at back, popular good value home-cooked food (all day weekends) from baguettes up, bargain lighter lunch deal Mon-Fri and good Sun lunch, Wadworths 6X and guests, friendly helpful young staff; children and dogs (in bar) welcome, garden over road with play area, open (and food) all day weekends.

ASTON   SU7884
★**Flower Pot** (01491) 574721
Off A4130 Henley–Maidenhead at top of Remenham Hill; RG9 3DG Roomy red-brick country pub with nice local feel; snug traditional bar and airy back dining area, lots of stuffed fish and other taxidermy, roaring log fire, four well kept ales such as Brakspears and Ringwood, enjoyable reasonably priced food (not Sun evening)

from baguettes to fish and game, friendly service; very busy with walkers and families at weekends, dogs allowed in some parts, plenty of picnic-sets in large picturesque garden with rural views, Thames nearby, three bedrooms, open all day weekends.

BARKHAM   SU7866
Bull (0118) 976 2816
Barkham Road; RG41 4TL Traditional pub in the heart of the countryside, run by friendly Thai family; opened-up carpeted interior with dining area to one end, wide range of beers including Courage Best, Fullers HSB, Sharps Doom Bar and guests, popular food including good South-east Asian choices and tapas-style bar menu; Mon quiz; children welcome, picnic-sets in garden, open all day (till 8pm Sun).

BEECH HILL   SU6964
Elm Tree (0118) 988 3505
3.3 miles from M4 junction 11: A33 towards Basingstoke, turning off into Beech Hill Road after about 2 miles; RG7 2AZ Off the beaten track with countryside views; five rooms (one with blazing fire), modern barn-style restaurant and conservatory, varied menu, prompt friendly service, well kept ales such as Ringwood and Timothy Taylors, good choice of wines by the glass and decent coffee; children and dogs welcome, disabled access/loo, open all day, no food Sun evening.

BEENHAM   SU5868
Six Bells (0118) 971 3368
The Green; RG7 5NX Extended red-brick Victorian village pub with good food from landlord-chef including imaginative additions to standard pub menu, well kept West Berkshire Good Old Boy, Sharps Doom Bar and a guest such as Vale, friendly staff, two bar areas with armchairs and winter fires, dining conservatory; board games; children welcome at lunchtime, four well appointed bedrooms, closed Sun evening and Mon

lunchtime – new owners arrived as we went to press, reports please.

BISHAM
SU8585
Bull (01628) 484734
Marlow Road; SL7 1RR Old village dining pub with wide choice of good food including French and continental cuisine in classic restaurant (white tablecloths) and simpler menu in traditional oak-beamed bar, weekday set menus (not Dec), a couple of ales such as Brakspears and Greene King, well chosen wines, friendly helpful service; background music; pleasant garden.

CHADDLEWORTH
SU4177
Ibex (01488) 638311
Main Street; RG20 7ER Old brick and flint country pub saved from closure by the local community; enjoyable reasonably priced pubby food (not Sun evening, Mon) from sandwiches to good Sun roasts (unlimited veg), local ales (brewed in the village) and a couple of guests, friendly accommodating staff; live music and quiz nights, darts; children, muddy boots and paws welcome, tables on sheltered lawn and terrace, two bedrooms, open all day weekends, closed Mon lunchtime.

CHARVIL
SU7776
Heron on the Ford (0118) 934 0700
Lands End Lane/Whistley Mill Lane near Old River ford; RG10 0UE Refurbished 1930s Tudor-style pub under newish management (was the Lands End) on a small lane; Brakspears beers and enjoyable food from sandwiches up, open-plan bar with log fire, side snug and separate restaurant, helpful friendly service; occasional live music; children and dogs welcome, sizeable garden with terrace, good walks (check website for details) and numerous little lakes nearby, open all day weekends (till 6.30pm Sun).

CHEAPSIDE
SU9469
Thatched Tavern (01344) 620874
Off A332/A329, then off B383 at Village Hall sign; SL5 7QG Civilised dining pub with character and plenty of room for just a drink; top quality modern cooking (can be pricey) along with more traditional choices and weekday set lunch, lots of wines by the glass including champagne from extensive list, Fullers London Pride, a beer named for the pub and a guest ale, big inglenook log fire, low beams and polished flagstones in cottagey core, three smart dining rooms off; children welcome, dogs in bar, tables on terrace and attractive sheltered back lawn, handy for Virginia Water, open (and food) all day, busy on Ascot race days.

CHIEVELEY
SU4773
★Olde Red Lion (01635) 248379
Handy for M4 junction 13 via A34 N-bound; Green Lane; RG20 8XB Popular

traditional village pub with up to four well kept Arkells beers and good varied choice of generously served food at reasonable prices, welcoming attentive service, low-beamed carpeted bar with log fire, extended back restaurant; background music, TV; children and dogs welcome, wheelchair accessible throughout, small garden, five bedrooms in separate building, open all day weekends.

COOKHAM
SU8985
★Bel & the Dragon (01628) 521263
High Street (B4447); SL6 9SQ Smartly updated 15th-c former coaching inn; heavy beams, log fires and simple country furnishings in two-room front bar and dining area, hand-painted cartoons on pastel walls, more modern bistro-style back restaurant, emphasis on very good food (separate bar and restaurant menus) including weekend brunch, Rebellion IPA and a local guest, plenty of wines by the glass from extensive list, cocktails; children welcome, dogs in bar, well tended garden with tables on paved terrace, play area, five bedrooms, Stanley Spencer Gallery almost opposite, open all day, food all day Sun.

COOKHAM
SU8885
★White Oak (01628) 523043
The Pound (B4447); SL6 9QE Modernised red-brick restauranty pub with highly regarded interesting food including good value set menus, Mon steak night, large back area and several other parts set for eating, front bar serving ales such as Greene King and good range of wines by the glass, friendly efficient service; children welcome, sheltered back terrace with steps up to white wirework tables on grass, closed Sun evening, otherwise open all day.

COOKHAM DEAN
SU8785
★Jolly Farmer (01628) 482905
Church Road, off Hills Lane; SL6 9PD Refurbished 18th-c pub owned by village consortium; beamed rooms with open fires, five well kept ales such as Rebellion and Timothy Taylors, Weston's cider and good choice of wines by the glass, fairly pubby food including wood-fired pizzas, pleasant attentive service; well behaved children and dogs welcome, tables out in front and on side terrace, garden with large play area, open all day.

COOKHAM DEAN
SU8785
Uncle Toms Cabin (01628) 483339
Off A308 Maidenhead–Marlow; Hills Lane, towards Cookham Rise and Cookham; SL6 9NT Welcoming small-roomed local with simple modernised interior; five well kept ales such as Rebellion and Timothy Taylors, plenty of wines by the glass and enjoyable food from lunchtime sandwiches up, low beams (and doorways), wood floors and grey-green panelling, gleaming horsebrasses, open fire; background

music, TV; children allowed in eating areas, dogs in bar, seats out at front and in large back garden, peaceful country setting, open all day Sat, closes 9pm Sun and Mon.

CRAZIES HILL　　　　SU7980
Horns　(0118) 940 6041
Warren Row Road off A4 towards Cockpole Green, then follow Crazies Hill signs; RG10 8LY Welcoming 16th-c beamed village pub with landlady-chef's good food from lunchtime baguettes and traditional favourites up, Brakspears ales kept well and nice choice of wines by the glass, friendly helpful service, four rooms including raftered barn restaurant; children welcome, dogs in bar, big garden with play area and summer barbecues, open all day Fri and Sat, till 7pm Sun, closed Mon (Tues after bank holiday).

DATCHET　　　　SU9877
Royal Stag　(01753) 584231
Not far from M4 junction 5; The Green; SL3 9JH Ancient beamed pub next to church overlooking green; well kept Fullers London Pride and three Windsor & Eton beers, enjoyable food including weekday lunchtime sandwiches, good Sun roasts, friendly staff, log fire, antlers on walls; Tues quiz; children and dogs welcome, seats outside, open (and food) all day.

DONNINGTON　　　　SU4770
Fox & Hounds　(01635) 40540
Old Oxford Road; RG14 3AP Great food and great service at this family-owned pub (they also run a local butcher's and have a meat raffle every other Sun); well kept Fullers, Sharps and West Berkshire, decent wine range and good generously served food from pub favourites to grills, attentive young staff, dining room around to the left; TV, darts; children and dogs welcome, picnic-sets out in front, handy for M4 (junction 13) and A34, closed Sun evening, Mon, otherwise open all day.

EAST GARSTON　　　　SU3676
⋆ ## Queens Arms　(01488) 648757
3.5 miles from M4 junction 14; A338 and village signposted Great Shefford; RG17 7ET Friendly slate-roofed inn at the heart of racehorse-training country; opened-up bar with antique prints (many jockeys), wheelbacks around well spaced tables on bare boards, well kept Ramsbury, large friendly bar serving local ales, a wide selection of spirits and an extensive wine list, lighter dining area with more prints, good food from sandwiches and traditional choices up (pizzas Sun evening), friendly obliging staff; background music, TV for

racing, newspapers including *Racing Post*, children and dogs (in bar) welcome, seats on sheltered terrace, 12 attractively decorated bedrooms, good surrounding downland walks, fly fishing and shooting can be arranged, open all day.

EAST ILSLEY　　　　SU4981
Crown & Horns　(01635) 281545
Just off A34, about 5 miles N of M4 junction 13; Compton Road; RG20 7LH Welcoming brick and tile pub in racehorse-training country; rambling beamed rooms with log fires, enjoyable home-made food from sandwiches, pizzas and pub favourites up, five real ales and over a dozen wines by the glass, friendly staff; background music; children, dogs and muddy boots welcome, picnic-sets with parasols in pretty courtyard, 11 nicely decorated bedrooms (named after famous horse races) in modern extension around courtyard, open (and food) all day and busy on Newbury race days.

EASTBURY　　　　SU3477
Plough　(01488) 71312
Centre of village by stream; RG17 7JN Popular old whitewashed village dining pub with very good food from chef-proprietor, a couple of changing ales and over 40 gins, friendly efficient staff, open-plan interior with some modern touches including large back restaurant, two-way log fire; children welcome, dogs in bar, tables out on front deck, open till 4.30pm Sun, closed Mon.

ETON　　　　SU9677
George　(01753) 861797
High Street; SL4 6AF Flagship pub for Windsor & Eton Brewery (a ten-minute walk away); traditional beamed interior, open fire, half a dozen of their beers (tasting trays) from ornately carved oak counter, ample helpings of enjoyable pubby food, friendly helpful service; quiz every other Tues; children and dogs welcome, decked back terrace with seating booths, eight bedrooms, open (and food) all day, kitchen shuts 5pm Sun.

FINCHAMPSTEAD　　　　SU7963
Queens Oak　(0118) 996 8567
Church Lane, off B3016; RG40 4LS Welcoming country pub named for an oak planted by Queen Victoria on green opposite; largely open-plan interior with some updating by present licensees, well kept Brakspears and other Marstons-related beers, a dozen wines by the glass and decent range of other drinks, enjoyable food (all day weekends) from ciabattas and pub favourites up; Thurs quiz, some live music; children, walkers and dogs welcome, good-sized garden with play area, open all day (till 7pm Sun).

Virtually all pubs in this book sell wine by the glass. We mention wines if they are a cut above the average.

FRILSHAM   SU5573
Pot Kiln (01635) 201366
*From Yattendon take turning S, opposite
church, follow first Frilsham signpost,
but just after crossing motorway go
straight on towards Bucklebury ignoring
Frilsham signposted right; pub on right
after about 0.5 miles; RG18 0XX*
Tucked-away red-brick country dining pub
with good food including signature local
game; various eating areas and small bare-
boards bar with woodburner, West Berkshire
ales, several wines by the glass and maybe
a couple of real ciders; children and dogs
welcome, unobstructed views from seats in
big suntrap garden, outside pizza oven, nice
walks in nearby woods, open all day Sat, till
5pm Sun, closed Tues.

HAMPSTEAD NORREYS   SU5376
White Hart (01635) 202248
Church Street; RG18 0TB Friendly and
relaxed low-beamed village pub with three
linked rooms, fireside seating and good-sized
dining area, enjoyable sensibly priced
home-made food from lunchtime baguettes/
ciabattas up, a couple of well kept Greene
King ales and a guest, well chosen wines;
some live music and quiz nights; children
and dogs (in bar) welcome, back terrace and
garden, open all day weekends, closed Mon.

HOLYPORT   SU8977
Belgian Arms (01628) 634468
*1.5 miles from M4 junction 8/9 via
A308(M), A330; in village turn left
on to big green, then left again at war
memorial; SL6 2JR* Welcoming wisteria-
clad dining pub set back from village green;
opened-up low-ceilinged interior with well
spaced tables on stripped wood floor, good
food from snacks, sharing plates and pub
favourites up, well kept Brakspears and nice
range of wines by the glass, friendly attentive
service; background and live acoustic music
(first Fri of month); children welcome,
attractive garden overlooking pond, open all
day, food all day Sat (brunch from 9am).

HOLYPORT   SU8977
George (01628) 628317
*1.5 miles from M4 junction 8/9, via
A308(M)/A330; The Green; SL6 2JL*
Attractive 16th-c pub on village green with
colourful history and plenty of old-world
charm; open-plan low-beamed interior, cosy
and dimly lit, with nice fireplace, good food
from lunchtime baguettes and pub favourites
up, well kept Fullers London Pride, a couple
of Rebellion ales and 16 wines by the glass,
friendly helpful service; background music,

quiz first Mon of month; children and dogs
(in bar) welcome, paved terrace and grassy
beer garden, closed Sun evening, Mon.

HUNGERFORD   SU3368
John O'Gaunt (01488) 683535
Bridge Street (A338); RG17 0EG
Modernised 16th-c town pub with beamed
interior; enjoyable food in generous portions
from lunchtime sandwiches/wraps up, six
well kept mainly local ales including own
microbrews (tasting trays available), good
bottled range too and local cider, efficient
cheerful service; children and dogs welcome,
small sheltered garden, outdoor Tiki Bar,
open all day, food all day Sun.

HUNGERFORD   SU3368
Three Swans (01488) 682721
High Street; RG17 0LZ Bright and
welcoming former coaching inn in town
centre, with lower bar serving three well
kept ales such as Black Sheep and Ramsbury,
Somersby's cider, plenty of wines by the
glass and cocktails, good food from snacks
and pizzas up, helpful friendly service, large
panelled restaurant and coffee shop; children
and dogs (in bar) welcome, some tables out
at front, more in part-covered courtyard
behind, 25 bedrooms, open all day from 7am
(8am weekends) for breakfast.

HUNGERFORD NEWTOWN   SU3571
Tally Ho (01488) 682312
A338 just S of M4 junction 14; RG17 0PP
Traditional red-brick beamed pub owned by
the local community, friendly and welcoming,
with good food (not Sun evening) from
baguettes to specials and popular Sun lunch,
four well kept local ales such as Ramsbury
and West Berkshire, proper cider, log fire;
occasional music and quiz nights, children
and dogs welcome, a couple of picnic-sets out
in front, more tables on side terrace, three
bedrooms, open all day.

HURLEY   SU8281
Dew Drop (01488) 315662
*Small yellow sign to pub off A4130 just
W; SL6 6RB* Old flint and brick pub tucked
away in nice woodland setting; shortish
choice of food including good lunchtime
sandwiches, Brakspears and a guest ale, two
adjoining rooms (one with piano), log fire;
children and dogs welcome, pleasant views
from back garden, good local walks, open all
day Sat, till 6pm Sun, closed Mon.

HURLEY   SU8382
Hurley House (01628) 568500
A4130 SE, just off A404; SL6 5LH
Elegant up-to-date hotel with informal

Post Office address codings confusingly give the impression that some pubs are
in Berkshire, when they're really in Buckinghamshire, Oxfordshire or Hampshire
(which is where we list them).

civilised atmosphere; several different seating areas in big open-plan room including green leather chesterfields grouped in the centre, armchairs in front of a woodburner and some cushioned wall seats, Rebellion IPA, West Berkshire Good Old Boy and good wines by the glass, clubby feel dining rooms with green button-back leather banquettes and mustard-yellow chairs, candles on tables, highly rated modern food (not Sun evening and not cheap) including set lunch menu, afternoon teas; background music (live Fri evening), board games; children and dogs (in bar) welcome, carefully landscaped gardens, ten comfortable well equipped bedrooms, good breakfast, open all day (till 10pm Sun).

HURST SU7973

⋆**Castle** (0118) 934 0034
Church Hill; RG10 0SJ Popular old dining pub next to bowling green and owned by church opposite; very good well presented food (not Sun evening, Mon) from fairly priced varied menu including daily specials (Fri fish night), three well kept changing ales and plenty of wines by the glass, friendly efficient staff, beams, wood floors and old brick nogging, some visible wattle and daub, woodburners; children and dogs (in bar) welcome, picnic-sets out at front behind picket fence and in sunny back garden, open all day weekends, closed Mon lunchtime.

HURST SU8074

Green Man (0118) 934 2599
Off A321 just outside village; RG10 0BP Partly 17th-c pub with enjoyable food from sandwiches and baked potatoes up including stone-baked pizzas, well kept Brakspears and a couple of Marstons-related guests, a dozen wines by the glass, friendly service, dark beams and standing timbers, cosy alcoves, wall seats and built-in settles, log fires; children and dogs (in bar) welcome, sheltered terrace, picnic-sets under spreading oak trees in large garden with play area, open (and food) all day.

INKPEN SU3764

⋆**Crown & Garter** (01488) 668325
Inkpen Common: Inkpen signposted with Kintbury off A4; in Kintbury turn left into Inkpen Road, then keep on into Inkpen Common; RG17 9QR Fine old brick pub dating from 1640 with friendly welcome; ales such as Ramsbury Gold and West Berkshire Good Old Boy and Mr Chubbs, ten wines by the glass and a dozen malt whiskies, mix of upholstered dining chairs and simple tables, pale floorboards, cushioned wall seats and leather armchairs by an open fire, old suitcases, mirrors and modern artwork on contemporary paintwork, smart restaurant and good seasonal food with pub classics and more imaginative dishes; background music; children and dogs (in bar) welcome, seating on front terrace, ten comfortable bedrooms in separate building

with own garden, coffee shop, bike racks, disabled access, closed Mon, Tues.

KNOWL HILL SU8178

Bird in Hand (01628) 826622
A4, handy for M4 junction 8/9; RG10 9UP Updated Wadworths pub set back from the road; roomy interior with light beams, panelling, parquet floor and log fire in main area, four real ales and enjoyable reasonably priced food including some specials, pleasant efficient service, restaurant; background music, fruit machine; children and dogs (in bar) welcome, tables on front and back terraces, bedrooms (some in separate block), open (and food) all day.

LITTLEWICK GREEN SU8379

Cricketers (01628) 822888
Not far from M4 junction 9; A404(M) then left on to A4 – village signed on left; Coronation Road; SL6 3RA Welcoming old-fashioned village pub in charming spot opposite cricket green (can get crowded); three well kept Badger ales and good choice of wines by the glass, enjoyable pub food (not Sun evening) from lunchtime sandwiches to specials, traditional interior with three linked rooms, wood and quarry-tiled floors, huge clock above woodburner in brick fireplace; background music, TV; children and dogs welcome, pretty hanging baskets and a few tables out in front behind picket fence, open all day.

MAIDENHEAD SU8881

15 Queen Street (01628) 623800
Queen Street; SL6 1NB Refurbished bar-restaurant keeping traditional bare-boards interior (was the Hand & Flowers); well kept Brakspears, decent wines and good choice of other drinks including cocktails, highly rated food (booking advised) with emphasis on steaks, also set menu and bottomless brunch, friendly prompt service; background music, open all day (till 6pm Sun).

MAIDENHEAD SU8582

Pinkneys Arms (01628) 630268
Lee Lane, just off A308 N; SL6 6NU Updated dining pub with good food from weekly changing menu (can be pricey), pizzas only Mon and Tues, well kept ales (mainly Rebellion) and decent wines, friendly efficient service; outside gents', barn function room; children and dogs welcome, big garden, closed Mon lunchtime, otherwise open all day from midday.

MARSH BENHAM SU4267

Red House (01635) 582017
Off A4 W of Newbury; RG20 8LY Appealing traditional thatched pub with lunchtime sandwiches and pub favourites, fish and chips Thurs, friendly efficient service, well kept West Berkshire ales and a guest, lots of wines by the glass, afternoon teas, roomy bar with wood or flagstone floors,

logburner, separate restaurant, good cheerful service; background music, monthly quiz; children and dogs welcome, terrace and long lawns sloping to River Kennet water meadows, open (and food) all day.

NEWBURY   SU4766
Catherine Wheel (01635) 569897
Cheap Street; RG14 5DB Popular Tudor-style pub with mullioned windows, crenellations and a carriage entrance; simple furniture on bare boards or stone tiles, white-painted beams and grey panelled dados, central fireplace, five well kept ales along with good selection of craft beers and real ciders, plenty more in bottles/cans, also decent wines and good value food with emphasis on Pieminister pies, friendly helpful staff; children and dogs welcome, seats and separate gin bar in back courtyard, open (and food) all day, kitchen shuts 6pm Sun.

NEWBURY   SU4767
Lock Stock & Barrel (01635) 580550
Northbrook Street; RG14 1AA Modern Fullers pub approached down small alleyway and popular for its canalside (River Kennet) setting; low ceiling, light wood or slate flooring and painted panelling, lots of windows overlooking canal, varied choice of enjoyable sensibly priced food all day from sandwiches up, well kept Fullers/Gales beers, efficient friendly staff; occasional live music; children welcome, outside seating including heated patio and suntrap roof terrace looking over a series of locks towards handsome church, moorings, open all day (till midnight Fri, Sat).

PANGBOURNE   SU6376
Elephant (0118) 984 2244
Church Road; RG8 7AR Large handsome black and white inn with decorative elephants of all sizes in bars, dining room and seating areas; main bar has flagstone floor, log fire and antler chandeliers, leather-backed stools around counter serving Sharps, West Berkshire, a couple of real ciders and 16 wines by the glass, good choice of enjoyable food from lunchtime sandwiches to steaks cooked on an open fire, afternoon teas, friendly service; background music; children and dogs (in bar) welcome, big back garden with giant chess set and rattan-style sofas on raised terrace, individually styled bedrooms, charging point for electric vehicles, pretty Thameside village, open all day.

READING   SU7173
Alehouse (0118) 950 8119
Broad Street; RG1 2BH No-frills drinkers' pub with nine well kept quickly changing ales, craft kegs, lots of different bottled beers and real ciders/perries; small bare-boards bar with raised seating area, hundreds of pump clips on walls and ceiling, corridor to several appealing panelled rooms, some little more than alcoves, no food; open all day.

READING   SU7273
Fishermans Cottage
(0118) 956 0432 *Kennet Side – easiest to walk from Orts Road, off Kings Road; RG1 3HJ* White-painted pub tucked away in housing estate by canalised River Kennet; good tasty food including tapas and paella, four interesting changing ales along with various craft beers, friendly service, modern interior with airy conservatory; twice-monthly quiz and live music; children and dogs welcome, picnic-sets up by towpath, beach hut-style booths on back deck, open all day, kitchen closes 7pm Sun and all Mon.

READING   SU7073
Nags Head (07765) 880137
Russell Street; RG1 7XD Fairly basic mock-Tudor drinkers' pub just outside town centre attracting good mix of customers; a dozen well kept changing beers and 14 ciders, baguettes and pies (roasts on Sun), open fire, darts and cribbage; background and occasional live music, TV for major sports (busy on Reading FC match days); suntrap beer garden, open all day.

READING   SU7173
★ **Sweeney & Todd** (0118) 958 6466
Castle Street; RG1 7RD Pie shop with popular bar-restaurant behind (little changed in over 30 years); warren of private period-feel alcoves and other areas on various levels, enjoyable home-made food including their range of good value pies, cheery service, small bar with four well kept ales such as Adnams and Hook Norton, Weston's cider and decent wines; children welcome in restaurant area, closed Sun evening and bank holidays, otherwise open (and food) all day.

SHEFFORD WOODLANDS   SU3673
★ **Pheasant** (01488) 648284
Less than half a mile from M4 junction 14 – A338 towards Wantage, first left on B4000; RG17 7AA Handome and carefully updated country inn – a great all-rounder; interconnecting bar rooms with comfortable mix of furniture, contemporary paintwork, antiques and horse-related prints, photos and paintings, also a snug with upholstered armchairs and sofas, separate dining room; real ales from maybe Banks's, Gritchie, Marstons and Ramsbury, well chosen wine list, cocktails, interesting liqueurs and impressive choice of spirits, highly rated modern British cooking (special diets catered for); background music; children and dogs (in bar and bedrooms) welcome, seats in the garden with attractive views, 11 individually designed modern bedrooms in separate extension, open all day.

SHINFIELD   SU7368
Black Boy (0118) 988 3116
Shinfield Road (A327); RG2 9BP

Barons group pub well placed for the M4; contemporary beamed interior with bow-windowed front bar and spreading back restaurant, painted half-panelling, some high tables and lots of booth seating, modern artwork and a couple of gas woodburners, three real ales including Greene King and good range of wines/gins, popular food from baguettes and sharing plates through burgers and pub favourites up, friendly helpful staff; background music; children welcome, no dogs inside, back terrace with own bar and various covered seating areas, open all day.

SHINFIELD SU7367

★ **Magpie & Parrot** (0118) 988 4130

2.6 miles from M4 junction 11, via B3270; A327 just SE of Shinfield on Arborfield Road; RG2 9EA Unusual homely little roadside cottage, very popular locally; two cosy spic and span bars, warm fire and lots of bric-a-brac (miniature and historic bottles, stuffed birds, dozens of model cars, veteran AA badges and automotive instruments), Fullers London Pride and a local guest from small corner counter, weekday lunchtime snacks and evening fish and chips (Thurs, Fri), hospitable landlady; no credit cards or mobile phones; pub dogs (others welcome), seats on back terrace and marquee on immaculate lawn, open 12-7.30pm (later once a month when live jazz), closed Sun evening, Mon.

SHURLOCK ROW SU8374

★ **Shurlock Inn** (0118) 934 9094

Just off B3018 SE of Twyford; The Street; RG10 0PS Refurbished and extended 17th-c village dining pub (part of the small Rarebreed group – see Plough at Cobham, Surrey); high quality food from bar snacks and sharing plates up including signature steaks, well kept ales such as Sharps, Rebellion and local Stardust, nice wines, interesting gin range and cocktails, friendly engaging staff, log fire in double-sided fireplace, restaurant with open-view kitchen; background music; children and dogs (in bar) welcome, black metal furniture on terrace, lawned garden with picnic-sets and fenced play area, open (and food) all day, kitchen closes 6.30pm Sun.

SULHAMSTEAD SU6269

Spring (0118) 930 3440

Bath Road (A4); RG7 5HP Attractive former coaching inn (sister to George in Wraysbury) with spacious bar and balustraded upstairs dining area under the rafters; good variety of popular food from interesting sandwiches up, three real ales including West Berkshire and nice range of wines by the glass, friendly efficient staff; children and dogs (in bar) welcome, plenty of seats outside on terrace overlooking cricket club, open all day.

SUNNINGHILL SU9568

Belvedere Arms (01344) 870931

London Road; SL5 7SB Chic country dining pub on edge of Virginia Water and Windsor Great Park; wide choice of good interesting food including Weds evening set menu and weekend brunch, ales such as Fullers and Sharps, friendly helpful service; children and dogs welcome, nice outside gravelled seating area with stream, open (and food) all day.

SUNNINGHILL SU9367

Carpenters Arms (01344) 622763

Upper Village Road; SL5 7AQ Restauranty village pub run by French team; good authentic French country cooking, not cheap but they do offer a reasonably priced set lunch (Mon-Sat), nice wines including house pichets and well kept Sharps Doom Bar; no children in the evening, terrace tables and back garden, open all day, food all day Sun, booking recommended.

SUNNINGHILL SU9367

Dog & Partridge (01344) 623204

Upper Village Road; SL5 7AQ Bright contemporary décor and emphasis on good freshly made food from lunchtime sandwiches up including some vegan choices, friendly helpful staff, three real ales and a good range of wines; background music; children and dogs welcome, disabled facilities, part covered courtyard garden with central fountain, closed Mon, otherwise open all day, food till 6pm Sun.

SWALLOWFIELD SU7364

★ **George & Dragon** (0118) 988 4432

Church Road, towards Farley Hill; RG7 1TJ Popular and characterful country pub with attentive long-serving licensees; comfortable linked rooms with beams and standing timbers, nice mix of old dining chairs, settles and wooden tables, rugs on flagstones, big log fire, country prints on red or bare brick walls, well kept ales – perhaps Ringwood Razorback, Sharps Doom Bar and Youngs Bitter, quite a few wines by the glass, several gins and whiskies, tasty food from sandwiches up; children and dogs (in bar) welcome, garden with picnic-sets, good circular walk from pub, open all day.

THEALE SU6471

Fox & Hounds (0118) 930 2295

2 miles from M4 junction 12; follow A4 W, then first signed for station, over two roundabouts, then over narrow canal bridge to Sheffield Bottom; RG7 4BE Large Wadworths pub with enjoyable reasonably priced food (not Sun evening) from baguettes to specials, five well kept ales, Weston's cider, decent wines and coffee, friendly efficient service, L-shaped bar with dividers, traditional mix of furniture on carpet or bare boards including area with modern sofas and low tables, two open fires; pool and darts, Sun quiz; children and dogs welcome, outside seating at front and sides, lakeside bird reserve opposite, open all day Fri-Sun.

THREE MILE CROSS   SU7167
Swan (0118) 988 3674
A33 just S of M4 junction 11; Basingstoke Road; RG7 1AT Traditional pub built in the 17th c and later a posting house; four well kept ales including Loddon and Timothy Taylors, enjoyable fairly standard home-made food at reasonable prices, friendly efficient staff, two beamed and panelled bars, inglenook with hanging black pots, old prints and some impressive stuffed fish; large well arranged outside seating area behind, near Reading FC's Madejski Stadium and gets very busy on match days, closed Sun evening, otherwise open all day.

WALTHAM ST LAWRENCE SU8376
★**Bell** (0118) 934 1788
B3024 E of Twyford; The Street; RG10 0JJ Welcoming black and white 14th-c pub with well preserved timbered interior; good home-made food marked on blackboard from bar snacks up, cheerful attentive service, five well kept mainly local beers including Loddon, up to eight real ciders and plenty of wines by the glass, also good choice of whiskies; two compact connecting rooms, another larger one off entrance hall, warming log fires, daily newspapers; children and dogs welcome, pretty back garden with terrace and shady trees, open all day weekends, no evening food Sun-Tues.

WARGRAVE   SU7878
Bull (0118) 940 3120
Off A321 Henley–Twyford; High Street; RG10 8DE Attractive low-beamed 15th-c brick coaching inn run well by hospitable landlady; five smallish interconnected rooms, main bar with inglenook log fire, two dining areas (one up steps for families), good traditional home-made food from baguettes up, three well kept ales including Brakspears Bitter, friendly attentive staff; background music; well behaved dogs welcome, walled garden behind, four bedrooms, open all day weekends, no evening food Sun.

WEST ILSLEY   SU4782
Harrow (01635) 281260
Signed off A34 at E Ilsley slip road; RG20 7AR Appealing and welcoming family-run country pub in peaceful spot overlooking cricket pitch and pond; Victorian prints in deep-coloured knocked-through bar, some antique furnishings, log fire, good choice of enjoyable sensibly priced home-made food (not Sun or Mon evenings), well kept Greene King ales and nice selection of wines by the glass, afternoon teas;

children allowed in eating areas, dogs in bar, big garden with picnic-sets, more seats on pleasant terrace, handy for Ridgeway walkers, closed Mon lunchtime and maybe early Sun evening if quiet.

WHITE WALTHAM   SU8477
★**Beehive** (01628) 822877
Waltham Road (B3024 W of Maidenhead); SL6 3SH Attractive red-brick village pub with highly regarded food cooked by chef-patron including more affordable bar menu; several comfortably spacious areas with leather chairs around sturdy tables, neat bar with scatter cushions on built-in wall seats and captain's chairs, Rebellion IPA, Sharps Doom Bar and Timothy Taylors Landlord on handpump, good wine list and farm cider, airy restaurant with folding doors on to front terrace overlooking cricket field, friendly service; children and dogs (in bar) welcome, plenty of tables in bigger back garden, disabled access/loos, open all day Sat, till 6pm Sun, closed Mon.

WINDSOR   SU9676
Carpenters Arms (01753) 863739
Market Street; SL4 1PB Popular Nicholsons pub rambling around central servery; good choice of well kept ales and several wines by the glass, reasonably priced pubby food from sandwiches up including range of pies, sturdy pub furnishings and Victorian-style décor with two pretty fireplaces, family areas up a few steps, also downstairs beside former tunnel entrance with suits of armour; background music, sports TV; no dogs, tables out on cobbled pedestrian alley opposite castle, no nearby parking, handy for Legoland bus stop, open (and food) all day.

WINDSOR   SU9676
Two Brewers (01753) 855426
Park Street; SL4 1LB Small pub at the entrance to the Long Walk, a stone's throw from Windsor Castle; three cosy unchanging rooms, well kept ales such as Fullers London Pride, St Austell Tribute and Sharps Doom Bar, good choice of wines by the glass and enjoyable freshly made food from shortish mid-priced menu (tapas Fri and Sat evenings), friendly service, thriving old-fashioned pub atmosphere, beams, bare boards and open fire, enamel signs, posters and old photographs; background music, daily papers; no children inside, dogs welcome, seating out at front on pretty Georgian street, open all day, kitchen closes 7pm Sun.

WINDSOR   SU9576
Vansittart Arms (01753) 865988
Vansittart Road; SL4 5DD Friendly salmon-coloured Victorian local; three rooms with cosy corners and open fires, well kept Fullers/Gales beers, large helpings of enjoyable good value home-made food (all

day weekends); background music, sports
TV, pool; children and dogs welcome, part-
covered beer garden, open all day.

WOODSIDE   SU9270
Rose & Crown (01344) 882051
*Woodside Road, Winkfield, off A332
Ascot–Windsor; SL4 2DP* Attractively
updated dining pub; beamed bar with wood
flooring and logburner, other areas set for
their enjoyable food from sandwiches and
pub favourites up including deals and good
Sun roasts, attentive friendly service, three
well kept ales such as Greene King and
Timothy Taylors, lots of wines by the glass;
background music; children and dogs (in
bar) welcome, tables out at front and in side
garden, smallish car park (parking in lane
can be tricky), open (and food) all day.

WRAYSBURY   TQ0174
George (01784) 482000
Windsor Road (B376); TW19 5DE
Beamed dining pub (sister pub is Spring in
Sulhamstead) with good fairly priced food
from lunchtime sandwiches up (special

diets catered for), three real ales and
plenty of wines by the glass, friendly helpful
service, mix of wooden farmhouse-style
furniture on bare boards, wall lanterns and
painted half-panelling, armchairs by open
fire; background music; children and dogs
welcome, decked terrace with smart modern
rattan tables and chairs, open all day, food
all day Sun.

WRAYSBURY   TQ0074
Perseverance (01784) 482375
High Street; TW19 5DB Welcoming
old community village pub ('the Percy');
enjoyable good value home-made food from
sandwiches up including weekday set lunch
and Weds steak night, well kept Otter Ale
and three guests (maybe Sharps or Windsor
& Eton), real cider, decent choice of wines
by the glass and interesting selection of gins,
friendly helpful staff, beams and log fires
(one in inglenook); regular events including
quiz, live music and open mike nights, darts;
children till 9pm and dogs welcome, nice
back garden with weekend pizza oven, open
all day (till 8pm Sun), food all day Sat.

Buckinghamshire

KEY ★ Star Pub 🌟 Top Quality Food 🍺 Great Beer
🍷 Good Wines £ Bargain Meals 🛏 Good Bedrooms 🍴 Serves Food

ADSTOCK   SP7330 Map 4
Old Thatched Inn 🌟 🍷 🍺
(01296) 712584 – www.theoldthatchedinn.co.uk
Main Street, off A413; MK18 2JN

Well run dining pub with keen landlord, friendly staff, five real ales and good food

Set in an attractive village surrounded by rolling farmland, this is a pretty thatched place with consistently high standards. Our readers enjoy it very much. The small front bar area has low beams, sofas on flagstones, high bar chairs and an open fire. A dining area leads off with more beams and a mix of pale wooden dining chairs around miscellaneous tables on a stripped wooden floor; background music. Fullers London Pride, Hook Norton Hooky, Sharps Doom Bar and two guests on handpump served by the enthusiastic landlord, plus 16 wines by the glass and a large selection of malt whiskies and gins. A modern conservatory restaurant at the back has well spaced tables on bare boards, and the sheltered terrace has plenty of tables and chairs under a gazebo. Disabled access.

🌟 Interesting, up-to-date food (catering for gluten-free, vegan and other diets) includes Colston Bassett stilton salad with walnuts and pear, prawn cocktail, baked aubergine with tomato provençale and mozzarella, pan-roasted Cornish hake with fennel, capers and peas, wild mushroom pappardelle with mushroom sauce, confit leg of duck with oriental noodles, pak choi, spring roll and hoisin sauce, and puddings such as white chocolate pannacotta and sticky date pudding with toffee sauce; there's a set lunch on weekdays. *Benchmark main dish: crispy pork belly, creamed potatoes, garlic cabbage, fondant apple and cider gravy. Two-course evening meal £23.00.*

Free house ~ Licensee Andrew Judge ~ Real ale ~ Open 12-11; 12-10 Sun ~ Bar food 12-2.30, 5-9; 12-8 Sun ~ Restaurant ~ Children welcome ~ Dogs allowed in bar

BEACONSFIELD   SU9490 Map 2
White Horse 🍷 🍺
(01494) 360000 – www.brunningandprice.co.uk/whitehorse
London End; HP9 2JD

Bustling town pub with a wide choice of interesting drinks, rewarding food and attractive furnishings

This spacious pub, with a great location in the centre of town, usefully opens at 10.30am when they offer teas, hot chocolate and a good selection of coffees. Helpful, friendly staff serve St Austell Brunning & Price

Traditional Bitter plus Rebellion Roasted Nuts, Redemption Trinity, Timothy Taylors Boltmaker and other changing ales on handpump, 22 wines by the glass, a wide choice of gins, 20 brandies and 59 malt whiskies. Life revolves around the bar, and this area and the interlinked dining rooms offer plenty of room for both those wanting just a drink and a chat and others after the fine range of food. There are long, wall banquettes, leather dining and wooden chairs and chesterfield sofas and armchairs on polished boards, rugs or tiles. Horse prints, pictures and photographs line bare brick or painted walls, house plants of varying size are dotted about and shelves of books abound, while open fires and woodburning stoves keep things cosy in winter; board games. A favourite spot is the conservatory towards the back with its skylight and mass of tropical plants interspersed with pretty wicker light fixtures. There are a few tables outside at the front.

Good, bistro-style food includes sandwiches, charcuterie plate, crispy baby squid with sweet chilli sauce, beetroot and quinoa burger in a pretzel bun, butternut squash tortellini with sunblush tomato dressing, chicken, leek and ham pie, massaman fish and seafood curry with coconut rice, peanuts and sesame pak choi, rare roasted topside of beef with yorkshire pudding, and puddings such as triple chocolate brownie with chocolate sauce and vanilla ice-cream and crème brûlée. *Benchmark main dish: baked cod with lemon and parsley crumb and chilli and chive risotto £16.95. Two-course evening meal £23.00.*

Brunning & Price ~ Manager Rachel Perry ~ Real ale ~ Open 10.30am-11pm; 10.30am-midnight Fri, Sat; 10.30-10.30 Sun ~ Bar food 12-10; 12-9 Sun ~ Children welcome (but not in the bar after 5pm) ~ Dogs allowed in bar

BOVINGDON GREEN
Royal Oak ⭑☆ ⚲

SU8386   Map 2

(01628) 488611 – www.royaloakmarlow.co.uk

0.75 miles N of Marlow, on back road to Frieth signposted off West Street (A4155) in centre; SL7 2JF

Civilised dining pub with nice little bar, a fine choice of wines by the glass, real ales and imaginative food

Thoughtful extra touches enhance the tone at this bright and friendly pub: a bowl of olives on the bar, carefully laid-out newspapers and fresh flowers or candles on the tables. You'll find a fine choice of drinks, including locally brewed Rebellion IPA alongside a guest, perhaps from Windsor & Eton or Chiltern, on handpump, more than 30 wines by the glass (including sparkling wine, champagne and pudding wines), 40 or so gins and 15 malt whiskies – though most customers are here for the excellent food. Staff remain helpful and impressively efficient, even when busy. The low-beamed, cosy snug, closest to the car park, has three small tables and a woodburning stove in an exposed brick fireplace (with a big pile of logs beside it). Several other attractively decorated areas open off the central bar with half-panelled walls variously painted in pale blue, green or cream (the dining room ones are red). Throughout there's a mix of church chairs, stripped wooden tables and chunky wall seats, with rugs on the partly wooden, partly flagstoned floors, co-ordinated cushions and curtains, and a bright, airy feel. Background music. A sunny terrace with good solid tables leads to an appealing garden with pétanque, ping pong, badminton and swing ball; there's also a smaller side garden and a kitchen herb garden. They have a tipi for private events.

Delicious modern food includes crispy salt and pepper squid with sriracha mayonnaise, spiced coastal fishcake with sweet chilli and lemon, Moroccan-spiced vegetable curry with bulgar wheat, pickled cucumber and mint yoghurt, pork belly with spiced puy lentils, roast pepper, hummus and coriander dressing, sea bream fillet with saffron potatoes, braised fennel, cherry tomatoes and black olive and caper dressing, chickpea and split pea falafel burger with halloumi, marjoram yoghurt and sweet potato fries, and puddings such as warm chocolate and beetroot brownie with malted milk ice-cream and treacle ginger tart with clotted cream and citrus curd. *Benchmark main dish: bubble and squeak with oak-smoked bacon, poached egg and hollandaise sauce £13.75. Two-course evening meal £22.00.*

Salisbury Pubs ~ Manager Laura Porter ~ Real ale ~ Open 11am-midnight; 11-11 Sun ~ Bar food 12-2.30, 6-9.30; 12-3, 6-10 Fri, Sat; 12-9 Sun ~ Restaurant ~ Children welcome ~ Dogs allowed in bar

BRILL SP6513 Map 4

Pointer 🌟 ⚆ 🛏

(01844) 238339 – www.thepointerbrill.co.uk
Church Street; HP18 9RT

● ●

Buckinghamshire Dining Pub of the Year

Carefully restored pub with rewarding food, local ales and interesting furnishings; bedrooms

Unusually, this handsome place is a pub-cum-restaurant-cum-butchery business and all the meat comes from their own livestock herds and neighbouring farms; also, free-range eggs, home-baked bread and home-made pies, sausage rolls and so on (open 2.30-6.30pm Wednesday-Friday, 9am-2.30pm Saturday). The stylish bar has low beams, windsor chairs, elegant armchairs and sofas with brocaded cushions, open fires or woodburners in brick fireplaces and animal-hide stools by the counter. House ales come from XT Brewery, and there's a solid list of artisan spirits and liqueurs, and a thoughtfully curated wine list, all served by friendly, attentive staff. The airy and attractive restaurant has antique Ercol chairs around pale oak tables, cushioned window seats, rafters in a high vaulted ceiling and an open kitchen. French windows open on to the sizeable garden. Opposite this handsome inn is a red brick cottage which houses their eight restful, pretty bedrooms. Tolkien is said to have based the village of Bree in *The Lord of the Rings* on this pretty village.

Interesting, indulgent dishes include bubble and squeak with crispy bacon, poached eggs and hollandaise sauce, devilled chicken livers on toasted brioche, baked whole camembert to share studded with garlic and rosemary, ale-battered fish and triple-cooked chips, basil and pumpkin seed pesto linguine with roasted aubergine and toasted pumpkin seeds, and puddings such as citrus chocolate mousse and tiramisu with Tia Maria, chocolate crumb, coffee ice-cream and chocolate tuille. *Benchmark main dish: Pointer burger and skinny fries £15.95. Two-course evening meal £24.00.*

Free house ~ Real ale ~ Open 3-11pm Mon, Tues; 12-11 Wed, Thur; 12-midnight Fri, Sat; 12-9pm Sun ~ Bar food 12-2.30, 6.30-9 (9.30 Fri, Sat) ~ Restaurant ~ Children welcome ~ Dogs allowed in bar & bedrooms ~ Bedrooms: £120

FORTY GREEN SU9291 Map 2

Royal Standard of England ◖

(01494) 673382 – www.rsoe.co.uk
3.5 miles from M40 junction 2, via A40 to Beaconsfield, then follow signs to Forty Green, off B474 0.75 miles N of New Beaconsfield; keep going through village; HP9 1XT

Full of history and character, with fascinating antiques in rambling rooms, and good choice of drinks and food

This ancient red-brick inn appears regularly in films and television programmes such as *Endeavour* and *Midsomer Murders* – and it's easy to see why. Trading for nearly 900 years (do read the leaflet documenting its long history), it's an atmospheric trip back in time. The rambling rooms have some fine old features to look out for: huge black ship's timbers, lovely worn floors, carved oak panelling, roaring winter fires with handsomely decorated iron firebacks and cluttered mantelpieces. There's also a massive settle apparently built to fit the curved transom of an Elizabethan ship. Nooks and crannies are filled with a collection of antiques, including rifles, powder-flasks and bugles, ancient pewter and pottery tankards, lots of tarnished brass and copper, needlework samplers and richly coloured stained glass. Drinks include Chiltern Pale Ale, Hardy & Hansons Olde Trip, Rebellion IPA and Zebedee and Windsor & Eton Conqueror on handpump, a carefully annotated list of bottled beers, an array of gins, whiskies and rums, farm ciders, perry, Somerset brandy and a good choice of wines by the glass. You can sit outside in a neatly hedged front rose garden or under the shade of a tree; look out for the red gargoyle on the wall facing the car park.

Traditional, hearty food includes lunchtime baguettes, welsh rarebit and other snacks on toast (11.30am-5pm), Cornish oysters, moules marinière, fish pie, roast chicken with spiced red cabbage, liver and bacon with mash and onion gravy, pork belly with bubble and squeak and apple sauce, vegan mushroom and sherry steamed pudding with sautéed potatoes, and puddings such as sticky toffee pudding with caramel sauce, chocolate mousse and eton mess. *Benchmark main dish: fish and chips £15.95. Two-course evening meal £20.00.*

Free house ~ Licensee Matthew O'Keeffe ~ Real ale ~ Open 10.30-11 (10 Sun) ~ Bar food 11.30-10 (9 Sun) ~ Children welcome ~ Dogs welcome

FULMER
SU9985   Map 2

Black Horse

(01753) 663183 – www.theblackhorsefulmer.co.uk

Village signposted off A40 in Gerrards Cross, W of junction with A413; Windmill Road; SL3 6HD

Appealingly reworked dining pub, friendly and relaxed, with up-to-date food, exemplary service and pleasant garden; bedrooms

Adjacent to the attractive red-brick church, this is an extended 17th-c pub in a charming conservation village. There's a proper bar in the middle and two cosy areas to the left: low black beams, rugs on bare boards, settles and other solid pub furniture and several open log fires. Greene King IPA, Timothy Taylors Landlord and a guest such as St Austell Tribute on handpump, 30 wines by the glass and a dozen malt whiskies; staff are friendly and efficient even when pushed. Background music. The main area on the right is set for dining and leads to the good-sized suntrap back terrace where there's a summer barbecue bar; there are also picnic-sets on the lawn beyond. The two bedrooms are stylish and well equipped. The pub launched a farm shop during the coronavirus lockdown; open daily, it's been a big hit locally.

Some sort of good quality food is served all day from breakfast onwards: crispy squid with sweet chilli mayonnaise, Moroccan spiced chickpea and apricot tagine with jasmine rice, confit pork belly with apple and kohlrabi slaw and apple sauce, sharing boards, halloumi burger in a brioche bun with skinny fries, wild mushroom risotto with truffle oil, crispy bacon and hollandaise, half rotisserie-cooked chicken with fries, confit duck leg with balsamic and bacon lentils, fondant potato and orange jus, and puddings such as apple and rhubarb crumble with custard or vanilla ice-cream, passion-fruit crème brûlée and eton mess. *Benchmark main dish: beer-battered haddock and chips £14.75. Two-course evening meal £20.50.*

Greene King ~ Real ale ~ Open 8am-9pm; 8-7 Sun ~ Bar food 8am-9pm; 8-7 Sun ~ Restaurant ~ Children welcome ~ Dogs allowed in bar ~ Bedrooms

GRANBOROUGH
SP7625   Map 4

Crown ♀

(01296) 670216 – www.thecrowngranborough.co.uk

Winslow Road; MK18 3NJ

Perfect in good weather with several seating areas and an outside bar, and cosy in winter with open fires

This spacious former coaching inn has existed on this site for centuries. With plenty of space for both eating and drinking, the main bar is a long room with painted beams, high chairs at the counter and at elbow tables and a fire at one end; a second bar has sofas, more painted beams and a comfortable feel. There are three changing ales on handpump – perhaps Fullers London Pride, Marstons Pedigree and Sharps Doom Bar – 12 wines by the glass and 50 gins, served by friendly staff. The restaurant is a lovely room with a high pitched roof and oak beams, farmhouse and other chairs around solid tables on wooden boards and a woodburning stove in a sizeable fireplace; a smaller room is more intimate and similarly furnished; background music. In warm weather, take advantage of the cushioned, rattan-style sofas on the terrace, the wooden tables and chairs under parasols on gravel or the picnic-sets on the long lawn (where there's also a wooden climbing frame); summer barbecues.

Good food uses local, seasonal produce and includes sandwiches, deep-fried whitebait with curry mayo, grilled goats cheese with beetroot, candied walnuts and red onion jam, chicken pie with creamed potatoes and sautéed greens, pan-fried fillet of salmon with cheese and leek gnocchi and samphire, and puddings such as sticky toffee pudding with vanilla ice-cream and lemon posset with red fruit compote and ginger nut biscuit; Thursday is burger and pint night and there's brunch on Saturday (10.30am-2pm). *Benchmark main dish: beer-battered fish and chips £13.95. Two-course evening meal £20.00.*

Free house ~ Licensee Andy Judge ~ Real ale ~ Open 12-10 Wed-Fri; 12-11 Sat; 12-7 Sun ~ Bar food 12-2, 5-9 Wed-Fri; 12-9 Sat; 12-7 Sun ~ Restaurant ~ Children welcome ~ Dogs allowed in bar

GREAT MISSENDEN
SP9000   Map 4

Nags Head ⭐ ⌂

(01494) 862200 – www.nagsheadbucks.com

Old London Road, E – beyond Abbey; HP16 0DG

Well run and pretty inn with beamed bars, an open fire, a good range of drinks and modern cooking; bedrooms

Roald Dahl used this attractive creeper-clad inn as his local and the Roald Dahl Museum & Story Centre is a short stroll away. Built as three small cottages in the 15th c, it's a gently civilised place with creative food. There's a low-beamed area on the left, a loftier part on the right, a mix of small pews, dining chairs and tables on carpet and a log fire in a handsome fireplace. Rebellion IPA and a couple of guests such as Malt Missenden Pale Ale on handpump from the unusual bar counter (the windows behind face the road), over 30 wines by the glass from an extensive list, 15 malt whiskies,

30 gins and half a dozen vintage Armagnacs. As well as an outside dining area beneath a pergola, there are seats on the extensive back lawn. The six beamed bedrooms are well equipped and comfortable, and the breakfasts are very good.

 Impressive food includes blue swimmer white crab meat, home-smoked salmon, blinis and chive cream, mushroom feuilletée with calvados cream and julienned vegetables, charcuterie board (for two), pan-fried lamb cannon with compote of Mediterranean vegetables and red onion jus, crab thermidor with skinny fries, steamed sea bass fillet with ruby chard and beurre blanc with capers, bean and sweetcorn burger with home-made almond and barbecue sauce and fries, and puddings such as raspberry and bourbon vanilla crème brûlée and blueberry, pear and almond 'Bourdaloue' tart with coconut ice-cream. *Benchmark main dish: Tring beer-battered haddock fillet with skinny fries and home-made tartare sauce £16.45. Two-course evening meal £23.50.*

Free house ~ Licensee Adam Michaels ~ Real ale ~ Open 12-11; 8am-10pm Sun ~ Bar food 12-2.30, 6-8.30; 12-9 Sat; 12-7 Sun ~ Restaurant ~ Children welcome ~ Dogs allowed in bar ~ Bedrooms: £115

HEDGERLEY
SU9687 Map 2

White Horse ★ 🍺 £

(01753) 643225 – www.thewhitehorsehedgerley.co.uk

2.4 miles from M40 junction 2; at exit roundabout take Slough turn-off following alongside M40; after 1.5 miles turn right at T junction into Village Lane; SL2 3UY

Charming old place with lots of beers, home-made lunchtime food and a cheery mix of customers

This convivial country gem is many people's idea of an unspoilt English pub and it's hard to believe that it's so close to suburbia as it feels a world away. The cottagey main bar has plenty of character with beams, brasses and exposed brickwork, low wooden tables, standing timbers, jugs and other bric-a-brac, a log fire and a good few leaflets and notices about village events. A little flagstoned public bar on the left has darts, shove-ha'penny and board games. The fine range of real ales might include Rebellion IPA and up to seven daily changing guests, sourced from all over the country and tapped straight from casks kept in a room behind the tiny hatch counter. Also, craft ales in kegs or bottles, three farm ciders, a dozen wines by the glass, a similar number of malt whiskies and winter mulled wine. A canopied extension leads out to the garden where there are tables, lots of hanging baskets and occasional barbecues; a few tables in front of the building overlook the quiet road; disabled access. There are good walks nearby and the pub is handy for the Church Wood RSPB reserve.

 Lunchtime-only bar food includes good sandwiches, a salad bar with home-cooked quiches and cold meats, changing hot dishes such as soup, sausage or lamb casserole, and proper puddings such as plum sponge and bread and butter pudding. *Benchmark main dish: steak pie £7.95.*

Free house ~ Licensee Kevin Brooker ~ Real ale ~ Open 11-2.30, 5-10 Mon, Tues; 11-2.30, 5-11 Weds-Fri; 11-11 Sat; 12-10.30 Sun ~ Bar food 12-2 (2.30 Sat, Sun) ~ Children allowed in canopied extension area ~ Dogs allowed in bar

LITTLE MARLOW
SU8787 Map 2

Queens Head 🌟

(01628) 482927 – www.marlowslittlesecret.co.uk

Village signposted off A4155 E of Marlow near Kings Head; bear right into Pound Lane cul-de-sac; SL7 3SR

Pretty tiled cottage with good food and ales, friendly staff and appealing garden

'Marlow's little secret' says the website, 'a hidden treasure' says one of our readers: this attractive red-brick country pub is certainly charmingly tucked away, next to the church and opposite the manor house. The friendly, unpretentious main bar has simple but comfortable furniture on polished boards and leads back to a sizeable squarish carpeted dining extension with good solid tables. Throughout are old local photographs on cream walls, panelled dados painted brown or sage, and lighted candles. On the right is a small, quite separate, low-ceilinged public bar with Rebellion IPA and Sharps Doom Bar on handpump, several wines by the glass, quite a range of whiskies and gins and good coffee; neatly dressed efficient staff and unobtrusive background music. On summer days, the front garden (though not large) is a decided plus: sheltered and neatly planted, it has teak tables and quite closely arranged picnic-sets.

Highly rated food includes ploughman's and ciabattas, avocado and poached egg on sourdough, seared scallops with pea purée and black pudding crumb, cauliflower steak with halloumi and chickpea stew, sea bass fillet with confit fennel and brown shrimp butter, shoulder and rump of lamb with onions, butternut squash and jus, chargrilled rib-eye steak with béarnaise sauce, and puddings such as chocolate crémeux and bakewell tart with raspberry ripple ice-cream. *Benchmark main dish: herb-crusted cod with peas and celeriac chips £18.50. Two-course evening meal £25.00.*

Punch ~ Lease Daniel O'Sullivan ~ Real ale ~ Open 11-11; 11-10 Sun ~ Bar food 12-2.30, 6.30-9.30; 12-4, 6.30-9.30 weekends ~ Restaurant ~ Children welcome ~ Dogs allowed in bar

LITTLE MISSENDEN   SU9298   Map 4
Crown 🍺 £
(01494) 862571 – www.thecrownlittlemissenden.co.uk
Crown Lane, SE end of village, which is signposted off A413 W of Amersham; HP7 0RD

Long-serving licensees and pubby feel in little country cottage, with several real ales and straightforward food; attractive garden

Few pubs can boast of being run by the same lovely family for more than 90 years, and that's one of the reasons why coming here is special. All visitors, not just the loyal bunch of regulars, are warmly welcomed. The bustling bars in this traditional brick cottage are more spacious than they might first appear – and immaculately kept. There are old red floor tiles on the left, oak parquet on the right, built-in wall seats, studded red leatherette chairs and a few small tables and a winter fire. You'll find Otter Bitter and three quickly changing guests on handpump or tapped from the cask, ten farm ciders, summer Pimms, a good range of gins and several malt whiskies; darts and board games. A large attractive sheltered garden behind has picnic-sets and other tables, and there are also seats out in front. Bedrooms are in a converted barn (continental breakfasts in your room only). Dogs may be allowed inside if well behaved. No children. The interesting church in the pretty village is well worth a visit.

Honest lunchtime-only food (not Sunday) includes their famous 'Bucks Bite', a long list of sandwiches with home-made chutney, ploughman's, generous salads, jacket potatoes with various fillings, and smoked haddock and spring onion or cod and bacon fishcakes with a sweet chilli dip.

Free house ~ Licensees Trevor and Carolyn How ~ Real ale ~ Open 11-2.30, 6-11; 12-4 Sun ~ Bar food 12-2; not Sun ~ Bedrooms: £85.

SKIRMETT

SU7790 Map 2

Frog 🍴☆🍷🛏

(01491) 638996 – www.thefrogatskirmett.co.uk

From A4155 NE of Henley take Hambleden turn and keep on; or from B482 Stokenchurch–Marlow take Turville turn and keep on; RG9 6TG

Bustling pub with modern cooking, a fine choice of drinks, lovely garden, and nearby walks; bedrooms

This pretty Chilterns pub has been cared for by the same husband-and-wife team (chef and front of house, respectively) for 25 years. The public bar, with a winter log fire in the brick fireplace, is very much at the heart of the place. There are lots of little framed prints, a cushioned sofa and leather-seated bar stools around a low circular table on the wooden floor, and high bar chairs by the counter; background music. You'll find Rebellion IPA and two changing guest beers on handpump, 13 wines by the glass (including champagne) and a good choice of malt whiskies; service is friendly and attentive. The two dining rooms are quite different in style – one is light and airy with country kitchen tables and chairs, while the other is more formal with dark red walls, smarter dining chairs and tables and candlelight. Outside, a side gate leads to a lovely garden with a large tree in the middle and unusual five-sided tables that are well placed for attractive valley views. It's an enjoyable place to stay, with three comfortable bedrooms. There are plenty of nearby walks in the charming Chilterns countryside; the delightful Cobstone windmill is just down the road and it's only a few miles to Henley and the River Thames.

🍴 Rewarding food includes lunchtime baguettes, sharing boards, eggs benedict with parma ham, king prawns in tempura batter with chilli jam and sweet chilli noodles, baked stuffed squash with goats cheese, chicken breast with asparagus and mushroom risotto and rosemary sauce, smoked haddock on colcannon with a poached egg and grain mustard sauce, duck breast with pak choi, rösti potato and orange and Cointreau sauce, and puddings. *Benchmark main dish: calves liver and bacon with black pudding, mashed potato and red wine sauce £17.50. Two-course evening meal £22.50.*

Free house ~ Licensees Jim Crowe and Noelle Greene ~ Real ale ~ Open 11.30-3, 6-11; 12-10 Sun ~ Bar food 12-2.15 (2.45 Sun), 6-9.15; winter 12-4 Sun ~ Restaurant ~ Children welcome ~ Dogs allowed in bar ~ Bedrooms: £95

Also Worth a Visit in Buckinghamshire

Besides the fully inspected pubs, you might like to try these pubs that have been recommended to us and described by readers. Do tell us what you think of them: feedback@goodguides.com

AMERSHAM SU9597

Elephant & Castle (01494) 721049
High Street; HP7 0DT Twin-gabled local with good value tasty food including pub staples such as fish and chips, steak and ale pie and burgers, quick friendly service, three well kept ales such as St Austell or Adnams from U-shaped counter, low-beams, woodburner in large brick fireplace, conservatory; garden behind, children and dogs welcome, open (and food) all day.

AMERSHAM SU9597

Kings Arms (01494) 725722
High Street; HP7 0DJ Picture-postcard timbered inn (dates from the 1400s) in charming street, lots of heavy beams and snug alcoves, big inglenook, Brakspears, Rebellion and a guest, 14 wines by the glass and good range of enjoyable food from sandwiches up, afternoon teas, friendly helpful service, restaurant; background music, collection of board games; children and dogs (in bar) welcome, 35 bedrooms,

garden behind, open all day, food all day weekends.

ASHERIDGE   SP9404
Blue Ball (01494) 758305
Braziers End; HP5 2UX Popular little tile-hung country pub with opened-up interior; generous helpings of enjoyable good value food cooked to order including daily specials, well kept Adnams, Fullers, Tring and Youngs, real cider, friendly landlady and staff; children (till 6pm) and dogs welcome, large well maintained back garden, good Chilterns walking country, open all day, no evening food Sun or Mon.

ASTON ABBOTTS   SP8519
Royal Oak (01296) 681262
Off A418 NE of Aylesbury; Wingrave Road; HP22 4LT Welcoming part-thatched beamed pub, up to four real ales and generous helpings of enjoyable reasonably priced food; children welcome, sunny back garden, 4 bedrooms, quite handy for Ascott House (NT).

ASTON CLINTON   SP8712
Oak (01296) 630466
Green End Street; HP22 5EU Cosy and attractive part-thatched village pub; well kept Fullers ales and guests, enjoyable food from snacks up including signature hanging kebabs, friendly attentive service, beams and inglenook log fire; sports TV; children welcome and dogs in the bar area, picnic-sets in good-sized garden, open (and food) all day.

ASTWOOD   SP9547
Old Swan (01234) 391351
Main Road; MK16 9JS Part thatched 17th-c village pub with warm cosy atmosphere, good food including steaks from the family's butchers, blackboard specials and weekday set menu, well kept Adnams Southwold, Fullers London Pride and Greene King IPA, nice selection of wines, friendly helpful service, beams and gleaming flagstones, inglenook woodburner, separate dining area; children and dogs (in bar) welcome – their cocker spaniel is called Tessie, large garden, closed Sun evening, Mon.

AYLESBURY   SP8114
Hop Pole (01296) 482129
Bicester Road; HP19 9AZ Friendly well looked-after end-of-terrace pub brewing its own Aylesbury Brewhouse beers, also guests and traditional cider, enjoyable fairly priced food including sharing plates and grills, back restaurant; regular live music, Tues quiz; seats out at front behind metal fence, open all day Fri-Sun, closed Mon lunchtime.

AYLESBURY   SP8113
★ Kings Head (01296) 718812
Kings Head Passage (off Bourbon Street), also entrance off Temple Street; no nearby parking except for disabled;

HP20 2RW Handsome town-centre pub owned by the National Trust, all nicely low key but civilised; some beautiful early Tudor windows and stunning 15th-c stained glass in former Great Hall and three timeless carefully restored rooms with stripped boards, cream walls with little decoration, upholstered sofas and armchairs, high-backed cushioned settles and some simple modern furniture, Chiltern ales and guests kept well, enjoyable bar food (not Sun-Tues evenings), friendly helpful service; disabled facilities, teak seats in atmospheric medieval cobbled courtyard shared with arts and crafts shop, open all day.

BEACHAMPTON   SP7736
Mowgli at the Bell
(01908) 418373 *Main Street; MK19 6DX* Big low-beamed pub combined with Indian restaurant with pleasant view down attractive streamside village street; updated bar and dining area divided by woodburner, popular Indian food and Sunday roasts; up to four changing ales, good friendly service; children welcome, large garden with paved terrace, open all day (till 8pm Sun).

BEACONSFIELD   SU9588
Hope & Champion (01494) 685530
M40, Beaconsfield Services; HP9 2SE UK's first pub (Wetherspoons) in a motorway service area; spacious modern interior on two floors, five real ales including Sharps Doom Bar and enjoyable food from breakfast on, good fast service; TVs; children welcome, no dogs inside, disabled access to ground floor only, lots of seats and tables out overlooking lake with fountain, open (and food) all day from 6am.

BEACONSFIELD   SU9490
Royal Saracens (01494) 674119
1 mile from M40 junction 2; London End (A40); HP9 2JH Former coaching inn with striking timbered façade and well updated open-plan interior; bar area with comfortable seating on wood or tiled floors, massive beams and timbers in one corner, log fires, wide choice of enjoyable food from sandwiches and sharing plates up, well kept ales such as Fullers London Pride and Sharps Doom Bar, craft kegs and plenty of wines by the glass, large back restaurant; children welcome, modern furniture and seating booths in sheltered courtyard, open (and food) all day, busy at weekends when best to book.

BLEDLOW   SP7702
Lions of Bledlow (01844) 343345
Off B4009 Chinnor–Princes Risborough; Church End; HP27 9PE Great views from bay windows of relaxed take-us-as-you-find-us Chilterns pub; low 16th-c beams, ancient floor tiles, inglenook log fires and a woodburner, several well kept beers and enjoyable food including vegetarian dishes,

friendly helpful staff; well behaved children and dogs welcome, picnic-sets out in peaceful sloping garden with sheltered terrace, nice setting and good walks, open all day weekends in summer.

BLEDLOW RIDGE   SU7997
Boot (01494) 481499
Chinnor Road; HP14 4AW Welcoming village pub with fresh modern décor; good food from sandwiches, sharing plates and pub favourites up, well kept Rebellion ales and Sharps Doom Bar, several wines by the glass from extensive list, dining room with exposed rafters and large brick fireplace, friendly service; background music; children and dogs welcome, terrace and sizeable lawned garden, closed Mon, otherwise open all day (till 7pm Sun).

BOURNE END   SU8987
Bounty (01628) 520056
Cock Marsh, actually across the river along the Cookham towpath, but shortest walk – still over 0.25 miles – is from Bourne End, over the railway bridge; SL8 5RG Welcoming laid-back pub tucked away in outstanding setting on bank of the Thames (accessible only by foot or boat); collection of flags on ceiling and jumble of other bits and pieces, well kept Rebellion ales from boat counter, basic pub food including children's meals, back dining area, darts, background music inside and out; dirty dogs and muddy walkers welcome; new outside bar in summer with bar billiards and table tennis; picnic-sets with parasols on front terrace, play area to right, open all day in summer (may be boat trips), just weekends in winter and closes early if quiet.

BRILL   SP6514
★Pheasant (01844) 239370
Windmill Street; off B4011 Bicester–Long Crendon; HP18 9TG More or less open-plan with raftered bar area, three well kept ales including Timothy Taylors Landlord and Vale Best, good food (till 4pm Sun) from changing menu, charming attentive staff, dining areas with high-backed leather or dark wooden chairs, attractively framed prints, books on shelves; background music; children and dogs (in bar) welcome, seats out on raised deck with steps down to garden, fine views over post windmill (one of the oldest in working order), walks from the door, four comfortable bedrooms (two in former bakehouse), good breakfast (residents only), open all day.

BUCKINGHAM   SP6933
Villiers (01280) 822444
Castle Street; MK18 1BS Pub part of this large comfortable hotel with own courtyard entrance; big inglenook log fire, panelling and stripped masonry in flagstoned bar, beers from Hook Norton and Adnams plus a local ale, reliably good food from shortish

menu, afternoon tea in new tearoom and bar, competent friendly staff; snug with sofas, refurbished restaurant with banquette and more formal seating; background music; children welcome till 9pm, no dogs, terrace tables, open all day.

BUTLERS CROSS   SP8407
★Russell Arms (01296) 624411
Off A4010 S of Aylesbury, at Nash Lee roundabout; or off A413 in Wendover, passing station; Chalkshire Road; HP17 0TS Bright and homely 18th-c beamed pub, a former coaching inn and servants' quarters for nearby Chequers with bar and two dining areas, eclectic mix of stripped wooden tables and chairs, open fire and woodburner in inglenook, contemporary restaurant area, well kept local ales such as Chiltern and Tring along with Rebellion IPA, 15 wines by the glass, artisan gins and good freshly made food, friendly welcoming staff; background music; children and dogs allowed, pretty garden with suntrap terrace, well placed for Chilterns walks.

CHALFONT ST GILES   SU9895
Ivy House (01494) 872184
A413 S; HP8 4RS Old brick and flint coaching inn with U-shaped bar, wood or tiled floors, log fire, Fullers ales and a guest back beamed and flagstoned restaurant serving tasty home-made food, friendly staff; background music and occasional live music, Thurs quiz, children welcome, some seats out under covered front part by road, pleasant terrace and sloping garden, five comfortable bedrooms, good hearty breakfast, open all day (till 8pm Sun).

CHEARSLEY   SP7110
Bell (01844) 208077
The Green; HP18 0DJ Cosy traditional thatched and beamed pub on attractive village green; Fullers beers and good wines by the glass, sensibly priced food (not Sun or Mon evenings) from pubby choices up, friendly helpful service, inglenook with big woodburner; quiz (first Sun of month), bingo (first Tues); children in eating area, dogs welcome, plenty of tables in spacious back garden with heated terrace and play area, open all day weekends.

CHESHAM   SP9604
Black Horse (01494) 784656
Vale Road, N off A416 in Chesham; HP5 3NS Extended and refurbished black-beamed country pub; well liked traditional food (all day Sat, Sun till 6pm winter, 8pm summer) from sandwiches up, real ales including Bombardier, Courage Directors and Eagle IPA, craft beers and 19 wines by the glass, good friendly service, inglenook log fire; Tues quiz; children and dogs welcome, picnic-sets out in front and on back lawn, closed Mon, otherwise open all day (Sun till 8pm winter, 9pm summer).

CHESHAM   SP9501
Queens Head (01494) 778690
Church Street; HP5 1JD Popular corner
pub with two traditional beamed bars;
scrubbed tables and log fires, Fullers ales
and a guest kept well, good Thai food along
with modest range of pub staples, restaurant,
friendly staff and chatty locals; Thurs quiz,
sports TV, children and dogs welcome, tables
in small courtyard used by smokers, next to
little River Chess, open all day.

CLIFTON REYNES   SP9051
Robin Hood (01234) 711574
*Off back road Emberton–Newton
Blossomville; no through road;
MK46 5DR* Community-owned 16th-c
stone-built village pub; well liked food
(award-winning chef and restaurant), up to
three real ales and decent wine list, good
friendly service, dark beams, inglenooks
with woodburners in both bars, dining
conservatory; Northamptonshire skittles
table; children and dogs welcome, two-acre
back garden with terrace and summer
barbecues, riverside walks to Olney, closed
Mon and Tues lunchtime.

COLESHILL   SU9594
★Harte & Magpies (01494) 726754
*E of village on A355 Amersham–
Beaconsfield, by junction with Magpie
Lane; HP7 0LU* Busy roadside pub with
open-plan interior; collection of pews, high-
backed booths and distinctive tables and
chairs making for plenty of snug corners,
candles in bottles and lots of old patriotic
prints, ales such as Chiltern and Rebellion,
12 wines by the glass and popular food from
baguettes and pizzas up; children (not live
music evenings) and dogs welcome, picnic-
sets on terrace by wisteria-draped tree, more
tables in big sloping garden with sturdy
wooden play area, classic car meeting second
Tues of month (Apr-Sept), good surrounding
walks, open (and food) all day, Sun till 9pm.

COLNBROOK   TQ0277
Ostrich (01753) 682628
*1.25 miles from M4 junction 5 via A4/
B3378, then 'village only' road; High
Street; SL3 0JZ* Historic timbered inn
(12th-c origins) with gruesome history – tales
of over 60 murders; refurbished interior
blending modern furnishings with oak beams
and open fireplaces, three Shepherd Neame
ales and good choice of wines, enjoyable
sensibly priced food from sandwiches and pub
favourites up, friendly service, restaurant;
children welcome, 11 bedrooms, teak furniture
in courtyard, open (and food) all day including
breakfast/brunch for non-residents.

CUDDINGTON   SP7311
★Crown (01844) 292222
*Spurt Street; off A418 Thame–Aylesbury;
HP18 0BB* Refurbished 17th-c thatched
cottage; two low-beamed linked rooms with
big inglenook log fire, well kept Fullers
and guests and enjoyable fairly priced food
from burgers up (special diets catered for),
efficient friendly service, two-room back
dining area with country kitchen chairs
around mix of tables; children and dogs (in
bar) welcome; neat side terrace with modern
furniture and planters, picnic-sets in front,
open all day Sat/Sun, no food Sun evening.

DENHAM   TQ0487
Green Man (01895) 832760
Village Road; next to the Swan; UB9 5BH
Welcoming 18th-c red-brick pub in centre
of this lovely village; modernised beamed
bar with flagstones and log fire, five well
kept ales including Rebellion and Sharps,
good choice of popular food from baguettes
up, cheerful efficient service, conservatory
dining extension; children and well behaved
dogs welcome, pretty hanging baskets out at
front, sunny back terrace and garden, open
all day.

DENHAM   TQ0487
★Swan (01895) 832085
*Village signed from M25 junction
16; UB9 5BH* Wisteria-clad Georgian
dining pub (Little Gems group); stylishly
furnished bars with nice mix of antique and
old-fashioned chairs at solid tables, heavily
draped curtains, log fires, Rebellion IPA and
a guest, good sensibly priced wine list and
decent range of spirits, well liked food (all
day Fri-Sun) including blackboard specials
and Sat brunch from 9.30am, friendly staff;
background music, daily papers; children
and dogs (in bar) welcome, extensive floodlit
back garden with sheltered terrace, open
all day.

DINTON   SP7610
Seven Stars (01296) 749000
*Signed off A418 Aylesbury–Thame, near
Gibraltar turn-off; Stars Lane;
HP17 8UL* Pretty 16th-c community-owned
pub run by French landlady and popular
locally; inglenook bar, beamed lounge and
dining room, well kept Fullers, Rebellion and
Vale, extensive wine list on two blackboards,
consistently good fairly priced food cooked
to order from pub staples up (some French
influences), friendly service; children
welcome, no dogs inside, tables in sheltered
garden with terrace, pleasant village, closed
Sun evening.

DORNEY   SU9279
Palmer Arms (01628) 666612
*2.7 miles from M4 junction 7, via
B3026; Village Road; SL4 6QW*
Modernised and extended dining pub
in attractive conservation village, good
popular food (best to book) from snacks
and pub favourites to more restaurant-style
dishes, friendly efficient service, Greene
King ales kept well, lots of wines by the

glass (interesting list) and good coffee, open fires in civilised front bar and back dining room; background music, daily newspapers; children and dogs (in certain areas) welcome, disabled facilities, terrace overlooking Mediterranean-feel garden, enclosed play area, nice riverside walks nearby, open (and food) all day.

DORNEY SU9279

Pineapple (01628) 662353

Lake End Road: 2.4 miles from M4 junction 7; left on A4 then left on B3026; SL4 6QS Nicely old-fashioned pub recently refurbished with an added contemporary garden room, handy for Dorney Court (where the first English pineapple was grown in 1661); shiny low Anaglypta ceilings, black-panelled dados, leather chairs around sturdy country tables (one very long, another in big bow window), woodburner and pretty little fireplace, china pineapples and other decorations on shelves in one of three cottagey carpeted linked rooms on left, Fullers London Pride, Sharps Atlantic, a craft ale and guest, huge variety of signature sandwiches, roasts on Sun and new kitchen for stone-baked pizzas; background music, open mike night last Weds of month, games machine; children and dogs welcome, rustic seats on roadside verandah, round picnic-sets in garden, fairy-lit decking under oak tree, open (and food) all day.

EASINGTON SP6810

★ **Mole & Chicken** (01844) 208387

From B4011 in Long Crendon follow Chearsley, Waddesdon signpost into Carters Lane opposite Indian restaurant, then turn left into Chilton Road; HP18 9EY Creeper-clad dining pub with opened-up beamed interior; cream-cushioned farmhouse chairs around oak and pine tables on flagstones or tiles, a couple of dark leather sofas, church candles and good winter log fires, Chiltern ales, several wines by the glass and quite a few malt whiskies from slabby-topped counter; interesting modern food along with more affordable pubby dishes and set menu, good service; background music; children welcome, no dogs inside, seats on raised terrace and decked area with fine views, five recently refurbished elegantly furnished bedrooms, open all day.

EVERSHOLT SP9832

Green Man (01525) 288111

Church End; MK17 9DU Handsome brick pub owned by Candice Brown (2016 *Great British Bake Off* winner) and her brother Ben; quirky modern-rustic update with maroon and teal paintwork, comfortable old leather armchairs and sofas, a woodburning stove in a brick fireplace, books on shelves and fresh flowers, cosy and welcoming vibe; Blackpit Brewery Ale and a guest, Orchard Thieves cider, ten wines by the glass and

cocktails from plank-fronted bar counter, interesting pubby food including toasties, ham hock hash and daily vegan pie; children and dogs welcome, closed Mon and Tues, otherwise open all day.

FINGEST SU7791

★ **Chequers** (01491) 638335

Off B482 Marlow–Stokenchurch; RG9 6QD Ancient white-shuttered brick and flint pub with unspoilt public bar plus other neatly kept old-fashioned rooms with large open fires, horsebrasses, pewter tankards and pub team photographs, beers from Brakspears, traditional cider, decent wines by the glass and several malt whiskies, enjoyable country cooking, smart back dining extension; board games; children and dogs welcome, tables on terrace and in big beautifully tended garden with fine views over the Hambleden Valley, good walking country and opposite interesting church with unique twin-roofed Norman tower, open all day weekends, closed Mon/Tues.

FLACKWELL HEATH SU8889

Crooked Billet (01628) 521216

Off A404; Sheepridge Lane; SL7 3SG Steps up to cosily old-fashioned 16th-c pub; Brakspears and Youngs ales, reasonably priced traditional lunchtime food including sandwiches, charming landlord and friendly staff, eating area spread pleasantly through alcoves, low black beams and good open fire; lovely cottagey garden with nice views (beyond road), walks nearby.

FRIETH SU7990

Prince Albert (01494) 881683

Off B482 SW of High Wycombe; RG9 6PY Cottagey Chilterns local with low black beams and joists, high-backed settles, big black stove in inglenook and log fire in larger area on right, decent food from sandwiches up Mon-Sat, lunchtime only Sun – they ask you to book on Sat; well kept Brakspears ales, friendly service; children and dogs welcome, nicely planted informal side garden with views of woods and fields, good walks, open all day.

FRIETH SU7990

Yew Tree (01494) 880077

Signed off B482 N of Marlow; RG9 6PJ Brick-built village pub with good food including chargrills and daily specials, real ales such as Chiltern, Loddon, Rebellion and West Berkshire, lots of wines by the glass, helpful personable staff, well presented interior with light coloured beams and timbers, wood floors and log fires, attractive back restaurant, conservatory; background music; children, walkers and dogs (in bar) welcome, tables on front terrace and in garden behind, open all day Sat, till 9pm Sun, closed Mon and Tues, also closed two weeks in summer, two weeks in winter.

GAWCOTT SP6831
Crown (01280) 822322
Hillesden Road; MK18 4JF Welcoming
16th-c black-beamed village pub; popular
good value food, three well kept ales, Sharps
Doom Bar and two guests from herringbone
brick counter, restaurant area; background
music, Sky TV; children and dogs welcome,
long back garden with swings, open all day
(till 9pm Mon, 10pm Tues), no food Sun
evening, Mon.

GERRARDS CROSS TQ0089
★Three Oaks (01753) 899016
*Austenwood Lane, just NW of junction
with Kingsway (B416); SL9 8NL*
Civilised dining pub facing Austenwood
Common; two-room front bar with fireside
bookshelves, armchairs and sturdy wall
settles and comfortable banquettes, well kept
Fullers, Rebellion and several wines by the
glass, dining part with three linked rooms,
popular highly regarded food including short
set menu, attentive friendly young staff; soft
background music; children welcome, sturdy
wooden tables on flagstoned side terrace,
open all day.

GREAT BRICKHILL SP9029
Red Lion (01525) 261715
Ivy Lane; MK17 9AH Refurbished
roadside village pub; enjoyable fairly
traditional food including lunchtime
sandwiches, real ales from Caledonian
and Tring and maybe a local guest such as
Leighton Buzzard or Hornes, good friendly
service, log fire in small bar, restaurant with
woodburner; background music, quiz Sun
evening; children and dogs (in bar) welcome,
lovely views over Buckinghamshire and
beyond from enclosed back lawn, closed Mon,
open all day weekends, no food Sun evening.

GREAT HAMPDEN SP8401
★Hampden Arms (01494) 488255
*W of Great Missenden, off A4128;
HP16 9RQ* Friendly village pub opposite
cricket pitch; comfortably furnished rooms
(back one more rustic with big woodburner),
well kept Rebellion IPA and a couple of
guests, local cider and several wines by
the glass from small corner bar, enjoyable
reasonably priced pubby food including
one or two Greek dishes, cheerful efficient
service; quiz third Weds of month; children
and dogs welcome, seats in tree-sheltered
garden, good Hampden Common walks, open
all day Sat/Sun.

GREAT KINGSHILL SU8798
★Red Lion (01494) 711262
A4128 N of High Wycombe; HP15 6EB
Welcoming village pub across from cricket
green; contemporary décor and relaxed
informal atmosphere, well cooked locally
sourced brasserie-style food including fixed-
price menu, local beers such as Rebellion

and good value wine list, 'lobby' and cosy
little flagstoned bar with leather tub chairs
by log fire, spacious candlelit dining room;
well behaved children welcome, a few seats
out at front and behind, website has walks
from pub, closed Sun evening, Mon.

GREAT MISSENDEN SP8901
★Cross Keys (01494) 865373
High Street; HP16 0AU Friendly and
relaxed village pub dating from the 16th c;
unspoilt beamed bar divided by standing
timbers, traditional furnishings including a
high-backed settle, log-effect gas fire in huge
fireplace, well kept Fullers ales and often an
unusual guest, enjoyable fairly priced food
(not Sun evening) from burgers up (special
diets catered for), cheerful helpful staff,
spacious beamed restaurant; children and
dogs welcome, picnic-sets on back terrace,
open all day.

GREAT MISSENDEN SP8901
George (01494) 865185
High Street; HP16 0BG 15th-c drinkers'
pub reopened/refreshed in 2018; heavily
beamed and timbered split-level interior,
medley of circular and small square tables
on bare boards or quarry tiles, open fires
(one in inglenook), four changing ales, craft
beers and real ciders; no food or children;
regular live music; dogs welcome, open
midday-10pm Fri and Sat, till 9pm Sun,
3-9pm Mon-Thurs.

HAMBLEDEN SU7886
Stag & Huntsman (01491) 571227
Off A4155 Henley–Marlow; RG9 6RP
Friendly brick and flint pub in pretty
Chilterns village; chatty locals in busy little
bar, built-in cushioned wall seats and simple
furniture on bare boards, good selection of
well kept ales, several wines by the glass,
sizeable open-plan room with armchairs
by woodburner, dining room with pleasing
mix of wooden tables and chairs, hunting
prints and other pictures on floral wallpaper,
popular food from light meals and sharing
plates up; background music, darts; children
and dogs welcome, country garden and nice
walks nearby, comfortable bedrooms, open all
day (to 8pm Sun).

HUGHENDEN VALLEY SU8697
★Harrow (01494) 564105
*Warrendene Road, off A4128 N of High
Wycombe; HP14 4LX* Small cheerful
brick and flint roadside cottage surrounded
by Chilterns walks (leave muddy boots in
porch); traditionally furnished with tiled-
floor bar on left, black beams and joists,
woodburner in big fireplace, pewter mugs,
country pictures and wall seats, similar but
bigger right-hand bar with sizeable dining
tables on brick floor, carpeted back dining
room, tasty good value pub food (all day
Mon-Sat, till 6pm Sun) from sandwiches and
baked potatoes up including special diets,

Fullers London Pride, Rebellion IPA and a guest, quick friendly service; Tues quiz; children and dogs welcome, disabled access, picnic-sets out in front, play area, open all day Mon-Sat, closed Sun evening.

HYDE HEATH SU9300

Plough (01494) 774408

Off B485 Great Missenden–Chesham; HP6 5RW Extensively refurbished small prettily placed pub with a good range of ales, good choice of popular well priced food, real fires and cosy friendly atmosphere; picnic-sets on cricket green opposite, open all day, no food Sun evening/Mon.

ICKFORD SP6407

Rising Sun (01844) 339238

E of Thame; Worminghall Road; HP18 9JD Welcoming thatched local with cosy low-beamed bar, Adnams, Black Sheep, Marstons and a weekly guest, enjoyable reasonably priced home-made food including stone-baked pizzas, log fire; Tues quiz; children, walkers and dogs welcome, pleasant garden with picnic-sets and play area, handy for Waterperry Gardens, open all day Fri-Sun, closed lunchtimes Mon and Tues, no food Sun evening, Mon, Tues.

IVINGHOE SP9416

Rose & Crown (01296) 668472

Vicarage Lane, off B489 opposite church; LU7 9EQ Cosy and welcoming 17th-c red-brick pub; good food at sensible prices from sandwiches up, well kept Sharps, Tring and three local guests, friendly efficient service; children and dogs welcome, a couple of tables out at front, sunny beer garden behind, pleasant village, open all day, no food Sun evening, Mon.

LACEY GREEN SP8200

Black Horse (01844) 345195

Main Road; HP27 0QU Welcoming two-bar beamed village local; popular good value home-made food (not Sun evening, Mon) from baguettes up, breakfast from 9am Tues-Sat, four real ales including Brakspears and nice choice of wines by the glass, quotations written on walls, inglenook woodburner; darts, sports TV; children and dogs welcome, picnic-sets in garden with play area and aunt sally, open all day Thurs-Sun, closed Mon lunchtime.

LACEY GREEN SP8201

Pink & Lily (01494) 489857

A4010 High Wycombe–Princes Risborough, follow Loosley sign, then Great Hampden, Great Missenden sign; HP27 0RJ Friendly updated 18th-c pub in pretty setting; enjoyable food from lunchtime sandwiches and traditional choices up, four changing mainly local ales and several wines by the glass, pubby furniture and open fire in airy main bar, cosier side areas and conservatory-style extension, small tap room with built-in wall benches on red tiles, framed Rupert Brooke poem about the pub (he used to drink here) and broad inglenook, games room; occasional background music; children, dogs and muddy walkers welcome, big garden with heated deck, futuristic glass pods, play area and barbecue, open all day.

LACEY GREEN SP8100

Whip (01844) 344060

Pink Road; HP27 0PG Hilltop local with mix of simple traditional furnishings in smallish front bar and larger downstairs dining area, popular generously served pubby food, six interesting well kept ales (May beer festival with live music), traditional ciders, friendly helpful staff; background music, Tues quiz, sports TV; children and dogs welcome, tables in charming sheltered garden looking up to restored working windmill, open all day, no food Sun evening.

LEY HILL SP9901

★**Swan** (01494) 783075

Village signposted off A416 in Chesham; HP5 1UT Friendly well looked-after pub – once three 16th-c cottages; character main bar (some steps) with original features including low beams, standing timbers, antique range and inglenook log fire, nice mix of furniture and collection of old local photographs, St Austell Tribute, Timothy Taylors Landlord and Tring Side Pocket for a Toad, several wines by the glass and tasty reasonably priced food, raftered dining section with french windows to terrace and lawn; children welcome till 9pm, pretty summer hanging baskets and tubs, common opposite with cricket pitch and a nine-hole golf course, closed Sun evening, Mon.

LITTLE MARLOW SU8788

Kings Head (01628) 476718

Church Road; A4155 about 2 miles E of Marlow; SL7 3RZ Welcoming 16th-c brick pub refurbished not so long ago; low-beamed bar with traditional furnishings and log fire, well kept Rebellion IPA and guests from light-blue panelled counter, separate dining room and lofty garden room also set for eating, generous helpings of enjoyable fairly priced food from shortish but varied menu, friendly helpful staff; children and dogs welcome, a few picnic-sets out at front, large walled garden behind with modern terrace furniture, near the Thames and plenty of nice walks,

---

Post Office address codings confusingly give the impression that some pubs are in Buckinghamshire, when they're really in Bedfordshire or Berkshire (which is where we list them).

open (and food) all day, kitchen shut evenings Sun and Mon.

LITTLE MISSENDEN   SU9298
Red Lion   (01494) 862876
Off A413 Amersham–Great Missenden; HP7 0QZ Unchanging pretty 17th-c cottage with long-serving landlord; small black-beamed bar, plain seats around elm pub tables, piano squashed into big inglenook beside black kitchen range packed with copper pots, kettles and rack of old guns, little country dining room with pleasant décor, well kept Greene King IPA, Skinners Betty Stogs and Tring Side Pocket for a Toad, fair-priced wines, pubby food; live music Sat; children welcome, dogs in bar, picnic-sets out in front and on grass behind wall, back garden with little bridge over River Misbourne, two bedrooms, open all day Fri-Sun.

LITTLEWORTH COMMON   SP9386
Blackwood Arms   (01753) 645672
3 miles S of M40 junction 2; Common Lane; SL1 8PP Traditional little 19th-c brick pub tucked away in lovely spot on edge of beechwoods (features in the film *My Week with Marilyn*); sturdy mix of furniture on bare boards, roaring log fire, enjoyable home-made food (not Sun evening) from open sandwiches up, well kept Brakspears and guests, interesting selection of wines, friendly accommodating staff; children and dogs welcome, hitching rail for horses, nice garden and good local walks, closed Mon, otherwise open all day (till 7.30pm Sun).

LITTLEWORTH COMMON   SU9386
Jolly Woodman   (01753) 644350
2 miles from M40 junction 2; off A355; SL1 8PF Lived-in red-brick country pub with three well kept changing ales and generous helpings of reasonably priced home-made food, rambling multi-level beamed and timbered areas including snug, collection of old tools and other bric-a-brac, central woodburner; children and dogs welcome, small front terrace and nice garden, good site by Burnham Beeches, regular jazz nights (see website), open all day, closes 8pm Sun.

LONG CRENDON   SP6908
★ Eight Bells   (01844) 208244
High Street, off B4011 N of Thame; car park entrance off Chearsley Road, not 'Village roads only'; HP18 9AL Character 17th-c beamed pub, unassuming and unchanging, with good cheerful staff; little bare-boards bar on left; XT, Ringwood and changing guests from the cask, gins and summer cider and decent choice of wines; bigger low-ceilinged room on right with log fire and a pleasantly haphazard mix of tables and simple seats on ancient red and black tiles, good modestly priced food (not Sun

evening, Mon), daily papers, TV for sport, also a snug hidey-hole with just three tables devoted to the local morris men – frequent visitors; children and dogs welcome, well spaced picnic-sets in colourful little back garden, aunt sally, interesting village featured in TV's *Midsomer Murders*, open all day weekends, closed Mon lunchtime, from 6pm Sun.

LUDGERSHALL   SP6617
Bull & Butcher   (01844) 238094
Off A41 Aylesbury–Bicester; bear left to The Green; HP18 9NZ Nicely old-fashioned country pub under friendly management; bar with low beams in ochre ceiling, pews and wheelback chairs on dark tiles or flagstones, inglenook woodburner, Greene King IPA and local Vale Brewery ales, enjoyable fairly priced pubby food including weekday set menu (lunchtime/early evening), themed nights and popular Sun lunch (booking advised), back dining room; children and dogs welcome, seats out at front overlooking green with play area, circular walks from the door, open all day Wed-Sat, till 7pm Sun, closed Mon and lunchtime Tues.

MAIDS MORETON   SP7035
Wheatsheaf   (01280) 822903
Main Street, just off A413 Towcester–Buckingham; MK18 1QR Attractive 17th-c thatched local; traditional low-beamed bar with bare boards and tiled floors, two inglenooks, four well kept ales including Tring Side Pocket for a Toad, good fairly pubby food (not Sun evening), friendly service, conservatory restaurant; quiz first Sun of month; dogs allowed in bar, seats on front terrace, hatch service for pleasant enclosed back garden, closed Mon, otherwise open all day.

MARLOW   SU8586
Coach
West Street; SL7 2LS Sister dining pub (with one Michelin star) to Tom Kerridge's Hand & Flowers; very well liked food (no bookings) from open kitchen with rotisserie, good helpful service, compact interior with modern décor, bar area serving up to four changing ales and nice wines by the glass (maybe local fizz) from pewter-topped counter; silent TVs; open all day from 8am for breakfast.

MARLOW   SU8486
★ Hand & Flowers   (01628) 482277
West Street (A4155); SL7 2BP Restaurant-pub owned by celebrity chef Tom Kerridge; nice informal atmosphere in three linked beamed rooms all set for eating, high-backed leather-seated chairs and wall seats around chunky tables, bare boards or

---

Pubs close to motorway junctions are listed at the back of the book.

flagstones, fresh flowers and candles, first class food (not cheap and must book long in advance), professional service, conservatory bar with four real ales including one named for them, lots of wines by the glass from good list and specialist gins; children welcome, comfortable character bedrooms, Thames walks nearby, closed Sun evening.

MARLOW   SU8586
Two Brewers (01628) 484140
St Peter Street, first right off Station Road from double roundabout; SL7 1NQ Red-brick 18th-c beamed pub set just back from the river; fairly pubby food from snacks up, three well kept Rebellion and Sharps ales and more than 25 wines by the glass, various dining areas including upstairs room and cellar restaurant; children and dogs welcome, seats outside, open (and food) all day, kitchen closes 6pm Sun.

MARLOW BOTTOM   SU8588
Three Horseshoes (01628) 483109
Signed from Handy Cross roundabout, off M40 junction 4; SL7 3RA Much extended former coaching inn under friendly management; well kept Rebellion ales and enjoyable reasonably priced food including pizzas, beams and log fires, comfortable traditional furnishings with a contemporary twist on different levels; children and dogs (in bar) welcome, sheltered back garden, good walks nearby, open all day, till 6pm Sun.

MARSWORTH   SP9114
Red Lion (01296) 668366
Vicarage Road; off B489 Dunstable–Aylesbury; HP23 4LU Partly thatched 17th-c brick pub close to impressive flight of locks on Grand Union Canal; plain public bar on right with quarry tiles, straightforward furniture, log burner and small coal fire, Tring Side Pocket, Harveys Sussex Best, Fullers London Pride and good selection of guests, traditional food at reasonable prices, friendly service; vaulted ceiling area with leather sofas, raised section with dining tables, games area (bar billiards, darts and juke box); children and dogs welcome, picnic-sets out in front, back terrace with steps up to sizeable garden, more seats and old stocks on village green opposite, open all day weekends.

MILTON KEYNES   SP8737
Swan (01908) 679489
Newport Road, Woughton on the Green; MK6 3BS Spacious and picturesque timber-framed Chef & Brewer overlooking village green; beamed interior with good log fires and nice nooks and corners, enjoyable food from their usual extensive menu, Greene King ales and good wine choice; children welcome, plenty of seating in large garden, footpaths to nearby lakes, open (and food) all day.

MILTON KEYNES   SP8939
★Swan (01908) 665240
Broughton Road, Milton Keynes village; MK10 9AH Attractive thatched pub with interconnecting rooms mixing original features with contemporary furnishings; main beamed and flagstoned bar with plush armchairs by inglenook, high chairs and tables, cushioned banquette and chunky tables, a good selection of well looked-after ales, an extensive wine list, good popular food including weekday set menu, helpful friendly young staff, spreading restaurant with open kitchen and doors to outside dining area overlooking garden; well behaved children welcome, dogs in bar, open (and food) all day.

MOULSOE   SP9141
Carrington Arms (01908) 218050
1.25 miles from M1 junction 14: A509 N, first right signed Moulsoe; Cranfield Road; MK16 0HB Restaurant-pub in former Victorian farmhouse with elegant open-plan interior; good choice of well liked food from pub staples up including chargrilled meats sold by weight from refrigerated display, real ales such as Brakspears, 23 wines by the glass from extensive list and large range of whiskies and gins, welcoming helpful staff; children allowed, long pretty garden behind with giant chess set, 16 bedrooms in two adjacent blocks, open all day, food all day weekends.

NEWPORT PAGNELL   SP8743
Cannon (01908) 211495
High Street; MK16 8AQ Friendly down-to-earth little bay-windowed drinkers' pub serving several well kept reasonably priced ales; half-panelled interior with interesting military theme, room behind for live music and comedy nights; Tues quiz, TV, juke box; seats in small backyard, open all day.

NEWTON LONGVILLE   SP8431
Crooked Billet (01908) 373936
Off A421 S of Milton Keynes; Westbrook End; MK17 0DF Brick and thatch pub under newish management; comfortably modernised beamed interior with inglenook log fires, good food from pub classics up (they add a service charge), Greene King IPA, Abbot and guests, nice wines by the glass and decent choice of other drinks, efficient friendly service; children and dogs (in bar) welcome, disabled access/loo, plenty of tables in grassy garden, open all day, food till 6pm Sun.

NORTH MARSTON   SP7722
Pilgrim (01296) 670969
High Street; MK18 3PD Welcoming red-brick pub with comfortably modernised interior, beams, bare boards and woodburner, good food from shortish but varied and imaginative menu cooked by landlord-chef,

some themed nights including Turkish and Indian, well kept Chiltern, XT and a guest beer, Saxby's cider and decent range of wines by the glass, friendly efficient staff; live music (third Tues of month), quiz (last Tues); sloping back garden with country views over rooftops, interesting village church, open all day Sat, till 8pm Sun, closed Mon and lunchtime Tues.

OLNEY   SP8851

Bull (01234) 711470

Market Place/High Street; MK46 4EA Former 17th-c coaching inn (Apostrophe group) with spacious well renovated interior; Black Sheep, Youngs Bitter and guests from generously stocked bar, craft beers, big choice of spirits, 25 wines by the glass, decent choice of enjoyable food from sandwiches and deli boards up, sky-lit dining room with open kitchen, friendly young staff; children and dogs welcome, disabled loo (others upstairs), 13 bedrooms, tables in courtyard and big back garden, open all day from 7am (8am weekends) for breakfast.

OLNEY   SP8851

★ Swan (01234) 711111

High Street S; MK46 4AA Cosy little pub with beamed and timbered linked rooms; popular good value food from tapas through pub favourites and burgers to blackboard specials, up to six well kept/priced ales (including their own-named Swan Local) and plenty of wines by the glass from good list, friendly attentive service, cheery log fires, small back bistro dining room (booking advised); courtyard tables, open all day (till 7pm Sun).

OVING   SP7821

★ Black Boy (01296) 641258

Off A413 N of Aylesbury; HP22 4HN Extended 16th-c brick and timbered pub under same ownership as the Eight Bells at Long Crendon and Russell Arms in Butlers Cross; low heavy beams, log fire in enormous inglenook, steps up to snug stripped-stone area, four changing ales from Chiltern, Marlow, XT and others, and good choice of wines and gins, enjoyable food from sandwiches and pizzas up, good friendly service, modern picture-window dining room; children and dogs welcome, tables on spacious sloping lawns and terrace, expansive Vale of Aylesbury views, open (and food) all day except Mon, till 6pm (4pm) Sun.

PENN   SU9093

Old Queens Head (01494) 813371

Hammersley Lane/Church Road, off B474 between Penn and Tylers Green; HP10 8EY Stylish old pub with open-plan

rooms; well spaced tables and comfortably varied seating on flagstones or broad dark boards, stairs up to attractive two-level raftered dining room, enjoyable food (special diets catered for) including Sat brunch from 9.30am, Greene King ales, lots of wines by the glass and good choice of other drinks including wide range of gins, log fire in big fireplace; background music, daily papers, children and dogs (in bar) welcome, sunny terrace overlooking church, picnic-sets on sheltered L-shaped lawn, beechwood walks close by, open all day.

PENN STREET   SU9295

★ Hit or Miss (01494) 713109

Off A404 SW of Amersham, keep on towards Winchmore Hill; HP7 0FA Welcoming traditional village pub; heavily beamed main bar with leather sofas and armchairs on parquet flooring, horsebrasses and open fire, two carpeted rooms with interesting cricketing and chair-making memorabilia, more sofas, wheelback and other dining chairs around pine tables, good interesting food (highish prices) including daily specials, sharing platters; Badger Fursty Ferret and guest ales; background music; children and dogs (in certain areas) welcome, picnic-sets on terrace overlooking own cricket pitch, parking over the road, open all day.

PENN STREET   SU9295

Squirrel (01494) 711291

Off A404 SW of Amersham, opposite the Common; HP7 0PX Open-plan flagstoned bar with log fire, comfortable sofas and mix of other furniture, reasonably priced home-made pubby food (not Sun evening, Mon) including range of burgers and good children's meals, up to five well kept ales such as Rebellion, Wychwood, Vale and Tring, various craft beers and a proper cider, quick friendly service, bric-a-brac and cricketing memorabilia (village cricket pitch is opposite), sweets in traditional glass jars; live acoustic music Fri, monthly quiz; dogs and children welcome, covered outside deck with sofas, logburner and own servery, play area in big back garden, lovely walks nearby, closed Mon lunchtime, otherwise open all day.

PRESTWOOD   SP8799

Polecat (01494) 412514

170 Wycombe Road (A4128 N of High Wycombe); HP16 0HJ Major refurbishment not long ago for this former 17th-c hunting lodge; low-ceilinged bar, rugs and assorted tables and chairs on bare boards or red tiles, various stuffed animals (white polecats in one cabinet), good

---

open fire, five real ales including Malt and Rebellion, lots of wines by the glass and quite a few spirits, good food including wood-fired pizzas and Josper grills, glass-fronted dining extension with open kitchen; children and dogs (in bar) welcome, terrace and attractive big garden, large play area, open all day from 8am for breakfast.

PRINCES RISBOROUGH SP8104
Red Lion (01844) 344476
Whiteleaf, off A4010; OS Sheet 165 map reference 817043; HP27 0LL Traditional 17th-c family-owned pub in charming village; Sharps Doom Bar and a couple of guests, decent wines and good gin selection, enjoyable reasonably priced pubby food including popular steaks, flowers on tables, log fires, friendly efficient service; traditional games in snug; children, walkers and dogs welcome, seats out in front and in garden behind, extensive views over to Oxfordshire, handy for the Ridgeway trail, four bedrooms, open all day weekends, closed Mon.

QUAINTON SP7420
George & Dragon (01296) 655436
The Green; HP22 4AR Traditional flower-decked brick pub by village green; five well kept mainly local ales, Weston's cider and enjoyable reasonably priced food including blackboard specials and bargain OAP lunch Tues, friendly efficient staff, split-level bar, coffee shop/deli, post office facility Weds; quiz and bingo nights, darts; children welcome, tables outside with good view of windmill, handy for Buckinghamshire Railway Centre, open all day Sat, closed Mon.

STOKE GOLDINGTON SP8348
★ Lamb (01908) 551233
High Street (B526 Newport Pagnell–Northampton); MK16 8NR Chatty village pub with friendly helpful licensees, up to five real ales including Tring, proper ciders and good range of wines, generous helpings of enjoyable home-made food (all day Sat, not Sun evening) from baguettes to good value Sun roasts, lounge with log fire and sheep decorations, two small pleasant dining rooms, darts and table skittles in public bar; may be soft background music, TV; children, walkers and dogs welcome, terrace and sheltered garden behind with play equipment, bedrooms in adjacent cottage, closed Mon lunchtime, otherwise open all day (till 7pm Sun).

THE LEE SP8904
★ Cock & Rabbit (01494) 837540
Back roads 2.5 miles N of Great Missenden, E of A413; HP16 9LZ Overlooking village green and run by same friendly Italian family for over 25 years; much emphasis on their good Italian cooking including popular Weds evening pasta deal, Greene King, Sharps and a beer named for the pub, plush-seated lounge, cosy dining

room and larger restaurant; children welcome, dogs in bar, seats on verandah, terraces and lawn, good walks, open all day Fri and Sat.

THE LEE SP8904
★ Old Swan (01494) 837239
Swan Bottom, back road 0.75 miles N of The Lee; HP16 9NU Friendly tucked-away country pub, mainly 16th-c with attractively furnished linked rooms; heavy beams, flagstones and old quarry tiles, high-backed antique settles and window seats, log fire in inglenook cooking range, good reasonably priced food (not Sun evening, Mon) from sensibly short menu, three real ales including Chiltern and Sharps, 16 wines by the glass; children and dogs (in bar) welcome, big, spreading back garden with picnic-sets and contemporary seating around rustic tables, play area, good surrounding walks and cycling routes, open all day Fri and Sat, till 7pm Sun, closed Mon lunchtime.

TURVILLE SU7691
★ Bull & Butcher (01491) 638283
Valley road off A4155 Henley–Marlow at Mill End, past Hambleden and Skirmett; RG9 6QU Popular 16th-c black and white pub in pretty village (famous as film and TV location); two traditional low-beamed rooms with inglenooks, wall settles in tiled-floor bar, deep well incorporated into glass-topped table, Brakspears ales kept well and decent wines by the glass, enjoyable good value food cooked by chef-landlord, friendly staff; background music; children and dogs welcome, seats by fruit trees in attractive garden, good walks (Chiltern Way runs through village), open all day weekends and can get very busy.

WADDESDON SP7316
Long Dog (01296) 651320
High Street; HP18 0JF Renovated village pub with good food from open-view kitchen including lunchtime baps, friendly accommodating service, well kept ales and nice choice of wines by the glass, bar area with log fire; background music, live jazz every other Tues; children and dogs welcome, tables out front and back, very handy for Waddesdon Manor (NT), open all day, food all day weekends.

WEEDON SP8118
★ Five Elms (01296) 641439
Stockaway; HP22 4NL Cottagey thatched pub with two welcoming little bars; low beams and log fires, ample helpings of good fairly priced food cooked by landlord (best to book), nice wines, interesting large range of gins and a well kept changing ale, cheerful helpful service, old photographs and prints, separate compact dining room; games such as shove-ha'penny; children welcome (no under-9s in restaurant), dogs in bar, pretty

hanging baskets and a few picnic-sets out in front, attractive village, closed Sun evening and lunchtimes Mon, Tues.

WEST WYCOMBE · SU8394
George & Dragon · (01494) 535340
High Street; A40 W of High Wycombe; HP14 3AB Rambling hotel bar in preserved NT Tudor village; massive beams and sloping walls, big log fire, a good selection of well looked-after ales, good range of wines and enjoyable food from shortish menu, prompt friendly service; children and dogs (in bar) welcome, tables in nice garden, ten bedrooms (magnificent oak staircase), handy for West Wycombe Park (NT) and the Hell-Fire Caves, open all day, meals 12-6 Sun.

WESTON TURVILLE · SP8510
Chequers · (01296) 613298
Church Lane; HP22 5SJ Comfortably updated dining pub tucked away in attractive part of the village; low 16th-c beams, flagstones and large log fire, very good up-to-date food from chef-owner in bar or restaurant including set lunch, friendly helpful staff, well kept ales such as Rebellion and Sharps, wide choice of wines by the glass; children welcome (no under-6s after 4pm in restaurant but allowed in bar), no dogs, tables on large front terrace, closed Sun evening to Tues lunchtime, otherwise open all day.

WESTON UNDERWOOD · SP8650
Cowpers Oak · (01234) 711382
Signed off A509 in Olney; High Street; MK46 5JS Wisteria-clad village pub with enjoyable home-cooked food from bar snacks up (special diets catered for), Mon burger and pie night, set menu offers, well kept good choice of real ales, several wines by the glass, friendly helpful staff, beams, painted panelling and some stripped stone, nice mix of old-fashioned furnishings, two open fires, restaurant behind; background music, Mon quiz; children and dogs (in bar) welcome, small suntrap front terrace, more tables on back decking and in big orchard garden, fenced play area, open all day weekends (till 9pm Sun).

WHELPLEY HILL · SP9501
White Hart · (01442) 833367
Off B4505 Bovington–Chesham; HP5 3RL Cosy recently refurbished village pub; good home-made food, well kept interesting beers including Tring, and good selection of other drinks, friendly accommodating service, log fires; background music; children and dogs welcome, seats out at front and in big back garden, nice local walks, open all day (till 5pm Sun, closed Mon), can get crowded at weekends.

WINCHMORE HILL · SU9394
Plough · (01494) 259757
The Hill; HP7 0PA Village pub-restaurant with good Italian food from wood-fired pizzas up (landlord is from Campania); flagstones, low beams and open fires, linked dining area with polished wood floor, real ales and imported lagers, nice coffee, quick friendly service, little shop selling Italian wines and other produce; children welcome, tables on terrace and lawn overlooking green, pleasant walks nearby, open all day.

WINCHMORE HILL · SU9394
Potters Arms · (01494) 726222
Fagnall Lane; HP7 0PH Welcoming 17th-c pub close to the village green; ales such as Rebellion and Chiltern, enjoyable pubby food (not Sun evening) from sandwiches and panini up, Thai night Sat, good helpful service, some black beams, leather sofa and armchairs by inglenook log fire; popular comedy night last Thurs of month; children welcome, tables in fenced front garden, four bedrooms, open all day Sat, till 7pm Sun.

WINSLOW · SP7627
Bell · (01296) 714091
Market Square; MK18 3AB Fine old coaching inn, comfortable and atmospheric, with reasonably priced food including range of pies in beamed bar and popular carvery restaurant, Greene King ales, friendly welcoming staff, snug with historical photos and log fire; courtyard tables, 39 bedrooms (some with four-posters), open all day.

WOOBURN COMMON · SU9187
★Chequers · (01628) 529575
From A4094 at Bourne End roundabout, follow for Wooburn, then straight over next roundabout into Kiln Lane; OS Sheet 175 map reference 910870; HP10 0JQ Bustling hotel (former 17th-c coaching inn) with friendly low-beamed main bar, second bar to the left and light and airy restaurant; good range of well liked food from snacks and sharing plates up, Rebellion ales, a guest beer and a dozen wines by the glass from good list, fair range of whiskies and brandies too, afternoon teas; background music, TV; children and dogs (in bar) welcome, spacious garden set away from the road, 29 comfortable bedrooms, open (and food) all day.

Cambridgeshire

KEY ★ Star Pub 🌟 Top Quality Food 🍺 Great Beer
🍷 Good Wines £ Bargain Meals 🛏 Good Bedrooms 🍴 Serves Food

BALSHAM   TL5850   MAP 5

Black Bull 🌟 🍷 🍺 🛏

(01223) 893844 – www.blackbull-balsham.co.uk
*Village signposted off A11 SW of Newmarket, and off A1307 in Linton; High Street;
CB21 4DJ*

**Pretty thatched pub with bedroom extension – a good all-rounder –
and with well regarded food too**

You can be sure of a warm welcome from the friendly landlord at this
handsome black and white timbered building. The beamed bar spreads
around a central servery where they keep Adnams Ghost Ship, Greene King
IPA and Woodfordes Wherry on handpump, 19 wines by the glass from a
good list, ten malt whiskies, draught lager and interesting juices. Dividers
and standing timbers break up the space, which has an open fire (with
leather sofas in front of it), floorboards and low black beams in the front
section; furniture includes small leatherette-seated dining chairs.
A restaurant extension (in a listed barn) has a high-raftered oak-panelled
roof and a network of standing posts and steel ties. The terrace in front
of the pub has teak tables and chairs by a long, pleasantly old-fashioned
verandah and there are more seats in a small sheltered back garden. The
smart, comfortable bedrooms are in a neat single-storey extension. It's under
the same ownership as the equally good Red Lion at Hinxton.

🌟 The particularly good food includes sandwiches, pulled ham hock with pea
velouté and home-made piccalilli, mushroom and blue cheese tart, beer-battered
fish and chips, butternut squash with spinach, chickpeas, tomatoes, mashed potato and
pine nuts, rolled pork belly with black pudding mash and mustard sauce, duck breast
with orange-glazed chicory and plum sauce, and puddings such as apple pannacotta and
chocolate délice with winter berry gel and vanilla ice-cream; they also offer breakfasts
7.30-9am (8.30-9.30am weekends). *Benchmark main dish: steak in ale pie £14.00.
Two-course evening meal £23.00.*

Free house ~ Licensee Alex Clarke ~ Real ale ~ Open 7.30am-11pm; 8.30am-11pm Sat;
8.30am-10.30pm Sun ~ Bar food 12-2, 6.30-9; 12-2.30, 6.30-9.30 Fri, Sat; 12-3, 6-8 Sun ~
Restaurant ~ Children welcome ~ Dogs allowed in bar, restaurant & bedrooms ~
Bedrooms: £99-£134

Post Office address codings confusingly give the impression that some pubs are in
Cambridgeshire, when they're really in Bedfordshire, Lincolnshire, Norfolk
or Northamptonshire (which is where we list them).

BARTLOW TL5845 MAP 5

Three Hills 🛏

(01223) 890500 – www.thethreehills.co.uk

Off Camps Road, signed Ashdon, S Walden; CB21 4PW

Bustling little pub with good food and drinks choice and seats in riverside garden; charming bedrooms

In a tiny village, this country inn has been attractively modernised and is very much the community hub. It's a friendly place with a genuine welcome for all. Most customers head straight for the cosy beamed bar. Here you'll find chapel chairs and cushioned wall seats with scatter cushions around wooden tables, a woodburning stove, two or three changing ales on handpump from breweries such as Marstons, Wolf and Woodfordes, as well as 15 wines by the glass. This leads into a comfy snug with sofas and armchairs, books on shelves, a TV and a second woodburner. The light and airy restaurant with its apex ceiling and skylight windows has wicker bull's heads and modern artwork on the walls above contemporary seats and tables. You can also dine outside on the expansive terrace and enjoy the landscaped garden that runs down to the little River Granta. Six pretty, well equipped bedrooms are located in the pub or in a separate annexe. The inn is named for the interesting Roman burial mounds nearby.

🍴 The well presented and highly regarded food includes sandwiches, pizzas, smoked haddock kedgeree, harissa chicken wings with apricot chutney, battered fish of the day with triple-cooked chips, country vegetable pie with champ potato and tenderstem broccoli, pepper, caper and spring onion frittata, Moroccan chicken salad with couscous, and puddings such as lemon drizzle cake with passion-fruit sorbet and vanilla cheesecake with summer berries and meringue. *Benchmark burger with brioche bun and triple-cooked chips £14.50. Two-course evening meal £19.00.*

Free house ~ Emma Harrison ~ Real ale ~ Open 12-10.30 Tues-Thurs; 12-11.30 Fri, Sat; 12-6 Sun ~ Bar food 12-2.30, 6-9; 12-6 Sun ~ Restaurant ~ Children allowed in bar ~ Dogs allowed in bar ~ Bedrooms: £120

ELTON TL0894 MAP 5

Crown 🍽⭐ 🍷 🛏

(01832) 280232 – www.crowninnelton.co.uk

Off B671 S of Wansford (A1/A47), and village signposted off A605 Peterborough–Oundle; Duck Street; PE8 6RQ

Cambridgeshire Dining Pub of the Year

Pretty pub with interesting food, several real ales, well chosen wines and a friendly atmosphere; stylish bedrooms

This lovely golden-stone thatched pub is nestled in beautiful countryside with lovely walks nearby. That, coupled with the highly praised food, means it is perennially popular with readers. The softly lit, beamed bar has leather and antique dining chairs around a nice mix of chunky tables on bare boards, an open fire in a stone fireplace and good pictures and pubby ornaments on pastel walls. The beamed main dining area has fresh flowers and candles, and similar tables and chairs on stripped wooden flooring; there's a modern circular dining extension too. High bar chairs against the counter are popular with locals, and they keep a house beer (from Kings Cliffe Brewery), Greene King IPA, Oakham JHB and guest ales on handpump, well chosen wines by the glass and farm cider; background music and TV. Bedrooms are smart, comfortable and well equipped and the breakfasts are especially good. There are tables outside on the front terrace, and Elton Mill and Lock are nearby. To find the pub (it's on the edge of this charming village), follow the brown sign towards Nassington.

 Highly rewarding food – cooked by the landlord – includes sandwiches, wild mushroom and pine nut pâté with toast, breaded chicken escalope with smoked bacon, linguine with wild mushrooms, omelettes, aubergine, buckwheat and cashew tagine with coriander and cumin couscous, steak and mushroom in ale pie, smoked cod with leek and bacon pie topped with cheddar mash with buttered greens and roasted carrots, panko-coated roast lamb with purple sprouting broccoli, truffle mash and roasted roots, and puddings such as dark chocolate brownie with peanut butter, clotted cream and chocolate truffles and treacle sponge with home-made custard and salted caramel ice-cream. *Benchmark main dish: pork belly with crispy bacon, hash browns, apple purée and cider sauce £17.95. Two-course evening meal £24.00.*

Free house ~ Licensee Marcus Lamb ~ Real ale ~ Open 12-11; 12-9 Sun ~ Bar food 12-2, 6.30-9; 12-3 Sun; not Mon except for residents ~ Restaurant ~ Children welcome ~ Dogs allowed in bar ~ Bedrooms: £135-£220

HEMINGFORD GREY   TL2970   MAP 5
Cock

(01480) 463609 – www.cambscuisine.com/the-cock-hemingford
Village signposted off A14 eastbound, and (via A1096 St Ives road) westbound; High Street; PE28 9BJ

Imaginative food in pretty pub with extensive wine list, four interesting beers, a bustling atmosphere and a smart restaurant

This excellent pub located in a delightful village on the River Ouse is considered by many readers as their favourite – quite an accolade! One feature we particularly like in a place that serves first class food is that they've sensibly kept the public bar (on the left) for drinking only: there's an open woodburning stove on a raised hearth, bar stools, wall seats and a carver, and steps leading down to more seating. Real ales on handpump include Adnams Southwold and Brewsters Hophead, plus 25 wines by the glass mainly from the Languedoc-Roussillon region, eight gins (one very local) and Cromwell cider (made in the village). Other bar rooms have white-painted or dark beams and lots of contemporary pale yellow and cream paintwork, church candles, artworks here and there, and a really attractive mix of old wooden dining chairs, settles and tables. In marked contrast, the stylishly rustic restaurant on the right (you must book to be sure of a table) is set for dining, with pale wooden floorboards and another woodburning stove. There are seats and tables among stone troughs and flowers on the terrace and in the neat garden, and pretty hanging baskets. Disabled access. Sister pubs are the Crown & Punchbowl at Horningsea, Three Horseshoes in Madingley and Tickell Arms in Whittlesford (all in Cambridgeshire).

 Delicious food includes sandwiches, salmon pastrami with kohlrabi and samphire slaw, glazed pork cheek with pork bonbon, apple and caramelised onion purée, salt and pepper squid with shaved fennel and mayonnaise, squash ricotta torte with fennel and potato gratin, lamb, mint and cumin sausages, egg pappardelle with courgettes, peas, basil and hazelnut crumb, jerk tofu skewer with mixed bean salad and pineapple salsa, sirloin steak with a choice of sauce and chips, and puddings such as damson parfait with honeycomb and apple and quince sponge and vegan chocolate délice with passion-fruit and mango salsa and coconut brittle; they also offer a two- and three-course weekday set lunch. *Benchmark main dish: fillet of cod with roast fennel, romesco sauce, chive oil and sautéed potatoes £18.00. Two-course evening meal £25.00.*

Free house ~ Licensees Oliver Thain and Richard Bradley ~ Real ale ~ Open 12-3, 6-11; 12-3, 5-11 Fri; 12-11 Sat; 12-10.30 Sun ~ Bar food 12-2.30, 6.30-9; 12-2.30, 6-9.30 Fri, Sat; 12-8 Sun ~ Restaurant ~ Children welcome until evening when must be over 10 (in pub), over 5 (in restaurant) ~ Dogs allowed in bar

HINXTON
Red Lion 🎯 ⚭ 🍺 ⚮

TL4945 MAP 5

(01799) 530601 – www.redlionhinxton.co.uk

2 miles off M11 junction 9 northbound; take first exit off A11, A1301 N, then left turn into village – High Street; a little further from junction 10, via A505 E and A1301 S; CB10 1QY

16th-c pub with friendly staff, interesting bar food, real ales and a big landscaped garden; comfortable bedrooms

Nestled within a pretty conservation village, this historic, Grade-II listed pub features a low-beamed bar with a relaxed, friendly atmosphere. There are oak chairs and tables on bare boards, two leather chesterfield sofas, an open fire and an old wall clock. You'll find their own-label Red & Black Ale (from the local Nethergate Brewery) plus Adnams Ghost Ship, Woodfordes Wherry and a guest such as Crafty Beers Sixteen Strides on handpump, 17 wines by the glass, 15 malt whiskies and first class service. An informal dining area has high-backed settles, and the smart restaurant (with oak rafters and traditional dry peg construction) is decorated with various pictures and clocks. In warm weather, there's plenty of seating outside with teak tables and chairs on one terrace, huge parasols on a second terrace by the porch and picnic-sets on grass. There's also a dovecote and nice views of the village church. The Imperial War Museum at Duxford is close by. This is a nice place to stay in well equipped, pretty bedrooms in a separate flint and brick building; breakfasts are good. They also own the Black Bull in Balsham just up the road.

 Appetising food includes sandwiches, chilli, lime and parsley tiger prawns with soba noodles, black treacle-cured salmon with lemongrass and ginger purée, pickled beetroot and spring onion, beetroot and roast butternut squash wellington with new potatoes, sautéed cabbage and chestnuts, pork schnitzel with new potatoes and chorizo jam, steak and ale pie, Moroccan vegetable tagine with minted yoghurt, flatbread and rice, and puddings such as maple baked pears with granola and vegan vanilla ice-cream and sticky toffee pudding with butterscotch sauce. *Benchmark main dish: pan-fried hake fillet with chorizo cake, wilted spinach and crayfish cream sauce £18.00. Two-course evening meal £23.00.*

Free house ~ Licensee Alex Clarke ~ Real ale ~ Open 7.30am-11pm; 8.30am-11pm Sat; 8.30am-10.30pm Sun ~ Bar food 12-2, 6.30-9; 12-2.30, 6.30-9.30 Fri, Sat; 12-3, 6-8 Sun ~ Restaurant ~ Children welcome ~ Dogs allowed in bar & bedrooms ~ Bedrooms: £119-£139

HORNINGSEA
Crown & Punchbowl 🎯 🍺 ⚮

TL4962 MAP 5

(01223) 860643 – www.cambscuisine.com/the-crown-and-punchbowl

Just NE of Cambridge; CB25 9JG

Impressive food and thoughtful drinks choice in carefully refurbished old inn with seats outside; bedrooms

This characterful 17th-c former coaching inn retains plenty of original features and character, and many of our readers love it. The beamed bar has a woodburning stove in a brick fireplace, leather banquettes and rustic old chairs, stripped boards, terracotta walls and an attractively carved counter where they serve freshly carved ham and home-made pickles. Behind the bar they keep Adnams Southwold and Brewsters Hophead tapped from the cask and more than 20 wines by the glass (with a focus on the Languedoc-Roussillon region), home-made punches (alcoholic and non-alcoholic) and local cider. The timbered dining room has leather cushioned chairs around wooden tables on pale boards, wall panelling and candlelight. Another conservatory-style room has large windows and ceramic light fittings (a nod to the village's history as a centre for Roman pottery). There are country seats out in front of the pub, while the five guest bedrooms upstairs are well equipped, light and comfortable. Sister pubs are the Cock at Hemingford Grey, Three Horseshoes in Madingley and Tickell Arms in Whittlesford (all in Cambridgeshire).

Delicious food includes sandwiches, salmon pastrami with kohlrabi and samphire slaw, glazed pork cheek with pork bonbon, apple and caramelised onion purée, salt and pepper squid with shaved fennel and mayonnaise, squash ricotta torte with fennel and potato gratin, lamb, mint and cumin sausages, egg pappardelle with courgettes, peas, basil and hazelnut crumb, jerk tofu skewer with mixed bean salad and pineapple salsa, sirloin steak with a choice of sauce and chips, and puddings such as damson parfait with honeycomb and apple and quince sponge and vegan chocolate délice with passion-fruit and mango salsa and coconut brittle; they also offer a two- and three-course weekday set lunch. *Benchmark main dish: pan-fried sea bass fillet with courgette and basil purée and flageolet beans £17.00. Two-course evening meal £25.00.*

Free house ~ Licensees Oliver Thain and Richard Bradley ~ Real ale ~ Open 12-3, 6-11; 12-3, 5-11 Fri; 12-11 Sat; 12-10.30 Sun ~ Bar food 12-2.30, 6.30-9 (9.30 Fri, Sat); 12-3, 6.30-8.30 Sun ~ Restaurant ~ Children welcome ~ Dogs allowed in bar ~ Bedrooms: £120

HUNTINGDON   TL2471   MAP 5
Old Bridge Hotel 🏅 ⭐ 🍷 🛏

(01480) 424300 – www.huntsbridge.com

1 High Street; ring road just off B1044 entering from easternmost A14 slip road; PE29 3TQ

Proper bar in Georgian hotel with a splendid range of drinks, first class service and excellent food; individually styled bedrooms

This lovely ivy-clad townhouse hotel sits on the banks of the River Ouse, but also on the edge of the town centre. It's a special place to stay, run with thought and great care, with 24 luxurious bedrooms (some overlook the river) and excellent breakfasts. And while much emphasis is naturally on this side of the business, there's a proper little pubby bar at its heart with a wide mix of customers. This has a log fire, comfortable sofas and low wooden tables on polished floorboards, and Adnams Ghost Ship and two guest ales on handpump. They also have an exceptional wine list (up to 30 by the glass in the bar) and a wine shop where you can taste a selection of wines before you buy. Food is available in the big airy restaurant with floor-to-ceiling windows overlooking the garden, or in the bar/lounge. There are seats and tables on the terrace by the Great Ouse river, and they have their own landing stage.

Creative food includes sandwiches, salt-baked beetroot with mozzarella and pickled walnut purée, fillets of gurnard with clams, samphire, pancetta griddled potatoes and cider sauce, spiced parsnip soup with curry oil, vegan jalfrezi with rice and home-made mango chutney, and puddings such as roast pineapple with coconut ice-cream and Malibu syrup and chocolate cake with salted caramel ice-cream and candied almonds. They also serve afternoon tea (booking required). *Benchmark main dish: vegan 'steak' and chunky chips with watercress, fried cauliflower and satay sauce £16.95. Two-course evening meal £28.00.*

Huntsbridge ~ Licensee John Hoskins ~ Real ale ~ Open 11am-11.30pm ~ Bar food 11.30-9.15 (10 Fri, Sat) ~ Restaurant ~ Children welcome ~ Dogs allowed in bar & bedrooms ~ Bedrooms: £148

 MADINGLEY   TL3960   MAP 5

Three Horseshoes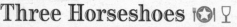

(01954) 210221 – www.cambscuisine.com/three-horseshoes
High Street; off A1303 W of Cambridge; CB23 8AB

Pretty pub with excellent food and wines, charming staff and seats in the garden

Situated in a quaint, romantic village just three miles from Cambridge city centre, this pretty thatched pub boasts light and attractive décor and an easy-going, friendly feel. It's a bustling and gently civilised place and the bare-boards bar has high-backed cushioned settles and a mix of nice old dining chairs around wooden tables, prints on pale paintwork and a woodburning stove. From the bar counter, friendly, courteous staff serve Adnams Southwold and a changing ale such as Brewsters Hophead on handpump and several good wines by the glass. The airy conservatory restaurant, overlooking the garden, has rattan-style and pale wooden chairs around plain tables on quarry tiles and parquet flooring, a long, brown button-back wall banquette and another woodburning stove. At the front of the building are solid benches and tables, and the sunny back terrace and lawn have picnic-sets and teak tables and chairs. Sister pubs are the Cock in Hemingford Grey, Crown & Punchbowl in Horningsea and Tickell Arms in Whittlesford (all in Cambridgeshire).

 Interesting, up-to-date food includes scallops with white bean purée, black pudding and red salsa, salad bowl of bulgar wheat, peas, radish, herbs and chickpeas with tahini and lemon dressing, goats cheese arancini with arrabiata sauce, haggis fritters with dijon mayonnaise, garlic-roasted butternut squash with shaved fennel, black olives and almonds, herb-crusted hake fillet with lemon roast potatoes and lemongrass butter, slow-cooked beef with dauphinoise potatoes and juniper sauce, and puddings such as peanut butter parfait with Malteser cookie crumb, whipped yoghurt and pickled strawberries, and chocolate pot with kirsch-soaked cherries and vanilla ice-cream; they also offer a two- and three-course set weekday lunch. *Benchmark main dish: beef burger on sourdough seeded bun with jalapeno beer cheese, fries and slaw £14.50. Two-course evening meal £26.00.*

Free house ~ Licensee Oliver Thain ~ Real ale ~ Open 12-3, 6-11; 12-3, 5.30-11 Fri; 12-11 Sat; 12-10.30 Sun ~ Bar food 12-2.30, 6.30-9; 12-2.30, 6-9.30 Fri, Sat; 12-8 Sun ~ Restaurant ~ Children welcome ~ Dogs allowed in bar

PETERBOROUGH   TL1899   MAP 5

Brewery Tap 🍺 £

(01733) 358500 – www.thebrewery-tap.com
Opposite Queensgate car park; PE1 2AA

Fantastic range of real ales including their own brews, popular Thai food and a lively, friendly atmosphere

Once an old labour exchange, this has been turned into a striking-looking open-plan and contemporary bar with particularly good own-brewed ales and Thai food – it's deservedly popular. It features an expanse of light wood and stone floors with blue-painted iron pillars holding up a steel-corded mezzanine level. Stylish lighting includes steel-meshed wall lights and a giant suspended steel ring with bulbs running around the rim. A band of chequered floor tiles traces the path of the long sculpted pale wood bar counter, which is boldly backed by an impressive display of bottles in a ceiling-high wall of wooden cubes. There's also a comfortable downstairs area, a big-screen TV for sporting events, background music and regular live bands and comedy nights. A two-storey glass wall divides the bar from the brewery, giving fascinating views of the two-barrel brew plan from which they produce their own Oakham Bishops Farewell, Citra, Inferno, JHB and seasonal ales; also, guest ales, quite a few whiskies and several wines by the glass.

The Thai food includes set menus and specials, as well as tom yum soup, chicken, beef, pork, prawn, duck and vegetable curries, stir-fried crispy chilli beef, gai yang (grilled chicken marinated in garlic, coriander and lemongrass with a sweet chilli sauce), various noodle dishes, all sorts of salads and stir-fries and five kinds of rice. *Benchmark main dish: pad thai noodles £9.60. Two-course evening meal £20.00.*

Own brew ~ Licensee Jessica Loock ~ Real ale ~ Open 12-11 (1am Fri, 2am Sat); 12-10.30 Sun ~ Bar food 12-2.30, 5.30-10.30; 12-10.30 Fri, Sat; 12-3.30, 5.30-9.30 Sun ~ Restaurant ~ Children welcome during food service times only ~ Dogs allowed in bar

REACH   TL5666   MAP 5

Dykes End 🍺

(01638) 743816 – www.dykesend.co.uk
From B1102 follow signpost to Swaffham Prior and Upware; village signposted; CB25 0JD

Attractive former farmhouse with popular food and seats outside

Villagers are lucky to have this handsome 17th-c pub on their doorstep by the church, while visitors are pleased to discover somewhere so charming after walking the nearby Devil's Dyke. Head first for the well stocked and simply decorated bar with kitchen chairs around stripped heavy pine tables on dark boards. House ales on handpump are Adnams Southwold and Timothy Taylors Landlord, with two regularly changing guests alongside a decent wine list and Adnams Wild Wave cider. In a panelled section on the left are a few candlelit dining tables, and on the right there's a step down to a red-carpeted part with black leather wall banquettes and dark wooden dining chairs and an open fire. There are picnic-sets in the front garden overlooking the village green.

As well as specialising in proper pies, the well liked food includes house pâté with caramelised nuts, sticky sesame chicken lollipops, whole baked garlic and rosemary camembert with ciabatta, grilled pork chop with charcuterie sauce, bubble and squeak and vegetables, nut roast and halloumi burger with skin-on fries, home-made beef burger with skin-on fries, and puddings such as strawberries and cream cheesecake with raspberry coulis and vanilla ice-cream and coppa amaretto. *Benchmark main dish: home-made steak and ale pie £12.50. Two-course evening meal £18.50.*

Free house ~ Licensee Simon Owers ~ Real ale ~ Open 12-2.30, 6-11; 12-11 Sat; 12-10.30 Sun ~ Bar food 12-2, 5.30-8.30; 12-3 Sun; not Mon ~ Restaurant ~ Children allowed but must be well behaved ~ Dogs welcome

Please let us know what you think of a pub's bedrooms: feedback@goodguides.com or (no stamp needed) Freepost THE GOOD PUB GUIDE, Random House Publishing, 20 Vauxhall Bridge Road, London SW1V 2SA.

THORNEY   TL2799 MAP 5
Dog in a Doublet 🌟
(01733) 202256 – www.doginad.co.uk
B1040 towards Thorney; PE6 0RW

Country inn with produce from own farm, tasty food and local ales, friendly service and seats outside; bedrooms

With plenty of good walks right outside the door and the River Nene and one of the biggest lock gates in Europe just across the road, this makes a fine setting for lunch. The bar has sofas, comfortable seats and an open fire. Ales on handpump change regularly, from breweries such as Heritage, and there are ten wines by the glass and three farm ciders. The restaurant leads off and has an open kitchen, solid wooden dining chairs around farmhouse tables, prints on red-painted walls and a monthly live pianist; background music and bar games. A deli counter offers their own produce and treats from further afield too. Outside, there are brightly painted picnic-sets under a gazebo. The eight bedrooms have vaulted ceilings and their own balconies, and they also have a campsite and farm.

 Enjoyable food uses free-range eggs, home-grown vegetables and home-reared pigs from their small farm and makes much use of the grill: courgette and flower stuffed with chive cream cheese, half or whole lobster mac and cheese, cured brisket in pho broth with veg and Thai herbs, 'hearth-style' Sunday roasts (including meat, fish, vegetarian and vegan options), and puddings such as sticky toffee pudding and passion-fruit and clotted cream crème brûlée with lavender shortbread; they also offer breakfasts (8.30-10.30am). *Benchmark main dish: fish and chips £14.00. Two-course evening meal £22.00.*

Free house ~ Licensees John McGinn and Della Mills ~ Real ale ~ Open 12-11; 12-9 Sun ~ Bar food 8.30-10am, 12-2.30, 5-9 Mon-Fri; 8.30-10.30am, 12-9 Sat; 8.30-10.30, 12-5 Sun ~ Children welcome ~ Dogs allowed in bar & bedrooms ~ Bedrooms: £

WHITTLESFORD   TL4648 MAP 5
Tickell Arms 🌟 ♟
(01223) 833025 – www.cambscuisine.com/the-tickell-whittlesford
2.4 miles from M11 junction 10: A505 towards Newmarket, then second turn left signposted Whittlesford; keep on into North Road; CB22 4NZ

Well run dining pub with good enterprising food and pretty garden

With its impressive choice of food, first class service and fine choice of drinks, it is easy to see why readers enjoy this pub so much. There are also some fine architectural features that are really worth looking at. The L-shaped bar has bentwood stools on floor tiles, ornate cast-iron pillars, a woodburning stove and (under bowler-hatted lampshades over the counter) Adnams Southwold and Brewsters Hophead on handpump, 25 fairly priced wines by the glass including champagne, and farm cider. There are also three porcelain handpumps from the era of the legendarily autocratic regime of the Wagner-loving former owner Kim Tickell. Tables in the dining room vary from sturdy to massive, with leather-cushioned bentwood and other dining chairs and one dark pew, and fresh minimalist décor in palest buff. This opens into an even lighter limestone-floored conservatory area, partly divided by a very high-backed ribbed-leather banquette. A side terrace has comfortable tables, and the secluded garden beyond has pergolas and a pond. Sister pubs are the Cock in Hemingford Grey, Crown & Punchbowl at Horningsea and Three Horseshoes in Madingley (all in Cambridgeshire).

🍴⭐ Interesting, up-to-date food includes scallops with white bean purée, black pudding and red salsa, salad bowl of bulgar wheat, peas, radish, herbs and chickpeas with tahini and lemon dressing, goats cheese arancini with arrabiata sauce, haggis fritters with dijon mayonnaise, garlic-roasted butternut squash with shaved fennel, black olives and almonds, herb-crusted hake fillet with lemon roast potatoes and lemongrass butter, slow-cooked beef with dauphinoise potatoes and juniper sauce, and puddings such as peanut butter parfait with Malteser cookie crumb, whipped yoghurt and pickled strawberries, and chocolate pot with kirsch-soaked cherries and vanilla ice-cream; they also offer a two- and three-course set weekday lunch. *Benchmark main dish: roast chicken breast with potato and herb terrine, smoked bacon and broad beans £16.75. Two-course evening meal £26.00.*

Free house ~ Licensees Oliver Thain and Max Freeman ~ Real ale ~ Open 12-3, 6-11; 12-11 Sat; 12-10.30 Sun ~ Bar food 12-2.30, 6.30-9; 12-2.30, 6.30-9.30 Fri; 12-3, 6-9.30 Sat; 12-3, 6-8 Sun ~ Restaurant ~ Children welcome until evening when must be over 10 (in pub), over 5 (in restaurant) ~ Dogs allowed in bar

Also Worth a Visit in Cambridgeshire

Besides the fully inspected pubs, you might like to try these pubs that have been recommended to us and described by readers. Do tell us what you think of them: feedback@goodguides.com

---

ABBOTS RIPTON   TL2377
Abbots Elm (01487) 773773
B1090; PE28 2PA Open-plan thatched dining pub (reconstructed after a major fire a decade ago); highly rated food from snacks and bar meals to interesting restaurant dishes using locally sourced and home-grown produce, extensive choice of wines by the glass including champagne, three well kept ales, good friendly service; children and dogs welcome, four bedrooms, open all day Sat, till 4pm Sun.

BABRAHAM   TL5150
George (01223) 837755
High Street; just off A1307; CB22 3AG Beamed and timbered 18th-c village pub set back from quiet road; decent choice of affordable home-made food from baguettes and pub favourites up, Greene King IPA and a couple of guests, friendly accommodating staff, bare-boards bar, carpeted restaurant and second dining/function room in adjoining barn; children welcome, tables in garden with terrace, open all day.

BARRINGTON   TL3849
Royal Oak (01223) 870791
Turn off A10 about 3.7 miles SW of M11 junction 11, in Foxton; West Green; CB22 7RZ Rambling thatched Tudor pub with tables out overlooking classic village green; heavy low beams and timbers, mixed furnishings, Greene King IPA and guests, Aspall's and Thatcher's ciders, good wine list and enjoyable food from pub favourites up, friendly helpful service, airy dining conservatory; background music, children and dogs welcome, classic car club meeting first Fri of month.

BOURN   TL3256
Willow Tree (01954) 719775
High Street, just off B1046 W of Cambridge; CB23 2SQ Light and airy dining pub with relaxed informal atmosphere despite the cut-glass chandeliers, sprinkling of Louis XVI furniture and profusion of silver-plated candlesticks; restaurant-style cooking (all-day Sun roast till 8pm), Woodfordes and a local guest, well chosen wines and inventive cocktails, friendly staff; live jazz Sun evening; children welcome, smart tables and chairs on back deck, grassed area beyond car park with fruit trees, huge weeping willow and tipi, closed Mon and Thurs, otherwise open all day.

BOXWORTH   TL3464
Golden Ball (01954) 267397
High Street; CB23 4LY Attractive partly thatched 16th-c village inn with pitched-roof dining bar, restaurant and small conservatory, emphasis on good fairly priced food from baguettes through pubby choices and grills to blackboard specials, friendly helpful service, well kept Bombardier, St Austell Tribute and a guest, 20 wines by the glass and good choice of whiskies and gins; children welcome, nice garden and heated terrace, pastures behind, ten quiet bedrooms in adjacent block, open all day, food till 4pm on Sun.

BRAMPTON   TL2170
Black Bull (01480) 457201
Church Road; PE28 4PF 16th-c and later with updated low-ceilinged interior; stripped-wood floor and inglenook woodburner in split-level main bar, restaurant with light wood furniture on tiles, popular well priced

pubby food including range of pies, four real ales, friendly efficient staff; children and dogs (in bar) welcome, garden with play area, open (and food) all day except Sun when kitchen shuts at 4pm.

BRINKLEY   TL6254
Red Lion (01638) 508707
High Street; CB8 0RA Old country pub set back from the road; painted beams, bare boards and inglenook log fire, Woodfordes Wherry and a couple of guests including Crafty Beers, good sensibly priced food from sandwiches up including some themed nights and Sun brunch, friendly service, restaurant; children and dogs (in bar) welcome, picnic-sets on lawn, campsite behind the pub, closed Sun evening, Mon and Tues.

BROUGHTON   TL2877
★ **Crown** (01487) 824428
Off A141 opposite RAF Wyton; Bridge Road; PE28 3AY Attractively tucked-away mansard-roofed dining pub opposite church; fresh airy décor with country pine tables and chairs on stone floors, some leather bucket seats and sofa, good well presented food (special diets catered for) from lunchtime sandwiches and pub favourites up, friendly service, four changing real ales such as Adnams and local breweries, restaurant; background music; children and dogs welcome, disabled access and facilities, tables out on big stretch of grass behind, open all day Sat, till 6pm Sun.

BUCKDEN   TL1967
★ **George** (01480) 812300
High Street; PE19 5XA Handsome and stylish hotel (former Georgian coaching inn) with bustling informal bar; fine fan beamwork, bucket chairs on parquet flooring, woodburner in carved stone fireplace, Adnams Southwold and a changing guest from zinc-topped counter, lots of wines including champagne by the glass, teas and coffees, popular brasserie with good modern food served by helpful enthusiastic young staff, also bar meals; background music; children and dogs welcome, tables under large parasols on attractive sheltered terrace with box hedging, 12 charming bedrooms named after famous Georges, smallish car park (free street parking), open all day.

BURWELL   TL5867
Anchor (01638) 743970
North Street; CB25 0BA Revamped 18th-c dining pub with good imaginative food cooked by chef-owner, Adnams, Greene King and Meantime ales and plenty of wines by the glass from an interesting list, helpful friendly service, restaurant, steps down to snug with books and board games; background music; children welcome till 9pm, dogs in bar, disabled loo, garden backing on to small river, closed Mon and Tues.

CAMBRIDGE   TL4658
★ **Cambridge Blue** (01223) 471680
85 Gwydir Street; CB1 2LG Friendly little backstreet local with a dozen or more interesting ales (some tapped from the cask – regular festivals), also six craft kegs, 200 bottled beers, up to seven ciders and over 70 whiskies, enjoyable well priced home-made food including seasonal specials, extended bar area with lots of breweriana and old advertising signs, attractive conservatory; children and dogs welcome, seats in back garden bordering cemetery, open all day, food all day weekends when it can get very busy.

CAMBRIDGE   TL4459
Castle (01223) 353194
Castle Street; CB3 0AJ Adnams range and interesting guest beers in bare-boards bar and other pleasantly simple rooms including snug and quieter upstairs area, good choice of pub food from sandwiches and snacks to blackboard specials, efficient friendly staff; background music, children and dogs welcome, part-covered walled back courtyard, open all day and very busy Fri and Sat evenings.

CAMBRIDGE   TL4658
Clarendon Arms (01223) 778272
Clarendon Street; CB1 1JX Welcoming backstreet corner local; pubby furniture on flagstones or bare boards, lots of pictures including local scenes, step down to back bar, Greene King ales and enjoyable home-made food from snacks to Sun roasts, friendly helpful service; children and dogs welcome, wheelchair access with help, seats in sunny back courtyard, open all day, no food Sun evening.

CAMBRIDGE   TL4657
Devonshire Arms (01223) 316610
Devonshire Road; CB1 2BH Welcoming Milton-tied pub with two busy linked bars, their well kept ales and guests, real cider, also great choice of bottled beers, decent wines and a dozen malts, enjoyable good value food (not Sun evening) from sandwiches and pizzas to grills, creaky wood floors, mix of furniture including long narrow refectory tables, architectural prints and steam engine pictures, woodburner in back bar; wheelchair access, handy for the station, open all day.

CAMBRIDGE   TL4458
★ **Eagle** (01223) 505020
Benet Street; CB2 3QN Once the city's most important coaching inn; rambling rooms with two ancient mullioned windows and the remains of possibly medieval wall paintings, two fireplaces dating from around 1600, lovely worn wooden floors and plenty of pine panelling, dark red ceiling left unpainted since World War II to preserve the

signatures of British and American airmen made with Zippo lighters, candle smoke and lipstick, well kept Greene King ales including Eagle DNA (Crick and Watson announced the discovery of DNA's structure here in 1953) and two guests, decent choice of enjoyable food served efficiently considering the crowds; children welcome, disabled facilities, heavy wooden seats in attractive cobbled and galleried courtyard, open all day.

CAMBRIDGE TL4558
Elm Tree (01223) 322553
Orchard Street; CB1 1JT Traditional one-bar backstreet drinkers' pub with welcoming atmosphere; seven well kept changing ales, wide range of Belgian bottled beers plus local cider/perry, friendly knowledgeable staff, no food, nice unspoilt interior with breweriana and other memorabilia; live music; wheelchair access, a few tables out at the side, open all day.

CAMBRIDGE TL4559
Fort St George (01223) 354327
Midsummer Common; CB4 1HA
Picturesque old pub (reached on foot only, no car parking nearby) in charming waterside position overlooking ducks, punts and boathouses; good value pubby food including traditional Sun lunch, well kept Greene King ales and decent wines by the glass, cheerful service, interior extended around old-fashioned Tudor core with oars on beams, historic boating photographs and open fire; children and dogs welcome, wheelchair access via side door but only to bar area (disabled toilet outside), lots of tables outside, open (and food) all day.

CAMBRIDGE TL4558
Free Press (01223) 368337
Prospect Row; CB1 1DU Unspoilt little backstreet pub with interesting décor including old newspaper pages and printing memorabilia (was printshop for a local paper); Greene King IPA, Abbot and Mild plus regularly changing guests, good range of wines by the glass, 25 malt whiskies and lots of gins and rums, tasty good value food, log fire, friendly atmosphere; TV for major sports, board games; children and dogs (in bar) welcome, wheelchair access, small sheltered paved garden behind, open all day.

CAMBRIDGE TL4557
Live & Let Live (01223) 460261
Mawson Road; CB1 2EA Popular backstreet corner pub with friendly relaxed atmosphere; five well kept ales including Nethergate and Oakham, proper cider and more than 100 rums, snacky food, panelled interior with sturdy varnished tables on bare boards, some steam railway and brewery memorabilia, old gas light fittings, cribbage and dominoes; dogs welcome, disabled access awkward but possible, closed Weds and Thurs lunchtimes.

CAMBRIDGE TL4458
Mill (01223) 311829
Mill Lane; CB2 1RX Fairly compact old pub in picturesque spot overlooking mill pond (punt hire); seven mainly local ales and proper cider from plank-topped servery, reasonably priced food including sandwiches and burgers, opened-up bar with bare boards, quarry tiles and some exposed brickwork, mix of old and new furniture including pews and banquettes, snug panelled back room; radiogram playing vinyl, Mon quiz, sports TV, children welcome, open (and food) all day.

CAMBRIDGE TL4458
Mitre (01223) 358403
Bridge Street, opposite St John's College; CB2 1UF Popular Nicholsons pub close to the river and well placed for visiting the colleges; spacious rambling bar on several levels, good selection of well kept ales and reasonably priced wines by the glass, their usual food including sandwiches and burgers, efficient friendly service; background music, children welcome, disabled access, open (and food) all day.

CAMBRIDGE TL4559
Old Spring (01223) 357228
Ferry Path; car park on Chesterton Road; CB4 1HB Extended Victorian pub, roomy and airy, with enjoyable home-made food from traditional choices up, friendly efficient service, well kept Greene King IPA, Abbot and four guests, plenty of wines by the glass and good coffee, mix of seating including sofas on bare boards, log fires, conservatory; background music; well behaved children welcome, no dogs inside, disabled facilities, seats out at front and on large heated back terrace, open all day, food all day weekends.

CAMBRIDGE TL4458
★**Pint Shop** (01223) 352293
Peas Hill; CB2 3PN Revamped former university offices on two floors; front bar with restaurant behind, parquet floors, grey-painted walls, simple furnishings and pendant lighting, Kirkstall Black Band Porter, Nene Valley Simple Pleasures, Oakham Citra and a couple of quickly changing guests on handpump plus up to 17 craft ales, a good choice of wines and around 100 gins, unusual food from bar snacks up cooked on charcoal grill, set menu options Mon-Fri, further dining room upstairs; ground-floor wheelchair access/loos, courtyard picnic-sets, handy for Cambridge Arts Theatre and Corn Exchange, open all day.

CAMBRIDGE TL4459
★**Punter** (01223) 363322
Pound Hill, on corner of A1303 ring road; CB3 0AE Former coaching inn (sister to the Punter in Oxford) with rambling series of informal rooms; pleasing mix of pews, elderly dining chairs and

Lloyd Loom on old dark boards, paintings and antique prints, small area down steps with candles on scrubbed tables, Adnams, Punter Blonde and two regularly changing guest ales, 15 wines by the glass, interesting fairly priced food from seasonal menu, good friendly service, raftered and flagstoned dining room; background jazz, board games; children and dogs welcome, tables in mainly covered courtyard with another bar/dining area in barn beyond, open all day.

CASTOR   TL1298
Prince of Wales Feathers
(01733) 380222 *Peterborough Road, off A47; PE5 7AL* Friendly stone-built local with half a dozen well kept ales including Castor, craft beers and proper cider/perry, good value food cooked by landlady including Thurs steak night, open-plan interior with dining area to the left; Sat live music, Sun quiz, pool, TV; children and dogs welcome, disabled access/loos, attractive front terrace, another at the back with large smokers' shelter, open all day, till late weekends, no food Sun evening.

CLAYHITHE   TL5064
Bridge Hotel (01223) 860622
Clayhithe Road; CB25 9HZ Fantastic riverside location with lovely views that you can enjoy from the large beer garden, this homely hostelry with characterful features such as old timbers, exposed brick, old wood floors and cream-painted wood-panelled walls is welcoming throughout all seasons; Greene King cask ales, craft beers and a good choice of wines are complemented by a good-value menu focusing on pub classics and tasty Sunday roasts; delightful strolls along the river, there's also a boat mooring facility and the Cam Sailing Club close by. Open 12-10 Sun-Thurs, 12-10.30 Fri, Sat.

CONINGTON   TL3266
White Swan (01954) 267251
Signed off A14 (was A604) Cambridge-Huntingdon; Elsworth Road; CB23 4LN Quietly placed 18th-c red-brick country pub; well kept Adnams and guests tapped from the cask, nine wines by the glass and good freshly made food (not Sun evening, Mon, Tues), friendly attentive service, traditional bar with tiled floor and log fire, restaurant extension, some old photographs and local artwork; children and dogs welcome, big front garden with play area, open all day.

DUXFORD   TL4746
★ John Barleycorn (01223) 832699
Handy for M11 junction 10; right at first roundabout, then left at main village junction into Moorfield Road;

CB22 4PP Charming 17th-c thatched and shuttered pub; heavy beams, standing timbers and brick pillars creating alcoves, nice old floor tiles, log fire and all manner of seating including some good antique farmhouse chairs, walls adorned with air force memorabilia, old clocks, china plates, copper pans and plenty of pictures, regularly changing ales from the likes of Burton Bridge, Fullers, St Austell and Timothy Taylors, good choice of wines by the glass, consistently good food from sandwiches and grazing boards up; background music; children and dogs (in bar) welcome, easy wheelchair access from back car park, hanging baskets and blue-painted picnic-sets on front gravel, more tables in garden behind, comfortable barn-conversion bedrooms, handy for Imperial War Museum, open all day.

DUXFORD   TL4745
Plough (01223) 833170
St Peters Street; CB22 4RP Popular early 18th-c thatched pub under newish management, clean and bright, with enjoyable home-made lunchtime food (not Mon), five real ales including Adnams and Everards, also a craft keg, four ciders/perries and good range of gins, friendly helpful service, woodburner in brick fireplace; games including darts and dominoes; children and dogs welcome, handy for IWM Duxford, open all day (from 2pm Mon).

ELLINGTON   TL1671
Mermaid (01480) 891106
High Street; PE28 0AB Popular village dining pub dating in part from the 14th c; highly praised imaginative Asian-influenced food (not Sun evening) from owner-chef including vegetarian and vegan menus, three changing real ales from brick counter, several wines by the glass from a good list, friendly obliging young staff, beams (some hiding coins left by US airmen), country furniture, woodburner, smallish dining rooms; background music (turned off on request); garden overlooking church, B&B available, no proper car park, open all day weekends (till 8pm Sun), closed Mon.

ELSWORTH   TL3163
George & Dragon (01954) 267236
Off A14 NW of Cambridge, via Boxworth, or off A428; CB23 8JQ Neatly kept dining pub with panelled and carpeted main bar opening on left to slightly elevated dining area with woodburner, garden room overlooking attractive terraces, more formal restaurant on right, wide choice of popular food including speciality fish/seafood, set menus and other deals, Greene King ales,

a guest beer and decent range of wines, welcoming attentive service; steps down to loos, children welcome, closed Sun evening and Mon.

ELSWORTH
TL3163

Poacher (01954) 267722

Brockley Road; CB23 4JS Welcoming 17th-c thatched and beamed corner local; well kept Woodfordes Wherry and a couple of guests from tiny servery, good reasonably priced traditional food (not Sun evening), friendly service, painted pine furniture on bare boards or tiles, open fire; background and some live music, monthly quiz, TV; children and dogs welcome (they have two huskies), a few picnic-sets out in front, more in back garden, good walks, open all day Sat, until 6pm Sun.

ELTON
TL0893

Black Horse (01832) 280591

Overend; B671 off A605 W of Peterborough and A1(M); PE8 6RU Honey-stone beamed dining pub with nicely updated and opened-up interior; popular generously served food cooked by owner-chef, friendly accommodating service, four real ales including Digfield, Greene King and a beer badged for them, decent wines; children welcome, dogs in bar; terrace and garden with views across to Elton Hall park and village church, open (and food) all day.

ELY
TL5479

Cutter (01353) 662713

Annesdale, off Station Road (or walk S along Riverside Walk from Maltings); CB7 4BN Beautifully placed riverside pub with bar, dining lounge and restaurant; enjoyable food from sandwiches and wraps up, friendly helpful service, well kept Sharps, Woodfordes and a guest from boat-shaped counter, nice wines by the glass and decent coffee, good views from window seats and terrace; quiz Mon; children welcome, dogs not allowed in restaurant area, moorings, open all day from 10am (food from midday).

ELY
TL5480

Lamb (01353) 663574

Brook Street (Lynn Road); CB7 4EJ Good choice of food in popular hotel's panelled lounge bar or restaurant, friendly welcoming staff, Greene King ales and plenty of wines by the glass; children and dogs welcome, close to cathedral, 37 clean comfortable bedrooms, good breakfast (for non-residents too), open (and food) all day.

ETTON
TF1406

Golden Pheasant (01733) 252387

Just off B1443 N of Peterborough, signed from near N end of A15 bypass; PE6 7DA Welcoming former Georgian farmhouse (a pub since 1964); spacious bar with open fire, good choice of real ales and other drinks, well liked food served by

friendly staff, back restaurant; TV; children welcome, no dogs inside, big tree-sheltered garden with play area, on Green Wheel cycle route, closed Mon, otherwise open all day.

FEN DRAYTON
TL3468

Three Tuns (01954) 230242

Eastbound on A14, take first exit after Fenstanton, signed Fen Drayton and follow to pub; westbound on A14 exit at junction 27 and follow signs to village on Cambridge Road; High Street; CB24 4SJ Well preserved thatched village pub with three more or less open-plan rooms; heavy moulded Tudor beams and timbers, log fires, mix of burgundy cushioned stools, nice old dining chairs and settles in bar, red-patterned carpet in dining room, well kept Greene King IPA, Old Speckled Hen and a couple of guests, a dozen wines by the glass, good reasonably priced pubby food including blackboard specials, friendly service; some quiz and live music nights; children and dogs (in bar) welcome, back garden with covered dining area and play equipment, open all day, till midnight Fri, Sat, till 6pm Sun, closed Mon.

FOWLMERE
TL4245

Chequers (01763) 209333

High Street (B1368); SG8 7SR Tasteful refurbishment for this popular 16th-c coaching inn – now sister pub to Green Man in neighbouring Thriplow; split-level rooms (one with inglenook), spacious conservatory and attractive upstairs timbered dining room; Greene King and two changing guests, excellent food (including their own pork) served by friendly and efficient staff; children and dogs welcome, lovely paved terrace and lawn behind; open (and food) all day, till 7pm Sun, closed Mon, Tues.

GRANTCHESTER
TL4355

★ Blue Ball (01223) 846004

Broadway; CB3 9NQ Traditional bareboards free house rebuilt in 1900 on site of much older pub (cellars remain); welcoming licensees (there's a list of publicans back to 1767), three real ales such as Adnams and Woodfordes, Aspall's ciders and decent choice of wines by the glass, affordably priced wholesome food, good log fire; traditional games including shut the box and ring the bull, newspapers and lots of books; children and dogs welcome, tables on small terrace with lovely views to Grantchester Meadows, two comfortable bedrooms, nice village, open all day (till 8pm Sun).

GRANTCHESTER
TL4355

Red Lion (01223) 840121

High Street; CB3 9NF Comfortable and spacious thatched pub with attractively modernised open areas including pitched-roof dining room, beams, timbers and panelling, popular food from shortish varied menu, well kept ales such as Greene King,

Nene Valley, Oakham and Woodfordes, lots of wines by the glass and some interesting gins including Cambridge distilled nearby; background music; children, dogs and muddy boots welcome, sheltered terrace and good-sized lawn with play area, easy walk to river, open (and food) all day.

GRANTCHESTER   TL4455
Rupert Brooke (01223) 841875
Broadway; junction Coton Road with Cambridge–Trumpington Road; CB3 9NQ Smartly presented restauranty pub; contemporary wood-clad extension at front with big windows, elegant dining chairs around polished tables on bare boards, back bar area and two-level restaurant, brasserie-style food from open kitchen including late lunch, a couple of real ales and 26 wines by the glass, 14 gins, afternoon tea (not Sun), good friendly service, upstairs club room and roof terrace; children and dogs (in bar) welcome, open all day (till 7pm Sun).

GREAT ABINGTON   TL5348
Three Tuns (01223) 891467
Off A1307 Cambridge–Haverhill, and A11; CB21 6AB Peacefully set 16th-c beamed village pub; low-backed settles on stripped-wood floors, open fires, three well kept changing ales and good authentic Thai food, welcoming landlord and friendly efficient staff; garden picnic-sets, nine well appointed bedrooms in modern block, open all day weekends.

HADDENHAM   TL4675
Three Kings (01353) 749080
Station Road; CB6 3XD Popular 17th-c village pub; enjoyable home-made food from sandwiches and pub favourites up including good Sun roasts and Thurs curry night, well kept Greene King IPA and two guest ales, friendly welcoming staff, log fire; children and dogs allowed, back courtyard, open (and food) all day.

HAIL WESTON   TL1662
Royal Oak (01480) 716712
High Street; just off A45, handy for A1 St Neots bypass; PE19 5JW Picturesque 17th-c thatched pub in pretty village near Grafham Water; cosy interior with beams, flagstones and inglenook log fire, three Adnams ales along with Sharps Doom Bar, enjoyable home-made food including set deal Weds and Thurs, helpful willing service, restaurant; background music (vinyl night third Weds of month), Sun quiz; children and dogs (in bar) welcome, picnic-sets in back garden with sandpit, good circular walks (ask for details), limited street

parking, closed Mon and Tues, otherwise open all day, no food Sun evening.

HARDWICK   TL3758
Blue Lion (01954) 789593
Signed off A428 (was A45) W of Cambridge; Main Street; CB23 7QU Attractive 18th-c split-level dining pub refurbished under newish management; good generously served food with a focus on fresh fish, can eat in bar or extended dining area with conservatory, three Greene King ales, friendly efficient young staff, white-painted beams and timbers, copper-canopied inglenook; children and dogs welcome, pretty little front garden, more seats on decking and lawn with play area, handy for Wimpole Way walks, closes 5pm Sun.

HELPSTON   TF1205
Blue Bell (01733) 252394
Woodgate; off B1443; PE6 7ED Renovated and extended 17th-c stone pub; enjoyable food from sharing plates and pub favourites up, three well kept ales, good range of wines and gins, friendly staff; children and dogs welcome, four bedrooms, open all day weekends, no food Sun evening; John Clare's cottage next door (open Fri, Sat and Mon).

HEMINGFORD ABBOTS   TL2870
★Axe & Compass (01480) 463605
High Street; village signposted off A14 W of Cambridge; PE28 9AH Spacious old thatched pub in pretty village; simple, beamed public bar with mate's chairs and stools around wooden tables on ancient floor tiles, two-way fireplace (not in use) into snug, woodburner here and in main room with more beams and standing timbers, tartan-patterned chairs and cushioned wall seats around nice old tables, local photographs, Sharps Doom Bar, Timothy Taylors Landlord and Woodfordes Wherry, local cider and 14 wines by the glass, well liked fairly priced food (all day Sat, not Sun evening, Mon) from pub favourites up, long dining extension; background music (occasional live music), quiz Tues, board games; well behaved children and dogs (in bar) welcome, disabled facilities, contemporary furniture on terrace, picnic-sets on grass, fenced play area, river walks, closed Mon lunchtime, otherwise open all day.

HEYDON   TL4339
★King William IV (01763) 838773
Off A505 W of M11 junction 10; SG8 8PW Rambling dimly lit rooms with fascinating rustic jumble (ploughshares, yokes, iron tools, cowbells and so forth) along with copperware and china in nooks

---

A star symbol before the name of a pub shows exceptional character and appeal. It doesn't mean extra comfort. Even quite a basic pub can win a star, if it's individual enough.

and crannies, some tables suspended by chains from beams, central log fire, Fullers, Greene King and Timothy Taylors, good choice of highly rated food including several vegetarian options, helpful staff; background music; children and dogs (in bar) welcome, picnic-sets in back garden with decked area overlooking fields, four bedrooms in separate building, open (and food) all day weekends.

HISTON   TL4363
★ **Red Lion**   (01223) 564437
High Street, off Station Road; 3.7 miles from M11 junction 1; CB24 9JD
Impressive choice of draught and bottled beers along with traditional cider/perry (festivals Easter/early Sept); ceiling joists in L-shaped main bar packed with beer mats, pump clips and whisky-water jugs, also fine collection of old brewery advertisements and enamel signs, enjoyable traditional food (not Fri, Sun evenings) including vegan and gluten-free choices, cheerful efficient service, log fires, comfortable brocaded wall seats, matching mate's chairs and pubby tables, extended bar on left (well behaved children allowed here) with darts, TV and huge collection of beer bottles, quiz night twice a month; mobile phones discouraged, no dogs inside; disabled access/facilities, picnic-sets in neat garden, limited parking, four bedrooms, open all day.

HOUGHTON   TL2772
Three Jolly Butchers
(01480) 463228   *A1123, Wyton; PE28 2AD* Popular 17th-c beamed pub with wide choice of enjoyable home-made food from bar and restaurant menus, friendly accommodating service, well kept ales including Greene King IPA and Sharps Doom Bar; background and live music, quiz nights, sports TV; well behaved children and dogs (in bar) welcome, covered back terrace with pool table, picnic-sets in large garden down to River Ouse (own moorings), pretty village and handy for Houghton Mill (NT), open (and food) all day, kitchen closes 4pm Sun.

HUNTINGDON   TL2572
King of the Belgians (01480) 52030
Main Street, Hartford; PE29 1XU
Traditional and welcoming little 16th-c beamed village local; four well kept changing ales, real cider and popular good value home-made food including stone-baked pizzas in bar or dining lounge; events including live music and quiz nights, charity beer/music festival in May, darts, shut the box and other traditional games, TV for major sports; children and dogs (in bar) welcome, rattan-style furniture on back terrace, open all day (till midnight Fri, Sat).

KEYSTON   TL0475
★ **Pheasant** (01832) 710241
Just off A14 SE of Thrapston; brown sign to pub down village loop road, off

B663; PE28 0RE Attractive thatched dining pub with pitched rafters under new chef/landlord – early reports suggest good food; spacious oak-beamed bar with open fires, country paintings on pale walls, three distinct dining areas, Adnams, Nene Valley and a guest beer, 17 wines by the glass including champagne, good service; children and dogs welcome, seats out at front and on back terrace, open all day Fri/Sat, closed Sun evening, Mon.

KIMBOLTON   TL0967
New Sun (01480) 860052
High Street; PE28 0HA Pink-painted village pub with cosy low-beamed front lounge, standing timbers and exposed brickwork, comfortable seats by log fire, narrower locals' bar serving Bombardier, Eagle IPA and a guest, several wines by the glass and decent range of gins, well liked food including tapas, friendly service, traditionally furnished dining room and airy conservatory leading to terrace with café-style furniture under giant umbrellas; background music, piano; well behaved children welcome away from bar, dogs allowed in bar, open all day, no food Sun or Mon evenings.

LEIGHTON BROMSWOLD   TL1175
Green Man (01480) 890238
Signed off A14 Huntingdon–Kettering; PE28 5AW Cosy traditional village pub with origins from the 13th c; four well kept changing ales and enjoyable good value hearty food, friendly long-serving landlady, plenty of unpretentious old-fashioned character with heavy low beams and inglenook log fire; events including live music and quiz nights, Northants skittles; children, walkers and dogs welcome, picnic-sets outside, closed Mon, Tues and Sun evening.

LITTLE SHELFORD   TL4551
Navigator (01223) 843901
2.5 miles from M11 junction 11: A10 towards Royston, then left at Hauxton, The Shelfords signpost; CB22 5ES
Attractive little 16th-c village pub with bar and small restaurant; beams, painted panelling and some exposed brickwork, open fire, good authentic Thai food, mainstream ales such as Adnams Ghost Ship, Sharps Doom Bar and Fullers London Pride and decent wines, friendly prompt service; children welcome, some picnic-sets outside on tarmac.

NEWTON   TL4349
★ **Queens Head** (01223) 870436
2.5 miles from M11 junction 11; A10 towards Royston, then left on to B1368; CB22 7PG Lovely traditional unchanging pub run by same welcoming family for many years – lots of loyal customers; peaceful bow-windowed main bar with crooked beams in low ceiling, bare wooden benches and seats built into cream walls, curved

high-backed settle, paintings and big log fire, well kept Adnams ales tapped from the cask, farm cider and simple food such as soup and sandwiches, small carpeted saloon, traditional games including table skittles, shove-ha'penny and nine men's morris; children on best behaviour allowed in games room only, dogs welcome, seats out in front by vine trellis.

OFFORD D'ARCY   TL2166
Horseshoe (01480) 810293
High Street; PE19 5RH Extended former 17th-c coaching house with two bars and restaurant; emphasis on their good food including popular Sun carvery, Sharps Doom Bar, a couple of guests and well chosen wines, friendly helpful service, beams and inglenooks; children welcome, dogs in snug (not Sun), lawned garden with play area, open all day Sat, till 9pm Sun.

ORWELL   TL3650
Chequers (01223) 207840
Town Green Road; SG8 5QL Village dining pub with good food (not Tues or Sun evenings) from pub favourites up including popular themed nights, well kept ales and decent choice of wines by the glass, friendly helpful staff; quiz every other Wed; children and dogs (in bar) welcome, disabled facilities, handy for Wimpole Estate (NT), open all day Fri and Sat, till 8pm Sun, closed Mon.

PAMPISFORD   TL4948
★**Chequers** (01223) 833220
2.6 miles from M11 junction 10: A505 E, then village and pub signed off; Town Lane; CB22 4ER Traditional neatly kept old pub with low beams and comfortable old-fashioned furnishings, booth seating on pale ceramic tiles in main area, low step down to bare-boards part, four real ales such as Greene King IPA and Woodfordes Wherry, well liked fairly priced pubby food, good friendly service; TV, children and dogs welcome, picnic-sets in small garden lit by black streetlamps, parking can be tricky, open all day (till 4pm Sun).

PETERBOROUGH   TL1998
★**Charters** (01733) 315700
Town Bridge, S side; PE1 1FP Interesting conversion of Dutch grain barge moored on River Nene; sizeable timbered bar on lower deck with eight real ales including Oakham (regular beer festivals), restaurant above serving good value pan-Asian food, lots of wooden tables and pews; background music, darts, quizzes, live bands (Fri and Sat after 10.30pm, Sun from 3.30pm); children

welcome till 9pm, dogs in bar, huge riverside garden (gets packed in fine weather), open all day.

PETERBOROUGH   TL1897
Coalheavers Arms (01733) 565664
Park Street, Woodston; PE2 9BH Friendly old-fashioned little flagstoned local near football ground (busy on match days); eight well kept ales and good range of bottled beers, traditional cider and several malt whiskies, basic snacks; Sun quiz, dogs welcome, pleasant garden behind, open all day Fri-Sun, closed lunchtime Mon-Thurs.

PETERBOROUGH   TL1898
Drapers Arms (01733) 847570
Cowgate; PE1 1LZ Roomy open-plan Wetherspoons in converted 19th-c draper's; ten well kept ales and their usual good value food served all day, prompt friendly service; TV; children welcome, open from 8am and can get very busy Fri, Sat evenings.

SPALDWICK   TL1372
George (01480) 890293
Just off A14 W of Huntingdon; PE28 0TD Former 17th-c village coaching inn with good food (till 7pm Sun) from bar snacks up, Timothy Taylors Landlord, Woodfordes Wherry and a guest, decent wines by the glass, friendly if not always speedy service, sofas in beamed bar, larger dining area including raftered part; children and dogs (in bar) welcome, seats out behind under parasols, open all day Fri-Sun.

ST IVES   TL3171
Oliver Cromwell (01480) 465601
Wellington Street; PE27 5AZ Homely, attractive Wells & Co two-bar pub in little street just back from the river; enjoyable good value lunchtime food such as steak and kidney pudding, half a dozen well kept changing ales, proper ciders and good choice of wines, friendly staff; background music (live Thurs), quiz first Tues of the month; small back terrace, open all day.

STAPLEFORD   TL4651
Rose (01223) 843349
London Road; M11 junction 11; CB22 5DG New management for this comfortable dining pub with good choice of popular fairly pubby food including set menus and Mon/Tues early bird deal, three well kept real ales, friendly uniformed staff, small low-ceilinged lounge with inglenook woodburner, roomy split-level dining area; steps up to lavatories; picnic-sets on back grass, open (and food) all day weekends.

Real ale may be served from handpumps, electric pumps (not just the on-off switches used for keg beer) or – common in Scotland – tall taps called founts (pronounced 'fonts') where a separate pump pushes the beer up under air pressure.

STILTON
TL1689

Bell (01733) 241066
High Street; village signposted from A1 S of Peterborough; PE7 3RA Lovely 17th-c coaching inn with a great deal of character: bow windows, sturdy upright wooden seats on flagstone floors, a big log fire in a handsome stone fireplace; bar-cum-dining area with changing ales such as Fullers London Pride, Greene King IPA and Old Speckled Hen on handpump, farm cider and good choice of wines by the glass, malt whiskies and gins; wide range of good food from snacks and sandwiches to interesting dishes in the restaurant, bar and courtyard; background music, board games and TV; bedrooms; open all day Sun.

SWAFFHAM PRIOR
TL5663

Red Lion (01638) 745483
B1102 NE of Cambridge; High Street; CB5 0LD Comfortable and welcoming 17th-c pub with well kept Batemans and guests, a dozen wines by the glass and enjoyable sensibly priced home-made food (not Sun evening, Mon, Tues), OAP weekday set lunch, helpful friendly staff, beams, old quarry tiles and brick fireplace, historic local photographs; quiz third Sun of month, darts, TV; children welcome, picnic-sets in back garden, interesting church and priory, open all day Sat, till 8pm Sun (later on quiz nights), closed lunchtimes Mon and Tues.

THRIPLOW
TL4346

Green Man (01763) 208855
3 miles from M11 junction 10; A505 towards Royston, then first right; Lower Street; SG8 7RJ Welcoming little roadside pub owned by the village (sister to Chequers in neighbouring Fowlmere); good food from shortish daily changing menu along with blackboard tapas, four well kept ales and decent wines by the glass, efficient friendly service; children and dogs welcome, picnic-sets on small grassy triangle in front, two circular walks from the pub, open (and food) all day.

UFFORD
TF0904

★White Hart (01780) 740250
Main Street; S on to Ufford Road off B1443 at Bainton, then right; PE9 3BH Friendly village pub dating from the 17th c, informal, chatty bar with wood floor and exposed stone walls, railway memorabilia, farm tools and chamber pots, high-backed settles and leather sofa by woodburner, well kept Fullers London Pride, Sharps Doom Bar and a couple of guests, several wines by the glass, good food from varied menu, beamed restaurant and small orangery; children and dogs welcome, three acres of gardens, 12 comfortable bedrooms, good breakfast, open all day (till 9pm Sun).

WHITTLESFORD
TL4648

Bees in the Wall (01223) 834289
North Road; handy for M11 junction 10 and IWM Duxford; CB22 4NZ Village-edge local with comfortably worn-in split-level timbered lounge, polished tables and country prints, small tiled public bar with old wall settles, darts, decent good value food from shortish menu, well kept Adnams Lighthouse and one or two guests, open fires; background and live music including folk club second Tues of month, small TV for major sports; children welcome, no dogs, picnic-sets in big paddock-style garden with terrace, bees still in the wall (here since the 1950s), closed all day Mon, lunchtimes Tues-Thurs (and Sat in winter), no food Sun evening or Tues.

Cheshire

ALDFORD
Grosvenor Arms ⭐ 🍷 🍺

SJ4259 MAP 7

(01244) 620228 – www.brunningandprice.co.uk/grosvenorarms

B5130 Chester–Wrexham; CH3 6HJ

Spacious place with impressive range of drinks, wide-ranging imaginative menu, good service, suntrap terrace and garden

Fine ornamental red and black brickwork and handsome half-timbering along with generous proportions speak to this pub's status as part of the Grosvenor Estate, but it has no airs and graces: inside, it's warm, charming and atmospheric, attracting a good mix of customers of all ages. There's a lot of interest and individuality in the spacious cream-painted areas that are sectioned by big knocked-through arches. A variety of floor finishes includes wood, quarry tiles, flagstones, black and white tiles, and the richly coloured Turkish rugs look well against these natural materials. Good solid pieces of traditional furniture, plenty of pictures and attractive lighting keep it all cosy. A handsome room has tall bookshelves lining one wall and they keep a good selection of board games. Well trained, attentive staff serve Phoenix Brunning & Price Original, Timothy Taylors Landlord, Weetwood Eastgate and guests such as Big Hand Seren, Salopian Oracle and Timothy Taylors Landlord Dark from a fine-looking bar counter, and they offer 20 wines by the glass from a knowledgeable list, more than 80 whiskies, 30 gins and farm cider. Outside is a large elegant suntrap terrace and a neat lawn with plenty of picnic-sets; the village green is opposite, and the route of a pleasant local walk is available to download from the website. Disabled access.

🍴 British food with Asian and Mediterranean influences changes frequently, but along with sandwiches might include Blacksticks Blue savoury cheesecake, Thai sesame fishcakes with spiced pineapple, carrot and edamame bean salad, chilli and lime marmalade, chicken and pistachio pastillas with apricot chutney and harissa yoghurt, charcuterie plate, king prawn satay with pineapple salsa, rice noodles and toasted peanut salad, grilled bream fillet with oven-roasted red onion, Appleby's cheese, potato and onion pie with home-made baked beans, braised shoulder of lamb with dauphinoise potatoes, red cabbage and red wine sauce, and puddings such as triple chocolate brownie with chocolate sauce and bread and butter pudding. *Benchmark main dish: smoked haddock and salmon fishcakes with tomato and onion salad £13.95. Two-course evening meal £22.50.*

Brunning & Price ~ Manager Justin Realff ~ Real ale ~ Open 11-11; 11-10.30 Sun ~ Bar food 12-9.30 ~ Children welcome ~ Dogs allowed in bar

ALLOSTOCK SJ7271 MAP 7
Three Greyhounds Inn ★◑ ♡
(01565) 723455 – www.thethreegreyhoundsinn.co.uk
*4.7 miles from M6 junction 18: A54 E then fork left on to B5803 into Holmes Chapel,
left at roundabout on to A50 for 2 miles, then left on to B5082 towards Northwich;
Holmes Chapel Road; WA16 9JY*

Relaxing, civilised and welcoming, with enjoyable food and drink all day

Our readers have long been impressed by this beacon of hospitality in its sea of green fields, and that looks unlikely to change. Staff are unfailingly welcoming, the choice of drinks is extensive and the food is highly regarded, and the former farmhouse has had a recent spruce-up outside and in to ensure it stays on top of its game. The rooms are linked by open doorways and the décor throughout is restful: candles and soft lighting, thick rugs on quarry tiles or bare boards, and dark grey walls hung with modern black-on-white prints. There's an appealing variety of wooden dining chairs, cushioned wall seats, little stools and plenty of plump scatter cushions around all sorts of tables; do note the one made from giant bellows. A smashing choice of drinks includes a dozen or so interesting wines by the glass, over 50 brandies and six local cider brandies, a farm cider and Three Greyhounds, Cheshire Cat, Byley Bomber, English Ales Black Hound Stout and a cider on handpump; unobtrusive background music and board games. Above the old farm barns is a restored private dining and party room called the Old Dog House. The big side lawn has picnic-table sets under parasols, with more tables on a decked side verandah with a Perspex roof. Shakerley Mere nature reserve is just across the road (you can walk around the mere). The pub is owned by Tim Bird and Mary McLaughlin of Cheshire Cat Pubs & Bars.

 Rewarding food includes weekday lunch specials, home-baked pork pie, sharing platters, seafood crockpot, duck liver and brandy pâté, ale-battered haddock, cod cheek, king prawn, salmon, mussel and bacon chowder, sweet potato, chickpea and roasted pepper curry, Yorkshire pork chop with black pudding mash, and desserts such as apple and blueberry crumble, boozy vanilla ice-cream and a cheeseboard with a port menu. *Benchmark main dish: home-made smoked fish pie £13.95. Two-course evening meal £21.00.*

Free house ~ Licensee James Macadam ~ Real ale ~ Open 10.30am-11pm; 10.30am-11.30pm Fri, Sat; 10.30-10.30 Sun ~ Bar food 12-9.15 Mon-Thurs; 12-9.45 Fri, Sat; 12-8.45 Sun ~ Children welcome (under-10s only before 7pm) ~ Dogs allowed in bar

ASTON SJ6146 MAP 7
Bhurtpore ★ ♡ ◈ £
(01270) 780917 – www.bhurtpore.co.uk
Off A530 SW of Nantwich; in village follow Wrenbury signpost; CW5 8DQ

Warm-hearted pub with some unusual artefacts and an excellent range of drinks (especially real ales); big garden

Licensee Simon George has such an encyclopaedic knowledge of beer that this comfortable red-brick pub has become a place of pilgrimage for connoisseurs of Britain's brewing scene – and he's a dab hand at cooking up a curry too. There are around 11 constantly changing real ales from all over the country, sourced and kept with love, among them the new brews from Salopian, Thornbridge and Red Willow, plus three interesting keg lagers. You'll also find dozens of unusual bottled beers, ciders, perries and farm cider, 140 different whiskies, 100 gins, 20 vodkas, 22 rums, carefully selected soft drinks and a dozen wines by the glass from a good list. The pub name commemorates the 1826 siege of Bhurtpore (a town in India) during which local landowner Sir Stapleton Cotton (later Viscount Combermere) was commander-in-chief. The connection with India also explains some of the quirky artefacts in the carpeted lounge bar – look out for the sunglasses-wearing turbanned figure behind the counter. There are also good local period photographs and some attractive furniture in the comfortable public bar; board games, pool, TV and games machine. Disabled access.

Locally sourced food includes lunchtime sandwiches and light meals, spicy lamb samosas, potato skins with bacon and cheese, beef lasagne with garlic bread, cod in beer batter, gammon with egg and breaded cheese and leek cakes and classic curries, plus puddings such as meringue roll with cream and raspberry filling and ginger pudding with toffee sauce. *Benchmark main dish: steak, kidney and real ale pie £12.25. Two-course evening meal £20.00.*

Free house ~ Licensee Simon George ~ Real ale ~ Open 12-11.30 Mon-Thurs; 12-midnight Fri, Sat; 12-11 Sun ~ Bar food 12-2, 5.30-9 Mon, Tues; 12-2, 5.30-9.30 Weds, Thurs; 12-9.30 Fri, Sat; 12-9 Sun ~ Restaurant ~ Children welcome until 8pm ~ Dogs allowed in bar

BARTHOMLEY SJ7752 MAP 7

White Lion £

(01270) 882242 – www.whitelion-barthomley.co.uk

M6 junction 16, B5078 N towards Alsager, then Barthomley signed on left; CW2 5PG

Timeless 17th-c village tavern with classic period interior, up to half a dozen real ales and good value lunchtime food

With its thatched roof, half-timbered exterior and blazing open fire, this timeless and unpretentious old pub is the perfect antidote to the modern tedium of the dreary M6. The bar has heavy oak beams dating from Stuart times, attractively moulded black panelling, prints of Cheshire on the walls, latticed windows and uneven wobbly old tables. Up some steps, a second room has another welcoming open fire, more oak panelling, a high-backed winged settle and a paraffin lamp hinged to the wall; shove-ha'penny. Local societies make good use of a third room. Banks's Sunbeam, Jennings Cocker Hoop and Sneck Lifter, Marstons Saddle Tank and Wainwright and a guest beer on handpump and eight wines by the glass served by genuinely friendly staff. The gents' are across an open courtyard. In summer, seats on cobbles outside offer nice views over the pretty village. The early 15th-c red sandstone church of St Bertoline (where you can learn about the Barthomley massacre) is worth a visit.

Honest pub food at good prices includes sandwiches, lamb henry with creamy mash, vegetable pie, sausage and mash, beer-battered fish, and puddings such as waffle with ice-cream and caramel sauce and sticky toffee pudding. *Benchmark main dish: ham, egg and hand-cut chips £7.95. Two-course evening meal £14.00.*

Marstons ~ Tenant Katy Hollins ~ Real ale ~ Open 12-11; 12-10.30 Sun ~ Bar food 12-2 Mon, Tues; 12-3 Weds-Fri; 12-6 Sat, Sun ~ Children welcome away from bar counter ~ Dogs allowed in bar

BOSTOCK GREEN SJ6769 MAP 7

Hayhurst Arms

(01606) 541810 – www.brunningandprice.co.uk/hayhurstarms

London Road, Bostock Green; CW10 9JP

Attractive pub with a marvellous choice of drinks, a wide range of rewarding food, friendly staff and seats outside

At the heart of Bostock both in terms of village life and its plum location hard by the village green, this former stables and coach house has been cleverly converted and extended. The long main bar is divided into different dining areas by elegant supporting pillars, and it's light and airy throughout: big windows, house plants, bookshelves, standard lamps, metal chandeliers and prints, old photographs and paintings arranged frame-to-frame above wooden dados. The varied dark wooden dining chairs are grouped around tables of all sizes on rugs, quarry tiles, wide floorboards and carpet, and three open fireplaces have big mirrors above them, with hefty leather armchairs to each side. A couple of cosier rooms lead off; background music and board games. Phoenix Brunning & Price Original and Weetwood Eastgate with guests such as Cheshire Lindow, Hawkshead Red and Partners Happy Daze on handpump, 25 wines by the glass, a good list of malt whiskies and 60 or so well chosen gins; staff are efficient and courteous. The outside terrace has good quality tables and chairs under parasols, and the village green opposite has swings and a play tractor.

Enjoyable modern food includes 'light bites' such as cheddar, leek and balsamic onion quiche and king prawn linguine with chilli, tomato and parmesan crisp, starters including smoked salmon with orange and beetroot salad and chicken liver pâté with apricot chutney, and main dishes such as crispy beef salad with sweet chilli sauce and roasted cashew nuts, roast duck breast with crispy leg croquettes, celeriac purée and cherry jus and sweet potato, aubergine and spinach Malaysian curry. Puddings include chocolate and orange tart with passion-fruit sorbet, crème brûlée with shortbread and summer pudding. *Benchmark main dish: grilled sea bass fillets with potato and shallot terrine and chervil and lemon cream sauce £16.95. Two-course evening meal £22.00.*

Brunning & Price ~ Manager Sean Parker ~ Real ale ~ Open 11-11; 11-10.30 Sun ~ Bar food 12-9.30; 12-10 Fri, Sat; 12-9 Sun ~ Children welcome ~ Dogs allowed in bar

BUNBURY　　　　　　　　　　　　　　　　　　　SJ5658　MAP 7

Dysart Arms 🍷 🍺

(01829) 260183 – www.brunningandprice.co.uk/dysart

Bowes Gate Road; village signposted off A51 NW of Nantwich; and from A49 S of Tarporley – coming in this way on northernmost village access road, bear left in village centre; CW6 9PH

Civilised chatty dining pub with thoughtfully laid-out rooms, enjoyable food and a lovely garden with pretty views

Although the interior of this commodious red-brick village local has been opened up, the neatly kept rooms still retain a cottagey feel as they ramble around the pleasantly lit central bar. Each room (some with open fires) is nicely furnished with an appealing variety of well spaced sturdy wooden tables and chairs, a couple of tall filled bookcases and just the right amount of carefully chosen bric-a-brac, properly lit pictures and plants. On a warm day, you'll need to arrive early if you want to bag one of the wooden tables on the terrace or a picnic-set on the lawn in the neatly kept and slightly elevated garden; the views of the splendid church at the end of this pretty village and the distant Peckforton Hills are lovely. You'll find the likes of Phoenix Brunning & Price Traditional, Timothy Taylors Boltmaker, Titanic Iceberg and Weetwood Eastgate on handpump, alongside a pleasing selection of over 20 wines by the glass, good ranges of gins and whiskies; background music and board games. Disabled access.

The day's tasty offerings kick off with an 'elevenses' menu of light, breakfasty dishes and include 'light bites' and afternoon tea. On the main menu, starters include summer vegetable risotto, five-spiced duck leg with spring onion, cucumber, hoisin sauce and pancakes and hummus with toasted flatbread, mains such as braised shoulder of lamb with new potatoes and rosemary gravy, pea and mint tortellini with garden pea velouté and asparagus, and rump steak with dijon mustard and tarragon butter, and puddings such as chocolate and orange tart with passion-fruit sorbet and triple chocolate brownie with chocolate sauce and vanilla ice-cream. *Benchmark main dish: steak and kidney suet pudding with mash and buttered greens £14.95. Two-course evening meal £22.00.*

Brunning & Price ~ Manager Stuart Groves ~ Real ale ~ Open 10-11 ~ Bar food 12-9 (9.30 Sat) ~ Children welcome ~ Dogs allowed in bar

BURLEYDAM   SJ6042   MAP 7

Combermere Arms ◀

(01948) 871223 – www.brunningandprice.co.uk/combermere

A525 Whitchurch–Audlem; SY13 4AT

Roomy and attractive beamed pub successfully mixing a good drinking side with imaginative all-day food

With some parts dating from the 1540s, this capacious, cream-painted inn offers lots of inviting nooks and crannies within its rambling yet intimate-feeling interior. The attractive, understated décor brings together antique cushioned dining chairs around dark wood tables, rugs on wood (some old, some new oak) and stone floors, prints hung frame-to-frame on cream walls, bookshelves and open fires. Friendly, efficient staff dispense Phoenix Brunning & Price Original from handpump, alongside farm cider and guests from breweries that might include Moorhouses, Plassey, Salopian and Timothy Taylors, plus fine ranges of gins and whiskies and 20 wines by the glass from an extensive list; board games and background music. Outside there are good solid wood tables and picnic-sets in a pretty, well tended garden.

Reliably good food includes sandwiches, chicken liver pâté with carrot and apricot baked camembert with candied walnuts and ciabatta croutons, vegetable parcels with chilli mango chutney, fried chicken breast with thyme fondant potato, sweetcorn purée and sherry sauce, rump steak sandwich with tarragon mayonnaise and fries, smoked haddock and salmon fishcakes, and puddings such as baked rhubarb cheesecake with stem ginger ice-cream, hot waffle with glazed bananas and honeycomb ice-cream and crème brûlée with shortbread. *Benchmark main dish: pork and leek sausages with mash, buttered greens and onion gravy £12.95. Two-course evening meal £22.50.*

Brunning & Price ~ Manager Lisa Hares ~ Real ale ~ Open 11.30-11; 12-10.30 Sun ~ Bar food 12-9 (9.30 Fri, Sat) ~ Children welcome ~ Dogs allowed in bar

BURWARDSLEY   SJ5256   MAP 7

Pheasant ★ ◉ ♀ ⌂

(01829) 770434 – www.thepheasantinn.co.uk

Higher Burwardsley; signposted from Tattenhall (which itself is signposted off A41 S of Chester) and from Harthill (reached by turning off A534 Nantwich–Holt at the Copper Mine); follow pub's signpost up hill from Post Office; OS Sheet 117 map reference 523566; CH3 9PF

Fantastic views and enjoyable food at this clever conversion of an old heavily beamed inn; good bedrooms

From its vantage point in the Peckforton Hills, the Pheasant offers sweeping views of the Cheshire plain and across to North Wales, along with top-end hospitality to locals, walkers and guests in its 12 country-chic bedrooms. The attractive low-beamed interior is airy and modern-feeling in parts, and the various separate areas have nice old chairs spread spaciously on wooden floors and a log fire in a huge see-through fireplace; quiet background music and daily newspapers. Friendly, helpful staff serve real ales such as Cheshire Brew Brothers Gold and Weetwoods Best, Cheshire Cat and Eastgate on handpump, around 20 wines by the glass, ten malt whiskies and local farm cider. From picnic-sets on the terrace, you can enjoy one of the county's most magnificent views; on a clear day with the telescope you can see as far as the pier head and cathedrals in Liverpool. Comfortable, character bedrooms are in the main building or an ivy-clad stable wing and make a great base for exploring the area. There are plenty of surrounding walks and the scenic Sandstone Trail passes nearby. Sister pubs are the Fishpool in Delamere and the Bears Paw in Warmingham.

 As well as lunchtime sandwiches, elevated pub food might include serrano ham, melon and burrata, prawn and crayfish cocktail with caviar, panzanella and ham hock terrine for starters, roast beef and trimmings (daily), hake with wild black rice, chorizo, sweetcorn velouté and tarragon vinaigrette and hand-crafted steak and ale pie for mains, and puddings such as raspberry and white chocolate cheesecake with raspberry sorbet and sticky toffee pudding. *Benchmark main dish: butter-poached chicken breast with creamed polenta, provençale vegetables, parmesan and basil oil £17.95. Two-course evening meal £24.00.*

Free house ~ Licensee Andrew Nelson ~ Real ale ~ Open 11-11 ~ Bar food 12-9.30; 12-10 Fri, Sat; 12-9 Sun ~ Restaurant ~ Children welcome ~ Dogs allowed in bar & bedrooms ~ Bedrooms: £105-£170

CHESTER
Architect ♀ ☕

SJ4066 MAP 7

(01244) 353070 – www.brunningandprice.co.uk/architect
Nicholas Street (A5268); CH1 2NX

Busy pub by the racecourse with interesting furnishings and décor, attentive staff, a good choice of drinks and super food

The titular architect is Thomas Harrison, who designed this dignified mansion as his own home, as well as Chester's landmark Grosvenor Bridge. It's connected by a glassed passage to a red-brick extension. Throughout, there are elegant antique dining chairs around a mix of nice old tables on rugs or bare floorboards, hundreds of interesting paintings and prints on grey, blue and teal walls, house plants and flowers on windowsills and mantelpieces, and lots of bookcases. The pubbiest part, with a more bustling feel, is the garden room where they serve Phoenix Brunning & Price Original and Weetwood Eastgate alongside guests such as Peerless Pale, Tatton Blonde and Timothy Taylors Boltmaker on handpump, a good choice of bottled craft beers, over 20 wines by the glass and impressive ranges of whiskies, rums and gins. As well as a friendly, easy-going atmosphere, you'll find open fires and armchairs tucked into cosy nooks, candelabra and big mirrors; background music and board games. Big windows and french doors look over a terrace, where there are plenty of good quality wooden seats and tables under parasols, and views over the Roodee racecourse.

Well executed modern dishes include sandwiches, satay king prawns, chicken liver pâté with carrot and apricot chutney, butternut squash, barley and spinach nut roast, honey-roasted ham and egg, chicken caesar salad, slow-braised ox cheek ragoût with pasta and parmesan, hake with prosciutto, chorizo, butter bean and spinach cassoulet, glazed duck breast with orange and carrot purée, duck croquette and red wine sauce, and puddings such as rhubarb and apple crumble with vanilla custard and crème brûlée; they also serve afternoon tea (2-5pm, book in advance). *Benchmark main dish: deep-fried cod in beer batter with chips, mushy peas and tartare sauce £14.95. Two-course evening meal £22.00.*

Brunning & Price ~ Manager Hannah Williams ~ Real ale ~ Open 10.30am-11pm Mon-Thurs; 10.30am-11.30pm Fri, Sat; 10.30-10.30 Sun ~ Bar food 12-9.30; 12-10 Fri, Sat; 12-9 Sun ~ Children welcome ~ Dogs allowed in bar

CHESTER
Mill 🍺 £   SJ4166 MAP 7

(01244) 350035 – www.millhotel.com
Milton Street; CH1 3NF

Big hotel with huge range of real ales, good value food and cheery service in sizeable bar; bedrooms

Housed in an 1830 corn mill, this chic modern hotel has an impressive range of facilities, including an excellent bar offering up to nine real ales on hand pump such as Castle Rock Harvest Pale, Phoenix Double Gold and Weetwoods Best; also, a dozen wines by the glass, a farm cider and 16 malt whiskies. You'll find a real mix of customers in the neatly kept bar which has some exposed brickwork and supporting pillars, slate-effect wallpaper, contemporary purple/grey upholstered seats around marble-topped tables on light wooden flooring, and helpful, friendly staff. A glass-walled dining extension has been added. One comfortable area is reminiscent of a bar on a cruise liner; quiet background music and unobtrusively placed big-screen sports TV. The hotel straddles the Shropshire Union Canal, with a glassed-in bridge connecting the two sections. Bedrooms are comfortable and rather smart. Disabled access.

There are several different menus, including afternoon tea, but the bar food includes sandwiches, whitebait, chicken caesar salad, roasted vegetable and butternut squash lasagne, rack of ribs with coleslaw, steak and mushroom in ale pie, gammon and pineapple, and a fish dish of the day. *Benchmark main dish: beer-battered fish and chips £10.95. Two-course evening meal £16.00.*

Free house ~ Licensee Chris Goulden ~ Real ale ~ Open 10am-midnight; 11am-midnight Sun ~ Bar food 9.30-9.30 ~ Restaurant ~ Children welcome until 9pm ~ Bedrooms: $87

CHESTER
Old Harkers Arms 🍷 🍺   SJ4166 MAP 7

(01244) 344525 – www.brunningandprice.co.uk/harkers
Russell Street, down steps off City Road where it crosses canal; CH3 5AL

Well run canalside building with a lively atmosphere, fantastic range of drinks and extremely good food

Right on the Shropshire Union Canal, this red-brick Victorian warehouse – once run as a chandler's by a certain Mr Harker – attracts cyclists and other towpath users, but given its central location it also buzzes with city life. The striking industrial interior with its high ceilings is divided into user-friendly spaces by brick pillars and offers fine, unimpeded views of the boats from the tall windows that run the length of the main bar. Walls are covered with old prints hung frame-to-frame, mixed dark wood furniture is set out in intimate groups on stripped-wood floors, there's a wall of bookshelves above a leather banquette at one end, and attractive lamps lend some warmth (as does the resident rescue dog, Ollie); board games. Cheerful staff serve ten cask ales including regulars Phoenix Brunning & Price Original and Weetwood Cheshire Cat Blonde and guests such as Castle Rock Harvest Pale, Peerless Oatmeal Stout, Rudgate Ruby Mild and Salopian Oracle plus a trio of craft beers, 130 malt whiskies, a well described wine list with 20 or so by the glass, 45 gins and a dozen farm ciders and perries. Disabled access.

 Modern British and international food includes roast tomato soup with herb oil and crème fraîche, halloumi chips with sweet chilli, chicken carbonara with smoked pancetta and a poached egg, steak burger with grilled bacon, coleslaw and fries, smoked haddock and salmon fishcakes, club sandwich, and puddings such as rhubarb and apple crumble tart and roasted pineapple with spiced oat granola and coconut ice-cream. *Benchmark main dish: chicken, ham and leek pie with mash, greens and tarragon and white wine sauce £13.95. Two-course evening meal £22.00.*

Brunning & Price ~ Manager Paul Jeffery ~ Real ale ~ Open 10.30am-11pm; 10am-11pm Sat; 10am-10.30pm Sun ~ Bar food 12-9.30; 10-9 Sun ~ Children allowed in bar; older children allowed in daytime ~ Dogs allowed in bar

CHOLMONDELEY

SJ5550 MAP 7

Cholmondeley Arms 🏆 ♀ 🍺 🛏

(01829) 720300 – www.cholmondeleyarms.co.uk

Bickley Moss; A49 5.5 miles N of Whitchurch. On satnav, enter Cholmondeley then Bickerton Road and this will bring you to the pub; SY14 8HN

Cheshire Dining Pub of the Year

Interesting pub with a decent range of real ales and wines, well presented food and sizeable garden; bedrooms

This former schoolhouse, now a pub and hotel, is a textbook example of how cherished historic buildings can be converted to serve their community in a new, imaginative way. Its pointed gables and ornate brickwork attract customers into an interior with plenty of architectural interest. The bar rooms have lofty ceilings and tall Victorian windows plus huge old radiators and school paraphernalia (hockey sticks, tennis rackets, trunks and so forth), armchairs by a fire with a massive stag's head above, big mirrors and all sorts of dining chairs and tables on warmly coloured rugs over bare boards; fresh flowers, church candles and background music. As well as an extraordinary number of gins (400 and counting), you'll find Cholmondeley Best (from Weetwood) plus a seasonal house ale such as School's Out, along with guests from the likes of Hobson and Snowdonia and a farm cider on handpump, and a dozen wines by the glass on a knowledgeably chosen list. A sizeable lawn (which drifts off into open countryside) has plenty of seating and there's more in front overlooking the quiet road. The bedrooms are in the old headmaster's house opposite and named after real and fictional teachers; the pictures dotted about actually did belong to former headmasters. Cholmondeley Castle Gardens are nearby. Disabled access. The pub is owned by Tim Bird and Mary McLaughlin of Cheshire Cat Pubs & Bars.

 Extremely good food with seasonal ingredients and specials includes sandwiches, meat and fish nibbles, a sharing plate, devilled kidneys on toast, goats cheese with roasted hazelnut and beetroot salad, wagyu burger, crispy cauliflower katsu curry, sea bass with nettle and pea shoot pesto, and desserts such as dark chocolate brownie, apple and toffee crumble and Cheshire Farm ice-creams. *Benchmark main dish: steak and kidney pie £14.95. Two-course evening meal £21.00.*

Free house ~ Licensee James Griffiths ~ Real ale ~ Open 11-11; 12-11 Sat; 12-10.30 Sun ~ Bar food 12-9.15 (9.45 Fri, Sat); 12-8.45 Sun ~ Children allowed in bar; no under-10s after 7pm ~ Dogs allowed in bar & bedrooms ~ Bedrooms: £105

It's very helpful if you let us know up-to-date food prices when you report on pubs.

COTEBROOK
Fox & Barrel 🌟

SJ5765 MAP 7

(01829) 760529 – www.foxandbarrel.co.uk
A49 NE of Tarporley; CW6 9DZ

Contemporary country dining pub brightened up by a recent refit

Built in the 1700s, this historic white-walled pub (supposedly named after a fox found hiding in a barrel in the cellar) has been given a classy update to bring more light into its capacious interior. The kitchen has had a refit too, allowing it to offer some sophisticated and complex dishes on its well thought-of menu. Both bar and dining room are broad, serene and spacious, with handsome grey panelling, bookcases and nicely designed seating, including refectory tables with modern candle stands in the dining room and some antique leather armchairs in the bar, all the better to enjoy the fire in the brick hearth. Four well kept beers are available on handpump from the likes of Weetwood and Storm, and there are over 40 gins, plus cocktails and a well conceived wine list featuring champagne and prosecco by the glass. Staff are smart and attentive. Outside, the front terrace has plenty of well presented tables and chairs under parasols and, at the back, there are picnic-sets on grass and some nice old fruit trees.

 Modern British food from a daily changing menu of local produce might include grown-up sandwiches, oysters, grilled padrón peppers, tandoori black bream, oxtail risotto, steamed Thai cod, twice-baked cheese soufflé, roast lamb rump with lamb hotpot, golden beetroot and wild garlic, salt-baked root vegetables, grills and puddings such as mango soufflé and apricot and whisky bread and butter pudding. *Benchmark main dish: poached chicken breast, home-made black pudding and bubble and squeak £15.75. Two-course evening meal £22.50.*

Free house ~ Licensee Richard Cotterill ~ Real ale ~ Open 12-11; 12-10.30 Sun ~ Bar food 12-9 (9.30 Fri, Sat) ~ Restaurant ~ Children welcome ~ Dogs allowed in bar & restaurant ~

DELAMERE
Fishpool ♀ 🍺

SJ5667 MAP 7

(01606) 883277 – www.thefishpoolinn.co.uk
Junction A54/B5152 Chester Road/Fishpool Road, a mile W of A49; CW8 2HP

Something for everyone in extensive, interestingly laid-out pub, with a good range of food and drinks served all day

A plain white façade (and yes, there's a pond) belies a beautifully designed interior. The clever layout combines a big, cheerful open main section plus plenty of other snug and intimate smaller areas, and the décor and furnishings are unusual and varied. A lofty central area, partly skylit and full of contented diners, has a row of booths facing the long bar counter, and numerous other tables with banquettes or overstuffed small armchairs on pale floorboards laid with rugs; then comes a conservatory overlooking picnic-sets on a flagstone terrace, and a lawn beyond. Off on two sides are many rooms with much lower ceilings, some with heavy dark beams, some with bright polychrome tile or intricate parquet flooring: William Morris wallpaper here, dusky paintwork or neat bookshelves there, sofas, armchairs, a fire in an old-fashioned open range, lots of old prints and some intriguing objects including carved or painted animal skulls; background music. Fishpool Best, Weetwood Cheshire Cat and Eastgate plus a guest such as Adnams Broadside on handpump, 15 or so wines by the glass, good cocktails and farm cider; unobtrusive background music

and upstairs lavatories. Disabled access. Sister pubs are the Pheasant in
Burwardsley and the Bears Paw in Warmingham.

🍴 As well as afternoon tea and quality own-made pizzas, the highly rated food
includes flatbreads and nibbles, starters such as curried salmon and smoked
haddock fishcake, truffle honey and goat's cheese mousse and tiger prawn pil pil, mains
including steak and onion pie, chilli con carne with beetroot tortilla chips, Thai red
curry and breaded Whitby scampi, and puddings such as double chocolate brownie with
chocolate sauce and various knickerbocker glories. *Benchmark main dish: classic
baked lasagne with garlic bread £15.00. Two-course evening meal £23.00.*

Free house ~ Licensee Andrew Nelson ~ Real ale ~ Open 11-11 ~ Bar food 12-9.30; 12-10
Fri, Sat; 12-9 Sun ~ Restaurant ~ Children welcome ~ Dogs allowed in bar

KELSALL
SJ5268 MAP 7
Morris Dancer 🍷 🍺
(01829) 701680 – www.brunningandprice.co.uk/morrisdancer
Chester Road (A54); CW6 0RZ

**Attractive contemporary pub with thoughtfully furnished bar and
dining rooms, a fine choice of drinks, rewarding food and seats
outside**

The grey-painted clapboard exterior of these converted stables conjures
a simple but stylish modern feel that continues indoors, with brick
walls, polished floorboards and exposed rafters. Although the carefully
extended building was designed to be mainly open-plan, there are areas
that feel cosy too. One room has a high apex ceiling, a woodburning stove
fronted by sturdy red leather armchairs and lined on either side by large
bookshelves. Other rooms have open fires, beams and timbering, antique-
style dining chairs and cushioned settles around polished tables of many
sizes and rugs on the floor. The walls are hung with hundreds of prints,
paintings and photographs and throughout there are mirrors, house plants
and elegant metal chandeliers. The Morris Dancer is a true village-centre
pub and the heart of the local community; check the website for regular
events. Friendly, efficient staff serve Phoenix Brunning & Price Original and
Weetwood Eastgate plus guests such as Castle Rock Session IPA, Hawkshead
Windermere Pale, Mobberley Road Runner, Severn Brewing Ruby Porter
and Tatton Blonde on handpump, 20 wines by the glass plus monthly guest
bottles, 20 malt whiskies and 150 gins; background music and board games.
In front of the pub are picnic-sets among pretty flowerbeds with more on a
back lawn by a play tractor. The sunny terrace has plenty of wooden chairs
and tables under green parasols.

🍴 Well executed food includes sandwiches, barbecue pulled pork croquettes, celeriac
slaw and sour apple purée, red pepper, pea and mint falafels, local pork sausages
with mash and onion gravy, game suet pudding, courgette, red pepper, aubergine and
spinach Malaysian curry, lamb, leek and potato hash with fried egg, and puddings such as
hot waffle with caramelised bananas and banoffi ice-cream and warm cherry bakewell
with cherry compote. *Benchmark main dish: crispy beef salad with sweet chilli sauce
and roasted cashew nuts £13.95. Two-course evening meal £22.50.*

Brunning & Price ~ Manager Ryan Martinez ~ Real ale ~ Open 10.30am-11pm; 10.30-10.30
Sun ~ Bar food 10.30-9.30 ~ Children welcome ~ Dogs allowed in bar

---

Post Office address codings give the impression that some pubs are in Cheshire,
when they're really in Derbyshire (and therefore included in that chapter) or in
Greater Manchester (see the Lancashire chapter).

KETTLESHULME

SJ9879 MAP 7

Swan

(01663) 732943

B5470 Macclesfield to Chapel-en-le-Frith, a mile W of Whaley Bridge; SK23 7QU

**Charming 16th-c pub known for fresh fish, good beer and
an attractive garden**

Long known for its excellent cooking, particularly its fish dishes and
renowned Sunday lunch (best to book in advance), this pretty white-
painted cottage suffered serious flooding in 2019 but is back and in great
form following renovations including a new dining room and a kitchen
upgrade. The dining conservatory is suavely modern in style, while the pub
interior remains snug and cosy, with latticed windows, very low dark beams,
timbered walls, antique coaching and other prints, ancient oak settles and
log fires. Marstons Bitter on handpump with a couple of guest beers such as
Wincle Waller, a thoughtful, varied wine list with several options by the glass,
30 gins and 15 malt whiskies served by courteous, friendly staff. The front
terrace has teak tables, while another two-level terrace has further tables and
steamer benches under parasols. The pub is handy for walks in the relatively
unfrequented north-west part of the Peak District National Park.

 As well as tip-top fresh fish dishes such as Scottish scallops with celeriac purée,
black pudding and pancetta, baked truffle and parmesan macaroni cheese
with garlic tiger prawns, bouillabaisse, fillet of turbot with jerusalem artichoke purée,
shiitake mushrooms and a truffle and brown butter, and chilli crab linguine made with
Cromer crab, you'll also find restaurant-quality vegetarian, vegan and meat dishes
including teriyaki, tamarind and chilli aubergine chargrilled in the new Josper oven,
aberdeen angus steak with field mushrooms, vine tomatoes and blackcurrant mustard,
venison three ways and veal, black pudding and mushroom suet pudding, plus open
sandwiches and puddings such as raspberry and apricot trifle and salted caramel
chocolate torte. *Benchmark main dish: fillet of halibut with langoustine bisque, leek
and potato champ and samphire £22.50. Two-course evening meal £28.00.*

Free house ~ Licensee Robert Cloughley ~ Real ale ~ Open 12-11.30; 12-4 Sun; closed Mon
~ Bar food 12-8.30; 12-4 Sun ~ Restaurant ~ Children welcome ~ Dogs allowed in bar

LOWER PEOVER

SJ7474 MAP 7

Bells of Peover

(01565) 722269 – www.thebellsofpeover.com
Just off B5081; The Cobbles; handy for M6 junction 17; WA16 9PZ

**Robinsons pub in pretty setting with real ales and interesting food;
lots of seating areas in the garden**

The Bells is picture-postcard pretty, a white-painted building with wisteria
coiling around its front door in a charming spot on a quiet cobbled
lane. The various rooms have beams, panelling and open fires that contrast
cleverly with contemporary seating ranging from brown leather wall
banquettes with scatter cushions to high-backed upholstered or leather
dining chairs around an assortment of tables on bare boards; plenty of prints,
paintings and mirrors on the walls. Robinsons Cumbria Way, Dizzy Blonde
and Unicorn on handpump and several wines by the glass served by helpful,
friendly staff; background music. In warm weather, head for the seats on
a front terrace overlooking the black and white 14th-c church; there's also
rattan-style furniture under a pergola on a side decked area and a spacious
lawn with picnic-sets spreading down through trees all the way to a little
stream. Major sporting events are sometimes shown out here on a big screen.

Food is creative and attractively presented, and includes a noteworthy vegan selection for every course; there's a new wood-fired pizza oven too. The menu includes some international classics such as nasi goreng, Thai green curry and Cajun halloumi stack, along with steaks, burgers, pies and fish served battered, pan-fried and with a chickpea tagine. For dessert, try a vegan dark chocolate torte with aquafaba meringue and raspberry sorbet, apple and berry crumble or sticky toffee pudding. *Benchmark main dish: chicken breast with sautéed wild mushrooms, mushroom purée and creamed kale £16.95. Two-course evening meal £24.00.*

Robinsons ~ Real ale ~ Open 12-11; 12-10 Sun ~ Bar food 12-9; 12-9.30 Fri, Sat; 12-8 Sun ~ Restaurant ~ Children welcome

MACCLESFIELD   SJ9271 MAP 7
Sutton Hall 🍺
(01260) 253211 – www.brunningandprice.co.uk/suttonhall
Leaving Macclesfield southwards on A523, turn left into Byrons Lane signposted Langley, Wincle, then just before canal viaduct fork right into Bullocks Lane; OS Sheet 118 map reference 925715; SK11 0HE

Historic building set in attractive grounds, with a fine range of drinks and well trained, courteous staff

Many of the fine 500-year-old features of this former manor house, convent and home to the Lucan family have been carefully restored and cleverly worked into the fabric of an up-to-date pub, managed to high contemporary standards. The hall at the heart of the building is especially noteworthy, in particular the entrance space. There's a charming series of rooms (a bar, a library with books on shelves and a raised open fire and dining areas) divided by tall oak timbers: antique oak panelling, warmly coloured rugs on broad flagstones, bare boards and tiles, lots of pictures placed frame-to-frame and two more fires. Background music and board games. The atmosphere is nicely relaxed and a good range of drinks includes Phoenix Brunning & Price Original and Wincle Lord Lucan and guests such as Pennine Black Forest, Rudgate Viking, Sharps Doom Bar and Titanic Iceberg on handpump, 20 or so wines by the glass from an extensive list and a wide selection of whiskies and gins; service is attentive and friendly. The pretty gardens have spaciously laid-out tables with umbrellas (some on their own little terraces), sloping lawns and fine mature trees.

The tempting food includes fancy sandwiches, a 'light bites' menu, starters such as cream of leek and potato soup, smoked salmon with orange and beetroot salad and five-spiced duck leg, and mains such as cod in beer batter with chips and mushy peas, crispy buttermilk chicken burger and braised shoulder of lamb with minted crushed new potatoes; among the desserts are sticky toffee pudding, triple chocolate brownie and crème brûlée. *Benchmark main dish: chicken, ham and leek pie with mash, buttered greens and white wine and tarragon sauce £14.95. Two-course evening meal £23.00.*

Brunning & Price ~ Manager Syd Foster ~ Real ale ~ Open 11-11 (10.30 Sun) ~ Bar food 12-9 (8 Sun) ~ Restaurant ~ Dogs allowed in bar

MARBURY   SJ5645 MAP 7
Swan 🍽️⭐ 🍷 🍺
(01948) 522860 – www.swanatmarbury.co.uk
NNE of Whitchurch; OS Sheet 117 map reference 562457; SY13 4LS

Carefully renovated village pub with attractive open-plan rooms, a thoughtful choice of drinks and food served by well trained staff, with seats on large terrace

Lovingly restored and extended a couple of years back, this handsome pub is at the heart of a picturesque Cheshire village, set between two meres and dotted with black and white buildings. There are two open-plan dining areas plus a large, light-filled restaurant and a long bar made from reclaimed school chemistry lab counters – it's all gently civilised, informal and chatty. Cushioned wooden dining chairs, leather-topped stools, suede wall seating and long, button-back benches are grouped around nice old tables on colourful rugs, polished floorboards or tiles, walls are hung with black and white photos and interesting prints, 2,000 books line shelves and house plants sit on windowsills. Woodburning stoves keep everything warm, and board games fuel conversation. Friendly, helpful staff serve Beartown Ursa Minor, Portland Stout, Stonehouse Station Bitter and Weetwood Southern Cross on handpump and there are a dozen good wines by the glass plus wine on tap that they import from France. Outside, good quality chairs, benches and tables fill a largeish terrace.

The enterprising modern menu changes daily and, alongside sandwiches, might include mussels with cider, pancetta and samphire, garden courgette and spring onion soup with home-made ricotta, Loch Duart salmon niçoise salad, beer-battered haddock with chips and mushy peas and leek, chestnut mushroom and cheshire cheese pot pie with braised red cabbage, and puddings such as chocolate, black cherry and ale cake with black cherry sorbet and summer fruit and elderflower pudding with elderflower ice-cream. *Benchmark main dish: Goosnargh chicken and black garlic kiev £16.00. Two-course evening meal £26.00.*

Free house ~ Licensee Tom Morgan-Wynne ~ Real ale ~ Open 11.30-11; 11.30-10.30 Sun ~ Bar food 12-9.30 (8.30 Sun) ~ Restaurant ~ Children welcome ~ Dogs allowed in bar

MOBBERLEY
SJ7879 MAP 7
Bulls Head 🌟 ▽ ◀
(01565) 873395 – www.thebullsheadpub.co.uk
Mill Lane; WA16 7HX

Terrific all-rounder with interesting food and drink and plenty of pubby character

A spirit of hospitality pervades this welcoming and well run pub, from its warm red-brick exterior to its friendly clientele and accommodating staff. A notably wide and well curated range of drinks includes house ales Bulls Head Best and Mobberley Wobbly plus three guests from local Cheshire microbreweries on handpump (useful tasting notes too), 15 wines by the glass, around 100 whiskies and local gins. Several rooms are furnished quite traditionally but with a touch of modernity: an unpretentious mix of wooden tables, cushioned wall seats and chairs on fine old quarry tiles, black and pale grey walls contrasting well with warming red lampshades, and pink bare-brick walls and pale stripped-timber detailing; also, lots of mirrors, hops, candles and open fires. Background music and board games. Dogs get a warm welcome (they're allowed in the snug) with friendly staff dispensing doggie biscuits from a huge jar. A circular walk to and from the pub is mentioned on the website. There are seats outside in the big garden. The pub is owned by Tim Bird and Mary McLaughlin of Cheshire Cat Pubs & Bars.

Very good food includes sandwiches (until 5pm), light weekday lunchtime snacks, 'sticky onion porkies', Cheshire pork pie, sharing plates, seafood crockpot, steak and Wobbly ale pie, sausages, mash and red cabbage, chicken breast burger and desserts such as Irish whiskey sticky toffee pudding, bakewell tart and apple and blackberry crumble. *Benchmark main dish: haddock in local ale batter with chips, tartare sauce and 'not so mushy' peas £14.50. Two-course evening meal £19.50.*

Free house ~ Licensee Stephanie Lylyk ~ Real ale ~ Open 12-11.30; 12-10.30 Sun ~ Bar food 12-9.30 (9 Sun) ~ Children welcome but no under-10s after 7pm ~ Dogs allowed in bar

MOBBERLEY

SJ7980 MAP 7

Church Inn ★ 🌟 ⛾ 🍺

(01565) 873178 – www.churchinnmobberley.co.uk

Brown sign to pub off B5085 on Wilmslow side of village; Church Lane; WA16 7RD

Friendly country pub with bags of character and a reputation for very good food and drink

From its handsome red-brick exterior to its pretty, characterful décor, this 'country tavern' exudes a restrained rustic charm much appreciated by our readers, who also enjoy its highly rated seasonal food. The small, snug interconnected rooms have all manner of nice old tables and chairs on wide floorboards, low ceilings and plenty of candlelight. The décor in soothing greys and dark green, with some oak-leaf wallpaper, is perked up by a collection of stuffed grouse and their relatives, and a huge variety of pictures; background music. Friendly, efficient young staff serve Mallorys Mobberley Best (local son George Mallory, lost near Everest's summit in 1924, is remembered in the church with a stained-glass window), Tatton Church Ale'Allujah and guests from local microbreweries on handpump, along with unusual and rewarding wines, with 12 by the glass. The award-winning Big Hill gin distillery is based at the pub, and both gin and wine tastings can be booked in the upstairs private dining room (also named after George Mallory). The sunny garden snakes down to an old bowling green with lovely pastoral views and a side courtyard has sturdy tables and benches. They give out a detailed leaflet describing a good four-mile circular walk from the pub, passing sister pub the Bulls Head en route. Dogs are welcomed in the bar with not just a tub of snacks on the counter, but maybe even the offer of a meaty 'beer'. The mainly medieval and Tudor St Wilfrid's Church is opposite. The pub is owned by Tim Bird and Mary McLaughlin of Cheshire Cat Pubs & Bars.

Interesting modern food includes lunchtime sandwiches, black pudding fritters and chutney, lamb and feta croquettes, potato and truffle soup, fish of the day, aberdeen angus burger, seasonal specials such as beetroot, feta and pistachio pie, roasted lamb rump with smoked marrow mash and pan-fried sea bass and salt-baked beetroot caesar salad, and puddings such as cherry soufflé with clotted cream and elderflower and honey pannacotta. *Benchmark main dish: featherblade of beef and caramelised onion pie £17.95. Two-course evening meal £22.50.*

Free house ~ Licensee Siobhan Youngs ~ Real ale ~ Open 12-11; 12-10.30 Sun ~ Bar food 12-9.15; 12-9.45 Fri, Sat; 12-8.30 Sun ~ Children welcome but no under-10s after 7pm ~ Dogs allowed in bar

MOBBERLEY

SJ7879 MAP 7

Roebuck 🌟 ⛾ 🛏

(01565) 873939 – www.roebuckinnmobberley.co.uk

Mill Lane; down hill from sharp bend on B5085 at E edge of 30mph limit; WA16 7HX

Interestingly renovated inn with a good range of drinks, enjoyable food and pretty multi-level garden; boutique-style rustic bedrooms

An appealing hybrid of pub, bistro and boutique hotel, with a nicely done shabby-chic-meets-luxury style, the Roebuck has added another string to its bow in the form of a wine and produce shop – a Covid-19 success story now here to stay. The décor mixes old shutters, reclaimed radiators, wood panelling and stripped brickwork, big gilt-edged mirrors, copper cooking pots and red and brick floor tiles. There's an open fire in the bar, chunky leather armchairs, lots of scatter cushions, an old trunk as a table, a two-way woodburner and an eclectic collection of art and photographs. Friendly staff serve Buck Bitter (named for the pub from Weetwood), Merlin Gold and Roebuck Best on handpump, a dozen wines and champagne by the glass, and a fine collection of liqueurs and aperitifs. The authentic-looking bistro has pots of herbs and candles in bottles on simple tables, café-style chairs and long leather wall banquettes; background music. To get to the garden you walk through the 'potting shed': upper and lower terraces, gazebos, herb beds and seats that range from rattan or elegant metal chairs to wooden benches and straightforward tables under parasols on decking or flagstones. The front of the building has a Mediterranean feel with gnarly olive and standard box trees, flowering window boxes and a couple of benches. The bedrooms have much character and colour and some have log burners; good breakfasts. A walking route is suggested on the website. The pub is owned by Tim Bird and Mary McLaughlin of Cheshire Cat Pubs & Bars.

🍽️ Appetising seasonal bistro food includes pizzas, small plates such as crispy fish tacos and garlic and tarragon chickpea fritters, tempura monkfish with Thai sweet and sour sauce, Peroni-battered haddock, steak burger with melted rarebit and spaghetti puttanesca, and desserts including baked chocolate pudding and meringue vacherin. *Benchmark main dish: half a roasted herb chicken and frites £16.00. Two-course evening meal £21.00.*

Free house ~ Licensee Kieran Garrihy ~ Real ale ~ Open 10am-10.30pm; 10am-11pm Sat; 10-10 Sun ~ Bar food 12-3, 6-9.15; 12-9.30 Fri, Sat; 12-8.45 Sun ~ Children welcome but no under-10s after 7pm ~ Dogs allowed in bar ~ Bedrooms: £125

MOTTRAM ST ANDREW   SJ8878   MAP 7
Bulls Head ♀ 🍺

(01625) 828111 – www.brunningandprice.co.uk/bullshead
A538 Prestbury–Wilmslow; Wilmslow Road/Priest Lane; E side of village; SK10 4QH

Smashing country dining pub with a thoughtful range of drinks and interesting food, plenty of character and well trained staff

The exterior of this village pub is attractive, with its pillared entrance and expansive windows, but its 'wow factor' is the dining zone, whose four levels stack up alongside or above one another, each with a distinctive décor and style. These vary from the informality of a sunken area with rugs on a tiled floor, through a comfortable library/dining room to another with an upstairs conservatory feel, and the last, with higher windows and more of a special-occasion atmosphere. The rest of the pub has an appealing and abundant mix of old prints and pictures, comfortable seating in great variety, a coal fire in one room, a blazing woodburning stove in a two-way fireplace dividing two other rooms and an antique black kitchen range in yet another. Phoenix Brunning & Price Original and guest ales such as Epic Hop Gun, Mobberley Maori, Peerless Eureka Blonde and Wincle Sir Philip on handpump, around 20 wines by the glass, 50 malt whiskies, 50 gins and several ciders, and an attractive separate tea-and-coffee station with pretty blue and white china cups, teapots and jugs. Also, background music, daily papers and board games. The lawn has plenty of picnic-sets beneath cocktail parasols. Disabled access.

🍴 From a well judged menu, the food includes classy sandwiches, 'light bites' such as smoked salmon and haddock fishcake, cream of leek and potato soup with granary bread, chicken liver pâté with apricot chutney, summer vegetable risotto, chicken, ham and leek pie with mash and buttered greens, pea and mint tortellini with pea velouté and asparagus, and desserts such as triple chocolate brownie and lemon cheesecake with raspberry ripple ice-cream. *Benchmark main dish: grilled sea bass fillets with potato and shallot terrine and chervil and lemon cream sauce £16.95. Two-course evening meal £23.00.*

Brunning & Price ~ Manager Ben Coverley ~ Real ale ~ Open 10am-11pm; 9.30am-11pm Sat, Sun ~ Bar food 12-9.30; 9.30-9.30 Sat; 9.30-9 Sun ~ Dogs allowed in bar

SANDBACH   SJ7560   MAP 7
Old Hall ♀ ☕

(01270) 758170 – www.brunningandprice.co.uk/oldhall

1.2 miles from M6 junction 17: A534 – ignore first turn into town and take the second – if you reach the roundabout double back; CW11 1AL

Lovely hall-house with plenty of drinking and dining space, real ales and imaginative food

This wonderful 17th-c manor house is Grade I listed both for its original half-timbered exterior and its little-altered interior, which, thanks to Brunning & Price's sensitive transformation, makes for a fine public house. The room to the left of the entrance hall is much as it's been for centuries, with a Jacobean fireplace, oak panelling and priest's hole, and it leads into the Oak Room, divided by standing timbers into two dining areas with heavy beams, oak flooring and reclaimed panelling. Other rooms in the original building have hefty beams and oak boards, two open fires and a woodburning stove; the cosy snugs are carpeted. The Garden Room is big and bright, with reclaimed quarry tiling and exposed A-frame oak timbering, and opens on to a suntrap back terrace with teak tables and chairs among flowering tubs. Throughout, the walls are covered with countless interesting prints, there's an appealing collection of antique dining chairs and tables of all sizes, and plenty of rugs, bookcases and plants. From the handsome bar counter, efficient and friendly staff serve regulars including Phoenix Brunning & Price Original alongside a changing and seasonal roster of guests, such as Hawkshead Mosaic and Mobberley Pancake (for Shrove Tuesday), some 20 good wines by the glass, plentiful malt whiskies and gins; background music, board games. There are picnic-sets in front of the building beside rose bushes and clipped box hedging.

Highly enjoyable food comes on several menus, including 'Elevenses', brunch and afternoon tea. Starters might include halloumi fries with tomato salsa, crispy baby squid and sweet chilli sauce and barbecue chicken wings, while typical mains are steak burger with grilled bacon, cheddar, spiced tomato mayonnaise and coleslaw, roast duck breast with crispy leg croquettes, celeriac purée and cherry jus and sweet potato, aubergine and spinach Malaysian curry, followed by puddings such as chocolate and orange tart with passion-fruit sorbet and crème brûlée with shortbread biscuits. *Benchmark main dish: braised feather of beef bourguignon with horseradish mash and buttered kale £16.95. Two-course evening meal £23.00.*

Brunning & Price ~ Manager Hannah Law ~ Real ale ~ Open 10am-11pm; 9.30am-11pm Sat; 9.30am-10.30pm Sun ~ Bar food 12-9.30; 12-9 Sun ~ Restaurant ~ Children allowed in bar ~ Dogs allowed in bar

THELWALL   SJ6587   MAP 7
Little Manor ♀

(01925) 212070 – www.brunningandprice.co.uk/littlemanor

Bell Lane; WA4 2SX

Restored manor house with plenty of room, well kept ales and tasty bistro-style food; seats outside

L ocal landowners the Percivals built this handsome house in 1660 and when the current owners discovered the family's coat of arms painted on an inside wall they adopted it as the pub's crest. Pride of ownership is also evident in the spruce exterior, hung with flowers, and the spacious interior, lovingly decorated in grey and blue heritage colours. Six beamed rooms are linked by open doorways to create plenty of nooks and crannies, with flooring ranging from rugs on bare boards through carpeting to some fine old black and white tiles. An appealing variety of seats includes antique dining chairs around small or large, circular or square tables plus leather armchairs by open fires (note the lovely carved wooden one); background music. Attractively lit, the décor includes hundreds of intriguing prints and photos, books on shelves and old glass and stone bottles on windowsills and mantelpieces; fresh flowers and house plants too. Phoenix Brunning & Price Original plus guests such as Coach House Cromwells Best, Hawkshead Windermere Pale, Lancaster Blonde and Timothy Taylors on handpump, around 20 wines by the glass, 60 gins and 60 whiskies. In fine weather you can sit at the chunky teak chairs and tables on the attractive terrace; some of them are under a heated shelter. Disabled access.

Popular modern food with good vegan and gluten-free options includes sandwiches, five-spiced duck leg with pancakes and trimmings, garlic and chilli king prawns, king prawn linguine with chilli, tomato and parmesan crisp, grilled sea bass fillets with potato and shallot terrine and chervil and lemon cream sauce, sweet potato, aubergine and spinach Malaysian curry, and desserts such as chocolate and orange tart with passion-fruit sorbet and sticky toffee pudding with toffee sauce and vanilla ice-cream. *Benchmark main dish: pork and leek sausages with mash, buttered greens and onion gravy £13.95. Two-course evening meal £22.50.*

Brunning & Price ~ Manager Jillian Dowling ~ Real ale ~ Open 10.30am-11pm; 10.30-10.30 Sun ~ Bar food 12-9.30 (9 Sun) ~ Children allowed in bar ~ Dogs allowed in bar

WARMINGHAM   SJ7161 MAP 7
Bears Paw 🍺 🛏
(01270) 526317 – www.thebearspaw.co.uk
School Lane; CW11 3QN

Nicely maintained and extensive Victorian inn with enjoyable food, half a dozen real ales and seats outside; bedrooms

T his spreading country inn is particularly known for the high quality of its food and service. All the interlinked bar rooms have plenty of individual character, but we particularly like the two little sitting rooms. These have panelling, fashionable wallpaper, bookshelves and slouchy leather furniture comfortably arranged beside woodburning stoves in magnificent fireplaces; stripped wood flooring and a dado keep it all informal. An eclectic mix of old wooden tables and some nice old carved chairs are well spaced throughout the dining areas, with lofty windows providing a light and airy feel and lots of big pot plants dotted about. There are stools at the long bar counter where cheerful, efficient staff serve Beartown Bears Paw (named for the pub) and a Weetwood ale suited to the season along with four regularly changing local guests on handpump, 15 wines by the glass and local cider; background music. A small front garden by the car park has seats and tables. Bedrooms are well equipped and the breakfasts are very good indeed. Disabled access. This is sister pub to the Pheasant in Burwardsley and the Fishpool at Delamere.

A fine choice of well regarded pub food with Asian accents includes daytime sandwiches, beef hash cake with fried egg and confit tomato, prawn cocktail, confit duck leg, roasted lamb rump, panko-coated chicken breast, sweet potato and pulled jackfruit burger, and puddings such as apple and almond tart, knickerbocker glories and warm chocolate brownie. *Benchmark main dish: slow-braised pork belly with black pudding and apple stuffing, spiced cassoulet, creamed potato and red wine jus £17.95. Two-course evening meal £23.00.*

Free house ~ Licensee Andrew Nelson ~ Real ale ~ Restaurant ~ Children welcome ~ Dogs allowed in bar & bedrooms ~ Bedrooms: £112

WHITELEY GREEN
Windmill ⭐ ☷ ▩

SJ9278 MAP 7

(01625) 574222 – www.thewindmill.info

Brown sign to pub off A523 Macclesfield–Poynton, just N of Prestbury; Hole House Lane; SK10 5SJ

Extensive relaxed country dining bar with big sheltered garden and enjoyable food

Most of this pub is given over to dining tables, mainly in a pleasantly informal, painted base/stripped top style, on bare boards; lunch is a particularly popular time to visit. The interior spreads around a big bar counter, its handpumps serving Storm ale and guests from breweries such as Adnams, Macclesfield, Mobberley, Sharps, Weetwood and Wincle; also, 14 wines by the glass served by friendly and helpful staff. One area has several leather sofas and fabric-upholstered easy chairs; another by a log fire in a huge brick fireplace has more easy chairs and a suede sofa; background music. The spreading lawns, surrounded by a belt of young trees, provide plenty of room for a great beer garden, with well spaced tables and picnic sets, and even a maze to baffle children. Middlewood Way (a linear country park) and Macclesfield Canal (Bridge 25) are just a stroll away.

Good, pleasing food made with local produce includes lunchtime sandwiches, sharing plates, home-made soup and crusty bread, parma ham-wrapped quail breast with wild mushrooms, sweet potato falafel, haddock in Storm ale batter, burgers, duck breast with potato terrine, parsnip and pineapple chutney, steaks, and desserts such as sticky toffee pudding, spiced plums with pannacotta and maple and pecan bread pudding with rum custard. *Benchmark main dish: fish pie with lobster sauce, grana padano mash topping and cauliflower cheese £13.50. Two-course evening meal £23.00.*

Mitchells & Butlers ~ Lease Peter and Jane Nixon ~ Real ale ~ Open 12-11; 12-10 Sun ~ Bar food 12-2.30, 5-9; 12-9.30 Sat; 12-7 Sun ~ Restaurant ~ Children welcome ~ Dogs allowed in bar

Also Worth a Visit in Cheshire

Besides the fully inspected pubs, you might like to try these pubs that have been recommended to us and described by readers. Do tell us what you think of them: feedback@goodguides.com

ALLGREAVE SU9767
Rose & Crown (01260) 227232
A54 Congleton–Buxton; SK11 0BJ
Welcoming 18th-c roadside pub in remote upland spot with good Dane Valley views and walks; renovated beamed rooms with wood floors and log fires, much enjoyed local food from sandwiches to traditional mains, half a dozen well kept regional ales such as Jennings Cumberland and Wincle Waller from the wood-clad bar; children and dogs welcome, lawned garden taking in the views, three bedrooms.

ALPRAHAM   SJ5759
Travellers Rest (01829) 260523
A51 Nantwich–Chester; CW6 9JA
Timeless four-room country local in same
family for three generations; friendly chatty
atmosphere, well kept Tetleys and Weetwood,
no food, leatherette, wicker and Formica,
some flock wallpaper, fine old brewery
mirrors, darts and dominoes; may be nesting
swallows in outside gents'; dogs welcome,
back bowling green, monthly quiz, closed
weekday lunchtimes (opens 6.30pm).

ASHLEY   SJ7784
Greyhound (0161) 871 7765
*3 miles S of Altrincham; Cow Lane;
WA15 0QR* Extended red-brick Lees pub,
their well kept ales, decent wines and
good choice of tasty reasonably priced food
including healthier and buffet options,
friendly service, smart greyhound-accented
décor, wood floors, log fire; fortnightly quiz
Tues, darts; children and dogs (in bar)
welcome, seats out on lawn and terrace,
handy for the station, open (and food)
all day.

AUDLEM   SJ6543
Lord Combermere (01270) 812277
The Square (A529/A525); CW3 0AQ
Modernised and opened up family-run pub
opposite village church; five well kept ales
from Timothy Taylors and guests such as Lees
and Sharps Doom Bar, generous helpings of
good sensibly priced food catering for gluten-
free diets (including pizzas), friendly helpful
staff, sofas, restaurant, music and quiz
nights, sports TV; children welcome, dogs in
bar, front terrace and back garden, handy for
Shropshire Union Canal, open all day (food
all day Fri-Sun).

BARBRIDGE   SJ6156
Barbridge Inn (01270) 528327
Just off A51 N of Nantwich; CW5 6AY
Spacious open-plan family dining pub by
lively marina at junction of Shropshire Union
and Middlewich canals; enjoyable food from
snacks (good sandwiches with 'breakfast'
fillings) and sharing boards to steaks,
friendly staff, three Weetwood ales including
one rebadged for the pub and one or two
guests, conservatory; background music;
dogs allowed in a couple of areas, waterside
garden with enclosed play area, moorings,
Santa breakfasts on Dec weekends, open
(and food) all day.

BARTON   SJ4454
★Cock o' Barton (01829) 782277
*Barton Road (A534 E of Farndon);
SY14 7HU* Stylish contemporary décor in
bright open skylit bar, cocktails, plenty of
wines by the glass and up to four real ales
including Stonehouse, Fri happy hour till
7pm, good choice of well liked up-to-date
food served by neat courteous staff, beamed

restaurant areas; background music; children
welcome (free main course for them on Sun),
tables in sunken heated inner courtyard with
canopies and modern water feature, picnic-
sets on back lawn, 14 bedrooms, open (and
food) all day from 8am for breakfast.

BIRKENHEAD   SJ3386
Refreshment Rooms
(0151) 644 5893 *Bedford Road E;
CH42 1LS* On the site of 19th-c
refreshment rooms for Mersey ferry workers
– present streamline-style building dates
from 1920s with memorabilia and features
such as a Cunard chandelier illustrating
Liverpool's maritime past; good rotating
selection of mainly local ales such as Big
Bog, Brimstage and Peerless and a house
beer from Lees (HMS Conway), Rosie's Welsh
cider and a couple of interesting lagers,
good competitively priced home-made food
including daily deals, friendly prompt service;
children and dogs welcome, beer garden at
back with play area, views across the Mersey
from out-of-the way riverside location, open
(and food) all day.

BOLLINGTON   SJ9377
Church House (01625) 574014
Church Street; SK10 5PY Friendly
traditional village pub on edge of the Peak
District – a good place to start or end a walk;
well liked home-made food including good
value set lunch, efficient friendly service,
well kept Adnams Southwold, Marstons
Wainwright plus a local guest perhaps from
Tatton or Weetwood, nice open fire, separate
dining room; children and clean dogs
welcome, picnic-sets in small beer garden,
five competitively priced bedrooms, good
breakfast, open all day weekends (food all
day Sun).

BOLLINGTON   SJ9377
Holly Bush (01625) 574573
Palmerston Street; SK10 5PW Cosy
Robinsons pub with listed mock-Tudor
exterior and panelled interior recently given
a low-key designer refurb; Robinsons ales and
a good range of other drinks including gin
of the week, home-made food from sharing
plates up, friendly helpful staff, original
panelling, parquet flooring and log fires;
occasional evening events such as discos and
live music, children welcome, dogs in bar,
open all day, kitchen shuts 7pm Sun.

BOLLINGTON   SJ9477
Poachers (01625) 572086
Mill Lane; SK10 5BU Traditional stone-
built village local prettily set in good walking
area, comfortable and welcoming, with tasty
pub food (all day Sun, not Mon) including
bargain two-course lunch deal and pie and
pint night Weds, well kept Storm, Weetwood
and three guests, good range of whiskies/
gins, efficient friendly service, log fire and
woodburner; occasional live music, quiz last

Sun of month; children and dogs welcome (dog towels), sunny back garden, open all day weekends, closed Mon lunchtime.

BOLLINGTON SJ9377
Vale (01625) 575147
Adlington Road; SK10 5JT Welcoming tap for Bollington brewery in 19th-c terrace row; their well kept beers on hand pump plus guest keg beers (tasters offered), two real ciders, Taddington Moravka lagers, enjoyable food (all day weekends) including range of locally made pies and daily specials, helpful efficient service, interesting photos, newspapers and books, roaring fire; quiz first Sun of month, community events; dogs welcome, picnic-sets in small beer garden just up the road, views of cricket on the ground behind, near Middlewood Way and Macclesfield Canal, open all day Fri-Sun.

BROOMEDGE SJ7086
Jolly Thresher (01925) 752265
Higher Lane; WA13 0RN Spacious well appointed dining pub with wide range of enjoyable food including healthy options, daily specials and good value set lunch (Mon-Fri, not Dec), well kept Hydes Lowry and Original (cheaper Mon), lots of wines by the glass and good choice of other drinks, restaurant and dining conservatory; Tues quiz; children and dogs (in bar) welcome, disabled access, tables on front terrace and in garden behind, open (and food) all day.

BROXTON SJ4858
Egerton Arms (01829) 782241
A41/A534 S of Chester; CH3 9JW Large neatly kept mock-Tudor dining pub; old polished furniture on wood or carpeted floors, lots of prints and books, log fires, wide choice of popular food oriented more towards dining than snacks, six well kept changing beers (four local and two national) and plenty of wines by the glass, efficient friendly staff; children and dogs welcome, wheelchair access, big garden with decking and play area, open all day.

CHELFORD SJ8175
★ Egerton Arms (01625) 861366
A537 Macclesfield–Knutsford; SK11 9BB Proudly independent local, large and rambling, with beams and nice mix of furniture including carved settles and wooden porter's chairs, grandfather clock, Tatton and up to six guest beers plus a couple of craft kegs, staff trained to recommend food/beer pairings, advocate of flourishing local food scene serving well made pub favourites such as good burgers, stone-baked pizzas and signature steaks, restaurant, steps down to little raftered games area with pool, darts and sports TV; quiz last Thurs of month; children and dogs welcome, picnic-sets on canopied deck and slate terrace, toddlers' play area, adjoining deli/coffee shop, open (and food) all day.

CHESTER SJ4066
★ Albion (01244) 340345
Albion Street; CH1 1RQ Classic Victorian corner pub proudly celebrating a bygone era with comfortable Edwardian décor and captivating WWI memorabilia (it's an official memorial site for the Cheshire Regiment); a couple of real ales on handpump, generously served 'trench rations' such as club and doorstep sandwiches and the likes of corned beef hash with pickled red cabbage, also veggie and gluten-free; open fire in Edwardian fireplace, 1928 Steck pianola, side dining room; monthly swing dance; dogs allowed in bar; two bedrooms; open all day Fri, may close early in evening if quiet.

CHESTER SJ4065
★ Bear & Billet (01244) 311886
Lower Bridge Street; CH1 1RU Ornately half-timbered 17th-c town house with lattice windows, an inn since the 18th c, now Grade I listed and part of the Market Town Taverns group; Okells beers and three changing guests plus good selection of wines and gins, reasonably priced pubby food including hot nibbles and a range of burgers, efficient service, atmospheric beamed bar with wood floor and panelling, open fire, scenes of old Chester in back dining part, further rooms above; quiz night and upstairs folk club (both Sun), five sports TVs; children and dogs welcome, courtyard seating, open (and food) all day, kitchen closes 7pm Sun.

CHESTER SJ4066
Boathouse (01244) 328709
The Groves, off Grosvenor Park Road; on River Dee five-minute walk from centre; CH1 1SD Single-storey pub on site of 17th-c boathouse with great River Dee views; Lees ales and decent choice of wines by the glass, short cocktail list, back bar serves premium gins and spirits, well priced pubby food from sandwiches and sharing plates up, seasonal and mini desserts; Weds quiz; children welcome, dogs outside only, disabled access/ facilities, tables and painted beach huts on paved terrace overlooking the water, little bridge to floating seating area, bedrooms in adjacent extension, open (and food) all day.

CHESTER SJ4065
★ Brewery Tap (01244) 340999
Lower Bridge Street; CH1 1RU Tap for Spitting Feathers brewery in interesting Jacobean building with 18th-c brick façade, external staircase up to lofty barrel-vaulted bar (former great hall) serving a couple of their well kept ales and five guest beers from cask, a cider, house lager plus interesting guests from keg and good choice of wines, reduced-price beers Weds from 5pm, hearty home-made food using local suppliers including Spitting Feathers' own farm (rare-breed pork), pews and other rustic furniture on flagstones, tapestries on walls, large

carved red-sandstone fireplace, also smaller plainer room; children and dogs welcome, no wheelchair access, open (and food) all day.

CHESTER SJ4166

★**Cellar** (01244) 318950

City Road; CH1 3AE Laid-back Canal Quarter beer specialist with six well kept ales ranging widely from local standards to strong stout to limited editions including their own collaboration with Marble, craft beers, real ciders and interesting selection of imports, decent wines and cocktails too, happy hour till 9pm weekdays, limited snacky food (free bacon sandwiches 12-6pm Sun), basement bar for private functions, interesting urinals made from repurposed kegs; sports TVs; a few pavement tables; closed Mon-Thurs till 3pm, otherwise open noon till late.

CHESTER SJ4571

Chester Fields (01244) 303100

A56, near junction with B5132, NE of Chester; CH2 4JR Restaurant pub in former barn with long views across fields from large garden and 'ski-style' huts for groups; two or three ales from local brewers such as Oaks and Weetwood, cocktail-savvy bar staff, menu of pub classics trad and modern from local ingredients, various daily deals; staff keen to please; pretty modern barn conversion with exposed brick walls, high A-frame ceiling and leather banquettes; monthly quiz; children and dogs welcome, open (and food) all day.

CHESTER SJ4066

Coach House (01244) 351900

Northgate Street; CH1 2HQ Well run 19th-c coaching inn next to town hall and close to cathedral; comfortable country-style lounge with central bar, well kept Marstons-related beers, decent choice of wines and gins, good fairly priced food including pub favourites from semi-open kitchen, prompt friendly service; children and dogs welcome, tables out in front, eight bedrooms, good breakfast, open (and food) all day, bar and breakfast from 10am, kitchen closes 8pm Sun.

CHESTER SJ4065

Cross Keys (01244) 344460

Duke Street/Lower Bridge Street; CH1 1RU Single-room Victorian corner pub with ornate interior; dark panelling, etched mirrors and heraldic stained-glass windows, button-back leather wall benches and cast-iron tables on bare boards, open fire, well kept Joules ales, a guest beer and good selection of gins, enjoyable sensibly priced pubby food, friendly service, upstairs

function room; background music; no dogs inside, seats out in front, closed Mon and Tues, otherwise open all day but kitchen may close early Sun.

CHESTER SJ4170

Oakfield (01244) 389710

Inside Chester Zoo; CH2 1LH Gorgeous red-brick manor house (Grade II listed), the former home of Chester Zoo's founders, now tastefully converted into a contemporary British pub and café/restaurant; two Weetwoods cask ales, worthwhile wine list, wide choice of locally sourced food plus afternoon tea; stunning interior including conservatory dining room, children welcome; views of gardens and some seats outside; open 10am-5pm daily.

CHESTER SJ4066

Olde Boot (01244) 314540

Eastgate Row N; CH1 1LQ Lovely 17th-c Rows building; long narrow bar with heavy beams, dark woodwork, oak flooring and flagstones, old kitchen range in lounge beyond, settles and oak panelling in upper area, well kept/priced Sam Smiths beers, cheerful service and chatty atmosphere encouraged by a ban on mobile phones and swearing, cash only; no children.

CHESTER SJ4066

Pied Bull (01244) 325829

Upper Northgate Street; CH1 2HQ Old beamed and panelled coaching inn with roomy open-plan bar, good own-brewed ales (brewery tours) along with guest beers and nice wines, also over 30 gins (tasting platters) and a good malt whisky selection, enjoyable fairly priced traditional food from sandwiches, baked potatoes and sharing plates up, meal deal including a bottle of wine Tues except Nov and Dec, friendly staff and locals, imposing stone fireplace, dining area in lighter and more contemporary style; children welcome, tables under parasols on enclosed terrace, handsome staircase up to 31 bedrooms, open (and food) all day, kitchen closes 8.30pm Sun.

CHESTER SJ4066

Telfords Warehouse (01244) 390090

Tower Wharf, behind Northgate Street near railway; CH1 4EZ Large converted canal warehouse designed in late 18th c by Thomas Telford, now a bar/restaurant/arts/music venue, half a dozen well kept interesting ales including Weetwood Cheshire Cat and Salopian Oracle, good variety of fairly priced food from sandwiches and snacks up, friendly efficient young staff, mixed clientele includes students, bare boards, exposed

---

brickwork and high ceiling, wall of windows overlooking the water, some old enamel signs and massive iron winding gear in bar, steps up to heavily beamed area with sofas, art gallery and restaurant; many events including monthly Mon quiz, gigs, salsa, bouncers on the door; tables out by canal; open all day (till late Weds-Sun).

CHRISTLETON SJ4465
Ring o' Bells (01244) 335422
Off A41; CH3 7AS Sleek and successful red-brick dining pub in the pretty village of Christleton, on the Shropshire Union Canal; ales from Weetwoods, Tatton, Cheshire Brew Brothers and Spitting Feathers (in the next village of Waverton), traditional pub fare (well liked Sunday lunch, two-for-one deals midweek) plus pizzas and modern and veggie/vegan favourites such as a buddha bowl, afternoon tea; lots of wood with stripped floorboards and carved bar plus bright conservatory dining room; wine tastings; professional and friendly staff; children and dogs (bar only) welcome; beer garden; open all day, food all day Sat, Sun.

CHURCH MINSHULL SJ6660
Badger (01270) 522348
B5074 Winsford–Nantwich; handy for Shropshire Union Canal, Middlewich branch; CW5 6DY Opened-up and modernised 18th-c coaching inn next to church in pretty village; broad range of good food from sharing boards and pub favourites up (check websites for good book-ahead offers), four well kept ales comprising own-badged Tatton Badger, Titanic Plum Porter and two changing guests, Mortimer's Orchard cider, interesting range of wines (some low-alcohol) and spirits, friendly helpful staff, bar with old quarry tiles and woodburner, lounge/dining area leading to conservatory with fairy lights; children and dogs (in bar) welcome, tables in garden, five attractive bedrooms, good breakfast, open (and food) all day.

COMBERBACH SJ6477
Spinner & Bergamot
(01606) 891307 *Warrington Road; CW9 6AY* Comfortable 18th-c beamed village pub named after two racehorses; good home-made food (smaller helpings available for some main courses), well kept Robinsons ales and nice choice of wines, pitched-ceiling timber dining extension, two-room carpeted lounge and tiled-floor public bar where dogs allowed, log fires; sports TVs; children welcome, small verandah, picnic-sets on sloping lawn, floodlit bowling green, open all day (food all day Sun till 7.30pm).

CONGLETON SJ8659
Horseshoe (01260) 272205
Fence Lane, Newbold Astbury, between A34 and A527 S; CW12 3NL Traditionally decorated 18th-c coaching inn set in peaceful countryside; three small blue-carpeted

rooms with decorative plates, copper and brass and other knick-knacks (some on delft shelves), mix of seating including plush banquettes and iron-base tables, log fire, well kept predominantly Robinsons ales, popular hearty home-made food at reasonable prices including good daily specials, friendly staff and locals; children welcome, no dogs inside, rustic garden furniture, heated outdoor 'rum shack', play area, good walks.

CONGLETON SJ8662
Young Pretender (01260) 273277
Lawton Street; CW12 1RS Under same ownership as the Old Dancer (Wilmslow) and Treacle Tap (Macclesfield); one-room former toyshop divided into smaller areas with local artwork on display, five well kept interesting ales served from casks on the bar plus ten keg fonts for European and craft beer and good selection of international draught/bottled beers, enjoyable beer-friendly food from snacks up including range of locally made pies; various events such as Sun quiz, brewery takeovers and film nights; children (till 8pm) and dogs welcome, open (and food) all day Fri-Sun, till 1am Fri and Sat.

COTEBROOK SJ5765
Alvanley Arms (01829) 760200
A49/B5152 N of Tarporley; CW6 9DS Welcoming roadside coaching inn, 17th-c behind its flower-decked Georgian façade, with updated beamed rooms, Robinsons ales, 20 wines by the glass, short gin list and good choice of other drinks, well liked fairly priced food from pubby menu, friendly helpful service; background music; children welcome, disabled access, garden with deck and large pond, pleasant walks, six comfortable bedrooms, good breakfast, open (and food) all day.

CREWE SJ7055
Borough Arms (01270) 254999
Earle Street; CW1 2BG No-frills drinkers' pub with up to ten well kept changing ales (maybe six microbrews), also good choice of continental beers and a couple of real ciders, friendly staff, two small rooms off central bar and downstairs lounge; occasional sports TV; picnic-sets on back terrace and lawn, open all day Fri-Sun, closed lunchtime other days.

CREWE SJ7055
Hops (01270) 211100
Prince Albert Street; CW1 2DF Friendly and relaxed Belgian-style café-bar on two floors; huge range of continental bottled beers (some also on draught), half a dozen interesting ales such as Rat Ratella and Shropshire guests and good range of ciders, snacky lunchtime food (Weds-Sat) and fun street-food events, proper coffee; children and dogs welcome, disabled access/loo, seats out at front, closed Mon lunchtime, otherwise open all day.

DISLEY   SJ9784
White Lion   (01663) 762800
Buxton Road (A6); SK12 2HA Welcoming
pub at east end of village under new
enthusiastic management; up to nine
changing ales might include Wainwright,
Butcombe and Ossett, short menu of
traditional pub classics including all-day Sun
breakfast, friendly staff; two new pool tables,
Thurs quiz; children and dogs (in one part)
welcome, closed Mon lunchtime, otherwise
open (and food) all day.

EATON   SJ8765
★ Plough   (01260) 280207
A536 Congleton–Macclesfield; CW12 2NH
Substantial and welcoming village pub with
beams, leaded bow windows and exposed
brickwork, cushioned wall and booth seats
and comfortable armchairs, woodburner in
big stone fireplace, four real ales such as
Shires and Storm, ten wines by the glass from
decent list and over 20 malt whiskies, classic
international and pub food dishes plus
sandwiches, friendly efficient staff, raftered
barn function room (moved here from Wales)
hosting many weddings; background music
(live Thurs), board games and occasional TV;
children and dogs (in bar) welcome, disabled
access, big tree-lined garden with tables
set for dining on covered deck, fine views of
Peak District fringes, appealingly designed
bedrooms in converted stable block, open
(and food) all day.

FADDILEY   SJ5852
Thatch   (01270) 524223
A534 Wrexham–Nantwich; CW5 8JE
Attractive thatched and timbered dining pub
dating from 15th c; low beams and open fires,
raised room to right of bar, back barn-style
dining room, Black Sheep, Timothy Taylors
Landlord and a guest such as Brains, popular
and nicely presented food from lunchtime
sandwiches up including fine own-made pies
($10 pie and pint deal Weds), friendly helpful
service; background music; children and dogs
(in bar and snug) welcome, nice country
garden with play area, open all day.

GAWSWORTH   SJ8869
★ Harrington Arms   (01260) 223325
*Off A536; Congleton Road/Church Lane;
SK11 9RJ* This unspoilt three-storey
building is still part of a working farm; low
17th-c beams, quarry-tiled and flagstoned
floors, snug corners and log fires, counter in
narrow space on right serving Robinsons ales,
a guest beer and good selection of wines and
whiskies, several unpretentious rooms off
with old settles and eclectic mix of tables and
chairs, lots of pictures on pale painted walls,
well liked hearty food from hot and cold

sandwiches to daily specials, friendly relaxed
atmosphere; background music (live folk
Fri); children and dogs (in bar) welcome,
benches out on small front cobbled area,
more seats in garden overlooking fields, lane
leads to one of Cheshire's prettiest villages,
Gawsworth Hall half a mile, open (and food)
all day weekends.

GOOSTREY   SJ7770
Crown   (01477) 532128
Off A50 and A535; CW4 8PE Extended
and opened-up 18th-c red-brick village pub;
beams and open fires, small conservatory,
good choice of enjoyable fairly pubby food
including good gluten-free, up to five well
kept Marstons-related ales, lots of wines by
the glass, cocktails, friendly efficient service
from young aproned staff; children and dogs
welcome, picnic-sets outside, close to Jodrell
Bank, open (and food) all day.

GRAPPENHALL   SJ6386
Parr Arms   (01925) 212120
*Near M6 junction 20 – A50 towards
Warrington, left after 1.5 miles; Church
Lane; WA4 3EP* Black-beamed pub in
picture-postcard setting with picnic-sets
out on cobbles by church, more tables on
small canopied back terrace; enjoyable
reasonably priced food from sandwiches and
baked potatoes to chargrills, also blackboard
specials, well kept Robinsons and good range
of other drinks from central bar, friendly
service, log fires; children and dogs (in one
area) welcome, open (and food) all day.

GREAT BUDWORTH   SJ6677
★ George & Dragon   (01606) 892650
*Signed off A559 NE of Northwich; High
Street opposite church; CW9 6HF*
Characterful building dating from 1722
(grand front part is 19th-c) in delightful
village; Lees ales kept well and plenty of
wines by the glass, wide choice (including
vegan menu and gluten-free puddings) of
rated home-cooked pub food, some quite
luxurious, dark panelled bar with log fire, hop
garlands and leather button-back banquettes,
back area more restaurant with wood floors
and exposed brickwork, some stuffed animals
and hunting memorabilia; children and dogs
(in bar) welcome, picnic-sets outside, open
(and food) all day.

KNUTSFORD   SJ7776
Dun Cow   (01565) 633093
*Chelford Road; outskirts of Knutsford
towards Macclesfield; WA16 8RH*
Comfortably opened-up country dining
pub arranged around central servery;
modern décor with cosy alcoves and log
fires, popular sensibly priced food from
sandwiches/ciabattas to daily specials, well

If we know a pub has an outdoor play area for children, we mention it.

kept Robinsons ales, friendly caring service; children and dogs welcome, good disabled access, tables on paved front and back terraces, open (and food) all day.

KNUTSFORD   SJ7578
Lord Eldon (01565) 652261
Tatton Street, off A50 at White Bear roundabout; WA16 6AD Traditional red-brick former coaching inn with four comfortable rooms (much bigger inside than it looks), friendly staff and locals, beams, brasses, old pictures and large open fire, well kept Tetleys and a couple of guests, no food; music and quiz nights, darts; dogs welcome, back garden but no car park, handy for Tatton Park (NT), open all day.

KNUTSFORD   SJ7578
Rose & Crown (01565) 652366
King Street; WA16 6DT Beamed and panelled 17th-c inn; very well liked trend-conscious food from sandwiches and sharing plates up, changing local ales, plenty of wines by the glass and some interesting gins, good friendly service, log fires in cosy bar and restaurant; live acoustic music Sun evening; children and dogs (in bar) welcome, outside bar and terrace, nine bedrooms, open (and food) all day.

LANGLEY   SJ9471
★Leather's Smithy (01260) 252313
Off A523 S of Macclesfield; OS Sheet 118 map reference 952715; SK11 0NE Isolated stone-built pub in fine walking country next to reservoir; well kept Theakstons and two or three guests, lots of whiskies, good locally sourced food (including vegan options) from sandwiches to blackboard specials, efficient friendly service, unfussy flagstoned bar and carpeted dining areas, beams, log fire and interesting local prints/photographs; children welcome, no dogs inside but muddy boots allowed in bar, picnic-sets in garden behind and on grass opposite, lovely views, open all day Sat, till 8pm Sun, closed Mon.

LITTLE BUDWORTH   SJ5867
Cabbage Hall (01829) 760292
Forest Road (A49); CW6 9ES Restauranty pub (part of the Pesto chain) specialising in good tapas-style Italian food ('piattini'), drinkers catered for in comfortable bar with parquet floor and real fire; real ales, cocktails and decent wines by the glass, also Italian-style afternoon teas, efficient friendly staff; children welcome, garden tables, open (and food) all day.

LITTLE BUDWORTH   SJ5965
Egerton Arms (01829) 760424
Pinfold Lane; CW6 9BS Proudly independent local, large and rambling, with beams and nice mix of furniture including carved settles and wooden porter's chairs, grandfather clock, Tatton and up to six guest

beers plus a couple of craft kegs, staff trained to recommend food/beer pairings, advocate of flourishing local food scene serving well made pub favourites such as good burgers, stone-baked pizzas and signature steaks, restaurant, steps down to little raftered games area with pool, darts and sports TV; quiz last Thurs of month; children and dogs welcome, picnic-sets on canopied deck and slate terrace, toddlers' play area, adjoining deli/coffee shop, open (and food) all day.

LITTLE LEIGH   SJ6076
Holly Bush (01606) 853196
A49 just S of A533; CW8 4QY Brick and timbered 17th-c thatched pub; good choice of well priced food, very friendly staff, Tetleys and a couple of mainstream guests, bar with open fire, restaurant extension; children welcome, no dogs inside, wheelchair access, courtyard tables and garden with play area, 14 bedrooms in converted back barn, open all day weekends (food all day Sun).

LOWER WHITLEY   SJ6178
Chetwode Arms (01925) 640044
Just off A49, handy for M56 junction 10; Street Lane; WA4 4EN Rambling low-beamed dining pub dating from the 17th c; good food including range of exotic meats cooked on a hot stone at your table, solid furnishings all clean and polished, small front bar with warm open fire, four real ales and good wines by the glass; well behaved children allowed (under-10s eat free early evening), limited wheelchair access, tables outside along with tipi (in summer) and own bowling green, open from 4pm (noon Sun), last food orders 8.30pm or by arrangement.

LYMM   SJ7087
Barn Owl (01925) 752020
Agden Wharf, Warrington Lane (just off B5159 E); WA13 0SW Popular extended pub in nice setting on Bridgewater Canal; Marstons Lancaster Bomber and Wainwright, Mobberley Route 97 and Thwaites Original, decent wines by the glass and some interesting gins, good choice of affordably priced traditional food including weekday OAP menu and Sun carvery, efficient service even when busy, friendly atmosphere; children and dogs (in one part) welcome, disabled facilities, moorings (space for one narrowboat), open all day.

LYMM   SJ6886
Church Green (01925) 752068
Higher Lane; WA13 0AP Popular dining pub with sleek interior and own vegetable garden, owned by celebrity chef Aiden Byrne; food can be very good from restauranty dishes to more affordable pubby choices, also children's and vegan menus, usually Jennings Cumberland and Marstons 61, pus Beavertown Neck Oil craft beer, carefully chosen wines and interesting gins, various dining areas including conservatory;

background music; disabled access/loos, pretty garden with heated side deck, open (and food) all day, breakfast from 10am (9am weekends), kitchen shuts 7pm Sun.

MACCLESFIELD   SJ9173
Snow Goose   (01625) 619299
Sunderland Street; SK11 6HN Quirky laid-back café-bar with feel of an alpine ski lodge; well kept Storm plus guest ales and a dozen interesting wines by glass or bottle, short menu of contemporary comfort food, bare-boards interior on three levels, woodburners, local artwork for sale, piano; background and live music, board games, crafts workshops; children and dogs welcome, balcony overlooking back garden, open all day and can get very busy.

MACCLESFIELD   SJ9173
Treacle Tap   (01625) 615938
Sunderland Street; SK11 6JL Simply but nicely furnished little bare-boards bar in former shop (same owners as the Young Pretender in Congleton and Old Dancer in Wilmslow); three interesting mainly local ales on constant rotation and good selection of bottled beers (particularly Belgian and German), other drinks too, short menu including meat/cheese platters and 'bowl food'; regular events such as French conversation, open mike and musicians' sessions and a stitch'n'bitch night; children welcome till 8pm, open (and food) all day Fri-Sun, from 4pm other days.

NANTWICH   SJ6452
★Black Lion   (01270) 628711
Welsh Row; CW5 5ED Historic black and white pub with plenty of character, saved after closure in 2019 by new capable management, open fire, good food (not Sun evening, Mon) from pubby menu, three well kept Weetwood ales and two or three guests, good friendly service, upstairs rooms with old wooden tables and leather sofas on undulating floors; children welcome, dogs in courtyard Hop Room, open all day Fri-Sun and can get busy.

NANTWICH
★Ebenezer's   SJ6552
Castle Street; CW5 5BA Popular town-centre bar devoted to craft ales and beers in former Methodist church; eight ale taps with swiftly changing occupants ranging widely in style and provenance (Salopian is a regular), real cider too, gins including home-made, wide and knowledgeable range of craft brews in keg, can and bottle, no food; run and patronised by friendly enthusiasts; occasional live music; a few seats outside; opening times vary.

NANTWICH   SJ6552
Vine   (01270) 619055
Hospital Street; CW5 5RP Black and white fronted pub dating from the 17th c; gently

modernised interior stretching far back with steps and quiet corners, coal fire, five to eight ales (cheaper Mon) including Hydes, 16 wines including by the glass, 25 gins and popular good value dishes from conventional pub food menu, friendly staff and locals, background music, sports TVs, darts; children and dogs welcome, small sunny outside seating area behind, open all day, food till 8pm (6pm Sun).

NESTON   SJ2976
Harp   (0151) 336 6980
Quayside, SW of Little Neston; keep·on along track at end of Marshlands Road; CH64 0TB Tucked-away little two-room country local on Dee estuary; five or so well kept ales such as Timothy Taylors, decent choice of bottled beers, wines by the glass and some good malt whiskies, enjoyable simple pub food (not Sun evening, log fire, pale quarry tiles and simple furnishings, interesting old photographs, hatch servery to lounge; children and dogs allowed, garden behind and picnic-sets up on front grassy bank facing Dee Marshes, glorious sunsets with wild calls of wading birds, good walks, open all day.

NORLEY   SJ5772
Tigers Head   (01928) 788309
Pytchleys Hollow; WA6 8NT Friendly little village local near Delamere Forest; enjoyable good value home-made food (evening deals), well kept Weetwood and four guests, over 30 gins including their own Second Son; tap room and lounge, upstairs skittle alley/function room; pool, darts, sports TV; children and dogs welcome, some seating out in front, more on paved terrace behind, bowling green, open all day Fri and Sat, till 9pm Sun and Mon, closed lunchtimes Mon-Thurs.

PARKGATE   SJ2778
Boathouse   (0151) 336 4187
Village signed off A540; CH64 6RN Popular 1920s black and white timbered pub with attractive linked rooms; good choice of enjoyable food from sandwiches and snacks up, cheerful if not always speedy service, three well kept Hydes ales (cheaper on Mon), several wines by the glass, standard cocktails, big conservatory with great views to Wales over silted Dee estuary (RSPB reserve), may be egrets and avocets; children and dogs (in bar) welcome, seats out on decking, open (and food) all day.

PARKGATE   SJ2778
Ship   (0151) 336 3931
The Parade; CH64 6SA Far-reaching Dee estuary and Wales views from hotel's bow-windowed bar; well kept Brimstage Trappers Hat and local guests, several wines by the glass, over 50 whiskies and interesting range of gins, good modern home-cooked pub food including sandwiches (until 5pm), daily

specials and popular Sun roasts, friendly service, log fire; children welcome, no dogs inside, a few tables out at front and to the side, 25 bedrooms, open (and food) all day.

PEOVER HEATH   SJ7973
★ **Dog** (01625) 861421
Wellbank Lane; the pub is often listed under Over Peover instead; WA16 8UP
Newly refurbished traditional country pub with attractive rooms (sister to the Ship at Styal); good variety of popular food (classy sandwiches until 5pm), own-pickled cockles and clams, five ales including Weetwood and Dunham Massey, decent choice of wines by the glass and malt whiskies, friendly efficient staff; children welcome, dogs in front room, picnic-sets out at front and in pretty back garden, two-mile walk from here to the Jodrell Bank Discovery Centre and Arboretum, six bedrooms, open (and food) all day.

POYNTON   SJ9283
Cask Tavern (01625) 875157
Park Lane; SK12 1RE Popular refurbished Bollington pub with five of their well kept ales including Oat Mill stout, craft beers, real ciders plus a new ten-tap keg board and several wines by the glass including draught prosecco, friendly staff, some snacky cold food; Mon quiz, monthly Weds vinyl night; children and dogs allowed, open all day Fri-Sun, from 4pm other days.

STYAL   SJ8383
Ship (01625) 444888
B5166 near Manchester Airport; SK9 4JE Busy 17th-c beamed pub under same ownership as the Dog at Peover Heath; good variety of well liked food including popular Sun lunch, ales from Weetwood and guests, well conceived wine list with several by the glass, friendly helpful service, lots of alcoves and snugs, some stripped brickwork and painted panelling, open fire; children allowed until 9pm if well behaved, seats out at front and on back terrace, attractive NT village with good walks on the doorstep, open (and food) all day.

SUTTON   SJ9469
★ **Ryles Arms** (01260) 252244
Hollin Lane, Higher Sutton; SK11 0NN Popular dining pub in fine countryside; very good food from extensive menu including signature grills, ales such as Black Sheep and Wincle, decent wines and several whiskies, pleasant décor, hill-view dining room with french windows to terrace; children welcome, good bedrooms in converted barn, open all day.

SUTTON   SJ9273
★ **Sutton Gamekeeper**
(01260) 252000 *Hollin Lane; SK11 0HL*
Updated beamed village pub with simple décor and sophisticated 'field to fork'

food including good game (best to book), Dunham Massey, Wincle and a guest, good friendly service, warm open fire; children welcome, well behaved dogs in bar, metal furniture in fenced garden behind, closed Mon (except bank holidays), otherwise open all day till 10pm, food all day weekends (till 7pm Sun).

SWETTENHAM   SJ7967
★ **Swettenham Arms** (01477) 571284
Off A54 Congleton–Holmes Chapel or A535 Chelford–Holmes Chapel; CW12 2LF 16th-c country former nunnery in a pretty village setting, expertly run by longstanding licensees, with three interlinked dark beamed areas traditionally styled with brasses and old prints, polished copper bar, three woodburning stoves; friendly efficient staff serve several changing real ales such as Timothy Taylors Landlord and Wincle Burke's Special, well selected wines including several by the glass, satisfying food from local ingredients; croquet, classic car and vintage motorbike events in summer; children and dogs (in bar) welcome; tables on back lawn adjoining lavender meadow; near Quinta Arboretum; open (and food) all day.

WESTON   SJ7352
White Lion (01270) 587011
Not far from M6 junction 16, via A500; CW2 5NA Refurbished 17th-c black and white pub hotel; low-beamed lounge bar with slate floor, chesterfields and inglenook woodburner, three well kept ales including Salopian and good selection of wines, popular well presented food from sandwiches and smaller plates up, stylish restaurant, good helpful service, children allowed in eating areas, dogs in bar, lovely garden with bowling green (not owned by the pub), 17 mid-range bedrooms, open all day.

WHITEGATE   SJ6268
Plough (01606) 889455
Beauty Bank, Foxwist Green; OS Sheet 118 map reference 624684; off A556 just W of Northwich, or A54 W of Winsford; CW8 2BP Flower-bedecked country pub with bar and extended dining area; good, reasonably priced food (best to book) from lunchtime panini up, cheerful efficient service, four well kept Robinsons ales and plenty of wines by the glass; background music; no under-14s inside, well behaved dogs allowed in tap room, disabled access, picnic-sets out at front and in back garden, popular walks nearby, open (and food) all day.

WILMSLOW   SJ8481
Old Dancer (01625) 530775
Grove Street; SK9 1DR Long narrow beer pub with big glass windows to pedestrianised street (sister pubs are Young Pretender in Congleton and Treacle Tap in Macclesfield);

bare-boards interior with simple wooden furniture and padded benches, some striking murals, five well kept changing local ales, ten craft beers and a proper cider, wide range of bottled beers, decent coffee and good value pies, puds, wraps, burgers and hot nibbles, friendly staff, second bar/function room upstairs (not always open); regular events including music and film nights, traditional games, newspapers; children and dogs welcome, seats out in front, open all day (till 1am Fri, Sat).

WINCLE   SJ9665
⭐ **Ship** (01260) 227217
Village signposted off A54 Congleton–Buxton; SK11 0QE Friendly 16th-c stone-built country pub; bare-boards bar leading to carpeted dining room, old stables area with flagstones, beams, woodburner and open fire, good generously served food from well priced menu with good vegan section, four Lees ales plus a local guest and 20 or so wines by the glass, quick attentive service; children and dogs welcome, tables in side garden, good Dane Valley walks, open (and food) all day.

WRENBURY   SJ5947
Dusty Miller (01270) 780537
Cholmondeley Road; village signed from A530 Nantwich–Whitchurch; CW5 8HG Converted 19th-c corn mill with fine canal views from terrace and series of tall glazed arches in bar; spacious feel with banquettes, beige carpets and a mix of tables, old lift hoist up under the rafters, Robinsons beers, and good food (not Tues) from interesting menu including stone-baked flatbreads, friendly staff; background music; children and dogs welcome, disabled access/loos, farm shop, closed Mon, otherwise open all day.

Cornwall

KEY  ★ Star Pub   🌟 Top Quality Food   🍺 Great Beer

🍷 Good Wines   £ Bargain Meals   🛏 Good Bedrooms   🍴 Serves Food

---

DEVORAN   SW7938   Map 1

Old Quay 🍺

(01872) 863142 – www.theoldquayinn.co.uk

Devoran from new Carnon Cross roundabout A39 Truro–Falmouth, left on old road, right at mini roundabout; TR3 6NE

Light and airy bar rooms in friendly pub with four real ales, good wine, imaginative food and seats on pretty back terraces

---

Just 50 metres from the coast-to-coast Portreath to Devoran Mineral Tramways cycle path, this charming pub proves popular with cyclists and walkers. You can even arrive by boat – provided the tide is right – as it's just up the hill from Devoran Quay. The easy-going, roomy bar has an interesting woodburner set halfway up one wall, a cushioned window seat, wall settles and a few bar stools around just three tables on stripped boards, and bar chairs by the counter. Black Sheep, Sharps Atlantic and Doom Bar and Skinners Betty Stogs on handpump and good wines by the glass (including prosecco). Off to the left is an airy room with pictures by local artists (for sale), built-in cushioned wall seating, plush stools and a couple of big tables on the dark slate floor. To the other side of the bar is another light room with more settles and farmhouse chairs, attractive blue and white striped cushions and more sailing photographs; darts and board games. As well as benches outside at the front looking down through the trees to the water, there's a series of snug little back terraces with picnic-sets and chairs and tables. Nearby parking is limited unless you arrive early. Wheelchair access through a side door.

🍴 Good quality food using local produce includes lunchtime sandwiches, mussels in white wine with fries, roasted butternut squash with pesto, roasted pine nuts, feta and pomegranate finished with rocket and herb oil, burgers with toppings and triple-cooked chips, fish pie, rump steak, a choice of three curries, beer-battered catch of the day or halloumi, breaded scampi, and puddings such as sticky toffee pudding and lemon tart. *Benchmark main dish: beer-battered catch of the day £12.00. Two-course evening meal £18.00.*

Punch ~ Tenants John and Hannah Calland ~ Real ale ~ Open 11-11 ~ Bar food 12-3, 6-9 ~ Restaurant ~ Children welcome ~ Dogs allowed in bar & restaurant

---

GURNARDS HEAD   SW4337   Map 1

Gurnards Head Hotel 🌟 🍷 🛏

(01736) 796928 – www.gurnardshead.co.uk

B3306 Zennor–St Just; TR26 3DE

Interesting inn with lots of wines by the glass, good inventive food and wild surrounding walks; comfortable bedrooms

---

This informally civilised inn is under the same ownership as the Old Coastguard in Mousehole (also in Cornwall) and the Griffin at Felinfach (Wales). The bars and dining areas are painted in bold, strong colours with work by local artists on the walls, open fires, books on shelves, fresh flowers and all manner of wooden dining chairs and tables and sofas on stripped boards or rugs. They always have three hand-pulled Cornish ales, currently from the likes of Skinners, St Austell and new favourites Cornish Crown, Harbour Brewing and Rebel Brewing. Also, about 20 wines by the glass or carafe and a couple of farm ciders; background music. The large, enclosed back garden has plenty of seats. Disabled access on ground floor only. If you stay in the comfortable, well appointed bedrooms, you'll have fine views of the rugged moors or the Atlantic Ocean just 500 metres away.

Impressive seasonal food includes starters such as gazpacho soup, St Austell Bay mussels with white wine, garlic and parsley, ploughman's with Westcombe cheddar, pickles and soda bread; mains such as duck leg with mash and gooseberry chutney, red gurnard with katsu curry and courgette chutney, featherblade steak with fries and rocket, lemon sole with samphire and caper and brown shrimp butter, and puddings such as carrot cake with mascarpone and strawberry parfait with yoghurt and lime sorbet. *Benchmark main dish: hake with mussels, cucumber and dill £21.00. Two-course evening meal £29.50.*

Free house ~ Licensees Charles and Edmund Inkin ~ Real ale ~ Open 8-11 ~ Bar food all day ~ Restaurant ~ Children welcome ~ Dogs allowed in bar & bedrooms ~ Bedrooms: £150

 HELFORD
Shipwrights Arms
SW7526 Map 1

(01326) 231235 – www.shipwrightshelford.co.uk
Off B3293 SE of Helston, via Mawgan; TR12 6JX

17th-c waterside inn with seats on terraces, attractively decorated bars, friendly service and tasty food

---

Surrounded by walks including a long-distance coast path that goes right past the front door, this thatched pub's lovely position is a big draw in summer. Sit on one of the many terraces that drop down to the water's edge and you'll enjoy a view of the beautiful wooded creek (at its best at high tide). You can moor at their pontoon and get a foot-ferry from Helford Passage. The bars have quite a nautical theme, with old navigation lamps, ship models, appropriate artworks and even the odd figurehead; antique pine and oak furniture sits on slate or bare-boarded floors and cushioned window seats have pretty cushions. Stools line the counter where they keep St Austell Tribute and a couple of guests such as Skinners Porthleven and Proper Job on handpump, 24 wines by the glass, 16 gins and ten malt whiskies; there's an open fire in winter.

Good food includes sandwiches (until 5pm), local scallops with black pudding, peas and truffle purée, beer-battered haddock and chips, shell-on prawns with garlic aioli, whole tempura squid with chilli and mango salsa and halloumi fries, local pasties, pan-fried hake with crushed new potatoes, and puddings such as dark chocolate brownie with dark chocolate sauce. In summer, their outside pizza oven is used daily and there's fresh local lobster and crab sandwiches, while roasts are plentiful in winter. *Benchmark main dish: Goan seafood curry £17.00. Two-course evening meal £22.00.*

Free house ~ Licensees Roger and Laura Fergus ~ Real ale ~ Open 11-11 ~ Bar food 12-3, 6-9; not Sun evening in winter ~ Restaurant ~ Children welcome ~ Dogs allowed in bar & restaurant

HELSTON
SW6522 Map 1

Halzephron ♀ 🛏
(01326) 240406 – www.halzephron-inn.co.uk

Gunwalloe, village about 4 miles S but not marked on many road maps; look for brown sign on A3083 alongside perimeter fence of RNAS Culdrose; TR12 7QB

Bustling pub in lovely spot with tasty bar food, local beers and good nearby walks; bedrooms

This is a traditional whitewashed country pub overlooking clifftop fields to the sea. The bar and dining areas are neatly kept and have an informal, friendly atmosphere, some fishing memorabilia, comfortable seating, a warm winter fire in a woodburning stove and a good range of drinks: Sharps Doom Bar and Skinners Porthleven on handpump along with three guests, nine wines by the glass, 40 malt whiskies and summer farm cider. The dining gallery seats up to 30 people; board games. Picnic-sets outside look across National Trust fields and countryside. The pretty bedrooms have country views and there are lovely coastal walks in both directions. Disabled access. This makes a perfect lunch break after a visit to nearby Church Cove with its sandy beach or to Gunwalloe fishing cove just 300 metres away.

Popular food includes lunchtime sandwiches and ploughman's plus seafood chowder, Indian-spiced whitebait, baked camembert and whole roasted bulb of garlic with redcurrant jelly and toasted ciabatta, smoked haddock fishcake with curry mayonnaise, local faggots with mash and onion gravy, five bean and sweet potato chilli with nachos and vegan cheese, confit duck leg with oriental noodles, vegetables and home-made plum sauce, harissa-spiced chicken with Moroccan salad, beer-battered cod with chips, peas and home-made tartare sauce, and puddings such as strawberry eton mess and sticky toffee pudding. *Benchmark main dish: beer-battered cod and chips £14.50. Two-course evening meal £20.00.*

Free house ~ Licensee Claire Murray ~ Real ale ~ Open 11-11; 12-10.30 Sun ~ Bar food 12-2 (3 Sun), 6-9 ~ Restaurant ~ Children welcome ~ Dogs allowed in bar & bedrooms ~ Bedrooms: £100

LANLIVERY
SX0759 Map 1

Crown 🛏
(01208) 872707 – www.thecrowninncornwall.co.uk

Signposted off A390 Lostwithiel–St Austell (tricky to find from other directions); PL30 5BT

Chatty atmosphere in nice old pub, with traditional rooms and well liked food and drink; bedrooms

Situated just ten minutes by car from the Eden Project, this characterful white-painted long house dates in part back to the 12th c. A good mix of customers includes both visitors and locals. The main bar has a woodburning stove in a huge fireplace, traditional settles on big flagstones, church and other wooden chairs around all sorts of tables, old Cornwall photographs and boarded ceilings with beams. Sharps Doom Bar and Skinners Betty Stogs plus a guest such as Harbour IPA on handpump, several wines by the glass and local cider. A couple of other rooms have high-backed black leather dining chairs and built-in cushioned pews, there's another (smaller) woodburning stove and a simply furnished conservatory. The porch has a huge well with a glass top and the quiet, pretty garden has picnic-sets. The bedrooms (in separate buildings) are clean and comfortable and overlook the rustic garden; breakfasts are good.

🍴 Pleasing food includes lunchtime sandwiches, herb-marinated grilled halloumi with hummus and roasted walnuts, squid with garlic mayonnaise, crispy fried whitebait, home-made fishcakes with salad and chilli sauce, pan-fried hake with salsa, vegetables and crushed potatoes, local scallops with bacon and garlic butter, mushroom and spinach tart topped with blue cheese, and pub classics such as beer-battered cod and chips and ham, egg and chips. Desserts include brownies, lemon tart and champagne jelly. The Sunday roasts are popular. *Benchmark main dish: chicken breast with a chimichurri dressing, sautéed potatoes and vegetables £12.80. Two-course evening meal £19.00.*

Free house ~ Licensee Nigel Wakeham ~ Real ale ~ Open 11.30-11; 12-10.30 Sun ~ Bar food 12-2.30, 6-9 ~ Restaurant ~ Children welcome but no under-14s at the bar ~ Dogs allowed in bar & bedrooms ~ Bedrooms: £99

LONGROCK SW5031 Map 1
Mexico Inn
(01736) 710625 – www.themexicoinn.com
Riverside; old coast road Penzance–Marazion; TR20 8JB

Granite-stone pub with rustic charm, seasonal food cooked by both licensees and a merry atmosphere

The open-plan rooms of this characterful local free house include one with leather tub chairs and a chesterfield sofa around a woodburning stove, as well as dining rooms with wheelback and wooden chairs around nice antique tables on bare boards, bold aqua-green and orange paintwork and bookshelves. There are stools against the counter where they serve Cornish Crown Causeway, St Austell Harlequin and Skinners Lushingtons on handpump, several wines by the glass, local gin, farm cider and home-made pink lemonade and ginger beer; background music, darts and board games. At the front are a few picnic-sets, while the extended back garden has a terrace and a large area growing herbs; there are more seats here too. Readers are quick to praise this cheerful pub for its chatty, easy-going atmosphere, genuine welcome and enjoyable home-cooked food.

🍴 Cooked by the enthusiastic chef-patron, the good, high-quality food includes whitebait with harissa mayonnaise, chicken liver pâté with sticky fig and toast, curried cauliflower fritters, grilled mackerel with beetroot, green beans, potato salad and tomatoes, grilled sirloin with dauphinoise potatoes, garlic butter trencher, tomatoes, green beans and red wine jus, slow-cooked lamb ragout and merguez sausage with saffron rice, courgettes and zaatar, and puddings such as chocolate brownie with raspberries and pistachios and frozen coconut parfait with mango marinated strawberries. *Benchmark main dish: brisket and burger with toppings, pickles and chips £13.50. Two-course evening meal £20.00.*

Free house ~ Licensee Tom Symons ~ Real ale ~ Open 11.30-11.30 (midnight Fri, Sat); 12-11 Sun ~ Bar food 12-2, 6-9; 12-2.45, 5.30-8 Sun ~ Restaurant ~ Children allowed in restaurant ~ Dogs allowed in bar

'Children welcome' means the pub says it lets children inside without any special restriction. If it allows them in, but to restricted areas such as an eating area or family room, we specify this. Places with separate restaurants often let children use them, and hotels usually let children into public areas such as lounges. Some pubs impose an evening time limit – let us know if you find one earlier than 9pm.

LOSTWITHIEL

SX1059 Map 1

Globe ♀ ◼

(01208) 872501

North Street (close to medieval bridge); PL22 0EG

Traditional local with interesting food and drink, friendly staff and suntrap back courtyard

This rambling inn is situated near a quaint 13th-c church and ancient river bridge. The unassuming and friendly bar, which is long and narrow, has a mix of pubby tables and seats, local photographs on pale blue plank panelling at one end and nice, mainly local prints (for sale) on walls above a coal-effect stove at the snug inner end; there's also a small front alcove. The ornately carved bar counter, with comfortable leatherette stools, dispenses Sharps Atlantic and Original and Skinners Betty Stogs on handpump, ten reasonably priced wines by the glass, 20 malt whiskies and two local ciders; background music, darts, board games and TV. The sheltered back courtyard is not large but has some attractive and unusual plants, and is a real suntrap (with an extendable awning and outside heaters). Staff are friendly and welcoming. You can park in several of the nearby streets or the (free) town car park.

 From a seasonal menu, the reliably good food includes Fowey mussels in velouté or tomato marinière sauce, spinach falafels with tahini and pitta bread, seafood chowder, vegetarian or pork and beef burger with trimmings, barbecued ribs, battered cod and chips, breaded scampi, and puddings such as ginger and black treacle sponge and apple pie with smoked cheddar cheese. *Benchmark main dish: home-made lasagne £10.00. Two-course evening meal £18.00.*

Free house ~ Licensee William Erwin ~ Real ale ~ Open 12-11; 12-midnight Fri, Sat ~ Bar food 12-9; maybe 12-2, 6.30-8.30 out of season ~ Restaurant ~ Children welcome ~ Dogs allowed in bar ~ Bedrooms: £90

MOUSEHOLE

SW4726 Map 1

Old Coastguard ⚹ ♀ ⛱

(01736) 731222 – www.oldcoastguardhotel.co.uk

The Parade (edge of village, Newlyn coast road); TR19 6PR

Cornwall Dining Pub of the Year

Lovely position for civilised inn with an easy-going atmosphere, good choice of wines and first rate food; bedrooms

This well run inn on the edge of an old fishing village is a charming (and very popular) place to stay, with 14 comfortable bedrooms offering views towards St Michael's Mount and the Lizard. The bar rooms have boldly coloured walls hung with paintings of sailing boats and local scenes, stripped floorboards and an atmosphere of informal but civilised comfort. The Upper Deck houses the bar and the restaurant, with a nice mix of antique dining chairs around oak and distressed pine tables, lamps on big barrel tables and chairs to either side of the log fire, topped by a vast bressumer beam. St Austell Tribute and a couple of guests such as Padstow Windjammer on handpump, 25 wines by the glass or carafe, a big choice of gins, vodkas and whiskies, a farm cider and a good choice of soft drinks. The Lower Deck has glass windows running the length of the building, several deep sofas and armchairs, and shelves of books and games; background music. The garden is rather special, with tropical palms and dracaena, a path leading down to rock pools and seats on the terrace looking over the sea. Disabled access.

Breakfasts are highly regarded. Sister pubs are the Gurnards Head (also Cornwall) and the Griffin at Felinfach (Wales).

🍴 From a well judged menu, the modern food includes Cornish asparagus with Rosary goats cheese, romesco sauce and hazelnuts, cured scallops with pickled rhubarb, fennel and roe, crispy lamb with peas and anchovies, tempura courgette flower with English feta, spring vegetables and a duck egg, Porthilly mussels with white wine and garlic, hake and octopus with cannellini bean and seaweed broth and nduja mayonnaise, and puddings such as crème brûlée and marmalade iced parfait with dark chocolate; they also do a set Sunday lunch. *Benchmark main dish: lamb rump with olive oil potatoes, peas, sweetbreads, mint and spinach £22.00. Two-course evening meal £27.00.*

Free house ~ Licensees Charles and Edmund Inkin ~ Real ale ~ Open 8am-11pm ~ Bar food 12-3, 5.30-9 ~ Restaurant ~ Children welcome ~ Dogs allowed in bar & bedrooms ~ Bedrooms: £157

MYLOR BRIDGE   SW8137   Map 1
Pandora ♀
(01326) 372678 – www.pandorainn.com

Restronguet Passage: from A39 in Penryn, take turning signposted Mylor Church, Mylor Bridge, Flushing and go straight through Mylor Bridge following Restronguet Passage signs; or from A39 further N, at or near Perranarworthal, take turning signposted Mylor, Restronguet, then follow Restronguet Weir signs, but turn left down hill at Restronguet Passage sign; TR11 5ST

Idyllically placed waterside inn with lots of atmosphere in beamed and flagstoned rooms, and all-day food

This medieval thatched pub has rambling, interconnected rooms with low beams, beautifully polished big flagstones and three large log fires in high hearths (to protect them against tidal floods); also, cosy alcoves, cushioned built-in wall seats and chairs, maps, yacht pictures, oars and ships' wheels; church candles help with the lighting. There's also a back cabin bar with pale farmhouse chairs, high-backed settles and a model galleon in a big glass cabinet. St Austell Hicks, Proper Job, Trelawny and Tribute on handpump, 23 wines by the glass and 18 malt whiskies. Upstairs, the attractive dining room has exposed oak vaulting, dark tables and chairs on pale oak flooring and large brass bells and lanterns. Because of the pub's popularity, parking is extremely difficult at peak times – however, you can also reach it by walking or cycling along the estuary bordered by wild flowers or arrive (as some customers do) by boat. In fine weather you can sit with your drink on the long floating pontoon and watch children crabbing. Wheelchair access.

🍴 As well as breakfast (9.30-11am) and sandwiches (until 5pm), the popular all-day food includes local mussels with cream, cider, honey and spring onions, ham hock with spiced apple chutney and toasted focaccia, crayfish salad with avocado mayonnaise, ploughman's or vegan board, home-made burger in a brioche bun with chips, breaded scampi with chips, roast butternut squash risotto, and puddings such as pistachio and golden syrup sponge, strawberry cheesecake and toffee eton mess. Picnic boxes are also available. *Benchmark main dish: fish pie £14.25. Two-course evening meal £21.00.*

St Austell ~ Tenants John Milan and Steven Bellman ~ Real ale ~ Open 9.30am-11pm ~ Bar food 12-9.30 ~ Restaurant ~ Children welcome ~ Dogs allowed in bar

---

The 🍺 symbol shows pubs that keep their beer unusually well, have a particularly good range or brew their own.

PENZANCE
Turks Head
SW4730   Map 1

(01736) 363093 – www.turksheadpenzance.co.uk

At top of main street, by big domed building turn left down Chapel Street; TR18 4AF

Bustling atmosphere in well run pub with popular food and beer

There's been a Turks Head here for more than 700 years – though most of the original building was destroyed by a Spanish raiding party in the 16th c. The current incarnation is a cheerful, honest establishment that appeals to visitors as much as locals. The bar has old flat irons, jugs and so forth hanging from the beams, pottery above the wood-effect panelling, wall seats and tables and a couple of elbow-rests around central pillars; background music and board games. Sharps Doom Bar, Skinners Betty Stogs and a couple of guests on handpump, ten wines by the glass, a dozen gins and 12 malt whiskies. The suntrap back garden has big urns of flowers, seats under a giant parasol and a barbecue.

Pleasing food includes lunchtime sandwiches, greek salad, caesar salad, Newlyn crab salad, sweet potato, butternut squash and red lentil curry, Cornish seafood pie, gammon steak with fried egg and skin-on fries, lasagne, seafood tagliatelle, confit duck leg with braised red cabbage, roasted carrots and mustard mash, burger (vegan, cajun chicken or steak) in a brioche bun with skin-on fries, and puddings. *Benchmark main dish: beer-battered fish and chips £14.95. Two-course evening meal £24.00.*

Punch ~ Lease Jonathan and Helen Gibbard ~ Real ale ~ Open 11.30am-midnight; 12-11 Sun ~ Bar food 12-2.30, 6-10 ~ Restaurant ~ Children allowed in restaurant ~ Dogs allowed in bar ~ Bedrooms

POLGOOTH
Polgooth Inn
SW9950   Map 1

(01726) 74089 – www.polgoothinn.co.uk

Well signed off A390 W of St Austell; Ricketts Lane; PL26 7DA

Welcoming pub with plenty of space for eating and drinking, Cornish ales, well liked food and seats on big front terrace

Spacious and inviting, this old country pub just outside a small village also serves high quality food. The spreading, linked rooms have dark beams and timbering, open fires and woodburning stoves. Seating ranges from high-backed settles to tartan upholstered dining chairs, banquettes to nice farmhouse seats (all around wooden tables on carpet), and there are old agricultural tools and photos on painted or exposed-stone walls. St Austell Cornish Best, HSD, Proper Job, Tribute and a seasonal guest on handpump, Korev lager, good wines by the glass and a gin menu. A dining extension with country kitchen furniture has a modern woodburner against a black brick wall, contemporary lighting and french doors to the terrace. Outside, you'll find picnic tables with plenty of umbrellas on grass (some under an awning), separate dining booths and a steadily expanding kitchen garden. There's live music on Sunday afternoons in summer, and it's a short drive to the Lost Gardens of Heligan.

The interesting, seasonal food (using produce from their own garden) includes freshly baked rolls, crispy breaded butterflied sardines, pink peppercorn and dill-crusted goats cheese, Indian-spiced vegan 'brisket' with lentil dhal, giant smoked haddock fishcake with a soft poached egg and hollandaise, steak, tattie and turnip pie, salt and pepper squid, seafood bouillabaisse, fresh crab specials, and puddings such as lemon posset and sticky toffee pudding with toffee sauce and clotted cream. Also, Sunday roasts and Cornish cream teas available all day, every day.

Benchmark main dish: barbecue brisket of beef with coleslaw and chips £16.50.
Two-course evening meal £21.00.

St Austell ~ Tenant Alex and Tanya Williams ~ Real ale ~ Open 10am-11pm; 11-11 Sun ~
Bar food 12-9.30 ~ Restaurant ~ Children welcome ~ Dogs allowed in bar

POLKERRIS   SX0952   Map 1

Rashleigh

(01726) 813991 – www.therashleighinnpolkerris.co.uk
Signposted off A3082 Fowey–St Austell; PL24 2TL

Lovely beachside spot with sizeable sun terrace, six real ales and
quite a choice of food

This former fishermen's tavern has a smashing location, on the edge of
a fine little beach with a restored jetty and just off the South West Coast
Path (renowned for its striking scenery). Inside, the bar has comfortably
cushioned chairs around dark wooden tables at the front, and similar
furnishings, local photographs and a winter log fire at the back. There's
Padstow Pride and Windjammer, Skinners Betty Stogs, Timothy Taylors
Landlord and guests from Dartmoor, Sharps and Tintagel on handpump, plus
ten wines by the glass, three farm ciders and organic soft drinks; background
music. The splendid view from the restaurant and front terrace stretches
right away to the far side of St Austell and Mevagissey bays. There's plenty
of parking in either the pub's own car park or the large village one. The Eden
Project is a short drive away.

Changing food includes lunchtime sandwiches, halloumi chips, whitebait with
garlic mayonnaise, sea bream with new potatoes, a proper steak pie with mash
and gravy, Fowey river mussels, sun-blush tomato and brie quiche, vegan nachos with
veg chilli and vegan cheese, and puddings such as raspberry and white chocolate
cheesecake and sticky toffee pudding with clotted cream or ice-cream. *Benchmark*
main dish: beer-battered fish and chips £12.00. Two-course evening meal £18.00.

Free house ~ Licensees Jon and Samantha Spode ~ Real ale ~ Open 11-11 (10 winter) ~
Bar food 12-3, 6-9; summer snacks 3-5 ~ Restaurant ~ Children allowed in restaurant ~
Dogs allowed in bar

POLPERRO   SX2050   Map 1

Blue Peter

(01503) 272743
Quay Road; PL13 2QZ

Friendly pub overlooking harbour with fishing paraphernalia,
real ales and carefully prepared food

This family-run inn right by Polperro's busy harbour is known locally as
'the Blue'. Traditional furnishings include a small winged settle and a
polished pew, wooden flooring, fishing regalia, photographs and pictures by
local artists, lots of candles and a solid wood bar counter. There's St Austell
Tribute and Sharps Own plus up to three guests from Cornish or Devon
breweries on handpump and a growing choice of gins and rums, served by
the helpful, long-serving licensees. One window seat looks down on the
harbour, while another looks out past rocks to the sea. Background music
and board games. There are seats on the terrace outside and more in an
amphitheatre-style area upstairs. The pub is as enjoyable and as popular as
ever, so expect to find it packed at peak times. Note that families must use
the upstairs room only.

The reasonably priced food includes sandwiches (the crab is popular), crab bruschetta with lime and yoghurt dressing, salt and pepper squid, chickpea and vegetable burger with sweet chilli dipping sauce, tempura-style fish and chips, honey and cider roasted ham with eggs and pineapple chutney, a fresh fish dish of the day, a pie of the day, chicken tikka with minted rice, couscous-stuffed red pepper, and puddings. *Benchmark main dish: seafood platter £18.75. Two-course evening meal £21.00.*

Free house ~ Real ale ~ Open 11-11; 12-10.30 Sun ~ Bar food 12-2.30, 6-8.30; 12-9 in high season ~ Children in upstairs family room only ~ Dogs allowed in bar

PORT ISAAC   SX0080   Map 1
Port Gaverne Inn 🛏
(01208) 880244 – www.portgavernehotel.co.uk
Port Gaverne signposted from Port Isaac and from B3314 E of Pendoggett; PL29 3SQ

Bustling small hotel with a proper bar and real ales, well liked food in several dining areas and seats in the garden; bedrooms

This is a lovely spot just back from the sea in a small fishing cove, just round the headland from Port Isaac. The chatty bar has low beams, flagstones and carpeting, some exposed stone, a big log fire and St Austell Proper Job and Tribute, Skinners Betty Stogs and Timothy Taylors Landlord on handpump, nine wines by the glass, 40 gins, 20 malt whiskies and farm cider. The lounge has some interesting old local photographs. You can eat in the bar or in the 'Captain's Cabin', which is a little room where everything is shrunk to scale (old oak chest, model sailing ship, even the prints on the white stone walls). There are seats and tables under parasols at the front, with more in the terraced garden. The 15 individually furnished and comfortable bedrooms have plenty of character, though the stairs up to most of them are fairly steep (staff will carry your luggage). Many come here for lunch after blowing the cobwebs away on a walk along the splendid and usually bracing surrounding clifftops. The TV series *Doc Martin* is filmed in the village and surroundings.

 Good quality food includes lunchtime sandwiches, crab and lobster tart with apple, beetroot and cress, shell-on prawns with chilli gremolata, crispy cod cheeks with pickled vegetables and garlic mayonnaise, lamb chop with pomegranate, mint oil and curd, dry-aged local steaks with garlic butter, and puddings such as warm chocolate pudding with honeycomb and lime and orange crème catalan with crystallised pistachios. *Benchmark main dish: whole Cornish mackerel with courgette and basil aioli £16.00. Two-course evening meal £23.00.*

Free house ~ Licensee Jackie Barnard ~ Real ale ~ Open 11am-midnight ~ Bar food 12-2, 6-9 ~ Restaurant ~ Children welcome ~ Dogs allowed in bar & bedrooms ~ Bedrooms: £195

ST IVES   SW5441   Map 1
Queens 🛏
(01736) 796468 – www.queenshotelstives.com
High Street; TR26 1RR

Bustling inn with a spacious bar, open fire, real ales and tasty food; bedrooms

The summer window boxes and hanging baskets adorning this late Georgian inn in the heart of St Ives are quite a sight. Inside, the open-plan, spreading bar has a relaxed atmosphere, all sorts of wooden chairs around scrubbed tables on bare floorboards, tartan banquettes on either side of the

Victorian fireplace, a wall of barometers above a leather chesterfield sofa and some brown leather armchairs; also, fresh flowers and candles on tables and on the mantelpiece above the open fire. Red-painted bar chairs line the white marble-topped counter where they serve St Austell HSD and Tribute on handpump, 12 wines by the glass (including a local one), a good choice of gins and rums and farm cider; background music, board games and TV for sports events. Bedrooms are attractive, airy and simply furnished, with Cornish artwork on the walls and some period furniture. Plenty of regulars and visitors crowd into the bar here to enjoy the local ales and popular food – and it's handy for the harbour, too.

From a seasonal menu, good food includes sandwiches (until 3pm), crispy whitebait with lemon mayo, goats cheese and beetroot salad with balsamic dressing, vegetable lasagne, a choice of burgers with onion rings and chips, honey-roast ham and free-range eggs, local sausages with mash and onion gravy, chicken bhuna curry with rice and naan, and puddings such as sticky toffee pudding with clotted cream and apple, raisin and cinnamon crumble with vanilla ice-cream. *Benchmark main dish: beef stew with dumplings £13.50. Two-course evening meal £20.00.*

St Austell ~ Tenant Neythan Hayes ~ Real ale ~ Open 11-11 ~ Bar food 12-3, 6-9; 12-9 Sun ~ Children allowed in bar ~ Dogs allowed in bar ~ Bedrooms: £150

ST MERRYN   SW8874   Map 1

Cornish Arms

(01841) 532700 – www.rickstein.com/eat-with-us/the-cornish-arms
Churchtown (B3276 towards Padstow); PL28 8ND

Bustling pub with plenty of space in bar and dining rooms, real ales, popular food, friendly service and seats outside

Part of Rick Stein's Cornish empire, this is run as a traditional local pub – a place for good beer, unpretentious food and a laid-back atmosphere. The main door leads into a sizeable informal area with a pool table and plenty of cushioned wall seating; to the left, a light, airy dining room overlooks the terrace. There's an upright modern woodburner, photographs of the sea and former games teams, and pale wooden dining chairs around tables on quarry tiles. This leads to two more linked rooms with ceiling joists; the first has pubby furniture on huge flagstones while the end room has more cushioned wall seating, contemporary seats and tables and parquet flooring. There's also a dining room to the back. St Austell Proper Job, Trelawny and Tribute on handpump, a dozen wines by the glass, a local gin and a farm cider, background music, board games and TV. Service is friendly. The window boxes are pretty and there are picnic-sets on a side terrace and on grass. Disabled access.

Quite a choice of seasonal food includes Cornish crab sandwich, local sardines with tomato, garlic and thyme dressing, half-pint of prawns, ham, egg and chips, barbecue chicken salad, scampi in a basket, lemon sole goujons, Pondicherri cod curry, local rump steak with chips, and some classic desserts such as sticky toffee pudding and Cornish ice-creams. *Benchmark main dish: steak and ale pie with mash and summer vegetables £13.95. Two-course evening meal £20.00.*

St Austell ~ Tenant Siebe Richards ~ Real ale ~ Open 11.30-11 ~ Bar food 12-3, 5-9 ~ Children welcome ~ Dogs allowed in bar & restaurant

---

Bedroom prices are for high summer. Even then you may get reductions for more than one night, or weekends (outside tourist areas). Winter special rates are common, and many inns reduce bedroom prices if you have a full evening meal.

TREVAUNANCE COVE   SW7251 Map 1

Driftwood Spars 🍺 🛏️

(01872) 552428 – www.driftwoodspars.co.uk

Off B3285 in St Agnes; Quay Road; TR5 0RT

**Friendly inn with plenty of history, own microbrewery, a wide range
of other drinks and popular food; nearby beach; bedrooms**

This three-bar pub is close to a dramatic cove and beach, so it can get
pretty busy at peak times. The fine choice of drinks here served by
knowledgeable, friendly staff includes their own-brewed Driftwood Spars
ales plus guests from breweries such as Atlantic, Firebrand and Harbour
on handpump (they hold three beer festivals a year), plus 20 malt whiskies,
15 rums, 20 gins and several wines by the glass. The three small bars are
timbered with massive ships' spars (the masts of great sailing ships, many of
which were wrecked along this coast), and furnishings include dark wooden
farmhouse and tub chairs and settles around tables of different sizes, padded
stools by the counter, old ship prints, lots of nautical and wreck memorabilia
and woodburning stoves; table football. It's said that an old smugglers'
tunnel leads from behind the bar up through the cliff. The modern dining
room overlooks the cove. The 15 bedrooms are attractive and comfortable
and some have fine views. The summer hanging baskets are pretty and there
are seats in the garden, next to the Crib Shack – a blue-painted container
dispensing drinks and snacks. Disabled access.

🍴 A good choice of food includes sandwiches and wraps, sourdough bruschetta,
crispy fried whitebait, pea and mint arancini, Driftwood Spars ale-battered
fish and chips, burger in a brioche bun with ale mayonnaise, dressed Cornish crab,
half St Agnes lobster with chips and salad, teriyaki rice noodles with broccoli,
butternut squash, mushrooms and tomatoes, Sri Lankan chicken curry, and puddings
such as chocolate brownie with vanilla bean ice-cream and lemon tart with local
strawberries. *Benchmark main dish: beer-battered fish and chips £12.95. Two-course
evening meal £20.00.*

Own brew ~ Licensee Louise Treseder ~ Real ale ~ Open 11-11; 11-10 Sun ~ Bar food
12-2.30, 6-9; 12-8 Sun ~ Restaurant ~ Children welcome (over-14s only in the main bar) ~
Dogs allowed in bar, restaurant & bedrooms ~ Bedrooms: £125

Also Worth a Visit in Cornwall

Besides the fully inspected pubs, you might like to try these pubs that
have been recommended to us and described by readers. Do tell us what
you think of them: feedback@goodguides.com

ALTARNUN   SX2280
Kings Head (01566) 86241
Five Lanes; PL15 7RX Old beamed
village pub; two or three West Country ales
and generous helpings of reasonably priced
pubby food from jacket potatoes up including
popular Sun carvery, carpeted lounge set for
dining with woodburner, slate floor in public
bar with another fire, friendly staff and ghost
of former landlady Peggy Bray; background
music; children and dogs (in bar) welcome,
picnic-sets on front terrace and in small
patio, comfortable bedrooms, open (and
food) all day, handy for A30.

ALTARNUN   SX2083
⭐ **Rising Sun** (01566) 86636
*NW; village signed off A39 just W of
A395 junction; PL15 7SN* Tucked-away
16th-c pub with traditionally furnished main
bar, low beams, slate flagstones and several
woodburners, well kept Penpont St Nonnas,
Skinners Lushingtons and guests, real cider
and nice wines by the glass, highly rated food
including local seafood and daily specials,
home-made bread, good crab sandwiches
too, efficient friendly service, restaurant;
background music, pool; well behaved
children and dogs (in bar) welcome, seats
on suntrap terrace and in beer garden,

pétanque, camping field, nice village with beautiful church, open all day weekends.

ANTONY
SX4054

★ Carew Arms (01752) 814440

Off A374; PL11 3AB Welcoming family-friendly pub with wide floorboards and rustic wooden tables and an open fire, Exeter Avocet and St Austell Tribute on handpump and ten wines by the glass, highly regarded imaginative food with plenty of fish and seafood alongside burgers and steaks, friendly staff, old skittle area is now a cosy dining room; café and farm shop downstairs, dogs allowed in bar, open all day.

BODINNICK
SX1352

Old Ferry (01726) 870237

Across the water from Fowey; coming by road, to avoid the ferry queue, turn left as you go downhill – car park on left before pub; PL23 1LX Welcoming 17th-c inn just up from the river with lovely views from terrace, dining room and some of its 11 comfortable bedrooms; traditional bar with nautical memorabilia, old photographs and woodburner, back room hewn into the rock, well kept Sharps ales and at least one guest, nice wines, good food from lunchtime sandwiches up including daily specials and children's menu, helpful staff; good circular walks, lane by pub in front of ferry slipway is extremely steep and parking limited.

BODMIN
SX0767

Hole in the Wall (01208) 72397

Crockwell Street; PL31 2DS Former debtors' prison with masses of bric-a-brac including old rifles, pistols and swords (note the stuffed lion), beams and arched 18th-c stonework, coal fire, well kept Butcombe, Sharps and guests; and enjoyable food, friendly staff and regulars, upstairs dining/function room; Thurs quiz; children and dogs welcome, well planted courtyard garden with small stream, open all day.

BOSCASTLE
SX0991

★ Cobweb (01840) 250278

B3263, just E of harbour; PL35 0HE Cosily dim-lit two-bar pub with plenty of character, hundreds of old bottles and jugs hanging from heavy beams, two or three high-backed settles, flagstones and dark stone walls, nice log fire, well kept beers including St Austell Tribute, decent wine choice, wide selection of simple good quality food at bargain prices, quick friendly service, pub games, sizeable family room with second fire; dogs welcome, open all day.

BOSCASTLE
SX0990

★ Napoleon (01840) 250204

High Street, top of village; PL35 0BD Welcoming 16th-c thick-walled cottage at the top of this steep quaint village (fine views halfway up); cosy rooms on different levels, slate floors, oak beams and log fires, interesting Napoleon prints and lots of knick-knacks, good food including daily specials in bar areas or small restaurant, well kept St Austell ales tapped from the cask, Healey's cider and decent wines; traditional games; background music, sing-along Tues, quiz every other Weds and bingo on Fri in quieter months; children and dogs welcome, small covered terrace and large sheltered garden, open all day (food all day in season).

BOSCASTLE
SX0991

Wellington (01840) 250202

Harbour; PL35 0AQ Old hotel's long beamed and carpeted bar, good varied choice of fairly priced food including vegan menu (other special diets catered for), Cornish ales kept well, nice coffee and cream teas, roaring woodburner, upstairs gallery area for dining with a more upmarket evening menu (also available in the bar); Weds folk night, quiz first Mon of month; children and dogs (in bar) welcome, big secluded garden, bedrooms and apartments in adjacent mill, Museum of Witchcraft and Magic nearby, open all day.

CADGWITH
SW7214

★ Cadgwith Cove Inn (01326) 290513

Down very narrow lane off A3083 S of Helston; limited parking but nearby car park; TR12 7JX Friendly little pub in fishing cove with lovely walks in either direction; simply furnished front rooms with bench seating on parquet, log fires, local photos and nautical memorabilia, well kept Atlantic, Sharps, Skinners and a monthly changing guest ale, popular pubby food and a board of locally landed fish/seafood (can be pricey); background music, folk night Tues, local singers (sea shanties) Fri, TV, Cornish euchre and board games; children and dogs welcome, front terrace overlooking old fishermen's sheds, seven refurbished comfortable bedrooms with sea views, coastal walks, open all day.

CALSTOCK
SX4368

Tamar (01822) 832487

The Quay; PL18 9QA Cheerful and relaxed 17th-c local on the Tamar and overlooked by its imposing viaduct; recently renovated bar area with beams, dark stripped stone and newly revealed original flagstones; more modern back dining room, good straightforward food and well kept West Country ales including Sharps Doom Bar, reasonable prices and friendly prompt service; some live music, sports TV; children (away from bar) and well behaved dogs welcome (away from restaurant), nicely furnished

---

You can send reports directly to us at feedback@goodguides.com

terrace, hilly walk or ferry to Cotehele (NT), open all day in summer, all day Fri-Sun winter.

CHAPEL AMBLE SW9975
Maltsters Arms (01208) 812473
Off A39 NE of Wadebridge; PL27 6EU
Country pub-restaurant with good pubby food and Sun lunchtime carvery, friendly accommodating staff, ales such as Sharps Doom Bar, Weston's cider, beams, stripped stone and painted half-panelling, woodburner, modern back extension; quiz night Weds; children and dogs (on slate-floored area) welcome, seats outside.

CHARLESTOWN SX0351
Harbourside (01726) 67955
Part of Pier House Hotel; PL25 3NJ
Glass-fronted split-level warehouse conversion alongside the renovated Pier House Hotel (also worth a visit); great spot looking over classic little harbour and its historic sailing ships; St Austell ales and guests, popular reasonably priced food including burgers and pizzas, friendly efficient service; live music every Sat, sports TVs, pool; children and dogs welcome, interesting film-set conservation village with shipwreck museum, good walks, parking away from pub, open (and food) all day.

CHARLESTOWN SX0351
Rashleigh Arms (01726) 73635
Charlestown Road; PL25 3NJ Modernised 19th-c inn with public bar, lounge and dining area; five well kept St Austell ales and good wine choice, popular fairly priced food including Tues curry night and Thurs steak night, quick friendly service; background music, sports TV; children welcome, dogs in bar, disabled facilities, front terrace, eight bedrooms (some with sea views), ten more in nearby Georgian house, Grade-II listed car park (site of old coal storage yards), short walk to attractive harbour with tall ships, open (and food) all day.

COMFORD SW7339
Fox & Hounds (01209) 820251
Comford; A393/B3298; TR16 6AX
Rambling low-beamed roadside pub; stripped stone and painted panelling, rugs on flagstones, mix of old and new furniture, woodburners, good range of well liked freshly made food from pub favourites up including daily specials and Sun carvery, well kept St Austell ales; background music, pool and darts; children and dogs (on leads) welcome, disabled facilities, nice floral displays at front, picnic-sets in back garden, open (and food) all day in season.

CONSTANTINE SW7328
★Trengilly Wartha (01326) 340332
Nancenoy; A3083 S of Helston, signposted Gweek near RNAS Culdrose, then fork right after Gweek; OS Sheet 204 map reference 731282; TR11 5RP

Popular friendly inn in several acres of gardens, long low-beamed main bar with woodburner, Cornish beers and cider, good wines by the glass, 80 malt whiskies, well liked food using local fish and shellfish, cosy bistro, conservatory family room, table football, quiz and jamming nights; dogs welcome, terrace with ivy-clad pergola, other seats under large parasols, lots of surrounding walks, bedrooms, safari tents and stable facilities, should you decide to turn up on horseback, open all day weekends.

COVERACK SW7818
Paris (01326) 280258
The Cove; TR12 6SX Comfortable Edwardian seaside inn above harbour in beautiful fishing village; carpeted L-shaped bar with log fire serving well kept St Austell ales and Healey's cider, large relaxed dining room with nautical colour scheme and spectacular bay views, wide choice of enjoyable food from sandwiches to good fresh fish, Sun lunchtime carvery, helpful cheery staff, model of namesake ship (wrecked nearby in 1899); popular Weds quiz, pool, background music, children and dogs (in bar) welcome, more sea views from garden and the four bedrooms, limited parking.

CRACKINGTON HAVEN SX1496
Coombe Barton (01840) 230345
Off A39 Bude–Camelford; EX23 0JG
Extended old inn in beautiful setting overlooking splendid sandy bay (fine sunsets); much enjoyed food from shortish fairly priced menu (booking advised), up to four rotating Cornish ales and good choice of other drinks, efficient friendly service; occasional quiz nights in winter, pool and darts; children welcome, dogs in bar, picnic-sets on side terrace, lovely cliff walks, roomy bedrooms and a self-catering lodge, open all day.

CROWS NEST SX2669
Crows Nest (01579) 345930
Signed off B3254 N of Liskeard; OS Sheet 201 map reference 263692; PL14 5JQ Characterful and welcoming little 17th-c pub; well kept St Austell ales, decent wines and good home-made pubby food from sandwiches up, Thurs steak night, bowed beams hung with stirrups, brasses and so forth, exposed stonework and big open fire, chatty locals; quiz night last Weds of month, background music, outside loos; children and dogs welcome, picnic-sets on terrace by quiet lane, handy for Bodmin Moor walks, open all day weekends.

CUBERT SW7857
★Smugglers Den (01637) 830209
Off A3075 S of Newquay; TR8 5PY Big open-plan 16th-c thatched pub tucked away in small hamlet; enjoyable locally sourced food from pub classics to daily fish specials (and a separate Pizza & Grill restaurant

with large deck in summer months) and up to four beers, including St Austell Tribute, from barrel-fronted counter, several wines by the glass, friendly staff, neat ranks of tables, dim lighting, stripped stone and heavy beam-and-plank ceilings, West Country pictures and seafaring memorabilia, steps down to huge inglenook, another step to big side dining room, also a little snug area with woodburner; background music, children and dogs (in bar) welcome, small front courtyard and terrace (both decked) with nice country views, beer garden and play area, camping opposite, open all day in summer.

DULOE   SX2358
Plough (01503) 262556
B3254 N of Looe; PL14 4PN Popular restauranty pub with three country-chic linked dining rooms, woodburners, dark polished slate floors, good food using locally sourced produce (booking advisable), well kept St Austell, Sharps and summer guests, Cornish Orchards' cider and ten wines by the glass, friendly helpful service; unobtrusive background music; children and dogs welcome, picnic-sets on grass out by road, closed Tues lunchtime.

EDMONTON   SW9672
★ **Quarryman** (01208) 816444
Off A39 just W of Wadebridge bypass; PL27 7JA Welcoming busy family-run pub adjoining small, pretty separately owned courtyard complex of 20 self-catering holiday lets in Cornish stone cottages; three-room beamed bar with interesting decorations including old sporting memorabilia, enjoyable food from short but varied and frequently changing menu, well kept ales such as Exeter, Padstow and Skinners plus guests, decent wines by the glass, efficient friendly service; sports TV; well behaved children and dogs (on slate-floored area) allowed, picnic-sets in front and slate courtyard behind with fish pond, open all day.

EGLOSHAYLE   SX0071
Earl of St Vincent (01208) 814807
Off A389, just outside Wadebridge; PL27 6HT Pretty flower-decked beamed dining pub with over 200 working antique clocks (many chiming), also golfing memorabilia, art deco ornaments, old pictures and rich furnishings, woodburner, enjoyable traditional home-made food from sandwiches to steaks, St Austell ales and Healey's cider; background music, outside loos; well behaved children allowed, no dogs inside, lovely garden with picnic-sets.

FALMOUTH   SW8032
Beerwolf Books (01326) 618474
Bells Court, off Market St; TR11 3AZ Stairs up to intriguing pub-cum-bookshop hidden down little alley in centre of town; a former working men's club with raftered ceilings and eclectic mix of furniture on bare boards, large range of well kept changing beers and ciders, plus craft beers, decent coffee, no food but can bring your own, friendly laid-back atmosphere; games including table tennis and pinball; children and dogs welcome, two picnic-sets outside, open all day.

FALMOUTH   SW8033
Boathouse (01326) 315425
Trevethan Hill/Webber Hill; TR11 2AG Two-level pub with buoyant local atmosphere and harbour views, four well kept changing beers featuring some smaller Cornish brewers, good range of other drinks and enjoyable home-made food (booking recommended), including fresh fish/seafood and Sun roasts, friendly service; background and occasional live music; children (till 8.30pm) and dogs welcome (except dining room), tables outside on patio, closed weekday lunchtimes in winter, otherwise open all day.

FALMOUTH   SW8132
★ **Chain Locker** (01326) 311085
Custom House Quay; TR11 3HH Refurbished 16th-c pub in fine spot by inner harbour; St Austell ales, guest beers and nice wines by the glass, good food from sandwiches and sharing plates to fresh local fish/seafood, friendly efficient young staff, bare boards and flagstones in nautically themed bar with plenty to look at, woodburners, upstairs restaurant (they have a lift) with two balconies taking in the views; background music, friendly; well behaved children and dogs (in bar) welcome, quayside tables under parasols, six well appointed boutique bedrooms, open all day from 8am.

FALMOUTH   SW8033
★ **Chintz Symposium** 07538 006495
High Street/Brewery Yard; TR11 2BY Upstairs bar with Alice in Wonderland-inspired décor, welcoming and relaxed and run by three friends; wood floors, rafters, comfortable plain furniture and hot little stove, plenty of quirky features including pitched ceiling decorated with patchwork of wallpaper and prints, a gold room hidden behind a bookcase and loos with dinosaur and circus-tent themes; a couple of changing

---

local ales, plenty of bottled beers, Healey's cider and 15 wines by the glass from carefully chosen list, also good range of spirits (some Cornish ones), cheese and charcuterie boards, friendly service; live music (every Thurs, Fri and Sat evenings) and other events, board games; children and dogs (theirs is Pig) welcome, courtyard, roof terrace, open daily from 3pm; the Hand craft beer bar is below.

FALMOUTH
SW8032
Seven Stars
(01326) 312111
The Moor (centre); TR11 3QA Quirky 17th-c local, unchanging, unsmart and not for everybody; friendly atmosphere with chatty regulars, up to six well kept ales tapped from the cask including Bass, Sharps and Skinners, quiet back snug; no food or mobile phones; dogs (on leads) welcome, corridor hatch serving roadside courtyard, open all day.

FALMOUTH
SW8033
Star & Garter
(01326) 316663
High Street; TR11 2AF Updated open-plan dining pub in a smart Georgian town house, good-sized L-shaped bar with fine high views over harbour and estuary, house ale and a couple of guests plus whiskies and cocktails and a good choice of wine, two for one on house ales 4-7pm, excellent restaurant-style food, friendly service; three stylish apartments although no children or dogs allowed, open Thurs-Sat 6pm to late, Sunday roasts 12-5pm.

FALMOUTH
SW8032
Working Boat
(01326) 314283
Greenbank Quay, off Stratton Place; TR11 2SP Part of the Greenbank Hotel set by one of the up-river piers (town centre is a brisk ten minutes' walk); interior on varying levels with big windows overlooking the water, dark green walls and stripped plank wainscoting, some nautical touches and many interesting Falmouth pictures, black-tile or board floors, tables with candles in bottles, St Austell, Skinners and a couple of other real ales, decent wines by the glass and good fairly priced food, friendly efficient service; background music, quiz night Sun; children and dogs welcome, tables out overlooking the natural harbour, another good bar and restaurant in the hotel, open all day.

FLUSHING
SW8033
Royal Standard
(01326) 374250
Off A393 at Penryn (or foot-ferry from Falmouth); St Peters Hill; TR11 5TP Compact pub just back from the waterfront with bistro-bar feel; good fairly priced food from blackboard menu (Weds curry night, Fri stone-baked pizza in season), well kept local ales and ten wines by the glass, friendly helpful staff, open fire; background and occasional live music; children and dogs (on leads) welcome, picnic-sets on small

front terrace, garden behind with harbour views, open all day.

FOWEY
SX1251
★ King of Prussia
(01726) 833694
Town Quay; PL23 1AT Handsome quayside building with roomy upstairs bar and restaurant, bay windows looking over harbour to Polruan, good food from ciabattas and sharing plates up including specials, St Austell ales and sensibly priced wines, friendly helpful staff; background music; children and dogs welcome, partly enclosed outside seating area, six pleasant bedrooms (all with views), open all day.

FOWEY
SX1251
Lugger
(01726) 833435
Fore Street; PL23 1AH Centrally placed St Austell pub with good mix of locals and visitors (can get very busy); up to four of their well kept ales in spotless front bar with nautical memorabilia, small back dining area, generous helpings of enjoyable good value food including local fish, friendly helpful staff; children and dogs welcome, pavement tables, open all day.

FOWEY
SX1251
Ship
(01726) 832230
Trafalgar Square; PL23 1AZ Bustling 16th-c beamed pub with open fire in bare-boards bar, maritime prints, nauticalia and other bits and pieces, St Austell ales and good wines by the glass, steps up to dining room with big stained-glass window, popular food from sandwiches and pub favourites up; background music, floral displays at the front, children and dogs welcome, four bedrooms, open all day.

GERRANS
SW8735
Royal Standard
(01872) 580271
The Square; TR2 5EB Friendly little local (less touristy than nearby Plume of Feathers in Portscatho); narrow doorways linking plainly furnished carpeted rooms, a couple of well kept Cornish ales, Sharps cider and lager, short choice of well chosen wines, enjoyable pub food from sandwiches to local fish, old photographs on white plaster or black-boarded walls, brass shell cases and kitchen utensils, woodburner; children (away from bar) and dogs welcome, disabled access, sunny beer garden, opposite interesting 15th-c church (rebuilt in 19th c after fire), self-catering apartment; for sale, so could be changes.

GOLANT
SX1254
Fishermans Arms
(01726) 832453
Fore Street (B3269); PL23 1LN Partly flagstoned small waterside local with lovely views across River Fowey from front bar and terrace; good value generous pubby food and up to four well kept West Country ales, friendly service, open fire, interesting old photographs; fortnightly quiz Tues (winter

only); children and dogs (on flagstones) welcome, pleasant terrace areas, open all day in summer (all day Fri-Sun, closed Mon in winter).

Dolphin (01726) 882435
A390 St Austell–Truro; TR2 4RR Friendly St Austell pub under newish ownership with well kept ales and decent choice of wines, good generous pub food, two-level bar with black beams and some panelling, polished wood or carpeted floors, pubby furniture with a few high-backed settles, pictures of old Grampound, woodburner, darts, quiz Tues, fortnightly live music Sat and music quiz Sun, pool (tournament fortnightly Sun), TV; children welcome, dogs in bar, wheelchair access from car park, beer garden, handy for Trewithen House and Gardens; open all day.

★Ferry Boat (01326) 250625
Signed from B3291; TR11 5LB Busy old pub with terrace in lovely position by sandy beach; bar with bench seating and wicker chairs, built-in cushioned banquette wall seats and stripped tables on grey slates, large woodburner, St Austell Proper Job, Tribute and occasional guest, St Austell Korev lager, Healey's cider and ten wines by the glass, good food including local fish/seafood, friendly service, arched doorway to games room with pool; some live music; children and dogs welcome, summer ferry from Helford village across the water, can also hire small boats and arrange fishing trips, walk down from car park is quite steep, open all day (in season).

★Blue Anchor (01326) 562821
Coinagehall Street; TR13 8EL Many love this no-nonsense, highly individual, 15th-c thatched pub; quaint rooms off corridor, flagstones, stripped stone, low beams and well worn furniture, ancient back brewhouse still producing distinctive Spingo ales including Middle, a very strong Special and Bragget made with honey and herbs, no food but can bring your own (good pasty shop nearby), family room, traditional games and skittle alley, friendly local atmosphere; regular live music, Mon quiz; children (away from bar) and dogs (on leads) welcome, back garden with own bar, four bedrooms in house next door, generous breakfast, open all day.

Copley Arms (01503) 240209
A387 Looe–Torpoint; PL11 3HJ Friendly 17th-c village pub popular with passing tourists; focus on enjoyable reasonably

priced food from bar snacks to grills in linked carpeted areas, well kept St Austell ales and nice choice of wines, variety of teas and coffee, log fires, tables in cosy booths in one part, sofas and easy chairs in another; background and some live music, open mike and karaoke nights; children and dogs (in bar) welcome (they even stock doggie ice-cream), a few roadside picnic-sets by small River Seaton, fenced play area, five bedrooms, open all day.

Treguth (01637) 830248
Signed from Cubert, SW of Newquay; TR8 5PP Ancient whitewashed stone and thatch pub near large beach; cosy low-beamed carpeted bar with big stone fireplace, bigger dining room at back, three West Country ales and popular food cooked by landlord-chef, friendly service; regular live music, quiz, pool; children and dogs welcome, handy for campsites and popular with holidaymakers, open all day weekends.

Devonport (01752) 822869
The Cleave; PL10 1NF Lovely bay views from front bar of this popular pub in historic traffic-free village; well kept changing local ales and ciders, good food from French chef-landlord including fish/seafood (excellent Fowey mussels), nice sandwiches, Cornish pasties and afternoon cream teas too; friendly efficient service even at busy times, light airy modern décor, warming log fire; occasional live music; children and dogs welcome, tables out by sea wall, closed Tues during term time, otherwise open all day.

Lamorna Wink (01736) 731566
Off B3315 SW of Penzance; TR19 6XH Cleanly updated 18th-c granite pub with great collection of nauticalia; bar with pale wood furniture on slate floor, upholstered wall benches and woodburner, dining room with another woodburner, well kept Skinners and enjoyable good value food from shortish menu; children and dogs welcome, picnic-sets and play area outside, short stroll to beautiful cove and good coast walks, closed Sun evening; for sale as we went to press, so may be changes.

Lanivet Inn (01208) 831212
Truro Road; PL30 5ET Welcoming old stone pub with long L-shaped bar, dining end with woodburner and generous helpings of popular good value food (best to book) from sandwiches/wraps to daily specials, St Austell ales and guests, friendly efficient service;

We don't mention free wi-fi, because it's standard in most pubs these days – though not universal. And don't expect a good signal in remote rural locations.

background and live music, fortnightly quiz Tues, pool, darts and TV; children and dogs (in bar) welcome, seats out at front and in fenced garden, handy for Saints Way trail, unusual pub sign recalling days when village supplied bamboo to London Zoo's pandas, open all day weekends.

LELANT SW5436
Watermill (01736) 757912
Lelant Downs; A3074 S; TR27 6LQ Mill-conversion family dining pub; working waterwheel behind with gearing in dark-beamed central bar opening into brighter airy front extension, upstairs restaurant, Sharps Doom Bar, Skinners Betty Stogs and a guest, decent choice of good reasonably priced food including daily specials, helpful friendly staff; Weds quiz (winter); children welcome, dogs welcome downstairs, good-sized pretty streamside garden, open all day.

LIZARD SW7012
Top House (01326) 290974
A3083; TR12 7NQ Comfortable pub with friendly staff and regulars; tasty unpretentious home-cooked food from sandwiches and snacks to local fresh fish and Sunday roasts; four well kept St Austell ales; local sea pictures (some RNLI photographs), shipwreck relics and serpentine craftwork, warm log fire; TV, darts and pool; children and dogs (in bar) welcome, disabled access, sheltered terrace, eight bedrooms in adjoining building (three with sea views), good coastal walks, open (and food) all day in summer, food all day weekends in winter.

LIZARD SW7012
Witchball (01326) 290662
Lighthouse Road; TR12 7NJ Small friendly beamed pub – the most southerly pub in mainland Britain – popular with locals and visitors (booking recommended in season), good food from sandwiches and pizzas to fresh fish/seafood, good value Tues steak night, well kept ales such as Cornish Chough, St Austell and Skinners, Cornish cider, cheerful helpful staff; pool; children and dogs welcome, front terrace, open all day summer, closed winter lunchtimes Mon-Wed.

LOSTWITHIEL SX1059
Earl of Chatham (01208) 872269
Grenville Road; PL22 0EP Traditional 16th-c split-level pub with beams, bare stone walls and open woodburner, generous helpings of enjoyable home-made food including popular Sun lunch, St Austell ales and nice choice of wines, friendly staff; children and dogs welcome, terrace picnic-sets, bedrooms, open all day.

LOSTWITHIEL SX1059
Royal Oak (01208) 872552
Duke Street; PL22 0AG Welcoming old pub with bar, lounge and evening dining area, open fires, St Austell Tribute, Sharps Doom

Bar and guests, traditional cider, wines and cocktails, good generously served pub food including Sun carvery, amiable helpful staff; background and live music most Fri; children welcome, dogs in bar, terrace picnic-sets under large willow, six comfortable clean bedrooms, open all day.

LUDGVAN SW5033
White Hart (01736) 740175
Off A30 Penzance–Hayle at Crowlas; TR20 8EY Ancient stone-built village pub, friendly and welcoming, with well kept ales such as Sharps and Skinners, cocktail menu, enjoyable home-made food including blackboard specials, curry night alternate Tues, small unspoilt beamed rooms with wood and stone floors, nooks and crannies, woodburners; background and summer live music, quiz first Weds of month; children and dogs welcome, back garden with decked area, interesting church next door, open all day in season.

MANACCAN SW7624
New Inn (01326) 231301
Down hill signed to Gillan and St Keverne; TR12 6HA Refurbished part-thatched community-owned pub in attractive village setting; bar area with painted beam-and-plank ceiling, exposed stonework and blue/grey half-panelling, cushioned wall benches and other fairly traditional furniture on flagstones, log fire, garden room opening on to small terrace, up to three well kept changing ales (often Dartmoor Legend), good home-cooked local food served by friendly staff; children and dogs welcome, open all day (summer only).

MARAZION SW5130
Godolphin Arms (01736) 888510
West End; TR17 0EN Revamped and extended former coaching inn with wonderful views across to St Michael's Mount; light contemporary décor and modern furnishings, well liked food from small plates and burgers up, St Austell and Skinners ales, lots of wines by the glass and good coffee, friendly staff; children and dogs (in most areas) welcome, beachside terrace and upper deck, ten stylish bedrooms (most with sea view, some with balconies), good breakfast, open all day from 8am.

MARAZION SW5130
Kings Arms (01736) 710291
The Square; TR17 0AP Old one-bar 18th-c pub in small square, comfortable, cosy and welcoming with woodburner, good well presented food (best to book) including lunchtime sandwiches, local fish (popular beer-battered fish and chips also available for takeaway) from regularly changing menu, well kept St Austell ales, friendly helpful staff; Tues quiz; children and dogs (on leads) welcome, sunny picnic-sets out in front, open all day.

MAWGAN
SW7025
Ship (01326) 221240
Churchfield, signed off Higher Lane;
TR12 6AD Former 18th-c courthouse in
nice setting near Helford River on the Lizard
peninsula; high-ceiling bare-boards bar with
woodburner in stone fireplace, end snug and
raised eating area, emphasis on landlord's
good food including local fish/seafood and
seasonal game (best to book), takeaway fish
and chips Tues, well kept ales and decent
wine list, cheerful helpful young staff; well
behaved children and dogs welcome, garden
picnic-sets, closed lunchtimes and all day
Sun, Mon.

MAWNAN SMITH
SW7728
Red Lion (01326) 250026
W of Falmouth, off former B3291
Penryn–Gweek; The Square; TR11 5EP
Old thatched and beamed pub with cosy
series of dimly lit rooms including raftered
bar; enjoyable food from light lunches to
daily specials, friendly helpful service, well
kept ales such as Bath Gem, St Austell
Tribute and Skinners Betty Stogs, plenty
of wines by the glass and good selection of
rums, woodburner in huge stone fireplace,
country and marine pictures, stoneware
bottles/flagons and some other bric-a-brac;
children (away from bar) and dogs welcome,
disabled access, picnic-sets outside, handy
for Glendurgan (NT) and Trebah gardens,
open all day.

MENHERION
SX2862
Golden Lion (01209) 860332
Top of village by reservoir; TR16 6NW
Tucked-away little stone dining pub in nice
spot by Stithians Reservoir; beamed bar
and snug, woodburner, well kept St Austell
ales, decent wines by the glass and local gin,
good choice of tasty well presented English,
European and Asian food, friendly welcoming
staff, restaurant with lake view; children
and dogs welcome, wheelchair access using
ramps, disabled loo, attractive garden with
play area, good walks, camping, open (and
food) all day.

METHERELL
SX4069
Carpenters Arms (01579) 351148
Follow Honicombe sign from St Anns
Chapel just W of Gunnislake A390;
Lower Metherell; PL17 8BJ Steps up to
heavily black-beamed village local; huge
polished flagstones and massive stone walls
in cosy bar, carpeted lounge/dining area,
three well kept ales such as St Austell,
Sharps and Timothy Taylors Landlord, good
reasonably priced food (not lunchtimes Mon-
Thurs) cooked by landlord including stone-
baked pizzas Mon and Fri evenings, friendly
staff and regulars; live music; children and
dogs welcome, front terrace, handy for
Cotehele (NT), open all day Fri-Sun, from
2pm other days.

MEVAGISSEY
SX0144
★Fountain (01726) 842320
Cliff Street, down alley by Post Office;
PL26 6QH Popular low-beamed fishermen's
pub; slate floor, some stripped stone and a
welcoming log fire, old local pictures, well
kept St Austell ales and good reasonably
priced food including local fish/seafood,
friendly staff, back bar with glass-topped
pit (the remains of an old fish-oil press and
smugglers' hide), small upstairs evening
restaurant; children and dogs welcome,
sports TV, Mon night singing by Mevagissey
Male Choir, pretty frontage with picnic-sets,
three bedrooms, open all day in summer.

MEVAGISSEY
SX0144
Kings Arms (01726) 843904
Fore Street; PL26 6UQ Small
unpretentious pub tucked away behind the
harbour; four well kept Cornish ales and nice
wines from slabby-topped wooden counter,
much enjoyed interesting food (shortish
changing menu) cooked by chef-landlord,
own-baked bread and pasties, home-smoked
food, lobster in season, good friendly service;
background and maybe some acoustic live
music, board games; children and dogs
welcome (pub cats), opening times can vary.

MEVAGISSEY
SX0144
Ship (01726) 843324
Fore Street, near harbour; PL26 6UQ
16th-c pub with interesting alcove areas in
big open-plan bar, low beams and flagstones,
nautical décor, woodburner, fairly priced
pubby food (small helpings available) from
sandwiches to good fresh fish, well kept
St Austell ales, cheery uniformed staff; local
live music Sat, Tues quiz; children and dogs
(in the bar) welcome, five bedrooms, open all
day (food all day in summer).

MITCHELL
SW8554
★Plume of Feathers (01872) 510387
Off A30 Bodmin–Redruth, by A3076
junction; take southwards road then
first right; TR8 5AX Popular 16th-c
coaching inn with appealing contemporary
décor; several linked bar and dining rooms,
stripped beams and standing timbers, local
artwork on pastel walls, painted dados and
two open fires, good contemporary British
food from sandwiches up with some emphasis
on fish, Sharps, Skinners and St Austell ales,
several wines by the glass, bright impressive
dining conservatory with central olive tree;
background music; children (away from bar)
and dogs welcome, picnic-sets under parasols
in well planted garden areas, comfortable
stable-conversion bedrooms, open all day
from 8am.

MITHIAN
SW7450
★Miners Arms (01872) 552375
Off B3285 E of St Agnes; TR5 0QF Cosy
stone-built 16th-c pub with traditional small

rooms and passages, pubby furnishings and open fires, stories of smugglers and ghosts, fine old wall painting of Elizabeth I in back bar, good choice of popular reasonably priced food from sandwiches/baked potatoes up, St Austell, Sharps and Skinners kept well, friendly helpful staff; background music, board games; children and dogs (in bar areas) welcome, seating in sheltered front cobbled forecourt, back terrace and garden, open (and food) all day.

MORWENSTOW   SS2015
Bush (01288) 331242
Signed off A39 N of Kilkhampton; Crosstown; EX23 9SR 13th-c beamed pub in fine spot near coastal walks and surfing beaches; character bar with traditional pubby furniture on flagstones, horse tack and copper/brass knick-knacks, open fire in winter, two St Austell ales and a guest, real cider and several wines by the glass, reasonably priced pubby food from sandwiches up, friendly staff, various dining rooms, one in modern raftered extension overlooking garden; monthly folk music, fortnightly quiz Weds; children and dogs (in bar) welcome, picnic-sets and thatched cabanas on lawn, play area, bedrooms with sea views and a self-catering cottage, open (and food) all day.

MOUSEHOLE   SW4626
★ Ship (01736) 731234
Harbourside; TR19 6QX Busy harbourside pub with opened-up main bar; black beams and panelling, built-in wooden wall benches and stools around low tables on granite flagstones, sailors' fancy ropework, cosy open fire, separate dining space; St Austell ales and several wines by the glass, straightforward pubby food and pizza menu, maybe background music; children and dogs (in bar) welcome, bedrooms above or in next-door cottage (some overlooking the sea), best to park at top of this pretty village and walk down (traffic in summer can be a nightmare), Christmas harbour lights also worth a look, open all day.

NEWLYN   SW4629
★ Tolcarne (01736) 363074
Tolcarne Place; TR18 5PR Simply updated 18th-c quayside pub with highly rated food from chef-landlord, much emphasis on local fish/seafood (menu board changes daily), must book, woodburner, friendly efficient service, St Austell Tribute, Sharps Doom Bar and Skinners Lushingtons; live jazz Sun lunchtime; children and dogs welcome, picnic-sets on terrace (harbour wall cuts off view), good parking.

NEWQUAY   SW8061
Fort (01637) 875700
Fore Street; TR7 1HA Massive pub in magnificent setting high above surfing beach and small harbour; full St Austell

range and decent pub food from brunch onwards, friendly staff coping well at busy times, modernised open-plan areas with solid furnishings from country kitchen tables and chairs to comfy sofas, soft lighting, pool table, excellent children's soft-play area; great views from long glass-walled side section and sizeable garden with multi-level terrace and further play areas, open (and food) all day.

NEWQUAY   SW8061
Lewinnick Lodge (01637) 878117
Pentire headland, off Pentire Road; TR7 1QD Modern flint-walled bar-restaurant built into bluff above the sea – big picture windows for the terrific views; light airy bar with wicker seating, three or four well kept ales and plenty of wines by the glass, spreading dining areas with contemporary furnishings on light oak flooring, popular bistro-style food from shortish menu including catch of the day, pleasant relaxed atmosphere; children and dogs (in bar) welcome, modern seats and tables on terraces making most of the stunning Atlantic views, large airy sea-view bedrooms, open all day; same management as the Plume of Feathers in Mitchell.

NEWTOWN   SW7423
Prince of Wales (01326) 231247
The one off B3293, SE of Helston; TR12 6DP Flower-decked stone pub in tucked-away hamlet on the Lizard peninsula; beamed bar with pubby furniture on slate floor, woodburner, small restaurant, Cornish ales such as Penzance and St Austell, good well presented food cooked to order from shortish menu, £10 dinner deal Weds, friendly helpful service; darts, sports TV; children and dogs welcome, picnic-sets on back gravel terrace and lawn, bedrooms and summer camping, closed Mon lunchtime.

PADSTOW   SW9175
★ Golden Lion (01841) 532797
Lanadwell Street; PL28 8AN Old inn dating from the 14th c; cheerful black-beamed locals' bar and high-raftered back lounge with plush banquettes, well kept Sharps Doom Bar, Skinners Betty Stogs and a guest, good range of gins, enjoyable generously served food including reasonably priced bar lunches, evening steaks and fresh fish, popular Sun lunch, friendly helpful staff, coal fire and woodburner; pool in family area, background music, sports TV; dogs welcome, colourful floral displays at front, terrace tables behind, three good bedrooms, open all day (no food Sun evening) but check times in low season.

PADSTOW   SW9175
Harbour Inn (01841) 533148
Strand Street; PL28 8BU Attractive old-school pub just back from the harbour and a quieter alternative; long room with nautical bric-a-brac, pubby furnishings including

some high-backed settles, comfy sofas in front area, piano and woodburner, well kept St Austell ales and enjoyable generously served traditional food, friendly helpful staff; children and dogs welcome, open all day.

PADSTOW   SW9175
Shipwrights (01841) 532451
North Quay; PL28 8AF Long brick-built quayside pub with open-plan beamed and flagstoned bar; St Austell ales, decent wines and good food from lunchtime sandwiches and sharing plates up, friendly staff, further upstairs eating area; background music, pool, TVs and fruit machine; children and dogs welcome, a few tables out by the water, more in back suntrap garden, open all day.

PAUL   SW4627
Kings Arms (01736) 731224
Mousehole Lane, opposite church; TR19 6TZ Refurbished beamed local with cosy bustling atmosphere, enjoyable sensibly priced pub food from sandwiches, baked potatoes and basket meals up, curry night Fri, well kept St Austell ales, Healey's cider and good selection of gins; live music including Tues bluegrass; children and dogs welcome, a few picnic-sets out in front, four bedrooms, open all day in summer.

PELYNT   SX2054
Jubilee (01503) 220312
B3359 NW of Looe; PL13 2JZ Beamed 16th-c village inn; enjoyable locally sourced food from sandwiches up, well kept St Austell ales, Healey's cider and decent range of other drinks including Cornish rum and gin, spotless interior with interesting Queen Victoria mementoes (pub renamed in 1897 to celebrate her diamond jubilee), some handsome antique furnishings, log fires under copper canopies, separate bar with winter pool table and darts; children and dogs welcome except in restaurant, disabled facilities, large terrace, 11 comfortable bedrooms, open all day (food all day in summer, all day weekends in winter).

PENDEEN   SW3834
North (01736) 788417
B3306, opposite the school; TR19 7DN Friendly little creeper-clad village pub set back from the road; well kept St Austell ales and popular food including range of curries and good Sun roasts, single bar with interesting tin-mining memorabilia and woodburner; children and dogs welcome, boules in big back garden, four bedrooms and camping, good walks, short walk to Geevor Tin Mine, open all day.

PENDOGGETT   SX0279
Cornish Arms (01208) 880335
B3314; PL30 3HH Old beamed coaching inn dating from the 16th c; traditional oak

settles on front bar's polished slate floor, open fire and woodburner, well kept Sharps ales plus Cornish microbrew guest and several wines by the glass from good list, around 100 gins, enjoyable home-made food including sandwiches/panini, interesting burgers and two-course light lunch deal (Mon-Fri), friendly efficient service, dining room and proper back locals' bar; local acoustic Celtic group alternate Fri; children and dogs welcome, disabled access, distant sea view from terrace, seven bedrooms, open all day.

PENELEWEY   SW8140
★ Punchbowl & Ladle (01872) 862237
B3289; TR3 6QY Thatched dining pub dating from the 15th c, new owners recently refreshed interior in faintly nautical shabby-chic style, enjoyable food including pub classics, daily specials and Sun roasts, St Austell ales, Healey's cider and good wine and whisky selection, helpful friendly service; occasional live music, quiz, sports TV, children's playroom; dogs welcome, wheelchair access (not from small side terrace), handy for Trelissick Garden (NT), open all day.

PENZANCE   SW4730
Admiral Benbow (01736) 363448
Chapel Street; TR18 4AF Wonderfully quirky historic two-floor pub packed with interesting nautical paraphernalia from shipwrecks and full of atmosphere; St Austell Proper Job, Sharps Doom Bar and a guest such as Treens, German lagers, Healey's cider, and good selection of gins and rums; enjoyable pubby food (including local fish) from shortish menu, friendly staff, cosy corners, downstairs restaurant in captain's cabin style, second bar upstairs and nice view from back room; unobtrusive background music; children and dogs welcome (theirs is Sir Cloudesley), open all day.

PENZANCE   SW4730
Bath (01736) 331940
Cornwall Terrace; TR18 4HL Friendly well looked-after pub tucked away behind the seafront; linked rooms (bigger than it looks) with beams, some panelling and old photographs of Penzance, good range of beers, no food; pool, darts, sports TV, fruit machine; children (till 9pm) and dogs (on leads) welcome, delightful sunny beer garden, open all day weekends.

PENZANCE   SW4730
Crown (01736) 351070
Victoria Square, Bread Street; TR18 2EP Friendly little backstreet corner local with neat bar and back snug, own Cornish Crown beers and several wines by the glass, no food but can bring your own; live acoustic music Mon, quiz Tues, board games; children and dogs welcome, a few picnic-sets out in front, open all day.

PENZANCE SW4729
Dolphin (01736) 364106
Quay Street, opposite harbour after swing-bridge; TR18 4BD Old stone-built pub with enjoyable good value food including fresh fish, up to four well kept St Austell ales, Healey's cider and good wines by the glass, roomy bar on different levels, nautical memorabilia and three resident ghosts; pool (winter only); children and dogs welcome, pavement picnic-sets, three comfortable bedrooms with sea/harbour views, no car park (public one not far away), handy for Scillies ferry, open (and food) all day.

PERRANARWORTHAL SW7738
Norway (01872) 864241
A39 Truro–Penryn; TR3 7NU Large beamed pub with half a dozen linked areas, good choice of food including daily specials, fresh fish and Sun carvery, St Austell ales and several wines by the glass, cream teas, good friendly service, open fires, panelling and mix of furniture on slate flagstones, restaurant; background music, quiz nights; children and dogs welcome, tables outside, four comfortable bedrooms, good breakfast, open (and food) all day.

PERRANUTHNOE SW5329
★Victoria (01736) 710309
Signed off A394 Penzance–Helston; TR20 9NP Village pub with attractively furnished L-shaped bar, exposed joists, cosy corners and woodburner, Monty's Growler (named after the pub dog) from Cornish Crown, Sharps Doom Bar and weekly guests, over ten wines by the glass and good food cooked by landlord, separate restaurant; background music, board games; acoustic music twice a month; children and dogs (in bar) welcome, open fire in winter, tables in tiered garden in summer, South West Coast Path nearby, three cosy bedrooms, closed Sun evening (and Mon, Tues in winter).

PERRANWELL STATION SW7739
Royal Oak (01872) 863175
Village signposted off A393 Redruth–Falmouth and A39 Falmouth–Truro; TR3 7PX Traditional chatty village pub; carpeted black-beamed bar with paintings by local artists, candlelit tables in snug room behind, big fireplace, St Austell Proper Job, Sharps Doom Bar, Skinners Lushingtons and a guest, proper cider and several wines by the glass, hearty helpings of enjoyable home-cooked food including specials, good friendly service; quiz first Tues of month; children and dogs (in bar) welcome, picnic-sets out at front, more seats in back garden, good surrounding walks, open all day.

PHILLEIGH SW8739
★Roseland (01872) 580254
Between A3078 and B3289, NE of St Mawes just E of King Harry Ferry;

TR2 5NB In small hamlet handy for the King Harry Ferry and Trelissick Garden (NT); two cosy black-beamed bar rooms, one with flagstones, the other carpeted, wheelbacks and built-in red cushioned seats, horsebrasses, interesting old photographs and some framed giant beetles, woodburner, tiny lower area liked by locals, side restaurant too, well kept Skinners Betty Stogs, Sharps Doom Bar and a guest, nice wines by the glass and enjoyable home-made food, friendly helpful service; children and dogs (in bar) welcome – pub dog is Dilly, seats on pretty paved front terrace, may open all day weekends in high season.

POLPERRO SX2051
Crumplehorn Mill (01503) 272348
Top of village near main car park; PL13 2RJ Converted mill and farmhouse that started out as an Elizabethan counting-house; beams, flagstones and some stripped stone, snug lower bar leading to long main room with cosy end eating area, well kept Cornish ales, wide choice of popular food from snacks to blackboard specials (booking advised), friendly efficient service, log fire; children and dogs welcome, outside seating and working mill wheel, bedrooms and self-catering apartments, open all day.

POLPERRO SX2050
Three Pilchards (01503) 272233
Quay Road; PL13 2QZ Small low-beamed local behind fish quay; generous helpings of reasonably priced food from baguettes to good fresh fish, well kept St Austell Tribute, up to four guest beers, ciders and decent wines by the glass, efficient obliging service even when busy, lots of black woodwork, dim lighting, simple furnishings, open fire in big stone fireplace; weekend live music; children and dogs welcome, lovely views from terrace with own bar (up steep steps), open all day.

POLRUAN SX1250
Lugger (01726) 870007
The Quay; back roads off A390 in Lostwithiel, or foot-ferry from Fowey; PL23 1PA Popular waterside pub; steps up to cosy beamed bar with open fire and woodburner, well kept St Austell ales and good pub food including specials and Sun carvery, friendly efficient service, restaurant on upper level; children, dogs and boots welcome, not suitable for wheelchairs, good local walks, limited nearby parking (steep hill to main car park), two-bedroom holiday cottage; open all day.

PORT ISAAC SW9980
★Golden Lion (01208) 880336
Fore Street; PL29 3RB Popular well positioned 18th-c pub keeping friendly local atmosphere in simply furnished old rooms; bar and snug with open fire, window seats and balcony tables looking down on rocky harbour and lifeboat slip far below, upstairs

restaurant, enjoyable food including good local fish, well kept St Austell ales from well stocked bar, amiable helpful staff; background music, pool, darts; children and dogs welcome, dramatic cliff walks, open all day.

PORTHALLOW SW7923
Five Pilchards (01326) 280256
SE of Helston; B3293 to St Keverne, then village signed; TR12 6PP Sturdy old-fashioned stone-built local in secluded cove right by shingle beach at the midpoint of the South West Coast Path; lots of salvaged nautical gear, interesting shipwreck memorabilia and model boats, woodburner, four real ales such as St Austell, Bays, Dartmoor and Exeter, a nearby cider and enjoyable reasonably priced food including local fish (booking advisable in summer), friendly chatty staff, conservatory; children and dogs welcome, seats out in sheltered yard, five newly refurbished bedrooms (four with sea views), open all day Sun, closed in winter Mon lunchtime and Tues.

PORTHLEVEN SW6325
Atlantic (01326) 562439
Peverell Terrace; TR13 9DZ Friendly buzzy pub in great setting above the harbour; good value tasty food including bargain weekly OAP lunch, Fri pie night and Sun roasts; ales such as St Austell and Skinners from boat-shaped counter, Weston's cider, big open-plan lounge with well spaced seating and cosier alcoves, good log fire in granite fireplace, carpeted dining room with trompe l'oeil murals; live music/entertainment Sat evening, Mon quiz, Thurs bingo, TV for major sports, darts; children and dogs welcome, lovely bay views from raised front terrace, open all day.

PORTHLEVEN SW6225
Harbour Inn (01326) 573876
Commercial Road; TR13 9JB Large neatly kept pub-hotel in outstanding harbourside setting; expansive lounge and bar plus dining area with blue panelling and ropework, big public bar, well kept St Austell ales and good range of fairly pubby food from snacks and sharing boards up, well organised friendly service; unobtrusive background music (live Sat), Thurs quiz; children and dogs (in bar) welcome, picnic-sets on spacious quayside terrace, 15 contemporary well equipped bedrooms (some with harbour view), good breakfast, open (and food) all day.

PORTHLEVEN SW6225
★Ship (01326) 564204
Mount Pleasant Road (harbour) off B3304; TR13 9JS Friendly fishermen's pub built into cliffs, fine harbour views (interestingly floodlit at night) from seats on terrace and in knocked-through bar, five ales including Sharps Doom Bar and Skinners

Porthleven, honest bar food like good crab sandwiches and mussels, good service, log fires in big stone fireplaces, some genuine individuality, family room (converted from old smithy) with huge fire, candlelit dining room also looking over sea; background music, games machine; children welcome away from bar, dogs in bar, terraced garden with ample seating, open all day.

PORTHTOWAN SW6948
★Blue (01209) 890329
Beach Road, East Cliff; car park (fee in season) advised; TR4 8AW Popular easy-going bar (not a traditional pub) by stunning beach attracting customers of all ages; big picture windows looking across terrace to huge expanse of sand and sea, wicker and white chairs around pale tables on grey-painted floorboards, cream or orange walls, ceiling fans and some large ferns, ales from St Austell, Sharps and Skinners, several wines by the glass, cocktails and shots, various coffees, hot chocolates and teas, all-day summer food from 10am brunch on including nachos with toppings, burgers and stone-baked pizzas; background music (sometimes live); children and dogs welcome, open all day (till midnight Fri, Sat), closed evenings out of season and may shut all Jan and some of Feb.

PORTLOE SW9339
Ship (01872) 501356
At top of village; TR2 5RA Cheerful traditional local in charming fishing village; L-shaped bar with tankards hanging from beams, nautical bric-a-brac, local memorabilia and beer bottle collection, straightforward pubby tables and chairs on carpet, open fire, St Austell ales, cider/perry and six wines by the glass, generously served food from shortish menu, lunch and dinner daily; background music, sports TV, darts; children and dogs (in bar) welcome, sloping streamside garden across road, three comfortable bedrooms, beach close by.

PORTREATH SW6545
Portreath Arms (01209) 842259
The Square; by B3300/B3301 N of Redruth; TR16 4LA Modernised family-owned small Victorian bar-restaurant-hotel; good food including specials and themed nights in bar or restaurant, friendly attentive service, beers such as Bays, St Austell and Skinners, local cider and good range of other drinks; quiz first Sun of month, some live music, sports TV, pool; children and dogs welcome, seven bedrooms, well placed for coastal walks, open all day.

PORTSCATHO SW8735
Plume of Feathers (01872) 580321
The Square; TR2 5HW Largely stripped-stone coastal village pub with some sea-related bric-a-brac and pictures in two comfortable linked areas, also small side

bar and separate restaurant, St Austell ales and enjoyable reasonably priced pubby food, friendly staff; background music; children, dogs and boots welcome, disabled access (but steps to restaurant and gents'), picnic-sets out under awning, lovely coast walks, five recently refurbished bedrooms (two dog-friendly), open all day in summer (and other times if busy).

ROCK   SW9375
★ **Mariners** (01208) 863679
Rock Road; PL27 6LD Busy modern dining pub with lovely views of Camel estuary, light spacious ground-floor bar, bare stone or painted walls, simple chairs and stools around tables on bare boards, cushioned wall banquettes, woodburning stove and high chairs against the counter, Sharps Atlantic, Coaster and Doom Bar on handpump, farm cider and a good range of wines by the glass, extremely popular food with emphasis on fish/seafood; similarly furnished restaurant upstairs with huge folding glass doors to balcony, children and dogs welcome, seats on front terrace (or can sit on sea wall), open all day.

RUAN LANIHORNE   SW8942
★ **Kings Head** (01872) 501263
Village signed off A3078 St Mawes Road; TR2 5NX Country pub in quiet hamlet with interesting church nearby; relaxed small bar with log fire, Skinners and a guest, maybe farm cider, very well liked food especially local fish/seafood, dining area to the right divided in two, lots of china cups hanging from ceiling joists, cabinet filled with old bottles, hunting prints and cartoons, separate restaurant to the left; background music; children welcome (including in dining area if well behaved) and dogs in bar, terrace across road and nice lower beer garden, walks along Fal estuary, open all day, closed Mon, lunchtime Tues.

SENNEN COVE   SW3526
Old Success (01736) 871232
Cove Hill; Cove Road off A30; TR19 7DG Glorious Whitesand Bay view from this seaside hotel; beamed bar with lifeboat and other nautical memorabilia, log fire, St Austell ales from plank-fronted servery, generally well liked food including fresh local fish; background and some live music (Sat evening and open mike Sun), Thurs quiz, children and dogs (away from restaurant) welcome, sun terrace and picnic-sets at front, 23 comfortable recently refurbished bedrooms (ten in newly built block), popular with surfers, open and food all day.

ST BREWARD   SX0977
Old Inn (01208) 850711
Off B3266 S of Camelford; Churchtown; PL30 4PP Broad slate flagstones, low oak beams, stripped stonework and two massive granite fireplaces dating from the 11th c,

pubby furniture, local-artwork, ales such as Sharps and Tintagel, proper ciders and several wines by the glass, enjoyable good value food including popular Sun carvery, roomy extended restaurant with tables out on deck; background music, occasional quiz, darts, pool; children and dogs welcome, moorland behind (cattle and sheep wander into the village), open all day.

ST DOMINICK   SX4067
Who'd Have Thought It
(01579) 350214 *Off A388 S of Callington; PL12 6TG* Large comfortable country pub with popular reasonably priced home-made food (booking advised) including gluten-free and vegan choices, well kept St Austell ales, a guest beer and good value wine list, friendly competent service, superb Tamar views especially from conservatory, beams and open fire; live music and quiz nights; children and dogs (in bar) welcome, garden tables, handy for Cotehele (NT), open all day.

ST EWE   SW9746
Crown (01726) 843322
Pub signed from Kestle and Polmassick; PL26 6EY Tucked-away 16th-c village pub with thoroughly traditional décor; low black-painted beams, big slate flagstones and carpet, two fireplaces decorated with shiny horsebrasses, china in glazed corner cupboards, wheelback chairs, pews and a splendid high-backed settle, four St Austell ales kept well and good value food from light dishes up, bargain OAP lunch and fish and chips (including takeaway) Fri, back overflow dining room up steps; children and dogs welcome, disabled access/facilities, handy for Lost Gardens of Heligan.

ST ISSEY   SW9271
Ring o' Bells (01841) 540251
A389 Wadebridge–Padstow; Churchtown; PL27 7QA Traditional slate-clad 17th-c village pub with open fire at one end of beamed bar, pool table the other, well kept Courage Best, St Austell Tribute, Sharps Doom Bar and Skinners Betty Stogs, good choice of wines and whiskies, friendly service, enjoyable sensibly priced food (own vegetables and pork) in long narrow side dining room; live music; children and dogs welcome, decked courtyard with pretty hanging baskets and tubs, three bedrooms, car park across road, open all day weekends and can get packed in summer, closed weekday lunchtimes.

ST IVES   SW5140
Golden Lion (01736) 797935
Market Place, next to church; TR26 1RZ Refurbished 19th-c two-room pub with friendly relaxed atmosphere, Skinners Betty Stogs and guests, proper ciders and enjoyable good value pubby food from sandwiches and ploughman's up; background music and

jukebox, live music every weekend, sports TV, pool (not in July and Aug); children and dogs welcome, beer garden behind, open all day.

ST IVES　　　　　　　　　　　　SW5140
Lifeboat　(01736) 794123
Wharf Road; TR26 1LF Thriving family-friendly quayside pub with decent choice of generously served food from snacks up including fish/seafood, well kept St Austell ales, friendly busy staff, spacious modernised interior with harbour-view tables and cosier corners, nautical theme, open log fire; quiz Thurs, background music, sports TV; children and dogs (in bar) welcome, disabled access/facilities, five bedrooms and two self-catering apartments, open all day, breakfast from 8am.

ST IVES　　　　　　　　　　　　SW5441
Pedn Olva　(01736) 796222
The Warren; TR26 2EA Hotel rather than pub perched on rocky outcrop with fine views of sea and Porthminster beach (especially from tables on roof terrace); roomy bar with well kept St Austell ales and good food, separate restaurant, efficient friendly service; 30 comfortable bedrooms, dogs welcome (in bar), open all day.

ST IVES　　　　　　　　　　　　SW5140
★**Sloop**　(01736) 796584
The Wharf; TR26 1LP Busy low-beamed, panelled and flagstoned historic harbourside inn; St Ives School pictures and attractive portrait drawings in front bar, atmospheric dimly lit corners, booth seating in back bar, good choice of food from burgers and pies to lots of fresh local fish, quick friendly service, well kept Sharps, real cider and an own-label gin, upstairs evening restaurant; background and regular live music, TV; children (in dining area) and dogs (not in restaurant) welcome, beach view from roof terrace and seats out on cobbles, handy for Tate gallery, 22 bedrooms (some in separate buildings), open all day, breakfast from 9am.

ST IVES　　　　　　　　　　　　SW5140
Union　(01736) 796486
Fore Street; TR26 1AB Popular and friendly low-beamed local, roomy but cosy, with good value food from sandwiches and jacket potatoes to local fish, buy two steaks/roasts and get a free bottle of house wine, well kept Sharps Doom Bar, a guest beer and Healey's cider, gas fire, leather sofas on carpet, dark woodwork and masses of old photographs of St Ives; background and live music; children and dogs welcome, open all day.

ST JUST IN PENWITH　　　　SW3731
Kings Arms　(01736) 788545
Market Square; TR19 7HF Friendly 14th-c pub with three separate carpeted areas; granite walls, beamed and boarded ceilings, open fire, shortish menu of good home-made food, well kept St Austell ales

and decent coffee; background and live music (Tues), Weds quiz, board games; children and dogs welcome, picnic-sets out in front, open all day.

ST JUST IN PENWITH　　　　SW3731
★**Star**　(01736) 788767
Fore Street; TR19 7LL Low-beamed two-room local with friendly landlord and relaxed informal atmosphere; five well kept St Austell ales, Healey's cider, no food (can bring your own lunchtime sandwiches or pasties), dimly lit main bar with old mining photographs on dark walls, ceiling covered in flags, coal fire; nostalgic juke box, live Celtic music Mon, open mike Thurs, euchre; children (not in main bar) and dogs welcome; tables in attractive backyard with smokers' shelter, open all day.

ST KEW　　　　　　　　　　　　SX0276
★**St Kew Inn**　(01208) 841259
Village signposted from A39 NE of Wadebridge; PL30 3HB Popular 15th-c beamed pub next to village church; unchanging slate-floored bar with fire in old black range, two dining areas including neat restaurant with stone walls, winged high-back settles and other traditional furniture on tartan carpet, another log fire in stone fireplace, St Austell ales from cask and handpump, local cider and gin, well liked food (not Sun evening in winter) from lunchtime baguettes to good Sun lunch, friendly efficient service; live Celtic music every other Fri; children away from bar and dogs welcome, pretty flowering tubs and baskets outside, picnic-sets in garden over road, open all day in summer.

ST MAWES　　　　　　　　　　　SW8433
Idle Rocks　(01326) 270771
Tredenham Road; TR2 5AN Civilised waterfront hotel by edge of harbour; pleasant small bar area and separate lounge, two-tier restaurant looking on to terrace and sea, Sharps Doom Bar (bottled beers only in winter) and decent wines by the glass, good food from bar snacks up, friendly helpful staff; well behaved dogs (but no small children) allowed on sun terrace, smallish bedrooms overlooking the water are the best bet, open all day.

ST MAWES　　　　　　　　　　　SW8433
★**Rising Sun**　(01326) 270233
The Square; TR2 5DJ Light and airy pub across road from harbour wall; bar on right with end woodburner and sea-view bow window, rugs on stripped wood and a few dining tables, sizeable carpeted left-hand bar and conservatory, well prepared tasty food from local fish to good steaks, cream teas, well kept St Austell ales and nice wines by the glass, friendly young staff, buzzy atmosphere; background music; children and dogs welcome, awkward wheelchair access, picnic-sets on sunny

front terrace, comfortable bedrooms, open
(and food) all day.

ST MAWES   SW8533
St Mawes Hotel (01326) 270270
Marine Parade; TR2 5DN Harbourside
hotel's relaxed bar-restaurant; bare boards
and simple furnishings, woodburner,
enjoyable food from small plates and pizzas
up, St Austell Tribute and a summer guest,
nice wines and good Italian coffee, more
room upstairs with sofas, scatter-cushion
wall seats and second woodburner, narrow
balcony overlooking the sea, friendly helpful
staff; children welcome, a few tables out in
front, 25-seat 'Hidden Cinema', good if not
cheap bedrooms (lovely views), open all day.

ST MAWGAN   SW8765
★ Falcon (01637) 860225
*NE of Newquay, off B3276 or A3059;
TR8 4EP* A village inn since 1758; bar
with big fireplace, farmhouse chairs and
cushioned wheelbacks around an assortment
of tables on patterned carpet, antique
coaching prints and falcon pictures, three
changing ales on handpump, usually local,
and decent wines by the glass, enjoyable
reasonably priced food from sandwiches
up, friendly service, compact stone-floored
dining room; children (away from bar) and
dogs (in bar) welcome, picnic-sets (some
painted blue) in pretty garden with wishing
well, cobbled front courtyard, comfortable
bedrooms, open all day during school
holidays (all day weekends at other times).

ST TUDY   SX0676
★ St Tudy Inn (01208) 850656
Off A391 near Wadebridge; PL30 3NN
Landlady's good modern cooking is the
main draw here; bar with log fire in raised
hearth, cushioned window seats and mix
of tables and chairs on slate floors, Sharps
Doom Bar, St Austell Tribute and a beer
badged for the pub, a couple of ciders and
around 25 wines by the glass, informal dining
rooms with rugs on bare boards, farmhouse
and wheelback chairs, fresh flowers,
candlelight and another log fire; background
music; children and dogs (in bar) welcome,
picnic-sets under parasols at front, more
seats in garden, closed Sun evening,
otherwise open all day.

TIDEFORD   SX3459
Rod & Line (01752) 851912
Church Road; PL12 5HW Small old-
fashioned rustic local, an inn since 1678, set
back from the road up steps; St Austell and
Skinners kept well, nice food including good
fresh fish/seafood from blackboard menus,
friendly helpful service, angling theme
with rods and other bric-a-brac, low-bowed
ceiling, settles, good log fire; frequent live
music, darts and shove-ha'penny; children
and dogs welcome, tables outside, four well
appointed bedrooms, open all day.

TINTAGEL   SX0588
Olde Malthouse (01840) 770461
Fore Street; PL34 0DA Refurbished 14th-c
beamed pub; inglenook bar and restaurant;
good food (booking advised) including cream
teas and home-made cakes, three well kept
local ales including Tintagel, friendly helpful
service; children and dogs welcome, tables on
roadside terrace, seven bedrooms, nice walks,
open all day, no evening food Sun-Tues.

TOWAN CROSS   SW4078
Victory (01209) 890359
Off B3277; TR4 8BN Welcoming roadside
local, comfortable and relaxed, with four
real ales including St Austell and Skinners,
generous helpings of enjoyable well priced
food and good helpful service, open-plan
interior with nice unfussy country décor,
conservatory; woodburner; pool and euchre;
children and dogs welcome, beer garden,
camping, handy for good uncrowded beaches,
open all day.

TREBARWITH   SX0585
Port William (01840) 770230
Trebarwith Strand; PL34 0HB Lovely
seaside setting with glorious views and
sunsets, waterside picnic-sets across road and
on covered terrace, maritime memorabilia
and log fires inside, enjoyable food from
sandwiches and baked potatoes to daily
specials (they may ask to swipe a card before
you eat), St Austell ales; background music;
children and dogs welcome, eight well
equipped comfortable bedrooms, open all day.

TREBURLEY   SX3477
★ Springer Spaniel (01579) 370424
*A388 Callington–Launceston;
PL15 9NS* Relaxed country dining pub with
traditional bar with high-backed settle by
woodburner, further cosy room set for dining
and restaurant up some steps, very good
attractively presented food from imaginative
menu, Dartmoor Jail Ale and Sharps Doom
Bar on handpump, 16 wines by the glass and
cocktails, efficient aproned staff; background
music; children and dogs (in bar) welcome,
picnic-sets on side terrace, closed Mon,
otherwise open all day.

TREEN   SW3923
★ Logan Rock (01736) 810495
*Just off B3315 Penzance–Lands End;
TR19 6LG* Cosy traditional low-beamed
bar with good log fire, well kept St Austell
ales and tasty pub food from sandwiches and
pasties to nice steaks (booking advised),
small back snug with collection of cricketing
memorabilia (welcoming landlady eminent
in county's cricket association), family room
(no under-14s in bar); dogs welcome on leads,
pretty split-level garden behind with covered
area, good coast walks including to Logan
Rock itself, handy for Minack Theatre, open
all day in season and can get very busy.

TREGADILLETT   SX2983
★ **Eliot Arms** (01566) 772051
*Village signposted off A30 at junction
with A395, W end of Launceston bypass;
PL15 7EU* Creeper-covered pub with
series of small rooms, interesting collections
including 72 antique clocks, 700 snuffs and
hundreds of horsebrasses, also barometers,
old prints and shelves of books/china, fine
mix of furniture on Delabole slate from high-
backed settles and chaise longues to more
modern seats, open fires, well kept St Austell
Tribute, Wadworths 6X and a Scottish house
beer, big helpings of enjoyable pubby food,
friendly staff and chatty locals; background
music, darts, games machine; children and
dogs welcome, outside seating front and
back, lovely hanging baskets and tubs, two
bedrooms, open all day.

TREGONY   SW9244
Kings Arms (01872) 530202
Fore Street (B3287); TR2 5RW Light
and airy 16th-c village coaching inn; long
traditional main bar and two beamed and
panelled front dining areas, freshly painted
with new carpets; St Austell ales, Healey's
cider/perry and nice wines, enjoyable sensibly
priced pub food using local produce, tea and
coffee, prompt service and friendly chatty
atmosphere, two fireplaces, one with huge
Cornish range, pubby furniture on carpet or
flagstones, old team photographs, back games
room; children and dogs welcome, disabled
access, tables in pleasant suntrap garden.

TREMATON   SX3960
Crooked Inn (01752) 848177
Off A38 just W of Saltash; PL12 4RZ
Friendly family-run inn down long drive;
open-plan bar with lower lounge leading
to conservatory with lovely views; beams,
straightforward furnishings and log fire,
Cornish ales and decent wines by the glass,
good choice of popular freshly made food from
doorstep sandwiches to daily specials, Sun
lunchtime carvery, helpful service; children
and dogs welcome, terrace overlooking garden
and valley, play area, roaming ducks and
geese, 15 bedrooms, open all day.

TRURO   SW8244
★ **Old Ale House** (01872) 271122
Quay Street; TR1 2HD City-centre tap
for Skinners brewery, five of their ales plus
guests (some from casks behind bar), lots
of craft beers, West Country ciders and
several wines by the glass including country
ones, no food (can bring your own), good
cheerful service, dimly lit beamed bar with
engaging mix of furnishings, sawdust on the
floor, beer mats on walls and ceiling, some
interesting 1920s bric-a-brac, free monkey
nuts, upstairs room; live music Mon and
Sat evenings (and sometimes Fri); children
(away from bar) and dogs welcome, open all
day (till 1am Sat).

TRURO   SW8245
Rising Sun (01872) 240003
Mitchell Hill; TR1 1ED Comfortably
opened-up split-level dining pub up steep hill
from town centre with chesterfield armchairs
by woodburner in front bar; highly praised
food cooked by chef-owner, Skinners beers
along with Fullers London Pride, two guest
ales and one guest craft beer, well chosen
wines and interesting and extensive selection
of whiskies and gins, helpful friendly staff;
children and dogs (in bar) welcome, back
courtyard, parking can be tricky, closed Mon
in winter, otherwise open all day.

TYWARDREATH   SX0854
New Inn (01726) 813901
Off A3082; Fore Street; PL24 2QP
Welcoming 18th-c local in nice village
setting; St Austell ales and guests including
Bass tapped from the cask, good food in back
restaurant and conservatory, friendly relaxed
atmosphere; some live music; children and
dogs welcome, large secluded garden behind
with play area, open all day.

WAINHOUSE CORNER   SX1895
Old Wainhouse (01840) 230711
A39; EX23 0BA Popular roadside pub
under new management so changes afoot
including new menu; main flagstoned bar
with attractive built-in settle and stripped
rustic farmhouse chairs around mix of tables,
beams hung with old tools, horse tack,
copper pans and so forth, large woodburner,
simpler room off and dining room with high-
backed chairs around pale wooden tables and
another woodburner, Sharps beers; pool and
darts; children and dogs (in bar) welcome,
picnic-sets on side grass, bedrooms looking
towards the sea, South West Coast Path close
by, open (and food) all day.

WATERGATE BAY   SW8464
Beach Hut (01637) 860877
*B3276 coast road N of Newquay;
TR8 4AA* Great views from bustling modern
beach bar appealing to customers of all ages;
planked walls, cushioned wicker and cane
armchairs around scrubbed wooden tables,
corner snugs with banquettes and tile-topped
tables, weathered stripped-wood floor and
unusual sloping bleached-board ceiling, big
windows and doors opening to glass-fronted
deck with retractable roof, three real ales
including Skinners, decent wines by the
glass and lots of coffees and teas, enjoyable
modern international food served by friendly
young staff; background music; dogs welcome
in bar, easy wheelchair access, open all day
from 9am (10.30am-5pm in winter).

ZELAH   SW8151
Hawkins Arms (01872) 540339
A30; TR4 9HU Homely 18th-c beamed
local with up to four well kept ales such
as Bays, St Austell and Skinners, tasty

generously served food from sandwiches
to blackboard specials, friendly staff,
woodburner in stone fireplace, restaurant;
occasional live music and quiz nights;
children and dogs (except in new extension)
welcome, back and side terraces, three
bedrooms with plans for more.

ZENNOR SW4538
★ **Tinners Arms** (01736) 796927
B3306 W of St Ives; TR26 3BY Character
pub attracting good mix of locals and visitors;
long unspoilt bar with wood panelling and
granite floors, stripped pine, real log fire,
well kept Skinners and a house beer (Zennor
Mermaid) from Sharps, real cider, sensibly
priced wines and decent coffee, good food
from soup of the day to fresh local fish,
back dining room, polite helpful staff; Thurs
folk night; children, muddy boots and dogs
welcome, tables in small suntrap courtyard
and beer garden, lovely windswept setting
near coast path and village church with its
15th-c carved mermaid bench, five bedrooms
in building next door (good breakfast), open
all day.

ISLES OF SCILLY

ST AGNES SV8808
★ **Turks Head** (01720) 422434
The Quay; TR22 0PL One of the UK's most
beautifully placed pubs with idyllic sea and
island views from garden terrace – can get
packed on fine days; enjoyable food from
freshly made pasties (must be ordered by
11am) to local fish, well kept ales including
a house beer from St Austell, proper cider,
friendly licensees and good cheerful young
staff, nautical memorabilia in beamed and
flagstoned bar, carpeted dining room; Wed
quiz; children and dogs welcome, closed in
winter, otherwise open all day.

ST MARTIN'S SV9116
Seven Stones (01720) 423777
*Lower Town above Lawrence`s Flats;
TR25 0QW* Stunning location with sea and
islands views from this long single-storey
stone building (the island's only pub);
welcoming atmosphere and enjoyable food
from sandwiches to local fish, well kept St
Austell, Sharps and Skinners, five wines by
the glass, good range of gin and tonics; some
film and live music nights; children and dogs
allowed, lots of terrace tables, wonderful
walks, open all day in summer (Weds, Fri and
Sat evenings, all day Sun till early evening
in winter).

ST MARY'S SV9010
Atlantic (01720) 422323
*The Strand; next to but independent
from Atlantic Hotel; TR21 0HY* Spreading

and hospitable dark bar with well kept
St Austell ales and popular pubby food
including children's menu and special diets,
sea-view restaurant, low beams, hanging
boat and other nauticalia, mix of locals and
tourists – busy evenings, quieter on sunny
lunchtimes; background and live music, pool,
darts, games machines; dogs welcome in bar,
attractive raised verandah with wide views
over harbour, bedrooms in adjacent hotel.

ST MARY'S SV9010
Mermaid (01720) 422701
The Bank; TR21 0HY Splendid picture-
window views across town beach and harbour
from back restaurant extension, one low-lit
bar with lots of seafaring relics and ceiling
flags, woodburner, steps down to brighter
second bar with stone floor and boat counter,
enjoyable sensibly priced food including
children's choices, Sun carvery, well kept
Ales of Scilly, Sharps and Skinners, friendly
staff; background and some live music, pool;
dogs welcome in bars, open all day and
packed summer Weds and Fri when the gigs
(rowing boats) race.

ST MARY'S SV9110
Old Town Inn (01720) 422301
Old Town; TR21 0NN Nice local feel in
welcoming light bar and big back dining area,
wood floors and panelling, good freshly made
food (not Mon-Weds in winter) from changing
menu, efficient service even at busy times,
St Austell, Sharps, Ales of Scilly in summer and
guests, great range of ciders; monthly folk
club and other live music, cinema in back
function room, pool and darts; children and
dogs welcome, wheelchair access, tables in
garden behind and courtyard at front, three
bedrooms, handy for airport, open all day in
season (usually closed weekday lunchtimes
in winter).

TRESCO SV8815
★ **New Inn** (01720) 423006
New Grimsby; TR24 0QG Handy for
ferries and close to the famous gardens;
main bar with sea views, comfortable sofas,
banquettes, planked partition seating
and farmhouse tables and chairs, a few
standing timbers, boat pictures, collection
of old telescopes and model yacht, pavilion
extension with wicker seats on blue-painted
floors, Ales of Scilly and Skinners, a dozen
good wines by the glass, quite a choice
of spirits and several coffees, enjoyable
not especially cheap food including daily
specials, friendly young staff; background
music, board games, darts and pool; children
and dogs (in bar) welcome, seats on flower-
filled sea-view terrace, 16 bedrooms with
use of Tresco Island Spa including indoor
swimming pool and gym, open all day in
summer.

Cumbria

KEY    ★ Star Pub   🌟 Top Quality Food   🍺 Great Beer
🍷 Good Wines   £ Bargain Meals   🛏 Good Bedrooms   🍴 Serves Food

---

 AMBLESIDE   NY3704 Map 9
Golden Rule 🍺
(015394) 32257 – www.goldenrule-ambleside.co.uk
Smithy Brow; follow Kirkstone Pass signpost from A591 on N side of town; LA22 9AS

Simple town tavern with a cosy, relaxed atmosphere and real ales

This honest Lakeland local was recently recognised by outdoor gear retailer Mountain Warehouse as offering Britain's best post-walk pint. The walks in question are many and varied, at all levels of challenge, hillside and waterside, and the pint in question is on handpump from Robinsons: Cascade, Cumbria Way, Dizzy Blonde, Trooper and Wizard – or there's Weston's cider, along with various teas and good coffee all day. It's a straightforward place where little changes. The bar area has built-in wall seats around cast-iron-framed tables (one with a local map set into its top), horsebrasses on black beams, various pictures on the walls, a welcoming winter fire and a relaxed atmosphere. A brass measuring rule hangs above the bar (hence the pub's name). There's also a back room with TV (not much used), a room on the left with a games machine, and another room, down a couple of steps on the right, with lots of seating. The back yard has benches and a covered heated area, and the window boxes are especially colourful. There's no car park. Disabled access.

> 🍴 The scotch eggs and pork pies (if they have them) run out fast, so don't assume you will get something to eat.

Robinsons ~ Tenant John Lockley ~ Real ale ~ Open 11am-midnight ~ Children welcome away from bar before 9pm ~ Dogs allowed in bar

 AMBLESIDE   NY3703 Map 9
Wateredge Inn 🛏
(015394) 32332 – www.wateredgeinn.co.uk
Borrans Road, off A591; LA22 0EP

Lakeside inn with plenty of room both inside and out, six ales on handpump and enjoyable all day-food; good bedrooms

So close to Windermere that it has its own jetty and moorings, the Wateredge offers the kind of genuine hospitality in its bar, restaurant and bedrooms that turns customers into regulars. It's at the northern tip of the lake, with picnic sets dotting a large area of gravel and lawn, though in season you'll need to arrive early to bag one at the water's edge. Indoors is lovely too: the bustling, modernised bar has big picture windows, funky lampshades, tartan and leather tub chairs around wooden tables on flagstones and several different areas leading off with exposed-stone or wood-panelled walls and interesting old photographs and paintings. One cosy and much favoured room has beams and timbering, sofas, armchairs and an open fire. Real ales on handpump include Wainwrights and Cumberland plus four guests from the likes of Tirril, and they offer prosecco cocktails and winter mulled wine. Background music and board games. As you would expect, some of the rooms offer views of Windermere, and all have a fresh, appealing, country style. Solo travellers note: there's a range of single rooms. Disabled access.

 All-day pubby food is of high quality and runs from casual (burgers, nachos, fish or scampi and chips) to more special-occasion dishes such as minted lamb rump with chargrilled aubergines and swordfish steak on chive mash and lemon and basil sauce. Puddings include warm chocolate fudge cake, sticky toffee pudding and raspberry eton mess. *Benchmark main dish: battered haddock with chips, mushy peas and home-made tartare sauce £12.50. Two-course evening meal £18.00.*

Free house ~ Real ale ~ Open 11-11 ~ Bar food 12-4.30 (3.30 in winter), 5.30-8.30 ~ Children allowed in bar ~ Dogs allowed in bar & bedrooms ~ Bedrooms: £144

BOWNESS-ON-WINDERMERE
SD4096 Map 9
Hole in t' Wall
(015394) 43488 – holeintwall.co.uk
Fallbarrow Road, off St Martins Parade; LA23 3DH

Lively and unchanging town local with popular ales and friendly staff

As the oldest pub in Bowness, dating to 1612, the Hole in t' Wall has garnered a wealth of historical character. Its name is attributed to a hole in a wall knocked through by a thirsty blacksmith who couldn't wait for a pint, and it was once run by a champion wrestler described by Charles Dickens as a quiet-looking giant. There's plenty to look at in the character bar, and the split-level rooms have beams, stripped stone and flagstones, lots of country knick-knacks and old pictures, and a splendid log fire beneath a vast slate mantelpiece, with red walls and stools also warming up the dark-panelled room; upstairs, there some noteworthy plasterwork. There's Robinsons Dizzy Blonde, Hartleys XB, Smooth and Unicorn plus a couple of guest beers on handpump, thoughtfully curated lists of whiskies, gins and rums; juke box in the bottom bar. The small flagstoned front courtyard has sheltered picnic-sets and outdoor heaters.

 Bar food made on the premises includes sandwiches, jacket potatoes, pork pie and scratchings, country-style pâté, lasagne, fish pie and a curry of the day, and puddings such as sticky toffee pudding. *Benchmark main dish: lamb henry with chips or new potatoes, minted gravy, vegetables and mint sauce £12.25. Two-course evening meal £17.00.*

Robinsons ~ Tenant Susan Burnet ~ Real ale ~ Open 11-11; 11am-11.30pm Fri, Sat; 12-11 Sun ~ Bar food 12-2.30, 6-8.30; 12-8 Fri, Sat; 12-5 Sun ~ Children allowed in bar

BRIGSTEER
SD4889 Map 9
Wheatsheaf
(015395) 68938 – www.thewheatsheafbrigsteer.co.uk
Off Brigsteer Brow; LA8 8AN

Bustling pub with nicely decorated rooms, a good choice of food and drink, and seats outside

This is a well run, relaxed and charming pub housed in three linked cottages in a quiet village tucked beneath the barrow of Scout Scar on the edge of the Lyth Valley, famed for its damsons. The bar has a two-way log fire, carved wooden stools against the counter and Robinsons-related beers plus guests from the likes of Bowness Bay and Fell on handpump, a decent selection of wines by the glass and eight malt whiskies. There's an appealing variety of cushioned dining chairs, settles and window seats set around an array of tables on either flagstones or floorboards, walls hung with animal and bird sketches, cartoons or interesting clock faces, and retro lighting. Outside there are seats and tables along the front of the building and picnic-sets on raised terracing. They have six pretty rooms; breakfasts are hearty.

 Generous helpings of tasty food from local ingredients include starters such as tomato bruschetta with goats cheese, sourdough, basil and balsamic and ham hock fritters, mains such as cumberland sausage, slow-cooked beef brisket, Cumbrian chicken, leek and mushroom pie, fish and chips, Cumbrian lamb burger, and puddings such as salted caramel chocolate pot, lemon and blackberry posset and gluten-free sticky toffee pudding. Interesting hand-made pizzas too. *Benchmark main dish: lancashire cheese and caramelised onion pie £13.50. Two-course evening meal £21.00.*

Individual Inns ~ Managers Nicki and Tom Roberts ~ Real ale ~ Open 12-10 ~ Bar food 12-2.30, 6-8; 12-8 Sun ~ Restaurant ~ Children allowed in bar ~ Dogs allowed in bar ~ Bedrooms: £120

BROUGHTON MILLS
SD2190 Map 9
Blacksmiths Arms ★
(01229) 716824 – www.theblacksmithsarms.com
Off A593 N of Broughton-in-Furness; LA20 6AX

Unchanging 18th-c pub tucked away in the middle of nowhere, with log fires, friendly landlords and creative food

The simple, white-rendered frontage of this former farmhouse recalls its past as a basic beer house then a working inn, farm and smithy, and its interior is little changed since those days, with original oak beams in three of its four rooms, local slate floors and the original farmhouse range. It's considered historically significant, and poet Samuel Taylor Coleridge is recorded as having supped a pint here, but the Blacksmiths wears its status lightly, with a relaxed, friendly atmosphere, kitchen-style furniture and warm, experienced innkeepers. Three real ales such as Barngates Cracker, Cross Bay Halo and a local guest on handpump, a Cumbrian pilsner from Tirril, nine wines by the glass, 11 malt whiskies and summer farm cider; darts, board games and dominoes. The hanging baskets and tubs of flowers in front of the building are very pretty in summer, and there are seats and tables under parasols on the front terrace. The surrounding countryside is lovely and walks are peaceful.

Enjoyable food includes lunchtime sandwiches, classic pub fare such as gammon steak and cod and chips as well as more creative dishes including cep arancini with a truffle emulsion, pigeon breast with cauliflower purée, spiced aubergine tagine with apricot and rocket salad, lemon-baked cod loin with crispy capers and white wine and chive sauce, and duck leg confit with tomato concasse; desserts might feature seville orange posset with raspberry jelly and dark chocolate torte. *Benchmark main dish: slow-cooked pork belly with chorizo, peas, crackling, baby onions and honey glaze £15.95. Two-course evening meal £20.00.*

Free house ~ Licensees Mike and Sophie Lane ~ Real ale ~ Open 5-11 Mon; 12-11 Tue-Sat; 12-10.30 Sun; winter hours may differ ~ Bar food 12-2, 6-9; not Mon ~ Children welcome

CARLETON
NY5329 Map 9

Cross Keys

(01768) 865588 – www.thecrosskeyspenrith.co.uk

A686, off A66 roundabout at Penrith; CA11 8TP

Friendly pub with several connected seating areas, real ales and popular food

The current owners rescued the Cross Keys from closure some years back and have filled it with life, entertaining a bustle of customers particularly at lunchtime (when walkers refuel) and for TV rugby matches, and fielding teams in local darts, pool and dominoes leagues. The beamed main bar has a friendly feel, pubby tables and chairs on light wooden floorboards, modern metal wall lights and pictures on bare stone walls, and Theakstons Best and Mild on handpump along with a guest such as Wychwood Dirty Tackle. Steps lead down to a small area with high bar stools around a high drinking table and then upstairs to the restaurant: a light, airy room with big windows, large wrought-iron candelabras hanging from the high A-frame ceiling, solid pale wooden tables and chairs, and doors leading to a verandah. At the far end of the main bar there are yet another couple of small connected bar rooms with pub games; background music. There are views of the fells from the garden. This is under the same ownership as the Highland Drove in Great Salkeld.

Classic pub food supplemented by a specials board includes the likes of prawn cocktail, deep-fried camembert, grilled steaks and gammon, beer-battered haddock, cumberland sausage, burgers and sliders, chicken jalfrezi pie and sweet potato, feta and spinach strudel, and puddings such as Mississippi mud pie and rhubarb and custard crumble tart. *Benchmark main dish: steak and ale pie £13.00. Two-course evening meal £18.00.*

Free house ~ Licensee Paul Newton ~ Real ale ~ Open 12-3, 5-midnight; 12-3, 5-1am Fri; 12-1am Sat; 12-midnight Sun ~ Bar food 12-2.30, 6-9; 12-2.30, 5.30-9 Fri, Sat; 12-2.30, 6-8.30 Sun ~ Restaurant ~ Children welcome ~ Dogs allowed in bar

CARTMEL FELL
SD4189 Map 9

Masons Arms

(015395) 68486 – www.masonsarmsstrawberrybank.co.uk

Strawberry Bank, a few miles S of Windermere between A592 and A5074; perhaps the simplest way to find the pub is to go uphill W from Bowland Bridge (which is signposted off A5074) towards Newby Bridge and keep right, then left at the staggered crossroads – it's then on your right, below Gummer's How; OS Sheet 97 map reference 413895; LA11 6NW

Wonderful views, beamed bar with plenty of character, interesting food and a good choice of ales and wines; self-catering cottages and apartments

One of Cumbria's most charming addresses – Strawberry Bank – is home to one of its most appealing pubs. Prettily perched inside a hairpin bend a couple of miles east of Windermere, it has a heated and covered terrace with rustic furniture that offers stunning views of the Winster Valley. Inside, it's a warren of characterful little rooms. The main bar has low black beams in a bowed ceiling, and country chairs and plain wooden tables on polished flagstones. A small lounge has oak tables and settles to match its fine Jacobean panelling. There's also a plain little room beyond the serving counter with pictures and a fire in an open range and an upstairs dining room; background music and board games. There are Robinsons ales such as Cumbria Way and Dizzy Blonde plus local guests from the likes of Bowness Bay and Hawkshead, a good range of bottled beers both British and foreign, 14 wines by the glass, 18 gins and farm cider; service is friendly and helpful. They offer stylish and comfortable self-catering suites, cottages and apartments, some with their own terrace. Good walks all around; climb nearby Gummer's How for a quick route to great views.

🍴 The popular food includes hand-raised warm pork pie, smoked mackerel pâté with beetroot and horseradish chutney, Cartmel Valley smoked salmon with horseradish and lemon goats cheese mousse, Cumbrian beef burger, prosciutto-wrapped chicken stuffed with goats cheese, fish and chips, crispy potato gnocchi with roasted vegetables and feta cheese, and puddings such as sticky toffee pudding and chocolate pot. *Benchmark main dish: pie of the day £13.95. Two-course evening meal £21.00.*

Individual Inns ~ Manager Nicki Roberts ~ Real ale ~ Open 12-10 ~ Bar food 12-2.30, 5.30-8; 12-8 Sun ~ Restaurant ~ Children allowed in bar ~ Dogs allowed in bar ~ Bedrooms: £105

CLIFTON   NY5326   Map 9
George & Dragon 🍴 ⭐ ♟ 🛏
(01768) 865381 – www.georgeanddragonclifton.co.uk
A6; near M6 junction 40; CA10 2ER

Former coaching inn with local ales, well chosen wines, smashing food and seats outside; smart bedrooms

This country inn is on the Lowther Estate, enabling it to successfully espouse a field-to-fork policy in its newly revamped, highly regarded restaurant, which, like the bars here, is civilised and friendly. The relaxed reception room has bright rugs on flagstones, leather chairs around a low table in front of an open fire, and a table in a private nook to one side of the reception desk. The main bar area, through wrought-iron gates, has more cheerful rugs, assorted wooden farmhouse chairs and tables, grey panelling topped with yellow-painted walls, photographs of the Estate and of the family with hunting dogs, various sheep and fell pictures and some high bar stools by the bar counter. Three changing local ales on handpump from the likes of Hawkshead, Hesket Newmarket, Keswick, Lytham and Tirril, plus a craft beer, 20 wines by the glass from a fine list sourced from small producers (including vegan and organic bottles) and interesting local liqueurs; background music and TV. To the left of the entrance, the sizeable restaurant consists of four open-plan rooms: there are plenty of old pews and church chairs around tables set for dining, a woodburning stove and a contemporary open kitchen. Outside, chunky tables and chairs are set in a decoratively paved front area and in a high-walled suntrap courtyard. The 11 bedrooms are stylish and comfortable and breakfasts very good.

🍴 A bounty of local and own-grown produce is employed in a seasonal, creative menu, fairly priced. Dishes might include twice-baked cheese and spring onion soufflé with chive cream, spiced Ravenglass crab fritters with aioli, smoked duck and Askham saddleback pork pie, Lowther Estate venison hotpot with cabbage, shorthorn steak with dripping chips, sweet potato, chickpea and roast aubergine curry, and puddings such as strawberry and redcurrant trifle and sticky toffee pudding with clotted cream. *Benchmark main dish: Nord Vue Farm chicken and wild mushroom pasty with garden greens and truffle parmesan chips £16.00. Two-course evening meal £22.00.*

Free house ~ Licensee Charles Lowther ~ Real ale ~ Open 7am-11pm ~ Bar food 11-11; they also offer breakfasts from 8am ~ Restaurant ~ Children welcome ~ Dogs allowed in bar & bedrooms ~ Bedrooms: £100

CONISTON
SD3098   Map 9

Sun 🛏️ ✍️

(015394) 41248 – www.thesunconiston.com

Signed left off A593 at the bridge; LA21 8HQ

Extended old pub with a lively bar, plenty of dining space, a fine choice of real ales, well liked food and seats outside; comfortable bedrooms

---

This delightful gabled hotel, its name emblazoned on its handsome white façade, has been serving the Coniston public for four centuries, from packhorse drivers to the first railway tourists. While it is a real all-rounder, it's a pub at heart. The cheerful bar has up to eight real ales on handpump from the likes of Fell, Hawkshead, Keswick and Ulverston. Also, 11 wines by the glass, 20 or so malt whiskies, several gins and farm cider; service is friendly. There are beams and timbers, exposed stone walls, flagstones and a Victorian-style range – as well as cask seats, old settles and cast-iron-framed tables, quite a few Donald Campbell photographs (this was his HQ during his final attempt on the world water-speed record) and a good mix of customers (often with their dogs). Above the bar is another room with extra seating, more pictures, pool, darts and a TV for sport, and beyond that is a sizeable lounge. A large dining conservatory houses a daytime café. This is a fine spot and the dramatic mountain views are shared by seats and tables on the terrace and in the big tree-sheltered garden, as well as by the quiet and comfortable bedrooms. Cash is preferred at the bar.

 Rewarding food might include lunchtime rolls and sandwiches, haggis and black pudding fritters, honey and coriander chicken kebab with a dip, Mediterranean vegetable and pesto tart, beer-battered fish and chips, slow-braised lamb with mint marinade and red wine jus, sea bass on prawn, pea and parmesan risotto, and puddings such as chocolate brownie and crumble of the day. *Benchmark main dish: burger and chips £13.00. Two-course evening meal £20.00.*

Free house ~ Licensee Alan Piper ~ Real ale ~ Open 11-11 ~ Bar food 12-3, 5.30-8.30 ~ Restaurant ~ Children allowed in bar ~ Dogs allowed in bar & bedrooms ~ Bedrooms: £110

CROSTHWAITE
SD4491   Map 9

Punch Bowl ⭐ 🍷 ✍️

(015395) 68237 – www.the-punchbowl.co.uk

Village signed off A5074 SE of Windermere; LA8 8HR

Cumbria Dining Pub of the Year

Civilised dining pub with a proper bar and other elegant rooms, a fine wine list, impressive food and friendly staff; stylish bedrooms

---

It's well known for its accomplished reinvention of pub dining, and the addition of equally desirable rooms, but the Punch Bowl gives equal care and attention to its alcohol provision, and will always have room for the discerning drinker. The public bar has rafters, a couple of eye-catching rugs on flagstones, bar stools by the slate-topped counter, Barngates Tag Lag and a couple of other local ales on handpump, plus the kind of extensive and well curated wine list any serious food venue should aspire to, 15 malt whiskies and a local damson gin (we're in the UK's damson heartland here). To the right are two linked carpeted and beamed rooms with well spaced country pine furniture of varying sizes (including a big refectory table), and walls that are painted in restrained neutral tones with an attractive assortment of prints; winter log fire, woodburning stove, lots of fresh flowers and daily papers. On the left, the light and airy restaurant area has comfortable high-backed leather dining chairs and a wooden floor; background music. Tables and seats on a terrace garlanded with honeysuckle are stepped into the hillside and overlook the pretty Lyth Valley; there are lovely walks from the doorstep. The nine bedrooms are beautifully designed and well equipped and breakfasts first class. The Punch Bowl invested in a state-of-the art anti-pathogen air-conditioning system shortly after Covid-19 struck.

An award-winning menu served at gourmet level and utilising ingredients from the Punch Bowl's own farm and orchard is always evolving – most recently to include extended vegan and vegetarian options. Dishes might include twice-baked lancashire cheese soufflé, Stornoway black pudding with crispy egg and bubble and squeak, ham hock terrine, pan-fried scallops, dry-aged Creedy Carver duck breast, crab risotto, sea bass with sauce vierge, cauliflower with baby beetroot, tunworth cheese and parmesan, rack of Cumbrian lamb, and puddings such as lemon tart with damson sorbet and chocolate and orange crémeux. *Benchmark main dish: pork tenderloin with rhubarb, apple and sage and fondant potato £16.00. Two-course evening meal £25.00.*

Free house ~ Licensee Richard Rose ~ Real ale ~ Open 10am-11pm; 11-11 Sun ~ Bar food 12-3, 4-9.30 ~ Restaurant ~ Children welcome ~ Dogs allowed in bar ~ Bedrooms: £160

ELTERWATER
Britannia 🍺 🛏️

NY3204   Map 9

(015394) 37210 – www.thebritanniainn.com
Off B5343; LA22 9HP

Much loved inn surrounded by wonderful walks and scenery, with up to eight real ales and well liked food; bedrooms

This walkers' favourite gets packed out at peak times, but the friendly, efficient staff still find time to make you feel welcome, and there are plenty of tables outside, not to mention a village green for the congenial crowds to spill out on to. It's an unpretentious and rather special place set in spectacular scenery, with walks of every gradient from the front door. The small front bar has beams and a couple of window seats that look across to Elterwater through the trees, while the small back bar is traditionally furnished: thick slate walls, winter coal fires, oak benches, settles, windsor chairs and a big old rocking chair. There are two beers named for the pub – Britannia Blonde (from sister company Langdale Brewing) and Britannia Inn Special from Coniston – plus regulars Coniston Bluebird, Elterwater Gold and Jennings Neddy Boggle and another three Cumbrian guests on handpump; a dozen or so malt whiskies. The traditional lounge is comfortable, and there's also a hall and dining room. You'll find plenty of seats outside, and visiting dancers (morris and step and garland) come to perform in summer. Bedrooms are warm and simple, and come with local health club privileges.

Reliably good food includes sandwiches and rolls, potted crayfish tails in mace and chive butter, grilled haggis, minted braised lamb marinated in mint and honey, five-bean chilli, Bluebird-battered haddock and chips, plus puddings such as sticky toffee pudding and crème brûlée. *Benchmark main dish: Cumbrian steak, ale and mushroom pie £15.50. Two-course evening meal £22.00.*

Free house ~ Licensee Andrew Parker ~ Real ale ~ Open 10.30am-11pm ~ Bar food 12-5, 6-9 ~ Restaurant ~ Children allowed in bar ~ Dogs allowed in bar & bedrooms ~ Bedrooms: £150

If you know a pub is ever open all day, please tell us.

GREAT SALKELD   NY5536 Map 10

Highland Drove

(01768) 898349 – www.highlanddroveinnpenrith.co.uk

B6412, off A686 NE of Penrith; CA11 9NA

Cheerful pub with good food and fair choice of drinks, and fine views from the upstairs verandah; bedrooms

You'll find all the prerequisites for a country inn here: well kept ales, quality food and comfortable bedrooms, plus plentiful outdoor pursuits on the doorstep, including salmon fishing, cricket watching and cycle and walking paths. It's run by a father and son team and attracts a good mix of regulars and visitors. The chatty main bar has sandstone flooring, stone walls, cushioned wheelback chairs around a mix of tables and an open fire in a raised stone fireplace. The downstairs eating area has more cushioned dining chairs around wooden tables on pale wooden floorboards, stone walls and ceiling joists, and a two-way fire in a raised stone fireplace that separates this room from the coffee lounge with its comfortable leather chairs and sofas. It's best to book to be sure of a table in the upstairs restaurant. Theakstons Best and Mild and a guest such as Banks's Sunbeam on handpump, a dozen wines by the glass and around 30 malt whiskies; background music, darts, pool and dominoes. The lovely views over the Eden Valley and the Pennines are best enjoyed from seats on the upstairs verandah; there are also seats on the back terrace. This is under the same ownership as the Cross Keys in Carleton.

Generous helpings of well regarded food includes lunchtime sandwiches and salads, smoked salmon and mackerel mousse, black pudding wontons, gammon or rib-eye steak with chips, cumberland sausage with mash and onion gravy, fish and chips, battered Whitby scampi, sticky Guinness and marmalade lamb shank, and desserts such as raspberry crème brûlée and sticky toffee pudding. *Benchmark main dish: steak and ale pie £13.00. Two-course evening meal £20.00.*

Free house ~ Licensees Donald and Paul Newton ~ Real ale ~ Open 12-3, 6-1am; 12-1am Sat; 12-11 Sun ~ Bar food 12-2, 6-9; 12-2, 6-8.30 Sun ~ Restaurant ~ Children welcome ~ Dogs allowed in bar ~ Bedrooms: £90

HAWKSHEAD   NY3501 Map 9

Drunken Duck 🏵 � 🍺 🛏

(015394) 36347 – www.drunkenduckinn.co.uk

Barngates; the pub is signposted from B5286 Hawkshead–Ambleside, opposite the Outgate Inn and from north first right after the wooded caravan site; LA22 0NG

Stylish little bar, several restaurant areas, own-brewed beers and bar meals as well as innovative restaurant choices; stunning views and lovely bedrooms

This smart little inn with its own well established brewery (Barngates) sits prettily at a crossroads in scenic open country. Civilised, but friendly and relaxed, it's popular with our readers – and walkers – and can be busy, particularly at lunchtimes. The star attractions are the six Barngates ales on handpump including Brathay Gold, Cat Nap, Chesters, Cracker Ale and Red Bull Terrier; there are also two of their craft lagers, a stout and a weiss beer. They also offer 16 wines by the glass (including pudding wines) from a fine list, 25 malt whiskies and 17 gins (they add their own botanicals to some of these). There are bar stools by the slate-topped counter, leather club chairs, beams and oak floorboards, and old Lake District photographs on the walls.

The three restaurant areas are elegant and the new lounge area is a huge success offering morning coffee, afternoon tea, cocktails and so forth. The 13 individually designed bedrooms are first class. Sit at the wooden tables and benches on grass opposite the building for stunning views across the fells, and if you come in spring or summer the flowering bulbs are lovely. Please note: dogs are allowed in the bar only.

Food is first class with a daily changing menu with plenty of thoughtful plant-based options. Dishes might include rabbit dumplings in rabbit broth with kimchi, glazed beets with cashew labneh and watercress emulsion, venison loin with venison suet pudding, charred cauliflower and wild garlic, confit of abalone mushroom on wild garlic risotto with pine nuts, and puddings such as figgy toffee pudding and dark chocolate and orange mousse with blood orange sorbet. *Benchmark main dish: pork belly with black pudding, baked celeriac, truffle and crackling £24.00. Two-course evening meal £30.00.*

Own brew ~ Licensee Steph Barton ~ Real ale ~ Open 11-11; 12-10.30 Sun ~ Bar food 12-3.30, 6-8.45 ~ Restaurant ~ Children welcome ~ Dogs allowed in bar ~ Bedrooms: £125

INGS   SD4498   Map 9

Watermill 🍺 £

(01539) 821309 – www.watermillinn.co.uk
Just off A591 E of Windermere; LA8 9PY

Bustling, cleverly converted pub with fantastic range of real ales from own microbrewery; bedrooms

The family-run Windermere brewery, based at the Watermill, was a prime mover in the Lake District's brewing renaissance, and the kit they imported from Florida continues to produce some fine ales. There are ten of them on handpump in this former woodmill and joiner's shop, including A Bit'er Ruff, Bad Dog, Black Beard, Collie Wobbles, Dogth Vader, Golden Retriever, Isle of Dogs, Windermere Blonde and Shih Tzu Faced; also, decent selections of gins and malt whiskies. The two cleverly converted bars have woodburning stoves, and the Riverside Bar (where dogs are allowed) backs on to the River Gowan and has low-beamed ceilings, flagstones, a darts area and views into the brewery. The Smithy Bar has leather-backed seats, carpentry memorabilia and a sunny conservatory with views of the surrounding hills. The two outside seating areas, appreciated by cyclists and walkers, take in the views and the sound of the river. Bedrooms are dog-friendly and two have balconies; breakfasts are hearty. Disabled access (pub only).

Good, honest pub food includes hot and cold lunchtime sandwiches, breaded camembert, fishcakes, cheesy garlic bread, full Cumbrian breakfast (lunch only), cumberland sausage with mash and red onion gravy, game casserole, fish pie, chargrilled steaks, burgers (including a falafel version), and puddings such as apple crumble and raspberry crème brûlée. *Benchmark main dish: lamb hotpot £13.95. Two-course evening meal £19.00.*

Own brew ~ Licensee Alison Coulthwaite ~ Real ale ~ Open 11.15-11; 11.15-10.30 Sun ~ Bar food 12-9 ~ Restaurant ~ Children allowed in bar ~ Dogs allowed in bar & bedrooms ~ Bedrooms: £95

Please tell us if the décor, atmosphere, food or drink at a pub is different from our description. We rely on readers' reports to keep us up to date: feedback@goodguides.com, or (no stamp needed) Freepost THE GOOD PUB GUIDE, Random House Publishing, 20 Vauxhall Bridge Road, London SW1V 2SA.

KIRKBY LONSDALE

SD6178 Map 7

Sun 🍴◐ 🛏

(015242) 71965 – www.sun-inn.info

Market Street (B6254); LA6 2AU

White-painted stone inn on cobbled alley with character bar, local ales, good wines and enjoyable food; lovely bedrooms

This is a handsome stone-built market town in gorgeous Lune Valley countryside, convenient for the Lake District, the Yorkshire Dales and the Forest of Bowland. The inn backs on to the churchyard and dates from the 17th c – there's plenty of history to the place. The rambling beamed bar has flagstones and stripped oak boards, pews, armchairs and cosy window seats, paintings on cream walls and a woodburning stove. Hawkshead Bitter, Kirkby Lonsdale Monumental Blonde and Marstons Wainwright on handpump served by helpful, friendly staff. There are a couple of dining rooms (one is red-walled) with a two-way woodburning stove and leather banquettes; background music. Bedrooms are attractive, comfortable and warm and several are dog-friendly; dogs get a welcome pack and they offer dog walking and sitting too. Disabled access. Turner stayed here in 1818 when painting the picture known as 'Ruskin's View'. Thursday is market day.

First class food using the best local seasonal produce includes lunchtime sandwiches, glazed pork cheek with apple, celeriac and hazelnut, beetroot-cured trout, fried pollock, braised lamb shoulder with crushed potato, gnocchi with mushrooms, brie and courgettes, and puddings such as millefeuille and ginger cake. *Benchmark main dish: chicken supreme with herb mash, carrots and bacon sauce £14.25. Two-course evening meal £21.00.*

Free house ~ Licensees Jenny and Iain Black ~ Real ale ~ Open 11-11; 11-11 Sat; 12-10 Sun ~ Bar food 12-3, 6.30-9; snacks 3-6.30 ~ Restaurant ~ Children welcome ~ Dogs allowed in bar, restaurant & bedrooms ~ Bedrooms: £115

LANGDALE

NY2806 Map 9

Old Dungeon Ghyll 🍺 £

(015394) 37272 – www.odg.co.uk

B5343; LA22 9JY

Honest place in lovely position with real ales, traditional food and fine surrounding walks; bedrooms

At the head of the Langdale Valley, this friendly, straightforward inn has long been the haunt of Lake District sightseers and a centre for climbers. You can walk from the door to such summits as Scafell, Bow Fell and, of course, the Langdale Pikes, flanking Dungeon Ghyll Force waterfall, so it's no surprise that boots or muddy trousers are no bar to entering the Climbers Bar. Here, you can sit on seats in old cattle stalls by the big, warming fire and enjoy the fine choice of six real ales on handpump: Cumbrian Legendary Loweswater Gold, Hawkshead Pale, Jennings Cumberland, Theakstons Old Peculier and guests. Farm cider, good wines and several malt whiskies. It's a good place to stay, with 12 warm, attractive bedrooms, a plush residents' lounge and highly rated breakfasts. It may get lively on a Saturday night (there's a popular National Trust campsite opposite).

Generous helpings of tasty food make use of meat from Wall End Farm up the road and might include fish and chips, sausage and mash, chilli con carne, goat curry, and puddings such as sticky toffee pudding. Packed lunches available. *Benchmark main dish: pie of the day £7.95. Two-course evening meal £18.00.*

Free house ~ Licensee Neil Walmsley ~ Real ale ~ Open 11-11; 11-10.30 Sun ~ Bar food 12-9 ~ Restaurant ~ Children welcome ~ Dogs allowed in bar & bedrooms ~ Bedrooms: £125

 LEVENS   SD4987 Map 9

Strickland Arms

(015395) 61010 – www.thestricklandarms.com

4 miles from M6 junction 36, via A590; just off A590, by Sizergh Castle gates; LA8 8DZ

Friendly, open-plan pub with popular food, local ales and a fine setting; seats outside

Popular with locals for its quality food and congenial atmosphere, the Strickland Arms is also opposite the entrance to Sizergh Castle (NT) and convenient for the M6 and A6, so lunchtimes can get busy – it's best to book a table in advance. The mood is friendly and gently civilised, and the bar on the right has oriental rugs on flagstones, a log fire, local and national ales on handpump such as Bowland Hen Harrier, Bowness Bay Swan Blonde and Settle Blonde, and several malt whiskies and nine wines by the glass. On the left are polished boards and another log fire, and throughout there's a nice mix of sturdy country furniture, candles on tables, hunting scenes and other old prints on the walls, curtains in heavy fabric and some Staffordshire china ornaments. Two of the dining rooms are upstairs; background music and board games. The flagstoned front terrace has plenty of tables and chairs, and picnic-sets are arranged on a grassy area; disabled access and facilities. The pub is part of the small Ainscoughs group.

Rewarding food includes lunchtime sandwiches, nice nibbles (there's a cumberland sausage roll), chicken wings with blue cheese dip, fish pie, Lancashire lamb hotpot with pickled red cabbage, wild mushroom and sage pearl barley risotto, gammon steak with pineapple, egg and chips, burgers (beef, Cajun chicken or falafel), caesar salad in a parmesan taco, and puddings such as sticky toffee pudding with butterscotch sauce and vegan chocolate tart. *Benchmark main dish: pie of the day £14.00. Two-course evening meal £20.00.*

Free house ~ Licensee Michael Redmond ~ Real ale ~ Open 12-11; 12-10.30 Sun ~ Bar food 12-2.30, 5.30-8.30 Mon-Fri; 12-8.30 Sat; 12-8 Sun ~ Children allowed in bar ~ Dogs allowed in bar

LITTLE LANGDALE   NY3103 Map 9

Three Shires ★

(015394) 37215 – www.threeshiresinn.co.uk

From A593 3 miles W of Ambleside take small road signposted The Langdales, Wrynose Pass; then bear left at first fork; LA22 9NZ

Fine valley views from seats on the terrace, local ales, quite a choice of food and good service; comfortable bedrooms

The only pub in the beautiful Little Langdale Valley, the slate-fronted Three Shires attracts crowds of appreciative walkers and cyclists, along with lovers of beer, whisky and sweeping views. It's ringed by fells, and you can see up to the nearby Wrynose Pass, where the historical counties of Cumberland, Westmorland and Lancashire meet (hence the pub's name). Our readers continue to praise the genuine welcome and reliably high standards here. Most head straight for the slate-floored bar, with its stripped timbers, green Lakeland stone, William Morris wallpaper, antique oak carved settles, country kitchen chairs and Cumbrian photographs. Five real ales on handpump might include Barngates Goodhews Dry Stout, Bowness Bay

Swan Blonde, Coniston Old Man Ale, Cumbrian Legendary Loweswater Gold
and Hawkshead Bitter, and they also have over 50 malt whiskies, a decent
wine list and draught cider. The front restaurant has comfortable leather
dining chairs and a wood floor, and a snug leading off; the residents' lounge
has sofas and an open fire. Background music, TV and board games. There
is plentiful outdoor seating in the garden and on the verandahs and terrace,
offering stunning views to the fells above and partly wooded hills. The nine
pretty bedrooms have a fine outlook too. Disabled access to public rooms
(not to bedrooms).

Locally sourced food comes from seasonal menus and along with sandwiches
might include ploughman's, twice-baked lancashire cheese soufflé, pulled ham,
pea and rosemary croquette with roasted garlic and saffron aioli, beer-battered haddock
and chips, sweet potato, chickpea and spinach curry, sweet chilli and ginger vegetable
stir-fry, pan-fried pheasant breast, and puddings such as sticky toffee pudding with
fudge sauce and gingerbread vodka and toffee ripple ice-cream and apple and backberry
crumble. *Benchmark main dish: burger of the day with smoked cheese and chips
£13.50. Two-course evening meal £22.00.*

Free house ~ Licensee Anthony Guthrie ~ Real ale ~ Open 10.30-10.30; 10.30-11 Sat; 10.30-
10 Sun; check winter hours on website, closed Jan ~ Bar food 12-3, 6-8.45 ~ Restaurant ~
Children welcome ~ Dogs allowed in bar ~ Bedrooms: £136

LOWESWATER
Kirkstile Inn ★ 🍺 🛏

NY1421   Map 9

(01900) 85219 ~ www.kirkstile.com
*From B5289 follow signs to Loweswater Lake; OS Sheet 89 map reference 140210;
CA13 0RU*

**Fine location for this well run, popular inn with busy bar, own-brewed
beers, good food and friendly welcome; bedrooms**

Hunkered against the foot of Mellbreak Fell, this well run, extremely well
liked 16th-c inn is surrounded by stunning walks and also on the
popular C2C cycle route. The main bar has a cosy atmosphere thanks to a
roaring log fire, plus low beams and carpeting, comfortably cushioned small
settles and pews, partly stripped stone walls, board games and a slate shove-
ha'penny board. As well as their own-brewed Cumbrian Legendary Esthwaite
Bitter, Langdale, Loweswater Gold, Vanilla Oatmeal Stout and a seasonal
guest on handpump, they keep nine wines by the glass and 20 malt whiskies;
staff are kind and efficient. The stunning views of the peaks can be enjoyed
from picnic-sets on the lawn, from the very attractive covered verandah in
front of the building and from one of the rooms off the bar. The 11 newly
refurbished bedrooms are comfortable and breakfasts are especially good.
Dogs are allowed in the bar only and not during evening food service.

Very nicely cooked food includes quality sandwiches, locally smoked chicken,
serrano ham and parmesan salad with hazelnut pesto, steak and ale pie with
home-made chips or mash, venison and black pudding sausage with mustard and whisky
cream, spicy vegetable chilli, and puddings such as vegan chocolate brownie, sticky
toffee pudding and lemon pannacotta. *Benchmark main dish: slow-roasted Lakeland
lamb shank £18.00. Two-course evening meal £22.00.*

Own brew ~ Licensee Roger Humphreys ~ Real ale ~ Open 11-11 ~ Bar food 12-2, 6-9; light
bites 2-4.30 ~ Restaurant ~ Children allowed in bar ~ Dogs allowed in bar ~ Bedrooms: £120

A star after the name of a pub shows exceptional quality.
It means most people would think a special trip worthwhile.

NEAR SAWREY   SD3795   Map 9

Tower Bank Arms

(015394) 36334 – www.towerbankarms.com

B5285 towards the Windermere ferry; LA22 0LF

Well run pub with several real ales, well regarded bar food and a friendly welcome; nice bedrooms

This friendly, busy pub backs on to Beatrix Potter's farm, on the quieter side of Lake Windermere. It was already centuries old when Potter immortalised it in *The Tale of Jemima Puddle-Duck*, and the low-beamed main bar has plenty of rustic charm, with a rough slate floor, game and fowl pictures, a grandfather clock, a log fire and fresh flowers. Barngates Tag Lag, Cumbrian Legendary Loweswater Gold and Hawkshead Bitter and Brodies Prime on handpump, ten wines by the glass, ten malt whiskies and six farm ciders; board games and darts. There are pleasant views of the wooded Claife Heights from seats in the extended garden. The pretty bedrooms have a country outlook; breakfasts are good.

Popular food includes lunchtime sandwiches, potted chicken liver and pistachio pâté with cumberland sauce, crayfish tails with marie rose sauce, gnocchi with wilted spinach and mushrooms in creamy tarragon sauce, cumberland sausage with caramelised red onion gravy and apple and sage mash, chicken with tarragon, red wine, mushroom and onion sauce and rösti potatoes, beer-battered haddock with chips, pork medallions with brandy, green peppercorn and sage cream, bubble and squeak and apple fritter, and puddings such as chocolate brownie with berries and vanilla ice-cream and raspberry eton mess. *Benchmark main dish: honey-glazed lamb shoulder in rosemary, redcurrant and red wine gravy £17.95. Two-course evening meal £22.00.*

Free house ~ Licensee Anthony Hutton ~ Real ale ~ Open 12-11; 12-10.30 Sun; closed Mon Nov-early Feb ~ Bar food 12-2, 6-8 ~ Children welcome until 9pm ~ Dogs allowed in bar & bedrooms ~ Bedrooms: £98

RAVENSTONEDALE   NY7203   Map 10

Black Swan ⭐ ◻ 🛏

(015396) 23204 – www.blackswanhotel.com

Just off A685 SW of Kirkby Stephen; CA17 4NG

Bustling hotel with thriving bar, several real ales, enjoyable food and good surrounding walks

With lovely bedrooms, a reputation for quality innkeeping, a little shop selling local delicacies and gifts and walks straight from the front door (leaflets available), the Black Swan is a village inn full of country pleasures. The popular U-shaped bar has hops on the gantry, quite a few original period features, stripped-stone walls, high wooden stools by the counter, a comfortable tweed banquette, various dining chairs and little stools around a mix of tables and fresh flowers; the cosy small lounge has comfy armchairs and an open fire. You can eat in the bar or in two separate restaurants. Friendly, helpful staff serve Black Sheep Bitter, Timothy Taylors Boltmaker and a couple of guests from breweries such as Bowness Bay, Fell and Settle on handpump, a globetrotting list of a dozen wines by the glass or bottle, more than 30 malt whiskies, 25 gins and a good choice of fruit juices and pressés; background music, TV, darts, board games, newspapers and magazines. The tree-sheltered streamside garden across the road has picnic-sets and, sometimes, red squirrels. Bedrooms are well appointed and very comfortable (some have disabled access, others are dog-friendly), there are also three yurts too, and breakfasts are excellent. Disabled access.

As well as breakfasts, the delicious seasonal, local fare includes a picnic-style lunch menu of sandwiches and other finger-friendly fare, pea and courgette soup with a cheese scone, chicken liver pâté, smoked mackerel with gooseberry pickle, horseradish and croutons, chicken kiev with smoked celeriac mash and maple syrup, fish and chips, bream with grilled aubergine, mussels, fennel and almonds with tandoori sauce, and puddings such as passion-fruit and white chocolate slice with mango sorbet and Thornby Moor cheese plate. *Benchmark main dish: roast lamb with glazed faggot, onions and salt-baked swede £25.00. Two-course evening meal £30.00.*

Free house ~ Licensee Louise Dinnes ~ Real ale ~ Open 7.30am-midnight ~ Bar food 12-3, 5-9; 12-4, 5-9 Sun; snacks all day ~ Restaurant ~ Children welcome ~ Dogs allowed in bar & bedrooms ~ Bedrooms: £120

SEDBERGH
Black Bull 🛏
SD6592 Map 10

(015396) 20264 – www.theblackbullsedbergh.co.uk
Main Street; LA10 5BL

17th-c town inn with a relaxed atmosphere, up-to-date décor, friendly owners and rewarding food and drink; well appointed bedrooms

There are some beautiful walks straight from the front door here along the Dales Way (the Howgill Fells are nearby), so why not make a weekend of it and stay in the stylishly modern and comfortable bedrooms for a couple of nights – you can bring your dog with you too. Right on the high street, this welcoming old coaching inn has been smartly furnished and the contemporary décor inhabits the old building comfortably. Red leather banquettes and armchairs are close to the woodburning stove and wooden bar stools line the counter where friendly staff keep ales such as Black Sheep on handpump along with craft ales on keg; the wine list is knowledgeably compiled. Airy restaurant areas have floor-to-ceiling windows looking out to the street, sleek black leather wall seats and chairs around wooden tables on bare boards and interesting and rather lovely Japanese-style hanging moss plants. There are 18 bedrooms stylishly decorated in modern country colours, and the sunny back garden has seats and tables.

 Using the best local produce, native breeds, foraged ingredients and bread from its own bakery, the highly regarded, creative food teams influences from the Japanese background of head chef Nina Matsunaga with traditional British cooking. Dishes might include nibbles of swordfish beignets with fermented chilli mayonnaise, crispy brawn and beetroot, Howgill Hereford beef fillet with birch syrup, salsify, dukkah and bone marrow, lemon sole with woodland mushrooms and wild garlic, wild venison with quince and almond, and desserts such as Yorkshire rhubarb, semi-freddo and honeycomb, and sesame custard with miso mousse and milk. *Benchmark main dish: Herdwick lamb loin and shoulder with beetroot and elf cap fungus £18.95. Two-course evening meal £26.00.*

Free house ~ Licensees James Ratcliffe and Nina Matsunaga ~ Real ale ~ Open 11-11; 11-9 Sun ~ Bar food 9-11am, 12-3, 6-9 Wed-Sat; 9-11am, 12-3, 6-8 Sun ~ Restaurant ~ Children welcome ~ Dogs allowed in bar & bedrooms ~ Bedrooms: £130

STAVELEY
Beer Hall at Hawkshead Brewery 🍺
SD4798 Map 10

(01539) 825260 – www.hawksheadbrewery.co.uk
Staveley Mill Yard, Back Lane; LA8 9LR

Hawkshead Brewery showcase plus a huge choice of bottled beers, brewery memorabilia and tasty food

This is a spacious and modern glass-fronted building with a buzzy, beer-loving vibe. The main bar is on two levels with the lower level dominated by the stainless-steel fermenting vessels. From 14 handpumps, knowledgeable, friendly staff serve the full range of Hawkshead Brewery ales. These include Bitter, Brodies Prime, Dry Stone Stout, Lakeland Gold, Helles Lager, Red, Session IPA, Windermere Pale and seasonal beers; they hold regular beer festivals. There's also a good selection of craft ales, 40 bottled beers, 30 gins and 23 whiskies. There are high-backed chairs around light wooden tables, benches beside long tables and nice dark leather sofas around low tables (all on oak floorboards); a couple of walls are almost entirely covered with artistic photos of barley, hops and the brewing process. You can buy T-shirts, branded glasses and polypins and there are brewery tours. Parking can be tricky at peak times.

Snacky food might include cheesy yorkshire puds, venison chilli with sour cream and toasted pitta, and hotdogs and fries, followed by desserts such as sticky toffee pudding with ice-cream and malted milk pannacotta with stout cake. *Benchmark main dish: giant yorkshire pudding filled with ale-braised beef £7.50. Two-course evening meal £13.50.*

Own brew ~ Licensee James Taylor ~ Real ale ~ Open 12-9; 12-11 Fri, Sat; 12-10.30 Sun ~ Bar food 12-3 Mon-Thurs; 12-8.30 Fri, Sat; 12-6 Sun; maybe later in school holidays ~ Children allowed in bar ~ Dogs allowed in bar

STONETHWAITE
NY2513 Map 9

Langstrath 🍺 🛏️

(017687) 77239 – www.thelangstrath.com
Off B5289 S of Derwentwater; CA12 5XG

Nice little place in a lovely spot, popular food with a modern twist, real ales and good wines, and seats outside; bedrooms

As the walking cartoons and attractive Lakeland mountain photographs on its textured white walls attest, the Langstrath is well located for outdoor pursuits, with fells all around and both the Cumbrian Way and the Coast to Coast path close by. It's a friendly and civilised small inn and the neat, simple bar (at its pubbiest at lunchtime) has a welcoming log fire in a big stone fireplace, rustic tables, plain chairs and cushioned wall seats. There's Jennings Cocker Hoop and Cumberland and Keswick Gold plus a changing guest on handpump, 25 malt whiskies and several wines by the glass; background music. The restaurant has fine views and there's a cosy residents' lounge too (in what was the original 16th-c cottage). Outside, a big sycamore shelters several picnic-sets that look up to Eagle Crag. Disabled access (but not to the comfortable bedrooms).

Tasty food includes lunchtime baguettes, sandwiches and jacket potatoes, rainbow trout salad, slow-roasted shoulder of lamb, rump steak with shallot and brandy cream sauce, pheasant stuffed with wild boar and damsons, cumberland sausage with mustard mash, sweet potato and black bean burger, and puddings such as crumble of the day and blueberry sundae. *Benchmark main dish: steak and ale pie £16.00. Two-course evening meal £23.00.*

Free house ~ Licensees Guy and Jacqui Frazer-Hollins ~ Real ale ~ Open 12-10.30; closed Mon, all Dec, Jan ~ Bar food 12-4.30, 6-8.30; closed Mon ~ Restaurant ~ Children welcome but not in bedrooms ~ Dogs allowed in bar ~ Bedrooms: £130

TALKIN   NY5457 Map 10

Blacksmiths Arms £

(016977) 3452 – www.blacksmithstalkin.co.uk

Village signposted from B6413 S of Brampton; CA8 1LE

Neatly kept and welcoming, tasty bar food, several real ales and fine nearby walks; bedrooms

On the edge of the North Pennines AONB and within striking distance of Hadrian's Wall, this extended former smithy has plenty of walks nearby and just the warm welcome – and open fires – you could wish for on your return. Several neatly kept, traditionally furnished bars include a lounge on the right with upholstered banquettes and wheelback chairs around dark wooden tables on patterned red carpeting, with country prints and other pictures on the walls. The restaurant is to the left and there's also a long lounge opposite the bar, with a step up to another room at the back. You'll find Black Sheep and Hawkshead Bitter and Windermere Pale plus a weekly changing guest on handpump, 20 wines by the glass, 30 malt whiskies and a dozen gins; background music, darts and board games. A couple of picnic-sets are placed outside the front door with more in the back garden. The cottagey bedrooms are comfortable and the breakfasts good. Disabled access.

Honest food includes sandwiches, black pudding bonbons with peppercorn dipping sauce, duck spring rolls with soy dip, vegetable curry, beef stroganoff, liver and bacon casserole with mash, chicken and leek pie, salmon fillet with white wine sauce, rump steak with onion rings and chips, and puddings. *Benchmark main dish: beer-battered haddock and chips £9.95. Two-course evening meal £16.00.*

Free house ~ Licensees Donald and Anne Jackson ~ Real ale ~ Open 12-11.30; 12-midnight Sat ~ Bar food 12-2.30, 6-9 ~ Restaurant ~ Children welcome ~ Bedrooms: £80

THRELKELD   NY3225 Map 9

Horse & Farrier ⇔ £

(017687) 79688 – www.horseandfarrier.com

A66 Penrith–Keswick; CA12 4SQ

Well run and friendly inn with good food and drinks and lovely nearby walks; bedrooms

Hard by the slopes of Blencathra, this pretty longhouse inn wears its august old age with pride (it dates from 1688) while bestowing it with a fresh, country-kitchen charm in a recent refurb. The linked rooms have beams, a mix of wooden and prettily upholstered dining chairs around polished tables on bare boards, open fires, a sizeable woodburning stove and a handsome old range, prints on freshly painted walls and a partly stripped-stone restaurant. It's a Jennings house, so the likes of Cumberland and Sneck Lifter are on handpump along with a couple of guests perhaps from Keswick or Tirril, several wines by the glass and efficient, friendly service; background music. There are picnic-sets out to the side of the building and in the garden, and fine views towards the Helvellyn range. The lovely beamed bedrooms are freshly and attractively decorated.

Well regarded food includes lunchtime sandwiches, baked garlic mushrooms, salt and pepper calamari, curry of the day, fish and chips, steak, mushroom and ale pie, burger (beef, Cajun chicken or falafel) and chips, slow-roasted pork fillet with new potato, broccoli and butternut squash fricassée and red wine and thyme sauce, and desserts such as sticky toffee pudding and passion-fruit and

greek yoghurt pannacotta. *Benchmark main dish: beef lasagne £12.95.
Two-course evening meal £20.00.*

Jennings (Marstons) ~ Lease David Arkley ~ Real ale ~ Open 8am-midnight ~ Bar food 12-9
~ Restaurant ~ Children welcome ~ Dogs allowed in bar ~ Bedrooms: £110

ULVERSTON

SD3177   Map 7

Bay Horse � 🛏

(01229) 583972 – www.thebayhorsehotel.co.uk

*Canal Foot signposted off A590, then wend your way past the huge Glaxo factory;
LA12 9EL*

**Civilised waterside hotel with lunchtime and early evening bar food,
two real ales and a fine choice of wines; smart bedrooms**

The Bay Horse sits on the corner of land where the historic Ulverston Canal meets the estuary of the River Leven, overlooking Morecambe Bay, and it makes the most of its scenic vantage point. There are wide views from the picture windows of the recently redecorated conservatory restaurant and the french windows of the sea-facing hotel rooms. No surprise, then, that birdwatchers love this place, as do walkers and cyclists (bike storage is offered), but also special-occasion diners. While there's a relaxed atmosphere at lunchtime, this is quite a smart place with some lovely touches. Restaurant tables are candlelit (and sunsets often dramatic), the furniture is high quality, there's an open fire in the handsomely marbled grey slate fireplace and the background music is well reproduced; board games. Kind, helpful staff serve Jennings Cumberland and one other ale on handpump along with 16 or so wines by the glass (including champagne and prosecco) from a carefully chosen, interesting list of over 100 bottles. This is a fine place to stay and breakfasts are excellent.

Using the best local, seasonal produce, the well thought-of food includes a formal and often imaginative dinner menu, a 'light bites' menu available lunchtime and early evening and a quality afternoon tea. Other lunchtime choices are hot and cold sandwiches, duck liver pâté with quince and red chilli jelly, cantaloupe melon with parma ham, smoked Scottish salmon with treacle bread, minced pork, leek and lancashire cheese medallions with madeira sauce, bobotie (spiced minced lamb) with savoury egg custard, crab and salmon fishcakes with white wine and herb cream sauce, and puddings such as chocolate crème brûlée and bananas baked with apricot, vanilla, rum and raisin and served with cinnamon cream. *Benchmark main dish: Aberdeen Angus beef, mushroom and Guinness casserole with spiced red cabbage and white pudding mash £18.75. Two-course evening meal £24.00.*

Free house ~ Licensee Robert Lyons ~ Real ale ~ Open 9am-11pm; 9am-10.30pm Sun ~
Bar food 12-2 (sandwiches and light meals only), 6.30-8.30 Mon; 12-4, 6.30-8.30 Tue-Sun ~
Restaurant ~ Children welcome at lunchtime and over-9s for dinner in restaurant ~
Dogs allowed in bar & bedrooms ~ Bedrooms: £117

WITHERSLACK

SD4482   Map 10

Derby Arms ◖

(015395) 52207 – www.thederbyarms.co.uk

Just off A590; LA11 6RH

**Bustling country inn with well kept ales, good food and wine
and a genuine welcome; bedrooms**

It describes itself as 'a country pub with rooms' and it's a good modern example of that concept: the restoration is nicely done in restrained contemporary fashion, and the innkeeping is thoughtful down to the last detail. The six real ales on handpump might include Bowness Bay Swan Blonde, Cumbrian Legendary Loweswater Gold and Pennine Heartland, and they also offer a dozen wines by the glass, over 40 gins and over 20 malt whiskies. The main bar has sporting prints on pale grey walls, elegant old dining chairs and tables on large rugs over floorboards, and an open fire. A larger room to the right is similarly furnished (with the addition of some cushioned pews) and has local prints, another open fire and alcoves in the back wall full of nice knick-knacks. Large windows lighten the rooms, helped at night by candles in brass candlesticks; background and occasional live music, TV, darts and pool. There are two additional rooms; one has dark red walls, a red velvet sofa, sporting prints and a handsome mirror over the fireplace. The six bedrooms, some with roll-top baths, are handsome and fairly priced and there's plenty to do nearby – Sizergh Castle (National Trust), Levens Hall and good walks and cycling (bike storage is available) around the Southern Lakes and Dales.

🍴 Food includes lunchtime sandwiches, grilled goats cheese tartlet, black pudding stack, steak and ale pie, fish and chips in two sizes, chicken curry, cheese, onion and leek pie, wild mushroom risotto, and puddings from a short menu such as double chocolate brownie and a cheeseboard. *Benchmark main dish: Whitby wholetail scampi £12.95. Two-course evening meal £19.00.*

Free house ~ Licensee Jamie King ~ Real ale ~ Open 12-11.30; 12-midnight Sat ~ Bar food 12-2.30, 5.30-8.30; 12-9 Fri, Sat; 12-8 Sun ~ Children allowed in bar ~ Dogs allowed in bar ~ Bedrooms: £85

Also Worth a Visit in Cumbria

Besides the fully inspected pubs, you might like to try these pubs that have been recommended to us and described by readers. Do tell us what you think of them: feedback@goodguides.com

ALLITHWAITE   SD3876
★**Pheasant** (015395) 32239
B5277; LA11 7RQ Welcoming family-run pub on village outskirts; enjoyable freshly cooked food including blackboard specials and good Sun roasts, smaller appetites and special diets catered for, well kept Cumbrian Legendary Loweswater Gold, Tetleys Bitter and up to three guests, friendly efficient service, traditional bar with log fire, two dining areas off; Thurs quiz; children welcome (not in conservatory), dogs in bar, outside tables on deck with Humphrey Head and Morecambe Bay views, open (and food) all day.

ALSTON   NY7146
Angel (01434) 381363
Front Street; CA9 3HU Simple 17th-c inn on steep cobbled street of this charming small Pennine market town; mainly local ales and generously served food including daily specials, reasonable prices, timbers, traditional furnishings and open fires, friendly atmosphere; children and dogs welcome, tables in sheltered back garden, four bedrooms.

AMBLESIDE   NY4008
★**Kirkstone Pass Inn** (015394) 33888
A592 N of Troutbeck; LA22 9LQ Historic 500-year-old inn (Lakeland's highest pub) in rugged scenery at the top of the pass; flagstones, stripped stone and dark beams, lots of old photographs and bric-a-brac, open fires, enjoyable good value pubby food and well kept changing local ales, friendly efficient service; well behaved children and dogs (bar only) welcome, tables outside with stunning views to Windermere, wind powered, four bedrooms, basic bunkhouse, open all day in summer (till 6pm Sun), phone for winter hours.

APPLEBY   NY6819
★**Royal Oak** (01768) 351463
B6542/Bongate; CA16 6UN Attractive old beamed and timbered coaching inn on edge of town; Black Sheep plus three

---

Real ale to us means beer that has matured naturally in its cask – not pressurised or filtered. If possible, we name all real ales stocked.

guests from the likes of Loweswater and Hawkshead, friendly efficient staff, log fire in panelled bar, lounge with easy chairs and carved settle, traditional snug, quite smart restaurant serving international and pub classics (food all day Sat and Sun, also early bird and OAP deals); TV, darts and dominoes; children and dogs welcome (menus for both), terrace tables, ten bedrooms plus self-catering cottage, good breakfast; open all day (food all day Sat, Sun).

ASKHAM   NY5123
Punchbowl (01931) 712443
4.5 miles from M6 junction 40;
CA10 2PF Attractive 18th-c village pub on edge of green opposite Askham Hall (gardens open to public); spacious beamed main bar, locals' bar, snug lounge and dining room, open fires, three changing ales from the likes of Jennings, Wainwright and Tirril, good hearty food (all day weekends), friendly staff; children and dogs welcome, picnic-sets out in front and on small raised terrace, six bedrooms, open all day.

ASKHAM   NY5123
★ Queens Head (01931) 712350
Lower Green; off A6 or B5320 S of Penrith; CA10 2PF 17th-c beamed village pub (sister to the George & Dragon at Clifton – see Main Entries) recently bought and refurbished as part of Askham Hall Estate; handsome country-style décor with log fire, Loweswater plus a guest, whisky collection and fine wines, short menu of hearty food using local and own-garden produce, themed Fri dinners (best to book); children, dogs and walkers welcome, six bedrooms, open all day (food till 6pm, or 7.30pm for residents).

BAMPTON GRANGE   NY5218
★ Crown & Mitre (01931) 713225
Opposite church; CA10 2QR Old inn set in attractive country hamlet (*Withnail and I* was filmed around here); opened-up bar with comfortable modern décor and nice log fire, separate dining room, popular good quality home-made evening food from pub favourites up, three well kept changing local ales (two in winter), friendly staff; children and dogs welcome, good walks from the door, eight bedrooms, shut lunchtimes (open from 5pm), winter hours may vary.

BARBON   SD6282
Barbon Inn (015242) 76233
Off A683 Kirkby Lonsdale–Sedbergh;
LA6 2LJ Charmingly set 17th-c fell-foot village inn; comfortable old-world interior, log fires (one in range), some sofas, armchairs and antique carved settles, a couple of local ales, decent food from bar meals up, restaurant; children and dogs welcome, wheelchair access (ladies' loo is upstairs), sheltered pretty garden and terrace, good walks, ten bedrooms, open (and food) all day weekends; for sale as we went to press.

BASSENTHWAITE   NY2332
Sun (017687) 76439
Off A591 N of Keswick; CA12 4QP
White-rendered 17th-c village pub; rambling bar with low black beams and blazing winter fires in two stone fireplaces, built-in wall seats and heavy wooden tables, Banks's Bassenthwaite Beauty and Jennings Cumberland plus a seasonal guest, generous food served by friendly staff, cosy dining room; quiz last Sun of month; children and dogs welcome, terrace with views of the fells and Skiddaw, open all day Sun (no food 2.30-5pm), from 4pm other days

BASSENTHWAITE LAKE   NY1930
★ Pheasant (017687) 76234
Follow Pheasant Inn sign at N end of dual carriageway stretch of A66 by Bassenthwaite Lake; CA13 9YE
Delightful bar in elegant old coaching inn, with enjoyable bar food and a good range of drinks; Coniston Bluebird Bitter and Cumbrian Legendary Loweswater Gold on handpump plus four guests, many wines by the glass from a fine list, around 80 whiskies. Mellow polished walls, cushioned oak settles, hunting prints; hearty food served in bistro, restaurant and (lunch only) bar; children and dogs (bar only) welcome; garden with seats and tables overlooking woodland; comfortable bedrooms; open all day.

BEETHAM   SD4979
Wheatsheaf (015395) 64652
Village (and inn) signed off A6 S of Milnthorpe; LA7 7AL Striking old building with fine black and white timbered cornerpiece; opened-up recently refurbished interior with wood floors, stained-glass windows and back open fire, two well kept changing local ales, 20 wines by the glass and good range of whiskies and other spirits, enjoyable food including daily specials, friendly helpful service; children and dogs welcome, plenty of surrounding walks, pretty 14th-c church opposite, four bedrooms, open (and food) all day.

BOOT   NY1701
Boot Inn (019467) 23711
Aka Burnmoor; signed just off the Wrynose/Hardknott Pass road; CA19 1TG Beamed country inn with six Robinsons ales, decent wines and enjoyable home-made food including daily specials, friendly helpful staff, blazing log fire in bare-boards bar, conservatory; children and dogs welcome, garden with play area, lovely surroundings and walks, seven bedrooms, open (and food) all day.

BOOT   NY1701
★ Brook House (019467) 23288
From Ambleside, W of Hardknott Pass; CA19 1TG Lovely views and walks from this friendly family-run country inn; good sensibly

priced food from sandwiches to specials, up to ten well kept ales such as Barngates, Cumbrian Legendary, Hawkshead and Yates, decent wines and over 180 whiskies (guided tastings available), relaxed comfortable raftered bar with log fire and stuffed animals, smaller plush snug, peaceful separate restaurant; Sun quiz; children and dogs welcome, tables on flagstoned terrace, eight reasonably priced bedrooms, good breakfast (for nearby campers too), excellent drying room, handy for Eskdale miniature railway terminus, open all day.

BOOT
NY1901

Woolpack (019467) 23230
Bleabeck, midway between Boot and Hardknott Pass; CA19 1TH Last pub before the Hardknott Pass (or first one after); warm welcoming atmosphere in main walkers' bar and more contemporary café-bar, also an evening restaurant (Fri, Sat), good home-made food including tapas-style dishes, wood-fired pizzas, steaks and daily specials, up to eight well kept ales, real cider, serious wine list and vast range of vodkas and gins; regular events such as live music, Apr sausage and cider festival and Nov wine festival, pool room, big-screen sports TV; children and dogs welcome, mountain-view garden with play area, seven bedrooms, open (and food) all day.

BOUTH
SD3285

★ **White Hart** (01229) 861229
Village signed off A590 near Haverthwaite; LA12 8JB Cheerful old inn with popular generously served food, Black Sheep, Jennings Cumberland and Coniston Bluebird plus three changing local ales, 25 malt whiskies, local produce used in traditional pub menu plus inventive specials, friendly service, sloping ceilings and floors, old local photographs, farm tools and stuffed animals, two real fires; background music; children and dogs (in one part of bar) welcome, tables out at back, playground opposite and fine surrounding walks, four bedrooms and adjoining rental cottage, open all day, food all day Sun.

BOWNESS-ON-WINDERMERE
SD4096

Royal Oak (015394) 43970
Brantfell Road; LA23 3EG Family-run townhouse inn handy for the steamer pier; interconnecting bar, dining room and big games room, old photographs and bric-a-brac, open fire, half a dozen well kept ales such as Cumberland and Timothy Taylors, generous reasonably priced pub food from sandwiches to specials, friendly efficient service; pool, darts and TV; children and dogs (in main bar) welcome, tables out in front, eight bedrooms, open (and food) all day.

BRAITHWAITE
NY2323

Royal Oak (017687) 78533
B5292 at top of village; CA12 5SY Refurbished village pub with warm welcoming atmosphere; four well kept Jennings ales and hearty helpings of good value traditional food (smaller servings available) including recommended steaks, efficient helpful service, large L-shaped beamed bar, restaurant; background music, TV, board games; children welcome, no dogs during food service, ten bedrooms, open all day.

BROUGHTON-IN-FURNESS
SD2187

Black Cock (01229) 716529
Princes Street; LA20 6HQ Cosy low-beamed pub dating from 16th c; Stringers ales plus up to four guests and good home-cooked food including daily specials, friendly efficient service, log fire; some live music; children and dogs welcome, picnic-sets out in front and in attractive courtyard, five simple clean bedrooms, open all day.

BROUGHTON-IN-FURNESS
SD2187

Manor Arms (01229) 716286
The Square; LA20 6HY Friendly end-of-terrace drinkers' pub on quiet sloping square; up to eight well kept changing ales and good choice of ciders, flagstoned front bar with nice bow-window seat, two log fires, old photographs and chiming clocks, limited food such as rolls; pool, board games; children and dogs allowed, bedrooms, open all day.

BUTTERMERE
NY1716

Bridge Hotel (017687) 70252
Just off B5289 SW of Keswick; CA13 9UZ Welcoming and popular with walkers, hotel-like in feel but with two traditional comfortable beamed bars (dogs allowed in one), four well kept Cumbrian ales and good food, more upmarket menu in evening dining room; children welcome (not in restaurant after 7pm), fell views from brick terrace, 21 bedrooms and six self-catering apartments, open (and food) all day.

CARTMEL
SD3778

Cavendish Arms (015395) 36240
Cavendish Street, off the Square; LA11 6QA Former coaching inn with simply furnished open-plan bar, hop-strung beams and roaring log fire (even on cooler summer evenings), three or four well kept

---

'Children welcome' means the pub says it lets children inside without any special restriction. If it allows them in, but to restricted areas such as an eating area or family room, we specify this. Some pubs may impose an evening time limit. We do not mention limits after 9pm as we assume children are home by then.

ales such as Theakstons and Unsworth Yard, several wines by the glass and good range of gins, friendly staff, enjoyable regional food from short menu plus lunchtime baps and ciabattas, restaurant; children welcome, dogs in bar, tables out in front and behind by stream, nice village with notable priory church, racecourse, foodie scene and good walks, ten bedrooms – three more above their 'lifestyle' shop in the square – open (and food) all day.

CASTERTON   SD6379

★ **Pheasant** (015242) 71230

A683; LA6 2RX Welcoming 18th-c family-run inn with neatly furnished beamed rooms; woodburning stove, well regarded and nicely presented seasonal food, also lunchtime sandwiches and one or two pub favourites, well kept ales including a house beer brewed by Tirril, nice wines and several malt whiskies, friendly helpful staff, arched and panelled restaurant; children and dogs welcome, a few roadside seats, more in pleasant garden with Vale of Lune views, near church with notable Pre-Raphaelite stained glass and paintings, two golf courses nearby, ten comfortable bedrooms, closed Mon, otherwise open all day.

CASTLE CARROCK   NY5455

★ **Duke of Cumberland**

(01228) 670341 *Geltsdale Road; CA8 9LU* Popular and welcoming stone-built village-green pub; updated country kitchen-style interior with upholstered wall benches and mix of pubby furniture on stone floor, open fire, dining area with old farmhouse tables and chairs, two local ales and good food (all day weekends) including a couple of curries; children and dogs welcome, sunny picnic-sets out at front, guest room and self-catering apartment, good walks nearby, closed Tues, otherwise open all day (best to check winter hours).

COCKERMOUTH   NY1230

Castle Bar (01900) 829904

Market Place; CA13 9NQ Busy 16th-c pub on three floors; beams, timbers and other original features mixing with modern furnishings, six well kept local beers such as Cumbrian Legendary and Jennings (cheaper 3-7pm Mon-Fri, all day Sun), Weston's cider, enjoyable home-made food including good value Sun roasts in upstairs dining room or in any of the three ground-floor areas, efficient service from friendly young staff; sports TVs; children welcome, dogs downstairs, seats on sunny back tiered terrace, open all day in high season, from 3pm Mon-Thurs in winter.

CONISTON   SD3097

Black Bull (015394) 41335/41668

Yewdale Road (A593); LA21 8DU Bustling 17th-c beamed inn brewing its own good Coniston beers and lagers; back area (liked by walkers and their dogs) with

---

slate floor, more comfortable carpeted front part with log fire and Donald Campbell memorabilia, enjoyable food including daily specials, friendly helpful staff, lounge with Old Man of Coniston big toe (large piece of stone in the wall), restaurant (evenings); they may ask for a credit card if you run a tab; children welcome, plenty of seats in former coachyard, 15 bedrooms, open (and food) all day from 10am, parking not easy at peak times.

CROOK   SD4695

Sun (01539) 821351

B5284 Kendal–Bowness; LA8 8LA Welcoming end-of-terrace country pub; low-beamed bar with dining areas off, stone, wood and carpeted floors, log fires, enjoyable traditional food from sandwiches up including specials and regular deals, two or three changing ales; children welcome (games for them), dogs and muddy boots in some parts, seats out at front by road, open all day Weds-Sat, till 9pm Sun, closed Tues.

DENT   SD7086

George & Dragon (015396) 25256

Main Street; LA10 5QL Two-bar corner tap for Dent Brewery in cobbled street; their full range kept well plus a guest and real cider, old panelling, partitioned tables and open fires, enjoyable food from snacks up, friendly young staff, steps down to restaurant, games room with pool and juke box; sports TV, children, walkers and dogs welcome, ten bedrooms, lovely village, open all day.

DUFTON   NY6825

Stag (017683) 51608

Village signed from A66 at Appleby; CA16 6DB Traditional little 18th-c pub by pretty village's green; good reasonably priced home-made food and frequently changing well kept beers such as Cross Bay Citra and Stockport Ginger Tinge, two log fires, one in splendid early Victorian kitchen range in main bar, room off to the left, dining room; quiz every other Thurs, darts, Aug beer festival; children, walkers and dogs welcome, tables out at front and in back garden with lovely hill views, handy for Pennine Way, self-catering cottage, open all day weekends, closed weekday lunchtimes.

ENNERDALE BRIDGE   NY0716

Fox & Hounds (01946) 861373

High Street; CA23 3AR Popular village pub with updated beamed interior, bare boards and quarry tiles, upholstered wall benches and wheelback chairs around pubby tables, woodburners, local Ennerdale and up to four other well kept local ales, tasty reasonably priced home-made food including appealing vegetarian/vegan choices, friendly staff; children and dogs welcome, picnic-sets in streamside garden, three spacious bedrooms, handy for walkers on Coast to Coast path, open (and food) all day.

ENNERDALE BRIDGE NY0615
Shepherds Arms (01946) 861249
Off A5086 E of Egremont; CA23 3AR
Friendly well placed walkers' inn by car-free
dale; bar with log fire and woodburner,
up to five local beers and good generously
served home-made food, can provide
packed lunches, panelled dining room and
conservatory; board games, children and
dogs welcome, seats outside by beck, eight
bedrooms, good breakfast, open (and food)
all day in season.

ESKDALE GREEN NY1200
★ Bower House (019467) 23244
0.5 miles W of Eskdale Green; CA19 1TD
Comfortably modernised 17th-c stone inn
extended around beamed core; four regional
ales and enjoyable hearty food some using
own produce (all day Sun) in bar or biggish
restaurant, log fires, friendly atmosphere;
children and dogs welcome, play area in
sheltered garden, charming spot by cricket
field with great view of Muncaster Fell, good
walks, 20 bedrooms (some in converted
barn), open all day.

FAR SAWREY SD3795
★ Cuckoo Brow (015394) 43425
B5285 N of village; LA22 0LQ Renovated
300-year-old coaching house in lovely setting;
opened-up bar with wood floors and central
woodburner, steps down to former stables
with tables in stalls, harnesses on rough
white walls, even water troughs and mangers,
Coniston Bluebird, Loweswater Gold and
a changing local ale, hearty but refined
seasonal food served by friendly helpful staff;
background music; children, walkers and
dogs welcome, seats on nice front lawn,
14 bedrooms, open (and food) all day.

FAUGH NY5054
String of Horses (01228) 670297
*S of village, on left as you go downhill;
CA8 9EG* Welcoming 17th-c coaching
inn with cosy communicating beamed
rooms; log fires, oak panelling and
some interesting carved furniture, tasty
traditional and globally inspired food with
great vegetarian options, well kept local
beers such as Allendale and nice house
wines, handsome restaurant; background
music, sports TV; children welcome,
no dogs, a few picnic-sets out in front,
11 comfortable bedrooms, good breakfast,
closed lunchtimes and all day Mon.

FOXFIELD SD2085
★ Prince of Wales (01229) 716238
Opposite station; LA20 6BX
Unpretentious and popular real ale
champion; half a dozen good changing

examples may include some brewed here,
bottled imports and real cider too, huge
helpings of home-made food (lots of unusual
pasties), good friendly service, hot coal fire;
live music second/fourth Weds of month, pub
games including bar billiards, beer-related
reading matter; children and dogs welcome,
four reasonably priced bedrooms, open all
day Fri-Sun, from 2.45pm Weds, Thurs, closed
Mon, Tues; may be new people taking over as
we went to press.

GLENRIDDING NY3816
Travellers Rest (017684) 82298
*Back of main car park, at the top of the
road; CA11 0QQ* Friendly low-beamed
and panelled two-bar pub hard by the
fellside (nearest pub to Helvellyn), good
straightforward food and well kept ales such
as Hesket Newmarket and Jennings, good
warming drinks for winter walkers, simple
yet comfortable pubby décor, old local
photographs, real fire; Ullswater views from
terrace picnic-sets, children, walkers and
dogs welcome, open (and food) all day.

GOSFORTH NY0703
Gosforth Hall (019467) 25322
*Off A595 and unclassified road to
Wasdale; CA20 1AZ* Friendly well run
Jacobean inn with interesting history;
beamed and carpeted bar (popular with
locals), fine plaster coat of arms above
woodburner, lounge/reception area with huge
fireplace, four changing regional ales and
enjoyable home-made food including good
range of pies, restaurant; sports TV, children
and dogs welcome, also cycle-friendly, nice
big side garden, 22 bedrooms (some in new
extension), open all day.

GRASMERE NY3406
Travellers Rest (015394) 35604
A591 just N; LA22 9RR Welcoming
16th-c roadside coaching inn with attractive
creeper-clad exterior; traditional linked
rooms, settles, padded benches and other
pubby furniture on flagstone or wood floors,
old local photographs and open fires, well
kept Jennings ales, good selection of wines
and enjoyable reasonably priced food
including steak menu and specials, friendly
helpful service; background music, pool,
steps up to gents'; children, walkers and dogs
welcome, seats outside with fell views, ten
bedrooms, open (and food) all day.

GRASMERE NY3307
Tweedies (015394) 35300
Part of Tweedies Lodge; LA22 9SW Lively
properly pubby atmosphere in big square
hotel bar with good views; up to 20 well kept
beers (national but specialising in local
and Scottish, tasters available), ciders and

All Guide inspections are anonymous. Anyone claiming to be a Good Pub Guide
inspector is a fraud. Please let us know.

perries, lots of bottles too and plenty of wines by the glass, good service, traditional décor with hundreds of beer mats on display, log fire, sturdy furnishings in flagstoned dining room serving good hearty food including children's choices, also attractive restaurant; weekend live music, Sept beer/music festival; walkers and dogs welcome, picnic-sets out in large pleasant garden, 16 comfortable well equipped bedrooms, open (and food) all day.

GREYSTOKE   NY4430
Boot & Shoe (017684) 83343
By village green, off B5288; CA11 0TP
Cosy 17th-c two-bar pub in pretty 'Tarzan' village; low ceilings, exposed brickwork and dark woodwork, good generously served traditional food including blackboard specials, well kept Black Sheep and a couple of local microbrews such as Lancaster Blonde, bustling friendly atmosphere; Thurs quiz, live music; children welcome, dogs in bar, seats out at front and in back garden with good play area, on national cycle route, four bedrooms, open all day.

HARTSOP   NY4013
Brotherswater Inn (017684) 82239
On Kirkstone Pass Road, S of Patterdale; CA11 0NZ Cosy well run walkers' and campers' pub in magnificent setting at the bottom of Kirkstone Pass; four good local ales, whiskies and enjoyable sensibly priced food served by friendly helpful staff, woodburner, beautiful fell views across the lake from picture windows and terrace tables; children and dogs welcome, seven bedrooms, bunkhouse, campsite, yurts and tipis, open all day.

HAWESWATER   NY4914
Haweswater (01931) 713592
Lakeside Road; CA10 2RP Beautiful 1930s hotel in remote location overlooking reservoir; plenty of art deco detail in refurbished bar/bistro and separate evening restaurant, open fires, food from pub favourites up to more brasserie-style dinner menu, no handpulled ales (bottles only), friendly efficient service; children and dogs (in bar) welcome, attractive gardens with red squirrels and wonderful views, on Wainwright's Coast to Coast path, 17 bedrooms, open all day.

HAWKSHEAD   SD3598
Kings Arms (015394) 36372
The Square; LA22 0NZ Old inn with low ceilings, traditional pubby furnishings and log fire, well stocked bar serving local ales such as Cumbrian Legendary and Hawkshead, good variety of enjoyable food from lunchtime sandwiches (including gluten-free) to elevated comfort food classics, side dining area; children and dogs (in bar) welcome, terrace overlooking central square of this lovely Elizabethan village, eight bedrooms, self-catering cottages nearby, free fishing permits for residents on Esthwaite Water, open all day till midnight.

HAWKSHEAD   SD3598
Queens Head (015394) 36271
Main Street; LA22 0NS Black and white timbered pub in this charming village; low-ceilinged flagstoned bar with heavy bowed black beams, dark panelling and open fire, snug little room off and several eating areas, Robinsons ales, a guest beer and good range of other drinks, enjoyable food from pub favourites and pizzas up, friendly helpful staff; background music and TV; children and dogs welcome, seats outside and pretty window boxes, 13 bedrooms, self-catering cottage, open all day.

HAWKSHEAD   SD3598
Red Lion (015394) 36213
Main Street; LA22 0NS Friendly old coaching inn recently refurbished but still traditional in feel; original panelling, beams, slate floor and woodburner, well kept local ales such as Hawkshead and Bowness Bay, good traditional food from shortish menu; sports TVs; children (in designated dining areas) and dogs welcome, eight bedrooms (some sloping floors), open all day.

HAWKSHEAD   SD3598
Sun (015394) 36236
Main Street; LA22 0NT Steps up to welcoming 17th-c beamed inn settling down under attentive new management; simply furnished with bare boards and brick walls, big log fire, changing ales from local breweries such as Wychwood and Jennings, classy pub food, sizeable restaurant; live music (Fri), pool table, TV; children and dogs (in bar) welcome, tables out in small front courtyard, ten bedrooms, open all day, food every day but call to check sitting times.

HESKET NEWMARKET   NY3438
★ Old Crown (016974) 78288
Village signed off B5299 in Caldbeck; CA7 8JG Straightforward cooperative-owned local in attractive village; small bar with bric-a-brac, mountaineering kit and pictures, woodburner, good Hesket Newmarket beers brewed in barn behind (can book tours), hearty home-made food (not Mon), reasonable prices and friendly service, dining room and garden room; folk night Mon, juke box, pool, darts and board games; children and dogs welcome, lovely walking country away from Lake District crowds (near Cumbria Way), open all day Fri-Sun, closed lunchtimes other days.

KENDAL   SD5192
Riflemans Arms (01539) 241470
Greenside; LA9 4LD Old-fashioned local in village-green setting on edge of town, friendly regulars and staff, Greene King Abbot, Timothy Taylors Landlord and guests,

no food; Thurs folk night, Sun quiz, TV, pool and darts (regular matches); children and dogs welcome, closed lunchtimes Mon-Thurs, otherwise open all day, hours may change in winter.

Dog & Gun (017687) 73463
Lake Road; off top end of Market Square; CA12 5BT Neatly furnished beamed town pub; settles and stripped boards in one room, flagstones and larger tables in another, collection of striking mountain photographs, reasonably priced standard pub fare including signature goulash (served in two sizes and vegetarian version), Greene King ales plus several local and national guests, friendly helpful staff, log fire; occasional quiz nights; children till 9.30pm and dogs welcome, beer garden, open (and food) all day, can get very busy in season.

George (017687) 72076
St Johns Street; CA12 5AZ Handsome 17th-c coaching inn with open-plan main bar and attractive dark-panelled side room; old-fashioned settles and modern banquettes under black beams, log fires, six Jennings ales and a couple of guests kept well, ten wines by the glass, generous home-made food including local beef, lamb and game in season, friendly helpful service, restaurant; children welcome in eating areas, dogs in bar, 12 bedrooms, open all day.

Inn on the Square (0800) 840 1247
Market Square; CA12 5JF Hotel with contemporary Scandinavian-influenced décor; enjoyable bar in front and back bars or steakhouse restaurant, good choice of wines and cocktails, well kept ales such as Keswick, efficient welcoming service; children and dogs (in bar areas) welcome, 34 bedrooms, open all day.

Pheasant (017687) 72219
Crosthwaite Road (A66, 1 mile out); CA12 5PP Small 17th-c beamed roadside local; good choice of popular home-made food at reasonable prices, well kept Jennings and guests, efficient friendly service, open fire, dining room; children (if eating) and dogs (in bar) welcome, a few picnic-sets out at front, beer garden up steps behind, bedrooms, near ancient church of St Kentigern, open all day.

Royal Oak (017687) 73135
Main Street; CA12 5HZ Refurbished 18th-c coaching house; Thwaites ales, decent wines and good choice of popular food, friendly service; children and dogs

welcome, comfortable bedrooms, open (and food) all day.

Swinside Inn (017687) 78253
From A66, take turning for Portinscale, drive through the village, ignore right turn by a house in woods, take next right opposite postbox in wall, pub is about a mile; CA12 5UE Updated 18th-c pub in peaceful valley setting (don't use postcode for satnav); two bars and various dining areas, open fires, well kept ales including one named for them (Double Sunset), good reasonably priced pubby food from lunchtime sandwiches up, friendly helpful staff; background music; children and dogs (in some parts) welcome, tables in garden and on upper and lower terraces with fine views across to the high crags and fells around Rosedale Pike, six bedrooms, big breakfast, large car park, open all day, food all day except Sat, Sun in winter.

Orange Tree (01524) 271716
Fairbank B6254; LA6 2BD White-fronted family-run town pub serving beers from nearby Kirkby Lonsdale brewery, well kept guest ales too, a real cider and good choice of wines and bottled Belgian beers, carpeted beamed bar with central wooden servery, sporting cartoons and old range, hearty reasonably priced food in back dining room, efficient staff; children and dogs welcome, six comfortable bedrooms (some in building next door), open all day.

Fetherston Arms (01768) 898284
The Square; CA10 1DQ Busy old stone inn with cosy bar and various dining areas; enjoyable, well presented food at reasonable prices including good home-made pies, interesting range of well kept changing beers, friendly helpful staff; children and dogs welcome, picnic tables on back lawn, nice Eden Valley village.

Sticklebarn (015394) 37356
By car park for Stickle Ghyll; LA22 9JU Glorious views from this roomy and busy Langdale Valley walkers'/climbers' bar owned and run by the NT; up to six well kept changing ales, shortish choice of enjoyable home-made food (some meat from next-door farm), mountaineering photographs, two woodburners; many events including occasional live music, films, quiz, seasonal festivals; children, dogs and boots welcome, big terrace with verandah, outside pizza oven and fire pit, open (and food) all day, shuts in winter at 9pm (10pm weekends, closed January).

We say if we know a pub allows dogs.

LEVENS SD4885
Hare & Hounds (015395) 60004
Off A590; LA8 8PN Welcoming 16th-c village pub handy for Sizergh Castle (NT); five well kept changing local ales and good home-made pub food including burgers and pizzas, partly panelled low-beamed lounge bar, front tap room with open fire and further seating down steps, also a barn dining room; Weds winter quiz; children, walkers and dogs welcome, disabled loo, good views from front terrace, five bedrooms and self-catering, open (and food) all day.

LINDALE SD4180
★Royal Oak (015395) 32882
The Gill; LA11 6LX Nicely presented open-plan village pub with three distinct areas; very good freshly made food (best to book) including hyper-local products, friendly helpful staff, well kept Robinsons ales and a good range of wines; children welcome, small garden behind, open all day Fri-Sun, call to check other hours

LORTON NY1526
★Wheatsheaf (01900) 85199
B5289 Buttermere–Cockermouth; CA13 9UW Good local atmosphere in neatly furnished bar with two log fires and vibrant coloured walls inside and out, Jennings ales, regularly changing guests and several good value wines, popular home-made food (all day Sun) from sandwiches up, smallish restaurant (best to book), affable hard-working landlord and friendly staff; children and dogs welcome, tables out behind and campsite, caravans to rent, open all day Fri-Sun.

LOW HESKET NY4646
Rose & Crown (01697) 473346
A6 Carlisle–Penrith; CA4 0HG Welcoming 18th-c coaching inn with split-level interior; enjoyable home-made food including good vegetarian menu, Jennings Bitter and guest, good service, pitched-roof dining room with railway memorabilia and central oak tree; background music, TV; children welcome, closed Mon, Tues, most of Weds (open for drinks only from 8.45pm) and all lunchtimes except Sun.

LUPTON SO5581
★Plough (015395) 67700
A65, near M6 junction 36; LA6 1PJ Carefully refurbished inn, comfortable and relaxing, with spreading open-plan bars, beams, furniture and decoration in a mix of neutral colours, gentle fabric prints and textures, rugs on wooden floors, leather sofas and armchairs by woodburner, good creative food served by neat staff, local ales, several good wines by the glass;

background music; children and dogs (in bar) welcome, picnic tables in back garden, good surrounding walks, bedrooms, open (and food) all day.

MELMERBY NY6137
Shepherds (01768) 889064
A686 Penrith–Alston; CA10 1HF Comfortable and welcoming 18th-c split-level country pub; beamed and flagstoned bar with woodburner, barn dining room, good food cooked by landlord-chef including themed nights, three well kept ales such as Allendale, Hawkshead and Tirril; children and dogs welcome, a few tables out at front, closed Mon, other opening times seasonal but always open Weds-Sat evenings and all Sun.

MUNGRISDALE NY3630
Mill Inn (017687) 79632
Off A66 Penrith–Keswick, 1 mile W of A5091 Ullswater turn-off; CA11 0XR Part 17th-c pub in fine setting below fells with wonderful surrounding walks; neatly kept bar with old millstone built into counter, traditional dark wood furnishings, hunting pictures and woodburner in stone fireplace, well kept Robinsons ales and good range of malt whiskies, enjoyable traditional food in hearty portions, friendly staff, separate dining room; darts and dominoes, pool in winter; children and dogs welcome, wheelchair access, seats in garden by river, five bedrooms, open all day (food till 8pm).

NETHER WASDALE NY1204
★Strands (01946) 726237
SW of Wast Water; CA20 1ET Lovely spot below the remote high fells around Wast Water; own-brew beers and popular good value food from changing menu, well cared-for high-beamed main bar with woodburner, smaller public bar with pool and table football, separate dining room, pleasant staff and relaxed friendly atmosphere; background and occasional live music; children and dogs welcome, neat garden with terrace and belvedere, 14 bedrooms, good breakfast, open all day; for sale, so may be changes.

NEWBIGGIN NY5649
Blue Bell (01768) 896615
B6413; CA8 9DH Small L-shaped village pub, friendly and unpretentious, with a changing local ale and enjoyable pubby food cooked by landlady, fireplace on right with woodburner; darts and pool; children welcome, good Eden Valley walks, closed weekday lunchtimes.

NEWBY BRIDGE SD3686
★Swan (015395) 31681
Just off A590; LA12 8NB Substantial, stylishly comfortable spa hotel (extended

---

There are report forms at the back of the book.

17th-c coaching house) in lovely setting by River Leven and its fine old bridge; busy low-ceilinged bar with scrubbed tables on bare boards, cheerful upholstered dining chairs and window seats, small iron fireplace, stools against counter serving three changing local ales, contemporary pub menu, more space and another log fire towards the back, main hotel also has a sizeable restaurant; background music; children (till 7pm) and dogs (in bar) welcome, iron-work tables and chairs on riverside terrace, well equipped contemporary bedrooms plus luxury cottages, open (and food) all day from 10am.

PAPCASTLE   NY1131
Belle Vue (01900) 821388
Belle Vue; CA13 0NT Beamed corner pub-restaurant decorated in country-kitchen style; good well presented food including roasts and sandwiches at dinner, Cumbrian ales such as Jennings, decent wines and interesting selection of whiskies and gins, friendly helpful service; background music; children welcome, closed Mon.

PATTERDALE   NY3915
White Lion (017684) 82214
A592 opposite village shop; CA11 0NW Tall narrow roadside inn with ready market of walkers and climbers (can get very busy especially in season); large helpings of enjoyable pub food and well kept beers such as Marstons and Theakstons, friendly hard-working staff, traditional flagstoned bar, open fires; sports TV; children and dogs welcome, seven bedrooms (five ensuite), open (and food) all day.

POOLEY BRIDGE   NY4724
★Crown (017684) 25869
Centre of village; CA10 2NP Refurbished dining inn/hotel in lovely position on Ullswater with local ales, pleasing food and plenty of seating on two waterside terraces; various Thwaites ales, good range of mainly traditional food nicely done, genuinely welcoming staff; spacious interior with proper little bar with stools against rough hewn counter and dining area leading directly to ground-floor terrace with heaters, contemporary seating and lovely river views backed by fells; children welcome, dogs in bar & bedrooms, attractive bedrooms (room service), handy for Penrith and steamboat excursions on Ullswater, open (and food) all day.

RAVENSTONEDALE   NY7401
Fat Lamb (015396) 23242
Crossbank; A683 Sedbergh–Kirkby Stephen; CA17 4LL Isolated inn surrounded by great scenery and lovely walks; comfortable old-fashioned feel, pews in beamed bar with fire in traditional black range, interesting local photographs and bird plates, propeller from 1930s biplane over servery, menu of popular pub food

classics, can eat in bar or separate dining room (less character), one well kept ale such as Black Sheep or Pennine, decent wines and many malt whiskies, friendly helpful staff; background music; children and dogs welcome, disabled facilities, tables out by nature reserve pastures with hide, 12 bedrooms, open all day, food all day weekends.

RAVENSTONEDALE   NY7204
Kings Head (015396) 23050
Pub visible from A685 W of Kirkby Stephen; CA17 4NH Sizeable riverside inn with opened-up beamed rooms, rugs on big flagstones and attractive array of wooden chairs and cushioned settles, prints on grey-painted walls, double-sided woodburner and another log fire in raised fireplace, similarly furnished dining room, real ales such as Wainwright, short tempting menu (steak and stilton pie a standout), friendly staff, darts; background music; children and dogs (in bar) welcome, picnic-sets by the river, six comfortable clean bedrooms, good surrounding walks, open (and food) all day; new owners as we went to press, so may be changes.

ROSTHWAITE   NY2514
Scafell (017687) 77208
B5289 S of Keswick; CA12 5XB 19th-c hotel's big tile-floored back bar useful for walkers; handsome slate and blazing log fire, up to six well kept local ales in season, over 60 malt whiskies and simple tasty pub food including lunchtime sandwiches, more elaborate dining in restaurant, also afternoon teas, cocktail bar/sun lounge, friendly helpful staff; background music; children and dogs welcome, tables outside overlooking beck, 23 contemporary bedrooms, open all day.

RYDAL   NY3606
Glen Rothay Hotel (015394) 34500
A591 Ambleside–Grasmere; LA22 9LR Small 17th-c roadside hotel with cosy back Badger Bar, copper-topped tables, stools and benches, lots of interesting local prints, at least four well kept changing ales and varied choice of locally sourced food from good sandwiches up, beamed and panelled dining lounge with open fire, restaurant, friendly efficient service; unusual loos cut into the rock; children, walkers and dogs welcome, tables in pretty garden (resident badgers are fed at dusk), eight comfortable bedrooms, good breakfast, handy for William Wordsworth's house at Rydal Mount, open all day.

SANDFORD   NY7316
Sandford Arms (01768) 351121
Village and pub signposted just off A66 W of Brough; CA16 6NR Neatly modernised former 18th-c farmhouse in peaceful village; good choice of enjoyable food served by friendly helpful staff, L-shaped

part-carpeted main bar with stripped beams and stonework, two well kept changing ales, comfortable raised and balustraded eating area, more formal dining room and second flagstoned bar, woodburner; background music; children and dogs welcome, seats in front garden and covered courtyard, five bedrooms, closed Tues and lunchtime Weds.

SANTON BRIDGE   NY1101
Bridge Inn (019467) 26221
Off A595 at Holmrook or Gosforth; CA19 1UX Old inn set in charming riverside spot with fell views; bustling beamed and timbered bar, some booths around stripped-pine tables, log fire, up to ten well kept ales such as Jennings, enjoyable food (booking advised) including blackboard specials and Sun carvery, friendly helpful staff, separate dining room and small reception hall with open fire; background music, newspapers, World's Biggest Liar competition (Nov); children and dogs (in bar) welcome, seats outside by quiet road, plenty of walks, 16 bedrooms, open (and food) all day, breakfast for non-residents.

SATTERTHWAITE   SD3392
Eagles Head (01229) 860237
S edge of village; LA12 8LN Nice little pub prettily placed on edge of beautiful Grizedale Forest (visitor centre nearby); low black beams and comfortable furnishings, old tiled floor, woodburner, four well kept changing Cumbrian ales, popular pubby food from shortish menu including good home-made pies, friendly welcoming staff; occasional live music; children, dogs, bikers and muddy boots welcome, picnic-sets in attractive tree-shaded courtyard garden, open all day in summer, may shut Weds in winter.

SCALES   NY3426
White Horse (017687) 79883
A66 W of Penrith; CA12 4SY Traditional Lakeland pub in lovely setting below Blencathra; log fire in flagstoned beamed bar, little snug and another room with black range, three local ales and good pubby food; quiz Weds, board games; children and dogs welcome, picnic-sets out in front, bunkhouse, open (and food) all day.

SEATHWAITE   SD2295
Newfield Inn (01229) 716840
Duddon Valley, near Ulpha (not Seathwaite in Borrowdale); LA20 6ED Friendly 16th-c whitewashed stone cottage in quiet country setting; bar with unusual slate floor and interesting pictures, woodburner (new managers were refurbishing as we went to press), four well kept changing local beers and good reasonably priced home-made food from sandwiches up; children and dogs welcome, tables in nice garden with hill views and play area, good walks, open (and food) all day.

SEDBERGH   SD6592
Dalesman (01539) 621183
Main Street; LA10 5BN Stone-built inn with three modernised linked rooms; freshly made food from sandwiches and tapas up using Dales-reared meats, friendly prompt service, five well kept local ales, plenty of wines by the glass and good range of other drinks, stripped stone and beams, central woodburner; background music; children welcome, no dogs inside, chunky picnic-sets out in front by road, five bedrooms plus others off-site and a self-catering cottage, open (and food) all day, breakfast/brunch from 8am.

STAVELEY   SD4797
★ **Eagle & Child** (01539) 821320
Kendal Road; just off A591 Windermere–Kendal; LA8 9LP Popular black and white pub with big bay windows – as much a part of the village landscape as the fells behind it; chatty cheerful bar with plenty of separate areas, flagstones, log fires (one beneath an impressive mantelbeam), police truncheons, walking sticks, photos, prints, bric-a-brac and farm tools, also attractive upstairs dining room with a beamed ceiling; Hawkshead and five regularly changing ales on handpump, perhaps from Barngates, Bowness Bay, Coniston, Cumbrian Legendary and Fell, several wines by the glass, 25 malt whiskies, 30 gins and farm cider, well regarded pubby food including sandwiches and pies; background music; walkers, children and dogs (in bar) welcome, sheltered riverside garden with picnic-sets under parasols, plus more in second garden and good-sized back terrace, comfortable bedrooms and generous breakfasts, open all day.

TORVER   SD2894
Church House (015394) 49159
A593/A5084 S of Coniston; LA21 8AZ Friendly 14th-c coaching house; small bar with low beams and big log fire in sizeable stone fireplace under refurbishment at time of writing, enjoyable home-made food (all day weekends) from sandwiches and up, four ales from barrel-fronted counter, comfortable lounge and separate dining room; board games, occasional live music; children and dogs (in bar) welcome, pretty lawned garden, four bedrooms and two bunk rooms, also standing for five caravans/motor homes, good nearby walks to Coniston Water, open all day.

TORVER   SD2894
Wilson Arms (015394) 41237
A593; LA21 8BB Old family-run roadside inn with adjoining deli; beams, nice log fire and one or two modern touches, well kept Cumbrian ales and good locally sourced food cooked to order in bar or dining room, friendly service; children and dogs welcome, hill views (including Old Man of Coniston) from tables in large garden, seven bedrooms

and three holiday cottages, open (and food) all day, call to check winter hours.

TROUTBECK   NY4103
Mortal Man (015394) 33193
A592 N of Windermere; Upper Road; LA23 1PL Popular 17th-c Lakeland inn; beamed and partly panelled bar with cosy room off, log fires, four well kept local ales including a house beer from Old School Brewery, several wines by the glass and well liked food in bar and picture-window restaurant; folk night Sun, open mike Tues, quiz Weds, storytelling Thurs; children and dogs welcome, great views from sunny garden, lovely village and surrounding walks, bedrooms, open (and food) all day.

TROUTBECK   NY4103
★Queens Head (015394) 32404
A592 N of Windermere; LA23 1PW Popular 17th-c beamed coaching inn well restored after devastating 2014 fire; some original features remain such as the four-poster bar and stone fireplaces, but generally an airier feel with good quality oak furniture on wood and flagstoned floors, enjoyable sensibly priced food from hot or cold sandwiches and pub favourites up, well kept Robinsons ales, a dozen wines by the glass and good selection of whiskies/gins, friendly efficient service; background music; children, walkers and dogs welcome, seats outside with fine views across to Applethwaite Moors, ten comfortably refurbished bedrooms (some in barn opposite), open (and food) all day, kitchen shuts 7pm Sun.

TROUTBECK   NY3827
Troutbeck Inn (017684) 83635
A5091/A66; CA11 0SJ Former railway hotel with small bar, lounge and log-fire restaurant, a couple of well known local ales and good food from pub standards up, efficient friendly service; children and dogs (in bar) welcome, beer garden with picnic tables, seven bedrooms plus three self-catering cottages in converted stables, open all day weekends, from 2.30pm weekdays, winter hours may differ.

ULDALE   NY2436
Snooty Fox (016973) 71479
Village signed off B5299 W of Caldbeck; CA7 1HA Comfortable and welcoming two-bar village inn; ample helpings of good quality home-cooked food (not Weds) using local ingredients, up to four well kept changing ales, decent selection of whiskies, friendly attentive staff, fox hunting memorabilia; winter pool table; children welcome in dining areas, dogs in snug, nice

---

location with garden at back, two bedrooms, closed lunchtimes except Sun.

ULVERSTON   SD2878
★Farmers (01229) 584469
Market Place; LA12 7BA Convivial town pub, wine bar and restaurant opposite the market cross decorated in contemporary cocktail bar style with original fireplace, three quickly changing guests, a dozen wines by the glass, good varied choice of popular fair-priced food from baguettes and deli boards up, cocktail bar leading to big raftered dining area with seating booths on either side (children here only); background music, Thurs quiz; colourful hanging baskets and tubs on front terrace warmed by a fire pit, Thurs and Sat market days (pub very busy then), self-catering apartments/cottages nearby, open all day from 9am for breakfast.

ULVERSTON   SD2878
Mill (01229) 581384
Mill Street; LA12 7EB Converted 19th-c flour mill on three floors; ground-floor bar with huge waterwheel behind glass, mix of furniture including leather armchairs and sofas on wood floor, warming logburners, around ten real ales including Lancaster (brewery owns the pub), good wines and fine array of whiskies, gins and brandies, spiral stairs up to restaurant and second bar with terrace, very good well presented food from sandwiches and snacks up (in restaurant only Fri, Sat), evening cocktail lounge on top floor (Fri, Sat), friendly efficient young staff; live music and quiz nights; children and dogs welcome, open all day.

UNDERBARROW   SD4692
Black Labrador (015395) 68234
From centre of Kendal at town hall, turn left into Beast Banks signed for Underbarrow, then follow Underbarrow Road; LA8 8HQ Attractive country inn opened up into its raftered roof for light bright feel, mix of furniture including leather sofas on stone floor, woodburner, three changing local beers, good choice of enjoyable freshly prepared food including from lava rock grill, recently added dining extension; darts and pool table; children and dogs welcome, picnic-sets and covered balcony in garden, closed Tues.

WASDALE HEAD   NY1807
Wasdale Head Inn (019467) 26229
NE of Wast Water; CA20 1EX Mountain hotel notable for its stunning fellside and its role in the history of British climbing; roomy walkers' bar with pew-style

---

A star symbol before the name of a pub shows exceptional character and appeal. It doesn't mean extra comfort. Even quite a basic pub can win a star, if it's individual enough.

seating and welcoming log burner, up to six local ales and good choice of wines, ample helpings of enjoyable pubby food including Herdwick lamb and mutton in season; residents' bar, lounge and panelled restaurant; children and dogs welcome, several tables outside, nine bedrooms, self-catering apartments in converted barn and camping, open all day.

WETHERAL   NY4654
Wheatsheaf (01228) 560686

Handy for M6 junctions 42/43; CA4 8HD Popular 19th-c pub in pretty village; tartan-carpeted floor and fake-bookshelf wallpaper, three well kept local ales and enjoyable home-made food including daily specials, good friendly service; Tues quiz, sports TV; children and dogs welcome, picnic-sets in small garden, open all day, no food Mon, Tues.

WHITEHAVEN   NX9718
Gin & Beer It (01946) 329354

Market Place; CA28 7JB Friendly and relaxed little bar, pizzeria and bottle shop with wide variety of drinks including six or so interesting beers on tap (many more in bottles and cans), over 50 gins and decent range of wines by the glass, nice cheese/charcuterie boards as well as pizza and finger-food snacks, eclectic mix of furniture on original tiled floor, exposed stone and wood-clad walls; unobtrusive background music, board games; dogs welcome, closed Sun-Tues and lunchtimes.

WINDERMERE   SD4198
★Crafty Baa (015394) 88002

Victoria Street, beside the Queens; LA23 1AB Small atmospheric bar with great selection of craft beers on tap and in bottles (listed on blackboards), good range of other drinks too including decent coffee, enjoyable food from snacks to more substantial cheese and charcuterie combinations served on slates, knowledgeable staff, rustic décor with bare boards, exposed stone walls and log fire, recycled materials and plenty of quirky touches, lots more room upstairs and in new cosy extension serving real ales and pies; background and live music; dogs welcome, a few seats out at front, open (and food) all day.

WREAY   NY4349
Plough (016974) 75770

Village signed from A6 N of Low Hesket; CA4 0RL Welcoming 18th-c beamed pub in pretty village; modernised split-level interior with pine tables and chairs on wood or flagstone floors, some exposed stonework, woodburner, good choice of enjoyable freshly prepared food (not Mon) including specials, well kept Hawkshead and a couple of guests from brick-fronted canopied bar, efficient friendly service; Mon quiz; children welcome, closed Mon and Tues.

Derbyshire

KEY ★ Star Pub | 🌟 Top Quality Food | 🍺 Great Beer
🍷 Good Wines | £ Bargain Meals | 🛏 Good Bedrooms | 🍴 Serves Food

---

 CHELMORTON   SK1170 Map 7

Church Inn 🍺 🛏 £

(01298) 85319 – www.thechurchinn.co.uk

Village signposted off A5270, between A6 and A515 SE of Buxton; keep on up through village towards church; SK17 9SL

Cosy, convivial inn beautifully set in High Peak walking country, with good value food and well kept ales

Refreshing both locals and travellers since 1742, this is very much a traditional inn that is consistently praised by our readers. The long-serving, hands-on licensees keep the chatty, low-ceilinged bar spic and span with its open fire and built-in cushioned benches and simple chairs around polished cast-iron-framed tables (a couple still with their squeaky sewing treadles). Shelves of books, Tiffany-style lamps and house plants in the curtained windows, atmospheric Dales photographs and prints, and a coal-effect stove in the stripped-stone end wall all add a cosy feel. You'll find five beers on handpump, such as Abbeydale Moonshine, Adnams Southwold, Marstons Pedigree and Thornbridge Jaipur, and ten wines by the glass; there's darts in a tile-floored games area on the left and board games. The inn is opposite a mainly 18th-c church and is prettily tucked into woodland with fine views over the village and hills beyond from good teak tables on a two-level terrace.

🍴 Tasty food includes sandwiches, prawn cocktail, black pudding fritters with spicy home-made chutney, vegetarian mixed bean chilli, beef lasagne, chicken breast in stilton sauce, steak and kidney pie, salmon fillet with prawn and white wine sauce, and puddings. *Benchmark main dish: sirloin steak with onion rings and chips £16.50. Two-course evening meal £20.00.*

Free house ~ Licensees Julie and Justin Satur ~ Real ale ~ Open 12-3, 6-10; 12-10 Fri, Sat; 12-10 Sun ~ Bar food 12-2.30, 6-8.30; 12-8.30 Fri-Sun ~ Restaurant ~ Children welcome ~ Dogs allowed in bar

---

 CHINLEY   SK0382 Map 7

Old Hall ★ 🍺 🛏

(01663) 750529 – www.old-hall-inn.co.uk

Village signposted off A6 (very sharp turn) E of New Mills; also off A624 N of Chapel-en-le-Frith; Whitehough Head Lane, off B6062; SK23 6EJ

Fine range of ales and ciders in splendid building with lots to look at and good country food; comfortable bedrooms

You'll find a friendly welcome at this elegant pub boasting unusual and interesting architectural features. Even if you're just dropping in for a drink, do take a peek at the surprisingly grand dining room with its great stone chimney soaring into high eaves, refectory tables on a parquet floor, lovely old mullioned windows and a splendid minstrels' gallery. The warm bar (basically four small friendly rooms opened into a single area tucked behind a massive central chimney) contains open fires, broad flagstones, red patterned carpet, sturdy country tables and a couple of long pews and various other seats. There are eight handpumps, serving Marstons Wainright and seven guest beers, predominantly local, from breweries such as Abbeydale, Kelham Island, Marble, Peak, Phoenix, Storm, Thornbridge, Whim and Wincle. Also, two or three cask ciders as well as some interesting lagers on tap, 12 malt whiskies, 20 gins and a rare range of bottled ciders. All the wines on the regularly changing list are available by the glass. They hold a beer festival with music in September. The pretty walled garden has picnic-sets under sycamore trees. Some of the attractive bedrooms look over the garden and there are also a couple of self-catering cottages.

Rewarding food includes sandwiches, ham hock terrine, curried haddock fishcake with fennel slaw, whitebait, High Peak cheddar and caramelised onion pie, burger with toppings, coleslaw and chips, smoked bacon, pork and sage sausages with mash and red wine gravy, lancashire hotpot, duck breast with dauphinoise potatoes, beetroot and chard, baked harissa hake with haricot bean and tomato cassoulet, and puddings such as toffee crème brûlée and strawberry cheesecake with home-made ice-cream. *Benchmark main dish: steak in ale suet pudding £14.00. Two-course evening meal £20.00.*

Free house ~ Licensee Daniel Capper ~ Real ale ~ Open 12-11; 12-midnight Sat ~ Bar food 12-9 (7.30 Sun) ~ Restaurant ~ Children welcome ~ Dogs allowed in bar ~ Bedrooms: £115

FENNY BENTLEY   SK1750   Map 7
Coach & Horses
(01335) 350246 – www.coachandhorsesfennybentley.co.uk
A515 N of Ashbourne; DE6 1LB

Cosy inn with pretty country furnishings, roaring open fires and food all day

Located at the southern end of the Peak District National Park, this village inn is surrounded by beautiful countryside and makes a perfect base for exploring the area. The traditional interior here has all the trappings you'd expect of a 17th-c country coaching inn, from roaring log fires, exposed brick hearths and flagstone floors to black beams hung with pewter mugs, and hand-made pine furniture that includes wall settles with floral-print cushions. There's also a conservatory dining room and a cosy front dining room. Real ales from local breweries such as Dancing Duck, Derby, Marstons, Peak, Whim and Wincle are on offer, plus a couple of farm ciders and seven wines by the glass. The landlord is knowledgeable about malt whiskies and he stocks around two dozen; quiet background music. A side garden by an elder tree (with views across fields) has seats and tables, and there are modern tables and chairs under cocktail parasols on a front roadside terrace. It's a short walk from the Tissington Trail, a popular cycling/walking path along a former railway line (best joined at the nearby picture-book village of Tissington). No dogs allowed inside.

Well thought-of food from local suppliers includes chicken liver pâté with fruit compote, sharing deli board, wild mushroom and goats cheese herb crumble, seafood tagliatelle, chicken breast stuffed with chorizo with spicy tomato sauce, sweet potato, chickpea and spinach curry, sirloin steak with onion rings, chips and a choice of sauce, barnsley lamb chop with port, redcurrant and rosemary sauce, and puddings such as lemon meringue roulade and honeycomb and vanilla cheesecake. *Benchmark main dish: lamb casserole with herb dumplings £13.25. Two-course evening meal £21.00.*

Free house ~ Licensees John and Matthew Dawson ~ Real ale ~ Open 12-3, 6-10; 12-10 Sat, Sun ~ Bar food 12-2.30, 6-8.30; 12-8.30 Sat, Sun ~ Restaurant ~ Children allowed in bar

GREAT LONGSTONE   SK1971   Map 7

Crispin

(01629) 640237 – www.thecrispingreatlongstone.co.uk
Main Street; village signed from A6020, N of Ashford in the Water; DE45 1TZ

Spotlessly kept pub with emphasis on good, fair-priced food

This cosy, traditional pub near some of the Peak District's most popular attractions draws in all sorts: walkers, cyclists, horse riders, families, classic car clubs and more. Décor throughout is traditional: brass or copper implements, decorative plates, horsebrasses on beams in the red ceiling, cushioned built-in wall benches and upholstered chairs and stools around polished tables on red carpet – and a warming fire. A corner area (with a woodburning stove) is snugly partitioned off and there's a separate, more formal dining room on the right; darts, board games and maybe faint background music. There are Robinsons ales such as Dizzy Blonde, Double Hop, Trooper and Unicorn and a guest beer on handpump, Weston's Old Rosie cider and quite a choice of wines and whiskies. In warm weather there are seats in the garden and picnic-sets out in front (one under a heated canopy) set well back above the quiet lane. Disabled access.

Pubby food includes a two- and three-course lunchtime deal plus sandwiches, omelettes, home-made pies, beer-battered fish and chips, chilli con carne, curries, fish pie, dressed crab, steaks from the local butcher, and puddings. *Benchmark main dish: steak and kidney pie £13.95. Two-course evening meal £20.00.*

Robinsons ~ Tenant Paul Rowlinson ~ Real ale ~ Open 12-3, 6-11; 12-11 Sat, Sun ~ Bar food 12-2.30, 6-9 ~ Restaurant ~ Children allowed in bar ~ Dogs allowed in bar

HASSOP   SK2272   Map 7

Old Eyre Arms

(01629) 640390 – www.oldeyrearms.co.uk
B6001 N of Bakewell; DE45 1NS

Comfortable old farmhouse with long-serving owners, decent food and beer, and pretty views from the garden

This is an ideal spot for discovering Chatsworth House and Haddon Hall, which are both close by, as is the Monsal Trail cycling/walking path. However, this fine 17th-c coaching inn is a destination on its own. In summer, the hanging baskets at the front are lovely and the delightful garden (with its gurgling fountain) looks straight out to fine Peak District countryside. The low-ceilinged beamed rooms are snug and cosy with log fires and traditional furnishings that include cushioned oak settles, comfortable plush chairs, a longcase clock, old pictures and lots of brass and copper. The tap room, snug and lounge are similarly decorated with cushioned oak benches, old pictures and an impressive collection of brass and copper; the tap room also has a fine display of teapots. Abbeydale Deception, Peak Chatsworth Gold and Swift Nick, Sheffield Crucible Best and Thornbridge Crackendale and Lord Marples on handpump, good wines by the glass, 35 gins, 20 malt whiskies and farm cider; background music. Above the stone fireplace in the lounge is a painting of the Eyre coat of arms

🍴 A good choice of food includes roasted beetroot, roasted fig and goats cheese salad, treacle-cured salmon with soda bread, game pie with seasonal vegetables, local sausages and mash with onion gravy, seared lamb rump with hogget pie and dauphinoise potatoes, shepherd's pie, burger with toppings and onion rings, chicken kiev with coleslaw and frites, and puddings such as apple pie and crème anglaise and Bakewell pudding with ice-cream and fruit compote. *Benchmark main dish: fish, chips and peas £14.00. Two-course evening meal £21.00.*

Free house ~ Licensee Lee Burgin ~ Real ale ~ Open 12-11; 12-8 Sun; closed Mon ~ Bar food 12-4, 6-9; 12-8 Sun ~ Children welcome ~ Dogs welcome

HATHERSAGE
SK2380   Map 7

Plough 🏠◐ ♀ 🛏

(01433) 650319 – www.theploughinn-hathersage.co.uk

Leadmill; B6001 towards Bakewell; S32 1BA

Derbyshire Dining Pub of the Year

Comfortable dining pub with well presented food, beer and wine and seats in a waterside garden; bedrooms

Great food, as well as a warm welcome and a good choice of well kept ales and other drinks await you at this immaculately kept 16th-c inn in the heart of the Peak District National Park, with great climbing and walking nearby. There are bright tartan and oriental patterned carpets, rows of dark wooden chairs and tables plus a very long banquette, two woodburning stoves and grey walls hung with decorative plates. The neat dining room is slightly more formal. Abbeydale Moonshine, Bradfield Yorkshire Farmer and Eagle Bombardier on handpump, 25 wines by the glass from a good list and around a dozen malt whiskies; quiet background music. The seats on the terrace have wonderful valley views and the nine-acre grounds are on the banks of the River Derwent – the pretty garden slopes down to the water. There are seven well equipped bedrooms in a barn conversion and two shepherd's huts. Disabled access.

🍴 As well as hot and cold sandwiches (until 5.30pm), the first class food includes ham hock terrine with peach and rosemary chutney, sharing platters, pizzas, mushroom orzo with oyster mushrooms and watercress, chicken katsu curry with coconut rice and cucumber, carrot and ginger dressing, seared tuna niçoise salad, fillet of beef with horseradish mashed potatoes, artichokes and ceps, rack of lamb with goats cheese dauphinoise, spinach and tapenade, and puddings such as rhubarb and custard pannacotta and chocolate cake with boozy cherries and black cherry sorbet. *Benchmark main dish: beer-battered haddock with chips and peas £14.00. Two-course evening meal £25.00.*

Free house ~ Licensees Bob, Cynthia and Elliott Emery ~ Real ale ~ Open 11-11; 12-10.30 Sun ~ Bar food 12-9 ~ Restaurant ~ Children welcome ~ Dogs allowed in bar & bedrooms ~ Bedrooms: £120

HAYFIELD
SK0387   Map 7

Royal 🛏

(01663) 742721 – www.theroyalathayfield.com

Market Street; SK22 2EP

Big, bustling inn with fine panelled rooms, friendly service and thoughtful choice of drinks and food; bedrooms

This large handsome stone inn is very much a feature of this attractive village. The oak-panelled bar and lounge areas have open fires, a fine collection of seats from long settles with pretty scatter cushions through elegant upholstered dining chairs to tub chairs and chesterfields, and an assortment of solid tables on rugs and flagstones; house plants and daily papers as well. Howard Town Twenty Trees (brewed specially for the pub) plus guests such as Brakspears Oxford Gold, Jennings Cumberland, Marstons Wainwright and Wincle Lord Lucan on handpump, 11 wines by the glass, ten malt whiskies and two farm ciders; background music, TV and board games. Bedrooms are well appointed and comfortable and make an excellent base for exploring the Peak District; breakfasts are good too.

Pleasing food includes sandwiches (until 5pm), creamy garlic mushrooms on toasted ciabatta, salmon and spring onion fishcake with celeriac rémoulade, chicken satay with peanut sauce and sticky rice, sharing plates, macaroni cheese, a curry and a pie of the day, gammon with egg or pineapple fritter, salmon with lemon and chive butter, sirloin steak with peppercorn sauce, and puddings such as bakewell tart and a cheesecake of the day; steak night is Wednesday. *Benchmark main dish: steak in ale pie £11.95. Two-course evening meal £16.00.*

Free house ~ Licensees Mark and Lisa Miller ~ Real ale ~ Open 11-11; 11am-11.30pm Sat; 11am-10.30pm Sun ~ Bar food 12-8.30; 12-9 Sat; 12-7 Sun ~ Children welcome ~ Dogs allowed in bar ~ Bedrooms: £85

OVER HADDON
SK2066 Map 7
Lathkil 🍺 £
(01629) 812501 ~ www.lathkil.co.uk
Village and inn signposted from B5055 just SW of Bakewell; DE45 1JE

Traditional pub with long-serving owners (they've been here for 39 years), super views, a good range of beers and well liked food; bedrooms

This pub originally provided much welcomed refreshment for the Victorian lead miners working in Lathkill Dale; today, it provides the same for those exploring the Peak District National Park – including the beautiful dale itself. On the right as you enter, an airy room has a nice fire in an attractively carved fireplace, old-fashioned settles with upholstered cushions, chairs, black beams, a delft shelf of blue and white plates and some original prints and photographs. On the left, the sunny spacious dining area doubles as an evening restaurant and there's a woodburning stove. Peak Swift Nick and Whim Hartington Bitter with guests such as Bradfield Farmers Blonde, Kelham Island Easy Rider and Raw Brown Cow on handpump, a reasonable range of wines (including mulled wine and prosecco), 40 gins and a decent selection of malt whiskies; they hold a beer, cider and gin festival in September. Background music, darts, TV and board games. Dogs are welcome, but muddy boots must be left in the lobby. The views are spectacular and can be enjoyed from seats in the walled garden and from windows in the bar. Bedrooms are comfortable and breakfasts hearty.

Food includes sandwiches (until 5.30pm), cakes (available all day), crispy brie wedges, burgers, pizzas, scampi and chips, sea bass and lime fishcakes with new potatoes, sweet potato, chickpea and spinach curry, some evening-only dishes (such as gammon steak with fried egg and chips) and puddings. *Benchmark main dish: beef lasagne with garlic bread £10.50. Two-course evening meal £18.00.*

Free house ~ Licensee Alice Grigor-Taylor ~ Real ale ~ Open 11-11; 12-10.30 Sun ~ Bar food 12-3, 5.30-8 ~ Restaurant ~ Children welcome ~ Dogs allowed in bar & bedrooms ~ Bedrooms: £85

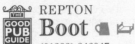

REPTON   SK3027

Boot 🍺 ⌂

(01283) 346047 – www.thebootatrepton.co.uk

Boot Hill; DE65 6FT

Refurbished village pub with simply furnished bar and dining rooms, well regarded food, own-brews and seats outside; bedrooms

This elegant, carefully restored 17th-c inn is ever popular with our readers. The bustling bar has beams and bare floorboards, high stools around equally high wooden tables, plush chairs and cushioned benches, and a good range of drinks that includes their own-brewed Boot Beer: Beast, Bitter, Clod Hopper, ESB, IPA, Repton Cross and Tuffers Old Boots. Also, a guest from another changing brewery and several wines by the glass served by friendly, efficient young staff. There's a dining room with antique-style chairs and tables and big doors that open on to the courtyard, plus a second room down a couple of steps with a woodburning stove. The split-level walled garden has wooden chairs and tables under parasols. The nine attractively furnished bedrooms are light, airy and comfortable; breakfast costs extra.

Interesting food includes breakfasts (8-11am weekdays, 8-10.30am weekends) and afternoon tea (booking required), flatbread with shredded lamb, tzatziki and pickled cucumber, coronation chicken terrine with curry mayonnaise, pickled raisins and coriander, pulled pork burger with pickles and skin-on fries, a pie of the day, corn-fed chicken breast stuffed with black garlic with parmesan arancini, lemon purée and onion sauce, roasted cod loin with peas, pancetta and smoked almond sauce, dry-aged steaks with roasted tomatoes, garlic mushrooms and triple-cooked chips, and puddings such as salted caramel tart with stem ginger ice-cream, and dark chocolate pannacotta with macerated cherries, nougat and candied almonds; they also offer a two- and three-course set lunch. *Benchmark main dish: fish and chips £13.95. Two-course evening meal £22.00.*

Free house ~ Licensee John Archer ~ Real ale ~ Open 8am-11pm ~ Bar food 12-2.30, 6-9; 12-7 Sun ~ Restaurant ~ Children welcome ~ Dogs allowed in bar ~ Bedrooms: from £75

STANTON IN PEAK   SK2364   Map 7

Flying Childers 🍺 £

(01629) 636333 – www.flyingchilders.com

Village signposted from B6056 S of Bakewell; Main Road; DE4 2LW

Top notch beer and inexpensive simple bar lunches in a warm-hearted, unspoilt pub; a delight

This traditional pub, ideal for exploring the many glories of the Peak District, evolved from several stone cottages. In the same family for many years, it's set in a beautiful steep stone village and is named after an unbeatable racehorse of the early 18th c. A snug little right-hand bar is the best place to enjoy your Bombardier and guests from breweries such as Abbeydale, Castle Rock and Matlock Wolds Farm on handpump, and several wines by the glass. This bar was virtually built for chat with its dark beam-and-plank ceiling, dark wall settles, single pew, plain tables, a hot coal and log fire, a few team photographs, dominoes and cribbage; background music. There's a bigger, equally unpretentious bar on the left. As well as seats out in front, there are picnic-sets in the well tended back garden. The surrounding walks are marvellous and both walkers and their dogs are warmly welcomed; they keep doggie treats behind the bar. Now that there is no longer a village shop, the pub does sell some produce.

🍴 Simple lunchtime-only food includes sandwiches and toasties, home-made soups (meat, vegetarian, vegan, gluten-free), vegan burgers, pasties (cheese and onion, mushroom or meat and veg) and afternoon tea. *Benchmark main dish: large bowl of soup £4.90.*

Free house ~ Licensees Richard and Sophie Wood ~ Real ale ~ Open 12-2 (3 weekends), 7-11 ~ Bar food 12-2 ~ Children in top end of bar only ~ Dogs allowed in bar

WOOLLEY MOOR
White Horse 🍴⭐ 🛏 ♀

SK3661   Map 7

(01246) 590319 – www.thewhitehorsewoolleymoor.co.uk
Badger Lane, off B6014 Matlock–Clay Cross; DE55 6FG

Attractive old dining pub in pretty countryside with good food and drinks; bedrooms

This lovely inn with smart bedrooms sits in the pretty hamlet of Woolley Moor on the outskirts of Ashover, with Ogston Reservoir just a couple of minutes' drive away. The pub is neat and uncluttered, and the bar, snug and dining room have wooden dining chairs and tables, stools and leather sofas on flagstoned or wooden floors, a woodburning stove (in the bar), an open fire (in the dining room) and boldly patterned curtains and blinds. Peak Bakewell Best Bitter and Chatsworth Gold and a guest such as Castle Rock Harvest Pale or Dancing Duck Ay Up on handpump, 17 gins and 13 wines by the glass. In the front garden you'll find picnic-sets under parasols on gravel, and boules. Each of the contemporary, well equipped bedroom suites has a private balcony and floor-to-ceiling windows that give splendid views over the Amber Valley.

⭐ Extremely good food includes crab cake with lemon and basil beurre blanc, home-cured bacon and cauliflower purée, sesame chicken with Asian slaw, bean cassoulet with baba ganoush and flatbread, chicken and tarragon pie with new potatoes and creamed leeks, salmon with noodles and ginger and coriander dressing, pan-fried hake in chorizo provençale sauce, and puddings such as white chocolate pannacotta with raspberry compote and meringue with caramelised lemon curd and lemon ice-cream. *Benchmark main dish: pork belly with spring onion mash and smoked bacon sauce £14.95. Two-course evening meal £20.00.*

Free house ~ Licensees David and Melanie Boulby ~ Real ale ~ Open 12-3, 6-11; 12-4 Sun ~ Bar food 12-1.45, 6-8; 12-3 Sun ~ Restaurant ~ Children welcome ~ Bedrooms: £119

Also Worth a Visit in Derbyshire

Besides the fully inspected pubs, you might like to try these pubs that have been recommended to us and described by readers. Do tell us what you think of them: feedback@goodguides.com

ALDERWASLEY   SK3153
Bear (01629) 822585
Left off A6 at Ambergate on to Holly Lane (turns into Jackass Lane) then right at end (staggered crossroads); DE56 2RD Unspoilt country inn with beamed cottagey rooms, one with large glass chandelier over assorted tables and chairs, another with tartan-covered wall banquettes and double-sided woodburner; other décor includes Staffordshire china ornaments, old paintings/engravings and a grandfather

clock; Bass, Thornbridge Jaipur and guests, several wines by the glass from a decent list, good selection of malt whiskies and more than 40 gins, enjoyable traditional food including good Sun carvery; children and dogs (in bar) welcome, seats in lovely garden, eight bedrooms and three self-catering cottages, open all day, food all day Fri-Sun.

ASHBOURNE   SK1846
Smiths Tavern (01335) 300809
St John Street, bottom of marketplace; DE6 1GH Traditional little pub stretching

back from heavily black-beamed bar through lounge to light and airy end room, up to seven well kept Marstons-related ales plus a weekend guest (tasting glasses available) and more than 30 whiskies, friendly knowledgeable staff, good pork pies; darts; children (until 9pm) and dogs welcome, open all day.

ASHFORD IN THE WATER   SK1969
Ashford Arms   (01629) 812725
Off A6 NW of Bakewell; Church Street (B6465, off A6020); DE45 1QB
Attractive 18th-c inn set in pretty village; decent reasonably priced food including OAP weekday lunch, well kept Black Sheep and two local guests, nice wines, restaurant and dining conservatory; children and dogs welcome, plenty of tables outside, eight comfortable bedrooms, open all day Sun (food till 6pm).

ASHFORD IN THE WATER   SK1969
★Bulls Head   (01629) 812931
Off A6 NW of Bakewell; Church Street (B6465, off A6020); DE45 1QB
Traditional 17th-c pub in attractive unspoilt village; cosy two-room beamed and carpeted bar with fires, one or two character gothic seats, spindleback and wheelback chairs around cast-iron-framed tables, local photographs and country prints on cream walls, four Robinsons ales and good choice of traditional food, friendly efficient service; background music; children and dogs welcome, overshoes for walkers, hardwood tables and benches in front and in good-sized garden behind with boules and Jenga, open all day weekends.

ASHOVER   SK3462
★Old Poets Corner   (01246) 590888
Butts Road (B6036, off A632 Matlock–Chesterfield); S45 0EW Friendly unpretentious local in character village taken over by Titanic Brewery in 2019; easy-going bar with mix of chairs and pews, open fire, small room off and french door to tiny balcony, Titanic ales (beer, gin and cider festivals Mar and Aug), Belgian beers, 12 ciders and good range of fruit wines and malt whiskies, straightforward food at fair prices, dining room; background and regular live music (mainly acoustic), quiz Weds; children (away from bar) and dogs welcome, wheelchair access/disabled loo, attractive bedrooms, holiday cottage sleeping up to eight, open all day, open all day; closed Mon, Tues.

ASTON-UPON-TRENT   SK4129
Malt   (01332) 799116
M1 junction 24A on to A50, village signed left near Shardlow; The Green (one-way street); DE72 2AA Comfortably

modernised village pub with enjoyable good value food (not Sun evening), well kept Bass, Marstons Shipyard, Sharps Doom Bar and three guests, friendly atmosphere; some live music, TV; children and dogs welcome, back terrace, open all day Fri-Sun, closed all Mon and Tues, lunchtimes Wed and Thurs.

BAMFORD   SK2083
Anglers Rest   (01433) 659317
Main Road (A6013)/Taggs Knoll; S33 0BQ Friendly community-owned pub with five good local beers and tasty home-made food including Fri evening fish and chips, traditional Sun lunch, also has a café and post office; some live music, poker, vinyl club, quiz Weds; children, walkers and dogs welcome, open all day.

BEELEY   SK2667
Devonshire Arms   (01629) 733259
B6012, off A6 Matlock–Bakewell; DE4 2NR Lovely 18th-c stone coaching inn in attractive Peak District village near Chatsworth House; original part with black beams, flagstones, stripped stone and cheerful log fires, contrasting ultra-modern bistro/conservatory, up to four well kept changing ales, several wines by the glass, more than 35 gins and nice range of malt whiskies, generally well liked food (can be pricey) including some pub standards; background music; children welcome, dogs in bar and some of the 18 bedrooms, open all day.

BELPER   SK3349
Bulls Head   (01773) 828898
Belper Lane End; DE56 2DL Spacious beamed village pub dating back to the 18th c; well kept Bass, Dancing Duck, Sharps Doom Bar and guest ale, good fairly traditional food at reasonable prices from sandwiches/baguettes up, friendly attentive staff, main bar plus snug with woodburner, gin/cocktail bar and garden room; children and dogs (in some parts) welcome, terrace seating, closed Mon, lunchtimes Tues and Wed, otherwise open all day, no food Sun evening, Mon.

BIRCHOVER   SK2362
Druid   (01629) 650424
Off B5056; Main Street; DE4 2BL Hospitable 17th-c stone pub at edge of village; traditional quarry-tiled bar with two woodburners, dining areas either side plus more modern downstairs restaurant and newish upstairs space, good well presented food from seasonal menu (special diets catered for) using local suppliers along with own lamb, eggs and honey, five changing ales, Aspall's cider and eight wines by the glass, friendly service; background music; children

---

We say if we know a pub has background music.

and dogs welcome, tables out in front on two levels, good area for walks, Nine Ladies stone circle nearby, open all day Fri and Sat, till 8pm Sun, closed Mon and Tues (hours may be extended in high season).

BIRCHOVER   SK2362
Red Lion (01629) 650363
Off B5056; Main Street; DE4 2BN
Welcoming early 18th-c stone-built pub; good value wholesome food including some Italian influences (landlord is Sardinian), Sun lunchtime carvery, they also make their own cheese and have a deli next door, Birchover ales (brewed here) and four ciders, glass-covered well inside, woodburners; acoustic music sessions and quiz nights; children and dogs welcome, nice rural views from outside seats, open all day Sat, till 8pm Sun, closed Mon, Tues and lunchtimes Weds-Fri.

BONSALL   SK2758
★**Barley Mow** (01629) 825685
Off A5012 W of Cromford; The Dale; DE4 2AY One-room stone-built village with friendly buoyant atmosphere; beams, pubby furnishings and woodburner, pictures and plenty of bric-a-brac, own Chickenfoot ales, local guests and real ciders, hearty helpings of good value popular food from short daily changing menu (be prepared to share a table); live music Fri and Sat, outside loos; children and dogs welcome, nice little front terrace, events such as hen racing and world record-breaking day, walks from the pub, camping, open all day weekends, closed Mon and lunchtimes Tues-Fri.

BONSALL   SK2758
Kings Head (01629) 822703
Off A5012 W of Cromford; Yeoman Street; DE4 2AA Welcoming 17th-c stone-built village local with two cosy beamed rooms; pubby furniture including cushioned wall benches on carpet or tiles, various knick-knacks and china, woodburners, three Batemans ales and enjoyable good value home-made food, restaurant; live music, darts; children and dogs welcome, seats out at front and in back courtyard, handy for Limestone Way and other walks, closed lunchtime, open all day Sun.

BRACKENFIELD   SK3658
Plough (01629) 534437
A615 Matlock–Alfreton, about a mile NW of Wessington; DE55 6DD Under new management with an upgrading programme underway, this modernised 16th-c former farmhouse is in a lovely setting; three-level beamed bar with woodburner, four well kept ales, plenty of wines by the glass and around 30 gins, good popular food including blackboard specials and daily deals, appealing lower-level restaurant extension, friendly attentive staff; open 10am for coffee and pastries; live music, quiz nights, beer garden with outdoor bar; children welcome,

dogs in certain areas, large neatly kept gardens with terrace. Open (and food) all day, till 1am Fri/Sat.

BRADWELL   SK1781
Bowling Green (01433) 620450
Smalldale, off B6049 at Gore Lane/Townend; S33 9JQ Popular and welcoming 16th-c village local with bar, restaurant and garden room extension; good choice of enjoyable reasonably priced pubby food, well kept ales such as Abbeydale, Adnams and Bradfield, log fires; children and dogs (in bar) welcome, lovely views from garden, bedrooms in separate building, open all day summer, from 3pm winter.

BRADWELL   SK1782
★**Samuel Fox** (01433) 621562
B6049; S33 9JT Hope Valley pub ideal for a pint and chat after walking in the Peak District, though many visit for the excellent modern British food cooked by the landlord; open-plan bar and interlinked dining room with red and dogtooth upholstered tub chairs around tables, several open brick fireplaces, also similarly furnished neat restaurant; Bradfield Farmers, Intrepid Blonde and Pennine Best Bitter on handpump, farm cider, 14 wines by the glass served by helpful, courteous staff; outdoor seating at the front, four quiet bedrooms, no dogs inside, wheelchair access, open evenings Weds-Sat, lunch Sun.

BRASSINGTON   SK2354
★**Olde Gate** (01629) 540448
Village signed off B5056 and B5035 NE of Ashbourne; DE4 4HJ Wonderfully unspoilt place – like stepping back in time; mullioned windows, 17th-c kitchen range with copper pots, old wall clock, rush-seated chairs and antique settles, beams hung with pewter mugs and shelves lined with embossed Doulton stoneware flagons, also a panelled Georgian room and, to the left of a small hatch-served lobby, a cosy beamed room with stripped settles, scrubbed tables and an open fire under a huge mantelbeam, Marstons, Thwaites and a guest, enjoyable fairly traditional food along with a vegetarian menu; cribbage and dominoes; well behaved children welcome, dogs in bar, benches in small front yard, garden with tables looking out over pastures, open all day Fri-Sun, closed Mon lunchtime, no food Sun evening.

BRETTON   SK2078
★**Barrel** (01433) 630856
Signposted from Foolow, which itself is signposted from A623 just E of junction with B6465 to Bakewell; can also be reached from either the B6049 at Great Hucklow, or the B6001 via Abney, from Leadmill just S of Hathersage; S32 5QD
Recently extended inn on edge of isolated ridge with fine views (on a clear day you can see five counties); stubs of massive knocked-

through walls divide the rooms into several spic and span areas, the cosy oak-beamed bar has gleaming copper and brass, patterned carpet and warming fire, ales from Marstons, real cider, several wines by the glass and 20 whiskies, enjoyable traditional food served by friendly staff; background music; well behaved children welcome, no dogs inside, seats on front roadside terrace and in courtyard garden, good walks, comfortable well appointed bedrooms, open all day, food all day Sun.

BUXTON SK0573

Gilberts (01298) 214071

High Street, on edge of Market Place; SK17 6ET Relaxed bar in former shop; solid rustic tables and chairs and some red leather chesterfields on bare boards, modern artwork and pendant lighting, woodburner, tractor-seat stools at corrugated-iron-fronted counter serving two or three well kept ales and a traditional cider, generous helpings of good freshly made food from sandwiches and sharing boards up, reasonable prices, friendly helpful staff; background and live music; children and dogs (theirs is Bruce) welcome, enclosed back terrace, open all day from 9am for breakfast, no food Sun evening.

BUXTON SK0573

Old Sun (01298) 937986

High Street; SK17 6HA Updated 17th-c coaching inn with several cosy linked areas; half a dozen well kept Marstons-related beers, good choice of wines by the glass and decent coffee, generous helpings of enjoyable home-made food including Tues pizza night, Thurs pie & pint and Fri fish, friendly accommodating staff, low beams, panelling, bare boards and flagstones, old local photographs, open fire and woodburner; background music, alternating quiz/open mike night Weds; children (till 9pm) and dogs welcome, tables out at front and in back garden with pizza oven, open all day, food all day weekends.

BUXTON SK0573

Tap House (01298) 214085

Old Court House, George Street; SK17 6AT Buxton brewery tap with their cask and craft range plus guests, also good selection of bottled beers, wines and spirits, tasty well priced food including some cooked in smoker, various interesting teas and coffees, friendly knowledgeable staff; daily newspapers; children and dogs welcome, a few seats outside, open (and food) all day.

BUXWORTH SK0282

Navigation (01663) 732072

S of village towards Silkhill, off B6062; SK23 7NE Inn by restored Bugsworth canal basin; half a dozen ales including from local microbreweries, good value pubby food from sandwiches up, linked low-

ceilinged rooms, canalia, brassware and old photographs, open fires, games room with pool and darts; background and live music; children (away from main bar), walkers and dogs welcome, disabled access, tables on sunken flagstoned terrace, six bedrooms, open (and food) all day.

CALVER SK2374

Derwentwater Arms (01433) 639211

In centre, bear left from Main Street into Folds Head; Low Side; S32 3XQ Elevated stone-built village pub with big windows looking over to cricket pitch; good fairly priced food (all day Sun) from pies, pizzas and pub favourites to daily specials, three well kept ales including Bass and Howard Town Hope, a dozen gins, friendly helpful service; children, walkers and dogs (in bar) welcome, terraces on slopes below (disabled access from back car park), next-door holiday cottage, open all day.

CASTLETON SK1582

★Olde Nags Head (01433) 620248

Cross Street (A6187); S33 8WH Small solidly built hotel dating from the 17th c; interesting antique oak furniture and coal fire in civilised beamed and flagstoned bar, adjoining snug with leather sofas, steps down to restaurant, well kept Bradfield Farmers Blonde, Sharps Doom Bar and several guests, nice coffee and good fairly priced pubby food including burgers and pizzas, friendly helpful staff; live music Sat; children and dogs (in bar) welcome, nine comfortable bedrooms, good breakfast, open all day.

CHESTERFIELD SK3670

Rose & Crown (01246) 563750

Old Road; S40 2QT Popular Brampton Brewery pub with their full range and changing guests, no food apart from Sun roasts, friendly helpful staff, spacious traditional refurbishment with leather banquettes, panelling, wood or carpeted floors, brewery memorabilia and cast-iron Victorian fireplace, cosy snug area; Tues quiz; tables outside, closed till 3pm Mon and Tues, otherwise open all day.

CHINLEY SK0482

Paper Mill (01663) 750529

Whitehough Head Lane; SK23 6EJ Under same management as next door Old Hall (see Main Entries); good selection of ales and craft kegs, plenty of bottled Belgian beers and couple of ciders, simple bar snacks along with good home-made pizzas (Thurs-Sun), also pop-up street-food kitchens, good choice of teas and coffees, friendly helpful staff, flagstones, woodburners and open fire, local artwork for sale; TV for major sports; children and dogs welcome, seats out at front and on split-level back terrace, plenty of good local walks, five bedrooms, open from 2pm Sat, all day Sun, closed weekday lunchtimes.

CRICH
SK3454
Cliff (01773) 852444
Cromford Road, Town End; DE4 5DP
Unpretentious little two-room roadside pub; well kept ales such as Blue Monkey, Dancing Duck and Sharps, generous helpings of good value straightforward food (not weekend evenings or Mon), friendly staff and regulars, two woodburners; quiz first Thurs of the month, occasional live music; children and dogs welcome, great views and walks, handy for National Tramway Museum, open all day weekends, closed weekday lunchtimes.

CROWDECOTE
SK1065
Packhorse (01298) 83618
B5055 W of Bakewell; SK17 0DB Small three-room 16th-c pub in lovely setting, welcoming landlord and staff, good reasonably priced home-made food from weekday light bites and sandwiches up, four well kept changing ales, split-level interior with brick or carpeted floors, stripped-stone walls, open fire and two woodburners; Thurs quiz, pool and darts; children and dogs welcome, tables out behind, beautiful views and a popular walking route, closed Mon, Tues.

DALBURY LEES
SK2637
Cow (01332) 824297
Just off Langley Common–Longford Road, off B5020 W of Derby; DE6 5BE Well reworked 19th-c beamed village pub/restaurant (sister to the Cock at Mugginton); good fairly priced food including sandwiches at lunchtimes and tapas-style dishes and other mains in the evenings; Bass, Timothy Taylors Landlord and good range of other drinks, friendly helpful service; background music, children and dogs welcome, 12 boutique bedrooms, open all day, Sun till 8pm.

DERBY
SK3635
Alexandra (01332) 293993
Siddals Road; DE1 2QE Imposing Victorian pub with two simple rooms; traditional furnishings on bare boards or carpet, railway prints and memorabilia, well kept Castle Rock and numerous quickly changing microbrewery guests, lots of continental bottled beers with more on tap, snack food such as pork pies and cobs; background music; children and dogs welcome, nicely planted backyard, 1960s locomotive cab in car park, four bedrooms, open all day.

DERBY
SK3635
Brunswick (01332) 290677
Railway Terrace; close to Derby Midland Station; DE1 2RU One of Britain's oldest railwaymen's pubs; up to 16 real ales including selection from own microbrewery, craft kegs, real ciders and good choice of bottled beers too, bargain food from generous sandwiches and snacks up, high-ceilinged panelled bar, snug with coal fire, chatty front parlour, interesting old train photographs and prints; live jazz upstairs first Thurs of month, quiz, darts, TV, games machine; dogs welcome, walled beer garden behind, open all day, no food Sun evening, Mon all day and Tues evening, limited choice on Derby County home match days.

DERBY
SK3435
Exeter Arms (01332) 605323
Exeter Place; DE1 2EU Victorian survivor amid 1930s apartment blocks and car parks; extended into next-door cottage, but keeping its traditional character including tiled-floor snug with curved wall benches and polished open range, friendly staff, well kept Dancing Duck, Marstons and at least two guests, good all-day food from large and varied menu; children and dogs welcome, open all day (till midnight Fri, Sat).

DERBY
SK3534
Falstaff (01332) 342902
Silver Hill Road, off Normanton Road; DE23 6UJ Big Victorian red-brick corner pub (aka the Folly) brewing its own good value ales, two friendly bars with interesting collection of memorabilia including breweriana, games room; children (till 6pm) and dogs welcome, outside seating area, open all day.

DERBY
SK3436
Five Lamps (01332) 348730
Duffield Road; DE1 3BH Corner pub with opened-up but well divided interior around central servery, wood-strip or carpeted floors, panelling, leather button-back bench seats and small balustraded raised section, over a dozen well kept ales such as Bass, Oakham, Peak and Marstons along with a house beer from Derby, real ciders, decent good value pubby food (not Sun evening); background music, TV; a few picnic-sets out in front, more on decked terrace, open all day (till midnight Fri, Sat).

DERBY
SK3536
Olde Dolphin (01332) 267711
Queen Street; DE1 3DL Quaint 16th-c timber-framed pub just below cathedral; four small dark unpretentious rooms including appealing snug, big bowed black beams, shiny panelling, opaque leaded windows, lantern lights and coal fires, half a dozen well kept predominantly mainstream ales, reasonably priced bar food and upstairs evening restaurant (Thurs-Sat); quiz and

---

If you know a pub is ever open all day, please tell us.

live music nights; children welcome if eating, dogs in bar, sizeable outside area for drinkers/smokers, open all day.

DERBY   SK3335
Rowditch (01332) 343123
Uttoxeter New Road (A516); DE22 3LL
Popular character local with its own microbrewery (well kept Marstons Pedigree and guests too), friendly landlord, two bars and attractive little snug on right, coal fire; no children, dogs welcome at weekends, occasional live music, pleasant back garden, closed weekday lunchtimes.

DERBY   SK3536
Silk Mill (01332) 365439
Full Street; DE1 3AF 1920s pub with central bar, lounge and skylit dining area, banquettes, cushioned stools and cast-iron-framed tables on wood floors, open fires, one or two quirky touches such as fish wallpaper, a stuffed crocodile and antler chandelier, good choice of real ales and ciders, several wines by the glass, good choice of spirits, enjoyable pubby food (all day weekdays, till 8pm Sun) from sandwiches up, friendly service; daily newspapers; open all day.

DERBY   SK3536
Tap (01332) 366283
Derwent Street/Exeter Place; DE1 2ED 19th-c Derby Brewing Co pub (aka Royal Standard) with unusual bowed end; ten real ales including five of their own from curved brick counter, lots of bottled imports and good selection of other drinks, knowledgeable staff, decent good value food (all day Sat, till 3pm Sun) from sandwiches and pizzas up, open-plan bare-boards interior with two high-ceilinged drinking areas, more room upstairs and roof terrace overlooking the Derwent; open all day (till 1am Fri, Sat).

EARL STERNDALE   SK0966
★ Quiet Woman (01298) 83211
Village signed off B5053 S of Buxton; SK17 0BU Old-fashioned unchanging country local in lovely Peak District countryside; simple beamed interior with plain furniture on quarry tiles, china ornaments and coal fire, well kept Marstons and guests, own-label bottled beers (available in gift packs), good pork pies; family room with pool, skittles and darts; no dogs inside, picnic-sets out in front along with budgies, hens, ducks and donkeys, you can buy free-range eggs, local poetry books and even hay, good hikes across nearby Dove Valley towards Longnor and Hollinsclough, small campsite next door with caravan for hire.

EDALE   SK1285
Old Nags Head (01433) 670291
Off A625 E of Chapel-en-le-Frith; Grindsbrook Booth; S33 7ZD Relaxed well used traditional pub at start of Pennine Way; good value food from sandwiches up including Sun carvery, a beer named for them plus three other well kept local ales, log fire, flagstoned area for booted walkers, airy back family room; background music, TV, pool and darts, Sept beer barrel race; dogs welcome, front terrace and garden, two self-catering cottages, open (and food) all day in summer, closed Mon and Tues in winter, can get very busy weekends.

ELMTON   SK5073
★ Elm Tree (01909) 721261
Off B6417 S of Clowne; S80 4LS Popular competently run country pub with landlord-chef's good fairly traditional food including weekday set lunch and afternoon teas, gluten-free and other special diets catered for, well kept small range of ales, several ciders and wide range of wines, friendly obliging service even when busy, stripped stone and panelling, log fire, back barn restaurant (mainly for functions); children and dogs (in bar) welcome, garden tables, play area, closed Tues, otherwise open (and food) all day till around 8pm (6pm Sun).

EYAM   SK2276
Miners Arms (01433) 630853
Off A632 Chesterfield to Chapel-en-le-Frith; Water Lane; S32 5RG Three-roomed 17th-c beamed inn with enjoyable food (not Sun evening, Mon lunchtime) from sandwiches up, Greene King and Theakstons ales, friendly efficient service; TV, background music; children, walkers and dogs welcome, picnic-sets out at front and in back garden, nice walks nearby especially below Froggatt Edge, seven bedrooms, open all day.

FOOLOW   SK1976
★ Bulls Head (01433) 630873
Village signposted off A623 Baslow–Tideswell; S32 5QR Friendly pub in pretty upland village by green; simply furnished flagstoned bar with interesting collection of photographs, four changing real ales, usually including one from Peak and well liked food from sandwiches up (more elaborate choices Sat evening), step down to former stables with high ceiling joists, stripped stone and woodburner, sedate partly panelled dining room with plates on delft shelves; background music; children, walkers and dogs welcome, side picnic-sets with nice views, paths from here out over rolling pasture enclosed by dry-stone walls, three bedrooms, open all day Tues-Sun, closed Mon.

FROGGATT EDGE   SK2476
★ Chequers (01433) 630231
A625, off A623 N of Bakewell; S32 3ZJ Roadside dining pub surrounded by lovely countryside; opened-up bar and eating areas, cushioned settles, farmhouse and captain's chairs around mix of tables, antique

prints, longcase clock and woodburner, good interesting food (all day weekends) along with more traditional choices, home-made chutneys and preserves for sale, Bradfield, Peak, Kelham Island and a guest ale, several wines by the glass, friendly helpful staff; background music; children welcome, no dogs inside, garden with Froggatt Edge escarpment up through woods behind, seven comfortable clean bedrooms, good breakfast, open all day.

GLOSSOP SK0394
Star (01457) 853072
Howard Street; SK13 7DD Unpretentious corner alehouse opposite the station; four or five well kept changing ales along with Weston's Old Rosie cider, no food, traditional layout including tiled and wood floors, tap room with hatch service, old local photographs; dogs welcome, open all day from 2pm (noon Sat, Sun).

GRINDLEFORD SK2378
Sir William (01433) 630303
B6001, opposite war memorial; S32 2HS Popular pub-hotel under welcoming management; good freshly made food from sandwiches up, Greene King ales and guests, friendly helpful service, restaurant; children, walkers and dogs (in a couple of areas) welcome, splendid view especially from terrace, eight comfortable bedrooms, open all day.

HARDWICK HALL SK4663
★Hardwick Inn (01246) 850245
Quite handy for M1 junction 29; S44 5QJ Popular golden-stone pub dating from the 15th c at south park gate of Hardwick Hall (NT); several endearingly old-fashioned linked rooms including proper bar, open fires, fine range of more than 200 malt whiskies and plenty of wines by the glass, well kept Black Sheep, Chatsworth Gold, Theakstons and a house beer (Bess of Hardwick) from Brampton, wide range of good reasonably priced bar food plus carvery restaurant (all day except shuts at 7pm Sun), long-serving licensees (in same family for three generations), efficient friendly staff; unobtrusive background music; children allowed away from bar areas, dogs in one part, tables out at front and in pleasant back garden, open all day.

HATHERSAGE SK2381
Bank House (01433) 449060
Main Road, centre of village; S32 1BB Busy restaurant-bar in converted bank; popular food from Mediterranean-influenced menu including tapas and pizzas, extensive range of wines, spirits and cocktails, a guest

ale on handpump with plenty more in bottles, cheerful efficient service, ground-floor bar, restaurant upstairs; open all day.

HATHERSAGE SK2381
★Scotsmans Pack (01433) 650253
School Lane, off A6187; S32 1BZ Friendly bustling inn equally popular with drinkers and diners; dark panelled rooms with lots of knick-knacks, upholstered stools and dining chairs, cushioned wall seats and assortment of tables, woodburner, five well kept Marstons-related ales, a dozen wines by the glass and good food from pub standards up, cream teas; background and some live music, quiz and bingo night Thurs, TV; picnic-sets on terrace overlooking trout stream, plenty of surrounding walks, five bedrooms, open all day.

HAYFIELD SK0388
Lantern Pike (01663) 747590
Glossop Road (A624 N) at Little Hayfield, just N of Hayfield; SK22 2NG Popular old roadside pub; traditional bar with warm fire and a few photos of the original *Coronation Street* cast (many were regulars along with series creator Tony Warren who based his characters on the locals), Timothy Taylors Landlord and a guest, decent pubby food; background and some live music; children welcome, tables on stone-walled terrace looking over towards Lantern Pike, plenty of surrounding walks on windswept moors, five bedrooms, open all day weekends, closed Mon.

HAYFIELD SK0387
Pack Horse (01663) 749126
Off A624 Glossop to Chapel-en-le-Frith; Market Street; SK22 2EP Modernised stone-built pub under welcoming licensees; good interesting food from landlord-chef using local suppliers, four well kept ales and decent choice of wines and gins, opened-up interior with some cosy areas, woodburners; background music, Weds quiz; children, walkers and dogs welcome, disabled access, a few picnic-sets out at front, closed Mon (except bank holidays when shuts Tues), otherwise open all day.

HOGNASTON SK2350
★Red Lion (01335) 370396
Off B5035 Ashbourne–Wirksworth; DE6 1PR Traditional 17th-c village inn with open-plan beamed bar; attractive mix of old tables, curved settles and other seats on tiles and ancient flagstones, three fires, Marstons Pedigree and guests, nice wines by the glass and good well presented home-made food from shortish menu, friendly service, dining conservatory; children and dogs welcome,

---

Half pints: by law, a pub should not charge more for half a pint than half the price of a full pint, unless it shows that half-pint price on its price list.

picnic-sets in field behind, boules, handy for Carsington Water, three good bedrooms, big breakfast, open all day Sun (food till 7pm).

HOLBROOK   SK3645
Dead Poets (01332) 780301
Chapel Street; village signed off A6 S of Belper; DE56 0TQ Friendly drinkers' local under new management; up to nine real ales, traditional ciders and good range of other drinks, lunchtime bar food such as cobs and pies, simple cottagey décor with beams, stripped-stone walls and broad flagstones, high-backed settles forming booths, big log fire, plenty of tucked-away corners, woodburner in snug, well behaved children allowed in conservatory; background music; dogs welcome, seats out at back, open all day Thurs-Sun.

HOPE   SK1783
★ Cheshire Cheese (01433) 620381
Off A6187, towards Edale; S33 6ZF 16th-c traditional stone inn with snug oak-beamed rooms on different levels; open fires, red carpets or stone floors, straightforward furnishings, up to five real ales such as Abbeydale, Bradfield and Peak, 12 malt whiskies and enjoyable food from sandwiches and pub favourites up plus special diets catered for, friendly service; Weds quiz, folk night third Thurs of month; children and dogs welcome, good local walks in the summits of Lose Hill and Win Hill or the cave district around Castleton, four bedrooms, limited parking, open all day weekends, closed Mon.

HOPE   SK1783
Old Hall (01433) 620160
Market Place, A625; S33 6RH Traditional 16th-c stone coaching inn; good pubby food from sandwiches to specials, five well kept real ales including Theakstons (beer festivals) and over 100 malt whiskies, friendly helpful staff, tea room; children and dogs (not in restaurant) welcome, sunny terrace, five comfortable bedrooms, open (and food) all day, breakfast from 8am (in tea room).

HORSLEY WOODHOUSE   SK3944
Old Oak (01332) 881299
Main Street (A609 Belper–Ilkeston); DE7 6AW Busy roadside local linked to nearby Bottle Brook and Leadmill microbreweries, their ales and guests plus weekend back bar with another eight well priced beers tapped from the cask, farm ciders too, basic snacks (can also bring your own food), beamed rooms with blazing coal fires; occasional live music; children and dogs welcome, hatch service to covered courtyard tables, nice views, open all day weekends, closed weekday lunchtimes till 4pm.

HURDLOW   SK1265
★ Royal Oak (01298) 83288
Monyash–Longnor Road, just off A515 S of Buxton; SK17 9QJ Bustling pub in

rural spot near High Peak Trail; two-room beamed bar with open fire, copper kettles, bed warming pans, horsebrasses and so forth, straightforward pubby chairs and tables, ales such as Buxton, Peak, Sharps and Thornbridge, proper ciders and good choice of wines by the glass, nice food including range of pies, friendly efficient service, dining room with traditional furniture on bare boards and another open fire, flagstoned cellar room perfect for a large group of diners; background music; children and dogs welcome, tables in terraced garden, self-catering barn with bunk bedrooms, campsite, open (and food) all day.

ILKESTON   SK4742
Dewdrop (0115) 932 9684
Station Street, Ilkeston junction, off A6096; DE7 5TE Large Victorian red-brick corner local in old industrial area, not strong on bar comfort but popular for its well kept beers (up to eight) such as Acorn, Blue Monkey and Oakham, simple bar snacks, back lounge with fire and piano, connecting lobby to front public bar with darts and TV, some Barnes Wallis memorabilia; children and dogs welcome, sheltered outside seating at back, walks by former Nottingham Canal, open all day weekends, closed weekday lunchtimes.

ILKESTON   SK4641
Spanish Bar (0115) 930 8666
South Street; DE7 5QJ Busy bar with half a dozen well kept/priced ales, traditional ciders and bottled Belgian beers, friendly efficient staff, evening overspill room; weekend live music, sports TV; dogs welcome, small back garden and skittle alley, open all day.

INGLEBY   SK3427
John Thompson (01332) 862469
NW of Melbourne; turn off A514 at Swarkestone Bridge or in Stanton by Bridge; can also be reached from Ticknall (or from Repton on B5008); DE73 7HW Own beers from the longest established microbrewery in the UK; comfortable neatly kept lounge with beams, old settles, button-back leather seats and sturdy oak tables, antique prints and paintings, log-effect gas fire, a couple of smaller cosier rooms off, simple good value lunchtime food including carvery, piano, TV and games in conservatory; background music; children welcome till 9pm, dogs in bar and conservatory, seats on lawns or partly covered terrace, pretty surrounding countryside, self-catering chalets, open all day weekends, closed Mon.

KING'S NEWTON   SK3826
Hardinge Arms (01332) 863808
Not far from M1 junction 23A, via A453 to Isley, then off Melbourne/Wilson Road; Main Street; DE73 8BX Bright spacious

old pub with enjoyable bar and evening restaurant food, well kept local ales and good range of wines, quick friendly service, chunky low beams, brick, wood and flagstone floors, woodburner; Sun quiz; children welcome in eating areas, handy for Donington Park and East Midlands Airport, bedrooms in converted stables, open all day Thurs-Sun, from 3pm other days.

KIRK IRETON   SK2650
★**Barley Mow** (01335) 370306
Village signed off B5023 S of Wirksworth; DE6 3JP Little-changed handsome Jacobean stone house with particularly kind landlady (here for more than 40 years, now increasingly taking a back seat); pubby-feeling small main bar with antique settles on tiles or built into panelling, shuttered mullioned windows, coal fire, another room with low beams, built-in cushioned pews, oak parquet and small woodburner, Whim Hartington IPA and four usually local guests, farm cider, cheap filled rolls and simple evening meals; no credit cards; children and dogs welcome, couple of benches out in front, good sized garden, community shop on premises, pretty hilltop village (you can walk to Carsington Water from here), bedrooms, nice breakfasts in flagstoned kitchen.

LADYBOWER RESERVOIR SK1986
Ladybower Inn (01433) 651241
A57 Sheffield–Glossop, just E of junction with A6013; S33 0AX Batemans pub handy for the huge nearby reservoir; their ales and a couple of guests, enjoyable pubby food from sandwiches up, friendly service, various traditionally furnished carpeted areas with cast-iron fireplaces, Lancaster Bomber pictures recalling the Dambusters' practice runs on the reservoir; background music, darts; children and dogs (in bar) welcome, picnic-sets out at front, seven annexe bedrooms, open (and food) all day.

LADYBOWER RESERVOIR SK2084
Yorkshire Bridge (01433) 651361
A6013 N of Bamford; S33 0AZ Busy inn a short stroll from Ladybower dam and close to Derwent and Howden reservoirs; beamed bar with woodburner, wheelbacks and other chairs around mix of tables on patterned carpet, copper items, china plates and various photographs and paintings, other areas including airy garden room with fine valley views, four ales such as Abbeydale, Bradfield and Peak, a decent choice of wines by the glass, generous helpings of popular pub food from sandwiches to grills, friendly service; background music; children welcome, no dogs at mealtimes, picnic-sets in paved courtyard, 14 comfortable bedrooms,

lovely surrounding walks, open all day, food served all day weekends.

LANGLEY MILL   SK4248
Thorn Tree (01773) 768675
Woodlinkin, Nottingham Road; NG16 4HG Updated roadside restaurant/pub (part of the Georges Tradition group) with great views over rolling country, good choice of enjoyable reasonably priced food including signature fish and chips and grills, three local ales, attentive friendly service, conservatory and deck taking in the view; children and dogs welcome, beer garden, open (and food) all day.

LITTLE LONGSTONE   SK1971
Packhorse (01629) 640471
Off A6 NW of Bakewell via Monsal Dale; DE45 1NN Long low building with three comfortable linked rooms; beams, open fires and pine tables on flagstones, well kept ales including Black Sheep and Thornbridge, good generously served home-made food from daily changing blackboard using fresh local produce (booking advised), affordably priced wine list, friendly accommodating service; Thurs quiz; children, dogs and hikers welcome (just off the Monsal Trail), terrace in steep little back garden, open (and food) all day weekends.

LITTON   SK1675
Red Lion (01298) 871458
Village signposted off A623, between B6465 and B6049 junctions; also signposted off B6049; SK17 8QU Welcoming traditional village pub; two linked front rooms with low beams, panelling and open fires, bigger stripped-stone back room, three or four well kept interesting, mainly local ales and enjoyable home-made food from sandwiches to daily specials; children (over 6) and dogs allowed, seats and tables in front with more on village green, good dales walks nearby, open all day.

LULLINGTON   SK2513
Colvile Arms (01827) 373212
Off A444 S of Burton; Main Street; DE12 8EG Popular 18th-c brick-built village pub; high-backed settles in simple panelled bar, cosy comfortable beamed lounge, well kept Marstons Pedigree and three guests, 30 or so gins, no food except cobs, pleasant friendly atmosphere; background music; children welcome till 7.30pm, dogs in bar, picnic-sets on sheltered back lawn, closed lunchtimes apart from Sun.

MAKENEY   SK3544
★**Holly Bush** (01332) 841729
From A6 heading N after Duffield, take first right after crossing River Derwent,

---

There are report forms at the back of the book.

then first left; DE56 ORX Unspoilt 17th-c
two-bar village pub (former farmhouse);
beams and black panelling, tiled and
flagstone floors, three blazing fires, one in
old-fashioned range by snug's curved high-
backed settle, well kept changing ales (some
served from jugs), craft beers and real cider,
enjoyable lunchtime food from rolls and
pork pies up, lobby with hatch service; beer
festivals and occasional live music; children,
walkers and dogs welcome, picnic-sets
outside, open all day.

MARSTON MONTGOMERY SK1338
Crown (01889) 591430
*On corner of Thurvaston Road and
Barway; DE6 2FF* Welcoming red-brick
beamed village pub, clean and bright, with
popular good value food, three real ales
including Marstons Pedigree and several
wines by the glass, friendly helpful staff,
restaurant; some live music; children and
dogs welcome, disabled access, terrace
tables, seven good bedrooms, open all day
weekends, food till 7pm Sun.

MATLOCK SK2960
Moca (01629) 583973
Dale Road; DE4 3LT Light café-style
bar with half a dozen or so well kept local
beers and snacky lunchtime food, friendly
knowledgeable staff, chunky pine furniture
on bare boards, black and white photographs
of musicians/bands; can fill up as not large;
dogs welcome, back terrace, open all day.

MATLOCK SK2960
Thorn Tree (01629) 580295
Jackson Road, Matlock Bank; DE4 3JQ
Superb valley views to Riber Castle from this
homely little 19th-c stone-built local; Bass,
Greene King, Nottingham, Timothy Taylors
and guests, simple well cooked food (Tues-
Fri lunchtimes till 1.30pm, Sun 5-6.30pm,
Weds pie night), friendly staff and regulars;
children and dogs welcome, tables outside
taking in the view, open all day Fri-Sun,
closed Mon lunchtime.

MAYFIELD SK1444
★ Rose & Crown (01335) 342498
*Main Road (B5032 off A52 W of
Ashbourne); DE6 2JT* Welcoming dining
pub with good attractively presented food
cooked by owner-chef, reasonable prices,
well kept Marstons Pedigree and nice range
of good value wines, efficient friendly service,
woodburner in beamed bar, restaurant;
children welcome, no dogs inside, terrace
tables under parasols, local walks, three
bedrooms, closed Sun evening, Mon and
Tues, food served 12-1.30pm, 6.15-8.30pm (no
lunchtime meals Weds, Thurs).

MIDDLE HANDLEY SK4078
Devonshire Arms (01246) 434800
Off B6052 NE of Chesterfield; S21 5RN
Welcoming 18th-c village dining pub under

newish management; freshly updated
modern décor in opened-up bar and
restaurant areas, enjoyable food from
sandwiches, sharing dishes and pub
favourites to burgers and steaks, three
local real ales, 20 or so wines and good
choice of gins and cocktails, friendly helpful
service; background and some live music;
children and dogs (in bar) welcome, tables
on front and side terraces, play area, seven
refurbished bedrooms, open (and food) all
day, kitchen closes 7pm Sun.

MILLERS DALE SK1473
Anglers Rest (01298) 871323
*Just down Litton Lane; pub is PH on
OS Sheet 119 map reference 142734;
SK17 8SN* Creeper-clad pub in lovely quiet
riverside setting; two bars and dining room,
log fires, Kelham Island, Peak and a couple
of guests, enjoyable uncomplicated food at
reasonable prices, cheery helpful service;
darts and pool; children welcome, muddy
boots and dogs in public bar, wonderful gorge
views and river walks (on the Monsal Trail),
self-catering apartment, open all day, food all
day Sat, till 8pm Sun.

MILLTOWN SK3561
Miners Arms (01246) 590218
*Off B6036 SE of Ashover; Oakstedge
Lane; S45 0HA* Spotless stone dining pub
with good freshly made food from well priced
daily changing blackboard menu (booking
advised), nice wines and one changing real
ale, log fires; children welcome, no dogs
inside, attractive country walks from the
door, closed Sun evening-Weds.

MILTON SK3126
Swan (01283) 704072
Just E of Repton; DE65 6EF Welcoming
flower-decked village pub under newish
family management; well kept Bass and
guests, nice range of gins and enjoyable food
including home-made pies, complimentary
cheeseboard Sun, comfortable homely
atmosphere; children and dogs (in bar)
welcome, garden behind, open all day
weekends, from 5pm other days.

MONYASH SK1566
★ Bulls Head (01629) 812372
B5055 W of Bakewell; DE45 1JH
Rambling stone pub with high-ceilinged
rooms, straightforward traditional
furnishings including plush stools lined
along bar, log fire, four real ales such
as Peak and Timothy Taylors Landlord,
restaurant with high-backed dining chairs
on heated stone floor, popular pubby food
(all day weekends) from sandwiches and
baked potatoes up, friendly service, small
back room with darts, board games and
pool; background music; children and dogs
(in bar) welcome, plenty of picnic-sets
under parasols in big garden, gate leading
to well equipped public play area, good

surrounding walks, open all day in high summer, all day Fri-Sun other times.

MOORWOOD MOOR SK3656
White Hart (01629) 534888
Inns Lane; village signed from South Wingfield; DE55 7NU Welcoming country inn with good seasonal food in bar and restaurant, helpful attentive staff, well kept Sharps Doom Bar, Timothy Taylors Landlord and a couple of local guests; more than 40 gins; children and dogs welcome, disabled access/loos, tables on attractive heated terrace, 17 modern bedrooms, open (and food) all day, kitchen closes 6.45pm Sun.

MUGGINTON SK2843
Cock (01773) 550703
Bullhurst Lane; N of Weston Underwood; DE6 4PJ Sister pub to the Cow at Dalbury Lees with nicely renovated traditional bar areas, beams and panelling, lots of pictures, old quarry tiles and cosy woodburners, steps down to large glass-fronted modern extension with mezzanine floor, good popular food from bar snacks, through pub favourites and some Asian choices to chargrills, also separate vegan and gluten-free menus, half a dozen well kept ales and good range of other drinks, efficient friendly service; children and dogs welcome, wheelchair access, plenty of tables in attractive walled gardens, outside summer bar, car park with electric charging points, good local walks, open all day, food all day (till 7pm Sun).

NEW MILLS SJ9886
Fox (0161) 427 1634
Brook Bottom Road; SK22 3AY Tucked-away old-fashioned country local in good walking area at end of single-track road; Robinsons ales and good value pub food (no credit cards), log fire; darts and pool; children and dogs welcome, lots of tables outside, open all day Fri-Sun.

NEW MILLS SK0086
Pack Horse (01663) 742365
Mellor Road; SK22 4QQ Popular and friendly stone-built country inn with lovely views across broad Sett Valley to Kinder Scout; Tetleys and three guests kept well, good quality food in traditional log-fire bar and restaurant; children welcome, no dogs inside, terrace and garden on different levels, 12 well equipped clean bedrooms, open (and food) all day.

NEWTON SOLNEY SK2825
Brickmakers Arms 07525 220103
Main Street (B5008 NE of Burton); DE15 0SJ Friendly end-of-terrace beamed pub owned by Burton Bridge Brewery; four of their well kept ales plus a guest from regional breweries, real ciders and plenty of bottled beers, no food, two rooms off bar, one with original panelling and delft shelf displaying jugs and plates, pubby furniture, built-in wall seats and coal fires, area with books; Mon quiz; dogs welcome, tables on terrace, open all day weekends (from 1pm Sat), closed weekday lunchtimes.

OCKBROOK SK4236
Royal Oak (01332) 662378
Off B6096 just outside Spondon; Green Lane; DE72 3SE 18th-c village local run by same friendly family since 1953; good value honest food (not Sun evening) from nice lunchtime cobs to steaks, well kept Bass and three or four interesting guests, real cider; tile-floored tap room, carpeted snug, inner bar, larger and lighter side room, nice old settle in entrance corridor; darts and dominoes, some live music; children welcome, dogs in the evening, disabled access, sheltered cottage garden and cobbled front courtyard, separate play area, open all day Fri-Sun.

OLD BRAMPTON SK3171
Fox & Goose (01246) 566335
Off A619 Chesterfield–Baslow at Wadshelf; S42 7JJ Fine panoramic views from this restored 14th-c pub; character beamed bar with traditional pubby furniture on large flagstones, woodburner in big stone fireplace, Black Sheep, Bradwell, Peak and a couple of guests, a dozen wines by the glass (regular wine tasting evenings), snug with more heavy beams, comfortable seating and small fire, good interesting food from sandwiches, Derbyshire tapas and sharing plates up, separate dining room and orangery restaurant taking in the views; children and dogs (in bar) welcome, tables under parasols on decked and terraced areas, open all day Thurs-Sat, till 6pm Sun, closed Mon-Weds.

OSMASTON SK1943
Shoulder of Mutton (01335) 342371
Off A52 SE of Ashbourne; DE6 1LW Beamed red-brick pub incorporating post office/shop; Marstons Pedigree and a guest or two, generous helpings of enjoyable home-made food (all day weekends) from sandwiches up, good friendly service; children welcome, no dogs inside, picnic-sets in attractive garden (farmland views), peaceful pretty village with thatched cottages, duck pond and good surrounding walks, open all day.

PARWICH SK1854
Sycamore (01335) 390212
By church; DE6 1QL Welcoming old village pub (some refurbishment); flagstoned bar with upholstered wall benches and woodburner, Robinsons ales, good reasonably priced home-made food including themed nights, efficient friendly service, a couple of back dining rooms, pub also houses the village shop; darts; children and dogs welcome, picnic-sets in small front courtyard, more on side grass, good walks nearby, open all day weekends.

PILSLEY SK2371

★**Devonshire Arms** (01246) 565405

*Village signposted off A619 W of Baslow,
and pub just below B6048; High Street;
DE45 1UL* Lovely tranquil little country
inn on the Chatsworth Estate; gentle
contemporary slant with wood-floored bar
and several fairly compact areas off (each
with own character – some steps), log fires in
stone fireplaces, comfortable seating and big
modern paintings, three well kept Peak ales,
a cider such as Lilley's and several wines
by the glass, enjoyable food from lunchtime
sandwiches up using Estate produce, friendly
staff; children and dogs welcome, a few
picnic-sets out at front, charging point for
electric vehicles in car park, Chatsworth
farm shop at the top of lane, bedrooms (some
with four-posters), open all day.

REPTON SK3026
Bulls Head (01283) 704422

High Street; DE65 6GF Lively village pub
(can get packed) with interesting décor in
various interconnecting bars; beams and
pillars, mix of wooden dining chairs, settles,
built-in wall seats and squashy sofas on bare
boards or flagstones, driftwood sculptures,
animal hides and an arty bull's head, log
fires, ales such as Marstons Pedigree, more
than 100 bottled beers and ciders, also
good selection of wines, gins and cocktails,
popular food including wood-fired pizzas
and range of grilled yakitori sticks, cheerful
staff, upstairs restaurant; background music;
children and dogs (in bar) welcome, sizeable
heated terrace with neatly set tables and
chairs under big parasols, open (and some
food) all day.

RIPLEY SK3950
Talbot Taphouse (01773) 742382

Butterley Hill; DE5 3LT Traditional
drinkers' pub with well kept selection of
its own Amber Ales and changing guests,
traditional ciders and good choice of
draught Belgian and bottled beers, friendly
knowledgeable staff, long narrow panelled
room with comfortable chairs, open fire in
brick fireplace; some live music, sports TV;
open from 5pm Mon-Thurs, 3pm Fri, 2pm
Sat, Sun.

ROWSLEY SK2565
★**Peacock** (01629) 733518

Bakewell Road; DE4 2EB Civilised
17th-c country hotel (former manor
house); comfortable seating in spacious
modern lounge, inner bar with log fire, bare
stone walls and some Robert 'Mouseman'
Thompson furniture, very good if not
cheap food from lunchtime sandwiches to
restaurant meals, Peak ales, nice wines and
well served coffee, pleasant helpful staff;
attractive riverside gardens, trout fishing,
15 good bedrooms.

SHARDLOW SK4430
Malt Shovel (01332) 792066

*3.5 miles from M1 junction 24, via A6
towards Derby; The Wharf; DE72 2HG*
Welcoming canalside pub in late 18th-c
former maltings; interesting odd-angled
layout with cosy corners and steps down to
snug, Marstons Pedigree and a beer badged
for the pub, very good value tasty food from
sandwiches and baked potatoes up including
popular breakfasts, evening meals Thurs
(Thai and English) and Fri (fish and chips)
only, quick friendly service, beams, panelling
and central open fire; live music Sun;
children and dogs welcome, lots of terrace
tables by Trent & Mersey Canal, pretty
hanging baskets, open all day.

SHARDLOW SK4429
Old Crown (01332) 792392

*Off A50 just W of M1 junction 24;
Cavendish Bridge, E of village;
DE72 2HL* Good value pub with half a
dozen well kept Marstons-related ales and
decent choice of malt whiskies, traditional
food (all day Sat, not Sun evening, Mon
evening) from sandwiches/baguettes up and
good value Sun lunch, beams with masses of
jugs and mugs, walls covered with other bric-
a-brac and breweriana, big inglenook; quiz
Mon, fortnightly live music Tues; children
and dogs welcome, garden with play area,
open all day.

SHELDON SK1768
★**Cock & Pullet** (01629) 814292

*Village signed off A6 just W of Ashford;
DE45 1QS* Charming no-frills village pub
with low beams, exposed stonework, some
flagstones and open fire, cheerful mismatch
of furnishings, large collection of clocks and
various representations of poultry (some
stuffed), well kept Sharps Doom Bar, Timothy
Taylors Landlord and a guest such as Peak,
tasty pub food from shortish menu including
popular Sun roasts, reasonable prices and
friendly efficient service; quiet background
music, pool in plainer public bar; children
and dogs welcome, seats and rockery on
pleasant back terrace, pretty village just off
the Limestone Way and popular all year with
walkers, clean bedrooms, open all day.

SHIRLEY SK2141
Saracens Head (01335) 360330

Church Lane; DE6 3AS Modernised late
18th-c dining pub in attractive village; good
range of well presented blackboard food from
pubby choices to more expensive restaurant-
style dishes, three Greene King ales, decent
wines and speciality coffees, simple country-
style dining furniture and two pretty working
art nouveau fireplaces; background music;
children welcome and dogs in bar area, pub
cat is Billy, picnic-sets out in front and on
back terrace; closed Mon, shuts 6pm Sun.

SOUTH WINGFIELD SK3755
Old Yew Tree (01773) 522942
B5035 W of Alfreton; Manor Road;
DE55 7NH Friendly 16th-c village pub,
no food except cobs on Sun lunchtime;
Bass, a local guest and a proper cider, log
fire, beams and carved panelling, separate
restaurant area; live music Sat, TV; children,
walkers and dogs welcome, some rattan-
style furniture out at the side, open all day
Fri-Sun, closed Mon.

SUTTON CUM
DUCKMANTON SK4371
Arkwright Arms (01246) 232053
A632 Bolsover–Chesterfield; S44 5JG
Friendly and relaxed mock-Tudor pub with
bar, pool room (dogs allowed here) and
dining room, all with real fires, good choice
of well priced food (not Sun evening), up to
eight changing ales, at least ten real ciders
and perries; TV, games machine; children
welcome, seats out at front and on side
terrace, open all day.

THORPE SK1650
Old Dog (01335) 350990
Spend Lane/Wintercroft Lane; DE6 2AT
Popular bistro-style village pub (former
18th-c coaching inn) with good food from
sensibly short menu including burgers and
hot dogs, four well kept changing ales often
from smaller breweries, friendly prompt
service, candlelit tables on flagstones,
woodburners; background music; children,
walkers and dogs welcome, covered eating
area outside, handy for Dovedale and
Tissington Trail, closed Mon, otherwise open
all day, food all day weekends (till 7pm Sun).

TICKNALL SK3523
Wheel (01332) 865168
Main Street (A514); DE73 7JZ Corner
pub under new management from late 2019;
contemporary décor in bar and upstairs
restaurant, traditional pub food such as
ploughmans, lasgagne and fish and chips;
Bass and Adnams Ghost Ship, friendly staff;
children and dogs welcome, outside area with
café tables on raised deck, near entrance to
Calke Abbey (NT).

TIDESWELL SK1575
Star (01298) 872725
High Street; SK17 8LD Friendly little
village pub with three well kept Marstons-
related ales, enjoyable traditional food and
reasonably priced wine list, quick cheerful
service, four compact rooms including lounge
with woodburner and dining room; Tues quiz,
Weds darts and dominoes; well behaved dogs

and children welcome, closed lunchtime
apart from Sun, no food Mon-Weds.

UPPER LANGWITH SK5169
Devonshire (01623) 747777
Rectory Road; NG20 9RF Popular dining
pub with several cosy modernised areas;
highly rated food (best to book) from
lunchtime sandwiches and pub favourites
up including a vegan menu, well kept Sharps
Doom Bar and three guests, decent wines,
friendly attentive service; children and dogs
(in bar) welcome, easy disabled access,
a few picnic-sets out at front, open all day
(till 7pm Sun).

WARDLOW SK1875
★Three Stags Heads (01298) 872268
Wardlow Mires; A623/B6465; SK17 8RW
Basic unchanging pub (17th-c longhouse) of
great individuality; old country furniture on
flagstones, heating from cast-iron kitchen
ranges, old photographs, locals in favourite
corners, well kept Abbeydale ales including
a strong house beer (Black Lurcher), proper
cider and lots of bottled beers, simple
food; no credit cards or mobile phones;
well behaved children and dogs welcome,
hill views from front terrace, good walking
country, open Thurs and Fri evenings and all
day weekends.

WHITTINGTON MOOR SK3873
Derby Tup (01246) 269835
Sheffield Road; B6057 just S of A61
roundabout; S41 8LS Popular Castle
Rock local with their ales along with named
guests from the likes of Adnams and Oakham,
also craft beers, up to seven ciders and
good range of other drinks; coal fire, simple
furniture and lots of standing room, two side
snugs; live music including jam session last
Mon of month; dogs welcome, seats out on
small back deck, open all day Sat, from 2pm
Sun, closed weekday lunchtimes.

WILLINGTON SK2928
Dragon (01283) 704795
The Green; DE65 6BP Renovated and
extended pub backing on to Trent & Mersey
Canal; good choice of enjoyable well
prepared food from sandwiches to grills,
vegan/vegetarian menu, microbrews from
sister pub the Boot at Repton (see Main
Entries), guest beers and good selection
of other drinks including 27 wines by the
glass, range of coffees and teas; some live
music, sports TV; children and dogs (not
in restaurant) welcome, picnic-sets out
overlooking canal (moorings), bedrooms in
attached cottage, open (and food) all day,
breakfast from 8am.

Post Office address codings confusingly give the impression that a few pubs are in
Derbyshire, when they're really in Cheshire (which is where we list them).

WINSTER
SK2460

★ **Bowling Green** (01629) 650219

East Bank, by Market House (NT);
DE4 2DS Traditional old stone pub
with good chatty atmosphere, character
long-serving landlord and welcoming staff,
enjoyable generously served food including
popular pies, at least three well kept
changing local ales and good selection of
whiskies, end log fire, dining area and family
conservatory (dogs allowed here too); nice
village with good surrounding walks, closed
Mon, Tues and lunchtimes apart from Sun.

WINSTER
SK2360

Miners Standard (01629) 650279

Bank Top (B5056 above village);
DE4 2DR Recently refurbished 17th-c
stone local, friendly and relaxed, with simply
furnished bar, snug and restaurant, four
well kept ales such as Bass and Marstons
Pedigree; good value pub food (not Sun
evening) including some vegetarian/vegan
choices, big woodburner and three log fires,
lead mining photographs and minerals, lots
of brass, a backwards clock, ancient well and
300-year-old original quarry tiles; background
music; children (away from bar) and dogs
welcome, attractive view from garden, three
bedrooms and campsite next door, interesting
stone-built village below, open all day.

YEAVELEY
SK1840

Yeaveley Arms (01335) 330700

On byroad S of Ashbourne; DE6 2DT
Charming village pub with good food (not
Sun evening) from fairly traditional menu,
well kept ales such as Adnams Ghost Ship,
Fullers London Pride and Timothy Taylors
Landlord, good whisky/gin selection,
helpful attentive service, slate-floor
bar with two-way woodburner, separate
restaurant; quirky gents' loo; children and
dogs (in bar) welcome, a few picnic-sets
out at front overlooking church, more
behind, open all day Sat and Sun, closed
Mon and lunchtime Tues.

Devon

KEY	★ Star Pub	🍽 Top Quality Food	🍺 Great Beer
🍷 Good Wines	£ Bargain Meals	🛏 Good Bedrooms	🍴 Serves Food

BRANSCOMBE
Fountain Head 🍺

SY1888 Map 1

(01297) 680359 – www.fountainheadinn.com

Upper village; W of Branscombe at Street; EX12 3BG

Friendly, unspoilt pub with local beers and tasty, fair priced food

Follow a narrow winding lane close to the church to find this lovely old pub. It dates back to the 14th c and remains steadfastly old-fashioned: the room on the left was once a smithy and has forge tools and horseshoes on high oak beams, cushioned pews and mate's chairs, and a log fire in the original raised hearth with its tall central chimney. There's Branscombe Vale Branoc, Golden Fiddle and Summa That on handpump, two local ciders and eight wines by the glass. On the right, an irregularly shaped snug room has another log fire, a white-painted plank ceiling with an unusual carved ceiling rose, brown-varnished panelling, a flagstone floor and local artwork for sale; darts and board games. You can sit outside on the front loggia and terrace listening to the little stream gurgling beneath the flagstoned path; barbecues and spit roasts may be held on Sunday evening from 6pm (end July-early September). Good coastal walks.

🍴 Well liked food includes sandwiches and toasties plus home-cured trout with pickled cucumber, dill and caper salad with horseradish mascarpone, ham hock, bacon and chicken terrine with piccalilli, home-cooked honey-roast ham and eggs, cauliflower cheese with crusty bread, lasagne, fresh fish dish of the day, chicken and ham with ginger, honey and mango salad, venison pie, 10oz rump steak with chips, and puddings. *Benchmark main dish: beer-battered fish and chips £12.00. Two-course evening meal £19.00.*

Free house ~ Licensee Jon Woodley ~ Real ale ~ Open 10-3, 6-11; 12-10.30 Sun ~ Bar food 12-2, 6.30-9; 12-2, 7-9 Sun ~ Restaurant ~ Children allowed in restaurant and away from main bar area ~ Dogs allowed in bar

BUCKLAND MONACHORUM
Drake Manor 🍺 🛏 £

SX4968 Map 1

(01822) 853892 – www.drakemanorinn.co.uk

Off A386 via Crapstone, just S of Yelverton roundabout; PL20 7NA

Nice small village pub with snug rooms, popular food, quite a choice of drinks and pretty back garden; bedrooms

This charming little pub is deservedly popular, with many visitors returning on a regular basis. Run by a friendly, long-serving landlady, it provides comfortable bedrooms and enjoyable, very fair value food. The heavily beamed public bar on the left has a chatty, easy-going feel, brocade-cushioned wall seats, prints of the village from 1905 onwards, horse tack and a few ship badges and a woodburning stove in a very big stone fireplace; a small door leads to a low-beamed cubbyhole. The snug Drakes Bar has beams hung with tiny cups and big brass keys, a woodburning stove in another stone fireplace, horsebrasses and stirrups, and a mix of seats and tables (note the fine high-backed stripped-pine settle with hood). On the right is a small beamed dining room with settles and tables on flagstones. Darts and board games. There's Dartmoor Jail Ale, Sharps Doom Bar and a guest from Exeter on handpump, ten wines by the glass, a dozen malt whiskies, 15 gins and three farm ciders; darts and board games. There are picnic-sets in the prettily planted and sheltered back garden and the front floral displays are much admired; morris men perform regularly in summer. They also offer an attractive self-catering apartment. Buckland Abbey (National Trust) is close by.

Good value food includes lunchtime baguettes and ploughman's, home-made fish cakes, roasted tomato, mozzarella and basil tart with fried halloumi and pine nut salad, fritto misto, breaded wholetail scampi, whitebait, calamari and fish goujons with fries, pea and lemon risotto with coconut milk and herbs, Cajun chicken breast with coleslaw, sriracha mayonnaise and fries, and puddings such as chocolate and cherry brownie with chocolate sauce and red berry sorbet and white chocolate mousse. *Benchmark main dish: pie of the day £13.00. Two-course evening meal £20.00.*

Punch ~ Lease Mandy Robinson ~ Real ale ~ Open 11.30-2.30, 6-11; 11.30-11.30 Fri, Sat; 12-11 Sun ~ Bar food 12-2, 6.30-9.30; 12-2.30, 6-9.30 Sat; 12-2.30, 6.30-9 Sun ~ Restaurant ~ Children allowed in restaurant ~ Dogs allowed in bar ~ Bedrooms: £50

CHAGFORD   SX7087 Map 1

Three Crowns 🛏

(01647) 433444 – www.threecrowns-chagford.co.uk
High Street; TQ13 8AJ

Stylish bar and lounges in ancient inn, conservatory restaurant and good food and drinks; smart bedrooms

There's a real sense of history to this thatched pub, parts of which date from the 13th c. Ancient and modern features blend cleverly together with massive beams and standing timbers, huge fireplaces with wood fires (lit all year), exposed stone walls, flagstones and mullioned windows, and a contemporary dining room with a glazed atrium. The building is decorated throughout with antique prints, photographs and polished copper kettles, pots and warming pans. The bar areas have leather armchairs and stools, built-in panelled wall seats and a few leather tub chairs. St Austell Proper Job and Tribute on handpump, Sandford Orchards cider, 20 wines by the glass, 22 gins, 14 malt whiskies and cocktails served by friendly, efficient staff; background music and board games. Sturdy tables and chairs are placed among box topiary in the south-facing courtyard garden. The stylish and well appointed bedrooms (21 in total) blend character with modern design. Parking is limited to superior rooms only, but there's also a nearby pay-and-display car park. Muddy boots and dogs are welcome.

Rewarding food includes sandwiches, sharing boards and ploughman's, scotch egg with smoked chilli chutney, mushroom tagliatelle, sirloin steak, grilled halloumi with charred courgette & aubergine stack, rump of lamb with summer vegetables and feta, greek salad, harissa and lime chicken thighs with couscous, fish of the day with chive beurre blanc, fillet of beef with chips, bearnaise sauce and salad, and puddings such as eton mess and fruit crumble with vanilla ice-cream. *Benchmark main dish: beer-battered fish and chips £14.00. Two-course evening meal £21.00.*

St Austell ~ Managers John Milan and Steve Bellman ~ Real ale ~ Open 10am-11pm; 10am-midnight Fri, Sat ~ Bar food 12-9 (9.30 Sat); 10am-noon snacks; 2.30-6pm sandwiches and cream teas ~ Restaurant ~ Children welcome ~ Dogs allowed in bar & bedrooms ~ Bedrooms: £155

COCKWOOD

SX9780 Map 1

Anchor

(01626) 890203 – www.anchorinncockwood.com
Off, but visible from, A379 Exeter–Torbay, after Starcross; EX6 8RA

Very popular dining pub specialising in seafood (other choices available), with up to six real ales

This village pub on the River Exe estuary has an enviable location, with much prized tables on the sheltered front terrace looking over the small harbour with its bobbing boats, swans and ducks. Inside, there are several small, low-ceilinged, rambling rooms with black panelling and good-sized tables in various nooks, a snug with a cheerful winter coal fire, and an extension made up of mainly reclaimed timber and decorated with over 300 ship emblems, brass and copper lamps and nautical knick-knacks. There are up to six real ales on handpump from West Country breweries such as Dartmoor, Exeter, Otter and St Austell with a couple of guests (they hold beer festivals at Easter and Halloween), 16 gins and 20 malt whiskies; background music, darts, cards and board games.

They pride themselves on fresh fish and seafood, including several mussel dishes, a shellfish platter to share, skate wing with black butter and whole grilled mackerel, but offer non-fishy choices too: sandwiches, gammon steak with pineapple and chips, chicken balti or five bean curry, Sunday roasts (including a veggie version), and puddings such as vanilla and rasberry pannacotta and home-made sticky toffee pudding. *Benchmark main dish: West Country mussels with cheddar and Devon cider sauce and chips £15.95. Two-course evening meal £22.00.*

Heavitree ~ Lease Malcolm and Katherine Protheroe, Scott Hellier ~ Real ale ~ Open 11-11; 11.30-10.30 Sun ~ Bar food 12-9 ~ Restaurant ~ Children allowed in restaurant and if seated away from the bar ~ Dogs allowed in bar

COLEFORD

SS7701 Map 1

New Inn

(01363) 84242 – www.thenewinncoleford.co.uk
Just off A377 Crediton–Barnstaple; EX17 5BZ

Ancient thatched inn with hospitable owners, good food and real ales; bedrooms

Dating back to the 13th c, the New Inn is undoubtedly one of the oldest 'new' inns around. You'll be sure of a cheerful greeting from the hands-on licensees – and also from Captain, the talkative Amazon blue parrot – and there are always plenty of chatty regulars. The U-shaped, thatched building has the servery in the 'angle' with interestingly furnished areas leading off it: ancient and modern settles, cushioned stone wall seats, some character tables (a pheasant worked into the grain of one) and carved dressers and chests. Also, paraffin lamps, antique prints on the white walls, landscape-decorated plates on one beam and pewter tankards on another. Dartmoor Legend, Otter Ale and a guest such as local Hunters Half Bore or Shepherd Neame Spitfire on handpump, local cider, eight wines by the glass and two dozen malt whiskies; background music, darts and board games. There are chairs and tables in an enclosed rear garden by the babbling stream. Bedrooms are peaceful and comfortable and the breakfasts are very good indeed.

The locally sourced and seasonal good food includes Creedy Carver duck, a pie of the day, cider-braised pork chops, pork and black pudding terrine, fillets of smoked salmon and smoked trout with smoked mackerel pâté, cauliflower gnocchi, celeriac and mushroom wellington, and puddings such as lime tart, maple and pecan bread and butter pudding and West Country cheeses. *Benchmark main dish: venison sausages with mash £13.95. Two-course evening meal £21.00.*

Free house ~ Licensee Dr Mark Smeed ~ Real ale ~ Open 12-3, 6-11 (10.30 Sun) ~ Bar food 12-2, 6.30-9 ~ Restaurant ~ Children welcome ~ Dogs allowed in bar ~ Bedrooms: £150

DALWOOD
ST2400 Map 1
Tuckers Arms 🍴

(01404) 881342 – www.thetuckersarms.co.uk
Village signposted off A35 Axminster–Honiton; keep on past village; EX13 7EG

13th-c thatched inn with friendly, hard-working licensees, real ales and interesting bar food

The colourful summer window boxes, hanging baskets and tubs outside this cream-washed and thatched medieval longhouse are really charming. Inside, you'll find a genuine welcome from the good-humoured staff. The flagstoned bar is very cosy, kept warm by a big inglenook log fireplace. Also, heavy beams, traditional furnishings including assorted dining chairs, window seats and wall settles, numerous horsebrasses and a cheerful, bustling atmosphere. The back bar has an enormous collection of miniature bottles and there's also a more formal dining room; lots of copper implements and platters. Branscombe Vale Branoc, Exeter Avocet and Otter Bitter on handpump, several wines by the glass and up to 20 malt whiskies; background music and a double skittle alley. There are seats in the garden, and the pub (the oldest building in the parish after the church) is surrounded by narrow high-hedged lanes and hilly pasture countryside.

Extremely good food includes lunchtime sandwiches, potted crab, pâté of the day, pumpkin and sage ravioli, local moules marinière, steak in ale pie, lamb rump with redcurrant and rosemary gravy, pork belly with apricot, cider and raisin chutney, beer-battered fish and chips, and puddings such as butterscotch and ginger pudding with salted caramel ice-cream and lemon meringue pie. *Benchmark main dish: fisherman's platter £10.50. Two-course evening meal £19.50.*

Free house ~ Licensee Tracey McGowan ~ Real ale ~ Open 11.30-3, 6.30-11.30 ~ Bar food 12-2, 6.30-9 ~ Restaurant ~ Well behaved children welcome ~ Dogs allowed in bar

EXETER
SX9192 Map 1
Fat Pig 🍺

(01392) 437217 – www.thefatpigexeter.co.uk
John Street; EX1 1BL

Enthusiastically run pub with own-brew beers, wide range of spirits, big-flavoured food and a buoyant atmosphere

This friendly and welcoming pub has a lively, cheerful feel, high quality food and a fine choice of drinks. The big-windowed bar is simply furnished: elegant stools against a mahogany counter, more stools and long cushioned pews by sturdy pale wooden tables on bare boards, an open fire in a pretty fireplace, blackboards listing food choices and lots of mirrors.

As well as their own-brewed Black Boar, Phat Nancys IPA and Tiny Ale and a changing guest on handpump, you'll find good wines by the glass, around 100 malt whiskies and a large selection of gins. There's also a red-painted conservatory with red quarry tiles, a happy jumble of hops and house plants, books and old stone bottles on shelves, more mirrors and long benches and settles with scatter cushions around rustic tables.

Robust and good food from a changing menu includes roast cod with prawn and chorizo paella and samphire, home-made spinach gnocchi with wild mushrooms, rocket and blue cheese cream, pork faggotts with greens, mashed potato and gravy, roast ham with new potatoes, green beans and parsley sauce, chargrilled pork chop in bourbon and vanilla marinade with spicy couscous salad, and puddings such as white chocolate mousse and chocolate and almond brownie. *Benchmark main dish: crispy smoked lamb shoulder with rosemary potatoes and harissa yoghurt £18.00. Two-course evening meal £22.00.*

Free house ~ Licensee Paul Timewell ~ Real ale ~ Open 5-11pm; 4-midnight Fri; 12-midnight Sat; 12-5 Sun ~ Bar food 5-9; 12-9 Sat; 12-4 Sun ~ Restaurant ~ Children allowed Sun lunchtime only ~ Dogs welcome

FROGMORE   SX7742   Map 1
Globe 🛏
(01548) 531351 – www.theglobeinn.co.uk
A379 E of Kingsbridge; TQ7 2NR

Extended and neatly refurbished inn with bar and several dining areas, real ales, popular food and seats outside; warm bedrooms

The surrounding South Hams countryside is very appealing and a lovely area to explore, so it makes sense to stay in the well equipped, comfortable bedrooms here – and breakfasts are generous. The neatly kept bar has a double-sided woodburner with horsebrass-decorated stone pillars on either side, another fireplace filled with logs, cushioned settles, chunky farmhouse chairs and built-in wall seats around a mix of tables on wooden flooring, and a copper diving helmet. Attentive staff serve ales from Otter Ale and Salcombe on handpump and several wines by the glass. The slate-floored games room has a pool table and darts. There's also a comfortable lounge with an open fire, cushioned dining chairs and tables on red carpeting, a big leather sofa, a model yacht and a large yacht painting – spot the clever mural of a log pile. Teak tables and chairs are arranged on the back terrace, with steps leading up to another level with picnic-sets; the summer window boxes are most attractive.

Food is well regarded and includes sandwiches, tapas, pizzas, beer-battered fish and chips, steak and local ale pie with roasted Mediterranean vegetables, pan-fried chicken breast with bacon and barbecue sauce, burger (beef or lentil and vegetable) with toppings and chips, vegan Penang curry with wild rice, and puddings. *Benchmark main dish: seafood pancake £15.95. Two-course evening meal £21.00.*

Free house ~ Licensees John and Lynda Horsley ~ Real ale ~ Open 12-11; ~ Bar food 12-2, 6-9 ~ Restaurant ~ Children welcome ~ Dogs allowed in bar & bedrooms ~ Bedrooms: £100

GEORGEHAM   SS4639   Map 1
Rock ⭐ ❢ �
(01271) 890322 – www.therockinn.biz
Rock Hill, above village; EX33 1JW

Beamed pub with smashing food, five real ales, plenty of room inside and out and a relaxed atmosphere

Five real ales and consistently good food are highlights at this friendly old pub. The big bustling bar is divided in two by a step. The pubby top part has half-planked walls, an open woodburning stove in a stone fireplace and captain's and farmhouse chairs around wooden tables on quarry tiles; the lower area has panelled wall seats, some built-in settles forming a cosy booth, old local photographs and ancient flat irons. Leading off here is a red-carpeted dining room with attractive black and white photographs of North Devon folk. Helpful young staff serve Sharps Doom Bar, St Austell Tribute, Timothy Taylors Landlord and two changing guests on handpump, local cider and more than a dozen wines by the glass; background music and board games. The light and airy back dining conservatory has high-backed wooden or modern dining chairs around tables under a vine, with a little terrace beyond. There are picnic-sets at the front beside pretty hanging baskets and tubs; wheelchair access.

Rewarding food with an emphasis on fish and seafood includes lunchtime ciabattas, smoked mackerel salad, burgers (beef, venison and wild boar, chicken or vegan) with toppings and chips, rack of barbecue ribs, Asian-style sea bass with potato cake, grilled half lobster with garlic butter, goats cheese salad, wild mushroom risotto, and puddings such as lemon posset and sticky toffee pudding with butterscotch sauce and ice-cream. *Benchmark main dish: River Fowey mussels £15.95. Two-course evening meal £22.00.*

Star Pubs & Bars ~ Lease Daniel Craddock ~ Real ale ~ Open 11am-11.30pm; 11am-midnight Sat; 12-11.30 Sun ~ Bar food 12-2.30, 6-9; 12-8.30 Sun ~ Restaurant ~ Children welcome ~ Dogs allowed in bar

HAYTOR VALE
Rock ★ 🌟 ♈ 🛏

SX7777 Map 1

(01364) 661305 – www.rock-inn.co.uk

Haytor signposted off B3387 just W of Bovey Tracey, on good moorland road to Widecombe; TQ13 9XP

Devon Dining Pub of the Year

Smart Dartmoor inn with lovely food, real ales and seats in pretty garden; comfortable bedrooms

This is an especially well run and civilised inn. Many of the casual lunchtime customers are walkers exploring Dartmoor National Park, but the pub also attracts those wanting a more formal evening meal and comfortable overnight stay. The two neatly kept, linked, partly panelled bar rooms have lots of dark wood and red plush, polished antique tables with candles and fresh flowers, old-fashioned prints and decorative plates, and warming winter log fires (the main fireplace has a fine Stuart fireback). Dartmoor Jail Ale and Exeter Avocet on handpump, 15 wines (plus champagne and sparkling rosé) by the glass and 20 malt whiskies. There's also a light and spacious dining room in the lower part of the inn and a residents' lounge. The large, pretty garden opposite has some seats, with more on the little terrace next to the pub. The nine beamed bedrooms are smart (with either garden or moor views) and are highly regarded by our readers, and breakfasts are excellent. There's also a self-catering holiday cottage next door. You can park at the back of the building. Dogs are allowed in the conservatory area and in some bedrooms.

First class food includes sandwiches, chicken and avocado with lemon mayo, wild garlic risotto with parmesan and white truffle oil, lamb and rosemary burger with mint mayonnaise and chips, roast cod with crab croquette, avocado purée, shaved fennel and lemon oil, roasted lamb rump with lamb pithivier, smoked aubergine and red wine jus, and puddings such as tonka bean cheesecake with amaretto ice-cream and chocolate marquise with soaked cherries and cherry sorbet; they also offer a two- and three-course lunch menu. *Benchmark main dish: rib-eye steak with roast cherry tomatoes and chips £22.95. Two-course evening meal £26.00.*

Free house ~ Licensee Christopher Graves ~ Real ale ~ Open 11-11; 11-10.30 Sun; may shut earlier in winter ~ Bar food 12-2.15, 6.45-9 (8.30 Sun); Jan, Feb, Nov 12-2.15, 6.30-7 ~ Children allowed away from main bar ~ Dogs allowed in bedrooms ~ Bedrooms: £149

IDDESLEIGH   SS5608   Map 1
Duke of York
(01837) 810253 – www.dukeofyorkdevon.co.uk
B3217 Exbourne–Dolton; EX19 8BG

15th-c thatched local with tasty food and a fair choice of drinks; bedrooms

If you enjoy simple, honest pubs, you'll feel right at home at this cob and stone village local, though it's not to everyone's taste. The unspoilt bar has plenty of chatty locals, rocking chairs, cushioned benches built into the wall's black-painted wooden dado, stripped tables and other simple country furnishings, banknotes pinned to beams, and a large open fireplace. Adnams Broadside, Bays Topsail and a guest ale tapped from the cask, several wines by the glass and three farm ciders. It can get pretty cramped at peak times. The dining room has a huge inglenook fireplace. Through a small coach arch is a little back garden with some picnic-sets. Bedrooms are clean but old-fashioned (and some may have no lock on the door); five are in the pub, with three more just a minute's walk away. Poet Ted Hughes was a regular, and Michael Morpurgo, author of *War Horse*, got the inspiration to write his novel after talking to World War I veteran Wilfred Ellis in front of the fire here over 30 years ago.

Bar food includes sandwiches, salt and pepper squid with sweet chilli dip, garlic mushrooms with stilton topping, beef or vegetable chilli, home-cooked ham and eggs, chicken and bacon lasagne, local sausages with mash and onion gravy, scampi with chips, slow-roasted pork belly with apple and cider sauce, beer-battered fish and chips, and puddings. *Benchmark main dish: steak and kidney pudding £13.95. Two-course evening meal £18.00.*

Free house ~ Licensee John Pittam ~ Real ale ~ Open 11-11; 11am-midnight Sat ~ Bar food 12-9.30; no food 3-5pm Mon-Weds in winter ~ Restaurant ~ Children welcome ~ Dogs allowed in bar & bedrooms ~ Bedrooms: £80

KINGSBRIDGE   SX7344   Map 1
Dodbrooke Inn ☖ £
(01548) 852068
Church Street, Dodbrooke (parking some way off); TQ7 1DB

Bustling local with friendly licensees, chatty locals and well regarded food and drink

This small terraced pub in a quiet residential area offers a genuine welcome to visitors. The friendly, long-serving licensees know what they are doing – they've been here for over 30 years. The traditional bar, with plenty of chatty regulars, has built-in cushioned stall seats and plush cushioned stools around pubby tables, some horse tack, local photographs and china jugs, a log fire and an easy-going atmosphere. There's Bass, Dartmoor Jail

Ale, Exeter Avocet and Sharps Doom Bar on handpump, local cider and eight wines by the glass. You can sit in the covered courtyard, which might be candlelit in warm weather.

🍽 Fair value food includes sandwiches, deep-fried whitebait with tartare sauce, scallops with crispy bacon, ham and eggs, beef stroganoff, sausage in a basket, minted lamb shank, popular speciality charcoal steaks (sirloin rump and fillet), and puddings. *Benchmark main dish: beer-battered fish and chips £9.75. Two-course evening meal £15.00.*

Free house ~ Licensees Michael and Jill Dyson ~ Real ale ~ Open 12-2, 5.30-11; 12-2, 7-10.30 Sun ~ Bar food 12-1.30, 5.30-8.30 ~ Children aged over 5 welcome

POSTBRIDGE
SX6780   Map 1

Warren House

(01822) 880208 – www.warrenhouseinn.co.uk

B3212 0.75 miles NE of Postbridge; PL20 6TA

Isolated 18th-c pub, ideal for a drink or meal after a moorland hike

This beautifully located pub is the perfect spot after a damp walk on Dartmoor. It's a straightforward and honest place, full of character. The cosy bar has simple furnishings such as easy chairs and settles beneath the beamed ochre ceiling, old pictures of the inn on partly panelled stone walls and dim lighting (powered by the pub's own generator); one of the open fires is said to have been kept alight since 1845. There's also a family room. They sell Black Tor Pride of Dartmoor, Otter Ale and changing guests such as Roam Sound Bitter and Summerskills Start Point on handpump, local farm cider and malt whiskies. The picnic-sets on both sides of the road have views overlooking moorland.

🍽 Bar food includes lunchtime ploughman's and baked potatoes, pasties, breaded king prawns with garlic dip, steak in ale pie, ricotta and spinach cannelloni, ham and chips, Spanish-style lamb in sherry, Mexican three-bean chilli with rice, smoked haddock and spring onion fishcakes, steaks with trimmings, and puddings such as chocolate fudge cake and sticky toffee pudding. *Benchmark main dish: rabbit pie £13.95. Two-course evening meal £19.00.*

Free house ~ Licensee Peter Parsons ~ Real ale ~ Open 11am-10pm; 12-10 Sun ~ Bar food 12-9; 12-8.30 Sun; 12-2.30 Mon, Tues in winter ~ Restaurant ~ Children in family room only ~ Dogs allowed in bar

SANDFORD
SS8202   Map 1

Lamb 🍺 🛏

(01363) 773676 – www.lambinnsandford.co.uk

The Square; EX17 4LW

16th-c inn with good food, thoughtful choice of drinks and seats in garden; well equipped bedrooms

You can expect a welcoming and friendly atmosphere at this former coaching inn. The charming linked beamed bar has red leather sofas beside a log fire, cushioned window seats, a settle and various dining chairs round a few tables on patterned carpet. Branscombe Vale Branoc and Powderkeg Speak Easy Translatlantic Pale with guests such as Dartmoor Jail Ale and Exmoor Antler on handpump, ten wines by the glass, four farm ciders, 20 gins (most are local) and 20 malt whiskies. The dining area has a woodburning stove, a cushioned wall pew, all manner of nice old wooden dining chairs and tables and quite a few mirrors. There's also a Tap Room with board games. There are rustic seats and tables and fairy lights in the cobbled, three-level garden, plus some picnic-sets on grass beyond the hedge. The eight bedrooms are comfortable, modern and well equipped. Nearby parking is at a premium, but the village car park is just a few minutes' walk up the small lane to the right.

Enjoyable food includes lunchtime ciabatta rolls, scallops with chorizo and red pepper, roast chicken thigh with pork bonbon and blue cheese mousse, broccoli and blue cheese tart with pepper purée and pickles, burgers with toppings and chips, duck breast with fondant potato and star anise, local lamb rack with dauphinoise potatoes and jus, 10oz rib-eye steak with garlic butter and chips, and puddings such as raspberry brûlée with blackberry buttercream and sticky toffee pudding with salted caramel ice-cream. *Benchmark main dish: fresh fish dish of the day £16.95. Two-course evening meal £21.00.*

Free house ~ Licensee Nick Silk ~ Real ale ~ Open 9am-11pm (midnight Sat); 9am-10.30pm Sun ~ Bar food 12-2.15, 6.30-9 ~ Restaurant ~ Children welcome ~ Dogs allowed in bar ~ Bedrooms: £94

SOUTH ZEAL SX6593 Map 1
Oxenham Arms 🛏
(01837) 840244 – www.theoxenhamarms.com
Off A30/A382; EX20 2JT

Wonderful 15th-c inn with lots of history, character bars, real ales, enjoyable food and big garden; bedrooms

This historic inn, first licensed in 1477, is full of stories and packed with character. It was originally a Benedictine monastery built to combat the pagan power of the Neolithic standing stone that still forms part of the wall in the room behind the bar (there's actually 20 feet of stone below the floor). The heavily beamed and partly panelled front bar has elegant mullioned windows and Stuart fireplaces, all sorts of chairs and built-in wall seats with scatter cushions around low oak tables on bare floorboards, and bar stools against the counter. The friendly staff serve Merry Monk (named for them from Dartmoor), Dartmoor Jail Ale and Teignworthy Gun Dog on handpump; also, seven wines by the glass, 70 malt whiskies, 25 ports, local mead and three farm ciders. A small room is equipped with beams, wheelback chairs around polished tables, decorative plates and another open fire. Imposing curved stone steps lead up to the four-acre garden, which has plenty of seats and fine views; there are more tables under parasols out in front. Some of the bedrooms have four-poster beds; Charles Dickens, snowed up one winter, wrote a lot of *The Pickwick Papers* here. This makes a good stop if you're travelling on the busy A30. You can also walk straight from the door on to Dartmoor and they provide details of walking tours.

Popular food includes lunchtime sandwiches, Devon minute rump steak with skinny fries, grilled tomato and mushroom, Brixham fish in their own beer batter with chips, mushy peas and home-made tartare sauce, butternut squash and sage ravioli with chilli and herb dressing, katsu chicken curry with rice, steak and ale pie, cauliflower, spinach and lentil dhal with rice, and puddings such as sticky toffee pudding, summer berry cheesecake and vanilla crème brûlée. *Benchmark main dish: steak in ale pie £12.95. Two-course evening meal £20.50.*

Free house ~ Licensees Simon and Lyn Powell ~ Real ale ~ Open 11-11; closed Mon ~ Bar food 12-3, 6-8.30; cream teas in afternoon ~ Restaurant ~ Children welcome ~ Dogs allowed in bar ~ Bedrooms: £134

SPREYTON   SX6996   Map 1

Tom Cobley

(01647) 231314 – www.tomcobleytavern.co.uk

Dragdown Hill; W out of village; EX17 5AL

Huge range of quickly changing real ales and ciders, and wide choice of food in friendly, busy village pub

There's masses of choice for beer lovers at this traditional old pub. Up to nine (and as many as 14 in the past) quickly changing real ales – well kept on handpump or tapped from the cask – include Dartmoor Jail Ale, Exeter 'fraidNot, Otter Ale, Plain Inncognito, St Austell Tribute and Teignworthy Gun Dog; also, up to ten farm ciders and perries. The comfortable bar (with its own thatched roof above the counter) has traditional furnishings, an open fire and local photographs and country scenes on the walls, and you can be sure of a genuine welcome from the hospitable landlord and his cheerful staff. A large back dining room has beams and similar décor. There are picnic-sets in the garden and more out in front by the quiet street. Several of the comfortable bedrooms have Dartmoor views. Disabled access.

Good quality, traditional food (special diets catered for) includes lunchtime sandwiches, pasties, ploughman's, omelettes, pâté with caramelised onion chutney, sweet potato and spinach curry, scampi and chips, lambs liver with bacon and onion gravy, chicken and mushroom pie with peas and chips, Thai prawn and cod fishcakes with chips, chicken curry, steak (rump or sirloin) with onion rings and chips, duck with home-made orange sauce, and puddings. *Benchmark main dish: steak in ale pie £11.95. Two-course evening meal £20.00.*

Free house ~ Licensees Roger and Carol Cudlip ~ Real ale ~ Open 12-3, 6-11 (midnight Fri, Sat); 12-4, 7-11 Sun ~ Bar food 12-2, 7-9 ~ Restaurant ~ Children welcome ~ Dogs allowed in bar & bedrooms ~ Bedrooms: £100

WIDECOMBE   SX7276   Map 1

Rugglestone

(01364) 621327 – www.rugglestoneinn.co.uk

Village at end of B3387; pub just S – turn left at church and NT church house, OS Sheet 191 map reference 720765; TQ13 7TF

Charming local with a couple of bars, cheerful customers, friendly staff, four real ales and traditional pub food

This appealing, wisteria-clad stone building has a picturesque setting, tucked away in a Dartmoor village beside a stream. An inn since the 1830s, it's just the place to refuel after enjoying a hearty walk in the surrounding countryside. The unspoilt bar has just four tables, a few window and wall seats, a one-person pew built into the corner beside a nice old stone fireplace (with a woodburner) and a good mix of customers. The rudimentary bar counter dispenses Moor beer (brewed just for them from Teignworthy), Dartmoor Legend and regional guests tapped from the cask; also, local farm cider and a decent small wine list. The room on the right is slightly bigger and lighter in feel, with beams, another stone fireplace, stripped-pine tables and a built-in wall bench; there's also a small dining room. To reach the picnic-sets in the garden you have to cross a bridge over a little moorland stream. Disabled access but no disabled loos. They have a holiday cottage available to rent.

Traditional food includes ploughman's, jacket potatoes, chicken liver pâté, deep-fried brie with redcurrant jelly, crispy whitebait, vegetable madras curry, beef and ale or steak and stilton pie, beer-battered haddock fillet with chips and peas, smoked trout salad with home-made coleslaw, and puddings. *Benchmark main dish: wholetail scampi with chips and peas £12.50. Two-course evening meal £18.00.*

Free house ~ Licensees Richard and Vicki Palmer ~ Real ale ~ Open 11.30-3, 6.30-11; 11.30-3, 5-11.30 Fri; 11.30am-midnight Sat; 12-11 Sun ~ Bar food 12-2, 6.30-9 ~ Restaurant ~ Children allowed in restaurant & away from bar area ~ Dogs allowed in bar

WOODBURY SALTERTON

SY0189 Map 1

Diggers Rest £

(01395) 232375 – www.diggersrest.co.uk

3.5 miles from M5 junction 30: A3052 towards Sidmouth, village signposted on right about 0.5 miles after Clyst St Mary; also signposted from B3179 SE of Exeter; EX5 1PQ

Bustling village pub with real ales, good food and seats in terraced garden

A former cider house, this place is 500 years old and very much the heart of the village. The main bar has antique furniture, local art on the walls and a cosy seating area by the open fire. A modern extension is light and airy and opens on to the garden. Ales include St Austell Proper Job and Tribute and Sharps Doom Bar on handpump, a selection of good quality wines and a full range of spirits; friendly new owners took over recently, and service is attentive and efficient. The window boxes and flowering baskets are pretty in summer and there are fine walks around Woodbury Common and in the surrounding Otter Valley.

Pleasing, good value food cooked from scratch mixes traditional dishes with more global fare; dishes include deep-fried whitebait, chicken wings in barbecue sauce, home-made aromatic fishcake with lime mayo, home-made beef lasagne, ham, egg and chips, burger (beef, Cajun chicken or falafel) with chips and slaw, Thai red chicken curry, slow-cooked Mongolian beef with noodles, Buddha bowl (roasted vegetables, grains, pickles, falafel and halloumi), and puddings such as fruit crumble and lemon drizzle cake. *Benchmark main dish: beer-battered fish and chips £11.00. Two-course evening meal £16.00.*

Heartstone Inns ~ Managers Arwen Beaton and Dan Kelley ~ Real ale ~ Open 12-3, 5.30-11; 12-11 Sat; 12-10.30 Sun ~ Bar food 12-2, 6-9; 12-8 Sun ~ Restaurant ~ Children welcome ~ Dogs welcome

Also Worth a Visit in Devon

Besides the fully inspected pubs, you might like to try these pubs that have been recommended to us and described by readers. Do tell us what you think of them: feedback@goodguides.com

ABBOTSKERSWELL　　　　SX8568
Court Farm (01626) 361866
Wilton Way; look for the church tower; TQ12 5NY Attractive neatly extended 17th-c longhouse tucked away in picturesque hamlet; various rooms off long beamed and paved main bar, good mix of furnishings, woodburners, well priced popular food (worth booking) including weekday lunchtime bargains, friendly helpful service, Bass, Otter and other beers, farm cider and decent wines; background music, pool and

darts; children and dogs (in bar) welcome, picnic-sets in pretty lawned garden, open all day, food all day Thurs-Sun.

APPLEDORE　　　　SS4630
Beaver (01237) 474822
Irsha Street; EX39 1RY Relaxed, well run harbourside pub with lovely estuary view from popular raised dining area; enjoyable reasonably priced food especially fresh local fish, prompt friendly service, good choice of West Country ales, farm cider, decent house wines and great range of whiskies;

background and some live music, quiz Weds, pool in smaller games room, TV; children and dogs (in bar) welcome, disabled access (but no nearby parking), tables on small sheltered water-view terrace.

Royal George (01237) 424138
Irsha Street; EX39 1RY Refurbished waterside dining pub; local beers, plenty of wines by the glass and good reasonably priced food from daily changing menu including fresh fish, friendly staff, superb estuary views from dining room and upstairs restaurant with balcony; children and dogs (downstairs) welcome, picturesque street sloping to the sea, a few picnic-sets out at front, four comfortably revamped bedrooms and self-catering cottage, open all day.

Ashill Inn (01884) 840506
M5 junction 27, follow signs to Willand, then left to Uffculme and Craddock on B3440; Ashill signed to left; pub in centre of village; EX15 3NL Popular 19th-c village pub, cosy and friendly, with well kept local ales and highly rated home-cooked food including daily specials (booking advised), reasonable prices, black beams, woodburner in stone fireplace, modern dining extension overlooking small garden; occasional live music, darts and skittles, TV; children welcome in bar area until 9pm, closed Mon lunchtime, no food Sun evening or Mon.

Durant Arms (01803) 732240
Off A381 S of Totnes; TQ9 7UP Traditional 18th-c village inn; enjoyable home-cooked food, four well kept ales including Noss Beer Works, good friendly service, slate-floored bar with stag's head above woodburner, china on delft shelf, other connecting rooms; occasional live music; children, walkers and dogs welcome, three bedrooms, open all day weekends, closed Mon lunchtime.

★Turtley Corn Mill (01364) 646100
0.5 miles off A38 roundabout at SW end of South Brent bypass; TQ10 9ES Converted watermill with series of linked areas; mix of wooden dining chairs and chunky tables on oriental rugs or dark flagstones, fat church candles, various prints and some framed 78rpm discs, woodburners, big windows looking out over grounds, Dartmoor, Otter and guests, nine wines by the glass and 30 malt whiskies, wide choice of brasserie-style food, friendly service; children and dogs (in bar) welcome, extensive garden with well spaced picnic-sets, giant chess set, small lake, ducks, chickens and peacocks, six bedrooms, open (and food) all day from 9am for breakfast.

Harbour Inn (01297) 20371
B3172 Seaton–Axminster; EX12 4AF Ancient thatched pub by estuary; updated heavily beamed bar rooms with bare boards, flagstones and some stripped-stone walls, huge inglenook, lots of model boats, old pictures, photographs and accounts of shipwrecks, other partitioned dining/seating areas including carpeted part with armchairs by woodburner, Badger ales and several wines by the glass, enjoyable food from sharing boards up; background music, Weds quiz; children and dogs (in bar) welcome, modern furniture on terrace, picnic-sets on grass, open (and food) all day.

Halfway (01395) 232273
A3052 Exeter–Sidmouth, junction with B3180; EX5 2JP Modernised roadside dining pub; well cooked food from fairly priced pub favourites up including home-made American-style burger, good fresh fish/seafood and Sun carvery, well kept Otter Bitter and St Austell Tribute, efficient friendly service, Dartmoor views from restaurant/conservatory and raised outside seating area; children and dogs (in bar) welcome, open all day.

★Swan (01398) 332248
Station Road; EX16 9NG Popular, well run beamed village inn with spacious bare-boards bar, woodburners in two inglenooks, three changing West Country beers, nice wines and fine choice of gins, very good food from interesting varied menu (both licensees are chefs), efficient friendly service; children and dogs welcome, three well appointed bedrooms, big breakfast, open all day, no food third Sun evening of month.

★Sloop (01548) 560489
Off A379/B3197 NW of Kingsbridge; TQ7 3AJ Welcoming 14th-c split-level pub close to fine beach and walks, popular and relaxed, with good mix of customers in black-beamed stripped-stone bar, country tables and chairs on flagstones, blazing woodburner, well kept St Austell Tribute, Proper Job and a guest, several wines by the glass and very nice food from sandwiches to good fresh fish, courteous helpful service, restaurant; background music; children and dogs (in bar) welcome, seats out at back, six bedrooms (some with sea views), open all day in summer.

Anchor (01297) 20386
Fore Street; EX12 3ET Sea-view inn with good choice of enjoyable food including local fish, Greene King, Otter and good value wines, open-plan interior with large eating

area, friendly staff; background music, sports TV, fruit machine; children well looked after, dogs welcome in bar, lots of tables in clifftop garden over road, six reasonably priced bedrooms, open (and food) all day.

BEESANDS
SX8140

Cricket (01548) 580215

About 3 miles S of A379, from Chillington; in village turn right along foreshore road; TQ7 2EN Pub-restaurant with pebbly Start Bay beach just over the sea wall; light airy New England-style décor with dark wood or leather chairs around chunky tables, stripped-wood flooring by the bar, carpet in the restaurant, some nautical bits and pieces including model boats, relaxed chatty atmosphere with a few tables kept for drinkers, Otter and St Austell ales, local cider and 14 wines by the glass, generally well liked food with emphasis on fish/seafood (worth booking – can be expensive); background radio, TVs; children and dogs (in bar) welcome, wheelchair access/loo, picnic-sets by sea wall, seven attractive bedrooms (some overlooking the sea), South West Coast Path runs through the village, open all day, food all day in high summer.

BELSTONE
SX61293

Tors (01837) 840689

A mile off A30; EX20 1QZ Popular small Victorian granite pub-hotel in peaceful village on edge of Dartmoor, family-run and welcoming, with long carpeted bar divided by settles, well kept ales such as Dartmoor and Teignworthy, over 60 malt whiskies and good choice of wines, enjoyable food from baguettes to specials, cheerful prompt service, restaurant and new outdoor Shed for burgers and beer; live music; children welcome and dogs (they have their own), disabled access, seats out on nearby grassy area overlooking valley, good walks, bedrooms, open all day weekends.

BISHOPS TAWTON
SS5629

★Chichester Arms (01271) 343945

Signed off A377 outside Barnstaple; East Street; EX32 0DQ Friendly 15th-c cob and thatch pub serving generous helpings of good well priced food from sandwiches/baguettes to fresh local fish, quick obliging service even when crowded, St Austell Tribute, Bombardier and a guest, decent wines, heavy low beams, large stone fireplace, restaurant; children and dogs welcome, awkward disabled access but staff very helpful, picnic-sets on front terrace and in back garden, open all day.

BOVEY TRACEY
SX8178

Cromwell Arms (01626) 833473

Fore Street; TQ13 9AE Welcoming 17th-c beamed inn with several areas including separate restaurant, popular good value food and up to five St Austell ales; quiz Tues, open mike Sun once a month; children and

dogs (in bar) welcome, disabled access/loos, small garden with decking and pergola, 14 bedrooms, open all day.

BRAMPFORD SPEKE
SX9298

Agricultural Inn (01392) 840043

Off A377 N of Exeter; EX5 5DP 18th-c local with new owners and new name (formerly the Lazy Toad); linked rooms with beams, standing timbers and slate floors, pubby furnishings and log fire, Exeter Avocet, Hanlons Yellow Hammer and Salcombe Seahorse on handpump and several wines by the glass, modern bistro food and traditional Sun roasts, street food outdoors Fri-Sun weather permitting; tables in courtyard (once used by the local farrier and wheelwright) and in walled garden, charming village of thatched cottages, good walks beside the River Exe and Devonshire Heartland Way, open all day, closed Mon.

BRANSCOMBE
SY2088

★Masons Arms (01297) 680300

Main Street; signed off A3052 Sidmouth–Seaton, then bear left into village; EX12 3DJ Popular old thatched pub near the sea in pretty village; rambling bar with slate floor, ancient ships' beams, comfortable seats, log fire in massive hearth, St Austell Proper Job, Tribute and guests, several wines by the glass, enjoyable fairly traditional food including sandwiches and daily specials, afternoon cream teas, friendly helpful staff, second bar with two-way woodburner and stripped pine, two smartly furnished dining rooms; children and dogs (in bars) welcome, quiet flower-filled front terrace with thatched-roof tables, side garden, neat comfortable bedrooms (some in converted cottages), open all day and can get very busy at peak times.

BRATTON CLOVELLY
SX4691

Clovelly (01837) 871447

From S (A30), turn left at church, pub is on the right; EX20 4JZ Friendly 18th-c village pub with cosy bar and two dining rooms; generous helpings of popular reasonably priced traditional food including specials, well kept Dartmoor, Sharps and a guest, cheerful staff, games room; may be live jazz second Mon of month; children and dogs welcome, 17th-c wall paintings in Norman church, open all day weekends.

BRAYFORD
SS7235

★Poltimore Arms No phone

Yarde Down; 3 miles towards Simonsbath; EX36 3HA Ivy-clad 17th-c beamed pub – so remote it generates its own electricity, and water is from a spring; good home-made evening food Thurs-Sat, also Sun lunchtime (best to book), two or three changing ales tapped from the cask, friendly helpful staff, traditional furnishings, woodburner in inglenook, two attractive restaurant areas separated by another woodburner, good country views; children and dogs (in bar) welcome, picnic-sets in side garden, shop and gallery, open all day.

BRENDON   SS7547
★ **Rockford Inn** (01598) 741214
Rockford; Lynton–Simonsbath Road, off B3223; EX35 6PT Homely and welcoming little 17th-c beamed inn surrounded by fine Exmoor walks and scenery; neatly linked rooms with cushioned settles, wall seats and other straightforward furniture, country prints and horse tack, open fires, good helpings of enjoyable sensibly priced pubby food, a couple of well kept ales such as Clearwater and Cotleigh tapped from the cask, Addlestone's and Thatcher's ciders, decent wines by the glass, lots of pump clips and toby jugs behind counter; background music, board games; children and dogs (in bar) welcome, seats across the road overlooking East Lyn river, seven well appointed bedrooms, open all day.

BRENDON   SS7648
Staghunters (01598) 741222
Leedford Lane; EX35 6PS Idyllically set family-run hotel with gardens by East Lyn river, can get packed, though quiet out of season; good choice of enjoyable reasonably priced food, up to six well kept ales such as Exmoor and St Austell, real cider, friendly efficient staff, bar with woodburner, restaurant; children, walkers and dogs welcome, riverside tables, 14 good value bedrooms, open all day weekends (and weekdays if busy).

BRIXHAM   SX9256
New Quay (01803) 883290
King Street; TQ5 9TW Early 18th-c pub tucked down side street; well kept changing West Country beers and ciders from board-fronted servery, good range of wines by the glass and gins, friendly helpful staff, beam and plank ceiling, spindleback chairs and mix of old tables on slate tiles, warming woodburner, fairly traditional menu using fresh local produce, upstairs restaurant with another woodburner and old town views; no children under 10, dogs welcome in bar, open all day Sun in summer, closed Mon-Weds and till 5.30pm Thurs-Sat.

BROADCLYST   SX9997
New Inn (01392) 461312
Wimple Road; EX5 3BX Friendly former 17th-c farmhouse with stripped brickwork, boarded ceiling, low doorways and log fires, enjoyable reasonably priced pubby food, Dartmoor, Hanlons, Otter and Sharps, restaurant; skittle alley; children and dogs welcome, garden with play area, open all day.

BROADHEMBURY   ST1004
Drewe Arms (01404) 841267
Off A373 Cullompton–Honiton; EX14 3NF Extended partly thatched

pub dating from the 15th c; carved beams and handsome stone-mullioned windows, woodburner and open fire, modernised bar area, five well kept local ales from the likes of Bays, Exmoor and Otter) and seven wines by the glass, enjoyable pubby food (not Mon, Tues or evening Sun), friendly helpful service, skittle alley; children and dogs (in bar) welcome, terrace seats, more up steps on tree-shaded lawn, nice setting near church in pretty village, open all day.

BROADHEMPSTON   SX8066
Monks Retreat (01803) 812203
The Square; TQ9 6BN Old pub next to the village school; black beams, wood floors and logburner in huge stone fireplace, cheerful welcoming staff, Dartmoor ales and enjoyable sensibly priced home-made food including daily specials, OAP lunch Thurs, fish and chips Weds evening, quiz every other Thurs, steps to sizeable dining area, also oak-framed dining extension; dogs welcome, bedrooms, closed Mon and Tues lunchtimes, no food Sun-Tues evenings.

BUCKFAST   SX7467
Abbey Inn (01364) 642343
Buckfast Road, off B3380; TQ11 0EA Lovely position perched on bank of River Dart; partly panelled bar with woodburner, three St Austell ales and Healey's cider, enjoyable reasonably priced pubby food from sandwiches, baguettes and pizzas up, Sun carvery, big dining room with more panelling and river views; background music; well behaved children and dogs (in bar) welcome, terrace and bedrooms overlooking the water, open all day.

BUCKLAND BREWER   SS4220
★ **Coach & Horses** (01237) 451395
Village signposted off A388 S of Monkleigh; OS Sheet 190 map reference 423206; EX39 5LU Friendly 13th-c thatched pub with heavily beamed bar (mind your head), comfortable seats, handsome antique settle and inglenook woodburner, smaller lounge with another inglenook log fire, Abbot Ale, Country Life Golden Pig, local ciders and several wines by the glass, decent food including home-made curries, small back games room (darts and pool) and skittle alley/function room; background music, occasional sports TV, games machine; children and dogs (in bar) welcome, picnic-sets on front terrace and in side garden, holiday cottage next door, closed Mon and Tues lunchtimes in winter.

BUTTERLEIGH   SS9708
Butterleigh Inn (01884) 855433
Off A396 in Bickleigh; EX15 1PN Traditional heavy-beamed country pub, friendly and relaxed with good mix of customers, enjoyable reasonably priced pubby food (not Mon) from baguettes up, Sun carvery, four well kept ales such as Cotleigh,

Otter, Hanlons and a guest, real ciders and good choice of wines, unspoilt lived-in interior with two big fireplaces, back dining room; children and dogs welcome, picnic-sets in large garden, four comfortable bedrooms, closed Sun evening, Mon lunchtime.

CADELEIGH   SS9107
★**Cadeleigh Arms** (01884) 855238
Village signed off A3072 W of junction with A396 Tiverton–Exeter at Bickleigh; EX16 8HP Attractive and friendly old pub owned by the local community; well kept ales from the likes of Exe Valley and Otter plus Powderkeg craft beers, Sandford Orchards cider, good locally sourced food (not Sun evening or Tues lunchtime) from regularly changing menu, carpeted room on left with bay-window seat and ornamental stove, flagstoned room to the right with high-backed settles and log fire in big fireplace, valley views from airy dining room down a couple of steps; background music, skittle alley; children and dogs welcome, tables on sunny terrace and gently sloping lawn, closed Mon.

CALIFORNIA CROSS   SX7053
California (01548) 821449
Brown sign to pub off A3121 S of A38 junction; PL21 0SG Neatly kept 18th-c or older beamed dining pub; red carpets, panelling and stripped stone, plates on delft shelving and other bits and pieces, log fire, good choice of enjoyable food from baguettes to steaks in bar and family area, popular Sun lunch (best to book), separate evening restaurant (Weds-Sun) and small snug, Dartmoor Best and Jail Ale and St Austell Tribute, traditional cider and decent wines by the glass, good friendly service; background music, children and dogs welcome, attractive garden and back terrace, open all day.

CHAGFORD   SX6987
Chagford (01647) 433109
Mill Street; TQ13 8AW Former coaching inn just off market square; main bar/dining room with understated modern décor; blue-painted half-panelling, mix of furniture including pine settles forming booths, local artwork, fresh flowers and woodburner, good food from changing menu featuring locally farmed Dexter beef, well kept ales such as Butcombe, Dartmoor and Otter, Symonds's and Thatcher's ciders, nice wines and proper coffee, friendly helpful staff; background music; children and dogs welcome, walled courtyard garden behind, three comfortable annexe bedrooms; new owners as went to press, so may be changes.

CHAGFORD   SX7087
Ring o' Bells (01647) 432466
Off A382; TQ13 8AH Welcoming old shuttered pub with good mix of locals and visitors; beamed and panelled bar, four well kept ales including Dartmoor and

enjoyable home-made food at fair prices, friendly attentive service, woodburner in big fireplace; some live music, well behaved children and dogs welcome, sunny walled garden behind, nearby moorland walks, four comfortable spotless bedrooms, good breakfast, open all day.

CHALLACOMBE   SS6941
Black Venus (01598) 763251
B3358 Blackmoor Gate–Simonsbath; EX31 4TT Welcoming 16th-c low-beamed pub; two or three well kept changing ales, Sandford Orchards cider and decent wines by the glass, enjoyable fairly priced food from sandwiches to popular Sun lunch, helpful chatty staff, pews and comfortable chairs, woodburner and big fireplace, roomy attractive dining area, games room with pool and darts; children and dogs welcome, garden play area, lovely countryside and good walks from the door, open all day in summer.

CHERITON BISHOP   SX7792
★**Old Thatch Inn** (01647) 24204
Off A30; EX6 6JH Attractive thatched village pub with welcoming relaxed atmosphere; rambling beamed bar separated by big stone fireplace, Dartmoor and a couple of guests, ciders such as Sandford's, good freshly prepared food including range of burgers, efficient friendly service, restaurant; quiz last Sun of month; children and dogs welcome, nice sheltered garden, open all day, no food Sun evening, Mon, Tues.

CHERITON FITZPAINE   SS8706
★**Ring of Bells** (01363) 860111
Off Barton Close, signed to village centre; EX17 4JG Renovated 14th-c thatched and beamed country pub; very good food cooked by landlord-chef including set menus (popular Tues auberge night), ales such as Branscombe Vale, Exe Valley and Teignworthy, local cider, friendly efficient service; children and dogs welcome (pub dog is Ruben), self-catering cottage, closed Mon, no food Sun evening.

CHILLINGTON   SX7942
Bear & Blacksmiths (01548) 581171
A379 E of Kingsbridge; TQ7 2LD Old refurbished pub with clean modern interior; landlord-chef's good food using local produce including some from own farm, three well kept ales, friendly helpful staff; children and dogs (in bar) welcome, tables set out on back terrace.

CHITTLEHAMPTON   SS6325
Bell (01769) 540368
Signed off B3227 S Molton–Umberleigh; EX37 9QL Family-run village inn on edge of square opposite historic church; decoratively tiled entrance to high-ceilinged bar with half-panelling and magnolia walls, lots of old photographs, animal heads and antlers, wooden pubby furniture, tasty good value

home-made food from sandwiches and pub favourites up, ales such as Cotleigh and Exmoor, ciders, outstanding range of whiskies and over 90 gins, cheerful hard-working young staff; children (away from bar) and dogs welcome, ramp for wheelchairs, disabled loos, shaded circular picnic-sets on front cobbles, nice sunny garden behind, three bedrooms, open all day Fri-Sun.

CHRISTOW   SX8385
★ **Teign House** (01647) 252286
Teign Valley Road (B3193); EX6 7PL
Former farmhouse in country setting; very good freshly made food from pub favourites up, also an Asian menu, three well kept local ales, cider and nice wines, friendly helpful staff, open fire in beamed bar, dining room; some live music; well behaved children and dogs welcome, garden and camping field, open all day.

CHUDLEIGH   SX8679
Bishop Lacey (01626) 854585
Fore Street, just off A38; TQ13 0HY
Old low-beamed former church house; three well kept West Country beers and enjoyable reasonably priced home-made food, cheerful obliging staff, two bars, log fire; children and dogs welcome, open all day.

CHULMLEIGH   SS6814
Red Lion (01769) 580384
East Street; EX18 7DD Nicely updated 17th-c coaching inn with beams and open fires, enjoyable fairly priced food including range of burgers and pizzas, St Austell, Sharps and a guest, friendly helpful service, darts; children welcome, five bedrooms, open all day Fri-Sun, closed lunchtimes Mon-Thurs.

CHURCHSTOW   SX7145
Church House (01548) 852237
A379 NW of Kingsbridge; TQ7 3QW
Attractive building dating from the 13th c; heavy black beams and stripped stonework, high-backed settle and other traditional furniture, copper pans hanging above woodburner in big inglenook, glass-covered well in one part, good home-made food including vegetarian options, summer pizzas and monthly curry night, St Austell ales and decent wines, friendly helpful staff; live folk evening first Thurs of the month, games such as table skittles in conservatory; children and dogs (not in restaurant) welcome, tables on big sunny terrace, closed out of season Sun evening, Mon.

CLAYHIDON   ST1615
Half Moon (01823) 680291
On main road through village; EX15 3TJ
Attractive old village pub with warm friendly atmosphere; good choice of popular home-made food from sharing boards up, well kept Bays Devon Dumpling and Otter, Healey's cider, good wine list, comfortable bar with

inglenook log fire; some live music; children and dogs welcome, picnic-sets in tiered garden over road, lovely valley views, closed Sun evening, Mon.

CLOVELLY   SS3124
Red Lion (01237) 431237
The Quay; EX39 5TF Rambling 18th-c building in lovely position on curving quay below spectacular cliffs; beams, flagstones, log fire and interesting local photographs in character back bar (dogs allowed here), well kept Country Life and Sharps, enjoyable food including good value set lunch, efficient service, upstairs restaurant; occasional live music; children and dogs welcome, 11 attractive bedrooms (six more in Sail Loft annexe), own car park for residents, open all day.

CLYST HYDON   ST0201
Five Bells (01884) 277288
W of village, just off B3176 not far from M5 junction 28; EX15 2NT Thatched and beamed dining pub (former 16th-c farmhouse); smartly updated interior with several different areas including raised dining part, assorted tables and chairs on wood or slate floors, woodburner in large stone fireplace, good food from pub favourites up, efficient friendly service, Otter ale and guests, Sandford Orchards cider and a dozen wines by the glass; children welcome, dogs in bar, disabled access/loo, cottagey garden with country views.

CLYST ST GEORGE   SX9888
St George & Dragon (01392) 876121
Topsham Road/A376, at roundabout; EX3 0QJ Spaciously extended open-plan Vintage Inn; low beams and some secluded corners, log fires, St Austell Tribute, Sharps Doom Bar and good choice of wines by the glass, their popular reasonably priced food, good service; children and dogs welcome, 21 bedrooms in adjoining Innkeepers Lodge, open all day.

CLYST ST MARY   SX9791
Half Moon (01392) 873515
Under a mile from M5 junction 30 via A376; EX5 1BR Popular old beamed pub near disused 12th-c bridge over the River Clyst; good home-made food at reasonable prices including daily specials (best to book), many dishes available in smaller helpings, three well kept ales and decent choice of wines by the glass, friendly helpful staff, bar and separate lounge/dining area, stone floors, some red plush seating and log fire; quiz or bingo night Sun (once a month); children and dogs welcome, disabled access, open all day Fri-Sun.

COCKWOOD   SX9780
★ **Ship** (01626) 890373
Off A379 N of Dawlish; EX6 8NU
Comfortable traditional 17th-c pub set back

from the estuary and harbour – gets very busy in season; good food including some fish specials, five ales such as Dartmoor and St Austell, friendly staff and locals, partitioned beamed bar with big log fire and ancient oven, decorative plates and seafaring memorabilia, small restaurant; background music; children and dogs welcome, nice steep-sided garden, open all day, food all day Sun.

COMBE MARTIN   SS5846
Pack o' Cards (01271) 882300

High Street; EX34 OET Unusual 'house of cards' building constructed in the late 17th c to celebrate a substantial gambling win – four floors, 13 rooms and 52 windows; snug bar area and various side rooms, three real ales such as Exmoor, St Austell and Wickwar, decent wines by the glass and good range of well liked food including children's choices and all-day Sun carvery, cream teas, friendly helpful service even at busy times, restaurant; dogs welcome, pretty riverside garden with play area, six comfortable bedrooms, generous breakfast, open all day.

COMBEINTEIGNHEAD   SX9071
Wild Goose (01626) 872241

Off unclassified coast road Newton Abbot–Shaldon, up hill in village; TQ12 4RA Friendly 17th-c family-run pub; spacious back lounge with beams and agricultural bits and pieces on the walls, five West Country ales and good freshly made food including daily specials, big fireplace in front bar, more beams, standing timbers and some flagstones, step down to area with another large fireplace, further cosy room with tub chairs; Sun quiz, Weds live music, TV projector for major sports; children and dogs welcome, nice country views from back garden, closed Mon.

COUNTISBURY   SS7449
Blue Ball (01598) 741263

A39, E of Lynton; EX35 6NE Welcoming heavy-beamed roadside pub in lovely rural setting; good range of generous local food in bar and restaurant, three or four real ales including Exmoor, decent wines and proper ciders, log fires; background music, TV; children, walkers and dogs welcome, views from terrace tables, good nearby cliff walks (pub provides details of circular routes), 15 comfortable bedrooms, open all day, food all day in summer.

CREDITON   SS8300
Crediton Inn (01363) 772882

Mill Street (follow Tiverton sign); EX17 1EZ Small friendly local (the 'Kirton') under long-serving landlady; well kept Hanlons Yellow Hammer and up to nine quickly changing guests (Nov beer festival), cheap well prepared weekend food, home-made scotch eggs at other times, back games room/skittle alley; open all day Mon-Sat.

CROYDE   SS4439
Manor House Inn (01271) 890241

St Marys Road, off B3231 NW of Braunton; EX33 1PG Friendly family pub with good choice of enjoyable food from lunchtime sandwiches to blackboard specials, four well kept West Country ales, cream teas, cheerful efficient service, spacious bar, restaurant and dining conservatory; background and live music, sports TV, games end with pool and darts, skittle alley; dogs welcome in bar, disabled facilities, attractive terraced garden with big play area, open all day.

CROYDE   SS4439
Thatch (01271) 890349

B3231 NW of Braunton; Hobbs Hill; EX33 1LZ Lively thatched pub near great surfing beaches (can get packed in summer); rambling and roomy with beams and open fire, settles and other good seating, enjoyable pubby food from sandwiches and baked potatoes up, well kept changing local ales, morning coffee, teas, cheerful young staff, smart restaurant with dressers and lots of china; background and live music; children in eating areas, dogs in bar, flower-filled suntrap terraces and large gardens shared with neighbouring Billy Budds, good play area, 17 simple clean bedrooms above the pub and nearby, self-catering cottage, open (and food) all day.

CULMSTOCK   ST1013
Culm Valley (01884) 840354

B3391, off A38 E of M5 junction 27; EX15 3JJ Friendly 18th-c pub with good choice of food from varied menu, four real ales including Otter, local cider and plenty of wines by the glass, country-style décor with hotchpotch of furniture, rugs on wood floors and some interesting bits and pieces, small front conservatory; occasional live music, children and dogs (in bar) welcome, totem pole outside, tables on raised grassed area (former railway platform) overlooking River Culm and old stone bridge, open all day Fri-Sun.

DARTINGTON   SX7861
★ Cott (01803) 863777

Cott signed off A385 W of Totnes, opposite A384 turn-off; TQ9 6HE Long 14th-c thatched pub with heavy beams, flagstones, nice mix of old furniture and two inglenooks (one with big woodburner), good locally sourced home-made food from traditional choices up in bar and restaurant, three well kept ales including St Austell, Old Rosie cider, nice wines by the glass, friendly efficient service; live music Weds and Sun; children and dogs welcome, wheelchair access (with help to restaurant), picnic-sets in garden and on pretty terrace, six comfortable bedrooms, open all day.

DARTMOUTH   SX8751
★ Cherub (01803) 832571
Higher Street; walk along riverfront,
right into Hauley Road and up steps
at end; TQ6 9RB Ancient building
(Dartmouth's oldest) with two heavily
timbered upper floors jettying over the street,
many original features including oak beams,
leaded lights and big stone fireplace, bustling
bar serving up to six well kept ales such as
Exeter, South Hams and a house beer brewed
by St Austell, enjoyable sensibly priced food
from pub favourites to blackboard specials,
efficient friendly service, low-ceilinged
upstairs restaurant; background music;
children welcome (no pushchairs), dogs in
bar, open all day.

DARTMOUTH   SX8751
Floating Bridge (01803) 832354
Opposite Upper Ferry; Coombe Road
(A379); TQ6 9PQ Popular pub in lovely
quayside spot; bar with lots of stools by
windows making most of waterside view,
black and white photographs of local boating
scenes, Dartmoor Jail Ale, Sharps Doom
Bar and St Austell Tribute, several wines by
the glass, enjoyable pubby food including
daily specials, bare-boards dining room with
leather-backed chairs around wooden tables;
children and dogs (in bar) welcome, pretty
window boxes, seats out by the river looking
at busy ferry crossing, more on sizeable roof
terrace, open (and food) all day.

DARTMOUTH   SX8751
★ Royal Castle Hotel (01803) 833033
The Quay; TQ6 9PS Much character and
many original features in this 300-year-old
waterside hotel; the two ground-floor bars are
quite different: oak-beamed Galleon bar (on
right) has a log fire in a Tudor fireplace, some
fine antiques and maritime pieces and plenty
of chatty locals; the Harbour bar (to left of
flagstoned entrance hall) is contemporary
and rather smart, with big-screen TV, St
Austell ales, plenty of wines by the glass and
well liked food from lunchtime sandwiches
and bar meals up, the Grill Room restaurant
overlooks the river; children welcome except
in Harbour bar, dogs allowed in bars and
stylish bedrooms, open (and food) all day
from 8am.

DITTISHAM   SX8654
★ Ferry Boat (01803) 722368
Manor Street; best to park in village
car park and walk down (quite steep);
TQ6 0EX Cheerful riverside pub with lively
mix of customers; beamed bar with log fires
and straightforward pubby furniture, lots of
boating bits and pieces, tide times chalked
on wall, flags on ceiling, picture-window view
of the Dart, at least three real ales such as
Otter and Sharps, a dozen wines by the glass
and good range of tasty home-made food
including pie of the day and various curries,

efficient service; background and some live
music, quiz night Thurs; children and dogs
welcome, moorings for visiting boats on
adjacent pontoon and bell to summon ferry,
good walks, open (and food) all day.

DODDISCOMBSLEIGH   SX8586
★ Nobody Inn (01647) 252394
Off B3193; EX6 7PS Atmospheric old
country inn, same owners as the Spoken in
Exmouth; beamed lounge with handsomely
carved antique settles, windsor and
wheelback chairs around all sorts of wooden
tables, guns and hunting prints in snug
area by one of the big inglenooks, a beer
named for the pub from Branscombe Vale
and a couple of guests, 150 wines by the
bottle and around 270 malt whiskies, good
food from shortish changing menu, friendly
service, more formal restaurant; children
welcome away from main bar (no under-5s
in restaurant), dogs allowed in bar, pretty
garden with rural views, local church worth
a visit for its fine medieval stained glass,
bedrooms, open all day.

DREWSTEIGNTON   SX7390
Drewe Arms (01647) 281409
Off A30 NW of Moretonhampstead;
EX6 6QN This pretty thatched village
pub, famed for its long-serving landlady (Britain's longest
serving landlady, Mabel Mudge) and unspoilt
nature including basic furnishings, original
serving hatch, good ales and straightforward
food, closed just as we went to press. We do
hope it is reborn – reports please.

DUNSFORD   SX8189
Royal Oak (01647) 252256
Signed from Moretonhampstead;
EX6 7DA Friendly comfortably worn-in
village pub; generous helpings of traditional
home-made food at reasonable prices, well
kept ales such as Otter and Greene King,
local cider, airy lounge with woodburner
and view from sunny bay, simple dining
room, steps down to pool room; background
and some live music; children and dogs (on
leads) welcome, sheltered tiered garden with
play area, various animals including donkeys,
miniature ponies, alpacas and guinea pigs,
good value bedrooms in converted barn.

EAST ALLINGTON   SX7648
Fortescue Arms (01548) 521215
Village signed off A381 Totnes–
Kingsbridge, S of A3122 junction;
TQ9 7RA Pretty 19th-c wisteria-clad village
pub; two-room bar with mix of tables and
chairs on black slate floor, half-panelling
and open fire, local ales, eight wines by the
glass, spacious restaurant with high-backed
dining chairs around pine tables and another
fire in stone fireplace, enjoyable well priced
traditional food cooked by landlord-chef
including separate vegetarian/vegan evening
menu, warm friendly service; background
and occasional live music; children welcome,

dogs in bar (food for them), wheelchair access, picnic-sets out at front with more on sheltered rear terrace, closed Mon and lunchtime Tues.

EAST BUDLEIGH   SY0684
Sir Walter Raleigh (01395) 442510
High Street; EX9 7ED Friendly little 16th-c low-beamed village local; well kept changing West Country beers and good traditional food, restaurant down step; children and dogs welcome, parking some way off, wonderful medieval bench carvings in nearby church, handy too for Bicton Park Botanical Gardens.

EAST DOWN   SS5941
Pyne Arms (01271) 850055
Off A39 Barnstaple–Lynton near Arlington; EX31 4LX Welcoming old pub tucked away in small hamlet; cosy carpeted bar with lots of alcoves, woodburner, good well presented food from traditional choices up, Exmoor, St Austell and a guest, nice choice of wines, flagstoned area with sofas, conservatory; background music; children and dogs welcome, small enclosed garden, good walks and handy for Arlington Court (NT), three comfortable bedrooms, open all day weekends, closed Mon lunchtime.

EAST PRAWLE   SX7836
Pigs Nose (01548) 511209
Prawle Green; TQ7 2BY Quirky 16th-c three-room pub, lots of interesting bric-a-brac and pictures, mix of old furniture with jars of wild flowers and candles on tables, low beams, flagstones and open fire, local ales tapped from the cask, farm ciders and enjoyable simple food including range of pies, small family area with unusual toys, pool and darts; background music, hall for live bands (landlord was 1960s tour manager); friendly pub dogs (others welcome and menu for them), tables outside, pleasant spot on village green.

EXETER   SX9390
Double Locks (01392) 256947
Canal Banks, Alphington, via Marsh Barton Industrial Estate; EX2 6LT Unsmart, individual and remotely located by ship canal; Youngs and local guests, Thatcher's and Aspall's cider (mulled cider and wine in winter); enjoyable pubby food from ploughman's to Sun roast (lunchtime only); background and some live music; children and dogs welcome, seats out on grass or decking with distant view to city and cathedral (nice towpath walk out), big play area, camping, open all day.

EXETER   SX9292
Georges Meeting House
(01392) 454250 *South Street; EX1 1ED* Interesting Wetherspoons in grand former 18th-c chapel; bare-boards interior with three-sided gallery, stained glass and tall

pulpit at one end, eight real ales from long counter, their usual good value food; children welcome, tables in attractive side garden under parasols, open all day from 8am.

EXETER   SX9292
★ Hour Glass (01392) 258722
Melbourne Street; off B3015 Topsham Road; EX2 4AU Old-fashioned bow-cornered pub tucked away in surviving Georgian part above the quay; good inventive food including vegetarian choices from shortish regularly changing menu, up to five well kept local ales (usually one from Otter), Burrow Hill cider, extensive range of wines and spirits, friendly relaxed atmosphere, beams, bare boards and mix of furnishings, assorted pictures on dark red walls and various odds and ends including a stuffed badger, open fire in small brick fireplace; background and live music; children (away from bar) and dogs welcome (resident cats), no pushchairs, open all day weekends, closed Mon lunchtime.

EXETER   SX9192
Mill on the Exe (01392) 214464
Bonhay Road (A377); EX4 3AB Former paper mill in good spot by pedestrian bridge over weir; spacious opened-up interior on two floors (each with bar), bare boards, old bricks, beams and timbers, three well kept ales including St Austell Tribute, good house wines and popular food from snacks and sharing boards up, all-day Sun carvery, large airy conservatory with feature raised fire, friendly atmosphere; children and dogs welcome, river views from balcony tables, spiral stairs down to waterside garden (summer barbecues), 11 bedrooms in attached hotel side, open (and food) all day.

EXETER   SX9292
Old Fire House (01392) 277279
New North Road; EX4 4EP Relaxed city-centre pub in Georgian building behind high arched wrought-iron gates; arranged over three floors with dimly lit beamed rooms and simple furniture, up to ten real ales from casks behind bar, 20 ciders and good choice of bottled beers and wines, bargain food including late-night pizzas; background music, live music weekends, open mike every other Thurs, and popular with young crowd (modest admission charge Fri, Sat night), Mon quiz; children welcome until 5pm, picnic-sets in front courtyard, open all day till late (3am Thurs-Sat).

EXETER   SX9292
White Hart (01392) 279897
South Street; EX1 1EE Rambling 15th-c inn close to the cathedral; various bars with heavy beams, oak flooring and some nice furnishings, inner cobbled courtyard, Marstons-related ales and good choice of reasonably priced food including deals and Sun carvery, friendly helpful staff;

background music; children welcome, 65 bedrooms (40 in back extension), open all day.

EXMINSTER SX9686

★ **Turf Hotel** (01392) 833128

From A379 S of village, follow the signs to the Swans Nest, then continue to end of track, by gates; park and walk right along canal towpath – nearly a mile; EX6 8EE Remote but popular waterside pub reached by 20-minute towpath walk, cycle ride or 60-seater boat from Topsham quay (15-minute trip); several little rooms – end one with slate floor, pine walls, built-in seats and woodburner, simple room along corridor serving Devonshire ales, local cider/juices and ten wines by the glass, interesting locally sourced food, friendly staff; background music, board games; children and dogs welcome, big garden with picnic-sets and summer barbecues, arrive early for a seat in fine weather, bedrooms and a yurt for hire, good breakfast, open all day in summer (best to check other times).

EXMOUTH SY0080

Bicton Inn (01395) 272589

Bicton Street; EX8 2RU Traditional 19th-c backstreet corner local with friendly buoyant atmosphere, up to eight well kept ales and a proper cider, no food; regular live music including folk nights, pool, darts and other pub games; children and dogs welcome, open all day.

EXMOUTH SX9980

Grapevine (01395) 222208

Victoria Road; EX8 1DL Popular red-brick corner pub on fringe of town centre; light and spacious with mix of wooden tables and seating on bare boards, own Crossed Anchors beers plus changing West Country guests, plenty of bottled imports and nice choice of wines by the glass, tasty American diner-style food from open kitchen, friendly service and relaxed atmosphere; background music, live bands Fri and Sat; children and dogs welcome, open (and food) all day.

EXMOUTH SY0080

Spoken (01395) 265228

Strand; EX8 1AL Relaxed corner bar under same ownership as the Nobody Inn at Doddiscombsleigh; quirky interior with eclectic mix of tables and chairs on wood floor, over 1,000 spirits including own gin, good selection of other drinks and popular Mediterranean food from breakfast on, friendly knowledgeable staff; pavement seats, children welcome, open all day from 10am.

EXTON SX9886

Puffing Billy (01392) 877888

Station Road/Exton Lane; EX3 0PR Attractively opened-up dining pub with light spacious interior; flagstones and woodburner in pitched-ceiling bar area, restaurant part with wood-strip flooring and second woodburner in two-way fireplace, some painted tables and chairs and upholstered wall benches, good food from sharing plates and pub favourites up, beers such as Bath, Bays and Otter, good selection of wines and gins, friendly attentive service; background music, quiz first Mon of month; children and dogs (in bar) welcome, tables out at front by road and on paved side terrace, handy for Exe Estuary cycle trail.

GOODLEIGH SS5934

New Inn (01271) 342488

Goodleigh Road; EX32 7LX Small village pub under welcoming long-serving licensees; low-beamed hop-hung bar with chatty locals on bar stools, well kept Sharps Doom Bar and a guest, wide blackboard choice of good reasonably priced food cooked by landlady including local game, log fire; children and dogs welcome, closed Tues (and Mon, Weds, Thurs lunchtimes).

HARBERTON SX7758

★ **Church House** (01803) 840231

Off A381 S of Totnes; next to church; TQ9 7SF Ancient village inn (dates to the 13th c) with unusually long bar; blackened beams, medieval latticed glass and oak panelling, attractive 17th- and 18th-c pews and settles, woodburner in big inglenook, well kept ales, local cider and ten wines by the glass, good fairly priced food (just pizzas Sun evening), friendly efficient service, separate dining room; quiz and live music nights; children and dogs welcome, sunny walled back garden, comfortable bedroom and new self-catering apartment, open all day Sun till 9pm, closed Mon and Tues lunchtimes.

HATHERLEIGH SS5404

Tally Ho (01837) 810306

Market Street (A386); EX20 3JN Friendly and relaxed old pub with own beers from back brewery plus a couple of guests; attractive heavy-beamed and timbered linked rooms, sturdy furnishings, big log fire and woodburner, good food from ciabattas up, restaurant, busy Tues market day (beer slightly cheaper then); background music, open mike night third Weds of month, darts; children and dogs welcome, tables in nice sheltered garden, three good value bedrooms, open all day.

HEMYOCK ST1313

Catherine Wheel (01823) 680224

Cornhill; EX15 3RQ Popular and friendly village pub with bar, lounge and restaurant; Otter and Sharps Doom Bar, Thatcher's cider and plenty of wines by the glass, good food (not Sun evening, Mon) from varied menu, fresh flowers on tables, leather sofas by woodburner, efficient service; occasional Sun quiz, darts, pool and skittle alley, children and dogs welcome, closed Mon lunchtime.

HONITON
★ Holt (01404) 47707
High Street, W end; EX14 1LA Charming
bustling little pub run by two brothers,
relaxed and informal, with just one room
downstairs, chunky tables and chairs on slate
flooring, shelves of books and coal-effect
woodburner, full range of Otter beers (the
family founded the brewery), bigger brighter
upstairs dining room with similar furniture
on pale floorboards, very good tapas and
other inventive food, well chosen wine list,
friendly efficient service; cookery classes
and some live music; well behaved children
welcome, dogs in bar, closed Sun, Mon.

SY1198

HOPE COVE
Hope & Anchor (01548) 561294
Tucked away by car park; TQ7 3HQ
Seaside inn on two floors; open kitchen
serving decent choice of popular food
from sharing plates to local fish, St Austell
ales and a West Country guest, several
wines by the glass, helpful amiable young
staff, flagstones and bare boards, two
woodburners, dining room views to Burgh
Island; background music; children and dogs
welcome, more sea views from tables on
decked balcony and terrace, 11 bedrooms,
open (and food) all day from 8am for
breakfast.

SX6740

HORNS CROSS
★ Hoops (01237) 451222
*A39 Clovelly–Bideford, W of village;
EX39 5DL* Pretty thatched and beamed
inn dating from the 13th c, friendly and
relaxed, with traditionally furnished bar,
log fires in sizeable fireplaces and some
standing timbers and partitioning, more
formal restaurant with attractive mix of
tables and chairs, some panelling, exposed
stone and another open fire, St Austell
Tribute and a guest, over a dozen wines by
the glass, generous helpings of enjoyable
fairly straightforward food using local
suppliers, cream teas; welcoming helpful
staff; may be background music; children and
dogs allowed, picnic-sets under parasols in
enclosed courtyard, more seats on terrace
and in three acres of gardens, 13 well
equipped bedrooms, open (and food) all day.

SS3823

HORSEBRIDGE
★ Royal (01822) 870214
*Off A384 Tavistock–Launceston;
PL19 8PJ* Ancient dimly lit local with dark
half-panelling, scrubbed tables on slate
floors, log fires and interesting bric-a-brac,
well kept Otter, St Austell and Skinners
direct from the cask, real cider and good
reasonably priced food, friendly service;
no children in the evening, dogs welcome,
picnic-sets on front and side terraces
in big garden, quiet rustic spot by lovely
old Tamar bridge, popular with walkers and
cyclists.

SX4074

IDE
Huntsman (01392) 272779
High Street; EX2 9RN Welcoming thatched
and beamed country pub; enjoyable fairly
pubby food from baguettes and sharing
boards up (more evening choice), two
sittings for Sun lunch, Butcombe, Exeter and
Sharps, friendly attentive service; children
and dogs welcome, picnic-sets in pleasant
garden, open all day Fri-Sun, no food Sun
evening.

SX9090

IDE
Poachers (01392) 273847
*3 miles from M5 junction 31, via A30;
High Street; EX2 9RW* Cosy beamed pub
in quaint village; Branscombe Vale Branoc
and five changing West Country guest ales
from ornate curved wooden bar, enjoyable
home-made food, mismatched old chairs and
sofas, various pictures and odds and ends,
big log fire, restaurant; occasional quiz;
dogs welcome (they have a boxer), tables in
pleasant garden with barbecue, open (and
food) all day, till late Fri, Sat.

SX8990

IDEFORD
★ Royal Oak (01626) 852274
2 miles off A380; TQ13 0AY
Unpretentious little 16th-c thatched
and flagstoned village pub; a couple of
changing local ales and generous helpings
of tasty well priced pubby food, navy theme
including interesting Nelson and Churchill
memorabilia, beams, panelling and big open
fireplace; children and dogs welcome, tables
out at front and by car park over road, closed
Mon lunchtime.

SX8977

ILFRACOMBE
George & Dragon (01271) 863851
Fore Street; EX34 9ED One of the oldest
pubs here (14th c) and handy for the
harbour; clean and comfortable with friendly
local atmosphere, ales such as Exmoor and
Sharps, decent wines and traditional food
including local fish, black beams, stripped
stone and open fireplaces, lots of ornaments,
china etc; background and some live music,
Tues quiz, no mobile phones; children and
dogs welcome, open all day and can get very
busy weekends.

SS5247

ILSINGTON
Carpenters Arms (01364) 661629
*Old Town Hill next to the church;
TQ13 9RG* Welcoming little 18th-c village
pub under newish management; L-shaped
room with painted beams and hefty
flagstones, comfortable seats by woodburner
in large stone fireplace, country-style tables
and chairs, enjoyable fairly traditional food
including stone-baked pizzas, three West
Country ales tapped from the cask; children,
walkers and dogs welcome, tables on pretty
front terrace, good surrounding walks, open
all day weekends, closed Mon lunchtime.

SX7876

INSTOW
SS4730
Boat House (01271) 861292
Marine Parade; EX39 4JJ Popular,
stylish and modern bar-restaurant by
huge tidal beach with views across to
Appledore; enjoyable food from light
lunches up including fish/seafood
specials, ales such as Sharps Doom Bar
and St Austell, decent wines by the glass,
friendly prompt service; good roof terrace;
children and dogs welcome, disabled
facilities, open all day.

KENN
SX9285
Ley Arms (01392) 832341
*Signed off A380 just S of Exeter;
EX6 7UW* Rambling old thatched dining
pub in quiet spot near the church; good range
of popular well presented/priced food using
local produce including blackboard specials,
smaller appetites and special diets catered
for, well kept West Country ales and decent
range of wines, friendly helpful staff, beams,
exposed stonework and polished granite
flagstones, log fires, restaurant and garden
room; children and dogs (theirs is Reggie)
welcome, terrace tables under parasols, open
all day, food all day weekends.

KENNFORD
SX9186
Seven Stars (01392) 834887
Centre of village; EX6 7TR Updated little
village pub with three West Country beers
and good food including pies and takeaway
pizzas, friendly atmosphere; quiz last Tues
of month, open mike night first Fri, pool,
darts and sports TV; children and dogs
welcome, closed Mon lunchtime, otherwise
open all day.

KILMINGTON
SY2698
New Inn (01297) 33376
Signed off Gammons Hill; EX13 7SF
Thatched local (originally three 14th-c
cottages), friendly and welcoming, with good
reasonably priced food including popular Sun
roasts, well kept Palmers ales; skittle alley
and boules court, monthly quiz; children and
dogs welcome, disabled access/loo (steps
in one part), large garden with tree-shaded
areas, closed Mon lunchtime, no food Sun
evening, Mon.

KILMINGTON
SY2798
★Old Inn (01297) 32096
A35; EX13 7RB Bustling 16th-c thatched
and beamed pub on edge of the village; well
kept ales such as Branscombe Vale and Otter,
decent choice of wines and enjoyable pubby
food including daily specials, welcoming
attentive service, small character front bar
with traditional games (there's also a skittle
alley), inglenook log fire in back lounge,
small restaurant; beer/cider festivals and
some live music; children and dogs welcome,
wheelchair access, terrace and lawned area,
open all day from 8am.

KING'S NYMPTON
SS6819
★Grove (01769) 580406
*Off B3226 SW of South Molton;
EX37 9ST* Welcoming 17th-c thatched
pub in remote conservation village; beamed
bar with lots of bookmarks hanging from
the ceiling, simple pubby furnishings on
flagstones, bare stone walls and a log fire,
three well kept West Country ales, eight
ciders, over 30 wines (including champagne)
by the glass and 60 or so malt whiskies, very
good home-cooked food (not Sun evening)
including daily specials, Tues night fish and
chips, restaurant; darts and board games,
well behaved children and dogs welcome,
self-catering cottage, nice surrounding walks,
closed Mon.

KINGSKERSWELL
SX8666
★Bickley Mill (01803) 873201
*Bickley Road, follow Maddacombe Road
from village, under new ring road,
W of Kingskerswell; TQ12 5LN* Restored
13th-c mill tucked away in lovely countryside;
rambling beamed rooms with open fires and
rugs on wood floors, variety of seating from
rustic chairs and settles to sofas piled with
cushions, modern art and black and white
photos on stone walls, good well presented
food including pub favourites from sensibly
priced menu, a couple of Bays ales and 11
wines by the glass, cheerful helpful service;
monthly jazz Sun lunchtime, children and
dogs (in bar) welcome, seats on big terrace,
also a subtropical hillside garden, well
appointed modern bedrooms, good breakfast,
open all day.

KINGSTON
SX6347
Dolphin (01548) 810314
*Off B3392 S of Modbury (can also be
reached from A379 W of Modbury);
TQ7 4QE* Peaceful and friendly 16th-c
inn with knocked-through beamed rooms;
traditional furniture on red carpeting, open
fire, woodburner in inglenook fireplace,
Butcombe and Dartmoor and a couple of
guests, a farm cider, straightforward food;
Mon darts, occasional live music; children
and dogs welcome, seats in garden, pretty
tubs and summer window boxes, quiet village
with several tracks leading down to the sea,
three bedrooms in building across road, open
all day weekends.

KNOWSTONE
SS8223
Masons Arms (01398) 341231
*Off A361 NW of Tiverton, follow signs to
Knowstone for 1.5 miles; EX36 4RY*
Thatched medieval dining pub known for
its first class food from chef-patron Mark
Dodson (one Michelin star) but many
locals pop in for a pint and a chat in small
low-ceilinged bar with beams, inglenook
log fire, rugs on flagstones, cushioned wall
seats and benches around rustic tables,
also snug with a woodburning stove and

airy modern dining room at the back with amazing painted ceiling; only one beer on handpump (Cotleigh Golden Seahawk), Winkleigh's cider and large selection of wines, imaginative modern food available à la carte and on two- and three-course set menus; dogs allowed in bar, picnic-tables under parasols at the front, closed Mon and Sun except first Sun in month.

LAKE SX5288

Bearslake (01837) 861334

A386 just S of Sourton; EX20 4HQ Rambling thatch and stone pub (former longhouse dating from the 13th c); leather sofas on crazy-paved slate floor at one end, other beamed rooms with stripped stone walls, woodburners, toby jugs, farm tools and traps, ales such as Otter and Teignworthy, decent wines and enjoyable food from separate bar and restaurant menus; quiz nights; children and dogs welcome, large sheltered streamside garden, Dartmoor walks, six comfortable bedrooms, closed Mon, Tues and evening Sun.

LANDSCOVE SX7766

Live & Let Live (01803) 762663

SE end of village by Methodist chapel; TQ13 7LZ Friendly open-plan village local with good food and well kept ales such as Dartmoor and New Lion, beams, exposed stonework and log fire; children and dogs welcome, tables on small front terrace and in little orchard across lane, good walks, bedrooms, closed Mon-Weds and evening Sun.

LIFTON SX3885

Arundell Arms (01566) 784666

Fore Street; PL16 0AA Good imaginative food in substantial country-house fishing hotel including set lunch, warmly welcoming and individual, with professional service, good choice of wines by the glass, morning coffee and afternoon tea; also adjacent Courthouse bar, complete with original cells, serving enjoyable fairly priced pubby food (not Sun evening, Mon) along with daily specials and children's meals, well kept Dartmoor Jail Ale and St Austell Tribute, darts and some live music; 25 bedrooms, useful A30 stop, open all day.

LOWER ASHTON SX8484

Manor Inn (01647) 252304

Ashton signposted off B3193 N of Chudleigh; EX6 7QL Friendly well run country pub with good quality reasonably priced food including lunchtime set menu and daily specials, well kept ales such as Dartmoor, Otter and St Austell, good choice of wines; open fires in both bars, back restaurant in converted smithy; children

and dogs welcome, disabled access, garden picnic-sets with nice rural outlook, open all day Sun (no evening food then), closed Mon.

LUPPITT ST1606

★ Luppitt Inn (01404) 891613

Back roads N of Honiton; EX14 4RT Unspoilt basic farmhouse pub tucked away in lovely countryside, an amazing survivor, run by chatty veteran landlady (almost a centenarian) with help from her granddaughter; corner servery and single table in tiny bar, another room (not much bigger) with fireplace and darts, cheap Otter tapped from a polypin, intriguing metal puzzles made by a neighbour, no food or music, lavatories across the yard; only open Thurs and Sat from 7.30pm.

LUSTLEIGH SX7881

★ Cleave (01647) 277223

Off A382 Bovey Tracey–Moretonhampstead; TQ13 9TJ Busy thatched pub in lovely Dartmoor National Park village; low-ceilinged beamed bar with granite walls and log fire, attractive antique high-backed settles, cushioned wall seats and wheelbacks on red patterned carpet, Dartmoor, Otter and a guest, good variety of enjoyable home-cooked food, efficient friendly service, back room (formerly the old station waiting room) converted to light airy bistro with pale wooden furniture on wood-strip floor, doors to outside eating area; children and dogs (in bar) welcome, more seats in sheltered garden, good circular walks, shuts around 6pm Sun, otherwise open (and food) all day.

LUTON SX9076

★ Elizabethan (01626) 775425

Haldon Moor; TQ13 0BL Popular tucked-away low-beamed dining pub (once owned by Elizabeth I, but much altered); wide choice of good well presented food including daily specials, two well kept ales and several reasonably priced wines by the glass, friendly attentive service; children and dogs (in bar) welcome, pretty front garden, open all day Sun.

LYDFORD SX5184

★ Castle Inn 01822 820242

Off A386 Okehampton–Tavistock; EX20 4BH Pink-painted Tudor inn next to the castle and church; traditional twin bars with big slate flagstones, bowed low beams and granite walls, high-backed settles and four inglenook log fires, notable stained-glass door and plenty of bits and pieces to look at; hearty helpings of popular well priced food, St Austell ales, guest beers and good wine selection, friendly helpful service, restaurant;

We don't mention free wi-fi, because it's standard in most pubs these days – though not universal. And don't expect a good signal in remote rural locations.

children and dogs welcome in certain areas, wheelchair access, seats out at front and in sheltered back garden, lovely NT river gorge nearby, eight bedrooms, open all day.

LYDFORD   SX5285
Dartmoor Inn (01822) 820221
Downton, A386; EX20 4AY Gently civilised inn, more restaurant-with-rooms and at its most informal at lunchtime with walkers from Dartmoor National Park; cheerful small bar with log fire, Otter Ale, St Austell Tribute and nice wines by the glass, good interesting food in several linked dining rooms with stylish contemporary décor; children and dogs (in bar) welcome, three well equipped pretty bedrooms (each with its own sitting area), usually open all day weekends and food Weds-Sun but hours may vary in summer.

LYMPSTONE   SX9984
Redwing (01395) 222156
Church Road; EX8 5JT Modernised dining pub not far from the church; comfortable seating on oak or black slate floors, well kept local beers such as Hanlons and St Austell, 19 wines by the glass and good freshly made food from ciabattas and pub favourites up, friendly attentive service, converted loft restaurant; children and dogs (in bar) welcome, terrace tables, attractive unspoilt village, open all day weekends.

LYMPSTONE   SX9884
Swan (01395) 270403
The Strand, by station entrance; EX8 5ET Old beamed pub with enjoyable home-made food including local fish and bargain weekday set lunch, split-level dining area with big log fire, Hanlons Yellow Hammer and four other West Country ales, short but well chosen wine list; occasional live music, pool, children welcome, picnic-sets out at front, popular with cyclists (bike racks provided), shore walks, open all day.

LYNMOUTH   SS7249
Rising Sun (01598) 753223
Harbourside; EX35 6EG Nice old pub in wonderful position overlooking harbour; beamed and stripped-stone bar bustling with locals and tourists, good fire, three Exmoor ales and a guest, popular food from comprehensive menu (emphasis on fish), upmarket hotel side with attractive restaurant; background music; well behaved children (till 7.30pm) and dogs (in bar) welcome, gardens behind, bedrooms in cottagey old thatched building, parking expensive during the day and scarce at night, open all day.

LYNTON   SS7248
Beggars Roost (01598) 753645
Manor Hotel; EX35 6LD Stone-built country pub with friendly relaxed atmosphere; enjoyable freshly made food and well kept ales including Exmoor and a house beer brewed by Marstons, helpful cheerful staff; children and dogs welcome, good bedrooms in hotel side, also camping next door, closed Jan, otherwise open all day.

LYNTON   SS7148
Cottage Inn (01598) 753496
B3234 just S; EX35 6NR Interesting place run by friendly licensees; wide choice of craft beers including own Fatbelly range, authentic evening Thai food (cooked by landlady) along with traditional Sun roasts, churchy Victorian windows, beamed and carpeted bar with woodburner, dining room overlooking West Lyn gorge; June music/ beer festival; children and dogs welcome, footbridge to wooded NT walks up to Watersmeet, bedrooms.

LYNTON   SS6548
Hunters (01598) 763230
Pub well signed off A39 W of Lynton; EX31 4PY Large Edwardian country inn set in superb Heddon Valley position down very steep hill by NT information centre; two bars one with woodburner, up to four ales including Exmoor and Heddon Valley (brewed for them locally), good range of other drinks and enjoyable well priced food from fairly pubby menu, efficient friendly service, dining room overlooking back garden; music nights, pool, board games; children and dogs welcome, four-acre grounds (roaming peacocks), great walks including to the sea, ten bedrooms, open all day.

MARLDON   SX8663
★Church House (01803) 558279
Off A380 NW of Paignton; TQ3 1SL Pleasant village pub dating from the 15th c; spreading bar with woodburner, unusual windows and some beams, dark pine and other dining chairs around solid tables, four real ales such as Dartmoor and Teignworthy, local cider, 16 wines by the glass and ten malt whiskies, other rooms including two restaurants (one in old barn), interesting much liked food, good service; background music, board games; children and dogs (in bar) welcome, picnic-sets on three carefully maintained grassy terraces behind.

MARSH   ST2510
Flintlock (01460) 234403
Pub signed just off A303 Ilminster– Honiton; EX14 9AJ Comfortable neatly maintained dining pub popular for its good value blackboard food including Sun lunches, special diets catered for, well kept Butcombe and Otter, decent choice of wines, friendly accommodating service, woodburner in stone inglenook, beams and mainly stripped stone walls, copper and brass; background music; children welcome, dogs in garden only, closed Mon.

MEAVY   SX5467
★ Royal Oak (01822) 852944
Off B3212 E of Yelverton; PL20 6PJ
Partly 15th-c pub taking its name from the
800-year-old oak on green opposite; heavy
beamed L-shaped bar with pews, red plush
banquettes, old agricultural prints and
church pictures, smaller locals' bar with
flagstones and big open-hearth fireplace,
separate dining room, good reasonably priced
food served by friendly staff, four well kept
ales including Dartmoor, farm ciders, a dozen
wines by the glass and several malt whiskies;
background music, board games; children
and dogs (in bar) welcome, picnic-sets out in
front and on the green, pretty Dartmoor-edge
village, open all day.

MEETH   SS5408
★ Bull & Dragon (01837) 811742
A386 Hatherleigh–Torrington;
EX20 3EP Welcoming 15th-c beamed and
thatched village pub; large open bar with
inglenook woodburner, well kept ales such
as Dartmoor and Exmoor, good reasonably
priced home-made food from shortish menu
plus some blackboard specials (booking
advised), charming helpful staff; children
and dogs welcome, at end of Tarka Trail cycle
route, closed Tues and Weds.

MILTON COMBE   SX4865
Who'd A Thought It (01822) 853313
Village signed off A386 S of Yelverton;
PL20 6HP Attractive 16th-c whitewashed
pub; black-panelled bar with some
interesting bits and pieces, traditional
furniture and woodburner, two separate
dining areas, good home-made food from
varied menu including set deal, friendly
efficient staff, four well kept ales, real cider
and decent choice of wines; background
and some live music; children and dogs
welcome, a few tables out in front, more in
back beer garden with stream, two bedrooms
in converted hayloft, open all day Sun,
closed Mon.

MOLLAND   SS8028
London (01769) 550269
*Village signed off B3227 E of South
Molton; EX36 3NG* Proper Exmoor
inn at its busiest in the shooting season;
two small linked rooms by old-fashioned
central servery, local stag-hunting pictures,
cushioned benches and plain chairs around
rough stripped trestle tables, Exmoor Ale,
attractive beamed room on left with famous
stag story on the wall, panelled dining room
on right with big curved settle by fireplace
(good hunting and gamebird prints),
enjoyable home-made food using fresh local
produce including seasonal game (not Sun
evening, no credit cards), small hall with
stuffed animals; fine Victorian lavatories;
children and dogs welcome, picnic-sets in
cottagey garden, untouched early 18th-c box

pews in church next door, two bedrooms,
closed Mon lunchtime.

MONKLEIGH   SS4520
Bell (01805) 938285
A388; EX39 5JS Welcoming thatched and
beamed 17th-c village pub with carpeted bar
and small restaurant; well kept Dartmoor
and a couple of guests, enjoyable reasonably
priced food including daily specials, themed
evenings and Sun carvery, friendly staff;
background music, quiz nights (monthly),
occasional live music, darts; children (till
9pm) and dogs welcome, wheelchair access,
garden with raised deck, views and good
walks, closed Mon (except bank holidays).

MORCHARD BISHOP   SS7607
London Inn (01363) 877222
Signed off A377 Crediton–Barnstaple;
EX17 6NW Prettily placed 16th-c village
coaching inn run by mother and daughter
team, thriving local atmosphere, good
generous home-made food (best to book
weekends), Fullers London Pride and a local
guest, helpful friendly service, low-beamed
open-plan carpeted bar with woodburner in
large fireplace, small dining room; pool, darts
and skittles; children and dogs welcome,
closed Mon and Tues lunchtimes.

MORELEIGH   SX7652
New Inn (01548) 821326
*B3207, off A381 Kingsbridge–Totnes in
Stanborough; TQ9 7JH* Cosy old-fashioned
country local with friendly landlady (same
family has run it for several decades); large
helpings of enjoyable home-made food at
reasonable prices including good steaks,
Timothy Taylors Landlord tapped from the
cask and a weekend guest, character old
furniture, attractive pictures and effective
inglenook log fire; opens from 6.30pm
(12-2.30, 7-10.30 Sun).

NEWTON ABBOT   SX8671
Olde Cider Bar (01626) 354221
East Street; TQ12 2LD Basic old-fashioned
cider house with plenty of atmosphere;
around 30 interesting reasonably priced
ciders (some very strong), a couple of
perries, more in bottles, good country wines
from the cask too, baguettes, pasties etc,
friendly staff, stools made from cask staves,
barrel seats and wall benches, flagstones and
bare boards; regular live folk music, small
back games room with bar billiards; dogs
welcome, terrace tables, open all day.

NEWTON ABBOT   SX8468
Two Mile Oak (01803) 812411
*A381 2 miles S, at Denbury/
Kingskerswell crossroads; TQ12 6DF*
Appealing two-bar beamed coaching inn;
black panelling, traditional furnishings
and candlelit alcoves, inglenook and
woodburners, well kept Dartmoor and Otter
tapped from the cask, nine wines by the

glass, enjoyable well priced pubby food from sandwiches and baked potatoes up (special diets catered for), decent coffee, cheerful staff; background music; quiz last Tues of month; children and dogs welcome, circular picnic-sets on terrace and lawn, open all day.

NEWTON FERRERS   SX5447
Dolphin (01752) 872007
Riverside Road East: Newton Hill off Church Park (B3186) then left; PL8 1AE Shuttered 18th-c pub in attractive setting; L-shaped bar with a few low beams, slate floors and open fire, well kept ales and good food cooked by landlord-chef, children welcome, terraces over lane looking down on River Yealm and yachts, can get packed in summer, parking limited.

NEWTON ST CYRES   SX8798
Beer Engine (01392) 851282
Off A377 towards Thorverton; EX5 5AX Former 19th-c railway hotel brewing its own beers since the 1980s; good home-made food including specials and popular Sun lunch, log fire in bar; children and dogs welcome, seats on decked verandah, steps down to garden, open all day, food all day Sun.

NEWTON TRACEY   SS5226
Hunters (01271) 858339
B3232 Barnstaple–Torrington; EX31 3PL Extended 15th-c pub with massive low beams and two inglenooks, popular reasonably priced food from pub standards up including choices for smaller appetites, well kept St Austell Tribute and Sharps Doom Bar, decent wines, friendly service, skittle alley/overflow dining area; soft background music; children and dogs welcome, disabled access using ramp, tables on small terrace behind, open all day weekends, food all day Sun till 7.45pm.

NOMANSLAND   SS8313
Mount Pleasant (01884) 860271
B3137 Tiverton–South Molton; EX16 8NN Informal country local with good mix of customers; huge fireplaces in long low-beamed main bar, happy mismatch of simple well worn furniture, candles on tables, country pictures, well kept ales such as Otter and guests, several wines by the glass, Sandford Orchards cider, good range of enjoyable freshly cooked food (special diets catered for), friendly attentive service, cosy dining room in former smithy with original forge, darts in public bar; background music; well behaved children and dogs welcome, back garden with play area, open (and food) all day.

NORTH BOVEY   SX7483
Ring of Bells (01647) 440375
Off A382/B3212 SW of Moretonhampstead; TQ13 8RB Popular 13th-c thatched inn restored after 2016 fire; low beams, bulgy walls and brick floors, woodburners (one in inglenook), much

liked food at fair prices from lunchtime sandwiches and traditional choices up, cask-tapped ales such as Dartmoor and Teignworthy, real cider and a dozen wines by the glass from good list, helpful friendly staff; quiz nights; children and dogs (in bar) welcome, picnic-sets and flower-filled troughs out at front, pretty Dartmoor village with lovely tree-covered green, good walks, five attractively refurbished bedrooms, open all day.

NOSS MAYO   SX5447
★Ship (01752) 872387
Off A379 via B3186, E of Plymouth; PL8 1EW Charming setting overlooking inlet and visiting boats (can get crowded in good weather); thick-walled bars with bare boards and log fires, four well kept ales such as Dartmoor and Noss Beer Works, good choice of wines and malt whiskies, popular food from varied menu, friendly efficient service, lots of local pictures and charts, books, newspapers and board games, restaurant upstairs; children and dogs (downstairs) welcome, plenty of seats on heated waterside terrace, parking restricted at high tide, open (and food) all day.

OKEHAMPTON   SX5895
Fountain (01837) 53532
Fore Street (just off A30); EX20 1AP Well run and welcoming former coaching inn; good food from snacks to daily specials, three or four well kept ales including Dartmoor and Sharps, cocktails, two bars and a restaurant; skittle alley; children and dogs welcome, seats out on decking, six bedrooms, open all day.

OTTERY ST MARY   SY0995
Volunteer (01404) 814060
Broad Street; EX11 1BZ Welcoming early 19th-c pub; traditional front bar with darts and open fire, four real ales tapped from the cask including Otter, more contemporary restaurant behind, good reasonably priced home-made food (not Sun evening), friendly service; upstairs loos; open all day.

PARKHAM   SS3821
★Bell (01237) 451201
Rectory Lane; EX39 5PL Thatched village pub reopened after devastating fire in 2017; three sympathetically renovated linked rooms (one on lower level), beams and standing timbers, cob walls, pubby furniture on slate or red patterned carpet, brass, copper and old photographs, grandfather clock, two woodburners and a range (they cook Sun roasts in it), well kept Dartmoor, Otter and Ringwood, 30 gins and a dozen malt whiskies, good reasonably priced home-made food; darts; well behaved children welcome, dogs in bar, disabled access/loo, picnic-sets on covered back terrace with fairy lights, closed Mon, Tues and shuts 4pm on Sun.

PARRACOMBE SS6644

★ **Fox & Goose** (01598) 763239
Off A39 Blackmoor Gate–Lynton;
EX31 4PE Popular and welcoming
Victorian pub with linked rooms; hunting
and farming memorabilia and interesting
old photographs, well kept Exeter, Exmoor
and Quantock ales, Winkleigh's cider and
several wines by the glass, good variety of
well cooked generously served food from
blackboard menus including local fish and
game, also takeaway pizzas, friendly helpful
staff, log fire, separate dining room; children
and dogs welcome, wheelchair access with
help, small front verandah, riverside terrace
and garden room, four bedrooms, open all
day in summer.

PAYHEMBURY ST0801

Six Bells (01404) 841261
Village signed from A373; leave A30 at
Honiton; EX14 3HR Welcoming 17th-c
village local; good range of well kept beers
such as Dartmoor and Sharps, generous
helpings of reasonably priced home-made
food from sandwiches to specials, friendly
helpful service, restaurant; skittle alley, pool;
children and dogs (in bar) welcome, open all
day Fri-Sun, closed Mon lunchtime, no food
Sun evening, Mon.

PETER TAVY SX5177

★ **Peter Tavy Inn** (01822) 810348
Off A386 near Mary Tavy, N of
Tavistock; PL19 9NN Old stone village inn
tucked away at end of small lane; bustling
low-beamed bar with high-backed settles on
black flagstones, mullioned windows, good
log fire in big stone fireplace, snug dining
area with carved wooden chairs, hops on
beams and various pictures, up to five well
kept West Country ales, Winkleigh's cider
and good wine/whisky choice, well liked food
from varied menu including OAP lunch (not
Sun) and early evening deal, friendly efficient
service, separate restaurant; children,
walkers and dogs welcome, picnic-sets in
pretty garden, peaceful moorland views, open
all day weekends.

PLYMOUTH SX4953

Bridge (01752) 403888
Shaw Way, Mount Batten; PL9 9XH
Modern two-storey bar-restaurant with
terrace and balcony overlooking busy
Yacht Haven Marina; enjoyable food from
sandwiches and pub favourites up, Dartmoor
Best, St Austell Tribute and nice range of
wines by the glass, impressive fish tank
upstairs; children welcome, well behaved
dogs allowed downstairs, open all day from
9am for breakfast.

PLYMOUTH SX4854

Dolphin (01752) 660876
Barbican; PL1 2LS Unpretentious
drinkers' pub with buoyant chatty atmosphere;
good range of well kept cask-tapped
ales including Bass and St Austell, open
fire, Beryl Cook paintings (even one of
the friendly landlord), no food but can bring
your own; dogs welcome, open all day.

PLYMOUTH SX4755

Fortescue (01752) 660673
Mutley Plain; PL4 6JQ Traditional
Victorian corner local with nine well kept
mostly changing ales and good range of
traditional ciders, no food apart from Sun
lunch, cellar bar/function room; Sun quiz,
Weds poker night, TV, fruit machine; dogs
welcome, seats on raised back terrace, open
all day.

PLYMPTON SX5455

Brook (01752) 297604
Longbrook Street; PL7 1ND Popular
community pub with enjoyable sensibly
priced home-made food and well kept local
beers, good friendly service, separate coffee
lounge; regular live music, line dancing and
tai chi, pool; children (till 9pm) and dogs
welcome, garden picnic-sets, closed Mon.

PLYMTREE ST0502

Blacksmiths Arms (01884) 277474
Near church; EX15 2JU Friendly 19th-c
beamed and carpeted village pub; good
reasonably priced food cooked by landlord,
three well kept changing local ales and
decent choice of wines by the glass; pool
room and skittle alley; children welcome,
dogs on leads (their leonberger is called
Jagermeister), garden with boules and play
area, open all day Sat, till 4pm Sun, closed
Mon, lunchtimes Tues-Fri.

PUSEHILL SS4228

Pig on the Hill (01237) 459222
Off B3226 near Westward Ho!;
EX39 5AH Extensively revamped
restaurants pub (originally a cowshed); good
choice of highly enjoyable, well presented
food (must book ahead), friendly helpful
service, Country Life and local guests, games
room with skittle alley; background music;
children and dogs (in bar) welcome, disabled
facilities, good views from terrace tables and
picnic-sets on grass, play area, boules, three
self-catering cabins, closed Mon and Tues.

RACKENFORD SS8518

Stag (01884) 881755
Pub signed off A361 NW of Tiverton;
EX16 8DT Well restored 12th-c thatched
pub with ancient cobbled 'tunnel' entry
passage between massive walls; three
changing local ales, real ciders and
interesting gin range, good freshly made
food using local ingredients including own
pork and lamb, low beams and some 17th-c
panelling with witches' marks, eclectic
mix of antique and contemporary furniture
including long oak refectory table and fine
high-backed settles either side of inglenook,

cosy room with sofas and another inglenook, bar area with polished concrete floor and glass-covered well; skittle alley in function room; children and dogs welcome, disabled access/loo, back terrace, closed Sun evening, Mon and Tues.

RATTERY SX7461

★**Church House** (01364) 642220

Village signposted from A385 W of Totnes, and A38 S of Buckfastleigh; TQ10 9LD One of Britain's oldest pubs with some parts dating from 12th c – look out for the spiral stone steps behind a little stone doorway on the left; characterful open-plan bar with beams and standing timbers, large fireplaces (one with a cosy nook partitioned around it), traditional pubby chairs and tables, window seats, prints and horsebrasses on plain white walls, also a dining room, lounge and purpose-built restaurant with a striking arched oak frame; Dartmoor Jail Ale, Exeter Avocet and Otter Bitter on handpump, 19 malt whiskies and a dozen wines by the glass, popular food from varied menu; picnic-sets at front and on large hedged-in lawn, courtyard garden with seating under parasols, children welcome, dogs in bar, open all day weekends.

RINGMORE SX6545

Journeys End (01548) 810205

Signed off B3392 at Pickwick Inn, St Anns Chapel, near Bigbury; best to park opposite church; TQ7 4HL Ancient village inn (dates from the 13th c) with friendly chatty atmosphere; character panelled lounge and other linked rooms, four local ales tapped from the cask, real cider, seven wines by the glass and well executed/presented food including some Thai dishes from good shortish menu (best to book in summer), log fires, family dining conservatory with board games; dogs (on leads) welcome throughout, garden with picnic-sets on gravel, old-fashioned street lights and decked area, attractive setting near thatched cottages and not far from the sea, open all day weekends (no food Sun evening), closed Mon.

ROBOROUGH SS5717

New Inn (01805) 603247

Off B3217 N of Winkleigh; EX19 8SY Tucked-away 16th-c thatched village pub, cheerful and busy, with well kept local ales, great range of ciders, several wines by the glass and 40 or so gins, enjoyable fairly priced food from varied menu, beamed bar with woodburner, tiny back room leading up to restaurant, friendly helpful staff; children and dogs welcome, seats on sunny front terrace, open all day Fri-Sun, closed lunchtimes Mon, Tues.

ROCKBEARE SY0195

★**Jack in the Green** (01404) 822240

Signed from A30 bypass E of Exeter; EX5 2EE Neat welcoming dining pub (most customers here to eat) run well by long-serving owner; first class food from interesting menu including excellent puddings, good friendly service, carpeted dining rooms with old hunting/shooting photographs and high-backed leather chairs around dark tables, big woodburner, also airy restaurant and club-like ante-room with two-way stove, comfortable sofas in flagstoned lounge bar, ales such as Amber, Butcombe and Otter, local cider, a dozen wines by the glass (over 100 by the bottle); background music; well behaved children welcome, no dogs inside, disabled facilities, plenty of seats in courtyard, open all day Sun, closed 25 Dec-5 Jan, quite handy for M5.

SALCOMBE SX7439

Fortescue (01548) 842868

Union Street, end of Fore Street; TQ8 8BZ Linked rooms with painted beams and half-panelling, rugs and pine furniture on quarry tiles, old local photographs and some stuffed fish, woodburners, decent pubby food including stone-baked pizzas, well kept ales such as Otter, Salcombe and Sharps, public bar with parquet floor, booth seating, games, TVs and machines; children welcome, courtyard picnic-sets, three bedrooms, open (and food) all day.

SALCOMBE SX7439

★**Victoria** (01548) 842604

Fore Street; TQ8 8BU Bustling town-centre pub with traditionally furnished beamed bar, huge flagstones and open fire in big stone fireplace, well kept Bath and St Austell ales including a beer named for the pub and a guest, several wines including champagne by the glass, a prosecco menu and around 25 gins, enjoyable food from good crab sandwiches up, other dining/drinking areas have stripped floorboards and nautical décor, more room upstairs, children and dogs (in bar) welcome, pretty summer window boxes and large tiered back garden with play area, chickens and budgies, quirky but comfortable Hobbit House bedrooms, no breakfasts (cafés and restaurants nearby), open (and food) all day.

SAMPFORD COURTENAY SS6300

New Inn (01837) 82247

B3072 Crediton–Holsworthy; EX20 2TB Thatched 16th-c pub in picturesque village; good food from landlord-chef including daily specials and a vegan menu, local ales tapped from the cask, proper cider and good range of wines, gins and champagnes, relaxed friendly atmosphere, beams and log fires; quiz last Weds of month; children and dogs (in bar) welcome, picnic-sets in garden.

SANDY PARK SX7189

Sandy Park Inn (01647) 432114

A382 Whiddon Down–Moretonhampstead; TQ13 8JW Hospitable little 17th-c thatched and beamed inn; cosy bar with wall settles and log fire, small dining room on left and inner snug, well kept Exeter Avocet, Dartmoor IPA and Otter Bitter, enjoyable simple food including range of pies, good friendly service; some acoustic live music; children and dogs welcome, nice back garden with country views, open from 4pm daily, no food Sun.

SHALDON   SX9372

Clifford Arms (01626) 872311

Fore Street; TQ14 0DE Attractive 18th-c open-plan pub on two levels; clean and bright, with good range of blackboard food including Thurs-Sat evening set menu, cream teas, up to four mainly local ales, lots of wines by the glass and cocktails, low beams and stone walls, wood or carpeted floors, log fire; regular live jazz; children over 5 welcome, café-style seating on front terrace, decked area behind with palms, pleasant seaside village, closed Mon, Tues and evening Sun, otherwise open all day from 8.30am.

SHALDON   SX9371

Ness House (01626) 873480

Ness Drive; TQ14 0HP Georgian hotel on Ness headland overlooking Teign estuary and well worth knowing for its position; comfortable two-room bar with mixed furniture on bare boards, log fire, Badger ales and decent wines by the glass, popular food in restaurant or small conservatory, afternoon teas; children welcome, no dogs, disabled facilities, terrace with lovely views, picnic-sets in back garden, nine bedrooms, open all day.

SHEBBEAR   SS4309

Devils Stone Inn (01409) 281210

Off A3072 or A388 NE of Holsworthy; EX21 5RU Neatly kept 17th-c beamed village pub reputed to be one of England's most haunted; seats in front of open woodburner, long L-shaped pew and second smaller one, flagstone floors, St Austell Tribute and a couple of local guests, decent wines and enjoyable food in dining room across corridor, plain back games room with pool and darts; children and dogs welcome (they have a rottweiler), picnic-sets on front terrace and in garden behind, next to actual Devil's Stone (turned by villagers on 5 Nov to keep the devil at bay), eight bedrooms (steep stairs to some), open all day Sun, closed Weds lunchtime.

SHEEPWASH   SS4806

Half Moon (01409) 231376

Off A3072 Holsworthy–Hatherleigh at Highampton; EX21 5NE Ancient inn loved by anglers for its seven miles of River Torridge fishing (salmon, sea and brown trout); simply furnished main bar, lots of beams, log fire in big fireplace, well kept ales such as Otter, St Austell and Sharps, several wines by the glass and tasty food from shortish sensibly priced menu (some gluten-

free options), friendly service, separate extended dining room; children and dogs welcome, 11 bedrooms (four in converted stables), tiny Dartmoor village off the beaten track, open all day.

SIDBURY   SY1496

Hare & Hounds (01404) 41760

3 miles N of Sidbury, at Putts Corner; A375 towards Honiton, crossroads with B3174; EX10 0QQ Large roadside pub popular for its highly thought-of daily carvery; spreading rooms with two log fires, heavy beams, red plush dining chairs, window seats and leather sofas around plenty of tables on carpet or bare boards, Otter and St Austell ales tapped from the cask, extensive wine list, newer dining extension with central fire; children welcome (no under-12s in bar), dogs in bar only, tables on decked area and in big garden with lovely views down Sid Valley to the sea, open (and food) all day.

SIDFORD   SY1389

Blue Ball (01395) 514062

A3052 just N of Sidmouth; EX10 9QL Handsome thatched pub in same friendly family for over 100 years; central bar with three main areas each with log fire, pale beams, nice mix of wooden dining chairs around circular tables on patterned carpet, prints, horsebrasses and plenty of bric-a-brac, well kept Bass, Otter, St Austell and Sharps, enjoyable bar food, chatty public bar; background music, board games, darts and skittle alley; children and dogs welcome, flower-filled garden, terrace and smokers' gazebo, coastal walks close by, bedrooms, open all day.

SIDMOUTH   ST1287

Anchor (01395) 514129

Old Fore Street; EX10 8LP Welcoming family-run pub popular for its fresh fish and other good value food, well kept Caledonian ales including one named for them, decent choice of wines, good friendly service, large carpeted L-shaped room with nautical pictures and aquarium, steps down to restaurant; darts; tables out in front, more in back beer garden with stage for live acts, open (and food) all day.

SIDMOUTH   SY1090

Bowd (01395) 513328

Junction B3176/A3052; EX10 0ND Popular thatched and beamed dining pub with enjoyable sensibly priced food (all day Sun) including daily carvery, a couple of Otter ales, friendly helpful staff, spacious flagstoned interior with standing timbers and alcoves; children and dogs welcome, plenty of seats in big garden, play area, open all day.

SIDMOUTH   SY1287

Dukes (01395) 513320

Esplanade; EX10 8AR More brasserie than pub, but long bar on left serves

Branscombe Vale and a couple of guests, good food specialising in local fish (best to book in the evening), friendly efficient young staff, linked areas including conservatory and flagstoned eating area (once a chapel), smart contemporary décor; big-screen TV, daily papers; children welcome, disabled facilities, prom-view terrace tables, bedrooms in adjoining Elizabeth Hotel, open (and food) all day (may be summer queues).

SIDMOUTH   SY1287
★ **Swan** (01395) 512849
York Street; EX10 8BY Cheerful old-fashioned town-centre local, well kept Youngs ales and enjoyable good value blackboard food from sandwiches up, friendly helpful staff, lounge bar with interesting pictures and memorabilia, darts and woodburner in bigger light and airy public bar with boarded walls and ceilings, daily newspapers, separate carpeted dining area; no under-14s, dogs welcome, flower-filled garden with smokers' area, open all day.

SILVERTON   SS9503
Lamb (01392) 860272
Fore Street; EX5 4HZ Traditional flagstoned local run well by friendly landlord; well kept Otter and a couple of guests tapped from stillage casks, inexpensive home-made pubby food including specials, separate eating area; quiz nights and other events, darts, skittle alley, children and dogs welcome, handy for Killerton (NT), open all day weekends.

SLAPTON   SX8245
Queens Arms (01548) 580800
Junction Sands Road and Prospect Hill; TQ7 2PN Smartly kept one-room village local with friendly staff and regulars, good value well balanced menu cooked by landlord, four real ales including Dartmoor and Otter, snug comfortable corners, roaring log fire, fascinating World War II photos and scrapbooks; quiz nights, live music, children and dogs welcome, lots of tables in lovely suntrap stepped garden, parking can be tricky at weekends.

SLAPTON   SX8245
★ **Tower** (01548) 580216
Church Road off Prospect Hill; TQ7 2PN Close to some fine beaches and backed by Slapton Ley nature reserve, this old inn has a low-beamed bar with settles, armchairs and scrubbed oak tables on flagstones or bare boards, log fires, three or four well kept West Country ales including one badged for them from St Austell, local cider and decent wines by the glass, good interesting food cooked by French chef, friendly accommodating service; children and dogs (in bar) welcome, wheelchair access to dining area (but not to lavatories), picnic-sets in pretty back garden overlooked by ivy-covered ruins of 14th-c chantry, comfortable bedrooms reached by external stone staircase, good breakfast, lane up to the pub is very narrow and parking can be tricky particularly at peak times, closed Sun evening (except July, Aug) and first two weeks of Jan.

SOURTON   SX5390
★ **Highwayman** (01837) 861243
A386, S of junction with A30; EX20 4HN Unique place – a quirky fantasy of dimly lit stonework and flagstone-floored burrows and alcoves, plenty of things to look at, one room a make-believe galleon; a couple of well kept local ales, proper cider and sometimes organic wines, lunchtime sandwiches, home-made pasties and platters (evening food mainly for residents), friendly chatty service; nostalgic background music, open mike nights, poetry evenings; children allowed in certain areas, outside fairy-tale pumpkin house and an old-lady-who-lived-in-a-shoe, period bedrooms with four-posters and half-testers.

STICKLEPATH   SX6494
★ **Devonshire** (01837) 840626
Off A30 at Whiddon Down or Okehampton; EX20 2NW Welcoming old-fashioned 16th-c thatched village local next to Finch Foundry museum (NT); low-beamed slate-floor bar with big log fire, longcase clock and easy-going old furnishings, stuffed animal heads, key collection, sofa in small snug, well kept low-priced ales tapped from the cask, Winkleigh's cider, good value sandwiches, soup and home-made pasties from the Aga (no evening meals), games room, lively folk night first Sun of month; dogs welcome, wheelchair access from car park, good walks nearby, open all day, closed Sun evening.

STOKE FLEMING   SX8648
Green Dragon (01803) 770238
Church Street; TQ6 0PX Freshened-up village local; beamed and flagstood interior with open fire, well kept ales such as St Austell and Otter, decent wines by the glass and enjoyable home-made food, friendly staff; background music; children and dogs welcome, tables on front terrace, small garden behind with play area, handy for South West Coast Path, best to check opening and food times.

STOKE GABRIEL   SX8457
Church House (01803) 782384
Off A385 just W of junction with A3022; Church Walk; TQ9 6SD Popular and welcoming early 14th-c pub; lounge bar with fine medieval beam-and-plank ceiling, black oak partition wall, window seats cut into thick butter-coloured walls, woodburner in huge fireplace, look out for the ancient mummified cat, well kept Sharps Doom Bar and a guest, enjoyable good value food, also little locals' bar; background music, Sun quiz; well behaved children and dogs welcome,

picnic-sets on small front terrace, old stocks (pub used to incorporate the village courthouse), limited parking, open all day.

STOKENHAM   SX8042
Tradesmans Arms (01548) 580996
Just off A379 Dartmouth–Kingsbridge; TQ7 2SZ Picturesque partly thatched 14th-c pub; traditional low-beamed cottagey interior with log fire, well kept West Country beers and decent wine list, good locally sourced food from lunchtime sandwiches to blackboard specials (booking advised), friendly attentive service, restaurant; children and dogs welcome, seats over lane on raised area looking down on village green, four nice bedrooms (they also have a self-catering apartment nearby), good breakfast.

TAVISTOCK   SX4874
★Cornish Arms (01822) 612145
West Street; PL19 8AN Chef-owner's highly regarded upscale pub food is a real draw here, can eat in bar or elegant dining room, comfortable seating and real fires, four well kept St Austell ales, good friendly service; children and dogs welcome, tables on split-level terrace, seven well appointed individual bedrooms, open all day.

TEIGNMOUTH   SX9372
Olde Jolly Sailor (01626) 772864
Set back from Northumberland Place; TQ14 8DE Town's oldest pub (said to date from the 12th c), comfortable low-ceilinged interior with stripped-stone walls, various nooks and crannies, well kept Fullers London Pride, Sharps Doom Bar and a couple of guests, generous helpings of tasty pub food (all day weekends), friendly welcoming staff; live music including Mon jazz monthly, sports TV; children and dogs welcome, seats in front courtyard, more behind with estuary views, open all day.

TEIGNMOUTH   SX9372
Ship (01626) 772674
Queen Street; TQ14 8BY Quayside pub with lovely estuary views from terrace picnic-sets; good reasonably priced food especially simply cooked local fish/seafood, five real ales including Bass, Otter and St Austell from brick-faced counter, bare boards bar with woodburner, back gallery restaurant; music festivals May/Aug; children and dogs welcome, open all day.

THORVERTON   SS9202
Thorverton Arms (01392) 860205
Village signed off A396 Exeter–Tiverton; EX5 5NS Spacious former coaching inn with five adjoining areas including log-fire

bar and restaurant, uncomplicated well cooked food at affordable prices (good fish and chips), Otter and Sharps Doom Bar, friendly helpful staff; live music, pool; children and dogs (in bar) welcome, wisteria-draped terrace and sunny garden, pleasant village, six comfortable bedrooms, good breakfast, open all day weekends, closed Sun evening and no food Mon, Tues.

THURLESTONE   SX6743
Village Inn (01548) 560382
Part of Thurlestone Hotel; TQ7 3NN Updated 16th-c pub attached to family-run hotel; wide choice of well liked food from open sandwiches and other snacks up, local beers and plenty of wines by the glass, friendly attentive service; background music; children and dogs welcome, picnic-sets out at front, handy for coast path, open all day weekends and in high season.

TIPTON ST JOHN   SY0991
★Golden Lion (01404) 812881
Pub signed off B3176 Sidmouth–Ottery St Mary; EX10 0AA Individually run beamed village pub with French chef-landlord doing good sensibly priced food using local fish, game and organic veg, light lunches and small helpings for children, well kept Otter and Sharps Doom Bar and good wine list, quick, friendly helpful service; attractive décor and furnishings mixing olde worlde with art deco and nouveau in spacious and relaxing two-part bar, subtle lighting, blazing log fire, quiet back restaurant; background music; well behaved children welcome, river walks nearby, garden and terrace tables with heaters.

TOPSHAM   SX9688
★Bridge Inn (01392) 873862
2.5 miles from M5 junction 30: Topsham signposted from exit roundabout; in Topsham follow signpost (A376) Exmouth, on the Elmgrove Road, into Bridge Hill; EX3 0QQ Very special old drinkers' pub (former 16th-c maltings painted in a distinctive pink), in landlady's family for five generations and quite unchanging and unspoilt; small characterful rooms and snugs, traditional furniture including a nice high-backed settle, woodburner, the 'bar' is landlady's front parlour (as notice on the door politely reminds customers), up to nine well kept ales tapped from the cask, simple food including good ploughman's, friendly staff and locals; live folk and blues, no background music, mobile phones or credit cards; children and dogs welcome, picnic-sets out overlooking weir.

TOPSHAM   SX9687
★**Globe** (01392) 873471
Fore Street; 2 miles from M5 junction 30; EX3 0HR Handsome carefully renovated former coaching inn blending original features with up-to-date touches; red-painted panelling in beamed bar hung with old prints, armchairs in a corner and suede tub and pubby chairs around dark tables on bare boards, small brick fireplace, second tartan-carpeted bar has pale panelling, traditional furniture and woodburner, St Austell ales and several wines by the glass, good choice of enjoyable food (including pizzas and separate vegan menu) from breakfast on, another log fire and huge candlesticks in elegant dining room; children and dogs (in bar) welcome, large terrace with parasol-shaded tables, individually decorated modern bedrooms, open (and food) all day.

TOPSHAM   SX9688
Passage House (01392) 873653
Ferry Road, off main street; EX3 0JN Relaxed 18th-c pub just back from the estuary shore; traditional black-beamed bar and slate-floored lower dining area, very good food (booking advised) from ciabattas to local fish, several well kept West Country ales, decent wines and some interesting gins, friendly attentive service; Tues quiz; children and dogs welcome, picnic-sets on terrace looking over moorings to nature reserve (lovely at sunset), open (and food) all day.

TORCROSS   SX8242
Start Bay (01548) 580553
A379 S of Dartmouth; TQ7 2TQ More fish and chip restaurant than pub, but does have Dartmoor and Otter ales, local wine and cider; very much set out for eating and exceptionally busy at peak times, staff cope well and food is generous and sensibly priced; wheelback chairs around dark tables, country pictures, some photographs of storms buffeting the building, winter coal fire, small drinking area by counter, large family room; no dogs during meal times, seats outside (highly prized) looking over pebble beach and wildlife lagoon, open all day.

TORQUAY   SX9265
★**Cary Arms** (01803) 327110
Beach Road: off B3199 Babbacombe Road, via Babbacombe Downs Road; turn steeply down near Babbacombe Theatre; TQ1 3LX Charming higgledy-piggledy hotel and spa reached down a tortuously steep lane (pay and display parking at bottom for non-residents); small, glass-enclosed entrance room with large ship lanterns and cleats, beamed grotto-effect bar overlooking the sea, rough pink granite walls,

alcoves, hobbit-style leather chairs around carved wooden tables, slate or bare-board floors, woodburner, Bays ale, Devon Rock and Devon Red ciders and nine good wines by the glass, enjoyable if not particularly cheap food; children and dogs (in bar) welcome, plenty of outside seating on various terraces, outside bar, steps down to quay with six mooring spaces, boutique-style bedrooms, self-catering cottages (glorious views) and chic beach huts and shore suites, open all day.

TORQUAY   SX9166
Crown & Sceptre (01803) 328290
Petitor Road, St Marychurch; TQ1 4QA Friendly two-bar local (in same family for over 40 years) with eight well kept ales such as Butcombe, Courage, Dartmoor, Hanlons and Harveys, three proper ciders and basic good value lunchtime food (not Mon, Tues), interesting naval memorabilia and chamber-pot collection; regular live music including Tues jazz and Fri folk; children and dogs welcome, sunny deck and garden.

TORQUAY   SX9163
Hole in the Wall (01803) 200755
Park Lane, opposite clock tower; TQ1 2AU Ancient two-bar local tucked away near harbour; enjoyable reasonably priced pubby food including good fresh fish, at least seven well kept ales such as St Austell, Butcombe, Otter and Sharps, real cider, good friendly service, smooth cobbled floors, low beams and alcoves, lots of nautical brassware, ship models and old local photographs, restaurant/function room; live music; children and dogs welcome, some seats in alley out at front, open all day and can get very busy at weekends.

TORRINGTON   SS4919
Black Horse (01805) 622121
High Street; EX38 8HN Popular twin-gabled former coaching inn; beams hung with stirrups in smallish bar, solid furniture and woodburner, lounge with striking ancient oak partition wall, back restaurant, five well kept ales including Courage and St Austell, generous helpings of tasty home-made food served by friendly staff; background music, darts and shove-ha'penny; children and dogs welcome, disabled access, three bedrooms, open all day.

TOTNES   SX8060
Albert (01803) 863214
Bridgetown; TQ9 5AD Unpretentious slate-hung pub near the river, small bar and two other rooms, low beams, flagstones, panelling, some old settles and lots of knick-knacks, friendly landlord brewing his own good Bridgetown ales, real cider and plenty of whiskies, honest reasonably priced pub food, friendly local atmosphere; quiz

---

We say if we know a pub has background music.

and music nights, darts, no dogs (theirs is Albert), paved beer garden behind.

TOTNES SX7960
Bay Horse (01803) 862088
Cistern Street; TQ9 5SP Welcoming traditional two-bar inn (15th c); half a dozen well kept ales including New Lion, ciders such as Sandford Orchards, simple lunchtime food; background and regular live music including good Sun jazz; children and dogs (on leads) welcome, attractive large garden behind, three bedrooms, good breakfast, open all day.

TOTNES SX8060
★ Royal Seven Stars (01803) 862125
Fore Street, The Plains; TQ9 5DD Handsome, well run hotel in centre of town and across from River Dart; companionable bar to left of interesting entrance hall, open fire, button-back banquettes and cushioned chairs around circular tables, stools against counter serving St Austell ales on handpump, farm cider, carefully chosen wines and interesting gins, dining rooms with lots to look at, good food from sandwiches and pub favourites up; children welcome, dogs in bar and bedrooms, disabled access, covered tables out at front among box-planted troughs, open (and food) all day from 8am.

TOTNES SX8059
★ Steam Packet (01803) 863880
St Peters Quay, on W bank (ie not on Steam Packet Quay); TQ9 5EW Spacious quayside pub overlooking the River Dart, popular for both eating and drinking; three distinct bar areas with polished floorboards, bare stone and brick walls, half-panelling and open fires, built-in wall seats, dark wooden chairs and leather-topped stools around traditional tables and comfortable sofas with scatter cushions, also conservatory restaurant; enjoyable bistro-like food plus sandwiches and breakfasts, friendly, efficient staff cope well at peak times; Dartmoor Legend, Roam Tavy Best Bitter, Salcombe Seahorse and Sharps Doom Bar on handpump, several wines by the glass and farm cider; background music, TV, large riverside terrace with seats under big parasols (arrive early if sunny), children welcome, dogs in bar, six comfortable airy bedrooms, open and food all day.

TUCKENHAY SX8156
Maltsters Arms (01803) 732350
Ashprington Road, off A381 from Totnes; TQ9 7EQ Popular old pub (once owned by celebrity chef Keith Floyd) in lovely quiet spot by wooded Bow Creek; good food from bar snacks to fresh fish specials, well kept Bays and three West Country guests, local ciders and great range of wines by the glass, friendly service, creek-view restaurant; background and some live music; children and dogs welcome, waterside terrace with

open-air bar, pontoon for visiting boats, six bedrooms (three with river views), open all day, food all day Fri-Sun during summer school holidays.

TYTHERLEIGH ST3103
Tytherleigh Arms (01460) 20214
A358 Chard–Axminster; EX13 7BE Modernised village dining pub dating from the 16th c; highly praised imaginative cooking (also some cheaper pubby dishes), ales such as Branscombe and Otter, well chosen wines, friendly professional service, bare boards bar with log fire, restaurant; well behaved children welcome (no under-5s in the evening), dogs allowed in bar, six comfortable bedrooms in converted stables, closed Sun evening out of season.

UGBOROUGH SX6755
Anchor (01752) 690388
Off A3121; PL21 0NG Newish management for this 17th-c beamed inn; bar with open fire, comfortable armchairs and dining chairs around mix of tables on wood floor, stools against planked counter serving Sharps Doom Bar, a guest beer and several wines by the glass, well regarded food, two-level restaurant with rattan dining chairs and wooden tables on flagstones in one part, more traditional dark wooden furniture in lower area, woodburner in big fireplace; background music, TV and board games; children and dogs (in bar) welcome, ten comfortable individually furnished bedrooms (four in courtyard cabins), open all day.

UGBOROUGH SX6755
Ship (01752) 892565
Off A3121 SE of Ivybridge; PL21 0NS Friendly dining pub extended from cosy 16th-c flagstoned core; well divided open-plan eating areas a step down from neat bar with woodburner, good food from bar meals up including blackboard specials (lots of fish), well kept Palmers, St Austell and a local guest, nice house wines, cheerful chatty staff; background music; children and dogs (in bar) welcome, tables out in front, open daily (timings may vary).

UPOTTERY ST2007
Sidmouth Arms (01404) 861252
Near the church; EX14 9PN Attractive 18th-c pub in pleasant village setting, roomy and comfortable, with helpful friendly staff, a couple of well kept Otter beers and a guest, proper cider, enjoyable good value traditional food; children and dogs welcome, small outside area, open (and food) all day.

WEARE GIFFARD SS4722
Cyder Press (01237) 425517
Tavern Gardens; EX39 4QR Welcoming village local with amiable landlord; impressive range of ciders, four real ales including a house beer from Timothy Taylors and some interesting gins, enjoyable fairly

priced home-made food (Weds-Sat and Sun lunchtime), black beams and timbers, inglenook woodburner; Tues folk night, Fri darts, monthly quiz; children (till 8.30pm) and dogs welcome, seats outside, beautiful countryside and handy for Tarka Trail, bedrooms, closed Mon and Tues lunchtimes, otherwise open all day (shuts Weds-Fri afternoons in winter).

WELCOMBE   SS2317
Old Smithy (01288) 331305
Signed off A39 S of Hartland; EX39 6HG
Cosy thatched and low-beamed country pub; open-plan bar with mix of wooden chairs at scrubbed pine tables, quirky 1960/70s retro décor; fairy lights and open fires, well kept local ales, traditional ciders and popular pubby food, good friendly service, more room upstairs; background and live music including monthly Mon folk night, quiz and pizza Thurs, various games; children and dogs welcome, lovely garden and setting by narrow lane leading eventually to attractive rocky cove, bunkhouse, closed Sun evening and lunchtimes Mon, Tues.

WEMBURY   SX5349
Odd Wheel (01752) 863052
Knighton Road; PL9 0JD Popular modernised village pub with five well kept West Country ales and good fairly traditional food from sandwiches/ciabattas up, reasonable prices including set lunch Mon-Fri, friendly helpful service, back restaurant; pool, darts, sports TV; children and dogs (in bar) welcome, seats out on decking, fenced play area, open (and food) all day weekends.

WESTON   ST1400
Otter (01404) 42594
Off A373, or A30 at W end of Honiton bypass; EX14 3NZ Big busy family pub with heavy low beams; good choice of enjoyable reasonably priced food (best to book) including menu for smaller appetites and two-for-one deals, carvery Thurs and Sun lunchtimes, cheerful helpful staff, well kept Otter ales and a guest, carpeted opened-up interior with good log fire; background music, pool; dogs allowed in one area, disabled access, picnic-sets on big lawn leading to River Otter, open (and food) all day.

WIDECOMBE   SX7176
Old Inn (01364) 621207
B3387 W of Bovey Tracey; TQ13 7TA
Busy dining pub with spacious beamed

interior; enjoyable fairly standard food at reasonable prices, well kept Badger, Dartmoor and a guest; Thatcher's cider, good friendly service, side conservatory with large central woodburner; children and dogs (in bar) welcome, nice garden with water features and pleasant terrace, wandering ducks and chickens, great walks from this pretty moorland village, Widecombe Fair second Tues of Sept, open (and food) all day, kitchen closes 5.30pm Sun.

WONSON   SX6789
Northmore Arms (01647) 231428
Between Throwleigh and Gidleigh; EX20 2JA Proper traditional old pub set in beautiful remote walking country; two simple old-fashioned rooms, log fire and woodburner, low beams and stripped stone, well kept ales such as Dartmoor tapped from the cask, farm cider and decent house wines, good reasonably priced food including popular Sun lunch (booking advised); walkers and dogs welcome, tables in garden.

YEALMPTON   SX5851
Rose & Crown (01752) 880223
A379 Kingsbridge–Plymouth; PL8 2EB
Central bar counter, all dark wood and heavy brass, leather-seated stools and mix of furnishings on stripped-wood floors, comfy sofa by woodburner, emphasis on popular bar and restaurant food, friendly attentive service, three St Austell ales, a dozen wines by the glass and decent coffee; children and dogs (bar area) welcome, tables in walled garden with pond, also a lawned area, eight well appointed bedrooms in separate building (dogs welcome), open (and food) all day.

LUNDY

LUNDY   SS1344
★ Marisco (01271) 870870
Get there by ferry (Bideford and Ilfracombe) or helicopter (Hartland Point); EX39 2LY One of England's most isolated pubs, yet surprisingly busy most nights; great setting, steep trudge up from landing stage, galleried interior with lifebelts and shipwreck salvage, open fire, St Austell ales, Weston's cider and reasonably priced house wines, good basic food using Lundy produce, friendly staff, books and games; no mobile phones; children welcome, tables outside, souvenir shop doubling as general store for the island's few residents, open (and food) all day from breakfast on.

Dorset

CERNE ABBAS   ST6601   Map 2
New Inn
(01300) 341274 – www.thenewinncerneabbas.co.uk
Long Street; DT2 7JF

Handsome former coaching inn with character bar, friendly licensees, local ales and inventive food; fine bedrooms

That famously endowed giant etched into the chalk hillside is just a walk away from this welcoming old inn, built centuries ago as a guest house for the nearby Benedictine abbey. Once you're ensconced, it's hard to drag yourself away. Original oak beams, mullioned windows and a pump and mounting block in the former coachyard add to its charms, and the bar has a solid oak counter, an attractive mix of old dining tables and chairs on slate or polished wooden floors, settles built into various nooks and crannies and a woodburner in the opened-up yorkstone fireplace. Palmers Copper, Dorset Gold, IPA and 200 on handpump, ten wines by the glass, several malt whiskies and local cider. The dining room is furnished in a similar style; background music. There are seats on the terrace and picnic-sets beneath mature fruit trees or parasols in the back garden. The ten bedrooms are smart and well equipped and located in either the charming 16th-c main building or a converted stable block. The whole package sits prettily in the chocolate-box village.

Nicely presented food makes good use of local produce and includes Dorset cheddar ploughman's, baked Somerset camembert with white onion jam and brioche (to share), goats cheese and caramelised onion tart with salsa verde, beer-battered cod and chips, chicken breast with wilted greens and mushroom cream, fish of the day with parmesan gnocchi, baby leeks and brown butter, and puddings such as clementine pannacotta and hazelnut roulade with cinnamon nougat, hazelnut brittle and fig ice-cream. *Benchmark main dish: dressed Portland crab with new potatoes or fries £18.00. Two-course evening meal £23.00.*

Palmers ~ Tenant Julian Dove ~ Real ale ~ Open 12-11; 12-10 Sun ~ Bar food 12-2.30, 7-9; 12-2.30, 6.30-9 Fri, Sat; 12-3, 7-8.30 Sun ~ Restaurant ~ Children welcome ~ Dogs allowed in bar & bedrooms ~ Bedrooms: £105

CHURCH KNOWLE

SY9381   Map 2

New Inn ♀

(01929) 480357 – www.newinn-churchknowle.co.uk

Village signed off A351 N of Corfe Castle; BH20 5NQ

Bustling pub with plenty of seating in various rooms, open fires, a thoughtful choice of drinks, good food and a friendly landlord

At the heart of this pretty Purbeck Hills village, the New Inn is a perfect place to rest after walking the coast path. This partly thatched 16th-c inn was once part of a working farm and has been run by Maurice Estop and his friendly team for 36 years. The main bar has an open fire in a stone fireplace, high-backed black leather dining chairs and cushioned wall settles around heavy rustic tables on red patterned carpet and quite a few stools against the counter; there's an interesting glass cabinet full of old medicine boxes and tins and quite a few horsebrasses. Ringwood Razorback, Sharps Doom Bar and a summer guest on handpump, six wines by the glass and farm cider; there's a wine shack from which you can choose your own wines, and also a wide choice of teas, coffees and local soft drinks. A similarly furnished dining room leads off here. There are picnic-sets on the lawn and camping available on the fields at the back of the pub (booking advised). The ruins of Corfe Castle (National Trust) are close by.

Popular, seasonal food includes sandwiches and daily fresh fish dishes (best to order lobster, dover sole or skate wings in advance). Among the dishes might be Dorset blue vinney soup, pan-fried scallops, garlic portobello mushrooms on toast, fish pie using six varieties of fish, whole grilled mackerel or sardines, pork belly with black pudding and red cabbage, traditional nut roast with yorkshire pudding, 28-day aged locally sourced steak with chips, and puddings such as plum and ginger crumble with ginger ice-cream and spotted dick with custard. *Benchmark main dish: steak and ale pie with chips £10.95. Two-course evening meal £19.00.*

Punch ~ Tenants Maurice and Matthew Estop ~ Real ale ~ Open 11-3, 6-11 (9 in winter); 12-3, 6-10 Sun ~ Bar food 12-2.15, 6-8.30; 12-3 Sun ~ Restaurant ~ Children welcome

EVERSHOT

ST5704   Map 2

Acorn ⭐ ♀ 🛏

(01935) 83228 – www.acorn-inn.co.uk

Off A37 S of Yeovil; DT2 0JW

Dorset Dining Pub of the Year

Fascinating old place in a pretty village with character rooms, friendly licensees and tasty food; bedrooms

Thomas Hardy may well have supped some Dorset ale in this venerable, 400-year-old inn: he certainly knew it, as he has his best-known heroine Tess Durbyfield (*Tess of the d'Urbervilles*) stop for breakfast next door on her mournful mission to see her errant husband's family. It's in some fabulous walking country for those who walk for pleasure rather than necessity. On chilly days, the log fires and low-beamed cosiness spark much joy. DBC Jurassic is a regular among the trio of frequently changing real ales on handpump, alongside 28 wines by the glass, 30 gins (including a gin of the month) and about 70 malt whiskies. A second bar has comfortable beige leather wall banquettes and little stools around tables set with fresh flowers, and a Turkish rug on nice old quarry tiles. This leads to a bistro-style dining room with ladder-back chairs around oak tables; the slightly more formal restaurant is similarly furnished. There's also a comfortable lounge with armchairs, board games and shelves of books and a skittle alley. Throughout are open fires, wood panelling, pretty knick-knacks, all manner of copper and brass items, water jugs, wall prints and photographs; background music, TV, board games and darts. A walled garden has picnic-sets under a fine beech tree. Each of the ten attractive bedrooms is individually decorated and has a Thomas Hardy theme.

 A thoughtful choice of good food mixes up-to-date fare with pub classics. Dishes include ploughman's, twice-baked crab and yarg soufflé with pickled samphire, deep-fried whitebait with home-made tartare sauce, roasted cod with lyonnaise potatoes and kale, rump of lamb with potato terrine, honey-roasted carrots and spinach and pea velouté, crispy mozzarella arancini with Mediterranean vegetables and watercress and spinach velouté, ham and eggs, beer-battered fish of the day with chips, and puddings such as chocolate mousse with strawberries and yoghurt ice-cream and sticky toffee pudding with candied orange and custard. *Benchmark main dish: spicy red chicken curry with crushed peanuts and coconut rice £15.00. Two-course evening meal £24.00.*

Free house ~ Licensee Natalie Legg ~ Real ale ~ Open 11-11; 12-10.30 Sun ~ Bar food 12-2, 7-9 ~ Restaurant ~ Children welcome ~ Dogs welcome ~ Bedrooms: £130

FARNHAM
Museum 🌟💷 🍷 🛏

ST9515 Map 2

(01725) 516261 – www.museuminn.co.uk
Village signposted off A354 Blandford Forum–Salisbury; DT11 8DE

Partly thatched smart inn with appealing rooms, brasserie-style food, real ales and fine wines; comfortable bedrooms

This is a great place for a post-ramble dinner and sleepover. The brasserie-style food is a big draw, and the bedrooms are pleasingly rustic and comfortable. There's a proper small bar with beams, flagstones, a big inglenook fireplace and quite an assortment of dining chairs around plain or painted wooden tables. Stools line the counter where friendly staff serve Ringwood Razor Back, Waylands Sixpenny 6d Best Bitter and a beer from Gritchie Brewing on handpump, ten wines by the glass, 20 malt whiskies, 30 gins and local spirits and ciders. This leads to a simply but attractively furnished dining room with cushioned window seats, a long, dark leather, button-back wall seat, similar chairs and tables on bare floorboards and quite a few photographs on patterned wallpaper. A quiet lounge has armchairs around a low table in front of an open fire, books on shelves and board games. Outside, the terrace has cushioned seats and tables under parasols. Four bedrooms are in the main building, four others in converted stables, and they also have a large thatched self-catering cottage, Mole's Cottage, which sleeps 16.

 Rewarding, modern food includes truffle mac 'n' cheese fritters, Scottish smoked salmon with fennel and watercress, beer-battered haddock and chips, seared bream fillet with new potatoes niçoise, roast cauliflower with Persian-spiced lentils, spinach, chickpeas and flatbread, pan-fried rump steak with chunky chips, field mushrooms and tomatoes, vegan burger with guacamole and fries, and puddings such as rhubarb and custard crumble pie, eton mess pavlova and lemon tart. *Benchmark main dish: chicken, tarragon and leek pie £14.00. Two-course evening meal £20.00.*

Cirrus Inns ~ Licensee Paolo Corgiolu ~ Real ale ~ Open 12-10.30; closed Mon, Tue ~ Bar food 12-3, 6-9 (9.30 Fri); 12-9.30 Sat; 12-8 Sun ~ Restaurant ~ Children welcome ~ Dogs allowed in bar & bedrooms ~ Bedrooms: £120

You can send reports directly to us at feedback@goodguides.com

KINGSTON   SY9579 Map 2

Scott Arms

(01929) 480270 – www.thescottarms.com

West Street (B3069); BH20 5LH

Magnificent views from a large garden, rambling character rooms, real ales, interesting food and an easy-going atmosphere; bedrooms

This is a lovely place on the Isle of Purbeck and perfect for refreshment – ginger beer or proper beer available – after making like the Famous Five and looking for treasure in nearby Corfe Castle (National Trust). The views from the well tended garden with its summer seating and kitchen are quite magnificent. The bar areas and dining room are on several levels with stripped stone and brickwork, flagstones and bare boards, beams and high rafters and open fires; seats range from sofas and easy chairs through all manner of wooden chairs around tables of varying sizes. Stairs lead up from the bar to a small minstrels' gallery-like area with sofas facing one another across a table. There's DBC Jurassic and Origin, and a guest such as Hop Back Crop Circle or Waylands Sixpenny 6d Best Bitter, on handpump, 11 wines by the glass and local cider; background music and board games. The four bedrooms named after local landmarks have splendid views and are delightfully appointed.

As well as the Jerkshak from Easter to September (the landlady is from Jamaica) for jerk chicken, curry mutton, ackee and saltfish and other Caribbean dishes, the varied food includes sandwiches, smoked mackerel pâté, calamari, grilled goats cheese salad with roasted aubergine, courgette and peppers, sharing boards, local sausages with mash and gravy, ham, egg and chips, free-range chicken with creamy wild mushroom sauce and dauphinoise potatoes, and puddings such as chocolate torte and Purbeck ice-creams. *Benchmark main dish: fish and chips £14.95. Two-course evening meal £20.00.*

Greene King ~ Lease Ian, Simon and Cynthia Coppack ~ Real ale ~ Open 11-10; 11-11 Sat ~ Bar food 12-2.30, 6-8.30; 12-8.30 weekends ~ Children welcome ~ Dogs allowed in bar ~ Bedrooms: £125

MIDDLEMARSH   ST6607 Map 2

Hunters Moon

(01963) 210966 – www.hunters-moon.org.uk

A352 Sherborne–Dorchester; DT9 5QN

Plenty of snug places to enjoy a pint in several linked areas, reasonably priced food and quite a choice of drinks; comfortable bedrooms

Its bucolic setting right in the middle of Dorset gives explorers the choice of Jurassic coast to the south or Hardyesque market towns to the north, and this lovely old inn is run by friendly licensees who are happy to advise on great days out. Staying over is a tempting option – there are eight attractive rooms, two of which are dog-friendly. The beamed bar rooms are filled with a great variety of tables and chairs on red patterned carpet, an array of ornaments from horsebrasses and other equine tack to pretty little tea cups hanging from beams, and lighting in the form of converted oil lamps; the atmosphere is properly pubby. Booths are formed by some attractively cushioned settles, walls are of exposed brick, stone and some panelling and there are three log fires (one in a capacious inglenook); background music, children's books and toys and board games. There's Butcombe Bitter, IPA Liberation and a local guest on handpump, farm cider and 16 wines by the glass. A neat lawn has picnic-sets with parasols. Breakfasts, if you do stay the night, are lovely.

 Crowd-pleasing, fairly priced food includes lunchtime sandwiches, pan-fried king prawns, caesar salad, field mushrooms with stilton and caramelised onions, a pie of the day, scampi and chips, a curry of the day, mixed bean, lime and coriander chilli with rice, cumberland sausages with mash and peas, and puddings such as crumble or cheesecake of the day and lemon and lime posset with chantilly cream and shortbread. *Benchmark main dish: burger (beef, game or chicken breast) with chips and coleslaw £11.00. Two-course evening meal £19.00.*

Enterprise ~ Lease Dean and Emma Mortimer ~ Real ale ~ Open 10.30-2.30, 6-10.30 (11 Fri); 10.30am-11pm Sat; 10.30-10.30 Sun ~ Bar food 12-2, 6-9; all day weekends ~ Children welcome ~ Dogs welcome ~ Bedrooms: £90

NETTLECOMBE SY5195 Map 2

Marquis of Lorne

(01308) 485236 ~ www.themarquisoflorne.co.uk
Off A3066 Bridport–Beaminster, via West Milton; DT6 3SY

Attractive country pub with enjoyable food and drink, friendly licensees and seats in big garden; bedrooms

A deservedly popular, cheerful pub with a double whammy of gorgeous, child-friendly garden and spectacular views over the soft Dorset hills topped by Eggardon, the site of an impressive 2,500-year-old hill fort. In warm weather, the pretty herbaceous borders, picnic-sets under apple trees and rustic-style play area are a popular stop-off point for family outings. Inside, the comfortable, bustling main bar has a log fire, mahogany panelling, old prints and photographs and neatly matching chairs and tables. Two dining areas lead off, the smaller of which has another log fire. A wooden-floored snug (liked by locals) has board games, table skittles and background music, and they keep Palmers Copper, 200 and IPA on hand pump in tip-top condition, with ten wines by the glass from a decent list and ten gins. The seven bedrooms are comfortably appointed; people tend to ask for ones with views of Eggardon.

 The landlord cooks pleasing food using seasonal local produce (much of it from the pub's own polytunnel). Dishes include soft herring roe with capers and parsley, roasted asparagus with roasted chicken jus and parmesan, Dorset scallops with black pudding, grilled vegetable lasagne with lovage pesto, lambs liver with bacon and mash, sticky beef with Indonesian-style salad, and puddings such as chocolate nemesis (gluten-free), waffle with bananas and toffee sauce, and Dorset apple cake. *Benchmark main dish: fillet of sea bass with crushed new potatoes and prawn velouté £14.00. Two-course evening meal £20.00.*

Palmers ~ Tenants Stephen and Tracey Brady ~ Real ale ~ Open 12-2.30, 6-11 ~ Bar food 12-2, 6-9 ~ Restaurant ~ Children welcome ~ Dogs allowed in bar ~ Bedrooms: £95

PLUSH ST7102 Map 2

Brace of Pheasants 🎖️ ♟ 🛏️

(01300) 348357 ~ www.braceofpheasants.co.uk
Village signposted from B3143 N of Dorchester at Piddletrenthide; DT2 7RQ

16th-c thatched pub with friendly service, popular food and pleasant garden; comfortable bedrooms

A highly recommended old thatched cottage tucked away down narrow, country lanes, with perfect walking country all around. The beamed bar has windsor chairs around good solid tables on patterned carpeting, a few standing timbers and a huge heavy-beamed inglenook at one end with a good warming log fire at the other. Cerne Abbas Ale and a guest such as Flack Manor Double Drop are tapped from the cask alongside a fine choice of wines with 20 by the glass, and two proper farm ciders. A decent-sized garden (the perfect play space for young pub dog Lucy) includes a terrace and a lawn sloping up towards a rockery. It's just the place for spending a weekend in attractive and comfortable bedrooms; our readers enjoy the annexe ones which are spotless and have their own little terrace. Breakfasts are first class.

Particularly good food from a daily changing menu with an emphasis on local suppliers includes trio of smoked fish with sweet beetroot relish, bubbling cheesy mushrooms, garlic and herb marinated venison steak with port and redcurrant sauce and confit garlic mash, beer-battered fish and chips, marinated goats cheese salad with walnuts, baby potatoes and beetroot, pan-fried duck breast with caramelised orange and madeira sauce and potato rösti, and puddings such as warm malva pudding with brandy glaze and stem ginger crème anglaise and flourless chocolate praline cake with chocolate sauce. *Benchmark main dish: pork loin steak with chorizo and apple stuffing and bubble and squeak £15.95. Two-course evening meal £22.00.*

Free house ~ Licensees Phil and Carol Bennett ~ Real ale ~ Open 12-3, 6.30-10.30; 12-3.30 Sun; closed Mon, Tue ~ Bar food 12-2.30, 7-9; 12-3 Sun ~ Children welcome ~ Dogs allowed in bar ~ Bedrooms: £119

SHERBORNE
ST6316 Map 2

Digby Tap 🍺 £

(01935) 813148 – www.digbytap.co.uk

Cooks Lane; park in Digby Road and walk round corner; DT9 3NS

Regularly changing ales in simple alehouse, open all day with very inexpensive beer and food

A perfect combination of old-style boozer, free-styling freehouse and thoroughly modern community (and boules/cricket) centre. You'll find customers from all walks of life enjoying the well kept beers and gratifyingly cheap food. The atmosphere is lively, chatty and warmly welcoming – both online (check out their Facebook page) and in real life – and the straightforward flagstoned bar with its cosy corners is full of understated character. The small games room has a pool table and a quiz machine, and there's also a TV room; mobile phones are discouraged. The splendid choice of beers on handpump, all inexpensive, includes Cerne Abbas Ale, Otter Bitter, Red Rock IPA and Teignworthy Neap Tide. Also, several wines by the glass and a choice of malt whiskies. Lovely Sherborne Abbey is just a stroll away, but there are many beauty spots where you can walk off your steak sandwich and pint of Otter (and still have change from a tenner).

Generous helpings of extraordinarily good value, straightforward food – lunchtime only – includes sandwiches and toasties, salmon and cream cheese bagel with chips, steak fajita with guacamole, sour cream salsa and chips, broccoli and cauliflower bake, and specials such as real ale cottage pie. *Benchmark main dish: creamy chicken, bacon and leek pie £7.00.*

Free house ~ Licensees Oliver Wilson and Nick Whigham ~ Real ale ~ Open 11-11; 12-11 Sun ~ Bar food 12-2; not Sun ~ Children welcome until 6pm ~ Dogs allowed in bar

We don't mention free wi-fi, because it's standard in most pubs these days – though not universal. And don't expect a good signal in remote rural locations.

WEST LULWORTH

SY8280

Castle Inn 🛏

(01929) 400311 – butcombe.com/the-castle-inn-dorset

B3070 SW of Wareham; BH20 5RN

Popular old inn, smartly updated, with a good mix of customers, cheerful atmosphere, real ales, well liked food and seats in garden; comfortable bedrooms

Recently refurbished, this pretty 16th-c thatched inn appeals to both locals and those staying for a few days. It's in lovely Isle of Purbeck countryside, close to Lulworth Cove, and there's plenty to do nearby. The open-plan bar and dining areas have retained some snugs and alcoves, and therefore some character, with wooden and painted church chairs around little tables on stripped boards, wooden armchairs on flagstones by the open fire and comfortable wall banquettes; children and dogs are welcome. Butcombe Original and three guest ales on handpump and 16 wines by the glass are served by friendly staff. There are plenty of picnic-sets at the front of the building, as well as more seats in the garden with views of the steep hillside. The dozen bedrooms (two are dog-friendly) are comfortable and boutique in style with a few quirky touches.

 Enjoyable food served all day includes steak baguettes, potted chicken, ham and herb terrine with sticky onion marmalade, sharing platter, River Fowey mussels in cider with leeks and bacon, various pub classics, pizzas, lentil, cauliflower and spinach curry, local trout fishcakes with spinach and poached egg, gammon with roasted pineapple, eggs and chips, and puddings such as triple chocolate brownie with espresso ice-cream and New York-style cheesecake with strawberries. *Benchmark main dish: beer-battered fish and chips £14.50. Two-course evening meal £20.00.*

Butcombe ~ Manager Simon Muckhtar ~ Real ale ~ Open 12-9, 12-10 Fri; 12-10 Sat; 12-8 Sun ~ Children welcome ~ Dogs allowed in bar ~ Bedrooms: £132

WEST STOUR

ST7822   Map 2

Ship 🌟 ♈ 🍺 🛏

(01747) 838640 – www.shipinn-dorset.com

A30 W of Shaftesbury; SP8 5RP

Civilised and pleasantly updated roadside dining inn offering a wide range of food and ales; bedrooms

Well run, warmly welcoming and surrounded by rolling pastureland, this is your perfect country pub. It has a relaxed, rustic style, not too fussy but the wood is polished and the bars orderly and well stocked. The neatly kept rooms include a smallish but airy bar on the left with cream décor, a mix of chunky farmhouse furniture on dark boards and big sash windows that look out on to bucolic farmland. In winter, a log fire is standard, as is the presence of two delightful Bedlington terriers, Douglas and Elliot, who trot in from the extensive and pretty garden for the warmth. The smaller flagstoned public bar has a good log fire and low ceilings. The house beer on handpump is Butcombe and there are two weekly changing guests: Hattie Browns (brewed down the road in Swanage) is a popular visitor, as are Palmers Copper and Waylands Sixpenny 6d Best. Also, 13 wines by the glass, 19 gins, a dozen malt whiskies and five farm ciders. During their summer beer festival they showcase a dozen beers and ten ciders, all from the West Country. On the right, two carpeted dining rooms with stripped pine dado, stone walls and shutters are similarly furnished in a pleasantly informal style, with some attractive contemporary cow prints; TV, numerous board games and background music. The five bedrooms are appealing and have lovely views of the surrounding countryside; breakfasts are particularly good.

 Highly enjoyable food includes lunchtime sandwiches, courgette, halloumi and herb fritters with cucumber and dill sauce, smoked haddock scotch egg with curried mayo, lamb koftas, roasted guinea fowl with pesto mash and aubergine caponata, king prawn and chorizo linguine, steak and chips, and puddings such as affogato, cranachan and elderflower, prosecco and raspberry jelly. *Benchmark main dish: ginger beer-battered hake with peas and chips £13.95. Two-course evening meal £21.00.*

Free house ~ Licensee Gavin Griggs ~ Real ale ~ Open 12-3, 6-11; 12-midnight Sat; 12-10 Sun; closed Mon ~ Bar food 12-2.30, 6-9; not Sun evening ~ Restaurant ~ Children welcome ~ Dogs allowed in bar ~ Bedrooms: £95

WEYMOUTH   SY6878 Map 2
Red Lion 🍺 £
(01305) 786940 – www.theredlionweymouth.co.uk
Hope Square; DT4 8TR

Bustling place with sunny terrace, a smashing range of drinks, tasty food and lots to look at

Fittingly for a pub that identifies so strongly with the Royal National Lifeboat Institute, the house bitter is called Lifeboat (named for the pub with 10p per pint going towards the RNLI), and the landlord keeps a timber-shivering number of rums (more than 100 at last count). This is the nearest pub to Weymouth RNLI and features numerous pictures and artefacts relating to the lifeboat crews and their boats. There's also DBC Jurassic (a local favourite) and guests from St Austell or Timothy Taylors on handpump, a dozen wines by the glass and 40 gins. The refurbished bare-boards interior, kept cosy with candles, has a cheerful, lively atmosphere, all manner of wooden chairs and tables, cushioned wall seats, some unusual maroon-cushioned high benches beside equally high tables, the odd armchair here and there, and plenty of bric-a-brac on stripped-brick walls. Some nice contemporary touches include the woven timber wall decorated with the names of strong beverages – guaranteed to raise the spirits – and loads of mirrors wittily overlapped; daily papers, board games and background music. On sunny evenings, the tables outside are worth bagging. The pub is a good source of information about the Weymouth area, and there's a downloadable pub walk on the website.

🍴 As well as lunchtime sandwiches, the well regarded food includes sharing platters (seafood and vegetarian), crab cakes, seafood chowder, whitebait, steak and Lifeboat ale pie with chips, chicken pie, vegetarian cottage pie, chicken club burger and chips, and puddings such as rum sundae (rum and raisin ice-cream layered with sticky toffee pudding and more rum) and sticky toffee and date pudding. *Benchmark main dish: pan-fried sea bass with new potatoes, greens and tomato salsa £13.95. Two-course evening meal £19.00.*

Free house ~ Licensee Brian McLaughlin ~ Real ale ~ Open 12-11; 12-10.30 Sun ~ Bar food 12-9; 12-8 Sun ~ Children welcome until 7pm

WIMBORNE MINSTER   SZ0199 Map 2
Green Man 🍺 £

(01202) 881021 – www.greenmanwimborne.com
Victoria Road, at junction with West Street (B3082/B3073); BH21 1EN

**Cosy, warm-hearted town tavern with well liked food and
Wadworths ales**

A cheerful, bustling place whose small linked areas have some timbering, tartan banquettes, wheelback and farmhouse chairs around pubby tables on parquet flooring or carpet, some William Morris-style wallpaper, horsebrasses and a high shelf of stone bottles. A woodburning stove keeps everyone toasty on cold days, and when the sun shines in the summer the flower displays out front and on the back terrace are a joy to behold over the rim of a pint glass. Friendly staff keep Wadworths 6X, IPA and Swordfish on handpump, and a farm cider. Darts, a silenced games machine and juke box; the Barn houses a pool table. Dog walkers are welcomed warmly – even dogs damp from a walk are offered a biscuit or two.

Excellent value food is served until 3pm. As well as popular all-day breakfasts, there are sandwiches, baguettes and jacket potatoes, satisfying Sunday roasts and reliable pubby lunch dishes such as burgers, scampi, beer-battered fish – all served with chips – and some daily specials, with ice-cream or cheese for afters. *Benchmark main dish: ploughman's with Dorset cheddar, pork pie and coleslaw £9.95.*

Wadworths ~ Tenants Katherine Twinn and Scott Valenti ~ Real ale ~ Open 12-11 Mon; 11-11 ~ Bar food 11-3; sometimes evenings, ring to check ~ Restaurant ~ Children welcome until 7pm ~ Dogs allowed in bar

WORTH MATRAVERS   SY9777   Map 2

Square & Compass

(01929) 439229 – www.squareandcompasspub.co.uk
At fork of both roads signposted to village from B3069; BH19 3LF

**Unchanging country tavern with masses of character, in the same
family for many years; lovely sea views and fine nearby walks**

The same family has run this fascinating and hospitable pub for more than a century. The local area's famously diverse geological history is celebrated in the pub's (free) fossil museum, the outside furniture is made of local stone and there's even a summer stone-carving competition in honour of the many chisel-wielders who come searching for treasure in the locality. A couple of simple rooms have straightforward furniture on flagstones and wooden benches around the walls, a woodburning stove, a stuffed albino badger and a loyal crowd of chatty locals. Regulars Hattie Browns HBA and Moonlite are on handpump and a couple of quickly changing guests, such as Hattie Browns Kirrin Island or Dog on the Roof and Trumans Zephyr, are tapped from the cask. This is the place to come for the taste of West Country orchards: up to ten farm ciders (such as Kiss Me Kate, Sat Down BeCider) are passed through the two serving hatches to customers in the drinking corridor; also, 20 malt whiskies. There's a fantastic view from the front terrace over the village rooftops down to the sea. There may be free-roaming chickens and other birds clucking around. Wonderful walks lead to some exciting switchback sections of the coast path above St Aldhelm's Head and Chapman's Pool – use the £2 honesty box 100 metres along the Corfe Castle road for parking if you're coming by car.

Bar food consists of pasties and pies (usually home-made but sometimes bought in, if it's really busy).

Free house ~ Licensees Charlie Newman and Kevin Hunt ~ Real ale ~ Open 12-11 ~ Bar food all day ~ Children welcome ~ Dogs welcome

Also Worth a Visit in Dorset

Besides the fully inspected pubs, you might like to try these pubs that have been recommended to us and described by readers. Do tell us what you think of them: feedback@goodguides.com

ANSTY
ST7603
Fox (01258) 880328
NW of Milton Abbas; DT2 7PN Tastefully redecorated 18th-c pub (owned by farm opposite) in pretty village in heart of Dorset; cosy bar popular with locals and visitors, with farmhouse chairs, stools and cushioned wall seats around tables on pale floorboards, real ales on handpump from Dorset breweries such as Cerne Abbas, Isle of Purbeck, Piddle and Wriggle Valley served by helpful staff, also dining rooms with traditional chairs and tables and well liked pubby food from baguettes up using own farm produce; children and dogs (in bar) welcome, sunny back garden with seats on grass and beneath a pergola, picnic-sets at front, 12 freshly redecorated bedrooms and lovely breakfasts, open all day.

ASKERSWELL
SY5393
★ Spyway Inn (01308) 485250
Off A35 Bridport–Dorchester; DT2 9EP Popular country local, once a smugglers' lookout, near Eggardon hill fort, one of the highest points in the region; unspoilt little rooms with cushioned wall and window seats, old photos, jugs hanging from beams and a Rayburn, also dining area with oak beams, timber uprights and woodburning stove and two smaller rooms; Otter Bitter and a guest from Cerne Abbas or Copper Street on handpump, nine wines by the glass, pleasing fair priced food including sandwiches; children and dogs (in bar) welcome, two comfortable bedrooms and good breakfasts, seats on back terrace and in garden with lovely views of downs and coast.

BLANDFORD FORUM
ST8806
Crown (01258) 456626
West Street; DT11 7AJ Civilised brick-built Georgian hotel on edge of town; spacious well patronised bar/dining area including snug with leather armchairs and roaring fire, full range of Badger ales from nearby brewery, numerous wines by the glass, cocktails, teas and coffee, good food from sandwiches and small plates up, separate restaurant; children welcome, dogs in bar, tables on big terrace with formal garden beyond, 27 refurbished bedrooms, open (and food) all day.

BOURNEMOUTH
SZ1092
Cricketers Arms (01202) 551589
Windham Road; BH1 4RN Well preserved Victorian pub near the station; separate public and lounge bars, tiled fireplaces and lots of dark wood, etched windows and stained glass, Fullers London Pride and two quickly changing guests, food includes bar snacks (home-made scotch eggs) and Sun roasts; quiz Tues, regular live music including folk, jazz and bands; children welcome, dogs in bar, picnic-sets out in front, open all day.

BOURNEMOUTH
SZ0891
Goat & Tricycle (01202) 314220
West Hill Road; BH2 5PF Interesting Edwardian local (two former pubs knocked together) with rambling split-level interior; Wadworths ales and guests from pillared bar's impressive rank of ten handpumps, real cider, reasonably priced pubby food, friendly staff; background music, Sun quiz; no under-18s, dogs welcome, good disabled access, part-covered yard, open (and food) all day.

BOURTON
ST7731
★ White Lion (01747) 840866
High Street, off old A303 E of Wincanton; SP8 5AT Welcoming low-beamed 18th-c stone pub, originally a series of cottages, in north of Dorset not far from Stourhead (NT); character interior with bare boards, flagstones, stripped stone, half-panelling and log fire in inglenook fireplace, traditional bar and two-level dining room with old wooden furniture, bow window seats, church candles and fresh flowers, Otter Amber and couple of guest beers such as Keystone Bedrock and Wriggle Valley Copper Hoppa on handpump, several wines by the glass, helpful staff, well liked rustic food; background music; children and dogs welcome, picnic-sets on back terrace and raised lawn, comfortable bedrooms, open all day.

BRIDPORT
SY4692
George (01308) 423187
South Street; DT6 3NQ Relaxed and welcoming old town pub; good food from open kitchen cooked by landlord-chef including daily specials, well kept Palmers and guests, decent wines by the glass, attentive friendly service; children and dogs welcome, disabled facilities, open all day (from 10am for brunch on Sat market day), closed Sun evening.

BRIDPORT
SY4692
Ropemakers (01308) 421255
West Street; DT6 3QP Long rambling town-centre pub with lots of pictures and memorabilia, well kept Palmers ales and enjoyable home-made food from sandwiches up (they cater for special diets), good friendly service; regular live music weekends, Tues quiz, cheese tasting second Wed of month; children and dogs welcome, tables in nicely planted back courtyard, open all day except Sun evening.

BRIDPORT SY4692

Tiger (01308) 427543

Barrack Street, off South Street; DT6 3LY
Cheerful and attractive open-plan Victorian
beamed pub with Sharps Doom Bar and
five quickly changing guests, real ciders, no
food except breakfast for residents, cocktail
bar open Fri and Sat evenings; darts, sports
TV, dogs welcome, seats in two heated
courtyards, seven bedrooms, open all day.

BUCKLAND NEWTON ST6804

Gaggle of Geese (01300) 345249

Locketts Lane; E end of village; DT2 7BS
Very family-friendly Victorian country pub;
Sharps Doom Bar and other well kept West
Country beers, good home-made food from
sandwiches up, log-fire in bar, separate
restaurant; live music and quiz nights, skittle
alley; dogs welcome, four acres of gardens
including terrace, orchard and pizza oven,
also soft play area, crazy golf and pygmy
goats, camping and shepherd's huts, closed
Mon, otherwise open (and food) all day, till
8pm (5pm) Sun.

BURTON BRADSTOCK SY4889

Anchor (01308) 897228

B3157 SE of Bridport; DT6 4QF Friendly
helpful staff in good restaurant serving local
fish and nice steaks, village pub part too with
blackboard choices from baguettes up, ales
such as Dorset, St Austell and Sharps, decent
wines by the glass, several malt whiskies and
gin menu; games including table skittles;
children and dogs (in bar) welcome, three
bedrooms, open all day.

BURTON BRADSTOCK SY4889

★Three Horseshoes (01308) 897259

Mill Street; DT6 4QZ Popular and
welcoming thatched pub near lovely sandy
beach; bar with sofas in bow windows, old
dining chairs and tables, built-in cushioned
wall seats, button-back armchairs by
woodburning stove, decorations including
bird prints, horsebrasses, mirrors and
farming implements, similarly furnished
dining room, well kept Palmers Copper,
Dorset Gold, IPA, Tally Ho, 200 and seasonal
guests on handpump, 12 wines (including
prosecco) by the glass, enjoyable food
including sandwiches using seasonal local
produce cooked by Dutch chef-landlord;
background music and board games; children
and dogs (in bar) welcome, rustic tables and
chairs out in front, more in back garden with
terrace, open all day in summer and gets
busy at peak times.

CERNE ABBAS ST6601

Royal Oak (01300) 341797

Long Street; DT2 7JG Creeper-clad
16th-c thatched village-centre pub; low black
beams, flagstones and rustic memorabilia,
nice log fire, well kept ales including local
Cerne Abbas, good home-made food using

local produce from lunchtime sandwiches
to daily specials, friendly helpful service;
some live music; children and dogs welcome,
small back garden, open all day Fri-Sun, may
close Tues in winter – best to check times
before you go.

CHEDINGTON ST4805

Winyards Gap (01935) 891244

A356 Dorchester–Crewkerne; DT8 3HY
Attractive dining pub surrounded by NT land
with spectacular views over Parrett Valley
into Somerset; enjoyable food including
Sun carvery, four well kept changing ales,
local ciders, friendly helpful service, bar
with woodburner, steps down to restaurant,
skittle alley/dining room; children and
dogs welcome, tables on front lawn under
parasols, good walks, four comfortable
bedrooms and two self-catering studios,
open all day weekends, closed Mon.

CHETNOLE ST6008

★Chetnole Inn (01935) 872337

Village signed off A37 S of Yeovil;
DT9 6NU Attractive country pub with
relaxed country kitchen feel, beamed bar
with wheelback chairs and pine tables on
huge flagstones and woodburning stove,
plus snug with leather sofa and another
woodburner, and airy dining room; Butcombe
Rare Breed, Wriggle Valley Golden Bear,
Ringwood Old Thumper and guest on tap, ten
wines by the glass, tempting food including
sandwiches, friendly staff; children and
dogs (in snug) welcome, three comfortable
bedrooms, delightful garden with picnic sets
overlooking rolling pasture, good walks in
lovely countryside, open all day weekends,
closed Mon, Sun evening.

CHIDEOCK SY4191

★Anchor (01297) 489215

Off A35 from Chideock; DT6 6JU
Delightful old pub in stunning location on
the beach beneath Golden Cap (highest cliff
on the south coast) by South West Coast
Path; character interior in three smallish
light rooms with padded wall seats, nice old
wooden chairs and stools around scrubbed
tables on bare boards, two woodburning
stoves (one under a huge bressumer beam),
tilley lamps, model ships and lots of historic
local photos; Palmers Copper, Dorset Gold,
IPA and guest ale on handpump, seven
wines by the glass, 25 gins, 40-plus rums and
cocktails, highly regarded food with focus
on fresh fish/seafood; background music;
children and dogs (in bar) welcome, three
smart stylish bedrooms overlooking the sea,
much prized tables on spacious front terrace,
open (and food) all day.

CHIDEOCK SY4292

George (01297) 489419

A35 Bridport–Lyme Regis; DT6 6JD
Welcoming thatched pub with cosy low-
beamed rooms; well kept Palmers ales, real

cider and popular straightforward food from shortish menu (also some daily specials), good service, warm log fires; background and some live music, monthly quiz; children and dogs welcome (pub dog is Ramsey), pretty walled garden with terrace and wood-fired pizza oven, closed Tues and Wed lunchtimes and Sun evening, otherwise open all day.

CHILD OKEFORD ST8213
Saxon (01258) 860310
Signed off A350 Blandford–Shaftesbury and A357 Blandford–Sherborne; Gold Hill; DT11 8HD Welcoming early 18th-c village pub under new management – changes include updated bar area with cosy log fire, new food menu (still with changing specials) and wine list; Butcombe, Otter and guest ales, two dining areas, efficient friendly service; board games and shove-ha'penny; children and dogs welcome, large attractive back garden and covered terrace; good walks on Neolithic Hambledon Hill, three comfortable bedrooms, open all day Sat, Sun.

CHRISTCHURCH SZ1593
Rising Sun (01202) 486122
Purewell; BH23 1EJ Comfortably modernised old pub and restaurant specialising in good authentic Thai and pan-Asian food, L-shaped bar serving Flack Manor Double Drop, Sharps Doom Bar and good choice of wines by the glass, pleasant helpful young staff; all weather terrace with palms and rattan furniture under large umbrellas, open all day.

CORFE CASTLE SY9681
Castle Inn (01929) 480208
East Street; BH20 5EE Welcoming little two-room pub mentioned in Hardy's *The Hand of Ethelberta*; up to three real ales and popular generously served food including Fri fish night, special diets catered for, accommodating friendly service, heavy black beams with fairy lights, exposed stone walls, flagstones and woodburner; background music; children welcome, no dogs inside, back terrace and big sunny garden with mature trees, steam train views, open all day.

CORFE CASTLE SY9682
Greyhound (01929) 480205
A351; The Square; BH20 5EZ Bustling picturesque old pub in the centre of this tourist village; three small low-ceilinged panelled rooms, steps and corridors, well kept ales such as Palmers, Ringwood and Sharps, local cider and good range of other drinks, nice food from ciabattas, light dishes and pizzas up, friendly staff coping well at busy times, traditional games including Purbeck longboard shove-ha'penny, family room; background and weekend live music;

dogs welcome, garden with large decked area, great views of castle and countryside, pretty courtyard opening on to castle bridge, open (and food) all day, best to book ahead in summer.

CORSCOMBE ST5205
Fox (01935) 892381
Towards Halstock: Hight Street into Fudge Street, L into Court Lane, L into Court Hill; DT2 0NS Very attractive thatched and rose-clad 16th-c country pub; beams, flagstones, built-in settles and log fires, well liked food using seasonal local produce, three well kept West Country ales, friendly efficient young staff, conservatory; regular live music, darts and skittles; children and dogs welcome (they have a labrador, Rudy, and a jack russell, Charlie), streamside lawn across lane, two annexe bedrooms (no breakfast), open all day Sun, closed Mon and Tues.

CRANBORNE SU0513
Fleur de Lys (01725) 551249
Wimborne Street (B3078 N of Wimborne); BH21 5PP New licensees for this attractive 16th-c inn (formerly Inn at Cranborne) with chatty relaxed atmosphere and rambling rooms with heavy beams; main bar has built-in wall seats and assorted chairs (farmhouse, wheelback, ladderback) on pale flagstones and woodburner in inglenook fireplace, also spreading dining areas with another woodburner, well kept Badger ales on handpump served by friendly helpful staff, highly rated food specialises in cooking with fire, in wood-fired oven or on grill; children welcome, dogs allowed everywhere, huge covered area for sheltered outdoor eating plus tables and chairs on gravel, nine bright bedrooms and excellent breakfasts (including for dogs and non-residents), on the edge of Cranborne Chase, open all day.

DEWLISH SY7798
Oak (01258) 837352
Off A354 Dorchester–Blandford Forum; DT2 7ND Welcoming red-brick village pub; two or three well kept local ales and enjoyable good value food including specials and popular Sun lunch, friendly helpful service, woodburner and open fire in bar; pool, Sun quiz; children welcome, good-sized garden behind, three bedrooms and self-catering cottage.

DORCHESTER SY6990
Blue Raddle (01305) 267762
Church Street, near central short-stay car park; DT1 1JN Cheery pubby atmosphere in long carpeted and partly panelled bar, well kept ales such as Cerne Abbas, Dartmoor, Palmers, St Austell

---

Post Office address codings confusingly give the impression that some pubs are in Dorset, when they're really in Somerset (which is where we list them).

and guest, local ciders, good wines and coffee, enjoyable simple home-made food (lunchtimes Weds-Sat, evenings Thurs-Sat), efficient friendly service; cribbage team; no under-14s, dogs welcome, good disabled access apart from one step, open all day Fri-Sun, closed Mon and Tues lunchtimes.

EAST CHALDON   SY7983
Sailors Return (01305) 854441
Village signposted from A352 Wareham–Dorchester; from village green, follow Dorchester, Weymouth signpost; note that the village is also known as Chaldon Herring; OS Sheet 194 map reference 790834; DT2 8DN Thatched village pub with five well kept ales such as Cerne Abbas, Flack Manor, Palmers, Otter and Ringwood, several ciders, short menu using local seasonal produce, Weds pie night, friendly attentive service, flagstoned bar and various dining areas; Tues winter quiz; children welcome, dogs in bar (no food in bar Fri evening), picnic-sets out at front and in side garden, useful for coast path, open all day weekends, closed Mon.

EAST MORDEN   SY9194
★Cock & Bottle (01929) 459238
B3075 W of Poole; BH20 7DL Popular extended dining pub with wide choice of good food including specials (best to book), separate traditional bar with open fire, well kept Badger ales and nice selection of wines by the glass, efficient cheerful service; children and dogs allowed in certain areas, outside seating and pleasant pastoral outlook, closed Sun evening.

EAST STOUR   ST8123
Kings Arms (01747) 838325
A30, 2 miles E of village; The Common; SP8 5NB Extended 17th-c inn serving locally sourced traditional pub food (special diets catered for) including popular all-day Sun carvery (best to book), real ales including Sharps Doom Bar, Aspall's cider, friendly efficient staff, open fire in bar, airy dining area with light wood furniture, Scottish pictures and Burns quotes; gentle background music; children and dogs (in bar) welcome, good disabled access, picnic-sets in big garden, bluebell walks nearby, three bedrooms, open all day Sun.

FIDDLEFORD   ST8013
Fiddleford Inn (01258) 472886
A357 Sturminster Newton–Blandford Forum; DT10 2BX Beamed roadside pub with three linked areas; modern charcoal paintwork blending with traditional furnishings, old flagstones, carpets and some exposed stone and brick, two-way woodburner, well kept ales, good traditional food including Sun carvery, friendly young staff; children and dogs welcome, big fenced garden, four bedrooms, open (and food) all day, kitchen closes 6.30pm Sun.

FONTMELL MAGNA   ST8616
Fontmell (01747) 811441
A350 S of Shaftesbury; SP7 0PA Imposing dining pub with rooms, much emphasis on the enterprising modern cooking, but also some more straightforward cheaper dishes (own rare-breed pork), good wine list, a house beer (Sibeth) from Keystone and two West Country guests, small bar area with comfy sofas and easy chairs, restaurant overlooking fast-flowing stream that runs under the building; garden across road with two wood-fired pizza ovens, six comfortable well appointed bedrooms, open all day from 10am.

GILLINGHAM   ST7926
Buffalo (01747) 823759
Off B3081 at Wyke 1 mile NW of Gillingham, pub 100 metres on left; SP8 4NJ Welcoming family-run local with Badger beers; two linked bars and restaurant serving generous helpings of popular well priced Italian food (best to book), friendly attentive service; background and some live music; children welcome, back terrace by car park, open till 7pm Sun, closed Mon lunchtime.

HINTON ST MARY   ST7816
White Horse (01258) 472723
Just off B3092 a mile N of Sturminster; DT10 1NA Welcoming traditional little village pub dating from the early 17th c; good varied choice of food including pizzas from wood-fired oven and fresh local fish/seafood (best to book), own-brew beers and decent house wines, unusual inglenook fireplace in cheerful bar, extended dining room; children, walkers and dogs welcome, picnic-sets in small well maintained garden, attractive setting, closed Sun evening, all day Mon.

HOLT   SU0304
Old Inn (01202) 883029
Holt Lane; beside the church; BH21 7DJ Updated red-brick Badger dining pub, their ales kept well and good range of wines and gins, tasty food including wood-fired pizzas and Mon steak night, quick friendly service, mix of pubby furniture on wood-strip floors, beams and log fire; children and dogs welcome, picnic-sets on front terrace, more tables in part-covered back garden, open all day weekends.

HURN   SZ1397
Avon Causeway (01202) 482714
Village signed off A338, then follow Avon, Sopley, Matchams sign; BH23 6AS Comfortable and spacious hotel/dining pub with enjoyable food from sandwiches and pub favourites up, well kept Wadworths ales, helpful staff, interesting railway decorations and coach restaurant (used for functions) by former 1870s station platform; children and dogs welcome, disabled access, nice garden

(some road noise) with play area, 12 good value bedrooms, near Bournemouth Airport (2 weeks' free parking if you stay before or after you fly), open all day, food all day Sun.

IBBERTON   ST7807
Ibberton (01258) 817956
Village W of Blandford Forum; DT11 0EN Welcoming 16th-c village pub in beautiful spot under Bulbarrow Hill; beamed and flagstoned bar with inglenook woodburner, three local beers and Dorset Orchards' cider from brick-faced servery, popular good value food including traditional choices, friendly helpful staff, two dining areas (one carpeted, the other where dogs allowed); children welcome, picnic-sets in front/side garden with stream, good walks, closed Mon, Tues and Sun evening.

LANGTON MATRAVERS   SY9978
Kings Arms (01929) 422979
High Street; BH19 3HA Friendly old-fashioned village local; ancient flagstoned corridor to bar, simple rooms off, one with a fine fireplace made from local marble, beers including Ringwood and enjoyable good value pubby food, cheerful helpful staff, splendid antique Purbeck longboard shove-ha'penny; children and dogs welcome, sunny picnic-sets outside, good walks including to Dancing Ledge, open all day.

LYME REGIS   SY3492
Cellar 59 (01297) 445086
Broad Street; DT7 3QF Flagstoned cellar bar with up to 14 real ales/craft kegs chalked on blackboard including their own Gyle 59 unfined beers, tasting trays available, snacks (can bring your own food too), friendly knowledgeable staff, shop above selling wide range of bottled/canned beers from home and abroad; outside seating area, well behaved children (until 7pm) and dogs welcome, open from noon weekends, 4pm weekdays, closed Mon (hours may change so best to check).

LYME REGIS   SY3391
Cobb Arms (01297) 443242
Marine Parade, Monmouth Beach; DT7 3JF Spacious recently refurbished restaurant-pub overlooking seafront, with well kept Palmers ales, decent wines and good choice of reasonably priced freshly cooked food (gluten-free options available), cream teas, quick service, a couple of sofas, ship pictures and marine fish tank, open fire; children and dogs welcome, disabled access (one step up from road), tables on small back terrace, well located next to harbour, beach and coastal walk, three bedrooms, open all day.

LYME REGIS   SY3391
Harbour Inn (01297) 442299
Marine Parade; DT7 3JF More eating than pubby with thriving family atmosphere; generally very well liked food from lunchtime sandwiches to local fish/seafood (not particularly cheap, booking advised in season), special diets catered for, Otter and St Austell ales, good choice of wines by the glass, tea and coffee, friendly service, clean-cut modern décor keeping some original flagstones and stone walls (lively acoustic), paintings for sale, sea views from front windows; background and occasional live music; dogs welcome, disabled access from street, tables on verandah and beachside terrace, open all day.

LYME REGIS   SY3492
Pilot Boat (01297) 443157
Bridge Street; DT7 3QA Popular bow-fronted pub with smart modern look near the waterfront; Palmers ales, good choice of wines by the glass and cocktails, enjoyable food including sandwiches, home-made pizzas and freshly caught fish/seafood, can eat in bar or separate restaurant with open kitchen, helpful friendly staff; Weds live music, Thurs quiz; children and dogs welcome, roof terrace, three boutique bedrooms (one with sea view), open (and food) all day from 8am.

LYME REGIS   SY3492
Volunteer (01297) 442214
Top of Broad Street (A3052 towards Exeter); DT7 3QE Cosy old-fashioned pub with long low-ceilinged bar, nice mix of customers (can get crowded), a well kept house beer from Branscombe Vale tapped from the cask and West Country guests, enjoyable modestly priced food in dining lounge (children allowed here), friendly young staff, roaring fires; dogs welcome, open all day.

MARNHULL   ST7719
Blackmore Vale (01258) 820701
Burton Street, via Church Hill off B3092; DT10 1JJ Atmospheric old stone-built village pub (was closed for a couple of years); three well kept local ales and decent food including Fri fish and chips, opened-up beamed and flagstoned bar with woodburner, more flagstones and oak flooring in cosy smaller bar with log fire; occasional live music, no mobile phones; walkers and dogs welcome, garden tables, open all day Sat, till 7pm Sun, closed Mon – but hours can vary, best to check.

MARNHULL   ST7818
Crown (01258) 820224
About 3 miles N of Sturminster Newton; Crown Road; DT10 1LN Part-thatched inn dating from the 16th c (the Pure Drop in Hardy's *Tess of the D'Urbervilles*); linked rooms with oak beams, huge flagstones or bare boards, log fire in big stone hearth in oldest part, more modern furnishings and carpet elsewhere, Badger ales, plenty of wines by the glass and over 50 gins, enjoyable generously served food including Sun carvery,

special diets catered for, good friendly service, restaurant; children welcome, peaceful enclosed garden, six bedrooms, open all day.

MARTINSTOWN   SY6488
Brewers Arms (01305) 889361
Burnside (B3159); DT2 9LB Friendly family-run village pub (former 19th-c school) with attractively updated interior; good reasonably priced home-made food from lunchtime baguettes to specials, vegan/vegetarian options and popular Tues curry night, real and craft ales from local breweries, children and dogs welcome, picnic-sets out at front and in courtyard, historic sheepwash pool nearby (start of the annual plastic duck race), good local walks, two bedrooms, closed Sun evening and Mon.

MILTON ABBAS   ST8001
Hambro Arms (01258) 880233
Signed off A354 SW of Blandford; DT11 0BP Nicely updated beamed pub in beautiful late 18th-c thatched village; recently refurbished bar and lounge, separate restaurant, well kept local ales and decent choice of wines, classic pub food including specials, special diets catered for, live music monthly, efficient friendly service; children welcome, dogs in bar, tables on front terrace, four bedrooms, open (and food) all day.

MOTCOMBE   ST8426
Coppleridge (01747) 851980
Signed from The Street, follow to Mere/ Gillingham; SP7 9HW Welcoming country inn (former 18th-c farmhouse) with traditional bar and various dining rooms, good home-made food from ciabattas and pub favourites up including some imaginative choices, Thurs steak night, ales such as Butcombe and decent wines by the glass, friendly helpful staff; children welcome, dogs in bar and garden room, ten spacious courtyard bedrooms, barn function room (popular wedding venue), 15-acre grounds with play area and two tennis courts, lovely views over Dorset countryside, open all day.

NORDEN HEATH   SY94834
Halfway (01929) 480402
A351 Wareham–Corfe Castle; BH20 5DU Cosily laid-out partly thatched 16th-c beamed pub halfway between Wareham and Corfe Castle; Badger beers, nice wines by the glass and enjoyable freshly cooked food including vegetarian dishes, good friendly service, front rooms with flagstones, stripped stone and woodburners, snug little side area, pitched-ceiling back room and new heated garden room; dogs welcome, picnic-sets on paved terrace and lawn, good nearby walks, open all day, food all day in school holidays.

OSMINGTON MILLS   SY7381
Smugglers (01305) 833125
Off A353 NE of Weymouth; DT3 6HF

Old partly thatched family-oriented inn set down from the road near the sea; well extended, with cosy dimly lit timber-divided areas, woodburners, old local pictures, Badger ales, guest beers and several wines by the glass, food generally good, service friendly and helpful; dogs welcome, picnic-sets on crazy paving in large outside area by little stream, thatched summer bar, lovely sea views from car park, useful for South West Coast Path, four bedrooms, open (and food) all day, can get busy.

PAMPHILL   ST9900
★Vine (01202) 882259
Off B3082 on NW edge of Wimborne: turn on to Cowgrove Hill at Cowgrove sign, then left up Vine Hill; BH21 4EE Simple old-fashioned place run by same family for three generations and part of Kingston Lacy Estate (NT); two tiny bars with coal-effect gas fire, handful of tables and seats on lino, narrow wooden stairs up to room with darts, a couple of real ales, local cider and foreign bottled beers, lunchtime bar snacks; quiet background music, no credit cards, outside lavatories; children (away from bar) and dogs welcome, verandah with spreading grapevine, sheltered gravel terrace and grassy area, Sept pumpkin and conkers festival.

PIDDLEHINTON   SY7197
Thimble (01300) 348270
High Street (B3143); DT2 7TD Spacious thatched pub with log fires and deep glassed-over well in low-beamed room; good freshly made food catering for special diets from baguettes up including range of burgers, well kept Palmers ales, friendly welcoming staff; background and live music; children and dogs (in bar) welcome, disabled facilities, valley views from garden with stream, open (and food) all day.

POOLE   SZ0391
Bermuda Triangle (01202) 748087
Parr Street, Lower Parkstone (just off A35 at Ashley Cross); BH14 0JY Quirky 19th-c bare-boards local on different levels; four well kept changing ales, two or three good continental lagers and many other beers from around the world, friendly staff, no food, dark panelling, snug old corners and lots of nautical and other bric-a-brac; background and some live music; no children and a bit too steppy for disabled access, new decked seating area outside, open all day Fri-Sun.

POOLE   SZ0190
Poole Arms (01202) 673450
Town Quay; BH15 1HJ Friendly 17th-c waterfront pub looking over harbour to Brownsea Island; one comfortably old-fashioned room with boarded ceiling and nautical prints, popular much enjoyed food (predominantly fresh fish/seafood) at fair prices, four well kept ales such as Ringwood

and St Austell, good service; outside gents';
no children, picnic-sets in front of the
handsome green-tiled façade, almost next
door to the Portsmouth Hoy, open all day.

POOLE   SZ0090
Portsmouth Hoy (01202) 673517
The Quay; BH15 1HJ Harbourside
nautical-themed pub with views to Brownsea
Island; old-world atmosphere with dark wood,
beams and bare boards, well kept Badger
ales and popular food including fresh fish,
friendly service; children and dogs welcome,
outside tables shared with the Poole Arms,
open all day.

POOLE   SZ0090
Rope & Anchor (01202) 675677
Sarum Street; BH15 1JW Split-level
Wadworths pub next to Poole Museum; good
food including fresh fish, well kept beers
and some nice wines by the glass, friendly
accommodating staff; background music
(live Fri), daily papers, children and dogs
welcome, seats on back terrace, open (and
food) all day.

PORTLAND   SY6873
Cove House (01305) 820895
*Follow Chiswell signposts – pub is
at NW corner of Portland; DT5 1AW*
Low-beamed traditional 18th-c pub in superb
position, effectively built into sea defences
just above the end of Chesil Beach, great
views from three-room bar's bay windows;
DBC Jurassic, Sharps Doom Bar and other
well kept beers, good freshly cooked food
including blackboard fish specials (booking
advised), friendly efficient service, steep
steps down to gents'; background music,
children and dogs welcome, tables out
by seawall, open all day, food all day at
weekends, check website for opening times
during the week.

PORTLAND   SY6872
George (01305) 820011
Reforne; DT5 2AP Cheery 17th-c
stone-built local (one of Portland's oldest
buildings); small beamed rooms with low
doorways, some tables carved with names
of generations of sailors and quarrymen,
interesting prints and mementoes, log fires,
well kept Greene King Abbot, guest beers
and real ciders, enjoyable pubby food from
baguettes and toasties up; weekend live
music, darts; children and dogs welcome,
picnic-sets in walled back garden, closed till
3pm Mon and Tues, otherwise open all day.

POWERSTOCK   SY5196
Three Horseshoes (01308) 485328
*Off A3066 Beaminster–Bridport via West
Milton; DT6 3TF* Tucked-away village pub

with cheerful cosy bar, stripped panelling,
windsor and mate's chairs around assorted
tables on bare boards, Palmers ales and
several wines by the glass, good freshly made
food including specials; children and dogs
welcome, picnic-sets on back terrace with
garden and country views, good surrounding
walks, three comfortable bedrooms, closed
Sun evening, Mon lunchtime.

PUDDLETOWN   SY7594
Blue Vinny (01305) 848228
The Moor; DT2 8TE Large modernised
village pub with beamed oak-floor bar and
restaurant, good choice of highly regarded
well presented food from lunchtime
baguettes up (booking advised), special
diets catered for, well kept ales, friendly
helpful young staff; children welcome, dogs
allowed in one part, terrace overlooking
garden with play area, open all day Fri-Sun,
no food Sun evening.

PUNCKNOWLE   SY5388
Crown (01308) 897711
*Off B3157 Bridport–Abbotsbury;
DT2 9BN* Welcoming 16th-c thatched
inn continuing well under new family
management; traditional locally sourced
food from sandwiches up, Palmers ales and
decent choice of wines by the glass, beams
and inglenook log fires; children and dogs
(in bar, garden and bedrooms) welcome,
disabled facilities, valley views from
peaceful pretty back garden, good walks,
two bedrooms, open all day Sat, till 6pm
Sun, closed Mon.

SANDFORD ORCAS   ST6220
★**Mitre** (01963) 220271
*Off B3148 and B3145 N of Sherborne;
DT9 4RU* Thriving tucked-away country
local with welcoming long-serving licensees;
three well kept changing ales and proper
ciders, wholesome home-made food (not
Mon) from good soup and sandwiches up,
flagstones, log fires and fresh flowers, small
bar and larger pleasantly homely dining
area; occasional open mike nights, games
including shove-ha'penny and dominoes;
children and dogs welcome, pretty back
garden with terrace, good local walks (on
Macmillan Way and Monarch's Way), closed
Sun evening, all Mon, Tues lunchtime.

SHAFTESBURY   ST8622
★**Grosvenor Arms** (01747) 850580
High Street; SP7 8JA Handy for the town
centre, this relaxed hotel has a civilised back
bar with sofas, armchairs and cushioned
settles, a woodburning stove and antlers on
partly panelled walls – a conservatory area
overlooking a central courtyard links this bar
with several dining rooms; Otter Bitter and

We say if we know a pub has background music.

a guest such as Wriggle Valley Golden Bear on handpump and 20 wines by the glass, well regarded food including sandwiches, pizzas and afternoon tea, friendly, helpful service; comfortable modern bedrooms, children welcome, dogs in bar and bedrooms, open (and food) all day.

SHAPWICK ST9301
Anchor (01258) 857269

Off A350 Blandford–Poole; West Street; DT11 9LB Welcoming red-brick Victorian pub owned by village consortium; popular freshly made food (booking advised) including blackboard specials and cream teas, vegan and other diets catered for, local ales, real cider, good friendly service, scrubbed pine tables on wood floors, pastel walls and open fires; children and dogs welcome, tables out in front, more in attractive back garden with terrace, outdoor wood-fired oven, handy for Kingston Lacy (NT), closed Sun evening, Mon, otherwise open all day.

STOBOROUGH SY9286
Kings Arms (01929) 552705

B3075 S of Wareham; Corfe Road opposite petrol station; BH20 5AB Popular part-thatched 17th-c village pub, well kept Isle of Purbeck, Ringwood and up to three guests, good fairly priced food in bar and restaurant from snacks and pub favourites up including some interesting specials, cheerful efficient staff; children and dogs welcome, disabled access/loos, flower-decked terrace and garden with play area, views over marshes to River Frome, open all day during summer school holidays (all day Fri-Sun at other times).

STOKE ABBOTT ST4500
★ **New Inn** (01308) 868333

Off B3162 and B3163 2 miles W of Beaminster; DT8 3JW Welcoming 17th-c pub in unspoilt thatched village with nice surrounding walks; well kept Palmers ales and good home-cooked local food including daily specials, woodburner in big inglenook, beams, brasses and copper, some handsome panelling, flagstoned dining room; children and dogs (in bar) welcome, wheelchair access, two attractive gardens, street fair third Sat in July, closed Sun evening, all Mon and Tues lunchtime.

STOURPAINE ST8609
White Horse (01258) 453535

Shaston Road; A350 NW of Blandford; DT11 8TA Traditional country local extended from early 18th-c core (originally two cottages); popular fairly pubby food including OAP deal, five well kept ales, traditional cider and over 70 gins, good friendly service, open-plan layout with pine tables on bare boards, woodburners, games part with pool, militaria display, also incorporates post office and village shop;

quiz, regular live music; dogs welcome in bar, seats out at front and on back decking, open all day, no food Mon evening.

STOURTON CAUNDLE ST7115
Trooper (01963) 362405

Village signed off A30 E of Milborne Port; DT10 2JW Pretty little stone-built pub under new management in lovely village setting (Enid Blyton's house opposite); friendly staff and atmosphere, a couple of well kept changing beers, a real cider and good range of gins, tiny low-ceilinged bar, stripped-stone dining room, darts, dominoes and shove-ha'penny, skittle alley, outside gents'; background music, folk night second Sun of month; children, walkers and dogs welcome, a few picnic-sets out in front, pleasant side garden and new back courtyard, camping (from 2021), closed Mon and Tues and lunchtimes Weds and Thurs, call for food times.

STRATTON SY6593
Saxon Arms (01305) 260020

Off A37 NW of Dorchester; The Square; DT2 9WG Traditional flint-and-thatch local; spacious open-plan interior with light oak tables and comfortable settles on flagstones or carpet, log fire, well kept Butcombe, Timothy Taylors Landlord and two guests, good value wines, tasty generously served food including deli boards and good choice of specials, pleasant efficient service, large comfortable dining section on right; background music, traditional games; children and dogs welcome, terrace tables overlooking village green, open (and food) all day Fri-Sun.

STUDLAND SZ0382
Bankes Arms (01929) 450225

Off B3351, Isle of Purbeck; Manor Road; BH19 3AU Historic 16th-c Purbeck stone inn at beginning of Jurassic Coast Path above fine beach, outstanding country, sea and cliff views from huge garden over road with lots of seating; comfortably traditional big bar with raised drinking area, beams, flagstones and large log fire, nine real ales including own Isle of Purbeck, local cider, decent wines by the glass and home-made food including pub classics; over-8s and dogs welcome, just off coast path near to Old Harry Rocks, can get very busy on summer weekends (parking in NT car park), ten bedrooms (Studland Bay views from front ones), open (and food) all day.

STURMINSTER MARSHALL SY9499
Golden Fox (01258) 857217

A350; BH21 4AQ Roadside country pub with popular good value food, up to three real ales such as Dartmoor and Hop Back, friendly helpful service, long comfortable beamed and panelled bar with log fire; games machines; children and dogs (in bar) welcome, terrace seating, open all day Fri-Sun, closed Tues.

STURMINSTER NEWTON ST7813
Bull (01258) 472435
A357, S of centre; DT10 2BS
Cosy thatched and beamed 15th-c pub, well
kept Badger ales and enjoyable good value
home-made food including daily specials,
friendly helpful staff, log fires; children and
dogs welcome, roadside picnic-sets, more in
small back garden, closed Sun evening, Mon,
otherwise open all day.

SWANAGE SZ0278
Red Lion (01929) 423533
High Street; BH19 2LY Popular and
unpretentious low-beamed local with great
choice of ciders and up to six well kept ales
such as Hop Back, Otter, Sharps and Timothy
Taylors, good value food including Weds curry
night and Fri steak night, quick friendly
service, brasses around log fire, restaurant;
background and some live music, pool, darts
and fruit machine; children welcome till
9pm, picnic-sets in garden with part-covered
terrace, five bedrooms in former back coach
house, open all day.

SYDLING ST NICHOLAS SY6399
Greyhound (01300) 341303
*Off A37 N of Dorchester; High Street;
DT2 9PD* Former coaching inn with beamed
and flagstoned serving area, woodburner in
brick fireplace, hops above counter, three
well kept changing ales and a couple of
proper ciders, carpeted bar with Portland
stone fireplace, painted panelling and
exposed stonework, popular food including
good value set lunch, friendly welcoming
staff, covered well in cosy dining room,
flagstoned conservatory; children and dogs
(in bar) welcome, picnic-sets in little front
garden, six comfortable bedrooms, open all
day Sat and Sun.

TARRANT MONKTON ST9408
★ Langton Arms (01258) 830225
*Village signposted from A354, then head
for church; DT11 8RX* Bustling thatched
pub in picturesque spot next to 15th-c
church; high-backed dining chairs around
wooden tables on flagstones, a cushioned
window seat and a few high chairs against
light oak counter, Flack Manor Double
Drop and guests, real cider and decent
choice of wines and whiskies, popular food
using meat from own farm, two connecting
beamed dining rooms with cushioned wooden
chairs around white-clothed tables, airy
conservatory; background music, board
games, skittle alley; children and dogs (in
bar) welcome, seats out at front and in back
garden with play area, bedrooms in brick
buildings around courtyard, open all day, food
all day weekends.

TOLPUDDLE SY7994
Martyrs (01305) 848249
Former A35 W of Bere Regis; DT2 7ES

1920s traditional village dining pub with
enjoyable home-made food including Mon
curry, Fri fish and chips and chips and Sun carvery,
cream teas, two or three Badger ales, friendly
accommodating staff, opened-up bare-boards
interior; background and live music, children
welcome, good disabled access, small front
terrace and garden behind, open (and food)
all day.

TRENT ST5818
★ Rose & Crown (01935) 850776
Opposite the church; DT9 4SL Partly
thatched pub across from lovely church; cosy
little right-hand bar with sofas in front of
open fire, bigger bar opposite has old wooden
tables and chairs on quarry tiles, Wadworths
ales, a guest beer and 20 wines by the glass,
good food from lunchtime sandwiches and
pub favourites to well presented restaurant
dishes, attentive friendly service, two other
interconnected rooms with pews, grandfather
clock and more fireplaces, simply furnished
back dining room; board games, children and
dogs welcome, parasol-shaded tables in back
garden with fine views, pretty bedrooms in
converted byre, excellent breakfast, open all
day.

UPLODERS SY5093
Crown (01308) 485356
Signed off A35 E of Bridport; DT6 4NU
Attractive stone-built village pub; log
fires, dark low beams, flagstones and mix
of old furniture including stripped pine,
grandfather clock, good traditional home-
made food using local suppliers, three
Palmers ales; background music; children
and dogs (in bar) welcome, tables in pretty
two-tier garden, closed Mon.

WAREHAM SY9287
Kings Arms (01929) 552503
*North Street (A351, N end of town);
BH20 4AD* Traditional thatched town local;
five well kept changing ales, real cider and
decent good value pubby food (till 6pm Sun),
friendly staff, back serving counter and two
bars off flagstoned central corridor, beams
and inglenook log fire, carpeted dining room
to the right, another at the back; some live
music, children and dogs welcome, steps up
to garden behind with circular picnic-sets
and smokers' shelter, open all day.

WAREHAM SY9287
Old Granary (01929) 552010
The Quay; BH20 4LP Fine old brick
building on bank of River Frome – can get
very busy; beamed snug by entrance opening
into main bar with brick walls and new oak
standing timbers, Badger ales and good wines
by the glass, enjoyable fairly standard food
at reasonable prices, friendly young staff,
restaurant area with connecting rooms,
also upstairs river-view dining room; quiet
background music; children and dogs (in
bar) welcome, seats out overlooking the

water and on covered roof terrace, boats for hire over bridge, limited nearby parking, open all day from 9am (10am Sun), food served from brunch on.

WAREHAM   SY9287
Quay Inn (01929) 552735
The Quay; BH20 4LP Comfortable 18th-c pub-restaurant in great waterside position; enjoyable food using locally sourced produce including cook-your-own meat on a hot stone, well kept Isle of Purbeck, Ringwood and Timothy Taylors, friendly attentive service, open fire; weekend live music; children and dogs welcome, front and rear terrace areas and picnic-sets out on quay (boat trips), market day Sat, three bedrooms, parking nearby can be difficult, open all day.

WAREHAM FOREST   SY9089
Silent Woman (01929) 552909
Wareham–Bere Regis; Bere Road; BH20 7PA Quaint old neatly kept dining pub divided by doorways and standing timbers; good choice of enjoyable food including daily specials, Badger ales kept well and plenty of wines by the glass, friendly helpful young staff, traditional furnishings, farm tools and stripped masonry; background music; no children inside, dogs welcome, wheelchair access, plenty of picnic-sets outside including a covered area, walks nearby, opening times vary during the year and it's a popular wedding venue, so best to check it's open.

WAYTOWN   SY4797
Hare & Hounds (01308) 488203
Between B3162 and A3066 N of Bridport; DT6 5LQ Attractive 18th-c country local up and down steps; friendly staff and regulars, well kept Palmers tapped from the cask, local cider, and generous helpings of enjoyable good value food (not Sun evening) including popular Sun lunch, open fire, two small cottagey rooms and pretty dining room; children and dogs welcome, lovely far-reaching Brit Valley views from sizeable well maintained garden with play area.

WEST BAY   SY4690
★ West Bay (01308) 422444
Station Road; DT6 4EW Relaxed newly refurbished inn a short stroll from the busy little harbour and not far from two unspoilt beaches (much visited since three *Broadchurch* TV series were filmed there); friendly simply furnished bar with wheelback and farmhouse chairs around wooden tables on bare boards, plus cosier carpeted dining area, Palmers ales and a seasonal guest, eight wines by the glass, good food with emphasis on fresh fish dishes (best to book); 100-year-old skittle alley; seating in large main garden and small side garden, quiet comfortable bedrooms, open all day in summer.

WEST BEXINGTON   SY5386
Manor Hotel (01308) 897660
Off B3157 SE of Bridport; Beach Road; DT2 9DF Relaxing quietly set restaurant with rooms, with long history and fine sea views; good choice of enjoyable food in beamed cellar bar, flagstoned restaurant or chic new garden room, well kept Otter, Addlestone's and Sheppy's cider and several wines by the glass, children welcome, dogs on leads (not in restaurant), charming well kept garden, close to Chesil Beach, 13 bedrooms.

WEST KNIGHTON   SY7387
New Inn (01305) 852349
Off A352 E of Dorchester; DT2 8PE Extended village inn dating from 1851, with carpeted bar and restaurant; good home-made food using local produce including daily specials and Sun carvery, special diets catered for, a couple of real ales such as Palmers , friendly efficient staff; skittle alley, pool; children welcome, dogs in bar, pleasant setting on edge of quiet village with farmland views, eight bedrooms, good breakfast, open all day Sun.

WEST LULWORTH   SY8280
Lulworth Cove (01929) 400333
Main Road; BH20 5RQ Modernised 400 year old inn on Jurassic Coast, with good range of enjoyable reasonably priced food from baguettes up, well kept Badger ales and several wines by the glass, friendly staff, seaside theme bar with bare boards and painted panelling; children and dogs welcome, picnic-sets on sizeable terrace, short stroll down to cove, 12 nautical themed en-suite bedrooms (some with sea-view balcony), open (and food) all day and can get very busy.

WEST STAFFORD   SY7289
Wise Man (01305) 261970
Signed off A352 Dorchester–Wareham; DT2 8AG Modernised 16th-c thatched and beamed pub near Hardy's Cottage (NT); open-plan interior with flagstone and wood floors, logburner, good food from imaginative varied menu, well kept Butcombe, Fullers and Timothy Taylors, decent choice of wines by the glass, friendly staff; children and dogs welcome, disabled facilities, plenty of seats outside, lovely walks nearby, open all day Sat, till 6.30pm Sun.

WEYMOUTH   SY6778
Boot 07809 440772
High West Street; DT4 8JH Friendly unspoilt characterful 14th-c tavern near the harbour; beams, bare boards, panelling, hooded stone-mullioned windows and coal fires, cosy gently sloping snug, ten well kept ales including Ringwood and other Marstons-related beers (tasting trays available), real cider and good selection of malt whiskies, no food apart from pork pies and pickled eggs

(regulars bring own food on Sun to share);
live music Tues, quiz Weds; disabled access,
pavement tables, open all day.

WEYMOUTH   SY6779
Handmade Pie & Ale House
(01305) 459342 *Queen Street; DT4 7HZ*
Friendly and relaxed place opposite the
station; wide range of good home-made
pies plus burgers and specials, six well kept
changing ales and plenty of ciders, more
dining space in upstairs raftered room;
children welcome, open (and food) all day.

WEYMOUTH   SY6878
Nothe Tavern (01305) 787300
Barrack Road; DT4 8TZ Updated 19th-c
red-brick pub a short walk from the busy
harbour area; enjoyable food from lunchtime
sandwiches and bar snacks up including daily
specials, some vegan choices and weekend
breakfasts, Brakspears, Ringwood and a dozen
wines by the glass, friendly efficient service,
restaurant with harbour and more distant sea
views; children and dogs (in bar) welcome,
more views from terrace, near Nothe Fort,
open all day, food all day Sun till 7pm.

WIMBORNE MINSTER   SZ0199
Minster Arms (01202) 840700
West Street; BH21 1JS Updated candlelit
corner pub with log fires, leather sofas and
an assortment of tables and chairs on wood
floors, three real ales and extensive choice
of wines by the glass, varied seasonal menu,
friendly service; live music; children and dogs
welcome, courtyard area with heaters, ten
modern comfortable bedrooms, open (and
food) all day.

WIMBORNE MINSTER   SU0100
Olive Branch (01202) 884686
*East Borough, just off Hanham Road
(B3073, just E of its junction with
B3078); BH21 1PF* Handsome townhouse
with various opened-up dining areas, one
with beams and view into kitchen, another
more canteen-like with long tables and
padded benches, popular food from range
of small plates through burgers up, special
diets catered for, relaxed atmosphere,
Badger beers in comfortable panelled
bar with woodburner, also a coffee bar;
Mediterranean-style garden, open all day,
closed Sun evening and Mon.

**WINTERBORNE
STICKLAND**   ST8304
Crown (01258) 881042
North Street; DT11 0NJ Popular thatched
and beamed village pub under welcoming
management; two rooms separated by
servery, smaller one with inglenook
woodburner, proper cider and good freshly
made food at sensible prices; children and
dogs welcome, pretty back terrace and steps
up to lawned area with village view, open all
day, till 7pm Sun, closed Tues.

**WINTERBORNE
WHITECHURCH**   ST8300
Milton Arms (01258) 880431
A354 Blandford–Dorchester; DT11 0HW
Modernised village pub with good sensibly
priced food including daily specials, three
well kept beers, friendly helpful staff;
children and dogs welcome, closed Sun
evening, otherwise open all day.

Essex

KEY ★ Star Pub 🍽 Top Quality Food 🍺 Great Beer

🍷 Good Wines £ Bargain Meals 🛏 Good Bedrooms 🍴 Serves Food

CHRISHALL TL4439 Map 5

Red Cow 🍺 🛏

(01763) 838792 – www.theredcow.com

High Street; off B1039 Wendens Ambo–Great Chishill; SG8 8RN

Thatched 14th-c pub with beamed rooms, four real ales, well liked food and seats in attractive garden; bedrooms

---

A bustling, well run local, with a neat and friendly bar and dining room with heavy beams and timbers, a woodburning stove and an open fire, all sorts of wooden dining chairs around tables of every size on bare floorboards, and a comfortable sofa and armchairs. Adnams Southwold and Woodfordes Wherry plus two guest beers such as Greene King Old Speckled Hen and Timothy Taylors Landlord on handpump, eight wines by the glass, Aspall's cider and cocktails; they hold a music and beer festival in May. Terraces have picnic-sets and the garden is pretty. Walkers enjoy the nearby Icknield Way, coming here for refreshment afterwards. There are five attractive, comfortable bedrooms in a restored thatched barn, and readers have been quick to voice their enthusiasm.

🍴 Pleasing food includes lunchtime ciabattas, smoked duck with spring onion and rocket salad and hoisin dressing, traditional prawn cocktail, home-made pie of the day (chicken and mushroom or ham and leek) with mash, steak burger with cheese, bacon, onion rings and home-made coleslaw, steaks with a choice of sauce, and puddings such as double chocolate brownie with salted caramel ice-cream and chocolate sauce and sticky toffee pudding with butterscotch sauce and vanilla ice-cream. *Benchmark main dish: home-cooked honey roast ham with fried eggs and chips £13.00. Two-course evening meal £23.00.*

Free house ~ Licensees Toby and Alexis Didier Serre ~ Real ale ~ Open 12-3, 6 (5.30 Fri)-midnight; 12-midnight Sat; 12-10 Sun ~ Bar food 12-2, 6-9; 12-2.30, 6-9 Sat; 12-3.30 Sun ~ Restaurant ~ Children welcome ~ Dogs allowed in bar ~ Bedrooms: £120

FEERING TL8720 Map 5

Sun 🍺

(01376) 570442 – www.suninnfeering.co.uk

Feering Hill; before Feering proper, B1204 off A12 just NE of Kelvedon; CO5 9NH

Striking 16th-c pub with six real ales, popular food and pleasant garden

---

You can expect a bustling atmosphere and a good mix of customers at this well run pub with a handsome frontage. The busy slate-floored bar has an easy-going feel and two big woodburning stoves (one in the huge central inglenook fireplace, another by an antique winged settle on the left). Throughout there are handsomely carved black beams and timbers galore, and attractive wildflower murals in a frieze above the central timber divider. The beers on handpump include Shepherd Neame Bishops Finger, Master Brew, Spitfire Gold and Whitstable Bay Pale plus a guest such as Isla Vale Hopping Mad, and they hold summer and winter beer festivals; also, 14 wines by the glass, 14 malt whiskies, 25 gins and eight rums, served by cheerful staff. A brick-paved back courtyard has tables, heaters and a shelter, and tall trees shade green picnic-sets in the garden beyond. The pub has its own small car park through an archway in the middle of the adjoining terraced houses.

A wide choice of food includes upmarket lunchtime sandwiches, venison carpaccio with parsnip crisps and purée, courgette, spelt and cumin fritter, salmon fillet with white crab and bacon crushed potatoes, slow-braised ox cheek with roasted garlic mash, chickpea, sweet potato and baby spinach balti with saffron rice, and puddings such as clementine posset with ginger biscuit and raspberry sorbet, a selection of Yorvale ice-creams and English cheeses. *Benchmark main dish: beef, mushroom and stilton pie with chips or new potatoes £15.00. Two-course evening meal £21.00.*

Shepherd Neame ~ Tenant Andy Howard ~ Real ale ~ Open 12-3, 5.30-11 (midnight Fri); 12-midnight Sat; 12-10.30 Sun ~ Bar food 12-2.30, 6-9 (9.30 Fri); 12-9 Sat; 12-8 Sun ~ Well behaved children welcome ~ Dogs allowed in bar & restaurant

 FULLER STREET   TL7416   Map 5

Square & Compasses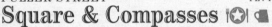

(01245) 361477 – www.thesquareandcompasses.co.uk

From A130/131 to Sudbury, Stansted and Chelmsford City Racecourse, follow sign to Great Leighs. Turn right into Boreham Road, pass Mill Lane. Left to Fuller Street/ Terling; CM3 2BB

Attractive surroundings, with two woodburning stoves, three ales and enjoyable food

Originally two farmers' cottages, this 17th-c pub retains many original features and has exposed beams, two woodburning stoves and an inglenook fireplace. 'A really great country pub' and 'perfect after walking the Essex Way' are just two positive reports from readers. Friendly staff serve Crouch Vale Brewers Gold and Maldon Drop of Nelsons Blood and Pucks Folly tapped from the cask, 23 wines by the glass, four ciders and home-made elderflower and lemon cordial; background jazz. The cosy beamed dining room features shelves of books, bottles and decanters against timbered walls, and an appealing variety of dining chairs around dark wooden tables set with linen napkins. Tables out in front on decking offer gentle country views.

Tasty food includes lunchtime sandwiches and pub classics such as fish pie, pork sausages with spring onion mash, and home-cooked ham with eggs and chips, seasonal dishes such as Essex skate wing with lemon parsley butter, and whole braised local partridge in cider with smoked bacon and garlic and juniper red cabbage, and puddings such as lemon tart with lemon syrup, spotted dick and custard and chocolate and orange torte with vanilla ice-cream. *Benchmark main dish: steak and ale pie £14.95. Two-course evening meal £21.00.*

Free house ~ Licensee Victor Roome ~ Real ale ~ Open 11.30-11; 12-midnight Sat; 12-11 Sun ~ Bar food 12-2 (2.30 Sat), 6-9; 12-5 Sun ~ Restaurant ~ Well behaved children welcome ~ Dogs allowed in bar

FYFIELD
Queens Head

TL5706   Map 5

(01277) 899231 – www.queensheadfyfield.co.uk
Corner of B184 and Queen Street; CM5 0RY

Friendly old pub with seats in riverside garden, a good choice of drinks and highly regarded food

This late 15th-c pub set in countryside has a prettily planted garden that runs down to the sleepy River Roding. In order to bag a seat here in good weather, customers tend to arrive early at the weekend – when the place is usefully open all day. The compact, low-beamed, L-shaped bar has exposed timbers, pretty lamps on nice sturdy elm tables and comfortable seating from wall banquettes to attractive, unusual high-backed chairs, some in a snug little side booth. In summer, two facing fireplaces have church candles instead of a fire; background music. Adnams Southwold and Ghost Ship and Franklins Citra IPA on handpump and 15 good wines by the glass. Our readers particularly like the enterprising food; the upstairs restaurant is more formal. Dogs are allowed in the garden.

Imaginative food includes scotch egg with mustard mayonnaise and bois boudran sauce, pan-roasted scallops with cauliflower, toasted hazelnuts and shallot dressing, skate with brown shrimp and caper beurre noisette and new potatoes, roasted spiced cauliflower masala dhal with onion bhaji and cucumber, coriander and onion salad, and puddings such as blackberry soufflé with gingernut biscuit ice-cream and chocolate mousse with chantilly cream, fresh berries and raspberry chocolate matchsticks. They also offer a two- and three-course set menu (not Saturday evening or Sunday). *Benchmark main dish: beef cheek and Guinness pie with mash, shallots, buttered savoy cabbage and beef jus £16.00. Two-course evening meal £27.00.*

Free house ~ Licensee Daniel Lamprecht ~ Real ale ~ Open 11-3.30, 6-11.30; 11-11.30 Sat; 12-8 Sun; closed Mon ~ Bar food 12-2.30 (4 Sat), 6.30-9.30; 12-6 Sun ~ Restaurant ~ Children welcome away from bar

HORNDON-ON-THE-HILL
Bell

TQ6783   Map 3

(01375) 642463 – www.bell-inn.co.uk
M25 junction 30 into A13, then left after 7 miles on to B1007, village signposted from here; SS17 8LD

● ●
Essex Dining Pub of the Year

Lovely historic pub with fine food and a very good range of drinks; individually styled bedrooms

This popular 15th-c coaching has been run by the same friendly family for more than 80 years. It's a first class all-rounder where customers are treated with great care and respect, and we've had nothing but glowing reports on it from our readers over the years. The heavily beamed, panelled bar maintains a strongly pubby appearance with high-backed antique settles and benches, rugs on flagstones and highly polished oak floorboards, and an open log fire. Look out for the curious collection of ossified hot-cross buns hanging along a beam in the saloon bar – the first was put there in 1906 to mark the day (a Good Friday) that Jack Turnell became licensee. The timbered restaurant has numerous old copper pots and pans hanging from beams. An impressive range of drinks includes Crouch Vale Brewers Gold, Greene King IPA, Leigh on Sea Cockle Row Spit and Renown and Sharps Doom Bar on handpump, 24 gins and over 114 well chosen wines (16 by the glass). Two giant umbrellas cover the courtyard, which has very pretty hanging baskets in summer. Centuries ago, many important medieval dignitaries would have stayed here as it was the last inn before travellers heading south could ford the Thames at Highams Causeway. Today, it remains a special place to stay with individually styled, thoughtfully equipped bedrooms of all sizes, from large and grand to small and cosy.

Impressive, up-to-date food includes pea, mint and ricotta wonton with courgette ribbons and nasturtium pesto, Maldon-cured smoked salmon with cucumber, horseradish and beetroot, lamb chump with broccoli tempura, black olive tapenade and mustard mash potato, cod with white wine and prawn velouté, parmentier potatoes and charred baby gem, and puddings such as chocolate marquise with toffee sauce, berries and chocolate soil, and peach melba baked alaska with hot apricot sauce. *Benchmark main dish: roasted chicken breast with bubble and squeak, caramelised cauliflower and chicken velouté £16.95. Two-course evening meal £24.00.*

Free house ~ Licensee John Vereker ~ Real ale ~ Open 11-11; 12-10.30 Sun ~ Bar food 12-1.45, 6.30 (6 Sat)-10; 12-2.30, 7-9.45 Sun ~ Children welcome ~ Dogs allowed in bar & bedrooms ~ Bedrooms: £82

HOWE STREET
Green Man 🔟 ♟

TL6914 Map 5

(01245) 408820 – www.galvingreenman.com
Just off A130 N of Chelmsford; CM3 1BG

Sizeable pub with up-to-date extensions, plenty of natural light, real ales, first class food, friendly staff and big garden

This charming 14th-c pub is owned by the Essex-born Galvin brothers – both exceptional chefs – so it's renowned for serving excellent award-winning food. But if you just want a drink and a chat, there's a cosy, timber-framed bar with proper character: flagstones or bare boards, an open fire, leather-topped stools, a button-back brown leather chesterfield, nice old wooden chairs around circular tables, a cushioned window seat and photos and prints on ochre walls. Also, Adnams Ghost Ship and Southwold on handpump, good wines by the glass, several malt whiskies, organic cider and a non-alcoholic juice of the day. Staff are attentive, friendly and helpful. The high-raftered dining rooms are divided by a two-way woodburning stove in a large brick fireplace. Big windows and glass doors provide plenty of natural light and the contemporary furnishings include modern lighting, and dark painted cushioned dining chairs and long button-back leather banquettes on either pale floorboards or flagstones; background music and TV. The 1.5 acres of garden, with the River Chelmer running along the bottom, has black metal furniture on a terrace and picnic-sets on grass. There are monthly wine dinners, regular music and garden events such as barbecues and a harvest festival.

Centred around locally sourced and seasonal ingredients, the inventive food includes sandwiches, Adnams Southwold Aylesbury duck liver parfait with quince purée and toasted brioche, pan-seared supreme of Atlantic cod with braised celery, puffed wild rice and curried mussels, Old Spot pork chop with smoked olive oil pomme purée, hispi cabbage and prune d'agen, beer-battered fish and chips, and puddings such as apple tarte tatin and coffee crémeux, hazelnut and Kahlúa ice-cream. Ask for details about children eating free in the school holidays. *Benchmark main dish: 'deluxe' Galvin beefburger with cheese, bacon and onion mayonnaise £16.50. Two-course evening meal £25.*

Galvin Pub Company ~ Licensees Chris and Jeff Galvin ~ Real ale ~ Open 11-11; 11-9.30 Sun ~ Bar food 12-4.30, 5-9 Mon-Thurs; 12-4.30, 5.30-10 Fri; 11.30-4.30, 5.30-10 Sat; 11.30-6 Sun ~ Restaurant ~ Children welcome ~ Dogs allowed in bar

LITTLE WALDEN

TL5441   Map 5

Crown 🍺 🛏 £

(01799) 522475 – www.thecrownlittlewalden.co.uk
B1052 N of Saffron Walden; CB10 1XA

Bustling old pub with a warming log fire, hearty food and real ales; bedrooms

This charming 18th-c beamed pub is very much the heart of the local community. There's a cosy, chatty atmosphere and a genuine welcome from the staff. The low-ceilinged rooms have traditional furnishings, floral curtains, bare boards or navy carpeting, cosy warm fires and an unusual walk-through fireplace. A higgledy-piggledy mix of chairs ranges from high-backed pews to little cushioned armchairs spaced around a good variety of closely arranged tables, mostly big, some stripped. A small red-tiled room on the right has two small tables. Three changing beers such as Adnams Broadside, Greene King Abbot and Woodfordes Wherry plus a guest ale are tapped straight from casks racked up behind the bar; TV, regular trad jazz nights and quiz. Tables on the terrace have views over the tranquil surrounding countryside. Staying overnight here means you can explore the area in comfort; breakfasts are excellent too. Disabled access.

Good quality food includes baguettes, devilled whitebait, creamy garlic mushrooms, four-cheese ravioli, smoked halibut, salmon and crayfish salad, honey-roast ham, battered fish and chips, pork fillet in spicy cajun sauce, chicken curry, and puddings such as eton mess and spicy apple crumble with custard, cream or ice-cream. *Benchmark main dish: steak and mushroom pie £11.00. Two-course evening meal £18.50.*

Free house ~ Licensee Colin Hayling ~ Real ale ~ Open 11.30-2.30, 6-11; 11.30-2.30, 6-11 Sat; 12-10.30 Sun ~ Bar food 12-2 Mon; 12-2, 6.45-9; 12-3 Sun ~ Restaurant ~ Children welcome ~ Dogs allowed in bar ~ Bedrooms: from £80

LITTLEY GREEN

TL6917   Map 5

Compasses 🍺

(01245) 362308 – www.compasseslittleygreen.co.uk
Village signposted off B1417 Felsted road in Hartoft End (opposite former Ridleys Brewery), about a mile N of junction with B1008 (former A130); CM3 1BU

Charming brick tavern – a prime example of what is now an all too rare breed; bedrooms

This picturesque Victorian pub is a classic country local. The friendly bar has brown-painted panelling and wall benches, plain chairs and tables on quarry tiles, and chat and laughter rather than piped music as the backdrop. There's a piano, darts and board games in one side room, and decorative mugs hanging from beams in another. A fine range of ales includes Bishop Nick Ridleys Rite (brewed in Braintree by the landlord's brother) and Crouch Vale Essex Boys Best Bitter, as well as three changing cask ales. Annual events include the Easter Steam Up! (steam engines), plus summer and Christmas beer festivals featuring dozens of beers. Also seven constantly changing ciders and perries, eight wines by the glass and a half dozen single malts. Picnic-sets sit out on the sheltered garden to the side and back, with a couple of long tables on the front cobbles by the quiet lane. There are five bedrooms in a modern block next to the pub.

A big blackboard shows the day's range of huffers: big rolls with a hearty range of hot or cold fillings. They also serve ploughman's, baked potatoes and sensibly priced dishes such as beer-battered cod and chips, a changing curry, chilli con carne and lasagne. They've recently started serving breakfast at the weekend. *Benchmark main dish: chicken curry with rice and poppadum £9.75. Two-course evening meal £15.00.*

Free house ~ Licensee Jocelyn Ridley ~ Real ale ~ Open 12-3, 5-11.30 Mon-Weds; 12-11.30 Thurs, Fri; 8.30am-11.30pm Sat, Sun ~ Bar food 12-2.30, 6-9 Mon-Thurs; 12-2.30, 5.30-9 Fri; 8.30-11am, 12-9 Sat; 8.30-11am, 12-8.30 Sun ~ Children welcome ~ Dogs allowed in bar ~ Bedrooms: £75

SOUTH HANNINGFIELD   TQ7497   Map 5
Old Windmill ♀
(01268) 712280 – www.brunningandprice.co.uk/oldwindmill
Off A130 S of Chelmsford; CM3 8HT

A forest of stripped standing timbers and open doorways have created cosy, rambling areas throughout this 18th-c pub. There's an agreeable mix of highly polished old tables and chairs, frame-to-frame pictures on cream walls, woodburning stoves and big pot plants. Deep green or dark red dados and a few old rugs dotted on the polished wood floors provide splashes of colour; other areas are more subdued with beige carpeting. Attentive young staff serve St Austell Brunning & Price Traditional and guests from breweries such as Crouch Vale, Leigh on Sea, Mighty Oak and Nethergate on handpump, a dozen wines by the glass and a good range of spirits including 50 different gins; background music. A back terrace has tables and chairs under parasols and plenty of picnic-sets on a lawn.

Good, modern food includes 'light bites', barbecue chicken wings, five-spiced duck leg with spring onion, cucumber, hoisin sauce and pancakes, summer risotto with broad beans, asparagus, radish and lemon, chicken, ham and leek pie with mash and buttered greens, beef bourguignon with horseradish mash and buttered kale, duck breast with crispy leg croquettes, celeriac purée and cherry jus, and puddings such as summer pudding, crème brûlée and Cheshire Farm ice-cream and sorbets. *Benchmark main dish: buttermilk chicken burger with bacon, garlic mayonnaise and fries £14.95. Two-course evening meal £22.00.*

Brunning & Price ~ Manager Nick Bryan ~ Real ale ~ Open 11.30-11; 12-10.30 Sun ~ Bar food 12-9; 12-9.30 Fri, Sat ~ Restaurant ~ Children welcome ~ Dogs allowed in bar

Also Worth a Visit in Essex

Besides the fully inspected pubs, you might like to try these pubs that have been recommended to us and described by readers. Do tell us what you think of them: feedback@goodguides.com

ARDLEIGH   TM0429
★**Wooden Fender** (01206) 230466
A137 towards Colchester; CO7 7PA
Extended old pub (former 17th-c staging post) with beams and log fires; good freshly made food from sharing plates through grills to daily specials, Greene King and guests, decent wines, friendly attentive service; children welcome in large dining area, dogs in bar, good-sized garden with play area, open all day Fri and Sat, till 9pm Sun, breakfast 7.30-11am Weds-Sun.

ARKESDEN   TL4834
Axe & Compasses (01799) 550272
Off B1038; CB11 4EX Comfortable part-thatched pub now run by two brothers; original part dating back to 1650 with low ceilings, original floor tiles and open fire

---

If you report on a pub that's not a featured entry, please tell us any lunchtimes or evenings when it doesn't serve bar food.

in brick fireplace, upholstered chairs, cushioned wall seats and settles, Old Speckled Hen, Timothy Taylors Landlord and Woodfordes, good choice of wines and malt whiskies, well liked food with some Greek influences (not Sun evening) served in converted stables with photographs of the pub and surrounding area, friendly efficient service; occasional live music; children welcome, benches out at front, more seats on side terrace, lovely village.

AYTHORPE RODING   TL5915
Axe & Compasses (01279) 876648
B184 S of Dunmow; CM6 1PP Attractive weatherboarded and part-thatched roadside pub, neatly kept and cosy, with beams, stripped brickwork and pale wood floors, modern furnishings, original part (on the left) has a two-way fireplace marking off a snug raftered dining area, popular food from light lunches up to roasts with all the trimmings, including deals and themed nights, special diets catered for, Fullers ale plus two guests and 13 wines by the glass; background and some live music, monthly quiz, board games; small back garden with stylish modern furniture, views across fields to windmill, open (and food) all day from 9am for breakfast.

BELCHAMP ST PAUL   TL7942
Half Moon (01787) 277402
Cole Green; CO10 7DP Quaint recently rethatched 16th-c beamed pub overlooking village green; good reasonably priced home-made food (not Sun evening, Mon) from varied menu, well kept Greene King IPA and guests, decent wines by the glass, friendly helpful staff, snug carpeted interior with woodburner, restaurant; Aug beer/music festival; children welcome, no dogs inside, tables out in front and in back garden, open all day weekends.

BIRCHANGER   TL5122
★ **Three Willows** (01279) 815913
Under a mile from M11 junction 8: A120 towards Bishop's Stortford, then almost immediately right to Birchanger Village; don't be waylaid earlier by the Birchanger Services signpost; CM23 5QR Welcoming village dining pub under new management since 2018; spacious carpeted bar with lots of cricketing memorabilia, well furnished smaller lounge, Greene King ales and good fairly traditional food cooked by landlord-chef including plenty of fresh fish, efficient friendly young staff; children welcome, dogs allowed in bar, picnic-sets out in front and on lawn behind (some motorway and Stansted Airport noise), play area, open all day Sat, till 7pm Sun.

BISHOPS GREEN   TL6317
Spotted Dog (01245) 231598
High Easter Road; CM6 1NF Pretty 18th-c thatched pub-restaurant in quiet rural

hamlet; very good food cooked by landlord-chef including more affordable set menu (not Fri, Sat evenings or Sun lunchtime), friendly attentive staff, Greene King IPA and a guest, contemporary beamed interior with high-backed leather chairs at well spaced tables; background music; children welcome, oak-wood garden furniture out behind picket fence, closed Sun evening, Mon and Tues.

BOREHAM   TL7409
Lion (01245) 394900
Main Road; CM3 3JA Stylish roadside bistro-bar with rooms; popular affordably priced food from snacks to daily specials, no bookings so may have to queue at busy times, several wines by the glass, bottled beers and up to six well kept changing ales, efficient friendly staff, conservatory; monthly comedy club; children welcome, no dogs inside, 23 comfortable bedrooms, open all day, food all day weekends.

BOREHAM   TL7509
Six Bells (01245) 467232
Main Road (B1137); CM3 3JE Family dining pub with several linked areas including inglenook bar, good affordably priced home-cooked food (smaller appetites and gluten-free diets catered for), well kept Greene King ales and a guest, polite helpful staff; no dogs inside, play area in good-sized garden, open (and food) all day weekends.

BRAINTREE   TL7421
King William IV (01376) 567755
London Road; CM77 7PU Small friendly drinkers' local with two simple bars, up to five real ales tapped from the cask including own Moody Goose brews, also proper ciders/perries and some unusual lagers, no food apart from snacks; regular events including beer festivals and music events; well behaved children and dogs welcome, picnic-sets in big garden, open all day Fri-Sun, from 3pm other days.

BRENTWOOD   TQ6195
Rose (01277) 218809
Chelmsford Road (A1023), Shenfield; CM15 8RN Updated beamed and timbered dining pub serving good fairly priced food (booking advised) from breakfast on, a couple of real ales including one badged for them and plenty of wines by the glass, friendly attentive young staff, cosy interior with woodburners and separate restaurant; children welcome, no dogs inside, terrace tables (some under cover), open all day from 8am (from noon Sun).

BURNHAM-ON-CROUCH   TQ9596
Ship (01621) 785057
High Street; CM0 8AA Relaxed 18th-c dining pub with good fairly priced food from imaginative snacks up, fish Fri, unlimited prosecco lunch Sat, local beers plus guests such as Harveys, decent wines and

cocktails (happy hour 6.30-8.30pm Fri, Sat), friendly helpful staff, bare-boards bar with grey-painted panelling and woodburner; background music; children welcome, some pavement seating, three comfortable boutique-style bedrooms, open (and food) all day.

BURNHAM-ON-CROUCH   TQ9495
White Harte   (01621) 782106
The Quay; CM0 8AS Cosy old-fashioned 17th-c hotel on water's edge overlooking yacht-filled River Crouch; partly carpeted bars with down-to-earth charm, assorted nautical bric-a-brac and hardware, other traditionally furnished high-ceilinged rooms with sea pictures on brown panelled or stripped brick walls, cushioned seats around oak tables, enormous winter log fire, beers from Adnams and Crouch Vale, generally well liked food; children and dogs allowed, outside seating jettied over the water, 19 bedrooms (eight with river view), open all day.

BURTON END   TL5323
Ash   (01279) 814841
Just N of Stansted Airport; CM24 8UQ Thatched 17th-c country pub; well kept ales including Greene King IPA and a beer badged for them, decent range of wines by the glass, enjoyable generously served food from lunchtime sandwiches and pubby choices up, friendly staff, black beams and timbers, quarry tiled floors, woodburner, pitched-roof dining extension; monthly quiz and charity events, sports TV; children welcome, tables out on deck and grass, open (and food) all day.

CASTLE HEDINGHAM   TL7835
Bell   (01787) 460350
St James Street (B1058); CO9 3EJ Beamed and timbered three-bar pub dating from the 15th c, unpretentious, unspoilt and run by the same family since the late 1960s; Adnams, Mighty Oak and guests tapped from the cask (July beer festival), popular pubby food along with Turkish specials, good friendly service; background and live music including lunchtime jazz last Sun of month, quiz Sun evening; dogs welcome, children away from public bar, garden with hops and covered area, handy for Hedingham Castle, open all day Fri-Sun.

CHATHAM GREEN   TL7115
Windmill   (01245) 910910
Chatham Green, pub signed from A131; CM3 3LE Beamed and timbered country dining pub with two attractive bedrooms

(one in adjacent stub of former windmill); good well presented food from chef-landlord, well chosen wine list, cocktails and a couple of ales from local breweries such as Bishop Nick and Mighty Oak, friendly helpful staff, cushioned wooden chairs around sturdy tables on bare boards or tartan carpet, some rustic bric-a-brac and woodburners; children and dogs welcome, tables out at front, closed Mon, Tues, open from 5pm Weds-Sat, from noon Sun.

CHELMSFORD   TL7006
Orange Tree   (01245) 262664
Lower Anchor Street; CM2 0AS Traditional two-room brick local with bargain lunchtime bar food, all-day breakfast Sat, Sun, steak and curry night Thurs; eight well kept ales (some tapped from the cask) including Elland, Mighty Oak and Oakham plus good bottled range, efficient service; quiz nights and other events, sports TV; dogs welcome in public bar, back terrace, handy for county cricket ground and can get very busy on match days, open all day (till midnight Fri).

CHIGWELL ROW   TQ4693
Two Brewers   (020) 8501 1313
Lambourne Road; IG7 6ET Spacious pub with welcoming relaxed atmosphere; assortment of tables and chairs and wall banquettes on flagstones or bare boards, heavy draped curtains, lots of pictures, photos and gilt-edged mirrors, two-way fireplace, good choice of real ales and wines by the glass, popular food from varied menu; children and dogs welcome, nice three-mile circular walk from the door, open (and food) all day.

CLAVERING   TL4832
★ Cricketers   (01799) 550442
B1038 Newport–Buntingford; CB11 4QT Busy dining pub with plenty of old-fashioned charm, inventive food and signed cookbooks by Jamie Oliver (his parents own it); main area with very low beams and big open fireplace, bays of deep purple button-backed banquettes and padded leather chairs on dark floorboards, split-level back part with carpeted dining areas and some big copper and brass pans on dark beams and timbers, five Adnams and Nethergate beers and 16 wines by the glass; background music; children welcome, attractive front terrace with rattan-style chairs around teak tables, 22 bedrooms, handy for Stansted Airport, open all day from 7am, food all day Sun.

'Children welcome' means the pub says it lets children inside without any special restriction. If it allows them in, but to restricted areas such as an eating area or family room, we specify this. Places with separate restaurants often let children use them, and hotels usually let children into public areas such as lounges. Some pubs impose an evening time limit – let us know if you find one earlier than 9pm.

COLCHESTER　　　　　　TL9924
Fat Cat　(01206) 577990
Butt Road/Alexandra Road; CO3 3BZ
Small sister pub to the Ipswich and Norwich
Fat Cats; eight well kept ales (including
their own) and wide range of other beers
all marked up on blackboard, enjoyable
inexpensive food (not Mon or Tues), friendly
helpful staff; music and food-based events,
Sun quiz, sports TV; children (mealtimes
only) and dogs welcome, open all day (no
food Sun evening, Mon, Tues).

COLCHESTER　　　　　　TL9925
Three Wise Monkeys
(01206) 543014　*High Street; CO1 1DN*
Popular centrally located bar on several
levels; ground floor serves half a dozen
changing ales, 15 craft beers and good
selection of other drinks including cocktails,
enjoyable food from well priced American
smokehouse menu, prompt friendly service,
another bar/dining area upstairs and above
that a live music/events venue, there's also
a basement gin bar (Thurs-Sat evenings);
open (and food) all day, shuts 1am Fri, Sat.

DANBURY　　　　　　TL7805
Bakers Arms　(01245) 227300
Maldon Road; CM3 4QH Pink-painted
community-run roadside pub with pleasant
informal atmosphere; well kept ales such as
Adnams, Wherry and two guests (May beer
festival), enjoyable food (not Sun evening
or lunchtimes Mon, Tues) including pizzas
and four sizes of fish and chips, welcoming
cheerful staff; children and dogs allowed
(they have a coonhound, harrier and great
dane), picnic-sets in back garden, open all
day (till 8pm Sun).

DEBDEN　　　　　　TL5533
Plough　(01799) 541899
High Street; CB11 3LE Welcoming village
pub serving Greene King and three guests
plus decent wines, beer/music festivals,
live music some weekends, monthly pub
quiz third Weds; good freshly made food
from landlord-chef including daily specials,
special diets catered for, cheerful helpful
service, restaurant, log fire; children and
dogs (in bar) welcome, fair-sized garden
behind, open all day Fri-Sun, closed Mon
and lunchtime Tues.

DEDHAM　　　　　　TM0533
★ **Sun**　(01206) 323351
High Street (B2109); CO7 6DF
Handsome yellow-painted Tudor coaching
inn in fine village at the heart of Constable
country; historic interior including panelled
lounge and split-level dining room with
exposed timbers, carved beams, smart
furnishings and splendid fireplaces,
Adnams, Crouch Vale and two guest ales
on handpump and impressive wine list
(many by the glass and carafe), enterprising

seasonal food including breakfast;
background music; children and dogs (in
bar) welcome, seven individually decorated
bedrooms, picnic-sets on quiet back lawn
with mature trees and view of church,
bicycles for hire, good walks and boating on
nearby River Stour, open all day.

DUNMOW　　　　　　TL6222
Angel & Harp　(01371) 859259
*Church Road, Church End; B1057
signposted to Finchingfield/The
Bardfields, off B184 N of town; CM6 2AD*
Comfortable old place with linked rooms
rambling around through standing timbers
and doorways, mix of seating including
armchairs, sofas and banquettes, stools each
side of free-standing zinc 'counter' serving
Nethergate, guest beers and 11 wines by the
glass, good range of popular food including
breakfasts and wood-fired pizzas (special
diets catered for), substantial brick fireplace
and some fine old floor tiles in low-ceilinged
main area, steps up to interesting raftered
room with one huge table, also attractive
extension with glass wall overlooking
flagstoned courtyard and grassed area
beyond; background music, beer festivals
and other events, quiz last Weds of month;
children and dogs (in bar) welcome, open
(and food) all day from 9am.

DUTON HILL　　　　　　TL6026
Three Horseshoes　(01371) 870681
*Off B184 Dunmow–Thaxted, 3 miles
N of Dunmow; CM6 2DX* Friendly
traditional village local; well kept Mighty
Oak and a couple of guests (late May Bank
Holiday beer festival), central fire in main
bar, aged armchairs by another fireplace in
homely left-hand parlour, lots of interesting
memorabilia, small public bar with darts
and pool, no food; open-air theatre in July;
dogs welcome, old enamel signs out at
front, garden with pond and views, closed
lunchtimes Mon-Thurs.

EARLS COLNE　　　　　　TL8528
Lion　(01787) 226823
High Street; CO6 2PA Restored village pub
dating from the 15th c, with recent addition
of large modern bar; Mediterranean-style
menu from tapas and wood-fired pizzas up,
well kept changing beers and interesting
wines (choose a bottle from their small shop
to drink in or take away); friendly service;
music and food-based events; children and
dogs welcome, courtyard tables, open (and
food) all day from 9am (10.30am Sun) for
breakfast.

EPPING FOREST　　　　　　TL4501
Forest Gate　(01992) 572312
Bell Common; CM16 4DZ Friendly open-
plan pub dating from the 17th c and run by
the same family for over 50 years; beams,
flagstones and panelling, big woodburner,
well kept Adnams and guests from brick-

faced bar, inexpensive pubby food (they also have a smart upmarket restaurant next door); darts, quiz last Sun of month; children and dogs welcome, tables on front lawn popular with walkers, four bedrooms in separate building, open all day.

FINCHINGFIELD   TL6832
Fox (01371) 810151
The Green; CM7 4JX Pargeted 16th-c building overlooking village duck pond; spacious beamed bar with exposed brickwork and central fireplace, flowers on tables, up to four changing local ales including two from Adnams, and good choice of wines by the glass, popular pubby food including Sun roasts (but not Sun evening), friendly helpful staff; background and some live music; children and dogs welcome, hanging baskets and picnic-sets in front, open all day.

FINGRINGHOE   TM0220
Whalebone (01206) 729307
Off A134 just S of Colchester centre, or B1025; CO5 7BG Old village dining pub with airy country-chic rooms; wooden chairs and tables on oak floors, fresh flowers and log fire, good seasonal pub food, four well kept beers including Adnams, friendly helpful staff, barn function room; background music; children and dogs welcome, charming back garden with peaceful valley view, front terrace, handy for Fingringhoe Wick nature reserve, open all day Sat, till 6pm Sun.

GESTINGTHORPE   TL8138
★ Pheasant (01787) 465010
Off B1058; CO9 3AU Refurbished country pub with old-fashioned character in small opened-up beamed rooms; settles and mix of other furniture on bare boards, books and china platters on shelves, woodburners in nice brick fireplaces, Adnams Southwold, a house beer from Woodfordes and an occasional guest, nine wines by the glass, good food using local and some home-grown produce including daily specials; occasional quiz and music nights; children and dogs (in bar) welcome, seats outside under parasols with views over fields, five stylish bedrooms, open all day (closed Mon), they also take days off Jan–May – so best to phone or check website.

GOLDHANGER   TL9008
★ Chequers (01621) 788203
Church Street; off B1026 E of Heybridge; CM9 8AS Friendly old village local with six rambling rooms including a spacious lounge with dark beams, black panelling and a huge sash window overlooking the graveyard of the fine church next door, a traditional dining room with bare boards and carpeting

and a games room with bar billiards, plus woodburning stove, open fire, TV and background music; six real ales (regular beer festivals) such as Adnams, Sharps and Woodfordes on handpump, farm ciders, 16 wines by the glass, ten malt whiskies and wide choice of popular fairly priced blackboard food; children welcome (not in tap room), dogs in bar, picnic-sets under umbrellas in the courtyard with a grapevine, open all day weekends, no food Sun evening.

GOSFIELD   TL7829
Kings Head (01787) 474016
The Street; CO9 1TP Tudor village pub refurbished and improved under newish owners; beams, standing timbers and other original features, main bar with handsome brick fireplace, three real ales such as Sharps, Greene King and a changing ale (Aug beer festival), good sensibly priced food (not Sun or Mon evenings) from baguettes up, efficient friendly service, well spaced tables in dining area opening into carpeted conservatory; some live music and quiz nights; children welcome, terrace with rattan-style seating, open all day.

GREAT BARDFIELD   TL6730
Vine (01371) 811822
Vine Street; CM7 4SR Victorian dining pub with highly rated well presented food from pub staples to monthly tasting menus, real ales such as Greene King and two guests, extensive wine list and some unusual gins, friendly helpful service, light airy décor with roaring log fire; monthly quiz, sports TV; children welcome, picnic-sets in good-sized garden (Aug beer festival), interesting village with links to notable artists (including Edward Bawden and Eric Ravilious), open all day.

GREAT BROMLEY   TM0824
Court House (01206) 250322
Harwich Road/Frating Road; CO7 7JG Popular modernised roadside pub, previously a courthouse dating from 17th c; carpeted bar with white-painted beams, good reasonably priced pubby food from lunchtime sandwiches to Sun roasts and occasional curry nights, four well kept changing ales including Shepherd Neame, friendly efficient service, restaurant and tea room; children welcome, bedrooms (some in motel-style building), closed Sun and Mon evenings, otherwise open all day.

GREAT BROMLEY   TM0627
Great Bromley Cross
(01206) 621772 *Ardleigh Road, just off A120 Colchester–Harwich; CO7 7TL* Welcoming updated community-owned

---

If we know a pub is cash-only, we say so. This is very rare: almost everywhere accepts credit and debit cards now.

country pub on crossroads; a couple of well kept changing ales such as Bishop Nick and Colchester, various gins and cocktails, low-priced food served Fri evening and on their regular events nights (live music, quizzes and so forth); Weds morning post office, library and coffee shop; children and dogs welcome, open Sun 12-3pm and Weds-Sat evenings.

GREAT CHESTERFORD TL5142
Crown & Thistle (01799) 530278
1.5 miles from M11 junction 9A; pub signposted off B184, in High Street; CB10 1PL Refurbished old pub under friendly management; decorative plasterwork inside and out, particularly around the early 16th-c inglenook, low-ceilinged area by bar serving ales such as Adnams, Fullers and Woodfordes, enjoyable Thai food and stone-baked pizzas in long handsomely proportioned dining room; children, walkers and dogs (in bar) welcome, picnic-sets out at front, more tables in suntrap back courtyard, closed Sun evening.

GREAT CHESTERFORD TL5142
Plough (01799) 531651
Off M11/A11 via B184; High Street; CB10 1PL Updated and extended 18th-c pub in peaceful village; popular fairly traditional food from sandwiches up, Tues evening fish and chips, Fri evening Mexican, special diets catered for, Greene King and two guest ales, a gin menu and good range of other drinks, friendly attentive service, timbered pitch-roof bar connecting to three restaurant areas; background music; children and dogs welcome, attractive well maintained garden, open all day Fri-Sun, food all day Sat, till 6pm Sun.

GREAT EASTON TL6126
Green Man (01371) 852285
Mill End Green; pub signed 2 miles N of Dunmow, off B184 towards Lindsell; CM6 2DN Popular well looked-after country dining pub down long winding lane; linked beamed rooms including bar with log fire, good food (best to book weekends) from pub favourites and tapas up, real ales such as Adnams, Greene King and Sharps (summer beer festival), decent wines by the glass and cocktails, friendly helpful service; background music; children welcome, dogs in bar, good-sized garden with terrace and play area, closed Mon, otherwise open all day (till around 7.30pm Sun).

GREAT HENNY TL8738
Henny Swan (01787) 267953
Henny Street; CO10 7LS Welcoming dining pub in great location on River Stour; well kept Adnams and a couple of guests, proper cider and plenty of wines by the glass, good food from separate bar and restaurant menus (booking advised), friendly efficient service; background music (live third Sun of month); children allowed in restaurant till

8pm, dogs in bar and lounge, disabled loos, terrace and waterside garden, rowing boats for hire, open all day, restaurant closed Mon.

GREAT WARLEY STREET TQ5890
Thatchers Arms (01277) 233535
Warley Road; CM13 3HU Old pub across from small village green; decent food from sandwiches and baked potatoes up, real ales including one badged for them, friendly young staff, red-carpeted black-beamed interior; may be background music; children, walkers and dogs welcome, picnic-sets outside, closed Mon, otherwise open all day (till midnight Fri, Sat), food all day Sat, till 5pm Sun.

HARWICH TM2632
Alma (01255) 318681
Kings Head Street; CO12 3EE Popular old seafarers' local just back from the quayside; highly rated food (best to book) from sharing plates up including good fresh fish/seafood, special diets catered for, well kept Adnams and good range of other beers, proper ciders and decent wines, friendly service; regular events nights (live music, quizzes and so forth); children and dogs welcome, cosy back courtyard, six bedrooms, open (and food) all day.

HASTINGWOOD TL4807
★**Rainbow & Dove** (01279) 415419
0.5 miles from M11 junction 7; CM17 9JX Pleasantly traditional low-beamed country pub dating from the 11th c (originally a small farmhouse) with three cosy rooms; built-in cushioned wall seats and mate's chairs around pubby tables, some stripped stonework, woodburner in original fireplace, three or four well kept changing ales, good choice of wines by the glass and enjoyable fairly priced food from sandwiches to popular Sun roasts, breakfast from 9am Sat, friendly helpful staff, barn function room; background music; children and dogs welcome, tables out under parasols, smallholding with rare-breed pigs, goats and chickens (own sausages and eggs), closed Sun and Mon evenings.

HATFIELD BROAD OAK TL5416
★**Dukes Head** (01279) 718598
B183 Hatfield Heath–Takeley; High Street; CM22 7HH Friendly buoyant village local with cosy seating areas around central woodburner and side servery, chunky stripped tables, armchairs and a sofa at one end, slightly more formal area at the back, cheerful prints amid creamy décor, background music and board games; Greene King IPA, Sharps Doom Bar and Timothy Taylors Landlord on handpump, good wine list, well regarded food served by cheerful staff; children welcome, dogs in bar, picnic-sets at front corner and teak tables under parasols on sheltered back terrace, open all day, food 6-8pm (noon-4pm Sun), closed Mon, Tues.

HATFIELD HEATH   TL5115
Thatchers   (01279) 730270
Stortford Road (A1005); CM22 7DU
Thatched and weatherboarded 16th-c dining
pub at end of large green; good food from
short but varied menu, well kept Greene
King IPA, St Austell Tribute and two guests
from long counter, several wines by the
glass, friendly attentive service, inglenook
woodburner, beams, some copper and brass
and old local photographs; background
music; children in back dining area, no dogs
inside, tables out in front behind picket
fence, open (and food) all day, till 9pm
(6pm) Sun.

HENHAM   TL5428
Cock   (01279) 850347
Church End; CM22 6AN Old timbered
building striking good balance between
community local and dining pub; enjoyable
well priced home-made food from fairly
pubby menu, Greene King IPA, a local beer
from Hadham, and Woodfordes, decent wines,
restaurant with leather-backed chairs on
wood floor, good open fires; quiz first Mon
of month, sports TV in snug; children and
dogs welcome, seats out at front and in tree-
shaded garden behind, open all day Fri and
Sat, till 7pm Sun.

HOWLETT END   TL5834
White Hart   (01799) 599030
*Thaxted Road (B184 SE of Saffron
Walden); CB10 2UZ* Comfortable and
well run pub-restaurant; two smartly set
modern dining rooms either side of small bar,
good generously served seasonal food from
sandwiches and pubby choices up, one real
ale (Nethergate) and nice choice of wines,
friendly helpful service; children welcome,
terrace and big garden, closed Sun evening,
Mon (open bank holiday lunchtime).

HULLBRIDGE   TQ8195
★Anchor   (01702) 230777
Ferry Road; SS5 6ND Lovely waterfront
pub surrounded by countryside and nature
reserve; contemporary décor and furnishings
in friendly bar and smart restaurant with
open kitchen, floor-to-ceiling windows, pale
leather dining chairs and very tall button-
back banquettes; perhaps Fullers London
Pride, Leigh on Sea Six Little Ships and
a guest ale on handpump, good wines by the
glass and cocktails, well executed brasserie-
style food including breakfast and brunch,
efficient staff; background music; dogs
allowed in bar, plenty of picnic-sets and other
seating outside on lawn and terrace by River
Crouch, open (and food) all day.

KIRBY LE SOKEN   TM2221
Ship   (01255) 679149
B1034 Thorpe–Walton; CO13 0DT
Refurbished 17th-c beamed pub with three
open fires, a wide choice of enjoyable good

value bar and restaurant food (all day Sat, till
4.30pm Sun), six real ales and a dozen ciders,
friendly helpful service; pétanque (alternate
Tues, plus Weds in summer), children and
dogs (in bar) welcome, disabled facilities,
picnic-sets and flowers on fenced front
terrace, garden and covered area behind,
open all day.

LANGHAM   TM0232
Shepherd   (01206) 272711
Moor Road/High Street; CO4 5NR Roomy
1920s village pub on crossroads; L-shaped
bar with areas off, wood floors and painted
half-panelling, large OS map covering one
wall, comfortable sofas, woodburner, well
kept beers such as Adnams, plenty of wines
by the glass and good selection of other
drinks, enjoyable fairly priced food including
set menu (Mon-Sat), Sun roasts, efficient
friendly service; occasional quiz and live
music nights; children and dogs (in bar)
welcome, side garden, open all day, food all
day Sat, till 5pm Sun.

LEIGH-ON-SEA   TQ8385
★Crooked Billet   (01702) 480289
High Street; SS9 2EP Steps up to homely
16th-c pub with waterfront views from
big bay windows, packed on busy summer
days when queues likely; half a dozen ales
including Adnams and Sharps plus craft
beers and gin menu, enjoyable standard
Nicholsons menu, log fires, beams, panelled
dado and bare boards, local fishing pictures
and bric-a-brac; background music; children
welcome, dogs outside only, side garden and
terrace, seawall seating over road shared
with Osborne's good shellfish stall (plastic
glasses for outside), pay-and-display parking
by flyover, open (and food) all day.

LITTLE BRAXTED   TL8413
Green Man   (01621) 891659
*Kelvedon Road; signed off B1389;
OS Sheet 168 map reference 848133;
CM8 3LB* Compact cream-painted village
pub opposite tiny green; modern décor with
old beams and log fires, enjoyable reasonably
priced traditional food from sandwiches
and baked potatoes up, over-55s set menu
and other deals, special diets catered for,
Greene King ales and a guest, Aspall's cider,
friendly helpful staff; children, walkers and
dogs welcome, picnic-sets out at front and in
pleasant sheltered garden, five-mile circular
walk from pub, open all day Sun, till 7pm Sun,
closed Mon evening.

LITTLE BROMLEY   TM1028
Haywain   (01206) 390004
Bentley Road; CO11 2PL Popular 18th-c
roadside pub; carpeted/flagstoned interior
with various cosy areas leading off main
bar, beams, exposed brickwork, painted
wainscoting and open fires, well kept Adnams
and a couple of guests, enjoyable food from
snacks to lava rock grills, friendly helpful

service; children, walkers and dogs welcome, small side garden, closed Sun evening to Tues, open (and food) all day Sat, breakfast from 9.30am Sat and Sun.

LITTLE TOTHAM
TL8811
Swan (01621) 331713
School Road; CM9 8LB Welcoming little village local with half a dozen well kept ales including Crouch Vale and Mighty Oak tapped from the cask, farm ciders/perry and good straightforward food served lunchtimes and Tues, Weds, Fri, Sat evenings; low 17th-c beams and log fire, back dining area, games bar with darts; live music and quiz nights, June beer festival; children, walkers and dogs welcome, disabled access, front lawned garden and small terrace, open all day, closed Mon lunchtime.

LITTLE WALTHAM
TL7013
White Hart (01245) 360205
The Street; CM3 3NY Handsome village pub with contemporary open-plan rooms; wood, slate and tartan-carpeted floors, seating from woven cane chairs through wall banquettes and cushioned window seats to upholstered armchairs, fireplaces (some piled high with logs), metal deer heads, antler chandeliers and candles in tall glass lanterns, four changing ales, good wines by the glass, cocktails, wide choice of popular reasonably priced food from sandwiches and snacks up including deals (special diets catered for), efficient friendly service; children and dogs (in bar) welcome, garden with cheerfully coloured metal chairs and parasols along with rattan-style seating and picnic-sets, open (and food) all day from 9am breakfast on.

LOUGHTON
TQ4296
Victoria (020) 8508 1779
Smarts Lane; IG10 4BP Chatty and welcoming flower-decked Victorian local; panelled bare-boards bar with small raised end dining area, five real ales including Sharps Doom Bar and Timothy Taylors Landlord, decent range of whiskies and good helpings of enjoyable home-made food from blackboard menu; children and dogs welcome, pleasant neatly kept front garden, Epping Forest walks, open all day.

MARGARETTING TYE
TL6801
★White Hart (01277) 840478
From B1002 (just S of A12/A414 junction) follow Maldon Road for 1.3 miles, then turn right immediately after river bridge, into Swan Lane, keeping on for 0.7 miles; The Tye; CM4 9JX Bustling country pub with open-plan but cottagey bars; dark timbers and painted wainscoting, mix of old wooden tables and chairs, woodburner with deer's head above, Adnams Broadside, Southwold and up to three guests tapped from the cask, 14 wines by the glass and over 100 gins, enjoyable

food from sandwiches and pub staples up, neat carpeted conservatory; background music, summer beer/music festivals, darts and board games; well behaved children welcome, dogs in bar, picnic-sets, dining pods and fenced duck pond outside, nice rural views, comfortable bedrooms, closed Mon, otherwise open (and food) all day; closed for refurbishment as we went to press – reports please.

MATCHING GREEN
TL5310
Chequers (01279) 731276
Off Downhall Road; CM17 0PZ Lively red-brick Victorian pub-restaurant in picturesque village; good traditional and Mediterranean-style food from lunchtime ciabattas and sharing plates up (special diets catered for), also more affordable fixed-price weekday lunch, Sat brunch, Sun roasts, friendly helpful staff, nice wines from comprehensive list, cocktails and well kept ales including Greene King; background music and occasional cabaret/music nights; disabled facilities, quiet spot overlooking large green, good local walks, open all day Fri-Sun, closed Mon except bank holidays.

MATCHING TYE
TL5111
Fox (01279) 731335
The Green; CM17 0QS Long 18th-c village pub opposite tiny green; decent range of popular well priced food, Greene King IPA, Shepherd Neame Spitfire and a guest (beer festivals), friendly welcoming staff, various areas including beamed restaurant and raftered barn room, comfortable dark wood furniture, brasses and woodburners; regular live music, TV; children welcome, garden, 12 bedrooms, open all day weekends.

MESSING
TL8919
★Old Crown (01621) 815575
Signed off B1022 and B1023; Lodge Road; CO5 9TU Bustling late 17th-c village pub near fine church; convivial carpeted bar with wheelback and farmhouse chairs around part-painted tables, open fire, ales such as Adnams and Crouch Vale (beer festivals), a dozen wines by the glass including champagne, highly regarded interesting food (not Sun evening), cheerful helpful service, two-room restaurant with white-painted chairs and rustic tables on bare boards, boating pictures on canary yellow or modern papered walls, another open fire; children and dogs (in bar) welcome, picnic-sets under parasols in back garden, more seats in front, deli behind the pub selling good local produce, open all day.

MISTLEY
TM1131
★Thorn (01206) 392821
High Street (B1352 E of Manningtree); CO11 1HE Popular for American chef-landlady's excellent food (especially seafood), but there's also a friendly welcome if you just want a drink or coffee; one

changing ale; high black beams give a clue to the building's age (Matthew Hopkins, the notorious 17th-c witchfinder general, based himself here), smart décor, though, is crisply up to date – bentwood chairs and mixed dining tables on terracotta tiles around central bar, cream walls above blue dado, colourful modern artwork, end brick fireplace with woodburner; newspapers and magazines, cookery classes; front pavement tables looking across to Robert Adam's swan fountain, interesting waterside village, 12 well appointed comfortable bedrooms (some in separate building), open all day from breakfast on.

MOUNT BURES   TL9031
Thatchers Arms (01787) 227460
Off B1508, Hall Road; CO8 5AT
Modernised country pub with oak beams and woodburners; good food cooked to order from lunchtime rolls to daily specials, four well kept ales including Adnams and Crouch Vale, cheerful helpful staff; background and some live music, occasional theatre and quiz nights, bar billiards; children and dogs welcome, picnic-sets out behind with peaceful Stour Valley views, open all day from 10am (11am Sun), food from noon till 9pm Mon-Thurs, 9.30pm Fri-Sat, 8pm Sun.

NORTH SHOEBURY   TQ9286
Angel (01702) 589600
Parsons Corner; SS3 8UD Timbered and partly thatched 17th-c pub by busy roundabout; Greene King and a couple of guests, popular food including daily specials and a vegan menu, small quarry-tiled entrance bar flanked by tartan-carpeted dining rooms, steps up to back bar with wood floor and some old local pictures, woodburner; background music; children and dogs allowed in certain areas, disabled facilities, seats out at front, open all day.

PAGLESHAM   TQ9492
Plough & Sail (01702) 258242
East End; SS4 2EQ Relaxed 17th-c weatherboarded dining pub in pretty country spot; popular fairly traditional food at affordable prices, well kept local ales, decent house wines, friendly service, low black beams and big log fires, pine tables, lots of brasses and pictures; background music; children welcome, front picnic-sets and attractive side garden with aviary, open all day Sat-Sun.

PELDON   TL9916
Peldon Plough (01206) 735808
Lower Road; CO5 7QR Welcoming little weatherboarded village pub with a couple of real ales such as Adnams and Greene King, decent wines by the glass and good choice of enjoyable pubby food, cheerful service, beams and woodburners, restaurant has become the lounge bar; regular quiz, children and dogs welcome (their friendly victorian

bulldog is Ponto), picnic-sets in back garden, shuts around 8pm Mon and Sun, also closed Mon lunchtime.

PELDON   TM0015
Peldon Rose (01206) 735373
B1025 Colchester–Mersea (do not turn left to Peldon village); CO5 7QJ Popular and friendly 14th-c inn with dark bowed beams, standing timbers and little leaded-light windows, some antique mahogany and padded leather wall banquettes, arched brick fireplace, a couple of Adnams ales along with Sharps Doom Bar, several wines by the glass and well liked home-made food (not Sun evening), cosy restaurant plus contrasting airy garden room; children (away from bar) and dogs welcome, plenty of seats in spacious garden with pretty pond, comfortable country-style bedrooms, open all day.

PLESHEY   TL6614
Leather Bottle (01245) 237291
The Street; CM3 1HG Quaint little two-room local in nice village with good walks nearby; Timothy Taylors Landlord and two local ales, enjoyable home-made food, curry night Thurs, friendly helpful staff, low ceilings and log fires; regular quiz and music events, children and dogs welcome, garden with play area, open all day.

PURLEIGH   TL8401
Bell (01621) 828348
Off B1010 E of Danbury, by church at top of hill; CM3 6QJ Cosy rambling beamed and timbered pub with fine views over the marshes and Blackwater estuary; bare boards, hops and brasses, inglenook log fire, well kept ales such as Adnams and Mighty Oak, plenty of wines by the glass (some local), good sensibly priced home-made food including specials, friendly staff; regular events from cribbage to films plus local art exhibitions in adjoining barn; children welcome, good walks (St Peter's Way), closed Sun evening, Mon (except bank holidays).

RIDGEWELL   TL7340
White Horse (01440) 785532
Mill Road (A1017 Haverhill–Halstead); CO9 4SG Comfortable beamed village pub with up to four well kept changing ales (some tapped from the cask), real ciders and decent wines by the glass, enjoyable food including lunchtime set menu, friendly service; background music and summer beer festival; well behaved children welcome, no dogs, tables out on terrace, modern bedroom block with good disabled access, closed Mon lunchtime, otherwise open all day, no food Sun evening.

SAFFRON WALDEN   TL5338
★ Eight Bells (01799) 522790
Bridge Street; B184 towards Cambridge; CB10 1BU Handsome Tudor pub with open-plan beamed bar with stylish modern

furnishings (more like a café than a pub); leather chairs around old wooden tables, upholstered wall banquettes with lots of cushions, painted standing timbers and bare boards, old brick fireplace and woodburner, flower paintings, mirrors and decorative plates on the walls; real ales include perhaps Woodfordes Wherry, ten wines by the glass and several malt whiskies, good inventive food, splendidly raftered and timbered back dining barn with modern furniture, more banquettes, antler light fittings and a woodburner; background music; children and dogs (in bar) welcome, garden with raised deck, nice walks nearby and handy for Audley End (EH), open all day, kitchen closes 6pm Sun.

SAFFRON WALDEN   TL5338
Kings Arms (01799) 522768
Market Hill; CB10 1HQ Steps up to chatty town-centre pub close to market square; five well kept ales and generous helpings of reasonably priced lunchtime food from sandwiches up, traditional multi-room interior on different levels, wooden beams, cosy open fire in back room; live music and quiz nights; children and dogs welcome, sunny beer garden behind, open all day.

SAFFRON WALDEN   TL5438
Old English Gentleman
(01799) 523595 *Gold Street; CB10 1EJ* Busy 19th-c red-brick pub in centre of town; bare boards, panelling and log fires, plenty of inviting nooks and crannies, well kept Adnams, Woodfordes and guests, plenty of wines by the glass and good choice of enjoyable lunchtime-only food from sandwiches and deli boards up, Sun roasts; friendly staff; background music; dogs welcome, part-covered heated terrace with modern furniture, open all day (till 1am Fri, Sat).

SOUTHEND   TQ8885
Pipe of Port (01702) 614606
Tylers Avenue, off High Street; SS1 1JN Cellar bar/wine merchants (not strictly a pub) with plenty of atmosphere, sawdust and candlelight, well liked food including signature pies and steaks, good value set menu (Mon-Sat), Sun roasts, excellent range of affordably priced wines and other drinks from craft beers to cocktails, friendly knowledgeable staff; regular wine tasting evenings; closed Sun evening and bank holidays.

SOUTHMINSTER   TQ9699
Station Arms (01621) 772225
Station Road; CM0 7EW Popular little weatherboarded local; unpretentious L-shaped bar with bare boards and panelling,

railway and brewery memorabilia, well kept Adnams Southwold and several guests such as Bishop Nick and Mighty Oak, Weston's cider, friendly chatty atmosphere; live blues third Sat of month, darts; back courtyard and barn with woodburner, open all day weekends (from 2pm Sat).

STANSTED   TL5125
Dog & Duck (01279) 812047
Lower Street; CM24 8LR Down-to-earth weatherboarded village pub run by friendly hard-working licensees; traditional beamed and carpeted lounge bar with well kept Greene King ales and guests, four different dining areas for their enjoyable reasonably priced food including good vegetarian choices and two-course OAP menu, Sun roasts; live music, quiz nights and other events, sports TV; children and dogs (in public bar) welcome, seats out on small front deck and in back garden, open all day, kitchen shuts 5pm Sun.

STOCK   TQ6998
Bakers Arms (01277) 840423
Common Road, just off B1007 Chelmsford–Billericay; CM4 9NF Popular open-plan beamed pub with good home-made food including some Mediterranean influences, friendly attentive service, four real ales such as Crouch Vale and Greene King, airy dining room with french windows to enclosed terrace, more seats out at front and in side garden; children welcome, open all day (food all day Fri-Sun).

STOCK   TQ6999
★Hoop (01277) 841137
B1007; from A12 Chelmsford bypass take Galleywood, Billericay turn-off; CM4 9BD Cheerful dining pub (once three weavers' cottages) with an open-plan bar with beams and standing timbers, pubby furniture and an upbeat atmosphere, also elegant dining room up in the timbered eaves with open fire in big brick-walled fireplace; good range of real ales including Adnams and regularly changing guests (beer/cider festival at end of May); children and dogs welcome in certain parts; newly refurbished beer garden with pretty flower borders, pizza oven, picnic-sets and covered seating area, limited parking, open all day, food all day Sat, closes 5pm Sun.

STOW MARIES   TQ8399
★Prince of Wales (01621) 828971
B1012 between South Woodham Ferrers and Cold Norton Posters; CM3 6SA Friendly atmosphere in this traditional weatherboarded pub; several little unspoilt low-ceilinged rooms, bare boards and log fires, conservatory dining area, half

a dozen widely sourced changing ales (beer festivals), bottled/draught belgian beers including fruit ones and a couple of ciders, enjoyable food (all day Sun) including home-smoked fish and meat, Thurs pizzas from wood-fired oven; regular events including live jazz (third Fri of month) and annual comedy festival; children in family room, terrace and garden tables, maybe summer barbecues, four good bedrooms in converted stable, open all day.

THEYDON BOIS   TQ4598
Bull (01992) 812145
Station Approach; CM16 7HR Cosy oak-beamed pub dating from the 17th c near the tube station; polished wood and carpeted floors, log fire, three well kept ales including Bombardier, several wines by the glass and good home-made food from sandwiches to blackboard specials (booking advised, particularly weekends), friendly staff; sports TV; children and dogs (in bar) welcome, paved beer garden, open all day, food all day Thurs-Sat, kitchen closed Sun evening.

TOOT HILL   TL5102
Green Man (01992) 522255
Off A113 in Stanford Rivers, S of Ongar, or A414 W of Ongar; CM5 9SD Traditional village pub refurbished to a good standard; large bar with comfortable seating and big log fire, three separate eating areas, Greene King IPA, two changing guest beers and several wines by the glass, good food from bar snacks up including several fish dishes, attentive friendly service; children and dogs welcome, attractive courtyard garden at front, four bedrooms, open all day.

UPSHIRE   TL4100
Horseshoes (01992) 712745
Horseshoe Hill, E of Waltham Abbey; EN9 3SN Welcoming Victorian village pub with small bar area and dining room; good food cooked by chef-landlord with some emphasis on fish, three well kept McMullens beers, friendly helpful staff; children and dogs (in bar) welcome, garden overlooking Lea Valley, more tables out in front, good walks, open all day, no evening food Sun or Mon.

WENDENS AMBO   TL5136
★Bell (01799) 540382
B1039 W of village; CB11 4JY Cottagey local with cheery bustle in low-ceilinged bars; brasses on ancient timbers, wheelback chairs at neat tables, winter log fire, Adnams, Oakham, Woodfordes and a guest, beer festival (Aug), real ciders and ten wines by the glass, well liked food (not Sun night), pizza van Thurs evening; background music; folk music first Weds of the month, children and dogs welcome, three-acre garden with seats under parasols

on paved terrace, pond leading to River Uttle, woodland walk and timber play area, pétanque pitch, open all day.

WICKHAM ST PAUL   TL8336
★Victory (01787) 269364
SW of Sudbury; The Green; CO9 2PT Old village dining pub by cricket green, attractive and spacious, with varied choice of well liked food served by friendly efficient staff, Adnams and guests from brick-faced counter, beams and timbers, leather sofas and armchairs, inglenook woodburner; background music, pool and darts; children welcome, dogs in public bar, picnic-sets in neat front garden, open all day Fri-Sun, closed Mon, no food Sun evening.

WIDDINGTON   TL5331
★Fleur de Lys (01799) 543280
Signed off B1383 N of Stansted; CB11 3SG Welcoming unpretentious low-beamed and timbered village pub; enjoyable locally sourced food (not Sun evening, Mon, Tues) in bar and dining room from sandwiches to very good (if pricey) steaks, OAP set lunch Weds and Thurs, well kept Adnams, Woodfordes and a couple of guests chosen by the regulars, decent wines, efficient friendly service, dim lighting, tiled and wood floors, inglenook log fire; pool and other games in back bar; children and dogs welcome, picnic-sets in pretty garden, open all day Fri and Sat, till 7.30pm Sun, closed Mon and Tues lunchtimes.

WIVENHOE   TM0321
Black Buoy (01206) 822425
Off A133; CO7 9BS Village pub owned by local consortium; open-plan partly timbered bare-boards bar; six well kept ales such as Adnams, Colchester, Crouch Vale and Mighty Oak, three craft kegs, Bad Apple cider and several wines by the glass, good sensibly priced home-made food (not Sun evening) from lunchtime sandwiches to daily specials, cheerful service, open fires, upper dining area glimpsing river over roofs; well behaved children and dogs allowed, seats out on brick terrace, two smart bedrooms up steep staircase, open all day (till 9.30pm Sun).

WOODHAM MORTIMER   TL8104
Hurdlemakers Arms
(01245) 225169 *Post Office Road; CM9 6ST* Small quietly placed traditional country local with low ceilings and timbered walls, five well kept changing usually local ales (beer festival in June) and good choice of ciders, generous helpings of enjoyable food from varied menu (special diets catered for), friendly service; children and dogs welcome, large garden with picnic-sets among trees and shrubs, play area and summer barbecues, open all day (till 9pm Sun), food all day weekends (till 7.30pm Sun).

Gloucestershire

BARNSLEY   SP0705   Map 4
Village Pub 🎖️ 🍷 🛏️
(01285) 740421 – www.thevillagepub.co.uk
B4425 Cirencester–Burford; GL7 5EF

Bustling pub with interesting food, a good choice of drinks and seats in the back courtyard; bedrooms

Perenially popular with both locals and visitors, this charming inn in the heart of a lovely Cotswold village has a friendly and relaxed atmosphere. Low-ceilinged bar rooms are smart and contemporary with pale and dark paintwork, exposed stone walls, flagstones and oak floorboards, heavy swagged curtains, plush chairs, stools and window settles around polished candlelit tables, three open fireplaces and country magazines and newspapers. There's a changing selection of ales such as Wye Valley Butty Bach and HPA on handpump, an extensive wine list with around a dozen by the glass and up to six farm ciders in summer; background music. The sheltered back courtyard has solid wooden furniture under parasols, outdoor heaters and its own servery. The six bedrooms are individually decorated and extremely comfortable and breakfasts are particularly good. The pub is owned by Barnsley House spa hotel across the road.

🎖️ Rewarding food includes confit duck with Asian salad, mandarin and sesame dressing, Thai-style crab cakes with lemon mayonnaise, tomato and courgette gratin with aubergine caviar, mushroom and butternut squash linguine with pesto, soused Cornish mackerel with pickled vegetables and sourdough, roast Loch Duart salmon with gremolata crust and summer vegetable fricassée, fish pie in thermidor sauce, battered haddock and chips, and puddings such as hibiscus pannacotta with mixed berries and lemon posset with white chocolate granola and raspberry. *Benchmark main dish: barnsley lamb chop with harissa potato wedges, chard and mint yoghurt £21.00. Two-course evening meal £25.00.*

Free house ~ Licensee Michael Mella ~ Real ale ~ Open 11-11; 11-10.30 Sun ~ Bar food 12-2.30, 6-9.30 (10 Fri); 12-3, 6-10 Sat; 12-9 Sun ~ Children welcome ~ Dogs allowed in bar ~ Bedrooms: £160

BLEDINGTON   SP2422   Map 4
Kings Head ⭐ 🎖️ 🍷 🍺 🛏️
(01608) 658365 – www.kingsheadinn.net
B4450 The Green; OX7 6XQ

Lovely 16th-c inn with atmospheric furnishings, super wines by the glass, real ales and delicious food; smart bedrooms

In a picturesque location opposite the green in a tranquil village, this smart yet cosy inn charms readers year after year – it's a winner in every way. It's a lovely place to stay, with six rooms above the inn itself and another six more spacious ones around a courtyard, all imaginatively and elegantly furnished; breakfasts are particularly good. Most people head first to the friendly, bustling main bar: ancient beams and other characterful furnishings (high-backed wooden settles, gate-leg or pedestal tables), a warming log fire in a stone inglenook, fine old flagstones and sporting memorabilia relating to rugby, racing, cricket and hunting. To the left, a drinking area has built-in wall benches, stools and dining chairs around wooden tables, rugs on bare boards and a woodburning stove. Attentive, welcoming staff serve Hook Norton Hooky and guests from breweries such as Butcombe, Prescott, Purity and Wye Valley on handpump, a super wine list with 15 by the glass, an excellent choice of malt whiskies and gins; background music, board games and cards. There are seats out in front and rattan-style armchairs around tables in the pretty back courtyard garden with a pagoda; maybe free-range bantams and ducks. The same professional licensees also run the Swan at Swinbrook (in Oxfordshire).

Local, organic produce is used for the impressive seasonal food. Dishes include open sandwiches, devilled lambs kidneys, pigeon breast with sour cherries, chicory, parmesan crumb and pigeon jus, goats cheese, fig and pear tart, sharing boards, caponata-stuffed courgette, red pepper and bean stew with green beans, burger of the day and chips, pork cutlet with star anise and carrot purée, salami, sprout flowers and jus, tiger prawn linguine with garlic, coriander and chilli, stone bass fillet with smoked pancetta, sun-dried tomatoes, pickled red onions and samphire, and puddings such as lemon posset with toasted meringue and shortbread and dark chocolate brownie with salted caramel sauce, raspberries and marshmallow. *Benchmark main dish: roast chicken, pork stuffing and mushroom pie with mash £15.50. Two-course evening meal £23.00.*

Free house ~ Licensees Nicola and Archie Orr-Ewing ~ Real ale ~ Open 12-11 ~ Bar food 12-2, 6.30-9; 12-2.30, 6-9.30 Fri, Sat; 12-3, 6.30-9 Sun ~ Restaurant ~ Children welcome ~ Dogs allowed in bar ~ Bedrooms: £100

BOURTON-ON-THE-HILL
Horse & Groom 🛏

SP1732   Map 4

(01386) 700413 – www.horseandgroom.info
A44 W of Moreton-in-Marsh; GL56 9AQ

Georgian inn with quite a choice of drinks and lovely views from seats outside; bedrooms

It's a delight to spend time at this handsome old place, whether you choose to sit in the lovely large garden with its fine country views or inside. The pubby bar is light, airy and simply furnished with a pleasing mix of farmhouse and other wooden chairs, settles, cushioned wall and window seats and tables on bare boards and a woodburning stove in a stone fireplace. Brakspears Bitter, Wye Valley Butty Bach and a changing guest on handpump, good wines by the glass, maybe a local farm cider and local gin. There are plenty of original features throughout; background music. Dining areas spread off from here, again with an attractive variety of dining chairs and rustic tables, rugs, snug little corners, an open fire and pale-painted or exposed stone walls. The five bedrooms are individually styled. It's best to arrive early to be sure of a space in the smallish car park. Batsford Arboretum is not far away.

Good seasonal food includes truffle mac 'n' cheese fritters, Scottish smoked salmon with shaved fennel and watercress, chicken, tarragon and leek pie with mash and buttered greens, seared bream fillet with Cornish new potato niçoise, British brisket burger and fries (also a vegan version), 8oz rib-eye steak with garlic parsley butter and chunky chips, and puddings such as rhubarb and custard crumble pie and sticky toffee pudding. *Benchmark main dish: beer-battered fish and chips £14.00. Two-course evening meal £21.00.*

Cirrus Inns ~ Licensee Abbie Davies ~ Real ale ~ Open 12-11; 12-10.30 Sun ~ Bar food 12-3, 6.30-9.30 (8.30 Sun) ~ Restaurant ~ Children welcome ~ Dogs allowed in bar & bedrooms ~ Bedrooms: £120

BROCKHAMPTON

SP0322   Map 4

Craven Arms

(01242) 820410 – www.thecravenarms.co.uk

Village signposted off A436 Andoversford–Naunton – look out for inn sign at head of lane in village; can also be reached from A40 Andoversford–Cheltenham via Whittington and Syreford; GL54 5XQ

Friendly village pub with tasty bar food, real ales and seats in a big garden

This cosy, family-run pub has loads of character, with low beams, roughly coursed thick stone walls and partly slate and partly wooden floors. The atmosphere is chatty and easy-going, and although it's been opened out to give a sizeable eating area off the bar servery, there's a feeling of several communicating rooms. What was a smaller lower bar has been enlarged to include a second bar counter. Throughout the furniture is mainly pine, with comfortable leather sofas, wall settles and tub chairs; also, farming implements, hand-presses, an open fire and a woodburning stove. Attentive staff serve local ales such as Bristol Beer Factory Fortitude, Prescott Hill Climb and Stroud Organic Pale Ale on handpump, eight wines by the glass and a farm cider; board games. Sliding doors now connect the restaurant with the large garden, with its lovely views and plenty of seats.

Rewarding food using local produce (with vegetarian, vegan, gluten-free and dairy-free options clearly marked) is cooked by the landlady's son and includes baguettes, gin-cured salmon with pickled fennel, smoked mackerel rillettes with pea shoots, chicken in a basket with chips, wild mushroom and nut loaf with crushed potatoes and celeriac purée, venison stew with creamy mash, overnight slow-cooked lamb with mash, pea purée, roasted roots and red wine jus, burger and chips, trout fillet with courgetti, charred leeks and dill hollandaise, and puddings such as chocolate tart with hazelnut and rose ice-cream and cashew and vanilla cheesecake with rhubarb compote. *Benchmark main dish: steak and ale pie with mash £15.00. Two-course evening meal £23.00.*

Free house ~ Licensee Barbara Price ~ Real ale ~ Open 12-3, 6-11; 12-5 Sun; closed Mon-Weds ~ Bar food 12-2, 6-9; 12-3 Sun ~ Restaurant ~ Children welcome ~ Dogs allowed in bar

CHEDWORTH

SP0512   Map 4

Seven Tuns ♀

(01285) 720630 – www.seventuns.co.uk

Village signposted off A429 NE of Cirencester; then take second signposted right turn and bear left towards church; GL54 4AE

Bustling, enjoyable little pub with good food and wine, several real ales and seats outside

Completely refurbished not so long ago, this 17th-c village pub tastefully incorporates new and old features, offers excellent food at reasonable prices and has an impressive range of drinks. No wonder it's so popular.

What was the upstairs skittle alley is now a rather smart restaurant with open rafters and an interesting menu. The downstairs linked rooms have original character with flagstone and wooden floors, restored furniture along with newer comfortable seating, and woodburning stoves. Drinks include their house ale Seven Tuns, Hook Norton Hooky, Otter Amber, Old Diary and a guest on handpump, farm cider, 14 wines by the glass from a large and thoughtful list and 23 whiskies, served by friendly, helpful staff; board games. You can sit outside at the front and back of the building; boules. Disabled access. Nearby walks are good but many customers are keen to visit the nearby Roman villa (National Trust).

Quite a choice of well regarded food includes sandwiches, tiger prawn caesar salad, pork, red wine and fennel sausage with pickles, breaded artichokes with green beans, olives and rocket, wagyu burger with black garlic ketchup and chips, smoked haddock risotto with black pudding, veal schnitzel with garlic and parmesan, courgette, cauliflower and squash tagine with couscous, and puddings such as chocolate terrine with honeycomb and praline sauce, and rhubarb posset with poached and jellied rhubarb. *Benchmark main dish: battered haddock and chips £15.00. Two-course evening meal £23.00.*

Youngs ~ Tenant Simon Willson-White ~ Real ale ~ Open 11-11; 11-midnight Sat ~ Bar food 12-3, 6-9.30; 12-9.30 Sat; 12-4, 6-9 Sun ~ Restaurant ~ Children welcome ~ Dogs allowed in bar

THE GOOD PUB GUIDE

CHELTENHAM — SO9422 Map 4

Old Courthouse

(01242) 500930 – www.brunningandprice.co.uk/oldcourthouse

County Court Road; GL50 1HB

Stunning conversion of a former courthouse on two levels with a fine choice of drinks and food

This grand two-storey pub has a real air of elegance with its large rooms with plush armchairs, built-in bookshelves and ornate chandeliers. That's not surprising, considering it was originally an Italianate-style courthouse. On the ground floor, what was the waiting room is now a big bar with cushioned wooden dining chairs around dark tables on rugs or parquet flooring, a central group of high chairs around equally high tables, a long, green leather, button-back banquette stretching down one wall, armchairs in front of open fires and lots of pictures; background music and board games. Friendly young staff serve St Austell Brunning & Price Traditional Bitter plus guests from breweries such as Cotswold Lion, Goffs, Hop Shed, Prescott, Purity and Wye Valley on handpump, 26 wines by the glass, 60 rums, 70 malt whiskies and a marvellous 144 gins. Leading off here are two small dining rooms with more open fires: one with blue décor and tartan-upholstered chairs and the other with lots of horse-racing prints and a dark red button-back leather wall banquette. At the top of the stairs, you pass under a vast chandelier to get to the handsome main courtroom. The raised, panelled seating area, largely unaltered, is surrounded by paintings of judges and looks down on a dining room with elegant marble pillars, leather chairs and wall seats, more paintings and a second bar counter. Throughout are the group's trademark bookshelves, house plants and church candles. Outside, a few tables and chairs are set out on the front pavement.

Appealing food includes sandwiches, cauliflower and chickpea falafel with coriander yoghurt, pulled pork croquettes with barbecue sauce, red cabbage and green chilli coleslaw, Sri Lankan curry with sweet potato, pak choi and coconut rice, cheshire cheese, potato and onion pie with carrot purée, roast parsnips and red wine sauce, mussels with bacon, leeks, cider and fries, pan-fried sea bass fillets with coconut and saffron velouté, sticky coconut rice and mango salsa, braised lamb shoulder with dauphinoise potatoes, carrot and swede mash and rosemary gravy, and puddings such as crème brûlée with shortbread biscuits and toffee apple sponge pudding. *Benchmark main dish: steak burger and chips £13.95. Two-course evening meal £23.00.*

Brunning & Price ~ Manager Dale Allison ~ Real ale ~ Open 10.30am-11pm; 10.30am-midnight Fri, Sat; 10.30-10.30 Sun ~ Bar food 12-9.30; 12-10 Fri, Sat; 12-9 Sun ~ Children welcome ~ Dogs allowed in bar

CHELTENHAM
Royal Oak

SO9624   Map 4

(01242) 522344 – www.royal-oak-prestbury.co.uk

Off B4348 just N; The Burgage, Prestbury; GL52 3DL

Bustling pub with popular food, several real ales and wine by the glass, and seats in the sheltered garden

The horse-racing pictures and posters adorning the walls of this upgraded yet traditional 16th-c village inn come as no surprise, since it's the closest pub to Cheltenham Racecourse. Always popular with racegoers, the congenial low-beamed bar has a comfortable mix of furnishings including antique wooden chairs and upholstered seating, parquet flooring, earth-toned and richly coloured walls, interesting pictures, and a woodburning stove in a stone fireplace. Helpful staff keep a couple of Butcombe beers plus two changing guests from Bespoke, Liberation or Timothy Taylors on handpump and ten wines by the glass; background music. The dining room tables are nicely spaced so that you don't feel crowded, and the skittle alley doubles as a function room. There are picnic-sets under parasols on the terrace and in the sheltered garden.

 Good quality food includes lunchtime sandwiches, potted chicken, ham and herb terrine, salt and pepper calamari with soy and chilli sauce, burger and chips, confit duck leg croquettes with pickled carrots and fennel and tarragon mayonnaise, trout fishcakes with spinach and poached egg, wild mushroom, ricotta and mozzarella lasagne with pickled fennel salad, lentil, cauliflower and spinach curry, spinach and ricotta ravioli with courgettes, and puddings such as white wine poached pear with blackberry sorbet and pistachio brittle and triple chocolate brownie with honeycomb and espresso ice-cream. *Benchmark main dish: beer-battered fish and chips £13.95. Two-course evening meal £20.00.*

Butcombe ~ Manager Thomas Wright ~ Real ale ~ Open 11-11; 12-10.30 Sun ~ Bar food 12-2, 6-9; 12-9 Fri, Sat; 12-8 Sun ~ Restaurant ~ Children welcome ~ Dogs allowed in bar

CIRENCESTER
Bear

SP0201

(01285) 653472 – butcombe.com/the-bear-inn-cirencester

Dyer Street; GL7 2PF

Bustling town pub with popular bar, real ales and wines by the glass, well liked food, helpful staff and seats out in front

This is the city's oldest coaching inn and has a strong local following – though visitors are welcomed just as warmly. For those popping in for a post-shopping drink, the relaxed but cheerful bar is the place to head for. Here you'll find leather armchairs in front of a modern woodburning stove in a huge fireplace, an attractive club-like area with button-back banquettes, books and plants on shelves, snug booths with more banquettes and windows looking out on to the street. Efficient, friendly staff serve Butcombe

Original and a couple of guests, a dozen whiskies, 15 gins and ten wines by the glass. The two-level dining room is furnished with Edwardian-style chairs around wooden tables on bare boards, a long cushioned settle, more bookshelves and an open fire. At the front of the building are plenty of seats and tables under parasols.

 Tasty food includes salt and pepper calamari with soy and chilli sauce, potted chicken, ham and herb terrine with sticky onion marmalade, spinach and ricotta ravioli with courgettes, beer-battered fish and chips, beef shin and ale pie, trout fishcakes with spinach and poached egg, lentil, cauliflower and spinach curry, and puddings such as apple and plum crumble with vanilla ice-cream and sticky date and toffee pudding. *Benchmark main dish: honey-roasted ham with eggs and piccalilli £14.95. Two-course evening meal £20.00.*

Butcombe ~ Manager Maddy Sinclair ~ Real ale ~ Open 12-11; 12-10 Sun ~ Bar food 12-3, 5.30-8.30 Mon-Fri; 12-9 Sat; 12-5 Sun ~ Children welcome ~ Dogs allowed in bar

COALEY
SO7701   Map 4
Old Fox
(01453) 890905 – www.oldfoxatcoaley.co.uk
The Street; GL11 5EG

Attractive old village local with good food and drink – the perfect stop on the Cotswold Way

This 300-year-old stone-built local sits in the centre of an attractive village surrounded by countryside. Lying on the Cotswold Way, it is, unsurprisingly, popular with walkers, cyclists and runners. Refurbished a couple of years ago, the single-room bar is dominated by a superb hewn-oak bar counter that divides it into separate distinct drinking areas; also a woodburning stove and flagstone flooring. There's Otter Bitter and up to five guests on handpump, three traditional ciders and a good choice of gins including examples from small-batch distillers. Service is efficient and friendly. Regular events include themed drink tastings, quiz nights, live music, beer pairings and special food evenings. There are pleasant outdoor seating areas to the front and side.

 The tasty, seasonal food – they describe it as 'traditional food with a twist of modernity' – includes sandwiches, smoked haddock and mussel chowder, roast squash, beetroot and roast onion salad with whipped goats cheese, nduja-crusted cod fillet with confit tomato, potato rösti and spinach and pea velouté, pan-roasted pork loin with lyonnaise potato and sauce diane, fennel- and ricotta-stuffed peppers with toasted pine nuts, couscous and tomato and parsley sauce, and puddings such as lemon posset with raspberry sorbet and shortbread and double chocolate sundae and brownie with fudge sauce. *Benchmark main dish: beef or chicken burger with coleslaw and chips £13.50. Two-course evening meal £20.00.*

Free house ~ Licensee Ellie Sainty ~ Real ale ~ Open 4-9pm Mon; 12-11; 12-11 Sat; 12-8 Sun ~ Bar food 12-2.30, 6-9 Tues-Sat; 12-3 Sun ~ Children welcome except in adults-only outdoor smoking area ~ Dogs allowed in bar

COOMBE HILL
SO8926   Map 4
Gloucester Old Spot ★ ◉ ◀
(01242) 680321 – www.thegloucesteroldspot.co.uk
Exit M5 junction 11 and use satnav GL51 9SY; access from junction 10 is restricted; GL51 9SY

Interestingly furnished country pub with much character, good ales and likeable food

This friendly, characterful pub manages to retain the feel of a country local, despite being close to Cheltenham. The quarry-tiled beamed bar has chapel chairs and other seats around assorted tables (including one in a bow-windowed alcove) and opens into a lighter, partly panelled area with cushioned settles and stripped kitchen tables. Changing beers from the likes of Bristol Beer Factory, Clavell & Hind, Otter, Purity, Stroud and Wye Valley, six decent wines by the glass, three farm ciders and their own-brand medium sweet perry are served by young, friendly staff. Decoration is in unobtrusive good taste, with winter log fires. A handsome baronial-style separate dining room (once a hunting lodge to nearby Boddington Manor) has similar country furniture, high stripped-brick walls, dark flagstones and candlelight; background music. Outside, there are chunky benches and tables under parasols on a terrace, with some oak barrel tables on brickwork and pretty flowers in vintage buckets and baskets; heaters for cooler weather and a smoker for smoked meats, fish and other treats.

Popular food includes filled rolls, seared pigeon breast with black pudding and honey-roasted beetroot, cheese soufflé with cream and nutmeg, buttermilk fried chicken with coconut dhal, burger with celeriac slaw and triple-cooked chips, crispy calamari with charred watermelon and feta, confit duck leg with smoked pork belly lardons, baby gem and mint salsa, and weekly changing seasonal puddings; they also offer a two-course weekday lunch menu. *Benchmark main dish: pork belly with smoked bacon and fennel stew £17.00. Two-course evening meal £23.00.*

Free house ~ Licensees Simon and Kate Daws ~ Real ale ~ Open 11-10; 11-11 Thurs-Sat ~ Bar food 12-2, 6-8.30 Mon-Thurs; 12-9 Fri, Sat; 12-8 Sun ~ Restaurant ~ Children welcome ~ Dogs allowed in bar

COWLEY   SO9714 Map 4

Green Dragon

(01242) 870271 ~ www.green-dragon-inn.co.uk
Off A435 S of Cheltenham at Elkstone, Cockleford sign; OS Sheet 163 map reference 970142; GL53 9NW

Inn dating from 1643 with character bars, separate restaurant, popular food, real ales and seats on terraces; bedrooms

Popular with those appreciating good food and drink and comfortable cottage-style accommodation, this attractive and well run stone-fronted country pub is so popular that you must book ahead to guarantee a table. The two beamed bars have a good mix of customers, plenty of character and a cosy, nicely old-fashioned feel; big flagstones, wooden floorboards, candlelit tables and winter log fires in two stone fireplaces. The furniture and the bar itself in the upper Mouse Bar were made by Robert 'Mouseman' Thompson craftsmen and have little mice running over the hand-carved tables, chairs and mantelpiece; there's also a small upstairs restaurant. Friendly staff keep a good range of drinks such as Butcombe Bitter, Cotswold Lion Golden Fleece, Hook Norton Old Hooky and seasonal ales like St Austell Jolly Holly on handpump, 15 wines by the glass, ten gins and ten malt whiskies; background music and a separate skittle alley. The nine bedrooms are comfortable and breakfasts are generous. The outside terraces have lots of seats and tables. Disabled access but not to bedrooms.

High quality food includes sandwiches, crayfish tail salad with marie rose sauce, pork and mushroom pâté with home-made chutney, soy and flaxseed schnitzel with tomato salsa, free-range chicken with succotash (sweetcorn, cannellini beans, onions, chilli and cream), vegetable curry, chargrilled pork loin steak with smoked bacon, oregano and white wine cream sauce, steak and kidney suet pudding, and desserts such as ginger sponge with custard and vanilla cheesecake with fruit coulis and chantilly cream. *Benchmark main dish: beef burger and chips £11.95. Two-course evening meal £21.00.*

Buccaneer Holdings ~ Manager Simon and Nicky Haly ~ Real ale ~ Open 11-10.30; 12-9.30 Sun ~ Bar food 12-2 , 6-8.30; 12-8.30 Sat; 12-8 Sun ~ Restaurant ~ Children welcome ~ Dogs allowed in bar ~ Bedrooms: £105

DIDMARTON   ST8187 Map 2
Kings Arms ♀ ⌂
(01454) 238245 – www.kingsarmsdidmarton.co.uk
A433 Tetbury road; GL9 1DT

Bustling pub with enjoyable food, a good choice of drinks, and pleasant back garden; bedrooms

This former coaching inn is simply but elegantly furnished, with little decorative touches such as church candles on shelves or in lanterns, antlers, prints and fresh flowers adding appeal and interest. Several knocked-through bar rooms work their way around a big servery (where there are high chairs and stools against the counter), with grey-painted half-panelling, armchairs by a log fire in a stone fireplace, settles and window seats with scatter cushions, bare boards here and flagstones and rugs there, and a mix of farmhouse chairs and benches around wooden tables of all shapes and sizes. There's also a restaurant with another open fire. Drinks include a changing selection of ales on handpump, such as Bath Ales Gem, Flying Monk Elmers, Otter Amber and Ringwood Boondoggle, nearly 20 wines by the glass and nine gins; darts. There are plenty of seats and picnic-sets in the pleasant back garden. The six dog-friendly bedrooms are individually furnished and comfortable and they also have self-catering cottages in a converted barn and stable block. The pub is handy for Westonbirt Arboretum. Disabled access.

Enjoyable food (with wood-fired pizzas in summer) includes truffle mac 'n' cheese fritters, crispy bacon, gem and avocado salad, seared bream fillet with Cornish new potato niçoise, roast cauliflower with Persian-spiced lentils, spinach and chickpeas, Moving Mountains vegan burger with vegan cheddar, guacamole and fries, chicken, tarragon and leek pie with mash and green, and puddings such as rhubarb and custard crumble pie and eton mess pavlova. *Benchmark main dish: crispy-battered haddock and chips £14.00. Two-course evening meal £22.00.*

Cirrus Inns ~ Licensee Mark Birchall ~ Real ale ~ Open 12-11; 12-9 Sun ~ Bar food 12-3, 6-9; 12-4 Sun ~ Restaurant ~ Children welcome ~ Dogs allowed in bar & bedrooms ~ Bedrooms: £70

DURSLEY   ST7598 Map 4
Old Spot ◀
(01453) 542870 – www.oldspotinn.co.uk
Hill Road; by bus station; GL11 4JQ

Unassuming and cheery town pub with a fine range of ales, regular beer festivals and good value lunchtime food

This bustling town local is renowned for its fine choice of drinks, including seven real ales on handpump – Uley Old Ric and Otter Bitter plus five guests such as Great Newsome Pricky Back Otchan, St Austell Trelawney, Stroud Tom Long and Wye Valley HPA; they also hold an annual beer festival. Also, 20 malt whiskies, 50 gins, three farm ciders, eight wines by the glass and artisan spirits. Staff are enthusiastic and helpful. The front door opens into a deep-pink small room with a lively mix of customers, stools on shiny quarry tiles beside a pine-boarded bar counter and old enamel beer signs on the walls and ceiling. Another little room leads off on the left towards the garden and a room to the right has lots of wooden benches and tables, with plenty of porcine paraphernalia throughout. The heated and covered garden has benches and parasols. Wheelchair access but no disabled loos.

 Reasonably priced food – at lunchtime only – includes doorstep sandwiches, smoked mackerel pâté, twice-baked goats cheese soufflé, cauliflower, squash and lentil curry, fish and chips, pork and apple sausages with creamed leeks and gravy, beef burger and chips, sweet chilli beef with stir-fried vegetables and noodles, and puddings such as double chocolate brownie with raspberry coulis and fruit crumble with custard. *Benchmark main dish: chicken tikka masala £14.00. Two-course evening meal £18.00.*

Free house ~ Licensee Ellie Sainty ~ Real ale ~ Open 12-11 ~ Bar food 12-3 ~ Children allowed in family room ~ Dogs allowed in bar

 EASTLEACH   SP1905 Map 4

Victoria

(01367) 850277 – www.thevictoriainneastleach.co.uk
Off A361 S of Burford; GL7 3NQ

Traditional stone pub in village with simply furnished bars, Arkells ales and decent food

Even by Cotswolds standards, this is a notably pretty and well maintained village with two fine old churches, a clapper bridge across the River Leach and this attractive little golden-stone pub. It's been the village tavern since 1856. The open-plan, low-ceilinged rooms cluster around the central servery, with cushioned window seats, leather armchairs and wheelbacks in the bar and more wheelbacks and cushioned settles in the dining room where there's also a log fire. Well kept Arkells 3B and a changing guest and seven wines by the glass are served by friendly staff; background and occasional live music, a pub quiz on the first Sunday of the month and board games. Seats and tables under parasols and picnic-sets at the front overlook the village. Disabled access but not to the loos. There are enjoyable surrounding walks and it's handy for Cotswold Wildlife Park.

 Cooked by the landlord, the pleasing food includes sandwiches, smoked local trout with crème fraîche and horseradish potato salad, saffron risotto with parmesan, pan-roasted hake with chorizo and creamed leeks, butternut squash, red onion, goats cheese and walnut tart, venison stew with dauphinoise potatoes, burger and fries, organic pork chop with apple sauce and pancetta, sirloin steak with peppercorn sauce and fries, and puddings such as lemon and yoghurt pannacotta and bread and butter pudding with clotted cream ice-cream. *Benchmark main dish: beer-battered haddock and chips £14.50. Two-course evening meal £21.00.*

Arkells ~ Tenants Tom and Maya Gabbitas ~ Real ale ~ Open 11-10.30; 11-6 Sun; closed Mon, Tues ~ Bar food 12-3, 5-9; 12-4 Sun ~ Restaurant ~ Children welcome ~ Dogs allowed in bar

 **EBRINGTON**   SP1839 Map 4

Ebrington Arms

(01386) 593223 – www.theebringtonarms.co.uk
Off B4035 E of Chipping Campden or A429 N of Moreton-in-Marsh; GL55 6NH

Nice old pub in attractive village with own-brewed ales, thoughtful choice of food and seats in the garden; bedrooms

Dating from around 1640, this attractive golden-stone inn has been at the centre of village life for centuries. The character bar and dining room have a log fire in a fine inglenook fireplace and a woodburning stove in a second fireplace (the ironwork is original) with armchairs beside it. Also, an airy bow-window seat, ladderback and farmhouse chairs and cushioned settles on old flagstones or bare boards, and fresh flowers and church candles. Real ales on handpump include their own-brewed Yubberton ales (Yubby Bitter, Yubby Goldie and the seasonal Yawnie Bitter) plus two local guests (maybe North Cotswold Moreton Mild, Otter Bitter or Wye Valley Dorothy Goodbodys stout), good wines from a thoughtful annotated list, nine gins, farm cider and winter mulled wine. Board games, bagatelle, shut the box and dominoes. Three tables in the bar are for owners with dogs. An arched stone wall shelters seats and tables under parasols on the terrace and picnic-sets line the lawn. The five well equipped, country-style bedrooms are very comfortable and breakfasts are good. Hidcote (National Trust) and Kiftsgate Court Gardens are both nearby. This is sister pub to the Killingworth Castle in Wootton (Oxfordshire).

🍽️ Enterprising food includes as much organic produce as possible: ox cheek with barbecue carrots and smoked mashed potato, confit trout with dill crème fraîche, barbecue summer squash with red onion, spring onion and tenderstem broccoli, beer-battered haddock and chips, lamb suet pudding with charred onions and date ketchup, whole plaice with sautéed potatoes, crispy capers and beurre noisette, and puddings such as baked lemon curd with strawberry and meringue, and peanut brittle and honey pannacotta with rhubarb and granola. Takeaway fish and chips on Friday 5.30-7pm. *Benchmark main dish: roasted Cornish cod with fennel, mussels and samphire chowder £18.00. Two-course evening meal £25.00.*

Free house ~ Licensees Claire and Jim Alexander ~ Real ale ~ Open 12-11; closed Mon, Tues ~ Bar food 12-2, 6-9; 12-3, 6-9 Sat; 12-3, 6-8 Sun ~ Restaurant ~ Children welcome ~ Dogs allowed in bar ~ Bedrooms: £150

FAIRFORD
Bull 🛏️

SP1501 Map 4

(01285) 712535 – www.thebullhotelfairford.co.uk
Market Place; GL7 4AA

Fine renovation of an old coaching inn with character bars and dining rooms and a thoughtful choice of good food and drink; bedrooms

This large and handsome former coaching inn combines old and new to great effect. Original beams, timbering and old stone walls and antique furniture blend cleverly with up-to-date touches including bold wallpaper, strongly coloured paintwork and bright scatter cushions. The room to the right of the entrance has vintage armchairs and a sofa in front of an open fire; opposite are two bar rooms with chapel chairs and settles, seats in a bow window and a vast bull's head above another open fire. You'll find other rooms up small staircases and through open doorways until you reach the dining rooms – one clad with reclaimed boards lined with large skulls and seating that consists of long button-back wall banquettes and modern dining chairs. Arkells beers such as 3B and Hoperation IPA on handpump, several wines by the glass, a dozen gins and 13 malt whiskies; background music and board games. Rustic tables and benches are set out at the front, with more seats in a courtyard garden. The 21 bedrooms are neat, comfortable and contemporary and breakfasts are well regarded. Disabled access. Do visit the church, dating to the 1490s and home to Britain's only set of intact medieval stained-glass windows. Sister pubs are the Five Alls in Filkins and the Plough at Kelmscott (both Oxfordshire).

🍴 Good, enjoyable food from a lengthy menu includes lunchtime sandwiches, black pudding fritters with apple, radish and tarragon salad, smoked salmon, leek and rarebit tart, slow-cooked pork belly in apple and cider with dauphinoise potatoes, butternut squash, sage and pine nut risotto, steak and kidney pie, beer-battered catch of the day and fries, slow-cooked Indian-spiced leg of lamb with green lentil dhal and coconut rice, a range of steaks, and puddings such as toffee apple pear crumble with crème anglaise and strawberry and Grand Marnier cheesecake with vanilla ice-cream; they also offer breakfast, morning coffee and afternoon tea to non-residents. *Benchmark main dish: ploughman's with pork pie, Wiltshire ham, cheddar, apple and celery £13.00. Two-course evening meal £22.00.*

Arkells ~ Tenant Steve Cook ~ Real ale ~ Open 12-11; 12-10.30 Sun ~ Bar food 12-2.30, 6-9.30; 12-3, 6-8.30 Sun ~ Restaurant ~ Children welcome ~ Dogs allowed in bar & bedrooms ~ Bedrooms: £120

FOSSEBRIDGE
SP0711 Map 4

Fossebridge Inn 🛏

(01285) 720721 – www.innatfossebridge.co.uk

A429 Cirencester to Stow-on-the-Wold; GL54 3JS

Handsome stone building in large riverside grounds with character bars, a thoughtful choice of food and drinks and friendly welcome; pretty bedrooms

Unsurprisingly, our readers are warmly enthusiastic about this 17th-c former coaching inn nestled in a pretty hamlet, with its good choice of food and drinks, elegant furnishings and lovely gardens. You'll find welcoming licensees at the helm and a cheerful mix of both locals and visitors. Stone arches divide the two original beamed bar rooms, which have both a woodburning stove and a log fire, stripped stone walls hung with copper implements and all sorts of nice old chairs, settles and cushioned wall and window seats around pale wooden tables on polished flagstones or bare boards. Butcombe Gold and Original, North Cotswold Windrush, Wadworths 6X and a beer named for the pub on handpump and 11 wines by the glass; background music and board games. The four acres of gardens include lawns running down to the River Coln, a large lake and plenty of picnic-sets under parasols. The seven bedrooms (named after Cotswold towns and villages) are individually furnished in a country style with modern bathrooms – and breakfasts are highly rated. As well as a two-mile circular stroll from the grounds you can walk up the glorious River Coln valley. Chedworth Roman Villa (National Trust) is not far away.

🍴 Good, enjoyable food includes breakfasts for non-residents (8.30-10am) and afternoon teas (3-5.30pm), plus sandwiches, country pâte with house chutney, pan-fried king prawns and chorizo, wild mushroom and basil tagliatelle with mascarpone cream sauce, hot chicken thigh curry with poppadums, chargrilled steak sandwich, sea bass with creamy white wine and parsley sauce, 10oz rib-eye steak with coleslaw and chips, and puddings such as sticky toffee pudding with clotted cream and apple and blackberry crumble with custard. *Benchmark main dish: cottage pie and a jug of gravy £12.50. Two-course evening meal £21.00.*

Free house ~ Licensee Dee Ludlow ~ Real ale ~ Open 12-11 ~ Bar food 12-9 ~ Children welcome ~ Dogs allowed in bar ~ Bedrooms: £120

GLOUCESTER
Café René ◨ £

SO8318 Map 4

(01452) 309340 – www.caferene.co.uk

Southgate Street; best to park in Blackfriars car park (Ladybellegate Street) and walk through passageway – pub entrance is just across road; GL1 1TP

Interestingly decorated bar with fair value food all day and good choice of drinks

This city-centre bar not far from the cathedral dates from the 17th c and has a subterranean feel, with black beams, dim lighting and no windows – plus stripped brick and timbering and an internal floodlit well with water trickling down into its depths. It is certainly different to many other places in the Guide. There's quite a choice of drinks: the long bar counter is made of dozens of big casks, and they keep four changing real ales tapped from the cask, such as Farr Brew The Best Bitter, Wickwar Falling Star and Wychwood Hobgoblin, plus farm ciders and a good choice of wines by the glass (decoration, including over the ceiling, consists mainly of great banks of empty wine bottles). Service remains friendly and efficient even when really pushed. One antique panelled high-backed settle joins the usual pub tables and wheelback chairs on carpet, and there's a sizeable dining area on the right. Well reproduced background music, a silenced games machine and big-screen TV (for rugby only). They have regular live music and hold a popular rhythm and blues festival at the end of July. There are picnic-sets under parasols out by the churchyard. To get here you walk down a flagstoned passageway beside the partly Norman church of St Mary de Crypt.

Some sort of food is served all day: lunchtime sandwiches, chicken liver pâté, sauteéd garlic mushrooms, Caribbean lamb curry with gungo rice and poppadum, sweet potato and black bean chilli with rice and avocado, sausages with mustard mash, greens and red onion gravy, chargrilled mixed grill, various pies (fish/chicken and mushroom/steak and ale/sweet potato, goats cheese and spinach) with chunky chips, and puddings such as lemon tart and chocolate fudge cake. *Benchmark main dish: 'Desparate Dan' burger and chips £10.95. Two-course evening meal £17.00.*

Free house ~ Licensee Paul Soden ~ Real ale ~ Open 11am-midnight (later Fri, Sat) ~ Bar food 12-9.30 ~ Children welcome ~ Restaurant

LOWER SLAUGHTER
Slaughters Country Inn ⊙ ♀ ⏤

SP1622 Map 4

(01451) 822143 – www.theslaughtersinn.co.uk

Village signposted off A429 Bourton-on-the-Water to Stow-on-the-Wold; GL54 2HS

Comfortable streamside inn with enticing food, real ales, attractive dining bar and fine grounds; smart bedrooms

With a lovely setting right by the River Eye, rustic interiors with roaring log fires and a stunning terrace for when the sun shines, this handsome stone building has all the ingredients of an idyllic Cotswold inn. The spacious grounds have tables and chairs under parasols on terraces and lawns that sweep down to the water. The spreading bar area has several low-beamed linked rooms with well spaced tables on polished flagstones, a variety of seats from simple chairs to soft sofas and warm log fires. You'll also find mullioned windows, shelves of board games, a few carefully placed landscape pictures or stuffed fish and an air of understated refinement. Service is first class. Wychwood Hobgoblin and a guest such as Brakspear on handpump, and 14 good wines by the glass. The smart evening restaurant looks over the lawn and the sheep pasture beyond. The 31 stylish and comfortable bedrooms make a fine base for exploring the area; some are in the main building, some in cottages across the courtyard.

 Tempting food includes pork pie with truffle mayo, smoked salmon with crispy capers and dill pickle, sharing platter, sweet potato and kale risotto, trio of Welsh Dragon sausages with creamed potato and gravy, moules marinière, saffron-spiced fish pie with mash, broccolini and toasted hazelnuts, chicken supreme with mushrooms, quinoa and pancetta, spiced buttermilk hake with roast fennel, new potatoes and gremolata, and puddings such as chocolate and Horlicks mousse with vanilla ice-cream and lemon drizzle, lemon curd, strawberries and basil gelato. Look out for special themed nights. *Benchmark main dish: beer-battered fish and chips £14.75. Two-course evening meal £23.00.*

Free house ~ Licensee Stephan Hardy ~ Real ale ~ Open 11-11 ~ Bar food 12-3, 6.30-9; 12-3 Sun; afternoon tea 12-5.30 ~ Restaurant ~ Children welcome ~ Dogs allowed in bar & bedrooms ~ Bedrooms: £140

NAILSWORTH
ST8699 Map 4

Weighbridge 🌟 🍷

(01453) 832520 – www.weighbridgeinn.co.uk
B4014 towards Tetbury; GL6 9AL

Bustling pub with cosy old-fashioned bar rooms, a fine choice of drinks and food, friendly service and sheltered garden

People love this pub for its famous two-in-one pies, which they've been serving for four decades. The relaxed bar with its good choice of drinks and the warm welcome from helpful staff are cherries on top of the cake (or pie?). Three cosily old-fashioned rooms have open fires, stripped stone walls and antique settles, country chairs and window seats. The black-beamed ceiling of the lounge bar is thickly festooned with black ironware – sheep shears, gin traps, lamps and a large collection of keys, many from the old Longfords Mill opposite the pub. Upstairs is a raftered hayloft with an engaging mix of rustic tables. Wadworths 6X and guest beers such as Clavell & Hind Blunderbuss, Prescott Hill Climb and Uley Old Spot Prize Strong Ale on handpump, 18 wines (and champagne and prosecco) by the glass, farm cider, 12 malt whiskies and 20 gins. A sheltered landscaped garden at the back has picnic-sets under umbrellas. Good disabled access and facilities.

 The renowned two-in-one pies (also available for home baking) come in a divided bowl – one half contains the filling of your choice (perhaps steak, kidney and stout, salmon in cream sauce, or root vegetables with beans and pulses in tomato sauce) with a pastry topping, the other half with home-made cauliflower cheese (or broccoli mornay or root vegetables). Also, lunchtime paninis and baked potatoes, lasagne, omelette, breaded brie wedges with cranberry sauce, pâté of the day, baked gnocchi in herby tomato sauce, chicken kiev, home-cooked ham and eggs, stew with dumplings, fish pie, and puddings such as dark chocolate mousse and sticky toffee pudding. *Benchmark main dish: two-in-one pie £14.80. Two-course evening meal £20.00.*

Free house ~ Licensee Mary Parsons ~ Real ale ~ Open 12-10.30; 12-11 Fri, Sat ~ Bar food 12-8.30; 12-9 Fri, Sat ~ Restaurant ~ Children welcome in upstairs dining room ~ Dogs allowed in bar

'Children welcome' means the pub says it lets children inside without any special restriction. If it allows them in, but to restricted areas such as an eating area or family room, we specify this. Some pubs may impose an evening time limit. We do not mention limits after 9pm as we assume children are home by then.

NEWLAND
SO5509 Map 4

Ostrich ★ ◉ ◀

(01594) 833260 – www.theostrichinn.com

Off B4228 in Coleford; or can be reached from the A466 in Redbrook, by turn-off at the England–Wales border – keep bearing right; GL16 8NP

Super range of beers in welcoming country pub, with spacious bar, open fire and good interesting food

This gently civilised pub is a beer-lover's paradise with an impressively large range of real ales always on offer. Whether you're a regular or a customer passing through, you'll get a genuine welcome from the charming landlady. The building dates mainly from the 16th c. The low-ceilinged bar is spacious but cosily traditional, with a chatty, relaxed atmosphere, a roaring log fire, creaky floors, window shutters, candles in bottles on the tables, miners' lamps on uneven walls, and comfortable furnishings that include cushioned window seats, wall settles and rod-backed country kitchen chairs. The fine choice of up to eight regularly changing real ales on handpump includes the likes of Exmoor Gold, Felinfoel Double Dragon, Greene King Abbot Ale, Hook Norton Old Hooky, Hop Back Summer Lightning, Shepherd Neame Spitfire, Uley Pigs Ear and Wye Valley Butty Bach; also, several wines by the glass, a couple of farm ciders and a good range of soft drinks. There are newspapers, board games and perhaps some quiet background jazz. The large pretty walled garden has seats and tables, with more out in front. All Saints church opposite, known as the Cathedral of the Forest for its unusual size, is worth a visit.

 Pleasing food includes ham hock terrine with piccalilli, Thai-style crab cakes with red pepper, smoked trout tart with pickled cucumber and dill, wild boar sausages with dauphinoise potatoes and red wine gravy, steak and ale pie, beef wellington with mushroom duxelles and port jus, ploughman's, pork ribs in a tangy sauce with garlic bread, corn-fed chicken with garlic and roquette risotto, daily specials, and puddings. *Benchmark main dish: salmon and spinach fishcakes with parsley sauce £14.50. Two-course evening meal £21.00.*

Free house ~ Licensee Kathryn Horton ~ Real ale ~ Open 12-2.30, 6.30-11 ~ Bar food 12-2.30, 6.30-9.30 ~ Restaurant ~ Children welcome ~ Dogs allowed in bar

OLDBURY-ON-SEVERN
ST6092 Map 2

Anchor ◀ £

(01454) 413331 – www.anchorinn-oldbury.co.uk

Village signposted from B4061; BS35 1QA

Friendly country pub with tasty bar food, a thoughtful range of drinks and a pretty garden with hanging baskets

In a pretty little village near the mouth of the River Severn, this inn offers a fine choice of good value food and drinks, served by hard-working, attentive staff. There might be Bass, Butcombe Original and St Austell Tribute on handpump, 11 wines by the glass, Tutts Clump Berkshire Diamond and two other farm ciders, 30 gins and 60 malt whiskies with helpful tasting notes. A neat lounge has black beams and stonework, cushioned window seats and a range of other wooden chairs, gate-leg tables, oil paintings of local scenes and a big log fire. The Village Bar has old and farming photographs on the walls, and there's a contemporary dining room towards the back of the building. In summer, the attractive garden is a real bonus with pretty hanging baskets and window boxes, and seats beneath parasols or trees; pétanque. You can walk to the River Severn (via the long-distance

Severn Way) and there are numerous footpaths and bridleways to explore. Wheelchair access to the dining room and a disabled lavatory.

 Enjoyable food includes ciabattas, king prawns in tempura batter, grilled halloumi and pesto with marinated artichokes and rocket, sharing platters, chargrilled lamb cutlets with greek salad, burger and fries, ham and free-range eggs, blue cheese and wild mushroom ravioli, chicken breast with mushroom and brandy sauce with dauphinoise potatoes, kashmiri lamb curry, flat-iron steak with fries, and puddings such as chocolate brownie with chocolate sauce and sticky toffee pudding. *Benchmark main dish: fish pie £12.95. Two-course evening meal £18.00.*

Free house ~ Licensees Michael Dowdeswell and Mark Sorrell ~ Real ale ~ Open 11.30-2.30, 6-10.30; 11.30-11 Sat; 12-10 Sun ~ Bar food 11.30-2 (2.30 Sat), 6-9; 12-3, 6-8 Sun ~ Restaurant ~ Children welcome but no under-12s in bar or lounge ~ Dogs allowed in bar ~ Bedrooms: £85

PAXFORD
SP1837 Map 4

Churchill Arms

(01386) 593159 – www.churchillarms.co

B4479, SE of Chipping Campden; GL55 6XH

Gloucestershire Dining Pub of the Year

Super food and drinks in golden-stone inn, attractive furnishings and seats outside; well equipped bedrooms

This 17th-c golden-stone inn has been carefully and attractively updated to create a destination dining pub with rooms. Make the most of it by sampling the first rate food and then staying overnight in one of the four stylish boutique bedrooms; breakfasts are good and hearty. The open-plan interior has painted beams and panelling, flagstone and wooden floors, a woodburner in an inglenook fireplace, cushioned settles and window seats and a medley of cushioned wooden dining chairs around pale tables, and big country photographs. Friendly, efficient staff serve Winston (named for them from North Cotswold) and a couple of regulars from Purity (usually Lawless and Longhorn) plus assorted guests from the same breweries on handpump and 21 wines from a good list. There are picnic-sets on a small front area and more seats in the gravelled back courtyard. Enjoyable surrounding walks.

 High class, beautifully presented food from a sensibly short menu, using local suppliers, is cooked by the chef-owner. Dishes might include seared Orkney scallop with avocado velouté, ham hock and chicken terrine with piccalilli, beetroot carpaccio with burrata, sea trout with tom kha gai, pak choi and clams, rump of Cotswold lamb with aubergine purée and confit tomato, beef wellington (for two), fish and chips, spinach and ricotta ravioli, and puddings such as white chocolate mousse with strawberry and lavender and crème caramel with blackberries. *Benchmark main dish: pork T-bone with crackling, mash, caramelised apple and pork jus £18.50. Two-course evening meal £27.00.*

Enterprise ~ Tenant Nick Deverell-Smith ~ Real ale ~ Open 12-11 ~ Bar food 12-3, 6-9; 12-8 Sun ~ Restaurant ~ Children welcome ~ Dogs allowed in bar ~ Bedrooms: £120

SELSLEY
SO8303 Map 4

Bell

(01453) 753801 – www.thebellinnselsley.com

Bell Lane; GL5 5JY

First rate food and a good drinks choice in golden-stone inn with friendly service and seats overlooking valley

This fine 16th-c village pub is ideal for walks along the Cotswold Way and on Selsley Common. The three interconnected bar rooms have beams, a woodburning stove and an open fire, wood-strip floors and modern dining chairs and tables in polished wood, with high chairs at the blue-painted bar counter. There's Stroud Budding, Wickwar BOB and a beer named for the pub on handpump, several wines by the glass including champagne, 18 malt whiskies and 100 gins – they have gin tasting trays, regular gin evenings and even offer overnight gin experiences. Service is friendly and helpful; the pub dog is called Bacchus. The garden room dining extension has retractable glass doors leading out to the terrace where picnic-sets enjoy spreading valley views. If you want to stay overnight, there are two comfortable modern bedrooms (dogs welcome for an extra charge).

The landlord cooks the accomplished, well presented food, which includes lunchtime sandwiches, smoked mackerel pâté, glazed leek, gruyère and tarragon fregola with crispy shallots, sesame chicken salad with beansprouts, Dorset crab tagliatelle, free-range chicken with celeriac, potato and mustard croquette, charred leeks and tarragon jus, seven-hour blade of beef with celeriac, parsley and potato purée, salmon and smoked haddock fishcake with broad beans, barbary duck breast with braised red cabbage and mustard mash, and puddings such as rose-scented crème brûlée with pistachio ice-cream and peanut butter parfait with caramelised bananas, banana bread and toffee. *Benchmark main dish: fish and chips £13.00. Two-course evening meal £23.00.*

Free house ~ Licensees Mark Payne and Sarah Natts ~ Real ale ~ Open 11-11; 11-8 Sun; 11-3, 5-11; 11-11 Fri, Sat; 11-8 Sun in winter ~ Bar food 12-2.30, 6-9; 12-3.30 Sun ~ Restaurant ~ Children welcome ~ Dogs allowed in bar & bedrooms ~ Bedrooms: £90

SHEEPSCOMBE   SO8910   Map 4

Butchers Arms £

(01452) 812113 – www.butchers-arms.co.uk

Village signed off B4070 NE of Stroud; or A46 N of Painswick (but narrow lanes); GL6 7RH

Cheerful pub with open fire and woodburner, plenty to look at, several real ales and enjoyable food; fine views

This is *Cider with Rosie* country – author Laurie Lee lived nearby and was a regular visitor to this historic 17th-c stone pub. Our readers also enjoy their visits very much, praising all aspects of the place. The bar has farmhouse chairs and stools around scrubbed tables, two big bay windows with cushioned seats, low beams clad with horsebrasses, and flooring that's half parquet and half old quarry tiles. Also, delft shelves lined with china, brass and copper cups, lamps and blow torches (there's even a pitchfork) and walls decorated with hunting prints and photos of the village and surrounding area. Leading off here is a high-ceilinged room with exposed stone walls hung with maps of local walks (there are many) and wheelback and mate's chairs around tables on bare boards. A cosy snug area has historic photos of the village and the area and a log-effect gas fire. Notorious from Bristol Beer Factory, a permanent fixture on the handpumps, is augmented by two changing guests from breweries such as Butcombe, Prescott, St Austell, Wye Valley and others. There are 16 wines by the glass and farm ciders; daily papers. The view over the lovely steep beechwood valley is terrific, and the seats outside make the most of it. Apparently, this area was once a royal hunting ground for Henry VIII.

Popular food at good prices includes lunchtime sandwiches, chorizo, potato and spicy cashew nut salad, chicken liver and port pâté with spiced plum chutney, sharing platters, beef lasagne, pork and leek sausages with grain mustard mash, cod, salmon and dill fishcakes with lemon mayonnaise, burger (beef or Mexican-style vegetarian) and chips, tomato and leek risotto, slow-cooked pork belly with celeriac mash, roasted carrots and apple and rosemary jus, and puddings. *Benchmark main dish: beer-battered fish and chips £11.00. Two-course evening meal £18.00.*

Free house ~ Licensees Mark and Sharon Tallents ~ Real ale ~ Open 12-10; 12-8 Sun ~ Bar food 12-2.30, 6-9; 12-9 Sat; 12-6 Sun ~ Restaurant ~ Children welcome ~ Dogs allowed in bar

TETBURY
ST8494 Map 4

Gumstool 🏵️ 🍷 🛏️

(01666) 890391 – www.calcot.co/dining/the-gumstool
Part of Calcot Manor Hotel; A4135 W of town, just E of junction with A46; GL8 8YJ

Civilised bar in smart hotel with relaxed atmosphere, super choice of drinks and enjoyable food; bedrooms

It's the lashings of style, attention to detail, impeccable service, great choice of drinks and first rate food that ensures the on-going popularity of this lively bar-brasserie attached to the very smart Calcot hotel and spa. The stylish and thoughtfully divided layout gives you the feeling of having a snug area more or less to yourself, without losing the friendly atmosphere of plenty going on around you. There are flagstones, elegant wooden dining chairs and tables, well chosen pictures and drawings and wooden 'stag's head and antlers' on mushroom-coloured walls, leather tub armchairs and stools and a neat row of copper cooking pans above the blazing log fire. From the long counter lined with modern chairs, they serve Butcombe Bitter and Wickwar BOB on handpump, around two dozen interesting wines by the glass and several malt whiskies; background music. The slightly sunken front courtyard has a few picnic-sets. The hotel's rooms and suites range from cosy to ultra-luxurious with families well catered for. Westonbirt Arboretum is not far away and Tetbury is renowned for its antiques shops.

Exceptional food includes beetroot and burrata salad with orange, hazelnut and watercress, twice-baked cheddar cheese soufflé, smoked salmon with celeriac and horseradish rémoulade, pork and sage sausages with mash, crispy shallots and onion gravy, sweet potato and bean curry with onion bhaji, pak choi and spring onion, lamb shank shepherd's pie, gilt-head bream with crushed new potatoes and masala velouté, pappardelle with roasted pepper, courgette and romesco sauce, and puddings such as raspberry bakewell tart and bread and butter pudding with toffee sauce and vanilla ice-cream. *Benchmark main dish: burger and skinny fries £16.00. Two-course evening meal £25.00.*

Free house ~ Licensees Paul Sadler and Richard Ball ~ Real ale ~ Open 12-11 ~ Bar food 12-2 (2.30 Sat), 6.30-9 ~ Children welcome ~ Bedrooms (hotel): £270

WINCHCOMBE
SP0228 Map 4

Lion 🍷 🛏️

(01242) 603300 – www.thelionwinchcombe.co.uk
North Street; GL54 5PS

Historic inn in fine town with drinking and dining spaces in character rooms, and seats on pretty terraces; warm, TV-free bedrooms

This attractive and bustling 16th-c coaching inn is set in the heart of a lovely town considered the 'walking capital' of the Cotswolds – making it the perfect base for exploring. The rustic-chic bar and dining areas have exposed golden-stone walls or portraits and gilt-edged mirrors on pale paintwork, armchairs, scatter cushions on wall seats, stools and elegant wooden dining chairs around mixed tables on flagstones, jugs of fresh flowers and plenty of big stubby candles. Marstons EPA, Prescott Grand Prix, Wye Valley Butty Bach and a changing guest on handpump, 17 good wines by the glass, 20 gins and ten malt whiskies served by smiling, courteous staff; daily papers, board games, TV and background music. Wood and metal seats and tables sit on various terraced areas among shrubs and climbers and there are more seats on grass. The eight bedrooms are individually decorated in a country style; two have their own staircases and one is in a converted hayloft. Sudeley Castle is within walking distance and Cheltenham Racecourse is nearby.

Good food includes lunchtime sandwiches, Scottish smoked salmon with watercress and shaved fennel, heritage tomato and buffalo mozarella salad, British brisket burger with ruby slaw and fries, vegan burger with vegan white cheddar, guacamole and fries, seared bream fillet with Cornish new potato niçoise, pan-fried 8oz rump steak with field mushroom, tomato and chunky chips, and puddings such as lemon tart with crème fraîche, rhubarb and custard crumble pie and eton mess pavlova. *Benchmark main dish: chicken, tarragon and leek pie with mash and buttered greens £14.00. Two-course evening meal £22.00.*

Cirrus Inns ~ Licensee Luke Buckle ~ Real ale ~ Open 12-11; 12-10 Sun ~ Bar food 12-3, 6-9 ~ Restaurant ~ Children welcome ~ Dogs allowed in bar & bedrooms ~ Bedrooms: £95

Also Worth a Visit in Gloucestershire

Besides the fully inspected pubs, you might like to try these pubs that have been recommended to us and described by readers. Do tell us what you think of them: feedback@goodguides.com

ALDSWORTH SP1510
Sherborne Arms (01451) 844346
B4425 Burford–Cirencester; GL54 3RB Rural pub (former 17th-c stone farmhouse) set down from the road and run by same family since 1984; enjoyable good value home-made food (can offer smaller helpings on some dishes), two or three changing ales and proper cider, friendly service, beams, stripped stone and log fire, smallish bar and big dining area, conservatory, games/function room; background music, film night first Mon of month; children and dogs welcome, disabled access, pleasant front garden with smokers' shelter, closed Sun evening, Mon (except bank holidays).

ALMONDSBURY ST6084
Bowl (01454) 612757
Church Road; 1.25 miles from M5 junction 16; from A38 towards Thornbury, turn left signed Lower Almondsbury, then right down Sundays Hill, then right; BS32 4DT Attractive traditional 16th-c inn boasting a long bar with thick stone walls, beams and roaring fires in winter; three Butcombe beers and one from Fullers plus a couple of guests and ten or so good wines by the glass, interesting menu including flatbread pizzas; 11 comfortable bedrooms, children welcome, patio, open all day, closes 6pm Sun.

AMBERLEY SO8401
Amberley Inn (01453) 872565
Steeply off A46 Stroud–Nailsworth – gentler approach from N Nailsworth; GL5 5AF Popular well located old stone inn with beautiful views and good local walks; two comfortable bars, snug and a more formal restaurant, well kept Stroud ales, nice wines and enjoyable locally sourced food from bar snacks up (special diets catered for), friendly helpful staff; children and dogs (in bar) welcome, side terrace and back garden, 13 bedrooms.

AMBERLEY SO8401
Black Horse (01453) 872556
Off A46 Stroud–Nailsworth to Amberley; left after Amberley Inn, left at war memorial; Littleworth; best to park by war memorial and walk down; GL5 5AL Two-bar pub with spectacular valley views from small conservatory and terraced garden; mix of pine furniture on wood and slate floors, exposed stone walls, modern artwork and two woodburners, up to five real ales including their own Amberley's Ale, Weston's cider and good range of whiskies and gins, enjoyable fairly traditional food (not Sun evening) at reasonable prices, amiable staff; children, walkers and dogs welcome, wheelchair access (highish step by gate), outside gents', picnic-sets on front grass, more in split-level back garden, parking can be tricky, open all day.

AMPNEY CRUCIS
SP0701

Crown of Crucis (01285) 851806
A417 E of Cirencester; GL7 5RS
Comfortably modernised roadside inn
with spacious split-level bar, beams and
log fires, good choice of enjoyable food
including competitively priced dish of the
day (weekday lunchtimes), Sharps Doom
Bar, a guest beer and decent choice of wines,
friendly helpful service; children and dogs
welcome, disabled facilities, tables out by
Ampney Brook with wooden bridge over
to cricket pitch, handy for Palladian Way
walkers, quiet courtyard bedrooms, good
breakfast, open (and food) all day.

ANDOVERSFORD
SP0219

Royal Oak (01242) 821426
*Signed just off A40; Gloucester Road;
GL54 4HR* Cosy 17th-c beamed village pub,
popular locally with lots of stripped stone,
galleried raised dining room beyond big
central open fire, well kept local and national
ales and more than a dozen wines by the
glass, good sensibly priced food including
sandwiches, burgers and vegetarian/gluten-
free menus, friendly welcoming staff; games
end with pool and darts, regular live music
and quiz nights; children and dogs welcome,
tables on back terrace, open all day.

APPERLEY
SO8627

Farmers Arms (01452) 780886
Lower Apperley (B4213); GL19 4DR
Popular extended country pub again under
newish management; beams, large open
fire and spacious split-level dining area,
Wadworths ales, several wines by the glass
and good home-made food, friendly helpful
staff; children and dogs welcome, picnic-sets
on terrace and in garden with nice rural
views, own chickens and pigs, one-bedroom
thatched holiday let, open all day.

ARLINGHAM
SO7110

Red Lion (01452) 740700
High Street; GL2 7JH Old village corner
pub owned by the local community; good
food from lunchtime sandwiches and pub
favourites up, Uley Bitter, their own ale and
guests, friendly staff, updated interior with
wood and carpeted floors, some beams;
children and dogs welcome, picnic-sets out
by the road, good circular walks listed on
website (not far from the River Severn),
closed Mon and lunchtime Tues, otherwise
open all day, food all day Sat, till 6pm Sun.

ASHLEWORTH QUAY
SO8125

Boat (01452) 700272
*Ashleworth signposted off A417 N of
Gloucester; quay signed from village;
GL19 4HZ* Tiny unpretentious old pub in
lovely spot on the banks of the Severn; front
parlour with mats on flagstones, built-in
settle by scrubbed deal table, elderly chairs
next to old-fashioned kitchen range, cribbage

and dominoes, back quarry-tiled dining
room with fireplace and a cosy snug, up
to ten mostly local ales and great range of
ciders, simple food such as basket meals and
burgers; live music and beer/cider festivals;
children, dogs and muddy boots welcome,
tricky for wheelchairs (friendly staff will
help), sunny crazy-paved front courtyard,
more seats to the side and on grass by river,
moorings, near interesting 15th-c tithe barn
(NT), open all day in summer apart from
Mon lunchtime (all day Fri-Sun, closed Mon
in winter).

AUST
ST5788

Boars Head (01454) 632278
*0.5 miles from M48 junction 1, off
Avonmouth Road; BS35 4AX* Cream-
painted 17th-c village pub with Marstons-
related ales, decent wines and well liked
food, linked rooms and alcoves, beams, some
stripped stone, flagstones and big fireplaces;
children and dogs (in bar) welcome,
wheelchair access, attractive sheltered
garden with covered area for smokers, handy
for the 'old' Severn bridge.

AVENING
ST8898

Bell (01453) 836422
High Street; GL8 8NF Welcoming
whitewashed country pub with proper locals'
bar and separate dining area, well kept
ales including Shepherd Neame Spitfire
and Wickwar, good authentic Indian food
(takeaways available); quiz first Sat of
month, sports TV; children, walkers and dogs
welcome, a few picnic-sets out at front, open
all day weekends, from 5.30pm other days,
no food Mon.

AVENING
ST8897

Queen Matilda (01453) 350305
B4014 Tetbury–Nailsworth; GL8 8NT
Friendly traditional stone-built village pub;
enjoyable fairly pubby food cooked by
landlord-chef including blackboard
specials, some authentic Thai curries
and popular Sun roasts, three changing
ales, good range of gins and decent
wines, helpful friendly service, wood
floors, exposed stonework, open fire and
woodburner; quiz last Thurs of month;
children and dogs welcome, a few picnic-
sets out at front, more in grassy back
garden, three comfortable barn-conversion
bedrooms, good breakfast, closed Sun
evening, Mon and lunchtimes (except Sun).

BIBURY
SP1006

★Catherine Wheel (01285) 740250
*Arlington; B4425 NE of Cirencester;
GL7 5ND* Attractive old dining pub in
beautiful chocolate-box Cotswold village;
enjoyable freshly made food (best to book
weekends) from sandwiches and pizzas up
including good local trout, well kept Hook
Norton Hooky, Stroud and a couple of guests,
Weston's cider, cheerful attentive young

staff, open-plan main bar and smaller back rooms, low beams, stripped stone and log fires, raftered dining room; children and dogs welcome, picnic-sets in front and in good-sized garden, handy for country and riverside walks, four bedrooms in separate building, open (and some food) all day.

BISHOP'S NORTON   SO8425
Red Lion (01452) 730935
Wainlode Lane; GL2 9LW Isolated red-brick pub on picturesque bend of the River Severn (prone to flooding), sister pub to Royal Exchange at Hartpury and Swan in Staunton; ales such as Butcombe and Wye Valley, proper cider and decent range of wines, gins and whiskies, enjoyable food (all day Sat, not Sun evening) from sandwiches and sharing boards up, also vegan; bar to the left of entrance, two snugs to the right, tiled/stripped-wood floors, blue/grey dados and woodburners in brick fireplaces, pubby furniture including pews, old photos and agricultural posters; background music (turned down/off on request), TV; children welcome, wheelchair access using portable ramp (friendly staff will help), picnic-sets on cobbled frontage, riverside garden across narrow road, adjacent campsite, good walks, open all day Fri and Sat, till 9pm Sun.

BLAISDON   SO7016
Red Hart (01452) 831717
Village signposted off A4136 just SW of junction with A40 W of Gloucester; OS Sheet 162 map reference 703169; GL17 0AH Bustling village pub with plenty to look at in flagstoned main bar and attractive carpeted restaurant; woodworking and farming tools on magnolia walls and hanging from beams, old photographs of prize farm stock, a framed inventory of the pub in 1903 and lots of books, pot plants and some interesting prints, candles on traditional tables, cushioned wall and window seats, well kept ales including Bespoke and Otter, Stowford Press cider and nine wines by the glass, popular food from sandwiches and traditional choices up; background music, board games; children welcome (family dining part), dogs in bar, wheelchair access, picnic-sets on terrace and in garden with play area, pretty summer window boxes, good surrounding walks, little church nearby also worth a visit.

BLOCKLEY   SP1635
Great Western Arms (01386) 700362
Station Road (B4479); GL56 9DT Simple little beamed pub under newish management; well kept Hook Norton ales, decent wines by the glass and good home-made food from varied menu, friendly efficient service, comfortable bar where dogs allowed, dining room; children welcome, paved terrace with lovely valley view, attractive village, open (and food) all day.

BRIMPSFIELD   SO9413
★Golden Heart (01242) 870261
Nettleton Bottom (not shown on road maps, so instead we list the pub under the name of the nearby village); on A417 N of the Brimpsfield turning northbound; GL4 8LA Traditional old roadside inn with low-ceilinged bar divided into five cosy areas; log fire in huge inglenook, exposed stone walls and wood panelling, well worn built-in settles and other old-fashioned furnishings, brass items, typewriters and banknotes, parlour on right with decorative fireplace leading into further room, well kept Brakspears and Hook Norton with guests such as Jennings, Stroud and Wychwood, several wines by the glass, popular sensibly priced food from extensive blackboard menu including several vegetarian/vegan options, friendly efficient staff; children and dogs welcome, seats and tables on suntrap terrace with pleasant valley views, nearby walks, open all day.

BROAD CAMPDEN   SP1537
★Bakers Arms (01386) 840515
Village signed from B4081 in Chipping Campden; GL55 6UR Beamed 17th-c stone pub in delightful Cotswold village; tiny character bar with stripped-stone walls and inglenook woodburner, half a dozen well kept ales such as North Cotswold, Wickwar and Wye Valley, simply furnished dining room serving popular pubby food (not Sun evening, Mon) plus blackboard specials; folk night last Weds of month and some Sun, board games; children (away from bar) and dogs (in bar) welcome, picnic-sets on terraces and in back garden, good nearby walks, open all day weekends, closed Mon lunchtime.

BROADWELL   SP2027
Fox (01451) 870909
Off A429, 2 miles N of Stow-on-the-Wold; GL56 0UF Atmospheric golden-stone pub set above broad village green; traditional furnishings in beamed bar with flagstones, stripped-stone walls and log fire, well kept/priced Donnington BB and SBA, good selection of wines and much enjoyed home-cooked food from shortish reasonably priced menu, friendly attentive staff, opened-up dining area; background music, darts and dominoes; children and dogs (in bar) welcome, picnic-sets on gravel in sizeable back garden, aunt sally, paddock for camping (ring for details), open all day Sat, closed Sun evening.

BUSSAGE   SO8804
Ram (01453) 883163
At Eastcombe, take The Ridgeway and first right The Ridge; pub is 500 metres on left; GL6 8BB Tucked-away Cotswold-stone local with roomy opened-up interior; good pubby food (not Sun evening) from lunchtime sandwiches to daily specials, well

kept ales from Butcombe, Greene King and St Austell, varied choice of wines, friendly helpful staff; soft background music; children and dogs (in bar) welcome, a few picnic-sets outside, good nearby walks, open all day Fri, Sat, till 8pm Sun.

CAMP SO9111
Fostons Ash (01452) 863262
B4070 Birdlip–Stroud, junction with Calf Way; GL6 7ES Open-plan dining pub with good sensibly priced food from varied menu, three or more well kept ales and nice range of wines by the glass, amiable helpful staff; background music; children and dogs welcome, rustic tables in attractive garden with part-covered terrace and play area, good walks, open (and food) all day.

CHARLTON KINGS SO9620
Royal (01242) 228937
Horsefair, opposite church; GL53 8JH Large 19th-c pub with clean modern décor; good food (all day weekends) in bar or dining conservatory, several well kept ales (tasting trays available) and decent wines, prompt friendly service; live music and quiz nights; children and dogs welcome, picnic-sets in garden overlooking church, open all day.

CHEDWORTH SP0608
Stump (01285) 720288
Fosse Cross – A429 N of Cirencester, some way from village; GL54 4NN Appealing rambling stone-built pub (formerly the Hare & Hounds) under new ownership; Hook Norton Old Hooky, Sharps Doom Bar and Theakstons ales, nice wines, own pizza oven and good quality pizza and pasta dishes, friendly efficient service, low beams and wood and flagstoned floors, bar made from reclaimed timbers, soft lighting, cosy corners and little side rooms, three big log fires, small conservatory; children welcome, disabled access/facilities, ten stylish courtyard bedrooms.

CHELTENHAM SO9421
★ Jolly Brewmaster (01242) 772261
Painswick Road; GL50 2EZ Popular convivial local with seven well kept changing ales and six ciders, friendly obliging young staff, open-plan linked areas around big semicircular counter, log fire; dogs welcome, coachyard and large garden with pretty cobbled areas and hand-made tables.

CHELTENHAM SO9522
Old Restoration (01242) 522792
High Street; GL50 1DX 17th-c beamed pub with extensive range of real ales and craft beers including three from Butcombe, enjoyable fair-priced food from sandwiches

to good Sun roasts, friendly helpful staff, open fires, games room with darts and pool; children (away from bar) and dogs welcome, open (and food) all day, from 8am Fri, Sat.

CHELTENHAM SO9624
Plough (01242) 361506
Mill Street, Prestbury; GL52 3BG Convivial thatched and beamed village local tucked away behind church; comfortable little front lounge with brick fireplace, upholstered wall benches in flagstoned back tap room, old local photographs and a grandfather clock by big log fire, corridor hatch serving two or three changing ales from stillage casks and proper ciders, enjoyable good value food including range of local pies, friendly service; perhaps live folk music Thurs; children and dogs welcome, picnic-sets in large back garden with own bar, play area and boules, open all day, no food Sun evening, closed Mon.

CHELTENHAM SO9422
Railway (01242) 522925
New Street; GL50 3QL Relaxed backstreet pub serving good authentic Thai food, real ales and craft beers from Arbor Ales, Bristol Beer Factory, Cotswold Brew Company, Stroud and others and decent selection of wines and gins, friendly helpful staff; Tues quiz; children and dogs welcome, part-covered terrace garden, open all day Fri-Sun, from 4.30pm other days.

CHELTENHAM SO9522
Sandford Park (01242) 690242
High Street; GL50 1DZ Former nightclub converted to a popular pub; three bar areas and upstairs function room, ten well kept changing cask ales along with craft and continental beers, several cask ciders and good value home-cooked food from hot dogs up (not Sun evening, Mon lunchtime), friendly staff; bar billiards; large back garden, open all day.

CHIPPING CAMPDEN SP1539
★ Eight Bells (01386) 840371
Church Street (one-way – entrance off B4035); GL55 6JG Lovely historic inn with cheerful bustling atmosphere; candlelit bar areas with massive timbers and beams, stripped-stone walls and log fires, cushioned pews, sofas and solid dark wood furniture on broad flagstones, ales such as Hook Norton, North Cotswold, Purity and Wye Valley from fine oak counter, also a couple of real ciders and seven wines by the glass, good food including lunchtime doorstep sandwiches, glass panel in dining room reveals church passage used by Catholic priests escaping the Roundheads; background music, board

games; well behaved children (not in bar after 7pm) and dogs (in bar) welcome, large terraced garden with striking views of almshouses and church, six attractive comfortable bedrooms, good breakfast, open all day.

CHIPPING CAMPDEN SP1539
Kings (01386) 840256
High Street; GL55 6AW Eclectic décor in 18th-c hotel's bar-brasserie and separate restaurant, good food from lunchtime sandwiches and pubby dishes to more upmarket choices, friendly attentive service, well kept Hook Norton Hooky and good choice of wines by the glass (can be pricey), afternoon teas, daily papers, traditional pub games and nice log fire; secluded back garden with picnic-sets and terrace tables, 19 comfortable bedrooms, open all day.

CHIPPING CAMPDEN SP1539
Noel Arms (01386) 840317
High Street; GL55 6AT Handsome 16th-c inn with beamed and stripped-stone bar, nice food from sandwiches to steaks, some good curries too from Sri Lankan chef (curry night last Thurs of month), well kept Hook Norton, local guests and good choice of wines by the glass, friendly efficient staff, coffee bar (from 9am), conservatory and separate restaurant; lunchtime jazz first Sun of month; children and dogs welcome, sunny courtyard tables, 28 well appointed bedrooms, good breakfast, open all day.

CHIPPING SODBURY ST7282
Horseshoe 01454 325658
High Street; BS37 6AH Welcoming unpretentious little pub in former stationers' making most of the space; seven well kept ales and six ciders, low priced pubby lunchtime food (not Sun, Mon), rolls, pies, pasties and Sun lunches, comfortable sofas and settles, another intimate room upstairs; occasional live music; dogs welcome, small pretty garden behind, open all day (till midnight weekends).

CIRENCESTER SP0202
Corinium (01285) 659711
Dollar Street/Gloucester Street; GL7 2DG Civilised and comfortable Georgian-fronted hotel (originally a 16th-c wool merchant's house); bar with good mix of tables on wood or flagstone floors, leather bucket seats by woodburner in stone fireplace, enjoyable fairly priced food from sandwiches to daily specials, three well kept local ales and decent wines, cheerful helpful young staff, restaurant; entrance through charming courtyard, wheelchair access with help, picnic-sets with umbrellas in attractive walled garden, 15 bedrooms.

CIRENCESTER SP0103
Drillmans Arms (01285) 653892
Gloucester Road, Stratton; GL7 2JY

Unpretentious two-room roadside local with welcoming long-serving landlady; well kept Eagle Bombardier and three quickly changing guests, basic lunchtime food only, low beams and woodburner; skittle alley, darts and pool; dogs welcome, tables out by small front car park, open all day Sat.

CIRENCESTER SP0202
Fleece (01285) 658507
Market Place; GL7 2NZ Carefully renovated old inn with various bars, lounges and airy dining areas; bare boards, contemporary pale paintwork, plenty of prints and fresh flowers, Thwaites ales and guests, two draught ciders, several wines by the glass and good selection of spirits and coffees and teas, well liked food from generous sandwiches up served by efficient courteous staff; children and dogs (in bar) welcome, terrace with white metal tables and chairs under parasols, 28 attractive well equipped bedrooms, hearty breakfast, open (and food) all day (Sun till 9pm).

CIRENCESTER SP0202
Golden Cross (01285) 652137
Black Jack Street, between church and Corinium Museum; GL7 2AA Bustling backstreet coaching inn with long thin bar, snug and skylit restaurant, enjoyable food at sensible prices including Sat brunch, well kept Arkells and good range of wines and whiskies, friendly service; occasional live music, sports TV; children and dogs welcome, rattan-style furniture in sunny courtyard garden, bedrooms and apartment, open all day (Sun till 9.30pm).

CIRENCESTER SP0201
Marlborough Arms (01285) 651474
Sheep Street; GL7 1QW Busy bare-boards drinkers' pub with eight well kept ales, also proper ciders and continental draught/bottled beers, friendly staff and good mix of customers, brewery memorabilia, pump clips and shelves of bottles, open fire; live music and quiz nights, sports TV, board games; enclosed back courtyard, open all day.

COATES SO9600
Tunnel House (01285) 770702
Follow Tarlton signs (right then left) from village, pub up rough track on right after railway bridge; OS Sheet 163 map reference 965005; GL7 6PW Character bow-fronted stone pub by entrance to derelict canal tunnel; rambling rooms with beams, exposed stonework and flagstones, good mix of furnishings and plenty to look at including old enamel signs, railway lamps, stuffed animals, even an upside-down card table fixed to the ceiling (complete with cards and drinks), sofas by log fire, Bristol Beer Factory, Ramsbury, Timothy Taylors and Uley, ciders such as Sandford Orchards, nine wines by the glass, enjoyable pubby food (not Sun evening) from baguettes to

daily specials, good friendly service, more conventional dining extension and back conservatory; background music; children and dogs welcome, disabled access/loos, impressive views from front terrace, large garden down to the canal, good nearby walks, open all day.

COLESBOURNE
Colesbourne Inn (01242) 870376
SO9913

A435 Cirencester–Cheltenham; GL53 9NP Gabled 19th-c roadside coaching inn; decent choice of popular food from sandwiches and sharing boards up, smaller appetites and gluten-free diets catered for, well kept Wadworths ales and plenty of wines by the glass, friendly service, linked partly panelled rooms, log fires, comfortable mix of settles, softly padded seats and leather sofas, candlelit back dining room; background music, TV; dogs welcome, views from attractive back garden and terrace, 14 bedrooms in converted stables, good breakfast (for non-residents too), open (and food) all day.

CROMHALL
Royal Oak (01454) 430993
ST6990

Tortworth Road; GL12 8AD Spacious old country pub under helpful friendly licensees; varied choice of popular reasonably priced food including set lunch and gluten-free menu (no food Mon or evening Sun), Keltek and a couple of guests such as Wickwar, good wine list, interesting split-level interior with log fires (one in inglenook), table built around illuminated medieval well in restaurant; children and dogs (in bar) welcome, wheelchair access to most areas, picnic-sets on paved terrace and grass, open all day except Mon when opens 6pm.

DYMOCK
Beauchamp Arms (01531) 890266
SO6931

B4215; GL18 2AQ Friendly parish-owned village pub with well kept changing ales, local ciders and good value traditional food, cheerful helpful staff, three smallish rooms, log fire; children and dogs welcome, pleasant little garden with pond, nearby walks among daffodils and bluebells, church with corner devoted to the Dymock Poets, closed Mon, no food Sun evening.

EASTINGTON
★**Old Badger** (01453) 822892
SO7705

Alkerton Road, a mile from M5 junction 13; GL10 3AT Traditionally furnished pub with spacious split-level interior with two log fires, pubby furniture including wall seats, settles and farmhouse chairs, quarry tiles and floorboards, various odds and ends such as stone bottles, bookshelves, breweriana and even a stuffed badger, good range of fresh food (not Sun evening) from sandwiches up including tapas, five changing regional ales from breweries such as Bath, Otter, Gloucester and Wickwar, well chosen wines,

a dozen malt whiskies and farm cider; nice efficient staff; children and dogs welcome, wheelchair access to top bar, tables in well landscaped garden with covered terrace, open all day.

ELKSTONE
Highwayman (01285) 821221
SO9610

Beechpike; A417 6 miles N of Cirencester; GL53 9PH Interesting 16th-c building with rambling interior; low beams, stripped stone and log fires, cosy alcoves, antique settles among more modern furnishings, good home-made food (gluten-free options) from lunchtime sandwiches up, Arkells beers and decent wines by the glass, friendly service; children and dogs welcome, disabled access, outside play area, closed Sun evening, Mon.

FORD
★**Plough** (01386) 584215
SP0829

B4077 Stow–Alderton; GL54 5RU 16th-c pub opposite famous stables and popular with the local horse-racing fraternity; beamed and stripped-stone bar with racing prints and photos, old settles and benches around big tables on uneven flagstones, oak tables in snug alcove, open fires and woodburners, Donnington BB and SBA, eight wines by the glass and a dozen malt whiskies, generous helpings of good reasonably priced food, charming service; background music, TV (for the races), darts; children and dogs (in bar) welcome, picnic-sets and pretty hanging baskets in front, large garden behind with play fort, comfortable clean bedrooms (some with views of the gallops), Cotswold Farm Park nearby, open all day Fri-Sun, food all day Sat, Sun, gets packed on race days.

FORTHAMPTON
Lower Lode Inn (01684) 293224
SO8731

At the end of Bishop's Walk by river; GL19 4RE Brick-built 15th-c coaching inn with River Severn moorings and plenty of waterside tables (prone to winter flooding); beams, flagstones and traditional seating, woodburners, enjoyable reasonably priced pubby food including summer Sun carvery, half a dozen well kept interesting beers, friendly helpful staff, restaurant, back pool room; children and dogs welcome, disabled facilities, five bedrooms and campsite, summer ferry from Lower Lode Lane, open all day Weds-Sun.

FRAMPTON COTTERELL
Globe (01454) 778286
ST6681

Church Road; BS36 2AB Popular white-painted pub next to church; large knocked-through bar-dining area with black beams and some stripped stone, usual furniture on parquet or carpet, woodburner in old fireplace, five well kept ales including Butcombe, Fullers and St Austell, Thatcher's ciders and well chosen wine list, enjoyable fairly priced pubby food, attentive friendly staff; background music; children and dogs welcome, wheelchair access via side door, disabled/baby changing facilities, big grassy garden with play area and smokers' gazebo, on Frome Valley Walkway, open all day.

FRAMPTON MANSELL SO9202
★ **Crown** (01285) 760601
Brown sign to pub off A491 Cirencester–Stroud; GL6 8JG Welcoming 17th-c country pub (former cider house) with pretty outlook; enjoyable food including daily specials, Clavell & Hind, Sharps, Stroud, Uley and a guest, three ciders and good choice of wines, friendly helpful young staff, stripped stone and heavy beams, rugs on bare boards, two log fires and a woodburner, restaurant; various events including notable bonfire-night fireworks; children and dogs welcome, disabled access, picnic-sets in sunny front garden, 12 bedrooms in separate block, open all day from midday, food all day Sun.

FRAMPTON ON SEVERN SO7407
Three Horseshoes (01452) 742100
The Green (B4071, handy for M5 junction 13, via A38); GL2 7DY Cheerfully unpretentious 18th-c pub by splendid green (longest in England); welcoming staff and locals, well kept Sharps, Timothy Taylors and Uley from small counter, proper ciders/perry too, good value home-made food including speciality pies; lived-in interior with parquet flooring, cushioned wall seats and open fire in large brick fireplace, quieter back lounge/dining room; folk nights, darts; children, walkers and dogs welcome, wheelchair access, picnic-sets out in front, garden behind with two boules pitches, views over River Severn to Forest of Dean, parking can be tricky (narrow road), open all day weekends.

FROCESTER SO7831
Frocester George (01453) 828683
Peter Street; GL10 3TQ Large refurbished Quality Inns pub on crossroads, bare-boards bar with modern furniture, light wood dados and big bay windows, some repro animal prints and oil-lamp fittings on off-white walls, warm woodburner in old fireplace, five cask ales such as Gloucester, Stroud, Uley and Wickwar, decent choice of ciders and extensive range of gins, good food from bar snacks and pub favourites to restaurant dishes, pleasant prompt service, can eat in bar, back annexe or restaurant; children and dogs welcome, wheelchair access via back door, part-covered courtyard, ten well equipped comfortable bedrooms, open (and food) all day.

GLASSHOUSE SO7121
★ **Glasshouse Inn** (01452) 830529
Off A40 just W of A4136; GL17 0NN Much extended beamed red-brick pub with series of small linked rooms; tiled or flagstoned floors, ochre walls and boarded

ceilings, appealing old-fashioned and antique furnishings, hunting pictures and taxidermy, cavernous black hearth with old iron pots etc, well kept ales including cask-tapped Butcombe and Sharps, Weston's cider, good reasonably priced wines, some interesting malt whiskies and a couple of decent gins, enjoyable home-made food from sandwiches and basket meals up (no bookings except Sun lunch), good friendly service, large flagstoned dining conservatory; background music; no under-14s (in bars) or dogs, good disabled access (but no loos), rustic furniture in neat garden with interesting topiary, flower-decked cider presses and lovely hanging baskets, nearby paths up wooded May Hill (NT), three self-catering lodges, closed Sun evening and Mon.

GLOUCESTER SO8318
Fountain (01452) 522562
Westgate Street; GL1 2NW Tucked-away 17th-c pub off pedestrianised street; seven well kept ales such as Bristol Beer Factory, Butcombe, Dartmoor and St Austell, craft beers, Thatcher's and Weston's ciders and a modestly priced wine list, good value pubby food from sandwiches and basket meals up, friendly chatty staff, open-plan carpeted bar with woodburner in handsome stone fireplace, some black beams and dark varnished dados, pubby furniture and built-in wall benches; background music; children (in certain areas) and dogs welcome, disabled access/loos, metal chairs and tables in flower-filled courtyard with big gates to Berkeley Street, handy for cathedral, open all day (food all day Fri and Sat, till 5pm Sun).

GLOUCESTER SO8218
Lord High Constable of England (01452) 302890 *Llanthony Warehouse, Llanthony Road; GL1 2EH* Popular Wetherspoons on east side of the docks; spacious and comfortable with high raftered ceiling, good range of real ales and craft beers, their usual well priced food, efficient service; TVs; children welcome, outside area overlooking canal, open all day from 8am.

GREAT RISSINGTON SP1917
★ **Lamb** (01451) 820388
Turn off A40 W of Burford to the Barringtons; keep straight on past Great Barrington until Great Rissington is signed on left; GL54 2LP Cotswold-stone village inn dating from the 18th c, bar with pubby furnishings including padded wall benches and sewing-machine tables on strip-wood floor, woodburner, leather chairs against counter serving well kept Brakspears, Wychwood Hobgoblin and a beer badged for the pub, decent wines by the glass and good choice of gins/malt whiskies, second woodburner in restaurant with collection of old agricultural tools, well liked interesting food along with sandwiches and a few pub standards, Weds steak day, friendly prompt

service; background music, TV; children, walkers and dogs (in bar) welcome, seats in sheltered hillside garden where Wellington bomber crashed in 1943 (see plaque and memorabilia), attractive circular walk, 13 bedrooms (four in converted outbuildings), open all day.

GRETTON   SP0130
Royal Oak (01242) 604999
Off B4077 E of Tewkesbury; GL54 5EP
Renovated old golden-stone country pub; bar with painted kitchen chairs, leather tub seats and pale wooden tables on bare boards or flagstones, open fires, airy dining room and conservatory, candelabras, antlers and big central woodburner, ales such as Purity, Ringwood, St Austell and Wye Valley, plenty of wines by the glass, popular food from pub favourites to specials; background music; children and dogs (in bar) welcome, wheelchair access (not to raised dining room), seats on back terrace with views over village to Dumbleton Hills and Malverns, play area and bookable tennis court, GWR steam trains run along bottom of garden in summer, open all day, food till 8pm Sun.

GUITING POWER   SP0924
★Farmers Arms (01451) 850358
Fosseway (A429); GL54 5TZ Nicely old-fashioned with stripped stone, flagstones, lots of pictures and woodburner, well kept/priced Donnington BB and SBA, wide blackboard choice of good honest food cooked by landlord including notable rabbit pie and reasonably priced Sun roasts, welcoming prompt service, carpeted back dining part; games area with darts, dominoes, cribbage and pool, skittle alley; children welcome, garden with quoits, lovely village and good surrounding walks, bedrooms.

GUITING POWER   SP0924
★Hollow Bottom (01451) 611111
Village signposted off B4068 SW of Stow-on-the-Wold (still called A436 on many maps); GL54 5UX Cosy old cottage popular with the racing fraternity; opened-up beamed bar with wooden flooring, horse-racing pictures and woodburner in unusual pillared stone fireplace, Butcombe Original and three changing ales, several wines by the glass and 15 malt whiskies, good gastropub food plus a few classics, pleasant attentive service, flagstoned dining areas with exposed stone walls, built-in cushioned wall seats and medley of tables; background music, TVs for racing; children and dogs (in bar) welcome, back garden has a decked area, heaters, fire pit and own thatched bar, views towards sloping fields and good nearby walks, five comfortable bedrooms (two in annexe), open all day.

HAM   ST6898
Salutation (01453) 810284
On main road through village; GL13 9QH
Welcoming unpretentious three-room country local; brasses on beams, horse and hunt pictures on Artex walls, high-backed settles, bench seats and other pubby furniture on tiled floors, six well kept local ales including own-brewed Tileys, 11 real ciders/perries and good range of bottled beers, limited choice of simple low-priced lunchtime food such as ham, egg and chips (own pigs, hens and potatoes), more ambitious weekend menus; folk night first Thurs of month and other live music, traditional games including shove-ha'penny, skittle alley; children and dogs welcome, wheelchair access (some tight doorways), grassy beer garden overlooking water meadows, well placed for Berkeley Castle, open all day weekends, closed Mon lunchtime.

HANHAM   ST6470
Chequers (0117) 329 1711
Hanham Mills; BS15 3NU Popular pub in lovely spot overlooking River Avon; enjoyable food from sandwiches and sharing plates up, Youngs ales, guest beers and interesting wines (plenty by the glass), efficient cheerful service, spacious up-to-date interior with various partitioned areas including snug with woodburner and comfortable seating by low tables, river views from large windows in flagstone and wood-floored bar/dining area, connecting carpeted restaurant; background music; children and dogs welcome, disabled access/loo, tables on riverside terrace, moorings, open (and food) all day.

HARTPURY   SO7924
Royal Exchange (01452) 700273
A417 Gloucester–Ledbury; GL19 3BW
Comfortable 19th-c country pub under same ownership as the Red Lion at Bishop's Norton and Swan in Staunton; modernised opened-up interior, flagstones, bare boards and carpet, two-way woodburner, popular reasonably priced food (all day Fri and Sat, not Sun evening) from sandwiches and sharing plates to chargrills and specials, Weds curry night, Wye Valley ales and guests, local cider/perry; quiz first Mon of month, sports TV; children and dogs (in bar) welcome, fine views from garden with terrace and covered deck, open all day Weds-Sun, closed Mon and Tues.

HAWKESBURY UPTON   ST7786
★Beaufort Arms (01454) 238217
High Street; GL9 1AU Unpretentious 17th-c pub in historic village; welcoming landlord and friendly chatty atmosphere, up to five well kept changing local ales and

---

Pubs close to motorway junctions are listed at the back of the book.

good range of ciders, popular pubby food (all available to take away), extended dining lounge on right with central woodburner, interesting brewery memorabilia and old local photographs, darts and skittles in bigger stripped-brick bare-boards bar with glass-topped well; well behaved children allowed, dogs in bar, disabled access/loos/parking, picnic-sets in grassed beer garden, on Cotswold Way and handy for Badminton Horse Trials, open all day.

HILLESLEY ST7689
Fleece (01453) 520003
Hawkesbury Road/Chapel Lane;
GL12 7RD Comfortably updated old stone-roofed pub owned by the local community; up to seven well kept mainly local ales with regulars such as Sharps Atlantic and Wye Valley Butty Bach, good wines by the glass and decent range of gins, enjoyable good value food including specials, friendly chatty staff and locals, bar with mix of pubby furniture, cushioned benches and wall seats, woodburner, steps down to dining room and snug; some live acoustic music; children, walkers and dogs welcome (leave muddy boots in porch), wheelchair access to bar only, back garden with play area and smokers' shelter, small village in lovely countryside near Cotswold Way, closed till 4.30pm Mon, Tues, otherwise open all day.

HINTON DYRHAM ST7376
★**Bull** (0117) 937 2332
2.4 miles from M4 junction 18; A46 towards Bath, then first right (opposite the Crown); SN14 8HG Welcoming 17th-c stone pub in nice setting; main bar with two huge fireplaces, low beams, oak settles and pews on ancient flagstones, stripped-stone back area and simply furnished carpeted restaurant, good food from pub standards to specials (eggs from own hens), well kept Wadworths ales; background music; children and dogs welcome, difficult wheelchair access (steps at front, but staff willing to help), seats on front balcony and in sizeable sheltered upper garden with play equipment, handy for Dyrham Park (NT), open all day Fri, Sat, close 6.30pm Sun.

IRON ACTON ST6883
Lamb (01454) 228265
B4058/9 Bristol–Chipping Sodbury;
BS37 9UZ Welcoming 17th-c former coaching house; well stocked bar serving ales such as Butcombe, St Austell and Wickwar, competitively priced wines and interesting gins, enjoyable good value food including lunchtime/early evening BOGOF deal, prompt pleasant service, low-ceilinged carpeted bar with dark varnished dados, rough-plastered cream walls and pubby furniture,

woodburners in huge stone fireplaces; unobtrusive background music, Mon quiz, pool and darts; children and dogs welcome, wheelchair access, picnic-sets on front terrace and in large grassy garden behind, open all day.

KEMBLE ST9899
Thames Head (01285) 770259
A433 Cirencester–Tetbury; GL7 6NZ Roadside pub with opened-up modernised interior around central servery; faux black beams, stripped-stone walls and some rough-boarded dados/wall seats, fairly rustic furniture on tartan carpet, shelves of books, stoneware jugs and a bust of Old Father Thames, intriguing little front alcove, two open fires, enjoyable fairly priced food, well kept Arkells and good value wines, friendly attentive staff; background music, skittle alley; children and dogs (in bar area) welcome, wheelchair access using ramp, disabled loo, tables outside, four simple bedrooms in converted stables, good breakfast, walk (crossing railway line) to nearby Thames source, open (and food) all day.

KILCOT SO6925
Kilcot Inn (01989) 720707
2.3 miles from M50 junction 3; B4221 towards Newent; GL18 1NG Attractive bay-windowed country pub under new ownership since July 2020; open-plan bar and dining areas with stripped beams, bare boards, dark flagstones, homely furniture and woodburners, Bombardier and Wye Valley Butty Bach on handpump, four draught ciders and perry, several malt whiskies, local wine, traditional country pub menu including game, Fri fish and Tues steak nights, special diets catered for, good friendly service, beams; background music and occasional live; children (large play area) and dogs welcome, picnic-sets in front, more in garden behind as well as straw-roofed tables, four comfortable bedrooms and good breakfasts, open all day from 7.30am.

KILKENNY SP0118
Kilkeney Inn (01242) 820341
A436, 1 mile W of Andoversford;
GL54 4LN Spacious beamed pub (used to be five stone cottages); stripped-stone and some plank-clad walls, wheelback, tub and leather dining chairs around tables on slate, wood or carpeted floors, open fire and woodburner, conservatory, ales such as Bombardier and Youngs, Weston's ciders and decent wines by the glass, well liked food from owner-chef including signature 'slow-cooked' dishes, gluten-free diets catered for, good friendly service; background music; children welcome, wheelchair access from

car park, tables out at front with lovely Cotswold views, more seating in landscaped back garden, one well appointed bedroom, closed Sun evening, Mon.

KINETON SP0926

Halfway House (01451) 850344

Signed from B4068 and B4077 W of Stow-on-the-Wold; GL54 5UG Welcoming 17th-c beamed village inn with enjoyable food including good burgers, well kept Donnington BB and SBA, Addlestone's cider and decent wines, separate dining area, log fire; pool and darts; children and dogs welcome, picnic-sets in sheltered back garden with pergola, good walks, bedrooms, open (and some food) all day.

KNOCKDOWN ST8388

Holford Arms (01454) 238669

A433; GL8 8QY Welcoming 16th-c beamed pub; bare-stone walls, flagstone or wood floors, leather sofas, armchairs and cushioned wall/window seats, candles on old dining tables, two woodburners (one in huge stone fireplace), cask-tapped ales including own Knockdown brews, also own Sherston's cider and apple juice, good wine list, enjoyable food from sandwiches up using local and home-grown produce, Mon steak night, pleasant helpful service; background and live music, skittle alley; children and dogs welcome, wheelchair access (no disabled loos), picnic-sets in side and back gardens, outside summer bar, six bedrooms, camping and glamping (in bell tents or wooden chalet), handy for Westonbirt Arboretum, Highgrove and Badminton Horse Trials, open all day Sat, Sun, from 4pm other days.

LEIGHTERTON ST8290

★ **Royal Oak** (01666) 890250

Village signposted off A46 S of Nailsworth; GL8 8UN Handsome early 18th-c mullion-windowed village pub; rambling beamed bar with two log fires, stripped stonework and pastel paintwork, mix of furniture including country pine, candles and fresh flowers on tables, ales such as Flying Monk, New Bristol, Uley and Wye Valley, traditional cider and several wines by the glass, very good food from interesting varied menu including some pub favourites and popular Sun lunch, helpful friendly service; children and dogs welcome, disabled access, sheltered side courtyard with teak and metal furniture, surrounding walks (on Monarch's Way) and handy for Westonbirt Arboretum, closed Sun evening, Mon.

LITTLETON-UPON-SEVERN ST5989

★ **White Hart** (01454) 412275

3.5 miles from M48 junction 1; BS35 1NR Sympathetically updated 17th-c farmhouse with three main rooms; nice mix of country furnishings, flagstones at front, huge tiles at the back, log fires (loveseat in inglenook), well kept Youngs ales and guests,

good range of other drinks including their own cider, popular food cooked by landlord from bar snacks and traditional choices to more adventurous specials, efficient service (may ask for a credit card before you eat); children (family dining room) and dogs welcome, wheelchair access, tables on front lawn looking over fields to the river, more behind in big orchard garden with roaming chickens and geese, walks from the door, open all day, food all day weekends.

LONGBOROUGH SP1729

Coach & Horses (01451) 830325

Ganborough Road; GL56 0QU Traditional little 17th-c stone local with up to three well kept/priced Donnington ales, Thatcher's cider and enjoyable good value pub food including basket meals, friendly landlord and staff, leather armchairs on flagstones, inglenook woodburner; background music, quiz last Sun of month, darts, dominoes and cribbage; children and dogs welcome, tables out at front looking down on stone cross and pretty village, two simple clean bedrooms, handy for Sezincote house and gardens, open all day Fri-Sun.

LONGFORD SO8320

Queens Head (01452) 301882

Tewkesbury Road (A38 just N of Gloucester); GL2 9EJ Partly timber-framed roadside dining pub; linked areas with attractive clubby décor including flagstoned bar area, generous helpings of very popular sensibly priced food (booking advised), Sharps and Wye Valley ales, good choice of wines and gins, efficient friendly service; no under-12s, open all day weekends.

LONGHOPE SO6720

Farmers Boy (01452) 470105

Boxbush, Ross Road; A40 outside village; GL17 0LP Popular roadside country pub extended around 17th-c core; Sharps Doom Bar and local guest ales, enjoyable range of food including signature pies, friendly service, beams, exposed stonework and wood floors, some bric-a-brac and logburner, steps down to restaurant and garden room with old well; background and live music, TV; children and dogs (in bar) welcome, picnic-sets and dining sheds (for social distancing) in pleasant garden, eight courtyard bedrooms, open all day.

LOWER ODDINGTON SP2326

★ **Fox** (01451) 870555

Signed off A436; GL56 0UR Attractively presented 16th-c creeper-clad inn with emphasis on their excellent food (can be pricey and must book), top notch service too, Hook Norton and a couple of guests such as Fullers London Pride and Timothy Taylors Landlord, Robinson's cider and well chosen wines (18 by the glass), series of relaxed country-style flagstoned rooms with assorted chairs around pine tables, candles and fresh flowers, log fires including inglenook woodburner; background music; children and dogs (in bar) welcome, tables under parasols at front, enclosed cottagey back garden and heated terrace, pretty village, three comfortable bedrooms.

LOWER SWELL   SP1725
Golden Ball (01451) 833886
B4068 W of Stow-on-the-Wold; GL54 1LF
Unassuming 17th-c stone-built village local surrounded by good walks; well kept Donnington ales (the attractive brewery is nearby), Thatcher's cider and well prepared/priced pubby food, good friendly service, neatly kept beamed interior with some cosy nooks, woodburner; background music, sports TV, darts; children and dogs welcome, small garden and raised deck/balcony, aunt sally, open all day weekends, no food Sun evening.

MARSHFIELD   ST7773
★ **Catherine Wheel** (01225) 892220
High Street; signed off A420 Bristol–Chippenham; SN14 8LR Attractive Georgian-fronted building in unspoilt village; high-ceilinged bare-stone front part with medley of settles, chairs and stripped tables, charming dining room with impressive open fireplace, cottagey beamed back area warmed by woodburners, well kept Butcombe, Stroud and a local guest, interesting wines and other drinks, enjoyable sensibly priced food from pub favourites up; darts and dominoes, live music last Thurs of month; well behaved children and dogs welcome, wheelchair access with help, flower-decked backyard, three bedrooms, open all day.

MAYSHILL   ST6882
New Inn (01454) 773161
Badminton Road (A432 Frampton Cotterell–Yate); BS36 2NT Popular largely 17th-c coaching inn with two comfortably carpeted bar rooms leading to restaurant, good choice of enjoyable generously served pub food at fair prices, friendly staff, three well kept changing ales such as Butcombe, Sharps and St Austell, Weston's cider and decent wines by the glass, log fire; children and dogs welcome, garden with play area, open all day Fri-Sun, food all day weekends.

MEYSEY HAMPTON   SU1199
★ **Masons Arms** (01285) 850164
Just off A417 Cirencester–Lechlade; High Street; GL7 5JT Bright and welcoming village inn under new management from August 2020; has had a contemporary revamp while keeping aspects of its 17th-c origins; traditional pub food, well kept Arkells ales and good wines by the glass, welcoming helpful staff, open-plan beamed bar with log fire, cushioned wall seat, church chairs and scrubbed oak tables, Cotswold stone or pale painted walls, restaurant; children and dogs (in bar and bedrooms) welcome, seating out on green, eight stylish

and well appointed bedrooms, open all day weekends from noon (from 8.30am weekdays with a break 3-5pm).

MICKLETON   SP1543
★ **Kings Arms** (01386) 438257
B4632 (ex A46); GL55 6RT Popular 18th-c honey-stone pub; good often imaginative food from lunchtime sandwiches to daily specials, real ales such as Bombardier and Wadworths 6X, proper cider and several wines by the glass from interesting list, friendly helpful staff, atmospheric open-plan beamed lounge with nice mix of comfortable chairs, soft lighting and good log fire, small locals' bar; background music; children and dogs welcome, circular picnic-sets under parasols in courtyard, more tables in sizeable garden, attractive village, handy for Hidcote (NT) and Kiftsgate Court Gardens, open all day.

MINCHINHAMPTON   SO8500
Old Lodge (01453) 832047
Nailsworth–Brimscombe – on common, fork left at pub's sign; OS Sheet 162 map reference 853008; GL6 9AQ Welcoming dining pub (former golf clubhouse and now part of the Cotswold Food Club group); civilised modern bistro feel with wood floors and stripped-stone walls, good food from pub favourites up, decent wines by the glass and four well kept changing beers, friendly helpful service; children and dogs (in bar) welcome, tables on neat lawn looking over NT common with grazing cows and horses, six bedrooms, open (and food) all day.

MINCHINHAMPTON   SO8801
Ragged Cot (01453) 884643
Cirencester Road; NE of town; GL6 8PE Attractively updated 17th-c Cotswold stone inn; front bar with open fire one end, woodburner the other, cushioned window seats and painted pine tables on wood-strip floor, connecting rooms including airy pitched-ceiling restaurant overlooking the garden, emphasis on their well liked (if not especially cheap) food from one or two pub favourites up, a beer badged for the pub along with two guests, decent range of wines; children and dogs welcome, outside café called 'the Shed', nine well appointed bedrooms.

MISERDEN   SO9308
Carpenters Arms (01285) 821283
Off B4070 NE of Stroud; GL6 7JA Welcoming traditional 17th-c country pub (used in the 2015 BBC adaptation of *Cider with Rosie*) with opened-up low-beamed bar; stripped-stone walls, log fire and woodburner, some interesting old photographs, Wye Valley Butty Bach, HPA and a guest, fine range of ciders and decent wines, generous helpings of popular reasonably priced food cooked by landlady using local/home-grown produce including good vegetarian choices,

also breakfast from 9am and afternoon teas, friendly helpful staff; Weds folk night, quiz Thurs; children and dogs welcome, seats out in front and to the side, popular with walkers and handy for Miserden Garden, open (and food) all day, kitchen closes 7pm Sun.

MORETON-IN-MARSH   SP2032

Black Bear (01608) 652992

High Street; GL56 0AX Friendly beamed and stripped-stone corner pub; bustling wood-floor bar with sports TVs and a couple of carved bears either side of log fire, well kept/priced Donnington ales, decent wines by the glass and good food from sensibly short changing menu, woodburner and light wood furniture in airy dining room; children welcome, open (and food) all day, kitchen closes 4pm Sun.

MORETON-IN-MARSH   SP2032

Inn on the Marsh (01608) 650709

Stow Road, next to duck pond; GL56 0DW Stone-built roadside pub with comfortable beamed bar; inglenook woodburner and some Dutch influences to the décor, chef-landlady is Dutch and cooks some good value national dishes alongside pub favourites, well kept Marstons-related beers and guests, cheerful welcoming staff, modern conservatory restaurant; background music from vintage vinyl or maybe landlord playing his guitar; children and dogs welcome, seats at front and in back garden, open all day weekends, closed Mon.

MORETON-IN-MARSH   SP2032

Redesdale Arms (01608) 650308

High Street; GL56 0AW Relaxed 17th-c hotel (former coaching inn); alcoves and big stone fireplace in comfortable solidly furnished panelled bar on right, darts in flagstoned public bar, three well kept ales, decent wines and coffee, enjoyable food from breakfast on served by courteous helpful staff, spacious child-friendly back brasserie and dining conservatory; background music, TVs, games machine; heated floodlit courtyard, 34 comfortable bedrooms (newer ones in mews), open all day from 8am.

MORETON-IN-MARSH   SP2032

White Hart Royal (01608) 650731

High Street; GL56 0BA Substantial 17th-c coaching inn with Charles I connection in centre of market town; cosy beamed slate-tiled bar with fine inglenook and nice old furniture, adjacent smarter panelled room with Georgian feel, separate lounge and restaurant, Hook Norton and a guest ale, good choice of wines and gins, well liked

---

food from sandwiches and pub favourites up including children's choices, friendly service; background music; courtyard tables, 28 bedrooms, good breakfast, open all day.

NAILSWORTH   ST8499

Britannia (01453) 832501

Cossack Square; GL6 0DG Large open-plan pub (part of the small Cotswold Food Club chain) in former manor house; popular pubby and bistro food including stone-baked pizzas (best to book evenings), friendly helpful service, well kept Hook Norton, Wadworths and guests, good choice of wines by the glass, big log fire; children welcome, picnic-sets in front garden, open all day (food all day weekends).

NAILSWORTH   ST8499

Egypt Mill (01453) 833449

Off A46; heading N towards Stroud, first right after roundabout, then left; GL6 0AE Converted 16th-c mill with working waterwheels; split-level brick- and stone-floor bar, stripped beams and some hefty ironwork in comfortable carpeted lounge, seating ranging from elegant dining chairs to cushioned wall seats and sofas, well kept ales, a dozen wines by the glass and enjoyable reasonably priced food including vegetarian/vegan options, good friendly service; background music; children welcome, plenty of tables in floodlit garden overlooking millpond, 32 well equipped bedrooms (some with fine beams and timbering), open (and food) all day.

NAUNTON   SP1123

★Black Horse (01451) 850565

Off B4068 W of Stow-on-the-Wold; GL54 3AD Welcoming locals' pub with well kept/priced Donnington BB and SBA, Weston's cider and popular home-made food from traditional pub favourites to daily specials such as seasonal game, friendly efficient service, black beams, stripped stone, flagstones and log fire, dining room; background music, darts and dominoes; children and dogs welcome, small seating area outside, charming village and fine Cotswold walks (walking groups asked to pre-order food), open all day Fri-Sun.

NETHER WESTCOTE   SP2220

★Feathered Nest (01993) 833030

Off A424 Burford to Stow-on-the-Wold; OX7 6SD Civilised former malthouse with largely stripped-stone bar up a few stairs, low beams and dark flagstones, carved settle among other carefully chosen furniture, saddle stools at counter serving ales such as Prescott and Purity and around a dozen

---

Please tell us if any pub deserves to be upgraded to a featured entry – and why: feedback@goodguides.com, or (no stamp needed) Freepost THE GOOD PUB GUIDE, Random House Publishing, 20 Vauxhall Bridge Road, London SW1V 2SA.

wines by the glass from an impressive list, high-raftered room leads off with sofas by vast log fire, smart two-level dining rooms, very good food and service; background music, TV; children and dogs (in bar) welcome, teak tables and wicker armchairs on paved terrace, heated shelter and spreading lawn bounded by floodlit trees, Evenlode Valley beyond, four well equipped individually decorated bedrooms, good breakfast, closed Tues and Weds, two weeks Feb, two weeks July and one week Oct, otherwise open all day.

NIBLEY   ST6982
Swan (01454) 312290
Badminton Road; BS37 5JF Part of small local pub group, friendly and relaxed, with good food from snacks to daily specials, Bath, Butcombe and Wadworths ales, real cider and over a dozen wines by the glass, good service, modernised interior with fireside leather sofas one side, dining tables the other, separate restaurant; background music; children and dogs (in bar) welcome, garden picnic-sets, open all day.

NORTH CERNEY   SP0208
★Bathurst Arms (01285) 832150
A435 Cirencester–Cheltenham; GL7 7BZ Handsome pink-painted 17th-c inn with beamed and panelled bar, attractive medley of old tables and chairs on flagstones, window seats and fireplace at each end (one is huge and has an open woodburner), oak-floored room leading off, Butcombe Bitter, St Austell Tribute and two guests, nine good wines by the glass and well liked food, restaurant with another woodburner; children and dogs (in bar) welcome, plenty of seats in attractively landscaped garden with River Chun running through it, lovely church opposite and handy for Cerney House Gardens, comfortably furnished bedrooms, open all day Fri-Sun (till 8pm Sun).

NORTHLEACH   SP1114
★Wheatsheaf (01451) 860244
West End; the inn is on your left as you come in following the sign off A429, just SW of the junction with A40; GL54 3EZ Smartly furnished characterful 17th-c coaching inn with friendly helpful service and good chatty atmosphere; airy linked bar and dining rooms with big windows, high ceilings, three open fires, flagstones and bare boards, attractive mix of furniture and interesting artwork, real ales from breweries such as Bath, Box Steam and Hook Norton, 20 wines by the glass from a fantastic list of around 300 and local cider, excellent restauranty food from breakfast (8-10am) onwards; background music and TV; children and dogs welcome, pretty back garden with plenty of seating, 14 comfortable individually styled bedrooms, lovely market town, open all day.

NORTH NIBLEY   ST7596
New Inn (01453) 543659
E of village itself; Waterley Bottom; GL11 6EF Former cider house in secluded rural setting popular with walkers; up to three well kept local changing beers served from antique pumps, fine range of ciders/perries (more in bottles) and enjoyable food from lunchtime sandwiches and ploughman's up, lounge bar with cushioned windsor chairs and high-backed settles, partly stripped-stone walls, simple cosy public bar (no children here after 6pm), cider festivals and other events (maybe local mummers); children and dogs welcome, hitching rail and trough for horses, picnic-sets and swings on lawn, covered decked area, two bedrooms, open all day weekends, closed Mon and lunchtime Tues.

OLD DOWN   ST6187
★Fox (01454) 412507
3.9 miles from M5 junction 15/16; A38 towards Gloucester, then Old Down signposted; turn left into Inner Down; BS32 4PR Tucked-away yet popular family-owned country pub; six well kept ales such as Bath, Butcombe, Fullers, St Austell and Sharps, Thatcher's and St Austell's Black Rat cider and several wines by the glass, good reasonably priced traditional food from baguettes up, low beams, carpeted, wood or flagstone floors, log fire, plain modern wooden furniture, dark green faux leather wall seats in bar, snug family room; dogs welcome, good disabled access (no loos), front and back gardens, long verandah with grapevine, play area, open all day.

OLD SODBURY   ST7581
Dog (01454) 312006
3 miles from M4 junction 18, via A46 and A432; The Hill (a busy road); BS37 6LZ Welcoming old pub with popular two-level carpeted bar, low beams, stripped stone and open fire, good reasonably priced food from sandwiches and baked potatoes to fresh fish and steaks, Sharps Doom Bar and three Wickwar ales kept well, friendly attentive young staff; children and dogs welcome, handy for Cotswold Way walkers, nice big garden with paved terrace, four annexe bedrooms, open all day.

PAINSWICK   SO8609
Falcon (01452) 814222
New Street; GL6 6UN Handsome stone-built inn dating from the 16th c; sympathetically updated open-plan layout with bar and two dining areas, tasty, popular food including daily specials, four well kept beers and good choice of fairly priced wines by the glass, friendly young staff; occasional live music; children and dogs welcome, 11 comfortable bedrooms, opposite churchyard famous for its 99 yews.

PARKEND
SO6107
Fountain (01594) 562189
Just off B4234; GL15 4JD 18th-c village inn by terminus of restored Dean Forest Railway; two well kept Wye Valley ales and guests such as Hillside and Greene King, Severn and Weston's ciders, wines in glass-sized bottles, enjoyable reasonably priced home-made food including Sun carvery and OAP weekday lunch deal, prompt service from friendly young staff, assorted chairs and settles in two linked carpeted rooms, pale wood panelling, old tools, bric-a-brac, photographs and framed local history information, open fire; Tues quiz, live music nights; children, walkers and dogs welcome, wheelchair access using ramps, disabled loo, grassy streamside beer garden, seven bedrooms and bunkhouse, open all day.

PARKEND
SO6308
Rising Sun (01594) 562008
Off B4431; GL15 4HN Perched on wooded hillside and approached by roughish single-track drive – popular with walkers and cyclists; open-plan carpeted bar with modern pub furniture, Wickwar BOB, three changing guests and real ciders, well priced straightforward food from sandwiches and baked potatoes up, friendly service; TV, occasional live music, lounge/games area (pool and machines); children and dogs welcome, wheelchair access with help, views from balcony and terrace tables under umbrellas, big woodside garden with play area and duck pond, self-catering accommodation, open (and food) all day.

PILNING
ST5684
Plough (01454) 632556
Handy for M5 junction 17 via B4055 and Station Road; Pilning Street; BS35 4JJ Fairly remote but thriving roadside local much extended over the years; Wadworths ales and Thatcher's ciders, good value pubby food including children's and OAPs' menus, cheerful efficient young staff, flagstone floors in the oldest part, polished wood and carpet elsewhere, dados and some old advertising pictures, log fires; live music and karaoke nights, pool and darts; dogs welcome (pub labrador is Bruiser), wheelchair access/loos, picnic-sets out at front and in large paddock with fenced-in play area, open all day, no food Sun evening.

POULTON
SP1001
Falcon (01285) 850878
London Road; GL7 5HN Popular bistro-feel village dining pub with highly regarded food from chef-owner including good value set lunch, well kept Hook Norton Old Hooky, a local guest beer and nice wines by the glass, friendly attentive service, neat modern interior with some old black beams, relaxed easy-going atmosphere; background music; well behaved children welcome, closed Sun evening, Mon.

QUENINGTON
SP1404
Keepers Arms (01285) 750349
Church Road; GL7 5BL Community local in pretty Cotswold village; cosy and comfortable, with stripped stone, low beams and log fires, friendly helpful landlord and staff, good fairly priced food in bar and restaurant from changing menu including daily specials and steak night, three well kept beers, such as Butcombe, Otter and St Austell, a dozen wines by the glass and interesting range of gins; quiz first Thurs of month; dogs welcome (their border collies are Denzil and Doris), picnic-sets out in front, four bedrooms, closed Mon and lunchtime Tues, food available Fri-Sun.

SALFORD HILL
SP2629
Greedy Goose (01608) 646551
Junction A44/A436, near Chastleton; GL56 0SP Old roadside country dining pub with contemporary interiors; enjoyable food from sandwiches and stone-baked pizzas up, three North Cotswold ales, friendly staff; children and dogs welcome, seats out at front and in back decked/gravelled area, campsite including wooden pods, open all day.

SAPPERTON
SO9403
★ Bell (01285) 760298
Village signposted from A419 Stroud–Cirencester; OS Sheet 163 map reference 948033; GL7 6LE Welcoming 250-year-old pub-restaurant with cosy connecting rooms around central bar; beams and exposed stonework, flagstone, wood and quarry-tiled floors, log fires, four well kept ales, plenty of wines by the glass and good choice of other drinks, much liked food (not Sun evening) from sandwiches, sharing boards and pub favourites to more ambitious choices, friendly knowledgeable service; children and dogs welcome, seats out in front and in back courtyard garden, tethering for horses, plenty of surrounding walks, closed Mon in winter, otherwise open all day.

SAPPERTON
SO9303
Daneway Inn (01285) 760297
Daneway; off A419 Stroud–Cirencester; GL7 6LN Quietly tucked-away 18th-c whitewashed pub; three linked rooms with bare boards or carpet, woodburner in amazing floor-to-ceiling carved oak dutch fireplace, also an inglenook, up to four Wadworths ales, traditional cider/perry and

---

We checked prices with the pubs as we went to press in summer 2020.
They should hold until around spring 2021.

enjoyable home-made food at fair prices, friendly staff, traditional games such as shove-ha'penny and ring the bull; children and dogs welcome, tricky wheelchair access (there are disabled loos), terrace tables and lovely sloping lawn, good walks by disused canal with tunnel to Coates, surrounding nature reserves, campsite with shepherd's hut, open (and food) all day except Sun.

SHIPTON MOYNE   ST8989

★ **Cat & Custard Pot** (01666) 880249

Off B4040 Malmesbury–Bristol; The Street; GL8 8PN Refurbished and extended early 18th-c pub in picturesque village; three real ales such as Flying Monk, Hook Norton and Wickwar, local ciders and interesting selection of whiskies and gins, decent wines by the glass too, good freshly made food at sensible prices including burgers and steaks, deceptively spacious inside with several dining areas, beams and bric-a-brac, hunting prints, cosy back snug, two-way woodburner; children, walkers and dogs welcome, front wheelchair access to most areas, disabled loos, picnic-sets in small front garden, handy for Beaufort Polo Club, Highgrove and Westonbirt Arboretum, six comfortable bedrooms, open all day.

SHURDINGTON   SO8318

Bell (01242) 862245

A46 just S of Cheltenham; GL3 4PB Friendly early 19th-c village pub with well liked fairly traditional pubby food from lunchtime sandwiches up, several local ales and good wines by the glass, attentive helpful staff, conservatory looking over cricket field; live music last Sat of month; children and dogs welcome, adjacent playground, open all day, no food Sun evening.

SLAD   SO8707

Woolpack (01452) 813429

B4070 Stroud–Birdlip; GL6 7QA Popular early 19th-c hillside village pub with lovely valley views; four unspoilt little connecting rooms, interesting photographs including some of Laurie Lee who was a regular (his books for sale), log fire, good imaginative food (highish prices) along with pub favourites, pizzas served Mon night, five well kept changing ales, local farm cider/perry and decent wines by the glass, friendly prompt service; some live music; children, walkers and dogs welcome, nice garden taking in the view, open all day (till 1am Fri, Sat), no food Sun evening, Mon lunchtime.

SLIMBRIDGE   SO7204

★ **Tudor Arms** (01453) 890306

Shepherds Patch; off A38 towards Slimbridge Wetlands Centre; GL2 7BP

Much extended red-brick roadside pub just back from canal swing-bridge; welcoming and popular with four mainly local ales, a couple of ciders/perries and good wines by the glass, also some interesting whiskies and gins, enjoyable well priced pubby food including basket meals, daily specials, prompt friendly service, linked areas with wood, flagstone or carpeted floors, some leather chairs and settles, comfortable dining room, conservatory; children and dogs (in back bar) welcome, disabled access/loos, tables on part-shaded terrace, boat trips, 16 annexe bedrooms, very close to Slimbridge Wetland Centre, open (and food) all day.

SNOWSHILL   SP0933

Snowshill Arms (01386) 852653

Opposite village green; WR12 7JU Unpretentious country pub in honeypot village – so no shortage of customers; well kept Donnington ales and reasonably priced straightforward (but tasty) food from sandwiches up, prompt friendly service, beams, log fire, stripped stone and neat array of tables, charming village views from bow windows, local photographs; skittle alley; children and dogs welcome, big back garden with stream and play area, handy for Snowshill Manor (NT), Cotswold Lavender farm and Cotswold Way walks.

SOMERFORD KEYNES   SU0195

Bakers Arms (01285) 861298

On main street through village; GL7 6DN Pretty little 17th-c stone-built pub with catslide roof; four well kept ales – maybe Butcombe Original, Fullers London Pride, Timothy Taylors Landlord and St Austell Proper Job – good choice of wines by the glass and enjoyable traditional food including burgers and basket meals, lots of pine tables in two linked areas, fire in big stone fireplace; children and dogs welcome, seats out at front and in garden with play area, lovely village, handy for Cotswold Water Park, open all day, food till 8.30pm (3pm Sun).

SOUTHROP   SP2003

★ **Swan** (01367) 850205

Off A361 Lechlade–Burford; GL7 3NU Creeper-clad 17th-c pub in pretty village and part of the Thyme company on the Southrop Manor Estate; chatty contemporary-rustic bar areas with simple tables and chairs on flagstones, open fire, stools at counter serving ales such as Clavell & Hind, Hillside, North Cotswold and Stroud, up to 15 wines by the glass from well chosen list, good imaginative food using Estate produce, helpful staff, two low-ceilinged dining rooms with tweed-upholstered chairs around nice mix of tables,

---

cushions on settles, rugs on flagstones, fresh flowers, candles and open fires; background music, TV, board games and skittle alley; children and dogs welcome, picnic-sets out at front, elegant metal furniture in sheltered walled garden, bedrooms, open all day.

STANTON
SP0634

★ **Mount** (01386) 584316

Village signposted off B4632 SW of Broadway; keep on past village on no-through road up hill, bear left; WR12 7NE Popular 17th-c pub with lovely views over village towards the Welsh mountains; heavy beams in low ceilings, flagstones and inglenook log fire, well kept Donnington ales, good wines by the glass and much enjoyed food from baguettes to daily specials, prompt friendly service despite the crowds, picture-window restaurant taking in the view; darts and board games; well behaved children and dogs welcome, wheelchair access via side door (no disabled loos), attractive terraced gardens, paddock across lane, good walks (Cotswold Way and Wyche Way nearby), open (and food) all day.

STAUNTON
SO7829

Swan (01452) 840323

Ledbury Road (A417), on mini roundabout; GL19 3QA Village pub owned by local farming family (they also have the Red Lion at Bishop's Norton and Royal Exchange in Hartpury); enjoyable well priced food from sandwiches up including Thurs steak night, ales such as Butcombe and Wye Valley, Weston's cider, bar with sofas and woodburner, spacious restaurant and modern conservatory, attached barn for functions; occasional quiz nights; children and dogs welcome, pretty garden, open all day Fri-Sun, closed Mon and Tues lunchtimes, no food Mon or evening Sun.

STAUNTON
SO5412

White Horse (01594) 834001

A4136; GL16 8PA Village pub on edge of Forest of Dean close to Welsh border, welcoming and relaxed, with good freshly prepared food in bar or restaurant including wood-fired pizzas, popular Sun lunch; well kept local ales such as Wye Valley and ciders, friendly helpful service; small shop; children and dogs welcome, disabled access, picnic-sets in good-sized garden with glamping pods.

STAVERTON
SO9024

House in the Tree (01242) 680241

Haydon (B4063 W of Cheltenham); GL51 0TQ Friendly old beamed and partly thatched pub; five real ales including Dartmoor, Sharps and perhaps Otter, Robinsons and Wychwood, traditional cider and decent wine list, well liked generously served food from baguettes to daily specials, good helpful service, rambling linked areas,

open fires; children and dogs welcome, plenty of tables in garden with good play area and pets corner, handy for M5 (junction 10), open all day, food all day Sat, till 6pm Sun.

STOW-ON-THE-WOLD
SP1925

Bell (01451) 870916

Park Street; A436 E of centre; GL54 1AJ Modernised creeper-clad dining pub with enjoyable food from breakfasts and bar snacks up, around 30 wines by the glass including champagne, well kept Youngs and a guest such as Purity, can eat in beamed and flagstoned bar with woodburner, or connecting dining areas; live acoustic music Sun evening; children and dogs welcome, picnic-sets outside, five well equipped bedrooms, eight more in nearby townhouse, open (and food) all day from 8am.

STOW-ON-THE-WOLD
SP1925

★ **Porch House** (01451) 870048

Digbeth Street; GL54 1BN Charming mainly 17th-c hotel with some striking features – there was some sort of inn here in 947; bar areas have beams (some draped with hops), flagstones or floorboards, exposed stone walls and open fireplaces, mix of tables, wooden and upholstered chairs, stools and settles, church candles, lanterns, books and stone bottles, also a cosy snug, a dining room and a conservatory, well kept Brakspears ales and a couple of guests, good wines by the glass and ten gins, imaginative food and attentive service; background music and board games; children and dogs (in bar and bedrooms) welcome, raised terrace with rattan chairs and cushioned wall benches around rustic tables, 14 stylish luxury bedrooms and particularly good breakfasts, open all day.

STOW-ON-THE-WOLD
SP1925

Queens Head (01451) 830563

The Square; GL54 1AB Traditional old Donnington pub overlooking the market square; their well kept/priced beers along with good well cooked pubby food, friendly chatty staff and buoyant atmosphere, stripped-stone front lounge, heavily beamed and flagstoned back bar with high-backed settles, coal-effect fire; background music; children (not in front bar) and dogs welcome, tables in attractive sunny back courtyard, open all day.

STOW-ON-THE-WOLD
SP1925

Talbot (01451) 870934

The Square; GL54 1BQ Relaxed one-bar pub in good position on market square; light airy décor with wood-clad walls and easy chairs by log fire, well liked/priced food from sandwiches and sharing plates to grills, four Wadworths ales, real cider and several wines by the glass, upstairs function room (and lavatories); background and live (Fri) music; children and dogs welcome, a few courtyard tables, open all day (till 6pm Sun).

STROUD   SO8505
Ale House (01453) 755447
John Street; GL5 2HA Fine range of well
kept beers and ciders/perries (third-of-a-pint
tasting glasses available), enjoyable food
including signature curries and good value
Sun lunch, main high-ceilinged part with sofa
by big open fire, other rooms off; live music
and quiz nights; well behaved children and
dogs welcome, small side courtyard with
café-style tables and chairs, farmers' market
Sat, open all day weekends.

SWINEFORD   ST6969
Swan (0117) 932 3101
A431, right on the Somerset border;
BS30 6LN Popular 19th-c roadside pub,
well kept Bath ales and guests, local ciders,
decent wines and good range of spirits
including Penderyn Welsh whisky and
Tarquin Cornish gin, enjoyable food from
lunchtime sandwiches up, efficient friendly
staff, updated interior with quarry tiles and
light wood floors, pastel walls and bluey-
green panelling, raised back dining area,
open fire; background music; children and
dogs welcome, wheelchair access to main bar,
picnic-sets out at front and in large grassy
garden with play area, open all day, food all
day weekends.

TETBURY   ST8893
Close (01666) 502272
Long Street; GL8 8AQ Contemporary bar
in old stone hotel, comfortable and stylish
with blazing log fire, enjoyable food from
sandwiches up, also brasserie and more
formal dining room, coffee and afternoon
teas, charming staff; children welcome,
tables in lovely garden behind, 20 luxurious
individually designed bedrooms, open all day.

TETBURY   ST8993
★ Royal Oak (01666) 500021
Cirencester Road; GL8 8EY Carefully
renovated golden-stone inn; rambling
open-plan bar with several snug areas and
roaring log fire, variety of chairs around dark
tables on wide floorboards, built-in green
leather wall seats and a few elbow tables,
five real ales including Butcombe, Moor and
Stroud from handsome carved counter, also
traditional cider, good choice of wines by
the glass and interesting spirits, upstairs
dining room with fine raftered ceiling, dark
polished furniture on more wide floorboards,
fresh flowers and candles, good food (not Sun
evening) including vegan options, friendly
helpful service; background and some live
music; children welcome till 8pm (unless in
restaurant), dogs in bar, disabled access/loos,
tables under parasols on terraces and lawn,
maybe Airstream trailer for Mexican street
food in summer, six good boutique bedrooms
across cobbled courtyard (book well ahead),
woodland walks from the door.

TETBURY   ST8993
Snooty Fox (01666) 502436
Market Place; GL8 8DD High-ceilinged
stripped-stone hotel lounge serving several
well kept local ales, a real cider and good
house wines, enjoyable all-day bar food
including breakfasts for non-residents
(9-11.30am) and afternoon teas (3-5.30pm),
leather sofas and elegant fireplace, nice side
room and anteroom, restaurant; background
music; children and dogs welcome, a few
sheltered tables out in front, 12 bedrooms.

TEWKESBURY   SO8932
Nottingham Arms (01684) 276346
High Street; GL20 5JU Popular old
black and white-fronted local; bare-boards
timbered bar with ales such as St Austell,
Sharps and Wye Valley, enjoyable home-made
food at reasonable prices including good Sun
lunch, friendly service, back dining room;
Sun live music, Thurs quiz; children and dogs
welcome, open all day.

TEWKESBURY   SO8932
Royal Hop Pole (01684) 274039
Church Street; GL20 5RT Wetherspoons
conversion of old inn (some parts dating from
the 15th c); their usual value-minded all-day
food and drink, good speedy service; terrace
seating and lovely garden leading down to
river, 28 bedrooms, open from 7am.

TODDINGTON   SP0432
Pheasant (01242) 621271
A46 Broadway–Winchcombe, junction
with A438 and B4077; GL54 5DT
Large stone-built roadside pub with modern
open-plan interior; tartan carpets, blue
panelled dados and log fire, Donnington
ales and generous helpings of tasty good
value food, friendly attentive staff; children
and dogs (in bar area) welcome, picnic-sets
outside, handy for preserved Gloucestershire
Warwickshire Steam Railway station, open all
day, breakfast (10-11am, not Mon), no food
Sun evening.

TOLLDOWN   ST7577
Crown (01225) 891166
1 mile from M4 junction 18 – A46
towards Bath; SN14 8HZ Cosy heavy-
beamed stone pub on crossroads; most
here for the good food (all day Sun) from
sandwiches and pub favourites to more
upmarket choices, special diets also catered
for, efficient welcoming staff, Wadworths ales,
Thatcher's cider, plenty of wines by the glass
and some decent gins, warm log fires, candles
on pine tables, wood, coir and quarry-tiled
floors, animal prints on green rough plaster
walls, some bare stonework; children and
dogs (in bar) welcome, disabled access/
loos, sunny beer garden, nine bedrooms in
building behind, handy for Dyrham Park
(NT) and Cotswold Way.

ULEY
ST7998

Old Crown
(01453) 860502

The Green; GL11 5SN Unspoilt 17th-c pub prettily set by village green just off Cotswold Way; long narrow room with settles and pews on bare boards, step up to partitioned-off lounge, five well kept local ales including Uley and Wye Valley, decent wines by the glass and small choice of well liked pubby food from baguettes up, friendly service, open fire; children and dogs welcome, a few picnic-sets in front and attractive garden behind, four bedrooms, open all day.

UPPER ODDINGTON
SP2225

★Horse & Groom
(01451) 830584

Village signposted from A436 E of Stow-on-the-Wold; GL56 0XH Welcoming 16th-c Cotswold-stone village inn; beamed bar with pale polished flagstones, stripped-stone walls and inglenook log fire, three real ales including Wye Valley, Dunkertons cider and plenty of wines by the glass, popular well cooked food from sensibly short but varied menu, can eat in bar, comfortable lounge or restaurant; background music; children and dogs (in bar) welcome, tables under parasols on terrace and in garden, bedrooms in main building and 'cottage', good breakfast, open all day.

UPTON CHEYNEY
ST6969

Upton Inn
(0117) 932 4489

Village signed off A431 at Bitton; BS30 6LY Friendly 18th-c stone-built village pub under new management; bar with wood or carpeted floors, two dining areas, one with woodburner in huge stone fireplace, the other with white panelling and pictures of old Bath, enjoyable home-made food from snacks up, well kept Badger ales, Thatcher's cider, pleasant hard-working staff; background music; children welcome, wheelchair access from back door, disabled loo (shared with ladies'), views of the Avon Valley from front terrace, open all day.

WESTON SUBEDGE
SP1241

★Seagrave Arms
(01386) 840192

B4632; GL55 6QH Nicely refurbished golden-stone inn-restaurant near the Cotswold Way; cosy little bar with ancient flagstones, half-panelled walls, open fire and chatty, informal atmosphere, two dining rooms with mix of furniture on wood floors and some striking paintings, smallish menu but with good imaginative well presented food using seasonal local produce, several changing ales and good wines (including fizz) by the glass, friendly efficient staff; background music, TV and board games; seating out at the front and in back garden, children and dogs (in bar and bedrooms) welcome, eight well equipped modern bedrooms (in main house or converted stables) and hearty breakfasts, open all day (food all day Sat).

WESTONBIRT
ST8690

★Hare & Hounds
(01666) 881000

A433 SW of Tetbury; GL8 8QL Substantial roadside hotel with separate entrance to pub; much liked food from snacks and sharing boards up, well kept Fullers ales, interesting ciders, lots of wines by the glass and good gin/whisky/rum selection (some locally distilled), coffee and afternoon teas, two bar areas and series of interconnecting rooms with polished wood floors, various pictures (including hares and hounds) and woodburner in two-way fireplace, more formal restaurant; background music; children welcome, muddy boots and dogs (there's a menu for them) in bar, disabled access/loos/parking, shaded wicker tables on front paved terrace, pleasant gardens, 42 bedrooms (some in outbuildings), convenient for the Arboretum, open all day and gets very busy (especially weekend lunchtimes).

WHITECROFT
SO6005

Miners Arms
(01594) 562483

B4234 N of Lydney; GL15 4PE Popular local with up to five changing ales, traditional cider and enjoyable sensibly priced food from lunchtime sandwiches up, rooms on either side of bar, woodburner and open fire, conservatory; background and some live music including jazz, skittle alley; children and dogs welcome, disabled access/loos, gardens front and back (one with stream), good local walks and handy for steam railway, self-catering cottage, open all day.

WILLERSEY
SP1039

Bell
(01386) 858405

B4632 Cheltenham–Stratford, near Broadway; WR12 7PJ Imposing neatly modernised 17th-c stone inn overlooking village green and duck pond; popular home-made food from bar meals up, Purity UBU and Mad Goose, prompt friendly service; children welcome, dogs in bar, lots of tables in big garden, good local walks (Cotswold Way), five bedrooms in outbuildings, open all day Sun.

WINCHCOMBE
SP0228

Corner Cupboard
(01242) 602303

Gloucester Street; GL54 5LX Attractive old golden-stone pub with enjoyable food (all day weekends) including curries in back dining room, four well kept ales, Sharps, Wickwar, Wye Valley and a guest, decent wines by the glass; comfortable stripped-stone lounge bar with heavy-beamed Tudor core, traditional hatch-service lobby, small side room with woodburner in massive stone fireplace; sports TV; children and dogs welcome, tables in back garden, handy for Gloucestershire Warwickshire Steam Railway and Sudeley Castle, open all day, food all day weekends.

WINCHCOMBE   SP0228
White Hart   (01242) 602359
High Street (B4632); GL54 5LJ 16th-c inn with big windows looking out over village street, mix of chairs and small settles around pine tables on bare boards, well kept ales such as Brains, Goffs, Otter and Sharps, wine shop at back (corkage added if you buy to drink on premises), also good choice by the glass, generally well liked food including specials, afternoon teas, good friendly service, separate restaurant; 11 comfortable bedrooms, children and dogs (in bar and bedrooms) welcome, open all day from 8am for breakfast.

WITHINGTON   SP0315
Mill Inn   (01242) 890204
Off A436 or A40; GL54 4BE Idyllic streamside setting for this mossy-roofed old stone inn, plenty of character with nice nooks and corners, beams, wood or flagstone floors, two inglenook log fires and woodburner, well kept/priced Sam Smiths tapped from the cask and ample helpings of traditional food including basket meals, four dining rooms, cheerful staff; children and dogs welcome, picnic-sets in big garden, splendid walks, open all day Sat in summer (closed Sun evening in winter), shut Mon lunchtime.

WOOLASTON COMMON   SO5900
Rising Sun   (01594) 529282
Village signed off A48 Lydney–Chepstow; GL15 6NU Traditional 17th-c stone village pub on fringe of Forest of Dean; generous helpings of good home-made food (some choices available in smaller servings), well kept Butcombe Rare Breed, Wye Valley Bitter and a guest, friendly service; children and dogs welcome, seats out at front and in large back garden, open all day during summer school holidays, otherwise all day Fri-Sun, closed Mon lunchtime.

Hampshire

AMPORT
SU2944   Map 2
Hawk Inn 🛏
(01264) 710371 – www.hawkinnamport.co.uk

Off A303 at Thruxton interchange; at Andover end of village just before Monxton; SP11 8AE

Relaxed rambling pub with contemporary furnishings, helpful staff and well thought-of food; bedrooms

Well placed for raptor enthusiasts – the famous Hawk Conservancy Trust is just down the road – this lovely village pub enjoys glorious views over Pill Hill Brook from its sandstone terrace. The open-plan front bar, with its brown leather armchairs and plush grey sofas by a low table, sisal matting on bare boards and a log fire in a brick fireplace, is our favourite spot for a relaxed drink. To the left, a tucked-away snug room has horse-racing photographs, shelves of books and a TV. Two dining areas have smart window blinds, black leather cushioned wall seating and elegant wooden chairs (some carved) around pale tables, big oil paintings on pale walls above a grey dado, and a woodburning stove; background music and board games. Black-topped stools line the counter, where courteous staff serve a changing roster of ales, such as Crafty Blind Side and Dark Star Hophead on handpump, and quite a few wines by the glass. Bedrooms are comfortable and stylish (one is reserved for guests with a small canine companion), and breakfasts are good.

🍴 Tasty food includes classic prawn and avocado cocktail, mushroom shawarma with vegan garlic mayo, burger (short rib, buttermilk chicken or vegan) with toppings and chips, a fish of the day, gnocchi with triple cheese sauce, basil and truffle oil, a range of steaks with a choice of sauce, caesar salad, and puddings such as dark chocolate brownie with chocolate sauce and ice-cream or sticky toffee pudding. *Benchmark main dish: ale-battered haddock and chips £14.50. Two-course evening meal £22.00.*

Upham ~ Manager Ryan Blandford ~ Real ale ~ Open 7.30am-11pm; 8.30am-11pm Sat; 8.30am-10.30pm Sun ~ Bar food 12-2.30, 6-9 (9.30 Fri, Sat) ~ Children welcome ~ Dogs welcome in bar & bedroom ~ Bedrooms: £81

BANK
SU2806   Map 2
Oak ☕
(023) 8028 2350 – www.oakinnlyndhurst.co.uk

Signposted just off A35 SW of Lyndhurst; SO43 7FD

Busy New Forest pub with friendly, efficient staff, popular food and interesting décor

A delightfully atmospheric pub just outside the self-styled 'capital' of the New Forest, whose bucolic atmosphere is enhanced by cushioned milk churns serving as bar stools, cosy lanterns and general hunting, shooting and fishing bric-a-brac adorning every corner and wall. The L-shaped bar has bay windows with built-in red-cushioned seats, and two or three little pine-panelled booths with small built-in tables and bench seats. The rest of the bare-boarded bar has low beams and joists, candles in brass holders on a row of stripped old and newer blond tables set against the wall. Fullers London Pride and two weekly changing guests on handpump and 14 wines by the glass; background music. There's always quite a mix of customers here, and as it's tucked away they tend to be walkers, cyclists and horse riders.

Quite a choice of food includes lunchtime sandwiches, celeriac and apple soup, garlic wild mushrooms with poached egg and hollandaise, sharing boards, slow-braised ox cheeks with potato purée, roasted shallots and cumin carrots, grilled polenta with roasted fennel, tomatoes, peppers and garlic, pan-roasted halibut with wild mushrooms, cavolo nero and verjus, and puddings such as baked rice pudding with fruit compote and chocolate tart with salted caramel and buffalo milk ice-cream. *Benchmark main dish: pappardelle with wild boar ragout, pecorino and truffle oil £14.50. Two-course evening meal £21.00.*

Fullers ~ Manager Matt England ~ Real ale ~ Open 11.30-11; 12-10.30 Sun ~ Bar food 12-5, 6-9 (8 Sun) ~ Children welcome during food service ~ Dogs allowed in bar

BAUGHURST
SU5860   Map 2
Wellington Arms ★ ⏷ ⌂
(0118) 982 0110 – www.thewellingtonarms.com
Baughurst Road, S of village; RG26 5LP

Hampshire Dining Pub of the Year

Delightful little country pub-with-rooms with hands-on, hard-working owners, exceptional cooking and a friendly welcome; character bedrooms

G arlanded with awards, this neatly appointed inn, standing in its own extensive well-tended grounds, embodies every rural charm a visitor could wish for – right down to productive bees and chickens contributing to the menu. Dog lovers will also be delighted by the resident pooches: Norfolk terriers Vincent and Ritchie. A thoughtful choice of drinks includes Longdog Bunny Chaser and West Berkshire Good Old Boy on handpump, 12 wines by the glass from a smashing list, farm ciders, good aperitifs and home-made elderflower cordial; background music. The dining room is attractively decorated with an assortment of cushioned oak dining chairs around a mix of polished tables on terracotta tiles, pretty blinds, brass candlesticks, flowers and windowsills stacked with cookery books. The garden has colourful herbaceous borders, teak tables and chairs under parasols and some picnic-sets. The food receives constant admiration from our readers, and this immaculately kept and pretty little spot is also a lovely place to stay, with four deeply comfortable and very well equipped bedrooms; breakfasts are first class: 'your breakfast eggs were either laid today or yesterday'.

Exceptional food (from a sensibly short and daily changing menu) uses their own vegetables and livestock (50 or so pedigree Jacob sheep graze in the field out back), honey from their own bees, herbs from next door and other carefully sourced produce, and is cooked by the chef-landlord Jason. Dishes include smoked salmon with radishes and avocado, twice-baked cheddar cheese soufflé on sautéed courgettes with parmesan, rope-grown mussels in white wine, parsley and cream, Baughurst House roe deer and root vegetables in red wine with a pastry lid and mash, smoked haddock, cod and salmon fishcake with sautéed samphire, whole roast partridge with sticky red cabbage, mash and parsnip crisps, and puddings such as marmalade sponge with egg custard and baked caramel custard with oranges and cinnamon syrup. They also offer a two- and three-course lunch. *Benchmark main dish: baked potato gnocchi with butternut squash £17.00. Two-course evening meal £30.00.*

Free house ~ Licensees Simon Page and Jason King ~ Real ale ~ Open 9-3, 6-10; 9-3, 6-11 Sat; 9-5 Sun; closed Mon ~ Bar food 12-1.30, 6.30-8; 12-1.30, 6-9 Fri, Sat; 12-3 Sun ~ Children welcome ~ Dogs allowed in bar, restaurant & bedrooms ~ Bedrooms: £125

BRANSGORE
Three Tuns 🏵️ ♀ 🍺

SZ1997   Map 2

(01425) 672232 – www.threetunsinn.com
Village signposted off A35 towards Lyndhurst and off B3347 N of Christchurch; 10 mins from Christchurch centre, opposite church; BH23 8JH

17th-c inn with proper old-fashioned bar with good beers, a civilised main dining area and inventive food

The very image of a country pub, with its neatly tended thatch and whitewashed exterior, this much loved place has all the low-ceilinged charm a New Forest rambler could ever need. It's very popular in summer, when you'll find lovely hanging baskets, picnic-sets on an attractive and extensive shrub-sheltered terrace and more tables on grass looking over pony paddocks; pétanque. Inside, on the right, is a separate traditional regulars' bar that seems almost taller than it is wide, with an impressive log-effect stove in a stripped-brick hearth, some shiny black panelling and individualistic pubby furnishings. The friendly, helpful licensees keep ten real ales, including their own-brewed Three Tuns beers, plus Exmoor Gold, Otter Amber, Purity Pure Gold, Ringwood Best Bitter and Fortyniner and other quickly changing guests on handpump (they also hold a beer festival in September), as well as Harrow Wood Farm local cider, five lagers on tap and 30 wines by the glass. A roomy, low-ceilinged and carpeted main area has a fireside 'codgers' corner' and a good mix of comfortably cushioned low chairs around a variety of dining tables. The Grade-II listed barn is popular for parties and weddings; board games and some live music. Disabled access and newly refurbished disabled loo. Electric car recharging points are available and glamping is planned for 2021.

🏵️ Creative food from a seasonal menu includes: sandwiches, home-made flowerpot bread (chef Colin Nash's speciality), Cornish mussels, Vietnamese vegetable salad, 'snail garden' (snails on forest moss with wild mushrooms, flowers and wild garlic), pan-fried calves liver with smoked bacon, mash and onion jus, Hengistbury Head sea bass and squid stew with coconut, coriander, lemon and ginger, Bransgorian venison cottage pie, liquorice lamb and 'allsorts' (beetroot, orange and fondant potato), wild mushroom spaetzle, and puddings such as cherry bakewell tart and vegan chocolate and pistachio terrine with seville orange sauce. *Benchmark main dish: steak and kidney pie with greens and mash £15.00. Two-course evening meal £23.00.*

Free house ~ Licensee Nigel Glenister ~ Real ale ~ Open 11-11; 11-11.30 Sat; 11.30-10.30 Sun ~ Bar food 12-9 ~ Restaurant ~ Children welcome ~ Dogs allowed in bar

---

'Children welcome' means the pub says it lets children inside without any special restriction. If it allows them in, but to restricted areas such as an eating area or family room, we specify this. Places with separate restaurants often let children use them, and hotels usually let children into public areas such as lounges. Some pubs impose an evening time limit – let us know if you find one earlier than 9pm.

CADNAM   SU2913   Map 2

White Hart ♀ ◖

(023) 8081 2277 – www.brunningandprice.co.uk/whitehartcadnam

Old Romsey Road, handy for M27 junction 1; SO40 2NP

New Forest pub with busy bar and dining rooms, a warm welcome, good choice of drinks and tasty food

---

One of the many popular hostelries in the New Forest, where peak tourist season brings a thirsty influx of walkers and riders. There's a cosy area with a woodburning stove in a nice old brick fireplace, rugs and comfortable leather armchairs; background music and board games. Various dining rooms lead off with more rugs on carpet or tiles, all manner of cushioned dining chairs and wooden tables, frame-to-frame country pictures and photographs on pale walls above painted wooden dados, house plants on windowsills, mirrors and elegant metal chandeliers. The bar has an open fire, stools and tables on parquet flooring and from the long curved counter, St Austell Brunning & Price Traditional Bitter, Flack Manor Double Drop and Hedge Hop, Hop Back Crop Circle and Minstrel and Itchen Valley Watercress Best on handpump, farm ciders, 20 good wines by the glass (including fizz), more than 60 gins and cocktails; staff are helpful and friendly. The spacious grounds, much extended, include a back terrace and garden with plenty of chairs and tables, and a children's play area with a jolly green vintage tractor, swings and a climbing frame.

 Good bistro-style food includes sandwiches and 'light bites', courgette and red onion bhaji, beetroot hummus, beef bao bun, fish pie, chicken, ham and leek pie with mash and spring greens, wild mushroom risotto, beer-battered cod and chips, sweet potato and spinach Malaysian curry, crispy beef salad, and puddings such as dark chocolate and orange tart and bread and butter pudding with apricot sauce. *Benchmark main dish: mushroom bourguignon pie with rosemary new potatoes and gravy £12.95. Two-course evening meal 22.00.*

Brunning & Price ~ Manager Steve Butt ~ Real ale ~ Open 11.30-11; 11.30-10 Sun ~ Bar food 12-9; 12-9.30 Fri, Sat ~ Restaurant ~ Children welcome ~ Dogs allowed in bar

---

DROXFORD   SU6018   Map 2

Bakers Arms ⦿ ◖

(01489) 877533 – www.thebakersarmsdroxford.com

High Street; A32 5 miles N of Wickham; SO32 3PA

Welcoming, opened-up and friendly pub with good beers, cosy corners and interesting cooking

---

A lovely, easy-going atmosphere reigns in this attractive old pub, in a pretty location not far from the River Meon. Local ales include Bowman Swift One and Wallops Wood – the brewery is only a mile away, so they're in perfect condition – plus ciders on handpump and ten wines by the glass from a short, carefully chosen list. The L-shaped, open-plan central bar is the main focus. Well spaced tables on carpet or neat bare boards are spread about with low leather chesterfields and an assortment of comfortably cushioned chairs at one end; a dark panelled dado, dark beams and joists and a modicum of country oddments emphasise the freshness of the crisp white paintwork. There's a good log fire, board games if more entertainment is required, and regular meal and movie events if you want to make a night of it. To one side, with a separate entrance, is the village post office. There are picnic-sets outside. The walks along and around the river are lovely.

🌟🍴 A wide choice of well regarded food includes home-made bread, baguettes with interesting fillings, gluten-free wraps and snacks such as truffled macaroni cheese and crispy crab wontons. Also, roasted pigeon breast or goats cheese with potato, parsley and pickled onion salad, mussels with white wine, herbs and cream, pork sausages with mash and onion gravy, chestnut, shallot and thyme tart with sautéed baby spinach, roasted lamb rump with creamed savoy cabbage, pea purée and roast potatoes, spiced black bean burger with fries, and puddings such as poached pear and ginger cheesecake and caramelised coconut rice pudding. *Benchmark main dish: Hampshire chalk-stream trout with fried potatoes and petits pois £17.50. Two-course evening meal £23.00.*

Free house ~ Licensees Adam and Anna Cordery ~ Real ale ~ Open 11.45-2.30 (3 Sat), 6-11; 12-6 Sun ~ Bar food 12-2, 6-9 (9.30 Fri); 12-2.30, 6-9.30 Sat; 11.45-5 Sun ~ Children welcome ~ Dogs allowed in bar

EVERSLEY
Tally Ho 🍷 🍺

SU7762   Map 2

(01189) 732134 – www.brunningandprice.co.uk/tallyho
Fleet Hill; RG27 0RR

Attractive pub with a busy bar and popular dining rooms, a good drinks list and rewarding food and seats outside

The Reverend Charles Kingsley, formerly of this parish, was scathing about Eversley (its peat bogs and ill-educated villagers), but then he may not have had access to this excellent pub. A former farmhouse, with lots of room both inside and out, the Tally Ho is the perfect start (and finish) for the Blackwater Trail walk. The main bar area, which is genuinely dog-friendly, has a few beams and standing timbers, wooden dining chairs and built-in window seats on rugs, bare boards and quarry tiles, house plants and glass bottles on windowsills and stubby candles. By the main door is a giant bellows made up as a table for newspapers and another window seat that's backed by guidebooks. One dining room leads off and two others have unusual slatted wooden walls, more large windows, a raised fireplace, similar tables and chairs on carpet and parquet flooring and a great many prints, cartoons and photographs on pale-painted walls. St Austell Brunning & Price Traditional Bitter plus guest beers from breweries such as Flack Manor, Longdog, Sambrook, Timothy Taylors and West Berkshire on handpump, 21 wines by the glass and some 55 gins; background music. There are lots of picnic-sets under white parasols on a lawn, with a few wooden tables and chairs by the front door. There are also swings and a play tractor.

🍴 Popular food includes sandwiches, leek and potato soup, summer risotto with broad beans, radish and asparagus, beetroot hummus with pitta bread, celeriac, wild mushroom and suet pudding with new potatoes and red wine gravy, smoked haddock and salmon fishcakes, braised shoulder of lamb with dauphinoise potatoes, carrot mash and rosemary gravy, and puddings such as apple and berry crumble, summer pudding with clotted cream and vegan ice-creams and sorbets. *Benchmark main dish: steak burger with fries and coleslaw £13.95. Two-course evening meal £23.00.*

Brunning & Price ~ Manager Jamie Rensch ~ Real ale ~ Open 10am-midnight; 12-10 Sun ~ Bar food 12-9; 12-9.30 Fri, Sat ~ Restaurant ~ Children welcome ~ Dogs welcome

---

Real ale may be served from handpumps, electric pumps (not just the on-off switches used for keg beer) or – common in Scotland – tall taps called founts (pronounced 'fonts') where a separate pump pushes the beer up under air pressure.

FACCOMBE
SU3958 Map 2
Jack Russell 🏮⭐ ♀ 🛏

(01264) 737315 – www.thejackrussellinn.com

Signed from A343 Newbury–Andover; SP11 0DS

Spacious brick pub with contemporary and old-style furnishings in bar and dining rooms, up-to-date food, friendly service and seats outside; dog-friendly bedrooms

With its irreproachable green credentials – water from a bore hole, electricity from a wind turbine and heating from a biomass boiler fuelled by Faccombe Forestry's cast-offs – the Jack Russell is top dog in the environmental stakes. The real top dogs, though, are the landlord's companions Barnie and Betty (not jack russells, but a spaniel and a labrador). And doggie guests are welcome in some of the very well equipped bedrooms (in a separate building or the pub itself). This is a lovely spot in the midst of fine walking country. A small entrance room with armchairs and an open fire leads into the bar, where there's an informal, almost club-like feel with leather button-back wall seats, panelled walls inlaid with A-Z cartoon characters, and kitchen chairs and stools on black and white floor tiles. Cheerful, efficient young staff serve Gritchie English Lore (Guy Ritchie's brewery), Ramsbury Gold and Ringwood Razorback on handpump and quite a few wines from a thoughtful list; background music and TV. The grey-panelled dining area, split up by blue-painted wooden partitions, has mustard-coloured leather banquettes and chunky wooden chairs around a mix of tables, parquet flooring, another open fire, bunches of dried flowers and contemporary lighting. A larger back restaurant has pale button-back sofas and white-painted chairs around wooden tables on carpet. Throughout are china plates and china dogs, books and board games. The garden has plenty of seats and tables and a pond.

 The imaginative seasonal food uses produce from the Faccombe Estate itself, including venison, game, vegetables and herbs. Dishes include Dorset blue vinney cheese, poached pear, chicory and radish salad, gilthead bream, chorizo, butter bean, mussel and clam stew, wild mushroom gnocchi with garlic and sage oil and Dorset black truffle, coffee and juniper-crusted venison with venison croquette, smoked fondant potato and cauliflower purée, and puddings such as rhubarb and stem ginger crumble with rhubarb and rosehip ice-cream and calvados crème brûlée with cinnamon doughnut. *Benchmark main dish: venison and red wine sausages with truffle mash and onion gravy £14.50. Two-course evening meal £23.00.*

Cirrus Inns ~ Licensee Ross Nicol ~ Real ale ~ Open 11-11; 11-10 Sun ~ Bar food 12-3, 6-9 (9.30 Fri, Sat); 12-7 Sun ~ Restaurant ~ Children welcome ~ Dogs allowed in bar & bedrooms ~ Bedrooms: £180

FREEFOLK
SU4848 Map 2
Watership Down 🏮⭐ ♀ 🍺 🛏

(01256) 892254 – www.watershipdowninn.com

Freefolk Priors, N of B3400 Whitchurch–Overton; brown sign to pub; RG28 7NJ

Cosy bar and open-plan dining rooms, five real ales, good food and pretty garden; bedrooms

An attractively refurbished old country inn, this free house stands at the foot of the North Wessex Downs. The wood-floored bar has stools by a pale oak counter, high stools next to an elbow shelf and five real ales on handpump sourced from within a 30-mile radius. They change regularly but may include Bowman Swift One, Flowerpots Bitter, Itchen Valley Hampshire Rose, Stonehenge Sign of Spring and West Berkshire Good Old

Boy, plus Purbeck cider and 16 good wines by the glass. Leading off here are two connected dining rooms with mate's chairs (some draped with animal skins) around chunky tables on more bare boards or old brickwork, and a woodburning stove in a raised fireplace; throughout, plants line the windowsills, and modern art and photos hang on pale paintwork above a grey-green dado. A conservatory with high-backed, cushioned wicker chairs around solid tables on floor tiles leads to a two-tiered terrace with seats and tables under big parasols. The large lawn has plenty of picnic-sets and views over the River Test Valley. Seven pretty bedrooms (named after characters from the novel *Watership Down*) offer inspiring views across the rolling downs; dogs are allowed in the four garden rooms.

Interesting food mixing British and international flavours includes goats cheese and thyme filo tart, cheesy nachos with pulled pork or smoked bean chilli, dry-aged beef brisket in sourdough bap with rosemary and garlic fries, slow-cooked Mexican-spiced pork burrito, katsu quorn and vegetable stir-fry with udon noodles, Spanish surf 'n' turf tacos with chorizo and tiger prawns and patatas bravas, and puddings such as salted caramel pain au raisin bread pudding with baked apple compote and coffee and hazelnut tiramisu. *Benchmark main dish: real ale-battered smoked cod with curried peas, triple-cooked chips and lemongrass and saffron aioli £14.50. Two-course evening meal £23.00.*

Free house ~ Licensee Philip Denée ~ Real ale ~ Open 12-3, 6.30-10.30; 12-11 Fri, Sat; 12-9.30 Sun ~ Bar food 8-9.30am, 12-2.30 (3 Sat), 6.30-9 Mon-Fri; 8-9.30am, 12-4 Sun ~ Restaurant ~ Children welcome ~ Dogs on leads allowed in bar, restaurant & bedrooms ~ Bedrooms: £145

FRITHAM
Royal Oak

SU2314 Map 2

(023) 8081 2606 – www.royaloakfritham.co.uk
Village signed from M27 junction 1; SO43 7HJ

Rural New Forest spot with traditional rooms, log fires, up to seven real ales and simple lunchtime food

There's a real down-on-the-farm feel to this appealing pub, and customers can immerse themselves in its bucolic charm if they fancy sleeping over in the shepherd's hut accommodation. The landlady's daughter runs Howen Farm, just next door, whose livestock you can watch grazing in the fields as you sup your ale. The three quite unchanging and neatly kept rooms are straightforward but full of proper traditional character, with black beams, prints and pictures celebrating local characters on the white walls, restored panelling, antique wheelback, spindleback and other old chairs and stools with colourful seats around solid tables on oak floors, and two roaring log fires. The back bar has books; darts and board games. Up to seven real ales are tapped from the cask including one named for the pub (from Bowman), Branscombe Vale Branoc, Flack Manor Double Drop, Hop Back Summer Lightning, Ringwood Best and Stonehenge Danish Dynamite. Also, nine wines by the glass (mulled wine in winter), 14 country wines, local cider and a September beer festival; service remains friendly and efficient even when the pub is packed (which it often is). Summer barbecues may be held in the neatly kept big garden, which has a marquee for poor weather and a pétanque pitch. There are three shepherd's huts available to rent. Dogs are welcome but must be on a lead.

Good value, farm-fresh food – served at lunchtime only – consists of excellent pork pies and sausage rolls made on the family farm next door (from their own outdoor-bred pigs), wholesome soups and quiches.

Free house ~ Licensees Neil and Pauline McCulloch ~ Real ale ~ Open 11-11;
12-10.30 Sun ~ Bar food 12-2.30 (3 weekends) ~ Children welcome ~ Dogs allowed
in bar ~ Bedrooms: £90

HIGHCLERE
SU4358 Map 2

Pheasant

(01635) 253360 – www.thepheasanthighclere.co.uk

Hollington Cross, Tothill service junction from A34; RG20 9SE

**Friendly country inn with character rooms, a good choice of drinks,
enjoyable food and seats in garden; bedrooms**

Assured of plenty of passing trade owing to its proximity to Highclere
Castle (location for TV series *Downton Abbey*), this a 17th-c rural
charmer. Formerly called the Yew Tree, in summer 2019 it gained new
owners and reverted to its original name. The main door opens into a heavy-
beamed character bar with leather tub chairs and a leather sofa in front of
a two-way fireplace housing a chiminea stove, and stools and high chairs
against the counter (church candles in chunky candlesticks to either side).
There's Penton Park Colonel Bob on handpump and good wines by the glass,
served by friendly, helpful staff. Leading off to the left is a room with antlers
and stuffed squirrels on the mantelpiece above an inglenook fireplace, books
piled on shelves, a pale button-back leather window seat, a mix of wooden
and painted dining chairs around nice old tables on red and black tiles or
carpet and, at one end, a tartan and leather wall banquette; background
music and board games. Dining rooms to the left of the bar, divided by hefty
timbers, have high-backed tartan seating creating booths and more wooden
or painted chairs around a mix of tables on flagstones or sisal carpet. Doors
lead to the garden where there's an outside bar and elegant metal and teak
seats and tables on gravel or raised decking. The eight bedrooms are well
equipped and comfortable (two accept dogs); breakfasts are good.

As well as breakfast, enjoyable food using seasonal local produce includes black
pudding scotch egg with own-made ketchup, tomato, mozzarella and lovage salad,
salt and pepper whitebait, roasted cauliflower, chickpea and lentil curry, pie and mash,
burger with fries and coleslaw, pan-roasted lamb with potato terrine, and puddings such
as ginger rice pudding with white chocolate and rhubarb and treacle tart with pistachio
ice-cream. *Benchmark main dish: spatchcock lemon and thyme poussin £14.00. Two-
course evening meal £21.00.*

Free house ~ Licensees Billy Callaway and Ryan Stacey ~ Real ale ~ Open 8am-11pm;
8.30am-11.30pm Sat; 8.30am-9pm Sun; closed Mon, Tues ~ Bar food 12-2.30, 6.30-9 Weds-Fri;
12.30-3, 6.30-9.30 Sat; 12-7.30 Sun ~ Restaurant ~ Children welcome ~ Dogs allowed in bar,
restaurant & bedrooms ~ Bedrooms: £130

HOOK
SU7153 Map 2

Hogget

(01256) 763009 – www.thehogget.co.uk

*1.1 miles from M3 junction 5; A287 N, at junction with A30 (car park just before
traffic lights); RG27 9JJ*

Well run and accommodating pub giving all-round good value

An inviting and amiable pub in the heart of down-from-London walking
territory: both the A30 and M3 are nearby. It does, however, also enjoy
a faithful local following, so lunchtimes here can be busy. It's a chatty pub
with a friendly atmosphere and the various comfortable rooms ramble
around the central servery, providing plenty of space for all. The wallpaper,

lighting and patterned carpet, plus high-backed stools and bar tables on the right at the back, give an easy-going and homely feel – as does the way the layout provides several smallish distinct areas. Ringwood Fortyniner and Razorback and Wychwood Hobgoblin on handpump, 14 wines by the glass plus prosecco and plenty of neatly dressed staff; daily papers, background music and books (often cookbooks) on shelves. A sizeable terrace has sturdy tables and chairs, including some in a heated covered area.

Tasty food includes baps and wraps, mac 'n' cheese balls, halloumi matchsticks with chilli sauce, cheesy nachos, barbecue ribs, sirloin steak with corn on the cob and rosemary fries, a wide range of Hogget burgers (including beef, halloumi with roasted peppers and hummus, vegan with dairy-free cheese and mayo), and puddings such as Malteser cheesecake, boozy chocolate torte and ice-creams. *Benchmark main dish: halloumi burger with grilled portobello mushroom and chipotle aioli £12.45. Two-course evening meal £19.00.*

Marstons ~ Lease Tom and Laura Faulkner ~ Real ale ~ Open 12-3, 5-11; 12-11 Sat; 12-8 Sun ~ Bar food 12-3, 5-9; 12-9 Sat; 12-8 Sun ~ Restaurant ~ Children welcome but not after 7pm Fri, Sat ~ Dogs allowed in bar & restaurant

HORDLE
Mill at Gordleton ♀ ⌂

SZ2996 Map 2

(01590) 682219 – www.themillatgordleton.co.uk
Silver Street; SO41 6DJ

Tucked-away inn with friendly bar, elegant dining rooms and pretty gardens; well equipped, comfortable bedrooms

The eight comfortable, individually furnished bedrooms in this charming country inn make a perfect base for exploring the area – it's on the edge of the New Forest, so there are plenty of nearby walks. The little panelled bar on the right is snug with a feature stove surrounded by logs, leather and Victorian-style chairs on parquet flooring, stools against the counter and courteous staff who serve Ringwood and other local ales on handpump, craft beers and 16 good wines by the glass. The dining rooms are gracious with well spaced tables on pale carpets and some interesting modern art on the walls and in glass cabinets. The gardens are really lovely, featuring an extensive series of interestingly planted areas looping about pools and a placid winding stream, and dotted with art objects. You'll find plenty of places to sit, from intimate pairs of chairs to teak or wrought-iron tables on the main waterside terrace (which is beautifully lit at night) and on grass.

As well as breakast for non-residents, the appealing food includes sandwiches, fried buffalo chicken wings, baked camembert (to share), mushroom shawarma with pickles, stone-baked pizzas, burgers, a range of steaks with a choice of sauce and side dish (including a vegan version with spicy cauliflower, salsa and sriracha mayo), half roast chicken with fries, a pie or fish of the day, and puddings such as sticky toffee pudding and dark chocolate brownie with chocolate sauce and vanilla ice-cream. *Benchmark main dish: pie of the day £13.50. Two-course evening meal £21.00.*

Upham ~ Tenant Mark Strode ~ Real ale ~ Open 11-11; 12-10.30 Sun ~ Bar food 12-2.15, 7-9.15; 12-3, 6.30-8.15 Sun ~ Restaurant ~ Children welcome ~ Dogs allowed in bar ~ Bedrooms: £180

Please tell us if the décor, atmosphere, food or drink at a pub is different from our description. We rely on readers' reports to keep us up to date: feedback@goodguides.com, or (no stamp needed) Freepost THE GOOD PUB GUIDE, Random House Publishing, 20 Vauxhall Bridge Road, London SW1V 2SA.

HURSLEY
Kings Head ♀ ⇔
SU4225   Map 2

(01962) 775208 – www.kingsheadhursley.co.uk

A3090 Winchester–Romsey; SO21 2JW

Creeper-covered pub with interestingly furnished rooms, well kept ales, good wines and enjoyable food; lovely bedrooms

This gracious red-brick pub on the Hursley Estate has eight comfortable bedrooms, all named after celebrated incumbents of the manor and its land – from Henry de Blois, original owner in the 12th c, to the Spitfire (Hursley House was control centre for the Spitfire programme during the war). The bar is pleasantly appointed: cushioned and shuttered window seats, high-backed plush green chairs and chunky leather stools around scrubbed tables on black floor slates, one high table with equally high chairs, and a raised fireplace with church candles on the mantelpiece above. Stools line the S-shaped, grey-painted counter where they serve Gritchie English Lore and Ringwood Razorback on handpump, 17 wines by the glass, 40 gins and ten malt whiskies. A character lower room has a rather fine brick wall, a woodburning stove and wall banquettes with leather and tartan upholstery, and cushioned settles on floorboards; background music, daily papers and board games. The smart courtyard garden has tables equipped with parasols and heaters for the typically mercurial British summer. The skittles alley can be hired for private events.

 Pleasing food using local seasonal produce includes mac 'n' cheese truffle fritters, crispy battered haddock and chips, vegan burger with avocado, vegan cheese and fries, pan-fried 8oz rump steak with field mushroom, tomatoes and chips, seared bream fillet with Cornish new potatoes niçoise, and puddings such as rhubarb and custard crumble pie and eton mess pavlova. *Benchmark main dish: chicken, tarragon and leek pie with mash and buttered greens £14.00. Two-course evening meal £21.00.*

Cirrus Inns ~ Licensee Liam Chamberlain ~ Real ale ~ Open 12-10.30 ~ Bar food 12-3, 6-9.30; 12-4 Sun ~ Restaurant ~ Children welcome ~ Dogs allowed in bar, restaurant & bedroom ~ Bedrooms: £100

HURSTBOURNE TARRANT
George & Dragon ♀ ⇔
SU3853   Map 2

(01264) 736277 – www.georgeanddragon.com

The Square (A343); SP11 0AA

15th-c coaching inn with local ales, classic pub food, and seats on a terrace; bedrooms

It's all very relaxed and friendly at this carefully renovated inn, where the beamed bar remains very much the focus, with its woodburning stove and comfortable seating. The helpful, convivial staff keep quality local ales on handpump: West Berkshire Brewery provides a couple – Good Old Boy and Mr Swift Pale Ale are favourites – plus one usually local guest, such as Andwell in Hook or Ramsbury near Marlborough. The wine list is also thoughtful: 18 wines by the glass and carafe from a carefully chosen list. Carpeted dining areas have mate's chairs and wheelbacks, cushioned banquettes line cosy window alcoves and a second woodburner ensures there are no chilly spots in winter. There are seats and tables on a small secluded terrace. The local walking is very pretty, and the G&D's nine comfortable, quiet bedrooms provide the opportunity to explore the area for a few days. Every other Saturday the pub hosts a morning market.

After consultation with the pub's many fans, the kitchen has returned to well executed pub classics, including own-made chicken nuggets, breaded whitebait, half a pint of prawns, Italian-style herby meatballs, superfood salads, calves liver and bacon with spring onion mash, a pie of the day and a catch of the day, and assorted burgers (beef, chicken, mushroom and goats cheese, vegan); also lunchtime sandwiches and pudddings. *Benchmark main dish: beer-battered cod and chips £13.95. Two-course evening meal £20.00.*

Free house ~ Licensee Patrick Vaughan-Fowler ~ Real ale ~ Open 11-9.30; 11-11 Fri, Sat; 11-6 Sun; closed Mon, Tues ~ Bar food 12-3, 5-8.30, 12-3, 5-9 Fri, Sat; 12-4 Sun ~ Children welcome ~ Dogs allowed in bar ~ Bedrooms: £80

 LITTLETON   SU4532 Map 2
Running Horse 🛏
(01962) 880218 – www.runninghorseinn.co.uk
Main Road; village signed off B3049 NW of Winchester; SO22 6QS

Carefully renovated country pub with several dining areas, woodburning stove in the bar, enjoyable food and cabana in garden; pretty bedrooms

This solid Hampshire pub was given a makeover in 2019 and now looks pretty modish, with its carefully polished chairs and tables, mirrors, bookshelves filled with handsome antique books, flagstoned or bare board flooring and a brick fireplace with a woodburning stove. A panelled alcove with banquettes is perfect for a tucked-away chat over a pint, or there are the leather-topped stools lining the bar counter, where they keep Crafty Blind Side, Loxhill Biscuit and a changing guest on handpump, 14 wines by the glass and a farm cider. Staff are courteous and friendly and the atmosphere is chatty and easy-going. The front and back terraces have seats and tables and there are picnic-sets on the back grass by a spreading sycamore, and a popular cabana with piled-up cushions to sit on. The 15 bedrooms are bright and cottagey with handsome, shabby-chic décor; the extensive breakfast menu is worth getting hungry for.

As well as breakfasts, popular food includes sandwiches, prawn and avocado cocktail, mushroom shawarma with pickles and vegan mayo, a pie of the day, a fish of the day, caesar salad with optional chicken, specials such as venison haunch with red cabbage and jus, and puddings such as dark chocolate brownie with ice-cream and a daily changing fruit crumble. *Benchmark main dish: local ale-battered fish and chips £14.50. Two-course evening meal £21.00.*

Upham ~ Licensee Jack Fuller ~ Real ale ~ Open 8am-10pm; 8am-11pm Sat; 8am-7pm Sun ~ Bar food 12-2.30, 6-9; 12-2.30, 6-9.30 Fri, Sat; 12-6 Sun ~ Restaurant ~ Children welcome ~ Dogs allowed in bar & bedrooms ~ Bedrooms: £120

LONGSTOCK   SU3537 Map 2
Peat Spade 🍸
(01264) 810612 – www.peatspadeinn.co.uk
Off A30 on W edge of Stockbridge; SO20 6DR

Former coaching inn with imaginative food, real ales and some sporting décor; bedrooms

There's a distinctly piscatorial vibe to this handsome country inn surrounded by rolling, lush countryside and just a few steps from the trout-filled River Test. Stuffed fish and hunting and fishing paintings hang on the walls. The walking (as well as the fly fishing) is fantastic round here, and the windows in the bar and dining room provide glorious views of the Test Way walking route. The pub has an interesting mix of dining chairs around miscellaneous tables on bare boards and candlelight. Crafty Blind Side and Hop Tipple on handpump, 12 wines by the glass, around 20 gins and 28 malt whiskies; background music, TV and board games. Seating on the terrace or in the garden ranges from modern rattan-style through traditional wooden chairs and tables to a sunken area with wall seats around a fire pit. Bedrooms are comfortable and well equipped, and dogs are allowed.

As well as breakfast and lunchtime sandwiches, the popular food includes fried buffalo chicken wings, panko-breaded squid with pico de gallo, ale-battered haddock with chips, a pie of the day and a fish of the day, gnocchi with triple cheese sauce, burger (short rib, chicken or vegan) and chips, caesar salad with chicken, steaks with a choice of classic sauce, and puddings such as chocolate tart, crumble of the day and lemon and forest fruits eton mess. *Benchmark main dish: pollo picante with fries and aioli or hot sriracha butter £13.50. Two-course evening meal £21.00.*

Upham ~ Manager Shelly Dias ~ Real ale ~ Open 5-11 Mon; 7-3, 5-11 Tues-Thurs; 7am-11pm Fri; 8am-11pm Sat; 8-7 Sun ~ Bar food 6-8.30 Mon; 12-2.30, 6-8.30 Tues-Fri; 12-8.30 Sat; 12-6 Sun ~ Restaurant ~ Children welcome ~ Dogs allowed in bar & bedrooms ~ Bedrooms: £98

LOWER FROYLE   SU7643   Map 2

Anchor 🍷 ⇖

(01420) 23261 – www.anchorinnatlowerfroyle.co.uk
Village signposted N of A31 W of Bentley; GU34 4NA

Plenty to look at in smart country pub, real ales and good wines; bedrooms

This cottagey, low-beamed inn is perfectly placed for a Hampshire Downs walk. The appealing bar has standing timbers, flagstones, log fires and candlelight, while the five comfortable, country-style bedrooms are perfect for hikers taking on the Pilgrims Way. Elsewhere, there are stripped wood floors, sofas and armchairs dotted here and there and a mix of attractive tables and dining chairs. Throughout are all sorts of interesting knick-knacks, books, copper items, horsebrasses and lots of pictures and prints on contemporary paintwork. High bar chairs line the counter where they keep Ringwood Fortyniner and Triple fff Altons Pride on handpump, 18 wines by the glass (including fizz) and a growing gin collection; background music and board games. Chawton Cottage (Jane Austen's house in which she wrote all six of her novels) is a ten-minute drive away.

Popular food includes lunchtime sandwiches, truffle mac 'n' cheese fritters, seared bream fillet with Cornish new potatoes niçoise, British brisket burger with ruby slaw and fries, roast cauliflower with Persian-spiced lentils, spinach, chickpeas and flatbread, 8oz rump steak with chips and garlic and parsley butter, chicken, tarragon and leek pie with mash and buttered greens, and puddings such as lemon tart and rhubarb and custard crumble pie. *Benchmark main dish: Moving Mountains vegan burger with vegan cheddar, guacamole and fries £14.00. Two-course evening meal £21.00.*

Cirrus Inns ~ Licensee Lee Hart ~ Real ale ~ Open 12-11; 11-11 Sat; 11-10.30 Sun ~ Bar food 12-3, 6-8.30 ~ Restaurant ~ Children welcome ~ Dogs allowed in bar & bedrooms ~ Bedrooms: £80-£150

Bedroom prices are for high summer. Even then you may get reductions for more than one night, or weekends (outside tourist areas). Winter special rates are common, and many inns reduce bedroom prices if you have a full evening meal.

LOWER WIELD

SU6339 Map 2

Yew Tree ⭐️ 🍷

(01256) 389224 – www.the-yewtree.org.uk

Turn off A339 NW of Alton at 'Medstead, Bentworth 1' signpost, then follow village signposts; or off B3046 S of Basingstoke, signposted from Preston Candover; or follow satnav to Hattingley Valley Vineyards (SO24 9AJ); SO24 9RX

Bustling country pub run by a friendly couple, relaxed atmosphere and super choice of wines and food; sizeable garden

A new husband (chef) and wife (front of house) team took over this popular, lively pub a few weeks before the coronavirus lockdown, but are doing well, winning praise from customers old and new for their warm welcome and enticing food. A small flagstoned bar area on the left has pictures above a stripped-brick dado, a ticking clock and a log fire. Lottie the pub dog sometimes snoozes in front of the latter. There's carpet around to the right of the serving counter (with a couple of stylish wrought-iron bar chairs), and miscellaneous chairs and mixed tables are spread throughout. Drinks include 15 wines by the glass from a well chosen list, local cider, a beer named for the pub (from Bowman) and Longdog Bunny Chaser on handpump and local Silverback gin. Outside, there's a front terrace with solid tables and chunky seats and a sizeable side garden with picnic-sets; there are pleasant views across the quiet lane to the cricket field and beyond. Some lovely wildlife-filled walks are nearby. Disabled access.

Enjoyable food from a varied menu includes baguettes, tacos (blackened haddock, spicy pork, jackfruit) with mango and chilli salsa and wasabi mayo, salt and pepper calamari, moules frites, slow-cooked shoulder of lamb with Greek salad and tzatziki, summer salads with local watercress, wood-fired pizzas, a curry of the day, vegetable tagliatelle with cashew nut pesto, and puddings such as lemon tart and Belgian chocolate torte. *Benchmark main dish: piri-piri chicken with salad and potatoes £13.50. Two-course evening meal £21.00.*

Free house ~ Licensees Matt and Jas Clarke ~ Real ale ~ Open 12-3, 6-11; 12-10.30 Sun ~ Bar food 12-2, 6.30-9 ~ Children welcome ~ Dogs allowed in bar

LYMINGTON

SZ3394 Map 2

Mayflower 🛏️

(01590) 672160 – www.themayflowerlymington.co.uk

Kings Saltern Road; SO41 3QD

Renovated inn with nautical décor, plenty of drinking and dining space, good food and drink and seats in garden; bedrooms

A seafaring theme dominates the décor at this jolly inn, where local salty seadogs congregate with holidaymakers from the glittering marina right next door. There are photographs of smart yachts and views of the western Solent, and sailing paraphernalia including model boats and ship's instruments displayed with pride. There's also much evidence of the historic vessel from which the pub takes its name, which weighed anchor in nearby Southampton in 1620 before the gruelling sea crossing ahead. The high-ceilinged front rooms have built-in wall seats and leather-seated dining chairs around dark wooden tables, candles and fresh flowers, patterned wallpaper or turquoise paintwork and logs piled neatly into the fireplace. Brakspear Gravity, Ringwood Razorback and frequently changing guests (Flack Manor is a favourite) on handpump and several wines by the glass, served by efficient young staff. Two rooms at the back have similar seats and tables, bookshelves and a raised woodburning stove; background music and

TV. There's a covered terrace and steps down to a lawn with heavy rustic tables and benches. The ocean-wave theme continues in the six airy, stylish bedrooms, some of which have coastal views.

🍴 The pleasing food is seasonal and strong on fish and seafood, including a highly prized fish pie. Other dishes include crispy bacon, gem and avocado salad, seared bream fillet with Cornish new potatoes niçoise, chicken, tarragon and leek pie with mash and buttered greens, pan-fried 8oz rump steak with field mushroom, tomatoes, watercress and garlic and parsley butter, Moving Mountains vegan burger with vegan cheese, guacamole and fries, roast cauliflower with Persian-spiced lentils, spinach, chickpeas and flatbread, and puddings such as lemon tart crème fraîche or sticky toffee pudding. *Benchmark main dish: crispy-battered haddock and chips £13.00. Two-course evening meal £21.00.*

Cirrus Inns ~ Licensee Terry Clautman ~ Real ale ~ Open 12-10.30; 12-10 Sun ~ Bar food 12-3, 6-9; 12-9 Sat; 12-8 Sun ~ Restaurant ~ Children welcome ~ Dogs allowed in bar, restaurant & bedrooms ~ Bedrooms: £200

MATTINGLEY

Leather Bottle 🍷 🍺

SU7357   Map 2

(0118) 932 6371 – www.brunningandprice.co.uk/leatherbottle
3 miles from M3 junction 5; in Hook, turn right-and-left on to B3349 Reading Road (former A32); RG27 8JU

Charming village inn with plenty of room in rambling areas, a fine choice of drinks and food and seats in garden

A typical Hampshire red-brick cottage that is now a reliable Brunning & Price pub. The small beamed rooms with open doorways and standing timbers have a satisfying rustic atmosphere, and rugs on nice old parquet floors and flagstones lend an antique vibe; the built-in cushioned wall settles and upholstered banquettes are designed for comfort. There are old-style dining chairs and stools around polished tables (each set with flowers and a candle) plus open fires and a woodburning stove, mirrors, prints and old photographs on the walls and glass bottles and house plants on the windowsills. Friendly, helpful and efficient staff serve Brunning & Price Traditional Bitter plus guests from breweries such as West Berkshire, Windsor & Eton and XT on handpump, 21 wines by the glass, around 45 gins and 30 whiskies; background music. The company's trademark play tractor sends out a 'families welcome' message, as do the wooden chairs and tables under green parasols and picnic-sets on grass.

🍴 The daily changing menu offers sandwiches and 'light bites', red pepper hummus with chilli and flatbread, garlic and chilli king prawns, summer vegetable risotto, barbecue chicken wings, beetroot and mint falafel with tzatziki, fattoush and vegan feta cheese, beer-battered cod and chips, pork and leek sausages with mash, buttered greens and onion gravy, Malaysian curry with sweet potato, aubergine and spinach, pak choi and coconut rice, and puddings such as chocolate and orange tart and lemon meringue roulade with raspberry sorbet. *Benchmark main dish: chicken, ham and leek pie with buttered greens and mash £15.25. Two-course evening meal £23.00.*

Brunning & Price ~ Manager Matthew Hutchings ~ Real ale ~ Open 11.30-11; 11.30-10 Sun ~ Bar food 12-9.30 ~ Children welcome ~ Dogs allowed in bar

We mention bottled beers and spirits only if there is something unusual about them – imported Belgian real ales, say, or dozens of malt whiskies. Do please let us know about them in your reports.

NORTH WARNBOROUGH
SU7352 Map 2

Mill House ♀ ◖

(01256) 702953 – www.brunningandprice.co.uk/millhouse

*A mile from M3 junction 5: A287 towards Farnham, then right (brown sign to pub)
on to B3349 Hook Road; RG29 1ET*

**Sizeable raftered mill with an attractive layout, modern food, good
choice of drinks and lovely waterside terraces**

A Grade-II listed watermill (the wheel was restored when Brunning &
Price took on these delightful old buildings), and a pleasure to explore.
There are several linked areas on the main upper floor with its heavy beams,
plenty of well spaced tables in different sizes and styles, coal-effect fires
in pretty fireplaces and a profusion of often interesting pictures. A section
of floor is glazed to reveal the rushing water and mill wheel below, and a
galleried section looks down into a dining room, given a more formal feel
by panelling. St Austell Brunning & Price Traditional Bitter plus guests such
as Ascot Racecard, Delphic Level Crossing, Longdog Lamplight Porter, Old
Pie Factory Pie in the Sky and West Berkshire Golden Age on handpump,
40 malt whiskies, 20 wines by the glass, over 100 gins and local farm cider;
background music and board games. Lovely grounds surround the building,
with lots of solid tables and chairs on terraces and picnic-sets on grass – and
the mill pond is a fabulous place for nature spotting. Handy for the M3.

🍴 Rewarding, bistro-style food includes chicken caesar croquettes, seasonal
vegetable risotto, hummus with pitta, braised shoulder of lamb with new potatoes
and buttered greens, fish pie, sweet potato, aubergine and spinach Malaysian curry, pork
tenderloin with colcannon potatoes and apple sauce, grilled sea bass fillets with potato
and shallot terrine, and puddings such as hot waffle with banana, toffee sauce and
honeycomb ice-cream and crème brûlée. *Benchmark main dish: king prawn linguine
with chilli and tomato £14.95. Two-course evening meal £23.00.*

Brunning & Price ~ Manager Ellie Moore ~ Real ale ~ Open 11.30-11; 12-10 Sun ~ Bar food
12-9; 12-9.30 Fri, Sat ~ Restaurant ~ Children welcome ~ Dogs allowed in bar

PETERSFIELD
SU7129 Map 2

White Horse ◖

(01420) 588387 – www.whitehorsepetersfield.co.uk

*Up on an old downs road about halfway between Steep and East Tisted, near
Priors Dean – OS Sheet 186 or 197 map reference 715290; GU32 1DA*

**Much loved old place with a great deal of simple character, friendly
licensees and fantastic range of beers**

A wonderful array of up to ten real ales are kept on handpump at this
unspoilt whitewashed old pub – one or two named for the pub, plus
Adnams Ghost Ship, Belvoir Rare Breed, Butcombe Bitter, Fullers London
Pride, Ringwood Boondoggle and Fortyniner and quickly changing guests;
lots of country wines, a dozen wines by the glass, 20 malt whiskies and
two farm ciders. They hold a beer festival in June and a cider festival in
September. The bars and dining room remain charming and idiosyncratic:
open fires, oak settles and a mix of dark wooden dining chairs, nice old
tables, sofas and armchairs, various pictures, farm tools, horsebrasses,
a couple of fireside rocking chairs and so forth. There are some rustic
seats outside on the gravelled area and camping facilities.

🍴 Reliably good food includes sandwiches, seasonal soups, halloumi sticks with
sweet chilli sauce, a pie of the day, smoked haddock, cod and salmon fish pie with
samphire and peas, beef and mushroom stroganoff, goats cheese and onion tart with

new potatoes, and puddings such as seasonal fruit eton mess and almond and pistachio tart with cardamom cream and roasted fig. *Benchmark main dish: braised beef stew and dumplings £14.50. Two-course evening meal £21.00.*

Fullers ~ Licensees William Young and Elizabeth Fogg ~ Real ale ~ Open 12-10; 12-11 Sat; closed Mon ~ Bar food 12-3, 6-8; 12-8 Sat; 12-6 Sun ~ Restaurant ~ Children welcome ~ Dogs allowed in bar

PORTSMOUTH
SZ6399   Map 2

Old Customs House 🍺 £

(023) 9283 2333 – www.theoldcustomshouse.com

Vernon Buildings, Gunwharf Quays; follow brown signs to Gunwharf Quays car park; PO1 3TY

Nicely converted historic building in a prime waterfront development with real ales and well liked food

The modern waterside complex of Gunwharf Quays is a really popular place for Pompey natives and the area's many tourists, so booking is advisable at lunch. This Grade-I listed, 18th-c former customs house has big windows and high ceilings, with nautical prints and photographs on pastel walls, coal-effect gas fires, unobtrusive lighting and well padded chairs around sturdy tables of varying sizes on bare boards; the sunny entrance area has leather sofas. Broad stairs lead up to a carpeted restaurant with similar décor. Fullers London Pride, ESB and Gales HSB, Dark Star Hophead and a couple of changing guests on handpump, a decent range of wines by the glass, 24 gins and good coffees and teas. Staff are efficient and the background music well reproduced. Picnic-sets out in front are just metres from the water; the bar has disabled access and facilities. The graceful Spinnaker Tower (170 metres high with a glass floor and stunning views from its observation decks) is just round the corner.

Crowd-pleasing food includes London Pride cheddar rarebit, honey and mustard chipolatas, beer-battered haddock and chips, plant burger with pickles and triple-cooked chips, spiced green lentil, cauliflower and spinach curry, rump steak and chips, and puddings such as chocolate brownie with Laverstoke Farm buffalo milk ice-cream and molasses, date and hops sticky toffee pudding. *Benchmark main dish: fried buttermilk chicken burger and chips £13.25. Two-course evening meal £20.00.*

Fullers ~ Manager Paul Stephens ~ Real ale ~ Open 9.30am-11.30pm; 9.30am-midnight Fri, Sat; 9.30am-10.30pm Sun ~ Bar food 9.30-11.30am, 12-9pm; 9.30-11am, 12-9.30pm Sat; 9.30-11am, 12-8pm Sun ~ Restaurant ~ Children welcome ~ Dogs allowed in bar

ROCKBOURNE
SU1118   Map 2

Rose & Thistle

(01725) 518236 – www.roseandthistle.co.uk

Signed off B3078 Fordingbridge–Cranborne; SP6 3NL

Homely cottage with hands-on landlord and friendly staff, informal bars, real ales and good food, and seats in garden

Once a pair of 16th-c cottages, this old pub has postcard-perfect thatch, a charming country garden and plenty of handsome old features including beams, timbers and flagstones. There are homely dining chairs, stools and benches around a mix of old pubby tables in the cosy bar, Butcombe Gold, Sharps Doom Bar and a changing local ale such as Flack Manor Double Drop on handpump, eight wines by the glass and Black Rat cider; background music and board games. The restaurant has a log fire in each of its two rooms (one in a big brick inglenook), old engravings and cricket prints and an informal and relaxed atmosphere; background music and board games. Benches and tables are arranged beneath lovely hanging baskets at the front of the building, with picnic-sets under parasols on grass; good nearby walks. This is a pretty village on the edge of the New Forest and Rockbourne Roman Villa is nearby.

 Well regarded food includes lunchtime sandwiches, breaded whitebait, tempura-battered vegetables, fishcake with salad and chilli jam, curried chicken with watercress and aioli, courgette and sweetcorn fritters with poached egg, a fish of the day with potato rösti and spinach, root vegetable cobbler with cheese scone, steak and kidney suet pudding, and desserts such as vodka-infused watermelon with strawberry compote and sorbet and blackberry, lemon and elderflower eton mess. *Benchmark main dish: burger and chips £13.75. Two-course evening meal £23.00.*

Free house ~ Licensee Chris Chester-Sterne ~ Real ale ~ Open 12-3, 6-10; 12-9.30 Sat; 12-5 Sun ~ Bar food 12-2, 6-8.30 Mon-Sat; 12-3 Sun ~ Restaurant ~ Children welcome ~ Dogs allowed in bar

ST MARY BOURNE
Bourne Valley ♀ ⇦

SU4250   Map 2

(01264) 738361 ~ www.bournevalleyinn.com
Upper Link (B3048); SP11 6BT

Bustling country inn with plenty of space, an easy-going atmosphere and enjoyable food and drink; good bedrooms

There are lovely walks around the Bourne Rivulet, a chalk tributary of the River Test that runs through the garden of this popular pub. Dogs and their walkers are warmly welcomed, including in the bedrooms. The bar areas have sofas, wooden dining chairs and tables on coir or bare boards, empty wine bottles lining shelves and windowsills, and a warm log fire. Ringwood Razorback, Ramsbury Gold and changing guests on handpump and 17 wines by the glass (including fizz) served by helpful, friendly staff; background music, board games and TV. There's also a deli counter for coffee and cake, afternoon tea and picnic hampers – popular with the fishing fraternity, for those peaceful hours spent on the riverbank. A large barn extension, with rafters, beams, rustic partitioning and movable shelves made from crates, has large tables surrounded by leather, cushioned and upholstered chairs, more coir carpeting, another open fire and doors that lead out to a terrace with picnic-sets and metal tables and chairs. The nine bedrooms are modern and comfortable.

The contemporary food uses local seasonal produce; game, including their very popular venison burger, features heavily in autumn. Other dishes include heritage tomatoes with mozzarella and basil vinaigrette, Scottish smoked salmon with watercress and shaved fennel, British brisket burger with ruby slaw and fries, seared bream fillet with Cornish new potatoes niçoise, chicken, tarragon and leek pie with mash and buttered greens, roast cauliflower with Persian-spiced lentils, spinach, chickpeas and flatbread, and puddings such as dark chocolate brownie and rhubarb and custard crumble pie. *Benchmark main dish: crispy-battered haddock and chips £14.00. Two-course evening meal £22.00.*

Cirrus Inns ~ Licensee Clare Cunningham ~ Real ale ~ Open 12-11; 12-6 Sun; closed Mon ~ Bar food 12-3, 6-9; 12-4 Sun ~ Children welcome ~ Dogs allowed in bar, restaurant & bedrooms ~ Bedrooms: £100

If we know a featured-entry pub does sandwiches, we always say so – if they're not mentioned, you'll have to assume they're not available.

STEEP

SU7525 Map 2

Harrow £

(01730) 262685 – www.theharrowinnsteep.co.uk

Take Midhurst exit from Petersfield bypass, at exit roundabout take first left towards Midhurst, then first turning on left opposite garage, and left again at Sheet church; follow over dual-carriageway bridge to pub; GU32 2DA

Unchanging, simple place with long-serving landladies, beers tapped from the cask, unfussy food and cottage garden; no children inside

Leaflets at this little country gem detail a four-mile circular walk on the South Downs – ideal for walking off one of the noteworthy ploughman's lunches that are its stock in trade. The Harrow remains as unspoilt as ever. There's no pandering to modern methods: no credit cards, no waitress service, no restaurant, no music and the rose-covered loos are outside. The same family have run it for almost 90 years and everything revolves around village chat. Adverts for logs sit next to calendars of local views (on sale in support of local charities) and news of various quirky competitions. The small public bar has hops and dried flowers (replaced every year) hanging from the beams, built-in wall benches on the tiled floor, stripped-pine wallboards, a good log fire in the big inglenook and wild flowers on scrubbed deal tables; dominoes. Bowman Swift One, Dark Star Hophead, Flack Manor Double Drop, Hop Back GFB, Langham Hip Hop and Ringwood Best are tapped straight from casks behind the counter, and they have local wine and apple juice; staff are polite and friendly, even when under pressure. The big garden has seats on paved areas surrounded by cottage garden flowers and fruit trees. The Petersfield bypass doesn't intrude much on this rural idyll, though you'll need to follow the directions above to find the pub. They sell honesty-box flowers outside to support local nursing charities. Wheelchair access but no disabled loos.

Honest food includes sandwiches, hearty soups, rare beef, home-cooked ham, cheddar, brie or stilton ploughman's, salads, hot scotch egg, quiches, and puddings such as lemon crunch cheesecake and winter treacle tart. *Benchmark main dish: ploughman's £11.50. Two-course evening meal £17.00.*

Free house ~ Licensees Claire and Denise McCutcheon ~ Real ale ~ Open 12-2.30, 6-11; 11-3, 6-11 Sat; 12-3, 7-10.30 Sun ~ Bar food 12-2, 7-9; not Sun evening ~ Dogs on leads allowed in bar

SWANWICK

SU5109 Map 2

Navigator

(01489) 572123 – www.thenavigatorswanwick.co.uk

Handy for M27 junction 9 – A27, by Bursledon Bridge; SO31 7EB

Bustling inn with cosy bar and plenty of dining space, helpful staff, popular food and local ales and seats outside; bedrooms

Its location near Swanwick Marina on the peaceful River Hamble means this place is popular with seafarers; in warm weather there are plenty of seats under large parasols, though no water views. A recent refurbishment has removed the conservatory and extended the dining area. The cosy bar has leather sofas by an open fire, church candles and fresh flowers, stools lining the bleached wooden bar counter and slate flooring and bare boards. Ringwood Fortyniner and a guest from the likes of Ascot and Bowmans on handpump and good wines by the glass; background music. The dining area has painted wall seats with colourful cushions, wall banquettes, cushioned wooden chairs around dark tables, woodstrip walls and yachting and photos of lighthouses. Some seating outside at the front. The 23 bedrooms are attractively decorated, smart and comfortable.

🍴 Well thought-of food includes lunchtime sandwiches, prawn and avocado cocktail, buffalo chicken wings, a range of stone-baked pizzas, 'buddha bowl' with brown rice, sesame, kale, avocado, carrot pickle, beetroot and roasted cauliflower, burgers (short rib, beef, chicken, vegan) and fries, various steaks (including a cauliflower version) with chips and a choice of sauce, and puddings such as dark chocolate brownie with sauce and ice cream and a daily fruit crumble. *Benchmark main dish: pie of the day £13.50. Two-course evening meal £21.00.*

Upham ~ Manager Nick Hall ~ Real ale ~ Open 7am-11pm; 8am-11pm Sat; 8am-10.30pm Sun ~ Bar food 8-10am, 12-2.30pm, 5-9pm Mon-Sat; 8-10am, 12-8pm Sun ~ Restaurant ~ Dogs allowed in bar & bedrooms ~ Bedrooms: £85

TOTFORD
Woolpack 🍷 🛏

SU5737   Map 2

(01962) 734184 – www.thewoolpackinn.co.uk
B3046 Basingstoke–Alresford; SO24 9TJ

Carefully refurbished rooms, plenty of character, first class food and drink and seats outside; lovely bedrooms

There is a teeny-weeny argument among the hamlets of the Home Counties as to which qualifies as the smallest in England. Totford lays one such claim. It is very bijou, sitting plum in the beautiful Candover Valley, which makes its handsome pub a popular landmark for walkers. As Boris the stuffed boar's head mounted on the wall would no doubt ruefully testify, it's also a big hit with the hunting, shooting and fishing crowd. The bar has an easy-going atmosphere, leather button-back armchairs, little stools and wooden chairs around a mix of tables on wide floorboards, and high chairs against the counter where they offer Ringwood Ramsbury and Razorback on handpump, 15 wines by the glass and a rather special bloody mary. Leading off here is a dining room with flagstones and carpet, a raised fireplace with guns, bellows and other country knick-knacks above it, and chunky tables and chairs. Throughout are rugs on flagstones, exposed brick and stonework, a few bits of timbering and beamery, church candles, lots of photographs, some cosy booth seating and high-back upholstered dining chairs and leather wall seats around a mix of tables. Outside, there are teak tables and chairs and picnic-sets on the terrace, on gravel and on grass, and distant views. There's also a play area. The seven delightful bedrooms are named after game birds; dogs are allowed. Gun cabinets and 'vegan and environmentally friendly British bath and body products' also puts the accommodation into a class of its own.

🍴 As well as pizzas from their outdoor wood-fired oven in summer, the pleasing food includes Scottish smoked salmon with watercress and fennel, truffle mac 'n' cheese fritters, crispy-battered haddock and chips, British brisket burger with ruby slaw and fries, pan-fried 8oz rump steak with chips and garlic and parsley butter, Sunday roasts (chicken or slow-roasted pork belly), and puddings such as rhubarb and custard crumble pie and sticky toffee pudding. *Benchmark main dish: chicken, tarragon and leek pie with mash and buttered greens £14.00. Two-course evening meal £22.00.*

Cirrus Inns ~ Licensee James Waterhouse ~ Real ale ~ Open 12-11; 12-10 Sun ~ Bar food 12-3, 6.30-9; 12-6 Sun ~ Restaurant ~ Children welcome ~ Dogs allowed in bar, restaurant & bedrooms ~ Bedrooms: £150

If we know a pub has an outdoor play area for children, we mention it.

WEST MEON

SU6424 Map 2

Thomas Lord 🛏

(01730) 829244 – www.thethomaslord.co.uk

High Street; GU32 1LN

Cricketing knick-knacks in character bar rooms, a smarter dining room, helpful staff, local beers, well thought-of food and pretty garden; bedrooms

The relaxed, friendly bar in this bustling pub has plenty of cricketing memorabilia (the place is named after the founder of Lord's Cricket Ground): bats, gloves, balls, stumps, photographs and prints, and even stuffed squirrels playing the game in a display cabinet above the counter. Also, a leather chesterfield and armchairs beside a log fire, wooden chairs and corner settles on parquet flooring. Beers include Crafty Ales IPA with guest appearances from Flowerpots and Triple fff, served by chatty, helpful staff. Another smaller room and the dining rooms have similar furnishings and open fires. The sizeable beer garden has lovely herbaceous borders, picnic-sets, an outdoor pizza oven and barbecue area, a chicken run and a kitchen garden – produce from which shows up on the menu. There are five well equipped wood cabins with french windows on to a little seating area, perfect for Hampshire staycations.

 Enjoyable food using local seasonal produce includes mushroom shawarma with pickles and rocket, panko-breaded squid, a fish of the day, gnocchi with triple cheese sauce, basil and truffle oil, beef, chicken or plant burger with fries, half roasted chicken with roasted garlic aioli, barbecue sauce or hot sriracha butter and skin-on fries, and puddings such as chocolate brownie, sticky toffee pudding and local ice-creams. *Benchmark main dish: haddock and chips £14.50. Two-course evening meal £21.00.*

Upham ~ Real ale ~ Open 8am-11pm; 8am-8pm Sun ~ Bar food 12-2.30, 5-8.30; 12-8.30 Sat; 12-6 Sun ~ Restaurant ~ Children welcome ~ Dogs allowed in bar & bedrooms ~ Bedrooms: £90

WINCHESTER

SU4829 Map 2

Wykeham Arms ⭐ 🍷 🛏

(01962) 853834 – www.wykehamarmswinchester.co.uk

Kingsgate Street (Kingsgate Arch and College Street are closed to traffic; there is access via Canon Street); SO23 9PE

Tucked-away pub with lots to look at, several real ales, many wines by the glass and highly thought-of food; pretty bedrooms

There's plenty to look at in this busy pub's characterful rooms, filled as they are with all sorts of curiosities; Victorian oak desks retired from Winchester College, collections of well thumbed books, walls hung with pewter tankards and numerous local prints and engravings. Elsewhere, there are kitchen chairs and deal tables with candles, leather banquettes and parquet and wooden flooring. On chilly days, you'll find crackling log fires – perhaps with Rolo, the pub's chocolate brown cockapoo, relaxing beside one of them. A snug room at the back, known as the Jameson Room (after the late landlord, Graeme Jameson), is decorated with a set of Ronald Searle 'Winespeak' prints. A second room is panelled. Fullers HSB, London Pride and Spring Sprinter, Gales Seafarers and a guest such as Flowerpots Goodens Gold on handpump, 33 wines by the glass, 15 malt whiskies, a couple of farm ciders and quite a few ports and sherries; the tea list is pretty special. There are tables outside in a covered back terrace and a small courtyard. With so much to see and do in this city and the surrounding area, the 14 attractive bedrooms seem especially tempting; some have four-posters and breakfasts are first class.

🍴⭐ Excellent food includes sandwiches, curried parsnip and apple soup, ham hock terrine with apple and fig chutney, smashed avocado with Isle of Wight tomatoes and poached egg, spiced cod with cauliflower purée, mango salsa and burnt spring onion, pearl barley and spelt risotto with butternut squash and goat's cheese, 12oz sirloin steak with béarnaise and triple-cooked chips, English garden salad with chicken, and puddings such as treacle tart and vanilla ice-cream and pear tarte tatin with toffee sauce. *Benchmark main dish: beef burger and triple-cooked chips £14.75. Two-course evening meal £22.00.*

Fullers ~ Manager Jon Howard ~ Real ale ~ Open 11-11; 11-10.30 Sun ~ Bar food 12-3, 6-9.30; 12-8 Sun ~ Restaurant ~ Children over 8 allowed in restaurant at lunchtime ~ Dogs allowed in bar & bedrooms ~ Bedrooms: £150

Also Worth a Visit in Hampshire

Besides the fully inspected pubs, you might like to try these pubs that have been recommended to us and described by readers. Do tell us what you think of them: feedback@goodguides.com

ALRESFORD   SU5832
Bell (01962) 732429
West Street; SO24 9AT Comfortable Georgian coaching inn (Grade II listed) with popular food including weekday fixed-price menu, up to five well kept changing ales and extensive choice of wines by the glass, fine selection of malt whiskies, bare-boards interior with scrubbed tables and log fire, hops and trophy heads (including a moose) in bar, separate smallish dining room; children and dogs welcome (resident spaniels are called Freddie and Teddy), attractive sunny back courtyard, six bedrooms, open all day (till 6pm Sun).

ALRESFORD   SU5831
Cricketers (01962) 422909
Jacklyns Lane; SO24 9LW Large pebble-dashed corner pub with modernised interior; good sensibly priced food including hugely popular Sun roasts, well kept beers and decent choice of wines by the glass, welcoming attentive staff, cricketing memorabilia and woodburner, separate dining area; occasional live music; children and dogs (in bar) welcome, sizeable garden with covered terrace, pizza oven and play area, open all day.

ALRESFORD   SU5832
Globe (01962) 733118
Bottom of Broad Street (B3046) where parking is limited; SO24 9DB Popular and welcoming old tile-hung pub (former coaching inn); enjoyable food (all day Sun) including weekday lunchtime/early evening deal, real ales including Nethergate and more than 20 wines by the glass, friendly staff; children and dogs welcome, nice garden

overlooking Alresford Pond, good riverside walks, open all day.

ALRESFORD   SU5832
Horse & Groom (01962) 734809
Broad Street; town signed off A31 bypass; SO24 9AQ Comfortable attractively updated Fullers pub with roomy well divided interior; their well kept ales and a local guest, enjoyable food from fairly compact but varied menu, friendly young staff, pale beams (some supported by iron pillars), exposed brickwork and log fires, bow window seats and a few stepped levels, back restaurant area; background and some live music, quiz Mon, daily newspapers, children and well behaved dogs welcome, small enclosed back terrace, open all day, food all day Sun till 7pm.

ALRESFORD   SU5832
Swan (01962) 732302
11 West Street; SO24 9AD Long narrow bar in 18th-c hotel (former coaching inn); painted panelling and some rustic stall seating, well kept ales such as local Alfreds, Itchen Valley and Sharps, decent wines, tea and coffee, popular reasonably priced food including breakfast (until 10.30am) and Sun roasts, efficient friendly service, two dining rooms (one more formal); children welcome, café-style table on terrace, 22 bedrooms.

AMPFIELD   SU4023
⭐**White Horse** (01794) 368356
A3090 Winchester–Romsey; SO51 9BQ Snug low-beamed front bar with candles and soft lighting, inglenook log fire and comfortable country furnishings, spreading beamed dining area behind, well kept Greene King, guest ales and several wines by the

glass, good food including all-day snacks, efficient service, locals' bar with another inglenook; background music; children and dogs welcome, pergola-covered terrace and high-hedged garden with plenty of picnic-sets, cricket green beyond, classic car meetings third Weds of month, good walks in Ampfield Woods and handy for Hillier Gardens, open all day.

BARTON STACEY   SU4341
Swan (01962) 760470
Village signed off A303; SO21 3RL
Beamed coaching inn with good affordably priced pubby food (not Sun evening, Mon) from lunchtime sandwiches up, three well kept ales, friendly owners and helpful young staff, bar with brick and timber walls, light wood flooring and inglenook log fire, back restaurant; board games, children and dogs welcome, picnic-sets on front gravel and lawned area, open all day Sat, till 6pm Sun, closed Mon.

BEAULIEU   SU3902
Montys Inn (01590) 612188
Almost opposite Palace House; SO42 7ZL
Attached to the regal Montagu Arms hotel, Montys has its own entrance and is a relaxed, simply furnished bar with panelling, bare floorboards, bay windows, a mix of pale tables surrounded by tartan-cushioned dining chairs and a winter log fire in a beautiful fireplace, also a smarter panelled dining room and tucked-away back garden; Ringwood Best and Fortyniner and a seasonal guest on handpump and several wines by the glass, served by cheerful, helpful staff, popular food using own kitchen garden produce from sandwiches and ploughman's to game; children and dogs welcome, open all day weekends.

BEAUWORTH   SU5624
Milburys (01962) 771248
Off A272 Winchester–Petersfield; SO24 0PB Traditional 17th-c tile-hung country pub named for nearby Milbarrow Down; beams, panelling and stripped stone, inglenook log fire (even on cooler summer days), massive 17th-c treadmill for much older incredibly deep well, galleried area, three changing ales and enjoyable reasonably priced simple food; skittle alley; children (in eating areas) and dogs welcome, garden with fine downland views, good walks, regular classic car meetings including TVR, two bedrooms, closed Sun and Mon evenings.

BENTLEY   SU7844
Star (01420) 23184
Centre of village on old A31; GU10 5LW Welcoming little early 19th-c village pub under new management; good reasonably priced food (smaller helpings available), Sharps Doom Bar, Triple fff Moondance and a guest, eight wines by the glass from decent list, good service, open fire in brick

fireplace, restaurant; quiz first Mon of month, newspapers; children and dogs welcome, garden with thatched gazebos, open all day, food all day Sun till 7pm.

BENTWORTH   SU6740
Sun (01420) 562338
Well Lane, off Station Road; signed Shaldon/Alton; GU34 5JT Creeper-clad 17th-c country tavern; unspoilt little beamed rooms with scrubbed deal tables, high-backed settles, pews and wheelback chairs on bare boards or brick floor, candles on tables, various pictures and knick-knacks, three log fires, good range of local real ales and enjoyable attractively presented food from shortish menu, friendly service; children and dogs welcome, seats out at front and in back garden, open (and food) all day Sun.

BISHOP'S SUTTON   SU6031
Ship (01962) 732863
B3047, on Alton side of Alresford; SO24 0AQ Old village corner dining pub revamped under present management; good food from pub favourites up including daily specials, three well kept changing ales, helpful friendly service, two-level bar with rugs on bare boards, woodburner, back dining room; children and dogs welcome, tables in garden, good walks and handy for Watercress Line, open all day Fri and Sat, till 7pm Sun, closed Mon.

BISHOP'S WALTHAM   SU5517
Barleycorn (01489) 892712
Lower Basingwell Street; SO32 1AJ Traditional 18th-c two-bar village local; popular generously served pub food at reasonable prices, good friendly service, well kept Greene King ales, a guest beer, decent wines and 50 gins, beams and some low ceiling panelling, open fires; well behaved children and dogs welcome, large garden and smokers' area at back, open all day.

BISHOP'S WALTHAM   SU5517
Crown (01489) 893350
The Square; SO32 1AF Spacious and attractively updated 16th-c beamed coaching inn; Fullers/Gales beers and popular fairly priced food from sandwiches to daily specials, cheerful helpful staff, bar area on the left with bare boards, comfortable seating and log fire, split-level dining room to the right with three further fireplaces; background music; children and dogs welcome, courtyard tables, opposite entrance to palace ruins, eight good bedrooms, open all day from 8.30am, food all day Fri-Sun.

BOLDRE   SZ3198
★ Red Lion (01590) 673177
Off A337 N of Lymington; SO41 8NE Relaxed New Forest-edge dining pub with five black-beamed rooms and three log fires; pews, sturdy cushioned dining chairs

and tapestried stools, rural landscapes on rough-cast walls, other rustic bits and pieces including copper and brass pans, a heavy horse harness and some ferocious-looking traps, old cooking range in cosy bar, well kept Ringwood and guests, very good home-made food from varied menu (worth booking), friendly service; dogs welcome, opposite village green with seats out among flowering tubs and hanging baskets, more tables in back garden, open all day Sun.

BRAISHFIELD SU3724
Wheatsheaf (01794) 368652
Village signposted off A3090 on NW edge of Romsey; SO51 0QE Friendly bay-windowed pub with four well kept beers and tasty home-cooked food, beams and cosy log fire; background music (live Thurs), sports TV, pool; children and dogs welcome, garden with play area and nice views, woodland walks nearby, close to Hillier Gardens, open all day.

BRAMBRIDGE SU4721
Dog & Crook (01962) 712129
Near M3 junction 12, via B3335; Church Lane; SO50 6HZ Bustling 18th-c pub with beamed bar and cosy dining room; enjoyable home-made food including separate gluten-free menu and Weds steak night, four real ales such as Bowman and Wadworths, several wines by the glass, gin parlour, friendly service; background music, fortnightly quiz Thurs; children and dogs welcome, disabled access/loos, garden with covered deck, pretty Itchen Way walks nearby, open all day Fri-Sun.

BRAMDEAN SU6127
Fox (01962) 771363
A272 Winchester–Petersfield; SO24 0LP Popular and welcoming 17th-c part-weatherboarded roadside pub; open-plan bar with black beams and log fires, well kept Sharps Doom Bar and guests, real ciders and several wines by the glass, ample helpings of good fairly traditional home-made food from sandwiches and sharing boards up, cheerful helpful staff; quiz first Mon of month; children and dogs welcome, walled-in terraced area and spacious lawn under fruit trees, three shepherd's huts, good surrounding walks, open (and food) all day Fri-Sun, kitchen closes 7pm Sun.

BREAMORE SU1517
Bat & Ball (01725) 512252
Salisbury Road; SP6 2EA Dutch-gabled red-brick roadside pub with two linked bar areas and restaurant; well kept Ringwood ales and enjoyable reasonably priced food, friendly service; regular live music; children and dogs welcome, pleasant large garden at the side (summer barbecues), Avon fishing and walks (lovely ones up by church and stately Breamore House), open (and food) all day.

BROCKENHURST SU3002
Huntsman (01590) 622225
Lyndhurst Road (A337); SO42 7RH Large modernised roadside inn; popular food from sandwiches and sharing plates up including wood-fired pizzas and chargrilled steaks, friendly service, three or four real ales such as Ringwood, cocktails and plenty of wines by the glass, coffee bar; skittle alley; children and dogs (in bar) welcome, decent-sized garden with part-covered terrace, 13 well appointed bedrooms, open (and food) all day.

BROOK SU2714
Bell (023) 8081 2214
B3079/B3078, handy for M27 junction 1; SO43 7HE Really a hotel with golf club, but has neat flagstoned bar with lovely 18th-c inglenook fire, well kept ales such as Flack Manor, Ringwood and Wychwood, good cider, plenty of wines by the glass and extensive range of gins, nice food too from snacks up, afternoon teas (perhaps with a glass of house champagne), helpful friendly uniformed staff, attractive restaurant; children and dogs (in bar) welcome, picnic-sets in big garden, delightful village, 28 comfortable bedrooms, open all day.

BROOK SU2713
★ Green Dragon (023) 8081 3359
B3078 NW of Cadnam, just off M27 junction 1; SO43 7HE Thatched New Forest dining pub dating from the 15th c; popular food from usual favourites to blackboard specials, well kept Wadworths ales and good range of wines by the glass, friendly helpful staff, linked areas with beams, log fires and traditional furnishings, lots of pictures and other bits and pieces including some old leather 'bends' showing brand marks of forest graziers; children and dogs (not in restaurant) welcome, disabled access from car park, attractive small terrace, garden with play area and paddocks beyond, picturesque village, open all day.

BROUGHTON SU3032
Tally Ho (01794) 301280
High Street, opposite church; signed off A30 Stockbridge–Salisbury; SO20 8AA Welcoming pub with light airy bar and separate eating area, four well kept ales including Ringwood and a house beer brewed in the village, good food from pub favourites up (more elaborate evening choice), friendly service; quiz and pizza nights; children welcome, charming secluded back garden, good walks, open all day.

BUCKLERS HARD SU4000
Master Builders House
(01590) 616253 *M27 junction 2 follow signs to Beaulieu, turn left on to B3056, then left to Bucklers Hard; SO42 7XB* Sizeable red-brick hotel in lovely spot

overlooking river in New Forest National Park; character main bar with heavy beams, log fire and simple furnishings, rugs on wood floor, mullioned windows, interesting list of shipbuilders dating from 18th c, ales such as Ringwood Best and Sharps Doom Bar, decent wine list, stairs down to room with fireplace at each end, enjoyable bar and restaurant food from sandwiches and pizzas up, afternoon teas, prompt friendly service; children and dogs welcome, picnic-sets on stepped terrace, small gate at bottom of garden for waterside walks, summer barbecues, 26 bedrooms, open (and food) all day.

BURGHCLERE   SU4660
Carpenters Arms (01635) 278251
Harts Lane, off A34; RG20 9JY
Welcoming little village pub (some recent refurbishment) with enjoyable reasonably priced food and well kept Arkells beers, helpful friendly service, good country views (Watership Down) from conservatory and terrace, log fire; background music; children, walkers and dogs welcome, handy for Sandham Memorial Chapel (NT) with its Stanley Spencer murals and Highclere Castle, eight comfortable annexe bedrooms, open all day, no food Sun evening.

BURLEY   SU2103
Queens Head (01425) 403423
The Cross; back road Ringwood–Lymington; BH24 4AB Large brick and tile Chef & Brewer dating partly from the 17th c; several updated rambling rooms, open fire, good choice of enjoyable reasonably priced food (order at bar) including deals, Greene King and local guests, helpful friendly staff; background music, fruit machine; children and dogs (in one area) welcome, plenty of space outside, car parking fee refunded at bar, pub and New Forest village can get packed in summer, open all day.

BURLEY   SU2202
White Buck (01425) 402264
Bisterne Close; 0.7 miles E, OS Sheet 195 map reference 223028; BH24 4AZ Lovely New Forest setting for this well run 19th-c mock-Tudor hotel; Fullers ales in long bar with two-way log fire at either end, seats in big bow window, comfortable part-panelled shooting-theme snug and spacious well divided dining area on different levels, good attractively presented food (some prices on the high side) and nice wines, helpful personable staff; background music; children and dogs welcome, terraces and spacious lawn with picnic-sets, excellent walks towards Burley itself and over Mill Lawn, good bedrooms, open all day.

CHALTON   SU7316
Red Lion (023) 9259 2246
Off A3 Petersfield–Horndean; PO8 0BG Largely extended timber and thatch country dining pub; interesting old core around inglenook (dates to the 12th c and has been a pub since the 1400s); well kept Fullers/Gales beers and a guest, popular food (all day weekends) from sandwiches and pub favourites up, friendly helpful service, back restaurant; children and dogs welcome, disabled access and facilities, nice views from neat rows of picnic-sets on rectangular lawn by large car park, good walks, nearby church also worth a visit and handy for Queen Elizabeth Country Park, open all day.

CHAWTON   SU7037
Greyfriar (01420) 83841
Off A31/A32 S of Alton; Winchester Road; GU34 1SB Tile-hung beamed dining pub opposite Jane Austen's House Museum; enjoyable food (not Sun evening) from lunchtime sandwiches and bar snacks up, Fullers ales, guest beers and good selection of gins, welcoming relaxed atmosphere with comfortable seating and sturdy pine tables in neat linked areas, open fire in restaurant end; quiz Sun; children and dogs welcome, small garden with terrace, good nearby walks, open all day.

CHERITON   SU5828
★ Flower Pots (01962) 771318
Off B3046 towards Beauworth and Winchester; OS Sheet 185 map reference 581282; SO24 0QQ Unspoilt 19th-c red-brick country local in same family since 1968; three or four very good value cask-tapped ales from on-site brewery, enjoyable reasonably priced home-made food (not Sun evening, Mon) including generous baps, range of casseroles and popular Weds curry night, cheerful welcoming staff, extended public bar with painted brick walls, tiled floor, open fire and glass-covered well, another straightforward but homely room with country pictures and small log fire; well behaved children and dogs welcome, seats on pretty front and back lawns (some under apple trees), vintage motorcycles Weds lunchtime (weather permitting), enjoyable local walks.

CHILBOLTON   SU3939
Abbots Mitre (01264) 860348
Off A3051 S of Andover; SO20 6BA 19th-c brick-built village pub; five well kept local ales from perhaps Andwell and Flack Manor and decent wines by the glass, popular food from sandwiches and pubby choices up including daily specials and Sun roasts, friendly service; children and dogs (in bar) welcome, wheelchair access, picnic-sets outside, River Test and other walks (circular one from the pub), open (and food) all day.

CRONDALL   SU7948
Plume of Feathers (01252) 850245
The Borough; GU10 5NT Attractive 15th-c brick and timber pub in picturesque village; good range of popular generously served food

from standards up, friendly helpful staff, well kept Greene King, some unusual guest beers and nice wines by the glass, beams and dark wood, red carpet, prints on cream walls, restaurant with log fire in big brick fireplace; soft background music; children welcome, picnic-sets in back terrace garden (bookable barbecues), three bedrooms, open all day Sun.

CROOKHAM   SU7952
Exchequer (01252) 615336
Crondall Road; GU51 5SU Welcoming smartly presented dining pub (part of the Red Mist group including the Royal Exchange at Lindford); popular food (can eat in bar or restaurant) from sandwiches and sharing boards to blackboard specials, burger night Mon, pie and pint night Tues, four well kept ales, cider and lager from local Hogs Back, also good choice of wines by the glass and interesting gins/cocktails, pleasant hard-working young staff, cosy woodburner, daily newspapers; children and dogs welcome, rattan-style furniture on split-level terrace, near Basingstoke Canal, open all day Fri and Sat, till 9.30pm Sun, food all day weekends.

DUMMER   SU5846
Queen (01256) 397367
Less than a mile from M3 junction 7; take Dummer slip road; RG25 2AD Comfortable well divided beamed pub with lots of softly lit alcoves; Courage, Fullers and a guest, decent choice of wines by the glass and popular food from lunchtime sandwiches and light dishes up, friendly service, big log fire, pictures of the Queen and some steeplechase prints; background music; children welcome in restaurant, picnic-sets under parasols on terrace and in back garden, attractive village with ancient church, open all day (closes 6pm Sun).

DUNBRIDGE   SU3126
Mill Arms (01794) 340355
Barley Hill (B3084); SO51 0LF Much extended 18th-c coaching inn opposite station; welcoming informal atmosphere in spacious high-ceilinged rooms, scrubbed pine tables, farmhouse chairs and several sofas on oak or flagstone floors, two log fires, local ales such as Flack Manor, enjoyable food, dining conservatory; darts and skittle alley; children and dogs (in bar) welcome, big garden, plenty of walks in surrounding Test Valley, six comfortable bedrooms, open all day (closes 8pm Sun).

DUNDRIDGE   SU5718
★Hampshire Bowman (01489) 892940
Off B3035 towards Droxford, Swanmore, then right at Bishop's Waltham signpost; SO32 1GD Chatty mix of customers at this homely relaxed country pub; five well kept local ales tapped from the cask (beer festival last weekend in July), ten or more traditional ciders and good value food (all day Fri-Sun)

from generous sandwiches and hearty pub dishes to specials, good cheerful service, stable bar and cosy unassuming original one; mobile phones discouraged; children and dogs welcome, tables on terrace and peaceful lawn, play equipment, hitching post for horses, popular with walkers and cyclists, open all day.

DURLEY   SU5116
Farmers Home (01489) 860457
B3354 and B2177; Heathen Street/Curdridge Road; SO32 2BT Comfortable red-brick beamed country pub, spacious but cosy, with two-bay dining area and restaurant, enjoyable food including good steaks and popular Sun lunch, friendly service, room for drinkers too with decent wines by the glass and three well kept ales including Gales and Ringwood, woodburner; children and dogs (in bar) welcome, large garden with pergola and play area, nice walks, open (and food) all day.

DURLEY   SU5217
★Robin Hood (01489) 860229
Durley Street, just off B2177 Bishop's Waltham–Winchester – brown signs to pub; SO32 2AA Quirky open-plan beamed pub with popular well prepared food from varied blackboard menu (order at bar), a house beer from Greene King and a couple of guests, nice wines, good friendly service, log fire and leather sofas in bare-boards bar, dining area with stone floors and mix of old pine tables and chairs, bookcase door to loos; background music; children and dogs welcome, disabled facilities, decked terrace, garden with play area, country views, open all day Sun.

EAST BOLDRE   SU3700
Turf Cutters Arms (01590) 612331
Main Road; SO42 7WL Small dimly lit 18th-c New Forest local behind white picket fence; lots of beams and pictures, nicely worn-in furnishings on bare boards and flagstones, log fire, enjoyable home-made food from ciabattas up (worth booking evenings/weekends), well kept Ringwood ales and a guest, friendly helpful service and chatty relaxed atmosphere; live music Fri evening, Sun afternoon; children and dogs welcome, picnic-sets in large back garden, enjoyable heathland walks, bedrooms in nearby converted barn, open all day.

EAST END   SZ3696
★East End Arms (01590) 626223
Back road Lymington–Beaulieu, parallel to B3054; SO41 5SY Simple friendly pub (owned by former Dire Straits bass guitarist); unfussy bar with chatty locals and log fire, Ringwood Best or Fortyniner and several wines by the glass, enjoyable freshly made food (not Sun evening) served by cheerful helpful staff, attractive dining room; occasional live music; children and dogs (in

bar) welcome, picnic-sets in terraced garden, five pretty cottagey bedrooms, open all day July-Sept (all day Fri-Sun rest of year).

EAST MEON   SU6822

Olde George (01730) 823481

Church Street; signed off A272 W of Petersfield, and off A32 in West Meon; GU32 1NH Atmospheric heavy-beamed village inn with good choice of well liked food including vegetarian and gluten-free options, Badger ales and decent selection of wines by the glass, cosy areas around central brick counter, inglenook log fires; children and dogs welcome, nice back terrace, five bedrooms, good breakfast, pretty village with fine church and surrounding walks, open all day Sun.

EASTLEIGH   SU4519

Steam Town Brewery

(023) 8235 9139 *Bishopstoke Road/ Dutton Lane; SO50 6AD* Brewpub with six of their beers along with guest ales and 16 craft kegs, also three ciders, decent wines and around 40 gins, good range of chargrilled burgers, friendly knowledgeable staff, industrial-style bare-boards interior with some reclaimed materials including factory light fittings, old train seats and a servery made from the side of a railway carriage; live music Weds-Sat; children and dogs (in bar) welcome, open all day, food all day Sat, till 6pm Sun.

EASTON   SU5132

Chestnut Horse (01962) 779866

3.6 miles from M3 junction 9: A33 towards Kings Worthy, then B3047 towards Itchen Abbas; Easton then signposted on right – bear left in village; SO21 1EG Comfortable 16th-c pub in pretty village of thatched cottages; open-plan but with a series of cosy separate areas, log fires, black beams and joists hung with jugs, mugs and chamber-pots, three Badger ales, plenty of wines by the glass and good selection of whiskies on right – bear left in food including home-made pizzas, Mon steak night and other offers, attentive friendly staff; background music; children and dogs (in bar) welcome, seats and tables on smallish sheltered decked area, summer tubs and baskets, walks in Itchen Valley, open all day Fri-Sun, food all day Sun.

ECCHINSWELL   SU4959

Royal Oak (01635) 297355

Ecchinswell Road; RG20 4UH Cosy and welcoming whitewashed village pub; bar with open fire, window seats and plush-topped stools around tables on wood floor, second room with another fire and airy dining room

with country kitchen chairs and mix of tables on light boards, three well kept ales and enjoyable fair value food, good friendly service; children welcome, picnic-sets on front terrace behind picket fence, more in large back garden running down to stream.

EMERY DOWN   SU2808

★**New Forest Inn** (023) 8028 4690

Village signed off A35 just W of Lyndhurst; SO43 7DY Well run 18th-c weatherboarded village pub in one of the best parts of the New Forest for walking; good sensibly priced home-made food including vegetarian choices, daily specials and popular Sun roasts (should book), friendly helpful uniformed staff, Ringwood and guests such as Flack Manor, real cider and several wines by the glass, coffee and tea; attractive softly lit separate areas on varying levels, each with own character, old pine and oak furniture, milk churn stools by bar, hunting prints and two log fires; background music; children and dogs welcome, covered terrace and nice little three-tier garden, four good value simple bedrooms, open (and food) all day, can get very busy weekends.

EMSWORTH   SU7405

Blue Bell (01243) 373394

South Street; PO10 7EG Friendly and relaxed little 1940s red-brick pub close to the quay; old-fashioned lived-in interior with nautical and other memorabilia, good choice of popular reasonably priced home-made food with emphasis on local produce including fresh fish (best to book), bar nibbles Sun lunchtime, well kept Sharps Doom Bar and a couple of guests such as Emsworth from brick and timber servery, helpful amiable staff; TV, daily newspapers; dogs welcome, seats on small front and side terraces, Sun market in adjacent car park, open all day.

EMSWORTH   SU7405

Coal Exchange (01243) 375866

Ships Quay, South Street; PO10 7EG Friendly little L-shaped Victorian local near harbour; well kept Fullers/Gales beers and guests, good value home-made lunchtime food (evenings Tues-Thurs including Weds pizza night), simple low-ceilinged bar with fire at each end; live music, children and dogs welcome, tables outside and smokers' shelter, handy for Wayfarers Walk and Solent Way, open all day Fri-Sun.

EMSWORTH   SU7505

Lord Raglan (01243) 372587

Queen Street; PO10 7BJ Traditional 18th-c flint pub with wide choice of enjoyable home-made food from daily changing menu, well kept Fullers/Gales beers, good friendly

We include some hotels with a good bar that offers facilities comparable to those of a pub.

service, log fire, restaurant; live music Sun evening, free wi-fi; dogs welcome, pleasant waterside garden behind with picnic-sets, open all day weekends.

EVERTON   SZ2994
Crown (01590) 642655
Old Christchurch Road; pub signed just off A337 W of Lymington; SO41 0JJ Quietly set restaurant-pub on edge of New Forest; highly thought-of food cooked by landlord-chef including daily specials, friendly service, Greene King, Ringwood and a guest, decent wines at sensible prices, two attractive dining rooms off tiled-floor bar, log fires; children welcome, wheelchair access possible, picnic-sets on front terrace behind picket fence and in small back garden, closed Mon.

EXTON   SU6120
★ Shoe (01489) 877526
Village signposted from A32 NE of Bishop's Waltham; SO32 3NT Popular brick-built country dining pub on South Downs Way; three linked rooms with log fires, good well presented food (best to book) from traditional favourites to more imaginative restaurant-style dishes including fresh fish and seasonal game, well kept Wadworths ales and a guest, several wines by the glass including local sparkling, good service from friendly young staff; children and dogs welcome, disabled facilities, seats under parasols at front, more in garden across lane overlooking River Meon (ice-cream shack summer weekends), open all day weekends.

FAREHAM   SU5705
Castle in the Air (01329) 280320
Old Gosport Road; PO16 0XH Open-plan Greene King pub by tidal Fareham Creek; their beers and guests kept well, enjoyable sensibly priced food including deals, good friendly service, flagstones and bare boards, large brick fireplace; live music and quiz nights; children and dogs welcome, terrace seating, open (and food) all day.

FAREHAM   SU5806
Cob & Pen (01329) 221624
Wallington Shore Road, not far from M27 junction 11; PO16 8SL Cheerful old corner local near Wallington River; four well kept ales including Hop Back, St Austell and Sharps, enjoyable well priced home-made food from sandwiches to specials, log fire; some live music, TV, darts; children and dogs welcome, large garden with play area and summer barbecues, open all day, no food Sun evening and winter Mon.

FARNBOROUGH   SU8756
★ Prince of Wales (01252) 545578
Rectory Road, near station; GU14 8AL Ten well kept ales including six quickly changing guests at this friendly Victorian local, three small linked areas with exposed brickwork, carpet or wood floors, open

fire and some antiquey touches, generous lunchtime pubby food at reasonable prices, also Mon curry night and Fri evening fish, good friendly service; quiz first Sun of month, wine evening Weds, live music monthly; well behaved children and dogs welcome, a few picnic-sets on front pavement, more seating on back terrace with smokers' gazebo, open all day Fri-Sun.

FAWLEY   SU4603
Jolly Sailor (023) 8089 1305
Ashlett Creek, off B3053; SO45 1DT Cottagey waterside pub near small boatyard and sailing club; good value straightforward bar food, Ringwood Best and a guest, cheerful service, mixed pubby furnishings on bare boards, raised log fire, second bar with darts and pool; children and dogs welcome, tables outside looking past creek's yachts and boats to busy shipping channel, good shore walks, well placed for the extensive woodland gardens at Exbury, famed for rhododendrons, open all day, no food Sun evening, Mon.

FROGHAM   SU1712
Foresters Arms (01425) 652294
Abbotswell Road; SP6 2JA Updated New Forest pub (part of the Little Pub Group); enjoyable good value food from lunchtime baguettes up, well kept Wadworths ales and a guest, good friendly service, cosy rustic-chic interior with rugs on wood or flagstone floors, woodburners in brick fireplaces, pale green panelling, mix of old and new furniture including settles and pews, antlers and grandfather clock; monthly quiz, ale and cider festival in Aug; children, walkers and dogs (in bar and on leads) welcome, picnic-sets out at front under pergola and on lawn, maybe ponies and donkeys, open all day weekends.

GOODWORTH CLATFORD   SU3642
Royal Oak (01264) 324105
Longstock Road; SP11 7QY Comfortably modern L-shaped bar with ales such as Flack Manor and Ringwood, nice wines by the glass and good pubby food from sandwiches up, friendly efficient staff; children welcome, picnic-sets in pretty dell-like garden, attractive Test Valley village and pleasant River Anton walks, closed Sun evening.

GOSPORT   SZ6198
Fighting Cocks (023) 9252 9885
Clayhall Road, Alverstoke; PO12 2AJ Welcoming modernised local in residential area; Wadworths ales and good choice of enjoyable pubby food at sensible prices including Sat breakfast from 9.30am, friendly helpful service, bar with some booth seating and upholstered wall benches, skylit dining room; Sun quiz, darts, TV, fruit machine; children and dogs in bar (welcome), big garden with play equipment, handy for Stokes Bay beaches, open all day, no food Sun evening.

GOSPORT   SZ6100
Queens Hotel 07974 031671
Queens Road; PO12 1LG Classic bare-
boards corner local that takes its beer
seriously – six real ales such as Fallen Acorn,
Ringwood and Youngs kept in top condition
by long-serving no-nonsense landlady,
popular Oct beer festival, three areas off bar,
good log fire in interesting carved fireplace,
sensibly placed darts, TV for major sports;
children allowed Sat afternoon only, no
dogs, open all day Sat, closed lunchtimes
Mon-Thurs.

GRAYSHOTT   SU8735
Fox & Pelican (01428) 604757
Headley Road; GU26 6LG Large village
pub with enjoyable food from sandwiches
up, Fullers/Gales beers and a guest, friendly
service, linked areas with comfortable
seating on wood or carpeted floors, open
fire in large fireplace, dining conservatory;
background and some live music, quiz Thurs,
sports TV, games machines; children and
dogs welcome, wheelchair access, tables on
paved terrace and lawn, fenced play area,
open all day, food all day Fri and Sat, till
6pm Sun.

GREYWELL   SU7151
Fox & Goose (01256) 702062
*Near M3 junction 5; A287 towards
Odiham, then first right to village;
RG29 1BY* Welcoming two-bar village pub
popular with locals and walkers; traditional
interior with country kitchen furniture and
open fire, enjoyable home-made pubby food
from good lunchtime sandwiches/baguettes
up, three well kept ales including Sharps
Doom Bar; open mike night third Mon of
month; children and dogs welcome, good-
sized back garden and camping field, River
Whitewater and Basingstoke Canal walks,
open all day.

GRIGGS GREEN   SU8231
Deers Hut (01428) 724406
Off A3 S of Hindhead; GU30 7PD
Popular old country pub with horseshoe bar
and several rustically furnished dining areas;
good if slightly pricey food from baguettes
and pub staples to daily specials, Sharps
Doom Bar, Youngs Bitter and a couple of
guests, good choice of other drinks, friendly
young staff; children welcome, attractive
woodland setting with picnic-sets on front
terrace and green, handy for walkers on
Shipwrights Way, classic car event (Father's
Day), open all day.

HAMBLE   SU4806
Bugle (023) 8045 3000
3 miles from M27 junction 8; SO31 4HA
Bustling little 16th-c village pub set just
back from the River Hamble; beamed and
timbered rooms with flagstones and polished
boards, woodburner in fine brick fireplace,
bar stools along herringbone-brick and
timber counter, a beer named for the pub
from Itchen Valley plus a couple of guests
(often Flack Manor), well liked food (all day
Sun); background music, TV; children and
dogs (in bar) welcome, picnic-sets on small
raised front terrace with views of boats
moored on river, open all day.

HAMBLE   SU4806
King & Queen (023) 8045 4247
*3 miles from M27 junction 8; High
Street; SO31 4HA* Popular with locals and
visiting sailors, this cheerful nautical-
themed pub has a simply furnished bar with
log fire at one end, three changing ales, good
wines, cocktails and some 30 different rums
(displayed in a rowing boat shelf unit), steps
down to two small dining rooms serving
generous helpings of enjoyable food from
sandwiches and pizzas up; children and dogs
welcome, planked tables and picnic-sets in
sunny front garden, open all day.

HAMBLE   SU4806
Victory (023) 8045 3105
High Street; SO31 4HA Split-level
18th-c red-brick pub with four well kept
ales and enjoyable reasonably priced bar
food including popular Sun lunch, cheerful
welcoming staff, nautical theme including
Battle of Trafalgar mural, beams and half-
panelling, wood, flagstone and carpeted
floors; live music, sports TV; children and
dogs welcome, rear terrace picnic-sets,
open all day.

HAMBLEDON   SU6716
★ Bat & Ball (023) 9263 2692
*Broadhalfpenny Down; about 2 miles
E towards Clanfield; PO8 0UB* Extended
dining pub opposite historic cricket pitch;
log fires and comfortable modern furnishings
in three linked rooms, lots of cricketing
memorabilia (the game's rules are said to
have been written here), Fullers ales and
enjoyable food from well priced snacks up,
panelled restaurant; children and dogs
welcome, tables on front terrace, garden
behind with lovely downs views, good walks,
open (and food) all day.

HAVANT   SU7106
Old House at Home
(023) 9248 3464 *South Street; PO9 1DA*
Black and white 17th-c pub next to church;
modernised two-bar interior with low beams
and nice rambling alcovey feel, enjoyable
sensibly priced food from sandwiches
and baked potatoes up, steak night Weds,
Fullers/Gales beers including seasonals,
friendly service; Tues quiz, juke box (some
live music), sports TV, fruit machines;
children (in smaller bar) and dogs welcome,
pretty jettied frontage with hanging baskets,
tables and smokers' shelter in back garden
with view of church, open all day, food all
day Fri and Sat, till 5pm Sun.

HAVANT   SU7106
Robin Hood   (023) 9248 2779
Homewell; PO9 1EE Traditional 18th-c
pub tucked away opposite church; opened-up
bar with beams and log fires, well kept
Fullers/Gales ales tapped from the cask, tasty
simple lunchtime food, friendly service; Tues
quiz, sports TV; dogs welcome, seats in small
back garden, open all day.

HAVANT   SU7206
Wheelwrights Arms   (023) 9247 6502
Emsworth Road; PO9 2SN Sizeable
stylishly decorated Victorian pub; five well
kept beers, decent wine list and enjoyable
pubby food from snacks and sharing plates
up, OAP lunch deal Mon-Fri, friendly service;
background and some live music, quiz night
(Havant a Clue) first and third Weds of
month; children and dogs welcome, shaded
tables out at front and in courtyard garden
behind, open all day, food all day Fri-Sun.

HAWKLEY   SU7429
Hawkley Inn   (01730) 827205
*Off B3006 near A3 junction; Pococks
Lane; GU33 6NE* Traditional tile-hung
village pub with views of South Downs, seven
well kept mainly local ales served from
central bar, open fires (large moose head
above one), rugs on flagstones, old pine
tables and assorted chairs, popular home-
made food from pub favourites up, friendly
staff; children and dogs welcome, covered
seating area at front, picnic-sets in big back
garden, useful for walkers on Hangers Way,
six comfortable bedrooms, open all day
weekends, no food Sun evening.

HAYLING ISLAND   SU7201
Maypole   (023) 9246 3670
Havant Road; PO11 0PS Sizeable two-bar
1930s roadside local; good reasonably
priced home-made pub food including
Fri fish night, Fullers/Gales beers kept
well, friendly service, parquet floors and
polished panelling, plenty of good seating,
open fires; Thurs quiz, darts; children and
dogs welcome, garden picnic-sets and play
equipment, closed Sun evening.

HECKFIELD   SU7260
New Inn   (0118) 932 6374
*B3349 Hook–Reading (former A32);
RG27 0LE* Rambling open-plan dining
pub with good reasonably priced food (all
day weekends) from sandwiches and baked
potatoes up, well kept Badger ales and
good choice of wines and whiskies, efficient
friendly service, attractive layout with some
traditional furniture in original core, two log

fires, restaurant; quiz last Thurs of month;
children welcome, good-sized heated terrace,
16 bedrooms in extension, open all day.

HERRIARD   SS6744
Fur & Feathers   (01256) 510510
*Pub signed just off A339 Basingstoke–
Alton; RG25 2PN* Light and airy Victorian
country pub with highly regarded food from
sharing plates and a burger menu up, four
well kept changing ales such as Hogs Back
TEA, Flack Double Drop and Itchen Valley
Pure Gold, Hampshire cider and good choice
of wines and gins, selection of Cuban cigars,
friendly efficient staff, smallish bar with
dining areas either side, pine furniture
on stripped-wood flooring, painted half-
panelling, two woodburners; background
music; children welcome, garden behind with
paved terrace, open all day (till 6pm Sun),
no food Mon.

HORSEBRIDGE   SU3430
John O'Gaunt   (01794) 388644
*Off A3057 Romsey–Andover, just SW
of Kings Somborne; SO20 6PU* Neatly
refurbished River Test village pub known
locally as 'the JOG'; L-shaped bar with mix
of furniture including armchairs on bare
boards, light wood dados, book wallpaper
either side of woodburner, popular good
value home-made food from baguettes up,
Ringwood Razorback and three guests, a
couple of real ciders and good selection
of gins, friendly helpful service; children,
walkers and dogs welcome, seats outside,
open all day, food all day weekends.

KEYHAVEN   SZ3091
★ Gun   (01590) 642391
Keyhaven Road; SO41 0TP Busy rambling
17th-c pub looking over boatyard and sea to
Isle of Wight; low-beamed bar with nautical
bric-a-brac and plenty of character (less
in family rooms and conservatory), good
fairly standard food including tasty crab
sandwiches, well kept ales such as Ringwood,
Sharps and Timothy Taylors tapped from the
cask, Weston's cider, lots of malt whiskies;
bar billiards; tables out in front and in big
back garden with swings and fish pond, you
can stroll down to small harbour and walk
to Hurst Castle, open all day Sat, closed Sun
evening.

KINGSCLERE   SU5258
Bel & Dragon   (01635) 299342
Swan Street; RG20 5PP Attractively
updated 15th-c beamed village inn, emphasis
on dining with well liked bar and restaurant
food including meat from their Josper oven,
weekend brunch, three real ales, own-label

Please tell us if any pub deserves to be upgraded to a featured entry – and why:
feedback@goodguides.com, or (no stamp needed) Freepost THE GOOD PUB GUIDE,
Random House Publishing, 20 Vauxhall Bridge Road, London SW1V 2SA.

gin, cocktails and good selection of wines by the glass including champagne; friendly helpful staff; children welcome, nine bedrooms, good surrounding walks, open all day, food all day Sun.

LANGSTONE   SU7104
★ **Royal Oak** (023) 9248 3125
Off A3023 just before Hayling Island bridge; Langstone High Street; PO9 1RY
Charmingly placed waterside dining pub overlooking tidal inlet and ancient wadeway to Hayling Island – boats at high tide, wading birds when it goes out; four Greene King ales and good choice of wines by the glass, reasonably priced pubby food from sandwiches up, spacious flagstoned bar and linked dining areas, log fire; children welcome in restaurant, dogs in bar, spacious garden with pond, good coast paths nearby, open (and food) all day from 10am.

LASHAM   SU6742
Royal Oak (01256) 381750
Beside church; pub signed from A339; GU34 5SJ Fairly tucked-away dining pub with much liked affordably priced food from pub standards up including weekday set lunch, three well kept local ales, friendly welcoming service, pristine interior with flagstoned bar and separate wood-floored restaurant; quiz third Thurs of month; children and dogs welcome, nice quiet garden by church, attractive village and good surrounding walks, open all day weekends, closed Mon.

LINDFORD   SU8036
Royal Exchange (01420) 488118
Liphook Road; GU35 0NX Red Mist pub with spacious bar and light modern dining room; enjoyable food from sandwiches and sharing boards to specials, four real ales including a house beer from Tilford, craft beers, plenty of wines by the glass and interesting selection of gins; children and dogs welcome, seats outside, open all day Fri-Sun, food all day Sun.

LINWOOD   SU1910
High Corner (01425) 473973
Signed from A338 via Moyles Court, and from A31; BH24 3QY Big rambling pub in splendid New Forest position at end of track; various areas including original log-fire bar, big back extensions for the summer crowds, nicely partitioned restaurant and lounge with verandah, good helpings of popular home-made food, well kept Wadworths ales and Weston's cider, friendly staff; children and dogs welcome, horses too (stables and paddock available), extensive wooded garden

with play area, seven comfortable bedrooms, open all day in summer (all day weekends other times).

LIPHOOK   SU8330
Links Tavern (01428) 723773
Portsmouth Road; GU30 7EF Spacious Fullers pub with comfortably modernised interior, plenty of connecting rooms and intimate spaces, four of their ales and wide choice of wines by the glass, enjoyable food from sandwiches and sharing boards up, friendly service; some live music; children welcome, picnic-sets on surrounding terraces and lawn, smokers' gazebo, pleasant woodland and lakeside walks at Foley Manor, open all day, food all day weekends.

LISS   SU7826
Jolly Drover (01730) 893137
London Road, Hill Brow; B2070 S of town, near B3006 junction; GU33 7QL Traditional 19th-c pub under long-serving licensees; neat carpeted beamed bar with a couple of chesterfields in front of brick inglenook, Sharps Doom Bar, Timothy Taylors Landlord and a dozen wines by the glass, generous helpings of enjoyable fairly priced food (puddings particularly good), friendly helpful service, two back dining sections; children welcome, teak furniture on terrace, picnic-sets on lawn, six barn-conversion bedrooms, closed Sun evening.

LITTLE LONDON   SU6259
Plough (01256) 850628
Silchester Road, off A340 N of Basingstoke; RG26 5EP Tucked-away local, cosy and unspoilt, with log fires, low beams and mixed furnishings on brick or tiled floors (watch the step), well kept Otter, Ringwood and interesting guests tapped from the cask, good value baguettes, no credit cards; bar billiards and darts; dogs welcome, attractive garden, handy for Pamber Forest and Calleva Roman remains, open all day.

LONG SUTTON   SU7447
Four Horseshoes (01256) 862488
Signed off B3349 S of Hook; RG29 1TA Welcoming unpretentious country pub with loyal band of regulars; open plan with black beams and two log fires, long-serving landlord cooking uncomplicated bargain food such as lancashire hotpot and fish and chips, friendly pair of publicans serving Palmers and maybe a guest ale; monthly quiz and jazz nights; children and dogs welcome, disabled access, small glazed-in front verandah, picnic-sets and play area on grass over road, pétanque, bedrooms with country views, closed Sun evening, Mon lunchtime.

If you report on a pub that's not a featured entry, please tell us any lunchtimes or evenings when it doesn't serve bar food.

LYMINGTON SZ3295
Angel & Blue Pig (01590) 672050
High Street; SO41 9AP Busy town-centre
Georgian inn; cosy right-hand room with
comfortable sofas and armchairs, rugs on
bare boards and an open fire, flagstoned
area and two beamed rooms to the left of the
entrance with old range in brick fireplace,
large boar's head and lots of books, back
bar has some nice old leather armchairs
by woodburner, four real ales including a
house beer from Ringwood, 16 wines by the
glass and cocktails, enjoyable brasserie-style
food; some live music; children and dogs (in
bar) welcome, terrace with seats under blue
parasols, 14 stylish modern bedrooms, open
(and food) all day.

LYMINGTON SZ3293
Chequers (01590) 673415
*Ridgeway Lane, Lower Woodside – dead
end just S of A337 roundabout W of
Lymington, by White Hart; SO41 8AH*
16th-c beamed pub with enjoyable food from
traditional favourites up (smaller helpings
available), Ringwood ales and good wines by
the glass, bare boards and quarry tiles, mix of
furniture including spindleback chairs, wall
pews and country pine tables, yacht-racing
pictures, woodburner; well behaved children
and dogs welcome, live cricket and rugby
on TV, tables and summer marquee in neat
walled back garden, good walks and handy
for bird-watching on Pennington Marshes,
open all day, food all day weekends.

LYMINGTON SZ3295
Kings Head (01590) 672709
Quay Hill; SO41 3AR Dimly lit old pub in
steep cobbled lane of smart small shops; well
kept Fullers, Ringwood, Timothy Taylors and
a couple of guests, several wines by the glass
and enjoyable uncomplicated food from
sandwiches up, pleasing mix of old-fashioned
furnishings in rambling beamed rooms, log
fire and woodburner; background music, daily
papers; children and dogs welcome, sunny
little courtyard behind, open all day and can
get very busy (food all day weekends).

LYMINGTON SZ3295
Monkey House (01590) 676754
Southampton Road (A337); SO41 9HA
Updated beamed dining pub with good
variety of well liked sensibly priced food from
open sandwiches up, five well kept local ales
and a dozen wines by the glass, pleasant
helpful staff, two rooms divided by a couple
of steps, lower one with high pitched ceiling,
log fires; background and Sun live music, TV;
children and dogs welcome, tables on paved
terrace and grass, two bedrooms, open all
day, food all day Sun.

LYNDHURST SU2908
Fox & Hounds (023) 8028 2098
22 High Street; SO43 7BG Big busy low-
beamed former coaching inn, comfortable
and much modernised with good food
including Tues burger night, well kept
Fullers/Gales beers and plenty of wines
by the glass, cheerful efficient service,
rambling opened-up interior with exposed
brick and standing timbers, rugs on wood
floors, log fires; regular live music, Mon
quiz, children and dogs welcome, disabled
facilities, murals and old enamel signs in
paved courtyard garden, open all day, food
all day weekends.

LYNDHURST SU2908
Waterloo Arms (023) 8028 2113
Pikes Hill, just off A337 N; SO43 7AS
Thatched 17th-c New Forest pub with low
beams, stripped-brick walls and log fire,
three regular beers and large selection of
ciders, enjoyable well priced pubby food
including blackboard specials, friendly staff,
comfortable bar and roomy back dining area;
live music last Sun of month; children and
dogs welcome, terrace and nice big garden,
open (and food) all day.

MAPLEDURWELL SU6851
★ Gamekeepers (01256) 322038
*Off A30, not far from M3 junction 6;
RG25 2LU* Dark-beamed dining pub with
good upmarket food from regularly changing
blackboard menu (not cheap and they add
a service charge), also some pubby choices
and lunchtime baguettes, welcoming helpful
landlord and friendly efficient staff, three
well kept local ales including Andwell, good
coffee, a few sofas in flagstoned and panelled
core, well spaced tables in large dining room;
background music, TV; children and dogs
(in bar) welcome, terrace and garden, lovely
thatched village with duck pond, good walks,
open all day weekends.

MARCHWOOD SU3809
Pilgrim (023) 8086 7752
*Hythe Road, off A326 at Twiggs Lane;
SO40 4WU* Extremely pretty pub created
from three thatched 18th-c cottages, well
kept Fullers/Gales beers and decent wines,
popular menu catering for all tastes, friendly
helpful staff, open fires; children and dogs
welcome, tree-lined garden with circular
picnic-sets, 14 good-looking bedrooms in
building across car park.

MEONSTOKE SU6120
Bucks Head (01489) 877313
*Village signed just off A32 N of Droxford;
SO32 3NA* Opened-up tile-hung pub in
lovely village setting with ducks on pretty
little River Meon; stone floors and log fires,
popular food from sandwiches to blackboard
specials and sourdough pizza, three well kept
ales including Greene King, good friendly
service; children and dogs welcome, small
walled gardens either side, one overlooking
river, good walks, five bedrooms, open all day
Sat, till 6pm Sun.

MILFORD-ON-SEA   SZ2891
Beach House   (01590) 643044
Park Lane; SO41 0PT Civilised well
placed Victorian hotel-dining pub owned by
Hall & Woodhouse; restored oak-panelled
interior with plenty of fine original features,
entrance hall bar serving Badger First Gold,
Tanglefoot and a guest, nice wines by the
glass and enjoyable sensibly priced food from
lunchtime sandwiches and sharing boards to
specials, friendly helpful service, magnificent
views from dining room (note the arty stags'
heads) and terrace; children welcome, dogs
in bar, grounds down to the Solent looking
out to the Needles, 15 bedrooms, open (and
food) all day.

MINSTEAD   SU2810
★ Trusty Servant   (023) 8081 2137
*Just off A31, not far from M27 junction
1; SO43 7FY* Attractive 19th-c red-brick
dining pub in pretty New Forest hamlet with
wandering cattle and ponies and plenty of
easy walks; two-room bare-boards bar and big
dining room, local pictures and hunting-
themed prints, open fires, well kept ales such
as Flack Manor, Ringwood and Sharps (Aug
beer festival), several wines by the glass,
good popular food from doorstep sandwiches
and pub favourites to local game, friendly
helpful staff, walkers, cyclists, children
and dogs welcome, terrace and big sloping
garden, interesting church where Sir Arthur
Conan Doyle is buried, five bedrooms, open
(and food) all day.

NEW CHERITON   SU5827
★ Hinton Arms   (01962) 771252
A272 near B3046 junction; SO24 0NH
Popular neatly kept country pub with
cheerful accommodating landlord and
friendly staff, three or four real ales including
a house beer from Bowman, decent wines
by the glass, large helpings of enjoyable
pub food from sandwiches to daily specials,
sporting pictures and memorabilia; TV
lounge, vintage car show Sept; well behaved
children and dogs welcome, pretty terrace and
big garden, profusion of colourful tubs and
hanging baskets, very handy for Hinton
Ampner House (NT).

NORTH GORLEY   SU1611
Royal Oak   (01425) 652244
*Ringwood Road; village signed off A338
S of Fordingbridge; SP6 2PB* Modernised
17th-c thatched and beamed New Forest pub;
three well kept ales including Ringwood, a
dozen wines by the glass/carafe and decent
range of gins, good popular food (not Sun
evening) from pub favourites up, attentive
friendly service, children and dogs welcome,
seats out at front behind picket fence and
in back garden, big duck pond over road,
closed Mon, otherwise open all day till 10pm
(8pm Sun).

NORTH WALTHAM   SU5645
★ Fox   (01256) 397288
*3 miles from M3 junction 7: A30
southwards, then turn right at second
North Waltham turn, just after
Wheatsheaf; pub also signed from village
centre; RG25 2BE* Well run traditional
flint pub with low-ceilinged bar; Andwell,
Brakspears, West Berkshire and a guest,
Aspall's cider (many more in bottles)
and good range of wines and whiskies,
padded country kitchen chairs on parquet
floor, poultry prints above dark dado, big
woodburner, good food from sandwiches/
baguettes to daily specials, larger separate
dining room with high-backed leather chairs
and blue tartan carpet; children and dogs
(in bar) welcome, picnic sets under parasols
in colourful garden with pergola walkway,
pretty window boxes and hanging baskets,
attractive walks including one to Jane
Austen's church at Steventon, open all day.

OVERTON   SU5149
★ White Hart   (01256) 771431
London Road; RG25 3NW Handsome 500-
year-old beamed inn with some contemporary
touches; cosy bar with open fire, carved
counter serving well kept beers, a dozen
wines by the glass and cocktails, two-level
dining room has a central woodburner
and there's another room with cushioned
wall seating, interesting up-to-date food
including lunchtime sandwiches; children
and dogs (in bar) welcome, suntrap garden
(heated awning for cooler days), comfortable
bedrooms in converted stable block, handy
for Laverstoke Mill (home to Bombay
Sapphire distillery), open all day.

OVINGTON   SU5631
Bush   (01962) 732764
Off A31 W of Alresford; SO24 0RE
Popular 17th-c country pub in charming
spot with streamside garden; low-ceilinged
bar, high-backed settles, pews and lots of
old pictures, log fire, well kept Wadworths
ales and good choice of wines by the glass,
enjoyable food from sandwiches and sharing
boards up, friendly service; children and
dogs welcome, good local walks, open all day
weekends, food all day Sun.

OWER   SU3216
Mortimer Arms   (023) 8081 4379
*Romsey Road, by M27 junction 2;
SO51 6AF* Pub-hotel under same ownership
as the New Forest Inn at Emery Down; cosy
informal bar with tables around three-sided
servery, more formal restaurant, well kept
ales such as Ringwood, a dozen wines by
the glass and some interesting gins, good
food from bar snacks and sharing plates to
specials, welcoming helpful service; events
such as themed food weeks and seasonal quiz
nights; children (till 7pm in bar) and dogs
welcome, picnic-sets in enclosed garden,

handy for Paultons theme park, 14 bedrooms, good breakfast, open (and food) all day.

PETERSFIELD   SU7423
Square Brewery (01730) 264291
The Square; GU32 3HJ Cheerful town-centre pub in modern-rustic style; three well kept Fullers ales and a guest, decent choice of wines and enjoyable sensibly priced food including good lunchtime sandwiches, wood floors, painted panelling and central woodburner; background music (live bands Sun), quiz last Thurs of month, salsa Fri; children and dogs welcome, seats out overlooking the square and in covered courtyard behind, open all day, no evening food Sat or Sun.

PETERSFIELD   SU7227
Trooper (01730) 827293
From A32 (look for staggered crossroads) take turning to Froxfield and Steep; pub 3 miles down on left in big dip; GU32 1BD Convivial pub with charming landlord and friendly staff; bar with cushioned dining chairs around dark wooden tables, log fire in a stone fireplace, photos of film stars, paintings by local artists, mirrors, candles and fresh flowers, Ringwood Best and a couple of guests from breweries such as Sharps and Hopback on handpump, seven wines by the glass, a dozen gins and seven malt whiskies, also a sun room and attractive raftered restaurant with good upmarket food; background music, board games, newspapers and magazines; children and dogs welcome, picnic-sets on lawn, neat bedrooms and very good breakfasts, lovely walks nearby, closed Sun evening.

PHOENIX GREEN   SU7555
Phoenix (01252) 842484
London Road, A30 W of Hartley Wintney; RG27 8RT Beamed 18th-c pub with timber dividers, rugs on bare boards and big end inglenook, good freshly made food from varied daily changing menu including speciality dry-aged steaks, four well kept ales, a couple of real ciders and 16 wines by the glass, good friendly service, back dining room; children and dogs (in bar) welcome, pleasant outlook from sunny garden with vine-covered pergola, open all day.

PILLEY   SZ3298
★ Fleur de Lys (01590) 672158
Off A337 Brockenhurst–Lymington; Pilley Street; SO41 5QG Attractive thatched and beamed village pub with 11th-c origins; highly regarded restauranty food from shortish menu (booking advised), Courage Directors, Sharps Doom Bar and

a guest, good wines, friendly helpful service, inglenook log fires; well behaved children and dogs welcome, pretty garden with old well, good forest and heathland walks, open all day Sat, till 6pm Sun, closed Mon.

PORTSMOUTH   SU6400
Brewhouse & Kitchen
(023) 9289 1340 *Guildhall Walk next to Theatre Royal; PO1 2DD* Popular mock-Tudor pub visibly brewing its own good beers, also decent choice of well priced food from sandwiches and small plates up, friendly helpful staff; children welcome, open (and food) all day.

PORTSMOUTH   SZ6399
Bridge Tavern (023) 9275 2992
East Street, Camber Dock; PO1 2JJ Maritime theme and good harbour views; flagstones, bare boards and lots of dark wood, comfortable furnishings, Fullers ales and a dozen wines by the glass, generous helpings of good sensibly priced food including plenty of fish dishes, upstairs dining rooms (more modern and airy); children welcome, painted picnic-sets on waterside terrace, open all day and busy with diners at weekends (kitchen closes 5pm Sun).

PORTSMOUTH   SU6501
George (023) 9275 3885
Queen Street, near dockyard entrance; PO1 3HU Spotless old inn (Grade I listed) with two rooms (one set for dining), log fire, glass-covered well and maritime pictures, well kept Greene King Abbot, Sharps Atlantic and Doom Bar, well priced food (not Sun evening, Mon lunchtime) from sandwiches up, good friendly service; eight bedrooms, handy for dockyard and HMS *Victory*, open all day.

PORTSMOUTH   SU6706
George (023) 9222 1079
Portsdown Hill Road, Widley; PO6 1BE Comfortable one-bar Georgian pub with friendly local feel (despite being surrounded by busy roads); seven well kept ales and good range of gins, popular pubby food including good ploughman's, helpful pleasant staff; live music Tues, quiz every other Sun; dogs welcome, picnic-sets on side terrace, views of Hayling Island, Portsmouth and Isle of Wight, hill walks across the road, open all day, closed (food) evenings.

PORTSMOUTH   SZ6399
Pembroke (023) 9282 3961
Pembroke Road; PO1 2NR Traditional well run corner local with good buoyant atmosphere, comfortable and unspoilt under

---

A star symbol before the name of a pub shows exceptional character and appeal.
It doesn't mean extra comfort. Even quite a basic pub can win a star,
if it's individual enough.

long-serving licensees, Bass, Fullers London Pride and Greene King Abbot from L-shaped bar, simple cheap food including fresh rolls, coal-effect gas fire; monthly live music, quiz every other Sun, darts; dogs welcome, open all day.

PORTSMOUTH   SU6300
Ship Anson (023) 9282 4152
Victory Road, The Hard (opposite Esplanade Station, Portsea); PO1 3DT
No-frills mock-Tudor pub close to dockyard entrance, spacious and comfortable, with well kept Greene King ales and a guest, generous pub food at bargain prices, also coffee and cakes, buoyant local atmosphere; fruit machines, sports TVs; children welcome, seats outside overlooking ferry port, very handy for HMS *Victory*, open (and food) all day.

PORTSMOUTH   SZ6299
Still & West (023) 9282 1567
Bath Square, Old Portsmouth; PO1 2JL
Great location with superb views of narrow harbour mouth and across to Isle of Wight, especially from glazed-in panoramic upper family area and waterfront terrace; nautical bar with fireside sofas, Fullers ales and good choice of wines by the glass, enjoyable all-day food from sandwiches and sharing plates to good fish dishes; background music; dogs welcome in bar, handy for Historic Dockyard, nearby pay-and-display parking, open from 10am (11.30am Sun).

RINGWOOD   SU1504
Railway (01425) 473701
Hightown Road; BH24 1NQ Traditional two-bar Victorian local with up to four well kept changing ales (usually one from nearby Ringwood), enjoyable home-made food including range of burgers, also vegan/vegetarian menu, friendly service; Thurs quiz, darts; children and dogs welcome, nice enclosed garden with play area, vegetable patch, ducks and chickens, open all day.

ROMSEY   SU3521
Old House at Home (01794) 513175
Love Lane; SO51 8DE Attractive 17th-c thatched pub surrounded by new development; friendly and bustling, with comfortable low-beamed interior, wide choice of freshly made sensibly priced bar food including popular Sun lunch, well kept Fullers/Gales beers and a guest, cheerful service; regular folk and jazz sessions; children and dogs (in bar) welcome, split-level attractive back terrace, open all day (no food Sun evening).

ROMSEY   SU3520
Three Tuns (01794) 512639
Middlebridge Street (but car park signed straight off A27 bypass); SO51 8HL
Good well presented food is the star at this old village pub but they do keep four beers

including Flack Manor, local cider and 11 wines by the glass; bar with cushioned bow-window seat, dark wooden tables on flagstones, beer mats pinned to the walls and church candles in fireplace, dining areas either side, one with a huge stuffed fish over another fireplace, the other with prints on yellow walls above a black dado, a few rugs scattered around, heavy beams and antler chandeliers; background music, board games, children and dogs welcome, back terrace with picnic-sets under parasols, more seats in front by the tiny street, open all day.

ROTHERWICK   SU7156
Coach & Horses (01256) 768976
Signed from B3349 N of Hook; also quite handy for M3 junction 5; RG27 9BG
Secluded much loved local with traditional beamed front rooms, well kept Badger ales and good choice of popular reasonably priced pubby food including specials, cheerful accommodating staff, log fire and woodburners, newer back dining area; children, dogs and muddy boots welcome, tables out at front and on back gravelled terrace overlooking fields, pretty flower tubs and hanging baskets, enjoyable walks, open all day Sat, until 6pm Sun, closed Mon (except bank holidays).

ROTHERWICK   SU7156
Falcon (01256) 765422
Off B3349 N of Hook, not far from M3 junction 5; RG27 9BL Welcoming open-plan country pub; good freshly made food, well kept ales and decent selection of wines and gins, friendly efficient service, rustic tables and comfy sofas in bare-boards bar, flagstoned dining area, log fires; quiz, comedy and live music nights, children and dogs welcome, disabled access, tables out in front and in back garden, open all day, food all day Sun.

SELBORNE   SU7433
Selborne Arms (01420) 511247
High Street; GU34 3JR Old-fashioned 17th-c beamed village pub; character tables, pews and deep settles made from casks on antique boards, good range of local ales and popular food from lunchtime baguettes up, big log fire, carpeted dining room with local photographs; quiz and live music nights; children welcome, no dogs inside, garden with arbour and terrace heated by logburner, orchard and play area, zigzag path up the Hangers Way, handy for Gilbert White's House, open all day weekends.

SHEDFIELD   SU5613
Samuels Rest (01329) 832213
Upper Church Road (signed off B2177); SO32 2JB Cosy village local overlooking cricket pitch; well kept Wadworths ales and generous helpings of enjoyable sensibly priced home-made food, nice eating area away from bar, conservatory; some live music

including folk night third Weds of month, pool and darts, children and dogs (in bar) welcome, good sized garden, lovely church nearby, open all day, food all day weekends (till about 6pm Sun).

SHEDFIELD   SU5513
Wheatsheaf (01329) 833024
A334 Wickham–Botley; SO32 2JG
Friendly extended traditional local; well kept/priced Flowerpots and guests tapped from the cask, proper cider, short sensible choice of enjoyable bargain lunches (evening food Tues and Weds), good service; live music Sat, darts; children and dogs (in bar) welcome, nice little back garden, handy for Wickham Vineyard, open all day.

SHERFIELD ENGLISH   SU3022
Hatchet (01794) 322487
Romsey Road; SO51 6FP Beamed and panelled 18th-c pub with good choice of popular fairly priced food including two-for-one steak deal (Tues, Thurs evenings), four well kept ales and good wine choice, friendly hard-working staff, long bar with cosy area down steps, woodburner, more steps up to second bar with darts, TV and juke box; monthly quiz; children and dogs (on leads) welcome, outside seating on two levels, play area, open all day weekends.

SOBERTON   SU6116
White Lion (01489) 877346
School Hill; signed off A32 S of Droxford; SO32 3PF Attractive unchanging 17th-c pub in nice spot opposite raised village green; enjoyable home-made food from baguettes up, four well kept ales including Bowman and Sharps, good range of wines by the glass, friendly efficient service, low-ceilinged bar with built-in wall seats and open fire, separate small restaurant; children and dogs welcome, sheltered garden and suntrap terrace, good walks nearby, stable-conversion bedrooms, open all day, food all day Sun.

SOPLEY   SZ1596
Woolpack (01425) 672252
B3347 N of Christchurch; BH23 7AX Pretty 17th-c thatched and beamed pub with rambling open-plan bar; well kept Ringwood Razorback, Sharps Doom Bar and a guest, Thatcher's cider and good choice of wines by the glass, enjoyable traditional food such as cod and chips served in newspaper, daily specials and range of sandwiches/wraps, modern dining conservatory overlooking weir; children and dogs (menu for them) welcome, terrace and charming garden with weeping willows, duck stream and footbridges, open (and food) all day.

SOUTHAMPTON   SU4314
Butchers Hook (023) 8178 2280
Manor Farm Road; SO18 1NN One-room micro-pub in former Bitterne Park butchers (some original features remain including

tiling); changing cask and keg beers from scaffold stillage (no bar), good bottled range too and real cider, gins and some wines; friendly helpful service, no food (can bring your own); board games; well behaved dogs welcome, a few bench seats out in front, closed Mon, Tues and lunchtimes Weds-Fri, open all day Sat from 1pm, Sun from 2pm, gets packed at busy times.

SOUTHAMPTON   SU4111
★Duke of Wellington (023) 8033 9222
Bugle Street (or walk along city wall from Bar Gate); SO14 2AH Striking half-timbered building dating from the 14th c (cellars even older); heavy beams and fine log fire, up to eight well kept Wadworths ales (tasting trays available), plenty of wines by the glass and good fairly priced food, friendly helpful service; background music and some live jazz (Fri); children welcome, sunny streetside picnic-sets, handy for Tudor House & Garden, open all day.

SOUTHAMPTON   SU4213
Rockstone (023) 8063 7256
Onslow Road; SO14 0JL Popular relaxed place with well liked generous food from signature burgers to street food (booking advised), good variety of real ales, craft beers and ciders from well stocked bar, friendly hard-working staff; some live music; children welcome, seats out at front, open (and food) all day (till 1am Sat).

SOUTHAMPTON   SU4213
White Star (023) 8082 1990
Oxford Street; SO14 3DJ Modernised opened-up bar with crescent-shaped banquettes, panelling and open fires, wood or stone floors, comfortable sofas and armchairs in secluded alcoves by south-facing windows, bistro-style dining area serving good up-to-date food along with pub favourites, Fullers ales and nice choice of wines by the glass, efficient attentive staff; background music; sunny pavement tables on pedestrianised street, 13 boutique bedrooms, open all day from 7am (8.30am weekends) for breakfast.

SOUTHSEA   SZ6699
Artillery Arms (023) 9273 3610
Hester Road; PO4 8HB Traditional two-bar Victorian backstreet local; half a dozen well kept ales including Triple fff, no food apart from rolls on match days (near Fratton Park), friendly atmosphere; Mon quiz, sports TV, pool and darts; children and dogs welcome, garden with play equipment, open all day.

SOUTHSEA   SZ6698
Eastney Tavern (023) 9282 6246
Cromwell Road; PO4 9PN Bow-fronted corner pub just off the seafront, spacious and comfortable, with various eating areas (plenty of room for drinkers too), popular good value food including Weds burger night

and Thurs curry (reduced menu Mon),
Sharps Doom Bar and a couple of local
guests, decent choice of wines by the glass,
good cheerful service; Tues quiz, live music
occasional Fri, sports TV; children and dogs
welcome, seats in courtyard garden, nearby
parking difficult, open all day.

SOUTHSEA   SZ6499

★ **Hole in the Wall** (023) 9229 8085
Great Southsea Street; PO5 3BY Friendly
unspoilt little local in old part of town, six
interesting well kept/priced ales including
Flowerpots Goodens Gold, four craft kegs
and good range of bottled beers, real cider/
perry, speciality local sausages and other
simple good value food (evenings Tues-Sat,
lunchtime Fri), nicely worn boards, dark
pews and panelling, old photographs and
prints, hundreds of pump clips on ceiling,
little snug behind the bar and sweet shop;
dogs welcome, small outside area at front
with benches, side garden, open all day
from 4pm (noon Fri, 2pm Sat and Sun).

SOUTHSEA   SZ6499

King Street Tavern (023) 9307 3568
King Street; PO5 4EH Victorian corner
pub in attractive conservation area with
fine tiled façade; four well kept Wadworths
ales and a couple of guests, craft kegs and
two proper ciders, enjoyable good value food
from smokehouse/barbecue menu, friendly
atmosphere; occasional live music including
Irish folk, big-screen sports TV; children
welcome, courtyard tables, open all day Fri
and Sat, till 7pm Sun, closed lunchtimes
Mon, Tues (and Weds in winter).

SOUTHSEA   SZ6498

Meat & Barrel (023) 9217 6291
Palmerston Road; PO5 3PT Sizeable
bar-restaurant with a fine range of real ales
and craft beers, tasters offered by friendly
knowledgeable staff, enjoyable food including
wide range of burgers and various sausage
and mash combinations; children welcome,
open all day.

SOUTHSEA   SZ6499

Wine Vaults (023) 9286 4712
*Albert Road, opposite King's Theatre;
PO5 2SF* Bustling Fullers pub that attracts
a young crowd with several chatty rooms
on different floors; main panelled bar with
long plain counter and pubby furniture on
bare boards, seven well kept ales and decent
choice of food including pizzas and burgers,
good service, separate restaurant; occasional
live music, sports TV, table football; children
and dogs (in bar) welcome, smokers' roof
terrace, open (and food) all day.

SOUTHWICK   SU6208

Golden Lion (023) 9221 0437
*High Street; just off B2177 on Portsdown
Hill; PO17 6EB* Spotless two-bar 16th-c
beamed pub (where Eisenhower and
Montgomery came before D-Day) under
welcoming ebullient landlord; up to seven
well kept local ales including two from
Southwick using barley from surrounding
fields, four ciders and a dozen wines by the
glass, good locally sourced home-made food
(not Sun or Mon evenings) from snacks up
in bar and dining room, cosy lounge with
Tues jazz; good outside loos; children and
dogs welcome, picnic-sets on side grass,
picturesque Estate village with scenic walks,
next to Southwick Brewhouse shop/museum
(over 250 bottled beers), open all day Sat,
till 7pm Sun.

SPARSHOLT   SU4331

Plough (01962) 776353
*Village signposted off B3049
(Winchester–Stockbridge), a little W
of Winchester; SO21 2NW* Neatly kept
dining pub under newish ownership; main
bar with interesting mix of wooden tables
and farmhouse or upholstered chairs, old
farm tools on walls and ceiling, Wadworths
ales and good choice of wines by the glass,
generally well regarded food from blackboard
menu, dining tables on the left looking
over fields to woodland; children and dogs
welcome, disabled access/facilities, plenty
of seats on terrace and lawn, play fort, open
all day.

STOCKBRIDGE   SU3535

Greyhound on the Test
(01264) 810833 *High Street; SO20 6EY*
Civilised inn-restaurant on the River Test
with highly regarded interesting food, not
cheap but they do offer a good value set
lunch, three real ales including a house beer
from Ringwood, nice choice of wines and
whiskies, friendly efficient staff, log fires
each end of bay-windowed bar (restaurant
to the right), dark low beams, scrubbed old
tables on woodstrip floor, evening candles;
children and dogs allowed, charming
riverside garden behind, ten bedrooms, good
walks and fly fishing, open all day.

STOCKBRIDGE   SU3535

Three Cups (01264) 810527
High Street; SO20 6HB Lovely low-beamed
building dating from 1500, updated and
added to yet keeping country inn feel; some
emphasis on dining with lots of set tables,
but also high-backed settles and rustic bric-
a-brac, three well kept ales and nice wines
by the glass, good food from shortish menu
including one or two pub favourites, friendly
service, back 'orangery' restaurant extension;
children and dogs welcome, charming
streamside garden with vine-covered terrace,
eight bedrooms (ones at back are quieter),
open all day.

STOCKBRIDGE   SU3535

★ **White Hart** (01264) 810663
*High Street; A272/A3057 roundabout;
SO20 6HF* Spacious village-edge pub

with pleasantly busy divided beamed bar, attractive décor with antique prints, oak pews and other seats around pine tables, decent choice of enjoyable food from bar snacks to daily specials, well kept Fullers/Gales beers, good friendly service, comfortable restaurant with open fire (children allowed); dogs in bar, terrace tables and nice garden, 24 bedrooms (ten recently added), open (and food) all day.

SWANMORE   SU5716
Brickmakers (01489) 890954
Church Road; SO32 2PA Large 1920s pub in centre of village, friendly and relaxed, with four well kept ales, decent wines and good food cooked by landlord-chef including popular Sun roasts and OAP weekday lunch deal, cheerful efficient service, leather sofas by log fire, pitched-roof dining area with local artwork; Tues quiz, some live music; children and dogs welcome (pub dog is Rosie), garden with raised deck, nearby walks, open (and food) all day.

SWANMORE   SU5815
Rising Sun (01489) 896663
Droxford Road; signed off A32 N of Wickham and B2177 S of Bishop`s Waltham, at Hillpound E of village centre; SO32 2PS Welcoming 17th-c brick coaching inn; low-beamed carpeted bar, comfortable seating by log fire, pleasant roomier dining area with brick barrel vaulting in one part, a house beer from Flack Manor along with Flowerpots Goodens Gold and a local guest, good range of wines by the glass and enjoyable reasonably priced home-cooked food including daily specials, friendly speedy service; children and dogs (in bar) welcome, picnic-sets on side grass with play area, King's Way long-distance path nearby, closed Sun evening.

SWAY   SZ2898
Hare & Hounds (01590) 682404
Durns Town, just off B3055 SW of Brockenhurst; SO41 6AL Comfortable New Forest family dining pub with hearty helpings of home-cooked food including daily specials, well kept ales such as Itchen Valley, Ringwood and Timothy Taylors, good friendly service, some low beams and central log fire; background music, Sun quiz; children and dogs welcome, picnic-sets and play frame in neatly kept garden, open all day.

TICHBORNE   SU5730
★ Tichborne Arms (01962) 733760
Signed off B3047; SO24 0NA Welcoming old-fashioned thatched free house dating from 1423 (rebuilt in the 1930s) at the edge of this quiet little village; half-panelled bare-boards bar with interesting pictures and other odds and ends, candlelit pine tables and raised woodburner, four regular beers including Palmers and local guests tapped from cooled casks, real cider, good fairly

traditional home-made food (not Sun or Mon evenings, booking advised), friendly attentive service, locals' bar with piano, darts and open fire; children and dogs welcome, sheltered terrace and large peaceful garden with water meadow views, close to Wayfarers Walk and Itchen Way, open all day Sat, till 7.30pm Sun.

TITCHFIELD   SU5305
Queens Head (01329) 842154
High Street; off A27 near Fareham; PO14 4AQ Welcoming early 17th-c family-run pub with enjoyable home-made food and four well kept changing ales; cosy bar with old local pictures, window seats and warm winter fire in central brick fireplace, small dining room; Sun quiz, function room for nostalgic dinner-dance and theatre nights; children welcome, picnic-sets in prettily planted backyard, pleasant conservation village near nature reserve, walks to coast, open all day.

TITCHFIELD   SU5405
Wheatsheaf (01329) 842965
East Street; off A27 near Fareham; PO14 4AD Welcoming old pub with small bow-windowed front bar and large back restaurant extension, good food including small-plates menu, Tues steak night and popular Sun roasts, five well kept ales such as Flowerpots and Palmers, log fires; background music, live acoustic music first Mon of month; terrace tables behind, open all day, food all day Sat, till 7pm Sun.

TWYFORD   SU4824
★ Bugle (01962) 714888
B3355/Park Lane; SO21 1QT Modern dining pub with good enterprising food (highish prices) from daily changing menu, also lunchtime sandwiches and snacks, well kept ales such as Bowman and Flowerpots, nice wines by the glass, attentive friendly young staff; background music; children and dogs (in bar) welcome, seats on attractive verandah, good walks nearby, three country-style comfortable bedrooms, open all day, no food Sun evening.

TWYFORD   SU4824
Phoenix (01962) 713322
High Street (B3335); SO21 1RF Cheerful open-plan local with raised dining area and large inglenook log fire, jovial long-serving landlord and friendly attentive staff, eight well kept ales including Greene King, good value wines and big helpings of enjoyable food from reasonably priced traditional menu; background music, sports TV, quiz nights, skittle alley; children welcome, side terraces, open all day in summer.

UPHAM   SU5320
Brushmakers Arms (01489) 860231
Shoe Lane; village signed from Winchester–Bishop's Waltham downs road, and from B2177; SO32 1JJ

Welcoming low-beamed village pub; L-shaped bar divided by central woodburner, cushioned settles and chairs around mix of tables, various brushes (once made here) and related paraphernalia, little back snug, enjoyable locally sourced home-made food, Bowman, Flack Manor, Flowerpots and a guest, good choice of wines; regular quiz and folk music; children and dogs welcome, big garden with picnic-sets on sheltered terrace and tree-shaded lawn, good nearby walks, open all day weekends, closed Mon lunchtime.

UPPER CLATFORD   SU3543
Crook & Shears (01264) 361543
Off A343 S of Andover, via Foundry Road; SP11 7QL Cosy and welcoming 17th-c thatched pub; well kept Otter and Ringwood ales, Thatcher's cider and reasonably priced traditional food (not Sun evening, Mon) from baguettes to enjoyable Sun roasts, also Tues steak night, friendly attentive service, open fires and woodburner, small dining room, back skittle alley with own bar; children and dogs welcome, pleasant secluded garden behind, closed Mon lunchtime.

UPPER FARRINGDON   SU7135
Rose & Crown (01420) 587001
Off A32 S of Alton; Crows Lane – follow Church, Selborne, Liss signpost; GU34 3ED Early 19th-c tile-hung village pub freshened up under welcoming new management; L-shaped bar with bare boards and log fire, local ales, plenty of wines by the glass and nice range of gins, good food (not Sun evening) from pub favourites up including Mon steak night, friendly helpful service, back dining room; children and dogs welcome, wide views from attractive garden, open all day Sat, till 9pm Sun.

UPTON   SU3555
Crown (01264) 736044
N of Hurstbourne Tarrant, off A343; SP11 0JS Popular old country pub with good imaginative food from bar snacks up, two or three changing regional ales and well chosen wines by the glass including English fizz, friendly helpful service, nice log fire, coffee lounge, restaurant and conservatory, also recently added farm shop; children and dogs (in bar) welcome, small garden and terrace, closed Mon and Tues, otherwise open all day, weekend brunch from 10am.

UPTON GREY   SU6948
Hoddington Arms (01256) 862371
Signed off B3349 S of Hook; Bidden Road; RG25 2RL Nicely updated 18th-c beamed pub; good food from varied menu (not Sun evening), three well kept ales and ten wines by the glass, friendly staff; events including live music, movie nights and beer/cider festivals; children and dogs welcome, large enclosed garden with terrace, quiet

pretty village with interesting Gertrude Jekyll garden, good walking/cycling, open all day Fri-Sun.

VERNHAM DEAN   SU3456
George (01264) 737279
Centre of village; SP11 0JY Rambling open-plan 17th-c beamed and timbered pub with notable eyebrow windows, some exposed brick and flint, inglenook log fire, well kept Flack Manor, Greene King, Hop Back and a guest, popular home-made food (not Sun evening) including notable curries and smaller lunchtime dishes, good friendly service; children and dogs welcome, pretty garden behind, lovely thatched village and fine walks, open all day (Sun till 6pm).

WALHAMPTON   SZ3396
Walhampton Arms (01590) 673113
B3054 NE of Lymington; aka Walhampton Inn; SO41 5RE Large comfortable Georgian-style family roadhouse handy for Isle of Wight ferry; popular well priced food including carvery (Sun and Mon) in raftered former stables and two adjoining areas, pleasant lounge, Ringwood and Flack Manor ales and traditional cider, cheerful helpful staff; curry/quiz night first Fri of month; attractive courtyard, good walks, open (and food) all day.

WALTHAM CHASE   SU5614
Black Dog (01329) 832316
Winchester Road; SO32 2LX Old brick-built country pub with low-ceilinged carpeted front bar, three well kept Greene King ales and a guest, over a dozen wines by the glass and enjoyable well priced food (all day Sun) from baguettes and basket meals up including weekday offers, cheerful helpful service, log fires, extended back restaurant; some live music, sports TV, beer festivals; children and dogs welcome, tables under parasols in good-sized neatly kept garden with deck, play area and colourful hanging baskets, open all day weekends.

WELL   SU7646
★Chequers (01256) 862605
Off A287 via Crondall, or A31 via Froyle and Lower Froyle; RG29 1TL Appealing low-beamed country dining pub; very good restaurant-style food (some quite pricey) including fresh fish/seafood, also brasserie menu and lunchtime sandwiches, Badger ales kept well and good choice of wines, wood floors, panelling and log fires; bench seating on vine-covered front terrace, spacious back garden overlooking fields, open (and food) all day.

WEST TYTHERLEY   SU2730
Black Horse (01794) 340308
North Lane; SP5 1NF Compact unspoilt village local with welcoming chatty atmosphere; traditional beamed bar with a couple of long tables, woodburner in big

fireplace, four mainly local ales and a real cider, nicely set dining area serving enjoyable reasonably priced food including good Sun roasts; monthly quiz Thurs, skittle alley; children, walkers and dogs welcome, open all day Sun till 7pm, closed Mon.

WHERWELL   SU3839
Mayfly (01264) 860283
Testcombe (over by Fullerton, not in Wherwell itself); A3057 SE of Andover, between B3420 turn-off and Leckford where road crosses River Test; OS Sheet 185 map reference 382390; SO20 6AX Busy red-brick pub in wonderful spot overlooking fast-flowing River Test; spacious beamed and carpeted bar with fishing paraphernalia, rustic pub furnishings and woodburner, well kept Fullers ales and extensive range of wines by the glass, popular food (must book for a good table) from sandwiches up, amiable staff coping well with the crowds, conservatory; background music; well behaved children and dogs welcome, plenty of riverside picnic-sets on terrace and grass, open (and food) all day.

WHERWELL   SU3840
White Lion (01264) 860317
B3420; SP11 7JF Early 17th-c multi-level beamed village inn, popular and friendly, with good choice of enjoyable food including signature pies and daily specials, well kept Sharps, Timothy Taylors and a local guest, ciders such as Orchard Pig and several wines by the glass, cheery helpful staff, comfy leather sofas and armchairs, dining rooms either side of bar; curry/stew night Mon, background music; well behaved children and dogs welcome, teak furniture in sunny courtyard, Test Way walks, three bedrooms, open all day Sat, till 9pm Sun, closed Mon (except bank holidays).

WICKHAM   SU5711
Greens (01329) 833197
The Square, at junction with A334; PO17 5JQ Civilised restaurant place with clean-cut modern décor, small bar with leather sofa and armchairs on light wood floor, extensive wine choice and a couple of real ales, obliging young staff, step down to split-level balustraded dining areas with good imaginative food along with more traditional choices and lunchtime set menu; background music; children welcome if eating, pleasant lawn overlooking water meadows, closed Sun evening, Mon.

WINCHESTER   SU4829
Bishop on the Bridge
(01962) 855111 *High Street/Bridge Street; SO23 9JX* Popular 19th-c red-brick Fullers pub by the River Itchen; their well kept beers (not cheap) and enjoyable food from sandwiches to daily specials, good friendly service, opened up traditional bare-boards interior; children and dogs welcome, attractive back terrace overlooking the river, open all day.

WINCHESTER   SU4828
★ Black Boy (01962) 861754
B3403 off M3 junction 10 towards city, then left into Wharf Hill; no nearby daytime parking – 220 metres from car park on B3403; SO23 9NP Wonderfully eccentric décor at this chatty old-fashioned pub, floor-to-ceiling books, lots of big clocks, mobiles made of wine bottles or spectacles, variety of stuffed animals including a baboon, donkey and dachshund, two open fires, orange-painted room with big oriental rugs on red floorboards, also a barn room with open hayloft, five well kept local ales, real cider and good selection of gins (weekend gin bar), decent straightforward home-made food (not Sun evening, Mon) from sandwiches up, cheerful service; table football and board games; supervised children and dogs welcome, slate tables out in front and seats on attractive secluded terrace, ten bedrooms in adjoining building, open all day.

WINCHESTER   SU4829
Golden Lion (01962) 865512
Alresford Road; SO23 0JZ Welcoming 1930s flower-decked pub on outskirts; generous helpings of enjoyable food from standard choices up (they cater for special diets including vegan), well kept Wadworths beers and ten wines by the glass, friendly attentive service, comfortable interior with modern back conservatory overlooking garden; live bluegrass last Tues of month; children and dogs welcome, open all day Sun.

WINCHESTER   SU4830
Hyde Tavern (01962) 862592
Hyde Street (B3047); SO23 7DY Cosy 15th-c gabled pub with welcoming chatty atmosphere in two wonderfully old-fashioned bars, well kept ales and a couple of proper ciders, no food (can bring your own), open fire; regular live music including folk nights, storytelling and writers' workshops, monthly quiz Sun, Father's Day beer festival; steps down to cellar bar and secluded garden, open all day weekends, shut weekdays till 5pm.

WINCHESTER   SU4829
★ Old Vine (01962) 854616
Great Minster Street; SO23 9HA Popular big-windowed town bar with four well kept ales including Alfreds, plenty of wines by the glass and decent range of whiskies, high beams and worn oak boards, larger dining side and modern conservatory (young children here only), good variety of food from sandwiches and pub staples up, efficient friendly service even though busy; background music; dogs welcome in bar, wheelchair accessible using ramp (no access to lavatories), by cathedral with a few pavement seats, more tables in partly

covered back terrace, charming bedrooms (some with cathedral views), open all day.

WINCHESTER   SU4728
Queen (01962) 853898
Kingsgate Road; SO23 9PG Cottagey twin-gabled pub with microbrewery in attractive setting opposite College cricket ground; cosy interior with bare boards and log fire, up to ten well kept beers including own brews (tasting trays available), enjoyable sensibly priced home-made food from sandwiches, bar snacks and sharing plates up, good friendly service, step to restaurant; May beer/cider/music festival; children and dogs (in bar) welcome, paved front terrace and large garden behind, open all day.

WINCHESTER   SU4729
St James (01962) 861288
Romsey Road; SO22 5BE Smallish corner pub (Little Pub Group) with attractively refurbished split-level interior; bare boards and flagstones, pews and wheelback chairs by scrubbed pine tables, some leather armchairs, painted panelling and a Victorian fireplace, plenty of pictures and other odds and ends, Wadworths ales, craft beers and good selection of wines by the glass, enjoyable food from sharing plates up including Mon burger night and Weds pie night, weekend brunch, gluten-free diets catered for, good friendly service; background

and some live music (jazz monthly), quiz Tues; children and dogs welcome, pleasant little terrace behind, open all day.

WINCHESTER   SU4829
Willow Tree (01962) 877255
Durngate Terrace; no adjacent weekday daytime parking, but Durngate car park is around corner in North Walls; a mile from M3 junction 9, by Easton Lane into city; SO23 8QX Popular 19th-c riverside pub; cosy pubby bar to the left with open fire, larger smarter restaurant to the right, well liked food from sandwiches and snacks up, four changing ales, well priced cocktails and several wines by the glass, friendly staff; quiz and live music; children and dogs welcome, lovely waterside garden (summer wood-fired pizzas), Winnall Moors nature reserve over the road, closed Sun evening, Mon, otherwise open all day.

WOOTTON   SZ2497
Rising Sun (01425) 610360
Bashley Common Road; BH25 5SF Busy well run New Forest pub; good fairly pubby food from light dishes to daily specials, efficient friendly service, five real ales including Flack Manor and Greene King, wide range of wines; children and dogs welcome, large garden with good adventure playground, roaming ponies, open (and food) all day.

Herefordshire

KEY ★ Star Pub 🌟 Top Quality Food 🍺 Great Beer
🍷 Good Wines £ Bargain Meals 🛏 Good Bedrooms 🍴 Serves Food

CAREY   SO5631 Map 4
Cottage of Content 🌟 🛏
(01432) 840242 – www.cottageofcontent.co.uk

Village signposted from good back road betweeen Ross-on-Wye and Hereford E of A49, through Hoarwithy; HR2 6NG

Country furnishings in a friendly rustic cottage with interesting food, real ales and seats on terraces; bedrooms

The look and feel of this medieval cottage set near the River Wye is totally charming. There's a multitude of beams, country furnishings such as stripped-pine kitchen chairs, long pews beside one big table and various old-fashioned tables on flagstones or bare boards and genuinely welcoming staff. Hobsons Best and Wye Valley Butty Bach on handpump, seven wines by the glass, a gin list and local cider and perry. Outside, picnic-sets can be found on the flower-filled front terrace and in the rural-feeling garden at the back. The five bedrooms are quiet and the breakfasts are good.

🌟 Highly thought-of food cooked by the landlord includes sandwiches, assorted tapas dishes, potato gnocchi in tomato and basil sauce, smoked salmon and smoked mackerel pâté roulade with pickled fennel and ginger salad, Thai green vegetable curry with saffron rice, griddled Hereford beef steak with chips and a choice of sauce, vegetarian wellington with mushrooms, spinach and brie, fish of the day, roast lamb rump with sun-dried tomato and herb-crushed potatoes, braised red cabbage and damson jus, and puddings such as tiramisu cheesecake and chocolate peanut butter tart with spiced rum and mixed berry coulis. *Benchmark main dish: chicken breast stuffed with mozzarella with Mediterranean vegetables, garlic and rosemary crushed sweet potatoes and pesto £16.50. Two-course evening meal £22.00.*

Free house ~ Licensees Richard and Helen Moore ~ Real ale ~ Open 12-2.30, 6.30-10.30; 12-2.30, 5.30-11 Fri; 12-2.30, 6.30-11 Sat; 12-3 Sun ~ Bar food 12-2, 6.30-9; 12-2 Sun ~ Restaurant ~ Children welcome ~ Dogs allowed in bar ~ Bedrooms: £85

LITTLE COWARNE   SO6050 Map 4
Three Horseshoes 🍷
(01885) 400276 – www.threehorseshoes.co.uk

Pub signposted off A465 SW of Bromyard; towards Ullingswick; HR7 4RQ

Bustling country pub with good food and drink and friendly staff; bedrooms

Known affectionately by regulars as 'The Shoes', this charming inn is set in the heart of the countryside. The L-shaped, quarry-tiled middle bar has hop-draped beams, upholstered settles, wooden chairs and tables, old local photographs above a woodburning stove, and local guidebooks. Opening off one side is the garden room with wicker armchairs around tables, and views over an outdoor seating area; leading off the other side is the games room, with pool, darts and cribbage. Wye Valley Bitter, Butty Bach and HPA on handpump, Herefordshire-made cider/perry from the likes of Celtic Marches, Oliver's, Robinsons and Weston's, ten wines by the glass and home-made elderflower cordial. A popular Sunday lunchtime carvery is offered in the stripped-stone, raftered and spacious restaurant extension. There are well sited tables and chairs on the terrace and in the neat, prettily planted garden. The two bedrooms are reached by outside stairs. Disabled access. As we went to press, the long-standing licensees, the Whittalls, announced their retirement after 30-plus years, so there may be changes.

Using some home-grown produce and making all their own chutneys, pickles and jams, the well thought-of food includes lunchtime sandwiches, crab and lime fishcakes, prawn and haddock smokies, sirloin steak with pepper sauce, burgers, butternut squash and spinach tikka masala and rice, goats cheese, leek, celery, apple and walnut filo parcel, and puddings such as home-made ice-cream. *Benchmark main dish: pan-fried chicken breast with cider and mushroom sauce £13.50. Two-course evening meal £19.00.*

Free house ~ Licensees Richard and Janet Abell ~ Real ale ~ Open 11-3, 6.30-11; 12-4 Sun ~ Bar food 12-2, 6.30-9.30 ~ Restaurant ~ Children welcome ~ Dogs allowed in bar ~ Bedrooms: £90

ROSS-ON-WYE
SO5924   Map 6
Kings Head 🛏
(01989) 763174 – www.kingshead.co.uk
High Street (B4260); HR9 5HL

Welcoming bar in well run market-town hotel with real ales and tasty food; good bedrooms

This welcoming, ancient pub has a fantastic atmosphere. The little beamed and panelled bar on the right has traditional pub furnishings, including comfortably padded bar seats and an antique cushioned box settle, stripped floorboards and a couple of black leather armchairs by a log-effect fire. Wye Valley Bitter, Butty Bach and HPA on handpump, three farm ciders, 16 gins, 15 malt whiskies and several wines by the glass at sensible prices. The beamed lounge bar on the left, also with bare boards, has some timbering, soft leather armchairs, padded bucket seats and shelves of books, and there's also a big carpeted dining room; background music, TV and board games. A sheltered back courtyard has plenty of contemporary tables and chairs for warm weather. The 15 bedrooms are all on the first or second floor, and there's no lift.

Appetising food includes confit duck and sesame spring rolls with chilli jam, mussels, battered haddock with peas and chips, Herefordshire sirloin steak, pistachio and spinach stuffed chicken breast, vegan butternut squash, sweet potato and broad bean curry with rice and poppadums, and puddings such as orange and brandy bread and butter pudding and chocolate torte with raspberry sorbet. *Benchmark main dish: oven-baked salmon fillet with chargrilled Mediterranean vegetables £15.95. Two-course evening meal £22.00.*

Free house ~ Licensee James Vidler ~ Real ale ~ Open 11-11; 12-10.30 Sun ~ Bar food 12-2, 5.30-9 ~ Restaurant ~ Children welcome ~ Dogs allowed in bar & bedrooms ~ Bedrooms: £90

SYMONDS YAT   SO5616   Map 4

Saracens Head ◖ ⌂

(01600) 890435 – www.saracensheadinn.co.uk

Symonds Yat E; HR9 6JL

Lovely riverside spot with seats on waterside terraces, a fine range of drinks and interesting food; comfortable bedrooms

This is a charming pub known for its fantastic riverside location. Plenty of chatty customers create a buoyant atmosphere in the flagstoned bar, where you'll find Sharps Doom Bar, Wye Valley Butty Bach and HPA and guests such as Kingstone Llandogo Trow, Ledbury Gold and Swan Gold on handpump, 13 wines by the glass, 40 vodkas, 20 malt whiskies and several ciders; TV, background music and board games. A cosy lounge and a modernised bare-boards dining room have fine old photos of the area and fresh flowers in jugs. There are lots of seats on terraces beside the River Wye – best to get here early in warm weather to bag one. The nearby Forest of Dean offers plenty of walks. One way to reach the inn is via the little hand-ferry (pulled by one of the staff). Most of the nine rooms have river views and breakfasts are good. Disabled access to the bar and terrace.

Well regarded food includes sandwiches and baguettes, charcuterie sharing board, superfood salad, Jamaican jerk beef short ribs with Jack Daniels barbecue sauce, sweet potato fries and sweetcorn fritters, steak (sirloin or rib-eye) with chips and a choice of sauce, roasted venison loin with braised red cabbage, charred broccoli and dauphinoise potatoes, beetroot falafel with butternut squash, halloumi and pomegranate dressing, and puddings such as eton mess and lemon posset with raspberry coulis. *Benchmark main dish: barbecue pulled pork burger with chips £15.50. Two-course evening meal £28.00.*

Free house ~ Licensees PK and CJ Rollinson ~ Real ale ~ Open 11-11; 11-10.30 Sun ~ Bar food 12-2.30, 6.30-9 ~ Children welcome but not in bedrooms ~ Dogs allowed in bar ~ Bedrooms: £130

TILLINGTON   SO4645   Map 6

Bell ◖

(01432) 760395 – www.thebelltillington.com

Off A4110 NW of Hereford; HR4 8LE

Relaxed and friendly pub with a snug character bar opening into civilised dining areas – good value

This cosy, inviting pub serves quality food at a reasonable price. The snug parquet-floored bar on the left has assorted bucket armchairs around low, chunky, mahogany-coloured tables, brightly cushioned wall benches, team photographs and shelves of books; the black beams are strung with dried hops. Wye Valley Bitter and Butty Bach on handpump, cider made on site, eight wines by the glass and locally produced spirits from Chase, all served by notably cheerful staff; daily papers, background music and board games. The bar opens into a comfortable bare-boards dining lounge with stripy plush banquettes and a coal fire. Beyond that is a pitched-ceiling restaurant area with more banquettes and big country prints; through slatted blinds you can see a sunken terrace with contemporary tables, and a garden with teak tables and picnic-sets. Disabled access.

The standard of food is high and includes open sandwiches, prawn tempura, mac 'n' cheese, pan-fried sea bass fillet with new potatoes and walnut pesto, slow-roasted pork belly with roast potatoes and gravy, honey roast ham with egg and chips, sweet potato and spinach curry, and desserts such as sticky toffee pudding and raspberry and white chocolate brûlée. *Benchmark main dish: steak and vegetable suet pudding pie £13.95. Two-course evening meal £20.00.*

Free house ~ Licensee Glenn Williams ~ Real ale ~ Open 12-10.30; 12-11 Sat; 12-9 Sun ~ Bar food 12-2.30, 6-9; all day Fri, Sat; 12-3 Sun ~ Children welcome ~ Restaurant ~ Dogs allowed in bar

TITLEY   SO3359   Map 6

Stag 🌟 🍷 🛏

(01544) 230221 – www.thestagg.co.uk

B4355 N of Kington; HR5 3RL

Herefordshire Dining Pub of the Year

Exceptional food in three dining rooms, real ales and a fine choice of other drinks, and seats in the two-acre garden; comfortable bedrooms

Run by the same husband (chef) and wife (front of house) for 20 years, the Stagg has a deserved reputation for its excellent and inventive food; as a result, most visitors are here to dine. However, there is also a pubby and convivial little bar with friendly, chatty locals and a good choice of drinks. As well as a gently civilised atmosphere, furnishings are deliberately simple: high-backed elegant wooden or leather dining chairs around a medley of tables on bare boards, candlelight and (in the bar) 200 jugs hanging from the ceiling. Courteous, warmly welcoming staff serve Ludlow Gold and Wye Valley Butty Bach on handpump, 18 house wines by the glass (plus a carefully chosen bin list), interesting soft drinks, a long list of enterprising cocktails and mocktails, local cider and perry, 16 local gins and several whiskies. The two-acre garden has seats on a terrace and a croquet lawn. Bedrooms are either above the pub or in a Georgian vicarage four minutes' walk away; super breakfasts. The inn is surrounded by good walking country and is handy for the Offa's Dyke Path.

🌟 They use their own eggs and home-grown vegetables and fruit (when available) for the delicious food that includes sandwiches on home-made bread, scallops with celeriac, apple and hazelnuts, local snails with parsley purée, ham, mushroom and garlic croutons, a couple of pubby choices such as pork sausages with mash and onion rings, roast cauliflower with cauliflower purée and cauliflower couscous, curry oil and parmentier potatoes, cod fillet with fennel, shrimps, parsley and lemon butter, lamb rump and slow-cooked shoulder with jerusalem artichokes and dauphinoise potatoes, beef fillet with mushroom purée, red wine shallots and chips, and puddings such as three crème brûlées (vanilla, coffee and cardamom) and bread and butter pudding with home-made ice-cream and prunes.

Free house ~ Licensees Steve and Nicola Reynolds ~ Real ale ~ Open 12-3, 6.30-11; 12-3.30 Sun; closed Sun evening, Mon, Tues, one week Feb, one week June, two weeks Nov ~ Bar food 12-2, 6.30-9; 12-2.45 Sun ~ Restaurant ~ Children welcome ~ Dogs allowed in bar & bedrooms ~ Bedrooms: £110

UPPER COLWALL   SO7643   Map 4

Chase

(01684) 540276 – www.thechaseinnmalvern.co.uk

Chase Road, brown sign to pub off B4218 Malvern–Colwall, first left after hilltop on bend going W; WR13 6DJ

Gorgeous sunset views from garden of nicely traditional tavern, and good drinks

This attractive country pub has stunning views across Herefordshire as far as the Black Mountains and the Brecon Beacons – the seats and tables on a steep series of small, pretty terraces behind the pub make the most of this outlook. The bars have a companionable atmosphere, a great variety of seats (from a wooden-legged tractor seat to a carved pew) and tables, an old black kitchen range and plenty of decorations – china mugs, blue-glass flasks, lots of small pictures. Four well kept ales are tapped from the cask, including Bombardier, Exmoor Gold and a couple of guests such as Hobsons Twisted Spire and Purity Mad Goose, and friendly staff also serve nine wines by the glass, 15 gins, six malt whiskies and a farm cider; board games. There are good walks in the vicinity.

Food has been more elaborate in the past but currently is limited to sandwiches, hot rolls (bacon, beef with gravy or barbecue pulled jackfruit) with home-made chips, and honey roast ham, egg and chips. *Benchmark main dish: beef and ale pie £12.30.*

Free house ~ Licensee Duncan Ironmonger ~ Real ale ~ Open 12-3, 5-11; 12-11 Sat; 12-10.30 Sun ~ Bar food 12-2 (2.30 weekends), 6.30-9 ~ Children welcome ~ Dogs allowed in bar

UPPER SAPEY
Baiting House 🛏
SO6863   Map 4

(01886) 853201 – www.baitinghouse.co.uk
B4203 Bromyard–Great Witley; WR6 6XT

Bustling inn with bars and dining rooms, local ales and a thoughtful choice of food with seats outside; bedrooms and lodges

This smartly refurbished 19th-c country inn on the Worcestershire border sits at the top of a hill above the Teme Valley. The bars have flagstones and wood-strip flooring, a woodburning stove, cushioned settles, stools and window seats and friendly, helpful staff who serve five well kept ales including Wye Valley and guests from Hobsons and Ludlow on handpump, several wines by the glass, local cider and a good choice of gins. The dining areas (dogs are allowed in one of these) are traditionally furnished with more bare boards and flagstones. There are seats, tables and picnic-sets on a back brick terrace and raised lawn, surrounded by fields. There's a wide range of well equipped and comfortable accommodation to choose from: bedrooms of varying sizes in the pub itself, and six new large 'meadow rooms' and three contemporary wooden lodges (with kitchens) in the grounds, a short walk from the pub; the lodges and some of the meadow rooms have a hot tub.

Well thought-of modern food includes chicken liver parfait with toasted brioche, twice-baked cheddar soufflé, crispy ham hock with chive mayonnaise, brisket of beef with parsley emulsion, beef fat onions and potato rosti, mushroom risotto with hazelnut pesto, sea bream with confit tomatoes and triple-cooked chips, roasted cauliflower with potato gnocchi, truffle pesto and mushroom ketchup, and puddings such as chocolate crèmeux with vanilla ice-cream and mango kulfi with lime meringue and coconut sorbet. *Benchmark main dish: slow-cooked lamb shoulder with red pepper and goats cheese £16.00. Two-course evening meal £26.00.*

Free house ~ Licensees Andrew and Kate Cornthwaite ~ Open 4-11 Mon; 12-11 Tues-Sun ~ Bar food 12-2, 6-8.30; not Mon ~ Restaurant ~ Children welcome ~ Dogs allowed in bar, restaurant & bedrooms ~ Bedrooms: £126

Post Office address codings confusingly give the impression that a few pubs are in Herefordshire when they're really in Gloucestershire or even Wales (which is where we list them).

WOOLHOPE

SO6135   Map 4

Crown

(01432) 860468 – www.thecrowninn.pub

Village signposted off B4224 in Fownhope; HR1 4QP

Chatty village local with fine range of local ciders and perries, and popular food

This welcoming pub is a cider lover's dream. The long-serving landlord makes four ciders (and keeps a couple of guests too) and serves around two dozen bottled ciders and perries from within a 15-mile radius. They also hold regular weekend events with live music, beer, cider and perry. Also, Ledbury Bitter and Wye Valley Butty Bach and HPA on handpump and several wines by the glass. The bar has painted farmhouse and other wooden chairs, upholstered settles and rustic tables on wooden flooring, an open fire and two woodburning stoves, some standing timbers and stools against the bar counter; background music, darts and board games. There's a garden bar with marvellous views and outdoor cooking on special nights. Seven new bedrooms are available through Airbnb. Disabled access.

Pleasing food includes sandwiches, fig, mozzarella and prosciutto salad, baked camembert with garlic and rosemary (to share), roasted aubergine with babaganoush and quinoa, venison chilli con carne, hake, chorizo and bean cassoulet with spring beans, ox cheek burger with monterey jack cheese and fries, Mediterranean vegetable quiche, and puddings such as lavender brûlée, summer berry cheesecake and chocolate brownie with vanilla ice-cream. *Benchmark main dish: venison chilli con carne with rice £13.00. Two-course evening meal £19.00.*

Free house ~ Licensee Matt Slocombe ~ Real ale ~ Open 12-3, 5-10.30; 12-11.30 Sat; 12-10 Sun ~ Bar food 12-2, 6-9; 12-3 Sun ~ Restaurant ~ Children welcome ~ Dogs allowed in bar

Also Worth a Visit in Herefordshire

Besides the fully inspected pubs, you might like to try these pubs that have been recommended to us and described by readers. Do tell us what you think of them: feedback@goodguides.com

ALMELEY   SO3351

Bells (01544) 327216

Off A480, A4111 or A4112 S of Kington; HR3 6LF Welcoming old country local; original jug-and-bottle entry lobby and carpeted beamed bar with woodburner, second bar has been converted into village shop/deli; three well kept changing ales, traditional cider/perry and good honest home-made food from sandwiches up (not evenings except for Fri fish and chips night); children and dogs welcome, garden with summer tea hut, on Wyche Way long-distance path, open all day weekends.

AYMESTREY   SO4265

★ **Riverside Inn** (01568) 708440

A4110, at N end of village, W of Leominster; HR6 9ST Black and white inn with terrace and tree-sheltered garden making most of lovely waterside spot by ancient stone bridge over the Lugg; cosy rambling beamed interior with some antique

furniture alongside stripped country kitchen tables, warm fires, well kept Hobsons, Wye Valley and a guest, local ciders and well chosen wines by the glass, very good imaginative food from chef-patron using local rare-breed meat and own fruit and vegetables (bar snacks only Sun evening), friendly helpful staff; quiet background music; children welcome, dogs in bar, lovely circular walks, nine well appointed bedrooms including three new garden rooms, fly fishing for residents, good breakfast, closed Mon lunchtime, otherwise open all day.

BISHOPS FROME   SO6648

Green Dragon (01885) 490607

Just off B4214 Bromyard–Ledbury; WR6 5BP Welcoming early 17th-c village pub; four linked rooms with unspoilt rustic feel, beams, flagstones and log fires (one in fine inglenook), half a dozen ales, real ciders and enjoyable traditional food (Weds-Sat evenings and Sun lunchtime); children and dogs welcome, tiered garden with smokers' shelter, on Herefordshire Trail, closed weekday lunchtimes, open all day Sat and Sun.

BODENHAM   SO5454
Englands Gate (01568) 797286
On A417 at Bodenham turn-off, about 6 miles S of Leominster; HR1 3HU Attractive black and white 16th-c coaching inn; rambling interior with beams and joists in low ceilings around a vast central stone chimneypiece, sturdy timber props, exposed stonework and well worn flagstones (one or two steps), Wye Valley Butty Bach, HPA and a guest, local cider and well liked food from lunchtime sandwiches up including themed nights, friendly staff; background and occasional live music, monthly quiz, July beer/cider/sausage festival; children welcome, dogs in bar, tables under parasols on terrace and in pleasant garden, seven modern bedrooms in converted coach house next door, open all day, closed Mon-Weds.

BOSBURY   SO6943
Bell (01531) 640285
B4220 N of Ledbury; HR8 1PX Timbered village pub opposite the church; log fires in both bars, Otter, Wye Valley and a guest, three ciders and good choice of wines by the glass, dining area serving popular sensibly priced traditional food (not Sun evening, Mon, Tues) including Sun carvery, friendly staff; pool and darts; children and dogs welcome, large garden with covered terrace and play equipment, open all day Sun till 9pm, closed lunchtimes Mon-Thurs.

BRINGSTY COMMON   SO6954
Live & Let Live (01886) 821462
Off A44 Knightwick–Bromyard 1.5 miles W of Whitbourne turn; take track southwards at Black Cat inn sign, bearing right at fork; WR6 5UW Bustling 17th-c timber and thatch cottage (former cider house); cosy flagstoned bar with log fire in cavernous stone fireplace, pewter jugs hanging from low beams, old casks built into hop-strung counter serving three well kept ales including Wye Valley Butty Bach, local ciders/apple juice and decent wines by the glass, enjoyable fairly traditional food served by friendly staff, two dining rooms upstairs under steep rafters; children and dogs welcome, glass-topped well and big wooden hogshead used as terrace tables, peaceful country views towards the Malverns from picnic-sets and rustic benches in former orchard, handy for Brockhampton Estate (NT), open all day Sat, till 6pm Sun, closed Mon except bank holidays.

BROMYARD DOWNS   SO6755
★Royal Oak (01885) 482585
Just NE of Bromyard; pub signed off A44; HR7 4QP Beautifully placed low-beamed 18th-c pub with wide views; open-plan carpeted and flagstoned bar, log

fire and woodburner, dining room with huge bay window, well kept Malvern Hills, Woods Shropshire Lad, enjoyable traditional food including sandwiches and pies, friendly helpful service; background music, pool; children, walkers and dogs welcome, nice garden with front terrace and play area, good walks and Brockhampton Estate (NT) nearby, closed Sun evening, Mon (open all day bank holiday weekends).

CANON PYON   SO4648
Nags Head (01432) 830725
A4110; HR4 8NY Welcoming 17th-c timbered roadside pub; beamed bar with log fire, flagstoned restaurant and tearoom, three well kept changing ales and popular good value food from bar snacks up, pleasant attentive service; children and dogs (in bar) welcome, extensive garden with play area, open until 3pm Sat, till 6pm Sun, closed Mon and lunchtime Tues.

CLIFFORD   SO2445
Castlefields (01497) 831554
B4350 N of Hay-on-Wye; HR3 5HB Rebuilt and enlarged family pub retaining some old features including a glass-covered well; generous helpings of popular good value food and a couple of changing ales, friendly helpful staff, wood or carpeted floors, two-way stone fireplace with woodburner, restaurant; pool, darts and various community-based events; lovely country views, camping, open and food all day weekends (till 4pm Sun), closed Mon, Tues.

CLODOCK   SO3227
★Cornewall Arms (01873) 860677
N of Walterstone; HR2 0PD Wonderfully old-fashioned survivor in remote hamlet by historic church facing the Black Mountains; friendly stable-door bar with log fire each end, a few mats and comfortable armchairs on stone floor, lots of ornaments and knick-knacks, photos of past village events and other pictures, books for sale/exchange, games including quoits, cards, darts and devil among the tailors, bottled Wye Valley and cider, no food or credit cards; dogs welcome, open from noon weekends and 5.30pm weekdays.

COLWALL   SO7440
★Wellington (01684) 540269
A449 Malvern–Ledbury; WR13 6HW Welcoming roadside country pub; highly thought-of food from bar snacks and standards to imaginative restaurant dishes, well kept Goffs Tournament, a couple of guests and nice wines by the glass, friendly helpful landlord and staff, comfortably lived-in two-level beamed bar with red patterned carpet and quarry tiles, some built-in settles including unusual high-backed one framing a window, woodburner and open fire, spacious relaxed back dining area; occasional live music, daily newspapers;

children and dogs welcome, nice views from picnic-sets on grass above car park, good local walks, closed Sun evenings and Mon (shut all day Aug bank holiday Mon, occasionally open on other bank holidays for lunch).

DORSTONE   SO3141
★ **Pandy** (01981) 550273
Pub signed off B4348 E of Hay-on-Wye; HR3 6AN Ancient inn (12th-c origins) by village green; traditional rooms with low beams, stout timbers and worn flagstones, various alcoves and vast fireplace, several woodburners, Sharps Atlantic, Wye Valley Butty Bach and a house beer from Grey Trees, real ciders, enjoyable reasonably priced food (not Sun evening or Mon) from changing blackboard menu; children and dogs (in bar) welcome, large beer garden, walking maps available, closed lunchtimes except for Fri-Sun.

EARDISLEY   SO3149
Tram (01544) 327251
Corner of A4111 and Woodseaves Road; HR3 6PG Handsome old pub in a famous black and white village; beamed bar with local character, sturdy standing timbers and bare boards, also nicely worn tables and chairs, long cushioned pews, high-backed settle, old country pictures and interesting tram prints, small dining room, stylish outside gents' (wheelchair access to the restaurant but no disabled loos); three well kept ales including Wye Valley Butty Bach on handpump, three organic ciders and highly regarded food made with local produce; games room with pool and darts; covered terrace and sizeable garden with picnic-sets and pétanque, children welcome, dogs in bar, closed Mon, evenings Tues and Sun.

EWYAS HAROLD   SO3828
Temple Bar (01981) 240423
Village centre signed from B4347; HR2 0EU Popular creeper-clad Georgian inn run by welcoming family; good freshly made food from bar meals to interesting evening restaurant dishes, Wye Valley Butty Bach, HPA and two guests, local cider, modernised interior keeping original oak beams, flagstones and log fire; children and dogs (in bar) welcome, disabled access, three comfortable bedrooms, hearty breakfast, open all day, no evening food Sun, Mon; new owners as we went to press, so there may be changes.

GARWAY   SO4622
Garway Moon (01600) 750270
Centre of village, opposite the green; HR2 8RQ Attractive 18th-c pub in pretty location overlooking common; decent food

(not Mon) including popular Weds curry night served by friendly staff, well kept ales such as Butcombe, Kingstone and Wye Valley, proper ciders, beams and exposed stonework, woodburner in inglenook, restaurant; children, dogs and muddy boots welcome, garden with terrace and play area, three bedrooms, open all day weekends, closed lunchtimes Mon and Tues.

GOODRICH   SO5719
Hostelrie (01600) 890241
Pub signed from B4229, S of village; HR9 6HX Unusual village inn with turreted Victorian gothic façade; three well kept Wye Valley ales and decent choice of wines from brick and timber servery, sandwiches, pub favourites and other enjoyable food including blackboard specials and Mon curry night, can eat in bar or restaurant, good friendly service, traditionally updated and softly lit with painted panelling, beams and stripped stonework; children, dogs and muddy boots welcome, picnic-sets in attractive garden, bedrooms, near Goodrich Castle (EH) and Wye Valley Walk, open all day Fri-Sun, closed Mon lunchtime.

GORSLEY   SO6726
Roadmaker (01989) 720352
0.5 miles from M50 junction 3; village signposted from exit – B4221; HR9 7SW Popular 19th-c village pub run by group of retired Gurkhas; large carpeted lounge bar with central log fire, good Nepalese food here and in evening restaurant, also Sun roasts and other English choices, well kept ales such as Butcombe, efficient courteous service; quiz first Sun of month; children welcome, no dogs, terrace with water feature, open all day Sat and Sun, closed Mon.

HAMPTON BISHOP   SO5538
Bunch of Carrots (01432) 870237
B4224; HR1 4JR Spacious country pub by River Wye; good daily carvery and choice of other pubby food (all day weekends), cheerful efficient service, well kept Wye Valley Butty Bach, HPA, Sharps Doom Bar and a guest, local cider and a dozen wines by the glass, traditional dimly lit bar area with beams, stone walls, rugs on flagstone floors, horsebrasses and fishing prints, woodburner, airy restaurant; children and dogs welcome, disabled access/loo, garden with play area, open all day.

HAREWOOD END   SO5227
Harewood End Inn (01989) 730637
A49 Hereford to Ross-on-Wye; HR2 8JT Roadside pub in two connecting buildings; compact bar and a couple of bare-boards dining rooms, high-backed chairs around scrubbed-top tables, interesting collection

---

Pubs close to motorway junctions are listed at the back of the book.

of enamel signs on panelled walls, open fire, good choice of enjoyable home-made food from lunchtime sandwiches to grills including signature Harewood burger, three well kept ales and decent choice of wines, welcoming attentive staff; quiz last Sun of month, pool and TV, children, dogs and muddy boots welcome, nice garden and local walks, five bedrooms, closed Mon.

HEREFORD · SO5139
Barrels (01432) 274968
St Owen Street; HR1 2JQ Friendly 18th-c coaching inn popular with good mix of customers; former home to the Wye Valley brewery and up to seven of their very well kept/priced ales from barrel-built counter (beer/music festival end Aug), Thatcher's cider, cheerful efficient staff, no food; live jazz first Mon of month, Thurs quiz, juke box, sports TV, pool and darts; dogs welcome, large partly covered courtyard behind, open all day.

HEREFORD · SO5040
Beer in Hand 07543 327548
Eign Street next to church; HR4 0AP Friendly micropub with good range of cask and keg beers including local Odyssey from temperature-controlled stillage, more in bottles and decent selection of other drinks including wines and spirits, snacky food such as pickled eggs, evening pizzas Thurs, Fri, enthusiastic knowledgeable staff, wooden tables and chairs down each side of simple front room, part-divided back part with sofas and benches, some barrel tables in bar area with pump clips decorating the ceiling; quiz first Weds of month, board games, dogs welcome, narrow side terrace, open all day Fri and Sat, from 3pm Sun and 5pm other days.

HEREFORD · SO5039
Lichfield Vaults (01432) 266821
Church Street; HR1 2LR A pub since the 18th c in picturesque pedestrianised area near cathedral; dark panelling, some stripped brick and exposed joists, impressive plasterwork in large-windowed front room, traditionally furnished with dark pews, cushioned pub chairs and a couple of heavily padded benches, hot coal stove, charming Cypriot landlord and friendly staff, six well kept ales such as Adnams, Butcombe, Fullers and Sharps, enjoyable lunchtime food from sandwiches up including Greek dishes and good Sun roasts; faint background music, live blues/rock last Sun afternoon of month, TV for sports (particularly rugby), games machines, daily papers; children and dogs welcome, picnic-sets in pleasant back courtyard, open all day.

HOARWITHY · SO5429
New Harp (01432) 840900
Off A49 Hereford to Ross-on-Wye; HR2 6QH Open-plan village dining pub

with cheerful bustling atmosphere; good well presented local food from chef-landlord, friendly helpful service, ales such as Ledbury, Otter and Wye Valley, Weston's cider (maybe their own organic cider in summer), pine tables on slate tiles, bay-window seats and half-panelling, screened-off dining area with light wood furniture, a couple of woodburners; background and some live music, sports TV; children, walkers and dogs welcome, pretty tree-sheltered garden with stream, picnic-sets and decked area, little shop and Mon morning post office, unusual Italianate Victorian church nearby, open all day.

KILPECK · SO4430
★ Kilpeck Inn (01981) 570464
Village and church signposted off A465 SW of Hereford; HR2 9DN Neatly refurbished village inn at the centre of local life for 250 years with beamed, flagstoned bar with several tempting corners and two dining rooms with high panelled wainscoting; Ledbury Dr Rudi's Extra Pale and Wye Valley Butty Bach on handpump, seven wines by the glass, several gins (including local ones) and farm cider, interesting food cooked by chef-landlord from sandwiches up and set lunch menu; background music; children and dogs (in bar) welcome, picnic-sets on grass at back, four comfortable bedrooms and good breakfasts, Kilpeck Castle ruins and lovely Romanesque church nearby, also good surrounding walks including Offa's Dyke Path, open all day weekends, closes 5pm Sun.

KINGSLAND · SO4461
Corners (01568) 708385
B4360 NW of Leominster, corner of Lugg Green Road; HR6 9RY Comfortably updated, partly black and white 16th-c village inn with snug nooks and corners; log fires, low beams, dark red plasterwork and some stripped brickwork, bow-window seat and leather armchairs in softly lit carpeted bar, well kept Hobsons, Wye Valley and decent selection of wines, big side dining room in converted hay loft with rafters and huge window, enjoyable reasonably priced food from pubby choices up including meal deals, cheerful attentive service; children welcome, no garden, ten bedrooms in modern block behind (no lift to first floor).

KINGTON · SO3056
★ Olde Tavern (01544) 231945
Victoria Road, just off A44 opposite B4355 – follow sign to 'Town Centre, Hospital, Cattle Market'; pub on right opposite Elizabeth Road, no inn sign but 'Estd 1767' notice; HR5 3BX Gloriously old-fashioned with hatch-served side room opening off small plain parlour and public bar, plenty of dark brown woodwork, large windows, settles and other antique furniture on bare floors, gas fire, old local pictures, china, pewter and curios, four well kept local

ales such as Hobsons and Ludlow, Weston's cider, generous helpings of enjoyable home-made food (Thurs-Sun), friendly atmosphere; children and dogs welcome, little yard at back, open all day weekends, closed weekday lunchtimes.

KINGTON   SO2956
Oxford Arms (01544) 230322
Duke Street; HR5 3DR Traditional old-fashioned beamed inn; woodburners in main bar on left and dining area to the right, smaller lounge with sofas and armchairs, real ales such as Hobsons (beer festivals), good reasonably priced home-made food including Weds curry and Thurs steak nights, good friendly service; some live music, pool and darts; children and dogs welcome, terrace picnic-sets, bedrooms, open all day weekends, closed Mon and lunchtimes Tues-Fri.

KINGTON   SO2956
Royal Oak (01544) 231864
Church Street; HR5 3BE Welcoming 17th-c pub with enjoyable traditional food including good value Sun carvery, well kept Timothy Taylors Landlord and Wye Valley HPA, bar with darts and open fire, separate dining room; children and dogs welcome, back garden with (summer barbecues and live music), handy for Offa's Dyke walkers, three neat simple bedrooms, open all day weekends, closed weekday lunchtimes, no evening food Sun or Tues.

LEDBURY   SO7137
★Feathers (01531) 635266
High Street (A417); HR8 1DS Handsome black and white Tudor hotel with convivial bar-brasserie good for drinkers and diners; locals congregate in one end with hop-covered beams, stripped panelling and stools against counter serving often local ales on handpump, craft beers, good wine list, 40 whiskies and cocktails, main part for diners with flowers on tables, comfortable bays of banquettes and other seats, log fire, much enjoyed food from sharing plates and pub classics up, charming professional service, afternoon teas in sedate front lounge with another fire; children and dogs (in bar) welcome, tables under parasols on sheltered back terrace (lots of pots and hanging baskets), stylish bedrooms, good breakfast, open all day.

LEDBURY   SO7137
★Prince of Wales (01531) 632250
Church Lane; narrow passage from Town Hall; HR8 1DL Friendly old black and white local prettily tucked away down

narrow cobbled alley; seven well kept ales, foreign draught/bottled beers and real cider, knowledgeable staff, decent uncomplicated low-priced food from sandwiches up, beams, nooks and crannies and shelves of books, long back room; background music, live blues Thurs night and Sun afternoon, folk session Weds evening; dogs welcome, a couple of tables in flower-filled backyard, open all day.

LEDBURY   SO7137
Seven Stars (01531) 635800
Homend (High Street); HR8 1BN 16th-c beamed and timbered pub with enjoyable seasonal food (all day weekends) using local suppliers including produce from own farm, also a vegan menu, three well kept ales including Shepherd Neame and a dozen gins, friendly helpful staff, bar area with comfortable seating and cosy woodburner, dining room behind; children and dogs welcome, disabled access, walled back terrace, three comfortable bedrooms, open all day.

LEDBURY   SO7137
Talbot (01531) 632963
New Street; HR8 2DX Comfortable 16th-c black and white fronted coaching inn; carpeted log-fire bar with Wadworths ales and guests, plenty of wines by the glass and good fairly traditional food from sharing boards and lunchtime sandwiches up, gluten-free menu, friendly efficient service, oak-panelled dining room; courtyard tables, 13 bedrooms (six in converted stables), good breakfast, open all day.

LEINTWARDINE   SO4073
Lion (01547) 540203
High Street; SY7 0JZ Restored inn beautifully situated by packhorse bridge over River Teme; helpful efficient staff and friendly atmosphere, good well presented food from varied menu including some imaginative choices (can be pricey), Tues steak night, restaurant and two separate bars (both with woodburners), well kept beers such as Ludlow and Wye Valley and a dozen wines by the glass, afternoon teas; children welcome, dogs allowed in top bar only, safely fenced riverside lawned garden with play area, eight attractive bedrooms, can arrange fishing trips, open all day (may shut early Sun in winter).

LEINTWARDINE   SO4073
★Sun (01547) 540705
Rosemary Lane, just off A4113; SY7 0LP Interesting 19th-c time warp: benches and farmhouse tables by coal fire in brick-floored front bar (dogs welcome here), three well

---

Please tell us if any pub deserves to be upgraded to a featured entry – and why: feedback@goodguides.com, or (no stamp needed) Freepost THE GOOD PUB GUIDE, Random House Publishing, 20 Vauxhall Bridge Road, London SW1V 2SA.

kept ales including Hobsons tapped from the cask (Aug beer festival), another fire in snug carpeted parlour, sandwiches, pork pies and perhaps a lunchtime ploughman's (can bring food from adjacent fish and chip shop), friendly staff and cheery locals; open mike night last Fri of month; pavilion-style extension at back with bar and garden room, open all day.

LEOMINSTER SO4959
★ **Grape Vaults** (01568) 611404
Broad Street; HR6 8BS Popular and friendly little two-room character pub; half a dozen well kept ales including Ludlow and tasty good value traditional food (no credit cards – ATM opposite), good cheerful service, two coal fires, beams and stripped woodwork, original dark high-backed settles and round copper-topped tables on bare boards, old local prints and posters, bottle collection, shelves of books in snug; live music Sun afternoon, occasional quiz nights; dogs welcome, open all day, no food Sun evening.

LINTON SO6525
Alma (01989) 720355
On main road through village; HR9 7RY Cheerful village local with up to five well kept ales from the likes of Butcombe, Ludlow and Oakham, Weston's cider and several wines by the glass, enjoyable pub food (not Sun, Mon) including specials, friendly service, front bar with woodburner, restaurant, pool in small back room; monthly quiz and open mike nights, also July music festival; children and dogs welcome, large garden behind with nice views, closed Mon lunchtime.

LUGWARDINE SO5441
Crown & Anchor (01432) 850630
Just off A438 E of Hereford; Cotts Lane; HR1 4AB Cottagey timbered pub dating from the early 18th c; ample helpings of enjoyable reasonably priced food, well kept Wye Valley and a guest, decent wines, good friendly service, various smallish opened-up rooms, inglenook log fire; children and dogs (in bar) welcome, seats in front garden, open all day weekends, food till 7pm Sun.

MICHAELCHURCH ESCLEY SO3133
★ **Bridge Inn** (01981) 510646
Off back road SE of Hay-on-Wye, along Escley Brook valley; HR2 0JW Black-beamed riverside inn delightfully tucked away down steep lane in attractive valley, run by hard-working licensees; homely easy-going bar with hops on dark beams, pine pews and dining chair around rustic tables, well kept Wye Valley Butty Bach and HPA, local farm cider and their own gin, two dining areas with local artwork, good home-made food including some unusual choices, friendly atmosphere; children welcome, seats out on large waterside terrace and

beer garden, camping, yurts and bedrooms in nearby farmhouse, good walks, open all day Fri-Sun, closed Mon lunchtime.

MUCH DEWCHURCH SO4831
Black Swan (01981) 540295
B4348 Ross-on-Wye to Hay-on-Wye; HR2 8DJ Roomy, attractive beamed local (partly 14th-c) with welcoming long-serving landlady; well kept Timothy Taylors Landlord and local guests, 12 ciders including Weston's, decent wines and enjoyable straightforward home-made food using local produce, log fires in cosy well worn bar and lounge/eating area, pool room with darts, TV and juke box; Thurs folk night; children and dogs welcome, seats on front terrace, open all day Sun.

MUCH MARCLE SO6634
Royal Oak (01531) 660300
On A449 Ross-on-Wye to Ledbury; HR8 2ND Roadside country dining pub with lovely views; good food from snacks and pub favourites up, meal deals Tues-Thurs, well kept Brakspears and Marstons Pedigree, friendly service, smallish bare-boards bar area, various dining sections including library room and large back function room; tribute bands and other live music, skittle alley; children and dogs (in bar) welcome, garden and terrace seating, two bedrooms, open all day in summer.

PEMBRIDGE SO3958
New Inn (01544) 388427
Market Square (A44); HR6 9DZ Timeless half-timbered ancient inn overlooking small black and white town's church; unpretentious three-room bar with antique settles, beams, worn flagstones and impressive inglenook, well kept changing ales, traditional cider and generous helpings of popular good value food including notable game pie, friendly service, quiet little family dining room; some live folk music, traditional games; no dogs inside, unsuitable for wheelchairs and loos downstairs.

PETERSTOW SO5524
Red Lion (01989) 730546
A49 W of Ross-on-Wye; HR9 6LH Roadside country pub with much enjoyed food cooked by landlord-chef (sensible prices and smaller appetites catered for), four well kept ales, Weston's cider and fruit cider, friendly staff, open-plan with large dining area and modern conservatory, log fires; quiz first Mon of month; children and dogs welcome, back play area, open (and food) all day except 3-6pm Sun.

PRESTON SO3841
Yew Tree (01981) 500359
Village W of Hereford; HR2 9JT Small tucked-away pub handy for River Wye; simple and welcoming, with a changing ale tapped from the cask and real cider, good value

home-made food including Fri steak night, beams and woodburner; some live music, pool, children and dogs welcome, bunkhouse, open all day weekends.

ROSS-ON-WYE   SO6024
White Lion (01989) 562785
Wilton Lane; HR9 6AQ Friendly riverside pub dating from 1650; well kept Wye Valley and a couple of guests, enjoyable traditional food (not Sun evening) from sandwiches up, good service, large fireplace in carpeted bar, stone-walled gaol restaurant (building once a police station); quiz second Thurs of month, children and dogs welcome, lots of tables in garden and on terrace overlooking the Wye and historic bridge, bedrooms and camping, open all day.

SELLACK   SO5526
★Loughpool (01989) 730888
Off A49; HR9 6LX Cottagey black and white country pub – some modernisation but keeping character; bars with beams and standing timbers, rustic furniture on flagstones, open fire and woodburner, well kept Wye Valley ales and a guest, local farm ciders/perries and several wines by the glass, landlord-chef's good attractively presented food from interesting menu including daily specials, back restaurant, friendly attentive service; well behaved children (during the day) and dogs (in bar) allowed, garden tables under parasols, good surrounding walks, closed Mon, Tues, Sun evening.

STAPLOW   SO6941
Oak (01531) 640954
Bromyard Road (B4214); HR8 1NP Popular roadside village pub with two snug bar areas; beams, flagstones and woodburners, four real ales and good choice of wines, open-kitchen restaurant serving good food from lunchtime sandwiches/ ciabattas up, cheerful helpful service; occasional live music; children and dogs welcome, garden picnic-sets, four comfortable bedrooms, open all day.

STAUNTON-ON-WYE   SO3844
Portway (01981) 500474
A438 Hereford to Hay-on-Wye, by Monnington turn; HR4 7NH Comfortable 16th-c beamed inn with good choice of popular well priced food, ales such as Ludlow, Sharps and Wye Valley, several wines by the glass, log-fire bar, lounge and restaurant; background music, TV, pool; children and dogs welcome, picnic-sets in sizeable garden among fruit trees, nine bedrooms, open all day.

STOCKTON CROSS   SO5161
Stockton Cross Inn (01568) 612509
Kimbolton; A4112, off A49 just N of Leominster; HR6 0HD Renovated half-timbered 16th-c drovers' inn (sister pub to the Baiting House – see Main Entries);

heavily beamed interior with inglenook woodburner, Wye Valley ales and guests, good choice of wines/gins and popular food (best to book) from daily changing menu, friendly accommodating staff; quiz third Tues of month; children and dogs welcome, picnic-sets in front garden and on gravel back terrace, handy for Berrington Hall (NT), closed Mon, otherwise open all day, no food Sun evening.

SUTTON ST NICHOLAS   SO5345
Golden Cross (01432) 880274
Corner of Ridgeway Road; HR1 3AZ Popular modernised pub with enjoyable good value food from ciabattas up, Wye Valley cask ales and guests from stone-fronted counter, good friendly service, clean décor, some breweriana, relaxed upstairs restaurant; weekend live music, juke box, pool and darts; children and dogs welcome, disabled facilities, no-smoking garden behind, pretty village and good surrounding walks, open all day Tues-Sun.

TRUMPET   SO6639
Trumpet Inn (01531) 670277
Corner A413 and A438; HR8 2RA Modernised black and white timbered pub dating from the 15th c; well kept Wadworths ales and plenty of wines by the glass, popular food from sandwiches up (some mains available in smaller helpings), efficient service, carpeted interior with beams, stripped brickwork and log fires, restaurant; children and dogs (in bar) welcome, tables in big garden behind, campsite with hard standings, open all day, closed Sun evening.

UPTON BISHOP   SO6326
★Moody Cow (01989) 780470
B4221 E of Ross-on-Wye; HR9 7TT Popular tucked-away dining pub with modern rustic décor; sandstone walls, slate floor and woodburner in L-shaped bar, biggish raftered restaurant and second more intimate eating area, highly regarded freshly made food from changing menu (can be pricey), three well kept changing ales and decent wines including some local ones, friendly service; children and dogs (treats for them) welcome, seats outside and garden growing own fruit/vegetables, closed Sun evening, Mon and Tues.

WALTERSTONE   SO3424
★Carpenters Arms (01873) 890353
Follow Walterstone signs off A465; HR2 0DX Charming unspoilt stone cottage with unchanging traditional rooms (known locally as the Gluepot – once you're in you don't want to leave); beams, broad polished flagstones, stripped-stone walls, ancient settles, a roaring fire in a gleaming black range, Wadworths 6X and a guest tapped from the cask, enjoyable straightforward food in snug main dining room with mahogany

tables and oak corner cupboards, another little dining area with old oak tables and church pews on more flagstones; no credit cards, outside loos are cold but in character; children welcome.

WELLINGTON HEATH   SO7140
Farmers Arms (01531) 634776
Off B4214 just N of Ledbury – pub signed right, from top of village; Horse Road; HR8 1LS Roomy open-plan beamed pub with enjoyable food (booking advised) including daily specials and various themed nights, Otter, Wye Valley Butty Bach and a guest, friendly staff; children and dogs welcome, picnic-sets on paved terrace, good walking country, open all day weekends, closed Mon (except bank holidays) and Tues lunchtime.

WEOBLEY   SO4051
Salutation (01544) 318443
Off A4112 SW of Leominster; HR4 8SJ Old beamed and timbered inn at top of delightful village green; enjoyable food cooked by chef-landlord from bar snacks up including set lunch/early evening deal, well kept Hobsons, Wye Valley and a local guest, Robinsons cider, friendly helpful service, bar and various dining areas, inglenook log fires; quiz/curry night first Weds of month; children welcome, sheltered back terrace, three bedrooms, good breakfast, open all day.

**WESTON-UNDER-
PENYARD**   SO6323
Weston Cross Inn (01989) 562759
A40 E of Ross; HR9 7NU Creeper-clad 19th-c roadside pub with good choice of enjoyable well priced food in bar or restaurant, Bass, Otter and a guest, Weston's cider, friendly helpful staff; children, walkers and dogs welcome, good-sized garden and play area, open all day Sat, no food Sun.

WHITBOURNE   SO7156
Live & Let Live (01886) 822276
Off A44 Bromyard–Worcester at Wheatsheaf; WR6 5SP Welcoming pub on southern edge of the village; good freshly made food (not Sun evening) from

blackboard menu including interesting specials, well kept ales such as Ludlow and Wye Valley, friendly helpful staff, beams and nice log fire, big-windowed restaurant; quiz second Sun of month; children welcome, garden with country views, open all day weekends, closed Mon lunchtime.

WIGMORE   SO4168
Oak (01568) 770424
Ford Street; HR6 9UJ Restored 16th-c coaching inn mixing original features with contemporary décor; highly regarded imaginative food (not Sun evening), Hobsons and guests, real cider and nice wines by the glass, good friendly service; children and dogs (in one part) welcome, two bedrooms, open all day Sun till 8pm, closed Mon, Tues and lunchtimes Weds-Sat.

WINFORTON   SO2946
Sun (01544) 327677
A438; HR3 6EA Welcoming village pub with enjoyable freshly cooked food (not Sun evening) including a couple of specials, Wye Valley beers and Robinsons cider, country-style beamed areas either side of central servery, stripped stone and woodburners; children and dogs welcome, garden picnic-sets, bedrooms, open all day weekends, closed Mon.

WOOLHOPE   SO6135
★Butchers Arms (01432) 860281
Off B4224 in Fownhope; HR1 4RF 16th-c low-beamed black and white pub surrounded by a pretty streamside garden with picnic-sets and new covered 'dining pods', built-in red-cushioned wall seats, farmhouse chairs and red-topped stools around a mix of old tables (some set for dining) on carpet, hunting and horse pictures on the cream walls and an open fire in the big fireplace; similarly furnished little beamed dining room, Breconshire Golden Valley, Wye Valley Bitter and Butty Bach and a couple of changing local beers on handpump, first-rate food cooked by the landlord using rare-breed meats and other carefully sourced produce; children and dogs welcome; usually closed Sun evening, Mon and Tues.

Hertfordshire

 BARNET   TQ2599   Map 5

Duke of York 𝖸 🍺

(020) 8440 4674 – www.brunningandprice.co.uk/dukeofyork

Barnet Road (A1000); EN5 4SG

Big place with reasonably priced bistro-style food and nice garden

This popular red-brick pub is set in spacious, pleasant gardens. Rather a grand building, the open doorways and stairs cleverly divide up the spreading rooms, while big windows and mirrors keep everything light and airy. There's a relaxed atmosphere and an eclectic mix of furniture on tiled or wooden flooring, hundreds of prints and photos on cream walls, fireplaces and thoughtful touches such as table lamps, books, rugs, fresh flowers and pot plants; background music. Served from an impressive counter by friendly staff, the fine range of drinks includes St Austell Brunning & Price Traditional Bitter plus guests from breweries such as Leighton Buzzard, Redemption, Sambrooks, Tring, Twickenham and Weltons on handpump, 20 wines by the glass, 30 gins and a large choice of whiskies. The garden is particularly attractive, with a range of seats, tables and picnic-sets on a tree-surrounded terrace and lawn, and a tractor in the popular play area.

🍴 Brasserie-style food includes sandwiches, chicken liver pâté with apricot chutney and granary toast, summer vegetable risotto with broad beans, radish, asparagus and lemon, a charcuterie board to share, maple and rosemary-roasted squash with herb and lemon quinoa and fennel salad, sweet potato, aubergine and spinach Malaysian curry with coconut rice and pak choi, steak burger with toppings, coleslaw and chips, slow-braised lamb shoulder with dauphinoise potatoes and gravy, and puddings such as triple chocolate brownie with chocolate sauce and vanilla ice-cream and lemon cheesecake with raspberry ripple ice-cream. *Benchmark main dish: beer-battered cod and chips £14.95. Two-course evening meal £22.00.*

Brunning & Price ~ Manager Justin Armstrong ~ Real ale ~ Open 11-11 (10.30 Sun) ~ Bar food 12-9 (9.30 Thurs-Sat) ~ Restaurant ~ Children welcome ~ Dogs allowed in bar

 FLAUNDEN   TL0101   Map 5

Bricklayers Arms 🌟 𝖸

(01442) 833322 – www.bricklayersarms.com

4 miles from M25 junction 18; village signposted off A41 – from village centre follow Boxmoor, Bovingdon road and turn right at Belsize, Watford signpost into Hogpits Bottom; HP3 0PH

Cosy country restaurant with fairly elaborate food; very good wine list

Surrounded by beautiful countryside and the rolling hills of the Chess Valley, it's hard to believe that this 18th-c pub is within such easy reach of London. Tucked away down winding lanes, this low brick and tiled pub is a civilised place for an excellent meal. It's mainly open-plan with stubs of knocked-through oak-timbered walls indicating the original room layout, and the well refurbished low-beamed bar is snug and comfortable, with a roaring log fire in winter. Stools line the brick counter where attentive staff keep Paradigm Touch Point, Tring Side Pocket for a Toad and a changing guest on handpump, an extensive wine list with 27 by the glass and a good choice of spirits; background music. In summer, the terrace and beautifully kept old-fashioned garden have seats and tables. Just up the Belsize road, a path on the left leads through delightful woods to a forested area around Hollow Hedge. The pub is just 15 minutes by car from the Warner Bros Studios where the *Harry Potter* films were made; you can tour the studios but must book in advance. Please note: dogs are allowed in the bar, but not on Sundays.

First class food includes duck liver parfait with red onion jam compote and melba toast, white crab meat with home-smoked salmon, chive cream and blinis, steamed sea bass with baby ruby chard and capers, pulled pork shoulder cooked in smoked cumin with red onion jus and Mediterranean vegetables, Tring beer-battered haddock with peas, salad and skinny fries, fillet of local beef with green peppercorn-flavoured brandy cream sauce, and puddings such as lemon and bourbon vanilla crème brûlée and white chocolate mousse with butter biscuit and peach melba top. *Benchmark main dish: duck confit with sweet and sour gooseberry jus £18.95. Two-course evening meal £28.00.*

Free house ~ Licensee Alvin Michaels ~ Real ale ~ Open 12-11; 12-midnight Sat; 12-10 Sun ~ Bar food 12-2.30, 6-8.30; 12-9 Sun and bank holidays ~ Restaurant ~ Children welcome ~ Dogs allowed in bar

FRITHSDEN
Alford Arms ⭐♟ ▢

TL0109 Map 5

(01442) 864480 – www.alfordarmsfrithsden.co.uk
A4146 from Hemel Hempstead to Water End, then second left (after Red Lion) signed Frithsden, then left at T junction, then right after 0.25 miles; HP1 3DD

Hertfordshire Dining Pub of the Year

Thriving dining pub with a chic interior, good food from imaginative menu and a thoughtful wine list

A meal in this attractive Victorian pub makes an ideal addition to a stroll in the lovely National Trust Ashridge Forest nearby – and walkers, dogs and children are all welcome. The elegant, understated interior has simple prints on pale cream walls, with blocks picked out in rich heritage colours, and an appealing mix of antique furniture from Georgian chairs to old commode stands on bare boards and patterned quarry tiles. A good mix of both drinkers and diners creates a cheerful atmosphere, and helpful staff serve Sharps Doom Bar and guest ales such as Chiltern Beechwood Bitter, Marlow Rebellion IPA and Tring Side Pocket for a Toad on handpump, 26 wines by the glass (including two sparkling ones) from a Europe-only list, 20 gins and 24 whiskies and bourbons; background jazz and darts. There are plenty of tables outside.

Creative food with an emphasis on local suppliers includes bubble and squeak with oak-smoked bacon, poached egg and hollandaise sauce, local goats cheese with roast beetroot, tomato panzanella salad with chargrilled courgette, king prawn linguine with smoked bacon, Bombay-spiced roast cauliflower with coriander couscous, pea pakoras and mint yoghurt, pan-roasted Cornish hake with peas, parmentier potatoes, tartare sauce and beer scraps, and puddings such as lemon posset with shortbread and elderflower strawberries and iced banana parfait with peanut crumble and chocolate sauce. *Benchmark main dish: free-range pork loin holstein with parmesan polenta chips, watercress and egg £17.00. Two-course evening meal £24.00.*

Salisbury Pubs ~ Lease Darren Johnston ~ Real ale ~ Open 11-11; 12-10.30 Sun ~ Bar food 12-2.30, 6.30-9.30; 12-3, 6-10 Fri, Sat; 12-9 Sun ~ Restaurant ~ Children welcome ~ Dogs allowed in bar

HERTFORD HEATH
TL3510 Map 5

College Arms 🌟 ♀

(01992) 558856 – www.thecollegearmshertfordheath.com
London Road; B1197; SG13 7PW

Light and airy rooms with contemporary furnishings, friendly service, good, interesting food and real ales; seats outside

With its hearty food, good choice of drinks and numerous events throughout the year, this is an enjoyable place that our readers return to on a regular basis. The bar has long cushioned wall seats and pale leather dining chairs around tables on rugs or wooden floorboards, and a modern bar counter where attentive staff serve quickly changing ales such as St Austell Tribute and Proper Job on handpump, a decent choice of wines by the glass and around 15 gins; background music. The snug area has more long wall seats with brown leather armchairs, a couple of cushioned pews and a wood-burning stove in an old brick fireplace. The elegant, partly carpeted dining room contains a real mix of antique-style dining chairs and tables. There are benches and tables among flowering pots on the back terrace and in the spacious, sunny garden.

🌟 Well executed food includes sandwiches, braised pig cheeks with mustard, cider sauce and parsnip crisp on sourdough, stuffed flat mushroom gratin and crusty bread, aubergine parmigiano with salad and fries, burger with toppings, slaw and fries, cumberland sausage and mash, Catalan fish stew, crab linguine, and puddings such as cheesecake of the week and lemon posset with poppyseed shortbread. *Benchmark main dish: beer-battered fish and chips £13.50. Two-course evening meal £19.50.*

Punch ~ Lease Andy Lilley ~ Real ale ~ Open 12-11; 12-midnight Fri; 9.30am-midnight Sat; 9.30am-8pm Sun ~ Bar food 12-3, 6-9; 12-9.30 Fri; 9.30-9.30 Sat; 9.30-6 Sun ~ Restaurant ~ Children welcome ~ Dogs allowed in bar

POTTERS CROUCH
TL1105 Map 5

Holly Bush 🍺 £

(01727) 851792 – www.thehollybushpub.co.uk
2.25 miles from M25 junction 21A: A405 towards St Albans, then first left, then after a mile turn left (ie away from Chiswell Green), then at T junction turn right into Blunts Lane; can also be reached fairly quickly, with a good map, from M1 junctions 6 and 8; AL2 3NN

Neat pub with gleaming furniture, well kept Fullers beers, good value food and an attractive garden

This attractive, tranquil 17th-c pub is tucked away in an idyllic hamlet – it's the ideal escape from the traffic-laden M25. The long, stepped bar has particularly well kept Fullers ESB, London Pride and Seafarers on handpump and several wines by the glass. There are quite a few antique dressers (several filled with plates), a number of comfortably cushioned settles, some antlers, a fox's mask, a fine old clock with a lovely chime, daily papers and (on the right as you enter) a big fireplace. In the evening, neatly placed candles cast glimmering light over darkly varnished tables, all sporting fresh flowers. The fenced-off back garden (the only place where dogs are allowed) has plenty of sturdy picnic-sets on a lawn surrounded by handsome trees.

Rewarding food includes sandwiches and platters, halloumi bites with sweet dipping sauce, smoked salmon with lemon crème fraîche, lamb koftas with tzatziki, chicken breast or beef burger with toppings, coleslaw and chips, cumberland sausages with mashed potatoes and gravy, smoked haddock fishcakes with roasted vine tomatoes, chilli con carne, and puddings such as cherry and almond tartlet and cinnamon-dusted Belgian waffle with maple syrup. *Benchmark main dish: steak in ale pie £13.50. Two-course evening meal £20.00.*

Fullers ~ Tenants Steven and Vanessa Williams ~ Real ale ~ Open 12-2.30, 6-11; 12-11 Sat; 12-5 Sun ~ Bar food 12-2 Mon-Weds; 12-2, 6-9 Thurs-Sat; 12-2.30 Sun ~ Children welcome until 7.30pm

PRESTON

Red Lion 🍺 £

TL1824   Map 5

(01462) 459585 – www.theredlionpreston.co.uk
Village signposted off B656 S of Hitchin; The Green; SG4 7UD

Homely village local with changing beers, fair-priced food and neat colourful garden

Perhaps one of the secrets to this pub's success is the fact that in 1982 it became the first pub in the country to be owned by the local community – and they've never looked back. It's a busy and cheerful place. The main room on the left has grey wainscoting, sturdy, well varnished furniture including padded country kitchen chairs and cast-iron-framed tables on patterned carpet, a generous window seat, fox hunting prints and a log fire in a brick fireplace. The somewhat smaller room on the right has steeplechase prints, varnished plank panelling and brocaded bar stools on flagstones around the servery; background music, darts and dominoes. Timothy Taylors Landlord and Tring Side Pocket for a Toad with guests such as Butcombe Original, Oakham JHB and Wolf in Sheeps Clothing on handpump, five farm ciders, seven wines by the glass (including an English house wine), a perry and winter mulled wine. A few picnic-sets on grass at the front face lime trees on the peaceful village green opposite, while the pergola-covered back terrace and good-sized sheltered garden with its colourful herbaceous border have seats and picnic-sets (some shade is provided by a tall ash tree). Check the website for details of circular walks from the pub.

Enjoyable home-made food from a changing menu includes sandwiches, sweet potato and spinach curry, prawns with garlic and chilli, wild mushroom, stilton and broccoli crumble, Asian-spiced sea bass, steak and red wine pie, chilli con carne, spiced lentil or lamb moussaka, moules frites, and puddings such as crème brûlée and passion-fruit pavlova. *Benchmark main dish: fish pie £12.50. Two-course evening meal £19.00.*

Free house ~ Licensee Raymond Lambe ~ Real ale ~ Open 12-3, 5-11; 12-midnight Sat; 12-10.30 Sun ~ Bar food 12-2, 6.30-8.30; not Sun evening, Mon ~ Children welcome ~ Dogs allowed in bar

---

We mention bottled beers and spirits only if there is something unusual about them – imported Belgian real ales, say, or dozens of malt whiskies. Please do let us know about them in your reports.

SARRATT

TQ0499 Map 5

Cricketers ♀ ◖

(01923) 270877 – www.brunningandprice.co.uk/cricketers

The Green; WD3 6AS

Plenty to look at in rambling rooms, up to six real ales, nice wines, enjoyable food and friendly staff; seats outside

This sizeable inn has cleverly created numerous little snugs and alcoves among its interlinked rooms, adding to its character and appeal. There are all manner of antique dining chairs and tables on rugs or stripped floorboards, comfortable armchairs or tub seats, cushioned pews, wall seats and two open fires in raised fireplaces; decoration includes cricketing memorabilia, fresh flowers, large plants and church candles. St Austell Brunning & Price Traditional Bitter plus guests from local breweries such as Chiltern, Malt, Paradigm (brewed in the village) and Tring on handpump, good wines by the glass, over 40 gins and 50 malt whiskies; background music and board games. Several sets of french windows open on to the back terrace where there are tables and chairs, with picnic-sets on grass next to a colourfully painted tractor. This is a pleasant village setting overlooking the green and duck pond.

 Interesting modern food includes sandwiches, smoked salmon with orange and beetroot salad, crispy baby squid and sweet chilli sauce, sweet potato, cauliflower, almond and chickpea tagine with couscous and tempura broccoli, chicken, ham and leek pie, Sicilian fish stew, pea and mint tortellini, and puddings such as summer pudding with clotted cream and sticky toffee pudding with toffee sauce. *Benchmark main dish: braised lamb shoulder with dauphinoise potatoes and rosemary gravy £18.95. Two-course evening meal £23.00.*

Brunning & Price ~ Manager Simon Walsh ~ Real ale ~ Open 11.30am-11pm; 11.30am-10.30pm Sun ~ Bar food 12-9; 12-9.30 Sat, Sun ~ Restaurant ~ Children welcome ~ Dogs allowed in bar

ST ALBANS

TL1308 Map 5

Prae Wood Arms ♀ ◖

(01727) 229090 – www.brunningandprice.co.uk/praewoodarms

Garden House Lane; AL3 6JZ

Spreading manor house in extensive grounds, with interestingly furnished rooms, plenty to look at, a pleasing range of drinks and modern food

This large, sprawling yet elegant pub, with its stone terrace overlooking extensive lawns that gently slope down towards the River Ver at the bottom of the gardens, remains an understandably popular choice with our readers. The five open fires here certainly keep this large and rather gracious pub warm in winter. The various chatty interconnected bar and dining areas have antique-style dining chairs and tables of every size and shape on bare boards, parquet and carpet, pale-painted walls that are hung with portraits, prints and huge mirrors, and elegant metal or glass chandeliers. Also, lots of books on shelves and house plants and stone and glass bottles on windowsills. Wooden stools line the counter where friendly, courteous young staff serve St Austell Brunning & Price Traditional Bitter with guests from breweries such as Arbor, Redemption, Salopian and Tring on handpump, 18 wines by the glass and 80 gins; background music and board games. The loos are upstairs.

A wide choice of modern food includes sandwiches, deep fried West Country brie with apricot chutney, braised ox cheek pie with roasted cauliflower, carrot purée and deep-fried kale, pea and mint tortellini with garden pea velouté and asparagus, pork and leek sausages with mash and onion gravy, steak burger with toppings, coleslaw and chips, Malaysian chicken curry with coconut rice and steamed pak choi, sea trout with baby spinach, fennel, gnocchi and tomato salsa, roast pork tenderloin with colcannon potato, and puddings such as lemon meringue roulade with raspberry sorbet and crème brûlée. *Benchmark main dish: beer-battered cod and chips £14.95. Two-course evening meal £24.00.*

Brunning & Price ~ Manager Rebecca Hall ~ Real ale ~ Open 11.30-11; 11.30-10 Sun ~ Bar food 12-9.30; 12-10 Fri, Sat; 12-9 Sun ~ Restaurant ~ Children welcome ~ Dogs allowed in bar

Also Worth a Visit in Hertfordshire

Besides the fully inspected pubs, you might like to try these pubs that have been recommended to us and described by readers. Do tell us what you think of them: feedback@goodguides.com

ALDBURY SP9612
Greyhound (01442) 851228
Stocks Road; village signed from A4251 Tring–Berkhamsted, and from B4506; HP23 5RT Picturesque village pub with some signs of real age inside; inglenook in cosy traditional beamed bar, more contemporary area with leather chairs, airy oak-floored back restaurant with wicker seats at big tables, Badger ales and 14 wines by the glass, generally well liked food from lunchtime sandwiches, sharing plates and pubby choices up, set menu Mon-Thurs; children welcome, dogs in bar, front benches facing green with whipping post, stocks and duck pond, suntrap gravel courtyard, eight bedrooms (some in newer building behind), open all day, food all day weekends (till 7.30pm Sun).

ALDBURY SP9612
★**Valiant Trooper** (01442) 851203
Trooper Road (towards Aldbury Common); off B4506 N of Berkhamsted; HP23 5RW Cheery traditional 17th-c village pub; appealing beamed bar with red and black floor tiles, built-in wall benches, a pew and small dining chairs around country tables, two further rooms (one with inglenook) and back barn restaurant, enjoyable generously served food (all day Sat, not Sun-Weds evenings), Chiltern, Tring and three guests, real cider and plenty of wines by the glass, friendly helpful staff; background music; children and dogs (in bar) welcome, enclosed garden with wooden adventure playground, well placed for Ashridge Estate beechwoods, open all day.

ALDENHAM TQ1498
Round Bush (01923) 855532
Roundbush Lane; WD25 8BG Cheery and bustling traditional village pub with plenty of atmosphere; two front rooms and back restaurant, popular generously served food at fair prices, well kept ales with regulars

Courage Directors, Eagle IPA and St Austell Tribute and one guest, friendly efficient staff; quiz first Mon of month, occasional live music and karaoke, darts; children, walkers and dogs welcome, big enclosed garden with play area, open (and food) all day.

ALLENS GREEN TL4517
Queens Head (01279) 723393
Village signed from West Road, Sawbridgeworth; CM21 0LS Friendly semi-detached village drinkers' pub owned by the local community; four well kept beers: Fullers London Pride, Mighty Oak Maldon Gold and two guests (many more at bank holiday beer festivals), also good range of ciders/perries, straightforward reasonably priced food; live music during beer festivals; dogs welcome, large garden, open all day weekends, closed lunchtimes Mon and Tues.

ARDELEY TL3027
Jolly Waggoner (01438) 861350
Off B1037 NE of Stevenage; SG2 7AH Cottagey beamed 16th-c pub in attractive tucked-away village with thatched cottages around the green; Buntingford Twitchell and a couple of guests from the likes of Adnams, Greene King and Leighton Buzzard on handpump, a good choice of wines by the glass and their own vodka distilled on-site, traditionally furnished bar with horsebrasses above the log fire, tartan-upholstered armchairs, high chairs against the counter, lots of nooks and corners, also restaurant extended into cottage next door with pleasing home-made food using their own meat and farm produce; darts and background music; picnic-sets on gravel and in lawned garden, children and dogs welcome, disabled access, open all day, food all day weekends – for sale as we went to press, so may be changes.

AYOT ST LAWRENCE TL1916
Brocket Arms (01438) 820250
Off B651 N of St Albans; AL6 9BT Attractive 14th-c country inn with low beams

and inglenook log fires, entrance corridor with bar on left and dining room to the right, good traditional food (special diets catered for), friendly helpful staff, six real ales such as Greene King, Nethergate and Sharps and own house beer brewed by Tring, wide choice of wines by the glass; live music including jazz and open mike nights, quiz second Sun of month; children welcome, dogs in bar, nice suntrap walled garden with play area, handy for George Bernard Shaw's house (Shaw's Corner – NT), six comfortable bedrooms, open all day, no food Sun evening.

BALDOCK · TL2433
Orange Tree · (01462) 892341
Norton Road; SG7 5AW Unpretentious old two-bar pub with up to 13 well kept ales including three regulars (Greene King Abbott and IPA and Tring Mansion Mild), four real ciders and large selection of whiskies, good value home-made food (all day Sat, till 6pm Sun) including range of pies and local sausages, friendly helpful staff; quiz Tues, folk club every other Weds, sports TV; children, dogs and muddy boots welcome, sizeable garden with play area, open all day Thurs-Sun.

BARKWAY · TL3834
Tally Ho · (01763) 848071
London Road (B1368); SG8 8EX Little village-edge pub with clean modern décor; mix of wooden furniture on light boarded floor, log fire in central brick fireplace, Greene King and three changing ales and good range of other drinks, limited menu of sandwiches, soup and bar snacks (may be fish and chip van or pop-up restaurants), friendly efficient staff; quiz second Weds of month; dogs and children welcome, decked seating area at front, picnic-sets and weeping willow in garden beyond car park, open all day Sat, 1.30-6pm Sun, from 4.30pm other days.

BENINGTON · TL3023
Bell · (01438) 869827
Town Lane; just past Post Office, towards Stevenage; SG2 7LA Traditional 16th-c pub in very pretty village; local beers such as Buntingford and Hadham and enjoyable Caribbean food (licensees are from Trinidad), low beams, sloping walls and large inglenook; occasional music nights and other events such as quiz every month; big garden with country views, handy for Benington Lordship Gardens, two cottages next door, open until 7pm Sun (food till 6pm), closed Mon, Tues and lunchtime Weds.

BERKHAMSTED · SP9907
Boat · (01422) 877152
Gravel Path, by bridge; HP4 2EF Cheerful open-plan Fullers dining pub in attractive canalside setting (can get packed in fine weather); their ales kept well and guests such as Haresfoot and Tring, good

choice of wines by the glass, cocktails, popular food from weekday lunchtime sandwiches and small plates to daily specials, mix of seating including padded stools and leather chesterfields on mainly parquet flooring, painted panelling and contemporary artwork, a couple of Victorian fireplaces; background music, live music last weekend of month; children and dogs welcome, french windows to paved terrace overlooking towpath and canal, moorings, open (and food) all day.

BERKHAMSTED · SP9807
Highwayman · (01442) 285480
High Street; HP4 1AQ Recently refurbished bustling town pub (White Brasserie Company) with plenty of room for both drinkers and diners; relaxed bar with big windows overlooking the street, upholstered and leather chairs around all sorts of tables, chic modern farmhouse themed decorations, well kept Sharps Doom Bar, Timothy Taylors Landlord and a guest such as St Austell Tribute, over 20 wines by the glass and well liked modern food from interesting French-influenced menu, cheerful helpful young staff; some live music, quiz Weds, sports TV, disabled access, children and dogs (in bar) welcome, back terraced garden, open (and food) all day.

BERKHAMSTED · SP9907
Rising Sun · (01442) 864913
George Street; HP4 2EG Victorian canalside pub known locally as the Riser; five well kept ales including one badged for them from Tring, more than 15 ciders/perries (four beer/cider festivals a year) and interesting range of spirits, two very small traditional rooms with a few basic chairs and tables and a coal fire, snuff and cigars for sale, no food apart from substantial ploughman's, friendly service; background music, children and dogs welcome, chairs out by canal and well worn seating in covered side beer garden, colourful hanging baskets, open all day.

BRAUGHING · TL3925
Axe & Compass · (01920) 821610
Just off B1368; The Street; SG11 2QR Nice pink-painted country pub in pretty village with ford; enjoyable freshly prepared food from varied menu, own-baked bread, well kept ales including Harveys and Weetwood and several wines by the glass, friendly staff, mix of furnishings on wood floors in two roomy bars, lots of old local photographs, log fires, restaurant with little shop selling home-made chutney and relish; well behaved children and dogs welcome, garden overlooking playing field, outside bar, usually open all day Thurs-Sun.

BRAUGHING · TL3925
Brown Bear · (01920) 822157
Just off B1368; The Street; SG11 2QF Steps up to traditional little low-beamed pub

with inglenook bar; three well kept changing ales and enjoyable home-cooked pubby food (not Mon or Tues) from ciabattas to good fish and chips, friendly staff, dining room with another good fire; Thurs quiz, monthly live music/open mike nights, games including darts, dominoes and shove-ha'penny; tricky disabled access, picnic-sets in garden behind with pizza oven, barbecue and pétanque, attractive village, open all day (till 6pm Sun, Mon, opens 3pm Mon, Tues).

BRAUGHING   TL3925
Golden Fleece (01920) 823555
Green End (B1368); SG11 2PE 17th-c village dining pub with good food (special diets catered for) from chef-landlady including some imaginative choices, popular tapas night and curry evenings, Adnams Southwold and local guests such as New River, plenty of wines by the glass, cheerful service, bare-boards bar and two dining rooms, beams, timbers and good log fire, pictures for sale; quiz nights, children welcome, circular picnic-sets out at front, back garden with metal furniture on split-level paved terrace, play area, open all day weekends (food till 6pm Sun).

BRICKET WOOD   TL1302
Gate (01923) 678944
Station Road/Smug Oak Lane; AL2 3PW Popular family pub freshened up under new management with good sensibly priced home-cooked food including pub favourites and pizzas, ales such as Adnams Ghost Ship, friendly service, bar with log fire and side dining area; monthly quiz; cyclists, walkers, children and dogs welcome, benches out front and garden (summer barbecues); other changes are planned including a more 'foodie' menu.

BURNHAM GREEN   TL2516
White Horse (01438) 798100
Off B1000 N of Welwyn; Whitehorse Lane; AL6 0HA Well supported village-green dining pub; mix of modern and traditional rustic décor including attractive 17th-c beamed core, good food from varied menu, two McMullens ales and two guests, friendly obliging service; monthly quiz; children and dogs (in bar) welcome, good-sized pretty garden behind with duck pond and play area, open all day (till 9pm Sun).

BUSHEY   TQ1394
Horse & Chains (020) 8421 9907
High Street; WD23 1BL New owners and a major refurbishment for this comfortably modernised pub plus a new menu with a South African slant (seafood sharing platters,

curries), well kept ales from breweries such as Tring, and good choice of wines by the glass, efficient friendly service, woodburner in big inglenook, kitchen view from compact dining room; sports TV; children and dogs welcome, open all day Fri-Sun, closed Mon.

BUSHEY   TQ1395
King Stag (020) 8950 2988
Bournehall Road; WD23 3EH Popular mock-Tudor Victorian pub tucked away in residential street; opened-up bare-boards interior, good choice of local beers along with a Greene King house ale, enjoyable food from local suppliers including weekday set lunch, Mon burger night and Weds steaks, friendly helpful service; variety of events; children and dogs welcome (menus for both), picnic-sets in back beer garden, open all day Sat, Sun, closed Mon, Tues.

BUSHEY   TQ1395
Swan (020) 8950 2256
Park Road; turning off A411; WD23 3EE Homely atmosphere in this traditional single-room terraced pub; well kept Black Sheep, Greene King, Timothy Taylors and Youngs, some snacky food, old photos and other memorabilia, coal fires; sports TVs, darts and board games; beer garden behind (outside ladies' loo), open all day.

CHAPMORE END   TL3216
Woodman (01920) 463339
Off B158 Wadesmill–Bengeo; pub signed 300 metres W of A602 roundabout; OS Sheet 166 map reference 328164; SG12 0HF Early Victorian local in peaceful country hamlet; plain seats around stripped pub tables, floor tiles or broad bare boards, working period fireplaces, two well kept Greene King ales and two guests poured from the cask, Thai and tapas menus Weds-Sat evenings, friendly staff, conservatory; children and dogs welcome, picnic-sets out in front under a couple of walnut trees, bigger back garden with fenced play area and boules, maybe summer Sun barbecues.

CHIPPERFIELD   TL0400
Cart & Horses (01923) 263763
Quickmoor Lane/Common Wood; WD4 9BA Smallish 18th-c wisteria-clad pub popular for its enjoyable generously served food including bargain specials, two or three well kept changing ales and good choice of wines by the glass, friendly staff; children and dogs welcome, picnic-sets in big garden with marquee and play area, nice surrounding countryside and walks, open all day.

Post Office address codings confusingly give the impression that some pubs are in Hertfordshire, when they're really in Bedfordshire, Buckinghamshire or Cambridgeshire (which is where we list them).

CHORLEYWOOD   TQ0294
Land of Liberty, Peace & Plenty (01923) 282226
Long Lane, Heronsgate, just off M25 junction 17; WD3 5BS Traditional 19th-c drinkers' pub in leafy outskirts; half a dozen well kept interesting ales and good choice of ciders/perries, snacky food such as pasties, simple layout, darts, skittles and board games; background jazz, TV (on request), no mobile phones or children inside; dogs welcome, garden with pavilion, open all day.

CHORLEYWOOD   TQ0295
Stag (01923) 282090
Long Lane, Heronsgate, just off M25 junction 17; WD3 5BT Open-plan Edwardian dining pub with good varied choice of food from sandwiches and tapas up, well kept McMullens ales and several wines by the glass, friendly attentive service, bar and eating areas extending into conservatory, woodburner in raised hearth; daily papers, children and dogs welcome, disabled access, tables on back lawn, open all day, food all day Weds-Sun.

CHORLEYWOOD   TQ0396
White Horse (01923) 283033
A404 just off M25 junction 18; WD3 5SD Black-beamed roadside pub with good food such as pizzas, tapas and panini, Greene King ales, friendly helpful staff, big log fire; sports TV; children and dogs (in bar) welcome, small back terrace, open all day.

COLNEY HEATH   TL2007
Plough (01727) 823720
Sleapshyde; handy for A1(M) junction 3; A414 towards St Albans, double back at first roundabout then turn left; AL4 0SE Part-thatched 17th-c dining pub; enjoyable interesting food from snacks up including vegan choices, four real ales, three proper ciders and wide selection of wines and gins, attentive friendly service, cosy low-beamed interior with two fireplaces; children and dogs welcome, front and back terraces, picnic-sets on lawn overlooking fields, open all day, no evening food Sun or Mon.

ESSENDON   TL2608
Candlestick (01707) 261322
West End Lane; AL9 6BA Peacefully located country pub run by father and son team; enjoyable pubby food, three well kept beers and several wines by the glass, relaxed friendly atmosphere, comfortable clean interior with faux black timbers, wood and carpeted floors and log fires; quiz nights; children and dogs welcome, plenty of seats outside, good walks, closed Mon and Tues, otherwise open all day.

GILSTON   TL4313
Plume of Feathers (01279) 424154
Pye Corner; CM20 2RD Old beamed corner pub with decent choice of well priced food (all day Fri and Sat, till 7pm Sun) including pizzas and cook-your-own meat on a volcanic rock, Courage Best, Adnams Broadside and local guests, good choice of wines by the glass, friendly if not always speedy service, carpeted interior with brass-hooded log fire; background music, children welcome, seats on terrace and fenced grassy area with play equipment.

GREAT AMWELL   TL3712
George IV (01920) 870039
St Johns Lane; SG12 9SW Pleasant 19th-c brick pub in pretty spot by church; good well presented food cooked by owner-chef from interesting snacks and pub staples up, occasional themed evenings, can eat in log-fire bar or back restaurant, well kept local beers Farr Brew Farr Apart and Hadham Oddy and a good choice of wines and gins, friendly helpful staff; quiz last Tues of month; attractive outside seating areas front and back, River Lea nearby, open all day Sat, till 6pm Sun, closed Mon (except 12-6pm bank holidays).

GREAT HORMEAD   TL4030
Three Tuns (01763) 289405
B1038/Horseshoe Hill; SG9 0NT Old thatched and timbered country pub-restaurant in lovely surroundings; enjoyable home-made food including blackboard specials, popular fish and chips night Thurs, Buntingford, New River and a couple of guests, good choice of wines by the glass and local gin, small linked areas, huge inglenook with another great hearth behind, back conservatory extension; monthly quiz, children, walkers and dogs welcome, nice secure garden, open all day Sun till 7pm, closed Mon apart from bank holidays.

HALLS GREEN   TL2728
Rising Sun (01462) 790487
NW of Stevenage; from A1(M) junction 9 follow Weston signs off B197, then left in village, right by duck pond; SG4 7DR Welcoming 18th-c beamed and carpeted country pub; enjoyable good value traditional food (not Sun evening) in bar or conservatory restaurant, well kept McMullens ales, friendly helpful service, woodburner

---

Real ale may be served from handpumps, electric pumps (not just the on-off switches used for keg beer) or – common in Scotland – tall taps called founts (pronounced 'fonts') where a separate pump pushes the beer up under air pressure.

and open fire; children and dogs (in bar) welcome, disabled access, big garden with terrace, boules and plenty for kids including swings and playhouse, open all day Sat and Sun, closed Mon.

HARPENDEN
TL1312

White Horse (01582) 469290

Redbourn Lane, Hatching Green (B487 just W of A1081 roundabout); AL5 2JP Smart up-to-date Peach group dining pub; chatty split-level bar (one side a former stables), stools by round tables, old parquet flooring and flagstones, some timbers and inglenook log fire, Greene King, Tring Side Pocket and a couple of guests, 17 wines by the glass from a comprehensive list and interesting range of gins, airy dining room with a swish mix of grey, yellow and red upholstered chairs, pews and cushioned wall seats around pale wooden tables on stripped boards, enjoyable food including weekday fixed-price lunch; background music, board games; children and dogs (in bar) welcome, contemporary tables and chairs under parasols on large flagstoned terrace, open (and food) all day from 9.30am breakfast on.

HATFIELD
TL2308

Eight Bells (01707) 272477

Park Street, Old Hatfield; AL9 5AX Attractive old beamed pub (two buildings knocked together) with Charles Dickens association; small rooms on different levels, wood floors and open fire, recently taken over by Farr Brew and the four beers include their own Our Greatest Golden and Our Most Perfect Pale, good value lunchtime food; live music Fri, games machine, children and dogs welcome, tables in backyard, open all day.

HATFIELD
TL2108

Harpsfield Hall (01707) 265840

Parkhouse Court, off Comet Way (A1001); AL10 9RQ Recently built aviation-themed Wetherspoons with large hangar-like interior; interesting décor using some old aircraft parts including a seating booth made from a jet engine housing, good range of beers and other drinks from long servery with time-zoned clocks in aeroplane windows, their usual good value food, friendly staff; TVs, children welcome, disabled access, tables on paved terrace, open all day from 8am.

HATFIELD
TL2308

Horse & Groom (01707) 264765

Park Street, Old Hatfield; AL9 5AT Friendly old town local with up to half a dozen well kept ales (beer festivals) and good value pubby lunchtime food, also Fri Thai night and Tues and Sat suppers (free if you buy a pint), dark beams and good winter fire, old local photographs, darts and dominoes; quiz Thurs, sports TV; dogs welcome, a few tables out behind, handy for Hatfield House, open all day.

HEMEL HEMPSTEAD
TL0411

Crown & Sceptre (01442) 234660

Bridens Camp; leaving on A4146, right at Flamstead/Markyate sign opposite Red Lion; HP2 6EY Traditional rambling pub, welcoming and relaxed, with well kept Greene King ales and several guests, generous helpings of good reasonably priced pubby food including Tues pie and pint night, cheerful efficient staff, dining room with woodburner; children and dogs (on leads) allowed, picnic-sets at front and in pleasant garden, good walks, open all day weekends, no food Sun evening.

HEMEL HEMPSTEAD
TL0604

Paper Mill (01442) 288800

Stationers Place, Apsley; HP3 9RH Modern canalside pub built on site of former paper mill; spacious open-plan interior with upstairs restaurant, Fullers ales and a couple of guests (usually local), food from sandwiches and sharing plates up, friendly staff, log fire; Mon quiz and live music nights, children welcome, tables outside on balcony and by the water, open (and food) all day.

HERTFORD
TL3212

Old Barge (01992) 581871

The Folly; SG14 1QD Red-brick bay-windowed pub by River Lee Navigation canal; clean quaint interior arranged around central bar, wood and flagstone floors, some black beams and log fire, well kept Marstons-related beers and five guests, real ciders/perries and enjoyable reasonably priced food (not Sun evening) from sandwiches up, friendly staff; background music, Sun quiz, music quiz last Thurs of month, games machines; children and dogs (in one part of bar) welcome, a few tables out in front, more to the side, open all day.

HERTFORD
TL3212

Old Cross Tavern (01992) 583133

St Andrew Street; SG14 1JA Chatty old red-brick pub popular for its half a dozen particularly well kept daily changing ales including own microbrews, also bottled Belgian beers and Aspall's cider, some snacky food such as pork pies, friendly staff and cosy relaxed atmosphere, open fires; May and Oct beer festivals; dogs welcome, small back terrace, open all day weekends, from 4.30pm other days.

HERTFORD
TL3212

Salisbury Arms (01992) 583091

Fore Street; SG14 1BZ Rambling 18th-c pub-hotel with three bars and smart restaurant; well kept McMullens ales, plenty of wines by the glass and good fairly priced food from sandwiches up, afternoon teas, efficient cheerful service, splendid Jacobean staircase to bedrooms; open all day.

HERTFORD HEATH
TL3511
Goat (01992) 535788
Vicarage Causeway; SG13 7RT Popular 16th-c low-beamed pub facing village green; generous helpings of enjoyable fair-priced food including deals, Greene King IPA and a couple of guests, friendly helpful staff, restaurant; quiz last Thurs of month, classic car meeting first Sun; children and dogs (in lower bar) welcome, picnic-sets out at front, open all day, no food Sun evening.

HIGH WYCH
TL4614
Rising Sun (01279) 724099
Signed off A1184 Harlow–Sawbridgeworth; CM21 0HZ Opened-up 19th-c red-brick village local; up to five well kept ales such as Adnams, Oakham and Woodfordes tapped from the cask, good home-cooked food, friendly staff and regulars, woodburner; walkers and dogs welcome, small side garden, closed Tues lunchtime.

HITCHIN
TL1828
Half Moon (01462) 453010
Queen Street; SG4 9TZ Tucked-away local freshened up a few years ago by friendly licensees; ten regularly changing well kept ales (beer festivals Apr and Oct) and good value pubby food from sandwiches up; quiz first Tues of month, some live music; children (till 8pm) and dogs welcome, back garden with terrace, open all day (till 1am Fri, Sat), kitchen closed Sun evening, Mon and Tues.

HITCHIN
TL5122
Victoria (01462) 432682
Ickleford Road, at roundabout; SG5 1TJ Popular wedge-shaped Victorian corner local; Greene King ales and four guests, enjoyable reasonably priced lunchtime food (also Mon and Fri evenings); events including beer festivals, live music and quiz nights, barn function room; children and dogs welcome, seats in sunny beer garden, open all day.

HUNSDON
TL4114
Fox & Hounds (01279) 843999
High Street; SG12 8NJ Village dining pub with good enterprising food from chef-landlord, not cheap but they do offer a weekday set menu, Adnams Southwold, a local guest and wide choice of wines by the glass, beams, panelling and fireside leather sofas, more formal restaurant with period furniture, bookcase door to lavatories; children welcome, dogs in bar, heated covered terrace, closed Sun evening, Mon.

LEY GREEN
TL1624
Plough (01438) 871394
Plough Lane, Kings Walden; SG4 8LA Small brick-built rural local, plain and old-fashioned, with chatty regulars, two well kept Greene King ales and a guest, simple low-priced food; live music Tues and Sat nights, children and dogs welcome, big informal garden with peaceful views, good walks nearby, camping, closed lunchtimes Mon and Tues, otherwise open all day.

LITTLE HADHAM
TL4322
Nags Head (01279) 771555
Hadham Ford, towards Much Hadham; SG11 2AX Popular and welcoming 16th-c country dining pub with small linked black-beamed rooms; enjoyable food from snacks to daily specials including good Sun roasts, close-set tables in cosy bar with three regular ales and decent wines, restaurant down a couple of steps; occasional quiz nights; children welcome in eating areas, dogs in main bar, tables out at front and two courtyard gardens behind, open all day Fri-Sun.

LONG MARSTON
SP8915
Queens Head (01296) 668368
Tring Road; HP23 4QL Welcoming beamed village local with enjoyable good value food from pub favourites up, well kept beers including Tring Side Pocket for a Toad and a couple of guests, helpful friendly service, open fire; children welcome, seats on terrace, good walks nearby, two bedrooms in annexe, open all day weekends, closed weekday lunchtimes, no food Sun evening and Mon-Weds.

MARSWORTH
SP9114
Anglers Retreat (01442) 822250
Startops End; HP23 4LJ Homely unpretentious pub near Tring Reservoirs and Grand Union Canal; smallish L-shaped angler-theme bar with stuffed fish and live parrot (Rosie), four well kept ales including St Austell Tribute, Tring Side Pocket for a Toad and two guests, wide choice of good value food from baguettes up, Mon pizza night, friendly welcoming staff; Thurs live music, Sun poker, outside gents'; children, walkers and dogs (in bar) welcome, side garden with tables under parasols, duck pond, aviary and an old tractor, bedrooms (some in separate building), open all day.

NUTHAMPSTEAD
TL4134
★Woodman (01763) 848328
Off B1368 S of Barkway; SG8 8NB Tucked-away thatched and weatherboarded village pub under long-serving family; 17th-c low beams/timbers and inglenook log fire, Adnams, Greene King and guests tapped from the cask, enjoyable home-made food (not Sun evening) from traditional choices up, friendly service, dining extension, interesting USAF memorabilia and outside memorial (near World War II airfield); children in family room with play area, dogs in bar, benches out overlooking tranquil lane, two comfortable bedrooms, open all day, closed Mon lunchtime.

PIRTON   TL1431
Motte & Bailey (01462) 712730
Great Green; SG5 3QD Welcoming
village-green pub with enjoyable food from
shortish list including set menu, real ales
such as Greene King, Sharps and Timothy
Taylors, good selection of wines and gins,
friendly helpful service; live music and quiz
nights; children and dogs welcome, picnic-
sets out at front behind picket fence, more
in back garden with play equipment, good
surrounding walks, open all day, no food Mon
or evening Sun.

POTTEN END   TL0108
Martins Pond (01442) 864318
The Green; HP4 2QQ Refurbished 19th-c
brick dining pub facing village green and
pond; popular freshly prepared food from
sandwiches up, well kept beers (including
local craft brewer Mad Squirrel), several
wines by the glass and decent range of
gins, friendly attentive staff, conservatory;
children and dogs (in bar) welcome, smallish
paved garden to the side, circular walks from
the door, open all day, food all day weekends
(until 6pm Sun).

REDBOURN   TL1011
Cricketers (01582) 620612
*3.2 miles from M1 junction 9; A5183
signed Redbourn/St Albans, at second
roundabout follow B487 for Hemel
Hempstead, first right into Chequer
Lane, then third right into East
Common; AL3 7ND* Well run and
extremely popular heart-of-the-village
pub serving imaginative freshly prepared
food; five well kept fast-changing ales
on handpump – Sharps Doom Bar, Tring
Side Pocket for a Toad and guests such
as St Austell Tribute and Tring Blinkers,
16 wines by the glass, farm cider, 17 gins,
ten malt whiskies, a new upstairs lounge
bar serving cocktails, prosecco and
gin; good mix of customers and helpful
service, children and dogs welcome, side
garden with seating opposite Redbourn
Common and walks nearby, open all day
Fri-Sun.

REDBOURN   TL1011
Hollybush (01582) 792423
Church End; AL3 7DU Picturesque pub
dating from the 16th c run by father and son
team; black-beamed lounge with big brick
fireplace and heavy wooden doors, larger
area with some built-in settles, Brakspears
and two guests, enjoyable reasonably
priced pubby food (not Sun evening) from
sandwiches and basket meals up, friendly
accommodating service; some live music,
darts; children and dogs (in bar) welcome,
picnic-sets in pleasant sunny garden (distant
M1 noise), pretty spot near medieval church,
open from 3pm Mon and Tues, otherwise
open all day.

REDCOATS GREEN   TL2026
Farmhouse (01438) 729500
Stevenage Road; SG4 7JR Large 15th-c
tile-faced building (part of the Anglian
Country Inns group) set in four acres of
grounds; good food from shortish but varied
menu (can be pricey), also fixed-price
Sun lunch and afternoon teas, Adnams
Southwold, plenty of wines by the glass
including champagne, friendly helpful staff,
conservatory restaurant; children and dogs
(in bar) welcome, 27 bedrooms (most in
converted outbuildings), open all day, no food
Sun evening.

RICKMANSWORTH   TQ0594
Feathers (01923) 770081
Church Street; WD3 1DJ Old pub quietly
set off the high street next to St Mary's
Church; beams, panelling and soft lighting,
well kept ales such as Fullers London Pride,
good wine list and varied choice of freshly
prepared food from sandwiches up, friendly
young staff coping well at busy times;
children allowed till 8pm, dogs in one side of
the bar, picnic-sets out behind, open all day.

RICKMANSWORTH   TQ0592
Rose & Crown (01923) 773826
*Woodcock Hill/Harefield Road, off A404
E of Rickmansworth at Batchworth;
WD3 1PP* Wisteria-clad 17th-c country
dining pub; enjoyable traditional home-
cooked food including range of burgers and
gluten-free menu, well kept Fullers London
Pride and a guest, friendly young staff, airy
dining room and conservatory, low beams
and open fires; quiz second Mon of month
and live music nights; children and dogs
welcome, large peaceful garden with views,
open all day.

RIDGE   TL2100
Old Guinea (01707) 660894
Crossoaks Lane; EN6 3LH Welcoming
modernised country pub with good pizzeria
alongside traditional bar; two regular ales
including St Austell Tribute, nice Italian
wines and proper coffee, open fire; children
and dogs (in bar) welcome, large garden
with far-reaching views, open all day (food
till 10pm).

ROYSTON   TL3540
Old Bull (01763) 242003
High Street; SG8 9AW Coaching inn dating
from the 16th c with bow-fronted Georgian
façade; roomy high-beamed bar, exposed
timbers and handsome fireplaces, plenty of
tables and some easy chairs on wood floor,
dining area with wall-sized photographs of
old Royston, enjoyable pubby food including
Sun carvery, well kept Greene King ales,
two guests and several wines by the glass,
helpful pleasant service; background music,
live folk second and last Fri of month, daily
newspapers; children and dogs (in bar)

welcome, suntrap courtyard, 11 bedrooms, open all day from 8am (till 1am Fri, Sat).

RUSHDEN   TL3031
Moon & Stars (01763) 288330
Mill End; off A507 about a mile W of Cottered; SG9 0TA Lovely cottagey low-beamed pub in peaceful country setting; well liked/priced food in bar or small dining room, three real ales including Greene King, friendly service; children and dogs welcome, large back garden, closed Sun evening, Mon.

SARRATT   TQ0499
★ Boot (01923) 262247
The Green; WD3 6BL Early 18th-c dining pub with good food (all day Sat, not Sun evening) from lunchtime sandwiches up, weekend breakfast (9.30-11.30am), three well kept ales and good choice of wines by the glass, friendly young staff, rambling bar with unusual inglenook, restaurant extension; children and (in some parts) dogs welcome, good-sized garden with polytunnel growing own produce, pleasant spot facing green, well located for Chess Valley walks, open all day.

SARRATT   TQ0498
Cock (01923) 282908
Church End: a very pretty approach is via North Hill, a lane N off A404, just under a mile W of A405; WD3 6HH Comfortably traditional 17th-c pub; latched back door opening directly into homely tiled snug with cluster of bar stools, vaulted ceiling and original bread oven, archway through to partly oak-panelled lounge with lovely inglenook log fire, red plush chairs at oak tables, lots of interesting artefacts and several namesake pictures of cockerels, Badger ales and decent choice of enjoyable food (not Sun evening), carpeted restaurant in converted barn; children and dogs (in bar) welcome, picnic-sets out at front looking over quiet lane towards churchyard, more on sheltered lawn and terrace with open country views, play area, open all day, closes 7pm Sun.

ST ALBANS   TL1406
Fighting Cocks (01727) 869152
Abbey Mill Lane; through abbey gateway – you can drive down; AL3 4HE Ancient octagonal building by River Ver; enjoyable pubby food (not Sun evening) cooked by landlord-chef, decent wines and up to nine well kept ales such as Hook Norton Hooky, Purity Ubu and Scottish Borders Foxy Blonde, friendly service (may be a wait at busy times), sunken Stuart cockfighting pit (now a dining area), low heavy beams, panelling and copper-canopied inglenook; some live

music, darts and board games; children and dogs welcome, attractive public park beyond garden, open all day.

ST ALBANS   TL1406
Garibaldi (01727) 894745
Albert Street; left turn down Holywell Hill past White Hart – car park left at end; AL1 1RT Civilised little Victorian backstreet local with well kept Fullers/Gales and a guest, good wines by the glass and popular Sun roasts (no other food), friendly staff; live music, sports TV, children and dogs welcome, picnic-sets on enclosed terrace, lots of window boxes and flowering tubs, open all day (from 2.30pm Mon, 1pm Tues-Thurs, noon Fri-Sun).

ST ALBANS   TL1506
Great Northern (01727) 730867
London Road; AL1 1PQ Welcoming nicely updated roadside pub; good attractively presented food from regularly changing menus including early evening set deal (useful for next-door cinema), four well kept beers including Black Sheep, good selection of wines and gins, efficient friendly service, July beer festival, quiz Tues, terrace tables, open all day Weds-Sun, closed lunchtimes other days, no food Sun evening, Mon.

ST ALBANS   TL1507
Mermaid (01727) 845700
Hatfield Road; AL1 3RL Bay-windowed pub with several seating areas (including window seats) arranged around central servery, six well kept ales, 15 ciders/perries and good selection of bottled beers, friendly knowledgeable staff, small menu serving Pieminister pies and some other food; background and live music, sports TV, darts; beer garden behind, open all day.·

ST ALBANS   TL1307
Six Bells (01727) 856945
St Michaels Street; AL3 4SH Rambling old pub with half a dozen well kept beers including Oakham, Timothy Taylors and Tring, reasonably priced home-made pubby food (not Sun evening) from lunchtime sandwiches up, cheerful helpful staff, low beams and timbers, log fire, quieter panelled dining room; some live music; children and dogs welcome, small back garden, handy for Verulamium Museum, open all day.

ST ALBANS   TL1406
White Hart Tap (01727) 860974
Keyfield, round corner from Garibaldi; AL1 1QJ Friendly 19th-c corner local with seven well kept ales including Timothy Taylors and Tring (maybe one from on-site microbrewery), decent choice of wines by the

---

If we know a pub has an outdoor play area for children, we mention it.

glass and reasonably priced home-made food (all day Sat and Sun); Weds quiz; children and dogs welcome, picnic-sets outside, open all day.

THERFIELD
TL3337

Fox & Duck (01763) 287246
Signed off A10 S of Royston; The Green; SG8 9PN Open-plan 19th-c bay-windowed pub in peaceful village setting with picnic-sets on small front green; good food (not Sun evening) from pub favourites up, Greene King and a couple of guests, friendly helpful staff, country chairs and sturdy stripped-top tables on stone flooring, smaller boarded area on left with darts, carpeted back restaurant; children and dogs welcome, garden behind with gate to park (play equipment), pleasant walks nearby, open all day weekends, closed Mon.

TRING
SP9211

Kings Arms (01442) 823318
King Street; by junction with Queen Street (which is off B4635 Western Road – continuation of High Street); HP23 6BE Cheerful brightly refurbished backstreet pub built in the 1830s; five well kept ales including Tring, real cider and decent choice of malt whiskies and gins, good value food (not Sun evening) from pub favourites up including daily specials, special diets catered for, stools around cast-iron tables, cushioned pews, some pine panelling and two warm coal fires (unusually below windows), separate courtyard restaurant (Fri-Sun); darts, children welcome, no dogs inside, open all day weekends.

TRING
SP9211

Robin Hood (01442) 824912
Brook Street (B486); HP23 5ED Welcoming traditional local with five Fullers/Gales beers and a guest kept well, good value pubby food (all day Sat), pop-up Thai restaurant Sun evening, friendly service, several well cared-for smallish linked areas, main bar with banquettes and traditional tables and chairs on bare boards or carpet, conservatory with woodburner; background music, Weds quiz; children welcome, dogs in bar, small back terrace, public car park nearby, open all day.

WATTON-AT-STONE
TL3019

Bull (01920) 831032
High Street; SG14 3SB Bustling 15th-c beamed coaching inn with impressive brick inglenook in pretty village; main bar has leather chesterfield and armchairs, dark wooden dining chairs and plush-topped stools on bare boards, contemporary paintwork and fresh flowers, comfortable relaxed atmosphere and friendly staff, also cosy room near entrance and elegantly furnished dining room; well kept ales such as Adnams Ghost Ship and Sharps Doom Bar, good wines, 15 gins and nice coffee, enjoyable food from

traditional choices up; children welcome, pleasant covered terrace with tables and chairs, garden with play area, open all day from 9.30am (noon Sun), closed Sun evening.

WESTMILL
TL3626

Sword Inn Hand (01763) 271356
Village signed off A10 S of Buntingford; SG9 9LQ Beamed 14th-c colour-washed pub in pretty village next to church; good food in bar and pitched-ceiling dining room from snacks to evening specials, cheerful attentive service, Greene King IPA and a guest from brick-faced counter, pine tables on bare boards or tiles, log fires; children and dogs (in one part of bar) welcome, attractive outside seating area, four comfortable bedrooms in outbuilding, open all day Fri, Sat, closed Sun evening.

WHEATHAMPSTEAD
TL1716

Cross Keys (01582) 832165
Off B651 at Gustard Wood 1.5 miles N; AL4 8LA Friendly 17th-c brick pub attractively placed in rolling wooded countryside; enjoyable reasonably priced pubby food (not Sun-Tues evenings) in bar and beamed restaurant including good Sun roasts, four well kept ales such as Adnams and Greene King, inglenook log fire; quiz second Mon of month; children, walkers and dogs welcome, picnic-sets in large garden with play area, three bedrooms, open all day Sat and Sun.

WIGGINTON
SP9310

Greyhound (01442) 824631
Just S of Tring; HP23 6EH Friendly village pub with good well presented food from varied menu including daily specials, three real ales and decent choice of wines, warm efficient service, woodburner in bare-boards bar, polished tables and leather chairs in connecting carpeted dining rooms; children and dogs welcome, back garden with fenced play area, handy for Ridgeway walks, three bedrooms, open (and food) all day except Sun when kitchen closes at 5pm.

WILDHILL
TL2606

Woodman (01707) 642618
Off B158 Brookmans Park–Essendon; AL9 6EA Simple tucked-away country local with friendly staff and regulars, two well kept Greene King ales and four guests, real cider, open-plan bar with log fire, two smaller back rooms (one with TV), straightforward weekday bar lunches (not Sun); darts; children and dogs welcome, plenty of seating in large garden.

WILLIAN
TL2230

Fox (01462) 480233
A1(M) junction 9; A6141 W towards Letchworth then first left; SG6 2AE Contemporary dining pub with pale wood tables and chairs on stripped boards or big ceramic tiles, paintings by local artists, good

inventive food along with more traditional choices including sandwiches, Adnams, Fullers, Woodfordes and two guests, good wine list (17 by the glass), attentive friendly young staff; background music, summer beer festival, TV; children and dogs (in bar) welcome, side terrace with smart tables under parasols, picnic-sets in good-sized back garden below handsome 14th-c church tower, eight bedrooms, open all day.

WILSTONE   SP9014
Half Moon (01442) 826410
Tring Road, off B489; HP23 4PD
Popular old village pub, clean and comfortable, with good value pubby food from sandwiches/panini up (best to book), well kept ales such as Malt, Sharps and Tring, friendly efficient staff, big log fire, low beams, old local pictures and lots of brasses; may be background radio, games including Scrabble, dominoes and darts; children and dogs welcome, some seats out in front and in good-sized back garden, handy for Grand Union Canal walks, open all day, no evening food Sun or Mon.

WINKWELL   TL0206
Three Horseshoes (01442) 862585
Just off A4251 Hemel–Berkhamsted; Pouchers End Lane, just over canal swing-bridge; HP1 2RZ 16th-c pub worth knowing for its charming setting by unusual swing-bridge over Grand Union Canal; low-beamed three-room core with inglenooks, traditional furniture including settles, a few sofas, ales such as Bombardier and Courage Directors, good selection of wines by the glass, food from British tapas to burgers (they may ask to keep a credit card while you eat), bay-windowed extension overlooking canal; music and comedy nights; children welcome, picnic-sets out by the water, open (and food) all day.

Isle of Wight

There are no Main Entries for the Isle of Wight this year. You might like to try these pubs that have been recommended to us and described by readers. Do tell us what you think of them: feedback@goodguides.com

ARRETON   SZ5386
White Lion (01983) 528479
A3056 Newport–Sandown; PO30 3AA
White-painted roadside pub (former coaching inn) in ancient village; beamed bar with stripped-wood floor and comfortable seats by log fire, Goddards Fuggle-Dee-Dum, Island Yachtsmans, Timothy Taylors Landlord and a guest, several wines by the glass, good choice of locally sourced food including sandwiches and home-made desserts, friendly attentive staff, restaurant; children, walkers and dogs welcome, pleasant terrace with view up to 12th-c church, good walks including to historic Arreton Manor, open all day.

BEMBRIDGE   SZ6488
Pilot Boat (01983) 872077
Station Road/Kings Road; PO35 5NN
The only pub on Bembridge Harbour, this appealing place is shaped like a boat, even down to the portholes; good food from sandwiches and burgers to local seafood, well kept Goddards and guests, friendly staff, restaurant area with woodburner and local artwork for sale; sports TV, darts; children and dogs welcome, disabled access, tables outside overlooking the water and in two pleasant sunny courtyards behind; shops and coastal walks nearby, five bedrooms (overnight cycle storage), open all day.

BEMBRIDGE   SZ6487
★Spinnaker (01983) 873572
Steyne Road; PO35 5UH Attractively refurbished Edwardian inn (part of the Inns of Distinction group); various bars, lounges and dining rooms all interconnected by open doorways yet retaining their individuality, interesting mix of furniture on wooden floors, armchairs and sofas beside open fires and a woodburner, some bold paintwork, photos and nautical memorabilia, real ales such as Goddards Fuggle-Dee-Dum and Marstons EPA and several wines by the glass, good imaginative food using island produce, afternoon teas; children and dogs (in bar) welcome, seats outside with views over Solent towards Portsmouth, 14 comfortable bedrooms, open all day from 9am for breakfast.

BONCHURCH   SZ5778
★Bonchurch Inn (01983) 852611
Bonchurch Shute; from A3055 E of Ventnor turn down to Old Bonchurch; opposite Leconfield Hotel; PO38 1NU
Quirky former stables with restaurant run by welcoming Italian family since 1984; congenial main bar with narrow-planked ship's decking and old-fashioned steamer-style seats plus family room and sun lounge with verandah, a couple of ales such as Bombardier tapped from the cask, decent wine list, popular bar food, good pizzas and Italian dishes, vegan menu, charming helpful service; background music, darts, shove-ha'penny and other games; children and dogs welcome, delightful continental-feel courtyard (parking can be tricky), holiday flat.

CARISBROOKE   SZ4687
★Blacksmiths (01983) 529263
B3401 1.5 miles W; PO30 5SS Family-run 400-year-old hillside pub just outside Carisbrooke and its famous castle (EH); airy bare-boards dining extension with superb Solent views, good pub food including vegetarian, vegan and gluten-free options (all day Sat, till 6pm Sun), scrubbed tables in neat beamed and flagstoned front bar serving Yates, a couple of guests and good choice of wines by the glass; children, dogs and walkers welcome (Tennyson Trail nearby), spectacular countryside views from terrace and garden down steps, play equipment, open (and food) all day.

COWES   SZ4995
Duke of York (01983) 295171
Mill Hill Road; PO31 7BT Welcoming inn usefully situated near the high street and ferry; at least two or three well kept ales and good choice of popular generously served pub food, lots of nautical bits and pieces, family room; children and dogs welcome, bedrooms, open all day.

COWES   SZ5094
★Lifeboat (01983) 292711
Britannia Way, East Cowes Marina (East Cowes and Cowes are two different towns; the main road into East Cowes is the A3021); PO32 6UB

Spacious modern bar-restaurant at the heart of East Cowes Marina with great views from large waterside terrace – hugely popular with the sailing fraternity; good value food including breakfast and daily specials, ales such as Goddards and at least one guest, decent wine list, friendly efficient staff; sports TV; children and dogs welcome (dogs get their own menu), open (and food) all day from 10am.

CULVER DOWN   SZ6385
Culver Haven (01983) 406107

Off B3395, seaward end of Culver Down, near Yarborough Monument; PO36 8QT Superb Channel views over the bays of Sandown, Shanklin and Bembridge and to mainland Portsmouth from this isolated clifftop pub on NT land; clean and modern with popular fairly priced home-made food, well kept changing ales such as Goddards, Timothy Taylors and Wadworths, several wines by the glass; friendly service, large restaurant; children and dogs welcome, small terrace, good walks (check website for maps), plenty of free parking.

FISHBOURNE   SZ5592
★ **Fishbourne Inn** (01983) 882823

From Portsmouth car ferry turn left into Fishbourne Lane (no-through road); PO33 4EU Attractive half-timbered mock-Tudor pub (part of the Inns of Distinction group) handy for the Wightlink ferry terminal; modern open-plan bar with tartan-upholstered banquettes and wooden chairs on slate flooring and woodburner, friendly staff serve Fullers Seafarer, Goddards Fuggle-Dee-Dum, St Austell Tribute and several wines by the glass; also comfortable lounge with large sofas and armchairs and smart airy dining room with chandeliers and house plants, pleasing food from sandwiches up; background music; children and dogs (in bar) welcome, outside seating area with picnic sets, five comfortable bedrooms, open and some kind of food all day from breakfast on.

FRESHWATER   SZ3487
★ **Red Lion** (01983) 754925

Church Place; from A3055 at E end of village by Freshwater Garage mini roundabout follow Yarmouth signpost, then take first real right turn signed to Parish Church; PO40 9BP Bay-windowed red-brick pub located in attractive area with great views of River Yar; well kept St Austell Proper Job, three guest beers and several wines by the glass, popular well priced food from daily changing blackboard menu using produce from their own garden, efficient friendly young staff, open-plan bar with country-style furnishings on flagstones or bare boards, woodburner, walkers, cyclists, children and dogs welcome, a couple of picnic-sets out front with view of church, more tables in back garden, good walking on nearby Freshwater Way, open all day.

GODSHILL   SZ5281
★ **Taverners** (01983) 840707

High Street (A3020); PO38 3HZ Welcoming 17th-c whitewashed pub in the thatched-cottage village of Godshill; good food with emphasis on fresh locally sourced produce (some home-grown), booking advised weekends, four well kept ales including Goddards and a house beer from Yates, Godshill's cider, plenty of wines by the glass and some interesting home-made liqueurs, good friendly service, spacious bar and two front dining areas, beams, bare boards, slate floors and woodburner; children and dogs welcome in certain parts, garden with terrace and play area, shop selling home-made and local produce, limited parking but free car park nearby, open all day, closed Sun evening (except bank and summer holidays).

GURNARD   SZ4796
Woodvale (01983) 292037

Princes Esplanade; PO31 8LE Large 1930s inn with splendid picture-window views of the Solent (stunning sunsets); good choice of food (special diets catered for) from sandwiches and baguettes to daily specials; Fullers London Pride, Ringwood Fortyniner and a couple of guests, good selection of wines by the glass, friendly staff; weekend live music, Mon quiz; children and dogs welcome, garden with terrace and summer barbecues, five bedrooms, open all day, food all day weekends.

HAVENSTREET   SZ5590
White Hart (01983) 883485

Off A3054 Newport–Ryde; Main Road; PO33 4DP Family-run old brick and stone village pub located near Isle of Wight Steam Railway; good choice of popular food from sandwiches up (special diets catered for), Ringwood and Goddards ales on rotation plus a guest, large selection of whiskies, friendly efficient service, cosy log-fire bar and carpeted dining area; children and dogs (not in evening) welcome, tables in secluded garden behind, open all day, food all day Sun.

NEWCHURCH   SZ5685
★ **Pointer** (01983) 865202

High Street; PO36 0NN Under recent new management, well run old two-room pub by Norman church; generous helpings of good fairly priced local food including blackboard specials (booking advised in season), well kept Fullers ales and two or three guests, friendly attentive service; children and dogs welcome, views from pleasant back garden, boules, open all day.

NEWPORT   SZ5089
Bargemans Rest (01983) 525828

Little London; PO30 5BS Family-run quayside pub with spreading bare-boards interior packed with nautical memorabilia; good choice of generous reasonably priced pubby food including vegetarian and gluten-free options,

Goddards, Ringwood and guests; frequent live music, children (away from bar) and dogs welcome, part-covered terrace overlooking River Medina, handy for town centre and Quay Arts Centre, open (and food) all day.

NEWPORT   SZ4989
Newport Ale House 07708 018051
Holyrood Street; PO30 5AZ Steps up to intriguing one-room pub in the heart of Newport; friendly chatty atmosphere, stools and leatherette bucket chairs on bare boards, half-panelling and some striking wallpaper, five well kept changing ales tapped from the cask by knowledgeable landlord, pies, rolls and sandwiches; regular live music, darts; dogs welcome, open all day.

NINGWOOD   SZ3989
★Horse & Groom (01983) 760672
A3054 Newport–Yarmouth, a mile W of Shalfleet; PO30 4NW Roomy carefully extended pub much liked by families; comfortable leather sofas grouped around low tables on flagstones, sturdy tables and chairs well spaced for relaxed dining, winter log fire, Greene King and a couple of guest beers (island ales served in summer) and good range of wines by the glass, enjoyable freshly made food (smaller appetites catered for), friendly welcoming staff; background music, games machine, board games, dogs allowed in bar, garden with well equipped play area including bouncy castle and crazy golf, nearby walks (well placed for Hamstead Trail), open all day from 9am for breakfast.

NITON   SZ5075
★Buddle (01983) 730243
St Catherines Road, Undercliff; off A3055 just S of village, towards St Catherines Point; PO38 2NE 16th-c former smugglers' haunt with characterful traditional bar rooms; heavy black beams, captain's chairs, wheelbacks and cushioned wall seats around solid wooden tables, big flagstones or carpeted floors, open fire in a broad stone fireplace with a huge black oak mantelbeam, a beer named for the pub plus Goddards Fuggle-Dee-Dum and Wight Squirrel and Yates Islander, Orchard Thieves cider, up to ten wines by the glass, enjoyable food from excellent sandwiches to specials and good fresh fish; background music; children and dogs welcome, picnic-sets on two stone terraces and in neatly kept sloping garden with fine sea views, great for walkers and nature lovers with coastal path nearby, open (and food) all day.

NORTHWOOD   SZ4983
Travellers Joy (01983) 298024
Off B3325 S of Cowes; PO31 8LS Friendly pub with simple contemporary interior; several well kept ales and enjoyable reasonably priced food from sandwiches and pubby choices to daily specials and Sun roasts, long bar with log fire, dining conservatory, pool room; Sun quiz and some live music;

children, walkers and dogs welcome, garden with pétanque and play area, open all day.

SANDOWN   SZ5984
Castle (01983) 403169
Fitzroy Street; PO36 8HY Friendly red-brick local serving six well kept beers such as Goddards, Shepherd Neame, Wadworths and Wychwood, carpeted interior with log fire and bric-a-brac (notable Halloween decorations); Sun quiz, darts, TV and fruit machine; children and dogs welcome, flower-filled back courtyard, a short walk to sandy beach and pier, open all day.

SEAVIEW   SZ5992
★Boathouse (01983) 810616
On B3330 Ryde–Seaview; PO34 5AW Extended blue-painted Victorian pub just across from the beach (sister to Spinnaker at Bembridge, Fishbourne Inn at Fishbourne and New Inn at Shalfleet); appealing bar with built-in wall seats, armchairs and leather pouffes, large model yacht on the mantelpiece above a woodburning stove, Goddards, Sharps Doom Bar and a guest, several wines by the glass and gins, also elegantly furnished dining rooms including one with a dinghy (complete with oars) leaning against the wall, well liked food from sandwiches to pub classics, friendly young staff; background music; children and dogs (in bar) welcome, picnic-sets on terrace overlooking the Solent, four airy sea-view bedrooms, open all day from 10am.

SEAVIEW   SZ6291
Seaview Hotel (01983) 612711
High Street; off B3330 Ryde–Bembridge; PO34 5EX Small civilised but relaxed Victorian hotel with two bars; traditional wood furnishings, seafaring paraphernalia and log fire in pubby bare-boards Pump bar, comfortable more refined front bar reminiscent of a naval wardroom, three well kept ales including Goddards, eight wines by the glass from good list, local gin and well executed pub fare, also first class upscale food in separate restaurant, pleasant helpful staff; background music; children welcome, dogs in bar, sea glimpses from tables on tiny front terrace, 13 bedrooms (seven in modern back annexe), self-catering cottage, good breakfast, open all day.

SHALFLEET   SZ4089
★New Inn (01983) 531314 *A3054*
Newport–Yarmouth; PO30 4NS Characterful whitewashed 18th-c former fishermen's haunt, still popular with visiting sailors (part of the Inns of Distinction group); good food including sandwiches and local fish/seafood, ale named for the pub (from Goddards), Hook Norton Old Hooky and a guest, several wines by the glass and a growing gin collection, rambling rooms with boarded ceilings, pubby chairs and scrubbed pine tables on stone or carpeted floors, log fires; background music; children and dogs (in bar)

welcome, seats on outside deck, a mile from Shalfleet quay and Newtown estuary and near the Yarmouth ferry, open all day.

SHANKLIN   SZ5881
★**Fishermans Cottage** (01983) 863882
Bottom of Shanklin Chine, accessed from far end of Shanklin Esplanade; PO37 6BN
Early 19th-c thatched cottage in terrific setting tucked into the cliffs on Appley beach, steep zigzag walk down beautiful chine; two cosy little rooms with low beams, flagstones and stripped-stone walls, old local pictures, fireplace with two-tier mantelpiece, Fullers London Pride and Yates Dark Side of the Wight and Islander, good value pub food focusing on fish/seafood with daily specials, friendly staff; background and some live music; children and dogs welcome, sun-soaked terrace overlooking sea, lovely walk to Luccombe, open all day in summer, but may shut early in bad weather, also closed Nov to mid-Feb (best to check times).

SHANKLIN   SZ5881
Steamer (01983) 862641
Esplanade; PO37 6BS Welcoming nautically themed beachfront bar, popular with families, good choice of enjoyable well priced food from snacks to daily specials, ales such as Goddards, Ringwood and Yates, friendly hard-working staff, mix of seating including cushioned pews and leather sofas on quarry tiles; live music most weekends; fine views across the sandy beach to the sea from part-covered two-tier terrace, five bedrooms, open all day.

ST HELENS   SZ6289
Vine (01983) 872337
Upper Green Road; PO33 1UJ Victorian red-brick local overlooking large village green (cricket in summer); enjoyable home-cooked food including stone-baked pizzas, well kept Sharps and guests, cheerful helpful staff; weekend live music, Weds quiz, pool and darts, children and dogs welcome, some seats out in front, play area across road, lovely coastal walks and beaches nearby, open all day, food all day weekends.

VENTNOR   SZ5677
Perks (01983) 857446
High Street; PO38 1LT Popular little bar packed with eclectic and interesting memorabilia behind shop-window front; well kept ales including Bass and occasional guests such as Adnams Broadside and Yates Golden Bitter, good range of wines, enjoyable well priced home-made lunchtime food from sandwiches and baked potatoes up, bargain OAP two-course lunch (evening food Fri and Sat only), fast friendly service; dogs welcome, open all day.

VENTNOR   SZ5677
★**Spyglass** (01983) 855338
Esplanade, SW end; road down is very steep and twisty, and parking nearby can

be difficult – best to use pay-and-display (free in winter) about 100 metres up the road; PO38 1JX Perched above the beach with fascinating jumble of seafaring memorabilia in snug quarry-tiled interior, very popular locally; Goddards, Ringwood and Yates ales, good choice of wines and popular food including fish/seafood dishes (good crab sandwiches), friendly helpful service; background music, live daily in summer; children welcome, dogs and muddy boots in bar, sea-wall terrace with fantastic views, coast walk towards Ventnor Botanic Garden, heftier hikes on to St Boniface Down and towards the eerie shell of Appuldurcombe House (EH), four sea-view bedrooms, open (and food) all day.

VENTNOR   SZ5677
Volunteer (01983) 852537
Victoria Street; PO38 1ES Welcoming one-room local as unusual as nearby Perks and under same management; five well kept changing ales (always one from an Isle of Wight brewery) and Dunkerton's organic cider, renovated interior with bare boards and carpet, upholstered seats, farmhouse chairs and cast-iron-framed tables, some military and Ventnor brewery memorabilia, Victorian tiled fireplace (electric fire); simple home-made food including sandwiches; background music, darts and the local game of rings; dogs welcome, no children, open all day.

WHITWELL   SZ5277
White Horse (01983) 730375
High Street; PO38 2PY Extended 15th-c whitewashed village pub with popular good value food from pub staples to daily specials (booking advised), four well kept changing ales, good friendly service, carpeted beamed bar with exposed stonework, restaurant; Mon quiz, pool, darts and traditional rings game; children and dogs welcome, picnic-sets among fruit trees in big garden with play area, open all day, food all day weekends.

YARMOUTH   SZ3589
Bugle (01983) 760272
The Square; PO41 0NS Charming 17th-c coaching house on Yarmouth's market square with long frontage and several linked rooms; chesterfields by open fire in low-ceilinged panelled lounge, farmhouse-style furniture in dining areas, books on shelves, restaurant with high-backed leather chairs around mix of tables on bare boards or carpet, generous helpings of enjoyable pub food including daily fresh fish, quick cheerful service, traditionally furnished bar with real ales such as Sharps and Timothy Taylors, conservatory; background music; children and dogs welcome, picnic-sets and lots of hanging baskets in large courtyard garden, seven bedrooms, handy for harbour and ferry, open (and some food) all day.

Kent

BIDDENDEN   TQ8238   Map 3
Three Chimneys 🍵 🍷 🛏

(01580) 291472 – www.thethreechimneys.co.uk

Off A262 at pub sign, a mile W of village; TN27 8LW

Pubby beamed rooms of considerable individuality, log fires, imaginative food and big, pretty garden; well appointed bedrooms

---

This characterful, cosy old inn is an ideal base for visiting the gardens at nearby Sissinghurst (National Trust). The small, low-beamed bar and dining rooms are civilised but informal with plenty of character. They're simply done out with plain wooden furniture and old settles on flagstones and coir matting, some harness and sporting prints on the stripped-brick walls and good log fires. Their own Chimneys Ale (from Goachers) plus Harveys Best on handpump, 18 wines by the glass from a good list, local Biddenden's cider and nine malt whiskies; background music in the restaurant. The candlelit bare-boards restaurant has rustic décor and french windows that open into an extended conservatory looking over seats in the pretty garden, where raised beds contain herbs and other produce for the kitchen. At the front of the building is an enclosed open-air dining courtyard. There are four comfortable bedrooms, each with their own terrace.

🍵 Highly thought-of food includes ploughman's, grilled mackerel fillet with salsa and garlic aioli, pigeon breast with celeriac purée and blackberries, hake fillet with cannellini beans, roasted cherry tomatoes and chorizo dressing, courgette and tomato ragoût with grilled halloumi, pork and sage sausages with creamed potatoes and port and red onion gravy, caramelised onion, courgette and tomato tartlet with grilled goats cheese and black olive tapenade, guinea fowl breast with braised peas, broad beans and Jersey Royal potatoes, and puddings such as dark chocolate délice on praline base with pistachio ice-cream and vanilla pannacotta with raspberry coulis. *Benchmark main dish: rib-eye steak with fries £23.95. Two-course evening meal £28.00.*

Free house ~ Licensee Craig Smith ~ Real ale ~ Open 11.30-11 ~ Bar food 12-9 (9.30 Sat) ~ Restaurant ~ Children welcome ~ Dogs allowed in bar ~ Bedrooms: £140

BRABOURNE   TR1041   Map 3
Five Bells 🍺

(01303) 813334 – www.fivebellsinnbrabourne.com

East Brabourne; TN25 5LP

Rural inn in pretty countryside with character bars, interesting décor, local ales and popular food; bedrooms

At the foot of the North Downs, this 16th-c inn is a fine place to spend a few days in comfortable bedrooms; lovely surrounding walks. Downstairs, the opened-up bars with hop-festooned beams, standing timbers and ancient brick walls, two open fires, all manner of dining chairs and tables on stripped boards, wall seats here and there with huge scatter cushions, and wooden stools at shelves and against the counter. Staff are helpful and friendly. Ales include their own house beer Pickled Egg Pale Ale, Old Dairy Summer Haze and a couple of changing locals such as Pig & Porter Skylarking and Tonbridge Blonde Ambition; also, Aspall's and Dudda's Tun ciders on draught and 16 well chosen wines by the glass. There are plenty of tables and chairs under cover out front. Décor in the four bedrooms is bold and idiosyncratic, with freestanding baths. Part of the Pickled Egg group, this is sister pub to the Radnor Arms in Folkestone, Duke William in Ickham and Woolpack in Warehorne (all in Kent).

Pleasing pubby food includes salt and pepper squid, whitebait with sriracha mayonnaise, ploughman's, roast chicken breast with caesar salad and poached egg, smoked frankfurter with sauerkraut and fries, rib-eye steak with grilled tomato, mushroom and chips, wood-fired pizzas, and puddings such as vanilla cheesecake and strawberries and black forest brownie with vanilla ice-cream. *Benchmark main dish: beer-battered cod with beef dripping chips and mushy peas £13.50. Two-course evening meal £20.00.*

Free house ~ Licensee Lee Corsi ~ Open 11-11; 11-midnight Fri, Sat; 11-10.30 Sun; closed Mon, Tues ~ Bar food 12-3, 5-8.30; 12-3, 6-9.30 Fri, Sat; 12-5 Sun ~ Children welcome ~ Dogs allowed in bar ~ Bedrooms: £100

CHIPSTEAD
George & Dragon 🏅❂ ♟

TQ5056   Map 3

(01732) 779019 – www.georgeanddragonchipstead.com
Near M25 junction 5; 39 High Street; TN13 2RW

Excellent food in popular village dining pub with three real ales, friendly, efficient service and seats in garden

It's no surprise our readers love the inventive menus and excellent food at this bustling and easy-going pub: licensee Ben James describes himself as a 'passionate, eccentric foodie' and framed magazine and newspaper articles by him about foraging and field-to-fork cookery adorn the walls. There's striking dragon-inspired wallpaper made especially for the pub, as well as antique tables and chairs on wide oak floorboards and a leather sofa facing the hearty fire. Upstairs is a sizeable timbered dining room with similar furnishings, and a cosy room that's just right for a private party. You'll find the pub's own George's Marvellous Medicine from Westerham and one or two guest ales on handpump, alongside 16 wines by the glass, a good rage of whiskies and cocktails – many people visit just for the espresso martinis. You can eat upstairs, downstairs or in the herb garden, and several seating areas outside have good quality tables and chairs under parasols.

Rewarding, hearty, seasonal food using local produce includes a daily set menu (not weekends) and very popular Sunday roasts. Dishes include harissa-roasted cauliflower with celeriac purée, toasted almond and diced apple, roasted sweet potato with puy lentil, spinach, caramelised onion and tomato salad with coconut, chilli and lime dressing, wild garlic and spinach risotto, burger with toppings and chips, rainbow trout with pine nut, egg and lemon dressing, pan-fried sea bass with crispy potatoes, bacon and sea purslane, seared venison haunch with jerusalem artichokes and truffle, and puddings such as peaches, raspberry, granola, puff pastry and clotted cream ice-cream and plum pie with vanilla custard and plum purée. *Benchmark main dish: steak sandwich £11.50. Two-course evening meal £21.00.*

Free house ~ Licensee Ben James ~ Real ale ~ Open 12-11; 12-10.30 Sun ~ Bar food 12-3
(4 Sat), 6-9.30; 12-8 Sun ~ Restaurant ~ Children welcome ~ Dogs allowed in bar

FOLKESTONE
TR2336 Map 3

Radnor Arms

(01303) 254435 – www.radnorarmsfolkestone.co.uk
Christ Church Road; CT20 2SX

**Bustling Victorian pub that also has some quieter cosy corners,
quirky décor and a good range of drinks**

Tucked away in a little backstreet, this is an interestingly renovated
Victorian pub that's proving a welcome addition to the town's pub scene.
There are several interconnected bar and dining rooms with quirky décor,
a friendly, bustling atmosphere and a fine choice of drinks (do note the
copper stills used for serving ales) that includes local suppliers such as beers
from Pig & Porter and Old Dairy, ciders from the Kent Cider Company and
wines from Gusbourne Estate. The entrance room has a modern cylindrical
woodburner and an open kitchen and this leads into the main serving area
with stools lining the copper-topped counter and a high shelf opposite, and
an open doorway into a couple of adjoining rooms. Here, you'll find another
woodburner, wood or leather dining chairs around polished tables on bare
boards, wall seating here and there, black and white photos of 1960s bands
and the local area, funky lamps, oars on the ceiling, wine bottles on shelves
and flowers in pots; there's an overspill room upstairs. Pale turquoise seats
and wooden tables fill the appealing cobbled courtyard garden that's hung
with lights and lanterns. This is part of the Pickled Egg group, along with
the Five Bells in Brabourne, Duke William in Ickham and Woolpack in
Wareborne (all in Kent).

Tasty pubby food includes broad beans with mint salt, black pudding scotch egg
with apple and apricot chutney, prawn cocktail, beef burger with ketchup, pickles
and fries, smoked frankfurter with sauerkraut, crispy onions and fries, beer-battered
cod and chips, wood-fired pizzas, and puddings such as cheesecake with strawberries
and a selection of ice-creams and sorbets. *Benchmark main dish: ploughman's
£13.95. Two-course evening meal £20.00.*

Free house ~ Licensee John Rodgers ~ Open 11-11; 11-midnight Fri, Sat; 11-10.30 Sun;
closed Mon, Tues ~ Bar food 12-3, 5-8.30; 12-3, 6-9.30 Fri, Sat; 12-5 Sun ~ Children welcome
~ Dogs allowed in bar

FORDWICH
TR1759 Map 3

George & Dragon ♀

(01227) 710661 – www.brunningandprice.co.uk/georgeanddragon
Off A28 at Sturry; CT2 0BX

**15th-c pub with a good choice of drinks, enjoyable food and
well trained staff**

Our readers find this handsome hostelry very homely, with its spreading
character rooms populated with lots of prints and paintings,
bookshelves, large mirrors, house plants and tankards. It's located on the
banks of the River Stour in Britain's smallest town. There are numerous
beams, timbers and open fires, and floors ranging from carpet, tiles and
flagstones to polished boards topped with rugs. You'll find an assortment
of nice old chairs and tables (one a giant bellows), button-back leather
armchairs, plush banquettes and little stools. Friendly, helpful staff serve
St Austell Brunning & Price Traditional Bitter plus guests from the likes of

Adnams, Canterbury Ales, Tonbridge and Wantsum on handpump, 17 wines by the glass, 34 whiskies and 49 gins. The lawn has plenty of picnic-sets plus Brunning & Price's hallmark play tractor. Disabled car park, access and loos. Howletts Wild Animal Park is nearby.

🍴 Good quality food includes sandwiches and 'light bites', pan-fried scallops with pea purée and shredded ham hock, chicken caesar croquettes, honey-roast ham and eggs, braised feather of beef bourguignon with horseradish mash and buttered kale, salmon and smoked haddock fishcake with poached egg, pea and mint tortellini with pea velouté and asparagus, Malaysian chicken curry with coconut rice and steamed pak choi, and puddings such as triple chocolate brownie with chocolate sauce and lemon cheesecake with raspberry ripple ice-cream. *Benchmark main dish: steak burger with bacon and fries £13.95. Two-course evening meal £22.00.*

Brunning & Price ~ Manager Diana Larfi ~ Real ale ~ Open 10am-11pm; 10am-10.30pm Sun ~ Bar food 12-9; 12-9.30 Fri, Sat ~ Restaurant ~ Children welcome ~ Dogs allowed in bar

ICKHAM   TR2258 Map 3
Duke William 🛏

(01227) 721308 – www.thedukewilliammickham.com
Off A257 E of Canterbury; The Street; CT3 1QP

Friendly pub with character rooms, good food and ales and seats in pretty garden; bedrooms

Set on the east bank of the River Stour, this attractive pub is nestled in a pretty village with thatched cottages and an 18th-c church. The spreading bar has huge oak beams and stripped joists, seats that range from brightly coloured bar stools and country kitchen style to cushioned settles with animal-skin throws, a range of tables on stripped wooden floors and a log fire with a low barrel table in front of it. Friendly staff serve three rapidly changing ales from breweries such as Old Dairy, Wantsum and Whitstable on handpump, eight wines by the glass and a good choice of gins and whiskies. The low-ceilinged dining room is similarly furnished and a conservatory looks over the garden and the fields beyond. Throughout, paintwork is contemporary, tables are set with fresh flowers and candles in stone bottles and there are interesting paintings, prints and china plates on the walls; background music and board games. Modern seats and tables are set under parasols on the partly covered terrace, with picnic-sets and a children's play area on grass. The four bedrooms (named after the owner's culinary heroes) are attractively and simply furnished, and breakfasts are generous.

🍴 Food is good, comes in generous portions and includes roasted red pepper hummus with sourdough, smoked chicken terrine with lardons and leek mayonnaise, fried plaice and tartare sauce bap, honey and mustard glazed ham with triple-cooked chips, roast chicken breast with caesar salad and poached egg, chargrilled pork cutlet with gnocchi and mushroom and tomato ragoût, and puddings such as rhubarb baked alaska and vanilla cheesecake with strawberries. *Benchmark main dish: burger with pickles and fries £13.95. Two-course evening meal £23.00.*

Free house ~ Licensee Mark Sargeant ~ Real ale ~ Open 11-11; 11-midnight Sat; 11-10.30 Sun ~ Bar food 12-3, 6-9; 12-3, 6.30-9.30 Fri, Sat; 12-5 Sun ~ Restaurant ~ Children welcome ~ Dogs allowed in bar ~ Bedrooms: £120

Please keep sending us reports. We rely on readers for news of new discoveries, and particularly for news of changes – however slight – at the fully described pubs: feedback@goodguides.com, or (no stamp needed) Freepost THE GOOD PUB GUIDE, Random House Publishing, 20 Vauxhall Bridge Road, London SW1V 2SA.

LANGTON GREEN

TQ5439 Map 3

Hare 🍷 🍺

(01892) 862419 – www.brunningandprice.co.uk/hare

A264 W of Tunbridge Wells; TN3 0JA

Edwardian pub with lots to look at, a fine choice of drinks and imaginative food

A combination of good, enterprising food, a wide range of drinks and imaginative lively décor lure customers back here on a regular basis. The high-ceilinged rooms are light and airy with rugs on bare boards, built-in wall seats, stools and old-style wooden tables and chairs, dark dados below pale-painted walls covered in old photographs and prints, romantic pastels and a huge collection of chamber-pots hanging from beams; background radio and board games. Cheerfully efficient young staff serve Greene King Abbot and IPA and two guests such as Bath Gem and Bedlam Benchmark on handpump, 21 wines by the glass, 59 malt whiskies, 42 gins and a farm cider. French windows open on to a big terrace with pleasant views of the tree-ringed village green. Parking in front of the pub is limited, but you can park in the lane to one side.

 Contemporary food includes sandwiches and 'light bites', smoked salmon with orange and beetroot salad with horseradish cream, vegetable risotto with broad beans, radish, asparagus and lemon, stilton, caramelised red onion and potato pie with redcurrant jus, braised shoulder of lamb with new potatoes and rosemary gravy, pork and leek sausages with mash and onion gravy, king prawn linguine with chilli and tomato, crispy beef salad with sweet chilli sauce and cashews, and puddings such as chocolate and orange tart with passion-fruit sorbet and hot waffle and caramelised banana with toffee sauce and honeycomb ice-cream. *Benchmark main dish: chicken, ham and leek pie with mash, greens and white wine sauce £14.95. Two-course evening meal £22.00.*

Brunning & Price ~ Manager Rebecca Bowen ~ Real ale ~ Open 11-11; 11-midnight Fri, Sat; 11-10.30 Sun ~ Bar food 12-9.30; 12-10 Fri, Sat; 12-9 Sun ~ Children allowed in bar ~ Dogs allowed in bar

PENSHURST

TQ5142 Map 3

Bottle House 🍽️⭐ 🍷

(01892) 870306 – www.thebottlehouseinnpenshurst.co.uk

Coldharbour Lane; leaving Penshurst SW on B2188 turn right at Smarts Hill signpost, then bear right towards Chiddingstone and Cowden; keep straight on; TN11 8ET

Country pub with friendly service, a good choice of drinks, tasty food and sunny terrace; nearby walks

This attractive, weatherboarded old country pub is a fine choice for a drink and a chat or a full-blown meal. Although the open-plan rooms are connected, there are nooks and crannies and standing timbers that give a sense of being separate and yet part of the chatty, bustling atmosphere. Pine wall boards and bar stools are ranged along the timber-clad copper-topped counter where they keep Larkins Traditional and a couple of guests such as Tonbridge Coppernob on handpump, 20 wines by the glass from a good list and local gin. There's also a hotchpotch of wooden tables (with fresh flowers and candles), fairly closely spaced chairs on dark boards or coir, a woodburning stove and photographs of the pub and local scenes; background music. Some walls are of stripped stone. The sunny, brick-paved terrace has plenty of teak chairs and tables under parasols, and olive trees in white pots. Good nearby walks.

🍴⭐ Pleasing food includes Thai crab cakes, greek salad, crayfish cocktail, a pie of the day with mash, seafood paella, piri-piri half chicken with corn on the cob, harissa halloumi salad, steak burger with skinny fries, roasted butternut squash risotto, pizzas, marinated swordfish steak with seared chicory and herby new potatoes, and puddings such as chocolate brownie with salted caramel sauce and vanilla ice-cream and frozen blackberry and apple yoghurt cake. *Benchmark main dish: slow-roasted pork belly with dauphinoise potatoes and apple and cider sauce £15.95. Two-course evening meal £22.00.*

Free house ~ Licensee Paul Hammond ~ Real ale ~ Open 11-11; 11-10.30 Sun ~ Bar food 12-10; 12-9 Sun and bank holidays ~ Restaurant ~ Children welcome ~ Dogs allowed in bar

---

PLUCKLEY
TQ9243 Map 3

Dering Arms 🍴⭐ 🍷
(01233) 840371 – www.deringarms.com

Pluckley station, which is signposted from B2077; or follow Station Road (left turn off Smarden Road in centre of Pluckley) for about 1.3 miles S, through Pluckley Thorne; TN27 0RR

Interesting building with carefully chosen wines, three ales and good fish and seafood dishes; bedrooms

This handsome inn was built in the 1840s as a hunting lodge on what was then the Dering Estate. It has an imposing stone frontage with mullioned arched windows and dutch gables. The high-ceilinged, stylishly plain main bar has a solid country feel with a mix of wooden furniture on flagstones, a roaring log fire in a big fireplace, country prints and some fishing rods. The smaller half-panelled back bar has similar dark wood furnishings, plus an extension with a woodburning stove, comfortable armchairs, sofas and a grand piano; board games. A beer named for the pub from Goachers and Goachers Gold Star Ale on handpump, six good wines by the glass from an unusually finely stocked cellar, local cider, 30 malt whiskies and 20 cognacs. There are three comfortable bedrooms. Classic car meetings (the long-serving landlord James has a couple of classic motors) are held here on the second Sunday of the month.

🍴⭐ First class fish and shellfish (oysters, prawns, lobsters, crab, skate wing, black bream, sea bass and more) are the stars here, though they do offer non-fishy choices too, such as interesting tapas, duck rillettes with ciabatta toast, venison steak with potato and celeriac purée and port sauce, confit duck with bubble and squeak potato cake and black cherry and ginger sauce and leg of lamb steak with peppers, black olives and couscous, plus puddings such as banana and vanilla ice-cream pancake and sticky toffee pudding with warm walnut sauce. *Benchmark main dish: salmon fishcakes with sorrel sauce £12.95. Two-course evening meal £22.00.*

Free house ~ Licensee James Buss ~ Real ale ~ Open 11.30-3, 6-11; 12-4.30 Sun ~ Bar food 12-2.30, 6.30-9; 12-3 Sun ~ Restaurant ~ Children welcome ~ Dogs allowed in bar ~ Bedrooms: $90

SEVENOAKS
TQ5352 Map 3

White Hart 🍷
(01732) 452022 – www.brunningandprice.co.uk/whitehart
Tonbridge Road (A225 S, past Knole); TN13 1SG

Well run coaching inn with lots to look at in character rooms, rewarding food and friendly, helpful staff

This large, welcoming inn on the edge of Sevenoaks is the perfect place for lunch after a visit to Knole (National Trust) and its huge deer park. The many atmospheric rooms are connected by open doorways and steps. You'll find log fires and woodburners, antique-style chairs and tables, rugs and bare floorboards and hundreds of prints and old photographs of local scenes or schools on cream-painted walls. Fresh flowers, house plants and candles too. Friendly, efficient staff serve St Austell Brunning & Price Traditional Bitter, Harveys Best and Old Dairy Blue Top plus guests from breweries such as Ruddles, Sharps, Timothy Taylors, Tonbridge and Westerham on handpump, around 20 good wines by the glass, a similar number of gins, 50 malt whiskies and a farm cider; daily papers, board games. At the front of the building are picnic-sets under parasols, with wooden benches and chairs around tables under more parasols on the back terrace.

Good quality modern cooking includes sandwiches and 'light bites', baked camembert with ciabatta croutes, crispy vegetable gyozas with spiced mango dip, scallops with butternut squash purée, crispy buttermilk chicken burger with fries, cauliflower, chickpea and sweet potato tagine with lemon and almond couscous, fish pie, pork tenderloin with creamy bacon and spring onion mash and cider jus, grilled sea bass fillets with potato and shallot terrine and chervil and lemon cream sauce, and puddings such as dark chocolate, Cointreau and orange trifle and triple-chocolate brownie with chocolate sauce and vanilla ice-cream. *Benchmark main dish: chicken, ham and leek pie with tarragon cream sauce £14.95. Two-course evening meal £22.00.*

Brunning & Price ~ Manager Tom Dennis ~ Real ale ~ Open 11.30-11; 12-11 Sun ~ Bar food 12-9.30; 12-10 Fri, Sat; 12-9 Sun ~ Children welcome away from bar until 7pm ~ Dogs allowed in bar

STALISFIELD GREEN

TQ9552 Map 3

Plough 🏵 🍺 🛏

(01795) 890256 – www.theploughinnstalisfield.co.uk

Off A252 in Charing; ME13 0HY

Kent Dining Pub of the Year

Ancient country pub with rambling rooms, open fires, interesting local ales and smashing food; bedrooms

With its rustic tables, old beams and blazing log fire in winter, coupled with excellent food and good choice of drinks, this a very welcoming place to spend a few hours. You can also spend the night: in individually designed, split-level suites in a purpose-built barn, with good views and tasty breakfasts. The relaxed hop-draped bar and dining rooms ramble around, up and down, with open fires in brick fireplaces, interesting pictures, books on shelves, farmhouse and other nice old dining chairs around a mix of pine or dark wood tables on bare boards, and the odd milk churn dotted about; background music. There are four Kentish ales on handpump from brewers such as Hopdaemon, Old Dairy, Ramsgate Gadds, Wantsum, Westerham and Whitstable (August beer festival), 16 wines by the glass, six local ciders and a wide selection of gins, malt whiskies and rums. There are picnic-sets on a simple terrace overlooking the village green below. They also have pitches for Camping and Caravanning Club members.

 Imaginative food using the best local produce and cooked by the landlord includes lunchtime rolls and seasonal daily specials, plus seared scallops with green beans, pickled fennel, pink grapefruit and caper beurre noisette, ham hock and chorizo terrine with celeriac rémoulade, Sicilian fish stew with fennel and saffron purée, burger with bacon jam, brie, slaw and chips, a pie of the day, Buccleuch fillet steak with cherry tomatoes, king oyster mushrooms, watercress salad and triple-cooked chips, and puddings such as coffee burnt cream with almond biscotti and poached pear and ginger cheesecake with crystallised ginger and honey yoghurt sorbet. *Benchmark main dish: beer-battered fish and chips £14.00. Two-course evening meal £23.00.*

Free house ~ Licensees Richard and Marianne Baker ~ Real ale ~ Open 12-3, 5-11; 12-11 Sat; 12-6 Sun ~ Bar food 12-1.45, 6-8.45; 12-2.30, 6-8.45 Sat; 12-3.30 Sun ~ Restaurant ~ Children welcome ~ Dogs allowed in bar & bedrooms ~ Bedrooms: £100

STONE IN OXNEY
TQ9428 Map 3

Ferry 🍺

(01233) 758246 – www.oxneyferry.com

Appledore Road; signed from Tenterden Road (B2080); TN30 7JY

Bustling small pub with character rooms, candlelight, open fires, real ales and popular food

A favoured haunt of smugglers in the 17th c, and located in a picturesque setting on the edge of Romney Marsh, this pretty cottage pub has plenty of room for both drinkers and diners. The chatty main bar has hop-draped painted beams, a green dado and stools against the counter where they serve a beer named for the pub (from Goachers), Harveys Best, Sharps Doom Bar and a guest such as Cellar Head IPA on handpump, 16 wines by the glass, farm ciders and 24 gins. To the right is a cosy eating area with wheelback chairs and a banquette around a few long tables, and a log fire in an inglenook with candles in wall sconces on either side. To the left of the main door is a dining area with big blackboards on red walls, a woodburning stove beneath a large bressumer beam and high-backed, light wooden dining chairs around assorted tables; up a couple of steps, a smarter dining area has modern chandeliers. Throughout there are wooden floors, all sorts of pictures and framed maps, a stuffed fish, beer flagons, an old musket and various brasses. Background and occasional live music, and TV, darts and pool in the games room. In warm weather, the tables and benches on the front terrace and seats in the back garden are much sought after; a river runs along the bottom and the sunsets can be lovely. Disabled access in the bar and on the terrace.

Tempting food includes devilled lamb kidneys on toast, moules marinière, vegan scallops with oyster mushrooms, squash and cauliflower purée, buttermilk chicken burger with spicy coleslaw and sweet potato fries, guinea fowl with tenderstem broccoli, roasted new potatoes and oyster mushroom sauce, glazed duck breast with parmentier potatoes, chargrilled chicory and sage and orange sauce, and puddings such as pavlova with forest fruit compote and vegan whipped cream and lemon posset with raspberries and redcurrants. *Benchmark main dish: seafood tagliatelle with prawns, crayfish tails and chorizo £19.45. Two-course evening meal £25.00.*

Free house ~ Licensee Paul Withers Green ~ Real ale ~ Open 11-11; 12-10 Sun ~ Bar food 12-3, 6-9; 11-9 Sat; 12-8 Sun ~ Restaurant ~ Children welcome ~ Dogs allowed in bar

TUNBRIDGE WELLS
TQ5839 Map 3

Sankeys 🏮🍴 🍷 🍺

(01892) 511422 – www.sankeys.co.uk

Mount Ephraim (A26 just N of junction with A267); TN4 8AA

Pubby bar, real ales, decent food and relaxed feel; downstairs brasserie (wonderful fish and shellfish) and seats on sunny back terrace

This lively, easy-going, street-level bar offers exceptional seafood, an unusually large choice of drinks and a homely interior decked out with lots of signs and memorabilia – no wonder it's so popular. Harveys

Best, Larkins Traditional and a local guest from the likes of Long Man and Tonbridge are well kept on handpump and there's a constantly changing range of craft beers, fruit beers, lagers and ciders, 30 wines by the glass and an extensive range of spirits, all served by helpful staff. Comfortably worn leather sofas, armchairs and pews sit around all sorts of tables on bare boards, and do note the particularly fine collection of rare enamel signs and antique brewery mirrors plus old prints, framed cigarette cards and lots of old wine bottles and soda siphons. There's a big flatscreen TV (for rugby only), background music and board games. Downstairs is a sizeable function room with french windows that lead out to an inviting suntrap deck.

🍽️ Good value, tasty food includes sandwiches, snacks such as cockles and devilled anchovies, shell-on Greenland prawns, garlic and chilli crevettes, fish soup with rouille, lobster (half, whole, thermidor), mussels cooked various ways, haddock and smoked salmon fishcakes with spinach and horseradish sauce and chips, burger (vegan, chicken, prawn, cod or beef) with toppings and chips, Cajun chicken salad, and puddings. *Benchmark main dish: seafood paella £19.95. Two-course evening meal £26.00.*

Free house ~ Licensee Matthew Sankey ~ Real ale ~ Open 12-11; 12-1am Thurs-Sat; 12-11 Sun ~ Bar food 12-3, 6-10; 12-10 Sat; 12-6 Sun ~ Restaurant ~ Children welcome ~ Dogs allowed in bar

ULCOMBE   TQ8550   Map 3
Pepper Box
(01622) 842558 – www.thepepperboxinn.co.uk
Fairbourne Heath; signposted from A20 in Harrietsham, or follow Ulcombe signpost from A20, then turn left at crossroads with sign to pub, then right at next minor crossroads; ME17 1LP

Friendly country pub with a fine log fire, well liked food, fair choice of drinks and seats in a pretty garden

This attractive white-painted old pub is just the place to relax after a good walk; indeed, the Greensand Way footpath is nearby. The location – nicely placed on high ground above the Weald – is very restful, and in warm weather the hop-covered terrace and shrub-filled garden are extremely welcoming. The homely bar has attentive and convivial licensees, standing timbers and a few low beams (some hung with hops), copper kettles and pans on windowsills, and nice horsebrasses on the fireplace's bressumer beam; two leather sofas are set beside the splendid inglenook fireplace with its lovely log fire. A side area, furnished more functionally for eating, extends into the opened-up beamed dining room with a range in another inglenook and more horsebrasses. Shepherd Neame Master Brew and guests such as Shepherd Neame Spitfire and Whitstable Bay Pale Ale on handpump and 16 wines by the glass; background music. The village church is worth a look.

🍴 Enjoyable food includes lunchtime sandwiches, tiger prawns in garlic, chilli and ginger butter, sloe gin pigeon with blackberry dressing, pork and mushroom stroganoff with tomato, paprika and basmati rice, a pie of the day, Thai fish curry with tiger prawns and crispy cod, duck breast with apple and calvados sauce and boulangère potatoes, roasted courgette with pepper, pine nut, breadcrumb and cheese stuffing, salmon fillet with braised lettuce, peas, samphire and crab, and puddings such as crème brûlée and sticky toffee pudding with ice-cream. *Benchmark main dish: cod in beer batter with chips and peas £12.50. Two-course evening meal £20.00.*

Shepherd Neame ~ Tenant Sophie Pemble ~ Real ale ~ Open 11.30-3, 6-11; 12-5 Sun ~ Bar food 12-2, 6.30-9.30; 12-3 Sun ~ Restaurant ~ Children allowed in bar (no under-8s in evening) ~ Dogs allowed in bar

WAREHORNE
Woolpack 🛏
TQ9832 Map 3

(01233) 732900 – www.woolpackinnwarehorne.com

Off B2067 near Hamstreet; TN26 2LL

In a pretty village and surrounded by sheep pastures with interestingly decorated bars, local ales, good food and seats outside; bedrooms

The interior of this part-weatherboarded 16th-c dining pub is interesting and full of character. The various connecting areas have beams, both an inglenook fireplace and a woodburning stove, walls (some boarded) hung with prints, old photographs, hops and ornate mirrors plus farming implements, fishing rods, oars and a boar's head. Seating ranges from all manner of wooden chairs and wall seats heaped with scatter cushions around tables of varying size on quarry tiles or old bricks. As well as Tonbridge and three changing regional ales served direct from the cask, there's local cider and good wines by the glass, and easy-going, friendly staff. Metal chairs and tables and long benches at the front of the building are interspersed by raised flower beds. Bedrooms are comfortable and quirky; some overlook the 15th-c village church. This is sister pub to the Five Bells in Brabourne, Radnor Arms in Folkestone and Duke William in Ickham.

Well thought-of pubby food includes salt and pepper squid with garlic mayonnaise, whitebait with sriracha mayonnaise, roasted red pepper hummus with sourdough, wood-fired pizzas, smoked frankfurter with sauerkraut, crispy onions and fries, beef burger and fries, roast chicken breast with caesar salad, poached egg and bacon crumb, and puddings such as vanilla cheesecake and strawberries, and chocolate brownie with vanilla ice-cream. *Benchmark main dish: beer-battered cod with beef dripping chips and mushy peas £13.50. Two-course evening meal £20.00.*

Free house ~ Licensees Alison and John Rogers ~ Open 11-11; 11-midnight Fri, Sat; 11-10.30 Sun; closed Mon, Tues ~ Bar food 12-3, 5-8.30; 12-3, 6-9.30 Fri, Sat; 12-5 Sun ~ Children welcome ~ Dogs allowed in bar ~ Bedrooms: £100

WHITSTABLE
Pearsons Arms ⭐🍴 🍷
TR1066 Map 3

(01227) 773133 – www.pearsonsarmswhitstable.co.uk

Sea Wall off Oxford Street after road splits into one-way system; public parking on left as road divides; CT5 1BT

Seaside pub with an emphasis on imaginative food, several local ales and good mix of customers

Appealing décor including driftwood walls, settles with scatter cushions, captain's chairs and leather armchairs on a stripped-wood floor, and carefully considered extra touches such as big flower arrangements on the bar counter, help make this welcoming beachside pub special. The two front bars are divided by a central chimney. You'll find a thoughtful range of drinks and interesting food, and there's plenty of space for enjoying both. Courteous staff serve Pearsons Arms (named for the pub from Adnams) and Sharps Doom Bar plus two guests such as Ramsgate Gadds Seasider and Timothy Taylors Landlord on handpump, 21 good wines by the glass and an extensive list of cocktails; background music and reguar live music nights. A cosy lower room has a bookcase mural and a couple of big chesterfields and dining chairs around plain tables on a stone floor. Up a couple of flights of stairs, the restaurant (overlooking the water) has mushroom-coloured paintwork, contemporary wallpaper, more driftwood and church chairs and pine tables on nice wide floorboards.

🍴 Highly regarded food includes sandwiches and small plates (salt and pepper squid, Whitstable rock oysters, grilled aubergine with basil pesto, mini chorizo sausages), plus pan-fried scallops with yuzu mayonnaise, roquefort and chicory salad with toasted walnuts, beef bourguignon, seafood platter, linguine with local crab, chilli and lime, lamb rump with pea, broad bean and feta ragoût and salsa verde, roasted basil gnocchi with ratatouille and pesto, and puddings such as blueberry pannacotta with blueberry gel and meringue, and sticky toffee pudding with caramelised banana and butterscotch sauce; they also offer a two- and three-course weekday set lunch. *Benchmark main dish: beer-battered fish with triple-cooked chips £16.00. Two-course evening meal £25.00.*

Enterprise ~ Lease Jake Alder ~ Real ale ~ Open 12-midnight; 12-11 Sun ~ Bar food 12-8; 12-6 Sun ~ Restaurant ~ Children welcome ~ Dogs allowed in bar

WINGHAM

TR2457 Map 3

Dog 🍴 ♀ 🛏

(01227) 720339 – www.thedog.co.uk
Canterbury Road (A257); CT3 1BB

Hands-on licensees in handsome old pub with first class food, local ales, friendly staff and seats on terrace; bedrooms

The clever addition of contemporary touches to the heavy beams and nice old brickwork of this medieval inn make it all the more appealing and attractive. The carpeted bar has a woodburning stove in an inglenook fireplace with armchairs grouped around in front, more armchairs against the walls, a cushioned window seat, dog motifs on the back of leather chairs and a white-painted piano; dotted about are fabric dogs, dog cartoons and prints on grey paintwork, pub games and daily papers. Swivelling wood stools line the counter where they keep Harveys Best and Whitstable Bay Pale Ale on handpump and nice wines by the glass; background music and board games. One part of the dining room has metal and animal-hide chairs and upholstered wall banquettes around wooden tables on wide floorboards, a few animal-hide stools by the bar and an open fire. An airy second room has a woodburning stove, high-backed tartan or leather chairs around more tables on flagstones and plants on windowsills. Outside on the terrace are modern grey or white chairs and tables and a gazebo. They have eight stylish, well equipped and individually styled bedrooms and breakfasts are particularly enjoyable.

🍴 Good, enterprising modern food includes sandwiches, soy-cured salmon with pickled cockles, lotus root and wasabi, mussels in cider cream sauce, chicken, bacon and avocado caesar salad, braised ox cheek with cauliflower purée, pea and broad bean pearl barley risotto, chicken supreme with ham croquette, fondant potato and sweetcorn, Moroccan-spiced lamb rump with couscous tabbouleh, chalk-stream trout with anchovy mayo and charred broccoli, and puddings such as hazelnut chocolate délice with cocoa nib tuile and cherry and almond tart; a fixed-price menu is available Monday to Thursday. *Benchmark main dish: battered haddock with triple-cooked chips £19.00. Two-course evening meal £34.00.*

Free house ~ Licensee Marc Brigden ~ Real ale ~ Open 11-11; 11-9 Sun ~ Bar food 12-2.30, 6.30-9; 12-5 Sun ~ Restaurant ~ Children welcome ~ Dogs allowed in bar ~ Bedrooms: £90

'Children welcome' means the pub says it lets children inside without any special restriction. If it allows them in, but to restricted areas such as an eating area or family room, we specify this. Places with separate restaurants often let children use them, and hotels usually let children into public areas such as lounges. Some pubs impose an evening time limit – let us know if you find one earlier than 9pm.

Also Worth a Visit in Kent

Besides the fully inspected pubs, you might like to try these pubs that have been recommended to us and described by readers. Do tell us what you think of them: feedback@goodguides.com

APPLEDORE   TQ9529
Black Lion (01233) 758206
The Street; TN26 2BU Bustling 1930s brick pub in attractive village; good generously served food (special diets catered for) including lamb from Romney Marsh and local fish, Goachers and four guests such as Black Sheep, Hastings Session Pale Ale, Rother Valley Level Best and Sharps Doom Bar, Biddenden cider, welcoming helpful staff, partitioned back eating area, log fire; background music, events such as bank holiday hog roasts; children welcome, tables out at front under parasols, good military canal walks, open all day, food all day Fri-Sun. *(Julie Swift)*

BARHAM   TR2050
Duke of Cumberland
(01227) 831396 *The Street; CT4 6NY*
Open-plan pub close to village green; enjoyable home cooking including good Sun roasts, well kept Harveys, Greene King, Black Sheep and a guest, friendly staff, plain tables and chairs on bare boards or flagstones, hops and log fire; quiz second Tues of month, sports TV, board games and darts; children welcome, dogs in bar, garden with boules and play area, three comfortable bedrooms, handy for A2, open all day, food all day weekends.

BEARSTED   TQ8055
Oak on the Green (01622) 737976
The Street; ME14 4EJ Well run dining pub with friendly bustling atmosphere (sister to the Old Mill at Kennington); two hop-festooned bar areas with bare boards and half-panelling, wide choice of home-made food including range of burgers, steaks and fajitas, Harveys Best, Shepherd Neame Spitfire and three guests, restaurant; they also own the smaller fish restaurant next door (closed Sun evening, Mon); children and dogs (in bar) welcome, disabled access, seats out at front under big umbrellas, open all day Fri-Sun.

BENENDEN   TQ8032
★**Bull** (01580) 240054
The Street; by village green; TN17 4DE
Relaxed informal atmosphere in bare-boards or dark terracotta-tiled rooms, pleasing mix of furniture, church candles on tables, log fire in brick inglenook, ales such as Hophead, Dark Star, Harveys and Larkins from carved wooden counter, Biddenden cider, more formal dining room, tasty generously served food including speciality pies and popular Sun carvery, friendly helpful staff; background music (live Sun afternoon

5-7pm); children and dogs (in bar) welcome, picnic-sets out in front behind white picket fence, back garden, three bedrooms, open all day Sat.

BETHERSDEN   TQ9240
George (01233) 820235
The Street; TN3 3AG Tile-hung village local with good buoyant atmosphere; well kept Harveys, St Austell, Greene King and two guests, generous sensibly priced food including good value carvery (Sun, Weds), large public bar with open fire, smaller lounge next to dining area; pool, darts, juke box; children and dogs welcome, open all day, no food Sun evening, Mon lunchtime.

BIDBOROUGH   TQ5643
★**Kentish Hare** (01892) 525709
Bidborough Ridge; TN3 0XB Good imaginative décor and food at this popular dining pub including set menus; leather armchairs around open fire in main bar, unusual stools made of corks, bookcase and suitcase wallpaper, a house beer from Tonbridge along with Harveys and a guest, 30 wines by the glass and good choice of other drinks, modern two-way woodburner in cosy middle room, second bar with seating booths and airy back restaurant with view into kitchen; background music; children welcome (under-5s eat free), dogs allowed in some areas, contemporary tables and chairs on deck overlooking lower terrace, open all day Sat, closed Sun evening, Mon, Tues.

BODSHAM   TR1045
Timber Batts (01233) 750083
Following Bodsham, Wye sign off B2068, keep right at unsigned fork after about 1.5 miles; TN25 5JQ Eccentric old rural pub under family ownership; traditional beamed bar with inglenook log fire, eclectic mix of furniture and masses of quirky bits and pieces including lots of taxidermy, three Kentish ales and four ciders, some evening food (Thurs-Sat); live music and DJ nights, bar billiards, pinball, board games; children and dogs welcome, lovely views over wide-spreading valley from garden with wandering chickens, camping, working forge next door (landlord is a blacksmith), closed Mon-Weds, open from 4pm Thurs and Fri, all day Sat, till 7pm Sun.

BOUGH BEECH   TQ4846
Wheatsheaf (01732) 700100
B2027, S of reservoir; TN8 7NU
Attractive 14th-c pub with emphasis on food including children's meals, five beers such as Westerham, Larkins and Harveys and good

choice of wines, beams and timbering, bare boards and log fires (one in a huge fireplace), high ceilinged dining room, more tables upstairs; dogs welcome, nice outside seating area and good walks including circular one around Bough Beech Reservoir, open all day (till 9.30pm Sun).

BOUGHTON ALUPH   TR0247
Flying Horse (01233) 620914
Boughton Lees, just off A251 N of Ashford; TN25 4HH Interesting old pub overlooking village cricket pitch; beams, panelling and inglenooks, stone-arched window and ancient glass-covered well, enjoyable food from sandwiches to grills including burgers and steaks, Fullers London Pride, Harveys Best and guests; background music, TV; children and dogs welcome, tables out at front and in spacious back garden, bedrooms, open all day from 8am for breakfast.

BOXLEY   TQ7758
Kings Arms (01622) 755177
1.75 miles from M20 junction 7; opposite church; ME14 3DR Cosy dining pub in pretty village at foot of the downs; largely 16th/17th-c, with good choice of popular food from lunchtime baguettes to weekly specials, four well kept ales including Fullers, Sharps and Harveys, welcoming helpful service, spic-and-span interior with low black beams, red chesterfields by big brick fireplace; background music, monthly quiz; children and dogs welcome, picnic-sets and play area in nice garden, good local walks, open (and food) all day.

BOYDEN GATE   TR2265
Gate Inn (01227) 860498
Off A299 Herne Bay–Ramsgate signed for Hillboro', Reculver, then left to Chislet; Chislet also signed off A28 Canterbury–Margate at Upstreet – keep right on to Boyden; CT3 4EB Rustic beamed pub with unpretentious quarry-tiled bar rooms; cushioned pews around character tables, attractively etched windows, old local photographs and double-aspect log fire, Shepherd Neame beers and occasional guest from tap room casks, popular sensibly priced home-made food from doorstep sandwiches to specials (must book at weekends), bare-boards restaurant in former bakery, woodburner; children and dogs (in bar) welcome, sheltered garden bounded by two streams, ducks and chickens, open all day weekends, no food Sun night.

BRASTED   TQ4654
Stanhope Arms (01959) 561970
Church Road; TN16 1HZ Welcoming old red-brick village pub next to the church; four real ales including Greene King and Black Sheep and well liked pubby food (not Sun evening, Mon, limited choice Tues), good service, cosy traditional bar with darts, bright cheerful restaurant with white tablecloths and napkins; children and dogs welcome (resident labradors), summer barbecues and bat and trap in back garden, open all day.

BRENCHLEY   TQ6841
★ Halfway House (01892) 722526
Horsmonden Road; TN12 7AX Beamed 18th-c inn with attractive mix of rustic and traditional furnishings on bare boards, old farm tools and other bric-a-brac, two log fires, friendly welcoming staff, up to a dozen well kept changing ales from breweries such as Kent, Goachers, Tonbridge, Long Man, Gun, Surrey Hills tapped from the cask (bank holiday beer/cider festivals end of May, Aug), enjoyable traditional home-made food including popular Sun roasts, two eating areas; quiz every other Weds, live music Thurs; children and dogs welcome, picnic-sets and play area in big garden, summer barbecues, two bedrooms, open all day, no food Sun evening.

BROADSTAIRS   TR3967
Charles Dickens (01843) 600160
Victoria Parade; CT10 1QS Centrally placed with big busy bar; decent choice of beers and wines, popular food from snacks to good local fish/seafood, breakfast from 10am (9am weekends), upstairs restaurant with fine sea views; Sat live music, sports TV; children welcome, tables out overlooking Viking Bay, almost next door to Dickens House Museum, open all day.

BROADSTAIRS   TR3868
Four Candles 07947 062063
Sowell Street; CT10 2AT Quirky, much enjoyed one-room micropub in former shop; good selection of local beers chalked on blackboard including own brews, Kentish ciders and wines, Canterbury cheeses and local pork pies, high tables and stools on sawdust floor, bucket lightshades and various odds and ends including pitchfork handles (the famous Two Ronnies sketch was inspired by a Broadstairs ironmonger); local cheese and pork pies, friendly chatty atmosphere; closed weekday lunchtimes, open all day weekends.

BROADSTAIRS   TR3967
★ Tartar Frigate (01843) 862013
Harbour Street, by quay; CT10 1EU Flint-faced harbourside pub dating from the 18th c; pleasantly old-fashioned bar with interesting local photographs and fishing memorabilia, hanging pots and brasses, log fire, well kept ales such as Ramsgate, Gadds lunchtime bar food (Mon-Sat) and very good fish/seafood in popular upstairs restaurant with fine Viking Bay views, also good value four-course Sun lunch with two sittings 12.30pm and 3.30pm, friendly hospitable staff; background and weekly live music including Weds folk session; open all day, no food Sun evening.

BROOKLAND TQ9724
Woolpack (01797) 344321
On A259 from Rye, turn right signposted
Midley where main road bends sharp
left, just after the expanse of Walland
Marsh; OS Sheet 189 map reference
977244; TN29 9TJ 15th-c cottage in heart
of Romney Marsh; lovely uneven brick floor
in ancient entrance lobby, quarry-tiled main
bar with low beams (thought to have come
from local wrecks) and massive inglenook,
carpeted dining room, generous helpings of
enjoyable reasonably priced home-made food
from sandwiches and baked potatoes up,
Shepherd Neame ales; may be background
radio; children welcome, picnic-sets in good-
sized gardens, summer barbecues, good local
walks, open (and food) all day weekends.

BURMARSH TR1032
Shepherd & Crook (01303) 872336
Shear Way, next to church; TN29 0JJ
Traditional 16th-c marshside village
local with smuggling history; three well
kept changing ales, nine cask ciders, good
straightforward home-made food at
reasonable prices including deals and gluten-
free options, friendly service, interesting
photographs and blow lamp collection, open
fire; bar games such as ring the bull; children
and dogs welcome, seats on side terrace,
holiday cottage by pub, closed Mon and Tues
(except bank holidays), open all day Sat, Sun
till 6pm.

CANTERBURY TR1458
Dolphin (01227) 455963
St Radigunds Street; CT1 2AA
Busy modernised dining pub under new
management with plenty of tables in light
spacious bar; enjoyable fairly traditional
home-made food from baguettes to popular
Sun roast, Sharps Doom Bar, Timothy Taylors
Landlord and guests, good choice of wines
including some country ones, friendly staff,
bric-a-brac on delft shelf, board games,
flagstoned conservatory; children welcome,
dogs at management's discretion, disabled
access, picnic-sets in good-sized back garden,
open all day (food all day Sat).

CANTERBURY TR1457
Foundry (01227) 455899
Stour Street; CT1 2NR This backstreet
brewpub has Canterbury Brewers beers
from visible microbrewery plus local guests
(tasting trays available), they also make their
own ciders and spirits, decent food (till 8pm,
9pm Fri, Sat, 6pm Sun) from sandwiches
and sharing plates up including burgers
and fajitas, helpful cheerful staff; children
welcome, no dogs, disabled access/loo, open
all day till midnight (till 10pm Sun).

CANTERBURY TR1557
Lady Luck (01227) 763298
St Peters Street; CT1 2BQ Quirky rock 'n'

roll bar with music-themed décor; real ales
such as Adnams, Sharps Doom Bar, craft
beers and good selection of other drinks
including a rum menu, enjoyable home-
cooked food with plenty for vegetarians/
vegans, good friendly service; regular
live bands and DJs, juke box, pool, daily
newspaper and board games; a couple of
pavement tables, more seats in beer garden
behind, open all day till 1am (till 2am Fri,
Sat, till 11pm Sun), food served till 7pm
(3pm Sun).

CANTERBURY TR1558
New Inn (01227) 464584
Havelock Street; CT1 1NP Friendly little
Victorian terraced local not far from the city
centre; seven well kept changing ales such
as Adnams, Kent, Black Sheep, Oakham,
Gads (tasters offered), a proper cider and
good range of whiskies, bare-boards bar with
woodburner, modern back conservatory,
no food; juke box and various games; dogs
welcome, seats in garden behind, nearby
parking can be difficult, open all day Fri-Sun.

CANTERBURY TR1457
Parrot (01227) 454170
Church Lane – the one off St Radigunds
Street, 100 metres E of St Radigunds car
park; CT1 2AG Ancient heavy-beamed pub
tucked down narrow part-cobbled street;
wood and flagstone floors, stripped masonry,
hops and three log fires, up to six real ales
including Shepherd Neame, good food from
open sandwiches up, extensive wine list,
friendly service, upstairs vaulted function
room; children welcome, nicely laid out
courtyard with central barbecue, open all day
from midday, food to 9pm Mon-Thurs, to 10pm
Fri, Sat, to 8.30pm Sun.

CANTERBURY TR1457
White Hart (01227) 765091
Worthgate Place, opposite tree-shaded
square off Castle Street; CT1 2QX
Popular little pub with friendly atmosphere;
Shepherd Neame ales and enjoyable well
priced food cooked by landlady including
some Italian dishes, opened up bare-boards
interior with woodburner in side room; quiz
nights; children and dogs welcome, large
garden behind (one of very few in the city),
open all day, food Fri-Sun.

CHARING TQ9551
Bowl (01233) 712256
Egg Hill Road; TN27 0HG Newly
renovated popular 16th-c pub high on the
downs (near Pilgrims Way) run by father
and daughter; beamed bare-boards bar with
inglenook log fire, tusky boar's head behind
dark-panelled counter serving good Kentish
beers such as Ramsgate Gadds, Hopdaemon,
Old Dairy, Whitstable Brewery and Wantsum,
carpeted dining area, enjoyable fairly
priced food (all day Sat, till 5pm Sun)
from lunchtime sandwiches/baguettes up

including range of burgers, friendly helpful service; July beer/cider/cocktail festival with live music; children and dogs welcome, chunky picnic-sets on heated front terrace, more tables in big lawned garden, good local walks, nine bedrooms, open all day.

CHARTHAM
TR1054
Artichoke (01227) 738316
Rottington Street; CT4 7JQ Attractive timbered pub (dates from the 15th c); generous helpings of enjoyable reasonably priced pub food (till 4.30pm Sun) from sandwiches and baked potatoes up, well kept Shepherd Neame ales, good service, carpeted log-fire bar, dining area with light wood tables (one built around a glass-topped well); quiz last Thurs of month, darts, board games, dominoes and bat and trap; children welcome, picnic-sets in back garden, closed Mon lunchtime, otherwise open all day.

CHIDDINGSTONE CAUSEWAY
TQ5247
Greyhound (01892) 870275
Charcott, off back road to Weald; TN11 8LG Red-brick village pub; well kept Larkins and a couple of guests, Chiddingstone and Dudda's Tun cider and good range of gins, enjoyable home-made food at reasonable prices (some produce from own farm), log fire; children, walkers and dogs welcome, picnic-sets out in front and in side garden, closed Mon, otherwise open all day (till 8pm Sun), no food Sun evening.

CHIDDINGSTONE CAUSEWAY
TQ5146
★Little Brown Jug (01892) 870318
B2027; TN11 8JJ Spacious open-plan Whiting & Hammond pub next to Penshurst station, comfortable bar and big dining extension, lots of pictures, prints, framed cigarette cards and maps on painted walls, big mirrors, candles on windowsills, bare boards and log fires, enjoyable food at sensible prices from sandwiches to full meals including pub classics and vegetarian/ vegan and smoked options, well kept Larkins Traditional and a couple of guests such as Timothy Taylors Landlord and Greene King Old Speckled Hen, decent wine list, smiling responsive service; board games, some live music; children welcome, dogs in front bar, terrace with seats and tables, picnic-sets on grass, dining huts for hire and children's play area, open (and food) all day, can get busy.

CHIDDINGSTONE HOATH
TQ4943
★Rock (01892) 870296
Hoath Corner on back road Chiddingstone–Cowden; OS Sheet 188 map reference 497431; TN8 7BS Welcoming and bustling little tile-hung cottage with undulating brick floor, simple furnishings and woodburner in fine brick inglenook, some quirky touches such as

curtains made from beer mats, well kept Larkins (brewed close by) and guests such as Long Man and Dark Star and good home-made food (not Sun evening) from varied menu including specials, large stuffed bull's head for ring the bull, up a step to smaller room with long wooden settle by nice table; walkers and dogs welcome, picnic-sets out in front and on back lawn, open all day (till 8pm Sun, closed Mon).

CHILHAM
TR0653
★White Horse (01227) 730355
The Square; CT4 8BY 15th-c pub in picturesque village square; handsome ceiling beams and massive fireplace with Lancastrian rose carved in the mantel beam, chunky light oak furniture on pale wood flooring and more traditional pubby furniture on quarry tiles, three well kept ales such as Timothy Taylor's Landlord and Fullers London Pride (Aug beer/cider festival), enjoyable varied food (all day Sat, to 8pm Sun), amiable helpful service; live music and quiz nights; children welcome, dogs in bar, handy for the castle, open all day.

CHILLENDEN
TR2653
★Griffins Head (01304) 840325
SE end of village; 2 miles E of Aylesham; CT3 1PS Attractive 14th-c beamed and timbered pub surrounded by nice countryside; gently upscale local atmosphere in two bars and flagstoned back dining room, big log fire, full range of Shepherd Neame ales, good wine list and decent choice of popular home-made food (all day Sat), attentive friendly service; no under-8s, dogs welcome, summer weekend barbecues in pretty garden, vintage car meetings first Sun of month, open all day.

CHIPSTEAD
TQ4956
★Bricklayers Arms (01732) 743424
Chevening Road; TN13 2RZ Attractive flower-decked pub (originally three cottages) overlooking lake and green, relaxed chatty atmosphere, well kept Harveys from casks behind long counter, good choice of popular fairly priced food from baguettes up including Mon steak night, Weds burger night, Fri fish night and Sunday roasts, cheerful helpful service, heavily beamed flagstoned bar with open fire and fine racehorse painting, larger back restaurant; Tues quiz and monthly live music; children and dogs welcome, disabled access/loo, seats out in front, closed Mon.

CONYER QUAY
TQ9664
Ship (01795) 520881
Conyer Road; ME9 9HR Renovated and extended 18th-c creekside pub owned by adjacent Swale Marina; bare boards and open fires, enjoyable home-cooked food, three changing ales such as Adnams and Old Dairy; children and dogs welcome, useful for boaters, walkers (on Saxon Shore Way) and birders, seats out at front.

COWDEN TQ4640

Fountain (01342) 850528
Off A264 and B2026; High Street;
TN8 7JG Good fairly priced food from
sandwiches up in attractive tile-hung village
pub; steep steps up to bar with well kept
Harveys and decent wines by the glass,
friendly helpful staff, beams, half-panelling
and old photographs, good log fire, mix
of tables in adjoining room, woodburner
in small back dining area, conservatory;
background music, quiz first Thurs of month;
children, walkers and dogs welcome, picnic-
sets on small terrace and lawn, pretty village,
open all day Sun but no evening food.

COWDEN TQ4642

★ Queens Arms (01342) 850598
Cowden Pound; junction B2026 with
Markbeech Road; TN8 5NP Friendly little
Victorian time warp known as Elsie's after
former long-serving landlady – present local
owner has thankfully kept things much the
same; two simple unpretentious rooms with
open fires, two well kept/priced ales from
Larkins and a guest, no food, darts, shove-
ha'penny and other traditional games, piano;
folk music, morris dancers and Christmas
mummers; dogs welcome, open 4-8pm
Mon-Sat, noon-4pm Sun

CRUNDALE TR0949

★ Compasses (01227) 700300
Sole Street; CT4 7ES Many people come
to this welcoming country pub for its
outstanding, imaginative food using locally
sourced ingredients, well kept Shepherd Neame
ales and maybe a guest, traditional interior
with hop-strung beams and woodburner in
brick inglenook, back restaurant; children and
walkers welcome, dogs in garden but not inside,
large garden with play equipment, closed Mon
(including bank holidays), otherwise open all
day (till 6pm Sun).

CUDHAM TQ4459

Blacksmiths Arms (01959) 572678
Cudham Lane S; TN14 7QB Popular
low-ceilinged local with five real ales such as
Adnams, Black Sheep, Courage and Sharps,
a good choice of wines by the glass and
enjoyable fairly traditional food at reasonable
prices, plenty of tables in eating area,
log fires, lovely views over wooded valley;
children and dogs (in bar) welcome, award-
winning flower-filled garden and lots of
colourful hanging baskets and window boxes,
open all day, no food Sun or Mon evenings.

DARGATE TR0761

Dove (01227) 751085
Village signposted from A299;
ME13 9HB Recently refurbished tucked-
away 19th-c restaurant-y pub; first class
food (not Wed evening or Sun evening)
cooked by chef-owner including set menus,
Shepherd Neame ales and good wines by the
glass, friendly efficient service, stripped-
wood tables on bare boards, some blue
half-panelling and old pictures of the pub,
woodburner in brick fireplace; children,
walkers and dogs welcome, sheltered garden,
open all day Fri and Sat, till 6pm Sun, closed
Mon, Tues.

DARTFORD TQ5272

Horse & Groom (01322) 290056
Leyton Cross Road; DA2 7AP Bright
refurbished pub next to Dartford Heath
with large bar with piano and restaurant
extension; Shepherd Neame ales, a dozen
wines by the glass and good food from
regularly changing menu including some
pub favourites, friendly service; live music;
children welcome, open all day.

DARTFORD TQ5473

Malt Shovel (01322) 224381
Darenth Road; DA1 1LP Cheerful 17th-c
waney-boarded pub with two bars and
conservatory; well kept Youngs, St Austell
and three guests, 14 wines by the glass and
good reasonably priced food from sandwiches
and sharing plates up, friendly helpful staff;
Mon quiz, some live music including folk
nights; children and dogs welcome, tables on
paved part-covered terrace, closed weekdays
until 3pm, open all day Sat, until 6pm Sun.

DEAL TR3751

Berry (01304) 362411
Canada Road; CT14 7EQ Small no-frills
local opposite old Royal Marine barracks;
welcoming enthusiastic landlord serving
up to 11 well kept ales such as Dark Star,
Redemption, Kent, Oakham and Harveys
(tasting notes on slates, regular beer
festivals), at least ten real ciders and
perries including Kentish farm cider, no
food, L-shaped carpeted bar with coal fire;
quiz second Fri of month, open mic nights,
darts teams, pool and some live music; dogs
welcome, small vine-covered back terrace,
open all day (from 3pm Tues).

DEAL TR3752

Bohemian (01304) 361939
Beach Street opposite pier; CT14 6HY
Seafront bar with five real ales such
as Harveys, Old Dairy, Dark Star and
Whitstable, and good choice of bottled beers,
extensive range of spirits too including 170
gins, popular traditional home-made food,
friendly helpful staff, L-shaped room with
mismatched furniture (some découpage
tables), polished wood floor, lots of pictures,
mirrors, signs and other odds and ends,

sofas and weekend papers, similar décor in upstairs cocktail bar with good sea views; background music; children and dogs welcome, sunny split-level deck behind and heated smokers' gazebo, open all day and can get very busy (particularly weekends).

DEAL   TR3752

Just Reproach   07432 413226

King Street; CT14 6HX Popular and genuinely welcoming micropub in former corner shop; simple drinking room with sturdy tables on bare boards, stools and cushioned benches, friendly knowledgeable service from father and daughter team, four changing small brewery ales tapped from the cask, also real ciders and some organic wines, locally made cheese, friendly chatty atmosphere; no mobile phones (fine for using them); dogs welcome, closed Sun evening.

DEAL   TR3753

Prince Albert   (01304) 375425

Middle Street; CT14 6LW Compact 19th-c corner pub in conservation area; bowed entrance doors, etched-glass windows and fairly ornate interior with assorted bric-a-brac, three changing local ales, popular food (Weds-Sat evenings) and Sun carvery in back dining area, friendly staff; dogs welcome, small garden behind, bedrooms, closed lunchtimes except Sun.

DEAL   TR3752

Royal   (01304) 375555

Beach Street; CT14 6JD Popular early 18th-c hotel right on the seafront; light and comfortable with plenty of casual drinkers in pubby bar, Shepherd Neame ales and good choice of enjoyable well priced food from sandwiches to fresh fish, friendly uniformed staff, restaurant; children and dogs (in bar) welcome, terrace overlooking the beach, 18 smart bedrooms (some with sea-view balconies), open (and food) 10am-9pm.

DEAL   TR3753

Ship   (01304) 372222

Middle Street; CT14 6JZ Traditional dimly lit two-room local in historic maritime quarter; five well kept/priced ales including Dark Star, Timothy Taylor, and Ramsgate Gadds served by friendly staff, no food, bare boards and lots of dark woodwork, stripped brick and local ship and wreck pictures, evening candles, cosy panelled back bar, open fire and woodburner; dogs welcome, small pretty walled garden, open all day.

DOVER   TR3241

Blakes   (01304) 202194

Castle Street; CT16 1PJ Small flagstoned cellar bar down steep steps; brick and flint walls, dim lighting, woodburner, its own Blakes Bitter from Dartford Wobbler Brewery plus Adnams Broadside and two changing

guests, farm ciders/perries, several wines by the glass and over 50 malt whiskies, good bar food from sandwiches up, panelled carpeted upstairs restaurant, friendly staff; well behaved children welcome, dogs in bar, side garden and suntrap back terrace, four bedrooms, open (and food) all day.

DUNGENESS   TR0916

Pilot   (01797) 320314

Battery Road; TN29 9NJ Single-storey, mid 20th-c seaside café-bar by shingle beach; well kept Adnams, Sharps and a guest, decent choice of good value food from enjoyable sandwiches to fish and chips, friendly efficient service (even when packed), open-plan interior divided into three areas, dark plank panelling (including the slightly curved ceiling), lighter front part overlooking beach, prints and local memorabilia, books for sale (proceeds to RNLI); background music; children welcome, dogs in garden only, picnic-sets in side garden, open (and food) all day till 10pm (9pm Sun).

DUNKS GREEN   TQ6152

★ Kentish Rifleman   (01732) 810727

Dunks Green Road; TN11 9RU Relaxing Tudor country pub with bare-boards bar and two carpeted dining areas; various rifles and guns on low beams, cosy log fire, well kept ales such as Harveys, Tonbridge, Westerham and Whitstable, enjoyable reasonably priced food from light meals to popular Sun roasts, Tues pie and pint deal, Fri fish and fizz deal, friendly efficient staff; children and dogs welcome, tables in pretty garden with well, good walks from the door, one bedroom, open all day, no food Sun or Mon evenings.

EAST PECKHAM   TQ6548

Man of Kent   (01622) 871345

Tonbridge Road; TN12 5LA Traditional tile-hung pub dating from the 16th c; low black beams, mix of pubby furniture on carpet or slate tiles, fresh flowers, big two-way woodburner in central fireplace, ales such as Harveys, Sharps, Timothy Taylors and Tonbridge, enjoyable well priced home-made food; children welcome, terrace seating by River Bourne, nearby walks.

EASTLING   TQ9656

Carpenters Arms   (01795) 890234

Off A251 S of M2 junction 6, via Painters Forstal; The Street; ME13 0AZ Partly 14th-c red-brick village pub; well kept Shepherd Neame ales and good reasonably priced pubby food from sandwiches and various ploughman's to daily specials plus Mon steak nights, Tues pie and a pint and Sunday roasts; friendly attentive service, big log fires front and back, oak beams and mix of old and new furniture on brick or bare-boards floors, vintage photographs of the pub and surroundings; some live music; children welcome, paved terrace with rattan-style furniture, open all day Sat, Sun.

EGERTON   TQ9047
Barrow House (01233) 756599
The Street; TN27 9DJ Stylishly refurbished
16th-c weatherboarded pub under same
ownership as the Milk House at Sissinghurst;
back bar with high beams and light stone
floor, inglenook log fire (plastered canopy
has signatures of World War II airmen), main
bar with more beams and timber partitions,
attractive wooden counter serving well kept
ales such as Harveys and Dark Star and good
choice of wines, enjoyable food from snacks
and sharing plates up, two-room restaurant
with bare boards, painted tables and antler
chandeliers, friendly staff; background and
some live music; children, walkers and dogs
welcome, disabled access via garden, three
smart and comfortable bedrooms, open from
9am, to 6pm Sun, Mon, to 10pm Tues-Thur, to
11pm Fri, Sat.

FAVERSHAM   TR0161
Bear (01795) 532668
Market Place; ME13 7AG Traditional late
Victorian Shepherd Neame pub (back part
dates from the 16th c); their ales kept well
and occasional guests, enjoyable low-priced
pubby food (not Fri-Sun evenings), friendly
relaxed atmosphere, locals' front bar, snug
and back dining lounge (all off side corridor);
quiz last Mon of month, darts; a couple of
pavement tables, open all day.

FAVERSHAM   TR0160
Elephant (01795) 590157
The Mall; ME13 8JN Traditional town
ale house, friendly and chatty, with four
or five good changing ales mainly from
smaller Kent brewers such as Hopdaemon
and further afield such as Rother Valley or
Mighty Oak, maybe a local cider too, no food
(can bring your own), single bare-boards bar
with central log fire and cosy seating areas,
dim lighting; juke box and some live music;
children and dogs welcome, peaceful suntrap
back garden with pond, open all day Sat, till
7pm Sun, from 3pm weekdays, closed Mon.

FAVERSHAM   TR0161
Sun (01795) 535098
West Street; ME13 7JE Rambling 14th-c
pub in pedestrianised street; unpretentious
feel in small low-ceilinged partly panelled
rooms, one with big inglenook, well kept
Shepherd Neame ales and enjoyable food
(not Sun evening) from sandwiches and pub
favourites up, smart restaurant attached;
background and live music (Fri); wheelchair
access negotiating small step, pleasant back
courtyard, 12 smart bedrooms, open all
day to 9pm Mon-Thurs, to 10pm Fri, Sat and
8pm Sun. Open from 8am for breakfast (for
residents).

FINGLESHAM   TR3353
★ Crown (01304) 612555
*Just off A258 Sandwich–Deal; The
Street; CT14 0NA* Neatly kept low-beamed
country local dating from the 16th c; good
value generous home-made food from usual
pub dishes to interesting specials, friendly
helpful service, Dark Star and a couple of
guests, softly lit split-level carpeted bar with
stripped stone and inglenook log fire, two
attractive dining rooms; children and dogs
welcome, lovely big garden with play area
and bat and trap, campsite with five hook-
ups, open all day Fri-Sun.

FOLKESTONE   TR2336
British Lion (01303) 251478
The Bayle, near churchyard; CT20 1SQ
Popular 18th-c flower-decked pub nestling
behind parish church; comfortable and cosy,
with four well kept ales such as Marstons
and a couple of real ciders, big helpings of
good value traditional food, friendly helpful
service; children welcome, tables out in
small yard.

FORDCOMBE   TQ5240
Chafford Arms (01892) 740267
*B2188, off A264 W of Langton Green;
TN3 0SA* Picturesque 19th-c tile-hung pub;
real ales including Harveys and Larkins, good
selection of wines and enjoyable food from
sandwiches and baguettes to imaginative
specials, helpful friendly staff, comfortable
lounge bar, dining room and locals' bar where
dogs allowed, three woodburners; children
welcome (menu for them), picnic-sets on
front terrace and in attractive sheltered back
garden with Weald views, 1930s telephone
box in car park, closed Sun evening, Mon,
otherwise open (and food) all day.

FORDWICH   TR1859
★ Fordwich Arms (01227) 710444
Off A28 in Sturry; CT2 0DB Interesting
1930s red-brick building by the River
Stour (the much older pub burnt down);
most customers here for young chef-
landlord's excellent modern food (not Sun
evening, Mon), but still drinkers in the
long parquet-floored bar where they serve
four real ales and good wines by the glass,
courteous friendly staff, simply furnished
panelled back dining room with open fire;
background music; children and dogs
welcome, tables on side lawn and riverside
terrace, the town hall opposite is thought to
be England's oldest, closed Mon, otherwise
open all day.

A star symbol before the name of a pub shows exceptional character and appeal.
It doesn't mean extra comfort. Even quite a basic pub can win a star,
if it's individual enough.

FRITTENDEN   TQ8141
Bell & Jorrocks (01580) 852415
Corner of Biddenden Road/The Street;
TN17 2EJ Simple 18th-c tile-hung village
local; two well kept ales, Black Sheep and
Harveys, plus two guests such as Fullers,
Tonbridge and Woodfordes (Easter weekend
beer festival), Weston's and Thatcher's
ciders, good home-made food (not Sun
evening, Mon, Tues), friendly welcoming
atmosphere, beamed interior with propeller
from German bomber above fireplace; regular
live music and other events, sports TV,
Kentish darts; children and dogs welcome,
closed Mon and Tues lunchtimes till 3pm,
otherwise open all day.

GOODNESTONE   TR2554
Fitzwalter Arms (01304) 840303
The Street; NB this is in E Kent not the
other Goodnestone; CT3 1PJ Old lattice-
windowed brick-built village pub; rustic
beamed bar with wood floor and open fire,
Shepherd Neame ales, enjoyable reasonably
priced pubby food, helpful cheerful service,
carpeted dining room with another fire;
darts; well behaved children and dogs
welcome, terrace with steps up to peaceful
garden, lovely church next door and close to
Goodnestone Park Gardens, three bedrooms
(steep stairs), open all day (to 8pm Mon), no
evening food Sun or Mon.

GOUDHURST   TQ7037
Green Cross (01580) 211200
East off A21 on to A262 (Station Road);
TN17 1HA Although they specialise in
excellent fish and shellfish here, there is a
properly pubby little two-roomed front bar
with a chatty atmosphere, Harveys Best and
half a dozen wines by the glass; hop-draped
beams, stripped floorboards and dark wooden
furnishings, wine bottles on windowsills,
brass jugs on a mantelshelf above the
fire, more formal main back dining room;
background music; children and dogs (in
bar) welcome, small side terrace, closed Sun
evening, Mon. Note: had not reopened after
lockdown at time of updating this edition of
the Guide.

GOUDHURST   TQ7237
Star & Eagle (01580) 211512
High Street; TN17 1AL Steps up to
striking medieval inn next to the church;
settles and Jacobean-style seats in old-
fashioned carpeted areas on different levels,
beams and log fires, good choice of enjoyable
food including some Spanish influences, well
kept ales such as Brakspears and Harveys,
15 wines by the glass, 14 gins including local
varieties, afternoon teas, friendly service,
restaurant; occasional live music; children
welcome, no dogs inside, tables out at back
with lovely views, attractive village, ten
character bedrooms, good breakfast, open
all day.

GROOMBRIDGE   TQ5337
★Crown (01892) 864742
B2110; TN3 9QH Charming tile-hung
Wealden inn with snug low-beamed bar; old
tables on worn flagstones, panelling, bric-a-
brac, fire in sizeable brick inglenook, well
kept Harveys, Larkins and a guest, enjoyable
pubby food (till 5pm Sun) from lunchtime
sandwiches up including plenty of gluten-free
options, good friendly service, refurbished
two-room restaurant with smaller inglenook;
background music; children and dogs (in bar
and snug) welcome, tables on narrow brick
terrace overlooking steep green, more seats
in garden behind, five bedrooms, handy for
Groombridge Place gardens, closed Mon.

HAWKHURST   TQ7531
★Great House (01580) 753119
Gills Green; pub signed off A229 N;
TN18 5EJ Stylish white-weatherboarded
restauranty pub (part of the Elite Pubs
group); good variety of well liked if not
always cheap food, Harveys Sussex Best and
guests from breweries such as Old Dairy,
Musket and Sharps from marble counter,
polite efficient service, sofas, armchairs and
bright scatter cushions in chatty bar, stools
against counter used by locals, dark wood
dining tables and smartly upholstered chairs
on slate floor beside log fire, steps down to
airy dining room with doors out to garden;
background and some live music; children
and dogs (in bar) welcome, open all day
(food all day weekends).

HAWKHURST   TQ7630
Queens (01580) 754233
Rye Road (A268 E); TN18 4EY Fine
Georgian-fronted inn (building actually
dates from the 16th c) set back from the
road; main bar with heavy beams and bare
boards, some high modern chairs and barrel
tables, armchairs either side of inglenook
woodburner, dining area and cosy snug, well
liked food from bar meals up, four ales such
as Harveys, Old Dairy, Rockin' Robin and
Sharps, 29 decent wines by the glass, good
friendly service, separate restaurant to left of
entrance with another inglenook; background
music; children welcome, tables out in front,
seven smart bedrooms with interesting
décor including family rooms, open all day,
breakfast for non-residents.

HEAVERHAM   TQ5758
Chequers (01732) 670266
Watery Lane; TN15 6NP Attractive 16th-c
beamed country pub; well kept Shepherd
Neame ales, decent wines by the glass and
enjoyable fairly traditional food at sensible
prices, friendly helpful service, public bar
with open fire, inglenook woodburner in
dining area, old timbered barn for functions;
children and dogs welcome, big garden, good
North Downs walks, open all day, no food
after 6pm Sun.

HERNE   TR1865
Butchers Arms (01227) 371000
Herne Street (A291); CT6 7HL The UK's
first micropub (converted from a butchers in
2005); up to half a dozen well kept changing
ales including Adnams and Old Dairy tapped
from backroom casks, tasters offered by
friendly former motorbike-racing landlord,
just a couple of benches and butcher's-block
tables (seats for about ten), lots of bric-a-
brac; dogs welcome, disabled access, tables
out under awning, open 12-1.30pm, 6-9pm,
closed Sun evening, Mon.

HERNHILL   TR0660
Red Lion (01227) 751207
*Off A299 via Dargate, or A2 via
Boughton Street and Staple Street;
ME13 9JR* Pretty Tudor pub by church and
attractive village green, some refurbishment
but keeping character; densely beamed with
antique-style tables and chairs on flagstones
or parquet, log fires, fairly traditional food
including pub classics, well kept ales such
as Sharps, Harveys and Shepherd Neame,
decent wines, friendly helpful staff, upstairs
restaurant; background and some live music;
children and dogs welcome, seats in front
and in big garden, closed Mon, Tues.

HEVER   TQ4743
Greyhound (01732) 862221
Uckfield Lane; TN8 7LJ Fully restored and
recently refurbished 19th-c country pub with
good popular food from sandwiches up, three
well kept ales including Harveys, friendly
efficient service, restaurant with more
adventurous menu; handy for Hever Castle,
five comfortable and spacious bedrooms,
closed Mon lunchtime in summer, no food
Sun evening in winter.

HEVER   TQ4744
Henry VIII (01732) 862457
By gates of Hever Castle; TN8 7NH
Predominantly 17th-c with heavy beams,
wide floorboards, some fine oak panelling
and inglenook fireplace, Henry VIII touches
to décor, emphasis on enjoyable fairly priced
food from pubby choices up, well kept
Shepherd Neame ales, friendly efficient
staff, restaurant; children and dogs welcome,
outside covered area with a couple of leather
sofas, steps down to deck and pondside lawn,
closed Mon, otherwise normally open all day
(but best to check), food till 7pm Sun.

HODSOLL STREET   TQ6263
Green Man (01732) 823575
*Signed off A227 S of Meopham; turn
right in village; TN15 7LE* Friendly
family-run village pub with traditional
furnishings in neat mainly carpeted rooms
around central bar; painted half-panelling,
old framed photographs and woodburner
in standalone fireplace, Harveys, Sharps,
Timothy Taylors and a guest, wide choice of
enjoyable blackboard food from sandwiches/
baguettes up; background music (live Sun),
quiz Mon; children and dogs welcome, picnic-
sets in front overlooking small green, more
tables and climbing frame on back lawn,
closed Mon, Tues.

HOLLINGBOURNE   TQ8455
Dirty Habit (01622) 880880
B2163, off A20; ME17 1UW Ancient dimly
lit beamed pub in same Elite Pubs group as
the Great House in Hawkhurst, Gun at Gun
Hill (Sussex) etc; four ales such as Harveys
and Sharps, several wines by the glass and
popular food including seasonal offers,
armchairs and stools on slate floor in main
bar area, panelled end room with mix of
tables and chairs, low-beamed dining room
and a further raftered eating area with brick
floor and woodburner; children welcome,
good outside shelter with armchairs and
sofas, on North Downs Way and handy for
Leeds Castle, open all day.

HOLLINGBOURNE   TQ8354
★Windmill (01622) 889000
*M20 junction 8, A20 towards Lenham
then left on to B2163 – Eyhorne Street;
ME17 1TR* Most people here for the
impressive food, but there's a small back bar
serving Sharps, local Musket and a guest,
19 wines by the glass; light and airy main
room with white-painted beams, animal skins
on bare boards and log fire in low inglenook,
mix of furniture including armchairs, heavy
settles with scatter cushions, red leather
banquette and dark wood dining tables and
chairs, two further dining rooms (steps up to
one), candles and fresh flowers; background
music (live Sun); children and dogs (in bar)
welcome, back garden with play area and
summer barbecues.

IDE HILL   TQ4851
Cock (01732) 750310
Off B2042 SW of Sevenoaks; TN14 6JN
Pretty village-green local dating from the
15th c, chatty and friendly, with two bars
(steps between), four ales including well
kept Greene King and a beer badged for
them, more than 20 whiskies, enjoyable good
value traditional food including notable steak
and kidney pudding, decent affordably priced
wine list, cosy in winter with inglenook log
fire; children and dogs welcome, picnic-
sets out at front, handy for Chartwell and
Emmetts Garden (both NT), nice walks
nearby, open all day.

IGHTHAM   TQ5956
George & Dragon (01732) 882440
The Street, A227; TN15 9HH Ancient
half-timbered pub with spacious modernised
interior; enjoyable food from pub favourites
up including daily specials and weekday set
menu, well kept Shepherd Neame ales and
decent wines, friendly staff, sofas among
other furnishings in long main bar, heavy-

beamed end room, woodburner and open fires, restaurant; children and dogs welcome, back terrace by car park, handy for Ightham Mote (NT), good walks, open all day Sat, food till 6pm Sun.

IGHTHAM COMMON   TQ5955
Old House (01732) 886077
Redwell, S of village; OS Sheet 188 map reference 591559; TN15 9EE Basic unchanging two-room country local tucked down narrow lane (no inn sign); beams, bare bricks and big inglenook log fire, half a dozen interesting changing ales from tap room casks, from favourites from well known breweries like Youngs, London Pride and Harveys, to smaller breweries like Dark Star and Bespoke, good selection of whiskies and gins, no food; darts; dogs welcome, closed weekday lunchtimes (opens 7pm) and may shut early if quiet.

KENNINGTON   TR0245
Old Mill (01223) 661000
Mill Lane; TN25 4DZ Updated and much extended early 19th-c dining pub (same owners as the Oak on the Green at Bearsted); good choice of popular food from sandwiches and snacks up, well kept ales and nice selection of wines, friendly helpful service; children welcome, plenty of terrace and garden seating, open all day Fri, Sat.

KINGSDOWN   TR3748
Kings Head (01304) 373915
Upper Street; CT14 8BJ Tucked-away split-level local with two cosy bars and L-shaped extension; black timbers, faded cream walls, woodburner, three changing real ales such as locals like Goachers and Ramsgate, popular reasonably priced food including blackboard specials and children's menu, friendly landlord and staff; background and occasional live music, a few vintage amusement machines and darts; dogs welcome, small side garden, skittle alley, open all day Sun, closed weekdays till 5pm.

KINGSTON   TR2051
Black Robin (01227) 830230
Elham Valley Road, off A2 S of Canterbury at Barham signpost; CT4 6HS 18th-c pub named after an infamous highwayman who was hanged nearby; Sharps and two guest usually Kentish ales, good helpings of enjoyable home-made food from shortish menu (can eat in bar or back restaurant extension), stone-baked pizzas to take away; background and live music including some established folk artists, sports TV; children and dogs welcome, disabled access, seats out on decking, open till 5pm Sun, closed Mon, Tues.

LADDINGFORD   TQ6848
Chequers (01622) 871266
The Street; ME18 6BP Friendly old beamed and weatherboarded village pub; good sensibly priced food from sandwiches and sharing boards up, some themed nights, well kept Adnams Southwold and three guests; events including ale and cheese festival Apr/May; children and dogs welcome, big garden with play area, shetland ponies in paddock, Medway walks nearby, one bedroom, open all day weekends.

LEEDS   TQ8253
George (01622) 861314
Lower Street; ME17 1RN Welcoming 17th-c tile-hung village pub; Shepherd Neame ales and good choice of enjoyable pubby food from blackboard menu including range of fajitas; sports TV, fruit machine; children and dogs welcome, picnic-sets out at front and in good-sized garden up steps, covered dining terrace, handy for Leeds Castle, open all day, kitchen closes 6pm Sun, 9pm other days.

LEIGH   TQ5446
Fleur de Lis (01732) 832283
High Street; TN11 8RL Modernised and opened-up brick pub in former 1855 cottage row; well kept ales such as Timothy Taylors, St Austell, Morland, Tonbridge and Whitstable along with a house beer (4 Jays) from Greene King, good fairly priced food including blackboard specials, friendly attentive staff; sports TV; children and dogs welcome, rattan furniture on back terrace, open all day Fri, Sat.

LEIGH   TQ5646
Plough (01732) 832149
Powder Mill Lane/Leigh Road, off B2027 NW of Tonbridge; TN11 9AJ Cosy, attractive opened-up Tudor country pub; lattice windows, hop-strung beams and parquet flooring, some cushioned pews and farmhouse chairs, massive grate in two-way inglenook, well kept Tonbridge Coppernob and up to three local guests, popular home-cooked food, friendly helpful staff, small flagstoned room behind servery with old mangle and darts; quiz third Thurs of month; children and dogs welcome, picnic-sets in garden with play area, old barn for weddings and other functions, open till 9pm, closed Mon.

LINTON   TQ7550
Bull (01622) 743612
Linton Hill (A229 S of Maidstone); ME17 4AW Comfortably modernised 17th-c dining pub; good choice of food from sandwiches and light dishes to pub favourites

---

If we know a pub is cash-only, we say so. This is very rare: almost everywhere accepts credit and debit cards now.

and grills, popular Sun carvery, fine fireplace in nice old beamed bar, carpeted restaurant, well kept Shepherd Neame ales, friendly efficient service; children and dogs (in bar) welcome, side garden overlooking church, splendid far-reaching views from back decking, two gazebos.

LITTLE CHART   TQ9446
Swan (01233) 840011
The Street; TN27 0QB Attractive 15th-c village pub with notable arched Dering windows, open fires and clean fresh décor in unspoilt front bar and good-sized dining area, flowers on tables, enjoyable home-made food including Tues curry night, well kept beers from Sharps, Old Dairy and others, and decent wines by the glass, friendly staff; Weds quiz, live music; children and dogs (in bar) welcome, nice riverside garden, open all day. to 10pm Sun, Mon.

LOWER HARDRES   TR1453
Granville (01227) 700402
Faussett Hill, Street End; B2068 S of Canterbury; CT4 7AL Spacious pub with contemporary furnishings in several linked areas, one with unusual central fire under large conical hood, also a proper public bar with farmhouse chairs, settles and woodburner, enjoyable food from baguettes and pub favourites to more restauranty dishes, good value set lunch and other deals, up to three Shepherd Neame ales including Master Brew, good choice of wines by the glass; background music, artwork for sale; children and dogs welcome, seats on small sunny terrace and in garden under large spreading tree, open all day.

LUDDESDOWNE   TQ6667
★ ## Cock (01474) 814208
Henley Street, N of village – OS Sheet 177 map reference 664672; off A227 in Meopham, or A228 in Cuxton; DA13 0XB Early 18th-c country pub under long-serving no-nonsense landlord; at least seven well kept ales such as Adnams, Goachers, Harveys, Shepherd Neame and Iron Pier, also some good German beers, snacky bar food, rugs on bare boards in bay-windowed lounge, beams and panelling, quarry-tiled locals' bar with settles, cask tables and other pubby furnishings, aircraft pictures, beer mats and bric-a-brac from stuffed animals to model cars, woodburners, back dining conservatory; music quiz fourth Mon of month, bar billiards and darts; no children inside or on part-covered heated back terrace, dogs welcome, large secure garden, good North Downs walks.

LYNSTED   TQ9460
Black Lion (01795) 521229
The Street; ME9 0RJ Welcoming early 17th-c village pub; well kept Goachers and good freshly made pubby food (all day Sat, not Sun evening) including blackboard specials, settles and old tables on bare

boards, log fires; some live music, pool; children and dogs welcome, well tended garden with play area, open all day.

MARDEN   TQ7547
Stile Bridge (01622) 831236
Staplehurst Road (A229); TN12 9BH Friendly roadside pub with homely dark wood furniture, wood-panelled walls and ceilings with bursts of colour (deep red and blue) and plenty of bric-a-brac and pictures; five well kept ales, Dark Star and Goachers and guests such as Oakham, also lots of bottled beers, real ciders and extensive range of gins (nearly 40, including local ones), good traditional food (not Sun evening) including vegan and gluten-free; regular live music; dogs welcome in bar, back garden and terrace, open all day.

MARKBEECH   TQ4742
Kentish Horse (01342) 850493
Off B2026 Hartfield–Edenbridge; TN8 5NT Attractive village pub (originally three cottages) next to the church, friendly and welcoming, with three well kept ales including Harveys and Larkins from brick counter, good value traditional food (not Sun-Weds evenings), friendly helpful staff, black beams and log fire in long carpeted bar, restaurant with pubby furniture and woodburner in large brick fireplace, french windows to terrace; folk night; children welcome, picnic-sets and fenced play area in garden, lovely views over Ashdown Forest.

MARTIN   TR3347
Lantern (01304) 852276
Off A258 Dover–Deal; The Street; CT15 5JL Pretty 17th-c brick pub (originally two farmworker's cottages) in lovely setting; small refurbished bar with low beams, stripped brick and cosy corners, extensive range of craft beers and real ales from copper-topped counter, decent wines by the glass, cocktails, enjoyable food from traditional choices up, friendly helpful service, soft lighting, log fires; background and some acoustic live music, shop selling home-made and local produce; children and dogs welcome, some tables out at front, more in good-sized back garden with big play house, open all day in summer, all day Fri-Sun winter.

MATFIELD   TQ6642
★ ## Poet at Matfield (01892) 722416
Maidstone Road; TN12 7JH Civilised 17th-c beamed pub-restaurant named for Siegfried Sassoon who was born nearby; highly regarded modern cooking from South African chef-patron including tasting menus (evenings Weds, Thurs) and very good value set menu (Tues-Fri lunch, Tues-Thurs dinner), ales such as Old Dairy, Tonbridge and Harveys, well chosen wines and more than 70 interesting craft gins, friendly professional service; garden with barbecue.

MATFIELD TQ6541

Star (01892) 725458

Maidstone Road (B2160); TN12 7JR
Creeper-clad pub close to the village
duck pond; beamed and bare-boards front
bar with three real ales such as Harveys,
enjoyable food (not Sun evening) including
signature home-made pies, friendly service,
restaurant in older back part with inglenook
woodburner; quiz second and fourth Thurs of
month, occasional live music; picnic-sets on
gravel terrace, open all day.

MEOPHAM TQ6364

★Cricketers (01474) 812163

Wrotham Road (A227); DA13 0QA
Whiting & Hammond pub in nice spot
overlooking cricket green; cushioned wall
settles, a mix of old-style wooden furniture
and a raised fireplace in the front bar,
and bookshelves, another fireplace, rugs
on bare floorboards and a sizeable dining
room beyond; busy and bustling, popular
reasonably priced food with some interesting
options, Caledonian Deuchars IPA and
around three guests such as Bexley Session
Golden Ale and Tonbridge Coppernob on
handpump, around a dozen wines by the
glass, good friendly service; children and
dogs welcome, tables out at front and in
back garden, open (and food) all day, from
9am weekdays.

MERSHAM TR0438

Farriers Arms (01233) 720444

The Forstal/Flood Street; TN25 6NU
Large early 17th-c pub owned by the local
community; beers from on-site microbrewery
including seasonal ales, decent choice of
wines and enjoyable home-made food from
bar snacks to daily specials, friendly staff,
opened-up interior with beams and log fires,
restaurant; July beer festival; children and
dogs welcome, pretty streamside garden
behind with pleasant country views, open
all day Weds-Sun.

NEWENDEN TQ8327

White Hart (01797) 252166

Rye Road (A268); TN18 5PN Popular
16th-c weatherboarded local; long low-
beamed bar with big stone fireplace, dining
areas off serving enjoyable reasonably priced
pub food including good Sun roasts, well
kept Harveys, Rother Valley and guests (July
beer/cider festival), friendly helpful young
staff, back games area with pool; background
music, quiz nights, sports TV; children and
dogs welcome, boules in large garden, near
river (boat trips to NT's Bodiam Castle), six
bedrooms, open all day.

NORTHBOURNE TR3352

Hare & Hounds (01304) 369188

*Off A256 or A258 near Dover; The
Street; CT14 0LG* Welcoming 17th-c
village pub with well kept Harveys and
Fullers, a guest beer and good choice of
wines from brick-faced servery, decent
pubby food, bare-boards and flagstoned bar
separated by a couple of archways, nice
log fire; children and dogs welcome, paved
terrace and garden with play area, open all
day Thurs-Sun.

OARE TR0163

★Shipwrights Arms (01795) 590088

*S shore of Oare Creek, E of village;
signed from Oare Road/Ham Road
junction in Faversham; ME13 7TU*
Remote marshland tavern with plenty of
character; three dark simple little bars
separated by standing timbers, wood
partitions and narrow door arches, medley
of seats from tapestry-cushioned stools
to black panelled built-in settles forming
booths, flags and boating pennants on
ceiling, wind gauge above main door (takes
reading from chimney), up to six beers,
including Kentish ones such as Goachers
and further afield such as Harveys,
tapped from the cask (pewter tankards
over counter), simple home-cooked food
lunchtime only except Fri, Sat; children
(away from bar area) and dogs welcome,
large garden with bat and trap, path
along Oare Creek to Swale estuary, lots of
surrounding bird life, closed Mon.

OARE TR0063

Three Mariners (01795) 533633

Church Road; ME13 0QA Comfortable
simply restored 18th-c pub with good food
including fresh fish and vegan, gluten-
free menus, Shepherd Neame ales and
plenty of wines by the glass, beams, bare
boards, antique wooden furniture and log
fire; children and dogs (in bar) welcome,
attractive garden overlooking Faversham
Creek, good walks.

PAINTERS FORSTAL TQ9958

Alma (01795) 533835

Signed off A2 at Ospringe; ME13 0DU
Welcoming weatherboarded and timbered
village local, homely and tidy, with well kept
Shepherd Neame ales, decent wines and good
value home cooking including notable steak
and kidney pudding, helpful service; children
and dogs (in bar) welcome, picnic-sets in
small enclosed garden with covered patio,
live music, play area over the road, campsite
nearby, no food Sun evening.

We mention bottled beers and spirits only if there is something unusual about them
– imported Belgian real ales, say, or dozens of malt whiskies. Do please let us know
about them in your reports.

PEMBURY   TQ6240
Camden Arms (01892) 822012
High Street (The Green); TN2 4PH
Substantial tile-hung inn opposite village
green; good generously served food from
extensive reasonably priced menu, Sun
carvery, five well kept ales such as Shepherd
Neame and Harveys and good choice of
wines, friendly welcoming staff, large
opened-up central bar with smaller dining
rooms off, beams, bare boards and flagstones,
various bits and pieces including landlord's
remarkable collection of Dinky Toys; sports
TV, occasional live music, children and dogs
welcome, tables on covered paved terrace,
picnic-sets on lawn, 15 bedrooms some with
four-posters, open (and food) all day.

PENSHURST   TQ5241
★Spotted Dog (01892) 870253
Smarts Hill, off B2188 S; TN11 8EP
Quaint weatherboarded pub first licensed
in 1520; heavy low beams and timbers,
attractive moulded panelling, big inglenook
fireplace, hops, horsebrasses and lots of
country pictures, traditional furniture on
bare boards or carpet, Harveys, Larkins,
Tonbridge and Youngs, several wines by the
glass, popular pubby food (not Sun evening);
children and dogs (in bar) welcome, terrace
seating on several levels with good views over
miles of countryside, open all day (till 9.30pm
Sun, 10pm Mon).

PETT BOTTOM   TR1652
Duck (01227) 830354
*Off B2068 S of Canterbury, via Lower
Hardres; CT4 5PB* Popular tile-hung pub
in attractive downland spot; long bare-boards
bar with scrubbed tables, pine panelling and
two log fires, good food cooked by landlord-
chef including weekday set lunch, friendly
attentive service, two or three well kept
beers such as Old Dairy and Romney Marsh
and 21 wines by the glass; children and dogs
welcome, seats and old well out in front,
garden behind where Ian Fleming used to
make notes for his James Bond books (see
blue plaque), camping nearby, closed Mon.

PETTERIDGE   TQ6640
Hopbine (01892) 722561
Petteridge Lane; NE of village; TN12 7NE
Unspoilt tiled and weatherboarded cottage
in quiet hamlet; two small rooms separated
by an open fire, traditional pubby furniture,
hops and horsebrasses, well kept Long
Man, Tonbridge and two guests, proper
cider and enjoyable good value home-made
food including wood-fired pizzas, themed
evenings, friendly staff, steps up to simple
back part with brick fireplace; dogs welcome

(pub cat is called Baxter), outside gents';
terrace seating, play area, open all day Sat,
Sun, closed Mon.

PLUCKLEY   TQ9144
Rose & Crown (01233) 840048
*Mundy Bois – spelled Monday Boys on
some maps – off Smarden Road SW of
village centre; TN27 0ST* Popular 17th-c
tile-hung pub with good classically English
food Weds-Sun (all day Sat and Sun) from
snacks to daily specials, three well kept beers
including Harveys and Whitstable, friendly
attentive service, main bar with massive
inglenook, small snug and restaurant;
background music, beer/music festival Aug;
children and dogs (in bar) welcome, pretty
garden and terrace with views, play area,
open all day.

RAMSGATE   TR3764
Artillery Arms (01843) 853202
West Cliff Road; CT11 9JS Old-fashioned
little corner local on two levels, chatty
and welcoming, with four or five well kept
interesting beers such as Ramsgate Gadds,
Thornbridge, Oakham and Moor, and
enjoyable food (all day weekends), artillery
prints/memorabilia and fine listed windows
depicting Napoleonic scenes; dogs welcome,
wheelchair access, open all day.

RAMSGATE   TR3764
Conqueror 07890 203282
*Grange Road/St Mildreds Road;
CT11 9LR* Cosy single-room micropub in
former corner shop; welcoming enthusiastic
landlord serving three changing ales direct
from the cask such as Ramsgate, Wantsum
and Dark Star, also local cider and apple
juice, friendly chatty atmosphere, large
windows and old photos of eponymous
cross-Channel paddle steamer; dogs welcome,
closed Sun evening, Mon.

ROCHESTER   TQ7468
Coopers Arms (01634) 404298
St Margarets Street; ME1 1TL Ancient
jettied building behind the cathedral; cosily
unpretentious with two comfortable beamed
bars, low-priced pub food from sandwiches
up and good range of well kept beers such as
Westerham and Tonbridge, list of landlords
back to 1543 and ghostly tales of a walled-up
member of the Coopers Brethren (mannequin
marks the spot); live music (Sun) and quiz
nights every other Tues; tables in attractive
courtyard, open all day.

ROLVENDEN   TQ8431
Bull (01580) 241212
Regent Street; TN17 4PB Welcoming
tile-hung cottage with woodburner in fine

We don't mention free wi-fi, because it's standard in most pubs these days – though
not universal. And don't expect a good signal in remote rural locations.

brick inglenook, high-backed dining chairs around rustic tables on stripped boards, built-in panelled wall seats, well kept Long Man and a guest such as Old Dairy, Stowford Press cider on tap, enjoyable food (not Sun evening) from pub favourites and pizzas up, pale oak tables in dining room; background music; children and dogs (in bar) welcome, picnic-sets behind picket fence at front and side, more seats in sizeable back garden, open all day, till 7pm Sun.

ROLVENDEN LAYNE   TQ8530
Ewe & Lamb   (01580) 241837
Maytham Road; TN17 4NP Characterful and cosy tile-hung village pub; beams, bare boards and log fires, three real ales including Harveys and more than 20 wines by the glass and 20 gins, good home-made food using local ingredients as much as possible including light lunch menu, daily specials and Sun carvery, good friendly service, back restaurant; some live music; children, walkers and dogs welcome, seats out at front behind picket fence, not much parking, open (and food) all day (Sun until 9pm).

SANDGATE   TR2035
Ship   (01303) 248525
High Street; CT20 3AH Long narrow corner pub with traditional nautical-theme bar and dining area at front and modern conservatory restaurant behind overlooking the sea, half a dozen cask-tapped ales including Dark Star, Greene King and Hop Back, real cider, decent wines and good range of gins, popular food with emphasis on local fish/seafood, affable long-serving landlord and friendly efficient staff; more good sea views from roof terrace and bedrooms, open all day.

SANDWICH   TR3358
Crispin   (01304) 621967
High Street; CT13 9EA Welcoming 15th-c corner pub next to medieval barbican and toll bridge; long timbered main room divided by open fire, four well kept ales including Adnams and Harveys and a house beer from local Mad Cat, good authentic Caribbean food along with more traditional choices; some live music; children and dogs welcome, seats out overlooking river, open all day, no food Sun evening.

SARRE   TR2564
Crown   (01843) 847808
Ramsgate Road (A253) off A28; CT7 0LF Historic 15th-c inn (Grade I listed) sandwiched between two main roads; front bar and other rambling rooms including restaurant, beams and log fires, well kept Shepherd Neame ales and decent fairly priced wines, own cherry brandy (pub known locally as the Cherry Brandy House), generous helpings of enjoyable locally sourced food from sandwiches up, good friendly service; children welcome,

side garden (traffic noise), comfortable surprisingly quiet bedrooms, open all day.

SEASALTER   TR0864
★Sportsman   (01227) 273370
Faversham Road, off B2040; CT5 4BP Informal restaurANTy pub just inside seawall – rather unprepossessing from outside but surprisingly light and airy; imaginative modern cooking using plenty of seafood (not Sun evening, Mon, must book and not cheap), good wine choice including English and a couple of well kept Shepherd Neame ales, knowledgeable landlord and friendly staff; two plain linked rooms and long conservatory, scrubbed pine tables, wheelback and basket-weave dining chairs on wood floor, local artwork; children welcome, plastic glasses for outside, wide views over marshland with grazing sheep and (from seawall) across to Sheppey, small caravan park one side, wood chalets the other, open all day Sun till 10pm.

SEVENOAKS   TQ5555
★Bucks Head   (01732) 761330
Godden Green, just E; TN15 0JJ Welcoming and relaxed old flower-decked pub with neatly kept bar and restaurant area, good freshly cooked blackboard food from baguettes to Sun roasts, well kept Shepherd Neame and a guest, beams, panelling and splendid inglenooks; children and dogs welcome, front terrace overlooking informal green and duck pond, pretty back garden with mature trees, pergola and views over quiet countryside behind Knole (NT), popular with walkers, closed Mon except bank holidays.

SEVENOAKS   TQ5355
Halfway House   (01732) 463667
2.5 miles from M25 junction 5; TN13 2JD Nicely updated old roadside pub with friendly staff and regulars; good competitively priced food from sensibly short blackboard menu, three changing ales from Westerham and Sharps, local wines and some interesting flavoured vodkas, upper bar with record deck and LPs (can bring your own), some live music too including ukulele club every other Mon; handy for the station, parking can be tricky, open all day except Mon-Weds.

SEVENOAKS   TQ5055
★Kings Head   (01732) 452081
Bessels Green; A25 W, just off A21; TN13 2QA Whiting & Hammond pub on village green; emphasis on eating but drinkers well catered for with six real ales on handpump, such as Dark Star, Old Dairy, St Austell and Tonbridge and 12 decent wines by the glass, spreading dining areas with a mix of cushioned dining chairs, button-back wall seats and settles around rustic or dark wooden tables on bare-board or tile floors, open fires, pictures on painted walls, house

plants, quick service from friendly chatty staff; children and dogs welcome, disabled access/facilities, large garden with bookable dining huts, open (and food) all day.

SHADOXHURST   TQ9737
Kings Head (01233) 732243
Woodchurch Road; TN26 1LQ Old family-run pub with clean updated interior; good value enjoyable food in bar and separate restaurant including blackboard specials, well kept Shepherd Neame and guests, friendly efficient staff, stripped pine tables on bare boards or quarry tiles, various bits and pieces including china, copper and brass, vintage photos and old horse tack, log fires; games area with pool, quiz last Sun of month; children and dogs welcome, tables on front terrace and in garden behind with play area, closed Sun evening, Mon.

SHIPBOURNE   TQ5952
★Chaser (01732) 810360
Stumble Hill (A227 N of Tonbridge); TN11 9PE Comfortably opened up Whiting & Hammond pub with linked rooms converging on large central island bar, stripped-wood floors, lots of pictures, pine wainscoting, old solid wood tables on rugs, shelves of books and open fires, well kept Morland, Larkins and two guests, decent wine and malt whisky choice, also good range of popular well executed food including pub classics and some more adventurous choices, helpful friendly staff, dark panelling and high timber-vaulted ceiling in striking school chapel-like restaurant; background music, board games; children welcome, dogs in bar, courtyard and small side garden, good local walks, open (and food) all day, can get very busy (best to book for Sunday lunch).

SHOREHAM   TQ5161
Kings Arms (01959) 523100
Church Street; TN14 7SJ Part-weatherboarded 16th-c pub in quaint unspoilt village close to the River Darent; cosy and unpretentious, with generous helpings of good honest food including Fri fish and chips, two or three well kept beers such as Harveys, Bombardier and Greene King, friendly helpful staff, log fire, plates and brasses, small restaurant area; children welcome, no dogs, picnic-sets outside on tarmac (some under cover), note the ostler's box (compete with mannequin) at the front, good local walks, open all day, no evening food Sun-Tues.

SHOREHAM   TQ5261
Olde George (01959) 522017
Church Street; TN14 7RY Traditional 16th-c pub opposite the church; low beams, uneven floors and cosy fires, two or three well kept changing ales such as Theakstons and enjoyable pubby food including bargain OAP lunch (Thurs, Fri), friendly attentive service, carpeted dining area to one side;

children, walkers and dogs welcome, picnic-sets by road, open all day.

SISSINGHURST   TQ7937
★Milk House (01580) 720200
The Street; TN17 2JG Bustling village inn near Sissinghurst Castle Garden (NT); bar on right with grey-painted beams and handsome Tudor fireplace fronted by plush sofas, wicker-faced counter serving Harveys and three guests, such as Dark Star, Tonbridge and Old Dairy, real cider, a good choice of wines by the glass and good range of whiskies and gins, restaurant to the left with small room off (perfect for a private party), good popular food including pizzas from outside oven; background music, daily papers; children and dogs (in bar) welcome, large side terrace with sturdy furniture under green parasols, garden picnic-sets and children's play hut by fenced-in pond, four comfortable well equipped bedrooms, open all day, closed Mon.

SMARDEN   TQ8642
Bell (01233) 770283
From Smarden follow Water Lane (between church and Chequers pub), then left at T junction; or from A274 take unsignposted turn E a mile N of B2077 to Smarden; TN27 8PW Old brick and tile country pub with series of cosy beamed rooms, enjoyable food from traditional choices up, Shepherd Neame ales and decent range of wines, good friendly service; picnic-sets in garden with own bar, closes 8pm Mon, otherwise open all day.

SNARGATE   TQ9928
★Red Lion (01797) 344648
B2080 Appledore–Brenzett; TN29 9UQ Unchanging 16th-c pub in same family for over 100 years; simple old-fashioned charm in three timeless little rooms with original cream wall panelling, heavy beams in sagging ceilings, dark pine Victorian farmhouse chairs on bare boards, an old piano and coal fire, local cider and four or five ales including Goachers tapped from casks behind unusual free-standing marble-topped counter, no food, bar snacks, traditional games like toad in the hole, nine men's morris and table skittles, friendly staff; children in family room, dogs in bar, outdoor lavatories, cottage garden, closed Mon.

SPELDHURST   TQ5541
★George & Dragon (01892) 863125
Village signed from A264 W of Tunbridge Wells; TN3 0NN Handsome pub based around a 13th-c manorial hall (lovely original features); entrance lobby with half-panelled room to the right, wheelback and other dining chairs, cushioned wall pew, small pictures and horsebrasses, doorway to another dining room with similar furnishings and second inglenook, bar to left of entrance has woodburner in small fireplace, high-

winged cushioned settles and other wooden furniture on stripped-wood floor, good range of well liked food from baguettes up, obliging friendly service, three well kept ales, several wines by the glass, raftered upstairs restaurant with fine king post; background music; children and dogs (in bar) welcome, teak furniture on front gravel terrace, covered back area and lower terrace with 200-year-old olive tree. Note: new owners (Elite Pubs) as we went to press, so there may be changes.

ST MARY IN THE MARSH   TR0627
Star (01797) 362139
Opposite church; TN29 0BX Remote fairly down-to-earth pub with Tudor origins; popular food (not Sun evening, Mon) from sandwiches up, five well kept ales including Shepherd Neame and Youngs and guests such as Ringwood, St Austell and Courage from brick-faced counter, friendly service, inglenook woodburner; quiz nights, live music nights; children and dogs welcome, tables in nice garden, beamed bedrooms with Romney Marsh views, lovely setting opposite ancient church (where Edith Nesbit, author of *The Railway Children*, is buried), popular with walkers and cyclists, open all day.

STAPLEHURST   TQ7846
Lord Raglan (01622) 843747
About 1.5 miles from town centre towards Maidstone, turn right off A229 into Chart Hill Road opposite Chart Cars; OS Sheet 188 map reference 785472; TN12 0DE Country pub with cosy chatty area around narrow counter, hop-strung low beams, two log fires and woodburner, mix of comfortably worn dark wood furniture, Goachers, Harveys and a guest, farm cider and perry, sandwiches and well liked reasonably priced home-cooked food, good wine list; children and dogs welcome, wheelchair access, tables on terrace and in the side orchard, Aug bank holiday onion festival, closed Sun.

STODMARSH   TR2160
★ Red Lion (01227) 721339
High Street; off A257 just E of Canterbury; CT3 4BA Tucked-away pub close to Stodmarsh National Nature Reserve; bar rooms with country kitchen furniture, plenty of candles and big log fire, Greene King IPA and a guest such as Adnams or Fullers tapped from the cask, Kentish Pip cider and eight wines by the glass, good food including Weds pie night, friendly helpful staff; background music, piano; children and dogs (in bar) welcome, tables – and wandering chickens! – in back garden, bedrooms, open all day summer, closed Sun evening, Mon.

SUNDRIDGE   TQ4855
White Horse (01959) 561198
Main Road; TN14 6EQ Refurbished

open-plan village pub with decent range of well liked food from sandwiches up including range of burgers, three real ales such as Adnams Southwold, Brakspears Special and Timothy Taylors Landlord, several wines by the glass, good friendly service, log fires and low beams, comfortable seating on wood floors; live music and quiz nights, children welcome, dogs in bar area, picnic-sets under parasols on fenced lawn, open all day, no food Sun evening.

SUTTON VALENCE   TQ8050
Plough (01622) 842555
Sutton Road (A274), Langley; ME17 3LX Roadside dining pub refurbished in 2020; main bar painted in shades of grey with mix of wooden and copper-topped tables, side bar and candlelit dining extension behind with view into kitchen, well kept local Rockin' Robin and a couple of guests such as Fullers London Pride or Harveys Sussex Best, several wines by the glass, enjoyable food from sandwiches and bar snacks to restaurantly choices, friendly relaxed atmosphere; live music Fri; children and dogs welcome, tables and vintage plough out at front behind picket fence, open all day (Sun till 8pm), closed Mon.

TENTERDEN   TQ8833
White Lion (01580) 765077
High Street; TN30 6BD Comfortably updated beamed and timbered 16th-c inn behind Georgian façade; popular food including Josper grills and pizzas from open kitchen, Marstons ales, good choice of other drinks including cocktails, big log fire, friendly helpful staff; background music; heated terrace overlooking street, comfortable well equipped bedrooms, open (and food) all day from 7am (8am Sat, Sun).

TEYNHAM   TQ9661
Plough (01795) 521348
Lewson Street; ME9 9JJ Picturesque 13th-c weatherboarded pub in quiet village; unpretentious split-level interior with low hop-strung beams and inglenook woodburner, friendly staff and atmosphere, Shepherd Neame ales, decent wines and enjoyable home-made food including popular Sun roasts; some live music, resident parrot called Bob; children and dogs welcome, front terrace behind picket fence, large well kept back garden with play area overlooking meadow, closed Sun evening, Mon.

TUDELEY   TQ6145
Poacher & Partridge
(01732) 358934 *Hartlake Road; TN11 0PH* Renovated in smart country style by Elite Pubs (Great House in Hawkhurst, Dirty Habit at Hollingbourne etc); light interior with feature pizza oven, wide range of food including daily specials, Tues steak night, ales such as Sharps Doom Bar, Harveys Sussex Best and Timothy Taylors Landlord,

good choice of wines by the glass, 14 gins and nine whiskies; live music including some afternoon jazz; children and dogs welcome, outside bar and grill, play area, nearby interesting church with Chagall stained glass (note roof paintings at pub's entrance), circular walks (leaflets provided), open (and food except Sun to 8pm) all day.

TUNBRIDGE WELLS TQ5837
Bull (01892) 263489
Frant Road; TN2 5LH Friendly 19th-c pub towards the southern outskirts of town; two modernised linked areas with one or two quirky touches, chunky pine tables and kitchen chairs on stripped-wood floor, a couple of leather sofas by open fire, well kept Shepherd Neame and good food cooked by chef-landlord from shortish menu; children (till 8.30pm) and dogs welcome, seats out on fenced roadside terrace, open all day.

UNDERRIVER TQ5552
★White Rock (01732) 833112
SE of Sevenoaks, off B245; TN15 0SB Attractive village pub with good food including vegan menu from pubby choices up (all day weekends, best to book), friendly helpful service, well kept Harveys, Tonbridge or Sharps and a beer badged for them, decent wines, beams, bare boards and stripped brickwork in cosy original part with adjacent dining area, another bar in modern extension with woodburner; background and some live music, darts, pool; children welcome, dogs may be allowed but do ask first, small front garden, back terrace and large lawn with boules and bat and trap, pretty churchyard, good walks nearby, open all day in summer, all day weekends winter.

UPNOR TQ7671
Ship (01634) 290553
Upnor Road, Lower Upnor; ME2 4UY Smallish mock-Tudor pub overlooking the Medway and boats; good home cooking including fish specials, Courage Best, Shepherd Neame Master Brew and guests, friendly staff, carpeted interior with marine knick-knacks; children and dogs welcome, picnic-sets out at front and in garden behind, open all day.

UPPER UPNOR TQ7570
Tudor Rose (01634) 714175
Off A228 N of Strood; High Street; ME2 4XG 16th-c pub down narrow cobbled street just back from the river and next to Upnor Castle (best to use village car park at top); cosy beamed rooms with

mix of old furniture and some nautical bits and pieces, Shepherd Neame ales and an occasional guest, popular pubby food (not Sun evening) from baguettes up, good friendly service; children welcome, seats out at front made from an old boat, large enclosed garden behind with arbour, open all day, till 8pm Sun.

WEALD TQ5250
★Windmill (01732) 463330
Windmill Road; TN14 6PN Popular and friendly village pub with new owners and a revamp; its own Weald Copper ale plus several well kept locals including Goachers, Battle, Larkins, Kent, Whitstable and others, local ciders and good fair-priced food from interestingly varied menu, attentive helpful service, traditional but recently opened up interior with etched windows and two fires, mix of seating including old pews and carved settles by candlelit tables, jugs and bottles on delft shelves, snug dining area; live music; children and dogs welcome, easy wheelchair access, nice quiet back garden, closed Mon, otherwise open all day Fri, Sat.

WEST MALLING TQ6757
Scared Crow (01732) 840408
Offham Road; ME19 6RB Cosy brick-built pub with good Mexican food along with pizzas and more traditional choices, well kept Adnams ales, friendly helpful service; background and some live music; children welcome, nice back garden.

WEST PECKHAM TQ6452
Swan on the Green (01622) 812271
Off A26/B2016 W of Maidstone; ME18 5JW Attractively placed brick and weatherboarded pub facing village cricket green; own-brewed Swan beers in relaxed open-plan beamed bar, stripped brickwork, bare boards and mixed furnishings, two-way log fire, enjoyable freshly made food (not Sun, Mon evenings) from varied menu, friendly efficient service; children and dogs welcome, next to interesting part-Saxon church, good walks including Greensand Way, shuts at 9.30pm Sun and Mon, and may close early other evenings if quiet.

WESTBERE TR1862
Old Yew Tree (01227) 710501
Just off A18 Canterbury–Margate; CT2 0HH Heavily beamed 14th-c pub in pretty village; simply furnished bare-boards bar with large inglenook log fire, enjoyable reasonably priced food from wide-ranging menu, Shepherd Neame Master Brew and

---

Please tell us if the décor, atmosphere, food or drink at a pub is different from our description. We rely on readers' reports to keep us up to date: feedback@goodguides.com, or (no stamp needed) Freepost THE GOOD PUB GUIDE, Random House Publishing, 20 Vauxhall Bridge Road, London SW1V 2SA.

a guest, friendly helpful staff; quiz first Weds of month, open mike last Weds of month; picnic-sets in garden behind, open all day weekends, closed Mon.

WESTGATE-ON-SEA   TR3270
Bake & Alehouse 07913 368787
Off St Mildreds Road down alley by cinema; CT8 8RE Friendly micropub in former bakery; simple little bare-boards room with a few tables (expect to share when busy), between five and eight well kept interesting ales tapped from the cask, real ciders (maybe a warm winter one – Monks Delight), Kentish wines, local cheese, sausage rolls and pork pies, friendly chatty atmosphere.

WHITSTABLE   TR1066
Black Dog
High Street; CT5 1BB Quirky micropub (former deli) with five changing ales and several artisan ciders tapped from the back room, friendly staff may offer tasters, snacky food, narrow dimly lit Victorian-feel bar with high tables and benches along two sides, intriguing mix of pictures and other bits and pieces on green walls, prominent chandelier suspended from red ceiling; eclectic background music and occasional folk sessions; open all day.

WHITSTABLE   TR1066
Old Neptune (01227) 272262
Marine Terrace; CT5 1EJ Great view over Swale estuary from this popular unpretentious weatherboarded pub set right on the beach (rebuilt after being washed away in 1897 storm); Harveys, Shepherd Neame and a guest, reasonably priced lunchtime food from shortish menu including decent fish and chips, friendly young staff; weekend live music; children and dogs welcome, picnic-sets on the shingle (plastic glasses out here and occasional barbecues), fine sunsets, can get very busy in summer, open all day.

WHITSTABLE   TR1066
Smack Inn (01227) 772910
Middle Wall next to Baptist church; CT5 1BJ Small Victorian backstreet local away from the tourist trail; two Shepherd Neame ales and shortish choice of enjoyable low-priced food including burgers and fish and chips, cheerful helpful staff, cosy interior arranged around central servery, panelling, stripped brickwork and log fire; regular live music, often in beach-themed back garden (barbecues); children and dogs welcome, open all day.

WICKHAMBREAUX   TR2258
Rose (01227) 721763
The Green; CT3 1RQ Attractive 16th-c and partly older pub in nice spot across green from church and watermill; enjoyable

home-made food, Greene King IPA and two guests such as Gadds, Courage, Fullers and St Austell (May/Aug beer festivals), local ciders on rotation, good wine list and lots of gins, friendly helpful staff, small bare-boards bar with log fire in big fireplace, dining area beyond standing timbers with woodburner, hop-strung beams, panelling and stripped brick; children and dogs welcome, enclosed side garden and small courtyard, open (and food) all day, kitchen closes 4pm Sun.

WILLESBOROUGH STREET   TR0341
Blacksmiths Arms (01233) 623975
The Street; TN24 0NA Beamed village pub dating in part from the 17th c; Fullers London Pride, Sharps Doom Bar, Harveys Sussex Best and a couple of guests, good traditional home-cooked food from sandwiches and snacks up, daily blackboard specials, friendly service, open fires including inglenook; children and dogs welcome, picnic-sets in good-sized garden with play area, handy for M20 (junction 10), open all day.

WROTHAM   TQ6159
Bull (01732) 789800
1.7 miles from M20, junction 2 – Wrotham signed; TN15 7RF Restored 14th-c coaching inn with large beamed bar and separate restaurant, matching tables and chairs throughout, enjoyable food from pubby dishes up including a smokehouse/ barbecue menu, real ales such as Dark Star and Old Dairy, craft kegs and good wine list, friendly efficient service; live music; children welcome, 11 comfortable bedrooms, open all day, food all day weekends.

WYE   TR0546
★Kings Head (01233) 812418
Church Street; TN25 5BN This welcoming former Victorian coaching inn, with its informal bare-boards bar has a mix of furnishings such as armchairs beside the fire and pale-painted high chairs beside the counter; a couple of Shepherd Neame beers including Whitstable Bay Pale Ale on handpump and 21 good wines by the glass; tasty menu from pub classics to more imaginative dishes; bedrooms; children and dogs allowed, disabled access, open all day, food all day Sat.

WYE   TR0546
New Flying Horse (01233) 812297
Upper Bridge Street; TN25 5AN 17th-c Shepherd Neame inn with beams and inglenook; enjoyable food including fixed-price menu in bar and restaurant, friendly accommodating staff; Sun quiz, occasional live music; children welcome, good-sized pretty garden with play area and miniature thatched pub (a former Chelsea Flower

Show exhibit), nine smart and contemporary bedrooms (some in converted stables), open (and food) all day.

WYE   TR0446

Tickled Trout (01233) 812227

Signed off A28 NE of Ashford; TN25 5EB
Popular summer family pub by River Stour; rustic-style carpeted bar with beams, stripped brickwork, stained-glass partitions and open fire, spacious conservatory/restaurant, ales such as Canterbury, Old Dairy and Sharps, Kentish ciders and several wines by the glass, friendly helpful staff; quiz nights, regular live music; children and dogs welcome, tables on terrace and riverside lawn, open (and food) all day.

YALDING   TQ6950

Walnut Tree (01622) 814266

B2010 SW of Maidstone; ME18 6JB
Old timbered village pub with split-level main bar with fine old settles, a long cushioned mahogany bench and mix of dining chairs on brick or carpeted floors, candles in bottles on chunky wooden tables, interesting old photographs, big inglenook log fire, up to five real ales such as Adnams, Harveys and Tonbridge, good choice of gins, good food from bar meals to more inventive restaurant dishes, Sun carvery, friendly prompt service, attractive raftered dining room; background and live music (every other Fri); children and dogs (in bar) welcome, paved back terrace, open (and food) all day, kitchen closes 6pm Sun.

Lancashire

with Greater Manchester, Merseyside and Wirral

KEY	★ Star Pub	⭐ Top Quality Food	🍺 Great Beer
🍷 Good Wines	£ Bargain Meals	🛏 Good Bedrooms	🍴 Serves Food

BARNSTON
Fox & Hounds 🍺

SJ2783   Map 7

(0151) 648 7685 – www.the-fox-hounds.co.uk

3 miles from M53 junction 3: A552 towards Woodchurch, then left on A551; CH61 1BW

Handsome early 20th-c pub gently renovated and serious about its food and drink

This spotless and efficiently run pub has retained the best of its original Edwardian features – separate snug, bar and lounge, fireplace, handsome wood- and glasswork, woodblock and quarry tile floors – enhanced by a newer conservatory and garden room set for dining. There are up six real ales on handpump: Theakstons Best and Old Peculier and Brimstage Trappers Hat plus interesting guests from brewers such as Salopian and Liverpool Brewing; also, more than 60 whiskies and 16 or so wines by the glass from a knowledgeable list chosen to complement the food. The main part of the roomy, bay-windowed lounge bar has built-in banquettes, straight-backed dining chairs around solid tables, carpets and plenty of old local prints. Tucked away opposite the serving counter is a charming little corner with an antique kitchen range and memorabilia to match. With its own entrance at the other end of the pub, a small locals' bar is worth a peek for its traditional layout and collection of horsebrasses and metal ashtrays; darts and TV. Next to it is a snug where children are allowed. There are some attractive light wood tables and chairs with parasols out in the flagstoned yard behind, dotted with colourful baskets and tubs. Disabled access and toilet.

🍴 The much praised seasonal food includes hot and cold sandwiches (until 5pm), spinach, carrot and potato pakoras, panko-crumbed smoked brie with candied walnuts, red apple and rocket salad, chorizo and black pudding hash with poached egg and welsh rarebit sauce, Bengali slow-cooked lamb shank infused in tomato, cardamom and turmeric with bombay potatoes, wild boar, smoked paprika and garlic meatballs in chorizo and butter bean ragout, roasted aubergine caponata with tomato ragout, melted goats cheese and rosemary roast potatoes, steak and ale pie, plus puddings such as local ice-creams and a cheeseboard with home-made piccalilli and an eccles cake. *Benchmark main dish: fish pie topped with cheddar and chive mash with green beans, savoy cabbage and chantenay carrots £15.50. Two-course evening meal £21.00.*

Free house ~ Licensee Mark Parry ~ Real ale ~ Open 12-11 ~ Bar food 12-9 ~ Children allowed in snug ~ Dogs allowed in bar

BASHALL EAVES
SD6943   Map 7

Red Pump

(01254) 826227 – www.theredpumpinn.co.uk

NW of Clitheroe, off B6478 or B6243; BB7 3DA

Beautifully placed pub with a cosy bar and first class food in contemporary, inviting dining rooms; bedrooms

With great walks in the surrounding Forest of Bowland and fishing on the nearby River Hodder, this picturesque country inn with bedrooms and camping is the pitstop of choice for hungry and weary outdoors enthusiasts. The eight individually decorated rooms have antique French beds, memory foam mattresses and powerful wetroom showers; there are also four yurts. The two inviting dining rooms and cosy, traditional central bar have had a light refresh and boast cushioned settles and wheelbacks on flagstones, bookshelves and log fires, and the convivial licensees create a cheerful, friendly atmosphere. Three regional beers on handpump change weekly and might include Black Sheep, Copper Dragon, Ilkley Gold or Lytham Blonde, plus 14 wines by the glass, around 35 gins and 30 whiskies; background music. There are lovely views of Pendle Hill and Longridge Fell from the seats on the front terrace and the newly landscaped garden.

Food is particularly good and includes pizzas from an outdoor wood-fired oven and a variety of 40-day dry-aged steaks from grass-fed cattle plus sandwiches, sharing platters (seafood or vegetarian), potted beef with rhubarb, ginger and mustard relish, devilled lambs kidneys, smoked haddock rarebit, Tuscan pork belly and bean stew, poached salmon thermidor, a pie of the day, aubergine, wild mushroom and tomato bake with tamarind bèchamel sauce, Irish stew with soda bread, and puddings; they also offer a two- and three-course set menu. *Benchmark main dish: sirloin banquet steak with melted cheese top and worcestershire sauce £26.00. Two-course evening meal £25.00.*

Free house ~ Licensees Frances and Jonathan Gledhill ~ Real ale ~ Open 3-9 Weds, Thurs; 12-11 Fri, Sat; 12-8 Sun; closed Mon, Tues ~ Bar food 6-8.30 Weds, Thurs; 12-2, 6-9 Fri, Sat; 12-5.30 Sun ~ Restaurant ~ Children welcome ~ Dogs allowed in bar & bedrooms ~ Bedrooms: £90

BAY HORSE
SD4952   Map 7

Bay Horse

(01524) 791204 – www.bayhorseinn.com

1.2 miles from M6 junction 33: A6 southwards, then off on left; LA2 0HR

18th-c former coaching inn with log fires, comfortable bar and restaurant, well regarded food, local ales and friendly staff

A characterful, gently civilised, family-run place with a series of small, rambling linked rooms including a cosily pubby beamed bar with cushioned wall banquettes in bay windows, lamps on windowsills and a warm log fire. Many customers are here to enjoy a good meal. The dining room has a woodburning stove and lovely views over the garden, where there are plenty of seats and tables. A new private dining space in a double-height converted barn with exposed stone walls is available for parties. Bowland Hen Harrier and Moorhouses Pendle Witches Brew on handpump, 12 wines by the glass, 15 malt whiskies and 20 gins served by friendly, efficient staff. Disabled access. It's a handy stopover for the nearby M6.

Cooked by the chef-owner, the highly regarded food includes baked Scottish scallops with cucumber, seaweed and orange butter, black pudding and caramelised apple scotch egg, sea bass with peas, potatoes, bacon and creamy brown crab meat sauce, chicken breast with peas, kale, charred onions and potato purée, roasted summer squash with tenderstem broccoli and charred onions, duck with green beans, mashed potato, chestnuts and burnt orange and port sauce, and puddings such as chocolate and peanut butter torte with caramel ice-cream and apricot bread and butter pudding with marmalade ice-cream. *Benchmark main dish: chicken breast with haggis and mustard and whisky sauce £18.50. Two-course evening meal £25.00.*

Free house ~ Licensee Craig Wilkinson ~ Real ale ~ Open 12-3, 6-10; 12-4, 6-11 Sat; 12-4, 6-9 Sun; closed Mon, Tues ~ Bar food 12-2, 6-9; 12-3, 6-8 Sun ~ Restaurant ~ Children welcome ~ Dogs allowed in bar

BISPHAM GREEN SD4813 Map 7

Eagle & Child

(01257) 462297 – www.eagleandchildbispham.co.uk

Maltkiln Lane (Parbold–Croston Road, off B5246); L40 3SG

Civilised pub with antiques, enterprising food, an interesting range of beers and appealing rustic garden

Friendly young staff and a warm welcome draw our readers to this well run rural all-rounder. There's Hawkshead Windermere Pale, Marstons Wainwright, Moorhouses White Witch and Thwaites Original on handpump, farm cider, ten wines by the glass, 35 gins and around 20 malt whiskies. Their popular beer festival is usually held on the early May Bank Holiday weekend. The largely open-plan bar is carefully furnished with several handsomely carved antique oak settles (the finest made in part, it seems, from a 16th-c wedding bedhead), a mix of small old oak chairs, an attractive oak coffer, old hunting prints and engravings and hop-draped low beams. Also, red walls, coir matting, oriental rugs on ancient flagstones in front of a fine old stone fireplace and counter. The pub dogs are called Beryl and Rolo; disabled access. The spacious garden has a well tended but unconventional bowling green; beyond is a wild area that's home to crested newts and moorhens. A handsome side barn houses a shop selling interesting wines and pottery, plus a proper butcher and a deli. This is part of the Ainscoughs group.

High quality food includes sandwiches, home-cured salmon with dill and juniper, heritage potato salad, sour cream and chives, Lancashire tart with black pudding, bacon, sausage, red onion jam and home-made brown sauce, chicken breast with garlic mashed potatoes, sweet chilli and mozzarella glaze and basil oil, lancashire cheese and onion pie with chips and home-made brown sauce, giant couscous salad with a choice of feta, chicken, sea bass or steak, and puddings such as sticky toffee pudding with vanilla ice-cream and rice pudding with raspberry jam. *Benchmark main dish: beer-battered fish and chips £13.95. Two-course evening meal £20.00.*

Free house ~ Licensee Peter Robinson ~ Real ale ~ Open 12-11; 12-10.30 Sun ~ Bar food 12-2, 5.30-8.30 (9 Fri); 12-9 Sat; 12-8 Sun ~ Children allowed in bar ~ Dogs allowed in bar & restaurant

FORMBY SD3109 Map 7

Sparrowhawk

(01704) 882350 – www.brunningandprice.co.uk/sparrowhawk

Southport Old Road; brown sign to pub just off A565 Formby bypass, S edge of Ainsdale; L37 0AB

Light and airy pub with interesting décor, good food and drinks choices and wooded grounds

A rather grand conversion of an old hotel, set in five acres of woods and parkland. In fact, a walk from the pub to coastal nature reserves might just yield red squirrels, still hanging on in this area. Bearing all the stylings of a well run Brunning & Price pub, the nicely proportioned open-plan rooms, spread out from the central bar, have plenty of interest: attractive prints on pastel walls, flowers, snug leather fireside armchairs in library corners, and seats and tables with rugs on dark boards by big bow windows. There's also a large, comfortably carpeted conservatory dining room; background music. Cheery, friendly young staff serve more than 40 gins, 30 whiskies and 19 wines by the glass, plus beers including Phoenix Brunning & Price Original, Salopian Oracle, Titanic Plum Porter and three guests on handpump. Outside, there's a flagstoned side terrace with sturdy tables, lawns with picnic-sets by swings and an old Fergie tractor, and scenic parkland views.

A wide choice of food includes sandwiches and 'light bites', summer vegetable risotto, ham hock hash cake with fried egg and piccalilli, Vietnamese-style ribs, braised shoulder of lamb with minted crushed new potatoes and rosemary gravy, sweet potato, aubergine and spinach Malaysian curry with coconut rice and pak choi, cumberland sausages with mash and gravy, and puddings such as hot waffle with boozy cherries and vanilla ice-cream and chocolate and orange tart with passion-fruit sorbet. *Benchmark main dish: chicken, ham and leek pie with mash, buttered greens and white wine and tarragon sauce £14.95. Two-course evening meal £22.00.*

Brunning & Price ~ Manager Iain Hendry ~ Real ale ~ Open 12-10 ~ Bar food 12-9 ~ Restaurant ~ Children welcome ~ Dogs allowed in bar

GREAT MITTON
Aspinall Arms 🍷 🍺
SD7138   Map 7

(01254) 826555 – www.brunningandprice.co.uk/aspinallarms
B6246 NW of Whalley; BB7 9PQ

Cleverly refurbished and extended riverside pub with cheerful helpful service and a fine choice of drinks and food

Scenically situated in the heart of the Ribble Valley, this riverside pub welcomes walkers, cyclists, anglers and a good mix of locals, dropping in and out all day. The various rambling rooms have seating that ranges from attractively cushioned old-style dining chairs through brass-studded leather ones to big armchairs and sofas around an assortment of dark tables. Floors are flagstoned, carpeted or wooden and topped with rugs, while the pale-painted or bare stone walls are hung with an extensive collection of prints and local photographs. Dotted about are large mirrors, house plants, stone bottles and bookshelves and there are both open fires and a woodburning stove. From the central servery, knowledgeable staff serve Phoenix Brunning & Price Original and Moorhouses Aspinall Witch (named for the pub) with guests such as Moorhouses Black Cat, Saltaire Blonde, Settle Jericho Blonde and Timothy Taylors Golden Best on handpump, 15 wines by the glass, 50 gins, an amazing 150 malt whiskies and a farm cider; background music and board games. Plenty of chairs and tables on a terrace and lots of picnic-sets in the extensive garden make the most of the waterside position.

Up-to-date food includes sandwiches and 'light bites', smoked salmon with orange and beetroot salad and horseradish cream, hummus with flatbread, five-spiced duck leg with spring onion, cucumber, hoisin sauce and pancakes, pea and mint tortellini with garden pea velouté and asparagus, braised feather of beef bourguignon with horseradish mash and kale, crispy beef salad with sweet chilli sauce and roasted cashew nuts, Appleby's cheshire cheese, potato and onion pie, and puddings such as eton mess and sticky toffee pudding with toffee sauce and vanilla ice-cream. *Benchmark main dish: buttermilk chicken burger with bacon, garlic mayonnaise and fries £14.95. Two-course evening meal £22.00.*

Brunning & Price ~ Manager Susanne Engelmann ~ Real ale ~ Open 10.30am-11pm;
10.30-10.30 Sun ~ Bar food 12-9.30; 12-9 Sun ~ Restaurant ~ Children welcome ~ Dogs
allowed in bar

MANCHESTER
SJ8297   Map 7

Wharf ♀ ◗

(0161) 220 2960 – www.brunningandprice.co.uk/thewharf
Blantyre Street/Slate Wharf; M15 4ST

**Big wharf-like pub with large terrace overlooking the water and a fine
range of drinks and food**

This appealing waterside spot by the Bridgewater Canal has a large
open-plan ground floor with a friendly, informal atmosphere and groups
of high tables and chairs, and a more formal restaurant upstairs. The big
front terrace has plenty of wood and chrome tables and chairs set round
a fountain, and picnic-sets overlooking the canal basin. Throughout there's
an appealing variety of dining chairs around dark wooden tables on rugs
and shiny floorboards, hundreds of interesting prints and posters on bare
brick or painted walls, old stone bottles, church candles and house plants on
windowsills and tables, plus bookshelves, armchairs and large mirrors over
open fires. Efficient, friendly staff serve Phoenix Brunning & Price Original
and Weetwood Cheshire Cat plus up to eight quickly changing guest ales on
handpump from breweries such as Beartown, Brightside, Rudgate, Squawk
and Titanic and local craft brewer Beatnikz, as well as farm cider, 16 wines
by the glass, 40 gins and 50-plus malt whiskies.

A wide range of popular food includes 'light bites', five-spiced duck leg with
spring onion, cucumber, hoisin sauce and pancakes, halloumi fries with tomato
salsa, cheshire cheese, potato and onion pie with carrot purée, kale and gravy, braised
shoulder of lamb with mashed potatoes, red cabbage and green beans, fish pie, pork and
leek sausages with mash, and puddings such as crème brûlée with shortbread and hot
waffle with caramelised banana and honeycomb ice-cream. *Benchmark main dish:
beer-battered fish and chips £14.95. Two-course evening meal £21.00.*

Brunning & Price ~ Manager Natasha Metcalfe ~ Real ale ~ Open 10am-11pm; 10am-
midnight Sat; 10am-10.30pm Sun ~ Bar food 10am-9.30pm; 10-10 Fri, Sat; 12-9 Sun ~
Restaurant ~ Children under 10 permitted until 9pm ~ Dogs allowed in bar

NETHER BURROW
SD6175   Map 7

Highwayman ♀ ◗

(01524) 273338 – www.brunningandprice.co.uk/highwayman
A683 S of Kirkby Lonsdale; LA6 2RJ

**Large and skilfully refurbished old stone house with country interior,
serving carefully sourced food; attractive gardens**

This is an imposing 17th-c stone building set among the rolling green hills
of the Lune Valley. Both the food and drink in this Brunning & Price
pub are highly regarded and there's always a friendly mix of customers.
The stylish and cosy flagstoned interior is nicely divided into intimate
corners, with a couple of large log fires, wooden, leather-seated or tartan
chairs around dark tables, button-back or leather wall banquettes and
a bustling atmosphere. There are some large photos on the walls and
interesting modern lighting. You'll find Phoenix Brunning & Price Original
plus Hawkshead Red, Kirkby Lonsdale Tiffin Gold, Lancaster Black and
Moorhouses Pendle Witches Brew on handpump, ten wines by the glass,
36 gins and 21 whiskies served by friendly, efficient staff; background music

and TV. French windows open out to a big terrace and lovely gardens with smart rattan-style furniture, taking in the pretty valley views.

🍴 Pleasing food using seasonal, local produce includes sandwiches and 'light bites', chicken liver pâté with apricot chutney, crispy baby squid with sweet chilli sauce, cauliflower fritters with curried mayonnaise, pea and mint tortellini with garden pea velouté and asparagus, gammon with chargrilled pineapple, egg and chips, salmon and smoked haddock fishcake, steak burger with grilled bacon, coleslaw and fries, and puddings such as summer pudding with clotted cream and lemon cheesecake with raspberry ripple ice-cream. *Benchmark main dish: braised lamb shoulder with roast potatoes and gravy £18.95. Two-course evening meal £22.50.*

Brunning & Price ~ Manager Aimee Sharples ~ Real ale ~ Open 12-11; 12-10 Sun ~ Bar food 12-8; 12-9 Fri, Sat ~ Restaurant ~ Children welcome ~ Dogs allowed in bar

PLEASINGTON
Clog & Billycock 🍷 ◖

SD6528   Map 7

(01254) 201163 – www.brunningandprice.co.uk/clogandbillycock
Village signposted off A677 Preston New Road on W edge of Blackburn; Billinge End Road; BB2 6QB

Wide range of good food and drink in appealing and well run stone-built village pub

Another member of the Brunning & Price family, this quaint and cosy 19th-c stone inn has been sympathetically extended. Several light and airy rooms run together with flagstoned floors, high ceilings with beams and joists and pale grey walls above a grey dado. There are laden bookshelves, mirrors, prints and pictures on pale painted walls, big house plants, wooden, plush upholstered or leather chairs and tartan banquettes around simple wooden tables, and an open fire and a fine old range. Helpful, friendly young staff serve Phoenix Brunning & Price Original and guests from breweries such as Bowland, Hawkshead, Moorhouses, Three B's and Timothy Taylors on handpump, eight wines by the glass, 40 rums, 50 malt whiskies and 60 gins; background music and board games. There's an appealing paved and awning-covered garden and terrace with benches, seats and tables and a fire pit. Disabled access.

🍴 Interesting, bistro-like food includes sandwiches and 'light bites', deep-fried brie with apricot chutney and candied walnuts, barbecue chicken wings, Sandham's lancashire cheese and onion pie with chips, crispy beef salad with sweet chilli sauce and roasted cashew nuts, chicken, ham and leek pie with mash and buttered greens, king prawn linguine with chilli and tomato, and puddings such as triple chocolate brownie with chocolate sauce and vanilla ice-cream and summer pudding with clotted cream and Cheshire Farm ice-creams and sorbets. *Benchmark main dish: deep fried cod in beer batter with chips, mushy peas and tartare sauce £14.95. Two-course evening meal £21.00.*

Brunning & Price ~ Manager Rob Broadbent ~ Real ale ~ Open 10am-11pm; 10am-10.30pm Sun ~ Bar food 12-9; 12-10 Fri, Sat ~ Children welcome ~ Dogs allowed in bar

PRESTON
Haighton Manor 🍷 ◖

SD5634   Map 7

(01772) 706350 – www.brunningandprice.co.uk/haightonmanor
Haighton Green Lane, Haighton; PR2 5SQ

Rather grand stone building surrounded by lawns and countryside with thoughtful drinks and food choice, and seats outside

This imposing 17th-c country house has been sympathetically restored by Brunning & Price, combining striking exposed stone walls with more homely touches. The bustling bar features an open fire, wooden chairs around a large farmhouse kitchen table, elegant metal chandeliers and stools against the counter. Various open-plan rooms lead off here with rugs on wooden floors, wall-to-wall prints, photographs and mirrors on pale walls above painted dados, more open fires, antique-style cushioned dining chairs around dark tables, and house plants and candles. One cosy character room has armchairs and chesterfield sofas on flagstones and bare stone walls, and there's a spacious conservatory dining extension. Cheerful staff serve Phoenix Brunning & Price Original plus guests such as Hawkshead Bitter, Lancaster Blonde, Moorhouses Black Cat, Pitchfork PG Steam and Timothy Taylors Landlord on handpump, more than 70 gins, 50 malt whiskies and ten farm ciders; board games. Good quality chairs, benches and tables under parasols are set out on a terrace surrounded by lawns with pleasant country views; there's the usual trademark tractor for children. Disabled access.

Appealing modern food includes sandwiches and 'light bites', garlic and chilli king prawns, chicken caesar croquettes with parmesan and anchovy salad, crispy vegetable parcels with spiced mango dip, roast duck breast with crispy leg croquettes, celeriac purée and cherry jus, steak burger with fries, braised feather of beef bourguignon with horseradish mash and buttered kale, cheddar, leek and balsamic onion quiche, cauliflower, chickpea and squash tagine with lemon and almond couscous, and puddings such as lemon cheesecake with raspberry ripple ice-cream and chocolate and orange tart with passion-fruit sorbet. *Benchmark main dish: braised shoulder of lamb with minted crushed new potatoes and rosemary gravy £18.95. Two-course evening meal £23.00.*

Brunning & Price ~ Manager Chris Humphries ~ Real ale ~ Open 12-11; 12-10.30 Sun ~ Bar food 12-9; 12-9.30 Fri, Sat ~ Restaurant ~ Children welcome ~ Dogs allowed in bar

SAWLEY   SD7746   Map 7
Spread Eagle 🛏

(01200) 441202 – www.spreadeaglesawley.co.uk
Village signed just off A59 NE of Clitheroe; BB7 4NH

Old coaching inn with good food, riverside restaurant and four real ales; bedrooms

With the Forest of Bowland and Pendle Hill nearby, there are plenty of good walks close to this attractive and well run old coaching inn in the heart of the Ribble Valley. Start with a stroll around the ruins of a 12th-c Cistercian abbey just over the road. The bar rooms have a pleasing mix of nice old and quirky modern furniture (anything from an old settle and pine tables to up-to-date low chairs upholstered in animal print fabric) and a rustic stone floor. Low ceilings, cosy sections, a warming fire and cottagey windows keep it feeling intimate. The dining areas are more formal, with modern stripes and a bookshelf mural; background music and board games. Young, efficient and friendly staff serve beers including Dark Horse Hetton Pale Ale and Robinsons Dizzy Blonde and Ribble Tickler, and a dozen wines by the glass. It's a favourite with dog walkers: pooches are allowed in both bar areas and get their own three-course menu including treats and dedicated drinks such as Pawsecco and a dog beer, Bottom Sniffer. The 11 bedrooms, some overlooking the river, are individually furnished and comfortable and breakfasts are good.

Reliable food includes lunchtime sandwiches, chorizo, new potato and chicken in paprika butter, carrot, beetroot and pea hummus, chicken liver pâté, fish and chips, slow-cooked lamb flank with root vegetables, cauliflower, chickpea and tomato tagine with couscous, cumberland sausage with mash and onion gravy, steak burger with toppings and chips, a pie of the day, and puddings. *Benchmark main dish: fish pie £12.95. Two-course evening meal £20.00.*

Individual Inns ~ Manager Greig and Natalie Barns ~ Real ale ~ Open 12-9 ~ Bar food 12-2, 5.30-8.30; 12-2, 6-9 Sat; 12-7 Sun ~ Restaurant ~ Children welcome ~ Dogs allowed in bar & bedrooms ~ Wi-fi ~ Bedrooms: £120

THORNTON HOUGH
SJ2979 Map 7

Red Fox � 🍺

(0151) 353 2920 – www.brunningandprice.co.uk/redfox
Liverpool Road; CH64 7TL

Sizeable pub with a fine choice of beers, wines, gins and whiskies, courteous staff serving enjoyable food and large back garden

Set back from the road, down a long drive surrounded by lawns and pleasant country views, this sprawling former country pile features a mix of cosy nooks and large, airy rooms. The spacious main bar is reached via stairs from the entrance: sturdy central pillars divide the room into smaller areas with high stools and tables in the middle, dark wooden tables and chairs to each side and deep leather armchairs and fender seats next to the large fireplace. This leads into a long, carpeted dining room with two rows of painted iron supports, hefty leather and wood chairs around highly polished tables and a raised fire pit; doors from here lead out to a terrace. Two additional dining rooms are similarly furnished, one with an elegant chandelier hanging from a fine moulded ceiling. Throughout there are photographs, prints and pictures covering the walls, big plants, stone bottles and shelves of books; background music and board games. Friendly, cheerful staff serve a fantastic range of drinks that includes Phoenix Brunning & Price Original plus guests such as Brightside Amarillo, Conwy West Coast Pale Ale, Cwrw Ial Limestone Cowboy, Hopback Crop Circle, Lancaster Black and Red and Oakham Inferno on handpump, 21 wines by the glass, 123 malt whiskies, more than 100 gins and ten farm ciders. At the back of the building there are terraces with good quality wooden chairs and tables under parasols, and steps down to picnic-sets around a fountain. Disabled access.

Well presented food includes sandwiches and 'light bites', smoked salmon with orange and beetroot salad and horseradish cream, chipolatas with honey and mustard, grilled sea bass fillets with potato and shallot terrine and chervil and lemon cream sauce, pork sausages with mash, buttered greens and onion gravy, pea and mint tortellini, crispy buttermilk chicken burger with bacon, garlic mayonnaise and fries, and puddings such as lemon meringue roulade with raspberry sorbet and chocolate and orange steamed sponge with white chocolate custard. *Benchmark main dish: beer-battered fish and chips £14.95. Two-course evening meal £22.00.*

Brunning & Price ~ Manager David Green ~ Real ale ~ Open 12-11; 10am-10.30pm Sun ~ Bar food 12-9; 12-9.30 Fri, Sat ~ Restaurant ~ Children welcome ~ Dogs allowed in bar

UPPERMILL
SD0006 Map 7

Church Inn 🍺 £

(01457) 820902 – www.churchinnsaddleworth.co.uk
From the main street (A607), look out for the sign for Saddleworth Church, and turn off up this steep narrow lane – keep on up; OL3 6LW

Community pub with big range of own-brew beers at unbeatable bargain prices and tasty food; children very welcome

This informal and friendly community local always attracts a cheerful crowd of happy customers, despite its remote setting. Home to the Saddleworth Brewery (situated at the side of the pub), the wonderful own-brewed ales on handpump and incredible value food are the main attractions, alongside extensive views across the moors. The big, unspoilt, L-shaped main bar has a cheerful, friendly atmosphere, high beams and some stripped stone, settles, pews, a good individual mix of chairs, lots of attractive prints, Staffordshire and other china on a high delft shelf, jugs, brasses and so forth. As well as their own beers, they have guests such as Copper Dragon, Donkeystone and Timothy Taylors. Some of their own seasonal ales are named after the licensee's children, only appearing around their birthdays; two home-brewed lagers on tap too. Unobtrusive background music. The terrace has magnificent valley views. The local bellringers arrive on Wednesdays to practise with a set of handbells kept here, and anyone can join the morris dancing on Thursdays. Children enjoy the menagerie of animals, and dogs are made to feel very welcome.

Honest, fair priced food includes sandwiches, prawn cocktail, spicy chicken wings, vegetable fajitas with sour cream, salsa and guacamole, home-made beef chilli, lamb shank in minted gravy, various home-made pies, salmon fillet with coriander crust and creamed leeks, gammon steak with egg or pineapple, and puddings such as apple crumble and jam roly poly. *Benchmark main dish: steak, mushroom and ale pie £10.50. Two-course evening meal £16.00.*

Own brew ~ Licensee Christine Taylor ~ Real ale ~ Open 12-10.30 ~ Bar food 12-2.30, 5-9 Mon-Fri; 12-9 Sat, Sun and bank holidays ~ Restaurant ~ Children welcome until 9pm ~ Dogs welcome

WHITEWELL
Inn at Whitewell ★ 🏵 ♀ 🍺 🛏

SD6546   Map 7

(01200) 448222 – www.innatwhitewell.com

Most easily reached by B6246 from Whalley; road through Dunsop Bridge from B6478 is also good; BB7 3AT

Lancashire Dining Pub of the Year

Rather grand old house with smartly pubby atmosphere, top quality food, exceptional wine list, real ales and professional, friendly service; luxury bedrooms

This elegant and sprawling manor house cuts an imposing silhouette against the surrounding landscape – it's situated high on the banks of the River Hodder, with spectacular views across the water to the Forest of Bowland. Visitors often choose to stay in one of its 23 lovely bedrooms or separate holiday cottage, the Piggeries: charming and individually furnished with beautifully restored bathrooms, several have open fires; breakfasts are excellent. The civilised bar rooms have handsome old wood furnishings, including antique settles, oak gate-leg tables and sonorous clocks, set off beautifully against powder blue walls neatly hung with big appealing prints. The pubby main bar has roaring log fires in attractive stone fireplaces and heavy curtains on sturdy wooden rails; one area has a selection of newspapers and magazines, local maps and guidebooks. There's a piano for anyone who wants to play, and board games. Early evening sees a cheerful bustle that later settles to a more tranquil and relaxing atmosphere. Drinks include a marvellous wine list of around 230 wines with 26 by the glass (there's also an excellent on-site wine shop), 24 whiskies, eight gins, a fine selection of soft drinks, and Black Sheep, Moorhouses Blonde Witch, Timothy Taylors Landlord and Tirril Ullswater Blonde on handpump. The riverside bar and adjacent terrace make the most of the scenic views, and they own several miles of trout, salmon and sea trout fishing on the river (picnic hampers on request). Limited disabled access.

🍴⭐ They bake their own bread, make jams and chutneys and use the best local produce including game in season. The delicious food includes lunchtime sandwiches, pressed ham hock with pickled baby carrots and piccalilli purée, home-cured salmon with dill and grain mustard dressing, potted crab with avocado purée and cucumber pickle, roast cannon of lamb with apricot, mint, smoked bacon, crushed peas and potato purée, fish pie, roast Goosnargh duck breast and leg croquette with braised cabbage and apple, Thai chickpea and vegetable curry, and home-made puddings; they serve afternoon tea too.

Free house ~ Licensee Charles Bowman ~ Real ale ~ Open 11am-midnight ~ Bar food 12-2, 7-9.30; 12-2, 6-9 Sun ~ Restaurant ~ Children welcome ~ Dogs welcome ~ Bedrooms: £170-£250

WORSLEY
Worsley Old Hall 🍷 🍺

SD7401 Map 7

(0161) 703 8706 – www.brunningandprice.co.uk/worsleyoldhall

A mile from M60 junction 13: A575 Walkden Road, then after roundabout take first left into Worsley Park; M28 2QT

Very handsomely converted landmark building, now a welcoming pub scoring high on all counts

This huge black and white timbered hall, with parts dating from the 16th c, has historic links to the construction of the nearby Bridgewater Canal. In fact, the Worsley Bridgewater Canal heritage area is a ten-minute walk away and RHS Garden Bridgewater (the largest gardening project in Europe) will open in 2021. The lovely, original architectural features of the pub include a gracefully arched inglenook and matching window alcove, handsome staircase, heavy beams and glowing mahogany panelling. The relaxed and chatty main area spreads generously around the feature central bar, where swift, friendly staff serve 21 good wines by the glass, more than 100 malt whiskies and 67 gins. Also, Phoenix Brunning & Price Original, Timothy Taylors Landlord and a beer named for the pub (from Facers) plus guests from breweries such as Beartown, Castle Rock, Dunscar, Howard Town, Inveralmond and Lancaster on handpump. There's also Brunning & Price's usual abundance of carefully selected prints, fireside armchairs, cushioned dining chairs and wooden tables and rugs on oak parquet flooring; board games and background music. On a sunny day, the seats and tables on the large flagstoned back terrace behind are quickly snapped up; there's also a barbecue area, a vast lawn beyond the fountain with picnic-table sets and views over the golf course.

🍴 Interesting modern food includes sandwiches and 'light bites', deep-fried brie with apricot chutney and candied walnuts, meze plate, roast duck breast with crispy leg croquettes, celeriac purée and cherry jus, Malaysian chicken curry with coconut rice and pak choi, rib-eye steak with dijon and tarragon butter, portobello mushrooms and chunky chips, pea and mint tortellini with garden pea velouté and asparagus, and puddings such as chocolate and orange tart with passion-fruit sorbet and summer pudding with clotted cream. *Benchmark main dish: chicken, ham and leek pie with mash, buttered greens and white wine and tarragon sauce £14.95. Two-course evening meal £22.00.*

Brunning & Price ~ Manager Ryan Maguire ~ Real ale ~ Open 12-11; 12-10.30 Sun ~ Bar food 12-9 ~ Restaurant ~ Children welcome ~ Dogs allowed in bar

Also Worth a Visit in Lancashire

Besides the fully inspected pubs, you might like to try these pubs that have been recommended to us and described by readers. Do tell us what you think of them: feedback@goodguides.com

BARLEY   SD8240
Pendle (01282) 614808
Barley Lane; BB12 9JX Friendly 1930s stone pub in shadow of Pendle Hill; three cosy rooms, two log fires and six well kept regional ales including Moorhouses, 15 wines by the glass, popular good value pubby food using local produce (lamb from family farm), conservatory; children and dogs welcome, picnic-sets on strip of lawn at front, small fenced play area across road by stream, lovely village and good walking country, bedrooms, open all day Fri-Sun.

BARTON   SD5137
Pickled Goose (01772) 802280
A6 N of Broughton; PR3 5AA Contemporary dining pub (formerly the Sparling) under new management and lightly refurbished, with enjoyable food including pub classics, quality real ales and good choice of wines by the glass, roomy bar with comfortable sofas and other seats, plenty of tables in linked areas off, wood and flagstone floors, modern fireplaces; handy for M6, open all day, closed Mon and Tues.

BELMONT   SD6715
Black Dog (01204) 811218
Church Street (A675); BL7 8AB Nicely set Holts pub with enjoyable traditional food including deals with vegan options, well kept beers and friendly staff, various modernised areas (some slightly raised), pubby furnishings including banquettes on light wood or carpeted floors, a couple of coal fires, picture-window dining extension; children and dogs (in bar) welcome, seats outside with moorland views over village, part-covered courtyard behind, good walks, three bedrooms, open (and food) all day.

BLACKBURN   SD6525
Oyster & Otter (01254) 203200
1.8 miles from M65 junction 3: A674 towards Blackburn, turn right at Feniscowles mini roundabout, signposted to Darwen and Tockholes, into Livesey Branch Road; BB2 5DQ Distinctive clapboard and stone building in modern New England style; open-plan interior with cushioned dining booths by big windows on one side, other cosy seating areas divided by shoulder-high walls and large central hearth, end part with comfy sofas, good food including signature fish/seafood from open kitchen, Marstons Wainwright, a guest ale and over 30 wines by the glass; background music; children welcome, seats on decking above road, open (and food) all day.

BOLTON   SD7112
Brewery Tap (01204) 302837
Belmont Road; BL1 7AN Two-room corner tap for Bank Top, their full range kept well and a guest, large range of traditional ciders, knowledgeable friendly staff, no food; quiet background music; children (until 7pm) and dogs welcome, disabled access, seats outside, open all day.

BRINDLE   SD5924
★ Cavendish Arms (01254) 852912
3 miles from M6 junction 29, via A6 and B5256 (Sandy Lane); PR6 8NG Traditional beamed village pub (dates from the 15th c) on corner adjacent to church; cosy snugs with open fires, stained-glass windows depicting the Battle of Brunanburh, carpets throughout, four Marstons-related ales, cocktails and good inexpensive home-made food including Thurs specials and Fri fish, afternoon tea Thurs-Sat, friendly helpful service, back dining room; Tues quiz; children and dogs (in tap room) welcome, heated canopied terrace with water feature, more tables in side garden, good walks, open (and food) all day weekends, closed lunchtimes Mon and Tues (no food those days or lunchtime Weds).

BURY   SD8313
Trackside (0161) 764 6461
East Lancashire Railway station, Bolton Street; BL9 0EY Welcoming busy station bar by East Lancs steam railway; bright, airy and clean with a dozen real ales, also bottled imports, real ciders and great range of whiskies, enjoyable lunchtime food (not Mon, Tues); quiz Tues, folk night last Thurs of month; children (till 7pm) and dogs welcome, platform tables under canopy, open all day.

CARNFORTH   SD5173
Longlands (01524) 781256
Tewitfield, about 2 miles N; A6070, off A6; LA6 1JH Popular family-run village inn; good food in bar and airy restaurant from pub favourites and flatbread pizzas up, four local beers, helpful friendly staff; live music; children and dogs welcome, bedrooms and self-catering cottages, Lancaster Canal and M6 nearby, open all day.

CHATBURN   SD7644
Brown Cow (01200) 440736
Bridge Road; BB7 4AW Welcoming recently refurbished village pub; opened-up interior with separate dining room, good well priced home-made food including weekly

specials, Marstons Wainwright and three guests, over 40 gins, friendly helpful service; children and dogs (in bar area) welcome, wheelchair access (ramp provided) and disabled loo (others upstairs), back garden with flagstone terrace, closed Mon, otherwise open all day, food all day weekends.

CHEADLE   SJ8588
James Watts (0161) 428 3361
High Street (A560); SK8 1AX Mock-Tudor pub owned by Hydes; fine range of cask and craft beer and extensive bottled world beer range (over 100), good choice of wines and other drinks too, food from snacks to various sharing combinations served on slates, friendly helpful staff; live acoustic music Mon and Thurs, quiz Sun; back terrace, open all day (till midnight Fri, Sat).

CHEADLE HULME   SJ8785
Church Inn (0161) 485 1897
Ravenoak Road (A5149 SE); SK8 7EG Popular old family-run pub with good food from varied menu including set deals, well kept Robinsons beers and nice selection of wines by the glass, gleaming brass on panelled walls, warming coal fire, back restaurant; live music most Sun evenings; children welcome, seats outside (some under cover), car park across road, open all day.

CLITHEROE   SD7441
Holmes Mill (01200) 407120
Greenacre Street; BB7 1EB Conversion of town's last working cotton mill; cavernous industrial interior keeping some of the old machinery, lovely flagged floor and plenty of recycled fixtures and fittings, walls fitted with leather benches and scrubbed plank tables, sturdy canteen chairs and high-backed stools elsewhere, vast U-shaped counter serving a minimum of 24 cask ales including six from Bowland (brewery visible behind glass partitions), good selection of enjoyable food including grills, also has a café, food shop and boutique hotel; background and some live music; picnic-sets outside along with covered seating in shipping containers, dogs welcome, open (and food) all day, till 8pm Sun.

CLITHEROE   SD7441
New Inn (01200) 423312
Parson Lane; BB7 2JN Traditional old-fashioned local with 11 well kept ales including Coach House and Moorhouses from central bar, friendly knowledgeable staff, cosy rooms with log fires; fortnightly Irish session (Sun afternoon) and other live music;

dogs welcome, seats out at front and in large area to rear, open all day.

COLNE   SD8940
Black Lane Ends (01282) 863070
Skipton Old Road, Foulridge; BB8 7EP Country pub tucked away in quiet lane; generous helpings of good sensibly priced food, three well kept real ales including Timothy Taylors Landlord and decent wine choice, cheerful attentive staff, long bar with spindleback chairs, padded wall benches and scrubbed tables, large fireplace partially separating small dining room with cast-iron range; children welcome, play area in back garden, nice views towards Wycoller from terrace, handy for canal and reservoir walks, open (and food) all day.

DENSHAW   SD9710
Printers Arms (01457) 874248
Oldham Road; OL3 5SN Above Oldham in shadow of Saddleworth Moor; modernised interior with small log-fire bar and three other rooms, popular good value food including bargain set menu (until 5pm or so Mon-Sat), Marstons Wainwright and Timothy Taylors Golden Best, several wines by the glass, friendly staff; children welcome, lovely views from two-tier beer garden, open (and food) all day.

DENSHAW   SD9711
Rams Head (01457) 874802
2 miles from M62 junction 22; A672 towards Oldham, pub N of village; OL3 5UN Sweeping moorland views from this popular roadside dining pub (don't be put off by the rather austere exterior); good food (all day Fri-Sun) including seasonal game and seafood, ales such as Timothy Taylors kept well and several wines by the glass, friendly service, four thick-walled little rooms, beam-and-plank ceilings, panelling, oak settles and built-in benches, log fires, coffee shop and adjacent delicatessen selling local produce; soft background music; children welcome, closed Mon and Tues.

DENTON   SJ9395
Lowes Arms (0161) 336 3064
Hyde Road (A57); M34 3FF Thriving 19th-c pub with own Westwood beers and local guests such as Crossbay and Prospect, jovial community-spirited landlord and helpful friendly staff, reasonably priced food including daily specials, bar with pool and darts, restaurant; children and dogs welcome, tables outside, smokers' shelter, open all day.

DIGGLE SE0007

Diggle (01457) 872741

*Village signed off A670 just N of
Dobcross; OL3 5JZ* Sturdy four-square
hillside pub in quiet spot just below the
moors overlooking Standedge Canal tunnel;
good value food from sandwiches and snacks
up, well kept ales such as Millstone and
Timothy Taylors, helpful staff; children and
dogs welcome, disabled access, picnic-sets
out among trees, four bedrooms, open
evenings only Mon-Fri, all day weekends.

DOLPHINHOLME SD5153

Fleece (01524) 791233

*A couple of miles from M6 junction 33;
W of village; Chipping Lane/Anyon
Road; LA2 9AQ* Extensively renovated
old stone inn (parts date from the 16th c);
various rooms including black-beamed
bar with rugs on flagstones and log fire
with unusual copper canopy, four well kept
regularly changing ales and decent wines by
the glass, popular sensibly priced food (not
Mon), friendly efficient service, dining lounge
with some modern booth seating and sofas in
front of woodburner, little shop selling local
produce; children and dogs welcome, modern
rattan-style furniture on terrace with Trough
of Bowland views, nine comfortable well
appointed bedrooms, good breakfast, closed
Mon lunchtime, otherwise open all day.

DUNHAM TOWN SJ7488

Axe & Cleaver (0161) 928 3391

School Lane; WA14 4SE Big 19th-c country
house converted into spacious open-plan
Chef & Brewer; good value popular food from
light lunchtime choices and sharing plates
up (best to book Sun lunch), three well kept
ales, friendly service; children welcome,
garden picnic-sets, handy for nearby Dunham
Massey (NT), open (and food) all day.

DUNHAM TOWN SJ7288

Vine (0161) 928 3275

Barns Lane, Dunham Massey; WA14 5RU
Tucked-away (but busy) old-fashioned village
local with friendly staff and regulars; well
kept/priced Sam Smiths ales and several
ciders, enjoyable generously served food
(not Sun evening, Mon), cosy bar and other
smallish rooms, coal fires in brick fireplaces;
children and dogs welcome, picnic-sets in
good-sized garden, handy for Dunham Massey
(NT), open all day.

EDENFIELD SD7919

Coach (01706) 825000

Market Street; BL0 0HJ Updated and
extended 19th-c dining pub; good food
including lunchtime express menu, three
real ales, over a dozen wines by the glass
and good range of gins, friendly young staff;
children and dogs (in bar) welcome, disabled
access/facilities, a few tables on front
pavement, open (and food) all day.

EGERTON SD7015

Cross Guns (01204) 291204

Blackburn Road (A666); BL7 9TR
Renovated 18th-c stone pub below the
moors; spacious cleanly updated interior
with beams, standing timbers, bare boards
and exposed stone walls, two snug areas to
the right with woodburners, bar constructed
from salvaged beams serving four well kept/
priced ales, over a dozen wines by the glass
and good choice of other drinks, popular
food including lunchtime sandwiches, pub
favourites and tapas, restaurant extending
into old stables, friendly staff; children
welcome, narrow fenced front terrace with
dog shower, open all day, food till 7pm Sun.

FENCE SD8237

Fence Gate (01282) 618101

*2.6 miles from M65 junction 13;
Wheatley Lane Road, just off A6068 W;
BB12 9EE* Imposing 18th-c dining inn with
good choice of enjoyable food, five real ales
from the likes of Bowland, Copper Dragon
and Moorhouses and several wines by the
glass, friendly service, panelled bar with
pewter counter and woodburner in large
stone fireplace, contemporary brasserie
plus various function rooms, look out for
their display of over 600 gins; background
and regular live music; children welcome,
rattan-style furniture out front, 24 bedrooms,
open all day.

FENCE SD8237

★**White Swan** (01282) 611773

Wheatley Lane; BB12 9QA Whitewashed
village dining pub with comfortably renovated
Victorian-style interior; Michelin-starred
food (not cheap) from short daily changing
menu, good friendly service, four well kept
Timothy Taylors ales from curved polished
wood servery, nice wines, own infused spirits
and good coffee, old pictures of the pub,
some antlers and stuffed animal heads, wall
lights and chandeliers, fireplace at each end;
children welcome, outside seating on two
levels with chunky wooden tables, closed Sun
and Mon except last Sun of month.

GISBURN SD8248

White Bull (01200) 415805

Main Street (A59); BB7 4HE Modernised
roadside pub with opened-up dining areas
either side of entrance, more room further
back to right of bar; taupe-painted walls and
stone-effect wallpaper, mix of dark furniture
on polished wood or flagstone floors, some
whitewashed beams and standing timbers,
enjoyable food (not Mon) from sandwiches,
sharing boards and pub standards up, Weds
steak night, well kept ales from semi-circular
counter with cherry wood top, friendly
service; children and dogs (in one section)
welcome, narrow access to large back car
park, grassy beer garden, eight comfortable
bedrooms, closed Mon lunchtime.

GOOSNARGH SD5636
Stags Head (01772) 861536
Whittingham Lane (B5269); PR3 2AU
Modernised old roadside dining pub; good
range of popular freshly made food at fair
prices, friendly helpful service, several well
kept ales such as Theakstons Best and Ossett
Yorkshire Blonde, lots of separate areas
including pitched-roof restaurant, open
fires; Thurs quiz, board games, TV; children,
walkers and dogs welcome, tables out in
pleasant garden with fenced play area, open
(and food) all day.

GREAT HARWOOD SD7332
Royal (01254) 876237
Station Road; BB6 7BA Popular Victorian
local with half a dozen well kept changing
ales and generous helpings of enjoyable pub
food, friendly staff; some live music, pool and
darts, sports TV; children welcome, partly
covered terrace, open all day.

GREENFIELD SD9904
King William IV (01457) 873933
Chew Valley Road (A669); OL3 7DD
Welcoming 19th-c village pub with eight
well kept ales including local Donkeystone,
Millstone and Pictish, enjoyable home-made
food (not Mon, Tues or lunchtimes Weds,
Thurs), helpful, friendly staff; Mon quiz,
sports TV; children and dogs welcome, tables
on walled front terrace, open all day.

GREENFIELD SD9904
Railway Hotel 07711 190374
*Shaw Hall Bank Road, opposite station;
OL3 7JZ* Friendly four-room stone pub
with half a dozen well kept mainly local
ales including Millstone, no food, old local
photographs and open fire; live music Thurs,
Fri and Sun, upstairs games room with pool;
children and dogs welcome, disabled access,
good views from beer garden of Saddleworth
hills, closed Mon, otherwise open all day.

HESWALL SJ2782
Jug & Bottle (0151) 342 5535
Mount Avenue; CH60 4RH Nicely updated
Victorian building with views through trees
of the Dee estuary and Welsh mountains
beyond; good-sized bar with wood and
flagstone floors, open fire, dining rooms off,
half a dozen well kept ales including Brains,
Brimstage and local brews, lots of wines
by the glass, good choice of popular fairly
priced home-made food from sandwiches and
sharing plates up, friendly attentive staff;
children and dogs welcome, teak furniture
on front deck and surrounding garden, nine
bedrooms upstairs, open (and food) all day.

HURST GREEN SD6837
★Shireburn Arms (01254) 826678
*Whalley Road (B6243 Clitheroe–
Goosnargh); BB7 9QJ* Welcoming 17th-c
hotel with peaceful Ribble Valley views from
big airy restaurant and neatly kept garden;
food from sandwiches and traditional dishes
to daily specials, leather armchairs, sofas and
log fire in beamed and flagstoned lounge bar
with linked dining area, two well kept ales
and several wines by the glass; daily papers;
children and dogs welcome, pretty Tolkien
walk from here, 21 comfortable bedrooms,
open all day from 7.30am for breakfast, food
served all day.

INGLETON SD6972
Masons Arms (01524) 242040
New Road (A65); LA6 3HL Welcoming
roadside village inn; stools and upholstered
chairs around mix of pubby tables on
wood-strip flooring, tartan-carpeted dining
end with woodburner, generous helpings
of hearty food from lunchtime hot or cold
sandwiches up (more evening choice), well
kept ales such as Sharps and four guests,
decent wine list with half a dozen by the
glass, good friendly service; children and
dogs welcome, three bedrooms, open (and
some food) all day.

IRBY SJ2586
★Irby Mill (0151) 604 0194
Mill Lane, off Greasby Road; CH49 3NT
Converted miller's sandstone cottage
(original windmill demolished 1898);
friendly and welcoming, with eight well kept
ales including Brains Rev James, Green
King Abbot and locals such as Peerless
and Weetwood, good choice of wines by
the glass and ample helpings of popular
reasonably priced food from sandwiches
up, efficient service, two low-beamed
traditional flagstoned rooms and extended
carpeted dining area, log fire, interesting old
photographs and history; children and dogs
welcome, tables on terraces and revamped
side area, good local walks, open (and food)
all day, gets crowded evenings/weekends
when parking limited.

LANCASTER SD4761
Borough (01524) 64170
Dalton Square; LA1 1PP Popular city-
centre pub; high ceilinged bar rooms with
chandeliers, leather chesterfields and elbow
tables on bare boards, some stained-glass
partitioning, eight real ales and lots of
bottled beers, several wines, big dining room
with booths along one side, decent food
including daily specials and vegan options;
upstairs comedy night Sun; children and dogs
welcome, nice little enclosed back garden,
bedrooms, open (and food) all day from 8am.

LANCASTER SD4761
Sun (01524) 66006
Church Street; LA1 1ET Hotel bar with ten
well kept ales including five from Lancaster,
more than 30 bottled/canned beers and good
choice of wines by the glass too, popular food
from sandwiches, sharing boards and pub
staples up, exposed stonework, panelling and

several fireplaces, conservatory; background music, TV; children welcome away from servery, tables on walled and paved terrace, 16 comfortable bedrooms, open all day (till 1am Fri, Sat).

LANCASTER
SD4761
Water Witch (01524) 63828
Parking in Aldcliffe Road behind Royal Lancaster Infirmary, off A6; LA1 1SU Attractive conversion of 18th-c canalside stables; flagstones, stripped stone, rafters and pitch-pine panelling, half a dozen well kept changing ales including Black Sheep, Cross Bay and Lancaster, 27 wines by the glass, wide choice of fairly traditional food from sandwiches and deli boards up including weekday deals, upstairs restaurant; Thurs quiz, children (in eating areas) and dogs welcome, picnic-sets out by water, moorings, open (and food) all day.

LITTLE ECCLESTON
SD4240
★ Cartford Inn (01995) 670166
Cartford Lane, off A586 Garstang–Blackpool, by toll bridge; PR3 0YP Riverside former coaching inn/boutique hotel with unusual four-level layout combining traditional and contemporary elements, four real ales including a house beer (Giddy Kipper) from Moorhouses, speciality bottled beers, 12 wines by the glass and interesting range of gins and whiskies, highly regarded imaginative food plus some pub favourites, restaurant, on-site shop, art gallery and delicatessen; children welcome (no under-10s after 8pm), garden tables looking out over tidal River Wyre (crossed by toll bridge), individually decorated bedrooms and two strikingly modern studio cabins, closed Mon lunchtime, otherwise open all day, food all day Sun.

LITTLEBOROUGH
SD9517
Moorcock (01706) 378156
Halifax Road (A58); OL15 0LD Long roadside inn high on the moors with far-reaching views; good food from sandwiches and pub favourites up in flagstoned bar or restaurant, Fri fish deal, four well kept beers; sports TV; terrace tables taking in the view, seven comfortable reasonably priced bedrooms, children welcome, open all day, food all day Fri-Sun, kitchen closed lunchtimes Mon-Weds.

LIVERPOOL
SJ3489
Baltic Fleet (0151) 709 3116
Wapping, near Albert Dock; L1 8DQ Unusual bow-fronted pub with six interesting beers including Wapping (brewed in the cellar), real ciders and several wines by the glass, simple well cooked/priced lunchtime food such as traditional scouse, bare boards, big arched windows, simple mix of furnishings and some nautical paraphernalia, fires in parlour and snug; background music, TV; children welcome in eating areas, dogs in bar, back terrace, open all day, no food Mon, Sun.

LIVERPOOL
SJ3589
Belvedere (0151) 709 0303
Sugnall Street; L7 7EB Unspoilt little 19th-c two-room pub with friendly chatty atmosphere, original features including etched glass and coal fires, well kept changing ales, good selection of bottled beers, real cider and fine choice of gins; dogs welcome, open all day.

LIVERPOOL
SJ3589
Cracke (0151) 709 4171
Rice Street; L1 9BB Friendly unchanging local with five well kept ales from Marstons and local brews, traditional cider, no food, small unspoilt bar with bare boards and bench seats, snug and a bigger back room with unusual Beatles diorama, local artwork and some photos of John Lennon who used to drink here; juke box; picnic-sets in sizeable tree-shaded back garden, open all day and popular with tourists.

LIVERPOOL
SJ3590
Crown (0151) 707 6027
Lime Street; L1 1JQ Well preserved and recently refurbished art nouveau showpiece – astonishing exterior; fine tiled fireplace and copper bar front, dark leather banquettes, panelling and splendid moulded ceiling, smaller back room with another good fireplace, impressive staircase sweeping up under cupola to handsome area with ornate windows, six craft beers on tap from BrewDog, Beavertown and Goose Island, good choice of bottled beers, cocktails and wide array of spirits, new menu of reasonably priced pubby food including pizza, burgers and vegan options; very convenient for the station, children welcome, open all day from 8am for breakfast.

LIVERPOOL
SJ3490
Dead Crafty Beer 07977 228918
Dale Street opposite the old magistrates' court; L2 5TF Craft beer bar with 20 on tap and over 150 in bottles, tasters offered by friendly knowledgeable staff, compact fairly basic interior with bare boards and exposed brickwork, bar made from flight cases; unisex loos downstairs; dogs allowed, open all day Fri-Sun, closed lunchtimes Mon-Thurs.

LIVERPOOL
SJ3589
Dispensary (0151) 709 2160
Renshaw Street; L1 2SP Small busy central pub under new management, worth knowing for its very well kept changing beers (up to ten) with regulars from Fernandes and Rat (Ossett) and Titanic, good choice of bottled imports too, bare boards and polished panelling, wonderful etched windows, comfortable raised back bar with fireplace (not used); background music; open all day (till midnight, 1.30am Fri, Sat).

LIVERPOOL　　　　　　　　SJ3490
Doctor Duncan (0151) 709 5100
St Johns Lane; L1 1HF Victorian pub with
several rooms including impressive back area
with pillared and vaulted tiled ceiling, open
fires and various apothecary cabinets, five
well kept ales and good value pubby food,
friendly helpful service; beer garden, open
all day.

LIVERPOOL　　　　　　　　SJ3589
Fly in the Loaf (0151) 708 0817
Hardman Street; L1 9AS Market Town
Tavern in former bakery; well kept Okells,
guest ales and several foreign beers from
long counter, also good selection of wines
and cocktails, decent food including
bar snacks and pizzas, efficient friendly
service, panelling and some raised sections;
background music; disabled loos (others
upstairs along with function room), open all
day, till midnight Fri, Sat.

LIVERPOOL　　　　　　　　SJ3490
Hole In Ye Wall (0151) 227 3809
Off Dale Street; L2 2AW Lightly
refurbished character 18th-c pub (the city's
oldest) with thriving local atmosphere in
high-beamed panelled bar; half a dozen
changing ales fed by gravity from upstairs
(no cellar as pub is on Quaker burial site),
extensive gin, whisky and rum range, no
food, friendly staff, plenty of woodwork,
stained glass and old Liverpool photographs,
coal-effect gas fire in unusual brass-canopied
fireplace; live music evenings Mon and last
Sat of month, traditional sing-along Sun,
sports TV; children allowed till 5pm, no dogs,
open all day.

LIVERPOOL　　　　　　　　SJ3490
Lion Tavern (0151) 236 9768
Moorfields, off Tithebarn Street; L2 2BP
Beautifully preserved ornate Victorian corner
pub; sparkling etched glass, large mirrors,
panelling and tilework, serving hatches in
central bar, two small back lounges one
with fine glass dome, eight changing beers
and extensive range of whiskies, simple
reasonably priced lunchtime food including
good pork pies, friendly staff; open all day.

LIVERPOOL　　　　　　　　SJ3590
Ma Egerton's Stage Door
(0151) 345 3525 *Pudsey Street, opposite
side entrance to Lime Street station;
L1 1JA* Victorian pub behind the Empire
Theatre named after former long-serving
landlady/theatrical agent; refurbished but
keeping old-fashioned character with green
leather button-back banquettes (note the
bell pushes), swagged curtains, wood floors,
panelling and a small period fireplace, lots

of celebrity pictures and other memorabilia,
a couple of changing ales and enjoyable food
including sharing plates and popular pizzas,
friendly staff; Mon quiz, Fri sing-along; open
all day.

LIVERPOOL　　　　　　　　SJ3589
Peter Kavanaghs (0151) 709 3443
*Egerton Street, off Catherine Street;
L8 7LY* Character Victorian pub popular
with locals and students; interesting décor
in several small rooms, old-world murals,
stained glass and all kinds of bric-a-brac (lots
hanging from ceiling), piano, wooden settles
and real fires, well kept Greene King Abbot
and guests, friendly licensees; open all day
(till 1am Fri, Sat).

LIVERPOOL　　　　　　　　SJ3589
Philharmonic Dining Rooms (0151) 707 2837
*36 Hope Street; corner of Hardman
Street; L1 9BX* Beautifully preserved
Victorian pub with wonderful period detail;
centrepiece mosaic-faced counter, heavily
carved and polished mahogany partitions
radiating out under intricate plasterwork
ceiling, main hall with stained glass of
Boer War heroes Baden-Powell and Lord
Roberts, rich panelling, mosaic floor and
copper panels of musicians above fireplace,
other areas including two side rooms called
Brahms and Liszt, the original Adamant
gents' is also worth a look, wide range of real
ales, several wines by the glass and extensive
range of gin and whisky, fair-priced food;
background music; children welcome till
7pm, open (and food) all day.

LIVERPOOL　　　　　　　　SJ3589
Roscoe Head (0151) 709 4365
Roscoe Street; L1 2SX Unassuming old
local with cosy bar, snug and two other
spotless unspoilt little rooms; well kept
Tetleys Bitter, Timothy Taylors Landlord
and four guests (tasting trays available),
friendly staff and regulars, hot pies available
all day, interesting memorabilia; Tues quiz
and traditional games, no background
music or games machine, open all day.

LIVERPOOL　　　　　　　　SJ3490
Ship & Mitre (0151) 236 0859
Dale Street; L2 2JH Friendly local with
fine art deco exterior and ship-like interior;
more than 200 draught and bottled beers
including ten unusual changing ales and
their own Flagship Beer (many beer
festivals), real ciders, decent choice of
good value food such as wraps, burgers and
all-day breakfast, free scouse after 5pm Weds,
upstairs function room with original 1930s
décor; Mon darts night, Thurs quiz, regular
tasting events; open all day.

Pubs close to motorway junctions are listed at the back of the book.

LIVERPOOL   SJ3490
★Thomas Rigbys (0151) 236 3269
Dale Street; L2 2EZ Spacious three-room Victorian pub; main bare-boards bar with iron pillars supporting sturdy beams, panelling and stained glass, up to eight cask beers including Okells and guests from long counter, also over 40 imported beers, back Nelson Room with impressive fireplace and an oak-panelled dining parlour where children allowed, enjoyable reasonably priced pubby food till early evening, efficient service; sports TV; disabled access (although some steps and downstairs lavatories), seats in spacious courtyard, open all day.

LONGRIDGE   SD6137
Corporation Arms (01772) 782644
Lower Road (B6243); PR3 2YJ Updated 18th-c roadside inn next to reservoir; good range of popular home-cooked food generously served and reasonably priced, well kept changing ales, plenty of wines by the glass, cheerful service and good welcoming atmosphere in three small linked rooms and restaurant; large garden, children welcome, five comfortable bedrooms, closed Mon, otherwise open (and food) all day.

LONGRIDGE   SD6037
Newdrop (01254) 878338
Higher Road, Longridge Fell, parallel to B6243 Longridge–Clitheroe; PR3 2XE Pleasant modernised dining pub in lovely moors-edge country with far-reaching views of Ribble Valley; good choice of reasonably priced food, decent wines and three well kept ales such as Timothy Taylors, friendly service; children welcome, open all day Sun, closed Mon and Tues.

LYDGATE   SD9704
★White Hart (01457) 872566
Stockport Road; Lydgate not marked on some maps and not the one near Todmorden; take A669 Oldham–Saddleworth, right at brow of hill to A6050 after almost 2.5 miles; OL4 4JJ Smart up-to-date dining pub overlooking Pennine moors; mix of locals (in bar or simpler end rooms) and diners in elegant brasserie with smartly dressed staff, highly regarded if not cheap food, Lees, Timothy Taylors plus four guests, 12 wines by the glass, old beams and exposed stonework contrasting with deep red or purple walls and modern artwork, open fires; children and dogs (in front lounge and snug) welcome, picnic-sets on back lawn making most of position, 16 bedrooms and separate cottage, open all day.

LYTHAM   SD3627
★Taps (01253) 736226
A584 S of Blackpool; Henry Street – in centre, one street in from West Beach; FY8 5LE Popular town pub just a couple of minutes from the beach; ten well kept ales including Greene King and a couple of proper ciders, simple good value lunchtime food (not Sun), friendly efficient staff, open-plan bar with wood or tiled floor, stripped brickwork and open fires (summer air-conditioning), dining area leading through to sunny terrace; TV for major sports, darts, fruit machine; children allowed till 7.30pm, small garden, parking nearby difficult (best to use West Beach car park on seafront, open all day.

MANCHESTER   SJ8498
Angel (0161) 833 4786
Angel Street, off Rochdale Road; M4 4BQ Friendly place on edge of the Northern Quarter; ten well kept ales including one badged for them, bottled beers and a couple of ciders/perries, piano in bare-boards bar, additional upstairs seating with two log fires and local artwork, no food; children (till 8pm) and dogs welcome, back beer garden, open all day.

MANCHESTER   SJ8398
Ape & Apple (0161) 839 9624
John Dalton Street; M2 6HQ Large open-plan pub with four well kept/priced Holts ales, guest beers and traditional bar food including deals and vegan options, comfortable seating on bare boards, carpet or tiles, lots of old prints and posters, upstairs restaurant/function room, friendly atmosphere; salsa dancing, comedy night, sports TV, games machines; children and dogs welcome, disabled access, central courtyard and roof terrace, open all day.

MANCHESTER   SJ8397
★Britons Protection (0161) 236 5895
Great Bridgewater Street, corner of Lower Mosley Street; M1 5LE Lively unpretentious pub with rambling rooms and notable tiled murals of 1819 Peterloo Massacre (took place nearby); plush little front bar with tiled floor, glossy brown and russet wall tiles, solid woodwork and ornate red and gold ceiling, two cosy inner lounges, both served by hatch, eight real ales including one named for the pub from massive counter with heated footrail, also over 300 malt whiskies, straightforward lunchtime food Mon-Fri; occasional storytelling and live music; children till 7pm, tables in enclosed back garden, handy for Bridgewater Hall concerts, open all day (very busy lunchtime and weekends).

MANCHESTER   SJ8498
Castle (0161) 237 9485
Oldham Street, about 200 metres from Piccadilly, on right; M4 1LE Restored 18th-c pub run well by former *Coronation Street* actor; simple traditional front bar, small snug, Robinsons ales and guests from fine bank of handpumps, Weston's Old Rosie cider; juke box, back room for regular live

music and other events, overspill space upstairs; nice tilework outside, open all day till late.

MANCHESTER SJ8497
Circus Tavern (0161) 236 5818
Portland Street; M1 4GX Traditional little two-room local; friendly staff serving well kept Robinsons and Tetleys from tiny corridor bar (or may be table service), leatherette wall benches and panelling, back room with football memorabilia and period fireplace; sports TV; open all day and can get crowded.

MANCHESTER SJ8398
City Arms (0161) 236 4610
Kennedy Street, off St Peters Square; M2 4BQ Friendly old-fashioned two-bar local sandwiched between two other pubs; eight well kept quickly changing ales including a mild and vegan or gluten-free option, up to eight real ciders, Belgian bottled beers and decent range of whiskies and gins, simple weekday lunchtime food, bare boards, panelling and button-back banquettes, coal fires; quiet background music, darts and dominoes; wheelchair access but steps down to back lounge, open all day (till 8pm Sun).

MANCHESTER SJ8397
Dukes 92 (0161) 839 8642
Castle Street, below the bottom end of Deansgate; M3 4LZ Friendly informal atmosphere in refurbished former stables overlooking canal basin; modern furnishings on light tiled floor, exposed brickwork, stairs up to stylish gallery bar leading to roof terrace, a couple of local ales such as Seven Bro7hers, decent wines and wide range of spirits (happy-hour cocktails Mon-Thurs), good food choice from bar snacks and pizzas up; background music, regular DJs and live music; children welcome till 8.30pm, no dogs inside, waterside tables on big terrace with outside bar/kitchen, open (and food) all day (till 1am Fri, Sat).

MANCHESTER SJ8194
Font (0161) 871 2022
Manchester Road, Chorlton; M21 9PG Relaxed split-level bar with eight changing ales, 16 craft kegs and extensive range of bottled beers, also six traditional ciders and fair-priced cocktails, enjoyable food from sandwiches and wraps to burgers and burritos; weekend DJs; children (till 8pm) and dogs welcome, seats out at front behind railings, open (and food) all day (till 1am Fri, Sat), popular with students.

MANCHESTER SJ8397
Knott Bar (0161) 839 9229
Deansgate; M3 4LY Modern glass-fronted café-bar under railway arch by Castlefield heritage site; seven well kept changing ales, also lots of craft beers and continental imports, pizza-based menu; background music; children welcome until 8pm, upstairs

balcony overlooking Rochdale Canal (dogs allowed here), open (and food) all day.

MANCHESTER SJ8497
Lass o' Gowrie (0161) 273 5822
36 Charles Street; off Oxford Road; M1 7DB Traditional tile-fronted side-street local refurbished a few years ago but keeping Victorian character; big-windowed bar with cosy room off, wood floors and stripped brickwork, pendant lighting, various pictures including black and white photos of old Manchester, three well kept Greene King ales plus local guests, simple bargain food such as home-made pies (not Sun), friendly service; some live music; balcony overlooking River Medlock, open all day weekends.

MANCHESTER SJ8499
★Marble Arch (0161) 832 5914
Rochdale Road (A664), Ancoats; centre of Gould Street, just E of Victoria station; M4 4HY Cheery pub with fine listed Victorian interior; long narrow bar with high ceiling, extensive glazed brickwork, marble and tiling, sloping mosaic floor and frieze advertising various drinks, old stone bottles on shelves, real ales including their own Marble beers (brewery visible from windows in back dining room – tours by arrangement), well liked home-made food including separate cheese menu; quiz Mon, background music, children welcome, small garden, open (and food) all day.

MANCHESTER SJ8398
★Mr Thomas's Chop House
(0161) 832 2245 *Cross Street; M2 7AR* Interesting late 19th-c pub with well preserved original features; generously served food including signature corned beef hash, ales such as Black Sheep and Timothy Taylors, decent range of wines by the glass from long list; front bar with panelling, old gas lamp fittings and framed cartoons, stools at wall and window shelves, back green-tiled eating areas have rows of tables on black and white Victorian tiles, archways and high ceilings; seats out at back, open (and food) all day.

MANCHESTER SJ8298
New Oxford (0161) 832 7082
Bexley Square, Salford; M3 6DB Red-brick Victorian corner pub with up to 20 well kept changing ales (chalked on blackboard), plus extensive range of draught and bottled continental beers, real ciders too, light airy feel in small front bar and back room, coal fire, low-priced basic food; quiz night, beer festivals, juke box; café-style seating out in square, open all day.

MANCHESTER SJ8398
★Oast House (0161) 829 3830
Crown Square, Springfields; M3 3AY Quirky mock-up of a Kentish oast house surrounded by modern high-rises; lofty

rustic interior with bare boards, timbers and plenty of tables, good selection of draught and bottled beers, wines and cocktails, enjoyable fairly priced food from deli boards to barbecues and rotisserie grills, friendly helpful young staff, busy cheerful atmosphere; background and nightly live music; children welcome, spacious outside seating area, open all day (till 2am Fri, Sat).

MANCHESTER SJ8398
Old Wellington (0161) 839 5179
Cathedral Gates, off Exchange Square; M3 1SW Tudor pub moved from Old Shambles Square during redevelopment; open-plan with original flagstones, panelling and gnarled timbers, small bar and dining area, restaurant and further bar on two floors above, half a dozen real ales (not cheap) and decent food from Nicholson's menu including range of pies, good friendly service; background music; children welcome, lots of tables out overlooking Exchange Square, open all day.

MANCHESTER SJ8397
★ Peveril of the Peak (0161) 236 6364
Great Bridgewater Street; M1 5JQ Vivid art nouveau external tilework and three sturdily furnished old-fashioned bare-boards rooms, interesting pictures, lots of mahogany, mirrors and stained or frosted glass, log fire, four changing ales from central servery, cheap basic lunchtime food; background music, TV, table football and pool; dogs welcome, pavement tables, open all day.

MANCHESTER SJ8498
Port Street Beer House
(0161) 237 9949 *Port Street; M1 2EQ* Former shop in Northern Quarter backstreet; fantastic range of draught and bottled craft beers along with well kept changing ales, knowledgeable staff, no food, can get very busy but more room upstairs; events such as 'meet the brewer' and 'tap takeovers'; open all day.

MANCHESTER SJ8397
Rain Bar (0161) 235 6500
Great Bridgewater Street; M1 5JG Bare boards and lots of woodwork in former umbrella works, Lees ales and plenty of wines by the glass, good choice of enjoyable fair value food from sandwiches to grills, friendly relaxed atmosphere, nooks and corners, coal fire in small snug, large upstairs bar/function room; background music; good back terrace overlooking Rochdale Canal, handy for Bridgewater Hall, open (and food) all day, shuts 8pm Sun.

MANCHESTER SJ8398
Sam's Chop House (0161) 834 3210
Back Pool Fold, Chapel Walks; M2 1HN Downstairs dining pub (offshoot from Mr Thomas's Chop House) with original Victorian décor; British food such as steak

and kidney pudding, corned beef hash and various grills served by formal waiters, well kept beers and good wine choice, a former haunt of LS Lowry (a bronze statue of him sits contemplatively at the bar), back restaurant with black and white tiled floor; background music; children welcome, some pavement tables, open all day.

MANCHESTER SJ8498
Smithfield Market Tavern
(0161) 425 6831 *Swan Street; M4 5JZ* Simply presented pub on edge of the Northern Quarter owned by Blackjack brewery, their ales and guests from six handpumps, also craft kegs, real cider and good selection of spirits, three main areas with vintage mismatched furniture on wood floors; occasional live music, traditional games including darts, shove-ha'penny and table skittles; dogs welcome, open all day weekends, from 4pm Mon, 2pm Tues-Fri.

MARPLE SJ9588
Ring o' Bells (0161) 427 2300
Church Lane; by Macclesfield Canal, bridge 2; SK6 7AY Popular old-fashioned canalside local with assorted memorabilia in four linked rooms; well kept Robinsons ales and good reasonably priced food; quiz nights and some live music including brass bands in the waterside garden; children welcome, own narrowboat, one bedroom, open all day.

MARPLE BRIDGE SJ9889
Hare & Hounds (0161) 427 4042
Mill Brow; from end of Town Street in centre turn left up Hollins Lane and keep on uphill; SK6 5LW Comfortable, civilised and well run stone-built country pub in lovely spot; good modern cooking including a grazing menu and popular Sun lunch, well kept Robinsons ales and nice wines, quite small inside (can get crowded), log fires; children and dogs (in bar) welcome, garden behind, open all day weekends (food till 7pm Sun), closed lunchtimes Mon-Thurs.

MELLOR SJ9888
Devonshire Arms (0161) 427 2563
This is the Mellor near Marple, S of Manchester; heading out of Marple on A626 towards Glossop, Mellor is next road after B6102, signposted off on right at Marple Bridge; Longhurst Lane; SK6 5PP Revamped Robinsons pub with well kept ales, decent range of wines by the glass and enjoyable fair priced pubby food from sandwiches and sharing plates up, good friendly service; children and dogs (in bar) welcome, garden with large part-covered pergola, open all day.

MELLOR SD6530
★ Millstone (01254) 813333
The Mellor near Blackburn; Mellor Lane; BB2 7JR Handsome and neatly kept 18th-c stone coaching inn, with central

bar with extensive panelling on both sides, well kept Thwaites ales and guests, a dozen wines by the glass, friendly staff, dining rooms with elegant painted wooden and pleasingly upholstered modern dining chairs and button-back wall seats around polished tables on carpet or parquet flooring, several log fires and attractive prints on pale paintwork; background music; side terrace with seats and tables under parasols; 23 bedrooms, open and food all day.

MORECAMBE   SD4264
Midland Grand Plaza
(01524) 424000 *Marine Road W;
LA4 4BZ* Classic art deco hotel in splendid seafront position; comfortable if unorthodox contemporary furnishings in spacious sea-view Rotunda Bar, rather pricey but enjoyable food from interesting Lancashire tapas to restaurant meals (popular and very good afternoon tea), good service; wide variety of events including 1930s vintage festival; children welcome, 44 bedrooms, open all day.

NEWTON   SD6950
★ Parkers Arms (01200) 446236
B6478 7 miles N of Clitheroe; BB7 3DY
Welcoming arch-windowed pub on edge of village; good locally sourced seasonal food from lunchtime sandwiches (home-baked bread) to imaginative specials, can eat in bar or restaurant, two changing ales, nice range of wines and decent coffee, pale green and cream walls, old oak boards or flagstones, upholstered window seats and open fires; children and well behaved dogs welcome, disabled access, lovely views from picnic-sets on front lawn, two bedrooms, closed Mon, Tues.

PARBOLD   SD4911
Windmill (01257) 462935
Mill Lane; WN8 7NW Opened-up and modernised beamed pub next to village windmill and facing Leeds & Liverpool Canal; mix of furniture on flagstone or oak floors including settles and some interesting carved chairs, candles on tables, animal prints on walls, good open fire, five well kept ales (some from own microbrewery), several wines by the glass and enjoyable food from pub favourites up, friendly young staff; Mon quiz; children and dogs (in snug) welcome, too many steps for wheelchairs, seats out in front behind railing and on back paved terrace, good local walks, open all day, food all day weekends.

PRESTON   SD5329
Black Horse (01772) 204855
Friargate; PR1 2EJ Listed ornate Victorian pub in pedestrianised street; splendid mosaic-tiled main bar serving eight well kept ales (Robinsons and guests), friendly helpful staff, panelling, stained glass and old local photographs, open fires, two

quiet cosy snugs, mirrored back area and upstairs function room; open all day from 10.30am (noon Sun).

RABY   SJ3179
★ Wheatsheaf (0151) 336 3416
Raby Mere Road, The Green; from A540 heading S from Heswall, turn left into Upper Raby Road, village about a mile further; CH63 4JH Up to nine well kept ales in pretty 17th-c black and white thatched pub, simply furnished rambling rooms with homely feel, cosy central bar and nice snug formed by antique settles around fine old fireplace, small coal fire in more spacious room, well liked reasonably priced bar food including good range of sandwiches/toasties, à la carte menu in large former cowshed restaurant, good friendly service, conservatory; children welcome, dogs in bar, picnic-sets on terrace and in pleasant back garden, open all day and gets very busy at weekends, no food Sun or Mon evenings.

RAMSBOTTOM   SD8016
Eagle & Child (01706) 824477
Whalley Road (A56); BL0 0DL Friendly roadside pub; generally well liked food from fairly ambitious menu using locally sourced produce including own vegetables, well kept Thwaites ales, real cider and decent choice of wines by the glass, good service; children and dogs welcome, orangery dining extension and interesting garden with valley views over roof tops to Holcombe Moor and Peel Tower, five owl-themed bedrooms (two with balconies), open all day Fri and Sat, till 7pm Sun.

RAMSBOTTOM   SD8017
★ Fishermans Retreat (01706) 825314
Twine Valley Park/Fishery signed off A56 N of Bury at Shuttleworth; Bye Road; BL0 0HH Remote yet busy pub-restaurant with highly regarded food (can be pricey) using produce from surrounding Estate and trout lakes (they can arrange fishing); mountain lodge-feel bar with beams and bare stone walls, five well kept ales, over 300 malt whiskies and dedicated whisky shop, good wine list, small family dining room and restaurant extension, helpful friendly staff; a few picnic-sets outside with lovely valley views, closed Mon, otherwise open (and food) all day.

RAMSBOTTOM   SD7816
Major (07775) 754612
Bolton Street; BL0 9JA Whitewashed end-of-terrace stone local under new management, with two carpeted bars, banquettes and other pubby furniture, old local pictures, two-way woodburner; up to five well kept ales including three guests from central bar, enjoyable home-made food, friendly helpful staff; children and dogs welcome, beer garden behind.

RAWTENSTALL   SD8213
Buffer Stops (0161) 764 7790
Bury Road; in East Lancashire Railway station; BB4 6EH Platform bar at Rawtenstall heritage station; five well kept ales, real cider/perry and selection of bottled beers, snacky food and pies, popular with locals and railway enthusiasts, good friendly service; children (in former waiting room) and dogs welcome, platform tables, open all day.

RILEY GREEN   SD6225
★ Royal Oak (01254) 201445
A675/A6061; PR5 0SL Extended old four-room pub (former coaching inn); popular freshly made food (all day Sat and Sun) from pizzas, burgers and pub favourites up, friendly efficient staff, five well kept ales including Thwaites and a guest from well stocked bar, low beams, ancient stripped stone and log fires, lots of nooks and crannies, comfortable dining rooms; children and dogs (in bar) welcome, picnic-sets at front and in side beer garden, short walk from Leeds & Liverpool Canal, footpath to Hoghton Tower, open all day.

ROCHDALE   SD8913
Baum (01706) 352186
Toad Lane (off Hunters Lane) next to the Rochdale Pioneers (Co-op) Museum; OL12 0NU Welcoming pub with plenty of old-fashioned charm in surviving cobbled street (new management but no major changes); seven well kept ales and lots of international bottled beers, good value food including tapas, cheerful young staff, bare boards, old advertising signs, conservatory; children and dogs welcome, seats in garden behind with pétanque, open all day (till midnight Sat).

ROMILEY   SJ9390
Platform 1 (0161) 406 8686
Stockport Road next to station; SK6 4BN Red-brick Victorian pub with airy opened-up interior; six mostly local ales including a well priced house beer, good value pubby food from sandwiches up, carpeted upstairs restaurant called Platform 2; occasional live music; children welcome, small decked seating area outside, open (and food) all day, kitchen closes 7pm Sun.

SALESBURY   SD6732
Bonny Inn (01254) 248467
B6245 Ribchester–Wilpshire; BB1 9HQ Opened up pub with light airy bar and split-level carpeted dining room, popular freshly made food including blackboard specials,

Thwaites ales and several wines by the glass, good service, back conservatory with fine Ribble Valley views; children and dogs (in bar) welcome, sturdy picnic-sets out in front under awning, more seats and views on terrace behind, open all day, food all day Sun.

SCARISBRICK   SD4011
Heatons Bridge Inn (01704) 840549
Heatons Bridge Road; L40 8JG Pretty 19th-c pub by bridge over Leeds & Liverpool Canal (popular with boaters); good value home-made food (not Sun evening, Mon, Tues), four cask ales including Black Cat and Tetleys, friendly welcoming staff, four traditional cosy areas and dining room; Tues quiz; children and dogs welcome, pretty hanging baskets, garden with play area and World War II pillbox (pub hosts two vintage military vehicle events during the year), open all day.

SILVERDALE   SD4675
Royal (01524) 702608
Emesgate Lane; LA5 0RA Village-centre pub with smallish parquet-floored bar, well kept local ales from light wood counter, sofa and armchairs by woodburner in stone fireplace, good reasonably priced food including breakfast from 10.30am, steak night Thurs, friendly helpful service, small front conservatory and upstairs dining room; daily newspapers; children welcome, no dogs inside, picnic-sets on terrace, two self-catering cottages, open and food all day.

STALYBRIDGE   SJ9598
Station Buffet (0161) 303 0007
The Station, Rassbottom Street; SK15 1RF Charming little Victorian buffet bar popular with locals and railway enthusiasts; period advertisements, old photographs of the station and other railway memorabilia on wood-panelled and red walls, fire below etched-glass mirror, includes former ladies' waiting room and part of the stationmaster's quarters with original ornate ceilings; five quickly rotating beers and some in bottles, real cider/perry, seven wines by the glass and ten malt whiskies, straightforward low-priced snacks and pies; children (in former waiting room) and dogs welcome, tables out on the platform, open all day.

STOCKPORT   SJ8990
★ Arden Arms (0161) 480 2185
Millgate Street/Corporation Street, opposite pay car park; SK1 2LX Cheerful Victorian pub in handsome dark-brick building; several well preserved high-ceilinged rooms off island bar (one very small

old-fashioned snug accessed via servery), tiling, panelling and two coal fires, sensibly priced food (not Sun) from sandwiches to specials, half a dozen well kept Robinsons ales, friendly efficient service; background and live music (Fri, Sat), Tues quiz, children and dogs welcome, tables in courtyard with smokers' shelter, open all day.

STOCKPORT SJ8990

Crown (0161) 429 6948

Heaton Lane, Heaton Norris; SK4 1AR
Busy but welcoming partly open-plan Victorian pub popular for its well kept changing ales (up to 11), also bottled beers and real cider, three cosy lounge areas off bar, bargain lunchtime food; frequent live music, pool and darts; dogs welcome, tables in cobbled courtyard, huge viaduct soaring above, open all day.

STOCKPORT SJ8892

Heaton Hops No phone

School Lane, off A6; SK4 5DE
Attractive non-blokey high-street tap house and bottle shop run with care and expertise; two cask ales (takeaway available in flagons) and eight keg lines, craft gins, sophisticated ciders and regularly updated craft ales in bottles and cans, no food; helpful staff; a couple of pavement tables in summer; opening hours vary.

STOCKPORT SJ8990

Magnet (0161) 429 6287

Wellington Road North; SK4 1HJ Busy pub with 14 changing ales including Watts from on-site brewery alongside 12 keg beers, real cider, extensive gin menu, pizza van Fri evenings; pool, darts and juke box; children (till 8pm) and dogs welcome, beer garden with two raised terraces, open all day Fri-Sun, from 4pm other days.

STOCKPORT SJ8990

Swan With Two Necks

(0161) 480 2341 *Princes Street; SK1 1RY* Traditional narrow pub with welcoming local atmosphere; front panelled bar, room behind with button-back wall benches, stone fireplace and skylight, drinking corridor, well kept Robinsons ales and decent lunchtime food from sandwiches up; children and dogs welcome, small outside area, open all day Fri-Sat.

TATHAM SD6169

Tatham Bridge Inn (01524) 221326

B6480, off A683 Lancaster–Kirkby Lonsdale; LA2 8NL Popular 17th-c pub with cosy low-beamed bar; well kept ales such as Tetleys and good range of enjoyable fair-priced food, friendly helpful staff, restaurant with woodburner; children and well behaved dogs welcome, large garden, camping, open all day except Weds and Thurs when closed 2-5pm.

TOCKHOLES SD6623

Black Bull (01254) 581381

Between Tockholes and Blackburn; BB3 0LL Welcoming 19th-c country pub on crossroads high above Blackburn; home to the Three B's Brewery with their good beers including Black Bull Bitter from brick-fronted counter (tasting trays available), no food, neat opened-up interior with dark blue patterned carpet and leaf wallpaper, cushioned wall seats and high-backed chairs, woodburner, snug to left of entrance with another fire; background music; seats outside (some under cover – including summerhouse), good views, open all day weekends, otherwise from 4pm, closed Mon, Tues.

TOCKHOLES SD6621

Royal (01254) 705373

Signed off A6062 S of Blackburn, and off A675; Tockholes Road; BB3 0PA Friendly old pub under new ownership with unpretentious little rooms and big open fires, four well kept ales from tiny back servery, new extension underway, well priced pubby food including some blackboard specials; children, walkers and dogs welcome, big garden with views from sheltered terrace, good walks including to Darwen Tower, open all day.

TODMORDEN SD9324

The Pub (01706) 812145

Lower part of Brook Street; OL14 5AJ Micropub/gin bar with cosy rustic décor; half a dozen well kept interesting ales from plank-faced servery and over 30 gins, helpful chatty staff, stools and window seats by small round tables, more room and loos upstairs; well behaved dogs welcome, open all day till 9pm (10pm Thurs, 11pm Fri, Sat).

TUNSTALL SD6073

★ Lunesdale Arms (01524) 236191

A683 S of Kirkby Lonsdale; LA6 2QN Attractive and stylish 17th-c dining pub; opened-up interior with bar, split-level restaurant and snooker room, lots of modern artwork, Marstons Wainwright and Timothy Taylors Landlord, good range of wines and gins, highly regarded Mediterranean-influenced food (best to book), friendly efficient service; children and dogs (in bar) welcome, pretty Lune Valley village, church has Brontë associations, open all day, food all day weekends.

WADDINGTON SD7243

Higher Buck (01200) 423226

The Square; BB7 3HZ Welcoming pub in picturesque village; smartly modernised open-plan interior with airy New England feel and nice mix of seating, good food including pub favourites (all day Sun till 8pm), well kept Thwaites from pine servery, good friendly service; background music;

children and dogs welcome, tables out on front cobbles and in small back courtyard, seven attractively refurbished bedrooms, open all day.

WADDINGTON SD7243

★**Lower Buck** (01200) 423342

Edisford Road; BB7 3HU Old stone village pub tucked away behind the church; four smartly presented little rooms, each with a warming coal fire, thriving front bar with scrubbed tables, large rug on bare boards and some stained-glass panelling, well kept real ales such as Bowland, Moorhouses and Timothy Taylors, several wines by the glass and enjoyable reasonably priced food from sandwiches up, friendly helpful service; daily newspapers; children and dogs welcome, picnic-sets out on front cobbles and in the sunny back garden, good Ribble Valley walks nearby, bedrooms and cottage, open all day, no food Mon except bank holidays.

WADDINGTON SD7243

★**Waddington Arms** (01200) 423262

Clitheroe Road (B6478 N of Clitheroe); BB7 3HP Character inn with four linked bars, left one snuggest with blazing woodburner in huge fireplace, other low-beamed rooms have fine oak settles, chunky stripped-pine tables and lots to look at including antique and modern prints and vintage motor-racing posters, tasty food, well kept Moorhouses and four guests, good choice of wines by the glass and a dozen malt whiskies; children and dogs welcome, seats out at front looking over to village church, also two-level back terrace and neat tree-sheltered lawn, six comfortable bedrooms, good walks in nearby Forest of Bowland, open all day.

WEST BRADFORD SD7444

Three Millstones (01200) 443339

Waddington Road; BB7 4SX Attractive old building, but more restaurant than pub, with all tables laid for owner-chef's highly praised food, four comfortable linked areas, beams, timbers and warming fires in two grand fireplaces, a couple of well kept local beers and good selection of wines, friendly efficient service; ten bedrooms in newish block, closed Mon, Tues.

WEST KIRBY SJ2186

White Lion (0151) 625 9037

Grange Road (A540); CH48 4EE Friendly proper pub in interesting 18th-c sandstone building; several small beamed areas on different levels, well kept and

quickly changing guests, coal stove; no children, steep steps up to attractive secluded back garden with fish pond, parking in residential side streets, open all day.

WHALLEY SD7336

★**Swan** (01254) 822195

King Street; BB7 9SN Modernised 17th-c former coaching inn with friendly staff and good mix of customers in spacious bar; a couple of Bowland ales plus Timothy Taylors Landlord, enjoyable food from fairly standard menu, further room with leather sofas and armchairs on bare boards; background music; children and dogs welcome, picnic-sets on back terrace and on grass strips by car park, six bedrooms, open (and food) all day.

WHEATLEY LANE SD8338

★**Sparrowhawk** (01282) 603034

Wheatley Lane Road; towards E end of village road, which runs N of and parallel to A6068; one way to reach it is to follow Fence signpost, then turn off at Barrowford signpost; BB12 9QG Comfortably civilised 1930s feel in imposing long black and white pub; oak panelling, parquet flooring and leather tub chairs, domed stained-glass skylight, six well kept ales from cushioned leatherette counter, nice wines by the glass and good food from sandwiches and light lunches up, friendly young staff; background and live music; children and dogs (in bar) welcome, heavy wooden tables on spacious front terrace with delightful views to the moors beyond Nelson and Colne, open all day.

WISWELL SD7437

★**Freemasons Arms** (01254) 822218

Village signposted off A671 and A59 NE of Whalley; pub on Vicarage Fold, a gravelled pedestrian passage between Pendleton Road and Old Back Lane in village centre (don't expect to park very close); BB7 9DF Civilised dining pub with three linked rooms; antique sporting prints on cream or pastel walls, rugs on polished flagstones, carved oak settles and variety of chairs around handsome stripped or salvaged tables, candles and log fires, ales such as Bowland and Moorhouses, more than 250 wines and highly regarded imaginative food (all day Sun till 6pm), efficient friendly service from uniformed staff, more rooms upstairs, cookery lessons; children and dogs (in bar) welcome, seating on flagstoned front terrace with heaters and awning, eight new bedrooms, open all day weekends, closed Mon.

'Children welcome' means the pub says it lets children inside without any special restriction. If it allows them in, but to restricted areas such as an eating area or family room, we specify this. Some pubs may impose an evening time limit. We do not mention limits after 9pm as we assume children are home by then.

WOODFORD SJ8882
Davenport Arms (0161) 439 2435
A5102 Wilmslow–Poynton; SK7 1PS
Popular red-brick country local (aka the
Thief's Neck) run by same family since 1932;
well kept Robinsons ales and enjoyable
lunchtime food from snacks up, friendly
service, snug rooms arranged around central
bar, log fires; sports TV; children and dogs
welcome, tables on front terrace and in nice
back garden with play area, open all day.

WRIGHTINGTON SD5011
Rigbye Arms (01257) 462354
*3 miles from M6 junction 27; off A5209
via Robin Hood Lane and left into High
Moor Lane; WN6 9QB* 17th-c dining pub
in attractive moorland setting, welcoming
and relaxed, with wide choice of good
sensibly priced food including game menu
cooked by long-serving landlord, hot and
cold sandwiches too, Mon meal deals, well
kept Timothy Taylors and two guests, decent
wines, several carpeted rooms including
cosy tap room, open fires, separate evening
restaurant (Weds-Sat, booking required);
children welcome, well behaved dogs in rear
bar), garden and bowling green, regular car
club meetings, open (and food) all day Sun.

WRIGHTINGTON BAR SD5313
Corner House (01257) 451400
B5250, N of M6 junction 27; WN6 9SE
Opened-up 19th-c corner pub-restaurant;
good food (all day weekends) from traditional
to more upscale choices, also meal deals and
daily specials, a couple of local ales and good
quality wines, plenty of tables in different
modernised areas; children and dogs
welcome, seats outside, monthly vintage/
classic car meetings, open all day.

Leicestershire

and Rutland

 ## BREEDON ON THE HILL   SK4022   Map 7
Three Horseshoes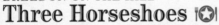
(01332) 695129 – www.thehorseshoes.com
Main Street (A453); DE73 8AN

Comfortable pub with friendly licensees and emphasis on popular food

This 18th-c dining pub started life as a farrier's. There's a stylishly eclectic feel to the interiors with a clean-cut bar, heavy worn flagstones, richly coloured walls and a log fire. Beyond the bar is a dining room with maroon walls, dark pews and tables, while a two-room dining area on the right has a comfortably civilised and chatty feel with big antique tables set quite close together on coir matting, and colourful modern country prints and antique engravings on canary yellow walls. Friendly staff serve Marstons Pedigree plus guest ales on handpump and decent house wines. There's also an idyllic garden. The farm shop sells their own and other local produce: eggs, jams, meat, smoked foods and chocolates. The hillside church is interesting to visit and Calke Abbey (National Trust) is not far away. Disabled access.

Enjoyable food includes chicken liver pâté with fruit chutney, grilled goats cheese with cranberry and walnut dressing, roast vegetable and chickpea casserole, blackened salmon with kale, corn and sweet potato, rib-eye steak with horseradish butter, chicken breast with stilton and mushroom sauce, venison and port steamed suet pudding, cod with braised cabbage and black pudding, and home-made desserts. *Benchmark main dish: Lincolnshire sausages and mash £10.50. Two-course evening meal £20.00.*

Free house ~ Licensees Ian Davison, Jennie Ison and Stuart Marson ~ Real ale ~ Open 12-2, 5.30-10; 12-3.30 Sun ~ Bar food 12-2, 5.30-9; 12-3.30 Sun ~ Restaurant ~ Children welcome ~ Dogs allowed in bar

 ## CLIPSHAM   SK9716   Map 8
Olive Branch
(01780) 410355 – www.theolivebranchpub.com
10 miles north of Stamford; from A1, take junction for B668; LE15 7SH

Leicestershire Dining Pub of the Year

A special place for a drink, a meal or an overnight stay

This perennially successful inn attracts a deservedly loyal following from both near and far, and has just celebrated its 20th anniversary. Formed from what were originally three labourers' cottages and a cowshed, it's an attractive, homely place. The various linked bar and dining rooms feel remarkably unstuffy, with dark joists and beams, rustic furniture, an interesting mix of pictures (some by local artists), candles on tables and a cosy log fire in a stone inglenook. Outside, tables, chairs and large plant pots sit on a pretty little terrace, sheltered in the crook of the two low buildings – new this year are canvas-roofed gazebos that allow for socially distanced dining. As well as a Grainstore beer named for the pub (Olive Ale), there are local Round Corner craft beers on tap, an enticing wine list (with at least 25 by the glass or carafe), a thoughtful choice of spirits, cocktails and several British and continental bottled beers. Service is efficient and genuinely welcoming; look out for their friendly springer spaniel, Alfie. A renovated Georgian house across the road from the main pub contains six individually decorated, restful bedrooms. As well as buying home-made jams and chutneys from the wine shop, you can order individual dishes to take away and order food for a dinner party at home. Disabled access.

The first rate, imaginative food makes good use of vegetables and herbs from their own kitchen garden, plus meat and cheese from local suppliers. They offer various fixed-price deals ranging from a two-course lunch menu to a seven-course tasting menu. Typical dishes include devilled whitebait, summer tomatoes, nasturtium and parmesan custard, haddock and chips, slow-cooked pork collar with aubergine caviar, smoked apple, hen of the woods and confit potato, girolle and Wiltshire truffle risotto with crispy parmesan, 28-day dry-aged sirloin with dripping chips and bearnaise sauce, and puddings such as Valrhona chocolate délice with carrot and sea buckthorn sorbet and poached Yorkshire rhubarb with pistachio curd. *Benchmark main dish: Burghley Park lamb shoulder with peas, alliums and smoked potato £22.50. Two-course evening meal £30.00.*

Free house ~ Licensee Ben Jones ~ Real ale ~ Open 12-3, 6-11; 12-11 Sat; 12-10.30 Sun ~ Bar food 12-2, 6.30-9.30; 12-2.30, 6.30-9.30 Sat; 12-3, 7-9 Sun ~ Restaurant ~ Children welcome ~ Dogs allowed in bar & bedrooms ~ Bedrooms: £180

GREETHAM   SK9314   Map 7
Wheatsheaf

(01572) 812325 – www.wheatsheaf-greetham.co.uk
B668 Stretton–Cottesmore; LE15 7NP

Friendly stone pub with interesting food, real ales, a dozen wines and seats in front and back gardens

Customers are welcomed to this stone pub by the friendly, hands-on and long-serving owners, the Craddocks. A pretty front garden, fenced off from the road, leads into the inviting interior with linked L-shaped rooms furnished with traditional settles and cushioned captain's chairs around tables of varying sizes, and wood-burning stoves. Brewsters Hophead, Grainstore Steelback IPA and Greene King IPA are served on handpump, alongside 17 wines by the glass (including fizz and pudding wines), 30 gins and home-made cordials. It's a good idea to book a table in advance for the popular restaurant. The games room has a TV, darts, pool, board games and background music. The pub dogs are a dachshund and a labradoodle, and visiting pooches are welcome in the bar. There are chunky picnic-sets on the front lawn and more seats on a back terrace by a pretty stream with a duck house; pétanque. You can buy the pub's own-made pickles, chutneys and chocolates. There's a ramp for wheelchairs.

The chef-landlady cooks the imaginative seasonal food, including fresh bread daily. As well as lunchtime sandwiches, dishes might include grilled quail with potato pancake, mussels, baked snails with garlic and parsley butter, wild mushroom and leek lasagne, fillet of sea bream with new potatoes and samphire, roast Gressingham duck breast with girolles and potato dauphinoise, crispy pork belly with spring onion mash and hispi cabbage, and puddings such as lemon verbena crème brûlée and boozy cherries with vanilla ice-cream and chocolate sauce. *Benchmark main dish: tiger prawns with home-made chips £17.50. Two-course evening meal £24.00.*

Punch ~ Lease Scott and Carol Craddock ~ Real ale ~ Open 12-3, 6-11; 12-11 Fri, Sat; 12-10 (8 in winter) Sun; closed Mon except bank holidays ~ Bar food 12-2 (2.15 Sat), 6.30-9; 12-2.45 Sun ~ Restaurant ~ Children welcome ~ Dogs allowed in bar

 PEGGS GREEN   SK4117   Map 7
New Inn £
(01530) 222293 – www.thenewinnpeggsgreen.co.uk

Signposted off A512 Ashby–Shepshed at roundabout, then turn immediately left down Zion Hill towards Newbold; pub is 100 metres on the right, with car park on opposite side of road; LE67 8JE

Intriguing bric-a-brac in unspoilt pub, friendly welcome, well liked food at fair prices and real ales; cottagey garden

Every inch of this welcoming village pub – run by the same friendly family since 1978 – is covered in appealing bric-a-brac. There are two cosy main rooms. The little room on the left, a bit like an old kitchen parlour (called the Cabin), has china on the mantelpiece, lots of prints and photographs, three old cast-iron tables, wooden stools and a small stripped kitchen table. The room to the right has attractive stripped panelling. The small back 'Best' room is good for private meetings and doubles as a gift shop selling home-made gifts (which sell for charity). The cheerful staff serve well kept ales such as Fullers London Pride and Marstons Pedigree plus a changing guest beer on handpump; background music and board games. There are plenty of seats in front of the pub, with more in the peaceful back garden. Do check the unusual opening and food service times carefully.

Themed food nights provided by local street-food vans – to eat in or take away – include fish and chips on Monday, pies on Tuesday, pizzas on Wednesday, US burgers on Thursday and 'loaded fries' on Friday; on Saturday, customers can bring their own food to eat in the pub.

Enterprise ~ Lease Maria Christina Kell ~ Real ale ~ Open 5.30-11 Mon-Thurs; 12-2.30, 5.30-11 Fri; 12-3, 6.30-11 Sat; 10-3, 7-10.30 Sun ~ Bar food 5.30-9 Mon, Weds, Thurs; 6-8 Tues; 12-2, 7-10 Fri; 12-2, 6-9 Sat; 10-2 Sun ~ Well behaved children welcome ~ Dogs allowed in bar

 SILEBY   SK6015   Map 7
White Swan
(01509) 814832 – www.whiteswansileby.co.uk

Off A6 or A607 N of Leicester; in centre turn into King Street (opposite church), then after mini roundabout turn right at Post Office signpost into Swan Street; LE12 7NW

Exemplary town local, a boon to its chatty regulars, with tasty home cooking and a friendly welcome

Mrs Miller has presided over this honest red-brick local since the 1980s. Set in the heart of the Soar Valley, it attracts walkers from Cossington Meadows and boaters moored at Sileby Marine. The décor has all the touches that mark the best of between-the-wars estate pub design from an art deco-tiled lobby to polychrome-tiled fireplaces, a shiny red Anaglypta ceiling and a comfortable layout of linked but separate areas including a small restaurant lined with books. There's plenty to look at among the bric-a-brac that includes decorative plates, numerous prints and hats-turned-lampshades. The staff are genuinely bright and cheerful. There are no cask ales, but plenty of bottled options such as Bombardier and Boddingtons, half a dozen wines by the glass and several gins. Mrs Miller also runs a successful catering business and offers a generous selection of takeaway frozen meals.

 Reasonably priced food includes creamy chicken, leek and bacon casserole, cumberland pie with minced beef, linguine with king prawns and lemongrass, baked cod in cheese sauce, nut roast with veggie gravy, pasta with Mediterranean vegetables in tomato sauce, and puddings such as blackberry and apple pie, treacle sponge and lemon meringue pie. *Benchmark main dish: beef cobbler £13.75. Two-course evening meal £18.00.*

Free house ~ Licensee Theresa Miller ~ Open 6-10; 6-11 Sat; 12-3.30 Sun; closed Mon ~ Bar food 6-8.30 Tues-Sat; 12-1.30 Sun ~ Restaurant ~ Children welcome ~ Dogs allowed in snug bar

SUTTON CHENEY
SK4100   Map 4

Hercules Revived

(01455) 699336 – www.herculesrevived.co.uk
Off A447 3 miles S of Market Bosworth; CV13 0AG

Attractively furnished bar and upstairs dining rooms, highly regarded food, real ales and helpful staff

Regular events at this welcoming 18th-c former coaching inn include wine-tasting lunches, floristry workshops and a gin festival. It's just as welcoming to those popping in for a pint and a chat as it is for diners coming for an enjoyable meal. The long bar has a relaxed, friendly atmosphere, brown leather wall seating, upholstered brown and white checked or plain wooden church chairs around various tables, rugs on wooden flooring, fresh flowers, prints and ornamental plates on creamy yellow walls and a large open fire; background music. There are high leather chairs against the rough-hewn counter, where they serve Church End What the Foxs Hat and Sharps Doom Bar on handpump, 23 wines by the glass and 25 gins. Upstairs, each of the interlinked, carpeted dining rooms has its own colour scheme and tartan dining chairs around dark wooden tables; one wall is a giant map of the area. Seating under parasols on the little back terrace with views across a meadow to the church. Dogs are allowed downstairs.

As well wood-fired pizzas from their outdoor oven in summer, the appealing, well presented food includes sandwiches, madeira-creamed garlic mushrooms on toast, beetroot, red onion and thyme tart, tomato and basil arancini, burgers (beef, chicken, falafel and field mushroom) with toppings and chips, lightly soda-battered fish and chips, rib-eye steak with a choice of sauce, oven-roasted hake with tenderstem broccoli and lemon buerre blanc, and puddings such as peach crumble with raspberry sauce and vanilla ice-cream and date and sticky toffee pudding; they also offer a weekday set lunch and a set dinner on Monday and Tuesday.

Free house ~ Licensee Oliver Warner ~ Real ale ~ Open 12-3.30, 6-11; 12-11 Sat; 12-5 Sun ~ Bar food 12-2.30, 6-9; 12-4 Sun ~ Restaurant ~ Children welcome ~ Dogs allowed in bar

SWITHLAND
SK5512   Map 7

Griffin

(01509) 890535 – www.griffininnswithland.co.uk
Main Street; between A6 and B5330, between Loughborough and Leicester; LE12 8TJ

A good mix of cheerful customers and well liked food in a busy, family-run pub

The streamside garden looking on to open fields is one of the many draws of this appealing village pub in the middle of Charnwood Forest. An attractive stone façade leads to beamed, communicating rooms with traditional woodburners, leather and upholstered banquettes and armchairs, some polished panelling, wooden floors and lots of bird prints. Stools line the counter where five cask ales including Everards Original are well kept on handpump. There are also wines by the glass from a good list, three farm ciders, 20 gins and several whiskies. There's a new roof over the courtyard, to allow for dining in all weathers, and more seats in the garden as well as painted picnic-sets outside the Old Stables; regular quiz and live music nights. The pub is handy for Bradgate Country Park and walks in Swithland Woods. Good wheelchair access and disabled facilities.

Enjoyable pubby food includes lunchtime baguettes and home-made flatbreads, salt and pepper squid, baked camembert wrapped in pancetta, grilled meats and burgers including brisket burger and vegan burger with beetroot and quinoa, Moroccan-style lamb tagine, salmon fillet with creamy crayfish, spinach and dill gnocchi, and puddings such as raspberry pannacotta, Belgian chocolate cheesecake and banoffi bread and butter pudding. *Benchmark main dish: beer-battered fish and chips £13.75. Two-course evening meal £20.00.*

Everards ~ Tenant John Cooledge ~ Real ale ~ Open 11-11; 10-midnight Sat; 10-11 Sun ~ Bar food 12-2.30, 5.30-9 Tues-Thurs; 12-2.30, 5.30-9.30 Fri, Sat; 12-8 Sun ~ Restaurant ~ Children welcome ~ Dogs allowed in bar

 WING

Kings Arms

SK8902 Map 4

(01572) 737634 – www.thekingsarms-wing.co.uk
Village signposted off A6003 S of Oakham; on the road between Manton and Morcott; Top Street; LE15 8SE

Former farmhouse with big log fires, super choice of wines by the glass and good modern cooking; bedrooms

This welcoming, early 17th-c stone-built inn in an attractive village comes with its own smokehouse, so you can be sure of a good meal. The neatly kept and inviting long main bar has two large log fires (one in a copper-canopied central hearth), various nooks and crannies, nice old low beams and stripped stone, and flagstone or wood-strip floors. Friendly, helpful staff serve four cask ales on handpump from the likes of Black Sheep, Courage, Grainstore and Skinners, almost three dozen wines by the glass, 16 gins, 12 malt whiskies and several home-made hedgerow liqueurs like sloe gin and elderflower vodka; dominoes and cards. There are seats out in front, and more in the sunny yew-sheltered garden. If you decide to stay over, you can choose from eight well equipped, pretty bedrooms in either the Old Bake House (the village's former bakery) or Orchard House (just up their private drive); breakfasts with home-made marmalade are particularly good. The car park has plenty of space. Do visit the medieval turf maze just up the road and it's only a couple of miles to one of England's two osprey hotspots.

Using produce from their own smokehouse, local game and home-made bread, pickles, chutneys and preserves, the excellent food includes sandwiches, smoked trout pâté, smokehouse platter (cured, smoked, fermented and air-dried meats), Exmouth mussels with white wine and cream sauce, sausages and mash with yorkshire pudding, Scottish wild boar with pub-orchard boozy pear, crab and cod fishcakes, butternut squash and sage risotto, and puddings such as vanilla crème brûlée and chocolate mousse with berries and chocolate brittle. They also offer a two- and three-course set lunch. *Benchmark main dish: partridge breast, confit rabbit leg and pheasant sausage with roasted roots and game chips £17.00. Two-course evening meal £23.00.*

Free house ~ Licensee David Goss ~ Real ale ~ Open 12-3, 6.30-10; 12-3, 6-midnight Sat; 12-3 Sun ~ Bar food 12-2, 6.30-8.30; 12-2, 6.30-9 Fri, Sat; 12-2 Sun ~ Restaurant ~ Children welcome until 9pm ~ Dogs allowed in bar & bedrooms ~ Bedrooms: £80

WYMONDHAM
SK8518   Map 7
Berkeley Arms 🏵

(01572) 787587 – www.berkeley-arms.co.uk

Main Street; LE14 2AG

Well run village pub with interlinked beamed rooms, a relaxed atmosphere and sunny terrace

Most customers are here to enjoy the hearty, home-cooked food, but the front-of-house welcome from the charming staff also plays a big part in this golden-stone inn's appeal. Surrounded by rolling Melton countryside, it's also a popular spot with cyclists and walkers. The rustic interior features beams adorned with dried hops and copper pans and plates, exposed-stone walls dotted with countryside prints and a bookshelf lined with pub and restaurant guides. At one end, two wing chairs and a leather sofa are set in front of a log fire. Drinks include Greene King IPA plus changing local guest ales on handpump, local cider, 30 gins, 15 whiskies and several wines by the glass. The dining areas are furnished in a kitchen style with light wood tables and red-cushioned chunky chairs. Outside, picnic-sets either side of the front entrance get the sun nearly all day long. The village's restored 200-year-old windmill is worth a visit.

🏵 Pleasing food, with lunchtime meal deals from Wednesday to Saturday, includes home-cured salmon gravadlax with horseradish mousse, black pudding, chorizo and duck scotch egg with celeriac slaw, rib-eye steak with chips, slow-cooked saddle of lamb with mash, beer-battered fish and chips, goats cheese and ratatouille wellington, pan-seared turbot with sautéed samphire and vermouth, lemon butter and dill sauce, Moroccan-spiced tomato and chickpea pie, and puddings such as vanilla and cider-infused poached apple and pear crumble and white chocolate and raspberry cheesecake. *Benchmark main dish: sausages with truffle oil mash £12.95. Two-course evening meal £20.00.*

Free house ~ Licensee Dipak Raxit ~ Real ale ~ Open 5.30-11 Tues; 12-3, 5.30-11; 12-11.30 Sat; 12-6.30 Sun; closed Mon ~ Bar food 12-1.45, 6.30-9 Weds-Sat; 12-3 Sun ~ Restaurant ~ Children welcome ~ Dogs allowed in bar

Also Worth a Visit in Leicestershire

Besides the fully inspected pubs, you might like to try these pubs that have been recommended to us and described by readers. Do tell us what you think of them: feedback@goodguides.com

AB KETTLEBY SK7519
Sugar Loaf (01664) 822473
Nottingham Road (A606 NW of Melton); LE14 3JB Cheerful beamed roadside pub popular with locals, modern open-plan bar and restaurant in glass-roofed conservatory; no-nonsense pub grub from baguettes and light lunches to daily specials, Sun roasts, pie and ale night Weds, ales such as Sharps Doom Bar and Timothy Taylors; background and occasional live music, TV, darts; children welcome, no dogs inside; seats on small side terrace and grass; open (and food) all day.

ASHBY-DE-LA-ZOUCH SK3516
Tap at No 76
Market Street; LE65 1AP High-street micropub, tap for Tollgate brewery (based at NT's Calke Abbey), plus guests, craft beers, ciders and wines by the glass, switched-on friendly staff, up-to-date interior with high tables, warehouse-style pendant lighting and good woodburner; snacks such as pork pies, sandwiches and cakes; walkers, cyclists and dogs welcome, over-18s only; open all day weekends, closed Mon and lunchtimes Tues-Fri.

BARROWDEN SK9400

Exeter Arms (01572) 747365

*Main Street, just off A47 Uppingham–
Peterborough; LE15 8EQ* Helpful
new owners for this former coaching inn
overlooking village green and duck pond;
stylish renovation with leather and tweed
upholstery, stone floors and woodburner,
ales such as Oakham, Shepherd Neame and
Timothy Taylors, country classic cuisine
including lunchtime sandwiches, outdoor
bar and grill on sunny weekends; picnic sets
at front with lovely views over the green and
Welland Valley, more tables in large back
garden with pétanque, good local walks,
children and dogs welcome, closed Sun
evening, Mon and lunchtime Tues.

BELMESTHORPE TF0410

Blue Bell (01780) 763859

*Village signposted off A16 just E of
Stamford; PE9 4JG* Cottagey 17th-c
stone pub in attractive remote hamlet, good
keenly priced home-made food and decent
range of well kept ales such as Grainstore
and Oakham, friendly welcoming staff,
comfortable dining areas either side of
central bar, beams and huge inglenook;
children and dogs welcome, seats in
garden, open all day weekends, closed Mon
lunchtime, no food Sun evening.

BELTON SK4420

Queens Head (01530) 222359

*4.4 miles from M1 junction 23: after
about 2.6 miles turn right off A512/
Ashby Road; Long Street/B5324; can
return to M1 junction 23A via A42;
LE12 9TP* Stylish 18th-c coaching inn
handy for East Midlands Airport; up-to-date
interiors with leather and suede seating and
dark-painted walls decorated with wooden
wine-crate labels, Charnwood, Timothy
Taylors and a guest ale, good food including
sandwiches and pub classics, steak nights
Sun-Tues, excellent service; darts; dogs
welcome (in bar and bistro), five smart
bedrooms, garden with tables shaded by
parasols, open all day.

BOTCHESTON SK4804

Greyhound (01455) 824421

*Main Street, off B5380 E of Desford;
LE9 9FF* Welcoming whitewashed village
pub (originally three cottages) with newish
owners and refreshed interiors with log fire
and artworks for sale; good reasonably
priced home-made food from sandwiches
and sharing plates up, Marstons-related ales
and decent choice of wines and gins, friendly
attentive service; skittle alley; children and
dogs (in bar) welcome, well kept garden with

play area, open all day Fri and Sat, till 7pm
Sun, closed Mon lunchtime, no food Mon and
Tues lunchtimes, Sun evening.

BRANSTON SK8129

Wheel (01476) 870376

Main Street near the church; NG32 1RU
New father and son team at this beamed
18th-c ironstone village pub set in
the picturesque Vale of Belvoir; smart
traditional interiors with log fires, ales
from maybe Adnams, Black Sheep or Castle
Rock, wines by the glass, classic pub food
including Sun roasts; background and
occasional live music, skittle alley; children
welcome, attractive garden, splendid
countryside near Belvoir Castle, open all
day (till 8pm Sun), closed Mon and Tues
lunchtimes, no food Mon evening.

BRAUNSTON SK8306

Blue Ball (01572) 722135

*Off A606 in Oakham; Cedar Street
opposite church; LE15 8QS* Pretty
17th-c thatched dining pub near Rutland
Water with good food (not Sun evening)
from ciabatta sandwiches and game pie
up, well kept ales including Marstons EPA,
decent choice of wines, friendly welcoming
staff, inviting interiors with leather sofas,
beamed ceilings, inglenook fireplace, log
fires and small conservatory; monthly jazz
Sun lunchtime; children and dogs (in bar)
welcome, painted furniture on outdoor
decking, attractive village, open all day Sat,
till 8pm Sun, closed Mon.

BRAUNSTON SK8306

Old Plough (01572) 722714

*Off A606 in Oakham; Church Street;
LE15 8QT* Comfortably opened-up black-
beamed village local; four well kept ales,
craft beers and good range of gins, enjoyable
food (not Sun evening) from ciabattas to
grills and themed nights including Tues pies,
Weds curry, Thurs burger and Fri fish and
chips, log fire, back dining conservatory;
children, dogs and muddy boots welcome,
tables in sheltered back garden with
pétanque, five bedrooms, handy for Rutland
Water, open all day.

BRUNTINGTHORPE SP6089

★ Joiners Arms (0116) 247 8258

*Off A5199 S of Leicester: Church Walk/
Cross Street; LE17 5QH* More restaurant
than pub with most of the two beamed rooms
set for eating, drinkers have area by small
light oak bar with open fire; civilised relaxed
atmosphere, candles on tables, elegant
dining chairs and big flower arrangements,
first class imaginative food served by efficient
friendly staff, set menu Tues evening and

We include some hotels with a good bar that offers facilities comparable
to those of a pub.

fish and chips Fri lunchtime, plenty of wines by the glass including champagne, one mainstream ale such as Greene King or Sharps; picnic-sets in front, closed Sun evening, Mon.

BUCKMINSTER SK8822
⋆ **Tollemache Arms** (01476) 860477
B676 Colsterworth–Melton Mowbray;
Main Street; NG33 5SA New management for this 19th-c stone-built village inn with rooms near Buckminster Park; boarded floors in linked areas with mix of wooden furniture including some small hand-made pews, armchairs by open fire in bar, leather sofas in library room off restaurant, pub favourites served on chopping boards, pensioners' lunch Thurs, ales including Fullers and Oakham, good choice of wines by the glass, cocktails and several malt whiskies; background music, TV; children and dogs (in bar) welcome, plenty of teak tables and chairs in sizeable garden, bedrooms; lovely village and handy for A1; open (and food) all day Sat, till 5pm Sun, closed Mon.

BURBAGE SP4492
Anchor (01455) 636107
Church Street; LE10 2DA Popular nautically themed drinkers' pub (locals call it the Yacht Club) with opened-up interior; beams, woodburners and some red plush, well kept Marstons-related ales, friendly staff, no food (maybe cobs on the bar); weekly live music and quiz nights, sports TV; dogs welcome, circular picnic-sets in sunken garden behind, pleasant village, open all day.

CALDECOTT SP8693
Plough (01536) 770284
Main Street; LE16 8RS Welcoming ironstone pub overlooking the green in Rutland village known for its thatched cottages, run by charming husband and wife team; new upholstery in carpeted bar with banquettes and small tables leading to spacious eating area, log fires, four well-kept changing beers, real ciders and wide range of popular inexpensive food with vegetarian options and blackboard specials, prompt service; children and dogs welcome; large gardens, closed weekday lunchtimes.

COLEORTON SK4016
Angel (01530) 834742
The Moor; LE67 8GB Friendly and homely with good range of enjoyable reasonably priced food (all day Sun) including carvery and blackboard specials, well kept beers such as Marstons Pedigree, hospitable attentive staff, beams and open fire; children welcome, tables outside, open all day Sun.

COLEORTON SK4117
⋆ **George** (01530) 834639
Loughborough Road (A512 E); LE67 8HF Much loved whitewashed village pub with traditional beamed bar and beer garden

whose countryside views extend all the way to Coleorton Hall; scatter-cushioned pews and wall seats, church candles on tables, dark panelled dado with local photographs above, shelves of books, leather sofa and tartan-upholstered tub chairs by woodburner, ales such as Leatherbritches and Marstons, several wines by the glass and good food from grilled meats to sharing plates and light lunches, friendly attentive staff; background music; well behaved children and dogs (in bar) welcome, wheelchair access and wheelchair-adapted loo, spreading back garden with sturdy furniture and play area, open all day Sat, till 8pm Sun, closed Mon.

CROXTON KERRIAL SK8329
Geese & Fountain (01476) 870350
A607 SW of Grantham; NG32 1QR Unpretentious family-run 17th-c coaching inn with rooms in the Vale of Belvoir that's popular with walkers and cyclists (secure bike racks); five real ales such as Grainstore, Oldershaw and Pheasantry, craft beers and extensive bottled range, organic wines, locally sourced food with a wide choice from sandwiches and pizzas up, big open-plan beamed bar with log fire; occasional live music, darts and library; children and dogs welcome, inner courtyard and sloping garden with views, seven good bedrooms in separate block, open all day, closed Jan.

DADLINGTON SP4097
Dog & Hedgehog (01455) 213151
The Green, opposite church; CV13 6JB Popular red-brick village dining pub noted for its good food including well liked Sun lunch, impressive vaulted-ceiling dining room, friendly staff and hands-on character landlord, rebadged ales from brewers such as Quartz and Tunnel, nice wines; children and dogs welcome, garden looking down to Ashby-de-la-Zouch Canal, closed Sun evening, otherwise open all day.

DISEWORTH SK4524
Plough (01332) 810333
Near East Midlands Airport and M1 junction 23A; DE74 2QJ Extended 16th-c beamed pub with well kept ales such as Bass, Marstons and Timothy Taylors, reasonably priced traditional food from home-made beef chilli to fish and chips (not Sun evening), friendly staff, spacious well divided restaurant and bar with wooden furnishings, log fires and eclectic pictures; children and dogs welcome, large paved terrace with steps up to lawn, handy for Donington Park race track, open all day.

EXTON SK9211
⋆ **Fox & Hounds** (01572) 811032
The Green; signed off A606 Stamford–Oakham; LE15 8AP New owners for this handsome 17th-c inn facing small village green; high-ceilinged candlelit lounge with comfortable seating and big stone fireplace,

well cooked/presented food including Weds steak night, Elgoods, Grainstore and a guest, nice wines by the glass, attentive service; soft background music, quiz night first Tues of the month; children welcome, dogs in bar, sheltered walled garden overlooking pretty paddocks, four luxurious bedrooms, handy for Rutland Water and the gardens at Barnsdale, closed Mon, otherwise open all day, till 9pm Sun.

FOXTON
SP6989

Foxton Locks (0116) 279 1515
Foxton Locks, off A6 3 miles NW of Market Harborough (park by bridge 60/62 and walk); LE16 7RA Busy place in great canalside setting at foot of spectacular flight of locks; large comfortably reworked L-shaped bar, popular no-nonsense food including gluten-free options, well kept ales including Timothy Taylors; some live music; children and dogs welcome, glassed-in dining 'terrace' overlooking the water, steps down to fenced waterside lawn, good walks, open (and food) all day.

GADDESBY
SK6813

Cheney Arms (01664) 840260
Rearsby Lane; LE7 4XE Friendly red-brick country pub set back from the road; bar with bare-boards and terracotta-tiled floor, well kept Everards and guests from brick-faced servery, open fires including inglenook in more formal dining room, big helpings of reasonably priced food (not Sun evening, Mon) from good lunchtime baguettes up; sports TV; children welcome, disabled access, walled back garden with pétanque, lovely medieval church nearby, four bedrooms, closed Mon lunchtime, otherwise open all day.

GILMORTON
SP5787

Grey Goose (01455) 552555
Lutterworth Road; LE17 5PN Popular bar-restaurant with good range of enjoyable freshly made food including lunchtime/early evening weekday set menu and Sun carvery, ales such as Sharps Doom Bar and several wines by the glass, good friendly staff, light contemporary décor, stylish wood and metal bar stools mixing with comfortable sofas and armchairs, woodburner in stripped-brick fireplace; modern furniture on terrace, closed Sun evening, otherwise open all day.

GLASTON
SK8900

Old Pheasant (01572) 822326
A47 Leicester–Peterborough, E of Uppingham; LE15 9BP Attractive much-extended stone inn with rooms in the heart of Rutland; beamed bar with leather sofas around an inglenook log fire and central brick servery, three real ales including Grainstore and Timothy Taylors, enjoyable good value food (not Sun evening), friendly helpful service, steps up to restaurant; bar billiards; children and dogs welcome, picnic-sets on pretty outdoor

terrace framed by foliage, bedrooms, open all day, no food Sun evening.

GREETHAM
SK9214

Plough (01572) 813613
B668 Stretton–Cottesmore; LE15 7NJ Traditional stone-faced village pub, comfortable and welcoming, with good home-made food including weekday deals, themed nights (curry, fish and chips) and breakfast from 9.30am Sat, traditional décor with bare-stone walls and dark wood furnishings; Black Sheep, Marstons Wainwright, and extensive list of gins, friendly service; quiz and live music nights; children and dogs welcome, tables in back garden, good local walks and not far from Rutland Water, open all day.

GUMLEY
SP6890

Bell (0116) 279 0126
NW of Market Harborough; Main Street; LE16 7RU Ceramic pint jugs hang from the ceiling of this beamed village pub whose friendly owners are happy to suggest local cycle paths; L-shaped bar with two log fires, Timothy Taylors Landlord, Woodfordes Wherry and guests, nine wines by the glass; fair-priced food including steak nights (Mon, Weds), set evening deal (Tues, Thurs) and Sun roasts, sports TV; children and dogs welcome, pretty terrace garden with pond, open (and food) all day weekends.

HALLATON
SP7896

★**Bewicke Arms** (01858) 555734
On Eastgate, opposite village sign; LE16 8UB Attractive 18th-c thatched dining pub in picture-perfect village; stylish contemporary interiors with bare-stone walls, vaulted-ceiling café and log fires, excellent interesting food using local ingredients, three changing ales, proper cider and well chosen wines; memorabilia from ancient inter-village bottle-kicking match (still held on Easter Mon); children and dogs welcome, wheelchair access, big terrace overlooking paddock and play area, three bedrooms in converted stables, shop, open all day.

HARBY
SK7531

Nags Head (01949) 869629
Main Street; LE14 4BN Popular old beamed pub in interesting Vale of Belvoir village; traditional beamed bar with log fires and spacious beer garden with picnic-sets and its own outdoor kitchen, good pubby food including burger menu and Tues evening deal and themed nights, perhaps Jennings Cumberland, Marstons Wainwright and a guest, warm service; regular live music, quiz nights and sports TV; children and dogs welcome, open all day Fri-Sun, closed Mon lunchtime, no food Sun evening.

HINCKLEY
Elbow Room 07900 191388
Station Road; LLE10 1AW Relaxed hipster vibe at this family-run micropub

calling itself an 'Ale & Cider House'; contemporary industrial décor with wood and metal bench seating, six ever-changing ales plus good selection of craft beers and ciders, over 50 gins, bar snacks such as scotch eggs and pork pies, friendly service, tables out front, open all day.

HINCKLEY SP4293
Railway (01455) 612399
Station Road; LE10 1AP Funky décor and young friendly staff at this brick pub owned by Steamin' Billy; their ales and guests from seven pumps, also draught continentals and real cider, sensibly priced food from sandwiches to burgers, Tues special deal, Thurs pie night, vaulted dining area and wood-panelled bar with eclectic wallpaper and board games bursting out of a vintage trunk; darts, live jazz; dogs welcome, beer garden behind, open all day and handy for the station.

HOBY SK6717
Blue Bell (01664) 434247
Main Street; LE14 3DT Attractive well run thatched pub; good range of popular realistically priced food from pub classics to sharing plates, salads and deli rolls (gluten-free options available), friendly attentive uniformed staff, four well kept Everards ales and two guests, lots of wines by the glass, open-plan and airy with beams, comfortable traditional furniture, old local photographs; background music, skittle alley and darts; children, walkers and dogs welcome, picnic-sets in valley-view garden with boules, open all day, food all day weekends.

HOUGHTON ON THE HILL SK6703
Old Black Horse (0116) 241 3486
Main Street (just off A47 Leicester–Uppingham); LE7 9GD Welcoming modernised village pub with enjoyable home-made food including pizzas, Sun roasts and vegan options, well kept Everards, decent wines by the glass and good range of other drinks, opened up split-level interior divided into distinct areas, mix of bare boards, tiles and carpet, some painted panelling, woodburner and open fire; lots of themed events from quiz nights to live rugby on TV; children and dogs (in bar) welcome, large back garden with countryside views and new children's play area, open all day Fri-Sun, no food Sun evening and Mon.

HUNGARTON SK6907
Black Boy (0116) 259 5410
Main Street; LE7 9JR Cheerful welcome at this famiy-run restaurany bar; attractive interiors with leather sofas, tartan upholstery and open fires, well priced food cooked to order by landlord-chef (weekend booking advised) including various themed nights, three changing ales, cheerful staff; background music; children welcome, picnic-sets on decking, boules pitch, closed Sun evening, Mon.

ILLSTON ON THE HILL SP7099
★Fox & Goose (0116) 259 6340
Main Street, off B6047 Market Harborough–Melton Mowbray; LE7 9EG Warm welcome from new landlords at this characterful village pub; two rooms keeping traditional feel with hunting pictures and assorted oddments including farming implements, stuffed foxes, woodburner and open fire, well kept Everards, a guest beer and decent choice of other drinks, popular good quality home-made food (not Sun evening, Mon, Tues) from lunchtime huffers up, cheerful helpful staff; children, walkers and dogs (in bar) welcome, disabled access, outside seating at front and side, Sept onion competition, open all day Weds-Sat, till 9pm Sun, closed Mon lunchtime.

KNIPTON SK8231
Manners Arms (01476) 879222
Signed off A607 Grantham–Melton Mowbray; Croxton Road; NG32 1RH Recent revamp for this handsome Georgian hunting lodge with rooms in the sought-after Vale of Belvoir; more restaurant than pub with elegant dining conservatory and bare-boards bar with log fire, reasonably priced and well presented food from sandwiches to fine dining, afternoon tea (with a pint) and popular Sun lunch, well kept ales such as Batemans, Bombardier and guests, nice choice of wines by the glass; background music; children and dogs welcome, terrace with ornamental pool, lovely views over pretty village, ten comfortable individually furnished bedrooms, open all day.

KNOSSINGTON SK8008
Fox & Hounds (01664) 452129
Off A606 W of Oakham; Somerby Road; LE15 8LY Attractive 18th-c ivy-clad village dining pub; beamed bar with antique furniture and curios, log fire and cosy eating areas, well liked food (best to book) from traditional choices to blackboard specials, Fullers London Pride, attentive friendly service; children (over 8) and dogs welcome, outdoor terrace brimming with flowers and cushioned benches, closed Sun evening, Mon and lunchtimes Tues-Sat. *(Sandra Morgan)*

LANGHAM SK8411
Wheatsheaf (01572) 869105
Burley Road/Bridge Street; LE15 7HY Atmospheric and relaxed family-run village pub with wide range of real ales including Greene King Abbot and gins (180 at the last count), smart contemporary décor in central bar flanked by dining areas with white and grey panelled walls, good generously served home-made food including vegetarian/vegan menu, friendly helpful staff; children and dogs welcome, seats on pleasant flower-decked terrace, closed lunchtimes Mon and Tues, otherwise open all day, food all day Sun.

LEICESTER SK5804
Blue Boar (0116) 319 6230
Millstone Lane; LE1 5JN Beer barrels are turned into tables and stools in this single room micropub; fine range of interesting beers on tap and in bottles including a house ale from Leatherbritches, also proper ciders and a dozen wines by the glass; some snacky food such as cobs and cheeseboards, young helpful staff, half-panelled walls with old Leicester maps, cellar visible through glass doors behind counter; dogs welcome, open all day.

LEICESTER SK5306
Forge (0116) 2871702
Main Street, Glenfield; LE3 8DG Well run popular whitewashed village pub handy for M1; traditional much-extended interior with exposed-stone walls in dining areas, Everards and guest ales, interesting wine list, modern pub food with European influences using locally sourced meat and certified sustainable seafood, weekday early bird menu, friendly helpful service; quiz; children welcome till 9pm, two attractive terraces with outdoor bar in summer months, open (and food) all day, no food Sun evening.

LEICESTER SK5804
Globe (0116) 253 9492
Silver Street; LE1 5EU One of Leicester's oldest pubs, this 18th-c inn is in the pedestrianised city centre; lots of woodwork in partitioned areas off central bar, bare boards and some Victorian mosaic flooring, mirrors and working gas lamps; four Everards ales, three guests, two real ciders and a large whisky selection; friendly staff; well priced food from bar snacks up including vegetarian/vegan menu, function room upstairs; background music (not in snug); children and dogs welcome, metal café-style tables out in front; open all day.

LEICESTER SK5803
Kings Head (0116) 254 8240
King Street; LE1 6RL Small drinkers' pub not far from rugby ground; well-kept ales including Black Country, craft beers, a couple of proper ciders and good gin range, no food apart from cobs, traditional décor and log fire; Thurs quiz, sports TV, newspapers and board games; raised back terrace and courtyard bar that's open on match days, open all day.

LEICESTER SK5804
★ Knight & Garter (0116) 303 3310
Hotel Street/Market Place S; LE1 5AW Red-brick dining pub with terrace overlooking new Green Dragon Square in city centre (same group as Rutland & Derby Arms); 14th-c origins but rebuilt in 1900s, leaded mullion windows combining well with new sleek contemporary décor including bare-brick walls, banquettes and leather upholstered chairs and stools around pale-wood tables,

moody lighting, separate restaurant (entry is through door disguised as a bookcase), good brasserie-style food with emphasis on steaks, also sandwiches and weekend brunch (from 10am), well kept real ales (usually Everards) and craft beers, cocktails and premium spirits from copper-topped bar, efficient and friendly staff; children welcome till 7pm, outdoor terrace with tables, open (and food) all day, closed Sun evening.

LEICESTER SK5804
Rutland & Derby Arms
(0116) 262 3299 *Millstone Lane; nearby metered parking; LE1 5JN* Smart modern city-centre bar; contemporary open-plan interior with long bar counter and quirky details such as lights from a Russian submarine; well kept Everards and guest craft beers, 16 wines by the glass and a good range of spirits, street-food cuisine including burgers and pizzas, excellent service; background and live music, sports TV, Mon quiz, annual cider and sausage festival; children welcome till 9pm, sunny courtyard with tables under parasols, more seats on Gin Garden roof terrace, closed Sun, otherwise open (and food) all day, till 1am Fri, Sat.

LEICESTER SK5804
★ Two-Tailed Lion (0116) 224 4769
Millstone Lane; LE1 5JN Pub and bottle shop in handsome red-brick building in central Greyfriars district; thoughtfully chosen real ales and craft beers from breweries such as Buxton, Cloudwater and local Framework – a changing blackboard lists the cask and keg beers available, nice wines and spirits too; on two floors with half panelling, marble-topped cast-iron tables, leather stools and banquettes and wall of plants in boxes, food limited to tasty bar snacks such as scotch eggs and pizza, knowledgeable and welcoming staff; regular events such as monthly beer tastings, home-brew clubs, quiz and food pairing nights; open all day Tues-Sat, closed Sun evening.

LONG WHATTON SK4823
★ Royal Oak (01509) 843694
The Green; LE12 5DB Smart village dining pub with rooms that's handy for Donington Park race circuit and East Midlands Airport; dining area and beamed-ceiling bar with tartan fabrics and exposed-brick walls, good well presented modern food along with pub favourites, set menu choices, Sun pie night and excellent breakfast, well kept ales such as Charnwood and St Austell, good wines by the glass from extensive list, friendly efficient staff; outdoor terrace with tables, 12 spotless bedrooms in two separate buildings behind pub, open all day.

LYDDINGTON SP8796
★ Old White Hart (01572) 821703
Main Street; Village signed off A6003 N of Corby; LE15 9LR Popular and welcoming 17th-c inn across from small

green; two cosy linked bars with log fires and heavy beams, cushioned wall benches and simple wooden furniture on tiled floors, some fine hunting prints, Greene King IPA and a guest, good food (not Sun evening in winter) including own sausages and cured meats (long-serving landlord is a butcher), midweek offers, efficient obliging service, attractive restaurant and small conservatory with rugs on strip-wood floors; children welcome, seats by heaters in pretty walled garden (dogs welcome here), eight floodlit boules pitches, well placed for Bede House (EH) and good nearby walks, 20 pretty bedrooms (six in nearby building), open all day, no food Sun evening in winter.

MANTON   SK8704
Horse & Jockey (01572) 737335
St Marys Road; LE15 8SU Colourful tubs and hanging baskets outside this popular early 19th-c pub on the Rutland Water cycle route (bike racks provided); updated low-beamed interior with modern furniture on wood or stone floors, logburner, well-kept ales such as Grainstore and Greene King plus a house beer (Fall at the First), decent fairly priced food from baguettes to blackboard specials, cheery service; background music; children and dogs welcome, outdoor picnic sets, Camping and Caravanning Club site, open all day in summer.

MARKET HARBOROUGH   SP7387
Beerhouse (01858) 465317
St Marys Road; LE16 7DX Micropub in converted furniture shop tucked away behind fish and chip shop; blackboard with a dozen real ales tapped from stillage, plenty of craft kegs and a couple of real ciders, friendly knowledgeable staff, snacks such as cobs, scotch eggs and pork pies, simple interior with connecting rooms; Mon quiz, some live music and comedy nights; dogs welcome, a few picnic-sets outside, closed lunchtimes Mon and Weds, all day Tues, otherwise open all day.

MARKET OVERTON   SK8816
Black Bull (01572) 767677
Teigh Road, opposite the church; LE15 7PW Attractive 17th-c stone pub with thatched roof in pretty village well placed for Rutland Water; good home-made food (booking advised) from pub staples up including Thurs steak night and Fri fish and chips, low-beamed, carpeted bar and two separate dining areas, woodburner and leather sofas, well-kept local ales along with some craft beers and wines by the glass, welcoming staff; quiz night last Thurs of month; children and dogs welcome, tables outside at front, two bedrooms, open till 6pm Sun, closed Mon.

MEDBOURNE   SP7992
★ **Nevill Arms** (01858) 565288
B664 Market Harborough–Uppingham; LE16 8EE Freshly refurbished stone-built

Victorian inn in idyllic village setting facing stream and little footbridge; modernised interiors with woodburners, stone inglenook, carpeted bar with beams and mullion windows, restaurant with rich décor and plush banquettes, excellent food from sandwiches up, well-kept ales including St Austell, craft kegs and good choice of wines by the glass, helpful staff; children and dogs (in bar) welcome, streamside picnic-sets, courtyard garden café (8.30am-5pm), ten bedrooms, some with four-poster beds, open all day.

MELTON MOWBRAY   SK7519
Anne of Cleves (01664) 481336
Burton Street, by St Mary's church; LE13 1AE Monks' chantry dating from the 14th c and gifted to Anne of Cleves by Henry VIII; heavy beams, flagstones and mullioned windows, tapestries, swords and other bits and pieces on ochre walls, chunky tables, character chairs and settles, log fire, well kept Everards and guests, decent wines and generously served food including famed local pork pies, small end dining room; background music; children and dogs welcome, tables in pretty little walled garden, open all day, no food Sun evening.

MELTON MOWBRAY   SK7518
Boat (01664) 500969
Burton Street; LE13 1AF Chatty and welcoming local with three well kept beers including Adnams and over 45 malt whiskies, no food except local pork pies, traditional bar with panelling and open fires, quiz nights and darts; dogs welcome, handy for the station, open all day Thurs-Sun (Fri from 2pm).

MOUNTSORREL   SK5715
Swan (0116) 230 2340
Loughborough Road, off A6; LE12 7AT Popular 17th-c former coaching inn with split-level interior; log fires, old flagstones and stripped-stone walls, good well priced food (best to book evenings) including monthly themed nights, friendly efficient staff, well kept ales such as Black Sheep and good choice of wines, neat dining areas; dogs welcome in bar, pretty walled back garden down to canalised River Soar, open all day weekends.

MOWSLEY   SP6488
Staff of Life (0116) 240 2359
Village signposted off A5199 S of Leicester; Main Street; LE17 6NT Gabled village pub with roomy fairly traditional bar; high-backed settles on flagstones, wicker chairs on shiny wood floor and stools around unusual circular counter, woodburner, ales such as Black Sheep, Exmoor and Wadworths, a dozen wines by the glass and decent whisky choice, well liked food with vegan/vegetarian options and set evening deal Weds-Fri; background music; well behaved children welcome (no under-12s Fri and Sat nights),

no dogs, seats out in front and on nice leaf-shaded deck, open Sun till 7pm, closed Mon (including bank holidays) and weekday lunchtimes.

NEWBOLD VERDON   SK4402
Windmill (01455) 824433
Brascote, via B582 (off A447 Hinckley–Coalville); LE9 9LE Modernised roadside country pub based on former mill house; cobbled back way into open-plan two-part bar, comfortable seats by woodburner, split-level restaurant with pitched ceiling, good food from baguettes up including set menus and themed nights, Greene King ales and guests, friendly efficient staff; background music; children welcome (they eat for free weekdays 12-1pm, 6-7pm), dogs in bar, picnic-sets in long narrow garden, open all day Sat, till 7pm Sun.

NORTH LUFFENHAM   SK9303
★ Fox (01780) 720991
Pinfold Lane; LE15 8LE Much loved stone pub in attractive village near Rutland Water; spotless interiors including flagstoned bar with woodburner, exposed walls in lounge with leather and tartan club chairs, spacious dining room, four well-kept ales and several wines by the glass from light wood servery, good quality food including sandwiches and pub favourites, friendly prompt service; darts and TV in upstairs snug; children and dogs welcome, large planters and picnic-sets under parasols on paved terrace, open all day weekends, closed Mon lunchtime.

OADBY   SK6202
★ Cow & Plough (0116) 272 0852
Gartree Road (B667 N of centre); LE2 2FB Converted farm buildings with extraordinary collection of brewery memorabilia in two dark back rooms – enamel signs and mirrors advertising long-forgotten beers, an aged brass cash register, furnishings and fittings salvaged from pubs and churches (there's some splendid stained glass behind the counter), own Steamin' Billy beers and several guests, two real ciders and a dozen malt whiskies, good generously served pubby food plus some interesting specials (booking essential weekends), long front extension and conservatory; background music, live jazz Weds lunchtime, TV, darts and board games; children and dogs (in bars and garden) welcome, picnic-sets on decked terrace, open all day, no food Sun evening.

OAKHAM   SK8508
Admiral Hornblower
(01572) 723004 *High Street; LE15 6AS* Attractive pub-hotel in historic Rutland town (sister to Finchs Arms in Upper Hambleton); former 17th-c farmhouse with several differently decorated areas, good imaginative food at sensible prices from interesting sandwiches and sharing boards up, special

diets catered for, three well kept ales, efficient friendly service; children and dogs welcome; seats out at front and in spacious side terrace with outdoor bar, ten bedrooms, substantial breakfast, open all day, food all day Sun, weekend brunch.

OAKHAM   SK8509
★ Grainstore (01572) 770065
Station Road, off A606; LE15 6RE Former Victorian grain store brewing its own good Grainstore beers on the upper floors above the down-to-earth bar (August Bank Holiday beer festival) – ten of its own beers on handpump and through swan necks with sparklers, 15 malt whiskies and several wines by the glass, warehouse-inspired décor with red metal pillars, bare-brick walls and cask tables, with huge glass doors pulled back in summer on to a terrace with picnic-sets, popular menu of pub classics plus themed nights and weekend breakfasts; games machine, darts, board games, giant Jenga, live music, comedy nights and open mike, brewery tours; children and dogs welcome, open all days, no food Sun evening.

OAKHAM   SK8608
★ Lord Nelson (01572) 868340
Market Place; LE15 6DT Handsome 16th-c pub overlooking main square of Rutland's county town; half a dozen rooms spread over two floors, imaginative furnishings including cushioned church pews, long oak settles and walls decorated with copper pans, vintage metal signs and plenty of prints (including of Lord Horatio, of course), Oakham JHB and guest ales from maybe Black Sheep, Caledonian and Fullers, 13 gins and 18 wines by the glass, tasty food including lunchtime ciabattas, pizzas, pub classics and weekend breakfasts; background music, board games; pretty outdoor terrace with hanging baskets and picnic-sets, children and dogs (except one dining room) welcome, open all day, food all day Sat and Sun.

OAKHAM   SK8508
Wheatsheaf (01572) 756124
Northgate; Church Street end; LE15 6QS Attractive and popular 17th-c local near church; well kept Everards and guests, good selection of wines by the glass and generous pubby food including lunchtime baguettes, burgers and Sun roasts, cheerful comfortable bar with open fires, quieter lounge, back conservatory; some live music; pretty suntrap courtyard, open all day Fri-Sun.

OLD DALBY   SK6723
★ Crown (01664) 820320
Debdale Hill; LE14 3LF Extended and cleverly revamped 17th-c creeper-clad pub (sister to Curzon Arms in Woodhouse Eaves and Windmill in Wymeswold); cosy rustic rooms in original part, plenty of reclaimed wood, nice old floorboards, flagstones and eclectic collection of old and new furniture,

shelves of books, advertising mirrors, even a stuffed hare holding a shotgun; Sharps Doom Bar and guests, three ciders, 14 wines by the glass and cocktails, popular interesting food along with more traditional choices and and wintertime Mon pie and Thurs steak nights; background and some live music, quiz last Tues of month, darts and board games; children welcome, dogs in bar, partly covered garden room leading to sunny terrace and lawn, open all day Fri-Sun, food till 6pm Sun.

QUENIBOROUGH   SK6412
Britannia (0116) 260 5675
Main Street; LE7 3DB Welcoming beamed village pub with good choice of well liked food including ciabattas, burgers and pizzas, Mon steak, Tues pie and Thurs Italian night, well kept ales such as Sharps and Timothy Taylors, several wines by the glass and over 20 gins, friendly helpful service, restaurant; Sun quiz; children and dogs welcome, picnic-sets out at front and in heated beer garden, open (and food) all day.

REDMILE   SK7935
★Windmill (01949) 842281
Off A52 Grantham–Nottingham; Main Street; NG13 0GA Old village pub with snug low-beamed bar, exposed brick and stone walls, sofas, easy chairs and log fire in large raised hearth, comfortable roomier dining areas with woodburners, monthly changing seasonal menu, well kept changing ales and nice choice of wines by the glass, efficient friendly staff; some pictures of 1980s TV series *Auf Wiedersehen Pet* being filmed here; children, walkers and dogs welcome, sizeable front terrace, pretty village with views towards Belvoir Castle, open all day Fri, Sat, till 6.30pm Sun, closed Mon.

ROTHLEY   SK5812
Woodmans Stroke (0116) 230 2785
Church Street; LE7 7PD Family-run 18th-c thatched pub (aka Woodies); good value weekday lunchtime food from sandwiches and ploughman's up (order at the bar), well kept changing ales and nice wines by the glass, friendly staff, beams and settles in front rooms, open fire, old local photographs and rugby/cricket memorabilia; sports TV; pretty hanging baskets and attractive garden with heated terrace and pétanque, open all day Sat.

RYHALL   TF0310
Millstone Inn (01780) 763649
Bridge Street; PE9 4HH Top-to-toe renovation for this Rutland village pub (formerly the Wicked Witch) with friendly new father and son team taking it back to its traditional roots and name; two changing ales, menu of bar snacks and pub classics plus curry and pie nights; upstairs games room with table football, pool and darts; children (with their own play area) and dogs (with their own doggie menu) welcome.

SADDINGTON   SP6591
Queens Head (0116) 240 2536
S of Leicester between A5199 (ex A50) and A6; Main Street; LE8 0QH Welcoming village pub with far-reaching countryside views; smart split-level interiors with flagstones and bare-brick walls, attractively presented food including pub classics and good value midweek menu, well kept Everards, a couple of guest beers and thoughtfully chosen wines by the glass (Fri happy hour 6-10pm); children welcome, garden with play area, farm shop (11.30am-4.30pm) offering everything from home-made pies to fabric alterations, closed Mon and Tues, otherwise open all day, food till 7pm Sun.

SEATON   SP9098
★George & Dragon (01572) 747418
Main Street; LE15 9HU High praise for this cosy 17th-c pub in unspoilt hilltop village with good views of Harringworth Viaduct; split-level interior with bar (former bakery) and separate candlelit restaurant with piano, bare stone and brick walls, church pew-style benches and leather sofas, Bass, Grainstore and a beer badged for them, excellent food with some pub classics and good Sun lunch, charming service; children and dogs (in bar) welcome, paved terrace with contemporary rattan tables and chairs, three bedrooms; closed lunchtimes Mon and Tues, otherwise open all day, no food Sun evening.

SHARNFORD   SP4891
Bricklayers (01455) 271799
Leicester Road; LE10 3PP Recent revamp for this welcoming 18th-c beamed and timbered village pub; big main bar, side lounge with woodburner and dining room in newer extension; ales such as Greene King and Sharps, decent choice of enjoyable reasonably priced pub food including Weds burgers, Thurs tapas/pizza night and popular Sun lunch (should book), friendly efficient staff; live music nights; children welcome, garden, handy for Fosse Meadows nature park, closed Mon, open all day Fri-Sat, till 8.30pm Sun.

SHAWELL   SP5480
White Swan (01788) 860357
Main Street; village signed down declassified road (ex A427) off A5/A426 roundabout – turn right in village; not far from M6 junction 1; LE17 6AG Attractive little 17th-c beamed dining pub; spotless contemporary interiors, dining room with glass atrium, wooden panelling and wine-fridge wall, good interesting food from landlord-chef along with some pub staples, local Dow Bridge ales and guests, lots of wines by the glass (wine tasting evenings and champagne breakfast Sat); children welcome, picnic sets on gravelled terrace,

open all day Sat (breakfast from 10am), closed Mon-Fri lunchtimes and Sun evening.

SHEARSBY SP6290
Chandlers Arms (0116) 247 8384
Fenny Lane, off A50 Leicester–Northampton; LE17 6PL Comfortable old creeper-clad pub in attractive village; six well kept ales including Dow Bridge, a summer cider and good value pubby food along with range of 'sizzling' dishes; background music, table skittles; children welcome, freshly renovated patio overlooking green, open Sun till 7pm, closed Mon and lunchtimes Tues-Thurs.

SHEPSHED SK4618
Horse (01509) 507006
Ashby Road; handy for M1 junction 23; LE12 9EF Modernised and extended pub with emphasis on dining; inglenook fireplace, light-wood beams and horse-inspired artefacts, popular well presented food from sandwiches up, cheerful attentive service, real ales such as Greene King Abbot and good choice of other drinks; some live music and quiz nights; children welcome, dogs in bar, garden and terrace with pizza oven, six courtyard bedrooms, open all day, no food Sun evening.

SOMERBY SK7710
Stilton Cheese (01664) 454394
High Street; off A606 Oakham–Melton Mowbray, via Cold Overton, or Leesthorpe and Pickwell; LE14 2QB Family-run ironstone pub with beamed bar/lounge, comfortable furnishings on red-patterned carpets, open fire and miscellaneous artefacts from country prints to plates, copper pots and even a stuffed badger; Grainstore, Marstons and guests, dozens of malt whiskies, popular reasonably priced pubby food along with daily blackboard specials; children and walkers welcome, no dogs (there's a friendly pub cat), seats on terrace, peaceful setting on edge of pretty village.

SOUTH LUFFENHAM SK9401
Coach House (01780) 720866
Stamford Road (A6121); LE15 8NT Charming new owners for this old roadside inn not far from Rutland Water; contemporary interiors with flagstoned bar, scatter cushions on short pews, log fire, modern dining room and new pool room, real ales including Timothy Taylors Landlord and local guests, plenty of wines by the glass; good interesting food cooked by the landlord including breakfasts; children and dogs (in bar) welcome, small back deck, seven bedrooms, open all day.

SPROXTON SK8524
Crown (01476) 861608
Coston Road; LE14 4QB Freshly repainted fairly compact 19th-c stone-built inn; comfortable interiors with light airy bar and woodburner, good reasonably priced food cooked by landlady, St Austell Tribute plus three guests and nice wines by the glass, welcoming service; children and dogs (in bar) welcome, sunny courtyard, attractive village and good local walks, three bedrooms, open all day Fri-Sun, closed lunchtimes Mon-Thurs.

STRETTON SK9415
★Jackson Stops (01780) 410237
Rookery Lane; a mile or less off A1, at B668 (Oakham) exit; follow village sign, turning off Clipsham Road into Manor Road, pub on left; LE15 7RA Attractive thatched former farmhouse with plenty of character in pretty Rutland village; meandering rooms and intimate enclaves filled with period features, black-beamed country bar with wall timbering and coal fire, smarter airy room to the right with mix of ancient and modern tables on dark blue carpet, corner fire, two dining rooms, one with stripped-stone walls and old open cooking range, thatched roof over later extension with beer garden; Grainstore ales, good range of wines by the glass and several malt whiskies; much liked food, warm friendly service; rare nurdling bench (a game involving old pennies), background music; children and dogs (in bar) welcome; closed Sun evening, Mon.

THORPE LANGTON SP7492
★Bakers Arms (01858) 545201
Off B6047 N of Market Harborough; LE16 7TS Civilised thatched restauranty pub with small bar; very good imaginative food (must book) from regularly changing menu including several fish/seafood dishes, cottagey beamed linked areas and stylishly simple country décor, a well kept ale from Langton (brewed in the village) and well chosen wines by the glass, friendly licensees and efficient service; no under-12s or dogs, picnic-sets in back garden with country views, closed Sun evening, Mon and weekday lunchtimes.

THRUSSINGTON SK6415
Star (01664) 424220
Village signposted off A46 N of Syston; The Green; LE7 4UH Smartly modernised 18th-c inn overlooking pretty village green; L-shaped bar with low stripped beams, broad floorboards, inglenook woodburner and unusual double-sided high-backed settle; Belvoir Star Bitter, a couple of guests and a good choice of wines by the glass; steps up to skylit dining room with banquettes and high-backed chairs; popular pubby food including lunchtime sandwiches and vegan options, Tues fish and chips, Weds steak and Thurs burger nights; background music, Sun quiz, TV; children and dogs (in bar) welcome; picnic sets on flagstoned terrace and side garden; nine well appointed bedrooms, open all day from 8am for breakfast.

UPPER HAMBLETON   SK8907
Finchs Arms (01572) 756575
Off A606; Oakham Road; LE15 8TL
17th-c stone inn on Rutland Water peninsula
(sister pub to the Admiral Hornblower
in Oakham); beamed and flagstoned bar
with log fires and old settles, five real ales
such as Castle Rock and Grainstore, good
selection of wines by the glass including
champagne, modern back restaurant
opening on to spacious hillside terrace
with lovely views over the water, well liked
food from ciabattas and sharing boards
up, also afternoon teas, friendly service;
children and dogs (in bar) welcome, good
surrounding walks, ten bedrooms, open all
day, food all day Sun.

UPPINGHAM   SP8699
Falcon (01572) 823535
High Street East; LE15 9PY Quietly
refined old ironstone coaching inn in
attractive market town close to Rutland
Water; oak-panelled bar, hand-carved
fireplace mantels and antiques, spacious
nicely furnished lounge and restaurant,
big windows overlooking market square;
good food from bar snacks up and popular
afternoon tea; own Uppingham Brewhouse
ales (newly opened brewery is behind the
hotel) and guests, efficient friendly service;
some live folk and jazz; children and dogs
(in bar) welcome, back garden with terrace,
smart bedrooms (some in converted stable
block); open all day.

UPPINGHAM   SP8699
Vaults (01572) 823259
Market Place next to church; LE15 9QH
Attractive old pub in sought-after Rutland
town (sister to adjacent Falcon hotel);
compact interiors with light contemporary
feel, beamed downstairs bar, two pleasant
upstairs dining rooms, popular reasonably
priced traditional food along with pizzas
and vegan and gluten-free options; own
Uppingham Brewhouse ales and guests,
several wines by the glass, friendly service;
background music, sports TV; children
and dogs welcome, tables out overlooking
picturesque square; four bedrooms (book via
Falcon), open all day.

WALTHAM ON THE WOLDS   SK8024
Royal Horseshoes (01664) 464346
Melton Road (A607); LE14 4AJ
Attractive sympathetically restored stone
and thatch pub with rooms overlooking
village green; traditional interiors with
interesting features including carved
wooden bar panels from Buckminster Hall,
two main rooms with beams and open fires,
good varied choice of generous reasonably
priced food, well kept ales from maybe
Castle Rock, Marstons, Sharps and guests,

carefully chosen wine list and some 30 gins;
darts; children welcome, no dogs inside,
courtyard tables, good value comfortable
bedrooms in annexe, hearty breakfast, open
all day weekends.

WHITWICK   SK4316
Three Horseshoes (01530) 484522
Leicester Road; LE67 5GN Takings are
still collected in a pint glass (there's no till)
at this unpretentious and unchanging brick
local known to customers as Polly's; long
quarry-tiled bar with old wooden benches
and open fires, tiny snug to the right, well-
kept Bass and Marstons Pedigree, no food;
piano, darts, dominoes and cards; outside
loos, open all day.

WOODHOUSE EAVES   SK5214
Curzon Arms (01509) 890377
Maplewell Road; LE12 8QZ Cheerful old
beamed pub in pretty Charnwood Forest
village (same group as the Crown at Old
Dalby, Windmill at Wymeswold etc); popular
food (not Sun evening) from lunchtime
sandwiches and pub favourites up, also Weds
steak night and weekday lunchtime/early
evening set menu, Sharps Doom Bar and a
couple of guests, several wines by the glass
and cocktails, welcoming though sometimes
overstretched service, attractive up-to-date
décor in linked areas; background music,
Tues quiz, TV; children, walkers and dogs
welcome, seating, picnic sets and
striped umbrellas on terrace and lawn, open
all day day Fri-Sun.

WOODHOUSE EAVES   SK5313
★Wheatsheaf (01509) 890320
*Brand Hill; turn right into Main Street,
off B591 S of Loughborough; LE12 8SS*
Brick and stone wisteria-clad country pub
with traditionally furnished beamed bar
areas with open fires and stained glass,
smartly refurbished dining rooms, ales such
as Adnams, Charnwood, Fullers and Timothy
Taylors, several wines by the glass and
generally well liked food, friendly service;
children and dogs (in bar) welcome, seats
outside in courtyard under parasols, open all
day Sat, closed Sun evening.

WYMESWOLD   SK6023
Windmill (01509) 881313
Brook Street; LE12 6TT Well liked
side-street village pub overlooking a brook
(sister to the Crown at Old Dalby and Curzon
Arms in Woodhouse Eaves); imaginative
décor with vintage trunks and leather-bound
books, enjoyable locally sourced food from
lunchtime snacks up including set menus,
Tues steak nights and Sun roasts; Sharps
Doom Bar and guest ales; children and dogs
(in bar) welcome, appealing back garden
with decked area, open all day Fri-Sun, no
food Sun evening.

Lincolnshire

BASTON

White Horse 🎯 🍷

TF1113 Map 8

(01778) 560923 – www.thewhitehorsebaston.co.uk

Church Street; PE6 9PE

Refurbished village pub with real ales, welcoming staff and good, popular food

This 18th-c pub has been painted blue and interestingly renovated using reclaimed farm materials that include the bricks in the bay window, the boards in the ceiling, some of the beams and the huge piece of sycamore that acts as the counter in the snug bar. The main bar has built-in wall seats with scatter cushions, windsor and farmhouse chairs and stools around all sorts of tables on wooden flooring, a woodburning stove in a brick fireplace (with big logs piled into another) and horse-related items on pale paintwork; background music, darts, TV and board games. The dining area is similarly furnished. Customers come from far and wide for both the impressive food and the wide choice of drinks; staff are friendly. Stools line the blue-painted counter where they keep Adnams Southwold, Nene Valley Blonde and a couple of guests, perhaps from Hopshackle and Youngs, on handpump, 12 wines by the glass, 14 gins and ten malt whiskies. There are seats and tables on a side terrace.

🎯 First class food includes sandwiches, game terrine with pickled girolles and spiced wine jelly, twice-baked gruyère cheese soufflé with parmesan crisp, tiger prawns with sweet chilli and lime, beetroot and feta burger with olive tapenade and chips, pork belly with spiced apple mash and parsnip crisps, chargrilled rib-eye, fish of the day, butternut squash, coconut and pine nut curry with cauliflower rice, and puddings such as chocolate posset with honeycomb and sweet cherry jelly and pear and honey tarte tatin with stem ginger sorbet. *Benchmark main dish: beef burger with tomato, mozzarella and basil pesto and chips £14.50. Two-course evening meal £22.00.*

Free house ~ Licensees Ben Larter and Germaine Stribling ~ Real ale ~ Open 4-11 Mon, Tues; 12-11 Weds, Thurs; 12-midnight Fri, Sat; 12-10.30pm Sun ~ Bar food 5.30-9 Tues; 12-2.30, 5.30-9 Weds-Fri; 9.30-9 Sat; 9.30-6 Sun ~ Restaurant ~ Children welcome until 9pm only ~ Dogs allowed in bar

'Children welcome' means the pub says it lets children inside without any special restriction. If it allows them in, but to restricted areas such as an eating area or family room, we specify this. Places with separate restaurants often let children use them, and hotels usually let children into public areas such as lounges. Some pubs impose an evening time limit – let us know if you find one earlier than 9pm.

HEIGHINGTON

TF0369 Map 8

Butcher & Beast ◖

(01522) 790386 – www.butcherandbeast.co.uk

High Street; LN4 1JS

Traditional village pub with pubby food and thoughtful choice of drinks

The lovely hanging baskets and tubs make quite a show at the front of this Batemans pub in summer. The terrific range of drinks chosen by the hands-on, hard-working licensees includes half a dozen real ales on handpump including Batemans XB, XXXB and seasonal ales, two farm ciders, eight wines by the glass, 30 gins and 20 malt whiskies. The simply decorated bar has a thriving atmosphere, comfortable wall banquettes, pubby furnishings and stools along the counter, while the snug has red-cushioned wall settles and high-backed wooden dining chairs. A beamed and extended dining room is neatly set with an attractive mix of wooden or painted chairs around chunky tables on floorboards, and there's a woodburning stove. Throughout, the cream or yellow walls are hung with old village photos and country pictures. The garden has a new patio area with a pergola and rattan-style furniture.

🍴 Tasty food includes creamy garlic mushrooms, chicken bites with barbecue sauce, crispy prawns with sweet chilli sauce, mushroom and pepper stroganoff with rice, Penang curry with coconut sauce, cauliflower and green beans, baked salmon in tomato sauce, chicken in apricot and stilton sauce, burger with toppings and relish, lambs liver and bacon casserole, squash, red onion and cranberry tagine, and puddings such as chocolate brownie fudge cake and sticky toffee pudding with toffee sauce. *Benchmark main dish: ham hock, chicken and leek pie £12.70. Two-course evening meal £20.00.*

Batemans ~ Tenants Mal and Diane Gray ~ Real ale ~ Open 12-11; 12-10.30 Sun ~ Bar food 5-8 Tues-Thurs; 12-8 Fri, Sat; 12-4 Sun; closed Mon ~ Restaurant ~ Children welcome away from bar ~ Dogs allowed in bar

HOUGH-ON-THE-HILL

SK9246 Map 8

Brownlow Arms ⭐ ♆ 🛏

(01400) 250234 – www.thebrownlowarms.com

High Road; NG32 2AZ

Lincolnshire Dining Pub of the Year

Refined country house with beamed bar, real ales and imaginative food; comfortable bedrooms

This attractive stone inn has been run with great care by the Willoughbys, husband and wife, for decades. The comfortable and warmly welcoming bar has beams, plenty of panelling, some exposed brickwork, local prints and scenes, a large mirror, and a pile of logs beside a big fireplace. The carefully arranged furnishings give the impression of several separate and cosy areas, with seating including elegant, stylishly mismatched upholstered armchairs; background music. Served by impeccably polite staff, the ales on handpump are Timothy Taylors Landlord and two guests, usually from Yorkshire Dales; also, 13 wines by the glass and 11 malt whiskies. The panelled dining room with its white-clothed tables and stripy upholstered chairs is a suitably smart setting for the seriously good food. There's also some seating outside on a fenced-off terrace with fields beyond. The five bedrooms are well equipped and comfortable and the breakfasts are very good. It's a delight to find yourself here after the tedium of the A1.

Delicious food includes sandwiches, Cromer crab and mascarpone toasties, moules marinière, twice-baked lincolnshire poacher souffle with creamed leeks, crispy onion and chives, wild mushroom risotto with parmesan crisp and truffle oil, braised ox cheek with bourguignon sauce and horseradish mash, Burghley Estate lamb cutlets, shepherd's pie, carrots and red currant jus, and puddings such as dark chocolate crémeux, chocolate soil, caramel and gingerbread and strawberry eton mess with champagne sorbet. *Benchmark main dish: pan-fried sea bream with sautéed potatoes, tomato, spinach and globe artichoke £20.95. Two-course evening meal £28.00.*

Free house ~ Licensee Paul Willoughby ~ Real ale ~ Open 6-11 Tues; 12-3, 6-11 Weds-Sat; 12-3 Sun; closed Mon ~ Bar food 6-9 Tues; 12-2, 6-9 Weds-Sat; 12-2.30 Sun ~ Restaurant ~ No under-8s in evening or Sun ~ Bedrooms: £110

INGHAM SK9483 Map 8

Inn on the Green

(01522) 730354 – www.innonthegreeningham.co.uk

The Green; LN1 2XT

Nicely modernised place with a happy atmosphere, thoughtfully prepared food and several ales

This stone pub overlooking the village green is a good all-rounder, run by experienced and established owners. Many customers are here for the excellent food, while the informal, pubby bar with its log fire is popular with locals. Here you'll find Sharps Doom Bar and three guests, such as local Ferry Ales, Milestone Welsh Dragons, Oldershaw Mosaic Blonde and Pheasantry Best Bitter and Roosters Buckeye, on handpump, ten wines by the glass, 20 malt whiskies and 40 gins, served by attentive staff. Several tables here may also be occupied by those enjoying the tasty food. The beamed and timbered dining room is spread over two floors, with lots of exposed brickwork, local prints and a warm winter fire; do book ahead to be sure of a table. The lounge between these rooms has leather sofas and background music and a bar counter where you can buy home-made jams, marmalade and chutney. They hold a quiz every other Wednesday. Dogs are allowed outside (and in the bar on days when there is no food service).

 Tempting food using some own-grown produce includes sandwiches, salmon fishcakes with home-made tartare sauce, pâté of the day with red onion marmalade, chickpea fritters with vegan churros, aubergine jam and pickled carrot, local sausages with chive mash and onion gravy, burger with toppings and fries, Persian-spiced lamb with flatbread and coleslaw, pulled pork hash with fried egg, mini paella, and puddings such as double chocolate brownie with salted caramel ice-cream and gooseberry and ginger eton mess; they also offer breakfast (9-10.30am) on the last Saturday of the month and a takeaway menu (evenings Thursday-Saturday, all day Sunday). *Benchmark main dish: roasted hake with pea, broad bean amd crème fraîche risotto £13.50. Two-course evening meal £20.00.*

Free house ~ Licensees Andrew Cafferkey and Sarah Sharpe ~ Real ale ~ Open 12-9 Tues, Weds; 12-10 Thurs, Sun; 12-11 Fri, Sat ~ Bar food 12-8.15 Thurs-Sat; 12-6.30 Sun ~ Restaurant ~ Children welcome until 9pm

STAMFORD TF0306 Map 8

George of Stamford

(01780) 750750 – www.georgehotelofstamford.com

High Street, St Martins (B1081 S of centre, not the quite different central pedestrianised High Street); PE9 2LB

Lovely coaching inn with traditional bar, several dining areas and lounges, excellent staff and top class food and drink; bedrooms

The most pubby part of this splendid historic hotel is the little York Bar at the front. It offers Adnams Broadside, Fullers London Pride and Grainstore Triple B on handpump, an exceptional list of 160 wines and ten malt whiskies; food choices here are simple. This main part of the building was erected in 1597 for Lord Burghley (whose nearby Elizabethan house is well worth visiting) and it is full of genuine character. The atmosphere throughout remains gently civilised and yet informal, and service is first class. The various areas are furnished with all manner of seats from leather, cane and antique wicker to soft sofas and easy chairs, and there's a room to suit every occasion. The central lounge is particularly striking with sturdy timbers, broad flagstones, heavy beams and massive stonework. Service is professional yet friendly. There's an amazing oak-panelled restaurant (jacket required) and a less formal Garden Room restaurant, which has well spaced furniture on herringbone glazed bricks around central tropical planting. Seats in the charming cobbled courtyard are highly prized and the immaculately kept walled garden is beautifully landscaped; there are also sunken lawns and croquet. Bedrooms are individually and thoughtfully decorated and breakfasts are splendid.

The simplest food option is the York Bar snack menu with sandwiches (their toasties are especially good), a proper ploughman's and a plate of smoked salmon with capers. Excellent food in the restaurants (with a separate vegan and vegetarian menu) includes moules marinière, beetroot carpaccio, truffled mushroom ravioli, half lobster with mild chilli sauce on spaghetti, calves liver with parsley mash and red onion marmalade, sweet potato gnocchi with wild garlic pesto, rack of Cumbrian lamb with roasted garlic, herb crust and dauphinoise potatoes, and puddings from their famous trolley such as orange and carrot syllabub and a classic sticky toffee pudding. *Benchmark main dish: sirloin steak sandwich £14.85. Two-course evening meal £30.00.*

Free house ~ Licensee Paul Reseigh ~ Real ale ~ Open 11-11; 11-10.30 Sun ~ Bar food all day ~ Restaurant ~ Children welcome ~ Dogs allowed in bar & bedrooms ~ Bedrooms: £250

STAMFORD   TF0307   Map 8

Tobie Norris 🍺

(01780) 753800 – www.kneadpubs.co.uk/the-tobie-norris
St Pauls Street; PE9 2BE

A warren of ancient rooms, a good period atmosphere, a fine choice of drinks, enjoyable food and seats outside

There's plenty of places to sit in this beautifully restored building, which dates from the late 13th c and was once a bell foundry. The charming series of small, characterful rooms have worn flagstones and meticulously stripped stonework, with a huge hearth for the woodburning stove in one room, and steeply pitched rafters in one of the two upstairs rooms. A snug end conservatory opens out to a narrow but sunny two-level courtyard with seats and tables. There's a wide variety of furnishings from pews and wall settles to comfortable armchairs, and a handsomely panelled shrine to Nelson and the Battle of Trafalgar. Attentive, friendly staff serve St Austell Tribute, Oakham Citra and local guests from the likes of Baker's Dozen, Hopshackle and Nene Valley on handpump, farm cider and 19 wines by the glass; board games and TV.

Enjoyable food includes focaccia sandwiches and pizza wraps, sharing boards, beetroot falafel with tzatziki, whitebait with paprika mayonnaise, sea bass with vegetable stir-fry and yuzu dressing, Indian-style burger with sag aloo and sweet onion bhaji, beer-battered fish and chips, pork belly with black pudding bubble and squeak, buttered greens, roasted carrots and cider jus, and puddings such as chocolate melting pot (for two) and lemon tart with winter berry compote and strawberry ice-cream. *Benchmark main dish: stone-baked pizza with a choice of toppings £10.95. Two-course evening meal £24.00.*

Knead Pubs ~ Licensee Matthew Williamson ~ Real ale ~ Open 10am-11pm; 10am-midnight Fri, Sat; 11-10.30 Sun ~ Bar food 12-2.30, 6-9 Mon-Thurs; 12-9.30 Fri, Sat; 12-8 Sun ~ Children welcome until 8pm ~ Dogs allowed in bar

Also Worth a Visit in Lincolnshire

Besides the fully inspected pubs, you might like to try these pubs that have been recommended to us and described by readers. Do tell us what you think of them: feedback@goodguides.com

ALLINGTON   SK8540
★**Welby Arms** (01400) 281361
The Green; off A1 at N end of Grantham bypass; NG32 2EA Friendly well run village inn; large simply furnished bar divided by stone archway, beams and joists, log fires (one in attractive arched brick fireplace), comfortable plush wall banquettes and stools, up to six changing ales, large selection of wines by the glass and plenty of malt whiskies, good locally sourced home-made food including blackboard specials, reasonable prices, can eat in bar or back dining lounge; children welcome, tables in walled courtyard with pretty flower-filled hanging baskets, picnic-sets on front lawn, comfortable bedrooms, open all day weekends.

ASLACKBY   TF0830
Robin Hood & Little John (01778) 440681 *A15 Bourne–Sleaford; NG34 0HL* Old mansard-roofed roadside country pub; split-level bar with beams, flagstones and woodburners, popular traditional food, daily specials, Timothy Taylors Landlord and guests, friendly staff, separate more modern oak-floored restaurant; children and dogs (in bar) welcome, tricky wheelchair access, large three-level outside terrace, open (and food) all day weekends.

BARHOLM   TF0810
Five Horseshoes (01778) 560238
W of Market Deeping; village signed from A15 Langtoft; PE9 4RA Welcoming old-fashioned village local, cosy and comfortable, with beams, rustic bric-a-brac and log fire, half a dozen well kept ales such as Adnams, Bass and Oakham, good range of wines, pizzas Fri and Sat evenings, summer barbecues and live music; pool room with TV; children and dogs welcome, large beer garden with play area and shady arbour, open all day weekends (from 1pm Sat).

BARNOLDBY LE BECK   TA2303
Ship (01472) 822308
Village signposted off A18 Louth–Grimsby; DN37 0BG Warm well furnished country pub with antiques and memorabilia in immaculate main lounge, good sensibly priced home cooking, fresh Grimsby fish, good Sunday lunch, friendly attentive service, well kept beers including Black Sheep Best Bitter, good range of wines, comfortable dining room, pleasant village setting, closed Sun evening and Mon.

BASSINGHAM   SK9160
Five Bells (01522) 788269
High Street; LN5 9JZ Cheerful old red-brick pub with well liked food including good value lunchtime set menu (Mon-Thurs), steak night (Weds) and fish night (Thurs), ales including Greene King and Sharps, and range of brandies, efficient friendly service, bare-boards interior with hop-draped beams, country furniture and cosy log fires, lots of brass and bric-a-brac, an old well in one part; well behaved children and dogs welcome, a few tables out in front fenced from road, open all day (food till 7pm Sun).

BELCHFORD   TF2975
★**Blue Bell** (01507) 533602
Village signed off A153 Horncastle–Louth; LN9 6LQ Popular 18th-c dining pub with cosy comfortable bar, Batemans XB and guests, good traditional and modern food (booking advised), efficient friendly service, restaurant; children and dogs welcome, picnic-sets in terraced back garden, useful base for Wolds walks and Viking Way (remove muddy boots), open all day Sun.

BICKER   TF2237
Red Lion (01775) 821200
A52 NE of Donnington; PE20 3EF Nicely decorated 17th-c village pub; enjoyable home-made food including set lunch and popular Sun carvery, also a Lincolnshire tapas menu, friendly helpful

service, Courage Directors, Greene King IPA, Adnams Southwold and a guest, bowed beams (some painted), exposed brickwork and half panelling, wood and flagstone floors, logburners, part-raftered restaurant; quiz first Weds of month; children welcome, dogs in bar, rattan-style furniture on brick terrace with pergola, lawned garden, open all day Sun till 7pm, closed Mon, Tues.

BILLINGBOROUGH   TF1134
★**Fortescue Arms** (01529) 240228
B1177, off A52 Grantham–Boston; NG34 0QB Beamed village pub with old stonework, exposed brick, panelling and big see-through fireplace in carpeted rooms, tables in bay windows overlooking high street, well kept ales such as St Austell and Sharps, enjoyable home-made food including occasional themed music nights, good friendly service even at busy times, Victorian prints, brass and copper, a stuffed badger and pheasant, dining rooms at each end; children and dogs welcome, picnic-sets and rattan-style furniture in sheltered courtyard with flowering tubs, useful big car park, open all day weekends.

BOSTON   TF3244
Mill (01205) 352874
Spilsby Road (A16); PE21 9QN Roadside pub under new management, reasonably priced food (not Tues) including some Italian choices and blackboard specials, Batemans XB and a guest; children welcome, tables out in front, open all day.

BOURNE   TF0920
★**Smiths** (01778) 426819
North Street; PE10 9AE Cleverly converted grocery store arranged over three floors; warren of interconnecting rooms with woodburners and open fires, walls hung with vintage enamel signs and mirrors, assorted items such as tilley lamps, pots, pans and cauldrons, even an old butcher's bike, Fullers London Pride, Oakham JHB and guests, nice wines by the glass and a dozen gins, good choice of enjoyable food including pizzas; background music, TV and games machine; children and dogs welcome, enclosed courtyard with metal tables and chairs, picnic-sets on grass and play area, open all day.

BURTON COGGLES   SK9725
Cholmeley Arms (01476) 550225
Village Street; NG33 4JS Three well kept changing ales in small beamed pubby bar with warm fire, generous helpings of good

reasonably priced home-made food, friendly accommodating staff, restaurant; children (till 8pm) and dogs welcome, farm shop, four comfortable modern bedrooms in separate building overlooking garden, handy for A1, open all day weekends.

CASTLE BYTHAM   SK9818
Castle Inn (01780) 411223
Off A1 Stamford–Grantham, or B1176; NG33 4RZ Friendly 17th-c beamed village pub; enjoyable pubby food and three well kept changing ales, fire in inglenook range (some food cooked here); events including quiz and live music; children and dogs welcome, farm shop, disabled access, tables on back terrace, open all day (from 4pm Mon).

CAYTHORPE   SK9348
Red Lion (01400) 272632
Signed just off A607 N of Grantham; High Street; NG32 3DN Popular 17th-c village pub recently refurbished and under new management; good fairly traditional home-made food, friendly helpful staff, well kept Adnams, a guest beer and sensibly priced wines, bare-boards bar with light wood counter, black beams and woodburner, modern restaurant; back terrace by car park, dogs welcome, well located for walking groups and cyclists, open all day weekends, closed Mon.

CHAPEL ST LEONARDS   TF5672
Admiral Benbow (01754) 871847
The Promenade; PE24 5BQ Small bare-boards beach bar in former shelter; ales including Black Sheep and two guests, foreign bottled beers and decent range of gin and other drinks, cakes and rolls plus dressed crab on peak weekends, friendly staff, cushioned bench seats, stools and barrel tables, lots of bric-a-brac and nautical memorabilia on planked walls and ceiling; children and dogs welcome, picnic-sets out on mock-up galleon, great sea views, open when the flag is flying.

CLAYPOLE   SK8449
Five Bells (01636) 626561
Main Street; NG23 5BJ Friendly brick-built village pub with good-sized beamed bar and smaller dining area beyond servery, well kept Tetleys and three mainly local guests, enjoyable reasonably priced home-made food including range of burgers, steaks and pizzas; pool and darts; children welcome, dogs in bar, grassy back garden with play area, four bedrooms, closed Mon and Tues lunchtimes, otherwise open all day.

Please keep sending us reports. We rely on readers for news of new discoveries, and particularly for news of changes – however slight – at the fully described pubs: feedback@goodguides.com, or (no stamp needed) Freepost THE GOOD PUB GUIDE, Random House Publishing, 20 Vauxhall Bridge Road, London SW1V 2SA.

CLEETHORPES TA3009
No 2 Refreshment Room
07905 375587 *Station Approach beneath the clock tower; DN35 8AX* Small comfortable station bar with well kept Hancocks HB, Rudgate Ruby Mild, Sharps Atlantic and Sea Fury and guests, three real ciders, friendly staff, interesting old pictures of the station, historical books on trains and the local area, no food apart from bar snacks and free Sun evening buffet; tables out under heaters, open all day.

CLEETHORPES TA3008
Nottingham House (01472) 505150
Sea View Street; DN35 8EU Seafront pub with lively main bar, lounge and snug, seven well kept ales including Oakham Citra, Tetleys Bitter and Timothy Taylors Landlord, good reasonably priced food from sandwiches and pub favourites up in bar or upstairs restaurant, helpful friendly staff; annual winter beer festival; children and dogs (in bar) welcome, bedrooms, good breakfast, open all day – new landlord as we went to press so may be changes.

CLEETHORPES TA3108
★ **Willys** (01472) 602145
Highcliff Road; south promenade; DN35 8RQ Popular mock-Tudor seafront pub enjoying panoramic Humber views; open-plan interior with tiled floor and painted brick walls, Bass and own good ales from visible microbrewery, also changing guests and Belgian beers, enjoyable home-made bar lunches at bargain prices, good mix of customers; children welcome, no dogs at food times, a few tables out on the prom, open all day (till 2am Fri, Sat).

COLEBY SK9760
Bell (01522) 813778
Village signed off A607 S of Lincoln, turn right and right into Far Lane at church; LN5 0AH Restauranty pub with very good food from owner-chef including early bird menu (Weds-Fri), welcoming staff, well kept Timothy Taylors and several wines by the glass (not cheap), bar and three dining areas; children over 8 welcome, terrace tables, village on Viking Way with lovely fenland views, open evenings Weds-Sat and lunchtime Sun.

DONINGTON ON BAIN TF2382
Black Horse (01507) 343640
Main Road; between A153 and A157, SW of Louth; LN11 9TJ Welcoming roadside village inn with two carpeted bars (back one with low beams) and restaurant, open fires and woodburner; good locally sourced food cooked by landlord-chef including daily specials, well kept changing ales and proper cider, games room with pool, darts and dominoes; children and dogs (in bars) welcome, picnic-sets in back garden, eight motel-style bedrooms, on Viking Way and handy for Cadwell Park race circuit, closed Mon lunchtime, Tues.

FOSDYKE TF3132
Ship (01205) 260764
Main Road (A17); PE12 6LH Useful roadside pub close to the River Welland; popular reasonably priced food from varied menu, also Sun carvery (two lunchtime sittings), a couple of Adnams beers and Batemans XB, friendly staff, boaty décor with quarry tiles, blue wainscotting and woodburner; children and dogs welcome, garden tables, open all day.

FULBECK SK9450
Hare & Hounds (01400) 273322
The Green (A607 Leadenham–Grantham); NG32 3JJ Converted 17th-c maltings overlooking attractive village green; modernised linked areas, easy chairs by bar's woodburner, highly regarded food from pub favourites up, friendly attentive service, four well kept ales and an affordable wine list, raftered upstairs function room; no dogs inside, terrace seating, eight good bedrooms in adjacent barn conversion, generous breakfast, open all day Sun till 8pm (food till 7pm).

GAINSBOROUGH SK8189
Eight Jolly Brewers (01427) 611022
Ship Court, Silver Street; DN21 2DW Small drinkers' pub in former warehouse; six interesting real ales, traditional cider and plenty of bottled beers, friendly staff and locals, beams and bare brick, more room upstairs; regular live music; seats outside, open all day.

GRASBY TA0804
Cross Keys (01652) 628247
Brigg Road; DN38 6AQ Welcoming country pub with lovely Wolds views (Lincoln Cathedral visible on a clear day); very good well presented/priced food from bar snacks and pub staples up (special diets catered for), bargain OAP menu 12-6pm Mon-Fri, well kept ales and good range of other drinks, cheerful efficient service; Tues quiz, live music some weekends, sports TV; children and dogs welcome, garden behind, handy for Viking Way walkers, open (and food) all day, kitchen closes 6.30pm Sun, 7pm Mon.

GREAT LIMBER TA1308
★ **New Inn** (01469) 569998
High Street; DN37 8JL Handsome place (Grade II listed) with a good mix of regulars and visitors; many are here for the impressive food but there's also a proper working bar with windsor chairs, red button-back wall seats and oak tables on pale floorboards, two fireplaces, shelves of books, also a two-part dining room, modern art, black and white photos and big mirrors throughout,

Theakstons Best plus guests such as Timothy Taylors Landlord and Bombardier on handpump, good selection of wines by the glass, interesting food using organic produce from the Brocklesby Estate (of which the pub is part); quiz, darts; children welcome in restaurant, dogs in bar and bedrooms, landscaped back garden with assorted seating, ten peaceful, comfortable bedrooms and excellent breakfast.

GREAT GONERBY   SK8938
Recruiting Sergeant (01476) 562238
High Street; NG31 8JP Friendly village pub with popular good value food cooked to order from lunchtime baguettes up, well kept Everards ales, comfortable back restaurant (separate menu); TV; children and dogs (in bar) welcome, disabled access/loo, open all day Fri-Sun, no evening food Sun and Mon, handy for A1.

HEALING   TA2110
Pig & Whistle (01472) 884544
Healing Manor, Stallingborough Road; DN41 7QF Pub attached to the Healing Manor Hotel; good food from bar meals up (cooked in the hotel kitchen), real ales including a house beer from local Axholme, extensive wine list and ample gins; children and dogs welcome (menus for both), 36-acre grounds, open (and food) all day.

KIRKBY ON BAIN   TF2462
★ Ebrington Arms (01526) 354560
Main Street; LN10 6YT Popular village pub with good value traditional food (not Mon, booking advised) and half a dozen well kept ales such as Adnams, Sharps and Timothy Taylors, friendly staff, beer mats on low 16th-c beams, carpets and banquettes, open fire, restaurant behind; darts; children and dogs welcome, disabled access/toilet, tables out in front by road, lawn to the side with play equipment, campsite next door, closed Mon lunchtime.

KIRMINGTON   TA1011
Marrowbone & Cleaver
(01652) 688335 *High Street; DN39 6YZ* Friendly 19th-c local owned by British motorcycle racer/presenter Guy Martin and his sister; enjoyable good value home-made food (all day Sun) from sandwiches to blackboard specials, three well kept ales including a house beer from Batemans and Sharps Doom Bar, newly refurbished with wooden flooring and log fire, flying and racing memorabilia, snug, dining conservatory; live music (usually last Sat of month), darts; children welcome, picnic-sets on side lawn, no food weekday lunchtimes, open all day.

LEADENHAM   SK9552
George (01400) 272251
Off A17 Newark–Sleaford; High Street; LN5 0PN Former coaching inn with comfortable old-fashioned two-room bar; well kept ales, several wines by the glass and remarkable range of over 700 whiskies, good choice of enjoyable food from fairly pubby menu including steaks, Sun carvery, friendly helpful service, restaurant; events including live music and comedy nights; children and dogs welcome, outside seating, six annexe bedrooms, open all day.

LINCOLN   SK9871
Dog & Bone (01522) 522403
John Street; LN2 5BH Comfortable and welcoming backstreet local with well kept Batemans, several guest beers, log fires, various things to look at including collection of valve radios, local artwork and exchange-library of recent fiction; background and live music, beer festivals; dogs welcome, picnic-sets on back terrace, open all day weekends, from 4.30pm other days (3.30pm Fri).

LINCOLN   SK9771
Jolly Brewer (01522) 528583
Broadgate; LN2 5AQ Popular no-frills pub with unusual art deco interior; half a dozen well kept ales, real cider such as Broadoak Moonshine, and decent range of other drinks, friendly staff; regular live music including Weds open mike night, darts; back courtyard with covered area, open all day, closed Mon.

LINCOLN   TF0854
Red Lion (01526) 321686
North Street, Digby; LN4 3LY Welcoming family-run village pub; comfortable beamed front bar, restaurant and a couple of other snug dining areas, good reasonably priced food cooked by chef-landlady, Weds steak night, changing ales, helpful friendly service; Sun quiz, pool, darts, pub games; children welcome, closed Mon and lunchtime Tues, no food Sun evening.

LINCOLN   SK9771
Strugglers (01522) 535023
Westgate; LN1 3BG Cosily worn-in beer lovers' haunt tucked beneath the castle walls, built in 1841 and once run by the local hangman (note the pub sign); half a dozen or more well kept ales including Greene King Abbot and Ossett Yorkshire Blonde, bare boards throughout with lots of knick-knacks and pump clips, two open fires (one in back snug); some live acoustic music; no children inside, dogs welcome, steps down to sunny back courtyard, cash only, open all day (till 1am Thurs-Sat).

If we know a pub is cash-only, we say so. This is very rare: almost everywhere accepts credit and debit cards now.

LINCOLN
SK9771
Victoria (01522) 541000
Union Road; LN1 3BJ Old-fashioned
local just outside the castle gates; simply
furnished tiled front lounge with pictures of
Queen Victoria, coal fire, half a dozen well
kept ales including Batemans, Castle Rock
and Timothy Taylors, foreign draught/bottled
beers and real cider, basic lunchtime food,
friendly knowledgeable staff and good mix of
customers (gets especially busy at lunchtime
and later in the evening); live music Sat;
children and dogs welcome, seats on terrace,
abutting castle walls play area, good castle
views, open all day till midnight.

LINCOLN
SK9771
Widow Cullens Well (01522) 523020
Steep Hill; just below cathedral; LN2 1LU
Ancient reworked building on two floors
(upstairs open to the rafters); well kept/
priced Sam Smiths beers and good value
pubby food including children's choices,
chatty mix of customers (busy evenings
and weekends), friendly service, beams,
stone walls and log fire, back extension
with namesake well; dogs welcome, terrace
seating, cash only, mobile phones banned,
open all day.

LINCOLN
SK9771
★ Wig & Mitre (01522) 535190
*Steep Hill; just below cathedral;
LN2 1LU* Civilised café-style dining pub
with attractive period features and plenty
of character; big-windowed downstairs bar,
beams and exposed stone walls, pews and
Gothic furniture on oak boards, comfortable
banquettes, quieter upstairs dining room
with views of castle walls and cathedral,
antique prints and caricatures of lawyers/
clerics, well liked food from breakfast on
including good value set menus, extensive
choice of wines by the glass from good list,
ales such as Everards Tiger, Oakham JHB
and a beer from own microbrewery, friendly
service; children and dogs welcome, open
from 8.30am.

LONG BENNINGTON
SK8344
Reindeer (01400) 281382
*Just off A1 N of Grantham – S end of
village, opposite school; NG23 5EH*
Modernised 17th-c roadside pub; enjoyable
fair value food (not Sun evening) from snacks
and pub favourites to daily specials, three
real ales including Timothy Taylors Landlord,
friendly staff, low painted beams, log fire in
stone fireplace; background music; children
and dogs welcome, white picnic-sets on
fenced front terrace, closed Mon and Tues,
otherwise open all day.

LONG BENNINGTON
SK8344
Royal Oak (01400) 281332
*Main Road; just off A1 N of Grantham;
NG23 5DJ* Popular local with spacious

open-plan bar, several wines by the glass
and good sensibly priced home-made food
including specials and popular Sun roasts,
friendly helpful staff; children welcome, seats
out in front and in big back garden, path for
customers to river, open all day Tues-Sat, till
7.30pm Sun, 6pm Mon.

MARKET DEEPING
TF1310
Bull (01778) 343320
Market Place; PE6 8EA Refurbished
and extended under present management,
but the heavy-beamed medieval Dugout
Bar remains, flagstone and oak floors,
woodburner in original stone fireplace, well
kept Everards and guests, generous helpings
of enjoyable reasonably priced food served
promptly by friendly staff; children welcome,
beer garden with own bar in converted
stable, play area, open all day from 11am
(noon Sun).

MARKET RASEN
TF1089
Aston Arms (01673) 842313
Market Place; LN8 3HL Popular market-
square pub serving generous helpings of
inexpensive food, John Smiths, Theakstons
and a guest, friendly staff, beamed bar,
lounge and games area; children and well
behaved dogs welcome, side terrace with
ramp access, open all day.

NORTON DISNEY
SK8859
Green Man (01522) 789804
*Main Street, off A46 Newark–Lincoln;
LN6 9JU* Old beamed village pub-
restaurant; highly rated food (booking
advised) including pub standards, Black
Sheep and Castle Rock ales, friendly,
helpful staff, opened-up modernised
interior; children welcome, tables in
spacious back garden, open all day, closed
Mon and Tues.

OASBY
TF0039
Houblon Arms (01529) 701086
Village signed off A52; NG32 3NB
Extensively renovated 17th-c inn; low beams,
exposed stonework and open fire, good bar
food to more upmarket (and expensive)
restaurant meal choices, Marstons-related
ales, plenty of wines by the glass and range
of cocktails, afternoon teas, friendly service;
well behaved children welcome, garden
area behind, four bedrooms with four-
posters, Bentley chauffeur service for guests
(advanced booking required), open all day
from 8.30am.

PINCHBECK
TF2326
Ship (01775) 711746
Northgate; PE11 3SE Popular thatched
and beamed riverside pub; cosy split-level
bar with warm woodburner, real ales and
enjoyable generously served food, friendly
helpful staff, restaurant; children and dogs
welcome, tables out on decking, open all day
Sat, closed Sun evening, Mon.

REVESBY   TF2961
Red Lion (01507) 568665
A155 Mareham–Spilsby; PE22 7NU
19th-c red-brick former coaching inn set
back from the road; ample helpings of
enjoyable home-made food from reasonably
priced pubby menu, Sun carvery, can eat
in comfortable lounge bar with open fire or
separate dining room, well kept Batemans
ales; games area with pool; children
welcome, tables out at front and on large side
lawn, four bedrooms, open all day.

SCAMPTON   SK9579
Dambusters (01522) 731333
High Street; LN1 2SD Welcoming pub
with several beamed rooms around central
bar; masses of interesting Dambusters and
other RAF memorabilia, generous helpings
of reasonably priced straightforward food
(not Sun evening) from shortish menu, also
home-made chutneys, pâté and biscuits for
sale, seven interesting ales including own
microbrews (ceiling covered in beer mats),
short list of well chosen wines, pews and
chairs around tables on wood floor, log fire
in big two-way brick fireplace, more formal
seating at back; children and dogs welcome
(their black labrador is Bomber), very near
Red Arrows runway viewpoint, closed Mon,
otherwise open all day (till 7.30pm Sun).

SKENDLEBY   TF4369
Blacksmiths Arms (01754) 890662
*Off A158 about 10 miles NW of Skegness;
PE23 4QE* Cottagey-fronted 17th-c pub
with cosy two-room bar, low beams and log
fire, view into the cellar from servery, well
kept real ales and enjoyable sensibly priced
food served by friendly staff, back dining
extension with deep well; children welcome,
Wolds views from back garden, closed Sun
evening, all day Mon and Tues lunchtime.

SKILLINGTON   SK8925
Cross Swords (01476) 861132
The Square; NG33 5HQ Welcoming
19th-c stone pub on crossroads in delightful
village; good sensibly priced food and well
kept ales such as Batemans and Timothy
Taylors; background music; children and dogs
welcome (they have a jack russell called
Rocco), three annexe bedrooms, open all day
Sat, closed Mon.

SOUTH FERRIBY   SE9921
Hope & Anchor (01652) 635334
Sluice Road (A1077); DN18 6JQ
Nautical-theme pub; bar, snug and back
dining area with wide views over confluence
of Rivers Ancholme and Humber (plenty
for bird-watchers), popular locally sourced
food (not Sun evening) from pub standards
to more restauranty choices including
dry-aged steaks (not cheap), Theakstons
and two guests, several wines by the glass
including champagne, good friendly service;
children and dogs welcome, disabled access/
loos, outside tables, open all day, food till
6pm Sun.

SOUTH RAUCEBY   TF0245
Bustard (01529) 488250
Main Street; NG34 8QG Modernised
19th-c stone-built pub with good food from
shortish but varied menu (can be pricey,
early evening discount on some dishes), well
kept Batemans, Loxley and a house beer
called Cheeky Bustard, plenty of wines by
the glass, friendly efficient staff, flagstoned
bar with log fire, steps up to bare-stone
restaurant (former stables); live jazz
monthly; children welcome, no dogs inside,
attractive garden, open all day Sat, closed
Sun evening, Mon.

SOUTH WITHAM   SK9219
Angel (01572) 768302
Church Street; NG33 5PJ Old stone pub
next to the village church with good value
pubby food including popular Sun carvery
and themed nights such as fish and chips last
Fri of month, well kept Fullers London Pride
and a guest; sports TV; dogs welcome, closed
lunchtimes Mon, Weds and Fri, handy for A1.

SPALDING   TF2422
Priors Oven 07866 045778
Sheep Market; PE11 1BH Friendly well
run micropub in ancient building (former
bakery); small octagonal room with vaulted
ceiling, island bar serving up to six well kept
changing ales and local cider, no food apart
from jars of nuts, spiral stairs up to loos and
comfortable lounge with period fireplace;
open all day, closed Mon.

STAMFORD   TF0207
**All Saints Brewery – Melbourn
Brothers** (01780) 752186
All Saints Street; PE9 2PA Well reworked
old building (core is a medieval hall)
with warren of rooms on three floors;
upstairs bar serving bottled fruit beers
from adjacent early 19th-c brewery and
low-priced Sam Smiths on handpump, food
from pub favourites up including set deals,
ground-floor dining area with log fire and
woodburner, top floor with leather sofas and
wing chairs; children and dogs welcome,
picnic-sets in cobbled courtyard, brewery
tours, open all day.

STAMFORD   TF0306
★**Bull & Swan** (01780) 766412
High Street, St Martins; PE9 2LJ
Handsome former staging post with three
traditional linked rooms; low beams and
bare boards, portraits on stone or painted
walls, several open fires and good mix of
seating including high-backed settles, leather
banquettes and bow-window seats, Adnams
Southwold, Sharps Doom Bar and guests, 20
wines by the glass and 30 malt whiskies, well
liked food from panini and sharing boards up,

helpful staff; background music; children and dogs welcome, tables in back coachyard with pizza shed, character bedrooms, open all day.

STAMFORD · TF0207
Crown (01780) 763136
All Saints Place; PE9 2AG Substantial well modernised stone-built hotel in same small group as the Tobie Norris (also in Stamford, see Main Entries); good choice of popular food using local produce (some from their own farm), prompt friendly service, well kept ales from the likes of Fullers, Oakham and Timothy Taylors (can be pricey), lots of wines by the glass and cocktails, decent coffee and afternoon teas, spacious main bar with long leather-cushioned counter, substantial pillars, step up to more traditional flagstoned area with stripped stone and armchairs, restaurant; background music; well behaved children and dogs allowed, seats in back courtyard, 28 comfortable bedrooms (some in separate townhouse), good breakfast, open (and food) all day.

STAMFORD · TF0207
★ Jolly Brewer (01780) 755141
Foundry Road; PE9 2PP Welcoming unpretentious 19th-c stone pub; six well kept ales including local breweries such as Baker's Dozen, traditional cider and wide range of interesting whiskies, low-priced simple food (weekday lunchtimes and Fri evenings), open fire in brick fireplace; regular beer festivals and fortnightly Sun quiz, sports TV, pool, darts and other games; dogs welcome, picnic-sets out at front, open all day (no food Mon).

STOW · SK8881
Cross Keys (01427) 788314
Stow Park Road; B1241 NW of Lincoln; LN1 2DD Village dining pub close to interesting Saxon minster church; bar with painted half-panelling, bottles and decorative china on delft shelving, woodburner, well kept local ales and good food cooked by chef-landlord including daily specials, friendly attentive service, restaurant; quiz nights and cooking demonstrations; children welcome, open all day weekends, closed Mon and Tues.

SURFLEET · TF2528
Mermaid (01775) 680275
B1356 (Gosberton Road), just off A16 N of Spalding; PE11 4AB Two high-ceilinged carpeted rooms, huge sash windows, banquettes, captain's chairs and spindlebacks, Adnams and a couple of guests, good choice of fairly standard food including weekly themed nights, restaurant; background music; children welcome, pretty terraced garden with summer bar and seats under thatched parasols, play area walled

from River Glen, moorings, two bedrooms, closed Sun evening, Mon lunchtime.

TATTERSHALL THORPE · TF2159
Blue Bell (01526) 342206
Thorpe Road; B1192 Coningsby–Woodhall Spa; LN4 4PE Ancient low-beamed pub (said to date from the 13th c) with friendly cosy atmosphere; RAF memorabilia including airmen's signatures on the ceiling (pub was used by the Dambusters), big open fire, well kept ales, nice wines and enjoyable well priced pubby food, small dining room; some live music; garden tables, closed Sun evening, Mon.

TETFORD · TF3374
White Hart (01507) 533255
East Road, off A158 E of Horncastle; LN9 6QQ Friendly bay-windowed village pub dating from the 16th c; pleasant bar with curved-back settles and slabby elm tables on red tiles, inglenook log fire, Bombardier, Brains Rev James and a couple of guests, good value generous pubby food, other areas including village shop; live music Thurs; children and dogs welcome, sheltered back lawn, bedrooms; open all day weekends, from 3.30pm weekdays.

THREEKINGHAM · TF0836
Three Kings (01529) 240249
Just off A52 12 miles E of Grantham; Saltersway; NG34 0AU Former coaching inn with big entrance hall, fire and pubby furniture in comfortable beamed lounge, also a panelled restaurant and bigger dining/function room, good choice of enjoyable home-made food including Thurs steak night, Bass, Timothy Taylors Landlord and guests; Weds quiz; children and dogs (in bar) welcome, sunny paved terrace and small lawned area, various car club meetings, closed Mon.

WAINFLEET · TF5058
★ Batemans Brewery (01754) 880317
Mill Lane, off A52 via B1195; PE24 4JE Circular bar in brewery's ivy-covered windmill tower; Batemans ales in top condition, well priced artisan bar food and pubby dishes, giant outdoor games, lots of brewery memorabilia and plenty for families to enjoy; dogs (on leads) welcome, entertaining brewery tours and shop, tables on terrace and grass, open 11-4pm (11.30am-3.30pm in winter).

WASHINGBOROUGH · TF0170
Ferry Boat (01522) 790794
High Street; LN4 1AZ Friendly old village pub with enjoyable traditional food including good value two-course weekday lunch, a couple of ales such as Bombardier Golden

---

We say if we know a pub allows dogs.

and Sharps; high-raftered central bar with low-beamed areas off including restaurant, bare-stone and stripped-brick walls, mix of furniture on wood floors, open fire; background and some live music, Weds quiz, games part with pool, darts and TV; children and dogs (in bar) welcome, beer garden, good river walks nearby, open all day.

WEST DEEPING   TF1009
Red Lion (01778) 347190
King Street; PE6 9HP Stone-built pub with long low-beamed bar, four well kept ales, often Fullers London Pride and local Hopshackle, popular freshly made food including baguettes and pub classics; monthly folk music and quiz night, children welcome, tables in back garden with terrace and fenced play area, vintage car/motorcycle meetings, open till 4pm Sun, closed Mon.

WILSFORD   TF0043
Plough (01400) 230304
Main Street; NG32 3NS Traditional old two-bar village pub next to church; beams and open fires, a couple of real ales, nice range of wines and good choice of well presented bar food (till 6pm Sun), pleasant friendly service, dining conservatory; pool and other games in adjoining room; children welcome, small walled back garden, good local walks, open all day Fri and Sun, closed Mon.

WITHAM ON THE HILL   TF0516
Six Bells (01778) 590360
Village signed from A6121, SW of Bourne; PE10 0JH Well restored Edwardian stone inn with smart comfortable bar; popular food including wood-fired pizzas, 'auberge supper' and set menus, three well kept ales, good friendly service; children and

dogs welcome, rattan-style furniture on front terrace, nice village, five bedrooms, good breakfast, open all day Sat.

WOODHALL SPA   TF1963
Village Limits (01526) 353312
Stixwould Road; LN10 6UJ Modernised country pub-restaurant on village outskirts; good locally sourced food from pub standards up, well kept Batemans XB and a beer badged for the pub from local Horncastle, friendly service, banquettes in smallish beamed bar, dining room with light wood furniture on wood-strip floor; children welcome, eight courtyard bedrooms, good views from garden, closed Mon lunchtime.

WOOLSTHORPE   SK8334
★ Chequers (01476) 870701
Woolsthorpe near Belvoir, signposted off A52 or A607 W of Grantham; NG32 1LU Friendly former coaching inn, dating back in part to 1640, in Vale of Belvoir with views of Belvoir Castle; heavily beamed main bar with two big tables, mix of seating including leather chairs and banquettes and huge boar's head above log fire in big brick fireplace, also dining area on the left, corridor leading to airy extended main restaurant and another bar, background music, well executed seasonal food, friendly well trained staff; Grainstore Rutland Bitter and three constantly changing guests, 30 wines by the glass, around 30 gins, good whisky selection, cocktails and farm cider; teak furniture outside plus picnic-sets on edge of pub's cricket field, four comfortable bedrooms in converted stables next door, children welcome, dogs in bar and some bedrooms, open all day, food all day weekends.

Norfolk

Kings Head 🍴 🍷 🛏

(01603) 744977 – www.kingsheadbawburgh.co.uk

Harts Lane; A47 just W of Norwich then B1108; NR9 3LS

Dating from the 17th c, this busy pub has much character, with small rooms that have plenty of low beams and standing timbers, leather sofas and an attractive assortment of old dining chairs and tables on wood-strip floors. There is also a light, airy bar area, a knocked-through open fire and a couple of woodburning stoves in the restaurant areas. Adnams Broadside, Lacons and a couple of changing guests on handpump, 14 wines by the glass, 20 gins (including five local ones) and eight malt whiskies; background music. There are seats in the garden and the pub is opposite a little green. Add in impressive food, helpful, friendly service and good accommodation, this is an enjoyable all-rounder. The six bedrooms are comfortable and pretty, and there are also two self-catering apartments. Portable disabled ramp but no loos.

🍴 Top notch food from a range of local suppliers includes sandwiches, chargrilled pigeon breast with black pudding potato cake, roasted chicory and crispy quail egg, smoked haddock kedgeree with spinach and poached egg, spiced falafel burger with barbecue pulled jackfruit, beetroot and apple slaw and skinny fries, honey-roast ham with fried duck egg, Norfolk seafood platter (crayfish, whitebait, treacle-cured salmon and pickled cockles), chargrilled lamb skewer with pickled red cabbage and tzatziki, and puddings such as rhubarb and custard millefeuille with rhubarb and ginger gin sorbet and banoffee fondant with caramelised banana and rum and raisin ice-cream. *Benchmark main dish: beer-battered fish and chips £15.00. Two-course evening meal £23.00.*

Free house ~ Licensee Anton Wimmer ~ Real ale ~ Open 11-11 ~ Bar food 12-2, 5.30-9; 12-3, 5.30-8 Sun ~ Restaurant ~ Children welcome ~ Dogs allowed in bar ~ Bedrooms: £110

White Horse 🛏

(01263) 740574 – www.whitehorseblakeney.com

Off A149 W of Sheringham; High Street; NR25 7AL

Near the quay in this charming former fishing village, this busy convivial place is popular with both locals and holidaymakers. The long, split-level bar has high chairs by the counter, button-back seats along the walls, simple dining chairs and tartan-upholstered armchairs around pine-topped tables and Adnams Broadside, Ghost Ship, Southwold and a seasonal ale on handpump, a dozen wines by the glass and six malt whiskies; background music and board games. The airy dining conservatory has modern art on planked walls, white rattan armchairs with colourful scatter cushions around pale-topped tables on floor tiles and big ceiling lanterns. A breakfast room is furnished in a similar style to the bar and there's a cosy lounge with sofas and armchairs in front of a small woodburning stove. In a suntrap walled terrace to the side you'll find black rattan-style furniture under large parasols. Some of the contemporary, attractive and comfortable bedrooms have views of the coastal marshes; breakfasts are highly rated. Dogs are allowed in one bedroom.

A wide choice of good food includes lunchtime sandwiches (not Sunday), Thai-style crab cakes with Asian slaw and chilli dip, smoked salmon and crayfish caesar salad, local crab with chilli and lime linguine, sweet potato and chickpea tagine with lemon couscous, local steak burger with binham blue cheese, smoked bacon and chips, sea bass fillet with tomato and beetroot salad, and grilled marinated chicken with greek salad, halloumi, tzatziki and hummus, and puddings such as lemon curd eton mess and banana and praline parfait with glazed banana and raspberries. *Benchmark main dish: pork sausages with mustard mash and crispy onions £16.00. Two-course evening meal £24.00.*

Adnams ~ Tenant Nick Attfield ~ Real ale ~ Open 11-11; 11-10.30 Sun ~ Bar food 12-2.30, 6-9; 12-2.30, 6-8.30 Sun ~ Restaurant ~ Children welcome ~ Dogs allowed in bar & bedroom ~ Bedrooms: £99

BURSTON
Crown

(01379) 741257 – www.burstoncrown.com
Village signposted off A140 N of Scole; Mill Road; IP22 5TW

This relaxed 16th-c south Norfolk pub has a choice of cosy nooks in which to eat and drink. In fine weather there are painted seats and tables on an outside terrace, as well as a secluded garden and a play area for children. The best place to sit on a cold day is on a comfortably cushioned sofa in front of the woodburning stove in a huge brick fireplace in the heavily beamed bar room; there are also stools by a low chunky wooden table, and newspapers and magazines. The public bar on the left has a nice long table and panelled settle on an old brick floor in one alcove, a pool table, and more tables and chairs towards the back near a dartboard. The simply furnished, beamed dining room has another large brick fireplace. The walls are hung with paintings by local artists. Adnams Broadside and Southwold and guests such as Humpty Dumpty Little Sharpie, Three Blind Mice Nothing Rhymes with Orange and Winters Best on handpump or tapped from the cask, ten wines by the glass and seven malt whiskies; background music, board games, dominoes and cards.

Rewarding food cooked by the landlord includes sandwiches, chicken liver parfait with white port and juniper berries and red onion marmalade, beetroot-cured salmon pâté with root vegetable slaw, spinach and ricotta dumplings with olive and rosemary polenta and tomato compote, rib-eye steak diane, grilled sea bream with braised fennel, fennel velouté and brown shrimp, Hyderabad lamb shank with rice, and puddings such as sticky toffee pudding with butterscotch sauce and vegan chocolate brownie with dairy-free ice-cream. *Benchmark main dish: beer-battered haddock and chips 12.90. Two-course evening meal £20.00.*

Free house ~ Licensees Bev and Steve Kembery ~ Real ale ~ Open 12-11; 12-10.30 Sun ~ Bar food 12-2, 6.30-9; 12-4 Sun; no food Sun evening, Mon ~ Restaurant ~ Children welcome ~ Dogs allowed in bar

CASTLE ACRE
TF8115 Map 8
Ostrich
(01760) 755398 – www.ostrichcastleacre.com

Stocks Green; PE32 2AE

Located beside the tree-lined village green and close to the remains of a Norman castle and a Cluniac priory (English Heritage), this former coaching inn dates back in part to the 16th c. The building itself contains many interesting features, such as original masonry, beams and trusses. The L-shaped, low-ceilinged front bar (on two levels) has a woodburning stove in a huge fireplace, lots of wheelback chairs and cushioned pews around pubby tables on a wood-strip floor and gold patterned wallpaper; there's a step up to an area in front of the bar counter where there are similar seats and tables and a log fire in a brick fireplace. Helpful staff serve Adnams Ghost Ship and Greene King Abbot, IPA and Morland Old Speckled Hen on handpump, around a dozen wines by the glass and several malt whiskies; background music, darts and board games. There's a separate dining room with another brick fireplace. The sheltered garden has picnic-sets under parasols. Bedrooms are warm and comfortable.

 Pleasing food includes lunchtime sandwiches and ciabattas, confit smoked duck with beetroot and egg salad, seared scallops with roasted red onions, pancetta and fondue sauce, sharing platters (meat, fish or vegetarian), roast artichoke, chicory and halloumi salad, pizzas with lots of toppings, smoked haddock with poached egg, asparagus and cheese sauce, confit duck leg with carrot purée and honey-roast parsnips and sweet potatoes, sirloin steak with chips and red onion marmalade, and puddings such as hot chocolate fondant with vanilla ice-cream and mixed berry pannacotta. *Benchmark main dish: slow-cooked pork belly and maple beef with sautéed cabbage and bacon £18.50. Two-course evening meal £23.00.*

Greene King ~ Tenant Carl Wade ~ Real ale ~ Open 10am-10.30pm; 10am-11.30pm Sat, Sun ~ Bar food 12-3, 6-9; 12-3, 6-10 Sat ~ Restaurant ~ Children welcome ~ Dogs allowed in bar ~ Bedrooms: £95

GREAT MASSINGHAM
TF7922 Map 8
Dabbling Duck
(01485) 520827 – www.thedabblingduck.co.uk

Off A148 King's Lynn–Fakenham; Abbey Road; PE32 2HN

This attractive village pub has cosy bars with leather sofas and armchairs, a mix of antique wooden dining tables and chairs on flagstones or stripped wooden floors, a very high-backed settle, 18th- and 19th-c quirky prints and cartoons, and plenty of beams and standing timbers; the three woodburning stoves are put to good use in winter. At the back of the pub is the Blenheim room, just right for a private group, and there's also a candlelit dining room. If the weather is warm you can sit on the front terrace and take in the pleasant setting (the village green and big duck ponds are opposite); there are also seats and a play area in the enclosed back garden. There's Adnams Broadside and Ghost Ship and Woodfordes Wherry and Nelsons Revenge on handpump, more than a dozen wines by the glass and the pub's own-brand Mucky Duck gin, served from a bar counter made of great slabs of polished tree trunk; background music, TV, darts and board games. The six bedrooms within the pub are named after famous local sportsmen and airmen from the World War II air base in Massingham; there are also three larger garden rooms. Wheelchair access.

 High quality food includes sandwiches, pheasant tacos with salsa verde, pink onions and avocado, seared tuna steak with kimchi, edamame beans and miso orange dressing, falafel burger with dukkah yoghurt, halloumi and veggie fries, beer-battered cod with dripping chips, Thai massaman curry, barbecue jerk salmon fillet with couscous salad, and puddings such as pear and apple gateau with brown butter pear and brown butter ice-cream and sticky toffee pudding with milk ice-cream and toffee sauce.There is also a wide-ranging pizza menu (served in the garden or as takeaway). *Benchmark main dish: rare-breed burger with toppings and dripping chips £13.50. Two-course evening meal £21.00.*

Free house ~ Licensee Dominic Symington ~ Real ale ~ Open 8am-11pm ~ Bar food 12-9 ~ Restaurant ~ Children welcome ~ Dogs allowed in bar & bedrooms ~ Bedrooms: £120

KING'S LYNN   TF6119 Map 8

Bank House ⭐ 🍷 🛏

(01553) 660492 – www.thebankhouse.co.uk
Kings Staithe Square via Boat Street and along the quay in one-way system; PE30 1RD

Dating from the early 18th c when it was built for a wealthy wine merchant, this fine quayside building became a branch of Gurneys (later Barclays) Bank in 1780 and remained so until 1869. Helpfully open and serving some kind of food all day, this well run place has a number of stylish rooms, including the elegant bar (once the bank manager's office) with sofas and armchairs, a log fire with fender seating, Barsham Bitter Old Bustard and a guest beer on handpump, 18 wines by the glass, a wide choice of gins, six whiskies, interesting vodkas, cocktails and a farm cider; background music. The restaurant has antique chairs and tables on bare boards, an airy brasserie has sofas and armchairs around low tables and a large brick fireplace, and two other areas (one with fine panelling, the other with a half-size billiards table) have more open fires. The atmosphere throughout is gently civilised but easy-going, and service is helpful and courteous. An outside area, flanked by magnificent wrought-iron gates, has fire pits for warmth on chillier evenings, and the riverside terrace (lovely sunsets) has an open-air cocktail bar in summer. Most of the dozen charming bedrooms overlook the river and breakfasts are first class. The Corn Exchange theatre and arts centre is just five minutes away. Sister pub is the Rose & Crown in Snettisham.

🌟◉🍴 A fine choice of interesting food includes sandwiches, smoked salmon bonbon with kale slaw and ponzu dressing, antipasti sharing platters, chickpea, broccoli, tomato, cashew, goji berry and pomegranate salad, mussels (French or English style), sweet potato and gorgonzola risotto with toasted pine nuts, duck breast with hasselback potatoes, sautéed baby turnips, pancetta and maple syrup, and puddings such as ginger pannacotta with passion fruit and brandy snap and rum-soaked sultana and white chocolate bread and butter pudding with crème anglaise. *Benchmark main dish: steak burger with toppings and fries £14.00. Two-course evening meal £24.00.*

Free house ~ Licensee Michael Baldwin ~ Real ale ~ Open 12-10 ~ Bar food 12-8 ~ Restaurant ~ Children welcome ~ Dogs allowed in bar & bedrooms ~ Bedrooms: £145

LARLING   TL9889 Map 5

Angel 🍺 🛏

(01953) 717963 – www.angel-larling.co.uk
From A11 Thetford–Attleborough, take B1111 turn-off and follow pub signs; NR16 2QU

This 17th-c former coaching inn has been run by the same friendly family since 1913 – they even have the original visitors' books from 1897 to 1909. The comfortable 1930s-style lounge on the right has squared panelling, cushioned wheelback chairs, a nice long cushioned panelled corner settle and some good solid tables for eating; also, a collection of whisky-water jugs on a delft shelf over the big brick fireplace, a woodburning stove, a couple of copper kettles and some hunting prints. Adnams Southwold and four guests from breweries such as Crouch Vale, Oakham, Orkney and Swannay on handpump, ten wines by the glass, 100 malt whiskies including locally distilled St Georges, 50 gins and a farm cider. The quarry-tiled, black-beamed public bar has a good local feel, with a juke box, games machine, board games and background music. There's a neat grassed area behind the car park with picnic-sets around a big fairy-lit apple tree and a fenced play area. It gets busy in warm weather, when customers visiting Peter Beales Roses or enjoying the lovely surrounding walks arrive for refreshment, and for the annual beer festival (August) with more than 100 real ales and ciders, live music and a barbecue. The five bedrooms are attractive and comfortable and their four-acre meadow is used as a caravan and camping site from April to September. Dogs are allowed in the garden, but not in the pub.

❙❙ Honest food includes sandwiches and jacket potatoes, home-made pâté with red onion chutney, crayfish and prawn marie rose, butternut squash and five bean chilli, various burgers with toppings and chips, smoked haddock mornay, gammon with egg or pineapple, 'smothered chicken' with bacon and cheese, vegetarian lasagne, lamb chops, mixed grill, and puddings such as chocolate fudge cake and local ice-creams and sorbets. *Benchmark main dish: pie of the day £12.00. Two-course evening meal £20.00.*

Free house ~ Licensee Andrew Stammers ~ Real ale ~ Open 10.30am-11pm; 10.30-10.30 Sun ~ Bar food 12-9.30 (10 Fri, Sat) ~ Restaurant ~ Children welcome ~ Bedrooms: £90

NORWICH
Fat Cat 🍺

TG2109 Map 5

(01603) 624364 – www.fatcatpub.co.uk

West End Street; on foot from city centre (1 mile) turn R down Nelson Street off Dereham Road; NR2 4NA

Heaven for real ale lovers, this cheerful town pub lies tucked away in a residential area just west of the city centre. With bare floorboards throughout, the no-nonsense furnishings include plain pine tables and simple solid seats, lots of brewery memorabilia, bric-a-brac and stained glass; board games. The knowledgeable Mr Keatley and his hospitable staff can help guide you through the extraordinary choice of 32 perfectly kept and quickly changing beers. On handpump or tapped from the cask in a stillroom behind the bar – big windows reveal all – are their own beers (Fat Cat Bitter, Honey Ale, IPA, Marmalade Cat, Tom Cat and Wild Cat), as well as guests such as Adnams Mosaic, Crouch Vale Yakima Gold, Dark Star American Pale Ale, Fullers ESB, Green Jack Mahseer, Greene King Abbot, Oakham Bishops Farewell and Citra and Timothy Taylors Landlord – and many more choices from across the country. You'll also find 15 draught lagers and craft ales, over 20 international bottled beers, ten malt whiskies, ten rums and 22 ciders and perries. There are pavement tables outside. No children under the age of 16.

❙❙ Bar food consists of filled rolls and good pies at lunchtime (not Sunday).

Own brew ~ Licensee Colin Keatley ~ Real ale ~ Open 12-11; 11-midnight Sat ~ No under-16s inside ~ Dogs allowed in bar

---

If we don't specify bar meal times for a featured entry, these are normally 12-2 and 7-9; we do show times if they are markedly different.

SALTHOUSE  TG0743 Map 8

Dun Cow 🌟 🍺

(01263) 740467 – www.salthouseduncow.com

A149 Blakeney–Sheringham (Purdy Street, junction with Bard Hill); NR25 7XA

Next to the village green, with a garden that overlooks the salt marshes and the North Sea beyond, this Dutch-gabled 18th-c pub has an enviable location. It's popular with both locals and visitors, and many customers return on a regular basis. The flint-walled bar consists of a pair of high-raftered rooms opened up into one area, with stone tiles around the counter where regulars congregate, and a carpeted seating area with a fireplace at each end. Also, scrubbed tables, one very high-backed settle, country kitchen chairs and elegant little red-padded dining chairs, with big sailing ship and other prints. Adnams Ghost Ship, Norfolk Brewhouse Moon Gazer Golden Ale and Amber Ale and Woodfordes Wherry on handpump, 19 wines by the glass and 14 malt whiskies. Picnic-sets on the front grass look out towards the sea and there are more seats in the sheltered back courtyard and the orchard garden beyond.

 With quite an emphasis on fresh fish, the very good food includes sandwiches (until 5pm), crispy fried crab and cod bonbons, grilled local shellfish with garlic butter, fennel and olive salad and fries, panko-fried tuna loin with marinated cucumber, wasabi and ginger, smoked fish platters, battered fish and chips, local rib-eye with beans and fries, harissa-roasted cauliflower with fattoush salad, linguine with local crab, chilli, mint and lime, and puddings such as chocolate brownie with vanilla ice-cream and chilled peach soup with raspberries and raspberry sorbet. *Benchmark main dish: Mediterranean fish stew £17.00. Two-course evening meal £23.00.*

Punch ~ Lease Daniel Goff ~ Real ale ~ Open 11.30-11 ~ Bar food 12-9 Children welcome ~ Dogs allowed in bar

SNETTISHAM TF6834 Map 8

Rose & Crown 🌟 ♟ 🛏

(01485) 541382 – www.roseandcrownsnettisham.co.uk

Village signposted from A149 King's Lynn–Hunstanton just N of Sandringham; coming in on the B1440 from the roundabout just N of village, take first left into Old Church Road; PE31 7LX

Norfolk Dining Pub of the Year

With well trained, friendly staff, a fine range of drinks, excellent food and stylish bedrooms it is hardly surprising that this lovely inn remains a firm favourite with so many customers. The two main bars have distinct character and simple charm, with an open fire and woodburning stove, old quarry tiles or coir flooring, upholstered wall seating and wooden tables and chairs, candles on mantelpieces and daily papers. There are stools against the bar where locals enjoy real ales such as Adnams Broadside and Southwold, Eagle IPA, Woodfordes Wherry and a regularly changing guest on handpump; also, a dozen wines by the glass, around 20 gins (including local ones), seasonal cocktails and jugs of sangria, local cider and fresh fruit juices. A small wood-floored back room has old sports equipment, the landlord's sporting trophies and photos of the pub-sponsored village cricket team. The civilised little restaurant (decorated in soft greys) has cushions and picture mounts with splashes of bright green and cream candles in antique brass candlesticks. At the back of the building, two rooms make up the airy Garden Room, with sofas, wooden farmhouse and white-painted dining chairs around a mix of circular and square tables, church candles in crown-shaped holders, attractive striped blinds and doors that lead to the pretty walled garden. Here there are plenty of contemporary seats and tables underneath parasols, outdoor heaters, colourful herbaceous borders and a wooden galleon-shaped climbing structure for children. The 16 bedrooms are spacious and individually decorated and breakfasts very good. Disabled lavatories and wheelchair ramp. Sister pub is the Bank House in King's Lynn.

Impressive food using the best local produce includes sandwiches, sticky miso aubergine with satay rice, Staithe Smokehouse salmon with pickled kohlrabi and salted cucumber, sweet potato and chickpea stew with babaganoush, burger with fries, Moroccan spiced roasted lamb loin with lamb tagine pie, sweet potato purée and crispy chicken skin, pan-seared sea bass fillet with salt and vinegar mash, caviar and cockle chowder and spring roll, caesar salad with stuffed chicken, parmentier potatoes and charred baby gem, and puddings such as baked nutmeg custard with poached rhubarb and ginger snap and toffee apple tart with vanilla ice-cream. *Benchmark main dish: beer-battered haddock and chips £14.75. Two-course evening meal £23.00.*

Free house ~ Licensee Anthony Goodrich ~ Real ale ~ Open 11-11; 11-10.45 Sun ~ Bar food 12-8.30; 12-9 Fri, Sat ~ Restaurant ~ Children welcome ~ Dogs allowed in bar & bedrooms ~ Bedrooms: £120

THORNHAM
Lifeboat 🍺 🛏

TF7343 Map 8

(01485) 512236 – www.lifeboatinnthornham.com
A149 by Orange Tree, then first left; PE36 6LT

Tucked away on a quiet lane behind the village church, this homely traditional inn has been providing food and shelter on the Norfolk coast for more than 500 years. The formal entrance hall has sofas and fender seats by a big open fire, there's another room with more sofas and a cylindrical woodburner and also a simply furnished dining room. There's a great deal of character in the rambling rooms here and plenty of space for eating and drinking. The main bar has beams, big lamps, brass and copper jugs and pans, cushioned window seats, chairs and settles around dark sturdy tables on quarry tiles and a woodburning stove; the antique penny-in-the-hole game is hidden under a bench cushion. A second bar, favoured by locals, is smaller, with some fine carving around the counter. Five real ales on handpump including Adnams Ghost Ship, Norfolk Brewhouse Moon Gazer Pintail and Woodfordes Mardlers Mild and Wherry, good wines by the glass and 15 gins; background music and board games. A quarry-tiled conservatory (used for eating) has fairy lights and steps that lead up to the back garden with grey-painted picnic-sets and a couple of cabanas; out in front are more picnic-sets. The 13 bedrooms, some with marshland views, are warm and comfortable and you can walk from here to the salt marshes about a mile away.

Good quality food includes sandwiches, crispy brie with cranberry sauce, prawn cocktail, pea and feta risotto with crispy onions, home-cooked ham and eggs, roast chicken caesar salad, fresh local crab salad, burger with toppings, coleslaw and skinny fries, sea bass with dill butter and crushed new potatoes, rump steak with peppercorn sauce, and puddings such as chocolate and pecan brownie with chocolate sauce and sticky toffee pudding with caramel sauce. *Benchmark main dish: beer-battered fish and chips £16.00. Two-course evening meal £23.00.*

Punch ~ Tenant Lee Bye ~ Real ale ~ Open 11-11 ~ Bar food 12-9 ~ Restaurant ~ Children welcome ~ Dogs allowed in bar & bedrooms ~ Bedrooms: £165

The 🍺 symbol shows pubs that keep their beer unusually well, have a particularly good range or brew their own.

THORNHAM

TF7343 Map 8

Orange Tree 🏠📷 ♀ 🛏

(01485) 512213 – www.theorangetreethornham.co.uk
Church Street/A149; PE36 6LY

Set back from the coast road in an attractive carrstone and chalk village, this cosy dining pub is close to marshes and mudflats full of birdlife. The sizeable pubby bar has white-painted beams, red leather chesterfields in front of a log fire, and flowery upholstered or leather and wooden dining chairs and plush wall seats around a mix of tables on wooden or quarry-tiled floors. Many customers enjoy staying in the 17 well equipped, comfortable and up-to-date rooms here – you can choose between the Courtyard, Old Bakery annexe and Manor Lodge, and breakfasts are good. Woodfordes Wherry and two guest beers on handpump, 37 wines by the glass, 21 gins and five ciders; background music and TV. A little dining room leads off here with silver décor, buddha heads and candles, and the two-part restaurant is simple and contemporary in style. The sunny front garden is pretty with lavender beds and climbing roses, lots of picnic-sets under parasols, outdoor heaters and a small smart corner pavilion. At the back of the building is another outdoor area with children's play equipment. Lovely walks all around. They're kind to dogs and have a doggie menu plus snacks.

 Rewarding food includes sandwiches, tempura prawns, pan-fried black pearl scallops with black pudding, pancetta, pea purée and pea shoots, caramelised shallot tarte tatin, sharing platters, prawn, chicken or vegetable tikka masala, grilled halloumi burger, southern-style buttermilk chicken burger with sweet potato fries, toppings and slaw, halibut with tarragon gnocchi, sautéed wild mushroom, mussel popcorn and caper hollandaise, 15-hour smoked rack of ribs with slaw and fries, and puddings such as sticky parkin pudding with poached pear, green cardamom ice-cream and candied pecans, black meringue with poached plums and apple crumble cheesecake. *Benchmark main dish: 48-hour home-smoked brisket burger with fries £15.45. Two-course evening meal £24.50.*

Punch ~ Lease Mark Goode ~ Real ale ~ Open 11-11; 12-10.30 Sun ~ Bar food 12-3, 6-9; all day weekends ~ Restaurant ~ Children welcome ~ Dogs allowed in bar & bedrooms ~ Bedrooms: £119

THORPE MARKET

TG2434 Map 8

Gunton Arms ♀

(01263) 832010 – www.theguntonarms.co.uk
Cromer Road; NR11 8TZ

Its location in a grand country house set in a 1,000-acre deer park is just one of several factors that makes this place unique. Walls adorned with quality art by the likes of Lucien Freud, Frank Auerbach and Paula Rego (the owner is an art dealer) adds to the enjoyment of staying or dining here. A large entrance hall leads to the simply furnished bar with dark pubby chairs and tables on a wooden floor, a log fire, a long settle beside a pool table and high stools against the mahogany counter where they serve Adnams Broadside and Southwold, Woodfordes Wherry and a guest beer on handpump, 19 wines by the glass, 16 malt whiskies and two ciders; staff are chatty and helpful. Heavy curtains line an open doorway into a dining room, where vast elk antlers hang above a big log fire (they often cook over this) and there are straightforward chairs around scrubbed tables on stone tiles. A lounge, with comfortable old leather armchairs and a sofa on a fine rug in front of yet another log fire, has genuine antiques and standard lamps. The restaurant is more formal with candles and napery, and there are also two homely sitting rooms for hotel residents. Many of the walls are painted dark red and hung with assorted artwork and large mirrors; background music, darts, TV and board games. The 12 lovely bedrooms have many original fittings and views over Gunton Park, but no TV.

Robust food using Estate produce includes sandwiches (until 5pm), prawn and local crab salad with cucumber noodles and saffron aioli, pork belly with apple and peashoots, their own venison sausages with mash and onion gravy, chicken, bacon and leek pie, slow-roast lamb shoulder with bubble and squeak, shellfish with pickled samphire and sea purslane salad, well hung steaks or pork chops cooked over the open fire (not Sunday) with béarnaise sauce, cod fillet with purple sprouting broccoli and garlic pesto, and puddings such as chocolate truffle torte with griottine cherries and prune, armagnac and almond tart with clotted cream. *Benchmark main dish: venison stew £16.00. Two-course evening meal £23.00.*

Free house ~ Licensee Simone Baker ~ Real ale ~ Open 12-11; 12-10.30 Sun ~ Bar food 12-10 ~ Restaurant ~ Children welcome ~ Dogs allowed in bar & bedrooms ~ Bedrooms: £130

WARHAM   TF9441   Map 8

Three Horseshoes 🛏

(01328) 710547 – www.warhamhorseshoes.co.uk

Warham All Saints; village signed from A149 Wells-next-the-Sea to Blakeney, and from B1105 S of Wells; NR23 1NL

With gaslit bar rooms that have panelling and painted roughcast walls hung with china plates and royalist photographs, this old-fashioned flint and brick pub has plenty of charm. Padded leather or upholstered wall seats and kitchen chairs around rustic pine tables on quarry tiles and several Victorian fireplaces contribute to the bygone atmosphere. Adnams Ghost Ship, Woodfordes Wherry and a guest on handpump and 20 wines by the glass served through a hatch by friendly staff; darts, dominoes, shove-ha'penny, cards and board games. There's a courtyard garden with flower tubs, a terrace with metal chairs and tables and lawns with picnic-sets. Four stylish, comfortable bedrooms are next door in what was the post office; two more recently refurbished rooms are upstairs in the pub. Dogs are made welcome (they have a basset hound called Lola) and they hold a pie and pint festival on the August bank holiday.

The pub is well known for its traditional home-made pies such as beef and binham blue cheese or walnut, mushroom and stout (not Sunday). Other food options include filled rolls, roast beetroot, binham blue cheese and walnut salad, rabbit and pork terrine, chicken and cheddar croquettes with barbecue sauce, salt and pepper tofu with stir-fried vegetables and noodles, sausages with mash and onion gravy, beef burger with bacon and redcurrant jelly, beer-battered fish and chips, and puddings such as dark chocolate mousse with butterscotch sauce and pink prosecco jelly with raspberry sorbet. *Benchmark main dish: chicken, tarragon and bacon pie with parsley liquor £12.00. Two-course evening meal £19.00.*

Free house ~ Licensees Victoria and James Hadley ~ Real ale ~ Open 11-11; 12-11 Sun ~ Bar food 12-2.30, 6-9; 12-9 Sat; 12-8 Sun ~ Children welcome ~ Dogs allowed in bar & bedrooms ~ Bedrooms: £145

WOLTERTON   TG1732   Map 8

Saracens Head ⭐🅾🛏

(01263) 768909 – www.saracenshead-norfolk.co.uk

Wolterton; Erpingham signed off A140 N of Aylsham, on through Calthorpe; NR11 7LZ

Follow quiet country lanes a little way north of Blickling Hall and the market town of Aylsham to discover this elegant and gently civilised place. Built in 1806 in a striking Italianate style for Lord Walpole's estate, it's worth seeking out for its unique character and friendly atmosphere. The two-room bar is simple but stylish with high ceilings, light terracotta walls and tall windows with cream and gold curtains – all lending a feeling of space, though it's not large. There's a mix of seats from built-in wall settles to wicker fireside chairs, as well as log fires and flowers. Courteous staff serve Woodfordes Wherry and a changing guest such as Panther Red Panther on handpump and several wines by the glass. The windows look out on to a charming old-fashioned gravel stableyard with plenty of chairs, benches and tables. A pretty six-table parlour on the right has another big log fire. The five bedrooms are comfortable and up to date.

Top rated food includes chicken liver pâté with red onion marmalade, grilled fresh mackerel with poached rhubarb, roasted cauliflower with blood orange and hummus, savoury cheesecake with roasted squash, red onions and baby tomatoes, local venison loin with braised red cabbage and fondant potato, herb-crusted cod fillet with parsnip mash and lemon and white wine sauce, slow-cooked local pork belly with mashed potatoes and chickpea, tomato and chorizo stew, and puddings such as vanilla pannacotta with poached rhubarb and mixed berry pavlova. *Benchmark main dish: roast local lamb with pea and mint purée and dauphinoise potatoes £18.50. Two-course evening meal £23.00.*

Free house ~ Licensees Tim and Janie Elwes ~ Real ale ~ Open 11-3, 6-10.30; closed Mon lunch, Sun evening ~ Bar food 6.30-8 Mon; 12-2, 6.30-8.30; 12.30-2.30 Sun ~ Restaurant ~ Children allowed in bar ~ Dogs allowed in bar & bedrooms ~ Bedrooms: £110

WOODBASTWICK
Fur & Feather ◧

TG3214   Map 8

(01603) 720003 – www.woodfordes.com/brewery-tap
Off B1140 E of Norwich; NR13 6HQ

This charming pub in an attractive village on the edge of the Norfolk Broads was converted from what was originally a row of thatched cottage buildings. As you might expect, the ale here is perfectly kept as Woodfordes brewery is literally next door. Efficient, helpful staff dispense all the Woodfordes range – Bure Gold, Nelsons Revenge, Norfolk Nog, Reedlighter, Volt and Wherry – in addition to several guests, all tapped from the cask (taster flights of three different 1/3 pints are available); also, five craft beers from Woodfordes 52° North range, a dozen wines by the glass and 15 malt whiskies. The style and atmosphere are not what you'd expect of a brewery tap – it's set out more like a comfortable and roomy dining pub with wooden chairs and tables on tiles or carpeting, plus sofas and armchairs; background music. There are seats and tables in the pleasant garden where they keep chickens. You can also visit the brewery shop (and if you eat here, you get a 10% discount voucher for the shop).

Good food includes sandwiches and hot ciabattas(until 5pm), Cajun chicken with sweetcorn and sun-dried tomatoes, parsnip and chestnut wellington, sweet potato masala with coconut quinoa and onion bhaji, trio of sausages with bubble and squeak, beer-battered fish and chips, game and ale pie, chargrilled steaks, red mullet and green Thai curry, Norfolk white lady cheese tart with caramelised onions, spinach and hasselback potatoes, beef brisket with horseradish bonbons and honey-roasted beetroot, and puddings such as apricot and almond crumble with crème fraîche and blueberry pannacotta with meringue and poached berries. *Benchmark main dish: game and ale pie with steak chips £13.50. Two-course evening meal £20.00.*

Woodfordes ~ Tenant Daniel Pratt ~ Real ale ~ Open 10am-11pm; 10-10 Sun ~ Bar food 12-2.30, 5.30-8.30; all day in high season ~ Restaurant ~ Children welcome ~ Dogs allowed in bar

Also Worth a Visit in Norfolk

Besides the fully inspected pubs, you might like to try these pubs that have been recommended to us and described by readers. Do tell us what you think of them: feedback@goodguides.com

AYLMERTON TG1840
Roman Camp (01263) 838291
Holt Road (A148); NR11 8QD Large 19th-c mock-Tudor roadside inn with comfortable panelled bar, cosy sitting room off with warm fire and light airy conservatory dining room, decent choice of enjoyable sensibly priced food from sandwiches up, well kept Adnams, Greene King and guests such as Humpty Dumpty, friendly helpful service from uniformed staff; children welcome, attractive sheltered garden behind with sunny terraces and pond, 15 well appointed bedrooms including two accessible twins, substantial breakfast, open (and food) all day.

AYLSHAM TG1926
★ Black Boys (01263) 732122
Market Place; off B1145; NR11 6EH Small friendly hotel with imposing Georgian façade; informal open-plan beamed bar with comfortable seating and plenty of tables on carpet or bare boards, popular generously served food from snacks up including good Sun roasts, Adnams, Woodfordes, guest ales and 28 wines by the glass, friendly attentive staff coping well at busy times; children and dogs welcome, seats in front by marketplace, more behind, eight bedrooms, hearty cooked breakfast from 8am, handy for Blickling Hall (NT), open all day, food all day Fri-Sun.

BANNINGHAM TG2129
★ Crown (01263) 733534
Colby Road; opposite church by village green; NR11 7DY Welcoming 17th-c beamed pub in same family for 30 years; good choice of popular food (they're helpful with gluten-free and vegan diets), well kept Greene King, at least one local guest ale and decent wines, friendly efficient service, log fires and woodburners; events including annual Aug jazz festival and winter quiz nights (last Tues of month), TV; children and dogs welcome, disabled access, sheltered patio and garden for alfresco dining; open (and food) all day weekends.

BINHAM TF9839
Chequers (01328) 830297
B1388 SW of Blakeney; NR21 0AL Long low-beamed 17th-c local away from the bustle of the coastal pubs; comfortable bar with coal fires at each end, Adnams Southwold, Norfolk Brewhouse Moon Gazer Golden and guests, enjoyable pub food at reasonable prices, set menu on Weds, friendly staff; various games; Mon quiz night; children and dogs welcome, picnic-sets in front and on grass at the back,

interesting village with huge priory church, open all day weekends and bank holidays.

BLAKENEY TG0243
Kings Arms (01263) 740341
West Gate Street; NR25 7NQ A stroll from the harbour to this chatty 18th-c pub; three simple low-ceilinged connecting rooms and airy garden room, well kept Woodfordes Nelsons Revenge and guests, generous wholesome food from breakfast on; children and dogs welcome, big garden, four rooms and three 'flats', good reduction for longer stays, open (and food) all day from 9.30am (noon Sun).

BLICKLING TG1728
Bucks Arms (01263) 732133
B1354 NW of Aylsham; NR11 6NF Handsome Jacobean inn well placed by gates to Blickling Hall (NT); small proper bar, dining lounge with woodburner and smarter more formal restaurant with another fire, Adnams and Woodfordes ales, several wines by the glass and substantial helpings of enjoyable pub food with meat from local supplier, good friendly service; background music; children and dogs welcome, tables out on lawn, lovely walks nearby, four bedrooms, open all day, food all day Sun.

BODHAM STREET TG1240
Red Hart (01263) 588270
The Street; NR25 6AD Old family-run village pub with well liked fairly traditional home-cooked food from lunchtime ciabattas up, three real ales, friendly helpful service; occasional live music and quiz nights, sports TV, pool; children and dogs welcome (menus for both), garden picnic-sets, open all day.

BRAMERTON TG2905
Waters Edge (01508) 538005
Mill Hill, N of village, by river; NR14 7ED Clean modern pub-restaurant in great spot overlooking bend of River Yare; popular if not especially cheap food including daily specials (booking recommended in summer), limited bar menu with burgers and similar, ales such as Adnams and Woodfordes, plenty of wines by the glass, efficient friendly service; children welcome, wheelchair access, circular picnic-sets on waterside deck, moorings, open all day in summer, food all day Sun, closed Mon and Tues in winter.

BRANCASTER TF7743
Ship (01485) 210333
London Street (A149); PE31 8AP Popular roadside inn with compact bar with built-in cushioned and planked wall seats,

four local ales and plenty of wines by the glass from oak counter, several dining areas, well liked food from lunchtime sandwiches up, friendly helpful staff, contemporary paintwork throughout, nice mix of furniture on rugs and bare boards, bookcases, shipping memorabilia and lots of prints, woodburner; background music; children and dogs welcome, gravelled seating area with circular picnic-sets out by car park, nine attractive well equipped bedrooms (six dog-friendly), open all day, food all day Sun.

BRANCASTER STAITHE TF7944
★ **Jolly Sailors** (01485) 210314
Main Road (A149); PE31 8BJ
Unpretentious pub set in prime bird-watching area on edge of NT dunes and salt flats; chatty mix of locals and visitors in simply furnished bars, wheelbacks, settles and cushioned benches around mix of tables on quarry tiles, photographs and local maps on the walls, woodburner, Adnams and Woodfordes ales and local guests, several wines by the glass, sizeable back dining room with popular food including local fish, smokehouse specials and stone-baked pizzas (prices reasonable for the area), cheerful staff coping well at busy times (may ask for a card if running a tab); children and dogs welcome, plenty of picnic-sets and play equipment in peaceful back garden, ice-cream hut in summer, vine-covered terrace, open all day (food all day in season).

BRANCASTER STAITHE TF8044
★ **White Horse** (01485) 210262
A149 E of Hunstanton; PE31 8BY
Popular restauranty place, but does have proper informal front bar serving own Brancaster beers (also in bottles), guest ales, lots of wines by the glass (including a local rosé) and good range of gins, log fire, pine furniture, historical photographs and bar billiards, middle part with comfortable sofas and newspapers, splendid views over tidal marshes from airy dining conservatory and raised lounge, good bar and restaurant food including tapas and plenty of fish including Brancaster mussels and oysters, friendly efficient staff (may ask for a credit card if running a tab); children and dogs (in bar) welcome, seats on sun deck enjoying saltmarsh views, more under cover on heated front terrace, 15 nice bedrooms including eight garden rooms and one with its own telescope, coast path passes bottom of garden, open (and bar food) all day, breakfast from 9am.

BRISLEY TF9521
Brisley Bell (01362) 705024
B1145; The Green; NR20 5DW
Refurbished 17th-c pub in good spot on edge of sheep-grazed common (one of England's biggest); friendly atmosphere, various areas ranging from cosy beamed snug with large open fire to airy garden room, well

liked classic British food with a continental twist (not Sun evening), Adnams and local guests, nice wines and decent range of other drinks (Norfolk whisky/gin), friendly efficient service; events such as live music, charity auctions and quiz nights; children and dogs welcome, terrace and good-sized garden, six bedrooms in converted outbuildings including one fully accessible and two dog-friendly, closed Mon, otherwise open all day.

BROCKDISH TM2179
Old Kings Head (01379) 668843
The Street; IP21 4JY Light and airy old pub at centre of village; several well kept changing local ales, decent wines by the glass and over 140 gins, enjoyable food with Italian slant (stone-baked pizzas and pasta), friendly helpful staff, L-shaped beamed bar with comfortable leather sofa, tub chairs, pews and scrubbed wooden tables on bare boards, log fire, steps up to smaller seating area, café serving good coffee and cakes, maybe local artwork for sale; live music nights; popular with Angles Way walkers, dogs welcome in bar, a few tables out at the side, closed Mon, otherwise open (and food) all day, shuts 10pm Tues-Thurs, 9pm Sun.

BROOME TM3591
Artichoke (01986) 893325
Yarmouth Road; NR35 2NZ
Unpretentious split-level roadside pub with up to 12 well kept ales (some from tap room casks) including Adnams, Belgian fruit beers and excellent selection of whiskies, good traditional home-made food in bar or dining room, friendly helpful staff, wood and flagstone floors, log fire in big fireplace; dogs welcome, garden picnic-sets, smokers' shelter, good walks nearby, closed Mon, otherwise open all day.

BURNHAM MARKET TF8342
Hoste (01328) 738777
The Green (B1155); PE31 8HD Stylish hotel's character front bar with informal chatty atmosphere; leather dining chairs, settles and armchairs, wood-effect flooring, farming implements and cartoons on the walls, woodburner, well kept ales including Woodfordes, Aspall's cider, 25 wines by the glass from extensive list and several malt whiskies, enjoyable if not cheap food including lunchtime sandwiches (12-5pm), afternoon teas, elegant dining areas, bustling conservatory and smart airy back restaurant; children and dogs (in bar) welcome, attractive garden, luxurious bedrooms, other rooms in properties elsewhere in village, open all day from 8am.

BURNHAM MARKET TF8342
Nelson (01328) 738321
Creake Road; PE31 8EN Dining pub with varied menu from sandwiches and wraps to international dishes using local ingredients

in bar and restaurant, pleasant efficient staff, well kept Adnams Ghost Ship, Woodfordes Wherry and guests from pale wood servery, extensive wine list, L-shaped bar with leather sofas and armchairs, local artwork for sale; children and dogs welcome, terrace picnic-sets under parasols, seven bedrooms (two in converted outbuilding), open all day.

BURNHAM OVERY STAITHE   TF8444

★ **Hero** (01328) 738334

Wells Road (A149); PE31 8JE Spacious refurbished roadside pub (sister to the Anchor at Morston); good choice of well liked, often inventive food from sandwiches and snacks up (booking advised), three real ales such as Adnams and Woodfordes, decent wines and interesting range of gins, friendly young staff, large bar and separate pitched-ceiling restaurant, woodburners; children and dogs welcome, terrace seating front and back, three bedrooms, open all day from 9am.

CHEDGRAVE   TM3699

White Horse (01508) 520250

Norwich Road; NR14 6ND Welcoming pub with five well kept ales such as Adnams, Timothy Taylors and Youngs, decent wines by the glass, selection of gins and good choice of popular sensibly priced food (all day Sun) including vegan and gluten-free menus, daily specials and themed nights, friendly attentive staff, log fire and sofas in bar, restaurant, occasional steak nights; some live music, comedy nights, pool and darts; children and dogs welcome, garden picnic-sets, open from noon.

COCKLEY CLEY   TF7904

Twenty Churchwardens

(01760) 721439 *Off A1065 S of Swaffham; PE37 8AN* Informal pub in converted school next to church; two well kept Adnams ales and enjoyable well priced food including nice home-made pies, three linked beamed rooms, good open fire, no background music; no credit cards; children and dogs (particularly) welcome, very small unspoilt village.

COLTISHALL   TG2719

Kings Head (01603) 737426

Wroxham Road (B1354); NR12 7EA Dining pub close to River Bure and moorings; imaginative food from owner-chef (especially fish/seafood), also bar snacks, lunchtime set menu and children's choices, well kept Adnams and two guests, good wines by the glass, open fire, fishing nets and stuffed fish including a monster pike; background music; no dogs, seats outside

(noisy road), four bedrooms (two ensuite), open (and food) all day Sun.

COLTON   TG1009

Norfolk Lurcher (01603) 880794

Village signed from A47 at Blind Lane, W of Easton; NR9 5DG Family-run barn conversion in small village; friendly relaxed atmosphere in large comfortable beamed bar, some old enamel signs and other memorabilia, woodburner, four well kept changing local ales, decent wines and fine range of whiskies, good food including extensive specials board and vegetarian choices, restaurant, monthly jazz nights, also magicians; children and dogs welcome, terrace and big garden with lake, eight bedrooms, shuts 9pm Sun and Tues lunchtime.

CONGHAM   TF7123

Anvil (01485) 600625

St Andrews Lane; PE32 1DU Tucked-away modern country pub with welcoming licensees; wide choice of generously served home-made food (smaller helpings available) including good value Sun carvery, quick friendly service, three or more well kept ales (at least one local); live music and quiz nights; children welcome, no dogs inside, picnic-sets in small walled front garden, small caravan site, closed Mon, open all day Fri-Sun.

CROMER   TG2242

Red Lion (01263) 514964

Off A149; Tucker Street/Brook Street; NR27 9HD Substantial Victorian hotel with elevated views over the sea and pier; original features including panelling and open fires, up to 12 well kept local ales, a couple of ciders and decent wines in bustling bare-boards flint-walled bar, good food from sandwiches and sharing plates up, efficient friendly service, spacious restaurant and conservatory; background music; children and dogs welcome, disabled access/loos, tables in back courtyard, 14 comfortable bedrooms (some with sea view, all dog-friendly), open all day.

DEREHAM   TF9813

George (01362) 696801

Swaffham Road; NR19 2AZ Welcoming 18th-c inn/restaurant; enjoyable generously served food at fair prices including popular Fri steak night and some themed evenings, Adnams and Woodfordes ales, friendly helpful staff, panelled interior with decent sized bar, dining room and conservatory; children and dogs welcome, heated terrace, nine bedrooms, open all day.

A star symbol before the name of a pub shows exceptional character and appeal.
It doesn't mean extra comfort. Even quite a basic pub can win a star,
if it's individual enough.

DERSINGHAM TF6930
Coach & Horses (01485) 540391
Manor Road; PE31 6LN Friendly local
with well kept Woodfordes Wherry and up to
three guest beers, enjoyable food including
daily specials, cheerful efficient service, bar
and back dining room; Thurs quiz, some live
music; children and dogs (in bar) welcome,
painted picnic-sets in garden with play area
and pétanque, three bedrooms, open all day,
no food Sun evening.

DERSINGHAM TF6930
Feathers (01485) 540768
*B1440 towards Sandringham; Manor
Road; PE31 6LN* Carrstone former
coaching inn in village a mile from the
Sandringham Estate; two adjoining bars
(main one with big open fire), well kept
Adnams, Woodfordes and a guest, good
value food including enjoyable Sun lunch,
friendly helpful service, back dining room;
background music; children and dogs
welcome (there's a pub dog), large garden
with play area, patio, function room in
converted stables, five bedrooms as well as
a spacious apartment, open all day.

EAST RUDHAM TF8228
★ Crown (01485) 528530
*A148 W of Fakenham; The Green;
PE31 8RD* Civilised open-plan beamed pub
by village green; main room with log fire at
one end, wooden and brown leather dining
chairs around mixed tables on rugs and
stripped boards, Adnams, Woodfordes and
two guest beers, 20 wines by the glass, decent
choice of enjoyable food from sandwiches up,
friendly service, pubbier part with built-in
cushioned seats and high chairs against
handsome slate-topped counter, lower snug
towards the back and upstairs dining room
with high-pitched ceiling and woodburner;
children and dogs welcome, partial
wheelchair access (no disabled loos), seats
under parasols on front gravelled terrace, six
comfortable bedrooms, special 'food and stay'
packages for Fakenham race days, open all
day, food all day Sun.

EDGEFIELD TG0934
Pigs (01263) 587634
*Norwich Road; B1149 S of Holt;
NR24 2RL* Popular country pub with rooms;
Adnams, Norfolk Brewhouse, Woodfordes and
a house beer (also from Norfolk Brewhouse)
tapped from casks in tiled-floor bar, dining
areas either side, one split into stalls by
standing timbers and low brick walls, the
other light and airy with white-painted
floorboards, some interesting artwork, good
variety of seasonal well liked food including
Norfolk tapas, games room with pool and

table football, also children's playroom;
background music; dogs allowed in bar,
good wheelchair access, rustic furniture
on big covered front terrace, adventure
playground, boules, 19 bedrooms (seven with
spa facilities including sauna and outside
bath, three dog-friendly), open all day from
8am (breakfast for non-residents), food all
day Sun.

ELSING TG0516
Mermaid (01362) 637640
Church Road; NR20 3EA Welcoming
16th-c pub in quiet little village; L-shaped
carpeted bar with woodburner, well kept
Adnams, Woodfordes and guests tapped
from the cask, enjoyable home-made food
including good range of pies and suet
puddings (signature steak and kidney roly-
poly), Indian and Thai curries also available,
Tues steak night, friendly helpful service;
pool and other games such as dominoes and
shut the box; children and dogs welcome,
disabled facilities, handy for walkers on
Wensum Way, nice garden, 14th-c church
opposite with interesting brasses, no food
Mon lunchtime.

GELDESTON TM3991
Wherry (01508) 518371
The Street; NR34 0LB Welcoming little
red-brick village pub with enjoyable home-
made traditional pub food including bargain
OAP lunch (Mon, Weds, Fri), well kept
Adnams and decent wines by the glass, quiz
second Thurs of month, regular live music;
children and dogs welcome, pleasant garden,
good walks and handy for Rowan Craft Marina,
open all day, food till 6pm Sun.

GREAT BIRCHAM TF7632
Kings Head (01485) 578265
*B1155, S end of village (called and
signed Bircham locally); PE31 6RJ*
Handsome Edwardian hotel with cheerful
little bar; comfortable sofas, tub chairs and
log fire, three well kept local ales such as
Woodfordes, good range of wines, whiskies
and over 80 gins, lounge areas and airy
modern restaurant with varied choice of
much liked food from sandwiches and pub
classics to à la carte, afternoon teas, friendly
helpful staff; background music; children
and dogs welcome, tables out at front and
in back garden with nice country views, 12
comfortable bedrooms, some dog-friendly,
open all day.

GREAT CRESSINGHAM TF8401
★ Windmill (01760) 756232
*Village signed off A1065 S of Swaffham;
Water End; IP25 6NN* Shuttered red-brick
inn with interesting pictures and bric-a-brac
in warren of rambling linked rooms, plenty of

We say if we know a pub allows dogs.

cosy corners; wide choice of tasty food from sandwiches and burgers to chargrills, Sun roasts, a house beer (Windy Miller) brewed by Purity along with Adnams, Greene King and two guests, good choice of wines by the glass and extensive range of whiskies/gins, friendly efficient staff; background music, big sports TV in side snug, games room with pool and other pub games; children and dogs welcome, picnic-sets and good play area in large garden, caravan parking on two adjacent sites, 15 bedrooms, open all day from 7.30am for breakfast.

HAPPISBURGH   TG3831
Hill House   (01692) 650004
By village church; NR12 0PW Comfortable traditional 16th-c village pub with Arthur Conan Doyle association; heavy-beamed bar with woodburner in brick inglenook, half a dozen well kept ales including own Dancing Men brews, good reasonably priced food from sandwiches to locally sourced meat and fish, friendly landlord and staff, separate restaurant in converted stables, adjoining coffee shop and carvery; pool and darts, annual midsummer beer festival; children and dogs (not dining room) welcome, tables out front and back, bedrooms (one in former signal box), nice setting near the sea, open all day.

HARPLEY   TF7825
Rose & Crown   (01485) 521807
Off A148 Fakenham–King's Lynn; Nethergate Street; PE31 6TW Old village pub run well by friendly licensees; good generously served home-made food including popular Sun roasts, well kept Woodfordes Wherry and guests, Aspall's cider, modernised interior with open fires; children and dogs welcome, picnic-sets in garden, open (and food) all day.

HEYDON   TG1127
★Earle Arms   (01263) 587376
Off B1149; NR11 6AD Popular old Dutch-gabled pub overlooking green and church in delightfully unspoilt Estate village; well kept Adnams, Woodfordes and a guest, food from varied if not extensive menu using local fish and meat (gluten-free choices marked) including daily specials, decent wine list, old-fashioned candlelit bar with racing prints, some stuffed animals and good log fire, more formal dining room; children and dogs welcome, picnic-sets in small cottagey back garden, open all day Sun (no evening food then), closed Mon.

HICKLING   TG4123
Greyhound   (01692) 598306
The Green; NR12 0YA Popular little village pub with welcoming long-serving landlord; enjoyable fairly pubby food in bar and neat restaurant, snacks and sandwiches at lunchtime, Sun roasts, three or four well kept ales including Adnams, local cider, single

malts, nice open fire; sports TV; well behaved children and dogs welcome, seats out at front and in pretty back garden with covered terrace, handy for Hickling Broad and nature reserve, open all day.

HILBOROUGH   TF8200
Swan   (01760) 756380
Brandon Road (A1065); IP26 5BW Welcoming early 18th-c pub with good quality food including interesting blackboard specials and Sun carvery, also a gluten-free menu, up to four well kept beers and sensibly priced wine list, pleasant helpful staff, small back restaurant; children and dogs (in bar) welcome, picnic-sets on sheltered lawn, eight bedrooms including two apartments, open all day, food all day Fri-Sun.

HINGHAM   TG0202
White Hart   (01953) 850214
Market Place, just off B1108 W of Norwich; NR9 4AF Georgian-fronted coaching inn with character rooms arranged over two floors; beams and standing timbers, stripped floorboards with oriental rugs, mix of furniture including comfortable sofas in quiet corners, lots of prints and photographs, woodburners, galleried long room up steps from main bar with Egyptian frieze, upstairs dining/function room, good choice of enjoyable traditional pub food including menu for dogs, four real ales, lots of wines by the glass and cocktails; background music, bar billiards; children and dogs welcome, modern benches and seats in gravelled courtyard, pretty village with huge 14th-c church, five bedrooms (three dog-friendly), open all day, food all day weekends.

HOLKHAM   TF8943
★Victoria   (01328) 711008
A149 near Holkham Hall; NR23 1RG Upmarket yet informal, this well run pub close to lovely and immense Holkham Beach is owned by the Holkham Estate; proper bare-boards bar to left of main door serving well kept Adnams Bitter, Woodfordes Wherry and a guest and 20 wines by the glass, little drawing room to right (for guests only) with open fire and slightly old-fashioned homely furniture, large open restaurant area with mix of furniture, rugs on stripped floorboards, antlers and antique guns and sofas by big log fire, conservatory dining room leading to back courtyard and there's another sizeable outside seating area with own bar; enjoyable local seasonal food, good coffee, efficient polite service; children and dogs welcome, walks to nature-reserve salt marshes and sea, ten stylish bedrooms (dogs allowed) in pub itself and ten more (no dogs) in building opposite, open all day.

HOLME-NEXT-THE-SEA   TF7043
White Horse   (01485) 525512
Kirkgate Street; PE36 6LH Attractive old-fashioned place with warm log fires and

lots of nooks and crannies; ample choice of enjoyable inexpensive food including local fish and Brancaster mussels, friendly efficient service, Adnams, Greene King and decent wines, side extension; children and dogs welcome, small back garden, more seats out in front and on lawn opposite, play area, open all day.

HOLT   TG0738
Feathers (01263) 712318
Market Place; NR25 6BW Relaxed hotel in charming Georgian town with popular locals' bar comfortably extended around original panelled area, open fire, antiques in attractive entrance/reception area, good choice of enjoyable fairly priced food including blackboard specials, Mon Brancaster mussels, Tues steak and wine, Weds Thai and Thurs curry nights, good vegetarian choice, friendly accommodating service, Greene King ales and decent wines, good coffee, restaurant and dining conservatory for evening meals and Sun lunch; background music; children and dogs (in bar) welcome, 14 comfortable bedrooms, open all day.

HONINGHAM   TG1011
Honingham Buck (01603) 880393
Just off A47 W of Norwich; The Street; NR9 5BL Picturesque and smartly renovated 16th-c pub in village close to Norwich; beamed and timbered bar with flagstones and inglenook woodburner, four Lacons beers and plenty of wines by the glass including champagne, very good imaginative food from unusual snacks up, friendly attentive service, comfortable restaurant with upholstered chairs and banquettes; children welcome, seats on sheltered lawn, eight clean modern bedrooms in converted outbuildings, open all day, food all day Sun till 7pm.

HORSEY   TG4622
★Nelson Head (01493) 393378
Off B1159; The Street; NR29 4AD Red-brick country pub, nicely tucked away and unspoilt, with impressive range of beers (some tapped from the cask) such as Tombstone and Woodfordes, proper ciders and good sensibly priced bar food from sandwiches and snacks to daily specials, friendly chatty staff, log fire and lots of interesting bric-a-brac including various guns, small side dining room; quiet background music; children welcome, well behaved dogs (on leads) in bar, large beer garden in field opposite, good coast walks (seals in winter), open all day, no food Sun evening in winter.

HORSTEAD   TG2619
Recruiting Sergeant (01603) 737077
B1150 just S of Coltishall; NR12 7EE Light, airy and spacious roadside pub – busy and well run; good generously served

food from wraps and jacket potatoes up including well regarded fish dishes (booking recommended), efficient welcoming staff, up to half a dozen changing ales such as Adnams, Greene King, Timothy Taylors and Woodfordes, over 25 wines by the glass, big open fire; children and dogs welcome, terrace and garden tables, variety of local walks including along River Bure, five comfortable dog-friendly bedrooms, open all day, breakfasts from 8am (9am weekends).

HUNWORTH   TG0735
Bell (01263) 711151
Signed off B roads S of Holt; NR24 2AA Renovated 18th-c beamed pub (known locally as the Hunny Bell) under same ownership as the Duck at Stanhoe; neat bar with country chairs around wooden tables, stone floor and woodburner, cosy snug and high-raftered restaurant, enjoyable food from sandwiches and pubby choices to more restauranty dishes cooked by landlord-chef, five real ales such as Norfolk Brewhouse, Woodfordes and Yetmans, good choice of gins, whiskies and cocktails, friendly helpful service; children and dogs welcome, wheelchair access, tables on terrace overlooking village green, more seats in garden among fruit trees, open all day, food all day Sun.

ITTERINGHAM   TG1430
★Walpole Arms (01263) 587258
Village signposted off B1354 NW of Aylsham; NR11 7AR 18th-c country pub owned by local farming family; beamed and timbered open-plan bar with woodburner, stripped-brick walls and cushioned wooden dining chairs around dark tables on red carpet, Adnams Southwold, Woodfordes Wherry and a guest ale on handpump, several wines by the glass and quite a few gins, very good modern cooking using local suppliers is a mix of British and Spanish dishes including tapas, airy garden room-style restaurant plus another area with leather armchairs, friendly staff; background music; children and dogs (in bar) welcome, vine-covered terrace and two-acre landscaped garden, handy for Blickling Hall (NT), open all day Sat, closed Sun evening.

KING'S LYNN   TF6120
Crown & Mitre (01553) 774669
Ferry Street; PE30 1LJ Old-fashioned unchanging pub in great riverside spot; lots of interesting naval and nautical memorabilia, up to six well kept ales and good value straightforward home-made food, river-view back conservatory; no credit cards; well behaved children and dogs allowed, quayside tables.

KING'S LYNN   TF6119
Marriotts Warehouse
(01553) 818500 *South Quay; PE30 5DT* Bar-restaurant-café in converted 16th-c brick and stone warehouse; well priced food from

lunchtime sandwiches and light dishes up (greater evening choice), good value three-course weekday menu, decent range of wines, three real ales, cocktails, small upstairs bar with river views; children welcome, quayside tables, open all day from 10am.

LESSINGHAM
TG3928

Star (01692) 580510

School Road; NR12 0DN Popular little pub on outskirts of village; low ceilings and inglenook woodburner, two real ales and ample helpings of enjoyable reasonably priced food including daily specials and Sun roasts, warm friendly service, small back restaurant; children and dogs welcome, good-sized garden, two bedrooms in building behind, closed Mon, no food Sun evening.

LETHERINGSETT
TG0638

Kings Head (01263) 712691

A148 (Holt Road) W of Holt; NR25 7AR Country house-style dining inn under same ownership as the Jolly Sailors in Brancaster Staithe; rugs on quarry tiles, hunting/coaching prints and open fires, own Brancaster beer along with Adnams, Norfolk Brewhouse Moon Gazer and Woodfordes, 15 wines by the glass, food from good sandwiches and pubby choices up, bread baked with flour from local mill, burger night Thurs, 'fizz 'n chips Fridays', skylit bare-boards dining room with built-in wall seating, farm tools on cream-painted flint and cob walls, back area under partly pitched ceiling with painted rafters; background music, sports TV; children and dogs welcome, picnic-sets out at front and in big garden with play area, four bedrooms, open all day.

LYNG
TG0617

Fox (01603) 872316

The Street; NR9 5AL Old beamed village pub with several linked areas and separate restaurant; ample helpings of good inexpensive home-made food including Mon street-food menu, Tues themed night and midweek two-course lunch deal, Woodfordes and up to three guest ales, friendly staff; pool and giant chessboard in one part; children and dogs (in front bar) welcome, enclosed garden with view of church, open all day in summer apart from Mon lunchtime.

MARSHAM
TG1924

Plough (01263) 735000

Old Norwich Road; NR10 5PS Welcoming 18th-c inn with open-plan split-level bar; enjoyable food using local produce (special diets catered for) including good value set lunch, Adnams Southwold and local guests such as Humpty Dumpty, friendly helpful staff; sports TV, regular quiz and music nights; children welcome, dogs in garden only, comfortable bedrooms, close to Aylsham and Blickling Hall (NT), open all day, food all day weekends.

MORSTON
TG0043

★**Anchor** (01263) 741392

A149 Salthouse–Stiffkey; The Street; NR25 7AA Three refurbished rooms with pubby furniture, coal fires and woodburner, local 1950s beach photographs, prints and bric-a-brac, Greene King IPA, Woodfordes Wherry and a guest, 20 wines by the glass and 25 gins, contemporary airy extension leads to restaurant with local art on walls, enjoyable straightforward food all day (good local mussels); background music, darts and board games; children and dogs welcome, tables and benches in sheltered outdoor area at the front, wonderful bird-watching/walking, you can take seal-spotting trips from the nearby quay, open all day from 9am.

MUNDFORD
TL8093

Crown (01842) 878233

Off A1065 Thetford–Swaffham; Crown Road; IP26 5HQ Unassuming 17th-c pub opposite village green, with heavy beams, huge fireplace and interesting local memorabilia, ales such as Courage Directors and Woodfordes Wherry, over 50 malt whiskies, enjoyable generously served food from sandwiches to daily specials at sensible prices, friendly staff, spiral iron stairs to two restaurant areas (larger one has separate entrance accessible to wheelchairs), locals' bar with sports TV; children and dogs welcome, back terrace and garden with wishing well, 40 bedrooms (some in adjoining building), also self-catering accommodation, open all day.

NEATISHEAD
TG3421

White Horse (01692) 630828

The Street; NR12 8AD Multi-roomed red-brick village pub (sister to the Lion at Thurne); open fire in traditional quarry-tiled bar with unusual beer-glass lights hanging from ceiling, pump clips decorating the walls, good selection of cask and keg beers including ale from own Neatishead brewery and a large selection of gins, generally well liked food from ciabattas up, modern galleried restaurant extension with view into microbrewery; quiz nights and some live music, TV, darts; children and dogs (in main bar) welcome, small courtyard behind, very popular with boaters in summer (mooring nearby), open all day.

NEW BUCKENHAM
TM0890

Kings Head (01953) 861247

Market Place; NR16 2AN Family-run 17th-c pub by small green opposite medieval market cross; ales such as Adnams Southwold and generous helpings of popular reasonably priced pubby food with decent choice for vegetarians (booking advised), helpful service, modern open-plan bar with beams and inglenook, big back dining area; pool; five bedrooms, open all day, no food Mon or evening Sun.

NORTH CREAKE   TF8538
Jolly Farmers (01328) 738185
Burnham Road; NR21 9JW Former
coaching inn in charming flintstone village;
main bar with large open fire in brick
fireplace, mix of farmhouse and high-backed
leather dining chairs around scrubbed pine
tables on quarry tiles, Greene King Abbot,
Woodfordes Wherry and a guest or two, 11
wines by the glass and a dozen malt whiskies,
limited food, smaller bar with pews and
woodburner, another in dining room; children
and dogs welcome, plenty of seats on terrace,
self-catering cottage, closed Sun evening,
Mon and Tues.

NORTH TUDDENHAM   TG0413
Lodge (01362) 638466
Off A47; NR20 3DJ Popular modernised
dining pub; good sensibly priced food from
traditional choices up including burgers,
sharing dishes and good steaks, local beers
(just one in winter) such as Woodfordes
Reedlighter, friendly attentive service;
monthly quiz; children and dogs (in bar)
welcome, tables outside (some on deck),
closed Sun evening and Mon, otherwise open
(and food) all day.

NORTHREPPS   TG2439
Foundry Arms (01263) 579256
Church Street; NR27 0AA Welcoming
village pub with good reasonably priced
traditional food from generous sandwiches
up, good value set lunch, pizzas, well kept
Adnams Broadside, Woodfordes Wherry and
a couple of guests, decent choice of wines,
efficient friendly service, woodburner,
smallish comfortable restaurant; pool
and darts in separate area, live music Sun
afternoons; children and dogs welcome,
picnic-sets in back garden, open all day, no
food Sun evening.

NORWICH   TG2309
Adam & Eve (01603) 667423
*Bishopgate; follow Palace Street from
Tombland, N of cathedral; NR3 1RZ*
The oldest pub in Norwich dating from
at least 1240 when used by workmen
building the cathedral, has a Saxon well
beneath the lower bar floor and striking
Dutch gables (added in 14th and 15th c);
old-fashioned small bars with tiled or
parquet floors, cushioned benches built
into partly panelled walls and some antique
high-backed settles, well kept ales such
as Adnams and Wolf, Aspall's cider and
around 40 malt whiskies, traditional pubby
food (not Sun evening) from baguettes
up, friendly service; background music;
children allowed in snug till 7pm, no dogs

inside, picnic-sets out among pretty tubs
and hanging baskets, open all day.

NORWICH   TG2408
Coach & Horses (01603) 477077
Thorpe Road; NR1 1BA Light and airy
tap for Chalk Hill brewery (tours available)
with eight own brews plus guests, food from
baguettes up including lunch deals, Sat
brunch and imaginative weekly specials,
friendly staff, L-shaped bare-boards bar with
open fire, pleasant back dining area; sports
TVs, gets very busy on home match days;
disabled access possible (not to lavatories),
front terrace, open all day.

NORWICH   TG2210
Duke of Wellington (01603) 441182
Waterloo Road; NR3 1EG Rambling corner
local with huge range of well kept quickly
changing ales including Fullers, Oakham
and Wolf, many served from tap room casks,
foreign bottled beers too, no food apart from
sausage rolls and pies (can bring your own,
cutlery is provided) and weekend summer
barbecue, real fire; live music and Mon quiz
nights, Aug beer festival, traditional games;
well behaved dogs welcome, small back
terrace, open all day.

NORWICH   TG2308
Edith Cavell (01603) 765813
Tombland/Princes Street; NR3 1HF
Corner pub-restaurant named after the
gallant World War I Norfolk nurse; popular
if not especially cheap food with emphasis
on steaks cooked on hot rocks, three real
ales including a house beer from Wolf,
friendly helpful service, smallish bar, upstairs
restaurant (and loos); diagonally across
from Erpingham Gate leading into cathedral
green, open all day (till 1am Fri, Sat).

NORWICH   TG2310
Fat Cat Tap (01603) 413153
Lawson Road; NR3 4LF This 1970s
shed-like building is home to the Fat Cat
brewery and sister pub to the Fat Cat (see
Main Entries); good buzzy atmosphere, their
ales and up to 12 guests along with draught
continentals, lots of bottled beers and eight
or more local ciders/perries, no food apart
from chips (with or without toppings) and
good value cheeseboards to share, can also
bring your own; regular live music and quiz
nights; dogs welcome, children till 6pm, seats
out front and back, open all day.

NORWICH   TG2309
★ Kings Head (01603) 620468
Magdalen Street; NR3 1JE Traditional
Victorian local with good friendly atmosphere
in two simply furnished bare-boards bars

If you report on a pub that's not a featured entry, please tell us any lunchtimes
or evenings when it doesn't serve bar food.

(front one is tiny), up to 14 very well kept changing regional ales, good choice of imported beers and a local cider, no food except pork pies; bar billiards in back bar; dogs welcome, open all day until late.

NORWICH   TG2208
Plough (01603) 661384

St Benedicts Street; NR2 4AR Small city-centre pub owned by Grain, their ales and guests kept well, good wines and cocktails, food limited to sausage pie, cheeseboards and summer barbecues, simply updated split-level interior with bare boards and open fire; background music, occasional DJ; good spacious beer garden behind, open all day.

NORWICH   TG2308
Ribs of Beef (01603) 619517

Wensum Street, S side of Fye Bridge; NR3 1HY Comfortable and welcoming riverside pub; nine real ales including Oakham, two traditional ciders and good wine choice, generous well priced food such as burgers and wings, roasts on Sun (no food Sun evening), quick cheerful service, traditional carpeted bar with river views, smaller downstairs room; live music Sun, quiz every other Thurs, sports TV; children welcome, limited seats outside on narrow waterside terrace, open all day.

NORWICH   TG2308
St Andrews Brew House

(01603) 305995 *St Andrews Street; NR2 4TP* Interesting place visibly brewing its own good beers (can tour the brewery), also plenty of guest ales, craft kegs and bottled beers, utilitarian bare-boards interior with exposed ducting, rough masonry walls and eclectic mix of seating including some button-back booths, popular sensibly priced food from British tapas and sharing boards up including special theme nights, busy efficient staff, upstairs function room; background music, sports TV; children and dogs welcome, pavement tables, open all day.

NORWICH   TG2309
Wig & Pen (01603) 625891

St Martins Palace Plain; NR3 1RN Popular 17th-c beamed pub close to cathedral; half a dozen well kept local ales including Adnams, Wolf and Woodfordes, well priced wines and good value food from sandwiches up, Sun roasts, prompt friendly service; background music, sports TVs, spring beer festival; metal café-style furniture on large terrace at front, open all day (till 6.30pm Sun).

OLD HUNSTANTON   TF6842
Lodge (01485) 532896

Old Hunstanton Road (A149); PE36 6HX Old red-brick roadside pub with clean contemporary décor; popular food in bar or restaurant from pizzas and pub favourites up, vegan menu, afternoon tea, well kept local beers and good choice of wines by the glass, friendly helpful staff, plenty of seating on wood floors including booths and sofas by woodburner; sports TV, occasional live music; children and dogs (in bar) welcome, tables on covered terrace and small lawn, 16 good bedrooms, open all day.

OVERSTRAND   TG2440
Sea Marge (01263) 579579

High Street; NR27 0AB Substantial half-timbered sea-view hotel (former Edwardian country house) with separate entrance to spacious bar; enjoyable food from ciabattas to local seafood including weekday deal (till 6pm) on some main courses, Sun carvery, real ales and decent wines by the glass, light airy restaurant (more upmarket menu); children welcome, dogs in some areas, five-acre grounds with terraced lawns down to clifftop and steep steps to coast path and beach, 25 comfortable bedrooms, open (and bar food) all day.

OVERSTRAND   TG2440
White Horse (01263) 579237

High Street; NR27 0AB Comfortably modernised red-brick pub with good choice of well liked food in bar, dining room or barn restaurant (also used for functions), up to five well kept regional ales, local seafood, friendly attentive staff; background music, silent sports TV, pool; children and dogs welcome, picnic-sets out in front, more in garden behind with play equipment (may be bouncy castle), short walk to beach, eight bedrooms, open all day from 8am.

OXBOROUGH   TF7401
★Bedingfeld Arms (01366) 328300

Near church; PE33 9PS Attractively furnished Georgian dining inn peacefully set opposite Oxburgh Hall (NT); wood-floored bar with green leather chesterfields, tub chairs and window seats, open fire in marble fireplace with gilt mirror above, fresh flowers and candles, long counter serving Adnams Broadside, Woodfordes Reedlighter and a guest, ten wines by the glass, airy dining room has high-backed chairs around antique tables, wall seats with scatter cushions and bird prints on pale grey walls, good food including lunchtime sandwiches, stone-baked pizzas and Sun roasts; background music, TV for major sports; well behaved children welcome, dogs in bar, covered verandah extension, more seats in garden with view of church, ten bedrooms (five in coach-house annexe), good breakfasts, open all day, food all day Sat, Sun.

RINGSTEAD   TF7040
Gin Trap (01485) 525264

Village signed off A149 near Hunstanton; OS Sheet 132 map reference 707403; PE36 5JU Attractive 17th-c village pub (former coaching inn); original beamed bar with woodburner, farmhouse and mate's chairs around solid pine tables on bare boards, window seats, coach lamps on walls, Adnams, Greene King, Woodfordes and guests, 16 wines by the glass and more than 100 gins (one distilled for the pub by Bullards of Norwich), decent choice of food (including vegan menu) served by friendly staff; step up to quarry-tiled room with conservatory beyond, character back snug with red-painted walls and nice old floor tiles; children and dogs (except in restaurant and snug) welcome, picnic-sets and play area in back garden, more seats out in front, handy for Peddars Way, seven comfortable well equipped bedrooms (some in adjacent building), open all day.

ROYDON   TF7022
Three Horseshoes (01485) 600666
The Roydon near King's Lynn; Lynn Road; PE32 1AQ Updated brick and stone village pub under same ownership as nearby Congham Hall Hotel; pleasant pastel décor with simple wood furniture, stone-floor bar and split-level part-carpeted restaurant, woodburner in each, popular home-made food including good steaks from reasonably priced blackboard menu, OAP set lunch Mon-Fri, Greene King IPA and a couple of guests such as Woodfordes, friendly helpful staff; children and dogs (in bar) welcome, tables out at front, open all day, food all day weekends.

SCULTHORPE   TF8930
★Sculthorpe Mill (01328) 856161
Inn signed off A148 W of Fakenham, opposite village; NR21 9QG Welcoming dining pub in rebuilt 18th-c mill, appealing riverside setting with seats out under weeping willows and in attractive garden behind; light, airy and relaxed with leather sofas and sturdy tables in bar/dining area, good reasonably priced food from sandwiches to daily specials, attentive service, Greene King and guest ales, good house wines and selection of gins, upstairs restaurant; background music; children and dogs welcome, six comfortable bedrooms (up two flights of stairs), open all day, closed Mon.

SEDGEFORD   TF7036
King William IV (01485) 571765
B1454, off A149 King's Lynn–Hunstanton; PE36 5LU Homely inn handy for beaches and bird-watching; bar and dining areas decorated with paintings of north Norfolk coast, high-backed dark leather dining chairs around pine tables on slate tiles, log fires, Adnams, Greene King and Woodfordes, ten wines by the glass and well liked food from pub favourites up including blackboard specials, OAP lunch Tues-Thurs, curry night Tues, pie night Weds; magazines and daily papers; children (no under-4s in main restaurant after 6.30pm) and dogs (in bar) welcome, seats on terrace and under parasols on grass, also an attractive covered

dining area surrounded by flowering tubs; nine comfortable bedrooms (two dog-friendly), closed Mon lunchtime, otherwise open all day.

SHERINGHAM   TG1543
Crown (01263) 823213
East Cliff; NR26 8BQ Comfortable 1930s bay-windowed pub in good position overlooking the North Sea; five well kept ales including Adnams, Fullers and Sharps, decent choice of enjoyable reasonably priced pubby food, three connecting areas with panelling and some exposed brickwork, upholstered wall benches and other traditional furniture on patterned carpet; background music and live music, darts, TVs and fruit machine; children and dogs welcome, lots of picnic-sets on sea-view terrace, next to the Mo Museum, open (and food) all day except Sun when kitchen closes at 5pm.

SHERINGHAM   TG1543
Lobster (01263) 822716
High Street; NR26 8JP Almost on seafront and popular with both locals and tourists; friendly panelled bar with log fire and seafaring décor, wide range of ales including Adnams, Greene King and Woodfordes, two or three ciders and decent wines by the glass, generous reasonably priced bar food from good sandwiches up, restaurant with seasonal seafood including lobster and crab; some live music; children and dogs welcome, 17 bedrooms, open all day.

SHOULDHAM   TF6708
Kings Arms (01366) 347410
The Green; PE33 0BY Traditional 17th-c pub on village green; beams and flagstones, exposed-stone or red-painted walls hung with prints, homely mix of dining chairs and tables, a leather button-back sofa and inglenook woodburner, well kept ales such as Adnams, Beeston and Grain tapped from the cask and weekly changing guest ales, local cider, ten wines by the glass and decent range of gins and malt whiskies, enjoyable food (not Sun evening, Mon) including good Sun roasts, also has a café staffed by volunteers selling village-baked cakes and scones; background music, folk session third Sun of month, charity quiz night last Sun of month, classic car/motorcycle meetings first Sun of month; children and dogs (in bar) welcome, painted picnic-sets on grass, closed Mon lunchtime, otherwise open all day.

SOUTHREPPS   TG2536
★Vernon Arms (01263) 833355
Church Street; NR11 8NP Popular old-fashioned brick and cobble village pub, welcoming and relaxed, with good reasonably priced home-made food (booking advised), friendly helpful staff, good range of ales including well kept Adnams, Woodfordes and guests, decent choice of wines and malt whiskies, big log fire; darts and pool,

occasional live music; tables outside, children, dogs and muddy boots welcome, open all day, no evening food Sun or Mon.

STANHOE   TF8037
★ **Duck** (01485) 518330
*B1155 Docking–Burnham Market;
PE31 8QD* Smart pub with emphasis on good imaginative food (sister to Bell at Hunworth), airy bar with cushioned Edwardian-style chairs around wooden tables on dark slate floor, stools against fine slab-topped counter serving Adnams Ghost Ship, Elgoods Cambridge and a dozen wines by the glass, woodburner and modern artwork in small area off, two dining rooms with scatter-cushion wall seats, scrubbed tables and local seascapes; children and dogs (in bar) welcome, disabled access/loo, tables out on front gravel and under fruit tree in small garden, there's also a garden room with fairy lights and candles, comfortable well appointed bedrooms, good breakfast, open all day, food all day Sun.

STIFFKEY   TF9643
Red Lion (01328) 830552
A149 Wells–Blakeney; NR23 1AJ Popular old village pub; main bar with tiled floor and inglenook woodburner, cushioned pews and other pubby seats, Woodfordes ales, a dozen wines by the glass and some local gins, well liked food including lunchtime sandwiches, pubby choices, local fish/shellfish (Brancaster mussels), curry and pint night Weds, friendly service, two back dining rooms, one a flint-walled conservatory; children and dogs welcome, big partly covered gravelled courtyard, more tables on covered deck, ten dog-friendly bedrooms in modern block with own balconies or terraces plus two luxury suites, nearby coastal walks, open all day, food all day weekends.

STOW BARDOLPH   TF6205
Hare Arms (01366) 382229
*Just off A10 N of Downham Market;
PE34 3HT* Popular modernised village pub; bare-boards bar with traditional pub furnishings and log fire, Greene King ales and a couple of well kept guests, ten wines by the glass, generous helpings of enjoyable good value food (all day Sun) from sandwiches up, daily specials, three dining areas including converted coach house; children welcome in some parts, no dogs inside, plenty of seats in front and back gardens, maybe wandering peacocks, Church Farm Rare Breeds Centre nearby, open (and food) all day weekends.

SURLINGHAM   TG3107
Ferry House (01508) 538659
Ferry Road: far end by river; NR14 7AR Welcoming unpretentious pub by River Yare; well kept regional ales and hearty helpings of good inexpensive home-made food from baguettes up, helpful accommodating service,

central woodburner in brick fireplace; monthly live music; children and dogs welcome, very busy with boats and visitors in summer (free mooring), picnic-sets on waterside lawn, handy for RSPB reserve, open (and food) all day.

THOMPSON   TL9296
Chequers (01953) 483360
*Griston Road, off A1075 S of Watton;
IP24 1PX* Picturesque 16th-c thatched dining pub tucked away in attractive setting; enjoyable food including bargain weekday lunch offer and Sun set menu, regular themed nights, ales such as Greene King and Woodfordes, friendly atmosphere, series of quaint rooms with low beams, inglenooks and some stripped brickwork; children and dogs (in bar) welcome, seats out in front and in back garden with swing, three rooms in adjacent block, open (and food) all day Sun.

THORNHAM   TF7343
Chequers (01485) 512229
High Street (A149); PE36 6LY Updated 16th-c roadside inn under same owners as the nearby Lifeboat (see Main Entries); two front bar rooms with pale-painted beams, wooden chairs or cube seats around mix of wooden tables on carpet or painted floorboards, some local photographs, open fire, a few stools at counter serving two local ales and decent wines by the glass, well liked food including Norfolk tapas and 'light bites' up, cosy room off with sofas, armchairs and woodburner, modern back dining room; children and dogs welcome, painted picnic-sets out at front, more seating in back courtyard garden with a couple of cabanas, 11 comfortable modern bedrooms, open all day.

THURNE   TG4016
Lion (01692) 671806
The Street; NR29 3AP Revamped Victorian villa at end of Thurne Dyke – popular with boaters; choice of six real ales and six proper ciders, several wines by the glass and some 20 gins including a house one infused with hops, happy hour 5-7pm (4-7pm weekends), enjoyable fair priced food from burgers and pizzas to specials, two-course set lunch Mon-Fri, friendly efficient service, sizeable restaurant; monthly quiz and some live music; children and dogs (in bar areas) welcome, grounds with play area, plenty of moorings (fee charged from 4pm), open all day.

TUNSTEAD   TG2921
Horse & Groom (01603) 737555
*Granary Way off Market Street;
NR12 8AH* Welcoming thatched village pub with modernised beamed interior; enjoyable fairly priced food from pub favourites up including Thurs burger night and Sat steak night, well kept changing local beers such as Lacons and Woodfordes and good selection of

gins, cheerful helpful staff; darts team Mon, quiz Tues, live acoustic music Weds; children and dogs welcome, open all day, no food Sun evening.

WALSINGHAM   TF9336
Black Lion   (01328) 820235
Friday Market Place; NR22 6DB
Attractively renovated beamed village inn dating from the 15th c; nice mix of old furniture on flagstones or quarry tiles, shelves of books, farming tools and other bits and pieces including a tandem on one wall, woodburners and open fire, tractor-seat stools by counter serving well kept Adnams, Woodfordes and a guest ale, more than a dozen wines by the glass, good traditional home-made food with vegan and gluten-free menus, friendly service; background and some live music; children and dogs welcome, a few tables out at front, more on little terrace with old well, six comfortable bedrooms (two dog-friendly), open all day, food all day weekends.

WALSINGHAM   TF9336
Bull   (01328) 820333
Common Place/Shire Hall Plain;
NR22 6BP Quirky pub in pilgrimage village; lived-in bar with shelves of curious knick-knacks, pictures of archbishops and clerical visiting cards, a half-size statue of Charlie Chaplin, even a mirror ball in one part, three well kept changing ales and tasty reasonably priced food (not weekend evenings) with daily specials and Sun roasts, roaring fire, typewriter in snug, old-fashioned cash register in the gents'; TV; children welcome, courtyard and attractive flowery terrace by village square, dovecote stuffed with plastic lobsters and crabs, outside games room, close to Anglican shrine, enjoyable snowdrop walk in nearby abbey garden, five bedrooms, open all day.

WEASENHAM ST PETER   TF8522
Fox & Hounds   (01328) 838868
A1065 Fakenham–Swaffham; The
Green; PE32 2TD Traditional 18th-c beamed local well run by friendly family; bar and two dining areas (one with inglenook woodburner), Adnams, Woodfordes and changing guest ales and reasonably priced home-made food including good pies, steak night Thurs, pubby furniture and carpets throughout, brasses and lots of military prints; children and dogs welcome, big well maintained garden and terrace, closed Sun evening and Mon.

WELLS-NEXT-THE-SEA   TF9143
Bowling Green   (01328) 710100
Church Street; NR23 1JB Welcoming 17th-c pub in quiet spot on outskirts; Greene King, Woodfordes and a guest, generous helpings of reasonably priced traditional food including bargain OAP lunch Tues and Sun roasts, L-shaped bar with corner settles,

flagstone and brick floor, two woodburners, raised dining end; occasional live music, children and dogs welcome, sunny back terrace, two bedrooms in converted barn, also self-catering accommodation.

WELLS-NEXT-THE-SEA   TF9143
★Crown   (01328) 710209
The Buttlands; NR23 1EX Smart old coaching inn (part of Flying Kiwi group) overlooking tree-lined green; rambling bar on several levels with beams and standing timbers, grey-painted planked wall seats and brown leather dining chairs on stripped floorboards, ales such as Adnams and Woodfordes, 25 wines by the glass, good modern food including daily specials, afternoon teas, friendly accommodating staff, airy dining room and elegant more formal restaurant; background music; children and dogs (in bar) welcome, 12 bedrooms, open from 8am for breakfast, food all day Sun, can get very busy.

WELLS-NEXT-THE-SEA   TF9143
Edinburgh   (01328) 710120
Station Road/Church Street; NR23 1AE
Traditional 19th-c pub near main shopping area; three well kept ales including Woodfordes and good home-made food including blackboard specials, open fire, sizeable 'Ollies' restaurant, also 'lifeboat' dining room decorated in RNLI colours; background music; children and dogs welcome, disabled access, courtyard with heated smokers' shelter, three bedrooms, open all day.

WELLS-NEXT-THE-SEA   TF9143
★Globe   (01328) 710206
The Buttlands; NR23 1EU Handsome blue-painted Georgian inn on tree-lined green, a short walk from the quay; plenty of space and nice atmosphere in opened-up contemporary rooms, tables on oak boards, big bay windows, well kept Adnams beers, thoughtful wine choice and enjoyable food from lunchtime ciabattas up, wood-fired pizzas outside Weds-Sun in summer, regular steak nights, good friendly service; background and some live music; children and dogs welcome, attractive courtyard with pale flagstones, more seats at front overlooking green, 19 bedrooms (12 in courtyard annexe, seven dog-friendly) and nearby holiday house, open all day (breakfast for non-residents).

WEST ACRE   TF7815
Stag   (01760) 755395
Low Road; PE32 1TR Small family-run local with three or more well kept changing ales such as Humpty Dumpty Little Sharpie in appealing unpretentious bar, good value home-made food including set Sun lunch, neat dining room; quiz third Sun of month; attractive spot in quiet village, closed Mon, no food Sun evening.

WEYBOURNE

TG1143

Ship (01263) 588721

A149 W of Sheringham; The Street; NR25 7SZ Popular traditional 19th-c village pub; three well kept changing ales such as Norfolk Brewhouse Moon Gazer, decent wine choice and over 150 gins, big bar with pubby furniture and woodburner, two dining rooms, good reasonably priced home-made food (should book weekends) from lunchtime sandwiches through pub favourites to local fish/seafood; background music, monthly quiz; well behaved children welcome, dogs in bar, seats out at front and in sunny lawned garden at side, convenient for Muckleburgh military vehicle museum and Poppy Line heritage railway, open all day in season, no food Sun evening.

WIVETON

TG0442

★ Wiveton Bell (01263) 740101

Blakeney Road; NR25 7TL Busy pub very popular for its top notch food but also welcoming drinkers; mainly open-plan with some fine old beams, log fire, yellow walls and attractive mix of furniture on stripped-wood flooring, sizeable dining conservatory, ales such as Norfolk Brewhouse, Woodfordes and Yetmans, around 20 wines by the glass, friendly attentive service; children and dogs (in bar) welcome, picnic-sets on front grass looking across to church, new terrace and stylish wicker furniture on decked areas behind, well equipped character bedrooms (three have small terraces), also a self-catering cottage, open all day, food all day Sun.

WYMONDHAM

TG1001

★ Green Dragon (01953) 607907

Church Street; NR18 0PH Picturesque heavily timbered medieval pub with plenty of character; small beamed bar and snug, bigger dining area, interesting pictures, log fire under Tudor mantelpiece, five well kept changing ales such as Norfolk Brewhouse and Wolf (beer/cider festival May) and over 50 whiskies, generous helpings of popular good value food (best to book) including daily specials and gluten-free menu, friendly helpful staff, upstairs function room; quiz Thurs, open mike night third Sun of month, ukulele group first and third Tues; children and dogs welcome, garden behind with raised deck, near glorious 12th-c abbey church, open all day (food all day Fri-Sun).

Northamptonshire

FARTHINGSTONE

SP6155 Map 4

Kings Arms ☕ £

(01327) 361604

Off A5 SE of Daventry; village signed from Litchborough; NN12 8EZ

Individual place with cosy traditional interior, carefully prepared food and lovely garden

This charming and quirky pub, run by the same couple for over 25 years, attracts plenty of chatty customers, creating a friendly and relaxed atmosphere. The cosy flagstoned bar has a huge log fire, comfortable homely sofas and armchairs near the entrance, whisky-water jugs hanging from oak beams, and lots of pictures and decorative plates on the walls. A games room at the far end has darts, dominoes, cribbage, Northamptonshire table skittles and board games. The ever-changing beers are kept in top condition and might include Harveys Sussex Best, St Austell Trelawny and Woodfordes Wherry on handpump; also local ciders, gins and a short but decent wine list. Look out for the interesting newspaper-influenced décor in the outside gents'. The handsome gargoyled stone exterior is nicely weathered and very pretty in summer when the hanging baskets are at their best. There are seats on a tranquil terrace among plant-filled, painted tractor tyres and recycled art, and they've recorded over 200 species of moth and 20 different butterflies in the garden. This is a picturesque village and good walks nearby include the Knightley Way. It's worth calling ahead to check the opening and food times.

🍴 Served at weekend lunchtimes only, popular food includes sandwiches and baguetttes, cheese platters, filled yorkshire puddings, casseroles, and puddings such as gingerbread with hot maple syrup and meringues.

Free house ~ Licensees Paul and Denise Egerton ~ Real ale ~ Open 6.30-10.30 Tues-Thurs; 6.30-11.30 Fri; 12-10.30 Sat; 12-5.30 Sun ~ Bar food 12-2.15 or so weekends; maybe evening snacks ~ Children welcome ~ Dogs allowed in bar

FOTHERINGHAY

TL0593 Map 5

Falcon ●★ ♀

(01832) 226254 – www.thefalcon-inn.co.uk

Village signposted off A605 on Peterborough side of Oundle; PE8 5HZ

Northamptonshire Dining Pub of the Year

Upmarket dining pub with a good range of drinks and modern British food, and attractive garden

This handsome inn is nestled in a lovely village steeped in royal history – Richard III was born in Fotheringhay Castle in 1452 and Mary, Queen of Scots was executed there in 1587 (only the castle earthworks remain now). Run by a hands-on landlady, there are winter log fires in stone fireplaces, fresh flowers, cushioned slatback armchairs, bucket chairs and comfortably cushioned window seats and bare floorboards. The atmosphere is enjoyably civilised and warmly welcoming. The Orangery restaurant opens on to a charming lavender-surrounded terrace with lovely views of the splendid local church behind and the attractively planted garden; plenty of seats under parasols. The thriving little locals' tap bar has a fine choice of drinks including Bombardier, Sharps Doom Bar and a guest from local breweries (perhaps Digfield, Kings Cliffe, Nobbys or Oakham) on handpump, 17 good wines by the glass and eight malt whiskies; darts team and board games. The tranquil River Nene runs through the village and the church is worth a visit for its memorials to members of the House of York.

Excellent modern food from a seasonal menu makes good use of produce from local estates. Dishes include duck, cabbage and plum terrine, chalk-stream trout with tomato consommé jelly and wasabi leaf, Deene Park venison wellington with pommes purée, red cabbage and damsons, Burghley Estate lamb (cannon and deep-fried shoulder) with parsnips, black kale, sherry and apricot jus, roasted coley supreme with parsley and tarragon crumble, poularde clams, saffron potatoes and vermouth sauce, spinach, pine nut and feta roulade with watercress, apple and potato salad, and puddings such as strawberry eton mess and rum baba with vanilla chantilly and roast banana. *Benchmark main dish: beer-battered haddock and triple-cooked chips £14.50. Two-course evening meal £23.00.*

Free house ~ Licensees Madison Keys and Zak Perrin ~ Real ale ~ Open 12-11; 12-10.30 Sun ~ Bar food 12-2, 6-9; 12-3, 5.30-8 Sun (12-3 Oct-Apr) ~ Restaurant ~ Children welcome ~ Dogs allowed in bar

GREAT BRINGTON   SP6664   Map 4
Althorp Coaching Inn
(01604) 770651 – www.althorp-coaching-inn.co.uk
Off A428 NW of Northampton, near Althorp Hall; until recently known as the Fox & Hounds; NN7 4JA

Friendly golden-stone thatched pub with some fine architectural features, popular food, well kept real ales and sheltered garden

Set in a picturesque village, this beautiful old pub dates back to the 16th c and has an ancient bar with all the traditional features you'd wish for: from a dog or two sprawled by the huge log fire to old beams, sagging joists and an appealing mix of country chairs and tables (set with fresh flowers) on broad flagstones and bare boards; background music. Also, snug alcoves, nooks and crannies with some stripped-pine shutters and panelling, another log fire and an eclectic medley of bric-a-brac from farming implements to an old clocking-in machine and country pictures. There are plenty of happy customers keen to enjoy the thoughtful choice of food and drink, including Phipps India Pale Ale, St Austell Tribute, Sharps Doom Bar plus guest ales on handpump; also, eight wines by the glass, a dozen malt whiskies and farm cider; regular quiz and open mike nights. A function room is located in the converted stable block next to the lovely cobbled and paved courtyard (also accessible by the old coaching entrance) with sheltered tables and tubs of flowers. More seating is available in the charming garden.

Highly enjoyable food includes sandwiches, feta and mushroom fritters, moules marinière, salmon fillet, wild mushroom risotto, braised lamb shank, dressed Cromer crab and crayfish tail salad, scotch rib-eye, and puddings such as pavlova with strawberries and cream and chocolate brownies. *Benchmark main dish: braised lamb shank with red wine sauce, mashed potatoes and vegetables £14.50. Two-course evening meal £21.00.*

Free house ~ Licensee Michael Krempels ~ Real ale ~ Open 11-11; 11-midnight Sat; 11-10 Sun ~ Bar food 12-3, 6-9; 12-9 Sat; 12-7 Sun ~ Restaurant ~ Children welcome ~ Dogs allowed in bar

Also Worth a Visit in Northamptonshire

Besides the fully inspected pubs, you might like to try these pubs that have been recommended to us and described by readers. Do tell us what you think of them: feedback@goodguides.com

ABTHORPE — SP6446

★ **New Inn** (01327) 857306 *Signed from A43 at first roundabout S of A5; Silver Street; NN12 8QR* Traditional partly thatched country local run by cheery farming family; fairly basic rambling bar with dining area down a couple of steps, beams, stripped stone and inglenook woodburner; four well kept Hook Norton beers, Weston's cider and good pubby food (not Sun evening, Mon) using local produce including own meat; open mike night second Sun of month, quiz last Sun, darts and table skittles; children, dogs and muddy boots welcome, garden tables, bedrooms in converted barn (short walk across fields), open all day Fri-Sun, closed lunchtimes Mon and Tues.

ARTHINGWORTH — SP7581
Bulls Head (01858) 525637 *Kelmarsh Road, just above A14 by A508 junction; pub signed from A14; LE16 8JZ* Steps up to much extended black-beamed pub with various seating areas in L-shaped bar, pubby furniture and upholstered banquettes, woodburner, well kept Adnams and a couple of guests (May beer festival), enjoyable good value food, efficient cheery service, restaurant; background music, TV, darts and skittles; wheelchair access (from behind) and disabled loos, terrace picnic-sets, eight bedrooms in separate block, handy for Kelmarsh Hall, open all day weekends (food till 7.30pm Sun).

ASHBY ST LEDGERS — SP5768
Olde Coach House (01788) 890349 *Main Street; 4 miles from M1 junction 18; A5 S to Kilsby, then A361 S towards Daventry; village also signed off A5 N of Weedon; CV23 8UN* Handsome former farmhouse with opened-up right-hand bar, stools against counter serving Bombardier, Youngs Original and a monthly guest, 16 wines by the glass, several informal dining areas (food can be good), hunting pictures, large mirrors and an original old stove in one part; background music and TV; children welcome, dogs in bar, modern tables and chairs out in front, dining courtyard and back garden with picnic-sets among shrubs and trees, 17 well equipped contemporary bedrooms, interesting church and the nearby manor house was once owned by one of the Gunpowder plotters, open all day, food till 8pm Sun.

AYNHO — SP5133
Cartwright (01869) 811885 *Croughton Road (B4100); handy for M40 junction 10; OX17 3BE* Welcoming 16th-c coaching inn with linked areas; contemporary furniture on wood or tiled floors, some exposed stone walls, leather sofas by big log fire in small bar, Butcombe and Hook Norton Old Hooky, nice wines and good coffee, popular well presented food including set deals, friendly helpful staff; background music, TV, daily papers; children welcome, a few seats in pretty corner of part-cobbled coachyard, 21 bedrooms, good breakfast, pleasant village with apricot trees growing against old cottage walls, open all day.

AYNHO — SP4932
★ **Great Western Arms** (01869) 338288 *On B4031 1.5 miles E of Deddington, 0.75 miles W of Aynho, adjacent to Oxford Canal and Old Aynho station; OX17 3BP* Attractive old creeper-clad pub with series of cosy linked rooms; fine solid country tables on broad flagstones, golden stripped-stone walls, two-way woodburner, well kept Hook Norton and guests, good wines by the glass and good food

Please tell us if the décor, atmosphere, food or drink at a pub is different from our description. We rely on readers' reports to keep us up to date: feedback@goodguides.com, or (no stamp needed) Freepost THE GOOD PUB GUIDE, Random House Publishing, 20 Vauxhall Bridge Road, London SW1V 2SA.

cooked by landlord-chef from pubby choices up (separate gluten-free menu), friendly attentive young staff, elegant dining area on right, extensive GWR collection including steam locomotive photographs; background music; children and dogs welcome, white cast-iron furniture in back former stable courtyard, moorings on Oxford Canal and nearby marina, four bedrooms, open all day, food all day Sun.

BADBY SP5558

Windmill (01327) 311070

Village signposted off A361 Daventry–Banbury; NN11 3AN Attractive 17th-c thatched and beamed village pub; flagstoned bar with tiled fireplace in huge inglenook, another log fire in adjoining snug, three mainstream ales and a regional guest, good food from interesting varied menu including daily specials, welcoming helpful staff, back restaurant extension; background music; children and dogs welcome, picnic-sets out at front by small green, enjoyable walks (Badby bluebell woods close by), eight bedrooms, open all day in summer, all day weekends winter.

BARNWELL TL0584

Montagu Arms (01832) 273726

Off A605 S of Oundle, then fork right at Thurning/Hemington sign; PE8 5PH Attractive old stone pub in pleasant streamside village; two well kept Digfield ales (brewed close by) and a couple of guests, real ciders and 13 wines by the glass, happy hour Mon 6-7pm, good food including Weds evening two-course deal, cheerful staff, low beams, flagstones and log fire, back dining room, conservatory and cellar bar; children and dogs welcome, big garden with play area, enjoyable walks, open all day Fri-Sun.

BRAYBROOKE SP7684

Swan (01858) 462754

Griffin Road; LE16 8LH Thatched pub with popular sensibly priced food (not Sun evening) from pub favourites up, friendly attentive staff, Everards ales and good choice of other drinks (happy hour Fri 5.30-7pm), fireside sofas, soft lighting, beams and some exposed brickwork, restaurant; background music, quiz last Weds of month; children and dogs welcome, disabled facilities, pretty hedged garden with covered terrace, open all day Sat, closed Mon.

BRIXWORTH SP7470

Coach & Horses (01604) 880329

Harborough Road, just off A508 N of Northampton; NN6 9BX Welcoming early 18th-c thatched and beamed pub; enjoyable food from fairly straightforward menu plus more adventurous specials including seasonal game, lunchtime and early evening set deals, well kept Marstons-related ales, prompt friendly service, log-fire bar with small dining area off, back lounge; tables

on gravelled terrace behind, children and dogs welcome, five bedrooms in converted outbuildings, charming village with famous Saxon church, open (and food) all day Sun.

CHACOMBE SP4943

George & Dragon (01295) 711500

Handy for M40 junction 11, via A361; Silver Street; OX17 2JR Welcoming 17th-c pub with beams, flagstones, panelling and bare stone walls, two inglenook woodburners and deep glass-covered well, good popular food (not Sun evening) in three dining areas including various deals, Everards ales and a guest from brass-topped counter, several wines by the glass; background music, charity quiz first Sun of month; children and dogs (in bar) welcome, picnic-sets with parasols on suntrap terrace, pretty village with interesting church, open all day.

CHAPEL BRAMPTON SP7366

★Brampton Halt (01604) 842676

Pitsford Road, off A5199 N of Northampton; NN6 8BA Popular well laid-out McManus pub on Northampton & Lamport Railway (which is open some weekends) in much extended former stationmaster's house; railway memorabilia and train theme throughout, wide choice of enjoyable food from sandwiches to blackboard specials, meal deal Mon-Thurs, half a dozen well kept ales including Fullers, Sharps and St Austell (beer festivals), plenty of wines by the glass and good range of other drinks, cheerful attentive service even when very busy, large restaurant; background music, TV in bar; children welcome, no dogs inside, lots of tables in big garden with awnings and heaters, summer barbecues and marquee, pretty views over small lake, Nene Way walks, open (and food) all day.

CHARLTON SP5235

Rose & Crown (01295) 811317

Main Street; OX17 3DP Cosy 17th-c thatched village pub under welcoming family management; enjoyable reasonably priced home-made food and well kept ales such as Greene King and Timothy Taylors, good friendly service, beams and stripped stone, nice log fire; children, walkers and dogs welcome, back garden with picnic-sets and wisteria arbour, Cherwell Valley views, open all day Fri and Sat, till 6pm Sun, closed Mon.

CLIPSTON SP7181

Bulls Head (01858) 525268

B4036 S of Market Harborough; LE16 9RT Welcoming village pub with popular good value food (not Mon) served in bar and restaurant, Everards ales and up to four guests, log fire and heavy beams (coins inserted by World War II airmen); background music, Tues quiz, TV; children and dogs welcome, terrace tables, three comfortable bedrooms, open all day weekends, closed Mon lunchtime.

COGENHOE
SP8360
Royal Oak (01604) 890922
Whiston Road; NN7 1NJ Modernised beamed village pub with very good food (best to book) from varied menu including summer wood-fired pizzas, three real ales such as Hook Norton Hooky and St Austell Tribute, friendly helpful staff, open fire in bar, smallish restaurant; children welcome, picnic-sets on part-covered deck, steps down to garden with play area, open all day Fri and Sat, till 7.30pm Sun, closed Mon.

COLLINGTREE
SP7555
Wooden Walls of Old England (01604) 760641
1.2 miles from M1 junction 15; High Street; NN4 0NE Cosy thatch and stone village pub dating from the 15th c and named as a tribute to the navy; four well kept ales and good choice of wines by the glass, generous helpings of reasonably priced home-made food (not Sun evening, Mon), friendly staff, beams and open fire, Northamptonshire skittles in one room; background music, sports TV; children welcome, big back garden with part-covered terrace, closed Mon lunchtime, otherwise open all day.

COLLYWESTON
SK9902
★Collyweston Slater (01780) 444288
The Drove (A43); PE9 3PQ Roomy 17th-c main road inn with good popular pub food including themed evenings, three well kept Everards ales and decent selection of wines, friendly service, contemporary interior with brown leather sofas and easy chairs, smart modern two-part dining room plus some more informal areas, one with raised woodburner in dividing wall, beams, stripped stone and mix of dark flagstones, bare boards and carpeting; background music, TV, darts; children welcome, dogs in bar areas, teak furniture on flagstoned terrace, boules, three bedrooms, open all day, no food Sun evening.

COSGROVE
SP7942
Barley Mow (01908) 562957
The Stocks; MK19 7JD Friendly old village pub close to Grand Union Canal; well kept Everards ales and a guest, decent range of wines and enjoyable reasonably priced home-made food, beamed interior with various connecting areas, dark furniture on carpet or light stone floors, some half-panelling, two-way woodburner in stone fireplace; occasional live music, TV, children and dogs welcome, tables on terrace and lawn leading down to the canal, open all day, food all day weekends.

CRICK
SP5872
★Red Lion (01788) 822342
1 mile from M1 junction 18; in centre of village off A428; NN6 7TX Nicely worn-in stone and thatch coaching inn run by same family since 1979; charming traditional low-ceilinged bar with lots of old horsebrasses (some rare) and tiny log stove in big inglenook, straightforward low-priced lunchtime food, more elaborate evening menu (not Sun) including popular steaks, plenty for vegetarians too, Adnams Southwold, Bombardier and two guests, good friendly service; quiz last Sun of month; children and dogs welcome, picnic-sets on terrace and in Perspex-covered coachyard with pretty hanging baskets.

CRICK
SP5872
Wheatsheaf (01788) 823824
Main Road (A428, handy for M1 junction 18); NN6 7TU Ironstone pub with comfortable log-fire bar and large smartly furnished back restaurant, five well kept ales including one badged for them, good selection of ciders, wines and gins, popular food including bargain OAP set deal (Mon-Sat till 5pm), friendly efficient service; occasional live music and quiz nights; children and dogs (in bar) welcome, bedrooms, open (and food) all day.

CULWORTH
SP5447
Red Lion (01295) 760050
Off B4525 NE of Banbury; OX17 2BD Nicely restored 18th-c beamed dining pub at end of stone terrace; cosy and comfortable, with much liked food (must book) including good Sun roasts, attentive but not intrusive service from welcoming staff, up to four real ales and decent choice of wines; lovely garden behind, open all day Sun, closed Mon and Tues.

DUDDINGTON
SK9800
Royal Oak (01780) 444267
High Street, just off A43; PE9 3QE Stone-built inn on edge of pretty village; modern bar area with leather sofas and chairs on flagstones, panelling and log fire, three real ales from brick servery, restaurant with stone walls, wood floor and light oak furniture, decent food from pub favourites up including set menu (Mon-Thurs), gluten-free and vegan diets catered for; background music; children welcome, disabled facilities, tables on small grassy area at front, six bedrooms, open all day Fri-Sun.

EAST HADDON
SP6668
Red Lion (01604) 770223
High Street; village signposted off A428 (turn right in village) and off A50 N of Northampton; NN6 8BU Elegant golden-stone thatched hotel with sizeable dining room, log-fire lounge and bar, emphasis on their well presented fairly priced food from pub favourites to more restaurant choices, most tables set for dining, but they do keep Courage Directors and St Austell Tribute and offer around a dozen wines by the glass, efficient friendly service; background music; children welcome, attractive grounds including walled side garden, seven

comfortable bedrooms, good breakfast, open all day, food all day weekends.

EASTON ON THE HILL   TF0104
Blue Bell   (01780) 763003
High Street; PE9 3LR Stone-built village pub with good Italian food (not Sun evening, Mon), four changing ales including Grainstore and plenty of wines by the glass, friendly Italian licensees and staff, restaurant; some live music, pool and TV in games area, May beer festival; children and dogs welcome, picnic-sets in sheltered garden behind, closed Sun evening and Mon.

EYDON   SP5450
Royal Oak   (01327) 263167
Lime Avenue; village signed off A361 Daventry–Banbury, and from B4525; NN11 3PG Interestingly laid-out 300-year-old ironstone pub, some lovely period features including fine flagstone floors and leaded windows, small cosy snug on right with cushioned benches built into alcoves, seats in bow window, inglenook log fire, long corridor-like central bar linking three other small characterful rooms, Fullers London Pride, Hook Norton Hooky and Timothy Taylors Landlord, enjoyable food from pub favourites up (just evenings Fri-Sat and Sun lunchtime), friendly staff; children and dogs welcome, terrace seating, open all day Sat, closed lunchtimes Mon and Tues.

GRAFTON REGIS   SP7546
★ **White Hart**   (01908) 542123
A508 S of Northampton; NN12 7SR Thatched roadside dining pub with several linked rooms; well liked home-cooked food from lunchtime baguettes to daily specials, popular Sun roasts (best to book), Greene King Abbot and IPA, Aspall's cider and nice wines by the glass, friendly helpful staff coping well when busy, restaurant with open fire; background music; children and dogs welcome (they have a couple of boxers and a parrot), terrace tables and gazebo in good-sized garden, self-catering cottage, closed Mon.

GREAT BILLING   SP8162
Elwes Arms   (01604) 407521
High Street; NN3 9DT Thatched and low-beamed 16th-c village pub with two bars (steps between); wide choice of good value tasty food including weekday lunch deal, Adnams, Sharps and Wychwood Hobgoblin, friendly service, pleasant dining room where children allowed; background music, quiz Thurs and Sun, open mike night first Weds of month, sports TV, darts; no dogs, garden tables and nice covered decked terrace, play area, open all day, food all day Sat and till 5pm Sun.

GREAT OXENDON   SP7383
★ **George**   (01858) 452286
A508 S of Market Harborough; LE16 8NA

Modernised well run pub under same owners as the Joiners Arms at Bruntingthorpe (Leicestershire); small back bar with two Langton ales and a craft beer, all other areas for dining/pre-dining with bistro-style décor, very good well presented food from shortish but varied menu including a few specials, also good value three-course menu (Mon-Sat lunchtime, Mon evening), prompt friendly service from well turned out staff; children welcome, no dogs inside, paved terrace overlooking garden, eight bedrooms (four in annexe), open all day.

HACKLETON   SP8054
White Hart   (01604) 870271
B526 SE of Northampton; NN7 2AD Comfortably traditional 18th-c country pub; enjoyable sensibly priced food from pub favourites up, Fullers London Pride, Greene King IPA and a guest, friendly helpful staff, flagstoned bar with log fire, dining area up steps, beams, stripped stone and brickwork, deep illuminated well; background music, sports TV, pool and hood skittles; well behaved children and dogs welcome, disabled access, picnic-sets in sunny garden, open all day, no food Sun evening.

HARRINGTON   SP7780
Tollemache Arms   (01536) 711770
High Street; off A508 S of Market Harborough; NN6 9NU Pretty thatched and beamed Tudor pub under same ownership as the Red Lion at East Haddon; enjoyable food including sharing boards, pizzas and burgers, well kept Bombardier, Eagle IPA and three guests, good choice of wines by the glass, cocktails and a local artisan gin, friendly attentive staff; children and dogs (in bar) welcome, back garden with country views and play area, lovely quiet ironstone village, handy for Carpetbagger Aviation Museum, open all day weekends (till 9pm Sun).

HIGHAM FERRERS   SP9668
Griffin   (01933) 312612
High Street; NN10 8BW Welcoming 17th-c pub-restaurant (bigger than it looks) with enjoyable food including fresh fish and popular Sun carvery (till 3.30pm), five well kept rotating ales and good selection of wines and malt whiskies, comfortable front bar with log fire (note the stools), smart back restaurant and dining conservatory, friendly relaxed atmosphere; tables on heated terrace, open all day Fri-Sun.

HINTON-IN-THE-HEDGES   SP5536
Crewe Arms   (01280) 705801
Off A43 W of Brackley; NN13 5NF Stone-built village pub dating from the 15th c; enjoyable home-made food (not Sun evening) including vegetarian/vegan choices and monthly tapas evening, well kept Hook Norton Hooky, a beer named for the pub and a couple of guests, decent wines and over

20 gins, good friendly service, log fires; quiz every other Mon, film nights; children and dogs welcome, picnic-sets in garden, two comfortable bothy bedrooms, open all day summer (all day Fri-Sun, from 4pm other days in winter).

KETTERING   SP8778
Alexandra Arms (01536) 522730
Victoria Street; NN16 0BU Backstreet pub with up to 15 quickly changing ales kept well by knowledgeable landlord; basic opened-up bar with pump clips covering walls and ceiling, some snacky food, darts, hood skittles and TV in back games room; quiz night Weds; dogs welcome, a couple of picnic-sets out in front, small beer garden with benches behind, open all day (from 2pm Mon-Thurs).

KILSBY   SP5671
★George (01788) 822229
2.5 miles from M1 junction 18: A428 towards Daventry, left on to A5 – pub off on right at roundabout; CV23 8YE Welcoming pub handy for the motorway (shuts 3-5.30pm); wood-panelled lounge with plush banquettes and coal-effect gas stove opening into smarter comfortably furnished area, proper old-fashioned public bar, well kept Adnams, Fullers, Timothy Taylors and a guest, fine range of malt whiskies, good value enjoyable home-made food including daily specials and themed evenings; Sun quiz, free-play pool tables, darts, TV; children welcome if eating, dogs in bar, garden picnic-sets, six bedrooms.

KINGS SUTTON   SP4936
★White Horse (01295) 812440
The Square; OX17 3RF Attractively updated Cotswold-stone pub by village green; long, narrow pubby bar with farmhouse tables and chairs on flagstones, armchairs and tartan stools by an open fire and tall stools against the counter, two dining areas with hop-festooned beams, wooden and painted chairs, scatter cushions on wall and window seats and bare floorboards, highly rated creative cooking from chef-landlord with emphasis on local suppliers, well kept Brakspears Oxford Gold and guests, carefully chosen wine list, plenty of gins, cocktails, good friendly service; children and dogs (in bar) welcome, wheelchair access, front picnic-sets looking across green to impressive church, enjoyable nearby walks, closed Mon, otherwise open all day.

KISLINGBURY   SP6959
Cromwell Cottage (01604) 830288
High Street; NN7 4AG Sizeable dining pub tucked away near River Nene; comfortable modernised bar/lounge with some beams and open fire, Civil War-themed pictures, maps and a large mural on one wall, smart dining room, popular food (booking advised) from snacks to specials including weekend brunch from 9am, well kept changing ales and nice

wines, friendly staff; no dogs, plenty of seats on paved terrace, open (and food) all day.

KISLINGBURY   SP6959
Sun (01604) 833571
Off A45 W of Northampton; Mill Road; NN7 4BB Welcoming thatch and ironstone village pub; Greene King IPA, St Austell Tribute and Hoggleys Northamptonshire Bitter, enjoyable fairly traditional food including pizzas and some vegetarian/vegan options, L-shaped bar-lounge and small separate dining area; quiz last Sun of month and occasional live music, sports TV; children welcome, no dogs inside, disabled access, a few picnic-sets out at front, open all day weekends, no food Sun evening, Mon or lunchtime Tues.

LITCHBOROUGH   SP6353
Old Red Lion (01327) 830064
Banbury Road, just off former B4525 Banbury–Northampton; opposite church; NN12 8JF Attractive beamed pub with four cosy rooms; flagstoned bar with woodburner in big inglenook, three real ales such as Grainstore, Great Oakley and Merrimen, enjoyable reasonably priced pubby food (not Mon), friendly relaxed atmosphere, barn-conversion restaurant at back; table skittles, darts; children and dogs welcome, popular with walkers, terrace seating, open all day Sat, till 9pm Sun, from 2.30pm other days (4pm Mon).

LITTLE BRINGTON   SP6663
★Saracens Head (01604) 770640
4.5 miles from M1 junction 16, first right off A45 to Daventry; also signed off A428; Main Street; NN7 4HS Friendly old village pub with an appealing fresh look; good food from interesting varied menu (booking advised), well kept ales including Timothy Taylors Landlord and three guests, 12 wines by the glass and 18 gins, helpful efficient service, roomy U-shaped beamed bar with woodburner, dining room with tartan carpet and books; children welcome, dogs in bar (resident lurcher is called Ellie), disabled access, picnic-sets and rattan-style furniture out on gravel, country views and nearby walks, handy for Althorp House and Holdenby House, open all day, closed Mon, no food Sun evening.

LITTLE HARROWDEN   SP8671
Lamb (01933) 673300
Orlingbury Road/Kings Lane – off A509 or A43 S of Kettering; NN9 5BH Popular 17th-c pub in delightful village; split-level carpeted lounge bar with brasses on beams and log fire, dining area, good promptly served food including OAP lunch deal, three real ales and sensibly priced wine list; games room with hood skittles; background music; children welcome, small raised terrace and lawned garden, open all day weekends, no food Sun evening.

LITTLE HOUGHTON SP8059
Four Pears (01604) 890900
Bedford Road, off A428 E of Northampton; NN7 1AB Modernised pub owned by four local couples (hence the name); three well kept ales, several wines by the glass and decent coffee, enjoyable food (not Sun evening) from light dishes to daily specials, friendly service, good-sized bar, comfortable lounge with woodburner and separate restaurant; children and dogs welcome, spacious outside courtyard area, parking can be tricky (no car park, narrow village street), open all day from noon.

LODDINGTON SP8178
Hare (01536) 710337
Main Street; NN14 1LA Welcoming 17th-c stone-built dining pub with modernised interior; good fairly priced home-made food from baguettes up, five well kept ales such as Greene King, Gun Dog and Sharps; background music, TV, Sun quiz; children and dogs welcome, picnic-sets on front lawn, open all day weekends.

LOWICK SP9780
Snooty Fox (01832) 733434
Off A6116 Corby–Raunds; NN14 3BH Solidly built 17th-c village pub under newish family management; spacious lounge bar with woodburner in sizeable fireplace, stripped stone and handsomely moulded dark oak beams, leather sofas and easy chairs on big terracotta tiles, carved counter serving two well kept changing ales and a dozen wines by the glass, more formal dining rooms with chunky tables on pale wood floor, enjoyable food from pub favourites and pizzas up (some produce from own allotment), friendly helpful service; children and dogs (in bar) welcome, picnic-sets on front grass, play area, open all day weekends, closed Mon.

MAIDWELL SP7477
Stag (01604) 686700
Harborough Road (A508 N of Northampton); a mile from A14 junction 2; NN6 9JA Beamed dining pub now with coffee shop and new village shop; pubby part by bar with woodburner and extensive eating areas, good value traditional food served by friendly staff, well kept often local ales and good choice of other drinks; background music, sports TV; children and dogs (in bar) welcome, disabled facilities, picnic-sets on back terrace, good-sized sloping garden beyond, five bedrooms, not far from splendid Palladian Kelmarsh Hall and park, open all day Fri and Sun.

MOULTON SP7866
Telegraph (01604) 648228
West Street; NN3 7SB Welcoming old village pub with good popular food from sandwiches and home-made pizzas up, well kept Sharps and a couple of guests, log fire in bar, back restaurant extension; children welcome, open (and food) all day Fri and Sat, till 9pm (5pm) Sun.

NETHER HEYFORD SP6658
Olde Sun (01327) 340164
1.75 miles from M1 junction 16; village signposted left off A45 westbound; Middle Street; NN7 3LL Popular village pub with small atmospheric linked rooms; beams and low ceilings, rugs on parquet, red tiles or flagstones (steps between some areas), big inglenook log fire, assorted bric-a-brac including brassware, railway memorabilia, advertising signs and World War II posters, nice old cash till in one part, Banks's, Timothy Taylors and two guests, good range of gins and enjoyable well priced food from sandwiches and baguettes up, takeaway fish and chips Fri, games room with hood skittles and darts; background music, quiz night second Sun of month; children and dogs welcome, old farm equipment outside, open all day, no food Sun evening, Mon.

NORTHAMPTON SP7560
Albion Brewery Bar (01604) 946606
Kingswell Street; NN1 1PR Tap for revived 19th-c Albion Brewery (visible through glass partition, tours available); half a dozen Phipps ales in top condition plus a guest and local cider, also their own Kingswell gins, bar food Tues-Sun, friendly staff, pitched-ceiling bar with big windows and reclaimed fittings (many from closed Phipps pubs), traditional games including Northamptonshire skittles and bar billiards; live music (upstairs concert venue still planned); children and dogs welcome, disabled access/loo, open all day Fri and Sat, closed Sun evening, Mon lunchtime.

NORTHAMPTON SP7261
Hopping Hare (01604) 580090
Harlestone Road (A428), New Duston; NN5 6PF Spacious Edwardian pub-restaurant-hotel on edge of housing estate, contemporary and comfortable, with good well presented food from lunchtime sandwiches and pub favourites to more pricey restaurant dishes, lunchtime/early evening set menu Mon-Thurs, three well kept ales and a dozen wines by the glass including champagne, prompt friendly service; background music, daily newspapers; children welcome, tables out on deck, 20 comfortable modern bedrooms, good breakfast, open (and food) all day.

NORTHAMPTON SP7560
Lamplighter (01604) 631125
Overstone Road; NN1 3JS Welcoming Victorian corner pub in the Mounts area attracting good mix of customers; wide choice of regularly changing real ales, well priced generously served food, good vegetarian options, popular Sun roasts and Mon burger night; regular live music (open

mike Mon), quiz Weds; children welcome if eating, picnic-sets in heated courtyard, open (and food) all day.

NORTHAMPTON SP7559

★**Malt Shovel** (01604) 234212

Bridge Street; no parking in nearby street, use Morrisons central car park, far end – passage past Europcar straight to back entrance; NN1 1QF Bustling city-centre tavern with up to 13 real ales in tip top condition, regulars might include Hook Norton Old Hooky, Nethergate Melford Mild, Oakham Bishops Farewell and JHB and Phipps NBC India Pale Ale (regular beer festivals), also Belgian draught and bottled beers, farm ciders and impressive range of spirits, extensive collection of carefully chosen brewing memorabilia, knowledgeable, enthusiastic staff, bargain-priced pubby lunchtime-only food; darts, background music, regular live music including blues and folk, quiz; children and dogs welcome, disabled facilities, secluded back yard with tables and chairs and a smokers' shelter, open all day.

NORTHAMPTON SP7661

Olde England (01604) 603799

Kettering Road, near the racecourse; NN1 4BP Quirky conversion of Victorian corner shop over three floors (steepish stairs to upper level and down to cellar bar), ground-floor room with assorted tables and chairs on bare boards, 20 changing ales and similar number of ciders served from hatch on stairs, lots of pictures with medieval or Arthurian themes, plus the odd banner, boar's head and suit of armour, cheap food with more extensive choice weekends when pub at its busiest, friendly staff and broad mix of customers; cards and board games; children and dogs welcome, open all day Fri-Sun, closed lunchtimes other days.

NORTHAMPTON SP7660

Princess Alexandra (01604) 245485

Alexandra Road; NN1 5QP Revamped backstreet pub (near the town centre) calling itself a Craft Beer & Alehouse; spacious relaxed bars with pleasing modern décor, recycled timber, exposed brickwork and woodburner, wide range of changing beers and some interesting ciders, tasters offered by friendly knowledgeable staff, shortish menu including snacks and pizzas; children and dogs welcome, small garden behind, parking nearby can be difficult, closed Mon-Weds lunchtime, otherwise open all day (till 1am Fri, Sat).

NORTHAMPTON SP7560

Wig & Pen (01604) 622178

St Giles Street; NN1 1JA Long L-shaped beamed room with bar running most of its length; up to a dozen well kept ales (tasters offered) including Adnams, Fullers and Greene King, traditional ciders and good choice of bottled beers, whiskies and gins, generous helpings of reasonably priced pub food (not weekend evenings) from sandwiches and snacks up, friendly young staff; summer Tues jazz and other live music, weekend DJs, sports TVs; split-level walled garden behind, handy for Guildhall and Derngate Theatre, open all day (till 1am Fri, Sat) and busy on Saints rugby days.

OLD SP7873

White Horse (01604) 781297

Walgrave Road, N of Northampton between A43 and A508; NN6 9QX Popular and welcoming village pub; good sensibly priced food from shortish menu along with some interesting specials (booking advised), three well kept changing ales, craft beers, proper ciders and decent wines by the glass, friendly if not always fast service, additional dining area upstairs; quiz night first Thurs of month, live music last Fri; well behaved children and dogs welcome, garden and deck overlooking 13th-c church, outside pizza oven, open all day Fri and Sat, till 7pm Sun, closed Mon.

OUNDLE TL0388

Ship (01832) 586934

West Street; PE8 4EF Bustling down-to-earth pub run by two brothers; heavily beamed lounge to left of central corridor, cosy areas with mix of leather and other seats, sturdy tables and log fire in stone inglenook, well kept Brewsters, Fullers, Nene Valley and Timothy Taylors, eight wines by the glass and fair value pubby food (not Sun evening), charming panelled snug at one end, also bistro bar and terrace bar with pool, darts and sports TV; background and some live music; children and dogs welcome, series of small covered terraces (lit up at night), 14 bedrooms, open all day.

OUNDLE TL0388

Talbot (01832) 273621

New Street; PE8 4EA Hotel in handsome former merchant's house; various rooms including comfortably modernised bar serving a couple of real ales such as Digfield, enjoyable food from sandwiches and sharing plates up, good helpful service, restaurant; children welcome, seats in courtyard and garden, 40 bedrooms, open (and food) all day, breakfast from 7am.

RAVENSTHORPE SP6670

Chequers (01604) 770379

Chequers Lane; NN6 8ER Cosy old creeper-clad brick pub set among modern residential development; L-shaped bar and restaurant, well kept ales including Adnams, Black Sheep and St Austell, good choice of enjoyable reasonably priced food from light snacks to steaks and daily specials, banquettes, cushioned pews and sturdy tables, coal-effect fire; children and dogs welcome, partly covered side terrace, play area and separate building for Northamptonshire skittles, handy for Ravensthorpe Reservoir and Coton Manor Garden, open all day weekends.

ROCKINGHAM SP8691
Sondes Arms (01536) 772193
Main Street; LE16 8TG 16th-c pub under same owners as the Thornhill Arms at Rushton; tastefully updated beamed interior with wood and stone floors, modern furnishings and woodburner, popular good value home-made food including bargain set menus and carvery (check times), four real ales, helpful friendly staff; children and dogs welcome, courtyard picnic-sets, attractive views of Rockingham Castle and church, lovely village (except for traffic), open (and food) all day Sun, closed Mon evening Jan and Feb.

RUSHDEN SP9566
Station Bar (01933) 213066
Station Approach; NN10 0AW Not a pub but part of station HQ of Rushden Historical Transport Society (non-members can sign in for £1); bar in former ladies' waiting room with gas lighting, enamel signs and railway memorabilia, seven ales including Dark Star and Phipps, tea and coffee, filled rolls and perhaps some hot food, friendly staff; also museum and summer train rides, table skittles in a Royal Mail carriage; outside benches, open all day weekends, closed weekday lunchtimes.

RUSHTON SP8483
Thornhill Arms (01536) 710251
Station Road; NN14 1RL Busy family-run dining pub opposite lovely village's cricket green; enjoyable food (booking advised) including keenly priced set menu (weekday evenings, Sat lunchtime) and carvery (Sun, Mon evening), gluten-free menu too, up to four well kept ales such as Black Sheep and Sharps, smart high-beamed back restaurant and several other neatly laid-out dining areas, open fire; children welcome, garden with decked area, open (and food) all day Sun.

SHUTLANGER SP7249
★ **Plough** (01604) 864644
Main Road, off A43 N of Towcester; NN12 7RU Atractive dining pub with excellent food presented with real flair (booking advised), three real ales including St Austell Tribute, good choice of wines by the glass, cocktails (weekday happy hour 5-7pm), efficient friendly service, new community shop/café introduced during Covid-19 lockdown; painted picnic-sets on gravel terrace, nearby walks (dogs allowed in bar), closed Mon and Tues, otherwise open all day (Sun till 9pm, food till 4.30pm).

SPRATTON SP7170
Kings Head (01604) 847351
Brixworth Road, off A5199 N of Northampton; NN6 8HH Combination of brasserie, bar and coffee shop; pale flagstones and ancient stripped stonework mixing well with handsome new wood flooring and up-to-date décor, leather chesterfields, an antique settle and café chairs around stripped tables, woodburner in brick fireplace, Shepherd Neame Spitfire, well kept ales including Adnams and St Austell, eight wines by the glass, decent range of gins and cocktails, good popular food from light lunches up; background music; children and dogs (in bar) welcome, back courtyard with modern tables and chairs, open all day Fri-Sun, no food Sun evening (coffee shop 8.30am-5pm, closed Sun).

STANWICK SP9871
Duke of Wellington (01933) 622452
Church Street; NN9 6PS Welcoming 19th-c stone pub next to the church; fresh contemporary décor in split-level interior, good well presented food (not Sun evening) from lunchtime sandwiches and pub favourites up including vegan choices, real ales such as Greene King Abbot and IPA, craft beers and decent range of wines; background and occasional live music, Weds quiz; children welcome, picnic-sets out at front under parasols, more behind, open all day (till 10pm Mon-Thurs, 11pm Fri, Sat, 9pm Sun).

STAVERTON SP5461
Countryman (01327) 311815
Daventry Road (A425); NN11 6JH Beamed and carpeted dining pub with popular food from shortish menu including some interesting vegetarian and vegan choices, Bombardier, Hook Norton Hooky and a guest, restaurant; background music; children and dogs welcome, disabled access, tables out at front and in small garden behind, open (and food) all day Sun.

STOKE BRUERNE SP7449
Boat (01604) 862428
3.5 miles from M1 junction 15 – A508 towards Stony Stratford, then signed on right; Bridge Road; NN12 7SB Long thatched pub (run by the Woodward family since 1887) in picturesque canalside spot; traditional flagstoned bar with open fire, half a dozen well kept ales including Banks's Amber Bitter, Marstons Old Empire and Wychwood Hobgoblin, Thatcher's cider, enjoyable fairly standard food at reasonable prices from baguettes up, friendly service, more modern central-pillared back bar and bistro, comfortable upstairs bookable restaurant with separate menu (closed

---

If you know a pub is ever open all day, please tell us.

Mon, Sun evening); background music, Northamptonshire skittles; children and dogs welcome, disabled facilities, tables out by towpath opposite canal museum, shop for boaters and trips on own narrowboat, open all day from 9am for breakfast and can get very busy in summer, especially weekends when parking nearby difficult.

STOKE DOYLE   TL0286

★**Shuckburgh Arms** (01832) 272339
Village signed (down Stoke Hill) from SW edge of Oundle; PE8 5TG Relaxed 17th-c pub in quiet hamlet; four traditional rooms with some modern touches, low black beams in bowed ceilings, pictures on pastel walls, lots of pale tables on wood or carpeted floors, stylish art deco seats and elegant dining chairs, inglenook woodburner, well kept ales such as Nene Valley and guests (maybe Conwy Valley, Osset and St Austell), nicely selected wines and popular sensibly priced food including Thurs steak night, helpful attentive staff; soft background music; children welcome, disabled access/loos, garden with decked area and play frame, bedrooms in separate modern block, closed Sun evening, Mon and Tues.

SUDBOROUGH   SP9682

Vane Arms (01832) 730033
Off A6116; Main Street; NN14 3BX Old thatched pub in pretty village; low beams, stripped stonework and inglenook fires, well kept Everards Tiger and guests, enjoyable freshly cooked food served by friendly staff, restaurant; children and well behaved dogs (in bar) welcome, disabled loo, terrace tables, three bedrooms in nearby building, closed Sun evening.

SULGRAVE   SP5545

★**Star** (01295) 760389
Manor Road; E of Banbury, signed off B4525; OX17 2SA Recently refurbished handsome creeper-clad inn; woodburner in fine inglenook, working shutters, old doors and flagstones, mix of antique, vintage and retro furniture, polished copper and brass, Hook Norton ales, several wines by the glass and enjoyable food from short but varied menu, friendly service, dining room with working range, snug in former farmhouse kitchen; children and dogs welcome, huge back garden with picnic sets (aunt sally is played here), short walk to Sulgrave Manor (George Washington's ancestral home), three bedrooms named after racehorses, closed Sun evening, Mon.

THORNBY   SP6675

★**Red Lion** (01604) 740238
Welford Road; A5199 Northampton–Leicester; NN6 8SJ Popular old village pub with interesting range of well kept changing and often local ales including Nobbys, Langton and Oakham, very good home-cooked food (not Sun evening, Mon)

from standards up including notable steak and stilton pie, smaller helpings available for some lunchtime dishes, prompt friendly service, beams and log fire, lots of old local photographs, back dining area; children and dogs welcome, garden with picnic-sets, accommodation in converted barn, open all day weekends when can get very busy (booking advised), closed Mon lunchtime.

THORPE MANDEVILLE   SP5344

★**Three Conies** (01295) 711025
Off B4525 E of Banbury; OX17 2EX Attractive and welcoming 17th-c ironstone pub; well kept Hook Norton ales and good choice of enjoyable locally sourced food (not Sun evening, Mon), beamed bar with some stripped stone, mix of old tables and comfortable seating on bare boards, log fires, large dining room; background and live music, quiz first Tues of month, TV, hood skittles; children and dogs welcome, disabled facilities, tables in front, more behind on decking and lawn, open all day.

TOWCESTER   SP7047

Folly (01327) 354031
A5 S, opposite racecourse; NN12 6LB Early 18th-c thatched and beamed dining pub with highly rated food (booking advised) including more affordable set lunch, good selection of wines and a couple of well kept local beers such as Towcester Mill, friendly efficient staff, small bar with steps up to dining area; children (till 8pm) and dogs (in bar) welcome, tables out at back, open all day Sun till 9pm, closed Mon.

TOWCESTER   SP6948

Towcester Mill (01327) 437060
Chantry Lane; NN12 6YY Old mill tucked away behind market square surrounded by redevelopment; nice little bare-boards bar acting as tap for on-site brewery (tours available – book ahead), seven ales including a couple of guests, also good range of ciders, friendly knowledgeable staff, occasional evening food; live music, comedy and quiz nights in upstairs room; dogs welcome, big garden behind with seats by mill race and pond, closed lunchtimes Mon-Fri, and shuts at 8pm Sun and Mon.

TURWESTON   SP6037

Stratton Arms (01280) 704956
E of crossroads in village; pub itself just inside Buckinghamshire; NN13 5JX Friendly chatty local in picturesque village; five well kept ales including Otter and good choice of other drinks, enjoyable reasonably priced traditional food (Weds-Sun lunchtimes, Weds-Sat evenings), low ceilings and two log fires, small restaurant; background music, sports TV; children and dogs welcome, large pleasant garden by Great Ouse with barbecue and play area, camping, open all day, till 7pm Sun.

TWYWELL   SP9578
Old Friar (01832) 732625
Lower Street, off A14 W of Thrapston;
NN14 3AH Welcoming pub with enjoyable
food including set lunch menu and Sun
carvery, Adnams and a couple of guests,
modernised split-level interior with beams
and some exposed stonework; children and
dogs (in bar) welcome, garden with good play
area, open (and food) all day weekends.

UPPER BODDINGTON   SP4853
Plough (01327) 260364
Warwick Road; NN11 6DH 18th-c
thatched village inn keeping much of its
original character; small beamed bar, lobby with old local photos,
four real ales including Greene King and
Shepherd Neame, a dozen wines by the
glass and enjoyable fairly traditional food in
restaurant, snug or intimate 'Doll's Parlour'
named after former veteran landlady, friendly
efficient service, woodburners; quiz first Sun
of month, occasional live music and beer
festivals; children and dogs welcome, four
bedrooms (some sharing bathroom), open all
day weekends, no food Sun evening.

WALGRAVE   SP8072
Royal Oak (01604) 781248
Zion Hill, off A43 Northampton–
Kettering; NN6 9PN Welcoming old
stone-built village local; good fairly priced
food including set lunch menu and daily
specials, well kept Adnams, Greene King and
three guests, decent wines, friendly prompt
service, long three-part carpeted beamed bar,
small lounge and back restaurant extension;
live music and quiz nights, sports TV, darts
and Northamptonshire skittles; children
welcome, no dogs inside, small garden with
play area, open all day Sun.

WELFORD   SP6480
Wharf Inn (01858) 575075
Pub just over Leicestershire border;
NN6 6JQ Spacious castellated Georgian
folly in delightful setting by two Grand
Union Canal marinas; six well kept ales such
as Grainstore, Marstons and Oakham in
unpretentious bar, popular reasonably priced
food (all day Sun) including good steak and
kidney pudding and daily specials, helpful
friendly service, pleasant dining section;
children and dogs welcome, wheelchair
access (portable ramps) and disabled loo, big
waterside garden and good local walks, four
bedrooms, open all day.

WELLINGBOROUGH   SP8867
Coach & Horses (01933) 441848
Oxford Street; NN8 4HY L-shaped bar
adorned with breweriana including hundreds
of pump clips fixed to the beams; a dozen
well kept changing ales and ten craft beers,
14 ciders and 80 gins, good value pubby food
including pizza, friendly staff, comfortable
cosy atmosphere with open fire; sports TV; no
children but dogs welcome, disabled access,
beer garden, open all day (till 6pm Sun, 9pm
Mon), no food Sun evening, Mon or Tues.

WELTON   SP5866
White Horse (01327) 702820
Off A361/B4036 N of Daventry; behind
church, High Street; NN11 2JP Beamed
17th-c village pub on different levels; well
kept Purity, Oakham, Sharps and a couple
of guests, local cider and nice house wines,
reasonably priced food (not Sun evening, Mon,
Tues) including good value steak deal Weds-
Sat, roasts only on Sun, woodburners, separate
games bar with darts and skittles, small dining
room; fortnightly Sun quiz and some live
music; children and dogs welcome in one part,
attractive garden and terrace, open all day
Fri-Sun, closed Mon and Tues lunchtimes.

WESTON   SP5846
Crown (01295) 760310
The Weston N of Brackley; Helmdon Road;
NN12 8PX Handsome 16th-c stone-built
inn (ex-farmhouse); updated interior with
log fires, painted beams and exposed stone
walls, Hook Norton Hooky, Sharps Doom Bar
and Towcester Mill Race, well liked food from
sandwiches and good value pubby dishes to
more restaurany choices, Weds fish night,
good friendly service; children and dogs
welcome, five bedrooms, attractive village
handy for Canons Ashby (NT) and Sulgrave
Manor, closed Sun evening and lunchtimes
Mon and Tues.

WHITTLEBURY   SP6943
Fox & Hounds (01327) 858048
High Street; NN12 8XJ Double-fronted
19th-c village bar-restaurant; modern
interior with wood flooring and comfy
stylish seating, four well kept ales, nice
selection of wines and good well presented
food from sandwiches and sharing boards
up (separate bar and restaurant menus),
friendly helpful service; children and dogs
welcome, picnic-sets on suntrap gravel
terrace, handy for Silverstone, open all day
weekends, closed Mon.

YARDLEY HASTINGS   SP8656
★ Rose & Crown (01604) 696276
Just off A428 Bedford–Northampton;
NN7 1EX Spacious and popular 18th-c
dining pub in pretty village; flagstones, beams,
stripped stonework and quiet corners, step
up to big comfortable dining room, flowers
on tables, good well presented food from
interesting changing menu along with bar
snacks and pubby choices, efficient friendly
young staff, six well kept ales – Greene King
Abbot and IPA, Phipps IPA and three guests –
two draught ciders and decent range of wines;
background and occasional live music, daily
newspapers; children welcome till 9pm, dogs
in bar, tables under parasols in split-level
garden, boules, open all day (from 5pm Mon).

Northumbria

(County Durham, Northumberland and Tyneside)

KEY ★ Star Pub 🍽 Top Quality Food ☕ Great Beer
🍷 Good Wines £ Bargain Meals 🛏 Good Bedrooms 🍴 Serves Food

Lord Crewe Arms ★ 🍽 🍷 ☕ 🛏

(01434) 677100 – www.lordcrewearmsblanchland.co.uk
B6306 S of Hexham; DH8 9SP

Wonderful historic building, with unique Crypt bar, cosy dining rooms and spacious character restaurant; comfortable, well equipped bedrooms

It might sound like a pub, but the Lord Crewe is in fact a lovely hotel with a modern country style that maps harmoniously on to the historic building: it was built as a guest house for the neighbouring monastery in the 12th c and the architecture is remarkable. The Crypt bar is a medieval vaulted room with thick stone walls, lit by chandeliers and with family crests on the ceiling. There are high wooden stools by shelf tables and against the armour-plated counter, cushioned settles and plush stools around a few little tables, with Crewe Brew (named for the pub from Twice Brewed) and two other Northumbrian ales on handpump, more than a dozen wines by the glass, a notable gin list, expertly made cocktails and a tap cider. Locals, walkers and diners enjoying an aperitif mix easily here, welcomed by the genuinely friendly and helpful staff; board and outdoor games. The hotel has several eating areas, including the stone-flagged 'larders' area with a baronial fireplace, shaded picnic tables in the garden and the grand Bishop's Dining Room, which features a fine old wooden floor, cushioned wall seating and leather-cushioned dining chairs around oak-topped tables, fresh flowers, antlers on the walls and a large central candelabra. It's a real treat to stay in one of the 21 bedrooms, which range from cosy to luxury suites, some with their own woodburners; breakfast is excellent. Derwent Reservoir is nearby.

🍽 A 'bar bait' snacks menu (including haggis scotch eggs and reuben sandwiches) is served in the bar. You can also eat from the main restaurant menu, focused on seasonal local produce, which might include 'jambon persillé' ham hock with egg yolk dressing and sourdough toast, pear, stilton and walnut salad, dry-aged Northumberland sirloin steak with fries, whole grilled plaice with samphire and new potatoes, roasted artichokes with whipped taleggio potato and warm vegetable dressing, and puddings such as chocolate mousse with salted caramel and hazelnuts and apple and blackberry crumble with custard. Set Sunday lunch is served as a sharing platter for the table, and afternoon tea is available. *Benchmark main dish: braised Northumberland lamb shoulder with peas and broad beans £18.00. Two-course evening meal £29.00.*

Free house ~ Licensee Tommy Mark ~ Real ale ~ Open 7am-midnight ~ Bar food 12-9 daily
~ Restaurant ~ Children allowed in larders area ~ Dogs allowed in bar, larders area
& bedrooms ~ Bedrooms: £210

COTHERSTONE

NZ0119   Map 10

Fox & Hounds ★ 🛏 £

(01833) 650241 – www.cotherstonefox.co.uk

B6277; DL12 9PF

Bustling Georgian country inn with good food and real ales; bedrooms

Set on the green of a pretty Teesdale village, this is a genuine country
pub with warmly welcoming and helpful licensees who get the basics of
old-fashioned hostelry right every time: great food and ale and a good night's
sleep, in a timelessly relaxing atmosphere. The cheerful, simply furnished
beamed bar has a partly wooden floor (elsewhere it's carpeted), a good
winter log fire, cushioned wall seats and local photographs and country
pictures in various alcoves and recesses; look out for the mural of a fox
enjoying a jug of ale. Three local ales on handpump include Tirril 1883 and
there is a decent selection of gins and malt whiskies too. There are seats
outside on a terrace and quoits. The bright, clean and comfortable bedrooms
make a good base for exploring the area – Cotherstone is on the edge of the
North Pennine AONB and close to the Yorkshire Dales National Park, and
there are fine surrounding walks. Disabled access.

 Expertly home-cooked and good value food is made from local ingredients
including Teesdale lamb and beef, Cotherstone cheese from the village creamery,
and eggs, herbs and vegetables from 'dad's garden'. Dishes might include warm bacon,
wensleydale cheese and red apple salad, baked pot of prawns, leeks and mushrooms
in Cotherstone cheese cream with herb crust, steak, black pudding and ale pie with
chips, lambs liver in gravy with mustard mash and crispy bacon, French vegetable bake,
gammon, tomato and cheese melt, and puddings such as chocolate cream crunch and
sticky toffee pudding. *Benchmark main dish: beer-battered haddock with mushy peas
and chips £9.90. Two-course evening meal £17.00.*

Free house ~ Licensee Nichola Swinburn ~ Real ale ~ Open 12-2.30, 6-11; 12-3, 6-11 Sat;
12-3, 6-10.30 Sun ~ Bar food 12-2, 6-8.30 (9 Fri, Sat) ~ Restaurant ~ Children welcome until
9pm ~ Dogs allowed in bar & bedrooms ~ Bedrooms: £100

CRASTER

NU2519   Map 10

Jolly Fisherman

(01665) 576461 – www.thejollyfishermancraster.co.uk

Off B1339, NE of Alnwick; NE66 3TR

Stunning views, very good food and plenty of seasonal visitors

The sheer delight of enjoying quality fish and seafood at the ocean's edge in
Northumberland's kipper capital has brought the Jolly Farmer an enviable
reputation and plenty of customers. The simple, comfortably furnished bar
with its button-back banquettes, open brickwork and bare boards provides
a fire-warmed refuge for winter coast-path walkers, and the pine-furnished
upstairs restaurant has huge windows overlooking the water. In summer,
there are plenty of picnic tables on the grass outside with views to both sea
(look out for dolphins) and harbour – you will need to arrive early on busy
days to secure a good spot; background music. Black Sheep and Mordue
Workie Ticket and a changing guest on handpump are served by helpful,
welcoming staff. They have a couple of fishermen's cottages for rent, as
well as a café and gift shop opposite and a new fish and chip van. This is

a fine base for walkers and the route from here along the cliff to ruined Dunstanburgh Castle (English Heritage) is popular.

A short menu supplemented by evening specials is dominated by seafood. Sandwiches, including the signature crab, are served until 4pm and luxury sharing platter. Starters might include Lindisfarne oysters, queen scallop popcorn, Shetland mussels, kipper scotch egg and devilled crab toast; among the mains are salmon and haddock fishcakes, crab salad, whole Craster kipper, luxury fish pie, lobster salad, vegetable wellington, sirloin steak and pressed belly pork, and desserts include sticky toffee pudding and eton mess. *Benchmark main dish: seafood kebab £19.00. Two-course evening meal £22.00.*

Punch ~ Lease David Whitehead ~ Real ale ~ Open & bar food 11-8.30; 11-9 Fri, Sat; 12-7 Sun; shorter hours Nov-Mar ~ Restaurant ~ Children welcome ~ Dogs allowed in bar

DIPTONMILL
NY9261 Map 10

Dipton Mill Inn ★ ◖ £

(01434) 606577 – www.diptonmill.co.uk

Dipton Mill Road, S Hexham; village signed from B6306; NE46 1YA

Own-brew beers from on-site microbrewery, good value bar food and waterside terrace

In the grounds of this appealingly unchanged country pub is the Hexhamshire Brewery – both are owned by the same family. The brewery's output, including Blackhall English Stout, Devils Elbow, Shire Bitter, Wall Walker and Whapweasel, makes its way to six of the pub's handpumps, supplemented by two draught ciders (Weston's Old Rosie and a guest), 20 malt whiskies and a dozen wines by the glass. It's a quaint little place whose neatly kept snug bar has genuine character, dark ply panelling, low ceilings, red furnishings, a dark red carpet and two welcoming open fires. The sunken garden is peaceful and pretty, with attractive planting and seats on grass by a restored mill stream. Hexham Racecourse is not far away and there are also woodland walks nearby.

The appealing, good value food changes daily and, as well as sandwiches, might include soup of the day, dressed crab, haddock with tomato and basil, mince and dumplings, steak pie, bacon chop in cider sauce, tomato, bean and vegetable casserole, and puddings such as syrup sponge and a cake of the day; Saturday is Indian food night. *Benchmark main dish: chicken breast in sherry sauce £9.20. Two-course evening meal £14.00.*

Own brew ~ Licensee Mark Brooker ~ Real ale ~ Open 12-2.30, 6-11; 12-3 Sun ~ Bar food 12-2.30, 6.30-8.30; 12-2 Sun ~ Restaurant ~ Children allowed in bar ~ Dogs allowed in bar

DURHAM
NZ2742 Map 10

Victoria ★ ◖

(0191) 386 5269 – www.victoriainn-durhamcity.co.uk

Hallgarth Street (A177, near Dunelm House); DH1 3AS

Unchanging and neatly kept Victorian pub with royal memorabilia, cheerful locals and well kept regional ales; bedrooms

Close to the historic centre of Durham, this traditional family-run inn not only makes a great base for exploring the city but is well worth a visit in its own right. The original Victorian décor is still intact and it remains charming and unspoilt – just how the long-serving, attentive owners like it. Three small rooms, leading off a central bar, have mahogany, etched and cut glass and mirrors, colourful William Morris wallpaper over a high panelled dado, some maroon plush seats in little booths, leatherette wall seats and long narrow drinkers' tables. Also, coal fires in handsome iron and tile fireplaces, photographs and articles showing a real pride in the pub, lots of period prints and engravings of Queen Victoria, and Staffordshire figurines of her and the Prince Consort. Big Lamp Bitter is always available on handpump, along with four other well kept changing ales, most of them, such as Durham White Stout and Wylam Gold Tankard, from the Newcastle and Durham area. There's also more than 35 Irish whiskeys, 60 Scottish malts and fair-priced house wines; dominoes. Attractive bedrooms, hearty breakfasts and free off-street parking make this little gem a perfect base for a city break.

Toasted sandwiches only are available all day.

Free house ~ Licensee Michael Webster ~ Real ale ~ Open 11.45-11; 12-10.30 Sun ~ Children allowed in bar ~ Dogs allowed in bar & bedrooms ~ Bedrooms: £90

GILSLAND
NY6366   Map 10
Samson 🍺
(016977) 47880/(016977) 47962 rooms – www.thesamson.co.uk
B6318, E end of village; CA8 7DR

Friendly village pub in wonderful countryside, with cheerful atmosphere in cosy bar, local ales and enjoyable food; bedrooms

The Samson is named after a locomotive that once served the local station. That's closed now, and lots of customers arrive here on foot or by bike instead, via the Hadrian's Wall Path and Hadrian's Cycleway – this charming, unpretentious pub offers them a particularly warm welcome. The busy bar has woodburning stoves, cushioned settles, a squashy sofa, pubby tables and chairs on red-patterned carpeting and comfortable stools at the carved wooden counter. Allendale Adder plus one or two local ales (perhaps from Muckle or Wrytree), and several wines by the glass; they hold quiz nights, themed evenings and live music events year round. In the dining room are tweed-upholstered chairs around tables set on wide floorboards, and prints on green walls. There are picnic-sets on the back lawn, and four warm and attractive bedrooms that make a good base for exploring the area. They also have a self-catering cottage outside the village.

A long-established kitchen team uses local and own-grown produce in tasty pub dishes such as twice-baked cheddar soufflé, bangers and mash, chestnut and mushroom pie, lamb hotpot and tomato risotto, plus appealing desserts such as sticky toffee pudding and armagnac parfait served with their own fig compote. *Benchmark main dish: chicken, bacon and leek pie £11.95. Two-course evening meal £19.00.*

Free house ~ Licensees Liam McNulty and Lauren Harrison ~ Real ale ~ Open 12-10.30 ~ Bar food 12-2.30, 6-8.30 ~ Children welcome ~ Dogs allowed in bar ~ Bedrooms: £90

GREAT STAINTON
NZ3321
Kings Arms 🍽
(01740) 630873 – www.kingsarmsgreatstainton.co.uk
Glebe Road; TS21 1NA

High-class food cooked by the owner in bustling village pub

Refurbished and reopened by an enthusiastic chef-patron and his wife, this busy little place is in a quiet, leafy village. Most customers are here for the particularly good food, but there is also a small bar with leather armchairs, high chairs against the counter, bare floorboards and a friendly welcome. There's a couple of real ales on handpump and well chosen wines by the glass. A restaurant extension at the rear has button-back banquette wall seating, high-backed dining chairs around white-clothed tables on carpet, books on shelves and a few local pictures, and there's a woodburning stove. There are seats and tables outside at the front and to the side.

I◉I Imaginative food using the best local produce includes a good-value set menu, creative seasonal specials, all-day bar snacks including a couple of sandwiches and notably good vegetarian options. From the main menu, dishes include foie gras and black pudding with scrumpy apple and pineapple chutney, charred Scottish mackerel with pickled cucumber, watercress and horseradish, Whitby dressed crab, local venison with rainbow chard, wild mushrooms, medjool dates and honey-roast black fig, Hartlepool halibut with white asparagus, spinach, lobster ravioli and bisque, and puddings such as Yorkshire rhubarb and egg custard tart and hot dark chocolate fondant. *Benchmark main dish: pancetta-rolled pork fillet, confit belly and braised cheek with crackling, squash purée, caramelised apples and scrumpy reduction £21.00. Two-course evening meal £32.00.*

Free house ~ Licensee Paul Bussey ~ Open 5.30-11 Mon; 11.30-3, 5.30-11 Tues-Sat; 11.30-6 Sun ~ Bar food 12-3, 5.30-9 Tues-Thurs; 12-3, 5.30-9.30 Fri, Sat; 12-4 Sun; not Mon ~ Children allowed in bar

HEDLEY ON THE HILL
Feathers ★ I◉I ◖

NZ0759 Map 10

(01661) 843607 – www.thefeathers.net
Village signposted from New Ridley, which is signposted from B6309 N of Consett; OS Sheet 88 map reference 078592; NE43 7SW

Northumbria Dining Pub of the Year

Popular village tavern with imaginative food, interesting beers from small breweries and a friendly welcome

Making a virtue out of necessity, the Feathers' licensees Rhian and Helen created an outside kitchen, fire-pit barbecue and outside dining space for summer 2020's tentative steps out of Covid-19 lockdown. This illustrates not just their community spirit and hard-working, hands-on ethos, but their respected status on the contemporary dining scene – such outdoor feasting is of the moment. The interior is tiny but very well run and welcoming, with two neat, homely bars with open fires, tankard-hung beams, stripped stonework, solid furniture including settles, and old black and white photographs of local places and farm and country workers. There are three cask and four craft beers on handpump, including Allendale Wagtail and Hadrian Border Secret Kingdom, as well as a wide range of farm ciders, 30 or so wines by the glass, 38 malt whiskies, home-flavoured gins and home-produced cordials. They hold regular wine and beer evenings, festivals and other events (see the website for details); dominoes and board games. The picnic-sets at the front are a nice place to watch the world drift by.

I◉I First class food using only the best carefully sourced local produce from artisan producers and farmers includes home-cured rare-breed ox tongue pastrami with potato salad and pickled beetroot, baked duck egg with morel mushrooms, wild garlic and cream, roast cauliflower steak with warm cracked wheat, roasted tomato and pepper sauce, beer-battered fish and chips, rabbit, cider and wild mushroom pie, local roast mallard with marmalade and Cointreau and celeriac purée, slow-cooked rare-breed lamb with braised spelt, leeks, carrots and mint, and puddings such as almond and orange sponge with vanilla custard and dark chocolate brownie with candied walnuts and vanilla ice-cream.

Free house ~ Licensees Rhian and Helen Cradock ~ Real ale ~ Open 6-10.30 Mon; 6-11 Weds; 12-11 Thurs-Sun; closed Mon and Wed lunchtimes, all Tue; closed first two weeks Jan ~ Bar food 6-8.30 Weds; 12-2, 6-8.30 Thurs, Fri; 12-2.30, 6.30-8.30 Sat; 12-4.30 Sun ~ Children welcome

NEWTON
Duke of Wellington

NZ0364   Map 10

(01661) 844446 – www.thedukeofwellingtoninn.co.uk

Off A69 E of Corbridge; NE43 7UL

Big stone pub with modern and traditional furnishings, well kept ales, interesting drinks and highly thought-of food; bedrooms

Readers are regularly charmed by the attractive country setting of this honey-stoned inn, with fine views across the Tyne Valley and sheep grazing right up to the car park's fence. In the bustling bar with its built-in cushioned wall seats, farmhouse chairs and tables on honey-coloured flagstones, big woodburning stove and rustic bar stools against the counter, they serve Greene King IPA, Hadrian Border Tyneside Blonde and other local ales from the likes of High House and Wylam on handpump, a dozen wines by the glass, cocktails and a good choice of malt whiskies and gins; TV, darts, board games and daily papers. The L-shaped restaurant has elegant blue tartan-upholstered and wood dining chairs around pale tables on bare boards, modern art on exposed stone walls, and french windows that lead out to the attractive back terrace. Paintwork throughout is contemporary. The seven comfortable and well equipped bedrooms (a couple are dog-friendly) are popular with those exploring the area; breakfasts are hearty.

 As well as breakfasts (8-10am), the creative food might include twice-baked cheddar soufflé with parmesan cream, local cured meats, mackerel with white chocolate, horseradish and beetroot, steak and mushroom pie, fish and chips, burgers and steaks, braised pork cheek with sultana ragout, grain mustard croquette, braised leeks and caraway jus, truffled mushroom arancini with pea purée, salt-baked beetroot and charred corn, halibut with prawns, braised fennel and sea vegetables, and puddings such as cream pannacotta with berry compote and sticky toffee pudding with clotted cream ice-cream. *Benchmark main dish: lamb rump with fondant potato, pea and broad bean fricassée, confit tomato, braised gem lettuce and mint vinaigrette £18.00. Two-course evening meal £20.00.*

Free house ~ Licensee Rob Harris ~ Real ale ~ Open 8am-11.30pm ~ Bar food 12-9; 12-5 Sun ~ Restaurant ~ Children welcome ~ Dogs allowed in bar & bedrooms ~ Bedrooms: £140

NEWTON-BY-THE-SEA
Ship

NU2424   Map 10

(01665) 576262 – www.shipinnnewton.co.uk

Low Newton-by-the-Sea, signed off B1339 N of Alnwick; NE66 3EL

In a charming seafront square of fishermen's cottages with good simple food and own-brew beers; check winter opening times

Beguiled by its seaside setting, the Ship's proprietor, Christine Forsyth, came here from Hertfordshire over 20 years ago on impulse and her pub has since earned a reputation for own-brew beer, a fine crab sandwich, bags of character and a friendly welcome. Tables outside the row of converted fishermen's cottages look across the sloping village green and down to the sea and you can walk from here along the massive stretch of empty, beautiful beach with views all the way to Dunstanburgh Castle (English Heritage).

Inside, the plainly furnished but cosy bare-boards bar on the right has nautical charts on dark pink walls, while another simple room on the left has beams, bright modern pictures on stripped-stone walls and a woodburning stove in a stone fireplace. They brew their own beers on site and usually have four on handpump at any one time from a range of 18 or so – maybe Ship Inn Dolly Day Dream, Red Rye or Sea Dog stout – plus Black Sheep Bitter. It can get extremely busy at peak times, so it's best to book in advance, and be prepared for a queue for the bar. There's no nearby parking from May to September, but there is a car park up the hill.

🍴 Good locally sourced food ranges from lunchtime sandwiches (including hand-picked crab) and regional snacks such as kipper fish cakes, Jarvis pies and filled 'stottie' bread rolls to more expensive dinner choices. Perhaps local organic salami and chorizo with home-made piccalilli, kipper pâté with oatcakes, roast monkfish wrapped in parma ham with roast cherry tomatoes, rib-eye steak or roasted beetroot with goats cheese and hazelnut salad, and puddings such as honey and walnut tart with vanilla ice-cream and Doddington's Dairy berwick edge cheese with home-made apple chutney. *Benchmark main dish: Northumbrian lamb chops with roasted fennel, tenderstem broccoli and heritage potatoes £19.95. Two-course evening meal £25.00.*

Own brew ~ Licensee Christine Forsyth ~ Real ale ~ Open 11-11; 12-10 Sun; 11-5 Mon-Weds; 12-5 Sun in winter ~ Bar food 12-2.30 Mon-Weds; 12-2.30, 7-8 Thurs-Sat; 12-2.30 Sun ~ Children welcome ~ Dogs allowed in bar & restaurant

ROMALDKIRK
Rose & Crown ★ 🏵 ⌨

NY9922   Map 10

(01833) 650213 – www.rose-and-crown.co.uk

Just off B6277; DL12 9EB

18th-c coaching inn with accomplished cooking, attentive service and a fine choice of drinks; boutique-style bedrooms

This is a lovely, handsome old inn standing next to St Romald's Church on the edge of the village green – you can see the original stocks and water pump from the picnic-sets out front. The beamed bar area has old-fashioned seats facing a warming log fire, a Jacobean oak settle, a grandfather clock, brass hunting horns and old farm tools and black and white pictures of Romaldkirk on the walls. Black Sheep, Marstons Wainwright and a changing guest ale on handpump, seven wines by the glass from a good list, 20 malt whiskies and 16 gins. Another room has elegant pale oak country chairs and stools by a woodburning stove and there's an oak-panelled restaurant; background music. If you stay in one of the 14 comfortable, well equipped bedrooms (in the main building, the courtyard or Monk's Cottage), the owners provide an in-house guide for days out in the area, and a *Walking in Teesdale* book. Disabled access. The church is worth a look and the exceptional Bowes Museum and High Force waterfall are both nearby.

🏵 Using impeccably local produce, much of it from Teesdale, the kitchen turns out nicely conceived modern British food along with platters and more straightforward pub grub such as 'hog roast' sausages and mash. Dishes might include mushroom soup with wild mushroom and rosemary crouton, goats cheese salad with nectarines, fennel, walnuts and burnt orange dressing, grilled seabass with brown shrimps, sag aloo, toasted almonds and spring onion and coconut curry, beef bourguignon pie with glazed carrots, champ potato and tenderstem broccoli, roasted aubergine with ratatouille topped with toasted pine nuts and mozzarella, and puddings such as dark chocolate brownie and tonka bean pannacotta with summer berries and almond crumb. *Benchmark main dish: roast loin of Teesdale lamb with shepherd's pie, crushed peas and mint pesto £18.00. Two-course evening meal £25.00.*

Free house ~ Licensee Cheryl Robinson ~ Real ale ~ Open 11-10; 11-11 Sat ~ Bar food 12-2, 6-8.30 ~ Restaurant ~ Children welcome (no under-8s after 8pm) ~ Dogs allowed in bar & bedrooms ~ Bedrooms: £150

SEAHOUSES NU2232 Map 10
Olde Ship ★ ◑ ⇔ £
(01665) 720200 – www.seahouses.co.uk
Just off B1340, towards harbour; NE68 7RD

Lots of atmosphere and maritime memorabilia in busy little inn, with views across harbour to Farne Islands; bedrooms

A stone's throw from the picturesque little fishing harbour, the Olde Ship is all about celebrating Seahouses' nautical heritage, and offers a good range of ten ales to toast it with. You'll find a rich assemblage of maritime bits and pieces in the unchanging and old-fashioned bar: lots of shiny brass fittings, ships' instruments and equipment, a knotted anchor made by local fishermen, sea pictures and model ships (including fine ones of the North Sunderland lifeboat and the Seahouses' *Grace Darling* lifeboat). There's also a model of the *Forfarshire*, the paddle steamer that local heroine Grace Darling went to rescue in 1838 (you can read more of the story in the pub), and even the ship's nameboard. An anemometer takes wind-speed readings from the top of the chimney. It's all gently lit by stained-glass sea-picture windows, lantern lights and a winter open fire. Simple furnishings include built-in leatherette pews around one end, stools and cast-iron tables. Black Sheep, Born in the Borders Game Bird and Hadrian Border Farne Island Pale are among the regular ales on handpump; summer guests might include Allendale Pennine Pale, Firebricks Blaydon Brick or Tyne Banks Dark Brown; there's a good wine list, 35 gins and 70 malt whiskies; background music and TV. The battlemented side terrace (more fishing memorabilia out here) and one window in the sun lounge look across the harbour to the Farne Islands (as do some bedrooms). If you find yourself here as dusk falls, the beam of the Longstones lighthouse shining across the fading evening sky is a charming sight. The pub is not really suitable for children, though there is a little family room, and children are welcome in the beer garden (as are walkers), with its sea and harbour views. You can book boat trips to the Farne Islands at the harbour, and there are bracing coastal walks, notably to Bamburgh, the birthplace of Grace Darling.

Tasty food includes sandwiches (including crab), duck and orange pâté, smoked fish chowder, vegetable lasagne, crab salad, gammon with egg and pineapple, chicken and mushroom casserole, pizzas, Craster kipper with brown bread, and puddings such as lemon meringue pie and rum and raisin pudding. *Benchmark main dish: beer-battered fish and chips £9.75. Two-course evening meal £16.00.*

Free house ~ Licensees Judith Glen and David Swan ~ Real ale ~ Open 11-11; 12-11 Sun ~ Bar food 12-2.30, 7-8.30 ~ Restaurant ~ Children allowed in restaurant ~ Bedrooms: £100

STANNERSBURN NY7286 Map 10
Pheasant Inn £ ⇔
(01434) 240382 – www.thepheasantinn.com
Kielder Water road signposted off B6320 in Bellingham; NE48 1DD

Friendly village inn with quite a mix of customers, homely bar food and streamside garden; bedrooms

This honey-stone longhouse dates back to the mid-1600s, and has long been a focus for the community, first as a farm, later as the drop-off point for Royal Mail and since the 1980s as a family-run pub. In a quiet valley surrounded by forests, it's close to Kielder Water, convenient for Hadrian's Wall and can arrange fishing and bike hire for guests: the area is a cycling mecca. The charming low-beamed lounge has ranks of old local photographs on stripped stone and panelling, brightly polished surfaces, shiny brasses, dark wooden pubby tables and chairs and upholstered stools ranged along the counter; there are several open fires. A separate public bar is simpler and opens into another snug seating area with beams and panelling. The friendly licensees and courteous staff serve Timothy Taylors Landlord and one or two guests such as Allendale Wolf and Wylam Cascade on handpump, several wines by the glass, 40 malt whiskies and a couple of farm ciders. There are picnic-sets in the streamside garden, plus a pony paddock. The eight bedrooms are comfortable, breakfasts are good and they also have a self-catering cottage.

Enjoyable food made with produce as local as its own cottage garden includes sandwiches and packed lunches; also, twice-baked Northumberland cheese soufflé, red onion and goats cheese tartlet, hot-smoked salmon, new potato, fennel and french bean salad with horseradish dressing, Moroccan baked cod with roasted vegetable couscous, dressed local crab, game and mushroom pie, salmon, lemon sole, monkfish or sea bass with herb butter or light cream sauce, and puddings such as brioche and marmalade bread and butter pudding and bakewell tart.

Free house ~ Licensees Walter and Robin Kershaw ~ Real ale ~ Open 12-3, 6-11 ~ Bar food 12-2, 6-8 ~ Restaurant ~ Children welcome ~ Dogs allowed in bedrooms but not inside the pub ~ Bedrooms: £116

WARK
Battlesteads ★ 🏵 🍺 🛏

NY8676   Map 10

(01434) 230209 – www.battlesteads.com

B6320 N of Hexham; NE48 3LS

Eco pub with good local ales, fair value interesting food and a relaxed atmosphere; comfortable bedrooms

The owners of this attractive stone pub deep in the North Tyne Valley are extremely conscientious about the environment and gently weave their beliefs into every aspect of the business; they grow their own produce (and recycle food waste in a wormery), have a charging point in the car park for electric cars and use a biomass boiler. The nicely restored, low-beamed, carpeted bar has a woodburning stove with a traditional oak surround, comfortable, tartan-upholstered seats and easy chairs and some high chairs around an equally high table. You'll find a good range of drinks: 12 wines by the glass, 25 malt whiskies, 35 gins and a farm cider, plus Fyne Jarl and Hadrian Border Secret Kingdom with a couple of guests such as Hadrian Border Tyneside Blonde and Wylam Gold Tankard on handpump. Service is excellent; background music and TV. There's also a restaurant, a spacious conservatory and tables on the terrace and a Dark Skies observatory nearby. There are 22 comfortable bedrooms; some of the ones on the ground floor have disabled access.

Highly regarded food making good use of their own produce and on-site smokery includes sandwiches, tempura courgette flowers with goats cheese, chilli and honey, own-made charcuterie, pan-fried duck breast with charred cauliflower, black pudding 'prunes', savoury granola and cassis jelly, beer-battered haddock, roast vegetable jalfrezi, grilled salmon with king prawns, Moroccan-style hogget with spiced couscous and home-made harissa, and puddings such as blackcurrant cheesecake and chocolate brownie with chocolate sauce. There are also tasting menus including for vegetarians. *Benchmark main dish: rack of Cumbrian lamb with dauphinoise potatoes and star anise carrots (for two) £34.00. Two-course evening meal £20.00.*

Free house ~ Licensees Richard and Dee Slade ~ Real ale ~ Open 11-11 ~ Bar food 12-3, 6.30-8.30 ~ Restaurant ~ Children welcome ~ Dogs allowed in bar, restaurant & bedrooms ~ Bedrooms: £125

Also Worth a Visit in Northumbria

Besides the fully inspected pubs, you might like to try these pubs that have been recommended to us and described by readers. Do tell us what you think of them: feedback@goodguides.com

ACOMB　　　　　　　　　　NY9366
Miners Arms　(01434) 603909
Main Street; NE46 4PW Friendly little 18th-c village pub; good value traditional food (not Sun evening, Mon) including weekday set menu and popular Sun roasts, Hadrian Border Tyneside Blonde plus two guests, carpeted bar with comfortable settles and huge fire in stone fireplace, back dining area; quiz last Thurs of month; children and dogs welcome, a couple of tables out in front, more in back courtyard, open all day Sun, closed other lunchtimes.

ALLENDALE　　　　　　　　NY8355
Golden Lion　(01434) 683225
Market Place; NE47 9BD Friendly 18th-c two-room pub on the market square; beers from on-site microbrewery along with guests such as Allendales, enjoyable traditional food at reasonable prices, can eat in bar or upstairs restaurant, games area with pool and darts; regular live music; children and dogs welcome, Allendale Fair first weekend of June, New Year's Eve flaming barrel procession, bedrooms, open all day (till late Fri, Sat).

ALNMOUTH　　　　　　　　NU2410
★ Red Lion　(01665) 830584
Northumberland Street; NE66 2RJ Friendly 18th-c coaching inn with peaceful sheltered garden and raised deck giving wide views over the Aln estuary; black beams, classic leather wall banquettes and window seats in pleasant relaxed bar, old local photographs on dark mahogany brown panelling, cheerful fires, four well kept real/craft ales might include Credence, Cullercoats and Tempest(Oct beer festival), good wines by the glass and popular fairly pubby food from lunchtime sandwiches to restaurant-standard pub fare, stripped-brick restaurant with flagstones and woodburner; background and monthly live music, Tues quiz; children and dogs (in bar) welcome, seven comfortable well equipped bedrooms, open all day.

ALNWICK　　　　　　　　　NU1813
John Bull　(01665) 602055
Howick Street; NE66 1UY Chatty beer drinkers' pub – essentially the front room of an early 19th-c terraced house; good selection of well kept changing ales may include Brentwood Mild and Legacy, real cider and lots of bottled Belgian beers, also over 100 malt whiskies; Sat cheese club (but otherwise no food), folk session every other Mon, darts and dominoes; small beer garden, closed weekday lunchtimes.

ALNWICK　　　　　　　　　NU1913
Market Tavern　(01665) 602759
Fenkle Street; NE66 1HW Refurbished split-level pub in central position; handsome corner bar with clock, well kept ales such as Hadrian Border and Wainwright, decent wines by the glass, popular fairly priced food (steaks a speciality), friendly helpful service; children and dogs welcome, six bedrooms, open all day.

ALNWICK　　　　　　　　　NU1813
Plough　(01665) 602395
Bondgate Without; NE66 1PN Smart contemporary pub-cum-boutique hotel in Victorian stone building (under same management as the Jolly Fisherman at Craster – see Main Entries); Timothy Taylors Landlord and a guest, several wines by the glass and extensive range of gins, good food (not Sun evening) in bar, bistro or upstairs restaurant, friendly helpful staff; children and dogs welcome, pleasant streetside raised terrace, seven bedrooms, open all day.

ALNWICK　　　　　　　　　NU1813
Tanners Arms　(01665) 602553
Hotspur Place; NE66 1QF Welcoming little drinkers' pub with five well kept local ales and a decent glass of wine; flagstones and stripped stone, warm woodburner, plush stools and wall benches, small tree in the centre of the room; juke box and some live acoustic music, TV; dogs welcome, open all day weekends, closed weekday lunchtimes.

ANICK　　　　　　　　　　NY9565
★ Rat　(01434) 602814
Village signposted NE of A69/A695 Hexham junction; NE46 4LN Popular country pub with cosy traditional bar; coal fire in kitchen range, cottagey knick-knacks such as floral chamber-pots hanging from

beams, six well kept ales, one of them Wylam, real cider, a dozen wines by the glass, good well presented interesting food (not Sun evening), efficient service, conservatory; background music; children welcome, charming garden with dovecote, statues and lovely North Tyne Valley views, limited parking (you can park around the village green), open all day.

AYCLIFFE   NZ2822
★**County** (01325) 312273
The Green, Aycliffe; just off A1(M) junction 59, off A167 at West Terrace and then right to village green; DL5 6LX
Smart inn with comfortable open-plan rooms; seating from cushioned dining chairs to country kitchen, painted ceiling joists, striped carpet and log burner, highly regarded imaginative food in simply decorated restaurant, three real ales, a craft beer and 11 wines by the glass, friendly service; children welcome, no dogs inside, metal tables and chairs out at front facing green, seven attractive bedrooms, open all day, food all day Sun till 6pm.

BAMBURGH   NU1834
Castle (01668) 214616
Front Street; NE69 7BW Spic and span comfortably old-fashioned pub with generous helpings of reasonably priced food from good scampi to daily specials, friendly efficient service, two well kept ales from Born in the Borders and decent house wines, cheery part-panelled bar and expanded dining area, open fires (one in old range); children welcome, no dogs inside, circular picnic-sets in nice beer garden, open (and food) all day, close to Bamburgh Castle.

BAMBURGH   NU1834
Lord Crewe Arms (01668) 214243
Front Street; NE69 7BL Small hotel prettily set in Georgian building now with sleek modern interior; bar and restaurant with painted joists and panelling, bare stone walls and light wood floor, warm woodburner, a couple of well kept local beers from Alnwick and Anarchy, cocktails, good varied menu from lunchtime 'stottie' sandwiches up, friendly helpful staff; children over 11 and dogs (in one area) welcome, sheltered garden with castle view, short walk from sandy beach and Bamburgh Castle, seven comfortable bedrooms, open all day.

BARDON MILL   NY7566
★**Twice Brewed** (01434) 344534
Military Road (B6318 NE of Hexham); NE47 7AN Large busy inn, remote but well placed for fell-walkers and major Hadrian's Wall sites and next to the Sill youth hostel and discovery centre; up to half a dozen ales including some from on-site microbrewery including interesting brews like cherry milk stout, they also distil their own spirits, home-cooked pub food from sandwiches/panini

up, cheerful helpful service; woodburners; brewery tours, guided star-gazing; children and dogs welcome, disabled access, picnic-sets in back garden, 18 bedrooms, open (and food) all day.

BARRASFORD   NY9173
★**Barrasford Arms** (01434) 681237
Village signposted off A6079 N of Hexham; NE48 4AA Bustling sandstone inn with owner-chef's highly praised interesting food (not Sun evening), welcoming local atmosphere and friendly helpful staff, traditional log-fire bar with old photographs and bric-a-brac, up to three local ales such as Allendale, First & Last and High House Farm, two dining rooms, one with wheelback chairs around neat tables and stone chimneybreast hung with guns and nets, the other with comfortably upholstered dining chairs; background music, TV, darts; children welcome, plenty of nearby walks, handy for Hadrian's Wall, bedrooms, open all day weekends, closed Mon.

BEADNELL   NU2229
Beadnell Towers (01665) 721211
The Wynding, off B1340; NE67 5AY Popular pub-hotel recently reborn as a stylish boutique hotel; bistro-style bar-restaurant with parquet, banquettes and striking yellow-upholstered bar stools; sophisticated range of wine, spirits including own gin and cocktails plus two ales from Alnick and guests, good locally sourced pub food; children and dogs welcome; 18 bedrooms, open all day.

BEAMISH   NZ2154
Beamish Hall (01207) 233733
NE of Stanley, off A6076; DH9 0YB Converted stone-built stables in courtyard at back of hotel; popular and family-friendly (can get crowded), with five or six beers from own microbrewery (tours available), decent wines and enjoyable food from light lunches up, uniformed staff; regular events such as live music, barbecues and a summer festival; plenty of seats outside, big play area, open (and food) all day.

BEAMISH   NZ2055
Black Horse (01207) 232569
Red Row (off Beamishburn Road NW, near A6076); OS Sheet 88, map reference 205541; DH9 0RW Late 17th-c country dining pub with contemporary/rustic interior; heritage colours, beams, flagstones and exposed stonework, enjoyable food (not Sun evening) from sandwiches and pub favourites up, regular themed nights such as Italian, half a dozen well kept changing beers, cocktails and decent wines by the glass, afternoon teas (one for children), friendly attentive staff, cosy fire-warmed front room extending to light spacious dining area with central bar, more dining upstairs, airy conservatory; children welcome, dogs in bar, views from terrace, more tables on grass,

attractive bedrooms and suite/cottage rental, close to Beamish open-air museum, open all day from 9am for breakfast.

BERWICK-UPON-TWEED NT9952
Barrels (01289) 308013
Bridge Street; TD15 1ES Small friendly pub with interesting collection of pop memorabilia and other bric-a-brac, some eccentric furniture too including a barber's chair in bare-boards front bar, five well kept changing beers and range of foreign bottled beers, snacky food, red banquettes in back room; regular live acoustic sessions (often in basement bar) and good quality background music; children and dogs welcome, open all day.

CHATTON NU0528
Percy Arms (01668) 215244
B6348 E of Wooler; NE66 5PS Sympathetically updated stone-built country inn (same owners as the Northumberland Arms at Felton); good well presented food from standard dishes up in flagstoned log-fire bar or light panelled dining room (booking advised), six well kept ales, good whisky and gin choice, friendly helpful staff, open fire and woodburner; darts; children and dogs (in bar) welcome, picnic-sets on small front lawn, five well appointed bedrooms, good breakfast, quiet village with sweeping views of the Cheviot Hills, open (and food) all day.

CONSETT NZ1150
Travellers Rest (01207) 507555
Forster Street; DH8 7JU Renovated brick-built pub on two floors; bare-boards bar with farmhouse furniture, woodburner in big fireplace, good pubby food including blackboard specials, three changing ales, friendly attentive staff, upstairs galleried dining area; jukebox and TV; children welcome, picnic-sets in paved beer garden behind, open all day.

CORBRIDGE NY9964
Angel (01434) 632119
Main Street; NE45 5LA Imposing coaching inn at end of broad street in this attractive old town; best sense of building's age in separate lounge with oak panelling and a big stone fireplace, also look out for the fine 17th-c arched doorway in left-hand porch; airy modern bar serving six local ales including a Wylam house beer, Weston's cider; around 20 wines by the glass and numerous gins and malt whiskies, good food from varied menu plus own fish and chip shop, dining lounge and raftered restaurant; children and dogs (not in bar) welcome, tables out at front under parasols, comfortable bedrooms, parking for residents

but free car park on other side of the bridge, open (and food) all day.

CORBRIDGE NY9864
Black Bull (01434) 632261
Middle Street; NE45 5AT Rambling 18th-c beamed pub with four linked rooms; mix of traditional pub furniture including leather banquettes, wood, flagstone or carpeted floors, log fires (one in open hearth with gleaming copper canopy), ceramics collection in front room and information about Hadrian's Wall, decent reasonably priced pubby food, two Greene King ales and two guest beers and good choice of wines by the glass, efficient cheery service; children welcome, no dogs, seats out on two-level terrace, open (and food) all day.

CORNHILL-ON-TWEED NT8539
Collingwood Arms (01890) 882424
Main Street; TD12 4UH Comfortably updated Georgian stone hotel; nice little bar with decent wines, around 25 malt whiskies and a couple of well kept local ales, good reasonably priced food in adjoining dining room or more pricey restaurant, friendly helpful staff, open fires; children and dogs (in bar) welcome, tables out in lovely grounds, local fishing and shooting, 15 well appointed bedrooms (named after ships from the Battle of Trafalgar), good breakfast, open all day.

CROOKHAM NT9138
Blue Bell (01890) 820789
Pallinsburn; A697 Wooler–Cornhill; TD12 4SH Welcoming 18th-c roadside country pub; enjoyable freshly prepared food, three well kept ales and good selection of gins, friendly attentive service; quiz some Sun, dogs welcome in bar, comfortable clean bedrooms, good breakfast, open all day Fri-Sun.

DARLINGTON NZ2814
Number Twenty 2 (01325) 354590
Coniscliffe Road; DL3 7RG Long narrow Victorian pub with high ceiling, wood and carpeted floors and some exposed brickwork, a dozen or more quickly changing ales (tasters offered) including own Village Brewer range and real ciders, draught continentals and 20 wines by the glass, they also have an in-house distillery, snacky lunchtime food, good friendly service; open from 4pm Mon and Tues, all day Weds-Sat, 2-7pm Sun.

DINNINGTON NZ2073
White Swan (01661) 872869
Prestwick Road; NE13 7AG Large open-plan pub-restaurant popular for its wide range of good value food including gluten-

---

Half pints: by law, a pub should not charge more for half a pint than half the price of a full pint, unless it shows that half-pint price on its price list.

free menu, reasonably priced wines and a well kept changing ale, efficient friendly service even at busy times; background music; family area (children's menu till 5.30pm), no dogs inside, disabled facilities, orangery and attractive garden with pond, handy for Newcastle Airport, open all day Sun till 6pm.

DUNSTAN NU2419
Cottage (01665) 576658
Off B1339 Alnmouth–Embleton; NE66 3SZ Comfortable single-storey beamed inn; enjoyable reasonably priced food from local suppliers includes Craster kippers, up to three well kept ales such as Hadrian Border, restaurant and conservatory; sports TV, live music; children and dogs welcome, attractive garden with terrace and play area, ten bedrooms, short walk from Craster and Dunstanburgh Castle (EH) ruins, open all day.

DURHAM NZ2742
Dun Cow (0191) 386 9219
Old Elvet; DH1 3HN Unchanging backstreet pub in pretty 16th-c black and white timbered cottage; tiny chatty front bar with wall benches, corridor to long narrow back lounge, three well kept ales including Black Sheep and simple sandwichy food (not Sun evening), friendly staff; background and occasional live music, Mon quiz; children welcome in lounge area, no dogs, open all day.

DURHAM NZ2742
Head of Steam (0191) 383 2173
Reform Place, North Road; DH1 4RZ Hidden-away pub close to the river; modern open-plan interior on two floors, well stocked bar serving good range of changing ales, craft kegs, real ciders and a vast range of bottles and cans from around Durham, Britain, Belgium and the USA, new cocktail list, competitively priced food including burgers and pizzas, deals most days; background music (live upstairs); dogs welcome, outside tables, open (and food) all day.

DURHAM NZ2642
Old Elm Tree (0191) 386 4621
Crossgate; DH1 4PS Friendly old pub on steep hill across from the castle; two-room main bar and small lounge up steps, half a dozen well kept beers, reasonably priced home-made food, open fires, live folk music and quiz nights; dogs welcome, small back terrace, open all day.

DURHAM NZ2742
Shakespeare
Saddler Street; DH1 3NU Friendly refurbished 19th-c brick pub (bigger inside than it looks); fairly compact front bar incorporating former snug, larger back lounge and an upstairs spirits bar, well kept Caledonian Deuchars IPA, Fullers London

Pride and two guests, pubby lunchtime food; children (till 5pm) and dogs welcome, convenient for castle, cathedral and river, can get crowded (particularly weekends), open all day.

DURHAM NZ2742
Swan & Three Cygnets
(0191) 384 0242 *Elvet Bridge; DH1 3AG* Victorian pub in good bridge-end spot high above the river, city views from big windows and terrace; bargain lunchtime food and Sam Smiths ales, helpful friendly young staff, popular with locals and students, picnic tables by river, no phones inside and cash only; open all day.

EACHWICK NZ1069
Plough (01661) 853555
Stamfordham Road (extension of B6324), S of village; NE18 0BG Large refurbished stone inn tucked away in remote countryside; open-plan split-level lounge with comfortable furniture including sofas, tub and wing-back chairs on wood or carpeted floors, good choice of enjoyable food from snacks to specials, also evening Chinese menu, one or two well kept changing ales and fairly priced wines, separate restaurant; outside seating, three bedrooms, open all day Fri and Sat, till 5pm Sun, closed Mon, Tues.

EARSDON NZ3273
★ Beehive (0191) 252 9352
Hartley Lane; NE25 0SZ Popular well run 18th-c country pub with cosy linked rooms; low painted beams, soft lighting, woodburners and one or two quirky touches, three well kept hatch-served ales (tasting trays available), highly rated well priced home-made food (best to book weekends) from sandwiches, light dishes and sharing boards up, friendly service; background and some live music, TVs; children welcome, dogs in one area, picnic-sets out overlooking fields, summer bar and separate family garden with play area, also 'secret garden', open (and food) all day, till 8pm (6pm) Sun.

EDMUNDBYERS NZ0150
Punch Bowl (01207) 255545
B6278; DH8 9NL Small village's community local; three well kept ales from the likes of Firebrick and good choice of reasonably priced food including daily specials, friendly service; TV; children and dogs (in bar) welcome, fishing on nearby Derwent Reservoir (permits from the pub), six bedrooms, good breakfast, open (and food) all day.

EGLINGHAM NU1019
★ Tankerville Arms (01665) 578444
B6346 Alnwick–Wooler; NE66 2TX Traditional 19th-c stone inn with contemporary touches and cosy friendly atmosphere; beams, bare boards and some stripped stonework, banquettes and warm

fires, three ale taps, good wines, enjoyable nicely presented food from shortish menu, raftered split-level restaurant; children, walkers and dogs welcome, lovely country views from back garden, attractive village, three bedrooms, closed lunchtimes Mon, Tues, otherwise open (and food) all day.

ELLINGHAM NU1625
Pack Horse (01665) 589292
Signed off A1 N of Alnwick; NE67 5HA
Stone-built pub in peaceful village; masses of jugs hanging from beams in flagstoned bar, a long settle and upholstered stools around traditional tables, log fire, Black Sheep, Timothy Taylors and a guest from local Rigg & Furrow, good food (not Sun evening) using own produce including home-reared meat, bare-boards snug with stag's head above large stone fireplace, restaurant divided into two with high-backed chairs around pale tables on tartan carpet; background music, open mike night last Sun evening of month; children and dogs (in bar) welcome, picnic-sets in enclosed garden, five pretty bedrooms and self-catering cottage, open all day in summer and Sat, Sun year round.

EMBLETON NU2322
Dunstanburgh Castle Hotel
(01665) 576111 *B1339; NE66 3UN*
Comfortable hotel in attractive spot near magnificent coastline; good choice of enjoyable bar and restaurant food using local meat and fish, good vegetarian options too, efficient friendly service, local ales and decent wines, two lounges with open fires; children and dogs (in one lounge) welcome, seats in nice garden, good for Embleton Bay and Dunstanburgh Castle (EH), bedrooms and self-catering cottages, open all day.

EMBLETON NU2322
Greys (01665) 576983
Stanley Terrace off WT Stead Road, turn at the Blue Bell; NE66 3UY Welcoming old-school proper pub with carpeted bar and cottagey back dining room; enjoyable home-made food including crab sandwiches, eight or so well kept regional beers such as Alnwick; juke box, sports TV; children and dogs welcome, small walled back garden with village views from raised deck, open all day.

ESH NZ1944
Cross Keys (0191) 373 1279
Front Street; DH7 9QR Friendly 18th-c beamed village local under enthusiastic new management; hearty helpings of good well priced food (not Sun evening) including blackboard specials, real ales and craft beers, afternoon teas; children welcome,

hanging baskets out at front, good country views from behind; apartment to rent sleeping nine; closed Mon, otherwise open all day (but may shut if quiet).

FELTON NU1800
Northumberland Arms
(01670) 787370 *West Thirston; B6345, off A1 N of Morpeth; NE65 9EE* Stylish 19th-c inn across road from River Coquet (same owners as the Percy Arms in Chatton); roomy open-plan lounge bar with beams, exposed stone/brickwork and nice mix of furnishings including big sofas on flagstones, woodburner, bare-boards restaurant with mix of light wood tables, good sensibly priced food from bar snacks and standard dishes up (best to book), bread from their own bakery, three changing ales including Allendale and nice wines by the glass, friendly service; Thurs quiz; children welcome, dogs in bar, six good bedrooms, open (and food) all day.

FROSTERLEY NZ0236
★ **Black Bull** (01388) 527784
Just off A689 W of centre; DL13 2SL Unique in having its very own peal of bells (licensee is a campanologist); great atmosphere in three interesting traditional beamed and flagstoned rooms with coal fires (one in old range), landlord's own good photographs and three grandfather clocks, six handpumps dispensing well kept local ales and traditional cider/perry, carefully chosen wines, good range of malt whiskies, highly rated food using local and organic ingredients (best to book evenings and Sun lunch), friendly helpful staff; some acoustic live music; well behaved children and dogs welcome, attractive no-smoking terrace with wood-fired bread oven (sometimes pizza) and old railway furnishings (opposite steam line station), closed Sun evening, Mon, Tue, otherwise open all day.

GATESHEAD NZ2563
Central (0191) 478 2543
Half Moon Lane; NE8 2AN Unusual 19th-c wedge-shaped pub (Grade II listed) restored by the Head of Steam group; well preserved features including notable buffet bar, great choice of changing local ales, real ciders and lots of bottled beers, low-priced food from short menu, upstairs function rooms and roof terrace; some live music; dogs welcome, open all day.

GRETA BRIDGE NZ0813
★ **Morritt** (01833) 627232
Hotel signposted off A66 W of Scotch Corner; DL12 9SE Striking 17th-c country house hotel popular for weddings and the

---

'Children welcome' means the pub says it lets children inside without any special restriction; some may impose an evening time limit earlier than 9pm – please tell us if you find this.

like; pubby bar with big windsor armchairs and sturdy oak settles around traditional cast-iron-framed tables, open fires and remarkable 1946 mural of Dickensian characters by JTY Gilroy (known for his Guinness adverts), big windows looking on to extensive lawn, a couple of real ales including Timothy Taylors, good gin and wine lists, enjoyable bar and restaurant food, afternoon teas, friendly staff; background music; children and dogs (in bar and bedrooms) welcome, attractively laid-out split-level garden with teak tables and play area, open all day.

HALTWHISTLE   NY7166
Milecastle Inn (01434) 321372
Military Road; B6318 NE – OS Sheet 86 map reference 715660; NE49 9NN Sturdy stone-built pub on remote moorland road running alongside Hadrian's Wall; small carpeted rooms off beamed bar, brasses, prints and two log fires, up to three well kept ales (maybe just Big Lamp Prince Bishop in winter), popular home-made food (best to book weekends), friendly helpful service, small comfortable restaurant; children welcome, no dogs inside, tables and benches in big sheltered garden with stunning views, two self-catering cottages next door, open all day in summer.

HART   NZ4634
White Hart (01429) 265468
Just off A179 W of Hartlepool; Front Street; TS27 3AW End-of-terrace pub with ship's figurehead outside; fires in both bars (one in old range), enjoyable fairly traditional food (not Sun evening), two changing ales; children welcome, no dogs inside, open all day.

HAYDON BRIDGE   NY8364
General Havelock (01434) 684376
Off A69 Corbridge–Haltwhistle; B6319 (Ratcliffe Road); NE47 6ER Old darkly painted pub, a short stroll upstream from Haydon Bridge itself; L-shaped bar with open fire, piano and some Philip Larkin memorabilia, two well kept ales, decent choice of wines by the glass and enjoyable generously served food, stripped-stone barn dining room; children and dogs (in bar) welcome, terrace with fine South Tyne river views, closed Mon lunchtime.

HEXHAM   NY9464
Heart of Northumberland
(01434) 608013 *Market Street; NE46 3NS* Renovated old local with Timothy Taylors Landlord and four guests kept well, also craft beers, proper ciders and plenty of wines by the glass, well cooked reasonably priced food from pub favourites up, good cheerful service, traditional furniture on bare boards, some blue-painted panelling and exposed stonework, woodburner in big fireplace; live music

Thurs; children and dogs welcome, small outside seating area behind, open (and food) all day including brunch from 11am.

HIGH HESLEDEN   NZ4538
Ship (01429) 836453
Off A19 via B1281; TS27 4QD Popular Victorian inn with seven well kept changing ales and good food cooked by landlady (some interesting specials), sailing ship models, log fire; sea views over farmland from garden, six bedrooms in modern block, open all day Sun till 8pm, closed Mon and lunchtimes Tues-Sat.

HOLY ISLAND   NU1241
Crown & Anchor (01289) 389215
Causeway passable only at low tide, check times at www. visitnorthumberland.com/coast/holy-island/crossing-times; TD15 2RX Simply updated pub-restaurant by the priory; two well kept Hadrian Border ales plus one guest, good range of whiskies and gins and enjoyable food from changing blackboard menu cooked by landlord-chef, cosy bar with coal fire, more roomy back dining room; children and dogs (in bar) welcome, disabled access/loo, picnic-sets in grassy garden with lovely views, four bedrooms, open all day.

HOLY ISLAND   NU1241
Ship (01289) 389311
Marygate; TD15 2SJ Well positioned and busy in season; beamed bar with wood floors, stone walls and maritime memorabilia, big stove, steps down to carpeted lounge/dining area, popular pubby menu including fish/seafood (good crab sandwiches), Holy Island Blessed Bitter badged for them by Hadrian Border plus one or two guests, also 30 malt whiskies and their own gin; background music; children welcome and usually dogs (but do ask first), sheltered sunny garden, four bedrooms, may close at quiet times.

HORSLEY   NZ0965
Lion & Lamb (01661) 852952
B6528, just off A69 Newcastle–Hexham; NE15 0NS Friendly whitewashed 18th-c former coaching inn; main beamed and flagstoned bar with scrubbed tables, stripped stone and open fire, three mainly local beers and popular good value food, attentive service, bare-boards restaurant (pasta and pizza night Tues); darts, monthly quiz and some live music; children and dogs (in bar) welcome, Tyne views from attractive sunny garden with terrace and play area, open all day.

HURWORTH-ON-TEES   NZ2814
★ Bay Horse (01325) 720663
Church Row; DL2 2AA Popular dining pub (best to book, particularly weekends) with very good imaginative food, quite pricey but they do offer a fixed-price alternative (Mon-Thurs), also vegetarian and vegan menus and

children's meals, two regular (Black Sheep and Old Speckled Hen) and two changing ales, extensive wine list, efficient friendly young staff, sizeable bar with good open fire, restaurant, and another dining room upstairs; seats on back terrace and in well tended walled garden, charming village by River Tees, open all day.

HURWORTH-ON-TEES   NZ3110
Otter & Fish (01325) 720019
Off A167 S of Darlington; Strait Lane; DL2 2AH Pleasant village setting across road from the Tees; up-to-date open-plan layout with flagstones and stripped wood, brick fireplaces and church candles, nice mix of dining furniture, comfortable armchairs and sofas by bar, popular well presented local food including an early evening discount and decent vegetarian and children's choices (best to book, especially weekends), friendly helpful staff, a couple of changing ales and several wines by the glass; outside seating area, closed Sun evening.

LANGDON BECK   NY8531
Langdon Beck Hotel
(01833) 622267 *B6277 Middleton–Alston; DL12 0XP* Remote unpretentious inn with two cosy bars and spacious lounge; good choice of enjoyable generous food using local Teesdale beef and lamb, ales such as Great North Eastern Rivet Catcher and Marstons Wainwright, friendly helpful staff, interesting rock collection in display cases in 'geology room'; events such as traditional Easter 'egg jarping' with hard-boiled eggs and late May beer festival; children and dogs welcome, wonderful fell views from garden, walkers and cyclists welcome, well placed for walks including Pennine Way; seven bedrooms (some sharing bathrooms), open all day, closed Mon Oct-Easter.

LANGLEY ON TYNE   NY8160
Carts Bog Inn (01434) 684338
A686 S, junction B6305; NE47 5NW Isolated 18th-c moorside pub; heavy beams and exposed stone walls, spindleback chairs around mix of tables on red carpet, old photographs and nice open fire, enjoyable generously served food from sandwiches up including signature Bog Pie (steak and mushroom suet pudding) and popular Sun lunch (best to book), two or three well kept local ales, friendly efficient staff; pool and darts in games room, Aug beer and cider festival; children and dogs welcome, picnic-sets in big garden with views, open all day weekends, closed Mon, Tues, sometimes Weds lunch .

LONG NEWTON   NZ3716
Vane (01642) 580401
Darlington Road; TS21 1DB Restored 19th-c village pub – which, as we went to press, was fighting hard to stay open as the Tees Valley's first community pub; previously,

and hopefully again (but check before visiting), Black Sheep and a couple of guests, warm friendly service, solid dark dining tables and chairs, upholstered banquettes, cosy bar with log fire, good food from simple to more restaurant; background music, Sun quiz; children and dogs (in bar) welcome, picnic-sets in garden with far-reaching views across fields, three bedrooms, open all day Sun, closed Mon and lunchtime Tues, no food Sun evening.

LONGFRAMLINGTON   NU1301
Granby (01665) 570228
Front Street; NE65 8DP Welcoming old coaching inn run by same family for three generations; highly regarded food cooked by chef-landlord from well executed pub favourites to creative restaurant dishes, also good value set lunch and afternoon teas, one well kept real ale and several malt whiskies, comfortable traditional beamed interior with bar, lounge and small restaurant; children welcome, no dogs, five bedrooms, open (and food) all day.

LONGFRAMLINGTON   NU1301
Village Inn (01665) 570268
Just off A697; Front Street; NE65 8AD Friendly 18th-c stone inn arranged into three distinct areas; tasty freshly prepared pub food including good Sun carvery, own-brewed VIP beers along with local guests; Mon quiz; five comfortable bedrooms and three self-catering log cabins (just outside the village), open all day.

LONGHORSLEY   NZ1494
Shoulder of Mutton (01670) 788236
East Road; A697 N of Morpeth; NE65 8SY Comfortable and capacious pub and restaurant with good choice of enjoyable reasonably priced food from lunchtime baguettes up, popular and good value Sun carvery (must book in advance), three real ales, good selection of other drinks, welcoming staff; background music, TV, fruit machine; children and dogs (in bar) welcome, picnic-sets in back garden, two bedrooms, open all day, food all day Fri, Sat and till 6pm Sun.

LUCKER   NU1530
★ Apple (01668) 213824
Off A1 N of Morpeth; NE70 7JH Updated old stone-built pub in tiny village; very good food from pub favourites, burgers and chargrills to more upmarket choices, real ales including a house beer and one other from Alnwick plus nice wines, friendly engaging staff, logburner in bar's large fireplace, wood-strip floors and some exposed stonework, modern furnishings, roomy big-windowed dining area; children and dogs welcome, wheelchair access, circular picnic-sets on decking, two comfortable bedrooms, good breakfast, closes 8pm Sun, otherwise open all day.

MAIDEN LAW   NZ1749

Three Horseshoes (01207) 520900
A6067 N of Lanchester; DH7 0QT
Spacious roadside dining pub; enjoyable
good value food from varied menu including
several vegetarian options, pie night Tues
(made from scratch), Mexican evening Weds,
afternoon teas, neatly kept open-plan interior
with central beamed and quarry-tiled bar,
mix of cane chairs, leatherette sofas and tub
chairs, two-way woodburner, conservatory;
children welcome, disabled parking and
wheelchair access, garden with play area,
open all day Sat, till 5pm Sun, closed Mon.

MICKLETON   NY9724
★ Crown (01833) 640381
B6277; DL12 0JZ Bustling country pub
under friendly hands-on licensees; simply
furnished bars and dining areas, cushioned
settles, upholstered leather and wooden
dining chairs around all sorts of tables
on polished boards, country prints and
photographs, woodburner flanked by two
leather armchairs, a couple of cask ales,
several wines by the glass and good food from
lunchtime sandwiches and pub favourites to
more restaurranty choices; children and dogs
welcome, rustic picnic-sets in pretty lawned
garden with fine country views, one bedroom
and Caravan Club campsite, closed Mon-Weds,
otherwise open (and food) all day, kitchen
closes 4pm Sun.

MIDDLETON   NZ0685
Ox (01670) 772634
*Village signed off B6343, W of Hartburn;
NE61 4QZ* Welcoming unpretentious
Georgian country pub in small tucked-away
village; a couple of well kept local ales
and tasty straightforward home-made food
(served Thurs to Sun lunchtime); open fires;
children and dogs welcome, seats outside in
beer garden, handy for Wallington (NT), open
all day Sat (summer only) and Sun, from
4.30pm other days.

MIDDLETON ONE ROW   NZ3612
Devonport (01325) 332255
The Front; DL2 1AS Spacious and
attractively refurbished 18th-c hotel-
restaurant-bar under same ownership as the
Bay Horse at Hurworth-on-Tees; stone and
wooden floors, open fires, some distinctive
pictures on fashionable grey-green walls and
a dog-friendly bar, enjoyable bistro/pub food,
a couple of real ales and good selection of
wines and spirits, warm welcoming service;
children and dogs (in bar) welcome; beer
garden and sunny terrace, attractive spot
facing village green, eight comfortable
bedrooms with up-to-date bathrooms, good
breakfast, handy for Teesside Airport.

MILFIELD   NT9333
Red Lion (01668) 216224
*Main Road (A697 Wooler–Cornhill);
NE71 6JD* Comfortable and welcoming
18th-c coaching inn with good food from
chef-owner, smaller appetites and gluten-free
diets catered for, well kept ales such as Black
Sheep and Thwaites, a dozen wines by the
glass and decent coffee, friendly efficient
service; Weds quiz; children welcome, no
dogs inside, pretty garden by car park at
back, six bedrooms (some with fishing rod
storage), good breakfast, open all day.

MORPETH   NZ1986
Tap & Spile (01670) 513894
Manchester Street; NE61 1BH Cosy
two-room pub with up to eight well kept ales
including Castle Rock and Timothy Taylors,
Weston's cider, fruit wines and short choice
of good value lunchtime food, friendly staff,
traditional pub furniture and interesting old
photographs, quieter back lounge (children
allowed here) with coal-effect gas fire;
darts, board games; background and live
acoustic music Sun afternoon, sports TV; dogs
welcome in front bar, open all day Fri-Sun.

NETHERTON   NT9807
Star (01669) 630238
*Off B6341 at Thropton, or A697 via
Whittingham; NE65 7HD* Simple village
local run by charming long-serving landlady
(licence has been in her family since 1917);
cherished mid-20th-c interior in large high-
ceilinged room with wall benches and many
original features, friendly regulars, range of
bottled beers (only), no food, music, children
or dogs; only open evenings two days a week
(Fri, Sun, from 7.30pm).

NEWBROUGH   NY8768
Red Lion (01434) 674226
Stanegate Road; NE47 5AR Former
coaching inn with light airy feel; log fires,
flagstones and half-panelling, old local
photographs and some large paintings,
seasonal locally sourced food well priced
for the quality served in bar and two dining
areas, a couple of well kept local ales,
friendly efficient service, games room with
pool and darts, little shop selling local art/
craftwork; children and dogs (not at food
times) welcome, garden behind with decking,
good walks and on NCN cycle route 72, six
bedrooms, open all day (from 4pm Mon).

NEWCASTLE UPON TYNE   NZ2464
★ Bacchus (0191) 261 1008
*High Bridge E, between Pilgrim Street
and Grey Street; NE1 6BX* Smart,
spacious and comfortable pub in Sir
John Fitzgerald group with ocean

Virtually all pubs in this book sell wine by the glass. We mention wines
if they are a cut above the average.

liner-inspired décor; two-level interior with lots of varnished wood, pillars, ship and shipbuilding photographs, very well kept ales include regulars Fyne Jarl and craft beer Anarchy Blonde Star plus seven guests, also plenty of bottled imports, farm cider and splendid range of whiskies, gin pairings, decent coffee too, friendly helpful staff, no food; background music but quiet ambiance; disabled facilities, handy for the Theatre Royal, open all day and can get very busy.

NEWCASTLE UPON TYNE NZ2464
Bodega (0191) 221 1552
Westgate Road; NE1 4AG Majestic Edwardian drinking lit next to Tyne Theatre; eight real ales/craft beers including local house beer Almasty Creation and good range of bottled beers, no food, friendly service, snug front cubicles, spacious back area with two magnificent stained-glass cupolas; quiz Thurs, background music, four big-screen TVs (very busy on match days), darts; open all day.

NEWCASTLE UPON TYNE NZ2563
★ Bridge Hotel (0191) 232 6400
Castle Square, next to high-level bridge; NE1 1RQ Beautiful and spacious 19th-c pub in historic Sir John Fitzgerald group, next to Stephenson's Tyne bridge; high-ceiling, stained-glass windows, replica slatted snob screens and magnificent fireplace, ten handpumps pouring Sharps Doom Bar, own ale plus quickly changing guests, real cider, bargain lunchtime food (not Mon), great river views from raised back area, live music upstairs including long-standing Mon folk club; background music, sports TV; flagstoned terrace overlooking part of old town wall, heated area, open all day.

NEWCASTLE UPON TYNE NZ2563
★ Bridge Tavern (0191) 261 9966
Under the Tyne Bridge; NE1 3UF Bustling brewpub under same ownership as the Town Wall; airy interior with exposed brickwork and lots of wood, industrial-style ceiling, view into small-batch microbrewery at back producing cask and keg (joint venture with Wylam), ten or so beers including local guests (tasting trays available), generous helpings of well liked often unusual food (all day, till 7pm Fri-Sun) from snacks and sharing boards up, friendly helpful staff; background music; well behaved children and dogs allowed before 7pm, upstairs bar and good roof terrace, open all day (till 1am Fri, Sat).

NEWCASTLE UPON TYNE NZ2563
Broad Chare (0191) 211 2144
Broad Chare, just off quayside opposite law courts; NE1 3DQ Traditional feel yet relatively recent conversion; known for its British-leaning food from rated bar snacks such as crispy pigs ears and pork crackling to hearty main courses, four real ales including a house beer from Wylam (Writer's Block), good choice of bottled beers, wines and whiskies, bare-boards bar and snug, old local photographs, upstairs dining room; background music; children welcome till 7pm (later in upstairs dining room), next to Live Theatre, open all day (no food Sun evening).

NEWCASTLE UPON TYNE NZ2464
Centurion (0191) 261 6611
Central Station, Neville Street; NE1 5DG Glorious high-ceilinged Victorian décor with tilework and columns in former first-class waiting room, well restored with comfortable leather seats giving club-like feel, half a dozen real ales including from Great North Eastern, good value food till early evening; background music, big-screen sports TV; well behaved children and dogs welcome, heated outdoor patio, useful café-deli next door, open all day.

NEWCASTLE UPON TYNE NZ2464
City Tavern (0191) 232 1308
Northumberland Road; NE1 8JF Revamped half-timbered city-centre pub on different levels; up to ten real ales including a couple badged for them, decent wine list and around 60 gins, enjoyable food from reasonably priced varied menu, plenty of vegan and gluten-free choices, friendly staff; well behaved children and dogs welcome (menus for both), open (and food) all day, kitchen closes 7pm Sun.

NEWCASTLE UPON TYNE NZ2664
Cluny (0191) 230 4474
Lime Street; NE1 2PQ Bar-café-music venue in interesting 19th-c mill/warehouse; low-priced home-made USA-style food including various burgers and wraps, up to seven well kept ales, interesting selection of guest cans and bottles from the likes of Beavertown and Magic Rock, efficient friendly service, sofas in comfortable raised area with daily papers and art magazines, back gallery featuring local artists; background music and regular live bands (also in Cluny 2 next door); children (till 7pm) and dogs allowed, picnic-sets out on green, striking setting below Metro bridge, parking nearby can be difficult, open (and food) all day.

NEWCASTLE UPON TYNE NZ2365
Cosy Dove (0191) 260 2895
Hunters Road, Spital Tongues; NE2 4NA City fringe pub with opened-up interior blending contemporary and traditional features, leather sofas, black and white tiles and wood floors, log fire, good fairly priced casual food from open kitchen including range of 'build your own' burgers and grills, a beer badged for the pub plus a guest, good range of wines and gins plus Alnwick rum, friendly welcoming staff;

background music, quiz nights and sports TV; a few pavement tables, open all day, no food Sun evening.

★**Crown Posada** (0191) 232 1269
The Side; off Dean Street, between and below the two high central bridges (A6125 and A6127); NE1 3JE City's second-oldest pub, on the quayside just a few minutes' stroll from the castle; long narrow room with elaborate coffered ceiling, stained-glass counter screens and fine mirrors with tulip lamps on curly brass mounts (matching the great ceiling candelabra), long green built-in leather wall seat flanked by narrow tables, old photos of Newcastle and plenty of caricatures, six handpumps serving well curated local and northern ales such as Abbeydale and Hadrian Border Tyneside Blonde, may do sandwiches, heating from fat low-level pipes, music from vintage record player; well behaved children in front snug till 6pm, open all day (midnight Fri, Sat) and can get packed at peak times.

Cumberland Arms (0191) 265 1725
James Place Street; NE6 1LD Traditional 19th-c pub with unspoilt interior serving a dozen well kept ales both local (such as Northern Alchemy) and national along with good range of craft beers and six tap ciders, two annual beer festivals, limited choice of reasonably priced snacky food, friendly obliging staff, bare boards and open fires; board games, events most nights including regular folk sessions, film and quiz evenings; dogs welcome, tables out overlooking Ouseburn Valley, four bedrooms, open all day weekends, from 1pm Mon-Fri (winter hours may vary).

★**Free Trade** (0191) 265 5764
St Lawrence Road, off Walker Road (A186); NE6 1AP Splendidly straightforward unpretentious red-brick pub with outstanding views up river from big windows, terrace tables and seats on grass; up to seven real ales, traditional ciders and plenty of bottled/canned beers and whiskies, all knowledgeably chosen, good sandwiches/pies/pasties, warm friendly atmosphere, original Formica tables and coal fire; brewery takeovers, board games on Sun (alternate), free juke box; steps down to back room and loos; open all day.

Old George (0191) 260 3035
Cloth Market, down alley past Pumphreys; NE1 1EZ Gently updated 16th-c former coaching house in cobbled yard; painted beams and panelling, comfortable armchairs by open fire, five well priced ales including Bass plus craft ales,

plenty of wines by the glass and cocktails, good value food including deals, friendly staff; sports TV, background music at one end, open mike Thurs, courtyard DJs Sat and events, sports TV; children welcome, open all day (till 2am Fri, Sat).

Split Chimp
Arch 7, Westgate Road; NE1 1SA Two-floor micropub built into a railway arch; ground-floor bar with cask tables, stools, pews and leather sofas, five well kept ales, five craft beers (more in bottles) from around the UK, all regularly changed, real cider and some wines by the glass, snacky food, upstairs skittle alley; live music; open all day Fri and Sat, till 8pm Sun, from 3pm other days.

Town Wall (0191) 232 3000
Pink Lane; across from Central Station; NE1 5HX In handsome listed building with spacious bare-boards interior and graphic touches; dark walls, button-back banquettes and sparsely spaced tables, pictures in heavy gilt frames, half a dozen ales including a trio from Wylam, good choice of bottled beers and several wines by the glass, well priced and interesting food including pub favourites and Asian street snacks; background music, cinema room; well behaved children and dogs allowed, open all day (till 1am Fri, Sat), food till 7pm Fri-Sun, 9pm other days.

★**Joiners Arms** (01665) 576112
High Newton-by-the-Sea, by turning to Linkhouse; NE66 3EA Open-plan village pub-restaurant; flagstoned bar with big front windows and open fire, wood-clad dining area behind, well presented locally sourced Northumbrian and classic pub food from interesting sandwiches (stotties) and sharing plates up, a couple of local ales, one usually from Alnwick, carefully chosen wines; background music; children and dogs (in bar) welcome, picnic-sets out at front and behind, good coastal walks and several from pub door, five stylish bedrooms and a cottage, open all day.

Cook & Barker Arms
(01665) 575234 *Village signed from A1 Alnwick–Felton; NE65 9JY* Traditional stone-built country inn; rustic beamed bar with partly panelled walls, upholstered wall benches by pine and marble tables, bottles and bric-a-brac on delft shelf, fire in old range one end, woodburner the other, four real ales and several wines by the glass from extensive list, popular trad and modern food including several fish options and local estate produce, high tea, good-value weekday set lunch, friendly efficient staff, separate restaurant with exposed stonework

and raftered ceiling; background music; children welcome, dogs in snug and lounge, small outside seating area, 16 bedrooms, Boxing Day hunt starts here, open (and food) all day.

NORTH SHIELDS   NZ3668
Salty Sea Dog   07455 107470
Union Quay; NE30 1HJ Quirky little bar in the Fish Quay heritage waterfront; local ales, craft beers and great selection of gins and other spirits, popular tapas, snacks, fish/seafood and casual classics, friendly helpful staff; dogs welcome, some pavement seating, open all day (till 1am Fri, Sat).

NORTH SHIELDS   NZ3668
★Staith House   (0191) 270 8441
Fish Quay/Union Road; NE30 1HF Attractively furnished dining pub with seats outside on the North Shields docklands; Caledonian Golden XPA, Theakstons Lightfoot and a guest and a fish-friendly wine list to suit the good cuisine (charcuterie, ice-cream, bread and smoked dishes all prepared on-site), friendly staff, attractive interior blends stripped wood, brickwork and stone with a mix of chairs, tartan wall seating and wooden tables, slate flooring and bare boards, woodburner with candles on mantelbeam and old River Tyne photos; children welcome, open (and food) all day, closed Mon and Tues.

OTTERBURN   NY8992
★William de Percy   (01830) 520261
Jedburgh Road; NE19 1NR Former coaching inn with French-inspired shabby-chic décor; good food from sharing plates up including range of crêpes, a couple of real ales, continental beers and decent choice of wines and cocktails; background music; children and dogs welcome, lovely Mediterranean-style gardens with palms and fountain, eight glamorous bedrooms, more in adjoining Petit Chateau (popular wedding venue), open (and food) all day.

PIERCEBRIDGE   NZ2115
Fox Hole   (01325) 374286
B6275 N of village, or off A67; DL2 3SJ Friendly 19th-c roadside pub handsomely done out in contemporary style with well liked interesting food from fashionable lunchtime sandwiches and sharing plates up, Camerons Strongarm, Timothy Taylors Landlord and a guest, decent wine choice and extensive range of spirits, contemporary opened-up interior, woodburners, dining room with kitchen view; TV for major sports; children welcome (under-7s till 7.30pm), dogs in bar, tables on terrace and small lawn, open all day, food till 4pm Sun.

PONTELAND   NZ1773
★Blackbird   (01661) 822684
North Road opposite church; NE20 9UH Imposing ancient stone pub gently and

beautifully modernised; mix of furniture including several high tables and button-back banquettes, wood, slate and tartan-carpeted floors, striking old map of Northumberland and etching of Battle of Otterburn either side of fireplace, larger Tudor stone fireplace in unusual Tunnel Room, good popular food from bar snacks to restauranty dishes, half a dozen well kept local and national ales, cocktails and over 50 gins, friendly service; sports TV, occasional live music; children and dogs welcome, picnic-sets out at front, more tables on back lawn, open all day, food till 5pm Sun.

RENNINGTON   NU2118
★Horseshoes   (01665) 577665
B1340; NE66 3RS Comfortable and welcoming little family-run pub with nice local feel; a couple of well kept ales including Hadrian Border Farne Island, decent wines by the glass and ample helpings of enjoyable pubby food using local suppliers, friendly efficient service, simple well worn-in bar with flagstones, padded benches and woodburner, carpeted restaurant; darts; children welcome, picnic-sets out on small front lawn, attractive quiet village near coast, Aug scarecrow competition, closed Mon.

ROCHESTER   NY8497
Redesdale Arms   (01830) 520668
A68 3 miles W of Otterburn; NE19 1TA Isolated old roadside inn aka the First & Last (inn on the way to and from Scotland) surrounded by unspoilt countryside; enjoyable home-made food including daily specials, vegan and gluten-free diets catered for, Allendale and First & Last ales, friendly attentive staff; pleasant light interior, ten bedrooms, on edge of Dark Sky park, open (and food) all day.

SEATON SLUICE   NZ3477
Kings Arms   (0191) 237 0275
West Terrace; NE26 4RD Friendly old pub in pleasant seaside location perched above tidal Seaton Sluice Harbour; good range of real ales and enjoyable pubby food (not Sun evening) including gluten-free choices and blackboard specials, beamed and carpeted bar with old photographs and woodburner at each end, restaurant; children welcome, a few picnic-sets on sunny front grass, more seats in enclosed beer garden behind, open all day.

SEDGEFIELD   NZ3528
Dun Cow   (01740) 620894
Front Street; TS21 3AT Popular 18th-c village inn with low-beamed bar, back tap room and restaurant, extensive choice of enjoyable reasonably priced food including good Sun roast, four well kept changing ales such as Hambleton, Hook Norton and Otter, traditional decoration (stone and white walls, red carpets, quality wood furniture)

kept spic and span, children welcome, six comfortable bedrooms, open (and food) all day weekends.

SHINCLIFFE NZ2940
Seven Stars (0191) 384 8454
High Street N (A177 S of Durham); DH1 2NU Comfortable 18th-c village inn with River Wear walks from the door; good hearty food including home-made burgers, three well kept changing ales, coal-effect gas fire in lounge bar, panelled dining room; children welcome in eating areas, dogs in bar, some picnic-sets outside, bedrooms, closed Mon, otherwise open all day.

SLALEY NY9757
Rose & Crown (01434) 673996
Church Close; NE47 0AA Welcoming 17th-c pub owned by the village; enjoyable good value pubby food including grills (not Sun evening), High House Farm Nels Best plus other local ales such as Allendale, beams and log fires; Sun quiz; children and dogs welcome, garden with long country views, two bedrooms, open all day.

SLALEY NY9658
Travellers Rest (01434) 673231
B6306 S of Hexham (and N of village); NE46 1TT Attractive stone-built country pub, spaciously opened up, with farmhouse-style décor, beams, flagstones and polished wood floors, huge fireplace, comfortable high-backed settles forming discrete areas, friendly welcoming staff, enjoyable food (not Sun evening) in bar or quieter dining room, two real ales such as Black Sheep and Caledonian and a guest, perhaps from Twice Brewed; children and dogs welcome, tables outside and well equipped adventure play area, three good value bedrooms, open all day (closed Mon).

SOUTH SHIELDS NZ3567
Alum Ale House (0191) 427 7245
Ferry Street (B1344); NE33 1JR Welcoming 18th-c bow-windowed pub adjacent to the Shields ferry landing; open-plan bare-boards bar with fire in old range, a dozen well kept Marstons-related ales, no food; music and quiz nights; no children, seats on front deck overlooking the river, handy for South Shields market, open all day.

SOUTH SHIELDS NZ3566
Steamboat (0191) 454 0134
Mill Dam/Coronation Street; NE33 1EQ Friendly 19th-c pub on cobbled corner with nine well kept oft-changing ales plus craft ales from near and far, a real cider and a wide and expanding range of spirits including 50 rums, snacks only plus coffee at quiet times; lots of nautical bric-a-brac, beermats adorning the bar, raised seating area and separate lounge; near river and market, open all day.

STANNINGTON NZ2179
★Ridley Arms (01670) 789216
Village signed off A1 S of Morpeth; NE61 6EL Extended Fitzgerald pub with several separate areas; open fire and cushioned settles in proper front bar, stools along counter serving up to seven local ales such as Black Sheep and offerings from Anarchy and the Durham Brewery, around a dozen wines by the glass and good coffee, decent choice of nicely done reasonably priced food, pleasant helpful staff, several dining areas with upholstered bucket chairs around dark tables on bare boards or carpet, calming decoration with a few cartoons and portraits on cream, panelled or stripped-stone walls; background music; children welcome, good disabled access, picnic-sets out at front and on back terrace, open (and food) all day; handy for A1.

STANNINGTON NZ1881
★St Marys Inn (01670) 293293
Turn left in Stannington village and past the church, follow Green Lane to St Marys Lane; NE61 6BL Lovely rework of gabled red-brick Edwardian building with clock tower (admin block for former asylum); series of rooms, each with own character, wood floors throughout, interesting artwork and several woodburners, well executed food from bar snacks and pub favourites up, efficient friendly service, a house beer from Hadrian Border, guest ales and good wine (including organic) and whisky choices, decent coffee; children and dogs (in bar areas) welcome, attractive well appointed bedrooms, generous breakfast, useful for A1, open all day from 8am, kitchen closes 6pm Sun.

SUNDERLAND NZ4057
Ivy House (0191) 567 3399
Worcester Terrace; SR2 7AW Friendly Victorian corner pub off the beaten track; five well kept changing ales from interesting brewers such as Cullercoats, Torrside and Two by Two, plus a real cider, interesting bottled beers and good range of spirits, popular reasonably priced food from open kitchen including own-made burgers and pizzas; background and live music, quiz, sports TV; children and dogs welcome, special (non-alcoholic) beer for dogs; open (and food) all day.

THROPTON NU0202
Three Wheat Heads (01669) 620262
B6341; NE65 7LR Popular 18th-c village inn looking on to Simonside Hills; three well kept regional ales and decent choice of wines, generous portions of tasty food, friendly service, open fires (one in fine tall stone fireplace), lovely country views from dining room's big windows; children and dogs (in bar) welcome, disabled access, garden with play area, comfortable bedrooms and

good breakfast, handy for Cragside (NT), open (and food) all day.

TYNEMOUTH NZ3669
Hugos (0191) 257 8956
Front Street; NE30 4DZ Sir John Fitzgerald pub-bar with open-plan split-level interior, four changing ales, decent choice of wines by the glass and cocktails, reasonably priced food from shortish menu including sandwiches; Weds quiz, sports TV; children welcome, some pavement seating, open all day, no evening food Fri-Sun.

TYNEMOUTH NZ3668
Turks Head (0191) 257 6547
Front Street; NE30 4DZ Friendly traditional town pub with white-tiled exterior, four regular and four changing ales and three craft kegs, menu of US and pub standards, steps between two comfortable small bars, ancient stuffed border collie and accompanying sad story (the pub is known locally as the Stuffed Dog, and the house beer from Hadrian also bears the name); juke box, sports TVs, darts; open (and food) all day.

WARDEN NY9166
Boatside (01434) 602233
Village signed N of A69; NE46 4SQ Modernised old stone pub in attractive spot by bridge at confluence of the North and South Tyne rivers; enjoyable fairly priced food from varied menu, a couple of local ales, woodburner, ceiling beams, tartan carpet, good friendly service; sports TV; children and dogs (in bar) welcome, small neat enclosed garden, bedrooms in adjoining cottages (some self-catering), open all day, last food orders 7.30pm (6pm Sun).

WARENFORD NU1429
White Swan (01668) 213453
Off A1 S of Belford; NE70 7HY Handsome characterful stone house known for excellent unpretentious food, much of it from its own fields, turkey coop and pigsty; all-rounder bar with interesting spirits and three real ales (perhaps Alnwick, Rigg & Furrow), cushioned wooden seats around pine tables, warm fire in big stone fireplace, steps to an extension with comfortable dining sets and woodburning stove, cheerful service; children and dogs (in bar) welcome, bedrooms, open all day.

WARKWORTH NU2406
Hermitage (01665) 711258
Castle Street; NE65 0UL Rambling former coaching inn with good choice of home-made food including Sun carvery, Jennings, Marstons and guests, decent range of wines including a vegan red, friendly staff, quaint décor with fire in old range, small upstairs restaurant; background music (live Fri), Thurs quiz; children and dogs welcome, benches and hanging baskets out at front, attractive setting, bedrooms, open (and food) all day.

WELDON BRIDGE NZ1398
★Anglers Arms (01665) 570271
B6344, just off A697; village signposted with Rothbury off A1 N of Morpeth; NE65 8AX Handsome and capacious coaching inn nicely located by bridge over River Coquet; two-part bar with cream walls or oak panelling, shiny black beams hung with copper pans, profusion of fishing memorabilia, taxidermy and a grandfather clock, some low tables with matching chairs, sofa by coal fire, three changing ales from the region (Great North Eastern, Hadrian Border) and elsewhere in the UK (Sharps, Skinners), around 40 malt whiskies and decent wines by the glass, well liked generously served food, friendly helpful staff; background music, Thurs quiz; children and dogs (in bar) welcome, attractive garden with good play area, fishing rights, comfortable bedrooms/apartment, open (and food) all day.

WEST BOLDON NZ3460
Red Lion (0191) 536 4197
Redcar Terrace; NE36 0PZ Bow-windowed flower-decked pub with cosy linked areas with country kitchen and drawing room vibe; open fire in beamed bar, three real ales such as Theakstons from ornate wood counter, separate snug and conservatory dining room with unusual wood sculptures, good range of popular well priced food, friendly relaxed atmosphere; seats out on back decking, open all day.

WHALTON NZ1281
★Beresford Arms (01670) 775273
B6524; NE61 3UZ Refurbished pub-restaurant in attractive village; small bar area serving three real ales (at least one from a local brewery) and interesting range of gins, good variety of well liked fairly priced food including hot and cold sandwiches, friendly helpful staff, spacious carpeted restaurant; converted stables for events/functions; children and dogs (in bar) welcome, a few seats out at front, more in enclosed back garden, comfortable bedrooms, open all day.

WHITFIELD NY7857
Elks Head (01434) 345282
Off A686 SW of Haydon Bridge; NE47 8HD Extended old stone pub attractively set in steep wooded valley on the Whitfield Estate (known for its shoots): light and spacious, with bar and two dining areas, good value tasty food including local game, a couple of real ales and several wines by the glass, friendly helpful service; children and dogs (in bar) welcome, picnic-sets in small pretty front garden by little river, scenic area with good walks, ten bedrooms (some in adjacent cottage), open all day in summer.

WHITLEY BAY NZ3742
★ Left Luggage Room
Metro Station, Northam Road; NE26 3NR
Quirky micropub in Monkseaton metro
station; high vaulted ceiling and brick walls
left in original rough condition adding to the
character, mismatched wooden furniture
on boarded floor, old suitcases and trunks
stacked below bar counter, wide selection of
changing ales, craft beers and ciders curated
with expertise, good range of other drinks
including several whiskies and gins (all listed
on blackboards), snacks only (pork pies are
many and legendary), friendly knowledgeable
staff; dogs welcome, tables out on platform
(under canopy), open all day.

WYLAM NZ1164
★ Boathouse (01661) 853431
*Station Road, handy for Newcastle–
Carlisle railway; across Tyne from
village; NE41 8HR* Convivial two-room
pub with a dozen real ales, traditional
ciders and good choice of malt whiskies,
enjoyable Thai menu and some snacky food,
friendly knowledgeable staff, light interior
with one or two low beams and woodburner;
occasional buskers night, juke box, sports
TV; children and dogs welcome, seats
outside, close to station, river and George
Stephenson's Birthplace (NT), open all day
(evenings can be very busy).

WYLAM NZ1164
Ship (01661) 854538
Main Road; NE41 8AQ Genuine warm
welcome at this sizeable open-plan dining
pub; good individual cooking from owner-
chef including Sat steak night and Sun set
lunch (till 3.30pm), Theakstons Best and
Stout on handpump, plus craft beers such
as Caledonian Coast to Coast and well
chosen wine list; children and dogs welcome,
picnic-sets in beer garden, bedrooms, closed
lunchtimes Mon and Tues, otherwise open all
day (till 6pm Sun).

Nottinghamshire

KEY ★ Star Pub   🍴⭐ Top Quality Food   🍺 Great Beer

🍷 Good Wines   £ Bargain Meals   🛏 Good Bedrooms   🍴 Serves Food

---

CAYTHORPE   SK6845   Map 7
Black Horse
(0115) 966 3520

Turn off A6097 0.25 miles SE of roundabout junction with A612, NE of Nottingham;
into Gunthorpe Road, then right into Caythorpe Road and keep on; NG14 7ED

Quaintly old-fashioned little pub with simple interior and enjoyable homely food; no children

---

It's the down-to-earth simplicity that attracts people to this welcoming country local, which has been run by generations of the same family for 300 years. Little changes, thankfully – although the pub now has smart new indoor loos and accepts credit cards – and our readers enjoy their visits very much. The homely, uncluttered, carpeted bar has just five tables, along with brocaded wall banquettes and settles, decorative plates on a delft shelf, a few horsebrasses attached to the ceiling joists, and a coal fire. Cheerful regulars might occupy the few bar stools to enjoy the well kept Greene King Abbot, local Brewsters (Hophead or Marquis) and an example from Blue Monkey on handpump, six wines by the glass, 12 gins and half a dozen whiskies. Off the front corridor is an inner room, partly panelled with a wall bench running all the way round three unusual, long, copper-topped tables; there are several old local photographs, darts and board games. Down on the left, an end room has just one huge round table. There are seats outside. Accommodation including a caravan pitch is planned. The pub is close to the River Trent where there are waterside walks. No children.

🍴 Good value home-cooked food (you'll need to book a table in advance) includes sandwiches, prawn cocktail, mushrooms on toast, three-egg omelettes, lamb chops with creamed potatoes, gammon and eggs, fish in parsley sauce, and puddings such as sticky toffee pudding and treacle sponge with custard. *Benchmark main dish: fresh fish of the day and chips £13.00. Two-course evening meal £19.00.*

Free house ~ Licensee Sharron Andrews ~ Real ale ~ Open 12-2.30, 5.30-11; 12-5 Sun; closed Mon ~ Bar food 11.45-1.45, 6-8.30; 12-5 Sun; not Sat evening ~ Dogs allowed in bar

---

'Children welcome' means the pub says it lets children inside without any special restriction. If it allows them in, but to restricted areas such as an eating area or family room, we specify this. Places with separate restaurants often let children use them, and hotels usually let children into public areas such as lounges. Some pubs impose an evening time limit – let us know if you find one earlier than 9pm.

COLSTON BASSETT

SK6933 Map 7

Martins Arms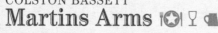

(01949) 81361 – www.themartinsarms.co.uk

Village signposted off A46 E of Nottingham; School Lane, near market cross in village centre; NG12 3FD

● ●

Nottinghamshire Dining Pub of the Year

Smart dining pub with impressive food, good range of drinks including seven real ales and attractive grounds

The imaginatively presented food, big choice of drinks and civilised surroundings make this special inn stand out. There's a comfortably relaxed atmosphere, warm logs fires in Jacobean fireplaces, fresh flowers and candlelight, and the smart décor includes period fabrics and colours, antique furniture and hunting prints; board games. The main elegant dining room is painted in a warm red with gold silk curtains. Neatly uniformed staff serve seven beers, such as Bass, Black Sheep, Greene King IPA, Jennings Cumberland, Marstons Pedigree, Ruddles County and Timothy Taylors Landlord on handpump, 22 wines by the glass or carafe (including prosecco, champagne and pudding wines) and a fair choice of whiskies and armagnacs. The lawned garden (with summer croquet and barbecues) backs on to National Trust parkland. Do visit the church opposite and Colston Bassett Dairy (just outside the village) which produces and sells its own stilton and Shropshire blue cheese.

Creative bar food includes sandwiches, ploughman's, crispy paprika whitebait, poached pigeon with stilton and grape salad, smoked duck salad with feta, cashews and miso dressing, twice-baked cheese soufflé, beetroot risotto with goats curd and apple, pork fillet with crispy wonton, pak choi, squid and chilli, hake with herb gnocchi, ham hock and peas, and puddings such as chocolate and lime pannacotta with roasted pineapple, lime purée and roasted pineapple sorbet. *Benchmark main dish: beef burger with stilton and truffle chips £15.00. Two-course evening meal £26.00.*

Free house ~ Licensees Lynne Strafford Bryan and Salvatore Inguanta ~ Real ale ~ Open 12-3, 6-11; 12-3.30, 6-11 Sat; 12-4, 7-10 Sun ~ Bar food 12-2, 6-9; not Sun evening ~ Restaurant ~ Children welcome

OXTON

SK6251 Map 7

Old Green Dragon £

(0115) 965 2243

End of High Street, next to Home Farm Stores; NG25 0SS

Down-to-earth local village pub with a fine choice of beers and hearty food

There's a proper emphasis on excellent beer, wholesome food and a welcoming atmosphere at this homely red-brick local. There's an ever-changing range of four to six cask ales on handpump on the solid oak bar – recent brewers have included Ashover, Geeves, Lenton Lane, Oakham, Shiny and Shipstones (check social media for regular updates) – as well as up to six ciders, 12 gins and a smattering of whiskies. Although the interior is open-plan, there are four distinct areas including a snug and a dining section. The menu offers honest pubby food in generous portions, with special themed nights from Wednesday to Friday. Service comes with a smile, children and dogs are welcome, and there's a sunny patio with seating at the front (though it's a bit close to the main road) as well as a small garden.

Straightforward, keenly priced food includes halloumi fries, stilton mushrooms, gammon steak with eggs, chargrilled steaks, Moroccan nut roast, vegan Penang curry, wholetail scampi, fish and chips, a pie of the day, burger and chips, sausages and mash, and puddings such as warm chocolate fudge cake and the always popular cornflake tart. *Benchmark main dish: beer-battered fish and chips £11.95. Two-course evening meal £17.00.*

Free house ~ Licensee Cloe Mellors ~ Open 5-10 Mon, Tues; 4-11 Weds, Thurs; 12-11 Fri, Sat; 12-10 Sun ~ Bar food 4-8 Weds, Thurs; 12-2, 5-8 Fri; 12-8 Sat; 12-4 Sun ~ Children welcome ~ Dogs allowed in bar

RADCLIFFE ON TRENT

SK6539 Map 7

Radcliffe

(0115) 933 1622 – theradcliffe.uk

0.3 mile N up Shelford Road from Radcliffe train station; NG12 1AW

Brightly decorated contemporary pub with four real ales, good food and large outside terrace

This bright and airy village pub situated a stone's throw from the red cliffs of the River Trent has a new lease of life, thanks to a comprehensive revamp from the team behind the reborn Railway at Lowdham (see Also Worth a Visit). It's quite a transformation, open plan but with distinctly different areas, with colourful contemporary décor that includes boldly patterned banquettes, blue and mustard suede and leather chairs around polished wood or metal-topped tables, funky lighting, wooden floorboards and seagrass carpeting. Oars are lined up on a bright blue wall and a collection of copper pans hangs from the ceiling. Friendly, chatty staff serve four real ales on handpump – perhaps Adnams Southwold, Black Sheep, Castle Rock Harvest Pale and Oakham Citra – as well as 13 wines by the glass, 20 gins and a similar number of whiskies. Outside at the back there's a spacious fenced-off terrace with teak tables and chairs beneath parasols and an outside bar, and beyond that grass with a children's play area.

 Good brasserie-style food include sandwiches, duck liver parfait with grilled focaccia, prawn and crayfish salad, roast cod with tenderstem broccoli, poached clams and patatas bravas, macaroni with ratatouille sauce, goats cheese and black olives, bavette steak with fries and confit tomato, curried cauliflower steak with red lentils, apple and golden raisins, and puddings such as raspberry frangipane tart with clotted cream, and lemon posset with blackberry sorbet and minted meringue. *Benchmark main dish: beer-battered haddock and chips £14.00. Two-course evening meal £21.00.*

Free house ~ Licensees David Hage and Mark Osborne ~ Open 12-10; 12-11 Fri, Sat; 12-8 Sun ~ Bar food 12-2, 5-8.30 Weds-Fri; 12-2.30pm Sat; 12-6 Sun ~ ~ Children allowed in bar ~ Dogs allowed in bar

UPPER BROUGHTON

SK6826 Map 7

Tap & Run

(01664) 820407 – www.tapandrun.co.uk

Main Road: A606 halfway between Nottingham and Melton Mowbray; LE14 3BG

Lively country pub combining a little cosiness with stylish décor and imaginative food

You'll be bowled over by this stylish pub that's set up equally well for casual dining or a relaxing drink and a chat. Straddling the Leicestershire/Nottinghamshire border in a hilltop village on the edge of the picturesque Vale of Belvoir, it's owned by England and Nottinghamshire cricketers Stuart Broad and Harry Gurney. Modern décor mixes modish paintwork in dark green and grey, walls of bare brick and metro tiles, tiled floors and a nice mix of wooden café and dining chairs and tables. Old photos and a large map cover one wall. There's a bar area with tub chairs, a leather sofa, stools by the polished wood counter and a brick fireplace with a woodburner, and also an attractive conservatory set for dining with large palms in pots. Friendly young staff serve well kept Charnwood Vixen, Timothy Taylors Landlord and a guest ale on handpump, along with a farm cider, 20 wines by the glass and a good range of gins, whiskies and rums. There's a patio and garden with seating.

¶ Rewarding food from a shortish menu mixes pub classics with more restauranty options. Dishes include crispy calamari salad, white stilton pannacotta with pickled walnut, mango and date, beef brisket pie with mash, duck breast with aubergine croquettes, pomegranate and tarragon salsa, wild mushroom pappardelle with spinach, courgette and corn fritter with fermented kale and corn chipotle, burger and chips, and puddings such as lemon custard tart with blueberries and clotted cream and chocolate fudge pie with orange mascarpone. A three-course set menu is available weekdays. *Benchmark main dish: beer-battered haddock and chips £13.95. Two-course evening meal £20.00.*

Free house ~ Licensees Stuart Broad and Harry Gurney ~ Open 12-10; 12-11 Fri, Sat; 12-6 Sun; closed Mon ~ Bar food 12-8.30; 12-5 Sun ~ Restaurant ~ Children welcome ~ Dogs allowed in bar

Also Worth a Visit in Nottinghamshire

Besides the fully inspected pubs, you might like to try these pubs that have been recommended to us and described by readers. Do tell us what you think of them: feedback@goodguides.com

AWSWORTH   SK4844
Gate (0115) 932 9821
Main Street, via A6096 off A610 Nuthall–Eastwood bypass; NG16 2RN
Renovated red-brick Victorian free house near site of once-famous railway viaduct; seven well kept changing beers and some snacky food, bar with woodburner, coal fire in lounge, friendly welcoming atmosphere; occasional live music and comedy nights, skittle alley; dogs welcome, disabled access/loo, back courtyard and roof terrace, open all day.

BAGTHORPE   SK4751
Dixies Arms (01773) 810505
A608 towards Eastwood off M1 junction 27, right on B600 via Sandhill Road, left into School Road; Lower Bagthorpe; NG16 5HF Friendly unspoilt 18th-c brick local with DH Lawrence connections; beams and tiled floors, well kept Greene King Abbot, Timothy Taylors Landlord and a guest, no food, entrance bar with tiny snug, good fire in small part-panelled parlour's fine fireplace, longer narrow room with toby jugs, darts and dominoes; live music Sat, quiz Sun, beer/folk festival June; children and dogs welcome, picnic-sets out at front, big garden and play area behind, open all day.

BEESTON   SK5236
Crown (0115) 925 4738
Church Street; NG9 1FY Everards pub with eight well kept ales such as Brewsters Hophead, Dancing Duck Nice Weather and Nottingham Rock Mild, a couple of craft beers, four real ciders/perries, whiskies, premium gins and a good choice of other drinks, friendly knowledgeable staff, no hot food but fresh cobs, pork pies and snacks; front snug and bar with slate and quarry-tiled floors, carpeted parlour, Victorian décor in lounge, beams, panelling and bric-a-brac; weekend live music, regular quiz nights and beer festivals; dogs welcome, terrace tables (some under cover), open all day.

BEESTON   SK5336
Star (0115) 854 5320
Middle Street; NG9 1FX Three-room inn with fine range of ten well kept changing ales from breweries such as Blue Monkey, Castle Rock, Dancing Duck, Oakham and Shipstones, real ciders and extensive choice of whiskies, friendly knowledgeable staff, good keenly priced pub food along with freshly baked pizzas; live music and quiz nights, separate games room with pool, darts and sports TV; children and dogs welcome, permanent marquee leading through to

heated terrace and large grassy garden with play equipment, eight good value bedrooms, open all day.

BEESTON   SK5336

★ **Victoria**   (0115) 925 4049

Dovecote Lane, backing on to the station; NG9 1JG Red-brick former station hotel attracting good mix of customers; up to 14 real ales including vegan and occasional gluten-free beers (regular beer festivals), two farm ciders, 120 malt whiskies and 30 wines by the glass, good sensibly priced food (order at bar) from varied blackboard menu including plenty for vegetarians, efficient friendly service, three fairly simple unfussy rooms with original long narrow layout (last one for diners only), solid furnishings, bare boards and stripped woodwork, stained-glass windows, some breweriana, open fires; live music and other events including July VicFest, newspapers and board games; children welcome till 8pm, dogs in bar, seats out on covered heated area overlooking platform (trains pass just a few feet away), limited parking, open (and food) all day.

BINGHAM   SK7039

Horse & Plough   (01949) 839313

Off A52; Long Acre; NG13 8AF Castle Rock pub in 1818 Methodist chapel near train station; low beams, flagstones and stripped brickwork, comfortable open-plan seating including pews, prints and old brewery memorabilia, their beers, guests and vegan beers (tasters offered), real cider and decent wine choice, enjoyable reasonably priced bar food and popular upstairs grill room with open kitchen, good friendly service; background music; children and dogs welcome, beer garden, disabled facilities, open all day.

BLYTH   SK6287

White Swan   (01909) 591222

High Street; S81 8EQ Old whitewashed pub opposite village green, comfortable and well maintained, with beams and exposed brickwork, mix of dining chairs and padded banquettes around assorted tables on flagstones or carpet, Black Sheep, Sharps Doom Bar and Timothy Taylors Landlord, enjoyable good value pubby food including vegetarian/vegan/gluten-free choices and Sun carvery, friendly welcoming staff; TV; children welcome, no dogs inside, tables out in front and in small back garden, open all day, no food Sun evening, Tues.

BUNNY   SK5829

Rancliffe Arms   (0115) 984 4727

Loughborough Road (A60 S of Nottingham); NG11 6QT Substantial old coaching inn with linked dining areas, enjoyable food including carvery (Mon evening, Weds, Sat and Sun), friendly welcoming staff, chunky country chairs around mixed tables on flagstones or carpet,

four well kept Marstons-related beers such as Jennings Cumberland in comfortable log-fire bar with sofas and armchairs; background music, TV; children welcome, no dogs inside, rattan-style furniture on outside decking, closed Mon.

CAR COLSTON   SK7242

Royal Oak   (01949) 20247

The Green, off Tenman Lane (off A46 not far from A6097 junction); NG13 8JE Good well priced often locally sourced traditional food (not Sun evening) in biggish 19th-c pub opposite one of England's largest village greens; well kept Marstons-related ales such as Courage, Bombardier and Wainwright, decent choice of wines by the glass, woodburner in lounge bar with tables set for eating, public bar with unusual barrel-vaulted brick ceiling; skittle alley; children and dogs welcome, picnic-sets on spacious back lawn, heated smokers' den, camping, open all day.

CAUNTON   SK7459

Caunton Beck   (01636) 636793

Newark Road; NG23 6AE Reconstructed low-beamed dining pub (on site of 16th-c tavern) made to look old using original timbers and reclaimed oak; scrubbed pine tables and country kitchen chairs, open fire, four ales such as Batemans, Oakham JHB and a couple of beers from sister pub's microbrewery (see Bottle & Glass at Harby), more than two dozen wines by the glass, generally well liked food from breakfast on, cheerful if not always speedy service; daily newspapers; children and dogs (in bar) welcome, seats on flowery terrace, handy for A1, open (and food) all day from 8.30am.

CAYTHORPE   SK6846

Old Volunteer   (0115) 966 5822

Caythorpe Road; NG14 7EB Village dining pub with good food, decent wines and four well kept ales, friendly helpful service, upstairs dining room with view over fields; children and dogs (in bar) welcome, seats out at front and on back deck, open (and food) all day, but may close early if quiet.

CUCKNEY   SK5671

Greendale Oak   (01623) 844441

A616, E of A60; NG20 9NQ Updated country pub with good all-day food (till 7pm Sun) from sandwiches to sharing plates and pub classics, eight real ales including two regulars from Everards and others from brewers such as Ashover and Joules, friendly helpful service, restaurant; background music; children welcome, no dogs inside, sturdy bench seating on front terrace, garden behind, open all day (till 1am Fri, Sat).

EDWINSTOWE   SK6266

Forest Lodge   (01623) 824443

Church Street; NG21 9QA Friendly 18th-c inn with enjoyable home-made food in pubby bar or restaurant, good service, five well kept ales including Bombardier and a house beer from Welbeck Abbey, beams and log fire; children welcome, 13 bedrooms, handy for Sherwood Forest.

EPPERSTONE SK6548
Cross Keys (0115) 966 9430
Main Street; NG14 6AD Recently refurbished dining pub with chef-proprietor's good well presented/priced food from regularly changing menu, three real ales including Nottingham and nice wines by the glass, friendly efficient service, woodburner separating lounge bar and restaurant; children welcome, muddy walkers and dogs in boot room, a few picnic-sets out at front, more in back garden with raised deck, pretty village and surrounding countryside, open (and food) all day, except Sun when kitchen closes at 6pm.

FARNDON SK7652
Boathouse (01636) 676578
Off A46 SW of Newark; keep on towards river – pub off Wyke Lane, just past the Riverside pub; NG24 3SX Big-windowed contemporary bar-restaurant overlooking the Trent, emphasis on food but they do serve a couple of changing ales, 24 wines by the glass and some interesting cocktails; main area with high ceiling trusses supporting bare ducting, simple modern tables and upholstered chairs, shallow step up to second similarly furnished dining area, good variety of food; background and some live music, July garden party with live bands; children welcome, wicker chairs around teak tables on heated terrace, own moorings, open all day.

FISKERTON SK7351
Bromley Arms (01636) 830789
Main Street; NG25 0UL Popular Trentside pub with modernised opened-up interior; fairly compact bar area with upholstered stools and leather armchairs/sofas, two-way fireplace, four well kept beers including Greene King, 18 wines by the glass, river-view dining part with upholstered chairs on patterned carpet (some matching wallpaper), enjoyable fairly priced food including set menu till 6pm (not Sun), friendly helpful service; background music; children welcome, rattan-style furniture on narrow walled terrace, picnic-sets by edge of wharf giving best views, open (and food) all day and can get very busy in summer.

GRANBY SK7436
★ Marquis of Granby (01949) 870621
Off A52 E of Nottingham; Dragon Street; NG13 9PN Friendly 18th-c pub in attractive Vale of Belvoir village; tap for Brewsters with

their well kept ales and interesting guests from chunky yew counter, no food, two small comfortable rooms, broad flagstones, some low beams, open fire; children and dogs welcome, open all day weekends, from 4pm Mon-Fri.

HARBY SK8870
Bottle & Glass (01522) 703438
High Street; village signed off A57 W of Lincoln; NG23 7EB Colourfully and comfortably furnished 19th-c pub with pair of bay-windowed front bars and restaurant extension; enjoyable food including set menu and blackboard specials, a couple of beers from on-site microbrewery along with a guest such as Black Sheep, good choice of wines, friendly service, open fire and woodburners; shop selling their bottled beers, general provisions and gifts; children welcome, dogs in bar, modern wrought-iron furniture on back terrace, picnic-sets on grass beyond and out at front, open (and food) all day, except Sun when kitchen closes 6pm, breakfast from 10am (9am weekends).

HOCKERTON SK7156
Spread Eagle (01636) 813322
Caunton Road; A617 Newark–Mansfield; NG25 0PL Village corner pub with compact interior with linked beamed rooms, a couple of woodburners, smallish bar area serving two real ales such as Black Sheep and decent choice of wines, generous helpings of good freshly made food from baguettes to daily specials, friendly accommodating staff; children welcome, dogs in one area, beer garden and separate deck, closed Mon and Tues, otherwise open (and food) all day.

KIMBERLEY SK4944
★ Nelson & Railway (0115) 938 2177
Station Road; handy for M1 junction 26 via A610; NG16 2NR Cheery Victorian beamed pub, popular and comfortable, with decent inexpensive home-made food from snacks to blackboard specials, four well kept ales including Greene King and guests such as Archers and Blue Monkey, mix of Edwardian-looking furniture, brewery prints (was tap for defunct Hardys & Hansons Brewery) and railway signs, dining extension; juke box, games machine and darts; children and dogs allowed, disabled access, nice front and back gardens, 11 good value bedrooms, proper breakfast, open all day, food all day Sat, till 6.30pm Sun.

KIMBERLEY SK5044
Stag 07934 043755
Nottingham Road; NG16 2NB Traditional 18th-c local with two cosy rooms, small central counter and corridor; low beams,

---

Post Office address codings confusingly give the impression that a few pubs are in Nottinghamshire, when they're really in Derbyshire (which is where we list them).

dark panelling, high-backed settles and some old Shipstones Brewery photographs, up to seven well kept ales including Adnams, Bass, Timothy Taylors and guest from perhaps Castle Rock or Thornbridge (beer festival first weekend Aug), no food apart from weekend rolls; Weds quiz and some live music, sports TV, table skittles, darts and dominoes; children and dogs welcome, wheelchair access from behind, front decking and attractive back garden with play area and summer barbecues, open all day Sat and Sun, from 4pm other days.

LANEHAM   SK8176

Ferry Boat (01777) 228350

Main Street, Church Laneham; DN22 0NQ
Welcoming early 19th-c country pub in quiet hamlet close to the River Trent; bar with nice log fire and three well kept beers such as Pheasantry and Southern Cross, enjoyable good value mainly pubby food (not Sun evening), friendly efficient service, restaurant; occasional live music; children and dogs welcome, disabled access, picnic-sets on raised front terrace, open all day weekends, closed till 3pm Mon-Thurs.

LAXTON   SK7266

Dovecote (01777) 871586

Off A6075 E of Ollerton; NG22 0NU
Red-brick dining pub under hard-working owners; cosy country atmosphere in three traditionally furnished eating areas, popular home-made food from sandwiches and light lunches to daily specials, also a children's menu, three well kept changing ales, proper cider and around 30 wines by the glass, friendly helpful staff; background music, no dogs inside, disabled access, small front terrace and sloping garden with views towards church, interesting village still using the medieval 'strip farming' system, two bedrooms, open all day Sat, Sun till 8pm (food till 6pm); handy for A1.

LOWDHAM   SK6745

Railway (0115) 966 3222

Longmoor Avenue, near the station; NG14 7DU Welcoming 19th-c village pub with clean modern décor (sister to Radcliffe in Radcliffe on Trent – see Main Entries); five real ales such as Castle Rock and Theakstons, 17 wines by the glass and 24 gins, shortish but varied choice of well liked/presented food cooked in open kitchen including good value set menu (lunchtime, early evening), friendly helpful staff; children and dogs welcome, chunky picnic-sets outside and play area, more seats on elevated back terrace, open all day, no food Sun evening.

MANSFIELD   SK5363

Railway Inn (01623) 623086

Station Street; best approached by viaduct from near Market Place; NG18 1EF Friendly traditional local; four changing ales, real cider and good low-priced

home-made food (till 5pm Sun), two little front rooms leading to main bar, another cosy room at back, laminate flooring throughout; some live music; children and dogs welcome, small courtyard and beer garden, handy for Robin Hood Line station and the newish bus station, open all day.

MAPLEBECK   SK7160

Beehive

Signed down pretty country lanes from A616 Newark–Ollerton and from A617 Newark–Mansfield; NG22 0BS Tiny beamed country tavern (the smallest in Nottinghamshire, and until the 1970s the smallest in the country) in nice spot, unpretentious and welcoming, with cosy front bar and slightly bigger side room, traditional furnishings and open fire, a couple of well kept changing ales, no food; children and dogs welcome, tables on small front terrace and grassy bank running down to stream, play area, opens 7pm weekdays and shuts 3.30pm Sun.

MORTON   SK7251

Full Moon (01636) 830251

Pub and village signed off Bleasby–Fiskerton back road, SE of Southwell; NG25 0UT Attractive old brick pub tucked away in remote hamlet close to the River Trent; modernised pale-beamed bar with two roaring fires, comfortable armchairs, eclectic mix of tables and other simple furnishings, up to five real ales, nine wines by the glass and cocktails, enjoyable sensibly priced food from ciabattas up including good value lunchtime/early evening set menu, afternoon teas, separate carpeted restaurant; background and some live music, board games; children and dogs (in bar) welcome, picnic-sets out at front, more on peaceful back terrace and sizeable lawn with sturdy play equipment, open all day Fri-Sun, no food Sun evening.

NEWARK   SK8054

Castle Barge (01636) 677320

Town Wharf next to Trent Bridge; NG24 1EU Old grain barge moored near the castle; top deck has enclosed dining area, below is cosy bar, four local beers (cheaper Thurs and Sun evenings), proper cider and cocktails (happy hour 5-8pm), good value straightforward food including stone-baked pizzas, friendly service; Weds quiz; children (not in bar) and dogs welcome, picnic-sets out on wharf, open all day.

NEWARK   SK7953

Just Beer (01636) 312047

Swan & Salmon Yard, off Castle Gate (B6166); NG24 1BG Welcoming one-room micropub tucked down alley; six or seven interesting quickly changing beers from brick counter, real cider/perry, limited range of other drinks, bright airy minimalist décor with some brewery memorabilia, half a dozen tables on stone floor, good mix of customers; darts, dominoes and board games; dogs welcome, open all day (from 1pm weekdays).

NEWARK   SK7953
★ **Prince Rupert** (01636) 918121
Stodman Street, off Castle Gate; NG24 1AW Timber-framed 15th-c pub near market, several carefully renovated small rooms on two floors, beams, exposed brickwork and many original features, characterful furniture including high-backed settles, assorted bric-a-brac, mirrors and old enamelled signs, open fires, airy conservatory with tricycles hanging from the ceiling, well kept Brains Rev James, Oakham JHB and four guests, plenty of wines by the glass, pubby food plus speciality pizzas with some unusual toppings, friendly staff, live music and open mike nights; children and dogs welcome, seats in small courtyard, open all day (till 1am Fri, Sat).

NOTTINGHAM   SK5739
★ **Bell** (0115) 947 5241
Angel Row; off Market Square; NG1 6HL Deceptively large pub with late Georgian frontage concealing two much older timber-framed buildings; front Tudor Bar with glass panels protecting patches of 300-year-old wallpaper, larger low-beamed Elizabethan Bar with half-panelled walls and maple parquet flooring, more heavy panelling and a 15th-c crown post in upstairs Belfry restaurant; around nine real ales including Greene King and Nottingham from remarkable deep sandstone cellar (can arrange tours), ten wines by the glass, reasonably priced straightforward bar food; background music, TV; children welcome in some parts, pavement tables, open (and food) all day (till 12.30am Fri, Sat).

NOTTINGHAM   SK5843
Bread & Bitter (0115) 960 7541
Woodthorpe Drive; NG3 5JL Welcoming pub in former suburban bakery (ovens remain); three bright and airy bare-boards rooms with brewery memorabilia, 11 well kept ales including Castle Rock and Fullers, good range of bottled beers, traditional cider and decent choice of wines, reasonably priced pubby food from cobs to specials, friendly staff; well behaved children and dogs welcome, open (and food) all day, kitchen closes 7pm Sun.

NOTTINGHAM   SK5739
Canalhouse (0115) 955 5060
Canal Street; NG1 7EH Converted wharf building with bridge over indoors canal spur (complete with narrowboat); lots of bare brick and varnished wood, huge joists on steel beams, long bar serving Castle Rock and five guests, well over 100 bottled beers and good choice of wines, sensibly priced food from snacks up including range of burgers;

background music; masses of tables out on attractive waterside terrace, open all day (till 1am Fri, Sat), food till 7pm Sun.

NOTTINGHAM   SK5739
Cock & Hoop (0115) 948 4414
High Pavement opposite Galleries of Justice; NG1 1HF Pub attached to the Lace Market Hotel; cosy panelled front bar with fireside armchairs and characterful décor, Castle Rock and several local guests, enjoyable fairly priced food from sandwiches to good Sun roasts including drink and dinner deals Weds-Sat, more room downstairs; children and dogs welcome, covered outside seating area, 42 bedrooms (ones by the street can be noisy at weekends), open (and food) all day.

NOTTINGHAM   SK5739
★ **Cross Keys** (0115) 941 7898
Byard Lane; NG1 2GJ Victorian city-centre pub on two levels; lower carpeted part with leather banquettes, panelling and chandeliers, upper area with old wooden tables and chairs and some bucket seats on bare boards, interesting pictures/prints, seven well kept beers including Navigation, good reasonably priced food from breakfast on, friendly service, upstairs function/dining room; sports TV; metal seats and tables outside, open all day from 9am.

NOTTINGHAM   SK5739
Fellows Morton & Clayton
(0115) 924 1175 *Canal Street (part of inner ring road); NG1 7EH* Flower-decked former canal warehouse; up to eight well kept mainly local ales, four real ciders and 14 wines by the glass, enjoyable food (till 7pm Sun) from snacks and sharing plates up including range of burgers, friendly staff, softly lit downstairs bar with alcove seating, wood floors and lots of exposed brickwork, pictures of old Nottingham, two raised areas and upstairs restaurant/function room; background music, sports TVs; children and dogs welcome, tables outside, open all day (till midnight Fri, Sat).

NOTTINGHAM   SK5542
Fox & Crown (0115) 942 2002
Church Street/Lincoln Street, Old Basford; NG6 0GA Range of Shipstones beers from the Little Star brewery behind this tucked-away pub, also guest ales, continentals and good choice of wines, restaurant area serving reasonably priced authentic Thai food (not Sun); events including quiz, live music and card nights, sports TV, games machines, pool and darts; disabled access/loo, tables on back terrace, open all day till 1am.

NOTTINGHAM   SK5642
Gladstone (0115) 912 9994
Loscoe Road, Carrington; NG5 2AW Welcoming mid-terrace backstreet local;

half a dozen well kept ales such as Castle Rock, Fullers, Oakham and Timothy Taylors, good range of malt whiskies too, comfortable lounge with collection of books, bar with old sporting memorabilia and darts; background music, sports TV; tables in small back garden among colourful tubs and hanging baskets, open all day weekends, closed weekday lunchtimes.

NOTTINGHAM SK5640
Hand & Heart (0115) 958 2456
Derby Road; NG1 5BA Unexceptional exterior but unusual inside with bar and dining areas cut deep into back sandstone; a house beer from Dancing Duck and around five guests, two real ciders and good wine and whisky choice, enjoyable fairly priced traditional food from sandwiches and snacks up, friendly helpful service, glassed-in upstairs room overlooking street; background music; children welcome till 7pm if eating, dogs in bar, open all day Fri-Sun, from 4pm other days, closed Mon, Tues.

NOTTINGHAM SK5739
★**Keans Head** (0115) 947 4052
St Marys Gate; NG1 1QA Cheery pub in attractive Lace Market area; fairly functional single room with big windows overlooking the street, simple wooden café furnishings on wood-strip floor, some exposed brickwork, red tiling and small fireplace, six real ales including Castle Rock, 11 craft kegs, draught Belgian beers and extensive bottled range, also 20 wines by the glass, over 60 malt whiskies and similar number of gins, teas/coffees, popular fairly traditional food (not Sun evening), friendly service; background music, daily papers, quiz Thurs; children welcome till 7pm, church next door worth visiting, open all day.

NOTTINGHAM SK5539
King William IV (0115) 958 9864
Manvers Street/Eyre Street, Sneinton; NG2 4PB Victorian corner local with plenty of character (aka the King Billy); well kept Oakham Bishops Farewell and Citra plus six guests mainly from local microbreweries such as Black Iris, Lincoln Green, Scribbler and Totally Brewed from circular bar, also craft beers and real cider, good fresh cobs and sausage rolls, friendly staff; Irish folk session Thurs, monthly quiz, silent sports TV, pool upstairs; dogs welcome, seats on roof terrace, handy for cricket, football and rugby grounds, open all day (from 2pm Mon).

NOTTINGHAM SK5740
★**Lincolnshire Poacher**
(0115) 941 1584 *Mansfield Road; up hill from Victoria Centre; NG1 3FR* Impressive range of drinks at this popular down-to-earth pub (attracts younger evening crowd), up to a dozen well kept ales including Castle Rock, lots of continental draught/bottled beers, half a dozen ciders

and over 70 malt whiskies, shortish choice of reasonably priced uncomplicated food; big simple traditional front bar with wall settles, wooden tables and breweriana, plain but lively room on left and corridor to chatty panelled back snug with newspapers and board games, conservatory overlooking large heated outside area; occasional live music; children (till 8pm) and dogs welcome, open all day (till midnight Thurs-Sat).

NOTTINGHAM SK5541
★**Lion** (0115) 970 3506
Lower Mosley Street, New Basford; NG7 7FQ Eleven real ales including Bass and Castle Rock and local guests such as Ashover, Black Iris, Nottingham and Shipstones from one of the city's deepest cellars (glass viewing panel, can be visited at quiet times), also plenty of craft beers and proper ciders, good well priced food including tapas, burgers, nachos and wraps (all day weekends); big open-plan room with feel of separate areas, bare bricks and dark oak boards, old brewery pictures and posters, open fires; regular live music including popular Sun lunchtime jazz, quiz Weds and Sun; children welcome till 6pm, no dogs, disabled facilities, garden with terrace and smokers' shelter, open all day.

NOTTINGHAM SK5739
Malt Cross (0115) 941 1048
St James's Street (pedestrianised) off Old Market Square; NG1 6FG Former Victorian music hall with high vaulted glass roof and gallery overlooking bar area; ornate iron pillars, chesterfield sofas and button-back seating booths on bare boards, good selection of drinks including some interesting real ales, decent well priced food from shortish menu, teas/coffees and daily newspapers; regular live music on small stage, Weds quiz; cellars converted into art gallery and workshops, ancient caves (tours available); open all day (till 9pm Sun).

NOTTINGHAM SK5739
Newshouse (0115) 952 3061
Canal Street; NG1 7HB Friendly two-room 1950s Castle Rock pub with striking blue tiled exterior; their ales and four changing guests, Belgian and Czech imports, decent lunchtime food, mix of bare boards and carpet, local newspaper/radio memorabilia, beer bottles on shelves, darts, table skittles and bar billiards; background music, big-screen sports TV; a few tables out in front, walking distance from both football grounds (busy on match days), open all day.

NOTTINGHAM SK6141
Old Volunteer (0115) 987 2299
Burton Road, Carlton; NG4 3DQ Imposing 19th-c community pub acting as tap for Flipside; five of their well kept ales and five guests, good range of whiskies, friendly helpful staff, some food including burgers;

live music and beer festivals; dogs welcome, picnic-sets on side terrace, open all day.

NOTTINGHAM   SK5739
Olde Salutation (0115) 947 6580
Hounds Gate/Maid Marian Way;
NG1 7AA Low beams, flagstones, ochre walls and cosy corners including two small quiet rooms in ancient lower back part, plusher modern front lounge, up to eight real ales including Castle Rock, Robinsons, Sharps and Wychwood and good choice of draught/bottled ciders, quickly served food till 8pm (6pm Sun, not Mon), helpful friendly staff (ask them to show you the haunted caves below the pub); background music, weekend live bands/DJs upstairs; open all day (till 3am Fri, Sat).

NOTTINGHAM   SK5739
★Olde Trip to Jerusalem
(0115) 947 3171 *Brewhouse Yard; from inner ring road follow 'The North, A6005 Long Eaton' signpost until in Castle Boulevard, then right into Castle Road; pub is on the left; NG1 6AD* Unusual rambling pub seemingly clinging to sandstone rock face, largely 17th-c and a former brewhouse for the hilltop castle; downstairs bar carved into the stone with some rocky alcoves, dark panelling and simple built-in seats, tables on flagstones, Greene King IPA, Hardys & Hansons Olde Trip and Nottingham Extra plus up to six guests (tasting trays available), good value food all day, efficient staff dealing well with busy mix of customers; popular little tourist shop with panelled walls soaring into dark cavernous heights; children welcome, seats and ring the bull in snug courtyard, open all day (till midnight Fri, Sat).

NOTTINGHAM   SK5640
Organ Grinder (0115) 970 0630
Alfreton Road; NG7 3JE Tap for Blue Monkey with up to nine well kept ales including guests, a couple of ciders and a perry, good local pork pies, open-plan bare-boards interior with woodburner; sports TV; well behaved dogs welcome, seats out behind, open all day.

NOTTINGHAM   SK5739
Pitcher & Piano (0115) 958 6081
High Pavement; NG1 1HN Remarkable lofty-roofed conversion of 19th-c church; popular all-day food including deals, good range of drinks from craft beers to cocktails including some Blue Monkey beers; some live music; children welcome, outside bar and terrace, open all day (till late Thurs-Sat).

NOTTINGHAM   SK5540
Plough (0115) 970 2615
St Peters Street, Radford; NG7 3EN Friendly 1930s local with own good value Nottingham ales brewed behind, also guest beers and several traditional ciders;

two bars (one carpeted, the other with terrazzo flooring), banquettes, old tables and chairs, bottles on delft shelving, coal fires; monthly blues and folk nights, Thurs quiz, TV, traditional games including outside skittle alley; dogs welcome, beer garden with covered smokers' area, open all day.

NOTTINGHAM   SK5344
Roebuck (0115) 979 3400
St James's Street (pedestrianised) off Old Market Square; NG1 6FH Light airy Wetherspoons conversion of 18th-c red-brick townhouse; high ceilings and some original features, extensive choice of well kept ales (tasting trays available), ciders/perry and good wine choice, their usual reasonably priced food from toasties up, Tues steak night, friendly staff, upper galleried area and enclosed roof terrace; muted TV; children welcome, disabled facilities, open all day from 8am.

NOTTINGHAM   SK5838
Trent Navigation (0115) 986 5658
Meadow Lane; NG2 3HS Welcoming tile-fronted Victorian pub close to canal and home to the Navigation Brewery; up to 13 cask ales including their own beers and guests along with ciders/perries, popular pubby food including daily deals; Sun quiz, sports TVs (pub is next to Notts County FC); children welcome, brewery shop at back, open all day, food all day Thurs-Sun.

NOTTINGHAM   SK5739
★Vat & Fiddle (0115) 985 0611
Queensbridge Road; alongside Sheriffs Way (near multi-storey car park); NG2 1NB Open-plan 1930s tap for next-door Castle Rock Brewery; varnished pine tables, bentwood chairs and stools on parquet or terrazzo flooring, some brewery memorabilia and interesting photographs of demolished local pubs, up to 13 real ales, bottled continentals, traditional ciders and over 30 malt whiskies, decent pubby food (not Sun evening), modern dining extension, visitors' centre with own bar; some live music; children and dogs welcome, picnic-sets out at front by road, open all day.

RADCLIFFE ON TRENT   SK6439
Horse Chestnut (0115) 933 1994
Main Road; NG12 2BE Smart pub with plenty of Victorian/Edwardian features; well kept Adnams, Woodfordes and four guests, craft beers and ten decent wines by the glass, sensibly priced home-made food (not Sun evening) including burgers, good pizzas and deal nights such as Tues curry and Thurs steak, friendly service, two-level main bar, parquet and mosaic floor, panelling, big mirrors and impressive lamps, handsome leather wall benches and period fireplaces; some live music; children and dogs welcome, disabled access, terrace seating, open all day.

RAMPTON   SK7978
Eyre Arms   (01777) 248771
Main Street; DN22 0HR Shuttered red-brick village pub with enjoyable good value food from chef-owner including extensive specials menu and weekday lunchtime bargains, well kept changing ales, friendly helpful service, dining area overlooking pleasant garden with play area, locals bar with pool; open all day.

RUDDINGTON   SK5733
Three Crowns   (0115) 846 9613
Easthorpe Street; NG11 6LB Open-plan pub known locally as the Top House; four well kept ales and very good Indian food in back Three Spices evening restaurant; open all day weekends, closed weekday lunchtimes.

SCAFTWORTH   SK6692
King William   (01302) 710292
A631 Bawtry–Everton; DN10 6BL Popular little red-brick country pub with friendly relaxed atmosphere; good well presented home-made food (best to book Sun lunch), Theakstons Best, a couple of guests and good choice of wines by the glass, bar, snug and two dining rooms with old high-backed settles, plain tables and chairs and log fires; background music; children and dogs welcome, seats on terrace and in big back garden running down to River Idle, swings, open all day, food till 8pm Sun.

SELSTON   SK4553
★ Horse & Jockey   (01773) 781012
Handy for M1 junctions 27/28; Church Lane; NG16 6FB Interesting pub on different levels dating from the 17th c; low heavy beams, dark flagstones, individual furnishings and good log fire in cast-iron range, friendly staff, Greene King Abbot and Timothy Taylors Landlord poured from the jug and up to four guests, real cider, no food, games area with darts and pool; folk night Weds, quiz Sun; dogs welcome, terrace and smokers' shelter, pleasant rolling countryside.

SOUTHWELL   SK7054
★ Final Whistle   (01636) 814953
Station Road; NG25 0ET Popular railway-themed pub commemorating the long-defunct Southwell line; ten well kept ales including Bass, Brewsters, Everards and Salopian (beer festivals), real ciders/perries, foreign bottled beers and good range of wines, snacky food such as pork pies; traditional opened-up bar with tiled or wood floor, settles and armchairs in quieter carpeted room, corridor drinking area, two open fires, panelling, lots of railway memorabilia and other odds and ends; quiz and live music nights (folk club third Thurs of month); children (till 9pm) and dogs welcome, back garden with wonderful mock-up of 1920s platform complete with

track and buffers, on Robin Hood Way and Southwell Trail, open all day.

SOUTHWELL   SK7053
Hearty Goodfellow   (01636) 919176
Church Street (A612); NG25 0HQ Welcoming open-plan cosy mock-Tudor pub; up to eight real ales, six real ciders and good range of house wines (12 by the glass), 11 gins, popular fairly straightforward food (till 7pm Sun) at reasonable prices, also takeaway fish and chips and pop-up fish/seafood restaurant in converted outbuilding, cheerful young staff, lots of polished wood, beams and two brick fireplaces; background and some live music, sports TVs; children and dogs welcome, covered terrace and nice big tree-shaded garden beyond car park, play area, handy for Southwell Workhouse (NT) and the Minster, open all day Fri-Sun.

STAUNTON IN THE VALE   SK8043
Staunton Arms   (01400) 281218
High Street, N of church on crossroads; NG13 9PE Attractive early 19th-c brick-built country inn; good well presented food from pub standards to more restaurant-style dishes, also lighter lunchtime choices and brunch from 10am Mon-Sat, Bass, Castle Rock and a guest, good range of wines and other drinks, efficient friendly service, L-shaped beamed bar with bare boards and open fire, steps up to dining area; children and dogs welcome, rattan-style furniture on front terrace, eight good bedrooms (and cottage), open (and food) all day.

TUXFORD   SK7471
Fountain   (01777) 872854
Lincoln Road on edge of village near East Coast railway line; NG22 0JQ Comfortably updated family dining pub-hotel with welcoming atmosphere; enjoyable affordably priced food (not Sun evening) from pub favourites, pizzas and grills to daily specials, local beers and ciders such as Springhead and Welbeck Abbey, friendly service; pool; picnic-sets out in fenced area, open all day Fri-Sun, closed lunchtimes Mon-Thurs.

UPTON   SK7354
★ Cross Keys   (01636) 813269
Main Street (A612); NG23 5SY 17th-c pub with rambling heavy-beamed bar, log fire in brick fireplace, own Mallard ales (brewed in Maythorne) and good home-made food from lunchtime sandwiches to specials, friendly staff, back extension; seats on decked terrace, handy for the Museum of Timekeeping (British Horological Institute), open all day Fri-Sun, closed Mon, lunchtimes Tues and Wed, no food Sun evening.

WEST BRIDGFORD   SK5838
Larwood & Voce   (0115) 981 9960
Fox Road; NG2 6AJ Open-plan dining pub (part of the small Moleface group); enjoyable

food in bar and restaurant area including some imaginative choices, afternoon teas, plenty of wines by the glass, cocktail menu and four well kept ales such as Black Sheep, Fullers London Pride, St Austell Proper Job and Sharps Doom Bar, attentive staff; sports TV; children welcome away from bar, seats out on raised deck with heaters, on edge of the cricket ground and handy for Nottingham Forest FC, open all day, from 10am weekends for breakfast.

WEST BRIDGFORD SK5938

Poppy & Pint (0115) 981 9995

Pierrepont Road; NG2 5DX Converted former British Legion Club backing on to bowling green and tennis courts; large bar with raised section and family area, around a dozen real ales including Castle Rock, a couple of ciders and decent food from breakfast on, friendly atmosphere; live music and other events (some in upstairs function room); dogs welcome, open all day from 9.30am (10am Sun).

WEST BRIDGFORD SK5837

Stratford Haven (0115) 982 5981

Stratford Road, Trent Bridge; NG2 6BA Traditional red-brick Castle Rock pub; bare-boards front bar leading to linked areas including airy skylit back part, up to 14 well kept ales on handpump, interesting bottled beers, proper ciders and good wine and whisky choice, reasonably priced pubby

food including Tues pie, Weds steak and blues and Thurs burger nights, friendly service; Sun quiz, live music and beer events; children (during the day) and dogs welcome, tables outside, handy for cricket ground and Nottingham Forest FC (busy on match days), open (and food) all day.

WEST STOCKWITH SK7994

White Hart (01427) 892672

Main Street; DN10 4EY Small country pub at junction of Chesterfield Canal and River Trent; own good Idle beers from next-door brewery plus guests, enjoyable well priced traditional food (not Sun evening) including blackboard specials and regular evening deals; live music Fri, pool and sports TV; children and dogs welcome, garden overlooking the water, open all day.

WYSALL SK6027

Plough (01509) 880339

Keyworth Road; off A60 at Costock, or A6006 at Wymeswold; NG12 5QQ Attractive 17th-c beamed village local; popular good value lunchtime food from shortish menu, cheerful staff, Bass, Greene King Abbot, Timothy Taylors Landlord and three guests, rooms either side of bar with nice mix of furnishings, big log fire; Tues quiz, pool; children welcome, dogs after 2.30pm, french doors to pretty terrace garden with potted palm trees, open all day.

Oxfordshire

ASCOTT UNDER WYCHWOOD   SP2918   Map 4
Swan 🍴 🛏

(01993) 832332 – www.countrycreatures.com/the-swan

Shipton Road; OX7 6AY

Former coaching inn in good walking country with boldly decorated bar and restaurant, well liked food and drinks and seats in garden

Extensively refurbished in 2019, this 16th-c coaching inn is in a lovely spot opposite the village church. The stylish interior has blue panelling, wood floors, limed beams and shuttered windows, and furniture includes easy chairs by an inglenook fireplace, prettily covered or wooden dining chairs around chunky pine tables and modern art on pale walls. The impressive array of drinks includes well kept Butcombe Best, Clavell & Hind Blunderbuss and Hook Norton Hooky, local and French ciders, 15 wines by the glass (including prosecco and champagne), several sherries, cocktails and a good choice of spirits. The restaurant, with its seagrass flooring, has some striking wallpaper, a woodburning stove and lavish flower arrangements. There are seats and tables in a back courtyard garden. The eight individually styled bedrooms are well equipped and comfortable; two are in an outbuilding. The inn is handy for the Oxfordshire Way and Wychwood Way. Sister pub is the Chequers in Churchill.

🍴 Quite a choice of enjoyable food includes interesting nibbles, pear and celery tart with stilton, wood pigeon with heritage carrots, raspberries and hazelnuts, grilled megrim sole with samphire, capers and brown shrimp, mutton or chicken and leek pie with mash, lamb rump with potato fondant, braised lettuce, peas and broad beans, pork belly with barbecue langoustine, sweetcorn and fennel, and puddings such as crème caramel with muscovado sponge and honeycomb and cherry parfait with almonds and Valrhona chocolate. *Benchmark main dish: double smoked brisket burger and fries £14.00. Two-course evening meal £23.00.*

Free house ~ Licensees Sam and Georgie Pearman ~ Real ale ~ Open 11.30-3, 5.30-11; 11.30-11.30 Sat; 11.30-10.30 Sun; closed Mon ~ Bar food 12-2.30, 6.30-9; 12-2.30 Sun ~ Children welcome ~ Dogs allowed in bar ~ Bedrooms: £120

ASTHALL   SP2811   Map 4
Maytime 🍴 🍷 🛏

(01993) 822068 – www.themaytime.com

Off A40 at W end of Witney bypass, then first left; OX18 4HW

17th-c former coaching inn with individually furnished bar and dining rooms, good food and wine and seats outside; smart bedrooms

An excellent range of drinks, coupled with an enticing menu and a lovely setting means that our readers greatly enjoy their visits to this golden-stone inn. The lofty, character bar has a lively feel, exposed roof trusses, flagstones, leather sofas, cushioned wall seats and stools against the counter where friendly staff serve two quickly changing ales on handpump, a couple of draught ciders, 47 good wines by the glass from a fine list, more than 150 gins, a good choice of other spirits and cocktails; background music and board games. Several white-painted, beamed rooms lead off on different levels with cushioned window seats, a mix of tartan upholstered and traditional wooden chairs around tables of varying size on black slates or bare boards, and pictures on painted or stone walls; one room has a glass ceiling. The pub's springer is called Alfie. The garden, with views of open countryside beyond, is charming: there are seats beneath large parasols on a terrace, picnic-sets on grass and a boules pitch. The six bedrooms are stylish and well equipped and breakfasts are highly rated. Enjoyable walks from the door.

Imaginative food includes sandwiches, wild boar scotch egg with nduja tomato sauce, beetroot-cured gravadlax with pickled cucumber, orange and chive cream cheese, buttermilk fried chicken with sriracha mayo and rocket salad, sharing boards, a pie of the day, Moroccan lamb rump with harissa couscous, roasted tomatoes and chickpea salsa, slow-roast pork belly with wholegrain mustard mash, spiced red cabbage and apple sauce, falafel burger with avocado, halloumi and skinny chips, and puddings such as plum frangipane with clotted cream and lemon tart with berry compote and crème fraîche. *Benchmark main dish: wild boar burger and skinny chips £16.00. Two-course evening meal £23.00.*

Free house ~ Licensee Dominic Wood ~ Real ale ~ Open 11-11 ~ Bar food 12-3, 6-9; 12-3, 6-8.45 Sun ~ Restaurant ~ Children welcome ~ Dogs allowed in bar ~ Bedrooms: £105

BANBURY
Olde Reindeer 🍺
SP4540 Map 4

(01295) 270972 – www.ye-olde-reindeer-inn-banbury.co.uk
Parsons Street, off Market Place; OX16 5NA

Rewarding town pub with a friendly welcome, real ales and decent food

This busy old tavern is dripping in history, while also offering a warm welcome, hearty food and well kept beer. The front bar has a pleasing, easy-going atmosphere, heavy 16th-c beams, very broad polished oak floorboards, a magnificent carved overmantel for one of the two roaring log fires and traditional solid furnishings; plenty of pictures on the walls and some interesting breweriana too. It's worth looking at the handsomely proportioned Globe Room used by Oliver Cromwell as his base during the Civil War. Quite a sight, it still has some lovely 17th-c carved dark oak panelling. Attentive staff serve Hook Norton Hooky, Hooky Mild, Old Hooky and a couple of seasonal guest beers on handpump, three craft beers from Hook Norton, 11 wines by the glass, eight gins, fruit wines and several malt whiskies. The little back courtyard has tables and benches under parasols, aunt sally and pretty flowering baskets. New owners were about to take over as we went to press, so there may be changes.

Honest, reasonably priced food includes lunchtime sandwiches and basket meals, baked rosemary camembert with garlic bread, Cajun chicken and chorizo burger with fries, ham and eggs, cumberland sausages with mustard mash, T-bone steak with onion rings, chips and a choice of sauce, mushroom and red wine stroganoff, sea bass with pan-fried new potatoes and chorizo, and puddings such as plum and apple crumble with custard and chocolate brownie with vanilla pod ice-cream and raspberries. *Benchmark main dish: beef burger and chips £12.95. Two-course evening meal £19.00.*

Hook Norton ~ Tenant Ian Thomas ~ Real ale ~ Open 11-11, 11-midnight Fri, Sat; 12-10.30 Sun ~ Bar food 12-3, 6-9; 12-3 Sun ~ Restaurant ~ Children allowed in bar ~ Dogs allowed in bar

BESSELS LEIGH   SP4501 Map 4

Greyhound 🍷 🍺

(01865) 862110 – www.brunningandprice.co.uk/greyhound
A420 Faringdon–Botley; OX13 5PX

Cotswold-stone inn with rambling rooms, a fine range of real ales, lots of wines by the glass and enjoyable food

This 400-year-old village pub has bags of character and atmosphere. The knocked-through rooms have individually chosen cushioned dining chairs, leather-topped stools and dark wooden tables grouped on carpeting or rug-covered floorboards and three fireplaces (one housing a woodburning stove). Also, all manner of old photographs and pictures covering the half-panelled walls, books on shelves, glass and stone bottles on windowsills, big gilt mirrors and sizeable pot plants. Wooden bar stools line the counter where efficient, friendly staff serve St Austell Brunning & Price Traditional Bitter, Loose Cannon Gunners Gold and Timothy Taylors Landlord with three guests such as Adnams Ghost Ship, Froth Blowers Piffle Snonker, North Cotswold Best and XT Three on handpump, 19 wines by the glass, around 75 gins, 30 rums and 88 whiskies; board games. By the back dining extension is a white picket fence-enclosed garden with picnic-sets under green parasols; the summer window boxes and hanging baskets are delightful.

Interesting food includes sandwiches, pan-fried scallops with pea purée and shredded ham hock, potted smoked mackerel with lemon jelly and pickled cucumber and samphire salad, crispy baby squid with sweet chilli sauce, crispy beef salad with sweet chilli dressing, lotus root crisps and cashews, burger with coleslaw and chips, fish pie (salmon, haddock and prawns), cauliflower, chickpea and squash tagine with lemon and almond couscous, slow-braised ox cheek ragoût with pasta and parmesan, and puddings such as lemon meringue roulade with raspberry ripple ice-cream and crème brûlée. *Benchmark main dish: pork and leek sausages with mash and buttered greens £13.95. Two-course evening meal £21.00.*

Brunning & Price ~ Manager James Ravenhill ~ Real ale ~ Open 11.30-11 ~ Bar food 12-9; 12-9.30 Fri, Sat ~ Children welcome ~ Dogs allowed in bar

CHARLBURY   SP3519 Map 4

Bull 🏅🍴 🍷 🛏

(01608) 810689 – www.bullinn-charlbury.com
Sheep Street; OX7 3RR

Handsome old inn with a civilised but informal atmosphere throughout, imaginative food and seats on terrace; lovely bedrooms

Mixing attractive original features with shabby-chic décor and contemporary pictures, wallpapers and furnishings, this 16th-c coaching inn has plenty of style and atmosphere. You'll find exposed stone and grey-painted panelled walls hung with colourful modern artwork, linen-cushioned seats with bright scatter cushions, painted wooden and upholstered dining chairs around simple tables on rugs or wooden floors and both a woodburning stove and an inglenook log fire. Fullers, Hook Norton and Wye

Valley ales on handpump from a bar made from an apothecary's chest painted peacock blue, plus 18 good wines by the glass and 14 whiskies served by friendly, helpful staff; background music and daily papers. The sunny back terrace has a vine-covered pergola. The eight bedrooms, including four in a converted barn, are individually decorated and comfortable.

 Tasty modern British food includes breakfasts for non-residents (8-11am), monkfish ceviche with red onion and lime, gin and beetroot-cured salmon with dill crème fraîche, Cotswold pork with tenderstem broccoli, butternut squash and chimichurri, beetroot risotto with pesto, a pie of the day, Brixham plaice with crab butter and samphire, minute steak with rocket and parmesan, lamb rump with truffle mash and minted sauce vierge, chicken milanese with garlic butter, and puddings such as dark chocolate with peanut brittle and salty caramel and apricot tarte tatin. *Benchmark main dish: burger with toppings and chips £14.00. Two-course evening meal £20.00.*

Free house ~ Licensees Charlie and Willow Crossley ~ Real ale ~ Open 8am-11pm; 8am-10pm Sun ~ Bar food 8am-9pm; 8am-6pm Sun ~ Restaurant ~ Children welcome ~ Dogs allowed in bar & bedrooms ~ Bedrooms: £99

CHAZEY HEATH
SU6979

Packhorse ♀ ☕

(0118) 972 2140 – www.brunningandprice.co.uk/packhorse
Off A4074 Reading–Wallingford by B4526; RG4 7UG

Attractive pub with interlinked bar and dining areas, a fine choice of drinks especially gin, rewarding food and seats outside

This welcoming pub is hidden down a steep, narrow lane in a tranquil village that influenced the landscape of *The Wind in the Willows* (author Kenneth Grahame lived not far away). Brick-built, the pub is a former farmhouse and dates back to the 17th c. The main bar has a raised inglenook fireplace with logs piled to each side and large brass platters above the bressummer beam, cushioned wall seating, antique-style dining chairs around mixed wooden tables, stubby candles and house plants. Other connected rooms are similarly furnished and throughout you'll find rugs, polished bare boards and carpeting, walls hung with prints, old photos and mirrors, books on shelves and stone and glass bottles. Friendly, well trained staff serve St Austell Brunning & Price Traditional Bitter plus guests such as Fullers London Pride, Glastonbury Session IPA, Loddon Hoppit and West Berkshire Good Old Boy on handpump, 21 good wines by the glass and almost 140 gins. In front of the pub are picnic-sets among flowering plants; in the back garden, wooden chairs and tables sit under giant parasols beside B&P's trademark play tractor. Gin and beer festivals are held in summer.

A wide choice of interesting food includes sandwiches and 'light bites', rabbit, leek and bacon pasty, cheese, potato and onion pie with carrot purée and gravy, braised feather of beef bourguignon with horseradish mash and buttered kale, Sri Lankan curry with sweet potato, butternut squash, red pepper and pak choi, cumberland pork sausages with mash and buttered greens, grilled sea bass fillets with potato and shallot terrine and chervil and lemon sauce, and puddings such as crème brûlée and lemon meringue roulade with raspberry sorbet. *Benchmark main dish: steak burger with coleslaw and chips £13.95. Two-course evening meal £22.00.*

Brunning & Price ~ Manager Sarah Livesey ~ Real ale ~ Open 11.30-11; 11.30-10.30 Sun ~ Bar food 12-9; 12-9.30 Fri, Sat ~ Children welcome ~ Dogs allowed in bar

It's very helpful if you let us know up-to-date food prices when you report on pubs.

CHURCH ENSTONE

SP3725 Map 4

Crown 🏵

(01608) 677262 – www.crowninnenstone.co.uk

Mill Lane; from A44 take B4030 turn-off at Enstone; OX7 4NN

Friendly country pub with helpful licensees, enjoyable food and well kept real ales; rooms

This handsome golden-stone inn sits in a tranquil hamlet at the edge of the Cotswolds. The food here is particularly good, so to be sure of a table it's best to book ahead. The smart, uncluttered, congenial bar has beams, cushioned window seats and dark farmhouse chairs around long tables on big flagstones, and an open fire; one of the owners is an artist and his work (for sale) adorns the walls. Stools line the counter where they keep Hook Norton Hooky Bitter and changing beers such as Sharps Doom Bar and Shepherd Neame Spitfire on handpump and 11 wines by the glass; board games. There's also a white-painted beamed dining room with high-backed wooden chairs around sturdy tables on a large, colourful rug or bare boards, as well as an airy, simply furnished conservatory. The front terrace has seats and tables overlooking the quiet lane, and there are more in the sheltered suntrap back garden. There are five attractive boutique-style rooms and a new self-catering cottage for those wishing to stay longer.

 Excellent food includes lunchtime sandwiches, lobster ravioli with lobster bisque, fennel and spring onion, ham hock terrine with rhubarb chutney, chicken wings with confit duck leg parcel, beetroot, watercress and candied walnuts, a home-made tart of the day, a pie of the day, assiette of lamb with caponata, runner beans and boulangère potatoes, sea bream fillet with baked polenta and red pepper salsa, baby artichokes, yellow courgettes, semi-dried tomatoes, giant couscous and pesto, and puddings such as tonka bean parfait with dark chocolate mousse, strawberries and arlette, and roasted peach tartlet with thyme cream, raspberry sorbet and meringue. *Benchmark main dish: roasted sea trout supreme with broccoli and roasted new potatoes £16.00. Two-course evening meal £24.00.*

Free house ~ Licensees George and Victoria Irvine ~ Real ale ~ Open 12-3, 6-11; 12-11 Sat; 12-6 Sun ~ Bar food 12-3, 6.30-9; 12-3 Sun ~ Restaurant ~ Children welcome ~ Dogs allowed in bar ~ Bedrooms: £120

CHURCHILL

SP2824 Map 4

Chequers 🏵 🍺

(01608) 659393 – www.thechequerschurchill.com

Church Road; B4450 Chipping Norton to Stow-on-the-Wold (and village signed off A361 Chipping Norton–Burford); OX7 6NJ

Simple furnishings in spacious bars and dining rooms, friendly relaxed atmosphere, up to six ales and popular food

The sumptuous furnishings of this appealing honey-coloured pub are a precursor to the impressive food and drink that awaits. The relaxed, friendly bar has an armchair and other comfortable chairs around an old trunk in front of an inglenook fireplace, some exposed stone walls, cushioned wall seats, and a mix of wooden and antique leather chairs around nice old tables on bare floorboards and flagstones. Rugs are dotted about and stools line the counter which is presided over by a big stag's head: there's Clavel & Hind Blunderbuss, Hook Norton Hooky, Gloucester Birdlip and Sharps Doom Bar on handpump, 17 wines by the glass (including champagne), 12 malt whiskies, mocktails and a farm cider; darts, newspapers and background music. At the back is a large extension with soaring rafters, large lantern lights, long button-back leather banquettes and other seating, while upstairs is another similarly furnished dining area and a room perfect for private gatherings. The landscaped and flagstoned back terrace has lots of good quality wooden chairs and tables and climbing plants. This is a pretty village and the church opposite is impressive and worth a visit. Wheelchair access. Sister pub is the Swan at Ascott under Wychwood.

Good modern food from a varied menu includes sandwiches, chargrilled harissa wild Scottish langoustine with burnt lime, burrata with pesto, toasted almonds and tomatoes, devilled kidneys on sourdough toast, various steaks with a choice of sauce, gnocchi with roasted red onion, chargrilled broccoli, pepper and green sauce, pan-roasted hake with nduja and chickpea stew with saffron aioli, lamb chops with romesco and grilled tenderstem broccoli, chicken paillard with Tuscan bread salad, and puddings such as apple and gooseberry crumble and chocolate, caramel and salted peanut pudding with vanilla ice-cream. *Benchmark main dish: chargrilled whole bream with fennel, orange and dill salad £18.00. Two-course evening meal £25.00.*

Free house ~ Licensees Sam and Georgie Pearman ~ Real ale ~ Open 12-11; 12-10.30 Sun ~ Bar food 12-3, 6-9.30 (10 Fri, Sat); 12-4, 6-9 Sun ~ Restaurant ~ Children welcome ~ Dogs allowed in bar

FILKINS

Five Alls
SP2304 Map 4

(01367) 860875 – www.thefiveallsfilkins.co.uk
Signed off A361 Lechlade–Burford; GL7 3JQ

Thoughtfully refurbished inn with enjoyable food, quite a range of drinks, a friendly welcome and seats outside; bedrooms

This pub has all the ingredients that most people look for in a classic pub: a good range of drinks, great food and an appealing, homely interior with beams, flagstones and floorboards augmented by thoughtful touches such as a real fire, candles and fresh flowers. The main bar has a cosy area with leather chesterfields grouped around a table by an open fire, an informal dining space with farmhouse chairs and cushioned pews around tables on bare boards and a nice little window seat for two. Stools line the counter where friendly staff serve a couple of Brakspears ales (perhaps Bitter and Oxford Gold), another from Ringwood and a guest on handpump, 15 wines by the glass, ten gins and seven malt whiskies. Décor in the dining room includes large old-fashioned portraits against unusual postage-stamp wallpaper, an attractive mix of chairs and tables plus modern artwork on pale-painted walls, candles and floral arrangements; traditional pub games, background music. The back terrace has chunky tables and chairs under parasols and there are a few picnic-sets at the front. The nine bedrooms (four above the pub, five in the garden) are comfortable and attractive. Sister pubs are the Plough at Kelmscott (also in Oxfordshire) and the Bull in Fairford (Gloucestershire). Disabled access.

Highly thought-of food includes sandwiches, scotch egg with celeriac rémoulade and garlic mayo, rare beef salad with truffle oil and parmesan shavings, crispy pork belly with fricassée of mushrooms, new potatoes and spring greens, beef and mushroom pie with caramelised root veg, risotto with broad beans, peas and pea purée, cheeseburger and fries, crispy duck leg with roast potato, heritage beetroot and bacon crumb, lamb kofta with dried fruit, chickpeas, couscous and tzatziki, and puddings such as sticky toffee pudding with butterscotch sauce and rhubarb and apple crumble with honeycomb ice cream; they also offer a set lunch (Monday-Thursday). *Benchmark main dish: pan-fried sea bream with crushed new potato, spinach and citrus sauce £18.00. Two-course evening meal £25.00.*

Free house ~ Licensee Steve Cook ~ Real ale ~ Open 12-11; 12-9 Sun ~ Bar food 12-2.30, 6-9.30; 12-3, 6-10 Fri, Sat; 12-3 Sun ~ Restaurant ~ Children welcome ~ Dogs allowed in bar ~ Bedrooms: £80

KELMSCOTT
Plough
SU2499 Map 4

(01367) 253543 – www.theploughinnkelmscott.com
NW of Faringdon, off B4449 between A417 and A4095; GL7 3HG

Lovely spot for tranquil pub with character bar and dining rooms, attractive furnishings and well regarded food; bedrooms

You'll get a warm welcome from the convivial licensee at this pretty little 17th-c inn tucked away in a lovely village by the upper Thames. The small, traditional, beamed front bar has ancient flagstones and stripped-stone walls along with a woodburning stove, seats against the counter and a village pub atmosphere. There are two Hook Norton beers (one named for the pub and a guest) on handpump, good wines by the glass and maybe farm cider. The dining room has elegant wooden or painted dining chairs around all sorts of tables, striped and cushioned wall seats, paintings on exposed stone walls, and rugs on the floor. Outside in the cottagey garden are seats and tables under parasols. The seven attractive bedrooms are light, comfortable and breakfasts good. The Oxfordshire Cycleway runs close by and the inn is a short walk from William Morris's former home, Kelmscott Manor (open Wednesdays and Saturdays April-October). This is sister pub to the Five Alls at Filkins (also in Oxfordshire) and Bull in Fairford (Gloucestershire).

Enjoyable food includes sandwiches, twice-baked double gloucester soufflé, quail eggs with celery salt, truffle mac 'n' cheese, sweet potato and squash curry, pork schnitzel with new potatoes, green beans and tenderstem broccoli, sea bream with seasonal vegetables, new potatoes and sauce vierge, linguine with chilli, oregano, olive oil and parmesan, cold poached salmon with garden herbs, new potato salad and herb mayo, flat-iron steak with tomatoes, peppercorn sauce and chips, and puddings such as summer berries eton mess and raisin and pear crumble with custard. *Benchmark main dish: beer-battered fish and chips £13.00. Two-course evening meal £22.00.*

Free house ~ Licensee Steve Cook ~ Real ale ~ Open 12-11; 12-6 Sun ~ Bar food 12-2.30, 6-9; 12-3, 6-9.30 Sat; 12-3, 6-8.30 Sun ~ Restaurant ~ Children welcome ~ Dogs allowed in bar ~ Bedrooms: £100

KINGHAM
Plough
SP2624 Map 4

(01608) 658327 – www.thekinghamplough.co.uk
Village signposted off B4450 E of Bledington; or turn S off A436 at staggered crossroads a mile SW of A44 junction – or take signed Daylesford turn off A436 and keep on; The Green; OX7 6YD

Friendly dining pub combining an informal pub atmosphere with highly regarded food; bedrooms

This pub is often busy, and it's easy to see why: well prepared food, a satisfying choice of drinks, attractive interiors and a delightful location overlooking the village green. The little bar has some bare stone walls, contemporary paintwork, nice old high-backed settles and cushioned chapel chairs on broad dark boards, candles on stripped tables and botanical prints; at one end is a big log fire, at the other a woodburning stove. A snug one-table area is opposite the servery where they keep Hook Norton Hooky and guests such as Goffs Jouster and Prescott Hill Climb on handpump,

16 wines by the glass, 14 malt whiskies, several gins and local cider; background music. The fairly spacious and raftered two-part dining room with similar furniture and colourful rugs is up a few steps. The six bedrooms are comfortable and pretty in a rustic-chic way (two have roll-top baths), and the breakfasts are good.

Excellent modern cooking includes salmon, avruga caviar, capers and shallot, half-pint of shell-on prawns with mayo, ploughman's, risotto primavera, Cornish moules marinière and fries, pan-roasted cod with spinach gnocchi, cauliflower, bacon and cabbage, rare-breed pork loin with onions, fish and chips, 8oz longhorn steak (rib-eye or flat-iron) with fries, watercress and béarnaise, and puddings such as apple tarte tatin with almond brittle and calvados ice-cream and lime and iced pomegranate parfait. Breakfast, morning coffee and afternoon tea are available to non-residents. *Benchmark main dish: venison and caramelised onion suet pie with mash £19.00. Two-course evening meal £27.00.*

Free house ~ Licensee Matt Beamish ~ Real ale ~ Open 11-11 ~ Bar food 12-9.30 ~ Restaurant ~ Children welcome ~ Dogs allowed in bar & bedrooms ~ Bedrooms: £165

KIRTLINGTON
SP4919   Map 4
Oxford Arms ⭐🍴 ♟
(01869) 350208 – www.oxford-arms.co.uk
Troy Lane, junction with A4095 W of Bicester; OX5 3HA

Civilised and friendly stripped-stone pub with enjoyable food using local produce and good wine choice

---

Quality food is a priority at this appealing dining pub, which focuses on using local produce as much as possible (around 85% of ingredients) including from its own organic kitchen garden. Chef-patron Mr Jones has been running the pub for 17 years now, and continues to do so with great care and attention. The long line of linked rooms is divided by a central stone hearth with a great circular stove, and by the servery itself – where you'll find Black Sheep and Timothy Taylors Landlord on handpump, an interesting range of wines, with 14 by the glass, nine malt whiskies, farm cider and organic soft drinks. Past the bar area with its cushioned wall pews, creaky beamed ceiling and age-darkened floor tiles, dining tables on parquet have neat high-backed chairs; beyond that, leather sofas cluster round a log fire at the end. Also, church candles, fresh flowers and plenty of stripped stone. The sheltered back terrace has teak tables under giant parasols with heaters, as well as white metal furniture and picnic-sets on neat gravel. The geranium-filled window boxes are pretty. Dogs must be kept on a lead. No under-12s. Disabled access.

The first class food includes Brixham crab and grilled local courgette tart, Wye Valley smoked mackerel with home-made pickled beetroot and crème fraîche, truffle and mushroom tortelloni with wild mushroom sauce and aged parmesan, vegan burger with vegan cheese, kitchen garden mixed leaves and triple-cooked chips, warm game salad with black pudding and blueberries, grilled lamb chop with herb and garlic butter and dauphinoise potatoes, monkfish, prawn and spinach madras curry with rice and mango chutney, and puddings such as flourless chocolate and hazelnut torte with rum and raisin ice-cream and warm fig and almond tart with vanilla ice-cream. *Benchmark main dish: wild sea bass with lemon oil £20.00. Two-course evening meal £27.00.*

Star Pubs & Bars ~ Lease Bryn Jones ~ Real ale ~ Open 12-2, 6-11; 12-3, 6-11 Sat; 12-3 Sun ~ Bar food 12-1.45, 6-8.45; 12-2.30 Sun ~ Restaurant ~ No children under 12 ~ Dogs allowed in bar & restaurant

LETCOMBE REGIS
Greyhound 🏮⭐️🍷🍺👜 SU3886 Map 2

(01235) 771969 – www.thegreyhoundletcombe.co.uk
Main Street; OX12 9JL

Refurbished pub with original windows and fireplaces, plenty of eating and dining space and seats outside; bedrooms

A good base for enjoying the fine surrounding walks and the chalk horse at nearby Uffington, this lovely red-brick village pub also offers a genuine welcome and rewarding food and drink. The bar is just the place for a pint by the woodburning stove, with simple furnishings that include pubby chairs and plush stools around a mix of tables on wide floorboards, and more stools against the counter. As well as four regularly changing real ales such as Little Ox Wipeout, Millstone Tiger Rut, North Cotswold Windrush Ale and West Berkshire Good Old Boy on handpump, you'll find 20 wines by the glass and ten gins; background music, TV and board games. The main dining room has lots of prints on pale walls, cushioned wooden dining chairs and settles with scatter cushions around solid tables and rugs on bare boards, with woodburning stoves at each end of the long room; one red-walled room has similar furnishings on quarry tiles. Picnic-sets with parasols sit outside on a back lawn. Bedrooms are light, well equipped and up to date (dogs are allowed in two of them). The pub offers four walking maps exploring some of the North Wessex Downs, and it's only a mile and a half to join the long-distance ancient Ridgeway Path.

 As well as lunchtime sandwiches, the highly regarded food includes twice-baked Gloucestershire cheddar soufflé with smoked haddock chowder, potted rabbit with mushroom crumb, apricot purée and pickled turnips, Cornish crab ravioli and bisque with crayfish, samphire, apple and coriander, slow-roasted aubergine with tamarind, roasted onion and white bean purée, roast cod with shallot purée, mussels, clams, sea vegetables and ale broth, pollock with fregola, squid, peppers, green olives, pickled lemon and saffron dressing, and puddings such as dark chocolate délice with raspberries and honeycomb and date cake with banana, hazelnuts, banana ice-cream and whisky caramel sauce. *Benchmark main dish: beer-battered fish and chips £16.00. Two-course evening meal £26.00.*

Free house ~ Licensee Catriona Galbraith ~ Real ale ~ Open 10am-11pm; 10-10 Sun ~ Bar food 12-2.30, 6-9 ~ Well behaved children welcome ~ Dogs allowed in bar & bedrooms ~ Bedrooms: £105

MILTON UNDER WYCHWOOD
Hare 🍷 SP2618 Map 4

(01993) 835763 – www.themiltonhare.co.uk
High Street; OX7 6LA

Renovated inn with linked bar and dining rooms, attractive contemporary furnishings, real ales, good food and seats in the garden

The rooms at this stylish golden-stone inn contain all manner of hare paraphernalia, including photos, paintings, statues, a large glass case with stuffed boxing hares, motifs on scatter cushions and so forth. There's a bar and a couple of little drinking areas warmed by a woodburning stove, with various dining areas leading off: wooden floors, dark grey or dark green painted or exposed stone walls, painted beams, big gilt-edged mirrors and seating that includes stools, wooden or leather dining chairs, long button-back wall seats and cushioned settles around tables of every size – each set with a little glass oil lamp. Splashes of bright colour here and there brighten things considerably. Stools line the counter, where friendly, well trained staff serve three real ales from breweries such as Butcombe and Hook Norton on handpump and 11 wines by the glass. The garden has tables, benches and chairs on a terrace and a lawn.

 They specialise in fresh fish and seafood from Cornwall including moules marinière, smoked mackerel pâté and grilled plaice with lemon and chive butter; also lunchtime sandwiches, ham hock and parsley scotch egg, potted Cotswold game with plum chutney and sourdough toast, lamb rump with savoy cabbage, pancetta and dauphinoise potatoes, chicken breast with spinach and basil gnocchi, Thai sweet potato, vegetable, coconut and almond curry, and puddings such as cherry bakewell tart and apple, pear and cinnamon crumble with vanilla ice-cream. *Benchmark main dish: venison and root vegetable pie with parsnip mash £18.50. Two-course evening meal £25.00.*

Free house ~ Licensees Sue and Rachel Hawkins ~ Real ale ~ Open 12-3, 5.30-11; 12-11 Fri, Sat; 12-10.30 Sun ~ Bar food 12-2.30, 6-9; 12-2.30, 6-9.30 Fri, Sat; 12-8 Sun ~ Restaurant ~ Children welcome but no under-12s in bar after 5pm ~ Dogs allowed in bar

OXFORD

Bear

SP5106   Map 4

(01865) 728164 ~ www.bearoxford.co.uk
Alfred Street/Wheatsheaf Alley; OX1 4EH

Delightful pub with two cosy character rooms, six real ales and well liked bar food

Dating from 1242, this city-centre Fullers pub is the oldest drinking house in the city, which means it has a lot of charm and character. The two small bar rooms are beamed and partly panelled with thousands of vintage ties on the walls, a winter coal fire and a chatty, bustling atmosphere. Friendly, helpful staff serve up to six real ales on handpump from a fine pewter bar counter: Fullers ESB, London Pride, Gales ESB, Shotover Scholar and a couple of changing guests. Staff are friendly and helpful; board games, sports TV, live music. A large terraced back garden has seats under parasols; they hold barbecues in summer.

 Bar food includes sandwiches, duck liver pâté with caramelised onion jam, black pudding hash and fried egg, burger (beef or vegan) with triple-cooked chips, butternut squash and sweet potato tagine with apricot and toasted almond couscous, tomato, sweet potato, chickpea and kidney bean ragoût, toulouse sausage, flageolet bean and smoked bacon casserole, rump steak with mushroom, tomato and chips, lamb shoulder shepherd's pie with red wine gravy, and puddings such as chocolate brownie with buffalo milk ice-cream and molasses and date and hops sticky toffee pudding with salted caramel ice-cream. *Benchmark main dish: beer-battered haddock and chips £14.75. Two-course evening meal £19.00.*

Fullers ~ Manager James Vernede ~ Real ale ~ Open 11-11; 11-midnight Fri, Sat; 11.30-10.30 Sun ~ Bar food 12-4, 5-9; 12-9 Fri, Sat; 12-6 Sun (barbecue 6-9 in summer) ~ Children welcome but no pushchairs inside ~ Dogs allowed in bar

OXFORD

Perch

SP4907   Map 4

(01865) 728891 ~ www.the-perch.co.uk
Binsey Lane, on right after river bridge leaving city on A420; OX2 0NG

Beautifully set inn with riverside gardens, local ales, popular food and friendly service

Despite being in the heart of the city, this popular historic inn manages to evoke an almost villagey feel. The efficient, helpful staff always cope well, with cheerful good humour. The heavily beamed bar has a huge, curved, red leather chesterfield in front of a woodburning stove, a very high-backed settle, little stools around tables and fine old flagstones. You'll find real ales from Hook Norton, Prescott, North Cotswold and other breweries on handpump and plenty of wines by the glass. Leading off here are the dining areas with bare floorboards, scatter cushions on built-in wall seats, wheelbacks and other chairs around light tables, a second woodburner with logs piled to the ceiling next to it and a fine brass chandelier. They hold an annual beer and cider festival, outdoor film evenings in summer and a folk festival. A partly covered terrace has seats and tables, there are picnic-sets on the lawn (which runs down to the River Cherwell and the Thames Path where there are moorings), a summer bar and an attractively furnished marquee. It's said that this might be one of the first places that Lewis Carroll gave public readings of *Alice in Wonderland*.

Enjoyable food (with a separate vegan menu) includes sandwiches, devilled whitebait, hot smoked salmon with beetroot and horseradish crème fraîche, sharing boards, roast chicken with radish, potato, apple and watercress salad, grilled fillet of Dorset trout with crushed new potatoes and crayfish, caper and tomato dressing, cheddar and ale-braised onion tart with wild nettle and almond pesto, and puddings such as dark chocolate brownie with hedgerow cream and caramel sauce and queen of puddings. *Benchmark main dish: Cornish fish and chips £14.95. Two-course evening meal £23.00.*

Free house ~ Licensee Jon Ellse ~ Real ale ~ Open 10.30am-11pm ~ Bar food 12-9.30 ~ Restaurant ~ Children welcome ~ Dogs allowed in bar

OXFORD
Punter ⭐

SP5005   Map 4

(01865) 248832 – www.thepunteroxford.co.uk
South Street, Osney (off A420 Botley Road via Bridge Street); OX2 0BE

Easy-going atmosphere in bustling vegetarian and vegan pub overlooking the water, with plenty of character and enjoyable food

Relaunched in 2020 with a completely vegetarian and vegan menu, this quirky pub is actually on Osney Island and has views over the Thames. Run by an enthusiastic landlord and his friendly staff, it's on two levels. The lower part has attractive rugs on flagstones and an open fire, while the upper room has more rugs on bare boards and a single big table surrounded by oil paintings (just right for a private group). Throughout are all manner of nice old dining chairs around an interesting mix of tables, art for sale on whitewashed walls and a rather fine stained-glass window. Greene King Morlands and XT and a changing guest beer on handpump from the tiled counter and a dozen wines by the glass; board games. The side terrace has a range of tables and chairs.

The popular and imaginative food includes grilled peaches with labneh, fried capers and rocket salad, twice-baked cheese soufflé with spinach and mustard cream sauce, king oyster and chestnut mushrooms with garlic and tarragon on toasted sourdough, meze board, jalapeño and sweetcorn bean burger with pineapple relish and charcoal brioche, goats cheese arancini with red pepper sauce and courgette salad, pea and green bean linguine alla genovese, cauliflower, courgette and naga chilli curry with coconut rice and toasted almonds, crispy chilli tofu stir-fry with udon noodles, kimchi and poached duck egg, and puddings such as strawberry and pistachio parfait and crème caramel with walnut and orange biscotti. *Benchmark main dish: almond, chickpea and courgette burger with avocado and rosemary fries £14.00. Two-course evening meal £19.00.*

Greene King ~ Lease Tom Rainey ~ Real ale ~ Open 12-11 ~ Bar food 12-3, 6-9.30; 12-9.30 Sat, Sun ~ Children allowed in bar ~ Dogs allowed in bar

OXFORD
Rose & Crown 🍷 ◖

SP5107 Map 4

(01865) 510551 – www.roseandcrownoxford.com

North Parade Avenue; very narrow, so best to park in a nearby street; OX2 6LX

Lively, friendly local with a fine choice of drinks and proper home cooking

This pub has had only 12 licensees since it opened in 1863 and the current ones have been here for 37 years now. It's no surprise they've not been in a hurry to leave, having given this straightforward-looking pub a great deal of atmosphere and individuality. The front door opens into a passage with a small counter and shelves of reference books for crossword buffs. This leads to two rooms: a cosy one at the front overlooking the street, and a panelled back room housing the main bar and traditional pub furnishings. A good mix of customers of all ages enjoy four well kept ales on handpump – Adnams Southwold, Hook Norton Old Hooky, Shotover Scholar and a guest ale, usually sourced locally – as well as an alcohol-free draught IPA, an extensive range of international bottled beers, around 35 malt whiskies and 20 wines by the glass (including champagne and sparkling wine). The pleasant back courtyard, with walls and heaters, can be covered with a huge awning; at the far end is a ten-seater dining/meeting room. Please note, no dogs or children.

🍴 Honest, reasonably priced food includes sandwiches and baguettes, falafel with hummus, pie and mash with thick gravy, niçoise or greek salads, breaded plaice with chips and mushy peas, salmon fillet with a sweet, smoky sauce, sirloin steak with peppercorn sauce or red wine gravy, and puddings such as apple pie or sticky toffee pudding. *Benchmark main dish: pint of sausages £13.00. Two-course evening meal £17.00.*

Free house ~ Licensees Andrew, Debbie and Adam Hall ~ Real ale ~ Open 11-11 ~ Bar food 12-2.30 (3 Sun), 6-9

SHILTON
Rose & Crown 🔴

SP2608 Map 4

(01993) 842280 – www.shiltonroseandcrown.com

Just off B4020 SE of Burford; OX18 4AB

Simple and appealing small pub with particularly good food, real ales and fine wines

Set in the heart of a lovely Cotswolds village, a couple of miles south of Burford, this traditional 17th-c inn offers a homely welcome. The chatty, bustling small front bar has an unassuming but civilised feel, low beams and timbers, exposed stone walls, a log fire in a big fireplace and half a dozen or so farmhouse chairs and tables on the red-tiled floor. There are usually a few locals at the planked counter where they serve rotating Hook Norton ales, Ramsbury Farmers Best and a regularly changing ale mainly from Butcombe, Loose Cannon or Cotswold Lion on handpump, along with ten wines by the glass, seven malt whiskies and farm cider. A second room, similar but bigger, is used mainly for eating, and has another log-burning fireplace. The attractive side garden has picnic-sets.

📶 Cooked by the chef-patron, the rewarding food caters for classic and contemporay tastes. Dishes include ciabatta sandwiches, smoked mackerel pâté with toast, gravadlax with dill and mustard sauce, aubergine, courgette and pepper caponata, lambs liver and bacon with mash, red Thai fish curry, pork stroganoff with rice, pressed lamb shoulder with greens and mash, ham, egg and chips, sirloin steak with garlic butter and chips, and puddings such as spotted dick with custard and blackberry and apple crumble. *Benchmark main dish: steak and mushroom pie £14.00. Two-course evening meal £21.00.*

Free house ~ Licensee Martin Coldicott ~ Real ale ~ Open 11.30-3, 6-10; 11.30-10 Sat; 12-9 Sun ~ Bar food 12-2 (2.45 Sat and bank holidays), 7-9; 12-2.45, 7-8 Sun ~ Restaurant ~ Children welcome lunchtime only ~ Dogs allowed in bar

SHIPLAKE
SU7779   Map 2

Baskerville 🗲★ ▾ ◖ 🛏

(0118) 940 3332 – www.thebaskerville.com
Station Road, Lower Shiplake (off A4155 just S of Henley); RG9 3NY

Emphasis on imaginative food but a proper bar too, interesting sporting memorabilia and a pretty garden; cosy, comfortable bedrooms

New owners arrived at this popular local spot in summer 2020 and promise to continue its emphasis on great food but in a more relaxed dining setting. The bar has a few beams, leather tub chairs and dining chairs around pine tables on oak floors or patterned carpet, plush red banquettes by the windows and a couple of log fires in brick fireplaces. Flowers and large house plants are dotted about, and the pale walls are hung with a fair array of signed rugby shirts and rowing memorabilia, oars, pictures and river maps (Henley is a 35-minute walk away via the Thames Path or a four-minute train journey); TV. Bar chairs line the light, modern counter where they keep Loddon Hoppit, Rebellion IPA and two guests on handpump, 13 wines by the glass from a thoughtfully chosen list, 50 malt whiskies and farm cider, all served by friendly, enthusiastic staff. The separate restaurant plays background music when it's quiet, and there's occasional live music too. The pretty garden has a covered barbecue area, teak furniture and picnic-sets under parasols. The four bedrooms are well equipped and comfortable and the breakfasts are excellent. Dogs are welcome everywhere except the restaurant, and even get their own 'beer'. Wheelchair access using a ramp; no disabled loos.

📶 Creative food includes lunchtime open sandwiches, tempura soft shell crab with chimichurri and crumpet crisps, moules marinière, octopus and heritage tomato salad, grilled flank steak with herb butter and chips, grilled smoked mackerel with black olives, crushed new potatoes and sauce verjus, wild boar ragoût with pappardelle, salt-baked beetroot with toasted barley, leaves and honey dressing, 'family feasts' such as whole roast chicken and salmon wellington (advance notice required), and puddings such as banana cake with baked figs and vanilla ice-cream and orange crème brûlée. *Benchmark main dish: grilled swordfish with piperade and salsa verde £19.50. Two-course evening meal £24.00.*

Free house ~ Licensee Simon Cromack ~ Real ale ~ Open 11-11; 12-10.30 Sun ~ Bar food 12-2.30, 6-9.30; 12-3.30 Sun ~ Restaurant ~ Children welcome but not in restaurant after 7pm Fri, Sat ~ Dogs allowed in bar & bedrooms ~ Bedrooms: £115

Please tell us if the décor, atmosphere, food or drink at a pub is different from our description. We rely on readers' reports to keep us up to date: feedback@goodguides.com, or (no stamp needed) Freepost THE GOOD PUB GUIDE, Random House Publishing, 20 Vauxhall Bridge Road, London SW1V 2SA.

SOUTH LEIGH

SP3908   Map 4

Mason Arms

(01993) 656238 – www.themasonarms.co.uk

3 miles S of A40 Witney–Eynsham; Station Road; OX29 6XN

Lovely countryside surrounds this highly thought-of inn with its inventive décor, thoughtful choice of food and drinks and attractive garden; well equipped bedrooms

The individual décor in this thatched 16th-c country inn-restaurant has plenty of quirky touches, such as decanter lampshades, floral wallpaper, neon signs, modern art and glass cabinets filled with knick-knacks. Furniture includes antique chairs and curved settles, old leather stools and velvet button-back wall banquettes with vividly coloured cushions – and there are also woodburning stoves and open fires, fat church candles and original floor tiles, flagstones and bare boards. It's all very creative and appealing. Helpful, friendly staff serve two well kept ales on handpump – Hook Norton Hooky and a guest, perhaps Cotswold Pale Ale or something from Wychwood – and a good selection of wines by the glass. Outside, the front courtyard has rustic chairs and tables and ancient-looking olive trees, while the garden has plenty of benches and picnic-sets. As well as eight bedrooms and suites (under the Artist Residence moniker), also decorated in a stylishly bohemian way, there's a cute shepherd's hut at the bottom of the garden.

Enjoyable food includes bloody mary prawn cocktail with avocado, scallops with white wine butter sauce and chives, sharing boards, beef burger with toppings and chips, grilled butternut squash, courgette, tenderstem broccoli, quinoa, pomegranate and hummus, lemon, thyme and garlic half chicken with house slaw, hake with roasted popper and butter bean stew, and puddings such as apple and pear crumble with vanilla ice-cream and white chocolate cheesecake with berry compote; there's also a daily set menu (5-6.30pm). *Benchmark main dish: fish and chips £15.00. Two-course evening meal £21.00.*

Free house ~ Licensees Charlie and Justin Salisbury ~ Open 8am-11pm; 8am-10pm Sun ~ Bar food 12-2.30, 6-9; 12-3, 6-9.30 Sat; 12-4, 6-9 Sun ~ Restaurant ~ Children allowed in restaurant ~ Dogs allowed in bar, restaurant & bedrooms ~ Bedrooms: £155

STANFORD IN THE VALE

SU3393   Map 4

Horse & Jockey

(01367) 710302 – www.horseandjockey.org

A417 Faringdon–Wantage; Faringdon Road; SN7 8NN

Bustling, traditional village local with real character, highly regarded and fair value food and well chosen wines; bedrooms

As you might have guessed from the name, this is racehorse-training country and the walls of this welcoming local pub are hung with big Alfred Munnings racecourse prints, card collections of Grand National winners and other horse and jockey pictures. The place is split into two sections: a contemporary dining area and an older part with flagstones, wood flooring, low beams and raftered ceilings. There are old high-backed settles and leather armchairs, a woodburning stove in a big fireplace and an easy-going atmosphere. There's a beer named for the pub (from Greene King), Ruddles Best and a changing guest on handpump, carefully chosen wines by the glass, 20 gins and a dozen malt whiskies; background music and board games. As well as tables under a heated courtyard canopy, there's a separate fenced garden with a few picnic-sets. Three bedrooms, housed in another building, are quiet and comfortable. Disabled access.

Quite a choice of popular food includes sandwiches, home-smoked trout pâté with wholemeal toast, king prawn skewer with sweet chilli and garlic, courgetti spaghetti with peppers, aubergine and onion in passata, stone-baked pizzas, breaded wholetail scampi with peas and chips, fish pie, crab macaroni cheese, steaks with onion rings, chips and a choice of sauce, and puddings such as chocolate pot with strawberries and chantilly cream and seasonal crumble with vanilla custard. *Benchmark main dish: beer-battered haddock and chips £12.95. Two-course evening meal £19.00.*

Greene King ~ Lease Charles and Anna Gaunt ~ Real ale ~ Open 11-3, 5-midnight; 11am-12.30am Sat; 12-11 Sun ~ Bar food 12-3, 6-9 ~ Restaurant ~ Children welcome ~ Dogs allowed in bar ~ Bedrooms: £85

SWINBROOK
SP2812   Map 4

Swan 🍽️⭐🍷🛏️

(01993) 823339 – www.theswanswinbrook.co.uk
Back road a mile N of A40, 2 miles E of Burford; OX18 4DY

Oxfordshire Dining Pub of the Year

Smart old pub with handsome oak garden rooms, antiques-filled bars, local beers and contemporary food; bedrooms

The flamboyant Mitford sisters grew up in Swinbrook and this inn belonged to 'Debo', the youngest sister, who became the Dowager Duchess of Devonshire. She died in 2014 but it still belongs to the Chatsworth Estate – look out for the Mitford family photographs blown up on the walls. It's a smart but cosy retreat in a lovely position by a bridge over the River Windrush. Some of the elegant and comfortable bedrooms are beside by the water, and the outdoor seats and picnic-sets share the same view. The little bar has simple antique furnishings, settles and benches, an open fire, and a stuffed swan (in an alcove); locals do drop in for a pint and a chat. A small dining room leads off from the bar to the right of the entrance, and there are also two garden rooms with high-backed beige and green dining chairs around pale wood tables and views across the garden and orchard. A new bar has been installed in the garden. Hook Norton Hooky Gold, North Cotswold Windrush Ale and Purity Bunny Hop on handpump, nine wines by the glass, farm ciders and local draught lager; staff are first class. Background music, board games and TV. The Kings Head in Bledington (Gloucestershire) is run by the same top notch licensees.

Excellent food includes lunchtime sandwiches, moules marinière, smoked ham hock terrine with piccalilli, salt and pepper squid with chorizo and tabbouleh, steak and red wine pie with chips and kale, fried polenta with courgettes, aubergine, halloumi and avocado, duck breast with peaches, parma ham, walnuts, raspberries, goats cheese and balsamic dressing, pan-fried sea bass with chorizo, fennel, samphire and crab bisque; and puddings such as vanilla cheesecake with poached peach and raspberry sorbet and lemon possett with plum and blackberry compote. *Benchmark main dish: Cajun-spiced beef burger with skinny chips £14.50. Two-course evening meal £23.00.*

Free house ~ Licensees Archie and Nicola Orr-Ewing ~ Real ale ~ Open 11-11 ~ Bar food 12-2, 6.30-9; 12-2.30, 6.30-9.30 Fri, Sat; 12-2.30, 6.30-8.30 Sun ~ Restaurant ~ Children welcome ~ Dogs allowed in bar ~ Bedrooms: £150

We mention bottled beers and spirits only if there is something unusual about them – imported Belgian real ales, say, or dozens of malt whiskies. Do please let us know about them in your reports.

TADPOLE BRIDGE

SP3200 Map 4

Trout ♀

(01367) 870382 – www.trout-inn.co.uk

Back road Bampton–Buckland, 4 miles NE of Faringdon; SN7 8RF

Busy country inn with waterside gardens, civilised bar and dining rooms and a fine choice of drinks and food; bedrooms

Sumptuously smart in places, and homely and cosy in others, this is an attractive inn dating from the 17th c. It's right on the bank of the Thames (there are moorings for six boats and seats and tables by the water), which means it gets pretty busy, especially in warm weather, when you'll need to book a table in advance. The bar has exposed stone walls, beams and standing timbers, two woodburning stoves with logs neatly piled to one side, leather armchairs and stools, scatter cushions on window seats, a large stuffed trout and bare boards and flagstones. Upholstered stools line the blue-painted counter where helpful staff serve a beer named for the pub (from Ramsbury), Loose Cannon Abingdon Bridge and guests such as Big Smoke Cosmic Dawn and Wychwood Hobgoblin on handpump, 15 wines by the glass from a varied and carefully chosen list, a growing number of gins and 12 malt whiskies; background music and board games. The dining rooms have green and brown checked chairs around a mix of nice wooden tables, fresh flowers and candlelight; the pale wood or blue-painted tongue-and-groove walls are hung with trout and stag prints, oars and mirrors. The six bedrooms are attractive and comfortable; three open on to a small courtyard and are suitable for dogs. The pub pooches are cockapoos Ernie and Toffee.

Pleasing food includes sandwiches, Scottish smoked salmon with watercress and shaved fennel, truffle mac 'n' cheese fritters, chicken, tarragon and leek pie with buttered greens and mash, burger and triple-cooked chips, roast cauliflower with Persian-spiced lentils, spinach, chickpeas and flatbread, and puddings such as rhubarb and custard crumble pie and pistachio cake with lemon curd, meringue and chocolate ice-cream. *Benchmark main dish: crispy-battered haddock and chips £14.00. Two-course evening meal £24.00.*

Cirrus Inns ~ Licensee Tom Brady ~ Real ale ~ Open 12-11 ~ Bar food 12-3, 6-9; 12-4 Sun ~ Restaurant ~ Children welcome ~ Dogs allowed in bar, restaurant & bedrooms ~ Bedrooms: £140

WOLVERCOTE

SP4809 Map 4

Jacobs Inn ⭐ ♀

(01865) 514333 – www.jacobs-inn.com

Godstow Road; OX2 8PG

Enjoyable pub with enthusiastic staff, simple furnishings, inventive cooking and seats in the garden

This is a consistently popular pub, judging by the bustling atmosphere that usually prevails. The simply furnished bar has leather armchairs and chesterfields, some plain tables and benches, wide floorboards, a small open fire and high chairs at the counter where they keep three changing beers such as Brakspear Gravity, Pedigree Amber and Wychwood Hobgoblin on handpump, 13 wines by the glass, a good choice of spirits and lots of teas and coffees; background music. You can eat at plain wooden tables in a grey panelled area with an open fire or in the smarter knocked-through dining room. This has standing timbers in the middle, a fire at each end and polished dark wood chairs and tables on floorboards; there are standard lamps, stags' heads, a reel-to-reel tape recorder and quite a few mirrors. Several seating areas outside have good quality tables and chairs under parasols, picnic-sets on decking, and deckchairs and more picnic-sets on grass. This is sister pub to the Woodstock Arms in Woodstock.

🍴 The interesting food (using home-reared pigs, free-range eggs and other local produce) includes sandwiches, halloumi and quinoa fattoush with mint, chimichurri and cherry tomatoes, pigeon breast with pickled wild mushrooms and shallot and orange dressing, salmon katsu with sticky rice, coq au vin with creamy mash and greens, smoked haddock and salmon fishcakes, crispy mackerel tacos with pepperonata and coriander, braised pork ribs with barbecue sauce and coleslaw, vegan burger with tomato and pickle, and puddings such as peach eton mess and strawberry cheesecake with white chocolate shortbread. *Benchmark main dish: chicken schnitzel with slaw and parmesan fries £15.00. Two-course evening meal £22.00.*

Marstons ~ Lease Damion Farah and Johnny Pugsley ~ Real ale ~ Open 10am-11pm; 10am-midnight Fri, Sat; 12-10.30 Sun ~ Bar food 12-3, 4-9; 12-9 Sat; 12-4 Sun ~ Restaurant ~ Children welcome ~ Dogs allowed in bar

WOODSTOCK

Woodstock Arms 🍴 ♀ 🛏

SP4416 Map 4

(01993) 811251 – thewoodstockarms.com
Market Street; OX20 1SX

Cheerful pub with bustling bar and dining room, highly regarded food, four real ales, big back courtyard and knowledgeable staff; bedrooms

In the centre of a vibrant Cotswold market town, within walking distance of Blenheim Palace, this is a lively and easy-going inn with a friendly air. The bar has a few leather winged chairs, wooden tables and chairs on patterned floor tiles or large rugs, hops on beams, bare stone walls, a log fire beneath a big copper hood and high chairs by the green-painted counter. There's a beer named for the pub, Greene King IPA, Old Speckled Hen and Timothy Taylors Landlord on handpump and good wines by the glass, served by cheerful staff. The hop-strung, dark beamed dining room has chunky tables and dark wooden chairs on parquet flooring, scatter cushions or animal hides on wall seating and a woodburning stove. The back courtyard has rustic benches and chairs and tables on flagstones, and there are a few seats out in front too. Bedrooms are comfortable, contemporary and compact. Sister pub is the Jacobs Inn at Wolvercote.

🍴 Food is enjoyable and includes good breakfasts (8am-noon) plus lunchtime sandwiches and baguettes, heritage beetroot with goats cheese, fennel and apple, crispy duck salad with soy and sesame dressing, butternut squash and sage risotto with parmesan and white truffle oil, double cheeseburger and fries, chargrilled cauliflower with pomegranate and coriander, a range of steaks (beef, chicken, swordfish and vegetarian), chicken breast stuffed with mushrooms with madeira cream sauce, and puddings such as vanilla and red berry cheesecake and salted caramel crème brûlée. *Benchmark main dish: chicken, leek and mushroom pie £14.50. Two-course evening meal £21.00.*

Greene King ~ Lease Damion Farah and Johnny Pugsley ~ Real ale ~ Open 8am-11pm; 8am-10.30pm Sun ~ Bar food all day ~ Restaurant ~ Children welcome ~ Dogs allowed in bar ~ Bedrooms: £110

> 'Children welcome' means the pub says it lets children inside without any special restriction. If it allows them in, but to restricted areas such as an eating area or family room, we specify this. Some pubs may impose an evening time limit. We do not mention limits after 9pm as we assume children are home by then.

WOOTTON
SP4320 Map 4

Killingworth Castle ⭐ 🛏

(01993) 811401 – www.thekillingworthcastle.com

Glympton Road; B4027 N of Woodstock; OX20 1EJ

Handsome stone pub with own-brew beers, good wines, pleasing food and pretty back garden; lovely bedrooms

Drinkers and diners are equally well provided for at this homely and welcoming inn, a few miles north of Woodstock. The bar has a woodburning stove at one end, benches and wall seats around wooden tables and plush-topped stools at the counter. This is where you'll find their own-brewed Yubberton Goldie, Yawnie and Yubby ales on handpump and guests from breweries such as North Cotswold, Little Ox, Shepherd Neame and Stroud plus a thoughtful wine list and a good range of gin and whisky – all served by friendly staff. The simply furnished and candlelit dining rooms have built-in wall seats as well as chapel and other chairs around rustic tables on more floorboards, and there's an open log fire. There are seats out in front of the inn, and a pretty back garden with picnic-sets under parasols. The eight boutique-style bedrooms, some on the ground floor, some on the first, are well equipped and most appealing. This is sister pub to the Ebrington Arms in Ebrington (Gloucestershire).

🌟 As well as breakfast, the highly regarded food using as much organic produce as possible includes beetroot tartare with goats cheese mousse and walnuts, pigeon breast with lentils, black pudding and saffron poached apple, pork belly with thyme mash, apple sauce and greens, beef bourguignon, cod with chorizo, kohlrabi, mash and caramelised cauliflower purée, roasted celeriac with split pea dhal, curly kale and pickled apple, and puddings such as chocolate fondant with peanut butter ice-cream and lime crème fraîche and poached peach with peach soup, blackcurrant sorbet and almonds. *Benchmark main dish: beer-battered fish and chips £15.00. Two-course evening meal £21.00.*

Free house ~ Licensees Claire and Jim Alexander ~ Real ale ~ Open 9am-11pm ~ Bar food 12-2, 6-9; 12-3.30, 6-9.30 Sat; 12-3.30, 6-8.30 Sun ~ Restaurant ~ Children welcome ~ Dogs allowed in bar & bedrooms ~ Bedrooms: £110

Also Worth a Visit in Oxfordshire

Besides the fully inspected pubs, you might like to try these pubs that have been recommended to us and described by readers. Do tell us what you think of them: feedback@goodguides.com

---

ABINGDON SU4997

Brewery Tap (01235) 521655
Ock Street; OX14 5BZ Former tap for defunct Morland Brewery; half a dozen well kept ales (beer festivals), proper ciders and good choice of wines, enjoyable well priced food (not Sun evening) from bar snacks to popular Sun roasts, stone floors and panelled walls, two log fires; juke box, background and weekend live music, Tues quiz, darts; children and dogs welcome, enclosed courtyard where aunt sally is played, three bedrooms and also a self-catering apartment over the road, open all day (till midnight Fri, 1am Sat).

ADDERBURY SP4735

⭐ **Red Lion** (01295) 810269
The Green; off A4260 S of Banbury; OX17 3NG Attractive 17th-c stone coaching inn with good choice of enjoyable well priced food (all day weekends) including deals, three Greene King ales such as Belhaven and Morland and decent range of wines, linked bar rooms with high stripped beams, panelling and stonework, big inglenook log fire, old books and Victorian/Edwardian pictures, more modern restaurant extension; background music, games area; children and dogs welcome, picnic-sets out on roadside terrace, 13 character bedrooms, good breakfast, open (and food) all day.

ALVESCOT   SP2704
Plough (01993) 842281
B4020 Carterton–Clanfield, SW of Witney; OX18 2PU Popular stone-built village pub with welcoming hands-on landlord; Wadworths ales, decent range of wines and enjoyable food from sandwiches and pub standards up including home-made pies and burgers, some choices available in smaller servings, friendly helpful staff; children and dogs (in bar) welcome, back terrace and garden with play area, open all day (till 10pm Sun-Thurs).

ARDINGTON   SU4388
Boars Head (01235) 835466
Signed off A417 Didcot–Wantage; OX12 8QA Modernised 17th-c timber-framed pub with good value popular food from daily changing menu (more evening choice), friendly attentive staff, four well kept ales such as Fullers London Pride, North Cotswold Windrush and one badged for them, low beams and log fires; background music (maybe live piano); children and dogs (in one area) welcome, terrace seating, peaceful attractive village.

ASHBURY   SU2685
Rose & Crown (01793) 710222
B4507/B4000; High Street; SN6 8NA Friendly 16th-c coaching inn with roomy open-plan beamed bar; three well kept Arkells beers and decent range of wines by the glass, enjoyable generously served food including pub classics and specials and popular Sun lunch (booking advised), polished woodwork, traditional pictures, chesterfields and pews, a raised section with oak tables and chairs, separate restaurant and games room (table tennis, pool and darts); background and occasional live music, sports TV; children and dogs welcome, disabled facilities, tables out at front and in back garden, lovely view down pretty village street of thatched cottages, well placed for Ridgeway walks, seven bedrooms, open all day Sat, till 7pm Sun, closed Mon lunchtime.

ASTON TIRROLD   SU5586
Chequers (01235) 850666
Aka Fat Frog; Fullers Road; village signed off A417 Streatley–Wantage; OX11 9EN Rustic brick-built dining pub (former Sweet Olive) with highly regarded quite restaurant food including tasting menus, also more affordable set lunch and popular Sun roasts, Hook Norton Hooky and St Austell Tribute, nice wines by the glass, friendly helpful service; monthly quiz; children and dogs (in bar area) welcome, wheelchair access, cottagey garden with play

area, closed Sun evening, Mon, lunchtimes Tues-Thurs, open all day Sat.

BANBURY   SP4540
Three Pigeons (01295) 275220
Southam Road; OX16 2ED Renovated 17th-c coaching inn (handy for town centre) with several small rooms surrounding bar; beams, flagstones, bare boards and gas woodburners (no logs because of part-thatched roof), good friendly atmosphere, well prepared food (all day weekends) from sandwiches to restaurant dishes, efficient unobtrusive service, four real ales such as Purity and Sharps, decent selection of wines by the glass and over 30 malt whiskies; children welcome, tables under parasols on paved terrace, well equipped up-to-date bedrooms, useful but limited parking, open all day, from 4pm Mon.

BECKLEY   SP5611
★Abingdon Arms (01865) 655667
Signed off B4027; High Street; OX3 9UU Old community-owned dining pub under new management in lovely unspoilt village; sympathetically refurbished beamed rooms including pitched-roof dining area, country furniture on bare boards, open fires, four regional ales such as Loddon, Shotover and XT, 16 wines by the glass and good range of gins, well regarded interesting food from shortish but varied menu, friendly accommodating service; background and some live music; children and dogs welcome, large garden dropping away from decked terraces, superb views over RSPB Otmoor reserve and good walks, open all day.

BEGBROKE   SP4713
Royal Sun (01865) 374718
A44 Oxford–Woodstock; OX5 1RZ Welcoming old stone-built pub with modernised bare-boards interior; good choice of enjoyable food from lunchtime sandwiches and pub favourites up, well kept Hook Norton and guests, good selection of wines by the glass, efficient friendly service; may be background music; children welcome, no dogs inside, tables on terrace and in small garden, open all day Sat, till 6pm Sun.

BICESTER   SP5822
Jacobs Plough (01869) 388101
North Street; OX26 6NB Smart stone-built village pub with open-plan bar and dining rooms; leather chesterfields by open fire, button-back wall seating, white-painted dining chairs around simple tables on bare boards and flagstones, antlers, various stuffed animals, pictures and mirrors on the walls, Belhaven, Hook Norton, Timothy Taylors and a couple of guests, good choice

of wines by the glass and wide range of spirits, enjoyable food including popular roasts, pub classics and more adventurous dishes, friendly helpful staff; seats outside in courtyard; comfortable cosy bedrooms, open (and food) all day.

BLEWBURY SU5385

Red Lion (01235) 850403
Nottingham Fee – narrow turning N from A417; OX11 9PQ Attractive red-brick downland village pub dating from the early 17th c; emphasis on owner-chef's highly regarded food from interesting varied menu including set lunch and evening deals, well kept Brakspears and good choice of wines from brick-faced counter, efficient service, dark beams, quarry-tiled floor and big log fire, separate dining area; children and dogs (in bar) welcome, wheelchair access, peaceful enclosed back garden, three bedrooms (Mole, Badger and Toad), good breakfast, closed Sun evening and Tues, otherwise open all day.

BRIGHTWELL SU5890

Red Lion (01491) 837373
Signed off A4130 2 miles W of Wallingford; OX10 0RT Bustling but welcoming 16th-c thatched village pub; three or four well kept ales such as Loddon and West Berkshire, decent wines and enjoyable good value home-made food including baguettes and popular pies, friendly efficient staff, two-part bar with snug seating by log fire, dining extension to the right; live music Sun, quiz last Mon of the month; children and dogs welcome, tables out at front and in back garden, closed Mon.

BRITWELL SALOME SU6793

⋆**Olivier at the Red Lion**
(01491) 613140 *B4009 Watlington–Benson; OX49 5LG* Brick and flint pub-restaurant with modernised bar and dining room in pastel greys; highly regarded food from French chef-patron including daily specials, efficient welcoming service, West Berkshire Mr Chubbs, a real cider and notably good choice of wines including ten by the glass; children welcome, seats in courtyard garden, closed Sun evening, Mon and Tues.

BROUGHTON SP4238

⋆**Saye & Sele Arms** (01295) 263348
B4035 SW of Banbury; OX15 5ED Attractive old stone house, part of the Broughton Estate (castle just five minutes away); sizeable bar with polished flagstones, cushioned window seats and dark wooden furnishings, Sharps Doom Bar, a couple of

guest beers and several wines by the glass, good food from sandwiches up including Weds steak night (free pudding), friendly service, two carpeted dining rooms with exposed stone walls, open fires, over 200 ornate water jugs hanging from beams; children welcome, no dogs inside, picnic-sets on terrace, neat lawn with tables under parasols, pergola and smokers' shelter, aunt sally, closed Sun evening.

BUCKLAND SU3497

⋆**Lamb** (01367) 870484
Off A420 NE of Faringdon; SN7 8QN Well run 18th-c stone-built dining pub in lovely village; highly praised interesting food cooked by chef-owner, can eat in low-beamed bar with log fire or restaurant, a couple of changing local ales and good choice of wines by the glass, also local gin and vodka, friendly helpful staff; well behaved children and dogs welcome, seats in courtyard and pleasant tree-shaded garden, enjoyable walks (well placed for Thames Path), three comfortable well equipped bedrooms, closed Sun evening, Mon.

BUCKNELL SP5525

Trigger Pond (01869) 252817
Handy for M40 junction 10; Bicester Road; OX27 7NE Cotswold-stone beamed pub opposite pond; small bar with dining areas either side, inglenook woodburner, conservatory, Wadworths ales and good choice of enjoyable food from sandwiches, pizzas and pub favourites up, helpful cheery staff, lots of humorous signs and notices; children and dogs welcome, tables out on colourful terraces, steps up to back lawn with more picnic-sets, closed Mon.

BURFORD SP2512

Angel (01993) 822714
Witney Street; OX18 4SN Long heavy-beamed dining pub in interesting 16th-c building, warmly welcoming with roaring log fire, good popular food from sandwiches and pub favourites up, Hook Norton ales and well chosen wines, TV; children and dogs welcome, large secluded garden, three comfortable bedrooms, open (and food) all day.

BURFORD SP2512

⋆**Highway** (01993) 823661
High Street (A361); OX18 4RG Comfortable 15th-c inn refurbished over last three years with notable float-glass windows in bar, can sit at long cushioned window seat overlooking street; ancient stripped stone mixing with grey/green walls and contemporary touches such as colourful

---

Post Office address codings confusingly give the impression that some pubs are in Oxfordshire, when they're really in Berkshire, Buckinghamshire, Gloucestershire or Warwickshire (which is where we list them).

artworks, second bar used as restaurant with another big window seat, two Hook Norton ales, ciders from Cotswold, lots of wines by the glass, good choice of malt whiskies; food from sandwiches up including pub classics and pies; background music; children and dogs (in bar) welcome, picnic-sets by pavement, 11 bedrooms, open all day but check for opening times during first two weeks of Jan.

BURFORD
SP2412
★ Lamb (01993) 823155
Village signposted off A40 W of Oxford; Sheep Street (B4425, off A361); OX18 4LR Fine 16th-c stone inn with civilised bustling atmosphere; cosy bar with armchairs on rugs and flagstones in front of log fire, china plates on shelves, Hook Norton Hooky and Wickwar Cotswold Way, extensive wine list (17 by the glass), 26 malt whiskies, traditional beamed lounge has polished floorboards, distinguished old chairs, oak tables and seats built into stone-mullioned windows, good seasonal food, separate restaurant; children welcome, dogs in bar (menu for them), teak furniture on pretty terrace leading down to neatly kept lawns, 17 well appointed bedrooms, open (and food) all day.

BURFORD
SP2512
Mermaid (01993) 822193
High Street; OX18 4QF Handsome 16th-c beamed dining pub with flagstones, stripped stone and good log fire, enjoyable food (all day weekends) at sensible prices including gluten-free menu and pie, fish and burger nights, friendly service, well kept Greene King ales and a guest, bay window seating at front, airy back dining room and upstairs restaurant, breakfasts till late and afternoon cream teas; background music (live Fri, Sat); children and dogs welcome, tables out at front and in courtyard behind, open all day.

CAULCOTT
SP5024
★ Horse & Groom (01869) 343257
Lower Heyford Road (B4030); OX25 4ND Pretty 16th-c roadside thatched cottage; L-shaped red-carpeted room with log fire in big inglenook (brassware under its long bressumer), plush-cushioned settles, chairs and stools around a few dark tables at low-ceilinged bar end, Black Sheep and three guests such as Church End and Goffs (July beer festival), decent house wines, popular food (booking essential) cooked by French owner-chef, also O'Hagans sausage menu, dining room at far end with jugs hanging on black joists, decorative plates, watercolours and original drawings, small side sun lounge; live music second Sun of month, shove-ha'penny and board games; well behaved over-5s welcome, awkward for disabled customers (some steps and no car park), picnic-sets in nice little front garden, closed Sun evening, Mon.

CHADLINGTON
SP3222
Tite (01608) 676910
Off A361 S of Chipping Norton; Mill End; OX7 3NY Friendly 17th-c country pub; bar with eating areas either side, beams, pubby furniture including spindleback chairs and settles, flagstones and bare boards, woodburner in large fireplace, well kept Sharps Doom Bar and two or three guests such as Courage Directors, Cotswold Lion Drover's Return and Chadlington Golden Ale (brewed in the village), Weston's cider and a dozen wines by the glass, enjoyable fairly traditional home-cooked food (not Sun evening), good service; occasional live music, winter quiz nights; well behaved children and dogs welcome, lovely shrub-filled garden with split-level terrace, good walks nearby, open all day.

CHALGROVE
SU6397
Red Lion (01865) 890625
High Street (B480 Watlington–Stadhampton); OX44 7SS Attractive beamed village pub owned by local church trust since 1637; good variety of freshly made food (not Sun evening) from sandwiches to blackboard specials, popular pudding evening second Tues of the month, well kept Butcombe, Fullers, Rebellion and two guests, friendly helpful staff, quarry-tiled bar with big open fire, separate carpeted restaurant; children and dogs welcome, nice gardens (front one borders stream), public car park across the road, open all day Sun.

CHARLTON-ON-OTMOOR
SP5615
Crown (01865) 331850
Signed off B4027 in Islip; High Street, opposite church; OX5 2UQ Updated 17th-c village local; relaxed atmosphere in bar and lounge, well kept Brakspears, Timothy Taylors and Vale, around 100 gins, no food; darts; children and dogs welcome, back garden where aunt sally is played, open all day Sat, till 7pm Sun, closed Tues and till 4pm other weekdays.

CHARNEY BASSETT
SU3794
Chequers (01235) 868642
Chapel Lane off Main Street; OX12 0EX Welcoming 18th-c village-green pub with spacious modernised interior; Brakspears and Wychwood ales, nine wines by the glass and enjoyable fairly priced food from lunchtime sandwiches/baguettes to steaks (booking advised), log fire; children and dogs (in bar) welcome, picnic-sets in small garden, three bedrooms.

CHECKENDON
SU6684
★ Black Horse (01491) 680418
Village signed off A4074 Reading–Wallingford; RG8 0TE Charmingly old-fashioned country tavern (run by the same family since the 1900s) tucked into woodland away from the main village; relaxing and

unchanging series of rooms, back one with Loose Cannon, Rebellion and West Berkshire, tapped from the cask, one with bar counter has tent pegs above the fireplace (they used to be made here), there's also a homely side lounge and another room beyond that, some snacky food such as baguettes and pickled eggs; no credit cards; well behaved children allowed, dogs outside only (unless small and on lead), seats on verandah and in garden, popular with walkers and cyclists, closed Sun evening in winter and may shut early if quiet.

CHIPPING NORTON SP3127
Blue Boar (01608) 643108
High Street/Goddards Lane; OX7 5NP
Spacious sympathetically revamped former coaching inn (first licensed in 1683); four well kept Youngs ales, lots of wines by the glass and good choice of popular sensibly priced food from bar snacks up, friendly helpful staff, woodburner in large stone fireplace, raftered back restaurant and airy flagstoned garden room; background and some live music, Weds quiz, darts, sports TV; children and dogs welcome, open (and food) all day.

CHIPPING NORTON SP3127
Chequers (01608) 644717
Goddards Lane; OX7 5NP Bustling town pub with three softly lit beamed rooms; flagstones and wood floors, panelling and exposed stone walls, inglenook log fire, seven mainly Fullers ales, 15 wines by the glass and enjoyable food from shortish menu, friendly staff, airy conservatory restaurant behind; TV; children and dogs (in bar) welcome, theatre next door, open all day, food all day weekends.

CHISELHAMPTON SU5998
Coach & Horses (01865) 890255
B480 Oxford–Watlington, opposite B4015 to Abingdon; OX44 7UX Extended 16th-c coaching inn with two beamed bars, big log fire, well kept Hook Norton and a guest, good choice of popular reasonably priced food, friendly obliging service, sizeable restaurant with polished oak tables and wall banquettes; background music; children welcome, neat terraced gardens overlooking fields by River Thame, some tables out in front, nine bedrooms in courtyard block, closed Sun evening, otherwise open all day.

CHOLSEY SU5886
Red Lion (01491) 599842
Cholsey–Wallingford road; OX10 9LG Old village pub under new management; decent choice of enjoyable food (not Sun evening, Mon) including burgers, moules frites and pub favourites, friendly helpful staff, Brakspears, guest ales and good range of gins; children and dogs welcome, picnic-sets out at front behind picket fence, more tables in back garden.

CHRISTMAS COMMON SU7193
Fox & Hounds (01491) 612599
Off B480/B481; OX49 5HL Old Chilterns pub in lovely countryside; spacious front barn restaurant serving enjoyable home-made food (including vegan options) from open kitchen, Brakspears, a guest beer and decent wines in two cosy beamed bar rooms, simply but comfortably furnished with bow windows, red and black floor tiles and big inglenook, snug little back room too; board games; children, walkers and dogs (in bar) welcome, rustic benches and tables out at front, open all day (till 7pm Sun).

CHURCH HANBOROUGH SP4212
Hand & Shears (01993) 875047
Opposite church; signed off A4095 at Long Hanborough, or off A40 at Eynsham roundabout; OX29 8AB Village pub doing well under new management; opened-up interior on different levels, L-shaped bare-boards bar, exposed stonework, some rustic half-panelling and a couple of cushioned window seats, sofa by log fire, Bombardier, Youngs Bitter and a guest from stone-faced counter, steps down to spacious part-raftered dining area divided by balustrades, enjoyable food, attentive friendly service; children welcome, closed Sun evening, Mon.

CLANFIELD SP2802
Clanfield Tavern (01367) 810117
Bampton Road (A4095 S of Witney); OX18 2RG Pleasantly extended 17th-c stone pub (former coaching inn); opened-up beamed interior keeping feel of separate areas, mostly carpeted with mix of pubby furniture including some old settles (built-in one by log fire), smallish bar with comfortable seating and woodburner in snug flagstoned area, Marstons-related ales and enjoyable food (not Sun evening) cooked by new chef-landlord, friendly if not always speedy service, more contemporary dining conservatory with Cotswold stone walls; background music; children and dogs welcome, picnic-sets on small flower-bordered lawn looking across to village green, open all day except closed Mon.

CLIFTON SP4931
Duke (01869) 226334
B4031 Deddington–Aynho; OX15 0PE Attractive 17th-c thatch and stone pub handy for M40; low beams and flagstones, log fire in vast fireplace, enjoyable food including good vegetarian choices and daily specials, well kept Hook Norton, Turpins and guests (maybe North Cotswold or Tring), friendly helpful service; walkers, children and dogs welcome, nice back garden, five comfortable bedrooms plus on-site camping and a shepherd's hut, opens 4pm Mon and Tues, otherwise open all day (till 7pm Sun).

CROWMARSH GIFFORD   SU6189
Queens Head (01491) 839857
The Street (A4130); OX10 8ER Ancient village pub with four well kept Fullers/Gales beers and good selection of wines, enjoyable food from varied (if fairly compact) menu including blackboard specials, good friendly service, oak-beamed bar and medieval dining hall; Mon quiz, children and dogs welcome, tables in large garden, open all day, food all day Sat, till 7pm Sun.

CUDDESDON   SP5902
Bat & Ball (01865) 874379
S of Wheatley; High Street; OX44 9HJ Old coaching inn with low beams (mostly painted), flagstones and wood floors, exposed stone/brickwork and lots of cricketing memorabilia, three well kept Marstons-related ales, decent wines and cocktails, enjoyable food from ciabattas and panini up, helpful friendly young staff, tables laid for dining throughout (feels more pubby at the front); background music; children and dogs (in bar area) welcome, sunny back terrace, seven bedrooms (some quite small).

CUMNOR   SP4503
Bear & Ragged Staff
(01865) 862329 *Signed from A420; Appleton Road; OX2 9QH* Extensive pub-restaurant (Peach group) dating from the 16th c; contemporary décor in linked rooms with wood or flagstone floors, painted beams, exposed stonework and log fires, well liked food (something available all day), five or six real ales such as Brakspears, Greene King and Loose Cannon, 16 wines by the glass, several gins and cocktails, airy garden room; background music; children and dogs (in bar) welcome, tables on sunny terrace, nine bedrooms (four in converted cottages), open all day from 8am for breakfast.

CURBRIDGE   SP3208
Lord Kitchener (01993) 772613
Lew Road (A4095 towards Bampton); OX29 7PD Modernised and extended roadside pub with wide range of food including gluten-free choices and signature pies, many dishes available in smaller helpings, Greene King Old Speckled Hen and a beer badged for the pub, several wines by the glass, good friendly service; live music Sat; children and dogs welcome, wheelchair access, closed Sun evening, Mon.

CUXHAM   SU6695
Half Moon (01491) 612165
4 miles from M40 junction 6; S on B4009, then right on B480 at Watlington; OX49 5NF 16th-c thatched and beamed pub in sleepy village surrounded by fine countryside; sensibly priced Italian-leaning food including popular pizzas, a couple of Rebellion ales, several wines by the glass and good coffee, friendly

accommodating staff; children and dogs welcome, nice garden behind, open (and food) all day.

DEDDINGTON   SP4631
Deddington Arms (01869) 338364
Off A4260 (B4031) Banbury–Oxford; Horse Fair; OX15 0SH Beamed and timbered 16th-c hotel in charming village with lots of antiques shops and good farmers' market (last Sat of month); well liked food in sizeable modernised back dining room or more traditional bar with mullioned windows, flagstones and log fire, four real ales including Adnams, Butcombe and Hook Norton, plenty of wines by the glass, friendly service; background music, TV for major sports; children welcome, no dogs inside, 27 comfortable bedrooms (some in modern courtyard annexe), nice local walks, open all day.

DENCHWORTH   SU3891
Fox (01235) 868258
Off A338 or A417 N of Wantage; Hyde Road; OX12 0DX Comfortable 17th-c thatched and beamed pub in pretty village; good sensibly priced food from extensive menu including Sun carvery (best to book), friendly efficient staff, a couple of changing ales and good choice of reasonably priced wines, plush seats in low-ceilinged connecting areas, two log fires, old prints and paintings, airy dining extension; children and dogs welcome, tables under umbrellas in pleasant sheltered garden with heated terrace, play area and aunt sally.

DORCHESTER-ON-THAMES SU5794
George (01865) 340404
Just off A4074 Maidenhead–Oxford; High Street; OX10 7HH Handsome 15th-c timbered hotel under new management in lovely village (both used for TV's *Midsomer Murders*); inglenook log fire in comfortably furnished beamed bar, good choice of enjoyable well presented food including vegan dishes, three or four real ales such as Loose Cannon and Sharps, cheerful efficient uniformed staff, high-raftered restaurant; background music; children welcome, 17 bedrooms, open all day.

DUCKLINGTON   SP3507
Bell (01993) 700341
Off A415, a mile SE of Witney; Standlake Road; OX29 7UP Pretty thatched and beamed village local; good value home-made food including OAP lunch deal and Sun carvery, Black Sheep, Greene King and St Austell ales, friendly service, big stripped-stone bar with scrubbed tables on flagstones, log fires and glass-covered well, old local photographs and farm tools, hatch-served public bar and roomy restaurant; background music, sports TV, pool; children welcome, seats outside and play area, five bedrooms, open all day, no food Sun evening.

DUNS TEW
SP4528

White Horse (01869) 340272
Off A4260 N of Kidlington; OX25 6JS
Former 17th-c coaching house set in attractive village; stripped brick and stonework, rugs on flagstones or wood floors, oak timbers and panelling, inglenook woodburners, up to three well kept ales including Greene King, 14 wines by the glass and enjoyable food, both pub classics and more unusual dishes, two dining rooms; children and dogs welcome, disabled access, teak tables on sunny paved terrace, 11 bedrooms in former stables, open all day.

EAST HAGBOURNE
SU5288

Fleur de Lys (01235) 813247
Main Road; OX11 9LN Welcoming 17th-c white-rendered village pub; open-plan timbered bar with log fire, half a dozen well kept changing ales including Morland and enjoyable pubby food from sandwiches to grills, good Sun lunch; live music including popular guitar night first Weds of month and folk night third Weds, quiz second Mon (not June-Sept), darts; children and dogs welcome, tables in back garden with marquee, open all day Fri-Sun, no food Tues, closed Mon.

EAST HENDRED
SU4588

★ Eyston Arms (01235) 833320
Village signposted off A417 E of Wantage; High Street; OX12 8JY
Popular dining pub with good mix of customers, relaxed atmosphere and impressive food including daily specials; several separate candlelit areas with low beams, caricatures of customers old and new by local artists, contemporary paintwork and modern country-style furnishings, flagstones and inglenook log fire, a few tables kept just for drinkers, Hook Norton, Wadworths and guests such as Sharps, 28 wines by the glass and decent range of whiskies and gins; background music, TV; children and dogs (in bar) welcome, picnic-sets outside overlooking the pretty lane, more seats in back courtyard garden, open all day (till 9pm Sun).

EATON
SP4403

Eight Bells (01865) 862261
Signed off B4017 SW of Oxford; OX13 5PR Popular old low-beamed pub with welcoming Irish landlord and relaxed local atmosphere; two small knocked-through bars with open fires and a dining area, well kept ales including Loose Cannon, several gins and good authentic Thai food, friendly helpful staff; live music including folk nights, darts; children and dogs welcome, pleasant garden with aunt sally, nice walks, open all day weekends, closed Mon and till 5pm Tues-Fri.

EPWELL
SP3540

★ Chandlers Arms (01295) 780153
Sibford Road, off B4035; OX15 6LH
Warmly welcoming little 16th-c stone pub with very good freshly made food (booking advised) from sandwiches and bar meals up, well kept Hook Norton Hooky and guests such as Fullers London Pride and Shepherd Neame Spitfire, proper coffee, bar with country-style furniture, two dining areas, good attentive service; live music, sports TV, darts; children welcome, no dogs, pleasant garden with aunt sally and summer entertainment, attractive out-of-the-way village near Macmillan Way long-distance path, open all day.

EWELME
SU6491

Shepherds Hut (01491) 836636
Off B4009 about 6 miles SW of M40 junction 6; High Street; OX10 6HQ
Popular extended bay-windowed village pub with beams, bare boards and woodburner; good home-made food (not Sun evening) from baguettes and snacks up, four mainly Greene King ales and good range of wines by the glass, friendly staff, back dining area; children, walkers and dogs welcome, terrace picnic-sets with steps up to lawn and play area, car park over the road, open all day.

EXLADE STREET
SU6582

★ Highwayman (01491) 682020
Just off A4074 Reading-Wallingford; RG8 0UA Whitewashed brick building (mainly 17th-c – some parts older) with interesting rambling layout; mix of furniture and two-way woodburner in beamed bar rooms, three well kept beers and plenty of wines by the glass, good freshly cooked food from landlord-chef including weekday set lunch, friendly efficient service, airy conservatory dining room; soft background music; children and dogs welcome, terrace and garden with fine views, closed Sun evening, Mon.

EYNSHAM
SP4209

Evenlode (01865) 882878
Old Witney Road; OX29 4PS Nicely renovated 1930s stone-built roadhouse; decent choice of well liked food including fixed-price menu, five Marstons-related beers and a dozen wines by the glass, coffee and afternoon teas, friendly if not always speedy service; TV; children and dogs welcome, wheelchair access, two terraces, seven bedrooms, open (and food) all day from 8am (9am weekends) for breakfast.

A star before the name of a pub shows exceptional atmosphere or quality. It means most people would think a special trip worthwhile.

FERNHAM SU2991

★**Woodman** (01367) 820643

A420 SW of Oxford, then left into B4508 after about 11 miles; village another 6 miles on; SN7 7NX 17th-c country dining pub with heavily beamed character main rooms, candlelit tables and a big open fire, also some newer areas, up to three changing ales, more than 20 gins, good choice of malt whiskies and decent selection of wines by the glass, good generously served food from sandwiches and pub standards up including Tues steak, Weds pie and Thurs burger nights, free minibus for eight or more local diners, friendly helpful service; background and some live music; children and dogs welcome, disabled access/loos, seats on small front lawn and heated back terrace, good walks below the downs, open all day Sun till 9pm, closed Mon.

FINSTOCK SP3616

★**Plough** (01993) 868333

Just off B4022 N of Witney; High Street; OX7 3BY Thatched and low-beamed village pub with long rambling bar; leather sofas by massive stone inglenook, pictures of local scenes and some historical documents, four well kept ales including Adnams Broadside, traditional cider, 14 wines by the glass, 15 gins including their own, and decent choice of whiskies, friendly landlord and staff, popular home-made pubby food (best to book) including deals, spacious dining room with candles on stripped-pine tables; soft background music, bar billiards; children and dogs (in bar) welcome, seats in neatly kept garden with aunt sally, woodland and River Evenlode walks, open all day Sat, closed Sun evening, Mon lunchtime.

FRINGFORD SP6028

Butchers Arms (01869) 277363

Off A421 N of Bicester; Main Street; OX27 8EB Welcoming partly thatched creeper-clad local in Flora Thompson's Candleford village; traditional food including good Sun roasts (three sittings, must book), four well kept real ales such as Black Sheep, Ringwood and St Austell, charming efficient service, unpretentious interior with L-shaped bar and back dining room, good log fire; children and dogs welcome, picnic-sets out at front beside cricket green, open all day.

FYFIELD SU4298

★**White Hart** (01865) 390585

Main Road; off A420 8 miles SW of Oxford; OX13 5LW Grand medieval hall with soaring eaves, huge stone-flanked window embrasures and minstrels' gallery, contrasting cosy low-beamed side bar with woodburner in large inglenook, fresh flowers and evening candles, civilised friendly atmosphere and full of history; good imaginative modern food (not Sun evening, best to book) cooked by licensee-chef

using home-grown produce, Loose Cannon and three guests such as Hook Norton and Sharps, 18 wines by the glass and several malt whiskies, cocktails too (Fri happy hour 5-6pm); background music; well behaved children welcome, elegant furniture under umbrellas on spacious heated terrace, lovely gardens, good Thames-side walks, open all day, closed Mon.

GODSTOW SP4809

★**Trout** (01865) 510930

Off A40/A44 roundabout via Wolvercote; OX2 8PN Pretty 17th-c Mitchells & Butlers dining pub in lovely riverside location (gets packed in fine weather); good choice of food from varied menu including vegan choices (booking essential at busy times), four beamed linked rooms with contemporary furnishings, flagstones and bare boards, log fires in three huge hearths, Brakspears, Sharps and Fullers, several wines by the glass, cocktails, friendly helpful staff; background music; children and dogs (in bar) welcome, plenty of terrace seats under big parasols, footbridge to island (may be closed), nunnery ruins opposite, car park fee refunded at bar, open (and food) all day.

GORING SU5980

★**Catherine Wheel** (01491) 872379

Station Road; RG8 9HB Friendly 18th-c village pub with two cosily traditional bar areas, especially the more individual lower room with its dark beams and inglenook log fire; popular home-made food (not Sun evening) from seasonal menu, well kept Brakspears and other Marstons-related ales, Aspall's cider and a dozen wines by the glass, back restaurant, notable doors to lavatories; background and some live music, monthly quiz, TV; children and dogs welcome, sunny garden with gravel terrace and summer pizza oven, handy for Thames Path, open all day.

GORING SU5980

John Barleycorn (01491) 872509

Manor Road; RG8 9DP Friendly low-beamed cottagey local with cosy unpretentious lounge bar and adjoining dining room; Brakspears and other Marston-related ales such as Ringwood, seven wines by the glass and popular good value pubby food (not Sun evening) from lunchtime sandwiches up, efficient cheerful service, public bar with log fire and bar billiards; children welcome, enclosed beer garden, short walk to the Thames, three bedrooms, open all day.

GORING SU5980

★**Miller of Mansfield** (01491) 872829

High Street; RG8 9AW Handsome former coaching inn with excellent – though not cheap – food cooked by chef-patron; simple, unfussy but smart décor in beamed bars, armchairs around open fires or in bay windows, plain wooden tables on bare boards, exposed stone and brick walls, a few prints and gilt-edged mirrors, ales such as Hook Norton, Sharps and West Berkshire, 16 wines by the glass from well chosen list, good choice of spirits including local gins, courteous staff, dining rooms with antique-style or contemporary chairs on more boards; background music; children and dogs (in bar) welcome, solid furniture in multi-level terraced garden, 13 individually decorated bedrooms, woodland walks nearby, open all day (till 9pm Sun).

GREAT TEW
SP3929

★ **Falkland Arms** (01608) 683653

The Green; off B4022 about 5 miles E of Chipping Norton; OX7 4DB Part-thatched 16th-c golden-stone pub in lovely village; unspoilt partly panelled bar with high-backed settles, stools and plain tables on flagstones or bare boards, lots of mugs and jugs hanging from beam-and-plank ceiling, interesting breweriana and dim converted oil lamps, shutters for mullioned lattice windows, log fire in fine inglenook, five Wadworths ales and two guests, proper cider and good selection of whiskies and gins, snuff for sale, locally sourced freshly made food, friendly service, separate dining room; folk night Sun; children and dogs welcome, tables out at front and under parasols in back garden, six bedrooms and cottage, open all day.

HAILEY
SP3414

Bird in Hand (01993) 868321

Whiteoak Green; B4022 Witney–Charlbury; OX29 9XP Attractive 17th-c extended stone inn with good food from fairly pubby menu (highish prices), well kept ales such as Hook Norton and Sharps and several wines by the glass, helpful friendly service, beams, timbers and stripped stone, comfortable armchairs on polished boards, large log fire, cosy corners in carpeted restaurant, lovely Cotswold views; parasol-shaded terrace tables, 16 bedrooms in modern block around grass quadrangle, open all day.

HAILEY
SU6485

★ **King William IV** (01491) 681845

The Hailey near Ipsden, off A4074 or A4130 SE of Wallingford; OX10 6AD Popular fine old pub in lovely countryside; beamed bar with good sturdy furniture on tiles in front of big log fire, three other cosy seating areas opening off, good freshly made food (not Sun evening) ranging from baguettes to specials, Brakspears and guests tapped from the cask, helpful friendly staff; children and dogs welcome, terrace and large garden enjoying peaceful far-reaching views,

good walking (Chiltern Way and Ridgeway), leave muddy boots in porch, open all day weekends in summer (closed Sun evening in winter).

HAMPTON POYLE
SP5015

Bell (01865) 376242

From A34 S, take Kidlington turn and village signed from roundabout; from A34 N, take Kidlington turn, then A4260 to roundabout, third turning signed for Superstore (Bicester Road); village signed from roundabout; OX5 2QD Extended old stone-built country inn; front bar with three snug rooms, lots of big black and white photoprints, sturdy simple furnishings, scatter cushions and window seats, a stove flanked by bookshelves one end, large fireplace the other, open kitchen (feature pizza oven) in biggish inner room, spreading restaurant with plenty of tables on pale limestone floor, inventive well liked food including cheaper weekday set menu, ales such as Hook Norton and Sharps, more than 30 wines by the glass, friendly service and cheerful buzzy atmosphere; background music; children and dogs (in bar) welcome, modern seats on sunny front terrace by quiet village lane, nine good bedrooms, open all day.

HANWELL
SP4343

Moon & Sixpence (01295) 730544

Main Street; OX17 1HW Refurbished stone-built pub in attractive village setting; good food cooked by owner-chef from pub favourites up including set menu choices, comfortable bar and dining areas with view into kitchen, well kept Bombardier and Courage, several wines by the glass from carefully chosen list; children welcome, disabled access, seats on back terrace, open till 6pm Sun.

HEADINGTON
SP5406

Butchers Arms (01865) 742470

Wilberforce Street; OX3 7AN Welcoming backstreet local attracting good mix of customers; bare-boards interior with roaring fire, well kept Fullers beers and good value tasty food including ciabattas, pub favourites and stone-baked pizzas; Sun quiz, occasional live music, dominoes, darts; children and dogs welcome, disabled access, heated terrace with smokers' shelter, open all day Fri-Sun.

HEADINGTON
SP5407

White Hart (01865) 761737

St Andrews Road, Old Town; OX3 9DL Traditional split-level 18th-c stone pub with smart interior facing the church; two

---

Real ale may be served from handpumps, electric pumps (not just the on-off switches used for keg beer) or – common in Scotland – tall taps called founts (pronounced 'fonts') where a separate pump pushes the beer up under air pressure.

well kept Everards ales and three changing guests, real cider, reasonably priced wines and enjoyable pubby food including range of pies, friendly staff; children welcome, delightful sunny back garden (May beer festival), open and food all day, kitchen closes 5pm Sun.

HENLEY
SU7682
Angel on the Bridge (01491) 410678
Thames-side, by the bridge; RG9 1BH
17th-c and worth knowing for its prime Thames-side position (packed during the regatta); small front bar with log fire, downstairs back bar and adjacent restaurant, beams, uneven floors and dim lighting, Brakspears ales and maybe a guest such as Ringwood, good choice of wines by the glass, enjoyable food from sandwiches and pubby choices up, cheerful efficient service; tables under parasols on popular waterside deck with own bar (plastic glasses here), moorings for two boats, open all day at least in summer.

HENLEY
SU7582
Argyll (01491) 573400
Market Place; RG9 2AA Comfortable traditional pub with panelled walls, wood flooring and suit of armour by the bar, well kept Greene King ales, a house beer called Midsomer Murders (the pub has featured in the TV series) and decent wines by the glass, enjoyable reasonably priced pubby food from sandwiches up, efficient friendly service; background music, TV; nice terrace garden behind and useful parking, open (and food) all day, till 6pm Sun.

HIGHMOOR
SU6984
★ Rising Sun (01491) 640856
Witheridge Hill, signposted off B481; OS Sheet 175 map reference 697841; RG9 5PF Welcoming 17th-c pub in small Chilterns village; cosy beamed bar with red and black quarry-tiled floor, comfortable sofa by inglenook woodburner, Brakspears Bitter and a couple of Marstons-related guests, a dozen wines by the glass, three linked eating areas with rugs and pubby furniture on bare boards, log fire, well liked food from baguettes up; background music; children and dogs (in bar) welcome, picnic-sets and white metal tables and chairs in pleasant back garden, good surrounding walks, open all day Fri-Sun, no food Sun evening.

HOOK NORTON
SP3534
Gate Hangs High (01608) 737387
N towards Sibford, at Banbury–Rollright crossroads; OX15 5DF Tucked-away homely old stone pub; cosy low-ceilinged bar with attractive inglenook and traditional furniture on bare boards, Hook Norton ales, side dining extension; background music; children and dogs (in bar) welcome, pretty courtyard and country garden, four bedrooms, camping, quite near Rollright Stones (EH), open all day.

ISLIP
SP5214
Red Lion (01865) 375367
High Street (B4027); OX5 2RX Part of small local group including the Jacobs Inn at Wolvercote and Woodstock Arms in Woodstock (see Main Entries for both); spreading bar and dining areas with cushioned wooden chairs, upholstered benches and wall seats around simple tables on bare boards, carpet or flagstones, some leather sofas and armchairs, two woodburners (one in a sizeable inglenook), Black Sheep, Sharps and Timothy Taylors, good choice of wines by the glass and enjoyable food from pub classics up including set lunch, friendly helpful staff; children welcome, tables and chairs outside in roped-off area, picnic-sets on lawn, open (and food) all day from 8am for breakfast.

KIDMORE END
SU6979
New Inn (0118) 972 3115
Chalkhouse Green Road; signed from B481 in Sonning Common; RG4 9AU Extended black and white pub by village church; beams and big log fire, enjoyable freshly made food, well kept Brakspears ales and small but decent range of wines by the glass, pleasant restaurant; children welcome, tables in large sheltered garden with pond, six bedrooms, open all day Thurs-Sat, till 8pm Sun, shuts 3-6pm Mon-Weds.

KINGHAM
SP2523
Wild Rabbit (01608) 658389
Church Street; OX7 6YA Revamped former 18th-c farmhouse (part of the Daylesford Estate); pristine look with limestone floors, exposed stone walls and lofty beams, antique country furniture and huge fireplaces, 17 wines by the glass from a long list, Hook Norton Hooky, Purity Mad Goose and guests, top notch modern cooking with emphasis on organic produce (not cheap and advice advised), floor-to-ceiling windows in spacious restaurant with kitchen view; children welcome, dogs in bar, paved front terrace with topiary rabbits and elegant furniture under cream parasols, 13 individually designed well appointed bedrooms, also five self-catering cottages nearby, open all day.

LANGFORD
SP2402
Bell (01367) 860249
Village signposted off A361 N of Lechlade, then pub signed; GL7 3LF 17th-c pub set in charming village; cosy flagstoned bar with Hook Norton Hooky, Sharps Doom Bar and a guest, several wines by the glass from good list, two heavily beamed dining rooms with traditional furniture on more flagstones, log fires, well liked varied choice of food from snacks and wood-fired pizzas up (best to book), pleasant helpful staff; children and dogs welcome, tables out at front and to the side, eight bedrooms, open all day.

LEWKNOR SU7197

★**Olde Leathern Bottel**

(01844) 351482 *Under a mile from M40 junction 6; off B4009 towards Watlington; OX49 5TW* Popular old village pub with two heavy-beamed bars; understated décor and rustic furnishings, woodburners (one in brick inglenook), well kept Brakspears, Marstons Pedigree and a guest, several wines by the glass and tasty pub food including specials, good friendly service, family room separated by standing timbers; dogs welcome, nice garden with lots of picnic-sets under parasols, play area, boules and aunt sally, handy for walks on Chilterns escarpment.

LITTLE MILTON SP6100

Lamb (01844) 279527

3 miles from M40 junction 7: A329 Thame–Wallingford; OX44 7PU Attractive little 16th-c thatched pub with dark beams, stripped stone and low windows, three interconnecting carpeted rooms on two levels, woodburner, good choice of enjoyable food (not Sun evening) from lunchtime sandwiches/baguettes up, wider evening choice, three well kept ales including Brakspears and Courage, decent range of wines, friendly attentive service; background music; children and dogs welcome, tables on paved back terrace and in pretty garden beyond car park, open all day Sun.

LONG HANBOROUGH SP4214

★**George & Dragon** (01993) 881362

A4095 Bladon–Witney; Main Road; OX29 8JX Substantial pub with original two-room bar (17th-c or older); low beams, stripped stone and two woodburners, Wells and Youngs ales and decent range of wines, roomy thatched restaurant extension with comfortably padded dining chairs around sturdy tables, wide choice of good food from sandwiches and snacks up, Thurs pie night, prompt friendly service; background music; children and dogs (in bar) welcome, large back garden with picnic-sets among shrubs, tables beneath canopy on separate sheltered terrace, summer barbecues, open (and food) all day.

LONG WITTENHAM SU5493

Plough (01865) 407738

High Street; OX14 4QH Welcoming 17th-c two-bar local with low beams, inglenook fires and lots of brass, two or three well kept ales including Butcombe, generous helpings of good reasonably priced food (not Sun evening) from sandwiches and traditional choices to interesting specials, efficient service, dining room, games in public bar; children and dogs welcome, two bedrooms, Thames moorings at bottom of long garden, play area, June music festival, open all day.

MAIDENSGROVE SU7288

Five Horseshoes (01491) 641282

Off B480 and B481, W of village; RG9 6EX Character 16th-c dining pub set high in the Chilterns; rambling bar with low ceiling and log fire, well liked food from changing menu including seasonal game, friendly service, well kept Brakspears and good choice of wines by the glass, airy conservatory restaurant; children and dogs (in bar) welcome, plenty of tables in suntrap garden with views of rolling countryside, good walks, open all day Sat, closed Sun evening, Mon and Tues.

MARSH BALDON SU5699

Seven Stars (01865) 343337

The Baldons signed off A4074 N of Dorchester; OX44 9LP Competently run, community-owned beamed pub on edge of village green; enjoyable food (all day Weds-Sat) including plenty of gluten-free and vegan choices, well kept Fullers London Pride and three mainly local guests, helpful friendly young staff coping well at busy times, modernised bar areas, seats by corner fire, raftered barn restaurant; monthly quiz and occasional live music; children, dogs and muddy boots welcome, seats outside overlooking fields and horses, open all day (till midnight Fri, Sat, 7pm Sun).

MILCOMBE SP4034

Horse & Groom (01295) 722142

Off A361 SW of Banbury; OX15 4RS Stone-built 17th-c pub at western edge of the village; generous servings of good freshly made food from lunchtime sandwiches up, Hook Norton and four changing ales and a dozen wines by the glass, friendly helpful service, inglenook woodburner in appealing low-beamed and flagstoned bar, back restaurant; children and dogs welcome, picnic-sets out in front, four bedrooms, good breakfast, handy for Wigginton Heath waterfowl and animal centre, usually open daily, closed Sun evening.

MINSTER LOVELL SP3211

★**Old Swan** (01993) 862512

Just N of B4047 Witney–Burford; OX29 0RN Upmarket 15th-c inn with much emphasis on hotel/restaurant side but also with unchanging tranquil little bar serving Brakspears Oxford Gold, North Cotswold Windrush Ale and Wychwood Hobgoblin, 15 good wines by the glass from a fine list, ten whiskies and quite a choice of teas and coffees, also several attractive low-beamed rooms with log fires in huge fireplaces, armchairs, sofas, dining chairs and antique tables, rugs on bare boards or ancient flagstones, antiques, prints and fresh flowers; accomplished modern cooking but currently limited to picnic boxes, pie menu and large selection of snacks; background music, board games; children and dogs (in bar) welcome, outdoor terrace with tables under parasols and 65-acre grounds with tennis, croquet and fishing on River Windrush, 15 characterful bedrooms.

MURCOTT   SP5815
★ **Nut Tree** (01865) 331253
Off B4027 NE of Oxford, via Islip and Charlton-on-Otmoor; OX5 2RE Despite its Michelin star, this 15th-c beamed and thatched place manages to keep a relaxed pubby atmosphere; first rate imaginative cooking (they also do sandwiches and cheaper bar food), good attentive but not intrusive service from friendly staff, well spaced tables with crisp white cloths, leather chesterfields in bar area, Vale beer badged for them and a couple of guests, 17 wines by the glass from an exceptional list; background music; children and dogs (in bar) welcome, terrace and pretty garden, unusual gargoyles on front wall (modelled loosely on local characters), closed Sun evening and Mon, otherwise open all day.

NORTH HINKSEY   SP4905
Fishes (01865) 249796
Off A420 just E of A34 ring road; N Hinksey Lane, then turn left opposite church into cul-de-sac signed to rugby club; OX2 0NA Popular brick and tile Victorian pub (Peach group) set in three acres of wooded grounds; extended open-plan interior with conservatory, good choice of food from sandwiches and deli boards up including gluten-free menu and weekday set menus till 6pm, well kept Greene King ales and a guest, plenty of wines by the glass, cocktails and nice selection of gins, friendly helpful staff; children welcome, dogs in bar and snug, tables out at front, on back deck and in streamside garden with summer barbecues and tipi, open (and food) all day from 9.30am for breakfast.

NORTH MORETON   SU5689
Bear at Home (01235) 811311
Off A4130 Didcot–Wallingford; High Street; OX11 9AT New management for this village pub dating from the 16th c; traditional bar with country pine furniture and fireside areas, small dining room to the right and larger extension (function room) beyond, lots of beams, carpeted floors, pictures on rough walls, smallish menu with pub staples, Timothy Taylors, a house beer from West Berkshire and a couple of local guests and a dozen wines by the glass; children and dogs welcome, nice back garden overlooking cricket pitch, pretty village, open all day Sat, Sun.

NORTHMOOR   SP4202
Red Lion (01865) 300301
B4449 SE of Stanton Harcourt; OX29 5SX Renovated 15th-c village pub owned by the local community; good range of well presented freshly made food using local

and home-grown produce, four or five real ales such as Brakspears, Loose Cannon and Vale and plenty of wines by the glass, friendly young staff, cosy atmosphere with heavy beams and bare stone walls, scrubbed tables, open fire one end, woodburner the other; children, walkers and dogs welcome, garden tables, three shepherd's huts available, open all day Sat, closed Sun evening, Mon.

OXFORD   SP5106
Chequers (01865) 727463
Off High Street; OX1 4DH Narrow 16th-c city-centre pub tucked away in courtyard down small alleyway; several areas on three floors with interesting architectural features, beams, panelling and stained glass, eight or so well kept ales including Sharps, St Austell and Thornbridge and enjoyable good value Nicholsons menu, afternoon tea; background music; walled garden, open (and food) all day.

OXFORD   SP5106
Eagle & Child (01865) 302925
St Giles; OX1 3LU Long narrow Nicholsons pub dating from the 16th c; two charmingly old-fashioned panelled front rooms with Tolkien and CS Lewis connections (the Inklings writers' group used to meet here and referred to it as the Bird & Baby), ales including Brakspears, Hook Norton and Sharps, enjoyable pubby food in stripped-brick dining extension and conservatory, can get busy but service remains good; children allowed in back till 8pm, open all day.

OXFORD   SP5105
Head of the River (01865) 721600
Folly Bridge; between St Aldates and Christ Church Meadow; OX1 4LB Popular riverside pub with spacious split-level bar with dividing brick arches, rugs on stone or wood-strip floors, open fire, well kept Fullers/Gales beers and good choice of wines by the glass, popular food from sandwiches and pub staples up, helpful friendly service; background music can be loud, daily papers, TV; tables on stepped waterside terrace, boats for hire and nearby Thames walks, 20 comfortable bedrooms, open all day from 7am.

OXFORD   SP5203
Isis Farmhouse (01865) 243854
Off Donnington Bridge Road; no car access; OX4 4EL Early 19th-c former farmhouse in charming waterside spot (accessible only to walkers/cyclists/boaters); relaxed lived-in interior with two woodburners, three beers from local Shotover and decent wines, sensibly priced food from shortish menu including afternoon teas, friendly if not always speedy service; background and weekend live music including Sun afternoon jazz, folk club second Fri of month; children and dogs welcome, terrace and garden picnic-sets,

short walk to Iffley Lock and nearby lavishly decorated early Norman church, open all day till 9pm (11pm Fri, Sat), closed Mon-Thurs in winter.

OXFORD · SP5006
Jam Factory (01865) 244613
Hollybush Row; OX1 1HU Bar/ restaurant/art gallery in former Frank Cooper's marmalade factory; good range of ales such as Loose Cannon Prescott and Purity, craft beers, 15 wines by the glass and various cocktails, well liked food including vegetarian/vegan choices and good value two-course lunch, relaxed friendly atmosphere; regular events such as music, poetry and film nights, art workshops and life drawing classes; children welcome, wheelchair access, large outdoor seating area, open all day from 8am breakfast on.

OXFORD · SP5106
Kings Arms (01865) 242369
Holywell Street/Parks Road; OX1 3SP Relaxed corner pub dating from the early 17th c opposite the New Bodleian Library; popular with locals and students (next-door Wadham College owns it), various cosy rooms up and down steps, lots of panelling and pictures, open fires, six well kept Youngs ales and guests, several wines by the glass, enjoyable pubby food from sandwiches up; children and dogs welcome, a few pavement tables, open (and food) all day.

OXFORD · SP5006
Lighthouse (01865) 204060
Park End Street; OX1 1HH Long narrow pub by Pacey's Bridge; modernised nautical-theme interior with wood floors (some steps), padded wall benches and stools at high tables, small front bar with fire in old range, other rooms leading back to restaurant, a couple of Wychwood ales, craft beers and cocktails, decent coffee too and good fairly priced food including tapas and good vegetarian/vegan options; french windows to small decked area overhanging Castle Mill Stream, open all day (till 1.30am Fri, Sat).

OXFORD · SP5006
Old Bookbinders (01865) 553549
Victor Street; OX2 6BT Dark and mellow family-run local tucked away in the Jericho area; friendly and unpretentious, with old fittings and lots of interesting bric-a-brac (some on the ceiling), six ales including Greene King and guests, decent choice of whiskies and other spirits, enjoyable French-leaning food including speciality crêpes and good value lunchtime/early evening set menu; shove-ha'penny and board games, Tues quiz, open mike night Sun; children, dogs and students welcome, some entertaining features such as multiple door handles to the gents', tables out on pavement, open all day, food all day Sun till 7pm.

OXFORD · SP5105
Royal Blenheim (01865) 242355
Ebbes Street; OX1 1PT Popular corner pub opened by Queen Victoria during her Golden Jubilee and now jointly owned by Everards, Titanic and White Horse; their well kept beers and guests, good value well presented pub food (till 5pm Sun) including some decent vegetarian/vegan options, friendly chatty staff, single airy room with raised perimeter seating; TV projector for major sports fixtures; open all day (till midnight Fri, Sat).

OXFORD · SP5106
Turf Tavern (01865) 243235
Bath Place; via St Helens Passage, between Holywell Street and New College Lane; OX1 3SU Interesting characterful pub hidden away behind high walls; small dark-beamed bars with lots of snug areas, up to ten constantly changing ales including Greene King, Weston's and Lilley's ciders, winter mulled wine, popular reasonably priced food from sandwiches up, pleasant helpful service; newspapers; children and dogs welcome, three walled-in courtyards (one with own bar), open (and food) all day.

PLAY HATCH · SU7477
Shoulder of Mutton (0118) 947 3908
W of Henley Road (A4155) roundabout; RG4 9QU Dining pub with low-ceilinged log-fire bar and large back conservatory restaurant, good food from landlord-chef including signature mutton dishes, well kept Greene King and a guest such as nearby Loddon, reasonably priced house wines, friendly service; children welcome, picnic-sets in carefully tended walled garden with well, closed Sun evening, Mon (and Tues evening Jan-June).

ROKE · SU6293
Home Sweet Home (01491) 838249
Off B4009 Benson–Watlington; OX10 6JD Wadworths country dining pub with several linked rooms; two smallish bars, heavy stripped beams, big central log fire and traditional furniture, carpeted room on right leading to restaurant area, well kept ales and good food including set lunch menu and popular Sun roasts, friendly accommodating staff; background music, Rokefest music/beer festival late May Bank Holiday; children and dogs welcome, seats in attractive low-walled front garden, open all day Sat, till 6pm Sun (food till 3.30pm), closed Mon.

ROTHERFIELD GREYS · SU7282
★ Maltsters Arms (01491) 628400
Can be reached off A4155 in Henley, via Greys Road passing Southfields long-stay car park; or follow Greys Court signpost off B481 N of Sonning Common; RG9 4QD Chilterns country pub with black-beamed front bar, comfortable wall

banquettes and woodburner, Brakspears and other Marstons-related beers, Aspall's cider and 16 wines by the glass, linked lounge and restaurant, good sensibly priced food from fairly pubby menu plus blackboard specials and themed food weeks (French, Italian etc), friendly service; background music; children and dogs (in bar) welcome, terrace tables under big heated canopy, picnic-sets on grass looking over paddocks and rolling countryside, good walks nearby and handy for Greys Court (NT), open all day.

ROTHERFIELD PEPPARD   SU7081
Unicorn (01491) 628674
Colmore Lane; RG9 5LX Attractive little country pub with bustling bare-boards bar with open fire, Brakspears Bitter and a couple of guests, enjoyable food including sandwiches, daily specials and deals, friendly service, separate dining room; Weds quiz and some live music, TV for major sports; children, walkers and dogs welcome, seats in back garden, open all day, no food Sun evening, closed Mon, Tues.

SHENINGTON   SP3742
Bell (01295) 670274
Off A422 NW of Banbury; OX15 6NQ Early 18th-c two-room pub in charming quiet village; good popular food cooked by landlord-chef, well kept Hook Norton Hooky, Sharps Doom Bar and a guest beer and good range of wines by the glass, friendly service, heavy beams, some flagstones, stripped stone and pine panelling, two woodburners; children welcome in eating areas, dogs in bar, picnic-sets out at front, good surrounding walks, open all day Sat, closed Sun evening to Weds lunchtime.

SHIPTON-UNDER-WYCHWOOD SP2717
Shaven Crown (01993) 830500
High Street (A361); OX7 6BA Ancient monastic building with magnificent lofty medieval rafters and imposing double stairway in hotel part's hall, separate beamed bar serving Hook Norton ales and several wines by the glass, good food from sandwiches and pubby choices up, helpful friendly staff, restaurant; background and occasional live music; children and dogs (in bar) welcome, peaceful central courtyard, seven bedrooms including one in former chapel with four-poster, closed Sun evening, otherwise open all day.

SHIPTON-UNDER-WYCHWOOD SP2717
Wychwood Inn (01993) 831185
High Street; OX7 6BA Former coaching inn run by mother and son team; contemporary décor in extended open-plan bar/dining area, more period character in flagstoned public bar with black beams and inglenook, four changing beers, plenty of wines by the glass and enjoyable food from sharing plates to grills, Mon burger night, friendly young staff, private dining room

in glassed-in coach entrance; TV for major sporting events; children and dogs welcome, picnic-sets on small terrace, five bedrooms, open all day.

SIBFORD GOWER   SP3537
Wykham Arms (01295) 788808
Signed off B4035 Banbury to Shipston-on-Stour; Temple Mill Road; OX15 5RX Cottagey 17th-c thatched and flagstoned dining pub; good food (not Sun evening) from light dishes up, friendly attentive staff, St Austell and two well kept changing ales and 23 wines by the glass, comfortable open-plan interior with low beams and stripped stone, glass-covered well, inglenook; children and dogs welcome, country views from big garden, lovely manor house opposite and good walks nearby, open all day Sun, closed Mon.

SOULDERN   SP5231
Fox (01869) 345284
Off B4100; Fox Lane; OX27 7JW Early 19th-c pub set in delightful village; open-plan beamed interior with woodburner in two-way fireplace, Timothy Taylors Boltmaker and guest ales such as Black Sheep, Hook Norton and Otter, several wines by the glass and good fairly priced food from shortish menu, friendly attentive service; regular quiz nights, Aug beer festival; terrace and walled garden, aunt sally, four bedrooms, open all day Sat, till 5pm Sun.

SOUTH NEWINGTON   SP4033
Duck on the Pond (01295) 721166
A361; OX15 4JE Roadside dining pub with small flagstoned bar and linked carpeted eating areas up a step; much enjoyed food from lunchtime baguettes up including some good vegetarian choices and popular Sun lunch, Hook Norton Hooky and a couple of guests, good range of wines and gins, also a driver-friendly drinks list, cheerful pleasant staff, lots of duck-related items, woodburner; children welcome, no dogs inside, spacious grounds with tables on deck and lawn, pond with waterfowl and little River Swere winding down beyond, open all day Sat, till 6pm Sun, closed Mon, Tues.

SPARSHOLT   SU3487
Star (01235) 751873
Watery Lane; OX12 9PL Modernised 16th-c dining pub with easy-going relaxed atmosphere; good up-to-date food along with more traditional choices and simpler lunchtime menu, friendly efficient service, dining rooms with pale farmhouse chairs around chunky tables on floorboards or big flagstones, hop-strung beams, open fire, ales such as Loose Cannon and Sharps and 15 wines by the glass in simply furnished bar; background music, board games; children and dogs welcome, seats in back garden, pretty village (snowdrops fill the churchyard in spring), eight comfortable barn conversion bedrooms, open all day.

STANTON ST JOHN   SP5709
Talk House   07926 249157
Middle Road/Wheatley Road (B4027 just outside village); OX33 1EX Attractive part-thatched dining pub; older part on left with steeply pitched rafters soaring above stripped-stone walls, mix of old dining chairs and big stripped tables, large rugs on flagstones; rest of building converted more recently but in similar style with massive beams, flagstones or stoneware tiles and log fires below low mantelbeams, good food from lunchtime sandwiches up, Fullers ales and over 20 wines by the glass; children welcome, inner courtyard with teak tables and chairs, a few picnic-sets on side grass, four bedrooms, open all day Fri, Sat, till 9pm Sun, closed Mon.

STEEPLE ASTON   SP4725
★ Red Lion   (01869) 340225
Off A4260 12 miles N of Oxford; OX25 4RY Cheerful village pub with neatly kept beamed and partly panelled bar, antique settle and other good furnishings, well kept Hook Norton ales and decent wines by the glass, enjoyable food from shortish menu including stone-baked pizzas, obliging young staff, back timber-framed dining extension; Mon quiz; well behaved children welcome till 7pm, dogs in bar, suntrap front garden with lovely flowers and shrubs, parking can be tricky, handy for Rousham House and Garden, open all day Sat, till 9pm Sun, closed Mon.

STEVENTON   SU4691
North Star
Stocks Lane, The Causeway, central westward turn off B4017; OX13 6SG Very traditional little village pub through yew tree gateway; tiled entrance corridor, main area with ancient high-backed settles forming booth in front of brick fireplace, three or four well kept ales from side tap room, hatch service to another room with plain seating, a couple of tables and coal fire, simple lunchtime food, friendly staff; children and dogs welcome, tables on front grass, aunt sally, open all day weekends, closed weekday lunchtimes.

STOKE LYNE   SP5628
Peyton Arms   07546 066160
From minor road off B4110 N of Bicester fork left into village; OX27 8SD Beautifully situated and largely unspoilt one-room alehouse run by character landlord (Mick the Hat); three very well kept Hook Norton ales from casks behind small corner bar, no food apart from filled rolls, inglenook fire, tiled floor and lots of memorabilia; no children or dogs; pleasant garden, closed Mon, Tues, opens 5pm Weds-Fri, 2-7pm Sat, Sun – but best to check in advance.

STOKE ROW   SU6884
Cherry Tree   (01491) 680430
Off B481 at Highmoor; RG9 5QA
Sympathetically updated 18th-c pub-restaurant (originally three cottages); enjoyable often interesting food from sharing plates to daily specials, Brakspears ales, good range of wines by the glass and more than 100 gins including local ones, helpful friendly staff, small linked rooms mainly set for dining, heavy low beams, stripped boards and flagstones; background music, TV in bar; well behaved children and dogs welcome, lots of tables in attractive garden, nearby walks, four good bedrooms in converted barn, open all day, no food Sun evening.

STOKE ROW   SU6884
★ Crooked Billet   (01491) 681048
Nottwood Lane, off B491 N of Reading – OS Sheet 175 map reference 684844; RG9 5PU Nice place, but more restaurant than pub; charming rustic layout with heavy beams, flagstones, antique pubby furnishings and fine inglenook log fire, crimson Victorian-style dining room, very good interesting food cooked by owner-chef using local and home-grown produce, cheaper set lunches Mon-Fri, helpful friendly staff, Brakspears Oxford Gold tapped from the cask (no counter), good wines, relaxed homely atmosphere; weekly live music often including established artists; children very welcome, big garden by Chilterns beechwoods, open all day, food all day weekends.

SUNNINGWELL   SP4900
Flowing Well   (01865) 735846
Just N of Abingdon; OX13 6RB Timbered pub in former 19th-c rectory; well liked food including British tapas, range of burgers and gluten-free menu, a couple of Greene King ales and a guest, good choice of wines; children welcome, dogs in bar, large heated raised terrace, more seats in garden with small well, open (and food) all day.

SUTTON COURTENAY   SU5094
Swan   (01235) 847446
The Green; OX14 4AE Red-brick 'Foodhouse & Bar' overlooking green; unfussy décor with grey-painted woodwork and white walls, plain modern wooden tables on quarry tiles, log fire, good well presented food including tapas, blackboard specials and Fri evening fish, stools at bar serving a couple of real ales such as Timothy Taylors Landlord, friendly staff; background music; children welcome, picnic-sets out at front and in enclosed back garden with play area, open all day Sat, till 6pm Sun, closed Mon.

SWERFORD   SP3830
★ Boxing Hare   (01608) 683212
A361 Banbury–Chipping Norton; OX7 4AP Old stone dining pub with highly regarded food including signature dry-aged steaks and daily specials, friendly attentive service, well kept Hook Norton and Timothy Taylors, good wines by the glass and several whiskies/gins such as local Cotswold,

attractive split-level interior with rugs on bare boards, white-painted beams and log fires; children welcome, lovely country views from neat garden, closed Sun evening to Tues lunchtime.

SWINFORD
SP4308
Talbot (01865) 881348
B4044 just S of Eynsham; OX29 4BT Spacious and comfortable 17th-c beamed pub; well kept Arkells tapped from cooled casks and good choice of wines, enjoyable well priced pubby food ranging from sandwiches and basket meals up including pizzas and weekday deals, Sun carvery, long attractive flagstoned bar with some stripped stone, cheerful log-effect gas fire; charity quiz second Mon of month; children and dogs welcome, garden with decked area overlooking Wharf Stream, nice walk along picturesque stretch of the Thames towpath, moorings quite nearby, 11 bedrooms, open all day.

THAME
SP7105
Cross Keys (01844) 218202
Park Street/East Street; OX9 3HP Friendly one-bar 19th-c corner local; eight well kept ales including own Thame beers (not always available) and half a dozen ciders, no food apart from scotch eggs and occasional cheese and wine nights but customers can bring their own; Weds quiz and regular comedy nights; courtyard garden, open all day weekends.

THAME
SP7005
James Figg (01844) 260166
Cornmarket; OX9 2BL Friendly coaching inn with four well kept ales such as Greene King, Purity, Sharps and XT, Aspall's cider and around ten wines by the glass, enjoyable good value food including pizzas and burgers, two-for-one deals Mon-Weds, log fire in brick fireplace with moose's head above, portrait of eponymous James Figg (local 18th-c boxer) and photos of more recent sporting champions, converted stables with own bar for music/functions; gets busier and noisier in the evening; children and dogs welcome, back beer garden, open (and food) all day, kitchen closes 6pm Sun.

THAME
SP7006
Thatch (01844) 214340
Lower High Street; OX9 2AA Characterful timbered and thatched 16th-c dining pub (Peach group); enjoyable food from deli boards to daily specials, three well kept ales such as XT, nice wines and some interesting gins, friendly service, cosy bar and appealing collection of little higgledy-piggledy rooms, heavy beams, old quarry tiles, flagstones and double-sided inglenook, smart contemporary furnishings and bold paintwork; children welcome, prettily planted terraced garden with tables under parasols, open (and food) all day.

THRUPP
SP4815
Boat (01865) 374279
Brown sign to pub off A4260 just N of Kidlington; OX5 1JY Attractive 16th-c stone pub set back from the southern Oxford Canal (moorings); modernised interior with low ceilings, bare boards and some ancient floor tiles, log fires and old coal stove, well priced home-made food including vegetarian options, specials and Sun carvery, four ales such as Greene King and Timothy Taylors, decent wines, dining room with *Inspector Morse* photos (pub featured in the TV series); children and dogs welcome, disabled facilities, plenty of tables in fenced back garden, open (and food) all day weekends, gets busy in summer.

TOOT BALDON
SP5600
★ Mole (01865) 340001
Between A4074 and B480 SE of Oxford; OX44 9NG Light open-plan restaurantary pub; very good if not cheap food (booking advised) including light lunch and weekly changing set menus, friendly attentive service, 21 wines by the glass and a couple of well kept ales from maybe Hook Norton and Loose Cannon, leather sofas by bar, neat country furniture or more formal leather dining chairs in linked eating areas including conservatory, stripped 18th-c beams and big open fire; background music; children welcome, no dogs inside, lovely gardens, open all day.

UFFINGTON
SU3089
Fox & Hounds (01367) 820680
High Street; SN7 7RP Welcoming beamed village pub; around five changing ales and good home-made food from shortish menu including Sun pizza, morning coffee and afternoon teas, friendly helpful staff, pubby furniture on quarry tiles or flagstones, woodburner in large stone fireplace, garden room extension with view of White Horse Hill; live music and quiz nights; children and dogs welcome, picnic-sets outside, handy for Tom Brown's School Museum, four ground-floor bedrooms, open all day, no food Sun evening and Mon.

WANTAGE
SU3987
Shoulder of Mutton (01235) 767158
Wallingford Street; OX12 8AX Renovated Victorian corner pub keeping character in bar, lounge and snug, ten well kept regularly changing beers, no food; quiz Mon, open mike Tues; seats in back courtyard, three comfortable affordably priced bedrooms, open all day.

WARBOROUGH
SU6093
Six Bells (01865) 858265
The Green S; just E of A329, 4 miles N of Wallingford; OX10 7DN Thatched 16th-c pub opposite village cricket green (both used in filming *Midsomer Murders*); a couple of

well kept Brakspears ales and a guest and good food (not Sun evening) from sharing boards to interesting specials, friendly staff, low beams and attractive country furnishings in small linked areas off bar, bare boards, stripped stone and big log fire; children and dogs (in bar) welcome, tables out in front and in pleasant orchard garden behind where aunt sally is played, open all day weekends, closed Mon.

WARDINGTON SP4946
Hare & Hounds (01295) 750645
A361 Banbury–Daventry; OX17 1SH
Comfortable and welcoming traditional village local, well kept Hook Norton and a guest, enjoyable home-made food including bargain OAP lunch, low-ceilinged bar leading to dining area, woodburner; quiz nights, coffee/dominoes mornings, darts; children and dogs welcome, garden with play area and aunt sally, open all day, till midnight Fri, Sat, 10pm Sun.

WATLINGTON SU6994
Fat Fox (01491) 613040
Shireburn Street; OX49 5BU Large centrally located 17th-c inn under new management; beamed bar with bare boards and open fire, three real ales including Brakspears and good choice of wines by the glass, well liked food from changing menu using local produce, friendly helpful staff, separate restaurant; children and dogs (in bar) welcome, Ridgeway walks, nine bedrooms (seven in converted back barn), good breakfast, handy for M40 (junction 3), open all day.

WESTON-ON-THE-GREEN SP5318
Chequers (01869) 351743
Handy for M40 junction 9, via A34; Northampton Road (B430); OX25 3QH
Extended thatched and beamed village pub with three areas off main bar; well kept Fullers ales, a dozen wines by the glass and decent range of gins from semicircular servery, good fairly priced food including sandwiches and snacks, chargrills and popular Sun carvery, breakfast from 10am, friendly attentive service, mix of traditional furniture on flagstone or parquet floors, some painted panelling; background music, children and dogs welcome, terrace and garden tables, overnight stops for motorhomes (book in advance), open all day from 2pm Sat, till 6pm Sun.

WHITCHURCH SU6377
Ferry Boat (0118) 984 2161
High Street, near toll bridge; RG8 7DB
Welcoming comfortably updated 18th-c pub; airy bar with log fire and separate restaurant, good choice of home-made food including stone-baked pizzas, real ales such as Sharps and Timothy Taylors, several wines by the glass; background music; well behaved children and dogs (in bar) welcome, café-style seating in courtyard garden, closed Sun evening, Mon.

WHITCHURCH SU6377
Greyhound (0118) 343 3016
High Street, just over toll bridge from Pangbourne; RG8 7EL Attractive former ferryman's cottage with small knocked-together low-beamed rooms; three real ales including Black Sheep, St Austell Tribute or Sharps Doom Bar and a guest, good value pubby food, friendly efficient staff; quiz first and third Thurs of month, live music; children and dogs welcome, small sheltered back garden, attractive village on Thames Path, open all day, no food Sun evening, Mon or Tues.

WITNEY SP3509
Angel (01993) 703238
Market Square; OX28 6AL Unpretentious 17th-c town local with wide choice of enjoyable well priced food from sandwiches up, Marstons-related ales including a house beer from Wychwood and an occasional guest, efficient friendly service even when packed, beams and open fire; background music (live weekends), sports TVs; lovely hanging baskets, back terrace with smokers' shelter, parking nearby can be difficult, open all day.

WITNEY SP3509
Fleece (01993) 892270
Church Green; OX28 4AZ Smartly presented town pub (Peach group); wide choice of good often imaginative food from sandwiches and deli boards up, fixed-price menu too (Mon-Fri 12-6pm), Greene King and a couple of guests, 17 wines by the glass, cocktails, good choice of gins, decent coffee, friendly helpful service, leather armchairs on wood floors, restaurant; background and occasional live music, daily papers; children and dogs (in bar) welcome, café-style tables out at front overlooking green, ten comfortable bedrooms, good breakfast, open (and food) all day from 9am.

WITNEY SP3509
Hollybush (01993) 708073
Corn Street; OX28 6BT Popular modernised 18th-c pub under same ownership as the Horseshoes across the road; front bar with woodburner in big fireplace, settles and window seats, various dining areas off, good food from sandwiches and deli boards up, weekday lunchtime set menu and other offers, three well kept ales including a house beer from Greene King and nice selection of wines, efficient friendly staff; background music; children and dogs welcome, open (and food) all day.

WITNEY SP3510
Horseshoes (01993) 703086
Corn Street, junction with Holloway Road; OX28 6BS Attractive 16th-c stone

gastropub with good freshly made food
(all day weekends) from pub favourites
up including gluten-free choices, weekday
set lunch and other deals, three changing
ales (maybe Black Sheep, Jennings and
Ringwood) and decent wines by the glass,
heavy beams, stripped-stone walls, oak floors
and log fires, separate back dining room;
children and dogs welcome, a few seats out at
front, tables on sunny paved terrace behind,
open all day.

WOLVERCOTE SP4909
Plough (01865) 556969
First Turn/Wolvercote Green; OX2 8AH
Two connecting buildings with comfortably
worn-in pubby rooms; armchairs and
Victorian-style carpeted bays in main lounge,
a well kept Greene King beer such as Hardys
& Hansons and a couple of guests, traditional
cider and decent wines by the glass, good
value enjoyable usual food in flagstoned
stables dining room and library (children
allowed here), bargain OAP lunchtime menu,
traditional snug, woodburner; dogs welcome
in bar, disabled access/facilities, picnic-sets
on part-decked terrace looking over rough
meadow to canal and woods, open all day
Fri-Sun.

WOODSTOCK SP4417
Black Prince (01993) 811530
Manor Road (A44 N); OX20 1XJ Old
pub with single low-ceilinged bar; timbers,
stripped stone and log fire, suit of armour,
good value home-made food (not Sun
evening) from sandwiches to specials, well
kept St Austell and three guests, friendly
service, newspapers, traditional pub games;
some live music, outside lavatories; children,
walkers and dogs welcome, tables in pretty
garden by small River Glyme, nearby right
of way into Blenheim parkland, open all day,
closes 7pm Sun.

WOODSTOCK SP4416
★ Kings Arms (01993) 813636
*Market Street/Park Lane (A44);
OX20 1SU* Bustling town-centre hotel with
unfussy bar attracting good mix of customers;
appealing variety of old and new furnishings
on stripped-wood floor, some black and white
photographs and a modern woodburning
stove, neat restaurant with high-backed
leather chairs around mix of tables on
black and white tiles, logs stacked either

side of another woodburner, Fullers/Gales
beers, a dozen wines by the glass and 35
malt whiskies, good food from varied menu;
background music; children and dogs (in
bar) welcome, café-style pavement tables,
15 bedrooms, open all day from 8am.

WOODSTOCK SP4416
Star (01993) 811373
Market Place; OX20 1TA Sizeable bustling
old inn; airy front part with bare boards and
big windows, lower ceilinged area with pale
stripped stone, boldly coloured walls and
comfortable seats on carpet, back part has
a profusion of beams, coal-effect stove and
an unusually wide antique settle; enjoyable
food from varied menu catering for special
diets, well kept ales such as Bombardier,
Courage Directors and Eagle IPA, good choice
of wines by the glass, friendly helpful staff;
background music, Tues quiz; sheltered
flagstoned courtyard behind, more seats out
in front, four bedrooms, open (and food) all
day from 8am.

WOOLSTONE SU2987
White Horse (01367) 820726
Off B4507; SN7 7QL Appealing partly
thatched black and white pub with
prominent gables and latticed windows;
stone flooring and two open fires in spacious
beamed bar, three Arkells ales and enjoyable
food from regularly changing menus
including wood-fired pizzas, friendly service,
restaurant; well behaved children and dogs
allowed, plenty of seats in front and back
gardens, secluded interesting village handy
for White Horse and Ridgeway Path (good
circular walk), six comfortable bedrooms,
open all day.

WYTHAM SP4708
White Hart (01865) 244372
Off A34 Oxford ring road; OX2 8QA
Renovated 16th-c country dining pub in
unspoilt preserved village; several areas with
log fires including converted stables, some
settles, handsome panelling and uneven
flagstones, good food (not Sun evening)
from lunchtime sandwiches to blackboard
specials, also vegetarian/vegan choices, cosy
bar with well kept Wadworths ales and lots
of wines by the glass, conservatory; children
and dogs welcome, courtyard tables, evening
barbecues Fri and Sat (weather permitting),
open all day (till 8pm Sun).

Shropshire

BASCHURCH
SJ4221 Map 7

New Inn

(01939) 260335 – www.newinnbaschurch.com

Church Road; SY4 2EF

Stylish and bustling village pub with several beers and very popular food; seats in attractive garden

---

There's plenty to like about this handsome whitewashed village pub in northern Shropshire: the enjoyable food, well kept ales, stylish interiors and friendly, laid-back vibe. The several interlinked rooms have been attractively modernised in a way that complements the nice original features including heavy oak beams and large brick fireplaces. The chatty bar has a woodburning stove, a leather sofa and armchairs, traditional dining chairs and stools around tables on quarry tiles and bare boards, and numerous prints on pale walls. Local ales on handpump include Salopian Shropshire Gold and Stonehouse Station Bitter and a weekly changing guest such as Loch Lomond Lost in Mosaic or Wye Valley Butty Bach, plus 12 wines by the glass and 20 gins, served by cheerful staff. The two dining rooms have logs piled into fireplaces, high-backed leather-seated chairs around light wood tables, candles in glass jars and lanterns, and fresh flowers. There are seats outside in a well tended garden. Partial disabled access.

Good food from an imaginative, varied menu includes sandwiches, pressed ham hock, chicken and black pudding terrine with scotch quail egg, smoked salmon roulade with herb blinis and dill and lemon cream, sharing platters including a vegan version, beer-battered haddock and chips, stir-fried vegetables on a sizzling skillet with basmati rice and a choice of toppings (teriyaki beef, king prawns, Cajun chicken, confit duck), falafel or steak burger and chips, various pizzas, and puddings such as lemon tart with berry compote and chantilly cream and sticky toffee pudding with vanilla ice-cream. *Benchmark main dish: steak and ale pot pie £12.00. Two-course evening meal £20.00.*

Free house ~ Licensees Chris and Ellie Conde ~ Real ale ~ Open 12-3, 6-11; 12-11 Fri, Sat; 12-7 Sun ~ Bar food 12-3, 6-9; 12-9 Sat; 12-5 Sun ~ Restaurant ~ Children welcome ~ Dogs allowed in bar

---

'Children welcome' means the pub says it lets children inside without any special restriction. If it allows them in, but to restricted areas such as an eating area or family room, we specify this. Places with separate restaurants often let children use them, and hotels usually let children into public areas such as lounges. Some pubs impose an evening time limit – let us know if you find one earlier than 9pm.

BRIDGNORTH

SO7192   Map 4

Old Castle £

(01746) 711420 – www.oldcastlebridgnorth.co.uk
West Castle Street; WV16 4AB

Relaxed and friendly town pub, with fair value pubby food, well kept ales and good-sized suntrap terrace

The Old Castle pub is a short walk from the old castle itself: all that's left is a 20-metre high remnant of the Norman tower, leaning at such an extraordinary angle that you expect it to topple at any moment. Walk through the gardens for marvellous views over the Low Town and the River Severn far below. There are fine views from the far end of the pub's sunny back terrace too – a pretty spot with picnic-sets, colourful hanging baskets, big pots of flowers and shrub borders. Inside, there's a low-beamed open-plan bar of proper character with tiles and bare boards, cushioned wall banquettes and settles around cast-iron-framed tables, and bar stools arranged along the counter where the friendly landlord and his helpful staff serve Hobsons Town Crier, Sharps Doom Bar and Wye Valley Butty Bach and HPA on handpump; background music and a big-screen TV for sports events. The generously served home-cooked food is very popular, so it's best to book. Wheelchair access through the front door to the top dining area; bar access through a side passage and door into their glass-roofed courtyard. No disabled loos.

Traditional food at fair prices includes sandwiches, baguettes and jacket potatoes, southern fried chicken dippers with barbecue sauce, chilli and cheese tortillas, steak and ale pie, burger (beef, Cajun chicken or portobello mushroom) and chips, sweet potato, red pepper and spinach lasagne, salmon, smoked haddock and prawn pie topped with cheesy mash, a range of steaks with mushroom and stilton or peppercorn sauce, and puddings. *Benchmark main dish: lamb shank with mash, peas and gravy £11.25. Two-course evening meal £19.00.*

Punch ~ Tenant Bryn Charles Masterman ~ Real ale ~ Open 11.30-11; 11.30-10 Sun ~ Bar food 12-3, 6-8.30 ~ Children welcome ~ Dogs allowed in bar & restaurant

CARDINGTON

SO5095   Map 4

Royal Oak

(01694) 771266 – www.at-the-oak.com
Village signposted off B4371 Church Stretton–Much Wenlock, pub behind church; also reached via narrow lanes from A49; SY6 7JZ

Heaps of character in well run and friendly rural pub with seasonal bar food and real ales

This is a pretty village in the heart of rural Shropshire, surrounded by great walking country: you can go straight from the pub to the summit of Caer Caradoc, a couple of miles to the west, and beyond that lies the moorland plateau of the Long Mynd. The front courtyard here takes full advantage of its beautiful position. Supposedly the county's oldest pub, the Royal Oak was first licensed in the 15th c and little has changed here over the centuries – it's much loved by locals and visitors. The rambling, low-beamed traditional bar has a roaring winter log fire, a cauldron, black kettle and pewter jugs in a vast inglenook fireplace, aged standing timbers from a knocked-through wall, and red and green tapestry seats solidly capped in elm; board games and dominoes (they have a pub team). Friendly staff serve Ludlow Best and Sharps Doom Bar with regularly changing local guests such as Sarah Hughes

Dark Ruby and Woods Shropshire Lass on handpump, a cask cider, eight wines by the glass from a good list, ten gins and several malt whiskies. A comfortable dining area has exposed old beams and studwork.

🍴 Proper home cooking using local produce from a seasonal menu includes sandwiches, ploughman's, salt and pepper calamari, wild mushroom arancini, venison liver and chilli pâté, smoked trout salad with beetroot, beef or panko-breaded halloumi burger with coleslaw and chips, chicken curry, game pie in red wine gravy, chilli (classic con carne or sweet potato and white bean), butternut squash and roasted red pepper lasagne, and puddings such as churros with chocolate sauce and ginger and black pepper pudding with toffee sauce. *Benchmark main dish: fidget pie (gammon cooked with spiced cider and apples) £12.95. Two-course evening meal £19.00.*

Free house ~ Licensees Steve and Eira Oldham ~ Real ale ~ Open 12-2.30, 6-11; 12-11 Sat; 12-9 (12-4 in winter) Sun; closed Mon ~ Bar food 12-2.30, 6-9 ~ Restaurant ~ Children welcome ~ Dogs allowed in bar & restaurant

CHETWYND ASTON

SJ7517 Map 7

Fox 🍷 🍺

(01952) 815940 – www.brunningandprice.co.uk/fox
Village signposted off A41 and A518 just S of Newport; TF10 9LQ

Civilised dining pub with generous helpings of well liked food and a fine array of drinks served by attentive staff

There's plenty of space at this well run pub, both inside and out, from the extensive garden and large car park to the spacious and spreading interiors (but with cosy corners too). The interconnected rooms (one with a broad arched ceiling) have plenty of tables of varying shapes and sizes and a mix of comfortable chairs on parquet, polished boards or attractive floor tiles. Numerous prints and photographs line the walls, there are three open fires and big windows and careful lighting contribute to the relaxed atmosphere; board games. Bar stools line the long bar counter where helpful, polite staff keep some 20 wines by the glass, 40 rums, about 130 gins, 60 malt whiskies, two farm ciders and St Austell Brunning & Price Traditional, Hop & Stagger Shropshire Pale, Woods Shropshire Lad and three quickly changing guests from the likes of Stonehouse, Titanic and Wye Valley on handpump. There's a private dining room upstairs and good disabled access. In warm weather, the garden is quite lovely, with seating on a sunny terrace, picnic-sets tucked into the shade of mature trees and extensive views across quiet country fields; play tractor and swings for children.

🍴 A wide choice of highly rated food includes sandwiches and 'light bites', classic prawn cocktail with marie rose sauce, baked camembert with apple, celery and walnut salad, beer-battered cod with chips and mushy peas, pork and leek sausages with mash and onion gravy, fish pie, Malaysian chicken curry with pak choi, cauliflower, chickpea and squash tagine with lemon and almond couscous, and puddings such as triple chocolate brownie with vanilla ice-cream and Cheshire Farms ice-creams and sorbets. *Benchmark main dish: steak burger with toppings and fries £13.95. Two-course evening meal £21.00.*

Brunning & Price ~ Manager Samantha Forrest ~ Real ale ~ Open 11-11; 11-10.30 Sun ~ Bar food 12-9.30; 12-10 Fri, Sat; 12-9 Sun ~ Children welcome ~ Dogs allowed in bar

Please tell us if the décor, atmosphere, food or drink at a pub is different from our description. We rely on readers' reports to keep us up to date: feedback@goodguides.com, or (no stamp needed) Freepost THE GOOD PUB GUIDE, Random House Publishing, 20 Vauxhall Bridge Road, London SW1V 2SA.

CLUN

SO3080   Map 6

White Horse 🍺 £

(01588) 418114 – www.whi-clun.co.uk

The Square; SY7 8JA

Bustling local with own-brewed and guest ales and good value traditional food; bedrooms

Very much the hub of this little village, this homely inn brews its own Clun beers, including Citadel, Loophole, Pale Ale and Solar. You'll find them all here on handpump, served by attentive staff, alongside guests such as Hobsons Best Bitter and Wye Valley Butty Bach; they also offer craft beers, 30 gins, several malt whiskies, wines by the glass and a couple of farm ciders. The cosy, low-beamed front bar is warmed in winter by an inglenook woodburning stove; from here, a door leads into a separate little dining room with a rare plank and muntin screen. The games room at the back has a TV, games machine, darts, pool, juke box and board games; occasional live music and open mike nights. There's also a small garden. The dog-friendly bedrooms are plainly furnished but comfortable. Good walks nearby.

Fairly priced, honest food includes baguettes, mackerel pâté, chilli chicken stir-fry, mushroom stroganoff, pork and cider casserole, chicken korma with rice, liver and bacon with mustard mash, salmon in butter and tarragon sauce, burger with toppings, onion rings and chips, gammon with egg and pineapple, sea bass fillet with tomato and basil sauce, and puddings. *Benchmark main dish: fish and chips £12.00. Two-course evening meal £20.00.*

Free house ~ Licensee Jack Limond ~ Real ale ~ Open 8am–midnight ~ Bar food 12-3, 6-9 ~ Restaurant ~ Children welcome until 10pm ~ Dogs allowed in bar & bedrooms ~ Bedrooms: £80

COALPORT

SJ7002   Map 4

Woodbridge 🍷 🍺

(01952) 882054 – www.brunningandprice.co.uk/woodbridge

Village signposted off A442 1.5 miles S of A4169 Telford roundabout; down in valley, turn left across narrow bridge into Coalport Road, pub immediately left; TF8 7JF

Superb Ironbridge Gorge site for extensive, handsomely reworked pub, an all-round success

This Brunning & Price pub has a striking location at the bottom of the steep and wooded Ironbridge Gorge, next to the mighty River Severn and opposite the little (originally wooden) bridge from which it gets its name. Tables and chairs at the front and side of the building look over the water, as do the picnic-sets on grass behind. The spreading series of linked rooms are comfortable and civilised with log fires and Coalport-style stoves, rugs on broad boards as well as tiles or carpet, black beams in the central part and plenty of polished tables and cosy armchair corners. A mass of pictures and prints, often of local scenes, line the walls and are well worth a look. Efficient, friendly staff serve St Austell Brunning & Price Traditional and regularly changing guests such as Enville Ale, Hobsons Spire, Salopian Shropshire Gold and St Austell Tribute on handpump, 20 wines by the glass and about 40 gins; background music and board games. You can walk from here along a disused railway path to reach Ironbridge itself, with its famous cast-iron bridge, the first in the world, erected in 1779.

Interesting, brasserie-style food (with a separate gluten-free menu) includes sandwiches and 'light bites', chicken caesar croquettes, crispy vegetable parcels with spiced mango dip, braised shoulder of lamb with crushed new potatoes and rosemary gravy, cauliflower, chickpea and squash tagine with lemon and almond couscous, chicken, ham and leek pie with mash and buttered greens, roast pork tenderloin with colcannon potato and apple purée, Malaysian chicken curry, and puddings such as chocolate and orange tart with passion-fruit sorbet and sticky toffee pudding. *Benchmark main dish: beer-battered cod and chips £14.95. Two-course evening meal £21.00.*

Brunning & Price ~ Manager Oliver Parrish ~ Real ale ~ Open 11.30-11; 11.30-midnight Sat; 11.30-10.30 Sun ~ Bar food 12-9.30; 12-10 Fri, Sat; 12-9 Sun ~ Restaurant ~ Children welcome ~ Dogs allowed in bar

IRONBRIDGE   SJ6703   Map 4
Golden Ball

(01952) 432179 – www.goldenballironbridge.co.uk
Brown sign to pub off Madeley Road (B4373) above village centre – pub behind Horse & Jockey, car park beyond on left; TF8 7BA

Low-beamed, friendly inn with popular food and drink; bedrooms

Tucked away among other historic buildings, this is the oldest pub in Ironbridge, dating back to 1728 – even older than the celebrated iron bridge itself. A list of landlords over the centuries is on display in the bar, which has old floorboards, padded pews, one or two black beams and a woodburning stove. There's Sharps Atlantic, Wye Valley HPA and a couple of guests on handpump, quite a few Belgian bottled ales, eight wines by the glass, several gins, rums and whiskies and a farm cider; background music, TV. There are more black beams, plain wooden tables and chairs, a tiled floor and a blackboard menu in the dining area. There's sheltered seating in a back garden and a front courtyard. You can walk from here down to the River Severn and beyond, but it's a pretty steep hike getting back up. The three bedrooms are comfortable and breakfasts are good.

Tasty food with vegetarian and vegan options includes lunchtime sandwiches, baked cod with roast chard and apple and cauliflower purée, cumberland sausages and mash, a range of home-made burgers, mixed bean cassoulet with confit duck leg, spinach and ricotta cannelloni, interesting pizzas such as Moroccan lamb with feta, pomegranate and mint or prawns with garlic, chilli and pea shoots, 8oz rib-eye steak with chips and sauce diane, and puddings such as apple and blackberry crumble and triple chocolate cheesecake. *Benchmark main dish: steak in ale pie £11.00. Two-course evening meal £20.00.*

Enterprise ~ Lease Jessica Janke ~ Real ale ~ Open 12-10.30; 12-11.30 Sat ~ Bar food 12-8.30; 12-6.30 Sun ~ Restaurant ~ Children welcome until 9pm ~ Dogs allowed in bar & bedrooms ~ Bedrooms: £70

LUDLOW   SO5174   Map 6
Charlton Arms

(01584) 872813 – www.thecharltonarms.co.uk
Ludford Bridge, B4361 Overton Road; SY8 1PJ

Fine position for popular pub with plenty of space for both drinking and dining and extensive terraces looking over the river; bedrooms

If you're sitting on the balcony at this attractive inn overlooking the River Teme and its massive medieval bridge, keep your eyes peeled for wildlife: kingfishers in spring and summer, and otters and swans in winter. Inside, the character bar has proper pubby tables and chairs on tiled and bricked floors, gluggle jugs along the gantry, a double-sided woodburner, and stools against the hop-hung counter where friendly staff serve five ales on handpump from local breweries such as Hobsons, Ludlow, Woods and Wye Valley, 15 wines by the glass, several gins and whiskies and a farm cider. The two rooms of the lounge (sharing a two-way woodburning stove) are comfortable and chatty with tub chairs, armchairs and high-backed black leather seats on pale wooden floors. The dining room also has views of the river and Ludford Bridge; background music and board games. The 12 bedrooms are well equipped and comfortable, and some have river views. It's a short walk uphill to the town centre and Ludlow Castle.

Enjoyable food includes lunchtime sandwiches, fish soup with rouille and croutons, rare-breed pork, cranberry and chestnut terrine with piccalilli and toasted sourdough, Thai-spiced octopus with avocado, bacon cheeseburger with barbecue sauce and skinny fries, stuffed chicken breast with ricotta, pine nuts, parma ham and fondant potato, braised short beef ribs with spring onion mash, haddock with crushed peas and chunky chips, 42-day dry-aged sirloin steak with peppercorn sauce and chips, and puddings such as roast plum and stem ginger fool and chocolate fondant with mint chocolate ice-cream. *Benchmark main dish: fisherman's pie £12.50. Two-course evening meal £21.00.*

Free house ~ Licensee Cedric Bosi ~ Real ale ~ Open 11am-11.30pm; 11am-midnight Sat; 12-10.30 Sun ~ Bar food 12-2.30, 6-8.30 ~ Restaurant ~ Dogs allowed in bar ~ Bedrooms: £100

LUDLOW
Church Inn 🍺 🛏
SO5174 Map 4

(01584) 874034 – www.thechurchinn.com
Church Street, behind Butter Cross; SY8 1AW

Splendid range of real ales and good food in character town-centre pub; bedrooms

The ground floor of this historic pub is divided into three appealingly decorated areas, with hops hanging from heavy beams and comfortable banquettes in cosy alcoves; the pulpit and pews come from a local church. A long central area has a fine stone fireplace, a chess table and board games, while the civilised lounge bar upstairs has high ceilings and big windows giving good views of St Laurence's church and the surrounding countryside. Friendly staff serve a fine range of real ales such as Hobsons Best, Ludlow Blonde and Gold, Salopian Darwins Origin, Woods Take 5 and a rotating guest on handpump, ten wines by the glass, 50 gins (including several local ones) and a farm cider; background music. There are picnic-sets in the back garden (which they share with the church). At the top of the building are four comfortable rooms with balconies and church views, and they also have nine smart rooms in their nearby Town House. Cedric Bosi (who owns the Church Inn with his brother Claude) also runs the Charlton Arms down the hill.

Rewarding food includes lunchtime sandwiches, breaded scampi with pineapple salsa and curry sauce, black pudding scotch egg, ploughman's, beer-battered haddock and chips, curry-roasted cauliflower steak with stir-fry quinoa and chimichurri sauce, pork chop with dauphinoise potatoes, cabbage and bacon, fisherman's pie, 8oz rump steak with onion rings and peppercorn sauce, and puddings such as lemon cheesecake with raspberry sorbet and crème brûlée. *Benchmark main dish: chicken, ham hock and mushroom pie with mash £12.50. Two-course evening meal £21.00.*

Free house ~ Licensee Matt Tommey ~ Real ale ~ Open 11-11; 11am-midnight Sat ~ Bar food 12-3, 6-9 ~ Restaurant ~ Children welcome ~ Dogs allowed in bar, restaurant & bedrooms ~ Bedrooms: £120

MAESBURY MARSH
SJ3125 Map 6
Navigation
(01691) 672958 – www.thenavigation.co.uk
Follow Maesbury Road off A483 S of Oswestry; by canal bridge; SY10 8JB

Hospitable canalside pub with warm welcome, cosy bar and local seasonal produce in a choice of dining areas

The friendly, long-running owners of the 'Navvy' and their cheerful, enthusiastic staff are keen to make everyone feel at home in this traditional pub next to the Montgomery Canal. The old-fashioned, quarry-tiled bar on the left has squishy brown leather sofas by an old-style black range and upholstered cask seats around some small tables. A couple of steps lead up beyond a balustrade to a carpeted area, with sofas and armchairs around low tables, and a piano (which does get used); off to the left is a dining area with paintings by local artists. The main dining room, with a low beamed ceiling and stripped stone walls, is beyond another small bar with a coal-effect gas fire and a striking row of carved choir stalls complete with misericord seats. Joules Slumbering Monk and Stonehouse Cambrian Gold and Station Bitter on handpump, about a dozen wines by the glass, nine malt whiskies (including one from Wales) and a farm cider (in summer); quiet background music and board games. There are picnic-sets with parasols beside the water.

 Using seasonal, local and free-range produce, the much liked food includes peppered smoked mackerel and horseradish salad, baked camembert with roasted garlic and cranberry sauce, pea and mushroom risotto, free-range ham with sautéed potatoes and creamy parsley sauce, sausages (pork, glamorgan or vegan) with mash, braised red cabbage and gravy, pan-fried sea bass fillets with sautéed potatoes, tomato sauce and broccoli, pork and chorizo meatballs with tomato sauce and spaghetti, beer-battered haddock or battered halloumi with peas and chips, Welsh beef steak with herb-crusted tomatoes, garlic mushrooms and chips, and puddings. *Benchmark main dish: crispy pork belly with apple mash, carrot and swede, black pudding and cider jus £13.50. Two-course evening meal £21.00.*

Free house ~ Licensees Brent Ellis and Mark Baggett ~ Real ale ~ Open 12-2, 6-11; 12-6 Sun; closed Mon, lunchtime Tues ~ Bar food 12-2, 6-8.30; 12-2 Sun ~ Restaurant ~ Children welcome ~ Dogs allowed in bar

NEENTON
SO6387 Map 4
Pheasant ⭐ 🍴 🛏
(01746) 787955 – www.pheasantatneenton.co.uk
B4364 Bridgnorth–Ludlow; WV16 6RJ

Community-owned village inn with a traditionally furnished bar and dining room, local ales and good food; seats in orchard garden

Halfway between Bridgnorth and Ludlow and within striking distance of some lovely walks, including Brown Clee Hill (Shropshire's highest), this charming inn is a fine spot to spend some time. It has three comfortable, simply furnished bedrooms, and breakfasts are first class. Rescued from dereliction some years ago, it's now a proper village pub, owned and run by the community, but with a warm welcome for visitors too – and restaurant-standard food. The cosy front bar has leather sofas and armchairs by a woodburning stove, rugs on tiles and stools by the counter where friendly, helpful staff serve four real ales on handpump from the likes of Enville, Hobsons, Hop & Stagger, Ludlow, Salopian and Wye Valley, 14 wines by the glass, several gins and farm cider; background music, board games. The dining room is in an airy, oak-framed extension at the back with a homely arrangement of cushioned chairs and wooden tables on bare boards. There are seats on a terrace with large parasols and heaters, picnic-sets on grass and under trees in the orchard and a children's play area; boules. Disabled access.

 The highly praised food includes crispy short rib fritters with smoked paprika mayonnaise, whitebait with tartare sauce, wild mushroom, garlic, pea and herb tagliatelle, pork and black pudding wellington with creamed cabbage and black garlic aioli, beer-battered haddock with mushy peas and chips, gnocchi with kale and hazelnut pesto and cherry tomatoes, pork fillet with crispy garlic sausage, savoy cabbage and fried egg, breaded Cornish cod katsu curry with pak choi, 8oz local sirloin steak with confit tomato, grilled mushroom and skin-on chips, and puddings such as damson bavarois with spiced damson jam and whisky chantilly and sticky toffee pudding with vanilla ice-cream. The Sunday roasts are very popular. *Benchmark main dish: breaded chicken schnitzel with fries and peppercorn sauce £17.00. Two-course evening meal £23.00.*

Free house ~ Licensees Mark Harris and Sarah Cowley ~ Real ale ~ Open 12-3, 6-11; 12-11 Fri, Sat; 12-8 Sun ~ Bar food 12-2.30, 6-9; 12-4 Sun ~ Restaurant ~ Children welcome ~ Dogs allowed in bar & bedrooms ~ Bedrooms: £110

NORTON
SJ7200   Map 4

Hundred House 🔘 🛏

(01952) 730353 – www.hundredhouse.co.uk
A442 Telford–Bridgnorth; TF11 9EE

Family-run inn with rambling rooms, lovely gardens, a good choice of drinks and rewarding food; comfortable bedrooms

With its delightful gardens and pretty bedrooms, this old red-brick inn is a very popular spot for special occasions, especially weddings, and has been run by the same friendly family for decades. Outside, you'll find old-fashioned roses, herbaceous borders, winding paths, a pond, statues and a big working herb garden (with around 50 varieties). Inside, the rambling bar rooms have a mix of interesting chairs and settles with long colourful patchwork leather cushions around sewing machine tables, beams hung with hops and huge bunches of dried flowers and herbs and jugs of fresh flowers. Winter log fires in handsome fireplaces include one with a large Jacobean arch and old black cooking pots. Steps lead up past a little balustrade to a partly panelled eating area. Real ales on handpump come from local breweries such as Hobsons, Sadlers, Three Tuns and Woods, plus 18 wines by the glass, a dozen malt whiskies, a growing choice of gins and a farm cider; background music and TV. The nine bedrooms (fittingly named after herbs) feature antique four-posters or half-testers, Victorian-style baths and rain showers and their trademark velvet-cushioned swing. Disabled access.

 Well regarded food includes sandwiches (until 5.30pm), ham, caper and parsley terrine with honey mustard pear and damson dressing, smoked salmon pâté, beetroot-cured salmon and fennel slaw, burger with toppings and fries, fish or cheese sharing platters, beer-brined partridge with crispy leg, braised cabbage, mash and caper and sage game jus, monkfish wth mussel and basil bisque, saffron rice cake and spinach, squash and sweetcorn fritters with roast cauliflower and chilli sauce, and puddings such as treacle tart with custard and honeycomb cheesecake with chantilly cream. *Benchmark main dish: roast lamb rump with Moroccan braised shoulder, confit potato and carrot and almond purée £20.95. Two-course evening meal £26.00.*

Free house ~ Licensees Henry, Stuart and David Phillips ~ Real ale ~ Open 11-11.15; 11-10.30 Sun ~ Bar food 7.30-9.30am, 12-8; 8-10am, 12-8 Sat, Sun ~ Restaurant ~ Children welcome ~ Dogs allowed in bar & bedrooms ~ Bedrooms: £100

SHIPLEY

SO8095   Map 4

Inn at Shipley 🍷 ☕

(01902) 701639 – www.brunningandprice.co.uk/innatshipley

Bridgnorth Road; A454 W of Wolverhampton; WV6 7EQ

Light and airy country pub with good range of beers and other drinks, interesting food and plenty of seating outside

This is a good spot for alfresco eating and drinking, with plenty of sturdy tables outside – some on a sizeable terrace with a side awning, others by weeping willows on the main lawn behind the car park, more on smaller lawns around the building. Inside the handsome red-brick building, a series of rambling rooms surround the large central bar; the various areas are interconnected but manage to also feel distinct and individual. A mix of dining chairs are arranged around assorted tables on rugs or polished floorboards, attractive pictures are hung frame-to-frame and big windows let in plenty of daylight; church candles, careful spotlighting and chandeliers add atmosphere. There are several woodburning stoves and log fires, including one in a big inglenook in a cosy, traditionally tiled, black-beamed end room and another by a welcoming set of leather armchairs. As is usual with Brunning & Price pubs, the atmosphere is chatty and informal, and staff are friendly and efficient. St Austell Brunning & Price Traditional, Enville Ale and Wye Valley HPA plus two or three rotating guests such as Ludlow Best and Sharps Doom Bar on handpump, 22 wines by the glass (including fizz), 80 malt whiskies, 70 gins and two farm ciders; background music and board games. There's a private dining room upstairs.

 A wide choice of pleasing food includes sandwiches, chicken liver pâté with apricot chutney, garlic and chilli king prawns, halloumi fries with tomato salsa, beer-battered cod and chips, grilled sea bass fillets with potato and shallot terrine and chervil and lemon cream sauce, chicken, ham and leek pie with mash and buttered greens, steak burger with toppings, coleslaw and fries, and puddings such as hot waffle with caramelised banana and banoffi ice-cream and Cheshire Farm sorbets and ice-creams. *Benchmark main dish: braised feather of beef bourguignon with horseradish mash £16.95. Two-course evening meal £22.00.*

Brunning & Price ~ Manager Simon Joyce ~ Real ale ~ Open 10.30am-11pm; 10.30-10.30 Sun ~ Bar food 12-9.30; 12-10 Fri, Sat; 12-9 Sun ~ Restaurant ~ Children welcome ~ Dogs allowed in bar

SHREWSBURY

SJ4812   Map 6

Armoury 🍷 ☕

(01743) 340525 – www.brunningandprice.co.uk/armoury

Victoria Quay, Victoria Avenue; SY1 1HH

Vibrant atmosphere in interestingly converted riverside warehouse with tempting all-day food

This massive red-brick bulding, built as a munitions warehouse in the late 18th c, was moved to its present site after the First World War. And what a good site it is: overlooking the broad River Severn and the Welsh Bridge, close to the Quarry park and near Shrewsbury's main shopping areas. The interior is pretty impressive with spacious open-plan rooms and long runs of big arched windows at the back with river views. Despite its size, the pub has a personal feel thanks to the judicious layout of furniture, interesting décor and cheerful bustle of customers and staff. A mix of wood tables and chairs are grouped on stripped-wood floors, the high brick walls display floor-to-ceiling books or masses of closely hung old prints, and there's a grand stone fireplace at one end. Colonial-style fans whirr away on the ceilings, which are supported by green-painted columns, and small wall-mounted glass cabinets display smokers' pipes. There's up to seven quickly changing and often local ales on handpump, such as St Austell Brunning & Price Traditional, Hop & Stagger Bridgnorth Porter, Montys Old Jailhouse and Wye Valley Hop, Skip & Jump, farm cider, 15 wines by the glass, over 60 malt whiskies and a similar number of gins. There are a few seats and tables outside at the front beneath lovely hanging baskets. There's no car park, but plenty of places to park nearby.

Interesting, reliable food includes sandwiches and 'light bites', crispy vegetable parcels with sweet chilli sauce, chicken caesar croquettes, pork and leek sausages with mash and onion gravy, beer-battered cod and chips, grilled sea bass fillets with potato and shallot terrine, braised shoulder of lamb with crushed new potatoes and rosemary gravy, cauliflower, chickpea and squash tagine with lemon and almond couscous, and puddings such as affogato and triple chocolate brownie with chocolate sauce. *Benchmark main dish: chicken, ham and leek pie with mash and buttered greens £14.95. Two-course evening meal £22.00.*

Brunning & Price ~ Manager Emily Periam ~ Real ale ~ Open 10am-11pm; 10am-midnight Fri, Sat; 10am-10.30pm Sun ~ Bar food 12-9.30; 12-10 Fri, Sat; 12-9 Sun ~ Children welcome ~ Dogs allowed in bar

SHREWSBURY
Boathouse ⌐

SJ4812   Map 6

(01743) 231658 – www.boathouseshrewsbury.co.uk
New Street/Quarry Park; leaving centre via Welsh Bridge/A488 turn into Port Hill Road; SY3 8JQ

Wonderful riverside position for busy pub, plenty of outside seating, nautical colours inside and well liked food and ales

This is a lovely spot overlooking the River Severn, with a fantastic outdoor terrace right next to the water that makes the most of the charming view – do arrive early on a sunny day if you want to sit at one of the parasol-shaded tables. The pretty little footbridge adjacent leads across the water to the Quarry park and the centre of Shrewsbury, where you'll also find highly rated sister establishment the Lion & Pheasant. The attractive interior has beams and timbering, pastel blue panelling, wooden chairs and cushioned settles around painted tables on bare boards, a woodburning stove and high chairs against the counter where cheerful staff serve five real ales on handpump, usually Salopian Oracle (the brewery is in town) and Wye Valley HPA plus guests from the likes of Hobsons and Three Tuns, eight wines by the glass, cocktails and an impressive gin selection. Note, no dogs inside. The separate Boatshed can be hired for private parties. The town holds lots of events, many of them based around the water, including the summer River Festival with pirates and coracle races.

Popular, brasserie-style food includes crispy baby squid with sweet chilli sauce, heritage beetroot, feta, pine nut and pesto salad, buttermilk chicken burger with Cajun slaw and skin-on fries, crispy beef salad with Asian beansprout salad and coriander crispy wontons, chargrilled bacon chop with black pudding, poached egg, new potatoes and hollandaise, red lentil and bean shepherd's pie with green beans, pan-fried sea bass fillet with crushed new potatoes, chorizo and black pepper butter, and puddings such as chocolate brownie and prosecco and blackcurrant cheesecake. *Benchmark main dish: Shropshire Gold-battered haddock and chips £14.95. Two-course evening meal £21.00.*

Free house ~ Licensees Jim Littler and the Chidlows ~ Real ale ~ Open 11-11 ~ Bar food 12-2.30, 6-9; 12-9 Fri-Sun ~ Restaurant ~ Children welcome

SHREWSBURY
SJ4912 Map 6

Lion & Pheasant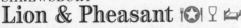

(01743) 770345 – www.lionandpheasant.co.uk

Follow City Centre signposts across the English Bridge; SY1 1XJ

Shropshire Dining Pub of the Year

Stylish bar and restaurant in comfortable, neatly updated and well placed town inn; bedrooms

This charming and attractive town-centre inn is a splendid place to stay, with 22 serene, comfortable and well equipped bedrooms and two self-catering apartments. Some rooms offer glimpses of the River Severn below the nearby English Bridge, and breakfasts are good. Shrewsbury's shops and attractions are all within walking distance, as is sister operation the Boathouse. The décor throughout is most appealing and cleverly combines original 16th-c features with contemporary touches. The big-windowed bar consists of three linked levels, the lowest of which has armchairs on dark flagstones by a big inglenook; elsewhere, there's a cushioned settee or two, but mostly there are designer metal chairs at sturdy stripped tables on dark floorboards. A few modern paintings, plentiful flowers and church candles brighten up the restrained cream and grey décor, as do the friendly staff and background music. The atmosphere is gently civilised but friendly. There are three real ales on handpump, perhaps Hobsons Twisted Spire, Salopian Oracle and Wye Valley Butty Bach or HPA, plus 14 wines by the glass and farm cider; new this year is a little wine bar and wine shop. Off quite a warren of corridors, the restaurant is in the older back part of the building with beams and timbering. There's also the lovely Crystal Room with its silver-edged mirrors and transparent chairs, perfect for a party or reception. Outside, there are seats and tables under cover in a gravelled courtyard with olive trees and flowering pots dotted about.

Delicious, carefully presented food using seasonal, local produce includes teriyaki cured salmon with cucumber, ginger and sesame tuille, chicken and duck liver parfait with red onion marmalade, buttered pollock with turnip fondant, haricot beans, tenderstem broccoli and mussel cream sauce, venison wellington with haunch ragoût, pomme dauphine and blackberries, wild mushroom risotto with Shropshire truffle, pan-fried duck breast with date purée, duck leg pomme anna, roast cauliflower and cavolo nero, and puddings such as banana soufflé with chocolate sorbet and lemon tart with Italian meringue and raspberry sorbet; they also offer a tasting menu (including a vegetarian version) and a set Sunday menu. *Benchmark main dish: 10oz sirloin steak with roast tomato, king oyster mushrooms and hand-cut chips £24.00. Two-course evening meal £28.00.*

Free house ~ Licensee Jim Littler ~ Real ale ~ Open 10.30am-11pm; 10.30am-midnight Sat ~ Bar food 12-3, 6-9; 12-9.30 Sat; 12-4, 6-8 Sun ~ Restaurant ~ Children welcome ~ Bedrooms: £135

Also Worth a Visit in Shropshire

Besides the fully inspected pubs, you might like to try these pubs that have been recommended to us and described by readers. Do tell us what you think of them: feedback@goodguides.com

ADMASTON SJ6313
Pheasant (01952) 251989
Shawbirch Road; TF5 0AD Modernised

19th-c red-brick pub fronting the road; enjoyable generously served pubby food (all day Sat, till 7pm Sun), three or four well kept ales including Purity and Wye Valley, decent range of wines, helpful service; background music, can get noisy; children welcome, no dogs during food times, garden with picnicsets and play area, open all day.

BISHOP'S CASTLE   SO3288
★Castle Hotel (01588) 638403
Market Square, just off B4385; SY9 5BN
Substantial coaching inn at top of historic market town; clubby little beamed and panelled bar with log fire, larger rooms off and another fire, well kept ales such as Hobsons and Three Tuns (brewed in the town), local cider, ten wines by the glass and 30 or so malt whiskies, popular food including afternoon tea served by friendly staff, handsome panelled dining room; background music; children and dogs welcome, pretty hanging baskets at front, garden behind with terrace seating and pergolas, good views and surrounding walks, 13 spacious bedrooms and new (2020) self-catering accommodation, useful big car park, open all day.

BISHOP'S CASTLE   SO3288
Six Bells (01588) 630144
Church Street; SY9 5AA Friendly unspoilt 17th-c pub, simple little bar with inglenook woodburner, old local photographs and prints, bigger room with mix of furniture on bare boards and another woodburner, usually Clun, Ludlow and Three Tuns beers, sandwiches only lunchtimes Mon-Sat, good value meals Thurs-Sat evenings, roasts Sun lunchtime; well behaved children and dogs welcome, open all day.

BISHOP'S CASTLE   SO3288
★Three Tuns (01588) 638797
Salop Street; SY9 5BW Extended old pub adjacent to unique four-storey Victorian brewhouse (a brewery is said to have been here since 1642); busy chatty atmosphere in public, lounge and snug bars, Three Tuns beers from old-fashioned handpumps, a dozen wines by the glass and good variety of tasty food (not Sun evening) from lunchtime sandwiches up, friendly young staff, modernised dining room done out in smart oak and glass; lots going on including usually fortnightly open mike night and film club; children and dogs welcome, open all day.

BOULDON   SO5485
Tally Ho (01584) 841811
W end of village, set back from road; SY7 9DP Welcoming tucked-away rural pub owned by group of villagers; good local beers such as Hobsons and Ludlow, enjoyable fairly priced food (not Mon or evening Sun) from sandwiches and light meals up, plainly furnished with rugs on quarry tiles and woodburner in big stone fireplace; darts and quiz night; children and dogs welcome, lovely country views from picnic-sets in garden, open all day weekends, closed Mon lunchtime.

BRIDGES   SO3996
★Bridges (01588) 650260
Pub signed from Pulverbatch–Wentnor road, W of Ratlinghope; SY5 0ST
Renovated beamed country pub (formerly the Horseshoes) owned by Three Tuns with their full range in excellent condition; bare-boards bar on the right, large dining room to the left, enjoyable fairly traditional home-made food including good ploughman's and daily specials, helpful friendly staff; occasional live music; children and well behaved dogs welcome, tables out by little East Onny river (some on raised deck), bedrooms in separate buildings, also camping and youth hostel nearby, great walking country, open (and food) all day, breakfast from 9.30am.

BRIDGNORTH   SO6890
★Down (01746) 789539
The Down; B4364 Ludlow Road
3 miles S; WV16 6UA Spotless roadside dining pub overlooking rolling countryside; enjoyable good value food (all day weekends) including popular daily carvery, efficient welcoming staff, four well kept ales such as Hobsons and Salopian; background music; children welcome, no dogs, nine comfortable bedrooms, open all day.

BRIDGNORTH   SO7193
Golden Lion (01746) 762016
High Street; WV16 4DS Friendly 18th-c coaching inn run by Holdens; five of their ales kept well and good range of gins, no food apart from cobs, separate lounge and public bar; sports TV; five comfortable individually decorated bedrooms with dedicated parking, good breakfast, open all day.

BRIDGNORTH   SO7192
★Railwaymans Arms (01746) 760920
Severn Valley Railway station, Hollybush Road (off A458 towards Stourbridge); WV16 5DT Chatty old-fashioned waiting room conversion at Severn Valley steam railway terminus, bustling on summer days; old station signs and train nameplates, superb mirror over fireplace, Bathams, Hobsons, Bewdley and plenty of other well kept ales along with a couple of proper ciders, bar snacks such as pork pies (can also bring food from the station café); children and dogs welcome, wheelchair access possible through side door (staff will help), tables out on platform, the train to Kidderminster (station bar there too) has an all-day bar and bookable Sun lunches, open all day.

BRIDGNORTH   SO7192
White Lion (01746) 763962
West Castle Street; WV16 4AB Fairly compact 18th-c two-bar pub with seven well kept ales including own Hop & Stagger brews, traditional cider and reasonably priced bar food such as home-made scotch

eggs and butcher-made pies, friendly helpful staff, comfortable carpeted lounge with open fire; regular events including folk club, storytelling and charity quiz; children and dogs welcome, lawned garden with terrace, four good value cosy bedrooms (no breakfast), usually open all day.

BRIDGNORTH
SO7093
Woodberry (01746) 762950
Victoria Road/Sydney Cottage Drive; WV16 4LF Welcoming dining inn with good choice of enjoyable locally sourced food, ales such as Enville and Hobsons, friendly efficient service; background music; children welcome, dogs not allowed inside, large garden with tables, nine comfortable bedrooms, good breakfast, closed Sun evening, otherwise open (and food) all day.

BROMFIELD
SO4877
★Clive Arms (01584) 856565
A49, 2 miles NW of Ludlow; SY8 2JR Civilised and recently refurbished bar-restaurant-hotel named after Clive of India who once lived here (part of Oakly Park Estate); much emphasis on their popular well presented food but also Hobsons and Ludlow ales, several wines by the glass and good bar snacks, friendly helpful service; smart dining room with wood-strip floor, door to bar and step down to raftered room with woodburner in huge fireplace; background music; children welcome, tables under parasols on secluded terrace, garden with fish pond, 18 bedrooms in separate building, Ludlow Farmshop next door and Ludlow Racecourse nearby, open all day.

BUCKNELL
SO3574
★Baron at Bucknell (01547) 530549
Chapel Lawn Road; off B4367 Knighton Road; SY7 0AH Modernised family-owned country inn, friendly and efficiently run, with enjoyable sensibly priced food cooked to order from pub favourites up, a couple of well kept local ales including Wye Valley, woodburner in carpeted bar opening into conservatory, pitched-roof dining room with small gallery, old cider press and grindstone, further Stable Bar with pool and TV where dogs allowed; children welcome, peaceful setting with lovely views from big garden, good walks from the door (check website for details), eight bedrooms including three chalets with hot tubs plus swimming pond, open all day Sat, till 6pm Sun, closed lunchtimes Mon-Thurs.

BURLTON
SJ4526
Burlton Inn (01939) 270284
A528 Shrewsbury–Ellesmere, near B4397 junction; SY4 5TB Welcoming attractively updated 18th-c inn; enjoyable pubby food and well kept Robinsons ales (maybe a guest), friendly helpful staff, beams, timbers and woodburner, comfortable snug, restaurant with garden room; children

and dogs (in bar) welcome, disabled access/facilities, seating on pleasant terrace, six comfortable well equipped bedrooms, open all day Sun (food till 7pm), closed Mon, lunchtimes Tues, Weds.

BURWARTON
SO6185
★Boyne Arms (01746) 787214
B4364 Bridgnorth–Ludlow; WV16 6QH Handsome Georgian coaching inn under welcoming management; good home-made food (not Sun evening, Mon, Tues), Ludlow and Wye Valley ales, Robinson's and Thatcher's ciders, friendly helpful service, separate restaurant and public bar (dogs allowed here); Burwarton agricultural show in August is a local highlight and worth a visit; children welcome, play area in pretty garden, two bedrooms, open all day weekends, closed Mon and Tues lunchtime.

CHURCH STRETTON
SO4593
Housmans (01694) 724441
High Street; SY6 6BX Buzzing and welcoming restaurant-bar with good wine, gin and cocktail lists plus two or three well kept ales, enjoyable range of food including tapas-style plates, some live music; children welcome, open all day Sat, till 5pm Sun, closed Mon.

CLAVERLEY
SO8095
Woodman (01746) 710553
B4176/Danford Lane; WV5 7DG Rural 19th-c red-brick dining pub; contemporary beamed interior arranged around central bar, good popular food (must book) using local produce including some from farm opposite, well kept Black Sheep and Enville, lots of wines by the glass and interesting range of gins, efficient service; terrace and garden tables, closed Sun evening, Mon.

CLUN
SO3080
Sun (01588) 640559
High Street; SY7 8JB Beamed and timbered 15th-c pub in peaceful village surrounded by lovely rolling countryside; traditional flagstoned public bar with inglenook woodburner, larger carpeted lounge with fragment of 17th-c wallpaper and set of fine old beer pumps, six well kept Three Tuns beers and good reasonably priced home-made food from varied menu, friendly helpful staff; children (in lounge), walkers and dogs (in bar) welcome, paved back courtyard, three bedrooms (one in converted outbuilding), open all day, no food Sun evening.

CLUNTON
SO3381
Crown (01588) 660265
B4368; SY7 0HU Welcoming community-owned country local; up to four well kept ales including Hobsons and Ludlow, traditional ciders and enjoyable home-made food (not Sun evening) from shortish menu, log fire in cosy flagstoned bar, carpeted dining

room and separate games room with pool and darts; children welcome in restaurant, dogs in bar, a few seats outside, open all day Fri-Sun, closed Mon-Thurs – but best to check times.

CORFTON   SO4985
Sun (01584) 861239

B4368 Much Wenlock–Craven Arms; SY7 9DF Lived-in and unchanging three-room country local with own good Corvedale ales, very friendly staff and Norman the long-serving landlord often busy in the back brewery, decent affordably priced pubby food from soup to steaks, lots of breweriana, basic quarry-tiled public bar with darts, pool and juke box, quieter carpeted lounge, dining room with covered well; children and dogs (in bar) welcome, good wheelchair access throughout and disabled loo, tables on terrace and in large garden with play area, spacious car park.

ELLERDINE HEATH   SJ6122
Royal Oak (01939) 250300

Hazles Road; TF6 6RL Friendly little country pub known locally as the 'Tiddly'; half a dozen well kept ales, real cider and good value straightforward food (not Mon, Tues or lunchtimes Weds-Fri), open fires; children and dogs welcome, good-sized garden, open all day.

GOLDSTONE   SJ7128
Wharf (01630) 661226

Off A529 S of Market Drayton, at Hinstock; keep on towards Cheswardine; TF9 2LP Clean and tidy pub by Shropshire Union Canal (Bridge 55) with moorings; Exmoor Gold, Joules Pale Ale, Sharps Doom Bar and a guest served from central bar, generous helpings of popular pub food at decent prices (best to book), good friendly service, winter fire; children welcome, no dogs inside, plenty of seats out by canal, on-site caravan park, open all day Fri-Sun.

GRINDLEY BROOK   SJ5242
Horse & Jockey (01948) 662723

A41; SY13 4QJ Extended 19th-c roadside pub with enjoyable good value food from varied menu including tapas-style dishes, eight well kept ales including a house beer from Woods named after resident chocolate labrador Blaze, teas and coffees, friendly helpful service, well divided open-plan interior with standing timbers and mix of furniture on wood or carpeted floors, woodburners and some interesting bits and pieces; children, dogs and muddy boots welcome, some tables outside, handy for Sandstone Trail and Llangollen Canal, open (and food) all day.

HIGHLEY   SO7483
Ship (01746) 861219

Severnside; WV16 6NU Modernised 18th-c inn set in lovely riverside location; pubby food including pizzas, steak nights (Tues, Thurs) and Sun carvery, five real ales such as Banks's and Hobsons; children welcome, disabled access and facilities, tables on raised front deck, handy for Severn Way walks and Severn Valley Railway, fishing rights, bedrooms and nearby camping, open (and food) all day.

HOPE   SJ3401
Stables (01743) 891344

Just off A488 3 miles S of Minsterley; SY5 0EP Hidden-away little 17th-c beamed country pub (former drovers' inn), friendly and welcoming, with enjoyable good value home-made food and a couple of well kept ales such as Three Tuns, log fires; dogs welcome, fine views from garden, two bedrooms and shepherd's hut, open all day weekends, closed weekday lunchtimes.

HOPTON WAFERS   SO6376
Hopton Crown (01299) 887101

A4117; DY14 0NB Attractive civilised 16th-c inn under same owners as the Admiral Rodney at Berrow Green (Worcestershire), Baiting House in Upper Sapey and Stockton Cross Inn near Kimbolton (both in Herefordshire); carpeted bar and two dining rooms with black beams, painted panelling, inglenook log fires and smart tartan upholstered dining chairs around dark tables, enjoyable food from shortish menu, real ales such as Ludlow and Wye Valley, cheerful helpful staff; children and dogs welcome, garden with terrace, duck pond and stream, 12 updated bedrooms (some in new adjoining building) and two self-catering cottages.

KNOCKIN   SJ3322
Bradford Arms (01691) 682358

B4396 NW of Shrewsbury; SY10 8HJ Sizeable neatly kept village local with notable three-faced roof clock; popular good value pubby food (best to book) with offers most nights and vegan menu, well kept Marstons-related beers, friendly welcoming staff, games rooms, TV; children and dogs welcome, garden behind by car park, open (and food) all day.

LEEBOTWOOD   SO4798
Pound (01694) 751477

A49 Church Stretton–Shrewsbury; SY6 6ND Thatched cruck-framed building dating from 1458; opened-up, extended and much modernised interior, core keeping hefty beams and woodburner in big fireplace, enjoyable reasonably priced pubby food from sandwiches up, real ales such as Greene King and Wye Valley, friendly helpful service; occasional live music; children and dogs (in bar) welcome, seats on flagstoned terrace and grass, open (and food) all day.

LEIGHTON   SJ6105
Kynnersley Arms (01952) 510233

B4380 5 miles W of Ironbridge; SY5 6RN

Successful newish management for this Victorian pub built on remains of an ancient corn mill; coal fire in opened-up bar, woodburner in connecting dining area, stairs to lower level containing mill machinery (there's also a 17th-c blast furnace), up to five well kept mainly local ales such as Salopian and Three Tuns, enjoyable pub food with a twist including pizzas and steaks, friendly helpful staff; background music, sports TV, pool; children and dogs welcome, enjoyable walks nearby, open all day, no food Sun evening.

LITTLE STRETTON   SO4491
★ **Green Dragon** (01694) 722925
Village well signed off A49 S of Church Stretton; Ludlow Road; SY6 6RE Popular village pub at the foot of Long Mynd; good reasonably priced fairly traditional food (also a vegan menu) in bar or small adjacent dining area (well behaved children allowed here), well kept ales such as Hobsons, Ludlow and Wye Valley, proper cider; friendly helpful staff, cosy beamed interior with warm woodburner, area for muddy paws and boots; tables outside and play area, handy for Carding Mill Valley (NT), open (and food) all day, best to book evenings.

LITTLE STRETTON   SO4492
★ **Ragleth** (01694) 722711
Village well signed off A49 S of Church Stretton; Ludlow Road; SY6 6RB Popular wisteria-clad 17th-c dining pub below Long Mynd and near Carding Mill Valley (NT); light and airy bay-windowed front bar with eclectic mix of old tables and chairs, some exposed brick and timber work, huge inglenook in heavily beamed public bar, four real ales such as Hobsons, Ludlow, Three Tuns and Wye Valley, good food from baguettes up including plenty of gluten-free and vegan dishes, cheerful attentive service; background music; children welcome, dogs in bar, lovely garden with tulip tree-shaded lawn and fenced-off play area, thatched and timbered church and fine hill walks nearby, open all day, food all day Sun, closed Mon.

LITTLE WENLOCK   SJ6507
Huntsman (01952) 503300
2.6 miles from M54 junction 7; Wellington Road; TF6 5BH Welcoming modernised village pub; enjoyable food from sandwiches/snacks and pub standards up, four well kept/priced changing ales and good selection of wines, black-beamed bar with stone floor and central log fire, restaurant has high-backed upholstered chairs at light wood tables and woodburner in big fireplace; children and dogs (in bar) welcome, terrace seating, bedrooms and self-catering cottage, handy for Wrekin walks, open (and food) all day, kitchen shuts 7pm Sun.

LOPPINGTON   SJ4729
Dickin Arms (01939) 233471
B4397; SY4 5SR Welcoming corner pub in pretty village; split-level interior with up-to-date country-style décor, beams, flagstones, some painted panelling and big woodburner in two-way brick fireplace, good freshly made food (not Sun evening, Mon) including tapas-style starters/snacks and good range of steaks, well kept local ales and plenty of other drinks, attentive friendly service; children welcome, dogs and muddy boots in Gun Room bar, open all day Fri, Sat, closed Mon lunchtime, no food Mon or evening Sun.

LUDLOW   SO5174
Blue Boar (01584) 878989
Mill Street; SY8 1BB Former coaching inn with lots of linked areas, well kept ales such as Black Sheep, Hobsons and Three Tuns, good choice of wines by the glass and enjoyable well priced home-made food (not Sun evening), friendly staff; Sitting Room upstairs hosts regular events including live music, quiz and book club; children and dogs welcome, back suntrap courtyard, open all day, closed Mon.

LUDLOW   SO5174
Queens (01584) 879177
Lower Galdeford; SY8 1RU Welcoming and popular family-run 19th-c pub; good reasonably priced food with Thurs fish night and emphasis on fresh local produce (booking advised, especially for Sun lunchtime), four well kept ales including Hobsons, Ludlow and Wye Valley, helpful friendly service, long narrow oak-floor bar, steps down to dining area with vaulted ceiling, modern furniture; some live music; children welcome (not in bar after 6pm), dogs allowed in one area, café-style seating on enclosed deck, courtyard bedrooms, open all day.

LUDLOW   SO5174
Rose & Crown (01584) 875726
Off Church Street, behind Buttercross; SY8 1AP Small refurbished Joules pub with 13th-c origins (retains many original features); six well kept ales from well stocked bar, good value pubby food (not Sun evening) using local suppliers, quick friendly service; live jazz and blues nights; children and dogs welcome, approached through passageway with a few courtyard seats at front, pretty location, open all day.

A star symbol before the name of a pub shows exceptional character and appeal. It doesn't mean extra comfort. Even quite a basic pub can win a star, if it's individual enough.

LUDLOW SO5175
Unicorn (01584) 873555
Corve Street, bottom end; SY8 1DU Small half-timbered 17th-c coaching inn; character bare-boards bar with beams and part-panelled walls, log fire, well kept ales such as Ludlow and Wye Valley, good wine list and enjoyable food cooked by owner-chefs (more restaurant evening choice), friendly service, back dining room; background music; children and dogs welcome, terrace among willows by river, bedrooms.

LUDLOW SO5174
Wheatsheaf (01584) 872980
Lower Broad Street; SY8 1PQ New management for this traditional 17th-c pub built into the medieval town gate; good reasonably priced food including daily specials and popular Sun lunch, a couple of Marstons-related ales and a guest, decent range of gins, welcoming helpful staff, dark beams, pubby furniture, exposed stonework and open fire; children and dogs welcome, a few seats out in front, five bedrooms, usually open all day, food all day weekends.

MAESBURY SJ3026
Original Ball (01691) 587360
Maesbury Road; SY10 8HB Old renovated brick-built country pub; hefty beams and woodburner in bar's central fireplace, Marstons Pedigree, Stonehouse Station Bitter and a guest, decent wines, enjoyable fairly traditional food (not Mon-Weds) including grills, Thurs steak night, friendly helpful staff; background and some live music, sports TV; children and dogs (in bar) welcome, disabled access, seats outside (some under cover), closed lunchtimes apart from Sun.

MARKET DRAYTON SJ6734
Red Lion (01630) 652602
Great Hales Street; TF9 1JP Extended 17th-c coaching inn acting as tap for Joules Brewery; back entrance into attractive modern bar with light wood floor and substantial oak timbers, traditional dark-beamed part to the right, updated but keeping original features with pubby furniture on flagstones, brewery mirrors and signs, woodburner, more breweriana in dining/function room to left featuring splendid 'Mouseman' Thompson carved oak panelling and fireplace; Joules Green Monkey, Pale Ale, Pure Blonde, Slumbering Monk and a couple of seasonal beers (tasting trays available), good selection of wines, fairly standard home-made food including Sun carvery till 4pm; children and dogs welcome, picnic-sets outside, brewery tours first Weds of month (must pre-book), open (and food) all day.

MARTON SJ2802
★ Sun (01938) 561211
B4386 NE of Chirbury; SY21 8JP

Welcoming family-run dining pub, clean and neatly kept, with high standard of cooking including seasonal game and good fresh fish, light and airy black-beamed bar with comfortable sofa and traditional furnishings, stove in big stone fireplace, Hobsons Best and several wines by the glass, chunky pale tables and ladder-back chairs in restaurant; children welcome, dogs in bar (but do ask first), front terrace, closed Sun evening to Weds lunchtime.

MUCH WENLOCK SO6299
Gaskell Arms (01952) 727212
High Street (A458); TF13 6AQ Substantial 17th-c coaching inn in pretty village with comfortable old-fashioned lounge divided by two-way fireplace, brassware and prints, well kept Wye Valley Butty Bach and a couple of local guests, enjoyable straightforward food served by friendly attentive staff, civilised beamed restaurant and separate locals' bar; background music; well behaved children allowed, no dogs inside, disabled facilities, spacious walled garden behind with covered terrace, 14 bedrooms (four in mews building, where dogs are allowed by arrangement), open all day.

MUCH WENLOCK SO6299
★ George & Dragon (01952) 727009
High Street; TF13 6AA Newish local owners for this very popular and welcoming traditional pub; quarry-tiled front bar with beams, antique settles and two attractive Victorian fireplaces, collection of memorabilia including old brewery advertisements and local photos, refurbished back dining room, five real ales including own George & Dragon Amber Ale, Greene King and St Austell, enjoyable well priced food including pizzas, pie and a pint night Tues, good friendly service; background and some live music, darts, sports TV; children and dogs (in bar) welcome, pay-and-display car park behind, open all day weekends, no food Sun evening.

MUNSLOW SO5287
★ Crown (01584) 841205
B4368 Much Wenlock–Craven Arms; SY7 9ET Former courthouse with imposing exterior and pretty rear façade showing Tudor origins; lots of nooks and crannies, split-level lounge bar with old-fashioned mix of furnishings on broad flagstones, bread oven by log fire, another fire in traditional snug, eating area with more beams, flagstones and stripped stone, also upstairs restaurant (weekends only), good food from sandwiches and sharing boards through pub standards to restaurant dishes, popular Sun lunch, steak nights Tues and Weds, ales such as Corvedale and Three Tuns, local bottled cider and nice wines, helpful efficient staff, friendly bustling atmosphere; background music; children welcome, level wheelchair

access to bar only where dogs allowed, three bedrooms, closed Sun evening, Mon.

NEWPORT
SJ7419

New Inn (01952) 812295
Stafford Road; TF10 7LX Modernised and extended Joules pub on crossroads; their beers and a guest from five handpumps, over 50 gins and good uncomplicated food (not Sun evening) served by friendly staff, attractive opened-up interior with some cosy corners, bare-brick and green-tiled walls, old metal advertising signs, quarry-tile flooring, log fire and woodburner; live music Sun evening, beer and gin festivals; children and dogs welcome, picnic-sets on covered terrace and on grass, open (and food) all day.

PICKLESCOTT
SO4399

Bottle & Glass (01694) 751252
Off A49 N of Church Stretton; SY6 6NR Remote 17th-c country pub with plenty of character in quarry-tiled bar and lounge/dining areas; low black beams, oak panelling and log fires, mix of old tables and chairs, good home-made food from baguettes up, Weds steak night, well kept ales such as Hobsons and Wye Valley, friendly helpful service; TV; children welcome, dogs in bar, seats on raised front area, good walks, bedrooms, open till 6pm Sun, closed Mon and Tues.

ROWTON
SJ3612

Windmill (01743) 884234
A458; SY5 9EJ Popular and welcoming 18th-c pub by Welsh border, in same family for nearly a century; nicely refurbished beamed bar with half-panelling, old photos, inglenook and a couple of dining areas off, good interesting food at sensible prices along with pub favourites, three well kept ales such as Hobsons, Salopian and Wye Valley, nice choice of wines; children and dogs (in bar) welcome, lovely panoramic country views from seats in back garden, closed Mon, Tues, open all day Sat, till 8pm Sun.

SHAWBURY
SJ5621

Fox & Hounds (01939) 250600
Wytheford Road; SY4 4JG Light and spacious 1960s pub; various opened-up areas including book-lined dining room with woodburner, rugs and assorted dark furniture on wood floors, cream-painted dados and lots of pictures, good fairly priced food from sandwiches and light lunches to daily specials, Weds pie night, four or five well kept ales such as Greene King and Rowton plus guests from maybe Purple Moose and Titanic, good choice of wines, efficient helpful service; disabled access/toilet; children welcome, picnic-sets on terrace and lawned area, open (and food) all day.

SHIFNAL
SJ74508

White Hart (01952) 461161
High Street; TF11 8BH Nine well kept ales including Salopian and Wye Valley in

this chatty 17th-c timbered pub, quaint and old-fashioned with separate bar and lounge, good home-made lunchtime food (not Sun) at reasonable prices, several wines by the glass and a proper cider, friendly welcoming staff; children and dogs (in bar) welcome, couple of steep steps at front door, back terrace and beer garden, open all day.

SHREWSBURY
SJ4912

Admiral Benbow (01743) 244423
Swan Hill; SY1 1NF Great choice of regional ales, also ciders/perries and bottled foreign beers: L-shaped room with separate snug, friendly staff; darts; no children, beer garden behind, closed Mon and lunchtimes except Sat.

SHREWSBURY
SJ4812

Bricklayers Arms (01743) 614646
Copthorne Road/Hafren Road; SY3 8NL Spotless 1930s suburban pub (walkable from the town centre) owned by Joules; their well kept beers and generous helpings of popular traditional food including good Sun lunch, cheerful efficient service, bare boards/carpet, panelling and green tilework, screens and gleaming stained glass, woodburner, old advertising signs and one wall with examples of different bricklaying patterns; children and dogs welcome, picnic-sets out in front, open (and food) all day Fri-Sun, from 4pm other days.

SHREWSBURY
SO4912

Coach & Horses (01743) 365661
Swan Hill/Cross Hill; SY1 1NF Relaxed beamed Victorian corner local off the beaten track; chatty wood-panelled bar, cosy little side room and back dining lounge, well kept Salopian, Stonehouse and guests, real cider, popular freshly made pubby food including Thurs fish night and Sun carvery; background music, quiz first Mon of month; children allowed in dining room, dogs in bar, open all day.

SHREWSBURY
SJ4913

Dolphin (01743) 247005
St Michaels Street; 0.5 miles N of station; SY1 2EZ Traditionally renovated 19th-c pub with friendly welcoming atmosphere; well kept Joules ales and guests, interesting international snacks and other reasonably priced food from short blackboard menu, compact bare-boards interior keeping original gas lighting and open fires, beer mats and Joules mirrors for decoration; music and quiz nights, darts; children and dogs welcome; seats on sunny back deck, open all day Fri-Sun, from 5pm other days.

SHREWSBURY
SJ4513

Ego at the Grapes (01743) 369621
Welshpool Road; SY3 5BH Part of the Ego chain of Italian-themed pub-restaurants; modern central bar with three distinct drinking areas, a couple of real ales,

17 wines by the glass and range of cocktails, popular mostly Mediterranean dishes including good value set menu, friendly helpful staff, restaurant occupies the left wing of the pub; children welcome, open (and food) all day.

SHREWSBURY   SJ4912
Golden Cross (01743) 362507
Princess Street; SY1 1LP Attractive town-centre inn first licensed in 1428; lots of old-world character blending with colourful shabby-chic décor, emphasis firmly on their highly praised food from lunchtime snacks up including plenty of vegan and gluten-free choices, good range of wines and a real ale such as Hobsons or Salopian, friendly helpful staff; children welcome, dogs too but do check first, five appealing bedrooms, no food Sun evening, Mon.

SHREWSBURY   SJ4912
Loggerheads (01743) 362398
Church Street; SY1 1UG Chatty old-fashioned local with panelled back room, flagstones, scrubbed-top tables, high-backed settles and coal fire, three other little rooms with lots of prints, bare boards and more flagstones, quaint linking corridor and hatch service for seven well kept beers, no food, friendly service; TV for major sports; dogs welcome (in some areas), open all day.

SHREWSBURY   SJ4912
Nags Head (01743) 362455
Wyle Cop; SY1 1XB Attractive old two-room pub, small, unpretentious and welcoming, with good range of well kept ales such as Hobsons, Timothy Taylors and Wye Valley, no food; TV and juke box; dogs welcome, garden behind with remains of ancient timbered building (now used as a smokers' shelter), open all day (till late Fri).

SHREWSBURY   SJ4812
Shrewsbury Hotel (01743) 236203
Mardol/Mardol Quay; SY1 1PU Partly open-plan Wetherspoons (former coaching inn) opposite the river; seven well kept/priced ales and their usual good value food, helpful friendly service; TVs for subtitled news; children welcome, tables out in front, 22 bedrooms (residents' car park), open all day from 7am.

SHREWSBURY   SJ4912
★**Three Fishes** (01743) 344793
Fish Street; SY1 1UR Timbered and heavily beamed 16th-c pub in quiet cobbled street; small tables on flagstones around three sides of central bar, old pictures, up to six well kept mainly local beers, good value

wines and enjoyable fairly priced traditional food (not Sun) from baguettes to blackboard specials, good friendly service even when busy; Mon quiz; dogs welcome, open all day Fri-Sun.

STIPERSTONES   SJ3600
★**Stiperstones Inn** (01743) 791327
Village signed off A488 S of Minsterley; SY5 0LZ Cosy traditional pub in fine walking country – some stunning hikes up the dramatic quartzite ridge of the Stiperstones; small carpeted lounge with comfortable leatherette wall banquettes and lots of brassware on ply-panelled walls, plainer public bar with darts, TV and fruit machine, open fires, a couple of real ales such as Three Tuns, various home-infused gins such as local whinberry, good value bar food usefully served all day, afternoon teas with freshly baked cakes and home-made jams, friendly helpful service; background music; children and dogs (in bar and garden) welcome, self-catering accommodation including newly refurbished converted chapel, open all day.

STOTTESDON   SO6782
Fighting Cocks (01746) 718270
High Street; DY14 8TZ Community pub in unspoilt countryside; plainly furnished split-level interior with carpet, low ceilings and log fire, up to five well kept mainly local ales, real ciders and decent gin selection, reasonably priced home-made food including pies, more dining space upstairs; regular live music; children and dogs (in bar) welcome, garden with play area and rural views, good walks, small shop behind, open all day weekends, closed Mon, lunchtimes Tues-Thurs.

UPTON MAGNA   SJ5512
Haughmond (01743) 709918
Pelham Road; SY4 4TZ Welcoming and stylish 'modern coaching inn'; bar with painted beams, oak-strip flooring/carpet and log fire, a house beer brewed by Marstons and two local guests from brick servery, good wine list and local gins, quality food in brasserie including tasting menus, village shop/café; children and dogs (in bar) welcome, great view to the Wrekin from attractive back garden, handy for Haughmond Hill walks and Attingham Park (NT), seven bedrooms (two dog-friendly) and self-catering option, currently closed Mon and Sun, but best to check.

WELLINGTON   SJ6411
Pheasant (01952) 260683
Market Street; TF1 1DT Town-centre pub with one long room; seven well kept ales

---

Post Office address codings confusingly give the impression that some pubs are in Shropshire, when they're really in Cheshire (which is where we list them).

including Everards Tiger and up to three from own Rowton brewery, two real ciders and enjoyable good value lunchtime food served till 4pm (not Sun), friendly helpful staff; no TV or games machines; children and dogs welcome, narrow courtyard behind, open all day.

WELSHAMPTON   SJ4335
Sun (01948) 710847
A495 Ellesmere–Whitchurch; SY12 0PH Extended roadside village pub; good choice of enjoyable reasonably priced food, Stonehouse Station Bitter and three guests, friendly attentive service; live music and quiz nights; children and dogs welcome, tables in fenced back garden, 15-minute walk to Llangollen/Shropshire Union Canal, three bedrooms, open (and food) all day.

WHITCHURCH   SJ5441
Black Bear (01948) 663800
High Street, at Church Street; SY13 1AZ Striking black and white timbered building (dating from 1662) opposite church; half a dozen well kept interesting beers including Salopian and Stonehouse, real cider and 15 wines by the glass, enjoyable good home-made food from sandwiches up, characterful interior and pleasant atmosphere; regular live music; children welcome (no under-10s after 7pm) and dogs in bar, open (and food) all day.

WHITCHURCH   SJ5441
Old Town Hall Vaults
(01948) 664682 *St Marys Street; SY13 1QU* Red-brick 19th-c Joules local (birthplace of composer Sir Edward German); four of their ales and a guest, enjoyable good value food from snacks up, main room divided into distinct areas with bar in one corner, oak panelling, stained glass, mirrors and signs, sturdy furniture including bench seating and cast-iron-framed tables, log fires, further room with glazed ceiling; outside listed gents'; dogs welcome, partly covered yard with barrel tables, open (and food) all day apart from Sun when kitchen shuts at 4pm.

WHITCHURCH   SJ5345
Willeymoor Lock (01948) 663274
Tarporley Road; signed off A49 just under 2 miles N; SY13 4HF Large opened-up family-run pub in picturesque spot by Llangollen Canal and Sandstone Trail; low beams, two log fires and sizeable collection of teapots and toby jugs, cheerful chatty atmosphere, half a dozen changing local ales such as Salopian, Stonehouse and Weetwood (fewer in winter) and several malt whiskies, good value pub food from sandwiches up; background music, games machine; children welcome away from bar, well behaved dogs in some areas, terrace tables, secure garden with good-sized play area.

Somerset

with Bristol

ASHCOTT ST4337 Map 1

Ring O' Bells 🍺 £

(01458) 210232 ~ www.ringobells.com

High Street; pub well signed off A39 W of Street; TA7 9PZ

Friendly village pub with homely décor in several bars, separate restaurant, tasty bar food and changing local ales

This traditional village pub, a great favourite with both locals and visitors, has been reliably well run by the same family for many years. The three main bars, on different levels, are all comfortable, with maroon plush-topped stools, cushioned mate's chairs and dark wooden pubby tables on patterned carpet, horsebrasses along the bressumer beam above a big stone fireplace and a growing collection of hand bells; background music and board games. Changing beers on handpump from small independent breweries include many from the West Country, such as Cheddar Potholer, Fine Tuned Pitch Perfect and Teignmouth Templer, plus nine wines by the glass, eight gins and local farm cider. There's also a separate restaurant, a skittle alley/function room and plenty of picnic-sets out on the terrace and in the garden. Disabled access. RSPB Ham Wall nature reserve is nearby.

🍴 Honest food includes sandwiches, ploughman's and jacket potatoes, Somerset brie fritters with cranberry sauce, seafood platter (to share), red kidney bean and mushroom bordelaise in red wine sauce, chicken breast with bacon, barbecue sauce and mozzarella cheese, spinach and feta cheese parcels, celery, almond and cashew nut roast with cheese sauce, pork chop with honey and wholegrain mustard sauce, and puddings such as blackcurrant cheesecake and a range of ice-cream sundaes. *Benchmark main dish: fresh grilled sardines with salad £11.00. Two-course evening meal £18.00.*

Free house ~ Licensees John and Elaine Foreman and John Sharman ~ Real ale ~ Open 12-2.30, 7-11; 12-3, 7-11 Sat; 12-3, 7-10.30 Sun ~ Bar food 12-2, 7-10 ~ Restaurant ~ Children welcome ~ Dogs allowed in bar

BATH ST7467 Map 2

Hare & Hounds

(01225) 482682 ~ www.hareandhoundsbath.com

Lansdown Road, Lansdown Hill; BA1 5TJ

Lovely views from back terrace with plenty of seating, relaxed bar areas, real ales, nice food and helpful staff

One of the big pluses of this attractive stone pub is the wonderful long view down over villages and fields from huge windows in the bar and from seats and tables on the decked back terrace. The atmosphere in the single long bar is relaxed and friendly, helped along by cheerful staff. Children are particularly made welcome, with a special menu, their own activity pack designed by the pub, and a play area in the garden. Décor is stylishly simple: chapel chairs and long cushioned wall seats around pale wood-topped tables on bare boards, a few striking pieces of art on pale walls above a blue-grey dado and an attractively carved counter where they serve a beer named for the pub (from Caledonian), Butcombe Bitter and a guest on handpump and 33 wines by the glass from a good list; background music. A bronze hare and hound sit at one end of the mantelpiece above a log fire, with a big mirror above. A little side conservatory is similarly furnished, with dark slate flagstones. The large neat garden has seats beneath a gazebo.

As well as pizzas from their new outside bar in summer, the well liked modern food includes sharing boards, harissa roast cauliflower with smoked sunflower seed purée, pickled red onion and dates, roast chicken with smoked butternut purée and charred sweetcorn, chargrilled miso aubergine with wild rice, burgers with toppings and fries, quinoa, freekah, broccoli and avocado salad, sirloin or rib-eye steak with a choice of sauce, and puddings such as lemon and elderflower posset with gooseberries and burnt Basque cheesecake with berries. *Benchmark main dish: beer-battered haddock and chips £14.50. Two-course evening meal £21.00.*

Bath Pub Company ~ Lease Joe Cussens ~ Real ale ~ Open 8.30am-11pm; 8.30am-10.30pm Sun ~ Bar food 8-11am, 12-9pm Mon-Fri; 9-11am, 12-9pm Sat; 9-10.45am, 12-8 Sun ~ Children welcome

BATH
Old Green Tree ◀

ST7564   Map 2

(01225) 448259
Green Street; BA1 2JZ

Tiny, unspoilt local with up to six real ales and lots of cheerful customers

A fixture of the city, loved by many because of its unpretentious straightforwardness, this charming little 18th-c tavern simply doesn't change – and we're all very grateful for that. There's oak panelling and low ceilings of wood and plaster, and just three small rooms. These include a comfortable lounge on the left as you go in – with walls decorated with wartime aircraft pictures (in winter) and local artists' work (in spring and summer) – and a back bar. The big skylight lightens things attractively. Half a dozen beers on handpump might include Green Tree Bitter (named for the pub from Blindmans Brewery) and Butcombe Original with guests such as Pitchfork Ales Pitchfork and Plain Inntrigue; also, seven wines by the glass from a nice little list with helpful tasting notes, 26 malt whiskies and a farm cider. The gents' is basic and down steep steps. No children and no dogs.

Lunchtime-only food includes doorstep sandwiches, soup, pâté, fish and chips, vegetable curry, burger with toppings and chips, ham, egg and chips, ploughman's, and sausage and mash with beer and onion gravy.

Free house ~ Licensee Tim Bethune ~ Real ale ~ Open 11-11; 12-6.30 Sun ~ Bar food 12-30; not Sun

> The details at the end of each featured entry start by saying whether the pub is a free house, or if it belongs to a brewery or pub group (which we name).

BISHOPSWOOD

ST2512   Map 1

Candlelight ★ ♀

(01460) 234476 – www.candlelight-inn.co.uk

Off A303/B3170 S of Taunton; TA20 3RS

Neat dining pub with a good choice of drinks, enjoyable food and seats in the garden; handy for A303

This 17th-c pub nestled in the heart of the Blackdown Hills is attractive inside and out, with imaginative food complemented by a good range of drinks. The neatly kept, interconnected dining rooms have exposed stone walls and pillars, wooden beams, church, farmhouse and antique dining chairs around solid rustic tables on polished floorboards, open fires and two woodburning stoves. High chairs line the bar counter where you'll find Otter Bitter and a guest on handpump, Otter Wildsider cider, 17 wines by the glass and a large choice of gins including their own Beau Gin. Outside, there are picnic-sets on decking and seats in the neatly landscaped garden. Dogs and walkers are welcome.

 Local produce is used in the interesting food, which includes sandwiches, Devon crab with passion-fruit sauce vierge and garden herbs, beetroot falafel with date and black garlic purée, chargrilled peach and sorrel pesto, roast pork belly with hispi cabbage, samphire, pea purée, filo-wrapped white pudding and hasselback potatoes, Cornish hake fillet with red pepper and basil risotto, puffed rice and salsa verde, rump or rib-eye steak, and desserts such as lemon possett and vanilla rice pudding with rhubarb compote, pink peppercorn shortbread and elderflower sorbet. *Benchmark main dish: beef burger with toppings and chunky chips £15.00. Two-course evening meal £25.00.*

Free house ~ Licensee Mike Rose ~ Real ale ~ Open 12-3, 6-11; 12-11 Sat; 12-6 Sun ~ Bar food 12-2, 7-9; 12-2.30, 6.30-9.30 Fri, Sat; 12-4 Sun ~ Children welcome ~ Dogs allowed in bar

BRISTOL

ST5873   Map 2

Highbury Vaults ◧ £

(0117) 973 3203 – www.highburyvaults.co.uk

St Michael's Hill, Cotham; BS2 8DE

Cheerful town pub with up to eight real ales, good reasonably priced food and friendly atmosphere

---

Close to Bristol University and the hospital, this convivial, bustling pub dating from the 18th c is popular with a wide range of customers, including visitors looking for a friendly local. The little front bar, with a corridor beside it, leads through to a series of small rooms: wooden floors, green and cream paintwork and old-fashioned furniture and prints (including royal family period engravings and lithographs in the front room). A model railway runs on a shelf the full length of the pub, with tunnels through the walls. The six quickly changing ales on handpump include several from Youngs plus guests such as Dorset Jurassic and St Austell Proper Job and Tribute; also, half a dozen wines by the glass and nine malt whiskies. They offer hot sausage rolls from the oven on Thursday and Friday evenings at 10pm; bar billiards, TV and board games. An attractive back terrace has tables built into a partly covered flowery arbour, and there's disabled access to the main bar (but not to the loos).

 Good value food includes sandwiches, burgers with toppings and sweet potato wedges, chicken, ham and leek pie with mash and greens, vegetable chilli with rice, oak-smoked mackerel with new potatoes and soft-boiled egg, chilli con carne, and

puddings such as sticky toffee pudding and assorted ice-creams. *Benchmark main dish: slow-braised beef chilli nachos £10.50. Two-course evening meal £16.00.*

Youngs ~ Manager Bradd Francis ~ Real ale ~ Open 12-midnight; 12-11 Sun ~ Bar food 12-2, 5.30-8.30; 12-5 Sun ~ Children allowed in bar until 9pm ~ Dogs allowed in bar

CHURCHILL
ST4459 Map 1

Crown 🍺 £

(01934) 852995 – www.crowninnchurchill.co.uk

The Batch; in village, turn off A368 into Skinners Lane at Nelson Arms; BS25 5PP

Unchanging small cottage with friendly customers and staff, super range of real ales and homely lunchtime food

Newcomers and regular vistors all love this place because it seems completely untouched by time. Seven real ales are tapped from the cask, including Bath Gem, Butcombe Bitter, Exmoor Ale, Palmers IPA, St Austell Tribute and a quickly changing guest; also several wines by the glass and four local ciders. The small and rather local-feeling room on the right, with a stone floor and cross beams, has a big log fire in a large stone fireplace and steps that lead up to another seating area. The left-hand room – which has a slate floor, window seats and a woodburner – leads to the Snug. The outside lavatories are basic. As well as garden tables at the front, there are more seats on the back lawn with hill views; the Mendip morris men visit in summer and some of the best walking on the Mendips is nearby. There isn't a pub sign outside, but no one seems to have a problem finding the place.

Traditional, lunchtime-only food includes sandwiches (the rare roast beef is popular), jacket potatoes, chilli con carne, ploughman's, beef casserole, cauliflower cheese, lasagne, and puddings. *Benchmark main dish: cottage pie £8.95.*

Free house ~ Licensee Brian Clements ~ Real ale ~ Open 11-11; 12-11 Sun ~ Bar food 12-2.30 ~ Well behaved children welcome ~ Dogs allowed in bar

CLAPTON-IN-GORDANO
ST4773 Map 1

Black Horse 🍺 £

(01275) 842105

4 miles from M5 junction 19; A369 towards Easton-in-Gordano, then right to Portbury; in Portbury turn left to Clapton-in-Gordano; follow Caswell Lane for 2.5km then turn right into Clevedon Lane; BS20 7RH

Unpretentious 14th-c pub with lots of cheerful customers, friendly service, real ales, cider and simple lunchtime food; pretty garden

A firm favourite with so many (us included), this is a proper rustic pub – and happily nothing has changed under the newish licensees. The partly flagstoned, partly red-tiled main room has winged settles and built-in wall benches around narrow, dark wooden tables, window seats, a big log fire with antique guns, stirrups and bits on the mantelbeam (and dozing dogs in front) and lots of humorous cartoons and photographs of the pub. A window in an inner snug retains metal bars from the days when this room was the petty sessions gaol; also, high-backed settles, lots of mugs hanging from black beams and numerous small prints and photos. A simply furnished room is the only place where children are allowed; background music. Butcombe Best, Courage Best, Exmoor Gold, Otter Bitter and an occasional guest on handpump or tapped from the cask, six wines by the glass and two farm ciders. The garden has rustic tables and benches, with more to one side of the car park. Paths from the pub lead up Naish Hill or to the Iron Age hill fort at Cadbury Camp and local cycle routes are within reach nearby. Wheelchair access but no disabled loos.

 Honest lunchtime-only food (not Sunday) includes hot and cold rolls and baguettes, daily specials such as steak and ale pie and lasagne, and occasional puddings. *Benchmark main dish: ploughman's £9.50.*

Enterprise ~ Lease John Beynon ~ Real ale ~ Open 12-9.30; 12-10.30 Fri, Sat; 12-9.30 Sun ~ Bar food 12-2.30; not Sun ~ Children allowed in family room only ~ Dogs allowed in bar

CORTON DENHAM ST6322 Map 2

Queens Arms

(01963) 220317 – www.thequeensarms.com
Village signposted off B3145 N of Sherborne; DT9 4LR

Somerset Dining Pub of the Year

Handsome 18th-c inn with super choice of drinks, interesting food and a sunny garden; comfortable, stylish bedrooms

Everyone mixes easily in this honey-coloured stone inn surrounded by glorious countryside. The bustling, high-beamed bar has rugs on flagstones and two large armchairs in front of an open fire, some old pews, barrel seats and a sofa, church candles and big bowls of flowers. There's also a couple of dining rooms, one of which has cushioned wall seats and chunky leather chairs around dark wooden tables, mirrors along one side and a drop-down cinema screen (screenings are held twice a month). They keep four regularly changing ales from breweries such as Bath, Cheddar, Exmoor and Otter on handpump, 22 wines (including champagne) by the glass from a carefully chosen list, more than 50 malt whiskies, 21 gins, unusual bottled beers from Belgium, Germany and the USA, cocktails and four local ciders and apple juices. The south-facing back terrace has teak tables and chairs under parasols, outdoor heaters for chillier weather and colourful flower tubs. There eight comfortable bedrooms with lovely country views and two self-catering cottages; breakfasts are particularly good. Cadbury Castle hill fort is not far away and there are fine walks nearby.

Tasty food includes marinated artichoke hearts with chilli and garlic olives, soused Cornish mackerel with pickled fennel, beef burger with toppings and chips, ploughman's, wild mushroom, spinach and feta wellington with peas and greens, pan-seared sea bass with parmentier potatoes, samphire, braised fennel, clams and lemongrass velouté, cider-glazed ham and eggs with pineapple and chips, pan-roasted Creedy Carver duck breast with greens, heritage carrots and duck-fat potatoes, and puddings such as raspberry ripple and white chocolate cheesecake with raspberry sorbet, and dark chocolate délice with orange sorbet and hazelnut crumb. *Benchmark main dish: ale-battered fish and triple-cooked chips £15.00. Two-course evening meal £22.00.*

Free house ~ Licensees Jeanette and Gordon Reid ~ Real ale ~ Open 8am-11pm; 8am-10.30pm Sun ~ Bar food 12-3, 6-9.30; 12-3, 6-9 Sun ~ Restaurant ~ Children welcome ~ Dogs allowed in bar & bedrooms ~ Bedrooms: £120

CROSCOMBE ST5844 Map 2

George

07892 699297/(01749) 342306 – www.thegeorgeinn.co.uk
Long Street (A371 Wells–Shepton Mallet); BA5 3QH

Warmly welcoming, family-run coaching inn with charming Canadian landlord, enjoyable food, good local beers and attractive garden; bedrooms

This 17th-c pub with rooms and a well tended garden is enduringly popular. You'll be made personally welcome by the licensees in the main bar where there's stripped stone, dark wooden tables and chairs and more comfortable seats, a settle by one of the log fires in the inglenook fireplaces and the family's grandfather clock; a snug area has a woodburning stove. They keep George & Dragon and King George the Thirst (both from Blindmans) and three guests from the likes of Bath, Cheddar, St Austell and Yeovil on handpump or tapped from the cask, four farm ciders, ten wines by the glass and home-made elderflower cordial. The attractive dining room has more stripped stone, local artwork and family photographs on burgundy walls and high-backed cushioned dining chairs around a mix of tables. There's Canadian timber and a pew reclaimed from the local church in the back bar, plus a family room with games and books for children; darts, board games, shove-ha'penny and a Canadian table game called crokinole. There are folk music, steak and curry nights, and the pub dog is called Pixie. An attractive, sizeable garden has seats on a heated and covered terrace, flower borders, a grassed area, a wood-fired pizza oven (used on Fridays) and chickens; there are also children's swings.

 Enjoyable food includes lunchtime sandwiches, baguettes and omelettes, panko-battered soft shell crab with fennel and chilli slaw, smoked haddock and dill fishcakes with anchovy and lemon mayonnaise, roast guinea fowl breast with bacon and leek rösti, grilled halloumi with chargrilled vegetables and wild rice salad, burger and chips, meat or vegetable lasagne, sirloin or rib-eye steak with tomato, mushroom and chips, and puddings such as poached pears in red wine and port with home-made vanilla ice-cream and chocolate brownie with chocolate sauce and Cointreau. *Benchmark main dish: pie of the day £13.95. Two-course evening meal £20.00.*

Free house ~ Licensees Peter and Veryan Graham ~ Real ale ~ Open 8am-3pm, 5-10pm; 8am-4pm Sun; closed Mon, Tues ~ Bar food 8-11am, 11.30am-2pm, 5-8pm; 8-11am, 11.30am-3pm Sun ~ Restaurant ~ Children welcome ~ Dogs allowed in bar ~ Bedrooms: £90

DULVERTON
Woods ★ ⑩ �

SS9127   Map 1

(01398) 324007 – www.woodsdulverton.co.uk
Bank Square; TA22 9BU

Smartly informal place with exceptional wines, real ales, first rate food and a good mix of customers

This special place is a hit with readers year after year. It draws a lovely mix of both drinkers and diners, and the atmosphere is gently civilised yet informally friendly. The pub is on the edge of Exmoor, so there are plenty of sporting prints on salmon pink walls, antlers and other hunting trophies, stuffed birds and a couple of salmon rods. By the bar counter are bare boards, tables partly separated by stable-style timbering and masonry dividers, and (on the right) a carpeted area with a woodburning stove in a big fireplace; daily papers and maybe unobjectionable background music. The marvellous drinks choice includes two or three beers tapped from the cask (such as Dartmoor Legend and Exmoor Ram), farm cider, many sherries and some unusual spirits – but it's the stunning wine list that draws the most attention. Mr Groves reckons he could put 1,000 different wines up on the bar and will open any of them (for a price) for just a glass. He's there every night and will happily chat to tables of restaurant customers about any wines they might be interested in. Big windows look on to the quiet town centre; there are a couple of metal tables on the pavement and a small suntrap courtyard at the back with a few picnic-sets.

The excellent food uses produce from their own farm: sandwiches, Cornish scallops with asparagus, bacon and shallot sauce, seared mackerel fillet with cucumber ribbons, chilli and lime, chestnut risotto with truffle oil, brill fillet with tiger prawns, new potatoes and pak choi, roast guinea fowl with wild garlic gnocchi, wild mushrooms, celeriac, tenderstem broccoli and white wine velouté, chargrilled rib-eye steak with fries, and puddings such as stem ginger pannacotta with poached rhubarb and apricot sorbet and sticky toffee pudding with toffee sauce and clotted cream ice-cream. *Benchmark main dish: grilled cod with new potatoes £15.00. Two-course evening meal £23.00.*

Free house ~ Licensee Patrick Groves ~ Real ale ~ Open 12-3, 6-11; 12-3, 7-11 Sun ~ Bar food 12-2, 6-9.30; 12-2, 7-9.30 Sun ~ Restaurant ~ Children welcome ~ Dogs allowed in bar

EXFORD

SS8538   Map 1

Crown 🛏

(01643) 831554 – www.crownhotelexmoor.co.uk
From Taunton A358 then B3224 to Exford, The Green; TA24 7PP

17th-c coaching inn with character bar, real ales and enjoyable food, and big back garden; bedrooms

Situated in one of Exmoor National Park's prettiest villages, this old inn is popular for its real ales, good food and welcoming atmosphere. A big fireplace houses a two-way woodburning stove, which warms the two-room bar and the lounge, and stuffed animal heads, hunting prints, hunting-themed plates and old photos of the area adorn the walls. Traditional furniture includes cushioned benches and pubby chairs around polished tables on bare boards, and there are stools against the counter where they serve Exmoor Ale and Gold and St Austell Tribute on handpump, 11 wines by the glass, ten malt whiskies, 20 gins and local farm cider; TV. A wall has been knocked through into what was the old residents' bar to create an informal lounge. At the front of the building are tables and chairs, with more on the back terrace; a stream threads its way past gently sloping lawns in the three-acre garden. Bedrooms are warm and comfortable and breakfasts are tasty. They're very dog-friendly and can arrange riding, fishing, shooting, hunting, wildlife-watching, cycling and trekking. Disabled access to bar.

Pleasing food includes sandwiches, smoked salmon and fennel salad with sliced avocado, ham hock and smoked chicken terrine with apple and cider chutney, battered halloumi with chips and mushy peas, roasted butternut squash risotto, sausage and mash with green beans and onion gravy, confit of duck leg with butter bean cassoulet, roasted chantenay carrots and dauphinoise potatoes, hake with chorizo and spinach in creamy fish velouté, and puddings such as raspberry panacotta with exotic fruit salad and lime sorbet and dark chocolate and salted caramel délice with vanilla ice-cream. *Benchmark main dish: beef and ale pie with bubble and squeak £14.95. Two-course evening meal £24.00.*

Free house ~ Licensee Sara Whittaker ~ Real ale ~ Open 12-11 (3-11pm Mon-Thurs; 12-11 Fri, Sat in winter) ~ Bar food 12-2, 6.30-9.15 ~ Restaurant ~ Children allowed in bar ~ Dogs allowed in bar & bedrooms ~ Bedrooms: £105

'Children welcome' means the pub says it lets children inside without any special restriction. If it allows them in, but to restricted areas such as an eating area or family room, we specify this. Places with separate restaurants often let children use them, and hotels usually let children into public areas such as lounges. Some pubs impose an evening time limit – let us know if you find one earlier than 9pm.

FROME
ST7747 Map 2

Archangel ♀

(01373) 456111 – www.archangelfrome.com

King Street; BA11 1BH

Ancient place with contemporary design, several eating and drinking areas, a bustling atmosphere, pleasing food and drink and courtyard seats; bedrooms

An inn since 1311, this colourful place, with its vibrant bar and multiple spaces for entertaining, exudes character, style and charm. The ancient and the modern are blended in a clever and effective way. Original beams and walls remain, but with touches of glass, steel, slate and leather throughout. The bar is bustling and convivial with wall banquettes, high tables and chairs, white-painted walls and a strip of blue neon lighting at ground level. Four beers including Box Steam Golden Bolt and Marstons Wainwright on handpump, 17 good wines by the glass and a large cocktail list. Stairs lead up to the restaurant with its glass-enclosed mezzanine cube, distressed walls, mustard yellow and pale green leather chairs around a mix of tables on big floorboards, high rafters lined with electric candles and a large carved angel on a plinth; background music. A long slate-floored passageway links this main part to a two-roomed snug area with big leather sofas and armchairs and an open fire, and a small, rather cosy dining room. The central courtyard has colourful tables and chairs and a Mediterranean feel. Disabled access.

Well regarded food includes sandwiches, smoked salmon with watercress and shaved fennel, pigeon breast with black pudding, parsnip and pickled red cabbage, beer-battered fish of the day with chips, roast cauliflower with Persian-spiced lentils, spinach chickpeas and flatbread, brisket burger with ruby slaw, baby gem and fries, pork fillet spare rib with salt-baked celeriac, onion and thyme, and puddings such as eton mess pavlova and dark chocolate brownie. *Benchmark main dish: chicken, tarragon and leek pie with mash and buttered greens £14.50. Two-course evening meal £21.00.*

Cirrus Inns ~ Licensee Tom Halloran ~ Real ale ~ Open 12-11; 12-midnight Fri, Sat; 12-6 Sun; closed Mon, Tues ~ Bar food 12-2.30, 6-9.30; 12-9.30 Sat; 12-4 Sun ~ Restaurant ~ Children welcome ~ Dogs allowed in bar & bedrooms ~ Bedrooms: £105

HINTON ST GEORGE
ST4212 Map 1

Lord Poulett Arms

(01460) 73149 – www.lordpoulettarms.com

Off A30 W of Crewkerne and off Merriott road (declassified – former A356, off B3165) N of Crewkerne; TA17 8SE

17th-c honey-coloured stone inn with a thoughtful choice of enjoyable food and drinks and pretty garden; attractive bedrooms

Attention to detail is the secret to this splendid pub: it's a fine old building furnished with beautiful antique furniture, serving delicious food made from the finest local ingredients and a carefully curated drinks list. Several linked character rooms have exposed stone or painted walls hung with portraits and mirrors, hop-draped beams, rugs on flagstones or bare boards and some lovely antique farmhouse, ladderback and windsor chairs and high-backed settles around fine oak or elm tables. There's a raised two-way fireplace, candles in brass sticks, a silver tea set, a grandfather clock and fresh flowers. You'll find a beer named for the pub and Timothy Taylors Landlord on handpump, 20 wines by the glass or carafe, home-made cordial, some interesting spirits and local bottled cider; background music, board games and table skittles. Outside, there are elegant metalwork chairs and tables in a Mediterranean-style gravelled area with flowering tubs, and a lawn with picnic-sets and wooden furniture; boules. The six bedrooms are comfortable and attractive. This is sister pub to the Talbot at Mells (also in Somerset) and the Beckford Arms at Fonthill Gifford (Wiltshire).

Highly regarded food from a seasonal menu includes roasted heritage carrot salad with Somerset feta and ras el hanout dressing, potted ham hock with toast, Somerset rarebit with leaf salad, baba ganoush with grilled flatbread, tabbouleh and roasted peppers, rump steak with bloody mary butter and chips, roast and pickled cauliflower with split pea dhal, River Exe mussels in cider, and puddings such as lemon posset with raspberries and shortbread and mascarpone cheesecake cream with local strawberries and pistachios. *Benchmark main dish: cider-battered fish and chips £14.75. Two-course evening meal £22.00.*

Free house ~ Licensees Dan Brod and Charlie Luxton ~ Real ale ~ Open 8am-11pm; 11am-10.30pm Sun ~ Bar food 8-9.30am, 12-3pm, 6-9.30pm ~ Children allowed in bar ~ Dogs allowed in bar & bedrooms ~ Bedrooms: £95

HOLCOMBE   ST6649   Map 2

Holcombe Inn

(01761) 232478 – www.holcombeinn.com

Off A367; Stratton Road; BA3 5EB

Charming inn with cosy bar, a wide choice of drinks and good food; lovely bedrooms

New owners have revamped this popular inn, putting extra focus upon the food it offers, with tempting new menus making the most of produce from its own kitchen garden. The bar and dining areas have been repainted in attractive pale and dark greys, and there are new light fittings, blinds and curtains along with some lovely wooden and wrought-iron chairs in the restaurant. To the right of the main entrance is a snug with a sofa and armchairs around an open woodburning stove. To the left is the bar: fine old flagstones, window seats around pine-topped tables, and a carved wooden counter where they serve Bath Gem, Butcombe Original and Otter Ale on handpump, a good number of wines and champagne by the glass, 25 malt whiskies, cocktails and a thoughtful choice of local drinks (cider, vodka, sloe gin, various juices); board games and background music. A two-way woodburning stove also warms the dining room, which has partitions to create snug seating areas. Just off here is a little sitting area serving specialist teas and coffees. The terrace and side lawn make the most of the stunning sunsets. The 11 well equipped bedrooms (including three lodges) have views over peaceful farmland. Dogs are welcome everywhere except the restaurant, and in two of the lodges. Disabled access.

Highly praised food includes pan-fried scallops with mushroom, shallot and walnut, salt pork and pistachio terrine with spiced oranges, pan-fried hake with crab bisque and saffron potatoes, beetroot risotto with crispy leeks and pickled fennel, home-cooked honey-roast ham and eggs, duck à l'orange with gingerbread crumb and pak choi, cod with ratte potatoes, spinach, beetroot and horseradish purée and orange and chardonnay buerre blanc, and puddings such as plum parfait with gin berries purée, peanuts and pistachios and ginger pudding with marmalade ice-cream. *Benchmark main dish: burger and fries £16.00. Two-course evening meal £27.00.*

Free house ~ Licensees Caroline Gardiner and Alan Lucas ~ Real ale ~ Open 8am-11pm ~ Bar food 12-2.30, 6-9; 12-9 Sat, Sun ~ Restaurant ~ Children welcome ~ Dogs allowed in bar & bedrooms ~ Bedrooms: £130

HUISH EPISCOPI   ST4326   Map 1
Rose & Crown ◗ £
(01458) 250494
Off A372 E of Langport; TA10 9QT

17th-c pub with local cider and real ales, tasty food and a friendly welcome from long-serving licensees

This welcoming, down-to-earth thatched inn dating from the mid 17th c (known locally as 'Eli's' after the licensees' grandfather) has been run by the same family for 150 years. There's no bar as such, just a central flagstoned still room where drinks are served: Teignworthy Reel Ale and a couple of guests such as Fine Tuned Sunshine Reggae and Hanlons Yellow Hammer, local farm cider and Somerset cider brandy. The casual little front parlours, with their unusual pointed arch windows, have family photographs, books, cribbage, dominoes, shove-ha'penny and bagatelle and attract a good mix of both locals and visitors. A much more orthodox big back extension has pool, a games machine and a juke box. There are plenty of seats and tables in the extensive outdoor area and two lawns – one is enclosed and has a children's play area. There's also a separate skittle alley, a large car park, morris men (in summer), classic car and motorbike meets and an organic produce co-op on Friday evenings. Pub customers and Brit Stop members can camp (by arrangement) on the adjoining paddock. The site of the Battle of Langport (1645) and good river walks are nearby.

Fairly priced, home-made food includes sandwiches, good soups, cottage pie, nachos, vegetarian or meat bean chilli, pork, apple and cider cobbler, chicken in tarragon sauce, and puddings such as apple crumble and white chocolate and raspberry bread and butter pudding. *Benchmark main dish: steak in ale pie £9.20. Two-course evening meal £13.70.*

Free house ~ Licensees Maureen Pittard, Stephen Pittard and Patricia O'Malley ~ Real ale ~ Open 11.30-2.30, 5.15-11; 11.30-11.30 Fri, Sat; 12-10.30 Sun (closes 8.30pm Mon Oct-Mar) ~ Bar food 12-2, 5.30-7.30; not Sun or Mon evenings ~ Children weclome ~ Dogs allowed in bar

---

MELLS   ST7249   Map 2
Talbot ♀ ⇌
(01373) 812254 – www.talbotinn.com
W of Frome, off A362 or A361; BA11 3PN

Interesting old coaching inn with real ales and good wines, seasonal food and seats in courtyard; lovely bedrooms

This handsome former coaching inn has a relaxed, candlelit bar with assorted wooden tables and chairs on big quarry tiles, a woodburning stove in a stone fireplace, and stools (popular with locals) against the counter where friendly staff serve a beer named for the pub (from Keystone), Butcombe Original and a guest on handpump, 22 good wines by the glass and a farm cider. Two interconnected dining rooms have brass-studded leather chairs around wooden tables, a log fire with candles in fine clay cups on the mantelpiece above and lots of coaching prints on the walls; quiet background music and board games. Outside, the courtyard has metalwork chairs and tables. Off here, in separate buildings, are a rustic-feeling sitting room with a huge mural and vast glass bottles, and a grill room with a big open fire overlooked by 18th-c portraits. The eight bedrooms are smart and stylish, and breakfasts are good. This is an interesting and attractive feudal village; the walled gardens opposite the inn are very pretty and the poet Siegfried

Sassoon is buried in the lovely church. Sister pubs are the Lord Poulett Arms in Hinton St George (also in this chapter) and the Beckford Arms at Fonthill Gifford (Wiltshire).

As well as breakfast, up-to-date food includes pan-seared scallops with black pudding and celeriac purée, blue cheese and walnut arancini with walnut salad and truffle mayo, plaice with new potatoes and white bean, fennel and orange salad, lamb rump with purple-sprouting broccoli, Jersey Royals and salsa verde, sumac-roasted cauliflower with spiced sweet potato purée, pomegranate and toasted almonds, and puddings such as vegan coconut pannacotta with mango and pineapple salsa and orange polenta cake with honey and orange crème fraîche. *Benchmark main dish: beef burger and chips £14.50. Two-course evening meal £23.00.*

Free house ~ Licensee Matt Greenlees ~ Real ale ~ Open 8am-11pm; 8am-10.30pm Sun ~ Bar food 12-3, 6-9.30 ~ Restaurant ~ Children welcome ~ Dogs allowed in bar & bedrooms ~ Bedrooms: £120

MILVERTON
Globe

ST1225   Map 1

(01823) 400534 – www.theglobemilverton.co.uk
Fore Street; TA4 1JX

Handsome old place with good ales, quite a choice of tasty food and seats outside; bedrooms

You'll get hearty portions of good country cooking and a cheerful welcome at this family-run inn. The opened-up rooms have solid rustic tables surrounded by an attractive mix of wooden or high-backed black leather chairs, artwork on pale-painted walls above a red dado, and a big gilt-edged mirror above a woodburning stove in an ornate fireplace; background music. Bar chairs line the counter where they keep Exmoor Ale and two guests from the likes of Otter or Quantock on handpump, ten wines by the glass, and local farm cider in the summer. The sheltered outside terrace has raffia-style chairs and tables and cushioned wall seating under parasols. The two bedrooms are comfortable and breakfasts are continental.

Well liked food includes sandwiches, roasted butternut squash risotto with crispy sage, grilled goats cheese with pickled beetroot and toasted pine nuts, salt beef brisket with sourdough and pickles, burger with toppings, coleslaw and chips, steak and kidney pie with chips, Tuscan bean stew with rosemary, tomato, pine nuts and grilled polenta, confit duck leg with truffle mash and cherry sauce, and puddings such as cinnamon poached pear with stem ginger ice-cream and sticky toffee pudding with toffee sauce and clotted cream. *Benchmark main dish: slow-roasted honey-glazed pork belly £18.00. Two-course evening meal £22.00.*

Free house ~ Licensees Mark and Adele Tarry ~ Real ale ~ Open 12-3, 6-11; 12-3 Sun ~ Bar food 12-2, 6.30-9; 12-2 Sun ~ Restaurant ~ Children welcome ~ Dogs allowed in bar ~ Bedrooms: £70

PITNEY
Halfway House ◧ £

ST4527   Map 1

(01458) 252513 – www.thehalfwayhouse.co.uk
Just off B3153 W of Somerton; TA10 9AB

Bustling, friendly local with a fine choice of real ales, local ciders and simple food

With up to 11 ales on offer at any time, this popular, easy-going pub is a beer-lover's dream. It's an unpretentious village local with a cheery mix of customers in three old-fashioned rooms; there are communal tables, roaring log fires and a homely feel underlined by a profusion of books, maps and newspapers. Tapped from the cask, three regular beers – Hop Back Crop Circle, Otter Bright and Teignworthy Reel Ale – sit alongside six to eight guest beers and four farm ciders, a dozen malt whiskies and several wines by the glass; board games. Tables and chairs are set outside on the lawn. There's a self-catering cottage for hire.

Simple, fair priced food includes sandwiches, feta and sun-dried tomato tart, faggots with mash and onion gravy, Somerset baked goats cheese with toast and red onion jam, pork steak with scrumpy sauce and mash, chicken caesar salad, vegetable tagine, fish casserole and chilli beef. *Benchmark main dish: beer-battered fish and chips £10.50. Two-course evening meal £16.00.*

Free house ~ Licensee Mark Phillips ~ Real ale ~ Open 11.30-3, 4-11; 11.30-11 Sat; 12-11 Sun ~ Bar food 12-2, 6-8 Mon-Sat; 12-3 Sun ~ Children welcome ~ Dogs allowed in bar

PRIDDY
Queen Victoria £

ST5250   Map 2

(01749) 676385 – www.thequeenvicpriddy.co.uk
Village signed off B3135; Pelting Drove; BA5 3BA

Stone-built country pub with a friendly atmosphere, real ales and honest food, and seats outside

With bare stone walls, planked ceilings, flagstoned or slate floors and dark wood furniture, the various rooms and alcoves here are both cosy and full of character. There's an open fire in a big grate as well as a woodburning stove in a back bar, while the smarter dining room is half panelled and half painted. Horse tack, farm tools and photos of Queen Victoria adorn the walls. Furniture is traditional: cushioned wall settles, farmhouse and other solid chairs around all manner of wooden tables, a nice old pew beside a screen settle making a snug alcove, and high chairs next to the bar counter where they serve Butcombe Bitter and Rare Breed and a changing guest on handpump, six farm ciders, seven malt whiskies, nine gins and nine wines by the glass. There are plenty of seats in the front courtyard, with more across the lane where there's also a children's playground; the smokers' shelter is a converted dray wagon. Wheelchair access.

Food is traditional and fair priced: chicken liver and bacon pâté, beef and ale pie with potatoes and peas, cheddar and cherry tomato tart with chips and salad, a range of pizzas, burger and chips, wholetail scampi with chips and peas, chilli beef, smoked salmon and prawn salad, faggots with mash and peas, and puddings such as chocolate fudge cake and treacle sponge and custard. *Benchmark main dish: beer-battered fish and chips £11.50. Two-course evening meal £16.50.*

Butcombe ~ Tenant Mark Walton ~ Real ale ~ Open 12-11; 12-10.30 Sun ~ Bar food 12-3, 5-9; 12-9 Sat; 12-8 Sun ~ Children welcome ~ Dogs allowed in bar

ROWBERROW
Swan

ST4458   Map 1

(01934) 852371 – butcombe.com/the-swan-inn-somerset
Off A38 S of A368 junction; BS25 1QL

Spacious dining pub opposite the village pond with refurbished bars, local ale, enjoyable food, helpful staff and seats in garden; good bedrooms

On the edge of the Mendip Hills, these former miner's cottages now house a bustling inn that's particularly popular with walkers and cyclists. The modernised interior has linked bar and dining rooms with beams, exposed stonework, some booth seating and animal head wallpaper in one part, plus a woodburning stove in a large fireplace and a mix of wooden chairs, banquettes and cushioned wall seating on bare boards. Friendly staff serve Butcombe Original plus guest ales, 30 gins, 11 whiskies and a decent range of wines by the glass. There's a good-sized garden with picnic-sets and a children's play area. The nine newly furnished bedrooms are warm and comfortable; four are dog-friendly and in a converted barn.

Well liked food includes mussels in cider, leeks and bacon with Butcombe beer soda breads, potted chicken, ham and herb terrine with sticky onion marmalade, flatbread pizzas, lentil, cauliflower and spinach curry with soya yoghurt and crispy chickpeas, burger with toppings and chips, trout fishcakes with café de paris butter, spinach and poached egg, 28-day dry-aged steak with garlic butter and trimmings, and puddings such as sticky date and toffee pudding with toffee sauce and rum and raisin ice-cream. *Benchmark main dish: British cured meat and cheese sourdough pizza £11.95. Two-course evening meal £20.00.*

Butcombe ~ Manager Sam Priest ~ Real ale ~ Open 10-10; 9.30am-10pm Sat; 9.30am-7pm Sun ~ Bar food 12-3, 6-9 Mon-Fri; 9.30-11am, 12-3pm, 6-9pm Sat; 9.30-11am, 12-6pm Sun ~ Children welcome ~ Dogs allowed in bar & bedrooms ~ Bedrooms: £110

STANTON WICK
ST6162 Map 2

Carpenters Arms ⭐ ♟ 🛏

(01761) 490202 – www.the-carpenters-arms.co.uk

Village signposted off A368, just W of junction with A37 S of Bristol; BS39 4BX

Bustling, friendly dining pub with pleasing food, helpful staff and fine choice of drinks; comfortable bedrooms

Converted from a row of old miners' cottages and nicely situated in the heart of the Chew Valley, this attractive stone inn is full of character. It was refurbished in 2019 and the various bars and dining areas have button-back wall banquettes, sofas and armchairs, wooden and leather dining chairs around all sorts of tables, smart curtains, stripped stone walls, two woodburning stoves and a big log fire in an inglenook. Friendly, helpful staff serve Butcombe Original, Bath Gem and Sharps Doom Bar on handpump, 14 wines by the glass (and some interesting bin ends) and several malt whiskies; TV in the snug. The front terrace has picnic-sets and there are pretty flower beds, hanging baskets and tubs. The 13 bedrooms are quiet and comfortable and breakfasts are very good. There are enjoyable walks in the peaceful surrounding countryside.

Good food includes sandwiches, vegan pesto hummus with roasted seeds and flatbread, whole baked camembert with rosemary and honey, macaroni and cauliflower cheese, monkfish and tiger prawn Malaysian curry, cod and prawn fishcake with beetroot, fennel and watercress salad, roasted red pepper salad with avocado, date molasses and pumpkin seeds, roast chicken with smoked bacon, mushrooms, asparagus and parmesan mash, and puddings such as lemon and thyme possett and chocolate, orange and rum torte. *Benchmark main dish: cider-battered fish and chips £14.00. Two-course evening meal £22.00.*

Buccaneer Holdings ~ Manager Simon Pledge ~ Real ale ~ Open 11-11; 12-10.30 Sun ~ Bar food 12-2.30, 6-9.30; 12-9 Sun ~ Restaurant ~ Children welcome ~ Dogs allowed in bar ~ Bedrooms: £110

WATERROW
Rock 🍴🛏

ST0525 Map 1

(01984) 623293 – www.rockinnwaterrow.co.uk

B3227 Wiveliscombe–Bampton; TA4 2AX

Handsome inn with local ales, interesting food and a nice mix of customers; comfortable bedrooms

This 450-year-old pub on the southern fringes of Exmoor National Park is popular with both drinkers and diners – the atmosphere is easy-going and welcoming to all. The bar area has wheelback chairs and cushioned window seats around scrubbed kitchen tables on pale floorboards, sympathetic lighting and a woodburning stove in a stone fireplace. High black leather bar chairs line the copper-topped bar counter where they serve Otter Bitter, St Austell Tribute and a guest beer on handpump, 14 wines by the glass and local farm cider; TV, darts and board games. The elegant restaurant is up some steps with panelled walls painted pale grey, a large wicker stag's head and high-backed wooden chairs around chunky kitchen tables on more pale floorboards; there's also a snug with sofas and leather armchairs. In front of the building is a terrace with seating. Although parking by the inn is limited, there's more on the far side of the main road over the bridge. The eight bedrooms are tastefully furnished, warm and comfortable.

🌟🍴 First class food cooked by the landlord includes Somerset baked brie fondant, pan-fried wood pigeon breast with Ibérico chorizo, parsnip gnocchi with fresh spinach and baby leeks, veal sirloin grilled with wild mushrooms, hispi cabbage and truffle mash potatoes, cannon of lamb with creamed carrot, hispi cabbage and boulangère potatoes, Angus T-bone steak with red wine sauce and truffle chips, and puddings such as rhubarb crumble with Madagascan vanilla bean ice-cream and sticky toffee pudding with clotted cream. *Benchmark main dish: featherblade of beef with black garlic and treacle £17.00. Two-course evening meal £25.00.*

Free house ~ Licensees Daren and Ruth Barclay ~ Real ale ~ Open 6-11 Tues; 12-3, 6-11 Weds-Sat; 12-3 Sun; closed Mon ~ Bar food 6.30-9.30 Tues; 12-2, 6.30-9.30 Weds-Sat; 12-2 Sun ~ Restaurant ~ Children welcome ~ Children to be seated with adults ~ Dogs allowed in bar, restaurant & bedrooms ~ Bedrooms: £90

WRINGTON
Plough

ST4762 Map 2

(01934) 862871 – www.theploughatwrington.co.uk

2.5 miles off A370 Bristol–Weston, from bottom of Rhodiate Hill; BS40 5QA

Welcoming pub with bustling bar and two dining rooms, good food, well kept beer and seats outside

Set in a picturesque village and handy for both Cheddar Gorge and Bristol Airport, this is a much liked and well run pub. The bar is chatty and convivial with locals perched on stools against the counter where they keep Butcombe Original (the brewery is in the village), St Austell Tribute, Youngs Bitter and a guest on handpump and 18 wines by the glass, served by friendly and efficient staff. Two dining rooms (the one at the back has plenty of big windows overlooking the gazebo and garden) have open doorways, and throughout you'll find slate or wooden floors, beams and standing timbers, three winter fires, plenty of pictures on the planked or painted walls and all manner of high-backed leather, wooden dining or farmhouse chairs around tables of lots of different sizes. Also, fresh flowers, table skittles, a chest containing games. There are picnic-sets at the front and also on the back grass; boules. They hold a farmers' market on the second Friday of the month. This is sister pub to the Rattlebone at Sherston (Wiltshire). Disabled access and loos.

🍴 From a thoughtful menu, the food includes sandwiches, smoked haddock and mozzarella fishcakes with wilted spinach, caesar salad with chicken croquettes, grilled octopus with pho broth and warm Asian salad, sun-blushed tomato linguine with onion, chilli and garlic, burger with coleslaw and sweet potato fries, sirloin or gammon steak with chips, chicken or vegetable Thai green curry, and puddings such as lemon tart with raspberry sorbet and carrot cake with spiced raisin purée and vanilla ice-cream; Wednesday is steak night. *Benchmark main dish: pie of the day £12.50. Two-course evening meal £21.00.*

Youngs ~ Tenant Jason Read ~ Real ale ~ Open 12-3, 5-11 Mon-Thurs; 12-midnight Fri, Sat; 12-11 Sun ~ Bar food 12-2.30, 6-9.30; 12-5, 7-9 Sun ~ Restaurant ~ Children welcome ~ Dogs allowed in bar

Also Worth a Visit in Somerset

Besides the fully inspected pubs, you might like to try these pubs that have been recommended to us and described by readers. Do tell us what you think of them: feedback@goodguides.com

AXBRIDGE   ST4354
Lamb (01934) 732253
The Square; off A371 Cheddar–Winscombe; BS26 2AP Big rambling carpeted pub on the town square with heavy 15th-c beams and timbers, stone and roughcast walls, old settles and large stone fireplaces, unusual bar front with bottles set in plaster, two Butcombe beers and two guests, local ciders, well chosen wines and good coffee, enjoyable food (all day weekends) from sandwiches up; board games, table skittles and skittle alley, sports TV; children and dogs allowed, seats out at front and in small sheltered back garden, medieval King John's Hunting Lodge (NT) opposite, open all day.

BABCARY   ST5628
★ **Red Lion** (01458) 223230
Off A37 S of Shepton Mallett; 2 miles or so N of roundabout where A37 meets A303 and A372; TA11 7ED Handsome 17th-c thatched stone inn in pretty village; characterful and relaxed bar areas and dining room with large stone lion's head, dark red and ochre walls, nice mix of old furniture, exposed beams, flagstones and polished floorboards, woodburner and open fire; Exmoor, Otter and local guest, 18 wines by the glass, farm cider and cocktails, good food including pub classics and more restauranty choices, outdoor wood-fired pizza bar (summer weekends); newspapers, background music, board games, table skittles; children and dogs (in bar) welcome, six comfortable well equipped bedrooms in separate building, long garden with seating and play area, wheelchair access, handy for Fleet Air Museum and Haynes Motor Museum, open all day Fri-Sun.

BACKWELL   ST4969
George (01275) 462770
Farleigh Road; A370 W of Bristol; BS48 3PG Modernised and extended roadside dining pub (former coaching inn); enjoyable food in bar and restaurant from ciabattas to pizzas and daily specials, also a gluten-free menu, well kept Bath, Butcombe and St Austell, 19 wines by the glass; background music in some areas; children and dogs welcome, gravel terrace and lawn behind, seven bedrooms, open (and food) all day.

BARRINGTON   ST3918
Barrington Boar (01460) 259281
Opposite church; TA19 0JB Old stone-built dining pub in pretty village; good variety of well liked food (not Sun evening, Mon, Tues) from lunchtime sandwiches and light meals up, friendly helpful service, Exmoor, a beer badged for them and guests such as Bristol Beer Factory, Otter, Quantock and St Austell, Perry's cider, local gins, a good wine list including local varieties, updated interior with solid furnishings, wood and stone floors, logburners (boar's head above one); children and dogs welcome, picnic-sets out in front and in pleasant beer garden behind, four bedrooms, handy for Barrington Court (NT), open all day Sun till 9pm, closed lunchtimes Mon, Tues.

BARROW GURNEY   ST5367
Princes Motto (01275) 474608
B3130, just off A370/A38; BS48 3RY Cosy pub with Wadworths ales and guests such as Butcombe served from casks behind the bar, Weston's and Thatcher's ciders and nice wines by the glass, good food from lunchtime ciabattas and pub favourites to blackboard specials, also a vegan menu,

Thurs 'build your own pizza' and Fri fish and chips nights, log fire; children and dogs welcome, pleasant garden with terrace, handy for Bristol Airport, closed Sun evening and Mon, otherwise open all day.

BATCOMBE   ST6839
★**Three Horseshoes** (01749) 850359

Village signposted off A359 Bruton–Frome; BA4 6HE Handsome honey-stone inn with long narrow main room; beams, local pictures, built-in cushioned window seats and nice mix of tables, woodburner one end, open fire the other, Butcombe and guests, local ciders, around a dozen wines by the glass and several malt whiskies, well liked food (best to book, especially weekends), helpful friendly service, attractive stripped-stone dining room; children, walkers and dogs welcome, three simple but pretty bedrooms, lovely church next door, open all day Sat, till 6pm Sun, closed Mon.

BATH   ST7464
Bath Brew House (01225) 805609

James Street West; BA1 2BX Interesting spaciously converted pub visibly brewing its own James Street beers (brewery tours available), also guest ales and craft kegs, smallish menu from open kitchen, various events such as comedy nights and live music in upstairs room with own bar and sports TV; well behaved children and dogs allowed in some areas, sizeable split-level beer garden with covered eating area, summer barbecues, open (and food) all day Sat.

BATH   ST7565
Bell (01225) 460426

Walcot Street; BA1 5BW Long narrow split-level pub owned by the local community; nine real ales, traditional ciders and some basic good value food, lots of beer pump clips and gig notices, a couple of fires (one gas), bar billiards, table football and board games; packed and lively in the evening with regular live music and DJs; canopied garden, even has its own laundrette, open all day.

BATH   ST7564
★**Coeur de Lion** (01225) 463568

Northumberland Place, off High Street; BA1 5AR Tiny stained-glass-fronted single-room pub, simple, cosy and friendly, with candles and log-effect gas fire, well kept Abbey ales and guests, good well priced traditional food from snacks and baguettes up (vegetarian options), Christmas mulled wine, more room and loos upstairs; may be background music; tables out in charming flower-filled flagstoned pedestrian alley, open all day, food till 6pm.

BATH   ST7564
★**Crystal Palace** (01225) 482666

Abbey Green; BA1 1NW Spacious two-room Fullers pub; rugs on wood floors and comfortable mix of seating, panelled walls and groups of pictures, popular sensibly priced food from lunchtime sandwiches up, speedy friendly service, four well kept ales from plank-faced bar, log fire, garden room opening on to nice sheltered courtyard; background music, sports TV; children and dogs welcome, handy for Roman Baths and main shopping areas, open (and food) all day.

BATH   ST7464
Garricks Head (01225) 318368

St Johns Place/Westgate, beside Theatre Royal; BA1 1ET Tranquil and relaxed dining pub with good food including pre-theatre menu; bar with tall windows, wheelback and other chairs around wooden tables on bare boards, candles and a couple of sizeable brass chandeliers, gas-effect coal fire with fine silver meat domes on wall above, up to four interesting regional ales including house ale named for the pub from Stonehenge, real ciders and decent wines by the glass, proper cocktails, separate smartly set dining room; may be soft background jazz; children and dogs (in bar) welcome, pavement tables, open all day.

BATH   ST7464
Griffin (01225) 420919

Monmouth Street; BA1 2AP Nicely updated little corner pub now owned by St Austell; four well kept Bath and St Austell ales, craft beers and extensive range of spirits (particularly gins and tequilas), interesting freshly made food from small plates menu, good Sun roasts, friendly staff; children welcome, eight comfortably refurbished bedrooms, open all day, no food Sun evening, Mon, Tues.

BATH   ST7465
Hall & Woodhouse (01225) 469259

Old King Street; BA1 2JW Conversion of stone-fronted warehouse/auction rooms; big open-plan interior on two floors, steel girders and glass, palms and chandeliers, mix of modern and traditional furniture including old-fashioned iron-framed tables with large candles and some simple bench seating, parquet and slate floors, three Badger ales from full-length servery on the right, sweeping stairs up to another bar and eating area (disabled access via lift), roof terrace, decent choice of food from pub favourites to specials, helpful chatty staff; gets very busy with after-work drinkers when standing room only, open (and food) all day, closed Mon.

BATH   ST7465
★**Hop Pole** (01225) 446327

Albion Buildings, Upper Bristol Road; BA1 3AR Bustling family-friendly Bath/St Austell pub, their beers and guests kept well, decent wines by the glass and good choice of spirits, popular food from traditional favourites up in bar and former skittle alley restaurant, friendly helpful staff, settles and other pub furniture on bare boards in four linked areas; background music, quiz nights; dogs welcome, wheelchair access to main bar area only, pleasant two-level back courtyard, opposite Royal Victoria Park (great kids' play area), open all day (till sunset Sun).

BATH ST7465

★ **Marlborough** (01225) 423731

35 Marlborough Buildings/Weston Road; BA1 2LY Centrally placed busy pub; U-shaped bare-boards bar with flowers on tables, seating ranging from thick button-back wall seats to chapel, kitchen and high-backed dining chairs, a couple of ales such as Box Steam and Butcombe, traditional cider and lots of wines by the glass, well liked food from pub favourites up including some vegan choices, steak night, cheerful young staff; background music; children and dogs welcome, suntrap courtyard garden, open all day.

BATH ST7565

Pig & Fiddle (01225) 460868

Saracen Street; BA1 5BR Lively place (particularly weekends), recently refurbished, with four well kept Butcombe ales and fairly simple affordably priced food, friendly staff, bare-boards interior with two large open fires and collection of sporting memorabilia, steps up to bustling servery and little dining area, games part (darts and table football); live music and DJ nights, several TVs for sport; picnic-sets on big, heated terrace now made bigger, open all day, food till 8pm (6pm Sun).

BATH ST7565

Pulteney Arms (01225) 463923

Daniel Street/Sutton Street; BA2 6ND Cosy, cheerful and largely unspoilt 18th-c pub; Bath Gem, Timothy Taylors Landlord, Wye Valley HPA and two guests, Thatcher's cider, enjoyable freshly made food at sensible prices, traditional furniture on wooden floors, old gas lamps, woodburner and lots of Bath RFC memorabilia; background music, sports TV, darts; children (until 9pm) and dogs welcome, pavement tables and small back terrace, handy for Sydney Gardens and Holburne Museum, open all day Fri-Sun, no food Sun evening.

BATH ST7464

Raven (01225) 425045

Queen Street; BA1 1HE Small buoyant city-centre free house composed from two Georgian town houses; two well kept house ales from Blindmans and four guests, craft beers and one or two changing ciders, decent

wines by the glass too, limited choice of food including range of pies and sausages, quick friendly service, bare boards, some stripped stone and an open fire, newspapers, quieter upstairs bar; no under-14s or dogs; open (and food) all day.

BATH ST7364

Royal Oak (01225) 481409

Lower Bristol Road; near Oldfield Park station; BA2 3BW Friendly roadside pub with three of its own Ralphs beers (named after resident husky), Downton Chimera IPA and several guests, also bottled beers and range of ciders/perries, no food, two bare-boards bar areas with open fires; regular live music and monthly quiz; dogs welcome, side beer garden, open all day Fri-Sun, from 4pm other days.

BATH ST7464

Salamander (01225) 428889

John Street; BA1 2JL Busy city local with full range of well kept Bath ales, St Austell Tribute and good choice of wines by the glass, bare boards, black woodwork and ochre walls, popular food from sandwiches up (more choice evenings/weekends), friendly helpful young staff, upstairs restaurant with open kitchen; background music, daily papers; children till 8pm, no dogs, open all day (till 1am Fri, Sat), gets packed on Bath RFC days.

BATH ST7564

Sam Weller (01225) 474910

Upper Borough Walls; BA1 1RH Fairly simple little pub with four ales such as Abbey, Butcombe and St Austell, decent choice of wines by the glass and sensibly priced tasty food from sandwiches up, friendly service, cosy inside with big window to watch the world go by; light background music; open all day (till 6pm Sun).

BATH ST7565

★ **Star** (01225) 425072

Vineyards; The Paragon (A4), junction with Guinea Lane; BA1 5NA Unspoilt 16th-c city-centre pub with a real sense of its past, now tap for Abbey Ales with guests including Bass, several wines by the glass, 30 malt whiskies and Cheddar Valley cider; four small linked rooms served from single bar; many original features including traditional wall benches (one hard one known as Death Row), panelling, dim lighting and open fires, no food apart from rolls and Sun bar nibbles, live folk nights, Sun quiz, cribbage, shove-ha'penny and free snuff; children and dogs welcome, open all day.

Cribbage is a card game using a block of wood with holes for matchsticks or special pins to score with; regulars in cribbage pubs are usually happy to teach strangers how to play.

BATH   ST7365
Victoria Pub & Kitchen
(01225) 422563 *Upper Bristol Road;
BA1 3AT* Opened-up and modernised
gastropub opposite Royal Victoria Park; bar/
kitchen area with a couple of easy chairs and
small dining section, two further rooms (one
down steps) with mix of furniture including
some bench tables and old metal chairs,
polished wood floors, pale grey walls and
painted panelling, reclaimed floorboards
used to clad one part, Butcombe, Sharps,
St Austell and a guest, Thatcher's ciders and
good wines, much liked food at fair prices
including weekday lunchtime/early evening
deal, friendly helpful staff; background
music; children and dogs welcome, partial
wheelchair access, disabled loo, small decked
terrace and raised beer garden, open all day,
food all day Fri-Sun.

BATH   ST7564
Volunteer Riflemans Arms
(01225) 425210 *New Bond Street Place;
BA1 1BH* Friendly little city-centre pub
with leather sofas and a few close-set tables,
wartime/military posters, open fire, four well
kept ales from maybe Butcombe, Exmoor and
Sharps, a couple of draught ciders and good
value tasty lunchtime food, small upstairs
dining room and roof terrace; background
music; pavement tables, open all day.

BATH   ST7564
★White Hart (01225) 338053
Widcombe Hill; BA2 6AA Bistro-style pub
with scrubbed pine tables on bare boards,
candles and fresh flowers, good imaginative
if not cheap food, well kept Butcombe from
traditional panelled counter, proper cider
and plenty of wines by the glass, quick
friendly service; background and occasional
live music outside in summer; children and
dogs welcome, pretty beer garden, four
bedrooms (some sharing bathroom) and
dorm rooms at good rates, open all day
(Sun till 5pm).

BATHFORD   ST7866
Crown (01225) 852426
*Bathford Hill, towards Bradford-on-
Avon, by Batheaston roundabout and
bridge; BA1 7SL* Bistro pub with good
blackboard food (some French-influenced,
some more traditional); ales such as Bath,
Sharps and Timothy Taylors, nice wines,
friendly service; newspapers, board games;
children and dogs welcome, tables out in
front and in back garden with pétanque,
open all day.

BICKNOLLER   ST1139
Bicknoller Inn (01984) 656234
Church Lane; TA4 4EW Welcoming old
thatched pub nestling below the Quantocks;
traditional flagstoned front bar with plenty
to look at from horsebrasses to contemporary
artwork, side room and large back restaurant
with open kitchen, popular food from pub
favourites up, Tues fish and chips night, Sun
carvery (booking advised), friendly helpful
service, four well kept Palmers ales and a
couple of real ciders, skittle alley; children
and dogs (in bar) welcome, courtyard and
nice back garden, boules, attractive village,
open all day weekends.

BLAGDON HILL   ST2118
Lamb & Flag (01823) 421893
4 miles S of Taunton; TA3 7SL
Atmospheric beamed pub with traditional
furniture including some slab-topped tables
on bare boards or flagstones, woodburner
in two-way fireplace, three changing ales,
such as Black Bear, Exmoor and Otter,
three local ciders, decent wines by the glass
and a good choice of gins, good reasonably
priced home-made food (not Sun evening)
from sandwiches up, helpful friendly
service, galleried upstairs area, skittle alley;
background and occasional live music;
children and dogs welcome, picnic-sets in
nice garden with Taunton Vale views, open
all day.

BLEADON   ST3457
Queens Arms (01934) 812080
*Just off A370 S of Weston; Celtic Way;
BS24 0NF* Popular 16th-c beamed village
pub with enjoyable reasonably priced
food from lunchtime baguettes to steaks,
Butcombe and other well kept ales, friendly
service, stripped-stone back bar with
woodburner, winged settles and sturdy tables,
flagstoned restaurant; children and dogs
welcome, partial wheelchair access, picnic-
sets on pretty terrace, open all day, no food
Sun evening, Mon.

BRADFORD-ON-TONE   ST1722
White Horse (01823) 461239
*Fairly near M5 junction 26, off A38
towards Taunton; TA4 1HF* Popular
17th-c family-run village pub across from
the church; ample helpings of enjoyable
good value food from fairly pubby menu
including blackboard specials and weekday
light lunch deal, friendly helpful staff, well
kept ales such as Exeter, Hanlons, Otter
and St Austell, bare-boards bar with leather
sofas and armchair by woodburner, linked
dining areas; background and occasional
live music, Mon quiz, skittle alley; children
and dogs (in bar) welcome, picnic-sets in
nice garden (maybe Percy the peacock),
unusual glass pub sign, closed Sun evening,
Mon lunchtime.

BRISTOL   ST5773
Albion (0117) 973 3522
Boyces Avenue, Clifton; BS8 4AA Popular
former 17th-c coaching house tucked away in
backstreet courtyard; refurbished interior on
two floors (private dining upstairs), enjoyable
food from sandwiches and sharing plates up

including Mon steak night, well kept Bath and St Austell ales, lots of wines by the glass and good choice of other drinks, cheerful attentive service; background music; children and dogs welcome, tables and heaters out in front, open all day, food till 4pm Sun.

BRISTOL ST5773

Alma (0117) 973 5171

Alma Vale Road, Clifton; BS8 2HY
Two-bar pub with Butcombe Original, St Austell Tribute and two guests, Aspall's and Thatcher's ciders and several wines by the glass, good range of whiskies too, well liked imaginative food along with more standard choices including pizzas and good Sun roasts, friendly hard-working staff, dark panelled traditionally furnished front bars with wood flooring, more contemporary back room with bright modern wallpaper and local artwork, thriving upstairs theatre (10% food discount for ticket holders); background music (live Sun), easy wheelchair access to ground floor (no disabled loo), small paved terrace behind (closed late evening), open all day.

BRISTOL ST5873

Bank (0117) 930 4691

John Street; BS1 2HR Small proper single-bar pub, centrally placed (but off the beaten track) and popular with office workers; four changing local ales (may include a porter), a couple of real ciders and enjoyable well priced food till 4pm including sandwiches, burgers and one or two unusual choices, good Sun lunch too, comfortable bench seats, newspapers, books on shelf above fireplace; background and regular live music, sports TV, Tues quiz; children and dogs welcome, wheelchair access, tables under umbrellas in paved courtyard, open all day (till 1am Thurs-Sat).

BRISTOL ST5972

Barley Mow (0117) 930 4709

Barton Road; The Dings; BS2 0LF
Late 19th-c Bristol Beer Factory pub in old industrial area close to the floating harbour; up to eight well kept changing ales, excellent selection of craft kegs and bottled beers, proper cider and decent choice of wines by the glass, enjoyable good value food (not Sun evening) from short menu catering for vegetarians and vegans, cheerful chatty staff, wood floors, off-white walls and blue half-panelling, cushioned wall seats and pubby furniture, various odds and ends dotted about, open fire in brick fireplace; Tues quiz; disabled access, open all day (till 9pm Sun).

BRISTOL ST5872

Beer Emporium (0117) 379 0333

King Street opposite the Old Vic; BS1 4EF Unusual staircase down to bar-restaurant in vaulted cellars; long stone-faced counter under stained-glass skylight,

12 regularly changing cask ales as well as numerous craft beers (tasters offered) plus over 150 in bottles from around the world, good selection of malt whiskies and other spirits, interesting wine list, coffees and teas, Italian food including range of pizzas (vegetarians/vegans catered for), cheerful chatty staff; some live music; wheelchair access via lift, disabled loos, open (and food) all day (till 2am Mon-Sat), can get crowded; beer shop upstairs.

BRISTOL ST5872

BrewDog (0117) 927 9258

Baldwin Street, opposite church; BS1 1QW Corner bar serving own BrewDog beers and guests from other craft breweries (draught and bottled), tasters offered by knowledgeable young staff, limited but interesting selection of bar snacks and pizzas, starkly modern feel with exposed brick, stainless-steel furniture and granite surfaces, can get noisily busy; dogs welcome, children until 8pm, wheelchair access, open all day till midnight (1am Thurs-Sat).

BRISTOL ST5874

Chums (0117) 973 1498

Chandos Road; BS6 6PF Micropub in former corner shop; mismatched furniture on boarded floor, painted half-panelling and lots of local artwork for sale, pine-planked bar with ales from breweries such as Butcombe, Cheddar, Palmers and XT, real ciders/perries and range of bottled Belgian beers, also good quality wines and interesting spirits, some snacky food, friendly chatty atmosphere (mobile phones discouraged); live music Sat and alternating with quiz night Weds; dogs welcome, wheelchair access using ramp (staff will help), disabled loo, open all day Fri-Sun, from 4pm other days.

BRISTOL ST5872

Commercial Rooms (0117) 927 9681

Corn Street; BS1 1HT Spacious colonnaded Wetherspoons (former early 19th-c merchants' club) in good location; main part with lofty stained-glass domed ceiling, large oval portraits of Bristol notables and gas lighting, comfortable quieter back room with ornate balcony, note the unusual wind gauge above horseshoe servery; good changing choice of real ales, local ciders and expanding range of gins, nice chatty bustle (busiest weekend evenings), their usual food and low prices; ladies' with chesterfields and open fire; children welcome until 9pm (8pm Fri), no dogs, side wheelchair access and disabled facilities, open all day from 8am, and till late Fri, Sat.

BRISTOL ST5872

Cornubia (0117) 925 4415

Temple Street opposite fire station; BS1 6EN Recently refurbished tucked-away 18th-c pub with up to eight real ales including a good locally brewed house beer, also interesting bottled beers, farm ciders and perry, snacky food such as pasties and pork pies, friendly helpful service, walls and ceilings covered in pump clips, union jacks and other memorabilia, open fire and an aquarium for turtles; weekly quiz, live jazz; dogs welcome, not suitable for wheelchairs, picnic-sets in secluded front beer garden (summer barbecues and jazz Sun afternoons), boules pitch, closed Sun evening, otherwise open all day.

BRISTOL ST5772

Cottage (0117) 921 5256

Baltic Wharf, Cumberland Road; BS1 6XG Buzzing Butcombe waterfront pub dating from 1868 with great views across the harbour; bright nautical theme with blue and white tiles and bare wood flooring, blue panelled walls and a mix of typical pub furniture, three Butcombe ales, local cider, cocktails and good selection of wines by the glass, food includes pub classics, sharing dishes, fresh fish/seafood and daily specials; children welcome; open all day, food all day Fri, Sat.

BRISTOL ST5976

Drapers Arms

Gloucester Road; BS7 8TZ Welcoming one-room micropub in former draper's shop; up to eight well kept local and national beers tapped from the cask, proper ciders and decent wines by the glass, no food apart from bar snacks; donation to charity box if you use a mobile phone; open from 5pm (midday Sat) till 9.30pm.

BRISTOL ST5773

Eldon House (0117) 922 1271

Lower Clifton Hill, Clifton; BS8 1BT Extended terrace-end Clifton pub; mix of wooden tables and chairs on bare boards, circular stone-walled dining area with glazed roof, snug with original stained glass and half-door servery, well kept Bath plus guests (maybe Arbor, Box Steam, Bristol Beer Company or St Austell) and several wines by the glass, enjoyable food from lunchtime snacks to daily changing evening menu (pop-up kitchens), friendly staff; background and regular live music, other events including Mon quiz; children welcome till 8pm, dogs in bar, open (and some food) all day.

BRISTOL ST5872

Famous Royal Naval Volunteer

07487 242300 *King Street; BS1 4EF* 17th-c pub in cobbled street known to locals as 'the Volley', very wide range of draught and bottled British beers, ciders/perries and a good choice of wines by the glass, friendly knowledgeable staff, good interesting food in back restaurant; weekend live music, sports TV; dogs welcome, terrace seating, open all day.

BRISTOL ST5876

Gloucester Old Spot

(0117) 924 7693 *Kellaway Avenue; BS6 7YQ* Popular opened-up family-run pub; four well kept ales such as Butcombe, Exmoor, Ringwood, St Austell and Timothy Taylors from horseshoe servery, 16 decent wines by the glass and enjoyable reasonably priced food including pizzas and burgers, friendly prompt service, back bar and large parquet-floored dining lounge opening on to verandah and AstroTurf beer garden; background music, Tues quiz; children and dogs welcome, wheelchair access using portable ramp (staff will help, no disabled loos), play area with wendy house, open all day from 9am for breakfast.

BRISTOL ST5872

Golden Guinea (0117) 987 2034

Guinea Street; BS1 6SX Steps up to cosy backstreet pub with well kept changing ales, interesting craft beers and proper ciders, simple bargain home-made food, friendly staff, pews, wing armchairs, leather sofas and farmhouse tables on bare boards, some flock wallpaper and contemporary street art; live music (including Tues folk night), sports TV; dogs welcome, seats out in front and behind, closed till 4pm Mon-Weds, otherwise open all day from noon (2pm Sun).

BRISTOL ST5772

Grain Barge (0117) 929 9347

Hotwell Road; BS8 4RU Converted 100-ft barge owned by Bristol Beer Factory, their ales kept well and fair priced food (all day weekends) including good sandwiches, burgers and Sun roasts, great harbour views from seats out on top deck, tables and sofas in wood floor bar below, also a 'hold bar' for events and functions; children welcome, open all day.

BRISTOL ST5873

Green Man (0117) 925 8062

Alfred Place, Kingsdown; BS2 8HD Cosy local with country pub feel; bare boards and dark woodwork, two well kept Dawkins ales and four mostly local guests, real cider, several wines by the glass and around 60 gins, food served Weds-Fri evenings only including good burgers, also popular Sun roasts from 12.30pm, friendly staff; background and regular live music, Weds quiz; children and dogs welcome, wheelchair access with help, open from 4pm Mon-Thurs, 2pm Fri and Sat, midday Sun.

If we know a pub is cash-only, we say so. This is very rare: almost everywhere accepts credit and debit cards now.

BRISTOL ST5873
Horts City Tavern (0117) 925 2520
Broad Street; BS1 2EJ Imposing 18th-c
Youngs pub, their well kept beers along
with the likes of Bath and St Austell, good
fairly priced food (all day Fri-Sun) including
sharing boards and burgers, spacious interior
with big windows overlooking street, some
raised sections and side rooms, old pictures
of the city, 26-seat cinema at back (free film
Weds evening); background music, sports
TVs in cobbled courtyard, open all day
and at its busiest lunchtime/early evening.

BRISTOL ST5977
Inn on the Green (0117) 952 1391
Filton Road (A38), Horfield; BS7 0PA
Busy open-plan pub with up to 13 changing
ales, half a dozen ciders and good selection
of whiskies/gins, enjoyable generously served
food including daily deals, helpful friendly
staff, wood or slate floors, lots of mirrors
and old prints, modern pub furniture along
with sofas and armchairs, more screened
seating in former skittle alley dining area;
bar billiards and darts; children and dogs
welcome, disabled access/facilities, beer
garden with sheltered pool table and summer
table tennis, open (and food) all day.

BRISTOL ST5774
Jersey Lily (0117) 973 8590
Whiteladies Road; BS8 2SB Compact
corner pub with matt-black frontage; well
kept Wickwar ales and guests, decent wines
and good range of gins, enjoyable reasonably
priced food from shortish menu including
lunchtime ciabattas, sharing plates and
range of burgers, busy but attentive service,
painted dados and polished wood floors, some
high tables and stools, step up to part with
sofas and easy chairs; live acoustic music
Thurs, Sun quiz, sports TV; partial wheelchair
access, pavement seats and awning, decked
side area through arch, open all day.

BRISTOL ST5874
Kensington Arms (0117) 944 6444
Stanley Road; BS6 6NP Dining pub (aka
the Kenny) in centre of Redland; highly
regarded food at fair prices from chef-
patron, well kept Bristol Beer Factory ales
and guests, Thatcher's cider and plenty of
wines by the glass from comprehensive list,
happy hour 4.30-6.30pm Mon-Thurs, friendly
attentive staff; background music; children
and dogs welcome, disabled facilities (no
wheelchair access to dining room, but can
eat in bar), heated front terrace, open all day
except Mon.

BRISTOL ST5972
Kings Head (0117) 929 2338
Victoria Street; BS1 6DE Welcoming and
relaxed little 17th-c pub; traditional bar
with big front window and splendid mirrored
bar-back, corridor to cosy panelled snug

with serving hatch, toby jugs on joists, old-
fashioned local prints and photographs, five
well kept local ales including Fullers, Harveys and
Wye Valley, no food; a few pavement tables,
open all day.

BRISTOL ST5972
Knights Templar (0117) 930 8710
The Square; BS1 6DG Glass and steel
Wetherspoons very handy for Temple Meads
station; spacious carpeted room with raised
area, great range of beers from well stocked
bar, their usual reasonably priced food served
from breakfast till late, helpful staff; lots
of TVs; children welcome, disabled access/
loos, plenty of outside seating, open all day
from 8am.

BRISTOL ST5276
Lamplighters (0117) 279 3754
*End of Station Road, Shirehampton;
BS11 9XA* Popular 18th-c riverside
pub; well kept Bath, St Austell and a
guest, Thatcher's ciders, teas and coffees,
competitively priced fairly traditional food
(not Sun evening) including children's
choices, blackboard specials and Tues OAP
lunch deal, modern bar furniture on carpet
or bare boards, some faux leather sofas
and armchairs, pastel walls with darker
greeny-blue dados, bold patterned wallpaper
here and there, mezzanine dining area and
cellar bar (not always open); occasional live
music; wheelchair access, disabled loos/baby
changing, picnic-sets on paved front terrace,
limited parking nearby (beware high spring
tides), riverside walks, open all day.

BRISTOL ST5976
Lazy Dog (0117) 924 4809
Ashley Down Road; BS7 9JR Popular
local with two bar areas (one upstairs), ales
such as Bath, Bristol Beer Factory, Purity
and Wye Valley, local ciders, interesting
wines and good range of spirits, well liked
food including some unusual dishes, helpful
chatty staff, charcoal grey interior with wood
panelled alcoves, white marble-effect bar
counter, leather wall benches, sofas and
armchairs on light wood floors, family room
with metal furniture (children till 7pm); quiz
and comedy nights; dogs welcome, disabled
access/loos, seats out at front and in partly
decked back garden, open all day.

BRISTOL ST5772
Nova Scotia (0117) 929 7994
*Baltic Wharf, Cumberland Basin;
BS1 6XJ* Welcoming old local on south
side of floating harbour with views to
Clifton and Avon Gorge; five ales including
Caledonian and guests, Thatcher's ciders,
generous helpings of enjoyable pub food
(not Sun evening) from doorstep sandwiches
to blackboard specials, four linked
areas with striking turquoise, ochre and
brown colour scheme, nautical charts as
wallpaper, mahogany and mirrors, maritime

photographs and some murals, welcoming relaxed atmosphere; Mon folk night; wheelchair access with help through snug's door, no disabled loo, plenty of tables out by water, open all day.

BRISTOL ST5872

Old Duke (0117) 401 9661

King Street; BS1 4ER Corner pub named after Duke Ellington and festooned with jazz posters, good jazz/blues bands nightly and Sun lunchtime, up to six real ales such as Bath and Otter and a couple of ciders, simple food, usual pub furnishings; tables on pedestrianised cobbled street, open all day (till 1am Fri, Sat), gets packed evenings.

BRISTOL ST5872

Old Fish Market (0117) 921 1515

Baldwin Street; BS1 1QZ Popular Fullers pub in imposing brick-built former fish market; well kept ales, craft beers, a dozen wines by the glass and fine range of whiskies/gins from handsome wooden counter, enjoyable food including pizzas and pub classics, friendly relaxed atmosphere; background music, Sun live jazz from 7pm, sports TVs; children and dogs welcome, open all day (food all day weekends).

BRISTOL ST5772

Orchard 07405 360994

Hanover Place, Spike Island; BS1 6XT Friendly corner local with around five well kept stillaged ales including Otter, St Austell and more than 20 ciders/perries (they've been selling traditional ciders for more than 180 years), simple lunchtime food such as rolls, pasties and pork pies, woodburner, piano; Mon blues jam and Tues jazz; tables out in front, handy for SS *Great Britain*, open all day.

BRISTOL ST5672

Portcullis (0117) 973 0270

Wellington Terrace; BS8 4LE Compact pub in Regency terrace close to Clifton Suspension Bridge; five well kept ales including three from Dawkins, traditional cider and good range of wines and spirits, low-priced pubby food (not Weds, Thurs), friendly service, flame-effect gas fire, dark wood and usual pubby furniture, upstairs room leading to beer garden; occasional acoustic live music, board games; dogs welcome, children in upstairs room; tricky wheelchair access, open all day Sat, Sun, closed lunchtimes Mon-Thurs (also Fri in winter).

BRISTOL ST5772

Pump House (0117) 927 2229

Merchants Road; BS8 4PZ Spacious well converted dockside building (former 19th-c pumping station); charcoal-grey brickwork, tiled floors and high ceilings, good locally sourced food in bar and smart candlelit mezzanine restaurant, Butcombe

and a couple of guests such as Bristol Beer Factory, decent wines from comprehensive list and over 400 gins, good selection of rums and whiskies too, friendly staff and cheerful atmosphere; waterside tables, open all day (till midnight Thurs-Sat).

BRISTOL ST5872

Riverstation (0117) 914 4434

The Grove; opposite Hole in the Wall pub; BS1 4RB Modern harbourside bar-restaurant converted some years ago from a former police building; light and airy split-level bar/dining area with tiled and polished wood floors, mix of seating including sofas and squashy banquettes, good views from french windows opening on to waterside terrace, Youngs ales, Orchard Pig cider and several international bottled beers, good selection of wines, spirits and cocktails too, spacious upstairs restaurant with high curved ceiling and lots of glass, further terraces overlooking the water, well liked food from interesting varied menu including British classics and sharing boards, helpful staff; background music; limited wheelchair access, open (and food) all day.

BRISTOL ST5972

Seven Stars (0117) 927 2845

Thomas Lane; BS1 6JG Unpretentious one-room real ale pub near harbour (and associated with Thomas Clarkson and slave trade abolition), popular with students and local office workers; up to eight well kept changing ales (20 from a featured county on first Mon-Thurs of the month), some interesting malts and bourbons, dark wood and bare boards, old local prints and photographs, no food – can bring in takeaways; weekend acoustic music, pool, games machine; dogs welcome, disabled access (but narrow alley with uneven cobbles and cast-iron kerbs), open all day.

BRISTOL ST5872

Small Bar

King Street; BS1 4DZ Bustling real ale/craft beer pub with up to 31 cask and keg choices including own Left Handed Giant, all served in smaller glasses (up to two-thirds of a pint), good range of bottled beers too, enjoyable food such as burgers and hotdogs along with vegetarian/vegan choices, bare boards and flagstones, roughly exposed brickwork here and there and wood plank walls, some barrel tables and a couple of old fireplaces, upstairs area with armchairs, sofas and shelves of books; background music; cards only, no cash; open all day (till 1am Fri, Sat).

BRISTOL ST6375

Snuffy Jacks Ale House

(0117) 965 5158 *Fishponds Road; BS16 3TE* Micropub in former stationers; up to eight cask-tapped ales, real ciders and some good quality gins from planked servery, friendly knowledgeable staff, mismatching furniture including old church pews on wood-strip floor, vibrant blue walls hung with local artwork, bare pendant lighting; quiz, no mobile phones or food (bar nibbles Sun); dogs welcome, wheelchair access, open all day Sat, till 4.30pm Sun and from 5pm weekdays.

BRISTOL ST5872
Three Tuns (0117) 329 4310
St Georges Road; BS1 5UR Popular old ochre-coloured pub just behind City Hall; around five real ales including local Arbor, four craft kegs and interesting selection of bottled beers, also local ciders and good range of spirits, snacky food along with decent burgers and Sun roasts, prompt service, L-shaped bar with pine tables on bare boards, a couple of small leather sofas in alcoves, open fire in cast-iron fireplace with mirror above; background and live music, other events such as quiz, magic and movie nights; dogs welcome, wheelchair access (no disabled loo), steps down to small covered and heated terrace, near cathedral, no food Sun evening, closed Mon.

BRISTOL ST5971
Victoria Park (0117) 330 6043
Raymend Road; BS3 4QW Brick-fronted family dining pub in hilly residential part of the city, welcoming and friendly, with large opened-up L-shaped interior, mix of furniture including long refectory tables and old pews on stripped-wood floors, dark-grey walls hung with local artwork, modern pendant lighting, white tiled back bar with folding glass doors to splendid tiered garden (rooftop views over to Dundry Hill), three changing ales, Weston's ciders and good choice of other drinks, popular food from interesting blackboard menu (booking advised weekends), also sandwiches and pizzas; background music, quiz nights and book club; dogs welcome, tricky wheelchair access and no disabled loos, nearby parking at a premium, open all day.

BRISTOL ST5973
Volunteer (0117) 955 8498
New Street, near Cabot Circus; BS2 9DX Tucked-away local with good choice of changing ales/craft beers, a couple of ciders and decent wines by the glass, pop-up kitchens along with popular Sun roasts, friendly relaxed atmosphere; live music and beer festivals; children and dogs welcome, walled garden behind, open from 4pm Tues-Fri, from noon Sat, 1-9pm Sun, closed Mon.

BRISTOL ST5976
Wellington (0117) 951 3022
Gloucester Road, Horfield (A38); BS7 8UR Updated and opened-up 1920s red-brick pub on edge of Horfield Common; well kept Bath and St Austell, craft beers, local cider and appealing choice of other drinks including range of gins, enjoyable reasonably priced food till 10pm, pleasant efficient service, separate dining area opening on to sunny paved terrace and grassy beer garden; background music, drop-down screens for major sports, pool; children and dogs welcome, wheelchair access from back door (or front using ramp), disabled loos, popular boutique bedrooms (best to book early), open all day (from 8am weekends for breakfast).

BRISTOL ST5872
Wild Beer (0117) 329 4997
Gaol Ferry Steps, Wapping Wharf, behind the M Shed Museum; BS1 5WE Busy bar in new development overlooking the old docks; more than 20 craft beers (including Wild Beer) listed on blackboards and served in third, half and two-thirds of a pint glasses (tasters offered), interesting wines and good selection of whiskies/gins, reasonably priced food from snacks up, cheerful helpful staff, flagstones, pale green walls and floor-to-ceiling windows, exposed ducting and a large mural on one wall, a couple of steps up to dining area with open kitchen; background music; children welcome, disabled access/facilities, split-level terrace with deckchairs and picnic-sets, parking nearby difficult, closed Mon, Tues.

BROADWAY ST3215
Bell (01460) 52343
Broadway Lane; TA19 9RG Welcoming 18th-c stone-built village pub; opened-up interior with flagstones and log fires, enjoyable fairly priced locally sourced food, including wood-fired pizzas, Bath, Otter and St Austell ales, decent choice of wines (11 by the glass) and some interesting local gins, friendly attentive service; live band first Sun of month; children and dogs welcome, tables on front walled terrace, open all day (from 9am for breakfast Fri, Sat).

BURROW BRIDGE ST3530
King Alfred (01823) 698379
Main Road, by the bridge; TA7 0RB Old-fashioned pub with relaxed friendly atmosphere in flagstoned bar, three well kept ales such as Bristol Beer Factory, Butcombe and Otter, local ciders and decent wines by the glass, good generously served food from pub standards up including daily specials, comfortable dining room upstairs with view over River Parrett and Somerset Levels, roof terrace; live music and quiz nights; children and dogs welcome, self-catering cottage, open all day (till 9pm Sun).

BUTLEIGH ST5133
Rose & Portcullis (01458) 850287
Sub Road/Barton Road; BA6 8TQ Welcoming stone-built country pub with enjoyable good value home-made food (not Sun evening), four well kept ales and good range of local ciders, helpful friendly staff,

bar and airy dining extension; sports TV; children and dogs welcome, tables outside, closed Mon and Tues.

CASTLE CARY   ST6432
George (01963) 350761
Just off A371 Shepton Mallet–Wincanton; Market Place; BA7 7AH Old-fashioned thatched country-town hotel (former 15th-c coaching inn); popular front bar with big inglenook, bistro-bar and restaurant, enjoyable food from sandwiches up, Timothy Taylors Landlord, Wadworths 6X and a changing real ale and decent wines by the glass, friendly staff; children and dogs welcome, 17 bedrooms (some in courtyard), open all day.

CATCOTT   ST3939
Crown (01278) 722288
Off A39 W of Street; Nidon Lane, via Brook Lane; TA7 9HQ Roomy traditional old pub just outside the village; welcoming landlord and staff, enjoyable food including good Sun carvery (booking advised), three real ales such as Butcombe, Dartmoor and Exmoor, decent wines by the glass, cosy area by log fire; skittle alley and traditional pub games; children and dogs welcome, picnic-sets and play area out behind, closed Mon lunchtime.

CHARLTON HORETHORNE ST6623
★ ## Kings Arms (01963) 220281
B3145 Wincanton–Sherborne; DT9 4NL Bustling rather smart 19th-c inn; main bar with assortment of local art (all for sale) on dark walls, carved wooden dining chairs and pine pews around mix of tables, slate floor and logburner, cosy room off with sofas, dining room and more formal back restaurant, Butcombe Bitter and a couple of guests, local cider, 16 wines by the glass and decent range of whiskies/gins, good up-to-date food served by efficient friendly staff; children and dogs (in bar) welcome, attractive back courtyard with modern seating under parasols, croquet, ten comfortable well equipped bedrooms, good breakfast, open all day.

CHARLTON MUSGROVE   ST7229
Smithy (01963) 824899
B3081, 5 miles SE of Bruton; about a mile off A303; BA9 8HG Restored 18th-c pub under friendly licensees; bar with stripped stone, heavy beams and inglenook woodburner, rugs on flagstone/concrete floor, quirky mismatched furniture (some tables made from old cheeseboards), ales such as Abbott, Greene King and Ruddles from plank-fronted servery, well liked uncomplicated food (not Sun evening), intimate dining area overlooking garden, restaurant in former

---

skittle alley; background and monthly live music, quiz nights, TV for major sports; children and dogs welcome, open all day.

CHEDDAR   ST4653
White Hart (01934) 741261
The Bays; BS27 3QN Welcoming village local at the bottom of Cheddar Gorge; well kept beers from the likes of Butcombe, Cheddar and St Austell, traditional cider and enjoyable competitively priced food from good ploughman's to Sun carvery, log fire; live music, quiz third Weds of month; children and dogs welcome, picnic-sets out at front and in back garden with play area, open (and food) all day.

CHEW MAGNA   ST5861
★ ## Pony & Trap (01275) 332627
Knowle Hill, New Town; from B3130 in village, follow Bishop Sutton, Bath signpost; BS40 8TQ Michelin-starred dining pub in nice rural spot near Chew Valley Lake; excellent food from snacks and some lunchtime pubby choices through to beautifully presented expensive restaurant dishes (must book), professional friendly service, Butcombe, Cheddar and Sharps ales, extensive wine list and good choice of other drinks including cocktails, front bar with cushioned wall seats and built-in benches on parquet, old range in snug area on left, dark plank panelling and housekeeper's chair in corner, lovely pasture views from two-level back dining area with white tables on slate flagstones; children welcome, dogs in bar, modern furniture on back terrace, picnic-sets on grass with chickens in runs below, good local walks.

CHEWTON MENDIP   ST5953
Waldegrave Arms (01761) 241384
High Street (A39); BA3 4LL Friendly roadside village pub run by the same family for over 30 years; traditional food from sandwiches up including Sun roasts, four well kept ales from maybe Butcombe, Cottage and Slaters; quiz nights and darts leagues; dogs welcome in bar, colourful window boxes and hanging baskets, flower-filled garden behind, open (and food) all day Sun.

CHISELBOROUGH   ST4614
Cat Head (01935) 881231
Cat Street; leave A303 on A356 towards Crewkerne; take the third left (at 1.4 miles) signed Chiselborough, then left after 0.2 miles; TA14 6TT Character 15th-c hamstone pub with bar and two dining areas, flagstones, mullioned windows and two permanently lit woodburners (one in fine inglenook), well executed fairly traditional food cooked by landlady, a couple of ales such as Butcombe and Sharps; classical

---

background music; children and dogs (in bar) welcome, picnic-sets in lovely back garden, closed Sun evening, Mon.

COMBE FLOREY   ST1531
★ **Farmers Arms** (01823) 432267
Off A358 Taunton–Williton, just N of main village turn-off; TA4 3HZ Popular 14th-c thatched and beamed pub well restored after severe fire damage; good food from interesting varied menu including Josper grills, at least four real ales such as Exmoor, Otter and Quantock, proper ciders and good range of whiskies and gins, friendly helpful staff; some live music; children and dogs welcome, tables out under parasols, maybe wood-fired pizzas in summer, Evelyn Waugh lived in the village, as did his son Auberon, open all day (till 7pm Sun).

COMBE HAY   ST7359
★ **Wheatsheaf** (01225) 833504
Village signposted off A367 or B3110 S of Bath; BA2 7EG Country dining pub with good imaginative food; sofas on dark flagstones by big fireplace in central part, other informal areas with high-backed dining chairs around chunky modern tables on parquet or coir matting, contemporary artwork and mirrors with colourful ceramic mosaic frames (many for sale), some interesting knick-knacks on windowsills, ales such as Butcombe and Otter, real cider and 17 wines by the glass from a good list, fine selection of malt whiskies too, efficient friendly service; background music; children and dogs welcome, two-level front garden with fine view over the church and valley; good surrounding walks, spacious comfortable bedrooms, closed Sun evening and Mon (except bank holidays).

COMPTON DANDO   ST6464
Compton Inn (01761) 490321
Court Hill; BS39 4JZ Welcoming stone-built village pub in lovely setting; enjoyable home-made food (not Sun evening), well kept Butcombe, Sharps and a guest, wood-floored bar with dining area at each end (one down a couple of steps), two-way woodburner in stone fireplace; TV; children, walkers and dogs welcome, picnic-sets out in front, garden behind with boules, open all day.

CONGRESBURY   ST4363
Old Inn (01934) 832270
Pauls Causeway, down Broad Street opposite The Cross; BS49 5DH Popular low-beamed and dimly lit 16th-c local; deep-set windows, flagstones and huge fireplaces, one with stove opening to both bar and dining area, mix of old furniture including pews and upholstered benches, leather ceiling straps, good choice of enjoyable reasonably priced pubby food (not Sun evening, Mon or Tues), well kept Youngs and a couple of guests tapped from casks, Thatcher's cider and ten decent wines by the

glass; children and dogs welcome, tables in back garden with pétanque, open all day.

CONGRESBURY   ST4363
★ **Plough** (01934) 877402
High Street (B3133); BS49 5JA Popular old-fashioned character local – a pub since the 1800s; half a dozen well kept changing West Country ales such as Butcombe, Cheddar, Otter St Austell and Yeovil, ciders from Orchard Pig and Thatcher's, quick friendly service, generous helpings of well cooked food (not Sun evening) including daily specials, several small interconnecting rooms off flagstoned main bar, mix of old and new furniture, built-in pine wall benches, old prints, photos, farm tools and some morris dancing memorabilia, log fires; Sun quiz; no children inside, dogs welcome, wheelchair access from car park, garden with rustic furniture and boules.

CORFE   ST2319
White Hart (01823) 421388
B3170 S of Taunton; TA3 7BU Traditional 17th-c village pub; enjoyable sensibly priced pubby food (not Tues) including vegetarian options, curry night last Thurs of the month (booking advised), well kept ales such as Butcombe, Marstons and Otter, beams, woodburner and open fire; bar billiards, skittle alley; children and dogs welcome, open all day Sat, closed Tues lunchtime.

CORSTON   ST6764
Wheatsheaf (01225) 874518
A39 towards Marksbury; BA2 9HB Old mansard-roofed roadside pub with good food from varied menu including popular Sun roasts (must book), well kept Butcombe and Sharps, Thatcher's cider, friendly attentive service, cosy bar with comfortable seating by roaring woodburner, smart restaurant; children and dogs welcome, open all day Fri-Sun, closed Mon.

CRANMORE   ST6643
Strode Arms (01749) 880450
West Cranmore; signed with pub off A361 Frome–Shepton Mallet; BA4 4QJ Pretty stone dining pub (former 15th-c farmhouse) overlooking village duck pond; rambling beamed rooms with log fires in handsome fireplaces, carpeted or flagstone floors, country furnishings, enjoyable generously served food from snacks up, four Wadworths ales, Thatcher's cider and decent wines by the glass, good friendly service; children, walkers and dogs welcome, seats on front terrace, well placed for East Somerset Railway (steam trains), open all day weekends.

CROSS   ST4254
New Inn (01934) 732455
A38 Bristol–Bridgwater, junction A371; BS26 2EE Steps up to popular old roadside pub with well kept Otter and several guest

beers (maybe Bath, Bristol Beer Factory, Cheddar, Sharps), good choice of enjoyable fairly traditional food from baguettes and baked potatoes up (booking advised), friendly service, more dining space upstairs; children and dogs welcome (resident cocker is called Guinness), newspapers and pub games; views from nice hillside garden with play area, Aug bank holiday mower racing/beer festival, open (and food) all day, till midnight Fri, Sat.

CROWCOMBE ST1336
Carew Arms (01984) 618631
Just off A358 Taunton–Minehead; TA4 4AD Interesting 17th-c beamed country inn attracting good mix of customers; hunting trophies, huge flagstones and good inglenook log fire in small lived-in front bar, up to five well kept ales such as Exmoor, Otter, Quantock and St Austell, real cider and enjoyable home-made food (not Sun evening in winter), friendly service; children (in dining room), walkers and dogs welcome, tables in good-sized garden, outside skittle alley, six bedrooms, open all day in summer (all day Fri-Sun winter).

CURRY RIVEL ST3925
Firehouse (01458) 887447
Church Street; TA10 0HE Stylishly renovated village pub; light beams, exposed stonework and log fires, lots of colourful touches and areas with distinctly different décors, cosy bar with tractor-seat stools at counter serving four real ales including Butcombe, decent wines and cocktails, pubby food along with pizzas from feature oven, lunchtime/early evening deal (Mon-Fri), friendly helpful young staff, various dining areas including upstairs raftered room and cellar bar with fine 14th-c vaulted ceiling; live music and quiz nights; children welcome, circular picnic-sets on paved terrace, open all day.

DINNINGTON ST4013
Dinnington Docks (01460) 52397
NE of village; Fosse Way; TA17 8SX Freshened-up large rural local; enjoyable home-made food (some choices available in smaller helpings), well kept Butcombe and guests, farm ciders, friendly attentive staff, memorabilia of former railway and canal dock, log fire; some live music, TV for major sports, skittle alley; children and well behaved dogs on leads (theirs are Saffron and George) welcome, chunky picnic-sets in large garden behind, good walks, open all day (till 7pm Sun), no food Sun evening or Mon.

DITCHEAT ST6236
★ **Manor House** (01749) 860276
Signed off A37 and A371 S of Shepton Mallet; BA4 6RB Striking 17th-c red-brick village inn; unusual arched doorways linking big flagstoned bar to comfortable lounge and stone-walled restaurant, comfy old leather armchairs, red leather dining chairs around scrubbed wooden tables, open fires; well kept Exmoor Gold and Butcombe beers, enjoyable food from breakfast to pub classics, friendly helpful staff; children welcome, tables on back grass, handy for Bath & West Showground, seven stylish bedrooms, good breakfast, open all day.

DOULTING ST6444
Poachers Pocket (01749) 880220
Chelynch Road, off A361; BA4 4PY Popular village pub with enjoyable reasonably priced wholesome food including Sun roasts in three sizes (must book), well kept Butcombe and Wadworths, friendly attentive service, country furniture on flagstones or carpet, log fire in stripped-stone end wall, dining conservatory; skittle alley/function room; children and dogs welcome, back garden with nice country views.

DOWLISH WAKE ST3712
New Inn (01460) 52413
Off A3037 S of Ilminster, via Kingstone; TA19 0NZ Comfortable and welcoming dark-beamed village pub; enjoyable home-made food from sandwiches and pub favourites up including steak, pie and curry nights, well kept Butcombe and Timothy Taylors, local cider, friendly helpful staff, woodburners in stone inglenooks, pleasant dining room; quiz first Sun of the month; dogs welcome, attractive garden and village, Perry's cider mill and shop nearby, four bedrooms in separate annexe, closed Mon.

DULVERTON SS9127
Bridge Inn (01398) 324130
Bridge Street; TA22 9HJ Welcoming unpretentious single-room pub dating from 1845 next to River Barle; reasonably priced locally sourced food including snacks, sandwiches, pies and pub classics, four well kept ales such as Bath, Exmoor and St Austell and some unusual imported beers, around 20 gins, comfortable sofas, woodburner; children and dogs welcome, two terraces, open all day in summer.

DUNSTER SS9943
★ **Luttrell Arms** (01643) 821555
High Street; A396; TA24 6SG Lovely hotel in imposing 15th-c abbey building with medieval features remaining; main bar has huge fireplace, antique chairs, horsebrasses, swords and guns, copper kettles, a stag's head, an antler chandelier and country knick-knacks, also Old Kitchen Bar with meat hooks on beamed ceiling, another huge log fire and bread oven, Boot Bar and comfortable sitting room; Exmoor, Otter and a couple of guests, farm ciders and 25 good wines by the glass, excellent food including afternoon tea in more formal restaurant; board games; children and dogs (in bar and bedrooms) welcome, 29 opulent bedrooms (some with four-posters, antiques and carved

fireplaces), new beauty salon, charming garden with seating on lawns and terraces, this is one of Exmoor National Park's prettiest villages, open all day.

DUNSTER   SS9843

Stags Head (01643) 821229
West Street (A396); TA24 6SN Unassuming 16th-c roadside inn with friendly accommodating staff; popular food from sandwiches to blackboard specials, Exmoor, Otter and a guest, beams, timbers and inglenook log fire, steps up to small back dining room; children and dogs (in bar) welcome, long narrow garden behind, four comfortable simple bedrooms, open all day.

EAST HARPTREE   ST5453

Castle of Comfort (01761) 221321
B3134, SW on Old Bristol Road; BS40 6DD Former coaching inn set high in the Mendips (last stop before the gallows for some past visitors); hefty timbers and exposed stonework, cushioned settles and other pubby furniture on carpet, log fires, Butcombe, Sharps and a guest, ample helpings of reasonably priced traditional food including good steaks and vegan/gluten-free options, friendly staff; children and dogs (in bar) welcome, wheelchair access, large garden with raised deck and play area, fine walks nearby.

EAST HARPTREE   ST5655

Waldegrave Arms (01761) 221429
Church Lane; BS40 6BD Welcoming old recently restored beamed pub; well kept Butcombe, Sharps and a guest, decent wines and plenty of gins, good food from wraps and pub favourites up, rooms arranged around central bar, eclectic mix of furniture on wood or stone floors, log fires; some live music; children and dogs welcome, picnic-sets in attractive sheltered garden with play area, delightful village, open (and food) all day, kitchen closes 6.30pm Sun.

EAST LAMBROOK   ST4218

Rose & Crown (01460) 240433
Silver Street; TA13 5HF Stone-built dining pub spreading extensively from compact 17th-c core with beams and inglenook woodburner, enjoyable food from shortish menu, Palmers ales and 11 wines by the glass, friendly service, restaurant extension with glass-covered well, skittle alley, charity quiz third Sun of month; children and dogs (in bar) welcome, disabled access from the side, picnic-sets on neat lawn, opposite East Lambrook Manor Gardens, open all day Sat, closed Mon.

EVERCREECH   ST6336

Natterjack (01749) 860253
A371 Shepton Mallet–Castle Cary; BA4 6NA Welcoming former Victorian station hotel (line closed 1966); good choice of generously served food at reasonable

prices, cheerful helpful service, three changing ales, real cider and nice range of wines, long bar with eating areas off; children and dogs welcome, lots of tables under parasols in big neatly kept garden, five bedrooms, closed Sun evening.

EXFORD   SS8538

★ Exmoor White Horse (01643) 831229 *B3224; TA24 7PY* Popular and welcoming old creeper-clad inn; more or less open-plan bar with good log fire, high-backed antique settle among more conventional seats, scrubbed deal tables, hunting prints and local photographs, Exmoor ales, Thatcher's cider and over 200 malt whiskies, good locally sourced bar and restaurant food including Sun carvery; children and dogs welcome, tables outside by river, pretty village, Land Rover Exmoor safaris, 28 comfortable bedrooms, open (and food) all day.

FAULKLAND   ST7555

★ Tuckers Grave (01373) 834230
A366 E of village; BA3 5XF Tiny totally unspoilt place named after Edward Tucker who hanged himself nearby in 1747 and was buried at the pub crossroads; entrance opening into simple tap room with woodburner, casks of Butcombe and Thatcher's Cheddar Valley cider in alcove on left, lunchtime sandwiches on request and occasional evening meals, two high-backed settles facing each other across a single table in right, side room, snug lounge (Rose Room) with Victorian fireplace; monthly live music (The Stranglers even recorded a song about the pub!); shove-ha'penny, skittle alley, outside loos; well behaved children and dogs allowed, lots of tables and chairs on attractive back lawn with good views, summer barbecues, camping, open all day weekends, closed Mon-Weds lunchtimes.

FRESHFORD   ST7960

★ Inn at Freshford (01225) 722250
Off A36 or B3108; BA2 7WG 16th-c village pub in lovely spot across from River Frome; three well kept ales such as Box Steam, craft beers, local cider and good choice of wines by the glass, interesting whiskies and gins too, popular good value home-made food from varied menu including selection of small plates and lunchtime sandwiches, friendly efficient young staff; background music; children and dogs welcome, wheelchair access to bar area (steps to dining room) but no disabled loo, attractive tiered hillside garden overlooking valley with outside bar and barbecue, good riverside walks, open (and food) all day.

FROME   ST7748

Griffin (01373) 301251
Milk Street; BA11 3DB Recently revamped corner pub; bare-boards bar with etched glass and open fires, long counter

serving couple of Frome ales, lots of craft beers and good range of gins, rums and tequilas, street-food style menu with range of burgers and good veggie/vegan options; small garden, open all day Fri-Sun, from 4pm other days.

FROME   ST7747

Three Swans (01373) 452009

King Street; BA11 1BH Appealing and quirky 17th-c beamed pub; well kept Abbey Bellringer, Butcombe and a local guest, nice wines by the glass, sandwiches, toasties and pub classics on Sat lunchtime plus popular roasts on Sun (must book), good friendly service, more space in small upstairs room; children welcome till 7pm, dogs in bar (not after 8pm Fri, Sat), part-covered beer garden, open all day Fri-Sun, closed other days till 4.30pm.

HALLATROW   ST6357

★ Old Station (01761) 452228

A39 S of Bristol; BS39 6EN Former 1920s station hotel with extraordinary collection of bric-a-brac including railway memorabilia, musical instruments, postboxes, even half an old Citroën, eclectic mix of furnishings too; Butcombe ales, several wines by the glass and good choice of highly regarded food cooked by landlord-chef, Pullman carriage restaurant, cheerful helpful service; children and dogs (in bar) welcome, café-style furniture on decking, picnic-sets on grass, polytunnel growing own vegetables, five bedrooms in converted outbuilding (no breakfast), open all day Fri-Sun.

HASELBURY PLUCKNETT ST4711

★ White Horse (01460) 78873

North Street; TA18 7RJ Popular open-plan village dining pub; good enterprising food cooked by chef-landlord from bar snacks up including set menu choices, West Country ales such as Otter, St Austell and Teignworthy tapped from the cask, local ciders and good choice of wines by the glass, friendly efficient service, candlelit tables on flagstones or bare boards, leather sofa by inglenook log fire; children and dogs welcome, pretty back terrace with roses and old well, closed Sun evening, Mon and Tues.

HILLFARANCE   ST1624

Anchor (01823) 461334

Oake; pub signed off Bradford-on-Tone to Oake road; TA4 1AW Comfortable village pub with dining area off attractive two-part bar; four local ales such as Exmoor and St Austell, local ciders on tap, more than 30 malt whiskies and several gins, good choice of enjoyable fairly priced food including home-made pies and Sun carvery, friendly

atmosphere; children and dogs welcome, garden with play area, bedrooms, open all day Sun.

HINTON BLEWETT   ST5956

★ Ring o' Bells (01761) 451245

Signed off A37 in Clutton; BS39 5AN Charming and welcoming low-beamed stone-built country local opposite village green; old-fashioned bar with solid furniture including pews, log fire, enjoyable home-cooked food catering for vegan and gluten-free diets, obliging service, well kept ales such as Butcombe and Timothy Taylors, local cider and good wines by the glass, dining room; children, walkers and dogs welcome, nice view from tables in sheltered front courtyard, open all day Fri and Sat, till 9pm Sun, no food Sun evening.

HINTON CHARTERHOUSE ST7758

Rose & Crown (01225) 722153

B3110 about 4 miles S of Bath; BA2 7SN Refurbished 18th-c village pub with partly divided carpeted bar with fine panelling, cushioned wall seats and mix of chairs around chunky tables, woodburner in ornate carved stone fireplace (smaller one the other side), well kept Butcombe and a guest, several wines by glass and enjoyable fairly priced home-made food, long dining room and steps to lower area with unusual beamed ceiling; background music, board games; children and dogs welcome, terraced garden, six comfortable bedrooms, open all day.

HORSINGTON   ST7023

Half Moon (01963) 370140

Signed off A357 S of Wincanton; BA8 0EF Friendly 17th-c pub with light and airy knocked-through bars; beams, stripped stone and oak floors, inglenook log fires, decent sensibly priced pubby food, three well kept constantly changing ales, decent range of wines and 28 gins, evening restaurant, skittle alley; children and dogs welcome, disabled access, attractive sloping front garden and big back one, good walks nearby, six bedrooms in separate buildings behind, closed Sun evening and lunchtimes Mon-Fri, best to check winter hours.

HORTON   ST3214

★ Five Dials (01460) 55359

Hanning Road; off A303; TA19 9QH Smartly updated village pub run by friendly helpful licensees; popular fairly priced food including good steaks and fish dishes, Otter, Sharps and a guest, local ciders and well chosen wines by the glass, restaurant; children and dogs welcome, attractive enclosed terrace garden, six comfortable bedrooms, open all day Fri-Sun, closed Mon.

We don't mention free wi-fi, because it's standard in most pubs these days – though not universal. And don't expect a good signal in remote rural locations.

KELSTON
ST7067
Old Crown (01225) 423032
Bitton Road; A431 W of Bath; BA1 9AQ
Updated 15th-c pub (sister pub is the Inn at Freshford); four small rooms, beams and polished flagstones, carved settles and cask tables, logs burning in ancient open range, also woodburner and coal-effect gas fire, well kept Bass, Butcombe and guest, real cider, enjoyable good value food from shortish menu plus daily specials in bar or restaurant, sandwiches available till 6pm Mon-Fri; children and dogs welcome, wheelchair access with help, picnic-sets under apple trees in sheltered sunny back garden with covered deck, outside bar and barbecue, open (and food) all day, kitchen shuts 7pm Sun.

KEYNSHAM
ST6669
★ Lock-Keeper (0117) 986 2383
Keynsham Road (A4175 NE of town); BS31 2DD Welcoming riverside pub with relaxed worn-in feel and plenty of character; simple left-hand bar with big painted settle, cushioned wall benches and old local photographs, two more little rooms with assorted cushioned dining chairs, more photographs and rustic prints, Youngs ales with guests such as Bath and St Austell, Thatcher's ciders and good range of wines/spirits, popular well priced bar food from lunchtime ciabattas up, cheerful helpful young staff, light modern conservatory (quite different in style); background and occasional live music; children and dogs (in bar) welcome, disabled access/loos, rattan furniture and giant parasols on big heated deck overlooking water, steps down to picnic-sets on grass, outside bar/barbecue, pétanque, open all day and can get very busy.

KILVE
ST1442
Hood Arms (01278) 741114
A39 E of Williton; TA5 1EA Welcoming 17th-c village inn; well kept Exmoor, St Austell and a guest, good reasonably priced food including popular Sun lunch (booking advised), friendly helpful service, warm woodburner in beamed bar, carpeted restaurant; children and dogs welcome, ramp for wheelchairs, disabled loo, tables in back garden, bedrooms, closed Sun evening.

KINGSDON
ST5126
★ Kingsdon Inn (01935) 840543
At Podimore roundabout on A303, follow sign to Langport (A372) then right on B3151; TA11 7LG Pretty little thatched cottage; main quarry-tiled bar with woodburner, built-in cushioned wall seats and country chairs around scrubbed kitchen tables, steps up to carpeted, half-panelled dining area, Butcombe Bitter and guests such as St Austell or Teignworthy, local cider and 14 wines by the glass, very good imaginative food cooked by landlord, second dining area plus an attractive separate

restaurant with another woodburner; background classical music, TV; children and dogs (in bar) welcome, picnic-sets on lawn, herb garden, handy for the Fleet Air Arm Museum, three comfortable bedrooms, closed first week of Jan.

LANGPORT
ST4625
★ Devonshire Arms (01458) 241271
B3165 Somerton–Martock, off A372 E of Langport; TA10 9LP Handsome gabled inn (former hunting lodge) on village green; simple flagstoned back bar with high-backed chairs around dark tables, up to three West Country ales tapped from the cask, 11 wines by the glass and local cider brandy, stylish main room with comfortable leather sofas and glass-topped log table by fire, scatter cushions on long wall bench, church candles, elegant dining room with wooden and upholstered chairs and wood tables on broad boards, good interesting food from lunchtime sandwiches up (local suppliers listed), efficient friendly service; wheelchair access from car park, teak furniture out at front, pretty box-enclosed courtyard behind with water-ball feature, more seats on raised terraces, nine comfortable bedrooms, good breakfast, open all day Fri-Sun.

LANSDOWN
ST7268
Blathwayt Arms (01225) 421995
Next to Lansdown Golf Club and Bath Racecourse; BA1 9BT Hilltop stone pub with well prepared traditional food (not Sun evening) including themed nights, ales such as Butcombe and Otter from dark wood bar, also Symonds and Weston's cider, decent wines and good range of gins, pleasant prompt service, mix of carpeted, wood and stone flooring, simple furniture, some raised areas in bar and conservatory, local photos and a map of the Battle of Lansdown (Civil War); background music; children welcome, wheelchair access to most areas, disabled loo, racecourse view from garden, play area, open all day.

LITTON
ST5954
★ Litton (01761) 241554
B3114, NW of Chewton Mendip; BA3 4PW Extensively refurbished partly 15th-c stone pub; airy interior with wood and flagstone floors, main bar with long polished elm servery and mix of furniture including scrubbed tables, leather chesterfields and settles, good varied choice of food from snacks, sharing plates and bar meals up, friendly helpful staff, local ales, craft beers and ciders, plenty of wines by the glass, good range of gins, separate whisky bar with oak and copper-topped counter; background music; children and dogs welcome, wheelchair access from back entrance, disabled loos, courtyard seating with steps up to lawned area, also terrace overlooking River Chew, good reservoir walks nearby, 12 individually styled bedrooms, open all day.

LONG ASHTON ST5370

Bird in Hand (01275) 395222

Weston Road; BS41 9LA Painted stone dining pub with good modern food from seasonal menu including popular Sun roasts, well kept Bath Gem, St Austell Tribute and two guests, Ashton Press cider, nice wines and some interesting gins, friendly helpful young staff, spindleback chairs and blue-painted pine tables on wood floors, collection of old enamel signs, open fire and woodburner; children and dogs welcome, side terrace, parking can be tricky, open all day.

LONG ASHTON ST5370

Miners Rest (01275) 393449

Providence Lane; BS41 9DJ Welcoming three-room country pub, comfortable and unpretentious, with well kept Butcombe and Sharps, traditional ciders, generous helpings of simple inexpensive lunchtime food, cheerful prompt service, local mining memorabilia, log fire, darts; well behaved children and dogs welcome, wheelchair access possible, vine-covered verandah and suntrap terrace, open all day.

LOWER GODNEY ST4742

★Sheppey Inn (01458) 831594

Tilleys Drove; BA5 1RZ Although rather unprepossessing from the outside, this quirky fun place is full of character and surprisingly popular for its remote setting; contemporary feel with eclectic mix of furniture on bare boards including plastic chairs by chunky wooden tables, cushioned wall benches and some 1950s retro, various stuffed animals, old photographs, modern artwork and assorted kitsch, at least six ciders tapped from the barrel along with local ales (maybe Bristol Beer Factory and Dawkins) and craft beers, imaginative choice of well liked food, some cooked in charcoal oven, friendly staff, black beams and log fire, long dining area with high pitched ceiling; background and regular live music; children and dogs welcome, seats on deck overlooking small River Sheppey, three individually styled bedrooms, open all day weekends.

LUXBOROUGH SS9837

★Royal Oak (01984) 641498

Kingsbridge; S of Dunster on minor roads into Brendon Hills; TA23 0SH Welcoming atmospheric old inn set deep in Exmoor National Park; compact beamed bar with ancient flagstones, several fine settles, scrubbed kitchen tables and huge brick inglenook, back bar with cobbled floor, some quarry tiles and stone fireplace, cosy side room set for eating plus two further dining rooms, Exmoor and two or three changing guests, good food from pub favourites up including seasonal game; pool, board games in back room, also a radiogram with stack of old LPs; children and dogs (in bar) welcome, seats in lovely sunny back courtyard, nine

bedrooms, good walks nearby including Coleridge Way, closed Mon, otherwise open all day.

LYDFORD ON FOSSE ST5630

Cross Keys (01963) 240473

Just off A37; TA11 7HA Beamed and flagstoned pub with good traditional home-made food including Sun carvery, cheerful service, three well kept ales tapped from the cask such as Bristol Beer Factory, Downton, Otter and Twisted Oak, good selection of proper cider and 11 wines by the glass, connecting rooms (main dining area at front), chunky rustic furniture and log fires in substantial old fireplaces; live music, quizzes and other events in function room; children and dogs welcome, disabled access/loos, seats on covered terrace and in sunny garden, six comfortable well equipped bedrooms, camping field, popular with Fosse Way walkers, open all day.

MIDDLEZOY ST3732

George (01823) 698215

Off A372 E of Bridgwater; TA7 0NN Steps up to friendly 17th-c beamed village pub; well kept St Austell and a couple of guests such as Bath and Cheddar (Easter beer festival), proper ciders and decent choice of wines by the glass, simple home-made lunchtime food, more evening choice including good steaks, attentive welcoming staff, bare stone walls, flagstones and a couple of log fires; quiz, live music and bingo nights, pool, darts, skittle alley; children and dogs welcome, a few tables outside, three bedrooms, open Sun 2-7pm (no food), closed all day Mon, Tues and lunchtimes Weds-Fri.

MIDFORD ST7660

Hope & Anchor (01225) 832296

Bath Road (B3110); BA2 7DD Ivy-covered 17th-c pub near Colliers Way cycling/walking path and close to walks on the disused Somerset & Dorset railway; neatly kept open-plan interior with bar, heavy-beamed flagstoned restaurant with mix of dark wooden furniture and woodburner, modern back conservatory liked by families, enjoyable good value food including daily specials, up to three real ales, traditional cider and plenty of wines by the glass, courteous staff and relaxed atmosphere; dogs welcome in bar, seats on two-tier back terrace, open all day weekends.

MINEHEAD SS9746

★Old Ship Aground (01643) 703516

Quay West next to lifeboat station; TA24 5UL Friendly flower-decked Edwardian quayside pub owned by local farming family; Marstons-related ales, Thatcher's cider and good selection of wines and spirits, enjoyable food using own meat and other local produce, Sun carvery, cheerful efficient service even when busy, faux black beams decorated with beer pump clips and nautical ropework, lots of pictures, pubby furniture on carpeted or polished wood floors, window-seat views; live music Fri, juke box in bar; children and dogs welcome, wheelchair access via side door, disabled loo, picnic-sets out at front overlooking harbour, 12 bedrooms (sea views), open all day.

MONKSILVER   ST0737
Notley Arms   (01984) 656095
B3188; TA4 4JB Bustling pub in lovely village on edge of Exmoor National Park; open-plan bar rooms with log fires and woodburners, cushioned window seats and settles, appealing collection of old dining chairs around mixed wooden tables on slate tiles or flagstones, paintings on cream or panelled walls, flowers and church candles, tractor-seat stools by counter serving five beers including Exmoor and St Austell, proper cider, around 30 wines by the glass and 20 malt whiskies, good well presented food from pub classics (with a twist) to inventive restaurant dishes, helpful friendly service; background music; children and dogs welcome, neat garden with plenty of picnic-sets, heated pavilion and clear-running stream at the bottom, half a dozen attractive comfortable bedrooms in former coach house, good breakfast, open all day from 9am.

MONTACUTE   ST4917
Kings Arms   (01935) 822255
Bishopston; TA15 6UU Extended 17th-c stone inn set beautifully next to church; stripped-stone bar with comfortable seating and log fire, contemporary restaurant, three real ales including Timothy Taylors, nice house wines and well liked food from bar snacks to restaurant dishes, friendly courteous staff; background music, quiz nights; children welcome, pleasant garden behind, 15 bedrooms (most ensuite), handy for Montacute House (NT), open all day.

NAILSEA   ST4469
Blue Flame   (01275) 856910
Netherton Wood Lane, West End; BS48 4DE Small friendly 19th-c farmers' local with two unchanging lived-in rooms; well kept ales from casks behind bar, traditional ciders and some snacky food such as fresh rolls and pies, coal fire, pub games; outside gents'; sizeable informal garden, limited parking, open all day Thurs-Sun, closed lunchtimes Mon, Tues.

NORTH CURRY   ST3125
Bird in Hand   (01823) 490248
Queens Square; off A378 (or A358) E of Taunton; TA3 6LT Friendly village pub with cosy main bar, old pews, settles, benches and yew tables on flagstones, some original beams and timbers, good inglenook log fire, well kept local ales such as Cotleigh and Otter and decent wines by the glass, popular food from varied blackboard menu,

restaurant part; background music; children, dogs and muddy boots welcome, closed Sun-Tues.

NORTON ST PHILIP   ST7755
★ George   (01373) 834224
A366; BA2 7LH Wonderful building full of history and interest – an inn for more than 700 years; heavy beams, timbering and panelling, vast open fires in carved stone fireplaces, distinctive furnishings, plenty of 18th-c pictures, fine pewter and heraldic shields, dining room with wonderful pitched ceiling and tapestries, Wadworths ales and enjoyable food from varied menu including pub classics and gluten-free choices, good friendly service; children and dogs (in bar and bedrooms) welcome, appealing galleried courtyard and terraced garden with view of medieval church and cricket pitch, atmospheric bedrooms (some reached by Norman turret and more in B&B opposite), usually open all day.

ODCOMBE   ST5015
★ Masons Arms   (01935) 862591
Off A3088 or A30 just W of Yeovil; Lower Odcombe; BA22 8TX Thatched village pub with simple bar, joists and standing timbers, cushioned dining chairs around tables on patterned carpet, a couple of tub chairs and a table in former inglenook fireplace, steps down to dining room with woodburner; own-brewed Odcombe ales, real cider and 11 wines by the glass, good popular food from varied menu including wood-fired pizzas Thurs-Sun; children and dogs welcome, thatched shelter and picnic-sets in garden, also a vegetable patch, chicken coop and campsite, six well equipped bedrooms, holiday cottage and shepherd's hut, hearty breakfast, open all day Sun.

OVER STRATTON   ST4315
Royal Oak   (01460) 240906
Off A303 via Ilminster turn at South Petherton roundabout; TA13 5LQ Attractive 17th-c thatched dining pub with linked rooms; oak beams, flagstones and thick stone walls, scrubbed kitchen tables, pews and settles, log-effect gas fire, much enjoyed food cooked by landlord-chef from pub favourites up including daily specials, fair prices, well kept Badger ales and good wines, friendly attentive service; children and dogs (theirs is Alfie) welcome, wheelchair access, back garden with paved terrace, open (and food) all day weekends, closed Mon evening (although may open in summer).

PORLOCK   SS8846
★ Ship   (01643) 862507
High Street; TA24 8QD Picturesque old thatched pub with beams, flagstones and big inglenook log fires, popular reasonably priced food from sandwiches up, eight well kept ales such as Exmoor and Otter, traditional cider, friendly service, back dining room,

small locals' front bar with games, quiz night; children welcome, attractive split-level sunny garden with decking and play area, nearby nature trail to Dunkery Beacon, five bedrooms, open all day; known as the Top Ship to distinguish it from the Ship at Porlock Weir.

PORLOCK WEIR   SS8846

★**Ship** (01643) 863288

Porlock Hill (A39); TA24 8PB
Unpretentious thatched pub in wonderful spot by peaceful harbour – can get packed; long and narrow with dark low beams, flagstones and stripped stone, simple pub furniture, woodburner, six West Country ales including Exmoor and St Austell, real ciders, a perry and good whisky and soft drinks choice, enjoyable pubby food served promptly by friendly staff, games rooms across small backyard, also a tea room; background and occasional live music, TV; children and dogs welcome, sturdy picnic-sets out at front and side, good coastal walks, three bedrooms, limited free parking but pay-and-display opposite; calls itself the Bottom Ship to avoid confusion with the Ship at Porlock.

PORTISHEAD   ST4776

Hall & Woodhouse (01275) 848685

Chandlery Square, Portishead Quays Marina; BS20 7DF Striking contemporary building overlooking marina slipway, unusual steel and glass construction incorporating shipping containers; main entrance with old Admiralty charts, bar with floor-to-ceiling windows, exposed utilities and suspended copper-shaded lights, mix of furniture including refectory tables, easy chairs and sofas, bookshelves one end with old radios, ship's telegraph etc, woodburner, Badger ales, local ciders and good selection of wines/ spirits from plank-faced servery, enjoyable food from baguettes and sharing plates up, more elaborate menu in upstairs restaurant (lift) with reclaimed wood floors and open kitchen, helpful cheerful staff; children welcome, dogs in bar, disabled access and facilities, covered seating area outside, open all day from 9am for breakfast.

PORTISHEAD   ST4576

Windmill (01275) 818483

M5 junction 19; A369 into town, then follow Sea Front sign and into Nore Road; BS20 6JZ Busy dining pub perched on steep hillside with panoramic Severn estuary views; curving glass frontage rising two storeys (adjacent windmill remains untouched), contemporary furnishings, Fullers ales and a couple of guests, Thatcher's cider and plenty of wines by the

glass, decent range of enjoyable food from sandwiches and baked potatoes up (some main courses available in smaller helpings); children welcome, dogs allowed in bar, disabled access/facilities including chairlift, metal furniture on tiered lantern-lit terraces and decking, open (and food) all day.

PRIDDY   ST5450

★**Hunters Lodge** (01749) 672275

From Wells on A39 pass hill with TV mast on left, then next left; BA5 3AR
Welcoming farmers', walkers' and potholers' pub above Ice Age cavern, unchanging and in same family for generations; well kept local beers such as Butcombe and Cheddar tapped from casks behind bar, Thatcher's and Wilkin's ciders, simple cheap home-made food, low beams, flagstones and panelling, log fires in huge fireplaces, caving memorabilia and old lead mining photographs; no mobiles or credit cards; children and dogs in family room, wheelchair access, garden picnic-sets.

PRISTON   ST6960

Ring o' Bells (01761) 471467

Village SW of Bath; BA2 9EE
Unpretentious old stone pub with large knocked-through bar; good reasonably priced traditional food cooked by licensees using nearby farm produce, well kept Butcombe, quick friendly service, flagstones, beams and good open fire; regularly used skittle alley; children, dogs and muddy boots welcome, benches out at front overlooking little village green (maypole here on May Day), good walks, closed Mon and lunchtimes Tues-Thurs, no food Sun evening.

RICKFORD   ST4859

Plume of Feathers (01761) 462682

Very sharp turn off A368; BS40 7AH
Cottagey 17th-c local in pretty streamside hamlet; enjoyable reasonably priced home-made food including pizzas in bar and dining room, well kept Butcombe, Cheddar and a guest, local cider and good choice of wines, black beams and half-panelling, cast-iron tables, settles and other traditional furniture, log fires; table skittles, shove-ha'penny, darts and pool; well behaved children and dogs welcome, rustic tables on narrow front terrace, garden behind, charity duck race in July, five bedrooms, open all day.

RIMPTON   ST6021

White Post Inn (01935) 851525

Rimpton Hill, B3148; BA22 8AR Small modern dining pub straddling Dorset border (boundary actually runs through the bar); highly rated imaginative food from chef-owner including reworked pub favourites

---

We include some hotels with a good bar that offers facilities comparable to those of a pub.

and tasting menus, local ales and ciders, a dozen wines by the glass and interesting list of spirits including a milk vodka, friendly helpful staff, cosy carpeted bar area with leather sofas and woodburner, fine country views from restaurant and back terrace; children welcome, three bedrooms, closed Sun evening, Mon and Tues.

RODE   ST8053
Cross Keys (01373) 830900
High Street; BA11 6NZ Popular pub in former brewery; two bars and restaurant, old well in one part, enjoyable freshly made food (not Sun evening) including good value Fri steak night, well kept Butcombe and a couple of guests, proper ciders and decent range of gins, good friendly service; monthly comedy night; children and dogs welcome, large enclosed garden and terrace, three bedrooms, open all day weekends, closed Mon.

SALTFORD   ST6867
Bird in Hand (01225) 873335
High Street; BS31 3EJ Comfortable and friendly with busy L-shaped bar; four well kept ales such as Butcombe and Sharps, good choice of popular fairly priced food (all day weekends) from well filled rolls up, prompt cheerful service, pubby furniture including settles, back conservatory dining area; beer festival; wheelchair access at front (not from car park), picnic-sets down towards river, pétanque, handy for Bristol & Bath Railway Path, open all day, closed Mon.

SALTFORD   ST6968
Jolly Sailor (01225) 873002
Off A4 Bath–Keynsham; Mead Lane; BS31 3ER Worth knowing for its great River Avon setting by lock and weir; good range of food from bar snacks to authentic Indian curries, OAP set lunch Mon-Fri, four Wadworths ales, flagstones, low beams and two log fires, conservatory dining room overlooking the water; background and weekend live music, Thurs quiz; children and dogs (in bar) welcome, disabled access/facilities, paved lockside terrace, open (and food) all day.

SANDFORD   ST4159
Railway (01934) 611518
Station Road; BS25 5RA Owned by Thatcher's and extensively modernised; their full range of ciders, real ales such as Butcombe, plenty of wines by the glass and enjoyable food from shortish menu including good value set lunch and Thurs tapas, pleasant young staff, lofty flagstoned bar with long oak counter, comfortable bare-boards area off with exposed stone walls and open fire, attractive timber-framed dining extension; children and dogs welcome, outside seating on two levels, open all day Thurs-Sat, till 8pm Sun, closed Mon-Weds.

SHEPTON MONTAGUE   ST6731
★Montague Inn (01749) 813213
Village signed off A359 Bruton–Castle Cary; BA9 8JW Simply but tastefully furnished dining pub with welcoming licensees, popular for a good meal or just a drink; stripped-wood tables and kitchen chairs, inglenook log fire, nicely presented often interesting food including range of burgers from shortish menu plus a few specials, three well kept ales such as Bath and Wadworths, real ciders and good wine and whisky choice, helpful well informed young staff, bright spacious restaurant extension behind; children and dogs (in bar) welcome, disabled access, garden and large terrace with teak furniture, maybe Sun jazz in summer, peaceful farmland views, closed Sun evening.

SIMONSBATH   SS7739
★Exmoor Forest Inn (01643) 831341
B3223/B3358; TA24 7SH Welcoming 19th-c inn beautifully placed in remote countryside; split-level bar with circular tables by counter, larger area with cushioned settles, upholstered stools and mate's chairs around mix of tables, hunting trophies, antlers and horse tack, woodburner, generously served good traditional food alongside more imaginative choices including local game, well kept ales such as Clearwater, Exmoor and Otter, Weston's cider, good range of wines and malt whiskies, airy dining room, residents' lounge; children and dogs welcome, seats in front garden, fine walks along River Barle, own trout and salmon fishing, comfortable bedrooms and self-catering cottage, good breakfast, open all day in high season.

SOMERTON   ST4828
★White Hart (01458) 272273
Market Place; TA11 7LX Attractive smallish 18th-c stone-built pub on market square in lovely village; main bar with long wall seats with scatter cushions, stools around small tables and big mirrors, a couple of snug bars with leather sofas, armchairs and open fires, also rugs, church candles, contemporary paintwork and interesting lighting; Bath Gem, Cheddar Potholer, Otter Amber and local guest, local cider, varied imaginative menu including wood-fired sourdough pizzas, helpful service; background music, board games; children and dogs (in bar) welcome; eight stylish comfortable bedrooms, open (and food) all day from breakfast on.

SOUTH CHERITON   ST6924
White Horse (01963) 370394
A357 Wincanton–Blandford; BA8 0BL Renovated 17th-c roadside country pub under friendly family management; three well kept ales including St Austell, craft beers and decent range of wines by the

glass, good locally sourced home-made food (not Sun evening) in bar or restaurant (separate menus), cheerful service; some live music, quiz, skittle alley; children and dogs welcome, picnic-sets in small back garden, open all day Fri-Sun, from 5pm Mon-Thurs.

SOUTH STOKE ST7461
Pack Horse (01225) 830300
Off B3110, S edge of Bath; BA2 7DU Historic pub rescued from the developers by the local community; two sympathetically restored rooms separated by servery, main one with heavy black beam-and-plank ceiling, stone-mullioned windows, quarry-tiled floor and log fire in handsome stone inglenook, room on left with another fire, Butcombe and changing local beers, traditional cider and enjoyable reasonably priced food from sandwiches/snacks and pub favourites up, good friendly service, two further rooms upstairs; quiz Weds, some live music; children and dogs (downstairs) welcome, picnic-sets in nice garden with lovely valley views, good walks (route sheets available from the bar), limited parking, best to park at top of village and walk down, open all day Fri and Sat, no food Sun evening.

SPAXTON ST2336
Lamb (01278) 671350
Barford Road, Four Forks; TA5 1AD Welcoming simply furnished little pub at foot of the Quantocks; open-plan beamed bar with woodburner, at least three well kept beers such as Exmoor and Otter, enjoyable good value food (not Sun evening) including notable local steaks, pies and blackboard specials (booking advised); quiz last Sun of month; tables on lawn behind, dogs (on lead) welcome, open Tues-Sat evenings only, from 6.30pm.

STANTON DREW ST5963
Druids Arms (01275) 332230
Off B3130; BS39 4EJ Updated old pub in stone-circle village (there are some standing stones in the garden); linked flagstoned rooms with low black beams, bare stone walls and green dados, cushioned window seats and pubby furniture, candles here and there, open fires, tractor-seat stools by pale wood bar serving Butcombe and Sharps Doom Bar, Thatcher's cider and modest wine list, friendly service, enjoyable often creative food from bar snacks up (not Sun evening), Mon fish and chips, Weds steak night; occasional live music, darts; children and dogs welcome, front wheelchair access using portable ramp, picnic-sets out by lane and in garden backing on to 14th-c church, maybe summer bouncy castle, open all day.

STAPLE FITZPAINE ST2618
Greyhound (01823) 480227
Off A358 or B3170 S of Taunton; TA3 5SP Recently refurbished rambling country pub with small but interesting menu

at reasonable prices, well kept Badger ales and decent wines by the glass, welcoming helpful staff, cosy interior with flagstones and carpeting, stripped stone walls, dark beams, nice mix of old furniture and log fires; children and dogs welcome, seven bedrooms, good breakfast, open all day.

STOKE SUB HAMDON ST4717
Prince of Wales (01935) 822848
Ham Hill; TA14 6RW Traditional stone pub at top of Ham Hill with superb views; local cask-tapped ales, traditional ciders and good food from sandwiches and West Country deli boards up, summer pizzas from outside oven, friendly staff; children, dogs and muddy boots welcome, open (and food) all day, breakfast 9-11am.

TARR SS8632
★Tarr Farm (01643) 851507
Tarr Steps – narrow road off B3223 N of Dulverton; deep ford if you approach from the W (inn is on E bank); TA22 9PY Fine Exmoor position for this 16th-c inn above River Barle's medieval clapper bridge (lovely walks); compact unpretentious bar rooms with good views, leather chairs around slabby rustic tables, some stall and wall seating, game bird pictures on wood-clad walls, three woodburners, well kept changing ales such as Exmoor and St Austell and several wines by the glass, good food using local produce and themed cuisine nights, residents' end with smart evening restaurant, friendly helpful service, log fire in pleasant lounge with dark leather armchairs and sofas; children and dogs welcome, slate-topped stone tables outside making most of setting, extensive grounds, good bedrooms (no under-10s) in separate modern building, open all day but may be closed early Feb.

TAUNTON ST2525
Hankridge Arms (01823) 444405
Hankridge Way, Deane Gate (near Sainsbury's); just off M5 junction 25 – A358 towards city, then right at roundabout, right at next roundabout; TA1 2LR Interesting well restored Badger dining pub based on 16th-c former farmhouse – quite a contrast to the modern shopping complex surrounding it; different-sized linked areas, beams, timbers and big log fire, food from lunchtime sandwiches through pubby choices up, well kept (if pricey) ales and decent wines by the glass, friendly efficient young staff; background music; dogs welcome, plenty of tables in pleasant outside area, open till 4pm Sun.

TAUNTON ST2225
Plough (01823) 324404
Station Road; TA1 1PB Popular little pub with three or four changing local ales, racked ciders and good selection of wines by the glass, simple food including range of pies,

bare boards and panelling, candles on tables, cosy nooks and open fire, hidden door to lavatories; background and some live music, weekly quiz; children and dogs welcome, handy for station, open all day Fri-Sun, closed lunchtimes Mon-Thurs.

TAUNTON   ST2223
Vivary Arms   (01823) 272563
Wilton Street; across Vivary Park from centre; TA1 3JR Popular low-beamed 18th-c local (Taunton's oldest pub); good value fresh food from light lunches up in snug plush lounge and small dining room, Otter Bitter, Sharps Doom Bar and a guest and decent wines by the glass, friendly helpful young staff, interesting collection of drink-related items; pool and darts; lovely hanging baskets and flowers out at front, nice little garden behind, children welcome, open all day Sun, closed Mon lunchtime.

TIMBERSCOMBE   SS9542
Lion   (01643) 841243
Church Street; TA24 7TP Refurbished Exmoor-edge village pub; enjoyable food from shortish well priced menu, changing local ales from the likes of Bath, Exmoor and St Austell, traditional ciders and good selection of gins, friendly efficient service; quiz first Weds of month, games area with darts, pool and juke box; children and dogs welcome, open (and food) all day except Mon when it opens at 5pm.

TINTINHULL   ST5019
★ Crown & Victoria   (01935) 823341
Farm Street, village signed off A303; BA22 8PZ Handsome golden-stone inn useful for the A303; carpeted bar with farmhouse furniture and big woodburner, high bar chairs at light oak counter serving four well kept ales, good popular food from shortish but varied menu using free range/local produce, efficient friendly service, dining room with more pine tables and chairs, former skittle alley also used for eating, end conservatory; well behaved children welcome, dogs in bar, disabled facilities, big garden with play area, five bedrooms, handy for Tintinhull Garden (NT), open all day, closed Sun evening.

TRULL   ST2122
Winchester Arms   (01823) 284723
Church Road; TA3 7LG Cosy streamside village pub with good value generous food including blackboard specials, monthly curry night and popular Sun lunch, four West Country ales (beer festival Aug) and local ciders, friendly helpful service, small dining room; Sun quiz, occasional live music, skittle alley; dogs welcome, garden with decked area

and summer barbecues, five cosy bedrooms, open all day Fri, Sat.

TUNLEY   ST6959
King William   (01761) 470408
B3115 SW of Bath; BA2 0EB Family-run 17th-c coaching inn with good fairly priced pub food from baguettes to daily specials (smaller helpings available and plenty of gluten-free choices), some themed nights too, well kept ales such as Butcombe and St Austell, decent wines and good range of gins, friendly efficient staff, bar popular with locals, other room set for dining; courtyard tables, three comfortable bedrooms, open till 4pm Sun, closed Mon, Tues.

UPTON   ST0129
Lowtrow Cross Inn   (01398) 371220
A3190 E of Upton; TA4 2DB Welcoming remote pub dating from the 17th c; low-beamed bar with bare boards, flagstones and log fire, pine furniture in two carpeted dining areas, one with enormous inglenook, the other doubling as a games room (pool, darts, skittle alley), three well kept ales including Exmoor, proper ciders and more than 35 gins, good coffee, popular generously served home-made food; occasional live music; children and dogs welcome, picnic-sets in front garden, lovely surroundings, three bedrooms, camping next door (separately run), open (and food) all day.

VOBSTER   ST7049
Vobster Inn   (01373) 812920
Lower Vobster; BA3 5RJ Spacious old stone-built dining pub; enjoyable reasonably priced home-made food (special diets catered for), Butcombe, Ashton Press cider and nice wines by the glass, three comfortable open-plan areas with antique furniture, plenty of room for just a drink; children and dogs (on lead, in bar) welcome, seats on lawn, boules, four bedrooms (also yurts and shepherd's huts), closed Sun evening, Mon and Tues.

WASHFORD   ST0440
White Horse   (01984) 640415
Abbey Road/Torre Rocks; TA23 0JZ Welcoming and popular old beamed local dating from 1709; three well kept changing ales such as Sharps Doom Bar and St Austell Tribute, proper cider and enjoyable reasonably priced pubby food from baguettes to daily specials, can eat in bar or separate restaurant, log fires; pool, skittle alley; well behaved children allowed in restaurant, over-14s only in bar, dogs welcome, picnic-sets and large smokers' pavilion over road next to trout stream, field with interesting collection of fowl and goats, handy for visits

to Exmoor National Park and close to Cleeve Abbey (EH), seven bedrooms (three in newish timber lodge), open all day.

WATCHET ST0743
Pebbles (01984) 634737
Market Street; TA23 0AN Popular, welcoming and relaxed little bar in former shop near Market House Museum and the harbour; extensive range of regional ciders (tasters offered), three cask-tapped ales such as Exmoor, Otter and Timothy Taylors, good choice of whiskies and gins, large range of traditional ciders, cider brandies and other drinks, friendly helpful staff, no food but can bring your own (plates and cutlery provided, fish and chip shop next door); regular live music (some impromptu) including folk and jazz, sea shanty and poetry evenings; dogs welcome, no wheelchair access (high front step), open all day except Weds when it opens at 5pm.

WATCHET ST0643
Star (01984) 631367
Mill Lane (B3191); TA23 0BZ Late 18th-c beamed pub at end of lane just off Watchet harbour; main flagstoned bar with other low-ceilinged side rooms, some exposed stonework and rough wood partitioning, mix of traditional furniture including oak settles, window seats, woodburner in ornate fireplace, good selection of pubby food mostly sourced locally including fresh fish, four or five well kept West Country ales such as Butcombe, Cotleigh, Dartmoor and Exmoor, real cider and some interesting gins and rums, cheerful helpful staff; background music; children and dogs (on leads) welcome, wheelchair access to main bar, picnic-sets out in front and in sloping beer garden behind, handy for marina and West Somerset Railway, open all day Fri-Sun.

WEDMORE ST4347
New Inn (01934) 712099
Combe Batch; BS28 4DU Welcoming unpretentious village pub popular with locals and visitors alike; well kept Butcombe Original, Timothy Taylors Landlord and a guest, real cider and big helpings of enjoyable sensibly priced pubby food, comfortable dining area; skittle alley, darts, sports TV and lots of local events including penny chuffing, conker competitions and the Turnip Prize (for worst piece of local artwork); children and dogs welcome, open all day weekends, closed lunchtimes Mon, Tues.

WEDMORE ST4348
★Swan (01934) 710337
Cheddar Road, opposite Church Street; BS28 4EQ Charming 18th-c village dining pub; open-plan and stylish including main bar with wooden tables and chairs on floorboards, long wall seat, woodburning stove and large mirrors, other areas with rugs on flagstones, leather chesterfield, armchairs and chairs and an airy dining room; Cheddar Potholer, Otter Bitter and two guest beers on handpump, 16 wines by the glass, local gin and two farm ciders, excellent modern food using local suppliers, quick, friendly service; occasional live music; children and dogs (in bar) welcome, seven comfortable pretty bedrooms, terrace and lawn with seats and tables, open all day, food all day Tues-Sun.

WELLOW ST7358
Fox & Badger (01225) 832293
Signed off A367 SW of Bath; BA2 8QG Popular village pub with opened-up interior with flagstones one end, bare boards the other, woodburner in massive hearth, some snug corners, Butcombe and two guests, real ciders and good range of well liked food (booking advised weekends), friendly service; children and dogs welcome, picnic-sets in covered courtyard, usually open all day Fri and Sat, closed Sun evening – but best to call to check.

WELLS ST5546
★Fountain (01749) 672317
St Thomas Street; BA5 2UU Relaxed restaurant place with big comfortable bar, interesting, quite colourful and mixed décor and large open fire; good helpings of popular food here or in upstairs dining room (booking advised weekends), Butcombe and three guest ales such as Bath and Fullers, several wines by the glass, chatty attentive staff; unobtrusive background music, newspapers; well behaved children welcome, no dogs, pretty in summer with window boxes and shutters, handy for cathedral and moated Bishop's Palace, closed Sun evening, Mon lunchtime.

WEST CHINNOCK ST4613
Muddled Man (01935) 881235
Lower Street; TA18 7PT Friendly unassuming family-run pub in attractive rustic village; single bar with three well kept changing West Country ales, real cider and more than 50 malt whiskies, enjoyable straightforward food using local produce; skittle alley; children and dogs welcome, small garden, two bedrooms, open all day Fri-Sun.

WEST HUNTSPILL ST3145
Crossways (01278) 783756
A38, between M5 junctions 22 and 23; TA9 3RA Rambling 17th-c tile-hung pub with split-level carpeted areas, beams and log fires, nine well kept ales including Exmoor, Otter and Pitchfork (tasting trays available), good choice of enjoyable generously served food at reasonable prices (advance booking recommended), cheerful efficient staff; TV, occasional live music; children welcome and dogs (not Fri, Sat evenings in dining areas), disabled access/loo, garden with play area and heated smokers' shelter, eight bedrooms, open all day, till 1am Fri, Sat.

WEST MONKTON ST2628
Monkton (01823) 412414
Blundells Lane; signed from A3259;
TA2 8NP Popular village dining pub with
good choice of freshly made food including
some South African dishes (best to book
weekends); bare-boards bar with central
woodburner, snug and separate restaurant,
well kept Exmoor, Otter and Sharps, real
ciders, gins, cocktails and a dozen wines by
the glass, good service; children and dogs
welcome, wheelchair access from the front,
lots of tables in big garden bounded by
stream, play area.

WEST PENNARD ST5438
Red Lion (01458) 832941
A361 E of Glastonbury; Newtown;
BA6 8NH Traditional 16th-c stone-built
village inn; bar and dining areas off small
flagstoned black-beamed core, enjoyable
home-made food including pub favourites
and popular Sun roasts, vegan and gluten-
free diets catered for, Butcombe and guest
ales and good selection of gins, also a cider
using apples from own orchard, friendly
attentive staff, inglenook woodburner
and open fires; background and some live
music, skittle alley, pool; children and dogs
welcome, tables on large forecourt, good
nearby walks, nine bedrooms in converted
side barn, no food Sun evening or lunchtimes
Mon and Tues.

WIDCOMBE ST2216
Holman Clavel (01823) 421070
Culmhead, on ridge road W of B3170,
follow sign for Blagdon; 2 miles S of
Corfe; TA3 7EA Country local dating
from the 14th c, friendly and relaxed, with
good food from varied blackboard menu
(vegetarian and gluten-free diets catered
for), six real ales including Butcombe,
Fullers, Hanlons and Otter, own Tricky
cider, flagstoned bar with woodburner in
big fireplace, room off has a long dining
table (seats 24); some live music; children,
dogs and muddy boots welcome, handy for
Blackdown Hills, two comfortable bedrooms,
campsite next door, open all day Fri, Sat, to
8pm Sun, closed Tues.

WINCANTON ST7028
Nog Inn (01963) 32998
South Street; BA9 9DL Friendly old split-
level town pub; well kept Otter, Sharps and
a couple of guests, continental beers and
real cider, good reasonably priced traditional
food including Sun carvery (not summer),
Tues steak night and Weds pie and pint, bare
boards, carpet and flagstones, pump clips
on bar ceiling, log fires; background music,
knitting group Mon evening, quiz second Tues

of month, darts; well behaved children and
dogs welcome, pleasant back garden with
heated smokers' shelter, open all day.

WINFORD ST5262
Crown (01275) 472388
Crown Hill, off Regil Road; BS40 8AY
Popular old pub set deep in the countryside;
linked beamed rooms with mix of pubby
furniture including settles on flagstones or
quarry tiles, old pictures and photographs
on rough walls, copper and brass, leather
sofas in front of large open fire, enjoyable
generous home-made food (all day Sun) at
very reasonable prices, three real ales such
as Butcombe and good choice of wines by
the glass, friendly landlord and staff; table
skittles and skittle alley; children and dogs
welcome, wheelchair access with help, tables
out in front and in back garden, closed Mon
lunchtime, otherwise open all day.

WINSFORD SS9034
★ Royal Oak (01643) 851455
Off A396 about 10 miles S of Dunster;
TA24 7JE Prettily placed thatched and
beamed Exmoor inn dating from 12th c;
enjoyable often interesting home-made food
(greater evening choice), Exmoor and Otter
ales, West Country ciders and decent wine
list, friendly helpful staff, carpeted bar with
woodburner in big stone fireplace, large bay
window seat looking across to village green
and foot and packhorse bridges over River
Winn, restaurant and other lounge areas;
children and dogs (in bar) welcome, disabled
facilities, 12 good bedrooms, some with
four-posters.

WITHAM FRIARY ST7440
★ Seymour Arms (01749) 850742
Signed from B3092 S of Frome;
BA11 5HF Well worn-in unchanging
flagstoned country tavern, in same friendly
family since 1952; two simple rooms off
19th-c hatch-service lobby, panelled benches
and open fires, well kept Cheddar Potholer
and an occasional guest, Rich's local cider
tapped from back room, low prices, no
food but can bring your own; bar billiards,
darts and table skittles; children and dogs
welcome, picnic-sets in big garden by main
rail line, cricket pitch over the road, open
all day Sat, Sun, from 4.30pm other days.

WITHYPOOL SS8435
Royal Oak (01643) 831506
Village signed off B3233; TA24 7QP
This prettily placed 18th-c country inn
(where RD Blackmore stayed while writing
Lorna Doone) reopened in summer 2019
after major refurbishment; two bars with
straightforward furnishings, open fire and
woodburner and separate dining room,

Exmoor and a couple of guests on handpump, restauranty food from varied menu; quiz last Sun of month; children and dogs welcome (special menu provided for them), eight comfortable bedrooms (dogs allowed in some), open all day.

WOOKEY   ST5245
Burcott (01749) 673874
B3139 W of Wells; BA5 1NJ Beamed roadside pub with two simply furnished old-fashioned front bar rooms; flagstones, some exposed stonework and half-panelling, lantern wall lights, old prints, woodburner, two or three ales such as Hop Back and a real cider, enjoyable food from snacks up in bar and restaurant, small games room; soft background music; children welcome in restaurant, no dogs inside, front window boxes and tubs, picnic-sets in sizeable garden with Mendip Hills views, four self-catering cottages in converted stables, closed Sun evening, Mon.

WOOKEY HOLE   ST5347
Wookey Hole Inn (01749) 676677
High Street; BA5 1BP Open-plan family dining pub usefully placed opposite the caves; welcoming and relaxed with unusual contemporary décor, wooden and tiled floors, tables with paper cloths for drawing on (crayons provided), two woodburners, decent food from lunchtime sandwiches and pub favourites to blackboard specials, house beer Wook Ale brewed for the pub by Quantock and two changing local guests (maybe Cheddar and Glastonbury), several Belgian beers, ciders and perry, efficient friendly staff; background music; children and dogs welcome, pleasant garden with various sculptures, five individually styled bedrooms, open all day apart from Sun evening.

YARLINGTON   ST6529
Stags Head (01963) 440393
Pound Lane; BA9 8DG Old low-ceilinged pub tucked away by the church in tiny village; cosy bar serving three well kept ales such as Bath, Exmoor, Otter, Sharps and Yeovil, traditional ciders, good food from sandwiches and pub favourites to more restauranty choices, efficient friendly service, wood-floored restaurant with big log fire, high-backed chairs and feature cider-press table; background music, quiz every other Tues; well behaved children welcome, dogs in bar, small stream in sheltered back garden, good walks, closed Sun evening.

Staffordshire

BREWOOD
SJ8708 Map 4

Oakley ☐ 🍺

(01902) 859800 – www.brunningandprice.co.uk/oakley
Kiddemore Green Road; ST19 9BH

Substantial, cleverly extended pub with interesting food and drink and seats outside

There's a lot to see near this sizeable pub, making it a great choice for lunch or an evening meal. In fine weather, customers like to make use of the seats and benches among flowering tubs and raised flower beds on the spreading terrace behind the pub, overlooking a lake. Inside, partitioning and metal standing posts split larger areas in the open-plan rooms into cosier drinking and dining spaces and throughout there are the trademark house plants, books on shelves, elegant metal chandeliers and standard lamps, stubby candles and fresh flowers. Seating ranges from groups of leather armchairs to all manner of cushioned wooden dining chairs around character tables on rugs or bare boards, the walls (some half-panelled) are hung with hundreds of prints, and mirrors hang above open fires (some in pretty Victorian fireplaces). From the long counter, friendly, helpful staff serve Phoenix Brunning & Price Original and Wye Valley Butty Bach with guests such as Greene King Escapade and XX Mild, Salopian Oracle, Titanic Plum Porter and Weetwood Eastgate on handpump, 16 wines by the glass, 100 whiskies, 120 gins and 80 rums; board games. There's a rack outside for cyclists, and a circular walk from the pub to help you work up your thirst or appetite. Disabled parking and loos.

🍴 Nicely presented, tasty food includes sandwiches, smoked salmon with orange and beetroot salad with horseradish cream, crispy baby squid and sweet chilli sauce, roast duck breast with crispy leg croquettes, celeriac purée and cherry jus, pea and mint tortellini with garden pea velouté and asparagus, and puddings such as lemon tart with fresh raspberries and chantilly cream and chocolate and orange tart with passion-fruit sorbet. *Benchmark main dish: steak burger with grilled bacon, cheddar, spiced tomato mayonnaise, coleslaw and fries £13.95. Two-course evening meal £21.00.*

Brunning & Price ~ Manager John Duncan ~ Real ale ~ Open 12-11; 12-10.30 Sun ~ Bar food 12-9 Mon-Thurs, Sun; 12-9.30 Fri, Sat ~ Restaurant ~ Children welcome ~ Dogs allowed in bar

CAULDON

SK0749 Map 7

Yew Tree ★ £

(01538) 309876

Village signposted from A523 and A52 about 8 miles W of Ashbourne; ST10 3EJ

An extraordinary collection of curios in friendly pub with good value food, a resident tortoise and bargain beer – very eccentric

---

Get beyond the unassuming exterior and you enter a unique space that looks for all the world like a museum, filled with fascinating curiosities and antiques. The most impressive pieces are the working polyphons and symphonions which are 19th-c developments of the musical box, some taller than a person, each with quite a repertoire of tunes and elaborate sound effects. There are also two pairs of Queen Victoria's stockings, an amazing collection of ceramics and pottery including a Grecian urn dating back almost 3,000 years, penny-farthing and boneshaker bicycles and the infamous Acme Dog Carrier. Seats include 18th-c settles, plenty of little wooden tables and a four-person oak church choir seat with carved heads that came from St Mary's church in Stafford. Look out for the array of musical instruments ranging from a one-string violin (phonofiddle) through pianos and a sousaphone to the aptly named serpent. Look out too for Colin the resident tortoise, who likes to get out and about most days. Drinks are very reasonably priced, so it's no wonder the place is popular with locals. Burton Bridge Bitter, Rudgate Ruby Mild and a guest from Dancing Duck on handpump, six interesting malt whiskies, ten wines by the glass, ten gins and six farm ciders. Darts and table skittles. There are seats outside the front door and in the cobbled stableyard, and they also have a collection of vintage motorcyles and memorabilia. Electric hook-ups for motorhomes. Disabled access. The 'Yew Tree Inn (Side Out)' is a new addition for 2020, aiming to bring the remarkable décor and ambience of the pub into a large marquee with its own outside bar and solid floor, where they serve coffee and cakes along with the wide range of beers offered inside the pub.

An appealing bar menu, served all day, focuses on snacks and includes Staffordshire oatcakes, scotch eggs (including a vegan beetroot one), home-baked pies and cakes. *Benchmark main dish: hot pork bap £4.00.*

Free house ~ Licensee Dan Buckland ~ Real ale ~ Open 12-3, 6-11; 12-11 Sat; 12-10 Sun ~ Bar food 12-3, 6-8; 12-8 weekends ~ Children welcome away from bar area ~ Dogs allowed in bar

---

CHEADLE

SK0342 Map 7

Queens at Freehay 🌀

(01538) 722383 – www.queensatfreehay.co.uk

A mile SE of Cheadle; take Rakeway Road off A522 (via Park Avenue or Mills Road), then after a mile turn into Counslow Road; ST10 1RF

Gently civilised dining pub with real ales and attractive garden

---

This friendly pub draws in people for many reasons. Some come to enjoy the good food, but those who want a drink and a chat are made just as welcome. In warm weather, the attractive and immaculately kept little back garden is a fine place to sit among mature shrubs and flowering tubs. The neat rooms have some cottagey touches that blend in well with the modern refurbishments. The comfortable lounge bar has pale wood tables on stripped-wood floors, small country pictures and curtains with matching cushions. It opens via an arch into a simple light and airy dining area with elegant chairs and tables on tartan carpeting. Helpful staff serve Marstons

Bombardier and Timothy Taylors Landlord on handpump and ten wines by the glass. Disabled access. Handy for Alton Towers.

🍴⭐ Interesting food includes mushroom, black pudding and cheddar melt, aromatic crispy duck, chilli chicken, Staffordshire pork belly, Moroccan harissa chicken, home-made beef and merlot pie, vegetable tagine, leek, potato and stilton crumble, Staffordshire oatcakes filled with leeks and bacon, and puddings such as mango crème brûlée and raspberry amaretti.

Free house ~ Licensee Adrian Rock ~ Real ale ~ Open 12-3, 6-11; 12-3, 6.30-10.30 Sun ~
Bar food 12-2, 6-9.30; 12-2.30, 6.30-9.30 Sun ~ Restaurant ~ Children allowed in restaurant

ELLASTONE
Duncombe Arms ⭐ 🍷 🛏

SK1143 Map 7

(01335) 324275 – www.duncombearms.co.uk
Main Road; DE6 2GZ

Staffordshire Dining Pub of the Year

Nooks and crannies, a thoughtful choice of drinks, friendly staff and lovely food; seats and tables in large garden; bedrooms

Whether you're out for a walk or to have a very good meal, there's a warm welcome for all in this stylishly refurbished village pub. Amid beams and bare-brick, exposed-stone and painted walls covered with prints and photos of horses and big bold paintings of pigs, sheep, cows and chickens, there's somewhere interesting to sit, whatever the occasion. Also, open fires and woodburners, large clocks, fresh flowers and stubby candles on mantelpieces, in big glass jars and on the tables. Flooring ranges from carpet to flagstones, bare floorboards and brick. Furnishings are just as eclectic: long leather button-back and cushioned wall seats, armchairs, all manner of wooden or upholstered dining chairs and tables made from mahogany, pine and even driftwood. There's a beer named for the pub plus Marstons Pedigree and at least one guest on handpump, 36 wines by the glass from a fine list, 28 gins and 25 malt whiskies; background music. An appealing terrace has wooden or rush seats around tables under parasols, braziers for cooler evenings and a view down over the garden to Worthy Island Wood. The ten individually designed and well equipped bedrooms are in Walnut House just a few paces from the pub; they also have a self-catering cottage available to rent.

🍴⭐ Excellent food from regularly changing, seasonal menus includes whole grilled langoustines with sorrel and aioli, chicken liver parfait with plum chutney and toasted sourdough, potato gnocchi with garden peas, baby onions and Lincolnshire poacher cheese, burger with all the trimmings and skinny fries, veal chop with potato terrine, wild mushrooms and watercress, poached salmon with salt-baked celeriac and clam and seaweed butter, and puddings such as custard tart with caramelised apricots, sticky toffee pudding with salted walnut ice-cream and a plate of British cheeses. *Benchmark main dish: corn-fed chicken breast with chargrilled broccoli, rainbow chard and chicken butter sauce £19.00. Two-course evening meal £26.00.*

Free house ~ Licensees Johnny and Laura Greenall ~ Real ale ~ Open 12-11; 12-10 Sun ~
Bar food 12-2.30, 6-9; 12-2.30, 6-10 Fri, Sat; 12-4, 6-8.30 Sun ~ Restaurant ~ Children
welcome ~ Dogs allowed in bar & bedrooms ~ Bedrooms: £160

Bedroom prices are for high summer. Even then you may get reductions for more than
one night, or weekends (outside tourist areas). Winter special rates are common, and
many inns reduce bedroom prices if you have a full evening meal.

LONGDON GREEN
SK0813 Map 7

Red Lion ♀ ◗

(01543) 490410 – www.brunningandprice.co.uk/redlion

Hay Lane; WS15 4QF

**Large, well run pub with interesting furnishings, a fine range
of drinks, enjoyable food and spreading garden**

In summer, it's relaxing to sit and watch cricket matches on the village green opposite this handsome pub; there's also a large garden with seats and tables on a suntrap terrace, picnic-sets on grass, a gazebo and swings and a play tractor for children. The rest of the year, the bustling bar remains the heart of the place, with friendly, courteous staff serving a good range of drinks from it. You'll find Phoenix Brunning & Price Original and guests such as Blythe Bagots Bitter, Salopian Oracle and Shropshire Gold, Timothy Taylors Boltmaker and a seasonal ale from Wye Valley on handpump, 20 wines by the glass, 50 malt whiskies, 30 gins and two farm ciders. Spreading rooms and nooks and crannies lead off the bar in an interior that has been extended and thoughtfully opened up. One dining room has skylights, rugs on nice old bricks, house plants lining the windowsill, an elegant metal chandelier and a miscellany of cushioned dining chairs around dark wooden tables. Similar furnishings fill the other rooms, and the walls are covered with old photos, pictures and prints relating to the local area and big gilt-edged mirrors; background music and board games. Open fires include a raised central fire pit.

 A wide-ranging, inventive menu includes sandwiches, smoked salmon with potato pancake, beetroot and horseradish and chive crème fraîche, a charcuterie plate, chicken liver pâté with toasted ciabatta, Moroccan crispy lamb salad with couscous, marinated apricot and lemon and coriander yoghurt, mushroom bourguignon pie with olive oil mash, greens and red wine jus, and puddings such as baked apple charlotte with salted caramel ice-cream and bread and butter pudding with apricot sauce and clotted cream. *Benchmark main dish: steak and ale pie with mashed potatoes and buttered greens £14.25. Two-course evening meal £21.00.*

Brunning & Price ~ Manager Paul Drain ~ Real ale ~ Open 10.30am-11pm; 10.30-10.30 Sun ~ Bar food 12-9.30; 12-9 Sun ~ Restaurant ~ Children welcome ~ Dogs allowed in bar

SWYNNERTON
SJ8535 Map 7

Fitzherbert Arms ⭐ ♀ ◗

(01782) 796782 – www.fitzherbertarms.co.uk

Off A51 Stone–Nantwich; ST15 0RA

**Character rooms with interesting décor, local ales and rewarding
food; seats outside with country views**

This charming, village-centre pub is not only consistently well run and welcoming, but also thoughtfully renovated and offers a fine choice of drinks and pleasing food. Once through an impressive glass door, the bar sits to the right with a raised fireplace styled like a furnace along with blacksmith's tools and relics. Down a step to the left is the older part of the pub, with button-back leather armchairs beside a two-way fireplace, rugs on flagstones, hops and some fine old brickwork. They serve Fitzherbert Best (from Weetwood) and Swynnerton Stout (from Staffordshire) on handpump with a couple of guests from breweries within a 35-mile radius (such as Merlin, Spitting Feathers, Titanic and Weetwood); also, 16 good wines by the glass, 30 fantastic and carefully chosen ports with helpful notes (they hold port tasting evenings – phone for details), a dozen gins and a fine hand pull cider from Taunton. Staff are helpful and friendly. The beamed private dining room is similarly furnished with a nice mix of old dining chairs and tables, plus window seats with scatter cushions, gilt-edged mirrors, black and white photographs and chandeliers; background music and board games. Do look out for the glass-topped giant bellows and anvil tables, door handles made of historic smithy irons, and candles in old port bottles. Outside, a covered, oak-timbered terrace has contemporary seats around rustic tables, heaters, fairy-lit shrubs in pots and country views; there are more seats in a small hedged garden. There's a circular walk from the pub; dogs are greeted with a biscuit and bowl of water. The pub is owned by Tim Bird and Mary McLaughlin of Cheshire Cat Pubs & Bars.

Creative and enjoyable food includes candied beetroot and Ragstone goats cheese risotto, a signature sharing plate with home-baked pork pie, scotch egg, port and chicken liver pâté, scampi and half-pint of prawns, pan-fried calves liver with mashed potato and greens, pan-fried cod with peas, bacon and caper sauce, katsu chicken curry, smoked fish pie, and puddings such as salted caramel cheesecake with vanilla ice-cream and chocolate brownie with chocolate sauce and honeycomb ice-cream. *Benchmark main dish: steak and Swynnerton Stout pie with chips £14.95. Two-course evening meal £21.00.*

Free house ~ Licensee Carl Dilks ~ Real ale ~ Open 12-11; 12-10.30 Sun ~ Bar food 12-9; 12-9.30 Fri, Sat ~ Children welcome but no under-10s after 7pm (9pm in garden and terrace areas in summer) ~ Dogs allowed in bar

WRINEHILL SJ7547 Map 7

Hand & Trumpet

(01270) 820048 – www.brunningandprice.co.uk/hand/

A531 Newcastle–Nantwich; CW3 9BJ

Big attractive dining pub with a good choice of ales and wines by the glass, served by courteous staff

With its appealing menu and an excellent selection of drinks, this substantial pub is always filled with friendly customers. The linked open-plan areas work their way around the long, solidly built counter, with a mix of dining chairs and sturdy tables on polished tiles or stripped oak boards with rugs. There are nicely lit prints and mirrors on cream walls between a mainly dark dado, plenty of house plants, open fires and deep red ceilings. Original bow windows and a large skylight keep the place light and airy, and french windows open on to a spacious balustraded deck with teak tables and chairs, and a view down to ducks swimming on a big pond in the sizeable garden. Friendly attentive staff serve Phoenix Brunning & Price Original and Weetwood Eastgate with guests such as Peerless Pale, Salopian Oracle, Timothy Taylors Landlord and Wincle Indian Runner on handpump, as well as 20 or so wines by the glass, 15 rums, more than 50 gins and 35 whiskies; board games. Good disabled access and facilities.

Well liked, inventive food includes summer vegetable risotto with broad beans, radish, asparagus and lemon, halloumi fries with tomato salsa, five spiced duck leg with spring onion, cucumber, hoisin sauce and pancakes, braised feather of beef bourguignon with horseradish mash and buttered kale, sweet potato, aubergine and spinach Malaysian curry, king prawn linguine with chilli, tomato and parmesan crisp, and puddings such as chocolate and orange tart with passion-fruit sorbet and a British farmhouse cheeseboard with biscuits, chutney and celery. *Benchmark main dish: chicken, ham and leek pie with mash, buttered greens and white wine and tarragon sauce £14.95. Two-course evening meal £22.00.*

Brunning & Price ~ Manager Ryan Platt ~ Real ale ~ Open 12-11; 12-10.30 Sun ~ Bar food 12-9 Mon-Thurs; 12-9.30 Fri, Sat; 12-8.30 Sun ~ Children allowed in restaurant ~ Dogs allowed in bar

Also Worth a Visit in Staffordshire

Besides the fully inspected pubs, you might like to try these pubs that have been recommended to us and described by readers. Do tell us what you think of them: feedback@goodguides.com

---

ABBOTS BROMLEY   SK0824

Coach & Horses (01283) 840256

High Street; WS15 3BN Well cared for 18th-c village pub with good choice of popular home-made food (not Sun evening) from baguettes and pizzas up, Marstons Pedigree, St Austell Tribute and a guest, several wines by the glass; beamed bar with stone floor and button-back banquettes, dark wood pubby furniture in carpeted restaurant, log fire; quiz, darts; children and dogs (in bar) welcome, pleasant garden with circular picnic-sets, open all day Sun.

ALSAGERS BANK   SJ8048

Gresley Arms (01782) 722469

High Street; ST7 8BQ Popular and welcoming pub at top of Alsagers Bank with wonderful far-reaching views from the back; eight or more interesting ales from smaller breweries and half a dozen real ciders, ample helpings of good value pubby food (not Sun evening) including Tues pie/pizza and pint night and Thurs steak night; traditional slate-floor bar with beams and open fire, comfortable lounge, picture-window dining room taking in the view; Mon quiz (with free chip butties), occasional live music; walkers and dogs welcome, garden picnic-sets, Apedale Heritage Centre nearby, open all day Wed-Sun, otherwise from 3pm.

ALSTONEFIELD   SK1355

★**George** (01335) 310205

Village signed from A515 Ashbourne–Buxton; DE6 2FX Simply furnished family-run pub in pretty village overlooking small green; chatty bar with low beams and quarry tiles, old Peak District photographs and pictures, log fire; eight ales including Marstons and a dozen wines by the glass from copper-topped counter, really good imaginative food (booking essential) using some home-grown produce, friendly efficient service, small snug and neat candlelit dining room with farmhouse furniture and woodburner; children welcome (over-10s only in dining room), dogs allowed in bar at lunchtimes; picnic-sets out at front, more seats in big sheltered stableyard behind, closed Mon-Wed.

ARMITAGE   SK0716

Plum Pudding (01543) 490330

Rugeley Road (A513); WS15 4AZ Canalside pub and Italian restaurant; good food in bar and dining room including daily specials, well kept changing ales such as Bass and Worthingtons, friendly helpful staff; live music Fri, children welcome, no dogs inside, tables on waterside terrace and narrow canal bank, moorings, open (and food) all day.

BARLASTON   SJ8838

Plume of Feathers (01782) 373100

Station Road; ST12 9DH Modernised village pub owned by actor Neil Morrissey; well kept ales including a couple named for them (tasting paddles available), decent selection of gins and good home-made food at sensible prices, friendly attentive service, restaurant; Weds quiz; children (till 9pm) and dogs welcome, seats outside overlooking canal and bowling green behind, open (and food) all day, kitchen closes 7.30pm Sun.

BIDDULPH   SJ8959

Talbot (01782) 512608

Grange Road (N, right off A527); ST8 7RY Family dining pub in 19th-c stone building (Vintage Inn); their usual fair-value food from sandwiches and sharing plates up including weekday set menus, well kept ales such as Sharps and guests, decent choice of other drinks; raised two-way log fire in restaurant part, some secluded areas; background music; dogs welcome in tiled bar area, handy for Biddulph Grange (NT), open (and food) all day.

BLACKBROOK   SJ7638

Swan with Two Necks

(01782) 680343 *Nantwich Road (A51); ST5 5EH* Country pub-restaurant with smart modern décor in open-plan split-level dining areas; good well presented food (booking advised) from sharing boards up, Timothy Taylors Landlord, three guest ales and plenty of wines by the glass including champagne; background music; children welcome, tables in garden and on parasol-shaded deck, open (and food) all day.

BREWOOD   SJ8808

Swan (01902) 850330

Market Place; ST19 9BS Former coaching inn with two low-beamed bars and inglenook log fire; well kept Courage Directors, Wye Valley HPA and four guests such as Salopian and Burton Bridge, good selection of whiskies and gins, no food; upstairs skittle alley, Sun quiz, sports TV; dogs allowed, open all day.

BURTON UPON TRENT   SK2523

Burton Bridge Inn (01283) 536596

Bridge Street (A50); DE14 1SY Friendly down-to-earth local with six good Burton Bridge ales from brewery across old-fashioned brick yard; simple little front area leading into adjacent bar, plain walls hung with brewery memorabilia, small beamed and oak-panelled lounge with coal-effect gas fire, upstairs skittle alley, bar snacks only (pies, cold cobs); children (till 8pm) and dogs welcome, picnic-sets to rear, closed lunchtimes apart from Fri, Sat and Sun.

BURTON UPON TRENT   SK2423
★ **Coopers Tavern** (01283) 567246
Cross Street; DE14 1EG Traditionally refurbished 19th-c backstreet local tied to Joules – was tap for the Bass brewery and still has some wonderful ephemera including mirrors and glazed adverts; homely and warm with coal fire, straightforward front parlour, back bar doubling as tap room with their beers, up to half a dozen guests (including Bass) and good selection of ciders/perries, cheeseboards, sausage rolls, scotch eggs and pies only but can bring your own food (or take beer to next-door curry house); live music including monthly acoustic and open mike nights, folk Tues; children (till 7pm) and dogs welcome, small back garden; closed all day Mon, till 5pm Tues (and Wed in winter).

CHEDDLETON   SJ9752
Black Lion (01538) 360620
Leek Road, by the church; ST13 7HP Convivial bustling atmosphere at this 19th-c village local; Bass, Timothy Taylors Landlord and four guests plus Weston's cider, generous helpings of good traditional lunchtime food including popular Sun roasts and Fri night fish and chips, otherwise snacks such as local pork pies and cheese in the evening, friendly efficient staff; some live music, pool and darts; children and dogs welcome, seats out in front and in fenced back garden, open all day.

CHEDDLETON   SJ9751
Boat (01538) 360521
Basford Bridge Lane, off A520; ST13 7EQ Cheerful unpretentious canalside local handy for Churnet Valley steam railway, flint mill and country park; long bar with low plank ceiling, well kept Marstons-related ales and enjoyable honest food from sandwiches to steaks, dining room behind; live music; children welcome, dogs in bar, seats out overlooking Caldon Canal, open all day.

CODSALL   SJ8603
Codsall Station (01902) 847061
Chapel Lane/Station Road; WV8 2EH Converted vintage waiting room and ticket office of working station, comfortable and welcoming with well kept Holdens ales and a couple of guests, good value pubby food including blackboard specials (just cobs and pork pies Sun, Mon), lots of railway

memorabilia, open fire, conservatory; children and dogs welcome, disabled access, terrace seating, open all day.

CONSALL   SK0049
Black Lion (01782) 550294
Consall Forge, OS Sheet 118 map reference 000491; best approach from Nature Park, off A522, using car park 0.5 miles past Nature Centre; ST9 0AJ Traditional take-us-as-you-find-us place tucked away in rustic canalside spot by restored steam railway station; generous helpings of enjoyable pub food (just bar snacks and soup Sun evening-Weds), up to five well kept ales including Black Hole and several ciders, flagstones and good coal fire; occasional music and open mike nights, background music; children and dogs welcome, seats out overlooking canal, area for campers and shop for boaters, good walks, open all day and can get very busy weekend lunchtimes.

COPMERE END   SJ8029
Star (01785) 850279
W of Eccleshall; ST21 6EW Friendly 19th-c two-room country local; well kept Bass, Bombardier, Sharps and a couple of guests, decent choice of reasonably priced food from sandwiches up (not Sun evening), open fire and woodburner; occasional live music, quiz; children and dogs welcome, tables and play area in back garden overlooking mere, good walks, open all day weekends, closed Mon.

DENSTONE   SK0940
Tavern (01889) 739861
College Road; ST14 5HR Welcoming 17th-c stone-built pub with good food (not Mon or Tues) including freshly made pizzas (Fri, Sat evenings) and Sun lunch, well kept Marstons ales and guests plus good range of wines by the glass, pleasant service, comfortable lounge, dining conservatory; occasional live music, darts; children and dogs welcome, picnic-sets out at front among tubs and hanging baskets, beer garden, village farm shop and lovely church, open all day Fri-Sun, closed Mon lunchtime.

DRAYCOTT IN THE MOORS SJ9840
Draycott Arms (01782) 911030
Junction of Uttoxeter Road and Cheadle Road; ST11 9RQ Welcoming modernised pub with good sensibly priced food including selection of small tapas-style plates, Sharps Doom Bar and a guest, Aspall's cider, friendly attentive service, two-way woodburner separating bar and restaurant; darts; children and dogs (in bar) welcome, garden with covered area, open all day Sat, till 5pm Sun, closed Mon.

We include some hotels with a good bar that offers facilities comparable to those of a pub.

DUSTON SP7262
Hopping Hare (01604) 580090
Hopping Hill Gardens; NN5 6PF
Imposing red-brick former manor surrounded
by housing; largish bar adjacent to entrance,
log fires and lots of different dining areas,
well kept Adnams, Black Sheep and a guest,
good range of wines by the glass and highly
rated attractively presented food, including
set menu and breakfast; friendly efficient
service; children welcome, no dogs inside,
seats out on decking, 20 modern bedrooms,
open (and food) all day.

ECCLESHALL SJ8329
Old Smithy (01785) 850564
Castle Street; ST21 6DF Comfortable
pub-restaurant with clean modern décor;
good freshly made food from sandwiches and
sharing boards up, four fairly mainstream
ales and good choice of wines and other
drinks, friendly efficient staff; children
welcome, small outside seating area, open all
day, food all day Sat, till 7.30pm Sun.

ECCLESHALL SJ8329
Royal Oak (01785) 859065
High Street; ST21 6BW Restored beamed
coaching inn with colonnaded frontage;
well kept Joules ales and enjoyable locally
sourced food (daily lunch and evening
service, except Sun when kitchen shuts
4pm), friendly chatty staff; weekly live music;
children and dogs (in bar) welcome, beer
garden, open all day.

FLASH SK0267
Travellers Rest/Knights Table
(01298) 23695 *A53 Buxton–Leek;
SK17 0SN* Isolated main-road pub, one
of the highest in Britain; good reasonably
priced traditional food (not Sun evening),
four well kept ales and good selection of
wines, friendly service, beams, bare stone
walls and open fires, medieval knights theme;
children very welcome, no dogs inside, great
Peak District views from back terrace, classic
car meeting last Thurs of month, bedrooms,
closed Mon and Tues, otherwise open all day.

FRADLEY SK1414
Swan (01283) 790330
Fradley Junction; DE13 7DN Terrace-
row pub (aka the Mucky Duck) in good
canalside location at Trent & Mersey and
Coventry junction; Everards ales and guests,
enjoyable reasonably priced food including
pizzas and popular Sun carvery (no food Sun
evening), cheery traditional public bar with
woodburner and open fire, quieter lounge

and lower vaulted dining room (former
stable); Tues quiz, Thurs folk night, Sun open
mike; children and dogs welcome, waterside
tables, open all day.

GNOSALL SJ8220
Boat (01785) 822208
*Gnosall Heath, by Shropshire Union
Canal Bridge 34; ST20 0DA* Popular
little canalside pub run by friendly family;
comfortable first-floor bar with curved
window seat overlooking narrowboats,
four ales including Marstons and Banks's,
decent choice of reasonably priced pubby
food including vegetarian/vegan choices and
Tues evening meal deal, open fire; darts and
dominoes; children and dogs welcome, tables
out by canal, moorings and nice walks, open
all day weekends (no food Sun evening),
closed Mon lunchtime.

GNOSALL SJ8220
George & Dragon 07779 327551
High Street; ST20 0EX Welcoming
unpretentious little pub dating from the 18th c;
well kept Holdens Golden Glow, Woods
Shropshire Lad and three guests, four proper
ciders and decent range of other drinks,
just snacky food such as cobs and home-
made sausage rolls; simple interior with
woodburner and some quirky tables made
from old farming gear, dogs welcome, open
all day weekends, from 4pm weekdays.

HANLEY SJ8847
Coachmakers Arms 07876 144818
*Lichfield Street, opposite the bus station;
ST1 3EA* Chatty traditional 19th-c pub;
well kept Bass and three guests, snacky
food such as pork pies, four small rooms
and drinking corridor (some redecoration),
original seating and open fires; occasional
live music, darts; dogs welcome, open all day
weekends, from 4pm other days (2pm Fri);
new managers since May 2020 so may be
changes – reports please.

HIGH OFFLEY SJ7725
Anchor (01785) 284569
*Off A519 Eccleshall–Newport; towards
High Lea, by Shropshire Union Canal
Bridge 42; Peggs Lane; ST20 0NG* Built
around 1830 to serve the Shropshire Union
Canal and little changed in the century or
more this family has run it; two small simple
front rooms, one with a couple of fine high-
backed settles on quarry tiles, Wadworths 6X
and Weston's cider, sandwiches on request,
owners' sitting room behind bar; outbuilding
with semi-open lavatories (swallows may fly
through); no children inside, lovely garden

Post Office address codings confusingly give the impression that some pubs
are in Staffordshire, when they're really in Cheshire or Derbyshire
(which is where we list them).

with hanging baskets and notable topiary anchor, small shop, moorings (near Bridge 42), caravans/camping, closed Mon-Thurs in winter.

HIMLEY   SO8990
★ **Crooked House**   (01384) 238583
Signed down long lane from B4176 Gornalwood–Himley, OS Sheet 139 map reference 896908; DY3 4DA This famous Black Country pub is an extraordinary sight – building thrown wildly out of kilter by mining subsidence, one side 4-ft lower than the other and slopes so weird that things appear to roll up them rather than down; public bar (dogs allowed here) with grandfather clock and hatch serving Banks's and other Marstons-related ales, lounge bar, enjoyable food from chop-house menu including set deal, some local antiques in level extension, conservatory; children welcome in eating areas, large outside terrace, closed Mon and Tues, otherwise open all day (till 6pm Sun).

HULME END   SK1059
Manifold Inn   (01298) 84537
B5054 Warslow–Hartington; SK17 0EX Fairly isolated stone coaching inn near River Manifold; enjoyable traditional home-made food at reasonable prices, four well kept ales such as Leatherbritches and Marstons, pleasant friendly staff, log fire in traditional carpeted bar, adjacent restaurant and conservatory; background music, TV; children and dogs (in some parts) welcome, disabled facilities, tables outside, 11 bedrooms (eight in converted barns), self-catering cottage, good walks including Manifold Trail, cycling routes nearby, open (and food) all day.

LEEK   SJ9956
Earl Grey   (01538) 372570
Ashbourne Road; ST13 5AT Traditional little red-brick corner pub with split-level interior; a house ale brewed by Whim plus several other interesting changing beers (tasters offered), real ciders and decent range of whiskies/gins, friendly knowledgeable staff and good mix of customers, no food; juke box and some live music, weekly quiz; dogs welcome, open from 5pm Mon, 3pm Tues-Fri, all day Sat and Sun.

LEEK   SJ9856
Wilkes Head   07976 592787
St Edward Street; ST13 5DS Friendly no-frills three-room local dating from the early 18th c; five changing ales including Whim, four real ciders and good choice of whiskies, no food; juke box in back room and regular live music events including festivals organised by musician landlord; children allowed in one room (not really a family pub), dogs on leads (but do ask first), fair disabled access, large garden with stage, open from 3pm Mon, Tues and Thurs, otherwise open all day.

LICHFIELD   SK1109
Beerbohm   (01543) 898252
Tamworth Street; WS13 6JP Popular continental style café-bar; four real ales including a beer badged for them, plenty of international beers (draught and bottled, including gluten-free options) and good choice of other drinks, friendly knowledgeable staff, cosy bar with comfortable seating and iron-framed tables on wood floor, upstairs lounge, no food but can bring your own (plates and cutlery supplied), tea and coffee; background music; well behaved dogs welcome, closed Sun and Mon, otherwise open all day.

LICHFIELD   SK0705
Boat   (01543) 361692
A461; from A5 at Muckley Corner, take A461 signed Walsall; continue over M6 Toll bridge and take next right (Hilton) to return on dual carriageway; WS14 0BU Highly regarded imaginative food including tasting menus (not cheap) at this modernised restaurthe-pub; split-level interior with view into kitchen from skylit entrance, upholstered dining chairs at sturdy tables, woodburner in cosy bar area serving up to three changing ales and several wines by the glass, attentive friendly service; background music; small outside bar in garden with central raised deck, closed all Mon and Tues, lunchtime Wed, evening Sun, otherwise open all day.

LICHFIELD   SK1109
Duke of York   (01543) 898558
Greenhill/Church Street; WS13 6DY Refurbished old beamed pub with split-level front bar, smart lounge and converted back stables, inglenook woodburners, three Joules ales and guests, good food from bar snacks up served by pleasant staff, Sun carvery (till 4pm); bowling green, some live music; no children but dogs allowed, terrace picnic-sets, open all day.

LICHFIELD   SK1109
Horse & Jockey   (01543) 410033
Sandford Street cul-de-sac; WS13 6QA Traditional free house with eight very well kept ales including Holdens, Marstons, Timothy Taylors and Wye Valley, some lunchtime food such as pork pies, good friendly service; games room, sports TV; no under-21s, dogs welcome, small garden behind, open all day.

LITTLE BRIDGEFORD   SJ8727
Mill   (01785) 282710
Worston Lane; near M6 junction 14; turn right off A5013 at Little Bridgeford; ST18 9QA Dining pub in attractive 1814 watermill; decent sensibly priced food, three Greene King ales and a guest, good friendly service; Thurs quiz; children and dogs welcome, disabled access, nice grounds with

adventure playground and nature trail (lakes, islands etc), open (and food) all day.

LONGDON   SK0814
Swan with Two Necks
(01543) 491570 *Off A51 Lichfield–Rugeley; Brook Lane; WS15 4PN* Welcoming village pub with long low-beamed quarry-tiled bar, two-way woodburner and some leather wall benches, separate wood-floored lounge/restaurant with a couple of open fires, enjoyable fairly pubby food, Marston Pedigree, Sharps Doom Bar and two guests, good range of gins, friendly helpful service; children (away from bar) and dogs (in bar) welcome, garden with play area, open (and food) all day, kitchen shuts 7pm Sun.

MARCHINGTON   SK1330
Dog & Partridge (01283) 820394
Church Lane; ST14 8LJ Flower-decked 18th-c village pub with various beamed and tile-floored rooms; Bass, four changing guests (beer festivals) and more than ten craft beers, good food (not Sun evening) including themed nights and bargain two-course lunch, good value wines; attentive friendly staff, real fires and some interesting bits and pieces; background music (live Sun from 5.30pm), open mike second and last Thurs of month; children and dogs (in bar) welcome, tables under parasols in paved back terrace by car park, open all day weekends (closed Mon and Tues in winter).

MEERBROOK   SJ9960
Lazy Trout (01538) 300385
Centre of village; ST13 8SN Popular country dining pub with good sensibly priced food from regularly changing menu, friendly helpful staff, small bar area serving five well kept ales including Greene King from curved stone counter, good selection of gins too; log fire in comfortable dining lounge on right, another dining room to the left with quarry tiles, pine furniture and old cooking range; juke box, occasional live music; children welcome, dogs and muddy boots in some parts, seats out at front by quiet lane and in appealing garden behind (splendid views to the Roaches and Hen Cloud), small children's play area, good walks, open (and food) all day.

NEWBOROUGH   SK1325
Red Lion (01283) 576182
Duffield Lane; DE13 8SH Old pub facing church in quiet village; comfortable bar with open fire, three Marstons-related ales, Bass

and good choice of other drinks, enjoyable fair priced food from snacks up including signature rotisserie chicken, vegetarian and vegan options and set lunch, smallish dining room, friendly accommodating staff; children welcome, seats out at front, open all day, kitchen shuts 6pm Sun.

ONECOTE   SK0455
★ Jervis Arms (01538) 304206
B5053; ST13 7RU Cosy whitewashed country dining pub refurbished in 2017 under welcoming new management; up to five well kept changing ales, proper cider and good range of wines and gins, generous helpings of popular reasonably priced food including sandwiches and good.Sun roasts (till 7.30pm), friendly efficient service, woodburners in all three rooms, beams and some exposed stonework, settles and other country furniture on old quarry tiles or wood floors; occasional live music, darts; children and dogs welcome, streamside (River Hamps) garden with footbridge to car park, closed Mon, otherwise open (and food) all day.

PENKRIDGE   SJ9214
Littleton Arms (01785) 716300
St Michaels Square/A449 – M6 detour between junctions 12 and 13; ST19 5AL Cheerfully busy dining pub-hotel (former coaching inn) with contemporary open-plan interior; good variety of enjoyable well presented food from sandwiches and sharing boards to popular Sun roasts plus vegan menu, six well kept changing ales and appealing choice of wines/gins from island servery, afternoon teas, friendly accommodating staff; background music (live last Fri of the month); children and dogs (in bar area) welcome, terrace seating under parasols, ten bedrooms, open all day (till midnight Fri, Sat), breakfast from 7am Mon-Fri (8am weekends).

SANDON   SJ9429
Dog & Doublet (01889) 508331
B5066 just off A51; ST18 0DJ Sizeable Edwardian pub with various linked bar and dining areas, good choice of enjoyable food (special diets catered for) including early evening deal (weekdays 5-6.30pm) and Thurs steak night, well kept ales including Banks's, Marstons and Titanic, over 20 wines by the glass, cocktails and afternoon teas, friendly staff; background music, sports TV; children and dogs (in bar) welcome, tables on front paved terrace and in central courtyard, 11 bedrooms, open all day.

'Children welcome' means the pub says it lets children inside without any special restriction. If it allows them in, but to restricted areas such as an eating area or family room, we specify this. Some pubs may impose an evening time limit. We do not mention limits after 9pm as we assume children are home by then.

SEIGHFORD   SJ8725
Hollybush (01785) 281644
*3 miles from M6 junction 14 via A5013/
B5405; ST18 9PQ* Modernised and
extended beamed pub owned by the village;
good value locally sourced pubby food (not
Sun evening, Mon) from sandwiches and
light choices up, popular Sun carvery, ales
including Titanic and Everards; Sun quiz,
portable skittle alley; children and dogs
welcome, disabled access, beer garden, open
all day Fri-Sun.

SHEEN   SK1160
Staffordshire Knot (01298) 84329
Off B5054 at Hulme End; SK17 0ET
Welcoming traditional 17th-c stone-built
village pub; nice mix of old furniture on
flagstones or red and black tiles, stag's
head and hunting prints, two log fires in
hefty stone fireplaces, good interesting food
cooked by landlady (booking required),
a couple of well kept ales and reasonably
priced wines, friendly helpful staff; children
and dogs welcome, picnic-sets on terrace,
closed Mon, and may shut if quiet.

SHENSTONE   SK1004
Plough (01543) 481800
Pinfold Hill, off A5127; WS14 0JN
Village dining pub with clean modern
interior; enjoyable food from sandwiches,
sharing boards and pizzas up, plus weekday
breakfast (9-11am Fri-Sun) and themed
nights, ales such as Greene King and
Holdens, good range of wines and other
drinks including cocktails, friendly service;
children welcome, dogs allowed in bar, tables
out on front terrace, open all day, no food
Sun evening.

STAFFORD   SJ9323
Swan (01785) 258142
Greengate Street; ST16 2JA Refurbished
18th-c two-bar coaching inn; well kept
changing ales, craft beers, plenty of wines
by the glass and wide choice of other drinks
including cocktails, good bar and brasserie
food, coffee shop, friendly helpful staff; live
music Fri in courtyard garden, 31 bedrooms,
open (and food) all day.

STANLEY   SJ9352
Travellers Rest (01782) 502580
Off A53 NE of Stoke; ST9 9LX
Comfortable old village pub with large
restaurant/bar area; beams and some
exposed stonework, pubby tables and chairs
on patterned carpet, button-back banquettes,
brassware and knick-knacks, well kept
Bass, Marstons Pedigree and guests from
central servery, wide choice of reasonably
priced popular food including deals (booking
advised), friendly helpful service; children
allowed away from bar, no dogs inside, tables
out at front under parasols, self-catering
cottages, open all day, food all day weekends.

STOKE-ON-TRENT   SJ8649
Bulls Head (01782) 834153
St Johns Square, Burslem; ST6 3AJ
Old-fashioned two-room tap for Titanic with
up to ten real ales (including guests) from
horseshoe bar, also good selection of Belgian
beers, real ciders and wines; well cared-for
interior with varnished tables on wood
or carpeted floors, coal fire; monthly live
folk music, bar billiards and table skittles;
drinking area outside (may be barbecue if
Port Vale are at home), open all day Fri-Sun,
closed till 3pm other days.

STOKE-ON-TRENT   SJ8745
Glebe (01782) 860670
*35 Glebe Street, by the Civic Centre;
ST4 1HG* Well restored 19th-c Joules
corner pub, their ales, Weston's cider and
good reasonably priced wines from central
mahogany counter, William Morris-attributed
leaded windows, bare boards and panelling,
some civic portraits and big fireplace with
coat of arms above, wholesome bar food (not
Sun) and all-day deli counter, friendly staff;
live music Tues, open mike Thurs; children
and dogs welcome, benches in small garden,
quite handy for station, closed Mon evening,
otherwise open all day.

STOKE-ON-TRENT   SJ8647
Holy Inadequate 07771 358238
Etruria Old Road; ST1 5PE Drinkers' pub
with five well kept ales including Joules Pale
and maybe one from on-site microbrewery,
good range of British craft kegs, German
lagers and lots of bottled beers, snacky food
such as pies and scotch eggs, friendly staff;
dogs welcome, outdoor covered terrace, open
all day Fri-Sun, from 4pm other days.

STONE   SJ9034
Royal Exchange (01785) 812685
*Corner of Radford Street (A520) and
Northesk Street; ST15 8DA* End-of-terrace
pub owned by Titanic; their well kept ales
and several guests including Everards, snacky
lunchtime food (Fri and Sat only), also Mon
evening meal deal, friendly helpful staff,
three seating areas (steps) including outdoor
snug, two fires; occasional acoustic music
and monthly Tues quiz; dogs welcome, open
all day (till midnight Fri, Sat).

STOWE   SK0027
Cock (01889) 270237
*Off A518 Stafford–Uttoxeter; Station
Road; ST18 0LF* Elegant conversion of
old beamed pub opposite village church;
well executed international food, including
afternoon tea, served daily (except Mon),
split-level restaurant and small bar area
serving real ale and seven wines by the glass
from French list (mainly smaller producers),
friendly efficient service; well behaved
children welcome, a few tables outside and
country views from garden behind.

TAMWORTH   SK2004

Market Vaults (01827) 66552
Market Street next to Town Hall;
B79 7LU Friendly little pub but keeping
traditional character; front bar and raised
back lounge, dark oak, brasswork, etched and
stained glass, original fireplaces and some
interesting old photographs; well kept Joules
ales and guests, real ciders, bargain lunchtime
food and evening bar snacks; live music
Thurs evening; children (till 6pm) and dogs
welcome, nice garden behind, open all day.

TAMWORTH   SK2003
Tamworth Tap (01827) 319872
Market Street; B79 7LR Cosy brewpub
in former shop; own Tamworth ales and
guests, real ciders, bottled Belgian beers
and 80 gins, good mix of customers and
friendly atmosphere, more room upstairs;
no children, dogs welcome; occasional live
music, monthly quiz; tables out at front and
in back courtyard with view of the castle,
open all day weekends (till 9pm Sun), closed
Mon and lunchtimes Tues-Fri.

TRYSULL   SO8594
Bell (01902) 892871
Bell Road; WV5 7JB Extended 18th-c red-
brick village pub next to the church; cosy bar,
inglenook lounge and large high-ceilinged
back dining area, well kept Bathams, Holdens
and guests, reasonably priced wines and
decent food including Sun roasts; children
and dogs (in bar) welcome, paved front
terrace, no food Sun evening.

WATERFALL   SK0851
Red Lion (01538) 308279
From A523 at Waterhouses, take
Waterfall Lane; ST10 3HZ Welcoming
stone-built pub in quiet Peak village; log fires
in two linked rooms, three well kept ales and
enjoyable traditional food (not Sun evening);
occasional live music, darts; children and
dogs welcome, tables outside with lovely
country views, closed weekday lunchtimes,
open all day weekends.

WETTON   SK1055
Royal Oak (01335) 310287
Village signed off Hulme End–
Alstonefield road, between B5054 and
A515; DE6 2AF Old stone pub in lovely
NT countryside – a popular stop for walkers;
traditional bar with white ceiling boards
above black beams, pubby furniture on
quarry tiles and log fire in stone fireplace,
carpeted sun lounge, well kept ales such as
Heritage, Storm and Wincle, good selection
of gins and malt whiskies, enjoyable fairly
priced home-made food from sandwiches
to specials, friendly helpful staff; children,
dogs and muddy boots welcome, picnic-sets
in shaded garden, camping, open all day Sat,
until 6pm Sun (summer and winter hours
may vary).

WHEATON ASTON   SJ8512
Hartley Arms (01785) 840232
Long Street (canalside, Tavern Bridge);
ST19 9NF Popular roomy pub in pleasant
spot just above Shropshire Union Canal
(Bridge 19); good affordably priced food
from landlord-chef including OAP lunch deal
(Mon-Fri), Thurs grill night, Sun carvery,
monthly cheese club, well kept Banks's
and other Marstons-related beers, efficient
friendly service; monthly live music; children
welcome, no dogs, picnic-sets outside, open
all day.

WHISTON   SJ8914
Swan (01785) 716200
Whiston Road, W of Penkridge;
ST19 5QH Large rambling country pub;
beamed bar with quarry-tiled floor and open
fire, real ales such as Hobsons, Holdens
and Wye Valley, proper ciders, extended
tartan-carpeted dining lounge, good choice
of enjoyable reasonably priced food including
range of burgers, friendly staff; TV, pool and
darts; children and dogs welcome, grassy
garden with aviary and play area, open all day
weekends, closed Mon lunchtime.

Suffolk

 ALDEBURGH   TM4656   Map 5

Cross Keys

(01728) 452637 – www.adnams.co.uk

Crabbe Street; IP15 5BN

16th-c pub with seats outside near the beach, chatty atmosphere, friendly licensee and local beers; nice bedrooms

There are few better viewpoints of Aldeburgh's fine pebbled beach than the terrace of the Cross Keys, but it more than earns its place in our selection on its own merits too. Dating from 1540, it's very much a traditional pub, with a cheerful, bustling atmosphere in its low-ceilinged, interconnecting bars and a warm welcome from the attentive staff, as well as pubby furniture and roaring log fires in two inglenook fireplaces. Adnams Broadside, Ghost Ship, Southwold and a seasonal guest on handpump, along with a good choice of wines by the glass; background music. Three newly refurbished bedrooms offer rustic charm and modern facilities at a good price.

 Tasty, seasonal food includes sandwiches, home-made mackerel pâté, cod, prawn and chilli fishcakes with lemon mayonnaise, chilli con carne with local pulled beef brisket, warm salad of quinoa, roasted butternut squash, aubergine and spinach, good pies, various burgers, and desserts such as dark chocolate and date brownie with pistachio crumb and salted caramel ice-cream and glazed lemon tart. *Benchmark main dish: cheese-topped fish pie with prawns, salmon, smoked haddock and local market fish £13.50. Two-course evening meal £20.00.*

Adnams ~ Manager Emily Portsmouth ~ Real ale ~ Open 11-11 ~ Bar food 12-3, 6-9 ~ Children welcome away from bar ~ Dogs allowed in bar ~ Bedrooms: £110

BRANDESTON   TM2460   Map 5

Queen 🍴⊙

(01728) 685307 – www.thequeenatbrandeston.co.uk

The Street/Low Lane; IP13 7AD

Welcoming country pub with popular food, local ales, simple furnishings and seats in the garden; shepherd's huts

This attractive brick-built pub continues to win praise from our readers, not just for the creative food that it's known for but also for its devotion to the craft of hospitality in the round, from warm and engaged service to its contribution to village life. The open-plan rooms are simply decorated in modern country style with settles, built-in wall seats, grey-painted and cushioned dining chairs around rustic tables on stripped floorboards or quarry tiles, an open fire, a woodburning stove and a few wall prints. Three ales such as Adnams Ghost Ship, Earl Soham Brandeston Gold and Woodfordes Try-Umph on handpump, a dozen or so wines by the glass, fruit gins and home-made fruit cordials; background and occasional live music and board games. Community events include a Christmas crafts fair and autumn beer festival, and there's a deli and produce shop. Outside, teak tables and chairs sit among planter boxes on gravel. Their bell tent and two prettily furnished shepherd's huts behind the kitchen garden are comfortable, warm and great fun as accommodation.

🍴⭐ Good food includes gourmet lunchtime sandwiches, own-made savoury snacks such as steak slices, and menus that use local and seasonal ingredients (some of it grown in the kitchen garden) in simple but carefully conceived modern dishes. These might include Basque potato torta with mozzarella and piquillo peppers, black pudding scotch egg with apple and tamarind chutney, rump steak with braised short rib, duck-fat chips, wild mushrooms and cavolo nero, assorted burgers with fries, harbour catch with pink fir potatoes, courgette, capers and burnt butter, spanakopita with greek salad, hummus and tzatziki, and desserts such as apple pie and steamed marmalade pudding. *Benchmark main dish: pie of the day with mash, leeks and parsnips £12.95. Two-course evening meal £20.00.*

Free house ~ Licensee Harriet Aitchison ~ Open 12-3, 6-11; 12-11 Fri, Sat; 12-9 Sun ~ Bar food 12-2.30, 6-8.45 (12-9 Fri in summer); 12-4 Sun ~ Restaurant ~ Children welcome ~ Bedrooms:

BROMESWELL

Unruly Pig 🍴⭐ 🍷

TM3050　Map 5

(01394) 460310 – www.theunrulypig.co.uk

Orford Road, Bromeswell Heath; IP12 2PU

●●●

Suffolk Dining Pub of the Year

Dining pub with Adnams ales, a great wine list, creative food, an informal feel and attentive staff

A highly rated dining pub, the Unruly Pig is also notable for its expertly curated wine list. With almost all of the 60 varieties available by the glass, including vegan and organic options, it allows for satisfying explorations and food pairings. There are a few classic bottles for the buffs, but in general it's an eclectic and approachable mix – as are the customers in this friendly and relaxed place. The bar has button-back leather wall seats, black leather dining chairs, simple tables, rugs on floorboards, woodburning stoves and contemporary seats against the counter where charming, courteous staff serve Adnams Southwold and Mosaic on handpump, cocktails, home-made cordials and interesting non-alcoholic drinks for drivers. The various linked dining rooms have beams and standing timbers, modern art and photos of well known pop stars on painted panelling, more up-to-date leather chairs and banquettes and rugs on bare boards; background music. There are seats and tables under cream parasols on the front terrace and they have bicycle racks. The pub is just a few minutes' drive from Sutton Hoo (National Trust).

🍴⭐ An alumnus of Gordon Ramsay, head chef Dave Wall's fairly priced 'Britalian' food is technically accomplished, beautifully presented and big on taste. There is a set menu, a Saturday brunch and Sunday roasts in addition to an à la carte. As well as lunchtime sandwiches, dishes might include burratina with lovage and parsley pesto, duck liver parfait, octopus with nduja ravioli, ink and miso dressing, various burgers, braised beef shin ragoût with bucatini pasta and parmesan, risotto with courgette, basil, tomato, black olives and mozzarella, and puddings such as pannacotta with espresso, chocolate and caramel. *Benchmark main dish: whole grilled bream with brown crab hollandaise and tomato salad £19.00. Two-course evening meal £23.00.*

Punch ~ Lease Brendan Padfield ~ Real ale ~ Open 12-3.30, 6-10.30; 9-11 Sat; 12-10.30 Sun ~ Bar food 12-2.30, 6-9.30 Mon-Sat; 12-8 Sun ~ Restaurant ~ Children welcome ~ Dogs allowed in bar

CHELMONDISTON
TM2037 Map 5
Butt & Oyster

(01473) 780764 – www.debeninns.co.uk/buttandoyster
Pin Mill – signposted from B1456 SE of Ipswich; continue to bottom of road; IP9 1JW

Chatty old riverside pub with pleasant views, good food and drink and seats on the terrace

You will have a ringside seat for watching the boats and birds on the River Orwell at this simply but pleasingly decorated former bargemen's pub. Its terrace abuts the water, but its parasol-shaded picnic tables get busy quickly, so on a warm day it's best to arrive early or request a window table for a meal indoors. The half-panelled little smoke room is pleasantly worn and unfussy with a woodburner in a brick fireplace and high-backed and other old-fashioned settles on a tiled floor. There's also a two-level dining room with country kitchen furniture on bare boards, and pictures and boat-related artefacts on the walls above the wainscotting. Adnams Ghost Ship, Broadside Southwold and a seasonal ale tapped from the cask by friendly, efficient staff, several wines by the glass and local cider; board games. Disabled access. The annual Thames Barge Race (end June/early July) is fun. The car park can fill up pretty quickly.

As well as enjoyable fish dishes, the good trend-aware food includes nicely priced breakfasts, baguettes and ciabattas, falafel with roast beets and beetroot purée, roast chicken and bacon caesar salad, katsu chicken burger, lamb kofta with sweet potato fries, Asian-style 'poke' bowls with various toppings, red Thai vegetable or prawn curry, and puddings such as a cheesecake of the day and sticky toffee pudding. *Benchmark main dish: fritto misto of tempura prawns, calamari, whitebait, scampi, fries and sweet chilli £13.95. Two-course evening meal £20.00.*

Deben Inns ~ Lease Steve Lomas ~ Real ale ~ Open 9am-11pm ~ Bar food 9am-9.30pm ~ Restaurant ~ Children welcome ~ Dogs allowed in bar

HASKETON
TM2450 Map 5
Turks Head 🏮♈️

(01394) 610343 – www.theturksheadhasketon.co.uk
Top Road; follow village signs taking B1079 from second Woodbridge roundabout; IP13 6JG

This 17th-c building, with its two tall chimneys, has an architectural grace about it that the local couple who rescued it from closure a few years ago have reflected in the tasteful but simple interior design. The light, spacious rooms with their natural wood and stone floors have been enhanced with local art and made comfortable with upholstered wall banquettes, but otherwise left uncluttered. The bar has white-painted beams, a woodburning stove in a large fireplace and tall chairs at the pale oak counter; there's a snug with a woodburner (dogs are allowed here) and the high-raftered, airy dining room has RAF-blue paintwork and doors out to the terrace; there's background music, board games and a genuine welcome for all. Courteous staff serve Adnams Ghost Ship and Old Ale, Earl Soham Victoria Bitter, Fullers London Pride and a guest such as Captain Barlow (named for them from Greene King) on handpump, over 20 wines by the glass and as many gins. In warm weather, the three pétanque pistes are put to good use – as are the chairs and tables under large parasols on the terrace and the picnic-sets on the lawn, especially during summer drinks festivals. Many local walks and cycle rides are described on the website.

 The chef's Indian heritage and classic French training are reflected in the seasonal menu, which uses local produce. Wraps are available all the time, hot gourmet sandwiches at Wednesday to Friday lunchtimes; Sunday brunch and roasts are served in sittings. On the main menu, dishes might include sticky chicken wings with tamarind sauce, local duck liver pâté, dressed Cromer crab, butter chicken masala with dahl makhani, raita, roti and poppadum, 28-day hung Suffolk rib-eye or fillet steak with chips, primavera risotto, and puddings such as grilled pineapple with chilli, mint and vegan ice-cream and summer berry eton mess. *Benchmark main dish: Bengali monkfish curry with coconut rice, aubergine bhaji and tiger prawn pakora £19.00. Two-course evening meal £26.00.*

Free house ~ Licensee Jemima Withey ~ Real ale ~ Open 11-11 (4-8 Mon, Tues Jan, Feb); 11am-midnight Sat; 11-8 Sun ~ Bar food 12-3, 6-9; 10-3, 6-9 Sat; 12-3 Sun; no food Mon, Tues Jan, Feb ~ Restaurant ~ Children welcome ~ Dogs allowed in bar

IPSWICH   TM1844   Map 5
Fat Cat 🍺
(01473) 726524 – www.fatcatipswich.co.uk
Spring Road, opposite junction with Nelson Road (best bet for parking is up there); IP4 5NL

It's all about beer and atmosphere at this all-heart, no-frills bar, which is reliably stuffed with real ales and cheerful customers. Up to 17 real ales tapped from the cask or, in the case of Adnams, on handpump, come from East Anglia and around the UK, from both well known and smaller breweries, in styles mainstream and more esoteric. Both current and upcoming brews are listed on the website so you can plan your visits, and might include Fat Cat Golden, Fullers London Pride, Green Jack Trawlerboys, Mighty Oak Oscar Wilde Mild, St Austell Tribute or Three Blind Mice's unfined orange and vanilla Saison. There are also three craft beers on tap, several farm ciders, quite a few Belgian bottled beers and wines by the glass. The bars have a mix of café chairs and stools, unpadded wall benches and cushioned seats around kitchen tables, bare floorboards and lots of enamel brewery signs and posters; board games and shove-ha'penny. There's also a spacious back conservatory and several picnic-sets on the terrace and lawn. Very little nearby parking. Well behaved dogs are welcome but they must be kept on a lead. No children.

🍴 They keep a supply of filled rolls, scotch eggs (including a spicy version), Suffolk pastries and cheesy sausage rolls made in their small kitchen. They may be happy for you to bring or order in takeaway food, but check first.

Free house ~ Licensees John Keatley and Liz Pledge ~ Real ale ~ Open 12-11; 12-midnight Fri; 11am-midnight Sat ~ Bar food all day while it lasts ~ Dogs allowed in bar

LAXFIELD   TM2972   Map 5
Kings Head 🍺 🛏
(01986) 798395 – www.lowhouselaxfield.com
Gorams Mill Lane, behind church; IP13 8DW

Ancient, unspoilt thatched inn behind the church in a charming rural village; bedrooms

K nown locally as the Low House, this time-capsule of a pub has been little altered during the 400 years of its existence and still serves its ales direct from the cask. There's no bar counter: the helpful staff potter in and out of a cellar tap bar to pour your pints of Adnams, Earl Soham Victoria, Green Jack Golden Best and whatever other ales they choose to stock. (This is a free house, owned for the community by a small group of residents.) You can get other drinks too, including eight or so wines by the glass and a good few malt whiskies and gins. The interesting little chequer-tiled front room is dominated by a booth of high-backed settles next to an open fire topped by an old-fashioned stove, two other rooms have pews, old seats and scrubbed deal tables, and decorations consist of old prints and photographs. Outside, a neatly kept garden has colourful herbaceous borders, a perfectly mown lawn with picnic-sets, and a charming pavilion for cooler summer evenings (you can book to eat in here). Three attractive, comfortable and well appointed bedrooms are in the converted stables. They hold regular events such as morris and molly dancing, classic car days, speciality food nights, beer festivals, plays in the garden and music and art shows.

Good, popular food includes sandwiches, pâté, home-made beef burger with monterey jack cheese and fries, butterflied piri-piri chicken with sautéed potatoes, smoked haddock kedgeree, lamb tagine with tabbouleh, a quiche of the day with salad and new potatoes, and puddings. *Benchmark main dish: pie of the day £11.95. Two-course evening meal £18.00.*

Free house ~ Licensee Emma Turnbull ~ Real ale ~ Open 12-11; 12-7 Sun ~ Bar food 12-2 (3 weekends), 6.30-9; not Sun evening ~ Restaurant ~ Children welcome away from tap room ~ Dogs allowed in bar ~ Bedrooms: £85

SIBTON
White Horse ★ ⭐ ☖

TM3570 Map 5

(01728) 660337 – www.sibtonwhitehorseinn.co.uk
Halesworth Road/Hubbard's Hill, N of Peasenhall; IP17 2JJ

Particularly well run inn with nicely old-fashioned bar, good mix of customers, real ales and imaginative food; bedrooms

A t the junction of three country lanes in pretty little Sibton, surrounded by farmland, this inn with restaurant and rooms has a larder of local suppliers on hand to supply its highly rated kitchen, along with its own prolific kitchen garden. The food is good, then, but it's also a proper village pub with a strong local following and genuinely friendly, hands-on licensees. The appealing bar has a roaring log fire in a large inglenook fireplace, horsebrasses and tack on the walls and a red and black tiled floor, ales on handpump from regulars Adnams, Earl Soham and Green Jack plus guests, 17 wines by the glass and 20 malt whiskies served from an old oak-panelled counter. A viewing panel reveals the working cellar and its ancient floor, and they hold beer, theatre and music events during the summer. Steps lead up past an old, partly knocked-through timbered wall into a carpeted gallery, and there's also a smart dining room and a secluded (and popular) dining terrace. The big garden, with two covered heated terraces, has plenty of seats and attractive planting. The five bedrooms, housed in a separate building next door, are warm, contemporary and well equipped and breakfasts are good. Disabled access but not to the loos.

Impressive food, much of it made from scratch and with gluten-free options, includes sandwiches, a Friday night barbecue in summer and game in season. Dishes might include cured mackerel with fennel, grapefruit, pine nuts and rocket pesto, satay chicken with Asian salad and peanut sauce, roast salmon fillet with potato terrine, samphire and caper, lemon and crayfish butter, confit Gressingham duck breast with mustard gnocchi, bacon and red wine sauce, Suffolk chicken breast with chorizo, orzo pasta and pepperonata, vegetable curry with sweet potato bhaji, and puddings such as chocolate mousse with beetroot sponge, chocolate crèmeux, clotted-cream ice-cream and pear brunoise and whisky set cream with honeycomb, cranberry sorbet and oats. *Benchmark main dish: Blythburgh pork belly with dauphinoise potato, chard and tarragon sauce £15.25. Two-course evening meal £23.00.*

Free house ~ Licensees Neil and Gill Mason ~ Real ale ~ Open 6.30-11 Mon; 12-3, 6.30-11 Tues-Thurs; 12-3, 6-11 Fri, Sat; 12-4, 7-10.30 Sun ~ Bar food 6.30-9 Mon; 12-2, 6.30-9 Tues-Thurs; 12-3, 6-11 Fri, Sat; 12-2.30, 7-8.30 Sun ~ Restaurant ~ Children welcome but no under-8s in the evening ~ Dogs allowed in bar ~ Bedrooms: £110

 SOUTHWOLD TM5076 Map 5

Crown ♀ 🍺 🛏

(01502) 722275 – www.thecrownsouthwold.co.uk
High Street; IP18 6DP

Graceful old coaching inn with plenty of room for both drinking and dining, local ales, interesting wines and seats outside; good bedrooms

This lovely inn takes pride of place on Southwold's handsome high street and in Adnams' pub portfolio too, in its home town; tours of the nearby brewery and distillery are available. Of course, the majority of customers are here for the particularly good food and comfortable bedrooms, but our readers also like to come in just for a drink, in the informal and chatty back bar. Here you'll find oak panelling, bare floorboards and antique tables and chairs, with Adnams Bitter, Broadside and Ghost Ship on handpump, a broad range of wines by the glass including low-alcohol options and eight malt whiskies served by friendly staff; background music and board games. The elegant beamed front bar and dining room are light and airy with a curved high-backed settle and other dark varnished settles, kitchen chairs and bar stools and a carefully restored and rather fine carved wooden fireplace; daily papers. There are seats on the sheltered side terrace or outside at the front by the High Street. Bedrooms in varying degrees of luxury are well equipped and individually furnished, and the breakfasts are highly rated.

Superior seasonal and locally sourced pub food might include Adnams Copper House gin-cured salmon with soused cucumber and horseradish cream, Blythburgh pork belly 'scrumpets' with apple sauce, beetroot and kale salad with toasted walnuts, pickled walnut and black garlic dressing, slow-cooked local beef and Adnams Blackshore suet-crusted pie with mash, greens and pie shop liquor, Ghost Ship beer-battered fish and chips, and puddings such as dark chocolate and hazelnut pot with griottine cherries. *Benchmark main dish: North Sea cod fillet, butter bean, tomato and porcini casserole with cavolo nero £18.00. Two-course evening meal £25.00.*

Adnams ~ Manager Darren Spencer ~ Real ale ~ Open 11-11; 11-10.30 Sun ~ Bar food 12-3, 6-8 ~ Restaurant ~ Children welcome ~ Dogs allowed in bar ~ Bedrooms: £155

 SOUTHWOLD TM4975 Map 5

Harbour Inn ♀ 🍺

(01502) 722381 – www.harbourinnsouthwold.co.uk
Blackshore, by the boats; from A1095, turn right at the Kings Head, and keep on past the golf course and water tower; IP18 6TA

Great spot down by the boats with lots of outside tables and interesting interior; popular food with emphasis on local seafood

Right on the bank of the River Blyth, which separates Southwold and Walberswick, this Adnams-owned pub is especially enjoyable in warm weather, with picnic-sets on the terrace giving views of the boats on the estuary, and seats and tables behind looking across marshy commons towards the town. Inside, the back bar is nicely nautical with dark panelling and built-in wall seats around scrubbed tables, and cheerful staff serve good wines by the glass, along with Adnams keg offerings such as Kobold lager and Blackshore stout alongside Broadside, Ghost Ship, Southwold and a guest on handpump. The low ceiling is draped with ensigns, signal flags and pennants, and there's a quaint old stove, rope fancywork, local fishing photographs and even portholes with water bubbling behind them. The lower front bar, with a tiled floor and panelling, is broadly similar, while the large, elevated dining room has panoramic views of the harbour, lighthouse, brewery and churches beyond the marshes (and sometimes even a cruise liner). You can walk from here along the Blyth estuary to Walberswick (where the Bell is under the same excellent management) via a footbridge and return by rowing-boat ferry (when in season). Because of its marshy location, the pub can suffer from flooding in winter: there's a line painted high up on the front wall indicating how high the waters came up to during the disastrous floods of 1953. Now it has its own weather station to provide information for walkers and sailors.

Locally caught fish is the highlight, with choices such as fried herring milts on sourdough toast, salt-baked tiger prawns with gremolata and fig salsa, devilled whitebait, cod and prawn Goan curry with saffron rice and kiln-roasted salmon and prawn pesto linguine; also platters and good fish (cod, haddock or plaice) and chips. There are sandwiches and a few meat, vegetarian and vegan dishes too, such as smoked Suffolk ham with eggs and chips and red pepper or mushroom and halloumi-style vegan cheese wellington; puddings might include chocolate fudge sundae and baked vanilla cheesecake. *Benchmark main dish: cheddar-glazed fish pie £13.90. Two-course evening meal £21.50.*

Adnams ~ Tenant Mark Cooper ~ Real ale ~ Open 11-11; 11-10.30 Sun ~ Bar food 12-9 ~ Restaurant ~ Children welcome ~ Dogs allowed in bar

WALBERSWICK
Anchor 🎯 ☆ ♀ ⌂

TM4974   Map 5

(01502) 722112 – www.anchoratwalberswick.com
The Street (B1387); village signed off A12; IP18 6UA

This handsome blue-washed inn has contributed to the huge popularity of Walberswick among well heeled holidaymakers: during their 15 years of ownership, former London publicans Mark and Sophie Dorber have poured their expertise and energy into creating an exemplary destination venue for food, drink and accommodation, as well as acting as a village local. The simply furnished front bar, divided into snug halves by a two-way open fire, has big windows, heavy stripped tables on original oak flooring, sturdy built-in leather wall seats and enjoyable artworks on colour-washed panelling; there's a woodburner too, as well as daily papers and board games. Helpful, friendly staff serve Adnams Ghost Ship and Southwold on handpump (and some of their keg beers), along with over 50 bottled beers, a notable wine list with 20 or so options by the glass and an interesting selection of gins. They hold an oyster and beer festival in August (and other interesting events such as art exhibitions and Christmas fairs). An extensive turquoise-painted dining area stretches back from a small, cream-painted lounge. There are plenty of seats in the attractive garden, with an outdoor bar, pizza oven and occasional barbecue serving the flagstoned terraces. Six spacious, chalet-style rooms in the garden have views of either the water or beach huts and sand dunes, while you can hear the sea from the four bedrooms in the main house; dogs are allowed in some rooms. As well as the coast path, there's a pleasant walk northwards to Southwold.

Good food is made where possible from local ingredients, including produce from the Anchor's allotment. Options might include ploughman's, wood-roasted pigeon breast and bacon salad with quince dressing, a fish platter, lamb kofta, barberries, saffron Persian rice and braised aubergine, dressed Cromer crab, chickpea tagine, and puddings such as citrus cheesecake with bitter orange syrup and fresh cherries with dark chocolate truffles. Call to check if breakfast is available; it's good, if it is. *Benchmark main dish: smoked haddock, salmon and cod fishcake with new potatoes and creamed spinach £15.75. Two-course evening meal £24.00.*

Boudica Inns ~ Lease Mark and Sophie Dorber ~ Real ale ~ Open 8am-11pm ~ Bar food 12-3, 6-9 ~ Restaurant ~ Children welcome ~ Dogs allowed in bar & bedrooms ~ Bedrooms: £110

WALBERSWICK   TM4974   Map 5
Bell 🍷 🍺 🛏

(01502) 723109 – www.bellinnwalberswick.co.uk
Just off B1387; IP18 6TN

Interesting and thriving old inn with good food and drinks choice, friendly atmosphere and nice garden; cosy bedrooms

Walberswick is known for its crabbing, beach huts and low-key charm, and you'll find all of them in or near this characterful 600-year-old pub. The appealingly rambling bar has a chatty atmosphere, antique curved settles, cushioned pews and window seats, scrubbed tables and two huge fireplaces. The fine old flooring encompasses sagging ancient bricks, broad boards, flagstones and black and red tiles. Friendly staff serve good wines by the glass and Adnams Broadside, Southwold and Ghost Ship (apparently inspired by the shipwrecks along this stretch of coast, whose lost souls are said to haunt the Bell), along with a seasonal guest ale on handpump and Adnams craft beers; darts. The Barn Café is open during the school holidays for light snacks, cakes, teas and so forth. A big, neatly planted, sheltered garden behind has picnic-sets and the rolling sand dunes are a stroll away. The seasonal rowing-boat ferry to Southwold is nearby (there's also a footbridge a bit further off). Bedrooms, some with sea or harbour views, are attractively decorated, and breakfasts are good.

Satisfying food from a seasonal menu includes pan-fried cockles, clams and pancetta on sourdough toast, roasted cauliflower, pancetta and hazelnut quiche lorraine, chargrilled smoked aubergine steak with beetroot, feta cheese and quinoa salad and walnut sauce, hot-smoked salmon with sautéed wild mushrooms, butter beans, tenderstem broccoli and a soy and sesame dressing, harissa-spiced chicken with tomato, caper and chickpea couscous, and desserts such as sticky toffee pudding with butterscotch sauce and toffee fudge ice-cream and vegan rhubarb and ginger cheesecake with candied lemon. *Benchmark main dish: crispy pork belly with fondant potato, hispi cabbage and Adnams cider and mustard sauce £14.50. Two-course evening meal £20.50.*

Adnams ~ Tenant Tom Rutkowski ~ Real ale ~ Open 11-11; 11-10.30 Sun ~ Bar food 12-2.30, 5.45-9 ~ Children allowed in bar ~ Dogs allowed in bar & bedrooms ~ Bedrooms: £100

The 🍺 symbol shows pubs that keep their beer unusually well, have a particularly good range or brew their own.

WALDRINGFIELD
Maybush

TM2844 Map 5

(01473) 736215 – www.debeninns.co.uk/maybush
Off A12 S of Martlesham; The Quay, Cliff Road; IP12 4QL

Busy pub with tables outside by the riverbank; nautical décor and a fair choice of drinks and fair value food

With sweeping views from inside and out of the broad, tidal River Deben with its bobbing boats, this family-friendly pub is the perfect place to while away an afternoon. The welcoming interior and thoughtful provision of food (served all day) and drink (including good coffee) make it particularly enjoyable. The spacious knocked-through bar is divided into separate areas by fireplaces or steps; there's also a light, high-ceilinged extension. The comfortable, well kept interior has a maritime theme, with nicely displayed nautical antiques including an elaborate ship's model in a glass case, and attractive wallpaper featuring ships' charts and knot-tying diagrams. Adnams Ghost Ship and Southwold and a guest beer on handpump and a fair choice of wines by the glass; board games. The numerous picnic-sets on a terrace behind the pub overlook the water but do get snapped up quickly in warm weather. Disabled access. River cruises are available nearby, though you have to pre-book. There is a large pay-and-display car park (charges are refunded to pub customers).

Popular food consists of breakfast, sandwiches and picnic boxes and an appetising seasonal menu, with fish delivered daily. Dishes might include whitebait with roasted garlic mayonnaise, baked camembert, breaded wholetail scampi with chips, vegan Mediterranean vegetable lasagne with chips, local sausages and mash, dressed Cromer crab, and puddings such as bakewell tart and eton mess with Suffolk strawberries. *Benchmark main dish: Adnams beer-battered fish and chips £13.95. Two-course evening meal £21.00.*

Deben Inns ~ Lease Steve and Louise Lomas ~ Real ale ~ Open 9am-11.30pm ~ Bar food 9am-9.30pm ~ Restaurant ~ Children welcome ~ Dogs allowed in bar

Also Worth a Visit in Suffolk

Besides the fully inspected pubs, you might like to try these pubs that have been recommended to us and described by readers. Do tell us what you think of them: feedback@goodguides.com

ALDEBURGH TM4656
Mill (01728) 452563
Market Cross Place, opposite Moot Hall; IP15 5BJ Part-timbered seafront pub; split-level interior with cosy beamed areas, log fire and some RNLI memorabilia, tasty casual food including tapas, good fresh fish and US-style barbecue dishes such as ribs and brisket from in-house smoking oven, four Adnams ales and decent choice of wines by the glass; background and monthly live music; children (until 9pm) and dogs welcome; one sea-view bedroom; handy for the fishermen's huts, open all day, closed Mon.

ALDEBURGH TM4656
White Hart (01728) 453205
High Street; IP15 5AJ Friendly one-room

local in a quaint one-storey former reading room; high ceiling, panelled walls and stained-glass windows, scrubbed tables on bare boards, open coal fire in cast-iron fireplace, four Adnams ales plus two changing guests, decent wines by the glass, filled rolls only food except for summer pizzas from wood-fired oven in courtyard; occasional live music; no children inside, dogs welcome, open all day.

ALDRINGHAM TM4461
Parrot & Punchbowl
(01728) 830221 *B1122/B1353 S of Leiston; IP16 4PY* Welcoming much storied 16th-c country pub with atmospheric beamed and carpeted bar; good fairly priced casual/pubby food made with local produce including for special diets, well kept Adnams

Southwold and a couple of guests, two-level restaurant; occasional quiz nights; children and dogs (in bar) welcome, nice sheltered garden, also family garden with play area, closed Mon and Sun evening.

BADINGHAM   TM3068
White Horse (01728) 638280
A1120 S of village; IP13 8JR Welcoming low-beamed 15th-c inn; generous helpings of enjoyable reasonably priced food from standards up, Adnams and guests tapped from the cask, real ciders, craft lagers and good range of other drinks, inglenook log fire and a couple of woodburners; children, dogs and muddy boots welcome, nice rambling garden with summer pizza oven and neat bowling green, three timbered bedrooms, open all day Sun (food till 5pm, 6.30pm for pizza).

BARHAM   TM1251
Sorrel Horse (01473) 830327
Old Norwich Road; IP6 0PG Friendly open-plan beamed and timbered country inn with pink exterior and good log fire in central chimney, well kept ales including Adnams, popular home-made pubby food (all day weekends); children and dogs welcome, disabled facilities, picnic-sets on side grass with large play area, bedrooms in converted barn, open (and food) all day.

BARROW   TL7663
★**Weeping Willow** (01284) 771881
Off A45 W of Bury; IP29 5AB Gorgeously restored food-led venue blending the best of modern design, including a striking glass-walled dining room, with fine original features; Adnams Ghost Ship, Timothy Taylors Landlord and Woodfordes Wherry on handpump, good wines by the glass, over 20 gins and farm cider, well liked restaurant-style food including afternoon tea; background music, occasional special events like yoga days; terrace with seats under parasols gives on to lovely garden then a meadow, children and dogs (in bar) welcome, open all day, closed Tues.

BENTLEY   TM1138
Case is Altered (01473) 805575
Capel Road; IP9 2DW Friendly community-owned pub in charming village; Greene King plus three well kept local ales, snacky lunchtime food including sandwiches/ panini and good ploughman's, full Sun lunch and occasional themed evenings, long main bar with woodburner, smaller bar behind and sizeable dining room with another woodburner; regular events such as open mike, games and quiz nights; children and dogs (in bar) welcome, disabled access/ loos, nice fenced garden adjoining village playground, closed Mon and Tues.

BILDESTON   TL9949
★**Crown** (01449) 740510
B1115 SW of Stowmarket; IP7 7EB
Picturesque 15th-c timbered country inn; smart beamed main bar with leather armchairs and inglenook log fire, contemporary artwork in back area, ales such as Adnams and Greene King including seasonal editions along with good choice of wines, gins and cocktails, highly praised imaginative food from snacks and reworked pub favourites up including tasting menus, more formal dining room; children and dogs (in bar) welcome, disabled access and parking, tables laid for eating in appealing central courtyard, more in large beautifully kept garden with decking, 12 individually decorated bedrooms, open all day.

BILDESTON   TL9949
Kings Head (01449) 741434
High Street; IP7 7ED Small beamed village pub dating from the 17th c with own good beers (brewery behind – can be viewed by appointment) plus local guests, enjoyable well priced home-made food (served Fri evening to Sun lunchtime only), pleasant chatty staff, wood floor bar with inglenook woodburning stove; music evenings including Weds open mike, pub games night including darts Thurs with monthly quiz, May beer festival; children and dogs welcome, back garden with terrace and play equipment, open all day weekends, closed Mon, Tues and lunchtimes Weds-Fri.

BLAXHALL   TM3656
Ship (01728) 688316
Off B1069 S of Snape; can be reached from A12 via Little Glemham; IP12 2DY
Popular low-beamed 18th-c pub with important folk heritage in charming country setting; enjoyable unfussy food using prime ingredients at good prices in restaurant or bar, well kept Adnams Southwold and Woodfordes Wherry and a couple of local guests, real cider; regular live and communal music including folk sessions; children in eating areas, dogs in bar, eight chalet bedrooms, open all day.

BLYFORD   TM4276
Queens Head (01502) 478404
B1123 Blythburgh–Halesworth, opposite the church; IP19 9JY Beautiful 15th-c thatched pub on the edge of coastal nature reserve; Adnams ales and good freshly made food from varied but not overlong menu, very low beams, some antique settles, huge fireplace; children (play area) and dogs welcome, tables out at front and in big garden to the side, open all day, food all day weekends.

BRAMFIELD   TM3973
Queens Head (01986) 784214
The Street; A144 S of Halesworth; IP19 9HT Smartly restored village pub next to interesting church; various rooms with heavy beams, timbering and tiled floors, woodburner in impressive brick fireplace in

high-raftered dining room, Adnams and guest ales from Suffolk and Norfolk, including less well known ones, good gin list, painstakingly local and often imaginative food from deli boards up, special diets catered for, friendly service; children welcome, tiered garden, open (and food) all day.

BRENT ELEIGH   TL9348
⭑Cock (01787) 247371
A1141 SE of Lavenham; CO10 9PB Timeless little thatched country pub with salmon-pink exterior; well kept Adnams, Greene King and interesting local guests, proper cider and enjoyable traditonal food from short menu nicely cooked by landlady, cosy ochre-walled snug and second small room, antique floor tiles, lovely coal fire, old photographs of village (church well worth a look); darts, shove-ha'penny; well behaved children and dogs welcome, picnic-sets up on side grass with summer hatch service, one bedroom, open (and food) all day Fri-Sun.

BROCKLEY GREEN   TL7247
Plough (01440) 786789
Hundon Road; CO10 8DT Neat knocked-through bar with beams, timbers and stripped brick, scrubbed tables and open fire, well liked food from lunchtime sandwiches and pub standards up now includes tapas and stone-baked pizzas, Tues steak dinners and offers other weeknights, three changing ales from the likes of Mauldons and Woodfordes, good choice of wines by the glass and several malt whiskies/gins, friendly helpful service, restaurant; monthly quiz; children and dogs welcome, attractive grounds with peaceful country views, comfortable bedrooms, closed Mon and evening Sun.

BROME   TM1376
Oaksmere (01379) 873940
Rectory Road, off B1077; IP23 8AH Civilised 19th-c country house hotel on estate with extensive grounds and tree-lined drive, inside the well appointed beamed and timbered 16th-c bar leads to stylishly comfortable carpeted area; Adnams ales plus guests, expert wine list, sophisticated bar snacks and stylish gourmet restaurant using local produce and specialising in steaks, polished staff; children welcome, conservatory and grounds with play galleon, luxury bedrooms, open (and some food) all day.

BUCKLESHAM   TM2441
Shannon (01473) 659512
Main Road; IP10 0DR Extended and updated old village pub with great local atmosphere enthusiastically run by two brothers; enjoyable food from regularly changing menu including good pies and Sun roasts, Adnams ales and decent range of gins, friendly helpful service; live music, quiz nights, darts and board games; children and dogs welcome, seats out at

front behind picket fence, open all day weekends, closed Mon.

BUNGAY   TM3389
Castle (01986) 892283
Earsham Street; NR35 1AF Pleasantly informal 16th-c dining inn with good interesting food from chef-owner; opened-up beamed interior with restaurant part at front, two open fires, Earl Soham Victoria and a couple of craft beers from perhaps Bull of the Woods or Cliff Quay, nice choice of wines by the glass and several gins, afternoon teas, friendly efficient staff, french windows to pretty courtyard garden shaded by an Indian bean tree; children welcome, dogs in bar area, four comfortable bedrooms, closed Sun evening, Mon (also Tues evening in winter), otherwise open all day.

BUNGAY   TM3491
Green Dragon (01986) 892681
Broad Street; NR35 1EF Unpretentious 1930s corner pub brewing its own good well priced beers including hoppy bitters and a strong mild, brewery tours may be available on request, interesting snacks (Korean-style chicken wings, Gambian 'domoda' peanut and tomato stew) served Thurs-Sat 5-9pm, friendly local atmosphere; occasional live music; children and dogs welcome, tables on brick terrace, open all day (till 9pm Sun).

BURY ST EDMUNDS   TL8463
Dove (01284) 702787
Hospital Road; IP33 3JU Friendly 19th-c alehouse with rustic bare-boards bar and separate parlour, half a dozen well kept/priced mainly local beers and a couple of proper ciders, no food; folk sessions and other acoustic music, comedy nights; dogs welcome, some seats out at front, closed weekday lunchtimes.

BURY ST EDMUNDS   TL8564
⭑Nutshell (01284) 764867
The Traverse, central pedestrian link off Abbeygate Street; IP33 1BJ Simple timeless local with tiny interior (claims to be Britain's smallest pub); lots of interest including vintage bank notes, military and other badges, a wooden propeller and a great metal halberd, even a mummified cat (found walled up here) and companion rat, short wooden benches along shopfront windows and a cut-down sewing-machine table, Greene King ales, no food; background music; steep narrow stairs up to lavatories, children (till 7pm) and dogs welcome, open all day.

BURY ST EDMUNDS   TL8564
Old Cannon (01284) 768769
Cannon Street, just off A134/A1101 roundabout at N end of town; IP33 1JR Early Victorian town house brewing its own beers in the bar (two huge gleaming stainless-steel vessels and views up to balustraded malt floor above the counter,

brewery tours Mon mornings), Old Cannon Best, Gunners Daughter and own seasonal ales, also guests such as Adnams Southwold and good range of other drinks, enjoyable pubby food and barbecue (not Sun evening), assortment of old and new furniture on bare boards; well behaved children and dogs allowed, one apartment and seven comfortable bedrooms in old brewhouse across courtyard, open all day.

BURY ST EDMUNDS   TL8564
One Bull (01284) 848220
Angel Hill; IP33 1UZ Contemporary pub with own Brewshed beers, local guests and lovingly selected range of wines by the glass and bottle (a wine shop opened here in 2020), good restaurant-style food (all day Sat) from shortish menu, friendly attentive service; children welcome till 6pm in bar (8pm restaurant), closed Sun evening, otherwise open all day and can get very busy.

BURY ST EDMUNDS   TL8563
★**Rose & Crown** (01284) 361336
Whiting Street; IP33 1NP Cheerful black-beamed corner local under affable family management; particularly well kept Greene King ales and oft-changing guests, simple lunchtime home cooking (not Sun) at bargain prices, good games-oriented public bar, rare separate off-sales hatch; no young children, pretty back courtyard, open all day weekdays.

BUXHALL   TM9957
★**Crown** (01449) 736521
Off B1115 W of Stowmarket; Mill Road; IP14 3DW A pub of two distinct halves; steps down to cosy low-beamed bar on left with woodburner in brick inglenook, larger timbered dining area beyond with view of old windmill, well kept Adnams Broadside and nice choice of wines by the glass; light airy dining room to the right with its own bar and another woodburner, very good food from interesting menu with everything except the sausages made in-house (prices reflect this), charming service; children and dogs welcome, plenty of parasol-shaded tables on secluded terrace with views over open country (ignore the pylons), herb garden, closed Sun evening, Mon.

CAVENDISH   TL8046
★**George** (01787) 280248
A1092; The Green; CO10 8BA Restauranty 16th-c inn with contemporary feel in two bow-windowed front areas; beams and timbers, big woodburner in stripped-brick fireplace, well liked food from short but varied menu including snacks, 'mac & cheese Thursdays', Nethergate and plenty of good wines by the glass, Aspall's cider, back servery and further eating area, charming helpful staff; background music; children and well behaved dogs welcome, stylish furniture on sheltered back terrace, tree-shaded garden with lovely village church behind, four

bedrooms up rather steep staircase, good breakfast, closed Sun evening, otherwise open all day.

CHELSWORTH   TL9848
Peacock (01449) 743952
B1115 Sudbury–Needham Market; IP7 7HU Prettily set 14th-c dining pub in conservation village; cosy beamed bar with exposed brickwork, grandfather clock and inglenook woodburner, ales such as Adnams, Nethergate and Woodfordes, separate timbered dining room, good sensibly priced food including seasonal game, friendly service; occasional music and quiz nights; children and dogs welcome, bedrooms, picnic-sets in small side garden, open all day Fri, Sat, till 6pm Sun – for sale but still open and active at press time.

CHILLESFORD   TM3852
★**Froize** (01394) 450282
B1084 E of Woodbridge; IP12 3PU More restaurant than pub and only open during mealtimes (lunch Tues-Sun, 'supper' Fri, Sat); very good if not cheap food using carefully sourced local produce including seasonal game, served buffet-style from 'visual hot table' by chef-proprietor David Grimwood, nice wines by the glass and well kept Adnams, warmly welcoming service, little deli next to bar; occasional events including folk music; seats on terrace, no dogs inside – best to check if open before visiting.

CREETING ST MARY   TM1155
Highwayman (01449) 760369
A140, just N of junction with A14; IP6 8PD Attractively updated 17th-c pub with two bars and pleasant galleried barn extension; welcoming landlord and friendly relaxed atmosphere, popular freshly cooked food from landlady-chef, well kept Greene King IPA and guests, decent wines; unobtrusive background music; children welcome, no dogs inside, tables on gravel terrace and back lawn with pretty pond, closed Sun evening, Mon.

CRETINGHAM   TM2260
Bell (01728) 685419
The Street; IP13 7BJ Attractive and welcoming timbered old village pub; enjoyable traditional home-made food from sandwiches up to good fresh fish (landlord is a fisherman), well kept ales such as Adnams, Earl Soham and Grain, nice wines by the glass, bare-boards bar, dining tables in tiled second room with woodburner in big fireplace; regular live music; children and dogs (in snug) welcome, garden picnic-sets.

DUNWICH   TM4770
★**Ship** (01728) 648219
St James Street; IP17 3DT Once the haunt of smugglers and seafarers, now a welcoming beamed and timbered pub-hotel with a striking blue-painted interior in interesting

historic seaside village; enjoyable home-made food, well kept Adnams and three guests, nice wines by the glass, bare-boards bar, dining tables and settles in tiled second room with woodburner in big fireplace; regular live music; children and dogs (in snug) welcome, garden picnic-sets, 14 bedrooms, handy for Dunwich Museum and RSPB Minsmere, beach, lovely coastal scenery and good walks nearby, open (and food) all day.

EARL SOHAM   TM2263
Victoria (01728) 685758
A1120 Yoxford–Stowmarket; IP13 7RL
Simple two-bar pub popular with locals; well kept local ales mainly from Earl Soham (used to be brewed here, now made just across the road) and sister brewery Cliff Quay, reasonably priced home-cooked food, friendly service, kitchen chairs, pews and scrubbed country tables on bare boards or tiled floors, panelling and open fire; outside gents'; children and dogs welcome, seats out in front and on raised beach lawn, handy for the working windmill at Saxtead (EH).

EASTBRIDGE   TM4566
★ Eels Foot (01728) 830154
Off B1122 N of Leiston; IP16 4SN
Country local bordered by freshwater marshes with footpath to sea; split-level bar with light modern furnishings on stripped-wood floors, open fire, Adnams ales including seasonals, Aspall's cider, a dozen wines by the glass and several malt whiskies, high quality reasonably priced food from lunchtime sandwiches up, neat back dining room; live folk music Thurs and last Sun of month, darts, board games; children and dogs welcome, tables on terrace and in attractive big back garden with new pizza oven, quiet comfortable bedrooms in separate building (one has wheelchair access), Caravan and Motorhome Club site, handy for RSPB Minsmere, open (and food) all day Fri-Sun.

EASTON   TM2858
White Horse (01728) 746456
N of Wickham Market on back road to Earl Soham and Framlingham; IP13 0ED Attractive 16th-c village dining pub refurbished under same owners as the Anchor at Woodbridge; much liked food from pub favourites up, three well kept ales including Adnams and good choice of wines, friendly attentive service; children and dogs welcome, a few tables out at front, more in enclosed back garden with play area, open all day Fri-Sun, closed Mon.

EDWARDSTONE   TL9542
White Horse (01787) 211211
Mill Green, just E; village signed off A1071 in Boxford; CO10 5PX
Unpretentious red-brick pub with good green credentials (own wind turbine) with up to a dozen well kept ales including own Little Earth Project of barrel-aged sour beers, plus

unfined vegan beers, craft kegs and real ciders, various sized bars with beer mats, rustic prints and photos on the walls, second-hand tables and chairs, three woodburners, straightforward home-made food; quiz, live music, beer/cider festivals and various outdoor events, traditional games such as bar billiards and ring the bull; children and dogs welcome, terrace, smokers' shelter, makeshift picnic-sets on grass, two Scandinavian-style self-catering chalets plus campsite, closed lunchtimes Mon and Tues, otherwise open all day, no food Sun evening.

EYE   TM1473
Queens Head (01379) 870153
Cross Street; IP23 7AB Pretty cream-painted timbered pub in picturesque country town, three rooms, cottagey feel; Adnams and local guests such as Bullards tapped from the cask (July beer festival), a dozen wines by the glass and good fairly priced food (not Sun evening) cooked by landlord including fish specials, friendly accommodating staff, interesting local artwork, woodburner; background music, monthly quiz and Sun bingo, children and dogs (on leads) welcome, good outdoor facilities including bar, pizza oven, beer garden and play area, open all day (Sun till 9pm).

FELIXSTOWE   TM3134
Fludyers Arms (01394) 691929
Undercliff Road E; IP11 7LU Restored and extended Edwardian pub-hotel on seafront; opened-up bare-boards bar and several dining areas including panelled restaurant, Adnams Southwold, Woodfordes Wherry and guests, good food from bar snacks to upmarket restaurany choices, weekday set menu, friendly attentive service; jazz and some other live music; children welcome, sea views from modern heated front terrace, 14 bedrooms (more views) and mews apartment, open (and food) all day.

FELIXSTOWE FERRY   TM3237
Ferry Boat (01394) 284203
Off Ferry Road, on the green; IP11 9RZ
Nautical-themed 17th-c pub tucked between golf links and dunes near harbour, martello tower and summer rowing-boat ferry across River Deben; enjoyable food including range of fish dishes and some vegetarian options, fish and chips all day in summer in good weather, friendly efficient staff, well kept Adnams Southwold, Woodfordes Wherry and a guest, decent coffee, warm log-burning stove; background music; children and dogs welcome, tables out in front, on green opposite and in fenced garden, good coast walks, open all day weekends and gets busy in summer.

FRAMLINGHAM   TM2862
Station Hotel (01728) 723455
Station Road (B1116 S); IP13 9EE
Simple high-ceilinged bar with big windows,

scrubbed tables on bare boards, half-panelling and woodburner, candles and flowers, well kept Earl Soham ales and good choice of wines, popular freshly cooked food from interesting menu, also wood-fired pizzas Thurs-Sat evenings, friendly relaxed atmosphere, back snug with tiled floor; children and dogs welcome, picnic-sets in pleasant garden.

FRESSINGFIELD   TM2677

⋆**Fox & Goose** (01379) 586247

Church Street; B1116 N of Framlingham; IP21 5PB Relaxed dining pub in beautifully timbered 16th-c former guildhall next to church; highly regarded food from bar meals served in cosy informal heavy-beamed rooms to upscale fixed-price menus in upstairs restaurant, friendly efficient service, Adnams and a changing guest on handpump and a dozen good wines by the glass; soft background music; children welcome, disabled loos on ground floor, tables out by duck pond, closed Mon.

FRISTON   TM4160

Old Chequers (01728) 688039

Just off A1094 Aldeburgh–Snape; IP17 1NP Welcoming village pub with modernised L-shaped bar, well kept ales such as Morlands Old Speckled Hen and Woodfordes Wherry from brick-faced servery, enjoyable home-made food including daily specials, woodburner in brick fireplace; well behaved children and dogs welcome (resident scottie is Lucy), sunny back terrace, nice circular walks to Aldeburgh and Snape, open all day Sun till 7pm, closed Mon, Tues.

GREAT BRICETT   TM0450

Red Lion (01473) 657863

B1078, E of Bildeston; IP7 7DD Modernised and extended old beamed pub; very good exclusively vegetarian and vegan food at competitive prices (nothing for meat eaters), takeaway frozen meals, real ales such as Greene King, efficient friendly service; dogs welcome in bar, garden with deck and play equipment, closed Sun evening to Weds lunchtime.

GREAT GLEMHAM   TM3461

Crown (01728) 663693

Between A12 Wickham Market–Saxmundham and B1119 Saxmundham–Framlingham; IP17 2DA Early 19th-c red-brick village pub; four fireplaces and some nice old Suffolk furniture on wood and quarry-tiled floors, mostly local beers from old brass handpumps, good well priced food (not Tues) including pub favourites with a twist, lots of fish dishes and pizzas hand-made to order, back coffee

lounge with freshly baked cakes, friendly helpful staff; quiz third Tues of month, open mike last Thurs, darts, table skittles; well behaved children and dogs welcome, disabled facilities, cast-iron furniture on back lawn, closed Sun evening to Tues lunchtime, weekend breakfasts from 9am.

GREAT WRATTING   TL6848

Red Lion (01440) 783237

School Road; CB9 7HA Popular village pub with a couple of enormous old whale bones flanking the entrance; log fire in bar, plain carpets and burgundy upholstered seating, lots of copper and brass, well kept Adnams and generous helpings of enjoyable pubby food, friendly staff, restaurant; children and dogs welcome, large back garden with play equipment, open all day Sat.

GRUNDISBURGH   TM2250

Dog (01473) 735267

The Green; off A12 via B1079 from Woodbridge bypass; IP13 6TA Friendly pink-washed pub with cottage-style public bar; log fire, settles and dark wooden carvers around pubby tables on tiles, Adnams, Earl Soham, Woodfordes and a guest, craft beers and good range of other drinks, enjoyable casual food (all day Sun) from fresh local ingredients also evident in new own deli, lots of sweet and savoury home-baking too, carpeted lounge linking to bare-boards dining room; children and dogs welcome, picnic-sets out in front, more seats in wicker-fenced Mediterranean-feel back garden, play area, closed Mon, otherwise open all day.

HADLEIGH   TM0242

Kings Head (01473) 828855

High Street; IP7 5EF Modernised Georgian-fronted pub (building is actually much older) formerly (and sometimes still) known as the Kings Head; popular British food from breakfast on including some themed nights, lobster weeks July and Oct, well kept Adnams and guests, Aspall's cider, good wines, friendly helpful staff; children and dogs (in some areas) welcome, open all day from 9am (11am Sun), food till 7pm Sun.

HARTEST   TL8352

Crown (01284) 830250

B1066 S of Bury St Edmunds; IP29 4DH Old pub by church behind pretty village green; good restaurant-quality food (all day Sun) and new wood-fired pizzas, own Brewshed beers, plenty of good wines by the glass, friendly attentive staff, split-level beamed interior (note the coins left by departing World War I soldiers), good log fire in big fireplace; children (not in bar after 8pm) and well

---

If we know a pub has an outdoor play area for children, we mention it.

behaved dogs welcome, tables on big back lawn and in sheltered side courtyard, good play area, open all day.

HAUGHLEY   TM0262
★ **Kings Arms** (01449) 257120
Off A45/B1113 N of Stowmarket; Old Street; IP14 3NT Prettily timbered 16th-c village pub beautifully done up in comfortable café-bar style, winning accolades for its good food (not Sun evening) from light lunches to ambitious evening à la carte, Greene King beers (Abbot ale was named here by a landlord in 1950), also a guest, craft beers and decent choice of wines, friendly service, woodburner in big brick fireplace; children and dogs (in bar) welcome, back garden, open all day Fri and Sat, till 6pm Sun, closed Mon, Tues.

HAWKEDON   TL7953
Queens Head (01284) 789218
Off A143 at Wickham Street, NE of Haverhill; and off B1066; IP29 4NN Tudor pub in pretty setting looking down broad peaceful green to interesting village church; quarry-tiled bar with dark beams and ochre walls, plenty of pews and chapel chairs around scrubbed tables, armchairs by antique woodburner in huge fireplace, cheerful helpful staff, Adnams Southwold, Woodfordes Wherry and guests, proper cider/perry and knowledgeable wine and whisky lists, good food (not Mon, Tues) in dining area with country prints and a couple of tusky boars' heads; occasional live music and wine tastings; picnic-sets out in front, more on back terrace overlooking rolling countryside, vintage car meeting first Sat of month, open all day Fri-Sun, closed lunchtimes Mon-Thurs.

HORRINGER   TL8261
Beehive (01284) 736737
A143; IP29 5SN Handsome brick and flint village pub with cosy series of beamed rooms and a woodburner; ales from Adnams and Bishop Nicks, enjoyable fairly priced food including daily specials; quiz nights, some live music, pool, lots of events often with a street-food theme; children and dogs welcome, back terrace and raised lawn, handy for Ickworth House (NT), closed Sun evening, Mon and lunchtime Tues.

IPSWICH   TM1644
Dove Street (01473) 211270
St Helens Street; IP4 2LA Drinkers' pub with over 20 well kept quickly changing ales including their own brews (regular beer festivals), farm ciders, bottled beers and good selection of whiskies, low priced simple pub food, bare-boards bar, carpeted snug and back conservatory; children (till 7pm) and dogs welcome, disabled facilities, seats on heated covered terrace, two bedrooms over the road along with the brewery shop, open (and food) all day.

IPSWICH   TM1645
Greyhound (01473) 252862
Henley Road/Anglesea Road; IP1 3SE Popular 19th-c pub close to picturesque Christchurch Park; cosy front bar with corridor to larger lounge/dining area, several well kept Adnams ales and a couple of guests, good home cooking including bargain weekday lunch and daily specials, quick friendly service; occasional Sun quiz, sports TV (sponsors Ipswich Town academy); children welcome, picnic-sets under parasols on back terrace and now also in converted car park with pergola, open all day, food all day Fri-Sun.

IPSWICH   TM1747
Railway Inn (01473) 252337
Westerfield Road close to the station; IP6 9AA Popular split-level pub near level crossing with straightforward reasonably priced food (all day weekends) including daily specials and set menus, well kept Adnams ales and several wines by the glass; children and dogs (in bar) welcome, four bedrooms, outside tables and colourful hanging baskets, open all day.

IPSWICH   TM1744
Woolpack (01473) 215862
Tuddenham Road; IP4 2SH Welcoming red-brick pub dating from the 1600s, quite traditional inside with lots of wood; Adnams and four other well kept mainstream beers from around the UK, several wines by the glass and popular fairly pubby food, helpful accommodating service, two bars, snug and back dining area, corner with piano and board games; live music including jazz some Fri, quiz second Sun; children and dogs welcome, seats on heated front terrace, opposite Christchurch Park, open all day from 10am for breakfast.

KERSEY   TM0044
Bell (01473) 823229
Signed off A1141 N of Hadleigh; The Street; IP7 6DY Attractive 14th-c black and white pub in notably picturesque village with ford; popular home-made food from well priced fairly traditional menu including good fish specials Fri and Sat, Adnams and a couple of guests, friendly service, low-beamed carpeted bar with log fire, restaurant; children and dogs welcome, bench and flower troughs out at front, split-level terrace and garden behind, open all day, food till 7.30pm Sun, kitchen closed Mon evening.

KESGRAVE   TM2346
Kesgrave Hall (01473) 333741
Hall Road; IP5 2PU Luxury spa hotel in white mansion with comfortably modern bare-boards bar; Greene King and a couple of guests from granite-topped servery, several wines by the glass and cocktails, popular if pricey food cooked in brasserie's open

kitchen (no booking so best to arrive early), brunch, afternoon teas, children and dogs welcome, attractive heated terrace with huge retractable awning, sweeping grounds, 23 stylish bedrooms, open (and food) all day from 10am.

LAVENHAM   TL9149
★**Angel** (01787) 247388

Market Place; CO10 9QZ Handsome Tudor building in centre of delightful small town; long bar with inglenook log fire and some fine 16th-c ceiling plasterwork, relaxed feel with chesterfield sofas and armchairs, further dining areas and more heavy beams and panelling, popular food including pub favourites, pizzas and grills, well kept ales from Adnams and a guest, Aspall's cider, cocktails and good range of wines, friendly staff; children and dogs (in bar) welcome, sizeable back garden, eight good-value bedrooms, open all day from 8am for breakfast.

LAVENHAM   TL9149
Swan (01787) 247477

High Street; CO10 9QA Upmarket hotel with spa in series of handsome medieval buildings beautifully decorated inside and out in contemporary country style; appealing network of beamed and timbered rooms including tiled-floor inner bar, log fire, well kept Adnams and a guest, Aspall's cider, lots of wines by the glass from extensive list and good range of other drinks, well thought-of innovative food, can eat in bar, informal brasserie or lavishly timbered restaurant, afternoon teas, efficient friendly staff; children and dogs welcome, sheltered courtyard garden, 45 bedrooms, open all day.

LINDSEY TYE   TL9846
Lindsey Rose (01449) 741424

Village signposted off A1141 NW of Hadleigh; IP7 6PP Refurbished apricot-painted village pub in fields; main bar with low beams, standing timbers and huge open fire, second similarly furnished room and another big fireplace, good fairly priced food from shortish but varied menu plus lighter menu with sandwiches Mon-Weds, Adnams ales and a guest, friendly helpful staff; children and dogs welcome, a few picnic-sets out on front gravel, more on back lawn with play area, open all day (till 6pm Sun, 10pm Mon, Tues).

LONG MELFORD   TL8646
★**Black Lion** (01787) 312356

Church Walk; CO10 9DN Gently civilised hotel opposite village green; open fire and comfortable leather seats in back bar (liked by locals), stools by counter serving Adnams and Nethergate ales, cocktails/mocktails and about 30 well chosen wines by the glass, two dining rooms with portraits and gilt-edged mirrors on green walls, candlelit tables and

another log fire, good attractively presented food from shortish menu, afternoon teas, friendly efficient staff, also drawing room and conservatory; background music; children and dogs (in bar) welcome, front terrace and charming walled garden, comfortable well equipped bedrooms, the grand cathedral-like church is also worth a visit, open all day.

MELTON   TM2850
Olde Coach & Horses

(01394) 384851 *Melton Road; IP12 1PD* Modernised beamed former staging inn; good choice of enjoyable fairly priced food from snacks and sharing plates up (special diets catered for), ales including Adnams and guests, decent wines by the glass, good friendly service; children welcome, dogs in wood-floored area, tables out under parasols among colourful hanging baskets and planters, open (and food) all day.

MIDDLETON   TM4267
★**Bell** (01728) 648286

Off A12 in Yoxford via B1122 towards Leiston; also signposted off B1125 Leiston–Westleton; The Street; IP17 3NN Attractive part-thatched pub once the brewhouse for Leiston Abbey; traditional bar on left with log fire in big hearth, low plank-panelled ceiling, old local photographs, bar stools and pews, Adnams ales tapped from the cask, ten or so wines by the glass and enjoyable good value food (not Sun evening), informal two-room dining area on right has beams, bare boards and mix of painted farmhouse and wheelback chairs around wooden tables, further room with large table (ideal for a family) by woodburner; children and dogs welcome, picnic-sets and parasols at front, more in big back garden, pétanque and pretty summer hanging baskets, handy for RSPB Minsmere and coast walks, open all day Sun till 10pm.

MOULTON   TL6964
★**Packhorse** (01638) 751818

Bridge Street; CB8 8SP Civilised, stylish inn adjacent to delightful 15th-c bridge across the River Kennett; simply furnished split-level bar with wooden tables and chairs on bare boards, some scatter-cushion armchairs and two-way log fire, Fullers London Pride, Woodfordes Wherry and a couple of guests, cocktails/mocktails and a good range of wines, many by the glass, good interesting food (not cheap), opened-up dining rooms keeping cosy areas, candlelight and flower arrangements; children and dogs welcome, tables on terrace and lawn, smart up-to-date bedrooms and very good breakfasts, handy for Newmarket races, open all day.

NAYLAND   TL9734
★**Anchor** (01206) 262313

Court Street; just off A134 – turn-off S of signposted B1087 main village turn; CO6 4JL Friendly pub by River Stour with relaxed modern décor under same ownership as the Angel at Stoke-by-Nayland; bare-boards bar with assorted wooden dining chairs and tables, mirrors, panelling and feature wallpaper and a pretty fireplace at one end, Adnams, Marstons and three changing ales, many wines by the glass including four sparkling, enjoyable food including some home-smoked dishes, notably good vegan menu, two other rooms behind and steep stairs up to cosy restaurant; quiz first Mon of month, some live music; children welcome, dogs in bar, terrace tables overlooking river, three dining pods for hire on riverbank, open all day, food till 6pm Sun, cash not accepted.

NEWBOURNE   TM2743

Fox (01473) 736307

Off A12 at roundabout 1.7 miles N of A14 junction; The Street; IP12 4NY Pink-washed 16th-c pub decked in summer flowers; low-beamed bar with slabby elm and other dark tables on quarry-tiled floor, stuffed fox in inglenook, comfortable carpeted dining room, Adnams Southwold, guest ales and decent wines by the glass, popular food catering for special diets; background music; children and dogs (in bar) welcome, wheelchair access, attractive grounds with rose garden and pond, open (and food) all day, from 9am Sat, Sun for breakfast.

NEWTON   TL9140

Saracens Head (01787) 379036

A134 4 miles E Sudbury; CO10 0QJ Old beamed and timbered roadside pub; good choice of food including vegetarian options and generous Sun lunch, Adnams and Greene King beers, friendly attentive service; bar billiards; children and dogs welcome, garden overlooking pond and common/golf course, closed Mon, otherwise open all day, food till 6pm Sun.

ORFORD   TM4249

★ **Jolly Sailor** (01394) 450243

Quay Street; IP12 2NU Welcoming old pub near Orford Quay under mother and daughter team; several snug rooms with exposed brickwork, boating pictures and other nautical memorabilia, well kept Adnams beers and popular food from good sandwiches up, efficient cheerful service, unusual spiral staircase in corner of flagstoned main bar by brick inglenook, horsebrasses and local photographs; children and dogs welcome, back terrace and lawn with views over marshes, popular with walkers and bird-watchers, bedrooms, open all day weekends.

ORFORD   TM4249

★ **Kings Head** (01394) 450271

Front Street; IP12 2LW Friendly 13th-c village inn surrounded by fine walks and lovely coastline; snug main bar with heavy low beams, Adnams ales and the occasional

guest and several wines by the glass, good home-made food (not Sun evening) from lunchtime sandwiches to daily specials with a focus on fish, popular Sun roast (must book), dining room has old stripped-brick walls and ancient boards, woodburners; occasional live music and quiz nights; children and dogs welcome, three bedrooms, open all day Fri-Sun, closed Mon.

PETTISTREE   TM2954

★ **Greyhound** (01728) 746451

The Street; brown sign to pub off B1438 S of Wickham Market, 0.5 miles N of A12; IP13 0HP Village pub with two smallish well maintained traditional rooms with open fires, candlelight, low beams, chunky farmhouse chairs and cushioned settles around dark wooden tables on bare floorboards; Adnams Ghost Ship, Soham Victoria Bitter and a seasonal guest on handpump, a dozen or so wines by the glass, several gins and malt whiskies (particularly Speyside and island malts), interesting food with local and Scottish influences cooked by landlady, friendly service; children welcome in dining area, dogs in bar, picnic-sets with parasols in side and front gardens, peaceful setting next to church and pleasant nearby walks (some listed on website), closed Mon lunchtime.

POLSTEAD   TL9938

Cock (01206) 263150

Signed off B1068 and A1071 E of Sudbury, then pub signed; Polstead Green; CO6 5AL Beamed and timbered village local dating from the 16th c; bar with woodburner and country kitchen furniture, three real ales (usually including one from Greene King), good choice of wines and enjoyable home-made food, light and airy barn restaurant; background music; children, walkers and dogs welcome, disabled facilities, picnic-sets overlooking small green, shuts around 8pm Sun, closed Mon and Tues.

RAMSHOLT   TM3041

Ramsholt Arms (01394) 411209

Signed off B1083; Dock Road; IP12 3AB Lovely isolated spot right on the River Deben, modernised open-plan bar with log fire, enjoyable good value food (all day Sat, till 8pm Sun) from lunchtime sandwiches up, Adnams, a couple of guest beers and decent choice of wines by the glass; children and dogs welcome, plenty of tables outside taking in the view, nice walks and handy for Sutton Hoo (NT), open all day.

REDE   TL8055

★ **Plough** (01284) 789208

Village signposted off A143 Bury St Edmunds–Haverhill; IP29 4BE Quaint partly thatched pub known and loved for its good food and friendly owners at end of quiet green in tucked-away village; traditional low-beamed rooms kept spic and span, wheelback chairs and plush red wall banquettes around dark pubby tables, solid-fuel stove in a brick fireplace, three changing ales and several wines by the glass, well liked food (not Sun evening) from blackboard menu; background music; children welcome till 8pm, picnic-sets out at front and in sheltered cottagey garden, closed Mon.

ROUGHAM
TL9063

Ravenwood Hall (01359) 270345
Off A14 E of Bury St Edmunds;
IP30 9JA Country-house hotel set in seven acres of lovely grounds; two compact bar rooms, high ceilings, patterned wallpaper and large windows overlooking sweeping lawn with stately cedar, well kept Adnams, good choice of wines and malt whiskies, back area set for eating with log fire, wide range of food including afternoon tea, smokehouse dishes and pizza as well as more elaborate choices served by pleasant staff, comfortable lounge area with a few moulded beams and early Tudor wall decoration above big inglenook, separate more formal restaurant; background music; children and dogs welcome, teak furniture in garden, swimming pool and croquet, large enclosures for geese, pygmy goats and shetland ponies, 14 bedrooms, open all day.

SHOTTISHAM
TM3244

Sorrel Horse (01394) 411617
Hollesley Road; IP12 3HA Charming 15th-c thatched community-owned local; well kept Woodfordes and guests tapped from the cask, decent choice of home-made traditional food, attentive friendly young staff, good log fire in tiled-floor bar with games area (bar billiards), woodburner in attractive dining room; occasional live music; children and dogs welcome, tables out on sloping front lawn and in small garden behind, open all day weekends.

SNAPE
TM4058

Golden Key (01728) 688510
Priory Lane; IP17 1SA Welcoming village pub under same management as the nearby Plough & Sail; low-beamed lounge with old-fashioned settle and straightforward tables and chairs on stripped-wood or chequerboard tiled floor, woodburner, small snug and two cosy dining rooms, well kept Adnams ales, local cider and several wines by the glass, good well presented food from sandwiches to daily specials, cheerful efficient young staff; children and dogs welcome, two terraces with pretty hanging baskets and seats under parasols, handy for the Maltings concert hall complex, three refurbished bedrooms, open all day weekends.

SNAPE
TM3957

★ Plough & Sail (01728) 688413
The Maltings, Snape Bridge (B1069 S);
IP17 1SR Part of the Maltings complex, this former smugglers' haunt is run by twin brothers (one is the chef); mostly open-plan with good blend of traditional and modern furnishings, the original 17th-c core has country pine tables and chairs on terracotta tiles and open fire, there's a second cosy room with leather chesterfields by a woodburner, a simply furnished bar hall and spacious modern dining room with wood-strip floor and pitched ceiling, an additional restaurant is upstairs, Adnams and Greene King ales, several wines by the glass and good up-to-date food along with pub favourites (they do a pre/post-concert set menu); background music; children and dogs (in bar) welcome, some picnic-sets out at front, more tables on flower-filled terrace, open all day and can get packed.

SOMERLEYTON
TM4797

Dukes Head (01502) 730281
Slugs Lane (B1074); NR32 5QR
Nicely positioned red-brick pub (part of the Somerleyton Hall Estate); bare-boards bar with country furniture, painted panelling and woodburner in brick fireplace, four local ales, interesting wines and good selection of other drinks, well liked seasonal food from Estate's own farms, friendly attentive staff, dining extension; children and dogs welcome, tables in tree-shaded garden with rural views, a stiff walk up from River Waveney (moorings), open all day, no food Sun evening, Mon, Tues.

SOUTH ELMHAM
TM3385

St Peters Brewery (01986) 782288
St Peter South Elmham; off B1062 SW of Bungay; NR35 1NQ Beautifully but simply furnished manor dating from the 13th c (much extended in the 16th c); own St Peters beers on draught and in bottles (can arrange brewery tours), they also make their own cider, bar with dramatic high ceiling, elaborate woodwork and flagstoned floor, antique tapestries, woodburner in fine fireplace, two further rooms reached up steepish stairs, outside tables overlooking original moat, weddings and other events; the bar was closed and a new manager being sought when we went to press – arrangements may change.

SOUTHWOLD
TM5076

★ Lord Nelson (01502) 722079
East Street, off High Street (A1095);
IP18 6EJ Busy bow-windowed local near seafront with partly panelled traditional bar and two small side rooms, coal fire, light wood furniture on tiles, lamps in nice nooks and corners, interesting Nelson memorabilia including attractive nautical prints and fine model of HMS *Victory*, five well kept ales with at least three from Adnams, several wines by the glass and decent pubby food, good friendly service; board games; children (away from the bar) and dogs welcome, seats out in front with serving hatch and sidelong view of the sea, sheltered and heated back garden with Adnams brewery in sight, open all day.

SOUTHWOLD TM5076
Red Lion (01502) 723227
South Green; IP18 6ET Updated 17th-c beamed pub with big windows looking over green towards the sea; sturdy wall benches and bar stools on wood floor, well kept Adnams including seasonals, back room with mate's chairs, pews and polished dark tables, lots of framed black and white photographs, good range of popular food served by friendly staff, three linked dining rooms; background music (live Sun afternoon); tables out in front (dogs welcome here) and in small sheltered back courtyard, next to the Adnams retail shop, open all day.

SOUTHWOLD TM5076
Sole Bay (01502) 723736
East Green; IP18 6JN Busy single-room pub near Adnams Brewery; up to six of their cask ales kept well plus their lagers and stout and a good wine choice, cheerful helpful staff, enjoyable reasonably priced simple food including good fish and chips, airy contemporary interior with well spaced tables; sports TV; children and dogs welcome, disabled access/loos, picnic-sets outside, moments from sea and lighthouse, open (and food) all day.

SOUTHWOLD TM5076
Swan (01502) 722186
Market Place; IP18 6EG Upmarket Adnams-owned hotel dating from the early 17th c, stylishly revamped with colourful contemporary feel, their full range of a dozen ales kept well plus bottled beers, cocktails and good choice of wines and spirits including own gins, tasty modern pub food (not cheap) in Tap Room bar with comfy banquettes, industrial lightbulbs in raftered ceiling and teal-painted bar, fashionable restaurant food in showpiece Still Room with copper gin bar, book a day ahead for afternoon teas in front lounge; children welcome, no dogs inside, brewery tours, nice courtyard garden, 40 or so luxury bedrooms (some in separate block), open all day.

STOKE ASH TM1170
White Horse (01379) 678222
A140/Workhouse Road; IP23 7ET Sizeable 17th-c gabled coaching inn on crossroads; beams and inglenook fireplaces, generous helpings of enjoyable reasonably priced pub food, well kept ales such as Abbot, Adnams and Woodfordes, Aspall's cider, efficient friendly service; children welcome, good value bedrooms in modern annexe, open (and food) all day from 8am.

STOKE-BY-NAYLAND TL9836
★Angel (01206) 263245
B1068 Sudbury–East Bergholt; CO6 4SA Elegant 17th-c inn in lovely village in Constable country; lounge with handsome beams, timbers, stripped brickwork and armchairs around low tables, more formal room featuring deep glass-covered well, chatty bar with straightforward furniture on red tiles, well kept Adnams and Woodfordes, several wines by the glass and good range of gins, whiskies and cocktails, very well liked food including breakfast, Sat brunch, lunchtime set menu (not Sun), afternoon teas (not Sun, booking required), efficient friendly service; children and dogs (in some parts) welcome, seats on sheltered terrace, six individually styled bedrooms, good breakfast, open all day from 8am.

STOKE-BY-NAYLAND TL9836
★Crown (01206) 262001
Park Street (B1068); CO6 4SE High praise for all aspects of this smart dining pub: attractive modern furnishings, top notch imaginative food, well kept real ales and a great wine choice, well equipped bedrooms; thriving atmosphere around the bar counter with its ales from the likes of Crouch Vale, Harveys and Woodfordes, exceptional wine cellar strong on Burgundy with 30 by the glass, large round tables among smaller ones in eating area plus big woodburner and contemporary artwork; appealing smart-casual menu with wine suggestions, helpful and intelligent service; children and dogs (in bar) welcome, flagstoned back terrace with teak furniture, heaters and views over lightly wooded countryside, pretty village and good nearby walks, open all day.

STOWUPLAND TM0759
Crown (01449) 490490
Church Road (A1120 just E of Stowmarket); IP14 4BQ Prettily thatched pub set back from the road behind white picket fence; wood-framed interior blending traditional and contemporary features, well liked sensibly priced food from pub favourites up including good stone-baked pizzas (visible oven), real ales and a decent range of wines by the glass, friendly efficient service, bar with log fire, restaurant; children and dogs welcome, spacious garden, open all day, just pizzas Sun evening.

STRATFORD ST MARY TM0434
★Swan (01206) 321244
Lower Street; CO7 6JR Fantastic range of drinks and thoughtful cooking of local produce at this lovely timbered inn; Adnams and Timothy Taylor typically among three ales on handpump plus interesting guests such as Harvest Ale (made with pub's own-grown hops), also notable ranges of spirits, wines and artisan sherries; two beamed bars, one with log fire in Tudor brick fireplace, other with coal fire, eclectic range of furniture on parquet or stone floors, compact timbered back restaurant, board games; children and dogs (in bar) welcome, lots of outdoor seating in large garden including under willow trees by the River Stour, open all day, closed Mon, Tues.

STUTTON TM1434
Gardeners Arms (01473) 328868
Manningtree Road, Upper Street (B1080); IP9 2TG Cottagey roadside free house on edge of small village bedecked with paraphernalia; well kept Adnams Southwold and guests, good value home-made food including daily specials, friendly helpful service, cosy L-shaped bar with log fire, red-carpeted dining room and larger area stretching to the back; children and dogs welcome, two-tier back garden with pond, open all day Sun, closed Mon.

SUDBURY TL8741
Brewery Tap (01787) 370876
East Street; CO10 2TP Light bright corner tap for Mauldons brewery; their range and guests kept well, also Belgian fruit beers and good range of malt whiskies, some snacky food (can bring your own, cutlery provided); comedy club first Weds of month, quiz and live music nights, darts, cribbage and bar billiards; dogs welcome, picnic-sets on terrace, open all day, closed Mon.

SWEFFLING TM3464
White Horse (01728) 664178
B1119 Framlingham–Saxmundham; IP17 2BB Traditional little two-room country pub with woodburner in one room, range in the other, up to three well kept changing East Anglian beers served from tap room door, real cider and some interesting local wines and spirits, simple food such as ploughman's and locally made pies, friendly service; some live acoustic music, bar billiards, darts and other traditional games; children and dogs welcome, pretty little beer garden with rustic arbour, self-catering cottage and campsite including yurts, always open Fri-Mon evenings and Sun lunch, check about other times.

SWILLAND TM1852
Moon & Mushroom (01473) 785320
Off B1078; IP6 9LR Popular 16th-c country local serving four changing East Anglian beers direct from the tap room, old tables and chairs on quarry tiles, log fire, enjoyable good value home-made food sourced locally; quiz first Weds of month, occasional live music; children and dogs welcome, heated flower-filled terrace, closed Sun evening, Mon.

THORNDON TM1469
Black Horse (01379) 678523
Off A140 or B1077, S of Eye; The Street; IP23 7JR Welcoming 17th-c village pub with enjoyable fairly traditional food including curries and popular home-made pies, two changing well kept local ales such as Adnams, friendly helpful service, lots of timbering, stripped brick and big fireplaces; well behaved children and dogs (in bar) welcome, tables on lawn, country views behind, open all day Sun till 9pm, closed Tues.

THORNHAM MAGNA TM1070
Four Horseshoes (01379) 678777
Off A140 S of Diss; Wickham Road; IP23 8HD Extensive thatched dining pub dating from the 12th c; well divided dimly lit carpeted bar, ales from the likes of Grain and Greene King and good choice of wines and whiskies, enjoyable reasonably priced menu of pub standards, friendly helpful staff, very low heavy black beams, country pictures and brass, large fireplace and an old illuminated well; background music; children and dogs (in bar) welcome, disabled access, picnic-sets on big sheltered lawn and out front, handy for Thornham Walks and interesting thatched Norman church, seven comfortable bedrooms, open all day.

THORPENESS TM4759
★Dolphin (01728) 454994
Just off B1353; Old Homes Road; village signposted from Aldeburgh; IP16 4FE Extended and neatly kept dining pub with rooms in interesting seaside village (all built in the early 1900s); main bar with Scandinavian feel, pale wooden tables and assortment of old chairs on broad modern quarry tiles, log fire, well kept Adnams, gin list and several wines by the glass, appealing village store now occupies the snug, the airy dining room has country kitchen-style furniture and traditional panelling, enjoyable locally sourced food from shortish but interesting menu with good vegan provision, friendly service; background music, TV, children and dogs welcome, garden function room with living meadow roof, spacious garden with boules, three bedrooms, open all day, closed Mon lunchtime in winter.

THURSTON TL9165
Fox & Hounds (01359) 232228
Barton Road; IP31 3QT Rather imposing former 19th-c station inn; six well kept ales, usually Adnams Broadside, Greene King IPA and four guests, traditional furnishings in carpeted lounge (back part set for dining), ceiling fans and lots of pump clips, generously served reasonably priced pubby food (not Sun evening) including regular themed nights, friendly service, bare-boards public bar with pool, darts and machines; background and some live music, quiz and bingo nights; children and dogs welcome, picnic-sets on grassed area by car park and on small covered side terrace, pretty village, self-catering apartment, open all day.

TUDDENHAM TM1948
★Fountain (01473) 785377
The Street; village signed off B1077 N of Ipswich; IP6 9BT Popular dining pub in

nice village; several linked café-style rooms with heavy beams and timbering, stripped floors, comfy upholstered chairs around light tables, open fire, mirrors and prints (some by cartoonist Giles who spent time here after World War II), wide choice of well cooked food (all day Sun till 7pm) including set menus and blackboard specials, a couple of changing ales and good selection of wines by the glass; background music; no under-10s in bar after 6.30pm, dogs welcome, wicker and metal chairs on covered heated terrace, rows of picnic-style tables under parasols on sizeable lawn.

UFFORD   TM2952
★**Crown** (01394) 461030
High Street; IP13 6EL Broad mix of customers at this popular family-run pub-restaurant; good food from varied menu including lunchtime sandwiches, bar and dining areas with cushioned wooden chairs and leather banquettes around medley of dark tables, shelves of books, open fires in brick fireplaces, stools against counter serving ales such as Adnams and Earl Soham, nicely put together wine list with good options by the glass, friendly service; children and dogs (in bar) welcome, seats out at front, picnic-sets under parasols in back garden with play area, open all day weekends, closed Tues.

UFFORD   TM2952
White Lion (01394) 460770
Lower Street (off B1438, towards Eyke); IP13 6DW 16th-c village pub near quiet stretch of River Deben; home to the Uffa Brewery with their three beers and guests tapped from the cask (Aug beer festival), generous helpings of enjoyable home-made food, raised woodburner in large central fireplace, captain's chairs and spindlebacks around simple tables on quarry tiles; children and dogs welcome, nice views from outside tables, summer barbecues and wood-fired pizzas, camping, closed Sun evening and Mon lunchtime.

WANGFORD   TM4779
Plough (01502) 578239
Barnaby Green; A12 next to service station; NR34 8AZ Useful roadside stop with attractive stone-floored interior with blue wainscotting and central woodburner, enjoyable reasonably priced home-made food from sandwiches to daily specials, well kept Adnams and decent range of wines, friendly staff; children and dogs welcome, big beer garden with play area, five pleasant courtyard bedrooms and small campsite, open all day.

WENHASTON   TM4274
Star (01502) 478240
Hall Road; IP19 9HF Traditional 19th-c country pub with three small rooms; well kept Adnams Southwold, four guest beers, a proper cider and decent wines by the glass, beer festivals, enjoyable inexpensive home-made food (smaller appetites catered for), friendly helpful staff, old enamel signs and other bits and pieces, open fires, dining room with local artwork; pub games, Sun afternoon live music; children, dogs and muddy boots welcome, sizeable lawn with boules, nice views, camping (must pre-book), open all day Sun (no food then but customers bring their own).

WESTLETON   TM4469
Crown (01728) 648777
B1125 Blythburgh–Leiston; IP17 3AD Former coaching inn now a stylish and upmarket hotel-restaurant with chatty informal bar; country furniture on bare boards, lovely log fire in big brick fireplace, Adnams Southwold, Woodfordes Bittern and many wines by the glass from thoughtful list, several malt whiskies, also parlour with sofas and woodburner, dining room redecorated in recent refurb with striking modern prints of local wildlife and modern conservatory, food can be good; background music; children and dogs (in bar and some bedrooms) welcome, charming terraced garden, comfortable bedrooms (some in converted stables and cottages), near RSPB Minsmere; open all day.

WESTLETON   TM4469
White Horse (01728) 648222
Darsham Road, off B1125 Blythburgh–Leiston; IP17 3AH Traditional dutch-gabled brick pub with welcoming relaxed atmosphere; enjoyable pubby food including blackboard specials, up to five well kept Adnams ales, friendly attentive service, high-ceilinged bar with central fire, steps down to stone-floored back dining room; Tues quiz; children and dogs welcome, picnic-sets in cottagey garden, more out by village duck pond, near RSBP Minsmere.

WHEPSTEAD   TL8258
★**White Horse** (01284) 735760
Off B1066 S of Bury; Rede Road; IP29 4SS Welcoming partly 17th-c village pub; bar with woodburner in a low fireplace, stools around pubby tables on tiles, Woodfordes and guests from copper-topped counter; nicely cooked pub standards, linked dining rooms with country kitchen tables and chairs and cushioned wall seats; background

---

Post Office address codings confusingly give the impression that some pubs are in Suffolk, when they're really in Cambridgeshire, Essex or Norfolk (which is where we list them).

music; children and dogs welcome, tables under parasols on sheltered back terrace, picnic-sets and play area on grass, enjoyable surrounding walks, closed Sun evening, Mon (except bank holidays).

WINGFIELD   TM2276
De La Pole Arms (01379) 384983
Off B1118 N of Stradbroke; Church Road; IP21 5RA Welcoming 16th-c timbered pub opposite church; enjoyable food from sandwiches and deli boards to daily specials, home-made cakes, Sun carvery, well kept Adnams and Earl Soham and decent wines by the glass, good friendly service, beams, flagstones and quarry tiles, simple bar with log fire in big fireplace, raftered restaurant; children and dogs welcome, disabled access, tables under parasols on sunny terrace, closed Mon, otherwise open all day from 11am (till 7pm Sun).

WOODBRIDGE   TM2748
Anchor (01394) 382649
Quay Street; IP12 1BX Resplendently purple 18th-c corner pub on the quayside (sister to the White Horse at Easton); good food from shortish but varied menu with Asian influences, lunchtime sandwiches, well kept Greene King ales and decent wines by the glass, efficient friendly service, two-room bar and beamed back dining area, some nautical touches, log fires including woodburner in large fireplace; children and dogs welcome, seats out at front and on side terrace, open all day.

WOODBRIDGE   TM2648
Cherry Tree (01394) 384627
Opposite Notcutts Nursery, off A12; Cumberland Street; IP12 4AG Opened-up 17th-c pub (bigger than it looks) with eight well kept ales including Adnams (beer festivals), good wines by the glass and locally sourced reasonably priced food, friendly service, oak beams and two log fires, mix of pine furniture, old local

photographs; Thurs quiz; children and dogs (in bar) welcome, garden with play area, three bedrooms in converted barn, good breakfast (for non-residents too), open (and food) all day.

WOODBRIDGE   TM2748
Crown (01394) 384242
Thoroughfare/Quay Street; IP12 1AD Stylish 17th-c dining inn; well kept ales such as Adnams in glass-roofed bar (boat suspended above counter), lots of wines by the glass and cocktails, good imaginative food from light meals up, breakfast, brunch, afternoon teas (must book), pleasant young staff, various eating areas with contemporary furnishings; occasional live jazz; children and dogs (in bar) welcome, courtyard tables, ten well appointed bedrooms, open (and food) all day.

WOODBRIDGE   TM2749
Old Mariner (01394) 382679
New Street; IP12 1DX Traditional little side-street local with cosy bustling bar, well kept Adnams Ghost Ship, Fullers London Pride and a couple of guests, craft beers too, no food, friendly welcoming staff, log fire; children and dogs welcome, sunny back garden with street-food events in summer, open all day.

WOODBRIDGE   TM2749
Olde Bell & Steelyard
(01394) 382933 *New Street, off Market Square; IP12 1DZ* Ancient timber-framed pub with plenty of old-world character (the listed steelyard still overhangs the street); two smallish beamed bars and cosy dining room, beamed and simply furnished, log fire, well kept Greene King and guests from canopied servery, standard home-made food; traditional games including bar billiards, sports TV, free wi-fi; children and dogs welcome, disabled access, pretty lawned garden with blue picnic tables, open all day Fri-Sun.

Surrey

BUCKLAND

Pheasant ♀ 🍺

TQ2250 Map 3

(01737) 221355 – www.brunningandprice.co.uk/pheasant

Reigate Road (A25 W of Reigate); RH3 7BG

Busy roadside pub with a thoughtful range of drinks and food served by friendly staff, character rooms and seats on terrace and lawn

This elegantly extended country pub has a large garden with tables on a terrace and picnic-sets on grass protected by weatherproof parasols, plus a fire pit, meaning that the variable British summer is no bar to comfortable alfresco refreshment. The fine range of drinks includes St Austell Brunning & Price Traditional Bitter plus several guests such as Adnams Ghost Ship, Surrey Hills Shere Drop and Timothy Taylors Landlord on handpump, 24 wines by the glass, 60 whiskies and more than 70 gins. Various open-plan rooms are interconnected and split into cosier areas by timbering and painted standing pillars. A couple of dining rooms at one end, separated by a two-sided open fire, have captain's chairs and cushioned dining chairs around a mix of tables on bare boards or rugs; throughout there are wall-to-wall prints and pictures, gilt-edged mirrors, house plants, old stone bottles and elegant metal chandeliers. The busy bar has a long high table with equally high chairs, another two-way fireplace with button-back leather armchairs and sofas in front of it and stools against the counter; background music and board games. One dining room has a big open fire pit in the middle. There's a restored antique tractor outside (the Brunning & Price trademark) for children to play on.

🍴 Attractively presented food (with a separate gluten-free menu) includes a meze plate, garlic and chilli king prawns, halloumi fries with salsa, braised shoulder of lamb with crushed new potatoes and rosemary gravy, pea and mint tortellini with garden pea velouté and asparagus, steak burger with toppings and chips, cauliflower biryani with lentil curry and red onion bhaji, and puddings such as hot waffle and caramelised banana with toffee sauce and honeycomb ice-cream triple chocolate brownie. *Benchmark main dish: fish pie (smoked haddock, salmon and prawns) £16.95. Two-course evening meal £22.00.*

Brunning & Price ~ Manager Jo Kirby ~ Real ale ~ Open 10am-11pm; 9am-11pm Sat; 9am-10.30pm Sun ~ Bar food 12-9; 8am-10pm Sat ~ Restaurant ~ Children welcome ~ Dogs allowed in bar

The details at the end of each featured entry start by saying whether the pub is a free house, or if it belongs to a brewery or pub group (which we name).

CHIDDINGFOLD

SU9635 Map 3

Swan 🛏

(01428) 684688 – www.theswaninnchiddingfold.com

Petworth Road (A283 S); GU8 4TY

Open-plan, light and airy rooms in well run inn, with local ales, modern food and seats in terraced garden; bedrooms

---

Consistently cited as one of Surrey's most winsome villages, Chiddingfold is a popular refreshment spot for walkers and riders, who love the garden at this attractive tile-hung pub. It can get pretty busy at the weekends, so book a table if you want to eat. The bar has an open fire in an inglenook fireplace with leather armchairs in front and antlers above, wooden tables and chairs and cushioned wall seats on pale floorboards and leather-topped stools against the counter where they keep Crafty Brewing Crafty One and Otter Ale and a guest on handpump, 19 wines by the glass and a good choice of spirits. Staff are helpful and friendly. A dining room leads off here with modern chairs and chunky tables on more bare floorboards. The three-tiered terraced garden has plenty of seats and tables. The 11 well equipped and comfortable bedrooms make a good base for exploring the area – there's plenty to do: the Goodwood Estate and its many charms are a drive away and a six-mile walk from the village green takes in some beautiful timber-framed Wealden buildings, ancient churches and a donkey sanctuary.

Food (starting with breakfast) is enjoyable and includes classic prawn and avocado cocktail, fried buffalo chicken wings, a pie of the day (short rib, chicken or vegan) with toppings and fries, local ale-battered fish and chips, gnocchi with triple cheese sauce, fresh basil and white truffle oil, rib-eye steak with caramelised onions, grilled tomatoes, herby mushrooms, watercress and fries, and puddings such as dark chocolate brownie with chocolate sauce and vanilla ice-cream or crumble of the day. *Benchmark main dish: half roasted chicken with lemon and thyme and skin-on fries £13.50. Two-course evening meal £22.00.*

Upham ~ Managers Zach and Sinead Leach ~ Real ale ~ Open 8am-11pm; 9am-10pm Sun ~ Bar food 12-6, 6-9; 12-3, 6-9.30 Fri, Sat; 12-8 Sun ~ Children welcome ~ Dogs allowed in bar ~ Bedrooms: £150

CHIPSTEAD

TQ2757 Map 3

White Hart 🍷 🍺

(01737) 554455 – www.brunningandprice.co.uk/whitehartchipstead

Hazelwood Lane; CR5 3QW

Airy open-plan rooms, a thoughtful choice of drinks, wholesome food and friendly staff

---

Prettily placed for walks in Happy Valley and Farthing Downs, with lavender fields not far away, Chipstead is your idyllic commuter village. The White Hart takes pride of place on the village green, with soothing rural views (proximity to Croydon notwithstanding) from every window. It's a well run and popular pub, with a good number of besotted regulars and a smart but homely vibe. The excellent choice of real ales on handpump includes St Austell Brunning & Price Traditional Bitter and oft-changing guests such as Adnams Broadside, Firebird Parody (gluten-free), Surrey Hills Shere Drop and Twickenham Redhead, 20 wines by the glass, more than 50 gins and around 30 malt whiskies; background music and board games. The long room to the left is light and airy, with wall panelling at one end, a woodburning stove and numerous windows overlooking the seats on the pretty terrace. Throughout there's a fine mix of antique dining chairs and settles around all sorts of tables, rugs on bare boards, hundreds of interesting cartoons, country pictures, prints and photos of cricket and rugby teams, large ornate mirrors, old glass and stone bottles, clocks, books and plants.

Pleasing bistro-style food includes sandwiches, prawn cocktail with marie rose sauce, braised feather of boeuf bourguignon with horseradish sauce and kale, fish pie (smoked haddock, salmon and prawns), cauliflower, chickpea and squash tagine with lemon and almond couscous and flatbread, beer-battered cod and chips, Malaysian chicken curry with coconut rice and steamed pak choi, and puddings such as crème brûlée and lemon meringue roulade with raspberry sorbet. There's a separate gluten-free menu. *Benchmark main dish: chicken, ham and leek pie with mash and buttered greens £14.95. Two-course evening meal £22.00.*

Brunning & Price ~ Manager Jason Patterson ~ Real ale ~ Open 11.30-9.30; 11.30-9 Sun ~ Bar food 12-9.30; 12-10 Fri, Sat; 12-9 Sun ~ Restaurant ~ Children welcome ~ Dogs allowed in bar

CHOBHAM
White Hart ♀ ◀

SU9761   Map 2

(01276) 857580 – www.brunningandprice.co.uk/whitehartchobham
High Street; GU24 8AA

Brick-built village pub with cheerful customers and a thoughtful choice of food and drink

A bustling atmosphere and friendly service make this lovely old red-brick inn on the village green a standout success. The opened-up bar has white-painted beams, standing pillars, rugs on parquet or wide boards, an assortment of dark wooden dining chairs and tables, and armchairs beside two fireplaces; background music and board games. High chairs line the counter where cheerful, well trained staff serve St Austell Brunning & Price Traditional Bitter and guests such as Ascot Starting Gate, Park Brewery Two Storm Ruby, Reunion Minimalist and Tillingbourne Hop Troll on handpump, 20 wines by the glass, 40 gins and over 40 malt whiskies. An L-shaped dining room has a leather wall banquette and leather and brass-studded dining chairs around a mix of tables and numerous old photos and prints on exposed-brick or painted walls. There's also a comfortable dining room with similar furniture, carpeting and a big elegant metal chandelier. Outdoor seating with parasols is arranged in the little garden at the side.

A pleasingly wide-ranging menu (special diets catered for) includes 'light bites', garlic and chilli king prawns, halloumi fries with salsa, pan-fried scallops with pea purée and shredded ham hock, crispy beef salad with cashews, grilled sea bass fillets with potato and shallot terrine, pea and mini tortellini with garden pea velouté and asparagus, pork and leek sausages with mash and buttered greens, and puddings such as summer pudding with clotted cream and triple chocolate brownie with chocolate sauce and vanilla ice-cream. *Benchmark main dish: beer-battered cod and chips £14.95. Two-course evening meal £22.00.*

Brunning & Price ~ Manager Stan Morgan ~ Real ale ~ Open 11.30-11; 12-10 Sun ~ Bar food 12-9 ~ Restaurant ~ Children welcome but not in bar area after 5pm ~ Dogs allowed in bar

'Children welcome' means the pub says it lets children inside without any special restriction. If it allows them in, but to restricted areas such as an eating area or family room, we specify this. Places with separate restaurants often let children use them, and hotels usually let children into public areas such as lounges. Some pubs impose an evening time limit – let us know if you find one earlier than 9pm.

ELSTEAD

Mill at Elstead ♀

SU9044 Map 2

(01252) 703333 – www.millelstead.co.uk

Farnham Road (B3001 just W of village, which is itself between Farnham and Milford); GU8 6LE

Fascinating building with big attractive waterside garden, Fullers beers and well liked food

The River Wey flows underneath this beautifully located former watermill – you can see the preserved waterwheel rotating through a glass floor in the main bar. The terrace looks out over the water, and a millpond with waterfowl and willow completes the bucolic scene. Inside, a series of rambling linked bar areas on the spacious ground floor have large windows that make the most of the view; there's an upstairs restaurant too. You'll find brown leather armchairs and antique engravings by a longcase clock, neat modern tables and dining chairs on bare boards, big country tables on broad ceramic tiles, iron pillars, stripped masonry and a log fire in a huge inglenook. Fullers ESB and London Pride and guests from breweries such as Hogs Back on handpump, 21 wines by the glass, several malt whiskies and 30 gins; background music, board games and TV. 'Shakespeare in the Garden' is a popular summer diversion.

Well regarded food includes lunchtime sandwiches, chilli and garlic roasted squash with tahini dressing, Fullers London Porter smoked salmon, sharing platters, beef or vegan burger with toppings and fries, tomato, sweet potato, chickpea and red kidney bean ragoût with smashed avocado, blackened salmon with new potatoes, and puddings such as glazed lemon tart and bakewell tart with vanilla custard. *Benchmark main dish: beer-battered haddock and chips £14.25. Two-course evening meal £23.00.*

Fullers ~ Manager Rachel Watson ~ Real ale ~ Open 12-11; 12-10.30 Sun ~ Bar food 12-4, 5-9; 12-9 Sat; 12-7 Sun ~ Restaurant ~ Children welcome ~ Dogs allowed in bar

ESHER

Marneys

TQ1566 Map 3

(020) 8398 4444 – www.marneys.co.uk

Alma Road (one-way), Weston Green; heading N on A309 from A307 roundabout; after half a mile turn left into Lime Tree Avenue (signposted to All Saints Parish Church), then left at T junction into Chestnut Avenue; KT10 8JN

Country-feeling pub with good value food and attractive garden

The Marney family had a timber business in this area of Thames Ditton in the last century, and this pub – and the pond opposite – were named for them in 1994. There's good walking to be had on the wooded common nearby and the area feels pretty rural given its Greater London location (handy for Hampton Court Palace). It's a friendly place, with a faithful group of regulars. With its low beams, woodburning stove, scrubbed pine tables, pews, wooden chairs and cottagey curtained windows, it's pleasantly country kitchen in style. There's Fullers London Pride, Twickenham Naked Ladies and Youngs Bitter on handpump, 16 wines by the glass, several malt whiskies and perhaps horse-racing on the telly in the corner (like many pubs in the area, Marneys attracts a fair number of sports fans). The seats and wooden tables on the front terrace provide inspiring views over the common, village church and duck pond, and there's more seating on decking in the attractively planted sheltered garden.

Satisfying food includes smoked mackerel pâté with pickles and melba toast, roast beef carpaccio, pea and courgette risotto with basil oil, moule frites, pie (rabbit and bacon or vegan) and mash, seafood linguine, braised featherblade of beef with mash and green beans, and puddings such as sticky toffee pudding or banana parfait with coconut ice-cream, peanut praline and white chocolate shavings. *Benchmark main dish: curried cauliflower steak with saffron and coconut curry, pilau rice and onion bhaji £13.50. Two-course evening meal £22.00.*

Free house ~ Real ale ~ Open 11-11.30; 12-11 Sun ~ Bar food 12-2.30, 6-9; 12-3 Sun; pizza evenings 6-9pm Fri, Sat ~ Restaurant ~ Children welcome away from bar ~ Dogs allowed in bar

FOREST GREEN
Parrot ♀ 🍺

TQ1241 Map 3

(01306) 775790 – www.brunningandprice.co.uk/parrot
B2127 just W of junction with B2126, SW of Dorking; RH5 5RZ

Bustling pub in the Surrey Hills with plenty of space, a thoughtful choice of food and drinks, lots to look at and seats in the garden

A bit of a Tardis, this one: it seems bigger on the inside than its cottagey exterior suggests. Overlooking the village green and with its own lawn dotted with picnic sets, the Parrot is a very popular local pub. The vibe is welcoming, as is the fire pit – perfect for when you come in from a winter walk. The cosy bar area by the main door has a woodburning stove in an inglenook fireplace (plus a smaller two-way one in another knocked-through wall), leather button-back armchairs, small stools and rugs on flagstones. From the heavy panelled counter, helpful, friendly staff serve St Austell Brunning & Price Traditional Bitter plus guests such as Dark Star American Pale Ale, Hogs Back TEA, Odyssey Nirvana and Surrey Hills Gilt Complex and Shere Drop on handpump, 22 wines by the glass, 73 gins, more than 60 whiskies and a farm cider; background radio. The spreading eating areas are separated by open doorways and standing timbers, with a mix of cushioned wooden or leather dining chairs around polished tables on more rugs and floorboards. Throughout there are country prints and photographs on walls above oak dados, house plants large and small, shelves of books and old bottles, and elegant metal chandeliers. One room (just right for a private party) is lined with lovely parrot prints. French windows lead to a large terrace with plenty of chairs and tables.

The pleasing, regularly changing menu includes gluten-free and vegan choices and a couple of sandwiches. Typical dishes are halloumi fries with salsa, barbecue chicken wings, roast pork tenderloin with colcannon potatoes and apple purée, crispy buttermilk chicken burger and fries, wild mushroom risotto with truffle oil, braised shoulder of lamb with crushed new potatoes and rosemary gravy, and puddings such as summer pudding with clotted cream and Cheshire Farm ice-creams and sorbets. *Benchmark main dish: smoked haddock and salmon fishcake with tomato and spring onion salad £13.95. Two-course evening meal £22.00.*

Brunning & Price ~ Manager Duncan Moore ~ Real ale ~ Open 11.30-11; 11.30-10 Sun ~ Bar food 12-9 ~ Restaurant ~ Children welcome ~ Dogs allowed in bar & restaurant

HAMBLEDON
Merry Harriers 🛏

SU9639 Map 2

(01428) 682883 – www.merryharriers.com
Off A283; just N of village; GU8 4DR

Rural pub with real ales in cheerful bar, good food in dining rooms, seats in flower-filled garden and llamas; bedrooms

A community-minded village like Hambledon needs a great pub at its heart and it has a beauty in the Merry Harriers, with its warm and welcoming bar, varied accommodation and unusual llama treks. With 16th-c origins, it has beams, a huge inglenook log fire and pine tables on bare boards in the bar, with four well kept changing ales on handpump such as Andwell Gold Muddler, Crafty Brewing Crafty One and Surrey Hills Shere Drop, local cider, several wines by the glass from a thoughtful list that includes a local sparkler, served by helpful staff. The more formal dining rooms have an attractive mix of wooden chairs and tables on polished boards and woodburning stoves. There are seats out in front and in the big garden with boules, chess and a children's play area. If you want to stay over, there's plenty of choice: four comfortable rooms in the inn, six quiet garden rooms and five charming and well appointed shepherd's huts. The summer guided treks (including picnic hampers) with one of the eight resident llamas are popular and great fun. Good walks nearby.

Pleasing food uses local produce (some foraged) and includes goats cheese, beetroot and chicory salad with walnut dressing, moules marinière, sausage and mash with onion gravy, fish and chips, beef, chicken fajita or butternut squash and chickpea burger and chips, vegan chilli and rice, rib-eye or sirloin steak and chips, salmon fillet with tenderstem broccoli and Cajun or lemon butter sauce, and classic puddings such as chocolate brownie and lemon tart. *Benchmark main dish: ploughman's £14.50. Two-course evening meal £21.00.*

Free house ~ Licensee Peter de Savary ~ Real ale ~ Open 5.30-11 Mon; 11.30-11 Tues-Sat; 12-8 Sun ~ Bar food 6-9 Mon; 12-2.30, 6-9 Tues-Sat; 12-3.30 Sun ~ Restaurant ~ Children welcome ~ Dogs allowed in bar, restaurant & bedrooms ~ Bedrooms: £160

MILFORD
Refectory ◖

SU9542   Map 2

(01483) 413820 – www.brunningandprice.co.uk/refectory
Portsmouth Road; GU8 5HJ

Beamed and timbered rooms of much character, six real ales and other thoughtful drinks and well liked food

This is a delightful pub housed in a converted barn of disputed vintage, though it certainly looks pleasingly like an old banqueting hall. Renowned for its warm welcome, monthly dog walks and excellent array of drinks, it's a lovely community hub. The L-shaped, mainly open-plan rooms are spacious, with exposed stone walls, stalling and standing timbers creating separate seating areas, strikingly heavy beams and a couple of big log fires in fine stone fireplaces. A two-tiered and balconied part at one end has a wall covered with huge brass platters; elsewhere there are nice old photographs and a variety of paintings. Dining chairs and dark wooden tables are grouped on wooden, quarry-tiled or carpeted floors, and there are bookshelves, big pot plants, stone bottles on windowsills and fresh flowers. High wooden bar stools line the long counter where they serve St Austell Brunning & Price Traditional Bitter, Hogs Back TEA and four local guests on handpump, a dozen wines by the glass and more than 60 gins. The courtyard (adjacent to the characterful pigeonry) has teak tables and chairs. Wheelchair facilities and disabled parking. Perfectly placed for country walks, with or without dogs.

Enjoyable food includes sandwiches and 'light bites' (such as cheddar, leek and balsamic onion quiche), plus chicken caesar croquettes, baked camembert with apple, celery and walnut salad, grilled sea bass fillets with potato and shallot terrine, braised feather of boeuf bourguignon with horseradish mash and kale, beer-battered cod and chips, roast duck breast with crispy leg croquettes, celeriac purée and cherry jus, and puddings such as chocolate and orange tart and summer pudding with clotted cream. *Benchmark main dish: Malaysian chicken curry with coconut rice and pak choi £13.95. Two-course evening meal £22.00.*

Brunning & Price ~ Manager Michael Collins ~ Real ale ~ Open 10.30am-11pm; 12-10.30 Sun ~ Bar food 12-9; 12-9.30 Fri, Sat ~ Restaurant ~ Children welcome ~ Dogs allowed in bar

NORWOOD HILL
Fox Revived ♀ ◖

TQ2342   Map 3

(01293) 229270 – www.brunningandprice.co.uk/foxrevived
Leigh–Charlwood back road; RH6 0ET

Extended, well run pub with attractive bar and dining areas, super staff, interesting food and a fine range of drinks; seats outside

There are beautiful views over the Surrey hills from this attractive pub, despite its being not far from Gatwick Airport. Sitting outside at tables on a stone terrace you feel like you're in the heart of the countryside, and there's a nice five-mile walk from the front door (details on the website). The various open-plan dining areas and nooks are divided up by balustrading and standing timbers, creating cosier and more private spaces. Button-back armchairs and stools sit by open fires, antique-style and high-backed leather dining chairs are grouped around tables of varying size on rugs and bare boards, and the walls are hung with photos, prints and gilt-edged mirrors; also, big house plants, lots of books on shelves and elegant metal chandeliers. Courteous, helpful staff serve St Austell Brunning & Price Traditional Bitter and Surrey Hills Shere Drop plus guests such as Adnams Ghost Ship, Gun Scaramanga, Long Man Old Man and Timothy Taylors Boltmaker on handpump, 20 wines by the glass, 17 rums, 60 gins, 40 whiskies and farm cider; background music and board games.

Rewarding, bistro-style food (with a separate gluten-free menu) includes sandwiches, deep-fried West Country brie with apricot chutney and candied walnuts, summer vegetable risotto, garlic and chilli prawns, halloumi fries with salsa, beer-battered cod and chips, braised feather of beef bourguignon with horseradish mash and kale, grilled sea bass fillets with potato and shallot terrine, cauliflower, squash and chickpea tagine with couscous, and puddings such as triple chocolate brownie with chocolate sauce and vanilla ice-cream and lemon cheesecake with raspberry ripple ice-cream. *Benchmark main dish: steak burger with coleslaw and fries £13.95. Two-course evening meal £22.00.*

Brunning & Price ~ Manager David Chant ~ Real ale ~ Open 10.30am-11pm; 10.30-10.30 Sun ~ Bar food 12-9.30; 12-10 Fri, Sat ~ Restaurant ~ Children welcome ~ Dogs allowed in bar

OXTED
Haycutter ♀ ◖

TQ3951   Map 3

(01883) 776955 – www.brunningandprice.co.uk/haycutter
Tanhouse Road, Broadham Green; off High Street opposite Old Bell; RH8 9PE

Plenty of chatty dining rooms and bars, lots to look at, attentive staff serving a fine choice of drinks and food, and seats outside

The large main bar in this much extended, characterful pub is the focus of its many charms. There's an assortment of dining chairs around wooden tables on parquet flooring or large rugs, some high tables with equally high stools in one corner, and masses of photos and pictures on pigeon-grey walls. House plants and bookshelves and a long counter stretches along a back wall. Here, friendly staff serve St Austell Brunning & Price Traditional

Bitter plus Harveys Sussex Best, Surrey Hills Shere Drop, Timothy Taylors Landlord, Wantsum Montgomery and Westerham Hay Today on handpump, 24 wines by the glass, more than 120 gins and 80 whiskies. A quarry-tiled walkway leads towards the original building with a couple of small rooms leading off to each side with similar furnishings and décor; there's also a massive circular table surrounded by a dozen chairs plus a private dining room. Outside, a large paved area with raised flower beds has good quality tables and chairs under big parasols and there are picnic-sets on lawns. Dogs are welcomed with a bowl of water and maybe even a biscuit or two.

Interesting food from a regularly changing menu includes sandwiches and 'light bites', red pepper hummus with flatbread, chicken liver pâté, crispy vegetable parcels with spiced mango dip, roast duck breast with crispy croquettes, celeriac purée and cherry jus, Malaysian chicken curry with coconut rice and pak choi, braised feather of beef bourguignon with horseradish mash and kale, steak burger with coleslaw and chips, and puddings such as crème brûlée and chocolate and orange tart with passion-fruit sorbet. *Benchmark main dish: pork and leek sausages with mash and buttered greens £13.95. Two-course evening meal £22.00.*

Brunning & Price ~ Manager Christopher Little ~ Real ale ~ Open 11.30-11; 12-10.30 Sun ~ Bar food 12-9.30; 12-10 Fri, Sat; 12-9 Sun ~ Restaurant ~ Children welcome away from the front area ~ Dogs allowed in bar

RIPLEY

Anchor ⭐ 🍷

TQ0556   Map 2

(01483) 211866 – www.ripleyanchor.co.uk

High Street; GU23 6AE

Surrey Dining Pub of the Year

Stylish dining pub with first class food, real ales, friendly service and sunny courtyard

This attractive red-brick pub – once an almshouse dating back to the 16th c – has a gently civilised but easy-going and convivial atmosphere. Several low-ceilinged, interlinked rooms have heavy beams, slate floors and open fires and are decorated in a stylish, simple way that's immediately inviting. There are church chairs around polished tables in the bar, comfortable seating in the dining areas, contemporary paintwork or exposed brick walls and elegant flower arrangements; background music. You'll find Windsor & Eton Guardsman and guests such as Tillingbourne Falls Gold on handpump, 20 excellent wines by the glass, six gins (some local), six whiskies and cocktails. At the back a sunny courtyard with decking has cushioned wicker chairs and sofas.

The imaginative, monthly changing menu includes smoked haddock arancini with curried mayo, chalkstream trout with cucumber ketchup and lemongrass sauce, wood pigeon with roast beetroot and black pudding purée, beef tartare with confit egg yolk, halibut with hasselback potatoes, runner beans and tomato and chervil dressing, dill gnocchi with courgettes and girolle mushrooms, roast lamb rump with hispi cabbage, pea and pancetta casserole, and puddings such as blackberry soufflé with white chocolate and cardamom ice-cream and tonka bean brûlée with raspberry sorbet; they offer a weekday set lunch. *Benchmark main dish: braised pork belly with sand carrot, chorizo and white beans £18.00. Two-course evening meal £28.00.*

Free house ~ Licensee Michael Wall-Palmer ~ Real ale ~ Open 12-2.30, 5.30-11; 12-11 Sat; 12-9 Sun; closed Mon ~ Bar food 12-2.30, 5.30-9; 12-8 Sun ~ Restaurant ~ Children allowed in restaurant

SUNBURY

TQ1068 Map 3

Flower Pot 🛏

(01932) 780741 – www.theflowerpotsunbury.co.uk

1.6 miles from M3 junction 1; follow Lower Sunbury sign from exit roundabout, then at Thames Street turn right; pub on next corner, with Green Street; TW16 6AA

Handsome place with an appealing, contemporary bar and dining room, real ales and all-day food; bedrooms

An excellent refreshment stop after a Thames-side walk, this former coaching inn, its elegant façade picked out with wrought-iron balconies, has a villagey feel. The airy bar has leather tub chairs around copper-topped tables, high chairs upholstered in brown and beige tartan around equally high tables in pale wood, attractive flagstones, contemporary paintwork and stools against the counter; there's also a couple of comfortably plush burgundy armchairs. The bar leads into a dining area with pale blue-painted and dark wooden cushioned dining chairs around an assortment of partly painted tables on bare boards, artwork on papered walls and a large gilt-edged mirror over an open fireplace; candles in glass jars, fresh flowers, background music and newspapers. Brakspears Bitter, Ringwood Boondoggle and Youngs Special on handpump and 15 wines by the glass. A side terrace has wood and metal tables and chairs; in summer the hanging baskets are pretty. The eight bedrooms are smart and comfortable.

🍴 Highly thought-of food from a varied menu includes sharing boards, barbecue sticky ribs, salads (goats cheese, chicken and bacon, tandoori salmon), assorted pizzas and burgers, lamb kebab with couscous and salad, smoked haddock with new potatoes, spinach, poached egg and hollandaise, a pie of the day, vegetable lasagne with garlic bread, and puddings such as seasonal crumble with custard and tiramisu with forest fruit coulis. *Benchmark main dish: chicken burger with barbecue sauce and chips £13.95. Two-course evening meal £21.00.*

Authentic Inns ~ Tenant Simon Bailey ~ Real ale ~ Open 7am-11pm; 8am-11pm Sat, Sun ~ Bar food 12-3, 6-9; 12-9 Sat ~ Restaurant ~ Children welcome ~ Dogs allowed in bar ~ Bedrooms: £100

Also Worth a Visit in Surrey

Besides the fully inspected pubs, you might like to try these pubs that have been recommended to us and described by readers. Do tell us what you think of them: feedback@goodguides.com

ABINGER COMMON TQ1146

Abinger Hatch (01306) 730737
Off A25 W of Dorking, towards Abinger Hammer; RH5 6HZ Dining pub dating from the 17th c in beautiful woodland spot; spacious split-level interior with heavy beams and log fires, well cooked food from toasted bagels and sharing plates to blackboard specials, friendly if not always speedy service, Ringwood Razorback and three guests, decent wine; children and dogs welcome, some disabled access, picnic-sets in side garden, near pretty church and pond, open (and food) all day.

ALBURY TQ0447

Drummond Arms (01483) 202039
Off A248 SE of Guildford; The Street; GU5 9AG Modernised 19th-c pub in pretty village; four real ales such as Adnams, Courage and Hogs Back, good choice of wines and enjoyable food from sandwiches and sharing plates up, opened-up bar with leather chesterfields and log fire, parquet-floored dining room, conservatory; children welcome, pretty back garden by little River Tillingbourne, summer barbecues and hog roasts, pleasant walks nearby, 11 bedrooms, open all day, food all day Sun.

If we know a pub has an outdoor play area for children, we mention it.

ALBURY HEATH   TQ0646
William IV   (01483) 202685
*Little London, off A25 Guildford–
Dorking; OS Sheet 187 map reference
065468; GU5 9DG* Refurbished 16th-c
pub; rustic low-beamed bar with flagstones
and inglenook log fire, well kept ales such
as Surrey Hills, a dozen wines by the glass
and some interesting gins (including a
non-alcoholic one), good freshly made food
served by friendly accommodating staff,
restaurant area up steps, curry night Tues;
children and dogs (in bar) welcome, picnic-
sets in small front garden behind picket
fence, good walks, open all day (till 9pm
Sun), no evening food Sun.

ALFOLD   TQ0435
Alfold Barn   (01403) 752288
Horsham Road, A281; GU6 8JE
Beautifully preserved 16th-c building with
bar and restaurant; very good locally sourced
home-made food from daily changing
menu with some emphasis on fish/seafood
(Sun booking essential), friendly attentive
service, a beer or two from nearby breweries,
black beams and rafters, mixed furniture
on flagstones or carpet, log fires; children
welcome, dogs in garden only, closed Sun
evening, Mon, Tues.

ALFOLD   TQ0334
Three Compasses   (01483) 275729
Dunsfold Road; GU6 8HY Welcoming
450-year-old pub with good fairly priced food
(not Sun evening, Mon) in bar and restaurant
areas, three well kept ales such as Otter, big
log fire; children and dogs welcome, large
garden, on back lane to former Dunsfold
Aerodrome (now Dunsfold Park with little
museum), Wey & Arun Canal nearby, open all
day (till 9pm Sun).

BATTS CORNER   SU8140
Bluebell   (01252) 792801
Batts Corner; GU10 4EX Busy tucked-
away country pub with linked stone-floor
rooms, light fresh décor and mix of furniture
including sofas by big log fire, well kept
ales such as Frensham, Langham and Triple
fff, good home-made food from sandwiches
to popular Sun lunch (must book), also
weekday set lunch deal, helpful friendly
staff; children, walkers and dogs welcome,
attractive spacious garden with rolling views,
summer barbecues and good play area, handy
for Alice Holt Forest, open all day Sat, till
8pm Sun.

BLETCHINGLEY   TQ3250
Bletchingley Arms   (01883) 740142
High Street (A25); RH1 4PE Spacious
modernised Barons group pub with plenty
of opened-up areas (some steps) including
beamed part with flagstones and woodburner,
good choice of well prepared sensibly priced
food from snacks up, three real ales, plenty

of wines by the glass and interesting range of
gins, friendly staff; background music (live
last Fri of month), newspapers, sports TV;
children and dogs (in bar) welcome, outside
seating areas with own bar, beach huts and
good play area, open all day.

BLETCHINGLEY   TQ3250
Red Lion   (01883) 743342
*Castle Street (A25), Redhill side;
RH1 4NU* Modernised and well looked-after
beamed village dining pub, decent range of
good home-made food including gluten-free
and vegan menus, well kept Greene King ales
and a dozen wines by the glass, friendly staff;
quiz and live music nights; children welcome,
heated part-covered terrace, secret garden,
open (and food) all day.

BRAMLEY   TQ0044
★ Jolly Farmer   (01483) 893355
High Street; GU5 0HB Village pub run
by the same family since 1971; traditional
beamed interior packed with collections
of plates and old bottles, enamel signs,
sewing machines, antique tools and so forth,
timbered semi-partitions and open fire,
Crafty Brewing, Greene King and up to six
guests, a couple of summer ciders and over a
dozen wines by the glass, generous helpings
of fairly traditional food including good Sun
carvery (worth booking); background music,
quiz every other Weds, board games, children
and dogs (in bar) welcome, tables out by car
park, walks up St Martha's Hill and handy for
Winkworth Arboretum (NT), four bedrooms
and self-contained flat, open all day.

BROCKHAM   TQ1949
Inn on the Green   (01737) 845101
Brockham Green; RH3 7JS Restaurantly
pub facing village green (part of the small
Grumpy Mole group); good food from
traditional choices up including cook-your-
own steaks on a hot stone, helpful friendly
service, well kept Fullers London Pride and
Surrey Hills Shere Drop, several wines by the
glass, afternoon teas, conservatory; children
welcome, picnic-sets out at front, garden
behind, open all day, food all day weekends.

BROCKHAM   TQ1949
Royal Oak   (01737) 843241
Brockham Green; RH3 7JS Nice spot
on charming village green below the North
Downs; bare-boards bar and airy dining area,
three or four well kept ales such as Fullers
and Sharps, enjoyable home-made food from
burgers and pub favourites up, log fires; quiz
and live music nights; children and dogs
welcome, tables out in front looking across
to fine church, more seats in back garden,
handy for Greensand Way, open all day.

BROOK   SU9238
Dog & Pheasant   (01428) 682763
Haslemere Road (A286); GU8 5UJ
Popular pub looking across busy road to

cricket green; long beamed bar divided by standing timbers, cushioned wall settles, open fire in brick fireplace, four well kept ales such as Sharps from linenfold counter, plenty of wines by the glass and decent range of gins, dining area on right, further room to left with big inglenook, generally well liked food including a pie of the day and Weds grill night; children and dogs welcome, picnic-sets on back deck and grass, play equipment, open all day, food till 4pm Sun.

BURROWHILL   SU9763
Four Horseshoes (01276) 856257
B383 N of Chobham; GU24 8QP
Busy pub attractively set by village green; updated interior with beams and log fires, up to four well kept ales including Fullers London Pride and a Caledonian house beer (Shoes), popular interesting food from sandwiches and sharing boards up (best to book weekends, kitchen shuts 4.30pm Sun), cheerful helpful staff, dining extension; children, dogs and muddy boots welcome, tables out at front (some under ancient yew), also back terrace and garden with picnic-sets and deck chairs, open all day (till 7pm Sun).

CARSHALTON   TQ2764
Hope (020) 8240 1255
West Street; SM5 2PR Chatty community-owned mock-Tudor local in conservation area: Downton, Windsor & Eton and five guests, also craft kegs, real cider/perry and over 50 bottled beers, generous low-priced pubby food (limited evening choice); 1950s-feel U-shaped bar with open fire, lots of pump clips, larger back room with bar billiards; regular beer and cider festivals, board games; no under-14s, dogs welcome, disabled access/loos, garden, open all day.

CATERHAM   TQ3254
Harrow (01883) 343260
Stanstead Road, Whitehill; CR3 6AJ
Simple 16th-c beamed pub high up in open country by North Downs Way; L-shaped bare-boards bar and carpeted back dining area, several real ales (sometimes tapped from the cask) such as Fullers and Ringwood, well liked food including daily specials, friendly staff and good local atmosphere; Mon quiz, children and dogs welcome, garden picnic-sets, popular with walkers and cyclists, open all day, no food Sun evening.

CHARLESHILL   SU8844
Donkey (01252) 702124
B3001 Milford–Farnham near Tilford; coming from Elstead, turn left as soon as you see pub sign; GU10 2AT Old-fashioned beamed dining pub with enjoyable home-made food including weekday deals, up to three well kept changing ales and good choice of wines by the glass, prompt friendly service, conservatory restaurant; children and dogs welcome, attractive garden with paddock for much loved remaining donkey

Pip (Dusty sadly died in 2020), good walks, open all day weekends.

CHARLTON   TQ0868
Harrow (01932) 783122
Charlton Road, Ashford Common; off B376 Laleham–Shepperton; TW17 0RJ
Pretty little thatched pub thought to date from 1130; simple beamed and carpeted interior with inglenook, Greene King ales and well priced food from pubby choices to good authentic Indian dishes (takeaways available), side dining extension, some signed celebrity photos (Shepperton film studios nearby); sports TV; picnic-sets in flower-filled front area, more seats in bigger back garden, small car park across busy road, open all day.

CHARLWOOD   TQ2441
Half Moon (01293) 863414
The Street; RH6 0DS Old pub next to churchyard in attractive village; spacious L-shaped bar (front part open to original upstairs windows), well kept Sharps Doom Bar, St Austell Tribute and a guest, enjoyable sensibly priced traditional food from sandwiches up, friendly service, back dining room, occasional live music; children and dogs (in bar) welcome, picnic-sets in nice courtyard area, handy for Gatwick Airport, food all day weekends.

CHERTSEY   TQ0466
Olde Swan (01932) 562129
Windsor Street; KT16 8AY Former coaching house run by McLean Inns; generous helpings of popular reasonably priced food including pizzas, burgers and good Sun lunch, four well kept ales such as Marstons Wainwright and Sharps Doom Bar from well stocked bar, friendly efficient young staff, opened-up split-level interior with rugs on bare boards, candles on tables, comfortable seating and lots of pictures, mirrors and other bits and pieces; weekend live music; children and dogs welcome, attractive outside area, seven bedrooms, open all day, food till 6pm Sun.

CHIDDINGFOLD   SU9635
★**Crown** (01428) 682255
The Green (A283); GU8 4TX Lovely 700-year-old timbered building with strong sense of history; bar and linked dining rooms with massive beams (some over 2-ft thick), oak panelling, moulded plasterwork and fine stained-glass windows, magnificently carved fireplace, some nice antique tables along with cushioned wall seats, mate's and other pubby chairs, lots of portraits, simple split-level back public bar with open fire, up to five changing ales including Hogs Back and Ringwood and several wines by the glass, enjoyable often interesting food (all day Fri-Sun); quiz first Thurs of month; children welcome, dogs in some areas, seats out looking across village green to interesting

church, more tables in sheltered central courtyard, character creaky bedrooms, open all day Fri-Sun.

CHILWORTH   TQ0347
Percy Arms (01483) 561765
Dorking Road; GU4 8NP Extended stylishly decorated pub with two bustling bars; smaller one has logs neatly piled above woodburner, a long slate-topped table and L-shaped settle, flagstoned main room with tartan-cushioned chairs against counter serving Greene King ales (one named for the pub), a guest beer and 16 wines by the glass, interesting food including some South African specialities and good value set lunch (Mon-Fri), courteous efficient service, restaurant rooms to left of entrance with upholstered tub and high-backed chairs on bare boards or rugs, further dining rooms down steps; TV; children and dogs (in bar areas) welcome, two-part garden connected by bridge over little stream, play equipment, five comfortable bedrooms, open all day, food all day weekends.

CHIPSTEAD   TQ2555
Well House (01737) 830640
Chipstead signed with Mugswell off A217, N of M25 junction 8; CR5 3SQ Originally three 16th-c cottages (converted from tea rooms to pub in 1955); log fires in all three rooms, low beams and rustic décor, bric-a-brac and pewter tankards hanging from ceiling, well kept Fullers, Surrey Hills and a local guest, food from ciabattas up, friendly staff, small dining conservatory, resident ghost (Harry the Monk); occasional live music; children and dogs allowed (in bars, they have cats), large pleasing hillside garden with ancient well (mentioned in the Domesday Book), delightful country setting, open all day.

CHURT   SU8538
Crossways (01428) 714323
Corner of A287 and Hale House Lane; GU10 2JS Friendly down-to-earth local attracting good mix of customers; quarry-tiled public bar with small brick fireplace, saloon with wood floor, panelling and banquettes, good beer range (some served direct from the cellar) and three or four real ciders, enjoyable well priced pub lunches (not Sun) including locally made pies, evening food Weds only, cheerful staff; darts, TV; no under-10s inside, dogs welcome, open all day Fri, Sat.

CLAYGATE   TQ1563
Foley (01372) 462021
Hare Lane; KT10 0LZ Restored former coaching inn; pubby part at front with

wooden tables and chairs on bare boards, comfortable seats by Victorian fireplace, lots of interconnected sitting and dining areas leading off, Youngs well kept ales, plenty of wines by the glass and interesting range of spirits, good choice of coffees and teas too, enjoyable food from open kitchen; background music, sports TV, daily papers; children and dogs (in bar) welcome, seats on two-level part-covered terrace, 17 modern bedrooms, open (and food) all day including breakfast from 8am.

CLAYGATE   TQ1563
Hare & Hounds (01372) 465149
The Green; KT10 0JL Renovated 19th-c flower-decked village pub; good sensibly priced French food along with some pub favourites in bar or smaller restaurant, nice wines and well kept changing ales including local Brightwater, friendly caring service; regular live music; children and dogs welcome, disabled access/loo, tables on attractive front terrace and in small back garden with play area, open (and food) all day, kitchen closes 7pm Sun and Mon afternoon.

CLAYGATE   TQ1563
Platform 3 (01372) 462334
The Parade, next to Claygate station; KT10 0PB Tiny pub in converted taxi office acting as tap for the Brightwater brewery, a couple of their beers and often a guest, Claygate cider and good range of wines and soft drinks, no food apart from crisps and nuts; outside seating (there's no room inside), closed Mon-Weds, otherwise open 3-9pm, but weather/season dependent (best to check website/Twitter).

COBHAM   TQ1059
Plough (01932) 589790
3.2 miles from M25 junction 10; right off A3 on A245; in Cobham, right into Downside Bridge Road; Plough Lane; KT11 3LT Smartly updated beamed village pub, part of the small Rarebreed group (see Shurlock Inn, Shurlock Row, Berkshire); much liked food cooked in open kitchen from bar snacks to grills, real ales including a Caledonian house beer and St Austell Tribute, good wine list, interesting gins and cocktails, friendly helpful service, roaring log fire; background and live music; children and dogs (in more informal area) welcome, some outside seating, open (and food) all day, kitchen closes 6pm Sun.

COBHAM   TQ1159
Running Mare (01932) 862007
Tilt Road; KT11 3EZ Attractive old flower-decked pub overlooking green (can get very

---

Pubs close to motorway junctions are listed at the back of the book.

busy); well kept Fullers ales, guest beers and over a dozen wines by the glass, good food from varied menu including tapas, seafood and popular Sun lunch, efficient friendly service, two timbered bars and restaurant; children and dogs welcome, a few tables out at front and on rose-covered back terrace, open all day, no food Sun evening.

COLDHARBOUR   TQ1544
Plough (01306) 711793
Village signposted in the network of small roads around Leith Hill; RH5 6HD Former 17th-c beamed coaching house under welcoming licensees – also incorporates the village shop; own-brew Leith Hill beers and guests, proper cider and a dozen wines by the glass, good popular food (not Sun evening) in bar or restaurant; background music, TV, events in barn room such as live music, food fairs, bridge nights and French lessons; children, walkers and dogs welcome, seats out at front and on back terrace overlooking fields, six comfortable bedrooms, open all day (till 9pm Sun).

COMPTON   SU9646
★ Withies (01483) 421158
Withies Lane; pub signed from B3000; GU3 1JA Gently old-fashioned and civilised 16th-c pub on edge of Loseley Park; atmospheric low-beamed carpeted bar, some 17th-c carved panels between windows, splendid art nouveau settle among old sewing-machine tables, log fire in massive inglenook, well kept Adnams, Greene King, Hogs Back and Sharps, highly regarded food, efficient staff in bow ties; children welcome, no dogs inside, seats on terrace, under apple trees and creeper-hung arbour, flower-edged neat front lawn, seven comfortable bedrooms, handy for Watts Gallery, closed Sun evening.

CRANLEIGH   TQ0539
Richard Onslow (01483) 274922
High Street; GU6 8AU Busy Peach group pub with cheerful small bar, leather tub chairs and built-in sofa, slate-floored drinking area, ales including Greene King and Surrey Hills, a proper cider and ten wines by the glass, generally well liked food from deli boards up including weekday set menu, two dining rooms (open fires) and sizeable restaurant with pale tables on wood floor, modern flowery wallpaper and large windows overlooking the street; background music, board games; children and dogs (in bar) welcome, seats out at front and in terraced back garden, ten well equipped bedrooms, open (and food) all day from 7am (8am weekends) for breakfast.

DORKING   TQ1649
Cricketers (01306) 889938
South Street; RH4 2JU Chatty and relaxed little Fullers local with up to five well kept ales and simple weekday lunchtime

food, friendly service, some cricketing memorabilia on stripped-brick walls; events including monthly quiz, beer festivals, Scalextric championship and onion-growing competition, darts, sports TV; children allowed until early evening, nice split-level suntrap back terrace, open all day.

DORKING   TQ1649
Kings Arms (01306) 886496
West Street; RH4 1BU Rambling 15th-c pub (originally three cottages) in antiques quarter of historic market town; cosy split-level interior with low black beams and timbers, some old panelling and leaded windows, mix of furniture on bare boards, brick or tiled floors, Shepherd Neame ales and an occasional guest, decent choice of fair value food from sandwiches and wraps up, friendly service; background music (live Fri, Sat), quiz Mon, sports TVs, fruit machine; children welcome, tables in two courtyards behind, open all day, food all day Sat, till 5pm Sun.

DORKING   TQ1649
Old House (01306) 889664
West Street; RH4 1BY Bustling old Youngs pub with opened-up beamed interior; good food from bar snacks up (not Sun evening, Mon, Tues); friendly staff; dogs welcome, back terrace with heated beach huts, closed Mon lunchtime, otherwise open all day (till 8pm Sun).

DORMANSLAND   TQ4042
Old House at Home (01342) 836828
West Street; RH7 6QP Friendly 19th-c village pub; beamed bar with traditional furniture on parquet floor, two-way woodburner, Shepherd Neame ales and several wines by the glass from unusual barrel-fronted counter, good well priced traditional food (not Sun evening, Mon, Tues), restaurant with wood and stone floor, darts and TV in snug; some live music; children and dogs (in bar) welcome, tables out in front, open all day Thurs-Sun.

DORMANSLAND   TQ4042
Plough (01342) 832933
Plough Road, off B2028 NE; RH7 6PS Friendly traditional old pub in quiet village; well kept Fullers, Harveys and Sharps, Weston's cider and decent wines, good choice of enjoyable lunchtime bar food including specials and popular Sun roasts, Thai restaurant (Mon evening-Sat), log fires and other original features; charity quiz nights and some live music; children and dogs welcome, disabled facilities, good-sized garden, open all day, no food Sun evening.

DUNSFOLD   TQ0036
Sun (01483) 200242
Off B2130 S of Godalming; GU8 4LE Old brick pub with four rooms (brighter at the front), beams and some exposed

brickwork, scrubbed pine furniture, two massive log fires, five real ales such as Greene King, Sharps and Tillingbourne, decent wines and enjoyable reasonably priced home-made food including curry evening (second Sat of month) and popular Sun lunch (best to book), good friendly service; quiz night Sun, darts; children and dogs welcome, seats on terrace and common opposite, good walks, open all day, no food Sun evening.

EASHING SU9543
★**Stag on the River** (01483) 421568
Lower Eashing, just off A3 southbound; GU7 2QG Gently upmarket riverside inn (part of Red Mist group) with Georgian façade concealing much older interior; attractively opened-up rooms including charming old-fashioned locals' bar with armchairs on red and black quarry tiles, log fire in cosy snug beyond, Hogs Back TEA, one or two Marstons-related ales and a house beer from Tilford, Hazy Hog cider, plenty of emphasis on food with several linked dining areas including river room up a couple of steps, attentive courteous staff; children welcome, dogs in bar, extensive terrace with rattan and wood furniture under parasols (some by weir), picnic-sets on grass, seven bedrooms, open all day, food all day weekends.

EAST CLANDON TQ0551
★**Queens Head** (01483) 222332
Just off A246 Guildford–Leatherhead; The Street; GU4 7RY Busy attractively updated dining pub in same Red Mist group as Duke of Cambridge at Tilford, Stag at Eashing, Wheatsheaf in Farnham etc; well liked food (best to book) from light dishes to good daily specials, set lunch deal (Mon-Thurs), Red Mist house beer along with Surrey Hills and a couple of guests from fine elm-topped counter, also Hazy Hog cider and nice wines by the glass, efficient friendly service, comfortable linked rooms, woodburner in big inglenook; daily newspapers and silent TV in bar; children welcome, tables out in front and on side terrace, handy for Hatchlands Park (NT), open (and food) all day Fri and Sat, shuts 9pm (8pm) Sun.

EFFINGHAM TQ1153
Plough (01372) 303105
Orestan Lane; KT24 5SW Youngs pub with their well kept ales and a guest, plenty of wines by the glass and good home-made food, open interior around central bar, grey-painted beams, delft shelving and half panelling, wood floors, two coal-effect gas fires; children and dogs welcome (pub dog is Ruby), disabled access/parking, plenty of tables on forecourt and in pretty garden among fruit trees, well placed for Polesden Lacey (NT), open all day Fri and Sat, closed Sun evening.

ELSTEAD SU9043
Woolpack (01252) 703106
B3001 Milford–Farnham; GU8 6HD Comfortably modernised tile-hung dining pub run by Italian family; enjoyable home-cooked food including stone-baked pizzas and weekly themed nights, cask-tapped ales and decent wines by the glass, friendly efficient service, long main bar, restaurant, open fires; children welcome, garden with picnic-sets, open all day Sun.

ESHER TQ1364
Wheatsheaf (01372) 464014
The Green; KT10 8AG Early 19th-c dining pub with neat opened-up bar area; light wood flooring, a mix of furniture including sofas and easy chairs, lots of colourful artwork and a couple of Victorian fireplaces, four well kept beers including Surrey Hills and plenty of wines by the glass, good food from upscale bar snacks, sharing plates and traditional favourites to more enterprising restaurant dishes, friendly staff, high-ceilinged back dining extension with small outside eating area; background music, sports TV, daily newspapers; well behaved children till 7.30pm, dogs in bar, teak tables under parasols on front paved terrace looking across to green, open (and food) all day.

FARNHAM SU8545
Spotted Cow (01252) 726541
Bourne Grove, Lower Bourne (towards Tilford); GU10 3QT Welcoming red-brick dining pub on edge of town in nice wooded setting (good walks nearby); highly regarded food from pub favourites and sharing boards up (booking advised), three changing ales and decent range of wines, friendly helpful staff; children and dogs welcome, big garden, open all day weekends (food till 7.30pm Sun).

FETCHAM TQ1456
Bell (01372) 372624
Bell Lane; KT22 9ND Attractively modernised Youngs pub; their ales, guest beers and over 30 wines by the glass including champagne, good choice of other drinks including cocktails, well liked food from varied menu in bar or restaurant, friendly helpful staff; live music and other events; children and dogs welcome, tables out on gravel terrace, weekend burger shack, open (and food) all day.

FICKLESHOLE TQ3960
White Bear (01959) 573166
Featherbed Lane/Fairchildes Lane; off A2022 just S of A212 roundabout; CR6 9PH Long 16th-c country dining pub with lots of small rooms; beams, flagstones and open fires, tasty food from home-made classics up (order at the bar), four real ales including Brakspears; children and well behaved dogs welcome, picnic-sets and stone bear on front terrace, sizeable back garden

with pond and summer weekend burger shack, open all day, food till 7.30pm Sun.

GODALMING   SU9643
Star (01483) 417717
Church Street; GU7 1EL Friendly 17th-c local in pedestrianised cobbled street; cosy low-beamed and panelled L-shaped bar, up to 15 well kept ales (some tapped from the cask) and extensive range of ciders/perries, enjoyable food including range of burgers (only bar snacks in the evening), more modern back room; regular beer/cider festivals; heated terrace behind, open all day.

GRAYSWOOD   SU9134
Wheatsheaf (01428) 644440
Grayswood Road (A286 NE of Haslemere); GU27 2DE Welcoming family-run dining pub with light airy décor; enjoyable freshly made food in bar or restaurant, good range of well kept beers, friendly helpful staff; occasional live music, quiz first Tues of month; children and dogs welcome, disabled access, front verandah and side terrace, six bedrooms in extension, good breakfast, open all day Sun till 7pm.

GUILDFORD   SU9950
Stoke (01483) 504296
Stoke Road; GU1 4JN Popular Greene King pub with good choice of drinks and enjoyable reasonably priced food including burgers, fajitas and pizzas, plenty of deals, friendly helpful service; quiz nights, sports TV, pool; children and dogs welcome, disabled facilities, seats on side terrace, refundable car parking fee, open (and food) all day.

GUILDFORD   SU9949
White House (01483) 302006
High Street; GU2 4AJ Modernised Fullers pub in pretty waterside setting; their ales and good range of wines, fair-priced food from small plates up, sizeable bar with conservatory, upstairs rooms and roof terrace; children welcome, a few picnic-sets out by River Wey, open (and food) all day.

HASCOMBE   TQ0039
White Horse (01483) 208258
B2130 S of Godalming; GU8 4JA Spacious renovated pub with 16th-c origins; four well kept ales including Otter, decent wines by the glass and good food from traditional choices up, friendly efficient staff, scrubbed tables and pews in beamed bar, some old black and white photographs and farming memorabilia, various other linked rooms including smart pitched ceiling restaurant (separate more upmarket menu); children and dogs welcome in some parts, small front terrace and attractive back

garden, pretty village with duck pond, good walks and handy for Winkworth Arboretum (NT), open all day.

HEADLEY   TQ2054
Cock (01372) 377258
Church Lane; KT18 6LE Relaxed opened-up country pub in same group (Red Mist) as the Queens Head at East Clandon, Duke of Cambridge at Tilford etc; light modern interior (parts date from the 18th c) with open fires and comfortable seating, enjoyable food (all day weekends) from lunchtime sandwiches and sharing plates up, set lunch Mon-Thurs, a house beer and a couple of guests, plenty of wines by the glass from interesting list and some local gins; children and dogs (in one area) welcome, disabled access using lift from upper car park, terrace picnic-sets under parasols, attractive setting and good woodland walks, open all day.

HORSELL   SU9959
★ **Red Lion** (01483) 768497
High Street; GU21 4SS Spacious popular pub with airy split-level bar, comfortable sofas and easy chairs on wood flooring, clusters of pictures on cream-painted walls, Fullers London Pride and a couple of guests from long wooden servery, a dozen wines by the glass and good range of other drinks, well liked bistro-style food served by friendly staff, back dining rooms; newspapers; children allowed till 8pm, attractive tree-sheltered terrace, steps up to garden with picnic-sets and shelter, good local walks, open (and food) all day.

HORSELL COMMON   TQ0160
Sands at Bleak House
(01483) 756988 *Chertsey Road, The Anthonys; A320 Woking–Ottershaw; GU21 5NL* Smart contemporary pub-restaurant on edge of Horsell Common; grey sandstone floor (and bar front), brown leather sofas and cushioned stools, two dining rooms with dark wood furniture, woodburners, good well presented food (can be pricey), Hogs Back and Sharps, friendly attentive uniformed staff; background music, TV; children welcome, dogs in courtyard only, good shortish walk to sandpits that inspired HG Wells's *The War of the Worlds*, seven bedrooms, open all day (till 6pm Sun).

LALEHAM   TQ0568
★ **Three Horseshoes** (01784) 455014
Shepperton Road (B376); TW18 1SE Bustling dining pub near pleasant stretch of the Thames with several interconnecting rooms; bar with white walls and contrasting deep blue woodwork, easy-going mix of tables

---

Virtually all pubs in this book sell wine by the glass. We mention wines
if they are a cut above the average.

and chairs on bare boards, woodburner fronted by armchairs and squashy sofa, well kept Fullers/Gales beers and plenty of wines by the glass, highly regarded food (booking advised) from sandwiches and sharing plates up, efficient friendly young staff, dining areas with assorted tables and chairs, pictures and mirrors on grey walls; soft background music; children welcome till 8pm, attractive flagstoned terrace, picnic-sets on grass, open (and food) all day.

LEIGH   TQ2147
★ **Seven Stars** (01306) 611254
Dawes Green, south of A25 Dorking–Reigate; RH2 8NP Attractive tile-hung country dining pub; comfortable beamed and flagstoned bar with traditional furnishings and inglenook, Fullers, Harveys, Sharps and Youngs from glowing copper counter, several wines by the glass and enjoyable sensibly priced food, plainer public bar and sympathetic restaurant extension where children allowed; dogs welcome in bar areas, plenty of outside seating, open all day Sat, till 6pm Sun.

LIMPSFIELD   TQ4053
Bull (01883) 713469
High Street; RH8 0DR Old red-brick village pub bought and refurbished by the local community in 2017; stylish décor with modern artwork, mirrors etc on deep blue walls, banquettes and other comfortable seating on wood-strip floors, nice open fire, good often imaginative food (not Sun evening) from sharing boards up including set menu, three changing ales, craft beers and well chosen wines from marble-topped counter; children and dogs (in bar) welcome, tables out on back deck under heated parasols, closed Mon, otherwise open all day (till 8pm Sun).

MARTYRS GREEN   TQ0857
Black Swan (01932) 862364
Handy for M25 junction 10; off A3 S-bound, but return N of junction; KT11 1NG Spacious country dining pub with contemporary décor (utterly changed from its days as the 'Slaughtered Lamb' in the movie *An American Werewolf in London*); good freshly made food from sandwiches and pub favourites up, fine choice of wines and champagnes, real ales such as Greene King IPA, Surrey Hills Shere Drop and Timothy Taylors Landlord, friendly efficient service, log fire and underfloor heating; background music; children and dogs (in bar) welcome, plenty of outside tables, summer barbecues, open (and food) all day.

MICKLEHAM   TQ1753
King William IV (01372) 372590
Just off A24 Leatherhead–Dorking; Byttom Hill; RH5 6EL Steps up to small pub tucked away from the main road; well kept Hogs Back TEA, Surrey Hills Shere Drop

and a guest, enjoyable food from lunchtime sandwiches to blackboard specials, friendly attentive service, pleasant outlook from cosy plank-panelled front bar, carpeted dining area with grandfather clock and log fire; background music, live summer jazz outside (Sun 4.30-7.30pm); children and dogs welcome, plenty of tables in pretty terraced garden (some in open-sided timber shelters), lovely valley views, open (and food) all day.

MICKLEHAM   TQ1753
★ **Running Horses** (01372) 372279
Old London Road (B2209); RH5 6DU Popular and well run country inn renowned for its food – arrive early for a seat or parking space; stylish bar and separate restaurant with red leather tub chairs and banquettes in booths, lovely panelling, parquet flooring, log fire in an inglenook, racing cartoons and Hogarth prints on the walls, race tickets hanging from a beam; Brakspears Bitter and Oxford Gold, Fullers London Pride and a monthly guest beer and around 20 wines by the glass, friendly, helpful staff, excellent food from breakfast on; children and dogs (in bar and bedrooms) welcome, front terrace with lovely tubs and hanging baskets, peaceful view of the old church opposite, disabled facilities, eight smart bedrooms including separate gatehouse, open all day, food all day weekends.

MOGADOR   TQ2453
Sportsman (01737) 246655
From M25 up A217 past second roundabout, then Mogador signed; KT20 7ES Modernised and extended low-ceilinged pub on edge of Walton Heath (originally a 16th-c royal hunting lodge); well kept ales including Sharps and Youngs, good food from interesting varied menu, restaurant with raised section; children welcome (no pushchairs), dogs in bar, seats out on common, front verandah and back lawn, popular with walkers and riders, open (and food) all day.

OCKLEY   TQ1337
Punchbowl (01306) 627249
Oakwood Hill, signed off A29 S; RH5 5PU Attractive 16th-c tile-hung country pub with slabby Horsham stone roof; enjoyable good value pubby food, Fullers HSB, London Pride and a couple of guests, central bar with flagstones and low beams, inglenook log fire decorated with horsebrasses, carpeted restaurant on the left, second bar to the right; regular quiz nights; children and dogs welcome, picnic-sets in pretty garden, quiet spot with good walks including Sussex Border Path, open all day.

OUTWOOD   TQ3246
★ **Bell** (01342) 842989
Outwood Common, just E of village; off A23 S of Redhill; RH1 5PN Attractive 17th-c extended dining pub; smartly rustic

beamed bar with oak and elm furniture (some Jacobean in style), soft lighting, low beams and vast stone inglenook, Fullers London Pride, ESB and a guest, 20 wines by the glass and wide range of spirits, popular food from pub standards to good fresh fish (best to book, especially evenings when drinking-only space limited); background music; children and dogs (in bar) welcome, disabled access, well maintained garden looking out past pine trees to rolling fields, open all day, food all day weekends.

OUTWOOD TQ3146
Dog & Duck (01342) 844552
Prince of Wales Road; turn off A23 at station sign in Salfords, S of Redhill – OS Sheet 187 map reference 312460; RH1 5QU Relaxed beamed country pub with enjoyable fairly priced home-made food in bar or large two-part restaurant, four well kept Badger ales and good range of wines, friendly helpful service; children and dogs (in bar) welcome unil 8.30pm, sizeable garden with raised deck, fenced duck pond and play area (also circuit for motorised kids' jeeps), open all day (till 9pm Sun).

OXTED TQ4048
Grumpy Mole (01883) 722207
Caterfield Lane, Staffhurst Wood, S of town; RH8 0RR Popular and welcoming country pub – part of small group of same name; Greene King ales (including one badged for them), a guest beer and lots of wines by the glass, good food from sandwiches and pub staples up, afternoon teas, friendly obliging service, well divided bar and dining areas, open fire; children and dogs welcome, rattan-style furniture on paved terrace, picnic-sets on lawn, lovely views across fields, open all day.

PUTTENHAM SU9347
Good Intent (01483) 810387
Signed off B3000 just S of A31 junction; The Street/Seale Lane; GU3 1AR Convivial beamed village local with big log fire in cosy front bar, alcove seating, some old farming tools and photographs of the pub, Timothy Taylors, Hogs Back and guests, reasonably priced traditional food (not Sun evening, Mon) from sandwiches up, parquet-floored dining area; darts; well behaved children and dogs welcome, small sunny garden, good walks, open all day weekends.

REDHILL TQ2749
Plough (01737) 766686
Church Road, St Johns; RH1 6QE Popular early 17th-c pub with warm friendly local atmosphere; lots of bits and pieces to look at including copper and brass hanging from beamed ceiling, nice open fire, Fullers London Pride and three guests, enjoyable sensibly priced blackboard food (not Sun evening), good helpful service; Weds quiz; no under-10s inside, dogs welcome, back garden with covered area (barbecues and spit roasts), open all day.

REIGATE TQ2349
Black Horse (01737) 230010
West Street (A25); RH2 9JZ Popular and welcoming White Brasserie Co pub; emphasis on their highly regarded food including some pub favourites and set menu (Mon-Sat till 6.30pm), engaging professional service, well kept ales such as Harveys, Sharps and Timothy Taylors, over 20 wines by the glass and good selection of other drinks, modern flagstoned bar area and good-sized dining extension; children and dogs welcome, disabled access, tables on paved terrace and lawn, nice spot by heathland, open (and food) all day.

REIGATE HEATH TQ2349
★Skimmington Castle (01737) 243100
Off A25 Reigate–Dorking via Flanchford Road and Bonny's Road; RH2 8RL Nicely located small country pub with emphasis on good home-made food from baguettes up (can get very busy and best to book), well kept Harveys, St Austell and a couple of guests, a dozen wines by the glass, friendly efficient service, snug beamed and panelled rooms, log fires; children, dogs and muddy boots welcome, seats out on three sides (some heaters), open all day, food till 7.30pm Sun (9pm summer).

RIPLEY TQ0456
Seven Stars (01483) 225128
Newark Lane (B367); GU23 6DL Neat 1930s pub with various snug areas; enjoyable food from varied menu, real ales such as Greene King, Fullers, Sharps and Shepherd Neame, good wines and coffee, red patterned carpet, gleaming brasses and open fire; quiet background music; picnic-sets and heated wooden booths in well tended garden, river and canalside walks, closed Sun evening.

ROWLEDGE SU8243
Hare & Hounds (01252) 792287
The Square; GU10 4AA Popular village pub with friendly welcoming atmosphere; good honest home cooking and four well kept ales including Greene King Ruddles County, smallish eating area; children and dogs welcome, garden with tables on terrace and play area, open all day, no food Sun evening.

SEND TQ0156
New Inn (01483) 762736
Send Road, Cartbridge; GU23 7EN Traditional old beamed pub by River Wey

---

We say if we know a pub allows dogs.

Navigation; long bar and dining room, log fires, ales such as Adnams, Fullers, Hogs Back and Sharps, good choice of generously served food (all day weekends) from ciabattas to blackboard specials, friendly helpful service; quiz first Weds of month; children and dogs welcome, large waterside garden with moorings, open all day and can get very busy in summer.

SHACKLEFORD   SU9345
Cyder House (01483) 810360
Peper Harow Lane; GU8 6AN
Refurbished 1920s village pub in pleasant leafy setting; Badger ales, proper ciders/perry and nice selection of wines by the glass, good home-made food from lunchtime sandwiches and baked potatoes up, popular burger night Mon, airy linked areas around central servery, wood floors, log fire; quiz every other Mon; children and dogs welcome, back terrace with steps up to play area, good walks, open all day (till 7pm Sun).

SHALFORD   TQ0047
Queen Victoria (01483) 566959
Station Row; GU4 8BY Tile-hung, bay-windowed local with compact modernised interior around central bar, enjoyable reasonably priced food (not Sun evening, Mon) from lunchtime sandwiches up, smaller appetites catered for, well kept Otter, Timothy Taylors and a guest, woodburner; quiz every other Thurs, some live music, sports TV; well behaved children and dogs welcome, seats out at front and on back terrace, open all day.

SHALFORD   TQ0047
Seahorse (01483) 514351
A281 S of Guildford; The Street; GU4 8BU Gently upmarket Mitchells & Butlers dining pub with contemporary décor and comfortable relaxed atmosphere; wide range of food including vegan choices and set menu (from 6pm Tues, Weds), three well kept ales such as Hogs Back TEA and Sharps Doom Bar, good choice of wines and other drinks, cheerful young staff; children welcome, big garden with heated terraces, handy for Shalford Mill (NT), open (and food) all day.

SHAMLEY GREEN   TQ0343
Bricklayers Arms (01483) 898377
Guildford Road, S of the green; GU5 0UA Red-brick village pub with five well kept ales such as Harveys, Sharps and Surrey Hills, enjoyable pubby food (not Sun evening) including themed evenings, U-shaped layout (a couple of steps) with bare boards, carpets and flagstones, exposed brickwork and stripped wood, old local photographs, sofas by woodburner; quiz nights, pool, darts and TV; children and dogs welcome, a couple of picnic-sets out in front, more seats behind, open all day.

SHAMLEY GREEN   TQ0343
★ Red Lion (01483) 892202
The Green; GU5 0UB Friendly pub facing village green and cricket pitch with cheerful mix of both diners and drinkers; two interconnected bars are fairly traditional – wooden tables, chairs and cushioned settles on bare boards and red carpet, standing timbers, white walls, deep red ceilings and open fires; Harveys, Hogs Back and Sharps, several wines by the glass, gins and malt whiskies, good food including baguettes and pub classics; background music; children and dogs (in bar) welcome, hand-made rustic tables and benches outside at front, more seating on heated covered terrace and grass at back, open all day, food all day weekends.

SHEPPERTON   TQ0866
Red Lion (01932) 244526
Russell Road; TW17 9HX In nice position across from the River Thames; bistro-style renovation (oldest part has been a pub since the 18th c), good well presented food from varied regularly changing menu (can be pricey), Sat brunch and popular Sun lunch, Fullers London Pride and local Thames Side White Swan from well stocked bar, afternoon teas, friendly staff; children and dogs welcome, modern furniture on fenced front terrace, more seats over road on riverside deck, open all day.

SHERE   TQ0747
White Horse (01483) 202518
Shere Lane; signed off A25 3 miles E of Guildford; GU5 9HS Splendid 15th-c building (Chef & Brewer) with several rooms off small bar; uneven floors, massive beams and timbers, Tudor stonework, oak wall seats and two log fires (one in huge inglenook), interesting range of enjoyable food including deals, Greene King IPA and a couple of guests, Weston's cider and plenty of wines by the glass, good, friendly service; children and dogs (in bar) welcome, seats out at front and in big garden behind, beautiful film-set village, open (and food) all day.

STAINES   TQ0371
Bells (01784) 454240
Church Street; TW18 4ZB Comfortable and sociable Youngs pub in old part of town by St Mary's church; their well kept ales and a guest, decent choice of wines and good food (not Sun evening) from pub standards up, attentive friendly service, central fireplace; sports TV; dogs allowed in bar, disabled access, tables in nice back garden with heated terrace, limited roadside parking, open all day.

STOKE D'ABERNON   TQ1259
★ Old Plough (01932) 862244
Station Road, off A245; KT11 3BN Popular attractively updated 300-year-old pub; good freshly made food including daily

specials, Fullers beers, a couple of guests and plenty of wines by the glass, competent friendly staff, restaurant with various knick-knacks; newspapers; children (not in bar after 7pm) and dogs welcome, seats out under pergola and in pretty garden, open (and food) all day.

TADWORTH
TQ2355
★ Dukes Head (01737) 812173
Dorking Road (B2032 opposite common and woods); KT20 5SL Welcoming 19th-c pub, roomy and comfortably modernised, with popular generously served food from varied menu (booking advised), five well kept ales including Fullers, Youngs and a Morlands house beer (KT20), Aspall's cider, good choice of wines by the glass, helpful friendly staff, three dining areas and two big inglenook log fires; background music, Weds quiz; children welcome (no highchairs); dogs in some areas, lots of hanging baskets and plenty of tables in well tended terraced garden, open (and food) all day, till 8pm (6.30pm) Sun.

THURSLEY
SU9039
Three Horseshoes (01252) 703900
Dye House Road, just off A3 SW of Godalming; GU8 6QD Pretty tile-hung pub owned by village consortium; convivial beamed front bar with log fire, ales such as Hogs Back TEA and several wines by the glass, good food (not Sun evening) from pubby choice up, friendly helpful staff, restaurant and small shop; children, walkers and dogs welcome, attractive two-acre garden with nice views over common and Saxon church, play fort, open all day, till 9pm Sun.

TILFORD
SU8742
Duke of Cambridge (01252) 792236
Tilford Road; GU10 2DD Dining pub in same Red Mist group as the Queens Head at East Clandon, Stag at Eashing etc; nice food from varied menu including gluten-free and children's choices, good selection of wines and gins (some local), well kept ales such as Hogs Back and Surrey Hills along with a Tilford craft beer (brewed on-site), helpful service; May charity music festival; children and dogs welcome, terrace and garden with outside bar/grill, good play area, open all day, food all day Sun.

VIRGINIA WATER
SU9968
Rose & Olive Branch
(01344) 845653 *Callow Hill; GU25 4LH* Cosy unpretentious red-brick pub with good choice of nicely presented food including speciality pies and several vegetarian and gluten-free options, four core Windsor & Eton ales, decent wines, friendly busy staff; background music; children and dogs welcome, tables on front terrace and in garden behind, good walks, open (and food) all day weekends.

WALLISWOOD
TQ1138
Scarlett Arms (01306) 627243
Signed from Ewhurst–Rowhook back road, or off A29 S of Ockley; RH5 5RD Cottagey 16th-c village pub; low beams, two log fires (one in big inglenook) and simple furniture on flagstones, well kept Badger ales and enjoyable reasonably priced food (not Sun evening), friendly prompt service, various smaller rooms off main bar; background music, darts; children and dogs welcome, tables out at front and in garden under parasols, play area, good walks, closed Mon lunchtime, otherwise open all day.

WARLINGHAM
TQ3955
Botley Hill Farmhouse
(01959) 577154 *S on Limpsfield Road (B269); CR6 9QH* 16th-c country pub set in lovely cycling country high on the North Downs; low-ceilinged linked rooms up and down steps, fresh flowers and candles, popular locally sourced food from sandwiches and pub standards up (till 7pm Sun, booking advised), own Titsey beers from on-site microbrewery plus a couple of guests such as Pilgrim and Westerham tapped from the cask (tasters offered), a dozen wines by the glass, good friendly service, big log fire in one room, tea room selling local produce; children and dogs welcome, disabled access, terrace and garden with far-reaching countryside views, good local walks, open all day, Sun breakfast from 9am.

WEST CLANDON
TQ0451
★ Bulls Head (01483) 222444
A247 SE of Woking; GU4 7ST Comfortably old-fashioned village pub based around 1540s timbered hall-house; enjoyable good value pubby food (not Sun evening) including proper home-made pies, friendly helpful staff, Youngs, Hogs Back and Surrey Hills ales, small lantern-lit beamed front bar with open fire, some stripped brickwork, old local prints and bric-a-brac, simple raised back inglenook dining area, games room (darts and pool); children and dogs welcome, disabled access from car park, play area in neat little garden, close to fire-gutted Clandon Park (NT) and nice walks, open all day, closed Sun evening.

WEST CLANDON
TQ0452
Onslow Arms (01483) 222447
A247 SE of Woking; GU4 7TE Busy modernised pub with heavily beamed rambling rooms leading away from central bar; wooden dining chairs and tables on wide floorboards, painted panelling, all sorts of copper implements, hunting horns and pictures, leather chesterfields in front of open fire, four real ales including Surrey Hills and a beer named for the pub, 20 wines by the glass, good popular food from lunchtime sandwiches and sharing boards and traditional choices up; live music first Weds of month,

TV, daily papers; children (till early evening) and dogs (in bar) welcome, pretty courtyard garden with tables under parasols, open (and food) all day.

WEST END   SU9461

★**The Inn at West End**

(01276) 858652 *Just under 2.5 miles from M3 junction 3; A322 S, on right; GU24 9PW* Modern-looking pub (part of the Barons Pubs chain) with contemporary paintwork, upholstered and leather dining chairs around a mix of tables on bare floorboards, modern artwork and light fittings, also extended restaurant and lounge area, Dark Star Hophead, Fullers London Pride and Thurstons Horsell Gold, several wines by the glass and good gin cocktails, interesting food from breakfast on; children and dogs (in bar and bedrooms) welcome, a few tables at front by road, also courtyard garden with painted picnic-sets, a dozen comfortable bedrooms, open (and food) all day.

WEST HORSLEY   TQ0853

Barley Mow (01483) 282693

Off A246 Leatherhead–Guildford at Bell & Colvill garage roundabout; The Street; KT24 6HR Welcoming beamed village pub with well kept ales such as Fullers and Surrey Hills, decent wines and good Thai food (not Sun) along with more conventional lunchtime menu, log fires, barn function room; background music; children and dogs (in bar) welcome, spacious garden, open all day.

WEST HORSLEY   TQ0752

King William IV (01483) 282318

The Street; KT24 6BG Comfortable and welcoming early 19th-c village pub; low entrance door to front and side bars, beams, flagstones and log fire, back conservatory restaurant, good variety of food (not Sun evening) including gluten-free menu, five real ales such as Courage and Surrey Hills; background and occasional live music, quiz nights; children and dogs welcome, disabled access, small sunny garden with deck and play area, good for walkers, open all day.

WEYBRIDGE   TQ0765

Old Crown (01932) 842844

Thames Street; KT13 8LP Comfortably old-fashioned three-bar pub dating from the 17th c; good value traditional food (not Sun-Tues evenings) from sandwiches to fresh fish, Courage, Youngs and a guest kept well, good choice of wines by the glass,

friendly efficient service, family lounge and conservatory; dogs welcome, secluded terrace, steps down to suntrap garden overlooking Wey/Thames confluence, mooring for small boats, open all day.

WEYBRIDGE   TQ0664

Queens Head (01932) 839820

Bridge Road; KT13 8XS 18th-c pub in White Brasserie Co group; good food from open kitchen including well priced lunchtime/early evening set menu (not Sun), also a proper bar serving real ales and plenty of wines by the glass, friendly staff; soft background music, newspapers; children welcome, tables out on small front terrace, open (and food) all day.

WINDLESHAM   SU9264

Bee (01276) 479244

School Road; GU20 6PD Cosy village pub with good food from sandwiches and traditional favourites up including steaks cooked on a hot stone, four well kept ales and decent wines by the glass, friendly accommodating staff, bar area with painted panelling and open fire in small brick fireplace, back dining room; TV; children and dogs (in bar) welcome, picnic-sets on small front terrace and in garden behind with play area, open all day, no food Sun evening.

WITLEY   SU9439

White Hart (01428) 683695

Petworth Road; GU8 5PH Picture-book beamed Tudor pub; well kept St Austell Tribute, Youngs Bitter and a guest, craft beers, plenty of wines by the glass and extensive range of whiskies, popular food including signature home-smoked/chargrilled dishes, friendly accommodating staff, bar, restaurant and cosy panelled snug with inglenook (where George Eliot used to drink); children and dogs welcome, seats on cobbled terrace and in garden, nice walks nearby, open (and food) all day, till 6pm (4pm) Sun.

WONERSH   TQ0145

Grantley Arms (01483) 893351

The Street; GU5 0PE Popular 16th-c village pub; opened-up beamed and timbered bar with mix of new and old furniture on light wood floor, a couple of steps up to long pitched-roof dining area, four real ales and interesting wine list, good well presented food from lunchtime sandwiches up, former bakery for private dining, friendly accommodating young staff;

Please keep sending us reports. We rely on readers for news of new discoveries, and particularly for news of changes – however slight – at the fully described pubs: feedback@goodguides.com, or (no stamp needed) Freepost THE GOOD PUB GUIDE, Random House Publishing, 20 Vauxhall Bridge Road, London SW1V 2SA.

occasional live music and quiz nights, daily newspapers; children welcome till 7.30pm, dogs in bar, wheelchair access using ramp, attractive paved terrace, open (and food) all day.

WOOD STREET   SU9550
Royal Oak (01483) 235137
Oak Hill; GU3 3DA 1920s red-brick village local; up to six well kept ales and good value traditional home-made food (not Sun evening, Mon), friendly staff; music and quiz nights; children and dogs welcome, decent sized back garden with play area, open all day Fri-Sun, closed Mon lunchtime.

WORPLESDON   SU9854
Jolly Farmer (01483) 235897
Burdenshott Road, off A320 Guildford– Woking, not in village; GU3 3RN Old Fullers pub in pleasant country setting; their well kept ales in beamed and flagstoned bar with small log fire, enjoyable fairly traditional food from lunchtime sandwiches up, bare-boards dining extension under pitched roof; background music; children welcome and dogs (theirs is called Tyson), garden with parasol-shaded tables and pergola, open all day (till 9pm Sun).

WRECCLESHAM   SU8344
Bat & Ball (01252) 792108
Bat & Ball Lane, South Farnham; approach from Sandrock Hill and Upper Bourne Lane, then narrow steep lane to pub; GU10 4SA Fairly traditional pub tucked away in hidden valley; enjoyable food (all day weekends) from interestingly varied menu, special diets catered for, six well kept local ales and plenty of wines by the glass; live music including open mike last Thurs of month and June beer/music festival; children and dogs welcome, disabled facilities, attractive terrace with vine arbour, more tables and substantial play fort in garden, open all day and can get very busy in summer.

WRECCLESHAM   SU8244
Royal Oak (01252) 728319
The Street; GU10 4QS Buoyant 17th-c black-beamed village local; enjoyable good value home-made food (smaller helpings available for some main courses), steak night Weds, burgers Thurs, three well kept Greene King ales, friendly helpful staff, log fire; Sun quiz, sports TV, darts; children and dogs welcome, large garden with play area, open all day.

Sussex

KEY   ⭐ Star Pub   🍽️ Top Quality Food   🍺 Great Beer

🍷 Good Wines   £ Bargain Meals   🛏️ Good Bedrooms   🍴 Serves Food

---

BOLNEY TQ2623 Map 2

Bolney Stage 🍷 🍺

(01444) 881200 – www.brunningandprice.co.uk/bolneystage

London Road, off old A23 just N of A272; RH17 5RL

Historic pub of much character with plenty of drinking and dining space, lots to look at, a wide choice of drinks, interesting food and seats outside

This sizeable 16th-c black and white country dining pub is part of the Brunning & Price group. The bar and dining rooms are interconnected by open doorways and standing timbers to create separate areas that share the same bustling, friendly and informal atmosphere: heavy beams, assorted flooring including polished flagstones, old brickwork, bare boards and carpet (often topped with rugs), a two-way open log fire, and wooden stools against a rustic bar counter. Throughout there are handsome antique chairs, some cushioned and some leather, a medley of solid tables, lots of prints, portraits and mirrors on pale contemporary paintwork, elegant metal chandeliers and numerous house plants. St Austell Brunning & Price Traditional Bitter, Harveys Old Ale, Long Man Best Bitter, Timothy Taylors Landlord on handpump, 18 wines by the glass and around 40 gins. Staff are efficient and cheerful; background music. There are seats and tables on terraces and under a gazebo, a fire pit and picnic-sets on a lawn; also, a play tractor and an equipped play area for children. It's handy for the Bluebell Railway and Sheffield Park (National Trust).

🍴 Good, up-to-date food includes sandwiches, prawn cocktail with marie rose sauce, baked camembert with toasted ciabatta, pea and mint tortellini with garden pea velouté and asparagus, deep-fried cod in beer batter with chips, steak burger with coleslaw and fries, roast pork tenderloin with colcannon potato and apple purée, Malaysian chicken curry with pak choi, and puddings such as sticky toffee pudding with toffee sauce and vanilla ice-cream and triple chocolate brownie with chocolate sauce. *Benchmark main dish: fish pie (salmon, smoked haddock and prawns) £16.95. Two-course evening meal £24.00.*

Brunning & Price ~ Manager Mark Lavis ~ Real ale ~ Open 11-11; 11-10.30 Sun ~ Bar food 12-9; 12-9.30 Fri, Sat ~ Restaurant ~ Children welcome ~ Dogs allowed in bar

---

'Children welcome' means the pub says it lets children inside without any special restriction. If it allows them in, but to restricted areas such as an eating area or family room, we specify this. Places with separate restaurants often let children use them, and hotels usually let children into public areas such as lounges. Some pubs impose an evening time limit – let us know if you find one earlier than 9pm.

CHARLTON
Fox Goes Free ♀

SU8812   Map 2

(01243) 811461 – www.thefoxgoesfree.com

Village signposted off A286 Chichester–Midhurst in Singleton, also from Chichester–Petworth via East Dean; PO18 0HU

400-year-old pub with beamed bars, popular food and drink and big garden; bedrooms

This charming and historic little pub is full of character. The bar, the first of several cosy separate rooms, has old Irish settles, tables and chapel chairs and an open fire. Standing timbers divide up a larger beamed bar with a huge brick fireplace and old local photographs on the walls. A dining area overlooks the garden; it's popular with race-goers (Goodwood is nearby) and walkers, so it's wise to book a table in advance. A family extension is cleverly converted from horse boxes and the stables where the 1926 Goodwood winner was once housed; board games and background music. They keep a beer named for the pub (from Arundel) and guests such as Fownes Smokestack Lightning and Greene King Scrum Down on handpump, almost 30 wines by the glass (using a specialist wine preservation system), quite a few gins and Addlestone's cider. An attractive back garden has picnic-sets under apple trees and the lovely South Downs as a backdrop, and there are rustic benches and tables on the gravelled front terrace too. The five charming, country-style bedrooms are comfortable and breakfasts well regarded. Disabled ramps available. You can walk up to Levin Down nature reserve, or stroll around the Iron Age hill fort on the Trundle with huge views to the Isle of Wight; the Weald & Downland Living Museum and gorgeous West Dean Gardens are nearby too.

A wide choice of food includes lunchtime sandwiches (not Sunday), courgette and feta fritters with mint yoghurt dressing, moules marinière or à la crème, vegan curry, cumberland sausages with mash and red onion, burgers (salt marsh beef, lamb or sweet potato and beetroot) with toppings, harissa mayonnaise and chips, honey and mustard glazed ham with eggs and chips, a pie of the day, and puddings such as lemon posset with lychee and pomegranate coulis and red velvet brownie with home-made ice-cream. *Benchmark main dish: fish pie £14.75. Two-course evening meal £21.00.*

Free house ~ Licensee David Coxon ~ Real ale ~ Open 11-11; 11-midnight Sat; 12-11 Sun ~ Bar food 12-2.15, 6.15-9.45; 12-2.45, 6.15-9.30 Sun; reduced menu in afternoon ~ Restaurant ~ Children welcome ~ Dogs allowed in bar ~ Bedrooms: £109

CHILGROVE
White Horse ♀ 🛏

SU8214   Map 2

(01243) 519444 – www.thewhitehorse.co.uk

B2141 Petersfield–Chichester; PO18 9HX

Handsome coaching inn with a thoughtful choice of drinks, first class food and plenty of outside seating; bedrooms

Perched at the foot of the stunning South Downs, this whitewashed country inn does a fine job of satisfying both drinkers and diners. The bar area has a relaxed atmosphere, leather armchairs in front of a woodburning stove and daily papers on the light oak counter where friendly staff serve Tipsy Horse (brewed for the pub by Ringwood), Youngs Original, Dark Star Hophead and Marstons 61 Deep on handpump and 18 wines by the glass from a carefully curated list. Just off here, a room with leather button-back wall seats and mate's and other dark wooden dining chairs has all sorts of country knick-knacks: stuffed animals, china plates, riding boots, flower paintings, dog drawings, stone bottles and books on shelves. The dining room to the other side of the bar has a huge painting of a galloping white horse, a long suede wall banquette, high-backed settles creating stalls, elegant chairs, lots of mirrors and big metal chandeliers. Throughout, there are fat candles in lanterns, flagstones and coir carpet, beams and timbering, and animal skin throws; background music and board games. A two-level terrace has dark grey rattan-style seats around glass-topped tables under parasols among pretty flowering tubs; an area up steps has rustic benches and tables and there are picnic-sets on grass at the front. Each of the 15 comfortable, contemporary and light bedrooms has a little private courtyard (two have a hot tub). Good surrounding walks.

Interesting food includes sandwiches, confit duck bonbons with plum dipping sauce, ham hock terrine with pickles, crispy-battered haddock with chunky chips, pan-fried sea bass fillet with artichoke, leek and potato hash and cider butter sauce, British brisket burger with ruby slaw and fries, roasted squash and red Thai vegetable curry, pressed lamb shoulder with haricot bean casserole, sprouting broccoli and salsa verde, and puddings such as dark chocolate truffle torte and lemon meringue pie. *Benchmark main dish: chicken and ham pie with buttered greens and mash £14.00. Two-course evening meal £20.00.*

Cirrus Inns ~ Licensee Josh Nicolson ~ Real ale ~ Open 12-10.30 ~ Bar food 12-3, 6-9.30; 12-4 Sun ~ Restaurant ~ Children welcome ~ Dogs allowed in bar & bedrooms ~ Bedrooms: £200

COPTHORNE
TQ3240   Map 3

Old House ♀ ⇦

(01342) 718529 – www.theoldhouseinn.co.uk
B2037 NE of village; RH10 3JB

Charming old pub with plenty of character, real ales, enjoyable food and attentive staff; attractive bedrooms

Light and airy spaces adorned with reclaimed wood gives this converted farm workers' cottage a fresh and modern twist while evoking a rustic country kitchen. It's a higgledy-piggledy timbered building and you'll feel immediately welcomed on walking into the little entrance bar. There's a brown leather chesterfield sofa, armchairs and carved wooden chairs around all sorts of tables, a big sisal mat on flagstones, a decorative fireplace and nightlights. Courage Best, Ringwood Razorback and a guest beer on handpump, several good wines by the glass and a couple of huge glass flagons holding Sipsmith vodka and gin; staff are friendly and helpful. The nooks and crannies in the interconnected rooms leading off here are just as cosy. Off to the left is a charming small room with a woodburning stove in an inglenook fireplace and two leather armchairs in front, white-painted beams in a low ceiling (this is the oldest part, dating from the 16th c), cushioned settles and pre-war-style cushioned dining chairs around varying tables. A teeny back room, like something you'd find on an old galleon, has button-back wall seating up to the roof, a few chairs and heavy ropework. Dining rooms are beamed (some painted) and timbered with parquet, quarry tiles or sisal flooring, high-backed leather and other dining chairs, more wall seating and fresh flowers and candles; background music and board games. The terraced garden has heavy rustic tables and benches. If you're heading to or from Gatwick Airport, you might find the six smartly comfortable bedrooms in a converted barn rather useful.

Rewarding food includes lunchtime sandwiches, confit duck bonbons with plum dipping sauce, wild and portobello mushrooms on toast with garlic and parsley cream, truffle mac 'n' cheese fritters, steak, ale and suet pudding, British brisket burger with ruby slaw and fries, crispy-battered haddock and chunky chips, pan-fried sea bass fillet with artichoke, leek and potato hash and cider butter sauce, lamb, chickpea and chorizo pie, and puddings such as pear and almond tart with chocolate sauce and lemon meringue pie. *Benchmark main dish: lamb, chickpea and chorizo pie with buttered greens and mash £14.50. Two-course evening meal £21.00.*

Cirrus Inns ~ Licensee Robbie Higgs ~ Real ale ~ Open 12-10.30 ~ Bar food 12-3, 6-9.30; 12-4 Sun ~ Restaurant ~ Children welcome ~ Dogs allowed in bar, restaurant & bedrooms ~ Bedrooms: £110

DANEHILL
Coach & Horses

TQ4128 Map 3

(01825) 740369 ~ www.coachandhorses.co
Off A275, via School Lane towards Chelwood Common; RH17 7JF

Well run dining pub with bustling bars, a welcoming landlord, very good food and ales and sizeable garden

This attractive golden-stone pub has a fine setting on the fringes of Ashdown Forest. The big garden is rather special, with an adults-only terrace beneath a huge maple, picnic-sets and a children's play area on lawns and views of the South Downs. The little bar to the right has half-panelled walls, simple furniture on polished floorboards, a woodburner in a brick fireplace and a big hatch to the bar counter: Harveys Best and Long Man Best Bitter on handpump, local Black Pig farmhouse cider and eight wines by the glass including prosecco and Bluebell sparkling wine from Sussex. A couple of steps lead down to a half-panelled area with a mix of dining chairs around characterful wooden tables (set with flowers and candles) on a fine brick floor, and changing artwork on the walls. Down another step is a dining area with stone walls, beams, flagstones and a woodburning stove. The highly regarded food draws in plenty of customers.

Top rated food includes sandwiches, goats cheese arancini with beetroot purée, pork and black pudding croquettes, smoked chicken terrine with spiced date chutney, whole baked camembert with raspberry and red wine vinegar jam, provençale fish soup, beer-battered fish and hand-cut chips, local pork and herb sausages with mash and caramelised onions, whole baked sea bass with sea herbs and caper butter, and puddings such as apple and rhubarb crumble with ginger ice-cream and sticky toffee pudding. *Benchmark main dish: calves liver and bacon with bubble and squeak £15.00. Two-course evening meal £21.00.*

Free house ~ Licensee Ian Philpots ~ Real ale ~ Open 12-3, 5.30-11; 12-11 Sat; 12-10.30 Sun ~ Bar food 12-2, 6.30-9 (9.30 Fri); 12-2.30, 6.30-9.30 Sat; 12-3 Sun ~ Restaurant ~ Children welcome; rear terrace is adult-only ~ Dogs allowed in bar

DIAL POST
Crown

TQ1519 Map 3

(01403) 710902 ~ www.crown-inn-dialpost.co.uk
Worthing Road (off A24 S of Horsham); RH13 8NH

Tile-hung village pub with interesting food and a good mix of customers; bedrooms

Situated opposite the village green, this former staging inn has a bustling, beamed bar with a couple of standing timbers, brown chesterfield sofas and wingback chairs, pine tables and chairs on a stone floor and a small woodburning stove in a brick fireplace. Greyhound Good Ordinary Bitter, Hammerpot Mosaic Pale and Long Man Best Bitter on handpump are served from the attractive herringbone brick counter, alongside a local cider, ten wines by the glass plus prosecco, champagne, interesting soft drinks and farm cider. To the right of the bar, the restaurant (with more beams) has an ornamental woodburner in a brick fireplace, a few photographs, chunky pine tables and chairs, some cushioned pews and a shelf of books; steps lead down to an additional dining room; background music and board games. The pub dogs are called Chops and Polly. A newish dining conservatory is light and airy, and there tables and sofas in the back garden. Although many are here for the quality food, there are always lots of chatty drinkers too.

The quickly changing menu, using the best local, seasonal produce, includes crispy whitebait with lime, halloumi fries with tomato chilli jam, potted crayfish with fennel, cucumber and dill salad, macaroni and cheese fritter with goats cheese and tomato fondue, steak burger with toppings, coleslaw and chips, home-made pies, king scallops with crispy potatoes and café de paris butter, beer-battered haddock and chips, local venison loin with honey-roasted root vegetables, fondant potato and game jus, and puddings such as orange and almond cake with dark chocolate and honey sauce and chocolate and passion-fruit tart with berry coulis. *Benchmark main dish: chorizo pizza £12.50. Two-course evening meal £18.00.*

Free house ~ Licensees Penny and James Middleton Burn ~ Real ale ~ Open 12-3, 6-10; 12-4.30 Sun; closed Mon, Tues in winter ~ Bar food 12-2, 6-8; 12-3 Sun ~ Restaurant ~ Children allowed in restaurant ~ Dogs allowed in bar, restaurant & bedrooms ~ Bedrooms: £55

DUNCTON
Cricketers

SU9517   Map 3

(01798) 342473 – www.thecricketersduncton.co.uk
Set back from A285; GU28 0LB

Charming old coaching inn with real ales, popular food and suntrap back garden

The traditional bar of this popular country pub has a display of cricketing memorabilia, a few standing timbers, simple seating and an open woodburning stove in an inglenook fireplace. Steps lead down to a dining room with farmhouse chairs around wooden tables. Dark Star Partridge Best Bitter, Triple fff Moondance and a couple of guest beers on handpump, 12 wines by the glass and three farm ciders; board games. There are picnic-sets out in front beneath the flowering window boxes and more on decked areas and under parasols on grass in the picturesque back garden. The pub got its present name from its 19th-c owner John Wisden, the cricketer who published the famous *Wisden Cricketers' Almanack*. There are two well equipped and comfortable bedrooms in a converted stone barn behind the pub; breakfasts are highly rated. Petworth House and Park (National Trust) is a few miles away.

Well presented food from a shortish menu includes lunchtime sandwiches, crab, prawn and leek gratin with watercress, cheddar and ham ploughman's, home-made lamb koftas with flatbread, tzatziki and goats cheese, beef lasagne, ham, egg and chips, various burgers, sirloin steak with onion rings and chips, beer-battered fish and chips, and puddings such as eton mess and warm chocolate brownie with chocolate sauce and vanilla ice-cream *Benchmark main dish: home-made steak, ale and mushroom pie £13.95. Two-course evening meal £20.00.*

Free house ~ Licensee Martin Boult ~ Real ale ~ Open 11-11; 12-10.30 Sun ~ Bar food 12-2.30, 6-9; 12-9 weekends; cream teas 2.30-6 ~ Children allowed in restaurant ~ Dogs allowed in bar ~ Bedrooms: £95

We say if we know a pub has background music.

EARTHAM

SU9309 Map 2

George ♀ ◧

(01243) 814340 – www.thegeorgeeartham.com

Signed off A285 Chichester–Petworth, from Fontwell off A27, from Slindon off A29;
PO18 0LT

170-year-old pub in tucked-away village with country furnishings and contemporary touches, local ales and enjoyable food

Muddy dogs and children are welcome at this relaxed pub in the South Downs National Park. The light and prettily decorated bar has dining chairs around wood-topped tables on parquet flooring, a dresser with country knick-knacks, paintings on cream-painted walls above a grey-planked dado and stone bottles and books. The charming, heavily beamed restaurant has high-backed tartan chairs and pale settles on more floorboards, books on shelves and a huge wall clock; background music and board games. In cold weather, three open fires keep the pub warm. There's a beer named for the pub (from Otter) and guests from local breweries such as Arundel, Goldmark and Urban Island on handpump, plus four local craft beers and two artisan lagers. You can also enjoy 13 wines by the glass, over 40 gins and two cocktails on tap – passion-fruit martini and espresso martini. The large garden has picnic-sets on grass and seats and tables under a gazebo. Easy disabled access. If you want to work up an appetite before a visit, there are some lovely walks and cycle routes nearby in Eartham Wood and along the South Downs Way and an interesting section of Stane Street (the Roman road connecting Chichester to London).

Imaginative food includes sandwiches, breaded whitebait, mussels with bacon, cider and parsley, chicken liver pâté with pear, apricot and stem ginger chutney, breaded jackfruit with barbecue dipping sauce and roasted squash, confit pork belly with bubble and squeak and chinese cabbage, lamb rump with turnip and potato dauphinoise, broccoli and salsa verde, steak or halloumi burger, and puddings such as sticky toffee pudding with vanilla ice-cream and fruit crumble with custard. *Benchmark main dish: beer-battered fish and chips £13.50. Two-course evening meal £22.00.*

Free house ~ Licensees James and Anita Thompson ~ Real ale ~ Open 12-11; 12-6 Sun ~ Bar food 12-2.30, 6-9 (9.30 Fri, Sat); 12-4.30 Sun ~ Restaurant ~ Children welcome ~ Dogs allowed in bar & restaurant

EAST LAVANT

SU8608 Map 2

Royal Oak ♀ ⇌

(01243) 527434 – www.royaloakeastlavant.co.uk

Pook Lane, off A286; PO18 0AX

Bustling dining pub with interesting food, a thoughtful wine list and seats outside; stylish bedrooms

This white-painted little house is in a pretty downland village, just round the corner from the Goodwood Estate. There's a proper drinking area to the left of the door, with an open fire, a high, button-back wall seat and wooden chairs around a few tables on stripped wooden boards. There are stools beside the brick counter where helpful, friendly staff keep Long Man Copper Hop, Marstons Pedigree and a guest beer on handpump, 11 wines by the glass and a growing number of gins and malt whiskies; background music, board games. The open-plan dining areas to the right have crooked beams, upholstered armchairs, red button-back banquettes and cushioned wooden chairs around rustic tables on a fine old brick floor; also, hunting scenes and mirrors on the walls and a woodburning stove in one fireplace with a large lamp in another. An end room with green or black banquettes on floor tiles has a large wooden propeller from a World War I French fighter plane on a flint wall. There's are seats and tables beneath parasols on the flagstoned front terrace, with more seating on a stepped side terrace. The five bedrooms are charming and up to date, and you can walk up a couple of steps to fields with a view of the church to the left. The car park is just across the lane, where they also have a couple of self-catering cottages. Disabled access.

🍴 Enjoyable food includes lunchtime sandwiches, confit duck bonbons with plum dipping sauce, wild and portobello mushrooms on toast with garlic and parsley cream, crispy-battered haddock with chunky chips, pan-fried sea bass fillet with artichoke, leek and potato hash and cider butter sauce, steak, ale and suet pudding, roasted squash and red Thai vegetable curry, pan-fried 8oz rump and chips, and puddings such as pear and almond tart with chocolate sauce and lemon meringue pie. *Benchmark main dish: British brisket burger with ruby slaw and fries £12.50. Two-course evening meal £19.00.*

Cirrus Inns ~ Licensee James Baldry ~ Real ale ~ Open 12-11; 12-4 Sun ~ Bar food 12-3, 6-9.30; 12-4 Sun ~ Restaurant ~ Children welcome ~ Dogs allowed in bar, restaurant & bedrooms ~ Bedrooms: £110

ERIDGE GREEN
Nevill Crest & Gun ♀ 🍺

TQ5535 Map 3

(01892) 864209 – www.brunningandprice.co.uk/nevillcrestandgun
A26 Tunbridge Wells–Crowborough; TN3 9JR

Handsome old building with lots of character, plenty to look at, six real ales and enjoyable modern food

This 500-year-old farmhouse in extensive grounds, now part of the Brunning & Price group, has been cleverly extended and renovated to make the most of its original features alongside more modern elements. There are heavy beams (some carved), panelling, rugs on wooden floors and woodburning stoves and open fires in three fireplaces (the linenfold carved bressumer above one is worth seeking out). Also, all manner of individual dining chairs around dark wood or copper-topped tables, lots of pictures, maps and photographs relating to the local area, and windowsills crammed with toby jugs, stone and glass bottles and plants. The airy dining extension has big exposed rafters and windows on all sides. St Austell Brunning and Price Traditional Bitter plus Harveys Best, Long Man Long Blonde and Old Man, Sambrooks Pumphouse Pale Ale and three quickly changing guests on handpump, 24 wines by the glass, 150 gins and 40 malt whiskies; board games and background music. There are some picnic-sets on grass at the front, and plenty of good quality wooden tables and chairs on a back terrace.

🍴 An extensive choice of enterprising food, with gluten-free options, includes sandwiches, pan-fried scallops with pea purée and shredded ham hock, barbecue chicken wings, Malaysian chicken curry with coconut rice and steamed pak choi, pork and leek sausages with mash and onion gravy, grilled sea bass fillets with potato and shallot terrine, braised lamb shoulder with crushed new potatoes and rosemary gravy, and puddings such as triple chocolate brownie with chocolate sauce and raspberry ripple ice-cream and hot waffle and caramelised banana with toffee sauce and strawberry ice cream. *Benchmark main dish: crispy beef salad with sweet chilli sauce and roasted cashew nuts £13.95. Two-course evening meal £21.00.*

Brunning & Price ~ Manager Tom McGloin ~ Real ale ~ Open 11.30-11; 11.30-10.30 Sun ~ Bar food 12-9; 12-9.30 Fri, Sat ~ Children allowed in restaurant ~ Dogs allowed in bar

FIRLE

TQ4607 Map 3

Ram 🍽️ ⛺

(01273) 858222 – www.raminn.co.uk

Village signed off A27 Lewes–Polegate; BN8 6NS

Bustling country pub with open fires, character rooms, good food and drink and seats in garden; bedrooms

---

This 500-year-old brick and flint pub in a pretty downland village (all part of the Firle Estate) is full of character. The main bar has a log fire, captain's and mate's chairs and a couple of gingham armchairs around dark pubby tables on bare boards or quarry tiles, and gilt-edged paintings on dark brown walls. You'll find Harveys Best and guest beers such as Beachy Head South Downs Ale and Goldmark Liquid Gold on handpump, 21 wines by the glass and eight malt whiskies; service is welcoming and helpful. Leading off from here is a cosy bar with another log fire, olive-green built-in planked and cushioned wall seats and more dark chairs and tables on parquet flooring. Throughout, there are various ceramic ram's heads or skulls, black and white photos of the local area, candles in hurricane jars and daily papers; darts and traditional Sussex coin game toad in the hole. The back dining room is up some steps and overlooks the flint-walled garden where there are tables and chairs on gravel and picnic-sets on grass; there are more picnic-sets under parasols at the front. The five charming bedrooms are individually furnished and comfortable, and breakfasts good. There's always a cheerful crowd of customers here and as the pub is tucked away beneath the South Downs, it's especially busy with walkers at lunchtime. Charleston, home to the Bloomsbury Group, is a couple of miles away.

 Open from 9am for breakfast, the imaginative modern food uses seasonal produce from the Estate and other local suppliers. Dishes include nibbles such as padrón peppers, plus smoked ham hock and pea terrine, Thai-spiced salmon fishcake with squid ink aioli, Sussex smokie, ploughman's, crispy chicken burger with 'baconnaise', coleslaw and fries, 40-day dry-aged rump steak with fries, three-bean cassoulet with stuffed portobello mushroom and grape, walnut and watercress salad, and puddings such as raspberry crème brûlée with lemon shortbread biscuits, and fig and walnut cheesecake with apricot sorbet. *Benchmark main dish: grilled fish of the day with Jersey Royals and green beans £14.00. Two-course evening meal £21.00.*

Free house ~ Licensee Hayley Bayes ~ Real ale ~ Open 9am-11pm ~ Bar food 9am-9.30pm ~ Children allowed in restaurant ~ Dogs allowed in bar ~ Bedrooms: £180

FLETCHING

TQ4223 Map 3

Griffin 🍽️ 🍷 ⛺

(01825) 722890 – www.thegriffininn.co.uk

Village signposted off A272 W of Uckfield; TN22 3SS

Sussex Dining Pub of the Year

Busy, gently upmarket inn with a fine wine list, real ales, daily changing restaurant and bar menu and a big garden; pretty bedrooms

---

There's a civilised feel throughout this appealing village pub. The beamed and quaintly panelled bar rooms have blazing log fires, old photographs and hunting prints, straightforward close-set furniture including some captain's chairs, and china on a delft shelf. A small bare-boarded serving area is off to one side and there's another cosy bar with sofas and a TV. Harveys Best, Long Man American Pale Ale and a couple of guests from Cellar Head and Pig & Porter on handpump, plus 30 wines by the glass from a good list (including champagne, prosecco and sweet wine); they hold a monthly wine club with supper. There's a cheerful mix of customers and a lively atmosphere in the bar – the place is very much the focal point of this handsome village and can get packed at weekends. The two-acre garden (aka the 'Sussex Serengeti') has a stunning view over Sheffield Park (National Trust); the grass is dotted with tables and chairs under parasols, and there's more seating on a sandstone terrace. The outside bar, barbecue and wood oven are much used in summer, when there's also live music at weekends. The 13 bright and pretty bedrooms, spread across the main building, next door and a converted barn, are comfortable and breakfasts good. There are ramps for wheelchairs.

 First class food from a seasonal menu includes ham hock terrine with date and apple chutney, pan-fried prawns with toasted hazelnut and almond romesco and salsa verde, chickpea and squash curry with sweet potato bhaji, pan-roasted hake fillet with mussels, tomato and Pernod bouillabaisse, confit pork belly with lyonnaise potatoes and mustard sauce, 28-day rib-eye steak with chilli and garlic butter and fries, and puddings such as blackberry, apple and rhubarb crumble with vanilla crème anglaise and dark chocolate terrine with fresh cherries and chocolate sauce. *Benchmark main dish: Harveys beer-battered Newhaven cod with spiced pickled onions and chips £18.00. Two-course evening meal £27.00.*

Free house ~ Licensees James Pullan and Samantha Barlow ~ Real ale ~ Open 11-12.30am; 11am-1am Sat ~ Bar food 12-2.30 (3 Sat), 6-9.30; 12-3.30, 6-9 Sun ~ Restaurant ~ Children welcome ~ Dogs allowed in bar & bedrooms ~ Bedrooms: £120

GORING-BY-SEA TQ0904 Map 2
Highdown 🍷 🍺 🛏
(01903) 924670 – www.brunningandprice.co.uk/highdown
Littlehampton Road; BN12 6FB

Handsome pub in a fine spot with interconnected rooms, lots to look at, seats outside and a tea room; bedrooms

Now part of the Brunning & Price group, this substantial 19th-c flint house was once the home of the Stern family, who also created the adjacent Highdown Gardens out of an old chalk pit – they're particularly lovely in spring. The pub part is made up of several open-plan rooms, each with their own character and with plenty of space for both drinking and eating. There are long cushioned wall settles, turn-of-the-century-style dining chairs, chunky or high-backed leather seats around solid dark polished tables, rugs on bare floorboards, parquet, black and white floor tiles and carpet, and lots of prints and photos on flint or painted walls. One smallish room is panelled with handsome portraits and another has books on shelves. Throughout you'll find house plants of every size, table and standard lamps, elegant metal chandeliers, fresh flowers and candles, open fires in stone fireplaces and, in the hall, a two-way fireplace fronted by a couple of armchairs. There's an easy-going atmosphere helped along by friendly, efficient staff and a fine choice of drinks that includes St Austell Brunning & Price Traditional Bitter, Harveys Best and guests such as Gun Scaramanga Extra Pale and Langham Hip Hop on handpump, 20 wines by the glass, 130 gins and 40 whiskies; background music and board games. Outside at the front is a terrace with teak tables and chairs under parasols and picnic-sets on a lawn. Set further back, in a separate building, the tea room has simple tables and chairs on parquet flooring, flint walls, heavy beams, a glass counter filled with cakes and its own terrace with tables and chairs. The 13 modern bedrooms are well appointed and comfortable. You can walk straight from the pub on to the South Downs for far-reaching views and the sea is just four minutes' drive away.

As well as breakfast, the good contemporary food includes sandwiches, crispy baby squid with chilli sauce, deep-fried West Country brie with apricot chutney and candied walnuts, halloumi fries with tomato salsa, braised shoulder of lamb with crushed new potatoes and rosemary gravy, steak burger with coleslaw and fries, king prawn linguine with garlic and chilli, beef bourguignon with horseradish mash, sweet potato, aubergine and spinach Malaysian curry, and puddings such as hot waffle and banana with cinnamon ice-cream and triple chocolate brownie with chocolate sauce and vanilla ice-cream. *Benchmark main dish: beer-battered cod with mushy peas and chips £14.95. Two-course evening meal £22.00.*

Brunning & Price ~ Manager Tom Foster ~ Real ale ~ Open 7.30-11; 7.30-10.30 Sun ~ Bar food 7.30-10.30am, 12-9; 7.30-10.30am, 12-9.30 Fri, Sat ~ Restaurant ~ Children welcome ~ Dogs allowed in bar & bedrooms ~ Bedrooms: £135

HASTINGS
Crown 🏅 ☆ ♁ 🍺
TQ8109 Map 3

(01424) 465100 – www.thecrownhastings.co.uk
Park on seafront and walk up All Saints Street, Old Town; TN34 3BN

Informal and friendly corner pub with high quality food, local ales and simple furnishings

This cosy corner pub in the historic Old Town is just back from the seafront with its fishing boats and distinctive 'net shops' (tall black-painted wooden sheds). The simply furnished bar has bare boards, plain chairs around scrubbed wooden tables set with posies of flowers, a log fire and plenty of windows to keep everything light (despite the modishly dark paintwork). Stools line the windows where they keep two changing ales from local breweries such as Cellarhead, Old Dairy, Romney Marsh and Three Legs on handpump, several craft beers, a couple of local ciders, 14 good wines by the glass, 20 gins and 11 whiskies; service is friendly and helpful. There's a dining area at one end of the bar with scatter cushions on wall seats, mismatched chairs and some large tables. There are changing displays of local art (for sale). Dogs and children receive a genuinely warm welcome. There's some seating outside at the front beside the pavement. This is a smashing little pub and, once found, our readers return on a regular basis.

Inventive, up-to-date food from a seasonal menu makes great use of local suppliers including fish landed on Hastings beach (they also bake their own sourdough bread and churn their own ice-cream). Dishes might include smoked mackerel on a crumpet with pea and mint salad, crispy fried chilli beef shin with pickled kohlrabi, roast pork belly with potato salad, slaw and barbecue sauce, spiced aubergine rösti with romesco sauce, chilli and red pepper salsa, and puddings such as victoria sponge with braised fennel, fennel custard and liquorice caramel and own-made ice-creams and sorbets. *Benchmark main dish: pan-fried coley with dill mash and mussels £16.00. Two-course evening meal £21.00.*

Free house ~ Licensees Tess and Andrew Swan ~ Real ale ~ Open 10-10 ~ Bar food 12-5, 6-9 ~ Children welcome ~ Dogs welcome

HORSHAM
Black Jug ♁ 🍺
TQ1730 Map 3

(01403) 253526 – www.brunningandprice.co.uk/blackjug
North Street; RH12 1RJ

Busy town-centre pub with wide choice of drinks, attentive staff and rewarding food

There's a buoyant countrified atmosphere to this brick and tile-hung pub. To keep the mixed crowd of office workers, theatre-goers and couples happy, efficient, friendly staff offer a fine choice of drinks: Harveys Best and St Austell Proper Job on handpump with regularly changing guests, around 30 wines by the glass (including fizz), 200 malt whiskies, 60 gins, 30 rums, 30 bourbons and farm cider – and tasty, brasserie-style food. The single, large, early 20th-c room has a long central bar, a nice collection of sizeable dark wood tables and comfortable chairs on a stripped-wood floor, bookcases and plenty of interesting old prints and photographs above a dark wood-panelled dado on pale walls. A spacious, bright conservatory has similar furniture and lots of hanging baskets, while the flower-filled back terrace has plenty of garden furniture. Parking is in the council car park next door, as the small one by the pub is for staff and deliveries only.

Good, modern food includes sandwiches, pan-fried scallops with pea purée and shredded ham hock, chicken caesar croquettes with parmesan and anchovy salad, steak burger with coleslaw and fries, grilled sea bass fillets with potato and shallot terrine and chervil and lemon cream sauce, pork and leek sausages with mash, pea and mint tortellini with garden pea velouté and asparagus, and puddings such as chocolate and orange tart with passion-fruit sorbet and lemon meringue roulade with raspberry sorbet. *Benchmark main dish: chicken, ham and leek pie with mash and buttered greens £14.95. Two-course evening meal £22.00.*

Brunning & Price ~ Manager Ally Craig ~ Real ale ~ Open 11.30-11; 12-10.30 Sun ~ Bar food 12-9; 12-9.30 Fri, Sat ~ Children welcome till 5pm ~ Dogs allowed in bar

LURGASHALL
Noahs Ark ♀

SU9327   Map 2

(01428) 707346 – www.noahsarkinn.co.uk
Off A283 N of Petworth; GU28 9ET

Busy old pub in nice spot with neatly kept bar and dining rooms, real ales and pleasing food using local produce

This 16th-c beamed country pub, run by a friendly couple, is perfectly placed overlooking the village green and cricket pitch. A good, cheerful crowd fill the simple, traditional bar and the atmosphere is buoyant and easygoing. There's a mix of wooden chairs and tables on parquet flooring and an inglenook fireplace plus Greene King IPA, St Austell Tribute and a guest ale on handpump, 24 wines by the glass (including sparkling and dessert wines) and a good range of gins. Open to the top of the rafters, the dining room is spacious and airy with church candles and fresh flowers on light wood tables, and a couple of comfortable sofas facing each other in front of an open woodburning stove; background music and board games. The border terrier is called Gillie and visiting dogs may get a dog biscuit. There are tables in a large side garden. Wheelchair ramp but no disabled loo.

Well liked, contemporary food includes goats cheese and red onion tart with fennel, rocket and beetroot salad, salt-cod fritters with harissa mayo, spiced lamb koftas with tomato and zaatar salsa, cod, scallop and mussel stew with coconut milk, ginger, chilli and saffron aioli, halloumi burger with red pepper, mushroom, hummus and fries, slow-braised venison ragoût with pappardelle, blue cheese and truffle oil, and puddings such as chocolate marquise with raspberry chantilly and berries. *Benchmark main dish: ale-battered haddock with chips £14.50. Two-course evening meal £22.00.*

Greene King ~ Lease Henry Coghlan and Amy Whitmore ~ Real ale ~ Open 11am-11.30pm; 11-midnight Sat; 12-8 Sun ~ Bar food 12-2.30, 7-9.30; 12-4 Sun ~ Restaurant ~ Children welcome ~ Dogs allowed in bar

OVING
Gribble Inn

SU9005 Map 2

(01243) 786893 – www.gribbleinn.co.uk

Between A27 and A259 E of Chichester; PO20 2BP

Own-brewed beers in bustling village pub with popular bar food and pretty garden

At the heart of the quaint village of Oving, a few miles east of Chichester, this 16th-c thatched brick cottage was once home to a school teacher called Rose Gribble. It's been a microbrewery and pub for the last 40 years (brewery tours are available): their own-brewed beers on handpump might include Fuzzy Duck, Gribble Ale, Lazy Buzzard, Pig's Ear, Reg's Tipple and seasonal ales – plus 16 wines by the glass, 40 gins, 20 malt whiskies, 30 vodkas and unusual rums. The chatty bar features a lot of heavy beams and timbering, while the other linked rooms have a cottagey feel with sofas round two roaring log fires; board games. The barn houses a venue for parties. There are seats outside in a covered area and more chairs and tables in the pretty garden with its apple and pear trees.

As well as breakfasts from 9am (not Sunday), the enjoyable food includes goats cheese mousse with beetroot carpaccio and cheese straws, seared queen scallop and chorizo risotto with basil oil, sharing platters, root vegetable tagine with cauliflower couscous, pork and herb sausages with bubble and squeak, slow-braised oxtail with mustard mash and parsnip purée, beer-battered haddock and chips, 10oz rib-eye steak with portobello mushroom and chips, and puddings such as white chocolate and vanilla rice pudding with sloe-gin berry compote and layers of chocolate sponge, chocolate mousse and chocolate ganache. *Benchmark main dish: slow-roasted pork belly with mash, savoy cabbage and bacon £15.25. Two-course evening meal £20.00.*

Free house ~ Licensees Simon Wood and Nicola Tester ~ Real ale ~ Open 9am-11pm; 12-10 Sun ~ Bar food 9-9; 12-4 Sun ~ Restaurant ~ Children allowed in restaurant ~ Dogs allowed in bar

PETWORTH
Angel 🏠 ⭐ ♟ 🛏

SU9721 Map 2

(01798) 342153 – www.angelinnpetworth.co.uk

Angel Street; GU28 0BG

Medieval building with 18th-c façade, chatty atmosphere in beamed bars, friendly service and good, interesting food; bedrooms

The interconnected rooms of this historic coaching inn have been smartly refurbished but retain many of their original features. The front bar has beams, a log fire in an inglenook fireplace and an appealing variety of old wooden and cushioned dining chairs and tables on wide floorboards. It leads to the main room with high chairs by the counter where they keep Arundel Sussex Gold, Greyhound Blonde Bird and Langham Best on handpump, 25 wines by the glass from an extensive list and nine gins; board games. Staff are courteous and helpful, and the atmosphere convivial. There are also high-backed brown leather and antique chairs and tables on pale wooden flooring, the odd milk churn and french windows to a three-level terraced garden. A cosy and popular back bar, also with a log fire, is similarly furnished. This is the perfect place for lunch after a wander round this attractive market town, known for its antiques shops and Petworth House and Park (National Trust). The seven bedrooms (named after trees) are warm and comfortable and breakfasts are good; a three-bedroom Georgian town house is also available.

Appetising food includes crispy confit Creedy Carver duck with charred peaches, salt and pepper squid with smoked garlic mayo, heritage tomato salad with home-made herb ricotta, fishcake with poached egg and watercress soup, summer vegetable salad, burger with toppings and fries, pasta carbonara, organic flat-iron steak with vine tomato, garlic mushroom and triple-cooked chips, and puddings such as roasted peaches with lemon thyme, toasted almonds and vanilla ice-cream and dark chocolate délice with raspberry sorbet. *Benchmark main dish: beer-battered fish and chips £16.00. Two-course evening meal £22.00.*

Free house ~ Licensee Philippe Diez ~ Real ale ~ Open 8am-11pm ~ Bar food 8am-9pm ~ Children allowed in restaurant ~ Dogs allowed in bar ~ Bedrooms: £100

PETWORTH
SU9921 Map 2
Welldiggers Arms 🛏
(01798) 344288 – www.thewelldiggersarms.co.uk
Low Heath; A283 E; GU28 0HG

Bustling inn with character bar and airy dining room, four real ales and good wines, helpful service and seats on terrace; bedrooms

This 300-year-old country pub just outside Petworth is a good choice if you want to spend a few days exploring West Sussex and the South Downs National Park. It has 14 attractive and comfortable bedrooms, either in the pub or a separate annexe, and all with views – dogs are welcome too. The bar has a woodburning stove with long wooden slab tables to either side (each set with candles in brass holders and a plant) as well as wall banquettes and settles with scatter cushions, wheelback chairs, painted beams and stools against the counter where cheerful, attentive staff serve Youngs Original and two guest ales on handpump and good wines by the glass; background music. An end room is just right for a small group. The big, airy dining room at the back has spreading country views from large picture windows, wall settles and more wheelbacks and country kitchen chairs with pretty cushions around tables of all sizes on flagstones, and a busy open kitchen. French windows lead out to the terrace, largely enclosed by a marquee and furnished with teak tables and chairs.

 Interesting food includes sandwiches, confit duck bonbons with plum dipping sauce, truffle mac 'n' cheese fritters, Scottish smoked salmon with watercress and fennel, crispy-battered haddock and chips, pan-fried sea bass fillet with artichoke, leek and potato hash and cider butter sauce, chicken and ham pie with mash and buttered greens, roasted squash and red Thai vegetable curry, Moving Mountains vegan burger with vegan cheese and guacamole, and puddings such as dark chocolate truffle torte and lemon meringue pie. *Benchmark main dish: beer-battered haddock and chips £14.00. Two-course evening meal £20.00.*

Cirrus Inns ~ Licensee Antony Robertson ~ Real ale ~ Open 12-10.30 ~ Bar food 12-3, 6-9.30; 12-4 Sun ~ Restaurant ~ Children welcome ~ Dogs allowed in bar & bedrooms ~ Bedrooms: £200

RINGMER
TQ4313 Map 3
Cock 🍺 £
(01273) 812040 – www.cockpub.co.uk
Uckfield Road – blocked-off section of road off A26 N of village turn-off; BN8 5RX

Country pub with a wide choice of popular bar food, real ales in character bar, and plenty of seats in the garden

You'll find a warm welcome from the convivial licensees at this well run and consistently popular 16th-c coaching inn. The unspoilt bar has traditional pubby furniture on flagstones, heavy beams, a log fire in an inglenook fireplace, Harveys Best and a couple of guests on handpump from local breweries such as Downlands, Hollerboys and Old Dairy; also 14 wines by the glass, a dozen gins and a similar number of malt whiskies. There are also three dining areas; background music. Outside are lots of picnic-sets, on terraces and in the garden, with views across open fields to the South Downs. The owners' dogs are called Bailey and Tally, and visiting canines are offered a bowl of water and a chew. This is sister pub to the Highlands at Uckfield.

Rewarding traditional food at good prices includes lunchtime sandwiches and ploughman's, tiger prawns in garlic butter, deep-fried camembert with cranberry sauce, salt and pepper squid with garlic mayo, pork and leek sausages with mash and onion gravy, roasted vegetable lasagne, lambs liver and bacon, breaded wholetail scampi with chips, sea bass fillet with sautéed potatoes and watercress sauce, and puddings such as banoffi pie with honeycomb ice-cream and fruit crumble with custard. *Benchmark main dish: steak and ale pie with mash £12.50. Two-course evening meal £19.00.*

Ridley Inns ~ Licensees Ian, Val, Nick and Matt Ridley ~ Real ale ~ Open 11-3, 6-11; 11-11 Fri, Sat; 11-9 Sun ~ Bar food 12-2.30, 6-9; 12-9 Fri, Sat; 12-7.30 Sun ~ Restaurant ~ Children allowed in restaurant; no toddlers or highchairs in bar ~ Dogs allowed in bar

ROBERTSBRIDGE
TQ7323 Map 3

George 🛏

(01580) 880315 – www.thegeorgerobertsbridge.co.uk
High Street; TN32 5AW

Handsome inn with pleasing food and ales and seats in courtyard garden; bedrooms

There's a warm welcome for all from the friendly family (including Martha the dachshund) running this attractive 18th-c pub. The right-hand bar area has a log fire in a brick inglenook with a leather sofa and a couple of armchairs in front – just the place for a quiet pint and a chat – plus high bar stools by the counter where they serve Cellar Head Single Hop Pale, Dark Star Hophead and Harveys Best on handpump, good wines by the glass and a farm cider. The dining area is opposite with elegant high-backed tartan or leather chairs around a mix of tables (each with fresh flowers and a tea-light) on stripped floorboards and more tea-lights in a small fireplace; background music. The back terrace has plenty of seats and tables. The four bedrooms are comfortable and the breakfasts well regarded. The pub is in the centre of this bustling village.

Food is good and includes lunchtime sandwiches, ciabattas and Turkish-style flatbreads, a 'fishy board', salad bowl with prawns or roasted Mediterranean vegetables, home-made lamb kofta and grilled lamb rump with fruity couscous, home-cooked ham and eggs, burger (beef, chicken or halloumi) with chips, daily specials, and puddings such as chocolate brownie with chocolate sauce and vanilla ice-cream and lemon cheesecake with blueberry sauce. *Benchmark main dish: local fish and chips with home-made tartare sauce £13.00. Two-course evening meal £20.00.*

Free house ~ Licensees John and Jane Turner ~ Real ale ~ Open 12-11; 12-9 Sun ~ Bar food 12-2.30, 5-8; 12-4 Sun ~ Children welcome but must be accompanied by an adult at all times ~ Dogs allowed in bar ~ Bedrooms: £120

SALEHURST TQ7424 Map 3

Salehurst Halt 🍺 £

(01580) 880620 – www.salehursthalt.co.uk

Village signposted from Robertsbridge bypass on A21 Tunbridge Wells–Battle;
Church Lane; TN32 5PH

Well run country local in quiet hamlet with easy-going atmosphere,
real ales, well liked bar food and seats in pretty back garden

This friendly little free house is just half a mile from the A21 and near an
attractive old church. To the right of the door is a small bare-boards area
with a few tables and chairs, a woodburning stove and shelves of books. The
main bar has hops on beams, farmhouse and wheelback chairs, settles with
scatter cushions and scrubbed tables on floorboards; background music and
board games. Harveys Best and guests from breweries such as Cellar Head,
Dark Star, Long Man and Old Dairy on handpump, farm cider, several malt
whiskies and eight wines by the glass. There's also an upstairs private dining
room for hire. The charming, cottagey back garden has views over the Rother
Valley and there's a terrace with metal chairs and tiled tables under a vine-
covered arbour; outdoor table tennis.

Tasty food includes dishes such as moules marinière, chicken liver parfait with
tomato and chipotle chutney, slow-cooked roast pork with roast potatoes and
cider gravy, cottage pie, Thai red duck curry with Asian peanut salad, fish stew (bass,
red mullet and mussels), and puddings such as salted caramel torte with clotted cream
and bread pudding with butterscotch sauce. They also offer themed menus (Greek, for
example, with the likes of chicken souvlaki or spinach, mint and feta filo pie), burger
evenings, fish and chips Fridays, plus pizzas from the wood-fired oven once a week in
summer. *Benchmark main dish: double cheese burger and chips £11.50. Two-course*
evening meal £18.00.

Free house ~ Licensee Andrew Augarde ~ Real ale ~ Open 12-11; 12-10.30 Sun; closed Mon
~ Bar food 12-3, 6-9; 12-4 Sun ~ Children allowed in restaurant ~ Dogs allowed in bar

TICEHURST TQ6830 Map 3

Bell 🍷 🛏

(01580) 200300 – www.thebellinticehurst.com

High Street; TN5 7AS

Carefully restored inn with beamed rooms, real ales, popular food
and seats in pretty courtyard garden; bedrooms

In the heart of a busy village, this lovingly renovated old coaching inn has
a lot of history and character, especially in the heavily beamed main bar:
you'll find cushioned wooden dining chairs around nice wooden tables on
bare boards, an inglenook fireplace and quirky decorations such as a squirrel
in a rocking chair. There are stools by the counter where they serve Cellar
Head Single Hop Pale and Harveys Best on handpump, with guests including
Old Dairy, Pig & Porter and Romney Marsh, ten wines by the glass, local gin
and several malt whiskies. The dining room continues on from the bar and
is similarly furnished, with the addition of cushioned wall settles and an
eclectic choice of paintings on the red walls; background music. A separate
snug has comfortable sofas grouped around a low table in front of another
open fire, interesting wallpaper, a large globe, an ancient typewriter and
various books and pieces of china. What was the carriage room holds a long
sunken table with benches on either side (perfect for an informal party)
and there's a newly refurbished upstairs function room too. At the back
is a courtyard garden with seats and tables and built-in cushioned seating

up steps on a raised area. The seven bedrooms in the main building are comfortable and very individually decorated, while the four separate lodges each have their own little garden built around a fire pit.

🍴 Championing local produce and with Spanish influences, the well regarded food includes serrano ham with tomato compote, tiger prawn with curry mayo, roasted aubergine with anticucho sauce, roquito pepper and star anise honey, swordfish with mussels and red Thai sauce, Spanish octopus with confit potatoes and chipotle mayo, rib-eye steak with soy glaze, marinated baby chicken with smoked romesco and honey, and puddings such as lemon posset with raspberries and granola and strawberries with whipped cream and meringue. They also offer breakfast from 7am. *Benchmark main dish: burger with cheese, chorizo, pickles and jalapeño mayo £12.50. Two-course evening meal £19.00.*

Free house ~ Licensee Howard Canning ~ Real ale ~ Open 7am-midnight ~ Bar food 12-3, 6-9 (8.30 Sun) ~ Restaurant ~ Dogs allowed in bar, restaurant & bedrooms ~ Bedrooms: £95

TILLINGTON
Horse Guards ⭐ � ☖ SU9621 Map 2

(01798) 342332 – www.thehorseguardsinn.co.uk
Off A272 Midhurst–Petworth; GU28 9AF

300-year-old inn with beams, panelling and open fires in rambling rooms, excellent food and charming garden; cottagey bedrooms

This prettily set village dining pub, once three cottages, was frequented by members of the Household Cavalry in the mid 19th c, hence its name. It's well run and deservedly popular. The neatly kept, beamed front bar has a gently civilised atmosphere, country furniture on bare boards, a chesterfield in one corner and a fine view beyond the village to the Rother Valley from a seat in the big panelled bay window. High bar chairs line the counter where friendly, efficient staff serve Brolly Brewing Spanky McDanky and Firebird Heritage on handpump, 17 wines by the glass, home-made liqueurs and cordials and local farm juices. Other rambling beamed rooms have similar furniture on brick floors, rugs and original panelling and there are fresh flowers throughout; background music and board games. When the weather is fine, the leafy, sheltered garden has picnic-sets, day beds, deckchairs and even a hammock, and there's also a charming terrace. The three cosy country bedrooms are comfortable and breakfasts are good. Constable and Turner both painted the medieval church with its unusual spire; Petworth House and Park (National Trust) is nearby.

🍽️ The first class seasonal food (using some home-grown and foraged produce) includes sandwiches, heritage tomato gazpacho with smoked oil and pickled cucumber salsa, Hampshire pork chorizo with pickles and sourdough toast, set goats cheese cream with beetroot relish, elderflower jelly and sourdough crisp, lamb chump and bonbon with pea purée and broad beans, South Downs pigeon breasts with smoked baba ganoush, cumin couscous and charred broccoli, Rother Valley 10oz rib-eye steak and fries, and puddings such as semolina custard tart, strawberries, Sussex honey and candied pecans and sticky toffee pudding. *Benchmark main dish: smoked haddock with peas, coriander, soft egg and mango chutney £15.50. Two-course evening meal £24.00.*

Enterprise ~ Lease Sam Beard and Michaela Hofirkova ~ Real ale ~ Open 12-midnight ~ Bar food 12-2.30, 6.30-9 (9.30 Fri); 12-3, 6-9.30 Sat; 12-3.30 Sun ~ Children allowed in restaurant ~ Dogs allowed in bar & bedrooms ~ Bedrooms: £110

Bedroom prices are for a standard double room in high summer. Even then you may get reductions for more than one night, or weekends (outside tourist areas).

UCKFIELD

TQ4720 Map 3

Highlands

(01825) 762989 – www.highlandsinn.co.uk

Eastbourne Road/Lewes Road; TN22 5SP

Busy, well run pub with plenty of space, real ales and well thought-of food; seats outside

This large, spreading 1930s pub is popular with locals who flock here on Sundays for the roasts. Our favourite spot is around the bar counter: tartan-covered benches, high leather chairs around equally high tables and armchairs, and Harveys Best and two quickly changing local guests on handpump, a good selection of wines by the glass and a dozen malt whiskies. Service from friendly, helpful young staff is good. The restaurant on the right has painted rafters in high ceilings, big glass lamps and walls decorated with local photographs and animal pictures. Also, all manner of cushioned dining and painted farmhouse chairs, long chesterfield sofas, upholstered banquettes and scatter cushions on settles make tables on the part-carpeted, wooden flooring; background music. An end bar, liked by locals, has a games area and an open fire. At the front of the building is a two-level terrace – the sunny top half is used for dining while the lower decked area has sofas and more tables and chairs. This is sister pub to the Cock at Ringmer. Disabled access.

A wide choice of popular food includes sandwiches, baked camembert with garlic, pine nuts and thyme, fried squid with saffron aioli, lamb and beef kofta with Greek salad, prawn and crayfish cocktail, pork and leek sausages with mash and onion gravy, chicken parmigiana, home-cooked ham and eggs with chips, twice-cooked pork belly with bubble and squeak potato cake and red wine gravy, smoked haddock mornay with spinach and spring onion mash, and puddings such as ginger and treacle tart with custard and crumble of the day. *Benchmark main dish: beer-battered cod and chips £12.95. Two-course evening meal £21.00.*

Ridley Inns ~ Licensees Ian, Val, Nick and Matt Ridley ~ Real ale ~ Open 11-11; 11-9 Sun ~ Bar food 12-2.30, 6-9.30; 12-9 Fri, Sat; 12-5 Sun ~ Restaurant ~ Children allowed in restaurant; no under-18s after 8.30pm ~ Dogs allowed in bar

WEST HOATHLY

TQ3632 Map 3

Cat

(01342) 810369 – www.catinn.co.uk

Village signposted from A22 and B2028 S of East Grinstead; North Lane; RH19 4PP

16th-c inn with old-fashioned bar, airy dining rooms, local real ales, tempting food and seats outside; charming bedrooms

You'll get a genuine welcome from the hands-on licensees at this attractive country dining pub. The lovely old bar has beams, pubby tables and chairs on an old wooden floor, and a fine log fire in an inglenook fireplace. Harveys Best and Old Ale and guests such as Bedlam Hibernation, Firebird Parody Session IPA and Larkins Traditional on handpump, as well as two local farm ciders, local apple juice, more than 30 wines by the glass or carafe (plus six locally made sparkling wines) from a carefully chosen list and plenty of non-alcoholic choices. Look out for the glass cover over the 75-ft deep well. The light, airy dining rooms have a nice mix of wooden dining chairs and tables on pale wooden flooring, and throughout there are hops, china platters, brass and copper ornaments and a gently upmarket atmosphere. Glass doors from a contemporary-style garden room open on to a terrace with teak furniture. The cocker spaniel is called Harvey. The four bedrooms are comfortable and well equipped and breakfasts are particularly good. Disabled access. Parking is limited but there is a public car park 300 metres away. Steam train enthusiasts can visit the Bluebell Railway, and the Priest House in the village is a fascinating museum in a cottage endowed with an extraordinary array of ancient anti-witch symbols.

Local, seasonal produce is at the heart of the excellent food: sandwiches, pork belly nuggets with piccalilli ketchup, chickpea and coriander falafel with hummus, salt and pepper squid, harissa and dill Cornish mussels with beer bread, beer-battered hake and chips, honey-glazed duck breast with sweet and sour beetroot and savoy cabbage, parmesan-crusted skate wing with chive butter sauce, sesame and chilli tofu with broccoli, kale and cashew nuts, and puddings such as sticky toffee pudding with butterscotch sauce and chocolate fondant with salted caramel and crème fraîche sorbet. *Benchmark main dish: steak, mushroom and ale pie £17.00. Two-course evening meal £26.00.*

Free house ~ Licensee Andrew Russell ~ Real ale ~ Open 12-11; 12-10 Sun ~ Bar food 12-2, 6-9; 12-2.30, 6-9.30 Fri, Sat; 12-2.30, 6-8.30 Sun ~ Children over 7 welcome ~ Dogs allowed in bar & bedrooms ~ Bedrooms: £130

WITHYHAM
Dorset Arms ♀ ⇔

TQ4935 Map 3

(01892) 770278 – www.dorset-arms.co.uk
B2110; TN7 4BD

Friendly, bustling inn with beamed rooms, real ales and good wines, interesting food and seats in garden; bedrooms

This is a nicely refurbished late 16th-c pub with a Georgian façade. The friendly and informal beamed bar is to the left of the front door, with fender seats around an open fire, scatter cushions on a built-in wall seat, a couple of armchairs and a few simple seats and tables; darts. Harveys Best and a couple of guests from breweries such as Larkins and Long Man on handpump (guests change every couple of weeks), around 20 wines by the glass from a good list and a growing collection of gins, served by friendly, courteous staff. The dining room has a cottagey feel with pretty curtains, bookshelves on either side of a small fireplace, horse pictures, rosettes and pieces of china, a long red leather wall seat and wheelback and farmhouse chairs around white tables; board games. A small room leads off with high-backed red leather chairs around light tables, a big ornate gilt-edged mirror, antlers and a chandelier; a lower room with contemporary seats and tables has a retractable roof. Outside, there are seats on the front terrace and picnic-sets on grass, and steep steps lead up to a lawned garden with more picnic-sets. The nine bedrooms (three in the pub, three in the pretty Old School Cottage) are attractively decorated and comfortable. The pub is part of the Buckhurst Estate on the edge of Ashdown Forest and named after the Earls and Dukes of Dorset.

Enjoyable food includes sandwiches, guinea fowl, pigeon and smoked chicken terrine with farmhouse chutney, prawn cocktail, eggs benedict, fish and chips with tartare sauce, seafood linguine, sea bass with samphire, brown shrimps and cockles, salad niçoise, monkfish with serrano ham crisp and parmentier potatoes, côte de boeuf (for two) with fries and béarnaise sauce, and puddings such as lemon and lime posset and plum and apple crumble with cream or vanilla ice-cream. *Benchmark main dish: bavette steak with fries £14.00. Two-course evening meal £22.00.*

Free house ~ Licensee Simon Brazier ~ Real ale ~ Open 12-11; 12-10 Sun ~ Bar food 12-2.30, 6-9; 12-9 Sat; 12-8 Sun ~ Restaurant ~ Children allowed in restaurant ~ Dogs allowed in bar & bedrooms ~ Bedrooms: £115

Also Worth a Visit in Sussex

Besides the fully inspected pubs, you might like to try these pubs that have been recommended to us and described by readers. Do tell us what you think of them: feedback@goodguides.com

---

ALBOURNE TQ2514

Ginger Fox (01273) 857888

Take B2117 W from A23; pub at junction with A281; BN6 9EA Thatched country dining pub with simple rustic interior; highly regarded modern cooking at restaurant prices and popular Sun roasts (booking recommended), small bar area serving ales such as Bedlam, Dark Star and Long Man, plenty of wines by the glass from good list and farm cider, friendly professional service; children welcome, attractive garden with downs views, play area, open all day.

ALFOLD BARS TQ0333

Sir Roger Tichborne (01403) 751873

B2133 N of Loxwood; RH14 0QS Renovated and extended beamed country pub keeping original nooks and crannies; five well kept ales such as Dark Star, Hammerpot and Youngs from brick-faced servery, popular well presented food (all day Fri-Sun) from varied menu including pub classics and more imaginative dishes, friendly attentive service, flagstones and inglenook log fire, pitched-roof restaurant with french windows to garden; children and dogs (in bar) welcome, back terrace and large sloping lawn with lovely rural views, play area, good walks, open all day.

ALFRISTON TQ5203

★ George (01323) 870319

High Street; BN26 5SY Welcoming 14th-c timbered inn in lovely village; characterful interior with hop-hung ancient low beams and huge inglenook fireplace, popular home-made bar food including lots of good fish and fresh veg in lively public bar, intimate candlelit restaurant or garden dining room, well kept beers such as Courage Best, Fullers London Pride, Greene King Old Speckled Hen and Harveys Best, decent wines, hard-working staff; background music, board games; comfortable attractive bedrooms and good breakfast, charming flint-walled back garden, fine riverside walks down to Cuckmere Haven.

ALFRISTON TQ5203

★ Star (01323) 870495

High Street; BN26 5TA Handsome 13th-c timbered inn decorated with fine medieval carvings, the striking red lion on the corner (known as Old Bill) was probably the figurehead from a wrecked Dutch ship; heavy dark beams in front bar full of character, cushioned settles, stools and captain's chairs around log fire in Tudor fireplace, tankards over counter serving fine local ales and wines

by the glass, steps down to big two-level bar (one level has lovely herringbone brick floor), through to a further library with comfortable armchairs and woodburner, good seasonal locally sourced food served by friendly young staff; children and dogs welcome, 30 comfortable contemporary bedrooms, open (and food) all day – bought by a boutique hotel group in 2020 and under refurbishment as we went to press, so expect changes.

AMBERLEY SO0313

Black Horse (01798) 831183

Off B2139; BN18 9NL Pretty village pub with bare boards, Turkish carpets and teal painted walls; character main bar, garden room and restaurant with view into kitchen, log fires, highly thought-of food from interesting fairly short menu (booking advised), three real ales and well chosen wines, friendly attentive service; children welcome, attractive garden with downs view, seven bedrooms, parking can be tricky, open all day.

AMBERLEY TQ0211

Bridge (01798) 831619

Houghton Bridge, off B2139; BN18 9LR Comfortable open-plan dining pub with good mix of locals and visitors; pleasant bar and two-room dining area, candles on tables, log fire, wide range of popular reasonably priced food from good sandwiches up, well kept Harveys, Long Man and one guest, cheerful efficient young staff; children and dogs welcome, seats out in front, more tables in enclosed side garden, handy for the station, open all day.

AMBERLEY TQ0313

Sportsman (01798) 831787

Crossgates; Rackham Road, off B2139; BN18 9NR Popular 17th-c tile-hung pub with three rooms around central bar; well kept local ales such as Ballards, Goldmark, Hammerpot, Harveys and Listers plus St Austell Tribute from Cornwall, good value home-cooked food from sandwiches up, friendly staff, great views over Amberley Wildbrooks nature reserve from back conservatory (binoculars provided) and decked terrace; children and dogs welcome, pretty little front garden, good walks, five bedrooms (three taking in the view), open all day Sat, till 6pm Sun.

ANGMERING TQ0604

Lamb (01903) 774300

The Square; BN16 4EQ Updated 18th-c village coaching inn; popular food from varied menu including good value two-course lunch, ales such as Fullers and Listers from light wood servery, good choice of gins and wines by the glass, helpful friendly service, painted half-panelling and wood-strip floors, inglenook log fire in bar, raised woodburner in restaurant; children and dogs welcome, terrace seating, eight modernised bedrooms, open all day.

ARDINGLY   TQ3430
Gardeners Arms (01444) 892328
B2028 2 miles N; RH17 6TJ Cosy and relaxed 17th-c pub opposite South of England showground; enjoyable food (all day Sun) from sandwiches and pub favourites up, Badger ales, pleasant efficient service, linked rooms with standing timbers and inglenooks, scrubbed pine furniture on flagstones and broad boards, old local photographs, mural in back part; children and dogs welcome, disabled facilities, pretty terrace and side garden, handy for Borde Hill Garden and Wakehurst (NT), open all day.

ARLINGTON   TQ5507
Old Oak (01323) 482072
Caneheath; off A22 or A27 NW of Polegate; BN26 6SJ 17th-c former almshouse with L-shaped bar, beams, log fires and comfortable seating, well kept Harveys and Long Man, enjoyable traditional food from sandwiches to specials, afternoon teas; background music, old Sussex coin game toad in the hole played here; children and dogs welcome, circular picnic-sets out in front and in garden with play area, walks in nearby Abbots Wood, open all day (food all day weekends).

ARLINGTON   TQ5407
Yew Tree (01323) 870590
Off A22 near Hailsham, or A27 W of Polegate; BN26 6RX Neatly cared-for Victorian village pub under long-serving licensees; generous helpings of good home-made food (booking advised), well kept Harveys and Long Man, decent wines, prompt friendly service, log fires, hop-covered beams and old local photographs, darts in thriving bare-boards bar, bigger plush dining lounge and comfortable conservatory; children and dogs (in one area) welcome, big garden with play area, good local walks, open (and food) all day Sun.

ARUNDEL   TQ0208
Black Rabbit (01903) 882638
Mill Road, Offham; keep on and don't give up; BN18 9PB Riverside pub in lovely spot near wildfowl reserve, popular with families and can get very busy; long bar with eating areas at either end, good choice of reasonably priced food from sandwiches and sharing boards up, well kept Badger ales and decent wines by the glass, friendly service, various bits and pieces including stuffed fish, fishing rods and a rowing boat used in filming *Harry Potter and the Philosopher's Stone*, log fires; dogs welcome, covered tables and pretty hanging baskets out at front, extensive terrace across road overlooking River Arun, good walks, open (and food) all day.

ARUNDEL   TQ0107
Swan (01903) 882314
High Street; BN18 9AG Georgian inn's comfortably relaxed L-shaped bar, well kept Fullers/Gales beers and occasional guests, popular fairly priced food including set lunch and other deals, friendly efficient young staff, wood flooring, sporting memorabilia and old photographs, local artwork for sale, open fire, connecting restaurant; children and dogs (in bar) welcome, 14 bedrooms, no car park (pay-and-display opposite), open all day, breakfast for non-residents.

ASHURST   TQ1816
Fountain (01403) 710219
B2135 S of Partridge Green; BN44 3AP Attractive 16th-c pub with plenty of character; rustic tap room on right with log fire in brick inglenook, country dining chairs around polished tables on flagstones, opened-up snug has heavy beams and another inglenook, Harveys Best, guest beers and plenty of wines by the glass, well liked home-cooked food including blackboard specials, skittle alley/function room; children and dogs welcome, seats on front brick terrace, pretty garden with orchard and duck pond, open (and food) all day, kitchen shuts 4pm Sun.

BALLS CROSS   SU9826
★Stag (01403) 820241
Village signed off A283 at N edge of Petworth; GU28 9JP Cheery unspoilt 17th-c country pub; cosy flagstoned bar with log fire in huge inglenook, a few seats and bar stools, Badger beers, Weston's Old Rosie cider and several wines by the glass, second tiny room and appealing bare-boards cottagey restaurant, fishing rods, horse tack, country knick-knacks and old photographs, good fairly pubby food (not Mon or Sun evenings); darts and board games in separate room, outside loos; children and dogs welcome, seats out in front and in pretty back garden, open all day Sat, till 9pm Sun.

BARCOMBE CROSS   TQ4212
Royal Oak (01273) 400418
Off A275 N of Lewes; BN8 5BA Village pub with good mix of locals and visitors, well kept Harveys ales, reasonably priced wines and 20 malt whiskies, generously served food from bar snacks up with themed nights (kitchen closes Sun evening-Weds), long bar

---

If you know a pub is ever open all day, please tell us.

with restaurant attached, beams, bare boards and open fire; skittle alley; children and dogs welcome, a few tables out in front and in small tree-shaded garden, open all day Sat.

BARNS GREEN   TQ1227
Queens Head (01403) 730436
Chapel Road; RH13 0PS Welcoming traditional tile-hung village pub; generous helpings of popular home-made food including daily specials, five well kept ales such as Fullers, Harveys and local Hepworths, good range of wines by the glass; events include live music and quiz; children and dogs welcome, tables out at front and in back garden with play area, open all day, no food Sun evening.

BERWICK   TQ5206
Berwick Inn (01323) 870018
By station; BN26 6SZ Roomy beamed and carpeted pub with large lounge/eating area, downstairs restaurant and upstairs coffee shop, copperware and railway pictures, log fires, well kept ales such as Harveys, good choice of wines by the glass and popular enterprising food from shortish menu including some pub classics; children welcome, large garden behind, good walking/cycling, handy for Drusillas Park zoo, open all day (till 9pm Sun).

BILLINGSHURST   TQ0830
Blue Ship (01403) 822709
The Haven; hamlet signposted off A29 just N of junction with A264, then follow signpost left towards Garlands and Okehurst; RH14 9BS Unspoilt pub in quiet country spot; beamed front bar with wall benches and scrubbed tables on brick floor, inglenook woodburner, cask-tapped Badger ales served from hatch, good home-made food from pub favourites up, two small carpeted back rooms; bar billiards, darts, shove-ha'penny, cribbage and dominoes; children and dogs welcome, tables out at front and in side garden with play area, camping, closed Sun evening, Mon.

BILLINGSHURST   TQ0725
Limeburners (01403) 782311
Lordings Road, Newbridge (B2133/A272 W); RH14 9JA Friendly characterful local in converted row of cottages; three Fullers ales and generous helpings of enjoyable reasonably priced pubby food from snacks up, part-carpeted bar with horsebrasses on dark beams and inglenook at each end, chatty atmosphere; live music and quiz nights, bar billiards, TV; children and dogs welcome, picnic-sets in pleasant front garden with play area, campsite behind.

BILLINGSHURST   TQ0825
Olde Six Bells (01403) 782124
High Street (A29); RH14 9QS Picturesque partly 14th-c timbered pub; updated interior with large bar and split-level restaurant, flagstone and wood

floors, inglenook log fire, Fullers London Pride, Sharps Doom Bar and three guest ales, Thornbridge craft beers, enjoyable reasonably priced pubby food (not Sun evening) from baguettes and baked potatoes up; occasional live music, games room; children and dogs welcome, roadside garden and terrace, open all day.

BINSTED   SU9806
Black Horse (01243) 553325
Binsted Lane; about 2 miles W of Arundel, turn S off A27 towards Binsted; BN18 0LP Modernised 17th-c dining pub with good varied choice of food from sandwiches up, ales such as Harveys and local Listers, wood-floored bar and separate dining room; regular live music; children and dogs welcome, plenty of outside seating on terrace with covered well, lawn and in open-fronted cart lodge, valley views over golf course, closed Sun evening, Mon.

BLACKBOYS   TQ5220
★Blackboys Inn (01825) 890283
B2192, S edge of village; TN22 5LG Old weatherboarded inn set back from road; main bar to the right with beams, timbers, dark wooden furniture and log fire, locals' bar to left with lots of bric-a-brac, Harveys ales including seasonals, several wines by the glass and wide choice of enjoyable food (all day Sat, till 6pm Sun), panelled dining areas; background and some live music, quiz and traditional pub games nights; children and dogs (in bar) welcome, sizeable garden with seats under trees, on terrace and under cover by duck pond, good walks (Vanguard Way goes past the pub and Wealdway is close by), five bedrooms in converted stables, open all day.

BODIAM   TQ7825
Castle Inn (01580) 830330
Village signed from B2244; opposite Bodiam Castle; TN32 5UB Bustling country pub very handy for Bodiam Castle (NT); Shepherd Neame ales and a couple of guests, farm cider, good choice of wines, popular reasonably priced food from sandwiches up, friendly helpful service, plain tables and chairs in snug bar with log fire, back restaurant, occasional live music; children welcome, picnic-sets on large sheltered terrace, open all day, food all day weekends.

BOGNOR REGIS   SZ9201
Royal Oak (01243) 821002
A259 Chichester Road, North Bersted; PO21 5JF Old-fashioned two-bar beamed local (aka the 'Pink Pub' because of its bright exterior), well kept Shepherd Neame Spitfire and a guest such as Wadworths, shortish choice of popular reasonably priced food till 6.30pm (2.30pm Sun), friendly service; Thurs quiz and occasional live music, darts, bar billiards and sports TV; children and dogs

welcome, small outside patio and large car park, open all day.

BOLNEY
TQ2622
Eight Bells (01444) 881396
The Street; RH17 5QW Popular and welcoming family-run village pub with wide choice of good sensibly priced food from bar snacks up, breakfasts (7.30-11am Mon-Sat), OAP lunch (Weds, Thurs), efficient friendly young staff, well kept Harveys, a couple of guests and decent range of wines, brick-floored bar with eight handbells suspended above servery, second flagstoned bar and timbered dining extension, open fires, bar billiards, pool and darts, sports TV; children and dogs welcome, disabled facilities, tables out on deck under huge canopy, outside bar and play area, various events including Easter Mon pram race, three bedrooms in separate beamed cottage, open all day, no food Sun evening (or Mon in Jan).

BOSHAM
SU8003
★Anchor Bleu (01243) 573956
High Street; PO18 8LS Waterside inn overlooking Chichester Harbour; two simple bars with low ochre ceilings, worn flagstones and exposed timbered brickwork, lots of nautical bric-a-brac, robust furniture (some tables close together), up to six real ales and popular sensibly priced bar food, efficient friendly staff (they may ask for a credit card if you run a tab), upstairs dining room; children and dogs welcome, seats on front terrace and raised back one (access through massive wheel-operated bulkhead door), lovely views over sheltered inlet, can park by water but note tide times, church up lane depicted in Bayeux Tapestry, village and shore worth exploring, open all day and can get very crowded.

BOSHAM
SU8105
White Swan (01243) 696465
A259 roundabout; Station Road; PO18 8NG Spic and span 18th-c dining pub with sensibly priced blackboard food including daily specials, three well kept ales such as Dark Star, Hop Back and Upham, cheerful helpful service, good-sized flagstoned bar, restaurant behind with old bread oven, darts in snug, fortnightly quiz, sports TV; children and dogs welcome in certain areas, open all day, no food Sun evening.

BRIGHTON
TQ3104
★Basketmakers Arms
(01273) 689006 *Gloucester Road – the E end, near Cheltenham Place; off Marlborough Place (A23) via Gloucester Street; BN1 4AD* Cheerful bustling backstreet local run by long-serving landlord; Fullers beers and guests from eight handpumps, decent wines by the glass and over 100 malt whiskies (good range of other spirits too), well liked reasonably

priced food, two small low-ceilinged rooms, lots of interesting old tins, enamel signs, photographs and posters; background music; children (till 8pm) and dogs welcome, disabled access, a few pavement tables, open (and food) all day, shuts midnight Fri, Sat.

BRIGHTON
TQ3004
Brighton Beer Dispensary
(01273) 710624 *Dean Street; BN1 3EG* Popular little terraced pub owned by Southey, their ales and guests, craft beers and an extensive bottled range, hand-pulled ciders too, friendly knowledgeable staff, food provided by pop-up kitchens, small back conservatory, quiz nights; open all day and can get packed.

BRIGHTON
TQ3203
Bristol Bar (01273) 605687
Paston Place; BN2 1HA Kemptown pub overlooking the sea; well kept Harveys and plenty of wines by the glass, enjoyable fairly priced bistro-style food from open kitchen, friendly staff; children (at lunchtime) and dogs welcome, wheelchair access, open all day.

BRIGHTON
TQ3104
Colonnade (01273) 328728
New Road, off North Street; by Theatre Royal; BN1 1UF Small richly restored theatre bar with ornate frontage – note Willie the 19th-c automaton in small bay window; shining brass and mahogany, plush banquettes, velvet swags and gleaming mirrors, interesting pre-war playbills and signed theatrical photographs, three well kept ales including Fullers London Pride, good range of wines and interesting gins; downstairs loos; pavement seats overlooking Pavilion gardens, open all day.

BRIGHTON
TQ3004
Craft Beer Company
(01273) 723736 *Upper North Street; BN1 3FG* Busy corner pub with fine selection of interesting draught and bottled beers (five on cask, 22 keg lines and 200 in bottles and cans) served by friendly knowledgeable staff, enjoyable food (not Mon) limited to burgers and Sun roasts, simple L-shaped bar with raised back section; sports TV; closed Mon lunchtime, otherwise open all day (till 1am Fri, Sat).

BRIGHTON
TQ3004
Evening Star (01273) 328931
Surrey Street; BN1 3PB Chatty drinkers' pub attracting good mix of customers; simple pale wood furniture on bare boards, seven ales on handpump including Dark Star (originally brewed here) and lots of changing guests, keg and continental beers (in bottles too) and traditional ciders/perries, bar snacks, friendly staff coping well at busy times; background and some live music;

pavement tables, open all day and handy for the station.

BRIGHTON   TQ3203
Ginger Dog (01273) 620990
College Place, Kemptown; BN2 1HN
Restaurant Kemptown pub in same small group as the Ginger Pig (Hove) and Ginger Fox (Albourne); well regarded modern food from changing menu (not especially cheap), good wines, cocktails and local beers, well informed friendly service, fairly traditional bare-boards interior; children and dogs (in bar) welcome, open all day.

BRIGHTON   TQ2804
★Ginger Pig (01273) 736123
Hove Street; BN3 2TR Bustling place just a short walk from the beach; informal bare-boards bar area with plush stools and simple wooden dining chairs around mixed tables, armchairs and sofas here and there, Harveys Best and a guest, nice wines by the glass and interesting local spirits and soft drinks, raised restaurant part with long button-back wall seating and more wooden tables and chairs, enterprising modern food (highish prices) served by friendly attentive staff; background music; children welcome, 11 stylish ensuite bedrooms, open all day.

BRIGHTON   TQ3103
Hand in Hand (01273) 699595
Upper St James Street, Kemptown; BN2 1JN It may be Brighton's smallest pub, but the canary yellow exterior makes it hard to miss; own-brewed beers along with a local guest, plenty of bottled beers and real cider, dimly lit bar with a few tables and benches, tie collection and lots of newspaper cuttings on the walls, photographs including Victorian nudes on the ceiling, some snacky food, pie and mash on Thurs, cheerful service and colourful mix of customers; interesting background music (live jazz Sun), veteran fruit machine; dogs welcome, open all day and can get crowded.

BRIGHTON   TQ3004
Lion & Lobster (01273) 327299
Sillwood Street; BN1 2PS Red-painted backstreet pub spread over three floors (three bars and restaurant); softly lit interior with lots of pictures, well kept ales such as Dark Star and Harveys, extensive choice of well presented enterprising food (booking advised) including daily specials and a late-night menu, friendly efficient young staff; regular jazz evenings, sports TV; large terrace on two levels (can get very busy in summer), open (and food) all day, till 2am Fri and Sat.

BROWNBREAD STREET   TQ6714
Ash Tree (01424) 892104
Off A271 (was B2204) W of Battle; first northward road W of Ashburnham Place, then first fork left, then bear right into

Brownbread Street; TN33 9NX Tranquil 17th-c country local tucked away in isolated hamlet; enjoyable affordably priced home-made food including specials, good choice of wines and well kept ales such as Harveys Best, cheerful service, cosy beamed bars with nice old settles and chairs, stripped brickwork, interesting dining areas with timbered dividers, good inglenook log fire; children (in eating area) and dogs welcome, pretty garden, closed Sun and Mon evenings, otherwise open all day.

BURWASH   TQ6724
Rose & Crown (01435) 882600
Inn sign on A265; TN19 7ER Old tile-hung local tucked down lane (parking can be tricky) in pretty village; well kept Harveys ales, decent wines and enjoyable fairly priced food (not Sun or Mon evenings), friendly staff, very low beamed ceilings, pubby furniture on patterned carpet, inglenook log fire, restaurant to the left with another inglenook, glass-covered well just inside front door; monthly live music and quiz; children and dogs welcome, small side garden and pleasant back terrace, four bedrooms, handy for Batemans (NT), open all day (till 9pm Sun).

BURWASH WEALD   TQ6523
Wheel (01435) 882299
A265 Burwash–Heathfield; TN19 7LA Steps up to this historic village pub, opened-up bar area with beams, bare boards and inglenook log fire, mix of old tables and chairs, candles in bottles and some interesting old local photographs, well kept Harveys and Adnams, a guest beer and well chosen wines, good sensibly priced food from sharing plates up, friendly helpful service, a couple of separate dining areas; background music; children and dogs (in bar) welcome, seats out in front and in tree-shaded back garden, open all day.

BURY   TQ0013
Squire & Horse (01798) 831343
Bury Common; A29 Fontwell–Pulborough; RH20 1NS 16th-c roadside dining pub with very good attractively presented food, well kept Harveys, a guest ale and good choice of wines, several partly divided beamed areas, plush wall seats, hunting prints and ornaments, log fire; children welcome, no dogs inside, pleasant garden and terrace (some road noise), open (and food) all day Sun, closed Mon and Tues.

BYWORTH   SU9821
★Black Horse (01798) 342424
Off A283; GU28 0HL Popular chatty country pub with smart simply furnished bar, pews and scrubbed tables on bare boards, pictures and old photographs, open fire, four real ales including Flowerpots and Fullers, Cornish Orchards cider, enjoyable food (not Sun evening) from light lunchtime dishes

up, back restaurant with nooks and crannies and old range, spiral staircase to heavily beamed function/dining room, games area (pool and darts); occasional live music and other events; children welcome, dogs in bar, attractive garden with tables on steep grassy terraces, lovely downs views, one bedroom in converted stable, open all day.

CATSFIELD
TQ7213
White Hart (01424) 892650
B2204, off A269; The Green; TN33 9DJ
Friendly weatherboarded and beamed village pub; well kept Harveys and Sharps, good range of malt whiskies and gins, enjoyable reasonably priced traditional food, warm log fire, raftered dining room with pubby furniture and woodburner; some live music; children, walkers and dogs welcome, fenced garden, two bedrooms, open all day, no food Sun evening.

CHAILEY
TQ3919
Five Bells (01825) 722259
A275, 9 miles N of Lewes; BN8 4DA
Attractive old roadside pub with good food (not Sun evening) cooked by landlord-chef from bar snacks and pub favourites up, some themed evenings, four well kept ales including Harveys and decent choice of wines, friendly staff, different rooms and alcoves leading from low-beamed central bar, older-style furniture on bare boards or quarry tiles, inglenook log fire; board games; children and dogs welcome, pretty garden front and side, good surrounding walks, open all day (till 8pm Sun).

CHICHESTER
SU8605
Chichester Inn (01243) 783185
West Street; PO19 1RP Georgian pub with half a dozen local ales such as Dark Star, Harveys and Langham, good value pubby food from snacks up, smallish front lounge with plain wooden tables and chairs, sofas by open fire, larger back public bar; live music and other events such as comedy nights and beer festivals, sports TV, pool; courtyard garden with smokers' shelter, four bedrooms, open all day.

CHICHESTER
SU8504
Crate & Apple (01243) 539336
Westgate; PO19 3EU Smart dining pub with enjoyable food from shortish but varied menu, local ales such as Harveys and Long Man, good range of wines by the glass, cocktails, friendly helpful service, modern décor with simple tables and chairs on wood or stone floors, painted dados, leather sofas by woodburner; open mike and quiz nights; children welcome, sunny front terrace with umbrellas, more seats behind, open all day from 10am.

CHICHESTER
SU8604
Eastgate (01243) 774877
The Hornet (A286); PO19 7JG Welcoming town pub with light airy interior extending

back; Fullers/Gales beers and a guest, well cooked affordably priced food (not Sat, Sun evenings), cheerful prompt service, pubby furniture on bare boards or patterned carpet, woodburner; background and weekend live music, pool, darts and sports TV; dogs welcome, small heated back terrace, open all day.

CHICHESTER
SU8605
George & Dragon (01243) 785660
North Street; PO19 1NQ Bustling L-shaped bar with comfortable leather sofas on bare boards, open fire, Harveys Best, St Austell Tribute, Timothy Taylors Landlord and a guest, Weston's cider, reasonably priced food from ciabattas up including some smokehouse dishes and daily specials, friendly service, conservatory restaurant; children welcome, decked back terrace with café-style tables and chairs, ten bedrooms in converted stables, open (and food) all day, except Sun when kitchen closes at 4pm, closed Mon.

CHICHESTER
SU8605
Park Tavern (01243) 785057
Priory Road; PO19 1NS Popular pub in pleasant spot opposite Priory Park; good choice of Fullers/Gales beers and enjoyable reasonably priced pubby food (not Sun or Mon evenings), smallish front bar, extensive back eating area; live music and quiz nights; children and dogs welcome, open all day.

CHIDDINGLY
TQ5414
★Six Bells (01825) 872227
Village signed off A22 Uckfield–Hailsham; BN8 6HE Lively unpretentious village local run well by hard-working hands-on landlord; small linked bars with interesting bric-a-brac, local pictures and posters, old furniture, cushioned window seats and log fires, family extension giving much needed extra space, well kept Courage, Harveys and a guest, decent wines by the glass and a proper cider, enjoyable low-priced food; regular live music including blues/folk night every other Tues; dogs welcome in bar, seats out at back by big raised goldfish pond, boules, church opposite with interesting Jefferay Monument, open all day.

CHIDHAM
SU7804
★Old House at Home (01243) 572477
Off A259 at Barleycorn pub in Nutbourne; Cot Lane; PO18 8SU Neat 18th-c red-brick pub in remote unspoilt farm hamlet; good choice of popular food from open sandwiches up, several wines by the glass and at least four real ales including a house bitter from Langham, friendly service, low beams and timbering, log fire; children allowed in eating areas, tables on front terrace and in attractive back garden, Chichester Harbour walks nearby, open (and food) all day.

CHILGROVE   SU8116
Royal Oak (01243) 535257
Off B2141 Petersfield–Chichester, signed Hooksway; PO18 9JZ Unchanging little country pub run by same licensees for more than 30 years; two simple cosy bars with huge log fires, country kitchen furniture and cottagey knick-knacks, Bowman Wallops Wood, Exmoor Beast, Fullers HSB and a guest, good honest food at reasonable prices, homely dining room with woodburner, plainer family room; background and occasional live music, cribbage, dominoes and shut the box; dogs welcome in bars, picnic-sets under parasols in pretty garden, handy for South Downs Way walkers, closed Mon (except bank holidays) and evenings apart from Fri and Sat.

COCKING CAUSEWAY   SU8819
Greyhound (01730) 814425
A286 Cocking–Midhurst; GU29 9QH Pretty 18th-c tile-hung pub set back from the road; four well kept changing ales and popular good value home-made food including weekly steak and wine nights (booking advised), friendly helpful staff, open-plan but cosy beamed and panelled bar with alcoves, log fire, pine furniture in modern back dining conservatory; monthly quiz; children and dogs welcome, grassed area at front with picnic-sets and huge eucalyptus, sizeable garden and play area behind, open all day, food all day Sun.

COLEMANS HATCH   TQ4533
★ Hatch (01342) 822363
Signed off B2026, or off B2110 opposite church; TN7 4EJ Quaint and appealing little weatherboarded pub dating from 1430 on the edge of Ashdown Forest; big log fire in quickly filling beamed bar, small back dining room with another fire, popular freshly made food (not Sun evening) from varied menu, well kept Harveys, Larkins and one or two guests, friendly staff and good mix of customers including families and dogs; picnic-sets on front terrace and in beautifully looked-after large garden, not much parking so get there early to find a space, open all day weekends.

COOLHAM   TQ1423
★ George & Dragon (01403) 741320
Dragons Green, Dragons Lane; pub signed off A272; RH13 8GE Tile-hung cottage surrounded by fine countryside; cosy bar with massive unusually low beams (date cut into one is either 1577 or 1677), heavily timbered walls, traditional furniture and log fire in big inglenook, Chapeau Rouleur, Harveys Best and Skinners Betty Stogs, decent wines by the glass and enjoyable food (not evenings Sun or Mon), dining room with pale farmhouse chairs around rustic tables on wood floor, quiz nights; children and dogs (in bar) welcome, pretty garden, two attractive double bedrooms in converted outbuilding, open all day Fri-Mon.

COUSLEY WOOD   TQ6533
Old Vine (01892) 782271
B2100 Wadhurst–Lamberhurst; TN5 6ER 16th-c weatherboarded dining pub, linked rooms with heavy beams and open timbering, inglenook log fire, ales such as Harveys and Timothy Taylors, several wines by the glass and interesting Latin American food cooked by Ecuadorian chef-landlord; children and dogs welcome, picnic-sets on front terrace, closed Sun evening, Mon, otherwise open (and food) all day.

COWFOLD   TQ2122
Hare & Hounds (01403) 865354
Henfield Road (A281 S); RH13 8DR Small friendly village pub with popular good value pubby food and a couple of well kept ales including Harveys, beamed and flagstoned bar with log fire, little room off to the right, dining room to the left; children and dogs welcome, a couple of picnic-sets out in front, more seating on back terrace, open all day Fri-Sun.

CRAWLEY   TQ2636
Brewery Shades (01293) 514255
High Street; RH10 1BA Popular old tile-hung pub in town centre; ten well kept beers, including a house bitter from Hardys & Hansons, several ciders and good choice of other drinks, enjoyable all-day pubby food from sandwiches up including daily roasts, friendly helpful young staff, rambling interior on different levels; silent sports TV; children welcome, seats outside in pedestrianised area, open all day till 12.30am (1.30am Fri, Sat).

CROWBOROUGH   TQ5332
Boars Head (01892) 331070
Boars Head Road; pub signed from A26; TN6 3GR Old tile-hung pub with linked rooms including low-beamed bar and bright modern dining conservatory, log fires in big stone fireplaces, good choice of enjoyable food including daily specials, Harveys and local guests such as Larkins and Long Man, friendly efficient service; live music; children and dogs welcome, garden next to farm with outdoor stage, open all day (till 7pm Sun).

Cribbage is a card game using a block of wood with holes for matchsticks or special pins to score with; regulars in cribbage pubs are usually happy to teach strangers how to play.

CUCKFIELD TQ3025
Rose & Crown (01444) 414217
London Road; RH17 5BS Former 17th-c
coaching inn run by father and son team with
refurbished interiors, good if not particularly
cheap food from regularly changing menus
(not Sun evening, Mon lunch or Tues), early
evening discount before 7pm, well kept
Harveys and a guest, local Hepworth lager
and good choice of wines/gins; children and
dogs welcome, tables out in front and in nice
garden behind, open all day (till 9pm Sun).

DALLINGTON TQ6619
Swan (01424) 838242
Woods Corner, B2096 E; TN21 9LB
Old tile-hung roadside local with cheerful
chatty atmosphere; well kept Harveys and
a guest, decent wines by the glass and good
blackboard food including deals, efficient
friendly service, bare-boards bar divided
by standing timbers, old enamel signs (on
walls and floor), mixed furniture including
cushioned settle and high-backed pew,
candles in bottles, swan ornaments, big
woodburner, simple back restaurant with
far-reaching views to the coast; occasional
background music, board games; children
and dogs welcome, steps down to loos and
garden, open all day, may close early if quiet.

DELL QUAY SU8302
Crown & Anchor (01243) 781712
*Off A286 S of Chichester – look out for
small sign; PO20 7EE* 19th/20th-c beamed
pub in splendid spot overlooking Chichester
Harbour – best at high tide and quiet times
(can get packed on sunny days and parking
difficult); comfortable bow-windowed lounge
and panelled public bar, two log fires, well
kept Youngs Best and a couple of guests,
plenty of wines by the glass, enjoyable freshly
made food including fresh fish/seafood,
friendly efficient young staff; children and
dogs welcome, views from large waterside
terrace with crab and burger shack, nice
walks, open all day, food all day weekends.

DURRINGTON TQ1104
Park View (01903) 521397
Salvington Road; BN13 2JR Whitewashed
pub with refurbished interiors opposite
recreation ground; three well kept ales and
good fairly traditional food at fair prices from
sandwiches/wraps up, wood-fired pizzas and
barbecues in summer, friendly helpful staff;
live music and other events, sports TV, pool;
children and dogs welcome, large sunny
beer garden behind, open all day, no food
Sun night.

EAST ASHLING SU8207
Horse & Groom (01243) 575339
B2178; PO18 9AX Busy unpretentious
country pub run by long-serving landlord; five
well kept ales including Dark Star, Hop Back
and Youngs, decent choice of wines by the

glass and sensibly priced tasty food from open
sandwiches and baguettes up, unchanging
front drinkers' bar with old pale flagstones
and inglenook range, scrubbed trestle tables
in carpeted area, airy extension with solid
country kitchen furniture; children and dogs
allowed in some parts, garden picnic-sets
under umbrellas, 11 neat bedrooms (some in
barn conversion), open all day (closes 6pm
Sun evening).

EAST CHILTINGTON TQ3715
Jolly Sportsman (01273) 890400
*2 miles N of B2116; Chapel Lane – follow
sign to 13th-c church; BN7 3BA* Civilised
place with impressive modern cooking
from French chef including barbecues and
crab and lobster specials in summer; small
character log-fire bar for drinkers, local ales
such as Harveys, excellent range of malt
whiskies, cognacs and armagnacs and very
good wine list, smart but cosy restaurant
with contemporary light wood furniture and
modern landscapes, garden room; children
and dogs (in bar) welcome, rustic tables
under trees in front garden, more seats on
big back lawn with views towards the South
Downs, closed Sun evening, Mon.

EAST DEAN SU9012
Star & Garter (01243) 811318
*Village signed with Charlton off A286 in
Singleton; also signed off A285; PO18 0JG*
Brick and flint dining pub in peaceful village
setting; pleasant bar and restaurant with
exposed brickwork, panelling and oak floors,
furnishings from sturdy stripped tables
and country kitchen chairs through chunky
modern to antique carved settles, well kept
Sharps Doom Bar, a couple of guest ales and
several wines by the glass, good food including
local fish/seafood and some themed evenings,
friendly service; background music, quiz
nights; children and dogs (in bar) welcome,
teak furniture on heated terrace, steps down
to walled lawn with picnic-sets, near South
Downs Way, three bedrooms, open (and food)
all day, kitchen closes 6pm Sun.

EAST DEAN TV5597
★ Tiger (01323) 423209
Off A259 Eastbourne–Seaford; BN20 0DA
Attractive old pub overlooking delightful
cottage-lined sloping green; small beamed bar
with window seat, long cushioned wall bench
and other rustic tables and chairs, walls
hung with fish prints and a stuffed tiger's
head, open woodburner, five real ales such
as Harveys, Long Man and St Austell, proper
cider, nine wines by the glass and local gin,
step down to another little room with fine
high-backed curved settle, separate dining
room serving enjoyable fairly traditional food;
children and dogs (in bar) welcome, seats
on flower-filled terrace (can also sit on the
green), five comfortable bedrooms, walks to
the coast and along Seven Sisters clifftops,
open all day.

EAST HOATHLY   TQ5216
Kings Head (01825) 840238
High Street/Mill Lane; BN8 6DR Creeper-clad 17th-c pub on crossroads (was the village school); long open-plan room with wood floor, brick walls and log fire, pubby furniture including upholstered settles, own 1648 ales (brewed next door) plus Harveys Best, enjoyable reasonably priced traditional food; occasional quiz nights, TV; children and dogs welcome, steps up to walled back garden, open all day.

EASTBOURNE   TV6098
Bibendum (01323) 735363
Grange Road/South Street opposite Town Hall; BN21 4EU Roomy 19th-c corner pub with wine-bar feel; well kept ales such as Harveys and Long Man, several wines by the glass and interesting selection of gins, enjoyable varied choice of food from snacks up, friendly helpful staff, restaurant serving tasty pubby food; quiz nights; children and dogs welcome, seats out in front under awning, disabled access, open (and food) all day, food till 6pm Sun.

EASTBOURNE   TV5999
Lamb (01323) 720545
High Street; BN21 1HH Ancient inn arranged around central servery; lounge bar with sturdy beams and substantial stone fireplace, latticed bow windows and antique furnishings, steps down to half-panelled bare-boards dining area with mix of old tables and chairs and another big fireplace, well kept Harveys ales, good choice of wines and enjoyable home-made food at fair prices, friendly efficient service, internal glass-covered well and historic cellars; upstairs live music including folk club, also quiz and comedy nights, TV and darts in public bar; children and dogs welcome, by 12th-c church away from seafront, four refurbished bedrooms, open all day.

EASTBOURNE   TV6199
Marine (01323) 720464
Seaside Road (A259); BN22 7NE Comfortable spacious pub under long-serving licensees (well known for its extravagant Christmas decorations); panelled and carpeted bar, steps down to lounge with sofas, tub chairs and log fire, three well kept ales, good choice of wines and around 45 whiskies/brandies, generous helpings of good freshly made food including up to a dozen daily specials, back conservatory; children welcome, terrace and covered smokers' area, near the seafront, open (and food) all day Sun.

EASTBOURNE   TV6097
Pilot (01323) 723440
Holywell Road, Meads; just off front below approach from Beachy Head; BN20 7RW Busy corner inn with good fairly priced home-cooked food from lunchtime sandwiches up, well kept ales such as Harveys and Sharps, good selection of wines by the glass, friendly staff; children welcome, dogs in bar, seats out at front and in nice split-level beer garden behind, walks up to Beachy Head, four bedrooms, open all day, till 8pm Sun.

EASTERGATE   SU9405
Wilkes Head (01243) 543380
Just off A29 Fontwell–Bognor; Church Lane; PO20 3UT Small friendly red-brick local with two traditional bars and back dining extension; beams, flagstones and inglenook log fire, enjoyable reasonably priced blackboard food from sandwiches up, Adnams Southwold, several guest ales and proper cider; occasional live music, beer festivals, darts; children welcome, tables in big garden with play area, open all day.

ELSTED   SU8320
Elsted Inn (01730) 813662
Elsted Marsh; GU29 0JT Attractive and welcoming Victorian country pub, good interesting food from shortish regularly changing menu using local produce, three or four well kept ales and plenty of wines by the glass, friendly accommodating service, two log fires, nice country furniture on bare boards, old Goodwood racing photos (horses and cars), dining area at back; folk night first Sun of the month, quiz last Weds of month; children and dogs (in bar) welcome, downs-view garden with large part-covered terrace, four comfortable bedrooms, closed Mon lunchtime, otherwise open all day, restaurant closed Sun evening and Mon, but some snacky food available.

ELSTED   SU8119
★Three Horseshoes (01730) 825746
Village signed from B2141 Chichester–Petersfield; from A272 about 2 miles W of Midhurst, turn left heading W; GU29 0JY Good mix of customers and a congenial bustle at this pretty white-painted old pub; beamed rooms, log fires and candlelight, ancient flooring, antique furnishings and interesting prints/photographs, up to five real ales tapped from the cask such as Bowman, Flowerpots, Langham and Youngs, summer cider, highly rated food from extensive blackboard menu, good friendly service; children allowed, dogs in bar, two delightful connecting gardens with plenty of seats, lovely roses and fine South Downs views, maybe wandering chickens, good surrounding walks.

ERIDGE STATION   TQ5434
★Huntsman (01892) 864258
Signed off A26 S of Eridge Green; TN3 9LE 19th-c brick and tile country local; two cosy opened-up rooms with painted half-panelling and lots of old photographs and prints, mix of furniture on bare boards

including scrubbed pine, sofa in front of log fire, three well kept Badger ales and several wines by the glass, good home-made food (not Sun evening) from baguettes up, friendly helpful service, downstairs function/overflow room; children and dogs welcome, tables on fenced front terrace, picnic-sets in garden set down behind, next to Eridge train station with lots of cars parked on the road (but pub has its own parking), closed Mon, otherwise open all day.

EWHURST GREEN   TQ7924

★ **White Dog** (01580) 830264

Turn off A21 to Bodiam at S end of Hurst Green, cross B2244, pass Bodiam Castle, cross river then bear left uphill at Ewhurst Green sign; TN32 5TD Well run 17th-c inn in a fine spot above Bodiam Castle (NT) and quite handy for Great Dixter; bustling bar with beams, wood panelling, roaring log fire in inglenook fireplace and old brick or flagstoned floors, a beer named for the pub (from Hardys & Hansons), Harveys Best, Rother Valley Level Best and a guest from Tonbridge on handpump and 20 wines by the glass, also dining room and appetising food, cheerful relaxed atmosphere and attentive staff, disabled access; background music, games room with darts, board games and pool; walkers, children and dogs welcome, seating in big garden, three rooms and tipis for hire, open all day.

FALMER   TQ3508

Swan (01273) 681842

Middle Street (just off A27 bypass); BN1 9PD Long thin building with seating areas either side of small central bar, Palmers and four local guests, straightforward sensibly priced lunchtime food (evenings Thurs and Fri), barn function room; some live music, sports TV; dogs welcome, seats on little terrace, near Sussex University (student discounts), closed Mon, otherwise open all day, busy on Albion match days.

FERNHURST   SU9028

Red Lion (01428) 643112

The Green, off A286 via Church Lane; GU27 3HY Friendly 16th-c wisteria-clad pub tucked quietly away on edge of green; heavy beams and timbers, inglenook woodburner and attractive furnishings, good food (not Sun evening) from sandwiches/snacks up, well kept Fullers/Gales beers and a guest, decent wines, restaurant; children and dogs welcome, seats out in front and in back garden with well, walks from the door, open all day.

FERRING   TQ0903

Henty Arms (01903) 241254

Ferring Lane; BN12 6QY Popular 19th-c local with five well kept changing ales and a real cider, generous helpings of well priced food (can get busy so best to book), friendly staff, opened-up lounge/dining area, log fire,

separate bar with TV and games including bar billiards; children and dogs welcome, garden tables, play area, open (and food) all day.

FINDON   TQ1208

Gun (01903) 872 235

High Street; BN14 0TA Welcoming low-beamed pub with opened-up bar area and restaurant; very good food (not Sun evening) including burger night (Mon), French night (Tues) and popular Sun lunch, four well kept Marstons-related beers, friendly chatty staff, log fire; children and dogs (in bar) welcome, sheltered garden, attractive village below Cissbury Ring (NT), open all day (closed Mon daytime).

FISHBOURNE   SU8304

Bulls Head (01243) 839895

Fishbourne Road (A259 Chichester–Emsworth); PO19 3JP Former 17th-c farmhouse with traditional interior; copper pans on black beams, some exposed brickwork and panelling, paintings of local scenes, good log fire, four well kept Fullers/Gales beers from wood-faced bar, good choice of enjoyable reasonably priced food from lunchtime baguettes up, friendly efficient service, intimate dining room; background music; children and dogs (in bar) welcome, tables on small covered deck, four bedrooms in former skittle alley, interesting harbour walks and handy for Fishbourne Roman Palace, open all day weekends.

FITTLEWORTH   TQ0118

Swan (01798) 865154

Lower Street (B2138, off A283 W of Pulborough); RH20 1EN Pretty tile-hung dining inn; beamed main bar with mix of furniture including windsor chairs, high-backed stools and banquettes on wood flooring, wall of pictures and old pub sign one end, big inglenook log fire the other, ales such as Harveys and Langham, several wines by the glass and traditional cider, good food from pubby choices up in bar and separate panelled restaurant, efficient friendly staff; background music; children and dogs (in bar) welcome, plenty of tables on big back lawn, good walks nearby, 16 well priced comfortable bedrooms, open all day.

FRANT   TQ5835

Abergavenny Arms (01892) 750233

A267 S of Tunbridge Wells; TN3 9DB Attractively updated beamed dining pub; good freshly cooked food from varied menu including themed evenings, six well kept local ales such as Harveys, Larkins, Long Man and Tonbridge, good choice of wines by the glass and several interesting gins, friendly efficient staff, leather sofas by big woodburner in brick inglenook, three separate dining areas; background music, daily papers; children and dogs welcome, terrace seating on different levels, front part looking over road to Eridge Park (good walks), open (and food) all day.

FRIDAY STREET   TV6203
★ **Farm at Friday Street**
(01323) 766049 *B2104, Langney; BN23 8AP* Extended former farmhouse, now well run Whiting & Hammond pub with easy-going friendly atmosphere; open-plan rooms split by brick pillars into cosier areas, with sofas, stools and all manner of wooden dining chairs and tables on bare boards, pale flagstones, coir or carpet, also open fires, house plants, church candles, lots of prints, pictures and farming implements; well kept ales from Long Man and Timothy Taylors, good wines by the glass; two-level dining room with timbered walls, conical roof, glass partitions and open kitchen serving popular seasonal food; background music; children and dogs (in bar) welcome, picnic-sets on front lawn, open (and food) all day.

FULKING   TQ2411
Shepherd & Dog (01273) 857382
Off A281 N of Brighton, via Poynings; BN5 9LU 17th-c bay-windowed pub in beautiful spot below the South Downs; low beams, panelling and inglenook, fine range of real ales and craft beers including Downlands (brewed a couple of miles away), also bottled beers, ciders and plenty of wines by the glass, enjoyable food from light lunches up, friendly young staff; children and dogs welcome, terrace and pretty streamside garden with own bar (summer barbecues), straightforward climb to Devil's Dyke, open all day (till 8pm Sun).

FUNTINGTON   SU7908
Fox & Hounds (01243) 575246
Common Road (B2146); PO18 9LL Bustling old bay-windowed pub with updated beamed rooms; enjoyable food from sandwiches and snacks to daily specials, popular Sun carvery, well kept Timothy Taylors Landlord and guests, lots of wines by the glass and good coffee, friendly service, comfortable spacious dining extension; some live music and quiz nights; children and dogs (in bar) welcome, tables out in front and in walled back garden, open (and food) all day.

GRAFFHAM   SU9217
White Horse (01798) 867331
On road signed to Heyshott/Midhurst at W end of village; GU28 0NT Large stylish dining pub; highly rated restauranty food along with some more traditional choices, Sharps Doom Bar, local guests and plenty of wines by the glass, welcoming attentive service, bar/dining room and conservatory restaurant with South Downs views; children and dogs welcome, big back garden and terrace (maybe summer jazz), good local walks, six well appointed bedrooms in two courtyard blocks, open all day Sat, till 5.30pm Sun, closed Mon and Tues.

GUN HILL   TQ5614
Gun (01825) 872361
Off A22 NW of Hailsham, or off A267; TN21 0JU Big 15th-c country dining pub (part of the small Elite group) with enjoyable bistro-style food from sharing boards and pizzas up; large central bar with nice old brick floor, stools against counter, Aga in corner, small grey-panelled room off with rugs on bare boards, animal skins on cushioned wall benches and mix of scrubbed and dark tables, logs piled into tall fireplace, well kept ales such as Harveys and Timothy Taylors, decent wines by the glass, cocktails, two-room cottagey restaurant, beams and open fires, old bottles and glasses along gantry, gun prints and country pictures; background music; children welcome, picnic-sets in garden and on lantern-lit front terrace, Wealdway walks, open (and food) all day.

HANDCROSS   TQ2629
Red Lion (01444) 400292
High Street; RH17 6BP Extensive stylish dining pub; beamed bar with wood and polished stone floor, armchairs and long thickly cushioned banquette facing circular copper-topped tables, Harveys and Sharps, plenty of wines by the glass and good range of other drinks including cocktails, side area has some ancient recycled timbers and stripped tables on nice oak boards, another part with lower white-painted plank ceiling, contemporary furnishings and big two-way fireplace, good choice of popular well presented food from sandwiches, sharing plates and pizzas up, also a vegan menu, friendly service; background music; children and dogs (in bar) welcome, handy for Nymans (NT), open all day.

HARTFIELD   TQ4634
Gallipot (01892) 770008
B2110 towards Forest Row; TN7 4AJ Traditional stone and weatherboard country pub; long narrow beamed interior with central bar and fire at one end, good home-made food from pub classics up (not many tables so best to book), three well kept local beers such as Harveys and Larkins, friendly helpful staff; some live music; children and dogs welcome, pleasant sloping garden behind with good views, handy for Pooh Bear country, open all day.

HASSOCKS   TQ3115
Thatched Inn (01273) 842946
Ockley Lane/Grand Avenue; BN6 8DH Popular 1950s thatched pub among modern bungalows; good choice of enjoyable reasonably priced food in bar and extended restaurant, well kept Brakspears, Harveys and a guest, several wines by the glass, welcoming efficient young staff; local artwork for sale, pool, darts and fruit machine; children and dogs welcome, back garden, views towards the South Downs.

HASTINGS TQ8109
Dolphin 01424 434326
Rock-a-Nore, off A259 at seafront;
TN34 3DW Friendly tile-hung pub facing
the fishermen's huts; compact carpeted
interior with masses of fishing/maritime
paraphernalia, enjoyable food including
fresh local fish and Japanese nights, well
kept Dark Star, Harveys, Youngs and guests
plus craft beers; background and regular live
music, quiz Thurs; children (till 7pm) and
dogs welcome, raised front terrace, open all
day, no food weekend evenings.

HASTINGS TQ8209
First In Last Out (01424) 425079
High Street, Old Town; TN34 3EY
Congenial pub serving its own FILO beers
(brewed close by) and a guest ale, good
fairly priced food including some interesting
vegetarian/vegan choices, Indian thali
(Thurs), friendly helpful staff, open-plan
carpeted pub with 1970s Artex walls, dark
wood booths and feature central raised log
fire, lighter back dining room; regular live
music, quiz nights; open all day, no food
Sun evening.

HASTINGS TQ8110
Imperial
Queens Road; TN34 1RL Popular
Victorian corner pub (same owners as the
Lamb at Wartling) visibly brewing its own
craft beers, also several other keg beers
(tasters offered), proper ciders and range
of spirits, good wood-fired pizzas including
vegan; some live music; dogs welcome, closed
till 4pm Mon and Tues, otherwise open all
day (till midnight Fri, Sat).

HEATHFIELD TQ5920
★Star (01435) 863570
Church Street, Old Heathfield, off A265/
B2096 E; TN21 9AH Nice old country
pub next to church; ancient heavy beams,
built-in wall settles, window seats, panelling
and inglenook log fire, doorway to similarly
decorated room set up more for eating,
upstairs dining room with striking barrel-
vaulted ceiling, Harveys Best and guests,
eight wines by the glass and well liked
food; background music; children and dogs
welcome, seats in pretty garden with views of
rolling pasture dotted with sheep and lined
with oak trees, open all day.

HENFIELD TQ2115
George (01273) 492296
High Street; BN5 9DB Former coaching
inn dating from the 16th c; easy chairs
and stools in central bar area, Harveys,
Timothy Taylors and good wines by glass,
room to the left with open fire and portraits
on green panelled walls, dining room to
the right with heavy beams and inglenook,
decent food including weekend breakfasts
(booking recommended), friendly licensees

and helpful young staff; background music,
some live music; children and dogs (in bar)
welcome, disabled access/loo, seats in back
courtyard, eight bedrooms, open all day (till
8pm Sun).

HENLEY SU8925
★Duke of Cumberland Arms
(01428) 652280 *Down steep narrow*
lanes off A286 S of Fernhurst; GU27 3HQ
Pretty country cottage with two small low-
ceilinged rooms; big scrubbed oak tables on
brick or flagstoned floors, rustic decorations
and open fire, Harveys and a couple of
guests tapped from the cask, several wines
by the glass and much enjoyed food (not
Sun or Mon evenings), more modern dining
extension with sofas in front of woodburner;
background music, board games; well
behaved children and dogs (in bar) welcome,
seats and picnic-sets on decking and in big
tiered garden with trout ponds, beautiful
views, open all day.

HERMITAGE SU7505
★Sussex Brewery (01243) 371533
A259 just W of Emsworth; PO10 8AU
Bustling little 18th-c pub on the West Sussex/
Hampshire border; small bare-boards bar
with good fire in brick inglenook, simple
furniture, flagstoned snug, well kept Youngs
ales and guests, ten wines by the glass and
popular hearty food including speciality
sausages (even vegetarian ones), weekend
breakfasts 9-11am, small upstairs restaurant;
children and dogs welcome, picnic-sets in
back courtyard, open all day (food all day Sun
till 7.30pm).

HIGH HURSTWOOD TQ4925
★Hurstwood (01825) 732257
Hurstwood Road off A272; TN22 4AH
Although the main draw to this small country
pub is their excellent inventive food (must
book), they still attract some loyal local
drinkers; open-plan U-shaped interior with
beams and bare boards, high spindleback
chairs against counter serving Harveys and
Sharps, good wines by the glass and cocktails,
friendly attentive young staff, area by tiled
Victorian fireplace with sofas and armchairs,
dining tables set with red gingham napkins,
little plants and church candles, hunting
prints and other artwork above painted dado,
various lamps/lanterns and a piano (which
does get played); children and dogs (in bar
area) welcome, french windows to deck with
lawn beyond, open all day (till 6pm Sun).

HOOE TQ6910
Red Lion (01424) 892371
Denbigh Road; off B2095; TN33 9EW
Attractive old local behind screen of
pollarded lime trees – originally a farmhouse
but a pub since the 17th c; plenty of
original features including hop-strung
beams, flagstones and two big inglenooks,
generous helpings of popular home-cooked

food (worth booking), well kept Harveys, a guest and plenty of continental beers, good friendly service, main bar and back snug, overflow function room and further eating space upstairs; children and dogs welcome, wheelchair access, seats out at front and in garden behind, open all day, closes 8pm Sun and Mon.

HOUGHTON   TQ0111
★ **George & Dragon** (01798) 831559
B2139 W of Storrington; BN18 9LW
Brick and flint pub (former coaching house) with 13th-c beams and timbers in attractive bar rambling up and down steps, note the elephant photograph above the fireplace, lovely Arun Valley views from back extension, good fairly priced pubby food including popular Sun lunch (booking advised), Marstons-related ales and decent wines by the glass, friendly helpful service; background music; children and dogs welcome, tables on decked terrace taking in the view (they may ask for a credit card if you eat out here), charming sloping garden, good walks, open all day Fri and Sat, till 9pm Sun.

HUNSTON   SU8601
Spotted Cow (01243) 786718
B2145 S of Chichester; PO20 1PD
Modernised slate-faced village pub with beams, flagstones and big log fires; good choice of food (not Sun evening, Mon or Tues) including specials, Fullers/Gales beers, friendly helpful staff, small front bar, roomier side lounge with armchairs, sofas and low tables, airy high-ceilinged restaurant; maybe background music, darts; children (if eating) and dogs welcome, good disabled access, enclosed garden with play equipment, handy for towpath walkers, open all day.

HURSTPIERPOINT   TQ2816
New Inn (01273) 834608
High Street; BN6 9RQ Popular 16th-c beamed village pub; Harveys and a couple of guests, good wines by the glass and enjoyable food from pub favourites up, including local meats on the Josper charcoal grill and vegan choices, friendly staff, linked areas including oak-panelled back bar with log fire and more formal restaurant; quiz nights, sports TV; children and dogs welcome, enclosed garden with terrace and play area, open all day, no food Sun evening.

ICKLESHAM   TQ8716
★ **Queens Head** (01424) 814552
Off A259 Rye–Hastings; TN36 4BL
Friendly well run country pub, popular locally (and at weekends with cyclists and walkers); open-plan areas around big counter, high timbered walls and vaulted roof, old beer bottles on shelves, farming implements, a grandfather clock behind the bar and a bicycle over it, pubby furniture on patterned carpet, other areas with inglenooks and a separate back room, six well kept ales

including Greene King, Hardys & Hansons and Harveys, local cider, several wines by the glass and good choice of generous fairly priced food; background music (live 4-6pm Sun), occasional pub quiz; well behaved children (till 8.30pm) and dogs welcome, picnic-sets, boules and play area in peaceful garden, fine Brede Valley views, you can walk to Winchelsea from here, open (and food) all day.

ICKLESHAM   TQ8716
★ **Robin Hood** (01424) 814277
Main Road; TN36 4BD Friendly family-run beamed pub with buoyant local atmosphere; good value unpretentious home-made food (all day Sun) including blackboard specials, Mon steak night and Weds curry, well kept Greene King IPA, up to six guests and three proper ciders, hops overhead and lots of copper bric-a-brac, log fire, games part with pool, back dining conservatory; children and dogs (in bar) welcome, play area and boules in big garden, lovely view of Brede Valley, open all day Fri-Sun, closes 3pm Tues.

ISFIELD   TQ4417
Laughing Fish (01825) 750349
Station Road; TN22 5XB Bustling opened-up Victorian local with affable landlord and cheerful efficient staff; enjoyable good value home-cooked food (not Sun evening) including daily specials and themed nights, six real ales with three from local independents such as Burning Sky, Gun and Long Man, also two real ciders on tap and craft lagers, open fire; bar billiards and other traditional games; children and dogs welcome, disabled access, small pleasantly shaded walled garden with enclosed play area, field for camping, right by Lavender Line railway (pub was station hotel), open all day.

JEVINGTON   TQ5601
Eight Bells (01323) 484442
Jevington Road, N of East Dean; BN26 5QB Friendly village pub in good walking country; simple furnishings, heavy beams, panelling, parquet floor and inglenook, popular home-made food from sandwiches and good ploughman's up, well kept ales including Harveys; background music, some live, quiz nights; children and dogs welcome, front terrace and secluded downs-view garden, adjacent cricket field, open all day.

KINGSTON   TQ3908
Juggs (01273) 472523
Village signed off A27 by roundabout W of Lewes; BN7 3NT Tile-hung village pub with very low front door and heavy 15th-c beams, lots of neatly stripped masonry, sturdy wooden furniture on bare boards and stone slabs, log fires, smaller eating areas including a family room, food from sandwiches and pub standards up, Harveys and Shepherd Neame

ales, good wines and coffee; background music, quiz nights; children and dogs welcome, disabled access/facilities, lots of outside tables including covered area with heaters, tubs and hanging baskets, play area, nice South Downs walks, open (and food) all day Fri-Sun.

KIRDFORD
TQ0126
★ **Half Moon** (01403) 820223

Opposite church, off A272 Petworth–Billingshurst; RH14 0LT Attractive old tile-hung village pub owned by celebrity model Jodie Kidd; beamed bar on right with cushioned window seat, barrel stools and armchairs by woodburner, some nice old photos and hunting wallpaper, a couple of local ales and plenty of wines by the glass from blue-painted counter, two restaurant rooms with rustic planked wall seats, painted or wooden chairs around simple tables and fine inglenook fireplace, good interesting food (not Sun evening) including weekday set lunch and tasting menus, friendly staff, background music; tables on terrace and lawn, kitchen garden to one side overlooked by church tower, closed Mon and Tues, otherwise open all day (till 8.30pm Sun).

LEWES
TQ4110
Black Horse (01273) 473653

Western Road; BN7 1RS Bow-windowed pub with knocked-through bar keeping traditional feel, two log fires, wood floor, panelling and lots of old pictures, up to eight well kept ales including Greene King and beers from local breweries such as Bedlam, Burning Sky, Isfield, Downlands, Hastings and Long Man, interesting gins, enjoyable home-made food, friendly service; occasional live music and quiz nights, sports TV, bar billiards and coin game toad in the hole; children welcome, beer garden, open all day.

LEWES
TQ4210
Gardeners Arms (01273) 474808

Cliffe High Street; BN7 2AN Unpretentious little bare-boards local opposite Harveys brewery shop; lots of beer mats on gantry, homely stools, built-in wall seats and plain scrubbed tables around three narrow sides of bar, photos of Lewes bonfire night, well kept Harveys and five interesting guests, real ciders, some lunchtime food such as sandwiches, pasties and pies; background music, TV, darts; no children, dogs welcome, open all day.

LEWES
TQ4210
★ **John Harvey** (01273) 479880

Bear Yard, just off Cliffe High Street; BN7 2AN Bustling tap for nearby Harveys brewery, four of their beers including seasonals kept in top condition (some poured from the cask), small choice of enjoyable well priced traditional food including good Sun roasts, friendly efficient young staff, beamed and flagstoned bar with woodburner, huge

vat halved to make two snug seating areas, lighter room on left and upstairs restaurant/function room; some live music; children welcome in restaurant, dogs in bar, a few tables outside, open all day, no food Sun evening.

LEWES
TQ4110
★ **Lewes Arms** (01273) 473152

Castle Ditch Lane/Mount Place – tucked behind castle ruins; BN7 1YH Cheerful unpretentious little corner local; well kept Fullers/Gales beers and guests such as Harveys Best, around 30 malt whiskies and plenty of wines by the glass, generous helpings of enjoyable reasonably priced food including good Sun roasts; tiny front bar on right with stools along curved counter and bench window seats, two other simple rooms hung with photographs and information about the famous Lewes bonfire night; folk evenings, quiz nights and more obscure events such as pea throwing and dwyle flunking; children (away from front bar) and dogs welcome, picnic-sets on attractive split-level back terrace, open all day (till midnight Fri, Sat).

LEWES
TQ4110
Pelham Arms (01273) 476149

At top of High Street; BN7 1XL Popular 17th-c beamed pub with characterful rambling interior; well presented food (not Mon, booking advised) including some interesting vegetarian choices and meat/fish from on-site smokehouse, friendly efficient service, own Abyss beers and guests; children and dogs (in bar) welcome, small courtyard garden, closed Mon lunchtime, otherwise open all day.

LEWES
TQ4110
Rights of Man (01273) 486894

High Street; BN7 1YE Harveys pub close to the Crown Court; five of their well kept ales and enjoyable food including tapas and Sun roasts, Victorian-style décor with a series of booths and wood panelling, another bar at the back and roof terrace; background music; open all day, food till 6pm Sun.

LEWES
TQ4210
★ **Snowdrop** (01273) 471018

South Street; BN7 2BU Welcoming pub tucked below the chalk cliffs; narrowboat theme with brightly painted servery and colourful jugs, kettles, lanterns etc hanging from curved planked ceiling, wide mix of simple furniture on parquet floor, old sewing machines and huge stone jars, rather bohemian atmosphere; well kept local ales such as Bedlam, Gun and Harveys, a couple of ciders and enjoyable reasonably priced food from interestingly varied menu, nice coffee, cheerful efficient staff (may ask for a card if running a tab), more tables in upstairs room (spiral stairs) with bar billiards and darts; background and frequent live music;

dogs very welcome (menu for them), outside seating on both sides, pretty hanging baskets, open (and food) all day, kitchen shuts 6pm Sun, closed Mon.

LICKFOLD   SU9226
★ **Lickfold Inn** (01789) 532535
NE of Midhurst, between A286 and A283; GU28 9EY Tucked-away Tudor inn with impressive food in bars and upstairs restaurant; two easy-going downstairs rooms with heavy Tudor beams, chapel chairs, Georgian settles and nice old tables on fine herringbone brick floor, comfortable sofas by woodburner, three well kept ales such as Langham, a dozen wines by the glass and a good choice of gins, rums and whiskies, restaurant with upholstered chairs and dark polished tables on bare boards, more heavy beams and second woodburner; some live music; children and dogs (in bar) welcome, plenty of seating on terrace and in garden on several levels, closed Mon and Tues, otherwise open all day (till 7pm Sun), shuts for ten days in Jan.

LINDFIELD   TQ3425
Bent Arms (01444) 483146
High Street; RH16 2HP Surprisingly spacious 16th-c village coaching inn with low beams, timbers and some stained glass, most tables set for their popular affordably priced food including lunchtime sandwiches and ploughman's using own bread and daily changing set menu, three well kept Badger ales, friendly service; children welcome, sizeable back garden with covered area, eight bedrooms and cottage, open all day, no food Sun evening.

LITLINGTON   TQ5201
Plough & Harrow (01323) 870632
Between A27 Lewes–Polegate and A259 E of Seaford; BN26 5RE Neatly extended 17th-c brick and flint village pub; large beamed and wood-floored bar with smaller rooms off, candles on tables, brewery mirrors and old farming implements on the walls, snug with inglenook, half a dozen well kept ales including at least three from nearby Long Man, decent wines by the glass and good food from pub staples up, friendly efficient service; quiz nights, some live music; children and dogs welcome, attractive back garden, good walks (on South Downs Way), open all day.

LITTLEHAMPTON   TQ0202
★ **Arun View** (01903) 722335
Wharf Road; W towards Chichester; BN17 5DD In lovely harbour spot with busy waterway directly below windows; popular good value food (all day Sun) from sandwiches/ciabattas to good fresh fish, well kept Fullers and Long Man, guest beers and several wines by the glass, cheerful helpful staff, flagstoned and panelled back bar with banquettes and dark wood tables, large

dining conservatory; background music, TVs, pool; children and dogs welcome, disabled facilities, flower-filled terrace, interesting waterside walkway to coast, four bedrooms, open all day.

LITTLEHAMPTON   TQ0202
Steam Packet (01903) 715994
River Road; BN17 5BZ 19th-c corner pub just across from the Arun View; open-plan interior providing several separate seating areas, well kept ales such as Bedlam, Downlands, Fallen Acorn and Langham, enjoyable reasonably priced food including daily specials; regular live jazz; seats out in small area facing river, raised back garden, three bedrooms, closed Mon and lunchtime Tues, no food Sun evening.

LITTLEWORTH   TQ1921
Windmill (01403) 710308
Pub signed off B2135; village signed off A272 southbound, W of Cowfold; RH13 8EJ Brick and tile inn dating from the 17th c; two beamed and flagstoned bars, one with inglenook log fire, woodburner in the other, lots of old farming tools and so forth on walls and ceiling, enjoyable home-made food (all day weekends) from sandwiches and pub standards up, summer wood-fired pizzas, well kept Harveys ales and a couple of guests, restaurant; quiz nights, occasional live music, bar billiards, darts and TV; children and dogs welcome, picnic-sets in peaceful garden overlooking fields, bedrooms, open all day.

LODSWORTH   SU9321
Halfway Bridge Inn (01798) 861281
Just before village, on A272 Midhurst–Petworth; GU28 9BP Restaurant 17th-c coaching inn with characterful linked rooms; beams, wooden floors and log fires (one in polished kitchen range), good if not especially cheap food from interesting menu (also pub favourites and set lunch), ales such as Arundel, Langham and Sharps, wide range of wines by the glass, pleasant helpful staff; background music, newspapers; children and dogs (in bar) welcome, small back terrace, six bedrooms in former stables, open all day, food all day weekends.

LOWER BEEDING   TQ2225
★ **Crabtree** (01403) 892666
Brighton Road; RH13 6PT Family-run pub with green-painted Victorian façade but much older inside with Tudor beams and huge inglenook (dated 1537), front bar with green leather chesterfield, plush stools and just three tables, woodburner and fresh flowers, also a garden room and cosy interlinked dining rooms, well kept Badger beers and around 25 wines by the glass including Sussex fizz, several malt whiskies and local cider, good creative food (not Sun evening) using local seasonal produce, friendly service; board games; children and

dogs (in bar) welcome, lovely landscaped garden with picnic-sets, wendy house and fine country views, handy for Nymans (NT), open (and food) all day.

LYMINSTER   TQ0204
Six Bells (01903) 713639
Lyminster Road (A284), Wick;
BN17 7PS Unassuming 18th-c flint pub with opened-up bar and separate dining room; well kept Fullers London Pride and a guest, decent house wines and enjoyable sensibly priced food, friendly attentive staff, low black beams, wood floor and big inglenook with horsebrasses on bressumer, pubby furnishings; background music; children and dogs (in one area) welcome, terrace and garden seating.

MAREHILL   TQ0618
White Horse (01798) 872189
Mare Hill Road (A283 E of Pulborough);
RH20 2DY White-painted roadside country pub dating from the 15th c; several linked areas with beams, timbers and log fires, good reasonably priced food including daily specials, well kept Fullers/Gales beers and a guest such as Dark Star, several wines by the glass, friendly attentive staff, nice views from restaurant; some live music; children and dogs welcome, attractive garden behind, handy for RSPB Pulborough Brooks reserve, open all day.

MARK CROSS   TQ5831
★Mark Cross Inn (01892) 852423
A267 N of Mayfield; TN6 3NP Big Whiting & Hammond pub with bar and dining rooms on several linked levels; well kept Fullers, Harveys, Sharps and guests, good wines by the glass, enjoyable food served by friendly efficient young staff, attractive mix of dark wood tables and cushioned dining chairs, walls crowded with photographs, prints, paintings and old newspaper cuttings, also open fires, books, church candles and stone bottles; children and dogs (in bar) welcome; terrace with teak furniture and lawn with picnic-sets offering broad Weald views, children's play fort, open (and food) all day from 9am.

MAYFIELD   TQ5826
Middle House (01435) 872146
High Street; TN20 6AB Handsome 16th-c timbered inn (Grade I listed); L-shaped beamed bar with massive fireplace, several well kept ales including Harveys, local cider and decent wines, quiet lounge area with leather chesterfields around log fire in ornate carved fireplace, good choice of enjoyable food, friendly staff coping well at busy times, attractive panelled restaurant with modern

glass extension; background music; children welcome, no dogs inside, lovely country views from terraced back garden, bedrooms, open (and food) all day weekends.

MAYFIELD   TQ5927
Rose & Crown (01435) 872200
Fletching Street; TN20 6TE Pretty 16th-c weatherboarded pub set down lane from village centre; two cosy front rooms with coins stuck to low ceiling boards, bench seats built into partly panelled walls and simple furniture on floorboards, inglenook log fire, Harveys, a guest beer and several wines by the glass, food and service can be good, curry and burger nights, further small room behind servery and larger carpeted one down steps; children welcome, dogs in bar, raised front terrace and decked back garden, two bedrooms, open all day, food all day weekends, closed Mon and Tues.

MID LAVANT   SU8508
Earl of March (01243) 533993
A286 Lavant Road; PO18 0BQ Updated and extended with emphasis on eating, but seats for drinkers in flagstoned log-fire bar, well kept Harveys, Timothy Taylors and a guest, nice wines by the glass including champagne and English fizz, good well presented restaurant-style food (not cheap) along with some pub favourites and lunchtime sandwiches, pleasant staff; children and dogs welcome, delightful location and local walks, view up to Goodwood from neatly kept garden, open all day.

MILLAND   SU8328
Rising Sun (01428) 741347
Iping Road junction with main road through village; GU30 7NA Busy 20th-c red-brick Fullers pub; their ales and a guest such as Dark Star, varied choice of fresh well presented food from sharing boards and pub favourites up, also two-course lunch deal, friendly helpful staff, three linked rooms including cheery log-fire bar and bare-boards restaurant; live music first Fri of month, occasional quiz and curry night; children and dogs welcome, extensive lawns attractively divided by tall yew hedge, canopied heated terrace and smokers' gazebo, good walking area, open all day (Fri-Sun).

MILTON STREET   TQ5304
Sussex Ox (01323) 870840
Off A27 just under a mile E of Alfriston roundabout; BN26 5RL Extended country pub (originally a 1900s slaughterhouse) with magnificent downs views; bar area with a couple of high tables and chairs on bare boards, old local photographs, three well

kept local ales such as Long Man along with craft beers and cider and good choice of wines by the glass, lower brick-floored room with farmhouse furniture and woodburner, similarly furnished dining room (children allowed here), further front eating area with high-backed rush-seated chairs, food can be good from traditional choices up (meat from own organic farm and veg from kitchen garden), friendly service; dogs welcome in bar, teak seating on raised back deck taking in the view, picnic-sets in garden below and more under parasols at front, open all day.

NETHERFIELD TQ7118
Netherfield Arms (01424) 838282
Just off B2096 Heathfield–Battle; TN33 9QD Welcoming low-ceilinged 18th-c country dining pub; wide choice of enjoyable food including good specials and vegan dishes, friendly attentive service, decent wines and well kept ales such as Long Man, inglenook log fire, cosy restaurant; picnic-sets in lovely back garden, far-reaching views from front, closed Sun evening, Mon.

NETHERFIELD TQ7118
White Hart (01424) 838382
Darwell Hill, B2096; TN33 9QH Weatherboarded country pub with busy little front bar, cushions on built-in wall seats, log fire at one end, hops and country prints, stools by counter serving well kept Harveys and Sharps, lounge area with sofas and scatter cushions, huge stag's head and bookshelves, tasty food including OAP weekday lunch deal, friendly helpful staff, dining room has rush-seated chairs around dark tables on coir, some half-panelling and woodburner; children and dogs welcome, rattan chairs around tables out on gravel terrace, fine far-reaching views, closed Sun evening, Mon.

NEWHAVEN TQ4500
Hope (01273) 515389
Follow West Beach signs from A259 westbound; BN9 9DN Big-windowed pub overlooking busy harbour entrance; long nautical-themed bar with raised area, comfy sofas and open fires, well kept ales such as Dark Star and Harveys, upstairs dining conservatory and breezy balcony with even better view towards Seaford Head, good choice of generous well priced food, friendly staff; regular live music, quiz nights; children and dogs welcome, tables on grassed waterside area, open all day, food all day Sat, till 7pm Sun.

NUTBOURNE TQ0718
Rising Sun (01798) 812191
Off A283 E of Pulborough; The Street; RH20 2HE Unspoilt creeper-clad village pub dating partly from the 16th c (same owner for nearly 40 years); front bar with beams, exposed brickwork and woodburner, scrubbed tables on bare boards, some 1920s

fashion and dance posters, Fullers London Pride and three guests, enjoyable pubby food from lunchtime sandwiches up including daily specials, friendly service, second bar leading through to quarry-tiled restaurant, cosy back family room; background music (some live); dogs welcome, terrace with small pond and smokers' shelter, archway through to lawned area, closed Sun evening.

NUTHURST TQ1926
Black Horse (01403) 891272
Off A281 SE of Horsham; RH13 6LH Welcoming 17th-c country pub with plenty of character in its several small rooms; low black beams, flagstones/bare boards and inglenook log fire, enjoyable good value pubby food served by friendly attentive staff, four real ales including Harveys; quiz nights; children and dogs welcome, pretty streamside back garden, more seats on front terrace, open all day weekends.

OFFHAM TQ3912
Blacksmiths Arms (01273) 472971
A275 N of Lewes; BN7 3QD Popular open-plan dining pub in rural village; good food with Jamaican influences, well kept ales such as Harveys and Long Man, efficient friendly service, clean updated interior with a couple of woodburners, one in huge end inglenook; children and dogs welcome, french windows to terrace, four bedrooms (steep stairs), open all day (till 5pm Sun), closed Mon.

PARTRIDGE GREEN TQ1819
★ Green Man (01403) 710250
Off A24 just under a mile S of A272 junction – take B2135 at West Grinstead signpost; pub at Jolesfield, N of Partridge Green; RH13 8JT Relaxed gently upmarket dining pub with popular enterprising food cooked by chef-landlord, ales such as Sharps and well chosen wines by the glass including champagne, good friendly service; unassuming front area by counter with bentwood bar seats, stools and library chairs around one or two low tables, old curved high-back settle, main eating area widening into back part with pretty enamelled stove, pitched ceiling area on left, more self-contained room on right; children and dogs (in bar) welcome, cast-iron seats and picnic-sets under parasols in neat back garden, closed Sun evening, Mon and Tues.

PARTRIDGE GREEN TQ1819
Partridge (01403) 710391
Church Road/High Street; RH13 8JS Spacious 19th-c roadside village pub (former station hotel) run by father and daughter team; three Dark Star ales (brewery close by) and a couple of guests, enjoyable sensibly priced home-made food (not Sun or Mon evenings) from sandwiches and sharing plates up including deals, some main courses available in smaller helpings, friendly relaxed

atmosphere; sports TV; children and dogs welcome, garden with large terrace and play equipment, open all day.

PATCHING TQ0705
Fox (01903) 871299
Arundel Road; signed off A27 eastbound just W of Worthing; BN13 3UJ Neatly kept pub with generously served food including popular Sun roasts (best to book), quick friendly service even at busy times, two or three well kept local ales including Harveys, large dining area off roomy panelled bar, dark pubby furniture on patterned carpet, hunting pictures; quiet background music; children and dogs welcome, disabled access, colourful hanging baskets and good-sized tree-shaded garden with well laid-out seating, heaters and play area, open all day, closes 7pm Sun (food till 5.30pm).

PATCHING TQ0805
Worlds End (01903) 871346
Former A27 Worthing–Arundel, off A280 roundabout; BN13 3UQ Long roomy pub next to Patching Pond; good range of food from sandwiches and snacks up (smaller helpings available for some main courses), well kept Badger beers and lots of wines by the glass, efficient friendly service, opened-up beamed interior including large raftered barn-style dining room; children and dogs welcome, good-sized garden behind with paved terrace and play area, open (and food) all day, kitchen closes 8pm Sun.

PEASMARSH TQ8822
Horse & Cart (01797) 230034
School Lane; TN31 6UW Updated village pub with welcoming atmosphere; light beams and wood floors, red leather sofa and armchair by open fire, back restaurant separated by gas woodburner in two-way brick fireplace, good mix of seating from pews to banquettes, a beer badged for the pub from Romney Marsh along with local Three Legs, extensive wine list (several by the glass), good food from pub staples up, friendly helpful service; games including shove-ha'penny; children and dogs welcome, a couple of tables out at front with more on back terrace and lawn, outside bar and pétanque, four bedrooms, closed Sun evening and Mon lunchtime, otherwise open all day.

PETT TQ8713
Royal Oak (01424) 812515
Pett Road; TN35 4HG Friendly brick and weatherboarded village pub; roomy main bar with large open fire, well kept Harveys and a couple of changing guests, popular home-made food including several fish dishes, two dining areas, efficient helpful service; occasional live music and quiz nights, traditional games; dogs welcome, small garden behind, open all day, closed Mon and Tues, no food Sun evening.

PETT TQ8613
Two Sawyers (01424) 812255
Pett Road, off A259; TN35 4HB Meandering low-beamed rooms including bare-boards bar with stripped tables, tiny snug and restaurant down sloping passageway, open fires, well kept Ringwood, Sharps and guests, local cider/perry and wide range of wines, popular good value home-made food, friendly helpful service; background and some live music; children in restaurant and dogs in bar welcome, suntrap front courtyard, back garden with shady trees and well spaced tables, four bedrooms, open all day.

PETWORTH SU9719
Badgers (01798) 342651
Station Road (A285 1.5 miles S); GU28 0JF Restauranty dining pub with good up-to-date food from snacks and sharing plates up including fresh fish and seasonal game, can eat in bar areas or restaurant, friendly accommodating staff, a couple of changing ales and well chosen wines, cosy fireside area with sofas; over-5s allowed in bar's eating area, stylish tables and seats on terrace by water-lily pool, summer hog/lamb roasts, three well appointed bedrooms, good breakfast, open all day.

PETWORTH SU9721
Star (01798) 368114
Market Square; GU28 0AH Opened-up and refurbished old pub with well kept Fullers/Gales beers, decent wines and enjoyable food including pie and mash menu, friendly helpful service, log fire; children and dogs (in bar) welcome, bright conservatory and a few seats on terrace overlooking market square, open all day.

PETWORTH SU9722
Stonemasons (01798) 342510
North Street; GU28 9NL Attractive 17th-c low-beamed inn; enjoyable freshly made food from sandwiches up, including blackboard specials, Skinners Betty Stogs and guests, helpful friendly staff, opened-up modernised areas in former adjoining cottages, inglenook log fires; TV; children and dogs welcome, picnic-sets in sheltered back garden, five bedrooms, opposite Petworth House (NT) so can get busy, open (and food) all day, including breakfast 8.30-11am, kitchen shuts 6pm Sun.

PLUMPTON TQ3613
Half Moon (01273) 890253
Ditchling Road (B2116); BN7 3AF Enlarged beamed and timbered roadside dining pub; good food from pub favourites up, local ales and plenty of wines by the glass, log fire with unusual flint chimneybreast; background music; children and dogs (in bar) welcome, tables in wisteria-clad front courtyard and on back

terrace, big downs-view garden, good walks, open all day (till 6pm Sun).

POYNINGS   TQ2611
Royal Oak   (01273) 857389
The Street; BN45 7AQ Welcoming traditional 19th-c pub in rural setting; large beamed bar with smaller more intimate areas up steps, well kept Harveys and a guest from three-sided servery, enjoyable reasonably priced home-cooked food, summer barbecues, friendly efficient service, traditional furnishing, hanging hops and old photographs, paintings for sale, woodburner; children and dogs welcome, big garden with country/downs views, play area and barbecue, good walks, open (and food) all day.

RINGMER   TQ4512
Green Man   (01273) 812422
Lewes Road; BN8 5NA Welcoming 1930s roadside pub with busy mix of locals and visitors; six real ales from brick-faced counter including Greene King, wide range of generous good value food, efficient friendly service, long bar with log fire, large restaurant and conservatory; children and dogs welcome, terrace tables, more on lawn under trees, play area, open (and food) all day.

RODMELL   TQ4105
Abergavenny Arms   (01273) 472416
Back road Lewes–Newhaven; BN7 3EZ Welcoming beamed and raftered ex-barn; large open-plan bar with wood and tiled floors, several recesses and log fire in big fireplace, good selection of enjoyable home-made food (not Sun evening) from daily changing menu, steak night Thurs, well kept Harveys and one or more local guests, upstairs eating area, games room; occasional live music; children welcome, large two-level back terrace with painted picnic-sets, same village as Virginia Woolf's Monk's House (NT) and near South Downs Way, open all day.

ROWHOOK   TQ1234
★Chequers   (01403) 790480
Off A29 NW of Horsham; RH12 3PY Attractive 15th-c country pub; beamed and flagstoned front bar with portraits and inglenook log fire, step up to low-ceilinged lounge, well kept Harveys and guests, decent wines by the glass and good food from chef-landlord using local ingredients including home-grown vegetables, efficient service from friendly chatty young staff, separate restaurant; background music; children and dogs welcome, tables out on front terraces and in pretty garden behind, good play area, closed Sun evening, Mon and Tues.

RUSPER   TQ2037
Star   (01293) 871264
Off A264 S of Crawley; RH12 4RA Several linked rooms in this cosy 15th-c beamed coaching inn; well kept ales such as

Fullers, Greene King and Ringwood, decent food (all day Sun) from sandwiches and light meals up including some Greek and vegan dishes, wood floors, old tools on walls, fine brick inglenook; children and dogs welcome, small back terrace, open all day.

RYE   TQ9220
★George   (01797) 222114
High Street; TN31 7JT Sizeable hotel with popular beamed bar; mix of furniture including settles on bare boards, log fire, local ales such as Dark Star, Harveys and Old Dairy, continental beers on tap too, friendly helpful service from neat young staff, interesting bistro-style food and good selection of wines including local vineyards such as Chapel Down, big spreading restaurant to right of main door; maybe background jazz; children and dogs welcome, seats on pleasant back terrace, attractive bedrooms, open all day – being refurbished as we went to press.

RYE   TQ9220
★Globe   (01797) 225220
Military Road; TN31 7NX Small weatherboarded pub with quirky touches such as corrugated iron-clad walls, hanging lobster-pot lights and eclectic range of furniture from school chairs to a table made from part of an old fishing boat, even hay bale seats in one part, fresh flowers, candles and paraffin lamps, two log fires, good locally sourced food from open kitchen with wood-fired oven, interesting local ales and ciders (no bar counter), also some wines from nearby Chapel Down, shelves of home-made preserves for sale, quick cheerful service; unisex loos; children and dogs welcome, seats on side decking, Sat market, open all day.

RYE   TQ9220
★Mermaid   (01797) 223065
Mermaid Street; TN31 7EY Fine old timbered inn on famous cobbled street (cellars date from 12th c, although pub was rebuilt in 1420); civilised antiques-filled bar, Victorian gothic carved chairs, older but plainer oak seats and huge working inglenook with massive bressumer (ask about the priest hole and secret passages), Harveys, Sharps and a guest, good selection of wines, gins and malt whiskies, enjoyable bar food (not Sat evening) or more elaborate and expensive restaurant choices, efficient friendly service, reputedly haunted by five ghosts; background music; children welcome, seats on small back terrace, 31 bedrooms (most with four-posters), good breakfast, on-site parking, open all day.

RYE   TQ9120
★Standard   (01797) 225231
The Mint, High Street; TN31 7EN Ancient pub sympathetically opened up and renovated; moulded beams, exposed brickwork and panelling, brown leather and

farmhouse chairs at rustic tables on quarry tiles, candles and log fires (stag's head above one), four well kept ales including local Three Legs, good fairly priced food using local ingredients (fish from the harbour), nice wines and decent coffee, friendly accommodating staff; outside gents'; well behaved children and dogs welcome, picnic sets on small back terrace, five well appointed character bedrooms (more in their nearby café/bakery), open all day.

RYE   TQ9220
Waterworks Micropub
07974 941393 *Tower Street/Rope Walk; TN31 7AT* Micropub in interesting old building (former waterworks); friendly hard-working landlord serving eight well kept local beers and three or four real ciders (all marked-up on blackboard), also wines by the glass and some snacky food, furniture and other bits and pieces for sale; dogs welcome, open all day weekends, otherwise from 2pm, handy for the station.

RYE   TQ9220
★Ypres Castle (01797) 223248
Gun Garden; steps up from A259, or down past Ypres Tower; TN31 7HH Traditional tucked-away 17th-c pub; main bar with wall banquettes, assorted tables and chairs on bare boards and open fire, half a dozen well kept local beers and a couple of proper ciders, good reasonably priced food from pub favourites up, two dining rooms, friendly relaxed atmosphere; background music (some live); children and dogs welcome, lovely views from sheltered garden down over the River Rother, open all day.

RYE HARBOUR   TQ9419
William the Conqueror
(01797) 223315 *Opposite lifeboat station, bottom of Harbour Road; TN31 7TU* Welcoming harbourside pub under same ownership as the Royal Oak at Whatlington; three well kept Shepherd Neame ales and decent choice of wines by the glass, good reasonably priced food including local fish and some Greek dishes, friendly helpful staff, three main areas (ramp down to lower dining part), nautical-themed décor with framed charts and old local pictures, some wooden booth seating and cushioned benches on bare boards, log fires; background and occasional live music; children and dogs welcome, picnic-sets out in front, open all day (till 10pm Mon-Thurs, 9pm Sun).

SEDLESCOMBE   TQ7817
Queens Head (01424) 870228
The Green; TN33 0QA Attractive old tile-hung village green pub (watch out for the wandering geese); beamed central bar with armchairs on bare boards, some window seats and a huge cartwheel, Harveys, Sharps Doom Bar and a guest such as Old Dairy,

decent choice of wines by the glass, dining areas either side with open fires (one in large inglenook), good popular food from shortish menu (also blackboard specials), helpful friendly staff; maybe quiet background music; children and dogs welcome, picnic-sets in spacious side garden, open all day, food till 4pm Sun.

SHORTBRIDGE   TQ4521
Peacock (01825) 762463
Piltdown; OS Sheet 198 map reference 450215; TN22 3XA Old black and white country dining pub, civilised and welcoming, with dark beams, timbers and big inglenook, some nice old furniture on parquet floors, good food from ciabattas up, two or three well kept ales and decent wines by the glass, friendly attentive staff, restaurant; children and dogs welcome, tables out at front and in back garden, bedrooms, open all day Fri-Sun.

SIDLESHAM   SZ8697
★Crab & Lobster (01243) 641233
Mill Lane; off B2145 S of Chichester; PO20 7NB Restaurant-with-rooms rather than pub but does have a small flagstoned bar serving real ales, plenty of wines by the glass (including champagne) and light meals; stylish upmarket restaurant with good imaginative (and pricey) food including excellent local fish, competent friendly young staff; background music; children welcome, tables on back terrace overlooking marshes, smart bedrooms and self-catering cottage, open all day (food all day weekends).

SINGLETON   SU8713
Partridge (01243) 811251
Just off A286 Midhurst–Chichester; PO18 0EY Pretty 16th-c pub in attractive village setting; all sorts of light and dark wood tables and dining chairs on polished wood floors, flagstones or carpet, some country knick-knacks, open fires and woodburner, three well kept changing ales, several wines by the glass and enjoyable food (all day Sat, till 7pm Sun) from sandwiches up, cream teas (must book), friendly welcoming service; background and live music, monthly quiz; children and dogs welcome, plenty of seats under parasols on terrace and in walled garden, play area, handy for Weald & Downland Living Museum, open all day.

SLINDON   SU9708
Spur (01243) 814216
Slindon Common; A29 towards Bognor; BN18 0NE Roomy 17th-c pub with well kept ales such as Courage Directors and Sharps Doom Bar, good choice of popular sensibly priced food from bar snacks up, friendly staff, pine tables and two big log fires, large panelled restaurant, games room with darts and pool, also a skittle alley; quiz nights, some live music; children and dogs (in bar)

welcome, pretty garden (some traffic noise), good local walks, open all day Sun.

SMALL DOLE — TQ2112
Fox (01273) 491196
Henfield Road; BN5 9XE Busy roadside village pub with good choice of well liked/priced home-made food including popular weekday set menu, quick friendly service, well kept Harveys and one or two guests, cosy dining areas off long panelled bar, dark pubby furniture on wood or carpeted floors, pictures of plants, fish and hunting scenes; quiet background music; children and dogs welcome, disabled access, seats out at front and in tree-shaded garden with play area, open all day Sun, closed Mon.

SOUTH HARTING — SU7819
★ ### White Hart (01730) 825124
B2146 SE of Petersfield; GU31 5QB Sympathetically renovated 16th-c village inn; bars and dining area with beams and standing timbers, a couple of woodburners and open fire, nice mix of furniture on bare boards or flagstones, candles and fresh flowers, up to four well kept changing ales, about 20 wines by the glass and a dozen malt whiskies, good food including lunchtime set menu, Mon burger nights, pleasant service; live music and quiz nights; children and dogs (in bar) welcome, terrace and garden tables, handy for Uppark (NT), comfortable character bedrooms, open all day, breakfast for non-residents.

SOUTHWATER — TQ1528
Bax Castle (01403) 730369
Two Mile Ash, a mile or so NW; RH13 0LA Early 19th-c country pub with well liked/priced wood-fired pizzas, two or three well kept Ringwood ales, friendly staff, sofas next to big log fire, barn restaurant; background music; children and dogs welcome, pleasant garden, near Downs Link path on former railway track, shuts 7pm Sun, otherwise open (and food) all day.

STAPLEFIELD — TQ2728
Jolly Tanners (01444) 400335
Handcross Road, just off A23; RH17 6EF Split-level local by cricket green, welcoming landlord and pub dogs, two good log fires, padded settles and lots of china, brasses and old photographs, Harveys and guests (beer festivals), real cider, enjoyable pubby food including burgers, 'sizzling' dishes and blackboard specials, friendly chatty atmosphere; background music (live Sat), Mon darts, Weds bridge, Thurs quiz; children and dogs welcome, attractive suntrap garden, quite handy for Nymans (NT), open all day, food till 5.30pm Sun.

STAPLEFIELD — TQ2728
Victory (01444) 400463
Warninglid Road; RH17 6EU Pretty little shuttered dining pub overlooking cricket green (and London to Brighton veteran car run, first Sun in Nov); friendly welcoming staff, good choice of popular home-made food (all day Sat, till 5pm Sun) with smaller helpings for children, well kept Harveys Best and a guest, local cider and decent wines from zinc-topped counter, beams and woodburner; dogs welcome in bar, nice tree-shaded garden with play area, open all day Thurs-Sun.

STEDHAM — SU8522
Hamilton Arms (01730) 812555
School Lane (off A272); GU29 0NZ Village local run by friendly Thai family; standard pub food as well as popular Thai bar snacks and restaurant dishes (you can buy ingredients in their little shop), reasonably priced wines and four or more well kept ales; background and occasional live music; pretty hanging baskets on front terrace overlooking small green, nearby walks, five bedrooms, open all day Thurs-Sun, closed Mon.

STOPHAM — TQ0318
White Hart (01798) 874903
Off A283 E of village, W of Pulborough; RH20 1DS Fine old beamed pub by medieval River Arun bridge; well kept Harveys, Sharps and a guest, popular food cooked by chef-landlord including early evening set menu; children and dogs (in bar) welcome, waterside tables, open all day, no food Sun evening.

STOUGHTON — SU8011
Hare & Hounds (023) 9263 1433
Signed off B2146 Petersfield–Emsworth; PO18 9JQ Brick and flint country pub with good reasonably priced home-cooked food from baguettes up, several well kept ales such as Dark Star, Long Man and Otter, Weston's cider and good choice of wines by the glass, cheerful service, flagstones and big open fires, locals' bar with darts; quiz nights; children (in eating areas) and dogs welcome, tables on pretty front terrace and grass behind, lovely setting near Saxon church, good walks, open all day.

SUTTON — SU9715
White Horse (01798) 869191
The Street; RH20 1PS Refurbished 18th-c village inn; wood-floored bar with open brick fireplace at each end, wooden chairs around well spaced tables, also banquette seating, three well kept local ales and nice wines by the glass, good food (not especially cheap)

We don't mention free wi-fi, because it's standard in most pubs these days – though not universal. And don't expect a good signal in remote rural locations.

from lunchtime sandwiches and a few pub favourites up, friendly efficient service, restaurant area; children and dogs welcome, some seats out at front, more on back terrace, good surrounding walks and handy for Bignor Roman Villa, eight comfortable well appointed bedrooms, open all day, food till 4pm Sun.

THAKEHAM
TQ1017

White Lion (01798) 813141

Off B2139 N of Storrington; The Street; RH20 3EP Steps up to 16th-c pub in pretty village; heavy beams, panelling, bare boards and traditional furnishings, four changing ales including Fullers and Harveys, decent wines by the glass and well liked food (not Sun evening) including good selection of blackboard specials, efficient service, pleasant dining room with inglenook; children and dogs welcome, sunny terrace and small enclosed lawn, closed Mon, otherwise open all day.

TICEHURST
TQ6831

★ **Bull** (01580) 200586

Three Leg Cross; off B2099 towards Wadhurst; TN5 7HH Attractive 14th-c country pub popular with good mix of customers; big log fires in two heavy-beamed old-fashioned bars, well kept Harveys and a couple of guests, contemporary furnishings in light airy dining extension, friendly service; children and dogs welcome, charming front garden (busy in summer), bigger back one with play area, good PYO fruit farm nearby, four bedrooms, open all day.

TURNERS HILL
TQ3435

★ **Red Lion** (01342) 715416

Lion Lane, just off B2028; RH10 4NU Welcoming traditional country local; snug parquet-floored bar with plush wall benches and small open fire, steps up to carpeted dining area with inglenook log fire, cushioned pews and settles, old photos and brewery memorabilia, well kept Harveys ales and good home-made food (lunchtime only – must book Sun); occasional live music including open mike nights, quiz; children (away from bar) and dogs welcome, picnic-sets on side grass overlooking village, open all day weekends, no food Thurs apart from rolls.

UDIMORE
TQ8818

Plough (01797) 223381

Cock Marling (B2089 W of Rye); TN31 6AL Traditionally updated and extended 17th-c roadside pub; enjoyable freshly made food including tapas and good steaks, well kept Harveys and Three Legs, Curious Brew craft lager and decent choice of wines by the glass, friendly welcoming staff, U-shaped bar with wood and quarry-tiled floors, two woodburners; occasional live music; children and dogs welcome, tables on good-sized sunny back terrace, Brede Valley views, self-catering apartment,

open (and food) all day Fri, Sat, till 6pm (3pm) Sun.

UPPER DICKER
TQ5409

Plough (01323) 844859

Coldharbour Road; BN27 3QJ Extended 17th-c pub with small central beamed bar, seats by inglenook, two restaurant areas off to the left and step up to larger dining bar on right with raised section, well kept Harveys and Shepherd Neame, enjoyable food from pubby choices up, friendly young staff; background and occasional live music; children and dogs welcome, spacious garden with play area, open (and food) all day.

WALBERTON
SU9705

Holly Tree (01243) 553110

The Street; BN18 0PH Quirky grey-painted Victorian pub; enjoyable food, including Sun roasts (until 6pm), changing ales and decent wines, friendly young staff; quiz, some live music and other events, big-screen sports TV; children and dogs welcome, café-style furniture and planters on front terrace, open all day.

WALDERTON
SU7910

Barley Mow (023) 9263 1321

Stoughton Road, just off B2146 Chichester–Petersfield; PO18 9ED Popular red-brick country pub with well liked food including pizza and steak nights, five real ales such as Dark Star, Harveys and Ringwood, a dozen wines by the glass, friendly welcoming staff, two log fires in U-shaped bar with roomy dining areas; skittle alley; children and dogs welcome, large streamside back garden, enjoyable walks (Kingley Vale nearby) and convenient for Stansted Park, open all day Sat, till 6pm (food 4pm) Sun.

WALDRON
TQ5419

★ **Star** (01435) 812495

Blackboys–Horam side road; TN21 0RA Pretty pub in quiet village across from the church; beamed main bar with settle next to good log fire in brick inglenook, wheelbacks around pubby tables on old quarry tiles, several built-in cushioned wall and window seats, old local pictures and photographs, high stools by central counter serving well kept Harveys, Sharps and a guest, maybe own apple juice, good food including bar snacks, pubby dishes and specials, dining areas with painted chairs around pine-topped tables on parquet or bare boards, bookshelf wallpaper, chatty local atmosphere and friendly staff; quiz, live music and comedy nights; picnic-sets in pleasant back garden, small café and shop next door, closed Sun evening, Mon.

WARNHAM
TQ1533

Greets (01403) 265047

Friday Street; RH12 3QY Welcoming 15th-c beamed pub with appealing simple décor; stripped pine tables on uneven flagstones, inglenook log fire, lots of nooks and corners, well kept Harveys and a dozen wines by the glass, good choice of fairly traditional food at sensible prices, friendly helpful staff, convivial locals' side bar with leather ceiling straps; children welcome, garden tables, open (and food) all day weekends.

WARNHAM   TQ1533
Sussex Oak (01403) 265028
Just off A24 Horsham–Dorking; Church Street; RH12 3QW Cheerfully busy country pub with heavy beams and timbers, mix of flagstones, tiles, wood and carpeting, big inglenook log fire, well kept Fullers, Harveys and guests from carved servery, real cider and plenty of wines by the glass, enjoyable fairly traditional food (smaller helpings available); background music, quiz, darts; children and dogs welcome, disabled facilities/parking, picnic-sets in large garden, good local walks, open all day, food all day weekends.

WARNINGLID   TQ2425
★ Half Moon (01444) 461227
B2115 off A23 S of Handcross or off B2110 Handcross–Lower Beeding; RH17 5TR Bustling 18th-c inn with properly pubby atmosphere and popular modern food; lively locals' bar with bare boards and small fireplace, room off with oak beams and flagstones, steps down to dining areas with mix of wooden chairs, cushioned wall settles and old tables on floorboards, plank panelling and bare brick, also old village photographs, another open fire and glass-covered well, Harveys Best, Greene King Old Speckled Hen and a guest, around 18 wines by the glass, malt whiskies and a farm cider, helpful staff; children and dogs (in bar) welcome, picnic-sets on lawn in sizeable garden with spectacular avenue of trees, open all day weekends, no food Sun evening.

WARTLING   TQ6509
★ Lamb (01323) 832116
Village signed with Herstmonceux Castle off A271 Herstmonceux–Battle; BN27 1RY Popular family-owned country pub; small entrance bar with open fireplace, Harveys Best and a couple of local guests, several wines by the glass from good list, two-level beamed and timbered dining room to the left with inglenook woodburner, bigger back bar and restaurant, well liked food including blackboard specials, friendly service; children and dogs welcome, steps up to garden with chunky seats, six bedrooms, closed Sun evening, otherwise open all day.

WEST ASHLING   SU8007
Richmond Arms (01243) 572046
Just off B2146; Mill Road; PO18 8EA Village dining pub in pretty setting

near big millpond with ducks and geese; highly regarded imaginative food (quite pricey, best to book) from bar snacks up, also wood-fired pizzas cooked in a vintage van (Fri, Sat evenings), well kept Harveys ales and good wines by the glass, competent friendly staff; children welcome, two nice bedrooms, closed Sun evening, Mon and Tues.

WEST HOATHLY   TQ3632
Fox (01342) 810644
Hammingden Lane/North Lane, towards Sharpthorne; RH19 4QG Welcoming corner pub with good food (not Sun evening) cooked by landlord-chef, Harveys Best Bitter and a guest such as St Austell Tribute, decent wines and lots of gins, friendly accommodating service, slightly quirky décor with curtain pelmets made from old pallets, bottle lampshades and floor-to-ceiling column of books in the bar, cosy log fires; some live music and quiz nights; children and dogs welcome, pavement tables under parasols, closed Mon and Tues, otherwise open all day (till 9pm Sun).

WEST MARDEN   SU7713
Victoria (023) 9263 1330
B2146 2 miles S of Uppark; PO18 9EN Friendly village pub popular with downland walkers; good traditional food (not Sun evening) in beamed bar and small back restaurant, well kept changing ales (beer, cider and gin festivals), log fire; occasional live music; children and dogs welcome, attractive garden, open all day Sat, till 9pm Sun, closed Mon (except bank holidays).

WEST WITTERING   SZ8099
Lamb (01243) 511105
Chichester Road; B2179/A286 towards Birdham; PO20 8QA Modernised 18th-c tile-hung country pub; three Badger ales and enjoyable home-cooked food including popular Sun roasts (booking advised), bar with painted beams and timbers, assorted furniture on parquet including kitchen chairs and scrubbed pine tables, woodburner in brick fireplace, two bare-boards dining rooms, some interesting artwork; background music; children and dogs welcome, tables out at front and in small sheltered back garden with pizza oven and play area, open all day, food all day Sun till 8pm.

WESTFIELD   TQ8115
New Inn (01424) 752800
Main Road; TN35 4QE Popular village pub with light open-plan interior, pubby furniture including wheelback and captain's chairs on pale wood floors, sparsely decorated white walls, conservatory, four or five mainly local ales including a house beer from Long Man, enjoyable reasonably priced home-made food from weekly changing menu (till 7pm Sun, not Mon evening), cheerful helpful staff; children and dogs welcome, disabled access, seats out on gravel terrace, open all day.

WHATLINGTON   TQ7619
Royal Oak   (01424) 870492
A21 N of village; TN33 0NJ Welcoming
15th-c weatherboarded pub set down from
the road (sister to the William the Conqueror
in Rye Harbour); cosy split-level interior
with series of linked rooms, black beams
and log fires (one in brick inglenook),
deep well in another part, good reasonably
priced food including steak cooked on a
hot stone Fri evening and popular Greek
meze night Sat (landlady-chef is Cypriot),
well kept Long Man and Shepherd Neame,
decent wines by the glass, friendly helpful
service; background music, quiz; children
and dogs welcome, play area inside and in
back garden, boules pitch, open (and food)
all day Sat, till 6pm (4pm) Sun, closed Mon
and Tues.

WILMINGTON   TQ5404
Giants Rest   (01323) 870207
Just off A27; BN26 5SQ Popular early
20th-c country pub; long wood-floored bar
with adjacent open areas, simple furniture,
rural pictures and log fire, Long Man and a
couple of local guests, South Downs cider
(made in the village), enjoyable pubby food
including good home-made pies, friendly
service; wooden puzzles and games; children
and dogs welcome, picnic-sets on front grass,
surrounded by South Downs walks and village
famous for chalk-carved Long Man, two
bedrooms, open (and food) all day, kitchen
may shut early Sun evening if quiet.

WINEHAM   TQ2320
★ Royal Oak   (01444) 881252
*Village signposted from A272 and
B2116; BN5 9AY* Splendidly old-fashioned
local with log fire in big inglenook, jugs
and ancient corkscrews on very low beams,
collection of cigarette boxes and old bottles,
various stuffed animals including a stoat and
crocodile, Harveys Best and guests tapped
from stillroom casks, enjoyable home-
cooked food (not Sun evening), more bric-
a-brac and old local photographs in back
parlour with views of quiet countryside;
occasional folk music and morris men;
children away from bar and dogs welcome,
picnic-sets out at front, closed evenings
25 and 26 Dec, 1 Jan.

WISBOROUGH GREEN   TQ0626
Bat & Ball   (01403) 700199
Newpound Lane; RH14 0EH 18th-c
red-brick Badger dining pub set in six-acre
grounds; their ales and 20 wines by the glass
including champagne from counter faced
in wine boxes, short but varied choice of
well liked food, afternoon teas, connecting
beamed rooms with cosy corners and plenty
of rustic charm including high-raftered
restaurant, quiz nights; children and dogs (in
bar) welcome, pretty front garden with pond,
camping and shepherd's huts, handy for

Fishers Farm Park, open (and food) all day,
till 8pm (6pm) Sun.

WISBOROUGH GREEN   TQ0526
Cricketers Arms   (01403) 700369
*Loxwood Road, just off A272
Billingshurst–Petworth; RH14 0DG*
Attractive old pub on edge of village green;
well kept ales such as Harveys, St Austell
and Sharps, good choice of fairly priced food,
including specials and deals (fish and chips
night Mon), gluten-free diets catered for,
cheerful welcoming staff, open-plan with two
big woodburners and pleasing mix of country
furniture on parquet flooring, stripped-brick
dining area on left; occasional live music;
children and dogs welcome, tables out in
front, annual lawn mower race on the green,
open all day.

WISBOROUGH GREEN   TQ0525
Three Crowns   (01403) 700239
Billingshurst Road (A272); RH14 0DX
Family-run beamed village pub; enjoyable
freshly made food from lunchtime open
sandwiches and pub favourites up (they add
a service charge), Thurs grill night, well
kept Harveys, Shepherd Neame and four
guests, extensive choice of wines by the
glass and gins, afternoon teas; quiz nights;
children and dogs welcome (pub dog is Ted),
big tree-shaded back garden, closed Tues
(and Mon in winter), otherwise open all day,
till 9pm Sun.

WIVELSFIELD GREEN   TQ3519
Cock   (01444) 471668
North Common Road; RH17 7RH
Pleasant red-brick village pub; good choice
of enjoyable reasonably priced food, Harveys
and guests, helpful friendly staff, two bars
and restaurant, log fire; monthly quiz night,
darts, bar billiards, pool and sports TV;
children, walkers and dogs welcome, seats
out at front and in back garden, open all day,
food all day Fri and Sat, till 8pm Sun.

WOODMANCOTE   SU7707
Woodmancote   (01243) 371019
*The one near Emsworth; Woodmancote
Lane; PO10 8RD* Village pub with unusual
contemporary décor – plenty of quirky
touches; enjoyable popular food (advisable to
book) from sandwiches and sharing boards
up, three real ales including one badged
for the pub and several wines by the glass,
friendly welcoming staff, restaurant; acoustic
music Sun afternoon, quiz every other Tues;
children and dogs (in bar) welcome, seats
outside under cover, open (and food) all day,
weekend breakfasts 10-11.30am, kitchen
shuts 7pm Sun.

WORTHING   TQ1502
Corner House   (01903) 216463
High Street; BN11 1DJ Extended pub
with bright modern interior; comfortable
seating including some sofas around three

sides of central bar, four real ales, craft beers and good range of wines marked up on blackboard, enjoyable reasonably priced food (they may ask for a credit card if you run a tab) including pie and pint night; quiz; children and dogs welcome, paved and heated back terrace, open all day, no food Sun evening.

WORTHING   TQ1402
Egremont   (01903) 600064
Brighton Road; BN11 3ED Restored 19th-c pub near seafront; up to six real ales including Harveys and a couple from Hand badged for them, extensive range of interesting gins and enjoyable reasonably priced pubby food from ciabattas and sharing plates up, some lunchtime choices available in smaller helpings, friendly helpful staff, split-level mainly bare-boards interior arranged around central bar, one part laid for dining, mix of furniture including button-back banquettes, stools, sofas and some high tables, original Kemptown Brewery stained glass, old enamel signs and other interesting bits and pieces; quiz and live music nights, TV for major sports; children and dogs welcome, pavement picnic-sets, open all day.

WORTHING   TQ1502
Selden Arms   01903 523361
Lyndhurst Road, between Waitrose and hospital; BN11 2DB Friendly unchanging 19th-c backstreet local opposite gasworks; welcoming long-serving licensees, six well kept changing ales, craft kegs and extensive range of bottled Belgian beers (Jan beer festival), bargain lunchtime food (not Sun) including doorstep sandwiches and pies, comfortably worn interior with photographs of old Worthing pubs, pump clips on ceiling, log fire; occasional live music and quiz nights, darts; dogs welcome, open all day.

Warwickshire

with Birmingham and the West Midlands

KEY   ★ Star Pub   🍽 Top Quality Food   🍺 Great Beer
🍷 Good Wines   £ Bargain Meals   🛏 Good Bedrooms   🍴 Serves Food

ALDERMINSTER   SP2348   Map 4

Bell 🍷 🍺 🛏

(01789) 335671 – www.brunningandprice.co.uk/bell
A3400 Oxford–Stratford; CV37 8NY

**18th-c inn with sympathetically modernised character bars, a two-
storey restaurant, modern cooking and thoughtful choice of drinks;
bedrooms**

Following a major refurbishment in early 2020, this former Georgian
coaching inn is now a Brunning & Price pub. The large bar area and
many different sized rooms cleverly manage to create a contemporary feel
while incorporating some original features such as beams and standing
timbers. The cheery staff serve three regular ales – St Austell Brunning
& Price Traditional Bitter, Purity Gold and Hook Norton Old Hooky – and
four changing guests on handpump, real cider and around 25 wines by the
glass including champagne. Comfortable furnishings include a mix of old
wooden chairs and tables, upholstered sofas, cosy armchairs, high bar
chairs by the counter, rugs on polished wooden floors, a double-sided open
fire and a woodburning stove; background music. The stylish and modern
restaurant is on two levels. The lower floor, with stunning chandeliers, is
decorated in soft pastels and silvers and has folding doors leading out to the
terrace, while the upper floor has chairs around polished copper tables on
dark floorboards, seats on a balcony and panoramic views across the Stour
Valley; there's also a private dining room with its own decked area and lawn.
Outside, the appealing courtyard and garden have seats and tables looking
over water meadows and the valley. The eight bedrooms are well equipped
and comfortable.

🍽 Rewarding food includes nibbles and 'light bites', a meze plate, crispy baby
squid with sweet chilli sauce, rump steak sandwich, Malaysian chicken curry,
cauliflower, chick pea and squash tagine, king prawn linguine with chilli, pork and
leek sausages with mash and buttered greens, grilled sea bass with potato and chervil
terrine, and puddings such as summer pudding with clotted cream and hot waffle and
caramelised banana with honeycomb ice-cream. Vegetarian, vegan and gluten-free
options are available. *Benchmark main dish: roast duck with crispy leg croquettes,
celeriac purée and cherry jus £15.95. Two-course evening meal £22.00.*

Brunning & Price ~ Manager Rachael Perry ~ Real ale ~ Open 11.30-11; 11.30-10 Sun ~
Bar food 12-9.30; 12-10 Fri-Sat ~ Restaurant ~ Children welcome ~ Dogs allowed in bar ~
Bedrooms: from £105

ARMSCOTE
Fuzzy Duck 🏠⭐ 🍷 🛏

SP2444 Map 4

(01608) 682635 – www.fuzzyduckarmscote.com

Off A3400 Stratford–Shipston; CV37 8DD

Interestingly refurbished former coaching inn with real ales, a good wine list, inventive food and seats outside; bedrooms

Owned by the sister and brother team behind soap company Baylis & Harding, this sensitively remodelled 18th-c inn is far from an ugly duckling. Handy for Stratford-upon-Avon and surrounded by Cotswold countryside, it's a lovely place to stay and the bedrooms (each named after a species of duck) are extremely comfortable and well equipped; first class breakfasts too. The bustling bar has an open fire, high chunky leather chairs around equally high metal tables on flagstones, with more leather chairs against the counter where they serve Purity Mad Goose and a weekly guest such as Church Farm IPA on handpump, real cider, eight wines by the glass and cocktails (including the Pink Duck); a wall of glass-faced boxes holds bottles of spirits belonging to regular customers. Three interconnected dining rooms have a mix of dark wooden tables surrounded by leather and other elegant chairs on pale floorboards, a sofa here and there and a two-way woodburning stove in an open fireplace. Throughout, cartoons and arty photographs hang on pale or dark grey walls and flowers are arranged in big vases; background music and board games. At the back, another dining room (also used for private parties) leads to a decked terrace with basket-weave armchairs, cushioned sofas and small modern metal chairs and tables under large parasols; there's also a small lawn with fruit trees.

 Tempting food includes bread and nibbles (such as pork crackling with apple sauce), warm goats cheese and red onion jam tartlet with dressed rocket, Asian-inspired crispy duck salad with hoisin dressing, ale-battered cod and chips, wild mushroom, chive and parmesan ristto, 8oz fillet steak with chips and peppercorn sauce, and desserts such as vanilla pannacotta with strawberry sorbet and dark chocolate brownie with salted caramel ice-cream. At press time, they were offering just a set menu: two courses for £24, three for £27.

Free house ~ Licensees Adrian Slater and Tania Fossey ~ Real ale ~ Open 10am-11pm; 11-5 Sun ~ Bar food 12-3, 6-9; 12-4 Sun ~ Restaurant ~ Children welcome ~ Dogs allowed in bar, restaurant & bedrooms ~ Bedrooms: £120

ARROW
Arrow Mill 🍷 🍺 🛏

SP0856 Map 4

(01789) 333790 – www.brunningandprice.co.uk/arrowmill

Opposite gates of Ragley Hall, B49 5NL; B49 5NL

Splendid former mill, carefully extended with airy drinking and dining rooms, a large selection of drinks, rewarding food and sunny terrace; good bedrooms

Enjoying a spectacular, secluded riverside setting, overlooking Ragley Hall Estate, close to Stratford-upon-Avon and the Roman town of Alcester, this is a beautifully and thoughtfully transformed old mill. It's certainly worth looking around before you decide where to sit as the original mill workings are on show, along with high raftered ceilings, heavy beams and timbers, fine brickwork and open fires – and some windows look out over the mill pond with its family of swans. The rooms and corridors are furnished with antique-style dining chairs, colourful leather armchairs, cushioned settles and stools, all manner of wooden tables on polished floorboards, parquet and rugs, plus elegant metal chandeliers, hundreds of prints and photographs, shelves of books and big house plants. One area is like a sitting room and is much coveted by customers, while there is also a private function room upstairs with its own balcony. Quick, friendly staff serve St Austell Brunning & Price Traditional Bitter on handpump plus two guest ales (one from Purity and another from perhaps Hook Norton), more than 110 gins and 21 wines by the glass, including champagne. A carefully planted terrace has wooden chairs and tables under green parasols, and the River Arrow runs the length of the garden. The nine spacious, comfortable and up-to-date bedrooms make an ideal base for exploring the area.

Brasserie-style food includes sandwiches, wild mushroom risotto, barbecue chicken wings, smoked haddock and salmon fishcake, braised feather of beef bourguignon with horseradish mash, crispy beef salad with sweet chilli sauce and roasted cashews, pea and mint tortellini, and puddings such as chocolate and orange tart with passion-fruit sorbet and crème brûlée. Afternoon tea is also available, as well as vegetarian, vegan and gluten-free options. *Benchmark main dish: braised lamb shoulder with crushed new potatoes and rosemary gravy £18.95. Two-course evening meal £22.00.*

Brunning & Price ~ Manager Peter Palfi ~ Real ale ~ Open 11.30-11; 11.30-10 Sun ~ Bar food 12-10; 12-9.30 Sun ~ Restaurant ~ Children welcome ~ Dogs allowed in bar ~ Bedrooms: £95

BIRMINGHAM

Old Joint Stock 🍺 £

SP0686 Map 4

(0121) 200 1892 – www.oldjointstocktheatre.co.uk
Temple Row West; B2 5NY

Big bustling Fullers pie-and-ale pub with impressive Victorian façade and interior, and a small back terrace; own theatre

This is an impressively flamboyant setting for a pint and a pie – a Grade-II listed building opposite Birmingham Cathedral, with chandeliers hanging from the soaring pink and gilt ceiling, gently illuminated busts lining the top of the ornately plastered walls and a splendid cupola above the centre of the room. Photographs of its historic past as a library and the Birmingham Joint Stock Bank line the walls; there's also a big dining balcony reached up a grand sweeping staircase. It's notably well run: staff remain efficient and friendly, even when it's busy. You'll find Fullers London Pride, Olivers Island, HSB, Seafarers and a guest or two on handpump, Cornish Orchards Gold cider, 17 wines by the glass and 36 gins; background music. The small and colourful back terrace has nicely quirky seats, tables and heaters. There's a purpose-built, first-floor theatre and you can book a two-course pre-theatre meal in advance.

The popular food (special diets catered for) includes breakfasts plus sandwiches, small or sharing plates, crispy squid with coriander and chilli jam, dirty halloumi fries, Vietnamese spicy chicken wings, black pudding scotch egg, Fullers Frontier-battered haddock goujons, chicken madras, speciality home-baked pies, and puddings such as chocolate brownie sundae with buffalo milk ice-cream and caramelised apple pie with vanilla custard. *Benchmark main dish: steak and Fullers London Pride Pie with red wine gravy £15.00. Two-course evening meal £20.50.*

Fullers ~ Manager Auda Matuleviciute ~ Real ale ~ Open 11-11; 12-6 Sun ~ Bar food 12-9; 12-10 Thurs-Sat; 12-4 Sun ~ Restaurant ~ Children allowed until 6pm

Pubs close to motorway junctions are listed at the back of the book.

BIRMINGHAM
Physician ⚦ ◀

SP0585 Map 4

(0121) 272 5900 – www.brunningandprice.co.uk/physician

Harborne Road, Edgbaston; pay-and-display parking in Highfield Road behind pub; B15 3DH

Substantial, extended pub with plenty of drinking and dining space, super drinks, interesting food and friendly atmosphere; seats outside

This imposing white building was once home to the Birmingham Medical Institute (whose modern headquarters are now across the road) – hence its name. Friendly, well trained staff serve a fantastic range of drinks: Purity Mad Goose, St Austell Brunning & Price Traditional Bitter and Timothy Taylors Landlord on handpump plus three guests, proper cider, 20 wines by the glass, 80 gins, 50 rums and around 40 malt whiskies. Oozing historical grandeur, the high ceilings and big sash windows have been used to great effect. The interlinked areas of all shapes and sizes have leather armchairs in front of open fires, a medley of cushioned wooden dining chairs and mate's chairs around polished solid tables on bare boards, rugs or carpet, lots of old prints on pale-painted walls, large gilt-edged mirrors and big house plants, stone bottles and books on shelves, and lighting that ranges from table lamps to elegant metal chandeliers; background music. Two rooms can be used for private dining, while the airy garden room overlooks the terraces with their good quality wooden seats and tables under green parasols among blooming tubs and flowerbeds. Disabled access. Birmingham's lovely Botanical Gardens with their stunning glasshouses are nearby.

 Rewarding food with vegetarian, vegan and gluten-free options includes elevenses (served until noon), sandwiches and dishes such as baked camembert with candied walnuts and celery salad, pan-fried scallops with pea purée and shredded ham hock, sharing boards, Malaysian vegetable curry with coconut rice and pak choi, sea bass fillets with lemon cream sauce, roast pork tenderloin with colcannon potato, rib-eye steak with tarragon butter, mushrooms and chips, and puddings such as lemon cheesecake with raspberry ripple ice-cream and sticky toffee pudding with vanilla ice-cream. *Benchmark main dish: braised feather of beef bourguignon with horseradish mash and buttered kale £16.95. Two-course evening meal £22.00.*

Brunning & Price ~ Manager Lisa Rogers ~ Real ale ~ Open 11.30-11; 11.30-10.30 Sun ~ Bar food 12-9.30; 12-10 Fri, Sat; 12-9 Sun ~ Children welcome ~ Dogs allowed in bar

HAMPTON-IN-ARDEN
White Lion ◀

SP2080 Map 4

(01675) 442833 – www.thewhitelioninn.com

High Street; handy for M42 junction 6; B92 0AA

Popular village local with a good choice of ales; bedrooms

The church opposite this popular pub is mentioned in the Domesday Book. Once a farmhouse, it's been a pub since 1838 and offers a fine choice of real ales on handpump: Banks's Mild, Hobsons Best, M&B Brew XI, Skinners Betty Stogs and Wye Valley HPA plus guests, three real ciders and 12 wines by the glass. The carpeted bar is nice and relaxed, with a mix of furniture tidily laid out, neatly curtained small windows, low-beamed ceilings and some local memorabilia on the cream-painted walls; background music, TV and board games. The modern dining areas are fresh and airy with farmhouse, wheelback and cane chairs around a mix of tables on stripped floorboards. There is a neat hedged garden with picnic-sets and tables and chairs. The nine reasonably priced bedrooms are quiet and comfortable with bright décor. This is an attractive village.

Traditional French bistro and British pub grub includes lunchtime sandwiches, calamari with dijon mustard, deep-fried breaded brie with apricot chutney, croque madame and monsieur, whitebait with tartare sauce, omelettes, steak burger with coleslaw and chips, rump steak, traditional Sunday roasts, and puddings such as apple crumble with custard and sundae brownie. *Benchmark main dish: fish and chips £12.25. Two-course evening meal £20.00.*

Free house ~ Licensee Chris Roach ~ Real ale ~ Open 11-11; 12-10.30 Sun ~ Bar food 12-2.30, 6-9; 12-4 Sun ~ Restaurant ~ Children welcome ~ Dogs allowed in bar, restaurant & bedrooms ~ Bedrooms: £100

HUNNINGHAM   SP3768   Map 4

Red Lion ♀

(01926) 632715 – www.redlionhunningham.co.uk

Village signposted off B4453 Leamington–Rugby just E of Weston, and off B4455 Fosse Way 2.5 miles SW of A423 junction; CV33 9DY

Friendly pub with a good range of drinks and well liked food

This attractive-looking pub, one half painted white, the other in red brick, offers enviable views of the River Leam. Popular food and an appealing, open-plan interior draw plenty of customers to this friendly and gently civilised place. Cleverly divided up, the rooms have beams, pews with scatter cushions, an assortment of antique dining chairs and stools around nice polished tables on bare boards or flagstones (with a few big rugs here and there) and contemporary paintwork. A cosy room has tub armchairs around an open coal fire. Byatts Platinum Blonde, Church Farm IPA, Purity Pure UBU and Wye Valley Bitter on handpump and 17 wines by the glass; background music. Outside, looking across to the arched 14th-c bridge, is a sunny terrace with tables and chairs and beyond that an expansive area of grass with plenty of picnic-sets.

Rewarding food includes sandwiches and sharing boards, potted salmon, bruschetta, seared red mullet with white wine and saffron broth, egg noodles and crispy kale, burgers (choose from beef, chicken or falafel) with toppings and chips, spiced cauliflower jambalaya, and puddings such as apple and rhubarb crumble with custard and passion-fruit baked cheesecake. Vegetarian, vegan and gluten-free options are available, as well as themed meal deals. *Benchmark main dish: cassoulet £16.00. Two-course evening meal £23.00.*

Free house ~ Licensee Richard Merand ~ Real ale ~ Open 11-11; 11-10.30 Sun ~ Bar food 12-9 ~ Restaurant ~ Children welcome ~ Dogs allowed in bar

ILMINGTON   SP2143   Map 4

Howard Arms ⭐♀🛏

(01608) 682226 – www.howardarms.com

Village signed with Wimpstone off A3400 S of Stratford; CV36 4LT

Lovely mellow-toned interior, lots to look at and tasty food and drink; bedrooms

On a pretty village green, nestled beneath the Cotswold escarpment, lies this handsome 400-year-old golden-stone inn. The beamed and flagstoned rooms contain a pleasing mix of furniture from pews and rustic stools to leather dining chairs around all sorts of tables, rugs on bare boards, shelves of books, candles and a log fire in a big inglenook. There's Timothy Taylors Landlord and a beer from Purity on handpump with a changing guest (perhaps North Cotswold or Wye Valley), three real ciders, 19 wines by the glass (including dessert wines) and a fair choice of whiskies and brandies;

background music and board games. In warm weather, the big back garden is delightful, with picnic-sets under parasols, a colourful herbaceous border and an outdoor play area. The eight bedrooms, all different, are well equipped and comfortable (one is downstairs) and the breakfasts highly regarded. There are good walks on the nearby hills.

As well as breakfast, pleasing food (with special dietary requirements catered for) includes sandwiches, sharing boards, spiced lamb kofta kebab with pitta and tzatziki, butternut squash, chickpea and courgette tagine, a fish of the day, chicken breast with puy lentils, beech mushrooms and curly kale, beef sirloin with chips and peppercorn sauce, ale-battered haddock and chips, and puddings such as chocolate and mint pannacotta and baked vanilla cheesecake with raspberry sorbet. *Benchmark main dish: game and chestnut mushroom stew £14.50. Two-course evening meal £22.00.*

Free house ~ Licensee Pawel Sobiszek ~ Real ale ~ Open 7.30am-11pm; 8am-11pm Sat; 8am-10.30pm Sun ~ Bar food 12-4, 6-9; 12-8 Sun ~ Restaurant ~ Children welcome ~ Dogs allowed in bar ~ Bedrooms: £140

LONG COMPTON
SP2832 Map 4

Red Lion

(01608) 684221 – www.redlion-longcompton.co.uk
A3400 S of Shipston-on-Stour; CV36 5JS

Traditional character and contemporary touches in comfortably furnished coaching inn; bedrooms

This contemporary-styled, Grade-II listed historic coaching inn is a favourite with our readers – and their dogs. The spacious, charmingly furnished lounge bar with beams and some exposed stone has nice rambling corners with cushioned settles among pleasantly assorted and comfortable seats and leather armchairs; there are tables on flagstones and carpets, animal prints on warm paintwork and both an open fire and a woodburning stove. Friendly, attentive staff serve Goffs Jouster, Hook Norton Hooky and a changing guest ale on handpump, 15 wines by the glass (including sparkling and pudding wines), real cider and local gin. The simple public bar has darts, pool, a juke box, fruit machine and a TV; background music and occasional quiz nights. There are tables out in the big back garden, with a large play area for children. The lovely pub dog Bella explains why this establishment goes the extra mile for four-legged friends, even offering home-cooked pigs' ears as well as dog-friendly accommodation. The five bedrooms (another two are planned for spring 2021) are quiet and spotlessly kept and breakfasts are particularly good.

Quite a choice of rewarding food includes sandwiches, imaginative salads, chargrilled rump steak, salmon and cod fishcakes, sweet potato satay curry, twice-baked cheese soufflé, lamb chop with peas, roasted butternut squash and redcurrant jus, pan-fried sea bass with wilted spinach, provençale sauce and salsa verde, and puddings such as raspberry and hazelnut pavlova and steamed treacle sponge with custard. Vegetarian, vegan, gluten-free and dairy-free options are available. *Benchmark main dish: steak in ale pie £16.00. Two-course evening meal £23.00.*

Cropthorne Inns ~ Manager Lisa Phipps ~ Real ale ~ Open 10-3, 5-9; 10-10 Sat; 10-9 Sun ~ Bar food 12-2, 6-8; 12-2, 6-8.30 Sat; 12-8 Sun ~ Restaurant ~ Children allowed in bar ~ Dogs allowed in bar & bedrooms ~ Bedrooms: £110

The details at the end of each featured entry start by saying whether the pub is a free house, or if it belongs to a brewery or pub group (which we name).

PRESTON BAGOT   SP1765   Map 4

Crabmill ♀ ☕

(01926) 843342 – www.brunningandprice.co.uk/crabmill
A4189 Henley-in-Arden to Warwick; B95 5EE

Charming old mill with beamed, interlinked rooms, interesting décor, imaginative food and drinks choice and seats outside

Carefully refurbished and gently civilised, this is a rambling former cider mill with plenty of character. The relaxed bar has a woodburning stove at one end fronted by armchairs, cushioned wall settles and stools around a mix of tables on bare boards and a fine mix of drinks such as St Austell Brunning & Price Traditional Bitter, Timothy Taylors Boltmaker, Church Farm IPA and a guest such as Shakespeare The Bard's Best on handpump, 21 wines by the glass including fizz, 60 gins and 25 rums. Staff are efficient and friendly. The heavily beamed dining areas have button-back banquettes and cushioned wooden chairs around heavy tables and rugs on floorboards; further rooms are similarly furnished. Throughout there are big house and pot plants, elegant metal chandeliers, books on shelves, gilt-edged mirrors and lots of prints on the walls. The large, attractive garden has picnic-sets on grass, and wooden seats and benches under parasols on a terrace.

🍴 Enterprising food includes sandwiches and 'light bites', chicken caesar croquettes, meze plate, beetroot hummus with flatbread, goats cheese and roasted Mediterranean vegetable quiche, 7oz fillet steak with chips and peppercorn sauce, pork sausages with mash, buttered greens and onion gravy, cauliflower, chickpea and squash tagine with couscous, battered cod and chips, and puddings such as lemon meringue roulade with raspberry sorbet and Cheshire Farm ice-creams. Vegetarian, vegan and gluten-free options are available. *Benchmark main dish: fish pie (salmon, smoked haddock and prawns) £14.95. Two-course evening meal £22.00.*

Brunning & Price ~ Manager Andy Harris ~ Real ale ~ Open 11.30-11; 11.30-10 Sun ~
Bar food 12-9 ~ Restaurant ~ Children welcome ~ Dogs allowed in bar

SHIPSTON-ON-STOUR   SP2540   Map 4

Black Horse ☕ £

(01608) 238489 – blackhorseshipston.co.uk
Station Road (off A3400); CV36 4BT

16th-c pub with simple country furnishings, well kept ales, an extensive choice of Thai food and seats outside

This pretty old stone tavern is the only thatched building in Shipston and also its oldest pub, first licensed in 1540. From a central entrance passage, low-beamed, character bars lead off with some fine old flagstones and floor tiles and two open fires (one in an inglenook). There are also wheelbacks, stools, rustic seats and tables and built-in wall benches, half-panelled or exposed-stone walls, and plenty of copper kettles, pans and bedwarmers, horse tack and toby jugs. Friendly staff serve Prescott Hill Climb and Wye Valley Butty Bach as well as guests such as Courage Directors, Uley Pigs Ear or Youngs Special on handpump, eight wines by the glass, 18 gins and ten malt whiskies; background music, TV, darts and board games. The little dining room has pale wooden tables and chairs on bare boards. There are a couple of benches on the front cobbles, contemporary seats and tables on a partly covered, raised decked area at the back and picnic-sets on grass; in summer, the flowering baskets and tubs are lovely. Disabled access.

🍴 The nicely priced and popular food is Thai: tom yum soups, steamed dumplings, chicken satay and fishcakes, plus pad Thai and other noodle dishes and lots of curries and stir-fries with chicken, beef, pork, duck, lamb or seafood. There are also a couple of pub classics such as fish and chips or burger and chips. *Benchmark main dish: Thai green curry £9.50. Two-course evening meal £18.00.*

Free house ~ Licensee Gabe Saunders ~ Real ale ~ Open 6-11 Mon; 12-11 ~ Bar food 12-2, 6-10; not Mon ~ Restaurant ~ Children welcome ~ Dogs allowed in bar

WARMINGTON
Falcon ♀ ◗

SP4147   Map 4

(01295) 692120 – www.brunningandprice.co.uk/falcon
B4100 towards Shotteswell; OX17 1JJ

Carefully extended roadside pub with spreading bar and dining rooms, a fine choice of drinks and food, and seats outside

A large modern fire pit inside and sunny garden with deckchairs outside provide a warm welcome at this beautifully restored golden-stone inn, whatever the season. Built in 1770 to take advantage of what was a busy turnpike road, it's now part of the Brunning & Price group. The beamed interconnected bar and dining areas have a lot of character, with cushioned Edwardian-style chairs and leather armchairs grouped around a wide mix of tables on rugs and pale floorboards. Prints and photos cover pale-painted walls, there are books on shelves, mirrors over several open fires, and elegant metal chandeliers, house plants and stone bottles. Friendly young staff serve St Austell Brunning & Price Traditional Bitter and several guests such as Hook Norton Hooky and North Cotswold Green Man IPA on handpump, real cider, 20 wines by the glass, more than 100 gins and numerous malt whiskies; background music and board games. The large garden has good quality seats and tables under a gazebo.

🍴 With vegetarian, vegan and gluten-free options, the good brasserie-style food includes sandwiches and 'light bites', chicken liver parfait with carrot chutney, crispy vegetable parcels with spiced mango dip, smoked haddock and salmon fishcake with tomato and spring onion salad, warm crispy beef salad with sweet chilli sauce, lotus root and roasted cashews, chicken, ham and leek pie with tarragon sauce, 10oz rump steak with dijon and tarragon butter and chips, and puddings such as triple chocolate brownie with chocolate sauce and hot waffle with toffee sauce, caramelised banana and honeycomb ice-cream. *Benchmark main dish: steak burger with coleslaw and fries £13.95. Two-course evening meal £22.00.*

Brunning & Price ~ Manager Dale Allison ~ Real ale ~ Open 11.30-11; 11.30-10 Sun ~ Bar food 12-9.30; 12-10 Fri, Sat; 12-9 Sun ~ Restaurant ~ Children welcome ~ Dogs allowed in bar

WELFORD-ON-AVON
Bell ⭐◗ ♀ ◗

SP1452   Map 4

(01789) 750353 – www.thebellwelford.co.uk
Off B439 W of Stratford; High Street; CV37 8EB

Warwickshire Dining Pub of the Year

Enjoyably civilised pub with appealing ancient interior, excellent carefully sourced food, a great range of drinks and a pretty garden with table service

Providing refreshment for over 300 years, this handsome and historic pub is proud to count Shakespeare as one of its former customers. All aspects of this particularly well run pub are highly and consistently praised, and the professional, hands-on licensees work very hard to achieve this. The attractive interior has plenty of signs of the building's venerable age, and is divided into five comfortable areas, each with its own character. These range from the cosy terracotta-painted bar to a light and airy gallery room with antique wood panelling, solid oak floor and contemporary Lloyd Loom chairs. Flagstone floors, stripped or well polished antique or period-style furniture and three good fires (one in an inglenook) add warmth and cosiness. You'll find Greene King Old Speckled Hen, Hobsons Best, Purity Pure Gold and Pure UBU on handpump and 16 wines (including prosecco, champagne and sweet wine) by the glass; background music. In summer, the virginia creeper-covered exterior is festooned with colourful hanging baskets. The delightful back garden has solid teak furniture, a vine-covered terrace, water features and gentle lighting (dogs on leads are allowed here). Disabled access.

🅾️ The appealing food using local, seasonal produce includes sandwiches and ploughman's, imaginative salads, crispy fried whitebait, deep-fried brie with apricot and ginger compote, horseshoe gammon with pineapple or free-range eggs, lasagne, mixed grill, haddock and chips, sirloin steak with a choice of sauce and chips, and home-made puddings such as chocolate torte with chocolate ice-cream and sticky toffee pudding with vanilla ice-cream. *Benchmark main dish: steak pie £16.95. Two-course evening meal £23.00.*

Free house ~ Licensees Colin and Teresa Ombler ~ Real ale ~ Open 12-3, 5.30-10; 12-close Sat; 11.45am-close Sun ~ Bar food 12-2.30, 5.30-9; 12-9 Sat; 12-8 Sun ~ Children welcome

WORDSLEY
Roe Deer ♀ 🍺

SO8887 Map 4

(01384) 958640 – www.brunningandprice.co.uk/roedeer
Lawnswood Road, off A449; NW of Stourbridge; DY7 5QJ

Substantial early 19th-c building with carefully decorated, linked rooms, a wide choice of interesting drinks, good modern food and seats in spreading grounds

It's lovely to watch the sunset framed by ancient trees from the terrace or interior of this grand Regency-style building with its sweeping views across parkland and fields beyond. Built in the 1810s and once a family home known as Lawnswood House, it's a stylish newcomer to the Brunning & Price group with a large, friendly and easy-going bar at its heart. There are wooden stools by the panelled counter, seats and tables on bare boards and a fine range of drinks that includes St Austell Brunning & Price Traditional Bitter and guests such as St Austell Proper Job, Timothy Taylor Landlord and Wye Valley HPA on handpump, craft beers, proper cider, 21 wines by the glass, 65 gins, 45 whiskies and a dozen rums. Staff are quick and helpful, while Poppy the sprocker spaniel welcomes dogs to the bar. Civilised dining rooms (including two private ones) fan out from here with high ceilings and huge casement windows, leather-backed and cushioned wooden chairs and button-back banquettes around tables of all sizes on parquet, flagstoned and carpeted floors, open fires, elegant metal chandeliers, large house plants, and walls hung with gilt-edged mirrors and hundreds of prints. Outside, there's a spacious stone terrace with teak tables and chairs under parasols, plenty of picnic-sets on grass and tasteful deer garden ornaments.

🍴 Rewarding food (catering for special diets) includes sandwiches and 'light bites', beetroot risotto with watercress and toasted grains, crispy duck salad with hoisin, watermelon and cashews, lamb and feta croquettes, cauliflower fritters with curried mayonnaise, cheshire cheese, potato and onion pie with red wine jus, honey-roasted cold ham with eggs and chips, South Indian-spiced sea bass fillets baked in banana leaf with coconut sauce, slow roast pork belly with black pudding and colcannon mash, and puddings such as rhubarb and coconut fool and bread and butter pudding with clotted cream. Brunch is served 9-11am daily. *Benchmark main dish: steak and ale pie with mash and buttered greens £14.50. Two-course evening meal £22.00.*

Brunning & Price ~ Manager Jon Astle-Rowe ~ Real ale ~ Open 9am-11pm; 9am-10.30pm Sun ~ Bar food 9-11am, 12-9.30pm; 9-11am, 12-10pm Fri, Sat; 9-11am, 12-9pm Sun ~ Restaurant ~ Children welcome ~ Dogs allowed in bar

Also Worth a Visit in Warwickshire

Besides the fully inspected pubs, you might like to try these pubs that have been recommended to us and described by readers. Do tell us what you think of them: feedback@goodguides.com

ALCESTER   SP0857
Turks Head (01789) 765948
High Street, across from church;
B49 5AD Updated old town pub with good friendly atmosphere; small front room and another off corridor, well kept Wye Valley and three guests, craft and continental beers, local cider and decent choice of wines and whiskies, enjoyable food from sharing plates and pizzas up including good fish and chips, children and dogs welcome, tables in walled garden behind (mostly covered), open all day, no food Sun evening.

ALDRIDGE   SK0500
Turtles Head (01922) 325635
Croft Parade; off High Street; WS9 8LY
Friendly micropub in row of 1960s shops; simple drinking area with leather sofa and some tub chairs on light wood floor, four well kept/priced ales, proper ciders and decent choice of other drinks, snacky food such as rolls and pork pies (you can also bring your own food), very popular with locals; children and dogs welcome, closed Mon, otherwise open all day (till 9pm Sun).

ALVESTON   SP2356
Ferry (01789) 269883
Ferry Lane; end of village, off B4086 Stratford–Wellesbourne; CV37 7QX
Comfortable beamed dining pub with enjoyable food and well kept ales such as Black Sheep and Wye Valley, friendly staff; special beer and wine events; children and dogs welcome, nice spot with seats out at front (some on raised deck), open all day Sat, closed Sun evening, Mon.

ARDENS GRAFTON   SP1153
Golden Cross (01789) 772420
Off A46 or B439 W of Stratford, corner of Wixford Road/Grafton Lane; B50 4LG
Modernised 18th-c stone pub; beamed bar with dark flagstones, mix of furniture including chapel chairs and pews around kitchen tables, woodburner in big old fireplace, ales such as Bombardier, eight wines by the glass and tasty uncomplicated home-made food including deals and themed nights, friendly helpful service, attractive lounge with unusual coffered

ceiling, big mullioned bay window and log fire; background music; children and dogs (in bar) welcome, wheelchair access, back garden with sturdy rustic furniture on terrace and picnic-sets on lawn, nice views, open (and food) all day.

ASTON CANTLOW   SP1360
Kings Head (01789) 488242
Village signed off A3400 NW of Stratford; B95 6HY Attractive black and white Tudor pub with low-beamed bar on right, old settles on flagstones and woodburner in large inglenook, quarry-tiled main room with window seats, big country tables and white-painted chairs and benches, local ales from Purity, real cider, over 30 gins and several wines by the glass, enjoyable food from sandwiches and pub favourites up, historically famous for its duck suppers, friendly efficient service; background music; children welcome, dogs in bar, garden with picnic-sets, kitchen garden and spreading chestnut tree, open (and food) all day.

BARSTON   SP2078
★**Bulls Head** (01675) 442830
From M42 junction 5, A4141 towards Warwick, first left, then signed down Barston Lane; B92 0JU Unassuming and unspoilt partly Tudor village pub; well kept ales such as Adnams, Purity and Sharps, popular traditional home-made food (not Sun evening) from sandwiches to specials, cheerful helpful staff, log fires, comfortable lounge with pictures and plates, oak-beamed bar and separate dining room; children and dogs welcome, good-sized secluded garden, open all day Fri-Sun.

BARSTON   SP1978
★**Malt Shovel** (01675) 443223
3 miles from M42 junction 5; A4141 towards Knowle, then first left into Jacobean Lane/Barston Lane; B92 0JP
Attractive village dining pub with French café-style blue shutters; light and airy bar with cream, tan and blue paintwork and terracotta floor tiles, dining chairs and scatter-cushioned pews around stripped-top tables, cheerful fruit and vegetable paintings and plenty of happy customers, Bombardier and Sharps Atlantic and Doom Bar on

handpump, 20 or so wines by the glass and several malt whiskies, exemplary service and enticing modern food, also converted barn restaurant; background music; children and dogs (in bar) welcome, sheltered back garden with picnic-sets and a weeping willow, terrace and verandah with teak furniture, open all day, till 7pm Sun.

BINLEY WOODS SP3977
Roseycombe (024) 7654 1022
Rugby Road; CV3 2AY Warm and friendly 1930s pub with wide choice of bargain home-made food (not Mon evening, Sun), Bass and Greene King IPA; children welcome, big garden, plenty of parking, open all day Fri-Sun.

BIRMINGHAM SP0788
★ **Bartons Arms** (0121) 333 5988
High Street, Aston (A34); B6 4UP Magnificent listed Edwardian landmark standing alone among busy roads and modern development; impressive richly decorated linked rooms from the palatial to the snug, original tilework murals, stained glass and mahogany, decorative fireplaces, sweeping stairs to handsome upstairs rooms, well kept Oakham ales and interesting bottled beers from ornate island bar with snob screens, reasonably priced Thai food (vegan options available), good friendly service; regular live music; open all day.

BIRMINGHAM SP0686
Brasshouse (0121) 633 3383
Broad Street; B1 2HP Spacious bank conversion with enjoyable good value food from tapas, burgers and pizzas up, various deals, well kept Marstons-related ales and guests, good range of other drinks including craft beers, gins and cocktails, efficient friendly service; TV and games machines; children welcome in dining area till 6pm, seats out overlooking canal, handy for National Sea Life Centre, International Convention Centre and Symphony Hall, open all day (till 1am Fri, 2am Sat).

BIRMINGHAM SP0688
Clifden (0121) 523 7515
Great Hampton Street (Jewellery Quarter); B18 6AA New name (they dropped the 'Lord') and new look for this craft beer bar (mainly from Laine) in city centre; leather and wooden dining chairs around polished wood tables, interesting collection of urban street art including Banksy prints, bustling atmosphere, generous food from pizzas and burgers to Sun roasts (vegan options), friendly service; sports TVs (outside too), quiz and weekend DJs; plenty of beer garden-style seating in part-covered

courtyard with table tennis and table football, open all day (till 2am Fri and Sat).

BIRMINGHAM SP0786
Old Contemptibles (0121) 200 3310
Edmund Street; B3 2HB Spacious Edwardian corner pub (Nicholsons) with lofty ceiling and lots of woodwork, good choice of real ales and enjoyable well priced food, friendly efficient young staff; upstairs loos; no children, handy central location near Snow Hill station, limited outdoor seating, open all day (till 6pm Sun).

BIRMINGHAM SP0784
Old Moseley Arms (0121) 440 1954
Tindal Street; B12 9QU Tucked-away red-brick Victorian pub in Balsall Heath; five well kept ales such as Church End, Enville and Wye Valley (regular festivals), nice selection of gins and good value authentic Indian food (evenings and all day Sun); sports TVs, darts, pool; outside seating area, handy for Edgbaston cricket ground, open all day, closes late at weekends.

BIRMINGHAM SP0686
Pint Shop (0121) 236 9039
Bennetts Hill; B2 5SN Sister to the Pint Shop in Cambridge (see Main Entries); stylish refurbishment with bustling bar and upstairs restaurant, half a dozen real ales and 21 craft beers (listed on blackboard), also good choice of wines and around 100 gins, enjoyable food from open kitchen including burgers, pies, kebabs and some vegan choices, friendly knowledgeable staff; background music, sports TV; dogs welcome in bar, open (and food) all day, closes late Thurs-Sat.

BIRMINGHAM SP0384
Plough (0121) 427 3678
High Street, Harborne; B17 9NT Popular place with spacious modern interior (one or two steps); enjoyable food including stone-baked pizzas and chargrilled burgers, regular offers, well kept ales such as Purity and Wye Valley, plenty of wines by the glass and 50 or so whiskies, good coffee, friendly staff; background music, TVs and various events such as wine/gin tastings; well behaved children welcome, paved garden with covered area, open (and food) all day from 8am (9am weekends) for breakfast.

BIRMINGHAM SP0686
Post Office Vaults (0121) 643 7354
New Street/Pinfold Street; B2 4BA Two entrances to this simple downstairs bar serving 13 interesting ciders/perries, eight real ales including a house beer from Kinver (First Class Stamp) and over

---

If you stay overnight in an inn or hotel, they are allowed to serve you an alcoholic drink at any hour of the day or night.

350 international bottled beers, friendly knowledgeable staff, no food but can bring your own (plates and cutlery provided); bar billiards; handy for New Street station, open all day.

BIRMINGHAM SP0686

★ **Purecraft Bar & Kitchen**
(0121) 237 5666
Waterloo Street; B2 5TJ Attractive industrial-chic bar from Purity brewery with excellent range of eight cask and 16 craft beers, interesting bottled range too along with cocktails and a dozen wines by the glass, open kitchen serving good food all day (not Sun evening) from sandwiches and sausage rolls up (food/beer pairings), friendly helpful service; children welcome, open all day, closed Sun and Mon.

BIRMINGHAM SP0687

★ **Rose Villa** (0121) 236 7910
By clocktower in Jewellery Quarter (Warstone Lane/Vyse Street); B18 6JW Well preserved 1920s red-brick pub (Grade II listed); front saloon with gorgeous stained-glass windows leading through to splendid little skylit bar with floor-to-ceiling green tiles and massive tiled arch over fireplace, quirky touches here and there such as antler chandeliers and a red phone box, four or five well kept ales including Sharps Doom Bar, craft beers, ciders, cocktails and over 100 vodkas, reasonably priced food from American diner menu, also themed nights and deals; live music and DJs Fri, Sat night; children and dogs welcome, open all day, till late Fri and Sat.

BIRMINGHAM SP0686

Tap & Spile (0121) 632 5602
Gas Street; B1 2JT Refurbished canalside pub on three floors; main bar/restaurant downstairs opening on to the towpath, three real ales, proper cider, decent range of wines and enjoyable good value food including grills and pizzas, another bar upstairs (open till 4am) and cocktail lounge on top floor; children and dogs welcome, picnic-sets out by Gas Street canal basin, open all day.

BIRMINGHAM SP0686

★ **Wellington** (0121) 200 3115
,Bennetts Hill; B2 5SN Traditionally renovated high-ceilinged pub with 17 well kept interesting ales (listed on TV screens) including three from Black Country, real ciders, bottled beers and good range of gins/whiskies, they also have a vegan drinks menu and sell snuff, experienced landlord and friendly staff, no food but plates and cutlery provided if you bring your own, more room and roof terrace upstairs; regular beer festivals and quiz nights, folk

evening first and third Tues of month, no children, darts; open all day.

BRIERLEY HILL SO9286

★ **Vine** (01384) 78293
B4172 between A461 and (nearer) A4100; immediately after the turn into Delph Road; DY5 2TN Popular Black Country pub (aka the Bull & Bladder) offering a true taste of the West Midlands; down-to-earth welcome and friendly chatty locals in meandering series of rooms, each different in character, traditional front bar with wall benches, comfortable extended snug has solidly built red plush seats and there's a tartan-decorated back bar, well kept/priced Bathams from next-door brewery, a couple of simple low-priced lunchtime dishes, cobs and snacks the rest of the day; quiz nights, TV, games machine, darts and dominoes; children and dogs welcome, tables in backyard, open all day.

BROOM SP0853

★ **Broom Tavern** (01789) 778199
High Street; off B439 in Bidford; B50 4HL Spacious 16th-c brick and timber village pub, relaxed and welcoming, with good interesting food from chef-owners including weekly themed specials and excellent Sun roasts, four well kept ales such as Purity and Wye Valley, well chosen wine list with several by the glass, good attentive (but not intrusive) service, main room divided into two parts, one with cottage-style tables and chairs, the other with oak furniture, black beams and log fire, also a snug perfect for a group of diners; Mon quiz; children welcome, dogs in lower bar area, tables out on grass either side, handy for Ragley Hall, open all day, closed Mon, no food Sun evening.

CHERINGTON SP2836

Cherington Arms (01608) 685183
Off A3400; CV36 5HS 17th-c stone-built village pub; popular food (not Mon) from French landlord-chef including open sandwiches, pub favourites, blackboard specials and Sun carvery, well kept Hook Norton and a guest, welcoming efficient staff, beamed bar with log fire, separate dining room; regular live music; children and dogs welcome, tables on terrace and in big garden bordering River Stour, good nearby walks, open all day Fri and Sat, till 6pm Sun, closed Mon lunchtime.

CLAVERDON SP2064

★ **Red Lion** (01926) 842291
Station Road; B4095 towards Warwick; CV35 8PE Upmarket beamed Tudor dining pub with enjoyable food from sharing plates up, well kept Hook Norton and several wines

---

All Guide inspections are anonymous. Anyone claiming to be a Good Pub Guide inspector is a fraud. Please let us know.

by the glass, friendly efficient staff, log fires in linked rooms, back area with country views over heated terrace and gardens; children welcome, no dogs inside, closed Sun evening.

COVENTRY SP3279
Old Windmill (024) 7625 1717
Spon Street; CV1 3BA Friendly 15th-c pub with lots of tiny rooms (known locally as Ma Brown's); exposed beams in uneven ceilings, inglenook woodburner, seven well kept ales including Theakstons and Timothy Taylors, real ales, good local pork pies; juke box and occasional live music, sports TV, darts; dogs welcome, closed Mon lunchtime, otherwise open all day from noon (till midnight Fri, Sat), busy at weekends.

COVENTRY SP3379
Town Wall (024) 7622 0963
Bond Street, among car parks behind Belgrade Theatre; CV1 4AH Busy 19th-c city-centre local surviving among new-builds; eight well kept ales including Bass, Brains Rev James and Theakstons, Weston's cider, enjoyable good value pub food (not Sun evening, Mon) from lunchtime sandwiches up, unspoilt basic front bar and tiny snug, etched windows, bigger back lounge with actor/playwright photographs and pictures of old Coventry, open fires; big-screen sports TV, juke box; no children, dogs welcome in bar, closed Mon lunchtime, otherwise open all day.

EARLSWOOD SP1274
Blue Bell Cider House
(01564) 702328 *Warings Green Road, not far from M42 junction 4; B94 6BP* Welcoming 19th-c red-brick pub by Stratford Canal; roomy lounge, cosy bar and conservatory, good value generous food including popular Sun carvery, own-brew organic beers plus guests, traditional ciders, friendly helpful staff; open mike nights and Weds quiz; children and dogs welcome, plenty of outside seating, moorings, open all day.

EASENHALL SP4679
Golden Lion (01788) 833577
Main Street; CV23 0JA Bar in 16th-c part of busy hotel; white-painted beams, half-panelling and log fire, some original wattle and daub and fine 17th-c carved bench depicting the 12 apostles, a couple of real ales and good food including cook your own meat on a hot rock and Sun carvery, prompt friendly service, more formal restaurant; background music; children and small dogs welcome, disabled access/loos, tables on side terrace and spacious lawn, 17 well equipped bedrooms (some with four-posters), attractive walks, open (and food) all day.

EDGE HILL SP3747
★**Castle** (01295) 670255
Off A422; OX15 6DJ Crenellated octagonal tower built in 1742 as Gothic folly

(marks where Charles I raised his standard at the Battle of Edgehill); major renovation creating bar and four dining areas, plenty of original features including arched windows and doorways, beams and stone fireplaces, fantastic views (some floor-to-ceiling windows), good food (not Sun evening), also deli bar for sandwiches, coffee and afternoon teas (must book), well kept Hook Norton ales, Weston's cider, friendly helpful young staff; downstairs lavatories; children welcome, seats in lovely large garden with more outstanding views, beautiful Compton Wynyates manor house nearby, four bedrooms, parking can be tricky at busy times, open all day Sat, till 8pm Sun.

ETTINGTON SP2748
Chequers (01789) 740387
Banbury Road (A422); CV37 7SR Refurbished 18th-c dining pub; good fair priced food from sharing plates and pub favourites up (not Sun evening), three real ales including a beer badged for them, real cider, a dozen wines by the glass and some interesting gins and cocktails, efficient friendly service, modern décor in bar and restaurant areas, upholstered chairs around pale wooden tables on wood-strip flooring, lots of pictures and some bold floral wallpaper; children welcome, no dogs inside, attractive back garden, open all day Sat, till 8pm Sun, closed Mon.

FARNBOROUGH SP4349
Kitchen (01295) 690615
Off A423 N of Banbury; OX17 1DZ Golden-stone dining pub in NT village; bar with painted beams, wood floor and cushioned window seats, red woodburner in big fireplace, saddle- and tractor-seat stools at blue-panelled counter serving Purity ales and nice wines by the glass, good seasonal food from interesting if not especially cheap menu, some produce from own kitchen garden, two-room dining area, friendly helpful staff; background music; children and dogs (in bar) welcome, neat sloping garden with blue picnic-sets and pizza oven, local walks, open all day weekends, closed Tues, Weds and lunchtime Thurs.

FENNY COMPTON SP4152
Merrie Lion (01295) 771134
Brook Street; CV47 2YH Early 18th-c beamed village pub with four well kept beers (including one badged for them), real cider, decent range of wines and good freshly made food from pubby choices up, friendly welcoming atmosphere; fortnightly Weds quiz and other events; dogs welcome, tables outside, handy for Burton Dassett Hills Country Park, open all day.

FILLONGLEY SP2787
Cottage (01676) 540599
Black Hall Lane; CV7 8EG Popular country dining pub on village outskirts; good

value food including vegetarian menu, OAP lunch and early evening deal, beers such as Bass and St Austell, friendly service; back terrace and lawn overlooking fields, closes 6pm Sun evening.

FIVE WAYS
SP2270

★**Case Is Altered** (01926) 484206
Follow Rowington signs at junction roundabout off A4177/A4141 N of Warwick, then right into Case Lane; CV35 7JD Convivial unspoilt old cottage licensed for over three centuries; well kept ales including Old Pie Factory and Wye Valley served by friendly long-serving landlady, no food (can bring your own sandwiches), simple small main bar with fine old poster of Lucas Blackwell & Arkwright Brewery (now flats), clock with hours spelling out Thornleys Ale (another defunct brewery), and just a few sturdy old-fashioned tables and a couple of stout leather-covered settles facing each other over spotless tiles, roaring log fire, modest little back room with old bar billiards table (takes sixpences); no children, dogs or mobile phones; full disabled access, stone table on little brick courtyard, closes 7.30pm Sun.

FLECKNOE
SP5163

Old Olive Bush (01788) 891134
Off A425 W of Daventry; CV23 8AT Unspoilt chatty little Edwardian pub in quiet photogenic village; enjoyable traditional food cooked by landlady (Weds-Sat evenings, Sun lunchtime), well kept changing ales and decent wines, open fire in bar with stripped-wood floor, steps up to games room (table skittles), small dining room with etched windows and another fire; Thurs quiz, summer beer festival; children welcome, pretty garden, closed Tues and weekday lunchtimes.

FRANKTON
SP4270

Friendly (01926) 632430
Just over a mile S of B4453 Leamington Spa–Rugby; Main Street; CV23 9NY Popular 16th-c village pub living up to its name; three well kept ales including Greene King IPA and good reasonably priced traditional food (not Sun evening, Mon), two low-ceilinged rooms, open fire; children and dogs welcome, open all day weekends, closed Mon lunchtime.

GAYDON
SP3654

Malt Shovel (01926) 641221
Under a mile from M40 junction 12; B4451 into village, then over roundabout and across B4100; Church Road; CV35 OET Warm welcome at this bustling village pub; varnished mahogany floorboards and some carpeting linking entrance to bar, main area with high-pitched ceiling, milk churns and earthenware in lit above servery, woodburner, steps up to space with comfortable sofas and big stained-glass

window, dining room, five well kept ales, real cider and enjoyable food served by friendly staff; background music, TV; children and dogs (in bar) welcome, open (and food) all day, kitchen shuts 6pm Sun.

HALESOWEN
SO9683

Waggon & Horses (0121) 585 9699
Stourbridge Road; B63 3TU Popular refurbished and extended 19th-c red-brick corner pub; Black Country ales along with plenty of interesting guests (tasting trays available) and five real ciders, friendly knowledgeable staff, snacky food such as cobs and pork pies, sloping floor in narrow main bar, open fire; dogs welcome in some parts, open all day.

HAMPTON LUCY
SP2557

Boars Head (01789) 840533
Church Street, E of Stratford; CV35 8BE Welcoming two-room village pub with five changing ales, reasonably priced wines and enjoyable good value pubby food (all day Sat, not Sun evening), friendly helpful staff, updated interior with beams and log fires; darts, children and dogs welcome, seats in enclosed back courtyard, near lovely church and well placed for Charlecote Park (NT) and M40, open all day.

HARBOROUGH MAGNA
SP4779

Old Lion (01788) 833238
3 miles from M6 junction 1; B4112 Pailton Road; CV23 0HQ Stylishly modernised village pub; good food from pub favourites and pizzas to steaks, friendly attentive staff, well kept ales, nice choice of wines and over 80 gins; some live music, board games; children and dogs (in bar) welcome, terrace seating, open all day Thurs-Sat, closes 3pm Sun.

HATTON
SP2367

★**Falcon** (01926) 484281
Birmingham Road, Haseley (4.6 miles from M40 junction 15, A46 towards Warwick, then left on A4177 and keep on past Hatton); CV35 7HA Modernised dining pub with rooms around island bar, lots of stripped brickwork and low beams, tiled and oak-planked floors, good moderately priced food from sandwiches, sharing boards and pub favourites up, themed nights and deals, friendly service, well kept ales, nice choice of wines by the glass, gins and cocktails, barn-style back restaurant; children and dogs (in bar) welcome, disabled facilities, garden with heated covered terrace, bedrooms in adjacent building, open (and food) all day.

HATTON
SP2467

Hatton Arms (01926) 492427
A4177, by Grand Union Canal; CV35 7JJ Former 18th-c coaching inn (part of the Hatton Estate) above flight of 21 locks known as 'Stairway to Heaven', views from

sunny balcony and huge garden; spacious modernised interior with linked rooms, some beams and log fire, good popular food using Estate produce including sandwiches and pub favourites, also vegan and gluten-free menus, real ales such as Hook Norton, Purity and Wye Valley, ten wines by the glass, efficient friendly service; children welcome, good walks nearby, moorings, open (and food) all day, kitchen closes 7.30pm Sun.

HENLEY-IN-ARDEN SP1566
Bluebell (01564) 793049
High Street (A3400, off M40 junction 16); B95 5AT Impressive timber-framed dining pub with fine coach entrance; rambling old beamed and flagstoned interior with contemporary furnishings creating stylish but relaxed atmosphere, big fireplace, three well kept ales such as Purity, a dozen wines by the glass and highly regarded food with Mediterranean and Middle Eastern influences cooked by new chef-owner, friendly staff, coffee and afternoon teas; background music; children welcome until 8.30pm, dogs allowed in one part, tables out at front and on narrow back terrace, closed Mon except bank holidays, otherwise open all day, shuts 7.30pm Sun.

KENILWORTH SP2872
Clarendon Arms (01926) 852017
Castle Hill; CV8 1NB Family-run pub opposite castle and under same ownership as next-door Harringtons restaurant; several rooms off long bare-boards bar, up to five well kept ales and tasty reasonably priced pub food including range of burgers, cheerful staff, largish peaceful upstairs dining room; children and dogs (in bar) welcome, metal tables on small raised terrace, daytime car park fee deducted from food bill, open (and food) all day weekends.

KENILWORTH SP2872
Cross (01926) 853840
New Street; CV8 2EZ Smart 19th-c Michelin-starred restaurant-pub; first class skilfully cooked food (not cheap) including tasting menus and set lunch (Tues-Sun), lots of wines by the glass from impressive list, fine range of spirits and a couple of real ales such as Bombardier, friendly well informed staff, open-plan split-level interior with view into kitchen, front bar for drinkers; children welcome, terrace and small garden, no food Sun evening.

KENILWORTH SP2872
Old Bakery (01926) 864111
High Street, off A452; CV8 1LZ Small hotel's cosy two-room bar (popular with older customers); four well kept ales including Wye Valley HPA and good choice of wines, whiskies, gins and coffee, food Mon and Weds evenings only (till 7.30pm); disabled access to the rear, children and dogs welcome, 14 comfortable bedrooms, good English breakfast, open all day.

KENILWORTH SP2872
★ **Virgins & Castle** (01926) 853737
High Street; CV8 1LY Small snugs by entrance corridor and maze of intimate rooms off inner servery; flagstones, heavy beams and lots of woodwork, coal fire, two well kept Everards ales and guests, wines, gins, tea and coffee and a 'temperance bar' for non-acoholic options, good reasonably priced food including new breakfast menu (9am-noon), friendly service, games bar upstairs; children allowed in eating areas, dogs in some parts, disabled facilities, tables in sheltered garden, parking close by can be tricky, open all day.

LADBROKE SP4158
Bell (01926) 811224
Signed off A423 S of Southam; CV47 2BY Beamed country pub set back from the road; smallish bar with tub chairs by log fire, snug off with library wallpaper and another fire in little brick fireplace, three well kept ales and plenty of wines by the glass, very good food from pub favourites and grills up, also gluten-free choices and weekday set menu, airy restaurant with light oak flooring, friendly young staff; background music; children and dogs (in bar) welcome, a few picnic-sets out in front and on side grass, pleasant surroundings, closed Sun evening, Mon and Tues.

LAPWORTH SP1871
★ **Boot** (01564) 782464
Old Warwick Road; B4439 Hockley Heath-Warwick – 2.8 miles from M40 junction 1, but from southbound carriageway only, and return only to northbound; B94 6JU Popular upmarket dining pub near Stratford Canal; good range of food from enterprising menu, efficient cheerful young staff, well kept Purity and Sharps, upscale wine list with over 20 by the glass, stripped beams and dark panelling, big antique hunting prints, cushioned pews and bucket chairs on ancient quarry tiles and bare boards, warm fire, charming low-raftered upstairs dining room; background music; children and dogs welcome, tables on side terrace (some under extendable canopy), more seating on grass beyond with tipi, nice walks, open all day, food till 7.30pm Sun.

Please tell us if any pub deserves to be upgraded to a featured entry – and why: feedback@goodguides.com, or (no stamp needed) Freepost THE GOOD PUB GUIDE, Random House Publishing, 20 Vauxhall Bridge Road, London SW1V 2SA.

LAPWORTH SP1970
Navigation (01564) 783337
Old Warwick Road (B4439 SE); B94 6NA
Modernised beamed pub by the Grand Union
Canal; slate-floor bar with woodburner,
bare-boards snug and restaurant, well
kept Purity, Timothy Taylors, Wadworths
and a guest, unusually Guinness also on
handpump, decent wines and enjoyable
reasonably priced food from sandwiches
and other bar choices up, good Sun roasts;
children welcome, dogs in bar, covered
terrace and waterside garden, moorings,
handy for Packwood House and Baddesley
Clinton (both NT), open all day, food all day
weekends including breakfast from 10am.

LEAMINGTON SPA SP3165
Cricketers Arms (01926) 881293
Archery Road; CV31 3PT Friendly town
local opposite bowling greens; enjoyable
fairly priced food using meat from good
local butcher including popular Sun roasts
(till 6pm), well kept ales such as Timothy
Taylors from central bar, Weston's cider,
some panelling and cricketing memorabilia,
comfortable banquettes, open fires;
fortnightly quiz Mon, poker night Weds,
occasional live music, sports TV, darts;
children and dogs welcome, heated back
terrace, open all day.

LEAMINGTON SPA SP3265
★ Drawing Board (01926) 330636
Newbold Street; CV32 4HN Set over
two floors with quirky décor including
framed vintage comic books, pop art and
neon lighting, leather sofas, mismatched
dining chairs and rustic tables mixed with
contemporary furniture, house plants,
antlers, woodburning stoves and even
a bike; Old Pie Factory Elephant Wash,
Purity Bunny Hop and a guest, craft beers,
real cider, 16 wines by the glass, separate
bottle shop; creative food (not Sun evening)
from sandwiches and tapas up including
vegetarian, vegan and gluten-free options,
cheery atmosphere with hard-working
landlord and friendly young staff; background
music, TV, retro arcade games machine,
board games, old-fashioned children's
annuals; children and dogs welcome,
disabled access, open all day.

LEAMINGTON SPA SP3166
★ Star & Garter (01926) 359960
Warwick Street; CV32 5LL Bustling open-
plan town-centre pub (Peach group); bare-
boards bar with upholstered wall seats, blue
leather banquettes, red leather armchairs
and small wooden stools around mix of
tables, well kept real ales such as Greene
King Abbot and IPA, and Purity UBU, lots of
wines by the glass and good selection of gins/
cocktails, enjoyable food from sandwiches/
snacks to Sun roasts including vegetarian,
vegan and gluten-free dishes, open-kitchen

dining area with booths down one side,
steps up to second bar, friendly helpful
staff; background music; children and dogs
welcome, open all day.

LEEK WOOTTON SP2868
Anchor (01926) 853355
Warwick Road; CV35 7QX Pub-restaurant
with popular fairly pubby food including
range of burgers and daily specials, well kept
ales such as Bass, Hook Norton and Purity,
good selection of wines and soft drinks,
friendly service; background music; children
welcome, long garden behind with play area,
open all day Fri-Sun.

LIGHTHORNE SP3455
Antelope (01926) 651188
*Old School Lane, Bishops Hill; a mile
SW of B4100 N of Banbury; CV35 0BX*
Attractive early 18th-c stone-built pub
in pretty village setting; two neatly kept
comfortable bars and separate dining area,
beams, flagstones, exposed stonework and
big open fire, well kept Greene King IPA,
Sharps Doom Bar and a couple of guests,
enjoyable food from sandwiches up including
a vegan menu, takeaways, friendly efficient
service; children and dogs welcome, picnic-
sets out by well and on small grassy area,
open (and food) all day Fri-Sun.

LITTLE COMPTON SP2530
★ Red Lion (01608) 674397
*Off A44 Moreton-in-Marsh to Chipping
Norton; GL56 0RT* Low-beamed 16th-c
Cotswold-stone inn; well liked food cooked by
landlord-chef from fairly traditional menu,
Donnington ales and good choice of wines
by the glass, friendly helpful service, snug
alcoves, inglenook woodburner; darts and
pool in public bar; some live music, Weds
bingo; well behaved children welcome, dogs
in garden only, white-painted metal furniture
in pretty garden, comfortable bedroom, open
all day Fri and Sat, till 6pm Sun, closed Mon
and Tues.

LONG ITCHINGTON SP4164
Two Boats (01926) 812640
*A423 N of Southam, by Grand Union
Canal; CV47 9QZ* Traditional brick-built
pub with lovely canal views from window
seats in long picture-filled main room,
enjoyable generously served food from
good value pubby menu, four well kept
ales including Bombardier and Youngs,
friendly helpful staff; TV and darts in side
bar; children and dogs welcome, waterfront
terrace and moorings, open all day, no food
Sun evening.

LONGFORD SP3684
Greyhound (024) 7636 3046
*Sutton Stop, off Black Horse Road/
Grange Road; junction of Coventry
and North Oxford canals; CV6 6DF*
Cosy 19th-c canalside pub with plenty of

character; up to five well kept ales and good range of enjoyable food including home-made pies, friendly helpful staff, woodburner and two-way coal fire, unusual tiny snug; occasional live music; children and dogs (in bar) welcome, tables on attractive waterside terrace, nice spot (if you ignore the pylons), open all day.

LOWSONFORD SP1868

Fleur de Lys (01564) 782431

Off B4439 Hockley Heath–Warwick; Lapworth Street; B95 5HJ Prettily placed old pub by Stratford Canal; linked beamed rooms of varying sizes, log fires, enjoyable fairly priced food including range of pies and gluten-free menu, Greene King Abbot and IPA and a couple of guests, plenty of wines by the glass, cocktails, friendly helpful service; children and dogs (in lower bar) welcome, large waterside garden with play area, open (and food) all day, till 10pm (8pm) Sun.

LYE SO9284

★Windsor Castle (01384) 897809

Stourbridge Road (corner A458/A4036; car park in Pedmore Road just above traffic lights – don't be tempted to use the next-door restaurant's parking!); DY9 7DG Interesting range of well kept beers from impressive row of handpumps including own Sadlers ales (brewery tours available); central flagstoned part with bar stools by counter and window shelf overlooking road, several other rooms including 1920s-inspired gin bar, enjoyable home-cooked food (not Sun evening), burger night Weds, friendly service; children and dogs (in bar) welcome, disabled facilities, terrace and verandah seating, four bedrooms, handy for Lye station, open all day (from 9am Sat for breakfast), closed Mon.

NAPTON SP4560

Folly (01926) 815185

Off A425 towards Priors Hardwick; Folly Lane, by locks; CV47 8NZ Beamed red-brick pub in lovely spot on Oxford Canal by Napton Locks and Folly Bridge (113); three bars on different levels, mix of furnishings and two big fireplaces (one with woodburner), lots of interesting bric-a-brac, pictures and old photographs, good straightforward home-made food (not Sun evening), well kept ales including Hook Norton; sports TV, children and dogs welcome (left-hand bar only), open all day.

NETHER WHITACRE SP2292

Gate (01675) 481292

Gate Lane; B46 2DS Welcoming traditional community pub; good home-cooked food

including themed evenings, seven well kept Marstons-related ales, log-fire bar, lounge and dining conservatory; games room with pool and darts; occasional quiz nights; children and dogs (in bar) welcome, garden picnic-sets and play area, open all day, food all day weekends (till 7pm Sun).

NETHERTON SO9488

★Old Swan (01384) 253075

Halesowen Road (A459 just S of centre); DY2 9PY Victorian tavern full of traditional character and known locally as Ma Pardoe's after former long-serving landlady; wonderfully unspoilt front bar with big swan centrepiece in patterned enamel ceiling, engraved mirrors, traditional furnishings and old-fashioned cylinder stove, other rooms including cosy back snug and more modern lounge, own well priced ales and enjoyable good value bar food, upstairs restaurant (Sun lunchtime only); no under-16s, dogs allowed in bar, open (and food) all day.

NORTON LINDSEY SP2263

New Inn (01926) 258411

Main Street; CV35 8JA Popular village pub owned by the local community; enjoyable reasonably priced food (not Sun evening, Mon or Tues) including blackboard specials, booking advised, well kept ales such as Greene King, Purity and Windmill, good range of gins, coffee, friendly accommodating staff; monthly quiz; children and dogs welcome, back garden, open all day weekends (till 8pm Sun).

OFFCHURCH SP3665

★Stag (01926) 425801

N of Welsh Road, off A425 at Radford Semele; CV33 9AQ Popular 16th-c thatched and beamed village dining pub; oak-floored bar with log fires, ales such as Hook Norton and Purity, a dozen wines by the glass and good food (not Sun evening) from interesting menu including excellent steaks, friendly efficient young staff, more formal cosy restaurant areas with bold wallpaper, striking fabrics, animal heads and big mirrors; children and dogs (in bar) welcome, nice garden with rattan-style furniture on terrace, open all day.

OLD HILL SO9686

Waterfall (0121) 559 9198

Waterfall Lane; B64 6RG Unpretentious two-room local with tankards and jugs hanging from boarded ceiling, well kept Holdens and guests, good straightforward low-priced food, friendly atmosphere; dogs welcome, seats on small raised front area and in back garden, open all day.

A star symbol before the name of a pub shows exceptional character and appeal. It doesn't mean extra comfort. Even quite a basic pub can win a star, if it's individual enough.

OXHILL SP3149

★ **Peacock** (01295) 688060

Off A422 Stratford–Banbury; CV35 0QU
Popular stone-built pub in pretty village; good
varied menu including blackboard specials
(no food Sun evening), friendly attentive
staff, four changing ales and good selection of
wines by the glass, cosy beamed bar with big
solid tables and woodburner, half-panelled
bare-boards dining room; background music;
children and dogs (in bar) welcome, pleasant
back garden, closed Mon, otherwise open
all day.

RATLEY SP3847

Rose & Crown (01295) 678148

Off A422 NW of Banbury; OX15 6DS
Ancient golden-stone Grade-II listed pub,
charming and cosy, with five well kept ales
such as St Austell Tribute Bitter and Wye
Valley Butty Bach, blackboard list of wines,
enjoyable good value food (not Sun evening,
Mon) including daily specials, friendly
efficient staff, carpeted black-beamed bar
with woodburner each end, traditional
furniture and window seats, cosy snug;
background music, darts; children, walkers
and dogs welcome, tables on sunny split-level
terrace, aunt sally, near lovely church in
sleepy village, handy for Upton House (NT),
open all day Fri-Sun, closed Mon.

ROWINGTON SP1969

Tom o' the Wood (01564) 782252

*Off B4439 N of Rowington, following
Lowsonford sign; Finwood Road;
CV35 7DH* Spaciously modernised and
extended canalside pub; good home-cooked
food (not Sun evening) from sharing baskets
and stone-baked pizzas up, themed evenings
including Thurs pie night, well kept Greene
King IPA and guests, Weston's Rosie's Pig
cider, friendly staff, conservatory; live
music; children and dogs (not in restaurant)
welcome, tables on terrace and side lawn,
open all day (till 8pm Sun).

RUGBY SP5075

Merchants (01788) 571119

Little Church Street; CV21 3AN Open-
plan pub tucked away near main shopping
area, cheerfully busy, with nine well kept ales
including Nethergate, Oakham and Purity,
real ciders and huge selection of Belgian and
other bottled imports, regular beer/cider/
gin festivals, low-priced lunchtime food
including range of burgers, quite dark inside
with beams, bare boards and flagstones, lots
of pump clips and interesting breweriana;
background music (occasionally live),
monthly quiz, sports TVs; open all day, till
1am Fri, Sat.

RUGBY SP5075

Seven Stars (01788) 535478

Albert Square; CV21 2SH Traditional
19th-c red-brick local with 11 well kept ales
such as Everards, Gun Dog and Oakham,
friendly landlord and staff, main bar, lounge,
snug and conservatory, rugby memorabilia,
snacky food including home-made scotch
eggs, pie and pint night Weds; sports TV, darts
and board games; children (till 7.30pm)
and dogs welcome, café-style seating in part-
covered courtyard with murals, closed Mon
lunchtime, otherwise open all day.

RUSHALL SK0300

Manor Arms 07428 521730

Park Road, off A461; WS4 1LG
Interesting low-beamed 18th-c pub (on much
older foundations) by Rushall Canal; three
rooms in contrasting styles, one with big
inglenook, well kept Banks's ales from pumps
fixed to the wall (there's no counter), simple
snacky food, friendly staff; no card payments;
children, walkers and dogs welcome,
waterside garden with moorings, next to Park
Lime Pits nature reserve, open all day.

SEDGLEY SO9293

★ **Beacon** (01902) 883380

*Bilston Street; A463, off A4123
Wolverhampton–Dudley; DY3 1JE*
Plain old brick pub with own good Sarah
Hughes ales from traditional Victorian tower
brewery behind; cheery locals in simple
quarry-tiled drinking corridor, little snug on
left with wall settles, imposing green-tiled
marble fireplace and glazed serving hatch,
blackened range in sparse tap room on right,
also a dark-panelled lounge with sturdy red
leather wall settles and dramatic sea prints,
plant-filled conservatory (no seats), little
food apart from cobs; no credit cards or dogs;
children allowed in some parts including
garden with play area.

SHIPSTON-ON-STOUR SP2540

★ **George** (01608) 661453

High Street; CV36 4AJ Deservedly
popular town-centre hotel with splendid
Georgian façade; spacious opened-up interior
with several linked bar and dining areas
with appealing modern décor, bare brick
walls and wooden floors, enjoyable food
from reasonably compact menu including
lunchtime sandwiches, Brakspears Gravity
and Oxford Gold and a guest, over a dozen
wines by the glass, good range of other drinks
including Cotswolds Gin and Tonic, efficient
helpful service and easy-going atmosphere;
children and dogs (in bar) welcome, teak
tables and chairs in courtyard behind, 15 well
appointed bedrooms, open (and food) all day,
closes 9.30pm Sun.

SHIPSTON-ON-STOUR SP2540

Horseshoe (01608) 662190

Church Street; CV36 4AP Popular 17th-c
timbered local (former coaching inn)
refurbished under present management;
two-room carpeted bar with cushioned wall
seats, scrubbed tables and open fire, North
Cotswold and Wye Valley, Hogan's Panking

Pole cider, enjoyable traditional food including Sun carvery, can eat in bar or end dining room; children and dogs welcome, café-style tables and chairs on back terrace, open all day Fri-Sun, closed Mon.

SHUSTOKE SP2290
★ **Griffin** (01675) 481205
Church Road, a mile E of village; 5 miles from M6 junction 4; A446 towards Tamworth, then right on to B4114 straight through Coleshill; B46 2LB Unpretentious country local with ten well kept changing ales including own Freestyle (brewed in next-door barn), farm cider and country wines, standard lunchtime bar food (not Sun); cheery low-beamed L-shaped bar with log fires in two stone fireplaces (one a big inglenook), fairly simple décor, some elm-topped sewing trestles and a nice old-fashioned settle, conservatory (children allowed here); dogs welcome, picnic-sets on back grass with distant views of Birmingham, large terrace, play area and summer marquee (live music, beer/cider festivals), camping field, open all day Fri-Sun.

SHUSTOKE SP2290
Plough (01675) 481557
B4114 Nuneaton—Coleshill; B46 2AN Old-fashioned feel with rooms arranged around central bar; well kept Bass and four guests, flavoured gins, good choice of fairly straightforward food from sandwiches and baked potatoes up (special diets catered for), afternoon tea and themed food nights, friendly helpful staff, separate dining room, black beams, open fire and gleaming brassware; regular quiz nights (usually Mon), pool and darts, fruit machine; children and dogs welcome, disabled facilities, seats out at back plus stylish contemporary outdoor 'pod' for hire, open all day.

STOCKTON SP4365
Boat (01926) 812657
A426 Southam—Rugby; CV23 8HQ Fairly traditionally updated canalside pub with open-plan split-level interior (raised part mainly for dining); dark wood furniture on pale stone or stripped boards, woodburner in brick fireplace, brewery mirrors and advertising signs, bottles and jugs on delft shelf, a house beer from Nethergate, three guest ales and several craft beers, popular reasonably priced pubby food (not Sun evening), friendly staff; children and dogs (in bar) welcome, waterside picnic-sets under pergola, garden behind with play area, moorings, disabled access, open all day (till 10pm Sun).

STOCKTON SP4363
Crown (01926) 812255
High Street; CV47 8JZ Friendly village pub with generous helpings of popular straightforward food and four well kept ales

(maybe St Austell), restaurant in ancient barn, log fires; children and dogs welcome, garden with play area, open all day, no food Sun evening, closed Tues.

STOURBRIDGE SO9084
Duke William (01384) 440202
Coventry Street; DY8 1EP Popular and friendly Edwardian corner pub in semi-pedestrianised area; own Craddocks beers from on-site microbrewery (tours available) plus guests and draught/bottled imports, DogDancer and Thundering Molly ciders, good pie, mash and peas menu, traditional old Black Country feel with long corridor, open fire in bar and cosy snug; regular events including music, quiz and film nights (some in upstairs function room); no children, dogs welcome, beer garden behind, open all day.

STOURBRIDGE SO8983
Plough & Harrow (01384) 397218
Worcester Street; DY8 1AX Friendly little end-of-terrace bay-windowed local (sister to the nearby Duke William); well kept Craddocks ales and several guests, snacky food (nothing hot), cosy horseshoe bar with log fires and piano; live music and quiz nights; dogs welcome, no children inside, partly covered beer garden with woodburner, close to Mary Stevens Park, open all day.

STRATFORD-UPON-AVON SP2054
Dirty Duck (01789) 297312
Waterside; CV37 6BA Bustling 16th-c Greene King pub near the Memorial Theatre; their well kept ales, good choice of wines and enjoyable fairly priced food including deals (allow plenty of time for a pre-theatre meal), wood floors and panelling, lots of signed RSC photographs, open fire, modern conservatory restaurant (best to book weekends); children allowed in dining areas, dogs in bar, attractive small terrace looking over riverside public gardens which act as an overflow in summer, open (and food) all day.

STRATFORD-UPON-AVON SP2054
Garrick (01789) 292186
High Street; CV37 6AU Ancient pub with fine timbered frontage, heavy beams in irregularly shaped rooms, simple furnishings on bare boards or flagstones, well kept Greene King ales, proper cider and decent wines by the glass, fairly priced food from sandwiches and light dishes up, small back dining area; background music, TV, games machine; children and dogs welcome, open (and food) all day.

STRATFORD-UPON-AVON SP1955
Old Thatch (01789) 295216
Rother Street/Greenhill Street; CV37 6LE Cosy and welcoming 15th-c thatched pub on corner of market square; well kept Fullers ales, nice wines and popular fairly priced food including Sun carvery, rustic décor, beams, slate or wood floors, sofas and log fire,

back dining area; children and dogs welcome, covered tables outside, open all day.

STRATFORD-UPON-AVON SP2055
One Elm (01789) 404919
Guild Street; CV37 6QZ Modernised Peach group pub on two floors; well liked food from sandwiches and pub standards up (smaller helpings for children), Purity and guests, plenty of wines by the glass and good range of gins and cocktails, friendly efficient service; dogs welcome, seats out at front and in attractive paved courtyard behind, open (and food) all day.

STRATFORD-UPON-AVON SP1955
White Swan (01789) 297022
Rother Street; CV37 6NH Extensively renovated historic hotel (dates from 1450) with warren of connecting heavily beamed areas around central bar (one or two steps), good mix of seating including leather armchairs/sofas and antique settles, Shakespearean themed pictures and prints, oak-panelled dining room with two fine carved fireplaces and 16th-c wall painting of Tobias and the Angel, five Fullers/Gales beers, several wines by the glass and good choice of food to suit all tastes and occasions (breakfast from 8am Mon-Fri), quick friendly service; background music, daily newspapers; children and dogs welcome, seats out at front overlooking market square and to the side, character bedrooms, open (and food) all day.

STRATFORD-UPON-AVON SP1954
Windmill (01789) 297687
Church Street; CV37 6HB Near the striking Guild Chapel, this pub was first licensed in 1600 (there's a list of landlords back to 1720); updated interior with low beams and standing timbers, big fireplaces and wood and carpeted floors, Greene King, Purity and guests, good choice of enjoyable fairly priced food including range of burgers, various deals, friendly efficient staff; background music, sports TV, games machine; children welcome, courtyard tables, open (and food) all day.

STRETTON-ON-FOSSE SP2238
★ **Plough** (01608) 661053
Just off A429; GL56 9QX Popular and welcoming little 17th-c village local; central servery separating small bar and snug dining area, well kept North Cotswold, Sharps, Timothy Taylors, Wychwood and guests, Thatcher's and local Pearson's cider, good home-cooked food (not Sun evening) including blackboard specials, low oak beams, stripped-brick/stone walls and some flagstones, inglenook log fire; dominoes and cribbage; children and dogs (in new heated outdoor dining area) welcome, currently open all day Fri-Sun, closed Mon-Weds – but best to check.

SUTTON COLDFIELD SP1195
Brewhouse & Kitchen
(0121) 796 6838 *Birmingham Road; B72 1QD* Mock-Tudor pub with own microbrewery (tours and beer and gin tasting masterclasses available), eight real ales (mainly theirs) plus good range of craft kegs and bottled beers, around a dozen wines by the glass and enjoyable reasonably priced food from snacks, burgers and ribs up (menu suggests beer pairings), friendly helpful staff, spacious modern interior with plenty of different seating areas including boothed dining part; children and dogs welcome, open (and food) all day.

TANWORTH-IN-ARDEN SP1071
Warwickshire Lad (01564) 742346
Broad Lane/Wood End Lane, Wood End; B94 5DP Beamed country pub with good choice of enjoyable food cooked by landlord-chef, well kept ales such as St Austell, Silhill and Wye Valley, friendly service; children and dogs welcome, popular with walkers (bridleway opposite), seats outside, open all day, food all day Fri and Sat, till 6pm Sun, handy for M42 (junction 3).

TEMPLE GRAFTON SP1355
Blue Boar (01789) 750010
1 mile E, towards Binton; off A422 W of Stratford; B49 6NR Welcoming stone-built dining inn with good food from sandwiches and sharing plates up, well kept Banks's, Wychwood and a couple of guests, afternoon teas, beams, stripped stonework and log fires, glass-covered well with goldfish, smarter dining room up a couple of steps; occasional live music, sports TV; children and dogs welcome, picnic-sets outside, bedrooms.

TIDDINGTON SP2255
Crown (01789) 297010
Main Street; CV37 7AZ Family-friendly pub with good well priced food (smaller helpings available) and four well kept ales including Sharps Doom Bar, friendly staff, darts, pool and TV in side bar; monthly charity quiz night; dogs welcome, garden with play area, open all day Fri and Sat, no food Sun evening.

TIPTON SO9492
Mad O'Rourke's Pie Factory
(0121) 557 1402 *Hurst Lane, Dudley Road towards Wednesbury; A457/A4037; DY4 9AB* Eccentric décor and quirky food – mixed grill served on a shovel, and you're awarded a certificate if you finish their

---

Real ale to us means beer that has matured naturally in its cask – not pressurised or filtered. If possible, we name all real ales stocked.

massive Desperate Dan Cow Pie, other good
value food including Sun lunchtime carvery,
vegetarian, vegan and gluten-free options,
meal deals Mon-Thurs, well kept Lump
Hammer house beers (brewed by Enville)
and guests; background and weekend live
music, TV; children welcome, bedrooms, open
(and food) all day.

UFTON   SP3762
White Hart   (01926) 612976
*Just off A425 Southam–Leamington;
CV33 9PJ* Friendly old pub in elevated
roadside position next to church; modernised
beamed bar with log fire, high-backed leather
chairs and some booth seating, stripped-
stone walls, a few steps here and there, well
kept ales such as Purity and Slaughterhouse,
several wines by the glass, enjoyable good
value food with set menu and Thurs pie night,
efficient service; children and dogs welcome,
picnic-sets in hilltop garden with panoramic
views, closed Sun evening, otherwise open
(and food) all day.

UPPER BRAILES   SP3039
Gate   (01608) 685212
*B4035 Shipston-on-Stour to Banbury;
OX15 5AX* Traditional low-beamed village
local; well kept Hook Norton and a guest,
Napton cider and enjoyable reasonably
priced food from shortish menu, efficient
friendly service, coal fire; TV and darts;
children and dogs welcome, play area and
aunt sally in extensive back garden, pretty
hillside spot with lovely walks, comfortable
bedrooms, good breakfast, closed weekday
lunchtimes, no food Sun evening, Mon.

UPPER GORNAL   SO9292
★ **Britannia**   (01902) 883253
Kent Street (A459); DY3 1UX Popular
old-fashioned 19th-c local with friendly
chatty atmosphere (known locally as Sally's
after former landlady); coal fires in front
bar and time-trapped little back room with
its wonderful wall-mounted handpumps,
particularly well kept/priced Bathams, some
bar snacks including good local pork pies;
occasional live music, sports TV; children and
dogs welcome, flower-filled back courtyard,
open all day.

WALSALL   SP0198
Black Country Arms
(01922) 640588   *High Street; WS1 1QW*
Imposing building dating from the 17th c
with pillared frontage and big Georgian-style
windows; refurbished high-ceilinged bar
on different levels including mezzanine,
Black Country ales and many guests from
traditional wooden servery, also craft beers
and real ciders, enjoyable home-made pubby
food at bargain prices, good friendly service;
background and live music, quiz nights,
sports TV; children and dogs welcome, small
side terrace, open all day (till midnight Fri,
Sat), no food Mon or evenings Tues, Sun.

WARWICK   SP2864
★ **Rose & Crown**   (01926) 411117
Market Place; CV34 4SH Friendly bustling
town-centre inn (Peach group); sizeable
open-plan bar with big windows overlooking
the street, mix of seating from sofas with
colourful cushions to benches and cushioned
wall seats, winter open fire, also back dining
room with black and white celebrity photos
on pale walls, good choice of sensibly priced
food including gluten-free menu, well kept
ales such as Church Farm, Greene King and
Purity, good wines, cocktails and coffee,
cheerful efficient service; background music;
children and dogs (in front bar) welcome,
tables out on wide front pavement, 13 airy
comfortable bedrooms (eight in building
opposite), open (and food) all day from
7.30am (8.30am Sat, Sun) for breakfast.

WHATCOTE   SP2944
★ **Royal Oak**   (01295) 688100
*Upper Farm Barn; centre of village;
CV36 5EF* Beautifully restored part-
thatched golden-stone inn on the edge of
the Cotswolds – most customers are here to
enjoy the sublime Michelin-starred food, but
this is also a proper pub with regulars around
the bar and real ales on handpump; beams
and timbering, raftered ceilings, flagstones,
polished floorboards, a leather chesterfield
in front of an inglenook fireplace, farmhouse
or wheelback chairs around a mix of tables,
cushioned window seats, some stall-
type areas with oak settles and relaxed,
informal atmosphere, restaurant in modern
conservatory-style room with white leather
chairs and tall glass doors leading out to
rustic picnic-sets and wooden seats and
tables; currently open Thurs-Sun, closed
Mon-Weds and lunchtime Thurs.

WHICHFORD   SP3134
Norman Knight   (01608) 684621
*Ascott Road, opposite village green;
CV36 5PE* Sympathetically extended
beamed and flagstoned pub; four well kept
ales such as Goffs and Prescott, a couple
of proper ciders and good food (not Sun
evening, Mon) using local produce including
organic meat from the family farm, helpful
friendly service; monthly quiz, occasional
live music; children and dogs welcome,
picnic-sets on front lawn facing lovely village
green, aunt sally, four glamping pods and a
shepherd's hut, nice walks, open all day Fri,
Sat, till 6pm Sun, closed Mon lunchtime.

WILLEY   SP4885
Barn   (01788) 833810
Coalpit Lane; CV23 0SL Family-run pub-
restaurant in converted barn; own O'Neills
beers (view into the brewery) plus a guest,
decent range of wines and gins, enjoyable
reasonably priced food from sandwiches and
sharing boards to burgers and grills, Sun
carvery till 4pm, friendly helpful service,

more room in upstairs galleried area; occasional live music, beer/gin festivals; children and dogs welcome, terrace with country views, open (and food) all day Sat, closes 6pm Sun.

WILLOUGHBY   SP5267
Rose (01788) 891180
Just off A45 E of Dunchurch; Main Street; CV23 8BH Neatly decorated old thatched dining pub; low beam-and-plank ceiling, wood or tiled floors, some panelling and inglenook woodburner, good range of popular food cooked by chef-landlord with monthly tapas night, well kept ales and reasonably priced house wines, friendly attentive young staff; children and dogs welcome, disabled facilities, seating in side garden with gate to local park and play area, closed Sun evening, Mon and Tues.

WOLVERHAMPTON   SO9298
★ **Great Western** (01902) 351090
Corn Hill/Sun Street, behind railway station; WV10 0DG Cheerful pub hidden away in cobbled lane down from mainline station; Holdens and guests kept well, real cider and bargain lunchtime food (not Sun), helpful friendly staff, traditional front bar, other rooms including neat conservatory, open fires and interesting railway memorabilia; TV; children and dogs welcome, maybe summer barbecues in yard, open all day and busy with Wolves fans on match days.

WOLVERHAMPTON   SJ8901
Hail to the Ale 07846 562910
Pendeford Avenue/Blackburn Avenue; WV6 9JN One-room micropub in converted shop, six well kept/priced beers including Morton and several real ciders, off-licence, simple food such as pork pies and sausage rolls, warm friendly atmosphere; children (until 8pm) and dogs welcome, seats outside, closed Mon (except bank holidays) and Tues, otherwise open all day (till 5pm Sun).

WOOTTON WAWEN   SP1563
Bulls Head (01564) 795803
Stratford Road, just off A3400; B95 6BD Attractive black and white dining pub; Elizabethan beams and timbers, stone and quarry-tiled floors, log fires, decent choice of enjoyable fairly priced food from sandwiches up with gluten-free options, Marstons Pedigree, Ringwood Boondoggle and a guest, friendly staff; children welcome, dogs in bar, outside tables front and back, handy for one of England's finest churches and Stratford Canal walks, open all day, no food Sun evening.

Wiltshire

KEY   ★ Star Pub   🖈 Top Quality Food   🍺 Great Beer

♈ Good Wines   £ Bargain Meals   🛏 Good Bedrooms   🍴 Serves Food

---

 ALDBOURNE   SU2675   Map 2

Blue Boar 🍺 £

(01672) 540237 – www.theblueboarpub.co.uk

The Green (off B4192 in centre); SN8 2EN

Simple pubby furnishings in bar, cosy restaurant, decent food and seats outside by village green

Picnic-sets outside the front of this traditional pub make the most of its charming location opposite the village green, and the summer window boxes are lovely. Inside, the heavily beamed bar has a relaxed, chatty atmosphere helped along by cheerful staff and plenty of regulars. You'll find built-in wooden window seats, tall farmhouse and other red-cushioned pubby chairs on flagstones or bare boards, a woodburning stove in an inglenook fireplace with a stuffed boar's head and large clock above it, and horsebrasses on the bressumer beam; a noticeboard has news of beer festivals and live music events. Wadworths IPA, 6X and a guest beer such as Bath Gem on handpump, eight wines by the glass, 17 malt whiskies and a farm cider. The back restaurant is beamed and cottagey with standing timbers, dark wooden chairs and tables on floorboards and rugs, and plates displayed on a dresser.

🍴 Remarkably fair value, honest food includes lunchtime sandwiches, smoked mackerel pâté, crispy mushroom dippers with apricot and ginger chutney, home-made soups, chicken breast with white wine and tarragon sauce, root vegetable nut roast topped with goats cheese, 10oz local sirloin steak with red wine sauce, and puddings such as Baileys and dark chocolate cheesecake and banoffi pie with caramel sauce and vanilla ice-cream. *Benchmark main dish: pan-seared salmon fillet with lemon and parsley butter £9.75. Two-course evening meal £15.00.*

Wadworths ~ Tenants Michael and Joanne Hehir ~ Real ale ~ Open 11.30-3, 5.30-11.30; 11.30am-midnight Fri, Sat; 12-11 Sun ~ Bar food 12-2 (2.30 Fri, Sat), 6.30-9; 12-3 Sun ~ Restaurant ~ Children welcome ~ Dogs allowed in bar

 COMPTON BASSETT   SU0372   Map 2

White Horse 🖈 🛏

(01249) 813118 – www.whitehorse-comptonbassett.co.uk

At N end of village; SN11 8RG

Bustling pub with three ales, good wines by the glass, interesting food and seats in big garden; pretty bedrooms

It says a lot that despite being well off the beaten track this very rural pub is always busy – their secret might be the good beer, creative food and comfortable bedrooms. All in all, it's a real winner. The friendly, bustling bar has cushioned window and wall seats and settles, chunky wood and leather dining chairs around assorted tables on parquet flooring, a woodburning stove, and bar stools against the counter where they keep Box Steam Tunnel Vision, Ramsbury Gold and Three Daggers Blonde on handpump, 15 wines by the glass, 13 malt whiskies, a cocktail list, a good range of spirits including local gin and farm cider. The dining room has dark red walls and tiles at one end and bare floorboards and pale paintwork at the other; throughout there are beams and joists and miscellaneous antique tables and chairs. Also, there's another woodburning stove, and background music and board games. The large, neatly kept garden has picnic-sets and other seats, while the paddock is home to pigs, sheep and geese. The eight bedrooms (in a separate building overlooking the grounds) are attractive and well equipped and breakfasts are good. There are lovely surrounding walks and Avebury (National Trust) with its stone circle isn't far away.

 They make everything in-house and use their own vegetables and herbs as well as local, seasonal produce. The first class food includes River Exe mussels with pancetta, leek and cider cream and focaccia, game terrine with apricot chutney, duck breast with beetroot gratin, celeriac, wild mushroom tapenade, cavolo nero and macerated blackberries, skate wing with pak choi, mussels, Thai spiced broth and noodles, homity pie with roasted apple and goats curd, burger with coleslaw and fries, and puddings such as vanilla rice pudding with poached rhubarb, rhubarb sorbet and ginger crumble and pineapple upside-down cake with rum caramel and poached pineapple ice-cream. They also offer a two- and three-course set menu on weekdays. *Benchmark main dish: cod fillet with curried cauliflower and nut and bacon butter £17.00. Two-course evening meal £24.00.*

Free house ~ Licensee Kristian Goodwin ~ Real ale ~ Open 12-10; 12-9 Sun ~ Bar food 6-9; Sat 12-2.30, 6-9; 12-3, 6-8 Sun ~ Restaurant ~ Children allowed in bar ~ Dogs allowed in bar ~ Bedrooms: £85

CORSHAM
ST8670 Map 2
Methuen Arms 🏅 ♀ 🛏
(01249) 717060 – www.themethuenarms.com
High Street; SN13 0HB

Elegant hotel with professional, friendly staff, fine drinks list, imaginative food and pretty garden; smart bedrooms

In a bustling market town, this is a handsome Georgian inn with a good mix of customers. It's a civilised and friendly place and the little bare-boards front bar has built-in cushioned wall seats and a settle around various tables, a woodburning stove, Butcombe Original plus two guests, an excellent wine list with 21 by the glass and a dozen gins. A small dining room is furnished with plush chairs, a wall banquette and pretty botanical-themed prints, while the main restaurant is light and airy with pretty country flowers and candles on tables. Hung with fairy lights at night, the back courtyard is charming and has plenty of wicker seats. This is a lovely place to stay in 19 newly refurbished bedrooms that make a perfect base for exploring the area; two rooms are dog-friendly. The breakfasts are first class.

 Particularly good food using seasonal ingredients and produce from their own kitchen garden includes seared scallops with peas, crispy squid, ham hock and hollandaise sauce, confit duck leg with orange citrus and celeriac, home-grown vegetables with toasted almonds, garlic and chilli butter, roasted monkfish with curried green lentils, fennel and garlic nasturtium, braised beef boulangère with truffle, carrots and radish, beer-battered haddock and chips, and puddings such as chocolate mousse with pistachio cream and salted caramel and burnt passion-fruit cream with mango and coconut. *Benchmark main dish: burger with slaw and fries £16.00. Two-course evening meal £25.00.*

Butcombe ~ Manager Hannah Licquorish ~ Real ale ~ Open 7.30am-10pm Mon-Fri; 8am-6pm Sun ~ Bar food 7.30-10.30am, 11.30am-2.30pm, 6-9pm; 8-10.30am, 12-6pm Sun ~ Restaurant ~ Children welcome ~ Dogs allowed in bar & bedrooms ~ Bedrooms: £119

CRICKLADE
SU1093 Map 4

Red Lion 🍺 🛏

(01793) 750776 – www.theredlioncricklade.co.uk
Off A419 Swindon–Cirencester; High Street; SN6 6DD

16th-c inn with well liked food in two dining rooms, real ales, friendly, relaxed atmosphere and big garden; bedrooms

Despite being acquired by St Austell, this pub continues to run their on-site Hop Kettle microbrewery, cheerfully offering Proper Job and Tribute alongside three or four of their own brews, including Hop Kettle C.O.B., Element and North Wall and experimental offerings – Oyster Stout with seaweed, anyone? They also keep several farm ciders, 12 wines by the glass, ten malt whiskies and 15 gins. The traditional bar has stools by the nice old counter, wheelbacks and other chairs around dark wooden tables on a patterned carpet, an open fire and bric-a-brac on the stone walls such as stuffed fish, animal heads and old street signs. You can eat here or in the slightly more formal dining room, furnished with pale wooden farmhouse chairs and tables on parquet flooring and a woodburning stove in a brick fireplace. There are plenty of picnic-sets in the big back garden. The five bedrooms are comfortable and breakfasts good. Cricklade itself is charming or you can walk along the Thames Path, a mere 100 metres away.

Enjoyable, seasonal food includes dishes such as crispy salt and chilli squid, crispy skinned cod loin with wild mushrooms and crushed new potatoes, pine nut-crusted rack of lamb with salsa verde and butter bean cassoulet, Thai crab risotto, caramelised red onion and goats cheese tart with warm potato salad, assorted pizzas, and puddings such as chocolate brownie with ice-cream and whiskey, white chocolate and apricot bread and butter pudding. *Benchmark main dish: stone-baked pizza £9-£15. Two-course evening meal £19.00.*

St Austell ~ Tenant Darren Nash ~ Real ale ~ Open 12-11; 12-midnight Sat; 12-10.30 Sun ~ Bar food 12-2, 5.30-8.30; 12-8.30 Sat; 12-5 Sun ~ Restaurant ~ Children allowed in bar ~ Dogs allowed in bar & bedrooms ~ Bedrooms: £95

CRUDWELL
ST9592 Map 4

Potting Shed 🍴⭐ 🍷 🍺

(01666) 577833 – www.thepottingshedpub.com
A429 N of Malmesbury; The Street; SN16 9EW

Friendly dining pub with an interesting range of drinks and food, seats in the big garden and smart accommodation in sister hotel

This beautifully restored country pub has great beers, creative cuisine and a comfortable, relaxed atmosphere. Low-beamed rooms ramble around the bar with its bare stone walls, open fires and woodburning stoves (one in a big worn stone fireplace), mixed plain tables and chairs on pale flagstones, armchairs and a sofa in one corner and daily papers. Four steps lead up into a high-raftered area with wood flooring, and there's another separate, smaller room that's ideal for a lunch or dinner party. Also, lots of dog and country prints and more modern pictures, fresh flowers, candles and some quirky, rustic decorations such as a garden-fork door handle, garden-spade beer pumps and so forth. Butcombe Gold and Original, Ramsbury Gold and Stroud Budding Organic Pale Ale on handpump, as well as carefully chosen wines and champagne by the glass and home-made seasonal cocktails; background music and board games. Dogs may get treats and are welcomed everywhere. There are teak seats around cask tables among the weeping willows, a boules piste and a vegetable garden and orchard. Wheelchair access to the front door from the car park, and disabled loos. Sister business the Rectory Hotel is just a stone's throw away and provides smart accommodation in 15 lovely rooms and a cottage.

Imaginative, seasonal food using local ingredients includes twice-baked double gloucester soufflé with spinach, raw beef salad with rocket and capers, burrata and tomato salad with basil and olives, roasted cauliflower steak with red pepper and caper salsa, grilled tiger prawns with chilli and garlic butter, flat-iron chicken with chimichurri and fries, and puddings such as double chocolate brownie with vanilla ice-cream and lemon polenta cake with lemon curd and meringue. *Benchmark main dish: burger and fries £14.00. Two-course evening meal £22.00.*

Enterprise ~ Lease Alex Payne ~ Real ale ~ Open 11-11; 11-midnight Fri, Sat ~ Bar food 12-2.30, 6-9.30; 12-2.30, 6.30-9.30 Fri-Sun ~ Restaurant ~ Children welcome ~ Dogs allowed in bar, restaurant & bedrooms ~ Bedrooms: £175

EAST CHISENBURY   SU1352 Map 2

Red Lion

(01980) 671124 – www.redlionfreehouse.com

At S end of village; SN9 6AQ

Wiltshire Dining Pub of the Year

Country inn in peaceful village run by hard-working chef-owners, contemporary décor, an informal atmosphere and excellent food; fine bedrooms with riverfront decks

It's the superb food cooked by Mr and Mrs Manning (both are top chefs) that draws customers from far and wide, but this is also a proper pub where locals congregate by the bar for a pint and a chat. You'll find Ramsbury Blindside, Box and Stonehenge ales on handpump, 24 wines by the glass, home-made cordials, quite a range of gins and a dozen malt whiskies. One long room is split into different areas by brick and green-planked uprights. A big woodburner sits in a brick inglenook fireplace at one end; at the other is a comfortable black leather armchair, and in between are high-backed and farmhouse wooden dining chairs around various tables on bare boards or stone tiles, with pretty flowers and church candles dotted about. There's an additional dining area too and an upstairs private dining room; background music. Outside, the terrace and grassed area above it have picnic-sets and tables and chairs. They make their own dog treats and can organise a packed lunch for walkers. Just across the road from the pub is their boutique guesthouse, Troutbeck. The five well equipped and extremely comfortable bedrooms have private decks overlooking the River Avon and breakfasts are delicious; the bloody marys and bucks fizz are complimentary.

Faultless food using their own produce and home-reared pigs and chickens includes lunchtime sandwiches, scallop ceviche with burnt apple, jalapeños and dill, mussel tagliatelle with saffron, Pernod and chives, wild mushroom pithivier with chestnuts, truffle nage and crispy parmesan, herb-roasted guinea fowl with potato millefeuille, charred leeks and madeira velouté, turbot with saffron-braised potatoes, fennel, brown shrimps and sauce bourride, and puddings such as new york cheesecake with bay, rhubarb and iced Hendrick's and tonic and bitter chocolate tart with banana compote, coffee cream and hazelnut praline. Instead of Sunday lunch, they now run a very popular morning bakery selling doughnuts and croissants, with beers until 1.30pm. *Benchmark main dish: local venison with medjool date and juniper poivrade £27.00. Two-course evening meal £37.00*

Free house ~ Licensees Britt and Guy Manning ~ Real ale ~ Open 3-11 Tues, Weds; 9am-11pm Thurs-Sat; 9am-1.30pm Sun ~ Bar food 5.45-10.30 Tues, Weds; 11.45-2.30, 5.45-10.30 Thurs-Sat; bakery only 9am-1pm Sun~ Children welcome ~ Dogs allowed in bar & bedrooms ~ Bedrooms: £155

EAST KNOYLE   ST8731 Map 2
Fox & Hounds ♀
(01747) 830573 – www.foxandhounds-eastknoyle.co.uk
Village signposted off A350 S of A303; The Green (named on some road atlases), a mile NW at OS Sheet 183 map reference 872313; or follow signpost off B3089, about 0.5 miles E of A303 junction near Little Chef; SP3 6BN

Pretty village pub with splendid views, welcoming service, good beers and popular, enjoyable food

There are remarkable views over Blackmore Vale from the picnic-sets in front of this part-thatched old pub, with woods to walk in and the Wiltshire Cycleway passing close by. Inside, three linked areas on different levels are arranged around the central horseshoe-shaped server, with plentiful oak woodwork and flagstones, comfortably padded dining chairs around big scrubbed tables, a couple of leather sofas and two woodburners; the furnishings are all very individual and uncluttered. There's also a small, pale-painted conservatory restaurant. Butcombe Bitter, Hop Back Summer Lightning, Plain Sheep Dip and Triple fff Moondance on handpump, a dozen wines by the glass and Thatcher's farm cider; board games and skittle alley.

As well as lunchtime ploughman's (not Sunday), the appealing food includes deep-fried rosemary and garlic brie wedges with cranberry sauce, Japanese-style battered king prawns with sweet chilli sauce, beef and red wine casserole with mash, duck breast with port and redcurrant sauce, various pizzas, barbecue pork belly with rösti potatoes, slow-braised pork belly with cider and apple sauce, a catch of the day (available in large and small portions – the large is huge) with chips, and puddings such as lemon posset and warm pear and almond tart with vanilla ice-cream. *Benchmark main dish: Thai green curry £11.00. Two-course evening meal £20.00.*

Free house ~ Licensee Murray Seator ~ Real ale ~ Open 11.30-3, 5-11 ~ Bar food 12-2.15, 6.30-9; 12-2, 6.30-8.30 Sun ~ Children welcome ~ Dogs allowed in bar

FONTHILL GIFFORD   ST9231 Map 2
Beckford Arms
(01747) 870385 – www.beckfordarms.com
Hindon Lane; from Fonthill Bishop, bear left after tea rooms through Estate gate; from Hindon follow High Street signed for Tisbury; SP3 6PX

Handsome 18th-c inn with character bar and restaurant, unfailingly good food, thoughtful choice of drinks and an easy-going atmosphere; comfortable bedrooms

It's not always good news when a pub burns down, but ten years ago the Beckford Arms made the best of it by recreating its Georgian coaching inn stone by stone but brand-new, with its glorious countryside setting unchanged. With well equipped and comfortable bedrooms (and two self-catering lodges) this makes a great base for exploring the area; breakfasts are good and generous. The atmosphere is gently civilised but informal and friendly. The main bar has assorted wooden dining chairs and tables on parquet flooring, a huge fireplace and bar stools beside the counter where they keep an interesting range of drinks – including Butcombe Bitter, Keystone Phoenix (named for them) and Timothy Taylors Landlord on handpump, 15 wines by the glass, 20 malt whiskies, local farm cider, winter mulled wine and cider, and cocktails such as a bloody mary using home-grown horseradish. The cosy sitting room is stylish with comfortable sofas facing one another across a low table, an appealing built-in window seat among other chairs and tables, and an open fire in a stone fireplace with candles in brass candlesticks and fresh flowers on the mantelpiece. There's also a separate restaurant and private dining room. The mature rambling garden has seats on a brick terrace, hammocks under trees, games for children, a dog bath and boules. This is sister pub to the Bath Arms in Horningsham (also Wiltshire) and the Lord Poulett Arms at Hinton St George and the Talbot in Mells (both in Somerset).

 As well as breakfasts (8-9.30am), the enjoyable, imaginative food includes tomato gazpacho with basil sorbet and pine nuts, confit beetroots with goats curd, parley aioli and walnuts, ploughman's, beer-brined chicken breast with spelt risotto and nettle pesto, pan-fried cod with sweetcorn purée and black bean and tomato ragoût, 42-day aged rump steak with roasted red peppers and wild garlic butter, and puddings such as lemon parfait with pistachio meringue and rose jelly and rum and caramel affogato. *Benchmark main dish: beef burger with harissa mayo and chips £14.50. Two-course evening meal £23.00.*

Free house ~ Licensees Dan Brod and Charlie Luxton ~ Real ale ~ Open 8am-11pm; 11-10.30 Sun ~ Bar food 12-3, 6-9.30 (9 Sun) ~ Restaurant ~ Children welcome ~ Dogs allowed in bar & restaurant ~ Bedrooms: £120

GREAT BEDWYN

SU2764 Map 2

Three Tuns 🌟 �Υ

(01672) 870280 – www.tunsfreehouse.com

Village signposted off A338 S of Hungerford, or off A4 W of Hungerford via Little Bedwyn; High Street; SN8 3NU

Friendly village pub with first class food and local ales; seats outside

This well run village pub receives consistently high praise from our readers, thanks to its well kept beers and magnificently ambitious, daily changing menus. The beamed front bar is traditional and simply furnished with pubby stools and chairs on bare floorboards, an open fire, artwork by local artists on the walls and plenty of original features. They keep local ales such as Butcombe Original, Ramsbury Gold and Otter Bitter on handpump, 12 wines by the glass, several malt whiskies, gins, vodkas and a couple of farm ciders. French doors in the back dining room lead out to the garden where there are tables and chairs, an outdoor grill and boules. The Kennet & Avon Canal runs through the village and the pub is on the edge of Savernake Forest, which has lovely walks and cycle routes. Great Bedwyn train station is three minutes on foot.

 The marvellous food on a seasonal, daily changing menu is cooked by the chef-patron who makes everything in-house. Dishes might include scorched mackerel fillet with cucumber kimchi, rocket and coriander oil, vegetable, hazelnut and rocket ragoût with pasta and croutons, burger with toppings and chips, home-cooked local ham and eggs, guinea fowl with fregola, chorizo, tomato, spinach and gremolata, roasted hake with clam croquette and spring greens, confit chicken leg with smoked bacon, French-style peas and aioli, and puddings such as chocolate cheesecake with griottine cherries, pistachio brittle and cherry sorbet and fruit and nut chocolate 'salami'. *Benchmark main dish: bavette steak with bone marrow, chips and chimichurri sauce £18.00. Two-course evening meal £20.00.*

Free house ~ Licensees James and Ashley Wilsey ~ Real ale ~ Open 10-3, 6-11 Tues-Thurs; 10am-11pm Fri, Sat; 12-6 Sun; closed Mon ~ Bar food 12-2.30, 6.30-9.30 ~ Restaurant ~ Children welcome until 8pm ~ Dogs allowed in bar

GRITTLETON
Neeld Arms

ST8680   Map 2

(01249) 782470 – www.neeldarms.co.uk

From M4 junction 17, follow A429 to Cirencester and immediately left, signed Stanton St Quintin and Grittleton; SN14 6AP

17th-c village pub with a good mix of customers, popular food and drink and friendly staff; bedrooms

This popular and welcoming pub, run by the same friendly licensees for almost 20 years, is very much at the heart of village life, with changing real ales and a seasonal, varied chalkboard menu. The open-plan rooms have Cotswold-stone walls, contemporary colours on wood panelling and a pleasant mix of seating ranging from bar stools and traditional settles to window seats and pale wooden dining chairs around an assortment of tables – each set with fresh flowers. The little brick fireplace houses a woodburning stove and there's an inglenook fireplace on the right. Flying Monk Mighty Monk and St Austell Tribute are always on tap, while guests might include Flying Monk Habit and Moles Best; along with decent wines, these are served from the blue-painted panelled and oak-topped bar counter. The back dining area has another inglenook with a big woodburning stove and white-painted chairs and settles around solid tables; even here, you still feel thoroughly part of the action. The six bedrooms are neatly kept, comfortable and nicely priced. An outdoor front terrace has a few tables behind a low roadside wall.

Well regarded food with seasonal specials includes chicken liver, port and brandy pâté with onion marmalade, crayfish tails with bloody mary dressing, potted prawns, various meat pies, venison steaks, baked whole sea bass with cherry tomatoes and pesto, wild mushroom tagliatelle, sausages and mash, asparagus and spinach pancakes topped with gruyère, and desserts such as warm treacle tart with custard and fruit crumble of the day. *Benchmark main dish: beef and horseradish pie £12.00. Two-course evening meal £20.00.*

Free house ~ Licensees Charlie and Boo West ~ Real ale ~ Open 12-3, 6-11; 12-11 Sat, Sun ~ Bar food 12-2, 6.30-9.30; 12-2.30, 7-9 Sun ~ Restaurant ~ Children welcome ~ Dogs allowed in bar ~ Bedrooms: £75

HOLT
Toll Gate ♈

ST8561   Map 2

(01225) 782326 – www.tollgateinn.co.uk

Ham Green; B3107 W of Melksham; BA14 6PX

Bustling pub with woodburning stoves in attractive bars, real ales and popular food; airy bedrooms

This friendly 16th-c stone pub has real character, with welcoming, attentive staff and chatty locals quickly making visitors feel at home. The relaxed bar has seats by a woodburner and a mix of tables and chairs on pale floorboards. You'll find Box Steam Golden Bolt (the brewery is in the village), Butcombe Bitter and Rare Breed, Sharps Doom Bar and Tollgate Gold (named for them from Box Steam) on handpump, 18 wines by the glass from a good, regularly updated list (on Thursday evenings you can bring your own wine – no corkage), interesting gins and three farm ciders; background music and board games. The dining room leads off the bar with high-backed leather and other cushioned chairs and a second woodburner. Up a few steps, the high-raftered restaurant is similarly furnished with dark blue walls and church windows (this used to be a workers' chapel). The sunny paved back terrace has seats and tables; boules. Bedrooms, some of which are in their old farm shop, have open fires; there's also a holiday cottage for rent. Wheelchair access to main bar and dining area (but not to the loos). The Courts Garden is in the village and Great Chalfield Manor (both National Trust) is nearby.

Tasty food using local produce and fish delivered daily from Lyme Bay includes lunchtime rolls, Thai chicken salad, pan-fried tiger prawns, ploughman's (with a home-made scotch egg), various burgers, wild mushroom tagliatelle, 28-day aged sirloin steak, crispy chicken penang with coconut rice and carrot and coriander slaw, and puddings such as apple crumble and Oreo cheesecake. Vegetarian, vegan and gluten-free options are available. *Benchmark main dish: beer-battered fish and chips £14.00. Two-course evening meal £21.00.*

Free house ~ Licensees Laura Boulton and Mark Hodges ~ Real ale ~ Open 9.30am-11.30pm; 9.30am-midnight Sat; 9.30am-4.30pm Sun ~ Bar food 12-2, 6.30-9; 12-9 Sat; 12-2.30 Sun ~ Restaurant ~ Children welcome ~ Bedrooms: $80

HORNINGSHAM
Bath Arms ♀ 🛏

ST8041   Map 2

(01985) 844308 – www.batharmsinn.com
By tradesmen's entrance to Longleat House; BA12 7LY

Bustling pub with plenty of space, rustic furnishings, interesting food and real ales; stylish bedrooms

Set on the Longleat Estate, with fantastic views over woodland and the Avon Valley, this is a handsome old stone inn with a country atmosphere. The various bar and dining rooms are linked. One simple end room has an open fire and cushioned pews, wall seats and dining chairs around large tables on wide floorboards. This leads into a smaller dining room and on into the main bar, where there's another open fire, rustic tables and chairs and a long cushioned settle on rugs and bare boards, candles in big wooden candlesticks and paintings of fancy-plumaged birds. Butcombe Original, Keystone Hornings (named for the pub) and a guest on handpump, plus Thatcher's cider and 25 wines by the glass from a good list; background music, board and pub games. The restaurant is similarly furnished, with chandeliers and a big painting of a sultan. The 16 bedrooms (in the main pub or stable block) are light, airy and comfortable. A back garden has a two-level terrace with circular picnic-sets, with more at the front and on gravel under pollarded trees. Wheelchair access to bars is via a side door; accessible loos. Sister pubs are the Beckford Arms in Fonthill Gifford (also Wiltshire) and the Lord Poulett Arms at Hinton St George and the Talbot in Mells (both in Somerset).

Rewarding food includes beetroot-cured salmon with horseradish crème fraîche, pork, black pudding and smoked bacon terrine with pickled fennel, roasted butternut squash and quinoa salad, pan-fried sea bream with cauliflower, Jersey Royals and samphire, burger and fries, beetroot fregola with garlic spinach, whipped feta cheese and toasted walnuts, guinea fowl breast with mushroom purée and crispy polenta, and puddings such as lemon posset with berry compote and vanilla cheesecake with strawberry sorbet. *Benchmark main dish: cider-battered haddock and triple-cooked chips £14.50. Two-course evening meal £23.00.*

Free house ~ Licensees Dan Brod and Charlie Luxton ~ Real ale ~ Open 8am-11pm; 11-10.30 Sun ~ Bar food 12-3, 6-9.30 ~ Restaurant ~ Children welcome ~ Dogs allowed in bar, restaurant & bedrooms ~ Bedrooms: $120

LOWER CHUTE

SU3153 Map 2

Hatchet 🍺 ⌂

(01264) 730229 – www.thehatchetinn.com

The Chutes well signposted via Appleshaw off A342, 2.5 miles W of Andover; SP11 9DX

Neatly kept 13th-c thatched inn with a friendly welcome for all, real ales and enjoyable food; comfortable bedrooms

The Chutes are a cluster of surprisingly remote villages just north of Andover, but plenty of customers manage to find their way to this long thatched pub. The beamed bar has a splendid 16th-c fireback in a huge fireplace (and a roaring winter log fire), various comfortable seats around oak tables and a peaceful local feel; there's also an extensive restaurant. The convivial landlord serves Timothy Taylors Landlord and a couple of guests such as Hatchet (named for the pub from Greene King) and Otter Bitter on handpump, eight wines by the glass, 20 malt whiskies, 40 different gins and several farm ciders including a rhubarb variety; background music and board games. There are seats out on a terrace and the side grass, and a safe play area for children. The seven snug bedrooms make this a fine place to stay (dogs are welcome in a couple of rooms) and breakfasts are hearty.

 Tasty food includes lunchtime baguettes and toasties, as well as tempura prawns with sweet chilli sauce, farmhouse pâté with apricot chutney, mushroom and red pepper stroganoff, ham and eggs, beef bourguignon, calves liver and bacon with mash and onion gravy, chicken tikka masala with mango chutney, lamb shank with mint sauce and mash, salmon supreme with tarragon and hollandaise sauce, and puddings such as rhubarb crumble and custard and chocolate and coconut tart with cream. *Benchmark main dish: steak and ale pie £12.95. Two-course evening meal £19.00.*

Free house ~ Licensee Jeremy McKay ~ Real ale ~ Open 11.30-3, 6-11; 11.30-11 Sat; 12-4, 7-10.30 Sun ~ Bar food 12-2.15, 6-9.30; 12-3, 7-9 Sun ~ Restaurant ~ Children welcome ~ Dogs allowed in bar & bedrooms ~ Bedrooms: £85

NEWTON TONY

SU2140 Map 2

Malet Arms ⍟ 🍺

(01980) 629279 – www.maletarms.co.uk

Village signposted off A338 Swindon–Salisbury; SP4 0HF

Smashing village pub with no pretensions, a good choice of local beers and highly regarded food

There's genuine unspoilt character to this pub next to the little River Bourne and the village green. That, mixed with the warmth of the welcome from the long-running owners and chatty locals, makes it a rather special place. Low-beamed interconnecting and homely rooms have all sorts of tables of differing sizes with high-winged wall settles, carved pews, chapel and carver chairs, and lots of pictures of local scenes and from imperial days. The main front windows are said to be made from the stern of a ship, and there's a log and coal fire in a huge fireplace. The snug is noteworthy for its fantastic collection of photographs and prints celebrating the local aviation history of Boscombe Down, alongside archive photographs of Stonehenge festivals of the 1970s and '80s. At the back is a homely, red-painted dining room. Four real ales on handpump come from breweries such as Butcombe, Fullers, Hop Back, Itchen Valley, Palmers, Plain, Ramsbury, Stonehenge and Triple fff and they also have farm cider on tap, over 30 malt whiskies and ten wines by the glass; board games. There are seats on the small front terrace with more on grass and in the back garden. The road leading to the pub goes through a ford, and it may be

best to use an alternative route in winter when the water can be quite deep.
There's an all-weather cricket pitch on the green.

 Country cooking uses game from local shoots (some bagged by the landlord),
lamb raised in the surrounding fields and free-range local pork; they also have
a new smoker (for fish, meat and cheese). Dishes might include venison carpaccio with
truffle oil and parmesan, chicken liver pâté with onion marmalade, vegetarian cottage
pie, local sausages with mash and onion gravy, daily fish dishes, lamb shoulder with pea
purée and mash, crispy pork belly with sage and onion mash and scrumpy gravy, and
puddings such as treacle tart and rocky road chocolate crunch. *Benchmark main dish:
stalker's pie (venison) £13.50. Two-course evening meal £22.00.*

Free house ~ Licensees Noel and Annie Cardew ~ Real ale ~ Open 12-3, 6-11; 12-4 Sun
(also 6-10 bank holidays); closed Mon, Tues ~ Bar food 12-2.15, 6.30-9.15; 12-2.15 Sun ~
Restaurant ~ Children allowed only in restaurant or snug ~ Dogs allowed in bar

RAMSBURY
Bell 🍽️🛏️

SU2771   Map 2

(01672) 520230 – www.thebellramsbury.com
Off B4192 NW of Hungerford, or A4 W; SN8 2PE

**300-year-old coaching inn with a civilised feel, character bar and
dining rooms, and a thoughtful choice of both drinks and food;
spotless bedrooms**

This 300-year-old coaching inn is part of the Ramsbury Estate, which
operates its own well respected brewery and distillery nearby, and
showcases Ramsbury products. It's a lovely old heavy-timbered building,
smartly decorated with contemporary paintwork and furnishings; the
atmosphere throughout is gently civilised and informal. The two rooms of the
chatty bar have tartan-cushioned wall seats and pale wooden dining chairs
around assorted tables, country and wildlife paintings, interesting stained-
glass windows and a woodburning stove. Neat, efficient staff serve Ramsbury
Farmers Best, Gold and Flint Knapper and a changing guest on handpump,
a dozen wines by the glass, 20 malt whiskies and their own-distilled gin and
vodka. A cosy room between the bar and restaurant has armchairs and sofas
before an open fire, a table of magazines and papers, a couple of portraits,
stuffed birds and a squirrel, books on shelves and patterned wallpaper. Smart
and relaxed, the restaurant is similarly furnished to the bar with wooden
tables on bare boards or rugs, oil paintings and winter-scene photographs
on beige walls; fresh flowers decorate each table. A nice surprise is the
charming back café with white-painted farmhouse chairs. The garden has
picnic-sets on a lower terrace and raised lawn, with more on a little terrace
towards the front. The nine bedrooms (in the inn or the renovated coach
house) are smart, well equipped and restful.

 Imaginative seasonal food (under a new head chef) includes a bar food menu
with such dishes as burger and chips and vegetarian alternatives. There are
also regularly changing (and considerably more expensive) à la carte offerings, such as
burrata with charred squash and chicory, smoked salmon with Dorset blue vinny, walnut
and fig, Creedy Carver duck breast with duck leg pie, purple kale and hen of the woods,
and barbecued monkfish with tandoori-spiced carrots and carrot quinoa. Puddings
include sourdough treacle tart with miso ice-cream and carrot cake with candied orange
and mascarpone sorbet. *Benchmark main dish (bar food): stout-battered cod and
chips £15.00. Two-course evening meal £23.00.*

Free house ~ Licensee Alistair Ewing ~ Real ale ~ Open 12-2.30, 5.30-11; 12-2.30, 5.30-11
Sat; 12-3 Sun ~ Bar food 12-2.30, 6-9; 12-3 Sun ~ Restaurant ~ Children allowed in bar ~
Dogs allowed in bar & bedrooms ~ Bedrooms: £120

SHERSTON
ST8585 Map 2
Rattlebone

(01666) 840871 – www.therattlebone.co.uk

Church Street; B4040 Malmesbury–Chipping Sodbury; SN16 0LR

17th-c village pub with rambling rooms, real ales and good bar food using local and free-range produce; friendly staff

Three boules courts, a skittle alley, a popular bar and a menu that goes well beyond simple pub food attract a loyal customer base from far and wide. The rambling, softly lit rooms have beams, standing timbers and flagstones, pews, settles and country kitchen chairs around an assortment of tables, and armchairs and sofas by roaring fires. Flying Monk Elmers, St Austell Tribute and Timothy Taylors Landlord on handpump, 20 wines by the glass from a thoughtful list, local cider and home-made lemonade; background music, darts, board games, TV and games machine. The skittle alley and boules courts outside are often in use by one of the many pub teams; a boules festival is held in July, as well as mangold hurling (similar to boules, but using cattle-feed turnips) and other events. The two pretty gardens include an extended terrace, with wooden seating and parasols, where they hold barbecues and spit roasts. Wheelchair access.

Tempting food includes lunchtime sandwiches, pea, broad bean and asparagus risotto, shredded duck salad with hoisin sauce and cashews, vegan vegetable paella with crispy almonds and piquillo peppers, burger (beef or chickpea and halloumi) with onion rings and fries, pork schnitzel with fried egg, capers and anchovies, monkfish scampi and fries, and puddings such as summer berry eton mess with honeycomb and raspberry purée, and chilled watermelon with mango sorbet and fruit purée. Thursday is steak night. *Benchmark main dish: roast spatchcock chicken with garlic, thyme and sea salt and fries £14.50. Two-course evening meal £20.00.*

Youngs ~ Tenant Jason Read ~ Real ale ~ Open 12-3, 5-11; 12-midnight Fri, Sat; 12-11 Sun ~ Bar food 12-2.30, 6-9.30; 12-5 Sun ~ Restaurant ~ Children welcome ~ Dogs allowed in bar

SWALLOWCLIFFE
ST9627 Map 2
Royal Oak

(01747) 870211 – www.royaloakswallowcliffe.com

Signed just off A30 Wilton–Shaftesbury; Common Lane; SP3 5PA

Thoughtfully restored inn with light, fresh décor, well stocked bar, good seasonal food and seats in garden; bedrooms

There's a gently civilised atmosphere to this part-thatched village pub that has been stylishly refurbished by the local community. Period features such as flagstone floors have been retained, but the feel is contemporary, with light uncluttered paintwork setting off locally made pale oak chairs, benches and tables, with chesterfield sofas by an inglenook fireplace. A row of stools line the white planked counter where helpful staff serve Butcombe Cliffehanger and guests from Box Steam and Flying Monk on handpump, 14 wines by the glass, ten gins and local cider and perry. There's also a good choice of teas and coffee; board games. The conservatory dining room, beautifully beamed and timbered, shares the bar's contemporary look, with exposed green-oak beams and floor-to-ceiling windows. Doors open from here on to the terrace and garden, where there are rustic tables surrounded by chairs and benches. The six bedrooms are spotlessly clean, extremely comfortable and up to date; breakfasts are very good. There are plenty of surrounding walks and places to visit.

Enjoyable, imaginative food includes snacks (crispy polenta soldiers with mashed avocado, mini yorkshire puddings with mackerel pâté) plus slow-cooked beef croquettes with feta, sea bream tartare with sesame, nori and soy, roast venison with faggot, parsnip and pickled pear, butternut squash and cheddar dumplings, pub classics like burger and chips or rib-eye steak with grilled mushroom and chips, and puddings such as café latte pannacotta with amaretti and date and walnut sticky toffee pudding. There's also a weekday two- and three-course set menu. *Benchmark main dish: Cornish hake with bubble and squeak cake and poached egg £18.00. Two-course evening meal £24.00.*

Free house ~ Licensee Steve Radford ~ Real ale ~ Open 11am-11.30pm ~ Bar food 12-2.30, 6-9 (8.45 Sun) ~ Restaurant ~ Children welcome ~ Dogs allowed in bar & bedroom ~ Bedrooms: from £100

SWINDON
SU1384   Map 2

Weighbridge ◀

(01793) 881500 – www.weighbridgeswindon.co.uk

Penzance Drive; SN5 7JL

Stunning building with stylish modern décor, own microbrewery ales, well prepared food and friendly, well trained staff

Now called the Weighbridge Steakhouse & Bar (rather than Brewhouse), this stylish bar puts a modern twist on Swindon's industrial heritage. Built in 1906 and once a weighing station for trains, it's a light, airy brick building, with illuminated trees emphasising the sense of space, station clocks on the walls and upholstered, teal-coloured stools lining the bar. Six handpumps dispense their own Weighbridge beers with three regulars including Brinkworth Village and Pooleys Golden as well as seasonal brews, while friendly staff also serve cocktails and several wines by the glass. Smartly modern and open-plan, the dining room has a steel-tensioned high-raftered roof (the big central skylight adds even more light), attractive high-backed orange or teal chairs and long wall banquettes, with bare brick walls hung with black and white pictures of the building's past. There are some seats on an outside terrace.

 The menu has changed to reflect its new name, with a focus on 35-day dry-aged beef steaks in a range of cuts and weights with a choice of sauces and sides. Also panko-breaded squid with garlic aioli, fried chicken waffle, caesar salad, a fish of the day, burgers and chips including a vegan version, grilled half roast chicken, baby back ribs, and puddings such as banoffi pie and apple crumble. *Benchmark main dish: 8oz rump steak £16.00. Two-course evening meal £21.00.*

Upham ~ Real ale ~ Open 11.30-11 ~ Bar food 11.30-9.30; 11.30-8 Sun ~ Restaurant ~ Children welcome ~ Dogs allowed in bar

TOLLARD ROYAL
ST9317   Map 2

King John ⚿

(01725) 516207 – www.kingjohninn.co.uk

B3081 Shaftesbury–Sixpenny Handley; SP5 5PS

Pleasing contemporary furnishings in carefully opened-up pub, courteous, helpful service, good drinks and excellent food; pretty bedrooms

This friendly, civilised pub combines well kept real ales with an enticing menu, all in a lovely village setting on Cranborne Chase. The open-plan L-shaped bar has a log fire, nice little touches such as a pot of herbs and tiny metal buckets of salt and pepper on scrubbed kitchen tables, a screen made up of the sides of wine boxes, and candles in big glass jars. An attractive mix of seats takes in spindlebacks, captain's and chapel chairs (some built into the bay windows) plus the odd cushioned settle, and there are big terracotta floor tiles, lantern-style wall lights, hound, hunting and other photographs, and prints of early 19th-c scientists. A beer named for the pub (from Marstons), Gritchie English Lore and Waylands Sixpenny 6d Gold on handpump and wines from a good list. A second log fire has fender seats on each side and leather chesterfields in front, and there's also a stuffed heron and grouse; daily papers and background music. Outside at the front are seats and tables beneath parasols, with more up steps in the raised garden where there's also an outdoor kitchen pavilion. The eight bedrooms are comfortable and pretty.

🍴 Tasty food includes crispy bacon, gem and avocado salad, crab on toast, 8oz rump steak with field mushroom, tomato, chips and garlic and parsley butter, chicken, ham and leek pie with mash and buttered greens, brisket burger with ruby slaw and fries, seared bream fillet with Cornish new potato niçoise, and puddings such as sticky toffee pudding and dark chocolate brownie. *Benchmark main dish: haddock and chips £14.00. Two-course evening meal £20.00.*

Cirrus Inns ~ Licensee Monika Kulicka ~ Real ale ~ Open 12-11; 12-10 Sun ~ Bar food 12-2.30, 6.30-9.30; 12-2.30, 6-9 Sun ~ Restaurant ~ Children welcome ~ Dogs allowed in bar ~ Bedrooms: £120

Also Worth a Visit in Wiltshire

Besides the fully inspected pubs, you might like to try these pubs that have been recommended to us and described by readers. Do tell us what you think of them: feedback@goodguides.com

ALVEDISTON ST9723
Crown (01722) 780203
Off A30 W of Salisbury; SP5 5JY
Welcoming 15th-c thatched inn (reopened in 2018 after long closure); three very low-beamed, partly panelled rooms, two inglenooks, good fairly priced traditional food including signature steak and kidney pudding, four well kept local ales; darts and board games; children, walkers and dogs welcome, pretty views from attractive garden with terrace, good walks nearby, three comfortable bedrooms, generous breakfast.

BADBURY SU1980
Plough (01793) 740342
A346 (Marlborough Road) just S of M4 junction 15; SN4 0EP Busy country pub with wide choice of fairly priced food (all day weekends) including daily specials, well kept Arkells beers, decent wines and good range of gins, friendly service, spacious tartan-carpeted bar with log fire, light airy dining room; background music; children and dogs welcome, far-reaching views from tree-shaded garden, open all day, breakfast from 10am Mon-Sat, useful M4 stop.

BARFORD ST MARTIN SU0531
Barford Inn (01722) 742242
B3089 W of Salisbury (Grovely Road), just off A30; SP3 4AB Welcoming 16th-c coaching inn; dark panelled front bar with big log fire, well kept Badger ales and decent wines by the glass, other connecting rooms including beamed bare-brick restaurant, wide choice of popular reasonably priced food (not Sun evening), prompt friendly service; children and dogs welcome, wheelchair access (not to bar), disabled loo, tables on terrace and in back garden, four annexe bedrooms, good walks, open all day, closed Mon in winter.

BECKHAMPTON SU0868
Waggon & Horses (01672) 539418
A4 Marlborough–Calne; SN8 1QJ Handsome stone and thatch former coaching inn; decent choice of enjoyable fairly priced food (not Sun evening) including gluten-free options in open-plan beamed bar or separate dining area, well kept Wadworths ales, friendly service; background music; children and dogs welcome, pleasant raised garden with play area, handy for Avebury (NT), open all day.

BERWICK ST JAMES SU0739
★ Boot (01722) 790243
High Street (B3083); SP3 4TN Welcoming 18th-c flint and stone pub not far from Stonehenge; good locally sourced food (not Sun evening, Mon) from daily changing blackboard menu cooked by landlord-chef, friendly efficient staff, well kept Wadworths

ales and a guest, huge log fire in inglenook at one end, sporting prints over brick fireplace at the other, small back dining room with collection of celebrity boots; children and dogs welcome, sheltered side lawn, open 6-8pm Mon (12-3pm bank holidays), otherwise regular hours.

BERWICK ST JOHN   ST9422
★ **Talbot** (01747) 828222
Village signed from A30 E of Shaftesbury; SP7 0HA Unspoilt 17th-c pub in attractive village; simple furnishings and big inglenook in heavily beamed bar, Ringwood Best, Wadworths 6X and a guest, several wines by the glass, reasonable choice of popular home-made food including some vegetarian options, friendly service, restaurant; darts; children and dogs (pub has its own) welcome, seats outside, good local walks, closed Sun evening, Mon.

BIDDESTONE   ST8673
White Horse (01249) 713350
The Green; SN14 7DG Prettily placed 16th-c three-room local near the village duck pond; a couple of well kept ales, plenty of wines by the glass and enjoyable good value food (not Sun evening) from snacks up, friendly staff; children and dogs welcome, tables out at front and in back garden with clematis-covered pergola and play area, closed Mon.

BISHOPSTONE   SU2483
Royal Oak (01793) 790481
Cues Lane; near Swindon; at first exit roundabout from A419 N of M4 junction 15, follow sign for Wanborough then Bishopstone, at small sign on telegraph pole turn left; SN6 8PP Informal dining pub run by local farmers in pretty village below Ridgeway and White Horse; well liked seasonal food (including breakfast) from daily changing menu including properly hung home-reared steaks, Arkells beers, organic wines and good choice of whiskies and gins; mainly scrubbed-wood furnishings on bare boards or parquet, log fire on left and little maze of pews, refurbished upstairs dining area (same level as garden) with own bar and good disabled access/loos; children and dogs welcome, modern furniture on front deck, picnic-sets on grass and among trees, 12 bedrooms in separate building.

BOX   ST8168
Northey Arms (01225) 742333
A4, Bath side; SN13 8AE 19th-c stone-built dining pub; good food from snacks up including daily specials (fresh fish), children's menu and Tues steak night, up to four real ales and 18 wines by the glass from well stocked bar, friendly young staff, fresh contemporary décor with chunky modern tables and high-backed rattan chairs, open fire; background music; tables and play area in garden behind, ten well

appointed bedrooms, open (and food) all day from 8am for breakfast.

BOX   ST8369
Quarrymans Arms (01225) 743569
Pub signed from A4 at Box Hill in both directions; SN13 8HN Former local for Bath-stone miners with related photographs and memorabilia; well kept Butcombe and guests, generally well liked food (all day Fri-Sun) including daily specials, friendly staff; children, walkers and dogs welcome, picnic-sets on terrace with sweeping views, four bedrooms, open all day.

BRADFORD-ON-AVON   ST8261
Bunch of Grapes (01225) 938088
Silver Street; BA15 1JY Stylishly renovated bar-restaurant with highly praised contemporary food including set menu choices, local ales such as Butcombe, craft beers and plenty of well chosen wines, good coffee and cakes too, friendly efficient service, elegant upstairs dining rooms with modish paintwork, large windows, trendy lighting and interesting artwork; background music; children welcome, open all day from 9am Weds-Sun, closed Mon and Tues, shuts 7pm Sun.

BRADFORD-ON-AVON   ST8060
Cross Guns (01225) 862335
Avoncliff, 2 miles W of Bradford-on-Avon on Turleigh road, turn left for Avoncliff; park at dead end and walk across the bridge; BA15 2HB 16th-c pub with steeply terraced areas above the bridges, aqueduct and river; bare boards, stripped stone and inglenook log fire in opened-up low-beamed interior, real ales, local ciders and extensive range of spirits, children and dogs welcome, wheelchair access but no disabled loo, canal moorings nearby, open (and food) all day, till 8pm (7pm) Sun, but opening can be erratic – call ahead to check.

BRADFORD-ON-AVON   ST8261
Dandy Lion (01225) 863433
Market Street; BA15 1LL Comfortably modernised 18th-c pub (same owners as Greyhound in Bromham and George in Sandy Lane); bar with stripped-wood floor and painted panelling, steps up to snug, more room in carpeted upstairs dining room, Wadworths ales, over a dozen wines by glass and good reasonably priced home-made food from fairly pubby menu, friendly service; background music, board games; children and dogs welcome, open (and food) all day.

BRADFORD-ON-AVON   ST8161
★ **Dog & Fox** (01225) 862137
Ashley Road, just outside town; BA15 1RT Welcoming unpretentious two-room local on country outskirts; beams and painted half-panelling, well kept ales such as Butcombe, Courage and Timothy Taylors, four ciders and enjoyable affordably

priced pub food, central little serving hatch for garden drinkers, go left for small bareboards bar with darts, right into an area with comfortable seating next to woodburner, with carpeted dining area behind; children and dogs welcome, picnic-sets and play area in lawned garden, large car park, open all day Sat, Sun.

BRADFORD-ON-AVON ST8261

★**George** (01225) 865650

Woolley Street; BA15 1AQ Neatly updated 18th-c stone dining pub with highly regarded food including good value set menus and themed evenings (last Thurs of month – booking advised), also breakfast (from 9.30am) and afternoon teas (Fri-Sun, booking required), efficient friendly service, a house beer from Butcombe and a couple of guests, good choice of wines and whiskies; two smallish rooms either side of entrance (one with open kitchen), mix of tables and chairs on wood floors, pictures for sale, cosy back lounge bar with sofas and wing chairs by log fire; children and dogs welcome, attractive split-level back garden, two self-catering apartments, open all day Fri and Sat, till 6pm Sun.

BRADFORD-ON-AVON ST8261

★**Stumble Inn** (01225) 862115

Market Street; BA15 1LL Friendly two-room micropub; four changing ales (two tapped from the cask), craft beers and decent range of wines, no food; seating on settles and pews, old enamel signs and big fireplace; no TVs or background music, board games aplenty, children and dogs welcome, closed Sun, Mon and lunchtimes apart from Sat.

BRADFORD-ON-AVON ST8260

★**Timbrells Yard** (01225) 869492

St Margarets Street; BA15 1DE Extensive modern refurbishment for this old stone-built riverside inn; long bar with cube stools and chairs around mix of tables on stripped floorboards, scatter cushions on upholstered wall/window seats, woodburner in big stone fireplace, archway through to small seating area with armchairs and sofas, quirky, contemporary and friendly feel, steps up to airy river-view restaurant with open kitchen, beers such as Box Steam, Brotherhood, Camden Town, Cheddar and Otter, 16 wines by the glass, good choice of other drinks including local cider and some interesting gins, well liked food from all-day bar snacks up; children and dogs (in bar and bedrooms) welcome, tables out on paved terrace, 17 stylish and well equipped bedrooms, open from 7.30am for breakfast.

BRINKWORTH SU0184

Three Crowns (01666) 510366

The Street; B4042 Wootton Bassett–Malmesbury; SN15 5AF Old stone pub with beamed bar with cushioned wall settles

and sturdy mate's chairs around tables on patterned carpet, fireplace at each end, Butcombe Original and a couple of guests, Thatcher's and Weston's ciders, 15 wines by the glass, flagstoned conservatory restaurant and other spreading dining areas with shelves of bottles and a giant pair of bellows, good food from pub staples up including daily specials and weekend breakfasts, small shop; children welcome, dogs in bar (menu for them), tables under parasols on terrace, more seats in garden, open all day, no food Sun evening.

BROKENBOROUGH ST9189

★**Horse Guards** (01666) 822302

Signed from Malmesbury on Tetbury road; SN16 0HZ Well run 18th-c village dining pub with fresh modern décor; beams and some bare stone walls in cosy bar, large two-way woodburner, lower back part mainly for their good home-made food using local ingredients including seasonal game, well kept Uley and a guest, interesting wines from shortish list (most available by the glass), welcoming owners and friendly staff; children and dogs allowed, two comfortable bedrooms, closed Mon lunchtime.

BROMHAM ST9665

★**Greyhound** (01380) 850241

Off A342; High Street; SN15 2HA Popular and welcoming old dining pub (same owners as Dandy Lion in Bradford-on-Avon and George in Sandy Lane); bar with white-painted beams and light modern décor, snug area to the right, dining part to the left, wood and tartan-carpeted floors, woodburner, back restaurant with walk-across well, good reasonably priced food cooked by landlord-chef including weekday lunch deal, efficient friendly service, well kept Wadworths ales and wide choice of wines, upstairs skittle alley/overflow restaurant; background music; children welcome, dogs in bar, circular picnic-sets in large enclosed garden with play equipment, ample parking in square opposite, closed Sun evening, Mon, otherwise open all day.

BULKINGTON ST9458

Well (01380) 828287

High Street; SN10 1SJ Popular dining pub with modernised open-plan interior; good food from sandwiches and traditional favourites up, efficient friendly service, four real ales including Butcombe, Sharps and Timothy Taylors, well priced wines; background music; children and dogs (in bar) welcome, seating in garden, wheelchair access, closed Mon.

CASTLE COMBE ST8477

Castle Inn (01249) 783030

Off A420; SN14 7HN Handsome old pub in remarkably well preserved Cotswold village; beamed bar with big stone fireplace, padded bar stools and fine old settle, some vintage

French posters, ales such as Castle Combe and St Austell from oak servery, 18 wines by the glass including champagne, well liked traditional food served by friendly attentive staff, two snug lounges, formal dining rooms and big upstairs conservatory opening on to charming little terrace; children and dogs (in bar) welcome, tables out at front looking down idyllic main street, fascinating medieval church clock, 12 bedrooms, car park shared with next-door hotel, open all day from 9.30am (food from midday).

CASTLE COMBE ST8379
Salutation (01249) 782083
The Gibb; B4039 Acton Turville–Chippenham, near Nettleton; SN14 7LH Friendly old pub with traditional L-shaped bar, beams, stripped stone and woodburner in handsome fireplace, well kept Fortitude and a guest such as Flying Monk, good locally sourced food from regularly changing menu including bargain two-course weekday lunch, lofty thatched and timbered barn restaurant; children and dogs welcome, nice garden, open all day.

CHICKSGROVE ST9729
★ Compasses (01722) 714318
From A30 5.5 miles W of B3089 junction, take lane on N side signposted 'Sutton Mandeville, Sutton Row', then first left fork (small signs point the way to the pub in Lower Chicksgrove; look out for the car park); can also be reached off B3089 W of Dinton, passing the glorious spire of Teffont Evias church; SP3 6NB Popular 14th-c thatched inn with unchanging character bar; old bottles and jugs hanging from beams above the roughly timbered counter, farm tools and traps on stripped-stone walls, high-backed settles forming snug booths, flagstones and log fire, ales such as Butcombe, Keystone and Three Daggers, real cider and a dozen wines by the glass, good sensibly priced food (not Sun evening) from interesting menu; children and dogs welcome, quiet garden behind with terraces and courtyard, good surrounding walks, comfortable bedrooms and self-catering cottage, open all day (all day Sat, Sun in winter).

CHILMARK ST9732
Black Dog (01722) 716484
B3089 Salisbury–Hindon; SP3 5AH New owners as we went to press for this cosy and welcoming 15th-c beamed pub in pretty village just south of busy A303; several linked areas, cushioned window seats, inglenook woodburner and interesting photographs from around the world, has had good food with emphasis on fish/seafood (not Sun evening and Mon), three well kept Wadworths ales, friendly attentive service; children and dogs (in bar) welcome, disabled access, good-sized garden fenced from the road, open all day weekends.

CHILTON FOLIAT SU3270
★ Wheatsheaf (01488) 680936
B4192; RG17 0TE Delightful 17th-c thatched pub with eco/sustainable attitude, where the landlord (a *MasterChef* semi-finalist) cooks the 'upmarket peasant food' including popular wood-fired pizzas, and his wife runs front of house; carefully restored character rooms include a beamed bar and dining room with wheelbacks and mate's chairs, built-in settles and bow-window seats around dark tables on patterned carpets, a piano and woodburning stoves; local ales include one named for the pub (from Butts) plus Brunswick The Usual and Ramsbury Gold, 15 wines by the glass from all-organic list, home-made liqueurs, organic soft drinks and farm cider; darts, board games and background music, also live music, quiz nights and cookery classes; children and dogs welcome, picnic-sets on grass, disabled access.

CHIPPENHAM ST9173
Old Road Tavern (01249) 247080
Old Road, by N side of station; SN15 1JA Friendly old-fashioned 19th-c town pub; public bar and two-part lounge, half a dozen well kept ales including Bath, Otter and Wye Valley, straightforward lunchtime food Thurs-Sat; live music and comedy nights in side barn, pool; large secluded back garden, handy for station, open all day.

CHOLDERTON SU2242
Crown (01980) 629247
A338 Tidworth–Salisbury roundabout, just off A303; SP4 0DW Thatched low-beamed cottage with nicely informal eating areas in L-shaped bar; a couple of well kept changing ales, ciders such as Aspall's and Broadoak and good food (including buffalo) cooked to order by landlord-chef, separate restaurant; quiz first Weds of month, occasional live music, beer/cider festival Sept; children and dogs welcome, picnic-sets out at front and in garden with play area, open (and food) all day Sun.

CHRISTIAN MALFORD ST9678
Rising Sun (01249) 721571
Station Road; SN15 4BL Community-run village pub dating from the early 19th c; small beamed bar with wood floor, leather sofas by log fire, well kept Otter and seasonally changing ales, ciders on draught, carpeted restaurant with high-backed dining chairs around modern wooden tables, enjoyable well presented food, good friendly service; children and dogs (in bar) welcome, disabled loo, a few picnic-sets out at front, play area and boules in back garden, can be open all day but best to check Facebook page.

COLLINGBOURNE DUCIS SU2453
Tipple Inn (01264) 850050
High Street; SN8 3EQ Comfortable 18th-c village pub well cared for by friendly

landlord; three changing ales and fairly standard home-cooked food (not Sun or Mon evenings) from good baguettes up, woodburners in bar and smallish restaurant with light wood furniture and some vibrant artwork; quiz and live music nights, sports TV, pool, darts; children, walkers and dogs welcome, small roadside terrace with pretty hanging baskets, grassy garden behind beyond car park, one bedroom, closed Tues.

CORSHAM ST8770
Flemish Weaver (01249) 701929
High Street; SN13 0EZ Town pub in attractive 17th-c building revamped in quirky style with all kinds of bits and pieces; good food (not Sun evening) and four well kept ales including a Wadworths house beer, friendly enthusiastic young staff; some live music; children and dogs welcome, tables in intriguing back courtyard, open all day, closed Mon.

CORTON ST9340
★**Dove** (01985) 850109
Off A36 at Upton Lovell, SE of Warminster; BA12 0SZ Modernised and extended brick pub on edge of small Wylye Valley village not far from the A303; popular well prepared food from sandwiches and pub favourites to more enterprising dishes including generous fish boards, well kept Otter, Wadworths and local guests, Thatcher's cider and nice wines by the glass from comprehensive list, chatty helpful staff, opened-up rooms with flagstones and light oak boards, pale green dados and lots of animal pictures/figurines, flowers on good quality dining tables, log fires, sunny conservatory; children and dogs welcome, wheelchair access/loos, grassy beer garden sheltered by thatched cob wall, five stable-block bedrooms and self-catering cottage, open all day and can get very busy.

DEVIZES SU0061
Black Swan (01380) 727777
Market Place; SN10 1JQ Traditional 18th-c coaching inn with plenty of atmosphere refurbished under new management; quirky bare-boards interior with period street signs, antiques and interesting bits and pieces, candles and open fire, Wadworths ales and a guest, sensibly priced food (not Sun evening) from fairly pubby menu, friendly service; quiz last Thurs of month; children and dogs welcome, nice courtyard garden with own bar (weekend live music and DJs monthly), 12 bedrooms, open all day.

DEVIZES SU0061
British Lion (01380) 720665
A361 Swindon roundabout; SN10 1LQ Chatty little drinkers' pub with four well kept quickly changing ales and a proper cider, bare-boards bar with brewery mirrors and gas fire, back part with pool and darts; no food, dogs not allowed, large garden with heated shelter behind, open all day.

DEVIZES SU0061
Three Crowns (01380) 722331
Maryport Street; SN10 1AG Popular 17th-c town-centre pub with good food and well kept range of Wadworths and guest ales, cider from a couple of barrels behind the bar, efficient helpful staff; some live music; children and dogs welcome, lovely sunny courtyard garden and more seating on a roof terrace, open all day, food all day but no booking so there may be a wait.

DONHEAD ST ANDREW ST9124
★**Forester** (01747) 828038
Village signposted off A30 E of Shaftesbury, just E of Ludwell; Lower Street; SP7 9EE Attractive 14th-c thatched restaurant-pub in charming village; nice relaxed bar with stripped tables on wood floors and inglenook log fire, sofas and magazines in alcove, Butcombe Bitter, a guest beer and good selection of wines by the glass including champagne, highly regarded food (some emphasis on fresh fish/seafood), also lunchtime sandwiches, efficient friendly service, comfortable restaurant with well spaced country kitchen tables, second cosier dining room; children and dogs welcome, country views from good-sized terrace, can walk up White Sheet Hill and past the old and 'new' Wardour castles, closed Sun evening, Mon.

DOWNTON SU1721
Wooden Spoon (01725) 511899
High Street (A338 S of Salisbury); SP5 3PG Popular 18th-c red-brick pub with two bars; well kept ales and good reasonably priced food from blackboard menus, friendly efficient service, open fire, extensive banknote collection; children and dogs welcome, appealing garden behind, closes 9pm Sun.

EBBESBOURNE WAKE ST9924
★**Horseshoe** (01722) 780474
On A354 S of Salisbury, right at signpost at Coombe Bissett; village about 8 miles further; SP5 5JF Popular unspoilt village pub run by the same welcoming family for over 45 years; Bowman, Gritchie, Otter and guest beers tapped from chilled casks, real cider, generous helpings of good traditional home-cooked food served by friendly staff, neatly kept and comfortable character bar with collection of farm tools and bric-a-brac on beams, small restaurant and conservatory; children welcome away

---

We accept no free drinks or meals and inspections are anonymous.

from bar, dogs at landlord's discretion, seats in pretty little garden with views over Ebble Valley, play area, chickens and goat in paddock, good nearby walks, one bedroom, closed Sun evening, Mon.

EDINGTON   ST9353
★ **Three Daggers** (01380) 830940
Westbury Road (B3098); BA13 4PG
Smart but relaxed pub brewing its own good Three Daggers beers in farm shop opposite; open-plan beamed interior with leather sofas and armchairs at one end by woodburner, wide range of enjoyable food including two-course lunch menu, well chosen wines (plenty by the glass), helpful friendly service, candlelit restaurant with slate floor and two-way fireplace, stairs up to high raftered dining/function room, airy conservatory; background music, darts and board games; children and dogs (in bar) welcome, picnic-sets on grass, fenced play area, three bedrooms plus separate six-bedroom house and spa facilities, open all day.

ENFORD   SU14351
★ **Swan** (01980) 670338
Long Street, off A345; SN9 6DD
Attractive and welcoming thatched village pub; opened-up beamed interior with log fire in large fireplace, five well kept changing local ales and good locally sourced home-made food from lunchtime sandwiches and snacks up, prompt friendly service; darts and board games, beer/music festival Aug Bank Holiday; children, walkers and dogs welcome, seats out on small front terrace and in big landscaped back garden, gallows-style inn sign spanning the road, open all day weekends, closed Mon lunchtime.

FORD   ST8474
White Hart (01249) 782213
Off A420 Chippenham–Bristol; SN14 8RP Handsome 16th-c Marstons-managed country inn; beamed bars with bare boards or quarry tiles, dining and tub chairs, cushioned wall seats and button-back sofas, lots of prints on bold paintwork, open fire and woodburner, three real ales including Bath Gem and a beer badged for the pub, good range of other drinks (20 wines by the glass), much liked food from sandwiches/baguettes to signature steaks cooked in charcoal oven, friendly efficient staff; children and dogs (in bar) welcome, front courtyard and terrace, trout stream by small stone bridge, comfortable modern bedrooms, open (and food) all day.

FOXHAM   ST9777
Foxham Inn (01249) 740665
NE of Chippenham; SN15 4NQ Small tucked-away country dining pub with simple traditional décor: enterprising food strong on local produce along with more straightforward bar meals and themed nights, well kept ales such as St Austell

Tribute, nice choice of wines by the glass and good coffee, woodburner, more contemporary conservatory-style restaurant with kitchen view, own bread, chutneys, jams etc for sale; children and dogs welcome, disabled access and facilities, terrace with pergola, extensive views from front, two comfortable bedrooms, closed Sun evening, Mon.

FROXFIELD   SU2968
Pelican (01488) 682479
Off A4, Bath Road; SN8 3JY Modernised and extended 17th-c coaching inn; enjoyable home-made food from sandwiches and panini up, helpful friendly young staff, local ales such as Wickwar, comfortable relaxed atmosphere; children and dogs welcome, pleasant streamside garden with terrace and duck pond, Kennet & Avon Canal walks (bridge 90), eight bedrooms, open all day, no food Sun evening.

HANNINGTON   SU1793
Jolly Tar (01793) 762245
Off B4019 W of Highworth; Queens Road; SN6 7RP Old painted stone pub in pretty village; beamed bar with big log fire, steps up to flagstoned and stripped-stone dining area, good reasonably priced home-made food including popular Sun lunch (should book), well kept Arkells ales, friendly helpful service; children and dogs (in bar) welcome, picnic-sets on front terrace and in big garden with play area, four comfortable bedrooms, good breakfast, closed Mon lunchtime except bank holidays, no food Sun evening.

HEDDINGTON   ST9966
Ivy (01380) 859652
Off A3102 S of Calne; SN11 0PL Picturesque thatched village local dating from the 15th c; L-shaped bar with heavy low beams, timbered walls and inglenook log fire, traditional furniture on parquet floor, Wadworths ales tapped from the cask, good wine choice and enjoyable well priced food (just Sun lunchtime and Fri, Sat evenings), back dining room; darts; children and dogs welcome, wheelchair access (no disabled loo), picnic-sets out at front and in small side garden, open all day Fri and Sat, till 9pm Sun, closed Mon and lunchtimes Tues-Thurs.

HINDON   ST9132
★ **Lamb** (01747) 820573
B3089 Wilton–Mere; SP3 6DP Attractive 12th-c coaching inn in picturesque village; roomy log-fire bar, two flagstoned lower sections with long polished table, high-backed pews and settles, steps up to third, bigger area, well kept Youngs and a guest, several wines by the glass and good selection of malt whiskies, cocktails and Cuban cigars, enjoyable bar and restaurant food including sandwiches, afternoon tea and pub classics, friendly service, can get very busy; children and dogs welcome, tables on roadside terrace

and in garden across the road, 18 stylish bedrooms, open all day from 7.30am (8am weekends) for breakfast.

KILMINGTON ST7835
Red Lion (01985) 844263
B3092 Mere–Frome, 2.5 miles S of Maiden Bradley; 3 miles from A303 Mere turn-off; BA12 6RP NT-owned country pub with low-beamed flagstoned bar, cushioned wall and window seats, curved high-backed settle, woodburner in large fireplace at either end, well kept ales such as Butcombe and Wessex, traditional ciders and enjoyable home-made food including lunchtime sandwiches, newer big-windowed back dining area where children allowed; dogs welcome in bar, attractive big garden with fine views, White Sheet Hill (hang-gliding) and Stourhead gardens (NT) nearby, open all day Sat till 8pm, Sun till 5pm, closed Mon, Tues.

KINGTON ST MICHAEL ST9077
Jolly Huntsman (01249) 750305
3 miles from M4 junction 17; SN14 6JB Roomy 18th-c stone-built pub; Flying Monk, Moles and a local guest, proper cider and good home-made food from pub standards up, friendly service, carpeted interior with scrubbed tables, comfortable sofas and good log fire; occasional jazz and blues; children and dogs (in bar) welcome, bedrooms in separate block.

LACOCK ST9268
Bell (01249) 730308
E of village; SN15 2PJ Extended cottagey pub with warm welcome; local ales including house beers from Great Western and guest ales, traditional ciders, well chosen/priced wines and good selection of malt whiskies and gins, enjoyable generously served food from lunchtime platters, pub favourites and grills up, friendly efficient young staff, linked rooms off bar including more formal restaurant and bright airy conservatory; children and dogs (in bar) welcome, disabled access (not to conservatory) from car park, well tended garden with play area and smokers' shelter ('the Coughing Shed'), long views across Avon Valley, open (and food) all day weekends.

LACOCK ST9168
George (01249) 730263
West Street; village signed off A350 S of Chippenham; SN15 2LH Rambling old inn at centre of busy NT tourist village; low-beamed bar with upright timbers creating cosy corners, some flagstones and stone-mullioned windows, dog treadwheel in outer breast of central fireplace, lots of pictures including photos of *Cranford* and *Harry Potter* being filmed in the village, six mainly Wadworths beers and Weston's cider, lots of wines by the glass, popular sensibly priced food from sandwiches up, friendly

staff; background music; children and dogs welcome, tricky wheelchair access, pleasant courtyard with pillory and old well, picnic-sets on grass, open all day summer.

LACOCK ST9168
Red Lion (01249) 730456
High Street; SN15 2LQ Popular NT-owned Georgian inn; sizeable opened-up interior with log fire in large stone fireplace, bare boards and flagstones, roughly carved screens here and there and some cosy alcoves, well kept Wadworths ales, Thatcher's and Weston's ciders, enjoyable food from sandwiches and sharing plates up, friendly efficient service; background music; children and dogs welcome, wheelchair access to main bar area only, picnic-sets out on gravel, four modern bedrooms, open (and food) all day.

LACOCK ST9367
Rising Sun (01249) 730363
Bewley Common, Bowden Hill – out towards Sandy Lane, up hill past abbey; OS Sheet 173 map reference 935679; SN15 2PP Attractive old stone pub with three knocked-together simply furnished rooms; beams and log fires, Stonehenge and guest ales, several proper ciders and fairly traditional locally sourced food including daily specials, friendly attentive service; background and some live music; well behaved children and dogs (in bar) welcome, no wheelchair access, wonderful views across Avon Valley from conservatory and two-level terrace, outside bar and kitchen for light meals, three-bed apartment to rent, open all day in summer (all day Fri and Sat, till 6pm Sun), closed Mon.

LEA ST9586
Rose & Crown (01666) 822053
The Street; SN16 9PA Creeper-clad Victorian stone pub next to the village church; enjoyable good value food from sandwiches up with more restaurant food in evening, Arkells and guest ales kept well, over 20 gins, friendly efficient service, compact interconnecting rooms with mix of furnishings, log fires including two-way woodburner; children and dogs welcome, picnic-sets out at front and in large well maintained garden with paved terrace and play area, closed Mon, otherwise open (and food) all day, kitchen shuts 5pm Sun.

LITTLE SOMERFORD ST9784
Somerford Arms (01666) 826535
Signed off B4042 Malmesbury–Brinkworth; SN15 5JP Modernised village pub now owned by the community; opened-up interior with stone flooring, painted half-panelling and two-way woodburner, enjoyable food from pub classics up, three well kept changing ales, 15 gins, over a dozen wines by the glass, friendly helpful service; children and dogs welcome (pub dog is called Freddie), open all day, from 4pm Mon.

LOCKERIDGE SU1467
Who'd A Thought It (01672) 861255
Signed off A4 Marlborough–Calne, just W of Fyfield; SN8 4EL Attractive village pub-restaurant serving popular food with pub standards and more adventurous options, well kept Wadworths beers and decent wines including champagne by the glass, friendly service; children and dogs welcome, pleasant back garden with play area, lovely bluebell walks nearby, open all day weekends, closed Tues, no food Sun evening (shuts 9pm) – under new management (father and son team) after some problems, reports please.

LONGBRIDGE DEVERILL ST8640
George (01985) 840396
A350/B3095; BA12 7DG Popular updated and extended roadside free house; well kept ales and generous helpings of enjoyable freshly made food including Sun carvery, friendly helpful service, conservatory; quiz night Sun; children and dogs (in bar) welcome, big riverside garden with play area, 12 bedrooms, handy for Longleat, open all day, breakfast for non-residents from 8am Mon-Sat.

LOWER WOODFORD SU1235
Wheatsheaf (01722) 782203
Signed off A360 just N of Salisbury; SP4 6NQ Updated and extended 18th-c dining pub with airy open feel; decent choice of fairly priced food from sandwiches and sharing boards up, well kept Badger and guest ales, good wines and coffee, beams, panelling and exposed brickwork, mix of old furniture, log fire and woodburner; background music; well behaved children welcome in restaurant, muddy boots and dogs in bar, disabled loo and parking, fenced tree-lined garden with play area, pretty setting, open (and food) all day.

LUCKINGTON ST8384
Old Royal Ship (01666) 840222
Off B4040 SW of Malmesbury; SN14 6PA Friendly pub by village green; one long bar divided into three areas, ales such as Flying Monk and Sharps from central servery, also traditional cider and several wines by the glass, good range of food including some vegetarian options, neat tables, spindleback chairs and cushioned settles on dark boards, stripped masonry and small open fire; background music, skittle alley, quiz and theme nights; children welcome, plenty of seats in garden (beyond car park) with boules and play area, Badminton House close by, open all day weekends.

MANTON SU1768
Oddfellows (01672) 512352
Village signposted off A4 just W of Marlborough; High Street; SN8 4HW Popular country pub with horse-racing theme, under new management (formerly the

Outside Chance); three small linked rooms with hop-strung beams, flagstones or bare boards, plain pub furnishings such as chapel chairs and a long-cushioned pew, one room has a more cosseted feel with banquette seating, log fire in big main fireplace, wide choice of enjoyable food, Wadworths ales and eight wines by the glass; background music, board games; children and dogs welcome, covered outside area (heated in winter) for outdoor dining, more rustic furniture under ash trees in good-sized garden, private access to local playing fields and play area, open all day weekends.

MARDEN SU0857
★ Millstream (01380) 848490
Village signposted off A342 SE of Devizes; SN10 3RH Rather smart red-brick dining pub in leafy setting at top end of attractive village; highly regarded food cooked by landlady-chef including fish/seafood specials and good value Sun lunch (best to book), well kept Wadworths ales, friendly efficient young staff, appealing layout of linked cosy areas, beams and log fires, red-cushioned dark pews and small padded dining chairs around sturdy oak and other good tables, comfy sofas in one part; children and dogs welcome (resident pointers are Sophie and Francesca), disabled access/loos, neat terrace by entrance and big lawned garden down to tree-lined stream, 12th-c church worth a visit, closed Sun and Mon evenings.

MARKET LAVINGTON SU0154
Green Dragon (01380) 813235
High Street; SN10 4AG Rambling early 17th-c red-brick pub with light and airy interior; four well kept Wadworths ales, good value wines and enjoyable reasonably priced food from sandwiches and baked potatoes up, friendly welcoming staff; darts, pool, boules; children and dogs welcome, wheelchair access, large back garden with shelter, six bedrooms (four in converted outbuildings), hearty breakfast, open all day.

MARLBOROUGH SU1869
Lamb (01672) 512668
The Parade; SN8 1NE Bustling town local attracting good mix of customers; cheerful lived-in main bar with wall banquettes and wheelback chairs around wooden tables on parquet flooring, two-way woodburner, good home-made food lunchtimes and Fri evening, well kept Wadworths ales, ten wines by the glass and 15 malt whiskies, friendly staff; juke box (live music Sat), games machine, TV and darts; tables in pleasant courtyard, pretty summer window boxes, seven bedrooms, open all day.

MARSTON MEYSEY SU1297
★ Old Spotted Cow (01285) 810264
Off A419 Swindon–Cirencester; SN6 6LQ Civilised country pub with three well kept

ales including Skinners Betty Stoggs and maybe Bath or Otter, welcoming attentive staff, two open fires, light wood furniture and cosy sofas, rugs on bare boards and parquet, stripped stone walls, house plants, candles and plenty of cow ornaments and pictures, interesting home-made food as well as more traditional dishes; well behaved children and dogs (in bar) welcome, spacious garden overlooking fields, play area, two bedrooms, open all day.

MONKTON FARLEIGH   ST8065
Kings Arms   (01225) 859761
Signed off A363 Bradford-on-Avon to Bath; BA15 2QH New management and recent refurbishment for this imposing 17th-c wisteria-clad stone pub in lovely village; beamed bar with wood-strip floor and inglenook, zinc-topped counter serving three real ales and a traditional cider, enjoyable food from varied menu, parquet-floored restaurant; children and dogs welcome, seats in front courtyard, more in two-tier back garden with country views, bedrooms, open (and food) all day.

NESTON   ST8668
Neston Country Inn   (01225) 811694
Church Rise, Pool Green; SN13 9SN Welcoming unpretentious early 19th-c inn; good reasonably priced food cooked by landlord with some South African influences and themed nights, well kept Fullers London Pride and a couple of local guests, friendly helpful staff; book club second Thurs of month, quiz last Thurs, darts; children and dogs welcome, picnic-sets in back garden with gate to village playing field, four bedrooms, open all day Sat, till 9pm Sun, closed Mon lunchtime (Tues lunchtime after bank holiday).

NETHERHAMPTON   SU1129
★ **Victoria & Albert**   (01722) 743174
Just off A3094 W of Salisbury; SP2 8PU Cosy black-beamed bar in simple 16th-c thatched cottage; old-fashioned cushioned wall settles on ancient floor tiles, log fire, three well kept changing ales, proper cider and decent wines, welcoming helpful staff, popular home-made food from sandwiches up at sensible prices, restaurant; children and dogs welcome, hatch service for sizeable terrace and garden behind, handy for Wilton House and walks in the Nadder Valley, closed Sun evening.

NOMANSLAND   SU2517
Lamb   (01794) 390246
Signed off B3078 and B3079, Forest Road; SP5 2BP Lovely New Forest village-green setting (the county border runs through the pub); family run and popular with locals, decent choice of enjoyable home-made food from lunchtime baguettes up, popular Sun roasts, four changing ales and sensibly priced wine list, friendly staff,

log fire in traditional carpeted bar, small dining room, lots of bits and pieces to look at, games room with pool; TV; children and dogs welcome, tables on front terrace overlooking the green (with grazing ponies) and in colourful back garden, open all day Fri-Sun.

NORTON   ST8884
Vine Tree   (01666) 837654
4 miles from M4 junction 17; A429 towards Malmesbury, then left at Hullavington, Sherston signpost, then follow Norton signposts; in village turn right at Foxley signpost, which takes you into Honey Lane; SN16 0JP Civilised dining pub with three neat small rooms; beams, old settles and unvarnished wooden tables on flagstones, sporting prints and church candles, large fireplace in central bar, ales such as Butcombe and local Flying Monk, 30 wines by the glass from extensive list and over 60 gins, well liked food from sharing boards up, restaurant with woodburner; children and dogs welcome, hitching rail for horses, picnic-sets and play area in two-acre garden, suntrap terrace, closed Sun evening (also closed Mon and Tues in winter).

OGBOURNE ST ANDREW   SU1871
Silks on the Downs   (01672) 841229
A345 N of Marlborough; SN8 1RZ Popular restaurant-y pub with horse-racing theme; highly regarded food (best to book) from shortish but varied menu, Ramsbury Gold and a guest, proper cider and decent wines by the glass, helpful friendly service, stylish décor with mix of dining tables on polished wood floors, some good prints and photographs as well as framed racing silks; well behaved children allowed, no dogs inside, conservatory, small decked area and garden, closed Sun evening.

PEWSEY   SU1561
Waterfront   (01672) 564020
Pewsey Wharf (A345 just N); SN9 5NU Bar-bistro in converted wharf building next to canal; ample helpings of good reasonably priced food including daily specials, three well kept changing ales tapped from the cask in upstairs bar (can eat here too), good quality wines, efficient friendly staff; children and dogs (not downstairs) welcome, waterside picnic-sets, nice walks, parking fee to the Kennet & Avon Canal Trust, closed Mon lunchtime (and all Tues in winter), open all day Fri-Sun.

PITTON   SU2131
Silver Plough   (01722) 712266
Village signed from A30 E of Salisbury (follow brown signs); SP5 1DU Former 18th-c farmhouse; front bar with pewter and china tankards, copper kettles and toby jugs hanging from black beams, cushioned antique settles around rustic pine tables, counter made from carved Elizabethan

overmantel serving Badger ales and good range of wines by the glass, enjoyable food from pub standards up, back locals' bar, a couple of woodburners; skittle alley, some live music; children and dogs welcome, south-facing lawn with tables under parasols, more seats on heated terrace, two bedrooms, good nearby walks including Clarendon Way, open all day Sat, closed Sun evening, Mon.

POULSHOT   ST9760
Raven (01380) 828271
Off A361; SN10 1RW Attractive half-timbered pub opposite village green; two black-beamed carpeted rooms with cushioned wall benches and other pubby furniture, open fire, Wadworths IPA, 6X and several wines by the glass, enjoyable well priced pubby food including OAP weekday lunch offer, friendly helpful service; quiz nights; children and dogs (in bar) welcome, walled back garden with trees and shrubs, open all day Sun till 9pm.

REDLYNCH   SU2021
Kings Head (01725) 510420
Off A338 via B3080; The Row; SP5 2JT Early 18th-c pub on edge of New Forest; three or four well kept ales such as Hop Back and Ringwood, decent house wines and coffee, good value home-made food from pub favourites up, beamed and flagstoned main bar with woodburner in large brick fireplace, small conservatory; children, dogs and muddy boots welcome, picnic-sets out in front and in side garden, Pepperbox Hill (NT) walks nearby, open (and food) all day Sun, closed Mon lunchtime.

ROWDE   ST9762
★**George & Dragon** (01380) 723053
A342 Devizes–Chippenham; SN10 2PN Welcoming and well run 16th-c coaching inn with lots of character; two low-beamed rooms with large open fireplaces, wooden dining chairs around candlelit tables, antique rugs and walls covered with old pictures and portraits, Butcombe and guests, several wines by the glass, good food including daily fresh seafood from Cornwall; background music; children and dogs (in bar) welcome, seats in pretty back garden, Kennet & Avon Canal nearby, three comfortable bedrooms, closed Sun evening.

SALISBURY   SU1429
★**Haunch of Venison** (01722) 411313
Minster Street, opposite Market Cross; SP1 1TB Ancient jettied pub with small downstairs rooms dating from 1320, massive beams, stout oak benches built into timbered walls, log fires, tiny snug (the Horsebox) with pewter counter and rare set of antique taps for gravity-fed spirits, well kept Hop Back, guest beers and 130 malt whiskies, enjoyable food including various venison dishes, friendly staff, steep stairs to restaurant, halfway up is panelled room with splendid

fireplace and (behind glass) the mummified hand of an 18th-c card sharp; children and dogs (in bars) welcome, open (and food) all day.

SALISBURY   SU1429
New Inn (01722) 326662
New Street; SP1 2PH Much extended old building with massive beams and timbers; good choice of enjoyable fair priced food from pub staples up, three well kept Badger ales and decent house wines, flagstones, bare boards and carpet, chesterfields, quiet cosy alcoves, inglenook woodburner; children welcome, pretty walled garden with striking view of nearby cathedral spire, two bedrooms, open all day.

SALISBURY   SU1430
Wyndham Arms (01722) 331026
Estcourt Road; SP1 3AS Friendly red-brick corner local with full Hop Back range (brewery was originally based here), also a guest ale, bottled beers and country wines, no food, small front and side rooms, longer main bar; Thurs quiz, darts and board games; children and dogs welcome, open all day Thurs-Sun, from 4.30pm other days.

SANDY LANE   ST9668
George (01380) 850403
A342 Devizes–Chippenham; SN15 2PX Handsome 18th-c stone pub under same owners as the Greyhound at Bromham and Dandy Lion at Bradford-on-Avon; long simply furnished bar with wood floor, light blue dado and log fire, Wadworths ales and enjoyable pubby food with an Italian twist including daily carvery, airy back dining room with large woodburner, timber-framed conservatory; children welcome, tables on terrace and lawn, charming thatched village, Bowood Estate walks, closed Mon, otherwise open (and food) all day, till 7pm (6pm) Sun.

SEEND   ST9361
Barge (01380) 828230
Seend Cleeve; signed off A361 Devizes–Trowbridge; SN12 6QB Busy waterside pub with plenty of seats in garden making the most of boating activity on Kennet & Avon Canal (moorings); rambling interior with log fires, some unusual seating in bar such as painted milk churns, Wadworths and guest ales and extensive range of wines by the glass, decent choice of enjoyable well priced food including summer barbecues, efficient service; background music; children and dogs welcome, open all day.

SEMINGTON   ST8960
Somerset Arms (01380) 870067
Off A350 bypass 2 miles S of Melksham; BA14 6JR 16th-c coaching inn with long heavy-beamed bar and restaurant, four well kept local ales, real ciders and enjoyable pubby food (not Sun evening) from baguettes up including plenty of gluten-free choices,

friendly young staff; children and dogs welcome, picnic-sets in small garden behind, three bedrooms, short walk from Kennet & Avon Canal, open all day, breakfast from 9am.

SHERSTON ST8586
Carpenters Arms (01666) 840665
Easton Town (B4040); SN16 0NT
Friendly whitewashed roadside pub; ales such as Butcombe, Flying Monk and Sharps, Thatcher's ciders and decent reasonably priced wines, enjoyable food including weekday OAP lunch, Weds burger night and Sat steak/wine deal, small interconnecting rooms with low beams, stripped-stone or grey-painted walls, light-wood flooring, log fires, modern dining conservatory; background music, pool; children and dogs welcome, disabled access/loos, grassy garden with play area, open all day.

SOUTH WRAXALL ST8364
★ **Longs Arms** (01225) 864450
Upper S Wraxall, off B3109 N of Bradford-on-Avon; BA15 2SB Handsome old stone pub, with good seasonal food from convivial landlord-chef, three West Country ales (perhaps from Exmoor, Gritchie or Palmers), several wines by the glass, good range of gins and farm cider; clean and tidy décor in open-plan rooms with nice mix of furniture on flagstones, wood-strip or carpeted floors, woodburner, friendly efficient staff; background music; children and dogs (in bar areas) welcome, pretty walled back garden with raised beds and greenhouse, open all day Fri-Sun.

STEEPLE ASHTON ST9056
Longs Arms (01380) 870245
High Street; BA14 6EU Attractively presented 17th-c stone coaching inn with friendly local atmosphere; Sharps and Wadworths ales kept well, plenty of wines by the glass and very good locally sourced food from lunchtime sandwiches/ciabattas and home-made pizzas up, bar with lots of pictures and old photos, adjacent dining part, woodburner; children and dogs welcome, play area and boules in big garden, self-catering cottage, delightful village with fine church, open all day Fri-Sun.

STOURTON ST7733
Spread Eagle (01747) 840587
Church Lawn; follow Stourhead brown signs off B3092, N of junction with A303 W of Mere; BA12 6QE Busy NT-owned Georgian inn at entrance to Stourhead Estate; spacious interior with antique settles, solid tables and chairs, sporting prints and handsome fireplaces, well kept Butcombe, Wessex and interesting wines by the glass in flagstoned bar, fairly compact but varied menu, cream teas; background music; children and dogs (in some parts) welcome, wheelchair access (step down to dining areas), smart back courtyard with circular

picnic-sets, five bedrooms (guests can wander freely around famous gardens outside normal hours, picnic hampers available), open all day.

SUTTON VENY ST8941
Woolpack (01985) 840834
High Street; BA12 7AW Small well run 1920s village local with friendly chatty atmosphere; good food including some inventive dishes cooked by landlord-chef from blackboard menu (best to book), home-made chutneys, pickles etc for sale, a couple of Butcombe ales, sensibly priced wines by the glass and good selection of malt whiskies, efficient amiable service, modernised interior with compact side dining area screened from bare-boards bar, woodburner; background music; dogs welcome, attractive garden terrace, closed Sun evening, Mon.

TISBURY ST9429
Boot (01747) 870363
High Street; SP3 6PS Ancient and unpretentious village local under welcoming long-serving licensee; three well kept changing ales tapped from the cask, cider/perry, enjoyable reasonably priced pubby food including well liked range of pizzas, open fire; traditional pub games; dogs welcome, tables in good-sized back garden, closed Sun evening and lunchtimes Mon, Tues.

UPAVON SU1355
Ship (01980) 630313
High Street; SN9 6EA Large thatched pub with good choice of enjoyable home-made food including wood-fired pizzas (Thurs-Sat evenings) and Weds steak night, well kept changing ales such as Butcombe and Wadworths, a couple of traditional ciders and decent range of wines and whiskies, some interesting nautical memorabilia; occasional live music; dogs and muddy boots welcome, picnic-sets in front and on small side terrace, parking can be tricky, open all day.

UPTON LOVELL ST9441
Prince Leopold (01985) 850460
Up Street, village signed from A36; BA12 0JP Prettily tucked-away Victorian country pub; simply furnished bar with light wood floor, ales such as Butcombe and plenty of wines by the glass from hand-crafted elm counter, cosy snug leading off with shelves either side of open fire and comfortable sofas, two other linked rooms and airy back restaurant overlooking River Wylye (as do some balcony tables), well liked food from sandwiches and pub favourites up, friendly service; children and dogs welcome, outside bar in waterside garden, bedrooms, open all day Sat, till 8pm Sun, closed Mon.

UPTON SCUDAMORE ST8647
Angel (01985) 213225
Off A350 N of Warminster; BA12 0AG
Smartly updated 16th-c dining inn well

placed for Longleat; farmhouse tables and chairs and leather sofas by fire in bare-boards bar, Sharps Doom Bar, good wines by the glass and well liked Italian food including good value weekday set lunch, friendly helpful service, steps up to two dining rooms with white paintwork, timbered walls and leather dining chairs and banquettes; children and dogs welcome, picnic tables at back by car park, six well equipped comfortable bedrooms, open all day weekends.

URCHFONT   SU0357
Lamb (01380) 848848
The Green; SN10 4QU Welcoming part-thatched village local; well kept Wadworths ales and enjoyable good value pubby food from baguettes to blackboard specials, simply furnished with carpeted bar and another adjoining room; skittle alley, darts; children and dogs welcome, picnic-sets in grassy side garden, pétanque, smokers' shelter, open all day at weekends (till 9pm Sun, 6pm for food).

WARMINSTER   ST8745
Organ (01985) 211777
High Street; BA12 9AQ Former 18th-c inn (reopened 2006 after 93 years as a shop) – bigger inside than it looks; front bar, games room and skittle alley, welcoming owners and chatty regulars, three well kept regional ales including one badged for them (Sept beer festival), real ciders/perries, no food apart from bar snacks and cheeseboards but can bring your own; local artwork in upstairs gallery; quiz nights and occasional live music; no under-21s, dogs welcome, seats in sunny rear courtyard, open from noon Sat, 4pm other days.

WARMINSTER   ST8745
★ Weymouth Arms (01985) 216995
Emwell Street; BA12 8JA Charming backstreet pub with snug panelled entrance bar, log fire in fine stone fireplace, ancient books on mantelpiece, leather tub chairs around walnut and satinwood table, more seats against the walls, Butcombe, Wadworths 6X and half a dozen wines by the glass, second heavily panelled room with wide floorboards and smaller fireplace, candles in brass sticks, split-level dining room stretching back to open kitchen serving good food from pub favourites up, friendly helpful service; children and dogs (in bar) welcome, seats in flower-filled back courtyard, six comfortable well equipped bedrooms, closed lunchtimes Mon-Thurs, no evening food Sun.

WEST OVERTON   SU1368
Bell (01672) 861099
A4 Marlborough–Calne; SN8 1QD Early 19th-c roadside coaching inn; highly praised imaginative cooking from owner-chef using fresh local ingredients, also lunchtime sandwiches and some pubby choices, well

kept local beers including one named for the pub, good wines, attentive friendly service from uniformed staff, bar with woodburner (dogs allowed here), spacious restaurant beyond; background music; disabled access, nice secluded back garden with terrace and summer bar, country views, good walks nearby, closed Sun evening, Mon.

WESTBROOK   ST9565
Westbrook Inn (01380) 850418
A3102 about 4 miles E of Melksham; SN15 2EE Comfortably updated pub in small village; good home-cooked food from varied menu including stone-baked pizzas, Bath ales and a guest, plenty of wines by the glass, hands-on licensees and friendly well trained staff; Tues quiz; good-sized garden with decked terrace and play area, open (and food) all day.

WESTWOOD   ST8159
★ New Inn (01225) 863123
Off B3109 S of Bradford-on-Avon; BA15 2AE Traditional 18th-c country pub with linked rooms; beams, stripped stonework and log fires, scrubbed tables on slate floor, lots of pictures, highly rated good value food cooked by chef-owner from pub staples to more imaginative choices, ales from Bath and Wadworths, good service and cheerful buzzy atmosphere; children and dogs welcome, sturdy furniture and gazebo in paved back garden, pretty village with good surrounding walks, Westwood Manor (NT) in road opposite, closed Sun evening.

WHITLEY   ST8866
Pear Tree (01225) 704966
Off B3353 S of Corsham; SN12 8QX Attractive beamed dining pub (former 17th-c farmhouse) with plenty of contemporary/rustic charm in front bar, restaurant and airy garden room, good food from varied if not particularly cheap menu, three regional ales including Bath Gem, interesting wine list (many by the glass) and good range of other drinks, friendly attentive service; monthly comedy nights; children welcome, terrace and pretty garden, eight well equipped bedrooms (four in converted barn), open all day from 7.30am (8.30am Sun) for breakfast.

WILCOT   SU1461
Golden Swan (01672) 562289
Signed off A345 N of Pewsey, and in Pewsey itself; SN9 5NN Steeply thatched country pub near Kennet & Avon Canal, friendly and welcoming, with well kept Wadworths ales and popular good value food cooked by landlady, small bar with log fire, snug and dining room, also games room (pool and darts); quiz first Sun of month; children and dogs welcome, metal furniture on front grass, more tables and wandering chickens behind, field for camping, three good value bedrooms (not ensuite), open all day weekends.

WILTON   SU2661
⋆**Swan** (01672) 870274
The village S of Great Bedwyn; SN8 3SS
Popular light and airy 1930s pub; good well
presented food (not Sun evening) from
sharing boards and basket meals to daily
specials, two Ramsbury ales and up to
three local cask-tapped guests, real ciders
and good value wines from extensive list,
friendly efficient staff, stripped pine tables,
high-backed settles and pews on bare boards,
woodburner; children and dogs welcome,
disabled access, picnic-sets in front garden,
picturesque village with windmill, open all
day weekends.

WINGFIELD   ST8256
Poplars (01225) 752426
*B3109 S of Bradford-on-Avon (Shop
Lane); BA14 9LN* Appealing country pub
with warm friendly atmosphere, beams and
log fires, enjoyable sensibly priced food
from pub staples to interesting specials,
Wadworths ales (including seasonal) and
Weston's cider, airy family dining extension;
quiz first Sun of month; nice garden and own
cricket pitch.

WINSLEY   ST7960
⋆**Seven Stars** (01225) 722204
*Off B3108 bypass W of Bradford-on-
Avon; BA15 2LQ* Handsome bustling
village inn with low-beamed linked areas,
pastel paintwork and stripped-stone walls,
farmhouse chairs around candlelit tables on
flagstones or carpet, woodburner, good food
from pub favourites up including highly rated
Sun roasts, friendly attentive service, well
kept Palmers IPA and West Country guests,
proper cider; background and live music,
winter quiz; children and dogs (in bar)
welcome, wheelchair access using ramp to
most areas, disabled loo, tables on terrace
and neat grassy surrounds, bowling green
opposite, open (and food) all day Fri-Sun.

Worcestershire

BAUGHTON   SO8742   Map 4

Jockey 🍽️ 🍷

(01684) 592153 – www.thejockeyinn.co.uk

4 miles from M50 junction 1; A38 northwards, then right on to A4104 Upton–Pershore; WR8 9DQ

Elegantly redesigned pub with a fine choice of drinks, rewarding food, courteous staff and seats outside

---

A smart extended dining pub close to Croome (National Trust). The contemporary open-plan areas work well together and the smart dining rooms have high-backed upholstered chairs, long button-back wall seats, a mix of stylish tables, oak and flagstone flooring and décor that takes in an unusual woven hazel hurdle wall, deer antler chandeliers, oil portraits, horse-racing photographs, bookshelves, stubby candles in glass lanterns and old jockey saddles. Stools on flagstones line the counter in the beamed bar, where friendly, attentive staff serve Timothy Taylors and Wye Valley Butty Bach and HPA on handpump, and plenty of wines by the glass (including champagne and sweet wines) from the large glass walk-in wine cellar on display behind the bar; also, extensive cocktails and a large number of gins. Big studded leather armchairs, sofas and pouffes are grouped together and there's a ceiling-high stack of logs beside a welcoming two-way woodburning stove; background music. Outside, the attractive paved courtyard has glass-topped tables, dark wicker chairs and large heated parasols surrounded by bamboo and wild herbs in planters.

🍽️ Highly enjoyable food, showcasing the best local produce, includes goats cheese bonbons with sun-dried tomato and red pepper chutney, smoked duck salad with burnt coconut, orange, watercress and cashew nuts, porcini mushroom ravioli with wild mushrooms, white truffle cream and parmesan, dill and lemon-marinated salmon with asparagus, leeks and lemon beurre blanc, roast breast of guinea fowl with black truffle gnocchi, baby leeks, chestnut mushrooms and chive cream, rib-eye steak with a choice of sauce and triple-cooked chips, plus gourmet burgers, stone-baked pizzas and sharing platters. Puddings include chocolate and banana strudel with chocolate sauce and banana fudge ice-cream and strawberry and white chocolate cheesecake with strawberry compote; they also offer a two- and three-course set lunch. *Benchmark main dish: rack of lamb with provençale vegetables, olive tapenade, creamed basil and parmesan potatoes £19.50. Two-course evening meal £26.00.*

Free house ~ Licensee Rebekah Seddon-Wickens ~ Real ale ~ Open 11.30am-11pm;
11.30-11.30 Sat; 12-6 Sun ~ Bar food 12-9; 12-9.30 Fri, Sat; 12-4 Sun ~ Restaurant ~
Children welcome ~ Dogs allowed in bar

BRETFORTON
SP0943 Map 4

Fleece ★ ◀ £

(01386) 831173 – www.thefleeceinn.co.uk

B4035 E of Evesham: turn S off this road into village; pub is in central square by church; there's a sizeable car park at one side of the church; WR11 7JE

Marvellously unspoilt medieval pub owned by the National Trust; bedrooms

---

There's always something going on at this medieval pub, from the yearly asparagus festival to folk sessions, morris dancing and vintage car gatherings. Bequeathed to the National Trust in 1977, it draws curious visitors and loyal locals. The fine country rooms include a great oak dresser holding a priceless 48-piece set of Stuart pewter, two grandfather clocks, ancient kitchen chairs, curved high-backed settles, a rocking chair and a rack of heavy pointed iron shafts, probably for spit roasting in one of the huge inglenook fireplaces; two other log fires. Once a farm, it belonged to the same family for 500 years and many of these furnishings are original heirlooms. As well as massive beams and exposed timbers, there are worn and crazed flagstones (scored with marks to keep out demons) and plenty of oddities such as a great cheese press and set of cheese moulds and a rare dough-proving table; a leaflet details the more bizarre items. Purity Mad Goose, Uley Pigs Ear and Wye Valley Bitter with guests such as North Cotswold Moreton Mild and Wychwood Hobgoblin on handpump, nine wines by the glass, a similar number of malt whiskies and four farm ciders – including Ark cider made with their own orchard's apples; board games. The lawn, with fruit trees around a beautifully restored thatched and timbered barn, is a lovely place to sit, and there are more picnic-sets and a stone pump-trough in the front courtyard. Accommodation includes one room in the inn, a bow-topped caravan and a self-catering cottage.

Reliable food includes lunchtime sandwiches, sharing platters of meat and cheese, classic prawn cocktail, Thai halloumi skewers with chilli jam, devilled whitebait, sweet potato, mushroom and courgette pie, a selection of burgers with toppings, beer-battered haddock or halloumi with chips, chicken or vegetable balti with basmati rice, 30-day dry-aged sirloin steak with trimmings and a choice of sauce, and puddings such as eton mess, treacle tart and dark chocolate ale cake. *Benchmark main dish: steak and ale pie with chips £14.00. Two-course evening meal £20.00.*

Free house ~ Licensee Nigel Smith ~ Real ale ~ Open 10.30am-11pm; ~ Bar food 12-2.30, 6.30-9; 12-8 Sun ~ Children welcome ~ Dogs allowed in bar, restaurant & bedrooms ~ Bedrooms: £98

BROADWAY
SP0937 Map 4

Crown & Trumpet ◀ £

(01386) 853202 – www.crownandtrumpet.co.uk

Church Street; WR12 7AE

Honest local with good real ales and decent food; bedrooms

This cheerful and welcoming golden-stone pub is just behind the green. The beamed and timbered bar has a bustling, easy-going atmosphere, antique high-backed dark settles, large solid tables and a blazing log fire. You'll find North Cotswold Green Man IPA and Shagweaver, Stroud Tom Long and Timothy Taylors Landlord on handpump alongside ten wines by the glass, ten malt whiskies, 20 gins and farm ciders. There's an assortment of pub games including darts, Jenga, shut the box, dominoes and ring the bull; TV and background music. The hardwood chairs and tables outside are set among flowers on a slightly raised front terrace. Children over the age of seven are welcome. Disabled access and five stylish bedrooms. Broadway is a handsome town with many visitors, including walkers on the long-distance Cotswold Way.

 Remarkable value food includes lunchtime sandwiches, home-made pies, devilled whitebait, omelettes, locally made faggots and chips, venison and pork sausages with mash and onion gravy, fisherman's pie, gammon and egg, chicken breast with chorizo, parsnips and sautéed potatoes, sirloin steak with a choice of sauce and chips, and puddings such as spotted dick and treacle tart, both with custard; they also offer a pie and pudding deal. *Benchmark main dish: Worcester pie and mash with cheese and vegetables £9.95. Two-course evening meal £15.00.*

Laurel (Enterprise) ~ Lease Andrew Scott ~ Real ale ~ Open 10am-10.30pm; 10am-11.30pm Sat ~ Bar food 12-2.15, 5.45-9.15; 12-9.15 Fri-Sun ~ Children welcome (no under-7s) ~ Dogs allowed in bar ~ Bedrooms: £72

CHILDSWICKHAM   SP0738   Map 4
Childswickham Inn 🕸
(01386) 852461 – www.childswickhaminn.co.uk
Off A44 NW of Broadway; WR12 7HP

Bustling dining pub with highly regarded food, good drinks choice, attentive staff and seats in neat garden

A rural pub and restaurant in the north Cotswolds, situated in the idyllic village of Childswickham. Many customers come for the particularly good food after enjoying the extensive surrounding countryside. There's also a proper chatty bar with friendly regulars (often with their dogs). Also, leather sofas and armchairs and attentive staff serving Bombardier, Greene King Abbot Ale, Sharps Doom Bar and Wye Valley HPA on handpump, 16 wines by the glass (with Friday evening deals on champagne and prosecco), malt whiskies, a growing collection of gins and farm cider; background music. The main dining area is a bright conservatory with doors opening to the garden and high-backed, fabric-covered chairs at wooden tables on bare floorboards. There's more seating outside in the form of smart rattan furniture on a paved terrace shaded by large umbrellas. Lovely surrounding walks. Disabled facilities.

 Rewarding food includes ciabatta and brioche bun sandwiches, antipasti and seafood sharing platters, halloumi fries with chilli dip, smoked salmon and mackerel roulade with toasted focaccia, a range of pub classics including ham with eggs and hand-cut chips, beer-battered fish and chips, and lasagne, plus sea bass fillets with sesame sautéed pak choi, teriyaki roast new potatoes and tempura king prawns, and lamb rump with bubble and squeak, creamed spinach, roast baby carrots and rosemary jus. Desserts include chocolate fondant with salted caramel sauce and toffee ice-cream, and pear and almond tart with walnut and maple ice-cream. Thursday is steak night. *Benchmark main dish: pie and mash £13.50. Two-course evening meal £22.00.*

Star Pubs & Bars ~ Lease Carol Marshall ~ Real ale ~ Open 11.30-11.30; 11.30am-10.30pm Sun; closed Mon and Tues lunchtimes ~ Bar food 12-2, 6-9 Weds-Sat; 12-6 Sun ~ Restaurant ~ Children welcome ~ Dogs allowed in bar

CLENT   SO9279   Map 4
Fountain 🕸 ♟
(01562) 883286 – www.thefountainatclent.co.uk
Adams Hill/Odnall Lane; off A491 at Holy Cross/Clent exit roundabout, via Violet Lane, then right at T junction; DY9 9PU

Restauranty pub often packed to overflowing, with imaginative dishes and good choice of drinks

Awhitewashed country pub in the picturesque village of Clent. The long pattern-carpeted dining bar (consisting of three knocked-together areas) is fairly traditional, with teak chairs and pedestal tables and some comfortably cushioned brocaded wall seats. There are nicely framed local photographs on the rag-rolled pinkish walls above a dark panelled dado, pretty wall lights and candles on the tables (flowers in summer). The changing real ales on handpump include Brakspears Oxford Gold and Marstons EPA and Wainwright, and most of their wines are available by the glass; also farm cider, speciality teas and good coffees. Background music and skittle alley. There are tables outside on a decked area, which is the only area suitable for dogs. Disabled access.

Particularly good food includes sandwiches, tiger prawns in garlic butter, chicken liver parfait with onion marmalade, pumpkin seed and chestnut roast with parmentier vegetables, salmon fillet on egg noodles with Thai sweet chilli sauce and courgette ribbons, corn-fed chicken breast stuffed with sage and onion mousse with red wine sauce, half roast duck with orange and star anise reduction and caramelised orange, mixed grilled fish with seaweed butter, chargrilled steaks with a choice of sauce, and puddings such as chocolate délice and sticky date pudding with toffee sauce and vanilla ice-cream; they also offer a two- and three-course menu (Monday-Saturday lunchtimes and Monday-Thursday evenings 6pm and 6.30pm). *Benchmark main dish: lamb pot roast £19.95. Two-course evening meal £26.00.*

Marstons ~ Lease Richard and Jacque Macey ~ Real ale ~ Open 11-11; 12-8.30 Sun ~ Bar food 12-2, 6-9 (9.30 Fri, Sat); 12-6 Sun ~ Restaurant ~ Children welcome

CUTNALL GREEN
Chequers 🌟 ☿ SO8868 Map 4

(01299) 851292 – www.chequerscutnallgreen.co.uk
Kidderminster Road; WR9 0PJ

Bustling roadside pub with plenty of drinking and dining space in interesting rooms, and rewarding food

This country pub was built on the site of an old coaching inn and is a clever mix of ancient and modern. There are red-painted walls between beams and timbering, broad floorboards and weathered quarry tiles, and warm winter fires. Also, leather sofas and tub chairs, high-backed purple and red or ladder-back dining chairs around all sorts of tables, plenty of mirrors giving the impression of even more space, brass plates and mugs, candles and fresh flowers. Green Duck Blonde, Sharps Doom Bar and Wye Valley HPA on handpump and 14 wines by the glass. One elegant but cosy room, known as the Players Lounge, has photographs of the landlord Mr Narbett, who was once a chef for the England football team. The pretty garden has three 'beach huts' to hire (with their own menu), chairs with barrel tables and sofas as well as heaters and parasols. Disabled access. We always get plenty of enthusiastic reports from our readers about this well run, popular pub.

As well as weekend breakfasts (9-11am), the rewarding food includes sandwiches, crispy butternut squash and goats cheese arancini, rosemary and garlic box-baked camembert with red onion confit, Balinese chicken curry, pie of the day, ham and free-range eggs, stone-baked pizzas, panko-crumbed katsu chicken burger with sweet potato fries, beer-battered cod and chips, chargrilled fillet steak with oven-dried tomatoes and chips, and puddings such as espresso affogato with vanilla ice-cream and raspberry and limoncello crème brûlée with lemon curd eton mess. *Benchmark main dish: slow-cooked shoulder of Cornish lamb £18.95. Two-course evening meal £26.00.*

Free house ~ Licensees Roger and Jo Narbett ~ Real ale ~ Open 12-11; 12-10.30 Sun ~
Bar food 12-2, 6-8.30 (9 Sat); 12-2.30, 6-8 Sun ~ Restaurant ~ Children welcome ~
Dogs allowed in bar

ELDERSFIELD

SO8131   Map 4

Butchers Arms 🏅🛏️

(01452) 840381 – www.thebutchersarms.net

*Pub and village signposted from B4211; Lime Street (coming from A417, fourth road
on left), OS Sheet 150 map reference 815314; village also signposted from B4208 N of
Staunton; GL19 4NX*

Worcestershire Dining Pub of the Year

**16th-c pub with an unspoilt interior, local ales and carefully chosen
wines, excellent food and seats in garden**

This is an attractive, 16th-c red-brick cottage with a deliberately simple,
unspoilt little locals' bar – although it's the first-class food that draws
many customers. There is a rustic charm to both the bar and the dining
room, with black beamed low ceilings, knocked-through walls and standing
timbers, cream paintwork, plain but individual wooden chairs, pews and
some high-backed settles on bare boards or tiles and rustic tables. Also,
two woodburning stoves, hop bines and wall prints. High chairs line the
counter where friendly staff serve Wye Valley Butty Bach tapped from the
cask, 11 good wines by the glass including sparkling and pudding choices
and farm cider. The good-sized garden has seats on lawns and looks out on
to pasture; quoits. Disabled access. There's a self-catering cottage to rent
next to the pub.

 Creative, tasty food cooked by the landlord includes hot smoked salmon with
beetroot and horseradish rémoulade and pickled cucumber, watermelon and
goats curd salad with peas, mint and pine nuts, salt cod scotch egg with chorizo and
romesco sauce, Middle White pork faggots with peas, mash, onion and red wine jus,
aubergine and sugar snap curry with cashew and almond sauce and ginger, coriander
and basmati rice, and puddings such as chocolate ganache with griottine cherries,
salted caramel ice-cream and honeycomb, and gooseberry and elderflower fool with
shortbread. *Benchmark main dish: Cornish cod with mussels, saffron sauce,
sweetcorn and new potatoes £19.50. Two-course evening meal £26.00.*

Free house ~ Licensees Mark and Jo-Anne Block ~ Real ale ~ Open 6-11 Tue-Thurs; 12-3,
6-11 Fri, Sat; 12-3 Sun ~ Bar food 6-9 Weds, Thurs; 12-1.30, 6-9 Fri, Sat; 12-1.30 Sun ~
Restaurant ~ Children allowed if over 9 ~ Dogs allowed in bar ~ Bedrooms: £100

GUARLFORD

SO8245   Map 4

Plough & Harrow ♈

(01684) 218410 – www.brunningandprice.co.uk/ploughandharrow
B4211 E of village; WR13 6NY

**Spreading village-edge pub with attractively decorated interior,
interesting food and drinks and plenty of outside seating**

Terraces and lawns surround this extended, newly refurbished pub and
there are plenty of seats under parasols from which to enjoy the view of
the nearby Malvern Hills. Inside, you can sit in the old part of the building
with its history and character or in the new, light and bright dining areas. It's
open-plan throughout, but with appealingly cosy corners and nooks. There
are leather or wooden dining chairs around an assortment of tables on rugs
and bare boards, button-back wall banquettes and armchairs and several

open fires. Shelves are lined with old books, walls are hung with framed newspaper cuttings, motor racing pictures and mirrors, and there are elegant metal chandeliers and house plants large and small. Friendly and efficient staff serve a wide range of drinks, including Phoenix Brunning & Price Original, the Hop Shed's Frizzle, Timothy Taylors Boltmaker and Wye Valley Hopfather on handpump, 21 wines by the glass (including bubbly) and a wide range of whiskies hailing from Scotland to Japan.

Interesting, varied food includes smoked salmon with orange and beetroot salad and horseradish cream, five-spiced duck leg with spring onion, cucumber, hoisin sauce and pancakes, and crispy baby squid and sweet chilli sauce for starters, plus mains such as braised shoulder of lamb with new potatoes and rosemary gravy, king prawn linguine with chilli and tomato, grilled sea bass fillets with potato and shallot terrine and chervil and lemon cream sauce, pork and leek sausages with mash, buttered greens and onion gravy, and sweet potato, aubergine and spinach Malaysian curry with coconut rice and pak choi. Typical desserts are chocolate and orange tart with passion-fruit sorbet and sticky toffee pudding with toffee sauce and vanilla ice-cream. *Benchmark main dish: cod in beer batter with chips, mushy peas and tartare sauce £14.95. Two-course evening meal £22.00.*

Brunning & Price ~ Manager Josh Nicholson ~ Real ale ~ Open 11.30-11; 11.30-10 Sun ~ Bar food 12-9 (9.30 Fri, Sat) ~ Restaurant ~ Children welcome ~ Dogs allowed in bar

MALVERN   SO7845   Map 4
Nags Head ◖

(01684) 574373 – www.nagsheadmalvern.co.uk
Bottom end of Bank Street, steep turn down off A449; WR14 2JG

Delightfully eclectic layout and décor, a good choice of ales, tasty lunchtime bar food and warmly welcoming atmosphere

The front terrace and garden of this attractive whitewashed free house have picnic-sets, benches and rustic tables as well as parasols and heaters. With up to 15 regularly changing real ales on handpump to choose from here, there's always going to be an enthusiastic crowd keen to try the offerings served by knowledgeable, friendly staff. There might be Arbor Shangri-La, Banks's Bitter, Bathams Best Bitter, Exmoor Gold, Hobsons Twisted Spire, Hook Norton Hooky Mild, Purity Bunny Hop, Otter Bitter, Ringwood Wainwright and Woods Shropshire Lad. Also, five farm ciders, more than 30 malt whiskies, over 30 gins, ten bottled craft ales/lagers and ten wines by the glass including pudding ones. A series of snug, individually decorated rooms, separated by a couple of steps and with two open fires, have leather armchairs, pews sometimes arranged as booths and a mix of tables (including sturdy ones stained different colours). There are bare boards here, flagstones there, carpet elsewhere, plenty of interesting pictures and homely touches such as house plants, shelves of well thumbed books and daily papers; board games.

Much liked lunchtime food includes sandwiches, coconut dhal dumplings with Sri Lankan sauce, smoked trout with boiled egg and keta, caper and shallot dressing, omelettes, guacamole and mango salad with black beans and ginger and lime dressing, and beef and mushroom in ale pie, with evening meals (served in the barn extension dining room only) such as burger with toppings, coleslaw and chips, spicy jackfruit corn tacos (red cabbage, coriander, chimichurri sauce and lime), pork tenderloin with sautéed red chard and bacon, pesto-crusted cod loin with puy lentils, dried tomatoes and lime vinaigrette, rump of Welsh lamb with rosemary potatoes, roasted cherry tomatoes and salsa verde, and puddings. *Benchmark main dish: Whitby scampi with home-made chips and peas £12.00. Two-course evening meal £17.00.*

Free house ~ Licensee Alex Whistance ~ Real ale ~ Open 11am-11.15pm; 11am-11.30pm Fri, Sat; 12-11 Sun ~ Bar food 12-2.30, 6.30-8.30; 12-2.30, 7-8.30 Sun ~ Restaurant ~ Children welcome ~ Dogs allowed in bar & restaurant

NEWLAND
SO7948 Map 4

Swan

(01886) 832224 – www.theswaninnmalvern.co.uk
Worcester Road (set well back from A449 just NW of Malvern); WR13 5AY

Popular, interesting pub with well kept real ales and seats in the big garden

Inside this bustling, creeper-clad pub there's a dimly lit, dark-beamed bar that's quite traditional, with a forest canopy of hops, whisky-water jugs, beakers and tankards. Several of the comfortable and clearly individually chosen seats are worth a close look for their carving, and the wall tapestries are interesting. On the right is a broadly similar red-carpeted dining room and beyond it, in complete contrast, an ultra-modern glass garden room. From the carved bar counter, friendly staff offer five real ales on handpump including two regulars: Purity Mad Goose and Ringwood Fortyniner and three quickly changing guest ales; also, several wines by the glass, malt whiskies and four farm ciders; board games. The garden here is as individual as the pub, with a cluster of huge casks topped with flowers, a piano doing flower-tub duty and a set of stocks on the pretty front terrace.

Pleasing food includes lunchtime sandwiches, scotch egg, pickles and chips, ploughman's, chicken caesar salad, beer-battered fish (or tofu) with chips, mushy peas and home-made tartare sauce, and puddings such as berry trifle and chocolate cheesecake. *Benchmark main dish: burger with caramelised onions, coleslaw and chips £12.50. Two-course evening meal £18.00.*

Free house ~ Licensee Duncan Ironmonger ~ Real ale ~ Open 12-11.30 ~ Bar food 12-2.30, 6-8.30 ~ Restaurant ~ Children welcome ~ Dogs allowed in bar & restaurant

WELLAND
SO8039 Map 4

Inn at Welland

(01684) 592317 – www.theinnatwelland.co.uk
Just off A4104 between Upton upon Severn and Welland, signed for Hook Bank; WR13 6LN

Stylish contemporary country dining bar with good food and wines and nice tables outside

A 17th-c dining pub that's handy for the Three Counties Showground (home to the RHS Malvern Spring Festival and numerous other events). The neatly dressed, efficient staff serve a fantastic choice of wines by the glass – 43, including champagne, sparkling and an unusually wide range of pudding wines; also, Ledbury Gold and Wye Valley Butty Bach on handpump, mocktails, cocktails and quite a few gins. The rooms have a chatty, easy-going atmosphere, grey paintwork, a few carefully chosen modern prints and chairs upholstered in attractive fabrics, with beige flagstones in the central area, wood flooring to the sides and a woodburning stove at one end. The good-sized tidy garden, offering tranquil views of the Malvern Hills, has tables with comfortable teak or wicker chairs on a biggish sheltered deck or on individual separate terraces set into lawn. Disabled access.

Excellent food includes starters such as omelette arnold bennett, chicken liver parfait with smoked bacon jam and toasted focaccia, caramelised onion and

Godminster cheese soufflé with rosemary cream, and seared South Coast scallops with local sweetcorn and preserved lemon. Mains might be charcoal-grilled Herefordshire beef (rib-eye or fillet) with portobello mushroom, roasted tomatoes and chips, slow-cooked Old Spot pork belly with bramley apple ketchup, rainbow chard and pomme anna, chalk-stream trout with red pepper quinoa, pak choi and chilli, and hay-baked duck breast with potato fondant, chard and pickled rhubarb. Puddings include blackberry soufflé with granny smith sorbet and maple and pecan tart with almond milk sorbet. *Benchmark main dish: slow-cooked Old Spot pork belly with bramley apple ketchup, rainbow chard and pomme anna £19.90. Two-course evening meal £28.00.*

Free house ~ Licensees David and Gillian Pinchbeck ~ Real ale ~ Open 12-3, 5.30-11; 12-4 Sun; closed Mon ~ Bar food 12-2.30, 6-9.30; 12-2.30 Sun ~ Restaurant ~ Children welcome ~ Dogs allowed in bar

Also Worth a Visit in Worcestershire

Besides the fully inspected pubs, you might like to try these pubs that have been recommended to us and described by readers. Do tell us what you think of them: feedback@goodguides.com

ABBERLEY   SO7567
Manor Arms (01299) 890300
Netherton Lane; WR6 6BN Modernised country inn tucked away in quiet village backwater opposite fine Norman church; changing local ales and ciders, 20 wines by the glass and highly praised well presented food from seasonal menu including snacks and pub favourites, afternoon tea, helpful friendly service, open log fire; children and dogs welcome, two-level deck with lovely valley views, good walks (on Worcestershire Way), six bedrooms, open all day.

ALVECHURCH   SP0172
Weighbridge (0121) 445 5111
Scarfield Wharf; B48 7SQ Little red-brick pub (former weighbridge office) by Worcester & Birmingham Canal marina; bar and a couple of other small rooms, half a dozen well kept ales including Kinver Bargee Bitter and Weatheroak Tillermans Tipple (beer festivals), simple low-priced pubby food (not Tues, Weds); tables outside and marquee to keep off the rain.

ASHTON UNDER HILL   SO9938
Star (01386) 881325
Elmley Road; WR11 7SN Smallish pub perched above road in quiet village at foot of Bredon Hill; linked beamed rooms around bar, one with flagstones and log fire, steps up to pitch-roofed dining room with woodburner, well liked food including Weds pie night and Sun roasts, real ales such as Black Sheep and Greene King plus weekly guest ale, friendly welcoming staff; background music, TV and

games machine; children and dogs welcome, picnic-sets in pleasant garden, good walks (Wyche Way passes nearby), open all day, no food Sun or Mon evenings.

BELBROUGHTON   SO9277
Olde Horse Shoe (01562) 730460
High Street; DY9 9ST Popular old beamed corner pub; smallish stone-floored bar and separate restaurant; real ales such as St Austell and Wye Valley, well liked food (not Sun evening, Mon) including sharing plates, friendly service, open fires; children and dogs welcome, big back garden, closed Mon lunchtime, otherwise open all day.

BERROW   SO7835
Duke of York (01684) 833449
Junction A438/B4208; WR13 6JQ Bustling old country pub with two linked rooms, beams, nooks and crannies and log fire; change of ownership in late 2019 has seen a sensitive refurb and addition of second bar in Cider Press barn outside; ales include Wye Valley Butty Bach and a weekly guest, small back restaurant serving pub classics, excellent friendly service; children and dogs welcome, big garden behind with children's play area, handy for Malvern Hills.

BERROW GREEN   SO7458
Admiral Rodney (01905) 886181
B4197, off A44 W of Worcester; WR6 6PL Refurbished 17th-c beamed inn with two bars, snug and former stable block restaurant, good varied menu including pizzas and steaks with affordable set menu Mon-Thurs, well chosen wines by the glass

---

Post Office address codings confusingly give the impression that some pubs are in Worcestershire, when they're really in Gloucestershire, Herefordshire, Shropshire or Warwickshire (which is where we list them).

and over 20 gins, friendly helpful service; pool and sports TV in separate function room; children welcome, dogs in bar, tables on front and back terraces, pretty views and good walks, 12 newly decorated bedrooms, open all day.

BEWDLEY   SO7775

Hop Pole (01299) 401295

Hop Pole Lane; DY12 2QH Modernised 19th-c pub with country-chic décor and cast-iron range in dining area, three well kept Marstons-related ales and several wines by the glass, good choice of popular food (booking advised) from pub favourites to set menus and themed nights; regular live music and other events, children and dogs (in bar) welcome, seats on raised front terrace, vegetable garden to the side, back play area, open all day.

BEWDLEY   SO7875

Mug House (01299) 402543

Severn Side North; DY12 2EE 18th-c bay-windowed pub in charming spot by River Severn; good food including burgers, pizzas, fish and steaks, served in bar or more upmarket evening restaurant with lobster tank, six well kept ales such as Bewdley, Purity, Timothy Taylors and Wye Valley (May beer festival), log fire; children (daytime only) and dogs welcome, disabled access, glass-covered terrace behind, seven river-view bedrooms, open all day, no food Sun evening.

BIRLINGHAM   SO9343

Swan (01386) 750485

Church Street; off A4104 S of Pershore, via B4080 Eckington Road, turn off at sign to Birlingham with integral 'The Swan Inn' brown sign (not the 'Birlingham (village only)' road), then left; WR10 3AQ Pretty family-run thatched and timbered cottage; updated beamed quarry-tiled bar with woodburner in big stone fireplace, well kept ales from Malvern Hills and Wye Valley, real cider and good food from reasonably priced varied menu including fresh fish specials, friendly efficient service, dining conservatory; well kept back garden, handy for River Avon walks, closed Mon and Tues except bank holidays.

BRANSFORD   SO8052

★ Bear & Ragged Staff (01886) 833399

Off A4103 SW of Worcester; Station Road; WR6 5JH Civilised dining pub with relaxed and friendly bar thanks to welcoming, long-serving licensees and attentive staff, interconnecting rooms provide fine views of attractive rolling countryside, also more formal restaurant with proper tablecloths and linen napkins; warming open fire in winter, background music, board games; Hobsons Twisted Spire and a guest from Wye Valley on handpump, ten wines by the glass and several malt

whiskies, brandies and liqueurs, hearty portions of highly regarded food (using some home-grown produce) includes Thurs burgers and Fri fish and chips; attractive secluded garden and terrace, children welcome, dogs in bar, good disabled access and facilities, closed Sun evening.

BREDON   SO9236

Fox & Hounds (01684) 772377

4.5 miles from M5 junction 9; A438 to Northway, left at B4079, in Bredon follow sign to church; GL20 7LA Cottagey 16th-c timber and stone thatched pub with low beams, stone pillars and stripped timbers, wooden parquet or tiled floors, velvet upholstered chairs in contemporary colours around mahogany and cast-iron-framed tables, Donnington ales, decent wines by the glass and excellent food; background and some live music; children welcome, dogs in bar, outside picnic-sets and pretty hanging baskets, closed Mon, open from 5pm weekdays, all day weekends.

BROADWAS-ON-TEME   SO7555

Royal Oak (01886) 821353

A44; WR6 5NE Red-brick roadside pub with various areas including lofty dining hall; popular good value roasts and other enjoyable food, well kept ales such as Courage, Bombardier and Ringwood, decent wines by the glass, friendly helpful service; children welcome, no dogs inside, disabled access from the back, garden with play area, open (and food) all day.

BROADWAY   SP0937

Swan (01386) 852278

The Green (B4362); WR12 7AA Sizeable old Mitchells & Butlers dining pub with contemporary décor in several linked areas; popular sensibly priced food, three well kept ales such as Purity Mad Goose and Sharps Doom Bar, plenty of wines by the glass and good range of cocktails, polite friendly young staff; children welcome, tables under parasols on small front terrace looking over road to village green, open all day, food served all day.

CALLOW END   SO8349

Blue Bell (01905) 830261

Upton Road; WR2 4TY Popular Marstons local with two bars and dining area; their well kept ales and wide variety of reasonably priced food including lots of specials and themed nights, friendly welcoming staff, open fire; quiz last Thurs of the month, sports TV, pool and darts; children allowed, dogs in garden only, open all day.

CALLOW END   SO8349

Old Bush (01905) 830792

Off Upton Road (B4424); WR2 4TE Friendly black and white village local with well kept ales such as Butcombe, Hobsons and Wye Valley, enjoyable home-cooked food, cosy small areas around central bar, beams, woodburner and various memorabilia, separate dining room; live music including Aug blues festival; children and dogs welcome, nice garden with play area, camping, open all day.

CALLOW HILL SP0164
Brook Inn (01527) 543209
Elcocks Brook, off B4504; B97 5UD Modernised country dining pub with well liked locally sourced food including burgers, steaks and good home-made desserts, Marstons-related ales, friendly staff; tables out at front and in pleasant back beer garden, open all day.

CAUNSALL SO8480
Anchor (01562) 850254
Caunsall Road, off A449; DY11 5YL Traditional unchanging two-room pub (in same family since 1927), popular and welcoming, with five well kept ales such as Hobsons, Three Tuns and Wye Valley, traditional ciders and good value generously filled cobs, friendly efficient service; children and dogs welcome, large outside seating area behind, near Staffordshire & Worcestershire Canal.

CHADDESLEY CORBETT SO8973
Swan (01562) 777302
Off A448 Bromsgrove–Kidderminster; DY10 4SD Popular old local with friendly buoyant atmosphere; well kept Bathams and enjoyable good value pubby food including stone-baked pizzas, various rooms including high-raftered lounge bar; jazz and other live music, TV, games machine; children and dogs on leads welcome, picnic-sets in huge lawned garden with play area and country views, Aug classic car show and Sept cycle ride, handy for Harvington Hall, open all day.

CLAINES SO8558
Mug House (01905) 456649
Claines Lane, off A449 3 miles W of M5 junction 3; WR3 7RN Fine views from this ancient country tavern in unique churchyard setting by fields below the Malvern Hills; several small rooms around central bar, low doorways and heavy oak beams, well kept Banks's ales, simple lunchtime pub food including home-cured ham with egg and chips; no credit cards, outside loos; children (away from servery) and dogs welcome, open all day weekends.

CROPTHORNE SO9944
Bell (01386) 861860
Main Road (B4084); WR10 3NE Isolated rather stark-looking roadside pub with contrasting brightly modernised interior; painted beams, bare boards and colourful carpet in L-shaped bar, well divided seating areas (one down a couple of steps), log fire, small back conservatory, emphasis on dining with popular freshly made food including

good ploughman's, three changing ales, welcoming efficient service; background and occasional live music; open all day Sat, till 8pm Sun, closed Mon.

CROWLE SO9256
Chequers (01905) 381772
Crowle Green, not far from M5 junction 6; WR7 4AA Busy beamed dining pub in the small Epicure group; good food (some quite pricey) from pork pies at the bar to dry-aged steaks, well kept ales such as St Austell and Wye Valley, lots of wines by the glass and good range of other drinks, friendly attentive staff; children and dogs (in bar) welcome, open all day.

DEFFORD SO9042
★**Monkey House** (01386) 750234
A4104, after passing Oak pub on right, it's the last of a small group of cottages; WR8 9BW Tiny black and white thatched cider house, a wonderful time warp and in the same family for over 150 years; ciders and a perry tapped from barrels into pottery mugs and served by landlady from hatch, no other drinks or food (can bring your own); children welcome, no dogs, garden with caravans, sheds and small spartan outbuilding with a couple of plain tables, settle and fireplace, only open lunchtimes Fri, Sun and evenings Weds, Sat.

DODFORD SO9372
Dodford Inn (01527) 835825
Whinfield Road; B61 9BG Refurbished mid-19th-c red-brick country pub tucked away in six-acre grounds (aka 'The Pub in the Field'); up to four well kept ales including Wye Valley, good home-made food (all day Sat, not Sun evening) including sharing platters, friendly welcoming staff; children allowed, no dogs inside, nice views over wooded valley from terrace tables, good walks, open all day, till 8pm Sun.

DROITWICH SO8963
Gardeners Arms (01905) 772936
Vines Lane; WR9 8LU Individual place on the edge of town; cosy traditional bar to the right serving four changing ales, bistro-style restaurant to the left with red gingham tablecloths and lots of pictures (mostly for sale), well priced food from varied menu including range of good local sausages, pizzas and pies; regular live music and quiz nights, also themed food evenings, pool and darts; children and dogs welcome, outside seating areas on different levels below railway embankment with quirky mix of furniture, play area, camping, close to Droitwich Canal, open (and food) all day.

DROITWICH SO9063
Hop Pole (01905) 770155
Friar Street; WR9 8ED Heavy-beamed 18th-c local with panelled rooms on different levels; well kept Wye Valley beers

and a couple of guests, generous helpings of bargain lunchtime food including sandwiches, friendly staff and regulars; dominoes, darts and pool, occasional live music; children and dogs welcome, partly canopied back garden, open all day.

DROITWICH   SO9063
Talbot (01905) 773871
High Street; WR9 8EJ Traditional town-centre pub recently acquired by Stourbridge's Craddocks Brewery, pleasingly simple décor with wood-panelled bar, exposed brickwork, wooden floors and tables, a few pews; full Craddocks range on handpump, straightforward pub food (fish finger sandwich, pies, lasagne); dog friendly and children allowed till 7pm; outdoor partially covered courtyard, open all day.

DUNLEY   SO7969
Dog (01299) 822833
A451 S of Stourport; DY13 0UE Attractive creeper-clad roadside pub and restaurant; good choice of enjoyable reasonably priced food from light meals up, well kept Wye Valley and guests, friendly staff; pool, darts, children and dogs welcome, garden with play area and bowling green, three bedrooms, bar open all day weekends (from 5pm other days), restaurant open for lunch and dinner except Sun evening.

ECKINGTON   SO9241
Bell (01386) 750033
Church Street (B4080); WR10 3AN Modernised village dining pub with much liked food (special diets catered for) including the option of cooking your own exotic meat (kangaroo or crocodile, perhaps) on a hot stone, two well kept ales, efficient friendly service; quiz first Sun of month; children and dogs (in Farmers Bar) welcome, enclosed back garden, on Wyche Way long-distance path, four bedrooms, open (and food) all day weekends.

ELMLEY CASTLE   SO9841
Queen Elizabeth (01386) 710251
Signed off A44 and A435, not far from Evesham; Main Street; WR10 3HS Modernised old community-owned pub; central bar with wood floor and small brick fireplace, well kept Purity, Wye Valley and a couple of guests, steps down to beamed and flagstoned snug with inglenook log fire, two dining rooms, enjoyable reasonably priced food (not Sun evening, Mon) including themed nights, good friendly service; children and dogs welcome, tables out in courtyard, closed Mon lunchtime, otherwise open all day from 10am (till 8pm Sun).

EVESHAM   SP0344
Old Red Horse (01386) 442784
Vine Street; WR11 4RE Attractive 15th-c black and white coaching inn divided into two bars with beams, bare boards and open fires, three real ales, traditional ciders and enjoyable reasonably priced pub food and popular steak nights (Tues, Weds), good cheerful service; TV, darts and machines; children and dogs welcome, nice covered inner courtyard with small pond, five bedrooms, open all day, no evening food weekends.

FLADBURY   SO9946
Chequers (01386) 861854
Chequers Lane; WR10 2PZ Village inn dating from 1372 with bright modern design complementing historic features such as ceiling beams and an old cooking range (lit in winter); well kept Pershore ales and three guests, popular food including pizza from their wood-fired oven, restaurant to rear, friendly staff; walled garden with play area and views to Bredon Hill, seven rooms, open all day.

FLYFORD FLAVELL   SO9754
Boot (01386) 462658
Off A422 Worcester–Alcester; Radford Road; WR7 4BS Family-run traditional coaching inn with popular food, including two-course lunch deal, cook your own steak on a hot stone and blackboard specials, Fullers London Pride and Sharps Doom Bar, good friendly service, log fires in ancient heavily beamed and timbered core, modern conservatory, games room with pool and TV; background music; children, walkers and dogs (in bar) welcome, tables on split-level terrace and small lawned area, five bedrooms, open all day.

GRIMLEY   SO8359
Camp House (01905) 640288
A443 5 miles N from Worcester, right to Grimley, right at village T junction; WR2 6LX Simple unpretentious old pub (in same family since 1939) tucked away in appealing Severn-side setting (prone to flooding); well kept Bathams and guests, proper ciders and decent home-made pubby food (no credit cards), rambling interior with open fires, friendly relaxed atmosphere; some live music, darts; children and well behaved dogs welcome, attractive lawns (maybe wandering peacocks), own landing stage and small campsite, open all day.

HADLEY   SO8662
Bowling Green (01905) 620294
Hadley Heath; off A4133 Droitwich–Ombersley; WR9 0AR Popular refurbished 16th-c inn with beams and big log fire, well kept Wadworths ales and decent wines by the glass, good food (all day Sun) from sandwiches and deli boards up, comfortable back lounge and restaurant; children welcome, tables out overlooking own bowling green (UK's oldest), comfortable bedrooms, nice walks (footpath starts from car park), open all day.

HANBURY SO9662
Vernon (01527) 821236
Droitwich Road (B4090); B60 4DB
Former 18th-c coaching inn with
contemporary interior; much emphasis on
dining, but they also serve up to four real
ales including Mad Goose and a dozen wines
by the glass in beamed bar, nice food from
sharing plates, pub favourites and flatbread
pizzas up, good value OAP set lunch too,
friendly efficient service, restaurant with
kitchen view; children and dogs welcome,
modern terrace seating, five boutique-style
bedrooms, open all day.

HANLEY CASTLE SO8342
★ Three Kings (01684) 592686
*Church End, off B4211 N of Upton upon
Severn; WR8 0BL* Timeless, hospitable
and by no means smart – in same family
since 1911 and a favourite with those who
put unspoilt character and individuality
first; cheerful, homely tiled-floor tap room
separated from entrance corridor by
monumental built-in settle, equally vast
inglenook fireplace, room on left with darts
and board games, separate entrance to
timbered lounge with second inglenook
and blacked kitchen range, leatherette
armchairs, spindleback chairs and antique
winged settle, well kept Butcombe, Hobsons
and three guests, Weston's cider and around
75 malt whiskies, simple snacks including
good sandwiches; live music; children and
dogs welcome, wood and iron seats on front
terrace looking across to old cedar shading
tiny green, on Wyche Way long-distance path,
open daily 12-3pm and from 7pm.

HANLEY SWAN SO8142
★ Swan (01684) 311870
B4209 Malvern–Upton; WR8 0EA
Contemporary/rustic décor and furnishings
blending well with old low beams (some
painted), bare boards and log fire, extended
back part set for their good well presented
food (all day Sat, not Sun evening) from
sandwiches/baguettes and pub favourites to
more restauranty dishes (booking advised),
ales such as Hobsons, Lakehouse and Wye
Valley, seven wines by the glass, friendly
helpful staff, oak-framed conservatory;
children and dogs welcome, disabled access/
loos, seats out on paved terrace and grass,
nice spot facing green and big duck pond, five
comfortable good value bedrooms, open all
day, breakfast all week from 8am.

HIMBLETON SO9458
Galton Arms (01905) 391672
Harrow Lane; WR9 7LQ Friendly old
black and white bay-windowed country pub;
good food (not Sun evening, Mon) including
daily specials in split-level beamed bar or
restaurant, well kept ales such as Banks's,
Bathams and Wye Valley, woodburner; sports
TV; children and dogs welcome, picnic-sets

in small part-paved garden, children's
play equipment, local walks, open all day
weekends, closed Mon lunchtime.

HOLT HEATH SO8063
Red Lion (01905) 620600
Witley Road (A443/A4133); WR6 6LX
Modernised dining pub specialising in good
value food; bar with grey-painted beams,
high-backed dining chairs around wooden
tables and a woodburner, three real ales and
several rums, good friendly service, raftered
restaurant; pool, sports TV, fruit machine;
picnic-sets in lawned garden with decked
area, open all day, closes 6pm Weds and Sun.

HOLY CROSS SO9278
Bell & Cross (01562) 730319
*2 miles from M5 junction 3; A491
towards Stourbridge, then follow Clent
signpost off on left; DY9 9QL* Attractive
19th-c pub with historic charm, three dining
rooms with a bar and smoke room each
with a different feel, from snug and chatty
to bright and airy, and several coal fires,
popular modern British food, Timothy Taylors
Landlord, and Wye Valley HPA on handpump
and good wines by the glass in the bar, large
garden with plenty of seats on the spacious
lawn and terrace, open all day.

KEMERTON SO9437
Crown (01386) 725020
*4 miles from M5 junction 9, back road
Bredon–Beckford; GL20 7HP* Small 18th-c
pub in pretty village with flagstoned bar
and log fire, good freshly made food from
sandwiches up including sharing boards
and daily specials, ales such as Wye Valley,
local cider, hospitable landlord and cheerful
staff, separate restaurant; children and
dogs welcome, roadside tables and peaceful
courtyard garden behind, good walks over
Bredon Hill, four pleasant bedrooms, closed
Mon lunchtime, otherwise open all day.

KIDDERMINSTER SO8376
King & Castle (01562) 747505
*Severn Valley Railway station,
Comberton Hill; DY10 1QX* Neatly
recreated Edwardian refreshment room
in Severn Valley Railway terminus – steam
trains outside and railway memorabilia
and photographs inside; eight real ales
including Bathams, Bewdley and Hobsons,
three traditional ciders, cobs at the bar or
reasonably priced straightforward food in
adjacent dining room; children welcome, little
railway museum close by, busy bank holidays/
railway gala days, open (and food) all day.

KNIGHTWICK SO7355
★ Talbot (01886) 821235
*Knightsford Bridge; B4197 just off A44
Worcester–Bromyard; WR6 5PH* Nicely
placed 14th-c inn of great individuality
run by the same family for over 30 years,
interesting furnishings and good pictures

in opened-up heavily beamed bar, freshly made food not cheap but often exceptional, with some interesting recipes and using local ingredients and their own kitchen garden produce, also posher restaurant (same menu); decent wines and their own cider and attractively priced and helpfully described Teme Valley ales (beer festivals); children and well behaved dogs welcome, lots of outside tables, comfortable character bedrooms, good breakfast, own fishing on River Teme; open all day, on Three Choirs and Worcestershire Ways, very busy on its farmers' market day (2nd Sun of month, largely organic).

LONGDON   SO8434
Hunters Inn (01684) 833388
B4211 S, towards Tewkesbury; GL20 6AR Beamed and timbered country pub with stripped brickwork and log fires, enjoyable locally sourced food, real ales such as Donnington and Otter, local ciders and decent wines by the glass, friendly service, raftered dining area, good views; some live music and quiz nights, darts; children welcome, extensive well tended garden, campsite, open all day weekends, closed Mon and Tues.

LOWER BROADHEATH   SO8056
Dewdrop (01905) 640012
Bell Lane; WR2 6RR Popular dining pub with contemporary interior; much enjoyed food from sandwiches and snacks up including some pub favourites, ales such as Bathams and Woods, real ciders and a dozen wines by the glass, afternoon teas, friendly attentive service; children welcome, dogs in bar and part of restaurant, rattan-style tables and chairs out at front, nine bedrooms in separate buildings, handy for the Firs (NT) – Elgar's birthplace, open all day, food all day weekends, breakfast from 7am (8am Sat, Sun).

LULSLEY   SO7354
Fox & Hounds (01886) 821228
Signed a mile off A44 Worcester–Bromyard; WR6 5QT Friendly tucked-away country pub with well kept Wye Valley Butty Bach and guests, local cider and good choice of whiskies and gins, enjoyable sensibly priced food (all day Sat, not Sun evening) from sandwiches and pub snacks up, parquet-floored bar with open fire, dining area and sizeable conservatory; children and dogs welcome, tables in side garden, separate enclosed play area, nice walks (near Worcestershire Way), closed lunchtimes Mon and Tues, otherwise open all day.

MALVERN   SO7746
Foley Arms (01684) 580350
Worcester Road; WR14 4QS Substantial Georgian hotel (former coaching inn) owned by Wetherspoons, carpeted bar with booths and gilt-framed mirrors, friendly staff and usual good value, splendid views from main bar, sunny terrace; children welcome, 23 bedrooms, open all day from 7am.

MALVERN   SO7640
Malvern Hills Hotel (01684) 540690
Opposite British Camp car park, Wynds Point; junction A449/B4232 S; WR13 6DW Big comfortable lounge bar with oak panelling and woodburner, three well kept Wye Valley ales and a guest (two in summer), quite a few malt whiskies, enjoyable food here or in two more modern restaurants (one with lovely country views), good friendly service; background music; children (till 4pm) and dogs (in bar) welcome, terrace seating under parasols, cosy bedrooms, Iron Age hill fort British Camp opposite with views from top, open (and food) all day.

MALVERN   SO7746
Red Lion (01684) 564787
St Anns Road; WR14 4RG Tucked up a narrow lane near town centre; enjoyable food from sandwiches and baguettes up, also very good adjacent Thai restaurant (evenings Tues-Sat), well kept Marstons-related ales such as Ringwood, cheerful prompt service, modern décor with stripped pine, bare boards, flagstones and pastel colours; background music, darts; attractive partly covered front terrace, well placed for hill walks, open (and food) all day Sat, closed Sun-Fri lunchtimes.

MALVERN   SO7643
Wyche (01684) 575396
Wyche Road; WR14 4EQ Comfortable busy pub near top of Malvern Hills, splendid views and popular with walkers, Wye Valley and guests, decent range of affordable pubby food from sandwiches up including themed nights, good service; pool and games machine in one bar; children and dogs welcome, four bedrooms plus self-catering apartments, open all day, closed Mon.

OMBERSLEY   SO8463
★**Kings Arms** (01905) 620142
Main Road (A4133); WR9 0EW Imposing beamed and timbered Tudor pub; low-ceilinged brick-floored bar with built-in panelled wall seat and woodburner in large fireplace, three dining areas, steps down to one, another with Charles II coat of arms decorating the ceiling, good food and service, well kept Marstons-related ales and good selection of wines by the glass using 'Verre de Vin' wine preservation system; background music; children and dogs welcome, seats on tree-sheltered courtyard, colourful hanging baskets and tubs, open all day Fri-Sun.

PENSAX   SO7368
★**Bell** (01299) 896677
B4202 Abberley–Clows Top, Snead Common part of village; WR6 6AE

Mock-Tudor roadside pub built in 1883 with pubby tables on bare boards, two woodburners and a snug with open fire, good local atmosphere and six to eight real ales including Otter and Timothy Taylors and two guest ciders, popular good value food, separate refurbished dining room; regular live music and events, children and dogs (in bar) welcome, large garden with amazing views, open all day (closed Mon lunchtime).

PERSHORE   SO9445
Pickled Plum (01386) 556645
High Street; WR10 1EQ Modernised old pub with six well kept ales on handpump, four craft lagers and ciders, enjoyable generously served food at fair prices including lunchtime/early evening two-course deal and blackboard specials, quick friendly service, beams and log fires; Sun quiz, acoustic music session first Mon of month; children and dogs welcome, open all day Fri-Sun, food all day Sat.

SEVERN STOKE   SO8544
Rose & Crown (01905) 371249
A38 S of Worcester; WR8 9JQ Attractive 16th-c black and white pub, gently refurbished under present owners; low beams, good fire and various knick-knacks in character bar, some cushioned wall seats and high-backed settles among more modern pub furniture, quarry-tiled or carpeted floors, well kept Marstons-related ales, Weston's cider and decent choice of enjoyable sensibly priced food from sharing plates up, good friendly service, carpeted back restaurant; children (away from bar) and dogs welcome, picnic-sets in big garden with play area, Malvern Hills views and good walks, open all day in summer.

SHATTERFORD   SO7981
Bellmans Cross (01299) 861322
Bridgnorth Road (A442); DY12 1RN Welcoming 19th-c mock-Tudor dining pub; good well presented food cooked by French chef-landlord including weekday themed evenings, restaurant with kitchen view, Enville and a couple of guests from neat timber-effect bar, good choice of wines, teas and coffees; children welcome, picnic-sets outside, handy for Severn Woods walks, open all day weekends, no food Sun evening.

STOKE POUND   SO9667
Queens Head (01527) 557007
Sugarbrook Lane, by Bridge 48, Worcester & Birmingham Canal; B60 3AU Smartly modernised by the small Lovely Pubs group; fairly large bar with comfortable seating area, dedicated dining part beyond, good choice of food including sharing plates, wood-fired pizzas and charcoal spit-roasts, early evening discount (Mon-Fri) and two-for-one pizzas (Mon-Thurs), well kept ales such as Sharps and Wye Valley, large selection of wines from

glass-fronted store, helpful pleasant staff; live music Thurs; children welcome, waterside garden with tipi, moorings, good walk up the 30 locks of Tardebigge Steps, quite handy for Avoncroft Museum, open (and food) all day.

STOKE WORKS   SO9365
Boat & Railway (01527) 575597
Shaw Lane, by Bridge 42 of Worcester & Birmingham Canal; B60 4EQ Neat and tidy canalside pub; enjoyable good value home-cooked food including deals, Marstons-related ales, friendly helpful staff, large separate dining area overlooking the water; children (till 9pm) and dogs (in bar) welcome, narrow covered terrace, moorings, open (and food) all day, kitchen shuts 6pm Sun.

STOKE WORKS   SO9365
Bowling Green (01527) 861291
A mile from M5 junction 5, via Stoke Lane; handy for Worcester & Birmingham Canal; B60 4BH Friendly comfortable pub with grey wooden panelling and carpeted floors, enjoyable straightforward food at bargain prices (particularly good faggots), well kept Banks's ales and a Marstons guest, wall chart showing cost of a pint over the years; children welcome, big garden with play area and well tended bowling green, camping, open all day, no food Sun.

TENBURY WELLS   SO5966
Fountain (01584) 810701
Oldwood, A4112 S; WR15 8TB Timbered 17th-c roadside pub with big black-beamed bar, good choice of well prepared/priced pubby food, ales from Hobsons and sometimes Wye Valley, friendly helpful service; children and dogs welcome, a few picnic-sets out at front, more in lawned garden with play equipment, ten bedrooms (separate block), open all day, food all day Sat.

TENBURY WELLS   SO5968
Pembroke House (01584) 810301
Cross Street; WR15 8EQ Striking timbered building (oldest in town) with pubby beamed bar and two dining rooms, good popular food (not Sun evening, Tues, best to book) including themed nights, friendly efficient staff, Hobsons Best and a guest, woodburner, games area with pool, darts and TV; background and some live music; children and dogs (after 4pm) welcome, smokers' shelter and pleasant garden, open all day.

TENBURY WELLS   SO6468
★Talbot (01584) 781941
Newnham Bridge; A456; WR15 8JF Gently civilised coaching inn with relaxed atmosphere; mix of dark pubby, painted wooden and upholstered dining chairs around a variety of tables, leather tub chairs and sofas, quarry tiles, bare floorboards, open

fires and candlelight, plus bookshelves, old local photographs, standard lamps and some elegant antiques, background music, TV and board games; welcoming staff serve Hobsons Best, Wye Valley HPA and a weekend guest on handpump, local cider and good wines by the glass, and the well regarded food includes sandwiches (book in advance at weekends); attractive little garden terrace at rear near the spacious car park, thoughtfully decorated and well equipped bedrooms – the perfect base for exploring the lovely Teme Valley countryside, children allowed in restaurant, dogs in bar and bedrooms, open all day, no food Sun evening.

UPHAMPTON   SO8464
Fruiterers Arms (01905) 620305
Off A449 N of Ombersley; WR9 0JW
Friendly country local (looks like a private house, and has been in the same family since the mid 19th c), simple rustic Jacobean panelled bar and lounge with comfortable armchairs, beams and log fire, lots of photographs and memorabilia, well kept Wye Valley and a couple of local guests, farm cider/perry, snacky food such as rolls and pork pies; children allowed till 9pm, dogs in one area, back terrace and some seats out in front, open all day (from 1pm Tues).

WEST MALVERN   SO7645
Brewers Arms (01684) 561989
The Dingle, signed off B4232; WR14 4BQ
Attractive little two-bar beamed country local down steep path with stone walls, tiled floor and Victorian fireplace; well kept Malvern Hills, Wye Valley and up to five guests at busy times, good value pubby food, airy dining room; children, walkers and dogs welcome, glorious view from small garden, open all day.

WILLERSEY   SP1039
New Inn (01386) 853226
Main Street; WR12 7PJ Friendly old stone-built local in lovely village with a flagstoned bar and a raised quarry-tiled end section, some black beams, games room (pool and darts) and separate skittle alley, well kept Donnington ales and generous helpings of good value pub food (not Sun evening) from sandwiches up; background music, TV, children and dogs welcome, rattan-style tables and chairs outside, good local walks, open all day.

WORCESTER   SO8554
Cardinals Hat (01905) 724006
Friar Street; just off A44 near cathedral; WR1 2NA Dating from the 14th c with three small character rooms (one with fine oak panelling), sister to the equally historic Fleece in Bretforton (see Main Entries); five changing ales all from the Worcester area, real ciders and plenty of bottled beers, good bar snacks and cheese/meat platters, friendly well informed staff; children welcome,

pleasant little brick-paved terrace behind, four good bedrooms (continental breakfast), near cathedral, closed Mon lunchtime, otherwise open all day.

WORCESTER   SO8455
Dragon (01905) 25845
The Tything (A38); WR1 1JT Refurbished Georgian alehouse run by Church End Brewery; L-shaped carpeted bar with woodburner, six well kept Church End ales and a couple of guests, traditional cider and seven wines by the glass, snacky food such as pork pies and sausage rolls, friendly landlady, more room (and loos) upstairs; no children inside, dogs welcome, partly covered back terrace, open all day Fri-Sun, from 4pm other days. Handy for train station.

WORCESTER   SO8454
Farriers Arms (01905) 27569
Fish Street; WR1 2HN Welcoming and relaxed old timbered pub off the High Street; compact interior with bar and dining areas wrapping around central bar, enjoyable inexpensive lunchtime food and Sun roasts (evening food Thurs and Fri only), well kept ales such as Bombardier and St Austell Tribute, decent house wines, good cheerful service; pool, darts, TV and games machines; children welcome away from bar until 7pm, beer garden, two bedrooms but no breakfast, handy for cathedral, open all day and gets busy lunchtimes.

WORCESTER   SO8554
King Charles II (01905) 726100
New Street; WR1 2DP Small jettied Tudor building through which King Charles II escaped at the end of the English Civil War; heavy beams, fine panelling and woodburners in carved fireplaces, settles and pews on bare boards, up to eight well kept ales from Craddocks and associated Bridgnorth and Two Thirsty Brewers, traditional ciders, enjoyable range of Pieminister pies served with peas and different types of mash (limited range of other food), friendly helpful staff (ask them about the skeleton under the floor), more seating upstairs; open all day (food all day weekends).

WORCESTER   SO8455
Ounce (01905) 330460
The Tything (A38); some nearby parking; WR1 1JL The short frontage belies the long narrow series of small linked areas behind, dark flagstones and broad floorboards, stripped or cast-iron-framed tables, open fires, also an upstairs room, Sharps Doom Bar and a couple of Wye Valley beers, a dozen wines by the glass, cocktails, good food with emphasis on steaks (order by weight – from £1 per ounce on Tues and Weds), friendly helpful staff; background music; children and dogs (in bar) welcome, sunny backyard with decking, closed Mon, otherwise open all day (till 6pm Sun).

WORCESTER   SO8555
Plough (01905) 21381
Fish Street; WR1 2HN Traditional
corner pub with two simple rooms off
entrance lobby; six well kept interesting
beers including Hobsons and Malvern Hills,
local cider/perry and good whisky choice,
straightforward meals Fri-Sun lunchtimes
only; outside loos and small back terrace with
cathedral view, open all day.

WYRE PIDDLE   SO9647
Anchor (01386) 244590
Off A4538 NW of Evesham; WR10 2JB
Great position by River Avon with moorings,
decking on three levels, floodlit lawn and
view from airy back dining room, real ales
such as Purity Mad Goose, local Pershore
and Wye Valley, good food from sharing plates
and pub favourites to wood-fired pizzas, swift
friendly service; children and dogs welcome,
kitchen closed Sun evenings, otherwise open
(and food) all day.

Yorkshire

KEY ⭐ Star Pub   🍽 Top Quality Food   🍺 Great Beer

🍷 Good Wines   £ Bargain Meals   🛏 Good Bedrooms   🍴 Serves Food

---

BILTON IN AINSTY   SE4749   Map 7

Tickled Trout 🍽 🛏

(01423) 359006 – www.tickledtrout.co.uk

Off B1224 Wetherby–York; Church Street; YO26 7NN

Neatly kept country inn with first class licensees, character bar and dining rooms, very good food and seats in garden; bedrooms

This extended 16th-c inn a few miles from Wetherby Racecourse is beautifully maintained and family-run. The sizeable bar has a friendly, informal feel, an attractive mix of tables and chairs on rugs and flagstones, hops on beams, trout prints on the walls, books and china on shelves, some stuffed animals by a dresser and a couple of leather armchairs in front of an open fire (the mounted deer head above it is huge). One of the dining rooms has black button-back chairs around clothed tables on tartan carpet; the other has some unusual trout wallpaper. Staff are helpful and attentive. Real ales on handpump include Rudgate Jorvik Blonde and changing guests and there's a good choice of wines by the glass. The garden has enough space to include a dining tipi and a wood-fired pizza oven. The five bedrooms are comfortable and all have country views. Sister pub is the Wild Swan in Minskip (also in Yorkshire).

🍽 Highly thought-of food includes game terrine, tiger prawn and squid tempura, venison with dauphinoise potatoes and port jus, steak and ale pie, chicken breast with roasted root vegetables, wild boar sausages with crackling and apple compote, pan-fried trout with tenderstem broccoli and almonds, and puddings such as caramelised tarte tatin with vanilla ice-cream and Belgian chocolate délice with hazelnut nougat. *Benchmark main dish: fish and chips £13.95. Two-course evening meal £20.00.*

Free house ~ Licensee Karl Mainey ~ Real ale ~ Open 12-11; 12-7 Sun ~ Bar food 12-2.30, 5-9.30; 12-7 Sun ~ Children welcome ~ Dogs allowed in bar & bedrooms ~ Bedrooms: from £120

BLAKEY RIDGE   SE6799   Map 10

Lion 🍺 🛏

(01751) 417320 – www.lionblakey.co.uk

From A171 Guisborough–Whitby follow 'Castleton, Hutton-le-Hole' signposts; from A170 Kirkby Moorside–Pickering follow 'Keldholm, Hutton-le-Hole, Castleton' signposts; OS Sheet 100 map reference 679996; YO62 7LQ; YO62 7LQ

Spacious pub in fine moorland setting with popular food all day; bedrooms

Located at the highest point of the North York Moors, this family-owned 16th-c inn offers, as you might expect, some spectacular moorland views. Our readers make the most of the numerous walking and cycling opportunities on the doorstep (bike storage is available) by staying in one of the 13 comfortable bedrooms; breakfasts are first class. The low-beamed rambling bars have open fires, a few large high-backed rustic settles around cast-iron-framed tables, lots of small dining chairs, a nice leather sofa and stone walls hung with old engravings and photographs of the pub under snow (it's often cut off in winter – 40 days is the record so far). The fine choice of seven beers might include Black Sheep Best, Sadlers Peaky Blinder Pale Ale and Mud City Stout and Theakstons Summit alongside 13 wines by the glass and several malt whiskies; background music and games machine. The fascinating open-air Ryedale Folk Museum is a few miles away.

Generous helpings of hearty food from a long menu of pub favourites includes lunchtime sandwiches, garlic mushrooms, chicken goujons, mussels in creamy white sauce, lamb chops in minted gravy, grilled chicken breast with leek and bacon sauce, assorted steaks, burgers and pies, roasted vegetable jalfrezi, vegetarian nut roast, and puddings such as jam roly-poly with custard, chocolate nut sundae and strawberry cheesecake. *Benchmark main dish: steak and mushroom pie £14.50. Two-course evening meal £21.00.*

Free house ~ Licensees Barry, Diana, Paul and David Crossland ~ Real ale ~ Open 10am-11pm ~ Bar food 12-10 ~ Restaurant ~ Children welcome ~ Dogs allowed in bar ~ Bedrooms: £95

BRADFIELD
SK2290 Map 7

Strines Inn 🛏 £

(0114) 285 1247 – www.thestrinesinn.co.uk

Pub signed from A57 (first left, E of junction with A6013, Ladybower Reservoir), follow moorland road for 2.5km; with a map can also be reached more circuitously from Strines signpost on A616 at head of Underbank Reservoir, W of Stocksbridge; S6 6JE

Bustling inn in stunning scenery with hearty food and plenty of customers; bedrooms

Long a refuge for travellers crossing the moors between Sheffield and Manchester (it's a couple of miles north of Snake Pass), the Strines is just as warm and homely as it should be, and our readers love it, particularly for overnight stays. The three bedrooms have four-poster beds and a dining table (they serve breakfast in your room); two also offer views of Strines Reservoir. The main bar has black beams liberally decked with copper kettles and so forth, a coal fire in a rather grand stone fireplace, quite a menagerie of stuffed animals, and traditional wooden wall benches with red plush cushioning to match the carpet; background music. Two other rooms, to the right and left, are similarly furnished. Acorn Yorkshire Pride, Peak Ales Chatsworth Gold, Marstons Pedigree and a guest from Loxley on handpump and seven wines by the glass. There are plenty of picnic-sets outside, as well as swings, a play area and peacocks, chickens and geese. Disabled access. Built as a manor house in the 13th c, most of the present building dates from the 16th c. Its isolated position on the edge of the Peak District National Park means there are excellent surrounding walks.

Tasty, honest food at good prices includes sandwiches/paninis, garlic mushrooms, game and port pâté, ploughman's, giant yorkshire puddings with meat or vegetarian fillings and roast potatoes, broccoli, mushroom and stilton pasta bake, mixed grill, Cajun chicken breast and chips, vegetable lasagne with garlic bread, burger and chips, and puddings such as treacle sponge and lemon and elderflower cheesecake with cream, ice-cream or custard. *Benchmark main dish: giant yorkshire pudding with sausages, vegetables and roast potates £9.95. Two-course evening meal £16.00.*

Free house ~ Licensee Bruce Howarth ~ Real ale ~ Open 10.30am-11pm ~ Bar food 12-2.30, 5.30-8.30; 12-9 Sat; 12-8 Sun ~ Children allowed in bar ~ Dogs allowed in bar ~ Bedrooms: £95

BROUGHTON
SD9450 Map 7

Bull ♀ ◧

(01756) 792065 – www.brunningandprice.co.uk/bull

A59; BD23 3AE

Stone pub with interconnected bar and dining areas, a fine choice of drinks, interesting food and seats outside

This large, handsome roadside pub, part of the Brunning & Price group, has attractive rooms spreading out from the main bar area and is especially popular with families. There are rugs on flagstones, open log fires, plenty of prints and cartoons on the walls, a mix of wooden or high-backed leather dining chairs, button-back armchairs and cushioned wooden settles and wall seats and polished tables. Also, elegant metal chandeliers, mirrors, house plants and a bustling, friendly atmosphere. Helpful, efficient staff serve Phoenix Brunning & Price Original and changing guests such as Dark Horse Hetton Pale Ale, Lancaster Blonde, Listers Best Bitter and Timothy Taylors Boltmaker and Landlord on handpump, 18 wines by the glass, as many as 30 gins and almost 40 whiskies; board games. In warm weather you can sit at rattan-style chairs and tables on the attractive terrace in front of the building. Disabled access. There's a lot to do and see nearby, including exploring Broughton Hall Estate's 3,000 acres of beautiful countryside and parkland.

Brasserie-style food (with a separate gluten-free menu) includes sandwiches and 'light bites', a meze plate, chicken, ham and leek pie with mash and buttered greens, cauliflower, chickpea and squash tagine with lemon and almond couscous, pork and leek sausages with mash and onion gravy, beer-battered cod and chips, fish pie (salmon, smoked haddock and prawns), crispy beef salad with sweet chilli sauce and roasted cashew nuts, venison haunch with dauphinoise potatoes and blackberrry jus, and puddings such as chocolate and orange tart with passion-fruit sorbet and hot waffle with caramelised banana and honeycomb ice-cream. *Benchmark main dish: Malaysian chicken curry with steamed pak choi £14.95. Two-course evening meal £21.00.*

Brunning & Price ~ Manager Steve Larkin ~ Real ale ~ Open 10am-11pm; 10am-10.30pm Sun ~ Bar food 12-9; 12-9.30 Fri, Sat ~ Restaurant ~ Children welcome ~ Dogs allowed in bar

CONSTABLE BURTON
SE1690 Map 10

Wyvill Arms ⍟ ♀ ◧ 🛏

(01677) 450581 – www.thewyvillarms.co.uk

A684 E of Leyburn; DL8 5LH

Well run, friendly dining pub with interesting food, plenty of wines by the glass, real ales and efficient helpful service; bedrooms

People flock to this 18th-c former farmhouse on the edge of the Yorkshire Dales for many reasons: the splendid food, homely and welcoming atmosphere, comfortable accommodation, attractive surroundings… we could go on. The small bar area has a finely worked plaster ceiling incorporating the Wyvill family's coat of arms, a mix of seating and an elaborate stone fireplace with a warm winter fire. A second bar has been refurbished, but has kept the model train on a railway track running around the room. A reception area includes a huge leather sofa with space for eight people, another carved stone fireplace and an old leaded stained-glass church window partition. Both rooms are hung with pictures of local scenes. Theakstons Best and guest beers from Rudgate and Wensleydale are on handpump, plus a good choice of wines by the glass and nine malt whiskies; chess, backgammon and dominoes. There are several large wooden benches under sizeable white parasols for outdoor dining and picnic-sets by a well. The seven smart, comfortable bedrooms make a lovely base for exploring the beautiful area, and breakfasts are generous. Constable Burton Hall is opposite.

 The best local, seasonal produce is used in the highly enjoyable food, which includes lunchtime sandwiches, scallops with black pudding, smoked haddock, cod and salmon fishcake with poached egg and hollandaise, beef bourguignon with mash, Egyptian-style aubergine and red pepper stew topped with mozzarella, venison with highlanders pudding, fondant potato and redcurrant and blueberry sauce, lamb shank with mash, vegetable 'posh pot' with camembert, half crispy roast duck with black cherry sauce and pak choi, steak and onion pie with chips, 28-day aged sirloin or fillet steak with a choice of five sauces, and puddings. *Benchmark main dish: fish and chips with mushy peas £14.50. Two-course evening meal £21.00.*

Free house ~ Licensee Nigel Stevens ~ Real ale ~ Open 11-3, 5.30-11; 11-3, 6-10 Sun ~ Bar food 12-2.15, 5.30-9 ~ Restaurant ~ Children welcome until 8.30pm ~ Dogs allowed in bar ~ Bedrooms: £75

CRAYKE
Durham Ox 🍴⭐ 🍷 🛏
(01347) 821506 – www.thedurhamox.com
Off B1363 at Brandsby, towards Easingwold; West Way; YO61 4TE

SE5670 Map 7

Convivial inn with interesting décor in old-fashioned rooms, fine drinks and smashing food; comfortable bedrooms

Set within a lovely little village, this friendly 17th-c coaching inn is a good all-rounder, popular with both locals and visitors. The old-fashioned lounge bar has antique tables, seats and settles on flagstones and pictures and photographs on dark red walls; also, interesting satirical carvings in the panelling (Victorian copies of medieval pew ends), polished copper and brass and an enormous inglenook fireplace. The bottom bar contains an illustrated account of local history (some of it gruesome) dating from the 12th c, and a large framed print of the famous Durham Ox, which weighed 171 stone. The Burns Bar has a woodburning stove, exposed brickwork and large french windows that open on to a balcony. Drinks include Black Sheep Bitter, Timothy Taylors Boltmaker, York Guzzler and a guest on handpump, 20 wines by the glass, a dozen malt whiskies and interesting spirits including a locally made gin named for the pub; background and some live music and board games. In warm weather, head for the seats in the courtyard garden; there are views on three sides over the Vale of York, while on the fourth is a charming lookout to the medieval church on the hill – supposedly the very hill up which the Grand Old Duke of York marched his men. Bedrooms, at the rear of the pub with newly built terraces or in renovated farm cottages (dogs allowed here), are well equipped and spacious, and breakfasts are very good. Another self-catering cottage sleeps six. The nearby A19 leads straight to a park & ride for York city centre.

First class food includes lunchtime sandwiches, baked queen scallops with garlic and parsley butter and gruyère crust, harissa bean and butternut squash ragoût with new potatoes and greens, spicy pork belly with chilli, honey and sesame dressing on Asian salad, beef in ale pie with horseradish and suet scone dumpling, a seafood sharing platter, grilled pork chop with mustard mash, red cabbage and cider and apple gravy, and puddings such as warm banana, toffee and pecan pudding with cinnamon and vegan vanilla ice-cream and crêpes suzette; they also offer an early bird menu (not Saturday). *Benchmark main dish: roast chicken supreme with potato cake and greens £17.00. Two-course evening meal £25.00.*

Free house ~ Licensee Michael Ibbotson ~ Real ale ~ Open 12-10.30; 12-midnight Thurs-Sat ~ Bar food 12-2.30, 5.30-9 (9.30 Thurs-Sat); 12-4, 5.30-8.30 Sun ~ Restaurant ~ Children welcome ~ Dogs allowed in bar & bedrooms ~ Bedrooms: £120

EAST WITTON
SE1486 Map 10

Blue Lion

(01969) 624273 – www.thebluelion.co.uk

A6108 Leyburn–Ripon; DL8 4SN

Civilised dining pub with a proper bar, real ales, highly enjoyable food and courteous service; comfortable bedrooms

This delightful Georgian coaching inn has for many years been known to provide the highest quality food in exquisite surroundings. It's the perfect choice if you want to explore the Yorkshire Dales National Park, and the long-serving owners welcome damp dog walkers just as warmly as those out for a special meal. The big squarish bar is civilised but informal with soft lighting, high-backed antique settles and old windsor chairs on Turkish rugs and flagstones, ham hooks in the high ceiling decorated with dried wheat, teazles and so forth, a delft shelf full of bric-a-brac, plus several prints, sporting caricatures and other pictures; daily papers. There are three ales including Black Sheep Best on handpump, an impressive wine list including 12 (plus champagne) by the glass, 11 gins and 21 malt whiskies. The candlelit, high-ceilinged and elegant dining room has another open fire. Picnic-sets on the gravel outside look beyond the stone houses on the far side of the village green to Witton Fell, and there's a large, attractive back garden. The 15 comfortable bedrooms have pretty country furnishings; some are in the main house, others in converted stables across the courtyard (these are dog-friendly).

The imaginative, first rate food includes sandwiches, potted salt beef with mini yorkshire pudding, horseradish hollandaise sauce and chargrilled dill pickle, Yorkshire beef fillet carpaccio with pomegranate compote and beer bread croutons with truffle emulsion, wensleydale cheese and leek risotto, ox cheek and ale suet pudding with maple-glazed parsnips and colcannon potato, grilled halibut with new potatoes and buttered spinach, sage- and lemon-stuffed porchetta with croquette potatoes, rhubarb compote and cider velouté, cassoulet (Yorkshire duck, Morteau sausage, roasted tomatoes and white beans), and puddings such as green apple soufflé with salted caramel ice-cream and Valrhona chocolate fondant with sweet date purée and walnut ice-cream. *Benchmark main dish: smoked haddock with mushroom and leek cream, soft poached egg and gruyère glaze £21.50. Two-course evening meal £32.00.*

Free house ~ Licensee Paul Klein ~ Real ale ~ Open 11-11 ~ Bar food 12-2.15, 7-9.15; 12-9.15 Sun ~ Restaurant ~ Children welcome ~ Dogs allowed in bar & bedrooms ~ Bedrooms: £125

Bedroom prices given are for a standard double room in high season.

ELSLACK

SD9249 Map 7

Tempest Arms

(01282) 842450 – www.tempestarms.co.uk

Just off A56 Earby–Skipton; BD23 3AY

Busy inn with three log fires in stylish rooms, five real ales, good wines and well regarded food; bedrooms

Handy for the Pennine Way, this comfortable and stylish 18th-c stone inn on the edge of the Yorkshire Dales, a few miles from Skipton, has a cosy and welcoming feel. Attracting a good mix of customers, the bar and surrounding dining areas are full of character: cushioned armchairs, built-in wall seats with added cushions, stools, plenty of tables and three log fires (one greets you at the entrance and divides the bar and restaurant). Also, quite a bit of exposed stonework, amusing prints on cream walls, five real ales on handpump – Dark Horse Hetton Pale Ale, Timothy Taylors Landlord and three changing guests, 13 wines by the glass, 30 malt whiskies and 50 gins; background music and board games. Tables outside are largely screened from the road by a raised bank. The 21 comfortable, well equipped bedrooms make the ideal base for exploring the area; the surrounding walks are lovely. Disabled access.

Highly thought-of food includes sandwiches, smoked salmon with charred asparagus and spinach, creamy mushrooms topped with stilton, sharing platters, lamb burger with smoked bacon, harissa and mint yoghurt and chips, lasagne, vegetable curry with basmati wild rice, sea bass with tomato and chilli salsa and sautéed potatoes, shredded duck with crispy ginger, beansprouts, spring onions, cucumber, carrots and spiced plum sauce, chicken escalope with rösti potatoes, fish pie with cheesy mash, and puddings such as crème brûlée and sherry trifle. *Benchmark main dish: steak and ale pie £13.95. Two-course evening meal £21.00.*

Individual Inns ~ Managers Martin and Veronica Clarkson ~ Real ale ~ Open 11-11; 12-10.30 Sun ~ Bar food 12-2.30, 6-9; 12-7.30 Sun ~ Restaurant ~ Children welcome ~ Dogs allowed in bar & bedrooms ~ Bedrooms: £105

FELIXKIRK

SE4684 Map 10

Carpenters Arms

(01845) 537369 – www.thecarpentersarmsfelixkirk.com

Village signed off A170 E of Thirsk; YO7 2DP

Stylishly furnished village pub with spacious rooms, real ales and highly regarded food; lodge-style bedrooms

This very popular pub has taken advantage of the enforced closure in summer 2020 to have a revamp including tranquil colour schemes using pale green colours and leaf-patterned wallpaper, new furnishings and exposed brick and stone; bedrooms have been upgraded too. Spacious and relaxed, the older parts have dark beams and joists, a mix of tables and chairs, some upholstered, on big flagstones or carpet, and stools against the panelled counter where they keep Black Sheep Best, York Guzzler and a changing guest ale on handpump, farm cider, around 20 wines by the glass and a good choice of malt whiskies and gins. The snug seating area has armchairs in front of a double-sided woodburning stove. The red-walled dining room is furnished with antique and country kitchen chairs around scrubbed tables, and the walls throughout are hung with traditional prints, local pictures and maps; background music. On a raised decked terrace, lots of seats and tables overlook the landscaped garden, with picnic-sets at the front. The ten bedrooms, two in the main building, eight around a landscaped garden, are bright and contemporary. This is part of the Provenance Inns & Hotels group.

 Appetising food includes lunchtime sandwiches, prawn and crayfish salad, game pie with crispy bacon salad, sharing boards, wagyu burger with chips, butternut squash and sage ravioli, honey- and five spice-glazed duck breast with pumpkin and fondant potato, coriander and lime-griddled chicken with sweet potato fries and yoghurt dip, roast shallot tart with vegan feta and spinach, and puddings such as pear and almond crumble tart with toffee sauce and amaretto custard and lemon and mascarpone cheesecake with scorched meringue; they also offer an early bird menu (5.30-6.45pm). *Benchmark main dish: steak in ale pie £15.00. Two-course evening meal £22.00.*

Free house ~ Licensee Paulo Pinto ~ Real ale ~ Open 12-11 ~ Bar food 12-2.30, 5.30-9.30; 12-4, 5.30-8.30 Sun ~ Restaurant ~ Children welcome ~ Dogs allowed in bar & bedrooms ~ Bedrooms: £120

GRANTLEY
SE2369 Map 7

Grantley Bar & Restaurant 🍴⭐
(01765) 620227 ~ www.grantleyarms.com
Village signposted off B6265 W of Ripon; HG4 3PJ

Relaxed and interesting dining pub with good food

The friendly, hands-on licensees at this pleasant 17th-c pub ensure both regulars and visitors a genuinely warm welcome. There's an easy-going atmosphere in the front bar, which has beams, a huge fireplace built of massive stone blocks and housing a woodburning stove, traditional furnishings such as comfortable dining chairs and polished tables set with evening tea-lights and some of the landlady's own paintings of ponies and dogs. The back dining room has crisp linen tablecloths, decorative plates and more paintings, mainly landscapes. Theakstons Best and a guest ale on handpump, eight wines by the glass, eight malt whiskies, a local farm cider and attentive friendly service. Teak tables and chairs on the flagstoned front terrace have a pleasant outlook. After visiting nearby Fountains Abbey and Studley Royal Water Garden (National Trust), this is a top choice for lunch.

 The enjoyable food includes lunchtime sandwiches and omelettes, hot or cold trio of fish, chicken liver parfait with plum chutney, prawn cocktail with cucumber sorbet, butternut squash and feta cheese tart, mushroom wellington topped with sun-dried tomatoes, beef stroganoff, Thai green curry, and puddings such as caramelised lemon tart and apple and berry crumble with custard; they also offer a two- and three-course set lunch (not Sunday). *Benchmark main dish: pie of the week £14.75. Two-course evening meal £22.00.*

Free house ~ Licensees Valerie Sails and Eric Broadwith ~ Real ale ~ Open 12-3, 5.30-10.30; 12-3, 5.30-11 Fri, Sat; 12-10.30 Sun ~ Bar food 12-2, 5.30-9 (9.30 Sat); 12-3.30, 5.30-8 Sun ~ Restaurant ~ Well behaved children welcome

GRINTON
SE0498 Map 10

Bridge Inn 🍺 £
(01748) 884224
B6270 W of Richmond; DL11 6HH

Bustling pub with traditional, comfortable bars, log fires, real ales, malt whiskies and tasty bar food; neat bedrooms

Situated by the river in the heart of Swaledale in the Yorkshire Dales National Park, this welcoming traditional pub with its notably good food and beer is a godsend for thirsty walkers and cyclists – who will be glad to hear that flood defences are being installed to prevent a repetition of 2019's inundation. There's a relaxing, comfortable atmosphere, bow-window seats and a pair of stripped traditional settles among more usual pub seats (all well cushioned), a good log fire and Jennings Cumberland, Marstons Wainwright and always something from the Yorkshire Dales brewery on handpump; also, eight wines by the glass, 25 gins and farm cider. On the right, a few steps lead down to a room with darts and ring the bull. On the left, past leather armchairs and a sofa next to a second log fire (and a glass chess set), is an extensive two-part dining room with décor in cream and shades of brown, and a modicum of fishing memorabilia. The five bedrooms are neat, simple and comfortable, and breakfasts good. There are picnic-sets outside and the lovely church opposite is known as the Cathedral of the Dales.

 Tasty favourites prepared with modern flair might include squid rings in panko breadcrumbs, black pudding scotch egg, forest mushrooms on toasted ciabatta with hollandaise, roast pork belly with colcannon, pork shoulder bonbon and apple and cider sauce, steak and ale pie, beef burger, chickpea curry, Whitby scampi, and desserts such as peanut butter brownie, ginger pudding with toffee sauce and blackcurrant yoghurt ice-cream cake. At lunchtime you can also get good-value hot and cold sandwiches and snacks. *Benchmark main dish: stuffed chicken breast with new potato and chive cake and a Yorkshire cheese sauce £14.95. Two-course evening meal £19.00.*

Jennings (Marstons) ~ Lease Andrew Atkin ~ Real ale ~ Open 12-11 ~ Bar food 12-2.30, 6-9; 12-3, 6-9 Sat, Sun ~ Restaurant ~ Children welcome ~ Dogs allowed in bar & bedrooms ~ Bedrooms: £90

HALIFAX
Shibden Mill 🏮 ❦ ♨ 🛏

SE1027 Map 7

(01422) 365840 – www.shibdenmillinn.com

Off A58 into Kell Lane at Stump Cross Inn, near A6036 junction; keep on, pub signposted from Kell Lane on left; HX3 7UL

Yorkshire Dining Pub of the Year

Interesting 370-year-old building with a spreading bar, four real ales and inventive, top class bar food; luxury bedrooms

If the rustic charm of this restored 17th-c mill combined with contemporary luxuries weren't enough to win you over, the large choice of ales, wines and spirits and exemplary food surely will. The rambling bar has plenty of character and is full of nooks and crannies. Some cosy side areas have banquettes heaped with cushions and rugs, nicely spaced attractive old tables and chairs, and candles in elegant iron holders, all giving a feeling of real intimacy; also, old hunting prints, country landscapes and a couple of big log fires. You'll find a beer named for them (from Moorhouses), Little Valley Withens Pale Ale and a couple of changing guests on handpump, 29 wines by the glass from a wide list, 22 malt whiskies and 20 gins. There's also an upstairs restaurant; background music. The pleasant heated terrace has plenty of seats and tables, including a sweet 'tea shed', and the building is prettily floodlit at night. To make the most of the lovely surrounding countryside, our readers regularly stay in the 11 stylish, well equipped bedrooms; breakfasts are good and hearty. Shibden Hall, star of the recent TV series *Gentleman Jack* about Anne Lister, is nearby.

🍽 Highly accomplished food includes lunchtime sandwiches, cauliflower bhaji with roasted cauliflower velouté, guinea fowl with pork jowl bacon, celeriac, apple and truffle, halibut with kohlrabi, girolle mushrooms and brown shrimp and chicken butter sauce, squash gnocchi with tunworth cheese, sage, burnt butter and ramson buds, burger with toppings, beetroot slaw and skinny fries, cod loin with crushed ginger and spring onion potatoes and summer vegetables, pork belly with crispy pig head, langoustine, baby turnips, pork fat potatoes, toasted almonds and sherry sauce, and puddings such as damson iced parfait with apple, treacle and caramelised crumpet and white chocolate tart with raspberry, sorrel and torched chocolate; they also offer afternoon tea and a seven-course taster menu. *Benchmark main dish: sausage of the day with mash and onion gravy £16.00. Two-course evening meal £26.00.*

Free house ~ Licensee Glen Pearson ~ Real ale ~ Open 12-11; 12-11.30 Sat; 12-10.30 Sun ~ Bar food 12-2 (2.30 Fri), 5.30-9; 12-2.30, 5.30-9.15 Sat; 12-7.30 Sun ~ Restaurant ~ Children welcome ~ Dogs allowed in bar ~ Bedrooms: £140

HELPERBY
SE4370   Map 7

Oak Tree ⭐ ▯ ⌂

(01423) 789189 – www.theoaktreehelperby.com

Raskelf Road; YO61 2PH

Attractive pub with real ales in friendly bar, fine food in cosy dining rooms and seats on terrace; comfortable bedrooms

Often busy with contented customers, this is a popular inn with colourful décor and a satisfying range of good food and drink. The informal bar has a mix of wooden tables on old quarry tiles, flagstones and oak floorboards, prints and paintings on bold red walls and open fires; background music. Stools line the counter where they keep Black Sheep Best, Theakstons Best, York Guzzler and a guest beer on handpump, ten wines by the glass, nine malt whiskies and gin, and farm cider. The main dining room has a large woodburner in a huge brick fireplace, high-backed purple chairs around nice old tables on oak flooring, ornate mirrors and some striking artwork on exposed brick walls. French windows lead out to the terrace where there are plenty of seats and tables for summer dining. Upstairs, a private dining room has a two-way woodburner, a sitting room with boldly coloured sofas and doors leading to a terrace. The six modern bedrooms are comfortable and well equipped; one is dog-friendly. Disabled access. This belongs to the Provenance Inns & Hotels group.

⭐ As well as breakfasts (8-11am), the highly regarded food includes lunchtime sandwiches, roast scallops and sticky pork with apple and creamed celeriac, confit pheasant spring roll with spiced chutney, sharing boards, prawn and chorizo risotto with tomato vinaigrette, chicken in a creamy tarragon sauce with herbed roast potatoes, fillet of cod with pomme purée, roast cauliflower and mussels, braised beef in red wine jus, and puddings such as cherry and chocolate crème brûlée. *Benchmark main dish: steak in ale pie £15.00. Two-course evening meal £22.00.*

Free house ~ Licensee Elizabeth Richards ~ Real ale ~ Open 8am-11pm ~ Bar food 12-2.30, 5.30-9.30; 12-4, 5.30-8 Sun ~ Restaurant ~ Children welcome ~ Dogs allowed in bar & bedrooms ~ Bedrooms: £100

ILKLEY
SE1347   Map 7

Wheatley Arms ▯ 🍺 ⌂

(01943) 816496 – www.wheatleyarms.co.uk

Wheatley Lane, Ben Rhydding; LS29 8PP

Smart inn with a cosy bar, restful dining rooms, professional service and good food and drink; comfortable bedrooms

This large, gabled, sandstone inn retains a decidedly homely and friendly vibe, despite being deservedly busy much of the time – particularly at lunchtime with hungry walkers, as a result of its proximity to Ilkley Moor.

The interconnected dining rooms have all manner of attractive antique and upholstered chairs and stools and prettily cushioned wooden or rush-seated settles around assorted tables, rugs on bare boards, some bold wallpaper, various prints and two log fires; our readers like the smart garden room. One half of the locals' bar has tub armchairs and other comfortable seats, the other has tartan-cushioned wall seats and mate's chairs, with classic wooden stools against the counter where they keep Dark Horse Craven Bitter, Ilkley Mary Jane and a couple of changing guests on handpump. Also, 23 wines by the glass (including prosecco and champagne), a dozen malt whiskies and a farm cider; background music, board games and TV. There are seats and tables on the terrace. Individually decorated, the 12 well equipped, smart and comfortable bedrooms are much used by those exploring the area; some come with a private roof terrace.

Consistently good food includes breakfasts, sandwiches (until 5.30pm), chestnut mushrooms with garlic cream sauce on toasted sourdough, crumbled goats cheese and chives, steak and mushroom in ale pie, smoked salmon, coriander and lime fishcake with red pepper coulis, burger with toppings, coleslaw and fries, gammon steak with hand-cut chips, poached eggs and pineapple jam, spiced chickpea and sweetcorn fritter with pickled beetroot, cherry tomato and rocket salad, 10oz rib-eye steak with peppercorn sauce and chips, and puddings such as raspberry cheesecake and warm treacle tart. *Benchmark main dish: beer-battered fish and chips £13.00. Two-course evening meal £21.00.*

Individual Inns ~ Licensee Jonathan Brown ~ Real ale ~ Open 10am-11pm; 8am-11pm Sat; 8am-10.30pm Sun ~ Bar food 12-2, 5-8; 12-9 Sat; 12-7 Sun ~ Restaurant ~ Children welcome ~ Dogs allowed in bar & bedrooms ~ Bedrooms: £100

KIRKBY FLEETHAM
Black Horse ♀ ◖ ⛏

SE2894 Map 10

(01609) 749010 – www.blackhorseinnkirkbyfleetham.com
Village signposted off A1 S of Catterick; Lumley Lane; DL7 0SH

Attractively reworked country inn with well liked food, good drinks choice and cheerful atmosphere; comfortable bedrooms

If you're looking for a characterful country pub with nods to both its traditional roots and modern comforts, this won't disappoint. The long, softly lit beamed bar on the right has flagstones, cushioned wall seats, some little settles and high-backed dining chairs by the log fire at one end, Black Sheep Best, Ossett Yorkshire Blonde and Timothy Taylors Boltmaker on handpump, 15 gins, ten whiskies and 11 wines by the glass. A dining room towards the back is light and open, with big bow windows on either side and a casual contemporary look thanks to pastel garden settles with scatter cushions around tables painted pale green; background pop music. The neat sheltered back lawn and flagstoned side terrace have teak seats and tables, and there are also picnic-sets at the front; quoits. The 14 bedrooms are attractive and comfortable with plenty of antique charm, and breakfasts are good.

Pleasing food includes wild mushroom bordelaise with white wine and garlic cream sauce, baked queenie scallops with red chilli, lime and soy sauce and roasted peanut and spring onion crust, crispy pork belly with braised pig cheek, turnips, quince and fondant potato, seared calves liver with mash, grilled bacon and green beans, 28-day aged sirloin steak with triple-cooked chips and café de paris butter, cauliflower and potato gnocchi with chestnut mushrooms, blue cheese and crispy sage, and puddings such as elderflower pannacotta and strawberry textures and chocolate nemesis. *Benchmark main dish: beer-battered monkfish scampi with pea salsa and fries £14.95. Two-course evening meal £21.00.*

Free house ~ Licensee Steven Barker ~ Real ale ~ Open 12-11 ~ Bar food 12-2.30, 5-9; 12-8
Sun ~ Restaurant ~ Children welcome ~ Dogs allowed in bar & bedrooms ~ Bedrooms: £90

LEDSHAM

SE4529   Map 7

Chequers 🌟 ♟ 🍷

(01977) 683135 – www.thechequersinn.com

1.5 miles from A1(M) junction 42: follow Leeds signs, then Ledsham signposted;
Claypit Lane; LS25 5LP

**Friendly pub with hands-on landlord, log fires in several beamed
rooms, real ales and interesting food; pretty back terrace**

Conveniently close to the A1, this down-to-earth pub is eternally popular.
The several, small, individually decorated rooms have plenty of character,
with low beams, log fires, lots of cosy alcoves, toby jugs, plates and all sorts
of knick-knacks on the walls and ceilings (cricket fans will be interested
to see a large photo in one room of four Yorkshire heroes). From the little
old-fashioned, panelled-in central servery they offer Brown Cow Ledsham
Sessions, Leeds Best, Theakstons Best, Timothy Taylors Landlord and a
guest beer on handpump and eight wines by the glass. Occasional live music
events. The lovely sheltered two-level terrace at the back has lots of tables
among roses, and the hanging baskets and flowers are very pretty. RSPB
Fairburn Ings reserve is not far and the ancient village church is worth a visit.

Enjoyable food includes sandwiches, mussels in white wine with pickled shallots,
garlic and ciabatta, smoked duck with candied pumpkin seeds and coriander,
cured and smoked meats board, aubergine, chickpea and tomato stew with crushed baby
potatoes, sausages with mash and onion gravy, roasted sea trout with pea and crayfish
tail risotto, calves liver with caramelised onion mash, bacon and gravy, burger with
chips and coleslaw, and puddings such as strawberry trifle and Baileys double chocolate
cheesecake. *Benchmark main dish: chicken breast with creamed potato, pancetta,
shallot and thyme sauce £14.95. Two-course evening meal £21.00.*

Free house ~ Licensee Amanda Wraith ~ Real ale ~ Open 11-11; 12-6 Sun ~ Bar food 12-9;
12-5 Sun ~ Restaurant ~ Children welcome ~ Dogs allowed in bar

LEVISHAM

SE8390   Map 10

Horseshoe 🌟 🛏

(01751) 460240 – www.horseshoelevisham.co.uk

Off A169 N of Pickering; YO18 7NL

**Friendly village pub with super food, neat rooms, real ales and seats
on the village green; bedrooms**

This bustling pub sits at the head of a charming, unspoilt village, its
outdoor picnic tables occupying the triangular green opposite. Drinkers,
diners and overnight guests have nothing but praise for the capable
management and all-round high standards here. The lively bars have beams,
upholstered banquettes, wheelback and captain's chairs around a variety
of tables on polished wooden floors, landscapes by a local artist on the
walls and a log fire in the broad stone fireplace; an adjoining snug has
a woodburning stove, comfortable sofas and old photographs of the pub
and village. Black Sheep Best and guests such as Cropton Yorkshire Moors
and Timothy Taylors Golden Best on handpump, ten or so wines by the glass,
bottled Yorkshire ciders, local gins and a dozen malt whiskies are served
by courteous staff. There are more tables in the back garden, along with
eight of the Horseshoe's 14 clean, comfortable bedrooms (the rest are in the
main building); dogs are allowed in one of the garden rooms. The inn makes

an excellent base for exploring the North York Moors National Park; Levisham has a station on the scenic North Yorkshire Moors Railway line, and its historic church is worth a visit. Breakfasts are hearty. Sister pub is the Fox & Rabbit in Lockton, a couple of miles away.

With an emphasis on local suppliers, the well regarded food includes sandwiches, fishcakes with tartare sauce, brie and parma ham parcels with melba toast, Cajun chicken salad with chips, grilled gammon with fried egg and pineapple, butternut squash, leek and pine nut risotto, braised lamb shank with rosemary mash and mint gravy, slow-roasted pork belly with thyme mash, cider gravy and apple sauce, deep-fried Whitby haddock with mushy peas and chips, and desserts such as rhubarb syllabub and chocolate truffle torte. *Benchmark main dish: fisherman's pie with home-made chips £12.50. Two-course evening meal £20.00.*

Free house ~ Licensees Toby and Charles Wood ~ Real ale ~ Open 11-11; 11-10 Sun ~ Bar food 12-2, 6-8.30 ~ Children welcome ~ Dogs allowed in bar & bedroom ~ Bedrooms: £90

LEYBURN

SE1190   Map 10

Sandpiper 🏵 ⏨ 🛏

(01969) 622206 – www.sandpiperinn.co.uk
Just off Market Place; DL8 5AT

Appealing food plus a drinkers' bar in pretty inn, with a good choice of whisky; bedrooms

The couple who run this cottagey 17th-c pub have perfected their innkeeping skills during their two decades of residency, and it consistently wins praise for its warm atmosphere, attention to detail and equal care given to drinking and dining. The cosy bar, with its low ceiling, black beams and log fire, is popular locally and has a chatty, friendly feel; the most coveted seats are in the snug a few steps up. Beside the linenfold panelled bar counter are photographs of the Dales and a woodburning stove in a stone fireplace; to the left is the attractive restaurant with dark wooden tables on a warm red rug and glassware sparkling in candlelight. Black Sheep Best and one or two guests from Wensleydale on handpump, 50 malt whiskies, good wines by the glass and a dozen gins; background music. In good weather, you can enjoy a drink on the front terrace among the pretty hanging baskets and flowering climbers. The two bedrooms are comfortable and well equipped. The pleasant little market town of Leyburn is a gateway to the Yorkshire Dales National Park.

Excllent and creative modern British food cooked by the chef-patron includes lunchtime sandwiches, duck and ham hock terrine with textures of beetroot and herb salad, smoked salmon with pickled shallots, capers and charred lemon, tempura-fried prawns, squid and vegetables with sweet chilli sauce, double-baked vintage cheddar soufflé with creamed leeks, steamed skrei cod with Scottish mussels, purple sprouting broccoli and tagliatelle, roasted chump of Dales lamb with dauphinoise potatoes and jumbo cranberries, roasted vegetable and wild garlic berry risotto with oyster mushrooms and pine nuts, plus puddings such as deconstructed caramel shortbread with vanilla fudge and cinder toffee and rhubarb and almond tart. *Benchmark main dish: braised Wensleydale beef with creamed leeks, chantenay carrots and mash £17.75. Two-course evening meal £26.00.*

Free house ~ Licensees Jonathan and Janine Harrison ~ Real ale ~ Open 12-3, 6-11; 12-3, 6-9 Sun; closed Mon ~ Bar food 12-2.30, 6-8.30 ~ Restaurant ~ Children welcome ~ Dogs allowed in bar & bedrooms ~ Bedrooms: £110

You can send reports directly to us at feedback@goodguides.com

LINTON IN CRAVEN

SD9962 Map 7

Fountaine 🍺

(01756) 752210 – www.fountaineinnatlinton.co.uk

Off B6265 Skipton–Grassington; BD23 5HJ

Neatly kept pub with attractive furnishings, open fires, five real ales and popular food; bedrooms

Set in one of the most beautiful corners of the Yorkshire Dales, this friendly pub offers a warm welcome, hearty food and good ales and other drinks. The bars have beams and white-painted joists in low ceilings, some exposed stone walls, log fires (one in a beautifully carved heavy wooden fireplace), attractive built-in cushioned wall benches and stools around a mix of copper-topped tables, little wall lamps and quite a few prints on the pale walls. There's a cosy snug. A Robinson's ale, John Smiths Bitter, Tetleys Best and two guests on handpump, 13 wines by the glass, a good range of gins and malt whiskies served by efficient staff; background music, darts and ring the bull. The terrace, looking across the road to the duck pond, has teak benches and tables under green parasols, and the hanging baskets are most attractive. The five well equipped bedrooms are in a converted barn behind the pub. There's plenty of good walking and cycling nearby.

 The thoughtful menu includes sandwiches, pork pie with stilton and rocket salad, house-cured salmon with beetroot pannacotta, goats cheese and lemon oil, chicken wrapped in prosciutto with Mediterranean roasted vegetables, goats cheese and sautéed potatoes, vegetable and chickpea tagine, lancashire cheese and onion pie, smoked haddock with chickpeas, chorizo, sweet peppers and a poached egg, slow-roasted beef brisket in ale with mash and yorkshire pudding, Welsh lamb burger and chips, and puddings such as bakewell tart with ice-cream and chocolate fudge brownie. *Benchmark main dish: beer-battered haddock and chips £13.95. Two-course evening meal £20.00.*

Individual Inns ~ Manager Christopher Gregson ~ Real ale ~ Open 12-11; 12-10.30 Sun ~ Bar food 12-9 ~ Restaurant ~ Children allowed in bar ~ Dogs allowed in bar & bedrooms ~ Bedrooms: £100

LOCKTON

SE8488 Map 10

Fox & Rabbit £

(01751) 460213 – www.foxandrabbit.co.uk

A169 N of Pickering; YO18 7NQ

Popular country inn with fine views, a friendly atmosphere, real ales and well liked food

A perennially popular, creeper-clad country pub run by two brothers who understand the meaning of hospitality: the welcome here is always warm, the upkeep flawless and standards reliably high. The interconnected rooms have beams, panelling and some exposed stonework, wall settles and banquettes, dark pubby chairs and tables on tartan carpet, a log fire and an inviting atmosphere; fresh flowers, brasses, china plates, prints and old local photographs too. The locals' bar is busy and cheerful and there are panoramic views from the comfortable restaurant – it's worth arriving early to bag a window seat. Black Sheep Best, Cropton Yorkshire Moors, Marstons Wainwright and Timothy Taylors Golden Best on handpump, over a dozen wines by the glass and 12 malt whiskies; background music and pool. Outside are seats under parasols and some picnic-sets. The inn is in the North York Moors National Park, so there are plenty of surrounding walks, including to nearby Dalby Forest. This is sister pub to the Horseshoe in nearby Levisham.

Rewarding food includes hearty pub classics supplemented by more varied blackboard fare, plus sandwiches and a daily roast with trimmings. Dishes might include chicken liver and brandy pâté with chutney, pan-seared pigeon breast with sautéed new potatoes and chorizo, toad in the hole, steak and ale pie, beef lasagne with chips, salad and garlic bread, pheasant breast with dauphinoise potatoes, wild mushrooms and red wine sauce, Mediterranean pasta bake, and puddings such as lemon and lime cheesecake and crème brûlée. *Benchmark main dish: venison burger with Yorkshire blue cheese, onion marmalade, onion rings and chips £12.50. Two-course evening meal £18.00.*

Free house ~ Licensees Toby and Charles Wood ~ Real ale ~ Open 12-11; 12-10 Sun ~ Bar food 12-2, 5-8.30; light snacks 2-4pm ~ Restaurant ~ Children welcome ~ Dogs allowed in bar

MALHAM
Lister Arms ♀ 🍺 🛏
(01729) 830444 – www.listerarms.co.uk

SD9062 Map 7

Off A65 NW of Skipton; BD23 4DB

Friendly inn in fine countryside with cosy bars and dining room, enjoyable food and seats outside; comfortable bedrooms

At the foot of Malham Cove, in the heart of a charming village, this handsome stone inn is popular with walkers. But lovers of ale and food make a beeline for it too, as do many locals. One bar has a medley of cushioned dining chairs and leather or upholstered armchairs around antique wooden tables on slate flooring, with a big deer's head above the inglenook fireplace. A second bar has a small brick fireplace with logs piled to each side, rustic slab tables, cushioned wheelback chairs and comfortable wall seats. There's Thwaites Amber, Gold, IPA, Mild and Original on handpump plus three rotating local guests, 20 wines by the glass and Weston's farm cider. A woodburning stove stands in the fireplace of the airy dining room where there are swagged curtains and smartly upholstered high-backed and pale wooden farmhouse chairs around rustic tables on bare floorboards. The flagstoned and gravelled courtyard has seats and benches around tables under parasols – some overlook the small green at the front. It's a popular place to stay, with satisfyingly hearty breakfasts and a choice of 23 attractive, warm and comfortable bedrooms (some in the pub, others in the next-door cottage and more in the barn conversion).

Highly rated food includes breakfasts (8-10am) plus sandwiches, tempura king prawns with chinese leaf salad and satay dipping sauce, oven-baked brie with home-made focaccia, sharing platters, globe artichoke and asparagus gnocchi with sautéed wild mushrooms and puffed potatoes, tandoori chicken with braised coriander rice and curried squash purée, pork sausages with mash, red onion marmalade and gravy, haddock, salmon and king prawn fish pie with fennel béchamel, peas and parmesan creamed potatoes, assorted burgers with toppings and chips, and desserts such as sticky toffee and date pudding with salted caramel sauce and vanilla ice-cream and plum tarte tatin with blood orange sorbet. *Benchmark main dish: steak in ale pie £13.50. Two-course evening meal £21.00.*

Thwaites ~ Manager Darren Dunn ~ Real ale ~ Open 8am-11pm; 8am-10.30pm Sun ~ Bar food 12-9.30 (9 in winter) ~ Restaurant ~ Children welcome ~ Dogs allowed in bar & bedrooms ~ Bedrooms: £130

If we know a featured-entry pub does sandwiches, we always say so – if they're not mentioned, you'll have to assume they're not available.

MARTON-CUM-GRAFTON
Punch Bowl 🍽️☆ ♀

SE4263 Map 7

(01423) 322519 – www.thepunchbowlmartoncumgrafton.com

Signed off A1 3 miles N of A59; YO51 9QY

Old pub with character bar and dining rooms, real ales, interesting food and seats on terrace

This popular pub in a lovely village has had a thorough makeover, with the bar area remodelled, walls and settles in pale greens, new flooring, furniture and lighting, new tables and seating in the patio area and an upgraded garden. There are lots of original features to look for, including beams and timbering in the main bar where there's Black Sheep Best, York Guzzler and a guest such as Theakston Best on handpump, and a good choice of wines by the glass, malt whiskies and gins; background music. Open doorways lead to five separate dining areas, each with an open fire, heavy beams and an attractive mix of cushioned wall seats and wooden or high-backed red-leather dining chairs around antique tables on oak or tiled floors; there are crimson sofas and walls with photographs of vintage car races and racing drivers, sporting-themed cartoons and old photographs of the pub and village. Up a spiral staircase is a coffee loft and a private dining room. There are seats and tables in the back courtyard where they hold summer barbecues. This belongs to the Provenance Inns & Hotels group.

🍽️ Top quality food includes lunchtime sandwiches, goats cheese bonbons with plum chutney and candied hazelnuts, prawn and crayfish salad, game pie, beer-battered haddock and chips, honey- and five spice-glazed breast of duck with pumpkin and leeks, sea bass with king prawn and chorizo risotto, roast shallot tart with vegan feta and spinach, wagyu burger and chips, and puddings such as sticky toffee pudding and pear and almond crumble tart. *Benchmark main dish: steak in ale pie £15.00. Two-course evening meal £22.00.*

Free house ~ Licensee Paul Neesam ~ Real ale ~ Open 12-3, 5-11; 12-11 Fri, Sat; 12-10.30 Sun ~ Bar food 12-2.30, 5.30-9.30; 12-8 Sun ~ Children welcome ~ Dogs allowed in bar

MASHAM
Black Sheep Brewery 🍺

SE2281 Map 10

(01765) 680100 – www.blacksheepbrewery.co.uk

Brewery signed off Leyburn Road (A6108); HG4 4EN

Lively place with friendly staff, unusual décor in big warehouse room, well kept beers and popular food

This place is a beer-lover's dream, as you get to view the brewing process as well as sample a good range of Black Sheep beers. The bar is located in the huge upper warehouse where they keep Black Sheep Ale, Best, Golden Sheep and Riggwelter plus several other changing Black Sheep beers such as Special and Twilighter on handpump, several wines by the glass and a fair choice of soft drinks. The rest of the place is more like a bistro than a pub – the contemporary furnishings are light and attractive with high wooden chairs around equally high tables on stripped floorboards and a good deal of bare woodwork, with cream-painted rough stonework and green-painted steel girders and pillars; background music, TV and friendly service. The guided tours of the brewery are popular and a glass wall lets you see into the brewing exhibition centre; a shop sells beers and beer-related items from pub games and T-shirts to pottery and fudge. There are picnic-sets out on the grass.

Good quality food includes sandwiches, a choice of beef, vegan, chicken, cheese and halloumi burgers with chips and slaw, stone-baked pizzas, smoked half rack of ribs, smoked charred chicken wings, haddock and dill fishcakes, sharing plates, beer-battered haddock and chips, pesto pasta, paneer and vegetable pie with salad, braised beef brisket with mash and tenderstem broccoli, and puddings such as apple pie with vanilla ice-cream and chocolate brownie. *Benchmark main dish: steak in ale pie £14.00. Two-course evening meal £20.00.*

Free house ~ Licensee Jake Humberstone ~ Real ale ~ Open 10am-5pm Tues, Sun; 10am-11pm Weds-Sat; closed Mon ~ Bar food 12-2.30 Tues; 12-2.30, 6-9 Weds-Sat; 12-4 Sun ~ Restaurant ~ Children allowed in bar ~ Dogs allowed in bar

MINSKIP

Wild Swan 🌟 ☆ ♀
SE3965   Map 7

(01423) 326334 – www.wildswan.pub
Main Street; YO51 9JF

Renovated country pub with stylish but relaxed bar and restaurant, well kept ales, excellent food and seats in charming garden

Dating from 1832, this cosy, well run pub remains perennially popular with our readers. The heavily beamed bar is just the place for a cosy pint and a chat, with its traditional dark wooden chairs, cushioned settles and stools on rugs or bare boards and a couple of armchairs by the two-way open fire. This leads to an informal dining area with farmhouse chairs around scrubbed kitchen tables, pewter tankards on a delft shelf and a large stag's head; background music. Friendly, helpful staff serve Black Sheep Best and Timothy Taylors Boltmaker and Landlord on handpump, ten wines by the glass and ten local gins. There's also a plusher, carpeted restaurant furnished with tartan-upholstered dining chairs around more stripped farmhouse tables (each set with a church candle and flowers), sage-green walls hung with mirrors, decorative wickerwork and oil paintings, and an open kitchen; this shares the open fire with the bar. The flower-filled garden has plenty of seating. Disabled access and loos. Sister pub is the Tickled Trout in Bilton in Ainsty (also in Yorkshire).

🌟 Food is first class and cooked by the chef-owner, using local suppliers as much as possible: lunchtime sandwiches, tempura tiger prawn and soft shell crab with sweet chilli sauce, Yorkshire Dales beef tasting plate, spiced pumpkin and squash tartlet with salad, pollack with mussels, prawns and samphire bouillabaisse, cider roasted pork belly with home-made black pudding, mash and sloe gin cabbage, roasted chicken breast with butternut squash gnocchi and wild mushroom fricassée, and puddings such as gin-laced lemon possett with shortbread and apple crumble with custard. *Benchmark main dish: salmon fillet with sautéed new potatoes, roasted beets and crackling £15.95. Two-course evening meal £22.00.*

Free house ~ Licensee Karl Mainey ~ Real ale ~ Open 12-11; 12-9 Sun ~ Bar food 12-2.15, 5-9.15; 12-7 Sun ~ Restaurant ~ Children welcome ~ Dogs allowed in bar

MOULTON
Black Bull 🌟 ♀
NZ2303   Map 10

(01325) 377556 – www.theblackbullmoulton.com
Just E of A1, 2.5 miles E of Scotch Corner; DL10 6QJ

Character pub with a traditional bar, a large open restaurant, high quality food and courteous efficient service; bedrooms

Another successful member of the small Yorkshire-based Provenance Inns & Hotels group, which emphasises a warm welcome, community spirit and good food and drink from across the county at all its pubs. The bar has a convivial atmosphere, flagstones and some original panelling and leather wall seating, wooden chairs and bright tiled tables. Black Sheep Best, Hambleton White Boar and Theakstons Best on handpump, 14 wines by the glass, cocktails/mocktails and more than 20 malt whiskies. There's also a dining area with cushioned wooden chairs around a mix of tables on pale flagstones, a woodburner in a brick fireplace and wood stacked beside. The modern dining extension dominates the pub and has floor-to-ceiling windows, browny-orange upholstered dining chairs and numerous old pictures and maps, plus two large mirrors against slate grey walls; background music. Doors from here lead out to a neat terrace with modern seats and tables set among plants in planters and a striking wire black bull. There's also the James Herriot Room, for private dining.

Food is excellent and includes lunchtime sandwiches, prawn and crayfish salad, twice-baked cheese soufflé with celeriac and poached pear salad, wagyu burger with chunky chips, sage and chestnut gnocchi with truffle butter, sea bass fillet with king prawn and chorizo risotto, venison loin and braised shoulder crumble with smoked potatoes, roast spiced aubergine with vegan feta and pickled beetroot, and puddings such as rhubarb and almond tart with amaretto custard and vanilla pannacotta with poached peaches. *Benchmark main dish: aged steak and ale pie with chips £15.00. Two-course evening meal £22.00.*

Free house ~ Licensee Jill Loughborough ~ Real ale ~ Open 12-3, 5-11; 12-11 Fri, Sat; 12-8 Sun ~ Bar food 12-2.30, 5.30-9.30; 12-3, 5.30-8.30 Sun ~ Restaurant ~ Children welcome ~ Dogs allowed in bar

RIPPONDEN

Old Bridge 🍷 🍺

SE0419 Map 7

(01422) 822595 – www.theoldbridgeinn.co.uk

From A58, best approach is Elland Road (opposite the Golden Lion), park opposite the church in pub's car park and walk back over ancient packhorse bridge; HX6 4DF

Pleasant old pub run by a long-serving family with relaxed communicating rooms and well liked food

With the Calderdale Way passing right by this ancient pub, you'll find plenty of walkers enjoying its cosy comforts alongside locals and other visitors. There's no traditional pub sign outside, so to find it head for the church next door – do note the beautiful medieval bridge. It's been run by the same welcoming family since the 1960s. The three communicating rooms, each on a slightly different level, have oak settles built into window recesses in the thick stone walls, antique oak tables, rush-seated chairs and comfortably cushioned free-standing settles, a few well chosen pictures and prints on the panelled or painted walls and a big woodburning stove. Efficient, friendly staff serve Timothy Taylors Best, Golden Best, Landlord and Ram Tam on handpump, a couple of craft beers such as Vocation Bread & Butter, foreign bottled beers, 15 wines by the glass, a good choice of gins and malt whiskies and farm cider. Seats in the garden overlook the little River Ryburn. No dogs inside. Disabled access but no loos.

The ever-popular weekday lunchtime cold meat and salad buffet has been running since 1963 (soup and sandwiches are also available). Evening and weekend choices include scotch egg with home-made piccalilli, prawn and avocado cocktail, piri-piri lemon chicken salad, a pie of the day, fisherman's pie, sweet potato and spring onion frittata with wilted spinach, grilled halloumi and roast cherry tomatoes, slow-roasted lamb ragoût with tagliatelle, 10oz local sirloin steak with a choice of sauce, and puddings such as sticky toffee pudding and cheesecake. *Benchmark main dish: smoked haddock and spinach pancakes £14.00. Two-course evening meal £20.00.*

Free house ~ Licensees Tim and Lindsay Eaton Walker ~ Real ale ~ Open 12-3, 5-11;
12-11 Fri, Sat; 12-10.30 Sun ~ Bar food 12-2, 5-9; 12-2, 5-9.30 Fri, Sat; 12-4 Sun ~ Children
welcome until 8pm but must be seated away from bar

SANCTON
SE9039 Map 7
Star 🌟 ⚲ 🍺
(01430) 827269 – www.thestaratsancton.co.uk
King Street (A1034 S of Market Weighton); YO43 4QP

**Bustling bar and more formal dining rooms with accomplished food
and a friendly, easy-going atmosphere**

Standards at this village pub are reliably excellent, and the family that
run it are always seeking to improve things further, most recently with
a decorative revamp in summer 2020 and plans to open three bedrooms in
2021. There's a proper bar with proper beer, but by popular demand most
of the space is given over to dining: the Star's victory in the inaugural Great
Yorkshire Pudding challenge should tell you all you need to know about
the standard of the cooking and its local ethos. The bar has flagstones,
a woodburning stove and flying-geese wallpaper, along with a cheerful
atmosphere and ales on handpump from the likes of Great Newsome,
Old Mill and Wold Top, plus a serious wine list with good options by the
glass or carafe including prosecco and champagne, 40 gins and 15 malt
whiskies. The two more formal (though still relaxed) dining rooms have
carpet, comfortable high-backed dining chairs and banquettes and a suave,
restrained colour scheme, plus a woodburner each. Outside at the back are
picnic-sets. The pub is at the foot of the Yorkshire Wolds Railway heritage
line, and at lunchtime in particular there's a good mix of locals, walkers and
cyclists. Disabled access.

First class food with a focus on produce from Yorkshire includes pub favourites
and more imaginative choices, with a bar menu, a 'Yorkshire lunch' set menu
(not Sunday) and an à la carte. Dishes might include yorkshire pudding with braised
oxtail, caramelised onion, crispy sage and red wine jus, smoked haddock risotto with
a poached egg, cured and braised pig cheeks with smoked bacon jam, sage and onion
scone and poached quince, steak and ale pie with spiced red cabbage and hand-cut
chips, Black Sheep beer-battered haddock and chips, lincolnshire poacher cheese
and leek cake with butternut squash, sprouting broccoli, crispy leeks and a fried egg,
pan-roasted hake with coconut, curried squash, bombay potato terrine and shallot
bhajis, and puddings such as sticky parkin with toffee sauce, hazelnut brittle, toasted
oats and caramel ice-cream and plum and anise clafoutis. *Benchmark main dish: fish
pie with spinach, cheesy potato and fennel garden salad £15.95. Two-course evening
meal £28.00.*

Free house ~ Licensees Ben and Lindsey Cox ~ Real ale ~ Open 12-3, 6-11; 12-10 Sun;
closed Mon ~ Bar food 12-2, 6-9.30; 12-3, 6-8 Sun ~ Restaurant ~ Children welcome
until 9.30pm

THORNTON WATLASS
SE2385 Map 10
Buck 🍺 🛏
(01677) 422461 – www.buckwatlass.co.uk
Village signposted off B6268 Bedale–Masham; HG4 4AH

**Down-to-earth village pub with up to five real ales, a traditional bar
and function room, well liked food and popular Sunday jazz; bedrooms**

There's a lovely community atmosphere at this friendly, busy place formed
from a row of low stone cottages opposite the village green and cricket

pitch. The pleasantly traditional bar on the right has upholstered wall settles on carpet, a fine mahogany bar counter, local artwork on the walls and a brick fireplace; background music, darts and board games. A snug area with a woodburning stove overlooks the garden. The Long Room displays photos and trophies from Thornton Watlass cricket teams past and present, and is the venue for the Sunday afternoon jazz sessions. Black Sheep Best, Theakstons Best, Timothy Taylor Landlord, Wensleydale Falconer and a guest on handpump, nine wines by the glass and eight malt whiskies. The sheltered garden has a well equipped children's play area. The five bedrooms are well appointed and comfortable, and breakfasts are good. Wheelchair access with ramp.

Tasty food includes sandwiches, scallops with chorizo and hazelnut picada, chicken livers with toasted sourdough, caramelised onion and goats cheese tart, vegan chilli and rice, chicken korma, cod fillet with orange and dill crumb and hasselback potatoes, slow-cooked beef goulash with sour cream, fish and chips, chicken parmigiana, sea bass with lemon and dill butter, 10oz rib-eye steak with trimmings and chips, vegetarian or vegan bean pot, and puddings. *Benchmark main dish: steak in ale pie £12.95. Two-course evening meal £17.00.*

Free house ~ Licensees Victoria and Tony Jowett ~ Real ale ~ Open 12-11; 12-10.30 Sun ~ Bar food 12-2, 6-9; 12-3, 6-8.30 Sun ~ Restaurant ~ Children welcome ~ Dogs allowed in bar & bedrooms ~ Bedrooms: £120

WELBURN
Crown & Cushion ♀ ◀

SE7168   Map 7

(01653) 618777 – www.thecrownandcushionwelburn.com
Off A64; YO60 7DZ

Plenty of dining and drinking space in well run inn with real ales and good food – and seats outside

This attractive village inn, with green paintwork against honey-coloured stone, is popular with bird-watchers and walkers exploring the Howardian Hills, and also with locals who appreciate its unaffected charm and good field-to-fork cooking. The little tap room has rustic tables and chairs on wide floorboards, Black Sheep Best, York Guzzler and a guest beer on handpump, a decent choice of malt whiskies and gins, 20 wines by the glass and farm cider. The bar has an area set for casual eating, with large wooden tables and roaring open fires, while the two slightly more formal dining rooms downstairs have stone floors, exposed brickwork, touches of the trademark green and comfortable dining furniture. Contemporary tables and chairs on the outdoor terrace and picnic-sets below, with long-reaching views, are quickly snapped up, especially in warm weather. Convenient for Castle Howard, this is part of the Provenance Inns & Hotels group.

Sustainably sourced from local producers including the group's own kitchen garden, the enjoyable food might include twice-baked wensleydale cheese soufflé, prawn and crayfish salad, 21-day dry-aged steak with chunky chips, cod fillet with mussels, roast cauliflower and pomme purée, roast shallot tart with spinach, vegan feta and carrot top and pistachio pesto, steak and ale pie, Yorkshire wagyu burger and chunky chips, and desserts such as sticky toffee pudding with butterscotch sauce and cinder toffee ice-cream and affogato with biscotti. *Benchmark main dish: beer-battered haddock and chunky chips £14.00. Two-course evening meal £22.00.*

Free house ~ Licensee Martin Humphrey ~ Real ale ~ Open 12-11 ~ Bar food 12-2.30, 5.30-9; 12-8 Sun ~ Restaurant ~ Children welcome ~ Dogs allowed in bar & restaurant

WIDDOP
SD9531 Map 7

Pack Horse 🍺 £

(01422) 842803

The Ridge; from A646 on W side of Hebden Bridge, turn off at Heptonstall signpost (as it's a sharp turn, coming out of Hebden Bridge the road signs direct you around a turning circle), then follow Slack and Widdop signposts; can also be reached from Nelson and Colne, on high, pretty road; OS Sheet 103 map reference 952317; HX7 7AT

Friendly, family-run pub up on the moors with tasty food, real ales and plenty of malt whiskies

Over four centuries, this whitewashed moorland inn has been a beacon of warmth and hospitality for all sorts of people, from users of the old packhorse trails to builders of the nearby Widdop and Gorple reservoirs, and today's walkers and riders on the Pennine Way and Pennine Bridleway, which both pass nearby. Décor is simple and traditional: the snug, carpeted bar has winter fires, window seats cut into the partly panelled, stripped-stone walls (from where you can take in the beautiful views), sturdy furnishings and horsey mementoes. Well kept Black Sheep Best and Marstons Wainwright plus a couple of changing guests on handpump, over 100 single malt whiskies along with some Irish ones, and 14 or so wines by the glass are served by friendly, accommodating staff. There are seats outside in the cobblestoned beer garden and pretty summer hanging baskets. Plans to open three bedrooms should come to fruition in early 2021.

 Satisfying, fairly priced food includes sandwiches, yorkshire pudding filled with sausages, onions and gravy, rib-eye and other steaks with traditional sauces, lamb shank with mash and gravy, steak and ale pie, feta salad, and desserts such as sticky toffee pudding and ginger and rhubarb with custard. *Benchmark main dish: steak in Guinness pie £10.95. Two-course evening meal £18.00.*

Free house ~ Licensee Sara Hollinrake ~ Real ale ~ Open 12-2, 6-10 Weds-Fri; 12-10 Sat; 12-8 Sun ~ Bar food 12-2, 6-8.30; 12-7 Sun ~ Children welcome until 8pm ~ Dogs allowed in bar

YORK
SE5951 Map 7

Judges Lodging 🍷 🛏

(01904) 639312 – www.judgeslodgingyork.co.uk

Lendal; YO1 8AQ

Lovely place with a character cellar bar, several dining rooms, well liked food and outside seating; stylish bedrooms

If you fancy a few days exploring York, this traditional Georgian townhouse is a lovely place to stay, with 21 recently revamped, comfortable and well equipped bedrooms, both large and small; there are York Minster views across the rooftops from some. The bar is in the cellar (and open for drinks and food all day) with fine vaulted ceilings, upholstered dining chairs and sofas on big flagstones, Thwaites Amber, Gold, IPA, Mild and Original on handpump and 17 wines by the glass (including fizz). This leads to a dining room and on to a bright and airy garden room, both of which have green-painted farmhouse chairs around blonde wooden tables on pale floorboards. On the first floor is what they call the Medicine Cabinet – a bar/reception area for both hotel and dining guests – with quirky men's trouser-leg stools by the bar counter, grey button-back leather armchairs on either side of the fireplace and plaster judges' heads on Farrow & Ball paintwork. Leading off here are two more dining rooms with leather chesterfields and more upholstered chairs around a mix of tables on bare boards, painted panelling, tall window shutters, chandeliers, gilt-edged mirrors and some unusual wire sculptures – it's all very smart and civilised. There are modern seats and tables between lavender pots at the front of the building, white metal furniture beside the garden room, and traditional wooden chairs, tables and picnic-sets in the rear courtyard.

As well as breakfast and afternoon tea, the rewarding food includes sandwiches (until 5pm), tempura tiger prawns with fennel relish and apple and herb salad, crispy pork belly bites with barbecue sauce and pork crackling, sharing plates, chestnut mushroom, pearl onion and leek pie, moules frites, a range of steaks, mac 'n' cheese with basil pesto, 10oz gammon steak with fried duck egg, sweet pickled pineapple and thick-cut chips, and puddings such as black forest gateau with vanilla ice-cream and chocolate brownie with honeycomb ice-cream. *Benchmark main dish: classic 8oz steak burger with fries £14.70. Two-course evening meal £23.00.*

Thwaites ~ Lease Nik Haywood ~ Real ale ~ Open 11-11; 11-10.30 Sun ~ Bar food 12-10 ~ Restaurant ~ Children welcome ~ Dogs allowed in bar ~ Bedrooms: £175

YORK
Maltings 🍺 £   SE5951   Map 7

(01904) 655387 – www.maltings.co.uk
Tanners Moat/Wellington Row, below Lendal Bridge; YO1 6HU

Bustling, friendly city pub with cheerful landlord, interesting real ales and other drinks plus good value standard food

If you're looking for a down-to-earth pub with a large range of drinks and good value food in quirky surroundings, well, here it is. Interesting drinks kept by the convivial, hard-working landlord include Black Sheep Best, Roosters YPA, Treboom Yorkshire Sparkle, York Guzzler and three quickly rotating guests, often from local microbreweries, six continental beers on tap, four craft beers, lots of bottled beers, four farm ciders, 15 country wines and 22 whiskies from all over the world. The atmosphere is bustling and friendly and the eclectic décor is strong on salvaged junk: old doors for the bar front and much of the ceiling, a marvellous collection of railway signs and amusing notices, an old chocolate dispensing machine, cigarette and tobacco advertisements alongside cough and chest remedies, what looks like a suburban front door for the entrance to the ladies', partly stripped orange brick walls and even a lavatory pan in one corner; games machine. The day's papers are framed in the gents'. The pub is very handy for the station and also the National Railway Museum; nearby parking is difficult. Please note that dogs are allowed only after food service has finished.

Great value food – at lunchtime only – includes sandwiches and toasties, baked potatoes with lots of fillings, ploughman's, chip butties, mushroom and spinach lasagne, ham and egg, sausage and beans, beef in ale pie, chilli tacos and roast chicken and chips. *Benchmark main dish: fish and chips £8.25.*

Free house ~ Licensee Shaun Collinge ~ Real ale ~ Open 11-11; 12-10.30 Sun ~ Bar food 12-2; 12-4 Sat, Sun ~ Children allowed during mealtimes

---

Please tell us if the décor, atmosphere, food or drink at a pub is different from our description. We rely on readers' reports to keep us up to date: feedback@goodguides.com, or (no stamp needed) Freepost THE GOOD PUB GUIDE, Random House Publishing, 20 Vauxhall Bridge Road, London SW1V 2SA.

Also Worth a Visit in Yorkshire

Besides the fully inspected pubs, you might like to try these pubs that have been recommended to us and described by readers. Do tell us what you think of them: feedback@goodguides.com

ADDINGHAM   SE0749
Swan (01943) 430003
Main Street; LS29 0NS Popular local with linked rooms around central servery; flagstones and four open fires (one in fine old range), six well kept changing ales including Wainwright and guests such as Ilkley, Ossett and Wharfedale, good food from sandwiches/baguettes to daily specials, Tues fish and chips, Fri steak night, friendly helpful service (may be a wait at busy times); live bands Sat, quiz nights; children (games and toys for them) and dogs welcome, tables out by pavement, open all day, food all day, Sun till 7pm.

AINDERBY STEEPLE   SE3392
Wellington Heifer (01609) 775718
A684, 3 miles from A1; opposite church; DL7 9PU Modernised late 18th-c pub with four connecting rooms (some steps); flagstone and carpeted floors, comfortable scatter-cushion bench seating and sturdy tables, log fires, three beers including Black Sheep and wines from carved counter, enjoyable food including good value lunchtime/early evening set menu, restaurant at end of corridor; quiz nights, live music; children and dogs welcome, three well appointed bedrooms, open all day Sun (food till 7pm).

AINTHORPE   NZ7007
Fox & Hounds (01287) 660218
Brook Lane; YO21 2LD Traditional 16th-c pub in tranquil moorland setting with grazing sheep and wonderful views; comfortable beamed bar with open fire in unusual stone fireplace, three well kept changing ales and good choice of wines by the glass, generous fairly priced food including daily specials, friendly staff, restaurant, games room; children and dogs welcome (great walks from the door), seven bedrooms and attached self-catering cottage, open all day.

AISLABY   SE8508
Forge (01947) 811522
Main Road, off A171 W of Whitby; YO21 1SW Mellow-stone family-run village pub with opened-up interior, light wood floor, dark wood tables and chairs, upholstered wall benches and woodburner in brick fireplace, well kept ales such as Black Sheep from small central servery, good home-made food at sensible prices including popular Sun roasts served till 7pm, friendly accommodating staff; Tues quiz; children and dogs welcome, six bedrooms.

ALDBOROUGH   SE4166
Ship (01423) 322749
Off B6265 just S of Boroughbridge, close to A1; YO51 9ER Attractive 14th-c beamed village dining pub adjacent to medieval church; good food from sandwiches and pub standards up including early bird deal, cheerful helpful service, well kept Black Sheep and Theakstons, extensive affordably priced wine list, some old-fashioned seats around cast-iron-framed tables, lots of copper and brass, inglenook fire, candlelit back restaurant; children (till 9pm) and dogs welcome, a few picnic-sets outside, well placed for Roman remains and museum, open all day Fri-Sun, food till 6pm Sun, kitchen closed Mon (except bank holidays).

ALLERSTON   SE8783
Cayley Arms (01723) 859904
A170 Pickering–Scarborough; YO18 7PJ Long knocked-through bar with light wood and stone floors, two woodburners, upholstered captain's chairs, leather cushioned wall benches and some comfortable button-back armchairs, antlers on bare stone walls, Theakstons, Wold Top and a guest, generous helpings of good freshly made food in bar or restaurant, friendly helpful service; well behaved children and dogs welcome, picnic-sets at front and in back garden by brook, five well appointed bedrooms, open all day in summer, check website for other times.

APPLETON-LE-MOORS   SE7388
★ Moors (01751) 417435
N of A170, just under 1.5 miles E of Kirkby Moorside; YO62 6TF Traditional 17th-c stone-built village pub; beamed bar with built-in high-backed settle next to old kitchen fireplace, plenty of other seating, three changing regional ales such as Bradfield and Pennine and wide range of malt whiskies and gins, good sensibly priced food from sandwiches/ciabattas and pub favourites up including daily specials, dining room with leather chairs at polished tables, friendly helpful staff; background and occasional live music; children and dogs welcome, tables in lovely walled garden, country views and walks to Rosedale Abbey and Hartoft End, eight pleasant bedrooms, open all day.

APPLETREEWICK   SE0560
★ Craven Arms (01756) 720270
Off B6160 Burnsall–Bolton Abbey; BD23 6DA Character creeper-clad 16th-c beamed pub; cushioned settles and rugs on

flagstones, open fires (one in old range), gas lighting and lots of interesting pictures and bric-a-brac, up to eight well kept ales including cask-tapped Theakstons Old Peculier and a house beer from Dark Horse, real cider and several wines by the glass, enjoyable home-made food from hot or cold sandwiches up, friendly helpful service, small dining room and splendid thatched and raftered cruck barn with gallery; traditional pub games and occasional live music; children, dogs and muddy boots welcome (plenty of surrounding walks), wheelchair access, nice country views from front picnic-sets, more seats in back garden, shepherd's hut accommodation, open (and food) all day.

ARNCLIFFE · SD9371
★**Falcon** (01756) 770205

Off B6160 N of Grassington; BD23 5QE Basic ivy-clad no-frills tavern in lovely setting on village green; coal fire in small bar with vintage furnishings, well kept Timothy Taylors Boltmaker and a guest either from handpump or poured from stoneware jugs in central hatch-style servery, enjoyable traditional food from sandwiches up, attractive watercolours, sepia photographs and humorous sporting prints, back sun-room overlooking pleasant garden; quiz first Fri of month; children (till 9pm) and dogs welcome, four miles of trout fishing (permits available from the pub), walks in lovely surrounding countryside, six bedrooms (two with own bathroom), open all day in summer, all day Fri-Sun winter, food till 5pm Sun.

ASKRIGG · SD9491
Crown (01969) 650387

Main Street; DL8 3HQ Friendly open-plan local in James Herriot village; three areas off main bar, open fires (one in old-fashioned range), enjoyable simple pub food at reasonable prices, well kept ales such as Black Sheep, John Smiths and Theakstons; children, walkers and dogs welcome, tables outside, nearby self-catering barn conversion, open all day.

ASKRIGG · SD9491
Kings Arms (01969) 650113

Signed from A684 Leyburn–Sedbergh in Bainbridge; DL8 3HQ Popular 18th-c coaching inn freshened up under present friendly management; high-ceilinged main bar with flagstones, traditional furnishings and good log fire, a couple of well kept house beers from nearby Yorkshire Dales plus guests such as Black Sheep and Theakstons, several wines by the glass, enjoyable reasonably priced food including some evening offers, more modern restaurant with inglenook, games room in former barrel-vaulted beer cellar; background music, sports TV; children and dogs (in bar) welcome, side courtyard, bedrooms run separately as part of Holiday Property Bond complex behind, open (and food) all day.

AUSTWICK · SD7668
★**Game Cock** (01524) 251226

Just off A65 Settle–Kirkby Lonsdale; LA2 8BB Quaint civilised place in pretty spot below Three Peaks; friendly beamed back bar with bare boards and good log fire, well kept Thwaites ales, winter mulled wine and decent coffee, cheerful efficient staff, plenty of emphasis on French chef-owner's good fairly priced food including blackboard specials and themed nights, two restaurant areas and small conservatory-style extension; live music and traditional pub games; children, walkers, cyclists and dogs welcome, tables out at front and in back garden, five bedrooms, closed Mon till 3pm, otherwise open (and food) all day.

AYSGARTH · SE0188
Aysgarth Falls (01969) 663775

A684; DL8 3SR Creeper-clad moorland hotel with good food and welcoming accommodating service; well kept ales such as Black Sheep, Rudgate, Theakstons and Wensleydale in log-fire bar where dogs allowed, comfortable eating areas, some interesting ancient masonry at the back recalling its days as a pilgrims' inn; great scenery near broad waterfalls, 13 bedrooms, camping (adults only), open all day.

AYSGARTH · SE0088
George & Dragon (01969) 663358

Just off A684; DL8 3AD 17th-c posting inn with enjoyable home-made food from sandwiches up, two big dining areas and small beamed and panelled bar with log fire, well kept ales including Black Sheep, Theakstons and a house beer from Yorkshire Dales, good choice of wines by the glass; may be background music; children and dogs (in bar) welcome, nice paved garden, lovely scenery and walks, handy for Aysgarth Falls, bedrooms, open all day.

BAILDON · SE1538
Junction (07525) 006906

Baildon Road; BD17 6AB Friendly wedge-shaped local with three traditional linked rooms; at least four cask ales (five or six at weekends) including Tetleys and a couple of own Junction brews (July festival) and selection of premium and flavoured gins, no food; games area with pool and darts, live music Sun evening, quiz night Thurs, sports TV; two-level patio area and smoking shelter outside, open all day Fri-Sun, from 2pm other days.

BARDSEY · SE3642
Bingley Arms (01937) 572462

Church Lane; LS17 9DR Ancient pub with spacious lounge divided into separate areas, substantial beams and huge fireplace (priest holes in the chimney), well kept Ossett Yorkshire Blonde, Timothy Taylors Landlord and John Smiths Extra Smooth, good range of home-cooked food, afternoon teas, friendly staff, smaller public bar, upstairs raftered restaurant; children welcome, attractive terraced garden behind, lovely Saxon church nearby, open all day.

BARKISLAND   SE0419
★ **Fleece** (01422) 820687
B6113 towards Ripponden; HX4 0DJ
Large well renovated and extended 18th-c beamed moorland dining pub; good popular food including weekday set menu, Black Sheep, Timothy Taylors Boltmaker, and two guest beers and 17 wines by the glass, efficient friendly uniformed staff; background and some live music; children welcome, no dogs, front disabled access, lovely Pennine views from first-floor terrace and garden, summer barbecues, seven bedrooms, useful for M62, open all day from 8am for breakfast, food till 7pm Sun.

BARNSLEY   SE3400
Cock (01226) 744227
Pilley Hill, Birdwell; S70 5UD Welcoming village local set down from the road; reasonably priced home-made food (not Sun evening, Mon) and several well kept changing ales such as Black Sheep and Chantry, cheerful helpful staff, main bar with beams, stone floor and open fire, lounge and back dining room; children and dogs welcome, open all day.

BARNSLEY   SE3203
Strafford Arms (01226) 287488
Near Northern College, about 2.5 miles NW of M1 junction 36; S75 3EW Pretty stone-built village pub (Fine & Country Inns) with opened-up contemporary interior; well liked food from lunchtime sandwiches and platters to Josper grills, ales such as Black Sheep and Timothy Taylors, good range of wines and cocktails, friendly service, log fires including one in big Yorkshire range; Tues quiz; children welcome, no dogs inside, garden with play area, on Trans Pennine Trail and by entrance to Wentworth Castle, open (and food) all day.

BECK HOLE   NZ8202
★ **Birch Hall** (01947) 896245
Off A169 SW of Whitby, from top of Sleights Moor; YO22 5LE Tiny pub-cum-village-shop in beautiful steep valley village; two unchanging rooms with built-in cushioned wall seats, wooden tables, flagstones or composition flooring, unusual items like tube of toothpaste priced 1/3d and lots of pictures and photos; three well kept ales such as Black Sheep Best and North Yorkshire Beckwatter, local pies, cakes and bar snacks, exceptionally friendly service; dominoes and quoits; children (in small family room) and dogs welcome, benches

in streamside garden, self-catering cottage, good walks (one along disused railway) and handy for Thomason Foss waterfall, open all day summer, closed Mon evening and Tues in winter.

BEDALE   SE2688
Old Black Swan (01677) 422973
Market Place; DL8 1ED Popular old pub with attractive bay-windowed frontage; four well kept ales including Theakstons and John Smiths and generous helpings of good value food, friendly efficient staff, log fire; darts, pool, sports TV, occasional live music; children and dogs welcome, disabled facilities, pretty small covered back terrace, Tues market, open (and food) all day.

BEVERLEY   TA0339
★ **White Horse** (01482) 861973
Hengate, off North Bar; HU17 8BN Timeless place known locally as Nellie's; carefully preserved Victorian interior with basic tiled rooms huddled around central bar, brown leatherette seats (high-backed settles in one snug) and plain chairs/benches on bare boards, antique cartoons and sentimental engravings, gas lighting including chandelier, coal fires, bargain Sam Smiths beers and guests, friendly staff, more space upstairs; charity quiz Tues, games room; children (till 7pm) and dogs welcome, courtyard picnic-sets, open all day.

BEVERLEY   TA0239
Woolpack (01482) 867095
Westwood Road, W of centre; HU17 8EN Nice little pub that despite gaining new management several times in recent years – including this one – remains very popular; at end of 19th-c row of terrace cottages; up to six Marstons-related beers and guests, enjoyable traditional food, open fires and simple furnishings, brasses, knick-knacks and prints, cosy snug where dogs allowed; children welcome, benches out at front, small seating area behind, closed Mon, otherwise open all day (may shut early if quiet).

BINGLEY   SE1039
Brown Cow (01274) 564345
B6429 just W of junction with A650; BD16 2QX Open-plan pub in nice riverside spot; Timothy Taylors range and good choice of enjoyable generously served food, friendly staff; live music and quiz nights; children and dogs welcome, tables out on sheltered terrace, open all day.

BIRSTALL   SE2126
Black Bull (01274) 865609
Kirkgate, off A652; head down hill towards church; WF17 9HE Refurbished old stone pub opposite part-Saxon church; long row of small linked rooms, low beams,

painted panelling and log fire, real ales such as Black Sheep, Exmoor, Saltaire and York, proper cider and decent range of gins, low-priced food including burgers and pizzas, upstairs former courtroom used for functions; children and dogs welcome, picnic-sets on gravel terrace, open all day, food Weds-Sat evenings and Sun lunchtime.

BIRSTWITH   SE2459
★**Station Hotel** (01423) 770254
Off B6165 W of Ripley; HG3 3AG
Welcoming immaculately kept stone-built dales pub; bar, log-fire restaurant and garden room, very good home-made food from pub staples up including set deal (Mon-Sat till 6pm), four local ales such as Black Sheep, Copper Dragon, Timothy Taylors and Yorkshire Heart and 14 wines by the glass, friendly efficient staff; Mon quiz and monthly open mike night; children and dogs on lead (in bar) welcome, attractive back garden with smokers' shelter, picturesque valley, four bedrooms, open (and food) all day.

BISHOPTHORPE   SE5947
Woodman (01904) 706507
Village signed just off A64 York S bypass; Main Street; YO23 2RB Welcoming open-plan pub with good range of enjoyable classic food cooked by landlord-chef, four weekly changing regional ales and decent choice of wines by the glass, friendly efficient service, woodburner; background music; children and dogs welcome, seats out in front and in large back garden with play equipment, handy for York Racecourse, open all day, food all day weekends (till 6pm Sun).

BOLTON ABBEY   SE0754
Devonshire Arms (01756) 718100
B6160; BD23 6AJ Elegant and comfortable 18th-c hotel in wonderful position on edge of Bolton Abbey Estate; good if not cheap food from light meals up in bright and colourful modern brasserie-bar, contemporary paintings (some for sale) on roughcast walls, colourful armchairs around cast-iron-framed tables on pale wood floor, up to four well kept ales including Theakstons and good wines by the glass, afternoon teas, more formal restaurant; tables in spacious courtyard with extensive views, Estate and Strid river-valley walks, bedrooms in old and new wings, open all day.

BRADFIELD   SK2692
Old Horns (0114) 285 1207
High Bradfield; S6 6LG Old Thwaites pub in hill village with stunning views; good hearty food including bargain themed days and Sun carvery, can eat in part-flagstoned bar or carpeted pitch-roofed dining room, half a dozen well kept beers, friendly helpful staff; background music, Tues quiz, TV; children welcome, raised terrace taking in the view, picnic-sets and play area in garden, next to interesting 14th-c church,

good walks, open (and food) all day, kitchen shuts 7pm Sun.

BRADFORD   SE1533
Fighting Cock (01274) 726907
Preston Street (off B6145); BD7 1JE
Traditional bare-boards alehouse by industrial estate; a dozen well kept changing ales, foreign draught/bottled beers and up to seven well kept changing ales, friendly staff and lively atmosphere, all-day sandwiches plus good simple lunchtime hot dishes (not Sun), coal fires; dogs welcome, fenced-in garden opposite (beer festivals), open all day.

BRADFORD   SE1533
New Beehive (01274) 721784
Westgate; BD1 3AA Robustly old-fashioned five-room Edwardian inn; plenty of period features including gas lighting, big mirrors, interesting paintings and coal fires, changing ales (mostly from smaller brewers) along with continental bottled beers, welcoming staff and friendly atmosphere (busy on BCFC match days), weekend live music in cellar bar; pool and bar billiards; children (until 8pm) and dogs welcome, back courtyard, 17 simple bedrooms, open all day from around 3pm Fri, Sat, otherwise open from 6pm.

BRADFORD   SE1633
Sparrow (01274) 270772
North Parade; BD1 3HZ Bare-boards bar owned by Kirkstall; their ales and guests along with good range of craft kegs and bottled beers, friendly knowledgeable staff, snacky food, more tables in cellar bar; quiz, background and live music; children and dogs welcome, open all day Fri-Sun (till midnight Fri, Sat), from 4pm other days.

BRAMHAM   SE4242
Swan (01937) 843570
Just off A1 2 miles N of A64; LS23 6QA
Unspoilt and unchanging little local up steep hill from village square (aka the Top Pub); friendly atmosphere and good mix of customers, well kept ales such as Black Sheep and Leeds, no food, two coal fires; open all day Sat, from 4pm weekdays.

BRANTINGHAM   SE9329
Triton (01482) 667261
Ellerker Road; HU15 1QE Spacious comfortably refurbished and extended old stone pub; good choice of enjoyable home-made food in bar and restaurant, three local ales such as Theakstons and Black Sheep, prompt friendly service; children, walkers and dogs welcome, tables out at front and in sheltered back garden, open all day weekends (food all day Sat, till 6pm Sun), closed Mon.

BREARTON   SE3260
Malt Shovel (01423) 862929
Village signposted off A61 N of Harrogate; HG3 3BX Cosy but smart

16th-c dining pub with attractive heavily beamed rooms with some exposed stone walls, two open fires and woodburner, attractive mix of tables and chairs on wood or slate floors, some partitioning separating several eating areas, good food from lunchtime sandwiches and pub favourites up, Marstons, Rudgate, Theakstons and plenty of wines by the glass from linenfold oak counter, airy conservatory; children welcome, no dogs inside, tables under parasols in garden, pretty hanging baskets, circular walks from the door, closed Sun evening, Mon.

BRIDGE HEWICK   SE3370

Black-a-moor   (01765) 603511

Boroughbridge Road (B6265 E of Ripon); HG4 5AA Roomy family-run dining pub with good choice of popular home-cooked food including set menu, well kept regularly changing ales such as Rudgate and Theakstons and decent wines, friendly young staff, sofas and woodburner in bar area; children welcome, dogs in snug, five comfortable bedrooms, closed Mon, Tues, kitchen closed Sun evening.

BURN   SE5928

Wheatsheaf   (01757) 270614

Main Road (A19 Selby–Doncaster); YO8 8LJ Busy but welcoming 19th-c roadside pub; comfortable seats in partly divided open-plan bar with log fire, lots to look at including air force wartime memorabilia; gleaming copper kettles, polished buffalo horns and cases of model vans and lorries, half a dozen well kept ales including Timothy Taylors on rotation and guests from local breweries such as Brown Cow, Great Heck and Ossett, 20 malt whiskies and straightforward good value food; background and live music, Sun quiz, games machine, TV; children and dogs welcome, picnic-sets on terrace in small back garden, open all day (till midnight Fri, Sat), no evening food Sun, Mon or Tues.

BURNISTON   TA0193

Three Jolly Sailors   (01723) 871445

A171 N of Scarborough; High Street; YO13 0HJ Comfortable and welcoming village pub with wide range of enjoyable reasonably priced food from sandwiches up, OAP and children's menus, ales such as Black Sheep and Timothy Taylors Landlord, main bar, restaurant and conservatory, open fires; traditional pub games, live music, dogs welcome, tables under parasols in small side garden, handy for Cleveland Way and coastal walks, open (and food) all day.

BURYTHORPE   SE7964

★Bay Horse   (01653) 658302

Off A64 8.5 miles NE of York ring road, via Kirkham and Westow; 5 miles S of Malton, by Welham Road; YO17 9LJ Welcoming old stone pub with plenty of authentic character; cosy linked rooms

with warming fires, old brick and flagstone floors, traditional furniture with candles on tables, lots of bits and pieces on walls and hanging from beams, eight well kept ales including All Hallows (brewed at sister pub the Goodmanham Arms at Goodmanham) and guests from local breweries like Ossett and Theakstons, real ciders and generous helpings of good reasonably priced lunchtime food including some Italian dishes, evening meals till 7.30pm just Tues (steak night) and Fri, friendly caring service; children and dogs welcome, flat disabled access from car park, nice wolds-edge village with fine surrounding walks, open all day.

CARLTON   SE0684

Foresters Arms   (01969) 640272

Off A684 W of Leyburn; DL8 4BB Old stone pub owned by local co-operative; bar with dark low beams, flagstones and log fire, four well kept Yorkshire ales such as Black Sheep, Theakstons and Wensleydale, popular affordably priced food including evening pizzas, carpeted restaurant; events including fortnightly quiz and live music; children and dogs welcome, disabled access/ loos, a few picnic-sets out at front, pretty village in heart of Yorkshire Dales National Park, lovely views, three bedrooms, open all day Sat, closed lunchtimes Mon and Tues, no food Sun evening, Mon, Tues.

CARLTON HUSTHWAITE   SE4976

Carlton Inn   (01845) 501265

Butt Lane; YO7 2BW Cosy modernised beamed dining pub; good fairly priced food including daily specials and early bird menu, friendly helpful service, John Smiths and Theakstons, local cider, mix of country furniture including some old settles, open fire; children welcome, dogs in back bar area, garden picnic-sets, open (and food) all day Sat, Sun, closed Mon.

CARPERBY   SE0089

Wheatsheaf   (01969) 663216

A mile NW of Aysgarth; DL8 4DF Friendly early 19th-c inn set in quiet dales village and popular with walkers; cosy traditional bar with warming fire, three or four well kept ales such as Black Sheep, Jennings and Theakstons, enjoyable fairly priced home-cooked food, lounge and dining room; children and dogs welcome, 13 comfortable bedrooms (James Herriot spent his honeymoon here in 1941), good breakfast, lovely walks including to Aysgarth Falls, open all day.

CARTHORPE   SE3083

★Fox & Hounds   (01845) 567433

Village signed from A1 N of Ripon, via B6285; DL8 2LG Popular neatly kept pub run by same family since 1983 and emphasis on their very good well presented food; attractive high-raftered restaurant with lots of farm and smithy tools, ales such as

Timothy Taylors and Theakstons in L-shaped bar with two log fires, plush seating, plates on stripped beams and evocative Victorian photographs of Whitby, some theatrical memorabilia in corridors, good friendly service; background classical music; children welcome, handy for A1, closed Mon and maybe first week Jan.

CATTAL   SE4455
Victoria (01423) 330249
Station Road; YO26 8EB Bustling Victorian-themed dining pub with extensive choice of good attractively presented food, charming attentive service, well kept ales including one from local Rudgate named for the landlord, good value wines; children welcome, picnic-sets in gravelled back garden, open (and food) all day Sun, from 4pm Weds-Sat, shut Mon and Tues, convenient for the station.

CHAPEL-LE-DALE   SD7477
★**Old Hill Inn** (01524) 241256
B5655 Ingleton–Hawes, 3 miles N of Ingleton; LA6 3AR Welcoming former farmhouse with fantastic views to Ingleborough and Whernside; clean rustic interior, beams, wood panelling, log fires and bare-stone recesses, straightforward furniture on stripped-wood floors, pictures and some interesting local artefacts, Black Sheep, Dent and a guest, good wholesome food including lovely puddings (look out for the landlord's sugar sculptures), separate dining room and sun lounge, relaxed chatty atmosphere; children welcome, dogs in bar, wonderful remote surrounding walks, two bedrooms and space for five caravans, open all day Sat, closed Mon.

CLAPHAM   SD7469
New Inn (01524) 251203
Off A65 N of Settle; LA2 8HH Nicely renovated 18th-c inn facing the river in this famously pretty village; good food in bar or bistro from lunchtime sandwiches and snacks up, local ales of the likes of Bowland and Timothy Taylors, including one named for them from Settle, friendly staff, white and grey colour scheme, stone floors and three open fires; children and dogs welcome, tables out overlooking the water and on back terrace, walk to Ingleborough Cave or more adventurous hikes, 19 neat bedrooms and upmarket bunkhouse, open all day.

CLIFTON   SE1622
Black Horse (01484) 713862
Westgate/Coalpit Lane; signed off Brighouse Road from M62 junction 25; HD6 4HJ Friendly 17th-c inn-restaurant at the heart of this pleasant village; good interesting food (can be pricey) in front dining rooms, also some pubby dishes and set menu choices, efficient uniformed staff, open fire in back bar with beam-and-plank ceiling, well kept ales such as Timothy Taylors, good

range of wines; children and dogs (in bar) welcome, nice courtyard, 22 comfortable bedrooms.

CLOUGHTON NEWLANDS   TA0195
Bryherstones (01723) 870744
Newlands Road, off A171 in Cloughton; YO13 0AR Popular traditional stone pub; several interconnecting rooms including dining room up on right and flagstoned stable-theme bar on left, good fair priced food using local produce including dry-aged steaks, Timothy Taylors and guests, friendly efficient service, games room (pool and darts); children and dogs welcome, picnic-sets and play area in sheltered back garden, open all day Sun, closed lunchtimes Mon-Weds.

COLEY   SE1226
Brown Horse (01422) 202112
Lane Ends, Denholme Gate Road (A644 Brighouse–Keighley, a mile N of Hipperholme); HX3 7SD Popular roadside pub with good reasonably priced home-made food (all day Fri, Sat, not Sun evening), well kept Brakspears, Saltaire, Timothy Taylors Landlord and a guest, cheerful attentive staff, open fires, small back conservatory overlooking beer garden; children welcome, no dogs inside, open all day.

COLTON   SE5444
★**Old Sun** (01904) 744261
Off A64 York–Tadcaster; LS24 8EP Whitewashed 18th-c pub in pretty village; simply furnished bar with stools and small tables on bare boards, built-in window seats, five ales including Black Sheep, Timothy Taylors and guests, good selection of wines by the glass and good food cooked by landlord-chef, dining areas with solid wood and tartan-upholstered chairs around polished tables, exposed brickwork and log fires; background music, newspapers; children and dogs welcome, seats on sunny front terrace and in rambling garden, log cabin-style outside bar with pizza oven, country views, accommodation in converted outbuilding.

CONEYTHORPE   SE3958
★**Tiger** (01423) 863632
2.3 miles from A1(M) junction 47; A59 towards York, then village signposted (and brown sign to Tiger Inn); bear left at brown sign in Flaxby; HG5 0RY Spreading red-carpeted bar with hundreds of pewter tankards hanging from painted joists, padded wall seats, pews and settles around sturdy scrubbed tables, sage green paintwork, old prints, china figurines in one arched alcove, open fire, more formal back dining area, good sensibly priced food from pub favourites up including set deals, June lobster festival, well kept Black Sheep Bitter, Ilkley Mary Jane and Timothy Taylors Landlord and extensive range of wines, friendly helpful staff; background music;

children welcome, picnic-sets on front gravel terrace and on small green opposite, open (and food) all day.

COXWOLD · SE5377
Fauconberg Arms · (01347) 868214
Off A170 Thirsk–Helmsley, via Kilburn or Wass; easily found off A19 too; YO61 4AD Early 17th-c village pub with heavily beamed flagstoned bar, log fires in both linked areas (one in broad inglenook), some attractive oak chairs made by local craftsmen alongside more usual pub furnishings, old local photographs and copper implements, well kept Isaac Poad, John Smiths, Theakstons and a guest, good fairly traditional food at sensible prices, friendly service, elegant dining room; children welcome, dogs in bar, views from terrace over fields to Byland Abbey (EH), picnic-sets on front cobbles, eight comfortable bedrooms, open all day.

CRATHORNE · NZ4407
Crathorne Arms · (01642) 961402
Centre of village; TS15 0BA Village dining pub with good food (can be pricey) from sandwiches up including set menu choices, Yorkshire beers such as Black Sheep and Timothy Taylors and well chosen wines, friendly obliging staff, atmospheric linked rooms with lots of mirrors and pictures, log fires; sunny back courtyard, open all day (till 7.30pm Sun), closed Mon.

CRAY · SD9479
★ White Lion · (01756) 760262
B6160 N of Kettlewell; BD23 5JB Former drovers' inn set in lovely countryside high up on Buckden Pike (the highest pub in Wharfedale); beamed flagstoned bar with button-back leather chesterfields and armchairs in front of woodburner, cushioned window seat and shelves of books, simple little back room (good for wet dogs), three local ales such as Black Sheep Best and Wharfedale Blonde, eight wines by the glass, Yorkshire gins and good food with a modern twist from short but varied menu, attractive dining room with open fire; background music; children and dogs welcome, picnic-sets above the quiet steep lane or can sit on flat limestone slabs in the shallow stream opposite, nine comfortable bedrooms (some in converted barn), open all day.

CROPTON · SE7588
New Inn · (01751) 417330
Village signposted off A170 W of Pickering; YO18 8HH Modernised village pub with own Great Yorkshire beers and guests (can tour brewery Tues-Sat lunchtime for £7.50 – includes a pint; beer festival); bar with plush seating, panelling and small fire, restaurant and downstairs conservatory, enjoyable fairly straightforward food from sandwiches up, friendly staff; background music, TV, games

machine, darts and pool; well behaved children and dogs (in bar) welcome, garden picnic-sets, nine bedrooms, self-catering cottage and camping, open all day.

DACRE BANKS · SE1961
★ Royal Oak · (01423) 780200
B6451 S of Pateley Bridge; HG3 4EN Popular 18th-c stone pub with delightful Nidderdale views from the back; good traditional food (not Sun or Mon evenings) along with daily specials, themed food nights, burger night Tues, attentive friendly staff, up to four well kept changing ales such as Rudgate and Sharps, at least ten wines available (by the glass) and at least 15 gins, beams and panelling, log-fire dining room, games room with darts, dominoes and pool; background music, TV; children welcome in eating areas, no dogs, seats on front terrace and in back garden, three bedrooms, hearty breakfast, open all day.

DANBY · NZ7008
Duke of Wellington · (01287) 660351
West Lane; YO21 2LY 18th-c creeper-clad inn used by Duke of Wellington during Napoleonic Wars overlooking village green; three well kept Yorkshire ales such as Daleside and Whitby, enjoyable evening food from shortish menu; children and dogs (in main bar) welcome, clean tidy bedrooms, closed Mon lunchtime, open all day Fri-Sun.

DARLEY · SE1961
Wellington Inn · (01423) 780362
B6451; Darley Head; HG3 2QQ Extended 18th-c roadside stone inn with fine Nidderdale views; beams, tiles and big open fire in bar, modern restaurant with light wood floor and small conservatory, enjoyable freshly made food from sandwiches up including wood-fired pizzas and blackboard specials, Sun set lunch, well kept Black Sheep, Timothy Taylors and two guests, large collection of gins and other spirits, helpful friendly staff; pool and darts; children and dogs (in bar) welcome, seats on large grassed area, 12 comfortable bedrooms, good breakfast, open all day.

DEWSBURY · SE2622
Huntsman · (01924) 275700
Walker Cottages, Chidswell Lane, Shaw Cross – pub signed; WF12 7SW Cosy low-beamed converted cottages alongside urban-fringe farm; original features including an old range in the snug, agricultural bric-a-brac, brassware, plates and bottles on delft shelving, blazing woodburner, small front extension, three to six Yorkshire ales such as Timothy Taylors and Westgate and up to three local guests, well priced traditional home-made food (Thurs-Sat evening, till 4pm Sun), friendly staff and nice relaxed atmosphere; children welcome, no dogs inside, picnic-sets in side paddock, opens 5pm Tues-Sat, open all day Sun, closed Mon.

DEWSBURY   SE2421
West Riding Licensed
Refreshment Rooms (01924) 459193
*Station (Platform 2), Wellington
Road; WF13 1HF* Three-room early
Victorian station bar under same owners
as the Sportsman in Huddersfield; Timothy
Taylors Boltmaker and seven other well
kept changing ales (beer festival), foreign
bottled beers and farm ciders, extensive
whisky, bourbon, rum and gin ranges, good
value pizzas, lots of railway memorabilia and
pictures, coal fire; juke box and live music;
children till 7pm in two end rooms, disabled
access, on Transpennine Real Ale Trail, open
all day Fri-Sun.

DOWNHOLME   SE1197
★**Bolton Arms** (01748) 823716
*Village signposted just off A6108
Leyburn–Richmond; DL11 6AE* Stone-
built pub with wonderful Swaledale views
from garden and dining conservatory; simply
furnished carpeted bar down a few steps
with two smallish linked areas, plush wall
banquettes, collection of gleaming brass
and few small country pictures, log fire
in neat fireplace, two ales such as Black
Sheep, Timothy Taylors and Wensleydale, ten
wines by the glass and eight malt whiskies,
good food from lunchtime baguettes up;
background music; children welcome,
no dogs inside, two bedrooms sharing
a bathroom, closed Tues lunchtime.

EASINGWOLD   SE5270
George (01347) 821698
Market Place; YO61 3AD Neat market
town hotel (former 18th-c coaching inn) with
slightly old-fashioned feel; well kept Black
Sheep, Timothy Taylors and a guest, good
food in bar and restaurant from sandwiches
to daily specials, smaller appetites catered
for, helpful cheerful service; soft background
music; children and dogs (in bar) welcome,
disabled access, pleasant bedrooms and good
breakfast, open all day.

EAST MORTON   SE0941
Busfeild Arms (01274) 563169
Main Road; BD20 5SP Attractive
19th-c stone-built village pub (originally a
school); traditionally furnished beamed and
flagstoned bar with woodburner, Saltaire,
Tetleys, Timothy Taylors and a guest, fairly
priced food from sandwiches up, restaurant;
Thurs quiz, live music Sat, sports TV; children
welcome, dogs in bar (on lead), picnic-sets
on front terrace, three bedrooms, open all
day, food till 5.45pm Sun.

EAST WITTON   SE1487
★**Cover Bridge Inn** (01969) 623250
*A6108 out towards Middleham;
DL8 4SQ* Cosy and welcoming 16th-c
flagstoned/carpeted country local; well kept
Yorkshire-brewed ales such as Black Sheep,

Theakstons, Timothy Taylors and five guests,
real cider and enjoyable generously served
pub food at sensible prices, small restaurant,
roaring fires; children and dogs welcome,
riverside garden with play area, three
bedrooms, open all day.

EBBERSTON   SE8983
Grapes (01723) 859273
High Street (A170); YO13 9PA
Modernised old roadside pub; plenty of
emphasis on their good popular food
from traditional pub favourites to more
imaginative dishes, Greene King IPA and
Morland Old Speckled Hen, decent wines,
friendly helpful service; children, muddy
boots and dogs (in bar) welcome, closed Mon
and lunchtime Tues.

EGTON   NZ8006
★**Wheatsheaf** (01947) 895271
Village centre; YO21 1TZ 19th-c village
pub of character boasting wonderful views
of the North York Moors; interesting pictures
and collectables in small bare-boards bar
with fire in old range, very good generously
served food including daily specials, friendly
service, Black Sheep, Helmsley Striding
the Riding, Timothy Taylors Landlord
and a summer guest, several wines by the
glass, restaurant; children and dogs (in
bar) welcome, four bedrooms and adjacent
cottage, open all day weekends (no food Sun
evening), closed Mon.

EGTON BRIDGE   NZ8005
Horseshoe (01947) 895245
*Village signed off A171 W of Whitby;
YO21 1XE* Attractively placed 18th-c stone
inn; open fires and woodburners, high-
backed built-in winged settles, wall seats
and spindleback chairs, various odds and
ends including a large stuffed trout (caught
nearby in 1913), Theakstons Best and two
guests such as Bradfield Farmers Blonde
and Pennine A Good Try, popular food using
their own eggs and vegetables and locally
sourced meat; background and some live
music; children welcome, dogs in side bar
during mealtimes, seats on quiet terrace in
nice mature garden by small River Esk, good
walks (on Coast to Coast path), six bedrooms,
open all day Sun, food till 7pm.

EGTON BRIDGE   NZ8005
★**Postgate** (01947) 895241
*Village signed off A171 W of Whitby;
YO21 1UX* Moorland village pub dating
from 1860 next to railway station; good
imaginative food at fair prices including
fresh local fish (lots of blackboard menus),
well kept Black Sheep and a guest, friendly
helpful staff, traditional quarry-tiled bar
with beams, panelled dado and coal fire in
antique range, elegant restaurant; children
and dogs welcome, walled front garden with
picnic-sets either side of brick path, three
comfortable bedrooms.

EMBSAY   SE0053
Elm Tree (01756) 790717
Elm Tree Square; BD23 6RB Popular
open-plan beamed 17th-c village pub;
hearty helpings of good value food including
blackboard specials, Thurs pie night, four
well kept ales such as Bombardier and
Timothy Taylors, cheerful young staff; darts,
pool; comfortable bedrooms, handy for
Embsay & Bolton Abbey Steam Railway, open
all day Sun.

FACEBY   NZ4903
Sutton Arms (01642) 700382
Mill Lane/Bank Lane; TS9 7BW
Welcoming village dining pub at foot of
Cleveland Hills, clean and comfortable, with
low beamed central bar flanked by eating
areas, highly regarded freshly made food
(best to book) from pub favourites to more
restauranty choices including excellent
steaks, well kept ales and good selection
of wines, friendly attentive service; tables
on tiered front deck, simply furnished but
well appointed bedrooms, good hearty
breakfast, closed Sun evening, Mon, Tues and
lunchtimes apart from Sun.

FEARBY   SE1980
Black Swan (01765) 689477
Keld Bank; HG4 4NF Refurbished and
extended country pub; beamed bar with
dining area to the right, woodburner in pale
stone fireplace, Black Sheep, Theakstons
and a couple of regional summer guests,
several wines by the glass and good food
from varied menu including daily specials
(seafood and game festivals), friendly
helpful service, lovely valley views from back
restaurant (more rustic in style); children
welcome till 7pm, dogs in bar, 14 modern
bedrooms (12 in annexe), camping, open all
day summer (from 3pm weekdays, all day
weekends in winter).

FERRENSBY   SE3660
★ **General Tarleton** (01423) 340284
A655 N of Knaresborough; HG5 0PZ
Carefully renovated 18th-c coaching inn,
more restaurant-with-rooms than pub,
but there's an informal bar with sofas and
woodburner serving well kept Black Sheep,
Timothy Taylors Landlord and a dozen wines
by the glass; other open-plan rooms with low
beams, exposed stonework and brick pillars
creating alcoves, dark leather high-backed
dining chairs around wooden tables; first
class modern cooking from owner-chef along
with more traditional food and children's
menu, friendly well trained staff; seats in
covered courtyard and tree-lined garden,
pretty country views, 13 stylish bedrooms,
good breakfast.

FILEY   TA1180
Bonhommes (01723) 515325
The Crescent; YO14 9JH Friendly old-
fashioned bar with up to five well kept ales
including Isaac Poad and Rudgate and four
ciders, good value food (not Sun evening,
Mon); live music, karaoke, bingo and quiz
nights; children and dogs welcome, open
all day.

FINGHALL   SE1889
★ **Queens Head** (01677) 450259
Off A684 E of Leyburn; DL8 5ND
Welcoming dining pub dating from the 1700s;
log fire either end of low-beamed carpeted
bar divided by stone archway, settles making
stalls around big tables, four real usually
local ales, good food (not lunchtimes Mon-
Weds) from traditional favourites up, efficient
service, extended dining room with fine
country views; children welcome, no dogs
inside (except bedrooms), disabled access/
facilities, back garden with decking (same
view), three bedrooms.

GARGRAVE   SD9253
Masons Arms (01756) 749304
*Church Street/Marton Road (off A65
NW of Skipton); BD23 3NL* Traditional
beamed pub with welcoming local
atmosphere; opened-up interior divided
into bar, lounge and restaurant, log fire,
ample helpings of enjoyable home-made
food including traditional dishes and
sharing plates at very fair prices, Black
Sheep, Tetleys, Timothy Taylors and a guest,
real cider, 12 wines by the glass and good
selection of spirits from ornate counter,
efficient staff; live acoustic music first Fri
month in winter, quiz nights, darts; children
and dogs welcome, tables out behind
overlooking own bowling green, charming
village on Pennine Way and not far from
Leeds & Liverpool Canal, six barn conversion
bedrooms, open (and food) all day.

GIGGLESWICK   SD8164
★ **Harts Head** (01729) 822086
Belle Hill; BD24 0BA Refurbished
18th-c village inn under new management
(Thwaites); bar/lounge and restaurant, five
well kept Thwaites ales and mainly pub
classics, friendly helpful staff; occasional live
music; children and dogs (in bar) welcome,
picnic-sets on sloping lawn, seven bedrooms,
open (and food) all day.

GILLAMOOR   SE6890
★ **Royal Oak** (01751) 431414
Off A170 in Kirkbymoorside; YO62 7HX
18th-c stone-built dining pub in attractive
village at the gateway to the North York
Moors; good pubby food at sensible prices

We say if we know a pub has background music.

including sandwiches, vegetarian options, daily specials and two-course deal, friendly staff, ales such as Black Sheep and Copper Dragon, reasonably priced wines, roomy bar with heavy dark beams, log fires in two tall stone fireplaces (one with old kitchen range), overspill dining room where dogs allowed; children welcome, eight comfortable modern bedrooms, good breakfast, handy for Bransdale Moor walks, open all day.

GILLING EAST SE6176

★ **Fairfax Arms** (01439) 788212
Main Street (B1363, off A170 via Oswaldkirk); YO62 4JH Welcoming smartly presented pub in nice village; beamed bar with woodburner, Black Sheep, Tetleys and a couple of local guests from handsome oak counter, interesting wines by the glass, two-part carpeted dining room, good modern food (can be pricey) along with sandwiches, vegan options and pub favourites, neat attentive staff, orangery and outside seating area by floodlit roadside stream; well placed for Howardian Hills and North York Moors, 12 comfortable up-to-date bedrooms, good breakfast, open all day, food till 7pm Sun.

GILLING WEST NZ1805

White Swan (01748) 825122
High Street (B6274 just N of Richmond); DL10 5JG Welcoming 17th-c village inn with open-plan bar and dining room, modern décor and log fires, well kept ales including a Mithril house beer and good range of other drinks, much enjoyed food from interesting street-food starters to speciality burgers and dry-aged steaks, friendly staff; games room; children and dogs welcome, tables in courtyard, bedrooms, open all day (except Jan-Mar when closed Tues, Wed).

GOATHLAND NZ8200

Mallyan Spout Hotel
(01947) 896486 *Opposite church; YO22 5AN* Late 19th-c creeper-clad stone hotel; two bars and three spacious lounges, open fires, popular fairly priced food from pub favourites up, Black Sheep and a guest such as Timothy Taylors, good choice of wines, cocktails, spirits including modern gins, and malt whiskies, afternoon teas, friendly helpful staff, smart restaurant (separate menu); well behaved children welcome, dogs in one bar, lovely gardens and views, handy for namesake waterfall, 20 comfortable bedrooms, good breakfast, open all day.

GOODMANHAM SE8943

Goodmanham Arms (01430) 873849
Main Street; YO43 3JA Unpretentious little red-brick country pub (not to everyone's taste) with three traditional linked areas; beam-and-plank ceilings, some red and black floor tiles, mix of new and old furniture and plenty of interesting odds and ends, even

a Harley-Davidson, six real ales including at least two from on-site All Hallows microbrewery, real ciders, unfussy food from Italian owner (no starters), maybe a winter casserole cooked over the open fire, evening meals 5-7.30pm Mon and Weds (though may vary); folk night first Thurs of month, jazz/blues third Thurs, quiz every other Weds; children welcome, no dogs during food times, good walks (on Wolds Way), open all day.

GRANGE MOOR SE2215

Kaye Arms (01924) 840228
Wakefield Road (A642); WF4 4BG Modernised and opened-up roadside dining pub divided into three distinct areas (small area for drinkers); popular good value food including meal deal for two (not Sat evening, Sun, Mon), well kept Black Sheep and a guest and plenty of wines by the glass, efficient friendly service; children and dogs (in bar) welcome, some seats out at front, handy for National Coal Mining Museum, open all day weekends, no food Mon, till 7pm Sun.

GRASSINGTON SE0064

Foresters Arms (01756) 752349
Main Street; BD23 5AA Comfortable opened-up coaching inn with friendly bustling atmosphere; six well kept regional ales such as Black Sheep, Tetleys and Timothy Taylors, good hearty food (smaller appetites also catered for) including range of pizzas delivered by dumb waiter from upstairs kitchen, efficient cheerful service, log fires; popular Mon quiz, sports TV, darts and pool; children, walkers and dogs welcome, a few tables out at front, seven affordable bedrooms, good breakfast, open all day, food all day Sun.

GREAT AYTON NZ5610

Royal Oak (01642) 722361
Off A173 – follow village signs; High Green; TS9 6BW Popular early 18th-c village inn with good fairly priced food including blackboard specials, meal deals and themed nights, four well kept ales such as Theakstons and Timothy Taylors, bar with log fire, beam-and-plank ceiling and bulgy old partly panelled stone walls, traditional furnishings including antique settles, pleasant views of elegant green from bay windows, two linked dining rooms; children welcome, dogs in bar, comfortable bedrooms, handy for Cleveland Way, open (and food) all day.

GREAT BROUGHTON NZ5405

Bay Horse (01642) 712319
High Street; TS9 7HA Large creeper-clad dining pub in attractive village; wide choice of food including blackboard specials and good value set lunch, friendly attentive service, four real ales such as Camerons and Jennings, restaurant; children welcome (under-5s till 8pm), seats outside, open all day weekends.

GREAT HABTON
SE7576
⭐**Grapes** (01653) 669166
Corner of Habton Lane and Kirby Misperton Lane; YO17 6TU Popular and genuinely welcoming beamed dining pub in small village, homely and cosy, with highly praised cooking including fresh local fish and game (booking advised), a couple of well kept ales, good service, open fire, small public bar with darts and TV; background music; a few roadside picnic-sets, nice walks, open all day Sun, closed Mon and weekday lunchtimes.

HALIFAX
SE0925
Mill Bar & Kitchen (01422) 647494
Dean Clough; HX3 5AX Bar in former carpet mill; good choice of craft beers, wines and cocktails, burgers, grills, pizzas and pub classics, friendly efficient service; background music; handy for Northern Broadsides theatre, open all day Fri-Sun, closed Mon.

HALIFAX
SE0924
Three Pigeons (01422) 347001
Sun Fold, South Parade; off Church Street; HX1 2LX Carefully restored 1930s five-room pub (Grade II listed); original flooring, panelling and tiled fireplaces, art deco fittings, ceiling painting in octagonal main area, six ales including range of Ossett beers and guests including related Fernandes and Rat, friendly chatty staff; children and dogs welcome, darts, tables outside, handy for Eureka! Museum and Shay Stadium (pub very busy on match days), open all day Fri-Sun, otherwise from 4pm.

HARDRAW
SD8691
Green Dragon (01969) 667392
Village signed off A684; DL8 3LZ Traditional dales pub dating from 13th c and full of character; stripped stonework, antique settles and other old furniture on flagstones, lots of pictures and bric-a-brac, low-beamed snug with fire in original range, another in big main bar, five well kept ales including Timothy Taylors and Theakstons, enjoyable pubby food, small restaurant; children and dogs (in bar) welcome, tables in attractive courtyard, bedrooms, bunkhouse and self-catering, next to Hardraw Force (England's highest single-drop waterfall), open all day weekends.

HAROME
SE6482
⭐**Star** (01439) 770397
High Street; village signed S of A170, E of Helmsley; YO62 5JE Pretty 14th-c thatched pub-restaurant; bar with bowed beam-and-plank ceiling, plenty of bric-a-brac and interesting furniture including Robert 'Mouseman' Thompson pieces, well polished tiled kitchen range, log fire, four changing ales and plenty of wines by the glass, smart restaurant for chef-owner's highly regarded inventive cooking (not cheap), also snacks in cocktail bar and a coffee loft in the eaves, well trained helpful staff; background music; children welcome, seats on sheltered front terrace, more in garden, nine individual bedrooms in building across road, very good breakfast, no food Sun evening or Mon lunchtime.

HARPHAM
TA0961
St Quintin Arms (01262) 490329
Main Street; YO25 4QY Comfortable old village inn with enjoyable reasonably priced home-made food including specials, well kept Theakstons and Wold Top, efficient friendly service, bar and small dining room; sports TV, daily papers; children welcome, no dogs inside, sheltered garden with terrace and pond, on National Cycle Route 1, four bedrooms, open all day Sat, Sun, closed Mon and lunchtime Tues.

HARROGATE
SE3155
Coach & Horses (01423) 561802
West Park; HG1 1BJ Friendly bustling pub with up to eight good Yorkshire-brewed ales, 80 malt whiskies and over 40 gins, good range of wines too, enjoyable reasonably priced lunchtime food plus some themed evenings, comfortable interior arranged around central bar with booths and other cosy areas; regular Fri charity raffle, Sun quiz; no children or dogs, open all day – closed for refurbishment at press time.

HARROGATE
SE3157
Gardeners Arms (01423) 506051
Bilton Lane (off A59 either in Bilton itself or on outskirts towards Harrogate – via Bilton Hall Drive); HG1 4DH Stone-built 17th-c house converted into down-to-earth local; tiny bar and three small rooms, flagstone floors, panelling and old prints, roaring fire in big stone fireplace with tree-stump seat either side, cheap Sam Smiths OBB, no food; children and dogs welcome, picnic-sets out at front and in surrounding streamside garden, lovely peaceful setting near Nidd Gorge, open all day.

HARROGATE
SE2955
⭐**Hales** (01423) 725570
Crescent Road; HG1 2RS Classic Victorian décor in 18th-c gas-lit local close to the Pump Rooms; leather seats in alcoves, lots of pictures and stuffed birds, comfortable saloon and tiny snug, five ales including Greene King, Robinsons and a house beer from Daleside, simple good value lunchtime food (not Mon), friendly helpful staff; weekly

Pubs close to motorway junctions are listed at the back of the book.

live music; children welcome till 6pm, no dogs during food service, open all day (till 1am Thurs-Sat) and can get lively weekend evenings.

HARROGATE   SE2955
Old Bell (01423) 507930
Royal Parade; HG1 2SZ Market Town Tavern with eight real ales including Ilkley, Theakstons and Timothy Taylors, several craft beers and good selection of wines and gins, friendly helpful staff, fairly traditional food from sandwiches up, mix of furniture including iron-framed tables and leather tub chairs on wood floors, Anaglypta dado, servery made from an old mahogany dresser, some vintage sweet shop ads, further seating upstairs; children (if eating) and dogs (on lead) welcome, open all day.

HAWES   SD8789
White Hart (01969) 667214
Main Street; DL8 3QL Welcoming 16th-c coaching inn on cobbled street; emphasis on good fairly priced food, but also at least four well kept regional ales, friendly fast service, interesting panelled bar with fire in antique range, daily papers, restaurant; children and dogs welcome, five bedrooms, open all day.

HEADINGLEY   SE2736
Arcadia (0113) 274 5599
Arndale Centre; LS6 2UE Glass-fronted Market Town Tavern in former bank; eight changing regional ales, a couple of craft kegs and over 100 bottled beers, real ciders, good range of wines too, friendly knowledgeable staff, snacky food including good local cheese, stairs to mezzanine; no children, dogs welcome; closed Mon, Tues.

HEATH   SE3520
Kings Arms (01924) 377527
Village signposted from A655 Wakefield–Normanton – or, more directly, turn off to the left opposite Horse & Groom; WF1 5SL Popular old-fashioned gas-lit pub of genuine character; fire in black range (long row of smoothing irons on the mantelpiece), plain elm stools, built-in oak settles and dark panelling, three well kept Ossett beers (one named for the pub) and four guests, real cider, standard food (Weds-Sun), more comfortable extension preserving original style, two other small flagstoned rooms and a conservatory; summer folk events, Tues quiz; children and dogs (in bar) welcome, benches out at front facing village green (surrounded by fine 19th-c stone merchants' houses), picnic-sets on side lawn and in nice walled garden, usually open all day (may shut early if quiet).

HEBDEN   SE0263
Clarendon (01756) 752446
B6265; BD23 5DE Well cared-for modernised 18th-c inn surrounded by wonderful moorland walking country; bar, snug and restaurant, open fire, well kept ales such as Black Sheep, Timothy Taylors and Wensleydale, good range of enjoyable food (till 6pm Sun) from pubby choices up including local game and blackboard specials, cheerful relaxed atmosphere; Sun quiz, darts; children and dogs (in bar) welcome, farm shop, six bedrooms, open all day Fri-Sun.

HEBDEN BRIDGE   SD9922
Hinchcliffe Arms (01422) 883256
Off B6138; HX7 5TA Tucked-away stone-built pub in great walking country on the Calderdale Way and near Stoodley Pike; open-plan bar to the left, restaurant on right, three well kept ales and guest, 11 wines by the glass, very good food from daily changing menu cooked by chef-owner, friendly staff; children, dogs (in bar) and walkers welcome, a few seats out at front, picturesque setting close to stream and Victorian church, open (and food) all day, Sun till 10pm (6pm).

HEBDEN BRIDGE   SD9927
Old Gate (01422) 843993
Oldgate; HX7 8JP Popular colourfully furnished bar-restaurant with wide choice of good food served from 10am breakfast on, nine well kept ales such as Moorhouses and Saltaire, plenty of bottled beers and good range of wines by the glass including champagne, helpful friendly service, refurbished upstairs restaurant; occasional live music and comedy nights; children welcome, tables outside, open (and food) all day.

HEBDEN BRIDGE   SD9827
Stubbing Wharf (01422) 844107
About a mile W; HX7 6LU Friendly pub in good spot sandwiched between the Rochdale Canal and River Calder; popular good value food from sandwiches and light meals up, at least four regional ales such as Black Sheep, Saltaire and Timothy Taylors kept well, proper ciders, cheerful hard-working young staff; Thurs quiz; well behaved children and dogs welcome, adjacent moorings, open (and food) all day.

HELMSLEY   SE6183
Feathers (01439) 770275
Market Place; YO62 5BH Substantial old stone inn overlooking the market square; enjoyable food (all day Sat) from sandwiches and pub favourites up, well kept Black Sheep, Tetleys and a couple of local guests, 26 wines by the glass including sparkling, afternoon teas, good friendly service, several rooms with comfortable seats, walnut and oak tables (some by Robert 'Mouseman' Thompson, as is the bar counter), flagstones or tartan carpet, heavy medieval beams and huge inglenook; children and dogs (in bar) welcome, terrace tables, 22 bedrooms, open all day.

HELWITH BRIDGE SD8169
Helwith Bridge Inn (01729) 860220
Off B6479 N of Stainforth; BD24 0EH
Friendly unpretentious village local popular
with walkers; usually Three Peaks Helwith
Bridge Bitter and Ingleborough Gold plus
a Thwaites beer and a guest in flagstoned
bar, enjoyable reasonably priced pub food
including Thurs steak night, friendly if not
always speedy service, dining room with light
wood furniture on bare boards; children and
dogs welcome, camping and bunkhouse, next
to River Ribble and Settle–Carlisle railway,
open all day, food all day Sat, till 7pm Sun.

HIGH HOYLAND SE2710
Cherry Tree (01226) 382541
*Bank End Lane; 3 miles W of M1
junction 38; S75 4BE* Split-level
whitewashed village pub; four well kept
ales such as Acorn Barnsley Bitter and
Black Sheep Bitter, real cider, good range of
enjoyable generously served food (not Sun
evening), competitive prices and friendly
young staff, beams and open fire, dining
areas each end of bar and separate small
restaurant; background and some live music;
children, walkers and dogs welcome, front
roadside picnic-sets with lovely views over
Cannon Hall Country Park, open all day
Fri-Sun.

HOLMFIRTH SD1408
Nook (01484) 682373
Victoria Square/South Lane; HD9 2DN
Friendly tucked-away 18th-c local run by
same family for two generations; own-brew
beers, guest ales and low-priced food with
emphasis on burgers, no-frills bar areas with
flagstones and quarry tiles, big open fire;
juke box, pool; heated streamside terrace,
bedrooms, open all day, kitchen from 3pm
Mon-Thurs; they also have the refurbished
Nook Tap House bar-restaurant next door.

HOPPERTON SE4256
Masons (01423) 330442
Hopperton Street; HG5 8NX Village dining
pub with popular food from standards up, a
couple of real ales and excellent choice of
gins, friendly helpful staff, snug pubby bar
and extended restaurant with high-backed
leather chairs around mix of tables on tiled
floor, open fires; background music; children
and dogs (in bar) welcome, closed Mon
and Tues, no food Sun evening or Weds-Fri
lunchtimes.

HORBURY SE2918
Boons (01924) 280442
Queen Street; WF4 6LP Comfortably
unpretentious 18th-c coaching inn;
chatty and relaxed, with Timothy Taylors
Landlord and seven quickly changing
guests, real cider, pleasant young
staff, no food or children, rugby league
memorabilia, warm fire, back tap room

with pool, sports TV and fruit machine;
courtyard tables, open all day Sat, Sun.

HORBURY SE2918
Cherry Tree (01924) 262916
Church Street; WF4 6LT Victorian pub
with own good Horbury ales from attached
microbrewery plus guests, 12 decent wines by
the glass and well liked food (not Mon, Tues),
pubby and sharing plates at lunchtime, more
restaurant-style at dinner, smart modern
décor with mix of seating on wood floors
including upholstered stools and banquettes,
some beams, exposed brickwork and painted
dados, two logburners; background music, TV;
interesting 18th-c church opposite, open all
day, closed Mon, from 4pm Tues.

HORBURY SE2918
Cricketers (01924) 267032
Cluntergate; WF4 5AG Welcoming late
19th-c red-brick drinkers' pub with attractive
oak bar and restored stained-glass window
with Arts and Crafts lettering; Timothy
Taylors Landlord and seven changing guests,
also craft beers, real cider and good selection
of spirits, no food; open mike, quiz and folk
nights, beer festivals and tap takeovers; dogs
welcome, open all day Fri-Sun, from 4pm
other days.

HUBBERHOLME SD9278
★ George (01756) 760223
Dubbs Lane; BD23 5JE Ancient little
dales inn, beautifully placed and run by
warmly welcoming licensees; heavy beams,
flagstones and stripped stone, enjoyable
fairly priced home-made food (booking
advised) from lunchtime sandwiches (not
Sun) up, Mon pie night, well kept Black
Sheep, Theakstons and two guests, open fire,
perpetual candle on bar; outside lavatories;
children allowed in dining area, well-behaved
dogs in bar (pub jack russell is George),
terrace seating, River Wharfe fishing rights,
six comfortable clean bedrooms (three
in annexe), good breakfast, closed Mon
lunchtime and Tues, otherwise open all day
(best to check winter hours).

HUDDERSFIELD SE1416
Grove (01484) 430113
Spring Grove Street; HD1 4BP Friendly
two-bar pub with huge selection of bottled
beers (some gluten-free), up to 18 well kept/
priced ales and 15 craft kegs, real cider,
also an impressive range of whiskies and
other spirits, knowledgeable staff, no food
apart from interesting bar snacks, eclectic
collection of artwork and taxidermy; live jazz
and folk sessions; children (till 8pm) and
dogs welcome, back terrace, open all day Sat
and Sun, from 2pm other days.

HUDDERSFIELD SE1416
Rat & Ratchet (01484) 542400
Chapel Hill; HD1 3EB Popular split-level
pub with own-brew beers and plenty of guests

including Ossett, good range of ciders/perries too, pork pies and sausage rolls, friendly staff; darts, pinball machine, quiz nights and live music; open all day Fri-Sun, from 3pm other days.

HUDDERSFIELD SE1417
Sportsman (01484) 421929
St Johns Road; HD1 5AY Same owners as the West Riding Licensed Refreshment Rooms at Dewsbury; restored 1930s interior with lounge and two cosy side rooms, eight real ales and plenty of craft beers, friendly knowledgeable staff, pie menu served Fri-Sun; live music; dogs welcome, handy for station, open all day (till midnight Fri, Sat).

HUDDERSFIELD SE1415
Star (01484) 545443
Albert Street, Lockwood; HD1 3PJ Friendly unpretentious local with range of ten competitively priced ales kept well by enthusiastic landlady (in charge for two decades), continental beers and real cider too, beer festivals in back marquee, open fire; open all day weekends, closed Mon and lunchtimes Tues-Fri.

HUDSWELL NZ1400
George & Dragon (01748) 518373
Hudswell Lane; DL11 6BL Community-owned village pub, popular and welcoming, with enjoyable good value food from shortish menu including speciality home-made pies, five cask and five keg beers mainly from small local breweries such as Bad Co, Brass Castle, Northallerton and Small World, plus bottled beers and extensive range of whiskies; small shop and library, monthly live music/quiz nights, quoits pitch; children and dogs welcome, panoramic Swaledale views from back terrace, open all day Sat, no food Sun evening.

HULL TA1028
★Olde White Harte (01482) 326363
Passage off Silver Street; HU1 1JG Dating from the 16th c with Civil War history; carved heavy beams, attractive stained glass, oak panelling and two big inglenooks with frieze of delft tiles, well kept Caledonian, Theakstons and guests from copper-topped counter, 80 or so malt whiskies; old skull (found here in the 19th c and displayed in a Perspex case); children welcome, dogs in bar, heated courtyard, open all day.

HUNMANBY TA1077
Piebald (01723) 447577
Sands Lane; E of level crossing; YO14 0LT Comfortably renovated pub with well stocked bar and separate dining room, popular generously served food featuring more than 50 different pies, up to five real ales including a house beer from Greene King, friendly helpful staff; occasional live music; children and dogs (in bar) welcome, picnic-sets on side terrace and lawned

garden bordering railway line, camping, open (and food) all day.

HUTTON-LE-HOLE SE7089
Crown (01751) 417343
The Green; YO62 6UA Friendly village local overlooking pretty green with wandering sheep in classic coach-trip country; Black Sheep, Tetleys and a guest, decent wines by the glass and enjoyable home-made pubby food (till 6pm Sun), cheerful efficient service, opened-up bar with varnished woodwork, dining area; quiz first Sun of month; children and clean dogs welcome, Ryedale Folk Museum next door and handy for Farndale walks, three newish bedrooms, also small site for caravans, open all day (but closed Mon and Tues in winter).

ILKLEY SE1147
Bar t'at (01943) 608888
Cunliffe Road; LS29 9DZ Extended Market Town Tavern with Black Sheep, Okells, Ilkley, Timothy Taylors and guests and a good wine and bottled beer choice, enjoyable well priced pubby food from sandwiches and snacks up, friendly service, candlelit cellar dining area; upstairs loos; children (until 9pm) and dogs (not downstairs) welcome, back terrace with heated canopy, open all day, kitchen closes 6pm Sun, pub at 9pm.

ILKLEY SE1147
Flying Duck (01943) 609587
Church Street; LS29 9DS Old stone pub with nine well kept beers including own Wharfedale ales brewed in barn behind, tasters offered by friendly knowledgeable staff, shortish choice of enjoyable good value food (lunchtime Tues-Sun) including selection of light dishes (perfect for sharing), beamed and flagstoned bar with woodburner in large stone fireplace; quiz, live music and open mike nights; children and dogs welcome, first-floor terrace, open all day (till late Fri, Sat), closed Mon.

KEIGHLEY SE0641
Boltmakers Arms (01535) 661936
East Parade; BD21 5HX Small split-level character local, friendly and bustling, with full Timothy Taylors range and a guest kept well, traditional cider and several malt whiskies, lots to look at including brewing pictures and celebrity photos, coal fire; Tues quiz, live music nights, sports TV; small beer garden, short walk from Keighley & Worth Valley Railway, open all day.

KETTLESING SE2257
★Queens Head (01423) 770263
Village signposted off A59 W of Harrogate; HG3 2LB Popular stone-built village pub with very good well priced traditional food; L-shaped carpeted main bar, lots of close-set cushioned dining chairs and tables, open fires, little heraldic shields on

the walls along with 19th-c song sheet covers and lithographs of Queen Victoria, delft shelf of blue and white china, smaller bar on left with built-in red banquettes and cricketing prints, life-size portrait of Elizabeth I in lobby, well kept Black Sheep, Roosters and Theakstons, ten wines by the glass and good range of spirits, efficient friendly service; background music; children welcome, seats in neatly kept sunny back garden, benches in front by lane, eight bedrooms, open all day Sun.

KETTLEWELL   SD9672
Blue Bell (01756) 760230
Middle Lane; BD23 5QX Roomy knocked-through former coaching inn, popular and welcoming, with well kept Theakstons, Wharfedale and plenty of guest beers, generous helpings of enjoyable pubby food, friendly helpful service, low beams and simple furnishings, old country photographs, woodburner; Sun quiz, TV; children, walkers and dogs welcome, shaded picnic-sets on cobbles facing bridge over River Wharfe, six annexe bedrooms, open all day.

KETTLEWELL   SD9772
★ **Kings Head** (01756) 761600
The Green; BD23 5RD Welcoming old pub tucked away near church; flagstoned main bar with log fire in big arched inglenook, three well kept local ales and 12 well chosen wines by the glass, very good affordably priced food (all day Sun till 7pm) cooked by chef-landlord from pub favourites to imaginative restaurant dishes, efficient friendly service; children allowed, no dogs inside, six comfortable bedrooms (some quite small) named after kings, attractive dales village with good surrounding walks, closed Mon (Oct-end Mar), otherwise open all day.

KETTLEWELL   SD9672
Racehorses (01756) 317996
B6160 N of Skipton; BD23 5QZ Comfortable and friendly two-bar inn next to River Wharf (across from the Blue Bell); tasty sensibly priced home-made food and four well kept Timothy Taylors ales, log fires, separate dining areas; children and dogs (in some parts) welcome, front and back terrace seating, pretty village well placed for Wharfedale walks, parking can be tricky, 14 good bedrooms, open all day.

KILDWICK   SE0145
White Lion (01535) 632265
Priest Bank Road, next to church; off A629 Keighley–Skipton; BD20 9BH Two-bar stone pub; well kept ales such as Timothy Taylors and Saltaire and enjoyable food; children and dogs welcome, Aire Valley views from sunny garden, attractive village with good surrounding walks, near Leeds & Liverpool Canal, open all day Sat, Sun, closed Mon, Tues.

KIRKBY MALHAM   SD8960
Victoria (01729) 830499
South end of village; BD23 4BS Mid 19th-c flower-decked pub with sundial above entrance; flagstoned bar with open fire, snug and separate restaurant, well kept Dark Horse and guests, good wine choice and enjoyable freshly cooked food, friendly service; children, muddy boots and dogs welcome, picnic-sets out at front, lovely village with interesting church, good walks (close to Pennine Way), four bedrooms, open all day, closed Mon.

KIRKBYMOORSIDE   SE6986
George & Dragon (01751) 433334
Market Place; YO62 6AA Friendly 17th-c coaching inn; front bar with beams, stripped wood floor and log fire, well kept changing local ales and several malt whiskies/gins, decent choice of enjoyable generously served food including range of burgers, good service, more formal restaurant; background music and some live music; children and dogs welcome, front and back terraces, 20 bedrooms, Weds market, open all day.

KNAYTON   SE4388
Dog & Gun (01845) 537368
Moor Road, off A19; YO7 4AZ Well cared-for family-run pub, cosy and comfortable, with roaring fire at one end, tables laid for their popular home-made food, both traditional and international dishes (best to book) including blackboard specials and deals, ales such as Black Sheep and Timothy Taylors, good friendly service; children and dogs welcome (menus for both), heated outside seating area, open all day weekends, closed Mon and lunchtimes Tues-Fri.

LANGTHWAITE   NY0002
★ **Charles Bathurst** 0333 7000779
Arkengarthdale, a mile N towards Tan Hill; DL11 6EN Busy 18th-c country inn (sister to the Punch Bowl at Low Row); strong emphasis on dining and bedrooms, but pubby feel in long bar with scrubbed pine tables and country chairs on stripped floors, snug alcoves, open fire, Black Sheep, Theakstons and a local guest, several wines by the glass and good choice of popular interesting food, cheerful helpful staff, dining room with Robert 'Mousey' Thompson furniture and views of Scar House, several other eating areas; background music, TV, pool and darts; children welcome, dogs in bar, lovely walks from the door and views over village and Arkengarthdale, 19 smart bedrooms (best not above dining room), open all day; worth checking there are no corporate events/weddings before you visit.

LANGTHWAITE   NZ0002
★ **Red Lion** (01748) 884218
Just off Arkengarthdale Road, Reeth–Brough; DL11 6RE Proper pub dating from

17th c in charming dales village with ancient bridge; long-serving character landlady and homely old-fashioned atmosphere, lunchtime sandwiches, pasties and sausage rolls, a couple of well kept Black Sheep ales and a guest, Thatcher's cider, country wines, tea and coffee, well behaved children allowed lunchtime in low-ceilinged side snug, newspapers and postcards; the ladies' is a genuine bathroom; no dogs inside, a few picnic-sets out at front, good walks including circular ones from the pub – maps and guides for sale.

LASTINGHAM SE7290
★ **Blacksmiths Arms** (01751) 417247
Off A170 W of Pickering; YO62 6TL
17th-c pub in charming village opposite beautiful Saxon church; small bar with log fire in open range, tankards hanging from beams, traditional furnishings, well kept Theakstons and other regional ales, several wines by the glass and good sensibly priced mostly pubby home-made food (not Sun evening) including vegetarian and gluten-free choices, prompt friendly service, two dining rooms; background music, darts and board games; children welcome, no dogs inside, seats out at front and in back beer garden, three bedrooms, open all day.

LEALHOLM NZ7607
★ **Board** (01947) 897279
Off A171 W of Whitby; YO21 2AJ
18th-c pub in wonderful moorland village spot by wide pool of River Esk; homely bare-boards bar on right with squashy old sofa and armchairs by big black stove, three well kept changing ales (maybe Black Sheep and Theakstons), seven real ciders and more than 60 whiskies, good seasonal food using meat from own farm and other local produce, friendly helpful landlady; children, dogs and muddy boots welcome, secluded waterside garden with decking, bedrooms (good breakfast) and self-catering cottage, open all day.

LEAVENING SE7863
Jolly Farmers (01653) 658276
Main Street; YO17 9SA Friendly bustling village local with up to five regional ales and popular good value pub food (not Mon, Tues), front bar with eating area behind, separate dining room; some live music; children and dogs welcome, open all day weekends, closed weekday lunchtimes.

LEEDS SE2932
★ **Grove** (0113) 244 2085
Back Row, Holbeck; LS11 5PL Unspoilt 1930s-feel local overshadowed by towering office blocks; tables and stools in main bar with marble floor, panelling and original fireplace, large back room and snug off drinking corridor, eight well kept regional ales including Daleside Blonde, Weston's cider, lunchtime food (not Sat, Sun), friendly

staff; regular live music including Fri folk club; dogs welcome, open all day.

LEEDS SE3033
Kirkstall Bridge (0113) 278 4044
Bridge Road, Headingley–Kirkstall; LS5 3BW Welcoming traditionally renovated pub by bridge over River Aire; main bare-boards bar with lots of breweriana and other rescued items from closed pubs, well kept Kirkstall beers and several guests, generous helpings of reasonably priced food from deli boards and pizzas up, downstairs flagstoned bar (dogs welcome here) leading out to riverside garden; Weds quiz, some live music; handy for ruined Kirkstall Abbey, open (and food) all day, kitchen closes 5pm Sun.

LEEDS SE2932
Midnight Bell (0113) 244 5044
Water Lane, Holbeck; LS11 5QN
Leeds Brewery pub on two floors in Holbeck Urban Village; their ales and guests kept well, enjoyable home-made food, friendly staff, light contemporary décor mixing with original beams and stripped brickwork; children and dogs welcome, courtyard beer garden, open (and food) all day, kitchen shuts 7pm Sun.

LEEDS SE3033
Scarbrough (0113) 243 4590
Bishopgate Street, opposite station; LS1 5DY Nicholsons pub with ornate tiled façade; eight well kept changing ales, good wine choice, 22 whiskies, 21 gins, served by friendly helpful staff, enjoyable food including speciality pies and breakfasts; sports TV; open all day, busy lunchtime and early evening.

LEEDS SE3033
★ **Whitelocks** (0113) 245 3950
Turks Head Yard, off Briggate; LS1 6HB
Classic Victorian pub full of character (if a little worn around the edges); long narrow bar with fine tiled counter, grand mirrors, mahogany and glass screens, heavy copper-topped tables and red leather seating, coal fire, five well kept regional ales, real ciders and enjoyable food; children welcome, tables in narrow courtyard, open (and food) all day, can get crowded at lunchtime.

LINTHWAITE SE1014
★ **Sair** (01484) 842370
Lane Top, Hoyle Ing, off A62; HD7 5SG
Old-fashioned four-room pub unchanged in decades and offering 11 of its own-brewed Linfit ales; pews and chairs on rough flagstones or wood floors, log-burning ranges, dominoes, cribbage and shove-ha'penny, piano and vintage rock juke box; no food; children and dogs welcome, plenty of tables out in front with fine Colne Valley views, restored Huddersfield Narrow Canal nearby, open all day Fri-Sun, otherwise from 3pm.

LINTON　　　　　　　　SE3846

Windmill　(01937) 582209

Off A661 W of Wetherby; LS22 4HT
Character 16th-c inn on different levels,
dark beams and stripped stone, antique
settles around copper-topped tables on
carpeted floors, three log fires; enjoyable
food from traditional dishes up including
gluten-free, vegetarian and vegan menus,
pie night Weds, steak night Thurs, four ales
such as Theakstons Best and several wines
by the glass, friendly young staff, restaurant
and airy conservatory; background and
some live music, Thurs quiz; children and
dogs (in bar) welcome, sunny back terrace
and sheltered garden with pear tree
(raised from seed brought back from the
Napoleonic Wars), two annexe bedrooms,
open all day weekends, food all day Sat, till
6pm Sun.

LITTON　　　　　　　　SD9074

Queens Arms　(01756) 770096

Off B6160 N of Grassington; BD23 5QJ
Beautifully placed 17th-c whitewashed
stone pub; main bar with slate floor and
beam-and-plank ceiling, old photographs on
rough stone walls, coal fire, plainer carpeted
dining room with woodburner, four real ales
(maybe one from on-site microbrewery) such
as Wharfedale Blonde, good freshly made
food including range of pies, friendly efficient
staff; children and dogs welcome, plenty of
seats in two-tier garden, country views and
good surrounding walks, four bedrooms,
open all day, food till 5pm Sun, (closed Mon
in winter).

LOFTHOUSE　　　　　　SE1073

Crown　(01423) 755206

*Pub signed from main road; Nidderdale;
HG3 5RZ* Prettily placed dales inn, friendly
and relaxed, with hearty simple food from
sandwiches up, well kept Black Sheep, Dark
Horse and Theakstons, small public bar,
comfortable dining extension where children
allowed, open fire; outside gents'; dogs
welcome, nice garden and good walks from
the door, bedrooms.

LOW BRADFIELD　　　　SK2691

Plough　(0114) 285 1280

*Village signposted off B6077 and B6076
NW of Sheffield; New Road; S6 6HW*
Comfortably modernised old pub ideally
placed for some of South Yorkshire's finest
scenery; L-shaped bar with stone walls,
button-back banquettes and captain's chairs,
log fire in big arched fireplace, well kept
Bradfield ales and guests, real cider, good
value food from sandwiches up; background
music, Weds quiz, sports TV; children and
dogs welcome, seats on back verandah,
terrace and lawn, Damflask and Agden
Reservoirs close by, open (and food) all day,
kitchen shuts 7pm Sun.

LOW CATTON　　　　　　SE7053

Gold Cup　(01759) 371354

*Village signposted with High Catton off
A166 in Stamford Bridge or A1079 at
Kexby Bridge; YO41 1EA* Bustling village
pub under long-serving owners; cheerful
neatly kept bar, plenty of smart tables and
chairs on stripped-wood floors, open fire
at one end, John Smiths and Theakstons
kept well, enjoyable fairly priced home-
cooked food (smaller appetites catered for),
spacious restaurant with pleasant views over
surrounding fields; background music, pool;
children and dogs (in bar) welcome, pleasant
garden, paddock with ponies, pub also has
fishing rights on adjacent River Derwent,
open (and food) all day weekends, closed
Mon lunchtime.

LOW ROW　　　　　　　SD9898

Punch Bowl　0333 7000 779

B6270 Reeth–Muker; DL11 6PF 17th-c
country inn under same ownership as the
Charles Bathurst at Langthwaite; long
bare-boards bar with peaceful view over
Swaledale, stripped kitchen tables and a
variety of seats including armchairs and
sofa by woodburner, enjoyable food (menu
on huge mirror), well kept Black Sheep,
Theakstons and a guest beer and nice wines
by the glass, friendly staff, separate dining
room similar in style; children and dogs (in
bar) welcome, wide views from terrace set
above road, 11 comfortable bedrooms, good
breakfast, open all day.

LUND　　　　　　　　　SE9748

★Wellington　(01377) 217294

Off B1248 SW of Driffield; YO25 9TE
Smart busy pub with cosy Farmers' Bar
overlooking village green; beams, nicely
polished wooden banquettes and square
tables, log fire in quirky fireplace, plainer
side room with flagstones and wine-theme
décor, Yorkstone walkway to further room
displaying village's Britain in Bloom awards,
four well kept ales including Timothy Taylors
and Theakstons, good wine list and 25 malt
whiskies, highly rated well presented food
in restaurant or bistro dining area, friendly
efficient staff; background music, TV;
children welcome, dogs in some areas (but do
ask first), disabled access/loo, picnic-tables
in pretty back courtyard, closed Mon, Tues.

MALTBY　　　　　　　　NZ4613

Chadwicks　(01642) 590300

High Lane; TS8 0BG Beamed 19th-c
pub-restaurant; first rate food including
some cheaper lunchtime/early evening pub
favourites, set menus, good helpful service,
a changing local ale, several gins and
cocktails; wine tasting evenings, quiz nights;
wheelchair access, seats on front terrace,
closed Mon, lunchtime Tues, otherwise open
all day, no food Sun evening.

MANFIELD   NZ2213
Crown (01325) 374243
Vicars Lane; DL2 2RF Unpretentious
two-bar village local, friendly and welcoming,
with seven interesting ales including Bass
and Village Brewer White Boar, proper ciders
and enjoyable home-made food, open fires,
games room with pool and darts; some live
music; children and dogs welcome, picnic-
sets and caravan in part-lawned garden, good
walks nearby, open Thurs-Sun.

MARSDEN   SE0411
Riverhead Brewery Tap
(01484) 844324 *Peel Street, next to
Co-op; just off A62 Huddersfield–
Oldham; HD7 6BR* Owned by Ossett with
up to ten well kept ales (microbrewery
visible from bare-boards bar), real cider;
friendly bustling atmosphere, airy upstairs
beamed restaurant with stripped tables
(moors view from some) and open kitchen,
good choice of enjoyable food (till 7pm Sun,
just sandwiches Mon and Tues); background
and occasional live music, Tues quiz; children
and dogs welcome, a few tables out by river,
open all day.

MASHAM   SE2281
White Bear (01765) 689319
*Wellgarth, Crosshills; signed off A6108
opposite turn into town; HG4 4EN*
Comfortably updated beamed inn; small
public bar with full Theakstons range
kept well and several wines by the glass,
welcoming coal fire in larger lounge, decent
choice of food, from sandwiches/baguettes
up, afternoon teas, friendly efficient staff,
restaurant extension; background music;
children and dogs (in bar) welcome, terrace
tables, 14 bedrooms, open all day.

MIDDLESMOOR   SE0974
Crown (01423) 755204
*Top of Nidderdale Road from Pateley
Bridge; HG3 5ST* Remote unpretentious
inn under new management (but no changes
planned) with beautiful view over stone-built
hamlet high in upper Nidderdale; well kept
Black Sheep, Dark Horse and Theakstons,
several whiskies and simple wholesome
food, blazing fires in cosy spotless rooms,
old photographs and bric-a-brac, homely
dining room; children and dogs welcome,
small garden, seven good value bedrooms,
self-catering cottage and camping, open all
day Sat, Sun.

MIDDLETON TYAS   NZ2205
Shoulder of Mutton (01325) 377271
*Just E of A1 Scotch Corner roundabout;
DL10 6QX* Welcoming old pub with three
softly lit low-ceilinged rooms on different
levels, good freshly made food from
sandwiches, sharing boards and pub classics
up, Thurs steak night, Black Sheep Bitter and
a couple of guests, decent range of wines,

whiskies and gins, friendly helpful service;
quiz last Weds of month; children and dogs
(in bar) welcome, a useful A1/A66 stop, open
(and food) all day Sat, Sun.

MILLINGTON   SE8351
Gait (01759) 302045
Main Street; YO42 1TX Friendly 16th-c
beamed local; five well kept regional ales
(summer beer festival) and enjoyable
straightforward home-made food, nice mix
of old and newer furnishings, large map of
Yorkshire on the ceiling, big inglenook log
fire; fortnightly quiz Weds; children and
dogs welcome, garden picnic-sets, appealing
village in good wolds walking country, two
holiday cottages next door, closed Mon and
lunchtimes Tues-Thurs.

MIRFIELD   SE2017
Hare & Hounds (01924) 493814
*Liley Lane (B6118 2 miles S);
WF14 8EE* Popular Vintage Inn with
attractive open-plan interior divided into
several distinct areas (some steps), their
usual good choice of reasonably priced food
including weekday fixed-price menus, well
kept Black Sheep, Sharps and a couple
of guests, cheerful helpful staff, log fire;
children and dogs welcome, tables outside
with good Pennine views, open (and food)
all day.

MOORSHOLM   NZ6912
Jolly Sailor (01287) 660270
A171 nearly a mile E; TS12 3LN
Remotely placed dining pub set down from
the main road; good variety of enjoyable
food served by friendly staff, well kept
Black Sheep and a guest, long beamed and
stripped-stone bar, separate restaurant;
children and dogs welcome, outside tables
with moorland views, play area, open all day.

NEWTON-ON-OUSE   SE5160
★ Dawnay Arms (01347) 848345
Off A19 N of York; YO30 2BR 18th-c
pub with two bars and airy river-view dining
room; low beams and chunky masonry,
chunky pine tables and old pews on bare
boards or flagstones, fishing memorabilia,
open fire and inglenook woodburner, highly
regarded original food, also good lunchtime
sandwiches (home-baked bread), set menu
and interesting vegetarian choices, Black
Sheep, Timothy Taylors Landlord and two
guests, good range of wines by the glass,
friendly efficient service; children and dogs
(call first) welcome, terrace tables, lawn
running down to Ouse moorings, handy for
Beningbrough Hall (NT), closed Sun evening,
Mon (except bank holidays) and winter Tues.

NORTH RIGTON   SE2749
Square & Compass (01423) 733031
Hall Green Lane/Rigton Hill; LS17 0DJ
Much extended stone building with smart
modern interior; beamed bar serving four

or five well kept ales including Leeds Pale, Ossett Yorkshire Blonde and Theakstons Best, good range of bottled beers, 19 wines by the glass, cocktails and several gins and whiskies, well liked food from sandwiches, sharing boards and pizzas up, friendly efficient service by aproned staff, restaurant; quiz; children and dogs (in bar) welcome, tables out on tiered terrace, peaceful village, open (and food) all day.

NUN MONKTON   SE5057
★**Alice Hawthorn** (01423) 330303
Off A59 York–Harrogate; The Green; YO26 8EW Attractively renovated village pub next to one of Yorkshire's oldest working greens (cattle roam quite freely); cosy bar with comfortable seats and open fire, Black Sheep Best, Timothy Taylors Landlord and Yorkshire Heart Hearty Bitter (brewed in the village), a dozen wines by the glass, good imaginative food (not Sun evening, can be pricey) using local ingredients including some from own kitchen garden, elegant dining rooms divided by two-way open fire, snug (the oldest part of the building) leads off here with another log fire; children and dogs (in bar) welcome, plenty of tables outside, 12 bedrooms, closed Mon, Tues and evening Sun, otherwise open all day.

OLDFIELD   SE0138
Grouse (01535) 643073
Harehills; 2 miles towards Colne; BD22 0RX Comfortable old pub in undisturbed moorland hamlet; well kept Timothy Taylors ales, 15 gins and enjoyable food from light lunches to good steaks and daily specials, weekday deals, friendly attentive service; children and dogs (in snug) welcome, picnic-sets on terrace with lovely Pennine views, open (and food) all day.

OSMOTHERLEY   SE4597
Golden Lion (01609) 883526
The Green, West End; off A19 N of Thirsk; DL6 3AA Welcoming bustling atmosphere in this attractive 18th-c inn; roomy beamed bar with cushioned wall seats, pews and dining chairs around pubby tables, mirrors on white walls, woodburner, Timothy Taylors Landlord and three changing guests, a dozen wines by the glass, over 15 gins and 45 malt whiskies, good popular food from traditional choices up, two dining rooms; background music; children and dogs (in bar) welcome, benches out at front overlooking village green, more seats on back terrace, popular with walkers (on Cleveland Way and the 40-mile Lyke Wake Walk starts here), seven modern bedrooms, closed Mon and Tues lunchtimes.

OSMOTHERLEY   SE4597
Three Tuns (01609) 883301
South End, off A19 N of Thirsk; DL6 3BN Small stylish pub-restaurant with décor inspired by Charles Rennie Mackintosh; very

good freshly made food in bistro setting with pale oak furniture and panelling, friendly efficient service, flagstoned bar with built-in cushioned wall benches, stripped-pine tables and stone fireplace, well kept ales such as Timothy Taylors, good friendly service; children welcome, dogs in bar, seats out at front and in charming terrace garden, good nearby walks, comfortable bedrooms, closed Mon-Thur.

OSSETT   SE2719
★**Brewers Pride** (01924) 273865
Low Mill Road/Healey Lane (long cul-de-sac by railway sidings, off B6128); WF5 8ND Friendly traditional local with well kept Ossett, Rudgate and several guests, cosy front rooms and flagstoned bar, brewery memorabilia, open fires, good well priced food (not Sun evening) including Tues evening tapas, more upmarket weekend menu in upstairs Millers Restaurant; quiz and pie night Mon, live music first Sun of the month; well behaved children (until 8pm) and dogs welcome, big back garden, near Calder & Hebble Navigation, open all day.

OSSETT   SE2820
Old Vic (01924) 273516
Manor Road, just off Horbury Road; WF5 0AU Friendly four-room roadside pub; well kept Ossett ales and guests from seven pumps, real cider, competitively priced home-cooked food (not Sun evening, Mon), traditional décor with old local photographs, shelves of bottles and antique range; Tues quiz and some live music, pool, darts and sports TV; children and dogs welcome, open all day Fri-Sun, from 4pm other days.

OSSETT   SE2719
Tap (01924) 272215
The Green; WF5 8JS Cosy tap for Ossett Brewery; simple traditional décor with flagstones, bare boards and woodburner, mix of seating including upholstered banquettes and padded stools, photos of other Ossett pubs, their well kept ales and guests plus competitively priced wines by the glass, friendly relaxed atmosphere; children and dogs (on lead) welcome, small car park (other nearby parking can be difficult), open all day Thurs-Sun, from 3pm other days.

OTLEY   SE2045
Old Cock (01943) 464424
Crossgate; LS21 1AA Traditional two-room drinkers' pub with nine mostly local ales and a couple of ciders, also foreign beers and some gluten-free choices, no cooked food but good pork pies and sandwiches, more room upstairs; no under-18s, dogs welcome, open all day.

OTLEY   SE2047
★**Roebuck** (01943) 463063
Roebuck Terrace; LS21 2EY Smartly modernised 18th-c beamed pub; good food

from sandwiches and sharing plates up including range of hearty pies, Black Sheep and three changing local beers, plenty of wines by the glass, friendly efficient service, log fire and woodburner, raftered restaurant with exposed brick walls and mix of old furniture including pews on wood floor; children and dogs (in bar) welcome, wheelchair access, tables out on terrace and small lawn, open all day (closed Mon in winter), food till 6.30pm Sun.

OXENHOPE SE0335
Bay Horse (01535) 642921
Upper Town; BD22 9LN Bustling community pub run by friendly licensees, half a dozen well kept local ales including Timothy Taylors, no food; live music Weds and Thurs, open mike last Sat of month; children, walkers and dogs welcome, seats outside, open all day Sat and Sun, closed weekday lunchtimes.

OXENHOPE SE0434
Dog & Gun (01535) 643159
Off B6141 towards Denholme; BD22 9SN Spacious beautifully placed 17th-c moorland pub, smartly extended and comfortable, with wide choice of enjoyable generously served food from sandwiches to daily specials, cheerful staff, Timothy Taylors range and good selection of malt whiskies, beams, copper, brasses, plates and jugs, big log fire each end, padded settles and stools, glass-covered well in one dining area, wonderful views; quiz nights, theme nights, wine tastings; bedrooms in adjoining hotel, open all day weekends (food all day Sun).

PICKERING SE7983
Black Swan (01751) 798209
Birdgate; YO18 7AL Renovated 18th-c coaching inn with own Great British Breworks beers from on-site brewery, also guests, real ciders and good choice of wines/ gins, enjoyable home-made food from pizzas up, friendly staff, beamed bar with log fire, restaurant and separate cocktail bar; background music; children and dogs welcome, bedrooms, open all day.

PICKERING SE7984
White Swan (01751) 472288
Market Place, just off A170; YO18 7AA Civilised and welcoming 16th-c coaching inn run by same family for pushing four decades; cosy properly pubby bar, sofas and a few tables, panelling and log fire, Black Sheep, Timothy Taylors Landlord and a dozen wines by the glass, second bare-boards room with big bow window and handsome art nouveau iron fireplace, good food (everything made in-house, even ketchup), flagstoned restaurant and next-door deli, efficient friendly staff, residents' lounge in converted beamed barn; children and dogs (in bar) welcome, 21 bedrooms, open all day.

POOL SE2445
★White Hart (0113) 203 7862
Just off A658 S of Harrogate, A659 E of Otley; LS21 1LH Popular light and airy Mitchells & Butlers dining pub (bigger inside than it looks); good food from sharing plates and pizzas to more restauranty dishes, also fixed-price menu, friendly young staff, 25 wines by the glass including champagne, cocktails and three well kept ales, stylishly simple bistro eating areas, armchairs and sofas on bar's flagstones and bare boards, welcoming log fires and relaxing atmosphere; background music; children and dogs welcome, plenty of tables outside, open (and food) all day.

PUDSEY SE2037
Thornhill (0113) 256 5492
Town Gate – Blackett Street; LS28 5NF Updated 17th-c roadside pub with wide range of enjoyable food including sandwiches, pub favourites and burgers, five real ales such as Theakstons and plenty of wines by the glass, friendly efficient staff; quiz Tues and Thurs; children and dogs welcome, seats outside, open (and food) all day.

REDMIRE SE0491
Bolton Arms (01969) 624336
Hargill Lane; DL8 4EA Welcoming village dining pub (former 17th-c farmhouse); enjoyable fairly traditional food at reasonable prices, well kept Black Sheep and guests, efficient friendly service, woodburner in comfortable carpeted bar, attractive dining room; children and dogs welcome, disabled facilities, picnic-sets in small part-paved garden, good walks and handy for Wensleydale Railway and Bolton Castle, five bedrooms (two with views from shared balcony, others in converted outbuilding), open all day.

REETH SE0399
Black Bull (01748) 884213
B6270; W side of village green; DL11 6SZ Popular 17th-c village inn overlooking broad sloping green; Black Sheep, Theakstons and guests, enjoyable reasonably priced food including good Sun carvery, friendly helpful staff, traditional dark beamed flagstoned and carpeted L-shaped front bar, open fires, lovely dales views from dining room; juke box and some live music, pool and darts; children and dogs (in bar) welcome, tables out at front, bedrooms (also with views), open all day.

REETH SE0499
Buck (01748) 884210
Arkengarthdale Road/Silver Street; DL11 6SW Friendly 18th-c coaching inn adjacent to the village green; part-carpeted beamed bar with open fire, up to five well kept ales such as Black Sheep and Timothy Taylors, steps up to dining area serving

enjoyable fairly pubby food; some live music, July beer festival; children welcome, dogs in bar (theirs is Marley), a few tables out in front, hidden walled garden with play equipment, good walking country, ten comfortable bedrooms, open all day Fri-Sun.

RIPLEY   SE2860
Boars Head (01423) 771888
Off A61 Harrogate–Ripon; HG3 3AY
Informal and relaxed old hotel belonging to the Ripley Castle Estate; long bar-bistro with nice mix of dining chairs and tables, walls hung with golf clubs, cricket bats, some jolly cricketing/hunting drawings, a boar's head and interesting religious carving, Theakstons and other local ales, 20 wines by the glass and several malt whiskies, good food using Estate produce, afternoon teas, separate restaurant; children welcome, dogs in bar and bedrooms, pleasant little garden, open all day, food all day Sun.

RIPON   SE3171
One-Eyed Rat (01765) 607704
Allhallowgate; HG4 1LQ Small friendly drinkers' pub with seven well kept changing ales, draught continentals and traditional cider; roaring fire in long narrow bare-boards bar, back carpeted area with piano and TV projector for sports, no food; some live music, quiz nights and a couple of beer festivals; children and dogs (on lead) welcome, outside seating area, open all day Fri-Sun, from 5pm other days.

RIPON   SE3171
Royal Oak (01765) 602284
Kirkgate; HG4 1PB Centrally placed 18th-c coaching inn on pedestrianised street; smart modern décor, Timothy Taylors ales and guests kept well, nice choice of wines and good food from pub staples to more enterprising restauranty dishes, friendly efficient service, split-level dining area; background music; children and dogs (in bar) welcome, seats in courtyard with retractable awning, eight bedrooms, open (and food) all day from 8am.

RISHWORTH   SE0316
Booth Wood (01422) 825600
Oldham Road (A672); HX6 4QU
Welcoming beamed and flagstoned country dining pub; good range of enjoyable food including bargain classics/retro menu served lunchtimes Mon-Sat and till 7pm weekdays, well kept Bradfield Farmers Blonde, Holts Bitter and up to three guests, friendly staff, some leather sofas and wing-back chairs, two blazing woodburners; folk nights and other live music; children welcome.

ROBIN HOOD'S BAY   NZ9504
Bay Hotel (01947) 880278
The Dock, Bay Town; YO22 4SJ Old village inn perched on edge of the bay with fine sea views from cosy picture-window

upstairs bar (Wainwright bar downstairs open too if busy), four real ales including Theakstons, reasonably priced home-made food in bar and separate dining area from sandwiches to blackboard specials, log fires; background music, TV; children and dogs welcome, popular with walkers (at end of the 191-mile Coast to Coast path), lots of tables outside, three bedrooms, steep road down and no parking at bottom, open all day.

ROBIN HOOD'S BAY   NZ9505
★**Laurel** (01947) 880400
Bay Bank; village signed off A171 S of Whitby; YO22 4SE Charming little pub at bottom of row of fishermen's cottages in especially pretty and unspoilt village; beamed main bar with open fire, old local photographs, Victorian prints and brasses, Adnams and Theakstons ales, no food; background music, darts and board games; children in snug bar only, dogs welcome, open all day Fri-Sun, from 2pm other days.

ROBIN HOOD'S BAY   NZ9505
Victoria (01947) 880205
Station Road; YO22 4RL Clifftop Victorian hotel with great bay views; good choice of local beers such as Theakstons, Whitby and York from curved counter in traditional bar, enjoyable freshly made food here or in restaurant (separate evening menu), also a coffee shop/tea room, friendly service; children and dogs welcome, useful car park, play area and picnic-sets in big garden overlooking sea and village, comfortable bedrooms (some with panoramic views), good breakfast, open (and food) all day.

SANDAL   SE3418
Star (01924) 229674
Standbridge Lane; WF2 7DY Friendly buzzy atmosphere at this comfortable 19th-c local; well kept ales including own good Morton Collins microbrews (not always available), simple well priced lunchtime food (evening sharing plates); Tues quiz and some live music; children and dogs welcome, a few seats out at front, more in back garden with decked area, open all day.

SANDHUTTON   SE3882
★**Kings Arms** (01845) 587887
A167, a mile N of A61 Thirsk–Ripon; YO7 4RW Bustling village inn run by father and son with focus on enjoyable food; easy-going bar with modern ladder-back chairs around light pine tables, old photographs of the pub and unusual circular woodburner in one corner, three ales such as Black Sheep, 11 wines by the glass, efficient friendly service, two similar furnished dining rooms; background music, TV, darts and board games; children and dogs (in bar) welcome, beer garden and secure bike storage, bedrooms, open all day (can get packed on Thirsk race days), no food Sun evening.

SAWLEY   SE2467
Sawley Arms (01765) 620642
*Village signposted off B6265 W of
Ripon; HG4 3EQ* Popular village dining
pub with good variety of well liked food
from sandwiches and hot ciabattas up,
Timothy Taylors, Theakstons and a couple
of guest beers, a dozen wines by the glass,
welcoming helpful staff, comfortable
modernised interior with log fire and
conservatory; quiz first Sun of month;
children welcome, seats on terrace and in
attractive garden, close to Fountains Abbey
(NT), four bedrooms, open (and food) all
day, breakfast from 8.45am.

SCARBOROUGH   TA0588
Golden Ball (01723) 353899
Sandside, opposite harbour; YO11 1PG
Tall mock-Tudor seafront pub with good
harbour and bay views from highly prized
window seats (busy in summer), panelled
bar with good mix of visitors and locals, some
nautical memorabilia and open fire, well
kept low-priced Sam Smiths; family lounge
upstairs, tables out in yard, open all day.

SCARBOROUGH   TA0388
Stumble Inn 07837 716774
Westborough; YO11 1TS Simple one-room
micropub with friendly chatty atmosphere;
half a dozen well kept changing ales
and extensive range of ciders/perries,
knowledgeable landlord happy to offer
tasters, walls and ceiling adorned with
hundreds of pump clips; no food or under-18s,
dogs welcome (except Fri and Sat evenings);
café-style tables out on pavement, open all
day and handy for the station.

SCORTON   NZ2500
Farmers Arms (01748) 812533
Northside; DL10 6DW Comfortably
modernised little pub in terrace of old
cottages overlooking green; well kept Sharps
Doom Bar and a guest, decent wines and
good freshly made food including popular Sun
lunch, friendly accommodating staff, bar with
open fire, darts and dominoes, restaurant;
background music, fortnightly quiz; children
and dogs welcome, open all day weekends,
closed Mon lunchtime.

SCORTON   NZ2400
Heifer (01748) 811357
B1263; High Row; DL10 6DH
Welcoming beamed pub facing village
green; comfortably updated bar and back
restaurant, good food from varied menu
including sandwiches and vegetarian
choices, Fri steak night and other evening

deals, well kept Theakstons and Timothy
Taylors ales and decent range of wines and
gins, friendly helpful service; children and
dogs (in bar) welcome, closed Mon.

SCOTTON   SE3259
Guy Fawkes Arms (01423) 868400
Main Street; HG5 9HU Welcoming pub
in village where Guy Fawkes lived; very
popular food (booking advised) including
good value set lunch and early bird offer
Weds-Fri, well kept Black Sheep and three
local guests; children and dogs (in bar – ring
first) welcome, open from 4pm Mon and Tues
(no food those days), otherwise open all day,
kitchen closes 7pm Sun.

SETTLE   SD8163
Golden Lion (01729) 822203
*B6480 (main road through town), off
A65 bypass; BD24 9DU* Market town inn
with grand staircase sweeping down into
baronial-style high-beamed bar, lovely log
fire, second bar with bare boards and dark
half-panelling, lots of old local photographs
and another fire, well kept Thwaites, guest
ales and decent wines by the glass, good
value food from deli boards to specials,
helpful friendly staff; live music; children
and dogs welcome, courtyard tables,
14 bedrooms, open (and food) all day.

SETTLE   SD8263
Talbot Arms (01729) 823924
High Street; BD24 9EX Friendly
place with six well kept ales including
Theakstons and local brews such as Settle
and Three Peaks, real cider, reasonably
priced traditional food from sandwiches
up including some evening deals, pubby
furniture on carpet, woodburner in
impressive stone fireplace, parquet-floored
games area with pool and darts; live music,
quiz first Mon of the month; children and
dogs welcome, picnic-sets in two-level back
garden, open (and food) all day, convenient
for station.

SHEFFIELD   SK3487
Bath (0114) 249 5151
*Victoria Street, off Glossop Road;
S3 7QL* Victorian corner pub with well
restored 1930s interior; two rooms and a
drinking corridor, black and white floor tiles,
traditional wall benches and some leaded
light partitions, well kept Thornbridge and
guests, traditional ciders, 30 malt whiskies,
simple snacky food including hot roast
pork sandwiches Fri and Sat, friendly staff;
live jazz/blues/folk Weds, quiz Thurs; dogs
welcome, closed Sun and bank holiday Mon,
otherwise open all day.

If we know a pub is cash-only, we say so. This is very rare: almost everywhere
accepts credit and debit cards now.

SHEFFIELD SK3687
Fat Cat (0114) 249 4801
Alma Street; S3 8SA Cheerfully busy
little Victorian pub with up to a dozen
interesting beers on handpump including
next-door Kelham Island, also draught/
bottled continentals and traditional cider,
friendly knowledgeable staff, straightforward
bargain food (not Sun evening) also catering
for vegetarians/vegans/gluten-free; Mon quiz;
seats in back courtyard, open all day.

SHEFFIELD SK3588
Harlequin 07794 156916
Nursery Street; S3 8GG Welcoming
open-plan corner pub owned by nearby Exit
33, their well kept ales and great selection
of changing guests (beer festivals), also
bottled imports and more than 20 real ciders/
perries, 40 rums, 40 gins, 20 whiskies and
straightforward cheap food including Sun
roasts (no credit cards); weekend live music,
jazz night second Thurs of month, quiz Weds;
no under-18s after 3pm, dogs welcome,
outside seating, open all day.

SHEFFIELD SK4086
Kelham Island Tavern
(0114) 272 2482 *Kelham Island; S3 8RY*
Busy little pub with around 13 interesting
ales and good range of bottled beers, two
rooms with simple pubby furnishings,
decent lunchtime food; Mon quiz, folk night
every other Sun, children till 9pm and dogs
welcome, flower-filled back courtyard garden,
open all day.

SHEFFIELD SK3290
★ New Barrack (0114) 232 4225
Penistone Road, Hillsborough; S6 2GA
Friendly buoyant pub with nine real ales
including Castle Rock, traditional cider,
lots of bottled Belgian beers and good value
traditional food; comfortable front lounge
with log fire and upholstered seats on old
pine floors, another fire in tap room, function
room (own bar); live music and comedy and
film nights, pool, darts, sports TV; children
(till 9pm) and dogs welcome, attractive
little walled garden, parking nearby can
be difficult, closed lunchtimes Mon-Thur,
otherwise open all day.

SHEFFIELD SK3186
Ranmoor (0114) 230 1325
*Fulwood Road (across from church);
S10 3GD* Comfortable and welcoming
19th-c local; open-plan interior with etched
bay windows, large mirrors and period
fireplaces, four well kept ales including
Abbeydale and Bradfield, enjoyable food; quiz
night; two outside seating areas, open all day.

SHEFFIELD SK3487
Red Deer (0114) 272 2890
Pitt Street; S1 4DD Friendly traditional
backstreet pub among university buildings;

bigger inside than it looks with eight well
kept ales and a real cider from central bar,
good value food (all day weekends) from
sandwiches and snacks up and catering for
vegetarians/vegans; Tues quiz, live music,
comedy nights, board games; tables outside,
dogs welcome, open all day (till 1am Fri, Sat).

SHEFFIELD SK3185
Rising Sun (0114) 230 3855
Fulwood Road; S10 3QA Extended
community pub with 11 ales (several from
Abbeydale), traditional ciders and good
selection of craft beers, tasty fairly priced
food, friendly service; background music, quiz
Weds and Sun; children and dogs welcome, a
few tables out in front, more on back terrace,
open all day.

SHEFFIELD SK3586
Sheffield Tap (0114) 273 7558
Station, platform 1B; S1 2BP
Busy station bar in restored Edwardian
refreshment room, popular for its extensive
range of international beers on draught and
in bottles, also own Tapped ales from visible
microbrewery and plenty of guests including
Thornbridge, real ciders, knowledgeable
helpful staff, snacky food, spacious tiled
interior with vaulted ceiling; children (until
8pm) and dogs welcome; open all day.

SHEFFIELD SK3687
Wellington (0114) 249 2295
*Henry Street; by Shalesmoor tram stop;
S3 7EQ* Traditional little 19th-c corner pub;
well kept Neepsend ales and guests from
seven handpumps, proper cider, friendly
staff, coal fire in lounge, some photographs
of old Sheffield; tables out behind in pretty
courtyard, open all day Fri-Sun, from 3pm
Mon-Thurs.

SHEFFIELD SK3584
White Lion (0114) 255 1500
London Road; S2 4HT Terrace-row pub
dating from the late 18th c with various
small lounges and snugs off central corridor,
ten well kept changing ales (marked on
blackboard), traditional ciders and good
selection of whiskies, friendly relaxed
atmosphere; backgammon, board games,
darts, dominoes, cribbage, regular live music
in back room, Weds quiz; children and dogs
welcome, open all day from 4pm (noon Sat,
2pm Sun).

SHELLEY SE2112
★ Three Acres (01484) 602606
*Roydhouse (not signed); from B6116
towards Skelmanthorpe, turn left in
Shelley (signposted Flockton, Elmley,
Elmley Moor), go up lane for 2 miles
towards radio mast; HD8 8LR* Civilised
former coaching inn with emphasis on hotel
and dining side; beamed lounge bar with
bare boards and open fire, tankards above
counter serving well kept ales such as Black

Sheep and Timothy Taylors, 40 malt whiskies and up to 17 wines by the glass from serious list, several formal dining rooms, wide choice of good if expensive food from lunchtime sandwiches up, competent friendly staff; conferences, weddings and other events; children welcome, fine moorland setting and lovely views, smart well equipped bedrooms.

SHERIFF HUTTON   SE6566
Highwayman (01347) 878328
The Square; YO60 6QZ Friendly family-run pub with hearty helpings of good value home-made food (not Sun evening, Mon) from sandwiches and baguettes up, a house beer from Belhaven (Stand & Deliver), Theakstons Best and a guest kept well, beamed interior with bar, restaurant and games room (pool and darts); Thurs quiz, TV; children and dogs welcome, picnic-sets in big garden, attractive village with castle ruins and 12th-c church, open all day weekends, closed Mon lunchtime.

SHIPLEY   SE1437
Fannys Ale House (01274) 591419
Saltaire Road; BD18 3JN Extended bare-boards alehouse on two floors, cosy and friendly, with eight well kept beers including Timothy Taylors, bottled imports and traditional ciders, gas lighting, brewery memorabilia, log fire and woodburner; dogs welcome, handy for Salts Mill, closed Mon lunchtime, otherwise open all day and can get crowded weekend evenings.

SHIPLEY   SE1337
Salt Bar & Kitchen (01274) 582111
Bingley Road; BD18 4DH Cavernous glass-fronted tramshed conversion (former Hop) on edge of Saltaire World Heritage Site; high pitched ceilings with some rather grand chandeliers, raised seating areas and stairs up to gallery, well kept Ossett ales along with own brews from central curved counter, good choice of enjoyable food including sandwiches, sharing boards and wood-fired pizzas, friendly helpful service; live music and quiz nights; no under-18s after 7pm, dogs allowed in tap room, picnic-sets out at front among the old tram tracks, open (and food) all day Sat, Sun, otherwise from 4pm.

SICKLINGHALL   SE3648
Scotts Arms (01937) 582100
Main Street; LS22 4BD Popular 17th-c roadside village pub; enjoyable generously served food (all day weekends) including blackboard specials, rambling interior with interesting nooks and crannies, low beams, old timbers and log fires (one in lovely fireplace), four well kept mainstream ales, good wine range, friendly efficient staff; children and dogs welcome, wheelchair

access from behind, disabled loos, big garden with teak furniture on paved terrace, open all day.

SINNINGTON   SE7485
★Fox & Hounds (01751) 431577
Off A170 W of Pickering; YO62 6SQ Popular 18th-c coaching house in pretty village; carpeted beamed bar with two-way woodburner, comfortable seating, various pictures and old artefacts, well kept ales such as Abbeydale, Black Sheep and Marstons Wainwright, several wines by the glass, good attractively presented food with both pubby and more restaurant choices, friendly helpful service, lounge and smart restaurant; children and dogs (in bar) welcome, picnic-sets out at front and in garden, ten comfortable bedrooms.

SKIPTON   SD9851
Beer Engine 07834 456134
Albert Street; BD23 1JD Popular shop-front micropub with simple décor, interesting range of five changing ales, bottled imports and real ciders, good choice of wines by the glass too, friendly knowledgeable staff; occasional live music; children and dogs welcome, closed Mon and Tues, otherwise open all day.

SKIPTON   SD9851
Narrow Boat (01756) 797922
Victoria Street; pub signed down alley off Coach Street; BD23 1JE Popular pub down cobbled alley by the canal basin; interesting selection of eight real ales including Ilkley, Okells and Timothy Taylors, also fruit, wheat and other craft beers with some limited editions and exclusives, traditional cider/perry, leather-upholstered chairs, pews and stools around wooden tables on bare boards, upstairs quite smart galleried area with interesting canal mural, generous helpings of enjoyable food at fair prices; background music, folk night Mon, live music Thurs; children (if eating) and dogs welcome, picnic-sets under front colonnade, open all day, food all day Sat, till 6pm Sun.

SKIPTON   SD9851
Woolly Sheep (01756) 700966
Sheep Street; BD23 1HY Bustling narrow pub just off the High Street; extensive Timothy Taylors range kept well, guest ales too, premium lagers such as ABK weissbier on tap plus several wines by the glass and good choice of gins, mocktails and cocktails, friendly service; two beamed bars off flagstone passage, exposed brickwork, coal fire in stone fireplace, split-level dining area at the back serving enjoyable fairly priced food from pub standards up; children welcome, covered, fairy-lit courtyard

---

We say if we know a pub allows dogs.

and outside bar, 12 nice bedrooms, good breakfast, open (and food) all day, shuts 1am Fri, Sat.

SLEDMERE   SE9364
★ **Triton** (01377) 236078
B1252/B1253 junction, NW of Great Driffield; YO25 3XQ Handsome 18th-c inn near Sledmere House and its estate; open-plan bar with old-fashioned atmosphere, dark wooden furniture on tartan carpet, a multitude of clocks ranging from grandfather to cuckoo, lots of plates, paintings and pictures, suit of armour in one part, open fire, Greene King, Timothy Taylors, Tetleys and Wold Top, some 50 gins, big helpings of popular traditional food (only take bookings in separate restaurant), friendly helpful staff; children welcome till 8pm, tables on forecourt, no dogs, five good bedrooms, generous breakfast, open all day Sun till 9pm (food till 6.30pm), closed Mon.

SLINGSBY   SE6975
Grapes (01653) 628076
Off B1257 Malton–Hovingham; Railway Street; YO62 4AL Busy Georgian village pub with good sensibly priced food from traditional menu (not Sun evening), well kept Timothy Taylors and Theakstons on handpump and Elland Slingsby Pale tapped from the cask plus guests, cheerful staff, bare boards, flagstones and painted beams, nice mix of old furniture and some eye-catching features including a bar counter made from a church organ case and a tusky boar's head above one of the woodburners; monthly quiz and music nights; children and dogs (in bar and snug) welcome, tables (lots under cover) and pizza oven out behind, open all day Fri-Sun, closed Mon.

SNAITH   SE6422
Brewers Arms (01405) 862404
Pontefract Road; DN14 9JS Refurbished open-plan Georgian inn adjacent to Old Mill brewery and serving its ales; decent home-made food from lunchtime sandwiches and jacket potatoes to international and pub standards at dinner; friendly helpful staff; children welcome in eating areas (play area), picnic tables out at front and in back garden, six attractive well appointed bedrooms, open all day.

SNAPE   SE2684
★ **Castle Arms** (01677) 470270
Off B6268 Masham–Bedale; DL8 2TB Wisteria-festooned pub in pretty village; flagstoned bar with beams, open fire, cosy red armchairs, Marstons-related ales and enjoyable food from sandwiches up, friendly regulars and staff, dining room (also flagstoned) with dark tables and chairs and another fire; children and dogs (in bar and tap room) welcome, picnic-sets out at front among pretty plants and in courtyard, fine walks in Yorkshire Dales and on North York

Moors, nine good bedrooms in converted barn; open all day Sat, closed Mon lunchtime.

SOUTH DALTON   SE9645
★ **Pipe & Glass** (01430) 810246
West End; brown sign to pub off B1248 NW of Beverley; HU17 7PN Attractive tucked-away village pub with emphasis on landlord-chef's excellent Michelin-starred food (full menu available in the bar, including lunchtime sandwiches); beamed and bow-windowed bar, copper pans hanging above woodburner in sizeable fireplace, cushioned window seats and high-backed wooden dining chairs around mix of tables, Black Sheep, a house beer (Two Chefs) from Great Yorkshire and a couple of guests, discerning food-friendly wine list, 40 or so malt whiskies, friendly staff, contemporary area beyond with leather chesterfields and another woodburner leading to airy restaurant overlooking parkland; background music; children welcome, tables on lawn and front terrace, stylish bedrooms and suites, charming village with 62-metre church spire, closed Mon, otherwise open (and some food) all day, kitchen closes 4pm Sun.

SOUTH KILVINGTON   SE4284
Old Oak Tree (01845) 523276
Stockton Road (A61); YO7 2NL Spacious low-ceilinged family-run inn convenient for the A1 with three linked rooms and long back conservatory; ample choice of good honest food from sandwiches up (much of it locally sourced), three well kept beers including Theakstons, friendly staff; children and dogs (in bar) welcome, tables on terrace with steps down to sloping lawn, five bedrooms, open (and food) all day Sun.

SOWERBY BRIDGE   SE0623
Hogs Head (01422) 836585
Stanley Street; HX6 2AH Lovely warm atmosphere in this attractive brewpub in former 18th-c maltings with a strong all-round drinks offer; one large room with heavy beams, comfortable chesterfields, exposed brickwork, bare boards and big woodburner, brewery visible behind glass, five of their good beers and guests, no food; dogs welcome, open all day weekends, from 3pm Mon-Fri.

STANBURY   SE0037
Old Silent (01535) 647437
Hob Lane; BD22 0HW Square stone dining inn with courtyard and attractively refurbished bedrooms, convenient for Howarth and Brontë country; enjoyable good value food and a couple of Timothy Taylors ales, linked rooms with beams, flagstones, mullioned windows and open fires, restaurant and conservatory; children and dogs welcome, eight bedrooms (some with fireplaces and moorland views), open all day but check times as settling in under new management.

STAVELEY SE3662
Royal Oak (01423) 340267
*Signed off A6055 Knaresborough–
Boroughbridge; HG5 9LD* Popular pub
in village conservation area under friendly
management; beams, panelling and open
fires, broad bay windows overlooking small
front garden, well kept Black Sheep, Timothy
Taylors and two local guests, several wines by
the glass, good fairly priced food in bar and
restaurant; children and dogs welcome, open
all day, food till 7pm Sun.

STILLINGTON SE5867
★ Bay Tree (01347) 811394
*Main Street; leave York on outer ring
road (A1237) to Scarborough, first exit
on left signposted B1363 to Helmsley;
YO61 1JU* Cottagey pub-restaurant in
pretty village's main street; modern bar
areas with comfortable cushioned wall seats
and kitchen chairs around mix of tables,
central gas-effect coal fire, real ales such as
Black Sheep, several wines by the glass and
extensive range of gins, highly rated seasonal
modern British and pubby food, steps up to
country-chic dining area, larger conservatory-
style restaurant behind; background music;
children and dogs (in bar) welcome, wicker
furniture in garden and picnic-sets at front,
closed Sun evening and Mon.

STOKESLEY NZ5208
White Swan (01642) 714985
West End; TS9 5BL Good Captain Cook
ales brewed at this attractive 18th-c flower-
decked local; traditional L-shaped bar with
three relaxing seating areas, log fire, assorted
memorabilia and nice bar counter with carved
panels; Tues open mike, Weds quiz, Thurs live
music, beer festivals, darts and sports TV; no
children, dogs welcome, open all day.

SUTTON UPON DERWENT SE7047
★ St Vincent Arms (01904) 608349
*Main Street (B1228 SE of York);
YO41 4BN* Busy pub with up to seven well
kept ales plus rotating guests, over 20
wines by the glass and a menu of popular
pub classics supplemented by blackboard
specials, friendly efficient service; parlour-
style front bar with panelling, traditional
high-backed settles, copper-topped tables
and cushioned bow-window seat, gas-effect
coal fire, another lounge and separate dining
room; children and dogs (in bar) welcome,
garden tables, convenient for Yorkshire Air
Museum.

TAN HILL NY8906
Tan Hill Inn (01833) 533007
*Arkengarthdale Road, Reeth–Brough,
at junction Keld/West Stonesdale Road;
DL11 6ED* Basic old stone pub (Britain's
highest) in wonderful bleak setting on
Pennine Way and W2W cycle route – often
snowbound; full of bric-a-brac and interesting

photographs, simple sturdy furniture on
flagstones and an ever-burning log fire with
prized stone side seats, five well kept local
ales including one badged for them from
Tirril, good pubby food, family room; regular
live bands (major music festival planned
for July 2021); children and dogs welcome,
picnic tables and dining dome, bedrooms,
bunk rooms, campervan parking and wild
camping, wandering ducks and sheep
(Swaledale sheep show here last Thurs in
May), open (and some food) all day, can get
very crowded.

THIRSK SE4282
Golden Fleece (01845) 523108
Market Place; YO7 1LL Handsome brick
coaching inn; good food in bar, restaurant
and coffee shop from cakes, snacks and
sharing plates up including pub favourites
and stone-baked pizzas, breakfasts and
afternoon teas, friendly helpful service, ales
such as Black Sheep and Coach House, craft
beers and over 20 wines by the glass, good
range of gins too, clean contemporary décor
in bar and separate dining rooms, view across
marketplace from bay windows; children and
dogs (in some areas) welcome, part-covered
back courtyard, many bedrooms, open (and
food) all day.

THIXENDALE SE8461
Cross Keys (01377) 288272
*Off A166 3 miles N of Fridaythorpe;
YO17 9TG* Unspoilt country pub in deep
valley below the rolling wolds – popular
with walkers (there's a drying room); cosy
and relaxed L-shaped bar with fitted wall
seats, well kept Tetleys and a couple of
guests, generous uncomplicated blackboard
food; no under-14s or dogs inside, views
from big back garden, handy for Wharram
Percy earthworks, comfortable bedrooms
in converted stables, good breakfast, closed
Mon-Thurs lunchtimes (unless pre-booked
by walking group).

THOLTHORPE SE4766
New Inn (01347) 838329
Flawith Road; YO61 1SL Updated beamed
village-green pub with simple attractive
interior, log fires in bar and candlelit
restaurant; good food (special diets catered
for) from sandwiches and wood-fired pizzas
up including popular Sun lunch, Weds
evening pizza deal, Fri evening fish and
chips, a couple of ales, friendly helpful staff;
Sun quiz; bakery and small shop, children
welcome, closed Mon and lunchtime Tues.

THORNTON SE0933
Ring o' Bells (01274) 832296
*Hill Top Road, W of village, and N of
B6145; BD13 3QL* Former Wesleyan
chapel house in hilltop position with long
views towards Shipley and Bingley; series
of linked rooms including conservatory-like
area, pleasing contemporary pub décor, well

thought-of British food with modern touches from favourites up including vegetarian/vegan choices and good value set menu, beers such as Timothy Taylors Landlord from well stocked bar, friendly efficient service; children and dogs welcome, comfortable seating outside, closed Mon, otherwise open (and food) all day, kitchen shuts 6.30pm Sun.

THORNTON   SE0832
White Horse (01274) 834268
Well Heads; BD13 3SJ Deceptively large country pub popular for its wide choice of good food including early bird menu (till 6.30pm Mon-Thurs), five well kept Timothy Taylors ales, pleasant helpful staff, four separate areas, two with log fires, busy bustling atmosphere; children welcome, upstairs lavatories (disabled ones on ground level), also disabled parking, open all day, food all day weekends (till 7.45pm Sun).

THORNTON DALE   SE8383
New Inn (01751) 474226
The Square; YO18 7LF Friendly early 18th-c beamed coaching inn (packed weekend evenings); three well kept ales and good fairly traditional food cooked by landlord including evening specials and deals; children and dogs (in bar) welcome, courtyard tables, six bedrooms and self-catering cottage, pretty village on edge of Dalby Forest, open all day, food all day Sun.

THORNTON IN LONSDALE SD6873
Marton Arms (015242) 42204
Off A65 just NW of Ingleton; LA6 3PB Refurbished old pub opposite 13th-c church where Arthur Conan Doyle was married; half a dozen real ales and around 60 gins, generous helpings of enjoyable 'fork to field' food from sandwiches, snacks and pub favourites up, friendly staff, opened-up interior keeping beams and some exposed stonework, mix of wooden tables and chairs on polished wood floor, kitchen tables and rugs on flagstones in restaurant, logburner; background and some live music (Sat); children and dogs welcome, picnic-sets on front terrace and back lawn, great walking country, 11 comfortable bedrooms, open all day, food all day Fri-Sun.

TIMBLE   SE1852
★ Timble Inn (01943) 880530
Off Otley–Blubberhouses moors road; LS21 2NN Smartly restored 18th-c dining inn tucked away in quiet farmland hamlet; good food from lunchtime sandwiches and pub favourites up including well aged local beef (booking essential, can be pricey), ales such as Black Sheep, Ilkley and Saltaire; children welcome, no dogs at food times,

good walks from the door, 11 well appointed bedrooms, closed Mon and evening Tues.

TONG   SE2230
Greyhound (0113) 285 2427
Tong Lane; BD4 0RR Traditional low-beamed and flagstoned local by village cricket field; generous helpings of enjoyable good value food, can eat in bar or cosy dining room, well kept regional ales and several wines by the glass, efficient friendly service; children welcome, no dogs inside, tables outside, open all day.

TOPCLIFFE   SE4076
Angel (01845) 578000
Off A1, take A168 to Thirsk, after 3 miles follow signs for Topcliffe; Long Street; YO7 3RW Part of the West Park Inns group; softly lit bare-boards bar with log fire, four mainly local ales and a dozen wines by the glass, enjoyable food in carpeted grill restaurant including lunchtime/early evening deal, cheerful helpful service; background music, various themed food evenings and comedy night (usually first Tues of month); children welcome, nice garden, 16 bedrooms, open all day (food all day Sun till 8pm).

TOWTON   SE4839
Rockingham Arms (01937) 530948
A162 Tadcaster–Ferrybridge; LS24 9PB Comfortable 18th-c roadside village pub with good home-made food from lunchtime baguettes up, efficient friendly service, ales such as Black Sheep and Yorkshire Heart, back conservatory overlooking garden; children and dogs welcome, handy for Towton Battlefield, open all day, no food Sun evening.

ULLESKELF   SE5140
Ulleskelf Arms (01937) 835059
Church Fenton Lane; LS24 9DS Village pub recently renovated in pleasant contemporary style with nice upholstery, exposed brickwork and log burner, good home-made food including daily specials, guest street-food vendors and Mon pie night, three well kept ales such as Tetleys; background music, quiz and other events; children, walkers and dogs welcome, beer garden behind, open all day Sun, closed lunchtimes Mon and Tues – but call to check times.

WAKEFIELD   SE3417
Castle (01924) 256981
Barnsley Road, Sandal; WF2 6AS Popular roadside dining pub with good food including noteworthy vegan menu, four well kept changing ales, friendly staff and pleasant relaxed atmosphere, colourful modern décor in beamed rooms, all seating comfortably upholstered; unobtrusive

background music; children welcome, dogs in bar, rattan-style furniture on paved back terrace overlooking bowling green, also out front, open (and food) all day.

WAKEFIELD SE3320
Fernandes Brewery Tap
(01924) 386348 *Avison Yard, Kirkgate; WF1 1UA* Unremarkable exterior conceals inviting beer palace in former malthouse now owned by Ossett but still brewing rated Fernandes ales in the cellar, also interesting guest beers, bottled imports and traditional ciders; ground-floor bar with flagstones, bare brick and panelling, downstairs Bier Keller (evenings Fri, Sat) and original raftered top-floor bar with some unusual breweriana including old pub signs; quiz plus lots of beer and music events and a Feb rhubarb festival; no children, dogs welcome, open all day Fri-Sun, from 4pm other days.

WAKEFIELD SE3220
Harrys Bar
(01924) 373773 *Westgate; WF1 1EL* Cheery little one-room local with good selection of real ales and bottled beers, stripped-brick walls, open fire; live music Mon and Weds; small back garden, open all day Sun, from 5pm Mon-Thurs, 4pm Fri-Sat.

WALTON SE4447
Fox & Hounds
(01937) 842192 *Hall Park Road, off back road Wetherby–Tadcaster; LS23 7DQ* Popular dining pub with good reasonably priced food from sandwiches to specials (should book Sun lunch), well kept ales such as Black Sheep and Timothy Taylors, friendly thriving atmosphere; children welcome, handy A1 stop, closed Mon.

WALTON SE3517
New Inn
(01924) 255447 *Shay Lane; WF2 6LA* Open-plan village pub with friendly uniformed staff and buoyant atmosphere; seven well kept mainly local ales, many from Ossett including Yorkshire Blonde and seasonal offers, decent wines by the glass and some premium gins, extensive choice of good reasonably priced food from sandwiches and sharing plates up, stylish dining area in building behind with own terrace; music, food and drink events; children welcome, dogs in bar, seats out in front and in lawned garden, open (and food) all day.

WARLEY TOWN SE0524
Maypole
(01422) 835861 *Signed off A646 just W of Halifax; HX2 7RZ* Popular and welcoming village dining pub; generous helpings of good reasonably priced food from fairly traditional menu including lunchtime/early evening set deal (Tues-Fri), well kept ales such as Bradfield and Timothy Taylors, efficient friendly young staff, comfortable open-plan

interior with two-way woodburner; children welcome, open all day Fri-Sun, closed Mon lunchtime, food till 7.30pm Sun.

WASS SE5579
Stapylton Arms
(01347) 868280 *Back road W of Ampleforth; or follow brown sign for Byland Abbey off A170 Thirsk–Helmsley; YO61 4BE* Whitewashed village pub with two bustling bars, beams, flagstones and log fires, a couple of ales such as Helmsley and Theakstons, ten or so wines by the glass from extensive list, restaurant in 18th-c granary serving generous helpings of good freshly made food from lunchtime sandwiches to daily specials, friendly attentive staff; children welcome, no dogs, pretty village and surrounding countryside, near ruins of Byland Abbey (EH), three comfortable well equipped bedrooms.

WATH-IN-NIDDERDALE SE1467
★Sportsmans Arms
(01423) 711306 *Nidderdale road off B6265 in Pateley Bridge; village and pub signposted over hump-back bridge, on right after a couple of miles; HG3 5PP* Civilised and beautifully located hotel and restaurant with well priced rooms run by long-serving owners; although most emphasis on the excellent food and bedrooms, it does have a proper welcoming bar with open fire, well kept Black Sheep and Timothy Taylors, Thatcher's cider, lots of wines by the glass (extensive list) and 40 or so malt whiskies, also a highly rated ploughman's and other bar food, helpful hospitable staff, elegant dining room; background music; children welcome, dogs in bar, benches and tables outside, pretty garden with croquet, own fishing rights on River Nidd.

WEAVERTHORPE SE9670
Blue Bell
(01944) 738204 *Village signed off A64 Malton–Scarborough at Sherburn; Main Road; YO17 8EX* Upscale dining pub on village green, quite ornate in parts, with good attractively presented food and fine choice of wines (many by the glass including champagne), well kept Tetleys, Timothy Taylors and guest, good range of ports and whiskies, cosy cheerful bar with open fire, intimate back restaurant, friendly attentive staff; 12 bedrooms (six in annexe), interesting village, closed Sun evening, Mon and Tues lunchtime.

WEAVERTHORPE SE9771
Star
(01944) 738346 *Village signed off A64 Malton–Scarborough at Sherburn; YO17 8EY* Modernised village pub with enjoyable fairly priced food including stone-baked pizzas and good Tues curry night, a couple of well kept Wold Top ales, friendly service, pleasant bar with woodburner and small area for darts,

recently upgraded restaurant with fresh light feel, children and dogs welcome, picnic-sets on front grass by little stream, four updated bedrooms, closed Mon and lunchtimes (apart from Sun).

WENSLEY SE0989
Three Horseshoes (01969) 622327
A684; DL8 4HJ Old whitewashed village pub with neat beamed and flagstoned bar; five well kept ales including Theakstons and Wensleydale, enjoyable straightforward food at reasonable prices from sandwiches up (reduced menu Mon evening), friendly helpful service, woodburner and open fire; children and dogs welcome, lovely Wensleydale views from paved terrace, popular with walkers, open all day.

WEST TANFIELD SE2678
Bruce Arms (01677) 470325
Main Street (A6108 N of Ripon); HG4 5JH Smart dining pub (18th-c coaching inn) under same ownership as the nearby Bull; good restaurant-style food served by friendly attentive staff, 'fizzy Fridays' with champagne/prosecco and gourmet nibbles, well kept Theakstons and Timothy Taylors, local Thornborough cider, good range of wines, gins and malt whiskies; terrace tables, three comfortable bedrooms, good breakfast, closed Mon, Tues and Weds lunchtimes; B&B continued during 2020 covid restrictions but pub operations were on hold as we went to press.

WEST TANFIELD SE2678
Bull (01677) 470678
Church Street (A6108 N of Ripon); HG4 5JQ Busy pub in picturesque riverside setting (in 1699 it was formed out of a ferryman's cottage); simple décor in flagstoned bar and slightly raised dining area with dark furniture and floorboards, popular fairly standard food (all day Sat, till 7pm Sun), well kept Black Sheep and Theakstons; background and live music once or twice a month (Sun); children (away from bar) and dogs welcome, tables on terraces in attractive garden sloping steeply to River Ure and its old bridge, five bedrooms, open all day weekends.

WEST WITTON SE0688
Fox & Hounds (01969) 623650
Main Street (A684); DL8 4LP Welcoming traditional 17th-c local; central coal fire dividing bar from games area (darts and juke box), bottles on delft shelving, well kept Black Sheep, Theakstons, Yorkshire Dales and guests, Weston's cider, enjoyable reasonably priced pubby food from baked potatoes up, dining room with inglenook;

children and dogs welcome, open all day weekends.

WEST WITTON SE0588
★ **Wensleydale Heifer** (01969) 622322
A684 W of Leyburn; DL8 4LS Stylish restaurant-with-rooms rather than pub, but can pop in for a drink; excellent food with emphasis on fish/seafood and grills (not cheap and best to book), also lunchtime/early evening set menu, sandwiches and snacks, good wines, cosy dining bar with Black Sheep and a house beer brewed by Yorkshire Dales, much bigger and more formal restaurant, attentive helpful service; children welcome, dogs in some areas and bedrooms, 13 well equipped bedrooms (back ones quietest), generous breakfast, open all day.

WESTOW SE7565
Blacksmiths Arms (01653) 619606
Off A64 York–Malton; Main Street; YO60 7NE Updated 18th-c pub well run by local farming family; attractive beamed bar with woodburner in brick fireplace, nicely presented food including own baking from lunchtime sandwiches up, signature steaks matured on the premises, well kept beers such as Black Sheep and Theakstons, friendly helpful service, restaurant; children welcome, no dogs inside, picnic-sets on side terrace, holiday cottage behind, closed Mon, otherwise open all day.

WHITBY NZ8911
Abbey Wharf (01947) 600306
Market Place; YO22 4DD Steps up to airy modern bar-restaurant (former Burberry factory) with lots of glass and exposed timberwork; good selection of ales on handpump (perhaps Abbey Wharf, Sharps, Titanic) from well stocked tile-fronted bar, enjoyable food including signature fish/seafood (takeaway fish and chips available) and chargrills (they add a service charge), friendly staff, mezzanine floor with own bar; maybe weekend live bands; children and dogs welcome, small terrace overlooking harbour, open (and food) all day.

WHITBY NZ9011
Black Horse (01947) 602906
Church Street; YO22 4BH Small traditional two-room pub, much older than its Victorian frontage, and previously a funeral parlour and brothel; friendly and down to earth with five changing ales (often Adnams Southwold, Black Dog Rhatas, Whitby Whaler), small-batch craft beers, continental bottled beers and a proper cider, range of Yorkshire tapas, tins of snuff for sale; dogs welcome, four cosy bedrooms, open all day.

If you report on a pub that's not a featured entry, please tell us any lunchtimes or evenings when it doesn't serve bar food.

WHITBY   NZ9011
Duke of York (01947) 600324
Church Street, Harbour East Side;
YO22 4DE Busy pub in fine harbourside
position, great views and handy for the
famous 199 steps leading up to the abbey;
comfortable beamed lounge bar with
benches, red carpet and old photos, well
kept ales such as Helmsley, Ossett and
Whitby, decent wines and several malt
whiskies, enjoyable straightforward bar food
at reasonable prices; background music, TV;
children welcome, bedrooms overlooking
water, no nearby parking, open (and food)
all day.

WHITBY   NZ8911
Station Inn (01947) 600498
New Quay Road; YO21 1DH Welcoming
three-room drinkers' pub across from the
station and harbour with beams, exposed
brick and lots of wood; eight well kept ales
including Sharps, Timothy Taylors and
Whitby, craft beers, Weston's cider and good
wines by the glass, friendly mix of customers;
background and regular live music, quiz
Thurs, traditional games, TV for football, dogs
welcome, three bedrooms, open all day.

WHITBY   NZ9011
White Horse & Griffin
(01947) 604857 *Church Street;*
YO22 4BH Historic 17th-c coaching inn
now classy tavern with attractive rooms and
good local food especially fish; tall narrow
front bar with bare boards and a couple of
large chandeliers, ales such as Black Sheep
and Timothy Taylors, good wines and over 30
gins, steps down to low-beamed bistro-style
dining area with flagstones and log fire,
attentive staff; children and dogs welcome,
close to the 199 steps up to the abbey, ten
bedrooms and cottage, open all day.

WIGHILL   SE4746
White Swan (01937) 832217
Main Street; LS24 8BQ Fairly modern
village pub with two cosy front rooms and
larger side extension; three well kept
ales such as Sharps, Timothy Taylors and
Theakstons, good food from pub classics up
including monthly themed night, own bakery,
friendly helpful staff; children welcome,
dogs in bar and snug, wheelchair access with
help (steps down to loos), picnic-sets on side
lawn, closed Mon, otherwise open all day,
food till 6pm Sun.

WINTERSETT   SE3815
Anglers Retreat
Ferry Top Lane; WF4 2EB Unpretentious
rural local by Anglers Country Park and
popular with walkers, birders and fishermen;
small lounge and tiny flagstoned bar, three
well kept ales, no food, hospitable landlord
and friendly cheerful atmosphere; pleasant
side garden; children and dogs (not in

garden) welcome, open all day Sat, until 5pm
Sun, closed Tues.

WITHERNWICK   TA1940
Falcon (01964) 527925
Main Street; HU11 4TA Welcoming 18th-c
beamed corner pub; popular good value food
from traditional menu (Weds pie night), well
kept Tetleys and a guest; children allowed, a
few seats outside, closed Mon and lunchtimes
apart from Sun, no food Tues.

WOMBLETON   SE6683
Plough (01751) 431356
Main Street; YO62 7RW Welcoming and
well tended 15th-c village local with notably
good home-made food (not Mon, Tues),
efficient helpful service, ales such as Black
Sheep and Theakstons, bar area with teal
banquettes and carpet, restaurant with
flowers, woodburner and handsome wood
floors; quiz last Sun of month; tables outside,
open all day Fri-Sun, closed lunchtimes Mon
and Tues.

WORTLEY   SK3099
Wortley Arms (0114) 288 8749
A629 N of Sheffield; S35 7DB 18th-c
stone-built coaching adjacent to the church;
several comfortably furnished rooms; beams,
panelling and large inglenook, enjoyable food
(all day Sat) including decent vegetarian
options, three well kept ales perhaps from
Bradfield, Sharps and Stancill, and good
range of gins; occasional live music and quiz
nights; children welcome, and dogs in bar,
nice village about ten minutes from M1, open
all day (till 8pm Sun).

YORK   SE6051
Black Swan (01904) 679131
Peaseholme Green (inner ring road);
YO1 7PR Striking black and white Tudor
merchant's house; compact panelled front
bar, central hall with crooked floor and fine
period staircase, vast inglenook in black-
beamed back bar, good choice of real ales
from the likes of Rudgate, Theakstons and
Timothy Taylors, decent wines and generous
helpings of reasonably priced pubby food in
panelled restaurant with coffered ceiling;
background music, Thurs folk club, regular
comedy gigs; children welcome, two beer
gardens, useful car park behind, bedrooms,
open all day, no food weekend evenings.

YORK   SE6051
★ Blue Bell (01904) 654904
Fossgate; YO1 9TF Delightfully old-
fashioned little Edwardian pub; very friendly
and chatty, beer specialist with blackboard
menu of seven changing ales (commonly
Bradfield, Rudgate, Timothy Taylors and
Wold Top) with house IPA from Brew York,
three real ciders, some snacky food including
good pork pies, tiny tiled-floor front bar
with roaring fire, panelled ceiling and
stained glass, corridor to small hatch-served

back room, lamps and candles, pub games; soft background music; no children, dogs welcome, pavement seating, open all day (but maybe just for locals on busy nights due to its size).

YORK SE6051

★ **Golden Ball** (01904) 849040

Cromwell Road/Victor Street; YO1 6DU Friendly co-operative-owned Edwardian corner pub with four well preserved rooms; up to seven well kept ales from the likes of Acorn and Ainsty, no food apart from bar snacks, bar billiards, cards and dominoes; Sun folk night and other live music, quiz Tues, TV; lovely small walled garden with serving hatch, open all day weekends, closed weekday lunchtimes.

YORK SE6051

Golden Fleece (01904) 620491

Pavement; YO1 9UP Popular little city-centre pub with four well kept ales including Theakstons Old Peculier and enjoyable good value pubby food; long corridor from bar to comfortable back dining room (sloping floors – it dates from 1503), interesting décor and lots of ghost stories; background music and occasional folk evenings, sports TV; children allowed if eating, no dogs, four bedrooms (two with four-posters), open all day.

YORK SE6052

Guy Fawkes (01904) 623716

High Petergate; YO1 7HP Splendid spot next to the Minster (claims to be the birthplace of Guy Fawkes); dark panelled interior with small bar to the left, larger room to the right with roaring fire and atmospheric back restaurant lit by candles and gas wall-lights, half a dozen real ales such as Copper Dragon, Ossett, Phoenix and Saltaire, decent food from pub favourites up; courtyard tables, 13 bedrooms, open (and food) all day.

YORK SE6052

★ **House of Trembling Madness** (01904) 640009

Stonegate; YO1 8AS Unusual beer specialist – esoteric range of other drinks too – above own excellent off-licence; impressive high-raftered medieval room with collection of stuffed animal heads from moles to lions, eclectic mix of furniture including cask seats and pews on bare boards, lovely old brick fireplace, cask and craft beers from pulpit servery, also huge selection of bottled beers (all available to buy downstairs), good knowledgeable staff, reasonably priced hearty food including various platters; two self-catering apartments in ancient courtyard behind, open (and food) all day.

YORK SE6052

Lamb & Lion (01904) 654112

High Petergate; YO1 7EH Appealing Georgian inn next to Bootham Bar; five well kept local ales and nice wines by the glass, gin menu, good food from sandwiches and pub favourites to more restauranty choices, friendly helpful staff, bare-boards bar and series of compact rooms off narrow corridors; steep steps up to attractive paved garden below city wall and looking up to the Minster, bedrooms, open all day.

YORK SE6051

Phoenix (01904) 656401

George Street; YO1 9PT Friendly little pub next to the city walls with tiled exterior; proper front public bar and comfortable back horseshoe-shaped lounge, four well kept ales from Yorkshire brewers (perhaps Northern Monk, Saltaire and Timothy Taylors), decent wines and simple food, log fire; live jazz usually Mon, Weds, Fri and Sun, bar billiards; pretty beer garden, handy for Barbican, open all day.

YORK SE6051

Pivni (01904) 635464

Patrick Pool; YO1 8BB Serious beer pub ('world beer freehouse') with half-timbered black and white exterior; small narrow bar with five ale pumps dispensing the likes of Beatnikz Republic Brandy Snap and RedWillow Breakfast Stout, six keg taps with rotating occupants such as Möbru and Wild Beer, real ciders, many canned and bottled beers (some unusual choices), friendly knowledgeable staff, some snacky food and good coffee, more seats upstairs; Mon quiz, juke box and occasional live music; dogs welcome, close to the Shambles, open all day.

YORK SE6051

Punch Bowl (01904) 655147

Stonegate; YO1 8AN Bustling 17th-c black and white-fronted pub with good choice of well kept ales, decent wines and sensibly priced Nicholsons menu including breakfast, efficient friendly service, small panelled rooms off corridor, dining room at back with fireplace; background music; a couple of tables out by pavement, open (and food) all day.

YORK SE6052

Snickleway (01904) 656138

Goodramgate; YO1 7LS Interesting little traditional pub behind big shopfront window; lots of antiques, copper and brass, cosy fires, six well kept ales, some lunchtime food (not Sun) including good sandwiches, friendly

---

We mention bottled beers and spirits only if there is something unusual about them – imported Belgian real ales, say, or dozens of malt whiskies. Do please let us know about them in your reports.

service, stories of various ghosts including Mrs Tulliver and her cat; Tues quiz, live music; small terrace; open all day.

YORK   SE6052
Star Inn the City (01904) 619208
Museum Street; YO1 7DR Restaurant place – sister to the Star in Harome (and Whitby) – in wonderful central riverside setting – a former 19th-c pumping station with modern glass extension; good but not cheap food, beers including a house ale (Two Chefs) from Great Yorkshire, a guest such as Bad Seed, and Pilsner Urquell dispensed from two large copper tanks, good range of wines by the glass and cocktails, friendly service; open all day from 9.30am for breakfast.

YORK   SE6051
Swan (01904) 634968
Bishopgate Street, Clementhorpe; YO23 1JH Unspoilt 1930s pub (Grade II listed) near the city walls with lovely original décor and a warm, welcoming atmosphere; two small rooms either side of lobby bar, Half Moon, Tetleys, Timothy Taylors and four interesting guest ales, two changing craft beers, and ciders, friendly knowledgeable staff; pleasant little walled garden, open all day Fri-Sun, from 4pm Mon-Weds, 3pm Thurs.

YORK   SE6052
Three Legged Mare (01904) 638246
High Petergate, close to the Minster; YO1 7EN Compact beer drinkers' pub (aka the Wonkey Donkey) with well kept York Brewery ales, several varied and interesting guest beers from the locality and beyond (including craft) from mainstream (Black Sheep) to lesser known (Almasty, Cwtch, Turning Point) and up to 20 boxed ciders and perries, friendly helpful staff, no food; regular live music including folk and open

mike nights, Mon quiz, board games; children (till 7pm) and dogs welcome, disabled loo (others down spiral stairs), back terrace, open all day till midnight (11pm Sun).

YORK   SE6051
Walmgate Ale House
(01904) 629222 *Walmgate; YO1 9TX* 17th-c city-centre pub-cum-restaurant on three levels; ground-floor bar with half a dozen Yorkshire ales and good range of wines, snacks including sausage rolls and local cheeses, upstairs Chopping Block restaurant with Anglo-French menu choices and weekend brunch (from 9.30am), further loft dining area, good friendly service; children welcome, closed Mon, Tues lunchtime, otherwise open (and food) all day.

YORK   SE5951
Whippet (01904) 500660
Opposite Park Inn Hotel, North Street; YO1 6JD Classy steak and ale house set back from the river; good popular food including signature dry-aged steaks (plus seitan 'steak'), small bar area with four well kept ales from Yorkshire brewers such as Bad Co and Roosters, lots of wines by the glass, interesting cocktails and excellent range of gins, friendly well informed staff; no children, open all day.

YORK   SE5951
York Tap (01904) 659009
Station, Station Road; YO24 1AB Restored Edwardian bar at York station; high ceiling with feature stained-glass cupolas, columns and iron fretwork, bentwood chairs and stools on terrazzo floor, button-back banquettes, period fireplaces, great changing selection of 20 real ales and ciders from circular counter with brass footrail, also bottled beers listed on blackboard, good pork pies; seats out by platform, open all day.

London

KEY ⭐ Star Pub · 🍽️ Top Quality Food · ☕ Great Beer
🍷 Good Wines · £ Bargain Meals · 🛏️ Good Bedrooms · 🍴 Serves Food

CENTRAL LONDON
Map 13
Admiral Codrington 🍷
(020) 7581 0005 ~ www.theadmiralcodrington.co.uk
Mossop Street; South Kensington tube; SW3 2LY

Long-standing Chelsea landmark with easy-going bar and pretty restaurant, popular food and seats outside

There's a pleasing café feel and civilised but informal atmosphere at the well run, bustling 'Cod', tucked away down a small street in Chelsea. The central dark-panelled bar has high red chairs beside the counter with more around equally high tables on either side of the log-effect gas fire, button-back wall banquettes with cream and red patterned seats, little stools and plain wooden chairs around a medley of tables on black-painted floorboards, patterned wallpaper above a dado and a shelf with daily papers. There are ornate flower arrangements, a big portrait above the fire, several naval prints and quiet background music. Helpful staff serve Bombardier, Shepherd Neame Whitstable Bay and guests such as Sambrooks on handpump, 18 wines by the glass and a thoughtful range of spirits. The light, airy restaurant area is a total contrast: high-backed pretty wall seats and plush dining chairs around pale tables, an open kitchen, fish prints on pale blue paintwork, a second fireplace and an impressive skylight. A back garden has chunky benches and tables under a summer awning.

🍴 Well presented, enjoyable food includes truffle mac 'n' cheese fritters, pork and apple sausage rolls, seared bream fillet with Cornish new potato niçoise, chicken, tarragon and leek pie with mash and buttered greens, British brisket burger with ruby slaw, fries and onion relish, and puddings such as lemon tart with crème fraîche and rhubarb and custard crumble pie. *Benchmark main dish: crispy battered haddock and chips £14.00. Two-course evening meal £21.00.*

Cirrus Inns ~ Licensee Raphael Nebot ~ Real ale ~ Open 11.30-11; 11.30am-1am Fri, Sat; 12-10.30 Sun ~ Bar food 12-10; 12-9 Sun ~ Restaurant ~ Children welcome ~ Dogs allowed in bar

CENTRAL LONDON
Map 13
Alfred Tennyson 🍽️ 🍷
(020) 7730 6074 ~ www.thealfredtennyson.co.uk
Motcomb Street; Knightsbridge tube; SW1X 8LA

Spacious, civilised four-storey pub with good drinks choice, rewarding food and friendly, helpful service

The four airy, elegant floors here offer lots of enjoyable options for both drinking and dining. There are high stools around equally high shelf tables for chatting, cushioned wooden settles around dark tables on parquet flooring for dining and eclectic décor that encompasses Edward Lear illustrations and antique books on windowsills. Stools line the long wooden counter from which friendly, helpful staff serve Hammerton N1 and Sharps Doom Bar on handpump, 20 malt whiskies, cocktails and 32 wines by the glass. The upstairs restaurant has plush upholstered chairs and wooden tables on more parquet, large house plants and a huge mirror above an open fire. Above that is a loft room that's used for drinks parties. Outside on the front pavement are tables and chairs beneath a striped awning; there's disabled access to the bar but no disabled loos.

Good-looking modern food includes cured salmon with brown crabmeat, fennel, herb dressing and rye crisps, courgette flower with aubergine, heritage tomatoes and basil, a daily changing home-made pie, beef sirloin with fries and red wine jus, pan-fried cod with smoked roe, violet artichokes, sea herbs and lemon pickle, and puddings such as roasted banana and rum parfait with chocolate ganache and strawberry cheesecake with cherry sorbet and balsamic. *Benchmark main dish: pan-roasted chicken with Jersey Royals, chanterelles and tarragon velouté £21.00. Two-course evening meal £26.00.*

Cubitt House ~ Manager Tony Gualtieri ~ Real ale ~ Open 11.30-11; 11.30-11.30 Fri, Sat; 11.30-10.30 Sun ~ Bar food 12-10 Mon-Sat, 1.30-9.30 Sun ~ Children welcome ~ Dogs allowed in bar

CENTRAL LONDON   Map 13

Beau Brummell

(020) 8075 9477 – www.thebeaubrummell.co.uk
Norris Street; SW1Y 4RJ

Busy, chic dining pub with first class food and drink, efficient service and seats outside

Named after the original dandy who counted King George IV as a close friend, this stylish pub in the central courtyard of St James's Market, just round the corner from Piccadilly Circus, is the newest addition to the Cubitt House group. Huge glass windows keep it all light and airy; the open-plan bar has curved button-back banquettes, mustard yellow dining chairs and stools around wooden tables on parquet flooring, large glass chandeliers and modern artwork. Stairs lead up from here to the mezzanine dining room. Well trained, friendly staff keep everything running smoothly and the fine choice of drinks includes Hammerton N1 and XPA and Sharps Doom Bar on handpump, around 40 wines by the glass from an impressive list (including several English wines, fizz and dessert wines), British spirits (they support small producers and distillers) for their cocktail list, and a thoughtful choice of soft drinks. Seats on the terrace at the front get snapped up pretty quickly when the weather is favourable; dogs are allowed in the downstairs bar.

Well presented dishes using sustainable, locally sourced produce as much as possible include pork rillettes with spiced pumpkin chutney, cured trout with beetroot relish and dill crème fraîche, pigeon pastrami with pickles, flat-iron steak with tomato and caper dressing, fries and watercress salad, a pie of the day, heritage carrot and smoked almond wellington, confit pork belly with haricot beans and calvados jus, and puddings such as Yorkshire forced rhubarb eton mess and poached pear with candied almonds, chocolate brownie and ricotta ice-cream. *Benchmark main dish: burger and fries £16.00. Two-course evening meal £24.00.*

Cubitt House ~ Manager Tony Gualtieri ~ Open 9am-11.30pm Mon-Thurs; 9am-midnight Fri; 10am-midnight Sat; 11.30-10.30 Sun ~ Bar food 11.30-10 Mon-Sat; 11.30-9.30 Sun ~ Restaurant ~ Children welcome ~ Dogs allowed in ground-floor bar

CENTRAL LONDON
Coach Makers Arms 🔅🌟 🍷

Map 13

(020) 7224 4022 – www.thecoachmakersarms.co.uk
Marylebone Lane; Bond Street tube; W1U 2PY

Restored three-level pub in Marylebone with plenty of room for both eating and drinking, imaginative food and a thoughtful choice of wines and spirits

This thoughtfully restored Georgian pub just off Marylebone High Street is spread over several floors, but it's the bustling ground-floor bar that is the heart of the place. This has button-back banquette wall seats, high chairs around equally high tables, striking ceiling lights and friendly staff who serve Hammerton N1 and Sharps Doom Bar on handpump, several craft beers, over 30 wines by the glass and 20 malt whiskies; background music and TV. The alluring cocktail bar in the basement has beams and panelled walls, rich red or green plush seats and wall banquettes by simple tables, some modern art and drinks that include a seasonally changing cocktail menu. Head upstairs to the first floor to find the bright and airy dining room, with leather or elegant wooden chairs around assorted tables on dark floorboards, oil portraits and old photographs on the walls and stained-glass windows overlooking the Marylebone streets below – and a restful atmosphere. Disabled access to the bar but not to the loos.

 Beautifully presented and highly regarded food includes cured trout with Pimm's, gooseberries and horseradish, beef tartare with watercress mayonnaise and smoked egg yolk, pan-fried hake with clams, samphire and borlotti beans, beef rib-eye with chunky chips and béarnaise sauce, charred celeriac steak with blue cheese mousse, beer-battered haddock and chips, and puddings such as buttermilk and vanilla pannacotta with strawberry compote, pistachio and almond crumble and dark chocolate brownie with hot fudge sauce and malt ice-cream; they also offer two- and three-course set menus. *Benchmark main dish: dry-aged beef burger with fries £16.50. Two-course evening meal £25.00.*

Cubitt House ~ Manager Tony Gualtieri ~ Real ale ~ Open 11.30-11; 11.30am-midnight Fri, Sat; 11.30-10.30 Sun ~ Bar food 11.30-10 Mon-Sat; 11.30-9.30 Sun ~ Restaurant ~ Children welcome ~ Dogs allowed in bar

CENTRAL LONDON
Cross Keys 🍷

Map 12

(020) 7351 0686 – www.thecrosskeyschelsea.co.uk
Lawrence Street; Sloane Square tube (some distance away); SW3 5NB

Popular pub with a friendly bar, airy back restaurant, real ales and modern bar food

In a quiet street midway between Chelsea Embankment and the Kings Road, this gently civilised, bright Chelsea pub is popular with a lively crowd of customers for both the up-to-date food and good choice of drinks. The central counter has bar areas to each side with simple furnishings: distressed panelled walls, some exposed brickwork, a couple of open fires, framed tobacco postcards and display cases of butterflies, tankards on a rack, mirrors, industrial-style ceiling lights, and a mix of cushioned wooden dining chairs and wheelbacks around scrubbed tables on bare boards and stools against the counter. Friendly staff serve ales from Brakspears, Sambrooks, Trumans and Youngs on handpump, eight wines by the glass and 18 whiskies; background music. At the back, the airy conservatory-style dining room has button-back wall seating and similar chairs and tables.

🍴 Well presented, tasty food includes pork and apple sausage rolls, truffle mac 'n' cheese fritters, chicken, tarragon and leek pie with buttered greens and mash, tagliatelle with morels, asparagus and poached egg, Moving Mountains vegan burger and chips, roast cauliflower with Persian-spiced lentils, spinach and chickpeas, duck breast with confit leg pastilla, fondant potato, savoy cabbage and chicory, and puddings such as lemon tart with crème fraîche and peanut and chocolate stack with praline foam and vanilla ice-cream. *Benchmark main dish: crispy battered haddock and chips £14.00. Two-course evening meal £20.00.*

Cirrus Inns ~ Licensee James Hardesly ~ Real ale ~ Open 12-11; 12-midnight Fri, Sat; 12-10.30 Sun ~ Bar food 12-3, 6-10; 12-4, 6-10 Sat; 12-9 Sun ~ Restaurant ~ Children welcome but must leave bar area by 7pm

CENTRAL LONDON   Map 13

Grazing Goat ⭐ ♈ 🍽 🛏

(020) 7724 7243 – www.thegrazinggoat.co.uk
New Quebec Street; Marble Arch tube; W1H 7RQ

A good mixed crowd of customers, restful décor, a thoughtful choice of drinks and interesting food; bedrooms

This stylish Cubitt House gastropub is a welcome rest-stop amid the hustle and bustle of Oxford Street and Marble Arch. The bar has a large gilt-edged mirror above an open fire and plenty of spreading dining space with white cushioned and beige dining chairs around pale tables on bare boards, sage green or oak-panelled walls, ceiling lamps and lanterns and some goat memorabilia dotted about. Efficient, friendly staff serve Hammerton N1 and Sharps Doom Bar on handpump, Beavertown craft beers, more than 30 wines by the glass, 17 malt whiskies and cocktails. The upstairs restaurant is more formal with wood-panelled walls and large sash windows. Glass doors open on to the street where there are a few wooden-slatted chairs and tables. The eight bedrooms are modern and well equipped, with good bathrooms. Disabled access to the bar but not to the loos.

🍴 As well as breakfast (from 7.30am), the rewarding, nicely presented food includes salt and chilli squid, violet artichoke croquettes with chervil mayonnaise, beer-battered haddock and triple-cooked chips, pan-roasted chicken breast with tarragon dumplings and wild mushrooms, a daily home-made pie, various steaks, pan-fried hake with broccoli and trompette mushrooms, and puddings such as pineapple carpaccio with coconut sorbet and ginger and mint syrup, and apple pie with pecans, salted caramel and vanilla ice-cream. *Benchmark main dish: dry-aged beef burger with smoked cheddar and fries £16.50. Two-course evening meal £25.00.*

Cubitt House ~ Manager Tony Gualtieri ~ Real ale ~ Open 7.30am-11pm; 7.30am-10.30pm Sun ~ Bar food 7.30am-10pm Mon-Sat; 7.30am-9.30pm Sun ~ Restaurant ~ Children welcome ~ Dogs allowed in bar ~ Bedrooms: £159

'Children welcome' means the pub says it lets children inside without any special restriction. If it allows them in, but to restricted areas such as an eating area or family room, we specify this. Places with separate restaurants often let children use them, and hotels usually let children into public areas such as lounges. Some pubs impose an evening time limit – let us know if you find one earlier than 9pm.

CENTRAL LONDON

Map 13

Harp ◖

(020) 7836 0291 – www.harpcoventgarden.com

47 Chandos Place; Charing Cross tube/rail, Leicester Square tube; WC2N 4HS

At least ten real ales and lots of ciders and perries in bustling narrow pub

J ust off the eastern side of Trafalgar Square, this busy little local is a gem – and a favourite with many. The main draw, of course, is the choice of at least ten particularly well kept real ales on handpump: these change quickly but always include Harveys Best, Dark Star American Pale Ale and Hophead and Fullers London Pride, with guests sourced from all over the country. Also, around six farm ciders, a perry and quite a few malt whiskies. The pub pretty much consists of one long narrow, very traditional bar, with lots of high bar stools along the wall counter and around elbow tables, big mirrors on the red walls, some lovely stained glass and loads of interesting, quirkily executed celebrity portraits. If you're lucky, you may be able to snare one of the prized seats by the front windows. A little room upstairs is much quieter, with comfortable furniture and a window overlooking the road below. At any time of day, the pub is always packed; at peak times, customers are happy to spill out on to the pavement or the back alley. The hanging baskets are a particular delight in summer.

⏍ Bar snacks, served only at lunchtime, include sandwiches, pork pies and sausage rolls.

Fullers ~ Manager Paul Sims ~ Real ale ~ Open 10.30am-11.30pm; 10.30am-midnight Fri, Sat; 12-10.30 Sun ~ Bar food 12-2

CENTRAL LONDON

Map 13

Lamb & Flag ◖ £

(020) 7497 9504 – www.lambandflagcoventgarden.co.uk

Rose Street, off Garrick Street; Covent Garden or Leicester Square tube; WC2E 9EB

Historic yet unpretentious, full of character and atmosphere, with seven real ales and pubby food

M any of the customers here have been visiting this characterful old Covent Garden tavern for years, and thankfully nothing changes. The more spartan front room leads into a cosy, atmospheric, low-ceilinged back bar with high-backed black settles and an open fire. Fullers ESB, London Pride, Olivers Island and Gales Seafarers plus guests such as Anstey Ale Daydreamer, Castle Rock Harvest Pale and Dark Star Hophead on handpump, as well as several wines by the glass and 12 malt whiskies. The upstairs Dryden Room, where the main food service is available, is often less crowded and has more seats (though fewer beers). There's a lively and well documented history: poet John Dryden was nearly beaten to death by hired thugs outside, and Charles Dickens made fun of the Middle Temple lawyers who frequented it when he was working in nearby Catherine Street.

⏍ Well liked food runs from bar snacks and sandwiches (such as battered fish finger, baby gem and tartare sauce) through to traditional pub favourites such as fish and chips, burgers and Sunday roasts, vegetarian dishes including spiced green lentil, cauliflower and spinach curry, and desserts such as warm chocolate brownie with buffalo milk vanilla ice-cream and molasses, date and hops sticky toffee pudding. *Benchmark main dish: burger with cheese and triple-cooked chips £13.25. Two-course evening meal £22.00.*

Fullers ~ Manager Patrick Linn ~ Real ale ~ Open 11-11; 12-10.30 Sun ~ Bar food 12-10;
12-9 Sun ~ Restaurant ~ Children allowed in upstairs dining room only ~ Dogs allowed
in bar

CENTRAL LONDON   Map 13

Olde Mitre 🍺 £

(020) 7405 4751 – www.yeoldemitreholborn.co.uk

Ely Place; Chancery Lane tube, Farringdon tube/rail; EC1N 6SJ

**Unspoilt old pub with a lovely atmosphere, unusual guest beers
and bargain toasted sandwiches and pies**

You need to be in the know to track down this tucked-away and unspoilt
little spot – it's a real refuge from the modern city nearby. There's been
a tavern on this site since 1546, though the current building dates from 1782.
The cosy small rooms have lots of dark panelling as well as antique settles
and old local pictures (particularly in the popular back room where there are
more seats). It gets good-naturedly packed with the City suited-and-booted
between 12.30pm and 2.15pm, filling up again in the early evening, but in
the early afternoons and by around 8pm it's a good deal more tranquil. An
upstairs room, mainly used for functions, may double as an overflow area
at peak periods. Fullers London Pride, Olivers Island and Seafarers with
regular guests such as Adnams Broadside and Caledonian Deuchars IPA
on handpump, plus eight farm ciders and 13 wines by the glass. No music,
TV or machines – the only games here are cribbage and dominoes. There's
some space for outside drinking by the pot plants and jasmine in the narrow
yard between the pub and St Etheldreda's Church (which is worth a look).
Note the pub doesn't open on Sundays or bank holidays. The best approach
is from Hatton Garden, walking up the right-hand side away from Chancery
Lane; keep an eye out for an easily missed sign on a lamp-post that points the
way down a narrow alley. No children.

Bar snacks, served all day (not Saturday), are limited to scotch eggs, lamb
and mint pasties, various pies (steak and ale, pork), sausage rolls and really
good value toasties.

Fullers ~ Manager Judith Norman ~ Real ale ~ Open 12-10; closed Sun and bank holidays ~
Bar food 12-10 Mon-Fri

CENTRAL LONDON   Map 13

Orange 🏅 ♗ 🛏

(020) 7881 9844 – www.theorange.co.uk

Pimlico Road; Sloane Square tube; SW1W 8NE

**Sympathetically restored pub with simply decorated rooms,
thoughtful choice of drinks and up-to-date food; bedrooms**

Once a brewery, this handsomely restored four-storey Georgian inn is
dominated by a ground-floor bar with a lively, chatty and easy-going
atmosphere. There are high ceilings, wooden dining chairs around pale tables
on bare boards, an open fire at one end and a large carved counter where
friendly staff keep Hammerton N1 and Sharps Doom Bar on handpump,
over 30 wines by the glass, 17 malt whiskies, a cocktail list and home-
made syrups. The dining room to the right, usually packed with cheerful
customers, serves excellent breakfasts and is decorated with prints, glass
bottles and soda siphons, big house plants and a few rustic knick-knacks.
Upstairs, the linked restaurant rooms are similarly furnished, with vintage
French travel posters and circus prints on cream walls, more open fireplaces,

large glass ceiling lights, chandeliers and quiet background music. There are four comfortable, well equipped bedrooms, some pavement tables and disabled access to the bar but not to the loos.

Beautifully presented modern food from breakfast (served from 8am) through to dinner includes a small selection of wood-fired pizzas, burrata with broad beans, preserved lemon and tomato relish, pan-roasted lamb rump with spinach gnocchi, chanterelles and thyme jus, pan-fried haddock with Jersey Royals, artichokes, samphire and tomato and caper dressing, and puddings such as passion-fruit and lemon meringue pie and strawberry and vanilla custard with caramelised pastry and crème fraîche parfait. *Benchmark main dish: home-made pie of the day £16.50. Two-course evening meal £26.00.*

Cubitt House ~ Manager Tony Gualtieri ~ Real ale ~ Open 11.30-11 Mon-Thurs; 11.30am-midnight Fri, Sat; 11.30-10.30 Sun ~ Bar food 11.30-10 Mon-Sat, 1.30-9.30 Sun ~ Restaurant ~ Children welcome ~ Dogs allowed in bar ~ Bedrooms: £159

CENTRAL LONDON
Punchbowl ♀

Map 13

(020) 7493 6841 – www.punchbowllondon.com
Farm Street; Green Park tube; W1J 5RP

Bustling, rather civilised pub with good wines and ales, enjoyable food and helpful service

This tucked-away 18th-c Mayfair local (once owned by Madonna and Guy Ritchie) contains a number of attractive spaces, the nicest of which is probably at the back where several panelled booths have suede bench seating, animal-picture scatter cushions, some etched glasswork and oil candles on tables. Elegant spoked chairs are grouped around dark tables on worn floorboards, a couple of long elbow shelves are lined with high chairs and one fireplace has a coal fire while the other is piled with logs. At the front it's simpler, with cushioned bench seating and pubby tables and chairs on floor tiles. All sorts of artwork from cartoons to oil paintings line the walls and the ceiling has interesting old hand-drawn street maps; background music. Caledonian Deuchars IPA, a beer named for the pub (also from Caledonian) and Marstons 61 Deep on handpump, 17 wines by the glass from a well chosen list, and professional, friendly service. The smart dining room upstairs has plush furnishings, large artworks and a huge gilt mirror above a fireplace; there are private dining facilities too.

Nicely presented, British-focused food includes lunchtime sandwiches with fries, spiced pumpkin and pear soup, roast bone marrow with red wine jus, tempura soft shell crab with kimchi salad and sweet chilli sauce, torched mackerel with warm beetroot and potato and herb salad, duck and Toulouse sausage cassoulet, jackfruit and lentil pie with sweet potato mash and green beans, and puddings such as chocolate brownie with banana ice-cream and mulled wine-poached pears with gingerbread crumble and ice-cream. *Benchmark main dish: burger and chips £16.50. Two-course evening meal £25.00.*

Cirrus Inns ~ Licensee Andres Cabrera ~ Real ale ~ Open 11.30-11; 11.30-10 Sun ~ Bar food 12-10; 12-10.30 Fri, Sat; 12-9 Sun ~ Restaurant ~ Children welcome if seated and dining ~ Dogs allowed in bar

Please keep sending us reports. We rely on readers for news of new discoveries, and particularly for news of changes – however slight – at the fully described pubs: feedback@goodguides.com, or (no stamp needed) Freepost THE GOOD PUB GUIDE, Random House Publishing, 20 Vauxhall Bridge Road, London SW1V 2SA.

CENTRAL LONDON Map 13

Star

(020) 7235 3019 – www.star-tavern-belgravia.co.uk

Belgrave Mews West, behind the German Embassy, off Belgrave Square; Hyde Park Corner or Knightsbridge tube; SW1X 8HT

In summer, the front of this historic pub is covered with a dazzling array of hanging baskets and flowering tubs. Outside peak times, there's a peaceful, local feel to the spot, hidden away in a cobbled mews. Once past the floral façade, the small bar is pleasant, with sash windows, a wooden floor, stools by the counter, an open winter fire and Fullers ESB, London Pride and Olivers Island plus a couple of guest beers on handpump, 14 wines by the glass and a few malt whiskies; board games. An arch leads to the main seating area with well polished tables and chairs and good lighting; there's also an upstairs dining room. It's rumoured that this is where the infamous Great Train Robbery was planned.

Well liked food from the Fullers kitchen includes sandwiches, snacks such as pies, hummus with flatbread and buffalo chicken wings, main dishes including sausages and mash, chicken schnitzel with kohlrabi and pine nut and kale slaw, and squash, spinach and feta cheese wellington, and puddings such as marmalade and whisky bread and butter pudding with buffalo milk vanilla ice-cream. *Benchmark main dish: Fullers Frontier-battered fish and chips £14.25. Two-course evening meal £20.00.*

Fullers ~ Manager Ollie Coulombeau ~ Real ale ~ Open 11-11; 12-11 Sat; 12-10.30 Sun ~ Bar food 12-3, 5-9; 12-9 Sat; 12-4, 5-9 Sun ~ Restaurant ~ Children welcome ~ Dogs allowed in bar

CENTRAL LONDON Map 13

Thomas Cubitt

(020) 7730 6060 – www.thethomascubitt.co.uk

Elizabeth Street; Sloane Square tube, Victoria tube/rail; SW1W 9PA

Belgravia pub with a civilised and friendly atmosphere and enjoyable food and drink

Set over three floors and with outdoor seating in a cordoned-off area of the pavement, this is a stylish and busy place in well heeled Elizabeth Street, right at the heart of Belgravia. The ground-floor bar has miscellaneous Edwardian-style dining chairs around wooden tables on stripped parquet flooring, architectural prints and antlers on panelled or painted walls, open fires and lovely flower arrangements. Attentive staff serve Hammerton N1 and Sharps Doom Bar on handpump, over 30 wines by the glass, 17 malt whiskies, home-made syrups and cocktails. The more formal dining room upstairs has smart upholstered wooden chairs around white-clothed tables, candles in wall holders, a few prints, house plants and window blinds; background music and TV. In warm weather, the floor-to-ceiling glass doors are pulled back to the street. Disabled access to the bar but not to the loos.

Attractively presented, interesting food includes beef tartare with nasturtiums and confit egg yolk, smoked mackerel with cucumber and borage, pan-roasted lamb rump with roasted sweet potato, broad beans, chanterelles and pomegranate jus, dry-aged beef burger with toppings and fries, caramelised onion tart with creamed watercress and truffled buttermilk, and puddings such as strawberry and mascarpone pannacotta with pistachio and almond crumble and pineapple carpaccio with ginger, mint and coconut sorbet. *Benchmark main dish: beer-battered haddock and triple-cooked chips £17.00. Two-course evening meal £25.00.*

Cubitt House ~ Manager Tony Gualtieri ~ Real ale ~ Open 11.30-11; 11.30-10.30 Sun ~ Bar food 11.30-10; 1.30-9.30 Sun ~ Restaurant ~ Children welcome ~ Dogs allowed in bar

Map 12

NORTH LONDON
Holly Bush

(020) 7435 2892 – www.hollybushhampstead.co.uk

Holly Mount; Hampstead tube; NW3 6SG

Unique village local with good food and drinks, and lovely unspoilt feel

A timeless old favourite, this place was originally a stable block and is hidden away among some of Hampstead's most villagey streets. The old-fashioned front bar has a dark sagging ceiling, brown and cream panelled walls (decorated with old advertisements and a few hanging plates), open fires, bare boards and secretive bays formed by partly glazed partitions. The slightly more intimate back room, named after the painter George Romney, has an embossed red ceiling, panelled and etched glass alcoves, and ochre-painted brick walls covered with small prints; lots of board and card games. Fullers ESB, London Pride and Olivers Island plus a guest or two such as Adnams Ghost Ship and Liberation Ale on handpump, as well as 18 malt whiskies, 14 gins and 20 wines by the glass from a good wine list. The upstairs dining room has table service at the weekend, as does the rest of the pub on Sundays. There are benches on the pavement outside. There's disabled access to the ground-floor rooms.

Popular food includes sandwiches, grilled sardines with Isle of Wight tomatoes, burger with toppings and fries, 8oz rib-eye steak with béarnaise sauce and chips, courgette bread and butter pudding with tomatoes, artichokes and basil, grilled salmon with lemon hollandaise, and puddings such as poached berries with lime gel, hazelnut crumb and meringue and set Valrhona chocolate with honeycomb, raspberries and blackberry sorbet. *Benchmark main dish: chicken schnitzel with apple, fennel and watercress slaw £17.00. Two-course evening meal £25.00.*

Fullers ~ Manager Mariya Ivanova ~ Real ale ~ Open 12-11; 12-10.30 Sun ~ Bar food 12-4, 6-10; 12-8 Sun ~ Restaurant ~ Children welcome ~ Dogs allowed in bar & restaurant

Map 13

NORTH LONDON
Lighterman

(020) 3846 3400 – www.thelighterman.co.uk

Granary Square, Regent's Canal; King's Cross/St Pancras tube/rail; N1C 4BH

London Dining Pub of the Year

Spacious contemporary place with up-to-date décor and furnishings, wide range of drinks, interesting all-day food and good, quick service

Set across three floors in the redeveloped plaza behind King's Cross station, with views across the fountains in Granary Square and the adjacent Regent's Canal, this bar-restaurant is as ultra-modern and stylish as you'd expect. The ground-floor terrace and wraparound decking on the first floor have plenty of seats, benches and tables to make the most of the vista. Floor-to-ceiling windows and large folding doors in the open-plan bars keep it all very light and airy, while the minimalist, industrial-style décor encompasses contemporary chairs, bench seats and tables on wood-strip floors. High chairs line the counters where efficient, friendly staff serve Five Points Pale and Harbour Ellensburg Session IPA on handpump, several craft and bottled beers, 18 wines by the glass and seasonal cocktails; background music. Note: they don't accept cash.

 Imaginative and appealing food includes flatbreads with toppings, cauliflower fritters with turmeric sauce, 28-day dry-aged grass-fed Galloway rib-eye steak with watercress and skin-on fries, pan-fried trout with brown shrimp, kohlrabi slaw and sea vegetables, supergrain or beef burger with skin-on fries, and puddings such as dark chocolate parfait with orange and honeycomb and raspberry and elderflower eton mess with lemon curd and mint. *Benchmark main dish: fish and chips with crushed peas £16.50. Two-course evening meal £24.00.*

Open House London ~ Manager Brett Murray ~ Real ale ~ Open 12-11; 12-midnight Fri; 10am-midnight Sat; 10-10 Sun ~ Bar food 12-9.30; 12-10 Fri; 10-10 Sat; 10-8.30 Sun ~ Restaurant ~ Children allowed in restaurant ~ Dogs allowed in bar & restaurant

NORTH LONDON   Map 13

Princess of Wales

(020) 7722 0354 – www.lovetheprincess.com

Fitzroy Road/Chalcot Road; Chalk Farm tube via Regents Park Road and footbridge; NW1 8LL

Friendly place with three different seating areas, enjoyable food, wide choice of drinks and funky garden

This bustling Regency corner pub in Primrose Hill is an elegant spot set over three floors. An airy dining room sits above the ground-floor main bar, which is open-plan and light with big windows looking out to the street, wooden tables and chairs on bare boards and plenty of high chairs against the counter. Sambrooks Wandle and a beer named for the pub (the Princess of Ales, also from Sambrooks) plus a changing guest ale on handpump, 22 wines by the glass, about a dozen malt whiskies and good cocktails from the in-house mixologist. The smarter dining room has beige- and white-painted chairs, leather sofas and stools around wooden tables on more bare boards, big gilt-edged mirrors and chandeliers; two TVs. The Garden Room downstairs has a bar, three connected areas and access to the suntrap garden with its Bansky-style mural, framed wall mirrors and picnic-sets (some painted pink and purple) under parasols.

Well presented, modern food includes popcorn chicken with barbecue sauce, saltfish croquettes with tartare sauce, avocado and crayfish salad, salmon teriyaki with mixed peppers and broccoli, a home-made pie of the day, chicken curry, seafood linguine, a range of pizzas, and puddings such as raspberry and passion-fruit cheese cake and banoffi pie. There's also a separate vegan menu. *Benchmark main dish: half roast chicken with coleslaw and fries £15.00. Two-course evening meal £22.00.*

Free house ~ Licensee Lawrence Santi ~ Real ale ~ Open 11am-11.30pm; 10am-11.30pm Sat; 10am-11pm Sun ~ Bar food 12-10 ~ Restaurant ~ Children allowed in restaurant ~ Dogs allowed in bar

SOUTH LONDON   Map 12

Fox & Grapes 🏅🖈 ♟

(020) 8619 1300 – www.foxandgrapeswimbledon.co.uk

Camp Road; Wimbledon rail; SW19 4UN

Wide mix of customers for very popular pub with enjoyable food and drink; airy modern bedrooms

Not surprisingly, given its location on the edge of Wimbledon Common, this spacious 18th-c gastropub is extremely popular with walkers and their dogs at lunchtime. There's always a good mix of both drinkers and diners, and the efficient, friendly staff manage to keep things running smoothly, even when it gets busy. The large, roomy main bar, with a step between its two halves, has high ceilings with unusual chandeliers, all sorts of wooden and leather dining chairs around scrubbed or painted tables on stripped boards or parquet flooring, and built-in wall seats and settles with pretty scatter cushions. Sharps Doombar and changing guests such as Sambrooks Wandle and Wimbledon Common Pale Ale on handpump, 13 wines by the glass (plus two sparkling ones) and a few malt whiskies; background music. The three bright bedrooms are light, airy and pretty. Parking is pay-and-display. Sister pub is the Victoria in East Sheen.

A popular all-day menu includes dishes such as smoked and fresh salmon rillettes with toast, ham hock and smoked chicken terrine, burger (beef or vegan versions) and chips, bratwurst with smoked chilli jam, Swiss cheese and jalapeños, duck confit with celeriac purée and pickled red cabbage, roasted butternut squash risotto with red chicory and gorgonzola, and desserts such as 'Wimbledon mess' (smashed meringues and English strawberries) and sticky toffee pudding with toffee sauce and vanilla ice-cream. *Benchmark main dish: ale-battered fish and chips £15.00. Two-course evening meal £21.00.*

Jolly Fine Pub Group ~ Manager Daniel Britz ~ Real ale ~ Open 12-10 ~ Bar food 12-9; 12-7 Sun ~ Restaurant ~ Children welcome ~ Dogs allowed in bar ~ Bedrooms: from £125

SOUTH LONDON
Map 12

Guildford Arms

(020) 8691 6293 – www.theguildfordarms.co.uk
Guildford Grove/Devonshire Drive; Deptford Bridge tube/DLR; SE10 8JY

Stylish bar and restaurant on two floors with imaginative food, a relaxed atmosphere and courtyard garden

With a bow-fronted Georgian exterior, this corner pub in residential Greenwich is designed more for an excellent meal than a casual drink – though they do have a small bar where they keep two local beers on tap (perhaps from Brockley and Villages microbreweries), Umbrella cider (from north London), a good wine list and cocktails. The modern, open-plan bar has minimalist décor, contemporary chairs and tables on bare boards and high chairs by the counter and more by window shelves. The lower ground-floor dining room features an open charcoal-grill kitchen and leads out to a pretty outdoor space with seats and tables under parasols, trees and lighting spread across a terrace and garden. Upstairs, the restaurant is stylish, with abstract art and photographs of food producers on pale grey walls and dark chairs and tables on carpet.

Tasty, beautifully presented food includes vegetarian, fish and meat 'feasting menus' (for two), charcoal-grilled dishes such as prawn and monkfish skewers with basil mayo or spatchcocked chicken with chipotle and lemon and tomato salsa, bar food such as fish pie or burger and chips, seasonal salads, and puddings such as orange, almond and polenta cake with pomegranate and crème fraîche and plum, sloe and almond crumble. *Benchmark main dish: butterflied lamb with aubergine, dukkah and mint yoghurt £16.00. Two-course evening meal £22.00.*

Free house ~ Licensee Guy Awford ~ Real ale ~ Open 12-11; 12-11 Sat; 12-10.30 Sun ~ Bar food 12-4, 5.30-9 Mon-Thurs, Sun; 12-4, 5.30-9.30 Fri, Sat ~ Restaurant ~ Children welcome ~ Dogs allowed in bar

SOUTH LONDON
Map 12

Victoria

(020) 8876 4238 – www.victoriasheen.co.uk
West Temple Sheen; Mortlake rail; SW14 7RT

Bustling pub serving all-day food and drink with a leafy garden; comfortable bedrooms

With its leafy garden and proximity to the roaming deer, noisy parrots and grassy acres of Richmond Park (just a five-minute walk away), this is a marvellously bucolic place to stay in the capital. With a buzzing but informal atmosphere, the bar rooms have button-back leather sofas and simple chairs and tables on bare floorboards, candles in lanterns, decorative bright pink or stag's head wallpaper, and stools against the counter where friendly young staff serve Timothy Taylors Landlord, Wimbledon Common Pale Ale and a changing guest on handpump, 14 good wines by the glass and winter mulled wine. There's another room with chandeliers and a stag's head; background music. A conservatory-style dining room has comfortable modern leather chairs around tables of varying sizes on pale floorboards, and doors that lead into the walled (and heated) garden where good quality seats and tables are set out under parasols and there's a children's play area. The old stables have been converted into seven comfortable, colourful bedrooms; breakfasts are good. Disabled access but no disabled loos. This is sister pub to the Fox & Grapes in Wimbledon.

Good, interesting food includes breakfast and brunch at weekends. Dishes might include Asian prawn salad with edamame, bean shoots and roasted peanuts, scotch egg with courgette, rocket and runner bean salad, tomato, basil and mozzarella gnocchi with basil pesto, pan-fried whole Cornish lemon sole with samphire, capers and noisette butter, ale-battered fish and chips, and puddings such as baked custard, poached gooseberries and shortbread and chocolate mousse with salted caramel, chocolate soil and honeycomb. *Benchmark main dish: burger and chips £14.50. Two-course evening meal £21.00.*

Jolly Fine Pub Group ~ Manager Jake Smith ~ Real ale ~ Open 12-11; closed Mon, Tues; 12-9 Sun ~ Bar food 12-9; 12-7 Sun ~ Restaurant ~ Children welcome ~ Dogs allowed in bar & restaurant ~ Bedrooms: £110

WEST LONDON Map 12

Brown Cow ♀

(020) 7384 9559 – www.thebrowncowpub.co.uk
Fulham Road; Parsons Green tube; SW6 5SA

Busy pub with food and drinks served all day by cheerful staff

This airy, rustic-style pub is open (and serves food) all day, so there are always plenty of customers popping in and out. The open-plan bar is furnished and decorated in a minimalist style with wooden and cushioned dining chairs and leather-topped stools around rustic tables on bare boards, button-back wall banquettes, prints on pale painted walls, a few suitcases on racks, house plants and industrial-style ceiling lamps. From a small bar counter lined with stools, friendly staff serve Youngs Original and two or three other ales on handpump, good wines by the glass and a growing collection of gins; background music and TV. There are a couple of tables outside on a side road.

Enjoyable food, from weekend brunches to Sunday roasts, includes truffle mac 'n' cheese fritters, crispy bacon, gem and avocado salad, chicken, tarragon and leek pie with buttered greens and mash, roast cauliflower with Persian-spiced lentils, spinach and chickpeas, 8oz rump steak with garlic and parsley butter and chips, and puddings such as rhubarb and custard crumble pie and lemon tart with crème fraîche. *Benchmark main dish: British brisket burger with ruby slaw and fries £12.50. Two-course evening meal £20.00.*

Cirrus Inns ~ Licensee Conrad Allard ~ Real ale ~ Open 10am-midnight; 10am-10.30pm Sun ~ Bar food 10am-11pm; 10-9 Sun ~ Restaurant ~ Children welcome ~ Dogs allowed in bar

WEST LONDON

Map 12

Dove ♀ ◧

(020) 8748 9474 – www.dovehammersmith.co.uk

Upper Mall; Ravenscourt Park tube; W6 9TA

Character pub with a lovely riverside terrace, cosily traditional front bar and an interesting history

---

This old-fashioned riverside pub is much loved and has been for decades – the front snug in particular is very popular, and is in the Guinness World Records as having the smallest bar room at a mere 1.3 metres by 2.4 metres. The low-ceilinged main bar is cosy, traditional and unchanging, with black panelling, red leatherette built-in wall settles and stools around assorted tables and an open fire. It leads to a bigger, similarly furnished back room that's more geared to eating, which in turn leads to a conservatory. Fullers ESB, London Pride and their seasonal beers such as Olivers Island and Seafarers on handpump, and more than 20 wines by the glass including champagne and sparkling wine. Head down steps at the back to reach the verandah with its highly prized tables looking over a low river wall to the Thames Reach just above Hammersmith Bridge; a tiny exclusive area, reached up a spiral staircase, is a prime spot for watching rowers on the water. The pub has played host to many writers, actors and artists over the years (there's a fascinating framed list on a wall); it's said to be where 'Rule, Britannia!' was composed and was a favourite with Turner, who painted the view of the Thames from here, and with Graham Greene. The street itself is associated with the foundation of the arts and crafts movement – William Morris's Kelmscott House (open certain afternoons) is nearby.

 Popular food includes ham hock terrine with apple and fig chutney, grilled sardines with Isle of Wight tomatoes, artichoke and watercress, chicken schnitzel with apple, fennel, radish and watercress salad, corn-fed chicken with sautéed potatoes, burger (beef or vegan) and triple-cooked chips, and puddings such as set milk chocolate parfait with raspberries, honeycomb and raspberry sorbet and poached berries with verbena gel, burnt meringue and hazelnut crumb. *Benchmark main dish: battered haddock and triple-cooked chips £15.25. Two-course evening meal £22.00.*

Fullers ~ Manager Sonia Labatut ~ Real ale ~ Open 12-11; 12-10.30 Sun ~ Bar food 12-10; 12-9 Sun ~ Children welcome ~ Dogs allowed in bar

WEST LONDON

Map 12

Sands End ♀

(020) 7731 7823 – www.thesandsend.co.uk

Stephendale Road; Imperial Wharf rail; SW6 2PR

Simply furnished, bustling pub in a quiet street with interesting food and a thoughtful range of drinks; seats outside

---

A short stroll from Chelsea Harbour, this friendly Fulham dining pub is always busy with lots of well heeled young locals and visitors, offering an informal but gently civilised atmosphere. The open-plan bar features a mix of wooden dining chairs, the odd settle and cushioned wall seat and scrubbed pine, painted or polished wooden tables on bare boards. The dining area is quieter and more spacious; background music. From the solid, central counter, efficient staff serve Otter Bitter, Sambrooks Wandle and a couple of changing guest ales on handpump and 18 wines by the glass (including fizz). Upstairs is a private dining room. Outside, there are seats and tables at the front on the quiet residential street. Disabled access.

🍴 Enjoyable food includes pork and apple sausage rolls, truffle mac 'n' cheese fritters, seared bream fillet with Cornish new potato niçoise, thyme-roasted poussin with spicy potato wedges, caramelised lemon and aioli, flat-iron steak with a choice of sauce, crispy battered haddock and chips, roast cauliflower with Persian-spiced lentils, spinach and chickpeas, and desserts such as sticky toffee pudding and pear and pistachio tart with vanilla ice-cream. *Benchmark main dish: 8oz rump steak with chips and garlic and parsley butter £18.00. Two-course evening meal £24.00.*

Cirrus Inns ~ Licensee Susan Carrol ~ Real ale ~ Open 12-midnight; 10am-midnight Sat; 10am-10.30pm Sun ~ Bar food 12-4, 6-10; 10-8 Sun ~ Restaurant ~ Children welcome but no high chairs ~ Dogs allowed in bar

 WEST LONDON   Map 12
Windsor Castle
(020) 7243 8797 – www.thewindsorcastlekensington.co.uk
Campden Hill Road; Holland Park or Notting Hill Gate tube; W8 7AR

Genuinely unspoilt, with lots of atmosphere in tiny, dark rooms and lovely summer garden

Try to visit this unchanging pub at lunchtime when it's generally quieter than the evening and you can fully enjoy its charm. Three of the tiny unspoilt rooms have their own entrance from the street, but it's much more fun trying to navigate through the minuscule doors between them inside. There's a wealth of dark oak furnishings, sturdy high-backed built-in elm benches, soft lighting and a coal-effect fire. The panelled and wood-floored dining room at the back overlooks the garden. Marstons Pedigree, Sharps Doom Bar, Timothy Taylors Landlord and up to five guest beers on handpump, decent house wines, farm ciders and malt whiskies. The garden, on several levels, has tables and chairs on flagstones and feels secluded thanks to its high ivy-covered walls; there are heaters for cooler evenings.

🍴 Popular food includes duck liver parfait with apple, date and tamarind chutney, calamari with chilli and mango salsa, crispy pork belly with dauphinoise potato and red wine sauce, risotto with peas, asparagus and courgettes, marinated roast lemon and garlic chicken with truffled potatoes, vegan burger and chips, and desserts such as sticky toffee pudding with vanilla ice-cream and Belgian chocolate brownie with hazelnut ice-cream. *Benchmark main dish: beer-battered cod and triple-cooked chips £15.00. Two-course evening meal £22.00.*

Mitchells & Butlers ~ Manager Ian Constantine ~ Real ale ~ Open 12-11; 12-10.30 Sun ~ Bar food 12-10; 12-9 Sun ~ Restaurant ~ Children allowed in restaurant ~ Dogs allowed in bar

 OUTER LONDON   Map 12
Bell
(020) 8941 9799 – www.thebellinnhampton.co.uk
Thames Street, Hampton; Hampton rail; TW12 2EA

Bustling pub by the Thames with seats and heaters outside, real ales, a good choice of food and friendly service

The garden of this friendly riverside pub is a boon in summer, when the contemporary chairs and tables plus booth seating, heaters and barbecues are much appreciated by happy customers. Inside, there's a good vibrant atmosphere in the interconnected rooms: wooden dining and tub chairs around copper-topped or chunky wooden tables, comfortably upholstered wall seats with scatter cushions, mirrors, old photographs and lots of church candles. From the long panelled bar counter, helpful staff serve Sambrooks Wandle, Sharps Doom Bar and Timothy Taylors Landlord on handpump, Park Brewery Gallows Gold craft beer, 18 wines by the glass, ten gins and cocktails. Background music.

🍴 A wide range of popular food includes sandwiches, sharing plates and dishes such as wild boar liver, rum and ginger pâté, pan-fried turbot with sautéed potatoes, wild mushrooms and parsley cream sauce, slow-cooked lamb shank madras with rice, raita and flatbread, braised steak and Doombar ale hotpot with sautéed red and green cabbage, and various burgers, pizzas and steaks. Puddings include dark chocolate brownie with vanilla bean cream and summer fruit eton mess. *Benchmark main dish: chicken and mushroom pie with garlic mash and gravy £14.95. Two-course evening meal £23.00.*

Authentic Inns ~ Lease Simon Bailey ~ Real ale ~ Open 12-11; 12-midnight Fri, Sat ~ Bar food 12-3, 5.30-10; 12-10 Sat; 12-9 Sun ~ Restaurant ~ Children welcome ~ Dogs allowed in bar

OUTER LONDON
Mute Swan 🍷 🍺

Map 12

(020) 8941 5959 – www.brunningandprice.co.uk/muteswan
Palace Gate, Hampton Court Road; Hampton Court rail; KT8 9BN

Handsome pub close to the Thames with sunny seats outside, relaxed bar, upstairs dining room and imaginative food and drinks

Always busy and friendly, this spacious, well run Brunning & Price pub is just yards from the River Thames (though there's no view). The light and airy bar has four big leather armchairs grouped around a low table, as well as brown leather wall seats, high-backed Edwardian-style cushioned dining chairs around dark tables and rugs on bare boards. The walls are covered in interesting photographs, maps, prints and posters and there are sizeable house plants, glass and stone bottles on the windowsills and a woodburning stove; the atmosphere is informal and relaxed. St Austell Brunning & Price Traditional Bitter plus guests from breweries such as Adnams, Hogs Back, Park Brewery, Twickenham, Windsor & Eton and XT on handpump, a well chosen wine list with almost 50 choices by the glass, 70 gins, 80 whiskies, 20 rums and farm cider; staff are efficient and helpful. A metal spiral staircase – presided over by an elegant metal chandelier – leads up to the dining area where there are brass-studded caramel leather chairs around well spaced tables on bare boards or carpeting, and more photos and prints. The tables and chairs on the front terrace get snapped up quickly. The entrance to Hampton Court Palace is just across the road. There are a few parking spaces in front, but you'll probably have to park elsewhere.

🍴 Well regarded food includes sandwiches, smoked salmon with orange and beetroot salad, barbecue chicken wings, sweet potato, aubergine and spinach Malaysian curry, chicken, ham and leek pie, pea and mint tortellini with garden pea velouté and asparagus, pork and leek sausages with mash and onion gravy, chicken supreme with chorizo, sherry cream and cavolo nero, 10oz rib-eye steak with dijon and tarragon butter and chips, and puddings such as hot waffle with caramelised banana, toffee sauce and honeycomb ice-cream and dark chocolate torte with cherry sorbet. *Benchmark main dish: beer-battered fish and chips £14.95. Two-course evening meal £21.00.*

Brunning & Price ~ Manager Alessio Porti ~ Real ale ~ 11-11; 11am-midnight Fri Sat; 11-10.30 Sun ~ Bar food 12-9.30; 12-9 Sun ~ Restaurant ~ Children welcome in upstairs restaurant only ~ Dogs allowed in bar

---

If we don't specify bar meal times for a featured entry, these are normally 12-2 and 7-9; we do show times if they are markedly different.

OUTER LONDON   Map 3

Old Orchard ♀ ◖

(01895) 822631 – www.brunningandprice.co.uk/oldorchard

Off Park Lane, Harefield; Denham rail (some distance away); UB9 6HJ

Wonderful views from the front garden, a good choice of drinks and interesting brasserie-style food

On summer days, the front terrace and garden of this expansive pub are little pieces of paradise, offering stunning views down to the narrowboats on the canal way below and across to the lakes that are part of the conservation area known as the Colne Valley Regional Park – its own little piece of paradise for wildlife. Inside, the open-plan rooms have an attractive mix of cushioned dining chairs around all sizes and shapes of dark wooden tables, lots of prints, maps and pictures covering the walls, books on shelves, old glass bottles on windowsills and rugs on wood or parquet flooring. One room is hung with a large rug and some tapestries. There are daily papers to read, two cosy coal fires, big pot plants and fresh flowers. Half a dozen real ales on handpump served by friendly, efficient staff include St Austell Brunning & Price Traditional Bitter and frequently changing guests – the likes of Redemption Trinity, Tring Side Pocket for a Toad and XT Hop Kitty – plus 17 wines by the glass, 80 gins, 140 malt whiskies and farm cider. There's plenty of seating outside and space for children to run around, and a play tractor for them to climb on.

A daily changing menu of appealing dishes (special diets catered for) includes a vegetarian meze plate, chicken caesar croquettes, braised feather of beef bourguignon with horseradish mash and buttered kale, roast pork tenderloin with colcannon potato and apple purée, grilled sea bass fillets with potato and shallot terrine, chicken, ham and leek pie with mash and white chicken gravy, and puddings such as chocolate and orange tart with passion-fruit sorbet and summer pudding with clotted cream. *Benchmark main dish: fish pie (salmon, smoked haddock and prawns) £16.95. Two-course evening meal £23.00.*

Brunning & Price ~ Manager Alisha Craigwell ~ Real ale ~ Open 11.30-11; 11.30-10 Sun ~ Bar food 12-10; 12-9.30 Thurs-Sat; 12-9 Sun ~ Children welcome ~ Dogs welcome

Also Worth a Visit in London

Besides the fully inspected pubs, you might like to try these pubs that have been recommended to us and described by readers. Do tell us what you think of them: feedback@goodguides.com

CENTRAL LONDON

EC1

Bishops Finger (020) 7248 2341
West Smithfield; EC1A 9JR Welcoming little pub close to Smithfield Market; Shepherd Neame ales (including seasonals) and enjoyable pubby food from bar snacks and sharing boards up, can eat in bar or upstairs room; children welcome, seats out in front, closed weekends and bank holidays, otherwise open all day and can get crowded.

Butchers Hook & Cleaver
(020) 7600 9181 *West Smithfield; EC1A 9DY* Fullers conversion of bank and adjoining butcher's shop; their full range kept well and enjoyable pubby food including various pies, helpful efficient service, spiral stairs to mezzanine; children welcome, closed weekends, otherwise open (and food) all day, gets busy with after-work drinkers.

Coach (020) 3954 1595
Ray Street; EC1R 3DJ Smartly revamped Clerkenwell dining pub with very good French-inspired cooking from chef-owner; traditional oak-panelled front bar serving Timothy Taylors, three regularly changing guests and well chosen wines by the glass, airy pitched-roof back dining room with floor-to-ceiling glass overlooking small courtyard garden, more dining space

upstairs; occasional quiz; open all day, kitchen closes 6pm Sun.

Craft Beer Company
(020) 7404 7049 *Leather Lane; EC1N 7TR* Corner drinkers' pub with excellent selection of real ales and craft beers plus an extensive bottled range, good choice of wines and spirits too, stools by high tables on bare boards, big chandelier hanging from mirrored ceiling, food limited to snacks, more room upstairs; beer tastings and other events; closed Sun, otherwise open all day and can get very busy.

Dovetail
(020) 7490 7321 *Jerusalem Passage; EC1V 4JP* Fairly small and can get very busy with drinkers spilling into alleyway; specialises in draught/bottled Belgian beers and serves popular food including some Belgian and vegetarian/vegan dishes, efficient staff coping well at pub is at its busiest; occasional beer tastings; closed Sun, otherwise open all day.

Fox & Anchor
(020) 7250 1300 *Charterhouse Street, by Smithfield Market; EC1M 6AA* Beautifully restored late Victorian pub/boutique hotel with fine art nouveau façade, long slender bar with unusual pewter-topped counter, lots of mahogany, green leather and etched glass, small back snugs; Youngs ales and guests, enjoyable food from good breakfast onwards, friendly efficient staff; individual well appointed bedrooms, open all day from 7am (8.30am Sat, 11am Sun).

★ Jerusalem Tavern
(020) 7490 4281 *Britton Street; EC1M 5UQ* Atmospheric re-creation of a dark 18th-c tavern (1720 merchant's house with shopfront added 1810); tiny dimly lit bar with simple wood furnishings on bare boards, some remarkable old wall tiles, coal fires and candlelight, stairs to a precarious-feeling (though perfectly secure) balcony, plainer back room, St Peters beers tapped from the cask and in bottles, short choice of lunchtime food including sandwiches plus evening meals Mon-Weds, friendly attentive young staff; children allowed till 3pm, dogs welcome, seats out on pavement, open all day weekdays, closed weekends, bank holidays and 24 Dec-2 Jan; can get very crowded at peak times.

Ninth Ward
(020) 7833 2949 *Farringdon Road; EC1R 3BN* American-themed bar/grill (has sister restaurant in New York) with unusual New Orleans-inspired interior (quite dark), tasty food such as burgers and fried chicken, good range of craft and bottled beers, cocktails, friendly staff; background music; closed Sat lunchtime and Sun, otherwise open all day till late.

Old Fountain
(020) 7253 2970 *Baldwin Street; EC1V 9NU* Popular traditional old pub in same family since 1964; long bar serving two rooms, main carpeted part with wooden tables and chairs and padded stools, excellent range of real ales and craft beers chalked on blackboard (some brewed in the cellar), enjoyable good value food from open kitchen, friendly knowledgeable staff; function room for live music, darts; nice roof terrace; open (and food) all day, no food Sun evening.

Old Red Cow
(020) 7600 6240 *Long Lane; EC1A 9EJ* Cheerful little pub close to the Barbican and within sight of Smithfield Market; fine changing selection of cask, craft and bottled beers, tasters offered by friendly knowledgeable staff, decent range of wines and well liked food from pizzas to popular Sun roasts, modernised interior with larger dining room upstairs; open (and food) all day and popular with after-work drinkers.

Viaduct Tavern
(020) 7600 1863 *Newgate Street; EC1A 7AA* Grade-II listed pub opposite Old Bailey on site of Newgate Prison (a couple of cells survive below), big copper lanterns outside, fine ornate high-ceilinged Victorian interior with three or four snug areas, Fullers ales and good selection of gins from horseshoe bar, snacky food such as sausage rolls and toasties; popular with after-work drinkers, open all day, closed Sun.

EC2
Hamilton Hall
(020) 7247 3579 *Bishopsgate; also entrance from Liverpool Street station; EC2M 7PY* Showpiece Wetherspoons pub with flamboyant Victorian baroque décor mixing with contemporary bar counter and modern furniture; lots of real ales, decent wines and their usual food and competitive pricing, friendly staff coping well at busy times, good-sized comfortable mezzanine; silenced machines, screens showing train times; good disabled access, café-style tables and chairs out in front, open Mon-Sat from 7am, Sun from 9am, can get very crowded after work.

Lord Aberconway
(020) 7929 1743 *Old Broad Street; EC2M 1QT* Victorian feel with high moulded ceiling, dark panelling, some red leather bench seating and drinking booths, five well kept ales, reasonably priced Nicholsons menu, dining gallery; handy for Liverpool Street station, gets busy with after-work drinkers, open all day (till 6pm Sun).

EC3
★ Counting House
(020) 7283 7123 *Cornhill; EC3V 3PD* Spacious bank conversion retaining original Victorian character; grand ceiling with impressive glass dome, chandeliers, rich polished mahogany and mosaics, stairs up to galleried

seating area, well kept Fullers beers from island bar with four-sided clock, enjoyable food including range of pies, efficient friendly service; wheelchair access, 15 bedrooms, open (and food) daily.

East India Arms (020) 7265 5121

Fenchurch Street; EC3M 4BR Standing-room 19th-c corner pub popular with City workers; small single room with wood floor, half-panelling, old local photographs and brewery mirrors, well kept Shepherd Neame ales served by efficient staff, tables outside, closed weekends, otherwise open all day.

Hoop & Grapes (020) 7481 4583

Aldgate High Street; EC3N 1AL Originally 17th-c (dismantled and rebuilt 1983) and much bigger inside than it looks; long partitioned bare-boards bar with beams, timbers, exposed brickwork and panelling, mix of seating including some button-back wall benches, eight real ales and standard Nicholsons menu (popular at lunchtime), friendly efficient service; a few seats in front, open (and food) all day.

Jamaica Wine House

(020) 7929 6972 *St Michael Alley, Cornhill; EC3V 9DS* 19th-c red-stone pub (site of London's first coffee house) in warren of small alleys; traditional Victorian décor with ornate coffered ceiling, oak-panelled booths and bare boards, Shepherd Neame ales and wide choice of wines, food in bar or downstairs dining room until 5pm; friendly helpful service; quiz first Tues of month; busiest lunchtime/early evening, closed weekends.

Lamb (020) 7626 2454

Leadenhall Market; EC3V 1LR Stand-up bar with friendly staff coping admirably with hordes of after-work drinkers, dark panelling, engraved glass and plenty of ledges and shelves, Youngs ales and good choice of wines, corner servery for lunchtime food; spiral stairs up to small carpeted gallery overlooking market's central crossing, separate stairs to nice bright dining room (separate menu), also basement bar with shiny wall tiles; tables out under splendid Victorian market roof – crowds here in warmer months, closed Sun, otherwise open (and food) all day.

Ship (020) 7702 4422

Hart Street; EC3R 7NB Tiny one-room 19th-c City pub with ornate flower-decked façade; well kept St Austell and a couple of guests, craft beers and ten wines by the glass, lunchtime food including selection of bar snacks and signature burgers, meal/drink deals, friendly staff, limited seating and can get packed, upstairs dining room, spiral stairs down to lavatories; closed weekends, otherwise open all day.

Ship (020) 7929 3903

Talbot Court, off Eastcheap; EC3V 0BP Interesting Nicholsons pub tucked down alleyway; busy bare-boards bar with soft lighting and ornate décor, galleried dining area, friendly efficient staff, several well kept ales including St Austell house beer, well liked good value food; closed Sun, otherwise open all day, till 6pm Sat.

Swan (020) 7929 6550

Ship Tavern Passage, off Gracechurch Street; EC3V 1LY Traditional Fullers pub with bustling narrow flagstoned bar; their well kept ales and lunchtime sandwiches/burgers, friendly efficient service, neatly kept Victorian panelled décor, low lighting, larger more ordinary carpeted bar upstairs; silent TV; covered alley used by smokers, open all day Mon-Fri, closed weekends.

EC4

★ Black Friar (020) 7236 5474

Queen Victoria Street; EC4V 4EG Pub near Blackfriars station built on site of 13th-c Dominican priory; an architectural gem with some stunning Edwardian bronze and marble art nouveau work, inner back room (the Grotto) with low vaulted mosaic ceiling, big bas-relief friezes of jolly monks set into richly coloured Florentine marble walls, gleaming mirrors, seats built into golden marble recesses and opulent pillared inglenook, ironic verbal embellishments such as Silence is Golden and Finery is Foolish, and opium-smoking hints modelled into the front room's fireplace; six ales including Fullers, Sharps and Nicholsons (St Austell), plenty of wines by the glass, traditional food (speciality pies); children welcome if quiet, plenty of room on wide forecourt, open (and food) all day.

Cockpit (020) 7248 7315

St Andrews Hill/Ireland Place, off Queen Victoria Street; EC4V 5BY Plenty of atmosphere in this little corner pub near St Paul's Cathedral; as name suggests, a former cockfighting venue with surviving spectators' gallery; good selection of beers such as Adnams, St Austell and Shepherd Neame, lunchtime food; open all day.

★ Old Bank of England

(020) 7430 2255 *Fleet Street; EC4A 2LT* Sumptuous conversion of Grade I-listed Italianate building (former branch of Bank of England), splendid lofty bar with unusually high island bar counter, chandeliers, ornate plastered ceiling, lots of other areas off including balcony, McMullens cask ales, Rivertown on draught, decent wines, well presented popular food (including, appropriately for a venue situated between Sweeney Todd's barber shop and Mrs Lovett's pie shop, pies), always very popular – closed and under refurbishment as we went to press, reports please.

Old Bell (020) 7583 0216

*Fleet Street, near Ludgate Circus;
EC4Y 1DH* Flagstoned dimly lit 17th-c
tavern backing on to St Bride's Church;
elaborate stained-glass bow window, heavy
black beams; half a dozen or more well
kept changing beers from island servery
(tasting trays available), usual Nicholsons
food, friendly helpful staff, various seating
nooks with brass-topped tables, coal fire;
background music; covered and heated
outside area, open all day.

★ Olde Cheshire Cheese

(020) 7353 6170 *Wine Office Court, off
145 Fleet Street; EC4A 2BU* Best to visit
this 17th-c former chophouse outside peak
times as it can be packed (early evening
especially); soaked in history with warren
of old-fashioned unpretentious rooms, high
beams, bare boards and old built-in black
benches, Victorian paintings on dark brown
walls, big open fires, tiny snug and steep
stone steps down to unexpected series of
cosy areas and secluded alcoves, Sam Smiths
beers, all-day pubby food, look out for Polly
the parrot (now stuffed) who entertained
distinguished guests for over 40 years;
children allowed in eating area at lunchtime
only, closed Sun.

Olde Watling (020) 7248 8935

Watling Street; EC4M 9BR Heavy-beamed
and timbered post-Blitz replica of pub built
by Wren in 1668; interesting choice of well
kept beers, standard Nicholsons menu,
good friendly service, quieter back bar and
upstairs dining room; open all day weekdays
(till 8pm Sat, 6pm Sun).

Three Cranes (020) 3455 7437

*Garlick Hill, opposite Mansion House
tube; EC4V 2BA* Revamped City pub
under same ownership as the Coach (EC1)
and Hero of Maida (W9); dark blue and oak
panelled bar with beers such as Beavertown,
Portobello and Timothy Taylors, good range
of wines and other drinks, snacky food
including sharing boards, full meals in
upstairs grill room, good friendly service;
open all day weekdays, closed weekends.

SW1

Antelope (020) 7824 8512

Eaton Terrace; SW1W 8EZ Pretty little
flower-decked local in Belgravia; traditional
interior with bare boards, panelling,
wallpaper and etched windows, mix of
old and new furniture, interesting prints
and gas-effect coal fire in tiled Victorian
fireplace; well kept Fullers ales from island
bar, upstairs dining room serving decent
pubby food (all day weekends) including
popular Sun roasts; board games, daily
papers; children (if eating) and dogs
welcome, open all day and can get crowded
in the evening.

Buckingham Arms (020) 7222 3386

Petty France; SW1H 9EU Welcoming and
relaxed early 19th-c bow-windowed local;
Youngs ales and two guests from long curved
bar, good range of wines by the glass and
well liked pubby food, elegant mirrors and
dark woodwork, stained-glass screens, some
armchairs and upholstered banquettes,
unusual side corridor with elbow ledge and
small tables; background music, TV, monthly
quiz, Meet the Brewer nights; dogs welcome,
handy for Buckingham Palace, Westminster
Abbey and St James's Park, open all day, till
5pm Sun.

Cask & Glass (020) 7834 7630

Palace Street; SW1E 5HN Snug traditional
one-room pub with friendly atmosphere;
black panelling, button-back wall benches
and old prints, good range of Shepherd
Neame ales, lunchtime toasties; quiet corner
TV; a few tables outside under awning, handy
for Queen's Gallery, open all day, till 8pm Sat,
closed Sun.

Cask Pub & Kitchen

(020) 7630 7225 *Charlwood Street/
Tachbrook Street; SW1V 2EE* Spacious
simply furnished modern bar; excellent
choice of draught beers with over 300 more
in bottles, decent range of wines too, good
burgers, bar snacks and Sun roasts, friendly
knowledgeable staff, chatty atmosphere –
can get packed and noisy in the evening; Sun
live music, regular beer-related events such
as Meet the Brewer; some outside seating,
open all day, food all day weekends.

Clarence (020) 7930 4808

Whitehall; SW1A 2HP Popular beamed
corner pub (Geronimo Inn) with cheerful
quirky décor; Youngs and guest ales such
as St Austell Proper Job, decent wines by
the glass and good food from snacks up;
quick friendly service, well spaced tables
and varied seating including tub chairs and
banquettes, upstairs dining area; three TVs;
children welcome till 6pm (9pm upstairs),
pavement tables, open (and food) all day.

★ Fox & Hounds (020) 7730 6367

*Passmore Street/Graham Terrace;
SW1W 8HR* Small flower-decked pub in
backstreets below Sloane Square; well kept
Youngs ales and guests, friendly staff, warm
red décor with panelling, lots of old pictures,
prints and photographs, wall benches and
leather chesterfields, coal-effect gas fire,
back room with skylight; TV, pub quiz last
Sun of the month; open (and snacky food)
all day, can get crowded early evening.

★ Grenadier (020) 7235 3074

*Wilton Row; the turning off Wilton
Crescent looks prohibitive, but the
barrier and watchman are there to keep
out cars; SW1X 7NR* Steps up to cosy
old mews pub with lots of character and

military history, but not much space (packed 5-7pm); simple unfussy panelled bar, stools and wooden benches on bare boards, Greene King ales and guests from rare pewter-topped counter, famous bloody marys, well liked food (can be pricey) from bar snacks up including signature beef wellington, intimate back restaurant; children over 8 and dogs allowed, hanging baskets, sentry box and benches outside, open (and food) all day.

Grosvenor (020) 7821 8786
Grosvenor Road; SW1V 3LA Traditional pub across from river (no views), chatty and relaxed, with three well kept ales including Sharps and nice selection of wines, enjoyable reasonably priced pubby food including good Sun roasts, friendly staff; pool, darts, board games and TV; some tables out by road, secluded beer garden behind, open (and food) all day.

Jugged Hare (020) 7828 1543
Vauxhall Bridge Road/Rochester Row; SW1V 1DX Popular Fullers pub in former colonnaded bank; iron pillars, dark woodwork and large chandelier, old photographs of London, smaller back panelled dining room, outdoor terrace, stairs up to gallery; four well kept ales and straightforward reasonably priced food including range of pies, good friendly service; background music, TVs, silent fruit machine; open all day.

★ Lord Moon of the Mall
(020) 7839 7701 *Whitehall; SW1A 2DY* Popular Wetherspoons bank conversion; elegant main room with big arched windows looking over Whitehall, old prints and a large portrait of Tim Martin (the chain's founder), through an arch the style is more recognisably Wetherspoons with neatly tiled areas and bookshelves opposite long servery; ten real ales and their good value food (from breakfasts up); children (if eating) and dogs welcome, open all day from 8am (till midnight Fri, Sat).

Morpeth Arms (020) 7834 6442
Millbank; SW1P 4RW Victorian pub facing the Thames with view over to MI6 headquarters from upstairs Spying Room; etched and cut glass, lots of mirrors, paintings, prints and old photographs (some of British spies); well kept Youngs ales and guests, decent choice of wines and fair value pubby food, welcoming efficient staff, built on site of Milbank Prison and cells remain below; seats outside (and a lot of traffic), handy for Tate Britain and Thames Path walkers, open (and food) all day, can get very busy weekday evenings.

Nags Head (020) 7235 1135
Kinnerton Street; SW1X 8ED Unspoilt and unchanging little mews pub with no-nonsense plain-talking landlord; low-ceilinged panelled front room with

unusual sunken counter, log-effect gas fire in old range, narrow passage down to even smaller bar, well kept Adnams from 19th-c handpumps, uncomplicated food, theatrical mementoes and other interesting memorabilia including a what-the-butler-saw machine and one-armed bandit; no mobiles, live music first Sun of the month, individual background music; well behaved children and dogs allowed, a few seats outside, open (and food) all day.

Red Lion (020) 7930 5826
Parliament Street; SW1A 2NH Victorian pub by Houses of Parliament used by Foreign Office staff and MPs; divided bare-boards bar with showy chandeliers suspended from fine moulded ceiling, parliamentary cartoons and prints, Fullers/Gales beers and decent wines from long counter, good range of food including popular fish and chips, efficient staff, also clubby cellar bar and upstairs panelled dining room; outside bench seating, open all day (till 9pm Sun).

Red Lion (020) 7930 4141
Crown Passage, behind St James's Street; SW1Y 6PP Cheerful traditional little pub with colourful hanging baskets tucked down narrow passage near St James's Palace; dark panelling and leaded lights, upholstered settles and stools on patterned carpet, lots of prints, decorative plates and horsebrasses; well kept Adnams, St Austell and decent range of malt whiskies, lunchtime sandwiches (no hot food), friendly service, narrow overflow room upstairs; sports TV; closed Sun, otherwise open all day.

★ Red Lion (020) 7321 0782
Duke of York Street; SW1Y 6JP Pretty little flower-decked Victorian pub, remarkably preserved and packed with customers often spilling out on to the pavement; series of small rooms with profusion of polished mahogany, gleaming mirrors, cut/etched windows and chandeliers, striking ornamental plaster ceiling, Fullers/Gales beers and traditional lunchtime food; children allowed until 8pm, closed Sun and bank holidays, otherwise open all day.

Speaker (020) 7222 4589
Great Peter Street; SW1P 2HA Bustling chatty atmosphere in this unpretentious smallish corner pub (can get packed at peak times); well kept Timothy Taylors and guests, bottled beers and lots of whiskies, no food (BYO from local eateries); friendly staff, panelling, political cartoons and prints, notes here and there on etiquette; board games, no mobile phones, background music or children; open all day Mon-Fri, closed weekends.

St Stephens Tavern (020) 7925 2286
Parliament Street; SW1A 2JR Victorian pub opposite Houses of Parliament and Big

Ben (so quite touristy); brass chandeliers hanging from lofty ceilings, tall windows with etched glass and swagged curtains, gleaming mahogany, division bell for MPs and lots of parliamentary memorabilia, also charming upper gallery bar (may be reserved for functions), four well kept Badger ales from handsome counter with pedestal lamps, fairly priced traditional food including burgers and pies; open (and food) all day.

White Swan (020) 7828 2000
Vauxhall Bridge Road; SW1V 2SA
Roomy split-level corner pub spruced up by McMullens; their ales and guests, decent wines by the glass and enjoyable sensibly priced pubby food, friendly staff, large etched glass windows, bare boards and chandeliers; background music, sports TV; handy for Tate Britain, open (and food) all day and can get very busy at peak times.

Windsor Castle (020) 7834 7260
Francis Street; SW1P 1DN Traditionally restored 19th-c pub directly behind Westminster Cathedral (was the Cardinal); modern etched glass and rebuilt screened snugs matching the original architect's drawings, fine Victorian moulded ceiling, open fires, well kept/priced Sam Smiths beers and enjoyable good value food (not Sun) such as fish and chips and steak and kidney pudding, parquet-floored back dining lounge with half-panelled and papered walls, another bar upstairs (not always open); no children, open all day.

SW3
Coopers Arms (020) 7376 3120
Flood Street; SW3 5TB Refurbished 19th-c pub, a useful bolthole for King's Road shoppers (so can get very busy); comfortable bar with good mix of tables and upholstered chairs on stripped boards, large moose head on one wall, open fire, well kept Youngs ales, guest beers and good selection of other drinks including over 20 wines by the glass and cocktails, decent food from fairly pubby menu; Tues quiz, projector for major sports, board games; well behaved children till 7pm, dogs allowed in bar, courtyard garden, open (and food) all day.

Hour Glass (020) 7581 2497
Brompton Road; SW3 2DY Compact wood-floored bar with open brick fireplace, leather banquette at each end, stools along drinking shelf overlooking street, Harviestoun ales, well chosen wines and good whisky/gin range, snacky food through to burgers and pub classics, sharing boards and kids' menu, panelled upstairs dining room, friendly helpful service; handy for V&A and other nearby museums, open all day (till 9.30pm Sun), no food Sun evening to Tues lunchtime.

Surprise (020) 7351 6954
Christchurch Terrace; SW3 4AJ
Late Victorian Chelsea pub (Geronimo Inn) popular with well heeled locals; Sharps, Youngs and a house beer (HMS Surprise) from light wood servery, champagne and plenty of other wines by the glass, interesting food (all day weekends) including British tapas-style canapé boards; friendly service, soft grey décor and comfortable furnishings with floral sofas and armchairs on sturdy floorboards, stained-glass partitioning, a model ship or two, upstairs dining room, daily papers; benches out in front under awning, open all day.

W1
★Argyll Arms (020) 7734 6117
Argyll Street; W1F 7TP Popular and individual Nicholsons pub with three interesting little front cubicle rooms (essentially unchanged since 1860s), wooden partitions and impressive frosted and engraved glass, mirrored corridor to spacious back room, eight real ales from well stocked bar and good sensibly priced food, upstairs dining room overlooking pedestrianised street; background music, fruit machine; children welcome till 8pm, pavement tables, convenient for the Palladium, open (and food) all day.

Clachan (020) 7494 0834
Kingly Street; W1B 5QH Nicholsons corner pub behind Liberty (and once owned by them): ornate plaster ceiling supported by fluted pillars, comfortable screened leather banquettes, smaller drinking alcove up three steps; fine selection of real ales from handsome mahogany counter, affordably priced meals in upstairs dining room; open (and food) all day, can get very busy.

Crown & Two Chairmen
(020) 7437 8192 *Bateman Street/Dean Street; W1D 3SB* Popular Soho corner pub; large bright main room with smaller area off to the right, different height tables on bare boards, ten real ales and craft beers on rotation, enjoyable food (shortish menu) from sharing boards up including Sun roasts, upstairs dining room, good mix of customers (busy with after-work drinkers); pavement tables, open (and food) all day.

★Dog & Duck (020) 7494 0697
Bateman Street/Frith Street; W1D 3AJ
Bags of character in this tiny Soho pub – best enjoyed in the afternoon when not so packed; unusual old tiles and mosaics (the dog with tongue hanging out in hot pursuit of a duck is notable), heavy old advertising mirrors and open fire, seven real ales including St Austell and Sharps from unusual little counter and quite a few wines by the glass, enjoyable

---

We say if we know a pub allows dogs.

well priced food (Nicholsons menu) in cosy upstairs dining room where children welcome; background music; dogs allowed in bar, open (and food) all day with drinkers often spilling on to the pavement.

Flying Horse (020) 7636 8324

Oxford Street, near junction with Tottenham Court Road; W1D 1AN Ornate late Victorian pub with long narrow bar; old tiling, mirrors, stained glass, mahogany fittings and so forth, also three notable murals behind glass of voluptuous nymphs painted by Felix de Jong, leather button-back banquettes and other furniture on bare boards, up to seven real ales and over 20 gins, friendly service, another bar downstairs; background music; children welcome until 9pm, can get very busy at lunchtime, open all day.

French House (020) 7437 2477

Dean Street; W1D 5BG Small character Soho pub with impressive range of wines, bottled beers and unusual drinks, some draught beers but no real ales or pint glasses; lively chatty atmosphere (mainly standing room), theatre memorabilia, good if not cheap modern food from short daily changing menu (lunchtimes Mon-Fri, evenings Tues-Fri) in bar or upstairs restaurant (must book), attentive friendly staff; no music or mobile phones; can get very busy evenings with customers spilling out on to the street, open all day.

Grapes (020) 7493 4216

Shepherd Market; W1J 7QQ Genuinely old-fashioned corner pub with dimly lit bar; stuffed birds and fish in display cases, some old guns, red button-back banquettes, wood floors and coal fire, snug back alcove, six real ales including Fullers, Sharps and a house beer from Brains, good choice of Thai food (some English dishes too, including toasties) in upstairs restaurant, lots of customers (especially lunchtime/early evening) out on the square in good weather; children till 6pm weekdays in bar (anytime in restaurant), open all day.

★Guinea (020) 7409 1728

Bruton Place; W1J 6NL Lovely hanging baskets outside this tiny 17th-c Mayfair mews pub, standing room only at peak times, a few cushioned wooden seats and tables on bare boards, side elbow shelf and snug back area, old-fashioned prints, planked ceiling, Youngs beers and a couple of guests, good range of wines and whiskies, shortish choice of food (not Sun evening) including famous steak and kidney pie, also smart (and expensive) Guinea Grill restaurant; open all day (till 6pm Sun).

Prince Regent (020) 7486 7395

Marylebone High Street; W1U 5JN Victorian corner pub in Marylebone village;

spacious bare-boards bar mixing original features with modern chic, four changing ales, lots of craft beers on rotation, good range of wines and cocktails, enjoyable food from pub standards up; Mon quiz; children welcome, open (and food) all day.

Running Horse (020) 7493 1275

Davies Street/Davies Mews; W1K 5JE Stylish 18th-c Mayfair pub with open-plan bare-boards bar; appealing collection of dining chairs and cushioned settles around mix of tables, tartan armchairs in front of green-tiled fireplace, horse-racing prints on plain or navy-painted panelling; regular and changing ales such as Rebellion, lots of wines by the glass and good food from bar snacks up (prices on the high side), upstairs cocktail bar with button-back club chairs, brass chandeliers and more horsey prints; background music, projector showing live televised racing; seats and tables out on the pavement, open all day (till 8pm Sun).

Three Tuns (020) 7408 0330

Portman Mews S; W1H 6HP Large bare-boards front bar and sizeable lounge/dining area with beams and nooks and crannies, Greene King ales and guests, generous helpings of enjoyable reasonably priced pub food, good friendly staff and buoyant atmosphere; regular quiz, BT and Sky Sports; garden, open (and food) all day.

W2

Leinster Arms (020) 7402 4670

Leinster Terrace; W2 3EU Small traditional flower-decked pub close to Hyde Park, friendly and busy, with Fullers London Pride, three guest beers and well liked pubby food at sensible prices; sports TV; children and dogs welcome, a few pavement tables, open (and food) all day.

Mad Bishop & Bear

(020) 7402 2441 *Paddington station; W2 1HB* Fullers pub up escalator from station concourse; their beers kept well and good choice of wines, reasonably priced standard food quickly served including breakfast from 7.30am (10am Sun), airy interior with ornate plasterwork and mirrored columns, high tables and chairs on light wood or tiled floors, raised carpeted dining area with some booth seating; background music, games machines and TVs (including train times); tables out at front, open all day till 11pm (10.30pm Sun).

★Victoria (020) 7724 1191

Strathearn Place; W2 2NH Well run and restored bare-boards pub with lots of Victorian pictures and memorabilia, cast-iron fireplaces, gilded mirrors and mahogany panelling, brass mock-gas lamps above attractive horseshoe bar serving Fullers ales, guest beers and several wines by the glass, popular reasonably priced food from sandwiches and snacks up, friendly service and chatty relaxed atmosphere, upstairs has small library/snug and replica of Gaiety Theatre bar (mostly for private functions); quiet background music, TV; children and dogs welcome, pavement tables and pretty hanging baskets, open (and food) all day.

WC1

Bountiful Cow (020) 7404 0200
Eagle Street; WC1R 4AP Popular for its excellent burgers and steaks; informal bar with cow themed decoration, booth seating and raised area by the windows, chrome stools against counter serving ales such as Adnams and several wines by the glass, smallish upper room and larger downstairs dining room; background music, jazz nights; children welcome, closed Sun, otherwise open all day.

Calthorpe Arms (020) 7278 4732
Grays Inn Road; WC1X 8JR Friendly early Victorian corner local; well kept Youngs ales and guests such as Sambrooks and Twickenham, short choice of enjoyable low-priced food including sandwiches and Sun roasts, carpeted bar with plush wall seats, upstairs overspill dining/function room; Sat folk music and regular film and quiz evenings, sports TV; dogs welcome, pavement tables, open all day, no food Sun evening.

★Cittie of Yorke (020) 7242 7670
High Holborn; WC1V 6BN Splendid back bar rather like a baronial hall with extraordinary extended counter, 1,000-gallon wine vats resting above gantry, bulbous lights hanging from soaring raftered roof, intimate ornately carved booths and unusual triangular fireplace, smaller comfortable panelled room with lots of little prints of York, cheap Sam Smiths beers and reasonably priced bar and pubby food, popular with students, lawyers and City types but plenty of space to absorb the crowds; no mobiles, children welcome, closed Sun, otherwise open all day.

Harrison (020) 7278 3966
Harrison Street; WC1H 8JF Tucked-away 1930s red-brick corner pub; modernised bar with simple mix of tables and chairs on bare boards, sofas by woodburner, three real ales such as Sharps Doom Bar and enjoyable food from snacks up (plenty for vegetarians), good friendly service; nightly live music (mainly folk) in basement; pavement picnic-sets, four bedrooms, open all day, kitchen shuts 4-5pm weekdays.

Lady Ottoline (020) 7831 0008
Northington Street; WC1N 2JF Sympathetically refurbished 19th-c Bloomsbury pub; original fitted benches together with modern high tables and stools on bare boards, woodburner, various artworks including portrait of Lady Ottoline Morrell

who had associations with the Bloomsbury Set, four changing ales, over 40 gins and plenty of wines by the glass, enjoyable modern food from bar snacks up, attentive friendly service, upstairs dining room; TV; children (till 6pm) and dogs allowed, pavement tables, open all day (till 5pm Sun).

★Lamb (020) 7405 0713
Lambs Conduit Street; WC1N 3LZ Authentic 19th-c Bloomsbury pub with green-tiled frontage; bank of cut-glass swivelling snob screens around U-shaped counter, sepia photographs of 1890s actresses on ochre-panelled walls, traditional cast-iron-framed tables and button-back wall benches on stripped boards, snug little back room, Youngs ales and guests kept well, good choice of wines and malt whiskies, decent food from sandwiches, sharing boards, Sun roasts (until 9.30pm) and pub favourites up, helpful efficient service, function room upstairs; Sun quiz; children welcome till 5pm, seats in small paved courtyard behind, Foundling Museum nearby, open all day (till midnight Thurs-Sat) and can get very busy.

Museum Tavern (020) 7242 8987
Museum Street/Great Russell Street; WC1B 3BA Ornate high-ceilinged Victorian pub opposite British Museum; half a dozen well kept ales and several wines by the glass, standard Taylor Walker menu, friendly helpful staff; pavement tables, open (and food) all day and busy lunchtime/early evening.

★Princess Louise (020) 7405 8816
High Holborn; WC1V 7EP Splendid Victorian gin palace with extravagant décor – even the gents' has its own preservation order; gloriously opulent main bar with wood and glass partitions, fine etched and gilt mirrors, brightly coloured and fruit-shaped tiles, slender Portland stone columns soaring towards the lofty and deeply moulded plaster ceiling, open fire, good value Sam Smiths beers from long counter, competitively priced pubby food (not Fri evening or weekends) in quieter upstairs room; no children, open all day (till 6.45pm Sun) and gets crowded early weekday evenings.

Queens Head (020) 7713 5772
Acton Street; WC1X 9NB Small Victorian terraced pub attracting good mix of customers; wide ever-changing range of UK and European draught beers (plenty more in bottles), real ciders and extensive whisky choice, food such as pork pies and meat/cheese boards; friendly knowledgeable staff, traditional interior with wood floors, etched mirrors and listed wall tiles, skylit back part; board games, live piano Thurs and Sun, live jazz last Thurs of month; open all day.

Queens Larder (020) 7837 5627
Queen Square; WC1N 3AR Cosy little Bloomsbury corner pub also known as the

Queen Charlotte (it's where she stored food for her mentally ill husband George III, who was being cared for nearby); character bare-boards bar with cast-iron tables, wall benches and stools around U-shaped counter, theatre posters on dark panelled walls, Greene King ales and a well kept guest such as Redemption Hopspur, decent lunchtime pubby food delivered by dumb waiter from upstairs kitchen, friendly service; background music; dogs welcome, pavement picnic-sets, open all day.

Skinners Arms (020) 7837 5621

Judd Street; WC1H 9NT Richly decorated, with glorious woodwork, high stuccoed ceilings and ornate windows, lots of London prints on busy wallpaper, interesting layout including comfortable back seating area, open fire, Greene King and guests from attractive long bar, enjoyable home-made food; unobtrusive background music and muted TV; pavement picnic-sets, handy for British Library, closed Sun, otherwise open all day.

Union Tavern (020) 7278 0111

Lloyd Baker Street; WC1X 9AA Bright bare-boards Victorian corner pub with attractive period décor; beers such as Beavertown, Curious, Sambrooks and Trumans, lots of wines by the glass and some premium gins served from dark wood bar, much enjoyed food from varied menu including very good value lunchtime/early evening set deals, friendly helpful service; background music; children and dogs welcome, open all day, food most of the day too, weekend brunch from 10.30am.

WC2

Admiralty (020) 7930 0066

Trafalgar Square; WC2N 5DS Handsome naval-theme pub by Trafalgar Square; button-back leather seating booths by big windows, high stools and elbow tables, grand chandeliers and lots of interesting prints, Fullers/Gales beers from traditional counter, standard pub food including breakfast from 9am (10am Sun) and speciality pies, efficient friendly staff, grand steps up to mezzanine, also atmospheric vaulted cellar bar; children welcome, a few pavement tables, open all day from 9am (10am Sun).

Bear & Staff (020) 7321 0814

Bear Street; WC2H 7AX Traditional Nicholsons corner pub with half a dozen well kept changing ales and standard pubby food (including deals) from sandwiches and pies up, friendly staff, upstairs dining room named after Charlie Chaplin who was a customer; pavement tables under awning, open (and food) all day.

Chandos (020) 7836 1401

St Martins Lane; WC2N 4ER Busy bare-boards bar just off Trafalgar Square with snug cubicles and plenty of standing room (can get packed early evening), lots of theatre memorabilia on stairs up to more comfortable split-level lounge with opera photographs (the Coliseum is almost next door), low wooden tables, panelling, leather sofas and stained-glass windows; well kept/priced Sam Smiths beers and decent good value pub food; background music and games machines; children upstairs till 9pm, open all day from 9am (for breakfast).

Coal Hole (020) 7379 9883

Strand; WC2R 0DW Well preserved Edwardian pub adjacent to the Savoy; original leaded windows, classical wall reliefs and high baronial-style ceiling, good selection of changing ales from central servery, standard Nicholsons menu, galleried area at back and wine bar downstairs; sports TV; open all day and can get very busy.

Cross Keys (020) 7836 5185

Endell Street/Betterton Street; WC2H 9EB Flower-decked Covent Garden pub with fascinating interior; masses of photographs, pictures and posters including Beatles memorabilia, all kinds of brassware and bric-a-brac from stuffed fish to musical instruments, well kept Brodies ales, guest beers and decent wines by the glass, good lunchtime sandwiches and a few bargain hot dishes including generous Sun roast; fruit machine; gents' downstairs, cobbled area out at front with tubs of flowers, open all day.

Edgar Wallace (020) 7353 3120

Essex Street; WC2R 3JE Spacious open-plan pub dating from the 18th c; eight well kept ales and enjoyable good value traditional food from sandwiches and snacks up (until 3pm Fri), half-panelled walls and red ceilings covered in beer mats, interesting Edgar Wallace memorabilia and lots of old cigarette adverts and other signs, friendly efficient service, upstairs dining room; no laptops, a few tables in side alleyway, closed weekends, otherwise open all day.

George (020) 7353 9638

Strand; WC2R 1AP Timbered pub near the law courts with long narrow bare-boards bar, plenty of real ales including Greene King and four changing guests, a dozen wines by the glass, lunchtime food from sandwiches up, upstairs Pig and Goose bar-restaurant serving modern British food; open (and food) all day.

Knights Templar (020) 7831 2660

Chancery Lane; WC2A 1DT Good well managed Wetherspoons in big-windowed

---

If you know a pub is ever open all day, please tell us.

former bank; marble pillars, handsome fittings, chandeliers and plasterwork, bustling atmosphere on two levels, ever-changing range of well kept/priced ales, good wine choice and enjoyable bargain food, including breakfast, friendly efficient service; children allowed until 9pm, open all day Mon-Fri, till 7pm Sat, closed Sun.

Mr Foggs Tavern (020) 7581 3992

St Martins Lane; WC2N 4EA Themed around Jules Verne's Phileas Fogg; small Victorian-style bar with appropriate pictures and stuffed animals on panelled walls, unusual tiled toilets, masses of bric-a-brac hanging from ceiling including model boats, bird cages, brass instruments, even an old pram; craft beers and over a dozen wines by the glass from metal-topped servery, friendly staff in period dress, enjoyable food including bar snacks, sharing plates, pies and Sun roasts, atmospheric upstairs re-creation of 19th-c salon/gin parlour with swagged curtains, Chinese wallpaper and chaise longues, extensive selection of gins and cocktails; children until 5pm, open all day.

Nell Gwynne (020) 7240 5579

Bull Inn Court, off Strand; WC2R 0NP Narrow dimly lit old pub tucked down alleyway; character bare-boards interior with lots of pictures (some of Nell Gwynne) on papered walls, a few tables and bar stools but mainly standing room and drinkers spill outside at busy times, St Austell Tribute and three guests, some interesting bottled beers and extensive range of spirits, bar snacks and toasties, open fire; good juke box, TV, darts; open all day.

Porterhouse (020) 7379 7917

Maiden Lane; WC2E 7NA London outpost of Dublin's Porterhouse brewery, in heart of Covent Garden, their interesting beers along with guests and lots of bottled imports, good choice of wines by the glass and Irish whiskeys, decent pubby food including pizzas, friendly efficient staff, three-level labyrinth of stairs (lifts for disabled), galleries, gleaming copper ducting and piping, prominent open-work clock hanging from the ceiling and neatly cased bottled beer displays dotted about; background and live music, sports TVs (even in the gents'); tables on front terrace, open all day and can get packed evenings.

Salisbury (020) 7836 5863

St Martins Lane; WC2N 4AP Gleaming Victorian pub opposite the Coliseum with a wealth of cut-glass and mahogany, wonderfully ornate bronze light fittings and etched mirrors, some interesting photographs including Dylan Thomas enjoying a drink here in 1941, well kept ales and good range of food from bar snacks and sharing platters up, cheerful staff; steep stairs down to lavatories; children allowed till 5pm, seats in pedestrianised side alley, open (and food) all day.

★Seven Stars (020) 7242 8521

Carey Street; WC2A 2JB Characterful pub (at back of Law Courts) with three rooms, liked by lawyers and reporters, red walls of the two main rooms lined with caricatures of barristers and judges and posters of legal-themed British films, big ceiling fans, checked tablecloths, cosy atmosphere, third room in former legal wig shop next door – it still has original frontage and neat display of wigs in windows, Adnams as a regular with four guests, including Harveys Best and Sambrooks Wandle, good interesting bar food all day, look out for Tom Paine the po-faced pub cat; fills up very quickly but can stand outside, no children.

Ship (020) 7405 1992

Gate Street; WC2A 3HP Tucked-away Holborn pub with dimly lit bare-boards bar; leaded lights, panelling and plaster-relief ceiling, some booth seating, open fire, six real ales including a Caledonian house beer, good variety of gins and enjoyable bar food, upstairs candlelit restaurant (good separate menu), friendly service; background music, live jazz late Sun afternoons; open (and food) all day.

★Ship & Shovell (020) 7839 1311

Craven Passage, off Craven Street; WC2N 5PH Unusually split between two facing buildings, one side brightly lit with dark wood, etched mirrors and interesting mainly naval pictures, some stall seating and open fire, other smaller side (across 'Underneath the Arches' alley) has a cosily partitioned bar, well kept Badger ales, a guest beer and reasonably priced pubby lunchtime food from baguettes up, good friendly service; next to Charing Cross station, closed Sun, otherwise open all day.

Temple Brew House (020) 7936 2536

Essex Street; WC2R 3JF Popular basement bar near the Royal Courts of Justice with exposed concrete, bare boards and some booths, fine range of beers including some from on-site microbrewery, wide selection of wines by the glass and well liked food from sandwiches, small plates and burgers up (own smokehouse), friendly service from enthusiastic knowledgeable young staff; board games; no under-18s, some pavement seating, open (and food) all day.

Wellington (020) 7836 2789

Strand/Wellington Street; WC2R 0HS Traditional corner pub next to the Lyceum Theatre; long narrow split-level bar with moulded ceiling, etched glass and ornate mahogany servery, ten real ales including Adnams and Fullers, craft beers and several wines by the glass, usual Nicholsons menu from breakfast up, friendly staff, upstairs restaurant; sports TV; tables outside, open (and food) all day.

EAST LONDON

E1

Princess of Prussia (020) 7702 0723

Prescot Street; E1 8AZ Atmospheric pub keeping original Burton Brewery signage at front and a couple of large Victorian lanterns; cosy interior with lots of pictures and bits and pieces on shelves, open fire, four well kept Shepherd Neame ales and enjoyable pubby food (all day Sat), relaxed chatty atmosphere; nice terrace garden behind, closed Sun, otherwise open all day.

★ Prospect of Whitby (020) 7481 1095

Wapping Wall; E1W 3SH Claims to be oldest pub on the Thames dating from 1520 (although largely rebuilt after much later fire), was known as the Devil's Tavern and has a colourful history (Pepys and Dickens used it regularly and Turner came for weeks at a time to study the river views) – tourists love it; L-shaped bare-boards bar with plenty of beams, flagstones and panelling, Greene King and four changing ales served from fine pewter counter, good choice of wines by the glass, bar food and up more formal restaurant upstairs; hard-working staff; Weds quiz; children welcome (only if eating after 5.30pm), unbeatable river views towards Docklands from tables on waterfront courtyard, open (and food) all day.

Town of Ramsgate (020) 7481 8000

Wapping High Street; E1W 2PN Interesting old-London Thames-side setting; long narrow dimly lit bar with squared oak panelling, Fullers, Harveys, Youngs and a guest, good choice of traditional food including daily specials and deals, friendly helpful service; background music, Mon quiz; children (till 8pm) and dogs welcome, restricted river view from small back terrace, open (and food) all day.

Williams (020) 7247 5163

Artillery Lane; E1 7LS Busy Spitalfields pub with 14 real ales (predominantly from smaller London brewers), craft beers and proper ciders, decent choice of well liked food from snacks up, comfortable seating areas, photographs of old London breweries on exposed brick walls; background and some live music, sports TV, darts; open (and food) all day.

E2

Sun (020) 7739 4097

Bethnal Green Road; E2 0AN Updated 19th-c bar with good choice of local craft beers and other drinks including cocktails, Irish whiskeys (the largest selection in London, it claims) and poitín, food limited to bar snacks and cheese/meat boards; friendly helpful service, bare floorboards, exposed brickwork and some leather banquettes, padded stools around copper-topped counter with industrial lanterns above, regular live music (Sun and Mon) and DJs, monthly local brewery hook-ups, open all day (till 2am Thurs-Sat).

E3

Palm Tree (020) 8980 2918

Grove Road; E3 5BH Lone survivor of East End terrace bombed in the Blitz, tucked away in Mile End Park by Regent's Canal; two Edwardian bars with busy décor and lots of photos around oval servery, old-fashioned and unchanging under long-serving licensees, a couple of well kept ales, lunchtime sandwiches, good local atmosphere with popular weekend live music; cash only; open all day (till late Sat).

E7

Forest Tavern (020) 8503 0868

Forest Lane across from Forest Gate station; E7 9BB Part of the Antic group, with bare boards and exposed brickwork; six real ales including house Volden, craft beers and enjoyable food from pub favourites up, friendly staff; live music and DJ nights, Tues quiz, games including table football; children and dogs welcome, seats out on decking, open all day Fri-Sun, from 4pm other days.

E11

Red Lion (020) 8988 2929

High Road Leytonstone; E11 3AA Large 19th-c corner pub (Antic group) with plenty of quirky character; high-ceilinged open-plan interior with lots of pictures, mirrors, books and general bric-a-brac, ten changing ales, craft kegs and real ciders, enjoyable food including bar snacks and pub staples; bar billiards and table football, weekend music and DJs, Mon quiz, occasional comedy nights; children and dogs welcome, picnic-sets out at front and in good-sized back garden, open all day.

E13

Black Lion (020) 8472 2351

High Street, Plaistow; E13 0AD Beamed 18th-c coaching inn surviving among 20th-c development; up to four real ales including Mighty Oak and enjoyable well priced pubby food, friendly staff; sports TVs; picnic-sets in spacious garden, open all day, no food weekends or bank holidays (except before West Ham home matches).

E14

★ Grapes (020) 7987 4396

Narrow Street, Limehouse; E14 8BP Relatively unchanged since Dickens used it as a model for his Six Jolly Fellowship Porters in *Our Mutual Friend*; a proper traditional tavern with friendly atmosphere and good mix of customers, partly panelled bar with prints of actors, old local maps and pictures of the pub itself, elaborately etched windows, open fire, plates along a shelf, larger back area leading to small heated deck looking over the river towards Canary Wharf, Adnams, Black Sheep, Timothy Taylors and two guests, good value tasty bar food, upstairs evening restaurant (Mon-Sat) with more fine views; Mon quiz; no under-18s, dogs welcome in bar, open all day, food all day Sat, till 3.30pm Sun.

Gun (020) 7515 5222
Coldharbour; E14 9NS Welcoming dining pub with great views from riverside terrace of the O2 arena; smart front restaurant and partitioned bar, second flagstoned bar behind with antique guns and log fire, cosy dining room next-door, Fullers beers, guest ales and several wines by the glass, good modern food (not cheap); background music; children welcome till 8pm, garden with games and dedicated bar (open at weekends), open all day.

NORTH LONDON

N1

Camden Head (020) 7359 0851
Camden Walk; N1 8DY Comfortably preserved Victorian pub in pedestrianised Camden street; lots of fine etched glass and mahogany panelling, unusual clock suspended from ceiling, button-back leather wall seats and a few small booths, half a dozen well kept changing ales including Greene King from island bar, fairly priced pubby food (order at the bar); free nightly comedy club upstairs; children welcome till 7pm, no dogs, chunky picnic-sets on front terrace, open (and food) all day.

Craft Beer Company
(020) 7278 0318 *White Lion Street; N1 9PP* Flower-decked Victorian pub (now part of small London-centric chain) in Islington attracting mix of customers; ten cask beers and interesting extensive choice of draught/bottled beers along with good range of other drinks, bar snacks and burger menu (all day weekends), cosy and softly lit with dark green walls and wood-strip or red carpeted floors, high tables in main bar, low ones in adjacent areas, open fire; piano, occasional live acoustic music; small side garden, open all day Fri-Sun, from 4pm other days.

Drapers Arms (020) 7619 0348
W end of Barnsbury Street; N1 1ER Simply furnished Georgian townhouse in residential Islington; busy U-shaped bar with dark wooden tables and wheelback chairs on bare boards, gilt mirrors over fireplaces, bright green counter serving Harveys and two guests, British draught lagers and around 20 wines by the glass, enjoyable food from shortish but varied menu, stylish upstairs dining room with striking chequerboard-painted floor; background music; children

welcome (must be seated and eating after 6pm), dogs allowed in bar, nice paved back terrace with zinc-topped tables under large parasols, open all day.

Earl of Essex (020) 7424 5828
Danbury Street; N1 8LE Bright one-room bare-boards pub in centre of Islington with great choice of beers on draught (listed on boards) and in bottles, decent range of other drinks too, varied menu from small plates up including suggested beer pairings, friendly knowledgeable staff; back walled garden, open (and food) all day.

Hemingford Arms (020) 7607 3303
Hemingford Road; N1 1DF 19th-c ivy-clad pub near Caledonian Road filled with bric-a-brac and theatre posters; good choice of real ales from central servery, Thai evening food (from 2pm Sun), open fire, bare boards, button-back sofas, upstairs bar/function room; live music, quiz nights, sports TV, games machines; picnic-sets outside, open all day.

Islington Townhouse
(020) 3637 6424 *Liverpool Road/Chapel Market; N1 0RW* Corner pub owned by Hippo Inns; stylish modern décor over three floors, good selection of beers and other drinks including cocktails and over 20 wines by the glass, good sensibly priced food from assorted small plates up, Sat brunch, friendly engaging staff; Mon quiz, board games, background music; children welcome, open (and food) all day.

★**Parcel Yard** (020) 7713 7258
King's Cross station, N end of new concourse, up stairs (or lift); N1C 4AH Impressive restoration of listed Victorian parcel sorting office; lots of interesting bare-boards rooms off corridors around airy central atrium, pleasing old-fashioned feel with exposed pipework and ducting adding to the effect, back bar serving full range of well kept Fullers beers plus guests from long modern counter, plenty of wines by the glass, similar upstairs area with railway memorabilia and old and new furniture including comfortable sofas, food from bar snacks up, breakfast till 11.30am; power points to recharge phones/laptops, screens for train times, platform views; seats out at front, open all day from 8am (9am Sun).

Wenlock Arms (020) 7608 3406
Wenlock Road; N1 7TA Friendly old-fashioned corner local in Hoxton backstreet with excellent choice of real ales, craft beers and ciders from central servery, plenty of foreign bottled beers too, simple food such as toasties and pies; alcove seating and coal fires; darts; children (until 8pm) and dogs welcome, open all day.

N4
Faltering Fullback (020) 7272 5834
Perth Road/Ennis Road; N4 3HB
Friendly ivy-covered corner pub in Stroud
Green with two softly lit bars, lots of bric-
a-brac, Fullers London Pride and a couple
of guests, good value evening Thai food in
back room; background and live music, Mon
quiz, sports TVs, pool; nice outside area on
different levels, open all day.

N6
Red Lion & Sun (020) 8340 1780
North Road (B519); N6 4BE 1920s
Highgate village dining pub with good
variety of well liked food (can be pricey)
including some decent vegetarian choices,
also takeaway fish and chips, three real
ales such as Brains Rev James, Caledonian
Deuchars IPA and Timothy Taylors, lots
of wines by the glass (good list) and
extensive range of whiskies, cheerful
helpful service; well behaved children
and dogs welcome, tables on leafy front
terrace and in smaller back courtyard,
open (and food) all day.

N16
Railway Tavern (020) 3092 3344
*St Jude Street/King Henrys Walk; N16
8JT* 19th-c bow-fronted single-bar pub in
Dalston; half a dozen well kept ales along
with craft kegs and bottled beers, vegan
pizzas (evenings only), reasonable prices and
friendly relaxed atmosphere, some railway
memorabilia; Tues quiz, acoustic live music;
children and dogs welcome, a few pavement
tables, open all day weekends, from 4pm
other days.

NW1
★**Chapel** (020) 7723 2337
Chapel Street; NW1 5DP Corner dining
pub attracting equal share of drinkers (busy
and noisy in the evening); spacious rooms
dominated by open kitchen, smart but simple
furnishings, sofas at lounge end next to big
fireplace, a couple of Greene King ales and
good choice of wines by the glass, coffees
and teas, decent food from weekly changing
menu, friendly service; children and dogs
welcome, picnic-sets in sizeable back garden,
more seats on decking under heated parasols,
open all day.

★**Doric Arch** (020) 7388 2221
Eversholt Street; NW1 2DN Almost part
of Euston station and a welcome retreat
from the busy concourse; well kept Fullers
ales, guest beers and enjoyable well priced
pubby food from snacks and sharing plates to

specials, friendly efficient service, compact
bare-boards bar with railway memorabilia
and pretty Victorian fireplace, some button-
back bench seating and a cosy boothed
alcove, steps to raised back dining area;
background music, TVs (including train
times); open (and food) all day.

Euston Tap (020) 3137 8837
Euston Road; NW1 2EF Two small 19th-c
neoclassical lodges in front of Euston station;
around ten quickly changing real ales, along
with craft kegs, proper ciders and range of
bottled beers served from a green tiled bar,
knowledgeable staff, limited seating but more
space and lavatories up spiral stairs; outside
tables, open all day.

Metropolitan (020) 7486 3489
*Baker Street station, Marylebone Road;
NW1 5LA* Flight of steps up to this spacious
Wetherspoons in impressively ornate pillared
hall (designed by Metropolitan Railway
architect Charles W Clark), lots of tables on
one side, very long bar on the other, around
ten real ales, good coffee and their usual
food, family area; open all day from 8am
(10am Sun).

Somers Town Coffee House
(020) 7387 7377 *Chalton Street (tucked
away between Euston and King's Cross/
St Pancras stations); NW1 1HS* Despite
its name (there was a coffee house here in
the 18th c) this is a busy pub with fine range
of well kept ales including Youngs and decent
choice of enjoyable food (gluten-free and
vegan diets catered for); spacious interior
with main wood panelled bar and open fires
on the ground floor, basement cocktail bar
(from 5pm) and upstairs private dining
rooms; background music; children and dogs
welcome, outside tables front and back,
open all day from 8am (10am weekends)
for breakfast.

Tapping the Admiral
(020) 7267 6118 *Castle Road; NW1 8SU*
Friendly local with fine range of well kept
ales mainly from London brewers, fairly
priced food including range of home-made
pies; quiz nights and live music, children
welcome till 7pm, heated beer garden,
open all day.

NW3
★**Flask** (020) 7435 4580
Flask Walk; NW3 1HE Bustling Hampstead
local with two traditional front bars
divided by unique Victorian screen, smart
banquettes, panelling and lots of little
prints, attractive fireplace; Youngs ales

A star symbol before the name of a pub shows exceptional character and appeal.
It doesn't mean extra comfort. Even quite a basic pub can win a star,
if it's individual enough.

and two guests, plenty of wines by the glass and maybe winter mulled wine, popular fairly pubby food from sharing plates up served all day weekdays and until 7pm Sun, good friendly service, dining conservatory; background music, TV, darts, board games, Tues quiz; children (till 8pm) and dogs welcome, conservatory, seats and tables in alley, open all day.

Spaniards Inn (020) 8731 8406

Spaniards Lane; NW3 7JJ Busy 16th-c pub next to Hampstead Heath; attractive and characterful low-ceilinged rooms with oak panelling, antique winged settles, snug alcoves and open fires; up to five real ales, several craft beers including locals and around 18 wines by glass, decent food from sandwiches and sharing boards up, dining room upstairs; charming garden with own bar (arrive early weekends as popular with dog walkers and families), car park also fills quickly and parking nearby difficult, open (and food) all day.

Washington (020) 7722 8842

Englands Lane; NW3 4UE Victorian corner pub in Belsize Park with plenty of original features; high moulded ceiling, ornate woodwork and tilework, etched glass and painted mirrors, mixed furniture on wood flooring including padded benches and button-back banquettes; stools around island bar serving five real ales, several craft beers and around 25 wines by the glass, enjoyable fairly traditional food at fair prices, friendly relaxed atmosphere; soft background music, Tues quiz and maybe other events in cellar bar; children and well behaved dogs allowed, open (and food) all day.

NW5
Southampton Arms 07375 755539

Highgate Road; NW5 1LE Popular simply furnished drinkers' pub near Parliament Hill; one long room with big front window, wall seats and stools around tables on bare boards, open fire, 18 handpulls with up to ten changing beers and good range of ciders, focus on independent breweries, simple food (pies, sausage rolls, baps), cash only; live piano some evenings, Mon quiz; small garden at back, handy for Hampstead Heath, open all day.

NW10
William IV (020) 8969 5955

Harrow Road; NW10 5JX Refurbished 19th-c corner pub in Kensal Green; four separate areas including main bar and dining room keeping original features, open fire, wood floors and painted panelling; wide range of craft ales from marble-topped servery, good fairly pubby food from short reasonably priced menu, Sat brunch menu, friendly staff; Sun quiz; children welcome, spacious garden with summer house, 15 bedrooms, open (and food) all day.

SOUTH LONDON

SE1
Dean Swift (020) 7357 0748

Gainsford Street; SE1 2NE Comfortably updated corner pub tucked away behind Tower Bridge; well kept changing ales, beers and several wines by the glass, good food from bar snacks to Sun roasts, upstairs restaurant; friendly well informed staff, sports TV; open (and food) all day.

Fire Station (020) 3727 5938

Waterloo Road; SE1 8SB Unusual fire station conversion, modern, busy and noisy, with two big knocked-through rooms, burger and pizza menu, changing ales and craft beers such as Beavertown, 14 wines by the glass and cocktails, friendly staff; background music; children welcome, a few tables out in front, handy for Old Vic theatre and Waterloo station, open (and food) all day from 7am (9am weekends) for breakfast.

Founders Arms (020) 7928 1899

Hopton Street; SE1 9JH Modern glass-walled building in superb location near Tate Modern – outstanding terrace with plenty of tables and views along Thames; Youngs ales, craft beers such as Beavertown and Camden, lots of wines by the glass, food served all day, tea and coffee from separate servery, wide range of customers including tourists, theatre- and gallery-goers spilling on to pavement and river walls, background music; children welcome (till 9pm Sun-Thurs, 8pm Fri and Sat) away from bar, dogs allowed on terrace, open 9am daily, till midnight Fri, Sat.

★ George (020) 7407 2056

Off 77 Borough High Street; SE1 1NH Tucked-away 16th-c coaching inn mentioned in *Little Dorrit*, owned by the National Trust and beautifully preserved; lots of tables in bustling cobbled courtyard with views of the tiered exterior galleries, series of no-frills ground-floor rooms with black beams, square-latticed windows and some panelling, plain oak or elm tables on bare boards, old-fashioned built-in settles, dimpled glass lanterns and a 1797 Act of Parliament clock, impressive central staircase up to a series of dining rooms and balcony, well kept Greene King ales, traditional food from bar snacks and sandwiches up; handy for Borough Market, children welcome away from bar, open (and food) all day.

★ Kings Arms (020) 7207 0784

Roupell Street; SE1 8TB Proper corner local tucked away amid terrace houses near Waterloo station, bustling and friendly, with curved servery dividing traditional bar and lounge, bare boards, open fire and various bits and pieces including old black and white photographs, decorative china and some local road signs; nine well kept changing beers and good choice of wines and malt whiskies, enjoyable reasonably priced Thai lunch and dinner service every day (till 6pm Sun), welcoming helpful staff, back extension with conservatory/courtyard dining area; Sun quiz, background music; children till 7pm, open all day.

★**Market Porter** (020) 7407 2495
Stoney Street; SE1 9AA Properly pubby no-frills place opening at 6am weekdays for workers at neighbouring Borough Market; up to ten unusual real ales (over 60 guests a week) often from far-flung brewers and served in top condition, food (all day and until 5pm Sun) in bar or upstairs lunchtime restaurant with view over market; particularly helpful friendly service; bare boards and open fire, barrels balancing on beams, simple furnishings, background music; children allowed weekends till 7pm, dogs welcome, gets very busy with drinkers spilling on to the street, open all day.

Rake (020) 7407 0557
Winchester Walk; SE1 9AG Tiny discreetly modern Borough Market bar with amazing bottled beer range in wall-wide cooler, also half a dozen continental lagers on tap and four real ales, light snacks available or you can bring your own food from the market stalls, good friendly service; decent-sized covered and heated outside area, open all day (until 8pm Sun).

Sheaf (020) 7407 9934
Southwark Street; SE1 1TY In cellars beneath the Hop Exchange with a tiny entrance that's easy to miss; brick vaulted ceilings and iron pillars, button-back benches, sofas and some high tables, lots of framed black and white photographs of former regulars, ten real ales and decent inexpensive pubby food; sports TVs; open all day.

Wheatsheaf (020) 7940 3880
Stoney Street; opposite Borough Market main entrance; SE1 9AA Updated Youngs pub directly below new railway bridge; their well kept ales with guests such as Beavertown, Camden Town and Meantime, good choice of wines by the glass and decent food from sandwiches and snacks up, cheerful busy atmosphere; live music; heated partially covered outside area, open (and food) all day from 9am (10.30am Sun, noon Mon).

White Hart (020) 7928 9190
Cornwall Road/Whittlesey Street; SE1 8TJ Backstreet corner pub near Waterloo station with friendly community bustle; interesting range of cask and craft beers, lots more in bottles and good selection of other drinks, sensibly priced up-to-date blackboard food along with pub standards, comfortable sofas on stripped boards,

fresh flowers on tables; background music; disabled facilities, open (and food) all day.

SE5

★**Crooked Well** (020) 7252 7798
Grove Lane; SE5 8SY Popular early 19th-c restaurant pub in heart of Camberwell; button-back sofas, wall seats and variety of wooden dining chairs and tables on bare boards, good food including vegan set menu and other deals, craft beers, a couple of real ales and plenty of wines by the glass, cocktails, happy hour 5-7pm daily, welcoming helpful staff, private dining/function rooms upstairs; children welcome, pavement picnic-sets, open all day weekends, 5-11pm Mon-Thurs.

SE8

Dog & Bell (020) 8692 5664
Prince Street; SE8 3JD Friendly old-fashioned Deptford local tucked away near the river (on the Thames Path); wood benches around bright cheerfully decorated L-shaped bar, open fire, up to half a dozen well kept ales including Fullers, bottled Belgian beers and reasonably priced pub food, prompt friendly service, dining room; live folk music, bar billiards, Sun quiz, TV; tables out in courtyard, open all day.

SE9

Park Tavern (020) 8850 3216
Passey Place; SE9 5DA Traditional Victorian corner pub off Eltham High Street; six well kept changing ales and 14 wines by the glass, log fire, friendly easy-going atmosphere, pub snacks, sandwiches and pubby mains served lunchtime; background music; pleasant little garden behind, open all day.

SE10

★**Greenwich Union** (020) 8692 6258
Royal Hill; SE10 8RT More like a bar than a pub with full Meantime craft range, over 150 bottled beers, unusual spirits and interesting choice of teas and coffees, enjoyable food from sharing plates and traditional favourites up, friendly prompt service, long narrow stone-flagged room with simple front area, wooden furniture, stove and daily papers, comfortable part with sofas and cushioned pews, booth seating in end conservatory; Weds quiz; well behaved children and dogs welcome, paved terrace with teak furniture and old-fashioned lamp posts, open (and food) all day, kitchen shuts 6pm Sun.

Pilot (020) 8858 5910
River Way, Blackwall Lane; SE10 0BE Early 19th-c pub surviving amid development around O2 arena; opened-up interior on three levels with roof terrace overlooking park, well kept Fullers/Gales beers, good choice of food (all day Fri, Sat, till 6pm Sun) from pubby choices and charcoal grills to daily specials;

background music and newspapers; dogs welcome, picnic-sets in front, more seating in enclosed back garden, ten well equipped boutique bedrooms, open all day.

Prince of Greenwich

(020) 8692 6089 *Royal Hill; SE10 8RT*
Victorian pub in Greenwich under warmly welcoming Sicilian owners; good Italian food from freshly made pizzas and pastas up, Fullers London Pride, Sharps Doom Bar and nice wines by the glass, quirky décor and unusual furnishings, lots of black and white jazz photos/posters (regular live jazz); Italian cinema club; children and well behaved dogs welcome, closed Mon, open from 4pm Tues-Fri, 12.30pm weekends.

SE11

Prince of Wales (020) 7735 9916

Cleaver Square; SE11 4EA Comfortably traditional little Edwardian pub in smart quiet Georgian square near the Oval; well kept Shepherd Neame ales and simple pub food from sandwiches up, warm friendly atmosphere, mismatched furniture on bare boards, open fire; pavement seats, pétanque set hire available to play in the square, open (and food) all day.

SE12

Lord Northbrook (020) 8318 1127

Burnt Ash Road; SE12 8PU Opened-up bare-boards Victorian corner pub near Lee station; good mix of seating including a couple of chesterfields by Victorian fireplace, contemporary paintwork and lots of pictures; well kept Fullers/Gales beers, decent food from shortish menu (all day weekends), friendly staff, conservatory; board games, Tues quiz, live music; children and dogs welcome, paved split-level back garden, some tables on pavement, open all day.

SE15

Ivy House (020) 7277 8233

Stuart Road; SE15 3BE Co-operative owned pub in Nunhead with eight real ales and good range of craft beers and ciders, well priced food (not lunchtimes Mon, Tues) including burgers, old-fashioned panelled interior, open fire; Weds quiz, stage in back room for live music, comedy and theatre nights, board games, variety of community events including knitting circle and yoga sessions; children (till 8pm) and dogs welcome, pavement picnic-sets, rack for cyclists, open all day.

Old Nuns Head (020) 7639 4007

Nunhead Green; SE15 3QQ Popular open-plan 1930s brick and timber pub on edge of small green; six changing ales and enjoyable

food provided by pop-up kitchens including burgers and street food, just roasts on Sun, cheerful efficient staff; music and comedy nights; children (till 8.30pm) and dogs welcome, back garden and a few seats out in front, handy for fascinating gothic Nunhead Cemetery, open all day (till 1am Fri, Sat), food from 6pm weekdays, noon weekends.

SE16

★ Mayflower (020) 7237 4088

Rotherhithe Street; SE16 4NF Cosy old riverside pub in Rotherhithe in unusual street with lovely early 18th-c church; generous food including upmarket daily specials and huge cheese selection, well kept Greene King Abbot and five guests, good value wines and decent coffee, friendly staff, black beams, panelling, high-backed settle and coal fires, nautical bric-a-brac, great Thames views from upstairs candlelit evening restaurant; background music, Tues quiz; children and dogs (in bar area) welcome, fun jetty/terrace over water (barbecues), handy for Brunel Museum, open (and food) all day.

SE20

Goldsmiths Arms (020) 8659 1242

Croydon Road, Penge; SE20 7TJ Popular and welcoming 19th-c pub just off Penge high street; bare-boards front bar with high ceiling and open fire, large room beyond mainly for dining, Purity Mad Goose, five guest beers and 11 wines by the glass, enjoyable good value food from shortish menu (order at the bar), friendly efficient young staff; background and weekend live music, Tues quiz, monthly open mike night; children (till 8pm) and dogs welcome, picnic-sets out at front and in large back garden, open all day Sat, Sun, from 4pm other days, no food Mon, Tues or after 6pm Sun.

SW4

Abbeville (020) 8675 2201

Abbeville Road; SW4 9JW Popular dining pub in same small group (Three Cheers Pub Co) as the Latchmere in Battersea; split-level interior including small mezzanine, bare boards, half-panelling and open fire, mix of old furniture, vintage prints and a stag's head; good food from short but varied menu, beers such as Meantime and Timothy Taylors, plenty of wines by the glass, cocktails; efficient friendly service; children and dogs welcome, pavement tables, open all day, food all day weekends.

Clapham Tap (020) 7498 9633

Clapham Manor Street; SW4 6ED
Friendly little end-of-terrace pub near Clapham High Street station with U-shaped bare-boards bar, six well kept ales including

---

Real ale to us means beer that has matured naturally in its cask – not pressurised or filtered. If possible, we name all real ales stocked.

Sambrooks, 16 craft beers and good range of gins and other spirits, enjoyable pubby food at reasonable prices; TVs, board games, area for table tennis, darts and other games; seats out at front and in back garden with artificial grass, open all day weekends, from 4pm weekdays.

Windmill (020) 8673 4578

Clapham Common South Side; SW4 9DE Large bustling pub by the common; contemporary front bar with quite a few original Victorian features, pillared dining room leading through to conservatory-style eating area, popular varied choice of food, Youngs ales and decent wines by the glass; background music (live Sat), Sun quiz; children and dogs welcome, tables under umbrellas along front, more seats in side garden with burger shack (during summer), 42 good bedrooms, open (and food) all day.

SW11

Eagle Ale House (020) 7228 2328

Chatham Road; SW11 6HG Welcoming unpretentious backstreet local just off Northcote Road and not far from Clapham Junction station; up to seven well kept/priced ales such as Harveys, Pilgrim and Surrey Hills, L-shaped carpeted bar with simple pubby furniture, shelves of books on either side of Victorian fireplace; some live music, big-screen sports TV; children and dogs welcome, back terrace with heated marquee, open all day weekends, from 4pm Mon-Thurs, 3pm Fri.

Fox & Hounds (020) 7924 5483

Latchmere Road; SW11 2JU Victorian pub with good Italian-influenced food (all day Sun, not Mon-Thurs lunchtimes), four real ales including St Austell and Sambrooks, several wines by the glass, spacious straightforward bar with big windows overlooking street, mismatched tables and chairs on bare boards, central servery and open kitchen behind; background music; children and dogs welcome, terrace picnic-sets, open all day Fri-Sun, closed Mon lunchtime.

Latchmere (020) 7223 3549

Battersea Park Road; SW11 3BW Popular Battersea corner pub (part of Three Cheers Pub Co) with award-winning theatre upstairs; open-plan bare-boards interior, Edwardian-style dining chairs, two-sided banquettes and red leather wall seats around wooden tables, sofas either side of log fire, big mirrors, model yachts, animal prints and posters, stools by counter serving Sambrooks and Timothy Taylors, 19 wines by the glass and cocktails, enjoyable food including pre-theatre set menu; quiz Mon, children (till 7pm) and dogs welcome, heated terrace with booths down one side and plenty of other seating, outdoor children's area, open all day, food all day Sat and Sun.

Westbridge (020) 7228 6482

Battersea Bridge Road; SW11 3AG Draft House pub serving Sambrooks and interesting constantly changing choice of real ales, craft beers and ciders served by friendly knowledgeable staff, tasting trays available, good reasonably priced food from open kitchen, can eat in bar or restaurant; background music (often blues/jazz), sports TV; small garden, open (and food) all day.

Woodman (020) 7228 2968

Battersea High Street; SW11 3HX Busy village-feel pub tucked behind cobbled Battersea Square; open-plan bare-boards and flagstoned interior with oak barrels and rustic look, Badger ales, Weston's Stowford Press cider and a dozen wines by the glass, enjoyable food from sharing boards up; good friendly service; TV for major sports; children and dogs welcome, partially covered back garden with heaters and wood-fired pizza oven, open (and food) all day weekends, from 4pm weekdays.

SW12

★ Nightingale (020) 8673 1637

Nightingale Lane; SW12 8NX Early Victorian local, cosy and civilised, with small front bar opening into larger back area and attractive family conservatory, well kept Youngs and guests, decent wines and enjoyable sensibly priced bar food, friendly service, open fire; Weds quiz; dogs welcome, nice secluded back beer garden, some pavement tables, open all day.

SW13

Bulls Head (020) 8876 5241

Lonsdale Road; SW13 9PY Imposing Victorian riverside pub in Barnes famous for its live jazz (since 1959) in back music room (nightly and Sun afternoon); three real ales including Sharps and Youngs from central servery, good range of food from bar snacks up, upstairs balconied restaurant, comfortable open-plan areas brightened up in Geronimo Inns' usual colourful modern style; children and dogs welcome, a few tables in small side courtyard, open (and food) all day.

Coach & Horses (020) 8876 2695

Barnes High Street; SW13 9LW Cosy long-established Youngs local (some refurbishment) with dark wood panelling and stained-glass windows; their well kept beers and a guest, decent fairly priced food from sandwiches and snacks up including range of burgers, friendly staff; sports TV; children and dogs welcome, long spacious back garden with artificial grass, open-sided huts and children's play area, open (and food) all day.

Red Lion (020) 8748 2984

Castelnau; SW13 9RU Roomy and comfortably refurbished 19th-c Fullers pub in Barnes; their well kept ales and guests plus good range of wines from central counter, varied choice of popular attractively presented food including blackboard specials, friendly staff, lofty back dining part has most character with big arched windows, impressive Victorian woodwork and domed stained-glass ceiling light, also front snug with gas-effect coal fire; TV; children and dogs welcome, disabled access/loo, covered patio and spacious garden to the back and side, open (and food) all day.

Watermans Arms (020) 8878 8800

Lonsdale Road, next to the Bulls Head; SW13 9PY Rverside pub (same owners as the Sussex Arms in Twickenham); extensive range of real ales and craft beers, plenty of wines by the glass and enjoyable good value food such as burgers, ribs and pizzas, more room and river-view balcony upstairs; background music, sports TV; open (and food) all day.

White Hart (020) 8876 5177

The Terrace; SW13 0NR Imposing 19th-c pub by Barnes Bridge with airy interior and verandahs offering fine Thames views; well kept ales including Bombardier and Youngs along with craft beers such as Camden Town and Meantime from island servery, good selection of wines by the glass, popular food in bar or upstairs restaurant with open kitchen and river-view balcony, friendly attentive staff; more seats on side terrace and by the towpath, open (and food) all day.

SW14

Plough (020) 8876 7833

Christchurch Road; SW14 7AF Attractive 18th-c pub tucked away in East Sheen near Richmond Park; fairly traditional bare-boards interior with pews and plush banquettes, well kept ales including Fullers London Pride and 20 wines by the glass from oak counter, generous helpings of popular home-made food, friendly staff; children and dogs welcome, tables under parasols on nice front terrace, open all day (till midnight Fri, Sat), food all day Sun.

SW15

Bricklayers Arms (020) 8246 5545

Down cul-de-sac off Lower Richmond Road near Putney Bridge; SW15 1DD Tucked-away little 19th-c Putney local; six Timothy Taylors beers and well kept changing ales, proper cider/perry and good selection of English wines, no food, efficient friendly staff, long L-shaped room with pitched-roof section, pine tables on bare boards, lots of pictures on painted panelling, log fire; background music, sports TV; open all day.

Half Moon (020) 8780 9383

Lower Richmond Road; SW15 1EU Good long-standing music venue (often folk) and comfortable open-plan bar areas furnished in Geronimo Inns' colourful style; Youngs and

a couple of guests from elegant curved bar counter, food from burgers and hot dogs to more elaborate choices and a brunch menu; nightly live music/comedy nights; large garden with burger shack, open (and food) all day.

Jolly Gardeners (020) 8789 2539

Lacy Road; SW15 1NT Slightly quirky bare-boards pub in residential Putney; gardening theme with trowels and watering cans on the walls, bucket lampshades, a reclining gnome and row of colourful heated sheds in the back garden, four changing ales and several other draught beers, good selection of wines, enjoyable varied choice of food from sandwiches and sharing boards up; Tues quiz, sports TV, newspapers; tables on front terrace with fairy lights, rear patio, open (and food) all day.

Telegraph

Telegraph Road; SW15 3TU Revamped country-style inn with garden tucked away on Putney Heath – new addition to the Brunning & Price group; due to the coronavirus pandemic, opening was delayed from spring 2020 to later in the year: expect B&P's usual winning formula of numerous real ales, good wine list, reliable brasserie-style food, efficient friendly staff, relaxed atmosphere and open-plan but cosy layout – reports please.

SW16

Earl Ferrers (020) 8835 8333

Ellora Road; SW16 6JF Streatham corner pub with opened-up bare-boards interior; Sambrooks and up to three changing well kept ales (tasters offered), enjoyable home-made food including popular Sun roasts, good friendly service; live music, DJs and quiz nights, pool and darts; children welcome, tables out at front and in beer garden, open all day weekends from 1pm, closed Mon and till 5pm Tues-Fri.

Railway (020) 8769 9448

Greyhound Lane; SW16 5SD Busy Streatham corner local with two big rooms; rotating ales from London brewers such as Belleville, Portobello and Sambrooks, good range of bottled beers and decent wines by the glass, enjoyable freshly made food (all day weekend), tea room serving pastries and brunch from 10am, friendly staff; events including Tues quiz, games night and monthly comedy nights (last Sun of month), board games; tables in walled back garden and on pavement, open all day (till 1am Fri, Sat).

SW18

Alma (020) 8870 2537

York Road, opposite Wandsworth Town station; SW18 1TF Corner Victorian pub-hotel with well kept Youngs and good choice of other beers and wines from island bar, sofas and informal mix of tables and chairs on wood floor, real fire, mosaic plaques and painted mirrors; wide range of good food from bar snacks up, back restaurant, friendly helpful staff; 23 bedrooms, open (and food) all day from 7am (8am weekends).

Cats Back (020) 8617 3448

Point Pleasant; SW18 1NN Traditionally refurbished 19th-c Harveys corner pub; four of their ales along with bottled beers, enjoyable food from sandwiches to Sun roasts, friendly staff; quiz night, upstairs events including live music, life drawing, film and comedy nights; open fire, partially covered beer garden with heaters, open all day.

Jolly Gardeners (020) 8870 8417

Garrett Lane; SW18 4EA Lively Victorian corner pub with L-shaped front bar; high-backed dining chairs around straightforward tables on pale floorboards, stools at high tables and at counter serving Beavertown Neck Oil, Belleville, By the Horns, Sambrooks and a wide range of wines by the glass, well regarded modern food (not Sun evening), dining area with open fire, friendly chatty staff, conservatory opening on to courtyard garden with heaters, summer barbecues; children and dogs (in bar) welcome, open all day, till 10pm Sun.

SW19

Alexandra (020) 8947 7691

Wimbledon Hill Road; SW19 7NE Busy 19th-c Youngs pub in Wimbeldon town centre; their well kept beers and guests from central servery, decent wine choice and enjoyable food from sandwiches and sharing boards to good Sun roasts, friendly attentive service, linked rooms with comfortable fairly traditional décor, more contemporary upstairs bar (burger menu); Mon quiz, sports TVs; tables out in mews and on attractive popular roof terrace, open (and food) all day.

Crooked Billet (020) 8946 4942

Wimbledon Common; SW19 4RQ Busy 18th-c pub popular for its position by Wimbledon Common (almost next door to the Hand in Hand); Youngs ales and guests, good choice of wines and generally well liked up-to-date food in open-plan bar or dining room, mix of wooden dining chairs, high-backed settles and scrubbed pine tables on oak boards, some interesting old prints, winter fire; Tues quiz, board games; children till 6pm in bar (later in restaurant), dogs welcome, open (and food) all day.

Hand in Hand (020) 8946 5720

Crooked Billet; SW19 4RQ Refurbished Youngs local on edge of Wimbledon Common; their ales and guests kept well, over 30 wines by the glass and good food from sharing plates, made-to-order pies and pub standards up, friendly helpful service, opened-up interior keeping cosy corners and original

character, log fire; Tues quiz; children and dogs welcome, front part-covered courtyard, benches out by common, open (and food) all day.

Sultan (020) 8544 9323

Norman Road; SW19 1BT Friendly 1950s red-brick drinkers' pub owned by Hop Back and hidden in a tangle of suburban roads; their well kept/priced ales, guest beers and real ciders, snacky food such as pork pies and toasties, scrubbed pine tables on patterned carpet, darts in public bar, small conservatory leading to walled beer garden (maybe summer barbecues); fortnightly quiz Tues, some live music; dogs welcome, open all day Thurs-Sun, from 3pm other days.

Woodman (020) 8286 4158

Durnsford Road; SW19 8DR Revamped 1930s pub behind railings; airy industrial-chic interior with bare boards and exposed brickwork, pendant lighting and fashionable metal chairs at small pale-wood tables, a couple of real ales and good range of interesting craft beers from planked servery, well liked food including burger night, friendly attentive young staff; Tues quiz, weekly live music; children welcome, garden, open all day.

WEST LONDON

SW6

★ Atlas (020) 7385 9129

Seagrave Road; SW6 1RX Busy ivy-clad pub with long simple bar; panelling and dark wall benches, mix of old tables and chairs on bare boards, brick fireplaces, four well kept ales, lots of wines by the glass and decent coffee, good if pricey Italian-influenced food (all day Sun); friendly service; background music, summer quiz Tues; children (till 7pm) and dogs welcome, side terrace with picnic-sets, open all day and busy with Chelsea supporters on match days.

Eight Bells (020) 7736 6307

Fulham High Street/Ranelagh Gardens; SW6 3JS Friendly traditional local tucked away near Putney Bridge; Fullers London Pride, Sharps Doom Bar and two guests, good value standard pub menu (all day Sun); sports TV; dogs welcome, seats outside under awning, close to Bishop's Park, open all day (from 10am) and busy with away supporters on Fulham match days.

Harwood Arms (020) 7386 1847

Walham Grove; SW6 1QP Popular Fulham restaurant-pub with top notch Michelin-starred food from fixed-price menus (not cheap), extensive wine list and a couple of well kept ales, opened-up informal bare-boards interior with all tables set for dining, stools at bar for drinkers; credit card required for booking (charge for late cancellations or no show); open all day (from 5.30pm Mon).

Malt House (020) 7084 6888

Vanston Place; Fulham Broadway tube; SW6 1AY Expansive refurbished Fulham pub dating from the 18th c; U-shaped bar with high ceilings and big windows, green leather button-back wall seats and dark wooden dining chairs around mix of tables, groups of sofas and armchairs on wood or tiled floors, pictures on panelled walls, Brakspears and a guest, nice wines by the glass and 11 malt whiskies, good varied choice of well liked food, helpful staff; children and dogs welcome, small paved back garden with candy-striped benches, pretty hanging baskets, fairy lights and candle-lit lanterns, comfortable airy bedrooms, open (and food) all day including breakfasts for non-residents.

White Horse (020) 7736 2115

Parsons Green; SW6 4UL Busy pub with modernised U-shaped bar; leather chesterfields and wooden tables on flagstone or wood floors, huge windows with slatted wooden blinds, winter fires (one in an elegant marble fireplace), Harveys Best and seven changing guests, fantastic choice of foreign bottled beers, some 20 wines by the glass and several malt whiskies, good up-to-date food, upstairs dining room (own bar) keeping Victorian character; children and dogs welcome, lots of tables on front terrace overlooking Parsons Green, open (and food) all day.

SW7

★Anglesea Arms (020) 7373 7960

Selwood Terrace; SW7 3QG Very busy 19th-c South Kensington pub, well run and friendly, with mix of old tables and chairs on wood-strip floor, panelling and heavy portraits, large brass chandeliers hanging from dark ceiling, several booths at one end with partly glazed screens, Greene King Abbott, and four guests, some 20 wines by the glass and good range of malt whiskies, well liked food from sharing plates up; steps down to dining room; children welcome, dogs in bar, picnic-sets on raised front terrace, open all day.

Hereford Arms (020) 7370 4988

Gloucester Road, opposite Hereford Square; SW7 4TE Traditional Fullers pub with opened-up bar; wooden furniture including some high tables on bare boards, chequered tiles around carved U-shaped counter serving their ales and a couple of guests, good food from bar snacks to blackboard specials, friendly staff; children welcome, disabled access, small outside drinking area, open (and food) all day.

Queens Arms (020) 7823 9293

Queens Gate Mews; SW7 5QL Popular Victorian corner pub with open-plan bare-boards bar; generous helpings of enjoyable good value home-made food, decent wines by the glass and good selection of beers including Sharps and St Austell, friendly helpful service; discreet background music and TV; children welcome, disabled facilities, convenient for Royal Albert Hall, open (and food) all day.

SW10

Fox & Pheasant (020) 7352 2943

Billing Road, off Fulham Road; SW10 9UJ Handsomely renovated pub in pretty little mews behind Stamford Bridge and Brompton Cemetery, owned by singer-songwriter James Blunt and his wife; rustic-chic makeover with toile de jouy wallpaper, leaded windows and three fireplaces, conservatory-style dining room (available for private parties), Hook Norton Hooky, St Austell Tribute and Timothy Taylors Landlord on handpump, 18 wines by the glass or carafe from carefully chosen list (plus champagne), Breton cider and cocktails, good gastropub food from pub classics up and all-day bar snacks; children and dogs welcome (pub dogs are Findlay and Bertie), open all day (from 4pm Mon), food all day weekends.

W4

★Bell & Crown (020) 8994 4164

Strand on the Green; W4 3PL Fullers local with great Thames views from back bar and conservatory; their ales and guests, good interesting food along with pub classics, efficient friendly service, panelling and log fire, lots of atmosphere and can get very busy weekends; children and dogs welcome, terrace and towpath seating, good riverside walks, open (and food) all day.

Bollo House (020) 8994 6037

Bollo Lane; W4 5LR Spacious 19th-c corner pub in residential Chiswick; four changing local ales and plenty of wines by the glass, cocktails (early bird deal Thurs), good variety of enjoyable food from snacks and small plates up, friendly relaxed atmosphere; background and occasional live music, Tues quiz, board games; children and dogs welcome, tables out at front behind wooden planters, open all day, food all day weekends.

Bulls Head (020) 8994 1204

Strand on the Green; W4 3PQ Cleanly updated old Thames-side pub (said to have served as Cromwell's HQ during the Civil War); seats by windows overlooking the water in beamed rooms (most tables set for dining), steps up and down, Greene King IPA and London Glory along with guests,

---

We accept no free drinks or meals and inspections are anonymous.

several wines by the glass and enjoyable food from pub favourites up, friendly efficient staff; background music; children and dogs (in bar) welcome, seats out by river, pretty hanging baskets, open (and food) all day.

City Barge (020) 8994 2148
Strand on the Green; W4 3PH Attractively furnished old riverside pub; light modern split-level interior keeping a few original features such as Victorian panelling and open fires, good choice of ales/craft beers and wines by the glass (prosecco on tap), interesting food from open kitchen including good fish choice; background music; children and dogs welcome, waterside picnic-sets facing Oliver's Island, deckchairs on grass and more formal terrace, open (and food) all day.

★ Duke of Sussex (020) 8742 8801
South Parade; W4 5LF Attractive Victorian local with unexpectedly large back garden, tables under parasols, nicely laid-out plants and carefully positioned lighting and heaters; simply furnished bar with some original etched glass, chapel and farmhouse chairs around scrubbed pine or dark wood tables, huge windows overlooking Acton Green, horseshoe counter serving ales such as Reunion, Sambrooks, Twickenham and Wimbledon, around 30 wines by the glass and 18 malt whiskies, interesting modern food including sharing platters, dining room with booths, chandeliers and splendid skylight; children and dogs (in bar) welcome, open (and food) all day.

Roebuck (020) 8995 4392
Chiswick High Road; W4 1PU Popular Victorian dining pub near Turnham Green tube with bare boards and high ceilings; front bar and roomy back dining area opening on to delightful paved garden, enjoyable well presented food (daily changing menu) from open kitchen, four real ales and good choice of wines by the glass; children and dogs welcome, open all day, food all day weekends.

Swan (020) 8994 8262
Evershed Walk, Acton Lane; W4 5HH Cosy 19th-c local with good mix of customers and convivial atmosphere; well liked Italian-influenced food along with more pubby choices, friendly helpful staff, a dozen or so wines by the glass, ales such as St Austell Tribute and decent selection of craft beers, two bars with wood floors and panelling, leather chesterfields by open fire; dogs very welcome, children till 7.30pm, picnic-sets on good spacious terrace, open all day weekends, from 5pm other days.

W6

★ Anglesea Arms (020) 8749 1291
Wingate Road; W6 0UR Bustling Victorian corner gastropub near Ravenscourt Park; bare-boards panelled bar with open fire,

five changing ales and 13 wines by the glass, very good food from short but interesting blackboard menu (not cheap), close-set tables in sky-lit bare-brick dining room, open fire, local artwork on display; children and dogs welcome, tables out by quiet street, open all day Fri-Sun, from 5pm other days, food all day Sun.

Blue Anchor (020) 3951 0580
Lower Mall; W6 9DJ Right on the Thames, a short walk from Hammersmith Bridge; two traditional linked areas with oak floors and panelling, four real ales including a house beer brewed by Nelsons, enjoyable food from light meals up and Sat brunch (from 10am), nice upstairs river-view dining room with balcony; weekly quiz, TV; disabled facilities, waterside pavement tables, open (and food) all day.

Carpenters Arms (020) 8741 8386
Black Lion Lane; W6 9BG Relaxed little corner dining pub in residential Hammersmith; highly regarded imaginative food including good value set lunch, fine too for just a drink with plenty of wines by the glass, cocktails and a couple of well kept changing beers, friendly staff and good mix of customers, simple bare-boards interior with open fire; dogs welcome, attractive garden, closed Mon lunchtime, otherwise open all day.

Hampshire Hog (020) 8748 3391
King Street; W6 9JT Spacious Hammersmith pub with light airy interior; plenty of emphasis on food from interesting if not extensive menu, good choice of wines including 50cl carafes, cocktails, ales such as Adnams and Fullers, prices can be high; background music; nice large garden with some seats under cover, closed Sun and Mon, otherwise open 4pm-midnight Weds-Fri, noon-midnight Sat.

Latymers (020) 8748 3446
Hammersmith Road; W6 7JP 1990s corner pub with modern bistro-feel bar, wood floor and padded wall benches, feature mirrored ceiling, well kept Fullers ales from blue-painted counter, back restaurant serving good fairly priced Thai food, friendly efficient staff; background music, board games, TV; children and dogs welcome, pavement seating, open all day.

Pear Tree (020) 7381 1787
Margravine Road; W6 8HJ Arts and crafts building (plenty of original features) tucked away behind Charing Cross Hospital; good pubby food from bar snacks up, well kept mainstream ales and good range of wines by the glass, efficient service, cosy softly lit interior with heavy drapes and open fires, cushions on well worn seating, fresh flowers, candles and crisp white evening tablecloths; background music, Sun quiz; dogs welcome,

pretty paved garden, five boutique-style bedrooms, open and food all day.

Queens Head (020) 7603 3174
Brook Green; W6 7BL Spacious Fullers pub dating from the early 19th c; cosy linked areas with beams and open fire, good menu from lunchtime sandwiches and bar snacks up, four well kept ales, craft beers and nice wines by the glass; Mon quiz; children and dogs welcome, big garden behind with children's play area, open (and food) all day.

Thatched House (020) 8741 6282
Dalling Road; W6 0ET New management for this spacious corner pub (Youngs' first); open-plan interior with their ales and guests from large grey-painted servery, rugs on bare boards, fresh flowers on mix of wooden tables, open fire, good food with some emphasis on fish, friendly staff, back conservatory with raised log-effect gas fire; paved garden and BBQ hut, open (and food) all day, Mon from 4pm (food from 5pm).

W7

Fox (020) 8567 0060
Green Lane; W7 2PJ Welcoming 19th-c open-plan local in quiet cul-de-sac near Grand Union Canal; several real ales including Fullers, St Austell and Timothy Taylors, craft beers and decent wines by the glass, popular well priced food (booking advised, especially Sun lunch), good friendly service, parquet flooring, panelling and stained glass, open fire; Thurs quiz, board games, live music Sat; children and dogs welcome, garden, open all day.

W8

Britannia (020) 7937 6905
Allen Street, off Kensington High Street; W8 6UX Smartly presented Youngs pub in Kensington with spacious front bar; their ales and two changing guests, good freshly prepared food including pub staples, pastel walls contrasting dark panelling, patterned rugs on bare boards, banquettes, leather tub chairs and sofas, steps down to back area with wall-sized photoprint of the demolished Britannia Brewery, dining conservatory beyond, spiral staircase up to overflow/function room; background and occasional live music, backgammmon club, sports TV; children and dogs welcome, side passage seats, wheelchair access (side passage to back part), open (and food) all day.

★ Churchill Arms (020) 7727 4242
Kensington Church Street; W8 7LN Bustling old pub between Kensington Gardens and Holland Park; crammed with bric-a-brac: countless lamps, miners' lights, horse tack, bedpans and brasses hanging

from ceiling, prints of US presidents and lots of Churchill memorabilia, a couple of interesting carved figures and statuettes behind central counter, five well kept Fullers ales, 18 wines by the glass and good value Thai food, spacious rather smart plant-filled dining conservatory; children and dogs welcome, some chrome tables and chairs outside, stunning display of window boxes and hanging baskets, open (and food) all day.

Princess Victoria (020) 7937 4534
Earls Court Road; W8 6EB Popular modern open-plan bar run by Spanish landlady; upholstered wall benches and light wood tables on bare boards, cushioned stools along servery, good choice of wines and cocktails, well liked food in upstairs dining room including tapas; live music/DJs some weekends; wooden tables out at front, open all day.

Scarsdale (020) 7937 1811
Edwardes Square; W8 6HE Popular easy-going Georgian pub in leafy Kensington square; scrubbed pine tables, simple cushioned dining chairs, pews and built-in wall seats on bare boards, oil paintings in fancy gilt frames, etched windows and some stained-glass screens, coal-effect gas fires; well kept Fullers ales and a guest, 19 wines by the glass and a dozen malt whiskies, enjoyable fairly pubby food from lunchtime sandwiches up; children (in dining area) and dogs welcome, seats and tables under parasols on attractive front terrace, open (and food) all day.

Uxbridge Arms (020) 7792 1362
Uxbridge Street; W8 7TQ Welcoming backstreet local with three traditional linked areas; well kept Caledonian Deuchars IPA (rebadged for the pub), Fullers London Pride, Sharps Doom Bar and a guest, good choice of wines and other drinks including cocktails, various meat and cheese boards, friendly helpful service, china, prints and old photographs; Sun quiz, some live music, sports TV, darts, board games; children and dogs welcome, a few seats out at front, open (and food) all day.

W9

Hero of Maida (020) 3960 9109
Shirland Road; W9 2JD Victorian corner pub under same owners as the Coach (EC1) and Three Cranes (EC4); zinc-topped counter serving house ale Timothy Taylors along with guests such as Sambrooks, carefully chosen wines by the glass and good range of other drinks, generally well liked food from Anglo-French menu (good prix-fixe menu), nicely refurbished interior keeping original features, high-ceilinged bare-boards bar with

---

We say if we know a pub has background music.

long blue-leather wall bench and other seats, lots of pictures, upstairs dining room; live music Thurs, Sun quiz; courtyard garden, five boutique-style bedrooms, open (and food) all day.

Prince Alfred (020) 7286 3287
Formosa Street; W9 1EE Well preserved ornate Victorian corner pub in Maida Vale with wonderful etched-glass frontage; five separate bar areas (lots of mahogany) arranged around central servery, snob screens and duck-through doors, Youngs ales, guest beers and good choice of wines by the glass, enjoyable food from sharing plates up in airy modern dining room with large central skylight, cellar function rooms; background music, Mon quiz; children and dogs welcome, few seats outside, open (and food) all day, Sat brunch from 10am.

Warwick Castle (020) 7266 0921
Warwick Place; W9 2PX Popular character pub in narrow street near Little Venice; comfortable Victorian-feel rooms including snug with open fire, good variety of food (all day Fri-Sun) from snacks and pub standards up, Greene King IPA and guests; Weds quiz; children and dogs welcome, flower-decked frontage and some tables out on pavement, open all day.

W12

Oak (020) 8741 7700
Goldhawk Road; W12 8EU Large refurbished Victorian pub serving interesting Mediterranean-influenced food including speciality wood-fired pizzas, good range of beers and wine, friendly staff; open (and food) all day weekends, from 6pm other days.

Princess Victoria (020) 8749 4466
Uxbridge Road; W12 9DH Imposing former gin palace with rather grand parquet-floored bar; groups of old prints on off-white walls, blue-painted panelling, comfortable leather wall seats and small 19th-c fireplace, ales such as Sambrooks and Timothy Taylors and some 40 craft beers from handsome marble-topped horseshoe counter, around 130 gins, cocktails and plenty of wines by the glass, food from snacks and pizzas up including weekday set lunch, friendly service, big dining room; Tues quiz, Weds open mike comedy, TV for major sports; children (till 8pm) and dogs (in bar) welcome, tables under large parasols on front cobbled terrace, also pretty back courtyard with white wrought-iron furniture, five bedrooms, open all day.

W13

Duke of Kent (020) 8991 7820
Scotch Common; W13 8DL Large Ealing pub built in 1929 (Grade II listed) with warren of interesting linked areas; mix of old and new furniture on wood floors, panelling and coal fires, several Fullers ales and guests,

good food from pub standards up, friendly helpful staff; live music Sun; children and dogs welcome, steps down to large garden with part-covered terrace, rows of tables and chairs on artificial grass, seating huts and play area, also an outside bar/barbecue, open (and food) all day.

W14

★**Colton Arms** (020) 3757 8050
Greyhound Road; W14 9SD Cosy Hippo Inns pub next to the Queen's Club tennis courts; small front Dot's Bar (named after former long-serving landlady) with handsomely carved high-backed oak bench, bare boards, painted panelling and log fire, Sharps Doom Bar, Timothy Taylors Landlord and more than 20 wines by the glass from copper-topped servery, extended skylit back dining area serving good variety of enjoyable food from snacks up, friendly young staff, some quirky touches including colourful stuffed birds in cages, other taxidermy and eclectic range of artwork; background music; little back terrace, open all day, food all day at weekends.

Crown & Sceptre (020) 7603 2007
Holland Road; W14 8BA Civilised Victorian corner pub with light airy interior; sofas, antique-style dining chairs and leather cube stools around wooden tables, rugs on bare boards, gas fire; Courage Directors, Youngs London Gold and a guest, plenty of wines by the glass and extensive range of whiskies and gins, enjoyable food from reasonably compact but varied menu; friendly service, cosy cellar bar with banquettes, candles in bottles and big prints on wood walls; background music, TV; children and dogs (in bar) welcome, pavement tables, comfortable boutique bedrooms, handy for Olympia, open all day from 7.30am.

★**Havelock Tavern** (020) 7603 5374
Masbro Road; W14 0LS Busy 19th-c corner dining pub with blue-tiled frontage on Brook Green; light airy L-shaped bar with plain unfussy décor, second smaller room behind, Sambrooks Wandle and guests, wide choice of interesting wines by the glass and good often imaginative food from short changing menu, friendly efficient service; children and dogs welcome, picnic-sets on paved terrace, open all day.

OUTER LONDON

BARNET
Black Horse (020) 8449 2230
Wood Street/Union Street; EN5 4BW Attractively updated 19th-c pub with eight real ales including own Barnet beers from back microbrewery, good range of food (all day weekends); children (till 7.30pm) and dogs welcome, terrace seating, summer gin garden, open all day.

Gate (020) 8449 7292

Barnet Road (A411, near Hendon Wood Lane); EN5 3LA Comfortably opened-up with country pub feel; beams and log fires, ample helpings of enjoyable popular food, well kept ales such as Greene King and Sharps, friendly service and atmosphere; children welcome, tables on sunny terrace, open (and food) all day.

Olde Mitre (020) 8449 6582

High Street; EN5 5SJ Small early 17th-c local (remains of a famous coaching inn); bay windows in low-beamed panelled front bar, back area on two slightly different levels, some bare boards and lots of dark wood, open fires, good choice of well kept ales including Adnams Southwold, Greene King Abbot and Timothy Taylors Landlord plus four changing, craft beers and decent wines, enjoyable pubby food, friendly service; Sun live music, sports TV, board games; children and dogs welcome, nice heated courtyard garden behind, open all day (till 1am Fri, Sat).

BECKENHAM

George (020) 8663 3468

High Street; BR3 1AG Refurbished weatherboarded pub with modern U-shaped interior; Greene King and five changing ales, craft beers and decent range of other drinks including cocktails, good choice of enjoyable reasonably priced food from snacks up, efficient friendly staff; live music, background music, sports TV and machines; children till 7pm, nice terrace garden to the side with huts and heaters, open all day.

BEXLEYHEATH

Robin Hood & Little John

(020) 8303 1128 *Lion Road; DA6 8PF* Small 19th-c family-run local in residential area, welcoming and spotless, with eight (including two changing) well kept ales such as Adnams, Bexley, Fullers and Harveys, popular bargain pubby lunchtime food (not Sun) with Italian specials; over-21s only, seats out at front and in back garden.

BRENTFORD

Black Dog (020) 8568 5688

Albany Road; TW8 0NF Popular late Victorian bare-boards corner pub; excellent choice of ales and craft beers (maybe one from their microbrewery), also five real ciders and carefully chosen wines, interesting varied menu including some good vegetarian/vegan choices, friendly knowledgeable staff; background music from vintage vinyl; children (until 8.30pm) and dogs welcome, attractive sunny beer garden, open all day, food all day weekends (booking advised).

Express (020) 8560 8484

Kew Bridge Road; TW8 0EW Two-bar Victorian pub on busy road north of Kew Bridge; traditional high ceilings, button-back banquettes and other pubby furniture on wood floors, lots of pictures and big mirrors, original fireplaces, ten real ales, including Bass and Harveys, several craft beers, proper ciders and good range of other drinks, enjoyable fairly priced food, friendly helpful staff; background music from vinyl collection, sports TV; large split-level back garden with heaters and artificial grass, open (and food) all day.

BROMLEY

Red Lion (020) 8460 2691

North Road; BR1 3LG Chatty backstreet local in conservation area; traditional dimly lit interior with wood floor, tiling, green velvet drapes and shelves of books; well kept Greene King, Harveys and guests, lunchtime food, good friendly service; darts, sports TV, tables out in front, open all day.

Two Doves (020) 8462 1627

Oakley Road (A233); BR2 8HD Popular Victorian local, comfortable and unpretentious, with cheerful staff and regulars, well kept Youngs and guests, snacky lunchtime food such as rolls and baked potatoes, modern back conservatory and lovely garden; sports TV; open all day Fri-Sun.

CHISLEHURST

Bulls Head (020) 8467 1727

Royal Parade; BR7 6NR Handsome refurbished pub-hotel (18th-c coaching inn); Youngs ales and lots of wines by the glass, good food from sandwiches and sharing boards up, afternoon teas, two bars and roomy restaurant; live music Sun, sports TV; children welcome, plenty of tables in back garden, 15 bedrooms, open (and food) all day.

Crown (020) 8467 7326

School Road; BR7 5PQ Imposing Victorian pub overlooking common; simple attractive interior with flagstoned bar and several dining areas, well kept Shepherd Neame ales and good quality food from sandwiches and traditional choices up, friendly helpful service; live music, open mike nights, sports TV; children welcome, terrace tables, pétanque, seven bedrooms, open all day.

CROYDON

Claret & Ale (020) 8656 7452

5 Bingham Corner, Lower Addiscombe Road; CR0 7AA Friendly one-room drinkers' pub; half a dozen changing ales including Palmers marked up on blackboard, real ciders and decent choice of other drinks, dark pubby furniture on woodstrip or red-carpeted floor, coarse plasterwork and faux black beams; some live music, sports TV; dogs welcome, handy for Addiscombe tram stop, open all day.

GREENFORD

Black Horse (020) 8578 1384

Oldfield Lane; car park is accessed by automatic gate to S side of pub, staff will give an exit code; UB6 0AS Spacious pub on two levels by Grand Union Canal; well kept Fullers ales, a dozen wines by the glass and decent choice of enjoyable reasonably priced food from sandwiches and snacks up, efficient friendly service; Tues karaoke, Thurs quiz, weekend live music, sports TV, darts and machines; children and dogs welcome, balcony tables overlooking canal and big garden fenced from towpath, open all day, food all day Fri-Sun.

HAMPTON
Jolly Coopers (020) 8979 3384
High Street; TW12 2SJ Friendly end-of-terrace Georgian local; four or five well kept ales and good choice of wines, well liked freshly cooked food (all day Sat) in back restaurant extension including good evening tapas and Sun lunch till 5pm; pretty terrace with climbing plants and summer barbecues, open all day.

HARROW
Castle (020) 8422 3155
West Street; HA1 3EF Edwardian Fullers pub in picturesque part (steps up from street); their well kept ales and guests, decent food from lunchtime sandwiches up including Thurs pie and craft beer night, several rooms around central servery, rugs on bare boards, lots of panelling, open fires, collection of clocks in cheery front bar, more sedate back lounge; live music Mon, quiz Tues; children and dogs welcome, nice garden behind with rattan furniture, open (and food) all day, Sat brunch from 10am.

★Hare (020) 8954 4949
Brookshill/Old Redding; HA3 6SD Carefully renovated old pub (White Brasserie Co) with attractive contemporary décor in bar and linked dining rooms; long counter serving Sharps Doom Bar, Timothy Taylors Landlord and several wines by the glass, also extensive range of gins and cocktails, good interesting food including set menu till 6.30pm (not Sun), stylish brasserie with rugs on bare boards and woodburner, two other dining areas, one perfect for a small group, church candles and modern artwork throughout; weekly quiz; children and dogs (in bar) welcome, some picnic-sets out at front, more seats in back garden with gazebo, open (and food) all day.

ISLEWORTH
Hare & Hounds (020) 8560 5438
Windmill Lane (B454, off A4 signed for Greenford); TW7 5PR Busy Edwardian pub in nice setting opposite Osterley Park and House (NT); spacious interior with connecting rooms including pitched-ceiling back dining extension, Fullers beers, decent wines and popular food from sandwiches and small plates up, friendly staff; Weds quiz, children and dogs welcome, disabled facilities, picnic-sets out at front on artificial grass, big garden behind with glass-covered

eating area, summer barbecues, play area, open (and food) all day.

London Apprentice (020) 8560 1915
Church Street; TW7 6BG Large Thames-side Taylor Walker pub; reasonably priced food from sandwiches up, well kept ales including Greene King and three changing guests, good wine choice, log fire, pleasant service, upstairs river-view restaurant; quiz Sun, live music Fri; children and dogs welcome, nice waterside terrace with tables and parasols, open (and food) all day.

KINGSTON UPON THAMES
Boaters (020) 8541 4672
Canbury Gardens (park in Lower Ham Road if you can); KT2 5AU Family-friendly pub by the Thames in small park; good selection of ales/craft beers, decent wines and varied choice of enjoyable food from changing menu, summer barbecue, friendly staff coping well at busy times, comfortable banquettes in split-level wood-floored bar; Sun evening jazz, Tues quiz, board games; dogs welcome, riverside terrace and balcony, parking nearby can be tricky, open (and food) all day.

Canbury Arms (020) 8255 9129
Canbury Park Road; KT2 6LQ Popular open-plan Victorian pub attractively revamped under new owners; comfortable seating including a button-back banquette in bare-boards bar with open fire and lots of modern artwork, stools by blue-painted counter serving four real ales such as Harveys and Park (brewed nearby), plenty of wines by the glass/carafe and cocktails, good food from sharing plates and pub favourites up, Sat brunch from 10am; friendly helpful staff, airy restaurant extension with skylights and big windows; newspapers, TV for major sports; children (till 7.30pm) and dogs (in bar) welcome, picnic-sets and rattan furniture on terrace behind metal railings, open (and food) all day.

Queens Head (020) 8237 8039
Richmond Road/Windsor Road; KT2 5HA Large refurbished red-brick Fullers pub; modern interior arranged around traditional wooden servery (rescued from another London pub), four real ales and good variety of enjoyable food from snacks up including some themed nights, helpful young staff; weekly quiz, Sun movie, background music; children welcome, part-covered front deck, paved back terrace with wooden planters, cabins and play area, ten bedrooms, open (and food) all day.

ORPINGTON
★Bo-Peep (01959) 534457
Hewitts Road, Chelsfield; 1.7 miles from M25 junction 4; BR6 7QL Popular country-feel dining pub; old low beams and enormous inglenook in carpeted bar,

two cosy candlelit dining rooms, airy side room overlooking lane and fields; three well kept ales including Sharps, good helpings of enjoyable food (not Sun evening) from traditional choices up, weekday afternoon teas, cheerful helpful staff; background music; children and dogs (in bar) welcome, picnic-sets on big brick terrace, open all day and a useful M25 stop.

Five Bells (01689) 821044

Church Road; just off A224 Orpington bypass; BR6 7RE Chatty 17th-c white weatherboarded village local; two separate bars and dining area, inglenook fireplace, well kept Courage, Harveys and a couple of guests, reasonably priced food from lunchtime sandwiches up, evening meals Thurs-Sat only; live music including jazz and open mike nights, quiz Tues, sports TV; children welcome, picnic-sets among flowers out in front, open all day.

Rose & Crown (01689) 869029

Farnborough Way (A21); BR6 6BT Civilised family-run pub with open-plan, interconnected rooms hung with frame-to-frame prints and pictures; five ales on handpump including one named for the pub (from Marstons), simple choice of good value bar food, good friendly service, interior filled with house plants, church candles, lots of mirrors, hundreds of books on shelves and three log fires with varied seating on bare boards or black and white tiles; child and dog friendly, big child-friendly garden with picnic-sets, beach huts and cabanas.

PINNER

Case is Altered (020) 8866 0476

High Road/Southill Lane; HA5 2EQ Attractive 17th-c pub in quiet setting adjacent to cricket ground; main bar, flagstoned snug and barn seating/dining area, open fire, Rebellion and guests, draught and bottled craft beers, lots of wines by the glass (can be pricey) and good range of other drinks, enjoyable food from sandwiches and snacks to charcoal grills from open kitchen, Sun BBQ 12-5pm, friendly staff; background music, weekly quiz; children and dogs welcome, nice front garden with outside bar (very popular in fine weather), handy for Eastcote House Gardens, open (and food) all day, kitchen shuts 6pm Sun.

RICHMOND UPON THAMES

Mitre (020) 8940 1336

St Marys Grove, just off the Upper Richmond Road; TW9 1UY Refurbished Victorian local with ten changing ales and four draught ciders/perries (tasters offered), wood-fired pizzas, friendly staff and pub dog

(others welcome), bare boards, chesterfields, leaded windows and woodburner; live music Sun, board games; children allowed, seats on small front terrace, outdoor screen, open all day weekends (until 8.30pm Sun), from 3pm other days.

New Inn (020) 8940 9444

Petersham Road (A307, Ham Common); TW10 7DB Attractive Georgian pub in good spot on Ham Common; unashamedly old-fashioned inside with very traditional décor, two open fires and a woodburner, well kept ales such as Adnams Broadside, Fullers London Pride and Youngs Bitter plus guests, decent pubby food including daily specials, friendly staff and good chatty atmosphere; children and dogs welcome, disabled facilities, picnic-sets out at front and in back courtyard, handy for Ham House (NT), open all day.

Princes Head (020) 8940 1572

The Green; TW9 1LX Spacious open-plan pub overlooking cricket green; low-ceilinged panelled areas off island servery, well kept Fullers ales and popular sensibly priced pub food from sandwiches up, coal-effect fire; background music, Thurs open mike, sports TV, daily papers; children allowed in certain areas, dogs welcome, circular picnic-sets outside, handy for Richmond Theatre, open (and food) all day.

White Cross (020) 8940 6844

Water Lane; TW9 1TH Lovely garden with terrific Thames outlook, seats on paved area, outside bar and boats to Kingston and Hampton Court; two chatty main rooms with local prints and photographs, three log fires (one unusually below a window), well kept Youngs and guests from old-fashioned island servery, 16 wines by the glass and enjoyable fairly pubby food from 10am breakfast and brunch on, also bright and airy upstairs room (where under-18s allowed) with pretty cast-iron balcony for splendid river view; background music, TV; dogs welcome, tides can reach the pub entrance (wellies provided), open (and food) all day.

White Swan (020) 8940 0959

Old Palace Lane; TW9 1PG Civilised little 18th-c pub with rustic dark-beamed bar, well kept Harveys, Otter, St Austell and one guest, generally well liked food including lunchtime sandwiches up, coal-effect fires, back dining conservatory and upstairs restaurant; soft background music; children (till 6.30pm) and dogs welcome, some seats on narrow paved area at front, more in pretty walled back terrace below railway, open all day.

Virtually all pubs in this book sell wine by the glass. We mention wines if they are a cut above the average.

ROMFORD

Golden Lion (01708) 740081
High Street; RM1 1HR Busy former coaching inn – dates from the 15th c and is one of the town's oldest buildings; enjoyable good value food from sandwiches, sharing plates and pub favourites up, Greene King ales, guest beers and decent range of other drinks, spacious beamed interior, more room upstairs; live music, sports TVs (even in the garden); children welcome, open (and food) all day.

Ship (01708) 741571
Main Road; RM2 5EL Friendly black and white pub built in 1762; low beams, panelling and woodburner in fine brick fireplace, Greene King, Sharps, Timothy Taylors and guests, enjoyable good value food (not weekend evenings) from sandwiches and sharing boards up; quiz Thurs, live music Sat; children and dogs welcome, picnic-sets on pavement and in back garden under parasols, open all day.

SURBITON

Antelope (020) 8399 5565
Maple Road; KT6 4AW Double-fronted Victorian pub with excellent choice of cask and craft beers including own Big Smoke unfined range from on-site microbrewery, several ciders too, tasty food including range of burgers and ribs; friendly knowledgeable staff, split-level bare-boards interior with comfortable mix of seating, grey-painted and tiled walls adorned with pump clips, open fire; background music from vinyl collection, board games; dogs welcome, paved back terrace with parasols, open (and food) all day.

TEDDINGTON

Kings Head (020) 3166 2900
High Street; TW11 8HG White Brasserie pub with comfortably updated front bar, easy chairs and button-back wall benches on bare boards, woodburner, a couple of snug rooms off, well kept changing ales, over 20 wines by the glass and good range of other drinks including cocktails, back dining part with similar décor and open kitchen, wide variety of enjoyable food from bar snacks up, good value set menu till 6.30pm (not Sun), courteous helpful staff; background music; children and dogs welcome, seats out at front and on enclosed back terrace, open (and food) all day.

TWICKENHAM

★Crown (020) 8892 5896
Richmond Road, St Margarets; TW1 2NH Popular Georgian pub with several large dining areas including splendid Victorian back hall; good food from sandwiches and sharing plates to restaur019 choices, three well kept ales and one changing guest, nice wines by the glass and good coffee; friendly efficient staff, open fire; newspapers; children till 7pm and dogs (in bar) welcome, sunny courtyard garden, open (and food) all day.

Sussex Arms (020) 8894 7468
Staines Road; TW2 5BG Traditional bare-boards pub with 15 handpumps plus ciders/perries from long counter, plenty in bottles too, simple food including good home-made pies, pizzas and burgers served all day (till 9.30pm Sun); friendly staff and welcoming atmosphere, walls and ceilings covered in beer mats and pump clips, open fire; background music from vinyl collection, some live acoustic music, Weds quiz; large back garden with boules, open all day.

White Swan (020) 8744 2951
Riverside; TW1 3DN 17th-c Thames-side pub up steep anti-flood steps; L-shaped bar with bare boards and cosy log fire, river views from prized bay window, five real ales including Twickenham and enjoyable fairly priced food (all day Sat, till 6pm Sun), friendly local atmosphere; Weds quiz (Sept-Apr), monthly acoustic live music, board games; children and dogs welcome, tranquil setting opposite Eel Pie Island with well used balcony and waterside terrace, open all day.

SCOTLAND

SHETLAND

ORKNEY

North Sea

WESTERN ISLES

LEWIS

HARRIS

NORTH UIST

SUTHERLAND

CAITHNESS

SOUTH UIST

SKYE

ROSS-SHIRE

BARRA

RUM

NAIRN

MORAYSHIRE

BANFFSHIRE

ABERDEENSHIRE

COLL

INVERNESS-SHIRE

KINCARDINE

TIREE

MULL

ARGYLL

ANGUS

COLONSAY

PERTHSHIRE

JURA

FIFE

KINROSS-SHIRE

STIRLINGSHIRE

CLACKMANNANSHIRE

DUNBARTON

ISLAY

RENFREW

W

E

LOTHIAN

MID

LANARK-SHIRE

BERWICK'

PEEBLES

ARRAN

SELKIRK

ROXBURGHSHIRE

AYRSHIRE

NORTHUMBERLAND

DUMFRIESSHIRE

KIRKCUDBRIGHT-SHIRE

WIGTOWNSHIRE

COUNTY DURHAM

CUMBRIA

Irish Sea

KEY ★ Star Pub 🎯 Top Quality Food 🍺 Great Beer
🍷 Good Wines £ Bargain Meals 🛏 Good Bedrooms 🍴 Serves Food

APPLECROSS   NG7144 Map 11

Applecross Inn ★ 🛏

(01520) 744262 – www.applecrossinn.co.uk

Off A896 S of Shieldaig; IV54 8LR

Isolated pub on famously scenic route on west coast, with particularly friendly welcome, real ales and good seafood; bedrooms

---

A popular spot, this inn is always packed with customers from all over the world and the atmosphere is lively and genuinely friendly; if you wish to stay here, you'll have to book months ahead. The exhilarating west coast drive to reach the inn is over the Bealach na Bà (Pass of the Cattle) and is one of the highest in Britain; do not attempt it in bad weather. The alternative route, along the single-track lane winding around the coast from just south of Shieldaig, has equally glorious sea loch (and then sea) views nearly all the way. The no-nonsense bar has a woodburning stove, exposed-stone walls, upholstered pine furnishings and a stone floor. There's Applecross Inner Sound and Sanctuary on handpump, over 50 malt whiskies, 25 gins, ten rums and a good, varied wine list (all are available by the glass); background music and board games. Tables in the shoreside garden enjoy magnificent views; there's an outdoor eating area for summer use and a retro food truck (Applecross Inn-Side Out) selling fish and chips and Applecross ices. Getting to this remote little gem is part of the experience and a memorable time awaits on arrival. Some disabled facilities.

🍴 Most people opt for the first class fresh local fish and seafood, which includes squat lobsters, creel-caught prawns, oysters, hand-dived scallops, fresh haddock, langoustines, a seafood platter and curried crab with mango, but they also offer sandwiches, local haggis flambéed in Drambuie topped with cream, duck breast with soy and honey marinade, beef chilli with rice, gammon and egg, spinach and potato curry, and puddings such as seasonal fruit crumble with custard and raspberry cranachan with almond praline. *Benchmark main dish: local prawns £22.00. Two-course evening meal £25.00.*

Free house ~ Licensee Judith Fish ~ Real ale ~ Open 11am-11.30pm; 11am-midnight Sat; 12.30-11 Sun ~ Bar food 12-9 ~ Restaurant ~ Accompanied under-16s allowed in the bar or outside until 9pm ~ Dogs allowed in bedrooms ~ Bedrooms: £100-£150

EDINBURGH   NT2574 Map 11

Abbotsford 🍺 £

(0131) 225 5276 – www.theabbotsford.com

Rose Street; E end, beside South St David Street; EH2 2PR

Busy city pub with period features, changing real ales, and bar and restaurant food

---

The atmosphere of this handsome bar in the centre of Edinburgh is invitingly lively. It's a classic of Edwardian pub design: long wooden tables and leatherette benches run the length of the dark wood-panelled walls, while high above is a rather handsome red and gold plaster-moulded ceiling. The hefty Victorian island bar is ornately carved from dark Spanish mahogany and highly polished; you'll find a find choice of drinks here, including six beers (five traditional founts, one handpull) such as Harviestoun Schiehallion, Mòr Calm & Wise and Stewarts 80/-, plus a selection of bottled US craft beers and around 80 malt whiskies. The smarter upstairs restaurant is impressive too. Little changes here, which is just how the wide mix of local customers like it.

🍴 Hearty food at good prices from snacks up includes beer-battered tiger prawns, nachos, smoked salmon with crème fraîche, haggis, neeps and tatties (vegetarian haggis too), sirloin steak, gammon steak with eggs and chips, Scottish beef burger with toppings, slow-cooked steak and ale pie with seasonal vegetables, roasted Mediterranean vegetable risotto with herb oil, and puddings such as Orkney ice-cream and Scottish cheeses with onion chutney and fruit. *Benchmark main dish: beer-battered haddock and chips £14.95. Two-course evening meal £21.00.*

Stewart ~ Licensee Robert Wilson ~ Real ale ~ Open 11-11; 11am-midnight Fri, Sat ~ Bar food 12-10 ~ Restaurant ~ Children over 5 allowed in restaurant; over-14s allowed in bar if dining with an adult until 5pm ~ Dogs allowed in bar

EDINBURGH NT2574 Map 11
Bow Bar 🍺 £
(0131) 226 7667 – www.thebowbar.co.uk
West Bow; EH1 2HH

Cosy, enjoyably unpretentious pub with an excellent choice of well kept beers

The warm welcoming interiors of this classic pub include walls covered with a fine collection of enamel advertising signs and handsome antique brewery mirrors, and there are sturdy leatherette wall seats and café-style bar seats around heavy narrow tables on the wooden floor. Expect a splendid range of drinks served by knowledgeable staff. From the rectangular bar with its impressive carved mahogany gantry, eight well kept real ales are dispensed from the tall 1920s founts on the counter; these include regulars such as Stewart 80/- and Tempest Pale Armadillo and five quickly changing guests from breweries such as Black Isle, Cromarty and Swannay, plus 13 craft beers. They hold regular beer festivals. Also on offer are over 400 malts, including five 'malts of the moment', a good choice of rums, 60 or so international bottled beers and 20 Scottish gins. Strong on traditional values, this is an honest pub and a bastion of simple stand-up drinking. No children.

🍴 Lunchtime-only food is limited to meat, vegetarian and vegan pies.

Free house ~ Licensee Mike Smith ~ Real ale ~ Open 12-midnight ~ Bar food 12-4 ~ Dogs allowed in bar

EDINBURGH NT2574 Map 11
Guildford Arms 🍺 £
(0131) 556 4312 – www.guildfordarms.com
West Register Street; EH2 2AA

Busy and friendly with spectacular Victorian décor, a marvellous range of real ales and good food

This is an easy-going, much loved bar with splendid Victorian décor (it was built in 1896) and a snug upstairs gallery restaurant with contrasting modern décor that gives a fine dress-circle view of the main bar below. It's opulently excessive, with ornate painted plasterwork on the lofty ceiling, dark mahogany fittings, heavy swagged velvet curtains and a busy patterned carpet. Tables and stools are lined up along towering arched windows opposite the bar, where knowledgeable, efficient staff serve ten well kept quickly changing beers such as Fyne Ales Jarl, Gun Project Babylon Pale Ale, Orkney Dark Island, Stewart Pentland IPA and Swannay Orkney IPA plus craft and continental beers. Also, several wines by the glass, 50 malt whiskies, a dozen rums and a dozen gins; TV and background music.

Tasty food at good prices includes lunchtime ciabattas and bar snacks such as spicy chicken wings, whitebait and beef chilli nachos plus soup of the day, pâté of the day, mushroom, spinach, brie and hazelnut wellington, sausages of the day with mash and onion gravy, steak and ale pie, haggis, neeps and tatties, Scottish beef burger with chips and coleslaw, and puddings. *Benchmark main dish: breaded haddock and chips £12.95. Two-course evening meal £20.00.*

Stewart ~ Lease Steve Jackson ~ Real ale ~ Open 11-11; 11am-midnight Thurs-Sat ~ Bar food 12 (12.30 Sun)-2.30, 5.30-9.30; 12-10 Fri, Sat snacks throughout afternoon except Fri, Sat ~ Restaurant ~ Children welcome in upstairs gallery if dining and over 5 ~ Dogs allowed in bar

EDINBURGH
Kays Bar ⬤ £

NT2574 Map 11

(0131) 225 1858 – www.kaysbar.co.uk
Jamaica Street West; off India Street; EH3 6HF

Cosy, enjoyably chatty backstreet pub with good value lunchtime food and an excellent choice of well kept beers

In days past, this pub was owned by John Kay, a whisky and wine merchant: wine barrels were hoisted up to the first floor and dispensed through pipes attached to nipples that are still visible around the ceiling light rose. A friendly little backstreet pub, it's surprisingly untouristy. Décor is simple, with large casks and vats arranged along the walls, old wine and spirits merchants' notices and gas-type lamps. Also, long, curving, well worn red plush wall banquettes and stools around cast-iron tables on red carpet, and red pillars supporting the red ceiling. A quiet panelled back room (a bit like a library) leads off, with a panelled pitched ceiling and a collection of books ranging from dictionaries to ancient steam-train books for boys; there's a lovely coal fire in winter and board games. Crucially, there's also a marvellous choice of drinks here including around seven real ales on handpump with four regulars – maybe Caledonian Deuchars IPA, Fyne Ales Jarl, Stewart Copper Cascade and Theakstons Best – plus more than 50 malt whiskies aged from eight to 50 years old including a changing 'malt of the moment', 20 gins and half a dozen wines by the glass. Sports TV. They hold a beer festival in August.

Good value lunchtime-only food includes stovies, pâté with toast, haggis, neeps and tatties, warm brie or prawn salads, beef or chicken curries, chilli con carne, steak pie, and puddings such as chocolate fudge cake. *Benchmark main dish: mince and tatties £5.50.*

Free house ~ Licensee Fraser Gillespie ~ Real ale ~ Open 11am-midnight; 11am-1am Fri, Sat; 12.30-11 Sun ~ Bar food 12-2.30; not Sun ~ Dogs allowed in bar

---

The details at the end of each featured entry start by saying whether the pub is a free house, or if it belongs to a brewery or pub group (which we name).

ELIE

NO4999   Map 11

Ship ⚓

(01333) 330246 – www.shipinn.scot

The Toft, off A917 (High Street) towards harbour; KY9 1DT

Busy seaside inn with stunning outlook, bustling bar, two-level dining rooms, tasty food and seats on the terrace; individually decorated bedrooms

The position of this pub is really special – by an expansive sandy bay between jutting headlands with oystercatchers and gulls much in evidence and maybe beach cricket (this is the only pub in Britain whose cricket team has a pitch on the beach). Picnic-sets on the outdoor terrace, which has its own bar, enjoy the lovely view. Inside, the bar is the heart of the place with armchairs to each side of an open fire, stools against the counter, interesting décor such as ropework lighting, oars and a ship's wheel, and welcoming staff serving up to four real ales on handpump, such as Caledonian Deuchars IPA, craft beers from the likes of St Andrews, 15 wines by the glass, a range of malt whiskies and Scottish gins. The attractive, half-panelled dining rooms have woodburning stoves, cushioned wooden chairs and pale tables on bare boards and seaside artwork. Four of the six light and airy, boutique-style bedrooms overlook the water. Sister pub is the Bridge Inn at Ratho.

 Tasty bar food using local and seasonal produce includes cullen skink, bangers and mash with crispy black pudding, root vegetables and onion jus, and burger with bacon, cheddar, slaw and chips. The restaurant menu offers beef and haggis fritters with crème fraîche, green chilli, coriander and parsley chutney, mackerel pâté with pickled cucumber, Shetland hake with braised chickpeas, chorizo, cherry tomatoes and chilli, Black Isle rib-eye with a choice of sauce, and puddings such as lime posset with strawberries and shortbread, raspberry eton mess and Isle of Arran ice-cream, sorbet or vegan ice-cream. *Benchmark main dish: beer-battered haddock and chips £14.95. Two-course evening meal £25.00.*

Free house ~ Licensees Graham and Rachel Bucknall ~ Real ale ~ Open 10.30am-11pm Mon-Thurs, Sun; 10.30am-midnight Fri, Sat ~ Bar food 12-8 ~ Restaurant ~ Children allowed in restaurant ~ Dogs allowed in bar & restaurant ~ Bedrooms: £180

GLASGOW

NS5765   Map 11

Bon Accord 🍺 £

(0141) 248 4427 – www.bonaccordpub.com

North Street; G3 7DA

Remarkable choice of drinks, a good welcome and bargain food

This traditional, often bustling bar has several linked rooms, all warmly understated with cream or terracotta walls, a mix of chairs and tables, a leather sofa and lots of bar stools on polished bare boards or carpeting. As well as more than 500 malt whiskies, the splendid drinks choice includes real ales (over 800 sold throughout the year) sourced from breweries across Britain and served from swan-necked handpumps, including Caledonian Deuchars IPA and nine daily changing guests, continental bottled beers, a farm cider and, in a remarkable display behind the counter, 50 gins, 20 rums and lots of vodkas. There's a TV, background music and board games, a pub quiz on Wednesday and live music on Saturday. Outside, there are circular picnic-sets on a small terrace, and modern tables and chairs set out in front. No dogs allowed inside.

Exceptionally good value food includes sandwiches, jacket potatoes, peppered mushrooms, giant yorkshire pudding filled with chicken breast, mash and pepper sauce, chilli con carne, all-day breakfast, Cajun chicken, assorted burgers, sirloin and rib-eye steaks, and puddings such as clootie dumpling and apple pie with custard. *Benchmark main dish: fish and chips £8.95. Two-course evening meal £14.00.*

Free house ~ Licensee Paul McDonagh ~ Real ale ~ Open 11-11 Mon; 11-midnight; 12.30-11 Sun ~ Bar food 11-8.45; 12.30-8.45 Sun ~ Children welcome until 8pm

GULLANE
NT4882 Map 11

Bonnie Badger 🔯 ▽ 🛏

(01620) 621111 – www.bonniebadger.com

Main Street; A198; EH31 2AB

Renovated inn with stylish décor, good choice of drinks, exceptional food and seats in terraced garden; well equipped bedrooms

This highly acclaimed inn – owned by the Michelin-starred chef Tom Kitchin – was updated a couple of years ago in an interesting Scandinavian/Scottish style. While food is obviously king here, there's always a warm welcome for those who just want a drink and a chat. The bar has high chairs against the counter, upholstered chairs around pubby tables on bare boards, and Belhaven 80/-, Harviestoun Sunburst Pale and a guest ale on handpump, craft beer such as Campervan Leith Juice, 28 wines by the glass, cocktails and 80 malt whiskies served by knowledgeable, friendly staff; pool table, board games, TV and background music. The main focus is on the dining room (originally the stables) which has its original sandstone walls, a high-raftered ceiling, a big open fireplace, panelling and seating that ranges from button-back wall banquettes to cushioned dark wooden dining chairs around pale-topped tables. A lounge has stylish, contemporary armchairs and sofas on chic pale floorboards. There are plenty of seats and tables outside on a two-level gravelled terrace, and an enclosed brazier. The 13 comfortable, modern bedrooms are in either the main building or two garden cottages across the courtyard – and it's all just a stroll from the beach and close to Muirfield golf course. Good wheelchair access.

 Excellent food following the nose-to-tail approach uses the best local, seasonal produce and gives a modern twist to pub classics. Dishes might include Loch Fyne oysters, chicken liver parfait with pickled cabbage, goats cheese tart, fish pie, roasted cod and shellfish in light curry sauce, spelt and lentil burger with chips, Borders grouse with girolles and game chips, half grilled lobster with garlic and parsley butter, and puddings such as chocolate fondant and pistachio ice-cream sandwich with berries. They also offer a fairly priced three-course set menu at lunch and early evening. *Benchmark main dish: steak pie with bone marrow £17.00. Two-course evening meal £27.00.*

Free house ~ Licensee Tom Kitchin ~ Real ale ~ Open 8am-11pm Mon-Thurs, Sun; 8am-1am Fri, Sat ~ Bar food 12-10 ~ Restaurant ~ Children welcome until 10pm ~ Dogs allowed in bar, restaurant & bedrooms ~ Bedrooms: £195

ISLE OF WHITHORN
NX4736 Map 9

Steam Packet

(01988) 500334 – www.thesteampacketinn.biz

Harbour Row; DG8 8LL

Waterside views from friendly inn with up to eight real ales and tasty food; bedrooms

This family-run inn sits right on the quayside in a pretty fishing village, close to the roofless remains of 14th-c St Ninian's kirk. It has large picture windows overlooking the bustle of yachts and inshore fishing boats and some of the seven bedrooms offer the same view. The comfortable low-ceilinged bar is split into two: on the right, plush button-back banquettes and boat pictures, and on the left, stools around cast-iron-framed tables on big stone tiles, and a woodburning stove in the bare stone wall; TV, board games and pool. They brew their own ales here at the Five Kingdoms Brewery and also keep Belhaven IPA, Fyne Ales Highlander, Greene King Old Speckled Hen and guests from other breweries such as Kelburn and Orkney on handpump, around 30 gins, 23 malt whiskies, nine wines by the glass and a couple of farm ciders. There's also a lower dining room with beams, high-backed dining chairs around square tables on wooden flooring plus another woodburner, a small eating area off the lounge bar, and an airy conservatory leading into the garden. Wheelchair access but no disabled loos.

Pleasing food includes vegetable curry, burger with onion rings and chips, prawn platter and other seafood options such as lobster, crab, sole and monkfish, sirloin steak with a choice of sauce, and puddings such as treacle sponge and vegan/gluten-free chocolate and vanilla brownies. *Benchmark main dish: beer-battered fish and chips £14.95. Two-course evening meal £20.00.*

Free house ~ Licensee Alastair Scoular ~ Real ale ~ Open 11-11; 12-11 Sun ~ Bar food 12-2.30, 4.30-9; 12-9 Fri-Sun ~ Restaurant ~ Children welcome except in public bar ~ Dogs allowed in bar & bedrooms ~ Bedrooms: £90

KILCHRENAN
Kilchrenan Inn 🛏

NN0323 Map 11

(01866) 833000 – www.kilchrenaninn.co.uk
B845, by road to Ardanaiseig; PA35 1HD

Close to the banks of Loch Awe with good food, Scottish drinks, friendly owners and seats outside; bedrooms

The stylish modern décor of this beautifully refurbished 18th-c inn (once a trading post) includes tartan-upholstered chairs and wall seats around simple tables on bare floorboards, grey and white paintwork and a woodburning stove. More tartan is used on the high chairs against the counter in the bar, where they keep Fyne Ales Easy Trail on handpump, nine wines by the glass, Scottish gins and several malt whiskies. The atmosphere throughout is relaxed and friendly. A dining room leads off and is similarly furnished, with up-to-date lighting and local artwork on planked walls. Outside in front of the inn are benches and tables, with picnic-sets arranged on the grass opposite. The three contemporary bedrooms are warm and comfortable; one of them, with a bunk bed, is suitable for families; breakfasts are highly rated. It's a beautiful drive to reach the inn along Loch Awe and then on to Ardanaiseig Gardens, and there's good walking, cycling and fishing nearby.

Enjoyable food includes lunchtime sandwiches, scotch egg with celeriac rémoulade and watercress, smoked fish board with toasted sourdough and lemon, vegetable burger with red onion, sriracha mayo and fries, pan-fried lemon sole with caper and lemon butter and samphire, chicken and ham pie with chantenay carrots and new potatoes, beer-battered haddock and fries, pea, mint and ricotta risotto, and puddings such as affogato, chocolate ganache pot and Scottish cheeseboard with chutney and oatcakes. *Benchmark main dish: roast rack of lamb with white onion purée, provençale vegetables and crispy new potatoes £17.50. Two-course evening meal £23.00.*

Free house ~ Licensees Phil Carr and Pip Pedley ~ Real ale ~ Open 5-10 Mon, Tues; 12-11 Weds, Thurs; 12-midnight Fri, Sat; 1-10 Sun (phone for winter closing time) ~ Bar food 6-8.30 Mon, Tues; 12-2, 6-8.30 Weds, Thurs; 12-2.30, 6-8.30 Fri, Sat; 1-7 Sun ~ Restaurant ~ Children welcome ~ Dogs allowed in bar & bedrooms ~ ~ Bedrooms: £130

MEIKLEOUR

NO1539   Map 11

Meikleour Arms ♀ ⚐

(01250) 883206 – www.meikleourarms.co.uk

A984 W of Coupar Angus; PH2 6EB

Beautifully furnished inn with genuinely welcoming, helpful staff and interesting food; lovely bedrooms

This charming 19th-c Perthshire inn is situated just beyond a spectacular 275-year-old beech hedge – the tallest in the world, no less (it was trimmed in 2019 for the first time in 20 years). The bar area has high chairs by the counter, painted chairs and sage green tweed banquettes by pale oak tables on flagstones, tree-pattern wallpapered or stone walls and a two-way woodburning stove; board games and background music. Ales include The Lure of Meikleour (from the Strathbraan Brewery), plus changing guests such as Caledonian Deuchars IPA and Strathbraan Head East, a thoughtfully chosen wine list with 11 wines by the glass and a 'wine of the month', 20 gins and over 50 malt whiskies. The main dining room is built in the style of a barn, with high rafters in an apex ceiling, wooden tables and chairs on more flagstones, and old family portraits and fly fishing touches on the walls (bare stone or with striking green wallpaper with a leaf and gold key design). There's also a private dining room, a country-style sitting room for residents and a drying room and tackle area for anglers. Seats in the garden and on a small colonnaded verandah (with more on a sloping lawn) have distant highland views. There are 11 elegant bedrooms and five cottages; three of the bedrooms have four-poster beds, and the downstairs rooms have wooden floors and are dog-friendly. It's part of the Meikleour Estate, and there's a lot to see and do nearby, including one of the best salmon beats in Scotland. Disabled access.

Using produce from the Estate (including venison and fish) and from their walled garden, the good, beautifully presented food includes sandwiches, moules marinière, twice-baked smoked cheddar soufflé with creamed leeks, steak and ale pie, kedgeree with smoked haddock and quail eggs, baked hake loin with tomato and shallot salsa, chargrilled chicken supreme with lemon and garlic marinade and new potatoes, venison steak and mini venison cottage pie, 28-day aged rump steak with a choice of sauce and chips, and puddings such as sticky toffee pudding, vanilla crème brûlée with Meikleour shortbread and Scottish cheese, chutney and biscuits. *Benchmark main dish: beer-battered Scottish haddock and chips £13.95. Two-course evening meal £22.00.*

Free house ~ Licensees Sam and Claire Mercer Nairne ~ Real ale ~ Open 10am-11pm ~ Bar food 12-11 ~ Restaurant ~ Children welcome ~ Dogs allowed in bar, restaurant & bedrooms ~ Bedrooms: £125

MELROSE

NT5433   Map 9

Burts Hotel 🏅 ♀ ⚐

(01896) 822285 – www.burtshotel.co.uk

B6374, Market Square; TD6 9PL

Scotland Dining Pub of the Year

Comfortable town-centre hotel with imaginative food and a fine array of malt whiskies; bedrooms

This delightful, family-run hotel has a welcoming bar as well as an elegant restaurant with swagged curtains, dark blue wallpaper and tables laid with white linen, if you're after a smarter dining experience. The 20 bedrooms, though quite small, are immaculate and comfortably decorated and make a lovely base for exploring; they also have a new self-catering cottage. Neat public areas are maintained with attention to detail. The red-carpeted bar has tidy pub tables between cushioned wall seats and windsor armchairs, Scottish prints on pale green walls, a woodburning stove and a long dark wood counter with three handpumps serving Born in the Borders Game Bird and changing ales (maybe Lowland Dryfe and Timothy Taylors Landlord), 12 wines by the glass from a good list, a farm cider, 25 gins and around 60 malt whiskies; background music. In summer you can sit out in the pleasant, well tended garden. Situated at the heart of an attractive border town, just a few steps from the ruins of Melrose Abbey and close to Abbotsford House, Sir Walter Scott's ancestral home, there's plenty to do nearby.

Using the best local, seasonal produce, the interesting food includes lunchtime sandwiches and light dishes (steamed mussels in white wine, thyme and shallot cream, salmon fishcakes with fennel and red onion slaw) as well as guinea fowl and apricot terrine with shallot and marmalade chutney, spiced lamb kofta kebabs with lime and cucumber crème fraîche, breaded or battered haddock and chips, mushroom and lentil bean burger, roasted monkfish tail with puy lentil casserole, curried butternut purée and cauliflower fritter, Borders lamb chops, vegetarian enchiladas topped with cheese and salad, and puddings such as frangipane tart with fruit coulis and fresh raspberries and American-style Nutella cheesecake with millionaire's mousse and hazelnut parfait. *Benchmark main dish: pan-fried fillet of salmon with tiger prawn risotto £17.95. Two-course evening meal £26.00.*

Free house ~ Licensees Nick and Trish Henderson ~ Real ale ~ Open 12-2; 6-9 ~ Bar food 12-2, 6-8 ~ Restaurant ~ Children welcome ~ Dogs allowed in bar & bedrooms ~ Bedrooms: $148

PLOCKTON

Plockton Hotel ★ 🏅📖

NG8033   Map 11

(01599) 544274 – www.plocktonhotel.co.uk
Village signposted from A87 near Kyle of Lochalsh; IV52 8TN

Well run small hotel with wonderful views, very good food with emphasis on local seafood and real ales; bedrooms

If you can, grab a table in the sea-front garden of this welcoming little hotel for a view out past Plockton's trademark palm trees to a shore lined with colourful flowering shrubs and across the sheltered anchorage to rugged mountains. The hotel is in the centre of this lovely Scottish National Trust village and part of a long, low terrace of stone houses. Half of the light, bright bedrooms have extraordinary views over Loch Carron, while the others, some with balconies, look over the hillside garden; breakfasts are good. The modern, comfortably furnished lounge bar has window seats with views of the harbour boats, as well as antique, dark red leather seating around neat Regency-style tables on a tartan carpet, and three model ships set into the woodwork and partly panelled stone walls. The separate public bar has board games, TV, a jukebox and background music. The well kept beers on handpump might include Belhaven Best, Glen Spean Red Revival, Isle of Skye Red and Orkney Raven, plus more than 20 malt whiskies, nine wines by the glass and a good selection of Scottish gins. There's a hotel nearby called the Plockton Inn, so don't get the two confused. Disabled access and loos, plus access to one bedroom.

IOI Fresh fish and shellfish play a big role here, with dishes including garlic crab claws, queen scallops and smoked bacon with garlic, sole and salmon parcels with prawn thermidor sauce, and sea bass with roasted butternut squash risotto; they also offer sandwiches, burgers, fish and chips, haggis and whisky starter, a vegetarian dish of the day, chicken breast stuffed with smoked ham and cheese with sun-dried tomato, garlic and cream sauce, venison with cumberland sauce, and puddings. *Benchmark main dish: langoustine platter £24.00. Two-course evening meal £21.00.*

Free house ~ Licensee Alan Pearson ~ Real ale ~ Open 11am-midnight ~ Bar food 12-2.15, 6-9 ~ Restaurant ~ Children welcome ~ Dogs allowed in bar ~ Bedrooms: £150

RATHO   NT1470   Map 11

Bridge Inn **IOI** ▢ 🍺

(0131) 333 1320 – www.bridgeinn.com

Baird Road; EH28 8RA

Canalside inn with cosy bar and airy restaurant, a thoughtful choice of drinks and enjoyable food; attractive bedrooms

The cosy bar of this charming 18th-c inn not far from Edinburgh has an open fire with leather armchairs to either side and a larger area with a two-way fireplace and upholstered tub and cushioned wooden chairs on pale boards around a mix of tables. Regular beers on handpump include Belhaven 80/-, Broughton Greenmantle and Inveralmond Lia Fail, among many other Scottish brewers, 15 wines by the glass and several malt whiskies. The pub is very much the heart of the village, attracting a good mix of customers and offering a warm welcome to all. The main restaurant is light and airy with up-to-date pale oak settles, antique-style chairs and big windows overlooking the Union Canal below. Seats on the terrace look out over the water and are quickly snapped up in warm weather. The four individually decorated and very comfortable bedrooms have fine views, and breakfasts are lovely. The Ship in Elie is under the same ownership.

IOI The quality food uses only Scottish meat and fish, some home-grown produce and their own pork and eggs from their free-ranging chickens and ducks. As well as breakfast (9-11am), options include sandwiches, crispy haggis bonbons with mustard mayo, grilled mackerel with tomatoes, cullen skink, sausage and mash with black pudding and crackling, salmon fillet with chorizo, potatoes and peas, duo of venison with stilton and broccoli purée, mushrooms and red wine jus, sweet potato gnocchi with wild mushrooms and spinach, and puddings such as chocolate brownie with buttermilk pannacotta and rhubarb sorbet and orange and caramel cheesecake with citrus sorbet. They have a separate gluten-free menu. *Benchmark main dish: pie of the day £15.50. Two-course evening meal £23.00.*

Free house ~ Licensees Graham and Rachel Bucknall ~ Real ale ~ Open 9am-11pm; 9am-midnight Fri, Sat ~ Bar food 9am-11am, 12-3, 5-9 Mon-Fri; 9am-11am, 12-9 Sat; 9am-11am, 12-8 Sun ~ Restaurant ~ Children welcome ~ Dogs allowed in bar ~ Bedrooms: £100

SHIELDAIG   NG8153   Map 11

Shieldaig Bar 🛏

(01520) 755251 – www.shieldaigbarcoastalkitchen.co.uk

Village signposted just off A896 Lochcarron–Gairloch; IV54 8XN

Wonderfully set contemporary bar with real ales and fresh seafood; tranquil bedrooms

This casual and appealing bar-restaurant on the edge of Loch Shieldaig is next door to the Tigh an Eilean Hotel and under the same ownership. It's on two storeys: the bar is below, with dining on the first floor, where there's also a decked balcony with a magnificent view of the loch and the fishing village. It's gently contemporary and nicely relaxed with timber floors, timber-boarded walls, shiny bolts through exposed wooden roof beams and an open kitchen. There's a couple of changing ales such as Strathcarron Golden Cow and Red Cow on handpump and up to a dozen wines by the glass; background music, TV, darts, pool and board games. Tables in the sheltered little courtyard are well placed to enjoy the gorgeous position, and there are a few picnic-sets on grass down by the water. If you wish to stay, the hotel has 11 comfortable bedrooms each with its own sitting area, but no TVs or telephones – to preserve the peace. Breakfasts are good and hearty. It's a brilliant base for spotting otters, sea eagles, seals and even the rare pine marten; the view over forested Shieldaig Island to Loch Torridon and then out to the sea beyond is stunning.

As well as shellfish straight from the jetty, the reliably good home-made food includes lunchtime sandwiches, cullen skink, moules marinière, hand-dived scallops and langoustines on generous platters, grilled goats cheese with rosemary and tomato salsa, pizzas from their wood-fired oven, battered haddock and chips, haggis, neeps and tatties, seafood stew, burger with coleslaw and chips, and puddings such as crème brûlée with Scottish raspberries and sticky toffee and date pudding with vanilla ice-cream and Scottish cheeses with oatcakes and chutney. *Benchmark main dish: seafood platter £21.00. Two-course evening meal £25.00.*

Free house ~ Licensee Cathryn Field ~ Real ale ~ Open 11-11 ~ Bar food 12-2.30, 6-8.30 ~ Restaurant ~ Children welcome ~ Dogs allowed in bar & bedrooms ~ Bedrooms: £160

SLIGACHAN
Sligachan Hotel 🍺 🛏

NG4930   Map 11

(01478) 650204 – www.sligachan.co.uk
A87 Broadford–Portree, junction with A863; IV47 8SW

Spectacularly set mountain hotel with walkers' bar and plusher side, all-day food and impressive range of whiskies

Unsurprisingly, this historic climbers' hotel on the Isle of Skye sits close to some of the most testing walks in Britain, with stunning scenery in every direction. The hotel itself dates from the 19th c. The huge main bar (aka Seumas' Bar) is modern and pine-clad: style-wise, it falls somewhere between a basic climbers' bar and the plusher, more sedate hotel side. It's spaciously open to the ceiling rafters and has geometrically laid-out dark tables and chairs; TV and board games. As well as their own-brewed Cuillin beers, including Eagle, Old Bridge and Pinnacle, they keep a guest on handpump plus an incredible display of over 400 malt whiskies at one end of the counter. It can get quite lively in here some nights, but there's also a more sedate lounge bar with leather bucket armchairs on plush carpets and a coal fire; background highland and islands music. The separate restaurant is in the hotel itself. The interesting little museum, well worth a visit, charts the history of the hotel and its famous climbers, with photographs and climbing and angling records. There are tables out in the garden and a big play area for children, which can be seen from the bar. The 21 bedrooms are comfortable, bright and modern, and there is also self-catering and bunkhouse accommodation and a campsite with caravan hook-ups during the summer months.

🍴 Some sort of food is on offer all day: cullen skink, boozy prawn cocktail with Misty Isle gin 'bloodymary' sauce, haggis bonbons with Talisker whisky and mustard mayo, falafel and spinach burger with smoky hummus, seafood platter, venison casserole, bean and lentil chilli with nachos, and puddings such as forest berry and vanilla custard crumble cake and sticky toffee pudding with butterscotch sauce. *Benchmark main dish: beer-battered haddock and chips £13.95. Two-course evening meal £21.00.*

Own brew ~ Gary Curley ~ Real ale ~ Open 9am-12.30am ~ Bar food 11-9 ~ Restaurant ~ Children welcome ~ Dogs allowed in bar & bedrooms ~ Bedrooms: £165

SWINTON
NT8347   Map 10

Wheatsheaf 🏵 ♇ 🛏

(01890) 860257 – www.eatdrinkstaywheatsheaf.com

A6112 N of Coldstream; TD11 3JJ

Civilised place with small bar for drinkers, comfortable lounges, top quality food and drinks and professional service; appealing bedrooms

This is a pretty village just a few miles from the River Tweed. While many customers come to enjoy the particularly good food served by attentive, friendly staff, there's also a little bar and informal lounges. Here they keep Belhaven IPA and a changing guest such as Tempest Ale on handpump alongside numerous malt whiskies, brandies and eight wines by the glass. There are comfortable plush armchairs, several nice old oak settles with cushions, a small open fire, sporting prints and china plates on the bottle-green walls in the bar and agricultural prints and fishing-theme décor on the painted or bare stone walls in the lounges. The dining room and front conservatory with its vaulted pine ceiling are carpeted, with high-backed slate-grey chairs around pale wood tables set with fresh flowers, while the more formal restaurant has leather high-backed dining chairs around cloth-covered tables; background music. Make the best of the surrounding rolling countryside by staying in the well equipped and comfortable bedrooms or the cottage; breakfasts are good and hearty.

🏵 As well as some traditional dishes, the creative food includes plenty of fresh local seafood, such as seared scallops with black pudding, samphire and citrus butter, langoustines and mussels. Other typical dishes include pigeon breast with parsnip purée and baby courgettes, vegetable moussaka, chicken breast with tarragon cream, roast venison loin with fondant potato, braised red cabbage, mushrooms and pancetta jus, duck breast with colcannon potatoes and raspberry jus, and puddings such as kiwi parfait with honey and ginger jelly, chocolate ice-cream and green tea genoise and vanilla rice pudding with home-made shortbread. *Benchmark main dish: beer-battered fish and chips £14.50. Two-course evening meal £20.00.*

Free house ~ Licensee Michael Lawrence ~ Real ale ~ Open 11-11; 11-midnight Fri, Sat ~ Bar food 12-2, 6-9; 12-2, 5.30-9 Thurs, Fri ~ Restaurant ~ Children welcome until 9pm ~ Dogs allowed in bar & bedrooms ~ Bedrooms: £140

Please tell us if the décor, atmosphere, food or drink at a pub is different from our description. We rely on readers' reports to keep us up to date: feedback@goodguides.com, or (no stamp needed) Freepost THE GOOD PUB GUIDE, Random House Publishing, 20 Vauxhall Bridge Road, London SW1V 2SA.

Also Worth a Visit in Scotland

Besides the fully inspected pubs, you might like to try these pubs that have been recommended to us and described by readers. Do tell us what you think of them: feedback@goodguides.com

ABERDEENSHIRE

ABERDEEN   NJ9305
Grill (01224) 583563
Union Street; AB11 6BA New owners in 2019 for this whisky bar in 19th-c granite building – don't be put off by the plain exterior, the remodelled 1920s interior is well worth a look; long wood-floored bar with fine moulded ceiling, mahogany panelling and button-back leather wall benches, ornate servery with glazed cabinets housing some of their 550 whiskies (some dating from the 1950s, and 30 from outside Scotland), five well kept ales including Fyne, basic snacks, no children or dogs, open all day.

ABERDEEN   NJ9406
★**Prince of Wales** (01224) 640597
St Nicholas Lane; AB10 1HF Individual and convivial old tavern with eight changing ales from very long counter; painted floorboards, flagstones or carpet, pews and screened booths, original tiled spittoon running length of bar, bargain hearty food; live acoustic music Sun evening, quiz Weds, games machines; children over 5 welcome if eating till 9pm; open (and food) all day.

ABOYNE   NO5298
Boat (01339) 886137
Charlestown Road (B968, just off A93); AB34 5EL Country inn with fine views across River Dee; bare-boards dining bar with contemporary paintwork, scatter cushions on built-in wall seats and woodburner in stone fireplace, model train chugging its way around just below ceiling height, good food from 8.30am breakfast on, three well kept changing ales, decent wines and some 30 malt whiskies, piano and another woodburner in back public bar, additional dining/function room upstairs; background music; 16 stylish well equipped bedrooms, children and dogs welcome, open all day.

BALMEDIE   NJ9619
Cock & Bull (01358) 743249
A90 N of Balmedie; AB23 8XY Friendly atmosphere and interesting décor in this country dining pub; good locally sourced food from sandwiches to daily specials, breakfast from 10am and afternoon teas (must book), beamed lounge bar with log fire, restaurant and conservatory; children and dogs (in lounge – special 'dog's dinner' menu) welcome, picnic-sets out front with distant sea view, enclosed play area, bedrooms in converted cottage, open (and food) all day.

BRAEMAR   NO1591
★**Fife Arms** (01339) 720200
Mar Road; AB35 5YN Large stunningly restored Victorian hotel packed with sumptuous furnishings, modern artwork and many quirky features; welcoming bare-boards bar with lots of pictures and taxidermy including a flying stag suspended over the counter, a couple of local beers such as Cairngorm and over 180 malt whiskies, well liked/priced food from short but varied menu, plenty of other areas (all worth seeing) including separate evening restaurant and cocktail bar, good service from uniformed staff; gardens overlooking River Clune, 46 individually themed bedrooms, children and dogs welcome, open (and food) all day.

OLDMELDRUM   NJ8127
Redgarth (01651) 872353
Kirk Brae, off A957; AB51 0DJ Good-sized comfortable lounge with traditional décor; two or three well kept beers and interesting range of malt whiskies (village has its own distillery, Glen Garioch), popular reasonably priced food, friendly attentive service, restaurant; lovely views to Bennachie, six bedrooms, children welcome, open and food all day Sun.

PENNAN   NJ8465
Pennan Inn (01346) 561201
Just off B9031 Banff–Fraserburgh; AB43 6JB Whitewashed building in long row of old fishermen's cottages, wonderful spot right by the sea (scenes from *Local Hero* filmed here); small bar with simple furniture and exposed stone walls, at least one real ale, no food, small gallery exhibiting work by local artists; three bedrooms, at foot of steep winding road and parking along front limited, open daily 3-9pm.

ANGUS

BROUGHTY FERRY   NO4630
★**Fisherman's Tavern**
(01382) 775941 *Fort Street; turning off shore road; DD5 2AD* Once a row of fishermen's cottages, this friendly pub is just steps from the beach; up to six well kept changing ales (summer beer festival) and good range of malt whiskies, comfortable lounge with coal fire, small snug and back dining area with another fire, popular fair priced pubby food from sandwiches up; sports TV; children and dogs welcome, disabled facilities, tables on front pavement,

more in secluded little walled garden, 12 bedrooms, open (and food) all day.

BROUGHTY FERRY   NO4634
Ship (01382) 779176
Fisher Street; DD5 2BR Waterfront pub with fine views over the Tay; dark nautical-feel plank panelling with brass fittings, red leather button-back banquettes and ornate plaster ceiling, woodburner and some old local photographs; beers such as Inveralmond and Timothy Taylors Landlord from impressive mahogany counter, enjoyable fairly priced food from bar snacks up including good fish and chips, upstairs restaurant, friendly accommodating service; one holiday cottage that sleeps four, dogs welcome in bar, open all day.

CLOVA   NO3273
Glen Clova Hotel (01575) 550350
B955 NW of Wheen; DD8 4QS Unpretentious climbers' bar in tucked-away 19th-c hotel; flagstones, bench seats and stone fireplace with woodburner, bric-a-brac and old photographs, a couple of well kept changing beers including own Clova Ale and local Burnside, 18 malts and plenty of wines by the glass; good food (same menu as the restaurant) using home-reared beef and lamb and venison from surrounding hills, friendly staff; children and dogs welcome, ten hotel bedrooms, nine garden lodges and eight 'steading rooms', glorious walks nearby, open all day.

MEMUS   NO4259
★**Drovers** (01307) 860322
N of Sheilhill; DD8 3TY Refurbished country pub-restaurant; very good attractively presented food from interesting menu, also more standard bar meals, vegan menu, friendly professional service, well kept Timothy Taylors Landlord and good selection of wines and whiskies, fairly traditional bar with fire in old range, more modern dining areas; children and dogs (in bar) welcome, peaceful country views from pretty orchard garden, play area, open (and food) all day.

ARGYLL

ARDFERN   NM8004
Galley of Lorne (01852) 500284
B8002; village and inn signposted off A816 Lochgilphead–Oban; PA31 8QN Family-run 17th-c drovers' inn on edge of Loch Craignish; cosy beamed and flagstoned bar with warming log fire, black panelling and unfussy assortment of furniture including settles, up to four real ales and 50 whiskies, good choice of food from lunchtime sandwiches up, lounge bar with woodburner and spacious picture-window restaurant; background music, small pool room, darts, games machine, sports TV; children and

dogs welcome, good sea and loch views from sheltered terrace and deck, seven bedrooms in extension, open evenings Mon-Fri, all day Sat and Sun.

BRIDGE OF ORCHY   NN2939
★**Bridge of Orchy Hotel**
(01838) 400208 *A82 Tyndrum–Glencoe; PA36 4AB* Spectacular spot on West Highland Way; very welcoming with good food in bar, lounge and smarter restaurant, decent choice of well kept ales, house wines and malt whiskies, open fires and interesting mountain photographs; dogs welcome, 32 good bedrooms across main building, airy riverside annexe and a cottage, open (and food) all day.

CAIRNDOW   NN1811
★**Cairndow Stagecoach Inn**
(01499) 600286 *Village and pub signed off A83; PA26 8BN* Historic 17th-c coaching inn in wonderful position on edge of Loch Fyne; good sensibly priced food including local venison and fresh fish, beers from nearby Fyne Ales and more than 40 malt whiskies (including a whisky of the month), friendly accommodating staff; children and dogs welcome, lovely peaceful lochside garden, 19 comfortable bedrooms, some in modern annexe with balconies overlooking the water, good breakfast, open (and food) all day.

CONNEL   NM9034
Oyster (01631) 710666
A85, W of Connel Bridge; PA37 1PJ 18th-c inn opposite former ferry slipway – lovely view across the water (especially at sunset); decent-sized bar (the Glue Pot) with friendly highland atmosphere, log fire in stone fireplace, Fyne and Caledonian Deuchars IPA, good range of wines, gins and malt whiskies, enjoyable food from pubby choices to local seafood, afternoon tea, friendly attentive service; sports TV; modern hotel part with 11 bedrooms and separate evening restaurant, open (and food) all day.

GLENCOE   NN1058
★**Clachaig** (01855) 811252
Old Glencoe Road, behind NTS Visitor Centre; PH49 4HX 18th-c climbers' and walkers' inn surrounded by the scenic grandeur of Glencoe; Boots Bar with up to 11 Scottish ales, over 400 malts and interesting range of 150 artisan gins, as well as vodkas and rums, from across Scotland, slate-floored snug with whisky barrel-panelled walls and open fire, lounge has mix of tables and booths, photos signed by famous climbers and local artwork, hearty food; background and live music, pool; children and dogs welcome, 23 comfortable bedrooms in adjoining hotel plus self-catering cottages, open (and food) all day.

INVERARAY NN0908

⋆**George** (01499) 302111

Main Street East; PA32 8TT Georgian hotel at hub of this appealing small town; pubby bar with exposed joists, bare stone walls, old tiles and big flagstones, antique settles, carved wooden benches and cushioned stone slabs along the walls, four log/peat fires, up to three changing ales such as Fyne Ales Jarl and Inveralmond Lia Fail, 120 malt whiskies, good food in bar or smarter restaurant, conservatory; children and dogs welcome; plenty of seats on well laid-out terraces, 17 bedrooms plus eight in adjacent house, Inveraray Castle and walks close by, can get packed in high season, open (and food) all day.

OBAN NM8530

Cuan Mor (01631) 565078

George Street; PA34 5SD Contemporary quayside bar-restaurant with exposed stone walls; over 100 malts, a couple of changing beers, cocktails and wide variety of enjoyable food including local fish and seafood such as fresh mussels; friendly service; children welcome, some seats outside, open (and food) all day.

OBAN NM8529

Lorne (01631) 570020

Stevenson Street; PA34 5NA Traditional Victorian pub tucked away behind the seafront; a well kept changing ale and good selection of whiskies and gins (many Scottish) from island servery with ornate brasswork, reasonably priced food including burgers and fish/seafood, good service; weekend live music and DJs, Weds quiz, TVs; children and dogs welcome, café-style tables and chairs in sheltered beer garden, open (and food) all day.

OBAN NM8530

⋆**Oban Inn** (01631) 567441

Stafford Street, near North Pier; PA34 5NJ Popular 18th-c pub with spotless beamed and slate-floored bar, well kept ales such as Fyne and good selection of malt whiskies including Oban, partly panelled upstairs dining bar with button-back banquettes around cast-iron-framed tables, coffered woodwork ceiling and little stained-glass false windows, good value hearty food served by friendly staff; background and regular live music; harbour view from walled terrace, dogs welcome, open (and food) all day.

OTTER FERRY NR9384

Oystercatcher (01700) 821229

B8000, by the water; PA21 2DH Old pub-restaurant in outstanding spot overlooking Loch Fyne; good food using local meat, cheese, fish and shellfish, well kept ales including Fyne from pine-clad bar, decent wine list, friendly staff; dogs welcome in bar; lots of tables out on spit, eight moorings for yachts, open all day (closed Tues, Weds).

PORT APPIN NM9045

Pierhouse (01631) 730302

In Appin, turn right at the Port Appin/ Lismore Ferry sign; PA38 4DE Beautiful location with views over Loch Linnhe to Lismore and beyond; smallish bar with good range of wines and beers, 100 malt whiskies and over 35 gins (many Scottish), excellent fish/seafood and other much liked food, picture-window restaurant enjoying the fine view, helpful friendly staff; children welcome, comfortable bedrooms, moorings for visiting yachts, open all day.

TAYVALLICH NR7487

Tayvallich Inn (01546) 870282

B8025; PA31 8PL Small single-storey bar-restaurant by Loch Sween specialising in good local seafood; pale pine furnishings on quarry tiles, local nautical charts, good range of whiskies and up to four well kept beers such as Fyne and Orkney, friendly atmosphere; background music (live first Fri of month); a few rustic picnic-sets on front deck with lovely views over yacht anchorage; children and dogs welcome, open all day in summer, open all day weekends, closed Mon in winter.

AYRSHIRE

SORN NS5526

Sorn Inn (01290) 551305

Village signed from Mauchline (A76); Main Street; KA5 6HU Restaurant-y pub in tiny conservation village; highly regarded imaginative food from brasserie dishes up in two restaurant areas, also smallish bar serving an Orkney ale, friendly staff; children and dogs (in bar) welcome, four comfortable well appointed bedrooms; open (and food) all day weekends, closed Mon.

SYMINGTON NS3831

Wheatsheaf (01563) 830307

Just off A77 Ayr–Kilmarnock; Main Street; KA1 5QB Single-storey former 18th-c posting inn, charming and cosy, with good food (must book weekends) including lunchtime/early evening set menu (plus specials and gluten-free options), efficient friendly service, log fire; children welcome, circular picnic-sets outside, quiet pretty village, open (and food) all day.

BERWICKSHIRE

ALLANTON NT8654

⋆**Allanton Inn** (01890) 818260

B6347 S of Chirnside; TD11 3JZ Well run 18th-c stone-built village inn with attractive open-plan interior; very good fairly priced food with emphasis on fresh fish/seafood from daily changing menu, a couple of well kept ales such as Born in the Borders, good wine list and 40 speciality gins, friendly efficient service, cosy bare boards bar with scatter cushions on bench seats, immaculate dining areas, log fire; background music; children and dogs (in garden) welcome, picnic-sets in sheltered beer garden and out front, appealing views, six comfortable bedrooms, open all day.

AUCHENCROW   NT8560
Craw (01890) 761253
B6438 NE of Duns; pub signed off A1; TD14 5LS Delightful little 18th-c pub in row of cream-washed cottages, friendly and welcoming, with enjoyable well presented food, up to five changing ales from smaller brewers and regular Timothy Taylors Landlord, good wine list, pictures on panelled walls, woodburner, more formal back restaurant; children welcome, tables out on village green and decking behind, three bedrooms and self-catering annexe, open all day Fri-Sun.

LAUDER   NT5347
Black Bull (01578) 722208
Market Place; TD2 6SR Recently refurbished whitewashed 18th-c inn with many original features; relaxed wood-panelled bar with interesting artwork and a couple of well kept ales, rustic bistro with mustard walls, leather armchairs and woodburner, fine Georgian-style dining room; sensibly priced food using local produce served daily from breakfast/coffee on and Sun roasts, friendly helpful staff; children and dogs (in bar) welcome, 12 well appointed bedrooms, open (and food) all day.

BORDERS

AYTON   NT9261
Hemelvaart Bier Café 07377 364266
High Street; TD14 5QL Welcoming continental-style village bar with plenty of community spirit; ten taps featuring local ales from likes of Tempest Brewery plus continental and American craft kegs, extensive range of bottled beers, interesting collection of gins too, friendly knowledgeable staff, enjoyable good value food (takeaway available) including range of burgers and locally made pies, also good coffee and home-made cakes; themed nights, regular live music, comedy evenings and other events; children and dogs welcome, open from 5pm Mon, Thurs, Fri, closed Tues, Weds, open from 1pm Sat, Sun.

DUMFRIES & GALLOWAY

LOCKERBIE   NY1382
Townhead (01576) 204627
Townhead Street; DG11 2AG Modernised

inn with good well presented food including OAP set lunch deal, can eat in bar or restaurant and they cater for special diets, no real ales (Belhaven Best), friendly helpful service; sports TV; children and dogs (in one area) welcome; nine comfortable well equipped bedrooms; closed Mon lunchtime, otherwise open all day.

DUMFRIESSHIRE

BARGRENNAN   NX3576
House O' Hill (01671) 840243
Off A714, road opposite church; DG8 6RN Small pub on edge of Galloway Forest; decent fair priced food from varied menu including daily specials, a couple of real ales such as Strathaven, decent wine list, afternoon teas, friendly helpful staff; children and dogs (in bar) welcome, two comfortable bedrooms and self-catering cottage, open all day weekends.

BEATTOCK   NT0702
Old Stables (01683) 300134
Smith Way; 0.25 mile from M74 junction 15; DG10 9QX Turreted 19th-c pub at edge of the village; Belhaven beers and bargain home-cooked food, friendly staff, bar and second railway-themed room with memorabilia from the old Beattock line (famous for its steep gradients); live music, big-screen TVs, pool and darts; children and dogs welcome, two bedrooms and parking for campervans, open all day.

DUMFRIES   NX9776
★ Cavens Arms (01387) 252896
Buccleuch Street; DG1 2AH Good generously served home-made food from pubby choices up, maybe nine well kept interesting ales and wide range of other drinks including fine choice of malts, friendly attentive service, civilised front part with lots of wood, drinkers' area at back with bar stools, banquettes and traditional cast-iron tables, more recently added lounge/restaurant; discreet TV; children over 14 welcome, no dogs; disabled facilities, small terrace behind, open (and food) all day, can get very busy.

DUMFRIES   NX9775
Globe (01387) 252335
High Street; DG1 2JA This town pub with strong Robert Burns connections reopened in 2019 after a comprehensive and sensitive restoration (tours of the poet's private rooms available, must pre-book); full of character with dark-panelling and antique furniture, small 17th-c snug and 1610 Restaurant with classic and modern Scottish dishes from short lunch menu to nine-course tasting menu, Lowland craft beers and impressive whisky collection, friendly service; open all day, closed Mon.

DUNBARTONSHIRE

ARROCHAR   NN2903
Village Inn (01301) 702279
*A814, just off A83 W of Loch Lomond;
G83 7AX* Friendly 19th-c lochside inn with
up to five well kept changing ales and good
range of other drinks, wide choice of popular
food (special diets catered for) including
evening set menu; heavy beams, bare boards,
panelling and roaring fire, steps down to
unpretentious bar; background music, sports
TV; children (in eating areas) and dogs
(in bar) welcome, tables out on deck and
lawn with lovely loch and hill views, neat
comfortable bedrooms (more spacious ones
in converted barn), open (and food) all day.

LUSS   NS3498
Inn on Loch Lomond
(01436) 860678 *A82, about 3 miles N;
G83 8PD* Large open-plan refurbished inn
across the road from Loch Lomond; decent
choice of enjoyable food including local fish
in bar and restaurant (takeaway available),
well kept beers, choice of wines by the glass
and good range of whiskies, friendly helpful
staff; children welcome, private jetty and
boat trips, contemporary bedrooms including
eight in waterside beach house, open (and
food) all day.

EAST LOTHIAN

GULLANE   NT4882
★ ## Old Clubhouse (01620) 842008
East Links Road; EH31 2AF Single-storey
half-timbered building in attractive position
overlooking Gullane Links; cosy bar and more
formal dining room, seating from wooden
dining chairs and banquettes to big squashy
leather armchairs and sofas, Victorian
pictures and cartoons, stuffed birds, sheet
music covers and other memorabilia, open
fires, enjoyable home-made food from
ciabattas up, Pentland IPA, Timothy Taylors
Landlord and a couple of guests, nice house
wines, friendly helpful service; children and
dogs (in bar) welcome, plenty of seats out at
front, open (and food) all day.

FIFE

CULROSS   NS9885
Red Lion (01383) 880225
Low Causeway; KY12 8HN Friendly
old pub in pretty NTS village; wide choice
of fair value food, a beer from Inveralmond
and several wines by the glass, beams and
amazing painted ceilings; seats outside, open
(and food) all day.

CUPAR   NO3714
Boudingait (01334) 208310
Bonnygate; KY15 4BU Bustling bar
with captain's and cushion-seated chairs
around dark tables on wood flooring, open
fire, high chairs against counter serving a
couple of changing ales, good choice of well
liked traditional food at reasonable prices
(takeaway available), afternoon teas, friendly
helpful staff; regular live music including
folk nights, quiz Weds; children and dogs
welcome, open (and food) all day.

INVERNESS-SHIRE

ARDGOUR   NN0163
Inn at Ardgour (01855) 841225
*From A82 follow signs for Strontian
A861 and take Corran Ferry across loch
to the inn; note that ferry does not sail
over Christmas period; PH33 7AA*
Traditional fairly remote roadside inn by
Corran Ferry slipway with fine Loch Linnhe
views; enjoyable food (from 5pm) and
decent beer and whisky choice, friendly
accommodating staff; children and well
behaved dogs welcome, a few tables outside,
11 bedrooms, open from 4pm.

AVIEMORE   NH8612
Cairngorm (01479) 810233
Grampian Road (A9); PH22 1PE
Large flagstoned bar in traditional turreted
hotel, lively and friendly, with Cairngorm ales
and good choice of other drinks; well priced
food from wide-ranging menu using local
produce, prompt helpful service, tartan-
walled and carpeted restaurant; daily live
music (not Tues when there's a quiz), sports
TV; children welcome, 32 comfortable smart
bedrooms (some with stunning views), open
(and food) all day.

CARRBRIDGE   NH9022
Cairn (01479) 841212
Main Road; PH23 3AS Welcoming
traditionally furnished hotel bar; three well
kept ales such as local Cairngorm and good
range of 70 whiskies including Tomintoul
served from the barrel, 40 Scottish gins,
popular home-cooked food, old local pictures,
warm coal fire, separate more formal dining
room; pool and sports TV; children and dogs
welcome, seats and tables out in front, 14
comfortable bedrooms, open all day.

DORES   NH5934
★ ## Dores (01463) 751203
B852 SW of Inverness; IV2 6TR
Traditional country pub with low ceilings
and exposed stonework in delightful spot on
the shore of Loch Ness; small attractive bar

If we know a pub has an outdoor play area for children, we mention it.

on right with up to four well kept changing Scottish ales and several whiskies, two-part dining area to the left serving good food from pub favourites up, friendly staff; children and dogs welcome, sheltered front garden, lots of picnic-sets out behind taking in the spectacular view, open (and food) all day, closed Mon in winter.

FORT WILLIAM   NN1274
Ben Nevis Inn (01397) 701227
N off A82: Achintee; PH33 6TE Roomy converted stone barn in stunning spot by footpath to Ben Nevis; good mainly straightforward food (lots of walkers so best to book), ales such as Cairngorm and Isle of Skye, prompt cheery service, bare-boards dining area with steps up to bar; live music (Tues in summer); children weclcome, dogs in beer garden, seats out at front and back, bunkhouse below, open all day Mar-Oct, otherwise closed Mon-Weds.

GLENFINNAN   NM9080
Glenfinnan House (01397) 722235
Take A830 off A32 to Glenfinnan, turn left after Glenfinnan Monument Visitors Centre; PH37 4LT Beautifully placed 18th-c hotel by Loch Shiel; traditional bar with well kept ales and over 50 whiskies, good food including fish/seafood and local venison, restaurant; rolling lawns down to the water, ornate comfortable bedrooms, may close in winter.

GLENUIG   NM6576
Glenuig Inn (01687) 470219
A861 SW of Lochailort, off A830 Fort William–Mallaig; PH38 4NG Welcoming inn set on the Sound of Arisaig; changing menu of great local food, real ales, organic wines and a wide range of Sottish gins and whiskies; dogs welcome, six bedrooms, ideally located for sea-kayaking and hill walking, open all year 4-9pm (food 6-8.30pm).

INVERMORISTON   NH4216
Glenmoriston Arms (01320) 351206
A82/A887; IV63 7YA Small civilised hotel dating in part from 1740 when it was a drovers' inn; bare-boards bar with stone fireplace and big old stag's head, a well kept beer such as Orkney and around 80 malt whiskies, good food here from lunchtime sandwiches up or in neatly laid-out restaurant with antique rifles, friendly staff; children and dogs (in bar) welcome, picnic-sets out at front, 11 bedrooms (three in converted outbuilding), handy for Loch Ness, open all day.

INVERNESS   NH6645
Black Isle (01463) 229920
Church Street; IV1 1EN Buzzy corner bar owned by Black Isle brewery, over 20 draught beers (listed on screens) plus extensive bottled range from slabby wood counter, long rustic tables, benches and mix of wooden

chairs on bare boards, full-length windows at front, some colourful murals and high ceiling with exposed ducting, good wood-fired pizzas, friendly knowledgeable staff; barrel tables and seats made from pallets on part-covered terrace, hostel-style bedrooms (private and shared), open (and food) all day.

INVERNESS   NH6644
Castle Tavern (01463) 718178
View Place, top of Castle Street; IV2 4SA Welcoming little stone-built pub with river and castle views; half a dozen mainly Scottish ales and fine whisky choice, good reasonably priced traditional food, informal upstairs restaurant; silent sports TV; children welcome, tables on heated front terrace, open (and food) all day.

INVERNESS   NH6645
Number 27 (01463) 241999
Castle Street; IV2 3DU Busy pub opposite the castle; friendly and welcoming, up to four changing ales and bottled beers, good choice of well liked/priced food including specials, restaurant at back; children welcome, open all day.

INVERNESS   NH6645
Phoenix Ale House (01463) 240300
Academy Street; IV1 1LX Popular 1890s bare-boards bar with fine oval servery, up to ten real ales and enjoyable reasonably priced food, neatly furnished adjoining dining room; sports TV; disabled access, open (and food) all day.

MALLAIG   NM6796
Steam (01687) 462002
Davies Brae; PH41 4PU Popular Victorian inn with good food including freshly landed fish/seafood (takeaway available), efficient friendly service, bar with open fire, split-level bare-boards restaurant; live music at weekends; children and dogs welcome (resident great dane), tables in back beer garden, six recently refurbished bedrooms, open all day.

WHITEBRIDGE   NH4815
Whitebridge (01456) 486226
B862 SW of village; IV2 6UN Traditional-style hunting, shooting and fishing hotel set in the foothills of the Monadhliath Mountains, popular and cheerful, with good traditional food, three well kept ales such as Cairngorm, Cromarty and Loch Ness and around 50 malts, two bars with woodburners, separate restaurant; well behaved dogs welcome, 12 bedrooms, open all day in summer, all day weekends in winter.

KINCARDINESHIRE

FETTERCAIRN   NO6573
Ramsay Arms (01561) 340334
Burnside Road; AB30 1XX Hotel with

tartan-carpeted bar and smart oak-panelled restaurant; well kept ales and a dozen malts including local Fettercairn, enjoyable fairly traditional food, friendly service; children welcome, picnic-sets in garden, attractive village (liked by Queen Victoria who stayed at the hotel), comfortable bedrooms, good breakfast, open all day Mon, Fri-Sun, from 5pm Tues-Thurs.

STONEHAVEN   NO8785
Ship (01569) 762617
Shore Head; AB39 2JY Whitewashed 18th-c waterside inn with bustling local atmosphere; good selection of changing beers and over 100 whiskies, well liked food in bar or modern restaurant, friendly staff; sports TV; children (till 8pm) and dogs (in bar) welcome, disabled access/loos, tables out overlooking pretty harbour, 11 bedrooms (many with sea views), open all day, food all day weekends.

KIRCUDBRIGHTSHIRE

CASTLE DOUGLAS   NX7662
Sulwath Brewery (01556) 504525
King Street; DG7 1DT Friendly bar attached to this small brewery (tours available); six of their ales in top condition along with bottled beers, limited food such as pies, stools and barrel tables, off-sales and souvenirs; dogs welcome, disabled access, open 10am-6pm Mon-Sat.

DALRY   NX6281
Clachan (01644) 430241
A713 Castle Douglas–Ayr; DG7 3UW Cheerful traditional inn with plenty of character; beams, dark woodwork and open fires, some large stuffed fish in display cases and other interesting bits and pieces, two well kept changing ales and good selection of other drinks, popular affordably priced food from lunchtime sandwiches and pub favourites up, friendly efficient service, woodburner in timbered restaurant with pitched ceiling; TV, fruit machine; children and dogs welcome, on Southern Upland Way; six modern bedrooms, open all day.

GATEHOUSE OF FLEET   NX6056
Masonic Arms (01557) 814335
Ann Street; off B727; DG7 2HU Spacious 18th-c dining pub; comfortable two-room pubby bar with traditional seating, pictures on timbered walls and stuffed fish above brick fireplace, Caledonian Deuchars IPA, Sulwath Galloway Gold and good choice of malt whiskies, enjoyable freshly made food from lunchtime sandwiches up, restaurant and stylish sun room with woodburner; background music (live Thurs), quiz Fri,

pool; children and dogs (in bar) welcome, picnic-sets under parasols in neatly kept sheltered garden with chiminea, more seats in front, open all day (may shut Mon, Tues in winter), food all day weekends.

HAUGH OF URR   NX8066
Laurie Arms (01556) 660246
B794 N of Dalbeattie; Main Street; DG7 3YA Welcoming 19th-c village pub with good local atmosphere; traditional furnishings and log fire in split-level carpeted bar, four well kept changing ales, decent wines by the glass and enjoyable reasonably priced home-made food including good steaks; friendly service, restaurant, games room with darts and pool; quiz first Fri of month; children and dogs (in bar) welcome, tables out at front and on sheltered terrace behind, open (and food) all day weekends.

KIRKCUDBRIGHT   NX6850
Selkirk Arms (01557) 330402
High Street; DG6 4JG Comfortable well run 18th-c hotel in pleasant spot by mouth of the Dee; tartan-carpeted lounge with open fire, up to three real ales including a house beer from local Sulwath, 20 malt whiskies and 15 gins, enjoyable food cooked to order in bistro and evening restaurant from pub standards up, afternoon teas (must book), friendly helpful service; background music; children and dogs (in bar) welcome, tables under parasols in neat lawned garden with 15th-c font, 16 well appointed bedrooms, open all day.

LANARKSHIRE

BALMAHA   NS4290
Oak Tree (01360) 870357
B837; G63 0JQ Family-run slate-clad inn on Loch Lomond's quiet side; beams, timbers and panelling, pubby bar with lots of old photographs, farm tools, stuffed animals and collection of grandfather clocks, log fire, good choice of enjoyable food from sandwiches and snacks up (no bookings), up to four changing Scottish beers and over 50 whiskies, restaurant, coffee shop and ice-cream parlour, village shop; children and dogs (in garden) welcome, plenty of tables outside around ancient oak tree; popular with West Highland Way walkers, attractive bedrooms, cottages and pods, open (and food) all day.

BIGGAR   NT0437
Crown (01899) 220116
High Street (A702); ML12 6DL Friendly old pub with good choice of enjoyable food from tapas-style plates and pizzas up, meal deals and good value Sun carvery, six cask ales (annual beer festival), 68 gins, open fire

---

It's very helpful if you let us know up-to-date food prices when you report on pubs.

in beamed front bar, panelled lounge with old local pictures, restaurant; live music every other Fri; children and dogs welcome, open (and food) all day.

Fintry (01360) 860224

Main Street; G63 0XA Community-owned 18th-c village pub with friendly relaxed atmosphere; beers from on-site microbrewery and enjoyable fairly priced home-made food, modernised interior with beams and two-way woodburner; ceilidh first Sat of month, quiz last Mon; children and dogs (in pool room) welcome, suntrap back garden, open (and food) all day.

★ Babbity Bowster (0141) 552 5055

Blackfriars Street; G1 1PE A Glasgow institution, this 18th-c former tobacco merchant's house changed hands in 2020 for first time in 30 years when long-standing, one-eyed landlord retired, now owned by large pub group; refurb to simply decorated light-filled interior with tall windows, dark wood tables and chairs, banquettes and attractive artwork, Caledonian Deuchars IPA, Fyne Ales Jarl and a changing guest on air-pressure tall founts and good collection of wines and malt whiskies, bistro-style food from lunchtime soup up; traditional live music Weds and Sat afternoons; children welcome if dining, terrace with string lighting, picnic-sets and parasols, six modern bedrooms, open (and food) all day.

Belle (0141) 339 2299

Great Western Road; G12 8HX Busy pub with wide mix of customers; leather-topped stools, modern and traditional chairs around all sorts of tables on polished wood floor, stags' heads and unusual mirrors on painted or exposed stone walls, open fire, American craft beers and European lagers, changing wine list; dogs very welcome, tables out on pavement and in tiny leafy back garden, open all day.

Drum & Monkey (0141) 221 6636

St Vincent Street; G2 5TF Busy Nicholsons bank conversion; lots of carved mahogany, granite pillars and ornate ceiling, island bar serving half a dozen real ales, over 20 gins and decent range of wines, good value food, quieter back area; children (till 8pm) and dogs welcome, open (and food) all day.

Pot Still (0141) 333 0980

Hope Street; G2 2TH Comfortable and welcoming little pub with over 700 malt whiskies including good value whisky of the month; traditional bare-boards interior with raised back part, button-back leather bench seats, dark panelling, etched and stained glass, columns up to ornately corniced ceiling, four changing ales and interesting bottled beers from nice old-fashioned servery, friendly knowledgeable staff, food limited to range of good value pies; silent fruit machine; can get packed, open all day.

St Louis (0141) 339 1742

Dumbarton Road, by the roundabout; G11 6RD Relaxed bar-café that has undergone recent facelift; simple but stylish décor, Williams Bros beers and enjoyable reasonably priced food including sandwiches and range of burgers, friendly staff; live music Sat, quiz Tues, monthly poetry night; dogs welcome, open (and food) all day from 9am (10am weekends).

State (0141) 332 2159

Holland Street; G2 4NG High-ceilinged bar with marble pillars and lots of carved wood including handsome island servery, half a dozen or so well kept changing ales, bargain lunchtime meals only, good atmosphere and friendly staff, armchairs among other comfortable seats, coal-effect fire in big fireplace, old prints and theatrical posters; background music (house blues band Tues), comedy night Sat, silent sports TVs, games machine; open all day, no food weekends.

Tennents (0141) 339 7203

Byres Road; G12 8TN Big busy high-ceilinged Victorian corner pub near the university; ornate plasterwork, panelling and paintings, traditional tables and chairs, stools and wall seating, a dozen well kept ales, craft beers and keenly priced wines from well stocked bar, wide range of good value food including deals; basement bar for weekend DJs, sports TVs; children and dogs welcome, open (and food) all day.

Three Judges (0141) 337 3055

Dumbarton Road, opposite Byres Road; G11 6PR Traditional corner bar with nine handpumps, regular Sharps Doom Bar plus eight other changing ales from small breweries across UK (they get through several hundred a year), friendly staff will offer tasters; live afternoon jazz last Sun of month, quiz night Sun, TV; dogs welcome, open all day.

MIDLOTHIAN

★ Sun (0131) 663 2456

A7 S; EH22 4TR Modernised former coaching inn opposite Newbattle Viaduct, surrounded by wooded area and close to the River Esk; bars carefully renovated with walls stripped back to the original stone (or with hunting-theme wallpaper), bare floorboards and refurbished fireplaces, cushioned built-in settles and good mix of other furniture, two changing ales on handpump from the likes of Cross Borders and Stewart, good wines by the glass, friendly staff; background music; children welcome in restaurant and dogs in bar, disabled access to restaurant only, seats in covered courtyard overlooking the garden (summer barbecues), also riverside decked area and coffee shop, six stylish bedrooms, open 9am-9pm, closes 7pm Sun.

EDINBURGH   NT2574
★**Café Royal** (0131) 556 1884
West Register Street; EH2 2AA Wonderful Victorian baroque interior – floors and stairway laid with marble, chandeliers hanging from magnificent plasterwork ceilings, superb series of Doulton tilework portraits of historical innovators (Watt, Faraday, Stephenson, Caxton, Benjamin Franklin and Robert Peel), substantial island bar serving well kept Greene King IPA and Stewart Pentland IPA plus five guest beers, several wines by the glass and 40 malts, very well liked food with emphasis on fresh seafood, good friendly service, the restaurant's stained glass is also worth a look (children welcome here); background music; open (and food) all day (till 1am Fri, Sat), can get very busy.

EDINBURGH   NT2574
Cloisters (0131) 221 9997
Brougham Street; EH3 9JH Friendly and interesting ex-parsonage alehouse with great range of changing beers (cask and keg), some 70 malt whiskies and several wines by the glass, good value food (all day Sat, not Mon), pews and bar gantry recycled from redundant church, bare boards and lots of brewery mirrors; lavatories down spiral stairs; no children, well behaved dogs welcome, open all day (till 1am Fri, Sat).

EDINBURGH   NT2573
Deacon Brodies (0131) 225 6531
Lawnmarket; EH1 2NT Atmospheric corner pub commemorating the notorious town councillor thief who was eventually hanged on the scaffold he'd designed; very busy bar with wonderfully ornate high ceiling, seven well kept ales including regulars Nicholsons Pale Ale (brewed by St Austell) and Stewart 80/-, decent selection of whiskies from long counter, reasonably priced Nicholsons menu in upstairs dining lounge where children allowed, friendly hard-working staff; background music, TV; open (and food) all day.

EDINBURGH   NT2573
Doric (0131) 225 1084
Market Street; EH1 1DE Welcoming 17th-c pub-restaurant with plenty of atmosphere; simple furnishings in small bar with wood floor and lots of pictures, four cask ales and good range of bottled beers, around 50 single malts, friendly staff, interesting modern food (must book) in upstairs wine bar and bistro, Sun roasts; live folk nights Fri, Sat; children welcome in bar till 4pm, restaurant till 9pm, handy for Waverley station, open (and food) all day.

EDINBURGH   NT2573
Ensign Ewart (0131) 225 7440
Lawnmarket, Royal Mile; last pub on right before castle; EH1 2PE Dimly lit olde-worlde pub handy for the castle (so gets busy); dark beams and bare boards, assorted pubby furniture including a barrel table, flintlock pistols and swords, big painting of Ewart capturing French banner at Waterloo, four well kept Scottish ales and extensive range of whiskies, straightforward bar food; background and traditional live music (nightly), TV, keypad entry to lavatories; open (and food) all day (till 1am Fri, Sat).

EDINBURGH   NT2472
Fountain (0131) 229 1899
Dundee Street; EH11 1AX Nicely updated pub with open-plan split-level interior; four or five draught beers from long well stocked bar, fairly priced food including brunch, good friendly service; children and dogs welcome, open (and food) all day.

EDINBURGH   NT2573
★**Halfway House** (0131) 225 7101
Fleshmarket Close (steps between Cockburn Street and Market Street, opposite Waverley station); EH1 1BX Tiny one-room character pub off steep steps; part carpeted, part tiled, with a few small tables and high-backed settles, lots of prints (some golf and railway themes), up to five well kept Scottish ales and good range of malt whiskies, limited choice of decent affordable food, friendly staff; dogs welcome, open (and food) all day.

EDINBURGH   NT2473
Hanging Bat (0131) 229 0759
Lothian Road; EH3 9AB Snug modern bar over three levels with own microbrewery, six real ales, craft kegs and plenty of bottled beers, food such as ribs and hot dogs; children welcome till 8pm, open (and food) all day.

EDINBURGH   NT2573
Inn on the Mile (0131) 556 9940
High Street; EH1 1LL Centrally placed pub-restaurant-boutique hotel in former bank; long high-ceilinged bar with booth seating, good selection of drinks including cocktails, well priced pubby food including

---

There are report forms at the back of the book.

Sun roasts, friendly efficient service; live music Tues, projector for major sports; children welcome, a few seats outside, nine stylish bedrooms, open (and food) all day from 8am (till 1am Fri, Sat), can be lively.

EDINBURGH NT2573

Jolly Judge (0131) 225 2669

James Court, by 495 Lawnmarket; EH1 2PB Small comfortable basement bar with interesting fruit and flower-painted wooden ceiling, welcoming relaxed atmosphere, three changing beers such as Belhaven Best and McEwans, good range of malts, lunchtime bar meals, log fire; quiz night Mon; no children, open all day.

EDINBURGH NT1968

Kinleith Mill (0131) 453 3214

Lanark Road (A70); EH14 5EN Old pub with contemporary bar; three well kept ales, 18 wines by the glass and 19 gins, enjoyable food from sandwiches and wraps up, friendly staff; sports TV, darts; children and dogs welcome, suntrap back garden, open (and food) all day.

EDINBURGH NT2573

Sandy Bells (0131) 225 2751

Forrest Road; EH1 2QH Small unpretentious place popular for its nightly folk music; up to eight Scottish ales and wide choice of whiskies, simple snacky food, good mix of customers and friendly atmosphere; open all day (till 1am Mon-Sat).

EDINBURGH NT2374

Scran & Scallie (0131) 332 6281

Comely Bank Road; EH4 1DT Well thought-of dining pub with very good traditional and seasonal food including weekday set lunch; bar has blue button-back wall seats, leather-topped stools and blue-painted chairs on bare boards, well kept Scottish ales, impressive collection of whiskies and house cocktails, sizeable dining area with painted brick walls, contemporary wallpaper and woodburner, helpful friendly service; TV; disabled access, children and dogs welcome, open all day.

EDINBURGH NT2872

Sheep Heid (0131) 661 7974

The Causeway, Duddingston; EH15 3QA Comfortably updated former coaching house in lovely spot near King Arthur's Seat, long history (dates from the 14th c) and some famous guests such as Mary, Queen of Scots; emphasis on dining but there is a cosy bar with fine rounded counter serving three well kept beers, enjoyable food from pizzas and burgers to more restauranty choices, also good value lunch menu, Sun roasts and children's meals, friendly staff; skittle alley; courtyard tables, dogs welcome, open (and food) all day.

EDINBURGH NT2574

★ Starbank (0131) 552 4141

Laverockbank Road, off Starbank Road, just off A901 Granton–Leith; EH5 3BZ Cheerful pub in a fine spot with terrific views over the Firth of Forth; long airy bare-boards bar with leather bench and tub seats, six well kept ales and good choice of malt whiskies, interesting food from sharing plates up in conservatory restaurant; live music and quiz nights, sports TV; children (till 9pm if eating) and dogs welcome, sheltered back terrace, parking on adjacent hilly street, open (and food) all day.

EDINBURGH NT2574

Stockbridge Tap (0131) 343 3000

Raeburn Place, Stockbridge; EH4 1HN Welcoming corner pub with traditional L-shaped interior, six interesting beers, over 60 malts and good reasonably priced food (not Mon or Tues); no children, dogs welcome, open all day.

EDINBURGH NT2676

Teuchters Landing (0131) 554 7427

Great Junction Street, Leith; EH6 6LU Interesting waterside pub in former ferry waiting room; great choice of whiskies and wines (listed on blackboard), five well kept ales such as Caledonian, Fyne, Inveralmond and Timothy Taylors, plus several craft beers, generous helpings of popular food (best to book, especially in summer for conservatory or floating terrace), friendly staff; TV for rugby; children and dogs welcome, open (and food) all day.

MORAYSHIRE

FINDHORN NJ0464

Crown & Anchor (01309) 690 243

Off A96; IV36 3YF Nice village setting adjacent to small sheltered harbour; enjoyable food including good fresh fish/seafood specials, a couple of real ales, more than 70 gins and around 100 whiskies, woodburner in cosy bar; sports TV; children allowed in conservatory and restaurant (till 8pm), outside seating (the 'Eatooterie') and smokers' shelter (the 'Smokooterie'), seven bedrooms, sand dune walks and good boating in Findhorn Bay, open all day, may close 3-5pm in winter.

NAIRNSHIRE

CAWDOR NH8449

Cawdor Tavern (01667) 404777

Pub signed from B9090; IV12 5XP Busy dining pub in lovely conservation village near Cawdor Castle; well kept Orkney ales, plenty of wines by the glass (comprehensive list) and good range of malt whiskies, freshly cooked food from traditional choices up, friendly staff, oak-panelled lounge with log fire, pool in public bar, restaurant; children and dogs (in bar) welcome, seats on front terrace, open (and food) all day in summer, closed 3-5pm Mon-Fri in winter.

PEEBLESSHIRE

INNERLEITHEN   NT3336
★**Traquair Arms**   (01896) 830229
B709, just off A72 Peebles–Galashiels; follow signs for Traquair House; EH44 6PD Old stone inn at heart of this pretty borders village; one of the few places serving Traquair ale (produced in original oak vessels in 18th-c brewhouse at nearby Traquair House), also Stewart and Tempest, over 40 malt whiskies, enjoyable traditional food (all day weekends), main bar with warm open fire, another in relaxed bistro-style restaurant, good mix of customers; background music, live music Sun and alternate Thurs; children and dogs (in bar) welcome, seats out at front and in attractive back garden, 16 bedrooms and two self-catering cottages, open all day.

PERTHSHIRE

BANKFOOT   NO0635
Bankfoot   (01738) 787243
Main Street; PH1 4AB Traditional coaching inn dating from 1760; two bars and restaurant, well kept local ales and enjoyable food cooked by landlady including Sun roasts, friendly helpful staff, open fires; live folk/acoustic night Weds; children and dogs welcome, six comfortable bedrooms, one self-contained apartment, open all day weekends, check website for winter hours.

BLAIR ATHOLL   NN8765
★**Atholl Arms**   (01796) 481205
B8079; PH18 5SG Sizeable Victorian highland house hotel with traditional Scottish feel; beamed Bothy bar serving four local Moulin ales and good well priced food, quick friendly service, cosy lounges and grand dining room with suit of armour and stag's head; children and dogs welcome, decent beer garden, 31 good value bedrooms and self-catering cottages, lovely setting near Blair Castle, open (and food) all day.

BRIG O' TURK   NN5306
Byre   (01877) 376292
A821 Callander–Trossachs, just outside village; FK17 8HT Beautifully placed byre conversion; slate-floored log-fire bar and roomier high-raftered restaurant, good popular food including local game and fish, a couple of changing Scottish ales and nice wines, friendly helpful staff; background music; children welcome, outside tables and boules piste, lovely walks, bike hire available (pre-book), open all day.

CALLANDER   NN6208
Old Rectory   (01877) 339215
Leny Road (A84); FK17 8AL Friendly 19th-c stone inn away from the town centre; cosy little bar with fine range of whiskies, well liked reasonably priced food in small adjoining restaurant including good Sun roasts, pleasant helpful staff; live music Weds and Sat, quiz second Tues of month; children and dogs welcome, four bedrooms, handy for Trossachs National Park, open all day.

DUNBLANE   NN7801
Tappit Hen   (01786) 825226
Kirk Street; FK15 0AL Small welcoming drinkers' pub across close from cathedral; four changing ales and good range of malt whiskies, friendly busy atmosphere; sports TV, fruit machine; children and dogs welcome, open all day.

DUNKELD   NO0243
Atholl Arms   (01350) 727219
Atholl Street (A923); PH8 0AQ Sizeable 19th-c hotel with brasserie, bistro and restaurant; open fires, well kept ales such as Inveralmond, excellent food including burgers, pizzas and some vegan choices, attentive and warmly friendly service; children and dogs welcome, beer garden across road running down to the River Tay, pavilion serving drinks and snacks, stylish bedrooms (six with river views), open (and food) all day.

DUNNING   NO0114
Kirkstyle   (01764) 684248
B9141, off A9 S of Perth; Kirkstyle Square; PH2 0RR Character 18th-c streamside pub with subtle ongoing renovations; log fire in snug bar, up to three real ales including one badged for them (Risky Kelt) and good choice of whiskies, enjoyable fairly priced home-made food from coffee and cake up (from 10am Weds-Fri), attentive friendly service, split-level stripped-stone restaurant behind; background and live traditional music (usually last Sun of month); children and dogs welcome, four bedrooms, open evenings Mon and Tues, all day Weds-Sun.

INCHTURE   NO2828
Inchture Hotel   (01828) 686298
Just off A90 Perth–Dundee; PH14 9RN Small creeper-clad 19th-c hotel in conservation village; updated lounge bar in fashionable greys with some exposed stonework and open fire, enjoyable well priced food here or in spacious conservatory restaurant, also bar snacks, local Abernyte bottled beers and good choice of wines by the glass, decent coffee, friendly efficient service, separate public bar; sports TV; children welcome, good value bedrooms, open (and food) all day.

KENMORE   NN7745

Kenmore Hotel (01887) 830205

A827 W of Aberfeldy; PH15 2NU Hotel
dating from the 16th c in pretty Loch
Tay village; comfortable traditional front
lounge with warm log fire (there's a poem
pencilled by Burns himself on the chimney
breast), dozens of malts helpfully arranged
alphabetically, friendly attentive staff,
modern restaurant with balcony, also back
bar and terrace overlooking River Tay with
enjoyable food from lunchtime soup and
sandwiches to grills, Inveralmond Ossian and
decent wines by the glass; pool and winter
darts, juke box, TV, fruit machine; children
and dogs welcome, 40 bedrooms plus lodges,
open (and food) all day.

KILMAHOG   NN6008

★Lade (01877) 330152

*A84 just NW of Callander, by A821
junction; FK17 8HD* Lively place
with plenty of character in several cosy
beamed areas; panelling and stripped
stone, highland prints and local artwork,
good home-made food from bar snacks
up (booking advised), three regular own-
brewed ales and around 40 malt whiskies,
big-windowed restaurant, friendly staff, shop
selling extensive range of Scottish bottled
beers; background and traditional live music
(weekends); children and dogs welcome,
disabled access/loo, terrace and pleasant
garden with fish ponds, open (and food) all
day (till 1am Fri, Sat, but may close early in
winter if quiet).

PERTH   NO1223

Greyfriars (01738) 633036

South Street; PH2 8PG Small comfortable
local in old part of town; up to four well kept
changing ales and good collection of whiskies
and gins, enjoyable lunchtime food (not Sun)
in bar or little upstairs dining room, friendly
welcoming staff; live music, sports TV; open
from 4pm Mon-Thurs, all day Fri, Sat, closes
6pm Sun.

PITLOCHRY   NN9163

★Killiecrankie Hotel (01796) 473220

Killiecrankie, off A9 N; PH16 5LG
Comfortable splendidly placed country
hotel with attractive panelled bar and airy
conservatory; well kept ales, more than 40
malt whiskies and well chosen wines, good
imaginative food served lunch and dinner
in bar or more formal evening restaurant,
friendly efficient service; children (in dining
area) and dogs welcome, four acres of
peaceful grounds with dramatic views, ten
bedrooms, open all day, closed Jan and Feb.

PITLOCHRY   NN9459

★Moulin (01796) 472196

*Kirkmichael Road, Moulin; A924 NE of
Pitlochry centre; PH16 5EW* Attractive
much-extended inn brewing its own good

beers in stables across the street; decent
wines by the glass and around 45 malt
whiskies, cheerfully busy down-to-earth bar
in oldest part with traditional character,
smaller bare-boards room and bigger
carpeted area with booths divided by stained-
glass country scenes, popular quickly served
food, separate restaurant; bar billiards and
1960s one-arm bandit; children and dogs (in
bar) welcome, picnic-sets on gravel looking
across to village kirk, good nearby walks,
15 well appointed comfortable bedrooms
and two self-catering cottages, open (and
food) all day.

PITLOCHRY   NN9358

Old Mill (01796) 474020

Mill Lane; PH16 5BH Welcoming family-
run inn (former 19th-c watermill) with
enjoyable food from breakfast, sandwiches
and sharing plates up, four changing real
ales including Inveralmond and Strathbraan,
traditional cider, good wine and whisky
choice, quick friendly service; weekend live
music; courtyard tables by Moulin Burn,
comfortable well equipped bedrooms, open
all day.

WEEM   NN8449

★Ailean Chraggan (01887) 820346

B846; PH15 2LD There's plenty to do
and see close to this little hotel; chatty
bar with good mix of customers, up to two
local Strathbraan ales and around 100
malt whiskies, popular locally sourced food
including Sun carvery, efficient friendly
service, adjoining neatly old-fashioned dining
room and a comfortable carpeted modern
lounge; children and dogs (in bar) welcome,
covered terrace and garden behind, views
stretching beyond the Tay to Ben Lawers (the
highest peak in this part of Scotland), five
comfortable bedrooms, open all day Thurs-
Sun, from 5pm Mon-Weds.

ROSS-SHIRE

BADACHRO   NG7873

★Badachro Inn (01445) 741255

*2.5 miles S of Gairloch village turn off
A832 on to B8056, then after another
3.25 miles turn right in Badachro to
the quay and inn; IV21 2AA* Superbly
positioned by Loch Gairloch with terrific
views from decking down to water's edge;
popular (especially in summer) with mix of
sailing visitors (free moorings) and chatty
locals, welcoming bar with interesting
photographs, An Teallach, Caledonian and
a guest ale, about 50 malt whiskies and good
selection of wines by the glass, quieter eating
area with large log fire, dining conservatory
overlooking bay, fairly priced food including
locally smoked fish and seafood; background
and live music; children and dogs welcome,
open all day.

DORNIE NG8826

Dornie Hotel (01599) 555205

Francis Street; IV40 8DT Friendly hotel with lovely views over Loch Long; lively bar with Isle of Skye Cuillin Beast and good value traditional food, pleasant restaurant specialising in popular local fish/seafood; children and dogs welcome, 11 bedrooms (book early), very handy for Eilean Donan Castle, open all day.

GAIRLOCH NG8075

Old Inn (01445) 712006

Just off A832/B8021; IV21 2BD Quietly positioned old drovers' inn by stream; up to six beers including own-brew ales, decent wines by the glass and some 20 malt whiskies, enjoyable food (not Sun evening) including local fish and game, relaxed locals' bar with traditional décor and woodburner, bistro/restaurant; background music (live Fri in summer), TV; children and dogs welcome, picnic-sets out by trees, bedrooms, open all day May-Aug, closed Dec-Feb.

GLENELG NG8119

★ Glenelg Inn (01599) 522273

Unmarked road from Shiel Bridge (A87) towards Skye; IV40 8JR Unpretentious mountain cabin-like bar in small (smarter) hotel reached by dramatic drive with spectacular views of Loch Duich to Skye; beams, wood-clad walls and big fireplace, simple tables and chairs, a couple of well kept ales (Dun brewery is in the village) and good fresh local food including seafood from daily changing menu, Sun roasts, friendly welcoming staff, dining room; regular live music; children and dogs welcome, lovely garden, fine views from some of the seven bedrooms, summer ferry to Skye, enjoyable nearby walks, open all day.

PLOCKTON NG8033

★ Plockton Inn (01599) 544222

Innes Street; not connected to Plockton Hotel (see Main Entries); IV52 8TW Close to the harbour in this lovely village; congenial bustling atmosphere even in winter, good fairly priced food with emphasis on local fish/seafood (some from own smokery), friendly efficient service, well kept changing beers such as Plockton Bay and good range of malts, lively public bar with traditional music Thurs (also Tues in summer); children welcome, seats out on decking, 14 bedrooms (seven in annexe over road) and good breakfast, open all day.

SHIEL BRIDGE NG9319

Kintail Lodge (01599) 511275

A87, N of Shiel Bridge; IV40 8HL Large bar adjoining hotel nestled down by Loch Duich; convivial bustle in season, two regular ales from Dun Brewing and Isle of Skye, plenty of malt whiskies, good food here and in restaurant/conservatory (weekends only

during winter) with magnificent view to Skye, friendly efficient service; children and dogs welcome, nine comfortable bedrooms and moorings for visiting yachts, good breakfast, open all day from Easter, phone for out-of-season hours.

ULLAPOOL NH1293

★ Ceilidh Place (01854) 612103

West Argyle Street; IV26 2TY More arty café-bar than pub, with gallery, bookshop and coffee shop; conservatory-style main area with mix of dining chairs around dark wood tables, cosy bar and other rooms filled with armchairs, sofas and scatter-cushioned wall seats, rugs on floors, woodburner, a beer from An Teallach, lots of wines by the glass and around 75 malt whiskies, tasty food (something available all day); regular jazz, folk and classical music, art exhibitions; children welcome till 7pm, tables on front terrace looking over houses to distant hills beyond natural harbour, comfortable bedrooms and bunkhouse, open all day.

ULLAPOOL NH1294

Morefield Motel (01854) 612161

A835 N edge of town; IV26 2TQ Modern family-run place, clean and bright, with cheerful L-shaped lounge bar, good food including local fish/seafood, three well kept changing ales including Loch Lomond and house-brew Feck Ale Left (Ullapool beer festival held here in October), decent wines and over 50 malt whiskies, large conservatory; background music, sports TV, pool and darts; children and dogs (outside of meal times) welcome, terrace tables, ten bedrooms, bike lock-up, open all day.

ROXBURGHSHIRE

ANCRUM NT6224

Cross Keys (01835) 830242

Off A68 Jedburgh–Edinburgh; TD8 6XH Early 19th-c terrace-row pub overlooking village green; chatty bar with good mix of customers and a dog or two by the open fire, minimal décor and simple furnishings, stools against counter serving Born in the Borders Foxy Blonde and Gold Dust, several wines by the glass and quite a few whiskies, well regarded often interesting food in second side bar or dining room with open kitchen, children and dogs welcome, seats out front and in back garden with gate leading down to Ale Water, open all day weekends (till 1am Sat), from 5pm weekdays.

KELSO NT7234

★ Cobbles (01573) 223548

Bowmont Street; TD5 7JH Small comfortably updated 19th-c dining pub just off the main square; friendly and well run with good range of food from pub standards to more enterprising dishes, local Tempest beers and decent range of wines/

malt whiskies, pubby furniture and open fire in bar, elegantly furnished restaurant with overspill room upstairs; folk music Fri evening; accommodation in one self-catering apartment, children and well behaved dogs welcome, disabled access, open all day (till late Fri, Sat).

KIRK YETHOLM   NT8328
★**Border** (01573) 420237
Village signposted off B6352/B6401 crossroads, SE of Kelso; The Green; TD5 8PQ Popular village inn facing green; welcoming traditional locals' bar with beams, flagstones and log fire, snug side rooms, up to three real ales, decent wines by the glass and numerous whiskies, good home-made food from extensive menu (all day Sun), friendly service, spacious dining room, lounge with another fire and neat conservatory; background music; children and dogs (in bar) welcome, sheltered back terrace, five well appointed comfortable bedrooms plus new self-catering cottage, good breakfast, at end of Pennine Way and start of Scottish National Trail, open all day.

ST BOSWELLS   NT5930
Buccleuch Arms (01835) 822243
A68 just S of Newtown St Boswells; TD6 0EW Civilised 19th-c sandstone hotel opposite village green; updated bar, comfortable lounge and bistro, good popular food from bar snacks up, charming service, two local ales such as Born in the Borders and Tempest, open fires; children and dogs (in bar) welcome, tables in attractive beer garden behind (plants for sale), 19 bedrooms, open (and some food) all day.

SELKIRKSHIRE

MOUNTBENGER   NT3324
Gordon Arms (01750) 82261
A708/B709; TD7 5LE Nice old inn – an oasis in these empty moorlands; a couple of real ales such as Belhaven and Born in the Borders; enjoyable reasonably priced pubby food cooked by landlord; acoustic music every third Sun of month from 3pm (there's a recording studio on site); children and dogs welcome, seven comfortable bedrooms, good walking country, open (and food) all day, closed Mon-Thurs in winter.

STIRLINGSHIRE

KIPPEN   NS6594
★**Cross Keys** (01786) 870293
Main Street; village signposted off A811 W of Stirling; FK8 3DN Cosy and gently civilised 18th-c inn; log fires in two bars, exposed stonework, bare boards or carpeting, built-in wall seating, wooden dining chairs and stools against counter serving a couple of Fallen ales (one brewed for the pub), a guest beer, 20 malt whiskies and a dozen wines by the glass, very good food (all day weekends, Sun roasts), including lighter lunch menu, friendly staff; background music, occasional folk nights; children (till 9pm) and dogs welcome, tables in garden looking across to the Ochil Hills, play area, three comfortable bedrooms, generous breakfast, open all day Fri-Sun.

THORNHILL   NS6699
★**Lion & Unicorn** (01786) 850204
Main Street (A873); FK8 3PJ Cosy pubby-feel bar with exposed stone walls, bare boards and stools lining the counter, carpeted front room traditionally furnished and set for dining, three log fires including one in massive 17th-c fireplace; enjoyable home-made food, a couple of changing ales including Belhaven and quite a few malt whiskies; games room with darts, pool, jukebox and TV; children (until 9pm) and dogs (in bar) welcome, picnic-sets in back garden, four bedrooms, open all day (till 1am Fri, Sat).

SUTHERLAND

KYLESKU   NC2333
★**Kylesku Hotel** (01971) 502231
A894, S side of former ferry crossing; IV27 4HW Remote but surprisingly busy hotel on shores of Loch Glendhu; bar with glorious mountain and loch view, well kept ales from the likes of Orkney and Windswept, nice wines by the glass and over 40 malt whiskies, wonderfully fresh seafood along with other good locally sourced food (booking advised), friendly accommodating staff, restaurant extension; children and dogs welcome, disabled access, tables outside taking in the view (seals and red-throated divers often in sight), good boat trips from hotel slipway, 11 comfortable bedrooms, open (and food) all day, closed in winter.

LAIRG   NC5224
★**Crask Inn** (01549) 411241
A836 13 miles N towards Altnaharra; IV27 4AB Remote whitewashed inn on single-track road through peaceful moorland; homely and welcoming with basic but comfortable bar, large stove, interesting books and harmonium, a couple of Black Isle ales (more in bottles), good simple food from toasties to three-course evening meals cooked by landlord including own lamb, friendly helpful staff, separate dining room; church services first Sat and third

---

We say if we know a pub allows dogs.

Thurs of month (pub is church-owned), live music first Sat of month; children and dogs welcome, four bedrooms, camping (no facilities), open all day.

WEST LOTHIAN

BO'NESS   NS9981
Corbie (01506) 825307
A904 Corbiehall; EH51 0AS Neatly furnished pub with up to six well kept beers such as Inveralmond and Orkney, over 60 malt whiskies, 80 gins and quite a choice of enjoyable food at fair prices, friendly staff; children and dogs (in garden) welcome, beer garden with play area, open (and food) all day.

LINLITHGOW   NS0077
★ **Four Marys** (01506) 842171
High Street; 2 miles from M9 junction 3 (and a little further from junction 4) – town signposted; EH49 7ED Named after Mary, Queen of Scots' four ladies-in-waiting and filled with mementoes of the ill-fated queen – pictures and written records, pieces of bed curtain and clothing, even a facsimile of her death-mask; L-shaped room with traditional and more modern seating on wood-block floor, mainly stripped-stone walls (some remarkable masonry in the inner area), elaborate Victorian dresser serving as part of the bar, seven well kept ales (taster glasses available, beer festivals), 70 malt whiskies and 45 gins, enjoyable reasonably priced food, friendly staff, tartan-carpeted dining area where children allowed till 9pm, enclosed beer garden (dogs allowed there), open (and food) all day.

WIGTOWNSHIRE

BLADNOCH   NX4254
Bladnoch Inn (01988) 402200
Corner of A714 and B7005; DG8 9AB Roadside pub across from Bladnoch distillery (tours available) in nice riverside setting; cheerful neat bar with eating area, separate restaurant, tasty pubby food from sandwiches up including Fri fish specials, Sat curry and Sun carvery, a couple of changing real ales, friendly obliging service; background music; children and dogs welcome, five good value bedrooms, open (and food) all day.

PORTPATRICK   NW9954
Crown (01776) 810261
North Crescent; DG9 8SX Popular seafront hotel in delightful harbourside village; enjoyable reasonably priced food including notable seafood and local game, efficient friendly service, two changing ales such as local Portpatrick, several dozen malts and decent wines by the glass, warm fire in rambling traditional bar with cosy corners, sewing-machine tables, old photographs and posters, attractively decorated early 20th-c

dining room opening through conservatory into sheltered back garden; background music, TV; children and dogs welcome, tables out front, 12 bedrooms, open (and food) all day.

STRANRAER   NX0660
Grapes (01776) 703386
Bridge Street; DG9 7HY Popular and welcoming 19th-c local; simple and old-fashioned with a couple of well kept ales such as Ayr and Portpatrick, over 60 malts; live music in bar or upstairs art deco room including bluegrass Fri; children and dogs welcome, courtyard seating, open all day.

Scottish Islands

ARRAN

BRODICK   NS0137
Wineport (01770) 302101
Signed off A841 at visitors centre; KA27 8DE Friendly pink-painted pub-bistro near Brodick Castle (NTS); well kept Arran Blonde (brewery next door) and a guest, decent food from blackboard menu catering for special diets, kitchen open all day in summer (11-5 out of season), modernised interior with open fire; children and dogs welcome, lots of picnic-sets on front lawn.

LAMLASH   NS0231
Pier Head Tavern (01770) 600418
A841; KA27 8JN Refurbished bayside pub with opened-up bar; enjoyable traditional food along with fresh seafood and some vegetarian choices, three real ales such as Arran and William Bros, good selection of malt whiskies and growing range of gins, efficient friendly service; live music Sat evening and Sun afternoon; roof terrace with views across Lamlash Bay to the Holy Isle, open all day.

BARRA

CASTLEBAY   NL6698
Castlebay Hotel (01871) 810223
By aeroplane from Glasgow or ferry from Oban; HS9 5XD Comfortable cheerful bar next to the hotel; popular food from sandwiches up, keg and bottled beers, also two-level lounge/restaurant with great harbour view, pleasant young staff; live music and comedy nights; decent bedrooms.

BUTE

ROTHESAY   NS0864
Black Bull (01700) 502366
W Princes Street; PA20 9AF Traditional comfortably furnished two-bar pub; three well kept changing ales and generous helpings of enjoyable reasonably priced food,

good friendly service; weekend live music, TV, pool; children welcome till 8pm, no dogs, opposite pier with its wonderfully restored Victorian gents', open all day and may serve food all day in summer, otherwise kitchen closed Mon, Tues and evening Weds.

COLONSAY

SCALASAIG   NR3893
★**Colonsay** (01951) 200316
W on B8086; PA61 7YP Stylish extended 18th-c hotel, a haven for ramblers, cyclists and birders; chatty bar is hub of the island and full of locals and visitors, comfortable sofas and armchairs on painted boards, pastel walls hung with interesting old islander pictures, log fires, Colonsay IPA, several wines by the glass and interesting selection of whiskies, relaxed informal restaurant overlooking the harbour, good food using home-grown produce (own oyster farm) including pre-ferry two-course offer (from 5.30pm; not Tues, Weds or Sat), friendly efficient service; children and dogs (in bar) welcome, nice views from garden, nine comfortable pretty bedrooms, backpackers' lodge and holiday cottages, closed Nov-Mar except Christmas and New Year, otherwise open all day (till 1am Sat).

GREAT CUMBRAE

MILLPORT   NS1554
Frasers (01475) 530518
Cardiff Street; KA28 0AS Small cheerful pub set just back from the harbour; bar with old paddle-steamer pictures and woodburner, back vaulted dining room, a couple of changing beers and enjoyable very reasonably priced pubby food, friendly staff; children welcome till 8pm, no dogs, tables in yard behind, open all day.

HARRIS

TARBERT   NB1500
★**Harris Hotel** (01859) 502154
Scott Road; HS3 3DL Large hotel in same family for over a century; small welcoming panelled bar with Hebridean brewed ales and fine selection of malt whiskies including some rarities, interesting food using local game and seafood, morning coffee and afternoon teas, they can also provide packed lunches, friendly accommodating staff, smart (but relaxed) airy restaurant; 23 comfortable sea-view bedrooms (some up narrow stairs).

ISLAY

BOWMORE   NR3159
★**Harbour Inn** (01496) 810330
The Square; PA43 7JR Attractively updated old whitewashed inn opposite the Bowmore distillery; lovely views of harbour and loch from dining room and conservatory, good fish/seafood and other locally sourced food, nice wines and a good selection of of Islay malts including some rarities, Belhaven keg beer, traditional snug bar with unusual barrel counter, friendly helpful staff; children and dogs (in bar) welcome, seven bedrooms.

PORT ASKAIG   NR4369
Port Askaig (01496) 840245
A846, by port; PA46 7RD Family-run inn on Sound of Islay shore overlooking ferry pier; snug, tartan-carpeted bar with good range of malt whiskies and local bottled ales, popular food using some home-grown produce, neat sea-view restaurant and traditional first-floor residents' lounge; regular live music; dogs welcome in bar, plenty of picnic-sets on waterside grass, 11 bedrooms and self-catering annexe, open (and food) all day.

PORT CHARLOTTE   NR2558
★**Port Charlotte Hotel**
(01496) 850360   *Main Street; PA48 7TU* Most beautiful of Islay's Georgian villages and in lovely position with sweeping views over Loch Indaal; exceptional collection of some 150 Islay malts including rarities, two changing local ales and decent wines by the glass, good food using local meat, game and seafood (packed lunches on request), civilised bare-boards pubby bar with padded wall seats, open fire and modern artwork, second comfortable back bar, neatly kept restaurant and roomy conservatory (overlooking beach); regular traditional live music; children welcome, garden tables, ten attractive bedrooms (most with sea view), open all day till 1am.

PORTNAHAVEN   NN1652
An Tighe Seinnse (01496) 860224
Queen Street; PA47 7SJ Friendly little end-of-terrace harbourside pub tucked away in this remote attractive fishing village; cosy bar with room off, open fire, good fairly priced food including local seafood, Belhaven keg beer and bottled Islay ales, good choice of malts; sports TV and occasional live music; can get crowded; open all day.

JURA

CRAIGHOUSE   NR5266
Jura Hotel (01496) 820243
A846, opposite distillery; PA60 7XU Family-run and in superb setting with views over the Small Isles to the mainland; bar, two lounges and restaurant, good food using local fish, seafood and game (breakfasts for non-residents if capacity allows), warm friendly service; garden down to water's edge, 17 bedrooms (mainly ensuite and most with sea view), camping.

MULL

DERVAIG   NM4251
★ **Bellachroy** (01688) 400314
B8073; PA75 6QW Island's oldest inn
dating from 1608; pub and restaurant food
including local fish/seafood, afternoon teas
and packed lunches, ales such as Isle of
Mull and good choice of whiskies and wines,
traditional bar with darts, attractive dining
area, comfortable residents' lounge with
games and TV; occasional live music and quiz
nights; children and dogs welcome, covered
outside area plus plenty of picnic-sets,
nice spot in sleepy lochside village, seven
comfortable bedrooms, open all year.

FIONNPHORT   NM3023
Keel Row (01681) 700458
A849; PA66 6BL Simply furnished bare-
boards bar with exposed stone walls and
woodburner, Caledonian Deuchars IPA and
several whiskies, generous helpings of tasty
pub food, friendly helpful staff, sea views over
to Iona from dining room's big windows; TV,
darts; children welcome, convenient for ferry,
open all day.

TOBERMORY   NM5055
Mishnish (01688) 302500
Main Street – the yellow building;
PA75 6NU Popular lively place right on
the bay; dimly lit two-room bar with cask
tables, old photographs and nautical/fishing
bric-a-brac, woodburner, little snugs, well
kept Belhaven and Isle of Mull, enjoyable
bar food, can also eat in next-door Mishdish
or (in summer) Italian restaurant upstairs;
background and live music, pool; beer garden
behind, 12 attractive bedrooms (some with sea
view), good breakfast, open all day till late.

ORKNEY

DOUNBY   HY3001
Merkister (01856) 771366
Russland Road, by Harray Loch;
KW17 2LF Fishing hotel in great location
on the loch shore; bar dominated by prize
catches, good food here and in evening
restaurant including hand-dived scallops and
local Aberdeen Angus steaks (specials and
vegetarian menu available), good friendly
service; 16 bedrooms, also good for walking
and birdwatching, open all day.

WESTRAY   HY4348
Pierowall Hotel (01857) 677472
Centre of Pierowall village, B9066;
KW17 2BZ Comfortable pub-hotel with
enjoyable home-cooked food from sandwiches
and snacks to good fresh fish (takeaways
available until 7.30pm; no food Tues evening
except for residents), bottled Orkney beers
and plenty of malts, lounge bar with warming
stove, public bar and separate restaurant; six

bedrooms (four ensuite) with bay or hill views,
tables out on front grass, handy for ferry.

SKYE

ARDVASAR   NG6303
Inn at Aird a' Bhasair
(01471) 844223 *A851 at S of island,*
near Armadale pier; IV45 8RS Wonderful
sea and mountain views from this peacefully
placed early 19th-c white stone inn (former
Ardvasar Hotel); much liked food using local
fish and meat, good selection of whiskies,
a craft keg such as Drygate Gladeye and
bottled beers from Isle of Skye, friendly
helpful staff, two bars, restaurant and games
room; background music, TV; children
welcome in eating areas, dogs in one bar,
tables outside, lovely walks, ten comfortable
bedrooms (front ones overlook the sound),
open all day Sat, Sun.

CARBOST   NG3731
★ **Old Inn** (01478) 640205
B8009; IV47 8SR Unpretentious waterside
pub with stunning views and well positioned
for walkers and climbers; simply furnished
chatty bar with exposed stone walls, bare-
boards or tiled floors, open fire, Cuillin ales
and a guest, traditional cider and quite a
few malt whiskies, tasty fairly priced food
using local fish/shellfish and highland meat;
background and regular live music, darts,
pool; children and dogs welcome, picnic-sets
on waterside terrace, bedrooms, bunkhouse
and family chalet also enjoying the views,
Talisker distillery nearby, closed afternoons
in winter, otherwise open (and food) all day,
breakfast 7.45-9.30am.

EDINBANE   NG3451
Edinbane (01470) 582414
Just off A850, signed for Meadhan
a Bhaile; IV51 9PW Friendly former
farmhouse with simply furnished bar, light
wood flooring and woodburner in stone
fireplace; well kept Isle of Skye and craft
beers, airy carpeted dining room serving good
attractively presented food including local
fish/seafood, friendly staff; live traditional
music (Sun); children and dogs welcome,
small garden with picnic-sets, six bedrooms,
open all day (check winter hours).

ISLE ORNSAY   NG7012
★ **Eilean Iarmain** (01471) 833332
Off A851 Broadford–Armadale;
IV43 8QR Smartly old-fashioned 19th-c
hotel in beautiful location looking over the
Sound of Sleat; cosy traditional bar with
panelling and open fire, well kept Isle of Skye
and good choice of vatted (blended) malt
whiskies including their own Gaelic Whisky
Collection (tastings in shop), good food here
or in charming sea-view restaurant, friendly
efficient service; associated gallery nearby
exhibiting work by local artists, traditional

background and live music; children welcome, outside tables with spectacular views, 16 comfortable bedrooms, open all day.

STEIN   NG2656
★ **Stein Inn** (01470) 592362
End of B886 N of Dunvegan in Waternish, off A850 Dunvegan–Portree; OS Sheet 23 map reference 263564; IV55 8GA Characterful 18th-c inn in tiny waterside hamlet with classic Hebridean views across Loch Dunvegan (great sunsets); unpretentious original public bar with flagstones, beam-and-plank ceiling, partly panelled stripped-stone walls and double-sided stove, up to three ales including Caledonian Deuchars IPA and a couple of local guests, ten wines by the glass, 130 malt whiskies, 18 gins, good service, wholesome food with local fish and meat; games area with pool, darts, board games, dominoes and cribbage, indoor play area for children

and showers for sailors; bedrooms and self-catering accommodation, children welcome, dogs in bar (not during food service) and bedrooms, benches outside, open all day, check winter times.

SOUTH UIST

LOCH CARNAN   NF8144
Orasay Inn (01870) 610298
Signed off A865 S of Creagorry; HS8 5PD
Wonderful remote spot overlooking the sea (lovely sunsets); good local food including fish/seafood, beef from own herd and vegetarian options, can eat in modern lounge or conservatory-style restaurant, friendly service, pleasant simply furnished public bar; seats outside on raised decked area, compact comfortable bedrooms (two with terraces), disabled access, children and dogs welcome, open all day in summer.

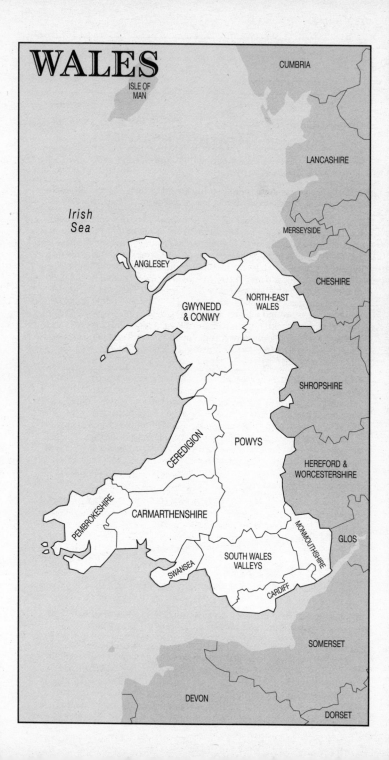

KEY	★ Star Pub	🍴 Top Quality Food	🍺 Great Beer
🍷 Good Wines	£ Bargain Meals	🛏 Good Bedrooms	🍴 Serves Food

ABERTHIN

ST0075 Map 6

Hare & Hounds 🍴 🍷

(01446) 774892 – www.hareandhoundsaberthin.com

1 mile NE of Cowbridge; CF71 7LG

First class food in smart, easy-going country pub, interesting drinks, helpful courteous service and seats in garden

This 300-year-old watering hole is a firm local favourite, relaxed and inviting, with hanging baskets at the front of the building and benches and picnic tables in the stone-walled garden. Expect the likes of Hancocks HB and Wye Valley HPA on handpump, plus 24 wines by the glass from a thoughtfully chosen list, local cider and home-made seasonal drinks such as damson gin, sloe gin and cherry brandy. The food cooked by the chef-landlord is excellent (they also have a bakery open Thursday to Sunday). Inside the stripped stone and whitewashed interior, you'll find mate's chairs and wheelbacks around wooden tables on bare boards, posies of flowers in vases, a dresser with home-made preserves, a woodburning stove in an inglenook fireplace, bookshelves with cookbooks and an open kitchen. There is background music (restaurant only) and darts. Disabled access. Sister pub is the Heathcock in Cardiff.

 The food is extremely good, with extensive use of seasonal and very local produce, from their own kitchen garden and smallholding as well as the surrounding Vale of Glamorgan. Typical dishes include Gower mussels with laverbread, house-smoked bacon and hispi cabbage, pork, prune and pistachio terrine, pan-fried skate with cockles, shrimp, salsify and brown butter, Torgelly Farm lamb hotpot and mint sauce (to share), roast pumpkin, squash and kale pappardelle, Middlewhite pork shoulder in cider and mustard sauce with confit potato, and puddings such as plum soufflé and rhubarb and almond tart with salted caramel and vanilla ice-cream. *Benchmark main dish: braised duck leg with bacon, wild garlic and mash £17.00. Two-course evening meal £26.00.*

Free house ~ Licensee Tom Watts-Jones ~ Real ale ~ Open 2.30-9 Mon, Tues; 12-11 Weds, Thurs; 12-midnight Fri, Sat; 12-10 Sun ~ Bar food 12-2.30, 6-9; 12-4 Sun ~ Restaurant ~ Children welcome but must leave bar by 7.30pm ~ Dogs allowed in bar

BEAUMARIS

SH6076 Map 6

Bull 🍴 🍷 🛏

(01248) 810329 – www.bullsheadinn.co.uk

Castle Street; LL58 8AP

Interesting historic inn with a rambling bar, stylish brasserie and restaurant; well equipped bedrooms in two different locations

Previous visitors to this dignified 15th-c inn have included Samuel Johnson and Charles Dickens. Nowadays, an amiable mix of customers fill the charming beamed bar, with its fine log fire and reminders of the town's past including a rare 17th-c brass water clock, a bloodthirsty array of cutlasses and even an oak ducking stool tucked into a snug alcove. Seats include comfortable low settles and leather-cushioned window seats, and there are lots of copper and china jugs. You're at the heart of historic Beaumaris here and close to the impressive castle. Courteous staff serve the likes of Bass, Sharps Doom Bar and local guests such as Purple Moose and Conwy on handpump, more than 20 wines by the glass (and 100-plus by the bottle), several cocktails and mocktails and a fine gin collection with interesting tonics. Board games too. A stylish brasserie (called Coach) serves an informal menu in relaxed surroundings and you can also dine outside in the adjacent courtyard. The five inn bedrooms are very well equipped; some are traditional, others more contemporary in style. There are further bedrooms in the boutique-style 17th-c Townhouse, which has disabled access.

Making the most of their surroundings by using local meat and fish, the beautifully presented food includes lunchtime sandwiches, crispy pig with mustard piccalilli, crackling and apple jam, Anglesey smoked salmon with celeriac rémoulade and soda bread, roast breast of herb-fed chicken with forestière sauce, leg croquette, Anglesey new potatoes and baby leeks, whole dressed Welsh crab with spiced fries and lemon aioli, 50-day dry-aged Welsh rib-eye steak with béarnaise sauce and chips, and puddings such as rum baba with vanilla cream and roasted pineapple carpaccio and millefeuille with mint poached raspberries. *Benchmark main dish: dry-aged Welsh beef burger with bacon jam, smoked cheddar and spiced fries £17.00. Two-course evening meal £25.00.*

Free house ~ Licensee David Robertson ~ Real ale ~ Open 11-11; 11-10.30 Sun ~ Bar food 12-9 ~ Restaurant ~ Children welcome ~ Dogs allowed in bar ~ Bedrooms: £90

BODFARI   SJ0970 Map 6
Dinorben Arms

(01745) 775090 – www.brunningandprice.co.uk/dinorbenarms
Short distance off A541 on B5429, near St Stephen's Church; LL16 4DA

Carefully extended village pub with interesting furnishings in open-plan bars, a fine choice of drinks and rewarding food

Far-reaching bucolic views, enjoyed from a spacious, partly covered terrace, from a grassy lawn and from a high tower set the tone for this whitewashed village pub prettily stationed beside the church. The large open-plan bar with pine furnishings and a contemporary feel has several cosier areas leading off, the oldest of which is heavily beamed and has antique settles, stone bottles on a delft shelf and a woodburning stove. There's a glassed-over well in one corner, a beautiful curved central wooden counter, leather armchairs grouped around one open fire (there are others), all manner of wooden dining chairs around tables on rugs or bare boards, elegant metal chandeliers, hundreds of prints on pale-painted or exposed stone walls, large house plants and sizeable gilt-edged mirrors. As for the ale, there's Phoenix Brunning & Price Original, maybe Facers North Star Porter and Timothy Taylors Boltmaker and guests from breweries such as Castle Rock, Conwy, Hafod, Purple Moose and Spitting Feathers on handpump, as well as lots of wines by the glass and a good choice of spirits.

Good brasserie-style food (with special diets catered for) includes a meze plate, smoked salmon with orange and beetroot salad, crispy baby squid with sweet chilli sauce, steak burger with coleslaw and fries, grilled sea bass fillets with potato and shallot terrine and chervil and lemon cream sauce, king prawn linguine, cauliflower, chickpea and squash tagine with couscous, braised feather of beef bourguignon with horseradish mash and kale, and puddings such as bread and bara brith butter pudding with apricot sauce and crème brûlée. *Benchmark main dish: pork and leek sausages with mash, greens and onion gravy £13.95. Two-course evening meal £22.00.*

Brunning & Price ~ Licensee John Unsworth ~ Real ale ~ Open 12-11; 12-10.30 Sun ~ Bar food 12-9; 12-10 Fri, Sat ~ Restaurant ~ Children welcome ~ Dogs allowed in bar

CARDIFF
Heathcock 🖈

ST1578   Map 6

(029) 2115 2290 – www.heathcockcardiff.com

Bridge Street; CF5 2EN

Simple décor in relaxed city street pub with highly thought-of food and drink and friendly staff; seats outside

Sister pub to the very successful Hare & Hounds in Aberthin, this bustling, friendly place is run along the same lines – part local pub and part informal dining room. The bar is half-panelled and simply decorated: in one corner there are some chunky leather stools and a leather wall banquette plus some elegant modern stools, high-backed farmhouse and other wooden chairs around a mix of tables on bare boards and a few high chairs against the counter where helpful staff serve up to four real ales on handpump from the Glamorgan and Wye Valley, a couple of craft beers/lagers, 13 wines by the glass and some interesting spirits including home-made fennel liqueur. The uncomplicated décor and mix of wicker and wooden chairs around chunky tables on more floorboards in the restaurant keeps the atmosphere easy-going and relaxed; a former skittles alley acts as an overflow area when things get really busy. There are picnic tables in the back garden among tubs of flowers.

🖈 Using local seasonal produce and making everything in-house including bread and pasta, the high quality food includes grilled mackerel with pear, horseradish and dill, braised rabbit leg pappardelle, roast haunch of venison with smoked bacon, red wine, cavolo nero and wild mushrooms, pan-fried hake with fennel, oxtail and cockles, steak and ale pie (for two), and puddings. They also offer an express two- and three-course set lunch (Monday-Wednesday). *Benchmark main dish: roast Torgelly Farm lamb with barley, celeriac and turnip £20.00. Two-course evening meal £26.00.*

Free house ~ Licensee Guy Ennever ~ Open 4-11.30 Tues-Thurs; 12-11.30 Fri, Sat; 12-7.30 Sun; closed Mon ~ Bar food 6-9 Tues-Thurs; 12-2.30, 6-9 Fri, Sat; 12-4 Sun ~ Children welcome ~ Dogs allowed in bar

COLWYN BAY
Pen-y-Bryn 🍷 🍺

SH8478   Map 6

(01492) 533360 – www.brunningandprice.co.uk/penybryn

B5113 Llanwrst Road, on southern outskirts; when you see the pub, turn off via Troon Road into Wentworth Avenue for the car park; LL29 6DD

Spacious, open-plan, one-storey building overlooking the bay with all-day brasserie-style food, a good range of drinks and obliging staff

Large windows at the back of this Brunning & Price pub look over the terrace and sizeable garden with their seats and tables out to sea and the dramatic Great Orme headland beyond Llandudno, framed in summer by award-winning flowering tubs and hanging baskets. A fine choice of drinks served by knowledgeable young staff includes Phoenix Brunning & Price Original, Purple Moose Snowdonia Ale and Timothy Taylors Boltmaker plus three quickly changing guests such as Castle Rock Elsie Mo, Jennings Cumberland and Montys Masquerade on handpump, well chosen, good value wines, prosecco and champagne (including almost 30 by the glass) and 40 malt whiskies; board games and background music. If you'd prefer to be inside rather than out, extending around the three long sides of the bar counter you'll find welcoming open fires, oriental rugs on pale stripped boards, a mix of seating and well spaced tables, shelves of books, a profusion of pictures, big pot plants, careful lighting and dark green, old-fashioned cast-iron school radiators.

🍴 The varied menu offers vegetarian, vegan and gluten-free options. Dishes include wild mushroom risotto, rump steak sandwich and fries, chicken caesar croquettes, five-spiced duck leg with hoisin sauce and pancakes, crispy beef salad with sweet chilli sauce and roasted cashew nuts, buttermilk chicken burger and fries, chicken, ham and leek pie with mash and buttered greens, sweet potato, aubergine and spinach Malaysian curry with coconut rice and pak choi, and puddings such as glazed lemon tart with raspberry sorbet and hot waffle and caramelised banana with toffee sauce and coconut ice-cream. *Benchmark main dish: beer-battered cod and chips £14.95. Two-course evening meal £22.00.*

Brunning & Price ~ Manager Sharon Brocklehurst ~ Real ale ~ Open 11-11; 11-10.30 Sun ~ Bar food 12-9.30; 12-9 Sun ~ Children welcome ~ Dogs allowed in bar

CRICKHOWELL

Bear ★ � ⛱

SO2118 Map 6

(01873) 810408 – www.bearhotel.co.uk
Brecon Road; A40 – at High Street; NP8 1BW

Convivial and interesting one-time coaching inn with a splendid, old-fashioned bar area warmed by a log fire and rewarding food and drink; comfortable bedrooms

This whitewashed, flower-fronted and thoroughly charming pub is one of Crickhowell's most striking buildings and has been welcoming guests for more than 500 years. The long-serving family currently in charge continue to offer a warm and genuine welcome to all. The bustling bar attracts a wide mix of customers. There are heavy beams, little plush-seated bentwood armchairs and handsome old cushioned settles, fresh flowers on tables, and a window seat that looks down over the market square. Next to the roaring log fire are a big sofa and leather easy chairs on oak parquet flooring with rugs and antiques including lots of pewter mugs and brassware, a longcase clock and interesting prints. Real ales on handpump include maybe Brains Rev James, Hancocks HB, Grey Trees Afghan Pale and Rhymney Export, alongside 30 malt whiskies, over 20 gins, local ciders, vintage and late-bottled ports and unusual wines (with at least ten by the glass). The reception rooms are comfortably furnished, and there are seats in the small garden. This is a particularly appealing place to stay, with a choice of 35 characterful bedrooms: the older ones in the main building have antiques, others are in a country style and the luxury ones have hot tubs and four-poster beds. Breakfasts are excellent. Disabled loos.

🍴 The enjoyable food makes good use of organic local produce and artisan makers in the Brecon Beacons, such as the Black Mountain Smokery, Welsh Venison Centre and Penderyn Distillery. Options include sandwiches, soups, salads, pan-fried wild sea bass with crushed new potatoes, mussels and saffron sauce, 30-day aged Welsh fillet steak with grilled mushroom, tomato and chips, potato gnocchi with roasted butternut squash and sage butter, Welsh beef burger with smoked bacon and rarebit in a potato bun with tomato chutney and chips, and puddings such as sticky toffee pudding with caramel sauce and vanilla ice-cream. *Benchmark main dish: pheasant medallions with olive oil mash, bacon-roasted brussels sprouts and madeira jus £16.00. Two-course evening meal £24.00.*

Free house ~ Licensee Stephen Hindmarsh ~ Real ale ~ Open 11-11; 12-11 Sun ~ Bar food 12-2.15, 6-10.30; 12-3, 7-9.30 Sun ~ Restaurant ~ Children welcome ~ Dogs allowed in bar & bedrooms ~ Bedrooms: £135

If we know a featured-entry pub does sandwiches, we always say so – if they're not mentioned, you'll have to assume they're not available.

DALE
Griffin ⭐

SM8105 Map 6

(01646) 636227 – www.griffininndale.co.uk

Just off B4327, by sea on one-way system; SA62 3RB

Friendly waterside pub with fresh fish and shellfish, local ales and an airy extension with lovely views

This strikingly located pub sits right by the water – its boast that it has one of the best sea-wall bars in Wales is true. The seats on the rooftop terrace (you can eat up here too) make the most of the lovely view of Milford Haven waterway, and there are delightful coastal walks to either side. The convivial licensees have created a cosy and inviting atmosphere, helped along by beams, wood panelling, traditional red quarry tiles and open fires. You'll find Brains Rev James, Evan Evans Cwrw Haf and Tenby Harbwr North Star on handpump, a well chosen wine list, local cider and malt whiskies (including a Welsh one); background music. There's also a modern, glass-fronted extension with its own stand-alone stove, and the big windows and doors open up the wonderful view of the coastline.

 The good food uses the best local produce, with the focus on impeccably fresh fish and shellfish from local fishing boats. Other dishes include sandwiches, salads, smoked mackerel pâté, Welsh lamb cawl, beef and stout puff pastry pie with chips, spicy prawn and mango curry, vegetable lasagne, gammon steak with mash and greens, and puddings such as sticky toffee pudding and chocolate orange torte. Takeaway menu available too. *Benchmark main dish: fish pie (white fish, salmon, smoked haddock and prawns) topped with Welsh cheddar mash £16.95. Two-course evening meal £22.00.*

Free house ~ Licensees Sian Mathias and Simon Vickers ~ Real ale ~ Open usually 12-11 – check website for winter times ~ Bar food 12-3, 5-9 ~ Restaurant ~ Children welcome

EAST ABERTHAW
Blue Anchor ◖ £

ST0366 Map 6

(01446) 750329 – www.blueanchoraberthaw.com

Village signed off B4265; Fontygary Road, at Port Road; CF62 3DD

Thatched character pub with a cosy range of small rooms, making a memorable spot for a drink

One of Wales's oldest taverns (dating back to the 14th c) greets you with its fetching thatched roof, low-beamed little rooms, open fires including one in an inglenook with antique oak seats built into the stripped stonework, and other seats and tables worked into a series of small, chatty alcoves. Outside, rustic seats shelter peacefully among tubs and troughs of flowers, with stone tables on a terrace, and a path leads invitingly from here to the shingle flats of the nearby estuary. The front bar has an ancient lime-ash floor and keeps regulars Brains Bitter, Theakstons Old Peculier, Wadworths 6X and Wye Valley HPA on handpump, alongside a frequently changing local guest from the Otley Brewery in Pontypridd, Celt Experience in Caerphilly, Vale of Glamorgan Brewery in Barry or Gower Brewery. Their cider range is courtesy of local producers Gwynt-y-ddraig. Unsurprisingly, the pub can get very full in the evenings and on summer weekends.

The pub has long cultivated a reputation for tasty food: nothing too fancy, but all well executed. Dishes include flaked smoked mackerel with lamb's lettuce and orange salad, ham hock terrine with piccalilli, crispy saffron arancini with mozzarella and garlic and herb mayonnaise, steak and Theakstons ale pie, beef fillet and mushroom stroganoff, Thai green chicken curry, spinach and ricotta ravioli, and desserts such as sticky toffee pudding with toffee sauce and vanilla ice-cream and plum and frangipane tart. *Benchmark main dish: deep-fried fillet of hake with mushy peas and chips £11.75. Two-course evening meal £19.00.*

Free house ~ Licensee Jeremy Coleman ~ Real ale ~ Open 11-11; 12-10.30 Sun ~ Bar food 12-2, 6-9; 12-3 Sun ~ Restaurant ~ Children welcome ~ Dogs allowed in bar

ERBISTOCK

Boat 🎯 ⚓ 🍷 🍺

SJ3542

(01978) 280205 – theboataterbistock.co.uk
Village signed off A539 W of Overton, then pub signed; LL13 0DL

Charming stone-built pub with interesting, carefully furnished rooms, a thoughtful choice of food and drink, friendly atmosphere and seats by the water

In a pretty setting almost alone by a church and on the banks of the River Dee, this is a lovely 17th-c golden-stone inn with seats and tables on a terrace overlooking the water. Inside, the beamed and flagstoned interior has been carefully refurbished while preserving its old-fashioned charm and easy-going country atmosphere. A rambling warren of rooms includes the chatty bar with armchairs next to a fine old range, a group of high chairs around a central, equally high barrel table and chairs by the counter where courteous, helpful staff serve five real ales on handpump such as Salopian or Weetwood with at least three regional beers (from Wales, Shropshire and Cheshire) and an impressive 30-plus wines by the glass; they also distil their own gin, the Spirit of Erbistock. There are more open fires, a woodburner and a varied and attractive mix of chairs, settles and built-in wall seats around polished tables on rugs and floorboards in the other dining areas. The walls (bare stone in part) are hung with mirrors, framed prints and photographs and a stag's head; do note the elegant antler chandelier.

🍴 The pub is clearly passionate about its food, which is attractively presented with local ingredients to the fore and an emphasis on game and fish. Typical dishes are pheasant and parsnip rösti with damson jam, salmon ballotine with poached egg, avocado purée, capers and pickled cucumber, Korean chicken, prawns and pak choi with noodles, roast hake with caper butter, crushed new potatoes and rainbow chard, wild mushroom pappardelle with garlic and sage cream, pub classics such as beer-battered fish and chips, steak burger and fish pie, and desserts such as sticky toffee pudding and popcorn pannacotta. *Benchmark main dish: lamb rump with fondant potato, peas, broad beans, feta and salsa verde £19.95. Two-course evening meal £25.00.*

Free house ~ Licensee Richard Johnson ~ Real ale ~ Open 11-10; 11-11 Fri, Sat; 12-10 Sun ~ Bar food 12-8.45; 12-9.15 Fri, Sat; 12-8 Sun ~ Restaurant ~ Children allowed in restaurant if seated with adults ~ Dogs allowed in bar

FELINFACH

Griffin 🎯 🍷 🍺 🛏️

SO0933 Map 6

(01874) 620111 – www.eatdrinksleep.ltd.uk
A470 NE of Brecon; LD3 0UB

Highly regarded dining pub with exceptional food, a fine range of drinks and upbeat rustic décor; inviting bedrooms

This distinctly upmarket and yet unpretentious place manages both its drinking and dining aspects very well, and for this reason wins heaps of praise from our readers. The back bar is quite pubby in an up-to-date way, with four leather sofas around a low table on pitted quarry tiles by a high slate hearth with a log fire – behind them are mixed stripped seats around scrubbed kitchen tables on bare boards, and a bright blue and ochre colour scheme with some modern prints; background music, board games and plenty of books. There's a good choice of ales from local breweries such as Brecon Brewing, Celt Experience, Montys, Rhymney, Waen and Wye Valley, plus a highly individual wine list with around 20 usually available by the glass and carafe (they also have their own wine shop) and a fine array of sherries, brandies and cider brandies. The two smallish front dining rooms are attractive. On the left: mixed dining chairs around mainly stripped tables on flagstones and white-painted rough stone walls, with a cream-coloured Aga in a stripped-stone embrasure. On the right: similar furniture on bare boards, large modern prints on terracotta walls and smart dark curtains. Dogs may sit with their owners at certain tables while dining. There are seats and tables outside. The seven bedrooms are comfortable even though small, and tastefully decorated: the hearty breakfasts are nicely informal. Good wheelchair access. Sister pubs are the Old Coastguard and Gurnard Head Hotel, both in Cornwall.

 The pub is known far and wide for its food, which is some of the region's best with much of the produce coming from their own kitchen garden. Typical dishes are crab beignets with mango salsa and curry ketchup, smoked duck with feta and pickled garden berries, barbecue sea bass with gooseberries and labneh, gnocchi with peas, girolles and spring onion, Middle White pork sausages with mash and greens, lamb belly with peas, courgette and fondant potato, and puddings such as strawberry eton mess and Welsh cheeses. The two- and three-course Sunday lunch is very popular. *Benchmark main dish: halibut with broad bean, pine nut and hazelnut fricassée and truffle £20.00. Two-course evening meal £28.00.*

Free house ~ Licensees Charles and Edmund Inkin and Julie Bell ~ Real ale ~ Open 11-11 ~ Bar food 12-2.30, 5.30-9 Mon-Sat; 12-3 Sun ~ Restaurant ~ Children welcome ~ Dogs allowed in bar & bedrooms ~ Bedrooms: £160

GRESFORD
SJ3453   Map 6
Pant-yr-Ochain ♀ ▥
(01978) 853525 – www.brunningandprice.co.uk/pantyrochain
Off A483 on N edge of Wrexham: at roundabout take A5156 (A534) towards Nantwich, then first left towards the Flash; LL12 8TY

Popular dining pub with good and diverse all-day food, a wide range of drinks and lovely lakeside garden

Journey down a long driveway to this black and white Victorian building, with its blaze of flower-filled gardens and carefully tended lawns stretching into the distance, and you'll feel like you've arrived at an elegant country mansion rather than a pub. Multiple eating and drinking areas including one set out as a library with floor-to-ceiling bookshelves, and another in a conservatory overlooking the grounds. There's a 16th-c inglenook fireplace and decoration throughout ranges between the intriguing, the stylish and the sumptuous, with numerous pictures and prints, house plants and old stone bottles. An impressive line-up of drinks served by well trained staff includes Phoenix Brunning & Price Original and guests such as Big Hand Seren, Brimstage Trappers Hat Bitter, Hawkshead Windermere Pale, Purple Moose Snowdonia Ale, Timothy Taylors Landlord and Weetwood Eastgate on handpump, an 80-strong malt whisky collection, 20 wines by the glass and several gins and rums. There are seats with parasols on the terrace and picnic-sets on the grass. Good disabled access.

Rewarding food (with a separate gluten-free menu) includes deep-fried West Country brie with apricot chutney, halloumi fries with tomato salsa, smoked salmon with orange and beetroot salad, roast duck breast with crispy leg croquettes, celeriac purée and cherry jus, beer-battered cod and chips, grilled sea bass fillets with potato and shallot terrine, braised shoulder of lamb with crushed new potatoes and rosemary gravy, beetroot, quinoa and soy bean burger and fries, and puddings such as chocolate and orange tart with passion-fruit sorbet and hot waffle and caramelised banana with toffee sauce and honeycomb ice-cream. *Benchmark main dish: fish pie (salmon, smoked haddock and prawns) £16.95. Two-course evening meal £22.00.*

Brunning & Price ~ Manager James Meakin ~ Real ale ~ Open 11-11; 11-10.30 Sun ~ Bar food 12-9.30; 12-9 Sun ~ Children welcome ~ Dogs allowed in bar

LLANARMON DYFFRYN CEIRIOG SJ1532 Map 6
West Arms 🌟 🛏️
(01691) 600665 – www.thewestarms.com
End of B4500 11 miles W of Chirk; LL20 7LD

Idyllic location for 16th-c inn with reliably good food and picturesque gardens; comfortable bedrooms

The friendly couple at the helm of this nicely updated former drovers' inn continue to make guests feel very welcome, just as it's been here since 1570. There are three quickly changing ales from Big Hand plus Timothy Taylors Landlord on handpump, at least a dozen wines by the glass, 20 malt whiskies and 40-odd gins. The comfortable back bar has antique settles, armchairs and a friendly, informal atmosphere, while the front lounge boasts an inglenook fireplace and original flagstones (five log fires keep everything nice and snug in winter). The restaurant is slightly more formal, but still has a relaxed, traditional feel; background music. In warm weather you can sit in the garden against a lovely backdrop of the Ceiriog Valley and Berwyn Mountains, and the pub makes a good base for exploring the area by foot, bike, car or horse. The 16 bedrooms are comfortable and well appointed and the breakfasts are highly regarded. It's very dog-friendly too.

 Food is good, seasonal and uses some home-grown produce and local game, meat and fish. As well as sandwiches, dishes include venison, pork and pistachio nut terrine, leek and caerphilly tart, a charcuterie board to share, five-spiced Gressingham duck breast with cabbage, bacon and rösti potato, a pie of the day, beer-battered cod and chips, burger (Welsh beef or vegan) with toppings and chips, sweet potato, pepper and red onion spiced roulade with roasted vegetables and herb butter sauce, plus puddings and afternoon tea. *Benchmark main dish: honey-glazed local lamb chops with roasted vegetable and potato terrine £19.00. Two-course evening meal £25.00.*

Free house ~ Licensees Nicky and Mark Williamson ~ Real ale ~ Open 9am-10pm Weds-Fri; 11-3 Sun ~ Bar food 12-2.30, 6.30-9 ~ Restaurant ~ Children welcome ~ Dogs welcome in bar & bedrooms ~ Bedrooms: £155

LLANDUDNO JUNCTION SH8180 Map 6
Queens Head 🌟 🍷
(01492) 546570 – www.queensheadglanwydden.co.uk
Glanwydden; heading towards Llandudno on B5115 from Colwyn Bay, turn left into Llanrhos Road at roundabout as you enter the Penrhyn Bay speed limit; Glanwydden is signed as the first left turn; LL31 9JP

Consistently good food served all day at comfortably modern dining pub

With all of northern Snowdonia within easy reach from here, this snug former wheelwright's cottage is not the most obvious pub choice hereabouts. Yet it is one of the best. Behind a modest-looking whitewashed exterior, the spacious yet intimate lounge bar has a mix of beams, rustic wooden tables and chairs, an open woodburning stove and fresh flowers. The choice of real ales on handpump frequently features local breweries Conwy and Purple Moose as well as Celt Experience from Caerphilly, plus 19 decent wines by the glass, several malt whiskies and good coffee. Food is king here, however: there is a good deal of it to choose from and it is popular – it's best to book a table in advance. There's a pleasant mix of seats and tables under parasols outside.

Using the best local, seasonal produce, the particularly good food has a decidedly meaty focus, but there are vegetarian/vegan options. Typical dishes include sandwiches (until 5pm), crispy confit duck leg with peas bonne femme and celeriac and white truffle purée, roasted pork belly with crispy quail egg, seared king scallops and butternut squash purée, beetroot pannacotta with goats cheese mousse, baby herb salad and candied walnut crumb, Moroccan-style lamb shank with roasted vegetable couscous, Conwy beer-battered haddock and chips, pan-seared stone bass with Thai-style coconut and king prawn laksa, vermicelli noodles and braised pak choi, chargrilled 10oz rib-eye steak with chips and café de paris butter, and puddings. *Benchmark main dish: Welsh black steak burger with Snowdonia beechwood cheddar, chipotle sauce, slaw and skin-on fries £12.95. Two-course evening meal £25.00.*

Stange & Co Pub Group ~ Lease Dan McLennan ~ Real ale ~ Open 12-11 ~ Bar food 12-9 ~ Restaurant ~ Children welcome

LLANELIAN-YN-RHOS
White Lion ♀

SH8676 Map 6

(01492) 515807 – www.whitelioninn.co.uk

Corner of Llanelian Road and Groes Road by Llanelian Park; signed off A5830 (shown as B5383 on some maps) and B5381, SE of Colwyn Bay; LL29 8YA

Bustling local with bar and spacious dining areas, tasty food, real ales and helpful staff

This beguilingly picturesque old village pub is tucked away at a crossing of narrow lanes in quiet hilly countryside above Colwyn Bay: if the several centuries' worth of history in the current building were not enough, know that a dwelling of some sort has been on this site for 1,200 years. There are two distinct parts to the pub, linked by a broad flight of steps, and each has its own cheery personality. Up at the top is a very spacious and neat dining area; at the other end is a traditional old bar with antique high-backed settles fitting snugly around a large fireplace, and flagstones by the counter. The likes of Marstons Saddle Tank and Weetwood Eastgate are on handpump, alongside farm cider, more than 25 wines by the glass, 15-plus gins including Welsh ones and ten malt whiskies, served by helpful staff. Off to the left is another dining room with jugs hanging from beams and teapots above the windows; background music and board games. An outdoor courtyard (also used for parking) has tables and chairs.

The popular food includes lunchtime sandwiches and hot baguettes, plus piri-piri garlic prawns, a pie of the day, chicken curry, fish pie, burger with toppings, home-made barbecue sauce and chips, chickpea and sweet potato coconut curry, goats cheese and walnut salad with honey and wholegrain mustard dressing, and puddings such as Belgian waffle with ice-cream and toffee sauce and apple pie. *Benchmark main dish: chicken breast with smoked bacon, cheese and mushrooms in a cider, rosemary and sage sauce with chips £13.95. Two-course evening meal £21.00.*

Free house ~ Licensee Simon Cole ~ Real ale ~ Open 11.30-3.30, 6-11; 11.30-3.30, 5-11
Fri, Sat; 12-10.30 Sun ~ Bar food 12-2, 6-9; 12-2, 5-9 Fri, Sat; 12-8.30 Sun ~ Restaurant ~
Children welcome

LLANFIHANGEL-Y-CREUDDYN   SN6676 Map 6
Y Ffarmers

(01974) 261275 – www.yffarmers.co.uk
Village signed off A4120 W of Pisgah; SY23 4LA

Traditional village pub with bar and dining areas, local ales and good food

Fully refurbished after a fire, this friendly modern pub remains the hub of the local community – but there's always a genuine welcome for visitors too. The bar has wooden kitchen chairs around rustic tables on pale floorboards and stools on black and red floor tiles against the counter, where charming staff serve two ales on handpump from the likes of local Grey Tree, Glamorgan or Mantle breweries, ciders and a decent selection of mainly old world wines. The room stretches around past a settle to the dining area with similar tables, button-back plush chairs and more floorboards. There's also a woodburning stove in a little fireplace. A sunken back terrace has seats and steps up to a lawn where there are picnic tables under parasols. The 13th-c village church is opposite.

Enjoyable food (takeaway only at time of writing) includes Llanfihangel lamb cutlets with couscous salad, ever-changing pies such as chicken and asparagus with mash and gravy, beer-battered fish and chips, beef lasagne, a choice of curries (maybe cauliflower, green bean and spinach or chicken makhani), and puddings such as peach and strawberry meringue roulade and salted caramel and ginger cheesecake. *Benchmark main dish: courgette and chickpea burger with coleslaw and chips £8.00. Two-course evening meal £14.00.*

Free house ~ Licensee Caitlin Morse ~ Real ale ~ Open & bar food 5-8.30 Weds; 12-2, 5-8.30
Thurs-Sat; 12-2 Sun – times may change, best to check ~ Restaurant ~ Children welcome ~
Dogs allowed in bar

LLANGOLLEN   SJ2142 Map 6
Corn Mill ♀ ☕

(01978) 869555 – www.brunningandprice.co.uk/cornmill
*Dee Lane, very narrow lane off Castle Street (A539) just S of bridge in Llangollen;
nearby parking can be tricky, may be best to use public car park on East Street/Parade
Street and walk; LL20 8PN*

Fascinating riverside building with fine views, personable young staff, super food all day and good beers

Quite a lot of the old mill workings, including the huge waterwheel (often turning), have been preserved at this impeccably restored watermill in Llangollen town centre: expect gleaming timber and tensioned steel rails, pale pine flooring on stout beams and lots of bare stone walls. There are good-sized dining tables, big rugs, thoughtfully chosen pictures (many with a water theme) and several pot plants. There are two serving bars. One, away from the water, has a much more local feel with regulars sitting on bar stools, pews on dark slate flagstones and daily papers. There are also seats on a raised deck in front of the pub overlooking the rushing mill race and rapids below; you can also watch steam trains arriving and leaving the station on the opposite riverbank. To drink: Phoenix Brunning & Price Original and Facers DHB on handpump with guests such as Facers North Star Porter,

Hawkshead Windermere Pale and Moorhouses Pendle Witches Brew, plus 15 wines by the glass, a good range of malt whiskies and farm cider.

🍴 Interesting food (with a separate gluten-free menu) includes sandwiches and 'light bites', deep-fried West Country brie with apricot chutney, halloumi fries with tomato salsa, pea and mint tortellini with pea velouté and asparagus, crispy beef salad with sweet chilli sauce, beer-battered cod and chips, braised shoulder of lamb with crushed new potatoes and rosemary gravy, sweet potato, aubergine and spinach Malaysian curry, and desserts such as triple chocolate brownie and bread and butter pudding. *Benchmark main dish: pork and leek sausages with mash and buttered greens £13.95. Two-course evening meal £21.00.*

Brunning & Price ~ Manager Andrew Barker ~ Real ale ~ Open 11-11; 11-10.30 Sun ~ Bar food 12-9.30; 12-9 Sun ~ Restaurant ~ Children welcome ~ Dogs allowed in bar

LLANMADOC   SS4493   Map 6

Britannia

(01792) 386624 – www.britanniagower.com

The Gower, near Whiteford Burrows (NT); SA3 1DB

Fine views from seats behind this popular pub with more in the big garden, well liked food and ales

Sitting out at a picnic table on the raised decked area with marvellous views over the Loughor estuary, it's easy to see why this family-run 18th-c pub on the winsome north coast of the Gower Peninsula fills up so quickly. In addition to the idyllic location, appealing outside space and lovely nearby walks, there's the refurbished beamed bar with a woodburning stove and plenty of space to enjoy a well kept pint – there's Gower Gold, Sharps Doom Bar and Wye Valley HPA on handpump. Also, several wines by the glass and friendly staff; background music, darts, TV and board games. The beamed restaurant – where seafood is an understandably important element, given the proximity of the beautiful coast – has attractive modern wooden tables and chairs on a striped carpet, paintings on exposed stone walls and another woodburning stove. There's a children's play area outside.

🍴 The good food is very popular and includes sandwiches, fresh local cockles and laverbread, smoked mackerel pot with crème fraîche and cucumber salsa, Welsh steak and ale pie with chips, beer-battered hake and chips, roast vegetable Thai curry with sticky rice and pak choi, traditional Welsh cawl, rib-eye or rump steak and chips, local salt-marsh lamb shank with mash and vegetable casserole, and puddings such as Penderyn whisky parfait and bread and butter pudding with mixed berries and crème fraîche; there's a separate vegetarian menu. *Benchmark main dish: Welsh lamb tagine with batch bread and jasmine rice £12.95. Two-course evening meal £21.00.*

Enterprise ~ Tenants Martin and Lindsey Davies ~ Real ale ~ Open 12-11 ~ Bar food 12-3, 6-8.30; 12-9 weekends ~ Restaurant ~ Children welcome ~ Dogs allowed in bar

MOLD   SJ2465   Map 6

Glasfryn ♀ 🍺

(01352) 750500 – www.brunningandprice.co.uk/glasfryn

N of the centre on Raikes Lane (parallel to the A5119), just S of the well signposted Theatr Clwyd; CH7 6LR

Busy bistro-style pub with inventive all-day food, nice décor and wide choice of drinks

This red-brick house set in beautiful lawned gardens is cleverly laid out inside to create plenty of nice quiet corners with a mix of informal, attractive country furnishings: rugs on bare boards, shelves of books, house plants, a warming fire and lots of close-hung homely pictures. Formerly judges' quarters for the local court and then a farm, it now dispenses the likes of Phoenix Brunning & Price Original, Facers North Star Porter, Hobsons Best, Muirhouse Pirates Gold, Purple Moose Snowdonia Ale, Timothy Taylors Boltmaker and Weetwood Cheshire Cat on handpump, alongside 20 wines by the glass, around 40 gins and huge selections of rum and malt whisky. The wooden tables on the large front terrace are a restful place to sit, providing sweeping views of the Clwydian Hills. Disabled access. Theatr Clwyd is just over the road.

Well regarded food (with a separate gluten-free menu) includes sandwiches, crispy baby squid with sweet chilli sauce, chicken caesar croquettes, smoked salmon with orange and beetroot salad, fish pie, south Indian-spiced sea bass fillets baked in banana leaf with coconut sauce, pork sausages with mash and buttered greens, sweet potato, aubergine and spinach Malaysian curry with pak choi, steak burger with toppings and fries, and puddings such as triple chocolate brownie with vanilla ice-cream and Cheshire Farm ice-creams and sorbets. *Benchmark main dish: braised shoulder of lamb with crushed new potatoes and rosemary gravy £18.95. Two-course evening meal £21.00.*

Brunning & Price ~ Manager Graham Arathoon ~ Real ale ~ Open 10.30-11; 10.30-10.30 Sun ~ Bar food 12-9.30; 12-9 Sun ~ Children welcome ~ Dogs allowed in bar

MONKNASH
Plough & Harrow ◨ £

SS9170   Map 6

(01656) 890209

Signposted 'Marcross, Broughton' off B4265 St Brides Major–Llantwit Major – turn left at end of Water Street on Heol Las; pub is then on the right; OS Sheet 170 map reference 920706; CF71 7QQ

Old building full of history and character, with a huge log fire and a good choice of real ales

A fine range of six real ales on handpump or tapped from the cask is served by the friendly landlord in this historic pub. These might come from breweries such as Bass, Glamorgan, Gower and Wye Valley; they usually hold beer festivals in August. There's also a good range of local farm cider and quite a few gins and malt whiskies. The unspoilt main bar with its massively thick stone walls used to be a scriptures room and mortuary (this was once part of a 15th-c monastic grange): there are ancient ham hooks in the heavily beamed ceiling, an intriguing arched doorway at the back, broad flagstones and a log fire in an inglenook fireplace with a side bread oven that's large enough to feed a village. The comfortably informal mix of furnishings includes three fine pine settles. The front garden has picnic tables. A beautiful walk from the pub leads through the wooded valley of Cwm Nash to the coast, revealing a spectacular stretch of cliffs around Nash Point.

The good, nicely priced food includes baguettes and ploughman's, salmon and coriander fishcakes with sweet chilli dip, sausages (vegetarian or smoked garlic, wild mushroom and pork) with new potatoes, mash or chips, vegan five bean chilli, pan-fried fresh mackerel fillets with sautéed potatoes and roast cherry vine tomatoes, chicken curry, butternut squash and sweet potato curry, beer-battered cod and chips, and desserts such as bread and butter pudding and sticky date pudding. *Benchmark main dish: steak and ale pie £10.95. Two-course evening meal £17.00.*

Free house ~ Licensee Andrew Naylor ~ Real ale ~ Open 12-11; 12-10.30 Sun ~ Bar food 12-2.30, 6-9; 12-5, 6-9 Sat; 12-5 Sun ~ Restaurant ~ Children welcome ~ Dogs allowed in bar

NEWPORT
Golden Lion ⌂

SN0539 Map 6

(01239) 820321 – www.goldenlionpembrokeshire.co.uk

East Street (A487); SA42 0SY

Attractive, friendly local, with tasty food and pleasant staff; well appointed bedrooms

A very attractive and popular inn in a charming seaside village, the Golden Lion offers a warm welcome in its genuinely pubby bar, where you'll find Sharps Doom Bar and a couple of guest ales from the nearby Bluestone Brewery on handpump, several malt whiskies, wines by the glass, 30 gins including Welsh gins and three ciders. There's also a cosy series of beamed rooms with distinctive old settles and a dining room with elegant blond oak furniture, whitewashed walls and potted plants. There's a TV, pool table, juke box, darts, games machine and board games, as well as background and regular live music. Staff are helpful. You can sit outside at the front or in a side garden. This coastal village makes a good base for exploring northern Pembrokeshire and the inn's 13 bedrooms are modern, comfortable and fair value (dogs can stay in the ground-floor ones). Good disabled access and facilities.

A fine choice of good food showcases local highlights of the culinary scene such as Preseli lamb (from the nearby Preseli Hills) and lobster from the local harbour. Dishes include sandwiches, smoked haddock and leek tart with crispy poached egg, sweet potato gnocchi with tomato and basil sauce, pork belly scotch egg with piccalilli gel, roasted barbecue half chicken with sweetcorn salsa and smoked bacon mac 'n' cheese, Thai green vegetable or chicken curry, 8oz Welsh rib-eye steak with fries, broad bean and spinach burger with chargrilled vegetables, harissa mayo and fries, and puddings such as lemon tart with berry compote and chantilly cream. *Benchmark main dish: haddock fillet in coriander and chilli tempura batter £16.50. Two-course evening meal £22.00.*

Free house ~ Licensee Daron Paish ~ Real ale ~ Open 12-midnight; 12-1am Sat ~ Bar food 12-2.30, 6.30-9 ~ Restaurant ~ Children welcome ~ Dogs allowed in bar & bedrooms ~ Bedrooms: £110

OLD RADNOR
Harp ⭘⌂

SO2459 Map 6

(01544) 350655 – www.harpinnradnor.co.uk

Village signposted off A44 Kington–New Radnor in Walton; LD8 2RH

Lovely inn in beautiful spot, with cottagey bar, tasty food and well kept ales; comfortable bedrooms

Our readers continue to heap praise on this charming hilltop inn with its friendly licensees and bags of ancient character. An old stone longhouse overlooking the heights of the Radnor Forest, it boasts slate floors, oak beams, antique settles and a roaring open inglenook fire. There are two well kept beers on handpump – regulars include Ludlow Gold, Salopian Darwins Origin and Oracle, Skinners Betty Stogs, Three Tuns XXX and Wye Valley HPA – as well as six wines and prosecco by the glass, local cider, local gins, vodkas and whiskies. Board games, cribbage, darts and quoits and lots of local books, maps and guides are provided for guests. A quieter dining area off to the right from the snug bar extends into another dining room with a woodburning stove. Tables outside maximise the glorious view, while the five spic and span bedrooms are highly sought after and share the same lovely outlook; good breakfasts too. Do visit the impressive village church and look for its early organ case (Britain's oldest), fine rood screen and ancient font.

Food is very well regarded with everything cooked fresh on the premises, and they're always happy to talk about the excellent local suppliers they use. Dishes include sandwiches, sticky sweet and sour pork belly pieces with Asian salad, goats cheese pannacotta with pickled beetroot and candied walnuts, king prawn tagliatelle in lemon, pea and courgette sauce, Hereford fillet steak with chips and garlic butter, falafel and beetroot tortilla wraps with pickled red cabbage, pan-roasted sea bass with a herb crust, sunblush tomatos and orzo pasta, and puddings such as summer berry and vanilla mascarpone cheesecake with vanilla ice-cream and pear and frangipane tart with apple sorbet. *Benchmark main dish: home-baked local ham with fried eggs and hand-cut chips £10.50. Two-course evening meal £21.00.*

Free house ~ Licensees Chris and Angela Ireland ~ Real ale ~ Open 6-11 Weds, Thurs; 12-3, 6-11 Fri, Sat; 12-3, 6-10.30 Sun; closed Mon except bank holidays, Tues ~ Bar food 6-9 Weds, Thurs; 12-2, 6-9 Fri, Sat; 12-2.30 Sun – opening and food hours may change, so do check ~ Restaurant ~ Children welcome ~ Dogs allowed in bar & bedrooms ~ Bedrooms: £130

OVERTON BRIDGE
Cross Foxes ♀ ◖

SJ3542 Map 6

(01978) 780380 – www.brunningandprice.co.uk/crossfoxes
A528 at River Dee 1.5 miles NW of Overton, near Erbistock; LL13 0DR

Terrific river views, contemporary food and an extensive range of drinks in bustling, well run pub

You can't beat the location of this expansive 18th-c coaching inn. It's set on a bend of the meandering, tree-fringed River Dee and next to a handsome stone bridge, with spectacular views from the terraces and grassy banks dipping down to the water. Grab a seat out here if you can. Inside, the ancient low-beamed bar has a red tiled floor, dark timbers, a log fire in a big inglenook and built-in old pews, and several dining areas are furnished with turkey rugs, large pot plants and frame-to-frame wall pictures. The airy dining conservatory also looks over the river. Helpful staff serve a fine array of drinks, including the likes of Brakspears Bitter, Jennings Cumberland, Marstons EPA and Ringwood Boondoggle on handpump, 16 wines by the glass, very impressive gin and malt whisky collections and a farm cider. Board games and newspapers too. There's a play tractor and swings in the garden to amuse the kids. This is beautiful Welsh Marches walking country.

The food meets the usual high Brunning & Price standard, with a separate gluten-free menu and plenty of options for vegans and vegetarians. Typical dishes are smoked salmon with orange and beetroot salad, hummus and pitta, garlic and chilli king prawn, pea and mint tortellini with garden pea velouté and asparagus, chicken, ham and leek pie with mash and buttered greens, spiced five bean chilli with tortilla chips, pork sausages with mash and red cabbage, 10oz rib-eye steak with mustard and peppercorn sauce and chunky chips, and puddings such as chocolate and honeycomb cheesecake with vanilla ice-cream and summer pudding. *Benchmark main dish: steak and ale pie with mash and gravy £14.95. Two-course evening meal £21.00.*

Brunning & Price ~ Manager Lynn Cunnah-Watson ~ Real ale ~ Open 11-11; 12-10.30 Sun ~ Bar food 12-9; 12-9.30 Fri, Sat ~ Children welcome ~ Dogs allowed in bar

PANTYGELLI
Crown ◉ ◖

SO3017 Map 6

(01873) 853314 – www.thecrownatpantygelli.com
Old Hereford Road N of Abergavenny; off A40 by war memorial via Pen Y Pound, passing leisure centre; Pantygelli also signposted from A465; NP7 7HR

Country pub in fine scenery, attractive inside and out, with good food and drinks

Step inside the dark flagstoned bar, with sturdy timber props and beams, a woodburner in a stone fireplace and a piano at the back and settle down to a pint of real ale on handpump from Bass, Rhymney and Wye Valley and a guest such as Tomos Watkin from the slate-roofed counter. Your thirst can be further quenched by several good wines by the glass and local organic apple juice and cider. The flower-filled terrace in front of this friendly, well run spot is ideal for clement days, with views from the lush valley to the hills, and there's also a smaller back terrace surrounded by lavender. Traditional it may be, but the four smallish, linked, carpeted dining rooms – the front pair separated by a massive stone chimneybreast – conspire with their thoughtfully chosen individual furnishings and lots of attractive prints by local artists to make for a thoroughly civilised ambience. Background music, darts and board games too.

🌟 The food is good and rewarding: tapas to share, king prawn, herring and smoked salmon salad, beef burger in a focaccia bun with home-made relish and chips, roasted vegetable risotto, steak and ale pie with chips, calzone pizza with prosciutto, mozzarella, roasted red peppers and capers, chicken madras curry with poppadum and naan, red Thai beef curry, and puddings such as rose crème brûlée and sticky toffee pudding with butterscotch sauce. *Benchmark main dish: sea bass poached in a paper parcel with kalamata olives, cherry tomatoes and aubergine £18.00. Two-course evening meal £22.00.*

Free house ~ Licensees Steve and Cherrie Chadwick ~ Real ale ~ Open 6-11 Mon; 12-2.30, 6-11 Tues-Fri; 12-3, 6-11 Sat; 12-3, 6-10.30 Sun ~ Bar food 12-2, 7-9; not Sun evening or Mon ~ Restaurant ~ Children welcome ~ Dogs allowed in bar

PENNAL
Riverside 🌟

SH6900   Map 6

(01654) 791285 – www.riversidehotel-pennal.co.uk

A493; opposite church; SY20 9DW

Carefully updated pub with tasty food and local beers, and efficient young staff; attractive guesthouse bedrooms

This pleasant inn (Glan yr Afon in Welsh) sits on the River Pennal just outside Machynlleth and just inside the southern boundary of Snowdonia National Park, so there are plenty of fine surrounding walks. Pleasing food is at the top of the agenda here, but there's a thoughtful range of drinks too, including real ales on handpump from Purple Moose, Salopian and Wye Valley, farm cider, a dozen wines by the glass and a huge array of malt whiskies and gins, served from a stone-fronted counter lined by high stools. The neatly furnished rooms have green and white walls, slate tiles on the floor, a woodburning stove, modern light wood dining furniture and some funky fabrics. There are seats and tables in the garden. Disabled access to restaurant (no disabled loos). They also run a charming Georgian guesthouse just down the road, with five comfortable bedrooms.

🌟 Enjoyable food includes lunchtime baguettes and sharing platters, Welsh rarebit, rollmop herring salad niçoise, spiced Mediterranean fish stew with chorizo, teriyaki salmon with noodle salad, 10oz Welsh sirloin steak with chips and peppercorn sauce, sea bass fillet with king prawns, samphire, sautéed potatoes and garlic and herb butter, and puddings such as crème brûlée and apple and blackberry crumble. *Benchmark main dish: steak burger with Welsh cheese, bacon, chilli relish and skinny fries £13.50. Two-course evening meal £21.00.*

Free house ~ Licensees Glyn and Corina Davies ~ Real ale ~ Open 3-11 Weds-Fri; 12-11 Sat; 12-10 Sun; closed Mon, Tues ~ Bar food 5-9 Weds-Fri; 12-2, 5-9 Sat; 12-3 Sun ~ Restaurant ~ Children welcome ~ Dogs allowed in bar & bedrooms ~ Bedrooms: £75

PONTYPRIDD
ST0790 Map 6

Bunch of Grapes 🏠 ☆ ♀ 🍺

(01443) 402934 – www.bunchofgrapes.org.uk

Off A4054; Ynysangharad Road; CF37 4DA

●●

Wales Dining Pub of the Year

Unpretentious, bustling gastropub with first class inventive food and fine drinks choice

Where to start with this highly praised 18th-c pub? Perhaps with the beers, where a seriously enviable list has been built up: Grey Trees Afghan Pale, North Riding Citra Pale, Oakham Citra, Salopian Dewdrops and Kashmir and Tenby Harbwr Pia Whanga on handpump, to name some of those regularly on offer. Also, five local craft keg beers, a couple of ciders and perries, 30 wines by the glass and over 20 small-batch gins, all served by knowledgable, friendly staff. The cosy bar has an informal, relaxed atmosphere, comfortable leather sofas, wooden chairs and tables, a roaring log fire, newspapers to read and background music. There's also a restaurant with elegant high-backed wooden dining chairs around a mix of tables and black and white local photo-prints taken by the landlord (an ex-professional photographer). A suntrap decked area has seats and tables. A new shop sells a good range of food, drink and household goods including fruit and veg boxes and their own-made bread. Disabled access.

🏵 The imaginative modern food is extremely good and very fairly priced. Dishes include sandwiches, pan-fried cockles, leeks, laverbread and pancetta on sourdough, smoked celeriac burger with sriracha and charcoal mayo, red cabbage slaw and chips, beer-braised short rib with roasted garlic and chive mash and lemon and ginger dressing, beetroot, mushroom, black bean and spinach pie, pan-fried hake with noodles, miso mushrooms and puy lentils, and puddings such as chocolate and avocado cake with plum compote and salted caramel and home-made ice-creams. *Benchmark main dish: confit duck leg with braised puy lentils, peas, spring onions, asparagus and sautéed new potatoes £13.00. Two-course evening meal £20.00.*

Free house ~ Licensee Nick Otley ~ Real ale ~ Open 11am-11.30pm; 11.45am-11pm Sun ~ Bar food 12-3, 6-9; 12-9 Fri, Sat; 12-3.30 Sun ~ Restaurant ~ Children welcome ~ Dogs allowed in bar

PUMSAINT
SN6540 Map 6

Dolaucothi Arms 🛏

(01558) 650237 – dolaucothiarms.co.uk

A482 Lampeter–Llandovery; SA19 8UW

Enjoyable inn with simply furnished bar and dining room, local beers and riverside garden; bedrooms

In the remote little village of Pumsaint, close to the Dolaucothi Roman Gold Mines, this whitewashed pub with its pretty garden is a welcome stop-off. Part of the Dolaucothi Estate and owned by the National Trust, it was once a drovers' inn and dates back to the 16th c. The chatty bar has comfortable armchairs and a sofa, red and black floor tiles and a welcoming woodburning stove. There are stone and glass bottles on the mantelpiece, local artwork on the walls and books of local and historic interest; darts and a children's corner with colouring books and board games; background music. The likes of Evan Evans, Gower, Purple Moose and Wye Valley are on handpump, along with several wines by the glass, local farm cider and a range of malt whiskies and gins. The terracotta-painted dining room has another woodburning stove, traditional local furniture that includes nice dining room chairs and tables on flagstones, and walls hung with local maps and old photos of the pub, village and Estate. The picnic tables in the neat garden overlook the Cothi River, where the pub has four miles of fishing rights. This is a warm and cosy place to stay, with three bedrooms (one is dog-friendly) complete with a half decanter of port and shortcake biscuits.

The food varies significantly between winter and summer. In winter, as well as sandwiches and jacket potatoes, dishes include beer-battered haddock and chips, red lentil, cannellini bean and vegetable cottage pie, scampi and chips, and assorted pizzas and burgers. In summer, they open a pop-up Mediterranean restaurant (called the Riviera); expect the likes of prosciutto crudo with melon, chicken liver, orange and Cointreau pâté, sea bass fillet in tomato, caper, anchovy and olive sauce, Spanish-style sirloin steak with chickpea, tomato, potato and kale casserole, and puddings such as Greek honey and almond cake. *Benchmark main dish: huevos rancheros £9.95. Two-course evening meal £19.00.*

Free house ~ Licensees Karen Charles and Clare Perry ~ Real ale ~ Open 4-11 Tues, Weds; 12-11 Thurs-Sat; 12-8 Sun; closed Mon ~ Bar food 5.30-8.30 Tues, Weds; 12.30-2.30, 5.30-8.30 Thurs-Sat; 12-2.30 Sun ~ Restaurant ~ Children welcome ~ Dogs allowed in bar ~ Bedrooms: £80

RAGLAN
Clytha Arms ★☆♀🍺🛏️

SO3609 Map 6

(01873) 840206 – www.clytha-arms.com

Clytha, off Abergavenny road – former A40, now declassified; 3 miles W of Raglan; NP7 9BW

Fine setting in spacious grounds, a relaxing spot for enjoying good food and impressive range of drinks; comfortable bedrooms

On the fringes of verdant Clytha Park – a serene location, now that the A40 bypasses to the north – stands this impressive country inn, becalmed amid its own beautiful, well cared-for grounds, with long heated verandahs and diamond-paned windows for customers to fully take in the garden views. Inside, there's a chatty, easy-going atmosphere and an interesting mix of customers. The bar and lounge are comfortable, light and airy, with nice old furniture, pine settles, window seats with big cushions, scrubbed wooden floors and open log fires; the contemporary restaurant is set with linen. A notable array of drinks includes regular Whoosh from Untapped a few miles down the road, plus four guests from the likes of Felinfoel Kingstone, Tenby Harbwr and Uley on handpump, an extensive wine list, lots of malt whiskies and various continental beers; they hold a cider and beer festival over the late May Bank Holiday weekend. You'll also find darts, bar skittles, boules, board games and a large-screen TV for rugby matches. There's pétanque and a play area in the garden. The three bedrooms (one with a four-poster bed) are comfortable and the Welsh breakfasts are good. The riverside path by the Usk is just a short stroll away.

Reliably high quality food includes, at the time of writing, pizzas on Wednesday night, a tapas menu (not Sunday) and various set menus, but this may change. Typical set menu dishes are leek and laverbread rissoles, chargrilled tuna salad niçoise, duck breast with beetroot, sage and garlic and rosemary potatoes, teriyaki chicken with sweetcorn fritters and avocado salad, lentil moussaka with Greek salad, venison and rabbit in red wine pie with mash or chips, smoked haddock with Y-Fenni cheese and champ potatoes, and puddings such as a daily changing cheesecake and blueberry and chocolate trifle. *Benchmark main dish: venison in rioja with paprika potatoes £12.00. Two-course evening meal £18.00.*

Free house ~ Licensees Andrew and Beverley Canning ~ Real ale ~ Open 12-3, 6-11;
12-11 Fri, Sat; 12-9 Sun; closed Mon lunchtime ~ Bar food 12.30-2.15, 7-9.30; 12.30-3.30 Sun
~ Restaurant ~ Children welcome ~ Dogs allowed in bar & bedrooms ~ Bedrooms: £90

ST GEORGE
Kinmel Arms 🟊 ♈ 🛏

SH9775   Map 6

(01745) 832207 – www.thekinmelarms.co.uk

Off A548 or B5381 SE of Abergele; 3 miles SE of Abergele; LL22 9BP

Bustling inn with a good choice of popular food, drinks and lovely position; bedrooms

This handsome 17th-c sandstone inn is usefully open to all from breakfast
through to dinner every day of the week (no food 11am-noon). It also
has four comfortable, contemporary bedroom suites, each with their own
decked area and evocative names such as Pebble and Driftwood, making it
a great base for exploring the delights of northern Snowdonia. The bar
has sofas on either side of a woodburning stove, a mix of traditional chairs
and tables on wooden flooring and seats against the counter where they keep
the likes of Brains Rev James, St Austell Tribute and Weetwood Cheshire
Cat on handpump, along with local regulars Conwy, Facers and Great Orme,
21 wines by the glass from a good list, 30 gins, 25 malt whiskies and farm
cider. The restaurant, with rattan chairs around marble-topped tables, has big
house plants and evening candles and twinkling lights; background music.
Afternoon tea is still served (not Sunday – book in advance) in the brilliant
tea room with its silver teapots and pretty bone-china cups. There are plenty
of picnic tables outside and the surrounding countryside is stunning, with
good walks right from the front door. Disabled access.

🟊 The very highly regarded food includes sandwiches, rabbit ravioli with black
pudding purée and ham velouté, stuffed figs wrapped in parma ham with
balsamic reduction, roast bone marrow with smoked sea salt toast, a pie of the day
with triple-cooked chips and gravy, burger with cured bacon, rarebit and fries, Menai
mussels in curry sauce, merlot of Welsh beef with wild mushroom, pancetta, green
beans and dauphinoise potatoes, pan-fried cod loin with asparagus and pea risotto, and
puddings. *Benchmark main dish: laverbread and leek risotto with goats cheese £13.95.
Two-course evening meal £25.00.*

Free house ~ Licensee Adam Williams ~ Real ale ~ Open 9am-11.30pm; 9am-10pm Sun ~
Bar food 9-11, 12-9 ~ Restaurant ~ Children welcome ~ Dogs allowed in bar ~ Bedrooms:
£175

STACKPOLE
Stackpole Inn 🟊 🛏

SR9896   Map 6

(01646) 672324 – www.stackpoleinn.co.uk

Village signed off B4319 S of Pembroke; SA71 5DF

Busy pub, a good base for the area, with enjoyable food and friendly service; comfortable bedrooms

If you're walking along this stunning stretch of the Pembrokeshire Coast
Path or visiting the nearby Bosherston Lily Ponds (at their best in June),
this inn is the perfect place to stop for refreshment – or you could take
advantage of its four spotless, comfortable bedrooms in order to explore
more of the hidden-away countryside hereabouts. The cottagey, ivy-clad
exterior fronted by a pretty garden dotted with picnic tables belies the
surprisingly modern interior, with ash beams, low ceilings and an appealing
mix of wooden and leather dining chairs and farmhouse tables. Brains Rev

James and Felinfoel Double Dragon are the regular fixtures on handpump, alongside local guests from the likes of Mumbles, Purple Moose, Tenby Harbwr and Tenby Brewing Co, at least nine wines by the glass from a good list and a decent malt whisky selection. Most of the interior space is given over to the dining – the food is well regarded.

The rewarding food showcases local produce while mixing innovation with tradition. Dishes include lunchtime ploughman's and filled rolls, Moroccan hummus dip with spiced nuts, seeds and flatbread, Welsh beef carpaccio with pistachio and port reduction, pan-fried fillet of hake, salmon or monkfish tail with crushed new potatoes, tenderstem broccoli and lemon sauce, tofu and vegetable katsu curry, beer-battered cod and chips, tagliatelle with Welsh beef and red wine ragoût, and puddings such as vanilla pannacotta with meringue and strawberries and a choice of Welsh cheeses. *Benchmark main dish: Welsh lamb cawl with Welsh cheddar and bread £11.00. Two-course evening meal £22.00.*

Free house ~ Licensees Gary and Becky Evans ~ Real ale ~ Open 12-11 (12-3, 6-11; 12-4 Sun in winter) ~ Bar food 12-8; 12-2.30, 6-9 Sun (12-2.15, 6.30-9; 12-2.30 Sun in winter) ~ Restaurant ~ Children welcome ~ Dogs allowed in bar ~ Bedrooms: £120

USK   SO3700   Map 6

Nags Head £

(01291) 672820 – www.nagsheadusk.co.uk

The Square; NP15 1BH

Traditional town-centre pub with a hearty welcome, good food and drinks

For more than 50 years, the genuinely welcoming Key family have looked after this venerable coaching inn, located in the heart of this picturesque market town opposite the clocktower. The traditional, cosy main bar has well polished tables and chairs packed under its beams (some of these have farming tools, lanterns or horsebrasses and harness attached), as well as leatherette wall benches and various sets of sporting prints and local pictures (look out for the original deeds to the pub), while tucked away at the front is an intimate little corner and, on the other side of the room, a passageway leading to a dining area. There's Brains Rev James and Sharps Doom Bar on handpump and 17 wines by the glass, served by hospitable staff. The seats outside at the front beneath the fantastic hanging baskets are an excellent spot for watching Usk town life pass by. The nearby church is well worth a look. The pub has no parking and note that nearby street parking can be limited. Disabled access.

Honest food at good prices using local meat and game in season includes grilled sardines, country pâté, home-made rabbit or steak pie, chicken in red wine with tomatoes, mushrooms and onions, faggots with mushy peas and onion gravy, breaded plaice, vegetarian and vegan options including leek and cheese sausages and chickpea and cauliflower curry, and specials such as poached Scottish salmon and guinea fowl in wine and fig sauce, plus puddings. *Benchmark main dish: rabbit pie £10.85. Two-course evening meal £19.00.*

Free house ~ Licensee Key family ~ Real ale ~ Open 10-3, 5.30-11; 10.30-2.30, 5.30-11 Sat; 10.30-2.30, 6-10 Sun ~ Bar food 11.30-2, 5.30-9 ~ Restaurant ~ Children welcome ~ Dogs allowed in bar

We checked prices with the pubs as we went to press in summer 2020. They should hold until around spring 2021.

Also Worth a Visit in Wales

Besides the fully inspected pubs, you might like to try these pubs that have been recommended to us and described by readers. Do tell us what you think of them: feedback@goodguides.com

ANGLESEY

ABERFFRAW   SH3568
Crown (01407) 840222
Bodorgan Square; LL63 5BX
Whitewashed village-square pub with at least two well kept changing ales from local breweries such as Conwy, Mona and Purple Moose, 40-odd gins and enjoyable home-made food including daily specials, quick friendly service; sports TV, quiz nights; well behaved children and dogs welcome, suntrap terraced beer garden behind with views towards the dunes, open 3-7pm Mon, Tue, all day Wed-Sun, food all day Sat (winter hours may vary).

MENAI BRIDGE   SH5773
Gazelle (01248) 713364
Glyngarth; A545, halfway towards Beaumaris; LL59 5PD Hotel and restaurant rather than pub in outstanding waterside position looking across to Snowdonia; main bar with smaller rooms off, up to three Robinsons ales kept well and good choice of wines and gins, enjoyable pubby food including sandwiches, baked potatoes, home-made pies and seafood; children and dogs (in bar) welcome, steep garden behind (and walk down from car park), eight bedrooms and three dog-friendly rooms in separate Menai Strait-facing annexe, slipway and mooring for visiting boats, closed Sun.

MENAI BRIDGE   SH5572
Liverpool Arms (01248) 712453
St Georges Road/Water Street; LL59 5EY Cosy nautical-themed boozer close to the quay and not far from the famous suspension bridge; four real ales including regulars Bass and Greene King Abbot, enjoyable home-made food with daily specials and Mon steak night, quick friendly service; quiz Weds and Sun; children welcome, part-covered terrace, open (and food) all day Fri-Sun.

MOELFRE   SH5186
Kinmel Arms (01248) 410231
Moelfre Bay; LL72 8HH Popular sea-view pub with nautical-theme interior, five Robinsons ales and ample helpings of enjoyable traditional food including sandwiches and jacket potatoes, friendly service; children and dogs welcome, picnic-sets on paved front terrace, open all day.

PENTRAETH   SH5278
Panton Arms (01248) 450959
Junction of A5025 and B5109; LL75 8AZ
Welcoming 18th-c roadside pub with spacious cleanly presented interior; enjoyable good value food (great pizzas) and three well kept ales including Purple Moose Glaslyn year-round; children and dogs (in bar) welcome, spacious back garden with play area, open all day in summer, food all day weekends.

RED WHARF BAY   SH5281
Ship (01248) 852568
Village signed off A5025 N of Pentraeth; LL75 8RJ Delightful whitewashed 18th-c pub right on Anglesey's east coast – fantastic views of miles of tidal sands; big old-fashioned rooms, nautical bric-a-brac, long varnished wall pews, cast-iron-framed tables and open fires, three well kept ales, 50 malt whiskies and decent choice of wines, enjoyable food including Conwy ale-battered haddock and chips and seafood chowder (may ask for a card if you run a tab); background music; children welcome in room on left, dogs in bar, limited disabled access, numerous outside tables, open (and food) all day.

RHOSCOLYN   SH2675
★ White Eagle (01407) 860267
Off B4545 S of Holyhead; LL65 2NJ Remote place rebuilt almost from scratch on site of an old pub; airy modern feel in neatly kept rooms, relaxed atmosphere and nice winter fire, Conwy, Weetwood and guests from smart oak counter, several wines by the glass, extensive choice of interesting locally sourced food including Menai Strait oysters and mussels, friendly helpful service, restaurant; children welcome, dogs in bar, terrific sea views from decking and garden, lane down to beach, open (and food) all day.

RHOSNEIGR   SH3272
Oystercatcher (01407) 812829
Just off A4080; LL64 5JP Modern glass-fronted Huf Haus building ensconced in dunes close to the sea, not really a pub (created as a restaurant/chefs' academy); sublime views from upstairs restaurant and bar with wide range of much enjoyed innovative food, well kept ales from breweries such as Conwy, Great Orme and Weetwood, decent choice of wines by the glass, good gins and rums, ground-floor coffee/wine bar serving lighter meals; children, walkers and dogs welcome, upper terrace with rattan sofas and colourful beach huts, full wheelchair access, open all day.

CARDIFF

CARDIFF ST1876
Cambrian Tap (029) 2064 4952
St Mary Street/Caroline Street; CF10 1AD
City-centre corner pub popular for its extensive range of Brains beers plus guests, 18 handpumps in total, several more bottled beers, friendly knowledgeable staff, nice home-made pies; open mike and comedy nights; dogs welcome, open all day.

CARDIFF ST1876
City Arms (029) 2064 1913
Quay Street; CF10 1EA City-centre alehouse decorated with pump clips from across the globe; Brains ales and several guests from Wales and beyond (some tapped from the cask), tasting trays available, also plenty of draught/bottled continentals and real cider, friendly knowledgeable staff, no food; some live music, darts; open all day (till 2am Fri and Sat), very busy on rugby match days.

CARDIFF ST1776
Cricketers (029) 2034 5102
Cathedral Road opposite Plasturton Place; CF11 9LL Victorian townhouse in quiet residential area backing on to Glamorgan CC; well kept Evan Evans ales and enjoyable freshly made food; jazz supper club Thurs; children welcome, sunny back garden, open (and food) all day, no food Sun evening.

COWBRIDGE SS9974
★ **Bear** (01446) 774814
High Street, with car park behind off North Street; signed off A48; CF71 7AF
Originally 12th-c but mainly Georgian coaching house in smart village; well kept ales, decent house wines and enjoyable food from sandwiches/wraps up, weekday set lunch, friendly helpful service; three attractively furnished bars with flagstones, bare boards or carpet, some stripped stone and panelling, big open fires, barrel-vaulted cellar restaurant; children and dogs (in one bar and some bedrooms) welcome, courtyard tables, disabled parking, open all day.

GWAELOD-Y-GARTH ST1183
Gwaelod y Garth Inn
(029) 2081 0408 *Main Road; CF15 9HH*
Meaning 'foot of the mountain', this stone-built village pub has wonderful valley views and is popular with walkers on the Taff Ely Ridgeway Path; upmarket well presented Welsh food (all day except Sun evening), friendly efficient service, own-brew beer along with Wye Valley and others from pine-clad bar, log fires, upstairs restaurant (disabled access from back car park); some live music Fri and Sat; table skittles, pool, juke box; children and dogs welcome, three bedrooms, open all day.

LLANBLETHIAN SS9873
Cross (01446) 772995
Off B4270; Church Road; CF71 7JF
Welcoming family-run former staging inn; freshly made hearty food from pubby choices up in bar or airy split-level restaurant, Brains, Wye Valley and guests, good choice of wines, woodburner and open fire; children welcome, dogs in bar, tables out on decking, open all day Weds-Sun (till 7pm Sun), closed Mon, Tue.

LLANCARFAN ST0570
Fox & Hounds (01446) 781287
Signed off A4226; can also be reached from A48 from Bonvilston or B4265 via Llancadle; CF62 3AD Comfortably modernised village pub in charming streamside setting by interesting church with medieval wall paintings; cosy chatty bar with woodburner, Glamorgan and Wye Valley ales and 19 wines by the glass from stone-faced counter, excellent modern food including some pub favourites and vegetarian choices, friendly accommodating staff; children and dogs (in bar) welcome, tables on covered terrace, clean comfortable bedrooms and good breakfast, handy for Cardiff Airport, open all day (from 3pm Mon-Thurs), food all day weekends.

PENARTH ST1771
Pilot (029) 2071 0615
Queens Road; CF64 1DJ End-of-terrace pub set high in residential area overlooking Cardiff Bay; good food including pub favourites and plenty of seafood from blackboard menu, well kept quickly changing ales, friendly welcoming staff; frequent live music, summer beer/cider festival; children and dogs allowed, tables out in narrow front area, open (and food) all day.

PENTYRCH ST1081
Kings Arms (029) 2089 0202
Church Road; CF15 9QF Ancient longhouse encompassing cosy bar with log fire in sizeable brick fireplace, beams and other 17th- or 18th-c features; Brains ales, guest beers and 14 wines by the glass, good food cooked by chef-owner including blackboard specials, comfortable lounge and restaurant; quiz nights, sports TV; children and dogs welcome, plenty of seats on terrace and lawn, summer barbecues, open all day, closed Mon lunchtime.

NEWPORT ST3188
Olde Murenger House
(01633) 263977 *High Street; NP20 1GA*
Fine 16th-c black and white timbered building; carefully restored split-level interior with ancient dark woodwork, leaded windows and traditional furniture on bare boards or carpet, Sam Smiths ales and enjoyable straightforward home-made food; open all day.

ST FAGANS   ST1277
Plymouth Arms (029) 2056 9173
Crofft-y-genau Road; CF5 6DU Stately
Victorian pub, now a rambling Vintage Inn
with log fires, panelling and local prints
in bustling linked areas, enjoyable food
including set menus, Sharps Doom Bar plus
local guests and decent wines by the glass;
lots of tables on extensive back lawn, handy
for National Museum of History, open (and
food) all day.

ST HILARY   ST0173
Bush (01446) 776888
*S off A48 E of Cowbridge, by church;
CF71 7DP* Cosily restored 16th-c thatched
and beamed stone pub; flagstoned main bar
with inglenook, bare-boards lounge and snug,
nice mix of old furniture, leather armchairs
and sofas around open fire; Bass, Greene
King Abbot, Hancocks HB and a guest,
Thatcher's cider and good wines by the glass,
enjoyable food including pizzas, burgers and
pies, friendly service; quiz nights and other
events; children and dogs (in bar) welcome,
some picnic-sets out at front, garden behind,
open all day.

TAFFS WELL   ST1283
Fagins (029) 2081 1800
Cardiff Road, Glan-y-Llyn; CF15 7QD
Terrace-row pub with interesting range
of cask-tapped ales, friendly olde-worlde
atmosphere, benches, pine tables and
other pubby furniture on flagstones, faux
black beams, woodburner, good value
straightforward food from lunchtime
baguettes up, restaurant; live music, sports
TV; children and dogs welcome, open all day
from 2pm (3pm Mon, noon Sat).

CARMARTHENSHIRE

ABERGORLECH   SN5833
Black Lion (01558) 685271
B4310; SA32 7SN Atmospheric 16th-c pub
in fine rural position; traditional stripped-
stone and black-beamed bar, pubby furniture
on old flagstones, woodburner, a couple
of local ales and good home-made food
including daily specials, dining extension/
coffee shop with farmhouse kitchen chairs
around mix of tables on bare boards,
local paintings and another woodburner;
background music; children and dogs (in
bar) welcome, delightful views of Cothi Valley
from riverside garden, nearby hiking and
mountain biking in Brechfa Forest, closed
Mon, otherwise open all day, no food Sun
evening.

BRECHFA   SN5230
Forest Arms (01267) 202288
Opposite church (B4310); SA32 7RA
Smart stone-built village inn; local beers and
enjoyable reasonably priced food including

daily specials and good vegetarian/vegan
options, friendly helpful staff, two beamed
bars, one with big inglenook and angling
theme (pub can arrange fishing on River
Cothi), the other in two sections, note Bob
the stuffed raven, also dining/function room
with pitched ceiling, chairs from St David's
cathedral and another log fire, former
patrons include Dylan Thomas; children and
dogs welcome, picnic-sets in back garden,
good walks and mountain bike trails, three
comfortable linked bedrooms (so not suited
to all), open (and food) all day weekends,
closed Mon.

CILYCWM   SN7540
Neuadd Fawr Arms (01550) 721644
*By church; 3 miles N of Llandovery;
SA20 0ST* Nicely placed 18th-c drovers' inn
among lanes to Llyn Brianne above River
Gwenlais; eclectic mix of old furniture on
huge slate flagstones, woodburners, good
seasonal food including Indian dishes and
own-reared lamb, bar and smaller dining
room (also afternoon and high tea Mar-Sept,
must book), one or two changing ales,
friendly helpful service; children and dogs
welcome, usually open all day Fri-Sun, closed
Mon-Thurs lunchtimes.

LLANDDAROG   SN5016
★Butchers Arms (01267) 275330
*On back road by church just off B4310;
SA32 8NS* Ancient whitewashed black-
beamed local with three intimate eating
areas off small central bar, popular food
including home-made pies, Felinfoel ales
tapped from the cask and nice wines by the
glass, conventional pub furniture, gleaming
brassware and open woodburner in biggish
fireplace; background music; children
welcome, tables outside and pretty window
boxes, closed Sun, Mon.

LLANDDAROG   SN5016
White Hart (01267) 275395
*Off A48 E of Carmarthen, via B4310;
SA32 8NT* 600-year-old thatched pub
brewing own Cole craft beers and ciders
using water from 90-metre borehole (brewery
tours available); comfortable lived-in beamed
rooms with lots of engaging bric-a-brac and
antiques including 17th-c carved settles
by huge log fire, interestingly furnished
high-raftered dining room with open kitchen,
generous if not cheap food, home-made jams
and chutneys for sale; background music;
children welcome, no dogs inside, disabled
access (ramps provided), picnic-sets on front
terrace and in back garden with play area,
closed Weds.

LLANDEILO   SN6226
Angel (01558) 822765
Rhosmaen Street; SA19 6EN Town-
centre local painted a distinctive eggshell
blue; comfortably furnished front bar with
four changing ales such as Evan Evans

from central counter, step up to popular back restaurant serving very good food at reasonable prices including a 'Llanpielo' pie of the day, friendly helpful staff; children welcome, walled beer garden behind, closed Sun evening.

LLANDOVERY · SN7634
Castle · (01550) 720343

Kings Road; SA20 0AP Popular hotel next to castle ruins; beams and antique furnishings, good attractively presented food from sandwiches to charcoal grills and daily fresh fish, afternoon teas, courteous efficient service, ales from Brains, Gower and Tenby Harbour; children and dogs welcome, picnic-sets on front terrace under parasols, 19 comfortable bedrooms, open (and food) all day (till 6pm Sun).

LLANDOVERY · SN7634
Kings Head · (01550) 720393

Market Square; SA20 0AB Early 18th-c beamed coaching inn; bar with patterned carpet, exposed stonework and large woodburner, well kept Gower Gold and Sharps Doom Bar plus a local guest from maybe Brecon or Glamorgan Brewing, enjoyable food from snacks and bar meals up, friendly service; children and dogs welcome, nine bedrooms (one on ground floor for disabled guests), open all day.

RHANDIRMWYN · SN7843
Royal Oak · (01550) 760201

7 miles N of Llandovery towards Llyn Brianne reservoir; SA20 0NY Friendly 17th-c stone-built hunting lodge set in remote, peaceful walking country; comfortable traditional bar with log fire, three well kept local ales, ciders and perries, good variety of popular sensibly priced food sourced locally, including wood-fired pizzas; children and dogs (in bar) welcome, hill views from pretty garden and four cottagey bedrooms, attached village shop, handy for Cambrian Mountains and Brecon Beacons, open all day, closed Sun evening and Mon lunchtime.

CEREDIGON

ABERAERON · SN4562
Cadwgan · (01545) 570149

Market Street; SA46 0AU Small late 18th-c pub opposite the harbour and named after the Norman castle that once stood in the town; exterior is painted mauve and lilac, interior is fairly basic with friendly regulars, well kept Hancocks HB and a couple of local guests such as Bluestone, nautical memorabilia and interesting old photographs, open fire, no food; sports TV; children and dogs welcome, pavement seats and little garden behind, closed Sun evening, Mon lunchtime.

ABERAERON · SN4562
★Harbourmaster · (01545) 570755

Quay Parade; SA46 0BT Charming small blue-painted hotel with long-established owners in prime spot by yacht-filled harbour; cheerful bar with brown leather wall banquettes, assorted tables and chairs on bare boards, and stools by zinc-topped counter serving ales such as Mantle and Purple Moose, local cider, 20 good wines by the glass, cocktails and several malt whiskies, also a dining room with blue leather chairs, sea-blue walls and seaside-inspired art, first class food including local fish/seafood, friendly efficient staff; children welcome, disabled access, 13 comfortable bedrooms in main building, warehouse and cottage (most overlook the harbour), good breakfast, open all day from 8am.

ABERYSTWYTH · SN6777
Halfway Inn · (01970) 880631

Pisgah – A4120 right out towards Devils Bridge; SY23 4NE Sweeping views from this beguiling whitewashed roadside country pub; beams and stripped stone, scrubbed tables, settles and wheelback chairs on flagstones, open fire and woodburner, Montys beers and enjoyable good value home-cooked food, friendly helpful service; games part with pool, darts and sports TV; children welcome (inside play area), dogs in bar, picnic-sets outside taking in the view, closed Mon, otherwise open (and food) all day.

BORTH · SN6089
Victoria · (01970) 871417

High Street (B4353); SY24 5HZ Stone-built pub backing on to the beach; popular reasonably priced food and well kept ales from Glamorgan, Sharps and Wye Valley, good friendly service, more space upstairs and sea-view balcony; sports TV; children and dogs (in bar) welcome, tables on back deck with superb coastal views and steps down to the shingle, open all day.

LAMPETER · SN5748
Black Lion · (01570) 422172

High Street; SA48 7BG Carefully refurbished 18th-c coaching inn, friendly and relaxed, with enjoyable pub food at reasonable prices, well kept ales from maybe Brecon Brewing and Grey Trees and decent wines by the glass; children welcome, dogs in bar and some of the comfortable bedrooms, hearty breakfast, open all day.

LLANGRANNOG · SN3154
Pentre Arms · (01239) 654345

On the front; SA44 6SP Friendly old seafront pub beautifully placed in this charming coastal village – magnificent sunset sea views from bar's picture window; three well kept ales such as Gales Seafarers and St Austell Tribute and good malt whisky selection, fairly standard food including steaks and often fresh fish, separate restaurant, pool room with TV and games machines; regular live music; children and dogs (in bar) welcome, seven bedrooms (some directly overlooking the small bay), staff will advise on dolphin-watching, handy for coast path, open all day.

LLANGRANNOG
SN3154

Ship (01239) 654510

Near the front, by pay & display car park entrance; SA44 6SL Just back from the bay with tables out by beachside car park; enjoyable food including lots of local fish/seafood and Thurs steak night, friendly helpful staff, well kept ales including regular Mantle and good selection of gins, bare-boards bar with big woodburner, further spacious upstairs eating area, games room; open mike evenings and other live music; children and dogs welcome, open all day and can get very busy in summer.

PENRHIWLLAN
SN3641

Daffodil (01559) 370343

A475 Newcastle Emlyn–Lampeter; SA44 5NG Contemporary open-plan dining pub with comfortable welcoming bar; sofas and leather tub chairs on pale limestone floor, woodburner, Hancocks HB and a local guest (maybe Glamorgan) from granite-panelled counter, two lower-ceilinged end rooms with big oriental rugs, steps down to a couple of airy dining rooms, open kitchen serving particularly good food (fish dishes and puddings a highlight); background music; children and dogs (in bar) welcome, nice decked area outside with valley views – best to check opening hours.

GWYNEDD & CONWY

ABERDARON
SH1726

Ty Newydd Hotel (01758) 760207

B4413, by the sea; LL53 8BE Smart seaside hotel with views over sandy Aberdaron Beach and Cardigan Bay; good choice of enjoyable food from bar snacks to Sun carvery, interesting local ales such as Cwrw Llŷn and Purple Moose, friendly helpful staff; panoramic terrace within feet of the waves, 11 bedrooms, traditional Welsh breakfast, open all day.

ABERDOVEY
SN6196

Penhelig Arms (01654) 767215

Penhelig station; LL35 0LT Harbourside location for this popular 18th-c hotel (formerly fishermen's cottages); traditional bar with warm fire in central stone fireplace, Brains ales, good choice of wines and malt whiskies, enjoyable reasonably priced traditional food, friendly service; children welcome, dogs allowed in bar and comfortable bedrooms (some have balconies overlooking estuary, ones nearest the road can be noisy), open (and food) all day.

BARMOUTH
SH6115

Myrddins (01341) 388060

Church Street; LL42 1EH Continental-style micropub-café with impressive selection of 40 craft beers including their own and many Welsh beers, both tapped from the cask and in bottles, generous helpings of enjoyable reasonably priced home-cooked food catering for vegetarian and gluten-free diets; children and dogs welcome, a couple of pavement tables, shuts at 8.30pm, closed Weds lunchtime – for sale as we went to press.

BETWS-Y-COED
SH7955

★ **Ty Gwyn** (01690) 710383

A5 just S of bridge to village; LL24 0SG Family-run former coaching inn with vibrant window boxes and red shutters; restaurant-with-rooms rather than pub (you must eat or stay overnight to be served drinks), but pubby feel in character beamed lounge bar with ancient cooking range, easy chairs, antiques, old prints and bric-a-brac, highly regarded interesting food using local produce including own fruit and veg, some themed nights, well kept ales, friendly professional service; background music; children welcome, plush bedrooms (some with four-poster beds and spa baths), holiday cottage, open all day.

BLAENAU FFESTINIOG
SH7041

Pengwern (01766) 762200

Church Square; LL41 4PB Unpretentious community-owned pub; changing ales from likes of local Conwy and Purple Moose in panelled bar, dining area serving good value food (not Sun evening), friendly local atmosphere; games room, live music; dogs welcome, fine views from back garden, seven bedrooms, open all day weekends, from 6pm Mon-Thurs, 5pm Fri.

CAERNARFON
SH4762

Bar Bach (01286) 673111

Greengate Street, near the castle; LL55 2NF Tiny bar, purportedly Wales's smallest, opposite Caernarfon Castle; simple furnishings, exposed stonework and small fire, three changing beers such as Hancocks and local Wild Horse, decent lunchtime food; sports TV; dogs welcome, open all day from 9am till 1.30am.

CAERNARFON
SH4762

★ **Black Boy** (01286) 673604

Northgate Street; LL55 1RW Busy traditional 16th-c inn with cosy beamed lounge bar, sumptuously furnished and packed with tables, additional dining room across corridor and dimly lit atmospheric public bar, exposed stonework and wall murals, mainly Welsh beers from likes of Cwrw Llŷn, Purple Moose and Tiny Rebel, nine wines by the glass and extensive selection of whiskies and gins, good generous food from sandwiches up including lunchtime set deal, efficient friendly service and lots of Welsh chat; background music, TV, disabled access (ramps) and loos, tables out on pedestrianised street, history-rich bedrooms (some in different buildings), open (and food) all day.

CAPEL CURIG SH7257
Bryn Tyrch (01690) 720338
A5, just SE of village; LL24 OEL
Family-owned roadside inn perfectly placed for mountains of Snowdonia; bistro-bar with open fire and amazing picture-windows views, Conwy Clogwyn Gold and Welsh Pride plus a guest, quite a few malt whiskies, comprehensive choice of good well presented food (not Mon lunchtime), second bar with big menu boards, leather sofas and mix of tables on bare boards; children, walkers and dogs welcome, steep little side garden, more seats on terrace and across road on expansive grassed area by River Llugwy, bright bedrooms, open all day in summer.

CAPEL CURIG SH7357
Tyn-y-Coed (01690) 720331
A5, 1 mile SE of village; LL24 OEE
Bustling family-owned B&B rather than pub across from River Llugwy in a stunning location below Moel Siabod, great surrounding walks and wild swimming; enjoyable home-made food using local produce, well kept Purple Moose and two guests, 50 whiskies and 30 gins, pleasant quick service, beams and log fires, pool room; children and dogs welcome, small garden either side, restored stagecoach over the road by car park, comfortable bedrooms, cycle storage and drying room, open all day Fri-Sun.

COLWYN BAY SH8579
Toad (01492) 532726
West Promenade; junction with Sea Bank Road; LL28 4BU Popular seafront pub overlooking the prom and beach; hearty choice of traditional food including fixed-price menu, pie night Weds, good wine list and real ales such as Jennings, friendly efficient service; children welcome, tables on front terrace beer garden, open (including food) all day.

CONWY SH7777
Albion Ale House (01492) 582484
Uppergate Street; LL32 8RF Unique collaboration between four Welsh breweries – Conwy, Great Orme, Nant and Purple Moose – who own and run this well preserved 1920s pub with its original back bar; their beers plus guests (tasting trays available) and good wine list, friendly staff, snacky food such as pies, three linked rooms with plenty of 1920s furnishings including stained glass and huge baronial fireplace, back part with serving hatch is quieter; dogs welcome, open all day.

DINAS MAWDDWY SH8514
★Red Lion (01650) 531247
Just off A470, opposite car park and public toilets; SY20 9JA Popular whitewashed tavern that's a great hit with hikers; two small traditional front bars including one with a blazing open fire, and more modern back extension with large terrace and picnic tables, great range of local ales from likes of Purple Moose, decent hearty food including much loved pies and Sunday carvery, friendly knowledgeable efficient service; children welcome, six simple bedrooms (four ensuite); pub named in Welsh (Llew Coch), perfectly located for exploring southern Snowdonia, open all day.

LLANBERIS SH6655
★Pen-y-Gwryd (01286) 870211
Nant Gwynant; at junction of A498 and A4086, ie across mountains from Llanberis – OS Sheet 115 map reference 660558; LL55 4NT Iconic mountaineers' inn (the 1953 Everest team used it as a training base) in fantastic mountain setting with marvellous views – a much loved Snowdonia institution; ivy-festooned farmhouse dating from 1810 and run by the same family since 1947, homely slate-floored log cabin bar with built-in wall benches and sturdy country chairs, plus a smaller room and a cosy panelled smoke room, fascinating climbing equipment and memorabilia throughout, Purple Moose ales and several malt whiskies; darts, pool, board games, bar billiards, table tennis and the hotel also has its own chapel, sauna and outdoor natural pool; children and dogs welcome, 18 comfortable bedrooms (some quite basic and not ensuite) with excellent traditional breakfast and communal dinner – at press time, open only for hotel guests, so call to check before visiting.

LLANDUDNO SH7882
Cottage Loaf (01492) 870762
Market Street; LL30 2SR Popular ex-bakery with three linked rooms including glass-roofed dining room; beams and bare stone walls, pleasing mix of traditional and modern décor, rugs on pale flagstones or bare boards; long wooden benches and tables, woodburners, decent home-made food from sandwiches to varied mains, Conwy Welsh Pride and local guest ales such as Great Orme, Nant and Purple Moose, good wine list, friendly service; teak furniture on front and back terraces, children welcome, open (and food) all day.

LLANFROTHEN SH6141
Brondanw Arms (01766) 770555
A4085 just N of B4410; LL48 6AQ Welsh-speaking village pub at end of short whitewashed terrace; main bar with exposed stone walls, slate floor and woodburning stove in large fireplace, pews and window

benches, old farm tools on the ceiling, snug with panelled booths and potbelly stove, long spacious dining room behind with contrasting red walls, good home-cooked food including carvery (Weds evening, Sun lunchtime), Robinsons ales and decent range of wines by the glass, friendly helpful staff; children and dogs welcome, wheelchair access (two long shallow steps at front), Snowdonia National Park views from garden with play area, camping and good nearby walks, handy for Plas Brondanw Gardens and not far from Portmeirion, closed Mon and lunchtime Tues.

LLANUWCHLLYN   SH8730
Eagles (01678) 540278
*B4403, just S of junction with A494;
LL23 7UB* Family-run and welcoming
stone-built pub with excellent reasonably
priced food using own farm produce, ales
such as Purple Moose; opened-up slate-floor
bar with log fire, beams and stripped stone,
back picture-window view of mountains
with Lake Bala in distance; sports TV;
children welcome, metal tables and chairs on
flower-filled back terrace, small shop (from
7.30am), caravan and camping park, usually
open all day.

MAENTWROG   SH6640
★**Grapes** (01766) 590365
*A496, just S of junction with A487;
LL41 4HN* Handsome 17th-c coaching inn;
lounge and main bar to the right serving
three real ales including Cwrw Llŷn and
Purple Moose, good choice of enjoyable
fairly priced pubby food, friendly helpful
staff, restaurant on the left and another
dining room behind with balcony overlooking
church, steps down to neat walled garden;
sports TV and pool in separate games room;
children welcome, picnic-sets on lawn,
play area, eight bedrooms (two in separate
cottages), Ffestiniog steam railway nearby,
open (and food) all day.

PENMAENPOOL   SH6918
George III (01341) 422525
*Just off A493 2 miles W of Dolgellau;
LL40 1YD* Inn dating from 1650 attractively
refurbished in 2019; lovely views over
Mawddach estuary from partly panelled
upstairs bar opening into cosy inglenook
lounge, beamed and flagstoned downstairs
bar, Robinsons ales, over 15 wines by the
glass and some interesting gins, good food
from varied menu till 5pm, friendly helpful
young staff, restaurant; children and dogs
welcome, sheltered terrace, ten bedrooms
(some in converted station – line now a
walkway), good walks nearby, open (and
food) all day.

PORTH DINLLAEN   SH2741
★**Ty Coch** (01758) 720498
*Beach car park signed from Morfa
Nefyn, then 15-minute walk; LL53 6DB*
Hugely popular former 19th-c vicarage in
idyllic location right on the beach with
wonderful views, far from roads and only
reachable on foot; bar crammed with nautical
and other memorabilia, simple furnishings,
coal fire, real ales including Purple Moose
and a craft beer (served in plastic as worried
about glass on the beach), simple lunchtime
bar menu, friendly service; children and
dogs welcome, open all day in season, check
opening hours in winter.

PORTHMADOG   SH5639
Australia (01766) 515957
High Street; LL49 9LR Purple Moose
brewery tap with their ales and some guests,
decent wines by the glass and tasty pub
food (not Mon, Tues), chunky contemporary
wooden furniture, beer barrel tables and
banquettes on bare boards; occasional quiz
and live music nights; children welcome,
seats outside, open all day.

PWLLHELI   SH3735
Whitehall (01758) 614091
Stryd Moch, at Lleyn Street; LL53 5RG
Whitewashed family-run pub-bistro in centre
of this Llŷn Peninsula market town; local ales
such as Cwrw Llŷn and good choice of wines,
popular freshly made food from lunchtime
ciabattas up, friendly staff, spiral stairs to
upstairs dining room; TV in bar; children
welcome, open all day (till late Fri, Sat).

RHYD DDU   SH5652
Cwellyn Arms (01766) 890321
A4085, at B4418; LL54 6TL Welcoming
18th-c village pub (same owners for over 30
years) not far below Welsh Highland Railway
top terminus; several real ales such as
Conwy and good choice of popular seasonal
food from home-baked rolls to blackboard
specials, friendly helpful staff, two cosy bars
with log fires, restaurant with woodburner;
children, walkers and dogs welcome,
spectacular Snowdon views from garden
tables and masses of hiking possibilities,
babbling stream just over wall, bedrooms
in pub plus self-catering farmhouses,
bunkhouses and campsite by Cwellyn Lake,
open all day.

ROWEN   SH7571
Ty Gwyn (01492) 650232
*1 mile W of B5106; S of Conwy;
LL32 8YU* Traditional 18th-c whitewashed
stone pub in charming village; well kept Lees
ales and enjoyable generously served food

A star before the name of a pub shows exceptional atmosphere or quality.
It means most people would think a special trip worthwhile.

including good Sun roasts, friendly service; children and dogs (in bar) welcome, picnic-sets out at front and in two pretty gardens (one with stream), good walking country, open all day weekends.

TREFRIW   SH7863
Old Ship (01492) 640013
B5106; LL27 0JH Well run old pub with nice staff and cheerful local atmosphere; much enjoyed locally sourced food from interesting menu, well kept local ales including Conwy and Purple Moose, good range of wines, malt whiskies and gins including local Aber Falls gin, log fire and inglenook woodburner; picnic-sets out by streamside garden, children welcome, open (and food) all day weekends, closed Mon except bank holidays.

TREMADOG   SH5640
Union (01766) 512748
Market Square; LL49 9RB Traditional early 19th-c stone-built pub in terrace overlooking square, cosy and comfortable, with quiet panelled lounge and carpeted public bar, exposed stone walls and woodburner, well kept ales such as Purple Moose, enjoyable pubby food including burgers and tapas, friendly staff, back restaurant; darts and TV; children and dogs (on lead in bar) welcome, paved terrace behind, open from 4pm daily.

TUDWEILIOG   SH2336
Lion (01758) 770244
Nefyn Road (B4417), Ll ŷn Peninsula; LL53 8ND Cheerful village inn with traditional furnishings in lounge bar and two dining rooms (one for families), enjoyable sensibly priced home-cooked food, real ales such as Purple Moose, decent wines and dozens of malt whiskies, growing gin collection too, quick friendly service; pool and board games in public bar; children and dogs welcome, large front garden, bedrooms, open all day weekends.

TY'N-Y-GROES   SH7773
★ **Groes** (01492) 650545
B5106 N of village; LL32 8TN 15th-c pub-hotel (supposedly the first licensed house in Wales) in picturesque setting overlooking Vale of Conwy and peaks of Snowdonia; rambling low-beamed thick-walled rooms with antique settles, clocks, portraits and other bits and pieces, large fireplace in back bar, Lees ales, 14 wines by the glass and decent range of malt whiskies, gins and ciders, enjoyable food from sandwiches up, can eat in bar, airy conservatory with its 30-year-old vine or smart restaurant; background music; children and dogs welcome, idyllic back garden, more seating out on narrow roadside terrace, wonderful views from well equipped bedroom suites (some have terraces or balconies), open (and food) all day.

MONMOUTHSHIRE

ABERGAVENNY   SO2914
Angel (01873) 857121
Cross Street, by town hall; NP7 5EN Comfortable late Georgian coaching inn; good local atmosphere in two-level bar, rugs on flagstones, big sofas, armchairs and settles, some lovely bevelled glass behind counter serving real ales such as Wye Valley, proper cider and good choice of wines and malt whiskies, well liked food, friendly helpful staff, attractive lounge (popular afternoon tea) and smart dining room; children and dogs (in bar) welcome, pretty candlelit courtyard, 35 bedrooms (some in other buildings), open all day.

ABERGAVENNY   SO3111
★ **Hardwick** (01873) 854220
B4598, off A40 at A465/A4042 exit – coming from E on A40, go right round the exit system, as B4598 is final turn-off; NP7 9AA More restaurant-with-rooms than pub and you'll need to book for owner-chef's highly rated imaginative food; drinkers welcome in refurbished bar serving Wye Valley and maybe locals Tudor and Untapped, local perry and a dozen wines by the glass, also a small plates menu, two dining rooms, one with beams, bare boards and a huge fireplace, the other in lighter carpeted extension, friendly service; no under-8s in restaurant after 8pm, parasol-shaded teak tables by car park, neat garden, eight bedrooms, open all day Weds-Sat, closed Sun evening.

CHEPSTOW   ST5394
Three Tuns (01291) 645797
Bridge Street; NP16 5EY Early 17th-c and a pub for much of that time; bare-boards interior with painted farmhouse pine furniture, a couple of sofas by woodburner, plates on dresser, local ales including Kingstone, ciders from nice wooden counter at unusual angle, reasonably priced lunchtime bar food including speciality pies, friendly staff; background and regular live music, quiz nights; children and dogs welcome, wheelchair access, attractive gravelled garden, bedrooms (one suitable for disabled guests), open all day.

GROSMONT   SO4024
Angel Inn at Grosmont
(01981) 240646 *Corner of B4347 and Poorscript Lane, by church; NP7 8EP* Small welcoming 17th-c local by Grosmont Castle on River Wye at border with England; rustic interior with simple wooden furniture, Wye Valley Butty Bach, a couple of guests and local cider, reasonably priced traditional food; pool room with darts, TV for rugby; no lavatories – public ones close by; dogs welcome, seats out by ancient market cross, back garden with boules, good local walks,

open all day Sat, Sun till 8pm, closed Tues and weekday lunchtimes.

LLANDENNY   SO4103
★**Raglan Arms** (01291) 690800
Centre of village; NP15 1DL
Well run dining pub with relaxed informal atmosphere; interesting freshly cooked food using local produce from highly decorated chef, good selection of wines and a changing real ale, friendly welcoming young staff, big pine tables in linked dining rooms leading to conservatory, log fire in flagstoned bar's handsome stone fireplace; children welcome, garden tables on flower-strewn terrace, closed Mon, Tues and evening Sun.

LLANGATTOCK LINGOED   SO3620
Hunters Moon (01873) 821499
N turn off B4521 at Caggle Street just E of Llanvetherine; NP7 8RR Attractive tucked-away countryside pub dating from the 13th c; beams, dark stripped stone and flagstones, woodburner, friendly licensees and locals, Wye Valley and Welsh ales tapped from the cask and enjoyable straightforward food, separate dining room; children and dogs welcome, tables out on deck, in garden and in charming dell with waterfall, glorious country on Offa's Dyke Path, four comfortable bedrooms, open (and food) all day.

LLANGYBI   ST3797
White Hart (01633) 450258
On main road; NP15 1NP Friendly village dining pub in delightful mainly 16th-c monastic building (part of Jane Seymour's dowry); pubby bar with roaring log fire, steps up to pleasant light restaurant, enjoyable food including daily specials and two-course weekday lunch deal, mainly Welsh ales and good choice of wines by the glass, afternoon teas; children welcome.

LLANISHEN   SO4703
Carpenters Arms (01600) 860812
B4293 8 miles N of Chepstow; NP16 6QJ Old cottagey family-run pub with hearty food including curries and pies, Friday coffee and cake morning, one changing real ale, friendly welcoming staff, comfortable bar/lounge, coal fire, back games room with pool; flagstoned terrace and little side lawn up steps, two self-catering cottages, closed Mon and lunchtime Tues, no food Sun evening.

LLANOVER   SO2907
★**Goose & Cuckoo** (01873) 880277
Upper Llanover signed up track off A4042 S of Abergavenny; cross river and after 0.5 miles take first left; NP7 9ER Quite remote whitewashed pub looking over picturesque valley just inside Brecon Beacons National Park; essentially one little rustically furnished room with woodburner in arched stone fireplace, small picture-window extension making most of the view, at least three well kept ales, 50 whiskies and generous helpings of simple tasty home-cooked food; live music, board games, cribbage and darts; children, walkers and dogs welcome, picnic-sets out on gravel below, bedrooms and self-catering, closed Mon, open all day Fri-Sun.

LLANTHONY   SO2827
★**Priory Hotel** (01873) 890487
Aka Abbey Hotel, Llanthony Priory; off A465, back road Llanvihangel Crucorney–Hay; NP7 7NN Magical setting for plain bar with pew seating in dimly lit vaulted crypt of graceful ruined Norman abbey, lovely in summer with lawns around and the peaceful border hills beyond, dramatic in winter often with snow; well kept Felinfoel Double Dragon and a couple of guests, enjoyable good value food (more restauranty in the evening), efficient service; children welcome but not in hotel part (seven non-ensuite bedrooms in restored abbey walls), no dogs, open all day weekends Apr-Oct, all day Tues-Sun July and Aug, closed in winter apart from Fri evening, Sat and lunchtime Sun.

LLANTRISANT FAWR   ST3997
Greyhound (01291) 672505
Off A449 near Usk; NP15 1LE Prettily set 18th-c country inn in lovely garden with fountain and splendid hill views, relaxed homely feel in three linked beamed rooms (steps between two), nice mix of furnishings and rustic decorations, Bass, Greene King Abbot and often local guests, good wines and enjoyable home cooking at sensible prices, friendly efficient service, pleasant panelled dining room, log fires; children welcome, muddy boots and dogs in one bar, disabled access, ten bedrooms in converted stable block, open (and some food) all day, shuts 6pm Sun.

LLANVIHANGEL CRUCORNEY   SO3220
Skirrid Mountain Inn
(01873) 890258 *Signed off A465; NP7 8DH* One of Britain's oldest pubs (claims to be Wales's oldest), dating partly from 1110 and a former courthouse – plenty of atmosphere and ghostly tales; ancient studded door to high-ceilinged main bar, exposed stone, flagstones and panelling, huge log fire, well kept ales and pubby food, separate dining room; children and dogs (in garden only) welcome, tables on terrace and small sloping back lawn, three bedrooms, open all day Sat, closed Mon lunchtime and Sun evening.

MAGOR   ST4287
Wheatsheaf (01633) 880608
A mile from M4 junction 23; Newport Road off B4245; NP26 3HN Welcoming white-painted pub with black beams and some exposed stonework, pubby furniture

on wood, flagstone or quarry-tiled floors, woodburner in big fireplace, ales such as Rhymney and Sharps, decent wines and 20 gins, well priced food from bar snacks to full meals, good friendly service, carpeted restaurant, pool and darts in tap room; frequent live music and quiz nights; garden with terrace, children and dogs welcome, wheelchair access (ramp for restaurant), open all day.

MAMHILAD   SO3004
Horseshoe (01873) 880542
Old Abergavenny Road at Croes-y-Pant Lane; NP4 8QZ Old beamed country pub with slate-floor bar; traditional pubby furniture and a couple of unusual posts acting as elbow tables, original Hancocks pub sign, ornate woodburner in stone fireplace, well kept ales including local Mad Dog, craft ciders, good fairly priced food from lunchtime baguettes to daily specials; children welcome, dogs away from dining area, lovely views particularly from tables by car park over road, open all day Fri-Sun.

PANDY   SO3322
Old Pandy (01873) 890208
A465 Abergavenny–Hereford; NP7 8DR Welcoming 17th-c beamed roadside pub on edge of the Black Mountains and popular with walkers; substantial portions of reasonably priced food from simple traditional menu, Wye Valley Butty Bach and HPA, friendly service; pool, darts, live music; children and dogs welcome, picnic tables on pretty terrace, adjacent bunkhouse, closed Mon lunchtime, open all day Fri-Sun.

RAGLAN   SO4107
Beaufort Arms (01291) 690412
High Street; NP15 2DY Smart but inviting hotel (former 16th-c coaching inn) with two character beamed bars, one with big stone fireplace and comfortable seats on slate floor, local ales such as Untapped, carefully sourced food including gluten-free options and good fish/seafood, light airy brasserie, friendly attentive service; background music, curry, pie and open mike nights; children and dogs (in bar) welcome, terrace tables, 16 bedrooms, open all day from 7am.

REDBROOK   SO5309
★Boat (01600) 712615
Car park signed on A466 Chepstow–Monmouth then 30m footbridge over Wye; or very narrow steep car access from Penallt; NP25 4AJ Beautifully set pub right on the River Wye and the Wales/England border, on Offa's Dyke path so attracts many walkers; local Wye Valley and Kingstone plus guests, real ciders and popular food from baguettes up including

different country-themed food nights, friendly helpful staff, stripped-stone walls, flagstones and woodburner; children and dogs welcome, seats in informal tiered suntrap garden with waterfall spilling down, open all day.

SKENFRITH   SO4520
★Bell (01600) 750235
B4521, 12 miles NE of Abergavenny; NP7 8UH Elegant 17th-c coaching inn close to Monnow River and handy for ruins of Skenfrith Castle (NT); main bar with inglenook fireplace and plenty of seating including comfortable sofas, bleached-oak counter serving ales such as Bespoke and Wye Valley, bottled local cider/perry, 15 wines by the glass from extensive list and good range of spirits, highly regarded contemporary food using some home-grown produce, friendly helpful staff, spacious restaurant; background music; children and dogs (in one bar) welcome, disabled access, terrace with good solid tables under parasols, steps up to sloping lawn, orchard area and neat kitchen garden, comfortable bedrooms named after fishing flies, open all day (closed one week in both Jan and Nov).

TAL-Y-COED   SO4115
Warwicks (01600) 780227
B4233 Monmouth–Abergavenny; though its postal address is Llantilio Crossenny, the inn is actually in Tal-y-coed, a mile or two E; NP7 8TL Pretty 17th-c wisteria-clad pub under enthusiastic welcoming management; softly lit beamed bar with friendly locals, good log fire in stone fireplace, settles and mix of other old furniture, horsebrasses and assorted memorabilia, a couple of well kept ales such as Hancocks and Otter, decent wines by the glass and good quality food cooked by landlady including daily specials, cosy little dining room; occasional live music; children welcome, dogs in bar, seats on front terrace and in neat garden, lovely countryside and surrounding walks.

TINTERN   SO5300
★Anchor (01291) 689582
Off A466 at brown sign for Tintern Abbey; NP16 6TE Historic building in wonderful setting next to magnificent Tintern Abbey ruins; bar with beams, flagstones and bare stone walls, original horse-drawn cider press (used when the grounds were the abbey's orchards), four real ales such as Kingstone, Otter and Wye Valley, good wines by the glass and local ciders, newish restaurant with stone walls, flagstones, elegant dining furniture and folding doors to terrace, airy orangery has best views (abbey is floodlit at night), well regarded

---

If you know a pub is ever open all day, please tell us.

food; children and dogs (in bar) welcome, picnics-sets on terrace and lawn, play area, River Wye just behind and lots of surrounding walks, open (and food) all day.

TRELLECK SO5005
Lion (01600) 860322
B4293 6 miles S of Monmouth; NP25 4PA Charming red-stone pub dating from 1580, open-plan bar with dining area to the left, one or two low black beams, mix of old furniture and two log fires, ales such as Wye Valley, wide range of enjoyable classic food at fair prices including takeaway pizzas; background music, open mike nights, traditional games; children and dogs welcome, tables out on grass and side courtyard overlooking church, self-catering cottage, open all day Fri-Sun, best to check for other times.

TRELLECK GRANGE SO5001
Fountain (01291) 689303
Minor road Tintern–Llanishen, 1 mile SE of village; NP16 6QW Welcoming traditional 17th-c drovers' pub; good food cooked by landlady using local produce from pub favourites to game specials and innovative curries, some themed nights, three well kept ales such as Glamorgan and Wye Valley, real cider, roomy low-beamed flagstoned bar with log fire; quiz, darts; children and dogs welcome, small walled garden, peaceful spot on small winding road, open all day weekends, closed Mon and lunchtimes Tues-Fri.

USK SO3700
Kings Head (01291) 672963
Old Market Street; NP15 1AL Popular 16th-c family-run inn, chatty and relaxed, with generously served traditional food and well kept beers from perhaps Fullers, Timothy Taylors and Wye Valley, friendly efficient staff, huge log fire in superb fireplace; sports TV; nine comfortable bedrooms, hearty Welsh breakfast, open all day.

NORTH-EAST WALES

CAERWYS SJ1373
Piccadilly (01352) 720284
North Street (B5122); CH7 5AW Slickly modernised pub-restaurant in building originally dating from 17th c; high-ceilinged bare-boards bar with raised central woodburner, dining room across corridor and spacious slate-floor restaurant behind with banquettes and light wood furniture, stairs up to further eating area, ample helpings of interesting fairly priced food prioritising local ingredients, up to four real ales such as Rev James or Doom Bar, gin bar with great array of gins, efficient friendly service; background and weekend live music; children welcome, partly covered side beer garden, open (and food) all day.

CARROG SJ1143
Grouse (01490) 430272
B5437, signed off A5 Llangollen–Corwen; LL21 9AT Welcoming little pub alongside River Dee by an ancient arched stone bridge, with superb river and valley views from covered flagstone terrace; several JW Lees ales and enjoyable reasonably priced food from sandwiches up, vegetarian/vegan and gluten-free diets catered for, friendly helpful staff, small bar with beamed dining area to the side; background music; children, walkers and dogs welcome, handy for Llangollen steam railway; open (and food) all day.

GRAIG FECHAN SJ1454
Three Pigeons (01824) 703178
On B5429 S of Ruthin; LL15 2EU Extended largely 18th-c whitewashed and beamed drovers' pub with wide choice of enjoyable sensibly priced food (all day weekends) from sandwiches and light dishes up, OAP lunch deal Weds, four rotating cask ales, local cider and many wines by the glass, friendly service, various nooks and corners, interesting mix of furniture and some old signs on the walls, great country views from restaurant over Clwydian Range hills; children and dogs (in bar) welcome, big garden with terrace and more of same views, good walks, two self-catering apartments, camping, open weekends, closed Mon.

HAWARDEN SJ3266
★**Glynne Arms** (01244) 569988
Glynne Way; CH5 3NS Golden-stone Georgian pub with friendly chatty local atmosphere; interconnecting character rooms with bare boards or parquet, a few bright rugs, mix of furniture including dark pubby chairs and blue or brown leather wall seats, mirrors, antlers, log-end wallpaper and framed posters, three open fires, enjoyable food from snacks to steaks using local produce (they also own the nearby Hawarden Estate farm shop), well kept ales such as Big Hand, Facers and Weetwood, several wines by the glass; background music, TV, board games; children and dogs (in bar) welcome, picnic-sets in back courtyard, open (and food) all day.

LLANARMON DYFFRYN CEIRIOG SJ1532
★**Hand** (01691) 600666
B4500 from Chirk; LL20 7LD Peaceful former farmhouse at heart of Upper Ceiriog valley with a dramatic setting close to the River Ceiriog and backed by the Berwyn Mountains; low-beamed bar with inglenook log fire, sturdy tables and a mix of seating including settles, wheelbacks and mate's chairs on carpet, old prints on the walls, real ales such as Stonehouse and Weetwood, seven wines by the glass and 20 malt whiskies, delicious, meticulously

prepared and popular food from pub classics up, woodburner in largely stripped-stone restaurant, quiet lounge and games room with darts and pool, spa; children welcome (not in bar after 8pm), dogs in some areas, picnic-sets on front terrace, more tables in garden, not far from Pistyll Rhaeadr (Wales's highest waterfall), elegant and spacious bedrooms, substantial breakfast, open all day.

LLANFERRES   SJ1860
Druid (01352) 810225
A494 Mold–Ruthin; CH7 5SN Extended 17th-c whitewashed inn set in fine walking country (Alyn Valley towards Loggerheads Country Park, or up Offa's Dyke Path to Moel Famau); views from broad bay window in civilised plush lounge and from bigger beamed back bar with two handsome antique oak settles, pleasant mix of more modern furnishings along with exposed stone walls and quarry-tiled area by log fire, Marstons-related ales, lots of malt whiskies and reasonably priced traditional food, games room with darts and pool; background music, quiz nights, TV; children welcome, dogs in bar, five bedrooms, open all day Fri-Sun.

LLANGOLLEN   SJ2142
Chainbridge (01978) 860215
2 miles NW Llangollen on B5103 by River Dee; LL20 8BS 19th-c hotel in great location fronting the River Dee rapids and with the Llangollen Canal behind, overlooks chain bridge and renovated steam railway; bar, lounge, restaurant and inviting outside spaces, decent food from sandwiches and pubby choices up, two or three well kept ales including Stonehouse Station Bitter and often Purple Moose; children and dogs welcome, 36 bedrooms (some with river-view balconies), good nearby walks, open all day.

MINERA   SJ2651
Tyn-y-Capel (01978) 269347
Church Road near St Mary's Church; LL11 3DA Attractive ancient coaching inn with origins in 13th c, once a stop-off for monks from Valle Crucis Abbey, hearty innovative food, up to four real ales including house beer Cat in the Capel (Facers); regular live music, quiz, sports TV; children and dogs (in bar) welcome, lovely hill views from terrace beer garden, park opposite with play area, open (and food) all day.

RUABON   SJ3043
Bridge End (01978) 810881
Bridge Street; LL14 6DA Proper old-fashioned real ale pub serving own McGivern ales (brewed here) alongside several guests and ciders, friendly staff and cheerful local atmosphere, some snacky food, black beams, open fires; Tues quiz, regular summer live music, beer festival Aug; children and dogs welcome, seats in garden, open all day Fri-Sun, closed Mon.

PEMBROKESHIRE

ABERCYCH   SN2539
★ Nags Head (01239) 841200
Off B4332 Cenarth–Boncath; SA37 0HJ Friendly and homely tucked-away riverside pub with dimly lit beamed bar; woodburner in big fireplace, stripped-wood tables on flagstones, clocks showing time around the world and numerous beer bottles on shelves, ales from local microbreweries like Bluestone and Mantle and enjoyable pubby food including daily specials, various other connecting rooms, one with a suspended coracle; background music, darts; children and dogs welcome, benches (some under cover) in part-paved part-grass garden overlooking river (pub has fishing rights), play area with wooden castle, three comfortable bedrooms, closed lunchtimes Mon-Thurs.

ANGLE   SM8603
Hibernia (01646) 641517
B4320; SA71 5AT Welcoming village pub with good reasonably priced home-made food and ales such as Brains Rev James, traditional bar with open fire, more modern dining room; some live music, sports TV, pool; children and dogs welcome, bedrooms, open all day in high summer, otherwise closed Mon, Tues and lunchtimes Weds, Thurs.

BOSHERSTON   SR9694
St Govans Country Inn
(01646) 661311 *Off B4319 S of Pembroke near turn-off for Bosherston Lily Ponds; SA71 5DN* Delightful find and surprisingly busy pub (for out-of-the-way location); big modernised open-plan bar, cheery and simple, changing ales such as Evan Evans and well priced pubby food with focus on seafood, curry nights, murals of local beauty spots, log fire in large stone fireplace; background music, TV, games machine and pool (winter only); children and dogs welcome, picnic-sets on small front terrace, good value bedrooms (residents' parking), beach and cliff walks, open all day in season (all day weekends at other times).

BROAD HAVEN   SM8614
★ Druidstone Hotel (01437) 781221
N on coast road, bear left for about 1.5 miles then follow sign left to Druidston Haven; SA62 3NE Cheerfully informal and eccentric rambling country house hotel in striking spot above the sea, individual, relaxed and with terrific views; inventive cooking using fresh local ingredients (best to book), helpful efficient service, cellar bar with at least one Welsh ale tapped from the cask, regulars from Bluestone, Brains and Caffle, wine list includes Welsh options, ceilidhs and folk events, friendly pub dogs (others welcome); attractive high-walled garden, all sorts of sporting activities from

boules to sand-yachting, good walks nearby, ten spacious homely bedrooms and five self-catering cottages, open all day.

CAREW   SN0403
Carew Inn (01646) 651267
A4075, just N of A477; SA70 8SL
Stone-built pub with appealing cottagey atmosphere; unpretentious small panelled public bar, nice old bentwood stools and mix of tables and chairs on bare boards, small dining area, spacious lounge bar, warm open fires, two changing beers such as Brains Rev James and enjoyable generously served food including Tues curry and Thurs steak nights, regular barbecues, two upstairs dining rooms with leather chairs at black tables; background music, dominoes, darts; children and dogs (in bar and lounge) welcome, enclosed back garden with play equipment, view of imposing Carew Castle ruins and remarkable 9th-c Celtic cross, four bedrooms in adjacent building, open all day, bar meals Mon-Sat.

COSHESTON   SN0003
Brewery Inn (01646) 686678
Just N of A477 at Slade Cross; SA72 4UD
17th-c stone-built village pub with nicely furnished flagstoned bar; good choice of enjoyable food including vegetarian options, a locally brewed house beer and a guest (often Brains Rev James, big range of gins, helpful friendly service; Weds quiz and some live music; children and dogs welcome, open all day Fri-Sun, closed Mon.

CRESSWELL QUAY   SN0506
★Cresselly Arms (01646) 651210
Village signed from A4075; SA68 0TE
Simple unchanging alehouse overlooking tidal creek on Cresswell River; plenty of local customers in two old-fashioned linked rooms, built-in wall benches, kitchen chairs and plain tables on red and black tiles, open fire in one room, Aga in the other with lots of china hanging from high beam-and-plank ceiling, third more conventionally furnished red-carpeted room, house beer Caffle Quay Ale plus Hancocks, Sharps and a rotating guest; no children or dogs, seats outside making most of the view, you can arrive by boat if tide is right, open all day in summer.

CWM GWAUN   SN0333
★Dyffryn Arms
Cwm Gwaun and Pontfaen signed off B4313 E of Fishguard; SA65 9SE
Classic rural time warp known locally as Bessie's after the much loved veteran landlady (her farming family have run it since 1840 and she's been in charge for well over a third of that time); reopened after fire in 2019 and just the same as ever; well kept Bass served by jug through hatch, low prices, lovely outside view and little beer garden, walks in nearby Preseli Hills, open more or less all day (may close if no customers).

DINAS   SN0139
Old Sailors (01348) 811491
Pwllgwaelod Beach; from A487 in Dinas Cross follow Bryn-henllan signpost; SA42 0SE Whitewashed shack-like building in superb and remote position, snuggled down into the sand by isolated cove below Dinas Head; good local fish/seafood (often crab and lobster), also snacks, coffee and summer cream teas, Brains Barry Island IPA, Gwynt Y Ddraig cider and decent wine, maritime bric-a-brac; children welcome, no dogs inside, picnic-sets in walled garden overlooking beach with views across to Fishguard, bracing walks, open all day Weds-Sat, closed Mon (except bank holidays) and evenings Tues and Sun.

FISHGUARD   SM9537
Fishguard Arms (01348) 872763
Main Street (A487); SA65 9HJ Tiny and brightly painted bay-windowed terrace pub with friendly community atmosphere, cosy front bar with unusually high counter serving well kept/priced Bass direct from the cask, back snug with woodburner and panelling, traditional games, darts and sports TV, no food; smokers' area out behind, open all day.

FISHGUARD   SM9537
Royal Oak (01348) 218632
Market Square, Upper Town; SA65 9HA Welcoming upper town pub with stripped beams, exposed stonework and slate flagstones, plaque commemorating defeat of bizarre French raid in 1797 (peace treaty was signed in the pub), well kept changing ales and farm cider from carved servery, good choice of popular fairly priced pubby food, friendly prompt service, big picture-window dining extension; folk night Tues, quiz Thurs; children and dogs welcome, pleasant terrace with view down to Lower Town bay, open all day.

FISHGUARD   SM9637
Ship (01348) 874033
Newport Road, Lower Town; SA65 9ND Traditional 18th-c terrace-row pub near the old harbour – a proper unchanging local gem; dark interior with beams and coal fire, lots of boat pictures, model ships and other memorabilia, ales include Bass, Felinfoel and Hancocks, no food; some live music; children and dogs welcome, front door directly on to the road (careful as you leave), open all day weekends, closed Mon, Tue and lunchtimes Weds-Fri.

JAMESTON   SS0699
Tudor Lodge (01834) 871212
A4139, just E of Jameston; SA70 7SS Friendly whitewashed inn just off main road, close to the coast; two bars with open fire and woodburner, a couple of well kept ales such as Brains Rev James and Sharps Doom Bar, several wines by the glass, decent choice

of hearty food, Tues curry and Thurs steak night, airy dining room with painted beams and high-backed chairs, open fire; children welcome, play area and plenty of picnic-sets in garden, five stylish comfortable bedrooms, open (and food) all day weekends, from 4pm weekdays.

LITTLE HAVEN   SM8512
Saint Brides Inn (01437) 781266
St Brides Road; SA62 3UN Appealing blue and white pub just 20 metres from Pembrokeshire Coast Path; neat beamed and stripped-stone bar and linked carpeted dining area, traditional furnishings, log fire, interesting well in back corner grotto thought to be partly Roman, Banks's, Marstons and local ales like Caffle, enjoyable bar food including fresh fish and other local produce, nice staff; background music and TV; children welcome, no dogs inside, seats in sheltered suntrap terrace garden across road, open all day in summer.

LITTLE HAVEN   SM8512
★Swan (01437) 781880
Point Road; SA62 3UL Attractive old pub overlooking bay; traditional oak-floored bar with mix of furniture including cask tables, a couple of leather armchairs by open fire at one end, woodburner the other, snug with one large table suitable for ten diners, ales such as Brains Rev James and regular Pembrokeshire guests, extensive choice of wines, good locally sourced food including fish/seafood, friendly helpful staff; background and some live music; children welcome, dogs in bar, sea views from raised heated terrace with rattan-style furniture, enjoyable walks along coast, no food Mon or Sun evening.

LLANSTADWELL   SM9404
Ferry House (01646) 600270
Church Road at Newton Road, Hazelbeach; SA73 1EG Neatly kept, traditionally furnished inn by the Cleddau estuary with great views; good food including local fish, Sharps Doom Bar, timber-framed dining conservatory making most of the view; children and dogs welcome, picnic-sets on waterside terrace, summer pontoon for visiting boats, six comfortable bedrooms, open (and food) all day, no food Sun evening.

MATHRY   SM8831
Farmers Arms (01348) 831284
N of junction of A487 and B4331; SA62 5HB Popular pub with traditional beamed bar; Felinfoel Double Dragon and two guests, several gins and ample helpings of enjoyable good value pubby food (all day Sat), including standout burger and curry selection, friendly staff and locals, large dining conservatory; background music, TV, games machine, pool, darts; children welcome, dogs in bar, nearby campsite, open all day.

NEWCHAPEL   SN2239
Ffynnone Arms (01239) 841800
B4332; SA37 0EH Welcoming 18th-c beamed pub with enjoyable traditional food including popular Sun carvery, special diets catered for and some produce home-grown, Hancocks HB and Wye Valley plus local guests from maybe Gwaun Valley and Mantle, local cider and afternoon teas in season, two woodburners; darts, pool and table skittles; disabled facilities, picnic-sets in small garden with pond, open weekday evenings, from 3pm Sat and noon Sun.

NEWPORT   SN0539
Castle (01239) 820742
Bridge Street; SA42 0TB Welcoming old pub with divided bar – one part panelled with open fire, the other with pool, darts, juke box and projector for major sports; wide choice of enjoyable home-made food from lunchtime sandwiches and baguettes up, ales such as Wye Valley and local guests like Bluestone, pleasant service, restaurant; some live music; children and dogs welcome, three bedrooms (one has four-poster), handy for Parrog estuary walk (good for bird-watchers), open all day.

NEWPORT   SN0539
Royal Oak (01239) 820632
West Street (A487); SA42 0TA Sizeable 18th-c pub with good traditional food plus lots of authentic curries (takeaway service available, also for fish and chips), well kept ales, friendly helpful staff, lounge with eating areas, separate stone and slate bar with pool, upstairs dining room; children welcome, no dogs, some tables outside, easy walk to beach and coast path, open (and food) all day.

PEMBROKE DOCK   SM9603
Shipwright (01646) 682090
Front Street; SA72 6JX Little blue-painted end-of-terrace pub on waterfront overlooking estuary; enjoyable home-made food and a couple of well kept ales, friendly efficient staff, bare-boards interior with nautical and other memorabilia, some booth seating; children welcome, five minutes from Ireland ferry terminal, open all day.

PORTHGAIN   SM8132
★Sloop (01348) 831449
2 miles N off A487 (St David's– Fishguard) – turn off at Croesgoch; SA62 5BN Very popular (nigh-on legendary) 18th-c tavern snuggled down in delightful cove-hugging village wedged tightly between headlands on Pembrokeshire Coast Path – fine walks in either direction; plank-ceilinged bar with lobster pots and fishing nets, ship clocks, lanterns and some relics from local wrecks, decent-sized eating area with simple furnishings, well liked bar food from sandwiches to good steaks and fresh

fish, three real ales such as Evan Evans and Hancocks HB, separate games room; quiz last Thurs of month, summer live music; seats on heated terrace overlooking harbour, self-catering cottage in village, no dogs, open all day, from 9.30am for breakfast Sat, Sun.

ST DAVID'S SM7525
Farmers Arms (01437) 721666
Goat Street; SA62 6RF Bustling old-fashioned low-ceilinged pub by cathedral gate; cheerful and unpretentiously pubby with bar on left and dining room to the right, open fire, up to four well kept ales from central servery including Evan Evans, decent food (summer only) from sandwiches to specials, friendly staff and atmosphere; TV for major sports, pool; children and dogs welcome, cathedral view from large tables on big back suntrap terrace with own bar, open (and food) all day summer, closed weekday lunchtimes in winter.

ST DOGMAELS SN1646
Ferry (01239) 615172
B4546; SA43 3LF Picturesque pastel-blue waterside pub with spectacular views of the Teifi estuary from attractively furnished picture-window dining extension, good freshly made food especially seafood, Brains ales and several wines by the glass, pleasant attentive staff, character bar with pine tables and leather sofas, interesting old photographs and local artwork; background music; children, walkers and dogs welcome, plenty of room outside on linked decked areas, own jetty/moorings and at start of Pembrokeshire Coast Path, open (and food) all day, closed Mon lunchtime.

TREFIN SM8332
Ship (01348) 831445
N off A487 at Croes-Goch or Penparc; Ffordd y Felin; SA62 5AX Well positioned traditional little pub just up from coast path; popular well priced food and a couple of interesting changing beers, friendly service, dining extension; occasional quiz and live music nights, pool; children welcome, lovely view from back garden, open all day.

POWYS

BEGUILDY SO1979
Radnorshire Arms (01547) 510634
B4355 Knighton–Newtown by St Michael's Church; LD7 1YE Lovely 17th-c black and white beamed country pub with enjoyable good value food (not Sun evening) including game, ales such as Ludlow, Stonehouse and Beguildy Gold (badged for them), friendly helpful service,

inglenook woodburner; quiz, pool; no dogs inside, picnic-sets on front terrace and in beer garden, closed Mon (except bank holidays).

CILMERY SO0051
Prince Llewelyn (01982) 552694
A483; LD2 3NU Country pub under friendly licensees; plush dining chairs and button-back banquettes in dining room, woodburner in carpeted bar, a couple of real ales and enjoyable food including seafood summer specials; children and dogs welcome, garden and lovely surrounding walks, open evenings Tues-Sun.

CRICKHOWELL SO2118
Dragon (01873) 810362
High Street; NP8 1BE Welcoming old family-owned inn, more hotel-restaurant than pub but with neat small bar serving Felinfoel Double Dragon and couple of local ales, stone and wood floors, sofas and armchairs by open fire, enjoyable traditional food with plenty of local ingredients from likes of Welsh Venison Centre and Black Mountain Smokery in tidy dining room, steak nights, good friendly service; children and dogs welcome, 15 bedrooms, open (and food) all day.

CRICKHOWELL SO1919
Nantyffin Cider Mill
(01873) 810775 *A40/A479; NP8 1SG* Former 16th-c drovers' inn facing River Usk in lovely Black Mountains countryside – charming views from tables on lawn; bar with solid furniture on tiles or carpet, woodburner in broad fireplace, a couple of Felinfoel beers, craft ciders, gin and whisky from nearby Glanusk Estate, several wines by the glass too, open-plan main area with beams, standing timbers and open fire in grey stonework wall, high-raftered restaurant with old cider press, good fairly pubby food at reasonable prices; background music, TV; children and dogs (in bar) welcome, play area in garden, handy for Tretower Court and Castle, closed Mon and Tues (also Weds in winter), open all day Thurs-Sun.

DERWENLAS SN7299
★**Black Lion** (01654) 703913
A487 2 miles SW of Machynlleth; SY20 8TN Cosy 16th-c country pub with extensive range of good well priced popular food including daily specials and separate vegan menu, friendly staff, real ales such as Wye Valley Butty Bach, decent wines, heavy black beams and timbering, thick walls, carpet over big slate flagstones, log fire; background music; garden behind with play area and steps up into woods, limited parking, closed Mon.

Real ale to us means beer that has matured naturally in its cask – not pressurised or filtered. If possible, we name all real ales stocked.

DOLFOR SO1187
Dolfor Inn (01686) 626531
Inn signposted up hill from A483 about 4 miles S of Newtown – slightly N of A489 (Newtown Bypass);
SY16 4AA Hospitable tucked-away hillside inn; cosy carpeted beamed bar with woodburner in stone fireplace, well kept ales including Ludlow Best plus guests from brick-faced counter, dining room with another woodburner in inglenook, enjoyable generously served food at fair prices including lunchtime sandwiches and afternoon teas; pool, darts and TV in games area; children and dogs welcome, good views from terrace, six comfortable bedrooms (two sharing bathroom), open all day Fri and Sat, closed Tues.

FELINFACH SO0933
Plough & Harrow (01874) 622709
Village and pub signed from A470, 4 miles N of Brecon; LD3 0UB Small village pub originally local blacksmith's house under welcoming long-serving licensees; simple bar, comfortable lounge area with woodburner and dining room, well kept Sharps Doom Bar and guests, good simple home-made food at reasonable prices; three bedrooms, children and dogs welcome, open evenings only from 6pm (7pm Sun).

GARTHMYL SO1999
Nags Head (01686) 640600
A483 at B4385; SY15 6RS Smart red-brick Georgian roadside inn with nicely updated interior; good food from sandwiches, sharing plates and pub favourites up, real ales such as Montys and Three Tuns, well chosen wines, helpful service from friendly uniformed staff, comfortable slate-floor bar with large two-way woodburner, pitched-roof dining room; children and dogs welcome, tables under parasols on paved back terrace, towpath walks along Montgomery Canal, five good bedrooms, open (and food) all day.

GLADESTRY SO2355
Royal Oak (01544) 370586
B4594; HR5 3NR Friendly old-fashioned village pub on Offa's Dyke Path; simple stripped-stone slate-floored walkers' bar, beams hung with tankards and lanterns, carpeted lounge, open fires, ales from likes of Three Tuns and Wye Valley; children welcome, dogs in bar, sheltered sunny back garden, four bedrooms, camping, best to check opening hours.

GLASBURY SO1839
Harp (01497) 847373
B4350 just N of junction with A438; HR3 5NR Welcoming 18th-c pub with good traditional food (not Mon, just pizzas Sun evening) including blackboard specials, Wye Valley ales, U-shaped beamed interior with

woodburner; children and dogs welcome, terrace and garden sloping invitingly down to River Wye, four bedrooms, open all day Fri-Sun, closed lunchtimes Mon, Tues.

HAY-ON-WYE SO2242
Blue Boar (01497) 820884
Castle Street/Oxford Road; HR3 5DF Old ivy-clad pub with character bar: cosy corners, dark panelling, pews and country chairs, open fire in Edwardian fireplace, well kept ales such as Brains Rev James and Timothy Taylors Landlord, organic bottled cider and several wines by the glass, decent food in long café/dining room with another open fire; background music; children and dogs welcome, tables under parasols in beer garden, open all day from 9am for breakfast.

HAY-ON-WYE SO2342
Old Black Lion (01497) 820841
Lion Street, opposite Bear Street; HR3 5AD 17th-c inn with comfortable low-beamed bar, country chairs at scrubbed pine tables, painted dados and original fireplace, real ales such as Evan Evans and Wye Valley from hop-strewn bar, local cider and broad range of whiskies too, well liked innovative food, friendly helpful service; live jazz; children and dogs (in one area) welcome, sheltered back terrace, ten character bedrooms (some above bar), hearty breakfast, usually open all day.

KNIGHTON SO2872
Horse & Jockey (01547) 520062
Wylcwm Place; LD7 1AE Whitewashed ivy-clad pub (former 14th-c coaching inn) popular locally; good well priced food from traditional choices to daily specials, can eat in bar or adjoining restaurant, local ales such as Wye Valley Butty Bach; children and dogs welcome, tables in pleasant courtyard, eight well-appointed bedrooms, handy for Offa's Dyke Path, open all day.

LIBANUS SN9926
Tai'r Bull (01874) 622600
A470 SW of Brecon in Tai'r Bull village; LD3 8EL Old roadside village pub; traditional bar with woodburner in large stone fireplace, Sharps Doom Bar and Wye Valley Butty Bach, home-made food available in bar or separate restaurant; children and dogs (in bar) welcome, great views of Pen-y-Fan from small flower-bedecked front terrace, five bedrooms, open all day Weds-Sun, closed till 5pm Mon and Tues.

LLANFIHANGEL-NANT-MELAN SO1958
Red Lion (01544) 350220
A44 9 miles W of Kington; LD8 2TN Attractive beamed and stripped-stone 16th-c roadside pub; roomy main bar with flagstones and woodburner, carpeted restaurant and front sun porch, tasty reasonably priced food, well kept changing ales, friendly service, back bar with another woodburner; children

and dogs welcome, can arrange horse stabling, country views from pleasant garden, four bedrooms, self-catering, campervans welcome in car park overnight, handy for Radnor Forest walks and near impressive waterfall, open (and food) all day Fri, Sat and Sun lunch.

LLANGATTOCK SO2117
Horseshoe (01873) 268773
Hillside Road at Park Drive; NP8 1PA
Busy attractively refurbished old inn; bar with flagstones, exposed stonework and some beams, button-back leather wall banquettes and other traditional furniture, two woodburners, more seating in back pitched-ceiling room with bare boards and pine dresser, Brains Rev James and Wye Valley Butty Bach, well liked food, friendly helpful service; TV; children and dogs welcome, comfortable bedrooms, open all day.

LLANGEDWYN SJ1924
Green Inn (01691) 828234
B4396 E of village; SY10 9JW
Old country dining pub (dating from 18th c) with modernised interior, various snug corners and good mix of furnishings including oak settles and comfy sofas, woodburner, real ales such as Three Tuns and enjoyable well priced pubby food including pizza and steak nights, friendly helpful staff; children and dogs welcome, picnic-sets in huge garden over road running down towards River Tanat, closed Mon, open all day weekends.

LLANGENNY SO2417
Dragons Head (01873) 810350
N of village, by bridge; NP8 1HD
Welcoming wisteria-clad pub tucked away in pretty valley and popular with hikers; local Rhymney plus a couple of guests and decent wines by the glass, good freshly cooked food, two-room bar with low beams, exposed stonework, snug feel and mix of traditional seating including leather chesterfields by big woodburner, lots of framed photographs and other bric-a-brac, two dining areas; children and dogs welcome, seats in garden and over lane by stream, small campsite nearby, closed Mon and till 6pm Tues-Fri.

LLANGORSE SO1327
Castle Inn (01874) 658819
B4560; LD3 7UB Friendly little whitewashed local with good generously served food cooked by landlady including range of pies, burgers and pizzas, ales such as Brains Rev James and Felinfoel Double Dragon, attentive helpful service; children and dogs welcome, open evenings Thurs-Sun (until 7pm Sun).

LLANGYNIDR SO1519
Coach & Horses (01874) 730245
Cwm Crawnon Road (B4558) 5 miles W of Crickhowell; NP8 1LS Rose-pink country dining pub dating from 16th c; well

kept ales and enjoyable food cooked by chef-owner plus separate deli, beams, stripped stone and big log fire, restaurant; children and dogs (in some areas) welcome, picnic-sets and play area across road in fenced garden by canal lock, four bedrooms, open all day, till 3pm Sun.

LLANIDLOES SN9584
Crown & Anchor (01686) 412398
Long Bridge Street; SY18 6EF Friendly largely unspoilt town-centre pub known locally as Ruby's after landlady who ran it for 50 years; Wye Valley plus guests such as Purple Moose, chatty locals' bar, lounge, snug and two other rooms separated by central hallway; pool and games machine; open all day Fri, Sat, from 2pm other days.

LLANWRTYD WELLS SN8746
Neuadd Arms (01591) 610236
The Square; LD5 4RB Large 19th-c hotel (friendly and by no means upmarket) in Britain's smallest town, brews its own good value Heart of Wales beers in back stable block (up to ten on at a time), enjoyable straightforward home-made food, log fires in lounge and small tiled public bar still with old service bells, restaurant, games room; well behaved dogs welcome in bars, a few tables out at front, 20 bedrooms (front ones can be noisy), very good walking area, novel events such as bog snorkelling and man v horse nearby, open all day from 9am.

MALLWYD SH8612
Brigands (01650) 511999
A470 by roundabout in village; SY20 9HJ Sizeable 15th-c beamed coaching inn with gently civilised atmosphere; well kept changing ales and enjoyable food from bar snacks up, popular morning and afternoon teas, friendly efficient staff; children and dogs welcome (dog-friendly beer available), extensive lawns with lovely views, can arrange fishing on River Dovey, nine character bedrooms, some with beams and four-poster beds, open all day.

MONTGOMERY SO2296
★ Dragon Hotel (01686) 668359
Market Square; SY15 6PA Striking and impeccably preserved timber-framed 17th-c hotel (former coaching inn) in quiet little town below ruined Norman castle; beamed back bar on two levels, four well kept ales including town's own Montys, craft beers and nice choice of wines by the glass, good food including baguettes, pub favourites and Mediterranean-influenced dishes, friendly helpful staff, front bistro-style restaurant with central two-way fireplace; unobtrusive background music; children and dogs welcome, 20 comfortable well equipped bedrooms, swimming pool (residents only), open all day.

PAINSCASTLE   SO1646
★ **Roast Ox** (01497) 851398

*B4594, off A470 Brecon–Builth Wells
or from A438 at Clyro; LD2 3JL* Well
restored pub with beams, flagstones and
stripped-stone walls, appropriate simple
furnishings and some rustic bric-a-brac, huge
antlers above open fire, ales tapped from
the cask and good range of ciders and malt
whiskies, popular freshly made food including
good fish and chips, friendly quick service;
children and dogs (in bar) welcome, picnic-
sets outside, attractive surrounding hill
country, eight comfortable neat bedrooms;
closed Mon, Tues, check winter hours.

PENCELLI   SO0925
Royal Oak (01874) 665396

B4558, 4.5 miles SE of Brecon; LD3 7LX
Straightforward country pub with two small
bars; low beams and log fires, assorted
furniture on flagstones, Brains Rev James
and a couple of guests, enjoyable home-made
pubby food including Sun roasts in bars
or small dining room; children and dogs
welcome, garden backing on to Monmouth
& Brecon Canal (moorings), lovely canalside
walks and handy for Taff Trail, open all day.

RHAYADER   SN9668
★ **Triangle** (01597) 810537

*Cwmdauddwr; B4518 by bridge over
River Wye, SW of centre; LD6 5AR*
Interesting little 16th-c drovers' pub
with buoyant local atmosphere; good value
pubby food (best to book evenings) from
shortish menu, regulars Brains Rev James
and Hancocks HB plus guests and reasonably
priced wines, friendly staff, dining area with
nice view over to River Wye; darts; children
and dogs (in bar) welcome, picnic-sets on
small front terrace, self-catering cottage
opposite, parking can be difficult, closed
lunchtimes Mon-Weds.

SOUTH WALES VALLEYS

KENFIG   SS8081
Prince of Wales (01656) 740356

*2.2 miles from M4 junction 37; A4229
towards Porthcawl, then right when dual
carriageway narrows on bend, signed
'Maudlam, Kenfig'; CF33 4PR* Ancient
local with plenty of individuality by historic
sand dunes; well kept ales including Bass
and Sharps Doom Bar, decent wines and good
choice of malts, generous straightforward
food including pizzas and Penclawdd cockles
served by friendly staff, chatty panelled room
off main bar, log fires, stripped stone and lots
of wreck pictures, restaurant and upstairs
overspill room; TV for rugby; dogs welcome in
bar, handy for nature reserve (June orchids),
usually open all day, no food Sun evening.

PENDERYN   SN9408
Red Lion (01685) 811914

*Off A4059 at Pontbren Llwyd, then
up Church Road (narrow hill from T
junction); CF44 9JR* Friendly 12th-c
stone-built pub (former drovers' inn) set
high in lovely walking country; dark beams,
flagstones and blazing log fires, antique
settles and interesting bits and pieces
including some military memorabilia, good
range of real ales (maybe Bass, Brains
and Fullers) and ciders tapped from the
cask, also whiskies and other spirits from
nearby Penderyn distillery, highly regarded
imaginative food (best to book); children and
dogs (in bar) welcome, great views from big
garden, open (and food) all day, closed Mon
lunchtime.

SWANSEA

BISHOPSTON   SS5789
Joiners Arms (01792) 232658

*Bishopston Road, just off B4436 SW of
Swansea; SA3 3EJ* Thriving 19th-c stone
local with own good value Swansea ales
along with well kept guests, ample helpings
of enjoyable freshly made pub food, friendly
staff, unpretentious quarry-tiled bar with
massive solid-fuel stove, comfortable lounge;
TV for rugby; children and dogs welcome,
open all day (from 3pm Mon and Tues).

BISHOPSTON   SS5889
Plough & Harrow (01792) 234459

*Off B4436 Bishopston–Swansea; SA3
3DJ* Cleanly modernised and renovated
old pub with L-shaped bar and restaurant;
good imaginative food from chef-owner from
lunchtime sandwiches to tasting menus
showcasing wide range of local produce,
ales such as Brains Rev James and plenty of
wines by the glass, helpful courteous service;
occasional quiz; open all day Fri-Sun, from
4pm Mon-Thurs.

LLANGENNITH   SS4291
Kings Head (01792) 386212

*Clos St Cenydd, opposite church; SA3
1HX* Extended 17th-c stone-built inn with
wide choice of popular food (best to book)
including Thai, Vietnamese and Indian
dishes, pizzas and daily specials, local Gower
beers, extensive range of gins and very good
malt whisky choice, friendly staff; pool and
games machines in lively public bar – back
bar quieter with dining areas; children
(throughout) and dogs (in lower bar)
welcome, large terrace with village views,
good walks, not far from large campsite, great
surfing and beautiful sandy beach (Rhosili),
bedrooms in separate modern buildings,
open (and food) all day, breakfast for non-
residents.

MUMBLES
SS6287
Pilot
07897 895511
Mumbles Road; SA3 4EL Friendly 19th-c
seafront local with half a dozen well kept
ales including some from own microbrewery,
slate-floored bar with boat suspended from
planked ceiling, woodburning stove, no food;
TV; dogs welcome till 9pm, open all day.

PENYCAE
SN8313
Ancient Briton
(01639) 730273
Brecon Road (A4067); SA9 1YY
Friendly opened-up roadside pub; nine ales
from far and wide plus three ciders and
enjoyable reasonably priced home-made food;
children and dogs welcome, seats outside
and play area, four bedrooms, campsite
(good facilities including disabled loo and
shower), superb walking country and handy
for Dan-yr-Ogof caves, Henrhyd Waterfall and
Craig-y-Nos Country Park, open all day.

REYNOLDSTON
SS4889
King Arthur
(01792) 390775
Higher Green, off A4118; SA3 1AD
Cheerful pub-hotel with timbered main
bar, country-style restaurant and nautically
themed family dining area (games room with
pool in winter); good fairly priced traditional
food from sandwiches and pub favourites up,

ales such as local Gower Gold kept well,
log fires and country house bric-a-brac,
buoyant local atmosphere in the evening;
background music; tables out on green, play
area, 18 bedrooms and self-catering cottage,
open (and bar food) all day, breakfast for
non-residents.

SWANSEA
SS6492
Brunswick
(01792) 465676
Duke Street; SA1 4HS Large rambling
local with traditional pubby furnishings,
lots of knick-knacks and local artwork, good
value popular food (served daily weekdays,
just lunchtimes at weekends), half a dozen
well kept ales tapped from cask, friendly
helpful service, regular live music; no dogs,
open all day.

THREE CROSSES
SS5694
Poundffald
(01792) 931061
Tirmynydd Road, NW end; SA4 3PB
Appealing 17th-c beamed and timber-framed
pub; farmhouse, mate's and attractively
upholstered chairs around wooden tables
on patterned carpet, woodburner, Sharps
Doom Bar and guest ales, enjoyable pubby
food from baguettes up; sports TV in separate
bar; regular quiz evenings; dogs welcome,
picnic-sets under parasols on terrace, open
(and food) all day.

A little further afield

Besides the fully inspected pubs, you might like to try these pubs that have been recommended to us and described by readers. Do tell us what you think of them: feedback@goodguides.com

Channel Islands

GUERNSEY

FOREST
Deerhound (01481) 238585
Le Bourg; GY8 0AN Spacious roadside dining pub with modern interior; Liberation ales and good selection of wine by the glass, popular food from lunchtime baguettes up, friendly service; children welcome, sunny sheltered terrace with parasols, handy for the airport, open all day.

KING'S MILLS
★**Fleur du Jardin** (01481) 257996
King's Mills Road; GY5 7JT Lovely 15th-c country hotel in pretty walled garden; low-beamed bar with log fire, Liberation ale and guests, local cider and plenty of wines by the glass, very good attractively presented food from tapas to sizzling platters, afternoon teas, friendly helpful service, restaurant; background music; children and small dogs welcome, plenty of tables on back terrace, solar-heated swimming pool, 15 stylish, contemporary bedrooms, open all day.

ST MARTIN
Les Douvres (01481) 238731
La Fosse; GY4 6ER Sister hotel to the Fleur du Jardin at King's Mills; popular beamed bar with country pub feel, three changing ales and plenty of wines by the glass, decent range of enjoyable fairly priced food including ploughman's, burgers and pizzas, friendly helpful staff; garden with swimming pool ('dip and dine' lunch and dinner), 19 elegant bedrooms, good breakfast, open all day.

ST PETER PORT
Ship & Crown (01481) 721368
Opposite Crown Pier, Esplanade; GY1 2NB Bustling old town pub with bay windows overlooking harbour, which features in the *Guernsey Literary and Potato Peel Pie* book and film; interesting photographs (especially of World War II occupation, also boats and local shipwrecks), decent bar food from sandwiches up, Liberation ales and guests, welcoming prompt service even when busy, more modern-feel Crow's Nest brasserie upstairs with good views; sports TVs in bar; open all day from 10am (noon Sun) till late.

JERSEY

ROZEL
★**Rozel** (01534) 869801
La Vallée de Rozel; JE3 6AJ Country pub by the sea with a lively traditional bar that's popular with locals, original granite fireplace with copper plating, Fullers London Pride, Sharps Doom Bar and local Liberation on handpump, La Mare Branchage farm cider, also good wines by the glass and several gins, highly regarded food from sandwiches up, friendly staff, smarter restaurant upstairs and additional seating on an elevated terrace; children and dogs (in bar) welcome, open all day, no food Sun evening or Mon.

ST AUBIN
Boat House (01534) 747141
North Quay; JE3 8BS Modern steel and timber-clad quayside building with great views (window tables for diners); bar serving well kept local ales and several wines by the glass, good food ranging from small plates to seafood platters to share, efficient young staff, airy upstairs restaurant (separate menu); balcony and decked terrace overlooking harbour, well positioned for St Aubin's Bay, open all day, food all day Fri-Sun.

ST AUBIN
★**Old Court House Inn**
(01534) 746433 *Harbour Boulevard; JE3 8AB* Attractively updated and prettily positioned historic harbourside inn; bustling bar with low beams, granite walls and open fire, other rambling areas including bistro, popular generously served food from sandwiches and pubby choices to good fresh fish/seafood, well kept Liberation ales and

15 wines by the glass, handsome upstairs restaurant with lovely views across the bay to St Helier, efficient service; children welcome, front deck overlooking harbour, more seats in courtyard behind, ten comfortable well equipped bedrooms, open all day (food all day in summer including breakfasts 7-10am).

ST AUBIN

Tenby (01534) 741224

Le Boulevard, towards St Helier; JE3 8AB Randalls pub overlooking the harbour; large bar and several other rooms, decent choice of food (all day Sun) from sandwiches and wraps to good seafood, a couple of real ales such as Skinners, Stowford Press Cider and half a dozen gins, helpful service; children welcome, disabled access/loos, seats out on small front deck under awning, more on paved side terrace, open all day.

ST BRELADE

Old Smugglers (01534) 741510

Ouaisne Bay; OS map reference 595476; JE3 8AW Unpretentious historic pub just up from Ouaisne beach with black beams, built-in settles and log fires, up to four well kept ales, proper cider and enjoyable traditional food, friendly service, restaurant; occasional live music, sports TV, darts, cribbage and dominoes; children and dogs welcome, sun porch with coast views, open all day in summer, food all day weekends.

ST HELIER

Cock & Bottle (01534) 722184

Royal Square; JE2 4WA Big lively outside eating area in Royal Square with lovely hanging baskets, rattan tables and chairs under parasols, heaters and blankets for cooler evenings; pleasantly old-fashioned and pubby inside with upholstered settles and small stools in front of large fireplace, well kept Liberation ales and wide choice of good food from sandwiches and wraps through pub favourites and bistro choices to summer seafood menu; open all day, kitchen closes 7pm Fri and Sat, 4pm Sun.

ST HELIER

Halkett (01534) 732769

Halkett Place; JE2 4WG Spacious modernised pub-cum-bar close to tree-lined square; two Liberation ales, a guest beer and 17 wines by the glass, fairly priced food from sandwiches/wraps and pubby choices up; DJs Fri and Sat, TVs; sliding door opening on to pavement, open all day, no food Sun evening, closed Mon.

ST HELIER

★ Lamplighter (01534) 723119

Mulcaster Street; JE2 3NJ Small friendly pub with eight well kept ales, good range of ciders and nearly 200 malt whiskies from long pewter-topped counter, traditional décor with tankards and pump clips on heavy timbers, some old gas light fittings, only food

is snacks such as pork pies; darts and sports TV; dogs welcome, wheelchair access (no disabled loos), interesting patriotic façade (the only union flag visible during Nazi occupation), open all day.

Isle of Man

DOUGLAS   SC3875

Rovers Return (01624) 676459

Church Street; IM1 3LX Old-fashioned popular pub tucked down alleyway with good mix of customers; mainly Bushys ales but some mainland guests, generous straightforward lunchtime food (not weekends), friendly staff, several rambling bars, back room filled with Blackburn Rovers memorabilia (landlord is a supporter), also fire brigade paraphernalia (beer pumps formed from old brass hose nozzles); rock juke box, TV, pool and darts; no children, fire in winter, outdoor tables in summer, open all day.

LAXEY   SC4382

Shore Hotel (01624) 861509

Old Laxey Hill – at the bottom of the hill just before the bridge; IM4 7DA Friendly nautically themed village pub brewing its own Old Laxey Bosun Bitter, good value wines by the glass and enjoyable pubby food including nice vegetarian options; children welcome, tables set out by lovely stream, nice walk to Laxey waterwheel, two bedrooms, good breakfast, open all day.

PEEL   SC2484

Creek (01624) 842216

Station Place/North Quay; IM5 1AT In lovely setting on the ancient quayside opposite the House of Mananman heritage centre, very busy at peak times; wide choice of highly thought-of food including fish, crab and lobster fresh from the boats, good local kippers too, up to ten well kept changing ales (always some from Okells), nautical-themed lounge bar with etched mirrors and mainly old woodwork; TVs and weekend live music in public bar; children welcome, tables outside overlooking harbour, open (and food) all day from 10am.

PORT ERIN   SC1969

Falcon's Nest (01624) 834077

Station Road; IM9 6AF Friendly family-run hotel overlooking the bay, enjoyable food including local fish/seafood and Sun carvery, up to five well kept ales and over 60 malt whiskies, traditional Top Bar with conservatory and open fire, restaurant and separate sports bar (own street entrance) with TV, darts and pool; monthly live music, children welcome until 9pm, 34 bedrooms, many with sea view, also eight self-catering apartments, handy for steam rail terminus, open all day.

Pubs that serve food all day

We list here all the Main Entry pubs that have told us they serve food all day, even if it's only one day of the week. The individual entries for the pubs themselves show the actual details – do to check with the pub too as opening hours can fluctuate, especially in current circumstances.

Bedfordshire
Wootton, Legstraps

Berkshire
Hare Hatch, Horse & Groom
Peasemore, Fox
Sonning, Bull

Buckinghamshire
Beaconsfield, White Horse
Bovingdon Green, Royal Oak
Forty Green, Royal Standard
   of England
Fulmer, Black Horse
Granborough, Crown
Great Missenden, Nags Head
Cambridgeshire
Huntingdon, Old Bridge Hotel
Peterborough, Brewery Tap

Cheshire
Aldford, Grosvenor Arms
Allostock, Three Greyhounds Inn
Aston, Bhurtpore
Bostock Green, Hayhurst Arms
Bunbury, Dysart Arms
Burleydam, Combermere Arms
Burwardsley, Pheasant
Chester, Architect
Chester, Mill
Chester, Old Harkers Arms

Cholmondeley, Cholmondeley
   Arms
Cotebrook, Fox & Barrel
Delamere, Fishpool
Kelsall, Morris Dancer
Kettleshulme, Swan
Lower Peover, Bells of Peover
Macclesfield, Sutton Hall
Marbury, Swan
Mobberley, Bulls Head
Mobberley, Church Inn
Mobberley, Roebuck
Mottram St Andrew, Bulls Head
Sandbach, Old Hall
Thelwall, Little Manor
Warmingham, Bears Paw

Cornwall
Gurnards Head, Gurnards Head
   Hotel
Lostwithiel, Globe
Mylor Bridge, Pandora
Polgooth, Polgooth Inn
Polperro, Blue Peter
St Ives, Queens
Trevaunance Cove, Driftwood
   Spars

Cumbria
Ambleside, Wateredge Inn
Bowness-on-Windermere,
   Hole in t' Wall

Cartmel Fell, Masons Arms
Clifton, George & Dragon
Ings, Watermill
Kirkby Lonsdale, Sun
Langdale, Old Dungeon Ghyll
Staveley, Beer Hall at Hawkshead
  Brewery
Threlkeld, Horse & Farrier
Witherslack, Derby Arms

Derbyshire

Chelmorton, Church Inn
Chinley, Old Hall
Fenny Bentley, Coach & Horses
Hathersage, Plough
Hayfield, Royal
Repton, Boot

Devon

Chagford, Three Crowns
Cockwood, Anchor
Iddesleigh, Duke of York
Postbridge, Warren House

Dorset

West Lulworth, Castle Inn
Weymouth, Red Lion
Wimborne Minster, Green Man
Worth Matravers, Square &
  Compass

Essex

Feering, Sun
Fyfield, Queens Head
Little Walden, Crown
Littley Green, Compasses
South Hanningfield, Old Windmill

Gloucestershire

Cheltenham, Old Courthouse
Cheltenham, Royal Oak
Cirencester, Bear
Cowley, Green Dragon
Didmarton, Kings Arms
Fossebridge, Fossebridge Inn

Gloucester, Café René
Nailsworth, Weighbridge
Sheepscombe, Butchers Arms

Hampshire

Bransgore, Three Tuns
Cadnam, White Hart
Eversley, Tally Ho
Hook, Hogget
Longstock, Peat Spade
Mattingley, Leather Bottle
North Warnborough, Mill House
Portsmouth, Old Customs House
Rockbourne, Rose & Thistle
Swanwick, Navigator
Herefordshire
Tillington, Bell
Upper Sapey, Baiting House

Hertfordshire

Barnet, Duke of York
Hertford Heath, College Arms
Sarratt, Cricketers
St Albans, Prae Wood Arms

Kent

Biddenden, Three Chimneys
Fordwich, George & Dragon
Langton Green, Hare
Penshurst, Bottle House
Sevenoaks, White Hart
Stalisfield Green, Plough
Stone in Oxney, Ferry
Tunbridge Wells, Sankeys
Whitstable, Pearsons Arms

Lancashire

Barnston, Fox & Hounds
Bashall Eaves, Red Pump
Formby, Sparrowhawk
Great Mitton, Aspinall Arms
Manchester, Wharf
Nether Burrow, Highwayman
Pleasington, Clog & Billycock

Preston, Haighton Manor
Thornton Hough, Red Fox
Uppermill, Church Inn
Worsley, Worsley Old Hall

Leicestershire
Swithland, Griffin

Lincolnshire
Baston, White Horse
Ingham, Inn on the Green
Stamford, Tobie Norris
Stamford, George of Stamford

Norfolk
Great Massingham, Dabbling Duck
King's Lynn, Bank House
Larling, Angel
Salthouse, Dun Cow
Snettisham, Rose & Crown
Thornham, Lifeboat
Thorpe Market, Gunton Arms
Warham, Three Horseshoes
Woodbastwick, Fur & Feather

Northumbria
Blanchland, Lord Crewe Arms
Craster, Jolly Fisherman
Newton, Duke of Wellington
Nottinghamshire
Upper Broughton, Tap & Run

Oxfordshire
Bessels Leigh, Greyhound
Charlbury, Bull
Chazey Heath, Packhorse
Kingham, Plough
Milton under Wychwood, Hare
Oxford, Bear
Oxford, Perch
Oxford, Punter
Wolvercote, Jacobs Inn
Woodstock, Woodstock Arms

Shropshire
Baschurch, New Inn
Chetwynd Aston, Fox
Coalport, Woodbridge
Ironbridge, Golden Ball
Shipley, Inn at Shipley
Shrewsbury, Armoury

Somerset
Stanton Wick, Carpenters Arms

Staffordshire
Brewood, Oakley
Cauldon, Yew Tree
Longdon Green, Red Lion
Swynnerton, Fitzherbert Arms
Wrinehill, Hand & Trumpet

Suffolk
Chelmondiston, Butt & Oyster
Southwold, Harbour Inn
Waldringfield, Maybush

Surrey
Buckland, Pheasant
Chiddingfold, Swan
Chipstead, White Hart
Chobham, White Hart
Elstead, Mill at Elstead
Forest Green, Parrot
Milford, Refectory
Norwood Hill, Fox Revived
Oxted, Haycutter

Sussex
Bolney, Bolney Stage
Eridge Green, Nevill Crest & Gun
Firle, Ram
Goring-by-Sea, Highdown
Horsham, Black Jug
Petworth, Angel
Ringmer, Cock
Uckfield, Highlands
Withyham, Dorset Arms

Warwickshire

Alderminster, Bell
Arrow, Arrow Mill
Birmingham, Physician
Birmingham, Old Joint Stock
Hunningham, Red Lion
Long Compton, Red Lion
Preston Bagot, Crabmill
Shipston-on-Stour, Black Horse
Warmington, Falcon
Welford-on-Avon, Bell
Wordsley, Roe Deer

Wiltshire

Cricklade, Red Lion
Swindon, Weighbridge
Tollard Royal, King John
Worcestershire
Broadway, Crown & Trumpet
Guarlford, Plough & Harrow
Malvern, Nags Head

Yorkshire

Blakey Ridge, Lion
Bradfield, Strines Inn
Broughton, Bull
Elslack, Tempest Arms
Grinton, Bridge Inn
Halifax, Shibden Mill
Ilkley, Wheatley Arms
Ledsham, Chequers
Linton in Craven, Fountaine
Widdop, Pack Horse
York, Judges Lodging

London

Central London, Alfred Tennyson
Central London, Beau Brummell
Central London, Coach Makers Arms
Central London, Cross Keys
Central London, Lamb & Flag
Central London, Olde Mitre
Central London, Punchbowl
Central London, Thomas Cubitt
North London, Holly Bush
North London, Lighterman
North London, Princess of Wales
South London, Victoria
West London, Dove
West London, Windsor Castle
Outer London, Mute Swan
Outer London, Old Orchard

Scotland

Applecross, Applecross Inn
Edinburgh, Guildford Arms
Edinburgh, Abbotsford
Elie, Ship
Glasgow, Bon Accord
Gullane, Bonnie Badger
Meikleour, Meikleour Arms
Ratho, Bridge Inn
Shieldaig, Shieldaig Bar
Scottish Islands
Sligachan, Sligachan Hotel

Wales

Beaumaris, Bull
Colwyn Bay, Pen-y-Bryn
Gresford, Pant-yr-Ochain
Llandudno Junction, Queens Head
Llanelian-yn-Rhos, White Lion
Llangollen, Corn Mill
Llanmadoc, Britannia
Mold, Glasfryn
Overton Bridge, Cross Foxes
Pontypridd, Bunch of Grapes

Pubs near motorway junctions

The number at the start of each line is the number of the junction. Detailed directions are given in the Main Entry for each pub. We also give the name of the chapter where you'll find the text.

M1

13: Woburn, Birch (Bedfordshire) 3.5 miles

M3

1: Sunbury, Flower Pot (Surrey) 1.6 miles

3: Chobham, White Hart (Surrey) 4 miles

5: North Warnborough, Mill House (Hampshire) 1 mile; Hook, Hogget (Hampshire) 1.1 miles; Mattingley, Leather Bottle (Hampshire) 3 miles

M4

9: Bray, Crown (Berkshire) 1.75 miles

13: Curridge, Bunk (Berkshire) 3 miles; Chieveley, Crab & Boar (Berkshire) 3.5 miles; Peasemore, Fox (Berkshire) 4 miles

M5

10: Coombe Hill, Gloucester Old Spot (Gloucestershire) 1 mile

19: Clapton-in-Gordano, Black Horse (Somerset) 4 miles

30: Woodbury Salterton, Diggers Rest (Devon) 3.5 miles

M6

16: Barthomley, White Lion (Cheshire) 1 mile

17: Sandbach, Old Hall (Cheshire) 1.2 miles

18: Allostock, Three Greyhounds Inn (Cheshire) 4.7 miles

19: Mobberley, Bulls Head (Cheshire) 4 miles

33: Bay Horse, Bay Horse (Lancashire) 1.2 miles

36: Levens, Strickland Arms (Cumbria) 4 miles

M11

9: Hinxton, Red Lion (Cambridgeshire) 2 miles

10: Whittlesford, Tickell Arms (Cambridgeshire) 2.4 miles

M25

5: Chipstead, George & Dragon (Kent) 1.25 miles

10: Ripley, Anchor (Surrey) 3.6 miles

18: Flaunden, Bricklayers Arms (Hertfordshire) 4 miles

21A: Potters Crouch, Holly Bush (Hertfordshire) 2.3 miles

M27

1: Cadnam, White Hart (Hampshire) 0.5 mile; Fritham, Royal Oak (Hampshire) 4 miles

M40

2: Hedgerley, White Horse (Buckinghamshire) 2.4 miles; Forty Green, Royal Standard of England (Buckinghamshire) 3.5 miles

M42

6: Hampton-in-Arden, White Lion (Warwickshire) 1.25 miles

M50

1: Baughton, Jockey (Worcestershire) 4 miles

M53

3: Barnston, Fox & Hounds (Lancashire) 3 miles

M60

13: Worsley, Worsley Old Hall (Lancashire) 1 mile

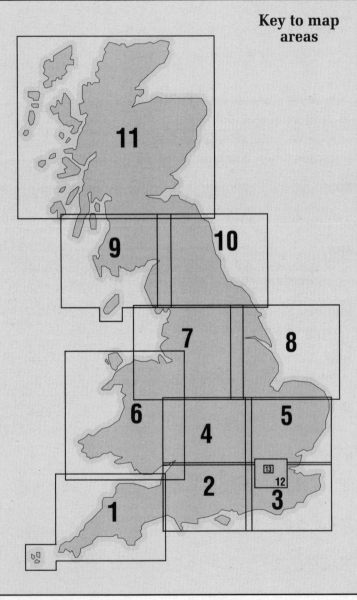

Key to map areas

11

9 10

7 8

6

4 5

2 13 12

1 3

Reference to sectional maps

—— Motorway   ● Main Entry

—— Major road   ◉ Main Entry with accommodation

----- County boundary   ■ Place name to assist navigation

MAPS

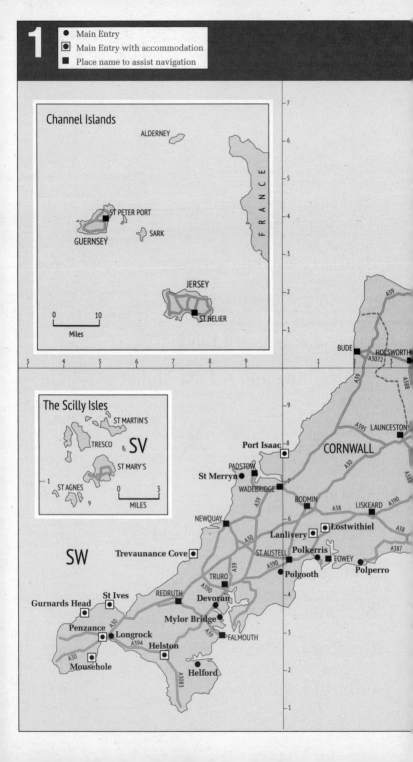

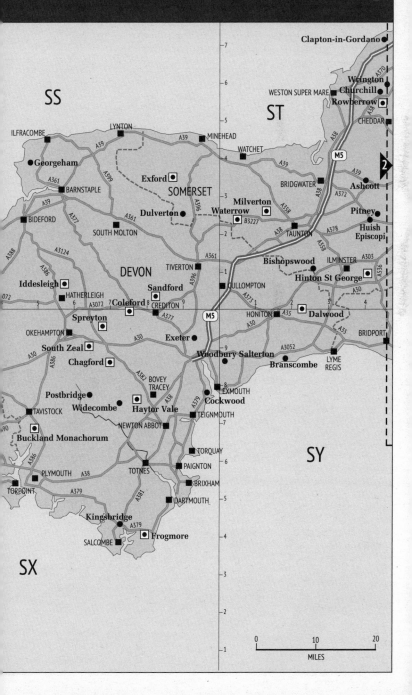

1

Clapton-in-Gordano

SS

W<del>r</del>ington
Churchill
Rowberrow

WESTON SUPER MARE

ST

CHEDDAR

ILFRACOMBE

LYNTON

MINEHEAD

WATCHET

M5

A39

A39

A39

A370

A38

2

Georgeham

A361

A599

Exford

SOMERSET

BRIDGWATER

A372

Ashcott

A39

A38

BARNSTAPLE

A39

A377

Dulverton

A361

A396

Milverton
Waterrow

B3227

Pitney

A358

Huish
Episcopi

BIDEFORD

A388

A3124

A361

SOUTH MOLTON

TAUNTON

A358

A378

A358

A356

A30

Iddesleigh

HATHERLEIGH

072

5

DEVON

A386

A3072

TIVERTON

A361

A396

6

Coleford

CREDITON

Sandford

7

8

CULLOMPTON

Bishopswood

ILMINSTER

A303

Hinton St George

A35

Spreyton

A377

9

A371

M5

1

2

3

4

HONITON

A35

Dalwood

OKEHAMPTON

A30

Exeter

A30

A3052

BRIDPORT

South Zeal

A386

A382

Chagford

BOVEY
TRACEY

Woodbury Salterton

9

Branscombe

LYME
REGIS

Postbridge

Widecombe

Haytor Vale

A38

A382

EXMOUTH

Cockwood

TEIGNMOUTH

8

7

TAVISTOCK

NEWTON ABBOT

Buckland Monachorum

90

A386

TORQUAY

SY

PLYMOUTH

A38

TOTNES

PAIGNTON

6

TORPOINT

A379

A381

BRIXHAM

DARTMOUTH

5

Kingsbridge

A379

Frogmore

SALCOMBE

4

SX

3

2

1

0   10   20
MILES

● Main Entry
◉ Main Entry with accommodation
■ Place name to assist navigation

Tetbury ◉
◉ **Cricklade**
4
A419

Oldbury-on-Severn ◉
Crudwell ◉
GLOUCESTERSHIRE
Didmarton ◉
A46
A433
A429
M4 M5
Sherston ◉
MALMESBURY
Swindon ●
A3102
A361
A350
Grittleton ◉
M4
A346
A432
CHIPPENHAM
Compton Bassett ◉
A4
MARLBOROUGH
M5
Bristol ●
A420
A46
CALNE
A4
A363
A346
Bath ●
A4
Corsham ◉
A3102
DEVIZES
WILTSHIRE
Stanton Wick ◉
A37
A39
Holt ◉
MELKSHAM
A38
A368
MIDSOMER NORTON
A366
TROWBRIDGE
A342
A345
A342
East Chisenbury ◉
CHEDDAR ■
A367
Holcombe ◉
Mells ◉
A36
A360
A371
● **Priddy**
Frome ◉
A361
WARMINSTER
A345
Newton To
Croscombe ◉
WELLS ■
SHEPTON MALLET
SOMERSET
A361
A362
Horningsham ◉
A303
AMESBURY
A538
A30
GLASTONBURY
ST
A37
A371
A359
WYLYE
A36
A360
East Knoyle ◉
Fonthill Gifford ◉
SALISBURY
A303
A357
WINCANTON
Swallowcliffe ◉
A36
A372
West Stour ◉
Corton Denham ◉
SHAFTESBURY
A30
Tollard Royal ◉
Rockbourne ●
YEOVIL ■
A30
Sherborne ●
A357
A350
A354
FORDINGBRIDGE
Farnham ◉
Fritham ●
A30
A352
DORSET
A31
Evershot ◉
Middlemarsh ◉
BLANDFORD FORUM
A350
RINGWOOD
A356
Cerne Abbas ◉ ● **Plush**
A354
A31
Nettlecombe ◉
Wimborne Minster ●
Bransgore ●
A35
A31
A350
A338
BRIDPORT ■
A35
DORCHESTER
POOLE
CHRISTCHURC
A354
West Lulworth ◉
Church Knowle ◉
WAREHAM
BOURNEMOUTH
A353
A551
SY
Weymouth ●
Kingston ◉
SWANAGE
Worth Matravers ●

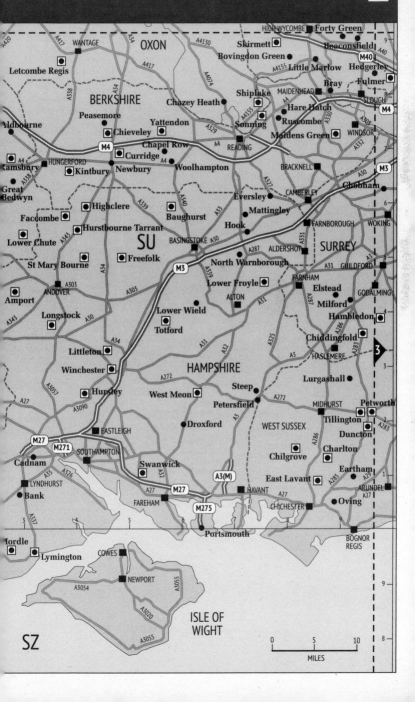

Main Entry
Main Entry with accommodation
Place name to assist navigation

BUCKS

M1   M11   5

M25   A127

Hedgerley   Harefield (see West London section)
M40   GREATER LONDON   Horndon-on-the-Hill
Fulmer   A13
UXBRIDGE   A128

BERKS   M4   TILBURY

M25   DARTFORD   GRAVESEND
STAINES   A2   ROCHESTER
M3   Sunbury   A2   M2
Esher
Chobham   M25   M20
M26   M20
WOKING   Ripley   M25   Chipstead   Chipstead   MAIDSTONE
A21   M25   Sevenoaks
GUILDFORD   Buckland   Oxted   WESTERHAM   TQ
DORKING   A25   TONBRIDGE
SURREY   REIGATE
Forest Green   Norwood Hill   Penshurst
M23   A264   Langton Green
Hambledon   Copthorne   Tunbridge
CRAWLEY   EAST GRINSTEAD   Wells
2   Horsham   Withyham   Eridge
West Hoathly   Green
Danehill   Ticehurst
HAYWARDS HEATH   CROWBOROUGH
Bolney   Fletching   Salehurst
Petworth   Uckfield   Robertsbridge
Dial Post   BURGESS HILL   EAST SUSSEX
WEST SUSSEX
Ringmer
ARUNDEL   LEWES   HAILSHAM   BEXHILL
WORTHING   Firle
Goring-by-Sea   BRIGHTON   NEWHAVEN
EASTBOURNE

TV

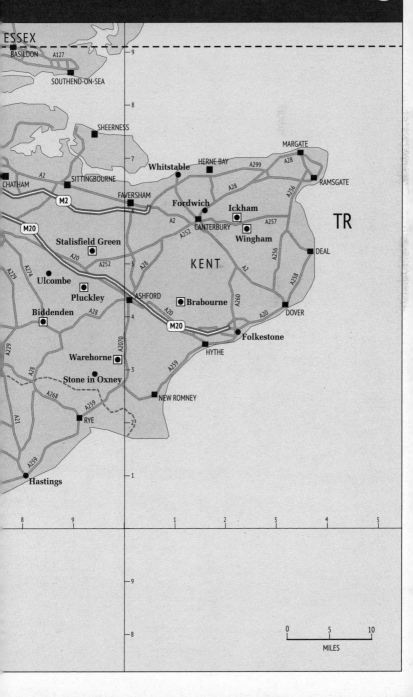

ESSEX

BASILDON   A127

SOUTHEND-ON-SEA

SHEERNESS

CHATHAM   A2

SITTINGBOURNE

M2

FAVERSHAM

Whitstable

HERNE BAY   A299

MARGATE

A28

RAMSGATE

A256

M20

Fordwich

A2

CANTERBURY

A252

Ickham

Wingham

A257

TR

A256

DEAL

Stalisfield Green

A20

A252

A28

KENT

A2

A258

Ulcombe

A274

A279

Pluckley

ASHFORD

Brabourne

A260

DOVER

A20

Biddenden

A28

M20

A2070

HYTHE

Folkestone

A229

Warehorne

A259

Stone in Oxney

A268

A259

NEW ROMNEY

A21

RYE

A259

Hastings

8   9   1   2   3   4   5

0   5   10

MILES

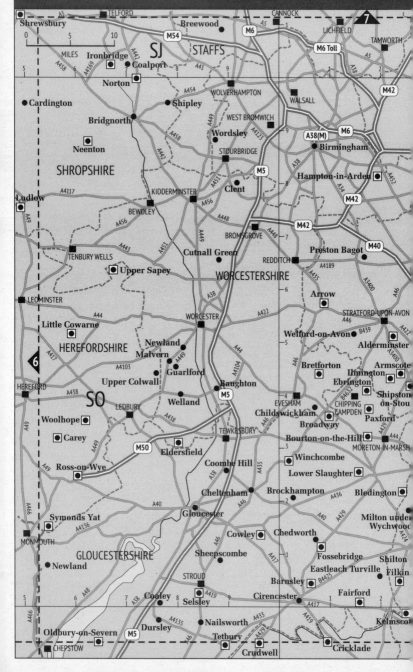

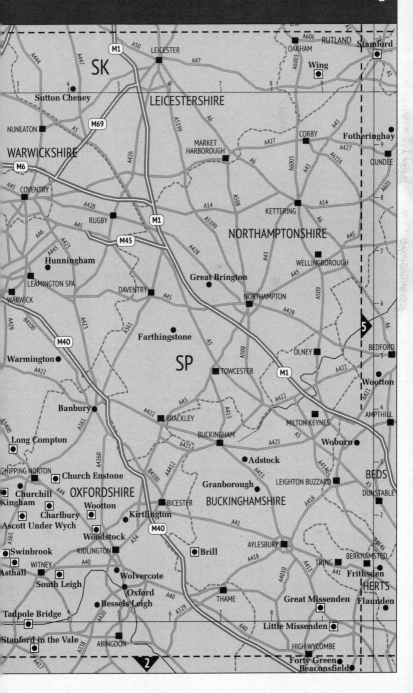

M1 A50 LEICESTER A47 RUTLAND A606 Stamford
OAKHAM A6003
SK Wing
A444 A447 A1
3 4 5 6 7 8 9
Sutton Cheney LEICESTERSHIRE
A5199 A6
NUNEATON M69 A5 MARKET CORBY A43 **Fotheringhay**
WARWICKSHIRE HARBOROUGH A427 A6116 A605 9
M6 A426 A6 A6003 A43 CUNDLE
A45 COVENTRY A428 A508 A14 8
A45 M1 KETTERING A14
RUGBY A5199 NORTHAMPTONSHIRE A6 A45 7
M45 A428 A43 WELLINGBOROUGH
Hunningham A46 A445 A425 A361 A5 **Great Brington** A509 A45 6
LEAMINGTON SPA DAVENTRY A45 NORTHAMPTON
WARWICK A428
A429 B4100 A508 BEDFORD 5
M40 **Farthingstone** A5 OLNEY A6
Warmington SP M1 A422
A422 TOWCESTER **Wootton**
A43 A422 A421
Banbury A422 BRACKLEY A413 MILTON KEYNES AMPTHILL 4
A361 BUCKINGHAM A421 A5 **Woburn**
Long Compton A260 A421 **Adstock** A413 A4146 BEDS 3
CHIPPING NORTON B4100 A412 **Granborough** LEIGHTON BUZZARD DUNSTABLE
Church Enstone BICESTER BUCKINGHAMSHIRE A418 2
Churchill A44 OXFORDSHIRE A41
Kingham **Charlbury** **Wootton** **Kirtlington** AYLESBURY A4146
Ascott Under Wych A34 M40 A4010 TRING BERKHAMSTED
Swinbrook **Woodstock** **Brill** A418 A41 **Frithsden**
WITNEY KIDLINGTON A40 A413 HERTS
Asthall A40 **Wolvercote** THAME **Great Missenden** **Flaunden**
South Leigh **Oxford** A40
Bessels Leigh A329 **Little Missenden**
Tadpole Bridge A420 5 6 7 8
Stanford in the Vale A338 HIGH WYCOMBE
A417 ABINGDON 2 **Forty Green**
Beaconsfield

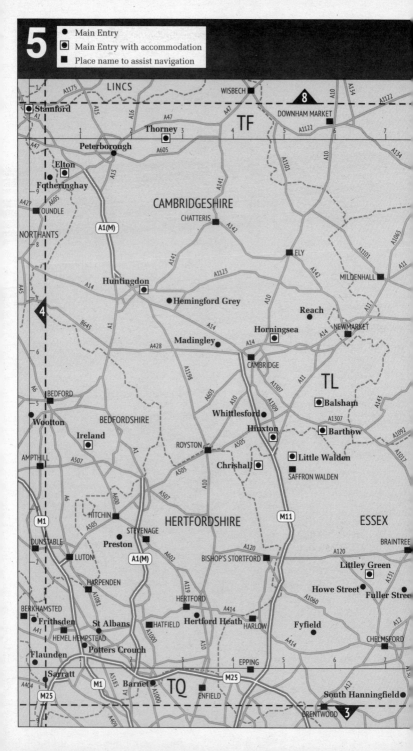

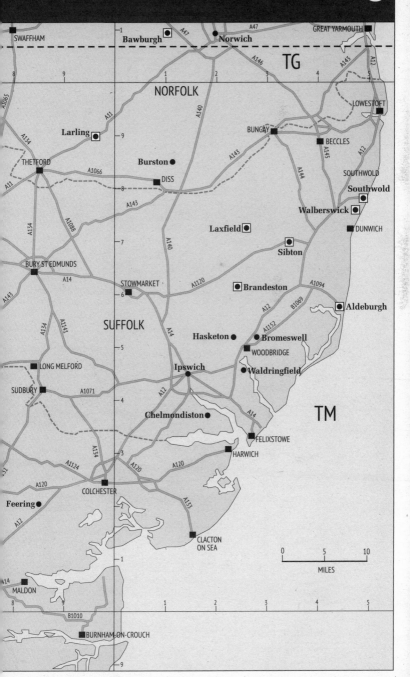

5

SWAFFHAM
Bawburgh
A47
Norwich
A47
GREAT YARMOUTH

TG

9

NORFOLK
A11
A140
A146
A143
LOWESTOFT
A12

A1065

Larling
9
BUNGAY
BECCLES
A145

A134
Burston
A143
SOUTHWOLD
A12

THETFORD
A1066
DISS
8
A144
Southwold
A11
A143
Walberswick
A1088
Laxfield
7
A140
Sibton
DUNWICH

BURY ST EDMUNDS
A1094
A134
STOWMARKET
6
A1120
Brandeston
B1069
Aldeburgh

A14
SUFFOLK
A12
A1152
A14
A154
A141
Hasketon
Bromeswell
WOODBRIDGE

LONG MELFORD
Ipswich
Waldringfield

SUDBURY
A1071
A12
TM
4

Chelmondiston
A14

A134
FELIXSTOWE
A1124
3
A120
HARWICH
A120
A120

COLCHESTER
A133

Feering
A12

CLACTON ON SEA

0   5   10
MILES

1

MALDON
A14

8

B1010

BURNHAM-ON-CROUCH
9

1   2   3   4   5

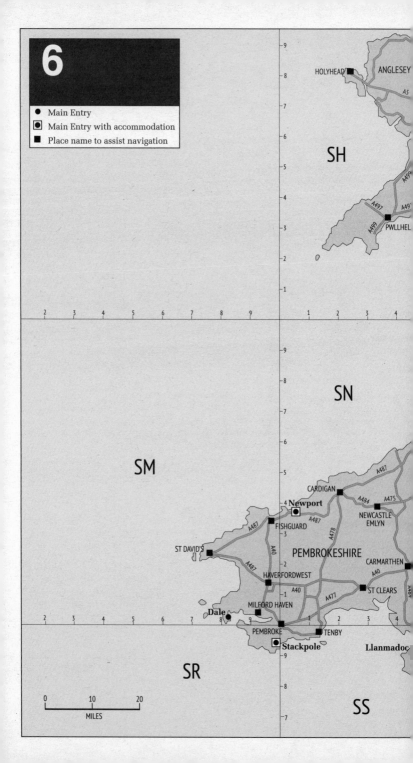

6

- ● Main Entry
- ◉ Main Entry with accommodation
- ■ Place name to assist navigation

HOLYHEAD ■   ANGLESEY
A5

SH

A497   *A49*
A499   PWLLHELI ■

SN

SM

A487
CARDIGAN ■
A484   *A475*
◉ **Newport**
A487   NEWCASTLE EMLYN ■
FISHGUARD ■
A487   *A478*
ST DAVID'S ■   **PEMBROKESHIRE**
A40   CARMARTHEN ■
A487   *A40*
HAVERFORDWEST ■   ST CLEARS ■
A40   *A477*   *A48*
MILFORD HAVEN ■
Dale ●
PEMBROKE ■   TENBY ■
◉ **Stackpole**   **Llanmadoc**

SR

SS

0   10   20
MILES

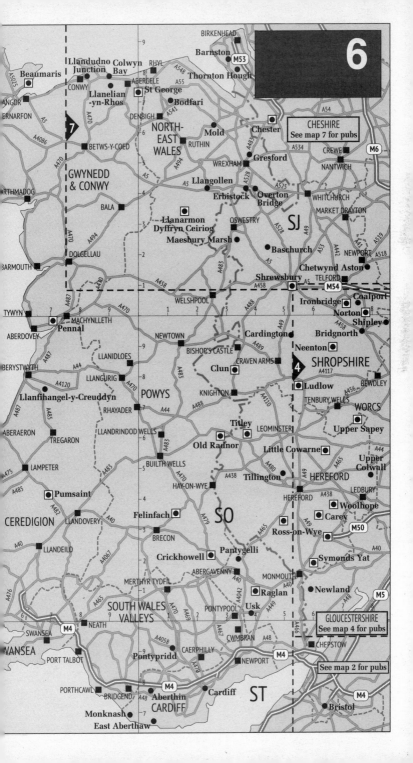

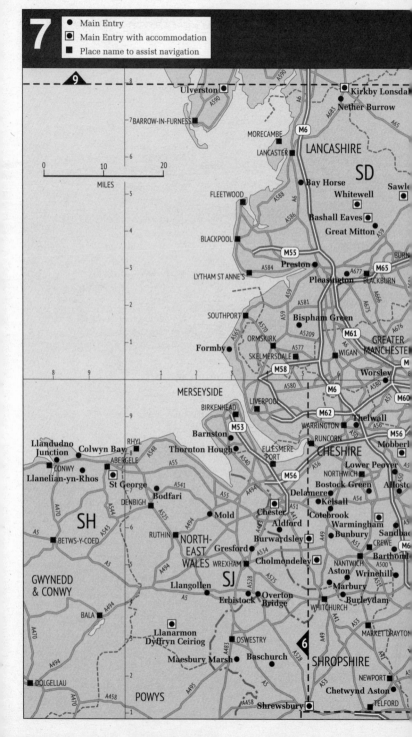

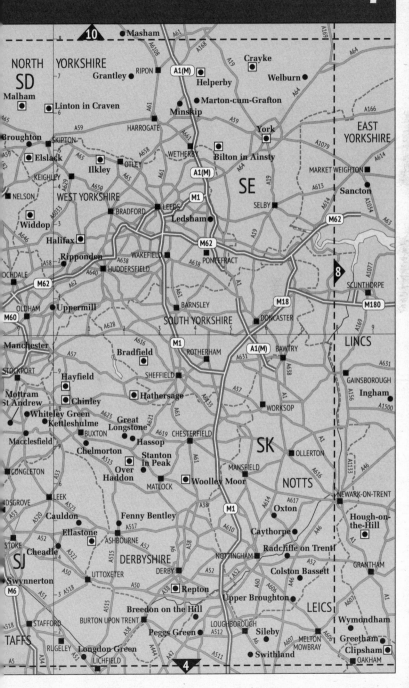

10 ● Masham   A61

NORTH YORKSHIRE   ● Crayke
SD   Grantley RIPON **A1(M)** ● Helperby   ● Welburn
● Malham   ● Linton in Craven   ● Marton-cum-Grafton
    Minskip   A166
● Broughton SKIPTON HARROGATE   ● York   EAST YORKSHIRE
● Elslack ● Ilkley OTLEY WETHERBY ● Bilton in Ainsty   MARKET WEIGHTON
● NELSON WEST YORKSHIRE   **A1(M)**   SE ● Sancton
● Widdop BRADFORD LEEDS **M1**   SELBY
● Halifax ● Ledsham   **M62**
● Ripponden WAKEFIELD   **M62**
ROCHDALE HUDDERSFIELD **M62** PONTEFRACT   **8** SCUNTHORPE
M62 OLDHAM ● Uppermill BARNSLEY   **M18** **M180**
M60   SOUTH YORKSHIRE DONCASTER
Manchester   **M1**   **A1(M)** BAWTRY LINCS
STOCKPORT ● Bradfield ROTHERHAM   GAINSBOROUGH
● Hayfield SHEFFIELD   ● Ingham
Mottram St Andrew ● Chinley ● Hathersage   WORKSOP
● Whiteley Green ● Great Longstone   SK
● Kettleshulme BUXTON CHESTERFIELD
Macclesfield ● Hassop   OLLERTON
● Chelmorton ● Stanton in Peak MANSFIELD   NOTTS
CONGLETON ● Over Haddon ● Woolley Moor   NEWARK-ON-TRENT
MATLOCK   Hough-on-the-Hill
LEEK ● Fenny Bentley **M1** ● Oxton
● Cauldon   A610 ● Caythorpe
● Ellastone ASHBOURNE   GRANTHAM
STOKE ● Cheadle   ● Radcliffe on Trent
SJ UTTOXETER DERBYSHIRE DERBY ● Colston Bassett
● Swynnerton ● Repton   LEICS ● Wymondham
M6 ● Upper Broughton
STAFFORD ● Breedon on the Hill LOUGHBOROUGH   ● Greetham
TAFFS BURTON UPON TRENT ● Peggs Green ● Sileby ● Clipsham
RUGELEY ● Longdon Green MELTON MOWBRAY OAKHAM
A5 LICHFIELD **4** ● Swithland

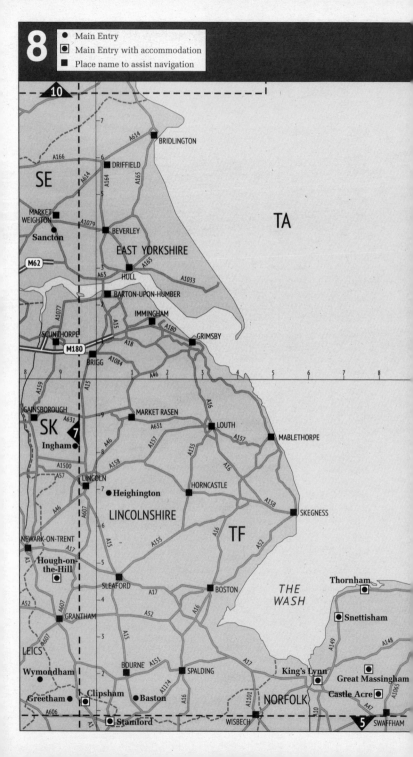

8
● Main Entry
◉ Main Entry with accommodation
■ Place name to assist navigation

10

SE

TA

A614
BRIDLINGTON
A166
A614
6
DRIFFIELD
A164
A165
5
MARKET WEIGHTON
A1079
BEVERLEY
Sancton
EAST YORKSHIRE
M62
A165
3
A63
HULL
A1033
A1077
BARTON-UPON-HUMBER
2
A15
IMMINGHAM
A180
SCUNTHORPE
GRIMSBY
M180
A18
A1084
BRIGG
A46

8   9   2   3   4   5   6   7   8

GAINSBOROUGH
A159
A631
SK   7
A15
MARKET RASEN
A16
A631
LOUTH
A157
MABLETHORPE
Ingham
A46
A157
A135
A1500
A158
A16
A57
LINCOLN
A46
A607
Heighington
HORNCASTLE
A158
SKEGNESS
NEWARK-ON-TRENT
LINCOLNSHIRE
TF
A17
A15
A155
A16
A52
Hough-on-the-Hill
6
A1
A52
A607
SLEAFORD
A17
BOSTON
THE WASH
Thornham
5
GRANTHAM
A16
Snettisham
A607
A15
A52
4
LEICS
A607
A15
A149
A148
Wymondham
3
BOURNE
A351
SPALDING
A17
King's Lynn
Great Massingham
Greetham
Clipsham
Baston
A16
A1174
A1101
Castle Acre
A1065
A606
2
A1
Stamford
WISBECH
NORFOLK
A47
5
SWAFFHAM
A10

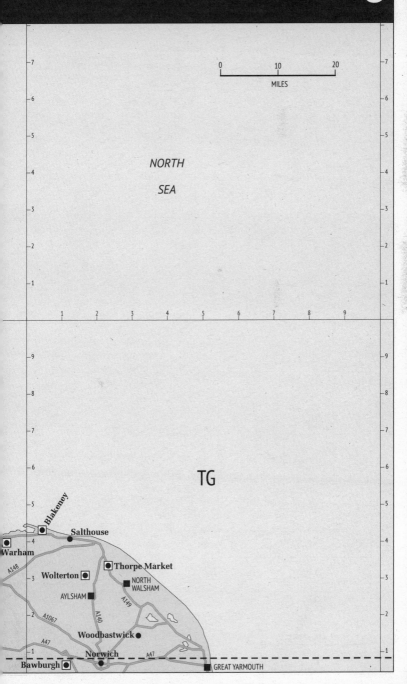

0   10   20

MILES

NORTH

SEA

TG

Blakeney

Salthouse

Warham

A148

Wolterton   Thorpe Market

NORTH
WALSHAM

AYLSHAM   A149

A1067   A140

A47   Woodbastwick

Norwich   A47

Bawburgh   GREAT YARMOUTH

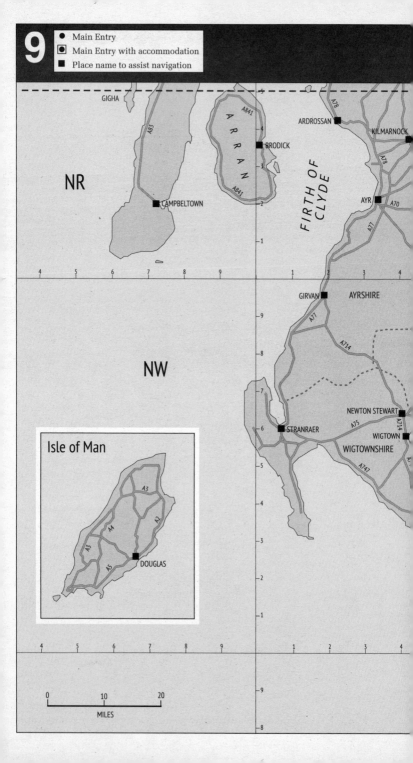

9
- Main Entry
- Main Entry with accommodation
- Place name to assist navigation

GIGHA

A841

A R R A N

A83

ARDROSSAN

KILMARNOCK

A78

BRODICK

FIRTH OF CLYDE

A78

NR

AYR

A70

CAMPBELTOWN

A841

A77

GIRVAN

AYRSHIRE

A77

A714

NW

NEWTON STEWART

A714

A75

STRANRAER

WIGTOWN

A77

WIGTOWNSHIRE

Isle of Man

A3

A2

A4

A747

A3

A5

DOUGLAS

0   10   20

MILES

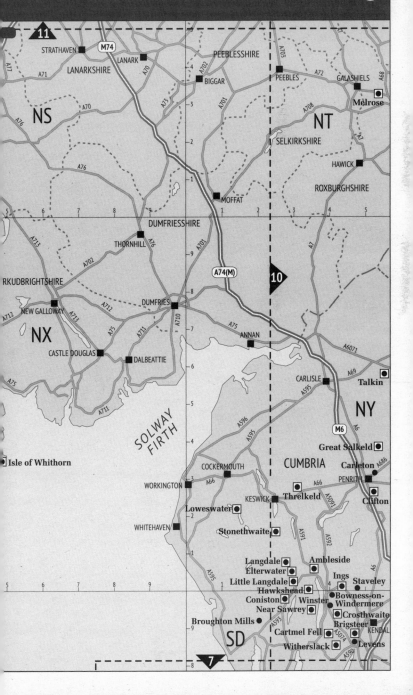

11

STRATHAVEN
M74
LANARK
LANARKSHIRE
A70
A71
A77
A76
A70
A70
NS

PEEBLESSHIRE
A702
BIGGAR
A701
A703
PEEBLES
A72
GALASHIELS
A68
Melrose
A708
NT
SELKIRKSHIRE
A7
HAWICK
ROXBURGHSHIRE

A76
A73
MOFFAT
DUMFRIESSHIRE
A701
A7

THORNHILL
A76
A702
A701
A74(M)
10

RKUDBRIGHTSHIRE
A712
NEW GALLOWAY
A713
A712
DUMFRIES
A710
A75
ANNAN
A6071

NX
A713
A75
A711
A711
CARLISLE
A595
A69
Talkin
NY

CASTLE DOUGLAS
DALBEATTIE
A75

SOLWAY
FIRTH
M6
A6

Isle of Whithorn
A596
A595
Great Salkeld
CUMBRIA
Carleton
A686
PENRITH
COCKERMOUTH
A66
A66
A591
Clifton
WORKINGTON
KESWICK
Threlkeld
Loweswater
Stonethwaite
A591
A592

WHITEHAVEN
A595
Langdale
Ambleside
Elterwater
Ings
Staveley
Little Langdale
Hawkshead
Bowness-on-
Coniston
Winster
Windermere
Near Sawrey
Crosthwaite
Broughton Mills
A595
Brigsteer
Cartmel Fell
A5074
KENDAL
SD
Witherslack
Levens
A590

7

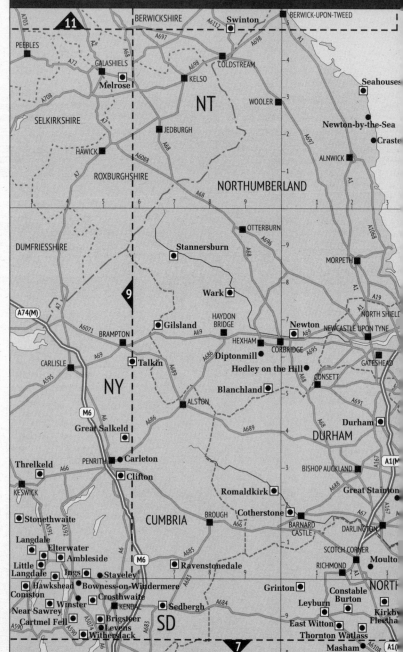

10
- ● Main Entry
- ◉ Main Entry with accommodation
- ■ Place name to assist navigation

11

BERWICKSHIRE

A703

A6112 Swinton

BERWICK-UPON-TWEED

A697

A1

PEEBLES

A68

GALASHIELS

A698

COLDSTREAM

A698

Seahouses

A7

Melrose

KELSO

NT

WOOLER

Newton-by-the-Sea

SELKIRKSHIRE

A7

JEDBURGH

A697

A68

A697

Craste

HAWICK

A6088

ALNWICK

A1

ROXBURGHSHIRE

NORTHUMBERLAND

A68

DUMFRIESSHIRE

OTTERBURN

A1068

9

Stannersburn

A696

MORPETH

A68

A74(M)

Wark

A7

A6071

Gilsland

HAYDON BRIDGE

Newton

NEWCASTLE UPON TYNE

NORTH SHIELD

BRAMPTON

A69

HEXHAM

A69

A695

A7

Diptonmill

CORBRIDGE

CARLISLE

A69

Talkin

A686

Hedley on the Hill

GATESHEAD

A595

NY

A689

Blanchland

A68

CONSETT

ALSTON

A691

A686

A689

Durham

Great Salkeld

A6

DURHAM

M6

A689

A167

Threlkeld

PENRITH

Carleton

A66

BISHOP AUCKLAND

A1(M

KESWICK

Clifton

A688

Great Stainton

Romaldkirk

A68

Stonethwaite

CUMBRIA

BROUGH

Cotherstone

A67

A167

Langdale

A592

A66

BARNARD CASTLE

DARLINGTON

Elterwater

Ambleside

SCOTCH CORNER

Little

A685

M6

Ravenstonedale

RICHMOND

Moulto

Langdale

Ings

Staveley

Grinton

NORTH

Hawkshead

Bowness-on-Windermere

A6

Constable

Coniston

Crosthwaite

A684

Leyburn

Burton

Near Sawrey

Winster

KENDAL

Sedbergh

Kirkby

Cartmel Fell

Brigsteer

A683

East Witton

Fleetha

A590

Levens

SD

Thornton Watlass

A1(

A590

Witherslack

A6

Masham

A6108

7

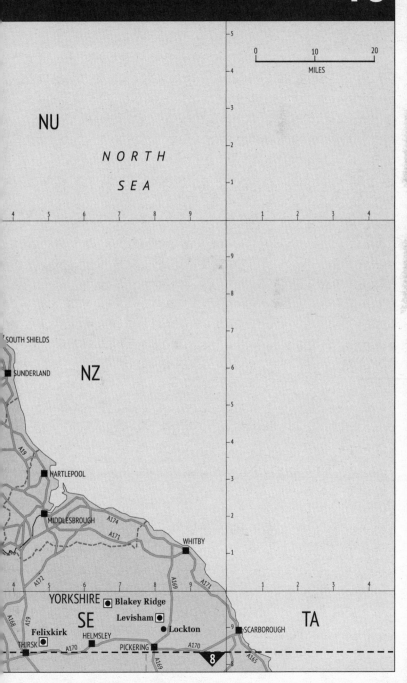

NU

N O R T H

S E A

0   10   20
MILES

4   5   6   7   8   9   1   2   3   4

SOUTH SHIELDS

SUNDERLAND   NZ

A19

HARTLEPOOL

MIDDLESBROUGH   A174

A171

WHITBY

4   5   6   7   8   9   1   2   3   4
A172   A169   A171

YORKSHIRE   ◉ Blakey Ridge

Levisham ◉

SE   ● Lockton

A168   A19   SCARBOROUGH   TA

Felixkirk   HELMSLEY

THIRSK   A170   PICKERING   A170

A169   ◆8◆   A165

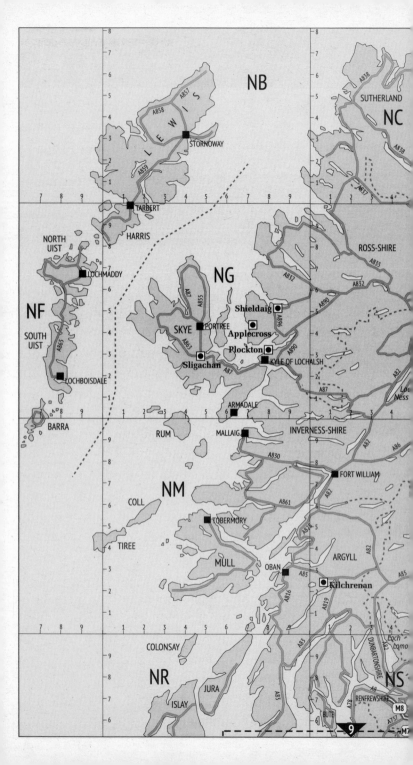

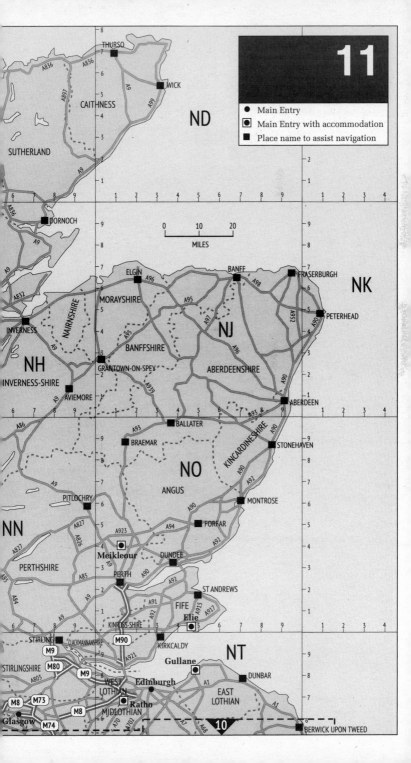

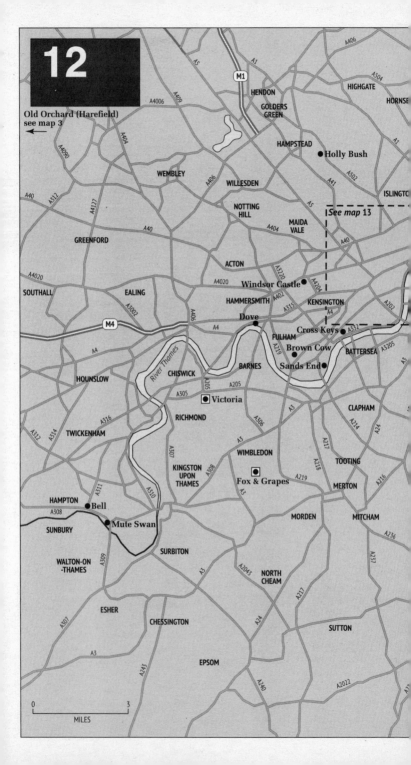

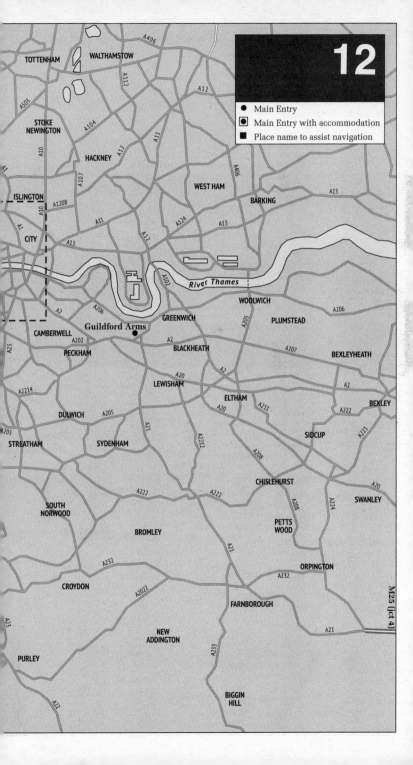

12

- ● Main Entry
- ◉ Main Entry with accommodation
- ■ Place name to assist navigation

River Thames

Guildford Arms

M25 (Jct 4)

TOTTENHAM
WALTHAMSTOW
STOKE NEWINGTON
HACKNEY
ISLINGTON
CITY
WEST HAM
BARKING
WOOLWICH
PLUMSTEAD
GREENWICH
CAMBERWELL
PECKHAM
BLACKHEATH
BEXLEYHEATH
LEWISHAM
ELTHAM
BEXLEY
DULWICH
SIDCUP
STREATHAM
SYDENHAM
CHISLEHURST
SWANLEY
SOUTH NORWOOD
BROMLEY
PETTS WOOD
ORPINGTON
CROYDON
FARNBOROUGH
NEW ADDINGTON
PURLEY
BIGGIN HILL

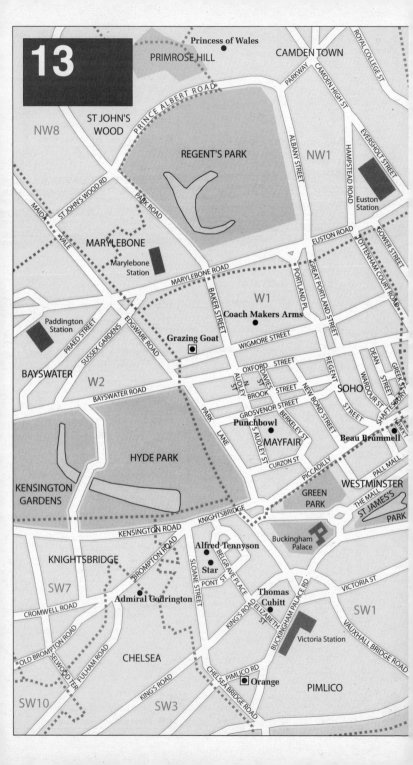

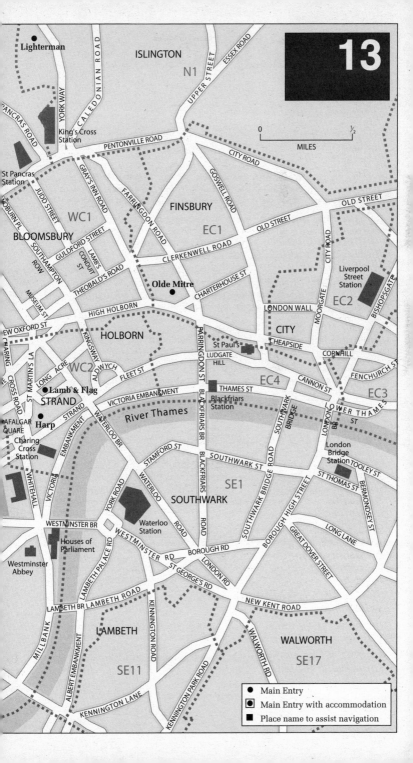

REPORT FORMS

We would very much appreciate hearing about your visits to pubs in this Guide, whether you have found them as described and recommend them for continued inclusion or noticed a fall in standards.

We'd also be glad to hear of any new pubs that you think we should know about. Readers' reports are very valuable to us, and sometimes pubs are dropped simply because we have had no up-to-date news on them.

You can use the cut-out forms on the following pages, email us at feedback@ goodguides.com or send us comments via our website (www.thegoodpubguide. co.uk) or app. We include two types of forms: one for you to simply list pubs you have visited and confirm that our review is accurate, and the other for you to give us more detailed information on individual pubs. If you would like more forms, please write to us at:

Freepost THE GOOD PUB GUIDE, Random House Publishing, 20 Vauxhall Bridge Road, London SW1V 2SA

If you would also like to continue to receive Good Pub Guide newsletters and offers from the Random House Group, please tick the box provided on the form.

Usually, the end of April is the cut-off date for reports for the next edition. We will, of course, use reports after this date, but your name will not appear in the Guide until the following year.

We'll assume we can print your name or initials as a recommender unless you tell us otherwise.

MAIN ENTRY OR ALSO WORTH A VISIT?
Please try to gauge whether a pub should be a Main Entry or in the Also Worth a Visit section (and tick the relevant box). Main Entries need qualities that would make it worth other readers' while to travel some distance to them. If a pub is an entirely new recommendation, the Also Worth a Visit section may be the best place for it to start its career in the Guide – to encourage other readers to report on it.

The more detail you can provide, the better. For example: how good the landlord or landlady is, what it looks like inside, the atmosphere and character, the quality and type of food, and which real ales are available and whether they're well kept, whether bedrooms are available, and how big/attractive the garden is. It's also helpful to know if children or dogs are welcome.

If the food or accommodation is outstanding, tick the FOOD Award or the STAY Award box.

If you're in a position to gauge a pub's suitability or otherwise for people with disabilities, do please tell us about that.

If you can, give the full address for any pub not currently in the Guide – in particular its postcode. If we can't find a pub's postcode, we can't include it in the Guide.

I have been to the following pubs in *The Good Pub Guide 2021* in the last few months, found them as described, and confirm that they deserve continued inclusion:

continued overleaf

PLEASE GIVE YOUR NAME AND ADDRESS ON THE BACK OF THIS FORM

Pubs visited continued..........

I would like to receive Good Pub Guide updates and offers from
The Random House Group. ☐

Your own name and address *(block capitals please)*

....

....

....

Postcode...

Please return to
Freepost THE GOOD PUB GUIDE,
Random House Publishing,
20 Vauxhall Bridge Road,
London SW1V 2SA

IF YOU PREFER, YOU CAN SEND
US REPORTS BY EMAIL:

feedback@goodguides.com

I have been to the following pubs in *The Good Pub Guide 2021* in the last few months, found them as described, and confirm that they deserve continued inclusion:

continued overleaf

PLEASE GIVE YOUR NAME AND ADDRESS ON THE BACK OF THIS FORM

Pubs visited continued..........

I would like to receive Good Pub Guide updates and offers from
The Random House Group. ☐

Your own name and address *(block capitals please)*

....

....

....

Postcode...

Please return to
Freepost THE GOOD PUB GUIDE,
Random House Publishing,
20 Vauxhall Bridge Road,
London SW1V 2SA

IF YOU PREFER, YOU CAN SEND
US REPORTS BY EMAIL:

feedback@goodguides.com

Report on (pub's name)

....

Pub's address

....

☐ YES MAIN ENTRY   ☐ YES WORTH A VISIT   ☐ NO don't include

Please tick one of these boxes to show your verdict, and give reasons, descriptive comments, prices and the date of your visit

☐ Deserves **FOOD Award**   ☐ Deserves **STAY Award**   2021:1

PLEASE GIVE YOUR NAME AND ADDRESS ON THE BACK OF THIS FORM

✂ ....

Report on (pub's name)

....

Pub's address

....

☐ YES MAIN ENTRY   ☐ YES WORTH A VISIT   ☐ NO don't include

Please tick one of these boxes to show your verdict, and give reasons, descriptive comments, prices and the date of your visit

☐ Deserves **FOOD Award**   ☐ Deserves **STAY Award**   2021:2

PLEASE GIVE YOUR NAME AND ADDRESS ON THE BACK OF THIS FORM

DO NOT USE THIS SIDE OF THE PAGE FOR WRITING ABOUT PUBS

Your own name and address *(block capitals please)*

By returning this form, you confirm your agreement that the information you provide in your review may be used by The Random House Group Ltd (or its assignees and/or licensees) in any media or medium whatsoever. Any personal details which you provide from which we can identify you are held and processed in accordance with the General Data Protection Regulation (GDPR), and details on how we process this personal data can be found in our Privacy Policy (https://www.penguinrandomhouse.co.uk/PrivacyPolicy/). **Your details will not be passed on to any third parties for their marketing purposes.**

I would like to receive Good Pub Guide updates and offers from The Random House Group. ☐

✂ ....

DO NOT USE THIS SIDE OF THE PAGE FOR WRITING ABOUT PUBS

Your own name and address *(block capitals please)*

By returning this form, you confirm your agreement that the information you provide in your review may be used by The Random House Group Ltd (or its assignees and/or licensees) in any media or medium whatsoever. Any personal details which you provide from which we can identify you are held and processed in accordance with the General Data Protection Regulation (GDPR), and details on how we process this personal data can be found in our Privacy Policy (https://www.penguinrandomhouse.co.uk/PrivacyPolicy/). **Your details will not be passed on to any third parties for their marketing purposes.**

I would like to receive Good Pub Guide updates and offers from The Random House Group. ☐